U0107919

新编

英汉双解词典

全新双色版

周全珍 ◎ 编著

四川辞书出版社

图书在版编目（CIP）数据

新编英汉双解词典：全新双色版 / 周全珍编著. —成都：
四川辞书出版社，2024.6
ISBN 978-7-5579-1540-7

Ⅰ.①新… Ⅱ.①周… Ⅲ.①英语－双解词典 ②双解
词典－英、汉 Ⅳ.①H316

中国国家版本馆 CIP 数据核字(2024)第 086017 号

新编英汉双解词典：全新双色版

XINBIAN YINGHAN SHUANGJIE CIDIAN：QUANXIN SHUANGSE BAN

周全珍　编著

责任编辑 / 李薇薇　雷　敏
封面设计 / 李其飞
责任印制 / 肖　鹏
出版发行 / 四川辞书出版社
地　　址 / 成都市锦江区三色路 238 号
邮政编码 / 610023
印　　刷 / 成都东江印务有限公司
开　　本 / 880 mm×1230 mm　1 / 32
版　　次 / 2024 年 6 月第 1 版
印　　次 / 2024 年 6 月第 1 次印刷
印　　张 / 30
书　　号 / ISBN 978-7-5579-1540-7
定　　价 / 78.00 元

前　言

Preface

　　本词典共收录英语单词、短语和扩展词近 50000 条。这些词条主要选自高等学校英语专业基础阶段教学大纲、现行全日制高级中学英语教学大纲和比较权威的英汉词典等。

　　本词典具有英汉双解的功能，不仅可以让使用者正确地理解每个单词和短语的含义，同时又能让使用者准确恰当地运用它们。本词典博采众长，融英语解释、汉语释义、例证、短语、派生词等为一体，设计新颖，例句丰富，实用性强，使用方便，是适合我国中学生、大学生及英语自学者使用的工具书，同时也可作为英语教师的教学参考书。

　　词典编写工作烦琐，虽然我们已力求审慎，但仍难免会存在疏漏或不足，恳请同行和读者不吝指正。

编　者

目 录
Contents

凡 例
Guide to the Use of the Dictionary

1.词条

1.1 词条按字母顺序排列,用黑正体印刷。

1.2 拼法相同但词源及词义不同的词,分立条目,在词的右上角标以 1、2、3 等数码。

1.3 一个词的不同拼写形式有两种表达方式:

1.3.1 拼法接近、按照字母顺序排列又较邻近的两种形式可以并列,将较常见的形式列在前面,次常见的列在后面,如:**gipsy,gypsy**/'ʤɪpsi/。

1.3.2 用圆括号括注有差异的字母,如 **acknowledg(e)ment**,表示该词有 acknowledgement 和 acknowledgment 两种拼写形式。

2.注音

2.1 词的读音一般紧接词条标出,音标符号置于双斜线号(//)内。

2.2 注音用最新国际音标。多音节词的重音符号置于其重读音节的音标符号之前,主重音符号置于上方,次重音符号置于下方,如:**mathematics**/ˌmæθəˈmætɪks/。可省略的音素用圆括号括出,如:**abhor** /əbˈhɔː(r)/中的/r/音。

2.3 一个词因词类或释义不同而发音不同时,在发音有变化的有关词类或释义前另行注音,如:**record** Ⅰ /rɪˈkɔːd/ *v.*…… Ⅱ /ˈrekɔːd/ *n.*……

2.4 当一个词有两种发音时,两种音分别标注,中间以逗号(,)分开,如:**abduct** /əbˈdʌkt,æbˈdʌkt/。

3.词类

3.1 词类用斜体英语缩写形式标注。词类缩写形式见 10 条。

3.2 一个词若有几种不同的词类功能,用黑正体罗马数码分别标注,如:**record** Ⅰ /rɪˈkɔːd/ *v.*…… Ⅱ /ˈrekɔːd/ *n.*……

3.3 前缀以及缩略语分别注以斜体英语缩写词 *pref.*(prefix)和 *abbr.*(abbreviation)。

4.词的屈折变化

4.1 不规则动词的变化形式置于词类之后,放在圆括号内。过去式和过去分词之间用逗号隔开,现在分词形式与过去形式之间用分号隔开。若过去式和过去分词形式相同,则不再重复标注;规则变化中需重复词尾辅音字母的形式,以简略形式予以注明,例如:**abet**/əˈbet/v. (-tt-)……

4.2 名词的复数不规则变化形式置于词类后,放在圆括号内以(*pl.*……)的形式标注。名词释义前若有(*pl.*)或(usually *pl.*),表示该名词在表示该义项时须用或常用复数形式。

4.3 形容或副词比较级和最高级的不规则变化形式置于词类后,放在圆括号内。比较级和最高级形式之间用逗号分隔。

5.释义

5.1 一个词有英语和汉语两种释义,英语释义后是汉语释义。

5.2 一个词有多个义项时,各义项前标以❶❷❸等序号。同一义项内意义较近的释义用逗号分隔,稍远的用分号分隔。

5.3 一个词有两种以上不同的词类功能,但释义用语大致相同时,也可合并释义。如:**aboard**/əˈbɔːd/*adv.& prep.*……在船(或飞机、车)上;上船;登机;上车。

5.4 释义中用 sb.,sb.'s 分别指"某人""某人的"。

5.5 释义中用 sth.指"某事""某物"。

6.例证

6.1 词条释义后收入词组或句子作为例证,例证后附汉语译文。

6.2 例证及译文均用白正体印刷;例证中出现词条用波浪号(~)代替,前后可替换或省略的词语置于圆括号内。如:**abandon**……~ oneself to drinking (grief) 酗酒无度(深陷悲痛)。

6.3 例证中 sb.,sb.'s,sth.的用法同 5.4、5.5。

6.4 同一个释义下有多个例证的,则例证之间以斜线号(/)隔开。

7.习语

7.1 习惯用语(包括复合词、成语、熟语和谚语)用黑正体印刷;习语中出现词条用波浪号(~)代替,前后可替换或省略的词语置于圆括号内。习语列在词的释义和例证之后,以平行号(‖)开始。

7.2 同一词条下的两条或数条习语,按字母顺序排列,并以斜线号(/)隔开;一条习语若有几个不同的释义,各义项前标以❶❷❸等序号。

7.3 习语中 sb.、sb.'s、sth.的用法同 5.4、5.5。

8.派生词

8.1 收在词条内部的派生词以平行号(∥)开始。派生词包含该词条的部分用波浪号(～)代替;若派生词的读音与词条的读音相差较大,则要注音。

8.2 收在词条内部的派生词注明词类和释义,部分派生词在释义后收入词组或句子作为例证。

8.3 同一词条下的两个或数个派生词,以斜线号(/)隔开。

9.若干符号的用法

9.1 双斜线号(//)用以标注读音。

9.2 斜线号(/)用以分隔同一个释义下的多个例证、多个习语或多个派生词。

9.3 平行号(∥)用以表示词条内习语部分或派生词部分的开始。

9.4 波浪号(～)用以代替词条。

9.4 圆括号(())用于:

9.4.1 注明词的屈折变化。

9.4.2 释义时的补充说明。

9.4.3 可以省略或替换的部分。

9.4.4 归并某些词的相近的释义或用法。

10.略语表

abbr.abbreviation 缩略语   *n*.noun 名词

adj.adjective 形容词   *num*.number 数词

adv.adverb 副词   *pref*.prefix 前缀

art.article 冠词   *prep*.preposition 介词

aux.*v*.auxiliary verb 助动词 *pron*.pronoun 代词

conj.conjunction 连词   *v*.verb 动词

int.interjection 感叹词   〈美〉美式英语

infinitive marker 动词不定式符号 〈英〉英式英语

Aa

A,a/ə,eɪ/, **an**/æn/

art. ❶ one（非特指的）一（个）：a foreign guest 一位外宾 ❷ any（一类事物中）任何一个：A bicycle has two wheels. 自行车有两个轮子。 ❸ to or for each 每一（个）：six kilometers an hour 每小时六千米 ❹ the same 同一（个）：things of a kind 同类的东西

aback/ə'bæk/

adv. backwards 向后 ‖ be taken ～ 吃惊：I was taken ～ by the sudden cry. 突如其来的哭声把我吓了一跳。

abacus/'æbəkəs/

n. a frame with beads sliding on wires, for doing arithmetic 算盘：The boy used an ～ to help him solve arithmetic problems. 那个男孩借助算盘解答算术题。

abalone/ˌæbə'ləʊni/

n. a sea mollusc with a spiral shell lined with mother-of-pearl 鲍鱼

abandon/ə'bændən/

Ⅰ *v.* ❶ give up；discontinue 放弃，终止：～ a plan 放弃（终止）一项计划/～ the idea of going there 打消去那儿的念头 ❷ leave completely，never to return 离弃，抛弃，遗弃：～ one's home 离弃家园/～ one's children 遗弃儿女/～ one's friend 抛弃朋友/～ a car on the motorway 将汽车丢弃在高速公路上 ❸（～ **oneself to sth.**）give oneself up entirely to sth. 沉溺于：～ oneself to drinking（grief）酗酒无度（深陷悲痛）Ⅱ *n.* complete lack of control or inhibition 放纵，无拘束：dance（shout，sing）with ～ 纵情地跳舞（喊叫，歌唱）

abandoned /ə'bændənd/

adj. completely uncontrolled，especially in a way that is thought to be immoral 无约束的，无度的，放荡的：～ behaviour 恣意放荡的行为

abase/ə'beɪs/

v. make（especially oneself）lose self-respect；make humble 贬低，降低（尤指自己的）身份

abashed/ə'bæʃt/

adj. not sure what to do or say（usually because of the behaviour or words of other people）困窘的，局促不安的（通常由于他人的言辞或举止所致）

abate/ə'beɪt/

v. ❶ make or become less 减少，减退，减轻；降低：The storm ～d at last. 风暴终于减弱了。 ❷ do away with（decree，obstruction，etc.）废除，撤销（法令等）；除去（妨碍等）❸（of winds，storms，sounds，pain，etc.）become less strong；decrease（风暴、声音、疼痛等）减少，减轻，减退：～ the noise 减轻噪声

abattoir/'æbətwɑː(r)/

n. a place where animals are killed for food 屠宰场

abbey/'æbi/

n. ❶ building(s) in which monks or nuns live 修道院 ❷ a church which used to be a part of an abbey（e.g. Westminster Abbey，London）（曾为大修道院一部分的）大教堂（例如：伦敦威斯敏斯特教堂）

abbreviate/ə'briːvɪeɪt/

v. make shorter（usually a word or phrase）简缩，缩写（通常指词或短语）：United Kingdom can be ～d to U.K. "United Kingdom"可缩写为"U.K."。

abbreviation/əˌbriːvɪ'eɪʃn/

n. a short form of a word or phrase（词或短语的）缩写：U. K. is the ～ of/for United Kingdom. "U. K." 是 "United Kingdom"的缩写。

ABC/ˌeɪbiː'siː/

n. ❶ the alphabet，as taught to children

A

（儿童学习的）字母（表）；children learning their ～ 学习 ABC 字母（表）的儿童 ❷ the simplest facts about sth. which have to be learnt first 基础知识；入门；初阶：classes in the ～ of cooking 烹饪入门课

abdicate /ˈæbdɪkeɪt/
　v. leave an important position（usually that of a king or queen）放弃重要职位（通常是王位）；退位；让位：He ～d the throne in favour of his brother. 他把王位让给弟弟。‖ abdication /ˌæbdɪˈkeɪʃn/ n. 让位

abdomen /ˈæbdəmən/
　n. the part of the body containing the digestive organs 腹部

abduct /əbˈdʌkt, æbˈdʌkt/
　v. carry sb. away against his will（usually by force）拐走（通常用暴力）；绑架‖ abduction n. 诱拐

aberrant /æˈberənt/
　adj. ❶ changed from what is usual, expected, or right 离开正路的，脱离常轨的：～ behaviour under the influence of drugs 毒品影响下的异常举止 ❷ not like the normal type 畸变的；变态的：an ～ example of a common insect 普通昆虫畸变的例子

aberration /ˌæbəˈreɪʃn/
　n. a departure from the right or usual course 偏离正道，脱离常轨

abet /əˈbet/
　v. (-tt-) encourage or give help to（a crime or criminal）教唆，怂恿；伙同（犯罪等）：The police say he aided and ～ted the thief in robbing the bank. 警方说他伙同该匪徒抢劫银行。

abeyance /əˈbeɪəns/
　n. (usually in **in/fall into** ～) disuse or lack of use, possibly only temporary (of a custom, law, rule, etc.)（习俗、法律、规则等的）中止，不为人遵循；暂缓：The custom has fallen into ～. 这风俗已不为人们所遵循。

abhor /əbˈhɔː(r)/
　v. (-rr-) hate sth. very much especially for moral reasons 憎恶，厌恶：～ cruelty to children 憎恨虐待小孩

abhorrent /əbˈhɒrənt/
　adj. horrible or disgusting 令人厌恶的；可恶的 ‖ abhorrence n. 憎恨，厌恶

abide /əˈbaɪd/
　v. (abided or abode) ❶ keep (a law, promise, etc.) 遵守（法律、诺言等）：～ by the rules of the game 遵守比赛规则 ❷ endure or bear 忍受；容忍

abiding /əˈbaɪdɪŋ/
　adj. lasting for a long time and unlikely to change 持久的；永久的：The experience left me with an ～ hatred of dogs. 这次经历使我从此永远讨厌狗。

ability /əˈbɪləti/
　n. ❶ the power or capacity to do sth. 能力；本领 ❷ cleverness；intelligence 聪明；智慧；才能；才智：a man of great ～ 很有才智的人

abject /ˈæbdʒekt/
　adj. contemptible；very miserable or unhappy 卑鄙的；凄苦的；可怜的：The people lived in ～ poverty. 人们过着赤贫的生活。

abjure /əbˈdʒʊə(r)/
　v. make a solemn promise, especially publicly to give up (an opinion, a claim, etc.)；solemnly renounce 公开宣布放弃（主张、权利等）：They ～d their religion. 他们郑重声明放弃自己的宗教信仰。

ablaze /əˈbleɪz/
　adj. ❶ on fire 着火的 ❷ very bright 光亮的：The house was ～ with light. 这房子灯光通明。❸ full of or overflowing with an emotion 情绪激动的：His followers were ～ with enthusiasm. 他的追随者情绪激昂。

able /ˈeɪbl/
　adj. ❶ having the power, skill or means to do sth. 有能力（或技能、手段）的：The boy is ～ to dress himself. 这男孩会自己穿衣服。/ I won't be ～ to finish my homework in an hour. 我不可能在一小时内做完作业。❷ clever；skillful；capable 聪明的；能干的：an ～ student 有才能的学生；an ～ person 能人

ablutions /əˈbluːʃnz/

A

n.(*pl.*) the act of washing oneself 沐浴，
盥洗：perform one's ～ 漱洗沐浴

ably/ˈeɪbli/
*adv.*in an able manner；skillfully 能干地；
巧妙地：She controlled the meeting very
～.她很干练地负责这次会议的进行。

abnegation/ˌæbnɪˈɡeɪʃən/
*n.*lack of concern for one's own wishes 自
制，克己

abnormal/æbˈnɔːml/
*adj.*not normal；not usual 不正常的，异常
的：～ behaviour 反常行为/an ～ fear of
snakes 极其怕蛇

abnormality/ˌæbnɔːˈmælti/
n. an abnormal feature, characteristic, or
occurrence, typically in a medical context
（尤指医学上的）异常（特征、特性或情
况）：a chromosome ～ 染色体异常

aboard/əˈbɔːd/
*adv.& prep.*on (to) or in (to) a ship, an
aeroplane, a bus or a train 在船（或飞机、
车）上；上船；登机；上车

abode/əˈbəʊd/
n. the place where one lives；one's home
住所：Welcome to my humble ～! 欢迎
光临寒舍! /a person with no fixed ～ 无
固定住所的人

abolish/əˈbɒlɪʃ/
*v.*put an end to；do away with completely
革除；彻底废除；取消：～ poverty (war)
消灭贫困（战争）/～ bad customs 革除坏
习俗/～ this tax 取消这种税

abolition/ˌæbəˈlɪʃən/
n. the action of abolishing system, practice, or institution 废除：the ～ of the
death penalty 废除死刑

abominable/əˈbɒmɪnəbl/
*adj.*causing great dislike；hateful 可恶的，
令人讨厌的：～ treatment of prisoners 对
犯人令人难以忍受的待遇/The food in
this hotel is ～.这家旅馆的饭菜糟透了。

abominate/əˈbɒmɪneɪt/
*v.*hate very much；abhor 憎恨；厌恶

abomination/əˌbɒmɪˈneɪʃn/
*n.*❶ a feeling of great hatred；disgust 憎
恨；厌恶 ❷sth. that causes hatred or disgust 令人厌恶的事物

aboriginal/ˌæbəˈrɪdʒənl/
Ⅰ*adj.* of or concerning people or living
things that have existed in a place from
the earliest times 土著的：an ～ civilization 土著文明 Ⅱ*n.* an aborigine 土著居
民；土人

aborigine/ˌæbəˈrɪdʒəni/
*n.*a member of a group, tribe, etc., that
has lived in a place from the earliest
times, especially in Australia 土著居民
（尤指澳洲土著）

abort/əˈbɔːt/
*v.*❶end a pregnancy too soon, so that a
baby cannot live 使(胎儿)流产；使堕胎：
The doctor had to ～ the pregnancy.医生
不得不打掉胎儿。❷give birth to a child
or young animal too early for it to survive
流产；小产 ❸end before an expected time
because of some trouble (使)中止，夭折：
The space flight had to be ～ed because
of difficulties with the computer.由于电
脑方面的故障，这次太空飞行不得不中
止。‖ abortion *n*. 人工流产；堕胎

abortive/əˈbɔːtɪv/
adj. failing to reach the result that was
intended；unsuccessful （计划等）流产的；
夭折的；未获成功的，失败的：an ～ at-
tempt to build a railway 一项落了空的修
建铁路计划/an ～ takeover bid 一次不成
功的收购出价

abound/əˈbaʊnd/
*v.*be plentiful；be rich；exist in great numbers or quantities 有许多，富于，富有，大
量存在：Arabia ～s in oil.阿拉伯盛产石
油。/The book ～s with good stories.这
本书里都是好故事。/Fish ～s in this lake.
这湖里鱼很多。

about/əˈbaʊt/
Ⅰ*prep.* ❶ round, near to 在……周围；
在……附近；在……身边 ❷here and there
到处；四处；在……各处：We walked ～ the
town.我们在城里四处走走。❸concerning
对于，关于：What are you talking ～? 你们
在谈什么？Ⅱ*adv.* ❶ near 周围；附近；到处
❷nearly, almost 大约；差不多：About 100
people were present on that day.那天大约有
100 人在场。❸approximately；near in time,

A

size, number, etc.(时间、尺寸、数量等)近于

above /əˈbʌv/

Ⅰ *prep.* ❶(of a place or position) higher than (位置、职位等)在……上面 ❷higher in rank or power than (地位)高于;(权力)大于 ❸too good for 太好而无法:~ reproach 无可指责❹higher or more than (a specified amount or norm) 高于;超出 (特定数量或标准):I'm a head ~ you.我比你高一个头。Ⅱ *adv.* ❶ in or to a higher place 在上面;以上 ❷on an earlier page or higher on the same page 上述,在上文:I want to quote something ~.我想引用上文中的一些东西。

aboveboard /əˌbʌvˈbɔːd/

adj. legal and honest 公开的;光明正大的:Don't worry, it's all open and ~.别担心,一切都是光明正大的。

abrade /əˈbreɪd/

v. wear away by hard rubbing 磨掉

abrasion /əˈbreɪʒn/

n. the process of rubbing away of a surface 表面磨损:an ~ of the skin 皮肤的擦伤处

abrasive /əˈbreɪsɪv/

Ⅰ *adj.* ❶ causing the process of wearing away of a surface 磨损的 ❷ causing annoyance or dislike; rough 招人讨厌的;粗暴的 Ⅱ *n.* a substance, such as sand, used for cleaning, polishing, or removing a surface 磨料(砂粒等)

abreast /əˈbrest/

adv. side by side 并列,并排,并肩:walk two ~ 两人并行行走 ‖ **keep(stay, be) ~ of (with) sth.** 及时了解新事物,跟上形势:be ~ of the news 及时获悉消息

abridge /əˈbrɪdʒ/

v. make (sth. written or spoken) shorter by using fewer words (文章、讲话等)压缩,删节:The book is ~d from the original.这书是原作的缩写本。

abridg(e)ment /əˈbrɪdʒmənt/

n. ❶ sth., such as a book or play, that has been made shorter 节本:an ~ for radio in five parts 供电台广播用的分五部分的节本 ❷ the act of making sth. shorter 节略,压缩

abroad /əˈbrɔːd/

adv. ❶in or to a foreign country 在国外;到国外:go ~ 出国 ❷ in all directions; widely 遍布;到处:The news soon spread ~.消息很快就传开了。

abrogate /ˈæbrəgeɪt/

v. put an end to the force of (a law, an agreement, etc.) 撤销;废除(法律、协议等):~ a law(a treaty) 废除法律(条约)

abrupt /əˈbrʌpt/

adj. ❶ very sudden and unexpected 突然的;出其不意的 ❷ bad tempered; unfriendly 粗鲁的;不礼貌的:His ~ reply hurt her.他粗鲁的回答伤害了她。

abscess /ˈæbsɪs/

n. a painful swelling in some part of the body, containing a thick liquid called pus 脓肿

absence /ˈæbsəns/

n. ❶the state or a period of being away or not present 不在,缺席;外出期,缺席的时间:~ from school (home) 缺课(离家)/ during one's ~ 在某人离开期间/an ~ of an hour 离开一小时 ❷a lack of sth.; the fact of being without sth. 缺乏;无:in the ~ of information 资料缺乏/~ of mind 心不在焉

absent

Ⅰ /ˈæbsənt/*adj.* not here, not present 不在的,缺席的:be ~ from work 不上班 ‖ **~-minded** *adj.* 心不在焉的 Ⅱ /əbˈsent/ *v.*(~ **oneself from**) not go to or be in a place 缺席;不到;不参加:He ~ed himself from the meeting.他没有到会。‖ ~ly *adv.* 心不在焉地

absentee /ˌæbsənˈtiː/

n. a person who is not present at a place where he or she is expected to be 缺席者:There were many ~s from the meeting.这次会议有很多人缺席。

absolute /ˈæbsəluːt/

adj. ❶complete; total 绝对的,完全的 ❷ not limited 不受限制(或约束)的 ❸definite and undoubted 明确的;不容置疑的 ‖ ~ness *n.*绝对

absolutely /ˈæbsəluːtli/

adv. ❶ completely; totally 完全地:I trust

her discretion ～.我完全相信她的判断。/It's difficult to cross the desert by car,but not ～ impossible.乘小汽车穿过沙漠是有困难,但并非完全不可能。❷ certainly 是那样;当然:"Do you think so?""Absolutely!""你认为是这样吗?" "当然!"

absolution/ˌæbsə'luːʃn/
*n.*❶release from sin,punishment or obligation(罪、惩罚、责任的)解除,免除;赦免 ❷a declaration of forgiveness for a sin 宣布赦罪

absolutism/'æbsəluːtɪzəm/
*n.*a political system or principle in which unlimited power is held by one ruler 专制主义(制度);独裁政治

absolve/əb'zɒlv,əb'sɒlv/
*v.*declare free from sin,guilt or responsibility 赦免……的罪;免除……的责任

absorb/əb'sɔːb,əb'zɔːb/
*v.*❶take or suck in 吸收 ❷attract the attention 吸引(注意力);使全神贯注 ❸(of a country or an organization) make (a smaller country or an organization) into a part of itself(国家或组织)把……并入;同化

absorbed/əb'sɔːbd/
*adj.*very interested in sth.or sb. so that you are not paying attention to anything else 被……吸引住;专心致志;全神贯注:She seemed totally ～ in the book.她好像完全被这本书迷住了。

absorbent/əb'sɔːbənt/
Ⅰ*adj.*that is able to absorb 有吸收能力的:put an ～ dressing on a cut 在伤口上敷上吸水性敷料 Ⅱ*n.*a substance or an item that absorbs liquid easily 吸收剂

absorbing/əb'sɔːbɪŋ/
*adj.*taking all one's attention;very interesting 非常吸引人的;引人入胜的:an ～ task 一项很吸引人的任务

absorption/əb'sɔːpʃən/
*n.*❶ the process or action by which one thing absorbs or is absorbed by another 吸收;合并:shock ～ 减震 ❷the fact or state of being engrossed in sth.吸引;专注:her ～ in the problems of the Third World 她对第三世界问题的专注

abstain/əb'steɪn/
*v.*stop using sth.;not use sth. (often for the sake of one's health) 禁绝;戒除(常为了健康):～ from alcohol 戒酒

abstemious/əb'stiːmɪəs/
*adj.*not taking too much food,drink,etc. (饮食等)有节制的

abstinence/'æbstɪnəns/
n. the practice of not taking too much food,drink,etc.(饮食等方面的)节制

abstract
Ⅰ/'æbstrækt/*adj.*existing in thought and separated from what is real or concrete 抽象的:～ art 抽象艺术 Ⅱ/'æbstrækt/*n.* ❶ a shortened form of a statement, speech, etc. 摘要;概括 ❷ an abstract painting,drawing,or other work of art; an abstract term or idea 抽象艺术作品;抽象名称(或概念) Ⅲ/əb'strækt/ *v.* ❶ make a shortened form (of a statement, speech,etc.) by separating out what is important 摘录;节录 ❷steal 偷窃

abstracted/æb'stræktɪd/
adj. not noticing what is happening or deep in thought 分心的;出神的 ‖ ～ly *adv.*心不在焉地

abstraction/æb'strækʃn/
*n.*❶an idea of a quality considered separately from any particular object or case 抽象(化);抽象概念 ❷the state of not noticing what is happening;being absent-minded 出神;心不在焉

abstruse/əb'struːs/
*adj.*difficult to understand 深奥的;难懂的:an ～ theory 深奥的理论

absurd/əb'sɜːd/
*adj.*unreasonable;foolish;ridiculous 不合理的,愚蠢的,可笑的:an ～ suggestion (mistake) 不合理的建议(可笑的错误) ‖ absurdity *n.* 荒唐可笑(的事)

abundance/ə'bʌndəns/
*n.*a copious supply or great amount ;plenty 丰足;大量:an ～ of skilled workers 大量的熟练工人/food in ～ 充足的食物

abundant/ə'bʌndənt/
*adj.*more than enough;plentiful 丰富的;充裕的:The country has ～ supplies of

A

oil and gas.这个国家的石油和天然气供应非常充足。‖ ～**ly** *adv.*大量地 ‖ ～**ly clear** 非常明白：She made it ～ly clear that she wanted me to leave.她非常清楚地表示，她要我离开。

abuse

Ⅰ/ə'bjuːz/*v.* ❶ make bad use of; use wrongly 滥用；妄用 ❷ treat badly; speak very roughly to 虐待；凌辱；辱骂 Ⅱ /ə'bjuːs/ *n.*❶ the improper or wrong use of sth.; misuse 滥用；妄用 ❷cruel and violent treatment; insulting and offensive language 虐待；凌辱；辱骂 ❸bad practice of custom 陋习；弊病

abusive/ə'bjuːsɪv/

*adj.*using or containing unkind, cruel, or rude language 辱骂性的；骂人的 ‖ ～**ly** *adv.*辱骂地/～**ness** *n.*滥用；咒骂

abut/ə'bʌt/

v.(of land or buildings)lie next to or touch on one side （土地、房屋等）邻接，紧靠：Their garden ～s on ours.他们的园子紧挨着我们的园子。

abysmal/ə'bɪzməl/

*adj.*very bad; extreme; utter 很坏的；极度的：～ food 很差的食物/ ～ ignorance 极度的无知

abyss/ə'bɪs/

*n.*a very deep hole 深渊，深坑

academic/ˌækə'demɪk/

Ⅰ*adj.*❶referring to schools, colleges or scholarship 学校的；学院的；学术性的 ❷ very theoretical, of little practical use 纯理论的；不切实际的：an idea which is of ～ interest only 一个仅有理论意义的想法 Ⅱ*n.*a scholar; a person who teaches in a university 学者；大学教师

academy/ə'kædəmi/

*n.*❶ a school for higher special training （高等）专科院校 ❷a society for cultivating art, literature, etc.of which membership is an honour 研究院；学会：the Chinese Academy of Sciences 中国科学院

accede/æk'siːd/

*v.*agree to; say yes to 同意；答应：He ～d to any request.他有求必应。

accelerate/ək'seləreɪt/

*v.*❶(cause to) become faster (使)加快：～ the heartbeat 使心率加快/The car suddenly ～d.汽车突然加速。❷(cause to) happen earlier (使)提早发生：The bad weather ～d our departure.天气不好，我们只得提早启程。

acceleration/əkˌselə'reɪʃn/

*n.*increase in the rate or speed of sth.加速；加快：a car with good ～ 加速性能好的汽车

accelerator/ək'seləreɪtə(r)/

*n.*❶the instrument in a machine or vehicle (especially a car)which is used to increase its speed 加速器；加速装置；油门：He put his foot down hard on the ～.他用劲踩油门踏板。❷a machine for making particles move very quickly 粒子加速器

accent

Ⅰ/'æksent/*n.*❶a stress given to a syllable or word in speech (音节或单词的)重音；重读：This word has its ～ on the third syllable.这个单词的重音在第三个音节上。❷an individual, local or national way of pronunciation 口音，土音：a strong American ～ 很重的美国口音 ❸a special emphasis 注重；强调：a biology course with an ～ on laboratory work 注重实验的生物学课程 Ⅱ /æk'sent/ *v.*pronounce with an accent 重读：Accent the word "academy" on the second syllable.重读"academy"的第二个音节。

accented/'æksentɪd/

*adj.*❶spoken with or characterized by a particular accent 带口音的：He spoke in slightly ～ English.他说英语时稍微有些口音。❷(of a word or syllable) stressed (词或音节)重读的

accentuate/æk'sentʃueɪt/

*v.*pronounce a word or syllable with special force or emphasis 以重音读出，重读

accept/ək'sept/

*v.*❶ take or receive sth.offered 接受：～ an invitation 接受邀请 ❷ admit; recognize; agree to; believe 承认；认可；相信

acceptable/ək'septəbl/

adj. ❶ worth accepting; pleasing or satisfactory 值得接受的；合意的：His work is ~.他的工作是令人满意的。❷ welcome 受欢迎的：It would be very ~ as a present. 它会作为礼物大受欢迎的。‖ **acceptably** *adv.* 可接受地；合意地

acceptance/ək'septəns/
n. ❶ the act of accepting or being accepted 接受；收受；承认；认可 ❷ favour; approval 赞同；赞成：gain ~ for one's ideas 使某人的想法获得赞同 ❸ (in business) an agreement to pay (商业上)承兑(票据等)

access/'ækses/
n. ❶ a way to enter a place 入径；通路 ❷ the opportunity to use sth. 使用机会：have easy ~ to sth. 容易得到某物 ‖ ~ **road** *n.* (干道的)支路/~ **speed** *n.* (计算机)存取速度/~ **time** *n.* (计算机)存取时间

accessible/ək'sesəbl/
adj. ❶ easy to reach, enter, or obtain sth. 容易达到的；易接近的；易取得的：The island is ~ only by boat. 这岛只有乘小艇才能去。❷ easy and friendly to talk to 随和的；平易近人的：A manager should be ~ to his/her staff. 经理应该让职员感到平易近人。

accession/æk'seʃn/
n. the act of taking up one's post 就职；就任；即位：~ to power 掌权

accessory/ək'sesəri/
n. sth. which is added to the main thing (especially parts of a motorcar such as lights, windscreen wipers, radio, etc.; parts of a woman's costume such as shoes, hat, handbag, etc.) 附件；附属品(尤指汽车的附件，如车灯、自动雨刷、收音机等；妇女装束的配饰，如鞋子、帽子、手提包等)

accident/'æksɪdənt/
n. sth.unfortunate and undesirable 意外事件；偶然事件；事故：a traffic ~ 交通事故 ‖ **by** ~ 偶然地/**without** ~ 平安无事地

accidental/ˌæksɪ'dentl/
adj. happening or done unexpectedly or by chance 偶然的；意外的；无意的：an ~ visit 一次偶然的访问

acclaim/ə'kleɪm/
v. applaud loudly for 向……欢呼，为……喝彩：The crowd ~ed him a hero. 人群欢呼着称他为英雄。‖ **acclamation** *n.* 欢呼；喝彩

acclimatize/ə'klaɪmətaɪz/
v. become or make sb. or sth. accustomed to a change of climate or surroundings (使)适应；(使)习惯；(使)服水土：John soon became ~d to the heat in India. 约翰很快就适应印度的炎热。

accommodate/ə'kɒmədeɪt/
v. ❶ supply with lodgings, or food and lodgings 提供住宿(或膳宿)：I can ~ you for a few nights.你可以在我这儿留宿几晚。❷ have (enough) room for (足以)容纳：The car can ~ five passengers. 这辆车可载五名乘客。❸ make suitable; adapt 使适合(应)：~ our plans to their arrangements 使我们的计划与他们的安排一致 ❹ supply; help to sb. 提供帮助：~ someone with money 借钱给某人

accommodating/ə'kɒmədeɪtɪŋ/
adj. willing to help or fit in with other people's wishes or demands 与人方便的；乐于助人的

accommodation/əˌkɒmə'deɪʃn/
n. ❶ a place to live or work in (house, flat, hotel room, etc.) 住处；办公处(房子、房间、旅店等)：The travel agent fixed up our ~.旅行社为我们安排了住处。/ office ~ 办公用房/the high cost of rented ~ in London 伦敦昂贵的租用房 ❷ the settling of a disagreement 和解：efforts to reach an ~ with the US over imports 为在进口货物方面同美国达成和解所做的努力

accompaniment/ə'kʌmpənɪmənt/
n. ❶ sth. which is used or provided with sth. else, especially in order to improve it 伴随物；附属物：A green salad makes a good ~ to this dish. 一碟生拌凉菜是这道菜的上好配菜。❷ music played at the same time as singing or to support another instrument (歌唱等的)伴奏：play a piano ~ 弹钢琴伴奏/The election results were announced to the ~ of loud cheering.在一片欢呼声中宣布了选举结果。

A

accompanist/əˈkʌmpənɪst/

n. a person who plays a musical accompaniment 伴奏者

accompany/əˈkʌmpəni/

v. ❶ go with sb. as a companion 陪伴,陪同:The Prime Minister's wife accompanied him when he visited the northern region.首相夫人陪同首相巡视北部地区。 ❷ play music while someone sings or plays on a different instrument 为……伴奏:John accompanied his wife on the piano.约翰为他的妻子作钢琴伴奏。

accomplice/əˈkʌmplɪs/

n. a person who helps sb. else to do sth.(especially sth. wrong) 同谋,帮凶

accomplish/əˈkʌmplɪʃ/

v. carry out successfully 完成,实现,做成功:He ~ed a great deal during his first year.他在第一年里取得很大的成就。 ‖ ~ed *adj.* 有造诣的;有技艺的(尤指在音乐、舞蹈、谈吐等方面):Jane is a very ~ed dancer.珍妮是一个技巧娴熟的舞蹈演员。 / ~ment *n.* 造诣;技艺

accord/əˈkɔːd/

Ⅰ *v.* ❶ give or grant sb.(welcome, praise, etc.)给予(欢迎、称颂等) ❷ be harmonious or agree with sth.符合;(与……)一致 Ⅱ *n.* ❶ agreement or harmony 一致;和谐 ❷ a treaty or agreement(between countries)(国家之间的)协定,条约 ‖ of one's own ~自愿地;主动地

accordance/əˈkɔːdəns/

n.(in ~ with)according to 依照;根据:in ~ with the rules(an order, one's wishes)根据规章(根据一项命令,遵照某人的意愿)

according/əˈkɔːdɪŋ/

adv.(~ to)❶ in a manner corresponding or conforming to 按照;依照:cook the rice ~ to the instructions 按照说明煮饭 ❷ in proportion or relation to 视……而定,按照:Salary will be fixed ~ to experience.按照资历确定薪金。

accordingly/əˈkɔːdɪŋli/

adv. ❶ as the stated circumstances suggest 相应地,按照:I'm an adult and I expect to be treated ~.我是个大人了,希望

像对待大人一样对待我。 ❷ consequently;therefore 因此,于是:He was asked to go, and ~ he left at once.人家请他走,于是他马上就离开了。

accordion/əˈkɔːdɪən/

n. a musical instrument that is pressed in from each side so that the air in the middle part is forced through holes that can be opened and closed to produce different sounds 手风琴

accost/əˈkɒst/

v. go and speak to a stranger(especially in a public place and in a troublesome or unpleasant way)跟陌生人搭讪(尤指在公共场所进行的令人厌烦或不愉快的攀谈):A stranger ~ed me in the street yesterday and asked for money.昨天在街上一位陌生人跟我搭讪并向我要钱。

account/əˈkaʊnt/

Ⅰ *n.* ❶ a record or statement of money(to be)paid or received 账,账目 ❷ an arrangement that sb. has with a bank for keeping and taking out of money, etc. 账户 ❸ a report or description of an event, person, etc.(关于事件、人物等的)报道,叙述,描写 ❹ reason;cause 原因,理由 ‖ by all ~s 据说;大家都说/on ~(货物)赊账;(钱)部分支付/on ~ of 因为/on no ~ 决不/on one's own ~ 靠自己(的钱财)Ⅱ *v.* ❶ provide a satisfactory record, especially of money received and paid out 说出(钱等的)用途 ❷ be an explanation of 说明(原因等);是……原因 ❸ consider or regard 认为;看作:We ~ her a clever girl.我们认为她是个聪明的女孩。/call to ~ 要求做出解释 ‖ ~ing *n.* 会计(学);结账,结算;账单

accountable/əˈkaʊntəbl/

adj. responsible;having to give an explanation for one's actions;answerable 负有责任的;(对自己的行动)有解释义务的:If anything happens to the car, I will hold you ~.这辆车要是出什么问题,我就唯你是问。/Should the police be more ~ to the public? 警方该不该对公众负有更大的责任?

accountancy/əˈkaʊntənsi/

n. the work or profession of an accountant

会计工作：a degree in ～ 会计学位

accountant/əˈkaʊntənt/

n. a person whose profession is to control and examine the money accounts of businesses 会计；会计师

accredit/əˈkredɪt/

v. ❶ give credit to sb. for sth. 相信；认可：He was ～ed with being one of the world's fastest sprinters. 他被公认为世界上最快的短跑选手之一。❷（～ sth. to sb.）attribute an action, saying, or quality to 把(行动，言论，特性)归于：The discovery of distillation is usually ～ed to the Arabs. 蒸馏法通常被认为是阿拉伯人发现的。❸(of an official body) give authority or sanction to sb. or sth. when recognized standards have been met (官方机构)授权，批准 ❹ give official authorization for (sb., typically a diplomat or journalist to be in a particular place or to hold a particular post)任命，委派(某人，尤指外交官或记者)：the ambassadors ～ed to Baghdad 派驻巴格达的大使

accredited/əˈkredɪtɪd/

adj. ❶ officially representing one's government in a foreign country, with official permission to be sth. 对外代表本国政府的；官方认可的 ❷ having the power to act for an organization 得到(某一组织)授权的：an ～ representative of the firm 公司的授权代表 ❸ officially recognized as reaching a certain standard or quality 公认为合格的；达到标准的：～ milk from a herd of healthy cows 由一群健康奶牛生产的合格牛奶

accrue/əˈkruː/

v. increase in size or amount (especially with reference to money) 增大；增多(尤指金钱)：A large sum should ～ to you by the end of the year. 到年底你会增加一大笔收入。

accumulate/əˈkjuːmjʊleɪt/

v. make or become greater in quantity 积累；积聚 ‖ **accumulation** *n.* 积聚物；堆积物：an accumulation of work while I was ill 我生病时积压下来的工作

accumulative/əˈkjuːmjʊlətɪv/

adj. increasing by successive addition 积累的；渐增的 ‖ ～**ly** *adv.* 累积地

accumulator/əˈkjuːmjʊleɪtə(r)/

n. ❶ a part of a computer where the results of what has been calculated are stored (电子计算机的)累加器 ❷ a type of battery which can take in new supplies of electricity so that it has enough power to keep working 蓄电池

accuracy/ˈækjərəsi/

n. the quality of being precise; exactness or correctness 精确(性)；准确(度)：the ～ of his account 他讲话的准确性/to throw darts with pinpoint ～ 掷飞镖准确到不差分毫

accurate/ˈækjərət/

adj. exactly correct 准确的；精确的：Her report of what happened was ～ in every detail. 她对发生的情况所做的报告准确反映了全部细节。/Is the station clock ～? 火车站的钟准吗？

accusation/ˌækjuːˈzeɪʃn/

n. a statement saying that sb. has done sth. illegal or wrong 指控；指责：make an (a false) ～ of murder against someone 诬告某人犯有谋杀罪

accuse/əˈkjuːz/

v. charge (someone) with doing wrong or breaking the law 控告；谴责：The police ～d him of murder. 警方告他谋杀。

accused/əˈkjuːzd/

adj. charged with doing sth. illegal or wrong 被指责的；被控告的：The company stands ～ of failing to safeguard the public. 这家公司被控告未能保护公众的利益。/The ～ (man) was asked to give his name. 被告被要求说出自己的姓名。/Several of the ～ were found guilty. 被告中有数人被判定有罪。

accustom/əˈkʌstəm/

v. make used to 使习惯：～ oneself to eating poor food 使自己习惯于食用粗劣食物 ‖ **be (get)**～**ed to** 习惯于：I am ～ed to looking after myself. 我习惯于自己照顾自己。/You must try to get ～ed to the work. 你必须设法适应这份工作。

A

accustomed/əˈkʌstəmd/
　　adj. ❶ in the habit of;used to 习惯于⋯⋯的:I'm not ~ to getting up so early.我不习惯于这样早起床。❷ regular;usual 惯常的:sitting in her ~ place at the head of the table 坐在她惯常坐的桌子首位

ace/eɪs/
　　n. ❶ a playing card with a large single symbol on it,ranked as the highest card (纸牌的)A 纸牌 ❷ a person who is very good at sth.能手,高手

ache/eɪk/
　　Ⅰ *v.* ❶ feel a continuous dull pain (连续隐隐地)疼痛:My head ~d badly.我头痛得很厉害。❷ be eager;long for 渴望:He ~s to see her again.他渴望能再见她一次。/~ for home 渴望回家 Ⅱ *n.* a continuous dull pain (连续隐隐的)疼痛:have a stomach~ 胃痛

achieve/əˈtʃiːv/
　　v. succeed in doing sth. or reaching a desired goal,level or standard 完成;实现;获得:~ success (one's purpose) 获得成功(达到目的)/~ wonders 创造奇迹

achievement/əˈtʃiːvmənt/
　　n. ❶ the process or fact of achieving sth. 完成;实现;获得:the ~ of one's purpose 目标的实现 ❷ sth. done successfully,especially by effort or skill 成就;成绩:He was awarded the Nobel Prize for ~s in physics.他因物理学方面的成就而获得诺贝尔奖。

acid/ˈæsɪd/
　　Ⅰ *adj.* ❶ sour 酸的;酸味的 ❷ (of a person's remarks) critical and severe (言辞)尖刻的 Ⅱ *n.* sth. which has a pH value less than seven,usually a liquid,can burn or sour the thing it touches 酸 ‖ ~ **rain** *n.* 酸雨 ‖ **acidic**/əˈsɪdɪk/*adj.* 酸的;酸性的

acidify/əˈsɪdɪfaɪ/
　　v. make sth. acid,or to become acid (使)酸化,变酸:Pollutants can ~ surface water.污染物质能使地表水酸化。

acidity/əˈsɪdɪti/
　　n. ❶ the level of acid in substances such as water,soil or wine (水、土壤或酒的)酸度 ❷ bitterness or sharpness in a person's

remarks or tone (人的话语或口吻)尖刻,尖酸:the cutting ~ in the voice 语气中带的尖酸

acidly/ˈæsɪdli/
　　adv. with bitterness or sarcasm 尖刻地,挖苦地:"Is it up to you to make that decision?"She asked ~."轮得着你来做出那个决定了么?"她挖苦道。

acknowledge/əkˈnɒlɪdʒ/
　　v. ❶ admit or accept 承认;接受 ❷ make known that one has received 告知收到 ❸ express thanks for 对⋯⋯表示感谢

acknowledg(e)ment/əkˈnɒlɪdʒmənt/
　　n. ❶ an act of accepting that sth. exists or is true,or that sth. is there (对事实、现实、存在的)承认:This report is an ~ of the problem.这个报告承认了问题的严重性。❷ an act or a statement expressing thanks to sb.;sth. that is given to sb. as thanks 感谢;谢礼

acme/ˈækmi/
　　n. the highest point of development,success,etc.(发展、成就等)顶点:the ~ of perfection 尽善尽美

acne/ˈækni/
　　n. a skin condition that produces spots or pimples,usually on the face of adolescents 粉刺;痤疮

acorn/ˈeɪkɔːn/
　　n. the nut or seed of an oak tree 橡树果实;橡子

acoustic/əˈkuːstɪk/
　　adj. ❶ of sound or the sense of hearing 声音的;听觉的:the ~ nerve 听觉神经 ❷ (especially of a musical instrument) making its natural sound,not helped by electrical apparatus (尤指乐器)原声的,不经过电子设备传声的:an ~ guitar 原声吉他

acoustics/əˈkuːstɪks/
　　n. ❶ the scientific study of sound 声学 ❷ the qualities of a place,especially a hall,which influence the way sounds can be heard in it (礼堂等的)音响效果,音质

acquaint/əˈkweɪnt/
　　v. make sb. familiar with or aware of sth. 使熟悉;使了解:~ oneself with the new

job 使自己熟悉新工作/～ someone with the new decision 把新决定通知某人/I'll ～ you with my wife when she arrives.我夫人来后我会介绍你与她认识。‖ **be (get, become)** ～**ed (with sb. or sth.)**(开始)熟悉;(开始)相识: be ～ed with the new rules 熟悉新规章/ Let's get ～ed (with each other).我们互相认识认识吧。

acquaintance/əˈkweɪntəns/
　*n.*❶knowledge of sth.熟悉;相识;了解:I have no ～ with him.我和他不相识。❷a person or persons one knows slightly 相识的人:He has a wide circle of ～s,but few real friends.他认识的人不少,但真正的朋友几乎没有。‖ **make the ～ of sb.**, **make sb.'s ～** 结识某人:Where did you make the ～ of the foreigner? 你在什么地方与那位外国人结识的?

acquiesce/ˌækwɪˈes/
　*v.*accept or agree sth.reluctantly without protest or argument 勉强同意;默许:He ～d in the arrangements which I had made.他勉强同意我所做的安排。

acquire/əˈkwaɪə(r)/
　*v.*gain or come to possess sth.,especially by one's own work,skill,or action,often over a long period of time (尤指通过个人的工作、技艺、行动等而)取得,获得,得到:I managed to ～ two tickets for the concert.我设法弄到了两张音乐会的票。/The company has recently ～d new offices in central London.公司最近在伦敦市中心得到了新的办公室。/to ～ a mannerism 养成独特的习惯

acquisition/ˌækwɪˈzɪʃn/
　*n.*❶the act of getting sth.获得:the ～ of knowledge (property) 知识的获得(财富的占有) ❷buying or obtaining assets or objects 资产购置,购得物,获得物:The house is one of his latest ～s.这栋房子是他最近添置的财产之一。

acquit/əˈkwɪt/
　v.(-tt-) ❶decide by a trial or investigation that sb. is not guilty of some crime or wrongdoing 宣判……无罪:He was ～ted of the robbery.他被宣判没有犯抢劫罪。❷do one's duty satisfactorily 履行;完成:He has ～ted himself very well in his

new job.他出色地完成了他的新任务。

acre/ˈeɪkə(r)/
　*n.*a unit for measuring the area of land (4,840 square yards or approximately 4,050 square metres) 英亩(等于 4840 平方码或约 4050 平方米)

acrid/ˈækrɪd/
　*adj.*❶ having a sharp, bitter smell or taste (气味等)辛辣的;刺激的 ❷ angry and bitter 愤怒刻薄的 ‖ **～ity**/əˈkrɪdəti/ *n.*辛辣,尖刻的批评/**～ness** *n.*辛辣;刻薄

acrimony/ˈækrɪməni/
　*n.*bitterness, as of feelings or words (态度、语言等的)尖刻,讥讽:They parted without ～.他们分手时没有相互反唇相讥。‖ **acrimonious**/ˌækrɪˈməʊniəs/ *adj.*尖刻的,讥讽的;激烈的:an acrimonious dispute 唇枪舌剑式的争辩

acrobat/ˈækrəbæt/
　*n.*an entertainer who performs difficult gymnastic feats 杂技演员

acrobatic/ˌækrəˈbætɪk/
　*adj.*of or like an acrobat;moving or changing position quickly and easily,especially in the air 杂技(似)的

acrobatics/ˌækrəˈbætɪks/
　*n.*❶the art and tricks of an acrobat 杂技 ❷ a group of acrobatic tricks considered as a performance 杂技表演

across/əˈkrɒs/
　I *prep.*❶from one side to the other side of sth. 横过;穿过 ❷ on the other side of sth.在……的对面:There is a bank ～ the street.街对面有家银行。‖ **come ～** 碰到/**put ～** 哄骗 II *adv.*from one side to the other side 横过;宽:Can you swim ～? 你能游过去吗? ‖ **get sb. ～** 使人理解/**put sth. ～** 讲清楚

act/ækt/
　I *v.*❶do sth.or take action 做事;(采取)行动:Act now before it is too late.趁还不太迟,马上行动。❷have an effect;work 奏效;起作用:The medicine ～s well.这药功效甚佳。❸behave (like) 表现,举止(像……):～ strangely (bravely) 行为古怪(表现英勇) ❹be an actor or actress;play the part of 演(戏);扮演;表演:He is

A

~ing (in) Othello tonight.他今晚扮演奥赛罗。❺ pretend to be 假装；～ calm (surprised) 装作冷静（假装吃惊） ‖ ～ as 担任，充当：～ as a guide 担任导游/ ～ for 代表；代理：He ~ed for me during my absence.我离开期间由他代理。/~ on(upon) ❶遵行：~ on one's advice 按某人的建议行事 ❷对……有作用（影响）：Water ~s on iron and makes it rust.水可作用于铁而使它生锈。 Ⅱ n.❶a thing being or to be done 行为；举动：a heroic ~ 英勇行为 ❷a main division of a play, an opera, etc.(戏剧、歌剧等的)幕：a two-~ play/a play in two ~s 两幕剧 ❸a formal decision；a law 正式决定；法令：pass an ~ 通过一项法令 ‖ in the ~ (of doing sth.)正在(做某事)：He was caught in the ~ of stealing a wallet.他在偷钱包的时候被抓住了。

acting¹ /ˈæktɪŋ/
　adj. appointed to carry out the duties of an office or position for a short time (在职务上)代理的：Our director is in hospital, but the ~ director can see you.我们的局长住院了，不过代理局长可以见你。

acting² /ˈæktɪŋ/
　n. the art or profession of representing a character, especially in a play or for a film or on television 表演；演戏；扮演

action /ˈækʃn/
　*n.*❶ the fact or process of doing sth. 行动，行动过程：a decisive ~ 果断的行动/ take ~ 采取行动/We need ~s, not words.我们需要行动而不是空话。❷a legal process 诉讼：bring(an) ~ against someone 对某人提出起诉 ❸a military engagement 作战，战斗：a naval ~ 一次海战/The general has seen ~ in three wars.这位将军在三次战争中参加过战斗。

actionable /ˈækʃnəbl/
　adj. giving enough cause for a charge in a court of law 可控诉的；可起诉的：I regard these allegations as ~.我认为对这些诬陷可以提出起诉。

activate /ˈæktɪveɪt/
　v. make active；cause to work or operate 使活动；刺激；启动：~ public opinion 使

舆论活跃/These push buttons ~ the elevator.这些按钮可启动这电梯。

active /ˈæktɪv/
　*adj.*❶ moving or tending to move about vigorously or frequently 活跃的；积极的 ❷ doing sth. regularly；functioning 定期进行的；起作用的 ❸ (of a verb or sentence) having the person or thing doing the action as the subject (动词或句子)主动的 ❹having a chemical effect 起化学作用的；活性的 ‖ ~ service *n.*现役 ‖ ~ly *adv.*积极地；活跃地/activist *n.*积极分子

activity /ækˈtɪvəti/
　*n.*❶a situation in which things are happening or being done(事情发生的)状况 ❷a thing (to be) done in order to achieve a particular aim (为达到一定目的而进行的)活动

actor /ˈæktə(r)/
　*n.*a man who acts in plays, films, on radio or television (戏剧、电影、电台或电视的)演员

actress /ˈæktrɪs/
　*n.*a female actor 女演员：She is a good ~.她是一个好演员。

actual /ˈæktʃʊəl/
　adj. existing as a real fact 实际的；现实的；事实上的

actuality /ˌæktʃʊˈæləti/
　*n.*❶the state of being real；existence 现实(性)；实在 ❷sth. that is real；a fact 事实；实际情况

actually /ˈæktʃʊəli/
　adv. ❶ (used to emphasize that sth. someone has said or done is surprising) in actual fact 实际上；居然，竟然：She says it's a good film, though she hasn't ~ seen it.她说这是部好电影,尽管她实际上并没有看过它。/Yes, I know he looks very young, but he's ~ 45.是的,我知道他看起来很年轻,但实际上他45岁了。/He not only invited me in but he ~ offered me a drink! 他不但请我进去,而且竟然请我喝了杯酒。❷used in conversation, sometimes when one is disagreeing or complaining, but often without any

real meaning（用于会话,有时是在不同意或不满意时使用,但常常并不具有实际含义）:You ～ owe me a little more than this.你欠我的可比这要多一些。/ "Yes, she's very nice.""Well,～, I don't like her very much." "是的,她是个好人。""唔,不过,我不是很喜欢她。"

actuate/ˈæktʃʊeɪt/

*v.*cause（sb.）to act;activate or motivate 使(某人)(行动);驱使;激励:He is ～d not by kindness but by ambition.他并非为好心所驱使,而是出于个人野心。

acuity/əˈkjuːəti/

*n.*fineness or sharpness,especially of the mind or the senses of sight or hearing (思维、视觉、听觉等的)灵敏,敏锐

acumen/ˈækjʊmen,əˈkjuːmən/

*n.*the ability to think clearly and quickly and to make correct decisions 敏锐;聪明;才干:He showed great business ～. 他很有业务才干。

acute/əˈkjuːt/

adj. ❶severe or intense 严重的;剧烈的:～ pain 剧痛/an ～ illness 急性疾病 ❷ having a perceptive understanding or insight 精明的;敏锐的:an ～ sense of hearing 敏锐的听觉/a very ～ criticism 一针见血的批评 ‖ ～ly *adv.*尖锐地;剧烈地

ad/æd/

*n.*a short form of advertisement（advertisement 的缩写形式)广告

adage/ˈædɪdʒ/

*n.*an old and well-known wise saying;proverb 格言;谚语

adagio/əˈdɑːdʒɪəʊ/

*n.*a piece of music played slowly 慢板;柔板乐章

adamant/ˈædəmənt/

adj. determined; unwilling to change one's decision or opinion 坚定不移的;固执的 ‖ ～ly *adv.*坚定不移地;固执地

adapt/əˈdæpt/

v. ❶ make or become suitable for new needs,different conditions,etc.使适应;使适合 ❷ change a book or play to make it become a film,TV play,etc.;rewrite 改编;改写 ‖ ～ation *n.*改编(本);改造(物);适应

adaptable/əˈdæptəbl/

*adj.*able to change so as to be suitable for new needs,different conditions,etc.能适应的;适应性强的

adaptor(-er)/əˈdæptə(r)/

n. ❶ a person who adapts a book,play or film 改编者 ❷ a plug that makes it possible to use more than one piece of electrical equipment from a single socket (电器的)多功能插头,多头插头 ❸ a device for connecting pieces of equipment that cannot be connected directly 连接器;适配器

add/æd/

v. ❶put sth. together so as to increase 增加;添加:～ a name to the list 在名单上添一个名字/The juice contains no ～ed sugar. 这种果汁没有加糖。❷ say or write further or in addition 进一步说 (写);继续说(写):May I ～ a point or two? 我可以补充一两点意见吗?/"And be sure to write," she ～ed. "别忘了写信。"她补了一句。❸put (numbers or amounts) together to form a total 把……加在一起(求出总数),做加法:～ 6 and 3 把 6 和 3 相加/～ the numbers up 把数字加在一起/learn to ～ 学习加法 ‖ ～ to 增加:～ to one's knowledge 增进知识/～ up to 合计(为):～ up to 120 总计为 120

added/ˈædɪd/

*adj.*existing in addition to what is usual or expected;further 附加的;增添的;额外的:The new system is not only cheaper, but has the ～ advantage of being much faster than the old one.新的系统不只是便宜,而且还有一个比旧系统快的额外好处。

addendum/əˈdendəm/

*n.*sth. that is added or is to be added,as at the end of a speech or book 补充;补遗;补编;附录

addict/ˈædɪkt/

*n.*a person who cannot stop himself from doing sth. or using sth. harmful 有瘾的

人：a drug ～ 吸毒上瘾的人

addicted/əˈdɪktɪd/

adj. ❶ dependent on sth., especially a drug and unable to stop having or taking it 有瘾的，上瘾的：It doesn't take long to become ～ to these drugs.服用这些毒品不要很长时间就会上瘾。❷devoted to a particular thing or activity 入了迷的；有嗜好的：My children are hopelessly ～ to television.我的几个孩子都成了电视迷，简直是不可救药了。

addiction/əˈdɪkʃn/

*n.*the state of being addicted or a habit to a particular substance, thing, or activity 吸毒成瘾；沉溺；癖好：the growing problem of heroin ～ among young people 年轻人吸食海洛因成瘾这一日益严重的问题

addition/əˈdɪʃn/

*n.*❶the process or action of adding sth. to sth.else 增加：～ to one's knowledge 知识的增进/The ～ of a baby to the family changed our lives.家中添了个婴儿改变了我们的生活。❷a thing or person added or joined 增添物；增加的人：an ～ to the family 家庭的新成员 ❸the process of calculating the total of two or more numbers 加法，加 ‖ in ～（to）此外；除……之外：I have some other things to do in ～（to this).此外，我还有些其他事情要办。

additional/əˈdɪʃənl/

*adj.*beyond what is usual；added 追加的；附加的；另外的：An ～ charge is made for heavy bags.重的行李要额外收费。/ one of the ～ requirements 额外的规定之一/～ evidence 补充的证据

additive/ˈædɪtɪv/

*n.*a substance, especially a chemical one, added in small quantities to sth.else, e.g. to add colour, taste, etc.添加物，添加剂：～-free foods 无添加剂的食品

add-on/ˈædˌɒn/

*n.*sth. that has been or can be added to an existing object or arrangement 附加物件

address/əˈdres/

Ⅰ*v.*❶speak to or make a speech to, especially in a formal way 向……讲话：～ the meeting 到会发言 ❷write on an envelope the name and address of the person, company, etc. that you are sending it to by mail 写(收信人)地址；姓名；致函 ‖ ～ oneself to 致力于 Ⅱ*n.*❶a formal speech or talk（to an audience）演说；讲话 ❷ the number of the building, name of the street and town, etc. where a person lives or to which letters, etc. may be sent 地址：～ book 通讯录

addressee/ˌædreˈsiː/

*n.*the person to whom a letter, parcel, etc., is addressed 收信人；收件人

adduce/əˈdjuːs/

*v.*give an example, evidence, reason, etc. to explain sth.or to show that sth.is true 举出(例证、证据、原因等)：Can you ～ any reason for his strange behaviour? 对于他的古怪行为你能给出什么解释吗?

adept/əˈdept/

*adj.*having great skill in doing sth. 熟练的；擅长的：He is very ～ at playing games.他善于做游戏。

adequate/ˈædɪkwət/

*adj.*enough or suitable 足够的；适合的：Though a bit too old he is still ～.尽管年纪大了点，但这工作他还是能胜任。/ I know no words ～ to express my thanks.我知道没有言语能充分表达我的感激之情。

adhere/ədˈhɪə(r)/

*v.*stick to sth.firmly 黏附；坚持；支持；忠于：～ to the contract 信守合同/This paint will ～ to any surface.这种油漆可黏附于任何表面。

adherence/ədˈhɪərəns/

*n.*the action of continuing to support or be loyal to sth., especially in spite of difficulties 信奉；坚持：～ to one's religious beliefs 坚持自己的宗教信仰

adherent/ədˈhɪərənt/

n. a person who supports a particular idea, political party, etc.信徒；拥护者；追随者

adhesion/ədˈhiːʒn/

*n.*❶ the state or action of sticking together or to sth. 黏附，黏合，胶着；坚持：～ to strict production timetables 坚持严格的生产时间表 ❷ the joining together of parts inside the body which should be separate（体内组织的）粘连

adhesive/əd'hiːsɪv/
I *n*. a substance such as glue that can stick or cause sticking 接合剂；胶布 II *adj*. that can stick or cause sticking 黏着的；有黏性的：～ tape 胶布

adjacent/ə'dʒeɪsnt/
adj. very close; touching or almost touching 毗连的；邻近的：The council offices are ～ to the library. 市议会各办公室就在图书馆旁边。

adjective/'ædʒɪktɪv/
n. a word that describes a noun or pronoun 形容词

adjoin/ə'dʒɔɪn/
v. be next to or very close to（another or each other）贴近，毗连，靠近：Our house ～s theirs. 我们的房子同他们的房子紧挨着。/～ing rooms 毗连的房间

adjourn/ə'dʒɜːn/
v. ❶ bring（a meeting, game, etc.）to a stop, especially for a short period or until a slightly later time 使（会议、比赛等）暂停；稍推迟：Shall we ～ this discussion until tomorrow? 我们暂时停止讨论，明天再进行好吗？ ❷ put off or postpone（a resolution or sentence）延迟，推迟（决议、宣判）❸（of a group of people）go to another place, especially for a rest（指一群人）换地方（尤指休息）：After the meeting we all ～ed to the pub. 会后我们全体转往小酒馆。‖ ～ment *n*. 体会；延期：The court met again after an ～ment of two weeks. 法庭休庭两周之后重新开庭。

adjudicate/ə'dʒuːdɪkeɪt/
v. act as a judge, e.g. in a competition or in an argument between two groups or organizations; decide about 裁决；裁定；评审：Who will ～ on this dispute? 谁来裁决这个争论？/～ a claim 裁定要求

adjunct/'ædʒʌŋkt/
n. ❶ a thing added to sth. larger or more important 附加物；附属物：The dictiona-ry is an essential ～ to the means of study. 字典是必不可少的学习工具之一。❷ a word or phrase that adds meaning to another word in a sentence or part of a sentence 修饰语，附加语：an ～ to the subject 主语的修饰语

adjust/ə'dʒʌst/
v. make a small change in sth. to make it better 调整；调节 ‖ ～able *adj*. 可调整的，可校准的/～ er *n*. 调节器/～ ment *n*. 调整；调节；校准

ad-lib/ˌæd'lɪb/
I *v*. (-bb-) perform or speak（music, words, etc.）without preparation 即兴表演：The actress forgot her lines but ～ bed very amusingly. 女演员忘记了台词，但是临时凑记了几句很有趣的话。 II *adv*.（ad lib）❶（speaking, playing, performing, etc.）without preparation（演讲、演奏、表演等）即兴地：a radio show in which people have to speak ～ for ten minutes on a given subject 临时给听众一个题目，请他即兴说十分钟的电台节目 ❷ without limit; freely 无限制地，自由地：a restaurant where you pay a fixed price and can eat ～ 付一定费用后就可随意进食的餐馆

adman/'ædmæn/
n. a member of the advertising profession 广告员，广告从业人员

administer/əd'mɪnɪstə(r)/
v. ❶ control and manage for the running of sth. 管理；支配 ❷ apply or put into operation 执行；施行；实施 ❸ give or provide sth. 给予

administration/ədˌmɪnɪ'streɪʃn/
n. ❶ the management or direction of the affairs of a business, government, etc. 管理；经营；行政 ❷ the government of a country, especially of a particular president or ruling party 行政机关；管理部门；（总统制国家的）政府 ❸ the act of giving a drug to sb.（药物的）施用

administrative/əd'mɪnɪstrətɪv/
adj. of or concerning administration 行政的；管理的：The job is mainly ～. 这个工作主要是行政性的。/～ responsibilities

A

行政责任

administrator/əd'mɪnɪstreɪtə(r)/

　*n.*a person whose job is administration 管理人员；行政官员；主管

admirable/'ædmərəbl/

　*adj.*deserving respect and approval；very good 值得钦佩的；值得赞美的；极好的：Saving the girl's life is an ～ thing to do. 把那女孩的生命挽救过来是一件大好事。

admiral/'ædmərəl/

　*n.*a naval officer with high rank 海军将官；海军上将

admiration/ˌædmə'reɪʃn/

　*n.*❶a feeling of respect or approval 敬佩，赞赏：～ for someone's courage 对某人胆量的钦佩/win sb.'s ～ 博得某人的赞赏 ❷a person or thing that causes admiration 令人钦佩的人；令人赞赏的事：He was the ～ of his friends.朋友们都钦佩他。

admire/əd'maɪə(r)/

　*v.*❶regard sb.or sth.with respect or approval 赞美；钦佩 ❷look at sth.or sb. with pleasure,etc.欣赏

admirer/əd'maɪərə(r)/

　*n.*❶a person who admires sb.or sth., especially a well-known person or thing 钦佩者；赞赏者：He is a great ～ of Picasso's early paintings. 他十分赞赏毕加索的早期作品。❷a man who is attracted to a woman and admires her 追求者，爱慕者（尤指爱慕女人的男人）

admissible/əd'mɪsəbl/

　*adj.*that can be accepted or considered 可采纳的；可接受的

admission/əd'mɪʃn/

　*n.*❶permission to go in 允许进入：No ～! 请勿进入！❷the cost of entrance 入场费 ❸a statement admitting that sth. is true 承认

admit/əd'mɪt/

　v.(-tt-)❶confess or agree to the truth of sth.,usually unwillingly（尤指勉强）承认：He ～ted his guilt.他承认犯了罪。/She ～ted that she had stolen the bicycle. 她承认偷了自行车。/I must ～, it's

more difficult than I thought it would be. 我必须承认，这比我想象的要困难得多。❷permit to enter；let in 允许入内：He was ～ted to hospital suffering from burns.他由于烧伤被送入医院治疗。❸leave a chance for being possible 容许有：The facts ～（of）no other explanation.这些事实不容许有别的解释。

admittance/əd'mɪtns/

　*n.*the right or fact of entering to a place 进入；允许进入

admittedly/əd'mɪtɪdli/

　*adv.*without denial 诚然；确实地；无可否认地：Admittedly, he works slowly, but his essays are always excellent. 应该承认,他写得很慢,但他的论文总是写得非常出色。

admixture/æd'mɪkstʃə(r)/

　*n.*a substance that is added to another in a mixture 混合物；混合剂

admonish/əd'mɒnɪʃ/

　*v.*warn or speak to sb.with gentle disapproval 警告；告诫；劝告 ‖ ～ment *n.*警告；训诫

admonitory/əd'mɒnɪtri/

　*adj.*of or being warning advice or gentle disapproval 劝告的；告诫的；轻责的：～ remarks 劝谏

adobe/ə'dəʊbi/

　*n.*a brick made of earth and straw dried in the sun,used as a building material 土坯，泥砖

adolescent/ædə'lesnt/

　*n.*a young person who is developing from a child to an adult 青少年 ‖ **adolescence** *n.* 青春期

adopt/ə'dɒpt/

　*v.*❶accept or take up to use 采纳，采取：～ a suggestion 采纳建议 /The board ～ed the proposal.委员会通过了该项提议。❷take（a child of other parents）into one's family as one's own 收养，领养：～ an orphan 领养一个孤儿

adoption/ə'dɒpʃn/

　n. ❶ the act of adopting a child 收养：If you can't have children of your own, why not consider ～? 如果你们不能生孩子,

为何不考虑收养（一个）呢？ ❷ the decision to start taking sth. for use 采用

adoptive /əˈdɒptɪv/
adj. as a result of having adopted a child 收养的：her ～ parents 她的养父母

adorable /əˈdɔːrəbl/
adj. charming or attractive 极可爱的；迷人的：an ～ child 可爱的小孩

adoration /ˌædəˈreɪʃn/
n. ❶ religious worship 宗教崇拜 ❷ a feeling of deep love and respect 敬慕；爱慕

adore /əˈdɔː(r)/
v. ❶ love or honour greatly 钟爱；敬重：She ～s her father. 她敬重父亲。 ❷ like greatly 非常喜爱：I ～ your hat. 我真喜欢你的帽子。 /～ playing football 非常喜欢踢足球

adorn /əˈdɔːn/
v. make more beautiful by decorating with flowers, jewels, etc. （用鲜花、珠宝等）装饰 ‖ ～ment *n.* 装饰；装饰品

adrift /əˈdrɪft/
adv. & adj. (usually with reference to ships and boats) moving without human control wherever taken by the winds and tides（通常指船只）漂泊地（的），漂流地（的）：go ～ 随波逐流 /He was ～ on the sea for three days. 他在海上漂泊了三天。

adroit /əˈdrɔɪt/
adj. clever in using one's hands or one's mind 灵巧的；机灵的

adulation /ˌædjuˈleɪʃn/
n. praise or admiration that is more than is necessary or deserved 恭维；奉承；谄媚：basking in the ～ of the crowd 沉浸于公众的恭维奉承之中

adult /ˈædʌlt, əˈdʌlt/
Ⅰ *adj.* fully grown; suitable for or typical of a fully grown person; mature 成年的；成年人的；成熟的 Ⅱ *n.* a fully grown person or animal, especially a person over an age stated by law（尤指达到法律规定成熟年龄的）成年人；成年动物 ‖ ～hood *n.* 成年

adulterate /əˈdʌltəreɪt/
v. make less pure or less good by adding sth. 掺杂；掺假

advance /ədˈvɑːns/
Ⅰ *v.* ❶ move forward in position, development, etc. 前进；进展；推进；促进 ❷ put forward (an advice, idea, theory, etc.) 提出（建议、看法、理论等）❸ cause to occur at an earlier date or time 使提前发生 ❹ raise (prices); promote (sb.) 提高（价格等）；提升（某人）❺ pay beforehand 预付 Ⅱ *n.* ❶ a forward movement; progress 前进，进展 ❷ the payment of money before it is due 预付；预付款 ❸ (*pl.*) attempts to gain someone's friendship, love, or favourable attention 讨好，接近；求爱的表示：She didn't respond to his ～s. 她对他的求爱表示没有做出反应。 Ⅲ *adj.* done, sent or supplied in advance 提前的；预先的：an ～ notice 预先通知 /an ～ copy of a new book 新书样本 ‖ in ～ beforehand 事先；预先；提前

advanced /ədˈvɑːnst/
adj. far on in life or in progress, etc. 年迈的；高级的；先进的

advancement /ədˈvɑːnsmənt/
n. ❶ an improvement or development 促进，发展；进步 ❷ the promotion of a person in rank 提拔，晋升

advantage /ədˈvɑːntɪdʒ/
Ⅰ *n.* ❶ sth. that may help one to be successful or to gain a favourable result 有利条件；优点 ❷ a favourable condition resulting from a particular course of action 优势；好处；利益 ‖ take ～ of 利用；欺骗 Ⅱ *v.* put in a favourable or more favourable position 处于更有利地位

advantageous /ˌædvənˈteɪdʒəs/
adj. helpful; profitable 有帮助的；有利的；有益的：The new process should be particularly ～ to small companies. 新的程序应该对小公司特别有利。

advent /ˈædvənt/
n. the coming or arrival (of an important event, person or thing)（重要事件、人物、事物的）出现，到来

adventure /ədˈventʃə(r)/
n. ❶ a journey, experience, etc., that is strange and exciting and often dangerous

冒险;冒险经历;冒险活动 ❷excitement and the willingness to take risks, etc. 冒险的刺激

adventurer/ədˈventʃə(r)/
*n.*❶ a person who enjoys adventures 冒险家 ❷ a person who hopes to gain wealth or a high social position by dishonest or dangerous means 投机分子

adventuress/ədˈventʃərɪs/
*n.*a female adventurer 女冒险家;女投机分子

adventurous/ədˈventʃərəs/
*adj.*❶eager for adventure;ready to take risks;daring 喜欢冒险的,有冒险精神的;胆大的 ❷ exciting and full of danger 充满危险的;刺激性的:an ～ life 冒险的生活/an ～ journey 惊险的旅行

adverb/ˈædvɜːb/
n. a word that gives information in a sentence about how, when, where, why, etc. 副词 ‖ ～ial *adj.*副词的

adversarial /ˌædvəˈseəriəl/
adj. (especially of political or legal systems) involving people who are in opposition and who make attacks on each other (尤指政治或法律制度)对立的;敌对的:the ～ nature of the two-party system 两党制的对抗性

adversary/ˈædvəsəri/
*n.*an opponent or enemy 对手;敌人

adverse/ˈædvɜːs/
*adj.*unfavourable;going against;opposing 不利的;有害的;逆的;反面的

adversity/ədˈvɜːsəti/
*n.*bad fortune;difficulties 不幸;厄运;困难:A good friend will not desert you in time of ～.好朋友不会在患难中弃你而去。/to meet with adversities 遭遇不幸

advertise(-ze)/ˈædvətaɪz/
*v.*❶make (a product, service or event) known to the public in a public medium 做广告宣传 ❷ ask for sb. or sth. by putting a notice in a newspaper, shop window, etc.登广告征求

advertisement/ədˈvɜːtɪsmənt/
*n.*a notice or announcement in a public medium telling people about a product,

service, event or job 广告:put an ～ in the paper 在报纸上登广告 /He's not a very good ～ for the driving school—he's failed his test six times! 他不是汽车驾驶学校的好广告——他六次考驾驶执照都没有合格!

advertising/ˈædvətaɪzɪŋ/
*n.*the activity or business of encouraging people to buy goods by means of advertisements 广告业;广告活动

advice/ədˈvaɪs/
*n.*❶ an opinion given to someone about what they should do in a particular situation 劝告,忠告;意见:Acting on her ～, I decided to give up smoking.遵照她的意见,我决定戒烟。/He gave them some good ～.他向他们提出了一些很好的意见。/Let me give you a piece of ～.我给你提一个意见吧。/If you take my ～, you won't tell anyone about this.你要是听我劝告的话,最好别向任何人透露此事。❷(especially in business)a letter or note giving information about delivery of goods, payment of money, etc.(尤指商业上有关货运、付款等的)通知书

advisable/ədˈvaɪzəbl/
*adj.*sensible;wise 可取的,可行的;明智的:It is ～ always to wear a safety belt when you're driving.开车的时候最好总是系着安全带。‖ advisability *n.*可取性,可行性;明智

advise/ədˈvaɪz/
v. ❶ offer suggestions about the best course of action to sb.建议:He ～d me to go home at once.他建议我马上回家。/ He ～d caution.他建议小心行事。❷recommend (sth.) 推荐(某物):The doctor will ～ which medicines are safe to take. 医生会推荐服用哪些药才安全。❸inform (sb.) about a fact or situation, typically in a formal or official way(尤指正式地或官方地)通知:Please ～ us of any change of address.如地址有变,敬请告知。

advisedly/ədˈvaɪzɪdli/
*adv.*after careful thought and purposely 深思熟虑地,有意地:She is behaving like a dictator — and I use the term ～.她的

所作所为活像个独裁者——我用这个词
是经过认真考虑的。

adviser /əd'vaɪzə(r)/
n. a person whose job is to give advice, especially to a government or business or (in the US) to students（政府、公司等的）顾问；（美国学校中指导学生选课等的）指导教师：the government's special ～ on the Middle East 政府的中东问题特别顾问

advisory /əd'vaɪzəri/
adj. having the power or duty to advise 有权进言的，提供咨询的：employed in an ～ capacity 以顾问身份受聘

advocacy /'ædvəkəsi/
n. ❶ the act of supporting an idea, way of life, person, etc.（对某种观点、生活方式、人物等的）支持，拥护，鼓吹 ❷ the profession or work of a lawyer 律师职业；律师工作

advocate /'ædvəkət/
Ⅰ *v.* speak in support of sth.; recommend 拥护；主张：～ a course of action 拥护某行动方针 /～ going to see the doctor 主张去看医生 Ⅱ *n.* ❶ a person who supports sth. or sb. 拥护者；支持者 ❷ a lawyer defending sb. in court 辩护律师

adze /ædz/
n. a sharp tool with the blade at a right angle to the handle, used for shaping large pieces of wood 手斧，锛子

aegis /'iːdʒɪs/
n. (under the ～ of) with the protection or support of 在……的支持(保护)下：a refugee programme under the ～ of the United Nations 由联合国赞助的难民安置计划

aerate /'eəreɪt/
v. ❶ charge a liquid with a gas under pressure 充气于(液体)：～d water 汽水 ❷ expose to air, or cause air to circulate through 使暴露于空气中；使通气

aerial /'eəriəl/
Ⅰ *n.* a wire used for receiving or sending radio waves（无线电）天线 Ⅱ *adj.* in or of the air 空中的；空气的：～ warfare 空战

aerobatics /ˌeərə'bætɪks/
n. the art of doing tricks in an aircraft, such as rolling over sideways or flying upside down 特技飞行；航空表演

aerobics /eə'rəubɪks/
n. a form of very active physical exercise which is usually done in a class with music and is intended to strengthen the heart and lungs 健身操

aerogramme /'eərəgræm/
n. ❶ an air-mail letter written on a single sheet of light-weight paper that folds and is sealed to form an envelope 航空邮件 ❷ a message sent by radio 无线电报

aeronautic /ˌeərə'nɔːtɪk/
adj. of or about the science or practice of all aspects of flight through the air 航空学的；航空的

aeroplane /'eərəpleɪn/
n. a flying machine; a plane 飞机（=〈美〉airplane）

aerosol /'eərəsɒl/
n. a container which squirts out a spray of a substance, such as furniture polish, when a knob is pressed 喷雾罐

aerospace /'eərəuspeɪs/
n. the branch of technology and industry concerned with both aviation and space flight 航空航天技术；航空航天工业：the ～ industry 宇航工业

aesthete /'iːsθiːt/
n. a person who has a highly developed sense of beauty, especially in art（尤指艺术方面的）审美家

aesthetic /es'θetɪk, iːs'θetɪk/
adj. referring to what is beautiful（especially in art, literature and music）（尤指艺术、文学和音乐方面）美的；审美的 ‖ ～s *n.* 美学

afar /ə'fɑː(r)/
adv. at a distance; far off 在远处；遥远地：I saw him from ～. 我从远处看到了他。

affable /'æfəbl/
adj. friendly; easy to talk to 友好的；易于交谈的

affair /ə'feə(r)/
n. ❶ an event described in a particular way 事；事情；事件 ❷ (*pl.*) events that are of

public interest and importance 公共事务 ❸a sexual relationship between two people not married to each other，especially one that lasts for some time 风流韵事；私通

affect/əˈfekt/

*v.*❶produce a change upon；have an effect on；act on 影响：The bad weather ～ed the growth of crops.坏天气影响了作物的生长。❷move or touch emotionally 打动；感动 ❸pretend to be feeling or thinking sth.假装：He ～ed surprise at the news.他听到这个消息，假装出一副吃惊的样子。❹attack or infect 侵袭；感染

affectation/ˌæfekˈteɪʃn/

n. behaviour which is not one's natural manner 不自然的行为；矫揉造作：She is sincere and quite without ～.她为人诚挚，毫不做作。/She's not really American — her accent is just an ～.她实际上不是美国人，她的美国腔是装出来的。

affected/əˈfektɪd/

*adj.*not real，natural，or sincere；showing affectation 不真实的；不自然的；不诚挚的；假装的；做作的：an ～ smile 假笑

affection/əˈfekʃn/

n. liking or loving feelings 喜爱；钟爱：show ～ to his friends 表现出对朋友的爱

affectionate/əˈfekʃənət/

*adj.*having or showing caring feelings and love 深情的；表示关爱的

affiliate/əˈfɪlɪeɪt/

Ⅰ*v.*(especially of a group)to join or connect(to a larger group) (尤指团体等)并入(更大的团体)；加盟：Our club is ～d with a national organization of similar clubs.我们的俱乐部加入了一个由同类俱乐部组成的全国性组织。Ⅱ*n.*a group or organization that is attached to another，especially a subsidiary (or part-owned) company controlled by a parent company 支会；分社；子公司；附属机构 ‖ **affiliation**/əˌfɪlɪˈeɪʃn/ *n.*隶属；隶属关系

affiliated/əˈfɪlɪeɪtɪd/

*adj.*closely connected to or controlled by

a group or an organization 隶属的：a government-～ institute 一家隶属于政府的研究所

affinity/əˈfɪnəti/

n. a close relationship between two persons or things 密切关系：There is an ～ between the Bantu languages.各种班图语之间都很相近。

affirm/əˈfɜːm/

*v.*❶ declare strongly and publicly in answer to a question or doubt 肯定；确认：The minister ～ed the government's intention to reduce taxes.部长确认政府有减税的意向。/ She ～ed that she was telling the truth. 她肯定自己说的是实话。❷ declare one's support for；uphold 宣称拥护；支持 ‖ ～ation/ˌæfəˈmeɪʃn/ *n.* 断言，肯定

affirmative/əˈfɜːmətɪv/

Ⅰ*adj.*❶agreeing with or consenting to a statement or request 同意的，赞成的：an ～ answer 赞同的回答 ❷stating that a fact is so；making an assertion 肯定的：～ sentences 肯定句 Ⅱ*n.*❶a statement of agreement with or consent to an assertion or request 同意，赞成 ❷a word used in making assertions or to express consent 陈述词，肯定词

affix/əˈfɪks/

*v.*❶ stick；attach 粘上；贴上：～ a stamp to an envelope 把邮票贴在信封上 ❷add to the end 添上；附上：～ a postscript 加一则附言

afflict/əˈflɪkt/

v. cause to suffer in the body or mind；trouble 使苦恼；折磨 ‖ ～ion *n.*苦恼；折磨；苦恼的事

affluent/ˈæfluənt/

*adj.*having a lot of money；rich 富裕的；丰富的

afford/əˈfɔːd/

v. ❶ have enough (time，money，space，etc.) or the means for 有时间做；支付得起；足以：I can't ～ the holiday.我无暇度假。/He can ～ (to buy) a new house.他买得起新房子。❷be able to do sth.without risk of serious consequences 担负得

起：I can't ～ to miss the train.这趟火车我误不得。/I can't～ any delay. 我一点也不能耽搁。❸provide or supply 提供；给予：A four-day work week will ～ us more leisure time.一周工作四天制可给我们更多的空闲时间。

affront/ə'frʌnt/
　Ⅰ n.a word or an act which publicly and intentionally insults sb. 蓄意当众侮辱；冒犯 Ⅱ v.insult or offend sb.or sth.冒犯，侮辱

afield/ə'fiːld/
　adv.far away,especially from home;to or at a great distance 远离(家乡等)；到(或在)远方：Don't go too far ～ or you'll get lost.别走得太远，要不然你会迷路的。/ We get a lot of tourists from Europe,and some from even further ～.我们这里有许多来自欧洲的旅游者，有些甚至来自更远的地方。

afire/ə'faɪə(r)/
　adj.& adv.on fire 燃烧着(的)，着火(的)：～ with enthusiasm 热情沸腾/He set the house ～.他放火把房子烧着了。

aflame/ə'fleɪm/
　adj.& adv.on fire;ablaze 着火(的)；燃烧着(的)：The house was ～.房子着火了。/ The gardens were ～ with red and orange leaves.绯红和橘黄色的叶子使那几个园子一片火红色。

afloat/ə'fləʊt/
　adv.& adj.on the sea,river,etc.在海上(的)，在河上(的)；漂浮地(的)

aforementioned/ˌəfɔː'menʃənd/
　adj.mentioned or named before or already 上述的，前述的：The car ～ belongs to the ～ Ms.Jones.这辆汽车是上述琼斯女士的。/The ～ was present at the trial.上述人员审判时都出庭了。

aforesaid/ə'fɔːsed/
　adj.=aforementioned

afraid/ə'freɪd/
　adj.❶full of fear;frightened 怕的，害怕的：She is ～ of snakes (the dark).她怕蛇(黑)。 ❷ (used to soften an unpleasant statement) filled with regret or concern 恐怕，担心的：You are wrong,I'm ～.恐怕你

错了。

afresh/ə'freʃ/
　adv.again 再，重新：start ～ 重新开始

Africa/'æfrɪkə/
　n. the second largest continent of the Earth 非洲(世界第二大洲)

African/'æfrɪkən/
　Ⅰ n.a person from Africa 非洲人 Ⅱ of or connected with Africa 非洲的

aft/ɑːft/
　adj.& adv.in or towards the stern of af boat or aircraft 在(向)船尾(的)；在(向)机尾(的)

after/'ɑːftə(r)/
　Ⅰ prep. ❶ later than; following in time (时间)在……以后：～ class 课后 ❷next in order to (顺序)跟在……后面，次于：After you.您先请。❸indicating sth. happening continuously or repeatedly (用于表示持续或重复性)(一个)接着(一个)：day ～ day 一天又一天 ❹as a result of; because of 由于，因为：I hate him ～ what he did to me.我因他对我的所作所为而恨他。❺in pursuit or quest 追求；探求：run ～ the thief 追踪窃贼 ❻in the manner or style of 仿照，依照：a painting ～ Qi Baishi 一幅模仿齐白石的画 Ⅱ conj.at a later time than (when) 在……以后：I arrived ～ she left.我在她走了以后到达。‖ ～**burner** n.(喷气发动机的)加力燃烧室；(内燃机的)后燃器/～**light** n.余晖；夕照/～**life** n.(迷信所说的)来世；下半生/～**sales service** n.售后服务/～-**shave** adj.& n.剃须后搽的(润肤香水)/～**shock** n.(地震的)余震/～**wit** n.事后聪明/～**word** n.跋；编后记

after-effect /ˌɑːftə'ɪfekt/
　n.an effect that follows after the primary action of sth. 后作用；后效；事后影响；余波；后果

afterglow /'ɑːftəgləʊ/
　n.light still glowing in the sky after sunset 夕照；晚霞

aftermath/'ɑːftəmæθ/
　n. the situation or consequences that follows an event,especially when unpleasant 后果；余波：the ～ of war 战后余殃

A

afternoon/ˌɑːftəˈnuːn/
  n. the time between midday and evening 下午；午后

afters/ˈɑːftəz/
  n. the part of a meal that comes after the main dish；dessert 餐后的甜食：What are we having for ～? 我们餐后用什么甜食？

afterthought/ˈɑːftəθɔːt/
  n. ❶ an idea that comes later 事后的想法 ❷ sth. added later, especially that was not part of the original plan（尤指原计划所没有的）增加的东西：The conservatory was an ～, added on to the building several years later. 暖房是该建筑物建成几年之后加盖的。

afterwards/ˈɑːftəwədz/
  adv. at a later time 以后；后来

again/əˈgen, əˈgeɪn/
  adv. ❶ once more；a second time 又一次；再一次：It was great to meet old friends ～. 见到老朋友太棒了。❷ returning to a previous position or condition 重，又（回到原处或先前情形）：She was glad to be home ～. 她很高兴又回到了家了。❸ used to introduce a further point that contrasts with what has just been said 再说，另一方面

against/əˈgenst, əˈgeɪnst/
  prep. ❶ in opposition to（反）对，逆：～ war 反对战争/～ the stream 逆流 ❷ close beside or in front of 倚；靠；在……的前面：stand a ladder ～ a wall 把梯子靠在墙上 ❸ as a contrast with 作为……的对照：The trees were black ～ the sky. 在天空的映衬下树木呈黑色。

agape/əˈgeɪp/
  adj. gaping, open-mouthed, especially because of surprise or wonder（尤指人因为吃惊、惊奇而）目瞪口呆的

agar/ˈeɪgɑː(r)/
  n. a jelly-like substance made from seaweed, used for bacterial cultures, etc. 琼脂

agate/ˈeɪgət/
  n. a very hard stone with patches or concentric bands of colour 玛瑙

age/eɪdʒ/
  Ⅰ *n.* ❶ time of life；number of years a person has lived 年龄 ❷ certain time in history 时期，时代 ❸（usually *pl.*）a long time 很长一段时间：We haven't seen you for ～s. 我们很久没有见到你了。Ⅱ *v.*（cause to）become old or mature（使）变老；（使）成熟 ‖ ～ group *n.* 年龄组（指同一年龄或年龄相近的人形成的群体）/～-long *adj.* 长久的；久远的：～-long struggle for freedom 为自由而进行的长期奋斗

aged/ˈeɪdʒɪd/
  adj. ❶ being of the stated number of years ……岁的 ❷ fully developed, especially in taste（味道等）醇厚的，芳香的 ❸ very old 年老的：the ～ 老年人

ag(e)ing/ˈeɪdʒɪŋ/
  Ⅰ *adj.* becoming old；rather old, especially older than is considered desirable or suitable 变老的；陈旧的：We need to replace some of this ～ office equipment. 我们需要把这套过时的办公室设备换掉一部分。/an ～ playboy 时下已经衰老的花花公子 Ⅱ *n.* ❶ the process of getting old 老化：a healthy diet which retards ～ 延缓衰老的保健饮食 ❷ the changes that happen (e.g. to wine, cheese, etc.) as time passes（酒、干酪等的）变陈，熟化

ageless/ˈeɪdʒlɪs/
  adj. never growing old or never showing signs of growing old 永不衰老的：an ～ song 一首永远有活力的歌曲/～ beauty 美颜永驻

agency/ˈeɪdʒənsi/
  n. ❶ a business or an organization that provides a particular service on behalf of others or for others 代理机构；服务机构；经销处：The company has agencies in many countries. 这家公司在许多国家有经销处。❷ a department or body providing a specific service for a government or organization 办事处，机构 ❸ action；power 作用；力量：by ～ of 由于……的作用；通过……的帮助

agenda/əˈdʒendə/
  n. a list of the subjects to be dealt with or

A

talked about at a meeting（会议的）议事日程：the first item on the ～ 第一项议程/The question of salary increases is high on the ～.增加薪金问题是要讨论的重要议程。

agent/'eɪdʒənt/

*n.*❶one who acts on behalf of or for another (in business, politics, etc.)（企业政治等的）代理人，代理商，经纪人：a land ～ 地产经纪人 ❷ means；a person or thing that acts 手段；行为者；起作用的人（或物）：a medical ～ 药剂/bleaching ～s 漂白因子

aggravate/'æɡrəveɪt/

*v.*❶make (a difficult situation)more serious or dangerous；make worse 使……加重；使……恶化；使……更坏：The lack of rain ～d the already serious shortage of food.干旱少雨使原来就很严重的粮食短缺问题更加严重。/Their debt problem was further ～d by the rise in interest rates.他们的债务问题因利率的提高而进一步恶化了。❷ make angry, especially by continual annoyance 惹恼；激怒：aggravating delays caused by heavy traffic 由交通拥挤造成的令人恼火的延误

aggregate/'æɡrɪɡeɪt/

Ⅰ *adj.* total 总的；合计的 Ⅱ *n.* ❶ the materials, such as sand and small stones, that are mixed with cement to form concrete（混凝土等的）集料，材料；骨料 ❷a total number or amount 总数；合计 Ⅲ *v.* ❶bring or come together into a group or mass（使）聚集 ❷ reach a total of；add up to 总计 ‖ in the ～ 总共

aggression/ə'ɡreʃn/

*n.*the act or tendency of starting a quarrel, fight, or war, especially without just cause 挑衅；侵犯；侵略：The military exercise was condemned as an act of ～.这次军事演习被谴责为一次挑衅行为。

aggressive/ə'ɡresɪv/

*adj.*❶ offensive；of or for attack 侵略的；侵犯的 ❷ quarrelsome；disposed to attack 爱寻衅的；好斗的；放肆的 ❸ pushing；not afraid of resistance 有进取心的；敢作敢为的

aggressor/ə'ɡresə(r)/

*n.*a person or country that begins a quarrel, fight, war, etc., with another, especially without just cause 挑衅者；攻击者；侵略者

aggrieved/ə'ɡriːvd/

*adj.*angry and unhappy because sb. has done sth. wrong to one 悲伤的；愤愤不平的；受委屈的：He was ～ at his friends' lack of interest in his success.他因朋友们对他的成功无动于衷而感到痛心。

aghast/ə'ɡɑːst/

*adj.*suddenly filled with great surprise, fear, and shock 大为震惊的；吓呆了的：She was ～, when she was told of her husband's huge gambling debts.她听到丈夫欠下大笔赌债，不由惊呆了。

agile/'ædʒaɪl/

*adj.*able to move easily and quickly 灵活的；敏捷的：She was still quite ～ despite her age.尽管她年事已高，但行动仍然很轻快。/an ～ mind 灵活的头脑

agitate/'ædʒɪteɪt/

*v.*ask very strongly that sth. should be changed and made better 强烈要求（改变或改善）；鼓动：The workers are agitating for higher wages and better conditions.工人们正在极力要求提高工资并改善工作条件。

agitation/ˌædʒɪ'teɪʃn/

*n.*❶ a state of anxiety or worry feelings 焦虑不安；忧虑：He was in a state of great ～.他处于异常焦虑之中。❷ a public protest, action, unrest, etc.for or against a political or social change 鼓动；骚动，煽动

agitator/'ædʒɪteɪtə(r)/

*n.*❶ a person who excites and influences public feeling, especially towards political change（尤指政治变革的）鼓动者，煽动者 ❷ a machine for shaking or mixing 搅拌器；搅拌机

ago/ə'ɡəʊ/

*adv.*before the present；in the past 以前：two centuries ～ 两百年前/long time ～ 很久以前

agonize/'æɡənaɪz/

*v.*make a long and anxious effort when

considering sth. or trying to make a decision 焦虑不已；苦苦思索

agonized/'ægənaɪzd/
*adj.*expressing great pain 痛苦的；She let out an ~ cry.她发出痛苦的叫喊声。

agonizing/'ægənaɪzɪŋ/
*adj.*causing great pain or anxiety 引起痛苦的；使焦虑的：an ~ decision 令人痛苦的决定 ‖ ~ly *adv.*苦闷地

agony/'ægəni/
*n.*very great pain or suffering of mind or body（身心的）极大痛苦：He lay in ~ until the doctor arrived. 在医生来到之前，他一直非常痛苦地躺在那里。/I was in an ~ of doubt.我疑虑不安，十分痛苦。

agrarian/ə'greəriən/
*adj.*concerning land, especially farmland or its ownership 土地的，耕地的；土地所有权的：a campaigner for ~ reform 土地改革的鼓吹者

agree/ə'griː/
*v.*❶ say"yes"；say that one will do sth. 允诺；答应；同意：They finally ~d to the plan.他们终于同意了该计划。/She ~d to buy me a dictionary. 她答应给我买一本词典。❷have the same opinion as sb.（与某人）持相同看法；同意；赞成：I ~ with you (about this).在这点上，我与你看法一致。/We ~d to leave as soon as possible.我们都认为应尽快离开。/They don't ~ on politics.他们对政治的看法不一。❸reach an understanding or agreement 达成谅解；达成协议：The two sides finally ~d on every point.最终双方在每一点上达成了协议。❹be consistent with 与……一致：The two statements do not ~ with each other.这两种说法不一致。❺be happy together 和睦相处：They ~ together all the time.他们一直相处得很融洽。❻be suitable（to）适合（于）：Long trips do not ~ with me.我不宜进行长途旅行。

agreeable/ə'griːəbl/
*adj.*❶ pleasant 令人愉快的：~ weather 宜人的天气 ❷ ready to agree 欣然同意的：Are you ~ to the suggestion? 你同意这项建议吗？ ❸acceptable or proper 可接受的；适合的 ‖ agreeably *adv.*愉快地；适合地

agreement/ə'griːmənt/
*n.*❶the act or state of sharing the same opinion or feeling 同意；一致：Their ~ about the matter surprised me. 他们对那事情的看法一致使我大为惊奇。/The meeting ended in friendly ~.会议在友好的意见一致的情况下结束。❷a promise or contract made with sb. 协议，契约：draw up an ~ 起草协议

agriculture/'ægrɪkʌltʃə(r)/
*n.*the science or practice of farming 农业 ‖ agricultural/ˌægrɪ'kʌltʃərəl/ *adj.*农业的

agronomist /ə'grɒnəmɪst/
*n.*a scientist who studies the relationship between crops and the environment 农学家

ah/ɑː/
*int.*a cry of surprise, pity, pain, joy, dislike, etc.（表示惊奇、怜悯、痛苦、喜悦、厌恶时发出的惊叹声）啊：Ah, there you are! 啊,你在这里呀!

aha/ɑː'hɑː/
*int.*a cry of surprise, satisfaction, amused discovery, etc.（表示惊讶、满足、发现可笑之事等时发出的喊声）啊哈：Aha, so it's you hiding there! 啊哈,原来是你躲在那里!

ahead/ə'hed/
*adv.*❶ in or into a forward position；in advance；before 在前面：Sharp turn ~. Drive carefully. 前面急转弯,行车小心。❷in or into the future 未来；今后：look ~ 向前看；展望未来 ❸in advance；earlier 预先；提前：They are ~ of times in their ideas.他们的思想走在时代的前面。❹in the lead 领先 ‖ ~ of time 提前

ahem/ə'hem/
*int.*a cough used to attract attention, give a slight warning, express doubts, etc.（用于引起注意、发出轻微警告或表示疑虑等的轻咳声）呃哼

aid/eɪd/
Ⅰ *n.*❶help 帮助，援助：materials in ~ of a foreign country 援外物资 ❷a thing or

person that is a source of help 辅助物；帮手：a hearing ～ 助听器 Ⅱ v. help or assist 帮助，援助：～ the old man with money 资助老人

AIDS /eɪdz/

abbr. the abbreviation for Acquired Immune Deficiency Syndrome 艾滋病（获得性免疫缺陷综合征）：an ～ victim 艾滋病患者/～ virus 艾滋病病毒

ail /eɪl/

v. ❶ be ill and grow weak 有病；生病：My grandmother is ～ing. 我祖母正患病。/ the country's ～ing economy 国家百孔千疮的经济 ❷ cause pain to；trouble 使痛苦；使苦恼：What ～s you? 是什么困扰着你?

aileron /'eɪlərɒn/

n. the movable back edge of the wing of an aircraft, used especially to keep the aircraft level or help it turn （飞机的）副翼

ailment /'eɪlmənt/

n. an illness, especially one that is not serious 疾病；小恙：He's always complaining of some ～ or other. 他总是抱怨自己的身体这儿不舒服，那儿不对劲。/a minor ～ 小病，微恙

aim /eɪm/

Ⅰ v. ❶ direct or point （a gun, blow, remark, etc.）at a target 瞄准；对准；针对：～ a gun at someone 把枪瞄准某人 ❷ direct one's efforts or purpose 致力（于），试图，目的（在于）：She is ～ing to be a writer. 她正致力于当一名作家。/We ～ to be visiting you soon. 我们打算不久去拜访你。Ⅱ n. ❶ the act of directing sth. at a target 对准；瞄准 ❷ purpose or intention 目的；意图：one's ～s in life 某人的生活目的

aimless /'eɪmlɪs/

adj. without any clear purpose or direction 无目的的；无目标的：his ～ life 他那漫无目的的人生/～ discussions 不着边际的讨论 ‖ ～ly *adv.* 无目的地/～ness *n.* 无目的性

air /eə(r)/

Ⅰ n. ❶ the mixture of gases that sur-

rounds the earth and which we breathe 空气；大气 ❷ the sky or the space above the ground 天空；空中 ❸ that part of a piece of music that is easily recognized and remembered；tune 歌曲；曲调 ❹ a special feeling or impression on sb. or sth. 感觉，印象 ❺（pl.）an annoyingly affected manner or attitude 趾高气扬 Ⅱ v. ❶ put into the open air or in a warm place 晾（衣服、被褥等）；烘干 ❷ let air into（a room）使（房间等）通气 ❸ cause others to know；show off 发表（意见、理论等）；炫耀 ‖ ～ bag n. 安全气袋/～ brake n. 气闸，风闸；（飞机的）减速板/～-conditioning n. 空调/～-cooled adj. 气冷的/～-cushion n. 气垫/～ drome n. 〈美〉飞机场/～ drop v.& n. 空投/～ field n. 飞机场/～ force n. 空军/～ gun n. 气枪/～ hostess n. 客机女服务员，空姐/～ letter n. 航空便笺/～ lane n. 航空路线/～ liner n. 大型客机，班机/～ lock n. 气塞（指阻挠管道中液体流动的气囊或气泡）；密封舱/～ man n. 航空兵；飞行员/～ mattress n. 充气床垫/～ miss n. 险些发生的撞机事故/～ plane n. 〈美〉飞机/～ pocket n. 气阱/～ port n. 机场，航空站，空港/～ pump n. 气泵，抽气机/～ raid n. 空袭/～ sick adj. 晕机的/～ taxi n. 出租飞机，短程小客机/～ terminal n. 航空终点站；机场大楼/～ traffic n. 空中交通/～worthy adj. 飞行性能良好的，适航的

airbase /'əbeɪs/

n. a base for military aircraft 空军基地

airborne /'eəbɔːn/

adj. ❶ carried in the air 空气传输的：～ pollutants 空气传播的污染物质 ❷（said about an aircraft）in flight after taking off （飞机）在空中的

aircraft /'eəkrɑːft/

n. an aeroplane, helicopter, or other flying machine 飞机，直升机；航空器

aircrew /'eəkruː/

n. the crew of an aircraft 全体机组人员

airing /'eərɪŋ/

n. ❶ the expression or discussion of opinions in front of a group of people（意见等的）公开发表，公开讨论：These are ideas I feel might be worth an ～. 这些是我认

A

为可能值得公开的一些想法。❷an exposure to warm or fresh air，for the purpose of ventilating or removing dampness from sth. 晾晒；通风

airless /ˈeəlɪs/

adj.❶stuffy；not ventilated 憋闷的；不通风的：a dusty，～ basement 满是灰尘的不通风的地下室 ❷ without wind or breeze；still 无风的；一动不动的：a hot，～ night 炎热无风的夜晚

airlift /ˈeəlɪft/

I *n*.an act of transporting supplies by aircraft，typically in a blockade or other emergency 空运；空投 Ⅱ *v*. transport（troops or supplies）by aircraft，typically when transportation by land is difficult 空运(部队，供给)：Helicopters were employed to ～ the troops out of danger.动用直升机将部队营救出来。

airline /ˈeəlaɪn/

n. ❶ an organization that provides a regular service of air transport for the public 航空公司 ❷a route which forms part of a system regularly used by aircraft 航线

airmail /ˈeəmeɪl/

n.the system of sending letters，etc.by air 航空邮递：Send it by ～.将它空邮寄出。

airship /ˈeəʃɪp/

n.a power-driven aircraft containing helium or another gas that is lighter than air 飞艇

airspace /ˈeəspeɪs/

n.the air above a country and subject to its control 领空，空域

airtight /ˈeətaɪt/

adj.not allowing air to enter or escape 密封的：Store the cake in an ～ container.把蛋糕存放在密封容器里。

airtime /ˈeətaɪm/

n.the time during which a radio or television programme is being broadcast（广播或电视节目的)播放时间

airwaves /ˈeəweɪvz/

n.radio waves that are used in broadcasting radio and television（广播、电视使用的)无线电波；波段：A well-known voice came over the ～.电波传来了一个大家熟悉的声音。

airway /ˈeəweɪ/

n.❶a regular route used by aircraft（飞机的)固定航线 ❷the passage by which air goes into the lungs，or a tube to supply air to the lungs in an emergency 气道；气管

airy /ˈeəri/

adj.❶open to the fresh air 空中的；通风的 ❷ seeming not to be related to real facts or conditions；impractical 空想的；不实际的；虚无缥缈的 ❸giving an impression of light gracefulness 轻盈的；轻快的 ❹unconcerned and not serious 轻率的；轻浮的 ‖ **airily** *adv*.无忧无虑地/**airiness** *n*.通风；活泼

aisle /aɪl/

n. a way between blocks of seats in a church，classroom，theatre，etc.（教堂、教室、戏院等里的)过道，通道

akin /əˈkɪn/

adj. having the same appearance，character，or nature；similar（外表、品质、性质等)相同的，同样的；类似的：His position in the Soviet system is roughly ～ to that of the US President's public relations adviser.他在苏联政府系统中的职位大致相当于美国总统的公共关系顾问。

alack /əˈlæk/

int.a cry expressing sorrow（表示哀伤的喊声)呜呼

alarm /əˈlɑːm/

I *n*.❶a loud noise or a signal that warns people of danger 警报 ❷any device，such as a bell，noise or flag，by which a warning is given 警报器 ❸ a feeling of fear or danger 惊恐 Ⅱ *v*.❶worry or frighten 使惊恐 ❷install sth. with a device which can send warning signals 给(某物)安装警报器

alarmist /əˈlɑːmɪst/

I *n*.a person who always expects danger，often without reason，and alarms other people with fears and warnings 惊慌失措者；大惊小怪者 Ⅱ *adj*. causing endless fear or worry 大惊小怪的：Don't be so

～—everything is under control. 别那么大惊小怪的，一切都在控制之中。

alas/ə'læs/

　　*int.*a cry of sadness or sorry（表示悲伤或遗憾）哎呀

album/'ælbəm/

　　*n.*a book with blank pages to keep photographs or stamps in, or for people to write their signatures in 影集；相片簿；集邮簿；签名纪念册

albumen/'ælbjʊmɪn/

　　*n.*❶ the white part of an egg 蛋白 ❷the protein contained in the white part of an egg 白蛋白

alcohol/'ælkəhɒl/

　　n. ❶ the strong liquid, found in drinks such as beer, wine, etc., which used as an industrial solvent and as fuel 酒精；乙醇 ❷ drinks which can make people drunk 酒精饮料

alcoholic/ˌælkə'hɒlɪk/

　　Ⅰ *adj.*of, containing or caused by alcohol 酒精的；含酒精的；由酒精引起的：～drinks 含酒精的饮料 Ⅱ *n.*one who suffers from a dependence on alcohol 酗酒者；嗜酒者

alcoholism/'ælkəhɒlɪzəm/

　　n. the diseased condition caused by the continued and habitual drinking of too much alcohol 酒精中毒

alcove/'ælkəʊv/

　　*n.*a small room opening out of a bigger room; a part of a big room divided from the main part in some way 凹室；（从大房间隔开的）小间

alert/ə'lɜːt/

　　Ⅰ *adj.*❶ quick to notice any dangerous or difficult circumstances 警惕的；警觉的 ❷quick to see and act; perceptive 活跃的；机灵的 Ⅱ *n.*❶a warning to be ready for danger 警报 ❷a state of being ready to deal with danger, especially after a warning 警戒状态 Ⅲ *v.*make sb. watchful and ready for possible danger 使警觉；使处于待命状态

alfresco/æl'freskəʊ/

　　adj. & *adv.*of or in the open air 露天（的），在户外（的）：We eat ～ in summer. 夏天我们在户外吃饭。/an ～ theatrical performance 露天戏剧演出

alga/'ælgə/

　　n.(*pl.*algae/'ældʒiː, 'ælgiː/) a water plant of very simple structure 海藻

algebra/'ældʒɪbrə/

　　*n.*a branch of mathematics in which sums are worked out using letters for numbers which are unknown 代数

algorithm/'ælgərɪðəm/

　　n. a list of instructions, especially to a computer, which are carried out in a fixed order to find the answer to a question, or to calculate a number, etc.演算法；运算法则；计算程序 ‖ ～ic /ˌælgə'rɪðmɪk/ *adj.* 算法的

alias/'eɪlɪəs/

　　Ⅰ *n.*a name which is not one's own(often used for dishonest purposes)（常用于不正当目的的）化名，假名 Ⅱ *adv.*used to indicate that a named person is also known under another name 别名地，化名地；又名:John Smith ～ Tom Brown 约翰·史密斯化名为汤姆·布朗

alibi/'ælɪbaɪ/

　　n. the statement or fact that one was somewhere else when a crime was committed at a certain place 不在犯罪现场的证词(或事实):have an ～ 有不在犯罪现场的证据

alien/'eɪljən/

　　Ⅰ *adj.*❶strange or unfamiliar 陌生的，不熟悉的:an ～ person 陌生人 ❷from another country or society; foreign 外国的；异域的:Lucy loves seeing ～ films.露西喜欢看外国电影。 ❸contrary to sth. 相反的 Ⅱ *n.*❶a person who is not a native person in the country where they live 外国人；外侨 ❷ being from another world 外星人；外星生物

alienate/'eɪlɪəneɪt/

　　*v.*cause（a person）to become unfriendly or isolated 使不和；使疏远:His sister was ～d from him by his unkindness.他为人刻薄，和妹妹疏远了。 ‖ **alienation** *n.*疏远

A

alight¹ /əˈlaɪt/
　adj. ❶burning 烧着的 ❷shining brightly 闪亮的

alight² /əˈlaɪt/
　v. get out of a vehicle, come down to the ground or to a resting place 下车；降落：He ~ed from the train. 他从火车上下来。

align /əˈlaɪn/
　v. come or bring into a straight line（使）排成一直线 ‖ ~ment *n.* 排成的直线；列队

alike /əˈlaɪk/
　Ⅰ *adj.* similar to each other 相似的；同样的：They are ~ only in appearance. 他们仅外表相像。Ⅱ *adv.* similarly；equally 相似地；一样地；平等地：A good teacher treats all his students ~. 一个好老师对所有学生能一视同仁。

aliment /ˈælɪmənt/
　n. sth. that nourishes；food 养料；食物

alimentary /ˌælɪˈmentəri/
　adj. connected with food or nutrition 饮食的；营养的：~ canal 消化道

alive /əˈlaɪv/
　adj. ❶continuing to live 活着的；在世的：His mother is dead, but his father is still ~. 他母亲过世了，但他父亲还健在。❷full of life；lively 充满生机的；活跃的：The old man seems to be more ~ than a lot of young people. 这老人似乎比许多年轻人还要活跃。‖ be ~ to 充分意识到，对……敏感：be ~ to the importance of health 充分认识到健康的重要/ be ~ with 充满

alkali /ˈælkəlaɪ/
　n. a substance which forms salts when joined to an acid, and turns litmus paper blue 碱

alkaline /ˈælkəlaɪn/
　adj. having the properties of an alkali, or containing alkali；having a pH greater than 7 碱性的

all /ɔːl/
　Ⅰ *adj.* ❶the whole number of；the whole extent or amount of 一切的；所有的；整个的；全部的 ❷the greatest possible a-mount of 尽量的；极度的：with ~ speed 以最高的速度 Ⅱ *adv.* ❶ entirely；quite 完全，十分 ❷much（接 the 和比较级）更加：You must study ~ the harder. 你应该更加努力学习。Ⅲ *pron.* everybody or everything 一切；全部；大家；全体 ‖ ~ at once 突然/~ of a sudden 突然/~ in ❶筋疲力尽的 ❷一切包括在内的/~ right 好，行/~ there 头脑清醒的/~ together 一道；同时 ‖ ~-important *adj.* 至关重要的，首要的/~-inclusive *adj.* 包括一切的/~-night *adj.* 通宵（服务）的/~-out *adj.* 全力的；没有保留的/~-purpose *adj.* 适于各种用途的/~-round *adj.* ❶全面的，多面的 ❷全能的，多才多艺的 ❸适于多种用途的；万能的/~-rounder *n.* 多面手；全能运动员/~-sided *adj.* 全面的/~-sidedly *adv.* 全面地/~-sidedness *n.* 全面性/~-time *adj.* ❶空前的 ❷全部时间的；专职的/~-weather *adj.* 适应各种气候的

allay /əˈleɪ/
　v. lessen the intensity of sth. 减轻；使和缓：~ sb.'s fear 减轻某人的忧虑/ ~ the pain of a disease 缓和病痛

allegation /ˌælɪˈɡeɪʃn/
　n. a claim or statement, which is not supported by proof, that sb. has done sth. wrong or illegal 宣称；指控；假说：~s of serious misconduct by government officials 有关政府官员严重渎职的说法/If the ~s against him prove correct, he will lose his job. 如果对他的这些指控证明是事实，他将失去那份工作。

allege /əˈledʒ/
　v. claim or assert that sb. has done sth. wrong or illegal without proof 无根据地说；宣称；断言（某人做坏事或违法的事）

allegiance /əˈliːdʒəns/
　n. faithfulness and duty（especially to a leader or an association that one is a member of）（尤指对领导或所属社团）忠诚

allegory /ˈælɪɡəri/
　n. a story, intended to teach a lesson, in which either abstract ideas(such as hate, beauty, faithfulness) or animals, appear as though they were human beings 寓言；讽

喻

allergic/ə'lɜːdʒɪk/

adj. ❶ having an allergy 患过敏症的；有过敏性反应的：He is ～ to fish.他对鱼肉过敏。❷ disliking intensely 厌恶的

allergy/'ælədʒi/

*n.*a condition in which one becomes ill or uncomfortable when brought into contact with sth. which usually does not affect other people(in this way) 过敏症，过敏性反应

alleviate/ə'liːvɪeɪt/

v. reduce (pain, suffering, difficulties, etc.)especially for a short time；relieve 减轻，缓和

alley/'æli/

n. a narrow street between or behind buildings in a town 小巷；胡同

alliance/ə'laɪəns/

*n.*a union, e.g. of states, groups (by treaty) 联盟；同盟

allied/'ælaɪd, ə'laɪd/

adj. ❶ joined together in agreement 联合的；同盟的 ❷ connected in some way 有关联的：Chemistry is ～ to physics. 化学和物理有关联。

alligator/'ælɪɡeɪtə(r)/

n. a large animal, rather like a crocodile, with a long nose and sharp teeth which is found mostly in rivers in tropical America 短吻鳄

allocate/'æləkeɪt/

*v.*give or distribute sth.to sb.or for a special purpose 分配；分派；配给

allocation/ˌælə'keɪʃn/

*n.*❶the act or process of allocating 拨给；分配；配给 ❷ a share or amount that has been allocated 配给物；配给量；份额

allot/ə'lɒt/

v.(-tt-) give as a share 分配，分给：Equal amount of money was ～ted to each.每个人分配相同数量的钱。‖ ～ment *n*.分配；配给物

allow/ə'laʊ/

*v.*❶permit sb.to do sth.准许，允许，许可：Passengers are not ～ed to smoke here. 乘客不准在此处吸烟。❷ let sb. have

sth. 给予；让某人得到某物：How much holiday are you ～ed? 你有多少天假？❸ let sth. be done or happen 容许发生 ❹set aside sth. for a special purpose (为某目的)留出，给出：I need to ～ about five hours for the flight.这次航班大概需要五小时。❺accept, admit or agree with sth. 接受；承认；同意：My parents have ～ed my sister's request for a new telephone. 父母同意了妹妹买新手机的请求。‖ ～ for 容许 ‖ ～able *adj*.允许的

allowance/ə'laʊəns/

*n.*a sum of money given regularly 津贴：A retired person can get an ～ of＄100 a month.退休者每月可得到 100 美元的津贴。

alloy/'ælɔɪ/

Ⅰ *n.* a substance made of two or more metals 合金 Ⅱ*v.* to mix one metal with something in lower value 把……铸成合金

allude/ə'luːd/

*v.*talk about sth. without mentioning it by name or directly 暗指；侧面提到：You mustn't even ～ to his father's illness. 你甚至连提都不能提他父亲的病。

allure/ə'lʊə(r)/

Ⅰ*v.*make sb. do sth. (possibly sth. bad) by offering sth.attractive 引诱；诱惑 Ⅱ*n.* attraction；charm 诱惑力；魅力 ‖ ～-ment *n*.诱惑的

alluring/ə'ljʊərɪŋ/

*adj.*attractive or appealing 诱人的；迷人的；有吸引力的：an ～ smile 迷人的微笑 ‖ ～ly *adv*.诱人的；妩媚地

allusion/ə'luːʒn/

n. an expression that is said or written about sth. indirectly, especially while speaking about sth. else 间接提及；影射；暗指；典故：She made several ～s to the previous government's failures. 她几次转弯抹角地提到了上届政府的种种失误。

allusive/ə'luːsɪv/

*adj.*containing allusions 暗指的；影射的；含典故的：an ～ style of poetry which is hard to understand 不容易读懂的富于典故的诗体

A

alluvial /ə'luːvɪəl/
adj. consisting of sand or mud left by rivers 冲积的；淤积的：～ soil 冲积土

alluvium /ə'luːvɪəm/
n. (*pl.* ～s or alluvia /ə'luːvɪə/) sand, mud, etc. left by flowing water 冲积层；淤积物

ally
Ⅰ /'ælaɪ/ *n.* a state, person, etc. allied to another 同盟国；同盟者 Ⅱ /ə'laɪ/ *v.* ❶ combine or unite by treaty, marriage, etc. 使结盟；使联姻 ❷ side with or support 拥护；支持

alma mater /ˌælmə'mɑːtə(r)/
n. ❶ the school, college, or university which one attended 母校 ❷ the song of a school, college, or university 校歌

almanac /'ɔlmənæk, 'ɔːlmənæk/
n. ❶ a book that is published annually containing information of that year about a particular subject or activity 年鉴 ❷ a book giving a list of the days of a year, together with information, especially in the form of tables, about the times of sunrise and sunset, changes in the moon, rise and fall of the sea, etc. 历书，年历（内容除日历外还说明日出日落时间、月亮的变化及潮汐等）

almighty /ɔːl'maɪti/
adj. ❶ having all power；powerful beyond measure 全能的，万能的：the Almighty 上帝 ❷ very great, enormous or serious 非常伟大的；巨大的；严重的

almond /'ɑːmənd/
n. the narrow, oval, light-brown nut 杏仁

almost /'ɔːlməust/
adv. very nearly；not quite 几乎，差不多：She is ～ as tall as her father. 她长得几乎与她父亲一样高了。

aloe /'æləu/
n. a tropical plant with thick sharp-pointed leaves and bitter juice 芦荟

aloft /ə'lɒft/
adv. high up, especially in the air or among the sails of a ship 在高处（尤指在空中或桅杆高处）：The flag was flying ～. 旗帜高高飘扬。

alone /ə'ləun/
adv. ❶ without any other people 单独地；独自地：He went ～. 他是一个人去的。❷（used after a noun or pronoun to emphasize one particular thing）only（用于名词或代词后以加强语气）仅仅，单，只：The shoes alone cost ＄300. 仅鞋子一项就花费 300 美元。‖ let ～ 更不用说

along /ə'lɒŋ/
Ⅰ *prep.* towards the end of 沿着：walk ～ a road 沿路步行 Ⅱ *adv.* ❶ onward 向前：move ～ 向前走 ❷ in company；together with 一起，随身：go ～ with sb. 与某人一起去／take a book ～ 随身带一本书

alongside /ə'lɒŋsaɪd/
prep. & *adv.* by or at the side（of）；side by side（with）在（……）旁边；沿（……）边，靠；并排：bring a boat ～ the wharf 使船靠码头／He walked ～ with his friend. 他与朋友并肩而行。

aloof /ə'luːf/
adv. & *adj.* at some distance from other people（usually in an unfriendly way）离开地（的）；远离地（的）（常指不友好）：stand oneself ～ from somebody 与某人疏远

aloud /ə'laud/
adv. ❶ in a voice that may be heard 出声地：read ～ 朗读 ❷ loudly 大声地

alpaca /æl'pækə/
n. ❶ a sheeplike animal of Peru, related to the llama（秘鲁产的）羊驼 ❷ a type of cloth made from the wool of the alpaca 羊驼呢

alpha /'ælfə/
n. the first letter（A, α）of the Greek alphabet, sometimes used as a mark for excellent work by a student 希腊字母表中的第一个字母（A, α）（有时用作学生作业优秀的符号）

alphabet /'ælfəbet/
n. ❶ a set of letters used in a language 字母表 ❷ the basic elements in a system 基本要素

alphabetical /ˌælfə'betɪkl/
adj. of, belonging to, or in the order of the alphabet 字母的；按照字母顺序的：In a dictionary the words are arranged in ～

order.词典里的单词是按照字母顺序排列的。‖ ~ly adv.按字母顺序地

alpine/'ælpaɪn/

adj.of or like high mountains 高山的：~ plants 高山植物/~ scenery 高山景色

already/ɔːl'redi/

adv.❶before or by this (that)time 已经：He was ~ there.他已在那里了。/They have ~ left.他们已离开了。❷(used in negative and interrogative sentences to express surprise) as soon or early as this (用于否定句或疑问句表示惊讶)就已经：Have you finished lunch ~? 你已吃过午饭? /Is it noon ~? 就到中午啦?

alright/ɔːl'raɪt/

adv.=all right 行；好；不错

also/'ɔːlsəʊ/

adv.in addition；besides；too 而且；此外；还；也：John is ~ coming to the party.约翰也来参加宴会。

altar/'ɔːltə(r)/

n. a table, stone or other raised object which is the most important place in a building where a religious ceremony is held 祭坛

altarpiece/'ɔːltəpiːs/

n.a painting or other work of art placed above and behind an altar (摆在祭坛后上方的)祭坛画，祭坛装饰

alter/'ɔːltə(r)/

v.change；become or make different (使)改变；(使)变化：Our appearance ~s as we get older.我们的外貌随年龄增长而改变。

alteration/ˌɔːltə'reɪʃn/

n.the action or process of altering or being altered 改动；更改；改变：The shirt needs ~.这件衬衣需要改一改。

alternate

Ⅰ/ɔːl'tɜːnət/*adj*.(of two things) happening by turns；first one and then the other 交替的；轮流的；交错 Ⅱ/'ɔːltɜːneɪt/ *v*.(cause to) follow by turns (使)交替；(使)轮流

alternative/ɔːl'tɜːnətɪv/

Ⅰ*adj*.providing a choice between two or more things 可供选择的；其他的：an ~ question

选择问句/~ routes 可供选择的路线 Ⅱ*n*. a choice between two or more things；one of the things to be chosen 选择；可选择的事物之一：He had no ~ but to go by train.他别无选择，只得乘火车去。

alternator/'ɔːltəneɪtə(r)/

n.an electric generator for producing alternating current 交流发电机

although/ɔːl'ðəʊ/

conj.❶in spite of the fact that；even if 虽然；不管；即使：Although the book is difficult to understand, it is interesting.这本书虽然不好理解，但是有趣。❷and yet；nevertheless；but 然而；可是：He said they were married, ~ I'm sure they aren't.他说他们已经结婚了，可是我肯定他们没结婚。

altimeter/'æltɪmiːtə(r)/

n.an instrument used, especially in an aircraft, for recording height (尤指飞机的)高度计(表)

altitude/'æltɪtjuːd/

n.(usually with reference to aeroplanes or mountains)height above sea level (海拔)高度：Mt Kenya has an ~ of over 5,000 metres.肯尼亚山海拔高度5 000米以上。

altogether/ˌɔːltə'geðə(r)/

adv.❶entirely；completely 完全地；全然地：an ~ different answer 完全不同的答复/This part of the sentence may be left out ~.该句的这一部分可全部略去。❷on the whole 总的来说；总之：Altogether, I'm glad it is over.总之，我很高兴，它结束了。❸with all included 总共：There were five of us ~.我们一共五人。

altruism/'æltruɪzəm/

n.the belief in concern for other people rather than yourself 利他主义

alum/'æləm/

n.a white mineral salt, hard and bitter-tasting, used medically, in dyeing, etc.明矾(用于医药、染色等)

alumin(i)um/ˌæljʊ'mɪnɪəm/

n.❶a light, silver coloured metal, used for making part of aeroplanes, saucepans, etc.铝 ❷the chemical element of atomic number 13(symbol：Al)铝元素(符号 Al)

A

alumni /ə'lʌmnaɪ/
n. the former male and female students of a school, college or university（统称）校友，毕业生：Harvard Alumni Association 哈佛大学校友会

always /'ɔ:lweɪz/
adv. ❶ at all times; on every occasion; forever 总是；永远：They ～ come late. 他们老迟到。/ I'll remember you ～. 我永远不会忘记你。❷ repeatedly 再三；老是：It's ～ raining there. 那儿老下雨。

AM /ˌeɪ 'em/
abbr. ❶ ante meridiem 午前，上午（= before noon）❷〈拉〉Artium Magister 文科硕士（= Master of Arts）❸ amplitude modulation 振幅调制

amanuensis /əˌmænju'ensɪs/
n. ❶ a person employed to write down what someone else is saying or to copy what someone else has written 记录员；抄写员；笔录者；文书 ❷ an assistant to write or copy for someone else 助手；秘书

amass /ə'mæs/
v. gather together a large amount of sth. (usually wealth, information, etc.) 积聚（通常指财富、信息等）：In his lifetime, he ～ed a large fortune. 他一生积累了一大笔财产。

amateur /'æmətə(r)/
I *n.* ❶ a person who does sth. because he enjoys doing it, and not for money or because it is not his job 业余爱好者 ❷ a person who does sth. unskillfully, because it is not his real job 外行 II *adj.* ❶ doing sth. just for interest without payment 业余的 ❷ not professional; unskillful 外行的；非专业的

amaze /ə'meɪz/
v. fill with great surprise or wonder 使惊愕；使大为惊奇：His performance ～d us. 他的表演令我们大为惊讶。

amazed /ə'meɪzd/
adj. filled with great surprise or wonder 吃惊的；惊异的：I was ～ at his calmness. 我对他的镇定感到吃惊。/ We were ～ to hear the news ～. 我们听到这个消息，都大为吃惊。/ You would be ～ how difficult it was. 你要是知道这是多么困难，会大为诧异的。/ an ～ expression on her face 她脸上吃惊的表情

amazement /ə'meɪzmənt/
n. a feeling of great surprise or wonder 惊愕；惊诧：She shook her head in ～. 她惊诧地摇了摇头。

amazing /ə'meɪzɪŋ/
adj. causing great surprise or wonder, especially because of quantity or quality; extraordinary（数量或质量等）惊人的；了不起的：The new car goes at an ～ speed. 新车跑起来快得令人吃惊。/ It's quite ～ that he should be so unaware of what's going on! 他对正在发生的事居然毫不知情，这实在叫人感到诧异。‖ ～ly *adv.* 令人惊讶地；惊奇地：an ～ly hot day 酷热的一天 / ～ly good 好极了

ambassador /æm'bæsədə(r)/
n. an important government official whose work is to live in a foreign country and conduct business with the government of that country on behalf of his own government 大使；使节

ambassadress /æm'bæsədrɪs/
n. ❶ the wife of an ambassador 大使夫人 ❷ a female ambassador 女大使

amber /'æmbə(r)/
n. ❶ a type of hard orange or yellow substance used for making jewellery and other ornaments 琥珀 ❷ a yellow light of traffic lights used as a cautionary singal 黄灯（信号）

ambience /'æmbɪəns/
n. the character, atmosphere or feeling of a place 氛围；情调；环境：This little restaurant has a pleasant ～. 这家小饭店的环境幽雅宜人。

ambient /'æmbɪənt/
adj. on all sides; completely surrounding 周围的；四周的：The equipment will function in ～ temperatures of up to 40℃. 这种设备要在周围温度达到40摄氏度时才发挥作用。

ambiguity /ˌæmbɪ'gju:ɪti/
n. ❶ the state of having more than two

possible meaning 歧义;一语多义：Write clear definitions in order to avoid ～.释义要写清楚以免产生歧义。❷the state of being difficult to understand or explain because of involving many different aspects 模棱两可;不明确：You must understand the ～ of my position.你必须理解我所处的位置不明确。

ambiguous/æmˈbɪɡjʊəs/
adj. ❶ having two or more different meanings 模棱两可的：The speaker gave an ～ reply.演讲人做出模棱两可的回答。❷ doubtful;not clear 不明确的;不清楚的

ambit/ˈæmbɪt/
n. the limit or range of power or influence (权力或势力的)界限,范围

ambition/æmˈbɪʃn/
n. a strong desire (to be, do sth. or for sth.) 志向;抱负;野心：His ～ is to be a journalist.他的志向是当个记者。

ambitious/æmˈbɪʃəs/
*adj.*❶having a strong desire for success, power,wealth,etc.有抱负的;有雄心的;有志气的;野心勃勃的：an ～ woman 一个有野心的女人 ❷ needing a lot of effort,money or time to do sth.费力的;耗资的;耗时的 ‖ ～ly *adv.* 雄心勃勃地/ ～ness *n.*不凡的抱负

ambivalent/æmˈbɪvələnt/
*adj.*having opposing feelings towards, or opinions about a person or thing 对人(或事)怀有矛盾看法的：an ～ attitude towards private enterprise 对私人企业所持的矛盾态度 ‖ ～ly *adv.* 犹豫不决地

amble/ˈæmbl/
v. (with reference to a person) walk or move at a slow, relaxed speed (指人)漫步,缓行：We ～d along the road together.我们一起沿着路慢慢地走。

ambulance/ˈæmbjʊləns/
n. a vehicle for carrying the sick or injured to hospital 救护车

ambush/ˈæmbʊʃ/
Ⅰ *v.* wait in hiding until one's enemies come past and then attack them by surprise 埋伏;伏击：The raiding party was

～ed in the forest.突击队在林中遭到伏击。Ⅱ *n.* a surprise attack by others waiting in a hidden place 袭击

amen/ɑːˈmen,eɪˈmen/
int. a word used at the end of a prayer, meaning "May it be so" or "May this prayer be granted"(祈祷的结束语)阿门(意为"但愿如此""诚心所愿")

amenable/əˈmiːnəbl/
*adj.*willing to take advice,listen to the opinions of other people,etc. 愿意听劝告的;肯接受意见的：The young prince was ～ to the advice of his elders.这年轻的王子能听从长辈们的劝告。

amend/əˈmend/
*v.*❶make changes in the words of (a rule or law) 修正(议案等) ❷make or become better by getting rid of faults;improve 改正;改进 ‖ ～able *adj.*可修正的;可改进的

amendment/əˈmendmənt/
n. a change that is made to improve a rule,law,statement,etc.(规则、法律、议案等)修正,改善;修正案

amends/əˈmendz/
n. sth. done to repair or pay for some harm, unkindness, damage, etc. 赔偿;赔罪

amenity/əˈmiːnəti,əˈmenəti/
n.(usually *pl.*) sth. which helps to make people's life more convenient or enjoyable 生活便利设施;生活福利设施

amiable/ˈeɪmiəbl/
*adj.*pleasant and well-intentioned;likable and friendly 和蔼可亲的;友好的;亲切的 ‖ amiability *n.*和蔼可亲/ amiably *adv.*和蔼可亲地

amicable /ˈæmɪkəbl/
*adj.*pleasant and friendly 心平气和的;友善的：an ～ relationship 和睦的关系 ‖ amicability *n.*友善/ amicably *adv.*友善地

amid/əˈmɪd/, **amidst** /əˈmɪdst/
*prep.*during;in the middle of 在……过程中;在……中：The team arrived ～ loud cheers.队伍在大声的欢呼声中到达。

amino acid/əˌmiːnəʊ ˈæsɪd/
n. any of several organic compounds

A

found in protein 氨基酸

amiss /ə'mɪs/

adj. wrong; not right 错误的：As soon as I entered the house, I felt that there was something ~. 我一走进屋子，就感到有什么事情不对头。

amity /'æməti/

n. a friendly relationship 友好；和睦：They lived in ~ with their neighbours. 他们和邻居和睦相处。

ammeter /'æmɪtə(r)/

n. an instrument for measuring an electric current in amperes 安培计；电流计

ammonia /ə'məʊnɪə/

n. ❶ a colourless, pungent gas used in fertilizers, cleaning fluids, etc. 氨 ❷ water solution of this gas 氨水

ammunition /ˌæmjʊ'nɪʃn/

n. ❶ a supply or quantity of bullets, shells, etc. 弹药，军火 ❷ information used to support one's argument（用作论证的）信息

amnesia /æm'niːzɪə/

n. illness in which a person cannot remember things 健忘症

amnesty /'æmnəsti/

n. pardon or forgiveness given by a government to people who have broken the law 大赦；特赦

among /ə'mʌŋ/, **amongst** /'əmʌŋst/

prep. ❶ surrounded by sb. 在……中间：He lived ~ his own people for ten years. 他在自己的人民中间生活了十年。❷ being a member or members in groups of things or people 系……中的一员；……之一：She was ~ the survivors. 她是幸存者之一。

amoral /ˌeɪ'mɒrəl/

adj. behaving or thinking in a way which does not recognize any difference between good and bad（行为或思想）没有道德观念的

amorous /'æmərəs/

adj. showing or having feelings of love; easily falling in love; concerned with love 恋爱的；多情的；有关爱情的

amorphous /ə'mɔːfəs/

adj. without definite shape, arrangement or order 无定形的；杂乱无章的；混乱的

amount /ə'maʊnt/

Ⅰ *v.* (~ to) be equal to; add up to 等于；合计；总共达：His words ~ to a refusal. 他说的话等于拒绝。/ The cost ~ed to $800. 费用共计 800 美元。Ⅱ *n.* ❶ the total quantity or sum 总数 ❷ a quantity of sth. 数量；数额：an ~ of time (information) 一段时间（一些信息）❸ a sum of money 金额

amour /ə'mʊə(r)/

n. an improper sexual relationship, especially one that is secret（秘密的）恋情，风流韵事

amp /æmp/

n. a unit for measuring electric current 安培（计算电流的单位）

amperage /'æmpərɪdʒ/

n. the strength of an electrical current measured in amps 安培数（电流强度）

amphibian /æm'fɪbɪən/

n. an animal, such as a frog, that is able to live both on land and in water（水陆）两栖动物

amphibious /æm'fɪbɪəs/

adj. ❶ able to live on land and in water 两栖的 ❷ by or for land and water 水陆协同的；水陆两用的：~ attack 水陆两用攻击 / ~ vehicle 水陆两用车辆

ample /'æmpl/

adj. ❶ quite enough 充裕的；足够的 ❷ large and accommodating 宽敞的 ‖ ~-ness *n.* 富裕；广大 / **amply** *adv.* 充足地；广大地

amplifier /'æmplɪfaɪə(r)/

n. an instrument, as used in radios and record players, that makes electrical current or power stronger, especially so as to make sound louder 放大器；扩音器；扬声器

amplify /'æmplɪfaɪ/

v. ❶ increase the strength of sth., especially sound coming through electrical instruments 放大，增强（声音）❷ increase in size, effect, etc., especially by explaining in greater detail 阐发；详述

amplitude/'æmplɪtjuːd/

　n.❶ the quality of being ample, especially great quantity; abundance 充足；丰富 ❷ largeness of space 广大；宽阔 ❸ the distance between the middle and the top (or bottom) of a wave such as a sound wave 振幅；波幅；幅度

ampoule/'æmpuːl/

　n. a small usually glass container for a hypodermic 安瓿（装注射液的小玻璃瓶）

amputate/'æmpjuteɪt/

　v. cut off a part or parts of the body for medical reasons（手术）切除；截（肢）

amulet/'æmjulɪt/

　n. an object worn in the belief that it will protect one against evil, disease, bad luck, etc. 护身符；驱邪物

amuse/ə'mjuːz/

　v.❶ make someone laugh or smile 逗（某人）笑 ❷ make one's time pass pleasantly 消遣

amusement/ə'mjuːzmənt/

　n.❶ the state of being amused; enjoyment 开心；愉悦；乐趣：I listened in ～. 我听得十分开心。/ To everyone's ～ the actor fell off the stage. 演员从舞台上跌了下来，把大家都逗乐了。❷ sth. that makes one's time pass pleasantly; diversion 消遣；娱乐：Big cities have theatres, films, football matches, and many other ～s. 大城市里有戏剧、电影、足球比赛以及许多其他的娱乐活动。‖ ～ **arcade** n.〈英〉娱乐场/～ **park** n.〈美〉游乐场

amusing/ə'mjuːzɪŋ/

　adj. making people laugh or smile; entertaining 逗笑的；供人消遣的：a likeable, ～ man 一个可爱有趣的人 ‖ ～**ly** adv. 有趣地；消遣地

anachronism/ə'nækrənɪzəm/

　n. a person, thing, or idea that is or appears to be in the wrong period of time 不合时代的人（或事物、观点）：Some people believe that the British House of Lords is an ～. 有些人认为英国的上议院是一种不合时代的东西。

an(a)emia/ə'niːmɪə/

　n. a medical condition in which a person does not have enough red corpuscles in the blood, resulting in pallor and weakness 贫血（症）

anaemic/ə'niːmɪk/

　adj.❶ suffering from anaemia 贫血的，患贫血症的 ❷ lacking forcefulness or spirit 没有活力的；无精打采的：an ～ performance 有气无力的表演 ‖ ～**ally** adv. 无精打采地

anaesthesia/ˌænɪs'θiːzɪə/

　n. the state of being unable to feel pain, especially as a result of injury, illness of the mind, drugs, etc.（对疼痛等的）感觉缺失，麻木；（由药品等造成的）麻醉状态

anaesthetic/ˌænɪs'θetɪk/

　n. a liquid or gas which makes a person unable to feel pain, either by making him become unconscious, or by affecting one part of the body only, used by a doctor or dentist before operating on a person 麻醉剂：local ～ 局部麻醉剂/general ～ 全身麻醉剂

anaesthetist/ə'niːsθətɪst/

　n. a doctor who gives an anaesthetic to a patient 麻醉师

anaesthetize/ə'niːsθətaɪz/

　v. make unable to feel pain by giving an anaesthetic, especially in order to perform an operation 使麻醉；施麻醉剂于

anal/'eɪnl/

　adj. of or near the anus 肛门的；近肛门的

analects/'ænəlekts/

　n.(pl.) collected literary excerpts 文选；论集

analgesic/ˌænæl'dʒiːsɪk/

　adj.(chiefly of a drug) relieving pain（主要指药剂）镇痛的；止痛的：an ～ drug 镇痛药；止痛药

analogous/ə'næləgəs/

　adj. similar in certain respects 相似的；类似的：He saw the relationship between a ruler and his subjects as ～ to that of father and children. 他认为统治者和臣民的关系可比拟成父亲和孩子的关系。‖ ～**ly** adv. 相似地；类似地

analogue/'ænəlɒg/

　n. sth. that is analogous to sth. else 相似

物;类似事情

analogy /ə'nælədʒɪ/

*n.*❶similarity or likeness 类似,相似 ❷a comparison between two things 类比: Shakespeare makes an ～ between the citizens of a country and the parts of a person's body.莎士比亚把一个国家的公民比作人体的各个部分。❸ a process of comparing the things with similar features to explain it 类推

analyse(-ze) /'ænəlaɪz/

*v.*❶study or examine sth. in order to understand or explain it 分析;分解;解析 ❷ psychoanalyse 心理分析 ‖ ～r *n.*分析者

analysis /ə'næləsɪs/

n. (*pl.* analyses /ə'næləsiːz/) ❶ the detailed examination of sth. by dividing it into its separate parts 分解;分析:The ～ of the food showed the presence of poison. 那食物经化验后表明有毒。❷ an examination of sth. together with thoughts and judgments about it 分析研究:Our ～ shows that the company's failure was caused by lack of investment.我们的分析研究表明,该公司所以失利,是由于投资不足。❸ psychoanalysis 心理分析 ‖ **in the final (last) ～** 最终;归根结底:In the last ～, the responsibility for this failure must lie with minister.归根结底,这次失败的责任应由部长承担。

analyst /'ænəlɪst/

*n.*❶ a person who makes an analysis, e.g. of chemical materials 分析者;化验员:a food ～ 食物化验员/a political ～ 政治分析家 ❷ a psychoanalyst 心理分析(医)师

analytic /ˌænə'lɪtɪk/

*adj.*using or skilled in using methods of careful examination, especially in order to separate things into the parts 分析的; (善于)用分析方法的:She has a very ～ mind.她有一个善于分析的头脑。/computer-based ～ techniques 借助电脑的分析技术

anarchic /ə'nɑːkɪk/

*adj.*of, like, or likely to cause anarchy, especially in lacking order or control 无政府状态的;无秩序的;混乱的:The situa-

tion in the country is becoming increasingly ～.这个国家的局势日益混乱。/an ～ style of painting 杂乱无章的绘画风格 ‖ ～ally *adv.*无政府主义地;混乱地

anarchism /'ænəkɪzəm/

n. the political belief that society should have no government, laws, police, etc. but should be a free association of all its members 无政府主义

anarchy /'ænəki/

*n.*a situation of disorder due to absence of law and government, so that each person does as he wishes (usually causing harm to other people) 无政府状态 ‖ anarchist *n.* 无政府主义者

anatomical /ˌænə'tɒmɪkl/

*adj.*of or concerned with anatomy 解剖 (学)的;an ～ description of the leg 腿的解剖说明 ‖ ～**ly** *adv.*解剖学上

anatomist /ə'nætəmɪst/

*n.*a person who studies anatomy 解剖学家

anatomy /ə'nætəmi/

*n.*❶ the dissection of a body or part of a person or animal to study the way it works or is built 解剖;剖析 ❷the scientific study of the bodies and body parts of people and animals 解剖学 ❸the body or body parts of a person or animal (人或动物)结构

ancestor /'ænsestə(r)/

*n.*❶ a person from whom one is descended 祖宗;祖先 ❷an early type of a modern animal or plant (动植物的)原种 ❸ an early form of a more developed machine, system, etc. (机械、制度等的)原型

ancestral /æn'sestrəl/

adj. belonging to or coming from one's ancestors 祖先的;祖传的

ancestry /'ænsestri/

n. a person's ancestors considered as a group or as a continuous line 祖先;世系: a woman of noble ～ 一个出身于贵族世家的女人 /Scottish ～ 苏格兰血统(世系)/to trace one's ～ 寻根

anchor /'æŋkə(r)/

Ⅰ *n.*❶ a piece of heavy metal, usually a

hook with two arms, at the end of a chain or rope, for lowering into the water to keep a ship from moving 锚：We sailed round the coast and dropped ～ in a pleasant little bay.我们绕着海岸航行,之后在一个景色宜人的小海湾抛锚停泊下来。/fishing boats riding, lying at ～ 抛了锚在海上漂浮的渔船 ❷ a person or thing that provides support and a feeling or safety 可以依靠的人(或事物),精神支柱;靠山 Ⅱ v. ❶ stop sailing and lower the anchor 抛锚停船 ❷ fix firmly in position (使)稳固,固定：～ the roof of a house 固定房顶 ❸ present and coordinate (a television or radio programme) 主持(电视、广播节目)

anchorage /'æŋkərɪdʒ/

n. ❶ a place where ships may anchor (船只)停泊处,抛锚处 ❷ a means of making sth. firm 固定方法：Rub the door with sandpaper to provide ～ for the next coat of paint.先用砂纸把门磨一磨,这样下一层油漆才粘得牢。

anchorite /'æŋkəraɪt/

n. a person who lives alone for religious reasons;hermit 隐士;隐居修道的人

ancient /'eɪnʃənt/

Ⅰ adj. ❶ belonging to the very distant past 古代的 ❷ very old 古老的;老式的 Ⅱ n. an old man 老年人

ancillary /æn'sɪləri/

adj.providing extra support to a main activity or organization 辅助的;补充的:～ services 辅助服务设施

and /ænd,ənd/

conj. ❶ connecting words, clauses, sentences (表示并列或对称关系,用来连接词、短语或句子)和;与;及;同;又;并;兼 ❷ then again; repeatedly, increasingly (强调连续、反复)接连:for hours ～ hours 很久很久 ❸ added to; plus (用来连接数词)加:Five ～ six is eleven.五加六是十一。❹ then; afterwards 然后;其后:She knocked on the door ～ went in. 她敲敲门,然后走了进去。❺ as a result of this (位于句首,用来承上启下)于是;而且:And you may now say that things are all right. 因此你现在可以说一切都是对的。

好。❻ expresses a result or explanation (表示结果或说明)就, 将：Water the seeds ～ they will grow.给种子浇水,它们就会发芽生长。

andante /æn'dænti/

Ⅰ n.a piece of music played rather slowly (乐曲的)行板 Ⅱ adj. & adv. (of music) played rather slowly 行板的(地);缓慢的(地)

android /'ændrɔɪd/

n. (in stories) a robot in a human form (故事中的)机器人

anecdotal /ˌænek'dəʊtl/

adj.of, containing, telling, or full of anecdotes 轶事的;趣闻的:an ～ lecture about his travels 有关他旅行趣闻的演说/The theory relies more on ～ evidence than genuine statistics.该理论依据的是一些传闻,而不是确实的统计数字。

anecdote /'ænɪkdəʊt/

n.a short interesting or amusing story about a person or an event 掌故;趣闻;轶事

anemometer /ˌænɪ'mɒmɪtə(r)/

n. a machine for measuring the strength or speed of wind 风力仪

anew /ə'njuː/

adv.again, or in a different way 重新;再：They started life ～ in America.他们在美国开始新生。

angel /'eɪndʒl/

n. ❶ a messenger from God, usually shown in pictures as a human being in white with wings (穿白衣服,有翅膀的人形)天使,上帝的使者 ❷ a person who is very kind, beautiful, etc.安琪儿,可爱的人

angelic /æn'dʒelɪk/

adj.❶ of or like an angel 天使的;天使般的 ❷ extremely beautiful or kind 极美丽的;极善良的 ‖ ～ally adv. 天使般地

anger /'æŋɡə(r)/

Ⅰ n. the fierce feeling of annoyance, displeasure or hostility 怒;怒火;怒气：be filled with ～ 满腔怒火 Ⅱ v.make sb. angry 使发怒;激怒：This ～ed him at first. 起初,这件事使他很生气。

A

angina /æn'dʒaɪnə/
n. a diseased condition of the heart, causing a sharp pain in the chest after strong physical exertion 心绞痛

angle[1] /'æŋgl/
Ⅰ *n.* ❶ the space between two lines that meet or cross each other 角；角度 ❷ a point of view 角度；方面 ❸ a particular way of considering a matter or question 观点，立场 Ⅱ *v.* ❶ turn or move at an angle 使转角度：~ a camera（摄影时）对角度 ❷ represent information, a report, etc. from a particular point of view 以某观点提供信息；从某一角度报道

angle[2] /'æŋgl/
v. ❶ fish (for trout, etc.) with a hook and bait 钓鱼 ❷ use tricks, hints, etc. in order to get sth.（用不正当手段）攫取，追逐

angler /'æŋglə/
n. a person who fishes with a rod and line 钓鱼人；垂钓者

Anglo- /'æŋgləʊ/
pref. English or British 英国的：~-French cooperation 英法合作

angora /æŋ'gɔːrə/
n. ❶ a type of goat or rabbit with long silky hair（一种有光滑柔软长毛的）安哥拉羊；安哥拉兔 ❷ woollen material or thread made from the hair of an angora rabbit 安哥拉兔毛织物；安哥拉兔毛线

angry /'æŋgri/
adj. ❶ filled with anger 生气的；发怒的：He is ~ with himself about it. 他为此正在与自己生气呢。/She was very ~ to hear the news. 她听到消息后十分气愤。❷ red and inflamed 红肿的；发炎的 ❸ stormy and threatening 狂风暴雨的；怒吼的

anguish /'æŋgwɪʃ/
n. severe pain, suffering, especially of mind 极度的痛苦；苦恼

angular /'æŋɡjʊlə(r)/
adj. ❶ having or forming an angle or angles 有角的；成角的 ❷ measured by an angle 用角度量的 ❸ lean and bony 骨瘦如柴的：an ~ basketball player 身材瘦削的篮球队员

animal /'ænɪml/
Ⅰ *n.* ❶ any living thing, especially one with four legs, which can feel and move about 动物；兽；牲畜 ❷ a person considered as behaving like a wild non-human creature 畜生般的人 Ⅱ *adj.* of or concerning of animals 动物的；野兽的

animate
Ⅰ /'ænɪmeɪt/ *v.* ❶ give life or excitement to 使有生命；使活泼；使生气勃勃：A smile ~d her face. 微笑使她显得容光焕发。❷ give the appearance of movement by showing pictures with slight difference rapidly one after one 把……制成动画 Ⅱ /'ænɪmət/ *adj.* having life; alive 有生命的；有生气的：Do you think ~ beings exist on Mars? 你认为火星上有生物存在吗？

animated /'ænɪmeɪtɪd/
adj. full of spirit and excitement; lively 栩栩如生的；生气勃勃的；活跃的

animation /ˌænɪ'meɪʃn/
n. ❶ excitement; spirit; liveliness 兴奋；生气；活跃：They were full of ~ as they talked about their holiday. 他们谈论起假期的事，兴奋不已。❷ the making of cartoons 卡通（动画）片的制作

animosity /ˌænɪ'mɒsəti/
n. strong hatred or dislike 憎恶；仇恨：I think that man feels great ~ towards you. 我想那个人对你怀有深仇大恨。

ankle /'æŋkl/
n. the part of the body between the foot and the leg 踝，踝关节

annals /'ænlz/
n. (*pl.*) ❶ a written account of events year by year in a chronological order 编年史 ❷ historical records; history 历史记载；历史 ❸ any journal containing reports of a society, etc.（学会等的）年报

annex /ə'neks/
v. take control and possession of a country, region, etc. 吞并，兼并（国家、地区等）

annexe /'æneks/
n. ❶ a building joined or added to a larger one 附属（或增建）建筑物：a hospital ~ 医院的附属建筑物 ❷ an additional part

of a document 附录

annihilate /əˈnaɪəleɪt/
v. destroy sth. entirely so that nothing is left 摧毁；消灭：The raiders ～d the village. 入侵者毁灭了那个村庄。

anniversary /ˌænɪˈvɜːsəri/
n. a date each year on which sth. happened in the past 周年纪念日

annotate /ˈænəteɪt/
v. write or give written notes adding more information or explaining sth. hard to understand 注释，注解：It is better to buy an ～d edition of Shakespeare plays. 买莎士比亚剧本最好买有注释的版本。

announce /əˈnaʊns/
v. ❶ tell people sth. officially; make known 宣布；宣告；发表 ❷ say that someone has come by calling out his name 通报……的来到 ❸ read (news) or introduce (a person or an act) on the radio, television, etc. 广播；播放 ❹ notify or inform sb. of sth. 通知 ❺ say sth. in a loud and serious way 宣称；声称

announcement /əˈnaʊnsmənt/
n. ❶ a statement making publicly known sth. that has happened or will happen 通告；布告；告示；声明：flight arrival ～s at the airport 机场关于班机到达的消息公告 /news ～ 新闻发布 /I've got an important ～ to make. 我有件重要的事情要宣布。 ❷ the act of publicly informing people about sth. 宣布；发表；通告：The ～ of the trade figures was delayed until after the election. 贸易数据推迟到选举以后公布。

announcer /əˈnaʊnsə(r)/
n. a person who reads news or introduces people, acts, etc., especially on radio or television (电台、电视台)广播员，播音员，节目主持人

annoy /əˈnɔɪ/
v. make rather angry; cause trouble to 使生气；使烦恼；烦扰：I was very ～ed with him about his rudeness. 对他的粗野无礼我十分恼火。 ‖ ～ance *n.* ❶烦恼 ❷讨厌的人；讨厌的东西

annoying /əˈnɔɪɪŋ/
adj. making sb. feel slightly angry 使恼怒的；使生气的；使烦恼的：～ habits 让人讨厌的习惯

annual /ˈænjuəl/
adj. happening, appearing, etc. every year or once a year 每年的；年度的

annuity /əˈnjuːəti/
n. ❶ a fixed sum of money paid every year for someone's rest life 年金 ❷ a form of insurance that provides such a regular annual income 年金保险；年金保险投资

annul /əˈnʌl/
v. stop or end completely (an agreement, law, rule, etc.) 取消，废除(协议、法令、规则等)

anode /ˈænəʊd/
n. the positively charged electrode 阳极；正极

anomalous /əˈnɒmələs/
adj. not following the usual or regular way; different from the others of a group 不规则的；异常的

anomaly /əˈnɒməli/
n. sth. which does not follow the normal rule or sth. which is different 反常；异常的事物：A school with no books in it would be an ～ these days. 如今没有藏书的学校是反常的。

anonymous /əˈnɒnɪməs/
adj. without a name, or with a name that is not made known 匿名的；无名的：He received an ～ gift. 他收到匿名礼物。/ This poem is ～. 这首诗没有署名。 ‖ anonymity /ˌænəˈnɪməti/ *n.* 匿名；无名

another /əˈnʌðə(r)/
adj. & pron. ❶ one more; an extra thing or person 又一；再一；另一(事物或人)：Would you like ～ drink? 还想喝一杯吗？/ I didn't say ～ word. 我没有再说一个字。 ❷ different; a different person or thing 另一；不同的(人或事物)：The room's too small. Let's see if they've got ～ one. 这房间太小。咱们看看是否另给找一间。/ moving from one place to ～ 从一地到另一地 ❸ a person or thing of a very similar type 类似的(人或事物)：

There'll never be ～ like him.不会再有像他那样的人物了。‖ one ～ 互相：give presents to one ～ 互赠礼品

answer/'ɑːnsə(r)/

Ⅰ *n.* ❶ a thing that is said, written, or done as a reaction of someone asking a question, sending a letter, etc.；reply 回答；答复；应答 ❷ sth. which is discovered as a result especially of thinking, calculating, etc.答案 Ⅱ *v.* ❶ say, write or do sth. as a reaction to a question or letter 回答；答复；应答 ❷ be responsible or to blame for 对……负责；因……受到谴责 ❸ be suitable；satisfy 符合，适合；满足：～ the needs of the market 满足市场的需要

answerable/'ɑːnsərəbl/

adj. ❶ able to be answered 可答复的；可驳斥的 ❷ having to explain or defend one's actions；responsible；accountable 应负责任的

ant/ænt/

n. a small insect that lives in highly organized societies 蚁 ‖ ～hill *n.* 蚁冢

antagonism /æn'tægənɪzəm/

n. active opposition or hostility 敌意；敌对；对立；对抗：the ～ between the two parties 两个党派之间的对立

antagonist /æn'tægənɪst/

n. a person who is hostile to sb. or sth.；an opponent 对立者；对手；敌手

antagonistic /æn₁tægə'nɪstɪk/

adj. showing or feeling antagonism, hostile 对立情绪的；对抗的；敌对的；敌意的 ‖ ～ally *adv.* 反对地

antagonize /æn'tægənaɪz/

v. make someone feel hostile towards you 使对立；使生气：Not wishing to ～ her further, he said no more.他不愿惹她更生气，便不再说话。

Antarctic/æn'tɑːktɪk/

adj. of the south polar regions 南极的；南极区的：the ～ Circle 南极圈/the ～ Continent 南极洲

ante/'ænti/

n. an amount that is risked in the card game of poker (赌纸牌下的)赌注：a ￡2 ～ 两英镑赌注

anteater /'æntiːtə(r)/

n. an animal with a long nose and a sticky tongue, which feeds on ants and termites 食蚁兽

antecedent/₁æntɪ'siːdnt/

Ⅰ *adj.* going or being before 先行的；先前的；在前的：the events ～ to the murder 谋杀案发生前的事情 Ⅱ *n.* ❶ a thing, event, etc., that goes before 前事；先例：the ～ of the automobile 汽车的前身 ❷ the word, phrase, or sentence to which a pronoun refers 先行词 ❸ (*pl.*) a person's ancestors or family and social background 祖先；身世；经历：a person of unknown ～s 一个来历不明的人

antechamber/'æntɪtʃeɪmbə(r)/

n. a small room leading to a larger one (通往较大房间的)前厅，外室

antedate/'æntɪdeɪt/

v. ❶ be earlier in history than (在历史上)比……为早，先于，早于：This old carriage ～s the invention of the car.这种老式四轮马车在汽车发明之前就有了。 ❷ write a date earlier than the date of writing on(a letter, cheque, etc.) (在信件、支票等上)填写比实际日期早的日期

antelope/'æntɪləʊp/

n. an animal with horns, found in Africa and Asia, which can run very fast 羚羊

antenatal/₁æntɪ'neɪtl/

adj. before the birth of a baby 出生前的：～ clinic 孕妇保健诊所

antenna/æn'tenə/

n. ❶ one of the two feelers on the head of an insect (昆虫的)触角 ❷ wire used in radio or television for sending or receiving radio waves；aerial (无线电或电视)天线

anterior/æn'tɪərɪə(r)/

adj. ❶ earlier (than)；before；prior 较……早的；在……以前的；先前的 ❷ (of a part of the body) nearer the front (身体部位)近前面(前部，前端)的

anteroom/'æntɪrʊm, -ruːm/

n. a small room leading into a bigger one 前室；接待室

anthem/'ænθəm/

n. ❶ a religious song to be sung in a church, especially by a choir, often with words taken from the Bible 赞美诗；圣歌 ❷ any ceremonial song of praise 颂歌；赞歌

anther/'ænθə(r)/
n. the part of a stamen that contains the pollen 花药（花的带花粉部分）

anthology/æn'θɒlədʒi/
n. a collection of poems or pieces of prose, or of both, by different writers, or a selection（诗、文、曲、画等的）选集 ‖ **anthologist** *n.* 选集的编者

anthrax/'ænθræks/
n. a serious disease which attacks cattle, sheep, and sometimes humans, typically affecting the skin and lungs 炭疽（病）

anthropoid/'ænθrəpɔɪd/
adj. ❶（of an animal）like a person（指动物）似人的：~ apes such as the chimpanzee and the gorilla 类人猿诸如黑猩猩和大猩猩等 ❷（of a person）like a monkey（指人）猴子似的

anthropologist /ˌænθrə'pɒlədʒɪst/
n. someone who studies anthropology 人类学家

anti-/'ænti/
pref. ❶ preventing 表示"防止" ❷ opposed to；against 表示"反的""逆的"

anti-aircraft/'æntɪˈeəkrɑːft/
adj. used in fighting against enemy aeroplanes 防空的：~ gun 高射炮

antibiotic/ˌæntɪbaɪˈɒtɪk/
n. a drug or medicine which works by destroying the germs causing an illness 抗生素：Penicillin is an ~. 盘尼西林是一种抗生素。

antibody/'æntɪbɒdi/
n. a substance produced in the body to fight against disease 抗体（身体中的抗病物质）

anticipate/æn'tɪsɪpeɪt/
v. ❶ think likely to happen；expect 预料；期望 ❷ do sth. before（someone else）抢……之先；占……之先 ❸ come or take place before an event or process expected for a later time 在……之前来到（或发

生）❹ guess or imagine in advance（what will happen）and take the necessary action in order to be ready 预见，预计（并做准备）

anticipation/ænˌtɪsɪˈpeɪʃn/
n. the act of anticipating 预期；预料；期望；抢先；占先：I had taken my coat and umbrella in ~ of rain. 我预料要下雨，所以带上了外套和雨伞。/The crowd waited outside the theatre in eager ~. 人群抱着热切的期望在剧院外面等候。

anticlimax/ˌæntiˈklaɪmæks/
n. a disappointing end to sth. 令人扫兴的结局；反高潮：The end of the story was an ~. 故事的结尾令人失望。

anticlockwise/ˌæntiˈklɒkwaɪz/
adj.&adv. in the direction opposite to the hands of a clock 逆时针方向的（地）

anticyclone/ˌæntiˈsaɪkləʊn/
n. an area of high atmospheric pressure 高气压；反气旋

antidote/'æntidəʊt/
n. ❶ a medicine which stops the effects of a poison 解毒药 ❷ anything which stops sth. bad or unpleasant 矫正方法；解除痛苦（或不愉快）的方法：Hard work is an ~ for unhappiness. 勤奋是消除悲伤的办法。

antifreeze/'æntifriːz/
n. a substance added to the water in the radiator of a car to prevent it freezing in cold weather 防冻剂；抗凝剂

antigen/'æntɪdʒən/
n. a substance such as a bacterium or virus which causes the body to produce antibodies to fight against disease 抗原（能使身体内产生抗体的物质）

antinuclear/ˌæntiˈnjuːklɪə(r)/
adj. opposing the use of atomic power and the production and storing of atomic weapons 反核的：an ~ demonstration 反核示威/the ~ movement 反核运动

antipathetic/ˌæntɪpəˈθetɪk/
adj. feeling, causing, or showing antipathy 厌恶的；反感的：He has always been strongly ~ to the views of the women's movement. 他对妇女运动的主张历来有

强烈的反感。‖ ～ally /-kli/ adv.引起反感地

antipathy /æn'tɪpəθi/
n. strong and unchanging feelings of dislike 厌恶;反感

anti-personnel /ˌæntɪ ˌpɜːsə'nel/
adj.(of bombs)intended to hurt people, not destroy property, by exploding into small pieces(炸弹)用于杀伤人的,杀伤性的

antiperspirant /ˌæntɪ'pɜːspərənt/
n. a chemical substance that helps to stop the skin from sweating 止汗剂

antiquarian /ˌæntɪ'kweərɪən/
Ⅰ n. a person who studies, collects, or sells antiquities or antiques 研究(或收藏,出售)古物的人 Ⅱ adj.of or concerning antiquities or antiques or people who study, collect or sell such things 古物的;研究(或收藏,出售)古物的:an ～ bookseller 古书商

antiquated /'æntɪkweɪtɪd/
adj.(usually of objects or ideas) old-fashioned or of no use(通常指物件或思想)废弃的;过时的;陈旧的

antique /æn'tiːk/
Ⅰ adj. of or connected with ancient times, especially ancient Rome or Greece 古代的(尤指古希腊或古罗马的)Ⅱ n. a piece of furniture, decorative object, jewellery, etc.that was made in an earlier period and that is rare or valuable 古物;古器;古玩

antiquity /æn'tɪkwəti/
n. ❶ the state of being very old;great age 古老;古;a building of great ～ 一座很古老的建筑物 ❷ a building, work of art, etc., remaining from ancient times, especially before the Middle Ages(尤指中世纪前流传下来的)古迹,古物:photograph the antiquities in the museum 为博物馆中的古物拍照

antiseptic /ˌæntɪ'septɪk/
Ⅰ adj. preventing the growth of germs and the spread of disease 防腐的;抗菌的 Ⅱ n. a substance which has this effect 防腐剂;抗菌剂

antisocial /ˌæntɪ'səʊʃl/
adj. ❶ against the ideas of what is good which most people in society have agreed on 反社会常理的 ❷ unfriendly;not wanting any friends 不友好的;孤僻的

antithesis /æn'tɪθəsɪs/
n. ❶ the opposite of sth. 对立;对照:Laughter is the ～ of tears.笑声是眼泪的反面。❷contrast 对比

antler /'æntlə(r)/
n.(usually pl.) one of the two horns of a deer 鹿角

antonym /'æntəʊnɪm/
n. a word that is opposite in meaning to another word 反义词

anus /'eɪnəs/
n. the opening of the body through which solid waste is sent out 肛门

anxiety /æŋ'zaɪəti/
n. ❶a state of being worried about what may happen 忧虑;担心;不安:his feelings of ～ 他焦虑的心情/cause ～ to someone 使某人忧虑 /The son is her constant ～.她儿子使她忧虑不已。❷ eager desire 渴望:～ for success 渴望成功

anxious /'æŋkʃəs/
adj. feeling anxiety;worried and frightened 忧虑的;担心的;焦心的;渴望的:She was ～ about your health.她担心你的身体。/I'm really ～ to see her.我真的急于想见她。‖ ～ly adv.不安地;忧虑地 /～ness n.焦虑

any /'eni/
Ⅰ adj. ❶ some;even the smallest number or amount 什么;一些:Any suggestions? 有什么建议吗? ❷every;(of more than two) no matter which 任何的;(三个或三个以上的人或物中)任一的:You may take ～ one of these.这些当中你可随便拿一个。Ⅱ adv.in the least;at all 一点儿也(不),丝毫:Is he ～ better today? 他今天好些了吗?

anybody /'enibɒdi/
Ⅰ pron. anyone;any person;all people 任何人:Has ～ seen him? 有什么人见过他吗? /I don't know ～ in the town.镇上

的人我一个都不认识。/Anybody can lift it.任何人都可把它举起来。Ⅱ *n.* a person of importance 重要人物

anyhow/ˈenɪhaʊ/

　adv. ❶ in any case；in spite of that；anyway 不管怎样；无论如何 ❷ carelessly；without regular orders 随随便便；马马虎虎

anyone /ˈenɪwʌn/

　pron. ❶ any person or people 任何人：There wasn't ～ there.那儿什么人都没有。/Does ～ remember him? 有谁记得他吗? ❷ a person of importance or authority 重要(或权威)的人：She wasn't ～ before 2002.2002 年之前她还是个无名之辈。

anything/ˈenɪθɪŋ/

　Ⅰ *pron.*any thing；whatever 任何事(物)：I'm sorry,I can't tell you ～.很抱歉,我什么也不能告诉你。/I wonder if she found ～. 我不知道她是否发现了什么。/Is there ～ in the room? 房里有什么东西吗? Ⅱ *adv.*in any way；at all 在任何方面；全然：Is this watch ～ like the one you lost? 这表和你遗失的那只有点相像吗? ‖ ～ but 决不；一点也不；与……正相反：He is ～ but polite.他这人一点也不讲礼貌。

anyway/ˈenɪweɪ/

　adv. ❶ in spite of everything；in any case；anyhow 无论如何；不管怎样；反正：It doesn't make much difference because we're going to be late ～.这没有多大关系,我们反正要迟到了。 ❷ (used when going on with a story, changing a subject in conversation,etc.) (用于继续讲述故事,改变话题等)反正：Well,～,I rang the bell.好吧,反正我按铃了。

anywhere/ˈenɪweə(r)/

　Ⅰ *adv.*in,at,or to any place 在(去)任何地方：I can't find my bike ～.我哪里也找不到我的自行车。/I've hardly been ～ since then.从那时以来,我几乎没有去过任何地方。‖ get (go) ～ 成功,进展：You'll never get ～ with that attitude.用那种态度,你将永无进展。Ⅱ *pron.*any place 任何地方：He hasn't ～ to stay.他无处可待。

apart/əˈpɑːt/

　adv. away from each other；to or on one side；separately 相隔；相距；除去；撤开；拆开：take a machine ～ 把机器拆开 ‖ **tell(know)** ～ 区别,分别：tell two things ～ 对两件东西加以区别

apartment/əˈpɑːtmənt/

　n. ❶ a set of rooms for living in,usually on the same floor of a building (常指在同一楼层的)公寓套房 ❷ (usually *pl.*) a room,especially a large or splendid one (尤指大而华丽的)房间

apathetic/ˌæpəˈθetɪk/

　adj. having no interest or feeling 冷漠的；无动于衷的

apathy/ˈæpəθi/

　n. lack of interest or feeling 冷漠；无感情：There is too much ～ about the need for further education. 人们普遍对深造不感兴趣。

ape/eɪp/

　Ⅰ *n.* a large monkey without a tail or with a very short tail, such as a gorilla or chimpanzee 无尾猿；类人猿 Ⅱ *v.* copy a person or a person's behaviour,manners, speech,etc.,especially in a stupid or unsuccessful way；imitate 模仿

aperitif/əˈperətɪf/

　n. a drink (usually alcoholic) which is taken before a meal to increase one's appetite 开胃酒

aperture/ˈæpətʃə(r)/

　n. a small hole,especially one which lets light come in(e.g.a camera has an aperture through which light passes to the film) (尤指透光线的)孔,隙；(照相机上的)光圈

apex/ˈeɪpeks/

　n.(*pl.*apices/ˈeɪpɪsiːz/ or ～es) the top or highest point of anything 顶,顶点

aphorism /ˈæfərɪzm/

　n. a short saying that states sth. true or wise 格言；警句

aplomb/əˈplɒm/

　*n.*self-confidence；belief in one's own abilities 自信；自持：do it with ～ 信心十足地做这事

A

apologetic /əˌpɒləˈdʒetɪk/
adj. wanting to apologize for sth.; expressing regret 道歉的；谢罪的；愧疚的：They were very ～ about the trouble they had caused.他们对所惹的麻烦深感愧疚。‖ ～ally *adv.* 道歉地；认错地

apologize /əˈpɒlədʒaɪz/
v. say you are sorry for sth. you have done 道歉；认错；谢罪：I ～d (to her) for stepping on her foot.我因踩了她的脚而（向她）道歉。

apology /əˈpɒlədʒi/
n. ❶ an expression of regret for a fault, wrong, etc. 道歉；认错；谢罪：He made an ～ to the teacher for what he had done.他就他的所作所为向老师认错。❷ explanation 解释；辩解：The writer's autobiography was really an ～ for the way he had lived.该作家的自传实际上是他对以往生活方式的辩解。

apostrophe /əˈpɒstrəfi/
n. the mark, as in John's book or I've read that book 所有格符号，省字号，撇号（即"'"）（如 John's book 或 I've read that book 中的"'"）

apothecary /əˈpɒθəkəri/
n. a person with a knowledge of chemistry who mixes and sells medicines; pharmacist 药剂师

apotheosis /əˌpɒθiˈəʊsɪs/
n. ❶ the raising of a person or thing to the highest possible honour and glory, or the state reached in this way（人或物）礼赞，崇拜；极点，顶峰；神化 ❷ the perfect example; quintessence 典范；最完美的榜样：Christ's mother is the ～ of womanhood.基督的母亲是女性的典范。

appal /əˈpɔːl/
v. fill with a strong feeling of dislike and shock 使厌恶恐惧；使震惊：The number of people killed on the roads ～s me.公路车祸死亡人数之多使我大为震惊。

appalled /əˈpɔːld/
adj. feeling or showing horror or disgust at sth. unpleasant or wrong 感到惊骇的；表示憎恶的：an ～ expression 惊恐的表情

appalling /əˈpɔːlɪŋ/
adj. ❶ causing fear and hatred; shocking; terrible 骇人听闻的；令人震惊的；可怕的：～ cruelty 骇人听闻的残忍 ❷ very bad 极坏的：an ～ waste 严重的浪费/～ food 糟透了的食物 ‖ ～ly *adv.* 骇人听闻地；令人毛骨悚然地：an ～ly bad driver 极差劲的司机

apparatus /ˌæpəˈreɪtəs/
n. (*pl.* apparatus or ～es) ❶ machines, tools, materials, etc., that work together for a particular purpose 器械；仪器；设备；装置 ❷ an organization or system made up of many parts 机构；组织 ❸ the organs in the body 器官

apparel /əˈpærəl/
n. clothing 衣服；服饰：the new ～ for this summer 今夏时装

apparent /əˈpærənt/
adj. ❶ easily seen or understood 明显的；显而易见的；明白的：His love for the child was ～.他对那孩子的钟爱是显而易见的。❷ seeming real or true but may not be 表面的；外表的：He was our ～ friend, but he actually did not help us.他表面上似乎是我们的朋友，但实际上并不帮助我们。

apparently /əˈpærəntli/
adv. ❶ it seems (that); according to what you have heard 似乎，看来，据……所知：I wasn't there, but ～ it was a good party.我当时不在，但据我所知，那聚会搞得很好。/Apparently they're intending to put up the price of electricity.看来他们要提高电费了。❷ it is clear (that) 显然：Apparently she never got my letter after all.显然，她始终没有收到我的信。

appeal /əˈpiːl/
Ⅰ *v.* ❶ make a serious and urgent request 恳求，呼吁：The speaker ～ed to his hearers for silence.那演讲者要求其听众安静。/The police ～ed for anyone with information to come forward to help them.警方呼吁知情人挺身而出协助他们。❷ look to (sb.) for support, help, etc. 求助（于）；诉诸：～ to one's teacher 向老师求助/～ to the law 诉诸法律 ❸ be attrac-

tive or interesting 有吸引力；引起兴趣：
The new toy ~s to the child.这新玩具引
起了孩子的兴趣。 Ⅱ *n.* ❶ a serious and
urgent request 恳求；呼吁：The ~ for
funds for the flooded towns was highly
successful.为遭洪灾城镇的资金募捐工
作十分成功。 ❷ the quality of being interesting or attractive 吸引力；感染力；魅
力：The game has lost its ~ for children.
这种游戏对孩子们已失去了吸引力。 /
artistic ~ 艺术感染力

appealing /əˈpiːlɪŋ/
adj. ❶ able to move the feelings 打动人
心的：the ~ eyes of a hungry dog 一条饿
狗的可怜眼神 ❷ attractive, pleasing or
interesting 有吸引力的；有趣的：What an
~ little baby! 多么讨人喜欢的婴儿！/
The idea of a free holiday is rather ~.免
费休假的主意颇有吸引力。

appear /əˈpɪə(r)/
v. ❶ come into sight；become visible；show
oneself publicly 出现；显露：A red sun ~ed
on the horizon. 一轮红日升起在地平线
上。 ❷ seem 看来：She ~ed very happy.
她看上去很愉快。 ❸ be published 出版

appearance /əˈpɪərəns/
n. ❶ an act or fact of becoming visible or
arriving 出现；来到；登台：the ~ of
spring 春天的到来 ❷ outward looks or
qualities 外表；外貌；外观；仪表：judge by
~ 以貌取人/He had the ~ of being un-
happy.他显出一副不高兴的样子。/the
~ of a house 房屋的外观

appease /əˈpiːz/
v. ❶ pacify（someone）by giving them
what is wanted（以满足需要来）抚慰；平
息 ❷ give a country sth. it wants to avoid
war 绥靖（满足另一国家的要求以避免战
争）‖ ~ment *n.*抚慰；绥靖

appellation /ˌæpəˈleɪʃn/
n. a name or title, especially one that is
formal or descriptive 名称，称呼

append /əˈpend/
*v.*add or join sth. written or printed onto
the end of a larger piece of written material 附加；增补：They ~ed their signatures to the statement. 他们在声明后签

上了自己的名字。

appendage /əˈpendɪdʒ/
n. sth. that is added to, connected to, or
hanging from something else that is larger or more important 附加物；附属物

appendicitis /əˌpendɪˈsaɪtɪs/
n. a disease in which the appendix becomes very painful 阑尾炎；盲肠炎

appendix /əˈpendɪks/
n. ❶ the part of the inside of the body below the stomach 阑尾；盲肠 ❷ some ex-
tra information found at the end of a
book or document 附录

appetite /ˈæpɪtaɪt/
n. ❶ a desire or wish to eat sth., especially
food 食欲，胃口：lose one's ~ 食欲不振
❷ a strong desire or wish 强烈的欲望 ‖
appetizing /ˈæpɪtaɪzɪŋ/ *adj.*引起食欲的

applaud /əˈplɔːd/
v. ❶ express approval or enjoyment（of）
by striking one's hands together 鼓掌以
示赞许，欣赏：They ~ed her perform-
ance.他们为她的表演叫好。/We ~ed
for his arrival.我们鼓掌欢迎他的到来。
❷ agree strongly with（极力）赞成，赞许：
They ~ed the new plan to save water.他
们十分赞成这一节水新方案。

applause /əˈplɔːz/
*n.*approval or praise, especially shown by
clapping or cheering 鼓掌；欢呼喝彩；赞
成；赞许：Loud ~ greeted his appearance.
热烈的掌声欢迎他登台。/His first no-
vel was worthy of ~.他的第一本小说值
得赞许。

apple /ˈæpl/
*n.*a round fruit with firm white flesh 苹
果：She ate the entire ~, core and all. 她
把整个苹果都吃了，连苹果心也吃光了。

appliance /əˈplaɪəns/
n. a device or instrument, especially one
operated by electricity and designed for
household use 器具（械），装置；（尤指）家
用电器：kitchen ~ 厨房电器/a medical
~ 医疗器械

applicable /ˈæplɪkəbl, əˈplɪkəbl/
*adj.*suitable to be used 适用的：This rule
is not ~ to government employees. 此项

规定不适用于政府雇员。

applicant/'æplɪkənt/

n. a person who asks for sth. formally 申请人

application/ˌæplɪ'keɪʃn/

n. ❶an act or way of putting to use 应用；实施；用法；用途：the ～ of a law 一项法令的实施/the ～ of science to farming 科学在农业上的应用/These new ～s interest me.这些新的用途使我感兴趣。 ❷a written or spoken request 申请；请求；申请书(表)：fill out an ～ 填申请表 /make an ～ for a passport 申请护照/on ～ (to) (向……)申请 ❸putting sth. (especially medicine) on；sth. put on (尤指药物)敷，贴，涂抹；涂敷物：the ～ of ointment to a burn 给烧伤部位涂抹软膏 ❹continued effort；close attention 勤奋；专注：work with great ～ 全神贯注地工作 ❺come into force or operation 生效 ❻a kind of software or programme for a special job 应用软件；应用程序

applied /ə'plaɪd/

adj. (said about a subject of study) used for a practical purpose (尤指学科)应用的，实用的：～ mathematics 应用数学

apply/ə'plaɪ/

v. ❶put sth. into use or position to serve its purpose 应用；实施；运用：～ this theory to production 把这个理论运用到生产中去 ❷have an effect 适用：This medicine doesn't ～ to children.这种药不适用于儿童。 ❸ask for；request sth. officially in writing 请求；申请：～ for a job 申请一份工作 ❹put or spread sth. on a surface 敷；涂抹 ❺work hard or study hard 努力工作；努力学习

appoint/ə'pɔɪnt/

v. ❶choose sb. for a position or job 任命；委任：We have decided to ～ a new teacher.我们已决定委派一位新教师。 /She's been ～ed as sales director.她被任命为销售部经理。 He was ～ed chairman. 他被任命为主席。 /I've been ～ed to run the overseas section. 我被指派经营海外部。 /A committee was ～ed to investigate these complaints.已任命一个委员会调查这些投诉。 ❷arrange or decide (es-pecially time or place when sth. will happen)约定，指定，决定(时间、地点)：The committee has ～ed a day in July for your case to be heard.委员会指定七月某一天审理你的案件。 /She wasn't there at the ～ed time.她没有在约定的时间到那里。 ‖ ～ee *n.* 被任命者；被委任者：a presidential ～ee 总统任命的人

appointment/ə'pɔɪntmənt/

n. ❶an act of choosing someone for a position or job 任命；委派 ❷an arrangement for a meeting at an agreed time and place 约会；约定

apportion/ə'pɔːʃn/

v. divide up and share out 分；分配；分摊：We must ～ the money fairly.我们必须把钱公平分配。 /It was difficult to ～ the blame for the accident between the two drivers.在这次车祸中，要分清两个司机的(过失)责任是很难的。 ‖ ～ment *n.* 分配；分摊

apposite/'æpəzɪt/

adj. exactly suitable to or directly connected with the present moment or situation 适当的；恰当的；切合的：an ～ remark 恰到好处的言辞

apposition/ˌæpə'zɪʃn/

n. an arrangement in which one simple sentence contains two or more noun phrases that describe the same person or thing and are used in the same way 同位，同格

appraisal/ə'preɪzl/

n. (a statement or opinion based on) act of appraising 评价；估计；鉴定：What's your ～ of the situation? 你对局势是如何估计的？/a system for the annual ～ of employees' work 每年对雇员工作进行评价的制度

appraise/ə'preɪz/

v. assess the value or quality of 评价；评估

appreciable /ə'priːʃəbl/

adj. enough to be noticed，felt or considerable 可以觉察到的，可感知的；可观的：an ～ amount 可观的数量 ‖ **appreciably** *adv.* 可察觉地；相当地

appreciate/ə'priːʃɪeɪt/

v. **❶** estimate the worth or quality of 鉴别；评价：～ small differences in color 鉴别细微的色差 **❷** value highly；think well of；enjoy 重视；赏识；欣赏：～ good wine 品尝美酒/Van Gogh's paintings were not ～d until after his death. 梵·高的画作在他去世后才受到人们的赏识。 **❸** be grateful for 为……表示感激：the gifts offered 感谢赠送的礼物 **❹** understand fully；recognize 充分理解；意识到：～ one's danger 意识到面临的危险 **❺** rise in value 增值：Land will continue to ～. 土地将不断增值。

appreciation /əˌpriːʃɪˈeɪʃn/
　n. **❶** understanding of the good qualities or worth of sth. 欣赏；鉴赏；赏识 **❷** a judgment of the worth or facts of sth. 正确评价；鉴别 **❸** a rise in value，especially of land or possessions 涨价；增值 **❹** the feeling of being grateful for 感激；感谢 **❺** full understanding；recognition 充分理解；意识

apprehension /ˌæprɪˈhenʃn/
　n. **❶** grasping；understanding 理解；领悟 **❷** the action of arresting sb. 逮捕；拘押 **❸** anxiety about sth. unpleasant may happen 恐惧；忧虑；担心；挂念

apprehensive /ˌæprɪˈhensɪv/
　adj. **❶** good at understanding 有理解力的；善于领会的 **❷** uneasy；worried 担心的；忧虑的 ‖ **～ly** *adv.* 担心地；理解地/**～ness** *n.* 忧虑感；领悟力

apprentice /əˈprentɪs/
　Ⅰ *n.* a person who is under an agreement to work for a fixed period at low wages，for a person who is skilled in a trade，in order to learn that person's skill 艺徒，学徒，徒弟；初学者，生手 Ⅱ *v.* make someone an apprentice 使当学徒：He ～d his son to a carpenter. 他让儿子学木匠。

apprenticeship /əˈprentɪʃɪp/
　n. the condition or period of having a job as an apprentice 学徒身份；学徒年限：The number of ～s has declined sharply in recent years. 近年来学徒的数量急剧下降。/At the end of your ～ your pay will be doubled. 你学徒期满后，你的工资将会增加一倍。

apprise /əˈpraɪz/
　v. inform or tell sb. of sth. 通知；告诉：He was ～d of our arrival. 我们通知他我们已经来了。

approach /əˈprəʊtʃ/
　Ⅰ *v.* **❶** come near to sb. or sth. in distance or time（在距离或时间上）靠近，接近：The spring is ～ing. 春天就要来了。 **❷** ask sb. for sth. or speak to sb. about sth.，typically with a request or proposal（多指为提要求或建议而）找……接洽；找……商量：She ～ed me for RMB 500. 她找我商量借 500 元人民币。 **❸** be close to sth. in amount，level or quality（在数额、水平或质量上）接近 **❹** solve a problem，task，etc. 着手处理；对付：How to ～ the task? 怎样完成这个任务呢？ Ⅱ *n.* **❶** a way of dealing with sth. 处理事情的方法 **❷** an approximation to sth. 接近 **❸** a road or other way leading to a place 通道；通路

approachable /əˈprəʊtʃəbl/
　adj. （said about a person）friendly and easy to talk to（指人）友好的，易攀谈的 ‖ **approachability** *n.* 易接近

appropriate[1] /əˈprəʊprɪət/
　adj. suitable or correct 适合的；恰当的；相宜的；得体的：at the ～ time 在适当的时候/～ remarks to the occasion 适合时宜的言论

appropriate[2] /əˈprəʊprɪeɪt/
　v. **❶** take sth. for one's own use without permission by stealing，by force，etc. 侵吞；挪用；占用：～ one's land 占用某人土地 **❷** take or give money for some purpose 拨（专款）：～ funds for education（a university）为教育（一所大学）拨专款

approval /əˈpruːvl/
　n. **❶** giving permission 批准：The proposal is subject to ～ by the shareholders. 这项建议须得到股东的批准。 **❷** a favourable opinion or judgment 赞成；同意：The audience showed its ～ by cheering loudly. 观众高声喝彩表示赞许。/I hope that the arrangements meet with your ～. 我希望这些安排得到你的同意。/The new proposals have won the ～ of the

A

board.新建议得到董事会的认可。

approve/ə'pruːv/

 *v.*❶agree officially to 批准；赞成；称许：Council ~d the financial budget.这个委员会批准了财政预算。❷（~ of）consider sth. good, right, wise, etc. 赞成；称许；同意：Do you ~ of his proposal? 你赞成他的建议吗？

approving/ə'pruːvɪŋ/

 *adj.*showing that you believe that sb. or sth. is good or acceptable 赞成的；同意的：He gave me an ~ nod.他向我点头表示同意。‖ ~**ly** *adv.*赞成地；表示同意地

approximate/ə'prɒksɪmət/

 Ⅰ*adj.*nearly correct but not exact 近似的；大约的 Ⅱ*v.* come near to sth. in amount, nature, etc.近似；接近：Your story only ~s to the real facts.你所说的仅仅是接近事实真相。

approximation/ə,prɒksɪ'meɪʃn/

 *n.*a result, calculation, etc., that is not exact but is good enough（计算等）近似的结果,近似值,概算：Could you give us a rough ~ of the likely cost? 你能给我们一个大概的成本价格吗？

apricot/'eɪprɪkɒt/

 *n.*a small, sweet, yellow fruit with a seed in the middle,growing in cool regions 杏

April/'eɪprəl/

 *n.*the fourth month of the year 四月

apron/'eɪprən/

 *n.*a piece of cloth or other material worn over the front of the body to keep one's clothes clean while working 围裙

apropos[1]/,æprə'pəʊ/

 adv.(used to introduce a new subject connected with what has just been mentioned) concerning or relating to or with reference to (用于引入与刚才话题有关的新话题)再说,至于,说到……：John was here yesterday；~he's got a new job. 约翰昨天来这里了。对了,他有了一份新工作。/Apropos (of) John's new job, what's his earning? 说起约翰的新工作,他挣多少钱?

apropos[2]/,æprə'pəʊ/

 *adj.*very suitable for the time or situation 适当的；及时的；恰当的：I thought her remarks were very ~.我认为她的话说得很合时宜。

apse/æps/

 n. the curved or many-sided end of a building, especially the east end of a church 半圆室；半圆形殿

apt/æpt/

 *adj.*❶exactly suitable；pertinent 恰当的；贴切的：an ~ answer 恰当的回答 ❷having a natural or habitual tendency to do sth.；likely 易于……的,有……倾向的：She is ~ to be ill in very cold weather.她在寒冷的天气里容易生病。‖ ~**ly** *adv.*适宜地；~**ness** *n.* 适合性；才能

aptitude/'æptɪtjuːd/

 *n.*a natural ability or skill, especially in learning 倾向；能力；才能：She has an ~ for languages.她有学习语言的天资。

aqualung/'ækwəlʌŋ/

 n. an apparatus that provides air for a swimmer under water, especially a container of special air that is carried on the back and has a tube that takes the air to the mouth or nose (尤指潜水者背在背上的)水肺,水中呼吸器

aquamarine/,ækwəmə'riːn/

 *n.*❶ a glass-like blue-green stone used for jewellery 海蓝宝石 ❷ the colour of this stone 蓝绿色；海蓝色

aquarium/ə'kweərɪəm/

 n. (*pl.* ~s or aquaria/ə'kweərɪə/) ❶ a glass container for fish and other water animals 玻璃养鱼缸；水族箱 ❷ a building(especially in a zoo) containing many of these containers for public visit 水族馆

aquatic/ə'kwætɪk/

 *adj.*living or happening in or on water 水生的；水中(或水上)的；水栖的：~ plants 水生植物/Aquatic sports include swimming and rowing.水上运动包括游泳、划船等。‖ ~**ally** *adv.* 水生地

aqueous/'eɪkwɪəs/

 *adj.*of, like, containing, or in water 水的；似水的；含水的；水中的

aquifer /'ækwɪfə/

*n.*a layer of rock that can hold or transmit water (岩石或土壤的)含水层,蓄水层

aquiline/'ækwɪlaɪn/

　*adj.*of or like an eagle 鹰的;似鹰的:An ～ nose is one that curves like an eagle's beak.鹰钩鼻是指像鹰嘴般弯曲的鼻子。/her sharp ～ profile 她那明显像鹰一般的面部轮廓

Arabic/'ærəbɪk/

　Ⅰ *adj.*of Arabia or the Arabs 阿拉伯的;阿拉伯人的:～ figures 阿拉伯数字 Ⅱ *n.*the Semitic language or writing of the Arabs,which is the main language of North Africa,the Middle East and Arabia 阿拉伯语

arable/'ærəbl/

　adj.(of land) suitable or used for growing crops (土地)适于耕作的,可耕的

arbiter/'ɑːbɪtə(r)/

　*n.*a person or group who has the power to judge or decide what will be done or accepted 仲裁人(机构),裁决人(机构):He is the ～ here on how people dress.他是这儿人们穿打扮的评判人。

arbitrary/'ɑːbɪtrəri/

　*adj.*❶based on one's own wishes or will, not determined by reason or principle 任意的;武断的:make ～ decisions 做武断的决定/an ～ choice 随意的选择 ❷uncontrolled by law; using power without restriction 不受法律约束的;专制的,独裁的:an ～ government 专制政府

arbitrate/'ɑːbɪtreɪt/

　*v.*judge or settle an argument by together choosing a person,etc.to make a decision 仲裁;裁决;公断:～ between two persons 在两个人之间做出公断 /Neither party would ～ the dispute.争执双方都不愿将其纠纷诉诸仲裁。

arbitration/ˌɑːbɪ'treɪʃn/

　*n.*the settling of an argument by the decision of a person or group that has been chosen by both sides 仲裁;公断:The workers agreed to go to ～ to settle their pay claim.工人们同意通过仲裁来解决他们的工资要求。

arbitrator /'ɑːbɪtreɪtə/

　*n.*an independent person or body officially appointed to settle an argument 仲裁人;仲裁机构

arboreal/ɑː'bɔːriəl/

　*adj.*of or living in trees 树木的;有关树木的;生活在树上的:～ animals 栖于树上的动物

arboretum /ˌɑːbə'riːtəm/

　n.(*pl.*～s or arboreta)a botanical garden where trees are grown for study and display (供科研、观赏的)树木园,植物园

arbour/'ɑːbə(r)/

　*n.*a sheltered place in a garden, usually made by making trees of bushes grow so as to form an arch (花园中长满蔓藤的)棚架,藤架;凉亭

arc/ɑːk/

　*n.*a part of a circle or a curved line 弧

arcade/ɑː'keɪd/

　*n.*a passage or street covered by a roof, usually with shops in the passage 店廊

arcane/ɑː'keɪn/

　*adj.*mysterious and secret;esoteric 神秘的;秘密的:～ knowledge 神秘的知识

arch/ɑːtʃ/

　Ⅰ *n.*❶a curved part of a bridge or building 拱;拱门;拱形结构 ❷sth. with this shape,especially the middle of the bottom of the foot 拱形;半圆形;牌楼;拱状物 Ⅱ *v.*form into an arch;form an arch or make into the shape of an arch 使成弓形

archaeologist /ˌɑːkɪ'ɒlədʒɪst/

　*n.*someone who studies archaeology 考古学家

archaeology /ˌɑːkɪ'ɒlədʒi/

　*n.*the study of ancient civilizations by digging for their physical remains and examining them 考古学

archaic/ɑː'keɪɪk/

　*adj.*old and no longer used 古体的;不再使用的

archbishop/ˌɑːtʃ'bɪʃəp/

　*n.*a priest in charge of the churches and bishops in a very large area 大主教:Archbishop Jones 大主教琼斯/His Grace the Archbishop of York 约克大主教阁下

arch-enemy/ˌɑːtʃˈenəmi/

　　n. ❶ a main enemy 主要敌人,大敌 ❷ the devil 撒旦,魔王

archer/ˈɑːtʃə(r)/

　　n. a person who shoots arrows from a bow, either as a sport or formerly in war 射箭运动员;(古代战争中的)弓箭手

archery/ˈɑːtʃəri/

　　n. the art or sport of shooting arrows 射箭术;射箭(运动)

archetype/ˈɑːkɪtaɪp/

　　n. ❶ the original model of sth., of which others are copies 原型 ❷ a perfectly typical example of sth. 典型 ‖ **archetypical** /ˌɑːkɪˈtɪpɪkəl/ *adj.* 典型的: the archetypical American tourist 典型的美国游客

architect/ˈɑːkɪtekt/

　　n. ❶ one who designs buildings, etc. 建筑师;the ~ of the building 这栋大楼的建筑设计者 ❷ a person who is responsible for planning or creating an idea or project (想法或计划的)缔造者,设计师

architecture/ˈɑːkɪˈtektʃə(r)/

　　n. ❶ the art and science of building, including its planning, making, and decoration 建筑学 ❷ the style or manner of building in a particular country or period of history 建筑物;建筑式样,建筑风格

archive/ˈɑːkaɪv/

　　n. (usually *pl.*) ❶ a place in which government documents and other official or historical papers are kept 档案馆;档案室 ❷ documents kept in such a place 档案

archivist/ˈɑːkɪvɪst/

　　n. a person who maintains and is in charge of archives 档案管理员

archway/ˈɑːtʃweɪ/

　　n. a passage or entrance under an arch 拱道;拱门

Arctic/ˈɑːktɪk/

　　Ⅰ *adj.* ❶ of or concerning the most northern part of the world 北极的;北极区的: the ~ Circle 北极圈/the ~ Ocean 北冰洋 ❷ extremely cold 极冷的 Ⅱ *n.* the regions around the North Pole 北极区

ardent/ˈɑːdnt/

　　adj. showing strong feelings or desires; passionate 热情的;热烈的: an ~ patriot 一位热忱的爱国者 ‖ ~**ly** *adv.* 热心地;热烈地

ardo(u)r/ˈɑːdə(r)/

　　n. great feelings of enthusiasm 激情,热情

arduous/ˈɑːdjuəs/

　　adj. needing hard and continuous effort; difficult 艰巨的;艰苦的: a long and ~ climb 漫长而吃力的攀登

area/ˈeərɪə/

　　n. ❶ a particular space or surface 空地;场地 ❷ the extent or measurement of a surface 面积 ❸ a region part of a town, country, etc. 地区;区域 ❹ the range or limits of a subject, activity, etc.(主题、活动等的)范围;领域

arena/əˈriːnə/

　　n. ❶ a circular or oval place, surrounded by seats, for athletic competitions(圆形或椭圆形的)体育场;sports ~ 运动场 ❷ any place where people fight or compete against each other(打斗或竞赛的)竞技场

arguable/ˈɑːgjuəbl/

　　adj. ❶ able to be supported with reasons 有论据的;可论证的: an ~ theory 可论证的理论 /It is ~ that the government has no right to interfere in this matter. 说政府无权干预这一事件是有论据的。❷ doubtful in some degree; questionable 有疑问的;可争辩的: an ~ decision 尚可争辩的决定 ‖ **arguably** *adv.* 可论证地,按理

argue/ˈɑːgjuː/

　　v. ❶ speak angrily to sb. because of diverging or opposite views 争吵;争执: I'm tired of arguing with him (about it); he never admits he's wrong. 我不愿再和他争论了,他从不认错。❷ give reasons for or against sth. 提供理由(赞成或反对): He is always arguing against me. 他老爱搬出理由来说我不对。/Let's not ~ the matter. 这件事我们不要辩论了。❸ show; prove 表示;证明: Her accent ~s that she was born abroad. 她的口音证明她是在国外出生的。/His appearance ~s him to be an African. 他的外貌说明他是非洲人。/This ~s her artistic

A

tastes.这证明了她的艺术鉴赏力。❹ persuade 说服；劝服：～ someone into selling his old car 说服某人去卖掉旧车/ ～ someone into an opinion 说服某人接受某种意见

argument /'ɑːgjʊmənt/

*n.*❶ an exchange of diverging or opposite views, especially an angry one 争论；争辩；争吵：They were having an ～ about whose turn it was to do the cooking.他们为该轮谁做饭而争吵不休。/They got into an ～ about politics.他们陷入了一场政治争论。❷ a reason given to support or disapprove sth. 论据；论点；理由：The committee listened to all the ～s for and against the proposal. 委员会听取了所有赞成和反对该提议的论据。/The risk of heart disease is a powerful ～ against smoking.吸烟有可能引起心脏病是反对吸烟的有力论据。❸ the use of reason to decide sth. or persuade someone 说理；辩论：We should try to settle this affair by ～, not by fighting.我们应以说理而不是打架的方式来解决这件事。❹ a short account of the story or subject of a book, poem, etc.; summary 梗概；概要；要旨

argumentative /ˌɑːgjʊˈmentətɪv/

*adj.*liking arguing a lot 好争论的：an ～ child 好争论的孩子 ‖ ～ly *adv.*好争论地；激辩地

arid /'ærɪd/

*adj.*dry; lacking water 干旱的；缺水的：The soil was very ～.这块地非常干旱。

arise /əˈraɪz/

*v.*❶stand up from sitting, kneeling, or lying 起来；升起 ❷come into being or begin to be noticed; appear 出现；呈现

aristocracy /ˌærɪˈstɒkrəsi/

*n.*❶the people of the highest social class, especially people from noble families who have titles of rank 贵族；贵族阶级；上层社会 ❷the finest, best, or most powerful members of any group or class 最优秀（最有权势）的人

aristocrat /'ærɪstəkræt/

*n.*a member of the aristocracy; a noble 贵族（成员）

aristocratic /ˌærɪstəˈkrætɪk/

*adj.*of, belonging to, or typical of the aristocracy 贵族的；有贵族特征的：an ～ family 贵族家庭

arithmetic /əˈrɪθmətɪk/

*n.*the type of mathematics that deals with the properties and manipulation of numbers 算术

arithmetical /ˌærɪθˈmetɪkəl/

*adj.*of or relating to arithmetic 算术的：an ～ calculation 算术运算 ‖ ～ly *adv.*算术上；用算术方法

ark /ɑːk/

n.(in the Bible **Noah's Ark**) the ship in which Noah and his family were saved from the great flood（《圣经》中诺亚及其家人在大洪水中获救的）诺亚方舟

arm /ɑːm/

Ⅰ *n.*❶ the part of the human body between the shoulder and the hand 臂；上肢：take her in one's ～s 把她抱在怀里/ under one's ～ 在腋下/keep sb. at ～'s length 避免与某人过分亲近/ ～ in ～ 手挽手 ❷sth. similar to an arm 臂状物：an ～ of a tree 树枝/ an ～ of a coat 衣袖 Ⅱ *v.*❶give weapons to; get weapons 武装：These countries are being ～ed for war.这些国家在戎装待阵。❷ prepare; provide 准备；提供：He is ～ed with a pair of glasses.他备有一副眼镜。

armada /ɑːˈmɑːdə/

*n.*a collection or fleet of armed ships 舰队：The Spanish Armada sailed to England in 1588.西班牙无敌舰队于 1588 年出征英国。

armadillo /ˌɑːməˈdɪləʊ/

*n.*a small animal which comes from the warm parts of the America, covered in hard bands of bonelike shell 犰狳（产于美洲的小动物，身上有骨质硬壳）

armament /'ɑːməmənt/

*n.*❶ the process of equipping military forces for war 武装备战 ❷(*pl.*)military weapons and equipment 军备，军事装备：～s race 军备竞赛

armband /'ɑːmbænd/

*n.*a band of material worn round the arm

A

to show the wearer's official position, or as a sign of mourning 臂章;(黑)臂纱

armchair¹ /ˈɑːmtʃeə(r)/

n. a comfortable chair with supports for the arms 扶手椅

armchair² /ˈɑːmtʃeə(r)/

adj. lacking practical or direct experience of a particular activity 只说不做的;空谈的:an ～ critic 不切实际的批评者

armed /ɑːmd/

adj. having or using weapons or armour 武装的;有……装备的:They were convicted of ～ robbery.他们被判犯有持枪抢劫罪。/Could the situation lead to ～ conflict? 这种局势会导致武装冲突吗? / She came to the meeting ～ with all the facts and figures to prove her case.她带着能证明她论点的所有事实和数据来出席会议。‖ ～ to the teeth 武装到牙齿

armful /ˈɑːmfʊl/

n. as much as you can hold in your arms 单臂(或双臂)一抱的量;一抱

armistice /ˈɑːmɪstɪs/

n. an agreement to stop fighting (usually to discuss peace) 停战;休战

armo(u)r /ˈɑːmə(r)/

n. ❶ a covering of metal worn by soldiers in old times to protect them 盔甲 ❷ the strong protective metal covering on modern vehicles of war 装甲

armo(u)red /ˈɑːməd/

adj. ❶ protected by armour 装甲的 ❷ having fighting vehicles protected by armour 配备有装甲车辆的:an ～ division 装甲师

armo(u)ry /ˈɑːməri/

n. ❶ a place where weapons and ammunition are stored 军械库 ❷ a supply of military weapons 军事装备

armpit /ˈɑːmpɪt/

n. a hollow under the arm at the shoulder 腋;腋窝;胳肢窝

armrest /ˈɑːmrest/

n. a padded or upholstered arm of a chair or other seat on which a sitter can comfortably rest the arms (椅子或其他座位的)扶手

arms /ɑːmz/

n. ❶ weapons of war 武器;军火:The government intends to cut expenditure on ～.政府打算削减军备支出。/They have 50,000 men under ～.他们有 5 万名处在备战状态中的士兵。/ The general called on the defeated army to lay down their ～.将军号召被打败的军队放下武器。/ They took up ～ in defence of their country.他们拿起武器保卫祖国。❷ a coat of arms 盾形纹章;盾徽 ‖ up in ～ 极力反对;强烈抗议:The women are up in ～ over their low rate of pay.这群妇女因不满低薪而愤怒抗议。

army /ˈɑːmi/

n. ❶ a large group of soldiers organized for fighting 军队:serve in the ～ 服役 ❷ the entire armed land forces of a country (一国的)陆军 ❸ a large group 大群:an ～ of tourists 一大群观光者

aroma /əˈrəʊmə/

n. a pleasant smell, usually of food or herbs (食物的)香味;(药草的)芳香

aromatherapy /əˌrəʊməˈθerəpi/

n. the use of aromatic plant extracts and natural oils for medicinal and cosmetic purposes (用芳香植物提取物和香精油来治疗和美容的)芳香疗法

aromatic /ˌærəˈmætɪk/

adj. sweet-smelling 有香味的;芳香的

around /əˈraʊnd/

Ⅰ *prep.* ❶ on all sides of;all round;surrounding 在……周围:The moon moves ～ the earth.月亮围绕地球运行。❷ so as to avoid or get past;round 绕过:steer a ship ～ reefs 使船绕过暗礁 ❸ near;about 在……附近;大约:He lives ～ London.他住在伦敦附近。/～ two o'clock 两点钟左右 Ⅱ *adv.* ❶ on all sides;about 在周围;在附近:He stood there and looked ～.他站在那儿四处张望。/We are waiting for you ～.我们在附近等你。❷ from one place to another;to various places 各处:The good news soon got ～.好消息很快就传开了。❸ measured in a circle 整整一圈;回转;迂回:The track is 400 metres ～.跑道一圈有 400 米长。/

Another autumn harvest season has come ~.又一个秋收季节来到了。

arouse/əˈraʊz/

v. awaken from sleep; make sb. having a particular feeling 叫醒；唤起，激起（感情）：The sleepy children were ~d by their father.那些打瞌睡的孩子被父亲叫醒。/ Her anger was ~d by his rudeness.她的愤怒是被他的无礼激起的。‖ a-rousal/əˈraʊzəl/唤起；激起

arrange/əˈreɪndʒ/

*v.*❶ put sth. in order 整理；排列 ❷ plan or organize sth. in advance 筹备；安排：They're ~d their wedding for next month.他们把婚礼安排在了下一个月。❸write or adapt a piece of music 谱写，改编（乐曲）

arrangement/əˈreɪndʒmənt/

*n.*❶ the act, process or result of putting sth.in order 整理；排列；布置：the ~ of the books 书籍的整理 ❷(usually *pl.*)a plan or preparation 筹备；安排：make ~s for a dance 筹备舞会 ❸a settlement or agreement 解决办法；协议；商定：come to an ~ 达成协议

array/əˈreɪ/

Ⅰ *n.*a collection of things arranged in order（排列整齐的）一批，一列 Ⅱ *v.*arrange a collection of things in order 布置；排列

arrears/əˈrɪəz/

n.(*pl.*) ❶ money that is owed and should have been paid earlier 逾期欠款 ❷work that has not yet been done 待完成的工作 ‖ be in ~ 拖欠；（工作等）落在后面；未完成进度：be in ~ with the rent 拖欠租金

arrest/əˈrest/

Ⅰ *v.*❶ seize sb. by the authority of the law 依法逮捕；拘留 ❷ put a stop to 阻止，抑制 ❸ catch sb.'s attention 吸引（注意力）Ⅱ *n.*the act or an example of arresting 逮捕；拘留 ‖ ~ing *adj.*引人注意的

arrival/əˈraɪvl/

*n.*❶ an act of arriving 到达；来到：the ~ of a train 火车到达 ❷ a person or thing that arrives or has arrived somewhere 到

达者；抵达物：late ~s 迟到者/ a new ~ 新来的人

arrive/əˈraɪv/

*v.*❶come to a place, especially to the end of a journey 到达；抵达；来临：~ in London 到达伦敦/A letter ~d for you yesterday.昨天你来了一封信。/Our vacation has ~d at last.我们的假期终于来到了。❷come to a decision, state, etc. 达成（决议等）；到达（某种状态等）：~ at manhood 进入成年 ❸ gain success or fame 成功；出名：a young actor who has ~d 一位功成名就的年轻演员

arrogance/ˈærəgəns/

n. the behaviour of a person when they feel that they are more important than other people, so that they are rude to them or do not consider them 傲慢；自大

arrogant/ˈærəgənt/

adj. showing very great pride; acting as though one thought that other people were much less important than oneself 骄傲自大的；傲慢的

arrogate/ˈærəgeɪt/

*v.*take or claim sth.without a proper or legal right 霸占；冒称；擅取：Having seized power in the country, he ~d to himself the right to change the law.他攫取了国家大权之后，便擅自修改了法律。

arrow/ˈærəʊ/

*n.*❶a thin, pointed stick shot from a bow 箭 ❷a mark or sign used to show direction or position 箭状物；箭号

arrowhead/ˈærəʊhed/

*n.*a pointed piece of stone or metal fixed to the front end of an arrow 箭镞；箭头

arsenal/ˈɑːsənl/

*n.*a building where guns and ammunition are stored or made, especially for the army 军械库；兵工厂

arson/ˈɑːsn/

*n.*the crime of setting fire to sth., especially buildings 纵火（罪）

arsonist/ˈɑːsənɪst/

*n.*a person who is guilty of arson 纵火犯；放火犯

art /ɑːt/

　　n. ❶ the expression or application of human creative skill and imagination, especially in painting, drawing or sculpture 艺术；美术 ❷ the skillful method of doing sth. 技术；技艺：the healing ～ 医术 ❸ things produced by art, especially paintings and sculpture 艺术品（尤指绘画与雕塑）：an exhibition of African ～ 非洲艺术（品）展览会

arterial /ɑːˈtɪəriəl/

　　adj. ❶ (of blood) sent from the heart in the arteries 动脉的：Arterial blood is bright red. 动脉血是鲜红色的。 ❷ (of road, railway, etc.) forming one of the chief parts of a large system（道路、铁路等）干线的：～ roads leading into London 通往伦敦的公路干线

artery /ˈɑːtəri/

　　n. the blood vessel which carries blood from the heart to the rest of the body 动脉

artful /ˈɑːtfl/

　　adj. cleverly deceitful; cunning 狡猾的；奸诈的：He's very ～ and usually succeeds in getting what he wants. 他很狡诈，因此常常能成功地达到目的。‖～ly *adv.* 狡猾地 /～ness *n.* 狡猾

article /ˈɑːtɪkl/

　　Ⅰ *n.* ❶ a piece of writing in a newspaper or magazine（报纸或杂志中的）文章；论文 ❷ a particular or separate item or object 物品；物件；商品 ❸ a complete separate part in a legal agreement, constitution, etc. 项目；条款 ❹ one of the words, a, an, or the, used before nouns 冠词：the definite ～ 定冠词 Ⅱ *v.* bind sb. to undergo a period of training 签约当见习员；进行见习培训

articulate /ɑːˈtɪkjʊlɪt/

　　Ⅰ *adj.* (of a person or their words) having or showing the ability to speak fluently and coherently（人或其言语）流利连贯的：She was not very ～. 她说话不怎么流利连贯。 Ⅱ *v.* ❶ say sth. clearly and distinctly 流利连贯地表达：She struggled to ～ her thoughts. 她竭力表明她的想法。 ❷ form a joint 形成关节：

This bone ～s with the next. 这块骨头与相邻的骨头形成关节。‖～ly *adv.* 流利连贯地/**articulation** *n.* 表达；发音；关节

artificial /ˌɑːtɪˈfɪʃl/

　　adj. ❶ made by humans, especially as a copy of sth. natural 人造的；人工的；假的：This drink contains no ～ flavouring or colouring. 这种饮料不掺人造香精和着色剂。/～ flowers 人造花/～ silk 人造丝 ❷ lacking true feelings; insincere 虚假的；不真挚的；矫揉造作的：She welcomed me with an ～ smile. 她以虚伪的微笑欢迎我。 ❸ happening as a result of human action, not through a natural process 人为的：High import taxes give their home-made goods an ～ advantage in the market. 高进口税使他们本国的产品在市场上取得人为的优势。‖～ly *adv.* 人工地；人为地；不自然地：Government subsidies have kept the price of food ～ly low. 政府给以补贴的办法人为地降低了食品的价格。

artillery /ɑːˈtɪləri/

　　n. ❶ large guns, especially on wheels or fixed in one place, e.g. on a ship or in a fort 炮；大炮 ❷ the part of the army that uses these weapons 炮兵

artisan /ˌɑːtɪˈzæn/

　　n. someone who does skilled work with their hands; craftsman 工匠，手艺人

artist /ˈɑːtɪst/

　　n. ❶ a person who produces works of art, especially paintings or drawings 艺术家；美术家 ❷ a person skilled at a particular occupation（某行业的）能手：He's no ordinary baker—he's an ～. 他是非同寻常的面包师——他简直是个艺术大师。 ❸ a performer such as a singer, dancer or actor 表演者 ❹ someone who is skilled in a particular activity, especially a bad one 擅长做某事（尤指坏事）的人：a rip-off ～ 神偷

artiste /ɑːˈtiːst/

　　n. a professional singer, actor, dancer, etc., who performs in a show 职业演艺人员；艺人

artistic /ɑːˈtɪstɪk/

　　adj. ❶ of art or artists 艺术（家）的；美术

(家)的：～ ability 艺术才华 ❷having or showing skill and taste in art 有艺术才能的；有艺术性的；有艺术鉴赏力的：The girl is very ～.这女孩很有艺术鉴赏力。

artistry/'ɑːtɪstri/

n. inventive imagination and ability; artistic skill 创作天赋；艺术才华；艺术性：the ～ of the violinist 小提琴家的艺术才华

artless/'ɑːtlɪs/

adj.❶simple；natural 单纯的；天真的；自然的；不做作的：Her love was as ～ as a child's.她的爱如同孩子般的天真质朴。❷lacking art, knowledge or skill 无艺术性的；无技能的；拙劣的：an ～ painting 一幅拙劣的画

artwork/'ɑːtwɜːk/

n. pictures and other visual materials included in a book or other publication（书刊等上的）插图，图片

arty/'ɑːti/

adj.seeming to be artistic or interested in the arts 冒充懂艺术的；附庸风雅的：～ lighting 故作艺术性的灯光照明

as/æz, əz/

Ⅰ *adv*.（used in comparisons and examples）equally；like（用于比较和举例）相同；像……：He's not ～ old ～ me. 他年纪没有我大。Ⅱ *conj*.❶ like, in the same way（表示比较）像……一样：The work is not so easy ～ you imagine.这工作不像你想象的那么简单。❷ in the way, in which（表示方式）按照；如同：state the facts ～ they are 如实地陈述事实 ❸ while, when（表示时间）当……的时候：As a young man, he lived in Japan.他青年时，住在日本。❹ because, since（表示原因）由于，鉴于：As he was not well, I decided to go without him. 因为他身体不好，我决定独自去了。❺（with so or such, showing a result）（与 so 或 such 连用，表示结果）如此……以至：So cold ～ to make swimming impossible.冷得不可能游泳。❻ though（表示让步）虽然，尽管：Much ～ I like it, I will not buy it.虽然我很喜欢这东西，但不想买它。Ⅲ *pron*.（used in "such ～" "the same ～", etc.）（用在"such ～""the same ～"等结构中）像……样的人（或物），凡是……的

人（或物）：My hometown is no longer the same ～ it was.我的家乡同过去不一样了。Ⅳ *prep*.in the condition of 作为：He is a target for terrorism ～ prime minister.首相，他是恐怖主义的目标。‖ ～ for 至于，就……方面说/～ from 从……时起/～ if（though）好像，仿佛/～ of 从……时起/～ to 至于；关于

ascend/ə'send/

v.climb, go or rise up 登高；上升；升高：He is the first person to ～ the mountain.他是第一个登上顶峰的人。‖ ～ing *adj*.上升的，向上的

ascendancy /ə'sendənsi/

n. the state of having great influence or being in control 支配地位；优势；影响：moral ～ 道德影响

ascent /ə'sent/

n.❶ the act of climbing or moving up；an upward journey 上升；升高；登高：The rocket steepened its ～.火箭飞速升空。❷a way up；an upward slope or path 上坡；上坡路

ascertain/ˌæsə'teɪn/

v.find out sth.in order to be certain；get to know 查明；弄清；确定 ‖ ～able *adj*.可查明的，可弄清的/～ment *n*.确定；发现

ascetic/ə'setɪk/

n. a person who does not allow himself any pleasures and comforts, usually for religious reasons 苦行者，禁欲主义者（通常出于宗教原因）

ascribe/ə'skraɪb/

v. think sth. to be the cause, reason, origin, etc. 把……归于：He ～d his failure to bad luck.他把自己的失败归咎于运气不好。

ash/æʃ/

n.❶powder left after sth. has burnt 灰（末）：plant ～ 草木灰/fly ～ 飞灰，烟灰 ❷（pl.）such powder together with the unburned remains 灰烬：The whole village was burnt to ～es.整个村庄被焚为一片灰烬。❸（pl.）the burnt remains of a human body 骨灰：Her ～es were scattered over the sea.她的骨灰撒在大海里。❹remains of sth. that has been destroyed

废墟

ashamed /ə'ʃeɪmd/

adj. ❶ feeling shame 害羞的；羞耻的；惭愧的；羞愧的：I am ～ of（myself for）having failed in English. 我为（自己）英语考试不及格而感到惭愧。/ I am ～ to have you as my friend. 交到你这个朋友，我感到羞耻。❷ not willing because of fearing shame 因害羞而不愿……的；羞（于）……的：He was ～ to ask her for help. 他不好意思向她求助。

ashen /'æʃn/

adj. of the colour of ash；pale grey 灰（白）色的：His ～ face showed how shocked he was. 他面如土色，说明他是多么震惊。

ashore /ə'ʃɔː(r)/

adv. on, onto, or to the shore 在岸上；向岸上：Passengers may go ～ at Kingston. 乘客可以在金斯顿上岸。

ashtray /'æʃtreɪ/

n. a container into which people who smoke put ash, cigarette ends, etc. 烟灰缸

Asia /'eɪʃə/

n. the largest continent in the world 亚洲：～ Minor 小亚细亚 / Southeast ～ 东南亚

Asian /'eɪʃn/

Ⅰ *adj.* of or relating to Asia or its people, customs, or languages 亚洲的；亚洲人的 Ⅱ *n.* a native of Asia or a person of Asian descent 亚洲人

aside /ə'saɪd/

Ⅰ *adv.* ❶ to the side 在旁边，在一边；到（或向）旁边，到（或向）一边：He laid the book ～ and talked with me. 他把书放在一旁和我谈了起来。❷ except for（暂且）撇开，除去：Joking ～, let's discuss the subject 不开玩笑（正经地说），我们来讨论下这个课题。Ⅱ *n.* ❶ words spoken by an actor to those watching a play, and not intended to be heard by the other characters in the play（戏剧等中的）旁白 ❷ a remark made or story told during a speech but which is not part of the main subject 离题的话 ‖ ～ from 除了……以外

ask /ɑːsk/

v. ❶ say or write sth. to obtain an answer or some information（询）问：Ask me if you're not sure. 如果你拿不准，来问我好了。/ I ～ed about her new job. 我询问了她新工作的情况。/ They ～ed me what was the matter. 他们问我出了什么事。/ He ～ed me the time. 他问我几点钟了。/ He ～ed if I could speak English. 他问我会不会说英语。❷ make a request for 要求，请求，央求：He ～ed（for）my advice. 他向我求教。/ He ～ed that his name（should）be kept secret. 他要求将他的名字保密。/ He ～ed to be given more work to do. 他请求多分配些工作给他做。❸ invite 邀请：～ him to stay for dinner 请他留下来用餐 ‖ ～ for trouble 自找麻烦 / for the ～ing 只需提出要求便能得到

askance /ə'skæns/

adv.（look ～ at sb.）look at sb. or sth. with suspicion or discontent（怀疑或不满地）看；瞟

askew /əs'kjuː/

adv. & adj. slightly crooked, not straight or level 歪斜地（的）；不正地（的）：Her hat was slightly ～. 她帽子戴得有点歪。

asleep /ə'sliːp/

adj. ❶ sleeping 睡着的 ❷ not being able to feel properly because the blood has not been flowing freely；numb 发麻的；麻木的：My arm is ～, probably, because I've been lying on it. 我的胳臂发麻，大概是一直被身子压住的缘故。

aspect /'æspekt/

n. ❶ a part or feature of a difficulty, question, subject, etc. to be particularly discussed；viewpoint（困难、问题等的）层面，方面；观点：There is another interesting ～ of this matter which needs thinking about. 这件事情还有一个令人关注的方面需要加以考虑。❷ appearance 外观；容貌：The house's ～ was dark and unattractive. 那栋房子外观灰暗，一点都不起眼。/ His ～ was frightening. 他的长相吓人。❸ the direction a thing faces in；the side or surface facing a given direction 方向，方位；（朝某一方向的）边，面：the eastern ～ of the house 房子朝东的一面 / The building has an eastern-facing

～.这栋楼有一面朝东。

asperity/æs'perəti/

　　*n.*the fact of roughness or severity,e.g.in speech,manner,or weather（说话、态度等的）粗鲁,刻薄,（天气的）严酷:He answered our questions with some ～.他回答我们的问题时态度很粗暴。/the asperities of a Russian winter 俄罗斯冬天的严寒

aspersions/ə'spɜ:ʃnz/

　　n.（*pl.*）unkind remarks or unfavourable judgments 诽谤;中伤;诬蔑:Are you casting ～ on my ability to drive? 你是不是故意使人对我的驾驶技术产生怀疑?

asphalt/'æsfælt/

　　Ⅰ *n.*a black material that is firm when it hardens,used for the surface of roads,roofs,etc.沥青;柏油 Ⅱ *v.*cover with asphalt 铺柏油

asphyxia/æs'fɪksɪə/

　　*n.*suffocation caused by lack of air in the lungs 窒息;闷死

asphyxiate/æs'fɪksɪeɪt/

　　*v.*make someone die from lack of oxygen 使窒息而死

aspiration /ˌæspə'reɪʃən/

　　*n.*❶a strong hope or ambition 愿望;抱负:the yawning gulf between ～ and reality 抱负与现实之间的鸿沟 ❷the action of pronouncing a sound with an exhalation of breath 发送气音;送气

aspire/ə'spaɪə(r)/

　　*v.*direct one's hopes and efforts to some important aim 渴望;追求

aspirin/'æsprɪn,'æspərɪn/

　　*n.*❶a drug which reduces pain or fever 阿司匹林(一种镇痛解热药) ❷a tablet or pill containing aspirin 阿司匹林药片(或丸)

aspiring /æs'paɪərɪŋ/

　　*adj.*wanting to be successful in life 有抱负的;有志向的:He came from an ～ working-class background.他出身于有抱负的工人阶级家庭。

ass/æs/

　　*n.*❶ an animal like a small horse with long ears 驴 ❷ a foolish person 蠢人,傻子

assail /ə'seɪl/

　　*v.*❶attack someone violently 攻击;袭击:He was ～ed with fierce blows to the head.他的头遭到猛烈殴打。❷disturb or upset sb. severely 困扰;使苦恼:She was ～ed by regrets.悔恨袭上她的心头。

assassinate/ə'sæsɪneɪt/

　　*v.*murder sb. by a sudden attack usually for a political reason (通常出于政治原因)暗杀;行刺 ‖ **assassination** /əˌsæsɪ'neɪʃn/ *n.* 暗杀;行刺/ **assassin** *n.* 暗杀者;刺客

assault/ə'sɔ:lt/

　　Ⅰ *n.*a violent attack,especially a sudden one (尤指突然的)攻击,袭击:The army launched a major ～ against the rebel town.军队向叛乱的城镇发动大规模的突然攻击。Ⅱ *v.*make a physical attack on 殴打,袭击:She was too shaken after being sexually ～ed to report the incident to the police.她遭到强暴后失魂落魄,竟没有向警方报案。

assay/ə'seɪ/

　　*v.*❶ test a substance, such as silver or gold to chemical analysis 化验,分析,鉴定(如金银含量) ❷ attempt sth. difficult 尝试(做难事):～ the impossible 尝试做不可能成功的事

assemblage/ə'semblɪdʒ/

　　*n.*❶ a group of people or a collection of articles 一群人;一批东西 ❷ the act of coming or putting together 组合,装配;收集,聚集

assemble/ə'sembl/

　　*v.*❶gather or bring sth. together; collect in one place 集合;聚集;集中:A large crowd ～d. 一大群人聚集在一起。❷ make sth. by putting pieces together 装配:This bookcase is very easy to ～.这个书架很容易装起来。

assembly/ə'sembli/

　　*n.*❶ a group of people, especially one gathered together for a special purpose (为某一目的) 聚集在一起的人 ❷(**Assembly**)the lower chamber in various American state legislatures 议会;(美国某些州的)州众议院 ❸ the process of gath-

A

ering together the parts of sth. collecting 装配；总成，组合

assent/əˈsent/

Ⅰ v. agree to；say yes to 同意，赞成：The committee ~ed to our proposals. 委员会同意我们的计划。Ⅱ n. agreement to sth.；permission 同意；许可

assert/əˈsɜːt/

v. ❶ state or express sth. clearly and forcefully 断言；声明：The student ~ed that he had not cheated at the exam. 那学生申明他考试没有作弊。/He ~ed that the climate was changing. 他断言气候在变。❷ defend or maintain rights，claims，etc. （对权利、要求等）维护，坚持：~ one's rights 维护权利

assertion/əˈsɜːʃn/

n. a forceful statement or claim 断言，声明；主张，断词：She could provide no evidence to back up her ~s. 她提不出依据来支持自己的主张。/He repeated his ~ that he was not guilty. 他一再坚称自己无罪。

assertive/əˈsɜːtɪv/

adj. expressing or tending to express firmly opinions or claims；showing a confident belief in one's own ability 断言的；肯定的；自信的；武断的：If you want to succeed in this business，you should be more ~. 如果你想在这一行取得成功，就必须更加果断。

assess/əˈses/

v. ❶ decide or fix the amount of (a tax，fine or other payment) 评定（征税、罚款等的）数额 ❷ calculate or estimate the value or amount of 评定价值（或金额）❸ evaluate or estimate the quality，importance or worth of 估算，估计（质量、重要性或价值等）

assessment/əˈsesmənt/

n. ❶ the act of assessing 评价，估计：a very perceptive ~ of the situation 对形势所做的一个非常敏锐的估计/What's your ~ of her chances of winning? 你估计她赢的机会有多大？❷ the value or amount at which sth. is calculated 核定额：my tax ~ for a year 我一年应纳税的

核定额

assessor/əˈsesə(r)/

n. ❶ a person whose job is to calculate the value of property or the amount of income or taxes（财产、收入、税收等的）估价员；评税员 ❷ a person who advises a judge or official committee on matters that demand special knowledge（在某种专业知识方面辅助法官或官方委员会工作的）技术顾问，助理

asset/ˈæset/

n. ❶ sth. valuable or useful which gives one an advantage 宝贵的东西；有用的东西：Good health is an ~. 健康就是财富。❷ (pl.) property which one owns 资产；财产：current ~s 流动资产

assign/əˈsaɪn/

v. ❶ give as a share；allocate (a job or duty) 分配；分派（工作或职责）：They ~ed those rooms to us. 他们把那些房间分给我们。❷ give（property，rights，etc.）to 把（财产、权利等）分给：The old man ~ed his property to his sons. 那老人把他的财产分给他的儿子们。❸ appoint sb. to a job or duty 委派；指派：I ~ed you (to) do the job，do it. 我把这工作分给你们，干吧。/The teacher ~ed his students to clean the classroom. 教师指派他的学生打扫教室。❹ put forward（as a time，place，reason，etc.）指定（时间、地点）；提出（理由）：The court ~ed a day for trial. 法庭指定了审判日期。

assignation /ˌæsɪɡˈneɪʃən/

n. an arrangement to meet，especially a secret one 幽会；约会

assignment/əˈsaɪnmənt/

n. ❶ a duty or piece of work that is given to a particular person（分配、指派的）工作，任务 ❷ the act of assigning 分配；指派

assimilate/əˈsɪmələɪt/

v. ❶ take（food）into the body and digest it；absorb ideas，knowledge，etc. 消化吸收（食物）；吸收（思想、知识等）：Some foods are ~d easily. 有些食物容易被吸收。❷ make or become a part of a country，or other group，especially in ways of behaving or thinking 同化：The USA has ~d people from many different countries.美国同化了来自许多不同国家的人。

assimilation/əˌsɪməˈleɪʃn/

*n.*❶ the act of assimilating or of being assimilated 消化，吸收；融合，同化 ❷ the changing of a speech sound because of the influence of another speech sound next to it (e.g.the p in cupboard) 语音的同化(如 cupboard 一词中的 p)

assist/əˈsɪst/

Ⅰ *v.*help sb. to do sth.帮助；支援：Scientists have ~ed us in the stamping out of this disease.科学家们帮助我们消灭了这种疾病。Ⅱ *n.*support or help 支持；援助

assistance/əˈsɪstəns/

*n.*help or support 帮助；援助：I gave ~ to him.我给了他帮助。/She came to my ~.她来帮助我。/Can I be of any ~ to you? 我能对你有什么帮助吗?

assistant/əˈsɪstənt/

*n.*a person who helps another in a job or piece of work, and is under that person's direction 助理；助手；副手：When the shop is busy he employs an ~.商店里忙的时候他就雇用一个店员。/a clerical ~ 文书助理/an ~ cook 助理厨师/the Assistant Director of Education in the London area 伦敦地区教育局副局长

associate/əˈsəʊʃɪeɪt/

Ⅰ *v.*❶ join in a relationship based on friendship, business, or a shared purpose; combine as friends or partners 使发生联系；使联合：They ~d themselves with a large company.他们与一家大公司联合。❷ make a connection between people or things in thought, memory, or imagination 把……联想起来：They always ~ China with the Great Wall.他们总是想起中国就联想到长城。Ⅱ *n.*❶ a person connected with another, especially in work；partner 合伙人；同事；朋友 ❷ a person given certain limited rights in an association(协会等的)准会员

associated/əˈsəʊʃɪeɪtɪd/

adj.(of a person or thing) connected with sb. or sth. else 有关联的；相关的：the risks ~ with taking drugs 与吸毒有关的危险

association/əˌsəʊsɪˈeɪʃn/

*n.*❶ a connection or cooperative link between things or persons 联合；联系；联盟；交往：Her English benefited through her long ~ with British children.她的英语得益于她长期与英国孩子的交往。❷ a connection in mind between people or things 联想 ❸ a group of persons joined together for some common purpose 协会；社团：a bar ~ 律师协会/an ~ of banks and bankers 银行协会

assort/əˈsɔːt/

*v.*❶ divide sth.into different sorts 把……分类(或归类) ❷ associate with sb. especially a bad company 与……为伍(尤指与坏人)：He is known to ~ with criminal types.人人都知道他与犯罪分子为伍。

assorted/əˈsɔːtɪd/

*adj.*of various kinds；mixed 各种各样的；混合的：~ chocolates 什锦巧克力

assortment/əˈsɔːtmənt/

*n.*a collection of different things or people 各种各样的人(或物)：an ~ of fresh flowers 各种鲜花

assume/əˈsjuːm/

*v.*❶ suppose to be the case 假定；假设：We should ~ him to be innocent before hearing the evidence against him.在听取他有罪的证词前我们应该假设他是无罪的。/He ~d that it was so.他想当然地认为它就是这个情况。❷take up；undertake 担任；承担：~ office 就职 ❸ take upon；adopt 呈现；采取：~ the defensive 采取守势 ❹pretend 假装：He ~d a look of happiness, in fact he was very sad.他假装快乐，但实际却很悲伤。

assumption/əˈsʌmpʃn/

*n.*❶ sth. that is taken as a fact or believed to be true without proof 假定，假设；设想：The results of the experiment shook the basic ~s of his theory.实验的结果动摇了他的理论的基本假设。/Let's work on the ~ that our proposal will be accepted.我们先假定我们的建议

A

会被采纳，就这样先干起来吧。❷ the act of taking or having power or responsibility（责任的）承担；（权力的）获取：the army's ～ of power 军队的夺权

assurance/ə'ʃɔːrəns/

*n.*❶certainty；confidence 确信；信心；把握：I have full ～ of her honesty. 对她的诚实我深信不疑。/She answered the teacher's questions with ～. 她很有把握地回答了老师的问题。❷excessive self-confidence；impudence 自大，狂妄：Mr. White had the ～ to claim that he could speak six foreign languages perfectly. 怀特先生狂妄宣称他能很熟练地讲六种外语。❸a statement made to assure sb. about sth. 保证，担保：I gave him an ～ that I would finish the work the next week. 我向他保证下周完成这项工作。

assure/ə'ʃɔː(r)/

*v.*❶say sth. positively with confidence 肯定地说；向……保证：I ～ you of his honesty. 我向你保证他忠诚可靠。/I ～ you (that) he is easy to teach. 我向你保证他容易教。❷cause sb. to be sure or to be certain 使确信；使放心：She ～d us of her willingness to work. 她使我们确信她愿意工作。❸ cover (a life) by assurance 保（人寿）险

assured/ə'ʃʊəd/

Ⅰ*adj.*❶having or showing certainty 确定的；有保证的 ❷confident in one's own abilities 自信的；确信的 Ⅱ*n.*(*pl.* assured) a person whose life has been insured 被保险人

astern/ə'stɜːn/

*adv.*at or towards the back or stern of a ship 在船尾；向船尾

asthma/'æsmə/

n. a disease which causes difficulty in breathing 哮喘；气喘

astigmatism/ə'stɪɡmətɪzəm/

*n.*the inability of the eye to see properly or clearly because of its shape 散光；散视

astir/ə'stɜː(r)/

adv.& *adj.*❶ awake and out of bed 起床地(的)：No one was ～ so early. 没有人这么早起床。❷ in a state of excitement 激

动地(的)；轰动地(的)；骚动地(的)：The ship was ～ with anxious passengers. 乘客们忧虑不安,全船一片乱哄哄

astonish/ə'stɒnɪʃ/

*v.*surprise sb.greatly 使惊异；使吃惊：The news ～ed everyone.这个消息使人震惊。

astonishment/ə'stɒnɪʃmənt/

*n.*great surprise or wonder 惊异,惊讶：To our ～ he actually arrived on time. 使我们大为惊讶的是他竟然准时到达了。/She stared in ～ at the document.她吃惊地盯着那文件。

astound/ə'staʊnd/

*v.*shock with very great surprise 使大为吃惊；使震惊

astounded/ə'staʊndɪd/

*adj.*very surprised or shocked by sth.感到震惊的；大吃一惊的：an ～ expression 大吃一惊的表情

astounding /ə'staʊndɪŋ/

*adj.*surprisingly impressive or notable 惊人的；令人惊骇的：The summit offers ～ views.顶峰让人看到惊心动魄的景色。

astray/ə'streɪ/

adv.& *adj.*away from the right path or way 迷路地(的)；入歧途地(的)，离开正道地(的)；犯错误地(的)：One of the sheep went ～ and got lost.一只羊迷路走失了。

astride/ə'straɪd/

adv.& *prep.*with one leg on each side 跨着；骑着；sit ～ a fence 跨坐在栅栏上

astringent/ə'strɪndʒənt/

Ⅰ*adj.*❶ able to tighten up the skin or stop bleeding 收敛(性)的；止血的：～ lotions 收敛性美容液 ❷ severe；bitter 严厉的；厉害的：～ criticism 严厉的批评 Ⅱ*n.*a substance or medicine that tightens up the skin and stops bleeding 收敛剂；止血药 ‖ ～ly *adv.*严格地；严厉地/**astringency** *n.*收敛性；严厉

astrology/ə'strɒlədʒi/

*n.*the art of observing the positions of the stars and telling how they influence human affairs 占星学,占星术

astronaut/'æstrənɔːt/

n. a person who is trained to travel in a

spaceship 宇航员,太空人

astronomer /əˈstrɒnəmə(r)/
　　n. someone who studies astronomy 天文学家

astronomical /ˌæstrəˈnɒmɪkl/
　　adj. ❶ concerned with astronomy 天文学（上）的 ❷ so large that we cannot imagine it（like the distance and sizes studied in astronomy）大得无法想象的,极大的(如天文学中所研究的距离和体积):an ～ distance 极远的距离/an ～ amount 巨大的数量 ‖ ～ly *adv.* 天文学上地;巨大地

astronomy /əˈstrɒnəmi/
　　n. the study of the sun, planets, stars and other objects in space 天文学

astute /əˈstjuːt/
　　adj. clever and able to see sth. quickly that is to one's advantage 敏锐的;精明的;聪明的;狡猾的:an ～ businesswoman 精明的女商人

asylum /əˈsaɪləm/
　　n. ❶ a hospital for people who are mentally ill 精神病院 ❷ any shelter or protection from danger 避难所

asymmetric(al) /əsɪˈmetrɪk(əl)/
　　adj. having two sides or parts that are not the same in size or shape 不对称的:a ～ shape 不对称的图形 ‖ **asymmetrically** *adv.* 不对称地/**asymmetry** /əˈsɪmətri/ *n.* 不对称

at /æt, ət/
　　prep. ❶ indicating a point in space (表示空间)在:～ the station 在车站 ❷ on or during a time (表示时间)在……时(刻):～ 6 o'clock 在 6 点/～ Christmas 圣诞节时 ❸ in a state of (表示状态)在……中:～ war 在交战中 ❹ used to express a relationship between an individual and a skill 在……方面:good ～ learning 善于学习的 ❺ used to denote a particular point or segment on a scale 以……:mass produce a kind of product ～ a low cost 以低成本大规模生产某种产品 ❻ used to indicate the cause 因为,由于:rejoice ～ others' achievements 为别人的成就感到高兴

atavistic /ˌætəˈvɪstɪk/
　　adj. following or imitating sth. done by a remote ancestor 返祖性的;回复到远祖的:～ fears and instincts 原始的恐惧和本能

atheism /ˈeɪθɪɪzəm/
　　n. the disbelief in the existence of God 无神论;不信神(的存在)

atheist /ˈeɪθɪɪst/
　　n. a person who does not believe in the existence of God 无神论者;不信神者:a confirmed ～ 一个坚定的无神论者

athlete /ˈæθliːt/
　　n. a person who practises athletics (田径)运动员

athletic /æθˈletɪk/
　　adj. ❶ of athletes or athletics 运动的;体育的;运动员的;体育家的 ❷ physically strong, with well-balanced proportions between the trunk and limbs 体格健壮的;行动敏捷的;活跃的 ‖ ～ally *adv.* 运动地;活跃地

athletics /æθˈletɪks/
　　n. (*pl.*) the practice of physical exercises and of sports demanding strength and speed, such as running and jumping 体育;(田径)运动

Atlantic /ətˈlæntɪk/
　　Ⅰ *n.* the Atlantic Ocean 大西洋:He sailed across the ～ in a canoe. 他划着独木舟渡过了大西洋。 Ⅱ *adj.* of or adjoining the Atlantic Ocean 大西洋的;大西洋沿岸的

atlas /ˈætləs/
　　n. a book of maps 地图册;图表集:a world ～ 世界地图册

atmosphere /ˈætməsfɪə(r)/
　　n. ❶ the air surrounding the earth 大气;大气层 ❷ the air in any place 空气 ❸ the feeling or the mood which one receives from a place or from particular conditions 气氛;氛围:He grew up in an ～ of love and trust. 他在充满着爱和信任的氛围中长大。 / There was an ～ of excitement in the theatre. 戏院里呈现一片令人激动的气氛。

atmospheric /ˌætməsˈferɪk/
　　adj. of or connected with the atmosphere

A

大气的,大气层的:～ pressure 大气压力/～ refraction 大气折射

atom /ˈætəm/

　　n. the smallest particle of a chemical element that can exist 原子 ‖ ～ **bomb** 原子弹/～ **bomber** 原子轰炸机

atomic /əˈtɒmɪk/

　　adj. of or concerning atoms, nuclear weapons, or nuclear energy 原子的;核武器的;核能的

atomizer /ˈætəmaɪzə/

　　n. an instrument that changes a liquid, e.g. a perfume, into a mist of very small drops by forcing it out through a very small hole 雾化器,喷雾器(如香水喷雾器)

atonal /eɪˈtəʊnl/

　　adj. of a piece of music not based on any ordered scale 无调的 ‖ ～**ly** *adv.* 无调地;不成调地 /～**ity** /ˌeɪtəʊˈnæləti/ *n.* 无调性

atrium /ˈɑːtrɪəm/

　　n. (*pl.* atria or ～s) ❶ the central court with an open roof of an ancient Roman house (古罗马建筑中无顶的)门厅;正厅 ❷ each of the two upper cavities in the heart that receive blood from the veins attached 心房

atrophy /ˈætrəfi/

　　v. (of body tissue or an organ) weaken and waste away, especially through lack of blood or lack of use (身体组织或器官)萎缩,衰退: The disease atrophied her leg. 疾病使她的一条腿萎缩了。/a boring repetitive job that atrophied my mind 使我智力退化的令人厌烦的重复性工作

attach /əˈtætʃ/

　　v. ❶ fasten sth. in position; fix or join 缚;系;连接 ❷ fasten (a related document) to another 附上(有关文件)

attache /əˈtæʃeɪ/

　　n. a person who is employed to the staff of an ambassador (大使馆)工作人员,随员,参赞: military ～ 大使馆或公使馆陆军武官/naval ～ 大使馆或公使馆海军武官

attachment /əˈtætʃmənt/

　　n. ❶ the act of attaching or being attached 连接;系: The case has a loop for ～ to your waist belt. 套子上有一个环可以系在皮带上。❷ sth. that is attached or forms an extra part of sth. 附件;附属物 ❸ affection or fondness 依恋;爱慕: a child's strong ～ to its parents 孩子对父母的强烈依恋

attack /əˈtæk/

　　Ⅰ *v.* ❶ use violence to hurt sb. 攻击;袭击 ❷ speak or write strongly against 非难;抨击 ❸ begin to deal with sth. with eagerness and determination (干劲十足地)投入,着手 ❹ make sb. suddenly ill (疾病)侵袭 Ⅱ *n.* ❶ an act of use violence intended to hurt sb. 攻击;袭击 ❷ writings, words or actions directed forcefully against a person, plan, etc., intended to hurt or damage 非难;抨击 ❸ a sudden and usually severe period of illness, especially one which tends to return (疾病等的)侵袭,发作

attain /əˈteɪn/

　　v. ❶ succeed in doing or getting sth. 达到;完成;获得 ❷ arrive at or reach 到达 ‖ ～**able** *adj.* 可达到的

attainment /əˈteɪnmənt/

　　n. ❶ success in doing or getting sth. 达到;完成;获得: the ～ of happiness 幸福的获得 ❷ sth. that has been successfully gained or learned, especially a skill 成就;造诣;学识;技能: The ability to speak Chinese was among his ～s. 他的技能之一是会讲汉语。

attempt /əˈtempt/

　　Ⅰ *v.* make an effort at; try 尝试;试图: The question was so difficult that he didn't even ～ it. 那个问题非常难,他甚至连试都没有试一下。/He ～ed to escape but failed. 他企图逃走,但失败了。Ⅱ *n.* ❶ an act of trying to do sth. 试图;企图;努力: We failed in our ～ to cross the river. 我们试图过河,但没有成功。❷ attack 攻击: make an ～ on a fortress 攻打要塞

attempted /əˈtemptɪd/

　　adj. (of a crime, etc.) that sb. has tried to do but without success (犯罪等)未遂的: an ～ murder 企图谋杀

attend /əˈtend/

A

v. ❶ be present at (an event or a meeting) 出席；参加：～ a meeting 参加会议/～ school 上学/ This party will be well ～ed.这个晚会将会有许多人参加。❷ look after；care for 照料；护理：～ to the door 看门/ ～ to the patient 护理病人 ❸ pay attention to 注意：Attend to your own business.别管闲事。❹ occur with or as a result of (作为结果)伴随：Such an act will be ～ed with ill effects. 这种行为将不会有好结果。

attendance/əˈtendəns/
n. ❶ the act or fact of attending, especially usually or regularly (尤指经常或定时定期的)出席，到场：Attendance at school is demanded by law. 法律规定儿童必须上学。/a poor ～ record 出席次数极少的记录 ❷ the number of people present 出席人数：an ～ of over 5,000 出席人数超过 5 000 ❸ the act of going with or being with sb. 伴随；随行；侍候；照顾：There is a doctor in ～ on the queen. 有一个医生在照顾女王。

attendant/əˈtendənt/
Ⅰ *n.* ❶ a person employed to look after and help visitors or customers in a public place (公共场所的)服务员，侍役：a car park ～ 停车场的服务员 ❷ a person who goes with and serves or looks after another 侍从；随从 Ⅱ *adj.* ❶ happening at the same time, as or as a result of sth. else 伴随的；随之而来的；附带的：One of the difficulties ～ on shift work is lack of sleep. 轮班工作带来的困难之一就是睡眠不足。/bad weather and its ～ problems 坏天气及随之而来的问题 ❷ on duty to help and look after someone 随侍的；侍候的；负责照顾的；服务的

attention/əˈtenʃn/
n. ❶ the act of directing one's mind (to sth. or sb.) 注意，留心：attract someone's ～ 引起某人的注意/You must pay ～ to your pronunciation. 你必须注意你的发音。❷ standing straight and still; a military command to come to such a position 立正姿势，立正口令：Attention! 立正! ❸ (usually *pl.*) a person's action trying to please sb. or to show interest in sb. 礼貌，

殷勤：He pays great ～s to that young lady. 他对那年轻女士大献殷勤。

attentive/əˈtentɪv/
adj. ❶ gaining or paying attention to sth. 注意的；留心的：an ～ listener 倾听者/～ audience 专心的观众/ He was very ～ to the lecture. 他很专心地听演讲。❷ attending to the comfort or wishes of others 体贴的；关心的：He was always ～ to his young sister. 他对他妹妹一直很关心。‖ ～ly *adv.* 专心地：They listened ～ly to the teacher. 他们专心地听老师讲解。

attest/əˈtest/
v. ❶ declare sth. to be true, especially by signing sth. (尤指通过签署某种文件)作证，证实，证明：～ a signature 见证签字 ❷ be proof of; demonstrate 作为……的证明；表明：His wealth ～ed his ability. 他的财富证明了他的才能。

attic/ˈætɪk/
n. the space in a building, especially a house, just below the roof, especially when made into a room or used for storage (屋顶下的)阁楼，顶楼

attire/əˈtaɪə(r)/
Ⅰ *n.* clothes, especially of a particular type (尤指特定式样的)衣服，服装：in formal ～ 穿着礼服 Ⅱ *v.* put on clothes; dress 穿着；盛装：～d in her academic robes 穿着她的大学学位服

attitude/ˈætɪtjuːd/
n. ❶ a position of the body; a posture 姿势 ❷ a way of feeling or thinking about someone or sth., especially as that influences one's behaviour 态度；看法

attorney/əˈtɜːni/
n. ❶ a qualified lawyer 律师 ❷ a person with legal authority to act for another in business or law 代理人：a letter of ～ 委任状/ power of ～ 代理权

attract/əˈtrækt/
v. ❶ cause the admiration, interest, or feelings of sb. 吸引，引起(赞赏、兴趣、感情等)：He was ～ed by her smile. 他为她的微笑吸引。/His new book has ～ed a lot of attention. 他的新书吸引了许多人的注意。❷ draw or pull towards oneself;

A

cause to come near 招引;吸引;引诱:A magnet ~s iron.磁石吸铁。/Flowers ~ bees.鲜花招引蜜蜂。/The company is trying to ~ overseas investors.这家公司试图吸引海外的投资者。/a proposal that ~ed widespread criticism 引起广泛批评的一个提案

attraction /əˈtrækʃn/
n. ❶ a force pulling things towards each other 引力:The ~ of the moon for the earth causes the tides.月亮与地球的引力引起潮汐。❷ a person or thing that attracts others 有吸引力的人(或事物):the chief ~ of the temple 这庙宇最引人注目之处

attractive /əˈtræktɪv/
adj. ❶ pleasing or appealing to the senses 有吸引力的;引人注目的;引人入胜的;诱惑人的:I find the idea of travel very ~.我觉得旅游这个主意很吸引人。/an ~ smile 动人的微笑 ❷ having good looks;pretty or handsome 漂亮的;英俊的:an ~ girl 一个漂亮的女孩

attribute /ˈætrɪbjuːt/
Ⅰ *n.* ❶ a quality of feature forming part of the nature 品质;属性:Kindness is one of his many fine ~s.他有许多好品质,其一是仁慈善良。❷ a symbol of a person or a thing (人或物)的特征,标志:The crown is an ~ of kingship.皇冠是王权的标志。Ⅱ *v.* ❶ consider sth. as being the result of or as coming from another thing 认为……是……的结果,归于:He ~d his success to good luck.他把他的成功归结于运气好。❷ think of as being written or made by 认为……是……写的(做的):This comedy has been ~ d to Shakespeare.这个喜剧被认为是莎士比亚写的。

attributive /əˈtrɪbjʊtɪv/
adj. (of adjectives or nouns) used before a noun to describe it (形容词或名词)用作定语的;修饰语的

attrition /əˈtrɪʃn/
n. an action which gradually makes sth. smaller,weaker,less useful,etc.磨损;消耗

atypical /eɪˈtɪpɪkl/
adj. not typical;different from what is usual 非典型的;不同寻常的:Her reaction to the drug was ~.她对这种药物的反应反常。‖ ~ly /-kli/ *adv.* 非典型地

auction /ˈɔːkʃn, ˈɒkʃn/
Ⅰ *n.* a public sale in which goods are sold to the person offering the highest price 拍卖:He sold it by ~.他把它拍卖掉。Ⅱ *v.* sell sth. at an auction 拍卖

auctioneer /ˌɔːkʃəˈnɪə(r)/
n. a person who is in charge of an auction and who calls out the prices as they are reached 拍卖人

audacious /ɔːˈdeɪʃəs/
adj. ❶ brave and ready to take a risk 大胆的 ❷ impudent and without any fear of authority 放肆的;鲁莽的

audacity /ɔːˈdæsəti/
n. ❶ daring bravery 大胆 ❷ daring rudeness;lack of respect 鲁莽;大胆无礼;放肆:How you have the ~ to say such a thing,I don't know! 你怎么胆敢说出这样的话,我真不明白!

audible /ˈɔːdəbl/
adj. loud enough to be heard 听得见的 ‖ ~ness *n.* 可听性/**audibly** *adv.* 可听见地

audience /ˈɔːdɪəns/
n. ❶ the group of people watching or listening to a performance, speech, television show, etc. 听众;观众:The lecturer draws large ~s.这位演说家吸引了许多听众。❷ a formal interview (given by a ruler) (统治者的)接见:Yesterday the king gave ~ to the American ambassador.昨天国王接见了美国大使。

audio /ˈɔːdɪəʊ/
adj. connected with or used in the broadcasting or receiving of sound that is recorded 声音的;录音的;声频的

audio-visual /ˌɔːdɪəʊˈvɪʒʊəl/
adj. involving both sight and sound,especially video 视听的:~ aids for the classroom 课堂视听教具

audit /ˈɔːdɪt/
Ⅰ *v.* check in detail the record of money received and spent to see that the record is correct 查(账) Ⅱ *n.* an examination of

this kind 审计;查账

audition/ɔː'dɪʃn/

*n.*a test given to an actor,etc.before he is given a part in a play（演员等被给予剧中角色前的）试演,试听

auditor /'ɔːdɪtə/

*n.*❶a person who conducts an audit 审计员;查账员 ❷a listener 听众;So low was his voice that the ∼s had to give it close attention.他的嗓音如此此低沉,听众们不得不非常仔细地听。

auditorium/ˌɔːdɪ'tɔːrɪəm/

*n.*the part of a theatre,concert hall,etc.in which the audience sits（戏院、音乐厅等的)观众席,听众席

auditory /'ɔːdɪtəri/

adj. to do with hearing 听觉的: the ∼ nerves 听觉神经

augment/ɔːg'ment/

*v.*become or make larger by adding sth.（使)增大;(使)扩大

august/ɔː'gʌst/

*adj.*noble and grand 尊严的,可敬的;庄严的,威严的 ‖ ∼**ly** *adv.*庄严地/∼**ness** *n.*庄严

August/'ɔːgəst/

*n.*the eighth month of the year 八月

aunt/ɑːnt/

*n.*❶the sister of one's father or mother, or the wife of one's uncle 姨母;姑母;伯母;婶母;舅母 ❷a woman who is a friend or neighbour of a small child or its parents 大娘;大妈;阿姨(对年长妇女的尊称)

aura/'ɔːrə/

*n.*effect or feeling that seems to surround and come from a person or place（人或地方的)气氛,气息,韵味: an ∼ of decay in the empty village 笼罩着这个荒无人烟村落的一种腐朽的气氛

aural/'ɔːrəl/

*adj.*of or related to the sense of hearing 听的,听觉的: an ∼ surgeon 耳科医生/ ∼ tests 听力检查

auricle/'ɔːrɪkl/

*n.*❶ the outside part of the ear 外耳,耳郭 ❷ either of the two spaces in the top

of the heart;atrium（心脏的)心房,心耳

aurora/ə'rɔːrə/

*n.*bands or arches of coloured light in the night sky seen either in the most northern parts of the world(aurora borealis or northern lights) or in the most southern parts(aurora australis or southern lights) 极光(如南极光和北极光)

auscultation/ˌɔːskəl'teɪʃn/

n. the act of listening to the sounds coming from the organs inside the body as a method of discovering the health 听诊

auspicious/ɔː'spɪʃəs/

adj. giving, promising, or showing signs of future success 预示成功的;吉兆的;吉祥的: an ∼ occasion 吉利的时辰

austere/ɒ'stɪə(r)/

*adj.*❶ severely and strictly moral; without comfort or enjoyment; serious 艰苦的,苦修的;严肃的 ❷ without decoration;plain 朴实无华的;简朴的 ‖ ∼**ly** *adv.*严格地;简朴地/∼**ness** *n.*严格;朴素

austerity/ɔː'sterəti/

*n.*❶the quality of being austere 苦行;禁欲 ❷sternness or severity of manner or attitude 严格,严厉;严肃 ❸a situation, especially one resulting from an intentional government plan in which there is little money for spending on comfort and enjoyment 紧缩,节制

authentic /ɔː'θentɪk/

*adj.*genuine;known to be true 可信的;真正的:an ∼ signature 亲笔签名 ‖ ∼**ally** *adv.*可靠地;真正地/ ∼**ity** *n.* 确实性;真实性

authenticate /ɔː'θentɪkeɪt/

*v.*prove that sth. is genuine 证明……是真实的;证实: These artifacts were ∼d from the Italian Renaissance.这些工艺品被鉴定为来源于意大利文艺复兴时期。 ‖ **authentication** *n.*证明;证实

author/'ɔːθə(r)/

Ⅰ*n.*❶ a writer of book,article,play,etc. 著作人;作家 ❷ a person who creates 创造者;创始人,发起人 Ⅱ*v.*create or begin sth.创造,创始

A

authoritarian /ɔːˌθɒrɪˈteərɪən/
adj. demanding strict obedience to authority and limiting personal freedom (国家)专制的；独裁主义的 ‖ ～ism *n.*独裁主义

authoritative /ɔːˈθɒrɪtətɪv/
adj. having a lot of authority；reliable 可信的；可靠的；clear，～ information and advice 明确可靠的信息和建议 ‖ ～ly *adj.*可信地；权威地

authority /ɔːˈθɒrəti/
n. ❶ the power or right to give orders and make others obey 权；权力：A father has ～ with his children.父亲有权管教孩子。❷ a person with special knowledge about a subject 专家；学术权威：He is a great ～ on grammar.他是语法权威。❸ (usually *pl.*) a person or an organization having power to control a special area or region 当局；官方：He's in the care of the local authorities.他归地方当局管。

authorize /ˈɔːθəraɪz/
v. give official permission for sth.or sb. to do sth.授权；批准；允许；认可 ‖ **authorization** *n.*授权；核准，认可/～d *adj.*核准的，许可的；公认的

autism /ˈɔːtɪzəm/
n. an illness of the mind，especially in children，in which the imagination becomes too important and good personal relationships cannot be formed 孤独症，自闭症

autistic /ɔːˈtɪstɪk/
adj. suffering from autism (患)孤独(自闭)症的：～ children 患有孤独症的儿童 ‖ ～ally *adv.*孤独地

auto /ˈɔːtəʊ/
n. (*pl.*～s) a car 汽车

autobiography /ˌɔːtəbaɪˈɒɡrəfi/
n. the story of sb.'s life written or told by himself 自传

autocracy /ɔːˈtɒkrəsi/
n. a system of government by a single person who can govern as he likes 专制政体；独裁 ‖ **autocratic** /ˌɔːtəˈkrætɪk/ *adj.*专制的；独裁的

autocrat /ˈɔːtəʊkræt/
n. ❶ a ruler who has absolute power 独裁者；专制统治者 ❷ a person who expects to be obeyed by other people and does not care about their opinions or feelings 专横的人；独断专行的人

autograph /ˈɔːtəɡrɑːf/
Ⅰ *n.* a person's name in her or his own writing (signature)，especially the signature of someone famous (尤指名人的)亲笔签名 Ⅱ *v.* (especially of a famous person) sign (a letter，statement，book，etc.) with one's own name to show that one has written it (尤指名人)在(信件、文件、书等)上亲笔签名

automate /ˈɔːtəmeɪt/
v. make (especially facility or industrial process) work by machinery with little or no work by people 使自动化：a fully ～d production line 全自动生产线

automatic /ˌɔːtəˈmætɪk/
adj. ❶ (of a machine) working or moving by itself (机器)自动的：～ telephone 自动电话/an ～ control system 自动控制系统 ❷ done or occurring spontaneously without conscious thought 无意识的；机械的：an ～ response 无意识的反应

automation /ˌɔːtəˈmeɪʃən/
n. the use or introduction of automatic equipment in a manufacturing or other process or facility 自动化

automobile /ˈɔːtəməbiːl/
n. a motorcar 〈美〉汽车

automotive /ˌɔːtəˈməʊtɪv/
adj. to do with motor vehicles 汽车的；机动车的：the ～ industry 汽车工业

autonomous /ɔːˈtɒnəməs/
adj. ❶ (of a country or region) having self-government，at least to a significant degree (国家或地区)自治的 ❷ (of a person) able to do things and make decisions without help from anyone else (人)自治的；有自主权的 ‖ ～ly *adv.*自治地；独立自主地

autonomy /ɔːˈtɒnəmi/
n. a condition in which a country or part of a country governs itself，instead of being governed by another country or by the central government 自治；自主

A

autumn/'ɔːtəm/

　　n. the season of the year between summer and winter when the leaves begin to fall from the trees and the crops are harvested 秋天,秋季(=〈美〉fall)

auxiliary/ɔːg'zɪlɪəri/

　　Ⅰ *adj.* providing supplementary help and support 辅助的;附属的;从属的:an ~ verb 助动词/ ~ troops 辅助部队 Ⅱ *n.* ❶ an auxiliary verb 助动词 ❷a helper or an assistant 辅助者,助手 ❸ additional troops used by a country at war 援军

avail/ə'veɪl/

　　Ⅰ *v.* be of use, of value or of help 有用;有利;有助:Money does not ~ on a desert island. 金钱在荒岛上没有有用处。‖ ~ oneself of 利用:I will ~ myself of the opportunity of speaking English. 我会利用这讲英语的机会。Ⅱ *n.* use;profit;advantage 用处;利益:without ~ 无益

available/ə'veɪləbl/

　　adj. capable of being used;that may be obtained 有用的;合用的:These tickets are ~ for a month. 这些票有效期一个月。

avalanche/'ævəlɑːnʃ/

　　n. ❶ a mass of snow amid ice which falls down a mountain 雪崩 ❷ anything which falls on one like an avalanche (雪崩似落下的)大量东西:an ~ of questions 连珠炮似的大量问题

avenge/ə'vendʒ/

　　v. take revenge for 替……报仇;报复:He swore to ~ his father on you. 他发誓要替他父亲向你报复。/They ~d themselves on the enemies. 他们向敌人报复。

avenue/'ævənjuː/

　　n. ❶ a road with trees on each side 林荫大道 ❷ a wide street in a town (城市中的)大街 ❸ a way or method 方法;手段;途径:~s to success 取得成功的途径

average/'ævərɪdʒ/

　　Ⅰ *n.* ❶ the result of adding several quantities together and dividing the total by the number of quantities 平均;平均数 ❷ a standard or level regarded as ordinary or usual 一般水平;中等水平 Ⅱ *adj.* ❶ calculated by making an average of a number of quantities 平均数的 ❷of the usual or ordinary kind 普通的;平常的 Ⅲ *v.* calculate the average of figures 计算平均数

averse/ə'vɜːs/

　　adj. opposed;not liking 反对的;不乐意的,不情愿的 ‖ ~ly *adv.* 反对地;不乐意地/ ~ness *n.* 厌恶;反对

aversion/ə'vɜːʃn/

　　n. ❶ a feeling of strong dislike or unwillingness 厌恶;讨厌;反感:She has an ~ to cats. 她讨厌猫。 ❷ a person or thing that causes this feeling 讨厌的人(或物):Housework is my pet ~. 我最讨厌做家务。/Smoking is one of my pet ~s aversions. 吸烟是我特别讨厌的事。

avert/ə'vɜːt/

　　v. stop sth. from happening 防止;避免:John's quick action ~ed a serious accident. 约翰动作敏捷,避免了一次严重事故。

aviation/ˌeɪvɪ'eɪʃn/

　　n. the flying in an aeroplane;the art or science of flying aeroplanes 航空;飞行术;航空学

avocado/ˌævə'kɑːdəʊ/

　　n. a type of pear-shaped green or black tropical fruit with soft pale flesh and a big stone 鳄梨(一种热带水果)

avoid/ə'vɔɪd/

　　v. ❶ keep or get away from doing sth. 回避;避免:~ the question 回避问题 ❷ contrive not to meet sb. or sth. 避开;躲开:~ danger 避开危险/~ the collision 避免相撞 ‖ ~ance *n.* 回避;避开

avoidable/ə'vɔɪdəbl/

　　adj. that can be prevented 可以避免的:Many deaths from heart disease are actually ~. 许多因心脏病造成的死亡实际上是可以避免的。

avoirdupois/ˌævədə'pɔɪz/

　　n. the system of weights in which the standard measures are the ounce, pound, and ton 常衡(以盎司、磅、吨为称量标准的衡制):16 ounces ~ 十六盎司(为一磅)的常衡制

A

avow/əˈvaʊ/

*v.*state openly；admit 公开声明；宣称；承认：The prisoner ～ed his guilt.这个罪犯承认了自己的罪行。/He ～ed that he was guilty.他承认他有罪。/Their ～ed aim is to overthrow the government.他们公开声明，他们的目的是推翻政府。‖ ～al *n.*声明

await/əˈweɪt/

*v.*❶ (of persons) wait for（人）等候；期待：We ～ your reply.我们等待你的答复。❷（of things）be in store for；be waiting for（事件等）等待（处理）；将降临到……身上：A hearty welcome ～s you.热烈的欢迎在等着你。

awake/əˈweɪk/

Ⅰ *v.*(awoke/əˈwəʊk/, awoken)❶ (cause to) stop sleeping；wake 唤醒；使醒：Don't ～ the sleeping child.别把孩子吵醒。❷ (cause to) become conscious or active 唤起；使觉悟；使奋发：He awoke to his opportunities.他觉察到了他的机会。Ⅱ *adj.*not asleep 醒着的：He isn't ～ yet.他还没有醒。

awaken/əˈweɪkən/

*v.*wake up 使醒；唤醒

awakening/əˈweɪkənɪŋ/

*n.*an act or a moment of becoming suddenly aware of sth.（突然的）领悟，认识，醒悟：The war came as a rude ～ to the hardships of life.战争让人猛然领悟到了生活的艰苦。

award/əˈwɔːd/

Ⅰ *v.*give or grant by official decision 判给；授予；颁发：She was ～ed the first prize.她荣获一等奖。/The judge ～ed him 50 pounds for damages.法官判给他50英镑赔偿损失。Ⅱ *n.*sth. given from the official decision，especially a prize in a competition 奖；奖品：the first ～ 一等奖

aware/əˈweə(r)/

*adj.*having knowledge or realization 知道的；意识到的；觉察到的：I was ～ of the fact.我知道了这事实。/He was ～ that I had resigned. 他知道我已经辞职了。/Are you ～ whether he is reliable or not? 你知道他是否可靠吗？

awareness/əˈweənɪs/

*n.*knowing sth.；knowing that sth. exists and is important；being interested in sth. 知道；认识；意识；兴趣：an ～ of the importance of eating a healthy diet 认识到健康饮食的重要性/environmental ～ 环境意识

away/əˈweɪ/

Ⅰ *adv.*❶at a stated distance in space or time（远）离：The place is two kilometers ～ from here.那个地方离这儿有两千米路。/The sports are two weeks ～.离运动会还有两个星期。❷so as to be gone or used up...去掉……：wash the dirt ～ 洗掉污垢/ Go ～! 滚开! ❸all the time；continuously 继续不断地：work ～ 连续干下去 Ⅱ *adj.*(of a sports match) played at the place,sports field,etc.,of one's opponent（球赛等）客场的，在对方场地进行的：home and ～ games 在主场和客场进行的比赛

awe/ɔː/

Ⅰ *n.*a feeling of respect mixed with fear and wonder 畏惧；敬畏；怕 Ⅱ *v.*fill with awe 威吓；使敬畏：They were ～d into silence by the enormous ancient buildings.他们看到这些庞大的古代建筑敬畏得说不出话来。

awesome/ˈɔːsəm/

*adj.*❶extremely impressive or daunting 惊人的；威慑的：the ～ power of the atomic bomb 原子弹的威慑力 ❷ very good；excellent 绝妙的；极佳的：The concert is truly ～! 音乐会真是棒极了!

awful/ˈɔːfl/

*adj.*❶ frightening；dreadful 令人畏惧的；可怕的；令人敬畏的 ❷ awe-inspiring 威严的；令人崇敬的 ❸ very great；very bad 极度的；非常的；极坏的 ‖ ～ly *adv.* 非常地；极度地，十分/～ness *n.*威严；可怕

awkward/ˈɔːkwəd/

*adj.*❶clumsy；having little skill 笨拙的；不熟练的：The boy is ～ with chopsticks.那男孩不会用筷子。/～ in action 行动笨拙 ❷not well designed for use 使用不便的：This is an ～ staircase.这楼梯上下不够方便。❸embarrassing 尴尬的：He was in an ～ situation.他陷入了尴尬处境。❹difficult to deal with；knotty 棘手的；难应付的；难处理的：A very ～ thing has happened.一件很棘手的事发生了。

awning /'ɔːnɪŋ/

*n.*a sheet of canvas or plastic stretched over a frame and fixed over a doorway or shop window as a protection against the sun or rain 雨篷；遮篷；天篷

axe/æks/

Ⅰ *n.*❶a large chopping tool with a heavy blade 斧 ❷(the ～)dismissal or redundancy 解雇；倒闭；被停业：When the business closes,30 staff will face the ～. 公司倒闭时，有 30 个员工面临被解雇。 Ⅱ *v.*❶to dismiss people or end a project suddenly 裁减；取消；解雇 ❷to have an axe to grind（用斧）砍

axial/'æksɪəl/

*adj.*❶forming or belonging to an axis 成

轴的；轴的；～ symmetry 轴对称/an ～ angle 轴角 ❷round an axis 轴向的：～ rotation 轴向旋转

axis/'æksɪs/

n.(*pl.* axes/'æksiːz/) ❶ a line round which a turning object spins；a political connection(not always an alliance) between two or more states 轴；轴线；轴心 ❷a line(e.g.across the middle of a circle) that divides a regular shape into two equal parts（把规则形状分成相等两部分的）中心线；中枢

axle/'æksl/

*n.*a rod or bar with a wheel on either end, around which the wheels turn or which turns with the wheels 轮轴；车轴；轴干；crank ～ 曲轴/a cross ～ 横轴

azure /'æʒə/

*adj.*bright blue in colour like a cloudless sky 天蓝色的；蔚蓝色的

Bb

babble/'bæbl/
Ⅰ *n.* a foolish or childish talking 愚蠢的谈话；幼稚的谈话 Ⅱ *v.* talk foolishly or childishly 傻里傻气地说；孩子般地说

babel/'beɪbl/
n. a scene of noisy and confused talking 混乱；嘈杂：What a ～! 多么嘈杂啊!

baboon/bə'buːn/
n. a large monkey of Africa and southern Asia with a doglike face 狒狒(一种大猴子，产于非洲及亚洲南部，面似狗)

baby/'beɪbi/
n. ❶ a very young child, especially one that cannot walk or talk yet 婴儿：A ～ cannot walk. 婴儿不会走路。/a ～ boy 小男孩 ❷ a very young animal 幼崽：a ～ monkey 幼猴

babysit/'beɪbɪsɪt/
v. to look after a child in its home while its parents are out 临时代为照看孩子：She was ～ting Sophie. 她在临时照看苏菲。

babysitter/'beɪbɪsɪtə(r)/
n. a person who looks after a child in its home while its parents are out 临时保姆；代人临时照看小孩的人

babyhood/'beɪbɪhʊd/
n. the period of time when one is a baby 婴儿期，幼小时期

babyish/'beɪbɪʃ/
adj. (especially of someone who is not a baby)like a baby 婴儿似的，孩子气的：It's ～ to cry about having a tooth out at your age. 在你这种年龄拔牙还哭哭啼啼的，真太孩子气啦。

bachelor/'bætʃələ(r)/
n. ❶ an unmarried man 未婚男子；单身汉 ❷ a person who has a bachelor's degree 拥有学士学位的人：a ～'s degree 学士学位/Bachelor of Arts 文学士/Bachelor of Science 理学士

bacillus/bə'sɪləs/
n. (*pl.* bacilli/bə'sɪlaɪ/) a rod-like bacterium, especially one of the types that cause disease 杆菌；细菌；病菌

back/bæk/
Ⅰ *n.* the part of a person's or animal's body that is the side opposite the chest, and goes from the neck to the bottom of the spine or the tail 背部；后面：Don't gossip behind his ～ but say nothing to his face. 不要当面不说，在他背后乱说。Ⅱ *adj.* toward the rear or farthest from the front 后面的；背面的：the ～ row 后排 Ⅲ *adv.* ❶ towards or at the back；away from the front 向后面；在后面：stand ～ 往后站/step ～ 向后退 ❷ in or into the place or position where sb. or sth. was before 回原处；溯至以前：come ～ 回来 ❸ in return；in reply 回复；作答：write ～ 回信/telephone someone～ 回电话 Ⅳ *v.* ❶(cause to) go backwards (使)后退：She ～ed the car into the gate. 她把汽车倒进大门里。❷ support and encourage, often with money；provide backing for (常指用钱)支持；撑腰：Several companies will ～ this plan. 有几家公司资助这项计划。‖ ～ and forth 来回地/～ down 退让；退回去/～ out (of) 收回(承诺等)；变卦/behind one's ～ 在背后；背着某人/break the ～ of 完成最困难的部分/get (have) one's own ～ 报仇；报复/go ～ on (upon, from) 丢弃(朋友)；食(言)；违(约)/hold ～ 停留；控制住/keep ～ 保留；忍住/on one's ～ 仰着；生病卧床/put ～ 延期；耽搁/put one's ～ into sth. 发愤(埋头)干/see the ～ of sb. 摆脱某人/set ～ 推迟；耽搁/take a ～ seat to 居……之后(占次要地位)/turn one's ～ on 不理；

背弃/with one's ～ to the wall 处于绝境

backache/ˈbækˌeɪk/

　　*n.*a pain in the back 背痛：suffering from (a) ～ 感到背痛

backbiting/ˈbækbaɪtɪŋ/

　　n. an unkind and unpleasant talk about someone who is absent 背后中伤：I didn't enjoy working there—there was too much ～.我不喜欢在那里工作，背后议论，流言蜚语太多。

backboard /ˈbækbɔːd/

　　*n.*❶a board placed at or forming the back of sth., such as a collage or piece of electronic equipment 托板；垫板 ❷(in basketball) an upright board behind the basket, off which the ball may rebound(篮球)篮板

backbone/ˈbækbəʊn/

　　*n.*❶the line of bones down the middle of the back 脊柱 ❷the chief support 支柱；骨干：They are ～s of the teaching group. 他们是教研组的骨干。❸ firmness；strength 骨气；勇气：He doesn't have enough ～.他没有足够的勇气。‖ to the ～ 彻底地：He is a German to the ～.他是个地道的德国人。

back-breaking/ˈbækbreɪkɪŋ/

　　adj.(of work) very hard and heavy (工作)累死人的，非常繁重的：a ～ job 繁重的工作

backchat/ˈbæktʃæt/

　　*n.*a rude talk in reply to someone 顶嘴；回嘴：Just listen to me! I don't want ～! 听我说就行了! 我不容许有人回嘴!

backdate/ˌbækˈdeɪt/

　　*v.*make sth. effective from an earlier date 从过去某个日期开始有效，将……追溯到(某年，某月)算起：The pay increase agreed in June will be ～d to January.6月同意增加的工资将从1月份算起。

backdrop/ˈbækdrɒp/

　　*n.*❶ a painted cloth hung across the back of a stage (舞台后部的)背景幕布 ❷ the conditions in which sth. happens；background 背景：The stormy political events of the 1930's provided the ～ for the film.这部影片是以20世纪30年代的政

治风暴为背景的。

backer/ˈbækə(r)/

　　*n.*someone who supports a plan, especially with money 支持者；赞助者；资助者：We'll stage the play as soon as we've found a ～.一旦我们找到资助者，我们就上演此剧。

backfire/ˌbækˈfaɪə(r)/

　　*v.*❶ (of a motor vehicle) make a loud noise because the explosion in the engine comes too soon (汽车引擎的)逆火，回火 ❷have an unexpected effect opposite to the effect intended 发生意外；产生事与愿违的后果：His plan ～d (on him), and he lost all his money.他的计划事与愿违，因此他的钱全亏掉了。

background/ˈbækgraʊnd/

　　*n.*❶the part of a painting or photograph that shows what is behind the main objects or people 背景：trees in the ～ of the picture 图画背景上的树 ❷past experiences(过去的)经历：She always prides herself upon her academic ～.她总是为她的学历而感到骄傲。❸the existing condition when sth.happens (发生某事的)背景情况：The riot took place against a ～ of widespread unemployment. 那次骚乱是在人们大量失业的情况下发生的。

backhand/ˈbækhænd/

　　n.(in games such as tennis) a stroke with the back of the hand turned in the direction of movement (网球的)反手击球：He's got an excellent ～.他具有高超的反手击球技术。

backhanded/ˌbækˈhændɪd/

　　*adj.*❶using or made with a backhand 反手击球的，用反手的 ❷(of a remark) indirect, especially sarcastic (话语)间接的，转弯抹角的，讽刺挖苦的：a ～ compliment 讽刺挖苦的恭维话

backing/ˈbækɪŋ/

　　*n.*❶help or support, especially with money 支持；帮助；资助：He's won the ～ of the Congress for his scheme.他的计划赢得了国会的支持。❷ sth. that is used to make the back of an object 衬垫物；背衬：(a) ～ of cardboard 硬纸板的衬背 ❸the

B

musical accompaniment that supports a singer or musician（音乐）伴奏

backlash/'bæklæʃ/

*n.*❶ a strong but usually delayed feeling of opposition among many people towards a belief or practice, especially towards a political or social development（对政治事件或社会发展的）强烈反应，对抗性反应：The continual rise in violent crime eventually provoked a ～ against the liberal gun-control laws.暴力犯罪不断增加，终于引起了对不严的枪支管制法的强烈不满。❷ a sudden violent backward movement 后冲，反撞；后坐力

backlog/'bæklɒg/

*n.*a number of business or work that have to be done but were not done at the proper time 积压未办的事；积压的工作：a ～ of work after the holidays 假日后积压的工作

backpack /'bækpæk/

*n.*❶a rucksack（箱形）背包 ❷a package of equipment carried on the back 背负在背上使用的装置

back-pedal/ˌbæk'pedl/

*v.*❶pedal backwards on a bicycle（骑脚踏车时）倒踩脚踏板 ❷change an earlier principle or draw back from some promised action 变卦；改变主意；出尔反尔；取消诺言：They promised to cut taxes,but they're beginning to ～ now.他们曾答应减税,但现在开始变卦了。

backslide/ˌbæk'slaɪd/

*v.*to become less good, work less hard, etc.,especially to go back to a worse condition after some improvement 滑坡；倒退；退步；故态复萌：I managed to keep off cigarettes for two months, but recently I'm afraid I've begun to ～.我设法戒了两个月烟,但遗憾的是最近我又开始抽起来了。

backsliding/'bæk'slaɪdɪŋ/

*n.*the situation when sb. fails to do sth. that they agreed to do and returns to their former bad behaviour 倒退；故态复萌

backspace/'bækspeɪs/

*n.*the part that one presses to make the movable part of a typewriter move back one or more spaces towards the beginning of the line（打字机的）退格键

backstage/ˌbæk'steɪdʒ/

*adv.*❶ behind the stage in a theatre,especially in the dressing rooms of the actors 在（戏院）后台；在演员化妆室：After the performance we were invited ～.演出结束后我们被请到后台。❷ in private；not seen publicly；secretly 秘密地；背地里；在幕后：That's what they say, but who knows what really goes on ～? 他们是这样说的；但谁知道幕后是怎么一回事?

backstairs/'bæksteəz/

Ⅰ*adj.*secret and perhaps unfair 秘密的；暗地里的；不公正的；不正当的：～ influence 暗中的影响力 Ⅱ *n.* (*pl.*) stairs at the back or side of a building 后（侧）楼梯

backstreet/'bækstriːt/

Ⅰ*n.*a small or minor street in a town 后街；小道 Ⅱ *adj.*done secretly or illicitly 秘密的；非法的

backstroke/'bækstrəʊk/

*n.*a way of swimming on one's back by moving first one leg and then the other backwards while kicking the feet 仰泳

backtrack/'bæktræk/

*v.*❶go back over the same path 走原路；由原路返回 ❷draw back from a former position,promise, etc.改变主意；取消诺言；变卦；出尔反尔：The government is already ～ing from its more expensive plans.政府业已开始撤回耗资较大的计划。

back-up/'bækʌp/

*n.*a thing or person ready to be used in place of or to help another 替代物；备用品；支援人员；后备人员：We won't be able to do it unless we have a lot of technical ～.此事要办成,非要有强大的技术后备力量不可。/ We have a ～ computer in case the main one breaks down.我们有一部备用的电脑,以防主机出故障。

backward/'bækwəd/

adj. ❶ towards the back or the starting-

B

point 向后的;倒的：have a ～ look 朝后看一看 ❷behind；late in development 落后的；进展缓慢的：This part of our country is still ～.我国的这个地区仍然很落后。/Because of his long illness,Smith is ～ in his studies.由于长期生病,史密斯的学习下降了。❸shy；reluctant；hesitating 羞怯的；不愿的；迟疑的：Although she is clever, she is ～ in giving her views.虽然她很聪明,但她羞于发表自己的意见。

backwards /ˈbækwədz/
*adv.*❶away from the front, towards the back 向后地 ❷with the back facing forwards 朝反方向；倒着 ❸in reverse order 反向地：Count ～ from 20.从 20 开始倒数。‖ **know sth.** ～ 了如指掌

backwash /ˈbækwɒʃ/
*n.*a backward flow of water（水波）反流,回浪

backwater /ˈbækwɔːtə(r)/
*n.*❶ a part of a river out of the main stream, where the water does not move（河流的）回水,死水,滞水 ❷a place not influenced by outside events or new ideas（不受外界事件或新思想影响的）落后地区,闭塞的地方：There aren't any good shops in this village, it's a real ～.这真是一个闭塞的村庄,连一家好的商店也找不到。/a cultural ～ 文化闭塞的地区

backwoods /ˈbækwʊdz/
*n.*❶（especially in North America）uncleared forest land far away from towns（尤指北美的）边远林区 ❷ a distant or backward area 落后的边远地区

backyard /ˌbækˈjɑːd/
*n.*❶ a yard behind a house, covered with a hard surface（屋子后面铺了硬地面的）后院 ❷ a yard behind a house, usually covered with grass；a back garden（常指有草皮的）后院;后花园：The children are playing in the ～.孩子们正在后花园玩耍。

bacon /ˈbeɪkən/
*n.*salted or smoked meat from the back or sides of a pig 咸肉;熏肉：cure the ～ 制熏肉

bacterium /bækˈtɪəriəm/
n.（*pl.* bacteria /bækˈtɪəriə/）one-celled living thing, too small to be seen without a microscope, sometimes a cause of disease 细菌：root nodule ～ 根瘤菌

bacteriology /bækˌtɪəriˈɒlədʒi/
*n.*the scientific study of bacteria 细菌学 ‖ **bacteriological** *adj.*细菌学的/**bacteriologist** *n.*细菌学家

bad /bæd/
adj.（worse, worst）❶ not good；not normal；evil 坏的；邪恶的；不道德的：lead a ～ life 过着邪恶的生活 ❷severe；serious 厉害的；严重的：I have a ～ headache. 我头痛得很厉害。❸ not pleasant；giving a terrible smell 令人不快的;（气味）难闻的：a ～ smell 臭味/～ weather 鬼天气 ❹unfit to eat because of decay；rotten 腐烂的；变质的：Fish easily goes ～ in hot weather.鱼在热天容易变质。‖ **be ～ for** 对……有害/**be taken ～** 生病/**be too ～** 真遗憾/**feel ～** 抱歉/**in a ～ way** 病重；倒霉/**not ～** 不错/**go from ～ to worse** 每况愈下,越来越糟

badge /bædʒ/
*n.*❶a small piece of metal or plastic with a picture or words on it, worn to show a person's occupation, rank, membership of a society 徽章；证章：a school ～ 校徽 ❷ a mark 标志：Chains are a ～ of slavery. 锁链是奴役的标志。

badger /ˈbædʒə(r)/
I *n.*a type of small animal with a white stripe on its nose, which lives in a hole in the ground and comes out at night 獾（鼻部有白条纹,居地穴,夜间出洞）**II** *v.*repeatedly ask for sth. or ask sb. to do sth. by putting pressure on sb.纠缠；烦扰

badinage /ˈbædɪnɑːʒ/
*n.*a playful joke or talk 开玩笑；打趣；戏弄；调侃：Enough of this ～, let's talk seriously.玩笑开够了,我们谈正经事吧。

badly /ˈbædli/
adv.（worse, worst）❶in a bad manner 坏；恶劣地：He behaved ～.他表现不好。❷to a great or serious degree；very much 严重地；非常地：My head ached ～ last

B

night.昨晚我头痛得厉害。‖ ～ off ❶ 穷的：He is now very ～ off.他现在境况 很不好。❷不足，缺少：He is ～ off for food.他缺少食品。

badminton/'bædmɪntən/
*n.*a tennis-like game played by 2 or 4 peo-ple who hit a small feathered object over a high net 羽毛球(运动)：play a game of ～ 打一场羽毛球

baffle/'bæfl/
Ⅰ *n.*a board or other means of controlling the flow of air, water, or sound coming into or going out an enclosed space 阻碍 体；挡板；隔板 Ⅱ *v.*❶be too difficult to understand or solve 困惑住；难住：One of the examination questions ～d me com-pletely.考试题目之一把我完全难住了。 ❷prevent sb.from doing sth.阻止；阻碍： They succeeded in baffling the enemy's plans.他们成功地阻挠了敌人的计划。

bag/bæg/
Ⅰ *n.*❶a container made of soft material (cloth, paper, plastics, leather, etc.) with an opening at the top 袋子；包；提包：a mail ～ 邮袋/a hand ～ 手提包 ❷all the birds, fish or animals shot or caught in one hunting trip 猎物袋；猎获物：They secured a good ～.他们获得了许多猎物。 ‖ **a ～ of bones** 骨瘦如柴的人或动物/ **give sb.the ～** 解雇(某人)Ⅱ *v.*(-gg-)❶ put into a bag or bags 装入袋子：～ (up) wheat 把麦子装进袋子 ❷kill or catch 杀 死；捕捉：They ～ged nothing.他们什么 也没捕到。

bagel/'beɪgl/
*n.*a ring-shaped bread roll 面包圈

baggage/'bægɪdʒ/
n. cases, bags, boxes, etc. of a traveller; luggage 行李：A porter carried our ～ out of the station.一个脚夫把我们的行李搬 出了车站。

baggy/'bægi/
*adj.*hanging in loose folds；not tight 宽松 下垂的；不紧绷的：His trousers were ～ at the knees.他裤子膝部宽松。

bagpipes/'bægpaɪps/
n. (*pl.*) a type of wind musical instru-ment found in Scotland and some other countries 风笛(见于苏格兰及其他某些 国家)

bail[1]/beɪl/
Ⅰ *n.*a sum of money which someone ac-cused of a crime or a friend or relative gives to a court of law so that he can be free until it is time for him to be put on trial.If he comes back to the court when it is time for him to be tried, the money is given back 保释金 ‖ **stand (go) ～ for sb.** 交钱保释某人 Ⅱ *v.*(～ sb.out) obtain sb.'s freedom by payment of bail 保释某 人

bail[2]/beɪl/
v.(～ out)❶ throw out of a boat the wa-ter that has got into it (to prevent the boat sinking) 舀掉(进入)船舱的水(使船 免于下沉)：～ out the boat 舀掉船舱的 水 ❷jump from an aeroplane with a par-achute 跳伞：When the aeroplane caught fire, the pilot ～ed out.飞机着火时，飞行 员跳伞。

bait/beɪt/
Ⅰ *n.*food or sth.like food used to attract fish, animals, or birds which are then caught (钓鱼、猎兽、捕鸟用的)饵，诱饵： The fish took the ～.鱼咬饵了。 Ⅱ *v.*put bait on a hook to catch fish, or in a trap to catch animals (在鱼钩或捕兽器上)装饵： He ～ed the hook with a worm.他在鱼钩 上套上一条蚯蚓作饵。

bake/beɪk/
*v.*❶cook in an oven (在炉中)烤；烘；焙： ～ bread 烘面包/～ cakes 烘糕饼 ❷ make or become hard by heating 烘干；烤 干：The sun ～d the ground hard.太阳将 地晒得坚硬。

baker/'beɪkə(r)/
*n.*a person who bakes bread and cakes, es-pecially in order to sell them in a shop 面包 师；制糕饼的人：I bought these buns at the ～'s shop.我在面包店买了这些小甜 圆面包。

bakery/'beɪkəri/
n. a place where bread and sometimes cakes are baked and sold 面包(糕饼)烘

房;面包(糕饼)店

balance/'bæləns/

Ⅰ *n*.❶ a condition of being steady 平衡;均衡:He lost his ～ and fell from the tree.他身体失去平衡,结果从树上摔下来了。❷ an instrument for weighing things 天平;秤:weigh sth.on the ～ 用天平称某物 ❸ the difference between two columns of an account 余额;结余:My bank ～ isn't large. 我银行的存款不多。/～ of trade 贸易差额 ‖ ～ of forces 力量对比/～ of payments 国际收支差额/keep（lose）one's ～ 保持(失去)平衡/out of ～ 失去平衡/strike a ～ 结算账目/keep ～保持平衡 ‖ ～ beam *n*.平衡木 Ⅱ *v*.❶ keep or put sth.in a steady state 保持平衡:In order to ～ their trade, they would have to reduce imports. 为了保持贸易平衡,他们将不得不减少进口。❷ compare two contrasting things 权衡;对比:We must ～ the benefits against the costs of medical insurance.我们要考虑医疗保险的利弊。

balanced/'bælənst/

adj.❶ giving equal attention to all sides or all opinions 公平的,合理的;均衡的,调和的:～ and impartial reporting of the election campaign 对竞选活动的公平公正的报道/a ～ judgment 稳健的判断 ❷ in which money spent and money earned are equal 收支平衡的:a ～ budget 收支平衡的预算 ❸ having or showing a firm sensible mind 心情平稳的;情绪稳定的;镇静的:She's very well ～.她情绪很稳定。

balcony/'bælkəni/

n.a ledge outside the window of the upper floor of a house surrounded by a wall or railing 阳台

bald/bɔːld/

adj.❶(of man) with little or no hair (on the head）;(of animals) hairless;(of land) without trees or bushes（人）秃头的;(动物)无毛的;(土地)光秃秃的,无草木的:a ～ bird 无羽毛的鸟/a ～ tree 没有叶子的树 ❷ without ornament; undisguised 无装饰的;不加掩饰的:～ facts 赤裸裸的事实

baldly/'bɔːldli/

adv.spoken plainly,without attempting to hide unpleasant facts 直言不讳地;直截了当地;不加掩饰地;赤裸裸地:To put it ～, if you don't stop smoking, you'll be dead in a year. 直率地说吧,你如果不戒烟,就只能活一年。

bale/beɪl/

Ⅰ *n*. a large bundle of goods packed (usually in canvas) ready for transport 包;捆:Cloth is packed in ～s.布匹包装成捆。Ⅱ*v*.make into or pack in bales 将……打包;捆扎:～ hay 捆干草

baleful/'beɪlfʊl/

adj.full of evil or wickedness 恶毒的,邪恶的

ba(u)lk/bɔːk/

v.refuse or be unwilling to use sth. or do sth. 拒绝;畏缩不前;犹疑不决:John ～ed at having to do any more work.约翰不情愿多干一点点儿活。

ball/bɔːl/

n.❶a round object used in play;anything of this shape 球;球状体:throw a ～ 投球 ❷a big party for people gathering for dancing 舞会:We were invited to a ～.我们应邀参加一次舞会。 ‖ get（set, start) the ～ rolling 使开始起来/keep the ～ rolling 使继续下去/play ～（with）开球;（与……）合作

ballad/'bæləd/

n. a type of poem or song which tells a story (usually a traditional story) 民谣;歌谣

ballcock/'bɔːlkɒk/

n.an apparatus for opening and closing a hole through which water passes,worked by a hollow floating ball which rises and falls with the level of the water 浮球阀;浮球栓;浮球旋塞

ballerina/ˌbæləˈriːnə/

n.a woman ballet dancer 芭蕾舞女演员

ballet/'bæleɪ/

n.❶a style of dancing in which a story is told without talking or singing 芭蕾舞;舞剧 ❷ the music for such this style of dancing 芭蕾舞音乐 ❸a group of ballet

B

dancers who work together（总称）芭蕾舞团；芭蕾舞演员：a member of the ～ 芭蕾舞团的一名演员

balloon/bəˈluːn/
I *n.* a bag or envelope filled with air, or with gas lighter than air 气球：The ～ floated off in the west.气球向西飘走了。II *v.* ❶ swell out or get bigger 膨胀；涨大：Her skirt ～ed in the wind.她的裙子在风中胀得像气球一样。❷ travel in a hot-air ballon as a sport 乘热气球飞行：They like to go ～ing at weekends.在周末他们喜欢乘气球飞行。

ballooning/bəˈluːnɪŋ/
n. the sport of flying in a balloon 乘气球飞行

ballot/ˈbælət/
I *n.* ❶ a sheet of paper used to make a secret vote（无记名）投票用纸；选票：They're counting the ～s now.他们正在计算选票。/The ～ boxes are sealed and taken to the City Hall.选票箱封好后送往市政厅。❷ the process or system of secret voting 无记名投票选举（制度）：The ～ is a vital part of the democratic process.无记名投票选举是民主化进程中一个极重要的部分。/The leaders were accused of rigging the ～.领导人被指控在选举中舞弊。❸ an occasion of voting or a chance to vote 投票表决；选举：The members have demanded a ～.会员要求投票表决。/a strike ～ 决定是否罢工的投票表决 /a postal ～ 邮递投票 ❹ the number of votes recorded; poll 投票总数，投票结果 II *v.* ❶ vote or decide secretly 无记名投票；通过投票选出（或决定）：They ～ed for the new chairman, but nobody knows the result yet.他们投票选举新主席，但还不知道选举结果。❷ find out the views of a group by holding a vote 通过投票了解（成员等）的意见：They'll have to ～ the membership before they can declare a strike.他们在宣布罢工之前，必须先通过投票了解全体会员的意见。

ballpark/ˈbɔːlpɑːk/
I *n.* ❶ a baseball ground 棒球场 ❷ a particular area or range（特定的）区域，范围 II *adj.* (of a price or cost) approximate; rough（价格、成本）近似的；大致的：The ～ figure is ＄400－500.大概为 400 到 500 美元。

ballpoint/ˈbɔːlpɔɪnt/
n. a pen with a tiny ball as its writing point, especially one using stiffer ink than a roller ball 圆珠笔

ballroom/ˈbɔːlruːm/
n. a large room used for dancing or formal occasions 舞会厅；宴会厅

balm/bɑːm/
n. ❶ a sweet-smelling oil or cream obtained from certain kinds of trees, used for soothing pain or healing（用以止痛或疗伤的）香油；香脂；香膏；止痛药膏 ❷ sth. that which gives peace of mind; consolation 安慰物；慰藉物：like ～ to someone's hurt feelings 如受伤心灵的一种慰藉

balmy/ˈbɑːmi/
adj. (especially with reference to winds) gentle and mild（尤指风）温和的；和煦的：a ～ breeze 温和的微风

balsa/ˈbɔːlsə/
n. a type of very light wood 轻木材

balustrade/ˌbæləsˈtreɪd/
n. a row of short posts or pillars supporting a rail or strip of stonework round a balcony or terrace（尤指阳台、平顶屋的）护栏，扶手

bamboo/bæmˈbuː/
n. a tall tropical plant of the grass family which has hard, hollow, jointed stems, which are used e.g. for making furniture 竹子：～ work 竹器/～ shoot 竹笋

ban/bæn/
I *v.* (-nn-) forbid sth., especially by law 禁止：Swimming is ～ned in this lake.禁止在湖内游泳。II *n.* an official prohibition 禁令：We have put a ～ on smoking.我们已经下令禁烟。

banal/bəˈnɑːl/
adj. very ordinary and containing nothing that is unusual or interesting 平庸的；乏味的：a very ～ remark 枯燥无味的话 ‖ ～ity *n.* 平常；乏味

banana/bəˈnɑːnə/

　　n. a type of curved fruit, yellow in colour 香蕉

band/bænd/

　　Ⅰ *n.* ❶ a thin flat strip of some material used especially to reinforce objects, fasten things together or as decoration 带子；绳子；箍条：a ～ for the head 头带 ❷ a radio range of frequencies 波段；频带：I have a seven-transistor, three-～ radio receiver. 我有一台七管三波段的收音机。❸ a group of persons who play music together 乐队：The ～ struck up a tune. 乐队开始奏乐。❹ a group of persons joined together with a common purpose 团伙；帮：a ～ of robbers 一伙强盗 Ⅱ *v.* ❶ tie with a band 用绳子捆(扎、绑)：He ～ed his shoes with a rope. 他用绳子把鞋系牢。❷ unite in a group 结合；联合：They ～ed themselves together. 他们自己联合起来了。

bandage/ˈbændɪdʒ/

　　Ⅰ *n.* a band of woven material to put round a wound or injury 绷带：Wrap the ～ round the injured leg. 用绷带包扎好受伤的腿。 Ⅱ *v.* bind a wound or injury with a band of woven material (用绷带)包扎：The nurse ～d up the wound of the patient. 护士把那位病人的伤口包扎起来了。

bandit/ˈbændɪt/

　　n. an armed robber, especially who attacks travellers 盗匪；土匪：a gang of ～s 一帮土匪

bandmaster/ˈbændˌmɑːstə(r)/

　　n. a man who conducts a military band, brass band, etc. (军乐、铜管乐队等的)乐队指挥

bandsman/ˈbændzmən/

　　n. a musician who plays in a military band, brass band, etc. (军乐队、铜管乐队等的)乐队队员

bandstand/ˈbændstænd/

　　n. a raised place, open at the sides but with a roof, for a band playing music in the open air (有顶盖的)室外音乐演奏台

bandy¹ /ˈbændi/

　　adj. (of the legs) curving outwards at the knees 膝向外弯曲的：～-legged 罗圈腿的

bandy² /ˈbændi/

　　v. exchange words when arguing with sb. 对吵：～ insults 互相漫骂

bane/beɪn/

　　n. ❶ poison 毒药：rat's ～ 灭鼠药 ❷ a cause of continual trouble 祸根；灾星；祸害：That car is the ～ of my life! 那辆车是我的祸根。‖ ～ful *adj.* 有害的；邪恶的

bang/bæŋ/

　　Ⅰ *n.* a sharp blow；a sudden loud, sharp noise 猛然撞击；突然的巨响：The firework went off with a ～. 焰火砰的一声冲出来了。 Ⅱ *v.* ❶ hit sharply, especially by accident；bump 猛击：She ～ed the keys of the piano. 她有力地弹着钢琴键。❷ make a sharp loud noise or noises 砰然作声：He ～ed the door shut behind. 他随手把门砰的一声关上了。

bangle/ˈbæŋgl/

　　n. a large ring of metal or other substance worn round the wrist or arm as an ornament 手镯

banish/ˈbænɪʃ/

　　v. ❶ send sb. away from a country as a punishment 放逐；流放 ❷ dismiss sth. from your mind 清除；废除：You must ～ all thoughts of failure. 你必须清除所有关于失败的想法。‖ ～ment *n.* 放逐；流放；充军

banister/ˈbænɪstə(r)/

　　n. (usually *pl.*) the rail and supports for the rail at the side of a staircase (楼梯的)栏杆

banjo/ˈbændʒəʊ/

　　n. (*pl.* ～s or ～es) a type of stringed musical instrument 班卓琴(一种弦乐器)

bank¹ /bæŋk/

　　n. the land along each side of a river or canal；the ground near a river 堤岸：the ～ of the river 河堤/the left ～ of the Seine 塞纳河左岸

bank² /bæŋk/

　　Ⅰ *n.* a place in which money is kept and paid out on demand, and where related activities go on 银行：withdraw money from the ～ 从银行提款 Ⅱ *v.* put or keep money in a bank 把钱存入银行：He ～s half his salary every month. 他每月把工资的一半存入银行。/ Where do you ～ with? 你在哪家银行存钱？‖ **～er** *n.* 银行家/**～note** *n.* 钞票

bankable / ˈbæŋkəb(ə)l /
adj. likely to make money for sb. 可赚钱的；可赢利的：The movie's success has made her six of the world's most ～ stars. 这部影片的成功使她成了世界上最有身价的明星之一。

banking / ˈbæŋkɪŋ /
n. the business of a bank or a banker 银行业：a career in ～ 银行业生涯/the international ～ system 国际银行业体制

bankroll / ˈbæŋkrəʊl /
Ⅰ *n.* a supply of money 资金；财源 Ⅱ *v.* supply money for or pay the cost of (a business, plan, etc.) 为……提供资金；资助

bankrupt / ˈbæŋkrʌpt /
Ⅰ *n.* a person unable to pay his debts 破产者：He declared himself a ～. 他宣告自己是个破产者。Ⅱ *adj.* unable to pay one's debts 破产的，无力还债的：The firm is ～. 该店已破产了。Ⅲ *v.* make sb. bankrupt 使某人破产：The fire ～ed him. 这场火灾使他破产了。

bankruptcy / ˈbæŋkrʌptsi /
n. the state of being bankrupt 破产；倒闭：There were ten bankruptcies in the town last year. 该市去年有十起破产事件。

banner / ˈbænə(r) /
n. ❶ a flag 旗帜；旗：the ～ of freedom 自由的旗帜 ❷ a long piece of cloth on which a sign is painted, usually carried between two poles 横幅

banquet / ˈbæŋkwɪt /
n. an elaborate meal, usually for a special event, at which speeches are made 宴会；盛宴：A ～ was given in honour of the distinguished scholar. 宴会是为这位著名的学者举行的。

banter / ˈbæntə(r) /
Ⅰ *n.* the friendly joking remarks（友好的）戏谑，打趣：The actress exchanged ～ with reporters. 女演员与记者互相开玩笑。Ⅱ *v.* speak or act playfully or jokingly 开玩笑；逗乐

bantering / ˈbæntərɪŋ /
adj.（of a way of talking）amusing and friendly（讲话方式）风趣的，诙谐的：There was a friendly, ～ tone in his voice. 他的声音流露出友好诙谐的语调。

baptism / ˈbæptɪzəm /
n. a ceremony or practice of most churches, in which drops of water are put on the head of a person, or in some cases, the person is put into the water as a sign that the person has become a member of the church 洗礼仪式；浸礼

baptize / bæpˈtaɪz /
v. ❶ perform the ceremony of baptism on 给……施行洗礼 ❷ admit as a member of the stated church by baptism 为……施行洗礼并吸纳入该教会：He was ～d a Roman Catholic. 他受洗礼成为罗马天主教徒。❸ give (sb.) a name at baptism 洗礼时给（某人）命名：She was ～d Sheila Jane. 她受洗礼时被命名为希拉·简。

bar / bɑː(r) /
Ⅰ *n.* ❶ a long piece of sth.; a hard, thick stick 条；杆；棒：an iron ～ 铁棒 ❷ a place where people can buy and have a particular kind of food or drink 酒吧；（饮食）服务部：a coffee ～ 咖啡馆/a cold-drink ～ 冷饮部/a snack ～ 快餐铺 Ⅱ *v.* (-rr-) ❶ fasten (a door, gate, etc.) with a bar or bars 上闩：He ～red all the doors of his house. 他把家里的门全上了闩。❷ obstruct 阻塞；阻碍：A high wall ～s the way into his garden. 一堵高墙挡住了他到花园的路。

barb / bɑːb /
n. a sharp point projecting away from the main point of a fishhook, arrow, etc.（鱼钩、箭等的）倒钩

barbarian / bɑːˈbeərɪən /
Ⅰ *n.* an uncultured or brutish person 野蛮人；未开化的人 Ⅱ *adj.* uncultured; brutish 野蛮的；未开化的：～ tribes 原始部落

barbaric / bɑːˈbærɪk /

adj.in the manner of barbarian;very cruel 野蛮的;未开化的;非常残忍的:～ punishment 残酷的处罚

barbarism/'bɑ:bərɪzəm/
 n.the state of being uncivilized 未开化状态;野蛮:living in ～ 过着未开化的生活

barbarity/bɑ:'bærəti/
 n.savage cruelty 残暴;野蛮性;暴行:hideous barbarities 穷凶极恶的残暴行为

barbarize/'bɑ:bəraɪz/
 v.make cruel and rough in manners 使变残暴;使变野蛮

barbarous/'bɑ:bərəs/
 adj.uncivilized;cruel and savage 未开化的;残忍的;野蛮的;粗野的:～ conduct 野蛮行为/～ treatment 残酷待遇

barbecue/'bɑ:bɪkju:/
 Ⅰ *n*.❶ a party or feast(usually in the open air)at which the food(usually meat)is cooked over an open fire 户外烧烤 ❷a metal frame for cooking meat,etc. over a fire 金属烤架 ❸food cooked in such a way 烤制食品 Ⅱ *v*.roast meat,etc. in this way 在烤架上烤肉:～d mutton cubes 烤羊肉串

barbed/bɑ:bd/
 adj.❶ with one or more bards or short sharp points 装有倒钩(倒刺)的;带刺的: a ～ hook 有倒刺的钩 ❷(of sth. spoken or written)sharp and unkind,especially in judging person,their ideas,etc.(言论)尖酸刻薄的:a ～ remark 尖刻伤人的话

barbell /'bɑ:bəl/
 n. a long metal bar to which discs of varying weights are attached at each end, used for weightlifting 杠铃

barber/'bɑ:bə(r)/
 n.a person(usually a man)who cuts men's hair and shaves as an occupation (以男性为服务对象的)理发师:Now young people go to the hairdresser's while old people go to the ～'s.现在年轻人喜欢上美容店,而老人则去理发店。

barbershop/'bɑ:bəʃɒp/
 n.a shop where a barber works 理发店

barbican/'bɑ:bɪkən/
 n.a tower for defence at a gate or bridge 碉堡;桥头堡

bard/bɑ:d/
 n.a poet 诗人:Shakespeare is sometimes called the Bard(of Avon).莎士比亚有时被称作(埃文河畔的)诗人。

bare/beə(r)/
 Ⅰ *adj*.❶ without clothing,covering,protection or decoration 赤裸的;空空的;没有保护的:fight with ～ hands 赤手空拳地搏斗 ❷basic;not more than 刚够的;仅能的:He earns a ～ living by writing. 他靠写作仅能维持生活。‖ **believe one's ～ word** 轻信某人/**lay ～** 揭发;暴露 Ⅱ *v*. uncover;reveal 揭开;暴露:～ one's head 脱帽/～ one's sword 抽出宝剑/～ one's heart 推心置腹/～ one's teeth 龇牙咧嘴

barefaced/beə'feɪst/
 adj.shameless 无耻的:tell a ～ lie 撒一个无耻的谎言

barefoot/'beəfʊt/
 adj.& *adv*.without shoes or other covering on the feet 光脚的(地);赤脚的(地): walk ～ 光着脚走路

barely/'beəli/
 adv.❶in a bare way 赤裸裸地;空泛地: ～ furnished room 几乎没有家具的房间 ❷almost not;only just;scarcely 仅仅;几乎没有;勉强:～ enough 勉强够/be ～ of age 刚成年/She had ～ time to catch the bus.她几乎来不及赶上公共汽车。

bargain/'bɑ:gɪn/
 Ⅰ *n*.❶an agreement made between two people or groups to do sth. in return for sth. else 协议;交易:He made a ～ with the buyer in a short time.他很快就与买主达成了协议。❷sth. for sale or bought for less than a ～ is really worth 便宜货:It's quite a ～ for only ＄100.100 美元就买下了,这真是个便宜货。‖ **drive a hard ～**(over)(为……)拼命讨价还价/**into the ～** 此外;另外/**make(strike)a ～(with)** (与……)成交/**it's(that's)a ～**(我)同意了 Ⅱ *v*.talk about the conditions of a sale,agreement,or contract;negotiate 讨价还价;洽谈条件;谈判:She likes ～ing in the free market.她喜欢在自由市场讨价还价。‖ **to ～ away** 廉价出售/**to ～**

B

for 预期;料到

bargaining /ˈbɑːgɪnɪŋ/

n. the discussion of prices, conditions, etc. with the aim of reaching an agreement that is acceptable 讨价还价;商谈;商讨: wage ～ 有关工资的谈判

barge /bɑːdʒ/

Ⅰ *n.* a large low boat with a flat bottom, used mainly for carrying heavy goods on a canal or river 驳船;平底船 Ⅱ *v.* bump heavily 碰撞;冲撞:～ into the table 撞桌子

baritone /ˈbærɪtəʊn/

n. ❶ a male singing voice between tenor and bass 男中音 ❷ a singer with such a voice 男中音歌唱家

barium /ˈbeərɪəm/

n. a silver-white, metallic chemical element 钡:～ meal 钡餐

bark¹ /bɑːk/

Ⅰ *n.* ❶ the cry made by dogs or foxes (狗或狐的) 吠声,叫声 ❷ a sound made by people laughing or coughing (人笑或咳嗽时发出的) 吠叫似的声音 Ⅱ *v.* ❶ give a bark or barks 吠叫: The dog ～s at strangers. 狗对陌生人吠叫。 ❷ say (sth.) in a sharp loud voice 咆哮;厉声说出: The officer ～ed out his orders. 军官以严厉而有威严的声音发出命令。

bark² /bɑːk/

Ⅰ *n.* the strong outer covering of a tree 树皮;木皮 Ⅱ *v.* ❶ take the bark off 剥去……的皮:～ a tree 剥树皮 ❷ scrape the skin off 蹭;擦破:～ one's leg 蹭破(擦破)了腿上的皮

barley /ˈbɑːli/

n. a grasslike grain plant grown as a food crop for people and cattle, and also used in the making of beer and spirits 大麦:～ corn 大麦粒

barmaid /ˈbɑːmeɪd/

n. a woman who serves drinks in a bar 酒吧女服务员;女招待

barman /ˈbɑːmən/

n. a man who serves drinks in a bar 酒吧男服务员;男招待

barmy /ˈbɑːmi/

adj. foolish or a little mad 愚蠢的;傻呵呵的: You must be ～ to go out playing football in a weather like this. 这样的天气还出去踢足球,你一定是疯了。

barn /bɑːn/

n. a farm building for storing crops and food for animals 谷仓;仓库

barnstorm /ˈbɑːnstɔːm/

v. travel from place to place making short stops to give theatre performances or make political speeches 巡回演出;巡回演说

barnyard /ˈbɑːnjɑːd/

n. an area of open ground around a barn 谷仓场院

barometer /bəˈrɒmɪtə(r)/

n. an instrument for measuring the pressure of the atmosphere 气压计(表):The ～ rises. 气压上升(表示天气要放晴)。

baron /ˈbærən/

n. ❶ a noble man with the lowest rank in the House of Lords 男爵 ❷ a very important and powerful business man 工业巨子;大王:an oil ～ 石油大王/beer ～s 啤酒大王

baroness /ˈbærənɪs, ˌbærəˈnes/

n. ❶ a woman who is the wife of a baron 男爵夫人 ❷ a woman who has the same rank as a baron 女男爵

baronial /bəˈrəʊnɪəl/

adj. ❶ of or related to a baron 男爵的;与男爵有关的 ❷ large, rich, and noble 富丽堂皇的;高贵的;豪华的:a ～ hall 富丽堂皇的大厅

baroque /bəˈrɒk/

adj. used to describe a style of art, architecture, etc. found in Europe from about 1600 to 1750 that has a great deal of ornaments and many curved shapes 巴洛克式的(1600 至 1750 年间欧洲的艺术、建筑等的风格,以装饰华丽、多曲面为特征)

barracks /ˈbærəks/

n. (*pl.*) buildings where soldiers live 兵营

barrage /ˈbærɑːʒ/

n. ❶ the heavy and continuous firing of big guns in battle 弹幕射击;火力网 ❷ a large dam on a river（often a dam connected with other development projects）堰，拦河坝

barrel/ˈbærəl/

　n. ❶ a round wooden container with curved sides and a flat top and bottom 木桶；琵琶桶：They bought a ～ of beer.他们买了一桶啤酒。❷the metal tube of a gun,revolver or pistol 枪管：a rifle ～ 一支来复枪管 ❸the part of a fountain pen that holds the ink 钢笔的吸墨水管：The ～ of the pen is broken.这钢笔的吸墨水管坏了。

barren/ˈbærən/

　*adj.*❶(of land) not good enough to produce crops（土地）贫瘠的，不毛的：～ land 不毛之地 ❷(of women or female animals) not able to produce children or young（妇女或雌性动物）不孕的；不育的：a ～ woman 不能生育的妇女 ❷(of a tree or plant) not producing fruit or seed（树或植物）不结果实的

barricade/ˌbærɪˈkeɪd/

　Ⅰ *n.*a barrier,especially one that is put up hastily across a door or street 路障；街垒 Ⅱ *v.*to block a door or street with such a barrier 设置路障；阻塞

barrier/ˈbærɪə(r)/

　n. sth. that is used to keep people or things apart or to prevent or control their movement 障碍(物)；栅栏；关卡：set up a ～ 设置障碍

barring/ˈbɑːrɪŋ/

　*prep.*except for 除……之外，除非：Barring any last-minute problems we should finish the job by tonight.除非最后一分钟出问题，否则我们今晚应能完成任务。

barrow/ˈbærəʊ/

　*n.*a small vehicle with one or two wheels used for carrying goods, usually pushed by hand（单轮或双轮）手推车

barter/ˈbɑːtə(r)/

　Ⅰ *v.*exchange goods or services for other goods or services rather than for money 易货贸易；物物交换；以货易货：～ rice for textiles 用大米换取纺织品 Ⅱ *n.*the action or system of bartering 易货贸易

（系统）：Payment can be made through ～.可以用易货方式来付款。

basalt/ˈbæsɔːlt/

　*n.*dark,tough,volcanic rock 玄武岩

base/beɪs/

　Ⅰ *n.*❶the lowest part of anything, especially the part on which sth. rests or is supported；the foundation 基部，基础，底部：The lamp stands on a circular ～.这盏灯装在一个圆形底座上。❷a substance into which other things are formed（混合物的）基本成分 ❸a starting place；headquarters 基地，总部：a naval ～ 海军基地 ❹line or surface on which a figure stands 底线，底面 Ⅱ *v.*build or place sth. as the foundation or starting point for sth. 以……为基础(或出发点)：On what did you ～ your calculation? 你的预测以什么为根据? Ⅲ *adj.*(of person,their behaviour, thoughts, etc.)low；dishonourable（人、行为、思想等）卑鄙的，卑贱的：His motives were ～.他的动机是卑鄙的。

baseball/ˈbeɪsbɔːl/

　*n.*❶a game played with a bat and ball between 2 teams of which the centre is 4 bases 棒球运动：play ～ 打棒球 ❷the ball used in this game 棒球

baseless/ˈbeɪslɪs/

　*adj.*without a good reason 无根据的；无缘无故的：～ fears 无根据的恐惧

baseline/ˈbeɪslaɪn/

　*n.*❶ a line or level used as a base, e. g. when measuring or making comparisons 基线；准线 ❷ the back line at each end of a court in games like tennis 底线(如网球场两端的球场界限)

basement/ˈbeɪsmənt/

　*n.*a room or rooms in a house which are below street level 地下室

bash/bæʃ/

　*v.*hit sb.very hard 重击；猛撞：He fell and ～ed his knee.他跌倒把膝盖磕了。

bashful/ˈbæʃfl/

　adj.(usually of children or young people) showing great discomfort and self-consciousness in the presence of other people；not knowing what to do or say in the

B

presence of other people（通常指小孩或年轻人）害羞的,忸怩的,拘谨的

bashing /ˈbæʃɪŋ/

n. ❶ violent physical assault 痛打 ❷ severe criticism 抨击;非难:press ～ 报界抨击

basic /ˈbeɪsɪk/

adj. of or at the base of foundation; fundamental 基本的;根本的:a ～ principle 基本原则

basically /ˈbeɪsɪkli/

adv. fundamentally 基本地;根本上:He is ～ a nice person. 他基本上是一个好人。

basics /ˈbeɪsɪks/

n. (*pl.*) the basic parts or principles of a subject, process, etc. 基础;基本原则(原理):The ～ of education are reading, writing, and simple arithmetic. 教育的基本训练包括读、写和简单运算。/We need to get back to (the) ～. 我们需要回到基本原则上来。

basil /ˈbæzəl/

n. a type of sweet-smelling plant (herb) used in cooking 紫苏;罗勒(一种带香味可用于烹调的植物)

basin /ˈbeɪsn/

n. ❶ a round, open dish of metal, pottery, etc. for holding liquids 盆:wash vegetables in a ～ 在盆里洗菜 ❷ an area of land from which water runs down into a river 盆地;流域:the Amazon Basin 亚马孙河流域/the Tarim Basin 塔里木盆地

basis /ˈbeɪsɪs/

n. (*pl.* bases /ˈbeɪsiːz/) ❶ the underlying support or foundation for an idea, argument, etc. 基础;根据:What is the ～ of your decision? 你这个决定的根据是什么? ❷ the most important part of a mixture (混合物的)主要成分:The ～ of the drink is orange juice. 这种饮料的主要成分是橘子汁。‖ **on the ～ of** 在……的基础上;on the ～ of morality 在道德的基础上

bask /bɑːsk/

v. lie and take pleasure in warmth and light 躺着晒太阳;取暖:He was ～ing in the sun. 他躺在太阳底下晒太阳

basket /ˈbɑːskɪt/

n. a light container made of narrow pieces of wood, plastic, etc. woven together, and used for carrying or holding things 篮子;篓子;筐子:a willow ～ 柳条做的篮子

basketball /ˈbɑːskɪtbɔːl/

n. ❶ a game played by two teams of five players each who try to throw a large inflated ball into basket fixed 10 feet. above the ground 篮球运动:They like ～. 他们喜欢篮球运动。❷ the ball used in this game 篮球:I have two ～s. 我有两个篮球。

bass¹ /beɪs/

Ⅰ *n.* ❶ the lowest male singing voice, or a singer with such a voice 男低音;男低音歌手 ❷ the lowest-pitched member of a group of similar musical instruments 低音(乐器) ❸ a bass guitar or double bass 低音吉他;低音提琴 Ⅱ *adj.* of the lowest pitch in music 低音的;低声调的

bass² /beɪs/

n. (*pl.* bass) an edible fish of the perch family 鲈鱼

bassinet /ˌbæsɪˈnet/

n. a baby's bed or carriage that looks like a basket, often with a covering at one end (婴儿)摇篮;(有篷盖的)婴儿车

bassist /ˈbeɪsɪst/

n. a person who plays the bass guitar or the double bass 低音吉他手;低音提琴手

bassoon /bəˈsuːn/

n. a musical instrument of the wood wind group, shaped like a large wooden tube 巴松管,低音管

bastard /ˈbɑːstəd/

n. a person whose mother and father were not married 私生子

bat¹ /bæt/

Ⅰ *n.* any of several types of specially shaped wooden stick used for hitting the ball in various games (棒球、板球等的)球棒;(网球、乒乓球等的)球拍 Ⅱ *v.* (-tt-) hit a ball with a bat 用球棒(或球拍)击球

bat² /bæt/

n. a small mouse-like animal that flies at

night and feeds on fruit and insects 蝙蝠：as blind as a ～ 瞎得跟蝙蝠一样；有眼无珠

batch/bætʃ/

　n. an amount or a number of things or people dealt with together 一批；一组：He received a ～ of telegrams. 他收到一批电报。/a ～ of loaves in the oven 在烤的一炉面包/a ～ of people 一批人

bated/'beɪtɪd/

　adj.（with ～ breath）hardly breathing at all（because of fear, interest, wonder, anxiety, etc.）（因恐惧、兴趣、惊奇、焦虑等时）屏息的：He waited for the news with ～ breath.他屏息、焦急地等待着消息。

bath/bɑːθ/

　Ⅰ *n.* an act of washing the body 洗澡：She takes a hot ～ every day.她每天都洗热水澡。Ⅱ *v.* give a bath to（sb.）；wash in a bath 洗澡；给……洗澡：She had to ～ the baby every day.她得每天给婴儿洗个澡。‖ ～house *n.*（公共）澡堂/～tub *n.* 澡盆；浴缸

bathe/beɪð/

　Ⅰ *v.* ❶ soak or wipe gently with liquid to clean or soothe, usually for medical reasons 浸洗；轻轻拭洗：Bathe your feet twice a day. 每天把脚放在水里浸洗两次。❷ go into the sea, a river, a lake, etc. for sport, swimming, to get cool（在海、河、湖等中）游泳消遣：I like to ～ in the sea.我喜欢在海里游泳。Ⅱ *n.* the act of swimming or spending time in the water 游泳；水浴 ‖ ～r *n.* 洗澡的人；游泳者

bathing/'beɪðɪŋ/

　n. the activity of going into the sea, a river, etc. to swim（到海、河等中）游泳；畅游：facilities for ～ and boating 游泳和划船设施 ‖ ～-suit *n.*（男子）游泳裤/sun-～ *n.* 日光浴

bathrobe/'bɑːθrəʊb/

　n. a garment like a loose coat worn before and after having a bath, etc. 浴袍；浴衣

bathroom/'bɑːθruːm/

　n. ❶ a room containing a bath and usually a toilet（通常有抽水马桶的）浴室 ❷ a

toilet 卫生间；厕所：Is there a ～ in this restaurant? 这家餐馆里有卫生间吗?

baths/bɑːðz/

　n. a public building with an indoor swimming pool or bathrooms（室内）公共游泳池、公共澡堂：the public ～ 公共浴室

batik/bə'tiːk, 'bætɪk/

　n. ❶ a method of printing coloured patterns on cloth by putting wax on the part that is not to be coloured 蜡染法 ❷ a piece of cloth treated in this way 蜡染布

baton/'bætn, 'bætɒn/

　n. ❶ a short thin stick used by a conductor to show the beat of the music（乐队指挥用的）指挥棒 ❷ a short thick stick used as a weapon by a policeman; a truncheon 警棍 ‖ dance to one's ～ 跟着某人的指挥棒转

battalion/bə'tæliən/

　n. an army unit made up of several companies 营；大队

batter/'bætə(r)/

　v. beat sth. hard and repeatedly 连续猛击：Someone was ～ing at the door.有人正在用力敲门。

battered/'bætəd/

　adj. ❶ injured by repeated blows or punishment（由于被连续击打或惩罚而）受伤的 ❷（of a thing）damaged by age and repeated use（物品由于长期重复使用）磨损的：a ～ old car 一辆破旧的老爷车

battering/'bætərɪŋ/

　n. a violent attack that injures or damages sb. or sth. 殴打；猛击：wife ～ 对妻子的暴力行为

battery/'bætəri/

　n. ❶ a device for producing an electric current 电池 ❷ a number of large guns used for war 炮组；炮列

battle/'bætl/

　Ⅰ *n.* a fight between enemies or opposing groups; a struggle 战斗；战役；斗争：Soon another ～ was fought, and the war continued.不久又进行了一次战斗，所以这场战争又延续下去了。‖ accept ～ 应战/give（offer）～ 挑战/give the ～ 认输/have（win, gain）the ～ 战胜/half the ～

B

成功的一半 Ⅱ v.struggle or fight 战斗；斗争：They ～d all night with the winds and the waves.他们与大风大浪搏斗了整整一晚上。/～ against poverty 与贫穷斗争 ‖ ～**front** n.前线/～**ground** n.战场

battlefield /ˈbæt(ə)lfiːld/
n.❶a piece of ground on which a battle is or was fought 战场 ❷a place or situation of strife or conflict 斗争领域：an ideological ～ 意识形态斗争领域

battleship/ˈbætlˌʃɪp/
n. the largest kind of warship with the biggest guns and heaviest armour 主力舰；战列舰

batty/ˈbæti/
adj.slightly mad；crazy or eccentric 有点疯的；疯疯癫癫的；古怪的

baud/bɔːd/
n. a unit used to express the speed at which information is sent to or from a computer, e. g. through a telephone line corresponding to one bit of information per second 波特（发报、数据传输速率单位）

bawdy/ˈbɔːdi/
adj.about sex in a rude funny way 淫猥的；猥亵的：～ jokes 淫猥的笑话

bawl/bɔːl/
v.shout or cry very loudly, usually in an impolite or unpleasant way)（通常指不礼貌或不高兴地）大叫，大喊：It is very bad manners to ～ at people in the street.在街上大声叫人是很不礼貌的。

bay/beɪ/
n.a part of the land curved inwards at the edge of the sea or a lake 湾；海湾 ‖ at ～ 处于走投无路的绝境：A beast at ～ will put up a desperate fight.困兽犹斗。

bayonet/ˈbeɪənɪt/
n.a long knife fixed to the end of a soldier's gun 刺刀：Bayonets were shining over the helmets of the soldiers. 刺刀在战士们的钢盔上面闪闪发光。

baz(a)ar/bəˈzɑː(r)/
n.(in Middle Eastern countries) a market place or group of shops (中东国家的)集市；市场

be/biː/
(am, is, are；was, were；been；being) Ⅰ v.❶used when you are naming people or things or describing them(提供名称或描述时用)就是；是：The sun is bright.阳光灿烂。/They are all ten years old. 他们都是十岁。❷become 成为：He wants to ～ a scientist.他想成为科学家。❸exist；occur；live 存在；有；生存：There was man on the earth long, long ago.很久很久以前地球上就有人类存在了。❹ happen；take place 发生；举行：When is the meeting to ～? 会议什么时候举行？Ⅱ aux. v.❶(used with a past participle to form the passive voice)(与过去分词构成被动语态)被：He was criticized by the teacher.他被老师批评了。❷(used with a present participle to form the progressive or continuous tense)(与现在分词构成进行时态)正：What are you doing? 你在干什么？❸(used with to-infinitive, to indicate duty, obligation, intention, arrangement or possibility, etc.)(和动词不定式连用表示责任、义务、意图、安排、可能性等)应当；可能：What am I to do? 我该怎么办？

beach/biːtʃ/
n.a shore of ocean, sea, or lake or the bank of a river covered by sand, smooth stones, or larger pieces of rock 海滩；湖滩；河堤：We often go to the ～ in summer.夏天我们常去海滩。‖ on the ～ 失业的；穷困潦倒的；在海滩上

beachhead/ˈbiːtʃhed/
n.an area on the shore of an enemy's land that has been taken by force and on which an army may land 滩头阵地；滩头堡

beachwear/ˈbiːtʃweə(r)/
n.clothing for wearing on the beach 海滩服装

beacon/ˈbiːkən/
n. a tall object or light on or near the shore, to act as a guide or warning to sailors 烽火；灯塔：an air ～ 航空信号/a ～ light 信标灯

bead/biːd/

B

n. ❶a small ball of wood, glass and other material with a hole through it for threading with others on a string or wire（空心）小珠子：The young lady wears a string of ～s.那位年轻妇女佩戴了一串珠子。❷a drop of liquid 液珠：His face was covered with ～s of sweat.他满脸都是汗珠。❸(*pl.*)a necklace made of such beads 珠子项链

beaded /ˈbiːdɪd/
　adj. ❶decorated with beads 饰以珠子的 ❷covered with beads of moisture 带着小滴液体的：His forehead was ～ with sweat.他额头上挂着汗珠。

beading /ˈbiːdɪŋ/
　n. a long narrow patterned piece of wood used for decorating walls, furniture, etc.（墙壁、家具等的）串珠状悬饰

beady /ˈbiːdi/
　adj.（especially of an eye）small, round, and shining, like a bead（尤指眼睛）小珠子般的，圆而亮的

beagle /ˈbiːgl/
　n. a smooth-haired dog with short legs and large ears, sometimes used in the hunting of hares 毕格尔犬（短腿大耳软毛的猎兔犬）

beak /biːk/
　n. the hard horny mouth of a bird 鸟嘴

beaker /ˈbiːkə(r)/
　n. ❶a large drinking vessel 大酒杯 ❷an open glass vessel with a lip, often used in laboratories for chemical experiments, etc.（用于实验室的）烧杯

beam /biːm/
　I *n.* ❶a long, heavy piece of square timber, ready for use in building 梁：a cross ～ 大梁 ❷a ray of light 光线：We enjoy seeing the glorious ～s of the rising sun. 我们喜欢观看旭日东升时的灿烂光辉。Ⅱ *v.* ❶send out light and warmth 发光；发热：The sun ～s brightly. 太阳光芒四射。❷smile happily or cheerfully 欣喜地微笑：Her face ～ed with delight. 她满面春风。❸ send out 发射；放；播送：The Voice of America programs are ～ed around the world.《美国之音》的节目向全

世界播送。

bean /biːn/
　n. a seed of any of various upright climbing plants, especially one that can be used as food 豆类：～ curd 豆腐 ‖ full of ～s 精神饱满 ‖ ～pod *n.* 豆荚/～stalk *n.* 豆茎

bear /beə(r)/
　v.（bore, borne or born）❶carry from one place to another; carry away; convey 运送；运走；携带；传运：～ a badge 佩戴徽章 ❷produce a crop of fruit 生产；结果：This tree ～s no fruit. 这棵树不结果。❸ tolerate; endure 忍受；忍耐；容忍；经受：I can't ～ the pain. 我无法忍受这种痛苦。❹support 承受；支撑：The ice is too thin to ～ your weight. 冰太薄，撑不住你的重量。❺give birth to 生育：She has borne him two sons. 她给他生了两个儿子。/ He was born in 1944. 他生于 1944 年。❻have; show 有；显示：This contract ～s your signature. 这份合同有你的签名。❼ take responsibility for 承担责任 ‖ ～ down 压倒；战胜/～ in mind 记住/～ on 关系到；影响/～ out 证实/～ witness 作证

bearable /ˈbeərəbl/
　adj. that can be borne or endured 忍得住的；受得了的：The climate is ～. 这气候是可以忍受的。

beard /bɪəd/
　n. hair on the face below the mouth, often including the jaws, and neck（下巴等上的）胡须；络腮胡子：grow a ～ 留胡子 ‖ ～ed *adj.* 留胡须的

bearer /ˈbeərə(r)/
　n. ❶a person or thing who bears or carries sth. 搬运工；挑夫；负荷者；运载工具：a litter ～ 担架兵 ❷a person who brings a letter or message 信差；送信人：the ～ of good news 传送好消息的人 ❸a fruit-producing tree or plant 结果实的植物：a good ～ 高产植物/a bad ～ 低产植物

bearing /ˈbeərɪŋ/
　n. ❶the way people behaves themselves; the way of standing or moving 行为；举止；（站、走等的）姿势：a man of noble ～ 举止高贵的人 ❷relation; aspect 关系；方

面：We must consider the question in all its ～s.我们必须从各方面考虑这问题。/It has some ～s on this subject,它和本题有些关系。❸the ability to suffer sth.忍受；忍耐：beyond all ～ 忍无可忍 ❹a direction in which a place lies 方向；方位：lose one's ～ 迷失方向 ❺the part of a machine in which moving parts turn 轴承：ball ～s 球轴承

bearish/'beərɪʃ/
*adj.*❶ rude；rough；bad-tempered 没礼貌的；粗鲁的；暴躁的 ❷ showing, expecting or tending to cause a fall in the prices of shares（证券交易）行情看跌的，熊市的

beast/biːst/
*n.*❶ a four-footed animal；a large bovine farm animal 四足兽；牲畜：The lion is the king of ～s.狮为百兽之王。❷a cruel or disgusting person 凶残的人：The workers hated that ～ of a boss.工人们恨透了那个可恶的老板。‖ ～ly *adj.*野兽（般）的；残忍的；令人厌恶的

beat/biːt/
Ⅰ *v.*(beat, beaten)❶ hit repeatedly 敲打：Waves ～ the shore.波浪冲击着岸边。❷ defeat or do better than sb.in a game or competition 击败；胜过：No one can ～ me at tennis.打网球谁也赢不了我。❸ make a regular sound or movement 规律作响；有规律地运动：My heart is ～ing fast.我的心跳得厉害。‖ ～ a retreat 败退/～ back 打退/～ down 击败/～ hollow 打得落花流水/～ one's brains 苦苦思索/～ time 打拍子/～ up 痛打；搅打（鸡蛋等）Ⅱ *n.*❶ a regular, rhythmic sound or movement 有节奏的声音；拍动，振动：the ～ of the pulse 脉搏跳动/～s of a drum 击鼓声 ❷ a main accent or rhythmic unit in music 节拍：follow the ～ in singing 按节拍唱歌

beaten/'biːtn/
*adj.*❶ (of metal) shaped by beating with a hammer（金属）锻打的，锤制而成的，被锤薄的：The doors of the palace were of ～ gold.宫殿的门包有金箔。❷ (of a path, track, etc.) given shape by the feet of those who pass along it（路、轨迹等）

被踏成的，走出来的：We followed a well-～ path through the forest.我们沿着一条人们踏出来的路穿过森林。‖ off the ～ track 不出名的；人迹罕至的；偏远的：Let's go somewhere off the ～ track this summer.今年夏天我们去人家不大去的地方吧。

beater/'biːtə(r)/
*n.*❶ sb. or sth. which hits or beats sb. or sth.else 打击者；拍打器；搅拌器：an egg ～ 打蛋器 /a carpet ～（清理）地毯的掸子/a wife ～ 打妻子的人 ❷ a person who drives wild animals or birds towards the guns of those waiting to shoot them（把野生动物或鸟赶向猎人枪口的）猎人助手

beating/'biːtɪŋ/
*n.*❶ an act of giving repeated blows, usually for punishment 打击；痛打（尤指为了惩罚）：He was given a severe ～.他被狠狠地打了一顿。❷ a defeat, especially in a game or competition（尤指在比赛中）失败，败北：The home side got quite a ～.主队遭到惨败。

beatitude/bɪ'ætɪtjuːd/
*n.*a state of great happiness or blessedness 至福，极乐

beautician/bjuː'tɪʃn/
*n.*a person whose job is to give beauty treatments (as to skin and hair) 美容师

beautify/'bjuːtɪfaɪ/
*v.*make sb. or sth. beautiful 使美丽，美化 ‖ **beautification** *n.*美化；装饰

beautiful/'bjuːtɪfl/
*adj.*giving pleasure or delight to the mind or senses 美的；美丽的；美观的；令人生美感的：a ～ face 美丽的面庞/～ weather 悦人的天气

beauty/'bjuːti/
*n.*❶the qualities that give pleasure to the senses or lift up the mind or spirit 美；美丽：Everyone must admire the ～ of a mother's love. 人人都必须赞叹母爱之美。/Beauty is only skin-deep.美貌是肤浅的。❷a beautiful woman；sth. beautiful 美女；美的东西：sleeping ～ 睡美人/Oh, what a ～! 啊，好漂亮！/These apples

B

are beauties.这些苹果真是太好了。

beaver/ˈbiːvə(r)/

   *n.*a type of small animal which lives both in water and on land and is known for its ability to dam up streams by using mud, twigs,etc.河狸

because/bɪˈkɒz/

   *conj.*for the reason that 因为:I do it ～ I like it.我喜欢,所以我就做。‖ ～ **of** 由于;因为/**not** ～ … **but** ～ 不是因为……,而是因为……

beckon/ˈbekən/

   *v.*make a sign with the hand 用手示意:He ～ed (to) us to follow him.他招手要我们跟着他。/He ～ed us nearer.他用手示意我们靠近些。

become/bɪˈkʌm/

   v.(became,become) ❶come or grow to be;begin to be 成为;变成:The custom has now ～ a rule.那习俗现在已成为规则。/He became a doctor.他成为医生。/He has ～ a famous man.他已成为名人。 ❷happen to 降临;遭遇:I don't know what has ～ of him.我不知道他的遭遇如何。/What will ～ of the children if their father dies? 如果他们的父亲死了,这些孩子的遭遇将怎样呢? ❸ be suitable for;look well on 适合;适宜;相称:That hat ～s you.那顶帽子很适合你。

becoming/bɪˈkʌmɪŋ/

   adj. ❶ (of colour, clothes, etc.) looking very good on the wearer (颜色、衣服等)合适的,相配的,好看的:Blue always looks very ～ on her.她穿蓝色的衣服总是很好看的。 ❷ proper or suitable;appropriate 适当的;适宜的:His laughter was not very ～ on such a solemn occasion.在如此严肃的场合,他的笑声不很得体。

bed/bed/

   *n.*❶ a piece of furniture to sleep on 床;床铺:a single (double) ～单(双)人床 ❷ the bottom of the sea, river, lake, etc. 海底;河床;湖底:The river ～ is dry.河床干涸了。‖ **go to** ～ 就寝/**make one's** ～ 铺床‖～**clothes** *n.*床上用品/～**time** *n.*就寝时间

bedding/ˈbedɪŋ/

   n. materials on which a person or an animal can sleep 寝具:protective ～ 防毒被垫

bedewed/bɪˈdjuːd/

   *adj.*made wet as with drops of water 被沾湿的;被滴湿的:cheeks ～ with tears 泪水沾湿了的双颊

bedfellow/ˈbedˌfeləʊ/

   *n.*❶ a person who shares a bed with another 同床者;共睡者 ❷ a companion or partner 同事;伙伴:Misfortune makes strange ～s.厄运使人萍水相逢。

bedlam/ˈbedləm/

   *n.*❶a wild noisy place or activity 乱哄哄的地方;喧闹:When the teacher was called away the classroom was a regular ～.当教师被叫走的时候,教室便喧闹不堪。 ❷a hospital for mad people 疯人院;精神病院

bedrock /ˈbedˈrɒk/

   *n.*❶the solid rock beneath loose soil 基岩 ❷the fundamental facts or principles on which an idea or belief is based 基本事实;基本原理:Honesty is the ～ of a good relationship.诚实是良好关系的基础。

bedroom/ˈbedrʊm/

   *n.*a room for sleeping in 卧室;寝室

bee/biː/

   n. a small, four-winged, stinging insect that produces wax and honey after gathering nectar from flowers 蜜蜂:a queen ～ 蜂王/working ～ 工蜂/keep ～s 养蜂

beef/biːf/

   I *n.* (*pl.* beeves/biːvz/) ❶the meat of farm cattle 牛肉 ❷a complaint 抱怨 II *v.* complain about sth.抱怨,发牢骚

beefsteak/ˈbiːfsteɪk/

   *n.*a thick piece of the best part of beef, usually without bones 牛排

beep /biːp/

   I *n.*a short high-pitched sound made by an electronic equipment or a car horn (电子装置或汽车喇叭发出的)嘟声 II *v.*produce such a sound 发出嘟声

beer/bɪə(r)/

*n.*❶ a type of bitter alcoholic drink made from grain 啤酒；draught ～ 生啤酒/dark ～ 黑啤酒 ❷ a glass or bottle of beer 一杯啤酒；一瓶啤酒；Two ～s, please. 请来两杯啤酒。

beeswax/'biːzwæks/

*n.*the wax made by bees, used for making furniture polish, candles, etc. 蜂蜡（用于制造家具擦光油、蜡烛等）

beet/biːt/

*n.*a plant with sweet root that is used as a vegetable 甜菜；red ～ 红甜菜

beetle/'biːtl/

*n.*an insect with hard, shiny wing covers 甲虫

beetroot/'biːtruːt/

*n.*the red root of beet, eaten in salads 甜菜根

befall/bɪ'fɔːl/

v.(befell, befallen)(usually of sth. bad) happen to（常指不好的事情）发生；降临；落到：What has ～en him? 他遭遇了什么事？/A misfortune has ～en. 发生了一件不幸的事。

befit/bɪ'fɪt/

v.(-tt-) be proper or suitable to 适合；适宜：He always travels first class, as ～s a person in his position. 他总是乘头等舱旅行，这样做适合他的身份。/a sober suit ～ting the occasion 一套适合那种场合的庄重朴素的服装

before/bɪ'fɔː(r)/

Ⅰ *adv.*❶ at an earlier time; in the past 以前；从前：Have you been here ～? 你以前来过这里吗？/ He had come here the day ～. 他是前一天来这里的。❷ in advance 在前面：He went ～ to see if the door was open. 他走在前头看门是否开着。Ⅱ *prep.*❶ in front of 在……的前面：He is standing ～ me. 他站在我前面。❷ earlier than 以前；早于……：the day ～ yesterday 前天/～ long 不久 Ⅲ *conj.*❶ previous to the time when 在……之前：Just ～ I left Shanghai I sent him a letter. 我离开上海前给他发了封信。/ Look ～ you leap.〈谚〉三思而后行。❷

rather than 宁愿……也不：I will die ～ I surrender. 我宁死不降。

beforehand/bɪ'fɔːhænd/

*adv.*ahead of time; in advance 预先；事先：You ought to have told me ～. 你本应该事先告诉我。/He had been ready to do so for several months ～. 几个月前他就已经准备好这样做。

befriend/bɪ'frend/

*v.*act as a friend to; be kind and helpful to 以朋友态度对待；亲近；帮助；照顾：She ～ed me in many ways. 她在很多方面都给予我帮助。

beg/beg/

v.(-gg-)❶ ask sb. for food, money, etc. 乞求；乞讨：He ～ged his bread from door to door. 挨家挨户乞讨。❷ ask sb. for sth. earnestly, or with deep feeling 请求；恳求：He ～ged his parents to forgive him. 他请求他的父母原谅他。‖ ～ for 请求得到/～（**your**）**pardon** 请再说一遍；请原谅/～ **the question** 回避正题/**go** ～**ging** 行乞

beget/bɪ'get/

*v.*❶（begat, begotten）become the father of 成为……之父；（父亲）生（子）：Abraham begat Isaac. 亚伯拉罕是以撒的父亲。❷（begot）produce; be the cause of 产生；引起；招致：Hunger ～s crime. 饥饿招致犯罪。

beggar/'begə(r)/

Ⅰ *n.*a person who lives by begging 乞丐；叫花子：He tossed a copper to the ～. 他丢了一个铜币给那乞丐。Ⅱ *v.*make sb. or sth. very poor 使贫穷；使匮乏：You'll ～ your family if you spend so much money on drink. 如果你花这么多钱喝酒的话，你会把你的家喝穷的。

beggarly/'begəli/

*adj.*much too little in amount; very poor 极少的；贫乏的：earn a ～ salary 挣得微薄的薪水

beggary/'begəri/

*n.*the state of being very poor 赤贫：They were reduced to ～ by the failure of their farm. 由于农场歉收，他们落到一贫如洗的境地。

begin/bɪ'gɪn/

v. ❶ start sth. or doing sth. 开始；启动：We began the project in May. 我们于 5 月份启动了这项工程。❷ start to happen or exist 起始；开始存在（或进行）：When does the meeting ～? 会议什么时候开始? ❸ to be sth. first, before becoming sth. else 起初是；本来是：He began as an actor before starting his business. 他先是当演员，后来做生意。❹ have sth. as the first part or the point where sth. starts（从……）开始；（以……）为起点：Each chapter ～s with a story. 每一章的开头都有一个故事。❺ start speaking 开始讲话 ❻ start or make sth. start for the first time 创始；创办：The school began in 1960. 这所学校创建于 1960 年。‖ **to ～ with** ❶ 起初；开始 ❷ 首先；第一点

beginner /bɪˈɡɪnə(r)/
n. a person still learning and without much experience 初学者：His book for the ～s in English is a best seller. 他那本供初学英语者用的书销路很好。

beginning /bɪˈɡɪnɪŋ/
n. the point at which sth. begins; the start; the origin 起点；开始；起源：at the ～ of the month（在）月初/She knows the subject from ～ to end. 她从头到尾了解这个题目。

begone /bɪˈɡɒn/
v. go away at once 立即走开：Begone with you! 你快快离去吧!

begrudge /bɪˈɡrʌdʒ/
v. ❶ give, do or pay sth. unwillingly, especially because it is unwanted or undeserved 勉强做；不乐意地付出；舍不得给：She ～d every minute taken from her work. 占用她工作的每一分钟，她心里都不痛快。/I ～ spending so much money on train fares. 我舍不得把这么多钱花在火车票上。❷ feel envy at 羡慕；嫉妒：We shouldn't ～ him his success. 我们不该嫉妒他的成功。

beguile /bɪˈɡaɪl/
v. ❶ charm or attract 迷住；诱惑：a beguiling smile 迷人的微笑 ❷ cause time to pass agreeably in a pleasant way 消磨（时间）；消遣：We ～d（away）the time by telling jokes. 我们讲笑话消闲作乐。❸

deceive; cheat 欺骗；哄骗：I was ～d by his flattery into trusting him. 我为他的恭维话所骗而信任了他。

behalf /bɪˈhɑːf/
n.（on/in ～ of, on/in sb.'s ～）for the interest of, on account of 为……；代表：I wrote him several letters on your ～. 我代表你向他写了几封信了。/He worked hard all his life in ～ of the poor people. 他整个一生都是在为穷苦大众的利益而努力工作。

behave /bɪˈheɪv/
v. ❶ act or conduct oneself 行为；举止；表现：～ well 行为好/Behave yourself! 规矩点! / The new fighters ～d gallantly under fire. 新战士在炮火下表现得很勇敢。❷（of machines, etc.）work or function（指机器等）工作；运转；开动：How is your new motor-car behaving? 你的新汽车开起来如何?

behavio(u)r /bɪˈheɪvjə(r)/
n. the way of behaving; the treatment shown towards others 行为；举止；态度：Tom won a prize for good ～ at school. 汤姆在学校里得到品行优良奖。/His ～ towards me shows that he does not like me. 他对我的态度显示他不喜欢我。

behead /bɪˈhed/
v. kill sb. by cutting sb.'s head off 砍头；斩首

behind /bɪˈhaɪnd/
prep. & adv. ❶ at the back of 在（……）后面：There's a swimming-pool ～. 后面有个游泳池。/She glanced ～ her. 她朝身后看了一眼。❷ slower in time, work, etc. 落后于；慢于：Don't fall ～. 不要落后。‖ **bars** 在监狱中；在牢房里/～ **one's back** 背着人；在背后/～ **the scenes** 在幕后/～ **the times** 过时；跟不上时代/～ **time** 晚点/**fall（lag）** ～ 落后/**leave** ～ 忘掉；留下 ‖ **～hand** *adj.* 延迟的；误期的；落后的

behold /bɪˈhəʊld/
v.（beheld）take notice or see sb. or sth. 看；目睹：～ the great city of Babylon 注视着伟大的巴比伦城

B

beholden/bɪˈhəʊldn/
adj. under an obligation（to）；owing thanks（to）对……感激的：We are much ~ to you for your help.我们对于你的帮助深为感激。

beige/beɪʒ/
adj. pale dull yellowish brown 米黄色的；淡棕色的

being/ˈbiːɪŋ/
n. ❶ existence 生存；存在：What is the aim of our ~？我们生存的目的是什么？❷a human creature 人：Men and women are human ~s.男人和女人都是人。‖ **come into** ~ 出现；产生；形成

belabour/bɪˈleɪbə/
v. ❶attack sb.with blows or words 攻击，袭击；抨击，责骂 ❷discuss a subject in too much detail 对……争论（或说明）过多；纠缠于：There is no need to ~ the point.没有必要对这一点多费口舌。

belated/bɪˈleɪtɪd/
adj. coming very late or too late 来迟的；误期的：a ~ apology 迟来的道歉 ‖ ~ly *adv.* 延迟地；延续地

belch/beltʃ/
Ⅰ *v.* ❶send out wind from the stomach noisily through the mouth 打嗝 ❷send out a large amount of smoke or flames 冒出，喷出（烟，火）：The front of the car was ~ing smoke.汽车的前面在冒烟。Ⅱ *n.* an act or sound of belching 打嗝；冒烟，冒火

belfry/ˈbelfri/
n. a tower or part of a tower in which bells hang 钟楼；钟塔

belie/bɪˈlaɪ/
v. give a false idea of sth.；fail to show the real thing 给人以……的错觉；掩饰：His happy face ~d his feeling of misery.他那快乐的脸掩饰了痛苦的感情。

belief/bɪˈliːf/
n. ❶ sth. accepted as true or real；sth. taught as part of a religion 信仰；信条：religious ~s 宗教信仰 ❷the feeling that sth.is real and true；trust；confidence 信任；相信；信心：the best of my ~ 在我看来/I haven't much ~ in his honesty.我对

他的诚实没有太大的信心。/He had no great ~ in his doctor.他不太信任他的医生。

believable/bɪˈliːvəbl/
adj. able to be believed 可信的；可信任的

believe/bɪˈliːv/
v. ❶ feel sure of the truth of sth.；be of the opinion（that）相信：Do you ~ his story？你相信他的话吗？❷think or suppose 认为：I ~ he is fit for this job.我认为他能胜任这项工作。❸ have trust in 信任；相信；信赖：Many people in the West ~ in Christianity.西方很多人信奉基督教。

believer/bɪˈliːvə(r)/
n. ❶ a person who has faith, especially religious faith 有（宗教）信仰者；信徒 ❷ a person who believes in sth. or sb.相信……的人：I'm a great ~ in fresh air as a cure for illness.我深信新鲜空气能治病。

belittle/bɪˈlɪtl/
v. cause to seem unimportant or of small value 轻视；贬低：We ~d the danger.我们不把危险看在眼里。/ Do not ~ what he has achieved.别小看他取得的成绩。

bell/bel/
n. ❶a round, hollow metal vessel which makes a ringing sound when struck 钟；铃：door ~ 门铃/electric ~ 电铃/ring the ~ 打钟/The church ~s are ringing.教堂的钟在响着。❷the sound of a bell 钟声；铃声：I heard the ~s from the village church.我听到村中教堂的钟声。/ There goes the ~.铃响了。❸sth. with the form of a typical bell 钟状物：~ flower 吊钟花

belle/bel/
n. a popular and attractive girl or woman 美女；美人；佳丽：the ~ of the ball 舞会之花，舞会上最美的女子

bellicose/ˈbelɪkəʊs/
adj. warlike；ready to quarrel or fight 好战的；好争吵的；好斗的

belligerent/bəˈlɪdʒərənt/
adj. fond of fighting or arguing 好战的；好斗的；好争吵的

bellow/ˈbeləʊ/
Ⅰ *v.* ❶ make a loud, deep noise（like a

bull）；shout；roar（牛等）吼叫；大叫；咆哮：He ～ed before the dentist had started.牙医还未动手他就大叫起来。❷utter loudly or angrily 大叫；怒吼：They ～ed out a drinking song.他们大声吼叫着唱饮酒歌。‖ *n.* the cry of a cow or bull；the cry of pain or anger 牛的吼叫声；咆哮；怒号；嚎叫

bellows/'beləʊz/
n.（*pl.*）an instrument for blowing air（e.g.used to make a fire burn more brightly）风箱（如用于鼓风助燃）

belly/'beli/
Ⅰ *n.* the part of the body containing the stomach and bowels 肚子；腹部 Ⅱ *v.*（usually of of sails）swell out when the wind blows（通常指船帆）张满：The ship's sails bellied out in the wind.船帆在风中张得鼓鼓的。

belong/bɪ'lɒŋ/
*v.*❶ be the property of 属于：This house ～s to him.这幢房子是属于他的。❷be a number of 是……的成员：What party do you ～ to? 你属于哪一个党派? ❸ fit a certain environment 适应（某种环境）：Does this chair ～ here? 这把椅子应该放在这里吗?

belongings /bɪ'lɒŋɪŋz/
*n.*a person's possessions 个人所有物；财物

beloved
Ⅰ /bɪ'lʌvd/*adj.*dearly loved 受爱戴的：～ of all who knew her 被所有认识她的人们所钟爱/He is ～ by all.他受大家的爱戴。Ⅱ /bɪ'lʌvɪd/*n.*a dearly loved person；darling 深受爱戴的人；亲爱的人：He wrote a sonnet to his ～.他写了一首十四行诗献给他亲爱的人。

below/bɪ'ləʊ/
Ⅰ *prep.*lower than 低于；在……以下：～ sea level 低于海平面 Ⅱ *adv.*at or to a lower level 在下面；向下：Don't throw the rubbish into the river ～.不要把垃圾扔到下面的河里。

belt/belt/
Ⅰ *n.*❶a band or strip of cloth or leather worn round the waist or over one shoulder 肩带；皮带；腰带：He wears a ～ round his waist. 他腰上系着一根皮带。❷an endless leather strap used to connect wheels and so drive machinery or carry things along 传动带；传送带：a fan ～ 风扇皮带 ❸ an area with particular characteristics 地带；区域：A great city ought to have a green ～ round it.一个大城市周围应有一片绿化地带。Ⅱ *v.*fasten with a belt；hit with a belt 用皮带系；用皮带抽打：The officer ～ed his sword on. 那军官将剑系在皮带上。

belted/'beltɪd/
*adj.*provided with a belt 有带子的：a ～ raincoat 有腰带的雨衣

bemoan/bɪ'məʊn/
v. express sorrow or disappointment because of 因……而表示忧伤（或失望）；悲叹；感叹：He ～ed his bitter fate.他自叹命苦。/She ～ed the lack of money for her new project.她为没有钱进行她的新项目而叹息。

bemused/bɪ'mjuːzd/
*adj.*unable to think or understand properly；confused 茫然的；发呆的；困惑的：a ～ expression 困惑的表情 /～ by（with）all the questions 被一大堆问题弄得茫无头绪

ben/ben/
*n.*a mountain or hill 山：Ben Nevis 尼维斯山

bench/bentʃ/
*n.*❶ a long seat of wood or stone 长凳；条凳：There are a lot of ～es by the lake.湖边有很多长凳。❷ a long worktable（木工、鞋匠等用的）工作台

bend/bend/
Ⅰ *v.*（bent）❶ cause to be out of a straight line or surface；force into a curve or angle（使）弯曲：The river ～s to the east.这条河折向东流。❷ become curved；make one's body curve forward down 弯腰；屈身：He bent down to pick up a coin.他弯腰拾起一枚硬币。‖ ～ **before**（**to**）向……屈服/～ **one's mind to** 专心于/ ～ **sb.to one's will** 使……屈从某人的意志/

B

be bent on 一心想（做某事）Ⅱ*n.* a curve or turn; a part that is not straight 弯道；转弯; 拐角:a ～ in the road 道路弯曲处

beneath/bɪˈniːθ/

adv. & *prep.* below or lower than; in a lower place 在……下面;低于;在下方: The ship sank ～ the waves. 船沉没在浪涛下面。/They saw the valley ～. 他们看见了底下的山谷。

benefaction /benɪˈfækʃən/

n. a donation or gift 捐赠;赠物

benefactor/ˈbenɪfæktə(r)/

n. a person who does good or who gives money for a good purpose 行善者;捐助人

beneficent/bɪˈnefɪsənt/

adj. doing good; kind or generous 行善的;仁慈的;宽厚的

beneficial/ˌbenɪˈfɪʃl/

adj. having good effect; favourable; helpful 有用的;有益的;有帮助的: Fresh air and good food are ～ to the health. 新鲜的空气和高质量的食品对健康有利。

beneficiary/benɪˈfɪʃəri/

n. a person who receives sth. (often money or property) 受惠者,受益人(常指接受金钱或财产者)

benefit/ˈbenɪfɪt/

Ⅰ*n.* an advantage or profit gained from sth.; good done or received 好处;益处;利益:I will get no personal ～ from it.我从中不会得到什么个人的好处。‖ **for the ～ of** 为了(……的利益)Ⅱ*v.* do good to; bring advantage to 有益于;有利于: Sports ～ our health. 体育运动有益于我们的健康。/He ～ed greatly from the deal.他从这笔交易中获益匪浅。

benevolent/bɪˈnevələnt/

adj. kind, liking to help other people 仁慈的;乐善好施的 ‖ **benevolence** *n.* 仁慈;善行

benign/bɪˈnaɪn/

adj. ❶(of certain diseases, etc.) not very harmful (疾病等)无大害的:a ～ tumour 良性肿瘤 ❷kind and gentle 和善的;温和的

bent/bent/

Ⅰ*adj.* ❶ made curved or crooked; not straight 弯的:a ～ pipe 一根弯管 ❷strongly inclined or determined 决心的;专心的:She is ～ on doing it.她决心要这件事。❸dishonest;corrupt 不正的;贪污受贿的:～ officials 贪官污吏 Ⅱ*n.* inclination or aptitude 倾向;爱好:She has a ～ for music.她爱好音乐。

benzene/ˈbenziːn/

n. a colourless liquid (C_6H_6) obtained chiefly from coal, that burns quickly and changes easily into a gas. It is used to make certain typed of engine run, and for cleaning 苯

bequeath/bɪˈkwiːð/

v. leave sth. to sb., especially after one dies 把……留给(尤指人死后):He ～ed a thousand pounds to his niece.他遗赠1000英镑给他的侄女。

bequest/bɪˈkwest/

n. sth. which is bequeathed 遗产;遗赠物

bereave/bəˈriːv/

v. (be ～d) be deprived of a relative or close friend by death 丧失(亲友):He was ～d of his wife and children.他丧失了妻儿。‖ ～**ment** *n.* (因死亡)丧失

bereaved /bɪˈriːvd/

adj. having recently suffered the death of a close relative 丧失亲友的:recently ～ families 刚刚痛失亲人的家庭

bereft /bɪˈreft/

adj. deprived of sth. 被剥夺的;失却的: They were ～ of hope.他们丧失了希望。

beret/ˈbereɪ/

n. a small round hat with no brim 贝雷帽,圆扁便帽

berry/ˈberi/

n. (often in compounds)a small fruit that grows on a bush (常构成复合词)浆果;莓

berserk/bəˈsɜːk/

adj. so angry that one seems to be mad 狂怒的 ‖ **go ～** 狂怒:The prisoner went ～ and wrecked the prison. 这囚犯狂怒起来,乱毁乱砸监狱。

berth/bɜːθ/

Ⅰ*n.* ❶a place on a ship or train where one

sleeps（轮船或飞机上的）卧铺 ❷a place where a ship anchors in a harbour, etc.停泊地；锚位 Ⅱ v. take a ship into a berth 使（船）停泊

beseech/bɪˈsiːtʃ/

v.（besought or beseeched）ask sb. for sth. in an anxious way 恳求；哀求

beset/bɪˈset/

v.（beset）surround and harass on all sides 包围；围困：The expedition was ∼ with dangers.这支探险队陷入重重危险。

beside/bɪˈsaɪd/

prep.at the side of；close to 在……旁边：He stands ∼ me.他站在我旁边。‖ ∼ oneself（with）（因……）若狂（发狂）/ be ∼ the point 离题；不中肯

besides/bɪˈsaɪdz/

Ⅰprep.apart from；in addition to 除……之外：Besides English, I have to learn another foreign language.除英语外，我还得学一门外语。 Ⅱadv.also；in addition 也；此外；而且：I don't like the colour of this suit and,∼, it is too expensive.我不喜欢这套衣服的颜色，而且它价钱也太贵。

besiege/bɪˈsiːdʒ/

v. ❶ surround an enemy town, city, etc. with soldiers in order to capture it 围困；围攻：Troy was ∼d by the Greeks for ten years.特洛伊城被希腊人围困达十年。 ❷surround and harass 围困；困扰：He was ∼d with requests. 他被一大堆要求弄得应接不暇。

besmear/bɪˈsmɪə(r)/

v. cover with dirty, sticky, or oily marks（以泥垢、油污）涂抹；弄脏：hands ∼ed with dirt 满是污垢的双手

besom/ˈbiːzəm/

n.a brush made of sticks tied together on a long handle 长柄扫帚

bespattered/bɪˈspætəd/

adj.marked all over with drops of li-quid；spattered 被泼溅的；溅污的：The windscreen of the car was so ∼ with dirt that it was difficult to see through it.汽车的挡风玻璃溅满了污泥，以至于很难看清外面的东西。

bespeak/bɪˈspiːk/

v.（bespoke, bespoken）show；be a sign of 显示；表示：The efficiency of the organization bespoke careful planning.这个组织的效率表明他们计划周密。

bespectacled/bɪˈspektəkld/

adj.wearing glasses 戴眼镜的

bespoke/bɪˈspəʊk/

adj.（of clothes）specially made to someone's measurements；made-to-measure（衣服）定做的

best/best/

Ⅰ adj.of the most excellent kind；very good 最优秀的；最好的：This is the ∼ film I have ever seen.这是我所看过的最好的影片。 Ⅱadv.❶ in the most excellent way 最好地：He works ∼ who is ∼ trained.受过最好训练的人工作得最好。 ❷ most；more than all others 最：I like skating ∼.我最喜欢滑冰。 Ⅲn. the most excellent or outstanding person or thing among several 最好的人（或物）：You 'd better wear your ∼ on formal occasion. 在正式场合，你最好穿上你最好的衣服。 ‖ be（the）∼ man 当傧相/the ∼ part of 大部分/as ∼ one can 尽量（好）地/ had ∼ 最好/at ∼ 至多/at one's ∼ 在极盛时期；处在最佳状态/do one's ∼ 尽力/（hope）for the ∼ 往好里（想）/get the ∼ of 打赢；占优势/make the ∼ of 尽量利用/ to the ∼ of one's ability 尽全力/ to the ∼ of one's knowledge（recollection, etc.）就自己所知（回忆等）/try one's ∼ 尽量/ with the ∼ 和别人一样好 ‖ ∼-seller n. 畅销书

bestow/bɪˈstəʊ/

v.give sth. to sb. as an offering 给予；赠予；授予：∼ a title and prize on someone 授予某人称号和奖金 ‖ ∼al n.赠予；赠品

bet/bet/

Ⅰv.（bet or -tt-）❶risk money on a race or on some other event of which the result is doubtful 打赌；赌钱；（下）赌注：Don't ∼ too much on this boxer.不要在这位拳击手身上下这么大的赌注。 ❷ be certain 敢肯定：I ∼ it rains.我敢肯定要下雨。 Ⅱn. the money that sb. risks in this way 赌金；赌注：He lost his ∼.他赌输了。 ‖ make a ∼（on）（对……）打赌/

B

you ～ 你可确信,当然

beta/'biːtə/

　　*n.*the second letter (B,β) of the Greek alphabet, sometimes used as a mark for good average work of a student 希腊字母表的第二个字母(有时用以表示学生的乙等成绩)

betake/bɪ'teɪk/

　　v.(betook, betaken) cause oneself to go to 去;往;赴:He betook himself to the palace to see the king. 他前往王宫觐见国王。

bethink/bɪ'θɪŋk/

　　v.(bethought)(～ oneself) think about; consider 想到;考虑:You should ～ yourself of your duty! 你应当考虑到你的职责!

betide/bɪ'taɪd/

　　*v.*happen to 降临于 ‖ woe ～ sb. 某人将要遭殃;某人将受惩罚:Woe ～ any pupil who comes in late. 哪个学生迟到就要倒霉。

betimes/bɪ'taɪmz/

　　*adv.*early; in good time 早;及时,适时

betoken/bɪ'təʊkən/

　　*v.*be a sign of 预示;显示……的征兆:black clouds that ～ a storm 预示着暴风雨即将来临的乌云

betray/bɪ'treɪ/

　　*v.*❶ be disloyal to 背叛;出卖:He ～ed his people.他背叛了他的人民。❷ make a secret known 泄露秘密:He ～ed the secret to the enemy.他把这个秘密泄露给敌人了。❸ be or give a sign of; show 流露;表现:Her red face ～ed her nervousness.她涨红的脸表明她内心的紧张。‖ ～al *n.*背叛;出卖;泄露;暴露

better/'betə(r)/

　　Ⅰ *adj.*❶ of higher quality, moral value, usefulness, etc. 较好的;更好的;更有用的:Fewer but ～.少而精。❷ partly or fully recovered from illness or injury 康复的;好转的:I feel ～ now.现在感觉好一些了。Ⅱ *adv.*in a more excellent manner 更;更好地:She speaks English ～ than I.她的英语比我讲得好。Ⅲ *v.*improve; do better than 提高;改善:～ the

working conditions 改善劳动工作条件 Ⅳ *n.*sth.or sb. better 较好的事物;较好者 ‖ no ～ than 和……一样/had ～ 最好/～ off 较富裕;景况更佳/all the ～ for ～ or worse 无论好坏;好歹/so much the ～ 反而更好

betting /'betɪŋ/

　　n. the action of gambling money on the outcome of a race, game, or other unpredictable event 赌博

between/bɪ'twiːn/

　　*prep.& adv.*in or into the space or time that separates (两者)之间;在中间:I can see no difference ～ A and B.我看不出 A 与 B 有什么区别。/a meeting with a short break ～ 中间有短暂休息的会议 ‖ come(stand) ～ 妨碍……关系/divide (share) ～ 两人分担/fall ～ two stools 两头失误/(read) ～ the lines (看出)字里行间的意思/in ～ 在它们中间;间隔

bevel/'bevəl/

　　Ⅰ *n.*the slope of a surface at an angle other than a right angle, usually along the edge of wood or glass 斜角;斜面 Ⅱ *v.* (-ll- or -l-)make a sloping edge on sth.切成斜角;斜削:～ed edges 切成斜角边

beverage/'bevərɪdʒ/

　　*n.*any sort of drink (e.g. milk, tea, beer) 饮料(如牛奶、茶、啤酒)

bevy/'bevi/

　　*n.*❶a large group or collection 一群:a ～ of girls 一群女孩 ❷flock of birds, especially quail 一群鸟(尤指鹌鹑):a ～ of larks 一群云雀

bewail/bɪ'weɪl/

　　*v.*express deep sorrow for, especially by or as if by weeping 悲伤;痛哭

beware/bɪ'weə(r)/

　　*v.*be on guard; take care 当心;谨防:Beware of pickpockets.提防扒手。/Beware of the dog.当心那条狗。

bewilder/bɪ'wɪldə(r)/

　　*v.*cause sb. to feel puzzled or confused 使迷惑;把……弄糊涂:He was so ～ed that he didn't know what to do.他茫然不知所措。‖ ～ment *n.*困惑;惊慌

bewildering /bɪ'wɪldərɪŋ/

adj. making you feel confused because there are too many things to choose from or because sth. is difficult to understand 令人困惑的;使人糊涂的:a ～ array 令人眼花缭乱的摆设

bewitch/bɪˈwɪtʃ/
v.❶work magic on 施妖术;迷惑;蛊惑 ❷attract;charm 迷人;令人心醉:a ～ing smile 迷人的微笑

beyond/bɪˈjɒnd/
Ⅰ*prep*.❶ at,on,or to the further side of 在……那边:The sun sets ～ the distant hills.太阳在远处的群山那边落下。❷exceeding 超过;超出:This question is ～ my power. 这个问题超出了我的能力。 Ⅱ*adv*.further on;at or to a distance 在远处:look ～ 往远处看

bi-/baɪ/
pref.twice;every two;having two of sth.二;两(倍);双:bilateral 双边的

biannual /baɪˈænjuəl/
adj.appearing or happening twice a year 一年两度的 ‖ ～ly *adv*.每半年地

bias/ˈbaɪəs/
Ⅰ*n*.prejudice;inclination 偏见;倾向性:He is without ～.他不偏不倚。/She has a ～ towards this plan.她倾向于这个计划。 Ⅱ*v*.(-s- or -ss-) make sb.come to a decision without allowing him to hear the full facts 使有偏见:He was ～ed against the plan from the beginning. 他一开始就对这项计划抱有偏见。/ The newspapers ～ed their readers against the new government.报纸使读者对新政府存有偏见。/He was ～ed towards the plan.他偏袒该项计划。

biased /ˈbaɪəst/
adj.inclined to favour one side rather than another 有偏见的;倾向性的:a ～ witness 有成见的证人

bib/bɪb/
n.a piece of cloth or plastic which is tied round a child's neck while he is eating (小孩吃东西时围的)围脖

Bible/ˈbaɪbl/
n.(the ～)the sacred writings of the Jews and the Christian Church 圣经:read the

～ 读《圣经》

bibliographer/ˌbɪblɪˈɒɡrəfə(r)/
n.a person who makes a bibliography 书目编著人;文献目录编著人;书志学家

bibliography/ˌbɪblɪˈɒɡrəfi/
n.a list of books and other writings about a particular subject or by a particular writer (关于某一学科的)书目;(某一作家的)作品目录

bibliophile/ˈbɪblɪəfaɪl/
n.a person who loves and collects books 珍爱书籍者;藏书家

bicameral /baɪˈkæmərəl/
adj.(said about a parliament) having two legislative chambers (议会)两院制的

bicentenary/ˌbaɪsenˈtiːnəri/
n.the celebration of sth. which happened 200 years ago 两百周年纪念

biceps/ˈbaɪseps/
n. the large muscle in the upper part of the arm 二头肌:His ～ is impressive.他臂力过人。

bicker/ˈbɪkə(r)/
v.quarrel about little things (为小事)吵嘴,争吵

bicycle/ˈbaɪsɪkl/
Ⅰ *n*. a two-wheeled vehicle which one rides by pushing its pedals with the feet 自行车:ride a ～ 骑自行车 Ⅱ*v*.ride a bicycle;travel by bicycle 骑自行车(旅行)

bid/bɪd/
Ⅰ*v*.(bid; bidding) (at an auction sale) make an offer of money (拍卖时)喊价;出价(购物):She ～ $100 for this painting.她出价 100 美元买这幅画。 Ⅱ*n*.a price offered at an auction 出价;喊价:He made the highest ～ for this painting.这张画他出价最高。

bidding /ˈbɪdɪŋ/
n. the offering of particular prices for sth.,especially at an auction (尤指拍卖中的)叫价,出价

bide/baɪd/
v. remain or stay somewhere 停留;居住 ‖ ～ one's time 等待良机:I'm planning to change my job,but I'm just bid-ing my time until the right opportunity comes

B

up.我打算换工作,不过得等到有合适的机会。

biennial /baɪˈenɪəl/
adj. ❶ (of an event) happening once every two years (事件)两年一次的 ❷(of a plant)living for two years and producing seed in the second year (植物)两年生的

bifurcate /ˈbaɪfəkeɪt/
v. (of roads, branches, rivers, etc.) divide into two branches or parts; fork (道路、树枝、河流等)分为两支(枝,部分);分岔

big /bɪg/
adj. ❶ large in size, degree, amount,, etc.(体积、程度、数量等)大的,巨大的: It's the world's ～gest computer company.它是全球最大的计算机公司。 ❷ grown-up 成年的,长大的: You're a ～ girl now. 你现在已长大成大姑娘了。 ❸ important; serious 重大的;严重的:Mary has made a ～ mistake.玛丽犯了一个严重的错误。 ❹ needing a lot of effort, money or time to succeed 庞大的;宏大的:They're full of ～ ideas.他们心怀大志。 ❺ popular; successful 受欢迎的;成功的:Orange is the ～ color this year.橘色是今年的流行色。 ❻ enthusiastic about sb. or sth. 热衷于……的;狂热的: I'm a ～ fan of him. 我是他的狂热追随者。 ❼ kind or generous 大方的;慷慨的:Our boss is a ～ man.我们的老板是个大方的人。‖ the ～ picture 整个局面;大局 / have a ～ mouth 爱泄露秘密;自吹自擂

bighead /ˈbɪghed/
n. someone who has too high an opinion of their own importance 自高自大的人

bight /baɪt/
n. ❶ a curve in a coast larger than, or curving less than, a bay 海岸线弯曲的部分;大湾 ❷ a loop made in the middle of a rope (绳子中间的)绳环,绳套

bigwig /ˈbɪgwɪg/
n. an important person 要人;显赫人物: government ～s 政府要人

bike /baɪk/
n. a bicycle or motorcycle 自行车;摩托车

bikini /bɪˈkiːni/
n. a very small swimming costume for women, consisting of two pieces 比基尼式女泳装;三点式女泳衣

bilateral /ˌbaɪˈlætərəl/
adj. on both sides; made by two opposing groups; having two sides 在两边的;双方的;有两边的:The two countries signed a ～ agreement on trade.两国签署了一项双边贸易协定。

bile /baɪl/
n. ❶ a bitter liquid produced by the liver to help the digestion of food 胆汁 ❷ anger or abomination 愤怒;憎恨

bilingual /baɪˈlɪŋgwəl/
adj. ❶ speaking or knowing two languages 说(或懂)两种语言的:Some children educated in foreign countries become ～. 一些在国外受教育的儿童能使用两种语言。 ❷ written in two languages 用两种语言写的:a ～ text 两种文字对照的课文

bilious /ˈbɪlɪəs/
adj. ❶ caused by too much bile 胆汁过多引起的:a ～ attack 胆汁病 ❷ sickly 令人厌恶的:a ～ colour 令人厌恶的颜色

bilk /bɪlk/
v. cheat sb., especially causing them to lose money; swindle 蒙骗(某人)(尤指使其丧失钱财)

bill /bɪl/
n. ❶ a banknote 钞票;纸币:a ten-dollar ～ 一张十美元的钞票 ❷ a written statement of charges for goods or services 账单:You have to pay the ～.你得付账。 ❸ a proposed law to be discussed by a parliament 议案;法案:This ～ will be brought to a vote.这项议案将提交表决。

billhook /ˈbɪlhʊk/
n. a tool consisting of a blade with a hooked point and a handle, used especially in cutting off branches of trees and cutting up wood for fires (剪枝、砍木柴用的)钩镰,钩刀

billiards /ˈbɪlɪədz/
n. a game played on a big special table with ivory balls and long sticks 台球戏

billing /ˈbɪlɪŋ/

n. ❶ the position, especially an important one, that sb. is advertised or described as having in a show, etc. (演员表上的) 排名, 演员名次: top ～ 领衔主演 ❷ the act of preparing and sending bills to customers 开具账单 ❸ the total amount of business that a company does in a particular period of time 营业额: ～s around ＄1 million 100 万美元左右的营业额

billion/ˈbɪljən/

n. ❶ one thousand millions 十亿 ❷ one million million 〈英〉一万亿

billow/ˈbɪləʊ/

Ⅰ*n.* ❶ a large wave 巨浪: the ～s of the Pacific 太平洋的巨浪 ❷ a rolling mass like a large wave, typically cloud, smoke or steam 翻滚的云团; 浓烟; 气浪 Ⅱ*v.* ❶ swell out 鼓起 ❷ rise and move in a large mass like a large wave 大量涌出

bimonthly/ˌbaɪˈmʌnθli/

adv.&adj. ❶ appearing or happening every two months 两月一次地(的): a ～ magazine 双月刊 ❷ appearing or happening twice a month 一月两次地(的)

bin/bɪn/

n. a large container, usually with a lid 大箱(通常有盖) ‖ dustbin *n.* 〈英〉垃圾箱

binary/ˈbaɪnəri/

adj. made up of two parts or things; double 一对的; 一双的; 双重的

bind/baɪnd/

v. (bound) ❶ tie or fasten sth. with rope 捆; 绑: They bound the thief with a rope. 他们用绳子把小偷捆了起来。 ❷ bandage (a wound) 包扎(伤口): The doctor bound up his wound. 医生为他包扎了伤口。 ❸ cause to obey, especially by a law or a solemn promise; put under an obligation 使受约束; 束缚: Both sides are bound by the contract. 双方都受合同的约束。 ‖ ～ oneself to do sth. 保证做/ ～ hand and foot 全身捆绑; 受约束/ be bound to do 一定/ be duty-bound to do 有责任做/ be bound up with 紧紧联系在一起

binder/ˈbaɪndə(r)/

n. ❶ a machine or person that binds

books (书籍的) 装订机, 装订者: Your book is still at the ～'s. 你的书仍在装订商那里。 ❷ a removable cover, especially for holding sheets of paper, magazines, etc. 活页封面; 活页夹 ❸ a substance that makes things stick together 黏合物

binding/ˈbaɪndɪŋ/

Ⅰ*n.* ❶ a book cover 书籍的封面: The ～ of this book is torn. 这本书的封面撕破了。 ❷ material sewn or stuck along the edge of sth., such as a dress, for strength or decoration (衣服等的) 镶边, 边饰, 滚条 Ⅱ*adj.* imposing a legal obligation on sb. 有约束力的; 应履行的: a ～ agreement 具有约束力的协议 / The contract is ～ on everyone who signed it. 所有签约者均应遵守合约。

bingo/ˈbɪŋgəʊ/

n. a game in which players mark off numbers on cards as the numbers are drawn randomly by a caller, the winner being the first person to mark off all their numbers 宾戈游戏

binoculars/bɪˈnɒkjʊləz/

n. (*pl.*) glasses which enable one to see things a long way away 双筒望远镜

binomial/baɪˈnəʊmiəl/

adj. composed of two terms 二项的; 二项式的

biochemistry/ˌbaɪəʊˈkemɪstri/

n. the science of the chemistry of living things 生物化学

biodegradable/ˌbaɪəʊdɪˈgreɪdəbl/

adj. able to be broken down into harmless products by the natural action of living things 可生物降解的: ～ packaging 可生物降解处理的包装材料

biographer/baɪˈɒgrəfə(r)/

n. a writer of biography 传记作者: Dr. Johnson's famous ～ James Boswell 为约翰逊博士写传的著名传记作家詹姆斯·鲍斯韦尔

biography/baɪˈɒgrəfi/

n. ❶ a person's life history written by an author 传; 传记: a Marx ～ 一本马克思传记 ❷ a branch of literature dealing with the lives of persons 传记文学

biological /ˌbaɪə'lɒdʒɪkəl/
adj. ❶ to do with biology 生物学的：the ~ sciences 生物科学 ❷（said about a detergent）containing enzymes（洗涤剂）加酶的 ‖ ~ly *adv.* 生物学上地

biologist /baɪ'ɒlədʒɪst/
n. a scientist who studies biology 生物学家

biology /baɪ'ɒlədʒi/
n. the science of life and living things 生物学：In ~ we study plants and animals. 在生物学中，我们研究植物和动物。

biome /'baɪəum/
n. a natural community of plants and animals, its composition being largely controlled by climate conditions 生物群落

biophysics /ˌbaɪəu'fɪzɪks/
n. the science which uses the laws and methods of physics to study biology 生物物理学

biosphere /'baɪəsfɪə/
n. the part of the earth's surface and atmosphere in which plants and animals can live 生物圈

biotechnology /ˌbaɪəutek'nɒlədʒi/
n. the use of living micro-organisms and biological processes in industrial and commercial production 生物科技

biotic /baɪ'ɒtɪk/
adj. of or having to do with life or living things 生命的；生物的

birch /bɜːtʃ/
n. ❶ any of several kinds of tree, common in northern countries, with smooth wood and thin branches 桦树：the white（silver）~ 白桦 ❷ the wood of this kind of tree 桦木

bird /bɜːd/
n. a creature with wings and feathers 鸟；飞禽：useful ~s 益鸟/ a ~ of prey 猛禽 ‖ ~s of a feather 一丘之貉/kill two ~s with one stone 一举两得

birth /bɜːθ/
n. ❶ being born；coming into the world 出生；诞生：the date of one's ~ 某人出生日期/the ~ rate 出生率/one's ~ certificate 出生证 ❷ the beginning of sth. such as a new idea or situation 起源；创始 ❸ origin or descent 出身；血统 ‖ by ~ 出生；生来/give ~ to 生；产生

birthday /'bɜːθdeɪ/
n. the anniversary of the day of one's birth 生日；诞辰：my 21st ~ 我的21岁生日 /a ~ party 庆祝生日的聚会 /Happy ~ to you 祝你生日快乐! ‖ in one's ~ suit 一丝不挂的；赤条条的

birthing /'bɜːθɪŋ/
n. the action or process of giving birth 分娩；生产

birthmark /'bɜːθmɑːk/
n. a usually red or brown mark on the skin at birth 胎记；胎痣

birthplace /'bɜːθpleɪs/
n. the place where someone was born or where sth. happened at first 出生地；发源地：Stratford-upon-Avon was Shakespeare's ~. 埃文河畔的斯特拉福是莎士比亚的出生地。/Cooperstown, New York, is said to be the ~ of baseball. 据说纽约州的库珀斯敦是棒球的发源地。

birthrate /'bɜːθreɪt/
n. the number of births for every 100 or every 1000 people in a particular year in a particular place 出生率：a ~ of three percent 100 3‰的出生率 /a rapidly increasing ~ 迅速增长的出生率

birthright /'bɜːθraɪt/
n. that which belongs to someone because of the family or nation they come from 与生俱来的权利；由于出生、国籍等而获得的权利：Freedom is our ~. 自由是我们与生俱来的权利。

biscuit /'bɪskɪt/
n. ❶ a flat, thin, crisp cake of many kinds, sweetened or unsweetened 〈英〉饼干：Give me a ~. 给我一块饼干。 ❷ a small soft round cake 〈美〉小软饼 ❸ a light-brown colour 浅棕色：I bought a pair of ~ shoes yesterday. 昨天我买了一双浅棕色的鞋子。

bisect /baɪ'sekt/
v. divide sth. into two parts 把……分为二

bisexual /baɪ'sekʃuəl/
Ⅰ *adj.* ❶ possessing qualities of both

B

sexes 具有雌雄两性特征的；雌雄同体的；两性的：a ～ plant 雌雄同株的植物 ❷ sexually attracted to both men and women 双性恋的 Ⅱ n. a person who is sexually attracted to both men and women 双性恋者

bishop/ˈbɪʃəp/
n. a clergyman of high rank who organizes the work of the Church in a city or district (基督教的)主教

bishopric/ˈbɪʃəprɪk/
n. the position of a bishop or the area that a bishop is in charge of 主教之职位；主教管辖的教区

bistro/ˈbiːstrəʊ/
n. (pl. ～s) a small simple restaurant 小餐馆

bit/bɪt/
n. a small amount or piece of sth. 一点；少许：a ～ of food 一点食物/wait a ～ 稍等一下/I am a ～ tired. 我有点累了。‖ ～ by ～ 一点点地；逐渐地/do one's ～ 尽力/to ～s 成为碎片/～s and pieces 零碎东西

bite/baɪt/
Ⅰ v. (bit, bitten) ❶ (of a person or animal) cut into sth. with the teeth 咬，啃：The girl bit into an apple. 女孩咬了一口苹果。❷ (of an animal or a person) use the teeth in order to inflict injury (动物，人)咬伤：Does the dog there ～? 那边的那条狗咬人吗？ ❸ (of a snake, insect, or spider) wound with a sting, pincers, or fangs (蛇)咬；(昆虫，蜘蛛)叮，蜇 ❹ (of an acid) corrode a surface (酸)腐蚀 Ⅱ n. ❶an act of cutting into sth. with the teeth 咬，啃 ❷a piece cut off by biting 咬下的一块 ❸a wound inflicted by an animal's or a person's teeth of by an insect or snake 咬伤；(虫的)叮，蜇；(蛇的)咬

biting/ˈbaɪtɪŋ/
adj. ❶ (of wind) so cold as to be painful (风)刺骨的：a ～ wind 刺骨的风 ❷harsh or cruel 犀利的，辛辣的，尖刻的：～ words 尖刻的话

bitter/ˈbɪtə(r)/
Ⅰ adj. ❶having a sharp, pungent taste or smell；not sweet 苦的；苦涩的：Good pills taste ～.良药苦口。❷ very sharp, causing pain or grief 辛酸的；痛苦的；抱怨的；生气的：a ～ life 痛苦的生活 ❸ piercingly cold 严寒的；刺骨的：a ～ wind 刺骨的寒风 Ⅱ n. (pl.) a bitter usually alcoholic mixture of plant products for mixing into drinks (掺入饮料中的)苦味配剂 ‖ ～ly adv. 悲痛地；厉害地/～ness n. 苦味；辛酸；苦难

bitter-sweet/ˌbɪtəˈswiːt/
adj. ❶ pleasant, but mixed with sadness 苦乐参半的：～ memories of childhood 对童年时代甜蜜而又辛酸的回忆 ❷ (of tastes or smells) bitter and sweet at the same time (味道或气味)又苦又甜的

bitty/ˈbɪti/
adj. consisting of or containing little bits or unconnected parts 七零八碎的；东拼西凑的；不连贯的：I thought the film was rather ～. 我认为那部影片有点儿七拼八凑。

bizarre/bɪˈzɑː(r)/
adj. very strange, unnatural 奇异的；古怪的

blabber/ˈblæbə(r)/
v. talk foolishly or too much 瞎说；胡扯；喋喋不休：I wish she'd stop ～ing (on) about her boyfriends. 我真希望她别再没完没了地讲她那些男朋友的事。

blabbermouth/ˈblæbəmaʊθ/
n. a person who tells secrets by talking too much 饶舌(而泄密)者；嘴巴不牢的人；碎嘴子

black/blæk/
Ⅰ adj. ❶of the very darkest colour due to the absence of or complete absorption of light；the opposite of white 黑色的，乌黑的：Her hair was ～.她的头发是黑色的。❷without light；completely dark 黑暗的；漆黑的：a ～ night 漆黑的夜晚 ❸ (of coffee or tea) served without milk (咖啡，茶)不加牛奶的，清的 ❹ belonging to a race of people who have dark skin；connected with black people 黑色人种的；黑人的：～ culture 黑人文化 ❺ without hope；very depressing 无希望的；令人沮

丧的: The future looks ～.前景显得很暗淡。Ⅱ n. ❶the very darkest colour, like night or coal 黑色 ❷a member of a race of people who have dark skin 黑色人种的人；黑人‖～ and blue 遍体鳞伤/～ and white 白纸黑字/call white ～ 颠倒黑白

blackboard /'blækbɔːd/
n. a dark board for writing on with chalk 黑板

blacken /'blækən/
v. ❶make sth. black, or to become black 使变黑；熏黑；使变暗: his ～ed teeth 他那被熏黑的牙齿 ❷damage a person's reputation 诋毁；给(某人)抹黑: His enemies tried to ～ his name.他的敌手企图败坏他的名声。

blacklist /'blæklɪst/
Ⅰ n. a list of people who are disapproved of 黑名单 Ⅱ v. put sb. on a blacklist 把……列入黑名单

blackmail /'blækmeɪl/
Ⅰ n. ❶an attempt to obtain money from a person by a threat to reveal information that will disgrace him 敲诈；勒索 ❷money got by blackmail 敲诈来的钱财 Ⅱ v. force sb. to make a payment of money for not making known sth. discreditable about him 敲诈；向……勒索: Did they ～ you yesterday? 昨天他们敲诈了你吗?

blackout /'blækaʊt/
n. ❶a period of darkness when no light must be shown; the extinguishing of all lights 断电；停电 ❷a temporary loss of consciousness 短暂意识丧失；短暂失去知觉 ❸prevention of the release of information 新闻管制；消息封锁: a total news ～ 全面的新闻封锁

bladder /'blædə(r)/
n. ❶an organ that is shaped like a bag inside the body which contains urine 膀胱 ❷a rubber bag inside a football (足)球胆

blade /bleɪd/
n. ❶the flat cutting part of a knife, sword, or other cutting tool or weapon 刀刃；刀口；刀片 ❷a long flat leaf of grass or grasslike plants such as wheat (草等的)叶片

blah /blɑː/
n. empty talk; nonsense 空谈；废话；瞎说: talking all kinds of ～ to her 和她说了一大堆废话

blame /bleɪm/
Ⅰ v. find fault with; say or think that sth. bad or wrong is caused by 归咎于；责备；埋怨: Don't ～ it on him.这事不要怪他。‖be to ～ for sth. 应该为某事受到责罚/～ sth.on sb. 把……归咎于某人 Ⅱ n. saying that sb.is responsible for sth.; responsibility for doing sth. badly 责备；责怪；(过失的)责任: He took the ～ for this failure.他承担这次失败的责任。‖put (lay) the ～ on 责备；责怪……/take (bear) the ～承担责任

blameless /'bleɪmlɪs/
adj. deserving no blame, innocent 无过错的；无可指责的: lead a ～ life 活得清白

blanch /blɑːntʃ/
v. ❶ make pale or white 使变白；使苍白: Age has ～ed his hair.年纪使他白了头发。❷(of a person) become pale with fear, cold, etc. (因恐惧、寒冷等)脸色煞白: ～ from fear 吓得脸色发白

bland /blænd/
adj. ❶without anything to attract attention 平淡的；乏味的 ❷(of food) smooth and easily digested and usually without much taste (食物)无刺激性的,易消化的,淡而无味的

blank /blæŋk/
Ⅰ adj. ❶with nothing written, printed or drawn on it 空白的: ～ pages 空白页 ❷without feeling, interest or expression 毫无表情的；不感兴趣的；茫然的: There was a ～ look on his face.他脸上毫无表情。Ⅱ n. space left empty or to be filled 空白；空白处: Fill in the ～s with proper verbs.用适当的动词填入空白处。

blanket /'blæŋkɪt/
Ⅰ n. ❶a thick, woollen covering especially used on beds 毛毯；毯子: The bed was covered with a ～.床上盖着一条毯子。❷sth. which covers like a blanket 像毛毯似的东西: a ～ of snow 像毛毯似的雪 Ⅱ v. cover sth. with a thick layer 以厚层盖,

B

覆盖：Snow ～ed the earth. 白雪覆盖着大地。

blare/bleə(r)/

I v.(of a horn or other loud sound-producing instrument) produce sounds loudly and unpleasantly (喇叭或其他高音器具) 刺耳地大声鸣响：The radio is blaring out (the news). 收音机高声响着(广播新闻)。/blaring car horns 发出刺耳声音的汽车喇叭　II n. the blare of a brass band 铜管乐队刺耳的吹奏声

blarney/ˈblɑːni/

n. the kind of talk that flatters and deceives people 谄媚；奉承话：Not so much of your ～! 不要再奉承了！

blast/blɑːst/

I n.❶a strong, sudden rush of wind 一阵风；狂风：When the window was opened, an icy ～ came into the room. 窗户打开，一股冷风吹进了房间。❷a sound made by a wind-instrument 汽笛声；管乐声：We heard a loud ～ of a steamer's whistle. 我们已经听到轮船响亮的汽笛声。❸an explosion 爆炸：a terrible ～ 可怕的爆炸　II v. blow up with explosives 炸开；炸掉：They are trying to ～ the rock away. 他们正在设法把这块石头炸掉。

blatant/ˈbleɪtnt/

adj.❶not trying to hide one's bad behaviour；shameless 公然的；无耻的：The student showed ～ disrespect for the rules of the college. 那个学生公然藐视学院的规章。❷noisy and boldly behaved 吵嚷的；喧扰的

blaze¹/bleɪz/

I n. bright flames in a fire 火焰；火灾：The firemen put out the ～ quickly. 消防人员很快就扑灭了大火。　II v. burn with bright flame；shine brightly and warmly 熊熊燃烧；发光；照耀：The sun ～d in the blue sky. 火红的太阳在蓝色的天空中照耀着。‖ blazing adj.燃烧着的；酷热的；烤人的

blaze²/bleɪz/

v.make marks along a trail for others to follow 在树干上做记号(指示道路)：He ～d a path for other hunters to follow in the forest.他在树上做出记号，为其他猎人引路穿过森林。

blazer/ˈbleɪzə(r)/

n. a loose-fitting jacket sometimes with the special sign of a school, club, etc., on it (有时带有学校、俱乐部等特殊标记的)宽松运动外衣

blazon/ˈbleɪzn/

I n.a coat of arms 盾形纹章；盾徽　II v. ❶ declare sth. loudly and publicly (公开)宣告，宣布 ❷ inscribe or paint an object with arms 在物体上镂刻(或绘制)纹章

bleach/bliːtʃ/

I v.cause to become white or pale, especially by means of chemicals or by the action of sunlight 漂白；晒白：～ the tablecloth 将桌布漂白　II n.a chemical used in bleaching 漂白剂

bleak/bliːk/

adj.❶exposed to cold winds 寒风吹袭的：The countryside here is very ～ in winter.在冬天，这乡间寒风凛冽。❷with very little hope of happiness 没有指望的；惨淡的：Without money, the future looked ～ for John. 约翰没有钱，看来他的前途黯淡。❸unhappy and unfriendly 不高兴的；冷漠的：When we arrived, we got a rather ～ welcome.我们到达时受到的迎接相当冷淡。

bleary/ˈblɪri/

adj.unable to see clearly (usually because of tiredness) (通常由于疲倦)视力模糊的

bleat/bliːt/

I v.❶make a sound like a sheep or goat (像羊)咩咩地叫 ❷complain in a low voice 低声抱怨　II n. the sound made by these animals 羊的叫声；咩咩的叫声

bleed/bliːd/

v.(bled) ❶lose blood as a result of injury or illness 出血；流血：If you cut your finger it will ～.如果你割破手指，它会流血。❷feel great distress 悲痛；伤心：Our hearts ～ for you.我们为你感到悲痛。❸draw blood from 自……抽血；放血：Doctors used to ～ people when they were ill. 昔时人们病了，医生常为他们放血。❹

B

force (sb.) to pay money unjustly 敲诈:
The blackmailers bled him for £500. 敲
诈者向他敲诈 500 英镑。

bleeding/'bli:dɪŋ/

adj.(used for giving force to an expression, especially of annoyance) bloody (用
于加强语气,尤表示非常厌烦)该死的,
讨厌的:What a ~ waste of time! 真是
白费时间!

bleep/bli:p/

Ⅰ *n.*a high, usually repeated sound sent
out by a machine to attract sb.'s attention
(机器所发出以引起人们注意的)哔哔声
Ⅱ *v.*❶ send out this kind of sound 发出
哔哔声 ❷ call sb. using a bleeper (用传
呼机)召唤(某人):They're ~ing you,
doctor.医生,他们正用传呼机叫你呢! ❸
prevent (a word or words) from being
heard on television or radio with beeps
(说话)被(电视或收音机中)哔哔声干扰
(盖过):The obscene words in the song
were ~ed (out).这首歌中的污秽歌词已
被哔哔声干扰掉。

bleeper/'bli:pə(r)/

*n.*a small machine which can be carried in
a pocket, fastened to clothing, etc. and
which bleeps when the attention of the
person wearing it is needed (可放进口袋
或挂在衣服上的)传呼机

blemish/'blemɪʃ/

Ⅰ *v.*spoil the appearance of sth.损害……
的美观;玷污;弄糟:a ~ed peach 一个有
伤痕的桃子 Ⅱ *n.*a mark, etc., that spoils
the beauty or perfection of sb. or sth.点;
污点;瑕疵:a ~ on someone's character
某人人格上的污点

blend/blend/

Ⅰ *v.*❶ mix two or more substances together 混合;掺杂:~ the flour and eggs
把面粉和鸡蛋搅和在一起 ❷ go well together 调和;协调:These two colours ~
well.这两种颜色配在一起很协调。Ⅱ *n.*a
mixture of different things or people 混
合物;混杂的人群

blender /'blendə/

*n.*a machine for mixing food or turning it
into liquid blessed (食品)搅拌机,搅拌器

bless/bles/

*v.*ask God's favour for;wish happiness or
favour to 祈求上帝保佑;祝福:God ~
you.上帝保佑你。 ‖ be ~ed with 幸运地
享有

blessing/'blesɪŋ/

n. ❶ prayer for God's favour;thanks to
God before or after a meal 祝福;祈祷:
Blessing upon you. 祝福你们。 ❷ anything that brings happiness or good fortune 幸事;喜事;幸福:What a ~ it is
you didn't travel on that airplane which
crashed yesterday! 你没有乘坐昨天失事
的那架飞机,多么幸运啊!

blight/blaɪt/

Ⅰ *n.*❶ a disease of plants that results in
the drying up and dying of the diseased
parts (植物的)枯萎病,病虫害 ❷ anything which spoils one's hopes,plans,etc.
使(希望、计划等)落空的事物 Ⅱ *v.*damage or spoil 破坏;挫折:The accident
~ed his life.这事故毁了他的一生。

blind/blaɪnd/

*adj.*❶ without the power to see 瞎的;失
明的:He is ~ in one eye.他一只眼睛失
明了。 ❷ reckless;thoughtless 盲目的;
无理智的:Blind worship of this idol must
be ended.对这种偶像的盲目崇拜应该停
止了。 ‖ ~ alley 死胡同/turn a ~ eye to
假装没看见 ‖ ~ly *adv.*盲目地/~ness *n.*
盲目性

blink/blɪŋk/

Ⅰ *v.*❶ shut and open the eyes quickly 眨
眼:~ the eyes 眨眼睛/~ at someone 对
某人眨眼示意 ❷ (of lights) shine in an
unsteady way (指光)闪烁不定:We saw
the lights of a steamer ~ing on the horizon.我们看见一艘轮船上的灯光在地平
线上闪烁着。Ⅱ *n.*❶ an act of blinking 眨
眼 ❷ a sudden quick gleam of light 闪烁:
a ~ of light 光线闪烁

blinkered/'blɪŋkəd/

*adj.*❶ (of a horse)wearing blinkers (马)
戴眼罩的 ❷ showing an inability to understand or accept anything beyond one's
own familiar ideas,customs,beliefs,etc.
狭隘的;有偏见的;片面的;保守的:~ o-

B

pinions 狭隘的见解

blinker/'blɪŋkə/
n.(*pl.*) pieces of leather put at the side of a horse's eyes to make it look straight a-head 马眼罩

blip/blɪp/
n. ❶ a very short sound produced by a machine, such as a radar apparatus or a machine that measures a sick person's heartbeat (仪器等发出的)极短促的哔哔声 ❷ a bright light flashing on a radar screen representing an object, often accompanied by such a sound 光点

bliss/blɪs/
*n.*perfect happiness; great joy 无上幸福; 非常快乐: domestic ~ 家庭的幸福

blissful /'blɪsfʊl/
*adj.*❶extremely happy; full of joy 极乐的;幸福的;欣喜若狂的: a ~ couple holding a baby 一对抱着婴儿、其乐融融的夫妻 ❷providing perfect happiness or great joy 使人幸福的;使人欣喜若狂的

blister/'blɪstə(r)/
Ⅰ *n.* a small bag-like swelling under the skin, filled with liquid, often caused by rubbing, burning, etc.水疱;水泡: get ~s on one's feet 脚上起泡 Ⅱ *v.* cause, get a blister or blisters on 起泡;(使)起泡: He is not used to manual work and his hands ~ easily.他不惯于用手工作,他的手容易起泡。/The sun has ~ed the paint on the door.太阳晒得门上的油漆都起了泡。

blistering /'blɪstərɪŋ/
*adj.*❶(said about heat) intense (热度)强烈的,剧烈的: the ~ heat of the desert 沙漠里的酷热 ❷(said about criticism) very severe (批评)猛烈的,严酷的: a ~ attack on the policy 对这一政策的无情抨击

blithe/blaɪð/
*adj.*happy and cheerful; not anxious 愉快的;无忧无虑的 ‖ ~ly *adv.*愉快地;无忧无虑地: He ~ly ignored me. 他怡然自得,不理我。

blitz/blɪts/
Ⅰ *n.* ❶ a (period of) sudden heavy attack, especially from the air 闪电般的猛烈袭击(尤指空袭);闪电战: During the ~ everyone used to spend the night in underground shelters. 空袭期间,大家常常到地下防空洞过夜。 ❷ a period of great activity for some special purpose (为某个特殊目的的)大规模行动: an advertising ~ 一次大规模的广告宣传/ Let's have a ~ on all these letters that need answering.我们对这些需要答复的信件来个闪电式的突击清理吧。 Ⅱ *v.* make blitz attacks on 对……进行猛烈空袭,以闪电战攻击: London was badly ~ed in 1940.伦敦于 1940 年遭到猛烈的空袭。

blizzard/'blɪzəd/
*n.*a snowstorm with a strong wind 暴风雪

bloat /bləʊt/
*v.*❶cause to swell with fluid or gas 使膨胀;使肿起;使鼓起: Her features were ~ed by drinking.她酗酒后变得面部浮肿。 ❷become swollen with fluid or gas 膨胀;肿起;鼓起: She suffered from abdominal ~ing.她因腹部鼓胀而受苦。

blob/blɒb/
*n.*a small round spot or object 小斑点;小圆块: A ~ of ice cream fell on her dress. 一小块冰激凌掉在她的衣服上。

bloc/blɒk/
*n.*a group of people or countries who act together in certain political activities 集团(在某些政治活动中一起行动的一群人或一些国家): There is an African-Asian ~ at the United Nations.联合国有个亚非集团。

block/blɒk/
Ⅰ *n.* ❶ any large, solid piece of wood, stone, etc.大块(石头、木头等): a ~ of ice 一大块冰/building ~s 积木 ❷ a large building divided into separate parts 大厦;大楼: a ~ of flats 公寓大厦/an office ~ 一座办公大楼 ❸the area or building surrounded by four streets in a town 街区: The shopping center is two ~s away.购物中心离这里两个街区。 ❹ obstruction; sth. that makes movement of flow difficult or impossible 堵塞;障碍物: There was a ~ in the pipe and the water couldn't flow away.管里有东西堵塞,水

B

流不走。Ⅱv.make movement impossible on or through sth.阻塞;拦阻;阻碍:The deep snow ~ed the road.积雪封住了道路。

blockade/blɒ'keɪd/
Ⅰn.the surrounding of a place by warships or soldiers to prevent people or goods from coming in or going out（用军事力量）封锁,禁运:raise (lift) a ~ (of)解除封锁/run a ~ 冲破封锁 Ⅱv.stop goods or people from reaching a place 封锁:~ the enemy harbour 封锁敌人港口

blockage/'blɒkɪdʒ/
n.sth. that blocks a pipe,tube,tunnel,etc.阻塞;阻碍:a ~ in the pipes 管道中的堵塞物

blood/blʌd/
n.❶the red liquid flowing throughout the body of man and the higher animals 血;血液:Their ~ was not shed in vain.他们的血没有白流。❷ the family origin or descent 血统 ‖ ~ **relation** n.血亲/~ **test** n.验血/~ **type** n.血型/~**shed** n.流血;杀戮

bloodless/'blʌdlɪs/
adj.❶looking pale,drained of blood 无血色的;苍白的 ❷without violence or killing 非暴力的;不流血的:a ~ coup 不流血政变 ❸lacking human emotion 无情的;冷酷的

bloodstream/'blʌdstriːm/
n.the blood circulating in the body 体内循环的血液;血流

bloody/'blʌdi/
adj.❶covered with blood 出血的;血迹斑斑的:a ~ hand 血淋淋的手 ❷with much bloodshed;cruel 流血过多的;残酷的:a ~ battle 残酷的战斗 ❸having the colour of blood 血红色的:The shirt is ~.这件衬衫是血红色的。

bloom/bluːm/
Ⅰn.❶a flower, especially of plants admired chiefly for their flowers 花（尤指观赏植物的花）:The tulips are in full ~ now.郁金香花现在盛开。❷the greatest beauty or perfection 青春;茂盛(时期):She was in the ~ of youth.她正在青春时

期。Ⅱv.be in flower;bear flowers 开花:The roses have been ~ing all summer.玫瑰花整个夏天一直都在开放。

bloomer/'bluːmə(r)/
n.a stupid mistake 大错;大失策;大败笔:I made a terrible ~.我犯了一个大错。

bloomers/'bluːməz/
n.(pl.)a woman's garment of short loose trousers gathered at the knee 灯笼裤

blossom/'blɒsəm/
Ⅰn.❶flowers, especially of a fruit tree （尤指果树的）花:apple ~s 苹果花 ❷ the condition or time of flowering 开花期:The cherry-trees are in full ~.这些樱花已盛开。Ⅱv.❶produce flowers 开花:The cherry-trees will ~ next month.这些樱花树下个月会开花。❷develop 成长;发育:He ~ed out as a first-rate athlete.他已成长为一流的运动员。

blot/blɒt/
Ⅰn.a mark caused by ink spilt on paper 污点;墨渍:He made some ~s on the book.他在书上弄了几点墨渍。Ⅱv.(-tt-) ❶ make a blot or blots on (paper with ink) 弄上墨污:He dropped his pen and ~ted his exam paper.他把钢笔掉落了,考卷上染上了墨渍。❷ dry up (wet ink) with blotting-paper（用吸墨纸）吸干墨水 ‖ ~ out 涂去;抹掉 ‖ ~ting paper n.吸墨纸

blotch/blɒtʃ/
n.a large roughly-shaped mark,especially on sb.'s face（尤指在脸上的）斑

blotchy/'blɒtʃi/
adj.covered in blotches 有斑点的;有污点的:her ~ face 她布满黑斑的脸

blotter/'blɒtə(r)/
n. ❶ a large piece of blotting paper against which writing paper can be pressed to dry the ink 吸墨纸 ❷ a book where records are written every day, before the information is stored elsewhere 临时记录簿;记事本:police ~ 警察临时记事本

blouse/blaʊz/
n.an outer garment from neck to waist, usually with sleeves, as worn by workmen

and sailors, or by women, kept in place at waist with a belt or band（工人、水手或妇女所穿的）短上衣

blow /bləʊ/

Ⅰ *v.* (blew, blown) ❶ (of the wind) move along; move sth. quickly and strongly in the air（风、空气）吹；刮: The wind blew hard. 刮大风了。 ❷ send air out of the mouth 吹气: He blew the dust off the shelter. 他把书架上的尘土吹掉。 ‖ ~ one's own trumpet（horn）自吹自擂/~ out 吹灭/~ over（风）吹过；停息/~ up 爆炸；发火；爆发 Ⅱ *n.* ❶ a sudden hard hit or shock 猛击；打击: He gave his opponent a hard ~ on the head. 他重重地打在对手的头上。 ❷ a shock or disaster that is upsetting, disapproving or damaging to sb. 打击: His death was a terrible ~ to us. 他的去世对我们是个很大的打击。 ‖ at（with）one ~ 一举；一下子/strike a ~ for（against）为（反对）……而战斗 ‖ ~ fly *n.* 绿头苍蝇/~ hole *n.* (鲸鱼等的)鼻孔；气孔/~ off *n.* 喷出/~ out *n.* 车胎爆裂/~ pipe *n.* 吹管；喷焊器/~ up *n.* 爆炸；(脾气等)爆发

blower /ˈbləʊə/

n. ❶ a device that creates a current of air 吹风机；送风机: a hot-air ~ 热风机 ❷ a telephone 电话

blubber /ˈblʌbə(r)/

n. the fat of whales and some other sea animals 鲸脂；海生动物脂肪

blue /bluː/

Ⅰ *adj.* ❶ having the colour of the clear sky or the deep sea 蓝色的；青色的；天蓝色的: It is painted ~. 它被漆成蓝色。 / His face was ~ with cold. 他的脸冷得发青。 ❷ sad and gloomy; depressed or depressing 忧郁的；沮丧的；悲观的: He looks ~. 他显得沮丧。 Ⅱ *n.* ❶ blue colour 蓝色: light ~ 浅蓝色 ❷ the sky or the sea 蓝天；海洋: fly into the ~ 飞上蓝天 ❸ a blue paint or pigment 蓝漆；蓝色染料

blueberry /ˈbluːbəri, ˈbluːberi/

n. (*pl.* -ies) a shrub with edible blue berries 越橘蓝色浆果；蓝莓

blueprint /ˈbluːˌprɪnt/

n. ❶ a design plan or technical drawing 蓝图；设计图 ❷ a detailed plan or scheme 规划；方案: a ~ for the privatization of health care 保健私有化方案

blues /bluːz/

n. ❶ a slow sad jazz song or tune, of black American folk origin 布鲁斯音乐，蓝调（源于美国黑人，节奏缓慢忧郁）❷ (the ~) the feelings of sadness or depression bluntly 忧郁；悲伤；沮丧: She's got the ~. 她变得忧郁了。

blunder /ˈblʌndə(r)/

Ⅰ *v.* ❶ move about uncertainly as if blind 瞎闯；乱闯；盲目行动: ~ into a wall 盲目乱动而碰着了墙壁/~ (up) on somone 偶然发现某人 ❷ make foolish mistakes 犯大错: Our leaders have ~ed again. 我们的领导们又犯了大错。 Ⅱ *n.* a stupid or careless mistake 大错误；愚蠢的错误；疏忽的错误: make a terrible ~ 铸成大错

blunt /blʌnt/

Ⅰ *adj.* ❶ not sharp 不锋利的: a ~ knife 钝刀 ❷ (of a person) speaking roughly and plainly, without trying to be polite or kind (指人)直率的，直言的，不客气的: He is a ~ man. 他是个直率的人。 Ⅱ *v.* make less sharp 使钝: If you try to cut stone with a knife, you will ~ the edge. 如果你试试以刀砍石，你就会把刀刃弄钝了。

blur /blɜː(r)/

Ⅰ *v.* (-rr-) make difficult to see sth. clearly 使模糊不清；使看不清: Tears ~red her eyes. 眼泪使她的眼睛模糊。 /The writing was ~red. 字迹被弄模糊不清。 Ⅱ *n.* ❶ a dirty spot or mark; a smear of ink 污点；污渍；墨水迹 ❷ sth. that cannot be clearly seen 一片模糊: The houses appeared as a ~ in the mist. 房屋在雾中呈现出一片模糊的景象。

blurred /blɜːd/

adj. ❶ not clear in outline, out of focus 模糊不清的: a ~ photograph 模糊的照片 ❷ difficult to distinguish 难以区分的: The boundary between right and wrong had become ~. 是与非的界限变得含混不清。

blurt/blɜːt/

　　v.tell sth.suddenly,often thoughtlessly 脱口而出：He ～ed out the news before he considered its effect.他脱口说出这个消息而没有考虑其后果。

blush/blʌʃ/

　　Ⅰ *v*.❶ become red (in the face) from shame or confusion 脸红；羞愧：～ at the thought of 一想到……就脸红/ I ～ for you.我替你脸红。❷be ashamed 羞于；惭愧：～ to own that...羞于承认…… Ⅱ *n*.a reddening of the face (from shame,etc.) (害羞等引起的)脸红：She turned away to hide her ～es.她转过身去掩饰她的脸红。

bluster/'blʌstə(r)/

　　v.complain or threaten in a noisy way 大声抱怨；蛮横威吓

blustery/'blʌstri/

　　adj.(of wind) noisy and violent 狂风大作的；呼啸的

board/bɔːd/

　　Ⅰ *n*.❶ a long thin flat piece of wood or other hard material, typically used for floors or other building purposes 板；木板 ❷ a flat piece of wood or other material used for a special purpose 板；牌；栏：a black ～ 黑板 ❸ a group of people who control sth.；a committee；a council 董事会；委员会；理事会：the ～of directors 董事会/the ～ of trade 贸易委员会 Ⅱ *v*.❶ cover up with boards 用木板盖：The floor was ～ed.地面已铺好木板。❷get on or into a ship (a plane, car, etc.) 上船(飞机、车等)：We ～ed the ship early this morning.我们今天清晨上了船。‖ on ～ 在船(或飞机等)上

boarder/'bɔːdə(r)/

　　n.❶a person who boards with sb.搭伙者；寄膳者：take in ～s for a living 以招收包伙为生 ❷a schoolboy or school-girl at a boarding-school 寄宿学校的学生：a day ～ 寄膳不寄宿的学生

boarding /'bɔːdɪŋ/

　　n.❶long,flat,thin pieces of wood used to build or cover sth. 木板；板材 ❷the procedure according to which pupils live in school during term time in return for

payment (学生)寄宿制 ❸the action of getting on or into a ship,aircraft,or other vehicle 上船；登机；上车

boast/bəust/

　　Ⅰ *v*.talk too much of oneself；praise oneself too much 自夸；吹嘘：He ～s of his wealth.他夸耀他的财产多。Ⅱ *n*.talking with self-satisfaction about sth. 夸耀 ‖ ～er *n*.吹牛皮的人/～ful *adj*.自夸的；自负的；爱吹牛的

boat/bəut/

　　n.a small vehicle for travelling across water 小船；艇：a fishing ～ 渔船/a sailing ～ 帆船 ‖ burn one's ～s 破釜沉舟/in the same ～ 处境相同 ‖ ～man *n*.船工

bob/bɒb/

　　v.(-bb-) move quickly up and down (使)上下跳动：The boats were ～bing on the water.那些小船在水面上随波起伏。/ ～ one's head up and down 频频点头

bobble/'bɒbl/

　　n.a small,often fluffy,ball of wool,etc. used for decoration (用于装饰的)小羊毛球,小绒球：cushions with ～ on them 带小绒球的坐垫 /a ～ hat 顶上饰有小绒球的帽子

bode/bəud/

　　v.be a good or bad sign for the future 预示……的吉(凶)：These early sales figures ～ well for the success of the book.本书的初步销售数字预示它的销路会很好。

bodily /'bɒdɪli/

　　Ⅰ *adj*.to do with the human body or physical nature bodily 身体的；躯体的：Children learned to control their ～ functions.孩子们学会了控制身体的官能。Ⅱ *adv*. by moving the whole of sb.'s body；by force 移动全身地；用力地：He lifted her ～ into the air.他把她整个人举到空中。

body/'bɒdi/

　　n.❶ the whole material part of a man or animal；the main part of a man or animal without the head,arms and legs 身体；躯体 ❷the main or central part of anything 躯干；主体 ❸ the dead body 尸体：They found the ～ of a woman in the valley.他

们在山谷里发现了一具女尸。❹ a group of persons who do sth.together 团体:The House of Commons is an elected ～.众议院是经选举产生出来的机构。‖ **keep ～ and soul together** 仅能维持生活;活命‖ ～**guard** *n.*警卫员;保镖

bog/bɒg/
Ⅰ *n.*the land which is wet and soft 沼泽地 Ⅱ *v.*(-gg-)(be ～ged down) be unable to move forward as though in a bog 停滞不前;陷入僵局: He was ～ged down in a mass of details.他被一大堆细节问题拖了后腿。‖ ～**gy** *adj.*沼泽般的

boggle/'bɒgl/
*v.*hesitate or be anxious at 犹豫;忧虑;焦虑

bogus/'bəugəs/
*adj.*false;untrue;pretending to be what it is not 伪造的;假的;假装的

boil/bɔɪl/
Ⅰ *v.*❶ (of a liquid or the vessel containing it) reach the temperature at which liquid changes into a gas 煮沸;烧开:～ing water 沸水 ❷ cause (a liquid or the vessel containing it) to reach this temperature 烧;煮:Will you ～ me some eggs? 给我煮几个鸡蛋好吗? ❸be very angry about sth.非常气愤 Ⅱ *n.*❶a certain temperature at which a kind of liquid is boiled 沸点 ❷the process of heating a liquid to the temperature 沸腾

boiler/'bɔɪlə(r)/
*n.*❶a metal container for heating liquids 煮器:This ～ is made of aluminium.这壶是用铝制的。❷a tank for making steam to heat buildings or drive engines 锅炉

boiling/'bɔɪlɪŋ/
*adj.*very hot 炽热的;很热的:a ～ hot day 酷热的一天

boisterous/'bɔɪstərəs/
adj.(of people's behaviour) noisy,cheerful and rough (行为)喧闹的,狂欢的

bold/bəuld/
*adj.*❶daring;courageous;adventurous 大胆的;无畏的;勇敢的:a ～ man 勇敢的人/a ～ action 大胆的行动 ❷in thick strokes 黑体;粗体 ‖ **make ～ to** 冒昧;大

胆

bolster/'bəulstə(r)/
Ⅰ *n.*a long pillow for a bed stretching from one side of a bed to the other 长枕头 Ⅱ *v.*give help and support to 帮助;支持:John's friends had to ～ up his courage.约翰的朋友不得不为他壮胆。

bolt/bəult/
Ⅰ *n.*❶ a metal fastening for a door or window (门、窗的)插销,闩 ❷ a screw with no point,which fastens through a piece of metal to hold things together 螺栓;螺钉 Ⅱ *v.*fasten with a bolt or bolts 上闩;用螺栓拴住:Is the door ～ed? 门闩上了吗?

bomb/bɒm/
Ⅰ *n.*a hollow metal ball or shell filled with gunpowder or some other explosive 炸弹:a tear gas ～ 催泪弹/an atom ～ 原子弹 Ⅱ *v.*attack with bombs 轰炸;投弹:The enemy planes ～ed the city.敌机轰炸了这座城市。

bombard/bɒm'bɑːd/
*v.*❶attack with fire from big guns 炮击;炮轰 ❷keep attacking continuously 不断抨击:The Members of Parliament ～ed the Prime Minister with questions.议员们连珠炮似的向首相提出质问。

bomber/'bɒmə(r)/
*n.*❶an aircraft used for bombing 轰炸机:This ～ was made in USA.这架轰炸机是美国制造的。❷ a soldier trained in bombing 投弹手

bombproof/'bɒmpruːf/
*adj.*giving protection against bombs 防弹的;避弹的:a ～ shelter 防空洞

bombshell/'bɒmʃel/
*n.*❶ a great and usually unpleasant surprise 令人震惊的事;突发的意外事件:The news of their divorce came as a ～ to us.他们离婚的消息使我们大吃一惊。❷ an extremely attractive woman 非常吸引人的女性:a blonde ～ 金发美人

bond/bɒnd/
*n.*❶sth. that unites two or more people or groups,such as a shared feeling or interest 纽带:a ～ of friendship 友谊的纽

带 ❷ an agreement or engagement that a person is bound to observe, especially one that has force in law; a document, signed and sealed, containing such an agreement 合约；契约；票据 ❸ a piece of printed paper issued by a government or a corporation acknowledging that money has been lent to it and will be paid back with interest 公债；债券

bondage /ˈbɒndɪdʒ/

n. slavery or captivity 奴役；束缚

bone /bəʊn/

n. the hard white material in the body of a person or animal 骨；骨头；骨骼: He broke a ~ in his leg. 他腿部骨折。‖ (**be**) **all ~ and skin** 瘦得皮包骨头 / **make no ~s about** 对……毫不犹豫 / **cut to the ~** 削减到最低限度 ‖ **~-deep** adj. 刻骨的

bonfire /ˈbɒnfaɪə(r)/

n. fire made in the open air 篝火，营火

bonnet /ˈbɒnɪt/

n. ❶ a hat tied under the chin (usually worn by women or children) （通常为妇女、儿童戴的）有带圆帽 ❷ the front part of a car covering the engine or the boot 〈英〉汽车罩

bonny /ˈbɒni/

adj. healthy looking; with a glow of health 健美的；容光焕发的: a ~ baby 健美的婴儿 / her ~ face 她健美的面庞

bonsai /ˈbɒnsaɪ/

n. (the art of growing) a plant in a pot that is prevented from reaching its natural size, especially a tree 盆景；盆栽（艺术）

bonus /ˈbəʊnəs/

n. an additional payment beyond what is usual, necessary, or expected, such as a share of profits paid to those who hold shares in or work for a business or are insured with an insurance company 额外的红利；奖金；额外津贴

bony /ˈbəʊni/

adj. ❶ of or like bone （似）骨的 ❷ (a person or part of the body) so thin that the bones can be seen 骨头突出的；瘦骨嶙峋

的；瘦得皮包骨的: his ~ fingers 他瘦骨嶙峋的手指 ❸ (of a fish eaten as food) having many bones （食用鱼）多骨（刺）的 ‖ **boniness** n. 骨瘦如柴

boo /buː/

Ⅰ n. & int. the noise made to show dislike (usually at a meeting) （表示厌恶的）嘘嘘声（通常指在会议上）Ⅱ v. make this noise 发出嘘嘘声: The crowd ~ed the Prime Minister. 群众向首相发嘘嘘声喝倒彩。

book /bʊk/

Ⅰ n. ❶ the printed pages attached together with a cover 书；本子: There are many ~s on the table. 桌上有许多书。 ❷ a number of things fastened together like a book 账簿；簿记: enter … in the ~s 把……记入账簿 ‖ **be at one's ~s** 用功学习 / **speak like a ~** 咬文嚼字 / **by the ~** 按常规 / **keep ~s** 上账；记账 / **speak by the ~** 说话确切 Ⅱ v. buy or arrange to have tickets, rooms, etc. 预订: ~ a ticket 预订票 ‖ **~ case** n. 书柜 / **~ keeper** n. 记账员 / **~ish** adj. 书生气的；文绉绉的 / **~ mark** n. 书签 / **~ seller** n. 书商 / **~ shelf** n. 书架 / **~ stall** n. 书摊；书亭 / **~ stand** n. 书摊 / **~ worm** n. 书呆子

booking /ˈbʊkɪŋ/

n. an act of reserving accommodation, a place, etc. or of buying a ticket in advance （座位、票等的）预订: Early ~ is essential. 提前订票是必要的。

booklet /ˈbʊklɪt/

n. a small thin book with paper covers 小册子

boom /buːm/

Ⅰ n. ❶ a sudden increase in trade and economic activity, , etc. （贸易和经济活动等的）激增，繁荣: a ~ in car sales 汽车销售额的剧增 ❷ a period when sth. such as a sport or a type of music suddenly becomes very popular and successful（某种体育运动、音乐等）突然风靡的时期 ❸ a loud deep sound 深沉的响声: The distant ~ of guns frightened the boy. 远处隆隆的炮声吓到了那个小男孩。 ❹ a long pole that carries a microphone or other equipment（麦克风）吊杆 Ⅱ v. ❶ make a loud deep sound 轰鸣；轰响：Outside, thunder ~ed.外面雷声隆隆。❷ say sth. in a loud deep voice 以低沉有力的声音说话：His voice ~ed out from the darkness.黑暗中传来他低沉有力的嗓音。❸ become bigger, more successful, , etc.迅速发展；激增；繁荣昌盛：Business is ~ing!生意兴隆！

boon/buːn/
  *n.*advantage；help 利益，好处；帮助：My new overcoat is a ~ in this cold weather.我的新大衣在这样冷的天气里很顶用。

boost/buːst/
  Ⅰ *v.*❶ speak favourably of or advertise sth., especially in order to persuade people to buy it 吹嘘；宣扬（尤指为了推销商品）❷push forward or upwards 往前推；往上推 ❸increase the power or speed of 增强；加速 Ⅱ *n.*❶acceleration or promotion 推动；促进 ❷increase or improvement 增长；提高

booster/ˈbuːstə(r)/
  *n.*❶ the first stage of a rocket or space craft, used to give initial acceleration and then jettisoned （火箭、飞船的）助推器：When the ~s have helped to lift a space station into orbit, they separate from it and return to Earth.助推火箭把太空站推入轨道后，就自行脱落返回地球。❷ an additional amount of a drug, to strengthen the effect of some of the same drug that was given earlier（增强药效的）附加剂量，加强剂：This injection will protect you against the disease, but after six months you'll need a ~.这种注射剂可以防止你得那种病，但半年后需要再注射以增加药力。❸ a person who is very much in favour of sth. or sb.热心支持者

boot/buːt/
  Ⅰ *n.*❶ an outer covering for the foot made of leather or rubber, covering the ankle（皮或橡胶制的）长筒靴，高靴：elastic-side ~s 边上装有松紧带的靴子/My ~s are too tight.我的靴太紧。❷a place for luggage in a coach or at the back of a motorcycle(客车、摩托车等的)行李箱 Ⅱ *v.*kick 踢：He ~ed a piece of stone off the side walk.他把一小块石头踢出人

行道。

booth/buːð/
  *n.*❶(at a market)a covered movable shop (市场上)有棚流动货摊，摊位：He is a dealer in small wares at a ~.他是个商人，摆摊经营小杂货。❷ an enclosed place for one person 单人小间：a telephone ~ 公用电话间

bootleg/ˈbuːtleg/
  Ⅰ *v.*(-gg-) ❶to smuggle alcohol 走私酒 ❷to make and sell sth. illegally 非法生产或销售 Ⅱ*adj.*sold or distributed illegally 非法生产或销售的：a ~ recording 盗版唱片

booty/ˈbuːti/
  *n.*goods and money taken from the enemy in war or stolen by robbers 战利品；赃物

booze/buːz/
  Ⅰ *n.*alcoholic drink 酒 Ⅱ*v.*drink alcoholic drinks 喝酒

border/ˈbɔːdə(r)/
  Ⅰ *n.*❶a strip around the edge of sth.包边 ❷the line dividing two states or countries 边界；国界：The criminal escaped over the ~.罪犯逃过了边界。Ⅱ*v.*be near to another country or region 与……接壤

borderland/ˈbɔːdəlænd/
  *n.*❶ land at or near the border of two countries 边境地带 ❷ a condition between two other conditions and like each of them in certain ways（介于两种状况之间的）边缘状态：the ~ between sleeping and waking 半睡半醒的蒙眬状态

borderline/ˈbɔːdəlaɪn/
  Ⅰ *n.*❶a boundary separating two countries or areas 边界线；国境线：the ~ between France and Germany on the map 地图上法国与德国的国境线 ❷a division between two distinct or opposite things 分界线 Ⅱ *adj.*only just acceptable in quality or as belonging to a category 不大合乎标准的，边缘的，不确定的：Ann will certainly pass the exam, but Susan is a ~ case.安考试肯定会及格，但苏珊的情况就难说了。

bore[1]/bɔː(r)/
  *v.*make a round hole or passage in sth. 钻

B

孔：~ for oil 钻孔取石油/~ a well for water 钻井取水

bore² /bɔː(r)/

I v.make sb. feel tired by being dull and uninteresting 使厌烦：It ~s me to death. 这件事把我烦透了。 II n. a person or thing that is dull and uninteresting 让人讨厌（或厌倦）的人（或事）：He is a perfect ~.他这人真讨厌。

boredom /'bɔːdəm/

n.the state of feeling bored；the quality of being very boring 厌烦；厌倦；无聊：This book helps to relieve the ~ of the winter evenings.这本书有助于打发冬日无聊的夜晚。

boring /'bɔːrɪŋ/

adj.dull and uninteresting 令人厌倦的；乏味的；无聊的：He has a ~ job in an office.他有一份乏味的办公室工作。

born /bɔːn/

adj.❶ existing as a result of birth 出生的：When were you ~? 你是什么时候生的？ ❷ destined to be 天生的：She's ~ ugly.她天生丑陋。

borne /bɔːn/

adj.❶（~ in on/upon）brought firmly to the consciousness of 意识到；完全认识到：Slowly it was ~ in on the citizens that the enemy had surrounded them.市民们渐渐地意识到敌人已经把他们包围了。❷carried as stated 由……所携带的（传播的）：water-~ diseases 由水传播的疾病 /Some plants have wind-~ seeds.有些植物靠风传播种子。

borough /'bʌrə/

n.a town or part of a large city which governs itself 自治市镇；区

borrow /'bɒrəʊ/

v.❶get or use sth. with intent to return it 借：I ~ed money of him. 我向他借了钱。/He neither ~s nor lends.他不借也不贷。❷adopt and use sth.as one's own 借用，引入：Many words in English have been ~ed from French.英语里许多单词是从法语来的。

borrowing /'bɒrəʊɪŋ/

n.the money that a company, an organiza-tion or a person borrows；the act of bor-rowing money 借款；贷款；借贷：High interest rates help to keep ~ down.高利率有助于控制借贷。

bosom /'buzəm/

n.❶a woman's breast；the part of dress covering this 乳房；衣服的胸部：She held the child to her ~.她把孩子紧紧地贴在怀里。/ She carried his letter in the ~ of her dress.她把他的信放在衣服胸部里面。❷the centre or inmost part, where one feels joy or sorrow 内心；衷心；胸怀：a ~ friend 知心朋友；心腹之交/Her ~ was torn by sorrow.因为忧愁她的心都碎了。❸ midst 其中：in the ~ of one's family 与家属在一起

boss /bɒs/

I n.a master；a person who controls or gives orders to workmen 主人；老板；工头；上司：He is fired by his ~.他被老板解雇了。 II v.give orders to 指挥；发号施令：He wants to ~ the show.他想指挥一切。

bossy /'bɒsi/

adj.too fond of giving orders 好发号施令的，专横的：a ~ person 好发号施令的人/She's an old ~-boots.她是个霸道的老太婆。

botanical /bə'tænɪkl/

adj.of or related to plants or botany 植物（学）的：a beautiful ~ garden with plants from all over the world 收集了世界各地植物的美丽的植物公园/~ drugs 植物性药物

botanize /'bɒtənaɪz/

v.study plant life and collect examples of plants 研究并采集植物

botany /'bɒtəni/

n.the science of the structure of plants 植物学 ‖ **botanist** n.植物学家

botch /bɒtʃ/

I v.repair badly；spoil by poor or clumsy work 拙劣地修补；笨手笨脚地弄坏：~ chair up 笨拙地修补椅子 II n.a piece of clumsy, badly done work 拙劣的工作：make a ~ of a party 把聚会搞得一团糟

both /bəʊθ/

B

*pron.*used for emphasis to refer two people or things, regarded and identified together 两者;双方:Hold it in ～ hands.用双手握住。/Both you and I want to go.我和你都想去。

bother/'bɒðə(r)/
Ⅰ *v.*❶ disturb;cause trouble to 打扰;麻烦:I'm sorry to have ～ed you.很抱歉,打搅你了。❷ worry;take trouble;be anxious 费心;烦恼:Don't ～ about him.别为他费心了。Ⅱ *n.*worry or trouble;sth. or sb.that carrys trouble 麻烦;烦恼;讨厌的事(或人):Don't get into such a ～ about small matters.别为了区区小事而如此烦恼。

bothersome/'bɒðəsəm/
*adj.*causing bother 引起麻烦的;讨厌的;令人为难的:～ demands 惹人讨厌的要求

bottle/'bɒtl/
Ⅰ *n.*a container with a narrow neck 瓶子:a ～ of wine 一瓶葡萄酒/an empty ～ 空瓶子 Ⅱ *v.*put a liquid into a bottle 把液体装进瓶中 ‖～neck *n.*狭窄路段

bottom/'bɒtəm/
*n.*❶ the lowest part of anything;the under part 底;底部;基础:the ～ of a well 井底/the ～ of the sea 海底 ❷ the last part;end 最后部分;尽头,末端:He is always at the ～ of the class.他总是班上最末一名。❸ the part of the body on which a person sits 屁股:He fell on his ～.他摔了个屁股蹲儿。‖ at the ～ of ……的根源/Bottoms up! 干杯! /from the ～ of one's heart 从心里,由衷地/get to the ～ of 弄清……的底细

bottomless /'bɒtəmlɪs/
*adj.*without a bottom,extremely deep 无底的;深不可测的

bough/baʊ/
*n.*a large branch coming from the trunk of a tree 大树枝:There are five birds on the ～.树枝上有五只鸟。

boulevard/'buːləvɑːd/
*n.*a wide street,often with trees on each side 林荫大道

bounce/baʊns/
*v.*spring or jump back after striking sth. hard;move up and down (使)弹回;(使)跳跃:～ a ball 拍球/A rubber ball ～s well.橡皮球弹力很好。/The car ～d along the bad road. 车在不平的路上颠簸而行。/The baby ～d up and down on the bed.婴孩在床上蹦跳。

bouncing/'baʊnsɪŋ/
adj.(especially of babies) healthy and active (尤指婴儿)健康活泼的

bouncy/'baʊnsi/
*adj.*❶ full of life and confidence,and eager for action 生气勃勃的;活跃的:a ～ person 精力充沛的人 ❷ that bounces well 弹性好的:a ～ ball 弹力好的球

bound[1] /baʊnd/
*adj.*❶ intending to go (to);going (to) 向……去的:The train is ～ for Guangzhou.这次列车开往广州。❷ be certain or sure that sth.will happen 必定的;一定的:As long as we work hard we are ～ to succeed.我们只要努力干,一定会成功。

bound[2] /baʊnd/
Ⅰ *v.*move or run in jumping movements 蹦跳:The boys ～ing with joy.那男孩高兴得蹦蹦跳跳。Ⅱ *n.*a jumping movement upward or forward 跳跃:With one ～ he reached the other side of the ditch.他纵身一跳就到了沟那边。‖ by leaps and ～s 飞速地

bound[3] /baʊnd/
*n.*a boundary;a limitation or restriction on feeling or action 界限,边界;限度,范围:beyond the ～s of one's knowledge 超出某人的知识范围 ‖ know no ～s 不知足;无限/out of ～s 禁止去;不容许/within ～s 在限度以内

boundary/'baʊndri/
*n.*a line that marks a limit;a dividing line 界限;分界线:This is the ～ between the two countries.这是两国间的分界线。

bounden/'baʊndən/
*adj.*rare necessary;obligatory 必要的;义不容辞的;分内的:～ duty 分内的义务

boundless/'baʊndlɪs/
*adj.*without limits 无限的;无边的;广阔的:Outer space is ～.外层空间是无边无

际的。

bounds/baʊndz/

n.the furthest limits or edges of sth.；the limits beyond which it is impossible or undesirable to go 界限；极限；限度；止境：You must keep your spending within ～.你花钱一定要有个限度。

bounteous/'baʊntɪəs/

adj.generous；abundant 慷慨的；丰富的：a ～ harvest 丰收

bountiful/'baʊntɪfl/

adj.generous；in large quantities 慷慨的；大量的：a ～ supply 充足的供应

bounty/'baʊnti/

n.❶generosity 宽大；慷慨 ❷sth. that is given generously 赏赐；赠品：the ～ of nature 大自然的赏赐 ❸money given by a government for some special act or service 奖励金；补助金

bouquet/bʊ'keɪ/

n.❶a bunch of flowers 花束：The girl is holding a ～ of red roses in her hand.这姑娘手里拿着一束红玫瑰。 ❷words of praise 恭维话，赞扬的话：He said ～s for me in front of the guests. 他在客人面前说了许多恭维我的话。 ❸the perfume of wine 酒香

bourgeois/'bɔːʒwɑː/

Ⅰn.❶ a capitalist who engages in industrial commercial enterprise 资产阶级 ❷a member of the middle class 中产阶级 Ⅱadj.❶being of the property-owing class 资产阶级的 ❷of, related to, or typical of the middle class 中产阶级的

bourgeoisie/ˌbʊəʒwɑː'ziː/

n.(the ～)the middle class 中产阶级：the national ～ 民族中产阶级

bout/baʊt/

n.❶a period of exercise, work, or other activity 一回；一次；一番；一阵：a wrestling ～ 摔跤之一回合/a ～ of fighting 一场战斗/a drinking ～ 一次饮宴 ❷an attack of illness 疾病的发作：a ～ of influenza 一次流行性感冒/bad coughing ～s 一阵剧烈咳嗽

boutique/buː'tiːk/

n.a small shop selling up-to-date clothes and other personal articles of the newest kind 精品店；时装商店

bovine/'bəʊvaɪn/

adj.like a cow or ox, especially in being slow-thinking and slow-moving 似牛的；迟钝的，缓慢的

bovver/'bɒvə(r)/

n.violence or threatening behaviour, especially by groups of young men (尤指青少年)打群架，斗殴，恐吓行为：a ～ boy 小流氓

bow/bəʊ/

Ⅰv.❶bend the head or body 弯；俯；鞠躬：They ～ed to the king.他们向国王鞠躬。 ❷bend 弯；俯：The man was ～ed with old age.这人因年老而弯腰驼背了。 ❸ submit or yield to another's wish or opinion 屈从；服从：We will never ～ to these unreasonable demands.我们决不会屈从这些无理要求。 ‖ ～ down to 向……卑躬屈膝(低三下四)/～ the neck (knee)低头屈膝 Ⅱn.an act of bending forward the head or the upper part of the body, especially to show respect 鞠躬；俯身：He made a low ～ to the statue.他向这尊雕像深深地鞠了一躬。 ‖ make one's ～ 首次亮相/take a ～ 鞠躬答礼；答谢

bowel/'baʊəl/

n.❶ the part of the alimentary canal below the stomach 肠子：move the ～s 通大便 ❷(pl.) the innermost part 内部；核心：in the ～s of the earth 地球的核心 ❸pity 同情；慈悲，怜悯：～ of mercy 慈悲的心肠

bowl/bəʊl/

n.a deep round container for holding sth.碗；钵：a rice ～ 一只饭碗/a ～ of rice 一碗饭

bowling/'bəʊlɪŋ/

n. the game of knocking down skittles with a heavy ball 保龄球

box¹/bɒks/

n.a container, usually with a lid, made of wood, cardboard, or metal, used for holding solids 箱；盒；匣：a wooden ～ 木箱/a pencil ～ 铅笔盒

box²/bɒks/

Ⅰ *v.*give sb.a blow with the open hand on ears;fight with fists,usually with thick gloves for sport 拳击;用拳打:They ～ed with each other for quite some time.他们彼此拳斗了好一阵子了。Ⅱ *n.*a blow with the open hand (on the ear) 一巴掌;一拳:I gave him a ～ on the ear.我打了他一耳光。

boxer/ˈbɒksə(r)/
*n.*a person who boxes 拳击家;拳击手:He was the best ～ in the country.他曾经是该国最好的拳击手。

boxing /ˈbɒksɪŋ/
*n.*a sport in which two people fight each other with their hands,while wearing very large thick gloves 拳击(运动)

boy/bɔɪ/
*n.*❶a male child or a young male person 男孩,少年:a ～ of ten 一个 10 岁的男孩 ❷a son (of any age) 儿子:He has two ～s and one girl.他有两个儿子和一个女儿。❸a male servant 男佣:a house ～ 男仆

boycott/ˈbɔɪkɒt/
Ⅰ *v.*join with others and refuse to have anything to do with or to trade with;refuse to handle 联合抵制;拒绝和……交易:These small countries tried to ～ the big country.这些小国企图联合抵制那个大国。Ⅱ *n.*a refusal to deal with (a firm,etc.) 拒绝与(商行等)打交道:They declared a ～ against the goods of that shop.他们宣布抵制那家商店的货物。

boyfriend /ˈbɔɪfrend/
*n.*a man or boy that sb. has a romantic or sexual relationship with 男朋友

boyish /ˈbɔɪʃ/
*adj.*like a boy 像男孩的;男孩般的:She looked ～ and defiant.她看起来像男孩,而且很倔强。‖ ～ly *adv.*稚气地;少年地

bra/brɑː/
n. an undergarment for supporting a woman's breasts 胸罩

brace/breɪs/
Ⅰ *n.*a piece of metal,wood,etc.used to hold things together 紧缚物,支撑物 Ⅱ *v.*

give support or strength 支柱;缚牢

bracelet/ˈbreɪslɪt/
*n.*a ring or chain of metal or other material worn round the wrist or arm (usually by women) (通常妇女戴的)手镯,臂镯

bracing /ˈbreɪsɪŋ/
adj.(especially of air) fresh and health-giving (尤指空气)令人心神清爽的,提神的:a ～ sea breeze 令人精神爽快的海风

bracken/ˈbrækən/
*n.*a type of coarse fern;a lot of ferns together 蕨(一种植物);一簇蕨

bracket/ˈbrækɪt/
*n.*a structure of metal,wood,or plastic,often in the shape of a right angle,fixed to a wall to support sth.,such as a shelf or lamp 支架;托架;撑架:We use ～s to hold up a shelf.我们用托架支撑搁板。

brag/bræg/
v.(-gg-) talk too proudly about oneself or one's possessions,etc.;boast 自夸;自吹自擂:He often ～ged of his achievements.他常吹嘘他取得的成就。

braid/breɪd/
*n.*❶ a narrow piece of material made by twisting several strands or pieces together;pieces of hair twisted together 编带;辫子 ❷ the material of this type put along the edges of clothing or used as decoration on clothing (衣服上的)穗带,镶边:His coat was covered with ～.他的外套饰有穗带。

Braille/breɪl/
*n.*a system of reading and writing invented for use by the blind,in which the letters are represented by raised dots which can be read by feeling them with the fingers 布莱叶盲文(供盲人用手指摸读、书写的点字体系)

brain/breɪn/
*n.*❶ the part inside the head of a person or animal, which thinks and feels; the centre of the nervous system 大脑;脑;智力,智慧:He has a sober ～.他脑子很清醒。❷the ability to think clearly,quickly and well;intelligence 脑力;脑筋:He has

no ～s.他没有头脑。/Use your ～s.你动一动脑筋吧。❸a clever person 聪明的人 ‖ beat one's ～s (out) 费尽思考/blow one's ～ out (用枪)把脑袋打得开花/have sth.on the ～ 老想着某事/rack one's ～s 冲昏头脑;使得意忘形 ‖ ～less adj.没有头脑的/～man n.谋士;参谋/～power n.智能;智囊/～sick adj.疯狂的/～trust n.智囊团;专家顾问组/～work n.脑力劳动

brainwash /'breɪnwɒʃ/
v.use mental pressure to force someone to reject old beliefs and accept new ones 对……实施洗脑;把思想强行灌输给

brainwave /'breɪweɪv/
n.❶an electrical impulse in the brain 脑电波 ❷a sudden clever idea (突发的)奇思;突然想到的妙计

braise /breɪz/
v.cook slowly in a container with a lid on, using very little water 炖;焖

brake /breɪk/
Ⅰ n.an apparatus for slowing or lessening movement and bringing to stop 刹车;制动闸:The driver put on the ～ suddenly.司机突然将车刹住。Ⅱ v.cause to slow down by using a brake 刹车;制动:He ～d (the car) by the street.他在街边刹住了车。

bran /bræn/
n.the crushed skin of wheat and other grain separated from the flour 麦麸;糠;谷皮

branch /brɑːntʃ/
Ⅰ n.❶ an arm-like part of a tree growing out from the trunk 树枝 ❷ a division or subdivision of a firm or an organization 分部;分公司;分支机构:Our company has set up ～es all over the country.我们公司在全国各地都设立了许多分公司。❸a smaller part from the main part,especially from the road,river or railway (常指道路、河流或铁路的)支路,支流,支线 Ⅱ v.send out;divide 分支;分岔:The road ～es here.这条路在这里分岔。‖ ～ out 发展;扩充

brand /brænd/
n.❶ a trademark; a particular kind of goods with such a mark 商标;牌子;Do you like this ～ of wine? 你喜欢这种牌子的酒吗? ❷ an iron,used red-hot for burning a mark into a surface; a mark made in this way 烙印;印记:This pencil-box has my ～ in it.这个铅笔盒里面有我的印记。‖ ～new adj.崭新的;全新的

brandy /'brændi/
n.a strong alcoholic drink made from wine 白兰地酒:two brandies with sodas 两杯加汽水的白兰地酒

brash /bræʃ/
adj.self-confident and impolite 傲慢的;无礼的

brass /brɑːs/
n.❶bright yellow metal made by mixing copper and zinc 黄铜;铜器:～ buttons 黄铜扣子/a ～ foundry 黄铜铸造厂/～plate 铜牌 ❷impudence 厚脸皮;无耻:How did he have the ～ to do that? 他怎么会厚颜无耻地去做那事?

brassy /'brɑːsi/
adj.(-ier,-iest) ❶like brass in color or sound 黄铜色的;(声音)似铜管乐器的 ❷loud and vulgar 喧闹的;嘈杂的 ‖ brassiness n.黄铜

brave /breɪv/
Ⅰ adj.without fear;having courage;ready to face danger,pain or suffering 勇敢的;无畏的:He is as ～ as a tiger.他勇猛如虎。Ⅱ v.have the courage to deal with some difficult things to gain sth.勇于做某事 ‖ ～ly adv.勇敢地;英勇地

bravery /'breɪvəri/
n.❶courage;the quality of being brave 大胆;勇敢;英勇:He was rewarded for his ～.他因勇敢而受奖。❷ splendour (of dress,etc.) (服装等)华丽:decked out in all their ～ 穿着他们最华丽的衣服

brawl /brɔːl/
Ⅰ n.a noisy fight or quarrel,often in a public place (在公共场所的)喧闹,斗殴,争吵 Ⅱ v.fight or quarrel in this way 打架;争吵

brawn /brɔːn/
n.❶muscle;strength 肌肉;体力:a job needing brains rather than ～ 需要脑力

B

而非体力的工作 ❷pickled meat of a pig 腌猪肉 ‖~y *adj.* 强壮的

brazen /ˈbreɪzn/

*adj.*❶bold and shameless 无耻的；恬不知耻的；厚颜无耻的 ❷made of brass or like brass 黄铜制的；像黄铜的

brazier/ˈbreɪzɪə(r)/

n. a metal framework like a basket with legs for holding burning coal or charcoal (金属)火盆，火钵

breach/briːtʃ/

Ⅰ*n.*❶an act of breaking the law or failing to do what one has promised to do (对法律的)违犯，破坏；毁约：a ~ of the peace in public 扰乱治安/ a ~ of contract 违反合同 ❷a gap or opening made by breaking down part of a wall, etc.(墙壁等的)破口，缺口 Ⅱ*v.*❶make a gap or opening in a wall,etc.使(墙壁等)有缺口 ❷not to keep an agreement or promise or fail to comply with rules, laws, etc.违反；违背

bread/bred/

*n.*❶common food made of flour or meal and usually raised with yeast and then baked 面包：brown ~ 黑面包/steamed ~ 馒头/a piece of ~ 一块面包/I bought a loaf of ~ from the baker.我从面包房买了一条面包。❷livelihood 生计：~ and cheese 普通食品；生计/He barely earns his ~.他勉强能够糊口。

breadth/bredθ/

n. the distance of measurement from side to side；width 宽度：The bridge is 100 metres in length and 15 metres in ~.桥长 100 米宽 15 米。

break/breɪk/

Ⅰ*v.*(broke, broken)❶ cause to separate into pieces by force；go or come into pieces 破碎；打碎；打破；折断：I broke a bowl.我打烂一个碗。❷ fail to observe 违背；违反：You are ~ing the law.你违法了。❸ interrupt 停止；中断；打断：~ the conversation 打断谈话/~ one's journey 中止某人的旅程 ❹beat the previous record for a particular achievement 打破(纪录)‖*n.*❶ an opening between two

or more things 间隔；缝隙 ❷a place where sth. especially a bone has broken 裂缝；裂口；破裂；骨折：There is a ~ in the pipe.这根管子有裂缝。❸ a short time when one stops doing sth.；a short rest from work 暂停；休息：We have a ~ between classes.我们有课间休息。‖~ away(from)突然离开，脱逃，脱离；与……决裂，改掉，破除/~ down 破除，毁掉，压倒，中止，停顿，(身体)垮了/~ in 闯入，打断/~ in on(upon)打扰；打断/~ into 破门而入；突然……起来/~ off 突然停止；中断/~ out 爆发，突然发生/~ up 打碎；驱散/~ with 与……绝交；破除 ‖~neck *adj.*危险的/~through *n.* 突破/~water *n.*防浪堤/~wind *n.*防风林；挡风墙/~able *adj.*&. *n.*易破碎的(东西)/~er *n.*激浪；拍岸巨浪

breakage/ˈbreɪkɪdʒ/

*n.*❶ an act of breaking 破裂；破损 ❷a broken place or part 破裂处：Have the workmen found the ~ in the water mains? 工人们找到了总输水管的破漏处吗？❸ broken articles 破损的物件：The hotel allows £150 a year for ~s.该旅馆每年备有 150 英镑的损失费。

breakaway/ˈbreɪkəweɪ/

Ⅰ*n.* becoming separate from a larger group 脱离；独立 Ⅱ*adj.*separated from a large group 脱离(群体)的

breakdown/ˈbreɪkdaʊn/

*n.*❶a failure in machinery, etc.(机器等的)故障，毛病：There was a ~ on the railway and all the trains were delayed several hours.铁路出了毛病，所有的火车均延误了数小时。❷collapse；weakening (体力)不支；病倒；衰弱：He is suffering from a nervous ~.他正患神经衰弱。❸a division by types or into smaller groups 分类：a statistical ~ of data 数据的统计性分类

breakfast/ˈbrekfəst/

Ⅰ*n.*the first meal of a day 早饭；早餐：at ~ 早餐时；在进早餐/have ~ 吃早饭/He hasn't eaten much ~.他早餐没有吃多少。Ⅱ*v.*eat breakfast 吃早点：~ on ham and eggs 早餐吃火腿鸡蛋

B

break-in/'breɪkˌɪn/
*n.*an illegal forced entry into a building or car,typically to steal sth. 非法闯入;破门而入

breakout /'breɪkaʊt/
*n.*a forcible escape, typically from prison 脱逃;越狱

breakthrough /'breɪkˌθruː/
*n.*a sudden and important discovery or development,especially in science (尤指科学上的)突破,重大成就

break-up/'breɪkˌʌp/
*n.*❶ an end to a relationship, typically a marriage (尤指婚姻关系)破裂 ❷a division of a country or organization into smaller autonomous units (国家或机构的)分裂,瓦解,解体:the ～ of the Soviet Union 苏联解体

breast/brest/
*n.*❶ either of the milk-producing parts of a woman 乳房:The baby is still at its mother's ～.这婴儿仍在吃奶。❷ the chest;the upper front part of the body between the neck and the stomach 胸;胸部;胸口:a ～ pocket 上衣前胸的口袋/beat one's ～胸顿足/a troubled ～ 心烦意乱 ‖ make a clean ～ of 坦白;和盘托出

breastfeed/'brestfiːd/
v.(breastfed) feed a baby with milk from the mother's breast (母亲)直接哺乳;(以母乳)喂奶

breath/breθ/
*n.*❶ air taken into and sent out of lungs 呼吸:draw a long ～ 做一次深呼吸/take a deep ～ 深深地吸一口气 ❷life 生命:I will work hard as long as I have ～只要我还有一口气,我就会拼命干。‖ catch one's ～ 喘息/hold one's ～ 屏息/lose one's ～ 喘不过气来/in a ～ 一口气,一举/in the same ～ 同时;can not be mentioned in the same ～ 不可同日而语/out of ～ 气喘吁吁/under one's ～ 轻声地/waste one's ～ 白费气力

breathable/'breθəbl/
adj.(of material used in making clothes) allowing air to pass through (衣料)透气的;Breathable,waterproof clothing is es-sential for most outdoor sports.大多数户外运动衣服必须透气且防水。

breathe/briːð/
*v.*❶ take air into your lungs and send it out again 呼吸:The air was so cold we could hardly ～.空气非常寒冷,我们难以呼吸。❷send air, smoke,etc.out of your mouth 呼出 ❸ say sth. quietly 低声说:"Follow me." she ～d.“跟我来。”她轻声说。❹ (of material or soil)admit or emit air or moisture (材料,土壤)透水,透气:Cotton clothing allows your skin to ～.棉织品能使皮肤透气。‖ ～ again 放宽心/～ your last 断气;死掉

breathing /'briːðɪŋ/
n. the process of taking air into and expelling it from the lungs 呼吸

breathless /'breθlɪs/
*adj.*❶out of breath,panting 气喘吁吁的 ❷ holding your breath with excitement (由于激动而)屏息的: He was ～ with shock.他震惊得屏住了呼吸。‖ ～ly *adv.*气喘地;屏息地

breathtaking /'breθˌteɪkɪŋ/
*adj.*very exciting,spectacular 激动人心的;动人心魄的

breed/briːd/
Ⅰ*v.*(bred) ❶ give birth to young;reproduce 生育;繁殖:Mice ～ quickly.老鼠繁殖很快。❷ keep (animals,etc.) for the purpose of producing young,especially in a controlled way 饲养,使繁殖:She bred a big fat pig.她喂了一头大肥猪。❸ educate,bring up 训练;教养:He was well bred in his childhood.他在童年时代受到了良好的教育。Ⅱ*n.*a kind or type of a thing or person 品种;类型:This is a new ～ of horse.这是新品种的马。‖ ～ in and in 同种繁殖;近亲结婚/～ out and out 异种繁殖 ‖ ～er *n.*饲养员

breeding /'briːdɪŋ/
*n.*good manners resulting from training or background 教养:a girl of good ～ 一个有良好教养的女孩

breeze/briːz/
*n.*a light gentle wind 微风:A ～ blew o-ver the lake.微风吹过湖面。

breezy /'briːzi/

adj.❶ pleasantly windy 轻风拂面的；有微风的：～ weather 惠风和畅的天气 ❷ merry, light and bright in manner 轻松自在的；怡然的：He has a ～ manner.他举止轻快活泼。

brethren /'breðrən/

n.(pl.) people who are members of the same society as yourself 同道；同仁

brevity /'brevəti/

n. shortness (of statements, human life, and other non-material things) 简洁；简短；短暂：Brevity is the soul of wit. 言以简洁为贵。

brew /bruː/

v.❶ make beer; make (tea or coffee) with hot water and prepare for drinking 酿酒；调制饮料：We ～ tea in boiling water.我们用开水泡茶。 ❷ be in preparation or ready to happen; develop 酝酿；即将发生：A storm is ～ing.风暴即将来临。 ‖ ～er n.酿酒者；酿酒商

brewery /'bruːəri/

n.a place where beer is brewed 啤酒厂；酿造厂

bribe /braɪb/

Ⅰ n.sth. given, offered, or promised to sb. in order to get him to do sth. in favour of the giver 贿赂：give a ～ 行贿 Ⅱ v.offer, give a bribe to 向……行贿；收买：～ a judge 贿赂法官/He had been ～d into silence.他接受贿赂保持沉默。

bribery /'braɪbəri/

n.the giving or offering of a bribe 行贿；贿赂；受贿

brick /brɪk/

Ⅰ n.❶ a clay moulded and baked by fire or sun, used for building purposes 砖；砖块：a house made of red ～s 一所红砖造的房子/a ～ wall 砖墙 ❷ a child's (usually wooden) toy, building block 积木 ❸ a thing shaped like a brick 砖状物：a ～ of icecream 一块冰砖 ❹ a generous or loyal person 慷慨的人；忠诚的人：She's real ～.她真是个好心人。 Ⅱ v.fill in, block or seal an opening with bricks 用砖围砌；用砖堵住：～ up a window 用砖将窗户堵住

brickwork /'brɪkwɜːk/

n.❶ a structure made of bricks 砖结构 ❷ (pl.) a place where bricks are made 砖厂；砖窑

bride /braɪd/

n.a woman on her wedding-day; a newly married woman 新娘；‖ bridal adj.新娘的；婚礼的

bridegroom /'braɪdgrum, -gruːm/

n.a man on his wedding day; a newly married man 新郎

bridesmaid /'braɪdzmeɪd/

n. a young woman or girl who helps a bride before and during the marriage ceremony 女傧相；伴娘

bridge /brɪdʒ/

Ⅰ n.a structure of wood, stone, steel, concrete, etc. carrying a road across a river, canal, railway, etc.桥；桥梁：They put up a ～ across the river.他们在河上建了一座桥。 Ⅱ v. build or form a bridge over sth. 架桥；建桥：The soldiers ～d the river quickly.战士们很快地在河上架起了桥。

bridle /'braɪdl/

Ⅰ n. leather straps that you put over a horse's head to control the horse 马笼头；缰绳：a horse without a ～ 一匹脱缰的马 Ⅱ v.put a bridle on(a horse); control or check 给(马)上辔头；控制；约束：～ a horse 给马系缰辔/～ one's temper 控制脾气 ‖ give the ～ to 放纵；放纵

brief /briːf/

Ⅰ adj.lasting only for a short time 短暂的；简短的：a ～ letter 一封简短的信/a ～ stay 短暂的逗留 Ⅱ n.a summary of the facts of the legal case prepared for a barrister 案情摘要：This is the ～ of the case.这就是那起案件的简要情况。 Ⅲ v. give essential information 简要说明：He ～ed us on the present situation.他简要地给我们介绍了当前的形势。 ‖ in ～简言之；简单地说 ‖ ～ly adv.简要地；简短地

briefcase /'briːfkeɪs/

n.a flat case for carrying documents 公文包；公事包

briefing /'briːfɪŋ/
n. ❶ a meeting for giving someone instructions or information 情况介绍会 ❷ the information or instructions given 简要说明；指令：This ~ explains the products and standards.这个简要说明介绍产品和标准。

brigade /brɪ'geɪd/
n. ❶ a large group of soldiers that forms a unit of an army 旅：the light ~ 轻骑兵旅 ❷ a group of people, usually with a special uniform, who have certain duties, such as putting out fires 工作队：a fire ~ 消防队/a shock ~ 突击队

bright /braɪt/
adj. ❶ giving out or reflecting much light；shining 明亮的；耀眼的；闪光的：a ~ day 晴朗的日子 ❷ having a vivid colour 鲜艳的：a bundle of ~ flowers 一束鲜艳的花 ❸ cheerful and happy；lit up with joy and hope 开朗的；欢快的：faces 愉快的面容/~ looks 高兴的神色/speak in a ~ voice 喜气洋洋地讲话 ❹ clever, quick-witted 聪明的；伶俐的：He is a ~ boy.他是个聪明的孩子。‖ ~ly *adv.*明亮地；鲜艳地/~ness *n.*明亮

brighten /'braɪtn/
v. (cause to) grow brighter or brighter 变亮；使发亮：The day ~ed. 天亮了。/These flowers ~ the room. 这些花使满室生辉。

brilliant /'brɪljənt/
adj. ❶ very bright；splendid；magnificent 光辉的；耀眼的：a ~ jewel 耀眼的珠宝/a ~ future 光辉的前程 ❷ very clever；outstanding；remarkable 聪明的；有才智的：a ~ young man 才华横溢的年轻人 ‖ **brilliance** *n.*光彩；光辉

brim /brɪm/
n. ❶ the edge of a cup, bowl, glass, etc. (杯、碗等的)边，缘：The glass is full to the ~.杯子满了。 ❷ the out-turned part of a hat, that gives shade 帽沿；帽檐：He wore a hat with a broad ~.他戴着一顶宽边帽。‖ ~ful *adj.*满溢的；洋溢着……的

brine /braɪn/
n. ❶ salt water, especially for pickling (腌食物的)盐水，咸水 ❷ seawater 海水

bring /brɪŋ/
v. ❶ come with sth. or sb. from somewhere else；cause (sb. or sth.) to be where the speaker is 带来；拿来；领来；取来：He brought me a glass of brandy.他给我端来一杯白兰地。 ❷ make sth. happen；cause to come 引起；导致：What ~s you here? 什么风把你吹到这儿来了？‖ ~ about 带来；造成/~ around 使改变思想；劝使；使恢复健康/~ back 带回；使回忆起；使恢复/~ down 击落；打倒；使降低/~ down the house 使全场轰动/~ forth 使产生；生(孩子)；开(花)；结(果)/~ forward 提出；提前；使涌现出/~ home (to) 使明白；使清楚/~ in 收；产生；挣得；引进/~ off 使成功；完成；救出/~ on 引起；导致；使发展/~ out 使显出；使明白；出版；生产/~ over 使看法转变/~ through 救活；使渡过困难/~ to 使苏醒/~ to an end (a close, a halt, etc.) 使结束(停顿，停止等)/~ to bear on 对……施加(压力、影响等)/~ to light 发现；让人知道/~ to pass 使发生；使成为事实/~ under 镇压，压制；使就范/~ up 提出；抚养；教育；呕吐

brink /brɪŋk/
n. the upper edge of a steep place, a sharp slope, etc.；the border of water 边缘；水边：the ~ of a pond 池塘边/the ~ of a precipice 悬崖边缘 ‖ on the ~ of 濒临；濒于

brisk /brɪsk/
adj. (of persons and movement) active；lively；quick-moving 轻快的；活泼的：a ~ walk 轻快的散步/a ~ trade 生意兴隆/a ~ wind 凉爽的风

bristle /'brɪsl/
Ⅰ *n.* a short stiff coarse hair 短而硬的毛：a toothbrush with stiff ~s 硬毛牙刷 Ⅱ *v.* ❶ (of hair) stand up (毛发)竖立：The dog was angry and ~d up.狗发脾气了，毛都竖立起来了。 ❷ react in an offended or angry manner 被激怒，发怒，生气：~ with anger 怒发冲冠 ❸ have plenty of (usually sth. unpleasant) (困难)重重：The work ~s with difficulties.这项工作

困难重重。

bristly /ˈbrɪsli/
*adj.*like or full of bristles 刚毛似的；布满刚毛的

brittle /ˈbrɪtl/
*adj.*hard but easy to break or snap 硬而易碎的；脆性的：Her bones became fragile and ～.她的骨头变得脆而易碎。

broach/brəʊtʃ/
*v.*begin to talk about sth.开始谈论；提出：He ～ed the subject of the summer holiday.他谈起暑假的事。

broad/brɔːd/
*adj.*❶wide；having a large distance from side to side 宽的；宽阔的：a ～ river 很宽的河/the ～ sea 宽阔的海洋/He has a ～ mind.他宽宏大量。❷including a great variety of people or things 广泛的 ❸general；without detail 概括的；粗略的 ❹large in area 开阔的 ❺clear or obvious 明确的，明显的 ‖ ～ **daylight** 大白天/in the ～ **sense** 广义而言

broadcast/ˈbrɔːdkɑːst/
Ⅰ*v.*(broadcast) send out or give as a radio (or television) presentation 广播；播送；播映：A special message was ～ this morning.今天早晨广播了一条特别消息。Ⅱ*n.*an act of sending sound and/or pictures by radio or television 广播；播送：Did you listen to the ～ of the football match? 你听了这次足球赛的广播吗？ ‖ ～**er** *n.*播音员/～**ing** *n.*广播；播音

broaden/ˈbrɔːdn/
*v.*make or become broad or broader 变阔；放宽；扩展：They have ～ed the road. 他们已加宽了路面。/We ～ed in experience by travelling. 旅行使我们增长了见识。

broadly/ˈbrɔːdli/
*adv.*❶in a broad way 宽阔地；敞开地；广泛地 ❷in a general way 总地；大体地：Broadly speaking, I agree with you. 总的来说；我同意你的说法。

broad-minded/ˌbrɔːdˈmaɪndɪd/
*adj.*having or showing willingness to respect the opinions of others even if very different from one's own 思想开明的；宽

宏大量的：a ～ man 一个宽宏大量的人

brocade/brəˈkeɪd/
*n.*a woven material richly ornamented with designs in raised gold or silver thread 锦缎；织锦

brochure/brəʊʃə(r)/
*n.*a small thin book，especially one giving instructions or details of a service offered for money 小册子：travel ～s 旅游小册子

broil/brɔɪl/
*v.*cook meat by using direct heat 烤；烧肉

broke/brəʊk/
*adj.*having no money，penniless；bankrupt 身无分文的；不名一文的；破产的：He is ～.他身无分文。/His firm has gone ～. 他的公司破产了。

broken/ˈbrəʊkən/
adj. ❶violently separated into parts or pieces 破碎的：a ～ cup 破杯子 ❷interrupted；disconnected 中断的；间断的：a ～ sleep 间断的睡眠 ❸damaged；not in working condition 损坏的；破损的：a ～ watch 一只破表 ❹(of an agreement or a promise)not kept or be breached 违反的；违背的

broker/ˈbrəʊkə(r)/
*n.*a person who acts for other people in buying and selling shares in business 经纪人；掮客

brokerage /ˈbrəʊkərɪdʒ/
*n.*❶the business of being a broker 经纪业务：a ～ firm 经纪公司 ❷a fee or commission charged by a broker 佣金；回扣

bromide/ˈbrəʊmaɪd/
*n.*any of several chemical compounds，used in medicine to calm excitement 溴化物(用作镇静剂)

bromine/ˈbrəʊmiːn/
*n.*a non-metallic element，compound of which are used in photographic and other chemicals 溴

bronze/brɒnz/
Ⅰ*n.*❶alloy of copper and tin 青铜(铜与锡之合金)：a ～ statue 铜像/the Bronze Age 青铜器时代 ❷a colour of bronze 古铜色；赤褐色 ❸a work of art made of bronze 青铜器：a fine collection of ～s

and ivories 所收藏的一批精制的青铜器及象牙制品 Ⅱ v. make（sth.）bronze in colour 使变成青铜色；a face ~d by the sun 晒成青铜色的脸 Ⅲ adj. made of or having the colour of bronze 青铜制的；青铜色的；古铜色的：a ~ vase 青铜花瓶

brooch /brəʊtʃ/
n. an ornament fastened by a pin, worn on a dress, etc.（别在女服上的）胸针，饰针

brood /bruːd/
Ⅰ n. the young birds hatched at one time in the nest 一窝，同窝幼雏：a ~ of chickens 一窝小鸡 Ⅱ v.❶sit on eggs as a female bird does 孵蛋：The hen ~s（on）ten eggs this time. 此次这母鸡孵蛋十个。❷think about sth. for a long time 沉思；思考：She sat in the corner and ~ed（over）her misfortune. 她坐在角落里，默默想着她的不幸。

brook¹ /brʊk/
n. a small stream 小溪

brook² /brʊk/
v. to tolerate sth. 容忍；忍受：He would ~ no argument. 他不允许有任何争辩。

broom /bruːm/
n. a large sweeping brush, usually with a long handle 扫帚：He swept the floor with a ~. 他用扫帚扫地。/A new ~ sweeps clean. 新官上任三把火。

broth /brɒθ/
n. soup（especially one made with meat）汤（尤指肉汤）

brother /ˈbrʌðə(r)/
n. a son of the same parents as another person; an unusually close friend; a member of the same club or group 兄；弟；弟兄；伙伴：an elder ~ 哥哥/a sworn ~ 结义兄弟

brotherhood /ˈbrʌðəhʊd/
n.❶the relationship of brothers 兄弟关系 ❷friendliness and companionship between men, or between people in general 手足情谊

brotherly /ˈbrʌðəli/
adj.❶of or like a brother 兄弟的；如兄弟的：~ affection 兄弟般的友爱 ❷friendly; kind 友爱的；亲切的：He talked to me

in a ~ way. 他亲切地和我交谈。

brow /braʊ/
n. the arch of hair above the eye; forehead 眉；眉毛；额：He sat there silently with knitted ~s. 他皱着眉头一言不发地坐在那儿。

brown /braʊn/
Ⅰ adj. having the colour of earth 棕色的；褐色的：~ paper 棕色包装纸；牛皮纸/~ sugar 红糖 Ⅱ n.❶the color of earth 棕色；褐色；咖啡色：leaves of various shades of ~ 各种深浅不同的棕色叶子 ❷brown clothes 棕色衣服：I like to wear ~. 我喜欢穿棕色衣服。Ⅲ v.（cause sth. to）become brown 使变成棕色（褐色）：His face was ~ed by the sun. 他的脸被太阳晒黑了。/The potatoes were ~ed in the pan. 马铃薯在锅里煎成褐色。

browse /braʊz/
Ⅰ v.❶（of cows, goats, etc.）feed by nibbling grass, leaves, etc.（牛、羊等）吃草：cattle browsing in the fields 在地里吃草的牛 ❷examine books in a casual, leisurely way 浏览（书刊）；随便翻阅：~ among books 浏览各种书籍 ❸search for information on computer, typically via Internet 尤指通过网络浏览信息 Ⅱ n.❶the act of feeding by continual nibbling grass, leaves, etc. 放牧；吃草 ❷the act of reading superficially 浏览：have a ~ in the bookshop 在书店里浏览一下

browser /ˈbraʊzə(r)/
n. a program with a graphical user interface for displaying HTML files, used to search the World Wide Web 浏览器：a Web ~ 网络浏览器

bruise /bruːz/
Ⅰ n.❶an injury to the body caused by a fall or a blow which does not break the skin 青肿；瘀伤：The ~ on his leg turned black and blue. 他脚上的瘀伤变成黑紫色。❷an injury to the outside of a fruit, vegetable, or plant（水果、蔬菜、植物等）碰损：The pear had ~s of dark spots. 这梨有碰伤的黑斑。Ⅱ v. cause an injury or hurt 使有淤伤；伤害：She ~d her forehead when she fell. 她摔倒时伤了额头。

brunch /brʌntʃ/

n. a late breakfast; an early lunch; or a combination of the two 晚吃的早餐;早吃的午餐;早午餐

brunt /brʌnt/
n. the chief part 主要部分; bear the ~ of an attack 在攻击面前首当其冲

brush /brʌʃ/
I *n.* a tool for cleaning, smoothing or painting, made of sticks, stiff hair, nylon, etc. 刷子;画笔: He painted the wall with a ~. 他用刷子粉刷墙壁。/a writing ~ 毛笔/a tooth ~ 牙刷/a hair ~ 发刷 II *v.* clean or smooth with a brush 刷;刷洗;刷掉: We ~ our teeth every morning and evening. 我们每天早晚都要刷牙。/He ~ed the dust off his coat. 他将衣上的尘土刷掉。‖ ~ **aside** 不予理会/~ **away** 刷掉;拂掉/~ **off** 刷掉;不理会/~ **up** (**on**) 温习;重新学习

brutal /ˈbruːtl/
adj. cruel and violent 残忍的;野蛮的: a ~ attack. 野蛮的袭击 ‖ ~**ity** *n.* 残忍;暴行/~**ly** *adv.* 残忍地;野蛮地

brute /bruːt/
I *n.* a savagely violent person or animal 残忍的人;野兽 II *adj.* unreasoning and animal-like 不理智的;人面兽心的;残忍的: He is an unfeeling ~. 他是个残酷无情的畜生。

brutish /ˈbruːtɪʃ/
adj. resembling or characteristic of a brute 粗野的;野蛮的: ~ behaviour 野蛮的行为 ‖ ~**ly** *adv.* 粗野地;残酷地

bubble /ˈbʌbl/
I *n.* a hollow ball of liquid containing air or gas 气泡;水泡: blow ~s in soapy water 在肥皂水中吹气泡 II *v.* send up bubbles; rise in bubbles; make the sound of bubbles 吹泡;起泡;发出冒泡的声音: When water boils it begins to ~. 水沸腾就冒泡。

bubbly /ˈbʌbli/
I *adj.* (bubblier, bubbliest) ❶ full of bubbles 多泡的 ❷ cheerful and lively 兴高采烈的 II *n.* champagne or sparkling wine 香槟酒

bucket /ˈbʌkɪt/
n. ❶ a type of container for liquids 吊桶;水桶;桶: a fire ~ 灭火水桶 ❷ the amount of a bucket contains 一桶之量: two ~s of oil 两满桶油

buckle /ˈbʌkl/
I *n.* a fastener for fastening a belt or strap, usually made of metal（通常用金属制成的）带扣,扣环 II *v.* ❶ be fastened or fasten with a buckle 扣住;用扣子扣住 ❷ (of metal) bend under a weight（金属受压而）弯曲

bud /bʌd/
I *n.* a leaf, flower, or branch, at the beginning of its growth 芽;花蕾: The flowers are now in ~. 花现正含苞待放。 II *v.* (-dd-) put out buds 发芽;萌芽: Trees begin to ~ in the spring. 树在春天开始发芽。‖ **in** ~ 发芽;含苞欲放/**nip in the** ~ 消灭在萌芽状态;防患于未然

Buddhism /ˈbʊdɪzəm/
n. an Asian religion based on the teaching of Siddhartha Gautama (or Buddha) 佛教

budget /ˈbʌdʒɪt/
I *n.* an estimate of probable future income and expenditure 预算: a family ~ 家庭收支预算/the state financial ~ 国家财政预算 II *v.* plan to save money for 做预算: ~ for the coming year 为明年做预算

budgetary /ˈbʌdʒɪtəri/
adj. connected with a budget 预算的: ~ control (policies) 预算控制(政策)

buffalo /ˈbʌfələʊ/
n. kinds of ox in Asia, Europe, and Africa（亚洲、欧洲、非洲等）水牛: water ~ 水牛

buffer /ˈbʌfə(r)/
I *n.* ❶ projecting pieces of metal on strong springs, placed on railway engines and at the end of railway lines, to lessen the shock if a railway engine does not stop when it should or if it is hit（铁道末端的）缓冲器 ❷ a thing or person which acts in the same way 缓冲物;缓冲者 II *v.* lesson or reduce the effect of sth. 缓解;减小

buffet[1] /ˈbʊfeɪ/
n. ❶ a meal where guests serve them-

B

selves 自助餐：a ～ lunch 自助午餐 ❷a room or counter selling light meals or snacks 快餐部；the station ～车站快餐厅

buffet² /'bʌfɪt/

v.hit or knock sth. violently 猛击；敲打：Our aircraft was ～ed by strong winds.我们的飞机受到强气流的冲击。

bug /bʌg/

n.❶a small, flat, ill-smelling, blood-suck-ing insect that infests dirty houses and beds 臭虫 ❷any small insect 〈美〉虫；小昆虫

bugle /'bjuːgl/

n. a musical instrument of copper or brass, used for military signals 军号；铜号；喇叭

bugler /'bjuːglə(r)/

n.a bugle blower 号手；司号兵

build /bɪld/

Ⅰ *v*.(built) ❶make by putting parts, mate-rial, etc.together 建筑；建造；建设：～ a house 建造房屋/～ a bridge 建筑桥梁/～ the country 建设国家 ❷create or de-velop sth. 创建；开发 ‖ ～ on（upon）把……建立于；依赖；指望/～ up 树立；逐步建立；锻炼 Ⅱ *n*.the shape and size of the human body 体形；体格

builder /'bɪldə(r)/

n.a person who builds, especially a con-tractor for building houses 建筑工人；施工人员；建设者

building /'bɪldɪŋ/

n.a house or other structure 房屋；建筑物：Do you see the large ～ over there? 你看见那边那幢大楼吗?

built-in /'bɪlt'ɪn/

adj.❶forming an integral part of a struc-ture 内置的；嵌在……内的：a worktop with a ～ cooker 内嵌煤气灶的工作台 ❷（of a characteristic）inherent；innate （特性）固有的；与生俱来的

bulb /bʌlb/

n.❶ a round root of certain plants（植物的）球茎：Onions grow from ～s.洋葱是由球茎生长的。❷ any object of this shape, especially the glass part of an elec-tric lamp that gives out light 球状物；(尤

指)电灯泡：the ～ of the eye 眼球/a light ～ 灯泡 ‖ ～ous *adj*.球茎状的

bulge /bʌldʒ/

Ⅰ *n*.❶a swelling of a surface caused by pressure from within or below 膨胀；凸出 ❷ a temporary increase in volume or numbers（体积、数目等的）暂时增加，暴增：population ～ 人口膨胀 Ⅱ *v*.swell be-yond the usual size 凸出；鼓起：His pock-ets were bulging with apples.他的口袋因装满苹果而胀得鼓鼓的。/He ～d his cheeks.他鼓起两颊。

bulk /bʌlk/

n.a great size, shape, mass or quantity 大体积；大量；大批：a man of large ～ 身材魁梧的人/～ buying 大量购买 ‖ in ～ 大批；大量；散装 ‖ ～y *adj*.庞大的；巨大的；笨重的

bull /bʊl/

n.the male of any animal in the cow fami-ly 公牛 ‖ a ～ in a china shop 乱闯祸的人；大老粗/take the ～ by the horns 不畏艰险 ‖ ～'s-eye *n*.靶心

bulldog /'bʊldɒg/

n.a type of small but strong and brave dog 牛头犬(一种小而勇猛的狗)

bulldoze /'bʊldəʊz/

v.❶clear an area with a bulldozer（用推土机）把……夷为平地 ❷force sb. to do sth. 强迫，威吓：He ～d them into accep-ting it.他强迫他们接受。

bulldozer /'bʊldəʊzə(r)/

n.a large vehicle for moving earth, etc.推土机

bullet /'bʊlɪt/

n.a shape piece of lead, usually coated with another metal, to be fired from a gun 子弹；枪弹：machine-gun ～s 机枪子弹

bulletin /'bʊlətɪn/

n.an official statement of news 公告；公报；布告：a news ～ 新闻公报/～ board 布告牌

bullish /'bʊlɪʃ/

adj.❶feeling confident and positive about the future 对未来有信心的；积极乐观的；in a ～ mood 满怀希望 ❷causing, or

B

connected with an increase in the price of shares (对股票价格)看涨的,牛市的:a ~ market 牛市

bully/ˈbʊli/

Ⅰ *n.* a person who uses his strength or power to frighten or hurt those who are weak 恶霸;暴徒;打手:play the ~ 横行霸道;欺软怕硬 Ⅱ *v.* use strength, etc., in this way 威吓;威逼;欺侮:~ one's way through 唬过去/You can't ~ me into doing it.你不能强逼着我做。

bum/bʌm/

n. ❶ the part of the body on which one sits 臀部;屁股 ❷ a habitual beggar or loafer 游荡者;乞丐;游手好闲的人

bumblebee/ˈbʌmblbiː/

n. a type of large bee 大黄蜂

bump/bʌmp/

Ⅰ *v.* hurt (one's head, etc.) by striking it against or on sth. 碰;撞:He ~ed his head against the wall. 他的头撞到了墙上。 Ⅱ *n.* ❶ a blow or knock 碰;撞:a ~ between two cars 两车相撞 ❷ a swelling on the body caused by such a blow (因碰撞造成的)肿块:He made a ~ on his head.他头上碰肿了一块。

bumper/ˈbʌmpə(r)/

Ⅰ *n.* a very full cup or glass 满杯 Ⅱ *adj.* usually large or abundant 丰盛的;大胜利的:a ~ harvest 丰收/~ crops 硕果累累的农作物

bumptious/ˈbʌmpʃəs/

adj. having too much confidence in one's own ability 高傲的;狂妄的

bumpy /ˈbʌmpi/

adj. (bumpier, bumpiest) full of bumps; causing jolts 不平的;多凸块的:a ~ road 崎岖不平的小路 ‖ bumpiness *n.*崎岖不平;颠簸

bun/bʌn/

n. ❶ a small sweet cake, often containing dried fruit 小甜面包;干果甜面包 ❷ hair twisted into a knot at the back of the head (扎在头后的)髻

bunch/bʌntʃ/

Ⅰ *n.* ❶ a number of things of the same kind fastened or growing together (一)

串;(一)束:a ~ of grapes 一串葡萄 ❷ a group (一)群:a ~ of sheep 一群羊 Ⅱ *v.* come or bring together into a bunch or bunches 聚成一簇;捆成一束:To keep warm,the sheep ~ed up in the shed. 为了保暖羊群在羊舍中挤在一起。/The florist ~ed the flowers and sold them at two dollars each ~.花匠把花捆成花束,每束售价两美元。 ‖ ~y *adj.*成束的

bundle/ˈbʌndl/

n. a number of articles fastened, tied, or wrapped together 捆;束;包:a ~ of chopsticks 一捆筷子/a ~ of clothes 一包衣服

bung/bʌŋ/

n. a piece of cork, rubber or other material, for putting in the hold in the side or end of a barrel 塞子;桶塞

bungalow/ˈbʌŋɡələʊ/

n. a house with only one storey 平房

bungle/ˈbʌŋɡl/

v. do sth. or make sth. very badly 把(事情)做糟,搞坏

buoy/bɔɪ/

Ⅰ *n.* an object which floats in the water, placed there to show hidden dangers to ships 浮标;浮筒 Ⅱ *v.* keep afloat; keep up 使浮起;支持;鼓励:~ up his hopes 激起他的希望

buoyancy/ˈbɔɪənsi/

n. the power to float or keep things floating 浮力:Salt water has more ~ than fresh water.海水比淡水浮力大。

buoyant /ˈbɔɪənt/

adj. ❶ able to float 能浮起的 ❷ cheerful and optimistic 轻松愉快的;乐观的:He was in a ~ mood. 他很乐观。 ‖ ~ly *adv.*有浮力地;心情愉快地

burden/ˈbɜːdn/

Ⅰ *n.* sth. to be carried; sth. difficult to bear 担子;负担;包袱:I don't want to add to your ~.我不想增加你的负担。 Ⅱ *v.* load or trouble 使负担:He is ~ed with a heavy debt.他负债累累。 ‖ ~some *adj.* 繁重的;累赘的

bureau/ˈbjʊərəʊ/

n. (*pl.* ~s or bureaux/ˈbjʊərəʊz/) ❶ a

government or municipal department or office 局;处;办公署;the Political Bureau of the Central Committee of the Communist Party of China 中国共产党中央委员会政治局/a travel ～ 旅行社/information ～ 新闻处 ❷ a writing desk with drawers (有抽屉的)办公桌,写字台 ❸ a chest of drawers for clothes, usually with a mirror (装着镜子的)衣柜,五屉柜

bureaucracy /bjʊəˈrɒkrəsi/
n. a government by paid officials not elected by the people, officials who keep their positions whatever political party is in power; this system of government 官僚政治;官僚主义

bureaucrat /ˈbjʊərəkræt/
n. an official who works in a bureau or government department, especially one who obeys the rules of his department with exercising much judgement 官僚;官僚主义者

bureaucratic /ˌbjʊərəˈkrætɪk/
adj. of or like a bureaucrat; carried on according to official rules and habits 官僚主义的;官僚政治的;官僚作风的:～ government 官僚政府

burette /bjʊəˈret/
n. a graduated glass tube with a tap at the bottom, for measuring small quantities of liquid or gas 滴定管;量管

burglar /ˈbɜːglə(r)/
n. a person who breaks into a house or building by night to steal or commit some other crime 夜贼;窃贼:Burglars broke into his house last night. 昨晚窃贼闯入他家里。

burial /ˈberɪəl/
n. the act, action, or ceremony of putting a dead body into a grave 安葬;埋葬;葬礼:a ～ case 棺材/a ～ ground 安葬地

burly /ˈbɜːli/
adj. (of a person) big and strong (人)粗壮的,魁伟的

burn /bɜːn/
I *v.* (burnt or burned) ❶ produce light 发光;发亮:The lights were ～ing all night. 这些灯整夜都亮着。❷ destroy,

damage, or hurt by fire, heat, or the action of acid 烧毁;烧伤:He ～ed his hand. 他烧伤了手。❸ be on fire or alight; be in flames; be hot; be capable of giving out light and heat 着火;点燃;烧着;照明:oil 烧油/～ coal 烧煤/～ a candle 点蜡烛 ‖ ～ **away** 烧着;烧掉/～ **down** 烧毁/～ **off** 烧掉/～ **out** 烧坏;烧光/～ **the candle at both ends** 过度劳累/～ **the midnight oil** 开夜车/～ **up** 烧掉,烧旺起来/～ **with** 有(强烈的情绪或要求)II *n.* an injury or a mark, made by fire, heat or acid 烧伤;灼伤:There are several ～s on his arms. 他双臂上有好几处烧伤。

burning /ˈbɜːnɪŋ/
adj. ❶ intense or extreme 强烈的;极度的:a ～ ambition 勃勃雄心 ❷ hotly discussed; vital 热烈争论的;十分重要的:a ～ question 当务之急

burnout /ˈbɜːnaʊt/
n. ❶ the reduction of a fuel or substance to nothing through use or combustion 燃尽;烧光:good carbon ～ 碳的充分燃烧 ❷ physical or mental collapse caused by overwork or stress (过劳或紧张导致的)精疲力竭,精神崩溃

burrow /ˈbʌrəʊ/
I *n.* a hole made in the ground and used as a home or shelter by rabbits, foxes, etc.(兔子、狐狸等在地下挖的)洞穴:Rabbits live in ～s. 兔子住在洞里面。II *v.* make (a hole, etc.) by digging 挖掘;打洞:～ a hole in the sand 在沙地里掘个洞

burst /bɜːst/
I *v.* (burst) ❶ (of a container) break suddenly and violently apart, especially as a result of an impact or pressure 爆炸;炸裂;崩裂:The boiler ～. 锅炉爆炸了。❷ begin doing sth. suddenly 突然发生;爆发:～ out laughing 突然大笑起来/～ into tears 突然大哭起来/～ with anger 勃然大怒/～ into the room 闯入房间 ‖ be ～ing to 急着要(做)/～ forth 突然出现(发出)/～ in (upon, on) 突然打断/～ upon 突然明白/～ open 猛然打开 II *n.* a sudden brief outbreak 突发;迸发:a ～ of laughter 一阵大笑/a ～ of cheers 一阵欢

呼

bury/'beri/

　v. put into the grave; hide sth. in the ground 埋葬；埋藏，掩藏：After the battle they buried the dead.战斗过后,他们埋葬了死者。‖ ~ **sb.alive** 活埋/ ~ **oneself in** (**be buried in**)专心致力于

bus/bʌs/

　I n. a large passenger vehicle, especially one serving public on fixed route 公共汽车：trolley ~ 电车/Shall we walk or go by ~? 我们是走路还是乘公共汽车？ II v.(-ss-) ❶travel by bus 乘公共汽车：We ~sed to work.我乘公共汽车上班。❷ transport by bus 用公共汽车运送：~ the children to school 用公共汽车把孩子送往学校

bush/buʃ/

　n. ❶ a low-growing plant with several or many woody stems coming up from the root 灌木；矮树：They hid in the ~es.他们藏在灌木丛中。❷a wild land that has not been cleared, especially in Australia or Africa（尤指澳大利亚、非洲）荒野‖ **beat about**（**around**）**the** ~旁敲侧击；说话拐弯抹角

bushel/'buʃl/

　n. a measure for grain and fruit（8 gallons）蒲式耳（计量谷类和水果的单位，相当于8加仑）：a Chinese ~ 一斗

bushy/'buʃi/

　adj. ❶covered with bushes 灌木丛生的 ❷thick and rough 浓密的：~ eyebrows 浓眉

business/'bɪznɪs/

　n. ❶ one's work or employment 商业；买卖；生意：It's a pleasure to do ~ with you.和你做生意很愉快。❷a particular money-earning activity or place,such as a shop 营业；商店；商号：He has a ~ there. 他在那里有家商店。❸work; duty; task 工作；职责；事务：What's your ~? 你的工作是什么？ / It's none of your ~.不关你的事。‖ **get down to** ~ 着手干/**have** ~ **with** 与……有关/**have no** ~ **to do** (**doing**) 无权干/**on** ~ 因公；办事/**mind one's own** ~ 莫管闲事

bustle/'bʌsl/

　I v.（cause to）move about quickly and noisily（使）匆忙：She ~d the children off to school. 她催促孩子们上学去。/ She is bustling about in the kitchen. 她在厨房不停地忙。 II n. quick and noisy movement 忙碌；熙攘：without hurry or ~ 不慌不忙

busy/'bɪzi/

　I adj. ❶having a great deal to do; not free 忙碌的；没有空闲的；工作繁忙的：be ~ with one's work 忙于自己的工作/be ~ doing something 忙于做某事/the ~ farming season 农忙时节/The bees are ~ collecting honey. 蜜蜂忙着采蜜。❷ full of people or activity 热闹的；繁华的：a ~ road 人来人往的街道/The shops are ~ before Christmas.商店在圣诞节都很热闹。❸full of work or activity 工作忙的：a ~ day 忙碌的一天❹in use; engaged 占用着的；没空儿的：The line is ~! （Line's ~!）电话占线！ II v. make oneself not free 使忙碌：~ oneself with some tasks 忙着工作/She busies herself (in) keeping the room in order.她忙着整理房间。

busybody/'bɪzɪbɒdi/

　n. a person who takes too much interest in the affairs of others 好管闲事的人

but/bʌt/

　I conj. ❶against what might be expected; in spite of this 而,相反；尽管如此：I'm poor ~ honest. 我虽穷但却诚实。❷ without it being the case that 若不：It never rains ~ it pours.不雨则已,一雨倾盆。 II prep. other than; except 除了：Who ~ a fool would do such a thing? 除了傻子外,谁会做这种事？ III adv. only; no more than 仅仅：He is ~ a child.他不过是个孩子。/We can ~ try.我们只能试试。

butcher/'butʃə(r)/

　I n. a person who kills, cuts up and sells animals for food 屠夫；屠户；肉贩 II v. kill violently, especially with a knife 屠宰；残杀

butler/ˈbʌtlə(r)/
n. a chief male servant in a house 男管家

butt/bʌt/
n. ❶a shooting-range; the targets and the mound of earth behind them 靶场; 靶子 ❷a person who is a target for jokes 笑柄; 抨击的对象: make a ～ of someone. 取笑某人

butter/ˈbʌtə(r)/
Ⅰ *n.* the yellow fat made from cream or milk 黄油; 奶油; 白脱油: spread ～ on bread 涂奶油于面包上 Ⅱ *v.* put butter on 涂黄油于……之上: ～ bread 把面包涂上黄油

butterfly/ˈbʌtəflaɪ/
n. an insect with four wings, often brightly coloured, and feelers 蝴蝶

buttock/ˈbʌtək/
n. either side of that part of the body on which one sits 臀部: the left ～ 左臀/ a smack on the ～s 打在屁股上的一巴掌

button/ˈbʌtn/
Ⅰ *n.* ❶a knob or round piece sewn onto clothing or other things used for fastening two parts together or decorating 纽扣; 扣子: He put on a coat with brass ～s.他穿着一件有铜扣的上衣。 ❷a button-like object used for controlling a machine, an apparatus, etc. or used as a handle or catch, either to take hold of, or to push, or to turn 按钮; 把手: press the ～ 按电钮 Ⅱ *v.* fasten (with a button or buttons) 扣(纽扣): He ～ed the top ～ of his shirt.他把衬衫最上面的纽扣扣起来了。/ This dress ～s at the back.这件衣服是背上扣扣的。‖ **～hole** *n.* 扣眼; 纽扣孔

buttress/ˈbʌtrɪs/
n. a support for a wall 扶壁; 支墩

buy/baɪ/
v. (bought) ❶obtain sth. by paying money for it 买; 购买: Jack bought a new car last week.杰克上个星期买了一辆新车。 ❷be enough to pay for sth. 够支付: Five yuan doesn't ～ much nowadays. 如今五块钱买不到多少东西了。 ❸persuade sb. to do sth. dishonest in return for money 买通; 收买; 贿赂: He can't be bought.他是收买不了的。 ❹obtain sth. by losing sth. else of great value 以……为代价: Her fame was bought at the expense of her marriage.她出了名, 却牺牲了她的婚姻。‖ ～ **off** 出钱免役; 收买/～ **out** 买下……的(全部产权)/～ **over** 收买; 贿赂/～ **up** 全买; 买光

buyer/ˈbaɪə/
n. ❶a person who makes a purchase 购买者; 买主 ❷a person employed to select and purchase stock or materials for a large retail or manufacturing business, etc.采购员

buzz/bʌz/
Ⅰ *v.* ❶make such a noise as bees do 发出嗡嗡声: The bees were ～ing among flowers.蜜蜂在花丛中嗡嗡作响。 ❷sound confusedly 发嘈杂声: The room ～ed with excitement. 室内发出兴奋的嘈杂声。 Ⅱ *n.* the noise made by bees (蜜蜂的)嗡嗡声

buzzard/ˈbʌzəd/
n. a vulture, especially a turkey vulture 兀鹫(尤指红头美洲鹫)

buzzer /ˈbʌzə/
n. an electrical device, similar to a bell, that makes a buzzing noise and is used for signalling 蜂鸣器

by/baɪ/
Ⅰ *prep.* ❶near; at or to the side of 靠近; 在……旁: ～ the window 靠近窗边 ❷past and beyond 通过; 经过: He walked ～ me quietly.他不声不响地从我旁边走过去了。 ❸ through the use or means of 通过; 靠; 用: Will you go there ～ train? 你将乘火车去吗? / The man makes a living ～ begging.这人以乞讨为生。 ❹not later than; before 不迟于; 在……之前: ～ the end of this term 在本学期末之前 ❺during 在……时间: They work ～ night.他们夜间工作。 Ⅱ *adv.* ❶ near 近旁: When nobody was ～, the old man felt lonely.老人身边没人时, 觉得很寂寞。 ❷ so as to go past 过去; 经过: I saw him pass ～.我见他走过去了。‖ ～ **all means** 必定/～ **and** ～ 不久; 一会儿/～ **and large** 大体上; 基本上; 总的说来/～ **far** 非常地; 甚; 最最/～ **chance** (acci-

dent）偶然地/~ leaps and bounds 快速地/~ means of 靠;借助/~ mistake 出于误会;弄错/~ no means 绝不;一点也不/~ oneself 独自/~ the side of 在……旁边/~ the way（~ the ~）顺便说起/~ turns 轮流/~ way of 取道;经由/side ~ side 紧靠;并/stand ~ 支持/take ~ surprise 突袭;出其不意攻击

bye-bye/ˈbaɪˈbaɪ/

Ⅰ n.（child's word for）sleep, bed（儿语）睡觉;床铺:go to ~s去睡觉 Ⅱ int.goodbye 再见

by(e)-law/ˈbaɪlɔː/

n.a law or regulation made by a local authority 地方法

bygone/ˈbaɪɡɒn/

adj.gone by; past 过去的;以往的:in ~ years 在以往的年代里

bypass/ˈbaɪpɑːs/

Ⅰ n.a road providing a secondary passage to be used instead of the main passage 旁路;岔道:take the ~ to avoid the traffic in the centre of the city 为避免市中心车辆而走旁道 Ⅱ v.go around 绕道;绕过:~ a city 绕过一个城市

by-product/ˈbaɪprɒdʌkt/

n.❶ sth. formed in addition to the main product 副产品:animal ~s 畜产品 ❷a

secondary result; a side effect 次要的结果;副效应:An increase in crime is one of the ~s of unemployment.犯罪案的增多是失业的副效应之一。

by-road/ˈbaɪrəud/

n.a side road; a road that is not much used 小路;僻路;旁道

bystander/ˈbaɪstændə(r)/

n.a person standing near, but not taking part in it when sth. happens 旁观者:an innocent ~ 无辜的旁观者

byte /baɪt/

n.a group of binary digits or bits（usually eight）operated on as a unit 字节

byway/ˈbaɪweɪ/

n.❶a smaller road or path which is not much used or known 小路;近道 ❷less important or well-known parts of a subject 较冷门的科目:~s of history 历史中较冷门的部分

byword/ˈbaɪwɜːd/

n.❶the name of a person, place, or thing that is taken as representing some quality, often bad 绰号;代号;别称;话柄:His name has become a ~ for cruelty.他的名字已成了冷酷无情的代词。❷a common saying or expression 谚语;俗语

Cc

cab/kæb/

*n.*❶a taxi 出租汽车；go by ～ 乘出租汽车去/take a ～ 乘出租汽车 ❷the part of a lorry where the driver sits（卡车的）司机台

cabal/kə'bæl/

*n.*a small group of people who make secret plans for（especially political）action（尤指政治）阴谋集团，秘密组织

cabaret/'kæbəreɪ/

n. entertainment（usually singing and dancing）given at a club，party，dance，etc.（在俱乐部、聚会、舞会等的）娱乐性表演（通常指歌舞）

cabbage/'kæbɪdʒ/

n. a round vegetable with many large green leaves 甘蓝；包心菜；卷心菜；Cabbage can be eaten raw.卷心菜可以生吃。

cabin/'kæbɪn/

*n.*❶ a small wooden house 简陋的小屋 ❷ a room on a ship or aeroplane 船舱；机舱‖～ **boy** 船舱（男）服务员/～ **class**（客轮）二等舱

cabinet/'kæbɪnɪt/

*n.*❶ a group of chosen members of a government，which is responsible for advising and deciding on government poling 内阁：The president asked the ～ members to state their views.总统请内阁成员发表各自的看法。❷a cupboard 橱柜‖～-**maker** *n.*组阁者/**shadow** ～ *n.*影子内阁

cable/'keɪbl/

Ⅰ *n.*❶a thick heavy metal rope used on ships（船用的）缆绳：The ship was held by two ～s.轮船被两条钢丝绳拴住了。❷ a set of wires that carries electricity，telephone signals，etc.电缆 ❸a message sent by electrical signals 电报：The mes-sage came by ～.这消息是由电报传来的。‖～ **car** *n.*缆车/～ **railway** *n.*缆车铁道 /～ **way** *n.*索道 Ⅱ *v.* send（a message）by cable 发电报：He ～d in reply.他发电报回答。

cacao/kə'kɑːəʊ，kə'keɪəʊ/

*n.*the seed of a tropical tree from which cocoa and chocolate are made；the tree on which this grows 可可豆；可可树

cack-handed/ˌkæk'hændɪd/

*adj.*awkward and unskilful；clumsy 笨手笨脚的

cackle/'kækl/

Ⅰ *n.*❶the noise made by a hen after laying an egg（母鸡下蛋后的）咯咯叫声 ❷a loud laugh which sounds like this 咯咯的笑声 Ⅱ *v.*❶make a loud unpleasant noise 咯咯叫 ❷laugh in a loud unpleasant way 咯咯地笑

cactus/'kæktəs/

n.（*pl.*～es or cacti /'kæktaɪ/）a type of plant often covered with prickles，growing in hot dry climates 仙人掌

caddy/'kædi/

*n.*a small box used for keeping tea in 茶叶盒；茶叶罐

cadge/kædʒ/

*v.*beg；get sth.without paying 乞求；占便宜：John is always cadging meals from his friends.约翰老是向朋友要饭吃。

cadre/'kɑːdə(r)/

*n.*❶a framework 骨架 ❷a highly trained and active member of political party or military force（政党或军队的）骨干，干部：We now need some new ～s of men and women.我们现在需要一批新的男女骨干。

cafe/'kæfeɪ/

n. a small restaurant where light meals

and drinks are served 小餐馆；咖啡馆

cafeteria/ˌkæfəˈtɪərɪə/
n. a place serving meals, in which people collect their own food and take it to their table (especially such a place in a college, school, factory, etc.) 自助餐厅（尤指在大学、学校、工厂等内部）

caffeine/ˈkæfiːn/
n. a substance found in coffee, etc. that makes you feel more active 咖啡因

cage/keɪdʒ/
Ⅰ *n.* ❶ a prison for animals or birds, made of wire, strong iron bars, or wood 笼：a bird in a ～ 笼中鸟 ❷ an open frame work forming the compartment in a lift 电梯梯厢 Ⅱ *v.* place or keep an animal in a cage 把（动物）关在笼中：After the tiger was caught, it was ～d. 那老虎被捉住后关进了笼子。

cagey/ˈkeɪdʒi/
adj. unwilling to talk freely or provide information （言谈）小心谨慎的；秘而不宣的：She's very ～ about her past life. 她对自己过去的生活守口如瓶。

cahoots/kəˈhuːts/
n. colluding or conspiring together, usually for a dishonest purpose （与……）合伙；（与……）勾结：The bank robbers and the police were in ～. 抢劫银行者与警察互相勾结。

cajole/kəˈdʒəʊl/
v. make sb. do sth. by using pleasing words or false promises 哄骗

cake/keɪk/
n. ❶ a sweet cooked food made of flour, fat and eggs 蛋糕：bake a ～ 烤蛋糕/have tea and ～s 吃茶点 ❷ a flattish compact mass of sth. 团；块：a ～ of soap 一块肥皂/a ～ of tobacco 一团烤烟

calamity/kəˈlæməti/
n. great and serious misfortune or disaster (e.g. a big earthquake or flood) 灾害；大灾难：natural calamities 自然灾害

calcify/ˈkælsɪfaɪ/
v. (cause to) become hard by the addition of lime (使)石灰质化，(使)钙化；(使)硬化

calcium/ˈkælsɪəm/
n. a chemical element, soft white metal found in chalk, milk, bones, etc. 钙

calculable/ˈkælkjʊləbl/
adj. able to be calculated or assessed 可计算的；可估计的

calculate/ˈkælkjʊleɪt/
v. ❶ find out by working with numbers; compute 计算：The scientist ～d the velocity of light. 那位科学家计算了光的速度。❷ estimate 估计：I ～d that we would spend two days finishing it. 我估计我们要花两天的时间做完这项工作。‖～ on 指望；期待

calculated/ˈkælkjʊleɪtɪd/
adj. intentionally planned to gain a particular result 故意的；蓄意的；有计划的：a ～ threat 别有用心的威胁/I took a ～ risk when I bought those shares. 我买那些股票时已把风险计算在内。

calculating/ˈkælkjʊleɪtɪŋ/
adj. making careful plans with the intention of bringing advantage to oneself, without considering the effects on other people 用尽心机的；工于心计的；有打算的：a cold, ～ criminal 一个冷酷而工于心计的罪犯

calculation/ˌkælkjʊˈleɪʃn/
n. ❶ the act or result of calculating 计算(的结果)；推断；预测；估计：These ～s are based on the latest statistics. 这些计算结果是以最近的统计数字为依据的。❷ care in planning, especially for one's own advantage 计谋；盘算；深思熟虑：He lied with cold ～. 他经过冷静的盘算后说谎了。

calculator/ˈkælkjʊleɪtə(r)/
n. a small machine which can perform calculations, such as adding and multiplying 计算器：a pocket ～ 袖珍计算器

calculus/ˈkælkjʊləs/
n. (*pl.* ～es or calculi/ˈkælkjʊlaɪ/) ❶ a branch of mathematics divided into two parts, differential calculus and integral calculus, that deal with variable quantities, used to solve many mathematical problems 演算；微积分：operational ～ 运

算微积 ❷a stone in some part of the human body 结石：biliary ～ 胆结石

calendar /ˈkælɪndə(r)/

*n.*❶a page or series of pages showing the days, weeks, months, of a particular year 日历；历书：a wall ～ 挂历 ❷a list of important dates or events 日程表：The general manager had a full ～ all day. 总经理的日程安排得满满的。

calf /kɑːf/

n. (*pl.* calves/kɑːvz/) ❶the young of cattle and some other animals 小牛犊；(其他动物的)仔：a deer ～ 鹿仔/a new panda ～ in the zoo 动物园里新生的小熊猫 ❷the part of the leg between the knee and the ankle 小腿

calfskin /ˈkɑːfˌskɪn/

n. leather made from the skin of the calf 小牛皮：～ boots 小牛皮靴子

calibrate /ˈkælɪbreɪt/

v. determine or correct the calibre or scale of a thermometer, gauge, or other graduated instrument 测量……的口径；标定……的刻度

calibration /ˌkælɪˈbreɪʃn/

n. ❶a set of degrees or measurement marks (测量器上的)刻度 ❷the act of calibrating 测量；标定

calibre /ˈkælɪbə(r)/

*n.*❶the inside diameter of a tube, gun, barrel, etc. (管子、枪、桶等的)口径：a small-～ rifle 小口径步枪 ❷the quality of mind or character 才能；才干：He is of high ～. 他卓有才能。

call /kɔːl/

Ⅰ *v.*❶ speak to sb. in a loud clear voice 大声说：The little boy ～ed out to the police for help. 那个小男孩向警察大声呼救。❷ make a short visit 拜访：I hope you'll ～ again. 我希望你再来。❸ telephone sb. (给某人)打电话：He ～ed me once a day. 他每天给我打一次电话。‖～ a spade 实事求是/～ back 回电话/～ by 顺访/～ for 来找(某人)；来取(某物)/～ forth 引起/～ it a day 到此为止/～ names 骂(人)/～ off 取消(活动)/～ on 拜访/～ the roll 点名/～ up ……打电

话 Ⅱ *n.*❶ a shout or cry 呼喊；叫声：I heard a ～ for help. 我听到呼救声。❷ a short visit 拜访：You must return his ～ soon. 你应该马上回访他。❸an attempt to ring someone on the telephone 打电话：There is a long-distance ～ for you. 有你的长途电话。‖～ box *n.* 公用电话亭/～ boy *n.* (旅馆)男服务员

caller /ˈkɔːlə(r)/

*n.*❶ a person who makes a short visit 访问者；来访者：John's a regular ～ here. 约翰是这里的常客。❷ a person making a telephone call, especially as addressed by the operator 打电话者(尤指接线员对打电话者的称呼)：I'm sorry, ～, the number's engaged 先生(女士)，很抱歉，电话占线。/An anonymous ～ warned the police about the bomb on the train. 一个匿名者来电话警告警方，说火车上有炸弹。❸ a person who calls out numbers in a game (游戏中)报数字的人

calligraphy /kəˈlɪɡrəfi/

n. handwriting 书法

calling /ˈkɔːlɪŋ/

*n.*❶ a strong urge of feeling of duty to do a particular kind of work；vocation 欲望；使命感；天职 ❷ a person's profession or trade 职业；行业

calliper /ˈkælɪpə/

*n.*❶ (*pl.*) an instrument consisting of two legs fixed together at one end, used for measuring thickness, the distance between two surfaces, and inner width (diameter) 测径规；卡钳；两脚规 ❷ metal supports fixed to the legs to help a person with weak legs to walk (装在腿上帮助腿力弱者行走的)金属支架

callisthenics /ˌkælɪsˈθenɪks/

n. physical exercises intended to develop healthy, strong, and beautiful bodies 健美(体)操；健身操

callous /ˈkæləs/

adj. having no feeling for the misfortune or suffering of others 无同情心的；硬心肠的

calloused /ˈkæləsɪd/

adj. (of a part of the body) having an area

of hardened skin（身体某部分）长胼胝的,长老茧的,有硬皮的

callow /ˈkæləʊ/

adj.（of a person or behaviour）young and without experience；immature（人或行为）幼稚的,缺乏经验的,不成熟的：a ～ youth 没有经验的青年

callus /ˈkæləs/

n. an area of thick hard skin 老茧；胼胝：～es on his hands 他手上的老茧

calm /kɑːm/

Ⅰ*adj.* ❶（of weather）not windy；（of sea）still（天气）无风的；（海洋）风平浪静的：After the storm, it was ～.暴雨过后,风平浪静。 ❷quiet, not excited；not showing fear, etc. 平静的；镇静的：She answered with a ～ voice.她以镇静的腔调回答。‖ ～belt *n.*无风带 Ⅱ*v.* make sb.or sth.become quiet and relaxed 使平静；使镇静：The mother ～ed her frightened child.母亲使受惊的孩子平静下来。/ The old woman finally ～ed down. 老妇人终于安静下来了。‖ ～ness *n.*平静

calorie /ˈkæləri/

n. ❶a unit of energy supplied by food 大卡,千卡(食物产生的热量值单位) ❷a unit for measuring a quantity of heat 卡路里(热量单位)

calve /kɑːv/

v. give birth to a young cow 生(小牛)

calorific /ˌkæləˈrɪfɪk/

adj. relating to or producing heat（热）卡的；产生热量的

camcorder /ˈkʌmkɔːdə(r)/

n. a combined video camera and sound recorder（便携式）摄像机；摄录影机

camel /ˈkæml/

n. a long-neck desert animal with one or two humps on it's back 骆驼：Camels are used for carrying loads in the desert.人们用骆驼在沙漠中运货物。

camellia /kəˈmiːliə/

n. a bush with a large sweet-smelling flower like a rose 山茶；山茶花

camera /ˈkæmərə/

n. a machine which takes photographs or movie pictures 照相机；摄影机：a film ～

电影摄影机

cameraman /ˈkæmərəmæn/

n. a person who operates a camera for films or television（电影或电视的）摄影师

camomile /ˈkæməmaɪl/

n. a plant with small sweet-smelling white and yellow flowers having medicinal qualities 洋甘菊；春黄菊：～ tea 甘菊茶

camouflage /ˈkæməflɑːʒ/

Ⅰ*n.* anything which hides sth. or changes its appearance so that it is not easily seen 伪装 Ⅱ*v.* hide sth.in this way 伪装；掩饰

camp /kæmp/

Ⅰ*n.* a place where people live for a time in tents or huts 营地 Ⅱ*v.* live in a tent 扎营；宿营：They ～ed in the valley.他们在峡谷中宿营。‖ go ～ing 进行野营 / in the same ～ 志同道合的 ‖ ～ bed *n.*行军床 / concentration ～ *n.*集中营 / summer ～ *n.* 夏令营

campaign /kæmˈpeɪn/

Ⅰ*n.* ❶ military operations, usually in one area 战役：The Germans were defeated in the ～ in North Africa.德国兵在北非的战役中被击败。 ❷ a planned course of action towards a special object 活动：The government has launched a ～ to increase production and practise economy.政府发起了一场增产节约运动。 Ⅱ*v.* take part in or go on a campaign 开展运动；参加运动：The whole country was ～ing against a war of aggression.举国上下正在开展一场反侵略的运动。

campanile /ˌkæmpəˈniːli/

n. a high bell tower which stands separately from any other building（独立的）钟楼

camper /ˈkæmpə(r)/

n. ❶ a person who camps 露营者 ❷ a motor vehicle big enough to live in when on holiday, usually having cooking equipment and beds in the back part 野营车(有床、厨房设备等供度假者使用的汽车)

campfire /ˈkæmpfaɪə(r)/

n. a wood fire made in the open air by

campers 营火；篝火

campground /'kæmpɡraund/

n. = campsite

camphor /'kæmfə(r)/

n. a strong-smelling white substance used medically and in the manufacture of celluloid 樟脑：a ～ ball 樟脑丸

campsite /'kæmpsaɪt/

n. a place, such as a field, used for camping in (野)营地

campus /'kæmpəs/

n. ❶ the grounds of a university, college, or school 校园：His home is on the ～ of the university. 他的家在那大学校园里。❷ a university; a separate branch of a university 大学；大学的校区：visit a ～ 访问一所大学

camshaft /'kæmʃɑːft/

n. a rod to which a cam is fastened 凸轮轴

can[1] /kæn, kən/

v. (could) ❶ be able to 能：He ～ touch the ceiling. 他能够到天花板。❷ know how to 会：He ～ run that machine. 他会使用那部机器。❸ have permission to; be allowed to 可以；允许：Can I speak to you a moment? 我可以和你说一会儿话吗？

can[2] /kæn/

I *n.* ❶ a round metal container for holding milk, coffee, oil, etc. (盛牛奶、咖啡、油等的) 容器：an oil ～ 油罐 ❷ contents of such a container 罐头：a ～ of beer 一听啤酒 II *v.* (-nn-) preserve by putting up in airtight containers 装于罐头内：He ～ned some fruit. 他将一些水果制成罐头。

canal /kə'næl/

n. a waterway dug across land for ships or small boats to go through 运河：the Suez Canal 苏伊士运河 / It is actually connected with Asia at the spot where the Suez Canal was dug. 它实际上是在开凿苏伊士运河的地方与亚洲连接。

canard /kæ'nɑːd/

n. a false report or piece of news 谣言；虚报；假新闻

canary /kə'neəri/

n. ❶ a small, yellow-feathered song-bird, usually kept in a cage 金丝雀 ❷ the light

yellow colour 淡黄色

cancel /'kænsl/

v. give up; call off 取消：She ～ed her trip to New York as she is lack of money. 由于缺钱，她取消了纽约之行。

cancellation /ˌkænsə'leɪʃn/

n. ❶ the act of cancelling 取消；勾销，注销：The ～ of the order for planes led to the closure of the factory. 购置飞机订单的取消导致这家工厂的倒闭。/ The flight is fully booked, but if there are any ～ we will let you know. 这班机的机票已预订一空，如有取消预订的，我们一定通知你。❷ the mark used when cancelling sth., such as a postage stamp 注销 (盖销) 记号

cancer /'kænsə(r)/

n. a disease caused by an uncontrolled division of abnormal cells in a part of the body 癌

cancerous /'kænsərəs/

adj. ❶ of or belonging to cancer 癌症的：a ～ indication 癌症征兆 ❷ suffering from cancer 患癌症的：a ～ liver 癌变的肝脏

candid /'kændɪd/

adj. open, honest, and sincere in manner; directly truthful, even when telling the truth is unwelcome 坦诚的；率直的；耿直忠厚的；直言不讳的：I would like your ～ opinion of these proposals. 我欢迎你对这些建议提出坦诚的意见。/ To be quite ～, I don't like your hairstyle. 说老实话，我不喜欢你的发型。‖ ～ ly *adv.* 坦率地：She talked quite ～ly about her unhappy marriage. 她对自己不愉快的婚姻谈得十分坦率。

candidacy /'kændɪdəsi/

n. the fact of being a candidate, especially for a political office (尤指政治性的) 候选人资格：He announced his ～ for the next presidential election. 他宣布了自己竞选下届总统的候选人身份。

candidate /'kændɪdət/

n. ❶ a person who wishes, or who is put forward by others, to take an office or position 候选人：There are three ～s for president. 有三位总统候选人。❷ a person taking an examination 考生：One hundred ～s passed the entrance examination. 100 名考生通过了入学考试。

candied/ˈkændɪd/
*adj.*covered with shiny sugar 糖渍的；蜜饯的：～ fruit 蜜饯水果

candle/ˈkændl/
*n.*a stick of hard wax, with a thread in the middle, which is lit to give light 蜡烛 ‖ ～**stick** *n.* 烛台

candlelight/ˈkændllaɪt/
*n.*the light produced by candles 烛光：We dined by ～.我们在烛光下用餐。

candlewick/ˈkændlˌwɪk/
*n.*cloth with a decorative pattern made of rows of raised short threads separated from other rows by bare material 有凸起花纹的织物：a ～ bedspread 有凸起花纹的床罩

cando(u)r/ˈkændə(r)/
*n.*the quality of being candid, saying what one thinks or knows without trying to hide anything 直率；坦白

candy/ˈkændi/
Ⅰ *n.*pieces of sugar in different shapes 糖果：two pieces of ～ 两块糖/a ～ store 糖果店 Ⅱ *v.*preserve (e.g. fruit) by boiling or cooking in sugar; form into sugar crystals 把(水果)制成蜜饯；成糖状：～ the oranges 将橘子制成蜜饯

candyfloss/ˈkændɪflɒs/
*n.*fine sticky often coloured sugar threads eaten as a sweet and usually on a stick 棉花糖

cane/keɪn/
Ⅰ *n.* ❶ a long, hollow, jointed stem of bamboo, sugar-cane, rattan, etc. (竹、甘蔗、藤等的)茎 ❷ a stick made from a came stem; a rod used for whipping 手杖；笞杖：On long walks the old man took along a ～.这老人走远路时带根手杖。Ⅱ *v.*beat with a cane 用笞杖鞭打：English schoolmasters used to ～ the boys as a punishment.英国教师从前常鞭笞学童作为惩罚。

canister/ˈkænɪstə(r)/
*n.*a small box (usually metal) with a lid, used for holding tea, coffee, etc. 罐；茶叶罐；咖啡罐

canned/kænd/
*adj.*❶(said about food or drinks) sealed in a can to preserve it (食物、饮料)罐装的，听装的 ❷(said about music) recorded for later reproduction (音乐)预先录好的

cannery/ˈkænəri/
*n.*a factory where food is put in tins 罐头食品厂

cannibal/ˈkænɪbl/
*n.*❶ a person who eats human flesh 食人者 ❷ an animal which eats the flesh of other animals of the same kind 同类相食的动物：Some fish are ～s.有些鱼是食其同类的。

cannibalize/ˈkænɪbəlaɪz/
*v.*take (a machine) to pieces to use the parts in other machines 拆卸利用，拆取(旧机器的零部件)：He ～d his old car to repair the new one.他拆旧车的零件来修理新车。

cannon/ˈkænən/
Ⅰ *n.*a large powerful gun, often fixed to the ground or onto a two wheeled carriage or, in modern times, fixed to an aircraft 大炮，加农炮；(飞机上的)机关炮：a 15th century ～ 15 世纪的大炮 Ⅱ *v.*hit or knock forcefully, especially by accident (尤指无意地)碰撞，相撞：She came running round the corner, ～ed into me, and knocked me over.她从拐角处跑过来，撞了我一个满怀，把我撞倒了。

cannonade/ˌkænəˈneɪd/
*n.*a continuous beady firing by large guns 连续炮击

canny/ˈkæni/
*adj.*❶ clever, careful, and not easily deceived, shrewd especially in money matters (尤指在钱财上)精明的，不易上当的，谨慎的 ❷ nice; good 好的；好看的，漂亮的：a ～ lass 漂亮的小女孩

canoe/kəˈnuː/
*n.*a long narrow boat, often made out of one tree trunk 独木舟：The two ～s were almost out of sight.那两只独木舟几乎看

C

不见了。/We crossed the lake by ～.我们乘独木舟过湖。

canon/ˈkænən/

*n.*❶a Church decree or law 教规；宗教法规 ❷a general standard or principle by which sth.is judged 标准；规范；准则：the ～s of conduct 行为准则/the ～ of art 艺术标准

canopy/ˈkænəpi/

*n.*covering(often supported by poles and usually made of cloth or wood) over a throne,bed,doorway,etc. 华盖；罩篷；天篷；遮阳

cantankerous/kænˈtæŋkərəs/

*adj.*bad-tempered and with the habit of being against what other people suggest 脾气不好的；爱抬杠的

canteen/kænˈtiːn/

n. ❶ a place (especially in a factory, school, military camp) where food and drink are sold and meals are bought and eaten (尤指工厂、学校、军事营地的)饮食部；食堂 ❷a small container in which water or other drink is carried 水壶；水罐：lift a ～ 提起水壶

cantilever/ˈkæntɪliːvə(r)/

*n.*a long projecting arm of metal fastened at one end only 悬臂；伸臂

canvas/ˈkænvəs/

*n.*❶a strong,coarse cloth used for tents, sails, bags, etc. and by artists for oil-paintings 粗帆布；画布 ❷an oil painting 油画：The priceless ～ was stolen from the art gallery.那幅无价的油画从画廊被偷走了。

canyon/ˈkænjən/

n. a deep, narrow valley with sides like cliffs(especially in America) (尤指在美洲的)峡谷

cap/kæp/

Ⅰ*n.*a sort of soft hat without a brim, but with a peak 帽子 Ⅱ*v.*(-pp-) put a cap on；cover the top of 给……戴帽；覆盖：Snow ～ped the mountains.雪覆盖了山顶。

capability/ˌkeɪpəˈbɪləti/

*n.*❶the power of doing things；fitness or

capacity 能力；才能 ❷undeveloped faculties 潜在的能力：The boy has great capabilities.那孩子有潜力。

capable/ˈkeɪpəbl/

*adj.*❶ gifted；able 有能力的：He seemed very ～.他似乎很有能力。❷skilful and effective, especially in practical matters 熟练的；卓有成效的：I don't believe you are ～ of winning the game.我不相信你能够赢得这场比赛。❸open to or admitting of sth. 可以……的；容许……的：The situation is ～ of improvement.局势可能会好转的。

capacious/kəˈpeɪʃəs/

*adj.*having a lot of space inside 宽敞的；容量大的：a ～ bottle 容量大的瓶子/a ～ mind 开阔的思想

capacitor/kəˈpæsɪtə(r)/

n. an apparatus that collects and stores electricity,as in a television set 电容器

capacity/kəˈpæsəti/

*n.*❶the ability to do things；the power of holding knowledge and ideas 能力：He has a great ～ for work.他的工作能力很强。❷ the amount that a container can hold 容量：The seating ～ of this theatre is 500.这家剧院可容纳 500 名观众。

cape¹/keɪp/

*n.*a covering for the shoulders and arms 披肩；短披风；短斗篷：wear a ～ 披斗篷

cape²/keɪp/

*n.*a high piece of land which goes out into the sea 岬；海角：the Cape of Good Hope 好望角

capillary/kəˈpɪləri/

*n.*a small, narrow tube, especially a very small blood-vessel 毛细管；毛细血管

capital/ˈkæpɪtl/

Ⅰ*n.*❶ a town or city where the government of a country, state or county is carried on 首都：Beijing is the ～ of China.北京是中国的首都。❷ a letter of the form and size that is used to begin sentences and names 大写字母：Begin every sentence with a ～.在每一个句子的开始，要用大写字母。❸ wealth；a valuable resource of a particular kind 资金；资本：

You need a lot of ～ to start up a new company.你需要许多资金开办一家新的公司。Ⅱ*adj.* ❶ (of a letter) written or printed in the form and size used to begin sentences and names（字母）大写的：～ letters 大写字母 ❷ punishable by death 应处死刑的：Murder can be a ～ offence. 谋杀可以被看作是死罪。❸ first-rate; excellent 一流的；极好的：He made a ～ speech.他做了一场精彩的演讲。

capitalism/ˈkæpɪtəlɪzəm/
　　n. an economic system in which a country's trade and industry are organized and controlled by the owners of capital 资本主义：monopoly ～ 垄断资本主义

capitalist/ˈkæpɪtəlɪst/
　　Ⅰ *n.* ❶ a person who controls much capital 资本家 ❷ a person who supports capitalism 资本主义者 Ⅱ *adj.* practising or supporting the principles of capitalism 资本主义的：the ～ system 资本主义制度/～ society 资本主义社会/a ～ country 资本主义国家

capitalize(-se)/ˈkæpɪtəlaɪz/
　　v. ❶ write or print with a capital letter 用大写字母书写（或印刷）：The names of the months are usually ～d. 月份的名称的首字母常用大写。❷ sell possessions to change them into money 变现；变卖资产：He ～d all his property. 他把他的全部财产变现。

capitation/ˌkæpɪˈteɪʃn/
　　n. a tax, fee, charge of the same sum per person 人头税；按人摊派的费用

capitulate/kəˈpɪtʃuleɪt/
　　v. surrender (on stated conditions)（有条件）投降，停止抵抗

cappuccino /ˌkæpuˈtʃiːnəu/
　　n. (*pl.* ～s) milky coffee made frothy with steam under pressure captivating 卡布奇诺咖啡

caprice/kəˈpriːs/
　　n. a sudden change of mind or behaviour that has no obvious cause; tendency to change suddenly without apparent causes 突变；反复无常

capricious/kəˈprɪʃəs/
　　adj. often changing, irregular; unpredictable 反复无常的；变化莫测的：The weather is so ～.天气如此多变。

capsize/ˈkæpsaɪz/
　　v. (with reference to ships and boats) turn over 使（船）倾覆；（船只）倾覆

capstan/ˈkæpstən/
　　n. a metal object for winding a rope (e.g. on a ship) 绞盘；起锚机

capsule/ˈkæpsjuːl/
　　n. a tiny soluble container for a dose of medicine 胶囊：He swallowed a ～.他吃下一粒胶囊。

captain/ˈkæptɪn/
　　n. ❶ the leader of a group of people, especially a sports team 首领；（尤指运动队的）队长：John is the ～ of the football team.约翰是足球队队长。❷ the chief person on a ship or airplane 船长；机长：The ～ refused to leave the ship while the danger lasted.危险未过时，船长拒绝离开轮船。❸ an officer of fairly high rank in the army or navy or air force 陆军上尉；海军上校；空军上尉：This lieutenant was promoted to ～.这位陆军中尉被提升为陆军上尉。

caption/ˈkæpʃn/
　　n. a short title or heading of an article in a periodical, etc.; words printed with a photograph or illustration, etc.; words on a movie film to explain the story（文章）标题；(图片、画面等)说明；解说词；（电影）字幕：put a ～ on an article 给文章加标题/the ～ of the drawing 图片说明

captious/ˈkæpʃəs/
　　adj. fond of finding fault, making protests, especially about unimportant points 吹毛求疵的；爱挑毛病的：a ～ woman 爱挑剔的女人

captivate/ˈkæptɪveɪt/
　　v. capture the fancy of; fascinate 迷惑；迷住：He was ～d by the girl.这女孩使他着了迷。

captive/ˈkæptɪv/
　　Ⅰ *n.* a person or animal that is caught 俘虏；捕获物：These ～s will be taken to

C

the rear areas.这些俘虏将被押往后方。
Ⅱ*adj.*❶taken or kept as a prisoner 被俘虏的:~ soldiers 战俘 ❷charmed 着迷的,被迷住的:her ~ beau 被她迷住的情郎

captivity/kæpˈtɪvəti/
n. the state of being captive 被俘(的状态),拘禁,囚禁;束缚: Many animals do not breed well in ~.许多动物一被关入笼中就繁殖得不好。/The hostages were released from ~.人质从囚禁中被释放出来了。

captor/ˈkæptə(r)/
n. a person who catches someone and holds him as a prisoner 俘虏者;捕捉者

capture/ˈkæptʃə(r)/
Ⅰ*v.*❶ catch, take or seize sb. or sth. by force, skill, trickery, etc. 抓住;捕获:We ~d a foreign spy.我们捉到了一个外国间谍。❷ take control of sth. by force from an enemy;win;gain (用武力从敌人手中)夺取;赢得;获得:The king's forces ~d the city.国王的军队占领了那座城市。Ⅱ*n.*❶ an act of seizing or taking 抓住;捕获: He was released yesterday, six months after his ~ by the terrorists.他被恐怖分子抓走六个月后,昨天获释。❷ an animal, a person or thing caught or taken 猎物;被捕获的人或物

car/kɑː(r)/
*n.*❶a road vehicle with four wheels and an engine, in which we can travel 小汽车:You can't park your ~ here.你不能把汽车停在此地。❷a railway carriage;a coach (火车)车厢;sleeping ~s 卧车厢 ‖ **baby** ~ *n.*微型汽车/**open** ~ *n.*敞篷车/**dining** ~ *n.*餐车/**sleeping** ~ *n.*卧车/**baggage** ~ *n.*行李车/**freight** ~ *n.*货车/**mail** ~ *n.*邮车

carafe/kəˈræf/
*n.*a container for wine, water, etc.酒壶;水壶

caramel/ˈkærəmel/
n. a type of sweet substance made from sugar which has been slightly burned 焦糖

carapace/ˈkærəpeɪs/

*n.*a protective hard shell on the outside of certain animals, such as crabs or tortoises (蟹或龟等的)甲壳

carat/ˈkærət/
*n.*a unit for measuring the quality of gold and the weight of jewels 开(黄金成色单位);克拉(宝石重量单位)

caravan/ˈkærəvæn/
*n.*❶a vehicle equipped for living in, typically towed by a car (活动房式的)拖车: take holidays in a ~ 在拖车里度假 ❷a group of merchants travelling together across deserts 沙漠上的商队

carbide/ˈkɑːbaɪd/
*n.*a compound of carbon 碳化物

carbohydrate/ˌkɑːbəʊˈhaɪdreɪt/
*n.*❶ a substance composed of carbon, hydrogen and oxygen 碳水化合物 ❷ this substance found in food, such as bread, which causes one to gain weight 糖类

carbon/ˈkɑːbən/
*n.*❶ a non-metallic element (symbol C) that occurs in all living matter, in its pure form as diamonds and graphite and in an impure form in coal and charcoal 碳 ❷ a piece of carbon paper or a carbon copy 复写的副本:How many ~s do you want? 你要打印几份复写本? ‖ ~ **paper** *n.*复写纸/~ **monoxide** *n.*一氧化碳

carbonic/kɑːˈbɒnɪk/
*adj.*of or containing carbon (含)碳的:~ acid 碳酸

carbuncle/ˈkɑːbʌŋkl/
*n.*❶a bright-red jewel 红宝石 ❷a red (usually painful) inflamed swelling under the skin 痈;炎肿

carcass/ˈkɑːkəs/
*n.*❶ the body of a dead animal, especially one which is ready to be cut up as meat 动物尸体(尤指屠宰后用作肉食的牲畜躯体) ❷ the decaying remains of sth., such as a car or a ship (废车船等的)残骸,骨架:Divers have found the ~ of a wrecked ship 100 miles from the coast.潜水员在离岸 100 英里处发现了一艘失事船只的残骸。❸ the body of a dead or living person 死尸;(人的)躯体

carcinogen/kɑːˈsɪnədʒen/
*n.*a carcinogenic substance 致癌物质

carcinogenic/ˌkɑːsɪnəˈdʒenɪk/
*adj.*causing cancer 致癌的：～ substances 致癌物质

card/kɑːd/
n. ❶ a playing card 纸牌：Now it's my turn to play the ～s.现在轮到我玩牌了。 ❷ a piece of stiff paper or thin cardboard, as used for various purposes 卡片：Here is my calling ～.这是我的名片。‖ **New Year** ～ 贺年片/**invitation** ～ 请帖/**visiting** ～ 名片/**membership** ～ 会员卡/**index** ～ 索引卡

cardboard/ˈkɑːdbɔːd/
*n.*a stiff, heavy paper material, used for making cards, boxes, etc.硬纸板：a box made of ～ 硬纸板做的箱子

cardiac/ˈkɑːdɪæk/
*adj.*of the heart or heart disease 心脏的；心脏病的：～ patient 心脏病患者

cardigan/ˈkɑːdɪgən/
*n.*a short woollen coat usually worn over a shirt 羊毛背心；羊毛衫(常穿在衬衫外面)

cardinal/ˈkɑːdɪnl/
Ⅰ *n.* an important priest of the Roman Catholic Church (天主教会的)红衣主教 Ⅱ *adj.* chief; most important; on which sth.depends 主要的；最重要的；基本的：a ～ idea 主导思想/the ～ numerals 基数词/a ～ principle 一条基本原则

card punch/ˈkɑːdpʌntʃ/
n. a machine that puts information onto cards in such a way that computers can read and understand it 打卡机

care/keə(r)/
Ⅰ *v.* ❶ feel interest, worry, or sorry, etc.; show concern 关心；操心；忧虑；介意：I don't ～ what they think. I shall go on just the same.我不在乎他们怎么想，我将一如既往。 ❷ be willing to 愿意；乐意：If you ～ to hear, I will tell it to you.如果你愿意听，我将把此事告诉你。 ❸ look after 照顾：She ～d for the children at home.她在家照料孩子。 ❹like 喜欢：Do you ～ for classical music? 你对古典音乐

感兴趣吗？ Ⅱ *n.* ❶ serious attention 小心；谨慎：Take ～ when you cross the road. 过街时要小心。 ❷ protection; charge 照顾；照管：The child was left in her ～.这小孩留给她照顾。 ❸a feeling of worry or anxiety; sth. that causes problems or anxiety 烦恼；忧虑；引起的烦恼的事；令人焦虑的事：He hasn't a ～ in the world.他无忧无虑。 ‖ ～ **of** 由……转交/**have a** ～ 当心/**medical** ～ 医疗/**take** ～ **of** 照顾

career/kəˈrɪə(r)/
Ⅰ *n.*❶the series of jobs that a person has in a particular area 生涯；经历：Lincoln's ～ as a statesman 林肯的从政生涯 ❷ profession; occupation 职业；专业：make teaching one's ～ 以教书为业 ❸ a run at full speed 急驶；飞奔：We were in full ～ when we struck the post.我们飞驰前进时撞在了那一根柱子上。 Ⅱ *v.* move quickly without control 失控飞驰

carefree/ˈkeəfriː/
*adj.*free from anxiety or responsibility 无忧无虑的；无牵挂的；不负责任的：the ～ days of the holidays 假期中的无忧时光/a ～ attitude 不负责任的态度

careful/ˈkeəfl/
adj. ❶ taking care; cautious 小心的；谨慎的：Be ～! 当心！ ❷showing attention to details; thorough 细心的；周密的；细致的：After ～ consideration, we decided to accept his request.经过慎重考虑，我们决定接受他的请求。 ‖ ～**ly** *adv.*细心地；小心地

careless/ˈkeəlɪs/
*adj.*❶ not careful 粗心的；欠思考的：He is ～ in his speech.他说话欠考虑。 ❷free from care or worry; unconcerned 不管的；不顾的：Don't be ～ with your money.在金钱方面，不要挥霍无度。 ‖ ～**ly** *adv.* 粗心地/～**ness** *n.*粗心大意

caress /kəˈres/
Ⅰ *n.*a loving touch or stroke 抚摩；爱抚 Ⅱ *v.*touch or stroke someone lovingly 爱抚；抚摩：She ～ed her daughter's forehead.她抚摩着女儿的前额。

C

caretaker/ˈkeəteɪkə(r)/
n. ❶ a person employed to look after a school or other usually large public building and to be responsible for small repairs, cleaning, etc. 看管者，管理员 ❷ a person who looks after a house of land when the owner is absent 看管（房地产的）人 ❸ a person who provides care, such as a parent, teacher, or nurse 照看人；保护人；监护人

careworn/ˈkeəwɔːn/
adj. showing the effects of grief, worry, or anxiety 饱经忧患的；因操心而憔悴的：the ～ face of the mother of a large poor family 一个贫困大家庭的母亲那饱经忧患的面容

carfare/ˈkɑːfeə(r)/
n. the fare that a passenger is charged for travelling in a bus, taxi, etc., within a town or city（市内公共汽车，计程车等的）车费

cargo/ˈkɑːɡəʊ/
n.(*pl*.～s or ～es)sth. carried on a ship or in an aeroplane（船上或飞机上所载的）货物：a ～ of cotton（oil）一船棉花（石油）/We sailed with a ～ of coal. 我们用船载煤。

caricature/ˈkærɪkətʃʊə(r)/
n. ❶ a picture description, imitation of a person's voice, behaviour, etc., stressing certain features to amuse or ridicule 讽刺画；漫画：Newspapers often contain ～s of well-known politicians. 报纸上经常刊登有关著名政治家的漫画。 ❷ the art of doing this 漫画艺术；漫画手法：He is skilled at ～. 他擅长漫画艺术。

caring/ˈkeərɪŋ/
adj. providing care and support, especially to people who need to be looked after 关心照顾人的；（尤指为老弱病者）提供帮助的：the ～ professions, such as nursing and social work 关心照顾人的职业，诸如医护和社会工作 /Is the government seen by the voters as a ～ government? 该政府在选民心目中是一个照顾国民的政府吗？

carload/ˈkɑːləʊd/
n. the number of people that can travel in a motor car 汽车载客量：a ～ of passengers 一车的乘客

carmine/ˈkɑːmɪn/
Ⅰ *adj*. deep red 鲜红色的；深红色的 Ⅱ *n*. deep red (colour) 鲜红色；深红色

carnal/ˈkɑːnl/
adj. of the body or fresh; sexual 肉体的；性欲的：～ desires 性欲/Carnal pleasures can destroy a man's soul. 好色可以毁身。

carnation/kɑːˈneɪʃn/
n. a type of flower with pink, white or red flowers which smell sweet 康乃馨；荷兰石竹

carnival/ˈkɑːnɪvl/
n. a public celebration, with processions, games, feasts, etc. (especially in Roman Catholic countries in the period before Lent)（尤指罗马天主教国家大斋节前举行的）狂欢节；嘉年华会

carnivore/ˈkɑːnɪvɔː/
n. an animal that feeds on the flesh of other animals 食肉动物

carnivorous/kɑːˈnɪvərəs/
adj. eating meat 食肉的：Lions and tigers are ～ animals. 狮子和老虎都是食肉类动物。

carol/ˈkærəl/
n. a religious song sung at Christmas time 圣诞颂歌

carp[1]/kɑːp/
n.(*pl*. carp) a type of freshwater fish used for food 鲤鱼

carp[2]/kɑːp/
v. make small and unnecessary criticisms; find small and unimportant faults or mistakes 找岔子；挑剔；吹毛求疵：He was always ～ing at the arrangements made by other people. 对于别人所做的安排，他总是爱挑剔。

carpenter/ˈkɑːpəntə(r)/
Ⅰ *n*. a person who does carpentry as a job 木匠，木工：The ～ is repairing the desks. 木匠在修理课桌。 Ⅱ *v*. do carpentry 做木工活

carpentry/ˈkɑːpɪntri/
n. the art of making things out of wood 木工业：work at ～ 干木工活儿

carpet /ˈkɑːpɪt/

Ⅰ *n.* a large mat used to cover the floor 地毯：a piece of ～ 一块地毯 Ⅱ *v.* cover with a carpet 铺上地毯：We ～ed the bedrooms. 我们在卧室里铺了地毯。

carport /ˈkɑːpɔːt/

n. a shelter for a car, with only a roof and one or two sides, often built against a side of a house （靠墙搭设的）敞篷式汽车间，停车棚

carriage /ˈkærɪdʒ/

n. ❶ a four-wheeled vehicle drawn by horses 四轮马车：The king's ～ was surrounded by crowds. 国王的马车被人群包围了。❷ a part of a train; a railway coach 车厢：Every railway ～ was full of passengers. 每一节车厢里坐满了乘客。

carrier /ˈkærɪə(r)/

n. ❶ a person or thing that carries goods, packages, and messages from one place to another 运送者；运输工具：a mail ～ 邮递员/Trains, buses, and ships are ～s. 火车、公共汽车和轮船都是运输工具。❷ a person or thing that passes diseases to others without himself or itself suffering from it 带菌者：Water and milk are often ～s of germs. 水和牛奶往往是病菌的媒介。❸ a military vehicle or ship which carries soldiers, planes, weapons, etc. 航空母舰：an aircraft ～ 一艘航空母舰 ❹ a usually metal framework fixed to a vehicle to hold bags, goods, etc. （车辆上的）载重架；货架

carrot /ˈkærət/

n. a yellow or orange-red root used as a vegetable 胡萝卜：Have some more ～(s). 请再吃点儿胡萝卜。

carry /ˈkæri/

v. ❶ support the weight of sb. or sth. and take them or it from place to place 拿；提；搬；扛；背；抱；运送：He was ～ing a suitcase. 他提着一只手提箱。❷ have sth. with you and take it wherever you go 携带；佩戴：People should not ～ controlled knives on them. 人们不应携带管制刀具。❸ contain and direct the flow of water, electricity, etc. 输送，传输，传送（水、电

等）：There is a pipeline ～ing oil in that field. 那片田地里有一条输油管道。❹ be infected with diseases 传播；传染：Flies can ～ a lot of diseases which affects humans. 苍蝇可传播危害人类的严重疾病。❺ be able to remember sth. 能记住；能回想起 ❻ support the weight of sth. 支撑；承载：A road bridge has to ～ a lot of traffic. 公路桥必须承载很多来往车辆。‖ ～ away 使激动得失去控制 /～ back to 使回忆起/～ into effect 实施；执行/～ on 进行；继续/～ out 实行；执行/～ through 进行到底；实现

carryall /ˈkærɪɔːl/

n. a large usually soft bag or case; a hold-all 大手提包；大袋子

carrycot /ˈkærɪkɒt/

n. a small boxlike container in which a baby can be carried 手提箱形的婴儿床

carsick /ˈkɑːsɪk/

adj. feeling sick or queasy from the motion of a car 晕车的 ‖ ～ness *n.* 晕车

cart /kɑːt/

n. ❶ a two-wheeled vehicle pulled by a horse, used to carry goods 两轮马车 ❷ a two-wheeled vehicle pulled or pushed by hand, used to carry goods 板车；手推车：The farmer pushed the ～ to the market. 农民推着板车走进集市。‖ put the ～ before the horse 顺序颠倒；本末倒置

cartel /kɑːˈtel/

n. a combination of independent often international companies intended to limit competition and increase profits 卡特尔，企业（同业）联盟（国际性公司之间为限制竞争和增加利润而结成的联盟）

carter /ˈkɑːtə(r)/

n. a person whose job is driving carts 马车夫；赶车人

cartilage /ˈkɑːtɪlɪdʒ/

n. a strong substance like elastic in the joints of the body; a particular structure made of this tissue 软骨；软骨组织

cartography /kɑːˈtɒɡrəfi/

n. the science or practice of planning and drawing maps 地图绘制学；地图绘制 ‖ **cartographer** *n.* 地图制图员；制图员 /**car-**

C

tographic *adj*.地图的；制图的

carton/ˈkɑːtn/

n.a cardboard container 纸板匣；纸箱

cartoon/kɑːˈtuːn/

n.❶a drawing in a newspaper or magazine that usually makes fun of a person or event 漫画：read political ~s 看政治性漫画 ❷a film using animation techniques to photograph a sequence of drawings 卡通片；动画片：Cartoons are very popular among children.动画片深受儿童们的喜爱。‖ ~**ist** *n*.漫画家；动画片画家

cartridge/ˈkɑːtrɪdʒ/

n.❶ a case made of metal or cardboard for holding gunpowder；a bullet 弹药筒；子弹 ❷ a roll of camera film 一卷照相软片；胶卷

carve/kɑːv/

v.❶ make sth. by cutting 雕刻；刻：He ~d a doll from a block of wood.他在一块木块上雕刻出一个洋娃娃。❷ cut (cooked meat) into pieces 切(肉)：Shall I ~ you another slice of chicken? 我再给你切一块鸡肉，好吗? ‖ ~ **up** 宰割；分割

carving /ˈkɑːvɪŋ/

n.a carved object or design 雕刻品；雕刻图案

cascade/kæsˈkeɪd/

n.❶a small waterfall 小瀑布 ❷anything that seems to pour or flow downwards 瀑布状物：Her hair fell over her shoulders in a ~ of curls.她的头发像瀑布一样垂在肩上。

case[1] /keɪs/

n.❶ an instance of a particular situation；condition 情况；情形：A similar ~ might happen again.同样的事可能再发生。❷ an example of disease；a person having a disease 病例；患者：All these ~s proved that his theory was right. 所有这些病例证明他的理论是正确的。❸ a special example，question to be decided in a lawcourt 案件；案情：This is a civil ~.这是一宗民事案件。‖ **in any** ~ 不管怎样/**in** ~ **of** 以防/**in no** ~ 在任何情况下都不/**in that** ~ 如果那样

case[2] /keɪs/

n.a container designed to hold or protect sth.盒；套；壳；罩；容器 ‖ **brief** ~ *n*.公文包/**pillow** ~ *n*.枕头套/**packing** ~ *n*.运货箱/**suit** ~ *n*.手提箱

cash/kæʃ/

Ⅰ *n*.money in coins or notes 现金：I have no ~ on me.我身上没带现金。Ⅱ *v*.exchange (a cheque or other order to pay) for the amount of money that it is worth 把(支票或其他汇票)兑换成现金：May I ~ the check? 我可以将这张支票兑换成现金吗?

cashier /kæˈʃɪə/

n.a person employed to receive and pay out money in a bank or to receive payments in a shop or business (商店、银行或商行的)出纳员，收支员

cashmere /ˌkæʃˈmɪə(r)/

n.a soft type of wool originally from the kashmir goat 开司米羊毛：a ~ sweater 一件开司米毛绒衫

casing/ˈkeɪsɪŋ/

n.a protective covering，such as the outer rubber covering of a car tyre (包在物体外面起保护)罩，壳，套，管，外胎：This wire has a rubber ~.这种导线外面包有一层橡胶。

casino/kəˈsiːnəʊ/

n.a building open to the public for gambling 赌场

cask/kɑːsk/

n.a barrel for storing liquids (装液体的)桶：a ~ of apple juice 一桶苹果汁

cassette/kəˈset/

n. a small plastic container holding tape that plays music when fitted into a cassette recorder or tape recorder 录音磁带盒，盒式录音磁带：~ tape recorder 盒式录音机

cassock/ˈkæsək/

n.a long heavy garment，usually black，worn by some priests and by people helping at religious services (教士等穿的，多为黑色的)法衣，长袍

cast/kɑːst/

v.(cast) ❶throw or drop 投；抛；撒；掷；扔：~ a net 撒网/ ~ a shadow 投影/ ~

C

anchor 抛锚 ❷assign a part to（an actor）；assign an actor to（a part）分派（演员）扮演角色；分派（角色）给演员：He was ～ for this part.他分派这个角色。❸give a vote 投票：～ a vote 投票 ❹pour（liquid metal）into a mould 浇铸：～ steel 浇铸钢材 ❺throw off；remove；get rid of 抛开；脱落；放弃：He ～ the problem from his mind.他把这个问题抛在脑后。/Let us ～ aside minor details.让我们抛开细节。

castigate /ˈkæstɪɡeɪt/
　*v.*criticize someone harshly 严厉责骂：He was ～d for not setting a good example. 他因未能树立好榜样而遭到训斥。‖ **castigation** *n.*严惩；苛评

castle /ˈkɑːsl/
　n. a building or group of buildings with thick walls and towers 城堡：The ～ stood on a hill.这座城堡在小山上。‖ ～ **in the air** 空中楼阁；想入非非

castrate /kæsˈtreɪt/
　*v.*cut off the testicles of a male human or animal 阉割

casual /ˈkæʒʊəl/
　I *adj.*❶ happening by chance 偶然的：a ～ meeting 偶然相见 ❷ informal；careless 随随便便的；漫不经心的：a very ～ person 一个非常随便的人 ❸not permanent 临时的；非经常的：The young man earned his living by ～ labour.那位年轻人靠做临时工谋生。Ⅱ *n.* ❶ informal shoes or clothes 便鞋；便服 ❷a worker working temporarily 临时工 ‖ ～**ly** *adv.* 漫不经心地

casualty /ˈkæʒʊəlti/
　*n.*❶an accident, especially one involving loss of life 事故；灾祸 ❷a person killed or seriously injured in war or in an accident（战争或事故的）伤员，亡者，遇难者：total casualties 伤亡总数

casuistry /ˈkæzjʊɪstri/
　*n.*false but clever use of arguments and reasoning especially when dealing with cases of conscience, law, or right and wrong behaviour 诡辩

cat /kæt/
　*n.*❶a small animal often kept as a pet or for catching mice 猫：When the ～s are away, the mice will play.猫儿不在，老鼠成精。❷a wild animal of the cat family 猫科动物 ‖ ～ **and dog life** 争争吵吵的日子/**let the ～ out of the bag** 泄露天机/**rain** ～**s and dogs** 下倾盆大雨

cataclysm /ˈkætəklɪzəm/
　*n.*a violent upheaval or disaster 大灾难；大灾变；大动乱 ‖ ～**ic** *adj.*灾变性的；大变动的

catacomb /ˈkætəkuːm/
　n.（usually *pl.*）series of underground galleries with opening along the sides for the burial of the dead 墓穴；陵墓

catalog（ue） /ˈkætəlɒɡ/
　I *n.*a list of names, places, etc.in a special order 目录 Ⅱ *v.*❶make a systematic list of 把……编成目录：Can you ～ the furniture you sell and send me a copy? 你能否把你们出售的家具编成目录送我一份？❷enter（an item）in the proper place in a list 把……编入目录分类：He went to a kind of closet and after a moment brought out a package, properly marked and cataloged by name and date. 他向一个壁橱走去，不一会儿拿出了个小包，这个小包按姓名和日期分类并做了标记。

catalyse /ˈkætəlaɪz/
　v. produce or accelerate a chemical reaction by catalysis 催化

catalyst /ˈkætəlɪst/
　n. sth. which helps a chemical change to take place without undergoing any change itself 催化剂

catapult /ˈkætəpʌlt/
　*n.*a piece of wood or metal, shaped like a letter Y, with a piece of rubber attached, used for shooting small stones 弹弓

catastrophe /kəˈtæstrəfi/
　*n.*a sudden happening that causes great suffering, misfortune, or ruin（突至的）大灾害；大灾难：The flood was a terrible ～ in which many people died.那次洪水真是一场可怕的大灾难，导致许多人丧生。

catcall /ˈkætkɔːl/
　*n.*a loud whistle or cry expressing disap-

C

proval or displeasure, made at the theatre, a sports match, etc.(表示反对或喝倒彩的)口哨声,嘘声,尖叫声

catch/kætʃ/

v.(caught) ❶stop and hold a moving object 接住;截住:The dog caught the stick in its mouth. 狗衔住了木棍。❷hold a liquid when it falls 接(落下的液体)❸take hold of sb. or sth. 抓住;握住:He caught hold of the most important chance in his life. 他抓住了人生中最重要的机会。❹capture a person or an animal 逮住;捕捉:How many fishes did you ~ today? 你今天捕到了几条鱼? ❺find or discover sb. doing sth., especially sth. wrong 当场发现:I caught the thief when he stole my cell phone. 小偷在偷我手机时,被我抓了个正着。❻to be in time to do sth.or for a bus, train, plane, etc. 及时做某事;赶上(汽车、火车、飞机等):I must go—I have a train to ~. 我得走了——我要赶火车。❼happen unexpectedly 突然遭受:She got caught in a thunderstorm when doing exercises in the park.她在公园运动时遇上了雷雨。‖ ~ fire 着火 /~ hold of 抓住 /~ one's eye 引起注意 /~ sight of 望见 /~ up with 赶上(某人)

catching/'kætʃɪŋ/

*adj.*❶(of a disease) infectious (疾病)传染的,传染性的 ❷(of an emotion or a mood) passing quickly from one person to another (情感或情绪)有感染力的:Her enthusiasm is ~.她的热情具有感染力。

catchy/'kætʃi/

*adj.*easily remembered 容易记住的:a ~ tune 易记的曲调

categorical/ˌkætə'gɒrɪkl/

adj. unconditional;made without any doubt in the mind of the speaker or writer 绝对的,无条件的;确信无疑的,明确的:a ~ statement/ 明确的声明/ The government has issued a ~ denial of this rumour.政府对这一谣言断然否定。‖ ~ly *adv.*断言地:He ~ly denied having seen it.他断然否认曾经看到过它。

categorize/'kætəgəraɪz/

*v.*put sth.in a category;classify 把……归类;把……列作:Participants were ~d according to age.参加者按年龄分组。/Her writing is very individual—it's difficult to ~.她作品的风格十分独特——很难将其归类。

category/'kætəgəri/

*n.*a class or division of people or things with particular features in common 类别,种类:The voters fall into three main categories.选民主要分为三类。

cater/'keɪtə(r)/

*v.*❶supply food 供应食物:He ~ed for two hundred guests at the party.他为宴会 200 位客人提供了食物。❷(~ to) try to satisfy a particular need or demand 迎合,设法满足(需要,要求):The radio and television have to ~ to many different types of interest and taste among the public.无线电广播和电视必须满足公众多种不同的兴趣和口味。

caterpillar/'kætəpɪlə/

*n.*the larva of a butterfly or moth 毛虫,蠋(蝴蝶或蛾的幼虫)

catfish/'kætfɪʃ/

n.(*pl.*~es or catfish) a large freshwater or sea fish with feelers like whiskers round the mouth 鲇鱼

cathedral/kə'θiːdrəl/

*n.*the main church of a district, under the care of a bishop 主教座堂;教区总教堂

catheter/'kæθɪtə(r)/

*n.*a thin tube that is put into passages in the body, used especially for putting in or taking out liquids 导(液)管

cathode/'kæθəʊd/

*n.*the negative pole of electric current 阴极,负极:~ rays 阴极射线

Catholic/'kæθəlɪk/

I *adj.*of Roman Catholic faith 罗马天主教的:Is he ~ or Protestant? 他信天主教还是新教? II *n.*a member of the Roman Catholic Church 天主教徒:Is he a ~ or Protestant? 他是天主教徒还是新教教徒?

catnap/'kætnæp/

I *n.*a short sleep during the day 瞌睡 II

v.(-pp-)to have such a sleep 打瞌睡

cattle/'kætl/

*n.*cows,bulls or oxen（总称）牛；牲畜：~ and sheep 牛羊/Cattle feed on grass.牛吃草。

catwalk/'kætwɔːk/

*n.*a narrow raised footway, especially along a bridge or round a large machine, or sticking out into a room for models to walk on in a fashion show（桥侧的）步行小道；(机器房中的)狭窄过道；(时装表演时模特儿走的)伸展台

caudal/'kɔːdl/

adj. of or at the tail or tail-end of the body 尾部；尾部的；在身体后端的

cauldron/'kɔːldrən/

*n.*a large pot used for cooking over a fire 大锅

cauliflower/'kɒlɪflaʊə(r)/

*n.*a type of vegetable like a cabbage with a white flower head 菜花

causal/'kɔːzl/

*adj.*having or showing the relationship of cause and effect 因果关系的；构成原因的：They denied that there was any ~ connection between unemployment and crime.他们认为失业和犯罪之间没有任何因果关系。

causality/kɔː'zælɪti/

*n.*the relationship between a cause and its effect；the principle that events have causes 因果关系；因果性；因果律

causation/kɔː'zeɪʃn/

n. ❶ the action of causing sth.导致；起因；惹起 ❷ the relationship of cause and effect；causality 因果关系；因果性；因果律

causative/'kɔːzətɪv/

adj. ❶ acting as a cause；producing an effect 起因的；成为原因的：one of several ~ factors in the company's failure 造成公司倒闭的几种原因之一 ❷（of a verb or verb form)showing that the subject of the verb is the cause of an action or state（动词或动词形式)使役的

cause/kɔːz/

I *n.*❶ a person or thing that makes sth.

happen 起因；根源：In our view, the root ~ of the crime problem is poverty and unemployment.依我们看，犯罪的根源是贫穷和失业。❷ a reason 理由；缘故：You have no ~ for complaint. 你没有理由抱怨。❸ an organization or idea for which efforts are being made（为之奋斗的)事业，目标，思想：Helping the poor is a worthy ~.扶贫济穷是有价值的事业。 II *v.*❶ make sth. happen, especially sth. bad or unpleasant 引起；造成：They believe inflation is ~d by big wage increases.他们认为通货膨胀是由大幅度增加工资造成的。❷ lead to；be the cause of 导致；使得：What ~d him to change his mind? 什么使他改变了主意?

causeway/'kɔːzweɪ/

*n.*a road built up above the surface of the land on either side（usually across swampy land)（通常指穿过沼泽地带的)堤道

caustic/'kɔːstɪk/

*adj.*❶able to burn or destroy living flesh 腐蚀性的；苛性的：~ soda 苛性钠 ❷ sharp；bitter；cutting 尖刻的；刻薄的；讽刺的：a ~ tongue 刻薄嘴

caution/'kɔːʃn/

I *n.*❶ care taken to avoid danger or mistakes；paying attention 谨慎；小心：You must exercise great ~ when operating the machine.操作机器时，你必须格外小心。❷ warning words 警告：The judge gave the prisoner a ~ and set him free. 法官给了那个囚犯一次警告，然后将他释放。II *v.*warn sb.about sth.警告；告诫

cautionary /'kɔːʃənəri/

*adj.*serving as a warning 劝告的；告诫的；警告的：a ~ tale 警世故事

cautious/'kɔːʃəs/

*adj.*being careful to avoid danger or mistakes 小心的；谨慎的：be ~ with money 用钱节俭 ‖ ~ly *adv.*谨慎地

cave/keɪv/

I *n.*a hollow space under the ground, especially one with an opening in the side of a hill 洞穴，(尤指)山洞：Crusoe looked about the ~, the floor and the wall were quite dry.克鲁索看看山洞四周,地面和洞壁都很干燥。/Many years ago, men lived in ~s.很久以前,人类过着穴居生活。Ⅱ v.(cause to) fall down and towards the centre 塌陷;陷落;使凹陷:The roof of the old house ~d in.那幢旧房的屋顶塌下来了。

cavern/ˈkævən/
n.a large deep cave 大山洞;大岩洞

cavernous /ˈkævənəs/
adj.large and dark, like a cavern 又大又黑的;像洞穴的

cavil/ˈkævl/
v. (-ll- or -l-) make unnecessary complaints against; find fault with 挑剔;吹毛求疵:~ at everything 事事挑剔/You could find nothing to ~ about.你什么毛病也挑不出来。

cavity/ˈkævəti/
n.an empty space or small hole within a solid body 腔;窝;洞:a ~ in a tooth 龋洞

caw/kɔː/
Ⅰ n.a cry of a raven, rook or crow 乌鸦的叫声;呱呱声 Ⅱ v.make this cry (乌鸦)叫,呱呱地叫

cease/siːs/
v.stop happening or existing 停止,结束;平息:They ~d talking. 他们停止了说话。/The rain has ~d. 雨停了。

ceasefire/ˈsiːsfaɪə(r)/
n.a signal to stop firing guns in war; a truce 停火;停战

ceaseless /ˈsiːslɪs/
adj.not ceasing, continuing constantly 不停的;不绝的;不断的 ‖ ~ly adv.不停地;不断地

cedar/ˈsiːdə(r)/
n.an evergreen tree with hard, red, sweet-smelling wood used for making boxes, pencils, fences, etc.雪松;A fire of ~ logs smells sweet.雪松木柴烧起来很香。

cede/siːd/
v.make an agreement to give land or other property or rights to another person or country; give up 割让(土地);转让(财产);放弃:~ a point in an argument 辩论中在某一点做出让步

ceiling/ˈsiːlɪŋ/
n.❶the upper surface of a room 天花板:There is a fly on the ~.天花板上有一只苍蝇。❷ the highest level 最高限度:price ~s 最高的限价

celebrate/ˈselɪbreɪt/
v.❶do sth. to show that a day or an event is special and important 庆祝:The people ~ the National Day. 人们欢庆国庆节。❷praise sb.or sth.赞颂:Today his words and deeds are ~d throughout the land.今天,他的言行受到举国称赞。

celebrated /ˈselɪbreɪtɪd/
adj.famous; well known 著名的;闻名的;驰名的:a ~ writer 著名作家

celebration/ˌselɪˈbreɪʃn/
n.❶ the act of celebrating sth. 庆祝:The ~ of our victory will last for a week.我们庆祝胜利的活动将持续一个星期。❷a special event organized to celebrate sth. 庆典;庆祝活动:a Saturday night ~ 周末庆祝活动

celebratory/ˌseləˈbreɪtəri/
adj.celebrating sth. or marking a special occasion 庆祝的;庆典的:a ~ dinner 喜庆宴会

celebrity/sɪˈlebrəti/
n.❶the state of being famous 著名;名声 ❷a famous person 知名人士;名人

celery/ˈseləri/
n.a small plant with long crisp light green stems eaten as a vegetable 芹菜:He dug up a head of ~.他从地里挖出一棵芹菜。

celestial/sɪˈlestɪəl/
adj.of the sky; of heaven 天的;天空的;天上的:The sun and the moon are ~ bodies.太阳和月亮都是天体。

celibate/ˈselɪbət/
adj.unmarried especially for a religious promise (尤指因宗教上的承诺而)独身的,不结婚的

cell/sel/
n. ❶ a very small piece of living substance, of which all plants and animals are made up 细胞;cancer ~s 癌细胞 ❷a small room in which a prisoner lives 单人牢房:The prisoner was locked in a ~.那

C

个囚犯被锁在一间单人牢房里。❸ an apparatus for making a current of electricity by chemical action 电池：My torch battery is made up of two ～s.我的手电电池由二节组成。

cellar/ˈselə(r)/
 *n.*a room under a house,used for storing things（especially fuel or wine）地下室（尤指贮藏燃料、酒类的地窖）

cellist /ˈtʃelɪst/
 *n.*a person who plays the cello 大提琴手；大提琴演奏者

cello/ˈtʃeləʊ/
 *n.*a type of stringed musical instrument played between the player's knees 大提琴

cellophane/ˈseləfeɪn/
 *n.*a transparent type of paper used for wrapping goods for sale 玻璃纸（用于包装商品出售）

cellular /ˈseljʊlə/
 *adj.*❶to do with cells；composed of cells 细胞的；由细胞组成的：～ structure 细胞结构 ❷（said about a fabric）woven with an open mesh that traps air and provides insulation（织物）网状的，网眼的：～ blankets 网眼毯 ❸（said about a telephone system）using short-range radio stations to transmit data（电话）蜂窝状的

Celsius/ˈselsɪəs/
 *adj.*referring to a system of measuring temperature,using 0 degrees for the temperature of melting ice,and 100 degrees for the temperature of boiling water 摄氏温度制的,摄氏的

cement/sɪˈment/
 Ⅰ *n.*❶ a powdery substance which becomes very hard when mixed with water, used for building 水泥 ❷a soft glue for sticking things 黏合剂 ❸sth. that unites people together for a common goal 凝聚力 Ⅱ *v.*❶ join or fill two things together with cement,glue,etc.（用水泥、胶等）黏接,胶金 ❷ join or fasten a relationship, an agreement,etc. firmly 加强,巩固：～ relations between our two countries 加强

我们两国间的关系

cemetery/ˈsemətri/
 *n.*a piece of land where dead people are buried 墓地,公墓

censor/ˈsensə(r)/
 Ⅰ *n.* an official who examines books，plays,etc.and cuts out any parts that are considered to be immoral（书籍、戏剧等的）审查员 Ⅱ *v.*examine and act upon as a censor 审查；检查：～ someone's mail 检查某人的信件

censure/ˈsenʃə(r)/
 *v.*express severe disapprove of sb.or sth. 指责；非难

census/ˈsensəs/
 *n.*an official count or survey of a population in a country 人口普查；人口调查：collect ～ data 收集人口普查数据

cent/sent/
 *n.*the unit of money worth the 100th part of a dollar or other decimal currency unit（货币单位）分：Have you got a 5-～ coin? 你有一个 5 分硬币吗?

centenary/senˈtiːnəri/
 Ⅰ *adj.*of a period of 100 years 一百周年的；一个世纪的 Ⅱ *n.* a period of 100 years；the 100th anniversary 一百周年；百年纪念：the ～ of the birth 诞辰一百周年纪念

centigrade/ˈsentɪɡreɪd/
 adj.＝Celsius

centigram /ˈsentɪɡræm/
 *n.*a metric unit of mass,equal to one hundredth of a gram 厘克；公毫

centimetre(-er)/ˈsentɪmiːtə(r)/
 *n.*a metric unit measure of length equal to one hundredth of a metre 厘米；公分

centipede /ˈsentɪpiːd/
 *n.*a small creature like an insect, with a long thin body and many legs 蜈蚣

central/ˈsentrəl/
 *adj.*❶in or at the centre or middle point；near or from the centre 在中央的；中心的；中央的；中心点的：a ～ station 中心车站 ❷principal；chief 主要的；重要的：the ～ character in a novel 小说中的主人公

centralism /ˈsentrəlɪzəm/

n. a policy of concentrating power or authority in one place 中央集权制（或主义）；集中制 ‖ **centralist** *n.* & *adj.* 中央集权主义者；拥护中央集权的

centralize /ˈsentrəlaɪz/

v. concentrate power or control in one central authority 集权控制；实行集中：a highly ～d system of government 高度中央集权的政府体制 ‖ **centralization** *n.* 集中化

centre(**-er**) /ˈsentə(r)/

I *n.* ❶ the middle point or part of sth. 中心；中央；中间：The tower is at the ～ of the town. 那座塔在城市的中心。 ❷ a place where a specified activity is concentrated（特定活动的）中心：Broadway is the theatrical ～ of the U.S. 百老汇街是美国的戏剧中心。 II *v.* ❶ place or be placed in the middle；bring to or come to one point 以……为中心；把……放在中心：He tried to ～ the picture on the wall. 他试图把那幅画挂在墙中间。 ❷ have sth. as a main subject or area of concern 以……为主题；把……作为集中点：She ～ed her attention on study. 她把精力集中在学习上。

centrifugal /senˈtrɪfjʊɡəl/

adj. moving away from a centre or axis 离心的 ‖ **-ly** *adv.* 离心地

centrifuge /ˈsentrɪfjuːdʒ/

n. a machine which, by rapid rotation, separates substances of different densities 离心机

centripetal /senˈtrɪpɪtl/

adj. moving or tending to move towards a centre 向心的

centrist /ˈsentrɪst/

n. a person with political views that are not extreme（政治上的）中间派，温和派

century /ˈsentʃəri/

n. ❶ a hundred years；one of the periods of 100 years before or after the birth of Jesus Christ 一百年；一个世纪；世纪：He has been dead for more than a ～. 他已逝世一百多年了。/ We live in the twenty-first ～. 我们生活在 21 世纪。 ❷ (in the cricket) 100 runs made by a batsman in one innings（板球中击球员一局所得的）百分：score a ～ 得百分

ceramic /sɪˈræmɪk/

I *adj.* (especially with reference to making or designing) of pottery；concerned with cups, plates, etc.（尤指制造或设计）陶瓷的；陶器的 II *n.* (*pl.* ～s) a pot or other articles made of clay hardened by heat permanently 陶瓷制品

cereal /ˈsɪərɪəl/

n. any grain crop used as food (e.g. wheat, corn, rice) 谷类食物（例如小麦、玉米、大米）

cerebellum /ˌserɪˈbeləm/

n. (*pl.* ～s or cerebella) a small part of the brain located in the back of the skull and controlling the movement of muscles 小脑

cerebral /ˈserɪbrəl/

adj. ❶ of the brain 脑的；大脑的：～ palsy 脑麻痹 ❷ intellectual；excluding the emotions 有理智的；不感情用事的：a rather ～ person 一个相当理智的人

cerebration /ˌserɪˈbreɪʃn/

n. the working of the brain；the act of thinking 大脑的作用（机能）；思想活动；思考

cerebrum /səˈriːbrəm/

n. (*pl.* ～s or cerebra /ˈserɪbrə/) the front part of the brain, concerned with thought and decision 大脑

ceremonial /ˌserɪˈməʊnɪəl/

adj. formal, as used for ceremonies 礼仪的；仪式的：～ dress 礼服/～ usage 礼仪上的惯例

ceremonious /ˌserɪˈməʊnɪəs/

adj. fond of or marked by ceremony or formality 讲究仪式的；拘礼的；隆重的：a ～ bow 毕恭毕敬的一鞠躬/a ～ person 拘泥礼节的人/a ～ welcome 盛大的欢迎

ceremony /ˈserɪməni/

n. ❶ an act or series of acts that includes formal or traditional actions 仪式；典礼：the opening ～ 开幕式 ❷ formal behaviour 礼仪；客套：There is no need for ～ between friends. 朋友间不必客气。 ‖

stand on ～（讲）客气

cert/sɜːt/

　　n. a certainty；sth. considered certain to happen 必然发生的事；绝对的事：It's a (dead) ～ that this horse will win the race.这匹马肯定会在这场比赛中获胜。

certain/'sɜːtn/

　　adj. ❶ specific but not named 某个的；某种的；某些的：I'm prepared to make ～ concessions.我准备做出某些让步。❷ having no doubt；sure 确实的；可靠的：There is no ～ cure for this disease.对于这种病，没有可靠的治疗方法。❸ sure to come or happen 有把握的；肯定的：I am not ～ whether he will come.我不敢肯定他会来。‖ for ～ 有把握地；肯定地/make ～ 弄清楚(情况)

certainly/'sɜːtnli/

　　adv. ❶without doubt；surely 必然地，无疑地：He is ～ a good man.他无疑是个好人。❷(used in answer to questions)yes；of course (用于回答问题)当然可以：—Can you lend me your pen for a while? —Certainly! ——你的钢笔可借给我一会儿吗? ——当然可以!

certainty/'sɜːtnti/

　　n. ❶a thing that is certain；an assured fact 必然的事；毫无疑问的事：the ～ of death in battle 战争必然有死亡 ❷ the state of being certain 确信；无疑：Answers to such questions would never be known with ～.这类问题永远不会有确切的答案。

certificate/sə'tɪfɪkət/

　　n. a written official document that may be used to prove a certain fact 证件；证书：This is your graduation ～.这是你的毕业证书。‖ birth ～ 出生证/health ～ 健康证/medical ～ 诊断书/marriage ～ 结婚证/death ～ 死亡证书

certification /ˌsɜːtɪfɪ'keɪʃən/

　　n. the act of certifying sth. 证明；鉴定：the medical ～ of the cause of death 为死因出具医学鉴定书

certify/'sɜːtɪfaɪ/

　　v. declare that sth. is true 证明；证实：the cause of her death 证明她的死因/I

～ that he is an honest man.我证明他是个诚实的人。/Her father was certified insane.她父亲被证明有精神病。

certitude/'sɜːtɪtjuːd/

　　n. the state of being or feeling certain；freedom from doubt 确实性；确定性；确信

cervical/sɜː'vaɪkl/

　　adj. ❶of the neck 颈(部)的 ❷of the cervix 子宫颈的：a ～ smear 子宫颈涂片检查

cervix/'sɜːvɪks/

　　n. the narrow necklike opening into the womb 子宫颈

cessation/se'seɪʃn/

　　n. a short pause or a stop (暂时)停止，休止，中断：a ～ of fighting with an enemy 休战 /a momentary ～ of breathing 呼吸暂停

cession/'seʃn/

　　n. the act of ceding or giving up land, property, or rights (领土的)割让；(财产、权力的)转让

cesspit/'sesˌpɪt/

　　n. an underground container or hole, in which waste from a building, especially body waste (sewage), is collected 污水坑；化粪池

chafe/tʃeɪf/

　　v. make (a part of the body) sore by rubbing against it 擦破；擦痛(身体某一部位)

chaff[1]/tʃɑːf/

　　n. ❶ the husks separated from grain before it is used as food 粗糠；谷壳 ❷ the dried grasses and plant stems used as food for farm animals 饲料；草料；秣

chaff[2]/tʃɑːf/

　　Ⅰ*v.* make fun of (someone) in a friendly way 对(某人)友善地开玩笑；(无恶意地)戏弄 Ⅱ*n.* friendly joking；banter (善意的)玩笑，戏弄

chain/tʃeɪn/

　　n. ❶ a row of metal rings joins together 链条 ❷ a series of connected things, etc.一系列；一连串：a ～ of revolts 一系列的反抗活动 ‖ ～ bridge *n.* 链式吊

桥/～ **reaction** *n*.连锁反应

chair/tʃeə(r)/

n.a seat with a back 椅子：He is sitting in a ～.他正坐在椅子上。‖ **arm** ～ 扶手椅/**easy** ～ 安乐椅/**folding** ～ 折叠椅/**rocking** ～ 摇椅/**revolving** ～ 转椅

chairman/'tʃeəmən/

n.(*pl*. chairmen) ❶ the person in charge of a meeting（会议）主席：He is ～ of the meeting.他是会议的主席。❷ the person in charge of a committee or company 委员会委员长；董事长

chairmanship/'tʃeəmənʃɪp/

n.the rank, position or period in office of chairman 主席的地位（或身份，任期）：a commission of inquiry under the ～ of a well-known judge 由一名著名法官担任主席的调查委员会

chairperson/'tʃeəpɜːsn/

n.a person who is in charge of a meeting or who directs the work of a committee or organization（主持会议、指导某个委员会或组织工作的）主席；议长；主持人

chairwoman/'tʃeəwʊmən/

n.(*pl*. chairwomen) a female chairperson 女主席；女议长；女主持人

chalk/tʃɔːk/

Ⅰ *n*.❶a soft white or grey rock (limestone) originally formed in ancient times from the shells of very small sea animals 白垩：Chalk is used for making lime.白垩用来做石灰。❷a material similar in texture, made into sticks for writing and drawing 粉笔：The teacher needed a box of colored ～.老师需要一盒彩色粉笔。Ⅱ *v*.write sth.with chalk 用粉笔写

challenge/'tʃælɪndʒ/

Ⅰ *v*.❶ invite sb.to enter a fight, competition, game, etc. 向……挑战；要求……比赛：I ～d him to a game of tennis.我要求他跟我赛一场网球。❷ question or dispute the truth or validity of sth.对……提出质疑：She ～d the justice of the new law.她对新法的公正性提出质疑。❸test the abilities of (a person or things) 对……考验：The new job ～d his skill.这项新的工作考验他的技能。Ⅱ *n*.an invita-tion to a game or contest；a call to a fight 挑战：He accepted the new ～.他接受了新的挑战。

challenging/'tʃælɪndʒɪŋ/

adj.needing the full use of one's abilities and effort；difficult, but in an interesting way 富有挑战性的；需要充分发挥能力的；困难而有趣的：a ～ problem 一个富有挑战性的难题 /She finds her new job very ～.她发现自己的新工作很有挑战性。

chamber/'tʃeɪmbə(r)/

n.a room, especially a bedroom 房间（尤指卧室）‖ ～ **music** 室内乐/～ **orchestra** 小型乐队

champ/tʃæmp/

v.❶ munch or chew enthusiastically or noisily 用力嚼；大声嚼：He ～ed on his sandwich.他大口嚼着三明治。❷(of a horse) make a noisy biting or chewing action(马)大声地咬，大声咀嚼

champagne/ʃæm'peɪn/

n.a kind of French wine which bubbles when the bottle is opened 香槟酒

champion/'tʃæmpɪən/

Ⅰ *n*.❶ a person or team that wins a game, a race, etc.；the best of all the players at a certain competition 冠军：My horse is the ～ of the race.我的马在竞赛中获得冠军。❷ a person who fights for or is in support of a belief 拥护者，斗争者：Is the Labour Party the great ～ of the working men? 工党是工人的拥护者吗？Ⅱ *v*.fight for or speak in support of a belief 支援，捍卫，为……而斗争

championship/'tʃæmpɪənʃɪp/

n.❶a contest for the position of champion in a sport or game, typically involving a series of matches（多指有系列比赛的）锦标赛 ❷ the position or title of being a champion 冠军位置；冠军头衔

chance/tʃɑːns/

Ⅰ *n*.❶ a suitable time or situation when you have an opportunity to do sth.机会：I give you one more ～.我再给你一次机会。❷a possibility of sth. happening 可能性：The ～s are a hundred to one that he will win.他成功的可能性只有百分之一。❸ the unplanned and unexpected course of events regarded as a power 机运;机遇:Chance had favoured her and she succeeded overnight.机遇终于来了,她很快就成功了。Ⅱ v.❶ take place or meet by chance 碰巧;恰好:We ~d to be out when she called.她打电话来时,我们碰巧出去了。❷ take a risk 碰碰运气;拿……冒险:You shouldn't ~ all your money at once.你不应该马上把所有的钱拿去冒险。‖ by ~ 碰巧/take a ~ 碰碰运气/~ it 碰运气;冒风险

chancel /'tʃɑːnsl/
  n.the area around and in front of the altar of a church,used by the priest and choir (教堂中牧师和唱诗班席次所在的)圣坛

chancellor /'tʃɑːnsələ(r)/
  n.❶ the head of government in Germany or Austria(德国或奥地利的)总理 ❷ the honorary head of a university in Britain 〈英〉大学名誉校长 ❸ a senior state or legal official 大臣;司法官 ❹ the head of some American universities (某些美国大学的)校长

chancy /'tʃɑːnsi/
  adj.risky;of uncertain result 冒险的;不可靠的;不确实的:That was a ~ thing to do;you could have been killed.那样做是很危险的,当时你很有可能送命的。/ We may be able to get tickets but it's a bit ~.我们也许能够弄到票,但不大靠得住。

change /tʃeɪndʒ/
  Ⅰ v.❶ become or make different 使变化;改变:That has ~d my idea.那使我改变了主意。❷ give or take one thing for another;exchange 兑换;交换:He ~d his dollars into francs.他把美元兑换成法郎。❸ leave and enter (different vehicles) in order to continue a journey 转车;换车:We ~d to another train.我们换乘了另一列火车。‖ ~ into 使……变为/~ one's mind 改变态度 Ⅱ n.❶ the act or result through which sth.becomes different 变化;转变:A great ~ took place in the village.这个村庄发生了巨大的变化。❷ the money given in exchange for the

same sum in larger units 零钱:I haven't any ~ in my pocket.我的口袋里没有零钱。‖ for a ~ 换换环境(花样等)

changeable /'tʃeɪndʒəbl/
  adj.❶ able to be changed 可改变的 ❷ changing frequently;unpredictable 变化无常的:~ weather 变化无常的天气

changeless /'tʃeɪndʒlɪs/
  adj.remaining the same 恒定的;不变的

changeover /'tʃeɪndʒ'əʊvə/
  n.a change from one system or situation to another (系统或形势的)改变,转变,更换:the ~ from a manual to a computerized system 由手工操作向计算机化系统的转换

channel /'tʃænl/
  n.❶ a narrow passage of sea,etc.海峡:the English Channel 英吉利海峡 ❷ a frequency band for radio 波道;频道:Which ~ do you like? 你喜欢听哪个频道? ❸ a medium for communication or the passage of information (交流或信息传播的)渠道,途径:The issue could be settled only through diplomatic ~s.这个问题只有通过外交途径才能解决。

chant /tʃɑːnt/
  Ⅰ n. an often-repeated tune to which psalms and canticles are fitted;several words to one note 圣歌;赞美诗 Ⅱ v.sing a chant;use a singing note (e.g. for a prayer in Church) 唱圣歌;唱诵

chaos /'keɪɒs/
  n.the state of complete disorder and confusion 混沌;混乱;一团糟:The strong wind left ~ behind it.狂风过后留下一片狼藉。/That country is now in ~.那个国家如今是一片混乱。/ The city was in a state of ~ after the earthquake.地震过后该市处于混乱状态。

chaotic /keɪ'ɒtɪk/
  adj.in a state of complete disorder and confusion 混乱的:The city traffic was ~.城市交通乱糟糟的。

chapter /'tʃæptə(r)/
  n.a main division of a book (书的)章,篇,回:By the end of the ~ you'll have guessed its meaning.到了这章的末尾,你

就会猜出它的意思。

char /tʃɑ:(r)/

v. (-rr-) ❶ make or become black by burning 烧炭;烧焦:Sugar ～s at 400℃.糖在 400 摄氏度烧焦。/The fire ～red the wood.火把树木烧焦了。❷ do some housework 打杂;做杂务: She goes out ～ring.她出去做打扫清洁的零工。

character /'kærəktə(r)/

n. ❶ the qualities which make a person different from another 个性,性格:He is a man of strong ～.他是一个个性很强的人。❷ a person in a book, play, etc. (图书、戏剧等中的)人物 ❸ a letter, sign, mark, etc. used in a system of writing or printing 字母;书写符号:Chinese ～s 汉语字体 ❹ the particular features of sth.特色 ❺ a good reputation 良好声誉

characteristic /ˌkærəktə'rɪstɪk/

Ⅰ *adj.* typical of a particular person, place or thing 特有的,独特的;具……特性的:～ generosity 特有的慷慨/It's ～ of him.这足以表示他的特性。Ⅱ *n.* a special feature or quality 特点;特征;特性;特色:Kindness is one of his ～s.亲切和蔼是他的特性之一。/An elephant's trunk is its notable ～.象的鼻子是它的显著特点。

characterize /'kærəktraɪz/

v. ❶ be characteristic of 是……的特征;以……为特征 ❷ describe the character of;portray 描述……的特性;描绘

charcoal /'tʃɑ:kəʊl/

n. a black substance, used as fuel, made by burning wood slowly in an oven with little air 炭;木炭:a stick of ～ 一根木炭

charge /tʃɑ:dʒ/

Ⅰ *v.* ❶ ask a price for sth. 收费;索价:How much do you ～ me? 你要收我多少钱? ❷ accuse sb. of sth. 控告;指责:I ～ this man with stealing goods.我指控这个人偷窃商品。❸ rush forward and attack sb.or sth.向……冲;冲锋:Suddenly the wild animal ～d at us.突然,那头野兽向我们猛冲过来。Ⅱ *n.* ❶ a price asked for goods or service 收费:The ～ for each visit is ＄10.每次参观收费 10 美元。❷ work given to sb. as a duty;a

thing or person given or entrusted to sb. to be taken care of 负责,管理;被托管物;受照管人 ❸ an accusation that a person has done wrong, especially that he has broken a law 罪名;控告:On what ～ do you arrest him? 你以什么罪名逮捕他? ❹ a sudden and violent attack 冲锋:The ～ was repulsed by the enemy.冲锋被敌人击退了。‖ bring a ～ against 控告/free of ～ 免费/in the ～ of 由……管/leave in ～ of 交由……照管/put sb.in ～ of 让某人负责/take ～ of 负责管理(照顾)……

charisma /kə'rɪzmə/

n. the quality which makes people feel devotion, admiration and loyalty towards one (引起公众爱戴效忠的)魅力

charismatic /ˌkærɪz'mætɪk/

adj. ❶ having great personal charm and influence 有超凡魅力的;有影响力的;有感召力的 ❷ (said about religious groups or worship) emphasizing gifts and abilities conferred by God, e. g. the gift of prophecy (宗教团体或宗教崇拜)蒙受神恩的;有特恩的(如有预言的天赋)

charitable /'tʃærətəbl/

adj. ❶ kind and generous, especially in giving help to the poor 仁慈的;慷慨的;慈悲为怀的 ❷ kind and sympathetic in judging others 宽容的;厚道的:I know he made a mistake, but let's be ～——he was tired at the time.我知道他出了错,但我们宽容点吧,他那时是累了。/Even on the most ～ analysis, it has not been a great success so far.即使根据最宽的标准来分析,到目前为止这还算不上成功。❸ concerned with giving help to people who are poor or in need 慈善的;行善的:a ～ institution 慈善机构/～ donations 慈善捐赠

charity /'tʃærəti/

n. ❶ help to the poor, the sick or anyone in need;love, kindness to others 施舍;仁爱;慈善;宽厚:live on ～ 靠施舍过活/a ～ school 贫民学校;免费学校/a ～ performance 义演/She was always very generous in her ～.她在慈善方面总是极为慷慨。❷ a society or organization for helping people in need 慈善团体：The Red Cross is a ～.红十字会是慈善机构。

charm /tʃɑːm/

I *n*. ❶ the power of pleasing or attracting people 迷人之处；招人喜欢的地方：He had great ～, every one liked him.他极有魅力，人人都喜欢他。❷ words or a thing that are said to be magic 魔法；符咒；有魔力的东西：The fairy godmother's magic ～ turned Cinderella's rags into a beautiful gown. 神话中教母的魔法可以将灰姑娘的破衣衫变成漂亮的礼服。Ⅱ *v*. ❶attract to get sth. or influence sb. 吸引；迷住 ❷ control or get sth. by using magic or as if by magic（用魔法或似有魔法）控制，得到

charming /ˈtʃɑːmɪŋ/

adj. pleasing or attractive 美丽的；可爱的，迷人的：What a ～ man! 多么讨人喜欢的小伙子!

charmless /ˈtʃɑːmlɪs/

adj. unattractive or unpleasant 缺乏魅力的；无吸引力的：a ～ structure 缺乏魅力的建筑物

chart /tʃɑːt/

I *n*.❶a sailor's map of the sea 航海图 ❷ an outline map giving special information 图表：a weather ～ 气象图 Ⅱ *v*. make a map 制图：～ the sea area between France and Britain 绘制法英两国之间的海域图

charter /ˈtʃɑːtə(r)/

I *n*.a written statement by some authority, giving sb. the power to do sth. 特许状 Ⅱ *v*.hire a bus, plane, train, etc. for a special purpose 包汽车（飞机、火车等）：The members of the club ～ed a plane to take them on holiday to France.俱乐部会员包机到法国度假。‖ ～ flight 包机旅行 ‖ ～ed *adj*. 有执照的：a ～ed accountant 特许会计师

chase /tʃeɪs/

v.❶ run after, try to catch up with 追逐：The hunter was chasing the wolf.猎人在追逐那只狼。❷ drive away 驱逐（出去），撵走：We must ～ the enemy from our country.我们应该把敌人从我国撵出

去。‖ ～ after 追赶；追逐

chasm /ˈkæzəm/

n.❶a very deep crack or opening in the surface of the earth or ice（地面或冰上的）宽深裂口；陷坑；断层 ❷a profound difference between people, viewpoints, attitudes, etc.巨大分歧；鸿沟：There was a deep political ～ between the two countries which nearly led to war.这两国之间存在的深刻政治裂痕使他们几乎发生战争。

chassis /ˈʃæsi/

n.❶ the frame on which the body and working parts of a vehicle are fastened or built（汽车等的）底盘，底座 ❷ the landing apparatus of a plane（飞机的）起落架，机架

chaste /tʃeɪst/

adj.pure in word, thought and deed 纯洁的；高雅的

chasten /ˈtʃeɪsn/

v. make someone realize they have done sth.wrong 使内疚；使懊悔：He felt ～ed and apologized. 他感到内疚并表示了歉意。

chastise /tʃæsˈtaɪz/

v.punish or reprimand someone severely 厉声训斥；严厉谴责：He ～d his colleagues for their laziness. 他厉声训斥同事们的怠惰。‖ ～ment *n*.惩罚；责罚

chastity /ˈtʃæstəti/

n.the state of being chaste 纯洁；高雅；贞节：defend one's ～ 保持贞操

chat /tʃæt/

I *v*.(-tt-) have a friendly talk 聊天，闲聊：The two old friends ～ted gaily while they met each other. 两位老朋友碰面后愉快地闲谈。Ⅱ *n*. a friendly talk about unimportant things 聊天：I had a ～ with an old friend on the street.我在街上跟一位老朋友闲聊了一会儿。

chatty /ˈtʃæti/

adj.❶fond of chatting 爱闲聊的；爱说话的：a ～ woman 长舌妇 ❷ having the style or manner of informal conversation 闲谈式的；闲聊的：a ～ letter 闲聊式的信

C

chauvinism/'ʃəʊvɪnɪzəm/
*n.*love of one's country, race, sex, etc. in a wild and unreasonable way; blind patriotism 狭隘的爱国主义; 沙文主义: male ～ 大男子主义

cheap/tʃi:p/
adj. ❶ low in price; costing little money 便宜的; 合算的: a ～ article 便宜货 ❷ of poor quality; worthless 低劣的; 不值钱的: a ～ novel 低劣的小说

cheapen /'tʃi:pən/
*v.*❶make sth. cheap, or become cheap 使降价; 使跌价: to ～ the cost of raw materials 降低原材料的成本 ❷ make sth. appear to have less value 使贬值; 贬低

cheat/tʃi:t/
Ⅰ *v.*❶be unfair or dishonest in order to get sth.; play tricks; act dishonestly 欺骗; 瞒哄: That shopkeeper ～s his customer.那个店主欺骗了他的顾客。 ❷ behave in a dishonest or deceitful way in order to win an advantage, especially in a game or an exam 作弊: Any student caught ～ing will be disqualified from the exam.任何被发现有舞弊行为的学生将被取消考试资格。 Ⅱ *n.* a person who cheats; a dishonest person 骗子: I saw you drop that card, you ～! 我看见你丢掉那张牌，你这个骗子!

check/tʃek/
Ⅰ *v.*❶ test or examine sth. in order to determine its accuracy, quality or condition 检查; 核对: Check the copy against the original.对照原文检查一下复印本。 ❷ hold back, cause to go slow or stop the progress of sth. 阻止; 遏止: He couldn't ～ his anger.他不能遏制自己的愤怒。 ‖ ～ **over** 检查一遍/～ **through** 查看, 校阅/～ **up** 检查, 调查 Ⅱ *n.*❶ an examination to make certain of accuracy, quality, or condition 检查, 核对: The plumber made a careful ～ of the pipes.管道工仔细地检查了一下管道。 ❷ a means of control or restraint 阻碍; 抑制: I advise you to keep a ～ on your temper.我建议你要忍住怒气。 ‖ ～**point** *n.*检查哨所

checker /'tʃekə/
*n.*❶a person or thing that verifies or examines sth. 查对者; 查对物; 检验人; 检验物 ❷a cashier in a supermarket 超市收银员

check-in /'tʃekɪn/
n. ❶ the place where you go first when you arrive at an airport, to show your ticket, etc. (机场的)登机手续办理处 ❷ the act of showing your ticket, etc. when you arrive at an airport (机场的)办理登机手续: Do you know your ～ time? 你知道办理登机手续的时间吗?

checklist /tʃek'lɪst/
n. a list of items required, things to be done, or points to be considered, used as a reminder 清单; 一览表

checkout /'tʃekaʊt/
n. ❶ a place where customers pay for goods in a supermarket (超市)收银台 ❷ the administrative procedure followed when a guest leaves a hotel at the end of their stay (客人离开旅店时的)结账

check-up /'tʃekʌp/
*n.*a routine medical or dental examination 体检; 口腔检查

cheek/tʃi:k/
*n.*❶ either side of the face below the eyes 面颊: A faint blush came into her ～.她的脸泛起了一阵红晕。 ❷ a bold talk or action 厚脸皮, 无礼的行为: That fellow has ～ enough for anything.那家伙很无耻, 什么事都做得出来。 ‖ ～y *adj.*厚脸皮的

cheep/tʃip/
Ⅰ *n.*the sound made by a small bird 小鸟的吱吱叫声 Ⅱ *v.*make a shrill squeaky sound 发出吱吱叫声

cheer/tʃɪə(r)/
Ⅰ *v.*❶ make or become happy 使高兴; 变得高兴: Your gift ～ed the orphan.你送的礼物使那孤儿高兴起来。 ❷ shout to show that you are pleased with sb. or sth. 欢呼; 喝彩: The audience ～ed him as he walked on stage.当他走向舞台时, 全体观众为他欢呼。 ‖ ～ **up** 高兴起来 Ⅱ *n.*❶ a shout of happiness or encouragement 欢呼; 喝彩 ❷ optimism or confidence 乐

观;信心 ‖ ～ly *adv.*高兴地;愉快地/～y
*adj.*愉快的;开朗的

cheerful/ˈtʃɪəfl/
 *adj.*❶full of cheer;glad 快乐的;高兴的:
She remained ～ throughout the trip. 在
旅途中她自始至终都很快乐。❷bring-
ing cheer pleasant;bright 令人快乐的;令
人愉快的:a ～ day 快乐的一天

cheerless /ˈtʃɪələs/
 *adj.*gloomy or dreary 阴郁的;沉闷的:
The room was ill-lit and ～.房间灯光昏
暗,让人压抑。

cheese/tʃiːz/
 *n.*a type of food made from thickened
milk 乳酪;干酪:a very good ～ 一块好
的干酪

chef/ʃef/
 *n.*a professional cook in a restaurant or
hotel,especially the chief cook (旅馆、饭
店的)厨师;主厨

chemical/ˈkemɪkl/
 Ⅰ *adj.*of, used in, or made by chemistry
化学的;化学上的;用化学方法得到的:
～ reaction 化学反应 Ⅱ *n.*a substance
used in or made by chemical process 化学
(制)品

chemist/ˈkemɪst/
 n. ❶ a scientist who does research in
chemistry 化学家 ❷ a person who is
qualified to sell medicines prescribed by a
doctor 药品商;药剂师

chemistry/ˈkemɪstri/
 n. ❶ the science which studies the substances or elements making up the
Earth, universe, and living things and
how these substances combine with each
other, and how they behave under different conditions 化 学 ❷ the chemical
structure and behaviour of a particular
substance 物质的化学组成(性质):the ～
of lead 铅的化学性质

chemotherapy/ˌkiːməʊˈθerəpi/
 *n.*the use of chemical substances to treat
and control certain diseases, especially
cancer (尤指对癌的)化学疗法,化学治疗

cheque/tʃek/
 *n.*a written order to a bank to pay money

支票 ‖ ～book *n.*支票簿;支票本

chequered/ˈtʃekəd/
 *adj.*full of ups and downs of fortune,with
a variety of incidents 多波折的;坎坷的;
盛衰无常的:a ～ career 饱经沧桑的一生

cherish/ˈtʃerɪʃ/
 *v.*❶ care for sth. tenderly; love 爱护;珍
视;钟爱: He ～es friendship. 他珍视友
情。❷ keep hope, love, or other deep
feelings firmly in mind 怀有;抱有:She
～ed no resentment. 她不抱怨恨。

cherry/ˈtʃeri/
 *n.*a small,yellow or red fruit with a stone
in the middle 樱桃

chess/tʃes/
 *n.*a board game for two players marked
with black and white squares 西洋棋;国
际象棋:Let's have a game of ～.我们下
一盘棋。

chest/tʃest/
 *n.*❶ the upper front part of the body,
where the ribs, lungs and hearts are 胸
膛;胸腔 ❷a large, heavy box used for
storing things 箱子;盒子:20 ～s of tea
20 箱茶叶

chestnut/ˈtʃesnʌt/
 *n.*❶ a type of large soft nut often eaten
roasted 栗子 ❷ the tree on which this
nut grows 栗树 ❸a deep reddish-brown
colour 栗色

chew/tʃuː/
 Ⅰ *v.*crush and grind food into little bits in
one's mouth 咀嚼;嚼碎:You must ～
your food well before you swallow it.食
物细嚼慢咽。 Ⅱ *n.*a sticky substance
sweetened and favoured for chewing 口香
糖;橡皮糖

chick/tʃɪk/
 n. ❶ a young bird, especially a young
chicken 小鸡;小鸟:Count your ～s before they are hatched.蛋尚未孵先数鸡。
(指过早乐观) ❷a little baby 小孩 ❸a
young woman 少妇

chicken/ˈtʃɪkɪn/
 *n.*❶a large bird that is kept for its eggs
or meat especially a young one 鸡(尤指
小鸡)❷meat from such a bird 鸡肉;Do

you like roast ～? 你喜欢吃烤鸡肉吗?

chief /tʃiːf/

I *n*. a leader or ruler of a people or community 元首,统帅,头领,酋长: the ～ of the tribe 酋长 II *adj*. ❶ main; most important 主要的;最重要的: Rice is the ～ crop in this area.水稻是这个地区的主要作物。❷first in rank 首席的,权力最大的 ‖ commander-in-～ *n*.总司令/editor-in-～ *n*.总编辑/～ engineer *n*.总工程师/～ delegate *n*.首席代表/～ conductor *n*.列车长

chiefly /'tʃiːfli/

adv. ❶ mainly; mostly 主要地;多半地: Air consists ～ of nitrogen.空气主要由氮组成。❷above all 首要地: They were ～ interested in making money. 他们主要是对赚钱感兴趣。

chieftain /'tʃiːftin/

n.❶ the chief of a clan or tribe 族长;酋长 ❷ the leader of a band of robbers 强盗的头目;匪首

chiffon /ʃɪ'fɒn/

n. a thin, transparent silk material used for scarves, veils, etc.雪纺绸;薄绸

chilblain /'tʃɪlblem/

n.a red sore or swelling on the hands or feet, caused by cold weather 冻疮

child /tʃaɪld/

n.(*pl*.children /'tʃɪldrən/) ❶a boy or girl 小孩;儿童;孩子: The disease is common among young children. 这种病在小孩中很常见。❷a son or daughter at any age 儿子;女儿

childbirth /'tʃaɪldbɜːθ/

n.the action of giving a birth to a baby 分娩;生孩子: She died in ～.她因生孩子而逝世了。

childhood /'tʃaɪldhʊd/

n.the period of being a child 童年(时代): He spent his ～ in hard work. 他在繁重的劳动中度过自己的童年。

childish /'tʃaɪldɪʃ/

adj.of, behaving like, suitable for a child; immature 儿童的;行为如儿童的;适于儿童的;幼稚的;act with ～ petulance 孩子般任性地行动/The little girl spoke in a

high ～ voice.这小女孩儿用尖尖的童声讲话。

childlike /'tʃaɪldlaɪk/

adj. like a child 孩子似的;天真的;～ games 儿童游戏/～ innocence 天真无邪

chill /tʃɪl/

I *n*.an unpleasant feeling of coldness 寒气;凉意:A ～ came over me.我身上一阵寒冷。II *v*.make or become cold (使)变凉:Our hearts ～ed when we heard the news.听到那条消息,我们的心都变凉了。

chilli /'tʃɪli/

n.(*pl*.～es)a dried hot-tasting pod of red pepper used in sauces or as a seasoning 辣椒

chilling /'tʃɪlɪŋ/

adj.frightening, usually because it is connected with sth. violent or cruel(常与残暴有关)令人恐惧的,令人害怕的:a ～ story 令人毛骨悚然的故事

chilly /'tʃɪli/

adj.(chillier, chilliest)❶ slightly or unpleasantly cold 寒冷的;阴冷的: It's ～ today.今天很寒冷。❷(said about a person or manner) aloof and unfriendly(人或举止)不友好的,冷淡的,冷漠的

chime /tʃaɪm/

I *n*.a musical sound of a bell (especially a bell in a church or clock)(尤指教堂或时钟的)钟声 II *v*. make melodious ringing sounds 发出和谐的钟声:The clock was chiming six when I came in.我走进来时,钟正敲六下。

chimney /'tʃɪmni/

n.❶ a structure through which smoke from a fire is carried away typically through the roof of a building 烟囱;烟筒;smoke like a ～ 烟瘾极大/～ sweeper 扫烟囱工人 ❷a glass tube that protects the flame of an oil-lamp from draughts (用以遮风的)油灯玻璃灯罩

chimpanzee /ˌtʃɪmpən'ziː/

n.an African ape, smaller than a gorilla 黑猩猩:Chimpanzees are very intelligent.黑猩猩很聪明。

chin /tʃɪn/

n.the part of the face below the mouth 下

巴;下颏:You move your ～ when you chew.你嚼东西时,下巴就要动。

china/'tʃaɪnə/
*n.*❶a hard white substance made by baking fine white clay at high temperatures 瓷料 ❷objects that are made of china 瓷器 ‖ ～ clay *n.*瓷土/～ ware *n.*(总称)瓷器

Chinese/'tʃaɪ'niːz/
Ⅰ*adj.*of belonging to China,its people or language 中国的:a ～ restaurant 一家中国餐馆 Ⅱ*n.*❶a native of China or person whose family was originally from China 中国人;华裔 ❷the language of China 中文;汉语:Foreigners find it difficult to learn ～.外国人觉得汉语很难学。‖ ～ cabbage *n.*白菜/～ lantern *n.*灯笼

chink/tʃɪŋk/
n.(especially in a wall or door)a narrow opening or crack (尤指墙壁或门上的)隙缝

chip/tʃɪp/
Ⅰ*n.*❶a small piece cut or broken off from wood,stone,china,etc. 木片;石片;渣;碎屑 ❷a thin piece of a potato,fruit,etc.(马铃薯、水果等的)薄片 Ⅱ*v.*(-pp-)cut or break a piece off;make into small pieces 切下(或碰坏)一片;把……切成碎片:All the plates have ～ped edges.所有这些盘子边上都有破损。

chirp/tʃɜːp/
Ⅰ*n.*a short,sharp sound made by some small birds and insects (鸟叫的)吱吱声;(虫鸣的)唧唧声:the ～s of cicadas 蝉的唧唧声 Ⅱ*v.*make short sounds;speak in a cheerful voice 发出吱吱声;兴高采烈地说:Some insects ～ out at night.有些昆虫在夜里叫。

chirpy/'tʃɜːpi/
*adj.*happy and cheerful;light-hearted 快活的;活泼的;轻松愉快的:a ～ little song 快乐的小调 / in a ～ mood 愉快的心情

chisel/'tʃɪzl/
*n.*a steel-edged tool for shaping wood,stone or metal 凿子;錾子

chit/tʃɪt/
*n.*a piece of paper with a few words written on it,used to show that one has permission to get sth. or to do sth.(用以证明持条人可以取得某物或做某事的)便条

chivalry/'ʃɪvəlri/
*n.*❶ (in the Middle Ages)the code of behaviour of knights (中世纪)骑士精神 ❷ polite and courageous behaviour of men,especially towards women (尤指男人对女人的)彬彬有礼

chives/tʃaɪvz/
n. (*pl.*) the long thin leaves of a plant with purple flowers,which taste like onions and are used to give flavour to food 细香葱,四季葱

chloride/'klɔːraɪd/
*n.*a compound of chlorine with another element 氯化物:sodium ～ 氯化钠/～ of lime 漂白粉

chlorine/'klɔːriːn/
n. a chemical element,a greenish-yellow,pungent-smelling poisonous gas,used as a sterilizing agent and in industry 氯;氯气

chocolate/'tʃɒklət/
*n.*❶a substance (powder or slab) made from cocoa 朱古力;巧克力 ❷drink or sweet made from this 巧克力饮料;巧克力糖:a box of ～s 一盒巧克力糖/eat ～s 吃巧克力糖 /a bar of ～ 一块巧克力 ❸a dark brown colour 赭色;深褐色

choice/tʃɔɪs/
Ⅰ*n.*❶ an act of selecting or making a decision 选择;抉择:Be careful in your ～ of friends.择友宜慎。 ❷ a person or thing chosen 被选择的人(或物):This is my ～.这是我所选择的。 ❸ a range of possibilities from which one or more may be selected 可选的范围:This shop has a large ～ of hats.这家商店有许多帽子可供顾客选择。Ⅱ*adj.*carefully selected;of high quality 精选的;高级的:She put on her ～ clothes.她穿上最好的衣服。

choir/'kwaɪə(r)/
*n.*a group of singers,especially one which sings in church 合唱团(尤指教堂中的唱诗班)

choke /tʃəʊk/

v. ❶ (of a person or an animal) be unable to breathe because of an constricted or obstructed throat or a lack of air (人或动物)窒息；噎住，呛住，哽住：The smoke almost ~d me. 这烟筒直让我透不过气来。❷ fill partly or completely a passage, space, etc. so that movement is difficult 充塞；填塞：The river is becoming ~d with sand. 泥沙堵塞了河流。❸ become speechless, especially because of strong emotion（尤指因感情激动而）说不出话来，哽咽：Anger ~s his words. 愤怒使他一时语塞。‖ ~ back 忍住/~ down 匆忙或费力地咽下去/~ off 使……突然中断/~ up 堵塞

choked /tʃəʊkt/

adj. angry or upset 生气的；发怒的；心烦意乱的：I was really ~ to hear he'd died. 听到他的死讯，我难过得说不出话来。

cholera /ˈkɒlərə/

n. an infectious and often fatal disease, common in hot countries, with vomiting and continual emptying of the bowels, often causing death from weakness 霍乱

cholesterol /kəˈlestərəʊl, kəˈlestərɒl/

n. a fatty substance in body tissue that can harden the arteries 胆固醇

choose /tʃuːz/

v. (chose, chosen) ❶ pick out or select sb. or sth. 选择；挑选：There is nothing to ~ between the two. 两者差不多，没有什么可挑的。❷ prefer；decide on a course of action 愿意；决定：~ death before surrender 宁死不屈

choosy /ˈtʃuːzi/

adj. (choosier, choosiest) taking a long time to choose, hard to please 精挑细选的；爱挑剔的；难以取悦的：She is very ~ about her clothes. 她对自己的衣着很讲究。

chop /tʃɒp/

v. (-pp-) ❶ cut sth. by hitting with an axe, knife, etc. 砍；劈：He was ~ping wood. 他正在砍柴。❷ cut sth. into small pieces 切碎：The cook ~ped the meat up before cooking it. 厨师在煮肉前把肉切

碎。‖ ~ at 向……砍去/~ down 砍倒/~ off 砍掉/~ up 切碎

chopper /ˈtʃɒpə(r)/

n. ❶ a person who chops 伐木者 ❷ a heavy tool with a sharp edge for chopping meat, wood, etc. 斧子；屠刀 ❸ a helicopter 直升机

choppy /ˈtʃɒpi/

adj. (choppier, choppiest) ❶ (said about the sea) slightly rough with a lot of short broken waves (海洋)波浪起伏的 ❷ having a disjointed or jerky quality 不连贯的，脱节的；不稳的 ‖ choppiness *n.* 波浪翻滚；不稳定

chopsticks /ˈtʃɒpstɪks/

n. (*pl.*) a pair of sticks used in some Asian countries for lifting food to the mouth 筷子：a pair of ~ 一双筷子/We are used to using ~ instead of knife and fork. 我们习惯用筷子吃饭而不用刀叉。

choral /ˈkɔːrəl/

adj. composed for or sung by a choir or chorus 合唱的；合唱团的

chorale /ˈkɔːrəl/

n. a song of praise to be sung in a church 赞美诗；圣歌：a Bach ~ 巴赫谱写的赞美诗

chord /kɔːd/

n. several musical notes played together 和弦

chore /tʃɔː(r)/

n. a routine task or job, especially in a house 零星工作（尤指家常杂务）

chorus /ˈkɔːrəs/

n. ❶ a large organized group of singers；a group of dancers or singers performing in a musical show 合唱队；（音乐剧）歌舞队：The ~ was (were) very good tonight. 今晚合唱团唱得非常好。❷ a part of a song that is sung by everyone after solo verses 合唱曲：a ~ for men's voices 男声合唱曲 ❸ sth. said or cried by many people together 齐声；异口同声：a ~ of praise 一片赞美声 /sing in ~ 合唱/read in ~ 齐声念 Ⅱ *v.* say a thing by different people at the same time 异口同声地说

Christ /kraɪst/

n. the title given to Jesus, now used as part of or as an alternative to his name 基督：Christians are the followers of ～.基督教徒就是基督的追随者。

christen/ˈkrɪsn/
v. ❶give a name to a child during the ceremony of baptism, by which the child is received into the Christian church（洗礼时）为受洗儿童命名 ❷give sb. or sth. a name 给……命名（或取名）

Christian/ˈkrɪstʃən/
Ⅰ *n.* a person who believes in the teachings of Christ 基督徒 Ⅱ *adj.* ❶of Jesus and the religion based on his teachings 基督教的：the ～ name 教名 ❷relating to Christians 基督教徒的

Christianity/ˌkrɪstɪˈænəti/
n. the Christian faith or religion, being a Christian 基督教；基督教徒的身份

Christmas/ˈkrɪsməs/
n. (also ～ **Day**) a yearly celebration of the birth of Jesus Christ, 25 December 圣诞节（12 月 25 日，略写作 Xmas）‖ ～ **tree** *n.*圣诞树/～ **card** *n.*圣诞卡/～ **Eve** *n.*圣诞前夕/～ **cake** *n.*圣诞蛋糕

chromosome/ˈkrəʊməsəʊm/
n. a tiny thread-like part of an animal or plant cell, carrying genes 染色体‖ **chromosomal** *adj.*染色体的

chronic/ˈkrɒnɪk/
adj. (of a disease or condition) continual, lasting for a long time（疾病或状况）慢性的，长期的：a ～ disease 慢性病

chronicle/ˈkrɒnɪkl/
Ⅰ *n.* the record of important or historical events in the order of their happening 年代记；编年史；记事 Ⅱ *v.* record events in the order of their happening 按事件顺序记载

chronological/ˌkrɒnəˈlɒdʒɪkl/
adj. arranged in the order in which a number of events happened 按年代次序排列的

chrysalis/ˈkrɪsəlɪs/
n. (*pl.*～es) an insect at a stage when it forms a sheath inside which it changes from a grub to an adult insect, especially a butterfly or moth 蛹（尤指蝶蛹、蛾蛹）

chuckle/ˈtʃʌkl/
Ⅰ *n.* a quiet laugh with closed mouth 轻声的笑；暗自的笑：She gave a ～ to herself at the joke. 她对那笑话暗自发笑。Ⅱ *v.* laugh quietly; laugh to oneself 低声轻笑；暗自笑：He ～d to himself as he read that funny story.他读那个有趣儿的故事时暗自发笑。

chuffed/tʃʌft/
adj. pleased or happy 满意的；喜欢的；高兴的：She's very ～ about her new job.她对新的工作十分满意。

chug/tʃʌg/
Ⅰ *v.* (-gg-) (of an engine or vehicle) move while making a low repeated knocking sound（引擎、机动车等）发出嘎嚓声前进：I heard the little car ～ along.我听到那辆小汽车突突地响着开过去了。/ They watched the old steam engine ～ging up the hill.他们望着那辆老式蒸汽机车咔嚓咔嚓地开上山坡。Ⅱ *n.* the chug of the motorboat 汽艇的突突声

chum/tʃʌm/
n. a close friend 好友：an old school ～ 老同学

chunk/tʃʌŋk/
n. a thick, solid piece or lump cut off a loaf, a piece of meat, etc. （厚）块：a ～ of wood 一块木头/The dog ate a ～ of meat.狗吃了一大块肉。

chunky/ˈtʃʌŋki/
adj. ❶ short, thick and solid 短粗而结实的 ❷ (of a person, especially a man) having a broad chest and strong-looking body, and not very tall（尤指男人）矮而壮实的 ❸ (of materials, clothes, etc.) thick and heavy（材料、衣服等）厚的，重的：a ～ woollen sweater 一件厚毛绒衫 / a ～ silver bracelet 沉甸甸的银镯 ❹ (of food) containing thick solid pieces（食品）大块的，厚片的：～ marmalade 含有橘子块的橘子酱

church/tʃɜːtʃ/
n. a building where Christians go to pray and worship 教堂：Our ～ has many activities.我们的教堂举办许多活动。

churlish/ˈtʃɜːlɪʃ/

　　*adj.*very bad-tempered and impolite 脾气暴躁的；没礼貌的

chute/ʃuːt/

　　n. ❶ a long, narrow, steep slope down which things may slide 斜槽；滑槽：a waste ～ 垃圾斜槽 ❷a parachute 降落伞

cicada/sɪˈkɑːdə/

　　*n.*a large insect with transparent wings. The male makes a loud shrill sound.蝉

cider/ˈsaɪdə(r)/

　　*n.*an alcoholic drink made from apples 苹果酒

cigar/sɪˈgɑː(r)/

　　*n.*a tight roll of tobacco leaves with a pointed end 雪茄烟

cigarette/ˌsɪgəˈret/

　　*n.*a thin paper tube of finely cut tobacco for smoking 香烟：She lit her ～.她点燃了香烟。

cinder/ˈsɪndə(r)/

　　*n.*a small piece of coal, wood, etc. partly burned, no longer flaming, and not yet ash 煤渣；炉渣；灰烬：fine ～s 细煤灰

cinema/ˈsɪnəmɑː, ˈsɪnəmə/

　　*n.*❶a place where people go to see films 电影院 ❷the art or industry of making films 电影艺术；电影工业：He's worked in the ～ all his life.他一生都在电影业工作。

cinnabar/ˈsɪnəbɑː/

　　n. ❶ a reddish mineral that is the chief source of mercury 朱砂；辰砂 ❷ the bright red colour of cinnabar 朱红色

cinnamon/ˈsɪnəmən/

　　*n.*❶the inner bark of an East Indian tree, used as a spice；its tree；肉桂；肉桂树❷a yellowish brown colour 黄褐色

cipher/ˈsaɪfə(r)/

　　n. ❶a system of writing in code, understood by certain people for whom the message is intended 密码 ❷an insignificant person or thing 无关紧要的人（或事）

circa /ˈsɜːkə/

　　prep.（used with dates）about, approxi-mately（与日期连用）大约：～ 1050 大约1050 年

circle/ˈsɜːkl/

　　Ⅰ *n.*❶ a round flat figure 圆；圆形 ❷a group of people or things arranged to form such a figure 一圈（人或物）：The children gathered round in a ～.孩子们围成一个圆圈。❸ a number of people who get together and have the same interests 圈子，集团：He has a large ～ of friends.他有一大群朋友。Ⅱ *v.*❶ surround 围住：The troop ～d the city.部队包围了城市。❷ move around；move in a circle 绕……运行；盘旋：The plane ～d around the airport before landing.飞机着陆前在机场上空盘旋了一阵。

circuit/ˈsɜːkɪt/

　　*n.*❶ a journey round from place to place 环行：It takes a year for the earth to make its ～ of the sun.地球绕太阳运行一周需时一年。❷ a path of an electric current 电路：A break in the ～ had caused the lights to go out. 由于电路中断，电灯熄灭了。

circuitous /sə(ː)ˈkjuː(ː)ɪtəs/

　　adj.（said about a route）longer than the usual way, indirect（路线）迂回的；绕道的；曲折的 ‖～ly *adv.*迂回地；曲折地

circuitry /ˈsɜːkɪtri/

　　*n.*a system of electrical circuits or the e-quipment forming them 电路系统；电路；电路装置

circular/ˈsɜːkjʊlə(r)/

　　*adj.*round like a circle；of a circle；moving in a circle 圆形的；环形的；循环的：a ～ ticket 环程客票/make a ～ tour around the world 环游世界的旅行/a ～ motion 圆周运动/a ～ explanation 迂回的说明

circulate/ˈsɜːkjʊleɪt/

　　*v.*move round from place to place or from person to person 传播；流通；循环：Traffic ～s in the streets of a city.车马在城市的路上穿梭来往。/The news was ～d through the room. 消息在房间里传开。/Blood ～s around the body.血液在身体内循环。

circulation/ˌsɜːkjʊˈleɪʃən/

C

*n.*❶ movement to and fro or around sth. 来回运行；循环 ❷ the number of copies of a newspaper or magazine usually sold 报刊流通量 ❸ the movement of blood around the body 血液循环

circumference/sə'kʌmfərəns/
*n.*❶ the outside edge around sth. 周围 ❷ the enclosing boundary round a circle 圆周(线)

circumscribe/'sɜːkəmskraɪb/
*v.*❶ draw a line round sth. 在……周围画一条线 ❷ confine the scope of; restrict 限制……的范围；划界；限制 ❸ draw (a figure) around another figure so as to touch as many points as possible 使外切；使外接

circumspect/'sɜːkəmspekt/
adj. very careful to avoid difficulty or danger 十分谨慎的；十分小心的

circumstance/'sɜːkəmstəns/
*n.*❶ conditions connected with an event or person 情况 ❷ financial condition 境遇(指经济情况)：My family is in easy ～s. 我的家人过着安逸的生活。❸ a fact that causes or helps to cause sth. to happen 事件；事实：His death is an unfortunate ～. 他的死是件不幸的事。‖ under (in) … ～s 在……情况下/under (in) no ～s 在任何情况下都不

circumstantial/ˌsɜːkəm'stænʃl/
*adj.*❶ giving full details 详细的；详尽的：a ～ report 详细报告 ❷ (of evidence) based on or consisting of details that strongly suggest sth. but do not provide direct proof (指证据) 根据情况的，旁证的：～ evidence 情况证据

circumvent/ˌsɜːkəm'vent/
v. find a way round a difficulty 设法回避；规避：In the end we managed to ～ the rules. 最后我们设法规避了那些规定。‖ ～ion *n.* 规避；绕行

circus/'sɜːkəs/
*n.*❶ a travelling show with performances by persons and trained animals 马戏；马戏团：a travelling ～ 流动马戏团 ❷ a place for public games and races 竞技场

cite/saɪt/

*v.*❶ call sb. to appear before a court of law 传讯；be ～d for contempt of court 因藐视法庭而被传讯 ❷ refer to; mention or bring up as an example 引述；引证；引用：～ an instance 举例/He ～d lines from the Bible. 他引用了《圣经》里的文字。

citizen/'sɪtɪzn/
*n.*❶ a person who belongs to a particular country and enjoys certain rights 公民：a Chinese ～ 中国公民/Many foreigners have become ～s of America. 许多外国人已成了美国公民。❷ a person who is resident in a particular place 居民

citizenship/'sɪtɪznʃɪp/
n. being a citizen; rights and duties of a citizen 公民身份；公民权利和义务：Citizenship brings duties as well as rights. 公民的资格包括权利和义务。

city/'sɪti/
n. a large and important town 都市；城市：the ～ of Beijing 北京市

civic/'sɪvɪk/
adj. of the official life and affairs of a city or its citizen 城市的；市政的；公民的：a ～ centre 市中心/～ rights 公民权利/～ duties 公民义务

civil/'sɪvl/
*adj.*❶ having to do with citizens or the state 公民的；国家的：We all have ～ rights and ～ duties. 我们都有公民的权利和义务。❷ not the armed forces 文职的；文官的：That country was ruled by a ～ government. 那个国家由文职政府统治。❸ polite and courteous 客气的；有礼貌的：The boy gave me a ～ answer. 那个男孩给我一个礼貌的答复。‖ ～ marriage *n.* 不在教堂举行的婚礼/～ war *n.* 内战

civilian/sɪ'vɪljən/
Ⅰ *n.* a person not in the armed services or the police force 平民；老百姓 Ⅱ *adj.* of, denoting, or relating to a person not belonging to the armed services or police 平民的；民间的；民用的

civility/sɪ'vɪlti/
n. (*pl.*-ies) politeness or an act of politeness 客气；礼貌：I hope we can treat each

other with ～ and respect.我希望我们能以礼相待,互相尊重。

civilization(-sation) /ˌsɪvəlaɪˈzeɪʃn/
n. ❶ the stage of human social development, especially one with a high level of art, religion, science, government, etc. and written language 文明:the ～ of mankind 人类的文明 ❷ the civilized states collectively 文明社会;文明国家

civilize(-se) /ˈsɪvəlaɪz/
v. bring from a savage or ignorant condition to a higher one 使开化;使文明:The Romans hoped to ～ all the tribes of Europe.罗马人希望把欧洲所有的部落都变文明。

civilized(-sed) /ˈsɪvɪlaɪzd/
adj. ❶ well-organized socially with a very developed culture and way of life 文明的;开化的:the ～ world 文明世界 ❷ having or showing polite and reasonable behaviour 有礼貌的;有教养的;举止得体的

claim /kleɪm/
Ⅰ *v.* ❶ ask for sth. as the rightful owner or as one's right (根据权利)要求;认领;索取:Has anyone ～ed this lost dog? 有人来认领这条迷路的狗吗? ❷ say that sth. is true 自称;声称;主张:Don't ～ to know what you don't know.不要强不知以为知。 ❸ deserve or need 需要;值得:This matter ～s our attention. 这事需要我们予以注意。 Ⅱ *n.* ❶ a demand for sth. as one's own by right 要求;索赔:a ～ for damages 赔偿损害的要求 ❷ the right to have or do sth. (对某事物的)权利,要求权:～ to property 对财产有要求权 ❸ a statement that sth. is true 声称;断言

claimant /ˈkleɪmənt/
n. a person who makes a claim 申请人;要求者;认领人:rival ～s to the throne 争夺王位的对手/Claimants of unemployment benefit should fill in this form.失业津贴申请人应填写本表。

clairvoyance /kleəˈvɔɪəns/
n. the power that some people are believed to have to be able to see future events or to communicate with people who are dead or far away 预见力;洞察力

clam /klæm/
n. a large shellfish,used as food 蛤;蚌

clamber /ˈklæmbə(r)/
v. climb with some difficulty, using the hands and feet 爬上;攀登:～ over a wall 爬过一道墙

clammy /ˈklæmi/
adj. cold and damp 冷而潮湿的:～ hands 又冷又湿的双手/～ walls 湿冷的墙壁

clamour /ˈklæmə(r)/
Ⅰ *n.* a loud confused noise or shout, especially of people complaining angrily or making a demand 吵闹;强烈要求;强烈抗议:make a ～ about trifles 为小事大吵大闹 Ⅱ *v.* demand sth. loudly and insistently 大声地要求或责难:The children ～ed to go skating.孩子们吵嚷着要去溜冰。 ‖ **clamorous** *adj.* 吵闹的;叫喊的

clamp /klæmp/
Ⅰ *n.* an appliance for holding things together tightly by means of screw 钳子;夹板 Ⅱ *v.* put a clamp or clamps on 夹住;夹紧:Clamp these two pieces of wood together.把这两块木头夹在一起。

clampdown /ˈklæmdaʊn/
n. a sudden action that is taken in order to stop an illegal activity 严禁,制止,取缔(非法活动):a ～ on drinking and driving 严禁酒后驾车

clan /klæn/
n. a large group of families which are all related to each other 宗族,氏族

clang /klæŋ/
Ⅰ *n.* the sound of one piece of metal object hitting another (撞击金属器物发出的)叮当声;当啷声:There was a ～ as he dropped the tools.当他把工具放下时,工具叮当作响。 Ⅱ *v.* (cause to)make a loud ringing sound, such as when metal is struck (使)发出铿锵声;(使)发出叮当声:The metal tool ～ed when it hit the wall.金属工具撞到墙上发出当的一声。

clanger /ˈklæŋə(r)/
n. a very obvious mistake or unintentionally foolish remark 明显的错误;疏忽;不

适当的话：She dropped a ～ when she mentioned his ex-wife.提到他的前妻时，她说了句不该说的话。

clangor/'klæŋə(r),'klæŋgə(r)/

*n.*a sound or repeated clanging（持续的）铿锵声，叮当声：the ～ of the bells 叮叮当当的钟声

clank/klæŋk/

Ⅰ *n.*a short loud sound of chains as the ship's anchor was lowered into the sea（船锚投入海中时锚链发出的）当啷声 Ⅱ *v.*(cause to)make a short loud sound,like that of a heavy metal chain being moved（使）发当啷声（如重铁链被移动时的声音）

clannish/'klænɪʃ/

adj.(of a group of people)closely united and tending not to trust or welcome people from outside the group（一伙人）自成一帮的,排外的

clansman/'klænzmən/

*n.*a member of a clan 宗族（氏族）的成员

clap/klæp/

Ⅰ *v.*(-pp-)❶ show approval by striking the hands together 鼓掌；拍手：The audience ～ped at the end of the play.演出结束时观众鼓掌。❷ hit sb.lightly with the open hand 轻拍：His boss ～ped him on the back approvingly.老板赞同地拍了拍他的背。 Ⅱ *n.*the sound of striking the hands together 拍；鼓掌：The audience gave him a ～.观众为他鼓掌。

clapper /'klæpə/

*n.*the part of a bell（called the tongue or striker）that hits the side of the bell to make a sound 钟锤；钟舌；铃舌

clarify/'klærɪfaɪ/

*v.*❶become or make sth.clearer or easier to understand（使）更清晰易懂；（使）澄清 ❷make sth.pure 净化；纯净

clarinet/ˌklærə'net/

n. a type of wind musical instrument played by blowing through it 单簧管

clarity /'klærɪti/

*n.*the quality being clear to see or understand 清晰；清楚；明确：For the sake of ～,each of these strategies is dealt with

separately.为清晰起见,每种策略分别处理。

clash/klæʃ/

Ⅰ *v.*❶(cause to)strike together suddenly（使）相撞 ❷happen at the same time and so interfere with each other；disagree 冲突；不合；相矛盾：～ with one's interests 与个人利益相矛盾/The evening party ～es with the football match.晚会与足球赛时间冲突了。 Ⅱ *n.*a loud noise by striking one metal object against another 碰撞声 ❷disagreement 冲突：a ～ of interests 利害冲突 ❸a mismatch of colours 颜色搭配不当：～ of colours 颜色的不协调

clasp/klɑːsp/

Ⅰ *v.*hold sth.closely or tightly 抱住,握住：The child ～ed the doll tightly.小孩紧紧抱住洋娃娃。 Ⅱ *n.*❶ a tight holding or embrace 握手；紧握；拥抱：He gave my hand a warm ～.他热情地握着我的手。 ❷ a metal fastener for holding two things or parts of one thing together 扣子；钩子：The bracelet has a gold ～.那只手镯上有一个金钩。

class/klɑːs/

*n.*❶ a group of students taught together 班 ❷a group people,animals or things having qualities of the same kind 种类；类别；等级：first-～ 一流的 ❸ a group of people at the same social or economical level 社会等级；阶级：Inequality of property breeds ～ conflict.财产的分布不均导致阶级矛盾。❹ a period of time during which pupils or students are taught together 课：What time does the next ～ begin? 下一节课什么时候开始?

classic/'klæsɪk/

Ⅰ *adj.*❶ of the highest quality；having a recognized value 最优秀的,经典的,一流的：a ～ novel 最佳小说 ❷ with reference to ancient Greece and Rome 古希腊和古罗马的 ❸(of art or literature)simple in style；without too much decoration（指艺术、文学）简朴典雅的,不事雕琢的 ❹remarkably and instructively typical 典型的：the ～ symptoms of flu 流行性感冒的典型症状 Ⅱ *n.*❶a work of literature,or a writer of the highest quality 经典;文学名著;大文豪:Hamlet has become a ～ 哈姆莱特已成经典。/ Shakespeare is a ～.莎士比亚是文学巨匠。❷(the ～) the literature of ancient Greek and Latin writers and philosophers(古希腊、古拉丁作家与哲学家的)古典著作

classical /ˈklæsɪkl/

*adj.*❶of or having to do with the literature,art,and life of ancient Greece and Rome 与古希腊(或古罗马)生活(或艺术、文学)有关的:～ architecture 古罗马建筑 ❷regarded as representing an exemplary standard;traditional and long established in form or style 标准的;传统的;经典的:～ physics 经典物理学/ a ～ folk dance 传统的民间舞蹈

classicism /ˈklæsɪsɪzm/

*n.*❶a style of art and literature that is simple and elegant and is based on the styles of ancient Greece and Rome.Classicism was popular in Europe in the 18th century.古典主义(基于古希腊与古罗马风格,18 世纪盛行于欧洲) ❷a style or form that has simple,natural qualities and pleasing combinations of parts 古典风格

classification /ˌklæsɪfɪˈkeɪʃən/

*n.*❶the process of classifying things 分类;归类;分级:the ～ of disease according to symptoms 根据症状对疾病的分类 ❷a category in which sth. is put 类别;等级;门类

classified /ˈklæsɪfaɪd/

*adj.*❶(of advertisements) arranged according to subject matter (广告)分类的 ❷(of information) officially secret and available only to specified people 《情报)机密的,保密的

classify /ˈklæsɪfaɪ/

*v.*❶arrange things in classes or groups 分类:Men in the post office ～ mail according to places where it is to go. 邮局人员将信件按到达地区进行分类。❷decide sb. or sth. belong to which group or type 界定

classmate /ˈklɑːsˌmeɪt/

*n.*a member of the same class in a school 同班同学

clatter /ˈklætə(r)/

I *v.*(cause sth. to) make a number of rapid short knocking sounds (使某物)发撞击声,发哐当声:The shutters ～ed in the wind.百叶窗在风中嚓啪作响。II *n.*❶a number of rapid short knocking sounds 连续而清脆的撞击声:the ～ of pots and pans 锅镬相碰的哐声 ❷the noise caused by people talking rapidly or a busy activity 喧嚷声;喧闹声:the busy ～ of the city 都市的喧闹声

clause /klɔːz/

*n.*❶a part of a sentence with its own subject and verb 子句;分句:main ～ 主句/ subordinate ～ 从句/object ～ 宾语从句 ❷a particular article in a law or contract (法律或契约的)条款:an additional ～ 附加条款

claw /klɔː/

I *n.*❶one of the sharp,hard points on the foot of an animal (动物的)爪,趾甲:A hen's ～ has three toes.母鸡的爪子有三只脚趾。❷pincers of a shell-fish (e.g. a lobster) (蟹等的)螯 ❸an instrument or device like a claw 似爪的工具 II *v.* scratch,tear,seize or pull sth. with claws or nails 抓;撕;搔;抓住:The cat ～ed and hissed in fear.猫害怕时便一面抓一面发出嘶嘶声。/She ～ed a hole in my shirt in her temper.她气得把我的衬衫撕了一个窟窿。

clay /kleɪ/

n. soft,sticky earth from which pots and bricks are made 黏土;陶土:white ～ 白黏土

clean /kliːn/

I *adj.*❶ free from dirt,marks or stains;not dirty 清洁的;干净的 ❷morally or sexually pure 正派的;纯洁的:They demanded the establishment of a ～ government.他们要求成立一个廉洁的政府。‖ a new broom sweeps ～ 新官上任三把火/do a ～ job 干得很出色/make a ～ breast of 坦白交代/make a ～ sweep of 彻底改变;大获全胜 II *v.* make sth. free from dirt,marks or mess especially by rubbing and often without water 把……弄干净;打扫:Clean your room now.现在把你的房间打扫干净。‖ ～ **out**(把房间、抽屉等)弄干净整齐/～ **up** 收拾整理;洗干净

cleaner/'kli:nə(r)/

　　*n.*❶a person who cleans 清洁工 ❷a machine, apparatus or substance used in cleaning 清洁器;吸尘器;除垢剂

cleaning/'kli:nɪŋ/

　　*n.*the work of making sth.clean 洗涤;扫除;清洗:general ～ 大扫除

cleanse/klenz/

　　*v.*make sth.thoroughly clear 弄清洁;使洗净:The nurse ～d the wound before stitching it.护士先把伤口洗干净才缝合。

clear/klɪə(r)/

　　Ⅰ *adj.*❶ easy to perceive or understand 清晰的;明白的:There is a ～ view of the sea from that hill.从那个山上,你可以清楚地看见大海。❷（of a substance）transparent（物质）透明的:Through the ～ water, we could see fish on the bottom.透过清澈的水,我们可以看见水底的鱼。❸ without cloud or mist 晴朗的:This afternoon will be cloudy,turning ～.今天下午的天气是阴转晴。❹ without any obstacles;having nothing in the way 没有障碍的;没有危险的:The road into town is now ～.通往城里的道路现在已畅通。‖ **be ～ of** 摆脱/**keep ～ of** 避开/**make ～** 讲清楚,表明 Ⅱ *adv.*❶ with clarity;distinctly 清晰地;清楚地:Sing it loud and ～.请唱大声一点、清楚一点。❷completely;all the way 完全地;一直地:The prisoner got ～ away.囚犯逃得无影无踪了。Ⅲ *v.*❶ take away things that are not wanted 清除;去掉:In winter,the streets sometimes have to be ～ed of snow.在冬天,街上的雪有时必须清除。❷ pass by or over（sth.）without touching（不接触地）通过,越过,穿过:The horse easily ～ed the fence.马很轻易越过了栅栏。❸（cause to）become clear（使）清澈;（使）变光亮;（使）变晴朗:After the storm the sky ～ed.暴风雨过后,天气晴朗起来。‖ ～ **away** 收走,清除/～ **up** 放晴 ‖ ～**ly** *adv.*清楚地,清晰地

clear-cut/'klɪə'kʌt/

　　adj. distinct; having clear outlines and meaning 明确的;具体的:～ ideas 思想明确

clearing/'klɪərɪŋ/

　　*n.*an area of land,in a forest without any trees on it 林中空地

cleavage /'kli:vɪdʒ/

　　n. ❶ the hollow between a woman's breasts 乳沟 ❷a split or division made by cleaving 劈开;分裂

cleave/kli:v/

　　v.（cleft or cleaved or clove,cleft or cleaved or cloven）❶ split or cut open 劈开;欲开:～an apple in two with a knife 用小刀将苹果切成两半 ❷ go through; make a way through sth.forcefully 穿过;开（路）:The airplane ～d the clouds.飞机穿过云层。/They ～d a path through the wilderness.他们在荒野中劈开一条路。

cleft/kleft/

　　n. a narrow opening, especially in the ground or in a rock（尤指地面或岩石中的）罅隙

clement /'klemənt/

　　*adj.*❶(of weather) mild（天气）温暖的,温和的 ❷(of a person or their actions) merciful（人或其行为）仁慈的,宽厚的

clench/klentʃ/

　　*v.*❶ press or squeeze sth.tightly 攥紧;咬紧:She ～ed her teeth. 她咬紧牙关。❷ hold sth.firmly 握紧;捏紧:He ～ed the steering wheel while the car was wobbling.车子摇摇晃晃时,他握紧方向盘。

clergy/'klɜ:dʒi/

　　*n.*the priests or ministers of or religion, especially of the Christian Church（基督教会正式任命的）牧师:The ～ are opposed to the plan.牧师们反对该计划。‖ ～ **man** *n.*(男)圣职人员

cleric/'klerɪk/

　　*n.*a Christian priest or minister 教士;牧师

clerical /'klerɪkl/

　　*adj.*❶ of the cleric 教士的;牧师的;神职

人员的 ❷ of or for a clerk 文书的；书记的

clerk /klɑːk/

n. a person who works in an office or bank to undertake administrative duties 职员；办事员；管账员

clever /ˈklevə(r)/

adj. ❶ quick to learn, think or understand；intelligent 聪明的：a ~ boy 聪明的男孩 ❷ having ability and skill 灵巧的：He is a ~ carpenter. 他是一个手巧的木匠。‖ be ~ at 擅长于/be ~ with 善于使用 ‖ ~ly *adv.* 聪明地；巧妙地/~ness *n.* 聪明

click /klɪk/

Ⅰ *n.* a sudden sharp sound like a light switch being turned on or off 咔嗒声 Ⅱ *v.* ❶ make this sound 发出咔嗒声 ❷ (of an idea, etc.) be understood suddenly (突然间) 理解 (主意等)

client /ˈklaɪənt/

n. ❶ a person who gets help or advice from a lawyer or any professional man 当事人；委托人 ❷ a customer (at a shop) (商店里的) 顾客

cliff /klɪf/

n. a steep face of rock, especially by the sea 悬崖

cliffhanger /ˈklɪfhæŋə(r)/

n. a tense and exciting ending to an episode of a story, leaving the audience anxious to know what happens next (故事等) 扣人心弦的) 悬念：The first part of the serial ended with a real ~. 这部连续剧的第一集以扣人心弦的悬念而告终。

climactic /klaɪˈmæktɪk/

adj. exciting；forming a climax 激动人心的；高潮的：the film's ~ scenes 电影的高潮场面

climate /ˈklaɪmɪt/

n. ❶ the weather conditions in a place 气候：I like dry ~. 我喜欢干燥的气候。 ❷ the general feelings or opinions of a group of people at a particular time 气氛：In a ~ of political unrest, a dictator can often seize power. 在政治不安定的气氛中，一个独裁者常能夺取政权。

climax /ˈklaɪmæks/

Ⅰ *n.* an event or point of greatest interest or importance (e.g. in a story or drama) 顶点；高潮 (如故事或戏剧中最有趣的地方)：as a ~ to the evening's entertainment 作为晚会的高潮 Ⅱ *v.* come to the most exciting or important part in sth. (使) 达到顶点 (高潮)

climb /klaɪm/

Ⅰ *v.* ❶ go up sth. towards the top 攀登；爬：We ~ed up the mountain this Wednesday. 这周星期三我们爬上了那座山。 ❷ move somewhere, especially with difficulty or effort (尤指吃力地向某处) 爬：Can you ~ down? 你能爬下去吗？ ❸ go up mountains or climb rocks as a hobby or sport 登山；攀岩：He likes to go ~ing in the morning. 他喜欢清晨去登山。 ❹ go higher in the sky 爬升；上升 ❺ slope upwards 倾斜上升 ❻ grow up (a wall, tree, or trellis) by clinging with tendrils or by twining 沿 (墙, 树, 格架) 攀缘向上 ❼ increase in value or amount 上升；增值：The paper's circulation continues to ~. 这份报纸的发行量在继续增长。 Ⅱ *n.* ❶ an act of climbing up a mountain, rock or large number of steps 攀登；爬阶梯：It is two hours' ~ to the summit. 爬到顶峰需要两个小时。 ❷ a mountain or rock which people climb up for sport (攀登的) 山, 岩 ❸ an increase in value or amount 增值；升值：the dollar's ~ against the euro 美元对欧元的升值 ❹ progress to a higher status, standard or position 提高地位；达到更高标准；晋升 ‖ ~ down 爬下来；认错

climber /ˈklaɪmə(r)/

n. one who climbs 攀爬者：a famous mountain ~ 著名的登山运动员

clinch /klɪntʃ/

Ⅰ *v.* ❶ settle sth. definitely 确定；决定；敲定：They wanted to impress him to ~ a business deal. 他们想打动他以便敲定一笔生意。 ❷ fasten sth. firmly 钉住；系牢 ❸ fight or grapple at close quarters 扭打 Ⅱ *n.* ❶ a fight at close quarters 扭打 ❷ an embrace 拥抱

cling /klɪŋ/

v.(clung) stick tightly; hold firmly; keep close to; stay close to sb. 坚持,墨守;握紧;黏着,紧贴;依恋,依附:～ to the rope 紧握绳子/～ to old ideas 墨守成规/Wet clothes ～ to the body. 湿衣服紧贴在身上。/ The ship clung to the coast. 船靠近海岸。

clinic/ˈklɪnɪk/
n. a place or hospital department where you get medical treatment 诊室;诊所: The ～ is near the station. 诊所在车站附近。

clinical /ˈklɪnɪkəl/
adj. ❶ relating to the treatment of patients 临床的;临诊的:～ medicine 临床医学 ❷ based on observed signs and symptoms (病况)引起明显症状的:～ death 临床死亡 ❸ (of a place) looking bare and hygienic (地方)空荡的,卫生的 ❹ (of a person or behaviour) unemotional, cool and detached (人或行为)冷淡的;无动于衷的: He watched her suffering with ～ detachment. 他无动于衷地看着她受苦。‖ ～ly *adv.* 临床地;干净地;冷静高效地

clink/klɪŋk/
Ⅰ *n.* a sharp sound like that made by drinking glasses knocking together (酒杯相碰时)叮当声 Ⅱ *v.* make sharp ring ing sound (使)发叮当声

clip/klɪp/
v.(-pp-) cut sth. with scissors or shears; make sth. short or neat 剪;剪短;修剪: a sheep 剪羊毛/He ～ped the boy's hair very short. 他把那男孩的头发剪得很短。

clipper/ˈklɪpə(r)/
n. ❶ (*pl.*) an instrument for clipping sth. 大剪刀,钳子: The ～s are on the table. 剪子在桌子上。 ❷ a sailing ship built for speed and used formerly especially in the sea trade; a fast air-liner 快船;快速飞机

clipping/ˈklɪpɪŋ/
n. a piece cut off or out of sth. 剪下物;nail ～ 剪下的指甲 / grass ～s 修剪下来的草/a newspaper ～s 剪报

clique/kliːk/
n. a group of people who keep together

because of interests which they have and who are unfriendly or unhelpful to other people 小集团;派系

cliquish/ˈkliːkɪʃ/
adj. of or like a clique; exclusive 小集团(似)的;派系的;排他(性)的

cloak/kləuk/
n. ❶ a loose outer garment, without sleeves 披风;斗篷 ❷ sth. used to hide or keep sth. secret 外衣;伪装: under the ～ of darkness 在黑暗的掩护下‖ ～room *n.* 衣帽间,小件物品寄存处

clobber[1]/ˈklɒbə(r)/
v. ❶ strike or attack sth. severely and repeatedly 狠揍;(不停地)猛打: I'll ～ you if you don't do what you're told. 你如不按所吩咐的去做,我就狠狠地揍你。/ The government's going to ～ the unions if they won't agree. 工会如果不同意,政府就将狠狠地制裁他们。 ❷ defeat sb. or sth. completely 彻底击败: They were absolutely ～ed in the game at last night. 他们在昨晚比赛中被彻底击败了。

clobber[2]/ˈklɒbə(r)/
n. ❶ the belongings that one carries around 随身带的东西: my fishing ～ 我随身带的渔具 ❷ clothes 衣服

clock/klɒk/
n. an instrument for measuring and showing time 钟: Did you wind the ～ up? 你给钟上发条了吗? ‖ around the ～ 二十四小时连着干/put the ～ back 把时钟往回拨/work against the ～ 拼命赶时间

clockwise/ˈklɒkwaɪz/
adv. in the same direction as the hands of a clock 顺时针旋转地: turn the lid ～ 顺时针地拧盖子

clockwork/ˈklɒkwɜːk/
n. a machinery that can usually be wound up with a key, and that is used especially in clocks and toys(尤指用于钟表和玩具上的)发条装置: The children played with their ～ trains. 孩子们在玩用发条开动的玩具火车。‖ like ～ 安稳地,顺利地;精确地;有规律地: The arrangement went ahead like ～. 事情安排得有条不紊。/ regular as ～ 经常地;极有规律地: He

visits us every Friday, regular as ～.他每个星期五都要来访,非常有规律。

clod /klɒd/

n. ❶ a lump or mass, especially of clay or earth 块;(尤指)土块,泥块 ❷ a stupid person; a fool 傻瓜;笨蛋

cloddish /ˈklɒdɪʃ/

adj. like a clod 傻头傻脑的;笨拙的:～ ignorance 愚昧无知

clog /klɒg/

Ⅰ *n.* ❶ a shoe with a wooden sole; a shoe carved out of a block of wood 木底鞋;木屐 ❷ a block of wood fastened to the leg of an animal to prevent its straying (绑在人或动物腿上以阻碍行动的)坠子,阻碍,障碍 Ⅱ *v.* (-gg-) (cause to) be or become blocked (使)阻塞;填塞:The pump won't work. It's ～ged up with dirty. 泵打不动了,被污物堵塞。/Don't ～ your memory with useless information. 不要给存储器装塞满无用的资料。

clone /kləʊn/

Ⅰ *n.* an animal or plant made from the cells of another animal or plant and therefore exactly like it 克隆 Ⅱ *v.* produce an animal or a plant as a clone of another 克隆动物(或植物)

close[1] /kləʊz/

Ⅰ *v.* ❶ move or cause to move so as to cover an opening (使)关闭;关上;闭上:Did you ～ all the doors and windows? 你把门和窗户都关上了吗? ❷ make the work of a shop, a store, etc. stop for a period of time 不开放;关门;关闭:The post office ～s at half past six. 邮局在六点半关门。❸ come to an end or bring to an end 结束:The pianist ～s the concert with a beautiful melody. 钢琴家以一曲优美的旋律结束了音乐会。‖ ～ **down** 关闭,倒闭/～ **in** 关在……里面/～ **up** 关闭,不开放 Ⅱ *n.* the end, especially of an activity or of a period of time 结束;末尾:The crowd began to leave before the ～ of the game. 比赛结束前,人群开始离去。‖ **bring to a** ～ 使……结束/**come to a** ～ 结束/**draw to a** ～ 快要结束,使结束

close[2] /kləʊs/

Ⅰ *adj.* ❶ near in relationship, friendship, or degree of connection 亲密的;紧密的:We must maintain ～ ties with the masses. 我们应该与群众保持密切的联系。❷ near or not far away in space or time 近的;靠近的:The church is ～ to the observatory. 教堂离天文台很近。Ⅱ *adv.* near; not far away 靠近;接近:He was following ～ behind. 他紧紧地跟在后面。‖ ～**ly** *adv.* 紧密地,密切地

closet /ˈklɒzɪt/

Ⅰ *n.* ❶ a small room for storing things 小房间;储藏室 ❷ a lavatory 盥洗室;厕所:water ～ 便所;厕所 Ⅱ *v.* shut up in a room for a private talk (关在房间)密谈:be ～ed with someone 同某人密谈

closing /ˈkləʊzɪŋ/

Ⅰ *adj.* coming at the end of a speech, a period of time or an activity (讲话、时段或活动)接近尾声的,结尾的,结束的:the ～ stages of the game 比赛的结束阶段 Ⅱ *n.* the act of shutting sth. such as a factory, hospital, school, etc. permanently (永久的)停业,关闭;倒闭

close-up /ˈkləʊsʌp/

n. a photograph taken at a close range and showing a lot of detail 特写照片;近景照片:a ～ of her face 表现她面部的一张特写照片/a picture of her face in ～ 以特写手法表现她脸部的一张照片

closure /ˈkləʊʒə(r)/

n. an act of closing or stopping 关闭;结束;终止

clot /klɒt/

Ⅰ *n.* ❶ a half-solid lump formed in the drying of certain liquids (especially blood) (尤指血)凝块 ❷ a stupid person 愚昧的人;傻瓜 Ⅱ *v.* (-tt-) become or make solid in this way (使)凝结

cloth /klɒθ/

n. ❶ a material made by weaving threads together 布;a piece of ～ 一块布料 ❷ a piece of material used for special purpose 有特殊用途的布:Pass the ～, please. I want to clean the windows. 请把抹布递过来,我想把窗子擦干净。‖ **table** ～ *n.* 桌布/**dish** ～ *n.* 擦盘子布

clothe/kləʊð/

v.put clothes on; supply clothes for 给……穿衣；为……提供衣服：be warmly ～d 穿得暖/He can barely feed and ～ his family.他仅能勉强使一家人有饭吃,有衣穿。

clothes/kləʊðz/

n.the things covering a person's body 衣服‖ sports ～ n.运动服/school ～ n.校服/maternity ～ n.孕妇服/baby ～ n.童装/～ hanger n.衣架/～ brush n.衣刷/～ line n.晒衣绳

clothing/ˈkləʊðɪŋ/

n.clothes 衣服；衣着：food,～ and shelter 衣食住/an article of ～ 一件衣服/Now they are all in their summer ～.他们现在都穿夏季服装。

cloud/klaʊd/

Ⅰ n.❶grey or white mist in the sky 云：There are so many grey ～s, I think it will rain today.天上有这么多的乌云,我看今天要下雨。❷a mass of smoke,dust or anything like a cloud 云状物：a ～ of dust 漫天尘土 ❸mass things in the air moving together 一群,一片：a ～ of flies 一群苍蝇 ❹sth. that causes unhappiness or fear 引起不愉快(或恐惧)的事情：a ～ of grief 愁云/The ～s of war were gathering.战争的乌云正在集聚。Ⅱ v.❶grow or become cloudy 布满乌云：The sky ～ed over. 天空乌云密布。❷(of sb.'s face) show worry, sorrow or anger (面部)显现忧虑,悲伤,愤怒：The boy's face ～ed.那个男孩一脸愁容。

cloudy/ˈklaʊdi/

adj.❶full of or covered with clouds 阴天的；多云的：It's ～ today. 今天是阴天。❷not clear or transparent 浑浊的；模糊不清的：～ ideas 模糊的想法/～ beer 浑浊的啤酒 ❸gloomy 阴郁的：a ～ mood 阴郁的情绪

clout/klaʊt/

Ⅰ n.❶a blow with the hand (用手的)一击 ❷the power or influence especially in politics or business (尤指政治或商业方面的)势力,影响 Ⅱ v.hit sth.or sb.hard with the hand 用手猛击

clove/kləʊv/

n.a spice made from the dried flower-buds of a tree growing in the tropics 丁香

clown/klaʊn/

Ⅰ n.a person(usually with a painted face and strange clothes) whose work is to do foolish things to amuse people (especially in a circus) 小丑(尤指马戏团中的小丑,通常脸涂油彩,着奇装异服) Ⅱ v.behave silly actions to make other people laugh 扮小丑；做出像小丑的举动

club/klʌb/

n.❶ a society of persons who meet together for a common purpose; the building or house used by such a society 俱乐部：He joined the local stamp ～.他加入了本地的集邮俱乐部。❷ a heavy stick of wood; a stick used in games (球)棍；警棍：The hooligan brandished a ～.那个流氓手里挥舞着棍棒。❸a black three-leafed figure printed on a playing card (纸牌中的)梅花：I have four ～s in my hand.我手里有四张梅花牌。

clunk /klʌŋk/

Ⅰ v.make a dull sound like thick metal objects hitting each other (金属碰撞)铿锵作响,发出沉闷声 Ⅱ n.such a sound 铿锵声；沉闷的金属敲击声

clue/kluː/

n.a thing that helps to find the answer to a problem 线索；提示：find a ～ to that case.找到有关那个案件的线索

clump/klʌmp/

n.a number of things close together(usually trees or plants) (常指树木或植物)一丛,一簇

clumsy/ˈklʌmzi/

adj.likely to drop things or move in an awkward way (行动)笨拙的；手脚不灵活的：You are ～! You've knocked over my cup of coffee! 你真笨! 你把我的咖啡打翻了!

cluster/ˈklʌstə(r)/

Ⅰ n.a number of things of the same kind growing or being close together in a group 一束；一簇；一团；一组：a ～ of flowers 一簇花/ They stood in ～.他们

C

密密麻麻地站在一起。Ⅱ v. gather or grow in one group or more groups 聚集；丛生：The boys ~ed together around the fire.那些男孩聚在火炉周围。

clutch/klʌtʃ/

Ⅰ v. take hold of sth. very tightly 紧紧抓住 Ⅱ n. ❶ a tight hold 紧握 ❷ the part of a car or similar machine which allows the power from the engine to be disconnected from the wheels; pedal which operates this part 离合器；离合器踏板

clutter/ˈklʌtə(r)/

Ⅰ v. make untidy 使乱糟糟地；使杂乱：These boxes have been ~ing up my garage for weeks.这些箱子乱七八糟地堆在汽车间里已经好几个星期了。Ⅱ n. an untidy condition 凌乱：His room is always in a ~.他的房间总是凌乱不堪。

cluttered/ˈklʌtəd/

adj. covered with or full of a lot of things or people, in a way that is untidy 杂乱的；凌乱的；挤满的：a ~ room 乱七八糟的房间

coach/kəutʃ/

Ⅰ n. ❶ a four-wheeled covered vehicle drawn by horses 四轮马车 ❷ a long-distance, single decked motorbus 长途公共汽车：We went there by ~.我们乘长途公共汽车去那儿。❸ a separate section of a train, that can carry many people 火车车厢：You can find him in the next ~.你在下一节车厢里能找到他。❹ a person who trains athletes for contests 教练：The football ~ and the basketball ~ are brothers.那个足球教练和那个篮球教练是兄弟。Ⅱ v. give special lessons 辅导（训练，学习）：She ~es me in French.她辅导我学习法语。

coagulate/kəuˈægjuleit/

v. (of a liquid, especially blood) change to a solid or semi-solid state（指液体，尤指血液）凝结

coal/kəul/

n. a black or dark brown mineral which is dug from the earth, which can be burnt to give heat, and from which gas and many other products can be made 煤；煤块

coalition/ˌkəuəˈliʃn/

n. an alliance of a number of groups, especially the joining of a number of political parties in order to form a government（尤指组成政府的政党的）联合，联盟

coarse/kɔːs/

adj. ❶ not smooth or soft; rough; of poor quality 粗糙的；粗劣的：~ material 粗糙的材料 ❷ not polite; rude 粗俗的；粗鲁的：Don't use ~ words before a lady. 在女士面前不要讲粗俗的话。❸ consisting of large articles 粗粒的

coarsen/ˈkɔːsn/

v. make sth. coarse, or to become coarse（使）变粗糙：His features had been ~ed by the weather.气候使他的颜面变得粗糙。

coast/kəust/

Ⅰ n. the land along the sea or ocean 海滨；海岸：on the ~ 在海岸上；沿岸/rocky ~ 岩岸/There are many ports along the ~ of our country.我国沿海有许多海港。Ⅱ v. go along or near the shore; slide down a slope 沿海岸航行；溜坡；滑行：The boy was enjoying ~ing along the slope on his bicycle.这男孩喜欢骑着自行车滑斜坡。

coastal/ˈkəustl/

adj. of or near the coast 靠近海岸的；临海的；沿海的：a ~ resort 海滨游乐胜地/~ waters 沿海水域/~ fishing 近海捕鱼

coastguard/ˈkəustgɑːd/

n. ❶ a naval or police organization that watches from the coast for ships in danger and attempts to prevent unlawful activity at sea（负责海岸救难、缉私等的）海岸警卫队 ❷ a member of this organization 海岸警卫队队员

coastline/ˈkəustlaim/

n. the outline or shape of a coast 海岸线；海岸地形（或轮廓）

coat/kəut/

n. ❶ a piece of clothing with sleeves and an opening in the front, which one can wear outside 上衣：She bought a ~ and a skirt.她买了一件上衣和一条裙子。❷ an outer garment with long sleeves, often fastened at the front with buttons and usually covering the body down to the knees, worn especially to keep warm or for protection 外衣, 外套, 大衣: It's very cold, so wear a ~.外面很冷, 穿上一件大衣吧。‖ **cut one's ~ according to one's cloth** 量布裁衣; 量入为出

coating/ˈkəʊtɪŋ/

n. ❶a thin layer or covering 薄层; 薄皮: two ~s of paint 两层漆 ❷cloth for coats 外衣料

coax/kəʊks/

v. ❶get sb. or sth. to do sth. by kindness or patience 哄诱; 劝诱: ~ a child to take its medicine 哄小孩吃药/ ~ a fire to burn 耐心地使火燃起来 ❷obtain sth. by gently persuading 靠哄而获得: She ~ed a smile from the baby.她哄得婴儿一笑。

cobble/ˈkɒbl/

Ⅰ *n.* (usually *pl.*) a stone worn round and smooth by water and used for paving（由水冲磨成圆而光滑用来铺路的）圆石, 鹅卵石 Ⅱ *v.* pave with these stones 用圆石铺（砌）路: Streets were first ~d in the 19th century.街道最初是在 19 世纪铺上卵石的。

cobra/ˈkəʊbrə/

n. a type of poisonous snake found in Africa and Asia 眼镜蛇

cobweb/ˈkɒbweb/

n. a fine network or single thread made by a spider 蜘蛛网; 蜘蛛丝

cocaine/kəʊˈkeɪn/

n. a powerful drug that some people take illegally for pleasure and sometimes used by doctors as a local anaesthetic 可卡因（用作毒品, 也可以做局部麻醉剂）

cochlea/ˈkɒklɪə/

n. (*pl.* cochleae) a spiral-shaped tube like part of the inner ear 螺旋状管（如耳蜗）

cock/kɒk/

n. ❶ an adult male chicken; a male bird 公鸡; 雄鸟: The ~ crowed in the farmyard. 公鸡在农家庭院里鸣叫。❷ a tap or valve controlling the flow of a liquid or gas in a pipe 旋塞: Turn the ~ to increase the flow of oil.打开旋塞增加油量。

cockerel/ˈkɒkrəl/

n. a young male chicken 小公鸡

cockroach/ˈkɒkrəʊtʃ/

n. a large brown insect often found in kitchens and near water pipes 蟑螂

cocktail/ˈkɒkteɪl/

n. a mixture of various alcoholic drinks（usually drunk before meals）鸡尾酒

cocky /ˈkɒki/

adj. slightly over-confident or arrogant 自以为是的; 傲慢自负的 ‖ cockily *adv.* 自以为是地; 趾高气扬地/cockiness *n.* 骄傲自大; 趾高气扬

cocoa/ˈkəʊkəʊ/

n. ❶ a dark brown powder made from crushed cacao seeds 可可粉 ❷hot drink made from this with milk or water 可可饮料: a mug of ~ 一杯可可

coconut/ˈkəʊkənʌt/

n. ❶ a large hard nut growing on a type of tropical tree 椰子 ❷ the sweet-tasting substance found inside the nut, used in cookery 椰肉（烹饪用）

cocoon/kəˈkuːn/

n. a silky covering in which some insects live at the stage of their life cycle before changing into the fully-grown insect 茧

cod/kɒd/

n. (*pl.* cod) a type of large sea fish, eaten as food 鳕鱼

coda/ˈkəʊdə/

n. ❶ an independent passage that ends a piece of music（乐曲、乐章的）结束乐段, 尾声 ❷ a partly independent passage that ends a work of literature（文学作品的）结尾, 结局

coddle/ˈkɒdl/

v. ❶treat sb. too tenderly 溺爱; 宠爱: His daughter has been ~d too much. 他的女儿太娇生惯养了。❷ cook sth. in water just below boiling point 用文火煮: ~ eggs 煮鸡蛋

code/kəʊd/

Ⅰ *n.* ❶a system of words, letters, figures, or symbols used to represent others, especially for the purposes of secrecy 密码; 代码: break a ~ 破译密码 ❷a system of

C

computer programming instructions 编码 ❸a set of moral principles or rules of behavior 道德准则；行为规范：Her parents asked her to obey a strict ~ of conduct. 她的父母要求她遵守严格的行为准则。❹a systematic collection of laws or statutes 法典；法规 Ⅱ v.❶assign a code to (sth.) for purposes of classification, analysis, or identification 为……编码 ❷ put a message into code so that it can only be understood by a few people 把……译成密码：All the intelligence agents are trying to ~ the military secrets. 情报人员正努力尝试把军事机密译成密码。❸ write a computer program 编程序；编码 ‖ international ~ 国际电码 /~ telegram 密码电报 / break a ~ 破一种密码

codify/'kəʊdɪfaɪ/
v.arrange laws, rules, etc.into a system 把……编成法典；编纂：~ the laws 编纂法典

coefficient/ˌkəʊɪ'fɪʃnt/
n.a measure of a particular property of a substance under specified conditions 系数：~ of expansion of steel 钢的膨胀系数

coexist /ˌkəʊɪg'zɪst/
v.exist at the same time 同时存在；共存：Different traditions ~ successfully side by side.不同的传统和谐地共存着。‖ ~ent adj.共存的；同时代的

coexistence/ˌkəʊɪg'zɪstns/
n.peaceful existence side by side of states with opposed political systems 共存；共处：peaceful ~ 和平共处

coffee/'kɒfi/
n. a drink made from the roasted and ground seeds of a certain plant 咖啡（粉末或饮料）‖ ~ bean n.咖啡豆/~ bar n.咖啡小吃店/~ house n.咖啡馆/~ pot n.咖啡壶/~ tree n.咖啡树

coffer/'kɒfə(r)/
n.❶a large strong box used to hold money or other valuable things in safety 保险箱 ❷(pl.) the funds or financial reserves of a group or institution 资金储备；金库：the ~s of a bank 银行的金库

coffin/'kɒfɪn/
n.a box in which a dead body is put 棺材；柩

cog/kɒg/
n.one of the teeth on the edge of a wheel in various machines（齿轮的）轮齿，钝齿

cogent /'kəʊdʒənt/
adj.logical and convincing 合乎逻辑的；有说服力的：a ~ argument 有说服力的争辩 ‖ ~ly adv.中肯地；有说服力地

cogitate/'kɒdʒɪteɪt/
v. think carefully and seriously about sth.；ponder 认真思考；深思熟虑

cognate/'kɒgneɪt/
Ⅰ adj.❶having the same source of origin 同族的；同源的；同系统的 ❷ related；having much in common 有联系的；同性质的 Ⅱ n.a word, etc. that has the same origin as another 同源词

cognition/kɒg'nɪʃn/
n. the mental action or process of acquiring knowledge and understanding through thought, experience, and the senses 认识；认知

cognitive/'kɒgnɪtɪv/
adj.of or about cognition 感知的；认识（力）的：~ psychology 认识心理学

cognizance/'kɒgnɪzəns/
n. knowledge；awareness 察觉；获知；认识：The judge has taken ~ of the new facts in your case.法官已经注意到你案件中的新事实。

cognizant/'kɒgnəzənt/
adj. having knowledge or information；aware 认知的；察知的：The judge said he was not fully ~ of the facts in the case.法官说他还不了解有关该案件的全部事实。

cogwheel/'kɒgwiːl/
n.a wheel with teeth round the edge that can move or be moved by another wheel of the same type 齿轮

cohere/kəʊ'hɪə(r)/
v. stick together；be or remain united；be consistent 黏合；连贯；一致：What he did failed to ~ with what he professed.他言行不符。‖ ~nce /kəʊ'hɪrəns/ n. 黏合性；连

贯性

coherent /kəʊˈhɪərənt/

adj. ❶ united as or forming a whole 结合在一起的 ❷（especially of speech, thought，ideas，reasoning）logical and clear，easy to understand（尤指演讲、思想、理念、推理）合乎逻辑的，清晰易懂的

cohesion /kəʊˈhiːʒn/

n. tendency to stick together；force with which molecules cohere 黏着；结合力，内聚性；凝聚力：Drops of liquid result from ～.液体的珠滴是由内聚力形成的。

coil /kɔɪl/

Ⅰ *n.* sth. arranged in a series of circles 圈形物 Ⅱ *v.* arrange sth. in the form of a coil 把……卷成圈

coin /kɔɪn/

Ⅰ *n.* a round piece of metal money 硬币 Ⅱ *v.* ❶ make metal into coins 铸造（钱币）：The government has decided to ～ new silver dollars.政府决定铸造新银元。❷ invent（especially a new word）创造，生造（新词）：Who ～ed that word? 谁生造了那个词？ ‖ false ～ 假币/～ **money** 发财；获大利/～ **one's brains** 动脑筋挣钱/**pay sb. back in his own ～** 以其人之道还治其人之身

coincide /ˌkəʊɪnˈsaɪd/

v. ❶ happen at the same time 巧合，恰巧一致：Her birthday ～s with the national day.她的生日恰巧是国庆节。❷（of ideas or opinions，etc.）be in agreement（想法、观点等）相同，一致：The judges did not ～ in opinion.裁判们的意见不一致。

coincidence /kəʊˈɪnsɪdəns/

n. ❶ the fact or process of happening at the same time or being in the same place 同时存在；并存 ❷ a remarkable occurrence of similar or corresponding events at the same time by chance 巧合；巧事

coincidental /kəʊɪnsɪˈdentl/

adj. ❶ resulting from a coincidence；done or happening by chance 巧合的；碰巧的；偶然的：It cannot be ～ that these years were a time of important new developments.这几年出现了新的重大发展绝非偶然。❷ happening or existing at the

same time 同时发生的；同时存在的 ‖ ～**ly** *adv.* 巧合地；一致地

coke /kəʊk/

n. a rough，light substance that remains when gas has been taken out of coal by heating it in an oven，used as a fuel in stoves and furnaces 焦炭；焦煤

colander /ˈkʌləndə(r)/

n. a dish with many small holes in the bottom，used in cooking to drain water from vegetables，etc. 滤锅，滤盆（上有许多小孔，烹饪时用以滤去蔬菜等的水）

cold /kəʊld/

Ⅰ *adj.* ❶ having a low temperature；not hot 冷的；寒冷的：It's very ～ outside.外面很冷。❷ not friendly or cheerful 冷淡的：His wife gave us a ～ reception.他的妻子冷淡地接待了我们。‖（have）～ **feet** 畏缩不前/**give the ～ shoulder** 冷淡对待/（kill sb.）in ～ **blood** 残酷无情地杀人/**make one's blood run ～** 使吓得要命/**pour ～ water on** 浇冷水，使泄气 ‖ ～ **current** *n.* 寒流/～ **cream** *n.* 冷霜/～ **wave** *n.* 寒潮/～ **war** *n.* 冷战 Ⅱ *n.* ❶ relative absence of heat；a low temperature 寒冷；冷：He is afraid of ～.他怕冷。/Don't go out in the ～ without a coat! 在这样寒冷的天气里穿上外衣才好出去。❷ a common illness that affects the nose and throat 感冒；伤风：catch（a）～ 伤风；感冒

cold-blooded /ˌkəʊldˈblʌdɪd/

adj. ❶ having blood that varies with the temperature（e.g. fish，reptiles）（指鱼类、爬行动物）冷血的：But for a ～ creature such as a frog or a snake it is a different matter.但对于冷血动物，像青蛙或蛇来说，可就不同了。❷（of persons，their actions）without feeling；pitiless（指人或其行为）冷酷的，无情的：a ～ murderer 残酷的凶手

coldness /ˈkəʊldnɪs/

n. ❶ the state of being cold 寒冷：Because of the ～ of the weather，we stay indoors.因为天气寒冷，所以我们待在室内。❷ no feelings；pitilessness 冷酷；无情

collaborate/kəˈlæbəreɪt/

v. ❶work together with others especially in literature 协作；合作；合著：The police and the army ~d to catch the terrorists. 警察和军队协作捉拿恐怖分子。❷work treasonably, especially with enemy forces 勾结；通敌：Anyone who ~d was shot.所有叛国通敌者都枪决了。

collaborative /kəˈlæbəreɪtɪv/

adj. produced or conducted by two or more parties working together 合作的；协作的：~ research 合作研究 ‖ ~ly *adv.* 合作地；协作地

collapse/kəˈlæps/

Ⅰ *v.* ❶ fall down or inwards suddenly; come or break into pieces 垮；塌；倒：The earthquake caused many buildings to ~. 地震使许多建筑物倒塌了。❷ fall down and become unconscious 昏倒；支持不住：If you work too hard, your health may ~.如果你太努力地工作，你可能会病倒。Ⅱ *n.* ❶ the act of collapsing 倒塌；崩溃：A heavy flood caused the ~ of the bridge. 洪水使这座桥倒塌了。❷ the sudden and complete loss of strength or will（身体或精神）垮下；支持不住；晕倒：He was in a state of ~.他的身体垮了。

collapsible/kəˈlæpsɪbl/

adj. that can be folded for easy storing 可折叠的：a ~ bicycle 折叠式脚踏车

collar/ˈkɒlə(r)/

Ⅰ *n.* ❶the part of clothes that fits round the neck 衣领；领：seize someone by the ~ 抓住某人领口／The ~ of his shirt was dirty.他衬衫的领子脏了。❷a leather or metal band put round the neck of an animal（动物颈上所系皮的或金属的）项圈 Ⅱ *v.* ❶ seize（sb.）tightly; take hold of roughly 扭住；抓住；揪住：The police ~ed him.警察抓住了他。❷take sth without permission 窃取；占取：Who's ~ed my pen? 谁拿走了我的钢笔？

collate/kəˈleɪt/

v. ❶ examine and compare（copies of books, notes, etc.）carefully in order to find the differences between them 对照；核对；校勘：~ two ancient manuscripts

校勘两本古代手稿 ❷ arrange the sheets of a book in the proper order before they are bound together（为装订按次序）整理（书页）

collateral/kəˈlætərəl/

Ⅰ *n.* valuable property promised to a lender if one is unable to repay a debt; security（举债的）担保物，抵押品：He offered his house as (a) ~ for the loan.他用自己的房子作为贷款的抵押。Ⅱ *adj.* ❶ additional but with less importance; secondary 并行的；附属的；附带的；伴随的；次要的：A ~ aim of the government's industrial strategy is to increase employment. 政府工业战略的一个附带目的是增加就业。／The bombs were aimed at military targets but there was some ~ damage to civilian areas.炸弹是针对军事目标的，但也给居民区造成了一些附带性的破坏。❷ descended from the same person but through different sons or daughters（亲戚）旁系的：Cousins are ~ relatives but brothers are directly related.堂（表）兄弟是旁系亲戚，而兄弟则是直系亲戚。❸ of or being collateral 附属担保的；抵押的

colleague/ˈkɒliːg/

n. persons working together and (usually) having similar ranks and duties 同事；同僚

collect/kəˈlekt/

v. ❶come or bring together in one place so as to form a group or mass; gather 收集，集中；聚集 ❷ask for or obtain payment of（money, taxes, rent, etc.）征收（金钱、税收、租金等）；募集（捐款等）：We're ~ing money for the famine victims.我们正在为灾民集资。‖ ~or *n.*收藏者

collected /kəˈlektɪd/

adj.（said about a person）calm and self-controlled（人）镇静的，泰然自若的：They look cool, calm, and ~.他们看上去冷静沉着，面不改色。‖ ~ly *adv.*冷静地；镇定地

collection /kəˈlekʃən/

n. ❶the process of collecting 聚集；积聚；集中；收取 ❷things collected systematically 收集物 ❸a number of things that have come together or been placed together 收藏品；搜集品 ❹money collected for a charity or at a church service (为慈善机构或做礼拜时的)募捐的钱

collective /kəˈlektɪv/
Ⅰ *adj*. to do with a group taken as a whole 集体的;共有的;共同的: a ～ approval 集体通过 Ⅱ *n*. a cooperative enterprise 合作社;集体企业 ‖ ～ly *adv*. 共同地;全体地

college /ˈkɒlɪdʒ/
n. a name given to various types of places of learning and also the staff and students of these institutions 学院,书院;大学内的学院;(美国)大学;学院的师生

collide /kəˈlaɪd/
v. ❶ come together violently; meet and strike; be in conflict 碰撞;猛撞;互相撞击;冲突: The two lorries ～d. 那两部货车相撞了。/ If the aims of two countries ～, there may be war. 如果两个国家的目标互相冲突,就可能发生战争。❷ disagree with sb. over sth. strongly such as ideas, opinions, etc. 冲突;矛盾;抵触

collision /kəˈlɪʒən/
n. ❶ an instance of one moving object or person striking violently against another (猛烈) 碰撞: The car was in ～ with a lorry. 这辆汽车撞上了一辆卡车。❷ an instance of conflict between opposing ideas, interests, or factions (观念、利益或派系间的)冲突,抵触: a ～ between two mutually inconsistent ideas 两种相互矛盾的观念之间的冲突

collude /kəˈl(j)uːd/
v. come to a secret understanding; conspire 暗中串通,勾结;共谋: Several people had ～d in the murder. 这起谋杀案是几个人串通制造的。

collusion /kəˈl(j)uːʒən/
n. a secret agreement between two or more people who are trying to deceive or cheat someone 密谋;勾结;串通 ‖ collusive *adj*. 共谋的

colonial /kəˈləʊnjəl/
Ⅰ *adj*. to do with a colony or colonies 殖民的;殖民国家的 Ⅱ *n*. someone who lives in a colony 殖民地当地人;殖民地居民

colonnade /ˌkɒləˈneɪd/
n. a line of stone columns forming part of a building 柱廊;一列柱子

colonize /ˈkɒlənaɪz/
v. take control of an area or a country that is not your own 把……变成殖民地;建立殖民地: The British first ～d North America in 17th century. 在 17 世纪英国人最先将北美洲开拓为殖民地。

colony /ˈkɒləni/
n. a country or territory that has been developed by people from another country 殖民地 ‖ colonialism *n*. 殖民主义;殖民政策 / colonist *n*. 殖民主义者

colo(u)r /ˈkʌlə(r)/
Ⅰ *n*. ❶ the quality that makes things look green, yellow, red, etc. 颜色: What ～ do you like? 你喜欢什么颜色? ❷ redness of the face 脸色;气色: She has very little ～. 她的脸上没有什么血色。❸ a substance (e. g. paint or dye) used to give colour to sth. (绘画或染色用的)颜料,色彩: Do you paint with water ～s or oil ～s? 你画水彩画,还是油画? ❹ a flag, badge, etc. that represents a team, country, ship, etc. (代表团队、国家、船等的)旗帜,徽章: They raised the ～s over the captured fort. 他们将旗帜升起在攻占的堡垒之上。‖ off ～ 感到身体有点不舒服 / change ～ 脸色变白,脸红 / lose ～ 变得苍白 / show one's true ～s 现原形 / under the ～ of 在……的借口下 / with flying ～s 成绩优异地,出色地 Ⅱ *v*. ❶ give colour to; put colour on 给……着色;染上颜色: She ～s her hair. 她把头发染了。❷ take on colour or change colour 变颜色: Her face ～ed as she was embarrassed. 她感到尴尬时脸变红了。‖ ～less *adj*. 没有颜色的;没有血色的

colo(u)rant /ˈkʌlərənt/
n. a dye or pigment used to colour things 染色剂;染料;颜料;着色剂

colo(u)rful /ˈkʌlə(r)fəl/
adj. ❶ full of colour 富于色彩的;颜色鲜艳的: a ～ array of flowers 一大批色彩鲜艳的鲜花 ❷ lively or exciting, with plenty of detail 生动的;绘声绘色的;丰富多

彩的：a ～ account 绘声绘色的描述 ‖
～ly adv.多彩地；绚烂地；丰富多彩地

colo(u)ring/'kʌlərɪŋ/

n.❶the way in which sth.is coloured 着色
❷a substance used to colour things 着色
剂，色素

column/'kɒləm/

n. ❶ a tall pillar supporting part of a
building, or standing alone 圆柱：The
dome was supported by white marble
～s.圆形屋顶由白色的大理石柱支撑。
❷anything similar to a column in shape,
appearance, or use 柱形物：A ～ of
smoke appeared above the hill.一柱烟出
现在山上。❸a section of a newspaper or
magazine regularly devoted to a particular subject or written by a particular person 报刊的一栏；专栏：Some newspapers
have eight ～s to a page.有些报纸一面有
8 个栏目。❹a large number of rows of
people、vehicles、etc.，following one behind the other 纵队：A ～ of soldiers
marched down the road.一队士兵沿着公
路行进。‖ ～ist n.专栏作家

coma/'kəʊmə/

n.a condition like a deep sleep，caused by
injury，disease or poison（由于外伤、疾
病、或中毒而引起的）昏迷：He went into
a ～ after swallowing a whole bottle of
sleeping pills.他吃了一瓶安眠药后就昏
迷过去了。

comb/kəʊm/

Ⅰ n.❶an object used for tidying，arrang-
ing，or straightening the hair usually consisting of a piece of plastic、metal、bone、
etc.with a row of thin teeth 梳子❷an act
of combing 梳；梳理：Your hair needs a
good ～.你的头发需要好好梳一下。Ⅱ
v.❶tidy，arrange，or straighten（especial-
ly the hair）with a comb 梳：The mother
～ed the child's hair.母亲给孩子梳头发。
❷ search（a place）thoroughly 彻底搜
查：The police ～ed the woods for the
missing boy.警察为了寻找失踪的男孩彻
底搜查了树林。

combat/'kɒmbæt/

Ⅰ n. fight；struggle 战斗；斗争；打斗：a
single ～ 一对一的打斗 Ⅱ v. fight；

struggle 战斗；斗争；打斗：The doctor
spent his life ～ing diseases.那位医生终
生与疾病做斗争。

combatant/'kɒmbətənt/

n.a person taking a direct part in fighting
战斗人员；格斗者；斗士；战士：In the last
war as many non-combatants as ～s were
killed.在上次战争中，非战斗人员与战斗
人员都有死亡。

combative/'kɒmbətɪv/

adj.ready and eager to fight or argue 好
斗的；斗志高昂的：a ～ spokesman for
right-wing policies 一位鼓吹右翼政策的
好斗的代言人

combination/ˌkɒmbɪ'neɪʃn/

n.❶the state of being joined or put together 合并；结合；联合；组合：His character is a ～ of strength and kindness.他
品性善良，性格坚强。❷a number of
people or things that combined or united
in a common purpose 结合体；联合体：A
～ of parties formed the new govern-
ment.各政党联合组成新政府。❸a piece
of undergarment covering body and legs
连裤内衣

combine/kəm'baɪn/

Ⅰ v.❶ unite；merge；form a group（使）结
合；联合；混合：Several factors had ～d to
ruin our plans.几种因素加在一起毁了我
们的计划。❷ put two or more different
things，features or qualities together 兼
有；兼备；使融合：The hotel ～s comfort
with convenience.这家旅馆既舒适又方
便。❸ do two or more things at the
same time 兼做；兼办：She has successfully ～d a career and her family.她成功
地兼顾了事业和家庭。❹ come together
to work or act together 合并；协力：You
should try to ～ learning with entertain-
ment.你应该把学习和娱乐结合起来。Ⅱ
n.❶a combine harvester 联合收割机 ❷a
group of people or companies acting together for a commercial purpose 集团；联
合企业

combustible/kəm'bʌstɪbl/

Ⅰ adj.catching fire and burning easily 易
燃的；可燃的：Petrol is highly ～.汽油极
易燃烧。Ⅱ n.a flammable substance 易

C

燃品

come/kʌm/

v.(came)❶ move towards or near to the speaker or a particular place 来：The bus is coming.公共汽车来了。❷ extend;arrive 伸到；达到：The dress ～s to her knees.这衣服长及她的膝部。❸ happen;take place;become seen;appear 发生；出现：What will ～,let it ～.要发生的事,让它发生好了。❹ become 变得;成为：His dream came true.他的梦想实现了。‖ ～ about 发生;造成/～ across 碰到/～ along 跟去;进展/～ around 到来;改变看法;恢复知觉/～ by 得到/～ clean 坦白交代/～ down 下降,跌价/～ down with 患上(某种传染性疾病)/～ for 来取/～ in 到来,进站/～ into being 开始存在/～ into blossom 开花/～ into conflict 和……发生冲突/～ into effect（force）开始生效/～ into fashion 开始时新/～ into power 开始执政/～ into sight 被……望见/～ into the open 开诚相见/～ near to 差一点就……/～ of 出生于(某种家庭),由……造成的/～ off 脱落,(洗)掉/～ on 进展;生长;上演;赶快/～ out 出版;开花;传出/～ over 来到;随便来访/～ through 经历(危险)活了下来/～ to 来到;加起来共计/～ to a climax 达到高潮/～ to a conclusion 作出结论/～ to a halt 停下来,停顿/～ to an end 结束/～ to blows 打起来/～ to life 活跃起来/～ to light 被发现,被大家知道/～ to nothing 没有结果/～ to one's senses 头脑清醒过来/～to pass 发生,成为事实/～ to sb.'s attention 受到某人注意/～ to sb.'s rescue 来援救某人/～ to the point 谈正题/～ together again 言归于好/～ up 走过来/～ up for 参加(竞选)/～ up to 达到(愿望、标准等),赶上/～ up with 提出/～ within view 进入视野

come-back/ˈkʌmbæk/

*n.*a successful return to a former position of strength or importance 复辟;复原;复位：Can he stage a ～? 他能东山再起吗？

comedian/kəˈmiːdɪən/

*n.*❶ an actor who plays comic parts in plays,broadcast and TV 喜剧演员 ❷a comedy writer 喜剧作家 ❸a person who

behaves in a comic way 丑角式人物：He's a real ～.他真是个滑稽人物。

comedy/ˈkɒmədi/

*n.*❶ a branch of drama that deals with everyday life and humorous events 喜剧：He prefers ～ to tragedy.他喜欢喜剧而不喜欢悲剧。❷ an amusing activity or incident in real life (真实生活中)有趣的事情：It was a ～ of errors.那是个喜剧性的错误。

comer/ˈkʌmə(r)/

n. one who arrives somewhere 来者;到者：the first ～ 首先来到的人/ the late ～s 迟到者

comet/ˈkɒmɪt/

*n.*a heavenly body looking like a star with a bright centre and a less bright tail that moves round the sun in an eccentric orbit 彗星：A ～ moves in orbit around the sun.彗星在轨道上绕着太阳转。

comfort/ˈkʌmfət/

Ⅰ *n.*❶ the state of being free from suffering,pain,etc.安逸,舒适：They began to seek ～ and enjoyment and fear hardship.他们开始贪图安逸、享乐,害怕吃苦。❷ help or kindness to sb.who is suffering sth.安慰：She finds ～ in her friends.她从朋友那儿得到安慰。❸ a person or thing that brings relief or help 使人得到安慰的人（或事）：This is a great ～ to me.这是我最大的安慰。Ⅱ *v.* give hope to 安慰 ‖ ～er *n.*安慰者/～ing *adj.*令人宽慰的

comfortable/ˈkʌmfətəbl/

*adj.*❶ having or providing comfort 舒适的;惬意的：a ～ chair 舒适的椅子 ❷ with no pain or worry 无痛苦的;没有忧虑的：The nurse made the sick man ～.护士使病人感觉到舒服。

comic/ˈkɒmɪk/

Ⅰ *adj.*❶ funny;humorous;having to do with comedy 滑稽的;幽默的：a ～ song 滑稽歌曲 ❷of comedy 喜剧的：a ～ opera 喜剧歌剧 Ⅱ *n.*❶a person who is funny or amusing,especially a professional comedian 喜剧演员;滑稽演员：He is a well-known ～.他是个著名的喜剧演员。

❷funny pictures 连环画：read the ～s 看连环漫画

coming/ˈkʌmɪŋ/

Ⅰ *n*. arrival；approach 到达；来到：The ～ of the new principal had everyone talking. 大家对新校长的到来议论纷纷。 Ⅱ *adj*. approaching；next 正在来到的；即将来到的：the ～ generation 下一代/in the ～ years 在未来的岁月里

comity/ˈkɒmɪti/

n. friendly, polite, and respectful behaviour and manners；courtesy 礼貌；礼让：～ of nations 国际礼让

comma/ˈkɒmə/

n. the sign, used in writing to divide up a sentence 逗号，逗点(，)

command/kəˈmɑːnd/

Ⅰ *v*. ❶give an authoritative order 命令：He ～ed the soldiers to attack. 他命令士兵进攻。❷control or restrain 控制：I advised him to ～ his temper. 我建议他控制自己的脾气。❸ have authority over；be in charge of 统率；指挥；管辖 Ⅱ *n*. ❶an order；a direction 命令：Who issued the ～ to fire? 谁发布命令开火的？❷the power to control；mastery 指挥：The army is under the king's direct ～. 部队由国王直接指挥。❸the part of the army under separate command 司令部：He worked at the German High Command. 他在德军统帅部工作。‖ at sb.'s ～ 听候差遣，由……掌握/by sb.'s ～ 根据……的命令/in ～ (of) 指挥，控制/take ～ of (开始)指挥

commandant/ˌkɒmənˈdænt/

n. a commanding officer, especially of military group or institution 指挥官；司令

commander/kəˈmɑːndə(r)/

n. a person who commands 指挥官；司令：a regiment ～ 团长/～-in-chief 总司令

commanding/kəˈmɑːndɪŋ/

adj. ❶(in military contexts) having a position of authority (军事用语)指挥的，统率的，：a ～ officer 指挥官 ❷possessing or giving superior strength 支配的；占优的；权力强大的：a ～ 13-6 lead 有着压倒性优势的 13 比 6 的领先 ❸indicating or expressing authority；imposing 有权威的；威严的；令人印象深刻的：His style is ～. 他的风度令人注目。

commando/kəˈmɑːndəʊ/

n. (*pl*. ～s or ～es) a soldier specially trained for carrying out quick raids in enemy areas 突击队员

commemorate/kəˈmeməreɪt/

v. keep or honour the memory of a person or event；be in memory of (things)纪念：The people built a monument to ～ the heroes. 人们建立纪念碑纪念英雄。

commemoration/kəˌmeməˈreɪʃn/

n. ❶the act of commemorating 纪念：in ～ of the battle of Waterloo 纪念滑铁卢战斗 ❷a ceremony or celebration in memory of a person or event 纪念会；纪念仪式；纪念活动

commence/kəˈmens/

v. begin；start 开始：～ doing work 开始做事/～ with this work 从这项工作开始/I have ～d learning Japanese. 我开始学日语。/The rainy season ～s now. 现在雨季开始了。

commencement/kəˈmensmənt/

n. ❶beginning 开始；开端：The ～ of the show was eagerly awaited. 人们急切地等待着演出开始。❷a ceremony at which degrees are conferred 学位授予典礼；毕业典礼：Commencement is an important day in a student's life. 毕业典礼是学生生涯中重要的日子。

commend/kəˈmend/

v. ❶entrust sth. for safekeeping to 把……交托给 ❷praise, speak favourably of 称赞；表扬；嘉奖：The teacher ～ed Tom for his neat work. 老师表扬汤姆的作业做得整洁。❸recommend 推荐：～ her to this position 推荐她胜任此工作岗位

commendation /ˌkɒmenˈdeɪʃən/

n. ❶praise 表扬；称赞：The book deserved the highest ～. 这本书应该得到最高度的赞扬。❷an award involving the giving of special praise 嘉奖

commensurate/kəˈmenʃərət/

adj. of the same size or quantity as sth. else；of the right size or quantity for sth.

（大小、数量上）同样的，相等的，旗鼓相当的：The danger of the journey was ~ with its importance. 此行危险的程度，正如其重要性。

comment /ˈkɒment/

Ⅰ *n.* a written or spoken opinion, explanation, or judgment made about an event, person, situation, etc. 评语；评论；意见：He made no ~ on the subject. 他对这个问题未做评论。Ⅱ *v.* make a comment; give an opinion 发表意见；提出看法：Everybody ~ed on her new hat. 每个人都谈论她的新帽子。

commentary /ˈkɒməntri/

n. a description spoken during a special event, match, etc. 解说词：a broadcast ~ 广播报道

commentate /ˈkɒmənˌteɪt/

v. report on an event as it occurs, especially for a news or sports broadcast; provide a commentary（尤指对新闻、体育）实况播音，实况报道，解说：He will ~ on live Monday matches. 他将对星期一的比赛进行现场实况报道。

commentator /ˈkɒmənteɪtə(r)/

n. a person who gives a commentary on the radio or television 实况评论员；解说员

commerce /ˈkɒmɜːs/

n. the buying and selling of goods and services; trade 商业，贸易：This country has grown rich because of its ~ with other nations. 这个国家因为与他国贸易而变得富裕。

commercial /kəˈmɜːʃl/

adj. of or for commerce 商业的；商务的：a ~ college 商学院/a ~ centre 商业中心 ‖ **commercialism** *n.* 商业主义/**commercialize** *v.* 使商业化；靠……赚钱

commiserate /kəˈmɪzəreɪt/

v. express pity; sympathize 同情；怜悯：She ~d with the losers on their defeat. 她对失败的一方表示同情。‖ **commiseration** *n.* 同情

commission /kəˈmɪʃn/

n. ❶ the act of giving authority to sb. to act for another 委托；代办：go beyond one's ~ 越权 ❷ money paid to a salesman for his services 佣金；酬金；回扣：He gets 20% ~ on everything he sells. 他所销售的所有东西都可得到 20% 的佣金。❸ a group of people specially appointed to perform certain duties 委员会

commissioner /kəˈmɪʃənə(r)/

n. ❶ a member of a commission, especially one with particular duties 专员；委员；政府特派员：a High Commissioner 高级专员 ❷ a local governor 地方长官

commit /kəˈmɪt/

v. (-tt-) ❶ do sth. bad or wrong 犯（罪）；干坏事：~ a big error 犯大错误/~ suicide 自杀/A robbery was ~ted last night. 昨晚发生了抢劫案。❷ send; entrust 交付；托付：~ the documents to someone for safe keeping 把文件交某人保管 ❸ make oneself responsible; undertake; bind (oneself) 答应负责；承诺；使（自己）受约束；牵累：be ~ted to revolutionary struggle 致力于革命斗争/He refused to ~ himself to any sort of promise. 他拒绝对任何许诺承担义务。

commitment /kəˈmɪtmənt/

n. a promise; a pledge or undertaking 承诺；保证：I don't want any ~s. 我不需要任何承诺。

committee /kəˈmɪti/

n. a group of people chosen to do a job 委员会：a standing ~ 常务委员会/the Central Committee of the Communist Party of China 中国共产党中央委员会/The football club ~ arranges all the matches. 足球俱乐部委员会安排所有的比赛。

commodity /kəˈmɒdəti/

n. ❶ a product or a raw material that can be bought and sold 商品：household commodities 家庭日用品/prices of commodities 物价 ❷ sth. useful 有用的东西

common /ˈkɒmən/

Ⅰ *adj.* ❶ usual and ordinary; happening or found often in many places 普通的；常见的：This bird is ~. 这种鸟很普通。❷ belonging to or shared equally by two or more 共同的，共用的：~ property 公共财产 ‖ ~ **ground** *n.* 共同利益；共同信念/

C

～ **knowledge** *n*.人所共知的事；常识／～ **sense** *n*.常识 Ⅱ *n*.an area of open land for public use 公用用地 ‖ ～**ly** *adv*.普通地；一般地

commonplace /ˈkɒmənpleɪs/
Ⅰ *adj*.ordinary or usual 平常的；平凡的；普通的 Ⅱ *n*.sth. that happens very often and not unusual 寻常的事物；普通的事物：Air travel is now a ～.如今，乘飞机是一件平常事。

commonwealth /ˈkɒmənwelθ/
n.❶an independent state or community, especially a democratic republic 国家；独立的政治共同体（尤指民主共和国）❷an aggregate or grouping of states or other bodies 联邦 ❸a community or organization of shared interests in a non-political field（非政治领域的、由共同利益组成的）团体，组织：the Christian ～ 基督教组织

commotion /kəˈməʊʃn/
n.a great and noisy confusion or excitement；violent uprising or disturbance 混乱；骚动；暴动；骚扰：cause a ～ 引起骚乱／You're making a great ～ about nothing.你无理取闹。

communal /ˈkɒmjunl/
adj.shared between the members of a group or community 公有的；共有的；公用的；共用的：a ～ kitchen 公用的厨房 ‖ ～**ly** *adv*.公有地；共同地；社区地

commune /ˈkɒmjuːn/
n.a group of people living together and sharing property and responsibility 公社：the Commune of Paris 巴黎公社

communicate /kəˈmjuːnɪkeɪt/
v.❶pass on ideas, feelings, thoughts, etc. 传达，传递（想法、感情、思想等）❷pass an illness 传染（疾病）❸share or exchange information, news, ideas, etc. with sb.交流信息（或消息、意见等）；沟通：～ with someone by letter 与某人通信／If you know English, you can ～ with people everywhere.如果你懂英语，你就可以与各地的人交流。

communication /kəˌmjuːnɪˈkeɪʃn/
n.❶the act of communicating 通信；传播；联系：Communication is difficult in some remote parts of this country.这个国家一些偏僻地区的通信很困难。❷the means of communicating 通信手段；通信设备：Communications were back to normal this morning.今天上午通信设备恢复了正常。❸a letter, message or call 书信；短信；电话

communicative /kəˈmjuːnɪkətɪv/
adj.willing to talk and give information 健谈的；乐意沟通的

communiqué /kəˈmjuːnɪkeɪ/
n.an official announcement（especially one made by a government）公报

communism /ˈkɒmjunɪzəm/
n.a theory or social system in which property is owned by all the people 共产主义

communist /ˈkɒmjunɪst/
n.a person who believes in or supports communism 共产主义者；共产主义的支持者

community /kəˈmjuːnəti/
n.a group of people having the same religion, race, occupation, etc. or with common interests 团体；共同体；社团：the Chinese ～ in New York 纽约的华侨界

commutation /ˌkɒmjuːˈteɪʃn/
n.❶the action or process of commuting a judical sentence 减刑：a ～ of the death sentence to life imprisonment 由死刑改为无期徒刑 ❷the act of making one kind of payment instead of another 交换；折换；代偿

commute /kəˈmjuːt/
v.❶exchange；change 交换；变换 ❷reduce a judical sentence 减刑；减轻处罚：The Governor ～d the convict's prison term.州长缩短了那个犯人的刑期。❸use a season ticket for travel to and from work every day 通勤；使用月（季）票乘车：She ～s from Cambridge to London.她每天乘火车来往于剑桥和伦敦之间。

compact /ˈkɒmpækt/
Ⅰ *adj*.❶smaller than that is usual 小型的；袖珍的：a ～ toy 袖珍玩具 ❷using or filling only a small amount of space 紧凑的；体积小的：The kitchen was ～.这间厨房空间狭小。❸ closely and firmly

packed together 紧密的；坚实的：～ earth 结实的泥土 ❹small and strong 矮小而健壮的：Jack had a ～ and muscular body.杰克个子矮小健壮。Ⅱ n. ❶ a small car 小汽车 ❷a small flat case containing face powder, a mirror, and a powder puff 带镜小粉盒 ❸an agreement between two or more people or countries 协定；协议；合约 Ⅲ v.press sth. together firmly 把……紧压在一起；压实：You should ～ the abstract of your paper.你应当紧缩你的论文摘要。

companion/kəmˈpænɪən/
n. ❶ a person who goes somewhere with or spends time with another, either because of friendship or by chance 伴侣；伙伴：～s in arms 战友/～s in misfortune 难友 ❷either of a pair or set of things；one thing that matches another 配对的物品之一 ❸(usually in titles) a book which explains how to do sth.；a handbook（常用于书名）指南，手册：the Motorist Companion《驾车指南》/the Gardener's Companion《园丁手册》

companionship/kəmˈpænjənʃɪp/
*n.*the state of being companions 友好；友谊；伴侣关系：a ～ of many years 多年的交情/enjoy someone's ～ 乐于与某人为友

company/ˈkʌmpəni/
*n.*❶the presence of another person；companionship 陪伴：He had no objection to my ～.他不反对我陪伴他。 ❷an organization made up of people who work together for purposes of business or trade 公司：Which ～ do you work for? 你在哪家公司上班？ ❸a number of persons working together 一伙人：A great ～ came to church.一伙人来到教堂。‖ be good ～适合交往/for ～ 陪伴；做伴/in 和……一道/in sb.'s ～ 和某人一道/keep ～（with）和……要好；伴随（一道）/keep sb. ～ 给某人做伴/part ～（with）（和……）分手，断绝来往

comparable/ˈkɒmpərəbl/
*adj.*that can be compared 可与相比的；比得上的：Her achievements are ～ with the best.她的成绩比得上最好的。

comparative/kəmˈpærətɪv/
*adj.*❶ having to do with comparison or comparing 比较性的；比较的：～ study 比较研究/～ linguistics 比较语言学 ❷measured or judged by comparing；relative 比较而言的；相对而言的：a ～ stranger 一个相对陌生的人/living in ～ comfort 生活得比较舒适 ❸(of an adjective or adverb)expressing a higher degree of a quality,but not the highest possible（形容词或副词）比较级的

compare/kəmˈpeə(r)/
*v.*❶ examine or judge one thing in relation to another in order to show the points of similarity or difference 比较：She ～d several samples of silk for a dress.她比较了好几种做衣服用的丝绸样品。 ❷describe as being alike 与……相比：My English cannot ～ with his.我的英语不如他。‖ can ～ with 能和……相比/～ notes 交换意见、情况等/～ to 把……比作/～d to 与……相比

comparison/kəmˈpærɪsn/
*n.*❶ a consideration or estimate of the similarities or dissimilarities between two things or people 比较；对照：The two movies invite ～ with one another.这两部电影很有可比性。 ❷an analogy 类比；比拟：a ～ of the brain to a computer 将大脑比作计算机 ❸the quality of being similar or equivalent 相似；类似；相等

compartment/kəmˈpɑːtmənt/
*n.*a division in a train；any of the separate parts into which an enclosed space is divided 火车车厢；分隔间：He sat in a second-class ～.他乘坐二等车厢。

compass/ˈkʌmpəs/
*n.*❶ an instrument with a needle that always points north 罗盘，指南针：mariner's ～ 航海罗盘/radio ～ 无线电罗盘 ❷ an instrument for drawing circles, measuring distance on a map, etc. 圆规；两脚规

compassion/kəmˈpæʃn/
n. sympathetic pity and concern for the suffering of others 怜悯；同情：be filled with ～ for someone 对某人十分同情/

have ～ on someone's sufferings 怜悯；同情某人的痛苦

compassionate /kəmˈpæʃənɪt/
adj. feeling or showing sympathy for people who are suffering 有同情心的；表示怜悯的 ‖ ～**ly** *adv.* 同情地；富有同情心地

compatible /kəmˈpætəbl/
adj. able or suitable to go together 和谐相处的；相容的：Those two people are not ～.这两个人合不来。/His ideas are not ～ with mine.他的主张跟我的主张格格不入。

compel /kəmˈpel/
v. (-ll-) force sb. to do sth. 强迫；迫使：be ～led to do 不得不做/The flood ～led us to turn back. 洪水迫使我们往回走。/You can't ～ obedience from us.你不能强迫我们顺从。

compelling /kəmˈpelɪŋ/
adj. bringing attention or admiration 引人注目的；令人赞赏的：a ～ movie 引人入胜的电影

compendium /kəmˈpendɪəm/
n. (*pl.* ～s or compendia) ❶ a concise and comprehensive summary of information about a subject 概要；概略 ❷ a collection of board games in one box 用具盒

compensate /ˈkɒmpenseɪt/
v. make a suitable payment；give sth. that makes up for a loss 赔偿；补偿：Nothing will ～ for the loss of one's youth.什么东西也弥补不了失去的青春。‖ compensation /ˌkɒmpenˈseɪʃn/ *n.* 补偿；赔偿；报酬；薪水

compete /kəmˈpiːt/
v. try to win sth. by defeating sb. else who is trying to do the same thing 竞赛；竞争；比赛：Some 2000 athletes ～d in 20 events.大约有 2000 名运动员参加了 20 个项目的竞赛。‖ ～ **against** 和……(竞)赛/～ **for** (和……)争夺，比赛…夺取/～ **with** 和……竞争，竞赛

competence /ˈkɒmpɪtəns/
n. ❶ the ability to do sth. successfully 能力；胜任：one's ～ for the task 对某项任务的胜任 ❷ (of a court, a magistrate) le-

gal capacity 权能；权限：exceed one's ～ 越权

competent /ˈkɒmpɪtənt/
adj. having the ability or skill to do sth. 胜任的；有能力的：We have to admit that he is a highly ～ man.我们必须承认他是一个大能人。

competition /ˌkɒmpəˈtɪʃn/
n. ❶ an event in which people compete with each other to find out who is the best at sth. 比赛；竞赛：chess ～s 棋类比赛/She came first in a drawing ～.她在绘画比赛中夺魁。❷ a situation of striving to gain or win sth. by defeating others engaged in the same attempt 竞争；对抗：keep trade ～ between two countries 在两国之间进行贸易竞争 ❸ a person who is competing against sb. 参赛者；竞争者：There was a lot of ～ for the job.有许多人竞聘此职。

competitive /kəmˈpetətɪv/
adj. in or for which there is competition 竞争的；竞争性的；比赛的：the ～ nature of business 做生意的天然竞争性/John's got a very ～ nature.约翰这个人天性好强。

competitor /kəmˈpetɪtə(r)/
n. a person who competes with another or others 竞争对手；敌手；比赛者：There were 10 ～s in the race.有 10 名选手参加赛跑。

compile /kəmˈpaɪl/
v. collect information and arrange (in a book list, etc.) 编纂；编辑：It takes years of hard work to ～ a good dictionary.编写一本好词典要花数年的辛勤劳动。‖ **compilation** *n.* 编写；收集/～**r** *n.* 编者

complacent /kəmˈpleɪsnt/
adj. smug or self-satisfied 自满的；沾沾自喜的：You can't afford to be ～ about security.你还不能对安全掉以轻心。‖ ～**ly** *adv.* 自满地；沾沾自喜地

complain /kəmˈpleɪn/
v. ❶ express displeasure 抱怨：He ～ed of his bad memory.他抱怨自己的记性不好。❷ state the presence of pain, illness, etc. 诉说(疼痛、疾病等)：He never

C

～ed about the pain.他从不说一声痛。

complaint /kəmˈpleɪnt/

n. ❶ the act of complaining 抱怨；诉苦：There is no reason for ～.根本没有理由抱怨。❷ a reason or cause for complaining 抱怨的理由：My only ～ is that there aren't enough hours in the day.我唯一要叫苦的就是白天没有足够的时间。

complement /ˈkɒmplɪmənt/

Ⅰ *n.* ❶ that which makes sth.complete 补足物；补充物：A fine wine is a ～ to a good meal.一顿美餐辅以美酒，便相得益彰。❷ the full number or quantity needed 全数；全量；定员：the ship's ～ 船的定员 ❸ word（s）complementing the predicate 补足语 Ⅱ *v.* add to or make complete 补足；补充

complementary /ˌkɒmplɪˈmentəri/

adj. supplying what is needed for complement 补足的；补充的；互补的：～ colours 互补色

complete /kəmˈpliːt/

Ⅰ *adj.* ❶ having all necessary, usual, or wanted parts；lacking nothing 全部的，完整的：Is this pack of cards ～? 这副牌是完整的吗? ❷ finished；ended 完成的：The first draft is ～.初稿已完成。❸ total；thorough 完全的；彻底的：The boxer achieved a ～ success.那个拳击手取得了彻底的成功。Ⅱ *v.* finish；bring to an end（especially sth. that takes a long time）；make perfect 完成；结束；完善：The railway is not ～d yet.那条铁路尚未修完。‖ ～**ly** *adv.* 完全地

completion /kəmˈpliːʃn/

n. an act of completing；the state of being completed 完成；完结；结束：Completion of this power station is expected in 2015.预计该发电站于 2015 年竣工。

complex /ˈkɒmpleks/

adj. made up of closely connected parts；difficult to understand or explain 复杂的；复合的；难以理解的：a ～ problem 复杂的问题/a ～ sentence 复合句

complexion /kəmˈplekʃn/

n. ❶ a natural colour, appearance of the skin, especially of the face 面色；气色；肤色：a good ～ 姣好的肤色 ❷ a general character or aspect of conduct, affair, etc. 特性；形势；局面：This victory changed the ～ of the war.这场胜利改变了战争的局势。

complexity /kəmˈpleksɪti/

n. ❶ the state of being formed of many parts；the state of being difficult to understand 复杂性；难懂：the ～ of the problem 这个问题的复杂性 ❷（*pl.*）a factor involved in a complicated process or situation 复杂因素；复杂情况：the complexities of society life 社会生活中的复杂因素

compliant /kəmˈplaɪənt/

adj. ❶（said about a person）willing to comply or obey（人）服从的，遵从的，顺从的 ❷ meeting a standard or requirement 依从的；遵照的；符合的：food which is ～ with safety regulations 符合安全规定的食品

complicate /ˈkɒmplɪkeɪt/

v. make（sth.）complex；make（sth.）more difficult to do or understand 使复杂；使难弄；使麻烦：This ～s matters.这使事情更麻烦了。

complicated /ˈkɒmplɪkeɪtɪd/

adj. difficult；not easy to do or understand 复杂的；难懂的；难理解的：a ～ plan 复杂的计划/a ～ puzzle 难解的疑团/This sentence is ～ in structure.这个句子结构复杂。/This question is too ～ for me.这个问题对我来说太复杂了。

complication /ˌkɒmplɪˈkeɪʃn/

n. ❶ the state of being complex, confused, difficult 错综复杂；纠纷 ❷ sth. that adds new difficulties 增加新困难的事物；新难题：a ～ that we had not expected 我们未曾预料到的新难题 ❸ a new illness, or new development of an illness, that makes treatment more difficult 并发病；并发症：influenza with ～s 流感并发症

complicity /kəmˈplɪsəti/

n. the act of taking part with another person in crime 同谋；共犯：～ in crime 同谋犯

compliment/ˈkɒmplɪmənt/

Ⅰ *n.* ❶ an expression of praise, admiration or approval 赞美的话；敬意：He paid her many ~s.他对她说了许多赞美的话。❷ (*pl.*) polite greetings 问候；道贺；贺词：Please give my ~s to your parents.请代我问候你父母。Ⅱ *v.* express admiration or approval 赞美；敬佩：We ~ed her on her skillful performance.我们钦佩她娴熟的技艺。

complimentary /ˌkɒmplɪˈment(ə)ri/

adj. ❶ expressing a compliment 祝贺的；表示敬意的；恭维的；赞美的 ❷ given free of charge 免费的；赠送的：~ tickets 赠票

comply/kəmˈplaɪ/

v. act in accordance with a demand, order, rule, etc.遵守；依从；服从：~ with safety regulations 遵守安全条例/We couldn't ~ with your request.我们无法满足你的要求。‖ **compliance** *n.*依从，顺从

component/kəmˈpəʊnənt/

n. one of the parts of which sth. is made up 组成成分，组件：This machine has 300 different ~s.这台机器有 300 个不同的组件。

compose/kəmˈpəʊz/

v. ❶ write or create a work of art, especially a piece of music or poem 创作（尤指作曲或作诗）：He spent his spare time composing poetry. 他在业余时间作诗。❷ make up 构成；组成：Twelve men ~ a jury.12 人组成一个陪审团。❸ calm or settle 使安详；平静下来：Compose yourself to read the book.静下心来读书。

composed /kəmˈpəʊzd/

adj. having one's feelings and expression under control; calm 镇静的；沉着的；泰然自若的 ‖ ~ly *adv.*镇静地；沉着地；自若地

composer /kɒmˈpəʊzə/

n. a person who writes music 作曲家

composite /ˈkɒmpəzɪt, ˈkɒmpəzaɪt/

Ⅰ *adj.* made up of a number of different parts or styles 合成的；混成的；复合的 Ⅱ *n.* sth. made by putting together different parts or materials 合成物；混合物；复合材料

composition/ˌkɒmpəˈzɪʃn/

n. ❶ the act of composing music, poetry, etc.创作；作曲 ❷ a piece of music or writing 作品（乐曲、文章）：a modern ~ 一支现代乐曲 ❸ the various parts from which sth. is made up 构成；成分：Scientists study the ~ of the soil.科学家研究土壤的构成。

compost/ˈkɒmpɒst/

n. a mixture of rotting vegetation, used in a garden to improve the soil 绿肥；混合肥料

composure/kəmˈpəʊʒə(r)/

n. complete control over one's feelings; calmness 泰然自若；镇静；沉着：behave with great ~ 态度极为镇定/Don't lose your ~.不要慌张。

compound/ˈkɒmpaʊnd/

Ⅰ *adj.* made up of different materials; having more combined parts 复合的，合成的：Soap is a ~ substance.肥皂是一种复合物质。Ⅱ *n.* a substance formed by the chemical combination of two or more elements 混合物；化合物：Water is a ~ of hydrogen and oxygen.水是氢和氧的化合物。

comprehend/ˌkɒmprɪˈhend/

v. ❶ understand sth. fully 理解；领会：He ~s geometry and algebra.他懂得几何和代数。❷ include 包括：The course will ~ all aspects of African culture.此课程将包括非洲文化的各个方面。

comprehension /ˌkɒmprɪˈhenʃən/

n. the action or capability of understanding sth.理解；领会；理解力：I have the least ~ of what he is trying to do.我对他正试图做的事完全不能理解。

comprehensive/ˌkɒmprɪˈhensɪv/

adj. of broad scope; including nearly all 综合的；全面的；广泛的：a ~ review 综合性复习/a man with a ~ mind of ideas 富有全面理解力的人

compress/kəmˈpres/

v. press together; force into a narrower space 压紧；压缩：~ cotton into bales 将棉花打成包/~ a speech into five minutes 把讲话压缩在五分钟之内

comprise/kəm'praɪz/

　　v.include;be made up of 包含;包括;由……构成:~ much matter in few words 言简意赅/The committee ~s seven persons.委员会由 7 人组成。

compromise/'kɒmprəmaɪz/

　　Ⅰ *n*.a settlement of a dispute by which each side gives up sth.it has asked for and neither side gets all it has asked for 妥协;和解;折中;让步:work out a ~ 拟定折中方案/We arrived at a ~ over the case.我们就该案子达成了某种妥协。Ⅱ *v*.❶ settle a dispute, etc. by giving up some of your demands when you disagree with sb.to make an agreement 与……妥协;和解:The government ~d with the workers.政府向工人妥协了。/We refused to ~ in this matter.我们在这个问题上拒绝妥协。❷bring (sb.or sth.) under suspicion by unwise behaviour,etc.受牵连;连累;危及:~ one's reputation 有损自己的名誉

compulsive/kəm'pʌlsɪv/

　　adj.❶acting from a compulsion 强迫性的;不由自主的:a ~ gambler 嗜赌成癖的赌徒❷extremely exciting or interesting 引人入胜的 ‖ ~ly *adv*.强制地;强迫地;引人入胜地

compulsory/kəm'pʌlsəri/

　　adj.that must be done because of a law or a rule（因法律或规则而）必须做的,强制的,强迫的:~ education 义务教育

compunction/kəm'pʌŋkʃ(ə)n/

　　n.a feeling of slight guilt or regret 内疚;愧疚;后悔,悔恨:He had lied to his father without ~.他向父亲撒了谎却毫无愧疚。

computation/ˌkɒmpjuˈteɪʃ(ə)n/

　　n.the act or process of calculating sth. 计算;计算过程

compute/kəm'pjuːt/

　　v. determine by calculation; count the number 估计;计算:~ the amount 估计数目/The boss ~d his losses at ＄50.老板估计他损失 50 美元。

computer/kəm'pjuːtə(r)/

　　n.a person who makes calculations;a cal-culating machine 计算者;计算机;电脑:~ language 计算机语言/~ science 电脑科学

computerize/kəm'pjuːtəraɪz/

　　v. ❶ process or store information by means of a computer 用计算机贮存（或处理信息）❷convert a process or set of machinery so that it can make use of or be controlled by a computer 使电脑化;使计算机化 ‖ **computerization** *n*.电脑化

comrade/'kɒmreɪd/

　　n.❶a friend 朋友;伙伴:They are ~s and are always together.他们是朋友,总是在一起。❷a fellow member of a union,po-litical party,etc.同志:~ Wang 王同志

concave/'kɒŋkeɪv/

　　adj. (especially of lenses) curving in-wards;having the shape of the inside of a circle or sphere（尤指透镜）凹的

concavity/kɒnˈkævɪti/

　　n.(*pl*.-ies)❶the state or quality of being concave 凹陷;凹度;凹性 ❷ a concave surface or thing 凹面;凹面物;凹处

conceal/kən'siːl/

　　v.hide; keep secret 隐藏;隐匿:He ~ed the sweets in his pocket.他把糖藏在衣袋里。/He ~ed himself behind the door.他藏在门后。/I do not ~ anything from my parents.我对父母不隐瞒任何事情。

concede/kən'siːd/

　　v.admit or agree that sth.is true or valid 承认,同意（某事属实或正确）:~ defeat 承认失败/~ a point in argument 在辩论中退让一步

conceit/kən'siːt/

　　n.too much pride in one's own power,a-bility,value,etc. 高傲,骄傲自大:He's full of ~.他十分自负。‖ ~ed *adj*. 自负的;骄傲自满的:a ~ed actor 一位自负的演员

conceive/kən'siːv/

　　v.❶form or devise in the mind;imagine;think out 想象;设想;想出;推测:~ a plan 想出一个计划/~ a hatred 怀恨/I can't ~ why you allowed the child to travel alone.我想不出你为什么让那孩子独自去旅行。/ We can't ~ of such a thing happening again.我们无法想象这种事情还会发生。❷(of a woman)become pregnant (妇女)怀孕:She ~d.她怀孕了。

concentrate/ˈkɒnsntreɪt/

v. ❶(cause to) come together in or around one place (使)聚集:The troops ~d near the station.部队在车站附近集合。❷direct (one's thoughts, efforts, attention, etc.) towards a particular activity or purpose 集中(思想,精力,注意等):You should ~ your attention on your work.你应该把精力集中在工作上。

concentrated/ˈkɒnsentreɪtɪd/

adj. ❶wholly directed to one thing; intense 全力以赴的;专心致志的;集中的:a ~ campaign 全力以赴的战役 ❷(of a substance or solution) present in a high proportion relative to other substances (物质或溶液)浓缩的: ~ fruit juice 浓缩水果汁

concentration/ˌkɒnsenˈtreɪʃən/

n. ❶the process of concentrating 专心;专注 ❷the ability to concentrate on sth.注意力:Tiredness affects your powers of ~.疲劳影响注意力的集中。❸the mass or amount of a substance contained in a specified amount of a solvent or in a mixture 浓度;含量

concentric/kənˈsentrɪk/

adj. having the same centre 同心的: ~ circles 同心圆

concept/ˈkɒnsept/

n. an idea of sth.; a general notion 观念;概念:A small baby has no ~ of right and wrong.婴儿没有是非概念。‖ **conceptualize**/kənˈseptʃʊəlaɪz/ *v.* 形成概念

conception/kənˈsepʃn/

n. ❶a general understanding; an idea 概念;观念;思想;见解:He's got a pretty strange ~ of friendship.他对友谊有一种非常独特的见解。❷the act of forming an idea, plan, etc. 设想;构思;构想 ❸the process of an egg being fertilized inside a woman's body 妊娠;怀孕

concern/kənˈsɜːn/

Ⅰ *v.* ❶have to do with sth.关系到,关于:This matter ~s all of us.这事与我们都有关。❷worry; make anxious 使担心;使忧虑:Her illness ~s me very much.她的疾病使我非常担心。Ⅱ *n.* ❶the thing of interest or important to sb.关注的事;关系重大的事:This is none of your ~.这不关你的事。❷anxiety; worry 忧虑;担心:There is no cause for ~.没有理由忧虑。‖ as far as … is ~ed 就……来说;就……而论/where … is ~ed 牵涉到…… 的时候

concerned/kənˈsɜːnd/

adj. ❶worried or anxious about sth. 担心的;忧虑的 ❷involved or interested in sth.感兴趣的;关切的;关注的

concerning/kənˈsɜːnɪŋ/

prep. about; to do with 关于;就:further revelations ~ his role in the affair 关于他在此事中所起作用的进一步揭露

concert/ˈkɒnsət/

n. an entertainment at which a number of pieces of music are played or sung 音乐会

concerted/kənˈsɜːtɪd/

adj. planned or done together by agreement; combined 一致的;共同的:a ~ effort 共同努力

concerto/kənˈtʃeətəʊ, kənˈtʃɜːtəʊ/

n. a piece of music written for a solo instrument or solo instruments and an orchestra 协奏曲

concession/kənˈseʃn/

n. ❶the act of conceding 让步:make a ~ to...对……让步 ❷the right given to do sth.special 特许权:an oil ~ 石油开采特许权

concise/kənˈsaɪs/

adj. saying a lot in few words 简洁的:a ~ letter 一封简要的信

conclude/kənˈkluːd/

v. ❶come to an end 结束:He ~d his speech.他结束了演讲。❷come to believe after thinking of known facts 得出结论:What do you ~ from the facts? 从这些事实中你得出什么结论? ❸establish an agreement with sb. formally and finally 达成协议

conclusion /kənˈkluːʒən/
n. ❶an end or finish of an event 结束;终结;结尾 ❷ the summing-up of an argument or text 结论;总结;结束语 ❸ the arrangement or settling of sth. (条约或协议的)订立,缔结:～ of the trade treaty 贸易条约的签署

conclusive /kənˈkluːsɪv/
adj. putting an end to all doubt or uncertainty;decisive or convincing 结论性的;不容置疑的;确凿的:～ evidence 确凿的证据 ‖ ～ly *adv.* 总结地;决定性地

concoct /kənˈkɒkt/
v. ❶prepare sth. by mixing various ingredients together 调制;调和:～ a splendid meal 调制佳肴 ❷invent a story, an excuse,a plot for a novel,etc.编造,虚构(故事、借口、小说情节等):～ an excuse for being late 编造迟到的借口

concord /ˈkɒŋkɔːd/
n. ❶agreement or harmony between people or groups 一致;和谐;协调:These neighbouring states had lived in ～ for centuries.这些相互毗邻的国家几个世纪以来一直和睦相处。❷a treaty 协定

concordance /kənˈkɔːdəns/
n. ❶ agreement 一致;和谐;协调 ❷ an alphabetical list of the words of a book with references to the passages in which they occur 词汇索引

concordant /kənˈkɔːdənt/
adj. in agreement;harmonious 一致的;和谐的;协调的

concrete /ˈkɒŋkriːt/
Ⅰ *adj.* real or solid 具体的;实在的;有形的:Our plans are not ～.我们的计划不具体。Ⅱ *n.* a building material made by mixing sand, very small stones, cement and water 混凝土:a ～ wall 混凝土墙

concur /kənˈkɜː/
v. (-rr-)❶agree 同意;赞同:The chairman ～red with the majority.主席赞成大多数人的意见。❷ happen or occur at the same time 同时发生;同时出现 ‖ ～rence *n.* 同意;一致;同时发生;同时出现

concurrent /kənˈkʌrənt/
adj. happening or occuring at the same time 同时发生的;同时出现的

condemn /kənˈdem/
v. ❶express very strong disapproval of sb. or sth. 谴责:Murder is ～ed by all reasonable people.谋杀受到所有理智的人的谴责。❷judge (a person) guilty 定罪,判处(徒刑):～ a murderer to life imprisonment 判处凶手无期徒刑 ‖ **condemnation** *n.* 谴责;判罪:condemnation of modern warfare 对现代战争的谴责

condensation /ˌkɒndenˈseɪʃən/
n. ❶ drops of water that form on a cold surface when warm water vapour becomes cool 凝结的水珠 ❷the process of a gas changing to a liquid (气体)冷凝,凝结 ❸a concise version of sth.,especially a text (尤指文章的)缩写(本),简写(本);节本;摘要

condense /kənˈdens/
v. ❶ (of a liquid) (cause to) increase in density or strength to become thicker (液体)凝缩,浓缩:～d milk 炼乳 ❷put (a piece of writing or speech) into fewer words 缩写(作品或演讲);使简洁:a ～d account of an event 一篇简要的叙述/A long story can be ～d into a few sentences.一篇长故事可以压缩为几句话。

condenser /kənˈdensə(r)/
n. ❶ an apparatus for converting gases or vapours to a liquid state 冷凝器 ❷ a lens for concentrating light rays on an area 聚光镜 ❸ an apparatus which stores electricity 电容器

condescend /ˌkɒndɪˈsend/
v. ❶behave in a way that shows you feel superior 显示优越感 ❷agree to do sth. even though you think it is beneath your dignity 屈尊;俯就:In the end they ～ed to come with us.最后他们屈尊跟我们一同过来。‖ **condescension** *n.* 傲慢态度;谦虚;屈尊

condescending /ˌkɒndɪˈsendɪŋ/
adj. behaving as though you are more important and more intelligent than other people 表现出优越感的;居高临下的:He has a ～ attitude towards the colleagues. 他对同事们总是居高临下。

condiment /ˈkɒndɪmənt/

n. a seasoning for food, such as salt or pepper. 调味品；佐料

condition /kənˈdɪʃn/

n. ❶ a state of being or existence 状况；状态：Weather ～s were good. 天气情况很好。❷ sth. on which another thing depends 条件：Ability and effort are ～s of success. 才能和努力是成功的条件。❸ (*pl.*) circumstances 情况；环境：What are ～s like in your country now? 你们国家现在的情况怎样？‖ in ～ 身体很好/out of ～ 身体不适/in good ～ 完好无损/on ～ that 条件是/on no ～ 绝不要

conditional /kənˈdɪʃənl/

adj. depending upon, containing a certain condition or conditions 含有条件的；有限制的：Her agreement to buy our house was ～ on us leaving all the furniture in it. 她同意买我们的房子，条件是我们要把家具都留在屋内。‖ ～ clause *n.* 条件从句

conditioner /kənˈdɪʃənə/

n. a substance put on sth. to improve its condition, such as a liquid for the hair 护发素；护发剂

condole /kənˈdəʊl/

v. express sympathy or regret at a loss, misfortune, etc. 慰问；吊唁；哀悼：I ～ with you upon the loss of your mother. 你母亲逝世，特向你表示慰问。

condolence /kənˈdəʊləns/

n. (usually *pl.*) an expression of sympathy or regret 吊唁；慰问：present one's ～s to 向……吊唁

condone /kənˈdəʊn/

v. forgive; allow some wrong action to go unpunished or be forgotten 宽恕；宽容：I cannot ～ the damage you have caused. 我不能宽恕你所造成的损害。

conducive /kənˈdjuːsɪv/

adj. likely to result in or lead to 导致……的；有助于……的：Exercise is ～ to good health. 锻炼有助于健康。

conduct /ˈkɒndʌkt/

v. ❶ direct or lead 引导；指导：～ tourists through a museum 陪同游客参观博物馆

❷ allow (heat, electric current, etc.) to pass through 传导（热、电流等）：Copper ～s electricity better than other materials. 铜比其他物质导电性能好。❸ control; direct 管理；指挥：～ an orchestra 指挥管弦乐队

conductor /kənˈdʌktə(r)/

n. ❶ a thing that conducts heat or electricity 导体；载体：a good ～ 良导体 ❷ a person who collects fares and sells tickets on a public vehicle 售票员 ❸ a person who directs a group of musicians （乐队）指挥

cone /kəʊn/

n. ❶ a solid object with a circular base and pointed tip 圆锥体 ❷ anything shaped like a cone 圆锥状东西：the ～ of a volcano 火山顶/an ice-cream ～ 蛋卷冰激凌 ❸ the fruit of certain trees(e.g.pine or fir) （松树或冷杉的）球果

confederate /kənˈfedərɪt/

Ⅰ *adj.* allied, joined by an agreement or treaty 联盟的；同盟的；联邦的 Ⅱ *n.* ❶ a member of a confederacy 同盟者；联合者 ❷ an ally or accomplice 帮凶；从犯

confederation /kənˌfedəˈreɪʃn/

n. a group of nations, societies, business firms, etc. that have joined together because of some interest or purpose which they share 同盟；联盟

confer /kənˈfɜː(r)/

v. (-rr-) ❶ give or grant (a degree, right, favour) 授予（学位、权利、恩惠等）：～ a medal on someone 授予某人奖章 ❷ consult or discuss 商议；讨论：～ with one's lawyer 与律师商谈

conference /ˈkɒnfərəns/

n. a meeting for exchanging opinions and ideas 会议；讨论会：arrange a ～ on elementary education 安排一次会议讨论初等教育问题

confess /kənˈfes/

v. ❶ say or admit (that one has done wrong); acknowledge 承认；供认；招认；招供：～ one's guilt 认罪 ❷ make one's sins known to a priest; (of a priest) listen to sb. doing this 向神父忏悔；（神父）听取……忏悔：The priest ～ed the criminal.

神父听取罪犯忏悔。

confession /kənˈfeɪʃn/

n. ❶ an admission of a crime or fault 认错；认罪：The accused man made a full ~.那被告完全认罪了。❷ an act of confessing one's sins to a priest（向神父的）忏悔：She went to ~ every Friday.她每星期五去忏悔。

confidant /ˌkɒnfɪˈdænt/

n. a person you confide in 知己；密友

confide /kənˈfaɪd/

v. ❶ tell（a secret, etc.）to sb.倾诉，吐露（秘密等）：He ~d to me that he had spent two years in prison.他向我吐露他坐过两年牢。❷ have trust or faith in 委托；交托；信赖：~ a task to someone 把工作委托给某人

confidence /ˈkɒnfɪdəns/

n. ❶ a belief in oneself or others or in what is said, reported, etc.; a belief that one is right or that one is able to do sth. 信心；自信：She lacks ~ in herself.她对自己缺乏信心。❷ the belief that one can have faith in sb. or sth. 相信；信赖：I have complete ~ in you.我对你完全信赖。❸ a secret which is confided to sb.知心话：The old friends exchanged ~s. 老朋友互吐衷肠。‖ in ~ 推心置腹地；说心腹话 /take sb. into one's ~ 对……说知心话 /with ~ 满怀信心地

confident /ˈkɒnfɪdənt/

adj. sure about oneself or about sth. 自信的；有信心的；有把握的：be ~ of success 确信成功 /I'm ~ that our team will win.我确信我们队会赢。/She gave me a ~ smile.她对我露出信赖的微笑。

confidential /ˌkɒnfɪˈdenʃəl/

adj. ❶ meant to be kept secret; said or written in confidence 机密的；保密的；秘密的 ❷ entrusted with private information 受信任的；委以机密的：a ~ secretary 机要秘书 ‖ ~ity *n.*机密性；保密性 /~ly *adv.*秘密地

configuration /kənˌfɪgəˈreɪʃn/

n. a shape or outline 轮廓；外貌；形状；外形：the ~ of the earth's surface 地球表面的形状

configure /kənˈfɪgə/

v. ❶ shape or put together in a particular form or configuration 使成形；装配；安装：The aircraft will be ~d as a VIP transport.这架飞机将被装配成运送贵宾的飞机。❷ arrange or order（a computer system or an element of it）so as to fit it for a designated task（计算机）配置；设定

confine /kənˈfaɪn/

v. ❶ keep sth. within limits 限制：Please ~ your remarks to the subject we are debating.请你讲话不要离开我们所讨论的题目。❷ shut or keep in a small space 禁闭；幽禁：He was ~d to prison for six years.他在监狱里关了六年。

confinement /kənˈfaɪnmənt/

n. ❶ the state of being confined or shut up 禁闭；监禁；关押 ❷ the time when a woman is giving birth to a baby 分娩；产期

confirm /kənˈfɜːm/

v. ❶ make certain; give proof of 证实；肯定：You must ~ your theory.你必须证实你的理论。❷ approve; make sth. effective formally 批准；认可；确认：~ a treaty 批准一个条约 ‖ ~ation *n.* 证实：We are waiting for ~ation of the news.我们正在等着证实此消息。

confiscate /ˈkɒnfɪskeɪt/

v. officially take sth. away from sb. 没收：The teacher ~d the book which the boy was reading in class.老师没收了男孩子在上课时候看的书。‖ confiscation /ˌkɒnfɪˈskeɪʃn/ *n.*没收；征用

conflict /ˈkɒnflɪkt/

n. ❶ a prolonged armed fight or struggle 武装斗争；战斗：Few ~s occurred along the borders.边境发生冲突的事件不多。❷ opposition; difference; argument 抵触；冲突；争论：in ~ with 与……相抵触

confluence /ˈkɒnfluəns/

n. ❶ flowing together; a place where two streams meet together and become one stream 合流；汇合处 ❷ movement in which people or things come together 群集

conform /kənˈfɔːm/

v. be in agreement with or comply with (generally accepted rules, standards, etc.) 使一致；使遵从；依从：You should ～ to the rules. 你应遵守规则。

conformation /ˌkɒnfɔːˈmeɪʃən/

n. the structure or form of a thing 构造；结构；形态

conformity /kənˈfɔːmɪti/

n. conforming to accepted rules or standards（对标准、规则的）遵守，顺从：～ to regulations 遵守规定

confound /kənˈfaʊnd/

v. ❶ cause surprise or confusion 使惊惶；使糊涂：The bad election results ～ed the government. 选举结果很糟，令政府惊慌失措。❷ mix up or confuse (ideas, etc.) 搞乱，混淆（概念等）：～ right with wrong 混淆是非／～ two things 把两桩事情混淆起来 ❸ defeat or overthrow (enemies, plans, etc.) 击败，挫败

confront /kənˈfrʌnt/

v. ❶ face and challenge an opponent or enemy 面对；面临；对抗 ❷ be present as sth. you have to deal with 降临于；临到（某人）头上：There are many problems ～ing us. 我们面临着许多问题。❸ face up to a problem and deal with it 面对，正视，处理（问题、困难）：There are too many problems to ～ all at once. 有太多问题，不能一次马上解决。❹ bring opponents face to face 对抗；对峙：They ～ed him with his accusers. 他们让他和控方对峙。‖ ～ation n. 对抗；对峙；冲突

confuse /kənˈfjuːz/

v. ❶ make sb. become unclear or perplexed about sth. 使混乱；迷惑：The road signs ～d the driver. 路标使司机感到迷惑。❷ mix up 混淆；弄混：I always ～ Australia with Austria. 我总是把澳大利亚和奥地利弄混。

confusion /kənˈfjuːʒn/

n. ❶ the act of confusing or mixing up 混淆：To avoid ～, the teams wore different colours. 为了避免混淆，各队穿着不同颜色的衣服。❷ the state of being bewildered or unclear in one's mind about sth.

困惑；迷惑；糊涂：His unexpected arrival threw everyone into ～. 他的突然到来使大家感到迷惑。‖ in ～ 处于混乱状态

congeal /kənˈdʒiːl/

v. change from liquid to solid (especially because of cold) 凝固；（尤指因冷而）凝结

congenial /kənˈdʒiːnɪəl/

adj. ❶ having the same interests and ideas, and therefore friendly（因兴趣、主张相同而）友好的；志趣相投的：a ～ companion 一个志趣相投的朋友 ❷ pleasant and suitable for oneself 惬意的；宜人的：～ surroundings 令人心旷神怡的环境

congenital /kənˈdʒenɪtl/

adj. existing in a person from birth 先天的：a ～ deformity 先天畸形 ‖ ～ly adv. 先天地；天生地

congested /kənˈdʒestɪd/

adj. ❶ too full or crowded 拥挤的；挤满的 ❷ (of an organ or tissue of the body) abnormally full of blood（身体器官或组织）充血的

congestion /kənˈdʒestʃn/

n. the state of being crowded and full of traffic 交通堵塞

congratulate /kənˈgrætʃuleɪt/

v. express pleasure at a person's success, good fortune, etc. 祝贺；庆贺：My father ～d me on passing the exam. 我爸爸祝贺我通过了考试。

congratulation /kənˌgrætʃuˈleɪʃn/

n. (usually pl.) words of joy and praise to sb. who has done well 祝贺；贺词：I offered him my ～s on his success. 我为他的成功祝贺。/Convey my ～s to him. （请）代我向他祝贺。

congregate /ˈkɒngrɪgeɪt/

v. come or bring together into a crowd or mass 聚集；会合；集合：People quickly ～d round the speaker. 人们迅速地围拢在演说者的四周。

congress /ˈkɒngres/

n. ❶ the elected law-making body of certain countries 国会：The matter will be discussed in ～ tomorrow. 这事明天将在国会讨论。❷ a series of meetings of representatives of societies, etc. for discussion 代表大会 ‖ ~**man** n.国会议员;众议员

conical /ˈkɒnɪkəl/
adj.cone-shaped 圆锥形的 ‖ ~**ly** *adv*.成圆锥形地

conjecture /kənˈdʒektʃə(r)/
Ⅰ *v*. guess;come to an opinion about some facts without having enough information 推测;猜想:Don't ~ about the outcome.不要对结果妄加猜测。 Ⅱ *n*.an opinion or conclusion formed on the basis of incomplete information 推测;猜想

conjunction /kənˈdʒʌŋkʃn/
n.❶a word that joins other words, clauses, etc. 连接词 ❷ the state of being joined 凑合;结合:a pleasing ~ of ability and beauty 能力与美貌的美满结合

conjure /ˈkʌndʒə(r)/
v.do tricks which seem to be magic, as a form of entertainment 变魔术,变戏法 ‖ **conjuror**, ~**r** *n*. 魔术师/ **conjuring** *n*. 魔术、戏法

connect /kəˈnekt/
v.❶be joined together(使)连接;联结:a ~ing door 连通两间房的门 ❷join sth.to the main supply of electricity, gas, water, , etc.or to another piece of equipment 使……连接;接通:I am waiting for the telephone to be ~ed.我在等待着接通电话。 ❸join a computer to the Internet or a computer network 使(计算机)连接(到互联网或计算机网络) ❹have a link with sb.or sth. 与……有联系(或关联):The two subjects are closely ~ed.这两门学科紧密相连。 ❺notice or make a link between people, things, events, etc. 注意到……有关联;把……联系起来 ❻arrive just before another leaves so that passengers can change from one to the other 衔接;联运:There's a ~ing flight at noon.中午有一趟联营航班。 ❼form a good relationship with sb. so that you can understand each other (与某人)建立良好关系:They didn't really ~.他们仍未真正建立起良好的关系。 ‖ ~ **up** 连起来;接上/ **be** ~**ed with** 与……有联系

connection /kəˈnekʃn/

n.❶the act of connecting or the state of being connected;a point where two things are connected;a thing which connects 联结,连接;连接点;连接物:a pipe ~ 管子接头/There's a strong ~ between smoking and heart disease.抽烟与心脏病有密切联系。 ❷(usually *pl*.)a person connected to others by a family relationship 亲戚:distant ~s 远亲 ‖ **in** ~ **with** 与……有关系

connective /kəˈnektɪv/
Ⅰ *adj*.connecting or linking things 连接的;联结的 Ⅱ *n*.a word that joins words or phrases or sentences 连接词;关联词

connote /kɒˈnəʊt/
v.❶(of a word) imply or suggest (an idea or feeling) in addition to the literal or primary meaning (词)意味着;有……的含义 ❷(of a fact) imply as a consequence or condition (事实)暗示;意味着……的结果(或条件):Laziness ~d failure.懒惰意味着失败。 ‖ **connotation** *n*.含义;隐含意义

conquer /ˈkɒŋkə(r)/
v.❶beat an enemy and take control of a country 征服;夺取:The town was ~ed by the enemy. 城镇被敌人夺取了。 ❷defeat or overcome problems, bad habits, etc.战胜,克服(困难,坏习惯等):She ~ed her shyness and spoke up.她克服了害羞的习惯大声说起话来。

conquest /ˈkɒŋkwest/
n.the act of conquering 征服;赢得:The Norman Conquest was in 1066.诺曼征服(即诺曼人征服英国)发生在 1066 年。

conscience /ˈkɒnʃəns/
n.the feeling inside one's mind;the moral sense of right and wrong 良心;良知;道德心:have no ~ 没有良心

conscientious /ˌkɒnʃiˈenʃəs/
adj.taking care to do one's work or duty as well as possible 认真的;负责的;尽责的;凭良心做的:a ~ teacher 尽责的教师 ‖ ~**ly** *adv*. 良心上地;尽责地,认真地

conscious /ˈkɒnʃəs/
adj. ❶ having all one's senses working and able to understand what is happen-

C

ing;not in a sleeplike state 有意识的;神志清醒的;有知觉的;He's not ~ yet after the accident.事故后他还没清醒过来。❷knowing, understanding or recognizing sth.;aware 意识到;察觉到;He wasn't ~ of having offended her. 他没有意识到自己已经冒犯了她。❸intentional 有意的;自觉的;Man is a ~ being.人是一种有意识的动物。‖~ly adv.有意识地;自觉地/~ness n.知觉;意识;觉悟

conscript /kən'skrɪpt/
Ⅰ n.a person made to serve in the armed forces by law 应征入伍者 Ⅱ v.make person serve in the armed forces by law 征召;征募

consecrate /'kɒnsɪkreɪt/
v.❶ carry out a ceremony which marks sb.or sth. as special for religious purposes (举行仪式)使某人(或某事物)神圣;~ a bishop church 使就主教圣职❷ keep sth. for a special purpose 奉献

consecutive /kən'sekjʊtɪv/
adj.following one after another continuously 连续的;three ~ days 连续三天

consensus /kən'sensəs/
n. a general agreement or feeling of a number of people 一致意见;共识

consent /kən'sent/
Ⅰ v.agree 同意;答应;~ to a proposal 同意一个提案/I asked my mother if I could go out,and she ~ed.我问妈妈我是否可以出去,她同意了。Ⅱ n.an agreement or permission 答应;同意;I had to get my mother's ~ before I went.我走之前必须得到我母亲的同意。

consequence /'kɒnsɪkwəns/
n.❶ sth. that follows from an action or set of conditions;a result 后果;结果 ❷ importance 重要性;This matter is of great ~ to all of us.这件事对我们都很重要。‖as a ~ 结果/as a ~ of 由于……的结果/take(bear) the ~s 承担后果

consequential /ˌkɒnsɪ'kwenʃəl/
adj.❶happening as a result or an effect of sth. 随之而来的;相应发生的;作为结果的;a loss of confidence and a ~ withdrawal of funds 丧失信心并因此撤资 ❷

important;significant 重要的;重大的;有重要意义的;The report discusses a number of ~ matters that are yet to be decided.这份报告讨论了许多有待决定的重大问题。

consequently /'kɒnsɪkwəntli/
adv. as a result; therefore 因此;所以;This poses a threat to agriculture and the food chain,and ~ to human health.这会对农业和食物链造成威胁,由此危及人的健康。

conservative /kən'sɜːvətɪv/
Ⅰ adj.❶ opposed to great or sudden changes 保守的 ❷ careful or cautious 谨慎的;稳健的 Ⅱ n.a member of the Conservative Party 保守党人

conservatory /kən'sɜːvətri/
n.a room or building(usually attached to a house)with glass walls,in which plants are kept and people enjoy the sun 温室;暖房

conserve /kən'sɜːv/
v.save sth.from loss or damage;keep sth. to be used when needed 保护;保存;We must ~ the natural resources of the country.我们必须保护国家自然资源。‖conservation n.保护;保存

consider /kən'sɪdə(r)/
v.❶ think carefully about sth. or about what to do 考虑;He never ~s others.他从不考虑别人。❷ regard as;think that sth.is true 认为;I ~ it as a great honour.我把它看作是一大荣誉。

considerable /kən'sɪdərəbl/
adj.notably large in amount, size, or extent 相当多的;相当大的;相当重要的 ‖considerably adv.相当大地;相当多地

considerate /kən'sɪdərət/
adj.thoughtful of others 体贴的;考虑周到的;~ behaviour 体贴的行为/He is ~ of others.他能为别人着想。

consideration /kənˌsɪdə'reɪʃn/
n.❶careful thought;thoughtful attention 考虑;思考;Please give careful ~ to this question.请仔细地考虑一下这个问题。❷thoughtful attention to or care for the wishes,needs,or feelings of others(为别

人)考虑;体贴,体谅: She ought to have more ～ for you.她应该多为你着想。**❸** a fact to be considered when making a decision 考虑的因素: Price and quality are two ～s in buying anything.无论买什么东西,价格和质量总是要考虑的因素。**❹**a payment for a service; reward 报酬: He is the sort of man who would do anything for a ～.他是这样一种人,只要有报酬任何事情都愿意干。‖ under ～ 在考虑中/in ～ of 考虑到;由于/on no ～ 在任何情况下都不/out of ～ for 出于对……的考虑/leave out of ～ 不予考虑;忽略/take into ～ 把……考虑进去;考虑到

considering /kən'sɪdərɪŋ/
prep. taking sth. into consideration 考虑到;就……而言;鉴于: It's very good ～ the conditions.就目前情况而言,这已经很好了。

consign /kən'saɪn/
v.**❶**send (goods, etc.) for delivery 运送;托运;寄售: The goods will be ～ed by rail.那些货物将由铁路托运。**❷**hand over; put into the care of sb. else 移交;托付: ～ an orphan to her care 将一个孤儿委托她抚养 ‖ ～ee *n*. 收件人;受托人

consignment /kən'saɪnmənt/
n.a batch of goods sent to someone 托付物;寄售物;托运物

consist /kən'sɪst/
v.**❶**(～ of) be composed or made up of 由……组成;由……构成: The team ～s of twenty men.队伍由 20 人组成。**❷**(～ in) have as an essential feature 以……为基本特色;在于: The beauty of the city ～s in its ancient buildings.这座城市的美就在于它那些古代的建筑。

consistent /kən'sɪstənt/
adj.**❶**in agreement or accordance 前后一致;始终如一: He's been a ～ friend to me.他始终是我的朋友。**❷**continually keeping to the same principles or course of action; having a regular pattern 与……一致的: What you say is not ～ with what you do.你的言行不一致。‖ ～ ly *adv*.一贯地;始终如一地

consistency /kən'sɪstənsi/

n.(*pl*.-ies)**❶**the thickness or firmness of a liquid or soft mixture 黏稠度;密实度;坚实度**❷**the state of being consistent 一致性;连贯性

console /kən'səʊl/
v. try to make sb. happier when he has suffered some loss or misfortune 安慰 ‖ consolation /ˌkɒnsə'leɪʃn/ *n*.安慰;慰藉: consolation prize 安慰奖

consolidate /kən'sɒlɪdeɪt/
v. become or make stronger or firmer (使)巩固: The army ～d the position which they had captured. 军队巩固他们占领的阵地。

consonance /'kɒnsənəns/
n.agreement or compatibility between opinions or actions 一致;协调:a rule in ～ with the people's customs 符合人们习惯的规定

consonant /'kɒnsənənt/
Ⅰ*n*.**❶** a sound which is not a vowel; a sound in which the breath is stopped in the mouth or throat in some way 辅音 **❷** a letter or symbol for such a sound 辅音字母 Ⅱ*adj*.in agreement 一致的;符合的

conspiracy /kən'spɪrəsi/
n.(*pl*.-ies) a plot formed by planning secretly with others 阴谋;密谋;共谋: conspiracies against the president 密谋反总统

conspicuous /kən'spɪkjʊəs/
adj.standing out so as to be clearly visible 显而易见的;显著的

conspire /kən'spaɪə(r)/
v.**❶** make plans with others,especially to commit an unlawful or harmful act 阴谋,密谋,共谋 **❷** act together to bring out some result 共同促成

constancy /'kɒnstənsi/
n.the quality of being constant or loyal 坚定不移;始终如一;忠诚;忠实: He admired her courage and ～.他钦佩她的勇气和忠贞。

constant /'kɒnstənt/
adj.**❶**fixed or unchanging; invariable 稳定的;不变的: He drove at a ～ speed.他开车的速度很稳。**❷**continually happening or repeated; regular 经常的;不断的:I

dislike these ~ arguments.我讨厌这些无休止的争论。❸ loyal; faithful 忠实的:He is ~ to his master. 他忠于其主人。‖ ~ly adv.经常地;不断地

consternation /ˌkɒnstəˈneɪʃn/
n.a great surprise and alarm or unhappiness 大吃一惊;惊恐

constipation /ˌkɒnstɪˈpeɪʃn/
n. the difficulty in passing waste matter out of the body 便秘 ‖ **constipated** /ˈkɒnstɪpeɪtɪd/ adj.便秘的

constituent /kənˈstɪtjuənt/
I adj. ❶ forming or helping to make a whole 组成的;构成的:the ~ parts of an atom 原子的成分 ❷ having the right to make or alter a political constitution 有权制订(或修改)宪法的:a ~ assembly 立宪会议 II n.❶ a person who has a parliamentary vote 选民 ❷ a component part 成分;要素

constitute /ˈkɒnstɪtjuːt/
v. make up; form 组成;构成:Twelve months ~ a year.十二个月为一年。

constitution /ˌkɒnstɪˈtjuːʃn/
n.❶ a general structure of a thing;the act or manner of constituting 构造;组成方式:the physical ~ of the sun 太阳的物理构造 ❷ a set of laws governing a country 宪法:The new ~ was pro-mulgated.新宪法颁布了。❸ a general physical structure and condition of a person's body 体格;体质:He jogs in the morning to build up a stronger ~.为了锻炼体质他早晨慢跑。‖ ~al adj.宪法的;合乎宪法的;体质上的

constrain /kənˈstreɪn/
v.❶make sb. do sth. by force 强迫;强制:I ~ed him to come.我迫使他来。❷ restrict or limit sth.or sb.限制;局限

constraint /kənˈstreɪnt/
n. ❶ a restriction or limitation on what you can do 限制;约束;束缚;局限 ❷a strained manner caused by holding back your real feelings 压抑;抑制;克制:At last we could relax and talk without ~.我们终于可以放松下来,无拘无束地谈话了。

constrict /kənˈstrɪkt/
v.fasten tightly so as to make smaller or prevent free movement 收缩;束缚:He felt ~ed by the rules.他感到受规则的束缚。

construct /kənˈstrʌkt/
v. ❶ build; make by putting together or combining parts 修建;建造:~ a large bridge 修建一座大桥 ❷ form sth. by bringing various conceptual elements together 构思;编写:a well-~ed novel 一部构思很好的小说

construction /kənˈstrʌkʃn/
n.❶ the act of constructing 建设;建筑:a warship under ~ 正在建造之中的战舰 ❷a building or other structure 建筑物;构造物:The ~ is very solid.这栋大楼的建造极为坚实。

constructive /kənˈstrʌktɪv/
adj. helping to construct; giving helpful suggestions 建设的;建设性的:a ~ criticism 建设性的批评

consul /ˈkɒnsl/
n.a man in an embassy in a foreign country who helps people of his own country 领事;an acting ~ 代理领事/If you are in trouble abroad you should see a ~.如果在国外遇到困难,你应该去找领事。

consulate /ˈkɒnsjulɪt/
n. the office or building where a consul works 领事馆

consult /kənˈsʌlt/
v.❶ seek information or advice from a person 请教;求教 ❷ discuss with 商议;商量:The two lawyers ~ed on the case.两个律师商议了那个案件。/~ with 与……商议 ❸ refer for information or suggestion to (a book, diary or watch) in order to ascertain sth.查阅;参考

consultant /kənˈsʌltənt/
n.❶a person who is qualified to give expert professional advice 顾问 ❷a senior hospital doctor or surgeon 顾问医师,会诊医师

consultation /ˌkɒnsəlˈteɪʃn/
n.❶the act of consulting 商量;协调;磋商:democratic ~s 民主协商 ❷a meeting

held to exchange opinions and ideas 磋商会；评议会：hold a ～ 举行协商会

consume /kən'sjuːm/

v. ❶ eat, drink or ingest 吃；喝 ❷ use up 消耗；耗尽：The big car ~d a lot of petrol. 那辆大轿车耗掉了许多油。❸ buy (goods or services) 购买，消费（商品或服务）❹ destroy by fire 烧毁：The fire soon ~d the wooden buildings. 大火很快烧毁了那些木房。

consumer /kən'sjuːmə(r)/

n. a person who buys goods or uses services 消费者；用户：Consumers are encouraged to complain about faulty goods. 要鼓励消费者对劣质商品投诉。

consumption /kən'sʌmpʃn/

n. ❶ using up or consuming of food, energy, materials, etc.；the quantity consumed （食物、能源、原材料等的）消费，消耗；消费量：production and ～ 生产和消费/ There's too great a ～ of alcohol in Britain. 英国酒的消费量太惊人。❷ pulmonary tuberculosis 肺病；肺结核

contact /'kɒntækt/

Ⅰ *n.* ❶ the state or condition of physical touching 接触：He came into ～ with many new ideas in the country. 他在那个国家接触到许多新思想。❷ the act of communicating with sb., especially regularly （尤指经常的）联系，联络：We must keep in ～ with him. 我们必须与他保持联系。Ⅱ *v.* communicate with sb. by telephone, mail, etc. 与……联系：I will ～ you. 我会跟你联络的。‖ **in ～ with** 与……有联系/**bring into ～ with** 使接触/**come into ～ with** 接触，碰上/**have ～ with** 接触到，和……有联系/**lose ～ with** 和……失去联系

contain /kən'teɪn/

v. ❶ hold or have within itself or as a part 有；包含；含有：His paper ～s no mistakes at all. 他的论文一点错误也没有。❷ hold back；keep under control or within limits 容纳；控制：How much does this bottle ～? 这只瓶子能装多少？

container /kən'teɪnə/

n. ❶ a box or bottle designed to contain sth. 容器 ❷ a large box-like receptacle of a standard design for transporting goods long distances by road, rail, sea, or air 集装箱

containment /kən'teɪnmənt/

n. the practice of keeping a hostile country or influence within its present limits 封锁；遏制：Many governments saw the ～ of terrorism as a global task. 许多国家的政府把遏制恐怖主义作为一项全球性任务。

contemplate /'kɒntempleɪt/

v. ❶ think very deeply about sth.（especially some religious subjects）沉思，冥想（尤指宗教问题）❷ gaze at sth. 注视；凝视 ❸ have in view as a probable though not certain intention 预期；打算：I am contemplating buying some new furniture. 我正打算买一些新家具。‖ **contemplation** *n.* 沉思；注视，凝视

contemplative /'kɒntempleɪtɪv/

adj. ❶ fond of contemplating things, thoughtful 沉思的：He regarded me with a ～ eye. 他若有所思地凝视着我。❷ devoted to religious contemplation 默念的；敛心默祷的

contemporary /kən'temprəri/

Ⅰ *adj.* ❶ modern；belonging to the present time 当代的：～ literature 当代文学 ❷ of or belonging to the same time 同时代的；同属于一个时期的；当时的：Scott was ～ with Byron. 司各特跟拜伦是同时代的。Ⅱ *n.* a person living at the same time or of the same age as another 同时代的人；同年龄的人

contempt /kən'tempt/

n. ❶ a lack of respect or admiration 轻视；轻蔑；藐视：I feel nothing but ～ for such dishonest behaviour. 对这种不诚实的行为，我觉得唯有嗤之以鼻。❷ a condition of being looked down upon or despised 受辱；丢脸；不光彩：bring someone into ～ 使某人受辱 ❸ disregard or disrespect；total disregard 不顾；不尊敬；不客气：show one's ～ of death 表现出不顾生死/treat someone with ～ 对某人不客气

contemptuous /kən'temptjʊəs/
adj. feeling or showing contempt 轻蔑的：She gave me a ～ look. 她鄙夷地看了我一眼。‖ ～ly *adv.* 轻蔑地

contend /kən'tend/
v. ❶ compete as in a race or against difficulties 竞争；奋斗；斗争；争夺：～ for first prize 争夺第一名/～ against drought 与干旱做斗争 ❷ assert or declare sth. in an argument 声称；主张

content[1] /kən'tent/
Ⅰ *adj.* satisfied；happy；not wanting more than one has 满意的；满足的：Are you ～ with your job? 你对你的工作满意吗？Ⅱ *n.* a state of satisfaction 满足；满意：live in peace and ～ 过着宁静满足的生活 Ⅲ *v.* make happy or satisfied 使满足：Nothing ～s her, she is always complaining. 没有什么能满足她，她总是抱怨。‖ ～ oneself with 满足于；对……感到满足/to one's heart's ～ 尽情地

content[2] /'kɒntent/
n. ❶ (*pl.*) those that are contained 内容；容纳物：the ～s of the box 盒子里装的东西 ❷ (*pl.*) a list of chapters in a book 书刊目录 ❸ the substance (of a book, speech, etc., as opposed to its form) (书籍、演说等的)内容：Do you approve of the ～ of the article? 你赞同此文的内容吗？

contention /kən'tenʃən/
n. ❶ the act of quarrelling or arguing 争吵；争执；争论：a long-standing ～ among physicists 物理学者之间长期存在的争论 ❷ an assertion made in arguing (争论中所持的)论点

contest
Ⅰ /'kɒntest/ *n.* a struggle or fight to gain control or advantage 争夺；竞赛，比赛：an oratorical ～ 辩论会/a musical ～ 音乐竞赛会/He entered the ～ for championship. 他参加了争夺冠军的比赛。Ⅱ /kən'test/ *v.* take part in competition, etc. to win 争夺；争取

context /'kɒntekst/
n. ❶ the words around a particular word or phrase, helping understanding (文章的)上下文 ❷ the background or envir-

onment of sth. 背景；环境

contiguous /kən'tɪgjʊəs/
adj. touching or adjoining 接壤的；共边的；接触的：The two countries are ～. 这两个国家接壤。

continent /'kɒntɪnənt/
n. one of the big land masses of the world 洲；大陆：Asia is the largest ～, covering one third of the earth's land area. 亚洲是最大的洲，占地球陆地面积的三分之一。

continental /ˌkɒntɪ'nentl/
Ⅰ *adj.* ❶ forming a continent, or to do with a continent (形成)洲的；(形成)大陆的 ❷ (Continental) to do with the mainland of Europe 欧洲大陆的 Ⅱ *n.* someone who lives in the mainland of Europe 欧洲大陆居民

contingency /kən'tɪndʒənsi/
n. uncertainty of occurrence；an event that happens by chance 偶然(性)；偶发事故；偶然事故：We must be prepared for all contingencies. 我们必须准备应付一切偶发事故。

continual /kən'tɪnjʊəl/
adj. repeated；frequent；uninterrupted 频繁的；连续的；不断的：～ rain 连绵不断的雨天/～ argument 喋喋不休的争吵/Continual dropping wears away the stone. 滴水穿石。

continuation /kənˌtɪnjʊ'eɪʃn/
n. ❶ continuing；starting again after a stop 连续；继续；持续：～ of study 继续学习 ❷ sth. which continues from sth. else 连续；续篇；延长(部分)：an exciting ～ of the story 该故事的精彩续篇

continue /kən'tɪnjuː/
v. ❶ keep existing or happening without stopping 持续；不断发生：The rain ～d falling all the night. 这场雨下了一晚上。❷ keep doing sth. without stopping 继续做；不停地干：Are you going to ～ with the project with Lucy? 你要继续和露西做这个项目吗？❸ go or move further in the same direction 走；移动；延伸：He ～d on his way. 他继续走他的路。❹ remain in a particular job or condition 留任；维持原状：She will ～ in her present job until

October.她将继续做她目前的工作直到 10 月。❺ recommence or resume after interruption(停顿后)继续,再开始:The TV play will ～ being played in next week.这部电视剧下星期继续开播。❻ carry on speaking after a pause or interruption (停顿或中断后)继续说:Continue your discussion after ten minutes' rest.十分钟休息后继续讨论。‖ ～ with 继续(干某事)

continuity /ˌkɒntɪˈnjuːəti/

n. ❶ the state of being continuous 连贯性;连续性;持续性:ensure ～ of electricity supplies 确保电力供给的连续性 ❷ the uninterrupted existence of sth.or succession of events 连贯的存在(或活动);连续的整体 ❸ the process of maintaining continuous action with consistent details in a film or television (电影或电视节目细节的)一致性,衔接

continuous/kənˈtɪnjʊəs/

adj. going on without stopping 继续的;不断的:The brain needs a ～ supply of blood.大脑需要不断地供给血液。

contort/kənˈtɔːt/

v. bend sth. so that it loses its proper shape 扭曲 ‖ ～ion *n.*扭曲;变形

contour/ˈkɒntʊə(r)/

*n.*a line on a map along which all places have the same height above sea level 等高线

contract

Ⅰ /kənˈtrækt/*v.*❶make an agreement 订约;承包:They have ～ed to build a railway.他们已签约承建一条铁路。❷ become liable for 对……负有责任 ❸catch or get (an illness) 染病;患病:～ an illness (bad habits)染患疾病(沾染恶习)/ ～ a severe fever 发高烧 ❹make or become smaller or shorter (使)收缩;弄窄;紧缩;缩短:Metals ～ when they become cool.金属遇冷则收缩。 Ⅱ /ˈkɒntrækt/*n.* ❶a formal agreement;an agreement to supply goods (at a fixed price) 合约;合同;(按固定价格提供货物的)契约:enter into a ～ with someone 与某人订立合同 ❷a signed paper on which the conditions of such an agreement are written 合同

书;契约书

contraction/kənˈtrækʃn/

*n.*❶contracting or being contracted 收缩;缩小;缩短;缩减:the ～ of the mercury in a thermometer 寒暑表中的水银收缩 ❷a short form of a word 词的缩约形式:Can't is the ～ of cannot. can't 为 cannot 的缩写词。

contractor/kənˈtræktə(r)/

*n.*a person or business firm that enters into contracts 承造者;立约者;承包商:engineering ～ 工程承包商

contradict/ˌkɒntrəˈdɪkt/

*v.*❶be opposite to;be contrary to 矛盾;相反;相抵触:The reports ～ each other. 这些报告互相矛盾。❷declare sth.or sb. to be wrong;deny 反驳;驳斥:Don't ～ me! 不要反驳我。

contradiction/ˌkɒntrəˈdɪkʃən/

*n.*❶a combination of statements,ideas,or features of a situation which are opposed to one another 矛盾;对立;抵触:There is a ～ between the two sets of figures.这两组数据相互矛盾。❷a person, thing, or situation in which inconsistent elements are present 自相矛盾的人(或事物、情况)

contrary/ˈkɒntrəri/

Ⅰ*adj.*completely different or wholly opposed 相反的:The result was ～ to what I had expected.结果与我原来预料的正好相反。 Ⅱ*n.*the opposite 相反;反面;相反事物:An examination of the facts proves the ～.仔细考察事实之后发现情况正好相反。 ‖ by contraries 相反地/ on the ～ 正相反/ quite the ～ 恰恰相反/ to the ～ 相反地

contrast

Ⅰ/ˈkɒntrɑːst/*n.* ❶ the comparison of objects or situations that are dissimilar, especially to show differences 对比;对照:There can be no differentiation without ～.有比较才有鉴别。 ❷ the difference between people or things that are compared 明显差别:The ～ between the two authors is remarkable.两位作者之间的差别是很明显的。 ‖ in ～ with (to)与……形成对照 Ⅱ /kənˈtrɑːst/ *v.* ❶ compare (two things or people) so that differences are made clear 使对比；使对照：Contrast these foreign goods with the domestic product.将这些外国货和本国货对比。❷ show a difference when compared 形成对照：His elegant clothes ~ed with his rough speech.他的粗鲁语言和他一身考究的服饰很不相称。

contribute /kən'trɪbjuːt/
*v.*❶help to cause or bring about sth.有助于；促成；促使 ❷join with others in giving help, money, etc. 捐助；捐献：Everybody ~d towards Jane's present. 大伙儿凑钱送了珍妮一份礼物。❸write（articles, etc.）and send in 投稿：~ a poem to a newspaper 向报社投一篇诗稿

contribution /ˌkɒntrɪ'bjuːʃn/
*n.*❶sth. done to help make another thing successful; any one of a number of individual efforts in a common endeavor 贡献；捐助：his ~s to science 他对科学的贡献/make ~s to 对······做出贡献 ❷money, things, etc. contributed 捐赠款，捐赠物：~ to the relief fund 对救济基金的捐款 ❸an article or other piece of writing submitted for publication in a collection（投的）稿件，交稿

contributor /kən'trɪbjuːtə(r)/
n. ❶ a person or thing that contributes sth. 捐献者；捐助者 ❷ a person who writes articles for a magazine or newspaper 撰稿者；投稿者 ❸a causal factor in the existence or occurrence of sth.促成因素

contributory /kən'trɪbjʊtəri/
*adj.*❶contributing to a result 促成的；促进的；起作用的 ❷ involving payments from the people who will benefit 需要受益人付钱的

contrivance /kən'traɪvəns/
n. ❶ an ingenious device 发明物 ❷ the process of contriving sth. 发明；创造 ❸a plan or scheme 计谋；计划

contrive /kən'traɪv/
*v.*cleverly manage to do sth. 发明；设计：He ~d to get an extra week's holiday.他巧妙地多争取了一周的假期。

control /kən'trəʊl/
Ⅰ *v.*(-ll-) ❶rule; have power over 控制；统治；管理；操纵：The government ~s the country.政府管理国家。/The policeman was ~ling the traffic.警察指挥着交通。❷hold down; keep in check 抑制；节制：~ one's anger 克制怒气/~ oneself 控制自己/Try to ~ your tongue.不要随便讲话。Ⅱ *n.*❶the power or authority to rule 统治权；控制权：The president has ~ over the armed forces.总统有统帅武装力量的权力。❷the act of controlling 控制；支配：price ~s 控制物价 ❸(*pl.*) a device used to control a machine 操纵装置；控制器：The pilot checked to make sure the ~s were working before he took off.飞行员首先检查控制器,确信没有毛病以后才起飞。

controversy /'kɒntrəvɜːsi/
n.(*pl.*-ies) a long argument or disagreement（尤指长期的）论争,争执,争吵,争议：The announcement ended a protracted ~.此项公告结束了一场旷日持久的争论。

contusion /kən'tjuːʒən/
n. a region of injured tissue or skin in which blood capillaries have been ruptured; a bruise 挫伤；撞伤；瘀伤；青肿

convene /kən'viːn/
v. call（persons）to come together（to hold a meeting, etc.）召集；集合(开会等)

convenience /kən'viːnɪəns/
*n.*❶the quality of being convenient 方便；便利：for ~ 为了方便起见/Come whenever it is to your ~.你什么时候方便,就什么时候来。❷ an apparatus, service, etc. which gives advantage to its user 方便的装置；便利设施：The house has all modern ~s.此屋具有所有现代化的设备。

convenient /kən'viːnɪənt/
adj. ❶ useful or suitable; not causing problems 有益的；合适的；方便的：The school is in a ~ place, near my home.这学校在我家附近,很方便。❷near; easy to reach 近便的；附近的：Our house is very ~ for the shops.我们的房子离商店

很近。

convention /kən'venʃn/
n. ❶a conference of members of a society, political party, etc., devoted to a particular purpose (社团、政党为某一特殊目的)会议，大会：a teachers'～ 教师大会 ❷formal agreements 协定；公约：the Geneva Convention 日内瓦公约 ❸a general consent (especially about forms of behaviour)；practice or custom based on general consent 惯例；习俗；常规：social～s 社会习俗/break away from～s 打破常规/By～ the deputy leader is always a woman.按照惯例这一领导人的副职总是由女子担任。

conventional /kən'venʃnl/
adj. ❶done or doing things in the accepted way；traditional 依照惯例的；墨守成规的；传统的；习惯的：～ methods 传统方法 ❷(of weapons) not nuclear (武器)非核的；常规的 ‖ ～ity *n.*惯例；习俗；常规 /～ly *adv.*照惯例；通常

converge /kən'vɜːdʒ/
v. move together and meet；tend to meet at a point 会聚；集中于一点：These two lines ～. 这两条线集中在一点。/The crowd ～d on the palace. 人群向宫殿集中。

conversation /ˌkɒnvə'seɪʃn/
n. a talk between two or more people 谈话；会话：have a ～ with him. 与他谈话/I met him in town and had an interesting ～ with him.我在城里碰见他，进行了一次有趣的谈话。/I had a long ～ with your teacher.我与你的老师进行了一次长谈。

converse /kən'vɜːs/
Ⅰ *v.* talk with sb. 谈话；交谈：～ with the President on the war 与总统谈论战争 Ⅱ *adj.*opposite or reverse 相反的；逆的：I hold the ～ opinion.我持相反的意见。 Ⅲ *n.*the opposite of another 相反；颠倒：In fact I believe the ～ to be true.实际上我认为反面意见倒是属实。

conversion /kən'vɜːʃn/
n. the process or action of changing or causing sth. to change from one form to another (使发生)转变，转换，转化：the ～ of food into body tissues 食物向身体组织的转化

convert
Ⅰ /kən'vɜːt/ *v.* ❶change sth. into sth. else 转变；变换：～ rags into paper 把破布变成纸/～ defeat into victory 转败为胜 ❷cause a person to change his belief, etc.使改变信仰：～ a man to Christianity 改变某人使其信仰基督教 Ⅱ /'kɒnvɜːt/ *n.*a person who has been converted, especially to a different religion 改变宗教者；皈依宗教者

convex /'kɒnveks/
adj. (especially of lenses) curving outwards, having the shape of the outside of a circle or sphere (尤指透镜)凸状的

convey /kən'veɪ/
v. ❶carry or take sth. from one place to another；transport 传导；运输；搬运；输送：～ goods from one place to another 把货物从一地运到另一地 ❷make (ideas, views, feelings, etc.) known to another person 传达，表达，转达(意思、见解、感情等)：～ one's deepest sympathy to... 向……表示深切的慰问/Words can't ～ my happiness. 言语无法表达我的喜悦。/Please ～ to him my best wishes.请向他转达我最美好的祝愿。

conveyance /kən'veɪəns/
n. ❶the action or process of transporting or carrying someone or sth. from one place to another 运送；载送；运输 ❷the action of making an idea, feeling, or impression known or understandable to someone (想法、感觉、感想的)表达，传达：Dance's ～ of meaning is complicated. 用舞蹈表达思想是很复杂的。

convict
Ⅰ /kən'vɪkt/ *v.* (of a judge, jury, lawyer, etc.) say or prove that somebody is guilty of a crime (指法官、陪审团、律师等)宣判……有罪；裁决……有罪；证明……有罪：The judge ～ed him of robbery. 法官判决他犯抢劫罪。 Ⅱ /'kɒnvɪkt/ *n.*a person in prison after being found guilty of a crime 犯人

conviction/kənˈvɪkʃn/

n. ❶ an act of convicting 定罪；裁决有罪；证明有罪：❷ a strong belief 深信；坚信：It's my ～ that you did not try hard enough.我深信你用功得不够。/He said it with ～.他深信不疑地说了这句话。

convince/kənˈvɪns/

v. ❶ make sb. feel sure about sth.；persuade sb. to believe sth.使(某人)相信；使(某人)信服；使(某人)确信：It was hard to ～ you that we couldn't afford a new car.真难使你相信我们买不起新汽车。❷persuade sb.to do sth.劝服

convincing /kənˈvɪnsɪŋ/

adj. ❶capable of causing someone to believe that sth. is true or real 有说服力的；令人信服的：a ～ argument 有说服力的论点 ❷(of a victory or a winner) leaving no margin of doubt；clear (胜利或获胜者)令人信服的；绝对的：England cruised to a ～ win over Ireland.英格兰队以绝对优势大胜爱尔兰队。‖ ～ly *adj.* 令人信服地；有说服力地

convoke/kənˈvəʊk/

v. call together；summon (a meeting) 召集；召开(会议等)：～ the new Parliament 召开新的国会

convulse/kənˈvʌls/

v. cause violent movements or disturbances 使剧烈摇动：He was ～d with laughter.他笑得前仰后合。‖ **convulsion** *n.*痉挛，抽搐

coo/kuː/

Ⅰ *n.*(*pl.*～s) a soft sound(e.g.made by a pigeon or by a baby)咕咕声(鸽子或婴儿等发出的柔和的声音）Ⅱ *v.*make a soft sound 发出咕咕的声音；喁喁细语

cook/kʊk/

Ⅰ *v.*❶ make food ready to eat 烹调；煮：Who will ～ the dinner? 谁来做晚饭呢? ❷ (of food) be heated so that the state or condition required for eating is reached 被烹调；被烧煮：Meat doesn't ～ as quickly as an egg.肉不像鸡蛋熟得快。Ⅱ *n.*a person who cooks 厨师；炊事员：His wife is a good ～.他的妻子很会做饭。‖ ～ **up** 做饭(饭菜)；编造，制造(麻烦)

cookery/ˈkʊkəri/

*n.*the art or skill of cooking 烹饪术；烹调法：～ lessons 烹饪课

cookie/ˈkʊki/

*n.*❶ a sweet biscuit 甜饼干：We had ～s and coffee.我们吃饼干喝咖啡。/chocolate-chip ～s 混有巧克力碎片的甜饼干 ❷ a person of a particular type 特殊类型的人：a smart ～ 聪明的人

cooking/ˈkʊkɪŋ/

*adj.*suitable for or used in cooking 烹调用的：～ sherry 烧菜用的雪利料酒/ ～ oil 烧菜用的油

cool/kuːl/

Ⅰ *adj.* ❶ pleasantly cold 凉爽的；凉快的：It's a ～ day today.今天天气很凉爽。/A ～ wind blew off the sea.一阵凉风吹过海面。❷ calm；not excited 冷静的：He was always ～ in the face of danger.在面对危险时他总是保持冷静。❸not showing interest or enthusiasm 冷淡的：They gave him a ～ reception.他们很冷淡地接待了她。Ⅱ *v.*❶make sth.less hot or become less hot (使)变冷；(使)凉下来：The rain ～ed the air.雨使空气变得凉起来。❷keep calm；calm down 冷静；平静：Her enthusiasm had ～ed.她的热情已经冷淡下来。‖ ～ **down** 凉快起来；冷静下来/～ **off** 凉快起来；冷淡下来

cooler /ˈkuːlə/

*n.*a device or container for keeping things cool 制冷装置；冷却容器

cooperate/kəʊˈɒpəreɪt/

v. ❶ work together for a particular purpose 合作：All the people in the village ～d to bring in the harvest.全村的人通力合作进行收割。❷ give help to sb. that needs help 协助；配合

cooperative /kəʊˈɒpərətɪv/

*adj.*❶willing to work helpfully with another person 合作的；协作的；同心协力的 ❷providing cooperation 协助的；配合的 ❸(of a business or farm)owned and run jointly by its members with the profits shared between them (农场、企业等)合作的

coordinate/kəʊˈɔːdɪnət/

Ⅰ*adj.*equal in importance 同等重要的：have

power ~ with the manager 与经理有同等权力 ‖ v. make coordinate; put into proper relation 使平等; 使同等; 调和; 协调: ~ one's movements when swimming 游泳时协调动作

cop /kɒp/
n. a policeman 警察

cope /kəʊp/
v. deal with sth. successfully 应付; 克服: She could not ~ with all the work. 她不能应付这一切工作。/ He had a lot of work, but he was able to ~. 他工作很多, 但他应付得开。

copious /ˈkəʊpjəs/
adj. in large amounts, plentiful 丰富的; 充裕的: She took ~ notes in the meeting. 她在会议上记了大量笔记。 ‖ ~ly *adv.* 丰富地; 充裕地

copper /ˈkɒpə(r)/
n. a reddish-brown metal; a coin made of copper 铜; 铜币: Copper is used to make electric wire and to make pennies. 铜用来做电线或造币。

copy /ˈkɒpi/
Ⅰ *n.* ❶ sth. made to be like another 抄本; 复制本; 副本: The secretary made a ~ of the document. 秘书将文件复制了一份。 ❷ one example of a book, newspaper, etc. of which many have been made (书报等的) 一本, 一份: Over one million copies of this book have already been sold. 这本书已销售100万册。 ❸ the material to be sent to a printer (供排字付印的) 稿子 Ⅱ *v.* ❶ make sth. like another exactly 复制; 复印 ❷ follow (sb. or sth.) as a standard or pattern; imitate 仿制; 模仿: You shouldn't ~ his weak points. 你不应该模仿他的缺点。 ❸ cheat by writing (exactly the same thing) as someone else 照抄; 抄袭: He was punished for ~ing. 他因抄袭而受到惩罚。 ‖ ~ down 记下来 / ~ out 抄录; 抄一份

copybook /ˈkɒpɪbʊk/
Ⅰ *n.* a book containing examples of handwriting for students to copy 习字帖; 描红簿 Ⅱ *adj.* commonplace; conventional; ordinary 老套的; 平庸的; 平凡的: a ~ maxim 陈腐的格言 / He was no ~ hero. 他是个非凡的英雄.

copyright /ˈkɒpɪraɪt/
n. the exclusive legal right, given to the originator or their assignee for a fixed number of years, to print, publish, perform, film, or record literary, artistic, or musical material, and to authorize others to do the same 版权

copywriter /ˈkɒpɪraɪtə(r)/
n. a writer who is to write words, especially for advertisements 撰稿员 (尤指撰写广告者)

coral /ˈkɒrəl/
Ⅰ *n.* a hard, red or white substance built on the sea bed by small creatures; sea organism that makes this substance 珊瑚 Ⅱ *adj.* like coral in colour, red or pink 珊瑚色的; 桃红色的: ~ lips 桃红色的嘴唇

cord /kɔːd/
n. ❶ a thick string or thin rope 细绳: He tied up the thief with (a) thick ~. 他用一根粗绳子将小偷捆起来。 ❷ (a piece of) electrical wire with a protective covering (一段) 电缆, 皮线 ❸ a part of the body looking like this (身体) 带状组织: vocal ~s 声带

cordial /ˈkɔːdɪəl/
adj. warm and sincere 诚恳的; 热诚的: a ~ handshake 热情的握手 / be ~ to his students 待学生诚恳

core /kɔː(r)/
Ⅰ *n.* ❶ the central part of certain fruits, containing seeds 果核; 核 ❷ the central or the most important part of anything 核心; 精髓; 要点; 本质: get to the core of the matter 直入事情的本质 / the ~ of the earth 地心 ‖ to the ~ 地地道道: He is honest to the ~. 他简直是诚实到家了。 Ⅱ *v.* remove the core of (fruit) 挖去……(水果的) 核: Core the apple, please. 请把苹果核挖掉。 Ⅲ *adj.* main or essential 主要的; 本质的; 基本的

coriander /ˌkɒrɪˈændə(r)/
n. the strong tasting leaves or seeds of a small plant, used for giving a special taste to especially Asian food 芫荽; 香菜

cork/kɔːk/

I *n*. ❶ the buoyant, light brown substance obtained form the outer layer of the bark of the cork oak 软木树皮 ❷ a round cover made of the above material or rubber or plastic fixed into the neck of a bottle (软木、橡胶等制成的)瓶塞 **II** *v*. cover a bottle with a cork 用瓶塞塞住：～(up) a bottle 塞住一个瓶子

corkage/ˈkɔːkɪdʒ/

n. the charge made by a hotel or restaurant for allowing people to drink wine which they have brought with them（对自带酒顾客收取的）开瓶费

corkscrew/ˈkɔːkskruː/

I *n*. an apparatus of twisted metal with a handle, used for pulling corks out of bottles（拔软木塞的）螺丝起子，瓶塞钻 **II** *adj*. shaped like a corkscrew; spiral 螺旋形的

corm/kɔːm/

n. the thick underground stem of certain plants, from which the flowers and leaves grow in the spring（植物的）球茎

corn/kɔːn/

n. any plant that is grown for its grain; the grain of these plants 谷物；谷粒‖～ **bread** *n*. 玉米面包/～ **cob** *n*. 玉米芯/～ **flakes** *n*. 玉米片/～ **flour** *n*. 玉米粉；棒子面/～ **stalk** *n*. 玉米秆

cornea/ˈkɔːnɪə/

n. the transparent outer coat of the eyeball 角膜

corner/ˈkɔːnə(r)/

I *n*. ❶ a point or an area where two or more edges, sides or surfaces of sth. join 角：the ～ of a magazine 杂志的一角 ❷ the area inside a room, box or similar space where its edges or walls meets 角落：at the ～ 在拐角处 ❸ a part of the world, especially a distant one 偏僻处；偏远地：They live in a remote ～ of England. 他们住在英国一个偏远的地方。‖ **in a tight** ～ 陷于困境/**cut** ～**s** 走捷径；找窍门/**drive**（**force**）**sb. into a** ～ 使陷于困境/**round**（**around**）**the** ～ 在拐角处；不远，就在前面 **II** *v*. ❶ put into a difficult position 使陷于困境：That question ～ed me. 那个问题使我陷入了困境。❷（of a vehicle, etc.）turn a corner（车辆等）转弯：My car ～s well even in bad weather. 即使在恶劣的天气，我的车子转弯也很灵。

cornet/ˈkɔːnɪt/

n. ❶ a brass musical instrument like a trumpet 喇叭；短号 ❷ a piece of light biscuit for holding ice cream（盛冰激凌用的）锥形脆薄饼

corny/ˈkɔːni/

adj. old-fashioned; often heard or repeated 陈旧的；陈词滥调的：his ～ jokes 他那陈旧而无聊的笑话

corporal/ˈkɔːpərəl/

I *n*. a rank of noncommissioned officer in the army, above lance corporal or private first class and below sergeant 下士 **II** *adj*. of the body 身体的；肉体的：～ punishment 体罚

corporate /ˈkɔːpərɪt/

adj. ❶ shared by members of a group 社团的；全体的；共同的：～ responsibility 共同的责任 ❷ forming a corporation 组成公司（或团体）的；法人的：a ～ body 法人团体

corporation/ˌkɔːpəˈreɪʃn/

n. ❶ a group of persons authorised to act as an individual（e. g. for business purpose）法人；法人团体：～ sole 单独法人/the British Broadcasting Corporation 英国广播公司（BBC）/～ law 公司法 ❷ a large company 大公司

corporeal /kɔːˈpɔːrɪəl/

adj. ❶ that can be touched; physical rather than spiritual 物质的；有形的；实体的：his ～ presence 他的大驾亲临 ❷ of or for the body 身体的；肉体的：～ needs 身体的需要

corps/kɔː(r)/

n.（*pl*. corps/kɔːz/）one of the technical branches of an army 技术兵种部队；特殊兵种部队：a marine ～ 海军陆战队

corpse/kɔːps/

n. a dead body of a human being 尸体；死尸

corpus/ˈkɔːpəs/

n. (*pl.* corpora/ˈkɔːpərə/ or ~es) ❶ a body, especially a dead one 身体(尤指尸体) ❷ a collection of writings or laws, especially the whole collection of a particular period,etc.(文献、法典的)全集:the ~ of civil law 民法全集 ❸ the substance of anything (任何事物的)主体

correct/kəˈrekt/

Ⅰ *adj.* true; right; proper 正确的;恰当的;合适的:do the ~ thing 处理恰当;做得对/make ~ decisions 做出正确决定/His answer is not quite ~.他的回答不太正确。Ⅱ *v.* ❶ make right; take out mistakes from 改正;校阅;纠正;矫正:~ mistakes 改正错误/~ a composition 修改作文 ❷point out the faults of 告诫;训诫:~ a child for disobedience 对小孩不听话进行训诫

correction /kəˈrekʃən/

n. ❶ the process of correcting sth. or of being corrected 改正的过程 ❷an alteration made to sth. to make it correct 纠正;改正

correlate/ˈkɒrəleɪt/

v. have or show a mutual relation or connection 有相互关系;相关:The results of this experiment do not ~ with the results of earlier ones. 这次试验的结果与以往试验的结果毫不相干。

correspond/ˌkɒrɪˈspɒnd/

v. ❶be in agreement with;suit 符合;相一致:His actions ~ with his words.他言行一致。❷be equal to; be similar 相等;相当:The American Congress ~s to the British Parliament. 美国的国会相当于英国议会。❸ exchange letters 通信:We have ~ed for some years.我们通信好些年了。

correspondence/ˌkɒrɪˈspɒndəns/

n. ❶ agreement or similarity 相符;一致;相似:a close ~ between the two accounts 这两篇报道非常相似 ❷ the act of exchanging letters or the letters exchanged 通信;信件:The girls continued their ~ throughout the summer.女孩子们整个夏季一直保持通信往来。/We

found it very difficult to read his ~.我们发现他的信件很难看懂。‖ in ~ with 与……有联系;和……相符 ‖ ~ college *n.* 函授学院

correspondent/ˌkɒrɪˈspɒndənt/

n. a journalist employed to provide news stories for newspapers or broadcast media 记者;通讯员:our Tirana ~ 本报驻地拉那记者/news from our own ~ 本报通讯消息

corridor/ˈkɒrɪdɔː(r)/

n. ❶a long narrow passage in a building or train 走廊;通道:at the end of the ~ 在走廊的尽头 ❷a narrow piece of land that passes through a foreign country 走廊(一国领土穿越他国国境内的狭长地带)

corrode/kəˈrəʊd/

v. wear away or damage by chemical changes 腐蚀:The metal was ~d by acid.金属被酸腐蚀了。/Iron ~s if it is not protected from the damp air.铁如果不加保护,在潮湿空气中会锈损。

corrosive /kəˈrəʊsɪv/

Ⅰ *adj.* tending to cause corrosion 腐蚀的;腐蚀性的 Ⅱ *n.* a substance having the tendency to cause corrosion 腐蚀性物质

corrugate/ˈkɒrəgeɪt/

v. bend into a series of folds 弄皱;起波纹

corrupt/kəˈrʌpt/

Ⅰ *adj.* ❶immoral;wicked;bad 不道德的;堕落的,邪恶的:a ~ film full of sex and violence 一部充满色情和暴力的影片/~ desire 邪恶的欲望 ❷ dishonest; open to bribery 不诚实的;贪赃的:a ~ official 贪赃枉法的官员 ❸ containing mistakes; different from the original 有错误的;与原文不同的:a ~ form of German 不标准的德语/ a ~ translation 与原文不同的译文 Ⅱ *v.* ❶ make or become morally depraved 腐蚀;贿赂;使……堕落:It's easy to ~ some politicians.有些政客很容易贿赂。/Bad company may ~ a good boy.坏同伴可能使好孩子堕落。❷ change the original form in a bad way 讹传;误译:The text was ~ed by careless copyist.原文被粗心的抄写者抄错了。‖ ~ible *adj.* 可贿赂的;易腐败的 /

~ion *n.* 腐败；堕落

cosine/'kəʊsaɪn/

*n.*the trigonometric function that is equal to the ratio of the side adjacent to an a-cute angle（in a right-angled triangle）to the hypotenuse 余弦

cosmetic/kɒz'metɪk/

Ⅰ*n.*（usually *pl.*）a substance used to the body, especially the face, to improve its appearance 化妆品；美容品 Ⅱ *adj.* de-signed to improve the appearance of the body, especially the face 化妆用的；美容的

cosmic/'kɒzmɪk/

*adj.*of the whole universe or cosmos 宇宙的；~ flight 宇宙飞行/~ radiation 宇宙辐射/Physics is governed by ~ laws. 物理学受宇宙法则的制约。

cost/kɒst/

Ⅰ*v.*（cost）❶ be obtainable at the price of；be worth；require the payment of 价值为；花费：The book ~s 50 fen. 这书价格为五毛。❷ result in the loss or injury of 使付出（代价）；需要付出：The victory ~s many lives. 这次胜利是牺牲许多生命换来的。Ⅱ*n.*❶ the price or the money to be paid when buying sth. 费用：The ~ of this hat was ＄100. 这顶帽子的价格为 100 美元。❷ that which is used, needed or given to obtain sth. 代价：What will the ~ be to me? 我将付出什么代价？❸the cost of taking a matter to a court of law, especially as ordered to be paid by the side that lost the case to the side that won it 诉讼费：She won the case and was awarded ~s. 她胜诉，因而获得了诉讼费的赔偿。‖ at a ~（of）以……的代价/at all ~s 不惜任何代价；无论任何

costly/'kɒstli/

*adj.*❶of great value；costing much 昂贵的；贵重的 ❷gained or won at a great loss 代价高的；付出很大代价的：the costliest war in our history 我国历史上损失最惨重的战争

costume/'kɒstjuːm/

*n.*❶ the style of dress 服装式样 ❷ clothes worn by an actor or actress in a play or film 戏装

cosy(-zy)/'kəʊzi/

*adj.*❶warm and comfortable 适意的；温暖舒适的；安逸的：a ~ little room 温暖舒适的小房间 ❷close and friendly 密切友好

cottage/'kɒtɪdʒ/

*n.*a small house in the country 乡村小屋；村舍‖ ~ hospital *n.*（乡村）诊疗所/~ industry *n.*家庭手工业/~ piano *n.*小型立式钢琴

cotton/'kɒtn/

*n.*a soft, white fibrous substance round the seeds of the cotton-plant, used for making thread, cloth, etc. 棉花

couch/kaʊtʃ/

Ⅰ*n.*a long seat on which one can sit or lie 长椅；长沙发；睡椅 Ⅱ*v.*❶（of animals）lie flat（either in hiding, or ready for a jump forward）（指动物）蹲伏，俯卧 ❷ express a thought, etc. in words 表达；措辞：The government refusal was ~ed in friendly language. 政府以友好的措辞表示拒绝。

cough/kɒf/

Ⅰ*v.*send out air from the lungs violently and noisily 咳嗽；咳嗽声：He ~s badly. 他咳嗽得很厉害。Ⅱ*n.*an act or sound of coughing 咳嗽：He gave me a warning ~. 他用咳嗽来提醒我注意。‖ ~ drops *n.* 咳嗽糖

could/kʊd, kəd/

*aux.v.*❶used to express possibility 可能：I ~ come tomorrow. 我明天可能来。/You ~ earn more if you work a little harder. 如果你工作再努力点，可能挣得更多。❷used to make a request politely（用于礼貌的请求）可以，能够：Could you please hold on a minute? 请等一会儿好吗？❸（suggesting a person should do sth. or behave in a certain way）should；ought to 本该；本应：You ~ at least have met me at the station. 最起码你该到车站接我。

council/'kaʊnsl/

*n.*❶a meeting held for consultation or ad-vice 会议：an emergency ~ 紧急会议/a family ～ 家庭会议 ❷a group of people appointed or elected to make laws, rules, or decisions, or to give advice 委员会；理事会；议会；顾问委员会：the State Council 国务院/the UN Security Council 联合国安全理事会/the governor's ～ 州长的顾问班子 ❸a group of people controlling a local government 政务委员会

counsel /'kaʊnsl/

Ⅰ n. (*pl.* counsel) ❶advice; opinions; suggestions 劝告，忠告；建议；意见：follow your ～ 听从你的劝告/The leaders met for ～ before coming to a decision. 作出决定前，领导人进行了协商。 ❷ a lawyer or lawyers giving legal advice 律师；法律顾问：Is ～ for the defence present? 辩护律师到庭了吗？ Ⅱ v. (-ll- or -l-) advice; recommend 劝告；建议：The doctor ～led operating at once. 医生建议马上动手术。/She ～led us to give up the plan. 她建议我们放弃这个计划。

counsel(l)or /'kaʊnsələ/

n. a person who has been trained to advise people with problems, especially personal problems (尤指针对私人问题的)顾问；辅导顾问

count /kaʊnt/

Ⅰ v. ❶ say or name number in order 数(数目)；点(数)：The child can't ～ yet. 那小孩还不会点数。 ❷ consider (sth. or sb.) to be 认为，看作：On the whole she ～ed herself a fortunate woman. 总的说来，她认为自己是一个幸运的女人。 ❸ be of worth or importance 起作用；重要：Every minute ～s. 每分钟都很重要。 ‖ ～ **against** 对……不利/～ **among** 把……算作一个/～ **as** 算作是/～ **for** 有价值；有重要性/～ **in** 把…算进去/～ **off** 挑出；点出；报数/～ **on** 指望；依靠/～ **out** 数清楚/～ **up** 加起来；算出总数 Ⅱ n. an act of counting; number got by counting 数；算：I may have missed one or two in the ～. 我在数数时也许漏掉了一两个。 ‖ **keep** ～ **of** 计数/**lose** ～ **of** 算不清确切数目/**take** ～ **of** 给予注意；计较 ‖ **less** *adj.* 无数的

countdown /'kaʊntˌdaʊn/

n. ❶ the process of counting numbers

backwards to zero before a precisely timed event, e. g. when launching a space rocket 倒数读秒；倒计时 ❷the period of time just before sth. important happens 大事临近的时期：the ～ to the wedding 婚礼的临近

countenance /'kaʊntɪnəns/

Ⅰ n. a person's face, or the expression on it 面容；脸色；面部表情 Ⅱ v. to allow sth. as acceptable or possible 认可；赞同：He was reluctant to ～ the use of force. 他不太同意使用武力。

counter /'kaʊntə(r)/

n. ❶a table or flat surface on which goods are shown, customers served, in a shop or bank 柜台 ❷(in compounds) a device for keeping count (in machinery, etc.) 计数器；speed-～ 计速器

counteract /ˌkaʊntə'rækt/

v. act against and make (action, force, poison) of less effect 抵抗；抵消；中和；消解：This drug will ～ the poison. 这种药可以解毒。

counterfeit /'kaʊntəfɪt/

Ⅰ adj. made in imitation of another thing in order to deceive 仿制的；伪造的：This painting is ～. 这幅画是伪造的。 Ⅱ v. copy (coins, handwriting, etc.) in order to deceive 伪造(货币、笔迹等) Ⅲ n. a forgery 伪造物；赝品

counterfoil /'kaʊntəfɔɪl/

n. the part of a cheque or receipt, which is kept as a record that the cheque, etc. has been given to sb. (支票或收据的)存根

counterpart /'kaʊntə pɑːt/

n. a person or thing exactly like, or closely corresponding to another 相似的人(或物)；配对物

country /'kʌntri/

n. ❶an area of land with clear borders in which people of one nation live 国家 ❷land which is not the town or city 田野；旷野：We watched the ～ out of the window. 我们从窗户里看到外边的田野。 ‖ ～**man** n. 同胞；乡下人

countryside /'kʌntrɪsaɪd/

n. land outside towns and cities, used for

farming or left unused;country areas 乡下；乡间；农村：settle down in the ～ 在农村安家落户

county/ˈkaʊnti/
n. a major division of a country or state 郡；县：～ court 郡法院

coup/kuː/
n. a sudden and violent action to end a government and set up another one 政变

couple/ˈkʌpl/
Ⅰ *n.* ❶ two people or things of the same kind that are together 两个（人或物）：I found a ～ of socks in my bedroom. 我在自己的卧室里找到了两只袜子。❷ two people who are married, engaged, or otherwise closely associated romantically or sexually 夫妻；情侣：They're a nice ～. 他们是一对好夫妻。❸ several people or things 几个人；几件事 Ⅱ *v.* fasten or join (two things) together 连在一起：Her name was ～d with his. 她的名字与他的连在一起。‖ ～**d with** 加上；外加

couplet/ˈkʌplɪt/
n. two successive lines of verse, equal in length and with rhyme 对联；对句；双行押韵诗：a heroic ～ 英雄叙事诗双行体

coupon/ˈkuːpɒn/
n. a ticket which gives the holder the right to receive or do sth. 公债券；配给票；赠品券：10p off if you use this coupon. 凭此券可优惠 10 便士。

courage/ˈkʌrɪdʒ/
n. the ability to do sth. dangerous or to face pain without showing fear 胆量；勇气 ‖ summon (pluck) up ～ 鼓起勇气 ‖ ～**ous**/kəˈreɪdʒəs/ *adj.* 勇敢的

course/kɔːs/
n. ❶ the way in which sth. progresses or develops 进展；过程；过程；经过：Wars have influenced the ～ of history. 战争影响了历史的进程。❷ a set of lessons or studies 课程：He takes a history ～ this term. 这学期他修了一门历史课。❸ an area of land set aside and prepared for racing,golf,etc. （赛马或高尔夫等的）场地：The race ～ is oval in shape. 赛马场呈椭圆形。‖ as a matter of ～ 理所当然的

事,自然地/in (during) the ～ of 在……中；在……的过程中/in (the) ～ of time (the years) 随着时间(岁月)的推移；经过相当时间/in due ～ 到一定时候；没经过太久/in the ordinary ～ of events (things) 在一般的情况下；通常/let sth. take (run) its ～ 听其自然/of ～ 当然；自然/run its ～ 自然地发展；经历其发展过程

court/kɔːt/
n. ❶ a place where judges and lawyers listen to law cases 法庭；法院 ❷ a place where a king or queen and the followers meet 宫廷；朝廷：He is a ～ correspondent. 他是一名报道皇室生活的记者。❸ a piece of ground marked for a sport 球场：the tennis ～ 网球场 ‖ hold ～ 开庭；上朝/pay ～ to 追逐；求爱/take sb. to ～ 控告某人 ‖ ～**yard**/ˈkɔːtjɑːd/ *n.* 庭院；院子

courteous/ˈkɜːtiəs/
adj. having good manners；polite 礼貌的；谦恭的：It was ～ of him to write a letter of thanks. 他很客气,写了一封感谢信。

courtesy/ˈkɜːtəsi/
n. ❶ courteous behaviour；politeness 谦恭；礼貌：a ～ visit 礼节上的访问 ❷ (*pl.*)a polite speech or action 有礼貌的话语（或行为）：Some people don't know the courtesies due to an old man. 有些人不知道如何尊敬老人。/I'll see that you get all the courtesies of the house. 我一定要让你受到我家的盛情款待。‖ by ～ of 由于……允许；出于……好意：The pictures were lent to us by ～ of the president. 这些画是经校长许可借给我们的。

cousin/ˈkʌzn/
n. ❶ a child of your uncle or aunt 堂（表）兄弟；堂（表）姐妹：I have two ～s. 我有两个堂（表）兄弟姐妹。❷ a distant relative 远亲

cover/ˈkʌvə(r)/
Ⅰ *v.* ❶ place (one substance or thing) over or in front of another 覆盖；遮盖：She ～ed her face with her hands. 她用手蒙住脸面。❷ travel (a certain distance) 走完(一段路程)：The cars ～ed 200 miles a day. 小汽车每天行驶 200 英里。❸ have as a size 占（多少面积）：The city ～ed ten square miles. 这座城市占地十平

方英里。❹ include;comprise;extend over 涉及;包含:His researches ~ed a wide field.他的研究涉及面很广。❺ protect 掩护;保护:Warships ~ed the landing of the planes.战舰掩护飞机登陆。❻ (of a journalist) report (what is said and done at meetings, on public occasions, etc.) 报道:This paper ~s sports thoroughly.这张报纸整版报道体育消息。‖ ~ **against** 为……进行保险/~ **up** 盖好;掩饰 Ⅱ n.❶sth. made to be put over,on or in front of sth. 盖子;套子:When the water boils,take the ~.水开时,把盖揭开。❷ the outside of a book 封面:This book needs a new ~.这本书要换一个新封面。❸ a thing which lies on,over or around sth.in order to protect or conceal it 覆盖物;遮盖物;掩盖物 ❹a shelter or protection sought by people 藏身处;掩护物:We tried to find ~ from the rain. 我们设法找一个避雨处。‖ **read from ~ to ~** 从头看到底/**take ~** 藏身/**under ~** 秘密地/**under ~ of** 在……的掩护下

coverage/ˈkʌvərɪdʒ/
  n.❶ the amount,extent or area included or covered 包含数量;覆盖程度;覆盖范围 ❷ the amount of protectio given by an insurance 承保范围 ❸ the reporting of events 新闻报道

covering/ˈkʌvərɪŋ/
  n.sth.that covers 遮盖物;覆盖物

coverlet/ˈkʌvəlɪt/
  n.a bedspread 床单;被罩

covert/ˈkʌvət/
  Ⅰ adj.secret or hidden;not openly shown or admitted 秘密的;隐藏的:~ dislike 隐藏的憎恶/~ activity by the CIA to undermine their government 中央情报局秘密颠覆他们政府的行动 Ⅱ n.a thick growth of bushes and small trees in which animals can hide (动物藏身的)树丛

covet/ˈkʌvɪt/
  v.desire eagerly especially sth. belonging to another person 贪求;垂涎;觊觎:He won the ~ed Lawson Award.他赢得人人都垂涎的劳森奖。/Never ~ wealth and power.不要贪求财富和权力。

covetous/ˈkʌvɪtəs/
  adj.too eager for wealth or property for someone else's possessions 贪婪的;垂涎的

cow/kaʊ/
  n.a fully grown female of any animal of the ox family, especially the domestic kind kept by farmers for producing milk 母牛‖ ~ **herd** n.放牛人/~ **house** n.牛舍/~ **hide** n.牛皮/~ **shed** n.牛棚

coward/ˈkaʊəd/
  n.a man who lacks courage;one who escapes from danger,difficulty or pain 胆小鬼;懦夫‖ ~**ly** adj. 胆小的

cowboy/ˈkaʊbɔɪ/
  n.a man who rides a horse and looks after cattle in America (美国的)骑马牧人,牛仔

crab/kræb/
  n. ❶ a kind of sea animals with flattened round body, hard shell, four pairs of legs and one pair of claws 螃蟹 ❷the meat of crab 蟹肉

crack/kræk/
  Ⅰ n.❶ a thin line where sth.is broken 裂缝 ❷ a sharp noise 噼啪声;爆裂声:The jug hit the floor with a terrible ~.瓶子撞在地上发出极大的破裂声。Ⅱ v.❶ break,but not into separate parts 破裂:The glass ~ed when he poured boiling water into it.他一往玻璃杯里倒开水,杯就爆裂了。❷ make a sharp noise,like gun 使发出爆裂声:The whip ~ed in the air.鞭梢在空中啪地一响。Ⅲ adj.first-rate 第一流的;顶呱呱的:a ~ football team 最好的足球队‖ ~ **up** (飞机,汽车等)撞坏,撞毁;衰退,垮掉;吹捧

cracker/ˈkrækə(r)/
  n.❶ a thin, flaky, dry biscuit (as eaten with cheese) 脆薄的饼干:cheese and ~s 干酪加饼干 ❷ a firework that makes cracking noises when set off 爆竹;鞭炮

cracking/ˈkrækɪŋ/
  adj.❶very good 极好的;出色的 ❷fast and exciting 快而令人兴奋的:The story rips along at a ~ pace.故事以激动人心的速度发展着。

crackle /ˈkrækl/

n. a series of small sharp sounds, such as the sound made by dry wood being burned 噼噼啪啪的响声

cradle /ˈkreɪdl/

n. ❶ a kind of small bed for a baby 摇篮 ❷ a place where sth. starts 发源地：Many people think of Italy as the ～ of art. 很多人认为意大利是艺术的发源地。

craft /krɑːft/

n. ❶ a trade needing special skill with one's hands（需要特殊手艺的）行业：the jeweller's ～ 珠宝行业 ❷ an art or skill 工艺；手艺：Translation is a ～. 翻译是一种技艺。❸ the skill in deceiving; cunning 诡计；骗术：Don't trust her; she is full of ～. 别信任她，她诡计多端。

craftsman /ˈkrɑːftsmən/

n. a male worker skilled in a particular craft（男性）手艺人；工匠；巧匠

craftsmanship /ˈkrɑːftsmənʃɪp/

n. ❶ the level of skill shown by sb. in making sth. beautiful with their hands 手艺；技艺 ❷ the quality of design and work shown by sth. that has been made by hand 精工细作：the superb ～ of the china 这些瓷器的一流工艺

crafty /ˈkrɑːfti/

adj.（craftier, craftiest）❶ cunning or deceitful 狡诈的；诡计多端的 ❷ ingenious 新颖独特的；巧妙的：a ～ idea 绝妙的主意 ‖ **craftily** *adv.* 狡猾地；熟练地

craggy /ˈkrægi/

adj.（craggier, craggiest）❶（of a cliff or rock face）steep or uneven（悬崖、岩面）粗糙的，不平的 ❷（of a man's face）rugged and rough-looking in an attractive way（男人的面孔）粗糙的，粗犷的 ‖ **cragginess** *n.* 崎岖；多峭壁

cram /kræm/

v.（-mm-）❶ fill with too many things; push into sth. so that it becomes too full 硬塞；塞满：He ～med the box with his papers. 他在箱子里塞满论文。/ He ～med the papers into the box. 他把论文硬塞进箱子里。❷ learn or cause to learn by heart in order to prepare for an examina-

tion 死记硬背；填鸭式地教（以应付考试）：The boys were ～ming for the examination. 男孩子们正在死记硬背应付考试。‖ ～ **full** *adj.* 填满的：The box was ～full of papers. 箱子里塞满了论文。

cramp /kræmp/

Ⅰ *n.* sudden pain and tightening of the muscles, caused by cold or overuse of the muscles 抽筋；痉挛 Ⅱ *v.* prevent easy movement; keep in a small space 阻碍；束缚，约束

crane /kreɪn/

n. ❶ a large bird with long legs and a long neck 鹤：We saw five ～s at the zoo. 我们在动物园里看到五只鹤。❷ a machine for lifting and moving heavy loads 起重机；吊车：Four ～s were being used on the new fifty-story building. 建造那座新的 50 层大楼时用了四台起重机。

crank¹ /kræŋk/

Ⅰ *n.* a handle of a machine 机器的曲柄 Ⅱ *v.* start a machine by using a crank 用曲柄开动机器

crank² /kræŋk/

n. a person with strong and unusual opinions 想法古怪的人

cranny /ˈkræni/

n. a small hole (especially in a wall or in a rock)（尤指墙上或崖石上的）小洞，缝隙

crash /kræʃ/

Ⅰ *v.* fall down or strike sth. violently 猛撞；坠毁：The plane ～ed shortly after taking off. 飞机起飞后不久就坠毁了。Ⅱ *n.* ❶ a violent collision, typically of one vehicle with another or with an object 坠毁；撞击：There was a serious car ～ this morning. 今天上午发生了一起严重的车祸。❷ a sudden loud noise as made by a violent blow, fall, break, etc. 轰隆响声；爆裂声：The tree fell with a great ～. 随着一声巨大的爆裂声，那棵树倒了下来。❸ ruin or collapse (e.g. in trade, finance) 失败；凋敝：The stock market ～ of 1929 ruined many people. 1929 年股票市场的凋敝导致了许多人破产。

crave /kreɪv/

v. ask earnestly for; have a strong desire

for 恳求；渴望：~ (for) fresh air 需要新鲜空气/ The tired boy ~d for rest.那个疲倦的男孩极想休息。

craving/'kreɪvɪŋ/

*n.*a strong wish or desire for sth. 渴望；强烈的欲望

crawl/krɔːl/

Ⅰ *v.*❶move slowly by dragging the body along the ground or on hands or knees 爬行；匍匐前进：The prisoner ~ed through a hole and escaped.那因犯从一个洞里爬出去逃跑了。❷move slowly 慢慢移动：The traffic ~ed through the city. 车辆缓缓穿过城市。Ⅱ *n.*❶the act of crawling 爬行；缓慢行进 ❷a style of swimming in which the arms make alternate overarm movements 自由式游泳

crayon/'kreɪən/

*n.*a soft coloured pencil, wax or chalk 彩色铅笔；蜡笔；粉笔：a picture in ~ 蜡笔画

craze/kreɪz/

*n.*sth. in which people have an interest, which is great but is not likely to last for a long time 狂热；(一时的)着迷：Everyone in the family had a ~ for Chinese food.家里每一个人都迷上中国菜。

crazy/'kreɪzi/

*adj.*❶mad, foolish 发疯的；发傻的：The noise is driving me ~.这噪声简直令我发疯。❷wildly excited or enthusiastic 热爱的；狂热的：She's ~ about singing.她狂热唱歌。‖ like ~ 拼命地

creak/kriːk/

Ⅰ *n.*a noise like that made by a door which needs oiling (门的)吱吱嘎嘎的声音 Ⅱ *v.*make this noise 吱吱作声：The wooden cart ~ed as it moved along.这辆板车走动时嘎吱嘎吱地响。‖ ~y *adj.* 吱吱嘎嘎的

cream/kriːm/

*n.*the fatty part of the milk that rises to the top 奶油：Butter is made from ~.黄油用奶油制成。

crease/kriːs/

Ⅰ *n.*a line made in cloth or paper by folding (布或纸的)折痕，皱折 Ⅱ *v.*make or

get a crease 起皱；起折痕：This cloth does not ~.这块布不起皱。

create/kriː'eɪt/

*v.*❶ make sth. happen or exist 创建；创立：~ more jobs for young people 为年轻人创造更多的就业机会 ❷cause sth. to happen as a result of one's actions 引起；引发 ‖ creator *n.*创造者；造物主

creation /krɪ'eɪʃən/

*n.*❶the act or process of creating sth. 发明；创造；创建 ❷ sth. which has been made or invented 创造物；作品

creative/kriː'eɪtɪv/

adj. having the power of creating new things 有创造力的；创造性的：~ imagination 创造性想象/ ~ writing 有创造性的作品

creature/'kriːtʃə(r)/

*n.*a living thing, person or animal 生物；人；动物：But for the cold-blooded ~s such as a frog or snake it is a different matter.但是对于冷血动物，诸如蛙、蛇，情况则不同了。/Birds are ~s which fly. 鸟是会飞的动物。

credence/'kriːdəns/

*n.*acceptance as true; belief 相信；信任：letter of ~ 介绍信/The newspaper are giving no ~ to his latest statement.报纸不相信他最近的声明。

credentials/krə'denʃlz/

n. (*pl.*)❶a person's qualifications and past achievements that make them suitable for sth. 资格；资历：Her ~ for the job are impeccable.她做这项工作是完全够格的。❷ documents that prove a person's identity or qualifications 证书；文凭：May I see your ~? 我能看下你的证书吗？

credibility /ˌkredɪ'bɪlɪti/

*n.*❶the quality of being believable or convincing 可靠性；可信性：The defendant's story lacks ~.被告的陈述不可信。❷the quality of being trusted and believed in 信任；相信；信誉

credible/'kredəbl/

*adj.*that can be believed；trust worthy 可信的；可信任的；可靠的：a ~ news report

值得相信的新闻报道/～ witnesses 可靠的证人

credit/ˈkredɪt/

Ⅰ *n*. ❶ belief in the truth of sth.; confidence 相信;信任:We gave ～ to his story.我们相信他讲的故事。❷good name; reputation 名誉;名望;名气:He is a man of highest ～.他是一位很有名望的人。❸ honour or approval that comes to a person,because of what he is or does 荣誉;功绩:The person who does the work should get the ～.干这份工作的人应受表扬。❹ the money in a person's bank account 存款 ❺sb.or sth.bring honour to others 添荣誉的人(或物):You are a ～ to the football team.你是一位为足球队争光的人。‖ **on ～** 赊账:You can buy things on ～ if your credit is good.如果你有信誉,就能赊购东西。/**to one's ～** ❶ 是某人的光荣:Much to his ～,the party was a great success.晚会开得很成功,这是他的光荣。❷属于:Young as he is,he already has five novels to his ～.尽管很年轻,他已写了五部小说。‖ ～ **card** *n*. 信用卡 Ⅱ *v*. believe; trust 相信;信任:Don't expect me to ～ such a strange tale.别以为我会相信这么离奇古怪的故事。

credulous/ˈkredjuləs/

adj.too ready to believe what one is told 轻信的:He is a ～ fool;he thought that I was telling the truth when I said I could do magic. 他是一个轻易受骗的人,我告诉他我会巫术,他竟信以为真。

creed/kri:d/

n.an official statement of religious beliefs 教义;信条

creek/kri:k/

n.❶ a narrow arm of water off the main stretch of water (河、海延伸至陆地的)细长小湾 ❷ a small river 小河;小溪

creep/kri:p/

v.(crept) ❶ move quietly,often with the body close to the ground 爬行;匍匐而行;微微地移动:Learn to ～ before you leap.先学爬后学跳。❷ (of the flesh) have the feeling that things are creeping over it 起鸡皮疙瘩;汗毛直竖:His story

made my flesh ～.他讲的故事使我毛骨悚然。‖ ～**er** *n*.爬行动物;爬虫;匍匐植物/～**y** *adj*.爬行的;令人毛骨悚然的

crest/krest/

n.❶ a tuft of feathers on a bird's head;a cock's comb 鸟冠;鸡冠 ❷ the top of a slope or hill;white top of a large wave 顶峰;浪头

crew/kru:/

n.all the persons working on a ship, aircraft,train,etc.(船、飞机或火车上的)全体工作人员:The ～ was small.乘务员人数不多。/The ～ are waiting for instructions from the ship's owner. 船员们等待着船主的命令。

crick/krɪk/

n.stiffness and pain in a part of the body (especially the neck) 肌肉痉挛(尤指颈部)

cricket/ˈkrɪkɪt/

n.a small brown insect that makes a noise which seems to go on all the time 蟋蟀: the chirping of ～s 蟋蟀唧唧叫声

crime/kraɪm/

n.❶a bad act that is against the law 罪行;犯罪:To steal is a ～.盗窃是一种犯罪行为。❷a foolish or useless action 失策;愚蠢行为:It would be an absolute ～ not to tell him the fact.不把事实真相告诉他,那是大错特错。

criminal/ˈkrɪmɪnl/

Ⅰ *adj*.❶of or being a crime 犯罪的;违法的:a ～ act 犯罪行为 ❷concerned with crime 刑事的:the ～ police 刑警队/～ law 刑法 Ⅱ *n*.a person who commits a crime or crimes 罪犯:The ～ was sentenced to death.那罪犯被判处死刑。

crimp /krɪmp/

v.❶ press material into small folds or ridges 使……起褶皱;将……弯成小褶 ❷make waves in hair with a hot iron 烫发

crimson/ˈkrɪmzn/

Ⅰ *n*.a deep red colour 深红色;绯红色 Ⅱ *v*.make or become crimson (使)变为深红色:The light from the fire ～ed the sky.火光把天空照得通红。

crinkle/ˈkrɪŋkl/

Ⅰ n. a small fold (especially in paper, cloth or skin)（尤指纸或布上的）褶痕；皱纹 Ⅱ v. make or get folds in（使）变皱：He ～d the paper. 他把纸弄皱了。

cripple/ˈkrɪpl/

Ⅰ n. one who is lame or physically or emotionally disabled 跛子；（身体、感情方面的）残废：an emotional ～ 感情上的残废 Ⅱ v. ❶ cause sb. not to walk normally any longer 使跛；使残废 ❷ damage；weaken 损坏；削弱：The attack ～d the enemy. 这次攻击削弱了敌人的战斗力。

crisis/ˈkraɪsɪs/

n. ❶ a time of difficulty or danger 危机：an economic ～ 经济危机 ❷ a turning point 转折点；关键时刻：Things are coming to a ～. 事情已经发展到了关键时刻。

crisp/krɪsp/

adj. ❶ hard, dry and easily broken 脆的；易碎的：～ potato chips 酥脆炸土豆片 ❷ fresh 新鲜的：～ cabbage 新鲜卷心菜 ❸ (of one's manners of speech, etc.) quick, clear, not hesitating（说话方式等）干脆的：a ～ manner of speaking 说话干脆利索 ❹ (of air, etc.) cool, dry and refreshing（空气等）清新的：～ air 清新的空气/a ～ autumn day 一个凉爽的秋日

criss-cross/ˈkrɪskrɒs/

adj. made or marked with lines that cross each other 互相交叉的

criterion/kraɪˈtɪəriən/

n. (pl. criteria/-riə/) a standard by which one can judge sth.（判断、评定的）标准，准绳：There are several criteria of a good school. 评定一所好学校有几条标准。

critic/ˈkrɪtɪk/

n. ❶ a person who says whether a book, film, play, piece of music, etc. is good or not, and gives reasons for his decision（usually in a newspaper or magazine）（通常指在报纸、杂志上对书籍、电影、戏剧、音乐发表评论的）评论家，批评家 ❷ a person who always notices the bad points and mistakes about anything 爱挑剔的人；吹毛求疵的人

critical /ˈkrɪtɪkəl/

adj. ❶ looking for or pointing out faults 批评的；批判性的；挑剔的：I'm sorry to be so ～. 如此挑剔，我很抱歉。❷ expressing judgements about books, art, music, etc.（对文艺作品）评论性的 ❸ at a point of crisis, very serious 严重的；可能有危险的：The patient's condition is ～. 病人的情况很危险。❹ having an important part to play in the success or failure of sth. 极重要的；关键的；至关紧要的：This is a ～ moment in his career. 这是他职业生涯中一个关键的时刻。 ‖ ～ ly adv. 批判性地；危急地；关键地

criticism/ˈkrɪtɪsɪzəm/

n. ❶ an unfavourable judgment or expression of disapproval 批评：I always think ～ is helpful. 我总觉得批评是有益的。❷ the forming and expressing of judgments about the good or bad qualities of anything, especially artistic work 意见；评论：I withdrew my ～. 我收回自己的意见。

criticize/ˈkrɪtɪsaɪz/

v. ❶ judge with disapproval；point out the faults of 批评；指责：His policies were severely ～d. 他的政策受到严厉的批评。❷ make judgments about the good and bad points of 评论；提意见：It's hard to ～ one's own work. 评论自己的作品是一件不容易的事。

crockery/ˈkrɒkəri/

n. plates, cups, dishes, etc. (usually those made of baked clay or china) 陶器；瓦器

crocodile/ˈkrɒkədaɪl/

n. a large animal with a long nose and a lot of sharp teeth, which lives in rivers in the tropics and which looks like a floating log 鳄鱼

crony/ˈkrəʊni/

n. a very close friend 知己；好友：He spends every evening drink in the pub with his cronies. 他每天晚上都跟知心朋友到酒馆喝酒。

crook/krʊk/

n. ❶ a long stick with a bent end used by a bishop or a shepherd 弯柄杖 ❷ any bent or curved thing or part 弯曲物；弯曲部

C

分：the ~ of the arm 臂弯 ❸a thief or swindler 小偷；骗子

crooked/ˈkrukɪd/

adj. ❶ not straight; twisted; bent 不直的；弯曲的：a ~ street 弯弯曲曲的街道 ❷ dishonest 不诚实；狡诈的：a ~ politician 不诚实的政客

crop/krɒp/

n. ❶ agricultural plants in the field 庄稼；作物 ❷ yearly or season's products of grain, grass, fruit, etc. 收成：This year's corn ~ will set a new record. 今年的谷物收成将会创新纪录。‖ in（out of）~ 在（没）耕种

cross/krɒs/

v. ❶ go from one side to the other; pass over 跨过；穿过：I ~ed the street. 我跨过了那条街。❷put or lie across 交叉：He sat down and ~ed his legs. 他坐下来交叉着腿。‖ ~ off 划掉／~ one's heart 向……保证／~ one's mind 想起／~ out 取消／~ over 投奔敌方／~ swords with 争论／~ one's fingers 祈求成功

crossbar/ˈkrɒsbɑː(r)/

n. a bar joining two upright posts, especially two goalposts, or the bar between the seat and handle bars of a bike（尤指球门的）横木；（脚踏车的）横梁

crossbreed/ˈkrɒsbriːd/

Ⅰ *v.* ❶ cause an animal or plant to breed with one of another breed 使杂交 ❷（of an animal or plant）breed with one of another breed（动植物的）异种交配，杂交 Ⅱ *n.* an animal or a plant which is a mixture of breeds（动植物的）杂种，杂交品种

crosscheck/ˌkrɒsˈtʃek/

v. make certain of the correctness of（a calculation, statement, etc.）e.g. by using a different method of calculation（以不同的方法）核对（计算结果等）；核查

cross-country/ˌkrɒsˈkʌntri, ˈkrɔːsˈkʌntri/

adj. & *adv.* ❶across fields or open country 越野的（地）：a ~ running 越野跑 ❷ from one part of a country to the other, especially not using main roads or routes （尤指通过越野）横越全国的（地）：~

train journeys 穿越全国的火车旅行

cross-current/ˈkrɒskʌrənt/

n. a current in the sea, a river, etc., moving across the general direction of the main current 交叉水流；逆流

crossing/ˈkrɒsɪŋ/

n. ❶an act of going across 横渡；横穿：the Atlantic ~ 横渡大西洋 ❷a place where sth. as a street, river, etc. may be crossed 横道；渡口 ❸ a place where two lines, roads, etc. cross 十字路口；交叉点：a level ~ 平交道口；平面交叉处

crossroads/ˈkrɒsrəudz/

n. ❶ a place where two or more roads cross one another 交叉路口 ❷a point at which a crucial decision must be made which will have far-reaching consequences 转折点；重大抉择时刻

crosswise/ˈkrɒswaɪz, ˈkrɔːswaɪz/

adj. & *adv.* in the form of a cross, with one thing crossing another 成十字形的（地）；交叉的（地）

crotch/krɒtʃ/

n. a place where a person's legs join; this place in a pair of trousers, etc.（人的）胯部；裤裆

crouch/krautʃ/

v. make the body close to the ground by bending the knees 蹲伏；弯身：She ~ed by the fire to get warm. 她在炉火边蹲下取暖。

crow/krəu/

Ⅰ *n.* ❶a large black bird with a harsh low cry 乌鸦：Crows sometimes eat most of the corn in a cornfield. 乌鸦有时能吃掉玉米地里的大部分玉米。❷ the sound of a cock 鸡鸣声：The ~ of the rooster woke me up. 雄鸡的鸣叫声把我吵醒。 Ⅱ *v.* ❶（of a cock）make a loud, shrill cry（公鸡）鸣叫：The rooster ~s every morning. 雄鸡每天早晨报晓。❷（of a baby）make sounds showing happiness（指婴儿）发笑声

crowbar/ˈkrəubɑː(r)/

n. a long piece of iron with a bent end, used for moving heavy objects, opening packing cases, etc. 弯头铁棍；铁橇

crowd /kraʊd/

I *n.* a large mass of people 人群;一群人 II *v.* come together in a a large mass;fill (a space) with people 挤入;涌入:They all ~ed into the cinema. 他们都涌进了电影院。‖ ~ **out**(**of**) 使不能容纳

crowded /'kraʊdɪd/

adj. ❶(of a place) full of people（地方）拥挤的,挤满人的:~ streets 拥挤的街道 ❷full of sth. 充满的;挤满的:a room ~ with books 堆满书籍的房间

crown /kraʊn/

I *n.* ❶ a circle worn on the head by a king or a queen 王冠:~ prince 王储 ❷a championship title 桂冠:He won the heavy-weight boxing ~ in 1985. 他获得了 1985 年重量拳击的桂冠。 II *v.* ❶ put a crown on a king or queen 加冕:We saw the archbishop ~ the queen. 我们看见大主教给女王加冕。 ❷ be or have at the top of 在……的顶上:Mist ~ed the mountain. 雾笼罩着山顶。 ❸ put a happy finishing touch to 以(胜利)结束;使圆满结束:Success ~ed his efforts. 他的努力终于得到成功。

crucial /'kruːʃl/

adj. very important,and coming at a time of great danger or difficulty 极重要的;严重关头的;关键性的:The Prime Minister has to make a ~ decision within the next few weeks. 今后几周内首相必须做出关键性的决定。

crude /kruːd/

adj. ❶not mature 未成熟的:~ fruit 未成熟的水果/Her paintings are rather ~, is not skilfully done. 她画画的技巧还不够熟练。 ❷rough 粗糙的:a ~ log 一根粗糙的木头 ❸in a natural state;unrefined 天然的;未提炼的:~ rubber 天然橡胶 ❹giving a general information of sth. simply 简略的;大概的

cruel /'kruəl/

adj. ❶liking to cause pain and suffering 残酷的;无情的:They are ~ to animals. 他们对待动物很残酷。 ❷painful;causing suffering 惨痛的;痛苦的:It was a ~ lesson. 那是一个惨痛的教训。‖ ~**ly**

adv. 残酷地

cruelty /'kruːəlti/

n. (*pl.*-ies) ❶ callous indifference to or pleasure in causing pain and suffering 残忍;残酷;残暴:They treated her with extreme ~. 他们极其残忍地对待她。 ❷behaviour which causes pain or suffering to a person or animal 残酷行为;残暴行为:We can't stand ~ to animals. 我们无法忍受对动物的残暴行为。

cruise /kruːz/

I *v.* sail from place to place 巡航;航行:~ along the shore 沿岸巡航 II *n.* a sea voyage 航行;巡游:make a round-the-world ~ 作环球航行

crumb /krʌm/

n. ❶small pieces of bread,cake,etc. 面包渣;碎屑:He fed ~s to the birds. 他用面包屑喂鸟。 ❷a very small amount of sth. 一点;少许:a ~ of comfort 一点安慰/~s of learning 点点滴滴的学问

crumble /'krʌmbl/

v. break or fall into small pieces;come to nothing;pass away 弄碎;粉碎;崩溃;灭亡;破灭:crumbling walls 断壁残垣/The cake began to ~ as soon as it was cut. 那块饼一切立刻就碎了。

crumple /'krʌmpl/

v. (cause to) be pressed or crushed into folds or creases 折皱;揉皱;压碎;压变形:He ~d the piece of paper in his hand. 他把那张纸片揉在手里。/The car ~d up when it hit the wall. 车子撞到墙上,变了形。

crunch /krʌntʃ/

I *v.* ❶ break sth. hard by biting noisily with the teeth 嘎吱嘎吱地嚼:He ~ed the apple. 他嘎吱嘎吱地嚼苹果。 ❷ crush or be crushed noisily 发出嘎吱嘎吱声:The hard snow ~ed under his feet. 他脚下坚实的雪嘎吱嘎吱响。 II *n.* ❶ the noise made by crunching 咬碎的声音;踩踏(或碾压)的声音 ❷ the moment of crisis 危急关头

crush /krʌʃ/

I *v.* ❶press hard or be pressed,so that there is breaking or injury 压碎;压榨;碾

碎;压坏:～ peanuts for oil 榨花生油/ The eggs have ～ed. 蛋压碎了。 /The bike was ～ed by a truck.自行车被卡车压坏了。 ❷(cause to)become full of folds (使)压皱;(使)变皱:The clothes have been badly ～ed in the trunk.衣服在皮箱里被压皱得不成形了。 ❸conquer; defeat 征服;平息;击溃:～ all opposition 制服所有的对手 ❹press;come crowding into 挤;挤入:The people ～ed in through the gates as soon as they were opened.大门一打开,人们一拥而入。 Ⅱn.❶an act of crushing 压碎;压倒;压榨 ❷a crowd of people pressed closely together, especially in an enclosed space 人群:There was such a ～ of people on the train that I could hardly breathe.火车上拥挤不堪,使得我喘不过气来。 ❸a drink made of juice of crushed fruit 果汁饮料:orange ～ 橘子汁

crust/krʌst/

Ⅰn.❶the hard-baked surface of a loaf; the outer covering (pastry) of a pie or tart 面包皮;馅饼的外皮;糕点外壳:rice ～s 锅巴 ❷the hard outer covering 硬外壳,硬表层:a ～ of ice 一层薄冰/the earth's ～ 地壳 Ⅱv.cover or become covered with a hard outer layer 硬壳覆盖;结成硬皮:Ice ～ed the lake.湖上结冰了。 / The snow ～ed over during the freezing weather. 雪在寒冷天气里结成一层冰。

crutch/krʌtʃ/

n.❶a long stick with a crosspiece at the top used under the arm to help a lame person to walk 拐杖:a pair of ～es 一副拐杖 ❷any moral support 精神上的寄托:Her son is her ～.她的儿子是她精神上的寄托。

cry/kraɪ/

Ⅰv.❶(of persons, animals, birds) make sounds that express feelings 叫;喊:～ aloud 大声叫喊/～ for mercy 叫喊求饶 ❷(of persons)weep;shed tears (with or without sound) (指人)哭泣;流泪:She cried bitterly.她哭得厉害。 /A baby can ～ as soon as it is born.婴儿一生下来就会哭。 ❸announce for sale;make known by calling out 叫卖:～ one's wares 叫卖

货物 Ⅱn.❶a loud sound of fear, pain, grief, etc.;a loud excited utterance of words (因恐惧、痛楚、悲伤等)哭叫,呼喊,呼声,哭声,哭诉,叫卖声:the ～ of a crow 乌鸦叫声/have a good ～ 痛哭一场/the ～ of a newspaper seller 卖报者的叫卖声 ❷watchwords or phrases used for a principle or cause 口号;标语:an e-lection ～ 选举口号

cryptic/ˈkrɪptɪk/

adj.secret;with a hidden meaning, or a meaning not easily seen 秘密的;难解的;意味深长的:a ～ remark 含意深远的评语

crystal/ˈkrɪstl/

Ⅰn.❶a substance that looks like glass;a piece of this substance 水晶;水晶制品:as clear as ～ 像水晶一样透明/a ～ wine glass 水晶酒杯 ❷a solid form of a substance which looks like crystal 结晶;晶体:Salt forms in ～s.盐结成晶体。 ❸glassware of best quality, made into bowls, vases, vessels, etc.(品质最好的)玻璃器皿 Ⅱadj.clear as crystal 水晶般的;透明的

crystallize/ˈkrɪstəlaɪz/

v.❶form crystals 结晶;晶化:When most liquids freeze they ～.大部分液体凝固后结晶。 ❷(of ideas or plans)become clear and definite in form (想法或计划)具体化,成形 ‖ **crystallization** n.结晶化;具体化

cube/kju:b/

Ⅰn.❶a solid figure with six equal square faces 正六面体 ❷sth.looking like this 立方形物体:a ～ of sugar 一块方糖 ❸the number got by multiplying itself twice 立方;三次幂 Ⅱv.calculate the cube of 求立方:4 ～d is 64.4 的立方是 64。

cubic/ˈkju:bɪk/

adj.❶cube-shaped 立方形的;立方体的 ❷denoting a unit of measurement equal to the volume of a cube whose side is one of the linear unit specified 立方的:30 billion ～ metres of water 300 亿立方米的水

cuboid/ˈkju:bɔɪd/

Ⅰ *adj*.more or less cubic in shape 立方形的;立方体的 Ⅱ *n*.a solid body with six rectangular faces 立方形;立方体

cuckoo/ˈkuku:/

n.(*pl*.~s) a bird which makes a sound like this word and which lays its eggs in the nests of other birds 布谷鸟;杜鹃

cucumber/ˈkju:kʌmbə(r)/

n. a long green-skinned vegetable with flesh 黄瓜

cuddle/ˈkʌdl/

Ⅰ *v*.hold close and lovingly in one's arms 使拥抱;使怀抱:~ one's baby 搂着孩子 Ⅱ *n*.the act of cuddling;a hug 拥抱;搂抱:run up to him for a ～ 跑向他去拥抱/give her mother a ～ 拥抱她母亲

cue[1]/kju:/

n.❶ a few words said by an actor,which are the signal for another actor to begin speaking (舞台上的)提示,暗示 ❷ a signal or sign to somebody that he should begin to do sth. (行动的)暗示

cue[2]/kju:/

n.a long stick used in the game of billiards 台球的球杆

cuff[1]/kʌf/

n.❶ the end of the sleeve of a coat or shirt at the wrist 袖口 ❷ the fold at the bottom of a trouser leg 裤脚的翻边 ‖ **off the ～** 即兴的;未经准备的:make a remark off the ～ 即席发言 ‖ **～link** *n*.(衬衫的)袖口扣

cuff[2]/kʌf/

Ⅰ *n*.a light blow to the head given with the hand (用手对头部的)轻轻拍打 Ⅱ *v*. hit sb. in this way 轻轻拍打头

cuisine/kwɪˈzi:n/

n.cooking or the style of cooking (especially in a hotel or restaurant, or in a country as a whole) 烹饪(尤指旅馆、酒店或某一国家的烹饪特色):French ～ is one of the best in the world.法国菜是世界上最好的烹饪之一。

culminate/ˈkʌlmɪneɪt/

v.reach the end point in some process 达到顶点:The long quarrel between Tom and his neighbour ~d in a fight.汤姆和

他邻居的口角最终发展到互相扭打。

cultivate/ˈkʌltɪveɪt/

v.❶prepare land for growing crops 耕;耕地:He ~d the field with a small tractor.他用小型拖拉机耕了地。❷plant;grow 种植;栽培:～ vegetables 种植蔬菜 ❸ develop 培养;养成:～ good habits 养成习惯

cultivated /ˈkʌltɪveɪtɪd/

adj.well-educated and well-mannered 有教养的;有修养的;举止文雅的

cultural/ˈkʌltʃərəl/

adj.of or having to do with culture 文化的;与文化相关的:a ～ institute 文化研究所

culture/ˈkʌltʃə(r)/

n.❶ a nation's or group of people's beliefs, accomplishments, behaviour patterns,customs,art and science in general 文明;文化:American ～ 美国文化/bring ～ to a backward nation 把文明带给一个落后民族 ❷ improvement of the body and mind through education and training (身体)锻炼;(心性)修养:physical ～ 体育

cumbersome/ˈkʌmbəsəm/

adj.large and heavy;difficult to use or move easily 笨重的

cumulative/ˈkju:mjʊlətɪv/

adj.getting larger by being added to 累积的:～ effect 累积的效果

cunning/ˈkʌnɪŋ/

Ⅰ *adj*.clever in deceiving 狡猾的:as ～ as a fox 像狐狸一样狡猾 Ⅱ *n*.cleverness in deceiving 狡猾;奸诈:He has a great deal of ~.他非常狡猾。

cup/kʌp/

n.❶a small bowl with a handle for drinking 杯子:wash the tea ～ 洗茶杯 ❷the amount that a cup will hold 一杯的量:a ～ of coffee 一杯咖啡 ❸a gold or silver bowl as a prize 奖杯;优胜杯:the school swimming ～ 学校游泳赛杯

cupboard/ˈkʌbəd/

n. a set of shelves enclosed by doors, where dishes,provisions,clothes,etc.may be stored 碗柜;食橱;衣柜

curable /ˈkjʊərəb(ə)l/
*adj.*able to be cured 能治愈的；可矫正：Most skin cancers are completely ～.大部分皮肤癌都可以完全治愈。

cupful/ˈkʌpfʊl/
*n.*the amount that a cup will hold 一满杯

curb/kɜːb/
Ⅰ *n.* ❶ a piece of leather or metal chain fastened under a horse's jaw and used to control the horse 马勒，马衔索(勒马的皮带或链带) ❷ anything which acts as a control in this way 抑制物；控制物 Ⅱ *v.* keep (feelings, etc.) under control 抑制；控制：You must learn to ～ your temper (情绪等)你要学会控制发火。

cure/kjʊə(r)/
Ⅰ *n.*❶restoration to health 病愈；痊愈：My ～ took seven weeks.我的病花了七个星期才治愈。❷ sth. that will end a problem or an illness 对策；疗法；药：Aspirin is a ～ for headaches.阿司匹林是治头痛的一种良药。Ⅱ *v.*❶eliminate a disease or injury with medical treatment 治愈：～ a man of a disease 治愈某人的病/～ an illness 治病/～ a child of bad habits 戒除孩子的恶习/The doctor ～d the pain in my back. 医生治好了我的背疼。❷solve a problem 解决(问题)

curio/ˈkjʊərɪəʊ/
*n.*an unusual and interesting object 古玩；古董；珍品

curiosity /ˌkjʊərɪˈɒsɪti/
n.(*pl.*-ies) ❶a strong desire to know or learn sth. 好奇心；求知欲：Filled with ～, she peered through the window.她满心好奇地透过窗户看。❷a strange or unusual object or fact 奇物；奇事：The museum is full of historical curiosities.这座博物馆有许多珍奇历史文物。

curious/ˈkjʊərɪəs/
*adj.*❶ wanting to know about sth. 好奇的：The baby was ～ about everything he saw.那婴儿对所见的一切都好奇。❷strange；unusual 奇怪的；奇特的；She has a ～ way of talking.她讲话的样子很怪。‖ ～ly *adv.*好奇地；感兴趣地

curl/kɜːl/
Ⅰ *n.*❶a small mass of hair twisting upwards 卷发 ❷ the state of having the shape of curl 卷曲状：keep one's hair in ～ 保持头发卷曲 Ⅱ *v.*cause (hair) to form a curl or curls 使(头发)卷曲，卷：I had my hair ～ed yesterday.我昨天去卷了发。/His hair ～s naturally.他的头发自然卷曲。

currency/ˈkʌrənsi/
*n.*a system of money used in a country 货币：a gold ～ 金币/foreign ～ 外币

current/ˈkʌrənt/
Ⅰ *adj.*❶ of the present time 现时的；当前的：～ events 时事 ❷ in common or general use 通用的；流行的：Some words are no longer ～.有些字不再通用。Ⅱ *n.* ❶ a continuous flow of water, air or any liquid 流；水流；气流：He swam with the ～.他顺流游泳。❷the flow of electricity through a wire, , etc.电流：He turned off the ～. 他把电关上了。❸ a general course or movement 趋势；倾向；潮流：It's foolish of you to go all along against the ～ of the times.你总是违背时代潮流，这是愚蠢的。‖ ～less *adj.*无电流的；无流的/～ly *adv.*普遍地；通常地；当前

curriculum/kəˈrɪkjʊləm/
n. (*pl.*-or curricula /kəˈrɪkjʊlə/) courses of study in a school, college, etc.(学校等的)课程：The ～ is overloaded.课程过多。‖ curricular *adj.*课程的

curry/ˈkʌri/
*n.*a type of food made with spices which taste very hot 咖喱

curse/kɜːs/
Ⅰ *n.*words, phrases or sentences calling for the punishment, injury or destruction of sth.or sb.诅咒；咒骂；骂人话 ‖ be under a ～ 被诅咒/call down (lay) a ～ upon sb.诅咒某人 Ⅱ *v.*use bad language against 诅咒；咒骂：He ～d the thief.他咒骂窃贼。‖ ～d /ˈkɜːsɪd/ *adj.*被咒骂的；该咒骂的；可恶的

cursory/ˈkɜːsə(r)/
*adj.*done in a hurry 粗略的；草率的：He took a ～ look at the title. 他粗略地看了

一下标题。

curtail/kɜː'teɪl/

*v.*make shorter or less 缩短；削减：I have had to ～ my spending.我不得不节约开支。

curtain/'kɜːtn/

*n.*❶a piece of cloth, etc. as hung up at a window, door, etc.窗帘；门帘 ❷a sheet of heavy material across the front of the stage in a theatre（舞台上的）幕布：The ～ falls and the play ends.幕布降下，全剧结束。‖ ～ **call** *n.*谢幕

curve/kɜːv/

Ⅰ *n.*a bent line having no angles；a rounded bend 曲线；弧形：a ～ in the road 一段弯路 Ⅱ *v.*(cause to) have the form of a curve；move in the course of a curve（使）弯曲；环行：The street ～s to left.这条街向左边弯。/He ～d the stick.他把这根棍子弄弯了。

cushion/'kuʃn/

*n.*a small bag filled with soft material inside, used for sitting, lying, kneeling, on or putting behind the back 垫子；坐垫；靠垫：a ～ of air 气垫

custard/'kʌstəd/

*n.*a sweet yellow substance made from milk and eggs and served with or as a pudding 牛奶蛋糊

custodian/kʌs'təʊdjən/

*n.*a guardian or keeper, especially of a public building 监护人；看守人；保管人

custody/'kʌstədi/

*n.*duty or work of protecting sth. or keeping sth. safe 监护权；保护；监禁：The police have the thief in ～.警方把小偷拘留起来。/The father asked for the ～ of his children when his wife left him.妻子离开他以后，做父亲的要求取得对孩子的监护权。

custom/'kʌstəm/

*n.*❶ usually and generally accepted behaviour among members of a social group 风俗；习惯：Social ～s vary greatly from country to country.社会习俗国与国之间大不相同。 ❷（*pl.*）import duties；a government department which collects these taxes 关税；海关：It took several minutes to get through the Customs.我们只用了几分钟就通过了海关检查。

customer/'kʌstəmə(r)/

*n.*❶a person who buys things, especially one who gives his custom to a shop 顾客；买主；主顾：The new shop across the road has taken away most of my ～s.路对面的那家新店夺去了我许多主顾。❷a person of fellow 家伙：an awkward ～ 难对付的家伙

cut/kʌt/

Ⅰ *v.*（cut；cutting）❶ divide, separate, wound, or make an opening with a sharp tool 切；割；割破；划破：Cut the meat into small pieces.把肉切成碎片。❷be capable of cutting 切起来；剪起来：This knife doesn't ～ well.这把刀切起来不快。❸ make short；make smaller in quantity, price, length, etc.；reduce 缩短；削减；减少：We must ～ the cost of education.我们必须削减教育费用。‖ ～ **across** 走捷径；穿过去/～ **at** 向……砍去/～ **away** 切除，剪掉/～ **back** 减少/～ **down** 削减；压缩/～ **in** 插嘴/～ **into** 插进来，参加/～ **off** 切断，停掉/～ **out** 删掉，剪下来/～ **out for** 适合做，是……的材料/～ **short** 打断（谈话）；中断（活动）/～ **a tooth** 长牙/～ **through** 穿过；穿透/～ **up** 切碎，破碎 Ⅱ *n.*❶an act of cutting；a piece of sth. that has been cut off 切割；划破；伤口：He bandaged the ～ on his face.他包扎了脸上的伤口。❷becoming shorter, less, lower, etc.降低；削减：I shall be pleased to see a ～ in prices.物价下降将令我十分高兴。

cute/kjuːt/

*adj.*❶ quick and clever 聪明的；伶俐的：It was ～ of you to spot that.你能把那个挑出来真是精细很。❷（of children or young women）pretty（指儿童或年轻女性）娇小可爱的

cutlery/'kʌtləri/

*n.*knives, forks and spoons used for eating food（西餐的）刀叉餐具

cutter/'kʌtə(r)/

*n.*❶ a person or thing that cuts 切割者；切削工人；切削器 ❷ a tailor who measures and cuts out the cloth (服装的)裁剪师

cybercafe/ˌsaɪbəˈkʌfeɪ/
n. a cafe with computers on which customers can use the Internet, send emails, etc.网吧；网咖

cyberspace/ˌsaɪbəˈspeɪs/
n.the imagined world in which communication between computers and on the Internet is described as occurring 网络空间

cycle/ˈsaɪkl/
Ⅰ *n*.❶ a series of events taking place in a regularly repeated order 周期：A ～ of the sun takes a year.太阳运转一个周期需要一年的时间。❷ the short form for bicycle or motorcycle 自行车；摩托车 Ⅱ *v*.ride a bicycle 骑自行车

cyclic /ˈsaɪklɪk/
adj.recurring in cycles or series 循环的；

周期的：the ～ processes of nature 自然界的循环过程

cyclone/ˈsaɪkləʊn/
n.strong winds which move in a circle around a still centre 旋风

cylinder/ˈsɪlɪndə(r)/
n.❶a long round empty or solid body 圆筒；圆柱体 ❷a container like this 圆柱形器皿 ❸a part of a machine within which a piston moves backwards and forwards 气缸

cynic/ˈsɪnɪk/
n.a person who think that people always have bad or selfish reasons for what they do, even if they seem to be acting in a good and kind way 愤世嫉俗者 ‖ ～al *adj*.愤世嫉俗的；冷嘲热讽的 /～ism /ˈsɪnɪsɪzəm/ *n*. 愤世嫉俗

Dd

dab/dæb/

　Ⅰ *n.* ❶a slight or light touch 轻拍；轻触 ❷a small quantity, especially of a soft or liquid substance（尤指软物或液体的）少量，些许 Ⅱ *v.* (-bb-) ❶ touch lightly or gently, usually several times 轻敷，轻擦，轻抚 ❷cover with light quick strokes and usually carelessly and incompletely（马虎地）涂，抹

dabble/ˈdæbl/

　v. ❶work at or study sth. without serious intentions 涉足；浅尝：～ in politics 涉猎政治 ❷move one's hands, feet, etc. playfully around in water 玩水；戏水：She ～d her toes in the river.她把脚趾浸在河里玩水。

dad/dæd/

　*n.*one's father 爸爸：Take me to the fun fair,～.爸爸，带我去游乐园吧。

dad(d)y/ˈdædi/

　n.(used especially by or to children) one's father（尤用于儿语）爸爸,爹爹

daffodil/ˈdæfədɪl/

　*n.*a type of yellow flower of early spring 水仙花

daft/dɑːft/

　*adj.*❶foolish; stupid 傻的；蠢的：Don't be so ～! 别发傻了! ❷crazy 疯狂的：go ～ 发狂

dagger/ˈdæɡə(r)/

　*n.*a short knife used as a weapon 匕首；短剑：at ～s drawn 剑拔弩张/He's at ～ drawn with his colleagues.他与同事们水火不相容。

daily/ˈdeɪli/

　Ⅰ *adv.* & *adj.* happening, appearing every day (or every weekday) 每日（的）；天天地（的）：～ life 日常生活/～ bread 生活必需品/ It appears ～.它每天出版。

　Ⅱ *n.*a newspaper published every day 日报：*China Daily* 中国日报

dainty/ˈdeɪnti/

　adj. small, pretty and delicate in appearance 秀丽的；娇美的；小巧玲珑的：a ～ little girl 秀丽的小姑娘/a ～ piece of furniture 精致的家具/～ flowers 娇艳的花朵

dairy/ˈdeəri/

　*n.*❶a building where butter, cheese, etc. are made 牛奶场：The ～ produces milk, cream, butter and cheese.这牛奶场生产牛奶、奶油、黄油和乳酪。❷ a shop where milk, butter, eggs, etc. are sold 乳品店‖～ cattle *n.*奶牛/～ farm *n.*乳品场 /～maid *n.*牛奶场女工/～man *n.*奶品商/～ products *n.*奶制品

dais/ˈdeɪɪs/

　*n.*a raised platform in a room for a speaker, lecturer or important person 讲台

daisy/ˈdeɪzi/

　*n.*a very common small flower, which is white around a yellow centre 雏菊

dally/ˈdæli/

　*v.*be slow to do sth. or waste time 慢吞吞地做；浪费（时间）：Don't ～ about or we'll be late.不要拖拖拉拉了，否则我们会迟到的。/They dallied over their food for a while.他们吃饭时磨蹭了一会儿。

dam/dæm/

　Ⅰ *n.*a wall built to keep water at a high level 堤；坝；水闸：It's the greatest ～ in our country.这是我国最大的水坝。Ⅱ *v.* (-mm-) ❶ build a dam across; hold back by means of a dam 筑水坝；用水坝拦挡：They are ～ming up the river.他们正在河上筑水坝。/To ～ a river is to build a wall across the river.在河上筑坝就是拦河修一道墙。❷ control 控制；抑制：～

up one's feelings 抑制自己的感情

damage/ˈdæmɪdʒ/

Ⅰ *n*.❶physical harm caused loss of value or usefulness 损害；损害：The storm did great ~ to the crops.这场暴风雨对农作物造成极大损害。/The insurance company must pay for the ~ to my property.保险公司必须赔偿我的财产损失。❷(*pl.*) the money that a person is ordered by a court to pay to another person for causing damage 赔偿金：She accused him for libel,and the court ordered him to pay her ~s of ￡1,500.她控告他诽谤,法庭责令他付1500英镑赔偿费给她。Ⅱ *v*.harm or spoil sb.or sth.损害；损坏：A lot of houses were ~d by fire.许多房屋被火烧毁。

damn/dæm/

v.❶ criticize (sth.) severely 指摘；谴责：His book was ~ed by the critics.他的书受到批评家的指责。❷ used when swearing at sb.or sth.to show that you are angry (表示愤怒)该死,混账：Damn it! 该死的! /Damn you! 你这混蛋! ‖~able *adj*.可恨的/~ation *n*.惩罚

damp/dæmp/

adj.slightly wet；wet on the surface 潮湿的：~ clothes 湿衣服/~ air 湿气/a ~ room 潮湿的房间

dampen/ˈdæmpən/

v.❶ make sth.wet 弄湿；使潮湿：The rain hardly ~ed the ground.这场雨连地面也没有打湿。❷ reduce the strength of (feelings,especially of happiness or keenness) (感情、欢乐、兴致)减弱；使扫兴：It was an unpleasant event and it ~ed our spirits for a while.那是一次不愉快的事件,使我们好一阵子都感到扫兴。

damper/ˈdæmpə(r)/

n.❶an influence that makes people feel sad or discouraged 令人沮丧的东西：The accident put a ~ on our party.这件意外事故使我们的聚会大为扫兴。❷a metal plate, door, etc., that can be moved to control the amount of air that reaches a burning fire and make it burn more or less brightly (调节空气控制炉火燃烧的)风门,节气闸

dance/dɑːns/

Ⅰ *v*.move the feet and body in a way that matches the speed or movements of music 跳舞；跳(某种)舞：Will you ~ with me? 你愿与我共舞吗？/To ~ a waltz.跳华尔兹。Ⅱ *n*.❶an act of dancing 跳舞；舞蹈：Shall we do a little ~? 我们跳跳舞好吗？/The waltz is a beautiful ~.华尔兹是种很美的舞蹈。❷a social meeting or party for dancing 舞会：Did you go to the ~ yesterday evening? 你昨晚去参加舞会了吗？

dancer/ˈdɑːnsə(r)/

n.a person who dances 舞蹈家；舞蹈演员

dandelion/ˈdændɪlaɪən/

n. a small, yellow flower which grows wild,and whose seeds fly in the air 蒲公英

dandruff/ˈdændrəf/

n.small white pieces of dead skin in the hair of the head 头皮屑

danger/ˈdeɪndʒə(r)/

n.❶ the possibility of suffering loss or harm 危险：in time of great ~ 在危急的时刻/a ~ signal 危险信号/There is always ~ of floods in a storm.暴雨常有洪水的危险。/He put his life in ~ when he ran across the busy street.他横穿繁华的马路十分危险。❷ sth.or sb.that causes harm or injury 危险的事物(或人物)：It's the ~ to us.对我们来说那是件危险的事。/The current in the river is a ~ to swimmers.湍急的河水对游泳者是一种威胁。

dangerous/ˈdeɪndʒərəs/

adj.able or likely to cause danger；harmful 危险的；有害的：a ~ journey 一次危险的旅行/A lion is ~ animal.狮子是危险的动物。/It's ~ to smoke.抽烟有害健康。/It is ~ to touch the electric wires.摸电线是危险的。

dangle/ˈdæŋgl/

v. hang loosely 垂着；悬挂：He ~d his arm over the back of the chair.他的手臂垂在椅背上。

dappled/ˈdæpld/

adj.marked with cloudy roundish spots of colour,or of sun and shadow 有斑点的；

斑驳的;有花斑的:a ～ horse 花斑马/the ～ shade of a tree 斑驳的树荫

dare/deə(r)/

I *aux.v.* be brave enough to (后接不带 to 的不定式,主要用于疑问、否定或条件 句) 敢,胆敢:How ～ you say such a thing! 你竟敢说出这些话来! / David ～ climb the tree. 大卫敢爬那棵树。/ She daren't tell her sister that she has lost her money. 她不敢告诉姐姐她丢了钱。/No one ～ speak of it. 没人敢谈这事。 II *v.* ❶ be bold or brave enough to do 敢(于):～ to think,speak and act 敢想,敢说,敢做/I didn't ～ to move. 我不敢动。/ He ～s to speak to me like that. 他竟敢那样跟我说话。/Does she ～ to go out alone at night? 她晚上敢一个人出去吗? ❷ have the courage to face; stand bravely against 敢于面对;敢于尝试:He will ～ any danger. 他敢于冒任何危险。 ❸challenge 向……挑战:The other boys ～ d him to dive from the bridge. 别的男孩挑动他从桥上跳水。‖ I ～ say(插入语)我想;我敢说:I ～ say he will arrive tonight. 我想他今晚会到了。/ You don't know anything about that matter,I ～ say. 恐怕你不知道那件事。 III *n.* sth. bold that you do because another person asks you 果敢行为;挑战;激将:He tried to ride on a cow for a ～. 他想骑到牛背上以示自己胆大。

daring/'deərɪŋ/

adj. ❶courageous 勇敢的;大胆的:a ～ person 勇敢的人 ❷bold in a new way 创新的:a ～ new art form 一种别具一格的艺术形式

dark/dɑːk/

I *adj.* ❶ partly or completely without light 黑暗的;暗的:It was ～ outside. 外面很黑。 ❷ tending towards black 深色的:～ blue 深蓝色 II *n.* the absence of light;darkness 黑暗;黑夜:The little girl is afraid of the ～. 这小女孩害怕黑暗。‖ before ～ 天黑前/after ～ 天黑以后/in the ～ 秘密地;不知情 ‖ ～ness *n.* 黑暗,黑夜;暗处

darken/'dɑːkən/

v. ❶make or become dark or darker (使)

变暗;(使)变黑:The sky was ～ing rapidly. 天空很快变暗。❷ make or become angry or unhappy (使)忧郁;(使)生气;(使)不快

darling/'dɑːlɪŋ/

I *n.* dear or loved person 心爱的人;亲爱的人;宠儿:My ～! 亲爱的! 宝贝! / Darling,go now,or you will be late. 亲爱的,现在走吧,不然你会迟到的。 II *adj.* greatly loved;dear 亲爱的;心爱的;可爱的:my ～ daughter 亲爱的女儿/What a little ～ dog! 多么可爱的小狗!

darn/dɑːn/

I *v.* repair a hole in cloth by weaving thread 织补;缝补:～ socks 织补袜子 II *n.* a place repaired by darning 织补;补丁;织补处

dart/dɑːt/

I *v.* ❶ move suddenly and quickly;rush 飞奔;急冲:He ～ed across the road. 他飞奔过了马路。/She ～ed into the shop. 她冲进店中。❷ throw or send out suddenly and quickly 投掷;射出:She ～ed an angry look at him. 她向他投以愤怒的一瞥。/The snake ～ed out its tongue. 那蛇吐出舌头。 II *n.* a sudden quick movement 飞奔;急冲:With a ～ he escaped from the room. 他一下子冲出房间。

dash/dæʃ/

I *v.* rush quickly;run suddenly and quickly 猛掷;猛冲:I must ～ or I'll be late. 我得猛跑,否则就要迟到了。 II *n.* a short race run at full speed 猛跑;猛冲:We made a ～ through the rain to the bus. 我们冒雨向公共汽车猛跑过去。/Cavalry rode off at a ～. 骑兵队急驰而去。

dashboard/'dæʃˌbɔːrd/

n. the instrument board in a car (汽车的)仪表板

data/'deɪtə,'dɑːtə/

n. information,details,facts,or figures about sth. 资料;论据;数据:a ～ book 参考书/～ bank 资料库;数据库/The ～ we have collected are not enough. 我们收集的资料不够。/ Scientists collect all kinds of ～ in their experiments. 科学家从试验中取得各种数据。/ The ～ is all ready for examination.考试的资料都准备好了。

database/ˈdeɪtəbeɪs/

*n.*a large collection of data that is stored in a computer system in such a way that it can easily be found by a computer user,same as data bank (电脑系统的)数据库,资料库

date/deɪt/

Ⅰ *n.*❶ the time,shown by the day of the month and sometimes the year 日期:～ of birth 出生日期/What's the ～ today? 今天是几月几日? ❷ a meeting that you have planned with sb.约会:He has a ～ with her this evening.他和她今晚有约会。 Ⅱ *v.*❶ write the date on;determine the time when sth.took place 写上日期:Your letter is ～d 3 June.你信上写的日期是 6 月 3 日。 ❷ go on or have an appointment (with sb. or each other) (和某人)约会:I'll ～ her for the dance.我将约她去跳舞。 ‖ **be (go) out of** ～ 过时/**be (bring sth.) up to** ～ (使)适于时代潮流;(使)直到现在/**to** ～ 到目前为止/～ **back to** 可追溯到…… ‖ ～**d** *adj.*过时的/～**able** *adj.*可鉴定时代的/～ **less** *adj.*无限期的;历久不衰

daub/dɔːb/

*v.*❶ paint in an unskilled way 乱涂;乱画 ❷ cover (sth. or somewhere) with sth. dirty or sticky 弄脏;乱涂:He ～ed jam all over his face.他的脸上沾满了果酱。/The people ～ the walls of their huts with mud.这些人在他们茅屋的墙上涂满了泥。

daughter/ˈdɔːtə(r)/

*n.*a girl child 女儿:We have a ～ and a son.我们有一个女儿和一个儿子。 ‖ ～-**in-law** *n.*儿媳

daunt/dɔːnt/

*v.*make someone afraid or discouraged 使畏惧;使胆怯:She didn't seem ～ed by the challenge ahead.在挑战面前,她似乎一点也不胆怯。 ‖ ～**ing** *adj.*使人畏惧的

dawdle/ˈdɔːdl/

*v.*waste time;move or do sth. very slowly 闲荡;虚度时光:Don't ～ away your time.不要虚掷光阴。

dawn/dɔːn/

Ⅰ *n.*❶the time when the sun rises 破晓;黎明:from ～ till dark 从早到晚/the ～ of civilization 文明的曙光/I woke up at ～.我黎明时醒来。/Dawn is a beautiful time here in the mountains.这一带山区的黎明美极了。 ❷ the beginning 开端:The book is about the ～ of civilization.这本书讲的是文明的开端。 Ⅱ *v.*❶grow light in the east in the morning 破晓;黎明;(天)亮起来:Day ～s in the east.东方破晓。/The day was ～ing.天渐渐亮起来了。 ❷come out;appear 显露;出现:Look! It ～ed.看! 它出现啦。 ❸begin to be understood or realized 开始认识到,开始了解;明白过来:The truth at last ～ed on her.她终于明白了真相。/The meaning suddenly ～ed upon me.我突然明白了这含义。 ❹begin;start 开始:～ing consciousness 开始醒悟/A new age ～ed with the invention of the computer.随着计算机的发明,一个新的时代开始了。/A new age for mankind is ～ing.人类的新时代已经开始。

day/deɪ/

*n.*❶the period of twenty-four hours that begins at midnight 一日(天);一昼夜:There are seven ～s in a week.一个星期有七天。 ❷the time when it is light;the opposite of night 白天:They worked ～ and night.他们夜以继日地工作。 ❸time or period 时代;时期:in my school-days 在我的学生时代/There were no guns and cannons in those ～s.那些年代还没有枪炮。 ‖ **all** ～ (**long**) 整天/**before** ～ 天亮前/**by** ～ 白天里/**the** ～ **after tomorrow** 后天/**the** ～ **before yesterday** 前天/**the other** ～ 几天前/～ **after** ～ 日复一日/～ **and night** 夜以继日/～ **by** ～ 一天天地/～ **in (and) out**(～ **in**,～ **out**) 天天;不断地/**from** ～ **to** ～ 一天一天地/**in a few** ～**s time** 几天后;不久/**in the old** ～**s** 在过去/**one** ～ (过去)某一天;(将来)总有一天/**some** ～ 将来有一天/**these** ～**s** 现今/**this** ～ **week (today week)** 上(下)周今日;上(下)星期这一天 ‖ ～**boy**,～ **girl** *n.*走读生

daybreak/'deɪbreɪk/

*n.*dawn;the first light of day 黎明;破晓: at ～ 黎明时/The boy can't wake up at ～.孩子在拂晓时醒不了。

daydream/'deɪdriːm/

Ⅰ *n.* a pleasant dreamlike set of thoughts while one is awake 白日梦: There are people who are fond of spinning ～s.许多人喜欢做白日梦。/She stared out of window,lost in ～s.她凝视着窗外,想入非非。Ⅱ *v.* have daydreams 做白日梦: Instead of working hard he always ～s.他不努力工作,却总在做白日梦。

daylight/'deɪlaɪt/

*n.*❶ the natural light of the sun 日光:～ lamp 日光灯/during ～ 在日间;在白天/ in the ～ 在日光下/in the broad ～ 在光天化日之下/It looks quite more different by ～ than at night.这东西白天看起来与夜里大不相同。❷ dawn;daybreak 黎明;破晓:at ～ (before ～)天亮前

dayroom/'deɪruːm/

*n.*a public room for reading,writing, and amusement in schools, military camps, hospitals, etc. during the day (学校、军队、医院等的)日间阅览室,日间康乐室,日间休息室

daytime/'deɪtaɪm/

n. the time between sunrise and sunset when there is light 白天;白昼: You can't see them in the ～.白天你不能看到它们。/Some animals sleep in the caves in the ～.有些野兽白天在山洞里睡觉。

daze/deɪz/

*v.*make confused or unable to think clearly 使眩晕;使茫然: He was ～d by a blow on the head.他头部受到一记猛击,一时天旋地转。

dazzle/'dæzl/

Ⅰ *v.* ❶ make a person unable to see because the light is too strong 耀眼;炫目;眼花:The light of the car ～d me on the dark road.在黑暗的马路上汽车的灯光使我眼花缭乱。/The sun ～d me. 阳光晃我眼睛。❷ cause to feel stupid or make unable to think clearly 眩惑;迷惑 He is ～d at success.他被成功冲昏了头脑。/

The splendid hall ～d all of us.辉煌的大厅使我们惊异不止。Ⅱ*n.*brightness that stops you from seeing clearly 耀眼;炫目: the ～ of light 耀眼的光/The theatre was a ～ of bright lights.这家剧院光线强烈,使人眼花缭乱。

dead/ded/

Ⅰ *adj.* ❶ not living 死的:a ～ man 死人/ a ～ tree 死树/～ flowers 凋谢了的花 ❷ not active; not working; unable to feel anything 无生命的;不运行的;失去知觉的: Rocks and metals are ～ matter.岩石和金属都是无生命的物质。❸ without movement or activity 静止的;静寂的: The valley is ～ at the moment.此刻这个峡谷死一般寂静。❹ complete;exact 完全的;精确的:come to a ～ stop 完全停止/a ～ calm 死寂 Ⅱ*adv.*completely;exactly 完全地;彻底地:The sportsman was ～ tired after the race.赛跑之后那位运动员累极了。/I am ～ sure that you are right.我绝对相信你是对的。Ⅲ *n.*(**the** ～)those who have died 死者

deaden /'dedn/

*v.*make pain or noise,etc.weaker 减弱(痛苦,噪声等):The doctor gave him drugs to ～ the pain.医生给了他止痛药。

deadline /'dedlaɪn/

n. the latest time or date by which sth. should be completed 最后期限;截止日期

deadlock /'dedlɒk/

Ⅰ*n.*a situation in which no progress can be made 僵持;僵局 Ⅱ*v.*to cause sth. to come to a point or situation where no progress can be made 陷入僵局:The negotiations are ～ed.谈判陷入僵局。

deadly /'dedli/

Ⅰ *adj.*(deadlier, deadliest) ❶ likely to kill;causing or able to cause death (可能)致命的,致死的:a ～ poison 致命的毒药 ❷extremely accurate or effective 极准的;有效的:His aim is ～.他瞄得极准。Ⅱ*adv.*❶as if dead 死一般地:～ pale 死一般地苍白 ❷extremely 极其;非常:I'm ～ serious.我是非常严肃的。‖ **deadliness** *n.*致命;深仇大恨

deadweight /'deɪdweɪt/
n. ❶ the weight of an inert person or thing 自重,静重,静负载 ❷ a heavy or oppressive burden 重负;重载 ❸ the dead load 静负荷 ❹ the weight of a vehicle without a load 车辆的自重

deaf /def/
adj. ❶ unable to hear anything or hear very well 聋的:～ and dumb 又聋又哑的/He can't hear you—he's ～.他听不见你说话——他是聋人。/Because I was ～,I could not learn to speak.因为聋,我不能学说话。 ❷ unwilling to listen 不愿听的:be ～ to advice 不听劝告/He turned a ～ ear to our requests for help. 他对我们请求帮助置之不理。

deafen /'defn/
v. make so much noise that it is difficult or impossible to hear the sounds for sb. 使聋;震耳欲聋:We were almost ～ed by the cheers of the students.学生们的欢呼声震得我们的耳朵发聋。

deal[1] /diːl/
n. (**a good/great** ～) ❶ much;a lot 大量;很多:He spent a good (great) ～ of money.他花了许多钱。 ❷ to a considerable extent 很:be a good ～ better 好得多

deal[2] /diːl/
I *n.* an agreement or arrangement in business or politics,especially one that is to the advantage of both sides 协议;交易;成交:The company has made a ～ with a buyer from France.这家公司和法国来的一个买主做了一笔买卖。/Well,it's a ～.好了,就这样成交了。 II *v.* ❶ give out 分配:I am going to ～ (out) these apples.我来分这些苹果。 ❷ buy and sell 买卖;经营:The shop ～s in jewels.这个商店经营珠宝。 ❸ do business or trade with 与……交易:Which company are you ～ing with? 你在和哪一家公司做生意? ❹ solve or cope with (affairs)处理;对待:How would you ～ with this affair? 你将如何处理这件事? /He is a man not easy to ～ with.他是个不易对付的人。‖～ **in** 做买卖;经营/～ **with** 处理;对待;对付;和……打交道;论述;涉及;与……有关

dean /diːn/
n. ❶ president;the head of a university department 院长;系主任:Do you know who is our ～? 你知道谁是我们的院长吗? /The ～ of Foreign Language Department is Zhang Hua.外语系主任是张华。 ❷ a clergyman at the head of a cathedral chapter 教长;主持牧师

dear /dɪə(r)/
adj. ❶ loved or cherished by sb.亲爱的;可爱的:He is my ～est friend.他是我最要好的朋友。 ❷ lovable;sweet 可爱的,美好的:What a ～ little child! 多么可爱的小孩! ❸ used in speech as a way of addressing a person in a polite way (用于礼貌称呼)亲爱的 ❹ used as the polite introduction to a letter (用于信件的礼貌抬头)亲爱的,尊敬的:My Dear Mr. Albert 阿尔伯特先生(阁下) ❺ greatly valued 昂贵的:That's a ～ shop.那个商店的东西都很昂贵。/Everything is getting ～er. 什么都在涨价。‖～**ness** *n.*亲爱;昂贵

dearly /'dɪəli/
adv. ❶ very much 非常;很:I would ～ love to come.我非常乐意来。 ❷ at great cost 高价地;昂贵地:She paid ～ for her mistake.她因犯错误而付出了巨大的代价。

death /deθ/
n. dying;ending of life 死亡:Her mother's ～ gave her a heavy blow.母亲的去世给她很大的打击。‖ **put sb. to** ～ 将某人处死/**bore sb. to** ～ 使某人厌烦透了/**burn to** ～ 烧死/**starve to** ～ 饿死/**work to** ～ 工作累得要死 ‖ ～**less** *adj.*不朽的/～**like** *adj.*死一般的/～**ly** *adj.*& *adv.*死一般的(地)

debate /dɪ'beɪt/
I *n.* a formal argument or discussion of a question,e. g. at a public meeting or in parliament 辩论:There will be a long ～ in parliament before the new law is passed.新法令通过以前,议会要先作一次长的辩论。 II *v.* have a discussion about 辩论:I am debating with him about (upon) this question.我和他就这个问题辩论哩。‖**debatable** *adj.*值得予以争论的;主权有争执的/～**r** *n.*辩论队员;善于(好)争辩者

debase /dɪ'beɪs/
　　*v.*❶reduce the quality or value of sth. 贬低；降低：The love episodes ～ the dignity of the drama. 爱情插曲冲淡了该戏剧的庄重性。❷make sb. less respected 败坏名誉 ‖ ～ment *n.*降低；贬值

debilitate /dɪ'bɪlɪteɪt/
　　*v.*make sb. very weak and infirm 使虚弱；使不坚定：a debilitating illness 使人虚弱的疾病

debit/'debɪt/
　　Ⅰ *n.*a note of money owed or spent by a person, in a record of money received and spent（账簿的）借方　Ⅱ *v.* remove an amount of money from a bank account to 记入（账户）的借方：The bank has ～ed the money to my account.银行把这一笔钱记在我账户的借方。

debt/det/
　　*n.*❶the money that one must pay to sb. else 债；欠款：I can not pay the ～ at present.我目前无法还这个债。❷a feeling that sb. has to the person who has helped or been kind to the body 恩情：a ～ of gratitude 人情债 ‖ be in（out of）～ 欠（不欠）债/get into（out of）～ 欠下（偿还）债款 ‖ **National Debt** *n.*公债 ‖ ～or *n.*负债者

decade/'dekeɪd/
　　*n.*a period of ten years；a group or series of ten 十年；十年的期间；十个组成的一组（或一系列）：the last ～ of the 19th century 19 世纪的最后 10 年/the first ～ of the month 上旬/a ～ of suggestions 十条建议/Prices have risen steadily during the past ～.在过去的十年间，物价一直在上涨。

decadence/'dekədəns/
　　*n.*falling from one level to a lower level 衰落：the ～ in literature and art 文学艺术的衰落 ‖ **decadent** *adj.*衰落的；颓废的

decay/dɪ'keɪ/
　　Ⅰ *v.*(cause to) go bad （使）腐烂；（使）腐败：The fruit ～ed in the damp weather. 这种水果在潮湿的天气里腐烂了。Ⅱ *n.* the destroyed parts of teeth 蛀牙；龋齿

deceit/dɪ'siːt/

*n.*❶ an act of deceiving；a dishonest act 欺诈；欺骗；欺骗人的行为：She is incapable of ～.她是绝不会欺骗的。❷ a dishonest trick 谎言；骗术：He got them to hand over all their money by a wicked ～.他用恶劣的骗术让他们把所有的钱都交给了他。

deceitful /dɪ'siːtful/
　　adj. deceiving people 欺骗的；欺诈的：Such an act would have been ～ and irresponsible.这样的行为本该是欺诈而不负责任的。‖ ～ly *adv.*欺骗地；虚伪地/～ness *n.*不诚实；欺诈

deceive/dɪ'siːv/
　　*v.*make sb.believe what is not true 欺骗：Don't try to ～ me, I know the truth. 别欺骗我，我知道真相。‖ **deception** *n.*欺骗/～r *n.*骗子

decelerate/diː'seləreɪt/
　　v. become or make sth. become slower （使）减速；（使）减缓

December/dɪ'sembə(r)/
　　*n.*the 12th month of the year 十二月：December is the last month in a year. 十二月是一年中最后一个月。

decent/'diːsnt/
　　*adj.*❶right and suitable；fit and proper；respectable 正派的；适当的；得体的：He behaved in a ～ manner.他举止得体。❷ satisfactory；fairly good 满意的；不错的：The poor girl never had a ～ clothes to wear.这可怜的小姑娘从未有过像样的衣服。❸kind 宽厚的；待人好的：It was very ～ of you to help the old lady.你真好，帮助了这位老太太。‖ ～ly *adv.*相当不错地；像样地/**decency** *n.*行为正当；端庄有礼

deceptive /dɪ'septɪv/
　　*adj.*misleading；giving a false impression 骗人的；误导的：Appearances can be ～.外表有可能是靠不住的。‖ ～ly *adv.*骗人地；误导地

decibel/'desɪbel/
　　*n.*a unit for the measurement of the loudness of sounds 分贝（测定音量的单位）

decide/dɪ'saɪd/
　　*v.*❶ reach a decision；make up one's mind

D

决定；决意：He has ～d to become a teacher.他决意做教师。❷ settle；give a judgement 解决；判断：We can ～ the question by experiment.我们用实验能解决这个问题。/The judge ～d the case.法官判决了这个案子。‖～ **against** 决定反对(不)……；做不利于……的决定‖ **in favour of** 决定支持……；做有利于……的决定/～ **on** 决定要……

decided /dɪˈsaɪdɪd/
adj. ❶ noticeable；definite 明显的；确定的：a ～ improvement 显著的进步 ❷ having clear and definite opinions；determined 观点鲜明的；坚定的；坚决的 ‖ ～**ly** *adv*.显然；肯定地；果断地；坚决地

decimal /ˈdesɪml/
Ⅰ *adj*.based on counting in tens or tenths 十进制的 Ⅱ *n*.a number expressed as a decimal fraction(e.g.0.7865) 小数(例如：0.7865)

decipher /dɪˈsaɪfə(r)/
v. ❶ find the meaning of a message written in a code or cipher 译解(密码) ❷ find the meaning of anything difficult to understand 解开(疑团)

decision /dɪˈsɪʒn/
n. ❶ a conclusion or resolution reached after consideration 决定；结论：come to a ～ 决定下来/ She could not make a ～ about the dresses.她决定不了要哪件礼服。/Under Freddie's leadership they came to a ～.在弗雷迪的领导下，他们做出了决定。❷ the ability to decide quickly 决断能力；果断：a man of ～ 果断的人/That man lacks ～.那人优柔寡断。/ She is a woman of ～.她是个果断的女人。❸ the action or process of deciding sth.or of resolving a question 决定；解决

decisive /dɪˈsaɪsɪv/
adj. ❶ showing determination and firmness；resolute 果断的；坚决的；有决断力的：You'll have to be more ～ if you want to do well in business.如果你想在商业上取得成就，你就必须更果断。❷ leading to a clear result；putting an end to a doubt 决定性的：They won the war after a ～ battle.一场决战后，他们取得了战争的胜利。❸ unquestionable 毫无疑问的；

明确的：a ～ advantage 明显的优势

deck /dek/
n.a floor or platform of a ship or bus 甲板；(公共汽车)层：Shall we go up on ～? 我们到甲板上去好吧？/the top of a double-～ bus 双层公共汽车的上层 ‖ **on ～** 在眼前；即将到来 ‖ ～ **chair** *n*.户外用帆布椅/～ **passenger** *n*.舱面乘客

declaim /dɪˈkleɪm/
v. ❶ make a speech；read aloud 演说；朗诵：He is ～ing.他正在演讲。/He ～s his poetry.他朗诵自己创作的诗。❷ forcefully protest against or criticize sth. 抨击；申斥：The play was bad；the newspapers all ～ed it.这出戏很糟，各报都加以抨击。

declamation /ˌdeklɪˈmeɪʃn/
n.the act or art of declaiming 慷慨激昂的演说；雄辩(术)

declaration /ˌdekləˈreɪʃn/
n. ❶ the act of making a formal statement；a formal statement representing sth.宣言；公告；声明：These events led to the ～ of war.这些事件导致了宣战。❷ a statement giving official information 申报(单)：Please make a written ～ of all the goods you bought abroad.请书面申报你在国外购买的全部物品。

declarative /dɪˈklærətɪv/
adj. making a statement or having the form of a statement 陈述的，叙述的：a ～ sentence 陈述句

declare /dɪˈkleə(r)/
v. ❶ make sth.known publicly and clearly 宣布；公告：I ～d this meeting closed.我宣告会议结束。❷ say sth. openly or firmly 郑重声称：The accused man ～d that he was not guilty.被告声称他是无罪的。‖ ～ **against** 表示反对/～ **for** 表示赞成/～ **war against**(on) 对……宣战

declared /dɪˈkleəd/
adj.openly admitted as 公开表示的；公开宣称的：a ～ supporter of the government 公开宣称支持政府的人/It's their ～ intention to increase taxes.他们公开宣称有增加税收的意图。

declination /ˌdeklɪˈneɪʃn/

n. ❶ the angle of a compass needle, east or west, from true north（指南针磁针的）偏差, 磁偏角：a ～ of 15 degrees 15 度的磁偏角 ❷ a formal refusal（正式的）谢绝

decline/dɪˈklaɪn/

Ⅰ*v.* ❶ slope downwards 向下倾斜：The road ～s sharply at this point. 此地道路形成陡坡。❷ go from a better to a worse position, or from higher to lower 缩小, 下降；衰退；恶化：Unemployment ～d to 2 percent. 失业率下降为 2%。/ His strength slowly ～d. 他的体力渐衰。/He spent his declining years in the country. 他在乡间度过晚年。❸ refuse a request or offer, usually politely；express unwillingness 辞谢：He ～d an invitation to dinner. 他辞谢了吃饭的邀请。Ⅱ*n.* a period or process of declining；the movement to a lower or worse position 衰落 ‖ **on the ～** 在衰落（衰退）中

declivity/dɪˈklɪvəti/

n. a downward surface or slope 倾斜面；斜坡

decode/ˌdiːˈkəʊd/

v. find the meaning of a message written in code 译解（密码）

decompose/ˌdiːkəmˈpəʊz/

v. (cause to) go bad or rotten and undergo chemical changes（使）腐烂；（使）变质；（使）分解 ‖ **decomposition**/ˌdiːkɒmpəˈzɪʃn/ *n.* 分解

decompress/ˌdiːkəmˈpres/

v. ❶ expand compressed data to the normal size 使（计算机压缩数据）解压 ❷ subject a diver to decompression 使（潜水员）减压

decontaminate/ˌdiːkənˈtæmɪneɪt/

v. remove poison, gas, radioactivity or other harmful substances from a place or thing 使消毒；消除（有害物质）

decorate/ˈdekəreɪt/

v. provide with sth. that is added because it is attractive or beautiful(not because it is necessary) 装饰：People like to ～ the house with holly at Christmas in western countries. 在西方国家, 人们在圣诞节喜欢用冬青装饰房子。‖ **decoration** /ˌdekəˈreɪʃn/ *n.* 装饰；装饰品 / **decorative** /ˈdekərətɪv/ *adj.* 适于作装饰的；装饰性的 / **decorator** *n.* 装饰工

decorous/ˈdekərəs/

adj. properly serious in manner according to the customs of society 礼貌得体的；端庄的：～ behaviour 彬彬有礼的举止

decoy/ˈdiːkɔɪ/

Ⅰ*n.* ❶ an artificial or real bird used to make other birds come near enough to be shot or caught 囮子；人造囮子 ❷ anything used in this way to lead a person into a certain position 圈套, 陷阱, 诱惑 Ⅱ*v.* ❶ shoot or catch a bird in this way 诱捕, 诱杀（鸟类）❷ lead a person into danger in this way 诱骗；诱入圈套

decrease/dɪˈkriːs/

Ⅰ*v.* become less in size, amount, strength, or quality；reduce 减少；降低；减轻：Decrease the dose of medicine as you feel better. 如果感觉好些, 就减少药的剂量。/His interest in it ～s gradually. 他在这方面的兴趣逐步减退。Ⅱ*n.* the process of reducing sth. in size, amount, strength, or quality；the amount reduced 减少；减少的量：There has been a ～ in our imports this years. 今年我们的进口减少了。/The ～ in sales was almost 20 percent. 销售额下降了差不多 20%。‖ **on the ～** 在减少中

decree/dɪˈkriː/

Ⅰ*n.* ❶ an official command or decision 命令；法令：issue a ～ 下令 ❷ a judgement 判决：the final ～ 最后判决 Ⅱ*v.* order sth. officially, with the force of law 颁布（法令等）：The governor ～d a day of mourning. 总督下令举行一天的哀悼。

decry/dɪˈkraɪ/

v. speak disapprovingly of；say bad things about（especially sth. dangerous to the public）非难；谴责；诋毁；贬抑：～ the violence of modern films 谴责现代电影中的暴力镜头

dedicate/ˈdedɪkeɪt/

v. give a lot of time and effort to a particular task or purpose 奉献；贡献：He ～d to

D

his motherland. 他为国捐躯。/He ~d his life to fighting corruption.他一生献身于和贪污腐败做斗争。‖ **dedication** /ˌdedɪˈkeɪʃn/n.奉献；贡献

deduce/dɪˈdjuːs/
*v.*determine or decide (sth.) from general principle 推论；推断：What do you ~ from these facts? 你从这些事实中能推引出什么结论？

deduct/dɪˈdʌkt/
*v.*take away (an amount, a part) from a total；subtract 扣除；减去：The cost of electricity consumption was ~ed from your salary.电费已从你的工资中扣除。‖ **~ible** *adj.*可扣除的

deduction/dɪˈdʌkʃn/
n. ❶ an amount that is deducted from sth.；the act or action of deducting 扣除额；扣除：She earned less money because of ~s from her wages.她赚得的钱少了，因为她的工资被扣除了一些。❷ the inference of particular instances by reference to a general law 演绎推理：Her ~ that he was dead that moment was correct.她关于他那时已经死亡的推论是正确的。

deductive/dɪˈdʌktɪv/
*adj.*reasoning from a general idea or set of facts to a particular idea or facts 推理的；推断的；演绎的：the ~ process 推理过程/~ reasoning 演绎推理

deed/diːd/
n. ❶ an action that is performed intentionally 行动；行为：Deeds are better than words.行动胜于言论。❷ action or performance 行动；行为：a heroic ~ 英雄事迹/do a good ~ every day 每天做一件好事 ❸ a written or printed agreement to show the ownership or rights 契约；契据

deem/diːm/
*v.*consider；have the opinion；judge 认为；视为；断定为：We would ~ it an honour if the minister agreed to meet us.假如部长同意接见我们，我们将引以为荣。They ~ed that he was no longer capable of managing his own affairs.他们认为他没有能力再处理自己的事务。

deep/diːp/
Ⅰ *adj.* ❶ going far down；reaching far from the surface or the outside edge 深的：The valley was ~ and there was a stream at the bottom. 山谷很深，谷底有一条小溪。/The river there is ten meters ~.该处河水深 10 米。❷ strong in colour (颜色)深的，浓的：~ red 深红色 ❸ strong in voice (声音)低沉的：~ voices 低沉的嗓音 ❹ (of sleep) profound (睡眠)深沉的：The boy is in a ~ sleep. 这个男孩正在酣睡。❺ felt strongly (感受)强烈的：~ sadness 深切的悲痛 Ⅱ *adv.*far down or in 深深地：He pushed his stick ~ into the mud.他把手杖深深地插入泥中。‖ **~-rooted** *adj.*根深蒂固的/**~-seated** *adj.*根源很深的 ‖ **~ly** *adv.*深深地；深入地

deepen/ˈdiːpən/
*v.*make or become deep or deeper 加深；深化：~ a colour 加深颜色/~ the well 把井挖深/~ the contradictions 加深矛盾/~ the red in the picture 加深画中的红色 /The economic crisis of the country is ~ing.该国的经济危机正在加深。/ Dusk is ~ing.暮色渐浓。

deer/dɪə(r)/
n. a four-legged animal which lives in woods 鹿：The ~ has two stomachs.鹿有两个胃。

deface/dɪˈfeɪs/
v. damage or spoil the appearance of 损坏……的外观：He ~d the library book by writing in it.他乱涂乱写污损了图书馆的图书。

defame/dɪˈfeɪm/
v. damage the good name of, usually by unfair means 破坏名誉；诽谤；中伤：The article is an attempt to ~ an honest man. 这篇文章旨在破坏一个诚实人的名誉。

default/dɪˈfɔːlt/
Ⅰ *v.*fail to pay a loan, perform a duty, or appear in a law court when required 拖欠；不履行；违约；未到庭 Ⅱ *n.* failure to pay a loan, perform a duty or appear in a law court 拖欠；违约；未到庭：judgement by ~ 缺席判决

defeat /dɪˈfiːt/

Ⅰ *v.* win a victory over; overcome 打败: Our team has ~ed our opponents. 我们球队打败了对手队。 Ⅱ *n.* losing a game, fight, war, etc. 击败; 失败: The uprising ended in ~. 这次起义以失败告终。

defect[1] /dɪˈfekt, ˈdiːfekt/

n. a fault 缺点; 瑕疵: This was his fatal ~. 这是他的致命缺点。

defect[2] /dɪˈfekt, ˈdiːfekt/

v. desert a political party, group, or country, especially in order to join an opposing one 背叛; 变节: The officer ~ed to another country. 这官员叛逃到了另一国家。 ‖ ~ion *n.* 叛变; 变节 / ~or *n.* 背叛者; 变节者

defective /dɪˈfektɪv/

adj. ❶ not working normally; faulty 有缺陷的; 有毛病的: ~ machinery 有缺陷的机器 ❷ (of a person) well below the average, especially in mind (指人) 心智不健全的, 智力低于正常标准的 ❸ lacking one or more of the usual forms of grammar 不完全变化的: "Must" and "can" are ~ verbs. must 和 can 是不完全变化动词。

defence(-se) /dɪˈfens/

n. ❶ the action of fighting against attack 防御; 保卫; 防护: national ~ 国防 / ~ works 防御工事 / air ~ 防空 / fight in ~ of our country 为保卫祖国而战 ❷ sth. that keeps away dangerous things or people 防卫物; 防御工事: coast ~ 海防 / The ~s of the city are strong. 这个城市的设防很牢固。 / The walls of York were strong ~s. 约克郡的城墙曾是坚固的防御工事。 ❸ arguments used in favour of an accused person; a lawyer acting for such a person (被告的) 答辩; 辩方: The lawyer produced a clever ~ for his client. 律师为他的当事人做出了巧妙的答辩。

defend /dɪˈfend/

v. ❶ protect sb. or sth. from harm or damage 保护; 保卫; 捍卫: The father tried to ~ boy from harm. 父亲尽力保护儿子使之免受伤害。 / A wrongly accused man has the right to ~ his reputation. 受到错误指责的人有权保护他的名誉。 ❷ speak or write in support of 为……辩护: The lawyer is ~ing him. 律师正在为他辩护。 ‖ ~ against (from) 保护……免受……

defensive /dɪˈfensɪv/

Ⅰ *adj.* used or intended to defend 防御用的; 防卫的; 守势的: ~ works 防御工事 / a ~ force 防卫力量 / a ~ treaty 防御条约 Ⅱ *n.* (on the ~) expecting or resisting attack 处于防御状态

defer /dɪˈfɜː(r)/

v. wait until later before doing sth. 推迟; 使延期: I have decided to ~ the meeting until next week. 我决定把会议延期到下周举行。

defiance /dɪˈfaɪəns/

n. a defiant behaviour or manner; open disobedience 违抗; 蔑视: His ~ of the law cost him his life. 公然违抗法律使他丧生。 / He went swimming in the sea in ~ of the warning sign. 他不顾警告标志到海里游泳。 ‖ in ~ of 不顾; 不服从 / bid ~ to 向……挑战 / set sth. at ~ 蔑视 (某物) ‖ defiant *adj.* 违抗的; 倨傲的 / defiantly *adv.* 不服地; 倨傲地

deficiency /dɪˈfɪʃnsi/

n. the quality of having none or not enough; a lack 缺乏, 不足; 短缺: Vitamin ~ can lead to illness. 身体缺少维生素就会生病。

deficient /dɪˈfɪʃnt/

adj. ❶ having none or not enough (of); lacking (in); inadequate 不足的; 缺乏的: a mentally ~ person 低能的人 / He is ~ in courage. 他缺乏勇气。 ❷ having some defects 有缺陷的

deficit /ˈdefɪsɪt/

n. an excess of debts over income; the amount of this excess 赤字; 亏空款额: Tax was low and state spending was high, resulting in a budget ~. 税率低而政府支出大, 结果出现预算赤字。

defile /dɪˈfaɪl/

v. destroy the pureness of sth. 弄脏, 污损: The animals ~d the water. 动物把水弄脏了。 / disgusting video films that ~ the minds of the young 污染青少年思想的不良录像影片

D

define /dɪˈfaɪn/

　v. ❶ state or show the meaning of words or phrases clearly 下定义；释义：A dictionary ～s words. 辞典给单词释义。❷ explain the exact qualities, limits, duties, etc. of sth. 限定；明确；规定：The constitution ～s the fundamental rights and duties of citizens. 宪法对公民的基本权利与义务有详细规定。/The mountain was clearly ～d against the eastern sky. 那山在东方天空的衬托下显得轮廓分明。‖ **definable** *adj.* 可阐释明白的；可下定义的

definite /ˈdefɪnət/

　adj. clearly known, seen, or stated; without any uncertainty 明确的；确切的；肯定的：I want a ～ answer. 我需要明确的答复。/Solids have ～ volume and shape. 固体具有一定的体积与形状。‖ ～ **article** *n.* 定冠词 ‖ ～**ly** *adv.* 明确地；干脆地 /**definitive** /dɪˈfɪnətɪv/ *adj.* 最后的；确切的；不容置疑的

definition /ˌdefɪˈnɪʃn/

　n. the statement of the meaning of a word 定义；释义：give a ～ 下定义 /You will notice that a dictionary often gives several ～s for one word. 你会注意到一本字典里对每个词常给出几个解释。

deflate /dɪˈfleɪt/

　v. let air or gas escape from a balloon, tyre, etc. 给（轮胎、气球等）排气，放气，泄气

deflation /diːˈfleɪʃn/

　n. ❶ the act of deflating or process of being deflated 抽气；放气；泄气；收缩 ❷ a decrease in the amount of money being used in a country, especially as a result of government policy, leading to less demand for goods, less industrial activities, and usually intended or likely to cause lower prices 通货紧缩

deflationary /diːˈfleɪʃnəri/

　adj. producing deflation of money or prices 通货紧缩的；物价降低的：～ policies 通货紧缩的政策

deflect /dɪˈflekt/

　v. cause sth. to turn away from a direction 使转向；使偏离：The ball hit the goalkeeper's boot and was ～ed into the goal. 球碰到守门员的靴子，折射进入球门。

deform /dɪˈfɔːm/

　v. change or spoil the shape or form of sth. 使变形；使成畸形：a structure 使结构变形

deformation /ˌdiːfɔːˈmeɪʃn/

　n. ❶ the process or result of changing and spoiling the normal shape of sth. 变形；畸形：Solid rock undergoing slow ～. 坚硬的岩石慢慢变形。❷ a change in the normal shape of sth. as a result of injury or illness 破相；残废：a ～ of the spine 脊柱的畸变

deformity /dɪˈfɔːmɪti/

　n. (*pl.*-ies) a deformed part of the body （身体的）畸形：children born with deformities 天生畸形的儿童

defraud /dɪˈfrɔːd/

　v. trick; cheat (a person) 诈骗：People who do not pay their taxes are ～ing the government. 不缴纳税收的人是在诈骗政府。/He ～ed me of the money. 他诈骗了我的钱。

defray /dɪˈfreɪ/

　v. pay the cost or expenses of sth.; supply the money needed for sth. 支付；支付费用

defrost /ˌdiːˈfrɒst/

　v. remove ice from; unfreeze 使去冰；使除霜；使解冻

deft /deft/

　adj. light, quick and clever (especially in using the hands in a job which needs skill) 熟练的，敏捷的，灵巧的

defuse /ˌdiːˈfjuːz/

　v. ❶ remove the fuse from (sth. explosive) so as to prevent an explosion 拆除（爆炸物）的引信：～ a bomb 拆除炸弹的引信 ❷ make less dangerous or harmful 减少……的危险（危害）性；缓和……的不安：～ a dangerous situation 缓和危险的局面

defy /dɪˈfaɪ/

　v. ❶ resist openly 违抗，蔑视，对……满不在乎：The soldier was determined to ～ his superior. 这士兵决心和他的上司对抗。/If you ～ the law, you may find yourself in prison.如果你蔑视法律,你就有可能坐牢。❷ be ready to fight against;challenge sb.to do sth.激,挑动(某人做他不愿或不会做的事): He defied his opponents to equal his record.他刺激其对手去平他的纪录。

degenerate/dɪˈdʒenəreɪt/

Ⅰ *v.* become worse in physical,mental or moral qualities 变坏;退化;堕落: Her health is degenerating rapidly.她的健康正迅速恶化。Ⅱ *adj.* having become worse in character,quality,etc. in comparison with a former state 变质的;堕落的;退化的:～ age 退步的时代

degrade/dɪˈɡreɪd/

*v.*❶ bring down in the opinion of others, in self-respect,or in behaviour 使堕落;使卑微:You ～ yourself when you tell a lie. 说谎会降低自己的身份。❷ reduce in rank or status 降级;降职:He was ～d for disobeying orders.他因不服从命令而被降级。

degree/dɪˈɡriː/

*n.*❶a step or stage in a scale or process 程度;阶段:She has a high ～ of intelligence.她很有智慧。❷ a unit of measurement for temperature or angle(温度、角度的单位)度:The thermometer rose ten ～s.温度计升高了 10 度。/A right angle has 90 ～s.直角为 90 度。❸a title given by a university 学位:the ～ of Master of Arts 文学硕士学位 ‖ by ～s 逐步地/in a … ～ (in … ～s) 在……程度上/to a … ～ 到……程度/to a high(highest) ～ 非常;极

dehydrate/diːˈhaɪdreɪt/

v. remove water from;dry 使脱水;使干燥:His body had ～d dangerously with the heat.他因受酷热身体脱水,情况危险。

deign/deɪn/

v. lower oneself to act or give sth. to people one considers unimportant 屈尊;惠顾:Now that she is rich and famous, she doesn't ～ to visit her former friends.既然她现在又有钱又有名气,便再也不愿屈尊去看望从前的朋友了。

dejected/dɪˈdʒektɪd/

adj. unhappy and upset 沮丧的

delay/dɪˈleɪ/

Ⅰ *v.*❶cause sb.to be slow or late 使延迟;使搁置:Heavy rain ～ed us.大雨使我们延误了时间。/The accident ～ed the train for twenty minutes.交通事故使火车晚点 20 分钟。❷ put off or postpone 推迟:We decided to ～ our holiday until the weather is better.我们决定把假期推迟到天气好些的时候。❸ move or take action slowly,especially on purpose 拖延;耽搁:I'm sorry that I've ～ed so long.对不起,我耽搁这么久。Ⅱ *n.*❶ the act of delaying or the state of being delayed 耽搁;延迟:You must start working without ～.你们必须马上开始工作。❷the time during which sth. or sb. is delayed 延迟的时间:a ～ of half an hour 延迟半小时 ‖ without ～ 立即;毫不迟延地

delegate

Ⅰ /ˈdelɪɡɪt/*n.* a person to whom sth. is delegated 代表:Each country sent three ～s to the meeting.每个国家派出三名代表参加会议。Ⅱ /ˈdelɪɡeɪt/ *v.* appoint as a representative 委派……为代表:I have been ～d to attend the meeting.我被委派作为参加会议的代表。

delegation /ˌdelɪˈɡeɪʃən/

*n.*❶a group of delegates 代表团:a ～ of teachers 教师代表团 ❷the act or process of delegating or being delegated 代表;授权

delete/dɪˈliːt/

v. strike or take out sth.written or printed 消去;删除:Several words have been ～d from his article by the teacher.老师删去了他论文中的几个字。‖ deletion *n.* 删除;删掉的词句

deliberate/dɪˈlɪbərət/

Ⅰ *adj.*❶ carefully considered;thoroughly planned;done on purpose;intentional 经过仔细考虑的;故意的;有意的:The government is taking ～ action to lower prices.政府正在采取经过仔细考虑的行动来降低物价。❷ done or acting in a careful and unhurried way 小心谨慎的:He walked with ～ steps.他走路小心翼翼。Ⅱ *v.* consider sth. carefully 仔细考

虑：He ～d his decision for several days. 他对其决定仔细考虑了好几天。‖ ～ly adv.有意识地

deliberation /dɪˌlɪbəˈreɪʃən/

n.❶long and careful consideration or discussion 深思，考虑；研究，审议：After much ～ they arrived at a compromise.再三考虑之后他们达成了妥协。❷careful movement or thought 缓慢；从容；审慎：He signed his name on the paper with ～. 他审慎地在文件上签上了自己的名字。

delicacy /ˈdelɪkəsi/

n.❶ the state or the quality of being delicate 柔和；精致；优美；娇弱；娇嫩；微妙；精密；灵敏；敏感：the ～ of colours 颜色的优美 /the ～ of health 身体的娇弱 / the ～ of hearing 听觉的敏锐 /a matter of great ～ 需要谨慎处理的事情 ❷ sth. pleasing to eat that is considered rare or costly 美味；好菜：the delicacies of the seasons 时菜 /That food is a great ～.那种食品堪称上等美食。

delicate /ˈdelɪkət/

adj.❶ fine；tender 精细的；娇嫩的：the ～ skin of a baby 婴儿娇嫩的皮肤/jewelry of ～ workmanship 手工精细的珠宝/ a long gown of ～ silk 柔软的丝长袍 ❷ easily broken or becoming ill 易损坏的；易生病的：A spider's web is very ～.蜘蛛网纤细易损。/a ～-looking woman 弱不禁风的女人

delicious /dɪˈlɪʃəs/

adj.pleasing in taste or smell；very satisfying 美味的；芬芳的；好吃的：What a ～ fruit！多好吃的水果！/The soup is ～. 汤味道很美。

delight /dɪˈlaɪt/

Ⅰ v.❶ please greatly 使高兴；使愉快：Her singing ～ed everybody.她唱的歌令人快乐。❷take great pleasure in doing sth. 喜欢；以……为乐：He ～s to tease little boys and girls.他喜欢逗小孩。Ⅱ n. great pleasure；joy 高兴；乐趣：I have read your letter with ～.我高兴地读了你的信。/The couple got a great deal of ～ from their children.孩子们给这对夫妇带来巨大的乐趣。/She took great ～ in making other people suffer.她以让别人

难受为乐。‖ take ～ in 乐于 ‖ ～ed adj.高兴的

delightful /dɪˈlaɪtfʊl/

adj.very pleasant 使人快乐的；令人愉快的：a ～ book 令人身心愉悦的书 ‖ ～ly adv.欣然地；快乐地

delimit /diːˈlɪmɪt/

v.draw the farthest point or edge 定界线；划界：The first chapter ～s his area of research.第一章讲述的范围是他所研究的领域。

delinquency /dɪˈlɪŋkwənsi/

n.wrong-doing；neglect of duty 犯罪；失职：juvenile ～ 少年犯罪

delinquent /dɪˈlɪŋkwənt/

adj.& n.(a person) doing wrong or failing to perform a duty 做错事的(人)；失职的(人)：～ behaviour 失职行为；犯罪行为

deliver /dɪˈlɪvə(r)/

v.❶bring hand over 送交；递送：We can ～ goods to your door.我们可以送货上门。/They ～ed an ultimatum to Japan. 他们向日本递交了最后通牒。❷ give a speech，talk，etc. or other official statement 发表；宣布；做(演讲，报告，陈述)；提出：He ～ed an important report at the meeting.他在会上做了一个重要的报告。❸give birth to a bady 分娩；生孩子 ‖ ～ance n.释放

delivery /dɪˈlɪvəri/

n.❶the action of delivering letters parcels or ordered goods 递送；交付；交货：～ of mail 送信 /How many deliveries are there in your town every day？你们的城里每天送几次信？❷ the manner of speaking 演讲技巧；口才：a poor ～ 讲得不好 /His sermon was good，but his ～ was poor.他的布道内容很好，可是口才很差。❸the process of giving birth to a child 分娩；出生：difficult ～ 难产

deliveryman /dɪˈlɪvrɪmən/

n.a man who delivers goods to people who have bought or ordered them，usually locally 送货员

delta /ˈdeltə/

n.an area of land where the mouth of a

river spreads out into several branches（河口数条支流形成的）三角洲

delude/dɪˈluːd/

*v.*make sb. believe sth. that is not true 欺骗；哄骗：Don't ～ yourself longer. 不要再自己骗自己了。/He ～d the children into following him.他哄骗得孩子们跟着他走。‖ delusion *n.*欺骗；迷惑/delusive *adj.*骗人的

deluge/ˈdeljuːdʒ/

*n.*❶ a great flood of water；a heavy rainstorm 大水；大暴雨 ❷ anything coming in great quantity like a flood of water 洪水般涌来的事物：a ～ of questions 大量的问题

deluxe/dəˈlʌks, dəˈluks/

*adj.*of very good quality and more expensive than usual 豪华的；华丽的：a ～ hotel 一家豪华旅馆/The ～ model costs a lot more.这种豪华型号要贵得多。

demand/dɪˈmɑːnd/

Ⅰ *v.*❶ ask for sth. firmly 要求：He ～ed an explanation.他要求得到一个解释。❷ need urgently 急需：This work ～s your attention without delay.这件工作急需你立即去做。Ⅱ *n.*the act of demanding；the claim and desire of people for particular goods or services 要求；需要：They refused to grant our ～s.他们拒绝应允我们的要求。/The supply exceeds the ～.供过于求。‖ in ～有需要；有需求/make ～s on (of)向某人提出要求；需要花费(某物)

demanding/dɪˈmɑːndɪŋ/

*adj.*needing a lot of attention and effort 很费心的；很费力的：A new baby and a new job can be equally ～.照顾新生儿和从事新工作一样费心费力。

demean/dɪˈmiːn/

*v.*lower oneself in dignity, reputation, etc. 降低身份；使贬低：He ～ed himself by doing such dirty and badly-paid work.他做这种又脏报酬又低的工作真是自贬身份。

demeanour/dɪˈmiːnə(r)/

*n.*the way of behaving 举止；行为：His ～ was very strange.他的举止很奇怪。

demented/dɪˈmentɪd/

*adj.*mad；violent and strange in behaviour 疯狂的；行为凶暴古怪的

demerit /dɪˈmerɪt/

*n.*a fault or defect 过失；缺点；短处：the merits and ～s of these proposals 这些建议的优缺点

democracy/dɪˈmɒkrəsi/

*n.*❶a system of government by the people, or by elected representatives of the people 民主政治；民主政体：What are the principles of ～? 民主政治的原则有哪些？❷ a country governed by its people or their representatives 民主国家：A true ～ allows free speech.真正的民主国家允许言论自由。❸ social equality and the right to take part in decision-making 民主精神：The teacher's ～ made him liked by all his pupils.这位教师的民主精神使他得到全体学生的爱戴。

democrat /ˈdeməkræt/

*n.*a person who believes in or works for democracy 民主主义者；民主人士

democratic/ˌdeməˈkrætɪk/

*adj.*❶of or favouring democracy 民主(主义)的：～ ideals 民主主义理想/a ～ country 民主国家 ❷believing in or practising the principle of equality 崇尚(或实施)平等原则的；主张民主的：The company is run on ～ lines, and all the staff are involved in making decisions.公司推行民主管理的方法，所有职工都参与决策。

democratize/dɪˈmɒkrətaɪz/

*v.*make democratic or more democratic 使民主化：～ the union's decision-making processes 使工会的决策程序民主化

demography/dɪˈmɒgrəfi/

*n.*the statistical study of population 人口统计学 ‖ demographer *n.*人口统计学家；人口学家/demographic /ˌdeməˈgræfɪk/ *adj.*人口结构的；人口统计的

demolish/dɪˈmɒlɪʃ/

v. ❶ destroy (especially a large structure)；pull or tear down 拆毁(尤指大建筑物)；摧毁；推翻：They're going to ～ that old factory.他们准备拆毁那家旧工厂。❷ prove an idea, concept or theory completely wrong 推翻（观点，理念，理论）：We've ~ed all her arguments. 我们已驳倒了她的全部论点。❸eat up 吃光：~ two big platefuls of chicken 吃光两大盘鸡肉

demon/'di:mən/

n. ❶ an evil spirit 恶魔；恶鬼；鬼：That child is a little ~.那孩子是个小捣蛋鬼。❷ a person with excellent strength, skill, etc.精力过人的人；技艺出众的人；高手：a ~ for work 工作不知疲倦的人/~ card-player 玩纸牌的高手

demonic/dɪ'mɒnɪk/

*adj.*by a demon or being a demon 受魔鬼影响的；魔鬼的：~ possession 魔鬼附身/a ~ spirit 恶鬼

demonstrable/dɪ'mɒnstrəbl/

*adj.*that can be clearly proved or shown 可论证的；可证明的；可表明的：a ~ fact 可加以证明的事实 ‖ **demonstrably** *adv.* 可论证地；明确地：But that idea is demonstrably false! 但是那个想法显然是错误的!

demonstrate/'demənstreɪt/

v. ❶ prove or make clear (a fact), especially by reasoning or providing examples 表明；证明：Recent events ~ the need for a change in policy.最近的事件表明，政策上需要有所改变。/How would you ~ that the world is round? 你如何证明世界是圆的？❷ take part in a public show of strong feelings or opinions, often with marching, big signs, etc.示威；游行示威：The workers ~d for better working conditions.工人们示威要求改善工作条件

demonstration /ˌdemənsˈtreɪʃən/

n. ❶ the showing of existence or truth of sth. by giving proof or evidence 证明；证实：a ~ of the connection between the several sets of figures 论证这几组数字间的联系 ❷ the outward showing of feelings 感情流露：~s of affection 爱意的表达 ❸ a practical exhibition and explanation of how sth. works or is performed 示范；演示：a ~ of the computer's functions 计算机各种功能的演示 ❹ a public meeting or march protesting against sth. or expressing views on a political issue 示

威集会；示威游行

demonstrative /dɪ'mɒnstrətɪv/

adj. ❶showing or proving sth. 示范的；演示的；证明的；证实的 ❷ expressing your feelings openly 公开表露感情的；感情外露的：a ~ greeting 热情的问候 ‖ ~ly *adv.*论证地

demoralize/dɪ'mɒrəlaɪz/

v. take away sb.'s courage, confidence, self-control, etc. 使无斗志；使意气消沉；使泄气：After losing three important battles, the army had become ~d.在三次重要战役都败北之后，这个部队士气十分低落。

demote/ˌdi:ˈməut/

*v.*make sb. to a lower rank or position 使降级，使降职：The soldier was ~d for failing to obey orders.这个士兵因不服从命令而被降级。

demure/dɪ'mɜ:(r)/

adj.(especially of young girls) quiet and rather afraid to talk to other people（尤指少女）娴静的，拘谨的，矜持的

den/den/

n. ❶ a place where a wild animal such as a lion or tiger lives（狮、虎等）兽穴 ❷ a place where a lion or tiger is kept at a zoo（动物园内狮、虎等的）兽笼 ❸ a room where one can be comfortable or work at one's hobbies 私人工作室；书房

denary/'di:nəri/

*adj.*of the number ten; having ten as the basis of reckoning; decimal 十的；以十作为计算基础的；十倍的，十进的

denial/dɪ'naɪəl/

n. ❶the action of declaring sth. to be untrue 否认 ❷a statement that a thing is not true 否认陈述，否认声明 ❸a refusal of a request or wish 拒绝

denim/'denɪm/

n. ❶a strong type of cotton cloth 斜纹粗棉布 ❷(*pl.*) trousers or overalls made of denim（蓝色斜纹粗布做成的）工装裤

denizen /'denɪzn/

*n.*a person, animal, or plant living or often present in a particular place 居民；居住

D

者：Monkeys are ~s of the jungle.猴子是在丛林里生活的动物。

denomination/dɪˌnɒmɪˈneɪʃn/

n. ❶ any branch of the Christian churches（基督教）教派，宗派：The service was attended by people of different ~s.不同教派的人们参加了这个礼拜仪式。❷ a type of unit measuring height，weight，money，etc.（长度、重量、货币等的）单位：Metres and centimetres are different ~s. 米和厘米是不同的长度单位。

denominator/dɪˈnɒmɪneɪtə(r)/

n. the number below the line in a vulgar fraction，for example 6 in 5/6 分母

denote/dɪˈnəʊt/

v. be a name of；mean 代表；表示：The word "tiger" ~s a certain kind of beast. "Tiger"一词代表一种兽类动物。/Dark clouds ~ a coming storm.乌云翻滚表示暴雨来临。‖ **denotation** *n.*表示；代表

denounce/dɪˈnaʊns/

v. ❶ publicly declare sth.to be wrong 指责；谴责；抨击：The newspapers ~d the new taxes.报界纷纷谴责新税收。❷ tell the police，etc. about a crime committed by someone 告发；揭发：He ~d Mr. Jones to the police. 他向警方告发了琼斯先生。

dense/dens/

adj. ❶ crowded together in great numbers 密集的：The crowd was so ~ that we could hardly move. 人群密集，我们几乎无法走动。❷（of liquids or vapour）not easily seen through（液体或气体）浓的；稠的：~ mist 浓雾 ‖ ~**ly** *adv.*密集地；稠密地

density/ˈdensəti/

n. ❶ the quality of being dense 浓密；稠密；密集：the ~ of a forest 森林的茂密 ❷ the relation of weight to volume 密度（质量与体积的关系）：Iron has a greater ~ than wood.铁比木头密度大。

dent/dent/

Ⅰ *n.*a small hollow place in the surface of sth. which is the result of pressure or of being hit 凹痕，压痕：A bullet made a ~ in the soldier's helmet.子弹在这个士兵

的头盔上打了个凹痕。Ⅱ *v.* make a hollow in（使）生凹坑：A taxi drove into my car and ~ed it.出租车把我的汽车撞了个痕。

dental/ˈdentl/

adj. of or related to the teeth 牙齿的：~ decay 蛀牙/a ~ surgeon 牙医

dentist/ˈdentɪst/

n. a person whose job is to take care of people's teeth 牙科医生

denture/ˈdentʃə(r)/

n.（*pl.*）a plate（fitted on the gums）of artificial teeth 一副牙齿；（尤指）一副假牙：a set of ~s 一副假牙

denude/dɪˈnjuːd/

v. ❶ make bare；strip（sth.）of its clothing or covering 使赤裸，使光秃；剥光：Most trees are ~d of their leaves in winter.多数树木在冬季都掉光了叶子。❷ lay（a rock or land）bare by removing what lies above，especially by erosion 使岩石裸露，使剥蚀：Land rapidly ~d by rain and river.受雨水和河流迅速剥蚀的土地。

deny/dɪˈnaɪ/

v. ❶ say that sth. is not true 否认；否定：He denied that he had attacked the old woman. 他否认曾袭击过这个老太太。/He said that I had stolen his bicycle，but I denied it.他说我偷了他的自行车，可是我不承认。❷ refuse a request 拒绝：He denies his wife nothing.他对他妻子有求必应。/ He denied my offer.他拒绝了我的提议。/ I could not ~ her request. I would sing a couple of songs.我无法拒绝她的要求，总是唱一两首歌给她听。

depart/dɪˈpɑːt/

v. ❶ leave，typically to start a journey 离开；起程；出发：The plane ~ed at 12 o'clock.飞机于 12 点起飞。/The ship ~s at noon. 这艘船在中午开出。❷ leave one's job or position 离职 ‖ ~ **from** 转移；离开

departed/dɪˈpɑːtɪd/

*adj.*dead 逝去的；死了的：the ~ 死者/our ~ heroes 我们的烈士

department/dɪˈpɑːtmənt/

*n.*any of the important divisions or branches of a government, business, college, etc. 部门；部；系；室：You mean that you'd like a job in a government ～? 你的意思是你喜欢政府部门的工作吗？/He is the dean of the Chinese Department. 他是中文系系主任。/the Department of Defense 国防部/the State Department（美国）国务院 ‖ ～ store n.百货公司

departure/dɪˈpɑːtʃə(r)/
n. ❶ the action of leaving and going to another place 离开；出发；起程：take one's ～ 出发/the time of ～ 出发时间 /his ～ from home 他的离家出走 /I haven't heard from her since her ～. 自从她离去后，我没有收到她的来信。 ❷ a deviation from an accepted or traditional course of action or thought 变更；背离：a new ～ for a folk singer 民歌手的新起点/His new work is a ～ from anything he wrote before.他的新作品与他以前写的都不同。

depend/dɪˈpend/
v. ❶ rely；trust 依靠；依赖：Children ～ on their parents for food and clothing. 儿童的衣食靠其父母。/Health ～s on good food, fresh air and enough sleep. 健康依赖于良好的食物、新鲜空气和足够的睡眠。 ❷ trust（usually a person）；have confidence in 信赖；指靠：The price ～s on quality. 价格视质量而定。 ‖ ～ on（upon）依靠；信赖/it（all）～s；that（all）～s 要看情况而定：I want to leave early but it ～s.我想早早离开，但还得看情况而定。

dependable/dɪˈpendəbl/
adj. able to be trusted；reliable 可信赖的；可靠的：She won't forget —she's very ～.她不会忘的——她非常可靠。/a ～ source of income 靠得住的经济来源

dependant/dɪˈpendənt/
n. a person who depends on someone else for food, clothing, money, etc. 受赡养者；受扶养的家属：Please state your name, age, and the number of ～s you have.请登记你的姓名、年龄以及供养的家属人数。

dependence/dɪˈpendəns/
n. ❶ the state of being dependent；inability to exist or operate without the help or support of sb. or sth. else 依赖；依靠：We need to reduce our ～ on oil as a source of energy.我们必须减少对石油作为能源的依赖。 ❷ trust；reliance 信任；信赖：I always place a lot of ～ on what she says. 我始终很信任她所说的话。 ❸ the need to have certain drugs regularly, especially dangerous ones；addiction 对药物（尤指毒品）的依赖；毒瘾

dependent/dɪˈpendənt/
adj. ❶ needing the help or support of sb. or sth. else 依靠的；依赖的：a child ～ on parents 依赖父母的孩子 /The country is heavily ～ on foreign aid. 这个国家大量依靠外国的援助。 ❷ that will be decided by 决定于……的；取决于……的：The size of the crowd is largely ～ on the weather.人数的多少主要取决于天气情况。

depict/dɪˈpɪkt/
v. represent or show in or as if in a picture 描写；描绘：The novel ～s the horrors of war. 这小说描写战争的恐怖。/The painting ～s the beautiful scenery of France in early spring.这幅画描绘了法国早春时节的美丽景色。

deplete/dɪˈpliːt/
v. use sth. by a large amount so that little or none is left 用尽；耗尽：Our supplies of food have been much ～d.我们的食品供给已用完了大部分。

deplorable/dɪˈplɔːrəbl/
adj. shockingly bad or regrettable 极差的，糟透的：His acting in the movie was ～.他在这部电影里的演技糟透了。 ‖ **deplorably** *adv.* 悲惨地；可叹地

deplore/dɪˈplɔː/
v. feel or express strong disapproval of sth. 公开谴责；强烈反对：We ～ racism in any form.我们谴责任何形式的种族歧视。

deploy/dɪˈplɔɪ/
v. make soldiers move into a line ready for a battle 部署（兵力）

depopulate/diːˈpɒpjuleɪt/
v. make or become less in population or number 减少……的人口；使人口减少：a

D

country ～d by disease 由于疾病而人口减少的国家

deport /dɪˈpɔːt/
v. expel（an unwanted person）from a country 驱逐出境；放逐：The spy was ～ed.这个间谍被驱逐出境。‖ ～ation n.（被）驱逐出境；（被）放逐

depose /dɪˈpəʊz/
v. make a king or other ruler leave his position 废黜（国王等统治者）：The army ～d the king and set up a republic. 军队废黜国王，建立了共和国。

deposit /dɪˈpɒzɪt/
Ⅰ v. ❶ put or set down；place 放置；搁：He ～ed his books on the desk.他把书放在桌子上。❷ put sth. into a bank, store or entrust for safe keeping 存放：He ～ed two hundred dollars in his savings account.他在他的储蓄户头上存了200美元。Ⅱ n. ❶ a sum of money stored in a bank account 存款：a current ～ 活期存款/a fixed ～ 定期存款/～ account 存款账户 ❷ a sum of money that is given as the first part of a larger payment 定金：The shopkeeper promises to keep the goods for me if I paid（left）a ～.店主答应，如果我付一点定金，他就可把那些货物给我留着。‖ ～or n.存款者；存户/～ary /dɪˈpɒzɪtəri/ n.保管人；储藏室

depot /ˈdepəʊ/
n. ❶ a storehouse；a place where soldier's goods are kept and new soldiers are trained 仓库；军需库；兵站：a service ～ 后勤仓库；修理站；服务站 /a supply ～ 给养仓库；给养站 ❷ a railway or bus station〈美〉火车站；公共汽车站

deprave /dɪˈpreɪv/
v. make bad or wicked in behaviour 使堕落：Do you believe that these films are likely to ～ young people? 你认为这些影片会使年轻人堕落吗？

depreciate /dɪˈpriːʃɪeɪt/
v. ❶ make or become less in value（使）贬值；跌价：Shares in this company have ～d.这家公司的股票已贬值了。/The price of TV sets has greatly ～d.电视机的价格大跌。❷ say that sth. has little value 贬

低；轻视：He ～s the value of exercise.他轻视锻炼的价值。‖ depreciation n. 贬值；轻视/depreciatory adj.贬值的；轻视的

depress /dɪˈpres/
v. ❶ press down 压下：Depress this button in case of fire.遇火灾时请按下此按钮。❷ cause to feel sad and without hope；discourage 使沮丧；使灰心：Rainy weather always ～es her.阴雨天总令她情绪低沉。/The bad news ～ed me all day.听到这个坏消息，我整天很沮丧。❸ cause（prices）to be lower；make less active 使跌价；使萧条：A rise in oil prices ～ed the car market.油价上涨导致汽车市场不景气。

depressed /dɪˈprest/
adj. ❶（of a person）in a state of general unhappiness or despondency（指人）沮丧的，消沉的 ❷（of a place or economic activity）suffering the damaging effects of a lack of demand or employment（指地方或经济活动）萧条的，衰退的：～ areas 经济萧条地区

depressing /dɪˈpresɪŋ/
adj. making you feel very sad and without enthusiasm 令人抑郁的；令人沮丧的；令人消沉的：Looking for a job these days can be very ～.如今求职有时会令人非常沮丧。‖ ～ly adv.沮丧地

depression /dɪˈpreʃn/
n. ❶ the state of sadness and low spirits 消沉；沮丧；抑郁；情绪低落：She was in a state of ～.她处于沮丧之中。❷ a hollow in the surface of sth. especially the ground 洼地；低凹地：The rain collected in several ～s on the ground.地面上一些低洼处积着雨水。❸ a period when business is depressed 萧条；不景气：economic ～ 经济萧条

deprivation /ˌdeprɪˈveɪʃən/
n. ❶ the lack of the basic benefits that most people have, such as a home and enough food 严重匮乏；赤贫 ❷ the lack of sth. that you need 丧失；缺乏：sleep ～ 睡眠缺乏

D

deprive/dɪˈpraɪv/

v. take away from; prevent from using or having sth. 剥夺；夺去：The prisoners are ~d of their rights as citizens. 囚犯被剥夺了公民权。/She has been ~d of sight. 她已经失明。

depth/depθ/

n. ❶ the degree of deepness; the distance from the top down 深；深度：What is the ~ of the well? 这口井有多深？/Water was found at a ~ of 40 feet. 人们在 40 英尺深处发现了水。❷ complexity and profundity of thought (思想的) 深度：This book shows the author's ~ of learning. 这本书显示了作者学问的深度。‖ **beyond (out of) one's ~** 没法理解；一窍不通/**in ~** 深入的(地)

deputation/ˌdepjuˈteɪʃn/

n. a group of people given the right to act or speak for others 代表团：A ~ from the railwaymen's union has gone to have talks with the Prime Minister. 铁路工会的代表团已前去和首相会谈。

depute/dɪˈpjuːt/

v. appoint (someone) to do sth. instead of oneself 指定(某人)为代表；使(某人)做代理人：I've been ~d to take charge of the shop while she's away at the conference. 她外出开会时，指派我负责管理这个商店。

deputy/ˈdepjuti/

n. a person appointed to act on behalf of or represent another 代理人；代表；副手：~ chairman 副主席/a ~ to the National People's Congress 全国人民代表大会代表/He is a ~ for Nanjing. 他是南京的代表。

derelict/ˈderəlɪkt/

adj. left or abandoned as unwanted or useless 荒废的；被弃置的：There were many ~ houses in the streets of the city. 该市的街道上有许多荒废的房屋。

derivative/dɪˈrɪvətɪv/

Ⅰ *adj*. derived from a source, not original 模仿的；缺乏独创性的：Their music is rather ~. 他们的音乐没有独创性。Ⅱ *n*. ❶ a thing that is derived from another 派生物；衍生物 ❷ a quantity measuring the

rate of change of another 导数

derive/dɪˈraɪv/

v. ❶ get; obtain 得到；获得：He ~s much pleasure from books. 他从书本中获得许多乐趣。❷ come from or originate 来源于；由……派生而来：Thousands of English words ~ from Latin. 成千上万的英语单词来源于拉丁语。‖ **derivation** /ˌderɪˈveɪʃn/ *n*. 获得；来源

descend/dɪˈsend/

v. come, fall, or sink from a higher to a lower level; go down 下来(去)；下落；下沉；使下去：The elevator ~ed slowly to the ground floor. 电梯慢慢地下到一层楼。/He ~ed the stairs. 他下楼了。‖ ~ **(be ~ed) from** 是……的后代；由……传下来的/~ **on (upon)** 突然来到；突袭/~ **to** 堕落到(做某事)；落到……的地步 ‖ ~**ed** *adj*. 后代的

descendant /dɪˈsend(ə)nt/

n. a person who is descended from another 子孙；后裔；后代

descent/dɪˈsent/

n. ❶ an action of coming or going down 下降；下来：the ~ of the balloons 气球的下落 /a gradual ~ 缓缓的下坡 /We began the ~ of the hill. 我们开始下山。❷ family origins 宗世血统；出身：of English ~ 祖籍英国 /an American of Chinese ~ 华裔美国人 /He is of good ~. 他出身名门。❸ a sudden attack 袭击：the invaders' ~ on the town 入侵者对该城镇的突然袭击

describe/dɪˈskraɪb/

v. ❶ give an account of what sth. or sb. is like 描述；叙述：She ~d the man she had seen. 她描述她看见过的那个人的模样。/Words can not ~ my joy. 言语不能形容我的快乐。❷ mark out or draw 标示；作图：~ a triangle 作三角图/The maths teacher ~d a circle on the blackboard with chalk. 数学教师在黑板上用粉笔画了个圈。

description/dɪˈskrɪpʃn/

n. a statement or account that describes sth. or sb. 描述；描写：The scenery was beautiful beyond ~. 这风景美得难以形

容。‖ **descriptive** *adj.*描写的;描述性的

desert¹ /'dezət/
*n.*a large sandy piece of land where there is very little rain and not much plant life 沙漠;不毛之地:the Sahara Desert 撒哈拉沙漠/～ island 荒岛

desert² /dɪ'zɜːt/
*v.*❶leave sb,without help or support 遗弃;抛弃:He ～ed his wife and went abroad.他遗弃了妻子,出国去了。/His family has ～ed him.他的家人与他断绝了关系。❷leave military service without permission 撤离(部队);开小差:The soldier ～ed.那士兵开了小差。‖ **～ed** *adj.*空的;无人居住的/～**er** *n.*逃兵;逃离工作岗位的人/～**ion** *n.*背弃;遗弃;逃亡

deserve /dɪ'zɜːv/
*v.*have earned by one's actions or character;be worthy of 应当得到;值得:She ～d the reward.她值得这样的奖赏。/Bad acts ～ punishment.恶行应当受到惩罚。‖ ～ **well** (**ill**) **of** 得好(恶)报/(**be**) **deserving of** 值得;应受到

deservedly /dɪ'zɜːvɪdli/
*adv.*according to what is deserved 应得地;恰如其分地;理所当然地:The actress is ～ popular.这位女演员为大众喜爱是理所当然的。

design /dɪ'zaɪn/
Ⅰ *n.*❶ a drawing or plan of sth.which is to be made 设计;方案;设计图:His ～ was exhibited in the show.他的设计在展览会上展出。/a ～ for a new aeroplane 一种新型飞机的设计 ❷ a general arrangement or planning of a picture,book,building,machine,etc.(图画、书籍、建筑机器等的)设计:This is a machine of excellent ～.这是一部设计得很好的机器。❸ a decorative pattern 装饰图案:This piece of cloth has a new ～.这段布图案新颖。❹ a plan or an intention 打算;意图 Ⅱ *v.*❶ make designs for 设计;画设计图:The engineer ～ed a new car.工程师设计了一种新车。❷ do or plan sth.with a specific purpose or intention in mind 专为某种目的(或意图)做:This dictionary was ～ed mainly for high school students.这本辞典主要是供中学生使用的。

‖～**ing** *n.*设计术/～**edly** *adv.*故意地;存心地

designate /'dezɪɡneɪt,'dezɪɡnət/
*v.*❶point out or call by a special name 标示;标出:The marks on his shoulder ～d the rank of an army officer.他的肩章标示其军阶。/Churches are ～d on the map by crosses.教堂在地图上用十字号标出。❷choose or name for a particular job or purpose 指定;指派;任命:He ～d Smith as his successor.他指定史密斯为他的继承人。‖ **designation** *n.*指定;任命

designer /dɪ'zaɪnə(r)/
*n.*a person whose job is to decide how things such as clothes,furniture,tools,etc.will look or work by making drawings,plans or patterns 设计者;构思者:a jewellery ～ 珠宝设计师

desirable /dɪ'zaɪrəbl/
adj.(of a thing or an object)worth having,doing,or desiring (指事物或物体)合乎需要的;称心如意的,令人渴望的:a ～ job 称心如意的工作

desire /dɪ'zaɪə(r)/
Ⅰ *v.*wish earnestly;long for strongly 渴望;很想要:I ～ pure love.我渴望得到纯洁的爱情。/Give her what she ～d.她想要什么就给她什么吧。Ⅱ *n.*a strong wish 强烈愿望;欲望;期望:He had little ～ to sleep.他很少睡意。/Their ～ for money has increased.他们的金钱欲望增大了。‖ **desirous** /dɪ'zaɪərəs/ *adj.*渴求的;极希望的

desk /desk/
*n.*a worktable,often with space inside for keeping books,pens,etc.书桌;写字台;办公桌:sit at the ～ 在写东西;在办公/There are some books on the big ～ in the classroom.教室里的讲桌上摆着一些书。

desolate /'desələt/
Ⅰ *adj.*❶empty and without people in 荒无人烟的;荒芜的;荒凉的:a ～ land 荒地 ❷ lonely and unhappy 孤寂的;凄凉的:She led a ～ life.她过着孤独寂寞的生活。Ⅱ *v.*make sb.feel lonely or sad 使感到凄凉;使悲伤:She was ～d to hear that

he was dead.听说他已去世,她感到忧伤。‖ ～ly adv.荒凉地/desolation n.荒废;孤寂

despair/dɪˈspeə(r)/

Ⅰ v.lose all hope or confidence 绝望;灰心丧气:Don't ～, things will get better soon.不要灰心,事情会很快好起来的。Ⅱ n.complete loss of hope or confidence 绝望;沮丧:He was filled with ～ when he read the examination questions.他一看到考试题目就感到绝望了。/I'm in ～.我已绝望。‖ the ～ of 令……失望的人(物)‖ ～ing adj.绝望的;导致绝望的

desperate/ˈdespərət/

adj.❶ ready for any wild act and not caring about danger,especially because of loss of hope;reckless(因绝望而)不顾一切后果的;亡命的:The ～ man jumped out of the window of the burning house.那个已不顾死活的人从起火的房屋窗口跳了出来。/a ～ criminal 亡命之徒 ❷(of a situation) extremely difficult and dangerous(情况)严重的;危急的:The state of affairs in that country is getting ～.该国的情况越来越严重。‖ ～ly adv.拼命地/desperation n.绝望;走投无路

despise/dɪˈspaɪz/

v.look down upon;consider worthless 轻视;蔑视;瞧不起:She ～s cheap clothes and will only wear the best.她对廉价衣服不屑一顾,只想穿最好的衣服。/They ～ lies and liars.他们鄙视谎言和说谎的人。

despite/dɪˈspaɪt/

prep.in spite of 不管;不顾:Despite the bad weather we enjoyed our holiday.尽管天气不好,我们仍然愉快地度过了我们的假期。/We lost ～ our efforts.尽管做了努力,我们还是输了。

despoil/dɪˈspɔɪl/

v.plunder or rob a place 掠夺;蹂躏(某个地方)

despondent/dɪˈspɒndənt/

adj.completely without hope and courage;feeling that no improvement is possible 灰心丧气的;意气消沉的:Mrs.Green is ～ about her husband's health.格林夫人对她丈夫的健康已经灰心了。‖ despondency n.失望;意气消沉/～ly adv.灰心丧气地

despot/ˈdespɒt/

n.a person who rules unjustly and cruelly 暴君;专制君主:an enlightened ～ 开明的君主

dessert/dɪˈzɜːt/

n.fruit or sweet food eaten at the end of a meal(餐末吃的)甜点

destination/ˌdestɪˈneɪʃn/

n.the place you are going to or sth.is sent to 目的地;终点;指定地点:The parcel was sent to the wrong ～.包裹被投错了地址。/It took us all day to reach our ～.我们用了整天的时间才到达目的地。

destiny/ˈdestɪni/

n.what is determined to happen;fate 命中注定的事;命运:decide the ～ of a lifetime 决定一生的命运 /It was his ～ to die in a foreign country.他命中注定客死异国。/Nobody knows his own ～.没有人知道自己的命运。

destroy/dɪˈstrɔɪ/

v.break to pieces;put an end to 摧毁;毁坏;毁灭:The fire ～ed the city.火灾摧毁了这座城市。/All his hopes were ～ed.他的一切希望都破灭了。‖ ～er n.破坏者

destruction/dɪˈstrʌkʃn/

n.the act or state of destroying or being destroyed 破坏;毁灭;被毁:The ～ of the railway was a big loss to the country.铁路被毁是这个国家的巨大损失。/The ～ by the earthquake was serious.地震造成的破坏很严重。‖ destructive adj.有破坏性的;带来破坏的

detach/dɪˈtætʃ/

v.take apart;separate 解开;分开;拆下:They ～ed a coach from the train.他们将一节车厢拆离开火车。‖ ～able adj.可分离的;可取下的/～edly adv.超然地

detached/dɪˈtætʃt/

adj.❶(said about a house) not joined to another(房子)单独的;独立的;不连接的 ❷free from emotion or bias;objective 客观的;公正的;无偏见的:Journalists need to remain ～.记者需要保持客观的

立场。

detachment /dɪˈtætʃmənt/

n. ❶freedom from emotion or bias 公正；客观；独立 ❷a group of soldiers, ships, etc. sent away from a larger group for a special duty 分遣队；支队；特遣小分队 ❸the act of detaching or being detached 分开；分离

detail /ˈdiːteɪl/

Ⅰ *n.* an individual feature, fact, or item 细节；详情：I like your plan, now tell me all the ~s. 我喜欢你的计划，请告诉我其全部细节。/Don't omit a single ~. 不要漏掉一点细节。/Please have me all the ~s of the accident. 请你告诉我这事故的详情。Ⅱ *v.* describe fully；give full details of 详细描述；详细说明：He ~ed my new duties to me. 他向我详细说明我的新职责。/a ~ed description 详细的描写 ‖ **go into ~(s)** 提供细节/**in ~** 详细地

detain /dɪˈteɪn/

v. keep back；keep under arrest 留住（不让走）；耽搁；拘留：The bad weather ~ed us for several days. 恶劣的天气耽搁了我们好几天。/The police ~ed the man to make further inquiries. 警察把这人拘留起来以做进一步侦讯。‖ **~ee** *n.* 拘留犯/**detention** /dɪˈtenʃn/ *n.* 拘留；扣押

detect /dɪˈtekt/

v. discover or investigate 查出；觉察出；侦查：The driver ~ed a fault in his car. 司机找出了车子的一个毛病。/Can you ~ an escape of gas in my kitchen? 你能觉察出我厨房里有煤气味吗？‖ **~able** *adj.* 可查明的；可觉察出的/**~ion** *n.* 查出；侦察/**~or** *n.* 检测器；探测器

detective /dɪˈtektɪv/

Ⅰ *n.* a special policeman that finds out who has done a crime 侦探：hire a private ~ 雇用一名私家侦探 Ⅱ *adj.* denoting a particular rank of policeman 侦探的；刑侦的：a ~ story 侦探小说

detention /dɪˈtenʃən/

n. ❶the action of detaining or being detained 拘留；扣押；监禁 ❷being kept in school after hours as a punishment （作为一种处罚的）课后留校

deter /dɪˈtɜː(r)/

v. (-rr-) prevent；discourage 阻止；阻拦：The bad weather ~red us from making the long journey. 恶劣的气候使我们无法长途旅行。

detergent /dɪˈtɜːdʒənt/

n. a substance other than soap, used for cleaning clothes or plates, cups, etc. 洗涤剂；洗衣粉

deteriorate /dɪˈtɪəriəreɪt/

v. make or become worse （使）变坏；恶化：The old man's health has ~d since the operation. 手术后老人的健康情况恶化了。‖ **deterioration** *n.* 恶化

determination /dɪˌtɜːmɪˈneɪʃn/

n. ❶firmness or purpose 决定；决心：come to a ~ 下决心/a man of ~ 有决断力的人/They have the ~ of winning the match. 他们有决心打赢这场比赛。❷the act of finding out or calculating 计算；测定：~ of the gold in a sample of rock 岩石样品中含金量的测定

determine /dɪˈtɜːmɪn/

v. ❶firmly decide；make up one's mind 下定决心；决意：He ~d to learn Greek. 他决心学希腊文。❷be the decisive factor in 造成；起决定性作用：Content ~s form. 内容决定形式。❸discover the facts about sth.；calculate sth. exactly 查明；测定 ‖ **determinant** *n.* 决定因素/**~d** *adj.* 决意的；下定决心的

detest /dɪˈtest/

v. hate sb. or sth. strongly 憎恶；极不喜欢：I ~ people who deceive and tell lies. 我憎恶欺骗和说谎话的人。‖ **~able** *adj.* 令人憎恶的/**~ation** *n.* 憎恶；嫌恶；讨厌；讨厌的东西

detour /ˈdiːtʊə(r)/

n. a road which is used when the usual road cannot be used；a journey made on such a road 弯路，迂回道；绕道，迂回：They had to make a ~ round the floods. 他们为避开洪水得绕道而行。

detract /dɪˈtrækt/

v. take sth. of value away from；cause to be or seem less valuable 去掉；减损（价值、功绩、名誉等）：It ~s nothing from his merit.这并未减损他的功绩。/The ugly frame ～s from the beauty of the picture.难看的画框损坏了这幅画的美。‖ ～**ion** *n*.减损;诽谤/～**or** *n*.诽谤者;诬蔑者

detriment/'detrɪmənt/

n.harm or damage 损害:My lack of education was a serious ～ to my career.我未受过正规教育严重妨碍了我的事业。‖ **to the ～ of** 有害于/**without ～ to** 无损(害)于 ‖ ～**al** *adj*.有损(害)的

devaluation/ˌdiːvæljuˈeɪʃn/

n.a reduction in the value of sth.especially in the exchange value of money (尤指货币等的)贬值;价值的降低:A further ～ of the pound may be necessary.英镑进一步贬值也许是必要的。

devalue/'diːvæljuː/

v.❶reduce the official value of a currency 使(货币)贬值:The government of Japan ～d the Japanese Yen.日本政府将日元贬值。❷reduce the worth or importance of 贬低,降低……的价值(或重要性):Let's not ～ his work unjustly.我们不能不公平地贬低他的作品。

devastate/'devəsteɪt/

v.destroy and make empty or ruined 摧毁;破坏;使荒废:The bomb ～d a large part of the city.这枚炸弹毁了该市大部分地区。‖ **devastation** /ˌdevəˈsteɪʃn/ *n*.毁坏;荒废

devastating/'devəsteɪtɪŋ/

adj.❶causing great destruction 毁灭性的;极具破坏性的 ❷causing great shock or grief 令人震惊的;引起极度忧伤的:～ news 令人震惊的消息

develop/dɪ'veləp/

v.❶(cause to) grow,increase or become larger or more complete (使)发展;(使)发育;(使)成长:The economy ～ed.经济发展了。/Plants ～ed from seeds.植物由种子发育而成。/They provide good material for ～ing reading skills.他们为提高阅读能力提供了良好的阅读材料。❷(cause to) become noticeable, visible or active (使)产生;(使)出现;(使)形成:That engine ～s a lot of heat.那马达产生大量的热。/A new class ～ed.一个新的阶级出现了。❸ bring out the economic possibilities of sth.,especially land or natural substances 开发(土地或自然资源):We must ～ the natural resources of our country.我们必须开发我国的自然资源。❹(cause to) appear on a film or photographic paper (使)显影 ‖ **a ～ed country** 发达国家/**a ～ing country** 发展中国家 ‖ ～**er** *n*.开发者;显影剂

development/dɪ'veləpmənt/

n.❶ the process of developing or being developed 成长;发育;发展;开发:the great ～ of our textile industry 我国纺织工业的巨大发展 /The ～ of this industry will take several years.这种工业的发展将要花费几年的时间。❷ a new event or stage which is the result of developing 新阶段;新发展:the latest ～ in the continuing crisis 持续危机中的最新发展/What are the latest ～s? 最近的发展情况怎么样？❸the process of treating a film or photographic paper to make a visible image 显像;显影:over ～ 过度显像/time ～ 定时显影

deviant /'diːvɪənt/

I *adj*.deviating from what is accepted as normal or usual 不正常的;异常的;偏离常规的:～ behaviour 偏常行为 **II** *n*.a person who deviates from accepted standards in beliefs or behaviour devolve 不正常的人

deviate/'diːvɪeɪt/

v. turn away from the right course or from the way that one is on 越轨,背离,偏离(常轨):He never ～d from complete honesty.他从来没有不诚实过。

device/dɪ'vaɪs/

n.❶a thing made or adapted for a special purpose 装置:He made a ～ for catching flies.他制作了一种可捕捉苍蝇的装置。/safety ～ 安全装置/mechanic ～ 机械装置 ❷a scheme;a trick 策略;诡计:by ～ of diplomacy 用外交策略

devil/'devl/

n.an evil spirit;the enemy of God 恶魔;恶人:Her family said she was possessed by ～s.她的家人说她是恶魔缠身了。‖

D

between the ～ and deep（blue）sea 进退维谷；进退两难‖～**ish** *adj*.恶魔似的/～**ment** *n*.恶作剧；恶迹；鬼脸气；怪事

devious/'di:vɪəs/
　adj. ❶ not straight or direct；not the shortest 弯曲的；迂回的：We travelled by a ～ route. 我们沿一条迂回的路旅行。❷ not completely honest 不太诚实的

devise/dɪ'vaɪz/
　v. think out；plan；invent 想出；设计；发明：She is trying to ～ a scheme of making money. 她正在力图想办法挣钱。/～ a secret code 设计一种密码

devote/dɪ'vəʊt/
　v.give all or most of one's time, energy, attention, etc. to sb. or sth. 完全奉献出；把……献给：He has ～d himself to the cure of cancer. 他毕生致力于癌症的治疗。‖～ **to** 献身于；致力于：You ～d too much time to this project. 你在这工程上耗时太多。

devoted/dɪ'vəʊtɪd/
　adj.very loving or loyal 挚爱的；忠诚的‖～**ly** *adv*.一心一意地；忠实地

devotion/dɪ'vəʊʃn/
　n.❶ the act of devoting；loyalty 献身；忠诚；热心：～ to duty 忠于职守 ❷ deep, strong love 深爱；挚爱；热爱：We're moved by his ～ to his students. 他热爱自己的学生，我们很受感动。

devour/dɪ'vaʊə(r)/
　v.❶eat very hungrily and greedily 狼吞虎咽 ❷ destroy 吞没；毁灭；Fire ～ed a huge area of forest. 大火吞没了大片森林。❸read or look at sth. with great interest 津津有味地看；如饥似渴地读：She ～ed the story. 她一口气看完那本小说。

devout/dɪ'vaʊt/
　adj.(of people) seriously concerned with religion；sincere 虔诚的；衷心的：His mother is a ～ Christian. 他母亲是个虔诚的基督教徒。/She is a ～ supporter of this plan. 她是这个计划的热诚支持者。‖～**ly** *adv*.虔诚地；衷心地

dew/dju:/
　n. small drops of water which form on cold surfaces during the night 露水：The glass is often wet with ～ in the summer morning. 夏天的早晨青草常为露水沾湿。

dewdrop/'dju:drɒp/
　n. a drop of dew or sth. that looks like that 露珠；露珠似的东西

dewy/'dju:i/
　adj.wet with or as if with dew (似)带露水的：She looked at him all dewy-eyed with love. 她用一双水汪汪的眼睛深情地看着他。

dexterity/dek'sterəti/
　n.quick cleverness and skill, especially in the use of the hands 灵巧；熟练：He showed great ～ in mechanical arts. 他在机械技艺方面表现得十分灵巧。

dexterous /'dekstərəs/
　adj.showing dexterity 敏捷的；灵巧的：She was ～ and did the tasks easy. 她很手巧，做这些事挺麻利的。‖～**ly** *adv*.巧妙地；敏捷地

diagnose/'daɪəgnəʊz/
　v. discover the nature of (a disease or fault) by making a careful examination 诊断：The doctor ～d his illness as a rare skin disease. 医生诊断他的病为一种罕见的皮肤病。

diagnosis/ˌdaɪəg'nəʊsɪs/
　n. (*pl*. diagnoses) a statement of the nature of a disease or other condition made after observing its signs and symptoms (对疾病的)诊断；(对其他情况的)判断

diagnostic /ˌdaɪəg'nɒstɪk/
　adj. concerned with the diagnosis of illness or other problems 诊断的；判断的：～ procedures 诊断程序

diagonal/daɪ'ægənl/
　n.a straight line going across from corner to corner 对角线

diagram/'daɪəgræm/
　n.a plan drawn to explain an idea, or how sth. works 图解；图表；示图：draw a ～ showing how the machine works 画图表示该机器如何工作 /a ～ of a rail network 铁路网示意图

dial/'daɪəl/
　Ⅰ *n*.❶the face of an instrument, such as a clock, showing measurements by means

of a pointer and figures 刻度盘；(钟、表、磅秤等的)面盘；the ～ of a watch 表面/the ～ of a compass 罗盘针面 ❷ the wheel on a telephone with numbered holes for the fingers, which is moved round when one makes a telephone call (电话机)拨号盘；a telephone ～ 电话机拨号盘 Ⅱ v. (-ll- or -l-) make telephone call (to) by using a dial or similar apparatus 拨电话；给(某人，某地)拨电话：Please ～ 114. 请拨 114。/Put in the money before ～ing. 拨电话前先把钱投进去。‖ ～ling code 电话区号/～tone 拨号音

dialect/ˈdaɪəlekt/

n. a spoken form of a language, found in a particular area of a country 方言；土语；地方话

dialogue/ˈdaɪəlɒg/

n. a conversation, especially in a book or play (尤指书或戏剧中的)对白，对话：Most plays are written in ～. 大多数戏剧都是用对话体写的。

diameter/daɪˈæmɪtə(r)/

n. the line going through the centre of a circle 直径，直径长度：Measure the ～ of the circle. 测量此圆的直径长度。‖ **diametrically** adv. 完全地：a diametrically opposite direction 完全相反的方向

diamond/ˈdaɪəmənd/

n.❶ a very hard, clear stone of pure carbon that is worth a lot of money 钻石；金刚石：a ring with a ～ in the centre 中间镶有钻石的戒指 /～ wedding 结婚六十周年纪念 ❷ a figure with four equal sides whose angles are not right angles 菱形 ❸ a suit of playing-cards marked with red diamond shapes (纸牌上的)红方块：Diamond is (are) trump(s). 方块是王牌。

diaper/ˈdaɪəpə(r)/

n. a piece of cloth put between a baby's legs and fastened at his waist 〈美〉尿布

diary/ˈdaɪəri/

n. a book for daily record of events, thoughts, etc. 日记；日记本；记事本：keep a ～ 记日记/write a ～ in English 用英

文写日记

dice/daɪs/

Ⅰ n. (pl.) small cubes of wood, ivory, bone, plastic, etc. marked with spots indicating numbers used in various games 骰子 Ⅱ v. cut vegetables, etc. into very small pieces 将(蔬菜等)切成小方块

dictate/dɪkˈteɪt/

v. say or read aloud to recorded or for others to write down 口授；让人听写：The manager ～d a letter to his secretary. 经理向秘书口授一封信。/The teacher ～d a passage to the class. 教师读一段文章让全班学生听写。‖ ～ to 下令；命令：I won't be ～d to you. 我不接受你的命令。‖ **dictation** n. 口授；听写：The pupils wrote at their teacher's dictation. 学生听写。

dictator/dɪkˈteɪtə/

n.❶ a ruler who has unlimited power, especially one who has taken control by force 独裁者；专政者 ❷ a domineering person 专横的人 ‖ ～ial adj. 独裁的；专政的；专横的

diction/ˈdɪkʃn/

n.❶ the choice of words and phrases to express meaning 措辞；遣词用字：His ～ is noted for its freshness and vividness. 他以遣词用字新颖生动见长。❷ the way in which a person pronounces words 发音：a clearly heard ～ 清晰的发音

dictionary/ˈdɪkʃənri/

n. a book which explains the words used in a language 字典；词典：look up (for) the word in the ～ 在字典中查字 /refer to (consult) a ～ 查阅字典/If you don't know the word, look it up in a ～. 你如果不认识这个单词，可以查词典。

dictum/ˈdɪktəm/

n. (pl. dicta or ～s)❶ a formal expression of an opinion 正式声明 ❷ a saying or maxim 格言；箴言

die/daɪ/

v. (died；dying) ❶ stop living 死；死亡：Flowers will ～ without water. 没有水植物就会枯死。/～ by drowning 溺死；淹死/～ in a traffic accident 死于车祸 ❷

cease to exist;disappear 逐渐过去;消失;
熄灭:The storm slowly ~d down.风暴
慢慢地过去了。/The music ~d in the
distance.音乐声渐渐远去而消失。❸
have a great wish for or to 极想;渴望:
She's dying to know where you've been.
她渴望知道你到哪儿去了。‖~away 逐
渐消逝/~ down 平息下来;熄灭/be dy-
ing for (to) 渴望着;迫切想要(某物或做
某事)/~ from 因……致死/~ in one's
bed 寿终正寝/~ of ... 因(患)……而死;
死于……/~ out 死光;灭绝/~ with
one's boots on 阵亡 ‖ dying wish n.遗言/
~hard n.死硬派;老顽固

diesel/'diːzl/
　　*n.*❶an oil-burning engine (used for e.g.
for buses and locomotives) in which fuel
is ignited by sudden compression 柴油
机;内燃机❷heavy fuel oil used in diesel
engines 柴油

diet/'daɪət/
　　*n.*❶the food you eat (日常)饮食;食物:
Too rich a ~ is not good for you.太油腻
的食物对你不好。/Cows have a ~ of
grass.牛以草为食。❷special food eaten
by people who want to get thinner,or for
medical (为减肥或因医疗原因)特定
饮食:The doctor put her on a ~.医生让
她限制食物。‖ be (go) on a ~(开始)节
食;减肥

differ/'dɪfə(r)/
　　*v.*❶be different 不同 ❷disagree 意见(看
法)不同:He and his boss ~ed constant-
ly.他和他老板总是有分歧。‖ ~from 与
……不同/~ with sb. about (on) sth. 在
(某事上)与(某人)意见相左

difference/'dɪfrəns/
　　*n.*❶the way a person or a thing differs
from another 不同;差别:There are many
~s between the two languages.这两种语
言之间有许多不同之处。❷the amount
by which one number is greater than another 差距:The ~ in temperature is 30
degrees.温差为 30 度。❸disagreement;
quarrel 意见分歧;争吵:Why can't you
settle your ~s and be friends again? 你
们何不消除歧见而言归于好? ‖ make a
~ between 区分对待/split the ~ 折中;

双方各让一半/make a ~ 有关系(影响);
起作用/make no~ 没有关系(影响);不
起作用

different/'dɪfrənt/
　　*adj.*❶ not the same 不同的: The two
boys are ~ in their tastes.这两个孩子的
兴趣不一样。/My house is quite ~ from
yours.我的房屋与你的相当不同。❷sep-
arate and individual 分别的;各种的:
They come from ~ parts of the country.
他们来自这个国家的不同地方。‖ ~
from 与……不同的

differential /ˌdɪfə'renʃəl/
　　I *adj.*❶of, showing, or depending on a
difference 差别的;以差别而定的;有区别
的 ❷relating to infinitesimal differences
(in the mathematics) (数学)微分的 II *n.*
❶a difference between amounts of things
差额❷a gear allowing a vehicle's driven
wheels to revolve at different speeds in
cornering 差动齿轮,差速器行星齿轮

differentiate/ˌdɪfə'renʃɪeɪt/
　　*v.*recognize or ascertain a difference between sth.or sb.;distinguish or discriminate 区别;区分:She ~s clearly between
right and wrong. 她明辨是非。/~ one
from another 把两者区别开来

difficult/'dɪfɪˌkəlt/
　　*adj.*❶not easy;needing effort or skill to
do or to understand sth. 困难的;难懂的:
All things are ~ to begin.万事开头难。/
He finds it ~ to stop smoking.他觉得戒
烟是件难事。❷(of people) not easy to
please or deal with (人)造成麻烦的;难
以讨好的:a ~ child 难侍弄的孩子

difficulty/'dɪfɪkəlti/
　　*n.*❶the state or quality of being hard to
do or to understand sth. 困难;艰难:He
did the work without ~.他毫不费力地做
完了工作。❷sth. hard to do or understand 难题;难处;困境:He keeps raising
difficulties over my new plan.他老是为难
我的新计划。/Here is a ~ for you to
get over.这里有个你要克服的困难。‖
get (run) into difficulties 陷入困境/**in a
~** 有困难/**out of a ~** 摆脱困境/**with ~**
困难地;吃力地

diffident /'dɪfɪdənt/

adj. ❶ having or showing a lack of confidence 羞怯的；缺乏自信的：He is ～ about expressing his opinions. 他对于表达自己的意见感到胆怯。/Don't be so ～ about your talents. 你对自己的天分不要那么缺乏自信心。❷ modest 谦虚的

diffuse

Ⅰ /dɪ'fjuːz/ *v.* spread out freely in all directions；disperse 传播；扩散：If a drop of ink is dropped into a bowl of water, it will ～ in the water. 如果将一滴墨水滴入一碗水中，它就会在水中扩散开来。/ ～ knowledge 传播知识/～ light 散射光线/～ heat 散热 Ⅱ /dɪ'fjuːs/ *adj.* ❶ spread out over a large area 散布的；漫射的：～ light 漫射光 ❷ using too many words and not keeping to the point 啰唆的；冗赘的：a ～ writer 文章啰唆的作者 ‖ **diffusion** *n.* 传播；散布；扩散；散射/**diffusive** *adj.* 普及的；扩散性的；散漫的

dig /dɪg/

v. (dug；digging) make a hole in the ground；move earth 挖；掘；刨：They are ～ging a tunnel through the hill. 他们正在开凿一条穿山隧道。/He dug a deep hole. 他掘了个深洞。‖ **at** 挖苦/～ **for** 挖寻/～ **in** 挖战壕；扎稳根；开始吃/～ **into** 开始吃；戳进；清查/～ **out** 掘出，找出/～ **over** 再想想/～**up** 挖到，翻挖

digest

Ⅰ /daɪ'dʒest/ *v.* ❶ change food in the stomach into the substances of a form that the body can use （使）消化：Some foods are ～ed more easily than others. 有些食物较其他的食物更易于消化。/ Cheese doesn't ～ easily. 干酪不易消化。❷ understand or assimilate sth. 领悟；理解：He read rapidly but ～ed nothing. 他读得很快，但什么也没有理解到。Ⅱ /'daɪdʒest/ *n.* a short account (of a piece of writing) which gives the most important facts 文摘；摘要 ‖ ～**ion** *n.* 消化力；消化/～**ive** *adj.* 消化的

digger /'dɪgə/

n. ❶ a person or an animal that digs 挖掘者；有挖掘习性的动物 ❷ a mechanical excavator 挖掘机

digit /'dɪdʒɪt/

n. ❶ any of the numbers from 0 to 9 (0−9 中的任何一个) 数字，数位 ❷ a finger or a toe 手指头；脚趾

digital /'dɪdʒɪtl/

adj. ❶ of or based on a system in which information is represented in the form of changing electrical signals 数字式的；使用数字的；数字信息系统的；数码的：a ～ sound recording 数码录音/ ～ computer 数字电子计算机 ❷ showing information in the form of numbers, rather than as a point on a scale, etc. 数字显示的：a ～ watch 数字显示式电子手表 /a ～ reading 数字显示的读数 ❸ of the fingers and toes 手指的；脚趾的

dignified /'dɪgnɪfaɪd/

adj. having or showing dignity 有尊严的；庄严的；威严的；高贵的：a ～ manner 庄重的举止/a ～ old man 威严的老人

dignify /'dɪgnɪfaɪ/

v. give respect or importance to (especially sth. that does not deserve it) 使有尊严；使高贵；把……夸大为；抬高……的身价：Don't try to ～ those few hairs on your face by calling them a beard! 别想把你脸上那几根毛说成是胡子来美化它！

dignity /'dɪgnəti/

n. ❶ the state or quality of being worthy of honour or being noble 尊贵；尊严；庄严：the ～ of labour 劳动神圣 /behave with ～ 举止庄重 /Although she is very poor, she has not lost her ～. 虽然很穷，但她没有失去自尊。❷ a high office or position 要职；高官：He may attain the ～ of the presidency. 他或许能升任总统呢。

digress /daɪ'gres/

v. turn aside from the subject which one is speaking or writing about, and deal with sth. else 离题；岔开话题：Don't ～ from the subject when lecturing. 讲课时不要岔开主题。

dike /daɪk/

n. =dyke

dilemma /dɪ'lemə, daɪ-/

n. a position in which one has to choose between two unpleasant things 进退两难

的困境;左右为难:The doctor was in a ~,should he tell his patient that he would probably not recover or should he tell a lie. 大夫左右为难,不知是该告诉病人说病大概治不好,还是不对病人说出实情。

diligence /'dılıdʒəns/
　　n. careful hard work or effort 勤勉;勤奋;刻苦;用功

diligent /'dılıdʒənt/
　　adj. hard-working;putting care and effort into what you do 勤奋的;勤勉的;孜孜不倦的:a ~ student 勤奋刻苦的学生 ‖ ~**ly** *adv.* 勤勉地;勤勉地

dilute /daɪ'ljuːt/
　　Ⅰ *v.* make (a liquid) weaker and thinner by mixing another liquid with it 稀释;冲淡:~ wine with water 用水把酒冲淡/~ a paint with oil 用油将油画颜料调稀 Ⅱ *adj.* that has been diluted 稀释了的;冲淡了的:~ acid 稀酸 ‖ **dilution** *n.* 稀释,冲淡;稀释物

dim /dɪm/
　　Ⅰ *adj.* ❶ not shining brightly 昏暗的;暗淡的:We can't read by such a ~ light. 我们无法在这么暗淡的灯光下看书。❷ not clear to be seen 模糊不清的;朦胧的:I saw a ~ shape of a man in the fog yesterday. 昨天我在雾中看到一个男人的模糊形象。‖ **take a ~ view of** 对……持悲观看法;对……不以为然 Ⅱ *v.* (-mm-) make or become less bright or clear (使)变昏暗;模糊:He ~med the car's headlights. 他把车头灯调暗。/Her eyes ~med with tears. 眼泪模糊了她的视线。‖ ~**ly** *adv.* 模糊地;隐约地/~**ness** *n.* 昏暗;模糊

dime /daɪm/
　　n. a coin of the US and Canada, worth 10 cents (美国、加拿大)一角银币

dimension /dı'menʃn, daɪ-/
　　n. ❶ a measurement in any one direction especially as used for establishing the position of sth. in space 度;(长、宽、高、厚)度:What are the ~s of this room? 这房间的长、宽、高是多少? ❷ the stated number of the size; the range of sth. 大

小;幅度;范围:a building of great ~s 巨大的建筑物/the ~s of the problem 问题涉及的范围

diminish /dı'mınıʃ/
　　v. make or become less or smaller (使)变小;减小;降低:His illness ~ed his strength. 疾病使他的体力下降。/The water in the river will ~ as the dry season comes. 随着旱季的到来河水将日渐减少。

dimple /'dımpl/
　　n. a small hollow in the chin or cheek, appearing when one smiles (微笑时出现在两颊的)酒窝,笑靥

dine /daɪn/
　　v. ❶ eat dinner 进餐:We decided to ~ out this evening. 我们决定今晚在外用餐。❷ give a dinner for 宴请:They are dining a prominent politician. 他们正在宴请一位重要的政治家。‖ ~ **in** 在家吃饭/~ **off** 吃(某种饭菜);吃(某人的饭)/~ **out** 出去吃饭

diner /'daɪnə(r)/
　　n. ❶ a person who dines 食客;就餐者;a restaurant capable of seating 100 ~s 可容纳 100 人就餐的餐馆 ❷ a dining car on a train (火车上的)餐车

dingy /'dındʒi/
　　adj. dark and dirty 又黑又脏的:a ~ room 又黑又脏的房间

dinky /'dıŋki/
　　adj. ❶ small and charming 小巧的;精致的:Look at that ~ little spoon! 瞧那把精致的小匙! ❷ small and unimportant 微不足道的:a ~ little room 不起眼的小房间

dinner /'dınə(r)/
　　n. ❶ the main meal of the day 正餐(午饭或晚饭):early ~ 午餐/late ~ 晚餐 /In England, ~ is usually at 8 p. m. 在英格兰,一般是晚上八点钟吃正餐。❷ a banquet 宴会:He was the guest of honour at the ~. 他是这次宴会的贵宾。

dinosaur /'daɪnəsɔː(r)/
　　n. a large extinct reptile 恐龙

dioxide /daɪ'ɒksaɪd/
　　n. an oxide formed by combining two atoms

of oxygen and one atom of another element 二氧化物：carbon ~ 二氧化碳

dip /dɪp/

I v. (-pp-) ❶ put sth. into a liquid and then take it out again 浸（泡）一会儿；沾湿：He ~ped his finger in the water. 他把手指在水中浸了一下。❷ go below a surface or level；slope downward（使）下降；下沉；倾斜：The sun ~ped below the horizon. 太阳沉入地平线下。/You should ~ the car's headlights when you meet another car at night. 晚上遇到另外的车辆时你应近光灯。‖ ~ **into** 浏览一下；随便翻阅；掏出 II n. the act of dipping or being dipped；a quick swim or bathe；a downward slope 浸；泡；倾斜：have (take) a ~ in the sea 在海水中泡一泡

diploma /dɪˈpləʊmə/

n. (pl. ~s or diplomata /-tə/) an educational certificate 毕业文凭；学位证书：a high school ~ 中学文凭/I have a ~ in English. 我有一张英语考试及格证书。

diplomacy /dɪˈpləʊməsi/

n. ❶ the art and practice of establishing and continuing relations between nations 外交；外交手段：He comes highly experienced in international ~. 在国际外交方面他具有丰富的经验。❷ the skill at dealing with people and getting them to agree 外交手腕：He exhibited remarkable ~ in handling the awkward situation. 在应付这种尴尬的处境时，他表现出卓越的外交手腕。

diplomat /ˈdɪpləmæt/

n. a person sent to work for his government in another country 外交官

diplomatic /ˌdɪpləˈmætɪk/

adj. of or having diplomacy 外交的；圆滑的；有技巧的：He has ~ privileges. 他有外交特权。/He is so ~ that he can get along with anyone. 他很会为人，和谁都处得好。‖ ~ **ally** adv. 外交上；圆滑地

dire /ˈdaɪə(r)/

adj. very serious or bad 极其严重的；危急的；极差的：a ~ situation 危急的形势/The film we saw was absolutely ~. 我们

看过的那部影片表演糟透了。

direct /dɪˈrekt, daɪ-/

I adj. ❶ straight；not turning 笔直的；径直的 ❷ going straight to the point；plain 直接的；不间断的；直达的：He got a ~ flight to Beijing. 他直飞北京。/the ~ result of the decision 该决定的直接后果/in ~ contact with someone. 与某人直接接触/~ action 直接行动 II adv. not stopping；not going a long way round 径直地：The train goes there ~. 这列火车直达该地。III v. ❶ show sb. the way；be in charge of sth. or sb. 指导；指挥；指示方向；指引；导演：Can you ~ me to the post office? 你能告诉我到邮局怎么走吗？/Who ~ed that film? 谁导演那部影片？❷ order；command 命令；指示：The officer ~ed him to return. 军官命令他回来。

direction /dɪˈrekʃn, daɪ-/

n. ❶ a course taken by a moving person or thing；a way that a person or thing looks or faces 方向；方位：in every ~ 四面八方/In which ~ are you going, north or south? 你去哪个方向，是南还是北？/The plane is flying in the ~ of Wuhan. 飞机正向武汉方向飞行。❷ guidance；order；command 指导；指挥：The experiment was made under the ~ of Professor Li. 实验在李教授指导下进行。❸ (usually pl.) information or instructions about what to do, where to go, how to do, etc. 指令；指示；说明书：He gave ~s to me about the work. 他向我发出工作指示。/Read the ~s before using this medicine. 使用此药之前请先看说明书。❹ the address of a receiver 收件人地址：The parcel was returned to the sender because the ~s were insufficient. 包裹因地址不详被退还给了寄件人。

directional /dɪˈrekʃənl/

adj. connected with direction in space 方向的；定向的

directive /dɪˈrektɪv, daɪ-/

I n. an official instruction or order 指示；命令：The management has issued a new ~ about the use of company cars. 公司管理部门发布了有关使用公司汽车的新指

示。Ⅱ *adj.* offering instructions 指示的

directly /dɪˈrektli, daɪ-/

adv. in a direct manner; without delay; exactly in a specified position 直接地；立即；完全；恰恰：He answered my question very ~. 他很直率地回答了我的问题。/ Directly I received his letter I went to see him. 我一收到他的信就去看他了。

director /dɪˈrektə(r), daɪ-/

n. ❶ one of senior managers who run a company 理事；董事；经理：He is one of the ~s of the company. 他是这个公司的一个董事。❷ a person who tells actors and actresses what to do in a play or a film 导演：The producer and the ~ quarrelled about the film. 电影制片人和导演对该影片发生了口角。❸ a controlling machine 指挥仪；控制器；引向器

directory /dɪˈrektəri/

n. (*pl.* -ies) ❶ a book containing a list of telephone subscribers, inhabitants of a district, members of a profession, business firms, etc. 名录；电话号码簿 ❷ a file containing a group of other files in a computer (计算机文件或按序的)目录

dirge /dɜːdʒ/

n. ❶ a slow sad song sung for a dead person 哀歌；挽歌；安灵歌 ❷ any slow sad song or piece of music 凄惨的歌曲(或乐曲)

dirt /dɜːt/

n. any substance like mud or soil to make sth. dirty 脏东西；泥土：His clothes were covered with ~. 他的衣服上尽是脏东西。/ He filled all the flower pots with ~. 他把花钵都装上泥土。‖ treat sb. like ~ 把(某人)看得一钱不值/fling (throw) ~ at (on) 说……的坏话；诬蔑 ‖ ~ road *n.* 砂土路/~ farmer *n.* 自耕农

dirty /ˈdɜːti/

Ⅰ *adj.* ❶ having dirt on it; not clean 脏的；不干净的：Repairing cars is a ~ job. 修车是件脏活。❷ concerned with sex in thought or talk 下流的；淫秽的：The press publishes ~ books. 该出版社出版黄色书籍。Ⅱ *v.* make or become dirty 弄脏；变脏：Don't ~ your new dress. 别把

你的新衣服弄脏了。/ White gloves ~ very easily. 白手套易脏。

disable /dɪsˈeɪbl/

v. make unable to do sth., especially take away power of action; wound 使失去能力；使伤残：An accident ~d her from dancing ballet. 一次事故使她失去跳芭蕾舞的能力。/ He was ~d in the war. 他在这次战争中(受伤)残废了。‖ ~d *n.* 残疾人/~ment *n.* 残废；使残废之物

disability /ˌdɪsəˈbɪləti/

n. ❶ a physical or mental condition that limits a person's movements or senses (身体或智力上的)残疾：~ pension 伤残抚恤金 ❷ a handicap 缺陷：His lack of training was a serious ~. 他缺乏训练是个严重缺陷。

disadvantage /ˌdɪsədˈvɑːntɪdʒ/

n. an unfavourable condition 不利之处；短处：It is a ~ not to be able to speak English. 不会说英语是个不利之点。/ His bad health is a great ~ to him. 身体不好是他的一大短处。‖ at a ~ 处于不利地位/to sb.'s ~ 对某人不利(的) ‖ ~ous /ˌdɪsædvənˈteɪdʒəs/ *adj.* 不利的；有害的

disagree /ˌdɪsəˈɡriː/

v. ❶ have a different opinion, fail to agree 不同意；不一致：After a long discussion, the two sides still ~d. 经长时间讨论之后双方意见仍不一致。/ The reports from Rome ~ with those from Paris. 来自罗马的报道与来自巴黎的报道不一致。❷ (of food, climate) have bad effects on (食物、气候等)不适合，有害：The climate ~s with me. 这种气候对我不适宜。‖ ~ment *n.* 意见不一；不同意；不一致

disagreeable /ˌdɪsəˈɡriːəbl/

adj. ❶ unpleasant or unenjoyable 讨厌的；令人不快的：a ~ smell 难闻的气味 ❷ unfriendly and bad-tempered 不友善的；脾气坏的：a ~ man 一个脾气不好的男人 ‖ disagreeably *adv.* 不愉快地；不友善地

disallow /ˌdɪsəˈlaʊ/

v. make an official decision not to allow or accept sth. 不允许；不接受；不承认：The referee ~ed the goal. 裁判裁决该球无

效。

disappear/ˌdɪsəˈpɪə(r)/

*v.*❶ go out of sight 消失；消散：The little boy ~ed around the corner.那小男孩在拐角处不见了。/The sun ~ed below the horizon.太阳在地平线上消失了。❷ be lost；become extinct 失踪；绝迹：A search is being carried out for the small boy who ~ed from his home on Monday. 正在寻找于星期一走出家门失踪的小男孩。/The police are look-ing for the man who ~ed yesterday.警察正在寻找昨天失踪的那个人。

disappoint/ˌdɪsəˈpɔɪnt/

*v.*fail to fulfil the hopes of sb.使失望：I'm sorry I ~ed you.对不起，我使你失望了。‖ ~ed *adj.*失望的；失意的：a ~ed man 失意的人/~ing *adj.*令人失望的：~ing news 扫兴的消息/~ment *n.*灰心，失望；令人失望的人（或物）：To my great ~ment, I did not get a letter from him. 使我大为失望的是，我没收到他的信。

disapprove/ˌdɪsəˈpruːv/

v. express an unfavourable opinion 不赞成；不以为然；不批准：Her parents ~ of her training for the theatre.她父母反对她做戏剧演员。/In fact they ~ very strongly.事实上他们强烈地表示反对。/ The court ~d the verdict.法院不批准陪审团的判决。‖ disapproval *n.*不赞成/disapproving *adj.*不赞成的；不以为然的/disapprovingly *adv.*不以为然地

disarm/dɪsˈɑːm/

*v.*❶ take away weapons from；reduce the size or give up the use of armed forces 缴械；解除……的武装；(国家)裁减军备；裁军：The policeman ~ed the thief.警察缴了小偷的凶器。/The superpowers are unlikely to ~ completely.超级大国是不可能彻底裁军的。❷ make sb.less suspicious,angry,hostile,etc.使减少怀疑；使息怒；化解敌意：I felt angry, but her smile ~ed me.我很生气，但她的微笑使我的怒气烟消云散了。

disarray/ˌdɪsəˈreɪ/

*n.*a condition in which things are not ar-ranged or organized properly 紊乱；混乱：Our army was in ~ after the battle. 战斗过后我军处于混乱状态。

disaster/dɪˈzɑːstə(r)/

*n.*a great or sudden misfortune；a terrible accident 不幸；灾害；灾难：The aircraft crash was a great ~.这次飞机失事是一场大灾难。

disastrous/dɪˈzɑːstrəs/

*adj.*❶ causing great damage 灾难性的：Lowering interest rates could have ~ consequences for the economy.降低利率可能给经济带来灾难性后果。❷ resul-ting in a complete failure 完全失败的 ‖ ~ly *adv.*灾难性地；悲惨地

disband/dɪsˈbænd/

v. break up (an organized group of peo-ple) 解散 (团体)：The six criminals agreed to ~.六名罪犯同意散伙。/The government ~ed all political parties.政府解散了所有的政党。

disbelief/ˌdɪsbɪˈliːf/

*n.*lack of belief；failure to believe 不信，怀疑；无信仰：He shook his head in ~.他怀疑地摇摇头。

disbelieve/ˌdɪsbɪˈliːv/

*v.*refuse to believe；be unable or unwilling to believe (in) 不相信；怀疑：We have no reason to ~ her.我们没理由怀疑她。/I ~ in his story.我不能相信他的话。

disc/dɪsk/

*n.*❶ any round flat thing 圆平物；圆盘；圆板；圆片：a metal ~ 金属圆盘/the sun's ~ 日轮/the moon's ~ 月轮 ❷ = disk ‖ ~-jockey/ˈdɪskdʒɒki/ *n.*唱片音乐节目主持人

discard/dɪˈskɑːd/

v. throw away；give up (sth. useless, and unwanted) 丢弃；抛弃：~ a broken radio 扔掉破收音机 /~ an old friend 抛弃老朋友

discharge/ˈdɪstʃɑːdʒ/

Ⅰ *v.*❶ allow (a liquid, gas, or other sub-stance) to flow out 排放出；流出；冒出；释放出：The factory ~s its waste into the river.工厂将废水排入河里。/The chimney ~s smoke.烟囱冒烟。❷ send (sb.) away；allow (sb.) to leave；dismiss 送(某人)离去；释放；解雇：The judge found him not guilty and ~d him.法官发现他无罪并将他释放。❸pay (a debt);perform (a duty) 偿还(债务);履行(职责):He ~d his liabilities.他还清了债务。Ⅱ *n.*❶ the action of allowing a liquid,gas,or other substance to flow out 排出;流出;放出:the ~ of gas from a container 气体从容器中逸出 ❷the act of allowing sb. to leave somewhere, especially sb.in a hospital or the army 获准离开;免职;出院;退伍:one's ~ from the army 退伍 ❸the act of performing a duty or paying a debt (职责的)履行;(债务的)清偿

discipline/'dɪsɪplɪn/
Ⅰ *v.*❶ train or develop,especially in obedience and self-control 训练;管教;使守纪律:The officer ~d the new soldiers.军官训练新兵。/You must learn to ~ yourself.你得学会自律。❷punish 处分,处罚:He was ~d for breaking school rules.他违反校规受到处分。Ⅱ *n.*❶a method of training to produce obedience and self-control 训练;管教:military ~ 军事训练 ❷a state of order and control gained as a result of this training 纪律;风纪:He is brave and has good ~.他不仅勇敢,而且纪律良好。❸punishment 惩罚,处分:the teacher's severe ~ 老师的严厉处分

disclaim/dɪs'kleɪm/
*v.*state that one does not have or accept;deny 放弃;否认:He ~ed responsibility for the accident.他否认在此次事故中负有责任。/She ~ed knowledge of the letter's contents.她否认知道信的内容。‖ ~**er** *n.*弃权声明

disclose/dɪs'kləʊz/
*v.*make sth. known;allow sth. to be seen 泄漏;透露;暴露:He ~d the truth.他说出真相。/~ a secret 揭露秘密/refuse to ~ one's name and address 拒不透露其姓名和住址 ‖ **disclosure** *n.*透露;说出;已揭露的秘密

disco/'dɪskəʊ/
*n.*a club or party at which people dance to pop music 迪斯科舞厅;迪斯科舞会

discolo(u)r/dɪs'kʌlə(r)/

*v.*spoil or change the colour of (使)变色;(使)褪色;玷污:Smoke and dirt had ~ed the walls.烟尘使得四壁污迹斑斑。

discomfort/dɪs'kʌmfət/
*n.*lack of comfort 不舒适;不适

discompose/ˌdɪskəm'pəʊz/
v. make (someone) lose control and become worried 使失常;使不安;使心烦意乱

disconnect/ˌdɪskə'nekt/
*v.*break the connection of or between sth. 断开;使不连接:An electric bell will not ring if you ~ its wires.如果把电线断开,电铃就不会响了。

disconnected /ˌdɪskə'nektɪd/
*adj.*not joined together in a logical way 无条理的;不连贯的:his ~ narrative 他那不连贯的叙述

disconsolate /dɪs'kɒnsəlɪt/
*adj.*unhappy at the loss of sth. 不开心的;郁郁寡欢的 ‖ ~**ly** *adv.*悲伤地;凄凉地

discontent/ˌdɪskən'tent/
Ⅰ *adj.*disgruntled;dissatisfied 不满的 Ⅱ *n.*lack of satisfaction;unhappiness 不满足;不满意:There was a lot of ~ among the workers.工人中不满情绪严重。Ⅲ *v.*make (someone) discontented 使不满意:~ you 使你不满意 ‖ ~**ed** *adj.*不满的;老不高兴的:/a ~ed look 一脸不满的神情/~**ment** *n.*不满

discontinue /'dɪskən'tɪnju(ː)/
*v.*stop doing or providing sth. 停止;终止;中断:The manufacturers have ~d that line.厂家已停止了那条生产线。‖ **discontinuance** *n.*废止;终止

discontinuity /ˌdɪsˌkɒntɪ'njuːətɪ/
*n.*a distinct break in physical continuity or sequence in time;the sharp difference of characteristics between parts of sth.不连贯,间断,中断;(事物不同部分性质上的)悬殊

discord/'dɪskɔːd/
n. disagreement between people 意见不合;不和:What has brought ~ into the family? 什么事情使得一家人不和? ‖ ~**ance** *n.*不一致;不和谐/~**ant** *adj.*不一

致的;不和谐的:～ant music 不和谐的乐曲

discount /'dɪskaʊnt/
Ⅰ *n*. the amount taken off a price 折扣:We give 10 percent ～ for cash.若付现金我们给 10%的折扣。Ⅱ *v*.take out a certain amount from a price;do not believe sth.or sb. completely 打折扣;不完全相信:You can ～ much of what he says.他说的话要大打折扣。‖ at a ～ 打折扣;不受重视

discourage /dɪ'skʌrɪdʒ/
v.❶ take away the courage or confidence of 使丧失勇气;使失去信心:Don't let one failure ～ you,try again.勿因一次失败而气馁,再试试看。❷ persuade sb. not to do sth. 阻挠(某种行动);劝阻(某人做某事):Strict laws were passed in an attempt to ～ crime. 为了阻止犯罪,通过了若干苛严的法律。/I ～d him from climbing the mountain without a guide.我劝他无向导不要去爬山。‖ ～ment *n*.气馁;挫折;障碍

discourse /'dɪskɔːs/
Ⅰ *n*.❶ a serious speech or piece of writing about a particular subject (关于特定专题的)演讲;讲道;论文:The priest delivered a long ～ on the evils of adultery. 牧师就通奸的罪恶做了冗长的讲道。❷ a serious conversation (严肃的)谈话,交谈:They passed the hours in learning ～. 他们在一起切磋学问度过了许多个小时。❸ a connected language in a speech or writing (讲话或文章中的)语段;话语:analyse the structure of scientific ～ 分析科学语域的结构 Ⅱ *v*. make a long formal speech about 讲述;论述;演讲:She ～d at length upon the relationship between crime and environment. 她详细论述了犯罪与环境之间的关系。

discourteous /dɪs'kɜːtɪəs/
adj.(of people or their behaviour) not polite;showing bad manners;rude (人或其行为)不礼貌的,失礼的,粗鲁的:It was ～ of you not to thank him.你不谢他是失礼的。

discourtesy /dɪs'kɜːtəsi/
n.an act of not being polite 无礼;失礼;粗鲁;不恭的言行:You showed great ～ by not asking him to sit down.你不请他坐是不礼貌的表现。

discover /dɪs'kʌvə(r)/
v.find out sth. for the first time;come to know or realize (sth.)发现;找出;了解到,意识到:Columbus ～ed America in 1492.哥伦布于 1492 年发现美洲。/ I ～ed that I had been cheated.我发现我受骗了。‖ ～able *adj*.可发现的/～er *n*.发现者

discovery /dɪs'kʌvəri/
n.the action or process of discovering or being discovered;sth. or sb. discovered 发现;被发现;发现的物(或人):Galileo's ～ of the truth about falling objects 伽利略关于落体真相的发现/ The ～ of oil in Shandong was exciting news.在山东发现石油是令人激动的新闻。/He made some important discoveries in science.他完成了一些重要的科学发现。

discredit /dɪs'kredɪt/
Ⅰ *v*. cause people to lack faith in;stop people believing in or having respect for 不相信;使(人)不相信;使不可信:I ～ all those rumors.我不相信所有这些传闻。/ Later research ～ed earlier theories.根据后来的研究,早先的理论不可信了。Ⅱ *n*.❶loss of belief,trust,or the good opinion of others 丧失信誉;丧失名誉;失去信心:His past lies threw ～ on his evidence.他过去说过假话(做过伪证),因此他提供的证明不可信。❷sb. or sth. that brings shame or loss of respect;a disgrace 败坏名声的人(或事);耻辱:He brought ～ on the whole family.他使全家人蒙上耻辱。

discreditable /dɪs'kredɪtəbl/
adj.(of behaviour) causing discredit;shameful (行为)有损信誉的,丢脸的,可耻的

discreet /dɪ'skriːt/
adj.careful and tactful in what one says and does;prudent 谨慎的;慎重的;考虑周到的:a ～ silence 谨慎的沉默/It wasn't very ～ of you to ring me up at the office.你在办公室给我打电话有点考虑欠周。

discrepancy /dɪsˈkrepənsi/

n. (*pl.*-ies) lack of agreement between things which should be the same 差异；不符合；不一致：There were several discrepancies between the witnesses' accounts. 证人们的证词有矛盾。

discrete /dɪˈskriːt/

adj. separate；distinct 分离的；各别的：The picture consisted of a lot of ～ spots of colour. 这幅画由许多互不相连的色点组成。

discretion /dɪˈskreʃn/

n. ❶ the ability or right to decide what is most suitable to be done 判断力；决定权：I leave this to your ～. 我把此事交给你定。❷ the quality of being discreet 谨慎；审慎：You must show ～ in choosing your friends. 你择友须审慎。‖ at the ～ of 由……来决定；按照……的意思 ‖ ～ary *adj.* 可自行决定的

discriminate /dɪˈskrɪmɪneɪt/

v. ❶ see or make a difference between things or people；distinguish 区别；不同对待：A teacher must not ～ against any pupils. 教师待学生必须一视同仁。❷ recognize the difference between people or things 区分 ‖ ～ against 歧视…… /～ between 区别对待/～ … from 把……和……加以区分/～ in favour of 对……予以优待 ‖ discrimination *n.* 区分；鉴别力；歧视：racial discrimination 种族歧视

discuss /dɪˈskʌs/

v. talk together about；argue about 讨论；商量；谈论：～ a question with sb. 与某人讨论一问题：Imagine you are in these situations, and ～ what you could do. 请商量一下，假若你们处在这种情况下你们能做些什么。‖ ～ion *n.* 讨论：We won't have more discussion about it. 我们不再讨论这个问题了。/be under discussion 在讨论中/come up for discussion 提出来讨论

disdain /dɪsˈdeɪn/

Ⅰ *n.* scorn；contempt 蔑视；鄙视：He treats his colleagues with ～. 他瞧不起同事。 Ⅱ *v.* think that sb. or sth. is unworthy of one's consideration 瞧不起；鄙视；不屑

于(做某事)：We ～ed to notice the insult. 我们不屑于计较这种侮辱。‖ ～ful *adj.* 鄙视的：be ～ful of (towards) someone 鄙视某人

disease /dɪˈziːz/

n. an illness or unhealthy condition caused by infection, a disorder, etc., but not by an accident 疾病；病：The business of doctors is to prevent and cure ～. 医生的职责就是防病和治病。/a chronic ～ 慢性病/an occupational ～ 职业病/an infectious ～ 传染病 ‖ ～d *adj.* 有病的

disengage /ˌdɪsɪnˈɡeɪdʒ/

v. ❶ (especially of parts of a machine) come loose and separate (尤指机器部件等)松开，脱开，解开 ❷ loosen and separate 使松开；使脱开；卸开；解除：Disengage the gears when you park the car. 停放汽车时要松开排挡。❸ (of soldiers, ships, etc.) stop fighting (士兵、战舰等)停止交战：The two sides ～ (themselves) after suffering heavy losses. 双方遭受惨重损失之后停火了。

disentangle /ˌdɪsɪnˈtæŋɡl/

v. ❶ remove knots and tangles from a string, rope, etc. 解开(绳、结等) ❷ find out the meaning or truth of sth. which is difficult to understand 弄清(奥秘，真相等)；解决(疑难问题)

disfigure /dɪsˈfɪɡə(r)/

v. spoil or damage the appearance of 毁损……的外表：He ～d the picture by throwing ink to it. 他把墨水泼到那幅画上，污损了画面。

disgorge /dɪsˈɡɔːdʒ/

v. ❶ throw out from the stomach through the mouth 吐出；呕出：The dog ～d the bone it had swallowed. 狗吐出已吞下的骨头。/chimneys disgorging smoke 喷吐着烟尘的烟囱 ❷ give up unwillingly (sth. stolen) 交出，交还(赃物)：They persuaded him to ～ the missing documents. 他们劝他交出那份不见了的文件。❸ (of a river) to flow out, pour out (江河)注入，流出：The Mississippi ～s (its waters) into the Gulf of Mexico. 密西西比河注入墨西哥湾。

disgrace /dɪsˈɡreɪs/

I *n*. shame or loss of honour and respect 丢脸；耻辱；不光彩：There need be no ～ in being poor. 贫穷并不足为耻。II *v*. bring shame and dishonour on；be a shame to 使丢脸；使蒙受耻辱；羞辱：She ～d her family by stealing. 她因偷窃丢了家人的脸。‖ **～ful** *adj*. 丢人的；可耻的

disguise /dɪsˈɡaɪz/

I *v*. change one's clothes or appearance in order not to be recognized 伪装；化装：She ～d herself as an angel for the party. 晚会上她们把自己化装成一个天使。II *n*. the art of changing appearance to make others not recognize you 化装；伪装：Nobody saw through his ～. 谁也没有看穿他的伪装。/His seeming friendship was a ～. 他表面上的友好只是一种伪装。‖ **in ～** 化了装的/**make no ～ of** 毫不掩饰

disgust /dɪsˈɡʌst/

I *n*. a strong feeling of dislike or profound disapproval 厌恶；嫌恶：He turned away in ～. 他厌恶地把脸转开。/To his ～, he saw a dead dog in the garden. 令他恶心的是，他在园里看到一只死狗。II *v*. cause to feel dislike or profound disapproval 使厌恶；使嫌恶：His behaviour ～ed everybody. 他的行为令每个人厌恶。/I'm completely ～ed with you. 我非常厌恶你。

disgusting /dɪsˈɡʌstɪŋ/

adj. extremely unpleasant 极糟的；令人不快的：a ～ habit 令人讨厌的习惯

dish /dɪʃ/

n. ❶ a little flat plate for food 盘子；碟子：a meat ～ 盛肉的盘子/a wooden ～ 木盘/a glass ～ 玻璃盘子 ❷ food which is prepared and ready to eat 一道菜：They serve both Cantonese and Pekinese ～es. 他们既供应粤菜也供应京菜。‖ **～ out** 分发/**～ up** 盛菜

dishearten /dɪsˈhɑːtn/

v. discourage；make less sure of success 使沮丧，使丧气；使失去信心

dishes /ˈdɪʃɪz/

n. all the plates, cups, knives, forks, etc. that have been used for a meal（就餐时用过的）餐具（包括盘、碟、杯、刀、叉等）：

Let's wash the ～. 我们来洗碗碟吧。

dishonest /dɪsˈɒnɪst/

adj. not honest 不诚实的；不老实的：The ～ boy cheated on the test. 那个不诚实的男孩考试作弊。‖ **～y** *n*. 不诚实

dishonour /dɪsˈɒnə(r)/

I *n*. a state of disgrace or shame；a person or thing that brings shame 耻辱；带来耻辱的人（或事）：He was a ～ to his family. 他是他家的耻辱。II *v*. bring shame upon 使蒙羞；玷辱 ‖ **～able** *adj*. 可耻的；不光彩的

disillusion /ˌdɪsɪˈluːʒn/

v. free from an illusion；tell or show the (especially unpleasant) truth to 使幻想破灭，使醒悟：I hate to ～ you, but your chances of winning are nil. 我很不愿意使你的幻想破灭，但你获胜实在无望。‖ **～ed** *adj*. 幻灭的；失望的：be ～ed with (at, about) 对……感到失望/**～ment** *n*. 醒悟

disinfect /ˌdɪsɪnˈfekt/

v. make sth. clean by destroying bacteria that may cause disease 消毒；杀菌：～ a room 给房间消毒 ‖ **～ion** *n*. 消毒；杀菌

disingenuous /ˌdɪsɪnˈdʒenjuəs/

adj. not open or sincere；slightly dishonest and untruthful 不真诚的；不坦率的：It was ～ of him to praise me just because he wanted help from me. 他只是为了想要我帮助而赞美我，真是有欠真诚。

disintegrate /dɪsˈɪntɪɡreɪt/

v. break up into small parts 碎裂；粉碎：The project ～d owing to lack of financial backing. 那个计划因缺乏财政支持而告吹了。/The family is starting to ～. 这个家庭开始破裂。

disinterested /dɪsˈɪntrəstɪd/

adj. ❶ willing or able to act fairly because one is not influenced by personal advantage；objective（因不涉及个人利益而）公正的；客观的；无偏见的；无私的：As a ～ observer, who do you think is right? 作为一名无偏见的观察者，你认为谁对呢？ ❷ not caring；uninterested（对……）不关心的；（对……）不感兴趣的：She seems completely ～in her work.

她似乎对自己的工作完全不感兴趣。

disjointed/dɪsˈdʒɔɪntɪd/
adj.(of words or ideas)not well connected;not following in reasonable order（言语、思想）不连贯的,支离破碎的,杂乱无章的：She gave a rather ~ account of the incident.她对该事件的报道相当支离破碎。

disk/dɪsk/
*n.*a flat circular piece of plastic used for storing computer information（计算机的）磁盘,磁碟

dislike/dɪsˈlaɪk/
Ⅰ*v.*not like;hate 不喜欢；讨厌：I ~ dishonest people.我不喜欢不诚实的人。/ She ~s climbing mountains.她不喜欢登山。Ⅱ*n.*a feeling of not liking 不喜欢；讨厌：She spoke of him with ~.她提到他时很反感。/have a ~ of monkey 讨厌猴子‖ **likes and** ~s 好恶／**take a** ~ **to** 开始讨厌

dislocate/ˈdɪsləkeɪt/
*v.*❶ put a bone in the body out of its proper position 使（骨头）脱位；使脱臼：He ~d his arm in a fall.他摔倒时胳膊脱臼了。❷ disturb;disarrange;put sth. out of order 扰乱,使紊乱;使混乱

disloyal/dɪsˈlɔɪəl/
*adj.*not loyal 不忠的；背叛的：be ~ to one's country 对国家不忠

dismal/ˈdɪzməl/
*adj.*causing or showing sadness 忧愁的；令人忧郁的；阴沉的：Why are you looking so ~? 你为何显得如此忧愁? /a ~ song 忧郁的歌/a ~ house 阴暗的房子/~ weather 阴沉的天气/~ news 令人沮丧的消息

dismantle/dɪsˈmæntl/
*v.*separate the parts which make up a whole 分解,拆开：He ~d his old car.他把他的旧车拆开了。/These chairs can be ~d for storage.这些椅子可以拆开收藏。

dismay/dɪsˈmeɪ/
Ⅰ*n.*a strong feeling of fear, anxiety and hopelessness 惊愕；惶恐；失望；气馁：He looked at me in ~.他惊愕地瞪着我。Ⅱ

*v.*fill with fear, anxiety, and disappointment,etc.使惊恐；使焦虑；使失望；使气馁：I was ~ed at the news.听到这个消息我十分惊愕。

dismiss/dɪsˈmɪs/
*v.*❶ discharge from employment or office 解雇；开除：He was ~ed for being lazy and dishonest.他因懒惰和不诚实而被解雇。❷ send away or allow to leave 解散；遣散：The teacher ~ed the class when the bell rang.铃声响了,教师让学生下课。‖ ~**al** *n.*解雇；撤职；解散

dismissive/dɪsˈmɪsɪv/
*adj.*considering a person, idea, etc. to be not worthy of attention or respect 对……轻视的；轻蔑的；鄙视的：He might have been less ~ of their talents if he could have seen their latest achievements.如果他看到他们最近的成就,他也许就不会那么小看他们的才干了。

dismount/dɪsˈmaunt/
*v.*❶ get down from a horse; get down from the bus（使）下马;（使）下车：The knight ~ed his opponent.这个武士把他的对手打下马来。/He ~ed near the village.他在村庄附近下了马。❷ unfold and unload（machines, guns）拆卸（机器）;卸（炮）：~ a gun from its carriage 从炮架上卸下大炮

disobey/ˌdɪsəˈbeɪ/
*v.*fail to obey（rules, a command or sb. in authority）不服从：Soldiers must never ~.军人以服从命令为天职。/~ one's mother 不听母亲的话‖ **disobedient** /ˌdɪsəˈbiːdɪənt/ *adj.*不服从的／**disobedience** *n.*不服从

disorder/dɪsˈɔːdə(r)/
*n.*lack of order;confusion 混乱；骚乱；紊乱：The burglars left the room in great ~.窃贼将这房间弄得乱七八糟。/The police went to the scene of the ~.警察到骚乱现场去。‖ ~**ly** *adj.*混乱的；秩序紊乱的

disordered /dɪsˈɔːdə(r)ed/
*adj.*showing a lack of order or control 杂乱的；混乱的；凌乱的：her ~ hair 她乱七八糟的头发 /a ~ state 混乱状态

disorient(**ate**) /dɪsˈɔːrɪent(eɪt)/

*v.*❶confuse someone and make them lose their sense of direction 使迷失方向：When she emerged into the street she was totally disorientated. 她一走到街上，就晕头转向。❷ make（someone）feel confused 使迷惑 ‖ disoriented, disorientated *adj.*不错所措的；迷失方向的

dispassionate /dɪˈspæʃənət/

adj. calm and impartial, not considering one's personal feelings and so able to decide what is right 冷静公正的；超然的；平心静气的

dispatch /dɪsˈpætʃ/

Ⅰ *v.*send off 派遣；发出：He ～ed his son to the shop to buy beer. 他打发儿子去店里买啤酒。/～ letters 发信 Ⅱ *n.*❶ the act of sending off or being sent off 打发；派出；发出：Hurry up the ～ of this telegram. 赶快发出这个电报。❷ a quick message, especially an official message or news report 政府公文；电讯：We received ～es from all parts of the world. 我们收到了世界各地发来的新闻电讯。‖ ～box *n.*公文箱

dispel /dɪˈspel/

v.(-ll-) drive away 驱散：The sun ～led the mist. 阳光驱散了薄雾。

dispense /dɪˈspens/

v. give out to；prodive sth. for people 分发；施予：The Red Cross ～d food and clothing to the sufferers. 红十字会给受难者分发食物和衣服。/～ justice 主持公道/～ charity to people 放赈 ‖ ～ with 不要；无需：He is well enough to ～ with the doctor's services. 他已痊愈，无需医生照顾了。

disperse /dɪˈspɜːs/

*v.*scatter in different directions；disappear 驱散；分散；散开；消散：The crowd ～d. 人群散了。/The wind ～d the clouds. 风吹散了乌云。

dispirited /dɪˈspɪrɪtɪd/

*adj.*unhappy and without hope 沮丧的；气馁的

displace /dɪsˈpleɪs/

*v.*❶take the place of sth. by pushing out 取代；挤掉：Television has ～d motion pictures as the most popular form of entertainment. 电视已取代电影成为最普及的娱乐形式。❷ force out of the usual place 移位：He ～d the computer from his bedroom to his reading room. 他把电脑从卧室移到书房。‖ ～ment *n.*取代；移位

display /dɪˈspleɪ/

Ⅰ *v.*❶ place or spread out sth. so that there is no difficulty in seeing 陈列；展示：Department stores ～ their goods in the window. 百货商店在橱窗里展示商品。❷ show signs of sth., especially a quality or feeling 显示，显露；表现 Ⅱ *n.* showing；performance 展示；表演：a ～ of skill 技术表演/a ～ of fruit 水果陈列品 ‖ on ～ 展出

displease /dɪsˈpliːz/

v. cause displeasure to；annoy 惹……生气；恼怒：His conduct ～d his teacher. 他的行为惹得他老师生气。‖ ～d *adj.*不高兴的/displeasing *adj.*使人不高兴的；令人生气的/displeasure /dɪsˈpleʒə(r)/ *n.*不高兴；生气：a frown of displeasure 因不满而皱眉

disposable /dɪˈspəʊzəbl/

*adj.*❶designed to be thrown away after it has been used 一次性的；用后即丢弃的：a ～ razor 一次性剃刀 ❷available to be used as needed, at your disposal 可随时使用的；可自由支配的 ‖ disposable *adj.*一次性的；用完即可丢弃的

disposal /dɪˈspəʊzl/

*n.*❶an action of getting rid of sth. 处理；处置；清理；去掉：the ～ of rubbish 垃圾的处理/The ～ of the difficulty pleased everybody. 困难的解决使人人都感到满意。❷ arrangement 布置；排列；安排：the ～ of business affairs 事务的安排 / the ～ of furniture in the room 室内家具的陈设 ❸the power or right to use sth. freely 使用权；支配权：the ～ of troops 兵力的部署/the ～ of the property 财产的分配

dispose /dɪˈspəʊz/

*v.*❶ place in good order；arrange 排列；布置：Man proposes, god ～s. 谋事在人，成

D

事在天．/The cruisers were ～d in line abreast.巡洋舰被布置成横队. ❷（～ of）finish with;get rid of;deal with 处理;除掉;解决: He ～d of his old furniture.他把旧家具处理掉。 ❸ （～ to） give a tendency to 使倾向于;使有意于: He is ～d to sudden periods of anger.他老喜欢突然发脾气。‖ ～r n.废物清除器

disposition/ˌdɪspə'zɪʃn/

n.❶ a person's inherent qualities of mind or character 性格;性情;气质: He has a very friendly ～.他的性情十分和善。 ❷ an inclination or tendency 倾向;意向 ❸ the action of arranging people or things in a particular way 安排;配置

disproportionate/ˌdɪsprə'pɔːʃənət/

adj.not equal in size or amount;too great or too little（大小或数量）不相称的;不均衡的;不成比例的

disprove/ˌdɪs'pruːv/

v.show that sth. is not true 证明……不成立;反驳

dispute/dɪ'spjuːt/

Ⅰ*v*.argue or debate (with or against sb.on or about sth.);disagree about or question the truth or correctness of 争论;辩论;质疑: It is ridiculous to ～ about such things.争论这样的问题真是可笑。Ⅱ*n*.a disagreement,argument or debate quarrel 争论;争端: The ～ grew more violent.争论变得更加激烈。/a border ～ 边界争端‖ beyond（all）～ 无可争辩的/in（under）～ 在争论中的/in ～ with 和……有争议‖ disputable *adj*.值得争论的;不能肯定的/disputatious /ˌdɪspjuː'teɪʃəs/ *adj*.好争辩的

disqualify/ˌdɪs'kwɒlɪfaɪ/

v.make or declare sb.unfit, unsuitable, or unable to do sth. 使某人不适合（不能,无资格）做某事: His health disqualified him from military service. 由于身体不好,他不能服兵役。‖ disqualification *n*.不适合;无资格

disquiet/dɪs'kwaɪət/

Ⅰ*v*.make anxious 使焦虑不安: His illness ～ed his wife.他的病使其妻子焦虑不安。Ⅱ*n*.anxiety 焦虑;不安: The news

caused ～ in the public.这一消息在公众中引起不安。

disregard/ˌdɪsrɪ'ɡɑːd/

Ⅰ*v*.pay no attention to;treat as unimportant or unworthy of notice 不理会;不重视;不尊重: He ～ed his father's advice and failed.他不理会他父亲的忠告,失败了。Ⅱ*n*.lack of proper attention to or respect for sb.or sth.漠视;忽视;蔑视: The government has shown a total ～ for the needs of the poor.政府对穷人的需求表现出完全漠视的态度。

disrepute/ˌdɪsrɪ'pjuːt/

n.loss or lack of people's good fame;bad repute 丧失名誉;坏名声: The hotel fell into ～ after the shooting incident.枪击事件发生后,这家旅馆便声誉扫地。/This pointless prosecution has brought the law into ～.这件无意义的起诉已为司法界招来恶名。

disrespect/ˌdɪsrɪ'spekt/

n.lack of respect or politeness 不敬;无礼: He meant no ～ by that remark.他说那句话并无不敬之意。‖ ～ful *adj*.不尊敬的;没礼貌的

disrupt/dɪs'rʌpt/

v. bring or throw (an event, activity or process) into disorder 扰乱;打乱: The special TV report ～ed regular programmes.专题报道节目打乱了正常的电视节目。‖ ～ion *n*.扰乱;破坏/～ive *adj*.扰乱的;捣乱性的

dissatisfy/dɪ'sætɪsfaɪ/

v.fail to satisfy;displease 令不满足;令不满意: The manager is dissatisfied with his work.经理对他的工作不满意。‖ dissatisfaction /ˌdɪˌsætɪs'fækʃn/ *n*.不满

dissemble /dɪ'sembl/

v.conceal your true feelings 伪装,掩藏（真实情感）: She was a very honest person who was incapable of dissembling.她是一个非常诚实的人,不会伪装。

dissent/dɪ'sent/

Ⅰ*v*.（～ from）have or express opinions which are opposed to official views, religious teaching, etc.持异议;不同意: I ～ from what he said.我不同意他的发言。

Ⅱ *n*.the holding or expression of opinions (意见的)不一致,分歧:express strong ～ 表示极不赞同‖～er *n*.持不同意见者

dissident /ˈdɪsɪdənt/
Ⅰ *adj*.not agreeing with others;refusing to accept the beliefs or leadership of others 持异议的;唱反调的;持不同政见的 Ⅱ *n*.a person who does not agree with others 持不同意见者

dissociate /dɪˈsəʊʃɪeɪt/
v.disconnect or separate (in thought,feeling);not associate with 分离;脱离:～ two ideas from another 把两个概念与另一个概念分开/ You cannot ～ a man from his words and deeds.你不能把一个人和他的言行分开。/He ～d himself from the committee's request.他否认与委员会的要求有关。

dissolute /ˈdɪsəluːt/
adj.unrestrained by convention or morality 放荡的;风流的

dissolution /ˌdɪsəˈljuːʃən/
n.❶putting an end to a marriage or partnership (婚姻关系的)解除;(合作关系的)终止 ❷formally ending a parliament or assembly (议会的)解散

dissolve /dɪˈzɒlv/
v.❶ (cause to) become liquid as the result of being taken into a liquid;melt 溶解;使溶解:Sugar ～s in water.糖溶于水。❷ disappear;bring or come to an end 消失;终止:The view ～d in mist.那景色消失在雾中。

dissuade /dɪˈsweɪd/
v.persuade sb. not to do sth.;make sb. agree not to do sth. by talking to him 劝阻,说服(某人)不做某事:I ～d him from borrowing the money.我劝他不要借钱。

distance /ˈdɪstəns/
n.a measure of space between two points,places,etc.;the state of being far off 距离;遥远:The town is a great ～ off.那城市很遥远。/the ～ of the sun from the earth 太阳与地球的距离/be a great ～ away 离得很远/within easy ～ of some place 离某处很近‖ at a (some) ～ 在一定远处/at a ～ of 在……远的地方/from

a ～ 从一定远处/in the ～ 在远处/keep at a ～ 保持一定距离;不很亲密/no ～ 很近

distant /ˈdɪstənt/
adj.separate in space or time;far off 遥远的;远处的:This is no ～ dream.这已不是遥远的梦。/～ music 远处的音乐声/at some far ～ time 在遥远的古代/past 遥远的过去/～ cousins 远房堂(表)兄弟(姐妹)/a ～ attitude 疏远的态度‖～ly *adv*.遥远地

distend /dɪˈstend/
v.(cause to) swell out by pressure from inside (使)膨胀;(使)胀大:a ～ed stomach 扩张的胃

distil /dɪˈstɪl/
v.make (a liquid)into gas and then make the gas into liquid 蒸馏;用蒸馏法提纯;蒸馏掉:～ed water 蒸馏水/～ out sth.将某物蒸馏掉‖～lation *n*.蒸馏;用蒸馏法制取(提纯)

distinct /dɪˈstɪŋkt/
adj.❶ easily heard, seen or understood 清晰的;明显的:The earth's shadow on the moon was quite ～.月球上的地球阴影十分清晰。/There is a ～ smell of dead mouse in the room.这房间里有明显的死老鼠的味。❷ separate;different 不同的;有区别的:Silk is ～ from rayon.蚕丝和人造丝不同。/a ～ question 一个不同的问题‖～ly *adv*.清晰地

distinction /dɪˈstɪŋkʃn/
n.❶ a difference or contrast 区分;差别:make a ～ between the two words 区分这两个词的差别 /She treated all her children alike without ～.她对待自己所有的孩子都一视同仁。❷excellence that sets sb.or sth.better than many others 卓越;杰出:people of ～ 知名人士 /a writer of ～ 杰出的作家 ❸a special mark,grade or award that is given to sb.奖赏;荣誉;卓越的成绩:an actor of ～ 有名的演员 /win ～s 得到荣誉 /graduate from college with ～ 以优异成绩从大学毕业 /He won many ～s of bravery and wisdom.他智勇双全获得了很高的荣誉。

distinctive /dɪsˈtɪŋktɪv/

adj. that distinguishes one thing from others 独特的；特别的；有特色的：The school has a ～ uniform.这个学校的校服很特别。

distinguish/dɪˈstɪŋgwɪʃ/

v.❶ recognize the difference between two things or people 区分；辨别：The twins are so much alike that it is impossible to ～ one from the other.这对孪生子像得使人无法分辨。/～ right from wrong 明辨是非 ❷ see,hear,or notice as being separate or distinct;recognize clearly 看清；听清；分清：I couldn't ～ the face of the man because it was too dark.因光线太暗我无法看清那人的脸。❸ be a characteristics that makes two things or people different 使区别于；使突出：What ～es a star from a planet? 恒星与行星何以区别？ ‖ ～able *adj*. 可区别的；看得清的：be easily ～able from someone 易与某人区分

distinguished /dɪsˈtɪŋgwɪʃt/

adj.❶ having a high reputation 权威的；受尊重的：a ～ author 一位德高望重的作家 ❷ noble and dignified in appearance or behaviour 高贵的；有尊严的

distort/dɪˈstɔːt/

v.twist out of the shape;give a false account of;twist out of the truth 扭曲；扭曲；使变形；曲解：a ～ing mirror 哈哈镜 /～ the facts 歪曲事实 /His face was ～ed with pain.他的脸因痛苦而扭曲。

distract/dɪˈstrækt/

v. take（persons or their attention）off sth.,especially for a short time 使转移注意力；使分心：The noise in the street ～ed me from my reading.街上的嘈杂声使我不能专心读书。 ‖ ～ion *n*.精神涣散

distress/dɪˈstres/

Ⅰ *n*.❶ a great pain,sorrow or anxiety（极度的）痛苦；忧伤；焦虑：She is in ～ about her father's illness. 她为父亲的病忧伤。 ❷ poverty 穷困；困苦：relieve ～ among the poor 解除穷人的困苦 ❸ a serious danger 危险：a ship in ～ 遇难船只 ❹ sth. that causes great suffering of the mind 使人痛苦的事：This is a great ～ to him.这是使他十分痛苦的事。 Ⅱ *v*.make sb.sad;cause unhappiness to 使痛苦；使难过：Don't ～ yourself. 不要担忧。 ‖ ～ing *adj*.使人痛苦(难受)的

distressed /dɪˈstrest/

adj.suffering from extreme anxiety,sorrow,or pain 焦虑的；悲伤的；痛苦的：the ～ relatives of the victims 受害人悲痛欲绝的亲属

distribute/dɪˈstrɪbjuːt/

v.❶ divide and give out 分配；分发：The teacher ～d the examination papers to the students.老师把试卷分发给学生。 ❷ spread out over an area 分布；散布：Troops were ～d all over the country.全国都布有军队。 /～ manure 施肥

distribution/ˌdɪstrɪˈbjuːʃn/

n. the action of sharing sth. out among a number of recipients 分配；分布：the ～ of prizes 奖品的分发 /the ～ of wealth 财富的分配 /a wide ～ 广泛的分布

district/ˈdɪstrɪkt/

n.a fixed division of a country,a city,etc., made for various official purposes 地区；行政区；管区：The city is divided into four ～s.这个城市划分为四个区。

distrust/dɪsˈtrʌst/

Ⅰ *v*.lack trust or confidence in;have little faith in 不信任：I don't make friends with people that I ～.我不和我不信任的人交朋友。 Ⅱ *n*.a feeling of not being able to trust sb. or sth.不信任：The child looked at the stranger with ～.小孩以不信任的眼光瞧着那生人。 ‖ ～ful *adj*.不信任的

disturb/dɪˈstɜːb/

v.❶ break the quiet,calm,peace,or order of 破坏安静(和平、秩序)；扰乱：A loud whistle ～ed the quietness of the forest. 一声响哨打破了林中的宁静。/～ the peace 扰乱治安 ❷ change the usual or natural condition of 干扰；打扰：May I ～ you for a moment? 能否稍稍打断你一下？ ❸ make (sb.) anxiously dissatisfied; worry 使心忧；使烦恼：The rumor ～ed the whole village.这谣言令全村人惶惶不安。 ‖ ～ance *n*.打扰；不安；骚乱

disturbed /dɪsˈtɜːbd/

   adj.(said about a person) suffering from emotional or psychological problems 心神不安的；心烦意乱的；精神紊乱的：～behaviour 失常的行为/He was deeply ～ by the news.这消息使他深感不安。

ditch/dɪtʃ/

   *n.*a long narrow channel dug in the fields or at the side of the road to carry off water 沟；渠：They dug a ～ at the foot of the hill last year.他们去年在山脚下挖了一条水渠。

dive/daɪv/

   v. ❶ jump into water with the head and arms going in first 跳水：He ～d from the bridge into the lake.他自桥上跳入湖水中。❷ go under water using breathing equipment 潜水：She ～d for pearls.她潜水探寻珍珠。❸ go quickly to a lower level；go down or out of sight suddenly 暴跌；俯冲：The eagle ～d to catch the hare.老鹰俯冲捕捉野兔。

diver/ˈdaɪvə(r)/

   *n.*a person who dives，especially one who works at the bottom of the sea in special clothing with a supply of air 跳水者，（尤指）潜水员

diverge/daɪˈvɜːdʒ/

   *v.*separate and go out in different directions 分叉；岔开：Their paths ～d at the fork in the road.他们在岔路口分道而行。‖ ～nce *n.*分歧；分散/ ～nt *adj.*发散的：～nt lens 发散透镜

diverse/daɪˈvɜːs/

   *adj.*different；various 各种不同的；多种多样的：People all over the world speak ～ languages.全世界的人讲多种不同的语言。

diversify/daɪˈvɜːsɪfaɪ/

   *v.*make or become different in forms，qualities，aims，or activities；vary （使）多样化：～ the products 使产品多样化

diversity /daɪˈvɜːsɪti/

   *n.*❶the state of being diverse 差异；不同；多样性：There was considerable ～ in the style of the paintings.这些画风格迥异。❷a range of different things 不同事物

divert/daɪˈvɜːt/

   v. ❶cause to turn aside or change from one use or direction to another 使转移：When the car crashed，the police ～ed the traffic.撞车时，警察指挥车辆改道行驶。/～ his attention from playing games 转移他玩游戏的注意力❷entertain or amuse 娱乐；消遣：～ oneself in singing 唱歌消遣 ‖ diversion *n.*转移；引开；消遣

divide/dɪˈvaɪd/

   v. ❶ separate or be separated into parts；keep apart or set apart （使）分开；划分；隔开：When the path ～s you must follow the left way.到了这条路的分岔处，你要走左边的路。/The river ～s my land from his.这条河将我的土地与他的土地分隔开来。/～ a thing in two 把东西分为两部分 ❷ separate and give out or share 分；分配：He ～d money among his sons.他将钱分给儿子们。❸find out how many times one number contains another 除：20 ～d by 5 is 4.20 除以 5 等于 4。

dividend /ˈdɪvɪdend/

   *n.*❶a benefit from an action 红利；回报；收益：This policy will pay ～s in the future.这项政策的好处将来会体现出来。❷a number that is to be divided by another 被除数

division/dɪˈvɪʒn/

   *n.*❶the action of separating sth.into parts 分开；分隔 ❷the distribution of sth.separated into parts 分配：a fair ～ 公平的分配 ❸a major unit or section of an organization （机构的）部分：the ～ of business 营业部/the sales ～ 销售部

divine/dɪˈvaɪn/

   Ⅰ*adj.*❶ of or like a god；sacred 神的；神圣的：Divine Service 敬神仪式 ❷ excellent in the highest degree；pleasing 很好的；超人的；悦人的：～ weather 好天气/You look simply ～，dear! 亲爱的，你看上去真美! Ⅱ*v.*❶ discover or guess by or as if by magical means 预测；占卜；预言：Astrologers claim to be able to ～ what the stars hold in store for us.占星学家声称能够卜出星球上都为我们储备了些什么。❷sense sth. by intuition 直觉；推测：～ a person's intention 识破某人的意图

diving /ˈdaɪvɪŋ/

n. ❶ the sport or activity of diving into water from a diving board 跳水 ❷ the sport or activity of swimming or exploring under water 潜水

divorce /dɪˈvɔːs/

Ⅰ *n.* the official ending of a marriage, especially as declared by a court of law 离婚；分离：This marriage ended in ～.这桩婚姻以离婚结束。/get a ～ from someone 与某人离婚/the ～ between religion and science 宗教与科学的分离 Ⅱ *v.* ❶ officially end a marriage between (a husband and wife) or to (a husband or a wife) 使离婚；同(丈夫或妻子)离婚：She ～d her husband. 她同丈夫离了婚。❷ separate 使分离；划分开：Is he still unable to ～ fantasy from reality? 他仍不能将幻想与现实分开吗？/～ religion and politics 使政教分离

divulge /daɪˈvʌldʒ/

v. make sth. secret known 泄露(秘密)：I can not ～ how much it cost.我不能把价钱泄露出来。

dizzy /ˈdɪzi/

adj. having an uncomfortable feeling in the head, as though things were moving 头晕目眩的；头晕眼花的：I felt ～ after travelling all day in the car.乘车旅行了一整天，我感到头晕目眩。

do /duː/

v. (did, done) ❶ used with another verb, especially to form questions or negatives, etc.(用作助动词，在疑问句、否定句等句中与主要动词连用)：I don't believe him. 我不相信他。/Didn't she sing well? 她不是唱得挺好吗？/Not only did he come, but he saw her.他不仅来了，而且见到了她。/Please ～ be seated.请务必坐下。/I ～ want to go with you.我一定要同你一道去。❷ used instead of another verb (用以替代另一动词以避免重复)："Did he come?""Yes, he did.""他来过吗？""是，他来过。"/He likes it, doesn't he? 他喜欢这个，是吗？❸ perform the actions that are necessary in order to complete (sth.) or bring it into a desired state 完成(某事)：You must ～ your

work well.你必须把工作干好。/～ business 做生意/～ repairs 搞修理/～ the reading 读书 ❹ combined with nouns in many senses (与名词连用，表达不同的动作)：He is ～ing economics at Beijing University.他在北京大学学习经济学。/～ an article 写篇论文/～ some copies 复制若干份/～ wonders 创造奇迹/～ the flowers 插花/～ a math problem 解数学题/～ one's hair 做头发/～ the dishes 洗碗碟/～ the room 收拾房间/～ one's face 脸部化妆/～ Hamlet 演哈姆莱特/～ sb. justice 公正待某人/～ a person well 待人好 ❺ finish 完成；结束：Will he ever be done? 他有没有完成的时候？/Is the meat done yet? 肉炖烂了没有？❻ suit; make progress or perform in a specified way 适合；进展：When in Rome, ～ as the Romans ～. 入乡随俗。/That won't ～.那不行。/The patient is ～ing well.病人情况良好。/That will ～! 那就行了！‖ ～ **away with** 废除；取消：These privileges must be done away with.必须取消这些特权。/～ **good** 做好事/～ **harm** 为害；有害处/～ **one's a favour (kindness, etc.)** 帮个忙/～ **one's best** 尽最大努力/～ **one's duty** 履行职责/～ **over** 重做；重新收拾/～ **up** 收拾；修理；装饰；打扮；包扎；系扣：We bought an old house and are ～ing it up.我们买了一所旧房，正在整修。/Do up the buttons on your shirt, please. 请把衬衫的纽扣扣好。/～ **with** 处置；想要；需要；有关系；就可以了：I don't know what to ～ with myself.我不知道自己该怎么办。/I could ～ with a cup of tea.我想要一杯茶。/I don't think you ought to have anything to ～ with him.我认为你和他不必有任何关系。/I can ～ with this.我有了这个就可以了。/～**without** 没有……也行；不用 ‖ ～**ing** *n.* 干的事；行为

dock /dɒk/

Ⅰ *n.* a place where ships are loaded, unloaded, or repaired 船坞；码头：go into ～ 进入船坞 Ⅱ *v.* (of a ship) come into dock (指船)进入船坞：This ship ～ed this morning.这艘船今天早上靠码头的。

docker /ˈdɒkə(r)/

n. a person who works at a dock, loading and unloading ships 码头工人

docket /ˈdɒkɪt/

Ⅰ *n.* a label or document describing the contents of sth., giving information about its use, etc. (载明内容、用途等的)标签，单据 Ⅱ *v.* describe in a docket 把……用标签加以说明：~ a parcel of goods 给一包货物加上说明标签

dockland /ˈdɒklənd/

n. the area around the docks in large port 港区；码头区：London's ~ by the Thames 伦敦泰晤士河边的码头区/~ development 码头区的开发

dockyard /ˈdɒkjɑːd/

n. a place where ships are built or repaired；a shipyard 造船厂；修船厂

doctor /ˈdɒktə(r)/

n. ❶ a person who has been trained in medical science 医生：see a ~ 看医生/an animal ~ 兽医/an army ~ 军医 ❷ a person who has received the highest degree given by a university 博士：Doctor of Philosophy 哲学博士：She gained a ~'s degree by studying hard. 她通过刻苦学习获得博士学位。

doctrine /ˈdɒktrɪn/

n. beliefs and teachings (of a church, political party, school of scientists, etc.) 教义；主义；学说：a matter of ~ 教旨问题/Marxist ~ 马克思主义

document /ˈdɒkjʊmənt/

Ⅰ *n.* sth. written or printed to be used as a record or in evidence 文件；文献；证书：official ~s 官方文件/~ of title 契据/a legal ~ 法律文件 Ⅱ *v.* prove or support sth. with documents 用文件证明；以文献为依据：The history of this area is very well ~ed. 这个地区的历史有充分的文献为依据。 ‖ ~ation *n.* (提供)证明文件

documentary /ˌdɒkjʊˈmentəri/

Ⅰ *adj.* ❶ consisting of documents 文件的；文献的；文件组成的：~ evidence 书面证据 ❷ giving a factual filmed report of a subject or activity 记录的；纪实的 Ⅱ *n.* (*pl.*-ies) a film giving information about real events 纪录影片

doddle /ˈdɒdl/

n. sth. that is very easy 轻而易举的事：That driving test was a real ~. 那次驾驶测验实在太容易了。

dodge /dɒdʒ/

Ⅰ *v.* ❶ avoid sth. by moving suddenly aside 躲闪；避开：~ a blow 躲开打击/~ about 东躲西藏/make a sudden ~ aside 迅速闪避一旁 ❷ avoid (a responsibility, duty, etc.) by a trick or in some dishonest way；evade 推托；逃避：~ military service 逃避兵役 Ⅱ *n.* ❶ a quick movement to avoid sth. 躲避；推托 ❷ a dishonest trick 骗人的诡计：He's up to all the ~s. 他诡计多端。

dodgem /ˈdɒdʒəmz/

n. a small electrically powered car with rubber bumpers all round in an enclosed space, often intentionally hitting other cars (游乐场中的)碰碰车，迷你电动车

dodgy /ˈdɒdʒi/

adj. ❶ not safe；risky；dangerous 不安全的；冒险的；危险的：a ~ plan 冒险的计划 /Don't sit on that chair；it's a bit ~. 别坐在那把椅子上，它有点儿不稳。 ❷ dishonest and unreliable 不诚实，不可靠的，狡诈的：a ~ person 狡诈的人

doe /dəʊ/

n. a female deer, rabbit or hare 母鹿；雌兔

doer /ˈduːə(r)/

n. a person who does things 做事的人；实行者；实干家：an evil-~ 作恶的人 /She's a ~, not just a thinker. 她不只是一个思想家，还是一个实干家。

dog /dɒg/

Ⅰ *n.* ❶ a common animal with four legs and a tail, kept as a pet or trained for work 狗：a police ~ 警犬/a hunting ~ 猎犬/a watch ~ 看门狗 Ⅱ *v.* (-gg-) keep close behind；follow 尾随；追随：~ a thief 跟踪小偷 ‖ die a ~'s death (die like a ~) 悲惨地死去；可耻地死去/go to the ~s 堕落；落魄/help a lame ~ over a stile 助人于危难之中；雪中送炭/lead a ~'s life 过悲惨的日子/It rains cats and ~s. 大雨倾盆。/~ days 酷暑天/~ paddle 狗刨式游泳

dogma/'dɒgmə/

n.(*pl.*~s or dogmata/'dɒgmətə/) an important belief or set of beliefs that people are expected to accept without reasoning 教义;教条:a political ~ 政治信条 ‖ ~**tic**/dɒg'mætɪk/ *adj.*教条的;武断的/~**tically** *adv.*教条地;武断地/~**tism** *n.* 教条主义

dole/dəʊl/

Ⅰ *v.*(~ **out**)give out in small amounts 少量地发放:He ~d out the food to the children.他把少量的食品分发给孩子们。 Ⅱ *n.* ❶ money given every week by the government to people without work（政府每周分发的）失业救济金:He's on the ~.他靠救济金生活。 ❷ sth. distributed 施舍物

doleful/'dəʊlfl/

*adj.*very miserable 非常可怜的;悲惨的

doll/dɒl/

Ⅰ *n.* ❶ a model of a baby or person, usually for a child to play with 洋娃娃;玩偶:My aunt gave me a ~.我姨妈给我一个漂亮的洋娃娃。 ❷ a pretty but empty-headed girl or woman 美丽而无头脑的女人:She's quite a ~! 她真是个漂亮而无头脑的女人。 Ⅱ *v.*dress (oneself) up smartly 漂亮地打扮自己:I'm going to get ~ed up for the party.我要打扮得漂漂亮亮地去参加宴会。

dollar/'dɒlə(r)/

*n.*a unit of money in the USA, Canada, and some other countries 元（美国、加拿大和某些其他国家的货币单位）:One ~ and eighty-seven cents was all she had saved.1 美元 87 分是她的全部积蓄。

dollop/'dɒləp/

n. ❶ a shapeless mass 一团;一块:a ~ of clay 一团黏土 ❷ a spoonful, especially of food（尤指食物的）一匙之量

dolly/'dɒli/

*n.*❶ (used especially by and to children)a child's doll（尤用作儿语）(玩具)娃娃 ❷ a flat frame on wheels for moving heavy objects, such as television or cinema cameras（移动重物用的）手推车;移动式摄像（摄影）机座台

dolphin/'dɒlfɪn/

*n.*a type of intelligent air-breathing sea creature with a beak-like snout and a curved fin on the back 海豚

domain/də'meɪn/

n. ❶ lands owned or controlled by one person, a government, etc. 领土;领地:His ~ extends for 20 miles in every direction.他的领地伸向四周 20 英里。 ❷ an area of activity, interest, or knowledge（活动、兴趣、知识的）领域,范围:the ~ of science 科学领域

dome/dəʊm/

*n.*a large rounded roof 大而圆的屋顶

domestic/də'mestɪk/

*adj.*❶of the home, family, household 家里的;家庭的:She's a very ~ sort of woman.她是个十分喜欢家庭生活的女子。/~ service 家务 ❷ not foreign, native 国内的;本国的;国产的:~ and foreign news 国内和国际新闻/~commerce (trade) 国内贸易/~ loans 内债/a ~ make 国产货 ❸ (of animals, etc.) kept by man（动物等）由人饲养的:Horses, cows and sheep are ~ animals.马、牛和羊是家畜。

domesticate/də'mestɪkeɪt/

*v.*make (an animal)able to live with people and work for them, especially on a farm or as a pet 驯养（动物）:Cows are ~d to provide us with milk.人们饲养奶牛来为我们提供牛奶。

domicile/'dɒmɪsaɪl/

*n.*a person's home; the place where a person lives or is considered to live for official purposes 住处,家;正式居住地,住所:His last known ~ was 10 New Street, Cambridge.他最近一次为人所知的住所是剑桥新街 10 号。

domiciled/'dɒmɪsaɪld/

*adj.*having one's domicile 有固定住所的;定居的:He does some work in the Middle East but is ~ in Britain for tax purposes.他在中东地区有些工作,但为了税务上的原因而把家安在英国。

dominance/'dɒmɪnəns/

*n.*the fact of position of dominating; pow-

D

er or controlling influence 支配(统治)地位;控制力;影响力：Our ~ of the market is seriously threatened by this new product.我们在市场上的优势受到这种新产品的严重威胁。

dominant /'dɒmɪnənt/
Ⅰ *adj.* ❶ most noticeable or important 最显著的;最重要的：Blue is the ~ colour in his later paintings.蓝色是他晚期油画中的主色。/Peace was the ~ theme of the conference.和平是大会的首要议题。❷ high and easily seen 高耸的;突出的：The Town Hall was built in a ~ position on a hill.市政厅建在山上一处居高临下的地方。❸ stronger than the other parts of a system or group（同一系统或类别中）有势力的,占优势的,支配的：The right hand is ~ in most people.大多数人的右手是优势手。/a ~ group in society 社会上占支配地位的团体 ❹ having control or authority;dominating 支配的;统治的;占优势的：a ~ personality 霸道的性格 ❺ (of groups of physical qualities passed on from parent to child) able to appear in the child even if only in the genes of one parent（遗传物质）显性的：Brown eyes are ~ and blue eyes are recessive.棕色眼睛是显性的,蓝色眼睛是隐性的。Ⅱ *n.* the fifth note of a musical scale of eight notes 全音阶的第五音

dominate /'dɒmɪneɪt/
v. ❶ have a commanding influence on 控制;支配：The strong usually ~ (over) the weak.强者通常统治弱者。❷ have the most important place or position (in);be the most obvious thing in a place 居于主位;高耸于：Sports,and not learning,seem to ~ (in) that school.那所学校看来是以运动为主,而不是以学习为主。/The building ~s the town.这座建筑物高耸于全城之上。

domination /ˌdɒmɪ'neɪʃn/
n. the act of dominating or the state of being dominated 支配;控制;统治;优势：After the leader died,rival parties struggled for ~ of the community.那位领导人去世后,互相抗衡的各个党派为取得对该社区的控制而争夺起来。

domineer /ˌdɒmɪ'nɪə(r)/
v. try to control other people,usually without any consideration of their feelings or wishes 专横;跋扈：a ~ing personality 专横的性格/He ~ed,and the rest of us hated it.他行事专横,我们大家都讨厌他这种作风。

domineering /ˌdɒmɪ'nɪərɪŋ/
adj. trying to control other people without considering their opinions or feelings 专断的;专横的：a ~ manner 专断的态度

dominion /də'mɪnɪən/
n. ❶ the power or right to rule 主权;统治权 ❷ the territory of a sovereign government 领土;领地;疆土：the vast ~s of the Chinese 中国的辽阔疆土

domino /'dɒmɪnəʊ/
n. (*pl.* ~s or ~es) a small flat oblong piece of wood or plastic with spots on one side,used in the game of dominoes 多米诺骨牌

donate /dəʊ'neɪt/
v. give money of goods,especially to a charity;contribute 捐赠：~ money to an orphanage 捐款给一所孤儿院 ‖ **donation** *n.* 捐赠;捐助款(物)：He made a donation of one million yuan to the Red Cross.他给红十字会捐赠 100 万元。

done /dʌn/
Ⅰ *adj.* ❶ carried out or completed 实现的;完成的：I'll be glad when this job is over and ~ with.这个工作彻底完成后我就高兴了。❷ (of food) cooked thoroughly (食物)煮透了的：The meat isn't quite ~ yet.这肉还不太熟。❸ no longer happening or existing 不再发生的;不再存在的 Ⅱ *int.* used to indicate that the speaker accepts the terms of an offer（用来表示说话人接受一项要约的条件）成交："I'll give you 1,000 for it." "Done!" "我出 1000 元买它。" "成交！"

donkey /'dɒŋki/
n. ❶ an animal like a small horse with long ears 驴：Donkeys are better than horses on mountain trails.走山间小路驴胜过马。❷ a stupid person 蠢人：He's a bit of a ~;he does silly things.他多少有

点蠢,尽干傻事儿。

donor/ˈdəʊnə(r)/

　　n. a person who donates（especially one who gives blood for use in hospitals）捐赠者(尤指献血者)

doodle/ˈduːdl/

　　v. make a drawing or pattern while thinking about sth. else 乱画；涂写；涂鸦：People sometimes ～ while they are listening to a lecture. 听讲座时人们有时会在笔记本上涂鸦。

doom/duːm/

　　Ⅰ *n.* death, destruction or any terrible and inevitable fate 毁灭；死亡；厄运：go to one's ～ 走向灭亡/send a man to his ～ 将一人处死　Ⅱ *v.* condemn to certain destruction or death 宣告……的毁灭；宣告……的死亡：From the start, the plan was ～ed to failure. 这个计划从一开始就已注定要失败。

door/dɔː(r)/

　　n. the entrance to a building or room；the flat piece of wood, metal, etc. which shuts the entrance 门；房门；柜门：The ～ opened and a man came out. 门开了,一个男人走了出来。/open the ～ 开门/knock at the ～ 敲门/the kitchen ～ 厨房门/the front ～ and the back ～ 前门和后门/answer the ～ 应声开门 ‖ at death's ～ 就要死了/at one's ～ 就在附近/from ～ to ～ 挨家挨户/next ～ 隔壁/out of ～s 在户外;露天的 ‖ ～bell *n.* 门铃/～keeper *n.* 看门人/～plate *n.* 门牌/～way *n.* 门口

dormant/ˈdɔːmənt/

　　adj. (especially of plants, volcanoes, animals, ideas, organizations, etc.) sleeping；not active but able to be active later on (尤指植物、火山、动物、想法、组织等)休眠的,蛰伏的,暂时静止的,暂停的

dormitory/ˈdɔːmɪtri/

　　n. a room for sleeping, with several beds 寝室；集体宿舍：Children sleep in dormitories when they live at school. 孩子们住校时,在集体宿舍就寝。

dorsal/ˈdɔːsl/

　　adj. of, on or near the back, especially of an animal (尤指动物的)背部的,背面的,近背部的：the ～ fin 脊鳍

dorsum/ˈdɔːsəm/

　　n. ❶ the back (of an animal)（动物的）背,背部 ❷ the part corresponding to or like the back 背状部分：the ～ of the hand 手背

dosage/ˈdəʊsɪdʒ/

　　n. the size or frequency of a dose of a medicine or drug (药的)剂量,服法：a ～ of 100 milligrams a day 每日 100 毫克的剂量

dose/dəʊs/

　　Ⅰ *n.* an amount of medicine to be taken at one time (药的)一剂,一服　Ⅱ *v.* give medicine to 给……服药

dossier/ˈdɒsɪeɪ/

　　n. a collection of papers giving information about a person, event or subject 卷宗, 档案：The police have a ～ on him. 他被警方记录在案。

dot/dɒt/

　　Ⅰ *n.* a small spot 小圆点；小点：The letter "i" has a ～ over it. 字母"i"之上方有个小圆点。　Ⅱ *v.* (-tt-) ❶ mark with a small spot or spots 打上小点 ❷ be scattered over 布满：Her face is ～ted with pimples. 她的脸上长满粉刺。/a ～ted line 虚线

dote/dəʊt/

　　v. (～ on) show much or too much fondness 娇宠,溺爱：She ～s on her children. 她溺爱自己的孩子。

doting/ˈdəʊtɪŋ/

　　adj. very or excessively loving and devoted 溺爱的：a ～ husband who thinks his wife will not do wrong 一位宠爱妻子并认为她不会做错事的丈夫

double/ˈdʌbl/

　　Ⅰ *adj.* ❶ twice as much as 两倍的：Her mother's weight is ～ hers. 她母亲的体重是她的两倍。/He did ～ work that day. 那天他干了两倍的工作量。❷ made for two persons or things 双人的；供两者用的：a ～ room 双人房间/a ～ bed 双人床 ❸ having two like things or parts 成双的；双合的：～ doors 双合门/a railway with a ~ track 双轨铁路/~ happiness 双喜 ❹having two different uses or qualities；dual 双重的；有两种不同用途的：a ~ purpose 双重的目的/a ~ meaning 双关的语义/~ duty 双重的职责/a man with a ~ character 双重性格的人/ a ~ personality 双重人格 Ⅱ n.❶ a number or amount twice as much 双倍：Four is the ~ of two.4 是 2 的两倍。❷a person or thing like another 一模一样的人(物)：She is the ~ of her sister.她同她的姐姐长得一模一样。Ⅲ v.❶ make or become twice as great (使)增加一倍：The baby ~d its weight in a year.这婴儿的体重在一年之内增加了一倍。❷ fold over 对折；折叠：He ~d his blankets because it was a cold night.因为那是一个寒夜，他把毯子折叠起来睡。‖ ~ one's fists 攥紧拳头/~ over with laughter 笑得前仰后合/~ back 折回来/~ over 折过来；弯曲身子/~ up 弯腰；两人同住一房；折叠；曲折 ‖ ~-breasted adj. 双排扣的/~-decker n.双层公共汽车；双层床；双层三明治(夹心面包)/~-edged adj. 双刃的 ‖ doubly adv.加倍地；双重地

doubt /daʊt/

Ⅰ n.a feeling of uncertainty；a reason for being unsure about 怀疑：I have some ~s about this being true.我有些怀疑这件事是否属实。/There is no room for ~.没有怀疑的余地。Ⅱ v.feel doubt about；be unsure of sth.；not believe 怀疑；不确定；不相信：I ~ if he will come.我不敢肯定他是否来。/You can ask him if you ~ my word.如果你不相信我的话，你可写信问他。‖ **beyond** (**all**) ~ 毫无疑问/**in** ~ 怀疑/**no** ~ 无疑地；当然/**without** (**a**) ~ 毫无疑问 ‖ ~**ful** adj.怀疑的；不能肯定的；值得怀疑的；不可靠的：She was ~ful of his good intentions.她怀疑他的好意。/He is a ~ful character.他是个不可靠的人。/~**fully** adv. 怀疑地：He looked at me ~fully.他用怀疑的目光看着我。

doubtless /ˈdaʊtlɪs/

adv.certainly；no doubt 肯定地；无疑地：Doubtless he'll solve the problem by himself.他肯定会自己解决这个问题。

dove /dʌv/

n.a kind of pigeon 鸽子：~ of peace 和平鸽

down /daʊn/

Ⅰ adv.❶ from a higher place to a lower place 向下；由上往下：The sun went ~. 太阳落山了。/fall ~ 落下；跌倒/jump ~ from the tree 从树上跳下/go ~ 走下去/climb ~ 爬下去/get ~ 下车/lie ~ 放下 ❷in or towards the south 在南方；向南方：go ~ to the south 去南方；南下 ❸ to a lower degree 下降；减少：Production has gone ~ this month.这个月生产下降了。/We should mark ~ the price. 我们应当把价格标低一些。/hold the spending ~ 减少开支/quiet ~ 安静下来/die ~ 熄灭(平息)/slow ~ 慢下来 ❹ (written) on paper 在纸上(写下)：Write these words ~ in your note books. 请把这些单词写在你的笔记本上。Ⅱ prep.from a higher to a lower level；along 向下；往下；沿：Look further ~ the hill.请往更远处山下看。/He ran ~ the hill.他跑下山去。/go ~ a river 顺河而下/walk ~ the street 沿街走去 Ⅲ v. bring, put, knock down 击倒；击落；投下；打败：He ~ed his opponent with three blows.他三下就击倒了对手。/~ tools (工人)停工；罢工 ‖ ~ **with** 打倒；放下/**up and** ~ 来回地/**up side** ~ 颠倒；倒过来

downer /ˈdaʊnə/

n.❶a depressant or tranquillizing drug 抑制药；镇静药 ❷sth. depressing 令人沮丧的事情：Not going for a picnic was a real ~.未能去野餐真让人很沮丧。

downfall /ˈdaʊnfɔːl/

n.❶a fall from prosperity or power 衰落；衰败；垮台：The scandal finally led to his ~.这桩绯闻最终使他身败名裂。❷sth. that causes this 衰落(衰败、垮台)的原因：Intractability was his ~.倔脾气是他败落的原因。

downgrade /ˈdaʊngreɪd/

v. reduce to a lower grade or rank 使降级；使降职：He's been ~d from manager to vice-manager.他已从经理降职为副经理。

download /ˌdaʊnˈləʊd/

v. transfer data from one system to another or to a disk 下载；下装：～ the software 下载软件

downright /'daʊnraɪt/

I *adj*. frank，direct 坦率的；直截了当的：He is a ～ sort of person. 他是个性格直爽的人。 II *adv*. completely 彻头彻尾地；完全地：～ foolish 愚蠢到家的/～ stupidity 愚不可及

downstairs /ˌdaʊn'steəz/

I *adv*. to，on a lower floor；down the stairs 到楼下；在楼下：go ～ 到楼下去/be waiting ～ 正在楼下等着 II *adj*. on a lower floor，especially the ground floor 楼下的；底楼的：the ～ part of the house 房子的底楼部分

downtown /ˌdaʊn'taʊn/

I *adv*. to or in the lower part of a town；to or in the main or business part of a town 去(在)城里；去(在)市中心区：go (be) ～ 去(在)市中心区 II *adj*. in the business centre of a town or city 市中心区的：～ streets 闹市街道/～ Manhattan 曼哈顿商业区

downward /'daʊnwəd/

adj. moving or leading to a lower place or level 往下的：a ～ slope 一段下坡/prices with a ～ tendency 有下跌趋势的物价/the ～ path to ruin 走向毁灭的道路

downwards /'daʊnwədz/

adv. towards what is lower 往下；向下：The monkey was hanging head ～ from the branch. 猴子头朝下倒挂在树枝上。/He laid the picture face ～ on the table. 他把那幅画反扣在桌上。

doze /dəʊz/

I *v*. sleep lightly 小睡；打盹；打瞌睡：The old man was dozing (off) under a tree. 老人正在树下打盹。/～ in the chair 坐在椅子里打瞌睡 II *n*. a short，light sleep 小睡；打盹：I have a ～ after lunch. 午饭后我要小睡一下。

dozen /'dʌzn/

n. (*pl*. dozen or ～s) a group or set of twelve 一打；12 个：five ～ socks 五打短袜/more than a ～ cats 十几只猫 ‖ ～**s of** 几十个(件)；许多：I have been there ～ s

of times. 我到那里去过很多次了。

dozy /'dəʊzi/

adj. ❶ feeling sleepy or lazy 想睡的；令人困倦的：a ～ feeling 困倦的感觉；/I'm feeling a bit ～ this afternoon. 今天下午我觉得有点困倦。 ❷ stupid；slow in understanding 愚笨的；迟钝的：a ～ boy 不开窍的男孩子

draft /drɑːft/

I *n*. ❶ a plan，design，or outline of sth. to be done 草稿；草案；草图：I've made a first ～ of my speech，but it still needs a lot of work. 我写好了一份演讲的草稿，但还需要做许多加工。/make a ～ for a new model car 画一种新型汽车的设计草图 ❷ a written order for payment of money by a bank (银行)汇票：a ～ for 500 pounds 一张 500 英镑的汇票 II *v*. make a draft of；prepare the outline or design of 起草；画出草图：～ a speech 草拟一份演说稿 ‖ ～**sman** *n*. (法案，议案)起草人，绘图员

drag /dræg/

v. (-gg-) ❶ pull along 拖；拉：～ a heavy box out of a cupboard 把一个重箱子从衣橱里拉出来 ❷ move or go slowly 慢慢地移动；拖延：Time ～ s when you are waiting for a bus. 当你等公共汽车时，感到时间过得很慢。/The performance ～ged. 节目拖得很长。 ‖ ～ **sb. down** 拖垮；整垮(某人)/～ **in** 扯进(某一话题)/～ **on (out)** 拖得很长；(时间)过得很慢/～ **up** 不必要地谈到……

dragon /'drægən/

n. a large imaginary creature with wings and a long tail(usually breathing fire) 龙

dragonfly /'drægənflaɪ/

(*pl*. -ies) an insect with a long thin body，often brightly coloured，and two pairs of large transparent wings 蜻蜓

drain /dreɪn/

I *v*. make water flow away；flow away 排出；流走：He dug a trench to ～ the water away from the field. 他挖了条沟把园田里的水排掉。/The water ～ed off. 水流走了。 II *n*. a means of draining，such as a ditch or underground pipe that carries

D

waste water away 排水装置；下水道；阴沟；排水沟：The ~s are blocked up.下水道被堵塞了。‖ ~pipe *n.*排水管

drainage /ˈdreɪnɪdʒ/
*n.*❶the process or means of draining 排水；放水：The area has poor ~.这个地区排水很差。❷a system of drains 排水系统

drama /ˈdrɑːmə/
*n.*stories that can be acted；plays 戏剧；剧本：I may do a ~ about him some day.有朝一日我可能要写个关于他的剧本。

dramatic /drəˈmætɪk/
*adj.*❶of or to do with drama 戏剧的，有关戏剧的；戏剧学的 ❷exciting and impressive 激动人心的；引人注目的；给人印象深刻的：a ~ victory 激动人心的胜利 ‖ ~ally *adv.*戏剧地；引人注目地

dramatics /drəˈmætɪks/
*n.*❶the study or practice of acting in and producing plays 戏剧艺术；戏剧表演 ❷exaggerated behaviour 戏剧性行为；夸张做作的举止

dramatist /ˈdræmətɪst/
*n.*a person who writes plays 剧作家；编剧：a TV ~ 电视剧编剧

dramatize /ˈdræmətaɪz/
*v.*❶make a story, etc. into a play 将（故事）改编成剧本 ❷make sth. seem more exciting 使戏剧化；戏剧性地表现：He tends to ~ things.他往往言过其实。‖ **dramatization** *n.*编剧；戏剧化

drape /dreɪp/
Ⅰ *v.*hang cloth loosely over sth. 把……悬挂；披：He ~d his coat over the back of his chair. 他把上衣披在椅背上。Ⅱ *n.* (usually *pl.*)a piece of cloth draped over sth., usually at a window or on the stage of a theatre 窗帘布；幕布 ‖ ~r *n.* 布商

drastic /ˈdræstɪk/
*adj.*having a strong effect 具有强烈效果的：He took ~ action to cure the disease. 他采取猛烈的措施治该病。

draught /drɑːft/
Ⅰ *n.*❶cold air coming into a room or other shut-in place 过堂风；空气流：Let's shut the window because I can feel a ~.

我们把窗户关上吧，我感到有股过堂风。❷a continuous act of swallowing 一饮；一服：drink at a ~ 一饮而尽 ❸the depth of water needed to float a ship （船的）吃水深度 Ⅱ *v.*=draft ‖ ~y *adj.*通风的；透冷风的

draw /drɔː/
Ⅰ *v.* (drew, drawn) ❶move by pulling after or behind 拖；拉(动)；拔(出)：The engine drew the train from the station.机车拉着火车离开了车站。/~ a bow 拉弓/~ the chair up to the table 把椅子挪到桌旁/~ one's sword 拔出剑来 ❷make a picture, especially with a pen or pencil （用钢笔、铅笔等）画；划(线)；绘制：He ~s well.他画得好。/~ a sketch 画张素描/~ a straight line 划条直线 ❸attract；extract 吸引；吸取；提取：Street accidents always ~ crowds.街上发生的事故总是吸引群众。/~ enemy fire by making a noise 用闹声引来敌人的炮火 ❹come to or arrive at a point in time 临；到：Spring is ~ing near.春天即将到来。/~ toward the shore 向岸边靠近 ❺obtain from a source 吸取；提取：~ water from a well 从井中打水/~ money from a bank 从银行取款 ‖ ~ a conclusion 得出结论/~ back 后退；退回；撤回：He will not ~ back from what he has promised.他允诺了的事，就不会再打退堂鼓。/~ in 变短；到达/~ sth.in 吸进；吸引；收回；收缩：The fisherman drew his net in. 渔夫收拢网。/~ into 使卷入……/~ near 临近/~ off 撤退；排除(水等)/~ on 来临/~ on sth.(sb.) 依靠；从……获得/~ out 逐渐变长/~ sth.out 使变长；拉长；取出(存款等)；拔出/~ up (车马等)停住；草拟；制定 Ⅱ *n.*❶a result with neither side winning 平局：The game ended in a 1∶1 ~.这场球赛打成1比1平局。❷a person or thing that attracts especially the public 有吸引力的人（或事物）：He is always a great ~ at political meetings.在政治会议上他总是个十分引人注意的人物。

drawback /ˈdrɔːˌbæk/
*n.*a disadvantage 缺点；不利条件：This is the major ~ of the new product.这是新

产品的一大缺点。

drawer /ˈdrɔːə/

n. ❶ a sliding box-like compartment in a piece of furniture 抽屉 ❷ a person who draws or designs sth. 制图人；图样设计人 ❸ the person who writes out a cheque 开票人；出票人

drawing /ˈdrɔːɪŋ/

n. ❶ a picture made with a pencil, pen, or crayon rather than paint（用铅笔、钢笔、蜡笔画的）图画，素描（画）❷ the art or skill of making drawings 构图（艺术）；制图（技巧）

drawl /drɔːl/

Ⅰ *v.* speak in a very slow and lazy way 拖腔拖调地说话 Ⅱ *n.* this way of speaking 拖腔

dread /dred/

Ⅰ *n.* great fear and anxiety; terror 畏惧；恐惧：He lives in constant ～ of poverty. 他经常生活在对贫困的恐惧中。/have a ～ of water 怕水 Ⅱ *v.* fear greatly; look forward to sth. with great fear 惧怕；害怕：I ～ the examination. 我害怕考试。

dreadful /ˈdredfl/

adj. ❶ causing great fear 可怕的；令人畏惧的：a ～ accident 可怕的事故 /a ～ story 可怕的故事 ❷ very bad; very unpleasant 非常糟糕的；令人不愉快的：～ weather 恶劣天气 /a ～ toothache 很厉害的牙疼 /There's been a ～ accident—two people have died. 发生了一件令人不愉快的事故——两人死了。

dream /driːm/

Ⅰ *n.* ❶ sth. that one seems to see or experience during sleep 梦：have a ～ 做梦 ❷ sth. imagined while awake; daydream 梦想；白日梦：Space travel used to be just a ～. 太空旅行过去只是一种梦想。Ⅱ *v.* (dreamed or dreamt) see, hear, think in sleep; have a picture or idea in one's mind while sleeping 做梦；梦见；梦想；幻想；I never ～t that such a thing could happen! 我做梦也想不到会发生这样的事！‖ ～ **of**（**about**）梦见 /not ～ **of** 绝不会 /～ **up** 设想出来；杜撰 ‖ ～**er** *n.* 做梦者；梦想家 /～**less** *adj.*（睡眠）无梦的；安详的 /～

-like *adj.* 如梦的 /～**y** *adj.* 梦幻的；蒙眬的

dreary /ˈdrɪəri/

adj. without cheer; gloomy; depressing 沉闷的；阴郁的；令人沮丧的：a ～ winter day 阴沉的冬日

drench /drentʃ/

v. make very wet 使浸湿，使湿透：We were ～ed by the rain. 我们被雨水淋透了。

dress /dres/

Ⅰ *n.* ❶ clothing in general (for both men and women), especially outer garments 衣服；服装；穿着：They like to wear their colourful national ～. 他们喜欢穿他们那五彩缤纷的民族服装。❷ an outer garment worn by a woman or girl, gown or frock 连衣裙：She wears a ～ for school. 她穿连衣裙上学。Ⅱ *v.* ❶ put on clothes 穿衣 ❷ wear clothes in a particular way 打扮 ❸ put clothes on to sb. 给……穿衣 ‖ ～ **up** 打扮 ‖ ～**er** *n.*（剧场）服装师；碗柜；梳妆台 /～**y** *adj.* 讲究衣着的

dressing /ˈdresɪŋ/

n. ❶ a bandage, plaster, ointment, etc. for a wound（伤口的）敷料 ❷ a sauce of oil, vinegar, herbs, etc. for a salad（拌色拉的油、醋、香料等）调料 ❸ the act of putting on clothes 穿衣；穿戴；打扮 ‖ ～ **room** *n.* 化妆室；更衣室 /～**-table** *n.* 梳妆台

dribble /ˈdrɪbl/

v. ❶ let saliva or liquid fall from the mouth 流口水 ❷ (in football) take (the ball) forward by means of short kicks（足球）运（球），盘（球），带（球）❸ (of liquid) fall in small drops（指液体）滴，淌

drift /drɪft/

Ⅰ *v.* ❶ (cause to) be carried slowly by wind or water 漂；漂流：The boat ～ed down the river. 小船顺流而下。/The logs are ～ed downstream to the mill. 原木随波逐流漂到工厂。❷ (of people) move casually or aimlessly（指人）漫无目标地移动，漂泊，流浪：He ～s from one job to another. 他盲目地不断更换工作。❸ (cause to) pile up under the force of the wind or water（使）吹积；（使）漂聚：leaves ～ed by the wind 风吹积起来的落

D

叶 Ⅱ *n.*❶ a continuous slow movement 漂流；飘游：the ～ of young people from the country to the city 年轻人从农村流向城市 ❷a mass of matter blown up by wind 吹积物：a snow ～ 吹积雪堆 ‖ ～**age** *n.*漂流；流量/～**er** *n.*流浪者

drill¹ /drɪl/
Ⅰ *n.*training in military exercises（军事）训练，操练：They were put to military ～. 他们接受军事训练。/ a ～ ground 练兵场 Ⅱ *v.*train (soldiers) in military movements 训练；操练：～ troops on a parade ground/在阅兵场训练军队/a well ～ed crew 训练有素的船员（乘务员）

drill² /drɪl/
Ⅰ *n.*a tool or pointed instrument for making holes in or through hard substances 钻子；钻孔器；钻床：a dentist's ～ 牙科医生的钻子 Ⅱ *v.*make a hole in sth. with a special fool or machine 钻孔：～ a hole in a wall 在墙上钻个洞

drink /drɪŋk/
Ⅰ *v.*(drank, drunk) ❶ take (liquid) into the mouth and swallow 饮；喝：I drank a cup of coffee. 我喝了杯咖啡。/He doesn't smoke or ～. 他不抽烟也不喝酒。/～ing water 饮用水 ❷ have an alcoholic drink 喝酒：Let's ～ to your health.我们为你的健康干杯。Ⅱ *n.*❶ a liquid for drinking；alcoholic liquid 饮料；酒：Give me a ～ of water. 给我一杯水。/He is fond of ～. 他喜欢喝酒。/soft ～ 清凉饮料/bottled ～s 瓶装饮料 ❷a quantity of liquid swallowed at one go(液体的)一口 ‖ ～ **in** 凝神倾听；欣赏；陶醉于……/～ **to** 为……干杯/～ **up** 喝完/be in ～ 喝醉了 ‖ ～**able** *adj.*可用的/～**er** *n.*饮者；酒徒

drip /drɪp/
Ⅰ *v.*(-pp-) fall down in drops 往下滴；滴水：The rain is ～ping from the tree.雨从树上滴下。/The tap is ～ping.水龙头在滴水。/Sweat was ～ping from his face. 汗从他的脸上滴下。/～ping wet 湿淋淋的 Ⅱ *n.*the action or sound of falling in drops 滴；滴水(液)声：There is a continuous ～ of water from the ceiling. 水从天花板上连续滴下。/We heard the ～ of a

leaky faucet.我们听到一个漏水龙头的滴水声。

dripping /ˈdrɪpɪŋ/
*adj.*extremely wet 湿淋淋的：～ wet hair 湿淋淋的头发

drive /draɪv/
Ⅰ *v.*(drove, driven) ❶ operate a motor-vehicle 驾驶：He ～s a taxi. 他开出租车。/The train is ～n by steam. 这火车用蒸汽开动。❷take (someone) in a vehicle 开车送(某人)：He drove me to the station.他开车送我去车站。❸ force to go 驱赶；驱使：He drove a cattle to market.他赶着一头牛去市场。❹ force a nail，etc.into sth. 钉：～ a nail into a board 把一颗钉子钉进板中 ❺force sb.to be (in a certain state)；cause sb.to do sth.逼迫；迫使：You'll ～ me mad. 你会把我逼疯。/His hunger drove him to steal food. 饥饿驱使他去偷食物。‖ ～**sth.in**（into）将(钉子)钉进；灌输(知识等)给/～ **sb. into** 迫使(某人)……/～ **off** 赶走 Ⅱ *n.*❶ a journey in a vehicle (especially for pleasure) 乘车出游；开车兜风：He often takes me for a ～. 他常开车带我去兜风。/It's a short ～ to the park. 开车很快就到公园。/an hour's ～ 一小时的行车路程 ❷a road for vehicles that connects a private house or garage with the street 车道(尤指穿过私宅院内或邻街停车库从的车道)：He built a ～ to his house.他修了一条车道通到他的房子。❸energy 精力；魄力；动力：He is clever, but he lacks ～.他很聪明，但缺乏干劲。‖ ～**r** *n.*驾驶员；司机；车夫；赶牲口的人/**driving** *adj.*驱动的；起推动作用的；驾驶的；猛烈的；driving licence 驾驶执照

drizzle /ˈdrɪzl/
Ⅰ *n.*rain which falls in very small drops 毛毛雨 Ⅱ *v.*rain in this way 下毛毛雨

droop /druːp/
*v.*bend or hang downwards through tiredness or weakness 低垂；下垂：The old man ～ed his head and began to murmur. 那老人低下了头，并开始细声细气地嘀咕。/The flowers ～ed soon after we picked them.我们把花摘下来以后，花很快就枯萎了。

drop/drɒp/

Ⅰ *n.*❶ a small round or pear-shaped mass of liquid（液）滴；珠：a ～ of water 水滴/a tear ～ 泪珠 ❷ a small amount of any liquid 很少量（液体）：Just a ～, then.那就来一点点吧。/only a ～in the ocean 沧海一粟 ❸ the act of going down; a sudden fall 落下；下降：a long ～ down into the hole 掉进洞中深处/a ～ in temperature 温度下降Ⅱ *v.*(-pp-)❶ let sth. fall; fall or let fall in drops（让）掉下；（让）倒下；（使）滴下：The apple blossom is beginning to ～.苹果花开始掉落。/The wet leaves ～ped water. 湿叶滴下水珠来。/～ anchor 抛锚 ❷ become lower or weaker 降低；下降；变弱；减轻：Please ～ your voice.请把声音放低点。/The wind ～ped.风小了。 ❸allow（sb.）to get out of a vehicle 让人下车：Please ～ me at the station.请让我在车站下车。 ❹ stop associating with; give up 同（某人）断绝关系 放弃：I have ～ped my piano lessons.我已不上钢琴课了。/He has ～ped all his old friends.他与老朋友都断了交往。 ❺leave out 删除；省掉；漏掉：You have ～ped a letter here.这里你漏掉了一个字母。 ‖ ～ back 后退；留在后面；下降/～ behind 落在后面/～ in 顺便来访；顺便走进（某处）/～ off 减少；下降；掉下；让……下车；打盹/～ out 退出；脱离；弃权 ‖～let *n.*小滴

dropper /'drɒpə/

*n.*a short glass tube with a rubber ball at one end, used for measuring out drops of liquid 滴管

droppings /'drɒpɪŋs/

*n.*the dung of animals or birds（动物、鸟的）粪

drought/draut/

n. a period of dry weather, causing a shortage of water 干旱

drown/draun/

*v.*❶ (cause to) die in water 淹死；把……淹死：The kitten fell into the pond and was ～ed.小猫掉进池塘里淹死了。/A ～ing man will catch at a straw.快要淹死的人会抓住一根稻草以图活命。 ❷ make（a sound）inaudible by making a

loud noise（声音）掩盖：The noise of the train ～ed his voice.火车的响声掩盖了他的声音。

drowsy/'drauzi/

*adj.*sleepy; half asleep; making a person feel sleepy 瞌睡的；半睡的；使人昏昏欲睡的：I'd just woken up and was still ～.我刚起床，可仍觉得困。/This drug can make you ～.这药能使人打瞌睡。

drug/drʌg/

Ⅰ *n.*❶a medicine for curing a disease 药；药物：The doctor gave me a new ～ for my headaches.医生给我开了一种治头痛的新药。 ❷ a chemical substance that affects the nervous system, especially a narcotic 麻醉药品；令人上瘾的东西；毒品：Heroin is a dangerous ～.海洛因是种危险的毒品。 Ⅱ *v.* (-gg-) administer a drug to sb.to induce stupor or insensibility 使服麻醉药；用药麻醉：a ～ged drink 加了（麻）药的饮料/a ～ged sleep 服麻醉剂引起的睡眠 ‖～gist *n.*药剂师/～store *n.*药房

drum/drʌm/

Ⅰ *n.*a hollow musical instrument played by beating; sth. shaped like a drum; a sound made by beating a drum 鼓；鼓状物；鼓声：beat a ～ 打鼓/beat the ～s for a new product 为新产品做宣传/beat the ～ for the new regime 替新政权鼓吹 Ⅱ *v.*(-mm-) beat or play a drum; beat repeatedly on sth. to make a sound 敲鼓；（连续敲击）使发出咚咚声：He ～med on the desk with his fingers.他用手指敲得书桌咚咚响。 ‖ ～sth. into 鼓吹/～ out 逐出/～ up 击鼓召集；招徕（顾客、生意等）；想出 ‖～beat *n.*鼓声；一击鼓/～fire *n.*连珠状炮火/～mer *n.*鼓手/～stick *n.*鼓槌

drunk/drʌŋk/

Ⅰ *adj.*unable to think or behave properly, through having had too much alcoholic drink 醉的；喝醉的：He's dead ～.他烂醉如泥。/I'm not ～ with joy.我没有陶醉在快乐之中。 Ⅱ *n.*a person who is drunk 醉酒者；醉鬼

dry/draɪ/

Ⅰ *adj.*❶ not wet; free from moisture 干

的；干燥的：The soil is too ~ for planting. 土壤太干，不能种东西。/~ air 干燥
空气/a ~ towel 干毛巾 ❷ without rain
干旱的；the ~ season and the rain season
旱季和雨季/~ weather 旱天 ❸ emptied
of water 没水的；干涸的：The well has
gone ~. 这井干涸了。/a ~ lake 没水的
湖/a ~ well 枯井/a ~ battery (cell) 干
电池 ❹ dull and uninteresting 干巴巴
的；枯燥无味的：a ~ book 枯燥无味的书
Ⅱ v. remove water from；make or become
dry 使脱水；变干；弄干；烤干；擦干：The
washing will ~ quickly on a sunny day
like this. 在这样的晴天洗过的衣物会干
得很快。/Dry your hands on a towel. 用
毛巾擦干你的手。/~ in the sun 在太阳
下晒干 ‖ (as) ~ as a bone 干巴巴的/
(as) ~ as dust 枯燥无味的；渴得要命的/
~ ice 干冰/~ land 陆地/~ off (out)
(使)完全变干/~ up (使)干涸 ‖ ~-clean
v. 干洗/~-eyed adj. 不流泪的；不表现悲
伤的

dryer, drier/'draɪə(r)/

n. sth. used to dry sth. else 干燥机：a hair
~ 头发吹风机/a clothes ~ 衣服干燥机

dual/'djuːəl/

adj. of two；having two parts 双的；双重
的 ‖ ~ carriageway n. 双行道

dub/dʌb/

v.(-bb-) put a new sound track on a film
originally made in another language 为
(译制片)配音：Many foreign films are
~bed when they are shown in England.
许多外国影片在英国上演时都经过译制
配音。

dubious/'djuːbɪəs/

adj. causing doubt；of uncertain value or
meaning 怀疑的；令人怀疑的；可疑的：I
feel ~ of his honesty. 我怀疑他的诚
实。/He is a rather ~ fellow who may
be a thief. 他是个颇为可疑的家伙，说不
定是个贼。/a ~ character 可疑的人物
/a ~ friend 不可靠的朋友/~ author-
ship 作者不明/~ behaviour 暧昧的行为

duchess/'dʌtʃɪs/

n. a wife or window of a duke 公爵夫人

duck/dʌk/

Ⅰ n. a common water-bird, domestic or
wild；a female of such a bird；such a bird
as food（家或野）鸭；母鸭；鸭肉：She
walks like a waddling ~. 她走路摇摇摆
摆像个鸭子。 Ⅱ v. ❶ move quickly down
or to one side 迅速低下；闪避：I
~ed my head to avoid being hit. 我赶快
低下头以免被击中。 ❷ push sb. quickly
under water for a short time 把……按入
水中：The big boy ~ed the small boy in
the swimming pool. 那大男孩将小男孩短
时浸入游泳池水中。 ‖ a ~'s egg 零分/a
lame ~ 跛脚鸭；行动失灵的人/take（to
sth.) like a ~ to water 毫无困难（疑虑）
地；自然地/like water off a ~'s back 一
点不起作用/~ out of 躲避；逃避 ‖ ~er
n. ❶ 潜水人 ❷ 养鸭人/~ing n. 闪避/
~ling n. 小鸭；嫩鸭肉

due/djuː/

Ⅰ adj. ❶ owed or owing as a debt or
right；requiring immediate payment 应付
的；欠的；到期的：The wages ~ to him
will be paid tomorrow. 欠他的工资明天
将付给他。/This bill is ~ today. 这张账
单今天到期。 ❷（especially showing arrangement made in advance) expected or
supposed to happen, arrive, etc. 预定要来
到的；预定的：What time is the steamer
~? 轮船应在什么时刻到达? /It's ~
here at 1：30. 它应在一点半到达此地。/
He is ~ to lecture twice tomorrow. 他预
定明天演讲两次。 ❸ proper, correct, or
suitable 适当的；恰当的；适宜的：after ~
consideration 经过适当的考虑/in ~
time 在适当的时机/pay ~ respect to
one's teachers 对老师给予应有的尊敬/in
~ course 及时地 Ⅱ n. sth. that rightfully
belongs or is owed to someone, especially
sth. non-material 应得之物：I don't like
him, but to give him his ~, he is a good
singer. 我不喜欢他，但说公道话，他是位
好歌手。/give the devil his ~ 对不喜欢
的人也要公平 ‖ be ~ for 应得到……的/
~ to 由于……；归因于……；归功于
……：The accident was ~ to his carelessness. 这次事故是由于他的疏忽造
成。/The flight was delayed ~ to bad
weather. 由于天气不好，飞机推迟起

飞。/The discovery is 〜 to Newton. 这一发现应归功于牛顿。

duel /dju:əl/

Ⅰ *n.* ❶ a formal fight between two people with swords or guns 决斗：challenge someone to a 〜 要求和某人决斗 ❷ any two-sided contest 双方竞争：a 〜 of wits 斗智 Ⅱ *v.* (-ll- or -l-) fight between two persons with swords or guns 决斗

duet /dju'et/

n. a song or piece of music for two people 二重唱；二重奏

duke /dju:k/

n. the title of a man from a very important family in Britain 公爵 ‖ 〜**dom** *n.* 公爵位

dull /dʌl/

adj. ❶ not bright or light；(of colour) lacking brightness 阴暗的；阴沉的；灰茫茫的；(颜色) 暗淡的，无光泽的：Yesterday was a 〜 day, with a cloudy sky. 昨天是多云的阴沉天。/ a 〜 colour 暗淡的颜色/〜 grey 暗灰色 ❷ slow in understanding；not sharp 笨的；迟钝的；不锋利的：a 〜 student 笨学生/a 〜 knife 钝刀/a 〜 answer 呆板的回答 ❸ uninteresting or not exciting；boring 枯燥乏味的；沉闷无聊的：The speech was so 〜 that I left early. 这次演讲十分枯燥无味，我早早地就离开了。

duly /'dju:li/

adv. punctually；properly 按时地；适当地；恰当地：The work was 〜 finished. 这项工作如期完成。/These proposals should be 〜 considered. 这些建议应适当地予以考虑。

dumb /dʌm/

adj. ❶ not able to speak 哑的；不会说话的：a school for the deaf and 〜 聋哑学校/〜 animals 不会说话的动物 ❷ unwilling to speak；silent 不肯说话的；沉默的：The class remained 〜 when the teacher asked a question. 当老师问一个问题时，全班皆沉默无言。/〜 show 哑剧 ‖ 〜**bell** *n.* 哑铃/〜**found** /dʌm'faʊnd/ *v.* 把……吓得目瞪口呆

dummy /'dʌmi/

n. ❶ sth. made to look like a person or thing 人体模型；仿造物：Shops which sell clothes often have dummies in the window. 服装店常常在橱窗里摆设人体模型作为衣服模特。❷ a rubber teat for a baby to suck 橡胶奶嘴

dump /dʌmp/

Ⅰ *v.* ❶ drop or unload (sth.) heavily or carclessly, in a rough pile 堆放；倾倒：No 〜ing here! 此处不准倒垃圾！❷ sell goods abroad at low prices 向国外廉价倾销 Ⅱ *n.* a place for dumping waste materials 堆放处；卸货场；垃圾站；垃圾倾倒场：a rubbish 〜 垃圾堆 ‖ (**down**) **in the** 〜**s** 沮丧的；忧郁的 ‖ 〜**er** (**truck**) *n.* 翻斗 (倾卸) 车

dumpling /'dʌmplɪŋ/

n. ❶ a ball made of flour, fat and water, boiled with meat and vegetables (由面粉、油和水混合与肉、蔬菜共煮的) 面团，饺子 ❷ a ball made of flour and water containing fruit. (水果等作馅的) 面团；水果布丁

dune /dju:n/

n. a low hill of sand heaped up by the wind (风吹积成的) 沙丘

dungeon /'dʌndʒən/

n. a room under ground, formerly used as a prison 地下室；地牢

dupe /dju:p/

Ⅰ *v.* cheat；make a fool of 欺骗；愚弄 Ⅱ *n.* a person who is tricked or cheated 受骗上当者

duplicate /'dju:plɪkət/

Ⅰ *v.* copy exactly 复制：Can you 〜 the document for me? 请替我复印一份文件好吗？/〜 a letter 复制信件 Ⅱ *n.* sth. that is exactly like another (与另一物) 一模一样的东西；复制品：Your jacket is a 〜 of mine. 你的夹克衫和我的一模一样。/a 〜 of the document 文件的复制件 Ⅲ *adj.* exactly like another made as a copy of sth. 完全相同的；副本的：a 〜 license 副本执照/〜 prints of a photograph 由同一张底片洗印出的相同的照片 ‖ **duplication** *n.* 复制；加倍/**duplicator** *n.* 复印机

durable /'djʊərəbl/

adj. able to last a long time and not become damaged or broken 耐用的：～ clothes 耐穿的衣服

duration /djʊ'reɪʃn/

n. the time during which sth. lasts 持续的期间：for the ～ of the holiday 在整个假期期间

during /'djʊərɪŋ/

prep. ❶ throughout；all through 在……整段时间内；在……整个过程中：Ice covers the lake ～ (the) winter. 冬季期间湖面为冰所覆盖。❷ at some time while sth. else is happening 在……过程中的某个时刻：He came to see me ～ my absence. 我不在时，他来看过我。

dusk /dʌsk/

n. the time just before it gets quite dark 薄暮；黄昏；傍晚：Put the car light on at ～. 黄昏时就把车灯打开。‖ ～y *adj.* 暗色的，肤色深的；朦胧的：the ～y races 深肤色人种

dust /dʌst/

Ⅰ *n.* fine dry earth or other matter 灰尘；尘土：The ～ was blowing in the streets. 街上尘土飞扬。/raise a cloud of ～ 扬起一股烟尘 Ⅱ *v.* ❶ clean dust from 掸去(抹去)灰尘：I ～ed the furniture. 我把家具上的灰尘掸掉。❷ cover with powder 撒上(粉末)：～ fertilizer on plants 给植物撒肥料 ‖ ～ and ashes 无用之物(粪土)/ bite the ～ 受伤倒地；倒毙；打输/ shake the ～ off one's feet 愤然离去；拂袖而去/ throw ～ in someone's eyes 蒙骗(迷惑)某人/ ～ off 重温，复习 ‖ ～cart *n.* 垃圾车

dustbin /'dʌstbɪn/

n. a bin for household rubbish (家用)垃圾桶，垃圾箱

duster /'dʌstə/

n. a cloth for dusting things 抹布；擦布

dustpan /'dʌstpæn/

n. a pan into which dust is brushed from a floor 畚箕

dusty /'dʌsti/

adj. (dustier, dustiest) ❶ covered with dust 布满灰尘的；灰尘覆盖的：a ～ road 尘土飞扬的路 ❷ (of a colour) dull or muted (颜色)暗的，土灰色的 ❸ uninteresting 枯燥无味的：a ～ old man 一个无趣的老家伙 ‖ **dustiness** *n.* 灰蒙蒙；尘污

dutiful /'djuːtɪfl/

adj. having a responsibility to；showing respect and obedience 忠于职守的；守本分的；恭敬的；孝顺的：a ～ son 孝顺的儿子

duty /'djuːti/

n. ❶ sth. that one ought to do in his job, by law, by morality, etc. 职责；责任；义务：When ～ calls, no man should disobey. 当有义务需要履行时，任何人都义不容辞。/His sense of ～ is very strong. 他的责任感很强。/the rights and duties of citizens 公民的权利和义务/do one's ～ 尽责；尽义务 ❷ money you pay at the customs on goods when they are brought into a country (某种)税；关税：customs duties 关税/death duties 遗产税/stamp ～ 印花税/import ～ 进口税 ‖ do ～ for (as) 起……作用，代替……/off ～ 下班；歇班/on ～ 在上班；值班；当勤 ‖ ～-free *adj.* 免税的/**dutiable** *adj.* 应上税的

dwarf /dwɔːf/

Ⅰ *n.* a person, animal, or plant that is much smaller than the usual one 侏儒；矮小的动物或植物：Snow White and the Seven Dwarfs is a charming story. 白雪公主与七个小矮人是个迷人的故事。Ⅱ *v.* ❶ stunt the growth or development of 影响发育 ❷ cause to look smaller than the usual one 使显得矮小；使相形见绌：The plants had been ～ed by the lack of water. 由于缺水，这些植物长得矮小。/The new tall building ～s all the little shops. 那座新建的大楼使所有的小商店相形见绌。

dwell /dwel/

v. (dwelt or dwelled) live；make one's home 居住；栖息：They dwelt in Chongqing during the war. 战争期间，他们住在重庆。/～ on an island 栖身岛上 ‖ ～ on (upon) 讲述(或思考，写)许多……；～ on (upon) the past 对过去的事考虑许多 ‖ ～er *n.* 居住者；居民/～ing *n.* 住处；住所

dwindle /'dwɪndl/

v. become steadily fewer, smaller or wea-

ker 逐渐减少（或变小，变差）；～ from...
to...从……逐渐减少到……/～ away
(in) to nothing 渐渐化为乌有/His
health ～d day by day.他的健康状况日益
恶化。

dye/daɪ/

Ⅰ *n.* the matter used in dyeing; colour
produced by dyeing 染料 Ⅱ *v.*give colour
to sth.or change the colour 染成……色；
染色；上色：She ～d her hair red.她把头
发染成红色。/His blood ～d the ground.
他的血染红了地面。/This cloth ～s eas-
ily.这种布容易上色。‖ ～**stuff** *n.*染料/
～**works** *n.*染场；染坊；染料厂

dyer/'daɪə(r)/

*n.*a worker who makes or gives colour to
sth.染工

dying/'daɪɪŋ/

adj. ❶ approaching death 垂死的；快死
的：He is a ～ man.他是一个快死的人。
❷ at death 临终的：Remember her ～
words! 记住她的临终遗言！

dyke/daɪk/

*n.*❶a long wall or embankment to hold
back water and prevent flooding 堤；坝；

堰 ❷a ditch for draining water from land
沟；壕沟；渠

dynamic/daɪ'næmɪk/

adj. ❶ of power and forces producing
motion 动力的；动态的 ❷ (of a person)
having great energy (人)精力充沛的，有
活力的：a ～ personality 精力充沛的人

dynamics/daɪ'næmɪks/

*n.*❶ the science that deals with objects or
matter in movement 动力学；力学 ❷ (in
music) changes of loudness（音乐中的）
力度变化，力度强弱法

dynamism/'daɪnəmɪzəm/

n.(of a person) the quality of being dy-
namic（人的）活力，精力，劲头

dynamite/'daɪnəmaɪt/

Ⅰ *n.*a very powerful explosive 烈性炸药
Ⅱ *v.*blow up with a very powerful explosive 爆破；用炸药炸毁

dynasty/'dɪnəsti/

*n.*a succession of rulers belonging to one
family;a period during which a particular
dynasty rules 王朝；朝代：the Ming Dynasty 明朝/～ history 朝代史

Ee

each/iːtʃ/

I *adj.& pron.* every person or thing in a group separately; every 每一（个）：Each child took a toy. 每一个孩子都拿了一个玩具。/Each has his merits. 各有所长。 II *adv.* for or to every one of a group 对（或给）每个：All the boys got a present ~. 所有的男孩都各自得到了一份礼物。

eager/ˈiːɡə(r)/

adj. full of strong interest or desire 热切的；渴望的：~ to succeed 急欲成功/We're ~ to know the truth. 我们迫切想知道真相。‖ ~ly *adv.* 急切地/~ness *n.* 渴望；热心

eagle/ˈiːɡl/

n. a large strong flesh-eating bird with a hooked beak and very good eyesight 鹰：The ~ was wheeling in the sky. 那只鹰在空中盘旋。

ear/ɪə(r)/

n. ❶an organ that you hear with 耳朵：My right ~ hurts. 我右耳疼。❷an ability to recognize, appreciate sounds, especially in music and languages 听力；辨音力：a keen ~ 敏锐的辨音能力 ‖ be all ~s 专心倾听/give one's ~s（to do sth. or for sth.）不惜任何代价/go in one ~ and out the other 左耳进右耳出/have（win）sb.'s ~(s) 获得某人的好感/over head and ~s 深陷/set（people）by the ~s 挑拨离间/turn a deaf ~ to 对……置之不理

eardrum/ˈɪədrʌm/

n. a tight thin skin inside the ear, which makes you able to hear sound 鼓膜；耳膜

eared/ɪəd/

adj. having ears that can be seen, or are of a particular kind 有……耳朵的，耳朵……的：the ~ seal 有耳朵的海豹/a pink-~ rabbit 粉红色耳朵的兔子/a sharp-~ little boy 一个耳灵的小男孩 / golden-~ corn 金黄色的玉米穗

early/ˈɜːli/

I *adv.* at or near to the beginning of a period of time; sooner than usual or than others 早；早先：~ in the morning 清早/~ in 1860 1860 年初/~ next year 明年初/die ~ in life 死得早/Man learned ~ to use tools. 人类很早就学会了使用工具。/I will have to get up ~ to go fishing tomorrow. 明天我要早些起床去钓鱼。 II *adj.* coming or happening at the beginning of a period of time 早的；早期的：~ rice 早稻/an ~ riser 早起的人/in the ~ spring（summer）在早春（初夏）/in my ~ days 在我幼年时期/an ~ bus 早班车/It's too ~ for bed. 现在睡觉还太早。/The ~ bird catches the worm.〈谚〉早起的鸟儿有虫吃。

earn/ɜːn/

v. ❶get money by working 挣得：He ~s ¥2,600 a month. 他每月挣 2 600 元。/He has ~ed a lot of money by working in the evenings. 他晚上干活赚了许多钱。/How much do you ~ a month? 你一个月挣多少钱？/The driver ~s £100 a week. 这个司机每周挣一百英镑。❷receive sth. for doing sth. good; get sth. that you deserve（使）得到；获得；赢得：~ fame 赢得名声/His works have ~ed him many friends. 他的著作为他赢得了许多朋友。❸get money as profit or interest on money you lend, or you have in a bank, etc. 获利，生息：How much interest will your savings ~ in this account? 你这个账户上存的钱能得多少利息？

earnest/ˈɜːnɪst/

I *adj.* very serious and sincere 认真的；诚挚的：an ~ person 一个认真的人/I'm in saying that. 我那样说是当真的。Ⅱ n. a thing intended or regarded as a sign or promise of what is to come 提示；保证

earnings /'ɜːnɪŋz/

n. ❶money obtained by working 工钱，收入：His ~ are not enough to support his family. 他的收入不够养家糊口。 ❷profits 利润：Our total ~ were about 4,000 dollars. 我们的总利润大约 4 000 美元。

earphones /'ɪəfəʊnz/

n. a piece of equipment worn over the ears that makes it possible to listen to music, the radio, etc. 耳机

earpiece /'ɪəpiːs/

n. ❶the part of a telephone or piece of electrical equipment that you hold next to or put into your ear so that you can listen 护耳片 ❷either of the two pieces of a pair of glasses which hold the glasses onto the ears 眼镜脚

earplug /'ɪəplʌg/

n. either of two pieces of soft material which are put into the ears to keep out water or noise (防水、防噪声的)耳塞

earring /'ɪəˌrɪŋ/

n. a piece of jewellery worn on the ear 耳环

earshot /'ɪəʃɒt/

n. (within/out of ~) within(beyond) the distance at which a sound can be heard 在听力范围之内(之外)

earth /ɜːθ/

Ⅰ n. ❶ (usually the ~) the planet where we live 地球：The ~ rotates around the sun. 地球环绕太阳旋转。 ❷ soil 泥土：plant the tree with ~ 用土栽树 Ⅱ v. cover with earth 用土掩盖：~ up the roots of a newly-planted shrub 用土埋住新栽灌木的根/She ~ed up the celery. 她给芹菜培上了土。 ‖ come down (back) to ~ 回到现实中/move heaven and ~ 竭尽全力

earthen /'ɜːθən/

adj. ❶made of earth 泥土做的 ❷ (said about a pot) made of baked clay (罐)用烧

过的黏土制造的，陶制的

earthly /'ɜːθli/

adj. ❶to do with the earth, or human life on it (与)地球(有关)的，(与)地球上人类生活(有关)的：Water is liquid at normal ~ temperatures. 水在正常的地球温度下是液态的。 ❷used to emphasize sth. 表示强调：There is no ~ reason to be afraid. 根本没有害怕的理由。

earthquake /'ɜːθkweɪk/

n. a strong and sudden shaking of the ground as a result of movements within the earth's crust or volcanic activity 地震：There was an ~ last year. 去年发生了地震。

earthworm /'ɜːθwɜːm/

n. a burrowing worm that lives in the soil 蚯蚓

earthy /'ɜːθi/

adj. (earthier, earthiest) ❶resembling or suggestive of earth or soil 似泥土的，有泥土特征的 ❷crude or vulgar 粗俗的；庸俗的；不文雅的：He has an ~ sense of humour. 他有些粗俗的幽默感。 ‖ earthiness n. 土质，土性；粗俗

ease /iːz/

Ⅰ n. the state of being comfortable and without worries or problems 安逸；轻松：a life of ~ 安逸的生活/He can lift the heavy stone with ~. 他可以轻松地举起这块大石头。 ‖ feel at ~ 感到轻松/ill at ~ 局促不安/take one's ~ 悠闲 Ⅱ v. become less serious or severe；relax one's efforts 放松；安心；缓和：You should first ~ yourself. 首先你得放松自己。

easel /'iːzl/

n. a frame for holding a picture while it is being painted 画架

easily /'iːzɪli/

adv. ❶without difficulty or effort 容易地，不费力地：She climbed the tree ~. 她轻而易举地爬上了树。 ❷without doubt 无疑：He is ~ the best singer among us. 他无疑是我们当中最好的歌手。 ❸very probably 很可能，多半：He may ~ be late today. 今天他多半会迟到。

E

east/iːst/

I *n.* the direction from which the sun comes up in the morning 东方：Our house faces ～.我们的房子朝东。/There is a strong ～ wind.东风很大。II *adj.* lying towards,at,in the direction of the east 东方的；向东的：He lives on the ～ coast.他住在东海岸。III *adv.* towards or in the east 向东方，在东方：The room faces ～, so we get the morning sun.房间朝东，所以上午有阳光。/The ship sailed ～.轮船向东方行驶。

Easter/'iːstə(r)/

n. the yearly celebration of the day when Christians commemorate the death of Christ and his return to life 复活节：～ Monday 复活节后的星期一

easterly/'iːstəli/

I *adj.* ❶in or towards the east 东方的；向东的；东部的 ❷(said about a wind) blowing from the east (风)从东方吹来的 II *n.*(*pl.*-ies) the wind blowing from the east 东风

eastern/'iːstən/

adj. of or in the east (在)东面的,(在)东部的：～ China 中国东部

eastward/'iːstwəd/

I *adj.* in an easterly direction 向东的：They followed an ～ course.他们沿着一条向东的路线行进。II *adv.*(also ～s) towards the east 向东

easy/'iːzi/

I *adj.* ❶not difficult 容易的；轻易做到的：Easy come, ～ go.〈谚〉来得容易,去得快。/To learn physics well isn't ～.学好物理是不容易的。/She is ～ to deal with.她很好相处。❷ comfortable and not worried 舒适的,舒服的：He has stopped working now and leads a very ～ life.他现在不工作了,过着非常安逸的生活。❸lacking anxiety or awkwardness; not embarrassed 悠然的；从容的：He has ～ manners.他的举止很潇洒。II *adv.* ❶in an easy manner 安适地；放松地：Take it ～.别紧张(放心好了)。/Go ～ here, the road is very rough.这儿得慢慢地走,

道路很不平。❷at ease；without effort 容易地；轻松地：Easier said than done.说起来容易做起来难。

eat/iːt/

v.(ate, eaten) ❶ take food into the mouth and swallow it；have a meal 吃；吃饭：I'm afraid he's ～ing too much.他恐怕吃得太多了吧！/～ up all the food 吃完了所有的食物 ❷destroy gradually 侵蚀；腐蚀‖～one's heart out 极为痛苦/～ one's words 收回所说的话

eatable/'iːtəbl/

I *n.*(*pl.*) food 食物；食品：Have you brought the ～s?你带吃的没有？II *adj.* fit to be eaten 可食用的；可吃的：The prison food was scarcely ～.监牢里的伙食几乎不能吃。

eaves/iːvz/

n.(*pl.*) the overhanging edges of a roof 屋檐

eavesdrop/'iːvzdrɒp/

v.(-pp-) listen secretly to a private conversation 偷听,窃听：She opened the door just enough to ～ on the conversation outside.她把门打开一道缝,刚好能偷听到外面的谈话。

ebb/eb/

I *v.*❶(of the tide) flow back from the land to the sea (指潮水)退,落：They swam till the tide began to ～.他们一直游到开始退潮。❷ grow less；become gradually weaker or fainter 减少；衰落：His fortune was beginning to ～.他的财产开始减少了。II *n.*❶the flowing out of the tide 退潮；落潮：the ～ and flow of the tide 海潮的落涨/The tide is on the ～.正在退潮。❷low state；decline or decay 衰退；衰落：My luck is on the ～.我的运气不好。

eccentric/ɪk'sentrɪk/

*adj.*❶strange；unusual 古怪的；异乎寻常的：～ behaviour 古怪的行为 ❷(of circles) not having the same point 不同圆心的

eccentricity/ˌeksen'trɪsəti/

n. eccentric behaviour 古怪行为；反常：

The man is famous for his eccentricities.
这个人以行为怪僻而出名。

echo/'ekəu/

I *n.*(*pl.*~es)❶a sound reflected or sent back 回声；回音：the ~es of our voices 我们的回声/This cave has a good ~.这山洞里回声很响。❷a person who repeated the words or opinions of another 应声虫；随声附和者：She's just her husband's ~.她只不过是她丈夫的应声虫。Ⅱ *v.*❶(of places) reflect back a sound (指地方)发出回声：The hills ~ed back the noise of the shots.群山回响着枪声。❷(of sounds) be sent back or repeated after the original sound has stopped (指声音)回响，回荡：Their shouts ~ed through the forest.他们的叫喊声在林中回荡。❸agree or repeat an idea or opinion 附和；重复：He ~es his brother in everything.他所有事都附和他哥哥。

eclectic/ɪ'klektɪk/

adj.(of people, methods, ideas, etc.) not following any particular system or set of ideas, but using parts of many different ones (人)兼收并蓄的；(方法、思想等)不拘一格的：The painter's style is very ~.这位画家的艺术风格博采众长。

eclipse/ɪ'klɪps/

I *n.*❶complete or partial darkening of the moon by the shade of the earth 月食；月全食：the lunar ~ 月食/the total moon ~ 月全食 ❷complete or partial darkening of the sun caused by the moon's passing between it and the earth 日食；日全食：the solar ~ 日食/the total solar ~ 日全食 ❸disappearence；the loss of one's right, fame, power, etc.(权利、名誉、地位等的)消失，丧失：He's suffering an ~.他声名尽失。Ⅱ *v.* cause an eclipse of (sth.)；cut off the light from；throw into the shade 引起日(月)食；蒙蔽；使失色：The moon ~d the sun.月亮遮住了太阳。

ecology/iː'kɒlədʒi/

n. the study of the relation of plants and animals to their environment 生态学 ‖ **ecologist** *n.*生态学家，生态学者

economic/ˌiːkə'nɒmɪk/

adj. connected with trade, industry and wealth；of economics 经济(上)的，经济学的：an ~ crisis 经济危机/the ~ base 经济基础

economical/ˌiːkə'nɒmɪkl/

*adj.*not wasteful；saving；thrifty 节约的，经济的，节俭的，节省的：He is ~ of his time.他很节约时间。/be ~ with fuel 节省燃料/an ~ person 一位节俭的人

economically/ˌiːkə'nɒmɪkli/

*adv.*❶not wastefully 节约地，节俭地：Mary dresses very ~ because she makes all her clothes herself.玛丽穿着节俭，衣服都是自己做的。❷in a way connected with economics 在经济(学)上：Economically speaking, the country is in a very healthy state.从经济学的观点来说，国家处于很兴旺的状态中。/Is the company ~ viable? 这家公司在经济上能独立发展吗？

economics/ˌiːkə'nɒmɪks/

*n.*the science of the production and distribution of goods or wealth 经济学：the ~ of publishing 出版经济学

economist/ɪ'kɒnəmɪst/

*n.*a person who studies and is skilled in economics 经济学家，经济专家

economize/ɪ'kɒnəmaɪz/

v. avoid waste；reduce one's expenses 节省，节俭：We have to ~ on water during the dry season.在旱季我们必须节约用水。

economy/ɪ'kɒnəmi/

*n.*❶the control and management of money, goods and other resources 经济：The ~ of this country is developing fast.这个国家的经济正快速增长。❷ careful management of available resources；freedom from waste 节俭：It is an ~ to do the cooking by ourselves.还是我们自己弄饭菜划算一些。

ecosystem/'iːkəusɪstəm/

*n.*the system made up of a group of animals, plants and bacteria and its physical and chemical environment, and the relationship between them 生态系(统)

ecstasy/'ekstəsi/

n.a state of very strong feeling, especially of joy and happiness 狂喜；出神，入迷：in an ～ of delight 欣喜若狂/be in (go into) ecstasies over sth.(开始)对某事物心醉神迷/He looked at her with ～.他看她看得出神。

ecstatic/ɪk'stætɪk/

adj.causing or experiencing great joy and happiness 狂喜的；入迷的：She was absolutely ～ when I told her the news. 当我把这个消息告诉她时，她兴奋极了。

eddy/'edi/

I *n*.(*pl*.-ies) a circular movement of air, water, dust, etc.(空气、水、尘土等的)旋涡，涡流：Eddies of dust swirled in the road.公路上尘土飞扬。Ⅱ *v*.(of air, water, dust, etc.)move in a circle；whirl (空气、水、尘土等)起旋涡；旋转

Eden/'iːdn/

n.(in the Bible) the garden where Adam and Eve lived before their disobedience to God 伊甸园；乐园

edge/edʒ/

I *n*.❶the part or place where sth.ends or begins or that is farthest from its centre 边缘：The factory is on the ～ of the city. 工厂坐落在城市的边缘。/the ～ of a bowl 碗的边缘 ❷the thin sharp cutting part of a blade, tool, etc. 刃；刀口 ‖ give sb.the ～ of one's tongue 训斥某人/have the ～ on sb.胜过某人/take the ～ off sth. 挫其锋芒 Ⅱ *v*.provide with an edge or border 加边

edging/'edʒɪŋ/

n.sth.that forms an edge or border 边缘；饰边：a white handkerchief with (a) blue ～ 一块镶蓝边的白手绢

edible/'edəbl/

adj.suitable for eating 可食用的：～ food 食品

edict/'iːdɪkt/

n.an official command by a person in authority 法令；敕令；诏书：obey the ～s of parliament 服从议会通过的法令

edify/'edɪfaɪ/

v.improve the mind or character of sb. 开导，启发：a most ～ing lecture 一次很有启迪性的讲座

edit/'edɪt/

v.prepare (another person's writing) for printing, broadcasting, etc., by deciding what shall be included or left out (为出版、广播等而)编辑，编选；剪辑：Edit a Shakespeare play for use in schools.编辑一本莎士比亚剧本以供学校使用。

edition/ɪ'dɪʃən/

n.❶ the form in which sth. is published 版本：a paperback ～ 平装本 ❷ all the copies of a book or newspaper issued at the same time (书或报纸的)一版印刷总数,版次：the first ～ 第一版/ the early morning ～ 早间版 ❸a particular version or broadcast of a regular radio or television programme (某固定广播电视节目的特殊的)一版，一期

editor/'edɪtə(r)/

n. a person who edits a book or newspaper,etc.(图书、报刊等的)编辑：a contributing ～ 特约编辑/the responsible ～ 责任编辑/the chief ～ 总编辑；主编/a sports ～ 体育栏编辑

educate/'edʒʊkeɪt/

v. give intellectual, moral and social instruction to；train 教育；训练：He was ～d at a very good school.他在一所很好的学校受过教育。‖ ～d *adj*.受过教育的/educator *n*.教师，教育工作者

education/ˌedʒʊ'keɪʃn/

n.the process of teaching and learning 教育：Is ～ free and compulsory in your country? 贵国是实行免费的义务教育吗? /The future of any nation depends on ～.任何国家的未来都取决于教育。‖ ～al *adj*.教育的/～alist *n*.教育家

efface/ɪ'feɪs/

v.rub out or remove；cause to fade 抹去；消除；冲淡：Time and weather had long ago ～d the inscription on the monument. 时间的推移和风雨的侵蚀早已使纪念碑上的字迹模糊不清了。/Time alone will

~ those unpleasant memories. 只有时间才会冲淡那些不愉快的记忆。

effect/ɪˈfekt/

I *n.* ❶a result or condition produced by a cause; sth. that happens when one thing acts on another 结果; 效果: The punishment has no ~ on him. 惩罚对他没什么影响。/Does the medicine have any ~? 这种药有什么效果吗? /The children were suffering from the ~s of the hot weather. 孩子们饱受天气炎热之苦。❷ an impression produced in the mind of a person 感受; 印象: sound ~s 音响效果 / The general ~ of the painting is overwhelming. 这幅画给人总的印象是很有气势。‖ in ~ 实际上/bring(carry, put)sth. into ~ 实行, 实施/come into ~ 实行; 开始实施/give ~ 使生效/take ~ 生效; 奏效/to the ~ that 大意是……/to the same ~ 有同样的意思 II *v.* cause; bring about; accomplish 产生; 引起; 实现; 取得: ~ a change 引起变化/~ one's purpose 达到目的

effective/ɪˈfektɪv/

adj. ❶ successful in producing a desired result 有效的, 奏效的, 产生预期效果的: take ~ measures 采取有效措施 ❷actual or existing 真正的; 实际的: the number of ~ members 实际成员人数

effectively/ɪˈfektɪvli/

adv. ❶in an effective way 有效地 ❷in fact; in effect 实际上, 事实上: Effectively, their response was a refusal. 实际上, 他们的答复是拒绝。/Chances of a settlement were ~ wrecked by this announcement. 和解的机会事实上被这项声明破坏了。

effectual/ɪˈfektʃuəl/

adj.(of an action) successful in producing the intended effect; effective (行动)奏效的, 收效的: ~ measures to combat unemployment 对付失业的有效措施

efficiency/ɪˈfɪʃənsi/

*n.*the ability to work well and quickly 效率: raise ~ 提高效率/labour ~ 劳动效率/Efficiency is very important for an organization. 对一个组织来说, 效率是极其重要的。

efficient/ɪˈfɪʃənt/

adj. working well and getting a lot of things done 有效力的; 有能力的: an ~ secretary 能干的秘书/an ~ way 有效的方法/an ~ new machine 效率高的新机器

effort/ˈefət/

n. ❶the strength and energy to do sth. 气力; 精力: a waste of time and ~ 时间和精力的浪费/Lucy must put more ~ into her work. 露西必须更加努力地工作。❷ an energetic attempt; struggle 努力; 奋斗: His ~s were much appreciated. 他的努力得到了大家的一致赞赏。❸the result of an attempt 努力的结果; 成就: It's a good ~. 这事干得不错。‖ ~less *adj.* 不费力的, 不需努力的/~lessly *adv.* 不费力地

effusion/ɪˈfjuːʒən/

n. an uncontrolled expression of strong feelings in speech or writing (语言、感情的)迸发; 无约束的表达: Her ~s of gratitude were clearly insincere. 她口口声声的感激显然并非出于真心。

effusive/ɪˈfjuːsɪv/

adj. ❶showing feeling in an unrestrained way 流露感情的; 溢于言表的: Her ~ welcome made us feel most uncomfortable. 她过分殷勤的欢迎使我们感到极不舒服。❷of or relating to the eruption of large volumes of molten rock (岩浆)喷发的, 喷出的 ‖ ~ly *adv.* 溢于言表地: He thanked them ~ly. 他向他们大表感恩戴德之情。/~ness *n.* 热情洋溢; 岩石喷发

e.g./ˌiːˈdʒiː/

abbr. for example 例如: They keep animals, ~ goats and cattle. 他们饲养家畜, 例如山羊和牛。

egg/eg/

n. a round or oval object laid by female birds, snakes, fish, or insects; ovum 蛋; 卵: We eat hen's ~s. 我们吃鸡蛋。/The hen laid a large brown ~. 这只母鸡下了一个棕色大蛋。/The male sperm fertilizes the female ~s. 雄性精子使雌性卵子

受精。

egghead/'eghed/

　　n. a clever, highly educated person in a particular area 学者;学究

eggplant/'egplɑːnt/

　　n. a plant with a large purple fruit, used as a vegetable 茄子

eggshell/'egʃel/

　　n. the hard outside part of an egg 蛋壳

ego/'egəʊ/

　　n. ❶ a person's sense of self-esteem or self-importance 自我,自尊,自负: He has an enormous ~. 他非常自负。/Is success good for one's ~? 成功对一个人的自尊有好处吗? /to boost someone's ~ by praising them 夸奖某人以增强他们的自尊 ❷(in Freudian psychology) the one of the three parts of the mind that is responsible for your sense of who you are (弗洛伊德心理学中构成心灵的三部分之一的)自我,意识的我

egocentric/ˌegəʊ'sentrɪk/

　　adj. thinking only about oneself rather than other people; selfish 以自我为中心的,自私自利的 ‖ ~**ally** *adv*. 利己地,自我中心地

egoism/'egəʊɪzəm/

　　n. ❶ the quality of always thinking about oneself and about what will be best for oneself; selfishness 自私,利己心 ❷ an ethical theory that people's moral behaviour should be based on what is most advantageous to themselves 利己主义,自我主义

egoist /'iːgəʊɪst, 'egəʊɪst/

　　n. a self-centred person 利己主义者;自我主义者 ‖ ~**ic** *adj*. 自私自利的;自我为中心的

egotism/'egəʊtɪzəm/

　　n. the practice of talking or thinking too much about oneself 自我吹嘘;自高自大;自负 ‖ **egotist** *n*. 自高自大者;自夸者

eight/eɪt/

　　num. the number 8 八 ‖ **have one over the** ~ 饮酒过量

eighteen /ˌeɪ'tiːn/

num. the number 18 十八 ‖ ~**th** *num*. 第十八

eighth /eɪtθ/

　　Ⅰ *num*. constituting number eight in a sequence; 8th 第八 Ⅱ *n*. each of eight equal parts of sth. 八分之一

eighty /'eɪti/

　　Ⅰ *num*. the number 80 八十 Ⅱ *n*. (the eighties) numbers, years or temperatures from 80 to 89 八十几;八十年代 ‖ **eightieth** *num*. 第八十

either/'aɪðə(r)/

　　Ⅰ *adj*. & *pron*. one or the other of two 两者之一(的);(两者中)任何一个(的): Either of them will be satisfactory. 两者中任何一个都会令人满意。/In ~ case, it's impolite to do that. 不管是两种情形中的哪一种,那样做都是不礼貌的。 Ⅱ *adv*. (with negative) used to indicate a similarity or link with a statement just made 也(用于否定句中): You're not in favour of it, and I'm not, ~. 你不同意,我也持否定态度。 Ⅲ *conj*. (~ ... or ...) used to show a choice of two things 不是……就是,或者……或者: He must be ~ mad or drunk. 他不是疯了就是醉了。

ejaculate /ɪ'dʒækjʊleɪt/

　　v. ❶ say sth. suddenly and sharply 突然说出,喊出 ❷(said about a man or male animal) eject semen from the penis at a sexual climax (男人或雄性动物)射精 ‖ **ejaculation** *n*. 突然说出(的话);射精

eject/ɪ'dʒekt/

　　v. throw or drive out in a violent way 强迫离开,驱逐: ~ sb. from the meeting 把某人逐出会场/ ~ sb. from the office 免某人的职

elaborate

　　Ⅰ /ɪ'læbərət/*adj*. involving many arranged parts or details carefully worked out and with a large number of parts and details 精巧的;复杂的;精心制作的: ~ plans 周密的计划/an ~ design 精心的设计 Ⅱ /ɪ'læbəreɪt/*v*. work out, explain or describe sth. in details 精心制作;详尽阐述;详细描述: ~ a system of logic 精心

搞出一套逻辑体系 ‖ ～ly *adv*.精巧地/～ness *n*.尽力,竭力/**elaboration** *n*.精巧

elapse/ɪˈlæps/
 v.(of time) go by; pass (时间)过去,消逝:Two years have ～d since we met last time.自从我们上次见面已经过去两年了。

elastic/ɪˈlæstɪk/
 adj.❶ (of an object or material) able to return to its original size or shape after being pulled or pressed (物品或材料)有弹性的:an ～ cushion 有弹性的垫子/an ～ rope 有弹力的绳子 ❷ (especially of plans or arrangements) able to be changed if the situation changes; not fixed (尤指计划或安排)可伸缩的;灵活的:This nation is carrying out an ～ diplomatic policy.这个国家实行的是一种弹性外交政策。

elasticity/ˌɪlæsˈtɪsəti/
 n.the quality that sth.has of being able to stretch and return to its original size and shape 弹性,弹力:high ～ 高弹性/price ～ 价格弹性

elated/ɪˈleɪtɪd/
 adj.filled with joy and happiness 兴高采烈的;喜气洋洋的:The ～ crowd cheered and cheered. 兴高采烈的人群不停地欢呼。/She seemed ～ at the news.她似乎对这个消息感到很兴奋。/We were all ～ to hear of the victory.听到我们胜利的消息,大家都感到欣欣鼓舞。

elation/ɪˈleɪʃn/
 n.a feeling of great happiness and excitement 喜气洋洋,兴高采烈

elbow/ˈelbəʊ/
 Ⅰ *n*.the outer point of the joint where the arm bends 手肘 Ⅱ *v*.push with the elbows 推进;用肘推:～ sb.aside 把某人挤在一旁/～ one's way through the crowd 在人群中挤过去 ‖ **out at one's ～** 靠近;在近旁

elder/ˈeldə(r)/
 Ⅰ *adj*.of a greater age of two (二者中)较年长的:my ～ sister 我的姐姐/his ～ son 他的(两个儿子中的)大儿子/Which brother did you see, the ～ or the youn-ger? 你见到了哪一个,是哥哥还是弟弟? /My ～ brother is a college student. 我哥哥是个大学生。Ⅱ *n*.(*pl*.) a person of or advanced sth. age 长者;前辈:We should respect our ～s.我们应该尊敬长辈。

elderly/ˈeldəli/
 adj.rather old; ageing 年老的;变老的:～ people 老年人

eldest/ˈeldɪst/
 adj.of the greatest age of three or more (三者或三者以上)最年长的;最老的:My ～ brother lives abroad.我的大哥住在国外。

elect/ɪˈlekt/
 Ⅰ *v*.❶choose sb.for an official position by voting 选举,推举:We ～ed Smith to be our chairman. 我们选举史密斯做我们的主席。❷choose or decide(to do sth.)选择,决定(做某事):She ～ed to go to the party tonight. 她决定参加今晚的聚会。Ⅱ *adj*.❶chosen or singled out 选中的;卓越的 ❷chosen for a position but not yet in office 当选而尚未就职的:the pres-ident ～候任总统

election/ɪˈlekʃn/
 n.the choosing of representatives by vot-ing 选举:an ～ campaign 竞选活动/a general ～ 大选;普选/There will be an ～ in that country next year.明年那个国家将举行一次选举。

elective/ɪˈlektɪv/
 adj.(of a position) for which the holder is chosen by election (职位)由选举产生的:The office of President of the U.S. is an ～ one, but the position of Queen of England is not.美国总统的职位是选举产生的,英国女皇的王位则不是。

elector/ɪˈlektə(r)/
 n.a person who has the right to vote in an election 有选举权的人,选民

electoral/ɪˈlektərəl/
 adj.concerning elections or electors 选举的;选举人的:Many people say the ～ system in this country should be changed.很多人都说该国的选举制度应该有所改

变。/～ systems（reforms）选举制度（改革）

electric /ɪˈlektrɪk/

adj. ❶ of, worked by, carrying or producing electricity 电的；电动的；带电的；发电的：an ～ current 电流/an ～light 电灯 ❷ very exciting 令人震惊的，令人兴奋的：His speech had an ～ effect upon all the listeners. 他的演说使听众极为兴奋。

electrical /ɪˈlektrɪkl/

adj. connected with, producing or using electricity 电的；发电的；用电的：an ～ engineer 电机工程师/～ apparatus 电力设备/This machine has an ～ fault. 这台机器有电力故障。

electrician /ɪˌlekˈtrɪʃ(ə)n/

n. a person whose job is to deal with electricity and electrical equipments 电工；电气技术员

electricity /ɪˌlekˈtrɪsəti/

n. ❶ a form of energy which is produced by various means（e.g. by a battery or generator）, carried usually through cables and wires, etc. for heating, lighting and driving machines, etc. 电；电能 ❷ a feeling of great excitement, especially one that spreads through a group of people 强烈的激情

electrics /ɪˈlektrɪks/

n. the system of wires that work in a house, car or an electrical apparatus（房屋、汽车或电力设备的）电力系统，电路：I don't know why the car won't start; perhaps it's a problem in the ～. 我不懂车子为什么发动不起来，也许问题出在电路上。

electrify /ɪˈlektrɪfaɪ/

v. ❶ make sth. to a system using electric power 使电气化：～ a railway system 使铁路系统电气化 ❷ charge sth. with electricity 使带电，充电：～ storage batteries 给蓄电池充电 ❸ cause sb. to feel excited and surprised greatly; shock sb. 使惊骇，使震惊：～ the audience 使观众震惊

electrode /ɪˈlektrəʊd/

n. a solid conductor through which electricity enters or leaves a vacuum tube 电极

electron /ɪˈlektrɒn/

n. a stable subatomic particle with a charge of negative electricity, found in all atoms and acting as the primary carrier of electricity in solids 电子

electronic /ɪˌlekˈtrɒnɪk/

adj. ❶ making use of transistors and microchips and other components that control electric currents 电子的 ❷ of or relating to electronics（与）电子学（有关）的：～ engineering 电子工程学 ❸ done by means of a computer network 通过网络的：～ banking 电子银行 ‖ ～ally *adv.* 用电子方法；用电子装置

electronics /ɪˌlekˈtrɒnɪks/

n. a branch of science and technology studying the development and use of electronic devices in transistors, computers, etc. 电子学

elegance /ˈelɪɡəns/

n. grace and beauty 优雅；优美；精美

elegant /ˈelɪɡənt/

adj. having the qualities of grace and beauty; stylish 文雅的；优美的：an ～ lady 淑女/ ～ manner 优雅的举止

elegy /ˈelədʒi/

n.（*pl.* -ies）a sorrowful or serious poem, typically a lament for the dead 哀歌；挽歌，挽诗

element /ˈelɪmənt/

n. ❶ a substance which has not so far been separated into simpler one by ordinary chemical methods 元素：Water is a compound containing the ～s hydrogen and oxygen. 水是含有氢和氧元素的化合物。 ❷ one of the parts which sth. is made up of; a necessary or typical part of sth. 要素；特色：Honesty is an important ～ in doing business. 诚信是做生意的一个重要因素。 ‖ ～al *adj.* 四大要素（土、水、气、火）的；自然的；基本的

elementary /ˌelɪˈmentri/

adj. simple and easy; basic; of the beginning stage 简易的，初步的，基本的，基础

的：the ～ rules of social conduct 社会行为的基本准则/ an ～ school 小学

elephant/ˈelɪfənt/

n. a type of large plant-eating mammal with a thick skin, ivory tusks and a long trunk 象

elevate/ˈelɪveɪt/

*v.*lift up or raise sth. to a higher position 提高，高举；抬起

elevator /ˈelɪveɪtə/

n. ❶ sth. that lifts or raises things 升降机，起卸机 ❷ the movable part of a hinged flap on the tailplane of an aircraft, used to control its attitude（飞机的）升降舵 ❸a lift in a building 电梯

elevation/ˌelɪˈveɪʃn/

*n.*❶the act of elevating or the state of being elevated 举起，提高；提升：The sergeant's ～ to lieutenant was deserved. 那中士被提升为中尉是当之无愧的。❷ height above sea-level 高度，海拔：The hill has an ～ of 4,000 feet. 这座山有4 000 英尺高。

eleven /ɪˈlevn/

Ⅰ *num.*the number 11, one more than ten 11，十一 Ⅱ *n.*a team of eleven players in cricket, football, etc.（板球、足球等）十一人队 ‖ ～th *num.&n.*第十一；十一分之一

elicit/ɪˈlɪsɪt/

v. get information, etc. from sb., often with difficulty 获悉；探出：～ information (an answer, the truth) 探知消息（获悉答复、探明真相）

eligible/ˈelɪdʒəbl/

*adj.*fulfilling the necessary conditions 合适的；合格的：He's ～ for the post. 他有资格担任这个职位。‖ eligibility *n.*合格；有资格/eligibly *adv.*可被选地；适当地

eliminate/ɪˈlɪmɪneɪt/

*v.*get rid of；remove 排除；消除；消灭：～ a possibility 排除一种可能性/～ mistakes 消灭错误

elimination/ɪˌlɪmɪˈneɪʃn/

*n.*the act of eliminating or state of being eliminated 消除，排除，淘汰：the ～ of unsuitable candidates 淘汰不合适的候选人

elite/eɪˈliːt/

*n.*a group of people considered to be the best in a particular society or group 杰出人物；精英：an educated ～ 受过良好教育的精英/the ～ of society 社会名流

ellipse/ɪˈlɪps/

*n.*a regular oval shape 椭圆

elliptical/ɪˈlɪptɪkl/

*adj.*❶of or having the form of an ellipse 椭圆的；椭圆形的 ❷of or showing ellipsis；having a word or words omitted 省略的；表示省略的

elm/elm/

n. a tall tree which has rough serrated leaves and propagates from root suckers, often found in cool northern regions 榆树；榆木

elope/ɪˈləʊp/

*v.*run away from one's parents in order to get married 私奔：The young woman ～d with the man she loved.这位姑娘与心爱的男人私奔了。

eloquent /ˈeləkwənt/

*adj.*fluently and expressively in speaking or writing 雄辩的，口才流利的；有表现力的 ‖ ～ly *adv.*善辩地；富于表现力地

else/els/

*adv.*❶besides；in addition 此外；别的：Do you have anything ～ to do? 你还有别的什么要做吗？❷ otherwise；if not 否则；不然：Be quick, or ～ you'll be late.快走，不然你会迟到的。

elsewhere/ˌelsˈweə(r)/

adv. somewhere else；at, in or to another place 在别处，向别处：Mr.and Mrs.Houston lived next door, but now they live ～. 豪斯顿夫妇原来住在隔壁，但现在他们住在别的地方。

elude/ɪˈluːd/

v. escape from sb. or sth., especially by means of a trick 躲避；逃避：～ observation 逃避观察/ ～ one's enemies 逃避敌人 ‖ elusive *adj.*逃避的

emaciated /ɪˈmeɪʃɪeɪtɪd/

adj. thin and weak because of illness or lack of food（因病或饥饿）瘦弱的，消瘦的

e-mail /ˈiːmeɪl/

n. messages distributed by electronic means from one computer user to one or more recipients via a network 电子邮件：We received thousands of ～s. 我们收到了成千上万封电子邮件。

emanate /ˈeməneɪt/

v. produce or show sth. 产生；显示；表现：He ～d confidence and power. 他表现出了信心和力量。

emancipate /ɪˈmænsɪpeɪt/

v. set someone free from slavery or some form of restraint 解放；使不受（法律、社会或政治的）约束：～d young women 获得解放的年轻妇女 ‖ **emancipatory** *adj.* 解放的；有助解放的

emancipation /ɪˌmænsɪˈpeɪʃn/

n. the act of emancipating or the state of being emancipated; release 解放：achieve the final ～ of all mankind 最终解放全人类

embankment /ɪmˈbæŋkmənt/

n. a wall made of earth or stone to support a road which is higher than the surrounding land, or to prevent the land beside a river being flooded 路基；河堤

embargo /ɪmˈbɑːɡəʊ/

Ⅰ *n.* (*pl.* ～es) an official order to stop trade, especially with another country 禁止贸易令；禁运：put (lay) an oil ～ on country 对某国实行石油禁运 Ⅱ *v.* put an embargo on sth. 禁止贸易；禁止船只出入

embark /ɪmˈbɑːk/

v. get onto a ship; put sth. onto a ship 乘船；将……装船：The soldiers ～ for Malta. 士兵们乘船去马耳他。 ‖ ～ **on**（**upon**）开始；从事

embarrass /ɪmˈbærəs/

v. cause to be ashamed or uncomfortable 使困窘，使窘迫：The young man was ～ed by lacking of money. 那位年轻人因缺钱而发窘。 ‖ ～**ing** *adj.* 令人窘迫的／

～**ingly** *adv.* 使人尴尬地

embarrassment /ɪmˈbærəsmənt/

n. ❶ the act of embarrassing or the state of being embarrassed 困窘，局促不安：ease one's ～ 缓解某人的困窘 ❷ a person or thing causing problems for sb. 使人困窘的人（或事）：financial ～s 经济拮据；财政困难／That nasty child is an ～ to his parents. 那个惹人讨厌的孩子令他父母感到难堪。

embassy /ˈembəsi/

n. a group of officials led by an ambassador who represent their government in a foreign country 大使馆；大使馆人员：go (come, send sb.) on an ～ 去（来，派某人）任大使／the Chinese ～ in Russia 中国驻俄罗斯大使馆

embed /ɪmˈbed/

v. (-dd-) fix sth. into a substance very firmly 牢牢嵌入，牢牢插入：The foundations of the bridge are ～ded in concrete. 桥基牢牢地嵌入混凝土中。

embellish /ɪmˈbelɪʃ/

v. make sth. more beautiful by adding decorations to it 装饰，布置

ember /ˈembə(r)/

n. (usually *pl.*) a small piece of coal or wood burning or glowing in a dying fire 余烬

embezzle /ɪmˈbezl/

v. use (money placed in one's care) in a wrong way for one's own benefit 贪污，侵吞：The bank manager ～d the money. 银行经理贪污了这笔款子。

emblem /ˈembləm/

n. an object which is the sign of sth. 象征；标记；徽章：The dove is an ～ of peace. 鸽子是和平的象征。

embody /ɪmˈbɒdi/

v. ❶ give a tangible or visible form to an idea, feeling, etc.（思想、感悟等）具体化；表现：Words ～ thought. 语言体现思想。／He embodies his idea in his speech. 他的思想体现在他的发言之中。 ❷ include; collect 包含；收录：This book embodies the works of many young writers.

这本书收录了许多青年作家的作品。

embolden/ɪmˈbəʊldən/

v. give courage or confidence to (sb.) 给(某人)壮胆；使(更)勇敢：The protesters were ~ed by the fact that the police were unarmed. 抗议者因警察没有带武器而壮了胆。/She smiled, and this ~ed him to speak to her. 她微微一笑，这使他壮起胆来跟她说话。

embolism/ˈembəlɪzəm/

n. the blockage of an artery or a vein caused by a clot of blood, an air-bubble, etc. (血管的)栓塞，栓子

embosom/ɪmˈbuzəm/

v. enclose or surround protectively 包围；怀抱；环绕：a village ~ed with hills 群山环绕的村庄

embosomed/ɪmˈbuzəmd/

adj. enclosed or surrounded 包围的，环绕的：a house ~ in trees (被)树木抱的房子

embrace/ɪmˈbreɪs/

Ⅰ *v.* ❶ take and hold (someone or each other) in the arms as a sign of affection 拥抱：The two brothers ~d and cried. 兄弟两人拥抱在一起哭了起来。❷ accept or support (a theory or belief) willingly and eagerly 支持，接受(理论或信仰)：The public ~ this new policy. 公众支持这一新政策。Ⅱ *n.* an act of embracing 拥抱：He held her to him in a warm ~. 他热情地拥抱她。

embroider/ɪmˈbrɔɪdə(r)/

v. sew a pattern or picture onto cloth 刺绣

embroidery/ɪmˈbrɔɪdəri/

n. (*pl.*-ies) ❶ the art or activity of embroidering 刺绣，绣花；刺绣艺术 ❷ embroidered cloth 绣制品

embryo/ˈembrɪəʊ/

n. ❶ an unborn or not hatched offspring animal, bird, etc. in the stage of development 胚胎 ❷ a thing at a rudimentary stage that shows potential for development 萌芽状态的事物；发展初期的事物

emend/ɪ(ː)ˈmend/

v. alter sth. written in order to remove mistakes 订正，改正(文稿) ‖ ~ation *n.* 校正；修订；修正

emerald/ˈemərəld/

n. a bright green precious stone; a colour like this stone 祖母绿；绿宝石；翠绿色

emerge/ɪˈmɜːdʒ/

v. come out or appear from inside or from being hidden 现出；出现：A moon ~d from behind the cloud. 月亮从云后露了出来。‖ ~nce *n.* 浮现；显露

emergency/ɪˈmɜːdʒənsi/

n. an unusual and dangerous situation in which one has to act quickly 紧急情况：An outbreak of fire or an accident is an ~. 失火或发生事故都是紧急情况。‖ ~ exit *n.* 太平门/ ~ ward *n.* 急诊室

emergent/ɪˈmɜːdʒənt/

adj. in the process of coming into being or becoming prominent 新兴的，兴起的：~ states 新兴国家

emery/ˈeməri/

n. a hard mineral used (especially in powdered form) for polishing, smooth-ing and grinding things (以粉末状用作磨料的)刚玉粉，金刚砂：~-paper, ~-cloth, ~-wheel 砂纸，砂布，砂轮

emigrant/ˈemɪɡrənt/

n. a person who leaves their own country to live in another country 移民

emigrate/ˈemɪɡreɪt/

v. go away from one's own country to another to settle there 移民：During the war, countless people ~d to other countries. 战争期间，无数的人移民到了其他国家。

eminent/ˈemɪnənt/

adj. ❶ (of people) well-known and respected (指人)著名的，杰出的：an ~ lawyer(scientist, general) 著名的律师(科学家、将军) ❷ greater than usual 非常的，非凡的；卓越的：~ honesty(intelligence) 非常诚实(非凡的智力) ‖ eminence *n.* 卓越，杰出；非凡

emissary/ˈemɪsəri/

n. a person who is sent with an official message or to do special work, often of a secret kind 特使，密使

emission/ɪ'mɪʃn/

n. the act of emitting; sth. emitted 发射，散发；射出物，散发物：the sun's ~ of light 阳光的照射/We've been receiving powerful radio ~s from a distant star system. 我们接收到从一个遥远的恒星系发射出的强大的无线电波。

emit/ɪ'mɪt/

v. (-tt-) produce and discharge 散发；发出；放射：~ a sound(a smell) 发出声音(气味)/~ radiation(light) 放射射线(光线)

emollient/ɪ'mɒlɪənt/

Ⅰ n. sth. especially a medicine that softens the skin and reduces pain when it is sore 润肤剂：This is a powerful ~ against sunburn. 这是一种防止太阳(光)灼伤的有效润肤剂。Ⅱ adj. ❶having the quality of softening or soothing the skin 柔肤的，润肤的 ❷soothing or calming 缓和的，安抚的：His ~ words calmed the situation down. 他那些安抚的话使事态缓和下来。

emotion/ɪ'məʊʃn/

n. any of the strong feelings of the human spirit 情感，情绪；激情：He spoke in a voice touched with much ~. 他以非常激动的声音说话。/full of ~s 充满激情

emotional/ɪ'məʊʃənl/

adj. ❶of the emotions 感情的，情感的，情绪的：He has ~ difficulties. 他有感情上的困扰。❷showing or causing strong feelings 表现强烈情感的；动人的：~ music 动人的音乐 ❸having feelings which are strong or easily moved 易激动的；易动感情的：an ~ woman 一位多愁善感的女子

emotionalism/ɪ'məʊʃnəlɪzəm/

n. the quality of feeling or showing too much emotion, and of allowing oneself to be controlled by it 多愁善感；感情用事

emotive/ɪ'məʊtɪv/

adj. causing strong feelings 引起强烈感情的；令人激动的：Capital punishment is a very ~ issue. 死刑是一个引起激烈争论的问题。

empathy/'empəθi/

n. the ability to imagine oneself in the position of another person, and so to share and understand that person's feelings 同情；同感，共鸣：As a rich and privileged person she has very little ~ with the people she claims to represent. 作为一个富有并有特权的人，她和那些她声称代表的人没有多少共鸣。

emperor/'empərə(r)/

n. the ruler of an empire 皇帝：Many years ago there lived an Emperor, who cared more for fine new clothes than for anything else. 许多年以前，有一位皇帝热衷于漂亮的新衣胜过其他一切。

emphasis/'emfəsɪs/

n. (pl. emphases/'emfəsiz/) special importance given to sth. 强调：Some schools lay (put) special ~ on language study. 一些学校特别注重语言的学习。

emphasize/'emfəsaɪz/

v. ❶place emphasis on; stress 强调，重视：The teacher ~d the importance of studying hard. 老师强调了努力学习的重要性。❷give extra force to a word or phrase 重读：Pronouns are not usually ~d. 代词通常不重读。

empire/'empaɪə(r)/

n. a group of states or countries under one ruler, usually an emperor or empress 帝国：A hundred years ago, Britain was a large ~. 一百年以前，英国是一个很大的帝国。

empirical/ɪm'pɪrɪkl/

adj. based on experiment or experience, not on theory 凭经验的；以实验(或经验)为依据的 ‖ ~ly adv. 以经验为主地

empiricism/ɪm'pɪrɪsɪzəm/

n. the system of working by empirical methods 经验主义，经验论 ‖ **empiricist** n. 经验主义者；经验论者

emplacement/ɪm'pleɪsmənt/

n. a special position prepared for a heavy gun or other military equipments to stand on 炮位，炮台；安置军事装备的阵地

employ/ɪm'plɔɪ/

E

v. ❶ give work to sb. and pay them for working for you 雇用：They ～d five workers.他们雇用了 5 名工人。❷ make use of sb.or sth.运用；采用：～ advanced technology 采用先进技术

employee/ɪmˈplɔii:/
n. the person who is employed 雇员，雇工，受雇者：The factory has two hundred ～s.工厂有 200 个职工。

employer/ɪmˈplɔɪə(r)/
n. the person who employs people 雇主：He is not a good ～.他不是一个好雇主。

employment/ɪmˈplɔɪmənt/
n. ❶ the state of being employed；the act of employing 就业；雇用：He left his home to look for ～.他离家去找工作。❷one's occupation 工作；职业：～ agency 职业介绍所

empress/ˈemprəs/
n. a female ruler of a country or several countries；the wife of an emperor 女皇；皇后

emptiness/ˈemptɪnəs/
n. ❶a feeling of being sad because nothing seems to have any value 空虚 ❷the fact that there is nothing or nobody in a place 空无；空旷：The silence and ～ of the house scared her.房子的空寂使她感到害怕。

empty/ˈempti/
Ⅰ *adj.* ❶ containing nothing 空的：an ～ bottle 空瓶 ❷without meaning or value 没有意义（或价值）的；空洞的；空虚的：My life feels ～ after children have left home.孩子们离家之后，我感觉生活很空虚。Ⅱ *v.*❶make sth.empty 清空，倒空，腾空：He emptied his pockets of their contents. 他把衣服口袋里的东西全都掏出来了。❷remove（the contents of）sth. and put them somewhere else 将（某物中的）东西取出置于别处：He emptied the waste paper onto the floor.他把废纸倒在了地板上。

emulate/ˈemjʊleɪt/
*v.*try to do as well as or better than；try to equal or surpass（a person or achieve-

ment）赶上，超过（人或成就）：She tried hard to ～ her classmates.她力争赶上她的同班同学。

emulation/ˌemjʊˈleɪʃn/
n. the act or state of emulating 竞争，竞赛，仿效：stimulate ～ and effort 刺激竞争与努力／The young man worked hard in ～ of his father.这位年轻人努力工作赶超他父亲。

emulsion/ɪˈmʌlʃn/
*n.*❶creamy liquid in which particles of oil are suspended 乳状液；乳浊液 ❷a type of paint in this form 乳化漆；乳胶漆

enable/ɪˈneɪbl/
*v.*make(sb.) able to do sth.；make (sth.) possible；give power or means to do sth. 使能够；使成为可能；使实现：Your help ～d me to finish the job.你的帮助使我能完成这项工作。

enact/ɪˈnækt/
*v.*❶make or pass a law 制定法律；颁布法令：as by law ～ed 如法律所规定 ❷perform（a play,etc.）on or as if on the stage of a theatre 演出（戏剧等）；展现：The beautiful view was ～ed before our eyes. 一片美景展现在我们眼前。

enactment/ɪˈnæktmənt/
*n.*❶the action of enacting；the state of being enacted 制定；颁布；规定；演出；扮演 ❷a law or a single provision of a law which has been made officially 法律；法令；法规；条例

encase/ɪnˈkeɪs/
*v.*surround or cover sth.in a case or close-fitting surround 包装，包裹：The machine was ～d in plastic. 这部机器包装在塑料壳内。

enchant/ɪnˈtʃɑːnt/
*v.*❶be very pleasant to sb.；be liked very much by sb. 使喜悦；使迷恋：She ～ed all her friends.她迷住了她所有的朋友。／The beautiful house ～ed everyone who saw it.这座美丽的房子使每个看见它的人都着了迷。❷ use magic on 施魔法于：The wizard ～ed the princess.巫士对公主施了魔法。‖ ～ing *adj.* 非常迷人的，令人

着魔的

encircle /ɪnˈsɜːkl/

　v. surround; form a circle round 包围; 环绕: a house ~d by (with) trees 一栋被树木环绕的房子/ The village was ~d by enemy forces. 村子被敌军包围了。

enclose /ɪnˈkləʊz/

　v. ❶ put a wall, fence, etc. to surround or close off on all sides 包围; 圈起: ~ the house with a fence 用篱笆将房子圈起来 ❷ put (sth.) in an envelope together with a letter 随信附上: Enclosed with my letter is my resume. 随信附上我的简历。

enclosure /ɪnˈkləʊʒə(r)/

　n. ❶ the act of enclosing a piece of land 圈地; 围绕; 围起; 封入: ~ of common land 圈用公地 ❷ a piece of land that is enclosed 圈占地, 圈用地: within a walled ~ 四周有墙的圈地 ❸ sth. that is put in with a letter 信中附件: The envelope contained a letter and 5 yuan as an ~. 信封里装着一封信, 还附有 5 元钱。

encompass /ɪnˈkʌmpəs/

　v. include or be concerned with (a wide range of activities, subjects, ideas, etc.) 包围; 包括: We're ~ed with doubts. 我们深感疑惑。

encounter /ɪnˈkaʊntə(r)/

　Ⅰ *v.* meet or have to deal with (sth. bad, especially a danger or a difficulty); be faced with 遭遇, 遇到 (困难或危险的事); 面临: One is sure to ~ many difficulties on the way to success. 在通向成功的道路上, 一个人肯定会遇到许多困难。Ⅱ *n.* a sudden meeting, usually either unexpected or dangerous (意外或危险的) 相遇, 遭遇, 冲突: an ~ action 遭遇战

encourage /ɪnˈkʌrɪdʒ/

　v. give hope, courage, support, etc. to (sb.) 鼓励: ~ a person to work harder 鼓励某人努力工作/ My friends tried hard to ~ me to go on with my experiment. 朋友们极力鼓励我继续我的实验。

encouragement /ɪnˈkʌrɪdʒmənt/

　n. ❶ the act of encouraging a person to do sth. 鼓励, 激励: He deserves greater ~.

他应得到更大的鼓励。❷ sth. that encourages sb. 起激励作用的事物: Their achievements were a great ~ to us. 他们取得的成就对我们是很大的鼓励。

encroach /ɪnˈkrəʊtʃ/

　v. (~ on/upon) intrude beyond the usual or proper limits 侵占, 侵犯: He always allows work to ~ upon his family life. 他总是让工作扰乱他的家庭生活。

encumber /ɪnˈkʌmbə(r)/

　v. make free action or movement difficult for; weigh down 妨碍; 牵累: be ~ed with a large family 为一大家子所累 ‖ **encumbrance** *n.* 阻碍物; 累赘; 负担

encyclopedia /ɪnˌsaɪkləˈpiːdɪə/

　n. a book or set of books dealing with every branch of knowledge, or with one particular branch, usually in alphabetical order 百科全书 ‖ **encyclopedic(al)** *adj.* 渊博的, 知识广博的/**encyclopedism** *n.* 百科全书的知识

end /end/

　Ⅰ *n.* ❶ the farthest or last part or point 末端; 终点: the ~ of a road 路的尽头/ the ~s of the earth 天涯海角; 天南地北 ❷ a small piece that remains after sth. has been used 剩余物; 残余: a cigarette ~ 烟蒂 ❸ a finish or termination of a state or situation 结束: at the ~ of a meeting 会议结束 ❹ death 死亡: The criminal will meet his ~ tomorrow. 这个罪犯明天就到了他的末日。❺ an aim or a goal 目的; 目标: the ~ that 其目的在于; 为了/ ~s and means 目的和手段 ‖ **at a loose ~** 无事可做/**on ~** 立起/**make ~s meet** 量入为出/**at an ~**; **at the ~ of** 结束/**come to an ~** 结束/**make (put) an ~ of sth.** 结束某物/**in the ~** 终于/**no ~ of** 很多/**without ~** 无尽的 Ⅱ *v.* (cause to) come to an end; finish 结束: Let's ~ our quarrel. 我们不要争吵了。/ I get hold of the wrong ~ of the stick. 我完全误解了。‖ **~ up (in/ with)** 以……而结束

endanger /ɪnˈdeɪndʒə(r)/

　v. put (sb. or sth.) in danger; make it possible that harm or damage will be caused 使处于危险之中; 危害, 危及: He ~ed our lives by setting fire to the house.他放火烧房危害我们的性命。/He ～ed his chances of success. 他已不可能成功。/ The sea turtle is an ～ed species.海龟是濒危物种。

endear/ɪnˈdɪə(r)/

*v.*cause to be loved or liked 使受喜爱：～ oneself to the audience 使自己受到观众的喜爱 ‖ ～ing *adj.*可爱的/ ～ingly *adv.*讨人喜欢地/ ～ment *n.*喜爱；钟爱

endeavour /ɪnˈdevə/

Ⅰ*v.*try hard to do or achieve sth. 努力，尽力：He is ～ing to be a good lawyer.他正努力成为一名优秀的律师。Ⅱ*n.*❶an attempt to achieve a goal 尝试；企图：an ～ to reduce serious injury 减轻严重损伤的尝试 ❷earnest and industrious effort, especially when sustained over a period of time 努力；勤奋：Enthusiasm is a vital ingredient in all human ～.热情是人积极进取的关键因素。❸an enterprise or undertaking 事业，活动：a political ～ 政治事业

endemic/enˈdemɪk/

adj.(especially of a disease)found regularly in a particular place (尤指疾病)地方性的：This chest disease is ～ among miners in this area.这种胸部疾病是流行于本地区矿工中的地方病。

ending/ˈendɪŋ/

*n.*the last part of sth. especially a book, story, etc.结尾，结局；末尾：Children like stories with happy ～s.小孩子喜欢结局圆满的故事。

endless/ˈendlɪs/

*adj.*❶ never finishing; having no end 永无休止的，无穷尽的：The journey seemed ～.这段路程似无尽头。/ I'm fed up with your ～ complaining.我受够了你没完没了的牢骚。❷(of a belt, chain, etc.) circular; with the ends joined (带、链等)环状的；两端连接的：The machine drives an ～ belt.这个机器带动一条环状带。

endorse/ɪnˈdɔːs/

*v.*❶declare one's approval or support 赞同；认可：I ～d his plan.我赞同他的计划。❷write one's name on the back of a cheque or other document to show that one accepts is as genuine 签名于(支票或其他文件)背面(以示认可)

endow/ɪnˈdaʊ/

*v.*give money, etc. to provide a regular income for (a hospital, college, etc.) 资助；捐赠：～ a school 捐助基金办学校/ He spent all his fortune ～ing a hospital. 他把所有的家产全部捐给了一家医院。‖ be ～ed with (courage, ability, spirit, etc.) 有(勇气、能力、精神等)

endowment /ɪnˈdaʊmənt/

*n.*❶ the action of endowing sth. or sb. 捐赠 ❷an income or form of property given or bequeathed to someone (赠给某人的)一笔款项(或财产) ❸a natural ability 天资，天赋

endurance/ɪnˈdjʊərəns/

*n.*the state or power to last 忍耐力；忍耐，持久：A long-distance runner must have ～.一个长跑运动员必须有耐力。‖ beyond/past ～ 不能再忍耐，忍无可忍：His cruelty is beyond ～.他的残酷令人无法忍受。

endure/ɪnˈdjʊə(r)/

*v.*bear (pain, suffering, etc.) patiently or for a long time 忍耐(痛苦、困难等)；容忍：～ a person 容忍某人/ ～ the heat 忍受炎热的天气/We must ～ to the end.我们必须坚持到底。‖ endurable *adj.*可忍受的/enduring *adj.*持久的/enduringly *adv.*耐久地，永久地

endways/ˈendweɪz/

*adv.*❶with the end forward；not sideways 竖着；末端朝上(前)：The table was pushed ～ through the door.那张桌子被侧着推出屋门。❷ with the end of one object touching that of another 两端相接地：The boy put the toy cars together ～. 那男孩把玩具汽车头尾相接地摆在一起。

enemy/ˈenəmi/

*n.*❶a person who is hated or opposed to someone 敌人；仇敌；敌手；反对者：the public ～ 公敌/the ～ planes 敌机/

Whales have few enemies. 鲸的敌人很少。/Frost is an ～ of flowers. 霜会危害花朵。❷(the ～) armed forces of a hostile nation 敌军：The ～ is defeated. 敌军被打败了。/ The ～ is (are) retreating. 敌军正在撤退。

energetic /ˌenəˈdʒetɪk/

adj. full of energy；full of force 精力旺盛的，精神饱满的，有力的：an ～ man 精力充沛的人/The more he worked, the more ～ he became. 他越干越有劲。

energize /ˈenədʒaɪz/

v. give energy and strength to 供给……能量；给予……活力：Food ～s you. 食物使你增添能量。

energy /ˈenədʒi/

n. ❶ the strength and vitality to sustain physical or mental activity 活力；干劲；精力：Such work demands much ～. 这样的工作需要花很多的精力。❷ (a person's) capacity for working 工作能力 ❸ the ability of matter to work 能；能量：electrical ～ 电能 ❹ a source of power used for driving machines, providing light and heat, etc. 能源：solar ～ 太阳能

enfeeble /ɪnˈfiːbl/

v. make sb. or sth. weak；cause to lose strength completely 使衰弱，使完全无力：The country was ～d by war, drought, and disease. 这个国家因战争、旱灾和疾病而衰落。

enfold /ɪnˈfəʊld/

v. enclose or surround sb. or sth., especially in one's arms 围住，抱住；拥抱：She ～ed the child lovingly in her arms. 她满怀爱意地把孩子抱在怀里。

enforce /ɪnˈfɔːs/

v. ❶ compel observance of sth., especially a law, rule or obligation 强迫遵守；强迫执行；强制履行(义务)：～ a law (rule) 实施法律(规则)/He ～d his will on the child. 他强令孩子执行他的命令。❷ give force or strength to 强迫；强调：～ a demand 坚持要求/He ～d his case with new evidence. 他用新证据支持他的诉讼。

engage /ɪnˈɡeɪdʒ/

v. ❶ be busy with；work at；take part in 忙于；从事 ❷ promise or enter into a contract to do sth. 允诺；担保：Can you ～ that you'll keep secret? 你能保证保密吗？❸ employ 雇用；聘用：～ an accountant 聘一名会计师 ❹ agree to marry 订婚：They are ～d. 他们订婚了。❺ attract 吸引：Her plight ～d our sympathy. 她的困境引起我们的同情。

engaged /ɪnˈɡeɪdʒd/

adj. ❶ busy；occupied 忙的，没空的：He told me he was otherwise ～. 他告诉我他在忙别的事。❷ having formally agreed to marry 已订婚的

engagement /ɪnˈɡeɪdʒmənt/

n. ❶ an agreement to marry 婚约：He has broken off his ～ to Ann. 他已与安解除了婚约。❷ a promise to meet or go out with sb.；appointment；date 约会：I have an ～ at nine tonight. 我今晚九点有个约会。❸ a formal promise 诺言，保证：The government has broken all its ～s. 政府背弃了所有的承诺。

engine /ˈendʒɪn/

n. ❶ a piece of machinery which converts power into motion 引擎；发动机：a car ～ 汽车引擎/This is a fast car—it has a big ～. 这是一部快车——它有一个大引擎。❷ the part of a train that pulls the rest 机车；车头：railway ～ 火车头/An ～ was moving towards the wooden bridge over the creek. 一辆机车正向着小河上的木桥驶去。

engineer /ˌendʒɪˈnɪə(r)/

Ⅰ *n.* a person who is professionally trained to plan the making of machines, roads, bridges, electrical equipment, etc. 工程师：a civil (mining) ～ 土木(采矿)工程师 Ⅱ *v.* plan and make as an engineer does 建造：The machine is well ～ed. 这机器造得很好。

engineering /ˌendʒɪˈnɪərɪŋ/

n. ❶ the science or profession of an engineer 工程学，工程：chemical ～ 化工 ❷ the planning, designing or construction of machines, buildings, etc. 设计，建造：The Queen admired the ～ of the new railway.女王称赞这条新铁路的建造。

English /ˈɪŋglɪʃ/

Ⅰ *n.* the language of England 英语：Queen's (King's) ～ 标准英语；纯正英语 Ⅱ *adj.* of England or its people 英国的；英格兰的；英格兰人的：the ～ 英国人 ‖ ～**man** *n.* 英国人

engrave /ɪnˈgreɪv/

v. cut or carve (words, designs, etc.) on the surface of a hard object 雕刻：～ a design on a metal plate 在金属板上刻图案 /a name ～d on a tombstone 刻在墓碑上的姓名 ‖ ～**r** *n.* 雕刻师 /**engraving** *n.* 雕刻术

engross /ɪnˈgrəʊs/

v. ❶ absorb completely the interest and attention of 使专心，使全神贯注：～ in one's work 全神贯注于工作 ❷ produce (a legal document) in its final or definitive form 正式写成 (法律文件)

engulf /ɪnˈgʌlf/

v. (of a natural force) surround and swallow up (指自然力量) 吞没：The stormy sea ～ed the small boat. 狂暴的大海吞噬了小船

enhance /ɪnˈhɑːns/

v. increase or further improve the value, quality, status or beauty of 提高；增强；增进：The manager wanted to ～ the reputation of the company. 经理想提高公司的声誉。

enigma /ɪˈnɪgmə/

n. a person, thing or situation that is intended to be difficult to understand 神秘的人；难解的事物；令人困惑的处境

enjoy /ɪnˈdʒɔɪ/

v. get pleasure from (things and experiences)；like 喜爱，乐于：Did you ～ your dinner? 这顿饭吃得愉快吗？ /We ～ talking to him. 我们喜欢同他交谈。 ‖ ～ oneself 感到快乐

enjoyable /ɪnˈdʒɔɪəb(ə)l/

adj. giving enjoyment, pleasant 令人愉快的，有乐趣的 ‖ **enjoyably** *adv.* 愉快地；有趣地

enjoyment /ɪnˈdʒɔɪmənt/

n. ❶ the pleasure, joy or satisfaction given by what is enjoyed 愉快；欢乐；享受：The book has given me great ～. 这本书给了我极大的享受。 ❷ the fact of having and using sth. 享受，享有：We are in the ～ of a happy life. 我们过着幸福的生活。 ❸ sth. enjoyed；sth. that gives joy and pleasure 乐趣，乐事：Hunting is his greatest ～. 打猎是他最大的乐趣。

enlarge /ɪnˈlɑːdʒ/

v. (cause to) grow larger or wider (使) 扩大：The school has decided to ～ the hall. 学校已决定扩建礼堂。 ‖ ～ **on** (**upon**) 详述 ‖ ～**ment** *n.* 放大，放大的照片

enlighten /ɪnˈlaɪtn/

v. cause to understand deeply and clearly, especially by making free from false beliefs 启迪；开导：～ sb. on sth. 就某事对某人作启发。/Can you ～ me on this subject? 你能帮助我弄明白这一问题吗？ ‖ ～**ment** *n.* 启蒙，开导

enlist /ɪnˈlɪst/

v. ❶ (cause to) join the armed forces (使) 从军；(使) 入伍：～ as a volunteer 当志愿兵 ❷ get help or support 获得 (帮助或支持)：I need to ～ your support. 我需要得到你的支持。 ‖ ～**ment** *n.* 征募，应征入伍

enliven /ɪnˈlaɪvn/

v. make more active, cheerful, or interesting 使活泼；使有生气：～ our life 使我们的生活富有生气

enmity /ˈenməti/

n. a feeling of hatred towards each other by enemies 仇恨，敌意

enormity /ɪˈnɔːməti/

n. ❶ a very serious and wicked crime 暴行；大罪行 ❷ great wickedness 极恶；凶恶

enormous /ɪˈnɔːməs/

adj. extremely large 巨大的；极大的：～ success 巨大的成功 /an ～ sum of money 巨额现金 ‖ ～**ly** *adv.* 巨大地，庞大地 /～**ness** *n.* 庞大，巨大

enough /ɪˈnʌf/

adj. & adv. as much or as many as may be

necessary 足够的(地);充分的(地):He does not have ～ money to go for travelling.他没有足够的钱去旅行。/This hall is large ～ to hold two thousand people. 这大厅大得足以容纳 2 000 人。‖ **more than** ～ 过多;太多/**sure** ～ 正如所料

enquire /ɪnˈkwaɪə/
v. ask for information from someone 打听,询问:He ～d about houses for sale.他探问有没有房子出售。/ He ～d her name.他打听了她的姓名。‖ ～ **after** 向……问好,问候:He ～d after his parents.他向她父母问好。/～ **for** 求见,找(某人)/～ **into** 调查;查究

enquiring /ɪnˈkwaɪrɪŋ/
adj. ❶ showing an interest in learning new things 爱打听的,好问的;爱探索的: an ～ mind 爱探究的头脑 ❷(of a look or expression) suggesting that information is sought (脸色或表情)探询的:The teacher sent her an ～ glance.老师询问地看了她一眼。‖ ～**ly** *adv.*怀疑地

enquiry /ɪnˈkwaɪəri/
n.(*pl.*-ies)❶a question asking for information 打听,询问;查问❷an investigation 调查

enrage /ɪnˈreɪdʒ/
v. make sb.very angry 使(人)发怒;激怒: Her behaviour ～d her husband. 她的行为使她的丈夫极为愤怒。/He was ～d by the rude remarks.他对那些粗暴的话极为愤慨。

enrapture /ɪnˈræptʃə/
v. fill sb.with intense delight 使欣喜若狂: The mother was ～d by the child who was sleeping in her arms so peacefully.孩子安静地睡在怀里,母亲心里乐滋滋的。

enrich /ɪnˈrɪtʃ/
v. make sb.or sth.rich or richer;improve by adding sth. 使丰富:Various kinds of activities ～ our life.各种各样的活动丰富了我们的生活。/ ～ oneself with knowledge 用知识充实自己‖ ～**ment** *n.* 丰富,改进

enrol(l) /ɪnˈrəʊl/
v. make (oneself or another person) offi-cially a member of a group (使)成为一员:He was ～ed in a famous university. 他被一所著名大学录取了。‖ ～**ment** *n.* 注册;登记

enroute /ɒnˈruːt/
adv. on the way;during the course of travelling 在途中:We stopped at Tokyo ～ from New York to Beijing.我们从纽约到北京的途中曾在东京停留。

enslave /ɪnˈsleɪv/
*v.*❶make a slave of 奴役,使成为奴隶 ❷ make sb.or sth.completely depend on sth. 使受控制:Her beauty ～d many young men.她的美貌令很多青年男子倾倒。

ensue /ɪnˈsjuː/
*v.*happen later;take place as a result 接着发生;接踵而来;因而产生;结果是:Si-lence ～d.接着是一片沉寂。/Bitter ar-guments ～d from misunderstanding. 这一误会引起了一场唇枪舌剑。

ensure /ɪnˈʃɔː(r)/
*v.*make (sth.) certain to happen 确定;确信:They said they could ～ your safety. 他们说他们可以保证你的安全。‖ ～ a-**gainst sth.** 保证不会发生(问题)

entail /ɪnˈteɪl/
v. involve (sth.) as a necessary or result 使成为必要;使成为必然:He bought a bigger house and this ～ed buying more furniture.他买了一座更大的房子,因此需要多买些家具。

entangle /ɪnˈtæŋgl/
*v.*❶make things become tangled 缠住,使纠缠:The bird had become ～d in the wire netting.那只小鸟被铁丝网缠住了。 ❷involve sb.in sth. complicated 使卷入,使陷入(复杂的境地):She found herself ～d in the case of murder so painfully.她发现自己极其不幸地牵连进那宗谋杀案里。‖ ～**ment** *n.*纠缠;牵连

entente /ɒnˈtɒnt/
*n.*❶an understanding or agreement be-tween nations or fractions 国家(或派别)之间的协议,协定:Two powerful groups are to fix the basis for an ～.两大集团将商定协议的基础。❷a group of states

that have made an agreement 盟国；协约国；the Entente (countries)（第一次世界大战时的）协约国

enter/ˈentə(r)/

v.❶ go or come into (a place) 进入：The manager ～ed the office. 经理走进了办公室。/～ the field of business 进入商业领域 ❷ join；become a member of；cause sb. to be admitted 加入：～ the Army 参军 ‖ ～ into sth. 开始处理某事/ ～ on (upon) 开始；着手/ ～ for 报名参加

enterprise/ˈentəpraɪz/

n.❶an organization，especially a business firm 企业：manage (conduct) an ～ 管理企业；a state (state-owned) ～ 国有企业 ❷willingness and initiative to take risks and do things that are difficult，new，or daring 首创精神；进取心；事业心：a man of ～ 有事业进取心的人 ‖ ～r n. 干事业的人；企业家

enterprising/ˈentəpraɪzɪŋ/

adj. showing initiative；adventurous 有进取心的；有创业精神的

entertain/ˌentəˈteɪn/

v.❶provide (sb.) with food and drink 款待：～ a friend to dinner 请朋友吃饭 ❷ provide (sb.) with amusement or enjoyment 使快乐；使娱乐：～ the audience with jokes 用笑话来娱乐观众

entertainment/ˌentəˈteɪnmənt/

n.❶a public performance or activity (at a theatre，circus，etc.) designed to entertain others（戏院、马戏团等）娱乐活动，文娱表演：The city offers many ～. 城里有许多娱乐活动。❷ the act of entertaining sb. 招待；款待；娱乐：After dinner，we all sit in front of the box for ～. 吃过饭，我们都坐在电视机前欣赏节目。

enthrone/ɪnˈθrəʊn/

v.❶install a king on a throne 使国王登基：The king was ～d with a great ceremony. 国王在盛大的庆祝活动中登基。❷give a high place to sb. in one's judgement or affection 给……以权位；崇拜，爱戴（某人）：He was a ruler ～d in the hearts of his subjects. 他是一位深受臣民

爱戴的君主。

enthuse/ɪnˈθjuːz/

v.make (sb.) interested and eagerly appreciative 使（人）热心于：What's she enthusing over this time? 她这次为什么事而这么热心？

enthusiasm/ɪnˈθjuːzɪæzəm/

n.❶a feeling of eager；liking for sth. or interest in sth. 热心，热忱，狂热 ❷sth. you are interested in 激发热情的东西，热衷的事物：Skiing is one of my ～s. 滑雪是我的爱好之一。

enthusiast/ɪnˈθjuːzɪæst/

n. someone who has a lot of enthusiasm for sth. 爱好者，热衷者：a sports ～体育爱好者

enthusiastic/ɪnˌθjuːzɪˈæstɪk/

adj. having or showing intense and eager enjoyment，interest，or approval 热心的；热情的；极感兴趣的：an ～ supporter 热心的支持者/an ～ welcome 热烈欢迎 ‖ ～ally adv. 热心地；满腔热情地

entire/ɪnˈtaɪə(r)/

adj. whole；complete 全部的；整个的：The ～ city was destroyed. 整座城市都被毁了。 ‖ ～ly adv. 整个地，全部地：He is ～ly ignorant of it. 他完全蒙在鼓里。/ ～ty n.完全；全部

entitle/ɪnˈtaɪtl/

v.❶ give a title or name to (a book，etc.) 取名：a book ～ed Story of Stone 一本名为《石头记》的书 ❷give a right to 有权利（干……）：The law ～s us to do it. 法律赋予了我们做这件事的权利。/He's ～d to form a company. 他被授权组建一个公司。 ‖ ～ment n.权利；津贴

entity/ˈentəti/

n. anything which exists independently 实在，实体

entrance¹/ɪnˈtrɑːns/

v. overcome，carry away (someone) as in a dream，with wonder and delight 使狂喜；使出神；使神魂颠倒：He was completely ～d by (with) the music. 他听音乐听得完全入了迷。

entrance² /'entrəns/

n. ❶ an opening that allows access to a place 入口：the front ～ 正门/the ～ to the railway station 火车站的入口处 ❷ the act of coming or going in 进入：Everyone rose at the manager's ～.经理一进来，大家都站起来了。/The music was played for the ～ of the dancers.随着舞蹈演员入场奏起了音乐。❸ the right or opportunity of entering somewhere or being a member of an institution or society 入场权；进入某地方或（加入某组织）的权力（或机会）：～ free 免费入场/No ～! 不准入内！/ He passed the ～ examination for the college.他通过了大学入学考试。

entrap /ɪn'træp/

v. (-pp-) arrest；make sb. or sth. into a trap；trick or deceive sb.诱捕；使陷入圈套；诱骗，欺骗：He felt he had been ～ped into marrying her.他感到同她结婚是中了圈套。

entreat /ɪn'triːt/

v. ask sb. earnestly 恳求，请求：He ～s both the patience and attention of the reader.他恳请读者既要耐心又要专注。/ He ～ed us to help him.他请求我们帮助他。

entreaty /ɪn'triːti/

n. an earnest humble request 恳求，乞求：All our entreaties were in vain, and he went away at dawn.我们所有的恳求都是徒劳的，他在天亮时就离开了。

entree /'ɒntreɪ/

n. ❶ the right or freedom to enter or join 入场权，进入（参加）许可：His wealth gave him an ～ into upper-class society.他的财富使他得以进入上层社会。❷ the main dish of a meal or a dish served before the main course in a formal dinner（正式宴会上的）主菜，主菜前的小菜

entrench /ɪn'trentʃ/

v. establish (oneself) firmly in a particular place or position, so that one cannot easily be moved 使（自己）牢固地处于特定位置；使处于牢固地位：He ～ed himself behind his newspaper and refused to speak to her.他躲在报纸后面，就是不肯同她说话。/He's completely ～ed in his political views.他毫不动摇地坚持自己的政治观点。

entrenched /ɪn'trentʃt/

adj. ❶ （of rights, customs, beliefs, etc.）firmly established, often in a way that is unreasonable（权利、风俗习惯、信仰等）确立的，根深蒂固的：You can't shift her from her ～ beliefs.你无法改变她根深蒂固的信仰。❷ （of a place that is being defended）protected by trenches（防守地点）用壕沟防护的

entrepreneur /ˌɒntrəprə'nɜː(r)/

n. a person who starts a company or arranges for a piece of work to be done, and takes business risks in the hope of making a profit 企业家；承包者 ‖ ～ial *adj.* 企业家的

entrust /ɪn'trʌst/

v. assign the responsibility for doing sth. to sb. 委托，交托：I ～ed you with the care of the child.我委托你照顾这个孩子。/I ～ed the child to your care.我把这个孩子委托给你照看。

entry /'entri/

n. (*pl.*-ies) ❶ the act of coming or going in 进入：Thieves had forced ～ into the building.盗贼强行进入那幢建筑。❷ a door, gate, or passage by which one enters 门口，通道：Don't leave your bike in the ～.别把自行车放在门口。❸ a person or thing that takes part in a contest 参赛者；参赛作品（或物品）：There were nearly 100 entries for the Marathon.将近100人参加了马拉松赛跑。❹ sth. written in a list, a book, etc. 条目，项目；记录：After making some entries in his notebook he went away.在笔记本上写了一些东西后，他就离开了。❺ the right of entering 进入权；进入许可：We can't go in—the sign says "NO ENTRY". 我们不可以进去——牌子上写着"禁止入内"。

entwine /ɪn'twaɪn/

v. twine one thing round another, interweave things 盘绕，缠绕；交错：The nations' histories were closely ～d.这些国家的历史有着千丝万缕的联系。

enunciate/ɪˈnʌnsɪeɪt/

　　*v.*❶express (ideas, opinions, etc.) clearly and firmly 清楚地表明；阐明：He is always willing to ～ his opinions on the subject of politics. 他总是愿意对政治问题发表意见。❷ say or pronounce words clearly 清晰地发音；清晰地念

envelop/ɪnˈveləp/

　　v. wrap up, cover or surround completely 包；裹；封住：～ oneself in a blanket 裹在毯子里／be ～ed in mist 烟雾缭绕

envelope/ˈenvələʊp, ˈɒnvələʊp/

　　n. a flat paper cover for a letter；any covering which contains sth. 信封；封皮；封袋：stick a stamp on an ～ 在信封上贴邮票／When I came home again last year, I found the ～ in a book. 去年我又回到家里时，在一本书里发现了那个信封。

enviable/ˈenvɪəbl/

　　adj. (sth.) arousing or likely to arouse envy 让人羡慕的；让人妒忌的：The company has an ～ reputation for reliability. 这家公司因可靠而享有令人羡慕的盛誉。／It's not an ～ task, trying to get the two sides to reach an agreement. 要想使双方达成一项协议，这可不是一件值得羡慕的工作。

envious/ˈenvɪəs/

　　adj. feeling or showing envy 嫉妒的，羡慕的：be ～ of sb.'s success 嫉妒，羡慕某人的成功／looking at sth. with ～ eyes 以羡慕的眼光看着某物

environment/ɪnˈvaɪərənmənt/

　　*n.*❶ the natural world in which people, animals and plants live 自然环境；生态环境 ❷ surroundings, or conditions, etc. affecting people's lives (生活)环境，条件

environmental /ɪnˌvaɪərənˈmentl/

　　*adj.*❶ relating to the natural world and the impact of human activity on its condition 自然环境的，生态环境的：Acid rain may have caused major ～ damage. 酸雨可能对环境造成了严重的破坏。❷ aiming or designed to promote the protection of the natural world 环保(性)的：～ tourism 环保旅游

environmentalist/ɪnˌvaɪərənˈmentlɪst/

　　n. a person who tries to prevent the environment from being spoilt 环境保护工作者

envoy/ˈenvɔɪ/

　　n. a person representing his government in a foreign country 使节；特使

envy/ˈenvi/

　　Ⅰ *v.* wish for that belonging to someone else 羡慕，忌妒 I ～ your good fortune. 我羡慕你的好运气。Ⅱ *n.* the feeling of disappointment and ill will at someone else's possessions, qualities or luck 忌妒，羡慕：My success excited his ～. 我的成功引起了他的忌妒。‖ ～ at sth. (of sb.) 忌妒某物(某人)

enzyme/ˈenzaɪm/

　　n. a substance produced by living cells, that affects the speed of chemical changes without itself being changed 酶：digestive ～ 消化酶/induced ～引导酶

epic/ˈepɪk/

　　Ⅰ *n.* a long poem of the deeds of heroes, or of a nation's past history 史诗；叙事诗：Homer's *Iliad* is a famous ～. 荷马的《伊利亚特》是一部著名的史诗。Ⅱ *adj.* having the features of an epic 史诗般的；具有史诗性质的

epidemic/ˌepɪˈdemɪk/

　　Ⅰ *n.*❶a disease occurring in a large number at the same time 流行病：an ～ of cholera 霍乱流行 ❷a widespread occurrence of an infectious disease (传染病)的流行，传播 Ⅱ *adj.* of, relating to, or of the nature of an epidemic 流行性的；盛行的

epidermal/ˌepɪˈdɜːməl/

　　adj. of or having to do with epidermis 表皮的，外皮的

epidermis/ˌepɪˈdɜːmɪs/

　　n. the outer layer of the skin 外皮；表皮(层)

epilog(ue)/ˈepɪlɒg/

　　n. the last part of a piece of literature, which finishes it off, especially a speech made by one of the actors at the end of a play 后记；尾声；收场白

episode/'epɪsəud/

　　n. an event, a situation, or a period of time in a chain of events, sb.'s life, a novel, etc. (人生的)一段经历；(小说的)片段；插曲：The novel deals with the romantic ~s of her early life. 小说涉及了她早年生活中几段浪漫情节。

epitome/ɪ'pɪtəmi/

　　n. an example which is typical of a group or quality 缩影，典型：the ~ of laziness 懒惰的典型

epitomize/ɪ'pɪtəmaɪz/

　　v. make or be an epitome of sth. 成为……的典型；是……的缩影

epoch/'i:pɒk/

　　n. a period of time in history, life, etc. marked by special events 纪元；时代：mark an ~ in science 开辟科学上的新纪元／an entire historical ~ 整个历史时代

equable/'ekwəbl/

　　adj. ❶ (of a person) of even calm temper; not easily annoyed (人)平和的，不易恼火的：I like working with Mary because she has such an ~ nature. 我喜欢与玛丽一道工作，因为她的性情很温和。❷ (of temperature) without great changes; even and regular (温度)变化小的，稳定的：Britain has quite an ~ climate; it seldom gets too hot or too cold. 英国的气候很稳定，很少有太热或太冷的时候。

equal/'i:kwəl/

　　Ⅰ *adj.* (of two or more) same in size, number, value, rank, etc. 同样的；相等的：~ pay 同酬／The two buildings are of the ~ height. 这两幢大厦一样高。／His watch is ~ to mine. 他的手表与我的一样。Ⅱ *n.* a person or thing considered to be the same as another 相等物；对手；匹敌者：She is the ~ of Mary in beauty. 她和玛莉一样漂亮。Ⅲ *v.* (-ll- or -l-) (of a size or number) to be the same as 等于：Three and three ~s six. 3 加 3 等于 6。

equality/ɪ'kwɒləti/

　　n. the state of being equal 平等，同等：They are fighting for the ~ of women. 他们在为争取妇女的平等而奋斗。／racial

~ 种族平等／~ of opportunity 机会均等

equalize/'i:kwəlaɪz/

　　v. ❶ make equal in quantity, size or degree, etc. 使平等，使相等：A small adjustment will ~ the temperature in the two rooms. 稍微调节一下就会使两个房间的温度相同。❷ make uniform in application or effect 均分，均摊：Our party's policy is to try to ~ the tax burden. 我们党的政策是试图均分税务负担。❸ reach the same score for both teams in sport (比赛中与对方)打成平手，拉平比分

equalizer/'i:kwəlaɪzə(r)/

　　n. ❶ a goal or point that makes one's score equal to the opponent in sport (比赛中)拉成平局的得分：England scored the ~ a few minutes before the end of the match. 英格兰队在比赛结束前几分钟进了一球，拉平了比分。❷ sth. which makes things equal or balanced 使相等者；使平衡者

equally/'i:kwəli/

　　adv. ❶ in the same manner; to an equal degree 相等地，同样地：They're both ~ fit. 他们两个都同样健壮(合适)。／They can both run ~ fast. 他们两个跑得一样快。❷ in equal shares 平均地，等分地：They shared the work ~. 他们把工作平分了。❸ (used to introduce a further comment on a topic) at the same time and having the same importance (用于引出对一个话题的进一步评论)同样地：We must help people to find houses outside the city, but ~, we must remember that some city people want to remain where they are. 我们必须帮助人们在城外找住房，但同样，我们还得记住有些城里人想留在原处。

equanimity/ˌekwə'nɪməti/

　　n. calmness of mind and temper, especially in difficult situations (尤指在困难中的)镇静，沉着：He received the bad news with surprising ~. 他接到这一坏消息时显得异常镇静。

equate/ɪ'kweɪt/

　　v. consider or make equal 视为相等：~

E

two quantities 使两量相等/You can't ~ the education system of Britain to that of Germany.你不能把英国教育制度与德国教育制度等同起来。

equation /ɪ'kweɪʒn/
n. ❶ a statement that two quantities are equal 等式,方程式: In the ~ $2x+1=7$, what is x? 在 $2x+1=7$ 这个方程式中,x 是多少? ❷ the state of being equal or equally balanced 相等,平衡: There is an ~ between unemployment and rising crime levels.失业人数和上升的犯罪数字趋于平衡。

equator /ɪ'kweɪtə(r)/
n. the imaginary circle round the middle of the earth, halfway between the North Pole and the South Pole 赤道: It is very hot near the ~.赤道附近非常炎热。

equatorial /ˌekwə'tɔːrɪəl/
adj. ❶ of or near the equator 赤道(附近)的: the ~ rain forest 赤道雨林 ❷ very hot 酷热的,炎热的: an ~ climate 炎热的气候

equidistant /ˌiːkwɪ'dɪstənt/
adj. equally distant 等距离的: Rome is about ~ from Cairo and Oslo.罗马到开罗和奥斯陆的距离大约相等。/Paris, Bordeaux, and Lyons are roughly ~.巴黎、波尔多和里昂相互间的距离大致相同。

equilateral /ˌiːkwɪ'lætərəl/
adj. (of a triangle) having all three sides equal (指三角形)等边的

equilibrium /ˌiːkwɪ'lɪbrɪəm/
n. the state of balance, mental or physical (身体或心理的)平衡

equip /ɪ'kwɪp/
v. (-pp-) supply with what is needed; fit out; furnish 供给;装备: The studio is ~ped with modern facilities.演播室装配了现代化设备。/ ~ a ship for a voyage 装备船只以便出航

equipment /ɪ'kwɪpmənt/
n. ❶ the set of things needed for a particular activity, especially an activity of a practical or technical kind (尤指实用或技术性的)设备,装备,装置: She set up

(tested) all her ~.她装配(测试)了全部器材。/to install video ~ 安装录像(影)设备/fire-fighting ~ 消防设备/The police found bomb-making ~ in the terrorists hideout.警方在恐怖分子的巢穴找到了制造炸弹的设备。❷ the process of equipping 配备(装备)过程

equitable /'ekwɪtəbl/
adj. fair and just 公平的,公正的: an ~ division of the money 金钱的合理分配/an ~ solution to the dispute 解决争端的公正办法

equity /'ekwəti/
n. fairness; the process of not treating sb. better than sb. else 公平;公正

equivalent /ɪ'kwɪvələnt/
Ⅰ *adj.* equal in value, amount, meaning, etc.相等的;等同的: be ~ to 等于,相当于/He changed his pounds for the (an) ~ amount of dollars.他把英镑兑换成等值的美金。Ⅱ *n.* a person, thing or amount that is equal to or corresponds with another 对等的人(或事物);对应的人(或事物);等值;等量: What is the ~ of this word in French? 这个词在法文里的对应词是什么?

era /'ɪərə/
n. a set of years which is counted from a particular point in time 纪元;时代: the Christian ~ 耶稣纪元/The ~ of space travel has begun.太空旅行的时代开始了。

eradicate /ɪ'rædɪkeɪt/
v. destroy, remove completely; tear out by the roots 摧毁;完全除去;根除: ~ a bad habit 根除坏习惯

erase /ɪ'reɪz/
v. rub out or remove sth., especially a pencil mark 擦掉: ~ the words 把字擦掉 ‖ ~r *n.* 橡皮擦;黑板擦

erasure /ɪ'reɪʒə/
n. the process of rubbing out or removing sth. 擦掉;消除;删除: the accidental ~ of important computer disks 计算机磁盘上的重要信息的意外删除

erect/ɪ'rekt/

Ⅰ *adj.* upright or straight; standing on end 竖起的；直立的；stand ～ 直立/with every hair ～ 毛发耸然 Ⅱ *v.* ❶ set into an upright position 竖立；～ a pole 竖起一根竿子 ❷ build sth.建立；建造；～ a monument 建立纪念碑 ❸ create or establish sth.；set up 创立；设立；～ trade barriers 设置贸易壁垒

erode/ɪ'rəʊd/

v. wear away gradually; destroy by taking away small pieces 侵蚀；腐蚀：The sea ～s the rocks.海水侵蚀岩石。

err/ɜː(r)/

v. make a mistake; do sth. wrong 犯错；出错：～ from the truth 背离真理/ ～ in observation(one's judgement) 观察(判断)方面出错

errand/'erənd/

n. a short journey made to carry a message, or to do or get sth. 差使；go on an ～ for sb. 为某人办某事/I've no time to run ～s for you.我没时间替你跑腿。

errant/'erənt/

adj. wandering away from the accepted course and behaving in a bad or irresponsible way 迷途的；偏离正道的；出格的；犯错误的：She went to London to bring back her ～ daughter.她到伦敦去把误入歧途的女儿领了回来。

erratic/ɪ'rætɪk/

adj. not regular; not always behaving in the regular way, and changing without any good reason 反复无常的；捉摸不定的；不稳定的：The singer gave an ～ performance.这名歌手未唱出水平。

error/'erə(r)/

n. ❶ a mistake 错误；过失：He often makes spelling ～s.他常犯拼写错误。❷ the condition of being wrong in belief or conduct 谬见；行为不正：He fell into ～.他误入歧途。‖ in ～ 弄错了的：I'm afraid he is in ～ (in saying that).我恐怕他(说那句话)是弄错了。

erudite/'eruːdaɪt/

adj. showing or having great knowledge or learning 博学的；饱学的；an ～ professor 博学的教授 ‖ **erudition**/ˌeruː'dɪʃn/ *n.* 渊博的知识

erupt/ɪ'rʌpt/

v. ❶ (especially of a volcano) burst out (尤指火山)喷发，爆发：This volcano has never ～ed in the last ten years.在过去十年中，这座火山从未爆发过。❷ break out suddenly and violently 突然发生：In Los Angeles, the neighborhood known as Watts ～ed into riots.在洛杉矶，一个叫作沃茨的街区爆发了骚乱。❸ (of spots, etc.)appear on the skin suddenly (指斑点等在皮肤上)突然出现：A rash has ～ed all over her back.她的背上出满了疹子。‖ ～**ion** *n.* 爆发；突然出现

escalate/'eskəleɪt/

v. increase in intensity or extent 上升；升级；加剧：Prices are escalating.物价正在上涨。/They ～d the case from a political crisis to an extensive constitutional collision.他们把事态从一次政治危机上升为大规模的宪法冲突。

escalator/'eskəleɪtə(r)/

n. a staircase which moves up or down on an endless belt 自动扶梯

escape/ɪ'skeɪp/

Ⅰ *v.* get free from 逃跑；逃脱：No one can ～ from the jail.没人能从监狱里逃跑。/ Gas is escaping from the pipe.管道在漏煤气。Ⅱ *n.* an act of getting free from sth. or somewhere 逃走；逃脱：～ from difficulties 逃避困难

escort

Ⅰ/'eskɔːt/*n.* a person or group of people or vehicles going with another or others to give protection or as a sign of honour 护送者；护卫队 Ⅱ/ɪ'skɔːt/*v.* go with (sb.) as an escort 护送；护卫：～ the cargo ship 为一艘货船护航

especial /ɪs'peʃəl/

adj. ❶ special or outstanding 格外的；特别的；特殊的；不一般的：of ～ interest 特别有兴趣 ❷ mainly suitable for one person or thing 独特的，独有的：for your ～ benefit 对你特别有利

especially/ɪ'speʃəli/

adv. ❶to a great degree; in particular 特别; 格外; 专门: I love cold drinks, ～ in summer. 我很爱喝冷饮, 特别是在夏天。/ She is ～ good at science. 她特别擅长科学。❷most of all 尤其: I would like a bicycle, ～ a blue one. 我想要辆自行车, 尤其是蓝色的。

Esperanto /ˌespəˈræntəʊ/
n. an artificial language invented in 1887 as a means of international communication 世界语(1887 年公布的一种人造国际语言)

espionage /ˈespɪɒnɑːʒ/
n. the practice of spying or of using spies 间谍活动

esplanade /ˌespləˈneɪd/
n. a level open space where people can walk along (供人散步的)广场, 空地

essay /ˈeseɪ/
Ⅰ *n.* a piece of writing, usually short and in prose, on a particular subject 文章; 散文; 小品文; 短评; 随笔: The students wrote ～s about the importance of education. 学生们写文章论述教育的重要性。Ⅱ *v.* try or attempt 试图; 企图: They ～ed the path of natural science. 他们曾努力探索过自然科学的道路。

essence /ˈesns/
n. ❶the most important feature or quality of sth. which makes a thing what it is 本质; 实质: The two things are the same in outward form but different in ～. 那两样东西外表相同, 但本质不同。❷the best part of a substance, taken out and reduced to a jelly, liquid, etc. 香精; 精华: meat ～ 肉汁

essential /ɪˈsenʃl/
adj. completely necessary for the existence, success, etc. of sth. 最重要的; 必要的: Water is ～ to life. 水是生命之源。/ It is ～ to have a good study habit. 有一个好的学习习惯是非常重要的。

essentially /ɪˈsenʃəli/
adv. ❶ basically; in reality, though perhaps not in appearance 本质上; 根本上: She's ～ a very nice person. 她本质上是个

和蔼可亲的人。❷ necessarily 必需地: "Must I do it today?" "Not ～." 这事我非今天做不可吗?"不必要。"

establish /ɪˈstæblɪʃ/
v. ❶set up; found 建立; 创立; 制定: ～ a state 建立一个国家 ❷settle or place (a person, oneself) in a position, place, etc. 使定居; 委任: They are now ～ed in their new house. 他们现在住在他们的新居内。❸achieve permanent acceptance for (a belief, claim, custom, etc.) 确立(信仰、要求、风俗等): destroy the old and ～ the new 破旧立新/Newton ～ed the law of gravity. 牛顿确定了万有引力定律。

establishment /ɪsˈtæblɪʃmənt/
n. ❶the process of establishing sth. 建立; 确立; 确定; 制定 ❷a business organization, public institution, or household 企业; 社会公共机构; 家庭: hotels or catering ～s 旅馆或饭店

estate /ɪˈsteɪt/
n. ❶an area or amount of land or property 地产: Estate business is a new economic activity in this country. 地产交易是这个国家的一项新的经济活动。❷ all the property owned by a person (一个人的全部)财产: real ～ 房地产, 不动产/personal ～ 私人财产 ‖ ～ agent *n.* 房地产经纪人

esteem /ɪˈstiːm/
Ⅰ *v.* ❶ respect and admire (especially a person) greatly 尊敬; 敬重: We all ～ our elders. 我们都敬重我们的长辈。❷ consider 认为: I ～ it quite unnecessary to go there. 我认为没必要去那儿。Ⅱ *n.* the respect and admiration for a person 尊敬, 敬重: hold someone in ～ 敬重某人/Since he behaved so badly he's gone down in my ～. 他表现非常恶劣, 使我对他的看法一落千丈。

estimable /ˈestɪməbl/
adj. worthy of great respect 值得尊敬的

estimate /ˈestɪmət/
Ⅰ *v.* judge or calculate the extent, value, size, quantity, etc. of sth. roughly; form an opinion about 评定; 估计; 判断: It is ～d

the earthquake caused 40,000 dollars of damage to the town.据估计,地震给这个镇造成了四万美元的损失。/We ～ that it will take us three years to fulfill this project.我们估算,完成这个项目需要三年的时间。Ⅱ n.a calculation or judgment of the extent,value,size,quantity,etc.,of sth.判断,估计:It's his ～ that...据他估计……

estimation/ˌestɪ'meɪʃn/
n.❶a judgment or opinion about the value or quality of sb.or sth.评价;判断:form a true ～ of sb.对某人做出正确的评价 ❷esteem 尊敬:After the victory,the victor gained notably in everyone's ～.胜利之后,战胜者明显受到大家尊敬。❸a judgement about the size,extent or quantity of sth.估计,估算

et cetera/ɪt'setərə,et'setərə/
adv.(usually abbreviated to etc.)and other things(通常缩写成 etc.)等等

eternal/ɪ'tɜːnl/
adj.❶lasting or existing forever;having no end 永恒的:～ life 永生/Our country will promise ～ prosperity.我们国家会永远繁荣富强。❷happening often and seeming never to stop 无休止的;永不停止的:I am tired of your ～ chatter.我讨厌你那没完没了的唠叨。‖ eternity n.永恒;来世

ether/'iːθə(r)/
n.a liquid which causes one to become unconscious when its vapour is breathed in 醚(一种麻醉剂)

ethereal/ɪ'θɪəriəl/
adj.❶of unearthly lightness and delicacy;like a spirit or fairy 虚幻的;轻飘的;缥缈的:The music has an ～ quality.这段曲子给人一种缥缈的感觉。/She has a ～ beauty.她有一种飘逸之美。❷heavenly or spiritual 天上的;非人间的;精神上的

ethic/'eθɪk/
n.a set of moral principles that control or influence a person's behaviour 道德规范;伦理标准:the Christian ～ 基督教伦理

ethical/'eθɪkl/
adj.❶connected with ethics 伦理的;道德的:The doctors' ～ committee decides whether it is morally right to perform certain operations.医德委员会裁决施行某些手术是否合乎道德。❷morally good or right 合乎道德的:I won't do it;it's not ～.我不干那事,那是不道德的。

ethically/'eθɪkli/
adv.❶in connection with ethics 与道德伦理有关地:Ethically(speaking),I think the operation was wrong.就道德来说,我认为动那次手术是错误的。❷in a morally good way 合乎道德地:I think he has behaved quite ～.我认为他的行为很合乎道德。

ethics/'eθɪks/
n.❶the science of moral principles 伦理学:Ethics is a branch of philosophy.伦理学是哲学的一个分支。❷moral principles that control or influence a person's behaviours 道德准则;伦理标准:medical ～ 医德

ethnic/'eθnɪk/
adj.with reference to a race or nation 种族的;民族的:There are many ～ groups in New York such as Italians,Poles,Irishmen,Swedes,etc.在纽约有许多族群,比如意大利人、波兰人、爱尔兰人、瑞典人等。

etiquette/'etɪket,'etɪkət/
n.formal rules for good behaviour 礼仪;礼节;成规:diplomatic ～ 外交礼节

euphemism/'juːfəmɪzəm/
n.a practice of using a more pleasant word or expression when referring to sth.unpleasant or embarrassing 委婉语;委婉说法

Europe/'jʊərəp/
n.the continent next to Asia in the east,the Atlantic Ocean in the west and the Mediterranean Sea in the south 欧洲:Eastern ～ 东欧/Western ～ 西欧

European/ˌjʊərə'pɪən/
Ⅰ adj.of or belonging to Europe or its people 欧洲的;欧洲人的:the ～ Com-

mon Market 欧洲共同市场 Ⅱ n. the native of Europe 欧洲人：The French, Germans, and Spaniards are ～s.法国人、德国人和西班牙人都是欧洲人。

euthanasia /ˌjuːθəˈneɪzɪə/
n.the act of causing someone to die gently and without pain, especially when they are suffering from a painful incurable disease or in a permanent coma 安乐死

evacuate /ɪˈvækjʊeɪt/
v.remove people from a place of danger to a safer place 疏散；转移；撤离：During the war, many people were ～d from the city. 战争期间，许多人被疏散撤离该市。

evade /ɪˈveɪd/
v.get out of the way of or escape from 躲避；逃避：～ criticism 逃避批评/ ～ military service 逃避兵役 ‖ evasion n.逃避/ evasive adj.逃避的；托词的

evaluate /ɪˈvæljʊeɪt/
v.form an opinion of the value , amount or quality of sth.；give an opinion of；estimate 评价；评估；估计

evaporate /ɪˈvæpəreɪt/
v.(of a liquid) change or cause to change into vapour (使)蒸发：Heat until all the water has ～d.加热至水全部蒸发。 ‖ evaporation /ɪˌvæpəˈreɪʃn/ n.蒸发，消失

evasive /ɪˈveɪsɪv/
adj.❶not willing to give a clear answer；not frank or straightforward 不直截了当的；含糊的；推诿的；推诿的 ❷seeking to avoid or prevent sth.躲避的；逃避的；规避的：take ～ action 采取回避行动 ‖～ly adv.推诿地；逃避地/～ness n.推诿；逃避

eve /iːv/
n.the day or evening before an event, especially a religious festival or holiday 前夕；前夜：Christmas Eve 圣诞节前夕，平安夜/New Year's Eve 除夕/on the ～ of victory 在胜利前夕

even /ˈiːvn/
Ⅰ adv.❶(used just before the surprising part of a statement, to add to its strength) which is more than might be expected 甚至；即使：He didn't ～ answer my letter. 他甚至没有回我的信。 ❷(used for making comparisons stronger) 更加；愈加：I'm ～ taller than you.我比你更高。 Ⅱ adj.❶flat, level, and smooth；forming a straight line 平坦的；平滑的：～ surface 平滑的表面 ❷(of things that can be measured and compared) equal 相等的：～ scores 相同的得分

evening /ˈiːvnɪŋ/
n.❶the end of the day and early part of the night(between about 6 p.m.and bedtime)(大约自下午六点到就寝时)傍晚，晚上：in the ～ 在傍晚/ on Sunday ～ 星期天晚上/ good ～ 晚安/ ～ dress 晚礼服 ❷a party, performance, etc. happening in the early parts of the night 晚会：an English ～ 英语晚会 ❸the last period, as of life 后期，末期：in the ～ of life 在晚年

evenly /ˈiːvənli/
adv.❶in a smooth, regular or equal way 平滑地；有规律地；均匀地；相等地：Make sure the paint covers the surface ～.要确保油漆均匀地涂在表面上。 ❷with equal amounts for each person or in each place 平均地；均等地：～ distributed 平均分配

event /ɪˈvent/
n.a thing that happens or takes place, especially an important, or unusual one 事件(尤指重要事件)：That ～ led to the Second World War.那个事件导致了第二次世界大战。 ‖ in the ～ 结果

eventful /ɪˈventfl/
adj.full of interesting or exciting events 充满大事的；多趣事的：He's led quite an ～ life. 他一生经历丰富。/We've had rather an ～ day.我们度过了不平凡的一天。

eventide /ˈiːvəntaɪd/
n.evening；the end of day 黄昏：at ～ 在傍晚

eventual /ɪˈventʃʊəl/
adj.(of an event) happening at last as a result (事件)最终发生的；结果的：The new computer system is expensive, but the ～ savings it will bring are very significant.新的计算机系统是昂贵的，但是

它最终将带来的节约是很可观的。/a research programme aimed at the ～ eradication of this disease 旨在最终消除这种疾病的研究计划

eventuality/ɪˌventʃʊˈæləti/

n.(*pl.*-ies) a possible event or result, especially an unpleasant one（尤指令人不快的）可能发生的事；可能出现的结果：We must be prepared for all eventualities.我们必须做好应付各种情况的准备。/This plan covers all eventualities.这项计划为可能发生的一切情况提供了答案。

eventually/ɪˈventʃʊəli/

*adv.*at last；in the end 最后，终于：After several attempts he ～ swam across.经过几次尝试，他终于游了过去。

eventuate/ɪˈventʃʊeɪt/

*v.*result in；happen as a result 导致；最终造成：A rapid rise in prices soon ～d in mass unemployment.物价迅速上涨，结果造成了大量失业。

ever/ˈevə(r)/

*adv.*❶at any time up to the present 曾经：Have you ～ been in an aeroplane? 你曾经坐过飞机吗？❷（used after a comparative or superlative for emphasis）（用于比较级或最高级后表示强调）以往任何时候：It is raining harder than ～.雨比以前下得更大了。/This is the best work you have ～ done.这是你所做的最好的工作了。❸（used in questions expressing astonishment or outrage for emphasis）（用于表惊讶或愤怒的疑问句，以示强调）竟然，究竟：What ～ do you mean? 你究竟是什么意思？‖ ～ afterwards 自此以后/for ～ 永远/yours ～（信的结束语）你永久的（朋友）

evergreen/ˈevəɡriːn/

Ⅰ *adj.*❶having green leaves all the year round 常绿的，常青的 ❷having an enduring freshness，success or popularity 经久不衰的；持久的 Ⅱ *n.*a plant that having green leaves all the year round 常青树，常绿植物，万年青

everlasting/ˌevəˈlɑːstɪŋ/

*adj.*❶lasting for ever；without an end 永久的；无穷尽的：They reached the zone of ～ snow.他们到达了常年积雪地带。❷unceasing；repeated too often 持续不断的；没完没了的：She was tired of his ～ complaints.她对他没完没了的牢骚感到厌烦。

evermore/ˌevəˈmɔː(r)/

*adv.*for all future time；always 始终；永久：He swore to love her (for)～.他发誓永远爱她。

every/ˈevri/

*adj.*❶（preceding a singular noun）used to refer to all the individual members of a set without exception（用于单数名词前）每个；每一：Every room has been painted.所有的房间都粉刷好了。❷all possible 所有可能的；完全可能的：You have ～ reason to do that.你完全有理由那样做。/ ～ other day 每隔一天/ ～ two days 每两天 ‖ ～ now and then 时常；有时/ ～ time 总是/in ～ way 在各方面

everyday/ˈevrɪdeɪ/

*adj.*used or happening every day；daily 每天的，日常的：～ life 日常生活/～ English 日常英语/an ～ occurrence 日常之事

everyone/ˈevrɪwʌn/

*pron.*every person 每个人；人人：You're great! I'm going to tell ～.你真了不起！我要对每个人说。

everything/ˈevrɪθɪŋ/

*pron.*❶all things 一切；所有的事物：Everything was destroyed.一切都毁了。/ I got ～ I needed in the market.我在市场上买到了我所需要的全部东西。❷the most important thing 最重要的事：Money isn't ～.金钱并不是最重要的事。

everywhere/ˈevrɪweə/

Ⅰ *adv.*in or to every place 各处；到处；处处：I looked ～ for my watch, but I couldn't find it.我到处寻找我的手表，但是找不到。Ⅱ *conj.*wherever 任何地方：Everywhere we go, people are much the same.无论我们走到哪里，人都差不多。Ⅲ *n.*every place 到处：Everywhere is cov-

E

ered with dust.到处都是灰尘。

evict/ɪˈvɪkt/

v.make a person leave a house or land by law（依法）驱逐，逐出：The owner of the house ～ed the people who did not pay their rent.房东把不付房租的人赶了出去。

evidence/ˈevɪdəns/

n.sth. such as facts，signs，or objects that give proof or reasons to make you believe or agree with sth. 证据；根据：Have you any ～ for this statement? 你说此话有无根据？‖ bear（give，show）～ of 有……的迹象

evident/ˈevɪdənt/

adj.clear；obvious 明显的；显然的；清楚的：It is ～ that you have done the job well.很明显你的工作做得很好。/ It is ～ that Alice has more than enough to eat.She is getting fat.很显然，艾丽丝吃得太多了些，她逐渐胖起来了。

evidently/ˈevɪdəntli/

adv.that can be seen or understood clearly；plainly or obviously 明显地；显然：He is ～ not well.他显然身体不舒服。

evil/ˈiːvl/

Ⅰ adj. morally bad or cruel；wicked；harmful 邪恶的；恶毒的；有害的：～ deeds 邪恶的行为/ ～ books 有害的书籍 Ⅱ n.❶ sin；wrong-doing 罪恶；邪恶：return good for ～ 以德报怨 ❷ sth.which is harmful or undesirable 丑恶现象；弊端：The government decides to do away with the six ～s throughout the country.政府决定在全国范围内扫除六害。

evocative/ɪˈvɒkətɪv/

adj.bringing memories and feelings 引起……记忆的，唤起……感情的：The taste of the cakes was ～ of my childhood.这些蛋糕的味道唤起了我对童年的回忆。/ an ～ smell 勾起回忆的气味

evoke/ɪˈvəʊk/

v.produce or call up 召唤；引起：～ admiration 引起羡慕/ ～ the spirit of contribution 号召奉献精神

evolution/ˌiːvəˈluːʃn/

n.❶ the development of plants，animals，etc.from very simple forms of life（动、植物等的）进化 ❷the process of change and development 演变；发展

evolve/ɪˈvɒlv/

v.❶develop gradually by a long continuous process 逐渐演变，逐渐 ❷ develop over successive generations as a result of natural selection 进化；演化：Man ～d from apes.人是由猿进化而来的。

exact/ɪɡˈzækt/

adj.correct in every detail；completely according to fact；precise 精确的；正确的：She gave us an ～ answer.她给了我们一个确切的回答。‖ ～ness n.精确

exacting/ɪɡˈzæktɪŋ/

adj.(of a person or a piece of work) demanding much care，effort，and attention（指人或工作）要求细致小心的，严格的；需要付出极大心力的：It was a day of ～ and tiring work. 这一天的工作既难又累。/～ standards of safety 严格的安全标准

exactitude/ɪɡˈzæktɪtjuːd/

n.the quality of being very accurate and exact 准确(性)；精确(性)

exactly/ɪɡˈzæktli/

adv.❶in an exact manner；to an exact degree 准确地；确切地：Your answer is ～ right.你的回答完全正确。❷（used to express agreement with what someone has said or emphasizing that it is right）（表示赞同或强调正确）正是；一点儿不错："You mean that you've known the truth? ""Exactly.""你是说，你已经知道真相了？""一点儿不错。"

exaggerate/ɪɡˈzædʒəreɪt/

v. represent sth. as being larger，greater，better，or worse than it really is 夸大，夸张

exalt/ɪɡˈzɔːlt/

v.give a higher rank or position to（sb.）提拔；提升：someone in an ～ed position 某人升职了

exaltation/ˌeɡzɔːlˈteɪʃn/

n.❶a feeling or state of extreme happiness（of success）兴奋；得意扬扬 ❷ the act of exalting sb. 提拔；晋升；提升

exalted/ɪgˈzɔːltɪd/

adj. ❶（of a person or his position）of high rank（指人或其地位）高贵的；崇高的：He felt very humble in such ~ company. 他与如此显贵的要人在一起感到非常卑下。❷ filled with exaltation 得意扬扬的

exam/ɪgˈzæm/

n. short for examination（examination 的简称）考试

examination/ɪgˌzæmɪˈneɪʃn/

n. ❶ the process of examining sb. or sth. 检查；调查：a medical ~ 体检 ❷ a formal test of a person's knowledge or ability by means of oral or written questions 正规考试 ❸ a formal questioning of a witness or an accused person in a law court 讯问

examine/ɪgˈzæmɪn/

v. ❶ inspect（sb. or sth.）in detail in order to test their nature or condition 检查；调查 ❷ give sb. a test to see how much knowledge they get about a subject 考核，测验（某人）‖ examiner *n.* 主考人

example/ɪgˈzɑːmpl/

n. ❶ a particular event or thing to show the meaning of a statement or rule；instance 实例：Please give me an ~. 请给我举一个实例。❷ a person or a person's behaviour that is worthy of being copied 模范，榜样：We should follow his ~. 我们应该以他为榜样。/set an ~ 树立榜样

excavate/ˈekskəveɪt/

v. dig；make by digging；uncover by digging 挖；挖掘；发掘：The archaeologists ~d an ancient city. 考古学家发掘出一座古城。‖ excavator *n.* 挖掘机，挖土机

exceed/ɪkˈsiːd/

v. ❶ go beyond what is necessary or allowed 超过；胜过；越出：~ the speed limit 超出限制时速/If your lorry ~s this weight, you cannot cross the bridge. 如果你的载重汽车超过这个重量，就不能过桥。❷ be more than 大于；多于：I don't know his exact speed, but it would

~ thirty miles an hour. 我不知道他的精确速度，但每小时会超过三十英里。/This city ~s that one. 这个城市比那个面积大。/This work ~s my ability. 这项工作超出了我的能力范围。

excel/ɪkˈsel/

v.（-ll-）be or do better than（others）；be very good at 胜过他人；超过他人，擅长于：My younger brother ~s his classmates in physics. 我弟弟在物理方面要好过他的同班同学。

excellence/ˈeksələns/

n. the quality of being outstanding or extremely good 优秀；卓越；杰出：awards for ~ 优秀奖

Excellency/ˈeksələnsi/

n.（*pl.* -ies）(**His, Your, etc.** ~) a title given to certain high officials of state, especially ambassadors, or of the Roman Catholic Church, or used in addressing them 阁下：Good morning, Your ~. 早上好，阁下。/ their ~ the French Ambassador 法国大使阁下

excellent/ˈeksələnt/

adj. very good；of high quality 优秀的；杰出的；卓越的；极好的：an ~ dancer 一位出色的舞蹈家/This is ~ work, Paul. 保尔，这是极好的工作。/His English is ~. 他的英语棒得很。

except/ɪkˈsept/

Ⅰ *prep.* other than；not including 除……之外：Everyone ~ me went there. 除了我之外，所有的人都去了。/Your article is very good ~ for a few grammar mistakes. 除了一些语法错误之外，你的文章非常好。Ⅱ *v.* take out；exclude 将……排除在外：I'm ~ed from the list. 我被排除在名单之外。

exception/ɪkˈsepʃn/

n. a person or thing that is not included 例外：Most children like sweets, but she is the ~. 大部分孩子都喜欢吃糖果，可是她例外。

exceptional/ɪkˈsepʃənl/

adj. unusual especially of unusually high quality, ability, etc.；not typical 特别的，

异常的;杰出的,优秀的:All her children are clever but the youngest girl is really ~.她的孩子都很聪明,但是那个最小的女儿尤为突出。/It was an ~ game.这是一场别开生面的比赛。/The firemen showed ~ bravery.消防队员表现了非凡的勇气。‖ ~ly adv.非常地;例外地

excerpt

Ⅰ /ˈeksɜːpt/ n.sth.selected;a short extract taken out of a film, broadcast, film or book 选录;摘录;节选;引用:~s from a novel 一部小说的摘录/I've seen a short ~ from the film on television.我从电视上看到了这部电影的一个简短的片段。Ⅱ /ekˈsɜːpt/ v.select (a short extract) from a book,etc.选录;摘录;节录

excess /ɪkˈses/

Ⅰ n.sth.which is greater in amount than what is normal or proper 过多之物,过量之物:He has an ~ of fluid in his body.他体液过多。/~baggage 超重行李 Ⅱ adj. extra or additional(to the usual or per-mitted amount)额外的;附加的:A company which makes high profits must pay ~ profits duty to the government.赢利高的公司须向政府交纳额外所得税。

excessive /ɪkˈsesɪv/

adj.more or greater than what is normal or necessary 过分的,过度的:He was drinking ~ amounts of wine.他喝红酒已过量了。‖ ~ly adv.过分地;极度地

exchange /ɪksˈtʃeɪndʒ/

Ⅰ v.give sth.and receive sth.(of the same type or equal value)in return 交换:I want to ~ my bike with his.我想用我的自行车来换取他的自行车。Ⅱ n. the act of exchanging 交换:We set up this sys-tem for the ~ of information.我们建立了这个体系是为了交流信息。

excite /ɪkˈsaɪt/

v. ❶ cause to lose calmness and have strong feelings, especially of expectation and happiness 激动;鼓舞:The crowd got very ~d at the news.这个消息使群众十分激动。❷ bring out or give rise to(a feeling or reaction)引发;激起:The king's cruelty ~d a rising of the people.

国王的残暴引起了一场暴动。/~ a riot 煽动暴乱 ❸cause(a part of the body)to be active 刺激(身体某部分):The patient had drugs that ~ the nervous system.这名患者服用了刺激神经系统的药物。‖ **excitable** adj.易激动的;易兴奋的

excited /ɪkˈsaɪtɪd/

adj. feeling or showing expectation, hap-piness;not calm 兴奋的;激动的:She's very ~ about getting a part in the film.她为能在电影中扮演一个角色而感到非常兴奋。/The scientists are ~ about the results of the experiment.科学家们为试验的结果兴奋不已。/The ~ children were opening their Christmas presents.兴奋的孩子们打开了他们的圣诞礼物。/Their new record is nothing to get ~ a-bout.他们的新唱片没什么了不起,不值得为之激动。

excitement /ɪkˈsaɪtmənt/

n.❶ the state of being excited 兴奋,激动:He has a weak heart, and should avoid ~.他心脏不太好,应当避免激动。❷ an exciting event 令人兴奋的事:Life will seem very quiet after the ~s of our holiday.在假期一阵兴奋之后,生活会显得很平静。

exciting /ɪkˈsaɪtɪŋ/

adj.causing excitement or interest 令人兴奋的;激动人心的:an ~ story 动人的故事/the most ~ news 最激动人心的消息/Skiing is more ~ than skating.滑雪比滑冰更令人兴奋。

exclaim /ɪkˈskleɪm/

v. speak or say loudly and suddenly, be-cause of surprise or other strong feelings (由于惊讶或强烈的感情而)惊叫,呼喊:The soldier ~ed in the dark:"Who's there?"那个士兵在黑暗中大声喝道:"谁在那儿?"

exclamation /ˌeksklə'meɪʃn/

n. yelling;speaking with sudden strong feelings 呼喊;惊叫;感叹:He gave a loud and angry ~.他生气地大声叫喊。‖ ex-clamatory adj.惊叹的;感叹的

E

E

exclude/ɪkˈskluːd/

v. ❶ prevent sb. or sth. from entering a place or taking part in sth.阻止；防止：~ a person from going in 阻止某人进入 ❷ not include sth. in what you are doing or considering 不包括；排除：We can ~ the possibility that he won't come.我们可以排除他不会来的可能性。/Buses run every hour, Sundays ~d.公共汽车每小时一班，星期天除外。

excluding/ɪkˈskluːdɪŋ/

prep. except；apart from 除……外，不包括：There were twenty people in the hotel，~ the hotel staff.旅馆内除了工作人员外，有二十人。

exclusion/ɪkˈskluːʒn/

n. the act or state of excluding or being excluded 拒绝；排斥：an attitude of ~ 排斥态度/His ~ from the tennis club hurt him very much.他被拒绝加入网球俱乐部一事严重地伤害了他的感情。

exclusive/ɪkˈskluːsɪv/

adj. ❶ not admitting or allowing other things, not true or valid if sth. else exists or is true 排除其他一切的；排斥性的；排他性的：The two schemes are mutually ~.这两个方案相互排斥。❷ intended or available only for certain people or not shared by anyone else 专用的，专有的；独有的，独占的：The hotel has ~ access to the beach.这家酒店有通向海滩的专用通道。❸（of legal terms）excluding anything that is not specified（条款）除外责任的 ❹（of a newspaper report）not published anywhere else（新闻报道）独家的 ‖ **-ly** adv.排外地；专有地；唯一地

excrement/ˈekskrɪmənt/

n. the waste matter excreted from the bowels, faeces 排泄物；粪便

excrete/ɪkˈskriːt/

v. discharge（solid or liquid waste matter）from the body 排泄；分泌：The skin ~s sweat.皮肤出汗。

excretion/ɪkˈskriːʃn/

n. ❶ the process of discharging of waste matter from the body 排泄；分泌：the ~ of sweat 出汗/the ~ of urine 排尿 ❷ waste matter that is discharged 排泄物：Sweat is an ~.汗是一种排泄物。

excretory/ekˈskriːtəri/

adj. of or having to do with excretion 排泄的；分泌的；有排泄功能的；排泄物的：The kidneys are ~ organs.肾是排泄器官。/No animal can live long with an impairment of its ~ function.动物排泄功能受到损害便不能活长久。

excursion/ɪkˈskɜːʃn/

n. a short journey for pleasure 短途旅行；远足：make an ~ to the seaside 去海滨旅行/a boating ~ 水上游览/a country ~ 乡间远足/a cross-country ~ 越野旅行/a scientific ~ 科学游览/We went on an ~ to the city.我们到城里去旅行。

excuse/ɪkˈskjuːz/

Ⅰ v. ❶ forgive sb. for a small fault or offence 宽恕；原谅：Excuse me for having kept you waiting so long.让你等了这么久，请原谅。/Such impoliteness can not be ~d.这样的无礼不能原谅。❷ free sb. from a duty or requirement 免除……的义务；免除对……的要求：They're ~d from paying taxes.他们可以不交税。Ⅱ n. a reason given to explain or defend one's conduct 辩解；托词：He's always making ~s for being late.他总是为他的迟到找借口。‖ **in ~ of** 为……辩解/**without ~** 无理由 ‖ **excusable** adj.可原谅的/**excusably** adv.可原谅地

execute/ˈeksɪkjuːt/

v. ❶ carry out or put sth. into action 实行；执行：This economic policy began to be ~d one year ago.这项经济政策是一年前开始实施的。❷ administer；put into effect 使生效：~ a will 使遗嘱生效 ❸ kill sb. as a legal punishment 处以某人死刑：The murderer will be ~d.谋杀犯将被处死。‖ **executant** n.执行者；演奏者

execution /ˌeksɪˈkjuːʃən/

n. ❶ the act of carrying out or performing sth. 实施；实行；执行：The idea was good, but the ~ was poor.这个主意倒不错，可实行情况不理想。❷ the act of killing sb. as a legal punishment 死刑的执行

executive /ɪgˈzekjətɪv/

Ⅰ *n*.❶a senior person or group of people with authority to manage a business organization 高级管理人员；经理 ❷ the branch of a government with responsibility for putting laws and decisions into effect 行政部门 Ⅱ *adj*.having the powers to put laws or decisions into effect 行政的：～ authority 行政当局

exemplify/ɪgˈzemplɪfaɪ/
v.be or make an example 举例说明，成为……的例子：This exemplifies what I mean.这正好作为我所说的一个实例。

exempt/ɪgˈzempt/
Ⅰ *v*.make（sb.or sth.）free from an obligation or liability imposed on others 免除：～ sb.from taxation（an exam）免除某人纳税（免考）Ⅱ *adj*.free from an obligation or liability imposed on others 被豁免的；被免除的：The enterprise is ～ from income tax for one year.这家企业可免交一年的所得税。‖ ～ion *n*.免除，豁免；免税

exercise/ˈeksəsaɪz/
Ⅰ *n*.❶activity set to practise or a skill 练习；训练：The pupils have to face a lot of ～s every day.学生每天要做很多练习。❷physical or mental activity carried out to stay healthy or become stronger 锻炼：morning ～ 早操/You should do more ～ to keep yourself healthy.为了保持身体健康，你应该多加运动。Ⅱ *v*.（cause to）take exercise 锻炼；运动：～ your mind 动脑筋

exert/ɪgˈzɜːt/
v.try one's best；put into use；use one's strength of body or mind 尽力；努力；运用；发挥：～ every effort（to do）尽一切力量（做某事）/She ～ed herself all year to earn good mark.她一年到头都很努力以求获得好分数。

exertion /ɪgˈzɜːʃən/
n.❶the process of exerting 运用；行使；发挥；施加：the ～ of authority 权力的行使 ❷a great effort 努力；尽力；费力：He was panting with the ～.他因使劲而在喘气。

exhale/eksˈheɪl/

v.breathe out the air or smoke 呼出；放出；呼气

exhaust/ɪgˈzɔːst/
Ⅰ *v*.❶ use up completely 用尽；耗尽：He is ～ed by the questions.他被这些问题弄得精疲力竭。❷ expel（gas or steam）from or into a particular place 排空（气体、蒸汽）：～ air from a room 把房子里的空气抽空 Ⅱ *n*. the pipe which allows unwanted gas，steam，etc.，to escape from an engine or machine 排气管 ‖ ～ion *n*.枯竭；耗尽

exhausted /ɪgˈzɔːstɪd/
adj.❶drained of one's physical or mental resources；very tired 疲惫不堪的；筋疲力尽的：I'm absolutely ～.我完全筋疲力尽了。❷（of resources or reserves）completely used up（资源、储备物）耗尽的；用光的：You cannot grow crops on ～ land.贫瘠的土地上种不了庄稼。‖ ～ly *adv*.筋疲力尽地；耗尽地

exhausting /ɪgˈzɔːstɪŋ/
adj.making you feel very tired 使人疲惫不堪的；令人筋疲力尽的 ：an ～ day at work 工作得筋疲力尽的一天

exhaustive /ɪgˈzɔːstɪv/
adj.very thorough；including all the possibilities 详尽的；彻底的；全面的：The police made an ～ search.警察进行了彻底的搜查。‖ ～ly *adv*.用尽一切地

exhibit/ɪgˈzɪbɪt/
Ⅰ *n*.an object or a work of art on public display 展品：Don't touch the ～s.不要触摸展品。Ⅱ *v*.❶show in public 陈列：～ the paintings in a museum 在博物馆举办画展 ❷show clearly a particular feeling, quality or ability 表现，显示，显出：The patient ～s great power of endurance.病人表现出了巨大的忍耐力。

exhibition /ˌeksɪˈbɪʃən/
n.❶a public display of works of art or other items in a museum or gallery 展览（会）；展出 ❷a display or show of feeling（感情的）展示；显露：an ～ of temper 性情的显露 ‖ to make an ～ of yourself 出洋相；当众出丑

exile/ˈeksaɪl/

v. force someone to leave their native country 流放，放逐

exist/ɪgˈzɪst/

v. be real or actual；have being；continue to live 存在；实有：This kind of creature began ～ing in the world 20,000 years ago. 这种生物早在两万年前就存在了。‖ ～ent *adj.* 存在的；现存的

existence/ɪgˈzɪstəns/

n. ❶ the state of being or being real 存在：When did the world come into ～? 这个世界是什么时候产生的？❷ a way of living 生活；生活方式：lead a dangerous ～ 过着危险的生活

existing /ɪgˈzɪstɪŋ/

adj. in existence or operation at the time under consideration；current 现有的；现行的；目前的：opponents of the ～ system 现行体制的反对者

exit/ˈeksɪt, ˈegzɪt/

Ⅰ *n.* ❶ a way out 出口，安全门：The ～ doors are open at the end of the performance. 演出结束时，出口都开了。❷ departure of an actor from the stage （演员）退场：The heroine makes her ～ from the stage. 女演员退场了。Ⅱ *v.* go out；(of an actor) leave (the stage) 退出；(尤指演员)退场：At the end of the third scene the actress ～ed. 第三幕结束时，那位女演员退场了。

exotic/ɪgˈzɒtɪk/

adj. coming from a foreign country (usually a distant one) 来自外国的(通常指遥远的外国)

expand/ɪkˈspænd/

v. ❶ make or become larger or more extensive；spread out 变大；扩大；扩充：We want to ～ our business. 我们想扩大生意。❷ become less reserved in character or behaviour 变得开朗些；变得愿意交谈 ❸ give more details to what you are talking 进一步阐述；详述 ‖ ～ in(into)扩大

expanse /ɪkˈspæns/

n. a wide area of open land, sea, or space 广阔区域；大片地区：the green ～ of the

forest 绿色的林海

expansion /ɪkˈspænʃən/

n. the process of expanding, an increase or extension 扩大；扩充；扩展：a period of rapid economic ～ 经济迅猛发展期

expansionism /ɪkˈspænʃənɪz(ə)m/

n. the policy of territorial or economic expansion 扩张主义；扩张政策

expansive /ɪkˈspænsɪv/

adj. ❶ covering a wide area in terms of space or scope；extensive or wide-ranging 广阔的；辽阔的；广泛的：～ coastal beaches 广阔的海滩 ❷ (of a person or their manner) generous and communicative because feeling at ease (人、态度)畅谈的；愿交往的：She felt ～ and inclined to talk. 她感到不拘束并愿意说话了。❸ tending towards economic or political expansion 扩展性的；扩张性的：～ economic policies 扩张性的经济政策

expect/ɪkˈspekt/

v. think or believe that sth. will happen 盼望；期待；料想：I ～ed you yesterday. 我昨天期盼着你。/Your parents have been ～ing a letter from you. 你父母一直在盼望你的信。/—Does he need help? —No, I ～ not. —他需要帮助吗？—我想不要。‖ ～ed *adj.* 预期的，预料的

expectancy /ɪkˈspektənsi/

n. (*pl.*-ies) the state of thinking or hoping that sth., especially sth. pleasant, will happen or be the case 期望；期待；期盼：They waited with an air of ～. 他们以一种期盼的神情等待着。

expectant /ɪkˈspektənt/

adj. ❶ expecting sth. to happen；hopeful 期待的；期盼的：The children are waiting for the fireworks to begin with ～ faces. 孩子们带着期盼的神情等待烟火表演。❷ (of a woman) pregnant (妇女)怀孕的 ‖ ～ly *adv.* 期望地，期盼地

expectation /ˌekspekˈteɪʃən/

n. ❶ a strong belief that sth. will happen 预计；预期：He is confident in his ～ of a full recovery. 他正满怀期待地等待着完全康复。❷ a belief that someone will or should achieve sth. 希冀，期望；指望：Students have high ～s for their future. 学生们对未来抱有很高的期望。

expedient /ɪkˈspiːdiənt/
Ⅰ *n*. a plan or idea which is convenient but considered improper or immoral 应急的办法；权宜之计 Ⅱ *adj*. convenient and practical to oneself but perhaps not correct or moral 方便实际的；权宜之计的：It would be ～ to help someone with such political influence. 帮助具有这种政治影响的人物可能是有利的。

expedite /ˈekspədaɪt/
v. make (a plan or arrangement) happen sooner or go faster 加速进程：～ the repairs to the roof 加速修理屋顶/That will ～ matters. 那将加速事情的进展。

expedition /ˌekspəˈdɪʃn/
n. ❶a journey done for a purpose, especially that of exploration or scientific research 旅行，出行（尤指探险或科学考察）❷the people who make such a journey 远征队；探险队

expel /ɪkˈspel/
v. (-ll-) ❶send away from a school or an organization as a punishment 开除；除名 ❷send out with force 用力排出

expend /ɪkˈspend/
v. spend or use up (money, time, energy, etc.) 花费；用光：～ all one's capital on equipment 将所有的资本用于设备/They ～ all their strength in (on) trying to climb out. 他们费尽力气想爬出来。‖ ～ sth. on (upon) sth.；～ sth. in doing sth. 把……花费在某物上（做某事）

expenditure /ɪkˈspendɪtʃə/
n. ❶the spending of money or other resources 花费；支出：the ～ of tax-payers' money 对纳税人的钱的使用/Work is the ～ of energy. 工作消耗体能。❷the amount spent 经费；费用；开支

expense /ɪkˈspens/
n. ❶spending of money；cost 花费；消费；开销：an ～ of time（energy）花费时间（精力）❷(usually *pl*.) money needed or used for sth. or in doing sth. 费用；经费；

……费；开支：travelling ～s 旅费/school ～s 学费/household（domestic）～s 家用；家庭开销/Expenses had been greater than she had calculated. 支出总比她预计的多。/Buying shoes for children can be a great ～. 为孩子买鞋可能是一大笔开支。

expensive /ɪkˈspensɪv/
adj. costing a lot of money 费用大的；昂贵的：an ～ education 费用昂贵的教育/too ～ for me to buy 太贵而使我买不起

experience /ɪkˈspɪəriəns/
Ⅰ *n*. ❶(the gaining of) knowledge or skill which comes from practice in an activity or doing sth. for a long time, rather than from books 经验：a mechanic of rich ～ 富有经验的机械师 ❷sth. that happens to one and has an effect on the mind and feelings 经历：He told us about his ～s in Africa. 他给我们讲述了他在非洲的经历。Ⅱ *v*. feel, suffer, or learn by (an) experience 经历：He ～d two wars during his life. 他一生中经历过两次战争。‖ ～d *adj*. 有经验的

experiment /ɪkˈsperɪmənt/
Ⅰ *n*. a scientific test made in order to learn sth. or prove the truth of an idea 实验：perform（carry out, undertake, do）an ～ 进行一项实验 Ⅱ *v*. do a scientific test 做实验：The teacher ～s with new methods. 老师用新方法进行了实验。‖ ～ation *n*. 实验；试验/～al *adj*. 实验的

expert /ˈekspɜːt/
n. a person with special skill or knowledge which comes from experience or training 专家；行家；能手：He is regarded as an ～ on baby education. 他被认为是幼儿教育专家。

expertise /ˌekspɜːˈtiːz/
n. the expert knowledge or skill in a particular field 专门知识；技术：I was surprised at his ～ in skiing. 他的滑雪技术使我大为惊讶。

expire /ɪkˈspaɪə(r)/
v. ❶die 去世；逝世 ❷send out；breath from the lung 呼气 ❸(of a period of

time) come to an end（期限）终止 ‖ ex-
piration/ˌekspɪˈreɪʃn/n.呼气；终结

expiry /ɪkˈspaɪəri/
 n.the time when sth. expires or is no longer valid 截止日期；期满：an ～ date 失效
日

explain/ɪkˈspleɪn/
 v.❶ show or tell sb. about sth. in a way
that makes it easy to understand 说明；解
释：Can you ～ the phrase to me? 你能向
我解释这个短语的意思吗? ❷ give a reason why sth. happens 说明……原因（或
理由）：He cannot ～ his absence. 他不能
解释清楚迟到的原因。 ‖ ～ sth.away 辩护

explanation/ˌekspləˈneɪʃn/
 n.a statement，fact，circumstance，etc. that
tells you why sth. happened 解释；说明：
What is your ～ for being late? 你对迟到
有何解释? /He didn't understand the
teacher's ～ of the text.他不明白教师对
课文的解释。/John could give no ～ for
being late.约翰对他的迟到做不出任何解
释。

explicit/ɪkˈsplɪsɪt/
 adj.clearly stated in detail 明确的；详述
的：I gave him ～ instructions. 我给了他
明确的指示。

explode/ɪkˈspləud/
 v. ❶（cause sth. to）burst with a loud
voice；blow up 爆炸：A plastic bomb ～d
in a park on Sunday.一颗塑料炸弹星期
天在公园内爆炸了。❷（of a person）
show sudden and violent emotion（人）爆
发，表露强烈感情：He ～d with anger.他
勃然大怒。

exploit[1] /ˈeksplɔɪt/
 n.a brave and exciting act 英勇的事迹，功
劳，功绩

exploit[2] /ɪkˈsplɔɪt/
 v.❶make full use of and get benefit from
（a resource）开发，充分利用（资源）：～ a
goldmine 开发金矿 ❷ benefit unfairly
from sb. by making them overwork and
not giving them much in return 剥削，榨
取：～ a person 剥削人 ‖ ～ation
/ˌeksplɔɪˈteɪʃn/ n.开发，开采；利用；剥削；

榨取

explore/ɪkˈsplɔː(r)/
 v.❶ travel into or through（a place）for
the purpose of discovery 勘探：Today
there are few places for people to ～.今
天,可供人们勘探的地方已不多了。❷
examine（especially a subject or ques-
tion）carefully in order to find out more
探求；探究：～ ways and means of solving
the question 寻求解决问题的方式方法/
～ latent possibilities 挖掘潜力 ‖ exploration n.探测；探究/exploratory adj.勘探
的

explorer /ɪkˈsplɔːrə(r)/
 n.a person who explores unknown places
in order to find out more 探险者；勘探者

explosion /ɪkˈspləʊʒən/
 n.❶a violent and destructive shattering
or blowing apart of sth.，as is caused by a
bomb 爆炸 ❷a sudden outburst of sth.
such as noise，light，or violent emotion，
especially anger 爆发（尤指怒气的迸发）：
an ～ of anger 怒气迸发 ❸a sudden
great increase 剧增；激增：a population
～ 人口的激增

explosive/ɪkˈspləʊsɪv/
 Ⅰ adj.❶able or likely to explode 会（引
起）爆炸的 ❷likely to cause violent and
dangerous reactions 可能引起争议（或冲
动）的：an ～ situation 可能引起过激反应
的形势 Ⅱ n.a substance that can explode
炸药，爆炸物 ‖ ～ly adv.爆发地；引起爆
炸地

export
 Ⅰ /ɪkˈspɔːt/v.send sth. out of the country
to another country for sale 输出；出口：
～ machinery 出口机械 Ⅱ /ˈekspɔːt/ n.
（pl.）sales of goods or services to other
countries 出口业：For the first time the
～s exceed imports.出口第一次超过了进
口。 ‖ ～able adj.可出口的/～ation n.
输出

expose/ɪkˈspəʊz/
 v.❶uncover；leave（sth.）unprotected；lay
open to（danger）使暴露；使面临（危险）：
～ one's skin to the sun 使某人的皮肤暴

露在阳光下/be ～d to all kinds of weather 经受风吹雨打/The soldiers ～d themselves too soon and failed to take the enemy by surprise.士兵们过早暴露目标,未能出其不意攻击敌人。❷ show for sale;display 展出;陈列:～ goods in a shop window 将商品陈列在橱窗里 ❸ make known or public 揭露;揭发:～ a plot (secret) 揭露阴谋(秘密) ❹ allow light to reach (film, etc.) 使曝光:～ a reel of film 使一卷胶片曝光

exposition /ˌekspəˈzɪʃən/
n. ❶ an explanatory account of a plan or theory (计划或想法的)阐述:an ～ of Marx's writings 对马克思作品的阐述 ❷ a large public exhibition 展览会;博览会

exposure /ɪkˈspəʊʒə/
n. ❶ the process of exposing sb. or sth. to air,cold,or harm 暴露;面临;遭受(伤害) ❷ the process of exposing film to the light so as to take a picture,or a piece of film exposed in this way 曝光;底片,胶片 ❸ publicity 关注;宣传

expound /ɪkˈspaʊnd/
v. explain by giving details 解释,阐述:～ an idea (a theory,a philosophy)阐述一种观点(理论,哲理)

express /ɪkˈspres/
I *v.* ❶ show or make known a feeling,opinion,or fact by words,looks or actions 表示;表达;表露:You should learn to ～ yourself. 你应当学会表达自己。❷ press or squeeze out (especially juices or oil) 压出,榨出(尤指汁液或油):The baby sucked milk ～ed from her mother's breast.婴儿吮吸着从母亲乳房里挤出的乳汁。❸ send (a letter,parcel,etc.) fast by special delivery 用快递寄出(信件、包裹等) II *n.* ❶ fast train that stops at few stations 特快列车 ❷ a service provided by the post office, railways, road services,etc. for carrying goods quickly (邮局、铁路、公路等部门提供的)快邮,速递:send goods by ～ 特快货运 ❸ a company that delivers goods quickly 捷运公司 III *adj.* ❶ clearly and definitely stated; explicit 清楚的;明确的 ❷ travelling or

operating at high speed 特快的;快速的:～ delivery 快递

expression /ɪkˈspreʃn/
n. ❶ the appearance of the face,showing one's feelings 表情:The ～ on her face shows that she is very excited.她脸上的表情表明她很激动。/an angry ～ 愤怒的表情 ❷ the process of showing feelings or thoughts in some way 表达;表露:He played the music with a lot of ～. 他以丰富的情感演奏音乐。❸ a word or group of words used to convey an idea 措辞;词语

expressive /ɪkˈspresɪv/
adj. ❶ expressing a lot of feelings or thoughts 富于表情的;富于表现力的:an ～ voice 富有表现力的声音 ❷ communicating the specified thought or feeling 表现(特定想法或感觉)的:a tone ～ of contempt 表现出轻蔑的语调 ‖ ～ly *adv.* 意味深长地;表现地;表示地

expropriate /eksˈprəʊprɪeɪt/
v. take sb.'s private property for the use of the public 征用:The government has ～d his land.政府征用了他的土地。

expulsion /ɪkˈspʌlʃn/
n. expelling or being expelled 驱逐;开除:an ～ order 驱逐出境的命令 ‖ **expulsive** *adj.*逐出的;开除的

exquisite /ˈekswɪzɪt, ɪkˈskwɪzɪt/
adj. very finely made or done; extremely beautiful or skillful 优美的;精致的:～ manners (grace) 优雅的举止(风度)/an ～ white fur coat 精美的白色皮大衣/～ objects 精品

extend /ɪkˈstend/
v. ❶ (of land, time) spread to cover a wider area or last longer (地域或时间)延伸,扩大,延长:～ a road 延长公路/The railway ～s far away.这条铁路延伸到很远的地方。❷ spread out the body at full length 伸展(身体) ❸ give sth.; offer 给予:Please ～ a warm welcome to them. 请给他们以热烈的欢迎。

extension /ɪkˈstenʃn/
n. ❶ the process or action of extending 延

伸;延长;伸展;扩大:The ~ of the garden will take several weeks.扩大那座花园需要几个星期。❷a part that is added to sth.to enlarge or prolong it 延伸部分;增加部分;扩建部分:We built an ~ onto the school,so now we have two more classrooms.我们扩充了学校的建筑,因此现在我们多了两间教室。/They decided to build an ~ to the school.他们决定扩建那所学校。/He added a two-room ~ to the house.他对那幢房子进行了两个居室的扩建。

extensive /ɪkˈstensɪv/

*adj.*❶occupying a large area 广阔的;广大的:an ~ garden 一个占地面积很大的花园 ❷large in amount or scale 数量大的;规模大的:an ~ collection of silver 大量收集的银子 ❸(of agriculture) obtaining a relatively small crop from a large area with a minimum of attention and expense (农业)粗放(经营)的:~ farming techniques 粗放耕作技术 ‖ ~ly *adv.*广阔地;广泛地;大规模地

extent /ɪkˈstent/

*n.*the size,scale or range of sth.宽度;区域;范围:be vast in ~ 范围大;广阔/a racing track 400 metres in ~ 400 米长的跑道/a vast ~ of a farm 广阔的农场/What is the ~ of your garden? 你的花园范围有多大?

exterior /ɪkˈstɪəriə(r)/

Ⅰ *adj.*relating to or coming from the outside 外部的;来自外部的/ ~ force 外部力量 Ⅱ *n.* the outside;the outer appearance or surface 外部;外面:paint the ~ walls of a house 给房子的外墙刷油漆

exterminate /ɪkˈstɜːmɪneɪt/

*v.*completely destroy or kill a large number of people or animals 灭绝;大量杀死:He ~d the rats on his farm.他在自己的农庄里灭鼠。

external /ɪkˈstɜːnl/

*adj.*❶connected with,coming from or located on the outside 外部的;外面的;外来的:the ~ walls of a house 房子的外墙/~ trade 对外贸易/~ debt of a country 国家的外债/This medicine is for ~

use only. 这药仅供外用。❷ relating to foreign countries 国外的;对外的:This newspaper doesn't pay enough attention to ~ affairs.这家报纸对国外事务不够重视。

extinct /ɪkˈstɪŋkt/

*adj.*❶no longer existing 绝种的;绝迹的:An ~ animal is one that once lived but does not exist now.绝种的动物是指从前有过而现在已不复存在的动物。❷ no longer active or alight 死的,不活动的;熄灭的:~ volcano 死火山

extinction /ɪkˈstɪŋkʃən/

*n.*❶ the state or process of making sth. extinct or becoming extinct 灭绝,绝种:the ~ of the great auk 大海鸦的灭绝。❷ the state or process of extinguishing sth. 消亡:the ~ of the state 国家的消亡

extinguish /ɪkˈstɪŋɡwɪʃ/

*v.*❶ put out (a light or fire) 熄灭:The firemen spent two days ~ing the fire.消防队员花了两天时间才扑灭了大火。❷ destroy sth.毁灭;消灭 ❸ pay off (a debt) 清偿(债务) ‖ ~er *n.*灭火器

extort /ɪkˈstɔːt/

*v.*get sth.by force or threat 强夺;敲诈,勒索:He ~ed money from the poor.他向穷人敲诈钱财。/He ~ed a promise from me.他逼我许诺。 ‖ ~ion *n.*敲诈;勒索;强夺/ ~ionate /ɪkˈstɔːʃənət/ *adj.* 要求过多的,要求过分的

extra /ˈekstrə/

Ⅰ *adj.*additional;beyond what is usual or necessary 额外的;附加的:Extra working hours should go with ~ money.额外加班应有加班费。Ⅱ *n.* sth. added,for which an extra charge is made 额外物:At this hotel a hot bath is an ~.在这家旅社洗热水澡要额外收钱。

extract

Ⅰ /ɪkˈstrækt/ *v.*pull or take out,especially with effort or difficulty 拔出:have a tooth ~ed 拔掉一颗牙/~ a bullet from a wound 从伤口处拔出子弹 Ⅱ /ˈekstrækt/ *n.*a short passage taken from a book,film or a piece of music 摘录;节选

extraction /ɪkˈstrækʃən/

   n. ❶ the action of taking out sth., especially using effort or force 拔出；提取：a dental ∼ 拔牙 ❷ the ethnic origin of someone's family 家世，祖系；血统：a woman of Spanish ∼ 一位西班牙血统的妇女

extractor /ɪkˈstræktə/

   n. a machine or device used to extract sth. 提取器，萃取器：a juice ∼ 榨汁机

extracurricular /ˌekstrəkəˈrɪkjʊlə(r)/

   adj. (especially of activities such as sports, music, acting) outside the regular course of study 课程以外的(尤指运动、音乐、表演等活动)：Football, dramatics and debating are ∼ activities in our high school. 足球、戏剧和辩论是我们中学里的课外活动。

extradite /ˈekstrədaɪt/

   v. hand over to the jurisdiction of his own country a foreigner accused or convicted of a crime 引渡(外国的罪犯)：The British Government ∼d the man wanted by the French police. 英国政府把法国警方通缉的那个男子引渡回法国。

extraordinary /ɪkˈstrɔːdnri/

   adj. more than what is ordinary; peculiar; strange 非常的；非凡的；特殊的；奇异的：an ∼ meeting 特别会议/∼ progress 极大的进步/∼ weather 反常的天气/an ∼ leader 杰出的领袖/What an ∼ story! 这故事真奇怪啊！/With ∼ strength the old man finished the race. 老人以非凡的体力跑完了全程。

extravagance /ɪkˈstrævəgəns/

   n. ❶ lack of restraint in spending money or use of resources 奢侈，铺张，挥霍：his reckless ∼ with money 他对钱财的大肆挥霍 ❷ a thing on which too much money has been spent or which has used up too many resources 奢侈品，奢华物 ❸ excessive elaborateness of style, speech, or action (式样、言辞或行为的)过于奢华；过度：the ∼ of the decoration 装饰的过于奢华

extravagant /ɪkˈstrævəgənt/

   adj. ❶ lacking restraint in spending money or use of resources 浪费的，奢侈的：The millionaire leads an ∼ life. 这个百万富翁过着奢侈的生活。 ❷ (of ideas, behaviour, and the expression of feeling) uncontrolled; beyond what is reasonable 过度的；过分的：∼ behaviour 过分的行为 ‖ ∼ly *adv.* 挥霍无度地

extreme /ɪkˈstriːm/

   Ⅰ *adj.* ❶ as far away as possible; remote 在尽头的；最远的：∼ penalty 极刑 ❷ at the furthest point 位于极点，位于末端的：He lives in the ∼ north of the country. 他居住于该国的最北端。 Ⅱ *n.* the greatest degree 末端；极度 ‖ go to (be driven to) ∼s 走向极端 ‖ ∼ly *adv.* 极其地/**extremist** *n.* 极端主义者/**extremity** *n.* 极点；末端

extricate /ˈekstrɪkeɪt/

   v. free someone from a difficulty which prevents him from moving 使摆脱，使解脱：He ∼d his friend from the chains. 他帮朋友挣脱了锁链。/He ∼d himself from debt. 他摆脱了债务。

extrude /ɪkˈstruːd/

   v. ❶ push out; force out; expel 挤出；压出；推出：He ∼d toothpaste from the tube. 他从牙膏管里挤出牙膏来。 ❷ shape (metal, plastics, etc.) by forcing through dies (将金属、塑料等)挤压成：Plastics material is ∼d through very small holes to form fibres. 塑料从细孔中挤压出来形成纤维。 ❸ stick out; protrude 伸出；突出

extrusion /ɪkˈstruːʒn/

   n. ❶ the act or process of extruding; the form or product produced by this process 挤压；挤压过程；挤压法；挤压的形状；压出品：∼ moulding 挤压模塑法/an ∼ press 挤压机 ❷ flowing out of lava onto the earth's surface; mass of rock formed by extrusion (熔岩的)喷出；熔岩喷出形成的大块岩石

exuberant /ɪgˈzjuːbərənt/

   adj. (of people and their behaviour) overflowing with energy and cheerful excitement; (of plants) growing luxuriantly

E

（人或其行为举止）生气勃勃的；充满活力的；（植物）茂盛的：～ crops 茂盛的农作物/children in ～ spirits 精力旺盛的孩子们‖ ～ly *adv.*生气勃勃地/exuberance *n.*旺盛的精力

exude/ɪgˈzjuːd/

　　v.(of moisture or a smell)come out,allow to come out,in small (from somewhere) slowly and steadily (使)水分渗出；(气味)散发出：Blood ～d through the bandage.血从绷带中渗出来。/His wound ～d blood.他的伤口渗出血来。

eye/aɪ/

　　Ⅰ *n.*❶the two organs on the face with that you sees with 眼睛：She has beautiful black ～s. 她有一双美丽的黑眼睛。❷sth.like an eye 似眼之物‖an ～ for an ～ 以牙还牙/～s right 向右看(口令)/if you had half an ～ 如果你稍加注意/in the ～s of 就……看来/under (before) one's very ～s 就在某人面前/up to the ～s in 埋头于/with an ～ to 指望/be in the public ～ 在公众场合露面/close one's ～s to 拒绝看/give sb.a black ～ 将某人打得鼻青脸肿/have an ～ for 判断；欣赏；着眼于/keep an ～ on 照看/make ～s at 向……送秋波/mind your ～ 当心/see ～ to ～ 完全同意/never take one's ～s off 永不停止注意/～ to ～ 赞同 Ⅱ *v.*look at or watch carefully 注视；审视：The police ～d me with a strange expression.警察用一种奇怪的神色盯着我。

eyeball[1]/ˈaɪbɔːl/

　　*n.*the whole of the eye,including the part hidden inside the head,which forms a more or less round ball 眼球：Don't read in a moving car or bus because the bumping and shaking make extra work for your ～ muscles.不要在行进中的小汽车或公共汽车上看书，因为车辆的颠簸摇

动会给眼球的肌肉增加额外的负荷。‖ ～ to ～(with)面对面；怒目相视；对峙：The two politicians confronted each other ～ to ～.两位政客怒目相视地争论着。/an ～-to-～ confrontation 面对面的对抗

eyeball[2]/ˈaɪbɔːl/

　　*v.*look directly at sb.or sth.打量；盯着看

eyebrow/ˈaɪbrau/

　　*n.*the arch line of hair above the eye 眉；眉毛：pluck one's ～ 拔眉毛

eyeful/ˈaɪful/

　　*n.*❶an amount of sth. such as liquid or dust that has been thrown,or blown into your eye 满眼 ❷a striking or attractive person or thing 悦目的人（或物）；美人；好看的东西 ‖ have (get) an ～ of sth. 一饱眼福

eyelash/ˈaɪlæʃ/

　　*n.*any of the small hairs on the edge of the eyelid 眼睫毛：She was wearing false ～es.她戴着假睫毛。

eyelet/ˈaɪlət/

　　*n.*a hole with a metal ring round it,which is made in material such as leather or cloth so that a rope or cord may be passed through it 孔眼；小孔(供穿线和穿绳用)

eyelid/ˈaɪlɪd/

　　*n.*the upper or lower covering of the eye 眼皮；眼睑：His ～ is swollen. 他的眼皮肿了。

eyesight/ˈaɪsaɪt/

　　*n.*the ability to see 视力：He has good ～. 他的视力很好。

eyewitness/ˈaɪˌwɪtnəs/

　　*n.*a person who has seen sth. happen and can describe it 见证人；目击者：Were there any ～es to the crime? 这桩罪案有没有见证人？

Ff

fable/ˈfeɪbl/

n. ❶ a story which teaches a moral lesson 寓言：The ～ *the Hare and the Tortoise* tells us not to be conceited.寓言《龟兔赛跑》告诉我们不要骄傲自满。❷ a story incorporating elements of legend and myth 传奇；神话：He likes to read ～. 他喜欢读神话故事。

fabric/ˈfæbrɪk/

n. ❶ the basic structure of a building；the essential structure of a society,an organization,etc.(建筑物的)结构；(社会、组织的)结构：The whole ～ of society was changed by the war.整个社会结构都被战争改变了。❷ woven material made by wool,cotton silk,etc.织物；布料：woollen (silk) ～ 毛(丝)织品

fabricate/ˈfæbrɪkeɪt/

v. ❶ make or construct sth.especially by putting parts together 制作；装配：He ～d all the furniture she bought yesterday.他把她昨天买的全部家具组装起来。❷ invent or concoct (a false story) 捏造；虚构：His biography published last month was ～d.上月出版的他的传记是虚构的。‖ **fabrication** *n.*构造；捏造

fabulous/ˈfæbjələs/

adj. ❶ very good；very big 很好的；很大的 ❷ strange；unusual and interesting；amazing 奇怪的；怪异的；惊人的

face/feɪs/

Ⅰ *n.* ❶ the front part of the head 脸；面：They are talking ～ to ～.他们在面对面地交谈。❷ the expression on the face 脸部表情：Their happy ～s comforted me.他们幸福的表情使我得到了安慰。❸ dignity；reputation 面子；威信：She didn't want to lose ～.In order to save her ～, she had to go away quietly.她不愿意丢脸。为了保全面子，她不得不悄然离去。

‖ make ～s 做鬼脸 Ⅱ *v.* ❶ be opposite sb.or sth.；have the face or front pointing towards sb.or sth.面向；朝：He sat facing her.他脸朝她坐着。❷ confront and deal with or accept 正视，面对；处理；接受：We must ～ difficulties and setbacks. 我们必须正视困难和挫折。

facet/ˈfæsɪt/

n. ❶ one of the sides of a precious stone which has been cut into shape 宝石的刻面 ❷ a part of sth.(某事物的)方面：There are many ～s to his character.他具有多面的性格。

facial[1]/ˈfeɪʃl/

adj. of the face 颜面的，脸部的：She bears a strong ～ resemblance to my sister. 她长得和我姐姐很像。

facial[2]/ˈfeɪʃl/

*n.*a beauty treatment in which the skin of the face is treated with various substances and may also be massaged 美容(包括脸部按摩)

facile/ˈfæsaɪl/

*adj.*easily done or achieved；not requiring much effort or skill (and often of a poor quality)容易做的；不费力的；轻率做出的；肤浅的：He made a ～ speech.他草率地做了一次演说。

facilitate/fəˈsɪlɪteɪt/

*v.*make an action easier 使更容易；促进：I decided to employ a secretary in order to ～ the work.为便于工作，我决定雇用一名秘书。

facility/fəˈsɪləti/

n. ❶ a quality which makes learning or doing things easy or simple 熟练；灵巧：She can speak Japanese with ～.她能熟练地说日语。❷ anything which makes doing sth.easier and more convenient 便利

F

条件;方便:In this city there are a lot of public health facilities. 这座城市里有许多公共保健设施。

facsimile /fæk'sɪməli/

n. an exact copy 复制本,摹本

fact /fækt/

n. ❶ sth. that has actually happened or is happening; sth. known to be or accepted as being true 现实;实情:We must seek truth from ～s, no matter what we do. 无论我们做什么,都必须实事求是。❷ things that are true rather than things that have been invented 真实的事物;真实情况:It's important to distinguish ～ from fiction. 把现实与虚构区分开来是很重要的。❸ a thing that is believed or claimed to be true 事实,真相:I disagree the ～s which you have listed. 我不同意你所列举的论据。‖ in ～ 实际上/as a matter of ～ 事实上

faction /'fækʃn/

n. a small group of people within a political party (政党内的)小派别,小集团

factor /'fæktə(r)/

n. ❶ any of the forces, conditions, influences, etc., that acts with others to bring about a result 要素;因素:Her diligence is an important ～ in her great success. 勤奋是她获得巨大成功的重要因素。❷ a whole number which when multiplied by one or more whole numbers, produces a given number 因子:2,3 and 5 are all ～s of 30. 2,3 和 5 都是 30 的因子。

factorize /'fæktəraɪz/

v. divide (a number or expression) into factors 把……分解为因子(因数)

factory /'fæktəri/

n. a place or building where goods are manufactured or assembled chiefly by machine 工厂;制造厂:an automobile (a clothing) ～ 汽车(服装)工厂 /She has lunch at the ～. 她在工厂吃午饭。

factual /'fæktʃuəl/

adj. concerned with fact; of the nature; of fact; real 事实的,真实的:the ～ aspects of the case 案情的事实方面/a ～ account 写实的报道

faculty /'fæklti/

n. ❶ a power of mind; a power of doing things 本领;才能:The girl has the ～ to learn painting easily. 这姑娘擅长学习绘画。❷ a group of departments concerned with a major division of knowledge in a university (大专院校的)系;科;院:This room is the office of the law ～. 这间房是法律系办公室。❸ the teaching or research staff in a university (of U.S.) (美国大学或学院的)全体教职员工:He was on the ～ there for over thirty years. 他在大学执教三十多年。

fad /fæd/

n. sth. that people have interested in only for a short period of time (风靡一时的)风尚;短暂的狂热:His interest in photography is only a passing ～. 他对摄影的爱好仅是一时的兴致。/the latest ～ 最新的时尚

fade /feɪd/

v. ❶ (cause to) lose brightness, colour, strength, freshness, etc. (使)凋谢;(使)枯萎;(使)褪色:Flowers ～ soon after they have been cut. 花摘下后很快就会枯萎。/The strong sunlight has ～d the window curtains. 强烈的阳光使窗帘褪色了。❷ disappear or die gradually 逐渐消失:All memory of her childhood ～d from her mind. 她童年的所有记忆渐渐从脑海中消失了。

fagged /fægd/

adj. extremely tired 疲惫不堪的

Fahrenheit /'færənhaɪt/

adj. of a thermometre on which 32° is the freezing point and 212° is the boiling point of water 华氏温度计的,华氏的:fifty degrees ～ 华氏 50 度(50°F)

fail /feɪl/

Ⅰ *v.* ❶ be unable to do sth. or do not succeed in doing sth. 失败:All our plans ～ed. 我们所有的计划都失败了。/I ～ed in persuading her. 我未能说服她。❷ be not enough 不足:The crops ～ed because of the drought. 由于旱灾,农作物都减产了。❸ lose strength; become weaker 衰退:She has been ～ing in health. 她的健

康状况越来越差。Ⅱ *n.* (without ～)emphasize that sth. always happens or an order or a promise 必定, 务必：Bring the book tomorrow without ～. 明天务必把书带来。

failing /ˈfeɪlɪŋ/

Ⅰ *n.* a flaw or weak point 弱点；缺点；短处：Pride is a terrible ～. 骄傲是一种可怕的弱点。Ⅱ *prep.* if a thing is not the case or does not happen 在……不在的情况下；若没有；若不是：Ask friends to recommend several persons or, ～ that, ask for a list in your local library. 请朋友推荐几个人, 如果办不到就向当地图书馆要一份名单。

failure /ˈfeɪljə(r)/

n. ❶ lack of success 失败, 不成功：His ～ to answer questions made the police suspicious. 他未能回答问题使警方怀疑起来。❷ a person or thing that fails 失败者；不成功的事：He was a ～ as a doctor. 作为一名医生他失败了。

faint /feɪnt/

Ⅰ *adj.* ❶ lacking strength；weak and dizzy 虚弱的；昏厥的：They felt ～ for lack of food. 他们饿得快要晕过去了。❷ not clear, dim 模糊不清的；暗淡的；无力的：There comes a ～ sound. 传来了微弱的声音。Ⅱ *v.* lose consciousness 昏厥：She ～ed when she saw the terrible scene. 看到这可怕的场面, 她晕倒了。

fair¹ /feə(r)/

n. ❶ a very large show of goods, advertising, etc. 博览会：I bought the dictionary at a book ～. 我在书展上买到了这本字典。❷ a market, especially one held at a particular place at regular periods for selling farm produce 集市；庙会：Peasants and artisans exchange their products at the ～ every ten days. 农民和工匠每 10 天赶集交换产品。

fair² /feə(r)/

adj. ❶ free from injustice, dishonesty, or self-interest 公正的；公平的：We didn't think that the judgement was ～. 我们认为该判决是不公正的。❷ moderately good；average 尚可；中等：Your oral English is good, but his is only ～. 你的英语

口语很好, 他的却是一般。❸ (of weather) good (天气) 晴朗的：How long will the ～ weather last? 晴朗的天气会维持多久？❹ (of the skin or hair) light in colour；not dark；blond (皮肤) 白皙的；(头发) 金黄的：The girl with blue eyes and ～ hair is very pretty. 那碧眼金发的姑娘非常漂亮。

fairly /ˈfeəli/

adv. ❶ to a moderately sufficient extent or degree 相当；还算：He has worked well. 他工作得不错。❷ in a way that is honest or just 公平地：treat sb. ～ 公平地对待某人

fairness /ˈfeənəs/

n. the quality of treating people equally or in a way that is reasonable 公正性；公平合理性：the ～ of the system 制度的公正性

fairy /ˈfeəri/

n. a tiny, graceful, imaginary being with magic powers 小妖精, 小仙女

fairy-tale

n. a story for children involving magical events and imaginary creatures 童话 (故事)

faith /feɪθ/

n. ❶ a strong belief；unquestioning confidence 信念；信任：I'm sure she'll get success. I've got great ～ in her. 我肯定她会成功。我对她有很大的信心。❷ a system of religious belief 宗教信仰：The Buddhism ～ is one of the three greatest religions in the world. 佛教是世界三大宗教之一。

faithful /ˈfeɪθfl/

adj. keeping faith, loyal and true (to sb., to a cause, to a promise, etc.) 忠实的；可靠的：a ～ translation 忠实于原文的译文 / be ～ to sb. 忠实于某人

faithfully /ˈfeɪθfəli/

adv. ❶ in a faithful manner 真心实意地：You promised ～ that you would come. 你真心实意地答应过要来的。❷ exactly 如实地：I copied the map ～. 我如实地复制了这张地图。❸ (Yours ～) the usual polite way of ending a formal letter, when addressing someone as Sir, Madam, etc. 忠实于您的(正式信件结尾所用的客套话)

faithless/'feɪθləs/

adj. disloyal; not deserving trust 不忠实的,不守信用的,背信弃义的: a ～ friend 一个不能信赖的朋友

fake/feɪk/

Ⅰ *v*. ❶ make sth. false or a copy of sth. with the intent to deceive 伪造,捏造: There wasn't a word of truth in what he said, the whole story had been ～d up. 他说的话没有一句是真的,整个故事都是捏造的。❷ pretend 假装: He is not sick, he's just faking 他没有病,他是装病。Ⅱ *n*. a person who makes deceitful pretenses; sth. that is a counterfeit 弄虚作假者; 假货; 赝品: The adventures of the spy turn out to be a series of ～s. 这个侦探的惊险活动原来都是虚构的。/ He looked like a postman but he was really a ～. 他看上去像个邮递员,但实际上是假冒的。Ⅲ *adj*. artificial; false 假的, 伪造的:～ money 假钱,假钞票

fall/fɔːl/

Ⅰ *v*. (fell, fallen) ❶ go down freely from a higher to a lower position or level, e. g. by losing balance or as a result of gravity 落下; 降落: In autumn, the dead leaves begin to ～ from the branches. 秋天,枯叶开始从树枝上飘落。❷ become lower in level, degree, or quantity (水平、程度或数量) 下降, 减弱: When a cold wave came, the temperature fell 10C° yesterday. 昨天寒潮一来,气温就下降了 10 度。❸ come or happen, as if by descending 正当(日子); 适逢: Christmas ～s on a Sunday this year. 今年的圣诞节正好是星期天。❹ hang loosely 下垂; 散落: Her hair ～s over her shoulders. 她的头发披在双肩上。❺ die in a battle 战死: The soldiers who had ～en in the war were buried here. 阵亡士兵都被掩埋在这里。❻ become 变成: My grandmother fell ill. 我奶奶生病了。/ He fell in love with the girl. 他爱上了这位姑娘。Ⅱ *n*. ❶ an act of falling 降落; 跌倒: He had a bad ～ and broke his left hand. 他跌得不轻,摔断了

左手。❷ autumn 秋天: I may be going abroad in the ～. 今年秋天,我可能会出国。❸ a waterfall 瀑布: The Victoria Fall is famous for its grandeur. 维多利亚瀑布以其壮观而著称。

fallacious /fə'leɪʃəs/

adj. containing a fallacy; faulty 谬误的:～ argument 谬误的论据 ‖ ～ly *adv*. 谬误地/～ness *n*. 谬误

fallacy/'fæləsi/

n. a belief which is untrue or based on unsound argument 谬见; 谬论; 谬误

fallible/'fæləbl/

adj. likely to make a mistake 易犯错误的

fallow/'fæləʊ/

adj. (of land) ploughed but not planted with seed (耕地)闲下来的,未经耕作的

false/fɔːls/

adj. ❶ not true or correct 错误的; 不老实的: The answer to the question is ～. 这个问题的答案是错误的。❷ not natural 人造的: He had his ～ teeth fixed in the hospital. 他在医院里镶了几颗假牙。‖ ～ly *adv*. 不真实地/～ness *n*. 不真实

falsify /'fɔːlsɪfaɪ/

v. (-ied) ❶ alter a document dishonestly 伪造; 篡改(文件) ❷ misrepresent facts 歪曲(事实) ‖ **falsification** *n*. 伪造; 篡改; 歪曲

falter /'fɔːltə(r)/

v. ❶ move, walk, or act in an uncertain or hesitating manner, from either weakness or fear 蹒跚; 跟跄; 踌躇; 犹豫: The sick man ～ed a few steps then fell. 那个病人摇摇晃晃地走了几步就摔倒了。/ He ～ed and lost his chance. 他犹豫不决,丧失了机会。❷ (of the voice) waver; (of a person) speak in a hesitating way or with a broken voice (声音)颤抖; 结巴地讲; 支吾地说: He ～ed out a few words. 他结结巴巴地说出几个字来。

fame/feɪm/

n. the condition of being well known 名声; 声誉: His ～ as a poet did not come until his death. 他死后才获得诗人的美誉。/ As time went on, Einstein's theory proved to be correct and by 1914 he had gained world 〜.随着时间的推移,爱因斯坦的相对论被证明是正确的,到了 1914 年,爱因斯坦已闻名世界。

famed/feɪmd/
adj.well known;famous 著名的;出名的: This area is 〜 for its natural beauty.这个地区以自然美景而闻名。/Marianne Welach, daughter of 〜 novelist Henry Welch 玛丽安娜·韦拉奇,著名小说家亨利·韦尔奇的女儿

familiar/fəˈmɪliə(r)/
adj.❶ well known to;often seen or heard 熟悉的;常见的;常听说的:Your face seems 〜.你面熟。❷ friendly and informal 友好的;不拘礼节的;I have a few 〜 friends here.这里我有几个亲密的朋友。‖ be 〜 with 通晓;熟悉 ‖ 〜ity *n*.熟悉;通晓/ 〜ize *v*.使熟悉

family/ˈfæməli/
n.❶ a group of parents and children living together as a unit 家庭:Every 〜 has a TV set in the village.这个村子里每家都有电视机。❷ all those people descended from a common ancestor 家族:the 〜 of York 约克家族 ❸ a group of related animals,plants,languages (动物、植物、语言的)类,属,科,族:animals of the cat 〜 猫科动物/ the Germanic 〜 of languages(including German, Dutch, English)日耳曼语系(包括德语、荷兰语、英语)❹ a famous or distinguished ancestry 名门望族:a man of a good 〜 出身名门望族的人 ❺ (collective noun)children (集合名词)子女:He has a large 〜.他子女很多。

famine/ˈfæmɪn/
n.❶ extreme scarcity of food in a region 饥荒:Many people die during 〜s every year.每年饥荒中都有很多人死去。❷ a particular shortage 严重的缺乏;奇缺:a coal 〜 煤荒

famous/ˈfeɪməs/
adj.❶ known by a lot of people 著名的;出名的:The museum is 〜 throughout the country.这个博物馆全国闻名。/The West Lake is 〜 for its scenery.西湖以其风景优美出名。/He is a 〜 novelist.他是一位著名的小说家。/The place is 〜

for its hot spring.这地方以温泉出名。❷ excellent;magnificent 极好的;擅长的;令人满意的:have a 〜 appetite 胃口很好

famously/ˈfeɪməsli/
adv.extremely well 非常好地:He is getting on 〜 at his new school.他在新学校的表现非常出色。

fan[1] /fæn/
Ⅰ *n*.a thing that you hold in the hand and wave to makes a current of air for cooling 扇子: In the bedroom an electric 〜 is hanging under the ceiling.卧室里的天花板下悬挂着电扇。 Ⅱ *v*.(-nn-) make a current of air by waving sth.扇:The old woman 〜ned her face with a sheet of paper.老太太用一张纸给自己脸上扇风。

fan[2] /fæn/
n.a fanatical supporter of sth.迷;狂热者: The football 〜s whistled and shouted aloud to cheer their team.足球迷大声呼叫、吹口哨来给他们队加油。

fanatic/fəˈnætɪk/
Ⅰ *n*.a person with excessive enthusiasm 狂热者:a religious 〜 宗教狂 Ⅱ *adj*.(also 〜al) too enthusiastic 狂热的:She's 〜 about keeping fit.她如醉如痴地注重健美。‖ 〜ally *adv*.狂热地/〜ism *n*.狂热;盲信

fancier/ˈfænsɪə(r)/
n.a person with special knowledge and interest of sth.especially birds, animals or plants 玩赏家;(尤指)饲养迷,园艺迷:a pigeon-〜 养鸽爱好者

fanciful/ˈfænsɪfl/
adj.❶ produced by the imagination;not based on reason of good sense 空想的,想象的:He had some 〜 notion about crossing the Atlantic in a barrel.他有一个不切实际的想法,即坐在一只木桶里横渡大西洋。❷ full of strange decorative details,decorated in an un-usual style 外表奇特的;花哨的;式样独出心裁的: 〜 designs 标新立异的设计 ‖ 〜ly *adv*.梦想地;奇异地

fancy/ˈfænsi/
Ⅰ *n*. ❶ imagination, especially in a free and undirected form 想象;幻想:Did you

really see a figure or was it only your ～? 你是真的看到了一个人影还是你的幻觉呢？❷ a hobby, especially one that is transient (尤指短暂的)爱好：I have a ～ for a swim. 我喜爱游泳。Ⅱ *adj.* decorative or brightly coloured; not ordinary; elaborate 颜色鲜艳的；花样的；精巧的；别致的：I like ～ diving. 我喜欢花样跳水。Ⅲ *v.* ❶ form a picture of; imagine 想象；设想：I ～ I heard a shot. 我好像听到了一声枪响。❷ have a liking for; wish for 喜爱；想要：I ～ that baby. 我喜欢那个婴儿。

fantasia /fænˈteɪzɪə/
n. ❶ a piece of music that does not follow any regular style 幻想曲 ❷ a piece of music made up of a collection of well-known tunes（名曲汇编的）集成曲，鸡尾乐曲

fantasize /ˈfæntəˌsaɪz/
v. form strange or wonderful ideas in the mind 想象，幻想：She ～d about winning the lottery. 她幻想自己中彩票。/ He ～d about meeting Marilyn Monroe. 他幻想与玛莉莲·梦露相遇。

fantastic /fænˈtæstɪk/
adj. ❶ imaginative or fanciful 幻想的；异想天开的 ❷ wild and strange; bizarre or exotic 奇异的；稀奇的；古怪的；～ shapes 奇形怪状 ❸ (of ideas, plans) impossible to carry out; remote from reality 不切实际的；实现不了的 ❹ very good; wonderful 非常好的；极妙的：a ～ meal 一顿极好的美餐 ‖ ～ally *adv.* 稀奇古怪地；极妙地

fantasy /ˈfæntəsi/
n. fancy or imagination, especially when extravagant 幻想：He lives in a world of ～ all day long. 他整天生活在幻想的世界里。

far /fɑː(r)/
Ⅰ *adv.* (farther, farthest; further, furthest) ❶ from, at, to or by a great distance 远：How ～ did you go? 你走了多远？/ They worked ～ into the night. 他们工作到深夜。❷ very much; by a great deal 很，极：She dances well, but her younger sister does ～ better. 她的舞跳得好，但她妹妹的更好。‖ as (so)

～ as 就……来说 / so ～ 迄今为止 Ⅱ *adj.* (farther, farthest; further, furthest) ❶ distant; remote 远(方)的；遥远的 ❷ more distant than another object of the same kind 较远的；更远的：A high tower stands on the ～ bank of the river. 在河的彼岸矗立着一座高塔。

fare /feə(r)/
Ⅰ *n.* ❶ the money charged for a journey (by bus, ship, taxi, etc.) 车费；船费；a tram ～ 电车费 / All ～s, please! 请买票！❷ a passenger paying to travel in a vehicle 乘客 ❸ food, especially as provided at a meal 伙食；食物：a bill of ～ 菜单 Ⅱ *v.* perform or get on with sth. 进行；进展：He ～s well. 他事事顺利。

farewell /ˌfeəˈwel/
Ⅰ *int.* goodbye 再会，再见：Farewell, my friends! 朋友们，再见！Ⅱ *n.* an act of parting; words said at departure 告别；道别；告别的话语：make one's ～s 辞行

farm /fɑːm/
Ⅰ *n.* an area of land and buildings for growing crops, raising animals, etc. 农场；饲养场：He has a large ～ in Australia. 他在澳大利亚有一个大农场。Ⅱ *v.* use land for growing crops, raising pigs, etc. 种田；务农；饲养牲口：After he retired, he ～ed in Latin America. 他退休后，在拉丁美洲搞农业。

farmer /ˈfɑːmə(r)/
n. a person who owns or manages a farm 农场主；牧场主，养殖场主：a sheep ～ 养羊场场主 / a coconut ～ 椰子园园主

farmhand /ˈfɑːmhænd/
n. a person who works on a farm; a farm labourer 农场工人

farmhouse /ˈfɑːmhaus/
n. the main house on a farm, where the farmer lives 农场住宅，农舍

farming /ˈfɑːmɪŋ/
n. the practice or business of being in charge of or working on a farm 农事，耕作；畜牧(养殖)(业)：new methods in dairy ～ 饲养乳牛的新方法

farmland /ˈfɑːmlænd/
n. land used or suitable for farming, espe-

cially cultivated land or pasture 农田,耕地;牧地

farmstead/'fɑːmsted/

*n.*a farmhouse and its surrounding buildings 农庄

farmyard/'fɑːmjɑːd/

*n.*a yard surrounded by farm buildings 农家宅院

farsighted/ˌfɑː'saɪtɪd/

*adj.*able to see the future effects of present actions 目光远大的,有远见的;有先见之明的:the government's ~ measures to combat the drugs problem 政府为解决吸毒问题所采取的卓有远见的措施

farther/'fɑːðə(r)/

Ⅰ *adj.*more distant 更远的:The market is on the ~ side of the river.集市在河的彼岸。Ⅱ *adv.*at or to a greater distance 更远的:I live in the suburb, ~ than you.我住在郊外,比你远。‖ **farthest** *adj.*&*adv.*最远(的)

fascinate/'fæsɪneɪt/

*v.*❶ charm or attract sb. greatly 深深吸引,迷住:The children were ~d by the toys in the shop windows.孩子们被商店橱窗里的玩具迷住了。/He is ~d with stamps. 他极喜欢邮票。❷ take away power of movement by a fixed look 使吓呆,蛊惑;(以眼神)震慑,使无法动弹:The snake ~d the frog. 蛇把青蛙吓呆了。

fascinating/'fæsɪneɪtɪŋ/

*adj.*extremely interesting and charming 有极大吸引力的;迷人的:a ~ old city full of ancient buildings 有着许多古老建筑的迷人的古城/I find her books quite ~.我发现她那些书很吸引人。

fascination /ˌfæsɪ'neɪʃ(ə)n/

*n.*❶ a very strong attraction that makes sth. very interesting 魅力;极大的吸引力:Water holds a ~ for most children.水对多数孩子都有极大的吸引力。❷ the state of being attracted to and interested in sb.or sth. 入迷;着迷:the public's enduring ~ with the Royal Family 公众对王室经久不衰的兴趣

fascism/'fæʃɪzəm/

*n.*a political system in which all industrial activity is controlled by the state, no political opposition is allowed, military strength is approved of, nationalism is strongly encouraged, and socialism is violently opposed 法西斯主义:Fascism trampled on human rights.法西斯主义践踏人权。‖ **fascist** *adj.*&*n.*法西斯主义的(支持者)

fashion/'fæʃən/

*n.*❶ a popular trend (of clothes, ornament, manners of behaviour, etc.) that which is most popular (服装、饰品、行为举止等的)时尚;时髦:Now it is the ~ for girls to wear skirts in summer.如今夏季姑娘们时兴穿裙子。❷ a manner or way of doing sth. 方式:He walks in a strange ~.他走起路来样子古怪。

fashionable/'fæʃnəbl/

*adj.*in fashion;popular 时髦的;流行的:a ~ lady 一位衣着入时的女士 ‖ **fashionably** *adv.* 时髦地;流行地

fast/fɑːst/

Ⅰ *adj.*❶ moving or able to move quickly 快的;迅速的:A ~ car runs along the street.一辆小轿车在街上疾驰。❷ (of a clock) showing a time in advance of the correct time (指钟表)走得快的:My watch is 5 minutes ~.我的表快五分钟。❸ firmly fixed and unlikely to move or change 牢固的:He made a rope ~ to the corner.他把绳子牢牢地固定在角上。❹ loyal;close 忠实的;亲近的:I'm your ~ friend.我是你忠实的朋友。❺ unfading 不褪色的:The color of my coat is ~.我上衣是不褪色的。Ⅱ *adv.*❶ firmly;tightly 牢固地;酣畅地:The baby is ~ asleep.婴儿睡得很香。❷ at a high speed 迅速地,快速地:The hare runs ~.野兔跑得很快。

fasten/'fɑːsn/

*v.*❶ make fast;fix firmly;tie or join together 系紧;钉牢;扣住;闩上:Please ~ all the windows. 请把所有的窗户都闩上。/Fasten your seat belt. 系紧安全带。/He ~ed (up) his coat.他扣上了衣服纽扣。❷ direct one's eyes, thoughts, attention,etc.upon sb. 把(眼睛、思想、注

意力)集中于：～ one's attention on sth. 把注意力集中在某事物上／He ～ed his eyes on the stranger.他把目光集中在那个陌生人身上。

fat /fæt/

I *n*. any oily materials found in animal bodies, especially when deposited as a layer under the skin or around certain organs 肉类,脂肪：Don't eat too much ～. 别吃太多的肥肉。II *adj*. ❶ covered with fat 肥胖的：She's ～, but her sister is lean.她很胖,而她的姐姐却很瘦。❷ thick and well-filled 厚的：He received a ～ letter.他收到一封厚厚的信。❸ rich; fertile 肥沃的：There are wide ～ lands in Northeast China.东北有广阔的沃野。‖ ～ness *n*.肥胖

fatal /'feɪtl/

adj. ❶ causing or resulting in death 致命的：He suffered from a ～ illness.他患了绝症。❷ bringing danger or ruin, or having unpleasant results 毁灭性的,不幸的：It is ～ to drive when you are very drunk.喝得烂醉时开车可是要命的。

fatalism /'feɪtəlɪzəm/

n. the belief that all events are predetermined and therefore inevitable 宿命论

fatality /fə'tæləti/

n. ❶ a death that is caused by accident, in war, or from disease(事故、战争、疾病引起的)死亡：It was a bad crash, but there were no fatalities. 这是一宗严重的撞车事故,但没有人死亡。❷ the quality of being fatal 致命性：New drugs have reduced the ～ of this disease.新药已经降低了这种疾病的致命性。/The ～ rate on our roads has been increasing.我们公路上的事故伤亡率一直在上升。❸ the belief or feeling of being decided by fate 命运；命数；天命

fatally /'feɪtəli/

adv. so as to cause death, ruin, or misfortune 致命地；灾难性地：～ wounded 受了致命伤／She was ～ attracted to him.她极其不幸地迷上了他。

fate /feɪt/

n. ❶ the unknown cause beyond a person control, regarded as predetermined by a supernatural power 命运；天数：I don't believe in ～. 我不相信命运。❷ a person's ultimate condition or the outcome of a particular situation for sb. or sth. 结局；结果：decide a person's ～ 决定某人的生死

fated /'feɪtɪd/

adj. destined by fate; doomed 命中注定的；命运决定的

fateful /'feɪtfl/

adj. showing an around certain organs important and decisive effect on future events 命运攸关的；决定命运的：the ～ night of the accident 发生事故的那个生命攸关的夜晚

father /'fɑːðə(r)/

n. ❶ a man in relation to his natural child or children 爸爸,父亲：John's ～ is a teacher, his mother is a teacher, too.约翰的父亲是教师,他的母亲也是教师。❷ (a title of address)priest(尊称)神父：Father Bill is an affable man.比尔神父是一个和蔼可亲的人。❸ an ancestors 祖先 ❹ the founder or first of sth. or doing sth.创始人；先驱：Edison is the ～ of the electric light. 爱迪生是电灯的发明者。 ‖ ～-in-law *n*.公公；岳父／～less *adj*.无父的／～ly *adj*.父亲(般)的／～land *n*.祖国

fatigue /fə'tiːg/

I *n*. ❶ great tiredness; exhaustion 极度疲劳：Some soldiers dropped with ～ during the long march.一些士兵在长途行军中因疲劳不堪而倒下了。❷ the tendency of metal or wood to break caused by continual use (金属或木材因长期使用造成的)疲劳：photoelectric ～ 光电疲劳 II *v*. make tired 使疲劳：The long journey ～d her.长途旅行使她疲劳不堪。

fatten /'fætən/

v. make sb. or sth. fat, or to become fat (使)长胖,长肥：The piglets are taken from the sow to be ～ed for market.这些小猪从母猪身边被带走,好育肥上市。

fatty /'fæti/

adj. (fattier, fattiest) like fat or containing fat 富含脂肪的；肥胖的；脂肪的

fault/fɔːlt/

 n. ❶ a bad or weak point, but not of a serious moral kind, in someone's character 缺点；毛病：Your only ～ is carelessness. 你唯一的缺点就是马虎。❷ a mistake or imperfection; sth. wrong or incorrect 错误；过失：It is your ～ that I am absent from the meeting because you failed to tell me about it yesterday. 我开会缺席都怪你，因为你昨天未能通知我。

faultless/'fɔːltləs/

 adj. without a fault; perfect 完美（无缺）的；无懈可击的：The dancers gave an absolutely ～ performance. 舞蹈家们的表演完美无瑕。

faulty/'fɔːlti/

 adj. having faults; not working or made correctly 有毛病（缺陷）的；错误的：a ～ connection in the electrical system 电路系统中一个有毛病的接头/～ reasoning 错误的推论

fauna/'fɔːnə/

 n. all the animals of a particular area or a particular time 动物区系；动物群

favour/'feɪvə(r)/

 Ⅰ *n.* ❶ an attitude of liking or approval 赞同；赞赏；好感：He did all he could to win her ～. 他尽力而为以求得她的欢心。❷ an act of kindness 恩惠；帮忙：Would you please do me a ～? 你能帮我个忙吗？‖ be in ～ of 赞同；支持/be out of ～ with 失宠 Ⅱ *v.* ❶ feel or show approval or preference for 垂青；赞同，赞成：Did he ～ your plan? 他赞成你的计划吗？❷ give more help, kindness, etc. to one person than to others 偏爱：A mother mustn't ～ one of her children more than the others. 做母亲的决不可偏爱一个孩子，亏待其他孩子。

favourable/'feɪvərəbl/

 adj. ❶ making people have a good opinion of sb. or sth. 给人好印象的：She made a ～ impression on us. 她给我们留下了好印象。❷ expressing approval 赞同的，赞成的；称赞的：～ comments 好评 ❸ to the advantage of sb. or sth. 有利的；促进的：～ economic conditions 有利的经济环境 ‖ **favourably** *adv.* 赞许地；顺利地；有利地

favourite/'feɪvərɪt/

 Ⅰ *adj.* liked more than others of the same kind; most loved 最喜爱的：Skating is my ～ sport. 滑冰是我最喜欢的运动。Ⅱ *n.* sth. or sb. that is liked or loved above all others 特别喜爱的人（或物）：I like all flowers but roses are my ～s. 花儿我都喜欢，但最喜欢的还是玫瑰。

fax/fæks/

 Ⅰ *n.* ❶ an exact copy of a document transmitted electronically 传真件 ❷ a machine used to transmit copies 传真机 Ⅱ *v.* transmit a document by this process 传真（文档）

fear/fɪə(r)/

 Ⅰ *n.* ❶ an unpleasant and usually strong feeling caused by the presence or expectation of danger 害怕：I walked quietly for ～ of waking the baby. 我静悄悄地走，害怕惊醒了孩子。❷ anxiety for the safety (of sb. or sth.) 担忧：Your ～ that he would be defeated was unnecessary. 你不必担心他会失败。Ⅱ *v.* ❶ be afraid of 害怕：Do you ～ the fierce dogs? 你怕猛犬吗？❷ feel anxiety or apprehension (for sb. or sth.) 担忧，担心（某人或某物）：You will win. Never ～. 你会赢的，不要担心。

fearful/'fɪəful/

 adj. ❶ causing fear; horrifying 可怕的；恐怖的；惧怕的：There has been a ～ accident and several people have been killed. 发生了一起可怕的车祸，有好几个人丧生。❷ feeling afraid; showing fear or anxiety 害怕的；担心的，担忧的

fearless/'fɪələs/

 adj. without fear 无畏的，勇敢的：a ～ mountaineer 无畏的登山运动员 ‖ ～**ly** *adv.* 勇敢地；大胆地 / ～**ness** *n.* 无畏；勇敢

feasible/'fiːzəbl/

 adj. possible or able to be done or carried out 可能的；可行的：a ～ idea 可行的想法

F

feast /fiːst/

I *n*.a meal with a lot of good food especially in celebration of sth.宴会;盛宴;筵席:What a ～ we had on the Eve of Christmas! 我们圣诞前夜吃的饭多丰盛啊! II *v*.❶ enjoy a big dinner 大吃大喝: He sat there ～ing (himself).他坐在那里大吃大喝。❷ take part in or make a large meal 参加宴会;宴请:I shall ～ my colleagues tomorrow.明天我将宴请我的同事们。

feat /fiːt/

n.a successful completion of sth.needing skill,strength or courage 技艺;伟绩:Man's first landing on the moon was a ～ of great daring.人类首次登月是一项极大的伟绩。/The circus acrobats performed ～s of dexterity and strength.马戏团杂技演员表演了灵巧与力量的技艺。

feather /'feðə(r)/

I *n*.one of the light coverings that grow from a bird's skin 羽(毛);翎毛:Feathers protect birds from cold and injury.羽毛保护鸟类不受寒冷及伤害。II *v*.decorate or supply sth.with feathers (给……)用羽毛装饰:The Indians ～ed their arrows to make them fly straight.印第安人在箭上装上羽毛,使箭能直飞。

feathery /'feðəri/

adj.❶ light and soft like feathers 轻软的;羽毛似的 ❷ covered with feathers 长满羽毛的,被羽毛覆盖的

feature /'fiːtʃə(r)/

I *n*.❶ the face as a whole 面貌:She has fine ～s.她容貌秀丽。❷ a characteristic or striking aspect of sth.特色;特征:A wide plain and rivers are the geographical ～s of this district.广阔的平原和众多河川是这个地区的地理特征。❸ a main film in a cinema programme 故事片;正片:It's a new colour ～.这是一部新彩色故事片。II *v*.❶ have as a prominent aspect 以……为特点:The house ～s a large garden.这幢房子的特点是有一个大花园。❷ include as a leading performer (电影)由……主演:This film ～s Charlie Chaplin.这部影片由查理•卓别林主演。

featureless /'fiːtʃələs/

adj.without any distinctive features 没有特色的;平淡无奇的:The scenery of the countryside is ～.这乡村的风景平淡无奇。

February /'februəri/

n.the second month of the year 二月

federal /'fedərəl/

adj.of or being a federation 联盟的;联邦的:The Federal Republic of Germany is in Western Europe.德意志联邦共和国在西欧。 ‖ ～ist *n*.联邦主义者

federation /ˌfedə'reɪʃn/

n.a group of states, united with one government which decides foreign affairs, defence, etc., but in which each state can have its own government to decide its own affairs 联邦政府

fee /fiː/

n.❶ a payment made to someone or public body for professional advice or service 费用,酬金:doctor's ～s 诊疗费/ a college admission ～ 大学入学报名费 ❷ money regularly paid for continuing services,especially to a school (尤指给学校的)固定费用,学费

feeble /'fiːbl/

adj.❶ lacking physical strength;weak; frail 虚弱的;乏力的;脆弱的:His pulse was very ～.他脉搏十分微弱。❷ failing to convince or impress;not showing determination 不具有说服力的;无力的;缺乏决心的:a ～ excuse 蹩脚的借口/a ～ attempt 不坚定的尝试

feed /fiːd/

I *v*.(fed) ❶ give food to;provide a supply of food for 喂(养);饲(养);供养;养:I have a large family to ～.我必须供养一大家人。❷ supply with material;supply sth.to sb.or sth. 供给(原料等);供应;输送:The moving belt ～s the machine with raw material.传送带把原料输入机器。❸ (of an animal) eat sth. (动物)吃东西,以……为食:The horses were ～ing quietly in the field.马在田野里安静地吃草。 ‖ ～ your face 大吃一顿;吃得过饱 II *n*.❶ an act of giving food,especially to animals and babies (尤指给动物或婴

F

儿的）喂食：The dog has two ~s a day. 这条狗一天喂两次。❷ a meal 一餐；一顿 ❸ food for animals 饲料：a bag of hen ~ 一袋鸡食

feedback /ˈfiːdbæk/
n. information about a product, etc. that a user gives back to its supplier, maker, etc. 反馈：The company welcomes ~ from people who use its goods. 该公司欢迎来自消费者的信息反馈。

feel /fiːl/
v. (felt) ❶ touch; examine by touching; try to find by touching 摸；触：The doctor felt my pulse. 医生为我把脉。❷ have a particular physical quality by touching 摸起来有……手感：Silk ~s soft. 丝绸手感柔滑。❸ give a sense of being; be conscious 感到；觉得：I felt happy when I met you. 我看见你很高兴。❹ have a particular opinion or attitude 认为；以为：I ~ that he will go there. 我想他会去那里的。

feeler /ˈfiːlə/
n. ❶ a long thin projection or organ on the bodies of certain animals, used to search for food or to test things by touching（某些动物的）触角，触须 ❷ a cautious question or suggestion put forward to test people's reactions 试探性问题：They were sufficiently depressed to put out peace ~s. 他们十分灰心丧气，试探性地提出和解。

feeling /ˈfiːlɪŋ/
n. ❶ the ability to feel things 触觉：He had lost all ~ in his legs. 他的腿已失去了知觉。❷ mental awareness or emotion 感受，感觉：a ~ of anger 愤怒的感觉 ❸ an idea or belief not wholly based on reason 想法；看法；信念：She had a ~ that someone was watching her. 她觉得有人在盯着她。❹ sensitivity; readiness to feel sympathy 情绪（化）；同情心：They seemed to show no ~ for the sufferings of others. 他们似乎对他人的痛苦毫无同情心。❺ an opinion or attitude 态度；意见：The ~ of the meeting was against it. 会议上的普遍意见是反对。❻ (*pl.*) the emotional side of a person's nature, as distinct from the intellectual side 情感；感情：I didn't mean to hurt your ~s. 我不是故意伤害你的感情。

feign /feɪn/
v. ❶ pretend to have a particular feeling or be ill, tired, etc. 假装；装作；佯装：~ illness 装病 /~ that one is mad 装疯 ❷ invent (a story or excuse) 虚构；杜撰；假造：~ an excuse 捏造借口

feint /feɪnt/
Ⅰ *n.* a false attack or blow made to draw the enemy's attention away from the real danger 佯攻，虚击 Ⅱ *v.* make a feint, especially by pretending to hit with one hand and then using the other 佯攻，声东击西：The boxer ~ed with his left, and then landed a heavy punch with his right. 那拳击手用左拳虚晃一招，然后重重地击出一记右拳。

feline /ˈfiːlaɪn/
Ⅰ *adj.* of or like a member of the cat family 猫（科）的；似猫的：Ⅱ *n.* a cat or other member of the cat family 猫；猫科动物：There is a ~ grace about the way she moves. 她走起路来轻柔无声。

fell /fel/
v. ❶ knock down 打倒：He ~ed his enemy with a single blow. 他一拳将敌人打倒。❷ cut down 砍倒：The woodman ~ed a tall pine tree. 伐木工人砍倒了一棵高大的松树。

fellow /ˈfeləʊ/
Ⅰ *n.* ❶ a man or boy 男人；小伙子：He is a nice ~. 他是一个棒小伙。❷ (*pl.*) a person in the same position or activity 同事；同伴；同类；伙伴：They were school ~s. 他们曾是同学。Ⅱ *adj.* of the same class, kind, etc. 同类的；伙伴的：The captain of a team organizes his ~ players. 队长是队友们的组织者。

fellowship /ˈfeləʊʃɪp/
n. ❶ friendly association with other people; companionship 交情；友谊 ❷ a society or group of people meeting to pursue a shared interest or aim 团体，协会；联谊会

female /ˈfiːmeɪl/
Ⅰ *adj.* ❶ of the sex that can bear off-

F

spring or produce eggs 母性的；雌性的：The hunter caught a ～ wolf.猎人逮住了一只母狼。❷ of women 女(性)的；妇女的：Sewing is considered a ～ occupation. 缝纫被公认为是妇女的职业。Ⅱ n.a female person,animal or plant 女性；母畜；雌性植物：Women and girls are ～s.妇女和女孩是阴性。

feminine/'femənɪn/

*adj.*❶ of or having the qualities suitable for a woman 女子气的：Jewelry and lace are mostly ～ belongings.珠宝和花边几乎都是女性的饰物。❷ for or belonging to the class of words that usually includes most of the words for females 阴性的：Tigress is the ～ noun for "tiger"."tigress"是"tiger"的阴性名词。

femininity/ˌfemə'nɪnəti/

n. the quality of being a woman 女子气质；阴柔

feminism/'femənɪzəm/

n. the advocacy or activity in support of the principle that women should have the same rights and chances as men 女权主义；女权运动 ‖ **feminist** *n.*女权主义者：the feminist movement 女权运动

fence/fens/

Ⅰ *n.* a barrier of wood or wire used to keep people and animals out of a place 栅栏；篱笆：The farmer built a ～ around the yard.农夫建起了围墙把庭院围了起来。Ⅱ *v.*❶ put a fence around 用栅栏围起：Farmers ～ their fields.农民常用篱笆把田地围起来。❷ fight with sword as a sport 击剑(运动)：The player ～d with his new sword.运动员用他的新剑参加击剑。

fencing /'fensɪŋ/

*n.*❶ a set of fences 栅栏；篱笆；围栏 ❷ the sport of fighting with long narrow swords 击剑运动

fend/fend/

v. ❶ with stand the force of sth.抵抗；抵挡：He ～ed off the blow.他避开这一拳。❷(～ for oneself) provide oneself, look after on without help 自己照顾自己，独自谋生

fender/'fendə(r)/

*n.*❶ a barrier that surrounds the wheels of a vehicle to block splashing water or mud 挡泥板 ❷ an object such as an old tyre,a lump of wood,etc., by the side of a boat to reduce friction against other things 船上的护舷材料(如旧轮胎、木块等) ❸ a metal frame in front of a fireplace 火炉围栏

ferment

Ⅰ /'fɜːment/*n.*❶ a substance capable of bringing about fermentation 发酵剂；酵母 ❷ excitement and unrest (especially political or social) (尤指政治或社会方面的)骚动：The country was in (a state of) ～.这个国家处于动荡之中。Ⅱ /fə'ment/ *v.*❶ undergo fermentation ,giving off a gas 发酵 ❷ excite;stir up 激起；煽动

ferocious/fə'rəʊʃəs/

*adj.*very angry and violent 暴怒的；凶猛的

ferocity /fə'rɒsəti/

n.(*pl.*-ies)the state or quality of being ferocious 凶残；凶猛；狂暴：The ～ of the storm caught them by surprise.这场风暴来势凶猛，让他们大为吃惊。

ferry/'feri/

*n.*❶ a place where there is a boat or other vehicle that carries people and goods across a river, channel, etc. 渡口：The children from the school waited at the ～ for the boat.放学的孩子们在渡口等船。❷ a boat which sails backwards and forwards across a narrow piece of water, carrying goods and passengers 渡船：Passengers can cross the river by ～.旅客可乘渡船过河。

fertile/'fɜːtaɪl/

adj. ❶ (of land)which produces or can produce good crops (土地)肥沃的：There are ～ fields in here.这儿土地肥沃。❷ (of a person's mind) inventive; full of suggestions,ideas,etc.(指人)有才智的：She is ～ in imagination.她想象力丰富。❸ (of living things) able to produce young or fruit 能繁殖的；有生育的：The farmer was surprised that the old pig was still ～.农夫对这只年老的猪仍能繁殖感到很惊讶。‖ **fertility** n.肥沃

fertilize /ˈfɜːtəlaɪz/
　　v.❶ make soil fertile or productive, especially by adding substances to it 给(土壤)施肥 ❷ introduce pollen into a plant or sperm into an egg or female animal so that it develops seed or young 使(卵、植物)受精;使(雌性动物)怀孕 ‖ **fertilization** n.施肥;肥沃;受精

fertilizer /ˈfɜːtəlaɪzə(r)/
　　n.a chemical or natural substance added to soil or land to increase its fertility 肥料

festival /ˈfestɪvl/
　　Ⅰ n.a day or time of religious or other celebration 节日;喜庆日: During the Spring Festival I always wear new clothes.春节期间我总是穿着新衣服。Ⅱ adj.of or suitable for a festival 节日的: Usually I send ～ greetings to my friends on Christmas Day.我通常在圣诞节向朋友们致以节日的问候。

festive /ˈfestɪv/
　　adj.joyous or exciting especially because of a holiday or celebration 喜庆的;欢庆的

festivity /feˈstɪvəti/
　　n.❶ the celebration of sth.in a happy way 欢庆 ❷ (pl.) joyful events that are organized in order to celebrate sth. 庆祝活动;庆典: the festivities on National Day 国庆节的庆祝活动

fetch /fetʃ/
　　v.❶ go for and bring back 去拿来: Please ～ me some water.请给我拿一些水来。❷ be sold for 卖得(若干价钱): The new house will ～ around＄1,000,000.这幢新房将卖得一百万美元。

fete /feɪt/
　　n.❶ a festival (often to collect money for a special purpose)(常为某一目的而筹款的)节日,喜庆日 ❷ an elaborate party (often outdoors)(户外的)游园会,联欢会

feud /fjuːd/
　　n.a quarrel between two people or two groups, families, etc. lasting a long time (两人、家族或部落等之间的)世仇,宿怨

feudal /ˈfjuːdl/
　　adj.of or relating to the system or the time of feudalism 封建制度的 封建时期的: The ～ system lasted for two thousand years in China.封建制度在中国延续了两千年之久。

feudalism /ˈfjuːdəlɪzəm/
　　n.the system in which people were given land and protection by people of higher rank and worked and fought for them in return 封建主义

fever /ˈfiːvə(r)/
　　n.❶ a body temperature that is higher than usual 发烧: I had a ～ yesterday.我昨天发烧了。❷ a disease marked by high temperature 热病: He suffered from scarlet ～ last year. 去年他曾患猩红热病。❸ a state of agitation or great excitement 激动不安;焦躁;极度兴奋: The player lost the game because he was in a ～ of impatience.由于极度急躁,运动员在比赛中输了。‖ ～ish adj.发热的;狂热的

fevered /ˈfiːvəd/
　　adj.❶ affected with a fever 发烧的,发热的: She mopped his ～ brow.她擦了擦他那发烧的额头。❷ highly excited 非常激动的;躁动不安的: ～ adolescent imagination 青春期躁动不安的想象

feverish /ˈfiːvərɪʃ/
　　adj.❶ having a fever; caused or accompanied by a fever 发烧的;发烧引起的 ❷ restless with excitement or agitation 激动的;焦虑不安的 ‖ ～ly adv.发热地;狂热地;兴奋地

few /fjuː/
　　Ⅰ adj.❶ (a ～)a small number(of) 几个的;少量的: A ～ people would go with you.有几个人会跟你一块儿走。❷ not many 没有几个的: Few people live to the age of 100. 活到一百岁的人很少。Ⅱ pron.not many; not enough 少数;没有几个: Few were in the classroom.教室里没有几个人。‖ no ～er than 多达;不少于

F

fiancé/fɪˈɒnseɪ/
  *n.*a man to whom a woman is engaged to marry 未婚夫

fiancée/fɪˈɒnseɪ/
  *n.*a woman that a man is engaged to marry 未婚妻

fib/fɪb/
  Ⅰ *n.*a small and not very important lie 小谎，无关紧要的谎言 Ⅱ *v.*(-bb-)tell such a lie 撒小谎

fibre(-er)/ˈfaɪbə(r)/
  *n.*any of the thin thread-like parts that together from many animal and plant growths such as wool, wood, or muscle 纤维：Some plant ~s are used for spinning and weaving into cloth.一些植物纤维用来纺织成布。

fibrous/ˈfaɪbrəs/
  *adj.*like or made of fibres 纤维(状)的：The coconut has a ~ outer covering.椰子有一个含纤维的外壳。

fickle/ˈfɪkl/
  *adj.*likely to change suddenly and without reason, especially in love or friendship；capricious（爱情、友情等）易变的；无常的：a ~ lover 靠不住的情人/The weather's so ~, one moment it's raining, the next the sun's out. 天气如此变化无常，一会儿下雨，一会儿出太阳。

fiction/ˈfɪkʃn/
  *n.*❶ sth.imagined or invented 虚构的事；捏造的事；杜撰：The newspaper's account of what happened was a complete ~.报纸对所发生的事情的报道完全是捏造的。❷ literature in the form of prose, especially novels that describes imaginary events and people 小说：works of ~ 小说作品

fictional/ˈfɪkʃənl/
  *adj.*belonging to fiction；told as a story 小说的；虚构的；捏造的：Jules Verne wrote a ~ account of a journey to the moon.儒勒·凡尔纳写了一本虚构的月球旅行记。

fictionalize/ˈfɪkʃənəlaɪz/
  *v.*write about (a true event) as if it were a story, changing some details, introducing imaginary characters, etc.把(真实的

事件)小说化；用小说的笔法写

fictitious/fɪkˈtɪʃəs/
  *adj.*untrue；or not real；being fabricated 假的；虚构的；捏造的：She invented a ~ boyfriend to put him off.她虚构出一个男朋友来拒绝他。/His account of the incident was totally ~.他对那个事件的叙述完全是虚构的。

fiddle/ˈfɪdl/
  Ⅰ *n.*❶ a violin 小提琴：play the ~ 拉小提琴 ❷ an act of defrauding or cheating 欺诈；欺骗 Ⅱ *v.*❶ play the violin 拉小提琴 ❷ move things aimlessly in one's fingers 无目的地用手指拨弄：He ~d about with his tie.他漫不经心地摆弄着领带。

fiddly/ˈfɪdli/
  *adj.*❶ needing delicate use of the fingers 需要手巧的：It's a very ~ job to get all wires back into their holes.要把所有这些电线弄回洞去，手要非常巧才干得了。❷ fiddling 琐细的，微不足道的：I can't be bothered with all these ~ details.我没有耐心过问所有这些琐碎的细节。

fidelity/fɪˈdeləti/
  *n.*❶ faithfulness；willingness to give support and help to sb. whatever the danger or difficulties 忠实；忠诚 ❷ accuracy；the ability to produce the same sound, shape, colour, etc.as an original 精确；逼真

field/fi:ld/
  *n.*❶ an area of land for growing crops or feeding animals 农田；牧场：The butterflies are flying in the ~.蝴蝶正在田野里飞着。❷ a piece of land for some special use 场地：The planes took off from the air ~.飞机从机场起飞了。❸ the place where people find oil, coal, gold, etc.（矿产）产地：We have opened several large oil ~ since 1950s.20 世纪 50 年代以来，我们开辟了几个大油田。❹ a particular brand of study or sphere of activity（学术或活动）领域，范围：He achieved splendid results in the ~ of medicine.他在医学领域取得了辉煌成果。

fieldwork/ˈfi:ldwɜːk/
  *n.*the scientific or social study done in the field, such as measuring and examining

things or asking people questions 野外考察；(社会研究的)实地考察

fiend /fiːnd/

n. ❶ a devil or evil spirit 恶魔，魔鬼 ❷ a wicked person 凶恶的人

fiendish /'fiːldɪʃ/

adj. ❶ fierce and cruel 残酷的，凶猛的：She has a ~ temper. 她脾气极坏。 ❷ extremely complex; not plain or simple 复杂的；不容易的；不简单的：a ~ plan (question) 难以处理的计划（难题）/He had worked out a plan of ~ complexity. 他已经制订出一项极度复杂的计划。‖ ~**ly** *adv.* 很；极：a ~ly difficult question 非常刁钻的难题

fierce /fɪəs/

adj. ❶ cruel 凶狠的；残忍的：The young man has a ~ look on his face. 这年轻人面容凶狠。 ❷ violent 狂暴的：The typhoon was so ~ that we could hardly stand up. 台风吹得太猛，我们简直站不稳。 ❸ intense 强烈的：He made a ~ speech, urging his fellows to fight. 他言辞激烈，力促伙伴去战斗。‖ ~**ly** *adv.* 残忍地／ ~**ness** *n.* 残忍

fiery /'faɪəri/

adj. ❶ flaming; looking like fire; hot as fire 燃烧的；似火的；火热的：a ~ sky 火红的天空 ❷ showing strong emotions, especially anger; quickly or easily made angry 易怒的；暴躁的；充满激情的；怒气冲冲的：a ~ temper 火爆的脾气／a ~ speech 激昂的演说

fifteen /ˌfɪf'tiːn/

num. ❶ the number 15 十五 ❷ a team of rugby players 橄榄球队：Tom plays in the second ~. 汤姆在第二橄榄球队打球。‖ ~**th** *num.* 第十五

fifty /'fɪfti/

num. the number 50 五十：the fifties 五十多岁，五十年代 ‖ **fiftieth** /'fɪftɪəθ/ *num.* 第五十

fig /fɪg/

n. soft, sweet, pear-shaped fruit, full of small seeds 无花果

fight /faɪt/

Ⅰ *v.* (fought) struggle with the hands or

with weapons; use physical force (as in war) 打仗；斗争：They ~ against the flood. 他们与洪水搏斗。 Ⅱ *n.* an act of fighting 战斗；搏斗：The two hooligans had a ~ in the street. 这两个小流氓在街上打了一架。

fighter /'faɪtə(r)/

n. ❶ someone who fights, in battle or for sport; a professional soldier or boxer 战士；格斗者；拳击手：a tireless ~ against racism 不知疲倦的反对种族主义的斗士 ❷ a small fast military aircraft that can destroy enemy aircraft in the air 战斗机，歼击机：a ~ pilot 战斗机驾驶员

figment /'fɪgmənt/

n. sth. imagined and untrue 虚构的事；臆造的东西

figurative /'fɪgərətɪv/

adj. (said about a word or expression) using or containing a figure of speech; metaphorical, not literal（词语或言语）比喻的；隐含的 ‖ ~**ly** *adv.* 形象地；比喻地

figure /'fɪgə(r)/

Ⅰ *n.* ❶ any of the number signs from 0 to 9 数字(尤指 0 至 9)：He has an income of six ~s. 他有六位数的收入。 ❷ the human shape considered from the point of view of being attractively thin 体形：I'm dieting to keep my ~. 我在节食以保持体形。 ❸ an often numbered drawing or diagram used in a book to explain sth. 图形；图表：See Figure 4 on page 1. 参看第一页插图四。 ❹ an important person 重要人物：Zhu Geliang is one of the best-known ~s in Chinese history. 诸葛亮是中国历史上最著名的人物之一。 Ⅱ *v.* ❶ imagine; picture mentally 想象：Figure the aftermath for yourself, I can't do anything for you. 想象一下你自己的后果吧，我无能为力。 ❷ calculate or work out 计算：Figure the sum total, I'll pay it up at once. 算一下总数，我一次付清。 ❸ consider; believe 认为：I ~ that practice makes perfect. 我认为熟能生巧。

filament /'fɪləmənt/

n. the piece of wire in an electric light bulb 电灯丝

F

file/faɪl/

I　*n.* ❶ a box, folder, etc. for storing papers in an ordered way, especially in an office 文件夹：Put these documents in the ～.把这些文件存档。 ❷ a steel tool with a rough surface, used for rubbing down, making smooth, or cutting through hard surfaces 锉（刀）：Yesterday I bought a nail ～ in the department store.昨天我在百货商店买了一只指甲锉。 ❸ a line of people one behind the other 行列：Citizens waited to buy food before the counter in single ～.市民们在柜台前排着队等候买食品。 Ⅱ *v.* ❶ place on or in a particular order 归档：The postman ～d the letters.邮递员把信件归了档。 ❷ rub or cut sth. with a file 锉：The turner ～d the spare parts of a machine with a flat ～.车工用扁锉锉平了机器的备件。 ❸ march in an orderly manner 列队行进：The cattle ～ into the field.牛群一头跟着一头走到地里去。

filing/ˈfaɪlɪŋ/

n. ❶ the act of putting documents, letters, etc. into a file 存档；归档 ❷ (*pl.*) very small pieces of metal, made when a larger piece of metal is filed 锉屑

fill/fɪl/

I　*v.* make sth. full of; become full of sth. （使）充满；装满：Fill this glass with wine.给这杯子斟满酒。/I'm ～ed with joy.我内心充满喜悦。/Fill in the blanks of the following sentences. 填充下列句子中的空白。 ‖ ～ **up** 装满；注满 Ⅱ *n.* an amount of sth. as much as one can eat or drink 饱满；充足：The dog ran to its water bowl and drank its ～.狗跑到水碗跟前喝了个够。

filler/ˈfɪlə/

n. sth. used to fill a cavity or to increase the bulk of sth. 填充物，填料

filling/ˈfɪlɪŋ/

n. ❶ a small amount of metal or other material used to fill a hole in a tooth（补牙的）填料：have a ～ at the dentist's. 在牙科诊所补一颗牙 ❷ food put inside a sandwich, cake, pie, etc.（三明治、蛋糕、馅饼等的）馅 ❸ soft material used to fill cushions, pillows, etc.（靠垫、枕头等的）填充物，填料

film/fɪlm/

I　*n.* ❶ a roll or sheet of thin flexible light sensitive material for use in photography 胶卷；软片：Jim is just putting a new roll of ～ into his camera.吉姆正好在往照相机里装一卷新胶卷。 ❷ a story or event recorded by a camera as a set of moving images and shown in a cinema or on television 电影；影片：I like to see colour ～s.我喜欢看彩色影片。 ❸ a thin covering 薄层：There's a ～ of mist outside before sunrise in spring. 春季日出前，户外通常有一层薄雾。 Ⅱ *v.* ❶ become or appear to become covered with a thin layer of sth. 变得朦胧：Tears ～ed her eyes.泪水模糊了她的双眼。 ❷ make a cinema or television film (of)（把……）拍成电影：We'll ～ this play.我们将把一剧本拍成电影。

filmy/ˈfɪlmi/

adj. (filmier, filmiest) thin and almost transparent 薄而几乎透明的：～ white voile 薄如蝉翼的白纱 ‖ **filminess** *n.* 薄膜状态

filter/ˈfɪltə(r)/

I　*n.* a coloured glass (as used on a camera lens) which allows light of certain wave lengths to pass through; (in radio) a device which separates alternating current of one frequency from others 滤光器；滤波镜；滤波器：The ～ in that telescope was broken by the boy.那个望远镜中的滤光器被这男孩弄破了。 Ⅱ *v.* (cause to) flow through a filter; purify (a liquid) by using a filter（使）过滤：The running water is ～ed through charcoal.自来水是用木炭过滤的。/The dross was ～ed from the solution.渣滓从溶液中滤出了。

filth/fɪlθ/

n. foul, disgusting dirt 肮脏，污秽：Go and wash off the ～ on your face.去洗掉脸上的脏东西。

filthy/ˈfɪlθi/

adj. ❶ disgustingly dirty 肮脏的 ❷ obscene; immorally foul 猥亵的，下流的：a ～ story 下流的故事

filtrate /ˈfɪltreɪt/

　　n. liquid that has passed through a filter 滤液

fin /fɪn/

　　n. ❶ one of the parts of its body which a fish uses for swimming 鳍 ❷ sth. shaped like a fin(e.g.on a bomb or rocket) 鳍状物(例如炸弹或火箭的安定翼)

final /ˈfaɪnl/

　　Ⅰ *adj.* ❶ last;coming at the end 最后的;最终的:The ～ decision was made after a warm discussion. 热烈讨论之后, 做出了最后的决定。❷ (of a decision, offer, etc.)that cannot be changed 决定性的:What was the ～ score of the football match? 足球比赛的结果怎么样? Ⅱ *n.* (usually *pl.*)❶ the last and most important examinations in a college course 期终考试:When do you take your ～s? 你们什么时候进行期末考试? ❷ the last and most important in a set of matches 决赛:We won the football ～s.我们赢了足球决赛。

finale /fɪˈnɑːli/

　　n. the last division of a piece of music or a musical show (音乐的)终曲;终场:That wonderful party made a fitting ～ to their visit.那次非常精彩的宴会使他们的访问圆满地结束了。

finality /faɪˈnæləti/

　　n. the fact of being an irreversible ending 不可逆转性;不可改变性;定局,终结:"No!"He said with ～."不,"他斩钉截铁地说。

finalize /ˈfaɪnəlaɪz/

　　v. bring (a plan, arrangement, etc.) into a finished and complete form 把(计划、安排等)最后定下来:The agreement between the two countries has now been ～.两国间的协定现在已经敲定。

finally /ˈfaɪnəli/

　　adv. ❶ at last 最终, 终于:After several delays,the plane ～ left at six o'clock.几经耽误,飞机最终六点钟起飞了。❷ as the last of a number of things;lastly 最后(一点):And ～,I'd just like to say this.最后,我想说说这件事。❸ so as not to

allow further change 决定性地;不可改变地:It's not ～ settled yet.这还没有最后决定。

finance /ˈfaɪnæns/

　　Ⅰ *n.* the commercial or government activity of providing funds and capital 财政;金融:The Minister of Finance made a report at the conference.财政部长在大会上做了一个报告。Ⅱ *v.* provide money for 供给经费:Usually parents ～ their children's college education in China.在中国通常由父母资助子女上大学。

financial /faɪˈnænʃl/

　　adj. relating to or involving money 金融的;财政的:in ～ difficulties 财政困难/The ～ situation seems to be much improved.财政状况看来有很大改善。

find /faɪnd/

　　Ⅰ *v.* (found)❶ discover sth. by searching;get sb.or sth.that was hidden,lost,or not known 找到:The missing child hasn't been found yet.那走丢的孩子还没有找到。❷ discover (sb. or sth.) to be, by chance or experience 发现:We dug 5 metres and then found water.我们挖了5米便发现了水。❸ obtain by effort 得出:Can you ～ the answer to this problem? 你能得出这道题的答案吗? ❹ become aware of by chance or experience 感觉;觉得:I found the new method effective. 我觉得新方法很有效。‖ ～ sb. out 查明;揭发/ ～ sth. out 问明;查出 Ⅱ *n.* sth. good or valuable that is found 珍贵的发现物:The antiquary made a ～ at antique auction.这古物收藏家在古董拍卖场上发现了珍贵文物。‖ ～ing *n.* 发现;找到;发现物;结果,结论

fine /faɪn/

　　Ⅰ *adj.* ❶ clear;bright;not raining 晴朗的:What a ～ day it is today! 今天天气多么晴朗! ❷ of superior grade or quality 精美的:This is a ～ carving.这是件精美的雕刻。❸ very thin or delicate 纤细的:Sand is ～r than gravel.沙比碎石更细。/ Thread is ～r than rope.线比绳细。❹ in good health or reasonably happy (身体)很好的;开心的:"How are you?""Fine, thanks.""你好吗?""很好,谢谢。"Ⅱ *adv.*

❶very well 很好：That skirt suits me ～. 那件裙子很适合我。❷ in a delicate way 细微地；精美地；难于察觉地：～-spun 细纺的 Ⅲ *n.*a sum of money that must be paid as a punishment for breaking a law or rule 罚金；罚款 Ⅳ *v.* punish sb. by a fine 处某人以罚款：She was ～d ＄300. 她被罚款 300 美金。

fineness /ˈfaɪnnəs/
n. ❶ the quality of being made of thin threads or lines very close together；the state or quality of being fine 纤细；精细度；精致 ❷ the quality of sth. 纯度；成色：the ～ of the gold 黄金的成色

finery /ˈfaɪnəri/
*n.*fine clothes or decorations 华丽的服饰；精致的装饰

finesse /fɪˈnes/
n. an ability to deal with difficult situations in a skilful way 手段；技巧；策略

finger /ˈfɪŋɡə(r)/
Ⅰ *n.*❶ one of the five end parts of the hand，especially one other than the thumb 手指（尤指拇指之外的指头）：There are five ～s (or four ～s and one thumb) on each hand.每只手有五个手指（四个手指和一个大拇指）。❷ the part of a glove that covers a finger（手套），指套 ❸ anything like a finger 指状物 Ⅱ *v.* touch or feel with the fingers 用手指触摸：He ～ed his chin.他用手指摸着下巴。

fingernail /ˈfɪŋɡəneɪl/
*n.*the nail on a finger 指甲

fingerprint /ˈfɪŋɡəprɪnt/
*n.*an impression or mark made on a surface by a person's fingertip，especially as used for identifying individuals from the unique pattern of whorls and lines 指纹，指印

finish /ˈfɪnɪʃ/
Ⅰ *v.* ❶ end；complete 结束；完成：～ school 毕业／～ a composition 做好文章／Every day I start work at 9:00 a.m. and ～ at 5:00 p.m.我每天上午九点开始工作，下午五点结束。/Have you ～ed reading the book? 你已读完那本书了吗? /The concert has just ～ed.音乐会刚结束。/

Have you ～ed with the dictionary? 这本词典你用完了吗? ❷ eat，drink or use what is left of sth.吃完；喝完；用完：We might as well ～ the cake；there isn't much left. 咱们索性把蛋糕吃完吧，也没剩多少了。❸ complete sth.or make sth. perfect 使……臻于完美；加工：I have a set of beautifully ～ed chinaware.我有一套加工精美的瓷器。❹ exhaust sb.completely 使某人筋疲力尽 ❺ destroy sb.or sth.毁坏；消灭：That fever nearly ～ed him off. 那次高烧险些要了他的命。 Ⅱ *n.*the end of sth.or the last part of sth. 结束；结尾；最后部分：fight the enemy to the ～ 和敌人战斗到底 ‖ ～ off 做完；吃光

finished /ˈfɪnɪʃt/
*adj.*❶ properly made and perfected 完美的，精致的：the ～ product 精致的产品/a very ～ performance 完美的表演 ❷ ended or brought to an end 完结（完成）了的，结束了的：The workmen were ～ by 7:00.工人们在七点以前收工。 ❸ no longer existing or happening 不再存在的；不再发生的：If the bank refuses to lend us the money，we're ～! 如果银行拒绝借钱给我们，我们就完蛋了!

finite /ˈfaɪnaɪt/
*adj.*❶ having limits or bounds 有限的：Human's understanding is ～.人类的理解力是有限的。 ❷ limited by number and person 受人称和数限制的，限定的："Am" is a ～ form of the verb "be"."Am"是动词"be"的一种限定形式。

fir /fɜː(r)/
*n.*a type of evergreen tree which has thin leaves shaped like needles 枞树；冷杉

fire /ˈfaɪə(r)/
Ⅰ *n.*❶ the hot，bright flames produced by things that are burning 火：The house was on ～.这栋房子失火了。❷ a mass of burning material，heat，etc. 炉火：There's a ～ in the next room.隔壁房间有炉火。❸ a destructive burning of sth. which destroys buildings，forests，etc. 火灾：A single spark can start a prairie ～. 星星之火，可以燎原。❹ the shooting by weapons，especially by guns；firing 射击；

开火：Cease ～! 停火! ‖ **catch**（**take**）～
着火/**set** ～ **to sth.** 纵火/**make a** ～ 生火 Ⅱ
v. ❶ (of a person or gun) shoot off bullets
射击；开火：The police ～d at the robbers.
警察朝强盗开火。❷ set fire to 点火；燃
烧：The soldier ～d a haystack. 士兵点燃了
干草堆。❸ make a fire 生火（炉子）：They
～d a furnace. 他们生了一炉火。‖ ～ **a-
larm** *n.* 火警/ ～ **man** *n.* 消防队员/ ～
place *n.* 壁炉

firecracker /ˈfaɪəˌkrækə(r)/
n. firework consisting of a small explosive
charge and fuse in a heavy paper casing
鞭炮，爆竹

firewall /ˈfaɪəwɔːl/
n. ❶ a wall or partition designed to check
the spread of a fire 防火墙，隔火墙 ❷ a
part of a computer network that prevents
unauthorized access (计算机的) 防火墙

firework /ˈfaɪəwɜːk/
n. a small device containing powder that
burns or explodes and produces bright
coloured lights and loud noises, used especially at celebrations 烟火；烟花：a ～(s)
display 放烟火

firing /ˈfaɪərɪŋ/
n. ❶ the action of setting fire to sth. 点
燃，引火：the deliberate ～ of a oil well
故意引燃油井 ❷ the discharging of a
gun or other weapon 开枪；开火；(武器
的) 发射 ❸ the dismissal of an employee
from a job 解雇，炒鱿鱼；革职：They are
protesting against the ～ of a colleague.
他们正在因一位同事被开除而抗议。

firm /fɜːm/
Ⅰ *adj.* ❶ solidly fixed in a place；not soft
or yielding to pressure 牢固的；稳固的；
坚硬的：You must hang the clock on a ～
nail or it will fall. 你得把钟挂在牢固的钉
子上，否则它会掉下来的。❷ not shak-
able or unlikely to change 坚定的：The
Chinese people are ～ in taking the road
of socialism. 中国人民坚决走社会主义道
路。Ⅱ *n.* an organization which sells or
produces sth. or provides a service which
people for 公司 ‖ ～**ly** *adv.* 坚定地/ ～**ness**
n. 坚定

firmly /ˈfɜːmli/

adv. in a firm manner 坚固地；坚定地；稳
定地：He held his son's hand ～ to be
sure that the boy did not bow either. 他紧
握儿子的手，以确保孩子也不鞠躬。/
The fence posts were fixed ～ in the
ground. 篱笆桩被牢牢地埋在地里。

first /fɜːst/
Ⅰ *num.* the one that happens or comes before all the others of the same kind 第一：
New Year's Day is the ～ day of the year.
元旦是一年的第一天。Ⅱ *adv.* for the initial time 第一；首次：She came ～ in the
race. 她赛跑得了第一。Ⅲ *n.* ❶ the beginning 开始；开端 ❷ the first person or
thing 第一名；第一个：They were the ～
to arrive at the meeting. 他们最早到会。
‖ ～ **of all** 首先/**at** ～ 起先/**from** ～ **to
last** 自始至终

fish /fɪʃ/
Ⅰ *n.* (*pl.* fish or ～es) a kind of cold-
blooded animal that lives in water 鱼；鱼
类：I caught two ～ in the pond yesterday. 我昨天在塘里捉到了两条鱼。Ⅱ *v.*
try to catch fish for food or as a form of
sport or recreation 捕鱼；钓鱼：My father
like to ～ all day in the river on Sunday.
星期天我父亲喜欢整天在河里钓鱼。

fisherman /ˈfɪʃəmən/
n. (*pl.* -men) a person who catches fish
for sport or his living 钓鱼者；渔民：Some
fishermen are unlucky. Instead of catching
fish, they catch old boots and rubbish. 有
些垂钓者不走运，没钓到鱼，却钓上破靴
子和垃圾。

fishery /ˈfɪʃəri/
n. (*pl.* -ies) ❶ a part of the sea where fishing is carried on 渔场 ❷ the business of
catching fish 渔业；水产业

fishy /ˈfɪʃi/
adj. ❶ smelling or tasting like fish 鱼腥
味的；鱼味的 ❷ causing a feeling of
doubt 可疑的：He felt there seemed to be
something ～ going on. 他觉得好像有可
疑的事情发生。

fission /ˈfɪʃn/
n. (usually of the breaking up of an atom
in a nuclear explosion) process of divid-

ing into several parts（原子核）裂变

fist /fɪst/

　　n. a tightly closed hand 拳头：He struck me with his ～. 他用拳头打我。/He shook his ～ at me in anger. 他愤怒地对我挥拳头。

fit[1] /fɪt/

　　Ⅰ *adj.* ❶ meeting adequate standards for a purpose 合适的；适宜的：This coat isn't ～ for me to wear. 这件大衣不适合我穿。❷ strong and healthy 健康的；身体好的：My grandfather is as ～ as a fiddle. 我祖父十分健康。Ⅱ *v.*(-tt-) ❶ be the right measure, shape and size for sb. or sth. 合身；合适：Does your new dress ～ well? 你的新衣穿着合身吗？ ❷ put into place 装配：Mr. Smith ～ted an air conditioner in his bedroom. 史密斯先生在自己的卧室里安装了一台空调。‖ ～ **in with** 顺应；适合

fit[2] /fɪt/

　　n. ❶ a sudden（usually short）attack of illness（病的）突然发作：He has a ～ of coughing. 他突然一阵咳嗽。❷ a sudden display of anger, etc.; outburst 一阵；突发（怒气等）：They were in ～s of laughter. 他们一阵又一阵地哈哈大笑。❸ the particular way in which sth. fits 合适：My coat is a good ～. 我的上衣很合身。‖ **by ～s and starts** 时冷时热地；间歇地

fitful /ˈfɪtfl/

　　adj. irregular; happening for short periods of time 间歇的，一阵一阵的，不规则的：～ showers of rain 一阵阵的大雨 ‖ ～**ly** *adv.* 断断续续地：He slept ～. 他睡睡醒醒。

fitment /ˈfɪtmənt/

　　n. a piece of fitted furniture（安装好了的）设备，家具：bathroom ～s 浴室设备

fitness /ˈfɪtnəs/

　　n. ❶ the state of being physically fit（身体）健康；健壮：They're doing exercises to improve their ～. 他们在做体操以增进健康。❷ the quality of being suitable 适合，恰当：No one questions her ～ for the job. 没有人对她能胜任这项工作表示怀疑。

fitted /ˈfɪtɪd/

　　adj. ❶ including（a part, piece of apparatus, etc.）配有（零件、附件等）的：Is the car ～ with a radio? 这辆车装有收音机吗？ ❷ fixed in a place 固定于一处的：～ carpet 固定的地毯 /～ cupboards 固定的碗柜

fitter /ˈfɪtə(r)/

　　n. ❶ a person who puts together, adjusts and repairs machines or electrical parts 装配工，修理工：a gas ～ 煤气装配工 ❷ a person who cuts out clothes and makes them the correct size for other people 试衣匠，试样裁缝

fitting[1] /ˈfɪtɪŋ/

　　adj. right for the purpose or occasion; suitable 恰当的；相称的；适合的：It is ～ that we should honour their memory. 我们纪念他们是适宜的。/It was ～ that he should be here to receive the prize in person. 他应该亲自来领奖才对。

fitting[2] /ˈfɪtɪŋ/

　　n. ❶ sth. necessary that is fixed into a building but able to be moved（房屋内的）设备，器材，家具：electric light ～s 电灯装置 ❷ an occasion when one puts on clothes that are being made for one, to see if they fit 试衣，试穿：I'm going for a ～ on Tuesday. 我星期二去试衣服。

five /faɪv/

　　num. the number 5，五 ‖ **fifth** /fɪfθ/ *num.* 第五

fix /fɪks/

　　Ⅰ *v.* ❶ fasten firmly in position 使固定；安装：Please ～ the world map on the wall. 请把这幅世界地图钉在墙上。❷ repair 修理：I had my broken watch ～ed. 我把我的破表送去修了。❸ arrange and establish（an exact time, place, price, etc.）, especially through agreement 确定；安排：Let's ～ a date for the next meeting. 让我们给下次会议订个日期吧。Ⅱ *n.* an awkward or difficult position 困境；窘境：If I can't pass the exam, I'll be in a ～. 如果我考试不及格，就会陷入困境。‖ ～ **up** 提供；安排

fixed /fɪkst/

*adj.*fastened;not movable or change-able 固定的;确定的,不变的:The tables are firmly ～ to the floor.这些桌子牢牢地固定在地板上。/That date is ～ now.现在日期已经确定。/He has very ～ ideas on this subject.在这个问题上他很坚持己见。

fixedly /ˈfɪksɪdli/
adv.(to look at sb. or sth.) steadily and continuously 目不转睛地:He stared ～ at the woman in black.他盯着看那个穿黑衣裳的女人。

fixity /ˈfɪksəti/
*n.*the quality of being fixed;firmness 固定性,稳定性:～ of purpose 目标的固定

fixture /ˈfɪkstʃə(r)/
*n.*❶ a fixed piece of furniture 固定家具:The fireplace is a ～.壁炉是固定家具。❷ sporting events fixed on an agreed date (定时举行的)体育比赛:The football team has a ～ on Sundays.这个足球队星期日有一场固定的比赛。❸ a person or thing that stays in one place,job, or other situation 固定于某种局面(或某地)的人(或物);固守于某职位的人:She has lunch in that restaurant so often that she is considered a ～.她常在那家餐馆吃午饭,因此被认为是那儿的常客。

fizz /fɪz/
Ⅰ *v.*make a sound like that of bubbles of gas coming out of a liquid 嘶嘶地响 Ⅱ *n.* ❶ this sound 嘶嘶声 ❷ an effervescent beverage 发泡饮料 ‖ ～y *adj.*嘶嘶作响的:a ～y drink 汽水

fizzle /ˈfɪzl/
*v.*end or fail in a weak and disappointing way 虎头蛇尾般地结束;夭折:His plans ～d out.他的计划结果夭折了。

flabby /ˈflæbi/
*adj.*fat with loose flesh 肥胖且松弛的

flaccid /ˈflæksɪd/
*adj.*not firm enough;weak and soft 软弱无力的:～ plant stems 萎蔫的茎秆

flag /flæg/
Ⅰ *n.*a coloured piece of cloth which is used as a sign 旗:At the top of the building there is a red ～.大楼楼顶有一面红旗。/Our national ～ is the Five-Starred Red Flag.我们的国旗是五星红旗。/The ～ fluttered in the breeze.旗帜在微风中飘扬。Ⅱ *v.*(-gg-) ❶ decorate with flags 用旗帜装饰:～ the house 用旗帜装饰房屋 ❷ signal to (sb.) or stop (a train, etc.) by waving a flag 用旗示意;用旗使(火车等)停下:～ down a train 挥动旗帜使火车停下来

flagpole /ˈflæɡpəʊl/
*n.*a long pole to raise a flag on, too large to hold in the hand 旗杆

flagrant /ˈfleɪɡrənt/
adj.(of sth. dishonest or bad) not hidden 罪恶昭彰的;明目张胆的;公然的:～ disobedience 公然违抗

flair /fleə(r)/
*n.*a natural ability to do sth. 天赋,才华:He has a ～ for mathematics.他在数学方面有天赋。

flake /fleɪk/
Ⅰ *n.*a small thin piece of sth., especially one that has broken off a larger piece 小薄片:～s of snow 雪片 Ⅱ *v.*come off in small thin pieces 以小片状剥落下来:The paint is flaking.这油漆斑驳脱落。

flame /fleɪm/
Ⅰ *n.*a hot bright stream of burning gas of a fire 火焰;火舌:The hospital was in ～s when the fire-engine arrived.消防车到达的时候,医院已经着火了。Ⅱ *v.* ❶ be a-flame or in flames 燃烧;焚烧:The fire ～d in the stove.火炉中升起火舌。❷ become red, bright, etc. by or as if by burning 照亮;使成火红色:The candles ～d brighter.烛光更加亮了。/Her cheeks ～d red.她的双颊变得通红。

flaming /ˈfleɪmɪŋ/
*adj.*very hot or bright 酷热的;鲜艳的;亮丽的:～ summer 酷热的夏天/ ～ red hair 亮丽的红发

flamingo /fləˈmɪŋɡəʊ/
*n.*a type of bird with long legs and neck and pinkish feathers 火烈鸟,火鹤,红鹤

flammable /ˈflæməbl/
*adj.*easily set on fire 易燃的:Pyjamas made from ～ material have been re-

moved from most shops.大部分商店都不再出售用易燃材料做的睡衣了。

flank/flæŋk/

　I *n*.❶ the side of a person or animal,between the ribs and the hip 腰窝：When fighting,I gave the enemy a heavy blow on the ～.格斗时,我在敌人的腰窝上猛击一拳。❷ the side of a building or mountain (山或建筑的)侧面：The outline of the ～ of the mountain against the horizon is clear.地平线衬托的山侧的轮廓清晰可辨。Ⅱ *v*. be placed beside sth. 在……的侧面：Tian'anmen Square is ～ed by the Great Hall of the People and the Museum of Chinese History.天安门广场的两侧是人民大会堂和中国历史博物馆。

flannel/ˈflænl/

　n.a soft,warm woollen cloth 法兰绒：It's a blanket made of ～.这是一条用法兰绒做的毯子。

flap/flæp/

　Ⅰ *n*.❶ a piece of sth.which hangs down or covers an opening (袋)盖；信封口盖：I stuck down the ～ of the envelope.我把信的封口粘住了。❷ a movement of a wing or an arm from side to side or up and down；the sound of sth.making such a movement (翅膀的)振动；(手臂的)挥动,振动声；挥舞声：I heard the ～ of wings.我听见了翅膀拍动的声音。Ⅱ *v*.(-pp-) wave up and down or from side to side 上下(或左右)移动；轻拍：The large, white sails,like wings of birds,～ped in the gentle wind.巨大、雪白的船帆,像鸟儿的翅膀在微风中拍打。

flare/fleə(r)/

　Ⅰ *n*.a bright but unsteady light or flame (摇曳的)光；(闪耀的)火光：The sentry saw the sudden ～ of a flashlight in the darkness.哨兵看见手电筒在黑暗中突然闪出亮光。Ⅱ *v*. ❶ burn brightly,but with an unsteady flame or for a short time (火光)闪耀；(摇曳着)燃烧：The candle began to ～ in the room.烛光开始在房间里摇曳。❷ suddenly become angry (突然)发火：Hearing the bad news, he ～d up.听到坏消息,他勃然大怒。

flash/flæʃ/

　Ⅰ *n*.❶ a sudden quick bright light 闪光：a ～ of lightning 闪电 ❷ instant；a short time 瞬间：She said that she would come back in a ～.她说她马上就回来。Ⅱ *v*.❶ shine very brightly for a short time；make a flash in this way (使)闪耀,闪光：The guard ～ed his torch into the dark hole. 卫兵用手电筒往黑洞里照。❷ move very fast 飞驰；掠过：A jet ～ed across the sky.一架喷气式飞机在空中掠过。

flashback/ˈflæʃbæk/

　n.❶ a scene in a film,play,etc.that goes back in time to show what happened earlier in the story (电影等的)闪回；(戏剧等的)倒叙：The events of his childhood are shown in (a) ～.他童年的往事是用倒叙来表现的。❷ a burst of flame moving rapidly back through a tube,into a container,etc.回烧,回火

flasher/ˈflæʃə(r)/

　n. sth.that flashes,such as a traffic signal or a light on a car 闪光物(如交通信号灯、车灯等)

flashgun/ˈflæʃɡʌn/

　n. a piece of equipment which holds a flashbulb and makes it work at the moment when the photograph is taken 闪光枪(引发闪光灯泡以配合拍摄的装置)

flashlight/ˈflæʃlaɪt/

　n.❶ a flashing light used for signals and in lighthouses (灯塔里的)闪光信号灯 ❷ a small electric light carried in the hand to give light；an electric torch 手电筒

flashpoint/ˈflæʃpɔɪnt/

　n.❶ a time or place at which anger or violence is about to break out (怒气、暴力等的)骤发之地；导火线；激化时刻：The port is a ～ between gangs.这座港口是两个帮派的纷争之地。❷ the temperature at which vapour from oil,etc.will ignite 闪点,燃点,引火点

flashy/ˈflæʃi/

　adj. unpleasantly big,bright,decorated, etc.,and perhaps not of good quality 华而不实的；俗气的：a large ～ car 华而不实的大轿车/cheap ～ clothes 便宜而俗气

的衣裳‖ **flashily** *adv.* 俗气地：flashily dressed 穿得俗不可耐的

flask/flɑːsk/
n. ❶ a type of bottle used in laboratories（实验室用的）烧瓶 ❷ a flat bottle for carrying in the pocket or fastened to one's belt,etc. 扁水瓶；扁酒瓶（便于放进口袋或挂在皮带上携带）❸ a vacuum container made in such a way that liquid put into it remains at the same temperature for a long time 保温瓶；热水瓶

flat/flæt/
Ⅰ *adj.* ❶ smooth and level；even 平坦的；平整的；光滑均匀的：The house has a ～ top. 这栋楼的屋顶是平的。 ❷ having a broad level surface but little height or depth 低的；漏的；浅的 ❸ complete；with no more argument 完全的；断然的：He gave a ～ refusal to my invitation. 他断然拒绝了我的邀请。 Ⅱ *n.* a group of living rooms on one floor 单元住房；套间：The building is divided into many ～s. 这栋楼房有许多套间。

flatly/'flætli/
adv. ❶ showing little interest or emotion 冷淡地 ❷ in a firm and unequivocal manner；absolutely 断然地，毫不迟疑地；绝对地：They ～ refused to accept our proposal. 他们断然拒绝我们的提议。 ❸ in a smooth and even way 平坦地；光滑地：He applied the paint～. 他平整地涂上颜料。

flatten/'flætn/
v. make or become flat（使）平坦：The hills ～ed（out）as they came near the sea. 丘陵地带越接近海边，地势越平坦。 /The blacksmith ～ed（out）a piece of metal by hammering it. 铁匠把一块金属锤平。

flatter/'flætə(r)/
v. ❶ praise（someone）too much or insincerely,especially in order to gain advantage 谄媚；奉承：She ～ed me about my cooking skill. 她奉承我厨艺。 ❷ give pleasure to 使得意：I feel greatly ～ed by your invitation. 蒙你邀请,不胜荣幸。 ‖ ～y *n.* 奉承；恭维

flaunt/flɔːnt/
v. behave in a bad or foolish way to make people take notice 炫耀,夸耀,夸示：She was ～ing her new clothes. 她正在炫耀她的新衣服。

flavo(u)r/'fleɪvə(r)/
n. ❶ the quality of a particular food or drinks as perceived by the taste buds（食物或饮料的）口味,味道,滋味：The jam has a delicious ～. 这果酱味道鲜美。 ❷ a particular quality or characteristic 特别风味：This novel has a humorous ～. 这篇小说有幽默风味。

flavo(u)ring/'fleɪvərɪŋ/
n. sth. used to give a flavo(u)r to food or drink 调味品,调味料,调味剂

flaw/flɔː/
n. ❶ a fault or a defect 缺陷,缺点,瑕疵：Greed is a ～ in her character. 贪心是她品格上的一个缺点。 ❷ a crack 裂纹；裂痕：There is a ～ in the old china plate. 古瓷盘上有一条裂纹。 ‖ ～ed *adj.* 有缺陷的,有裂纹的：This china is ～ed. 这件瓷器上有裂纹。

flawless/'flɔːlɪs/
adj. without a flaw and there fore perfect 无瑕的；完美的：a ～ performance 完美的表演 ‖ ～ly *adv.* 无暇地；完美地/ ～ness *n.* 完美无缺

flea/fliː/
n. a small jumping insect that feeds on human and animal blood 蚤 ‖ a ～ in one's ear 尖锐的批评；严厉的责难

fleck/flek/
Ⅰ *n.* a small patch of colour or light 小色斑；小光斑 Ⅱ *v.* mark or dot with small patches of colour or particles of sth. 给……饰以小色点；用小斑点点缀

flee/fliː/
v.（fled）run away from 逃走；逃离：The enemy troops fled in disorder. 敌军狼狈逃窜。 /Fleeing Germany, Einstein went first to France. 爱因斯坦逃离德国以后,先到了法国。

fleece/fliːs/
Ⅰ *n.* ❶ the woolly covering of a sheep or goat 羊毛 ❷ a soft fabric or a piece of clothing made from this 羊毛状织物 Ⅱ *v.*

F

swindle someone or deprive them of sth. by trickery（尤指用诈骗）诈取（某人）：We were ~d by a tout for tickets.我们被票贩子狠宰了一刀。

fleet/fliːt/

n. ❶ a group of warships, naval aircraft, etc. under one command 船队, 舰队：the second ~ 第二舰队 ❷ a group of buses, aircraft, etc. under one control 车队；机群

flesh/fleʃ/

Ⅰ *n.* the soft part consisting of muscle and fat between the skin and bones of animal or a human 肉：The Great Wall was made not only of stone and earth, but also of the ~ and blood of millions of men. 长城不仅是用石头与泥土筑成的, 而且是用数以百万计人的血肉筑成的。Ⅱ *v.* add more details or information to sth. 充实（某事物）；增加细节（或详情）：You need to ~ out your paper before you hand it in. 上交之前, 你的论文需要增加一些具体材料。

fleshly/ˈfleʃli/

adj. connected with physical and sexual desires 性欲的, 肉欲的：~ desires 情欲

fleshy/ˈfleʃi/

adj. ❶ having much flesh；fat 多肉的, 肥胖的：~ cheeks 丰腴的双颊 ❷ of or like flesh 肉的；似肉的：a ~ texture 肉质（肉样）结构

flex/fleks/

v. bend, move or stretch（one's limbs, etc.）屈伸, 活动（四肢）：He ~ed his stiff arm slowly. 他慢慢地弯曲他那僵硬的手臂。

flexible/ˈfleksəbl/

adj. ❶ easily bent without breaking 易弯曲的；柔韧的：Leather, rubber and wire are ~.皮革、橡皮和金属丝是柔韧的。❷ able to change to suit new conditions or situations 能适应新情况的；不变的；灵活的：For further reform and opening-up we need an economic policy that is more ~.为了进一步改革开放, 我们需要更为灵活的经济政策。‖ **flexibly** *adv.* 柔韧地/**flexibility** *n.* 柔韧性；灵活性

flick/flɪk/

Ⅰ *n.* ❶ a quick light blow 快速轻击；轻弹 ❷ a short sudden movement 短暂而突然的动作；猛然一动：He turned the pancake over with a strong ~ of his wrist.他手腕猛一抖就把饼翻了过来。Ⅱ *v.* hit sth. with a sudden quick movement 轻击；轻拍；轻弹；轻拂：He ~ed the horse with his whip.他用鞭轻抽他的马。

flicker/ˈflɪkə(r)/

Ⅰ *v.* burn unsteadily；shine with an unsteady light（火光）闪烁, 摇曳；忽隐忽现：The candle was ~ing in wind.烛光在风中忽隐忽现。Ⅱ *n.* light shining in an unsteady way（光）闪烁, 摇曳：In the ~ of a candle she seemed to see a figure.在摇晃的烛光中她似乎看见了一个人影。

flight/flaɪt/

n. ❶ the act of flying 飞；飞翔：I'm interested in studying the ~ of birds.我对研究鸟的飞翔很感兴趣。❷ a plane making a particular journey 航班：Flight No. 114 to Tibet is ready to leave.飞西藏的114航班即将起飞。❸ a series of stairs between two floors or landings 楼梯；阶梯：When he stepped downstairs, he fell down from a ~.当他下楼时, 从阶梯上摔了下来。❹ the act of running away 逃跑：The enemy were put to ~.敌人被打得四处逃窜。

flimsy/ˈflɪmzi/

adj. not strongly made or easily torn because of poor material（因质地差而）不结实的, 易撕破的, 易损坏的

flinders/ˈflɪndəz/

n.（*pl.*）small fragments or splinters 碎片, 破片：break sth. in ~ 打碎某物

fling/flɪŋ/

Ⅰ *v.*（flung）❶ throw sth. violently, angrily or hurriedly 扔；抛；投；掷：He flung a stone at the dog.他扔石头打狗。❷ put or push sb. or sth. quickly or roughly and forcefully 猛推；使劲地推开：~ the books on the floor 把书摔在地板上 /~ the door open 把门猛地推开 ❸ move（one's arms, legs, etc.）violently, hurriedly, and carelessly or angrily 急伸；挥动（手臂、腿等）；猛动（身体或身体部位）：He flung his arms into the air.他猛地伸

出双臂。Ⅱ *n.* ❶ the act of flinging; throw 扔;抛;掷 ❷ an impetuous act; a wild time 放纵;放肆:He had a few ~s in his younger days.他年轻时也曾有过几次风流韵事。

flint/ˈflɪnt/

n. ❶ a very hard type of stone 燧石:This layer of rock contains a lot of ~.这一岩层中有大量燧石。❷ a stone in a cigarette lighter, etc. which produces a spark when hit with a piece of steel (打火机等的)打火石

flip/flɪp/

v. (-pp-) move, push, or throw sth. with a sudden sharp movement (猛地)移动,弹,推,扔

flipper/ˈflɪpə(r)/

n. ❶ a broad flat limb of certain sea creatures (e.g. the seal) which helps it to swim (海豹等的)鳍状肢 ❷ a long piece of rubber attachment worn on the foot to help people to swim (游泳用的)橡皮脚蹼

flirt/flɜːt/

Ⅰ *v.* ❶ behave as though trying to attract sb. for amusement 调情;打情骂俏:She was ~ing with him. 她正在跟他打情骂俏。❷ think about sth. not very seriously 不认真考虑 He ~ed with the idea. 他并没有认真考虑这个主意。Ⅱ *n.* a person who habitually flirts 调情者 ‖ ~**ation** *n.* 调情;调戏

flit/flɪt/

v. (-tt-) move quickly and lightly from place to place 轻快地掠过:The birds were ~ting about in the trees. 鸟儿在树木间轻快地飞来飞去。

float/fləʊt/

Ⅰ *v.* be held on the surface of a liquid, or up in air move with moving liquid 漂浮;浮动:Wood can ~ on water. 木头能浮在水面。Ⅱ *n.* ❶ the act or process of floating 漂浮:Did you see the slow ~ of a sail on the river? 你见过帆船在河上缓缓漂行吗? ❷ sth. that floats, especially a piece of wood or other light object used on a fishing line or to support the edge of

a fishing net 漂浮物;鱼漂,浮子:A cork on a fish line is a ~.钓鱼丝上的软木是浮子。

floating/ˈfləʊtɪŋ/

adj. ❶ not fixed or settled in a particular place 不固定的;流动的,浮动的:London has a large ~ population. 伦敦的流动人口很多。❷ (of a body part) not properly connected or not in the usual place (身体部位)浮动的,不在正常位置的:a ~ kidney 游动肾

flock/flɒk/

Ⅰ *n.* ❶ a group of animals or birds that stay together (鸟、牛、羊)群:The dog can watch over a ~ of sheep. 这狗能看守一群绵羊。❷ a group of people; crowd 人群:Visitors came in ~s to see the new bridge. 成群的人来参观这座新桥。Ⅱ *v.* gather in large numbers; come or go in large numbers 群集;聚集;蜂拥:Birds of a feather ~ together. 物以类聚,人以群分。

floe/fləʊ/

n. a large mass of ice floating on the surface of the sea 大片浮冰,浮冰块

flog/flɒg/

v. (-gg-) ❶ hit many times very hard with a stick or whip 多次重打;抽打;鞭打 ❷ sell 出售 ‖ ~**ging** *n.* 重打

flood/flʌd/

Ⅰ *n.* ❶ the covering with water of a place that is usually dry; a great overflow of water 洪水;水灾:The soldiers are fighting against the mountain flood. 士兵们正与山洪搏斗。/The river is in ~.这条河泛滥了。❷ a large quantity or flow 大批;大量:I had a ~ of cards on Christmas Day.圣诞节那天我收到了一大堆贺卡。Ⅱ *v.* become so full that it spreads out 淹没;泛滥:The river ~ed the field in the rainy season.雨季,这条河淹没了田野。

floodgate/ˈflʌdgeɪt/

n. ❶ a gate used for controlling the flow from a large body of water 防洪闸(门),泄水闸(门) ❷ (open the ~) allow feelings to be suddenly expressed or action suddenly taken after being forcibly held back 让被强忍住的感情突然爆发;使硬被克制的行为突然发生:The new law opened the ~s as many more people suddenly applied for government aid.新的法律放开了限制,突然间越来越多的人向政府申请援助。

floodlight/ˈflʌdlaɪt/
Ⅰ n. a large electric light that produces a very powerful and bright beam of light, used for lighting the outside of buildings, football grounds, etc., at night 泛光灯,(泛光)探照灯;泛光(照明):a match played under ~s 在泛光灯下进行的比赛 Ⅱ v. (floodlit) light by using floodlights 用泛光灯照明:Buckingham Palace is floodlit at night.在夜里,白金汉宫被泛光灯照得通亮。

floor/flɔː(r)/
Ⅰ n. ❶ the surface on which one stands indoors; the surface nearest the ground 地面;地板:His wife scrubs the bedroom ~ every day.他的妻子每天都擦洗卧室地板。❷ all the rooms that are on the same level of a building 楼层:We live on the third ~.我们住在三楼。Ⅱ v. make sb. fall down by hitting them 击倒:The strong boxer ~ed his opponent with a heavy blow.这健壮的拳击手一记重拳把对手打倒了。‖ ~ing n.地板材料

flop/flɒp/
Ⅰ v. (-pp-) ❶ fall heavily and without much control over one's movements 沉重下坠;不由自主地倒下:He ~ped into a chair.他扑通一下坐在椅子上。❷ fail totally 彻底失败 Ⅱ n. a total failure 彻底失败:The new play was a ~.新戏彻底败了。

floppy /ˈflɒpi/
adj. (floppier, floppiest) hanging loosely, not firm or rigid 松散下垂的;耷拉的:a ~ hat 耷拉着的帽子 ‖ **floppily** adv. 下垂地;懒散地/**floppiness** n. 下垂;松懈;懒散

flora/ˈflɔːrə/
n. all the plant life in a particular area or at a particular period of time (某地区或某时期的)植物群

floral/ˈflɔːrəl/
adj. ❶ of flowers 花的 ❷ decorated with flowers 以花装饰的

florid/ˈflɒrɪd/
adj. ❶ (of the face) red in colour (脸色)红润的 ❷ with too much decoration 装饰过多的;华丽的

flounce/flaʊns/
v. move in an impatient or angry manner (不耐烦或生气地)暴跳,急走,猛冲:She ~d out of the room.她怒气冲冲地跑出房间。

flour/ˈflaʊə(r)/
n. wheat powder or grain powder 面粉;谷物粉

flourish/ˈflʌrɪʃ/
Ⅰ n. an impressive act or way of doing sth. 出色表现(或发挥):His poems were in full ~ at that time.那时,他的诗歌创作正处在鼎盛时期。Ⅱ v. ❶ grow vigorously 兴旺:His business is ~ing.他的生意兴隆。❷ wave about sth. to make people look at it (为引起注意)挥舞:She ~ed the flag joyfully.她高兴地挥动着旗子。

flourmill/ˈflɔːˈmɪl/
n. a place where flour is made from grain 面粉厂

floury/ˈflaʊəri/
adj. ❶ covered with flour 满是面粉的:She was making pastry and her hands were ~.她正在做糕点,手上沾满了面粉。❷ soft and rather powdery 松软而粉质的:~ potatoes 粉质的马铃薯

flow/fləʊ/
Ⅰ n. ❶ the action or fact of moving along in a steady continuous stream 流淌;流动:There is a constant ~ of water in the cavern.大岩洞中有水不断地流出。❷ the rise of the tide 涨潮:The tide is on the ~.正在涨潮。Ⅱ v. ❶ (of a liquid) move along steadily and continuously in a current or stream (液体)流;流动:The Yellow River ~s eastward to the sea.黄河东流入海。❷ (of the tide) rise (潮)涨:The tide began to ~ at the midnight.半夜涨潮了。‖ ~ing adj.流动的

flower/ˈflaʊə(r)/

I *n.* ❶ the part of a plant that produces seeds or fruits 花：The peach tree is in ~.这棵桃树在开花。❷ the finest or best part of sth. 最好部分：She is in the ~ of her age.她正处在青春时代。Ⅱ *v.* produce flowers；bloom 开花：Plum trees ~ early in spring.梅树在早春开花。‖ ~ing *adj.*开花的/ ~y *adj.*多花的；(辞藻)华丽的

flu/fluː/

*n.*a type of disease which is like a cold but more serious 流感(influenza 的简体)：Flu is common during the winter.流感是冬季的常见病。

fluctuate/ˈflʌktʃʊeɪt/

*v.*frequently change from higher to lower；rise and fall irregularly in number or amount (数量等)波动,涨落,起伏 ‖ fluctuation /ˌflʌktʃʊˈeɪʃn/ *n.*波动

flue/fluː/

n. a metal pipe or tube, especially in a chimney through which smoke or heat passes 烟道：The fire won't burn because the ~'s blocked up.炉火着不起来,因为烟道堵住了。

fluent/ˈfluːənt/

*adj.*able to speak easily, articulately 说话流利的：He is a ~ speaker. 他说话流利。/He made a ~ speech.他作了一次流利的演讲。‖ ~ly *adv.*流利地,通畅地/ fluency *n.*流畅,流利

fluid/ˈfluːɪd/

I *adj.* ❶ having the quality of flowing 流动的：The patient lives on ~ foods.病人靠流质食物为生。❷ unsettled；not fixed 不固定的：Though I settled down in this city, my ideas on the job were still ~.虽然我在这座城市安家落户,但我对工作的想法仍然未定。Ⅱ *n.*a liquid or a gas substance 流体；液体：Water is a ~.水是液体。

fluorescent/ˌflʊəˈresnt/

adj.(of a substance) having or showing fluorescence (物质)荧光的,发荧光的

fluoride/ˈflɔːraɪd/

n. a compound of fluorine and another substance 氟化物

fluorine/ˈflɔːriːn/

n. a chemical element which is a poisonous pale yellow gas and is very reactive 氟

flurry/ˈflʌri/

*n.*a small amount of snow, rain, etc. that just fails for a short time 一阵雪(或雨等)

flush/flʌʃ/

I *v.* ❶ become red in face；make face turn red (脸)发红：She ~ed when the man spoke to her.当那个男人对她说话时,她脸红了。❷ flow or rush suddenly 奔流：The brook was ~ing after a heavy rain. 一场大雨过后,小溪漫水了。❸ clean or wash with a flush of water 用水冲洗：She ~es the lavatory every day.她每天用水冲洗厕所。❹ (cause to)become excited (使)兴奋；(使)得意：The men were ~ed with success.那些人因成功而兴奋不已。Ⅱ *n.* ❶ a rush of blood to the face, reddening caused by this (脸的)晕红：The young man suffered from tuberculosis, so he always had an unhealthy ~.这年轻人患了肺结核,因此,脸上有不健康的晕红色。❷ a sudden feeling of anger, excitement, etc. 激动；兴奋：The woman had a ~ when she heard her son had found a job.这位妇女听说她的儿子已找到了一份工作时,激动不已。Ⅲ *adj.* ❶ exactly on a level (with)；even in surface 齐平的：The river is ~ with its banks after a continuous rain. 下了一场连绵雨后,河水齐岸了。❷ having plenty of money 富裕的：He was ~ when his business was successful.他的生意成功使他富了起来。

fluster/ˈflʌstə(r)/

I *v.*make sb. too excited or worried to be able to do sth. properly 使惊慌失措；使困惑 Ⅱ *n.*a condition of being flustered 困惑；惊慌失措：He is in a ~.他惊慌失措。

flute/fluːt/

*n.*a long slender, tubelike musical instrument 长笛

flutter/ˈflʌtə(r)/

Ⅰ v.❶ move the wings lightly and quickly 振翼；拍翅：The butterfly ~ed from leaf to leaf. 蝴蝶在叶间振翅飞舞。❷ wave back and forth, quickly and lightly 飘动；挥动：The flags were ~ing. 旗帜在飘扬。❸（cause to）move about in an excited, confused way 焦急地乱动；（使）坐立不安：She ~ed nervously about, going from room to room. 她紧张地在房子里走来走去。Ⅱ n.❶ a quick, light movement 飘动；振动；挥动；颤动 ❷ a state of nervous or confused excitement 心绪不宁；焦急；不安

flux/flʌks/

n. continuous movement and change 不断的改变；不停的变动：in a state of ~ 处于不断变化的状态中

fly/flaɪ/

Ⅰ n. a small flying insect with two wings 苍蝇：I hate flies because they contaminate food. 我讨厌苍蝇，因为他们污染食物。Ⅱ v.（flew, flown）❶ move or be moved through the air by means of wings 飞；飞行：Birds can ~ with their wings. 鸟能用翅膀飞行。❷ travel by aircraft 乘飞机旅行：I'm ~ing from London to Paris tomorrow. 我明天将从伦敦飞往巴黎。❸ pass rapidly；hurry；move at speed 飞跑；飞奔：A violent earthquake occurred in Tangshan city, soldiers flew to the rescue. 唐山市发生强烈地震时，战士们都飞速前往援救。

flyer /ˈflaɪə/

n.❶ a person or thing that flies 飞行者；飞行物 ❷ an animal or vehicle that moves very fast 快速移动的人（或物）：His free kick was a real ~. 他的任意球速度很快。❸ a small poster advertising an event 广告传单

flying[1]/ˈflaɪɪŋ/

adj.❶（of a jump）made after running（跑了几步后）纵身一跳的，横越的：The stream was several feet wide, but she took a ~ leap and got safely across. 这小溪有数英尺宽，但她纵身一跃，安全越过。❷ lasting a very short time 短暂的，匆匆的：It's just a ~ visit；We can't stay long. 这只是仓促的短暂访问，我们不能久留。

flying[2]/ˈflaɪɪŋ/

n. travelling by aircraft, as a means of getting from one place to another or as a sport（作为旅行或运动的）飞行：I don't like ~；it makes me feel sick. 我不喜欢飞行，它使我感到不适。/I'm terrified of ~；I'd rather go by sea. 我害怕坐飞机，我宁愿坐船。/a ~ club 飞行俱乐部

flyleaf/ˈflaɪliːf/

n. a page on which there is usually no printing, at the beginning or end of a book, fastened to the cover（书籍前后的）空白页，衬页，扉页

flyover/ˈflaɪəʊvə(r)/

n. a place where two roads or railways cross each other at different levels 立交桥；高架公路

flyswatter/ˈflaɪˌswɒtə(r)/

n. an instrument for killing flies, usually made of a flat piece of plastic or wire net fixed to a handle （苍）蝇拍

foam/fəʊm/

Ⅰ n.❶ a mass of very small bubbles on the surface of a liquid, on skin, etc. 泡沫：Soap ~ can remove the dirty on clothes. 肥皂泡沫能去掉衣服上的污垢。❷ a soft light rubber material, full of small holes 泡沫橡胶；海绵橡胶：A lot of things are made of ~ plastics. 许多东西是用泡沫塑料制成的。Ⅱ v. produce a mass of small bubbles 起泡沫：After you remove the lid of a bottle of beer, it ~s. 揭去啤酒瓶盖后，啤酒冒泡。‖ ~y adj. 泡沫的，泡沫似的

fob/fɒb/

v.(-bb-) deceive sb.；make sb. accept sth. which is false or worthless 欺骗某人；（用假货或劣质货）蒙骗某人：He ~bed me off with an excuse. 他找了一个借口蒙骗我。

focus/ˈfəʊks/

Ⅰ n.❶ the thing or person that people are most interested in 中心点：She became the ~ of attention at a fashion show. 这位模特儿在时装展览会上成了注意的焦点。❷ a meeting-point of rays of light, heat,etc.;a point or distance at which an object is most clearly seen by the eye or through lens 焦点;焦距:Before he took a photo,he adjusted the ～ of the camera. 他先调好照相机的焦距,然后拍照。Ⅱ v. ❶ pay particular attention to 集中;重视: At the party all eyes were ～ed on her.在聚会上,全部视线都集中在她身上。❷ arrange the lens in (an instrument) so as to obtain a clear picture (of) 焦点;调焦距:He ～ed the lens of a microscope.他调整显微镜以定焦距。

fodder/ˈfɒdə(r)/
*n.*food for cows, horses, sheep, etc. which has been stored 草料,饲料

fog/fɒɡ/
Ⅰ *n.*a thick cloud of tiny drops of water in the air which obscures or restricts visibility 雾:The ～ was thick and I couldn't see the road.雾很重,我看不见路。Ⅱ v. (-gg-) cover or be covered with fog or steam 起雾;被雾笼罩着:The windscreen has ～ged up.挡风玻璃已覆盖着一层雾气。/Steam has ～ged the bathroom mirror.水蒸气使浴室里的镜子雾气蒙蒙。

foggy/ˈfɒɡi/
*adj.*❶ full of or covered with fog 有雾的,雾茫茫的:a ～ evening 有雾的晚上 ❷ not clear;confused;puzzled 不清楚的;迷糊的,迷惑的:I have only a ～ idea of what you mean.我隐隐约约地知道一点你的用意。

fog(e)y/ˈfəʊɡi/
*n.*a slow usually old person who dislikes changes and does not understand modern ideas 老顽固,老保守:The judge was an old ～ and was completely out of touch with modern life.这位法官是个老顽固,完全脱离了现代生活。

foil[1]/fɔɪl/
*n.*❶ metal hammered into a thin sheet like paper 箔 ❷ a person or a thing which makes another seem better, more beautiful,more clever,etc. in contrast 陪衬的角色;衬托物

foil[2] /fɔɪl/

*v.*prevent sb. from doing sth. (especially sth. wrong) 阻止(尤指坏事):I ～ed the thief.我阻止了那小偷作案。/ I ～ed his attempt to steal the money.我使他要偷钱的企图不能得逞。

foist/fɔɪst/
v.(～ on) ❶ cause (sb. or sth. unwanted) to be borne or suffered for a time by (someone) 把……强加于……:They didn't invite him to go out with them but he ～ed himself on them.他们没有邀请他与他们同去,但是他硬是跟着去了。❷ pass or sell sth. which is false or worthless to sb.,especially by deceit 骗卖 (假货等):Don't trust that shopkeeper, he'll try to ～ damaged goods (off) on you.不要相信那个店主,他会拿已损坏的货品欺骗你。

fold/fəʊld/
Ⅰ *n.*a line made in material, paper,etc., by folding 褶;褶痕:Each ～ in the curtain should be of the same width.窗帘的每道褶应一样宽。Ⅱ v.❶ turn or press back one part of (sth.,especially paper or cloth) and lay it on the remaining part; bend into two or more parts 折叠,对折:I ～ed the letter and then put it into an envelope.我把信折好后放进信封里。❷ press (a pair of limbs) together 合拢,交叠:Sometimes we ～ our hands to give honor to someone.有时我们双手合上向某人致敬。❸ wrap;cover 包裹;笼罩:I ～ed some books up in paper.我将几本书用纸包起来。‖ ～er *n.*文件夹

foliage/ˈfəʊlɪɪdʒ/
n. leaves of a plant 叶子:Pollution has stripped the trees of their ～.污染使这些树掉了叶子。

folk/fəʊk/
Ⅰ *n.*people in general 人们:Town ～ here like to mock at country ～.这里的城里人爱嘲笑乡里人。Ⅱ *adj.*of the common people of a country;of a tribe 民间的:I like ～ songs very much.我非常喜欢民歌。

follow/ˈfɒləʊ/

v. **①** go or come after (in space, time or order);pursue steadily 跟随;追求:Follow me, please. 请跟我来。**②** go along 循 (路等):The Chinese people — the socialist road firmly. 中国人民坚定地走社会主义道路。**③** understand clearly 领会;听懂:My teacher speaks English so fast that I can't — him. 我的老师讲英语太快,我听不懂。**④** take as a guide, a leader or an example 遵循:We should — Lei Feng's example. 我们应该以雷锋为榜样,向他学习。‖ as —s 如下

follower /ˈfɒləʊə/
n. **①** a person who supports or believes in a person or cause 追随者;拥护者;爱好者;keen —s of football 足球迷 **②** a person who moves or travels behind sb. or sth. 跟在后面的人

following /ˈfɒləʊɪŋ/
Ⅰ *n.* a body of believers or supporters 拥护者,追随者:The local team has a large —. 当地这支球队有一大批拥趸。Ⅱ *adj.* about to be mentioned 下述的;下列的: Answer the — questions. 回答下列问题。Ⅲ *prep.* after or as a result of 在……以后;作为……的结果:Police are hunting for two men — a spate of robberies in the area. 在该地区发生一连串抢劫案后,警察正在搜捕两名男子。

folly /ˈfɒli/
n. foolish words or behaviours 傻话;蠢事;荒唐事

fond /fɒnd/
adj. **①** loving;tender 慈爱的:She is a — mother. 她是一位慈祥的母亲。**②** (— of) having an affection or liking for 喜爱的,喜欢的:I am not too — of dancing. 我不太喜欢跳舞。**③** (of a hope or a wish) not likely to happen (指希望或心愿)不可能实现的:This is only a — dream. 这只不过是黄粱美梦。‖ —ly *adv.* 爱怜地;痴想地

fondle /ˈfɒndl/
v. touch in a loving way 爱抚

food /fuːd/
n. sth. that living creature or plants take into their bodies to give them strength and help to develop and to live 食物;养料:Milk is the natural — for young babies. 奶是婴儿的天然食品。

fool /fuːl/
Ⅰ *n.* a person who behaves or speaks in a way that lacks intelligence or good judgement 愚人;傻瓜:He is no —. 他才不是傻瓜。Ⅱ *v.* trick or deceive (sb.) 胡闹;欺骗;愚弄:Stop —ing (about)! 不要再干愚蠢的事了!

foolery /ˈfuːləri/
n. silly or foolish behaviour 愚蠢的行为

foolhardy /ˈfuːlhɑːdi/
adj. foolishly daring;taking unwise risks; reckless 莽撞的;蛮干的:You were very — to jump off the bus while it was still moving. 公共汽车还在开你就跳下车,你也太莽撞了。

foolish /ˈfuːlɪʃ/
adj. lacking good sense or judgement unwise;silly;like a fool 傻的,愚笨的;傻瓜似的:She always asks some — questions. 她总是问一些可笑的问题。/It would be — for us to quarrel. 我们争吵是愚蠢的。‖ —ly *adv.* 愚笨地;无聊地

foolproof /ˈfuːlpruːf/
adj. **①** that cannot go wrong 错不了的,不会出毛病的:I've found a — way of doing it. 我找到了做那件事的万无一失的方法。/a — plan 万无一失的计划 **②** very simple to understand, use, work, etc. 十分简单明了的;容易使用的:a — machine 容易操作的机器

foot /fʊt/
Ⅰ *n.* (*pl.* feet) **①** the part of your leg that you stand on or walk 脚:I wear a new pair of leather shoes on my feet. 我脚上穿了一双新皮鞋。**②** the bottom of sth. 底部:There is a village at the — of the mountain. 山脚下有一个村子。**③** a measure of length equal to twelve inches 英尺:This rope is 2.5 feet long. 这条绳子有 2.5 英尺长。‖ on — 步行,走路 Ⅱ *v.* go on foot;walk 步行:Foot it! 走着去!

football /ˈfʊtbɔːl/
n. **①** a form of team game played by two teams of eleven players involving kicking and in some cases also handling a ball 足

球运动;橄榄球:I watched an exciting ～ match on TV last night.昨天夜里我在电视上看了一场精彩的足球比赛。❷ a large leather or plastic ball filled with air, used in these games 足球;橄榄球: My uncle bought me a ～.我叔父给我买了一个足球。

footbridge /ˈfʊtˌbrɪdʒ/
*n.*a bridge for pedestrians 人行桥,步行桥

foothold /ˈfʊthəʊld/
*n.*❶ a place wide enough to put a foot when climbing (攀登时踩脚的)立足处 ❷ a secure position from which further progress can be made (进一步发展的)据点,立足点: The company is attempting to gain a ～ in the European market.公司试图在欧洲市场站稳脚跟。

footmark/ˈfʊtmɑːk/
*n.*a mark made by a foot ;footprint 足迹,脚印: He often thought about the ～.Perhaps he had made it himself.他常常想到那只脚印,也许是他自己踩下的。

footnote /ˈfʊtnəʊt/
*n.*a note printed at the bottom of a page of a book 脚注

footprint /ˈfʊtprɪnt/
*n.*a mark left by a foot or shoe 脚印,足迹

footstep/ˈfʊtstep/
*n.*❶ the distance covered by one step 一步的距离:It's just two ～s away.仅仅两步远。❷ a footprint 脚印:The ～s of the thief were clearly marked on the chair.椅子上清楚地留下了小偷的脚印。❸ the sound of a person's step 脚步声: At midnight I heard ～s in the corridor, then a knock at the door.半夜里我听到走廊里有脚步声,随后是敲门的声音。

footwear/ˈfʊtweə(r)/
*n.*outer coverings worn on the feet, such as shoes, boots, etc. 鞋类: You can buy shoelaces in the ～ department.你能在商店售鞋部买到鞋带。

for/fɔː(r), fə(r)/
Ⅰ *prep.* ❶ having sth. as a purpose or destination (表示目的或去向)往, 向: The swimmers struck out ～ the shore. 游泳者奋力向岸边游去。❷ having sth.

as a reason or cause (表示原因)因为, 由于:What did you do that ～? 你为什么干那件事? ❸ considering the circumstances or in respect of 对于:It's dangerous ～ a small child to swim in the river alone.小孩子单独在河里游泳是危险的。❹ indicating the length of time (表示时间、距离)计, 达: The old man can walk ～ 5 kilometers an hour.这老人一小时能走5公里路。/I've lived in New York ～ ten years.我在纽约已经住了十年。❺ in place of;as a sign of 代替;代表:The letters PM stand ～ Prime Minister.字母PM代表首相。❻ in favour of;in support of;in agreement with 赞成:Are you ～ or against the bill? 你是赞成这个法案,还是反对呢? Ⅱ *conj.* (not used at the beginning of a sentence) because 因为;由于(不用于句首):He didn't go to party,～ he was busy with work.他没有参加晚会,因为他忙于工作。‖ as ～ 至于

forage/ˈfɒrɪdʒ/
Ⅰ *n.*❶ food supplies for horses and cattle (牛、马的)饲料;草料 ❷ a wide search over an area in order to obtain sth. especially food 搜寻,寻找(尤指食物) Ⅱ *v.* ❶ wander about looking for food or other supplies 搜寻(食物、粮食等):The campers went foraging for wood to make a fire.露营的人到处寻找生火的木柴。❷ hunt about or search, turning many things over 搜寻;查找:She ～d about in her handbag, but she couldn't find her ticket.她把手提包翻了个遍,但没有找到她的票。

foray/ˈfɒreɪ/
Ⅰ *n.*❶ a sudden rush into enemy territory, usually by a small number of soldiers, in order to damage or seize arms, food, etc.突袭;袭击:The officer sent a few of his men on a ～.军官派了一小队人去突袭。❷ a short attempt to become active in an activity that is quite different from one's usual activity (对新活动领域的)短暂尝试:After his unsuccessful ～ into politics,he went back to his law practice. 在参政初次涉足失利之后,他又回来当律师了。Ⅱ *v.* go out and attack enemy

country suddenly, especially in order to carry off food or other supplies（为了掠夺而）进行突袭

forbear /fɔːˈbeə(r)/
v. (forbore, forborne) refrain; restrain an impulse to do sth. 抑制；自制；忍耐；容忍：~ (from) complaining 不发牢骚

forbearance /fɔːˈbeərəns/
n. patience; self-control 耐心，自制：He showed great ~.他自制力很强。

forbearing /fɔːˈbeərɪŋ/
adj. patient and restrained 宽容的，能忍耐的：She has a ~ nature.她具有宽容的个性。

forbid /fəˈbɪd/
v. ❶ (forbade or forbad, forbidden) command sb. not to do sth.禁止；不许：~ sb. to leave 不许某人离开 /He is ~den to leave the house.他被禁止离开这个房间。/I ~ you to go out.我不许你出去。/His mother forbade him to swim in the river.他的母亲不许他在河里游泳。❷ make sth. difficult or impossible 妨碍，阻止（某事）：His unreasonable conduct forbade him to ask others for help.他的无理行为使他不可能得到他人的帮助。

forbidden /fəˈbɪdn/
adj. not allowed; prohibited 不允许的，被禁止的：Smoking is ~.严禁吸烟。/Forbidden City 紫禁城

forbidding /fəˈbɪdɪŋ/
adj. having a fierce, unfriendly or dangerous appearance 样子可怕的；令人生畏的；凶险的：She's very nice but because she has a ~ manner she's slow in making friends.她人很好，但态度严峻，所以不容易交上朋友。/The travellers' way was blocked by a ~ range of mountains.旅行者的去路被形势险恶的山峦阻挡了。

force /fɔːs/
Ⅰ *n.* ❶ a power, person or thing that has strong influences 力；力量：He overcame his bad habit by sheer ~ of will.他全凭意志力克服了他的坏习惯。❷ fierce or uncontrolled use of strength or violence 武力；暴力：The police had to use ~ to stop the crowd forward.警察不得不用武力阻止人群前进。❸ an organized body of armed or disciplined men 军队；部队：The Chinese People's Liberation Army consists of army, navy and air ~.中国人民解放军由陆、海、空军组成。❹ (of a rule, order, law, etc.) the state of being in effect, use, or operation（规章、命令、法律等的）生效；效力：Did the new law come into ~? 新法规生效了吗？Ⅱ *v.* ❶ use power to get or do sth.; oblige sb. to do sth. 强迫：He was ~d to leave his motherland.他被迫离开祖国。❷ make a way through or into by physical strength 施强力于；强行（撞开、通过等）：I had lost my key, so I had to ~ the door open.我钥匙掉了，只好破门而入。

forced /fɔːst/
adj. made or driven by force; done by unusual effort 强迫的，被迫的：~ march 强行军/ ~ landing 强迫降落

forceful /ˈfɔːsfl/
adj. (especially of a person or argument) strong and powerful（尤指人或论点）有力的：He made a ~ speech.他做了一次有力的发言。

forceps /ˈfɔːseps/
n. a medical instrument with two long thin blades joined at one end or in the middle, used for holding objects firmly 镊子，钳子

forcible /ˈfɔːsəbl/
adj. ❶ using physical force 强迫的；用暴力的：The police had to make a ~ entry into the house where the thief was hiding.警察不得不强行进入小偷藏身的那座房子。❷ (especially of a manner or speaking) strong and effective; powerful（尤指举止或讲话）强有力的；有说服力的：The burglary at her neighbour's house was a ~ reminder that she should lock up carefully every time she went out.她邻居家中的失窃，让她深刻的意识到，每次出门都应仔细锁好门窗。‖ **forcibly** *adv.* 用武力地；清楚地：Her ideas are always forcibly expressed. 她常常用令人信服的方式表达自己的意见。

ford /fɔːd/

Ⅰ *n*.a shallow place in a river where it is possible to walk across 浅滩 Ⅱ *v*.cross (a river, stream, etc.) by walking through the water 涉水而过(河流、溪涧)

fore /fɔː(r)/

Ⅰ *adj*.situated in the front 前面的: My seat is in the ～ part of the classroom.我的座位在教室的前部。 Ⅱ *adv*.in or towards the front part of a ship or aircraft 在(船或飞机的)前面;往(船或飞机的)前面: The captain went ～ to check the deck.船长走向船头去检查甲板。 Ⅲ *n*.the front part (of a ship or aircraft) (船或飞机的)前部: The sailor went to the ～.水手走向船头。

forearm[1] /ˈfɔːrɑːm/

n.the lower part of the arm between the hand and the elbow 前臂

forearm[2] /ˌfɔːrˈɑːm/

v.prepare for an attack before the time of need 预先武装;预做准备

forebear /ˈfɔːbeə(r)/

n.a person from whom one is descended; ancestor 祖先,祖宗: My ～s lived in the west of Scotland.我的祖先住在苏格兰西部。

forebode /fɔːˈbəud/

v.be a warning of (sth. unpleasant) 预示(灾祸等)

foreboding /fɔːˈbəudɪŋ/

n.a feeling that sth. bad is coming 对不详之事的预感: have a ～ about sth. 预感会发生不幸的事

forecast /ˈfɔːkɑːst/

Ⅰ *n*.a statement of future events, based on some kind of knowledge or judgment 预报;预测: The weather ～ on the radio says it will be cloudy tomorrow.广播电台气象预报说明天多云。 Ⅱ *v*.(～ or ～ed) predict or estimate what is going to happen at some future time especially with the help of some kind of knowledge 预报;预测: He ～s traffic accidents at the weekend.他预言周末会出交通事故。

forefather /ˈfɔːfɑːðə/

n.❶ a member of the past generations of one's family or people;an ancestor 祖先,

祖宗,前辈 ❷ a precursor of a particular movement 先驱,前人: the ～s of modern socialism 现代社会主义运动的先驱

forefinger /ˈfɔːfɪŋgə(r)/

n.the finger next to the thumb 食指

forefront /ˈfɔːfrʌnt/

n.(the ～) the foremost part 最前部: in the ～ of the battle 在战斗的最前线

foregoing /ˈfɔːgəuɪŋ/

adj.mentioned or stated earlier 以前的,前述的

foregone /ˈfɔːgɒn/

adj.(a ～ **conclusion**) a result that can be predicted from the start 预料中的必然结局

foreground /ˈfɔːgraund/

n.❶ the part of a view or picture nearest the observer 前景 ❷ the most noticeable position 突出的地位;最显著的位置: keep oneself in the ～ 突出自己

forehead /ˈfɒrɪd, ˈfɔːhed/

n.the part of the face above the eyes and below the hair 前额

foreign /ˈfɒrən/

adj.❶ to, from, of, or concerning a country or language that is not one's own or not the one being talked about or considered 外国的;来自外国的;外国语的: Foreign languages are taught in our school all the time.我们学校里一直教外语。 ❷ coming or introduced from outside;having no relation (to) 外来的;与……无关的: The surgeon cleaned the wound of ～ matter.外科大夫清除了伤口中的异物。

foreigner /ˈfɒrɪnə(r)/

n.a person from another country 外国人

foreleg /ˈfɔːleg/

n.a front leg of an animal (动物的)前腿

foreman /ˈfɔːmən/

n.(*pl*.foremen) a man in charge of a group of workers 工头,领班

foremost /ˈfɔːməust/

adj.the most prominent in rank, position or importance 最重要的;最杰出的;领先的: the ～ painter of the 19th century 十九世纪最重要的画家

forename /'fɔːneɪm/

n. a person's first name 名：Please check that your surname and ～s have been correctly entered.请核对你的姓名已正确输入。

forerunner /'fɔːrʌnə(r)/

n. ❶ a sign or warning of sth. to come 预兆，前兆：Swallows, the ～s of spring. 燕子，春天的前兆。 ❷ a person or thing who prepares the way for, or is a sign of the coming of someone or something else 先锋，先驱：She was a ～ of the modern women's movement. 她是现代妇女运动的先锋。

foresee /fɔː'siː/

v. (foresaw, ～n) see or know sth. in advance 预知，预见：We should have ～n the trouble months ago. 几个月前我们就应该预料到会有这种麻烦。/He ～s that things will go well. 他预知事情将会很顺利。/I can't ～ what will happen in the future. 我不能预见将来会发生什么事。

foreseeable /fɔː'siːəbl/

adj. that can be foreseen 可预见到的：It was a ～ accident. 那是一次可预见的事故。

foreshadow /fɔː'ʃædəʊ/

v. be a sign that sth. dangerous or unpleasant is coming 预兆，预示（会发生危险或不快的事）

foresight /'fɔːsaɪt/

n. an ability to know or guess what will happen in the future 先见之明，远见：The couple had the ～ to plan their retirement wisely.这对夫妇很有远见，精心安排了退休后的生活。

forest /'fɒrɪst/

n. a large area of land covered with trees and undergrowth 森林；林区：～s stretching for miles and miles 伸延无数英里的森林地带 /A large part of Africa is made up of thick ～.非洲的大部分地区都是森林。

forestall /fɔː'stɔːl/

v. do sth. with the aim of preventing another person from doing it（预先采取行动以）阻止；先发制人：～ problems 预先阻止问题发生

forested /'fɒrɪstɪd/

adj. covered in forest 满是森林的；林木覆盖的：The area is heavily ～ and sparsely populated.该地区森林茂密，人烟稀少。

forestry /'fɒrɪstri/

n. the science or practice of planting and managing forests 林学；林业

foretell /fɔː'tel/

v. (foretold) tell sth. beforehand 预言，预测：～ sb.'s future 预测某人的未来/Who can ～ how the world will end? 谁能预言世界将会怎样结束呢？

forethought /'fɔːθɔːt/

n. wise planning for future needs; consideration of what is to come 事先的考虑（或筹划）；深谋远虑：If you'd had the ～ to bring your raincoat, you wouldn't have got wet.你如果事先想到带雨衣，就不会被雨淋湿了。

forever /fər'evə(r)/

adv. ❶ for all future time 永远地；永久地：I shall remember that happy day ～. 我将永远记住那幸福的日子。/I hope you'll remain friends ～.我希望你们永远是朋友。 ❷ continually 总是；老是：The little boy is ～ asking questions.那小男孩老是问问题。

forewarn /fɔː'wɔːn/

v. tell sb. of some danger, etc. which is coming 预先警告

foreword /'fɔːwɜːd/

n. an introduction or preface to a book 前言，引言，序言：The ～ was written by a famous writer.此前言是一位著名作家写的。

forfeit /'fɔːfɪt/

Ⅰ *v.* lose sth. as a punishment or as a result of one's actions（因受罚或过失而）丧失 Ⅱ *n.* sth. lost in this way 丧失的东西；没收物

forge /fɔːdʒ/

Ⅰ *n.* ❶ a place with a fire where metal is heated very hot and then hammered into shape 铁匠铺：Horseshoes are made in a ～.马蹄铁是在铁匠铺里做的。 ❷ a furnace or hearth for melting or refining metal 熔铁炉,冶炼炉 Ⅱ*v.*❶ form metal by heating and hammering 锻造,铸造:~ an anchor 锻造铁锚 ❷ make an imitation or copy of (sth.) in order to deceive people 伪造;假冒:He ~d my signature. 他伪造我的签名。

forger/ˈfɔːdʒə(r)/

*n.*a person who forges money,papers,etc. (钱、文件等的)伪造者

forgery/ˈfɔːdʒəri/

*n.*a forged or copied document,signature, banknote or work of art; forging (文件、签名、钞票、艺术品的)伪造品,赝品;伪造,假冒:When he bought the picture he was told it was Rubens', but he later found out that it was a ~.他买下这幅画时,有人告诉他那是鲁宾斯的画,但后来他发现那是赝品。/They were sent to prison for ~.他们因伪造罪入狱。

forget/fəˈget/

v.(forgot, forgotten) ❶ lose from the memory; fail to remember or recall 忘记: I forgot all about it.我一点也记不得了。 ❷ put out of the mind; stop thinking about 不再去想:Let's ~ those unhappy events. 让我们不再去想那些不愉快的事情吧。

forgetful /fəˈgetfl/

*adj.*tending to forget things 健忘的;好忘事的:Grandma has become very ~ in recent years. 近年来奶奶变得十分健忘。‖~ly *adv.*健忘地;不注意地/~ness *n.* 健忘

forgive/fəˈgɪv/

v.(forgave,~n) stop feeling angry or resentful towards sb.; no longer have the wish to punish sb. for (an offence, a sin, etc.); pardon or show mercy to (sb.) 原谅,宽恕,饶恕(某人):~ sb. of his debt 免除某人的债务 /Forgive me for the wrongs I've done you. 原谅我冤枉你了。/To drop a tray of rings was bad, but that would be ~n.打翻一盘戒指虽然是坏事,但那还是可以原谅的。

forgiveness/fəˈgɪvnəs/

*n.*❶ the act of forgiving or state of being

forgiven 原谅,宽恕,饶恕:He asked God's ~ for his wrong-doings.他乞求上帝原谅他的过失。❷ willingness to forgive 宽厚之心

forgiving/fəˈgɪvɪŋ/

*adj.*willing or able to forgive 宽大的,宽容的,仁慈的:a gentle ~ nature 宽大仁慈的本性

for(e)go/fɔːˈgəʊ/

v.(forwent, forgone) decide not to have or do sth.especially that you would like to have or do 放弃(想做的事或想得到的东西):He decided to ~ sugar in his tea.他决定喝茶不加糖。

fork/fɔːk/

Ⅰ *n.*❶ an implement with two or more points,used for lifting food to the mouth 叉;餐叉:Europeans eat food with a knife and ~.欧洲人吃东西用刀和叉。❷ a farm or gardening tool for breaking up the soil, lifting dried grass, etc., having a handle with two or more metal points at one end 耙;草叉❸ a place where a road, river or tree branch, etc.divides into two parts (路、河流等)岔口;岔流:At the ~ you must take the right road.到三岔路口你必须走右边那条路。Ⅱ *v.*❶ lift, move, carry sth. with a fork 叉起;耙: Farmers must ~ the ground over before sowing wheat.农民下麦种前得先耙地。❷ (of a road, river, etc.) divide into two directions (路、河流等)分岔:The high way ~s just before the square.高速公路就在广场前分岔。

forked/fɔːkt/

adj. having one end divided into two or more points 叉状的;有叉的:Snakes have ~ tongues.蛇的舌头呈叉状。

form/fɔːm/

Ⅰ *n.*❶ the shape or outward appearance 外形;样子:We could just see the ~ of a ship in the darkness.我们只能看见在暗处有一艘船的影子。❷ a general plan or arrangement that sth. shows or expresses itself; kind or sort 种类;形式:Vapor, cloud,fog,sleet,snow,ice,frost are ~s of water.蒸汽、云、雾、霰、雪、冰、霜是水的不同形式。❸ a printed document with blank spaces in which to answer questions and give other information 表格：Yesterday I filled in a job application ～.昨天我填了一份求职申请表。❹ a class or year in British school（英国的）年级：My son is in ～ 2.我儿子上二年级。❺ (especially in sport) the state of a sports player with regard to their current standard of play 竞技状态：Before competition she was in good ～.比赛前她的竞技状态良好。❻ a long wooden seat, usually without a back 无靠背长木椅：There are a few ～s near the woods.靠近小树林有几条长木凳。Ⅱ v.❶ make up or produce, especially by combining parts 构成：The girl can ～ words and sentences correctly.这女孩能正确地构词和造句。❷ come or bring gradually into existence; develop 形成；养成：Good habits gradually ～ed in his life.他在生活中已逐渐养成了良好的习惯。❸ bring together parts or combine to create (sth.) 组织；建立：The revolutionary people ～ed the troops.革命人民组建起了这支部队。

formal /ˈfɔːml/
adj.❶ according to accepted rules or custom 正式的：The American President paid a ～ visit to China.美国总统正式访问了中国。❷ of the outward shape or appearance (not the content or matter) 形式上的：In some countries either king or queen is only a ～ head of state.在一些国家里，国王或女王都只是形式上的国家元首。

formalism /ˈfɔːməlɪzəm/
n. excessive obedience to prescribed rules and forms ceremonies, especially in art and religion（艺术、宗教等方面的）形式主义

formality /fɔːˈmæləti/
n.❶ the rigid obedience of rules and accepted forms of behaviour 拘泥形式，拘谨；遵守礼节：Even with close friends he observes a certain ～.即使与亲密的朋友在一起，他也要遵守某种程度的礼节。❷ a thing that you must do as a formal or official part of a legal process 正式手

续：There are a few formalities to be gone through before you enter a foreign country, such as showing your passport.进入外国之前要履行一些正规的手续，如出示你的护照。❸ sth. that is done as a matter of course and has lost its real meaning 形式上的俗套；必须履行的手续：The written part of the exam is just a ～; no one ever fails it.考试的笔答部分只是一种形式而已，没有人不及格。

formalize /ˈfɔːməlaɪz/
v.❶ put (an agreement, plan, etc.) into clear usually written form 使（协议、计划等）成书面文字形式：The agreement must be ～d before it can have the force of law.该协议必须写成文字才有法律效力。❷ give sth. a fixed structure or form 使正式；使具有一定形式：～ the arrangements for conference 把会议的各项安排确定下来

format /ˈfɔːmæt/
n.❶ the way in which sth. is arranged or set out 安排，布局，设计 ❷ the shape and size of a book, magazine, etc.（书刊的）版式，开本

formation /fɔːˈmeɪʃn/
n.❶ the action of forming or making 组成，形成，养成：The ～ of his teeth was irregular.他的牙齿不整齐。/the ～ of character 性格的形成 ❷ an arrangement of people, ships, aircrafts, etc.（人、船、飞机等的）排列，队形：The planes flew in ～.飞机编队飞行。/The soldiers were drawn up in battle ～.士兵们排成战斗队形。

formative /ˈfɔːmətɪv/
adj. causing sb. or sth. to have a certain type of nature 形成个性的：the ～ years of childhood 童年性格形成的时期

former /ˈfɔːmə(r)/
adj.❶ of an earlier period 原先的；以前的：When you make acquaintance with new friends, you shouldn't forget your ～ friends.当你结识新朋友时，不应该忘记过去的朋友。❷ denoting the first of two people or things just mentioned（两者中）前者的：Basketball and volleyball, I prefer the ～.篮球和排球，我比较喜欢前者。

formerly/ˈfɔːməli/

adv. in earlier times 以前；从前：Peru was ~ ruled by the Spanish. 秘鲁从前受西班牙人的统治。/Formerly he worked in a factory, but now he's a teacher. 从前他在工厂工作，可现在他是一名教师。

formless/ˈfɔːmləs/

adj. ❶ without shape 无形状的，无定形的：a strange ~ creature 一种奇异的无定形生物 ❷ lacking order or arrangement 无秩序的；杂乱的：The experimental music was rather ~. 这种实验音乐相当杂乱无章。

formula/ˈfɔːmjələ/

n.(*pl.*~s or formulae) ❶ a mathematical relationship or rule expressed in symbols or a set of chemical symbols showing the elements present in a compound and their proportions (数学)公式；(化学)分子式：The ~ for water is H_2O. 水的分子式是 H_2O。❷ a list of the chemical substances used in making a medicine, a fuel, a drink, etc., sometimes also including a description of how they are to be mixed 药方；(化学)配制方：The spy has stolen the secret ~ for new cordite. 间谍盗窃了新无烟火药的秘密配方。

formulaic/ˌfɔːmjuˈleɪk/

adj. containing or made up of fixed expressions or set forms of words (根据)公式的；公式化的，刻板的：~ poetry 形式刻板的诗歌

formulate/ˈfɔːmjuleɪt/

v. ❶ express in an exact or systematic way (确切或系统地)阐述(表达)：He took care to ~ his reply very clearly. 他注意非常清楚地作出系统的回答。❷ create or devise a plan, suggestion, etc. 规划，构想(计划、建议等)：The government is trying to ~ a new policy on Northern Ireland. 政府正力图制定一个对待北爱尔兰的新政策。

forsake/fəˈseɪk/

v.(forsook, forsaken) give up; break away from; desert 放弃；遗弃；抛弃；丢弃：~ bad habits 摒弃坏习惯 /~ one's wife and children 遗弃妻儿

forsooth/fəˈsuːθ/

adv. used to emphasize a statement, especially in order to show surprise (用于强调，尤表示惊讶)确实，无疑

forswear/fɔːˈsweə(r)/

v.(forswore, forsworn) make a solemn promise to give up or to stop doing (sth.) 发誓抛弃；坚决放弃：The priests of some religions must ~ possessions and marriage. 有些宗教的教士必须宣誓放弃财产和婚姻。/He forswore drinking. 他发誓戒酒。

fort/fɔːt/

n. a building erected for military defence 堡垒；要塞

forte/ˈfɔːteɪ/

n. sth. that sb. does well 长处；特长：Driving is his ~. 开车是他的特长。

forth/fɔːθ/

adv. ❶ from that time 从那以后：From that day ~, the lovers were never parted. 从那天起，这对情人从未分离过。❷ towards a place; forwards 向某处；向前：The captain of team came ~ and received a prize cup. 队长走上前来接受一只奖杯。‖ **back and** ~ 前前后后；来回 /**and so** ~ 等等

forthcoming/ˌfɔːθˈkʌmɪŋ/

adj. ❶ happening or appearing soon 即将到来的，即将出现的：the ~ holidays 即将到来的假日 ❷ ready or made available when needed 现成的；随要随有的：The funds we hoped for were not ~. 我们所期待的资金尚未拿到。

forthright/ˈfɔːθraɪt/

adj. saying what one thinks, without trying to hide anything 直率的；直截了当的

fortitude/ˈfɔːtɪtjuːd/

n. courage, endurance and self-control in facing pain, danger of difficulty 勇敢；坚忍不拔的精神

fortnight/ˈfɔːtnaɪt/

n. two weeks 两周：a ~'s holiday 一个为期两周的假期 / a ~ ago yesterday 从昨天算起两周前

fortress/ˈfɔːtrəs/

*n.*a place built with walls and defences 堡垒,要塞

fortunate/ˈfɔːtʃənət/
adj. favoured by fortune; lucky; prosperous; having, bringing, brought by good fortune 幸运的;运气好的;吉利的;带来好运的:be ~ all life 一生幸运 / You were ~ to escape being injured.你没有受伤真是幸运。

fortunately/ˈfɔːtʃənətli/
adv. by good chance; luckily 幸运地;幸亏:I was late in getting to the station, but ~ for me, the train was late too.我到火车站已经迟了,但幸好火车也误点了。/Fortunately, the fire was discovered soon after it had started.真幸运,火刚着起来就被发现了。

fortune/ˈfɔːtʃuːn/
n. ❶ chance; luck; fate 命运;运气:He strives without stop to better his ~.他不停地奋斗以改善自己的命运。 ❷ a great deal of money; wealth 财富:My grandfather was abroad and made a ~.我的祖父在国外发了财。

forty/ˈfɔːti/
num. the number 40 四十 ‖ **fortieth** /ˈfɔːtɪəθ/ *num.*第四十

forum/ˈfɔːrəm/
n. ❶ the public square or market place of ancient Rome(古罗马)集会的广场,公共集会点 ❷ any place for public discussion 讲坛,讨论会场:The letters page of this newspaper is a ~ for public argument.这家报纸的读者来信栏是一个大众论坛。

forward/ˈfɔːwəd/
Ⅰ *adj.* ❶ at or directed towards the front, the end, or the future 向前的:~ movement 向前运动 ❷ advanced or early in development 早的;早熟的:The apples are rather ~ this year because of drought. 由于干旱,今年苹果早熟。Ⅱ *adv.* ❶ onward so as to make progress 朝前方:Forward march! 开步走! ❷ towards the future; onward in time 将来:From this day ~(s) you must rely on yourself.从今以后你得自力更生。 ‖ **backwards and ~s** 来回地;前后地/**look ~ to** 期待;盼

望 Ⅲ *v.* ❶ help advance the development of 促进:The manager tried to ~ the production plan.经理尽力推进执行生产计划。 ❷ send or pass on (letters, parcels, etc.) to a new address 转寄(信件、包裹等):Please ~ my letters to my new address.请把我的信件转到我的新地址。Ⅳ *n.*(in sports such as football)one of the attacking players in a team(足球等)前锋:He is a ~ known by all of us.他是我们大家熟知的足球前锋。

forwards/ˈfɔːwədz/
adv. towards the front of a place; in advance; ahead 向前;朝前:rush ~ 冲向前/Take two steps ~.向前走两步。

fossil/ˈfɒsl/
n. remains of a very old plant, animal, etc., which has been kept from destruction in hard rock 化石

fossilize/ˈfɒsəlaɪz/
v.(cause to)become a fossil (使)变成化石;(使)石化:animal remains ~d in the rocks of the valley 河谷岩层中的动物石残骸 / ~d ideas 陈旧僵化的思想

foster/ˈfɒstə(r)/
v. ❶ care for or bring up sb.; develop (a feeling or idea in oneself) 照顾;抚养,养育;培养(感情、观念):She ~ed the children for several months.她照顾那些孩子好几个月了。 /~ the sick 照顾病人 /~ musical ability 培养音乐才能 ❷ encourage or promote the development of sth. 鼓励;激发;促进:We should ~ the child's talents.我们应该激发出孩子的才能。

foul/faul/
Ⅰ *adj.* ❶ very dirty; with bad smell 肮脏的;难闻的:There is a ~ stink in WC.厕所里有一股难闻的恶臭。 ❷ obscene or profane 卑鄙的;下流的:The wild boy speaks ~ language. 这个野孩子讲下流话。 ❸ wicked or immoral 罪恶的;邪恶的:Rape is a ~ crime.强奸是邪恶的罪行。 ❹ done contrary to the rules of a sport 犯规的:The ball was ~.这个球是犯了规的。 ❺ (of weather) rough; stormy (天气)恶劣的;暴风雨的:In May there is ~ weather in the country.五月里这个国家的天气极糟。Ⅱ *v.* ❶ (in sport)

commit a foul（体育运动中）犯规：He was sent off the field for ～ing.他因犯规被罚出场。❷ make dirty；pollute 使肮脏；污染：The factory ～ed the lake by sending out polluted water into it.这座工厂向湖里排放污水而使该湖受到污染。Ⅲ adv.unfairly；contrary to the rules 犯规地：He often played ～.他打球常犯规。Ⅳ n.an action that is against the rules of the game 犯规：One more ～ and you're out of the game.再犯一次规，你就要被罚下场。

found/faʊnd/

v.start the building of；lay the base of；establish 建立；创办：The new China was ～ed in 1949.新中国成立于 1949 年。

foundation/faʊnˈdeɪʃn/

n.❶ founding or establishing 建立，创立，建设：The ～ of Peking University took place in 1898.北京大学是 1898 年创办的。❷ the lowest load-bearing part of a building 地基：a stone ～ 石基 /Pisa Leaning Tower's ～ is just not deep or wide enough for the tower about it.比萨斜塔的地基负荷量，无论从深度还是宽度衡量都是不合乎标准的。❸ a principle，an idea or a fact that sth.is based on 基础；根据：lay the ～(s) of one's success 打下成功的基础

founder/ˈfaʊndə(r)/

Ⅰ n.the person who founds or establishes an organization，institution，etc.创立人，建立者 Ⅱ v.(of a ship) fill with water and sink（指船只）浸水沉没：The ship ～ed in the heavy sea.该船进水而沉在深海里。

foundry/ˈfaʊndri/

n.a factory where things are made from molten metal 铸造厂

fount/faʊnt/

n.the place where sth.begins or comes from；source 源，源头；源泉：That old man is a ～ of wisdom.那老人有无穷的智慧。

fountain/ˈfaʊntn/

n.❶ a natural or man-made spring of water 喷泉 ❷ a source origin of sth.根源；源

泉：the ～ of a river 江河的源头

four/fɔː(r)/

num.the number 4 四‖ on all ～s 趴在地上，四脚落地 /scatter to the ～ winds 撒向四面八方 /the ～ corners of the earth (country)世界各地(全国各地)

fourteen/ˌfɔːˈtiːn/

num.the number 14 十四‖ ～th/ˌfɔːˈtiːnθ/ num.第十四

fowl/faʊl/

n.(pl.～ or ～s)any bird that is kept for its meat and eggs 禽，家禽：the ～s of the air 飞禽 / keep ～ 养家禽 /roast ～ for dinner 供食用的烤禽

fox/fɒks/

Ⅰ n.a small doglike flesh-eating animal with a bushy tail 狐狸 Ⅱ v.deceive cleverly or baffle someone 欺骗；迷惑：He managed to ～ them by wearing a disguise.他设法戴着假面具欺骗他们。

foxy/ˈfɒksi/

adj.❶ like a fox in nature；not to be trusted 狐狸似的；狡猾的：Watch out！He's a bit of a ～ character！小心！他可生性有点狡猾。❷ like a fox in appearance 形似狐狸的，长得像狐狸的：She has rather ～ features.她的相貌颇似狐狸。❸ sexually attractive 妖艳的，性感的：She's a real ～ lady！她真是个迷人的女子。

fraction/ˈfrækʃn/

n.❶ a very small piece 碎片：She slipped on the floor and dropped a glass into ～s.她在地板上滑了一下，把一个玻璃杯摔碎了。❷ a small part or amount 少量；一点儿：In these days he only spent a ～ of his time at home.这些日子他在家里只待了很少的时间。❸ a division of a whole number 分数：1/2 and 1/3 are ～s.1/2 和 1/3 都是分数。

fractional/ˈfrækʃənl/

adj.❶ so small as to be unimportant 微不足道的，极少的，极小的：The difference between his wages and yours is only ～.他的工资与你的工资差不了多少。❷ of or being a fraction 分数的；小数的

fractionally/ˈfrækʃənəli/

*adv.*to a very small degree 极小地；极少地：If calculations in planning to send a spacecraft to the moon are even ~ incorrect, the project will fail.送太空飞船登月的计划在计算方面如果出一点差错，就会遭受失败。

fractious/ˈfrækʃəs/

adj.(especially of a child or an old or sick person) restless and complaining; bad tempered about small things and ready to quarrel (尤指小孩、老人或病人)易怒的，容易发脾气的，乖张的：Babies tend to be ~ when their new teeth are growing. 婴儿在长牙时往往容易发脾气。

fracture/ˈfræktʃə(r)/

Ⅰ *n.* the breaking of a bone 骨折 Ⅱ *v.* break or cause to break (使)破裂；(使)断裂

fragile/ˈfrædʒaɪl/

*adj.*easily broken; delicate 易碎的，易破的：~ china 易碎的瓷器

fragment/ˈfrægmənt/

Ⅰ *n.*a part broken off 碎片，断片，破片：She's trying to put the ~s of a broken vase together.她在试着将一只破花瓶的碎片拼起来。Ⅱ *v.* divide or break into pieces 破为碎片：The glass will ~ if hit by something hard.玻璃被硬器碰撞就会破为碎片。

fragmentary /ˈfrægməntəri/

*adj.*consisting of fragments 残缺不全的；不完整的：Excavations have revealed ~ remains of masonry.挖掘工作已经显露出砖石建筑的残破遗迹。

fragrance/ˈfreɪgrəns/

*n.*a pleasant smell 香味,香气,芳香

fragrant/ˈfreɪgrənt/

adj. having a pleasant smell 芳香的；香的：~ flowers 香花/ ~ memories 甜蜜的记忆

frail/freɪl/

adj. slender and not very strong; weak, especially in health 脆弱的，薄弱的，(尤指身体)虚弱的：a ~ child 一个体质虚弱的孩子

frailty/ˈfreɪlti/

*n.*❶ the quality of being frail 脆弱，虚弱

❷ a weakness of character or behaviour (性格或行为上的)弱点，缺点：I suppose laziness is one of the frailties of human nature.我认为懒惰是人性中的弱点之一。

frame/freɪm/

Ⅰ *n.*❶ the form or shape of a human or animal body (人、动物的)骨架,体格：My father is a man of heavy ~.我的父亲是个身材魁梧的人。❷ the support structure of a building, vehicle, etc.(建筑物、车辆等的)构架,支架：The bridge has a steel ~.这座桥的构架是钢制的。❸ the general ideas or system that forms the background to sth.总的思想,体系；体制；模式：the ~ of socialist society 社会主义社会的模式。❹ any of the single photographs that make up a film(影片的)一个镜头画面 Ⅱ *v.* ❶put or build a frame around sth.(给某物)镶框,做框：He ~d the picture this morning. 今天上午他给那幅画镶了一个框。❷ express sth. in words; compose or formulate 用文字表达；创作；拟定；制定：The referees ~d a set of rules about the game. 裁判们制定了该游戏的一套规则。❸ produce false evidence against (an innocent person) so that he appears guilty 诬陷；陷害：The criminal suspect said he had been ~d. 嫌疑人说他是被陷害的。

framework/ˈfreɪmwɜːk/

*n.*the part of a structure that gives shape and support 结构；框架：The engineers have just designed the ~ of a large suspension bridge.工程师们刚刚设计完一座大型吊桥的结构。

frank/fræŋk/

*adj.*expressing clearly one's thoughts and feelings 坦率的；坦白的；直率的：be ~ with you 老实跟你说；老实说 /If you want my ~ opinion, I don't think the plan will succeed.如果你要我直说，那么我认为这个计划不会成功。

frankly/ˈfræŋkli/

*adv.*❶ in an open and honest manner 直率地，坦诚地 ❷ speaking honestly and plainly 老实说：Frankly, I don't think your chances of getting the job are very good.老实说，我认为你获得这项工作的

机会并不大。

fraternal /frə'tɜːnl/

adj. of or like a brother 兄弟的；兄弟般的

fraternity /frə'tɜːnəti/

n. ❶ a society or group of men who work together or help each other in some way 兄弟会；互助会 ❷ such a group at a school or college 〈美〉学生联谊会 ❸ a feeling of friendship and mutual support within a group（团体内的）情谊，手足般友谊

fraud /frɔːd/

n. ❶ the crime of making sb. believe sth. which is not true, in order to get sth. from him 欺骗罪 ❷ a person or thing intended to deceive others not true 骗子；假货

fray[1] /freɪ/

n. fight or struggle 吵架；打架；冲突

fray[2] /freɪ/

v.（of cloth, rope, etc.）become or make worn so that there are loose threads（指布、绳索等）磨损，磨破，擦散：This cloth ～s easily. 这布太不经磨。

frazzle /'fræzl/

n. ❶ a condition of being completely tired in body and mind, owing to hard work or other difficulties（由于艰苦工作或其他困难而造成的）疲惫；筋疲力尽：I've been traveling round the shops all day, and I'm absolutely worn to a ～. 我逛了一整天商店，浑身精疲力竭。 ❷ a thoroughly burnt condition 烧烂；烤焦：He forgot about the food he was frying, and it got to a ～. 他忘记了所炸的食物，结果都烧焦了。

freak /friːk/

Ⅰ *n*. a plant, animal, person, etc. that is unusual and unnatural in form 畸形，怪物；有怪癖的人 Ⅱ *adj*. strange and unusual 反常的；怪异的：a ～ storm 反常的暴风雨

freckle /'frekl/

n. the small brown spot on human skin 雀斑；斑点

free /friː/

Ⅰ *adj*. ❶ not in the power of another person; not in prison; having personal rights 自由的：Everyone is ～ to air his opinion.

每个人都可以畅所欲言。 ❷ not busy; not working 不忙的；空闲的：Will you be ～ this weekend? 这个周末你有空吗? ❸ without payment; costing nothing; having no duty or charge 免费的；免税的：I got two ～ tickets for the lecture on stocks. 我弄到了两张听股票讲座的免费票。 ❹ ready to give; generous 大方的；慷慨的：He is very ～ with his money when he gambles. 他赌钱时是非常大方的。 ❺ too friendly; lacking in respect; not controlled by politeness 过分亲近的；轻浮的；不庄重的，不礼貌的：Don't be too ～ in formal situations. 在正式场合不要太随便。

Ⅱ *v*. make free 释放；使自由：I hope to ～ women from household drudgery. 我希望能把妇女从繁重的家务劳动中解放出来。

freedom /'friːdəm/

n. ❶ the state of being free 自由；自主：～ of speech 言论自由 /～ of religion 宗教自由 /～ of the press 出版自由 /After five years the prisoner was given his ～. 五年之后，犯人获得了自由。 ❷ the power to do, say, think, or write as one pleases（言论、行动等的）自由权：I was given the ～ of that house. 我那时可以随便用那所房子。

freely /'friːli/

adv. in a free manner 自由地；随意地：speak ～ 畅所欲言 /If he can not do this, he has not really grasped the spirit of the foreign language and can not use it ～. 如果做不到这一点，他就没有真正掌握这种外语的精神实质，也就不能运用自如。

freeman /'friːmən/

n. a person who, as an honour, has been given certain special rights in a city（享有某些特权的）荣誉市民：The famous politician was made a ～ of the City of London. 这位著名的政治家成为伦敦市的荣誉市民。

freestyle /'friːstaɪl/

n. ❶ a competition or method of swimming using the crawl stroke 自由式（游泳）：Which swimmer won the 100 metres ～? 哪位选手获得一百米自由式游泳冠

军? ❷ (in wrestling) the use of movements according to choice, not set rules 自由式(摔跤)

freethinker /ˌfriːˈθɪŋkə(r)/

n. someone who forms their opinions using their own powers of reasoning, and does not just accept official teachings, especially in religious matters (尤指宗教上的)自由思想家,思想自由的人

freeway /ˈfriːweɪ/

n. a divided highway for fast travelling on which usually no tolls are charged; expressway 快车道;高速公路

freewheeling /ˌfriːˈwiːlɪŋ/

adj. not greatly worrying about rules, formal behaviour, responsibilities, or the results of actions 随心所欲的;放任自流的

freeze /friːz/

v. (froze, frozen) ❶ become hard and often turn to ice 结冰;凝固: The water in the lake froze this winter. 湖里的水这个冬天结冰了。 ❷ be or feel very cold 感到极冷: I must put my overcoat on because I'm ~ing. 我都冻坏了,我得穿上我的大衣。 ❸ not allow (money or assets) to be used or exchanged for a period of time 冻结(财产、存款等): The money of the suspect would ~ for 3 years. 该嫌疑人的财产要冻结三年。 ‖ ~r *n.* 冷藏箱;冰室

freezing /ˈfriːzɪŋ/

adj. very cold; chilling 极冷的: It was ~ last night. 昨夜天气酷寒。/What ~ weather! 多冷的天气呀!

freight /freɪt/

Ⅰ *n.* goods carried by truck, ship, train, or aircraft (用车、船、火车或飞机运送的)货物;货运: A lot of ~ was piled up in the storehouse waiting for transport. 大批货物堆积在仓库待运。 Ⅱ *v.* send or carry goods by truck, train, ship or aircraft 寄送,运送(货物)

frenzy /ˈfrenzi/

n. the state of great excitement or fear, so mad that one cannot think or act properly (激动或恐惧引起的)狂乱

frequency /ˈfriːkwənsi/

n. ❶ the state of happening often 频繁: Serious disasters appear to be increasing in ~. 严重灾害似乎越来越频繁。 ❷ the rate at which sth. happens or is repeated 频率,频度;发生次数: This radio station broadcasts on 3 different frequencies. 这家广播电台用三种不同的频率广播。

frequent /ˈfriːkwənt/

Ⅰ /ˈfriːkwənt/ *adj.* found or happening often; habitual 时常发生的,经常的,习惯的: Hurricanes are ~ here in autumn. 在秋天此地时常有飓风。/He's a ~ visitor. 他是这儿的常客。 Ⅱ /frɪˈkwent/ *v.* visit a place often or habitually 常光顾,常去: He ~s bars. 他常去酒吧。/Frogs ~ wet places. 青蛙常在湿地。

fresh /freʃ/

adj. ❶ newly made, produced, gathered, grown, etc.; not tinned, frozen or preserved 新鲜的: These are ~ eggs. 这些是新鲜鸡蛋。 ❷ new or different; no previously known or used 新近的;新的: Is there any ~ news? 有什么新的消息吗? ❸ (of the air, wind, weather) cool, refreshing 凉爽的;清新的: Open the window. Let the ~ air in! 打开窗户,让新鲜空气进来! ❹ bright and attractive 鲜艳的;亮丽的: Children like ~ colors. 孩子们喜欢鲜艳的颜色。

freshen /ˈfreʃn/

v. renew; make fresh 使新鲜: The rain ~ed the flowers. 这场雨使这些花显得更加鲜艳。

freshly /ˈfreʃli/

adv. (usually before a past participle) recently; just lately (用于过去分词之前)新近,刚才: "This coffee smells good." "Yes, it's ~ made." "这咖啡味道很香。" "是啊,是新磨的。"/His shirts have been ~ washed and ironed. 他的衬衣刚刚洗熨过。

freshman /ˈfreʃmən/

n. a student in the first year at a high school, college, or university (中学、学院或大学的)一年级新生

freshwater /ˈfreʃwɔːtə(r)/

adj. of, living in, or being a river or inland

lake;not belonging to the sea 淡水的;生存于淡水的;非海水的: ～ fish 淡水鱼/ ～ lakes 淡水湖

friable/'fraɪəbl/
*adj.*easily crumbled 易碎的;易粉碎的: The dry soil was ～.干燥的土壤很易捏碎。‖ **friability** *n.*易碎性;脆性

friction/'frɪkʃn/
*n.*❶ the rubbing of one thing against another 摩擦:Matches are lighted by ～.火柴由摩擦而着火。 ❷ the force that slows the motion of things that touch 摩擦力: It is necessary to reduce ～ as much as possible.必须尽可能地减少摩擦力。 ❸ conflict or difference caused by a clash of wills, temperaments or opinions (因意愿、性情、见解不协调而引起的)对立;冲突;摩擦: political ～ between two countries 两国间政治上的不和

Friday/'fraɪdi/
*n.*the day of the week after Thursday 星期五:Today is ～.今天是星期五。

fridge/frɪdʒ/
*n.*a refrigerator 冰箱

friend/frend/
*n.*❶ a person that you know well and like 朋友:I've made ～s with him yesterday.昨天我和他交了朋友。 ❷ a person who supports an organization, a country or a cause by giving financial or other help;a person who supports a particular idea, etc.赞助者;支持者:the ～s of the hospital 这家医院的赞助者/a ～ of democracy 维护民主的人。

friendly/'frendli/
*adj.*of a friend; having the attitude of a friend; kind and willing to make friends 朋友似的;友好的;友善的:They have always been on ～ terms.他们一直保持友好关系。‖ **be ～ with sb.**与某人友好

friendship/'frendʃɪp/
*n.*a relationship of being friends 友谊;朋友关系:Real ～ is more valuable than money.真正的友谊比金钱更宝贵。

fright/fraɪt/
*n.*a feeling or experience of fear 惊吓;恐怖:I was filled with ～ when I saw a mad dog.我看见一只疯狗时大为惊恐。

frighten/'fraɪtn/
*v.*fill with fright or terror; alarm suddenly 使吃惊;使害怕;吓唬:～ the sparrows away 把麻雀吓走 /I was ～ed out of my wits.我被吓得魂不附体。

frightened/'fraɪtnd/
*adj.*in a state of fear; afraid 受惊吓的;害怕的:a ～ horse 一匹受惊的马/ be ～ at the thought of 想到……就感到害怕/ He was ～ of the fierce dog.他害怕这条猛犬。/I was ～ to look down from the top of the tall building.我害怕从高的建筑物顶上往下看。

frightening/'fraɪtnɪŋ/
*adj.*making you feel afraid 引起恐惧的;使惊恐的;骇人的: a ～ experience (thought) 可怕的经历(想法) ‖ ～**ly** *adv.* 引起恐慌地;令人恐惧地

frightful/'fraɪtfl/
*adj.*dreadful; terrible; shocking 可怕的,令人恐怖的:a ～ explosion 可怕的爆炸/ He had a ～ experience.他有过一段可怕的经历。

frigid/'frɪdʒɪd/
*adj.*❶ very cold 寒冷的 ❷ very unfriendly; showing no emotions 冷淡的;冷漠的

frill/frɪl/
*n.*❶a piece of cloth used as a decoration on a dress, etc.(服装的)饰边 ❷ anything unnecessary and used only as a decoration 不必要的装饰品;虚饰物

fringe/frɪndʒ/
*n.*❶ the hair covering the forehead 额前垂发,刘海儿 ❷ a strip of decoration made of loose threads on the edge of a dress, carpet, scarf, etc.(服装、地毯、围巾等的)穗,流苏,须边 ❸ the edge or outside of an area or a group (地区或群体的)边缘,外围:on the ～ of a group 在人群的外围

frisk/frɪsk/
*v.*search sb. to see whether he is carrying weapons, drugs, etc. by passing the hands over the body 搜身 ‖ ～**y** *adj.*活泼的;喜欢蹦蹦跳跳的

frizzy/'frɪzi/

F

adj.(of the hair) having small tight curls
（指头发）卷曲的

fro/frəʊ/
adv.(**to and ～**) backwards and forwards
来来回回

frog/frɒg/
n. a small animal that lives on land and in
water with long back legs for swimming
and jumping 蛙：A ～ is a helpful animal
that kills pests in summer.青蛙在夏季消
灭害虫,是有益的动物。

frogman /ˈfrɒgmən/
n.(*pl.*frogmen)a swimmer equipped with
a rubber suit, flippers, and breathing apparatus for swimming and working underwater 蛙人；潜水员

frolic/ˈfrɒlɪk/
Ⅰ *n.*any noisy and happy action 嬉戏,作
乐 Ⅱ*v.*behave noisily and happily 嬉戏,
闹着玩

from/frɒm,frəm/
prep. ❶ indicating the starting at the
stated place, position, or action（表示空
间的起始点）从；自：The thief jumps ～
the wall.小偷自墙上跳下。❷ indicating
the starting at the stated time, a process
or an event（表示时间的起始点）从……
起：He works hard ～ morning till night.
他从早到晚辛勤劳动。❸ indicating the
distance between two places（表示距离）
离：The snow mountain is ten miles ～
the village.雪山距村庄十里远。❹ indicating the source or provenance of sb. or
sth.（表示来源）来自,从……来：I re-
ceived a letter ～ my aunt.我接到了姑妈
的来信。/Blood was trickling ～ the
wound.血正从伤口里一滴一滴流出来。
❺ because of；as a result of；through（表
示原因）由于；因为：Eating nothing all
day long the child cried ～ hunger.整天
没吃东西,小孩饿得直哭。❻ indicating
protection（表示防止）防：He saved the
boy ～ drowning.他救了这即将淹死的孩
子。

front/frʌnt/
Ⅰ *adj.*of or at the front 前面的；正面的：
We entered the court through the ～

door.我们从前门走进法庭。Ⅱ *n.* ❶ the
most forward part of sth. 面面；前部：She
sat in the ～ of the cinema.她坐在电影院
的前排。/In ～ of the school there is a
playground.学校前面有一块操场。❷
the place where fighting takes place in a
war 前线：The troops are going to the ～.
部队正开赴前线。Ⅲ *v.*(of a building or
piece of land ）have the front facing towards 面前；朝向：The temple ～s the
south.这座庙宇朝南。

frontage/ˈfrʌntɪdʒ/
*n.*a part of a building or of land that stretches along a road, river, etc.（建筑物或土
地的）沿着街道（河流）伸展的部分；临街
（河、湖等）地：The shop has ～s on two
busy streets.这家商店的门面正对着两条
热闹的街道。/The boat-building compa-
ny is looking for a yard with a wide river
～.这家造船公司正在寻找一块临河的宽
广场地。

frontal/ˈfrʌntl/
*adj.*❶ of, at, or to the front 前面的,正面
的：The brain has two ～ lobes.大脑有两
个前叶。❷ (of an attack)direct or delivered from the front (攻击)直接的,从正
面发起的 ❸ of or being a weather front
气锋的：A new ～ system is moving towards Britain from the west.有一股新的
气锋系统正从西方向着英国移动。

frontier/ˈfrʌntɪə(r)/
*n.*a boundary between countries 国境,边
疆,边界：They were caught trying to
cross the ～.他们企图偷越国境时被逮住
了。

frost/frɒst/
Ⅰ *n.*❶ a weather condition at a temperature below the freezing point of water 严
寒天气；霜冻；冰点以下的天气：Frost has
killed some plants.严寒冻死了一些植物。
❷ a deposit of white ice crystals forms
on the ground or other surfaces when the
temperature drops below 0℃ 霜：The ～
melted when the sun rose.太阳出来了,
霜融化了。Ⅱ*v.*cover sth.or become covered with frost (使)蒙上霜,结霜：In
winter sometimes it ～s.冬天有时霜冻。

frostbite /ˈfrɒstbaɪt/

n. an injury to the tissue of the body caused by exposure to extreme cold 冻伤,冻疮 ‖ **frostbitten** *adj.*生冻疮的

frosted /ˈfrɒstɪd/
adj. ❶ covered with or as if with frost 结霜的,被霜覆盖的;似结霜的：the ～ garden 白霜覆盖的花园 ❷ (of glass or a window) having a translucent textured surface so that it is difficult to see through (玻璃、窗户) 磨砂的,毛面的

frosty /ˈfrɒsti/
adj. ❶ covered with frost 结了霜的：～ fields 结了霜的田野 ❷ very cold 严寒的：It was a very ～ morning.那是个霜冻的早晨。❸ unfriendly and cold in manner 不友善的;冷淡的：She gave me a ～ greeting.她冷淡地同我打了一个招呼。

froth /frɒθ/
n. small bubbles on the top of liquid (e.g. on a glass of beer) 泡沫 (如啤酒的泡沫)：I don't like beer with too much ～. 我不喜欢泡沫太多的啤酒。‖ ～**y** *adj.* 有泡沫的;泡沫状的

frown /fraʊn/
Ⅰ *v.* draw the eyebrows down over the nose, as you do when you are angry or thinking 皱眉;蹙额：He ～ed as he tried to work out the sum.他设法算出总数时,把眉头皱了起来。Ⅱ *n.* a facial expression or look characterized by such a furrowing of one's brows 皱眉头;蹙额：There was a deep ～ on her face.她的额头常常皱着。

frugal /ˈfruːɡl/
adj. careful, economical of food, money or expenditure; costing little 节俭的：You must be ～ of money.你必须节省金钱。

fruit /fruːt/
n. ❶ a part of a plant or tree that contains the seeds and is used as food (e.g. apples, bananas) 水果：You should eat more ～ so as to keep fit.为了保持身段,你应该多吃水果。❷ (the ～) the profit, result, or reward of labour, industry, study, etc. 结果;成果：His success is the ～ of his hard labour.他的成功是辛勤劳动的成果。

fruitful /ˈfruːtfl/
adj. ❶ bearing plenty of fruit 果实累累的 ❷ successful; producing good results 成功的;有收获的：a ～ meeting 一次成功的会议/ a ～ career 成功的事业

fruitless /ˈfruːtləs/
adj. ❶ producing no fruit 不结果实的 ❷ (of an effort) useless, unsuccessful, not bringing the desired result 白费的;无收获的;不成功的：～ efforts 徒劳

frustrate /frʌˈstreɪt/
v. defeat sb. or sb.'s effort 挫败：The bad weather ～d all our hopes of going for an outing.恶劣的天气打破了我们去郊游的希望。/be ～d in an attempt to do sth.欲做某事而遭受挫折

frustrated /frʌˈstreɪtɪd, ˈfrʌstreɪtɪd/
adj. ❶ feeling annoyed and impatient because you cannot do or achieve what you want 懊丧的;懊恼的;沮丧的：We all felt ～ at the lack of progress.没有进展,我们都感到懊丧。❷ (of a person) unable to follow or be successful in a particular career (人) 失意的：a ～ actor 失意的演员 ❸ prevented from progressing, succeeding, or being fulfilled 受挫的,落空的：Some parents may want the children to fulfil their own ～ dreams.有些父母可能希望他们的孩子能去实现自己未完成的梦想。

frustrating /frʌˈstreɪtɪŋ/
adj. causing you to feel annoyed and impatient because you cannot do or achieve what you want 令人懊恼的;令人沮丧的：It's ～ to have to wait so long.要等这么长时间,真令人懊恼。

frustration /frʌˈstreɪʃn/
n. defeat or disappointment 挫败;挫折;失望：embittered by numerous ～s 遭多次挫折

fry /fraɪ/
v. cook sth. or be cooked in hot fat or oil 油炸;油煎：The sausages are ～ing in the pan.香肠正在平底锅里煎着。/I shall ～ the fish for dinner.我将把这条鱼煎好供晚餐吃。‖ ～**pan** *n.*煎锅

fuel /ˈfjuːəl/

Ⅰ *n*. any material that is used for producing heat or power by burning 燃料：Wood,coal and oil can be used as ～.木头、煤和石油可做燃料。Ⅱ *v*. supply sth. with material that can be burnt to produce heat or power 给……提供燃料：Now most ships are ～ed with oil.目前大多数船舶以石油作为燃料。

fugitive/ˈfjuːdʒətɪv/

　　n.a person who runs away from a place, especially to avoid arrest 逃犯；逃亡者：a ～ from justice 逃犯

fulcrum/ˈfʊlkrəm/

　　n. the support on which a lever turns in raising sth. 支点，支轴：Use this stone as a ～ to lever out the stump. 以这石块作为支点，用杠杆把树桩撬起来。

fulfil/fʊlˈfɪl/

　　v.do or perform what is required or necessary 履行；完成：We must strive to ～ our due obligations.我们应努力履行我们应尽的义务。‖ ～ment *n*.完成；实现

full/fʊl/

　　Ⅰ *adj*. ❶ containing or holding as much or as many as possible；having a lot of a particular quality 满的；装满的；充满(某种品质)的：waste bins ～ of rubbish 装满垃圾的垃圾箱 Young people are ～ of vigour and vitality.年轻人朝气蓬勃。❷ complete with nothing missing 完全的；完整的：I copied the ～ text.我抄写了全文。❸ reaching the highest or greatest possible 尽可能多(大)；十足的：The train is running at ～ speed.火车正在全速前进。❹ (of a shape or sb. 's body) plump or rounded；fleshy 圆鼓鼓的；丰满的：The shop sold clothes for ～er figure.这家铺子出售胖人穿的衣服。Ⅱ *adv*. completely 十分；足足：They walked ～ 10 miles.他们步行了整整十英里。

fullness /ˈfʊlnəs/

　　n.the state of being full 装满，充满：several tins in different states of ～几个装得不一样满的铁皮罐 ‖ in the ～ of time 到时候，在适当的时候；最终

fully/ˈfʊli/

　　adv.completely；entirely 完全地：I don't

～ understand his reasons for quitting.我不完全明白他辞职的原因。/It will take ～ four days.那要花整整四天时间。

fumble/ˈfʌmbl/

　　Ⅰ *v*.move the fingers or hands awkwardly in search of sth. 乱摸；摸索：In the dark I ～d for the lost key.在黑暗中我摸索着寻找丢失的钥匙。Ⅱ *n*. the act of fumbling 摸索：The ～s of six blind men for the elephant are funny.六个瞎子摸象的动作很可笑。

fume/fjuːm/

　　Ⅰ *n*. ❶ (*pl*.) smoke or gas that smells strongly or is dangerous to breathe in (浓烈的或有害的)烟，气：The room is filled with ～s of cigars.房间里充满着雪茄烟的气味。❷ rage or fury 狂怒：Father was in a ～.父亲勃然大怒。Ⅱ *v*. ❶ give off smoke 冒烟；冒气：The burnt rubbish heap was still fuming.烧完了的垃圾堆仍在冒烟。❷ be very angry and restless 大为生气；大发雷霆：The manager ～d at the carelessness of his secretary.经理对秘书的粗心大意大发脾气。

fun/fʌn/

　　Ⅰ *n*. amusement；pleasure 娱乐；乐趣：They had a lot of ～ at the Spring Festival.春节期间，他们玩得痛快极了。‖ in (for) ～ 开玩笑地；为了好玩/make ～ of 取笑；开玩笑 Ⅱ *adj*. amusing or enjoyable；providing pleasure 有趣的；逗笑的：This game looks ～! 这个游戏好像很有趣！/ The actor wears a ～ hat. 那个演员戴着一顶滑稽的帽子。‖ ～fair *n*. 游乐场

function/ˈfʌŋkʃn/

　　Ⅰ *n*.a special duty (of a person) or purpose (of a thing) 作用；功能；职能；机能：the ～ of the heart 心脏的功能/ the ～s of a judge 法官的职责 Ⅱ *v*.work or act in the correct way 正常工作；起作用：The telephone does not ～ properly.这电话机有毛病。

functional /ˈfʌŋkʃənl/

　　adj. ❶ to do with a function or having a function (有……)机能的；(有……)作用的；(有……)目的的：There are important ～ differences between left and right brain.左脑和右脑在机能上有重要的不同之处。❷ working or operating; able to be used 在工作的;在运转的;(能)起作用的: The computer network is not yet fully ~.计算机网络暂时还未全面运作。❸ designed to be practical and useful rather than attractive or luxurious 实用的 ‖ ~ly adv.机能上地;功能上地

fund/fʌnd/
I n.❶ a large stock or supply of sth. 贮藏;贮存:a ~ of knowledge 丰富的知识 ❷ a sum of money available for a purpose 基金;资金:a relief ~ 救济基金 II v.provide money for an activity,organization,etc. 为(活动、组织)提供资金:a project ~ed by the government 一项政府出资的计划

fundamental/ˌfʌndə'mentl/
I n. (usually pl.) a central or primary rule,law,etc.on which a system is based 基本规律;基本原理;根本法则:Self-reliance and hard struggle are the important ~s in building socialism.自力更生、艰苦奋斗是建设社会主义的重要原则。II adj.being at the base or from which all else develops 基本的;根本的;基础的: The ~ purpose for me to learn English is to know the world affairs through it.我学英语的根本目的是通过它了解世界事务。‖ ~ly adv.基本地

funeral/'fjuːnərəl/
n.a burial or ceremony for a dead person 丧葬;葬礼:attend a ~ 参加丧(葬)礼

funerary /'fjuːnərəri/
adj.to do with a funeral or burial 丧葬的;与葬礼有关的: ~ ceremonies 丧葬仪式

funnel/'fʌnl/
n.❶ a type of tube with a wide mouth and a narrow bottom,used for pouring liquid,etc. into a container 漏斗 ❷ the part of a steamship or steam engine where smoke comes out (轮船或蒸汽机的)烟囱

funny/'fʌni/
adj.❶ amusing or causing laughter 滑稽的;逗乐的;有趣的:When I was a small

child,my grandfather often told me ~ stories.我小的时候,爷爷常给我讲好笑的故事。/This is a very ~ book.这是一本很有趣的书。❷ strange or curious; hard to explain 古怪的;奇怪的;难以解释的:There's something ~ about the telephone,it won't work this morning.这电话有点古怪,今天早上就是不好使。

fur/fɜː(r)/
n.❶ the soft thick hair covering certain animals (某些动物的)毛,软毛:There is thick ~ on a bear in winter.冬季,熊的躯体上披着厚厚的软毛。❷ the animal skin with the fur on it, especially when made into garments(动物的)毛皮;(尤指)毛皮衣服,裘皮衣服:All of them wear expensive ~ coats.他们都穿着昂贵的皮大衣。‖ ~ry adj.毛皮的,像毛皮的

furious/'fjʊəriəs/
adj.very angry and violent 狂怒的;猛烈的;狂暴的:a ~ man 大发雷霆的人/a ~ wind 狂风/ a ~ struggle 猛烈的斗争

furnace/'fɜːnɪs/
n. an apparatus in a factory, in which metals and other substances are heated to very high temperatures in an enclosed space 高炉;熔炉:Steel is melted in a blast ~.钢在高炉中熔化。

furnish/'fɜːnɪʃ/
v.❶ supply what is necessary for a special purpose 供给:The grocery ~ed people with food.这家食品杂货店供应食品。❷ put furniture in;supply with furniture (用家具)布置:The rooms of this hotel are luxuriously and artistically ~ed.这宾馆的房间布置得豪华、艺术。‖ ~ed adj.备有家具的/ ~ings n.家具和陈设品

furniture/'fɜːnɪtʃə(r)/
n.movable articles of a building or room, such as tables and beds 家具(总称):a piece of ~ 一件家具

furrow/'fʌrəʊ/
I n. ❶ a long narrow track cut by a plough in farming land when the earth is being turned over in preparation for

F

planting 犁沟：When the tractor runs across the field, there are ～s left behind. 当拖拉机驶过田野，它后面留下了犁沟。❷ a deep line or fold in the skin of the face, especially the forehead（脸上的）皱纹：There are many deep ～s all over the old man's sunburnt face.老人晒黑的脸上布满许多深深的皱纹。Ⅱ v.❶ make a rut, groove or trail in the ground or the surface of sth. 使出现车辙（或凹槽、痕迹）❷ mark or be marked with lines or wrinkles caused by frowning, worrying or concentration 有皱纹；使起皱纹：The old man looked at the sick dog with a ～ed brow.老人皱起眉头看着这只生病的狗。

further/ˈfɜːðə(r)/
Ⅰ adv.❶ at or to a greater distance or more distant point; farther 较远地；更远地：It's not safe to go any ～.再走远一些就不安全了。❷ more; to a greater degree or extent 进一步；在更大程度上；在更大范围内：The police decided to investigate ～.警方决定做进一步调查。❸ over a greater expanse of time（时间上）更远地：Think ～ back into your school time.再往前回想你的学生时光。Ⅱ v. help(sth.) advance or succeed 增进；促进：They'll do all they can to ～ your plan.他们将尽力促使你的计划成功。

furthermore/ˌfɜːðəˈmɔː(r)/
adv. in addition; moreover; besides 此外，再者：Furthermore, I should like to point out...此外，我想指出……

furthermost/ˈfɜːðəməʊst/
adj. located at the greatest distance from sth. 最远的：at the ～ end of the street 在街尾

furthest/ˈfɜːðɪst/
Ⅰ adj.❶ located at the greatest distance from sth.最远的❷ extremely remote 极其遥远的 Ⅱ adv. at or by the greatest distance 离……最远地

fury/ˈfjʊəri/
n. great anger 愤怒，盛怒：He couldn't speak for ～.由于愤怒他说不出话来。/ He flew into a ～.他勃然大怒。

fuse/fjuːz/
Ⅰ n. a small container with a short thin piece of wire, placed in an electric apparatus or system, which melts if too much electric power passes through it, and thus breaks the connection and prevents fires or other damage 保险丝：A ～ has burnt, causing all the lights in the teaching building to fail.保险丝烧了，教学大楼的全部电灯都熄灭了。Ⅱ v.❶ melt or cause metal to melt in great heat（使）熔化：Lead will ～ at a lower temperature than some other metals.铅的熔点比其他一些金属低。❷ join or become joined by melting 熔合：He ～d two pieces of wire together in his lab.他在实验室里熔合了两根铁丝。❸（cause to）stop working owing to the melting of a fuse（使）（电路）烧断：All the lights in the dormitory have ～d.保险丝烧断，宿舍里电灯全熄了。

fusion/ˈfjuːʒn/
n. the process of mixing or joining 混合；结合，联合：a ～ of various races 不同种族的融合/a ～ of various ideas 不同想法的结合

fuss/fʌs/
Ⅰ n.❶ an unnecessary or excessive expression of excitement, anger, impatience, etc.大惊小怪；小题大做：Stop all this ～! 不要大惊小怪！❷ an anxious nervous condition 焦虑；紧张：Don't get into a ～ about nothing. 别没事找事，自寻烦恼。Ⅱ v. disturb or bother 烦扰：Don't ～ me.别烦我。

fussy/ˈfʌsi/
adj.❶ full of or showing nervous excitement; worrying about little things 大惊小怪的；瞎忙的 ❷（of clothes, style, etc.）over ornamented; having too many unimportant details, etc.（衣服、风格等）过分装饰的

fusty/ˈfʌsti/
adj.❶（of room, box, clothes, etc.）having an unpleasant smell as a result of having been shut up for a long time, especially when not quite dry（房间、箱子、衣服等）有霉味的 ❷ not modern; old-fashioned 过时的；陈腐的；旧式的：We want to clear away all these ～ ideas about

education and bring in some up-to-date methods.我们要清除所有这些陈腐的教育观念,引进一些现代的教育方法。

futile/ˈfjuːtaɪl/
*adj.*producing no good results 无益的;无效的:They made a ~ search 他们白白搜寻了一番。

futon/ˈfuːtɒn/
*n.*a Japanese quilted mattress rolled out on the floor for use as a bed 蒲团,日本床垫

future/ˈfjuːtʃə(r)/
Ⅰ *n.* ❶ the time or a period of time coming after the present 将来;未来:The ~ must always be uncertain.未来的一切总是难以预料。 ❷ the possibility of being successful or surviving at a later time 前途;前景:Young people have bright ~. 年轻人前途光明。 ‖ in ~ 将来 Ⅱ *adj.* coming after the present 未来的;将来的:We believe in a ~ life.我们对未来的生活充满信心。

F

Gg

gab/gæb/
　　v. (-bb-) talk continuously and without thought 闲聊；喋喋不休

gabble/'gæbl/
　　Ⅰ *v.* speak quickly and indistinctly 急促不清地说话：The dying patient ～d to his family.垂危的病人跟他的家人急促不清地说话。Ⅱ *n.* words or word-like sounds spoken so quickly that they cannot be heard clearly 急促不清的话：I heard the ～ of excited children.我听到孩子们兴奋得说不清话。

gad/gæd/
　　v. (-dd-) wander aimlessly in search of pleasure 游荡，闲逛：She spent a few months ～ding about (Europe) before her exams.考试前，她（在欧洲）漫游了几个月。

gadabout/'gædəbaut/
　　n. a person who goes out for amusement 好游荡者，闲游者：She's become quite a ～ since she left home.她自从离家以后，变成了一个十足游手好闲的人。

gadgetry/'gædʒɪtri/
　　n. small machines or devices which do sth. useful 小型器械（或装置）：Their kitchen is so full of ～ that you can hardly move.他们的厨房里到处都是小巧的装置，多得几乎连走动的地方都没有了。

gaffe/gæf/
　　n. an unintentional social mistake or awkward 失礼；失言；失态：From the way she looked at me when I asked how much money she earned I realized I'd committed an awful ～.当我问她赚多少钱时，我从她看我的神情上知道自己严重失言。

gaffer/'gæfə(r)/
　　n. ❶ someone in charge of the lighting in making a cinema film （拍摄电影时负责灯光的）照明电工 ❷ a man in charge, especially in a factory 领班，工头 ❸ an old man 老头

gaggle/'gægl/
　　n. ❶ a flock of geese 鹅群 ❷ a group of noisy people who talk a lot 一群吵闹的人：A ～ of schoolgirls followed the tennis star to his car.一群七嘴八舌的女学生跟着网球明星一直到他的车跟前。

gaiety/'geɪəti/
　　n. ❶ a feeling, attitude or atmosphere of happiness 愉快；快活 ❷ (*pl.*) merry making；joyful, festive occasions 欢乐；狂欢；乐事：the gaieties of the New Year 新年的快乐

gaily/'geɪli/
　　adv. ❶ in a cheerful manner 欢乐地；愉快地；喜气洋洋地：she laughed ～.她快乐地笑了。❷ in an insensitive, thoughtless way 轻率地，欠思索地：They ～ went on talking after the film had started.电影开演后，他们还在毫无顾忌地讲话。

gain/geɪn/
　　Ⅰ *v.* ❶ obtain sth. useful, advantageous, wanted, profitable, etc. 获得：The scientist ～ed Nobel Prize for this year.这位科学家获得了今年的诺贝尔奖。❷ have an increase in 增添；增长；增加：The plane ～ed speed as it took off.飞机起飞后，就加速了。❸ (of a watch or clock) go fast by (an amount of time) （表、钟）走快：My watch ～s half a minute a day.我的表一天快半分钟。❹ reach (somewhere), especially with effort or difficulty （费力地）到达（某地）：We climbed a mountain with difficulty, at last, ～ed the top of the mountain.我们艰难地爬山，最后到达了山顶。Ⅱ *n.* ❶ (the act of making) a profit 获利：No ～s without pains.不劳则无获。❷ an increase in amount 增长；增

加；A fall into the pit, a ～ in your wit.吃一堑，长一智。

gainful /ˈɡeɪnfl/

adj. paid or profitable 有收益的；有报酬的；有利可图的：a ～ employment 有酬的工作 ‖ ～ly *adv.* 有利益地；有利可图地

gait /ɡeɪt/

n. a way or manner of walking or running 走相；步态；步法：an awkward ～ 难看的步态

gala /ˈɡɑːlə/

n. a special show, celebration or festival 节日；庆祝活动；演出

galaxy /ˈɡæləksi/

n. ❶ huge mass of millions of stars 星系：Our universe is made up of many galaxies. 我们的宇宙是由许多星系组成的。❷ (Galaxy) the extremely large group of stars and planets to which the Earth belongs and which is seen at night as a faint band of light across the sky 银河系

gale /ɡeɪl/

n. ❶ a strong wind 强风；大风；疾风：It is blowing a ～. 刮大风了。❷ a noisy outburst 一阵喧闹：～s of laughter 一阵阵笑声

gall /ɡɔːl/

n. ❶ bitter liquid made by the liver 胆汁：～ bladder 胆汁；胆囊 ❷ anything bitter; a bitter feeling 苦味；痛苦；怨恨：words full of venom and ～ 充满恶毒怨恨的话 ❸ rudeness; bad manners 粗鲁；无礼

gallant /ˈɡælənt/

adj. ❶ courageous 勇敢的：We need a ～ fighter. 我们需要一个勇敢的战士。❷ (of a man) attentive and polite to women (男子对女子) 献殷勤的：The young man is ～ to women. 这年轻人惯于对妇女献殷勤。

gallery /ˈɡæləri/

n. ❶ a room or building used to show collections of pictures, statues, or other works of art 美术作品陈列馆，画廊 ❷ the highest and cheapest seats in a theatre (剧院中票价最便宜的) 最高楼座 (的观众)

gallon /ˈɡælən/

n. a unit of measurement for liquids 加仑 (液量单位)：One ～ is eight pints, or 4.5 litres. 一加仑等于八品脱或四升半。

gallop /ˈɡæləp/

Ⅰ *n.* a fast gait of a horse (指马等) 飞跑；疾驰：go at a ～ 飞奔 Ⅱ *v.* do sth. in a hurry 匆匆地做：～ through one's work 急急忙忙赶完工作

galloping /ˈɡæləpɪŋ/

adj. increasing or changing very quickly 迅速增加 (变化) 的：The country is suffering from ～ inflation; the value of its money has halved in the past six months. 这个国家通货膨胀迅速恶化，货币在过去六个月贬值了一半。

gallows /ˈɡæləʊz/

n. a wooden framework on which to put criminals to death by hanging 绞刑架；绞台：come to the ～ 上绞架/send a man to the ～ 处某人绞刑

galvanize /ˈɡælvənaɪz/

v. ❶ coat (iron) with zinc to protect it from rust 电镀；镀锌：～d iron 镀锌铁皮 ❷ suddenly awaken or stimulate by electricity or shock (用电) 刺激；突然唤醒：The alarm bell ～d them into action 警铃声唤醒他们采取行动。

galvanometer /ˌɡælvəˈnɒmɪtə(r)/

n. an instrument for detecting and measuring a small electric current 电流计

gambit /ˈɡæmbɪt/

n. ❶ an action or remark intended to gain some advantage 开头一招；开局；开场白 ❷ (in chess) an opening sequence of moves in which a player deliberately sacrifices a pawn or other piece in order to gain a favourable position (国际象棋中为获得优势而采取的) 开局让棋法

gamble /ˈɡæmbl/

Ⅰ *v.* play games for chance of money; take risks of the chance for making a profit 赌博：He lost all his money gambling on the stock exchange. 他炒股票把钱输了个精光。 Ⅱ *n.* a risky matter or act 冒险：The travel to the South Pole is a ～. 去南极旅行是一次冒险。 ‖ ～r *n.* 赌徒

gambol/ˈɡæmbl/

v.(-ll- or -l-)jump or dance playfully like young animals or children（像小动物或小孩一样）蹦蹦跳跳,嬉戏

game/ɡeɪm/

n.❶ a form of play or sport 游戏：Hide-and-seek is a favorite children's ～.捉迷藏是孩子们都喜爱的游戏。❷(pl.) athletic contests 运动会：He intended to take part in the Olympic Games.他打算参加奥林匹克运动会。❸a single part of a set into which a match is divided,e.g.in tennis,bridge,etc.（网球、桥牌等的）一局,一场：She won 3～s.她赢了三局。❹ a trick or secret plan 诡计：He liked to play a double ～.他喜欢玩弄两面手法。❺ wild animals,birds,and fish which are hunted or fished for food,especially as a sport 猎物；野味：The hound smelt out the ～ and barked.猎犬嗅出了猎物就狂吠起来。

gamesmanship/ˈɡeɪmzmənʃɪp/

n.the art of winning by using the rules to one's own advantage without actually cheating（比赛中用以取胜而不算犯规的）绝招,花招,小动作

gang/ɡæŋ/

n.❶ an organized group of people working together（在一起工作的）队；组。❷ a group of criminals 犯罪团伙：The ～ are being hunted by the police.警方正在追捕这帮匪徒。

ganger/ˈɡæŋə(r)/

n.the foreman of a group of workers,especially building workers（尤指建筑工会的）工头,领班

gangland/ˈɡæŋlænd/

n.the world of organized and especially violent crime 歹徒充斥的地区；黑社会：A group of ～ bosses met to decide who would control which territory.一群黑社会头目聚在一起以决定由谁控制哪个地盘。

ganglion/ˈɡæŋɡliən/

n.(pl.～s or ganglia/ˈɡæŋɡliə/)❶ a mass of nerve cells 神经节 ❷ a (painful) swelling containing liquid 腱鞘囊肿

gangplank/ˈɡæŋplæŋk/

n.a wooden board which is used to make a bridge to get into or out of a ship or to pass from one ship to another（上下船用的）跳板,舷梯

gangster/ˈɡæŋstə(r)/

n.a member of an organized group of violence 歹徒；匪徒：a ～ film 盗匪影片

gangway/ˈɡæŋweɪ/

n.❶ opening in a ship's side；movable bridge from this to the land（轮船）梯口；舷门；舷梯；跳板 ❷ the passage between two rows of seats in a cinema,theatre,bus,or train；aisle（电影院、剧场、公共汽车、火车等座位间的）通路；过道

gap/ɡæp/

n.❶ an empty space between two objects or two parts of an object 缺口；裂缝：We can see the green field through a ～ in the wall.我们能从墙上的缺口看见绿色的田野。❷ a big difference between two groups of people,things,or sets of ideas 差距；分歧；间隔：There is a ～ between the two generations.两代人之间出现了代沟。

gape/ɡeɪp/

v.❶look at sb.or sth. in surprise or wonder,especially with the mouth open 张着大嘴呆看；张大嘴：The boy ～d at the large whale,horrified.男孩目瞪口呆地看着大鲸鱼,惊恐万状。❷ come apart or open widely 裂开

garage/ˈɡærɑːʒ,ˈɡærɪdʒ/

n.❶ a building in which motor vehicles can be kept 汽车房,车库：He drove his car to the ～.他把轿车开进了车库。❷ a place where motor vehicles are repaired and petrol and oil may also be sold 汽车修理厂：The driver stopped his car at the ～ to buy some petrol.司机把车停在汽车修理厂前以便买些汽油。

garb/ɡɑːb/

Ⅰ n.the clothes especially as worn by a particular kind of person（尤指不寻常的）服装；装束；制服：a man in clerical ～ 穿着牧师服装的人 Ⅱ v.provide with clothes or put clothes on 穿；装扮：

oneself as a sailor 打扮成水手模样/be ~ed in motley 穿着五颜六色衣服

garbage/ˈɡɑːbɪdʒ/

*n.*waste food put out as worthless, or for pigs, etc.; rubbish, refuse (of any kind) 垃圾；废物；剩饭残羹：~ can (truck) 垃圾箱(车)/The street is covered with old tins and other forms of ~.满街都是废弃的空罐头和其他各种废物。

garble/ˈɡɑːbl/

*v.*give an incomplete or confused account 曲解；篡改：The newspaper account of the minister's speech was completely ~d.报纸对部长演讲的报道完全是歪曲。

garden/ˈɡɑːdn/

Ⅰ *n.*a piece of land, often around or at the side of a house, which may be covered with grass or planted with flowers, fruit and vegetables (花、果、菜)园：He planted many beautiful flowers in his ~.他在花园里种了许多美丽的花。Ⅱ *v.*work in a park, keeping it tidy, making plants grow,etc.种花；种菜：He has been ~ing all day.他已做了一天的园艺工作。

gardener/ˈɡɑːdnə(r)/

*n.*a person who works in a garden, either for pay or as a hobby 园丁；园艺家；园林工人：*Song of the Gardeners*《园丁之歌》

gardenia /ɡɑːˈdiːniə/

n. a bush with shiny leaves and large white or yellow flowers with a sweet smell, also called gardenias 栀子花

gargle/ˈɡɑːɡl/

Ⅰ *v.*wash the throat with liquid by blowing through it at the back of the mouth 漱口，漱喉，含漱：I ~ every morning when I have a cold.我感冒时每天清晨漱口。Ⅱ *n.*the act of gargling; rinse liquid used for rinsing the mouth 漱口；含漱剂：Hot water with salt makes a good ~.热水加盐就是一种很好的含漱剂。

garish/ˈɡeərɪʃ/

*adj.*bright and showy; too brightly coloured 华丽而俗气的；过分鲜艳的：The room is spoilt by the ~ wallpaper.这房间因为贴了花花绿绿的墙纸而变得俗不可耐。

garland/ˈɡɑːlənd/

*n.*a woven circle of flowers or leaves used as a sign of victory 花环；花冠：carry away (gain, win) the ~ 比赛获胜

garlic/ˈɡɑːlɪk/

*n.*an onion-like plant with a strong taste and smell, used in cooking 大蒜：a clove of ~ 一瓣蒜/too much ~ in the food 食物中放太多的蒜

garment/ˈɡɑːmənt/

*n.*an article of dress 衣服：a new ~ 新衣服/~s of all kind(s) 各种服装

garnish/ˈɡɑːnɪʃ/

Ⅰ *v.* (usually of a dish of food) decorate with parsley or other ornamental foods (通常指一盘食物)加配菜；为(食物)添加饰菜：The cook ~ed the beef with onions.厨子用洋葱装饰牛肉。Ⅱ *n.* sth. used to decorate a dish of food (e.g.parsley, mint,etc.)配菜，装饰菜(如芫荽、薄荷等)

garrison/ˈɡærɪsn/

Ⅰ *n.*the military force stationed in a town or fort 驻军；卫戍部队；警卫部队 Ⅱ *v.* supply a town, etc. with troops; place troops,etc. on troops duty 驻防(城市)；守卫；配备(军队)：The government will ~ the coastal towns.政府将派军驻守沿海城镇。/The soldiers ~ed the town.士兵们守卫着这个城市。

gas/ɡæs/

*n.*❶ a substance like air, which is not solid or liquid and usually cannot be seen 气体；气态：Air is a mixture of ~es.空气是多种气体的混合物。❷ a substance of this type, especially natural gas, which is burnt in the home for heating and cooking and formerly also for light 煤气：Put the kettle on the ~.将壶放在煤气炉上。

gaseous/ˈɡeɪsɪəs/

*adj.*existing as or having characteristics of a gas 气态的；气体的；似气体的：a ~ mixture 气态混合物

gash/ɡæʃ/

Ⅰ *n.*a long, deep cut in the skin or in the surface of sth.(深长的)伤口：There was a ~ on his face.他的脸上有一道长而深

的伤口。Ⅱ *v.* wound with a large deep cut (伤口长而深地)划伤,砍伤:She ~ed her right hand on the broken cup.破杯子把她的右手划了一道长而深的口子。

gasket/'gæskɪt/

n. a ring or strip of soft material placed tightly between two parts of a joint in a pipe,etc. to prevent gas, steam, etc. from escaping 垫片,垫圈,密封垫

gasolene/'gæsəliːn/

n. petrol 〈美〉汽油:The enemy plane threw a ~ bomb and flew away. 敌机扔下了一颗汽油弹就飞走了。

gasometer /gæ'sɒmɪtə/

n. a large round tank in which gas is stored and from which it is distributed through pipes to users (多为圆柱形,金属的)储(煤)气罐

gasp/gɑːsp/

Ⅰ *v.*❶take one's breath suddenly and in a way that can be heard, especially because of surprise, shock, etc. 喘不过气来:The audience ~ed when the acrobats acted on the rope.杂技演员在钢丝上表演时,观众凝神屏息。❷breathe quickly,especially with difficulty,making a noise 气喘吁吁地说:He ~ed out the last word. 他气喘吁吁地说出了最后一句话。Ⅱ *n.* an act of gasping 气喘:I heard a ~ of surprise from the crowd.我听到了来自人群中的一声惊叹。

gate/geɪt/

n. ❶ a structure like a door in a wall, fence,etc.that can be closed 大门;城门;篱笆门;闸门:at the ~ 在大门口/The boy jumped over the ~ into the field. 男孩跳过栅门进入田野。❷ the total a-mount of money paid by the people entering to watch a sports match,etc.观众人数;门票收入:There was a ~ of thousands.观众有数千人。

gatehouse/'geɪthaʊs/

n. a small house built at or over a gate (e. g.at the entrance to a park or castle) (公园、城堡等大门旁的)门房,警卫室

gatekeeper/'geɪtkiːpə(r)/

n. a person who is in charge of the opening and closing of a gate 看门人

gatepost/'geɪtpəʊst/

n. a post beside a gate, from which the gate is hung or to which it fastens (大门的)门柱

gateway/'geɪtweɪ/

n. ❶ an opening in a fence, wall, etc., across which a gate may be put 入口;通道;门径 ❷ a way of reaching or gaining (especially sth. desirable) 途径,门路;方法,手段:Hard work is the ~ to success. 努力工作是通往成功之路。

gather/'gæðə(r)/

v. ❶ get or assemble together 聚集:Thousands of people ~ to celebrate the victory.成千上万的人集会庆祝胜利。❷ pick up and arrange together; collect 采集;收获:The farmers are ~ing wheat.农民正在收小麦。❸introduce information that you have found out,especially when you have found it out in an indirect way 推测,猜想:Did you ~ what the mad man was saying? 你听出这个疯子说的什么了吗?

gathering/'gæðərɪŋ/

*n.*❶a group of persons to gather in one place 集会,聚会:a small social ~ 小型的社交聚会 ❷a fold or pleat in a garment 衣褶

gaudy/'gɔːdi/

adj. bright and showy 华丽而俗气的:That's a ~ tie you are wearing.你打的领带太俗气了。

ga(u)ge/geɪdʒ/

Ⅰ *n.* ❶ an instrument for measuring (e.g.rainfall, strength of wind, size, diameter,etc.of tools,wires,etc.) 测量仪器:a rain ~ 雨量器/a screw ~ 螺旋规 ❷the distance between opposite wheels on a vehicle that runs on rails (铁路)轨距:broad (narrow) ~ 宽(窄)轨道 ❸accepted or approved instance or example of a quantity or quality against which others are judged or measured or compared standard measure;extent 规格;标准;尺度:take the ~ of 估计;度量 Ⅱ *v.* ❶ measure by means of a gauge 测量:~

the rainfall 测量雨量 ❷estimate;judge; guess 估计;判断;猜测

gaunt /gɔːnt/

adj. ❶（of a person）lean, haggard, as from hunger, ill-health or suffering 瘦削的;憔悴的:a ~ figure 枯瘦的身躯 ❷（of a place）grim or desolate 贫瘠的;荒凉的:a ~ hillside 荒凉的山坡

gauze /gɔːz/

n. a type of light, soft cloth with tiny holes in it or of wire for screening windows a-gainst insects, etc. 纱布;(金属等的)网纱:cotton ~ 棉纱布

gay /geɪ/

adj. ❶ cheerful;happy;full of fun 愉快的:We heard ~ music and laughter from the illuminating house. 我们听到灯火通明的房子里传来欢快的音乐和笑声。❷ bright or attractive, so that one feels happy to see it, hear it, etc. 明快的;轻快的;鲜艳的:Every day he gives her a bundle of ~ flowers.他每天给她送来一束艳丽的花。

gaze /geɪz/

Ⅰ *v.* look steadily, especially for a long time and often without being conscious of what one is doing 凝视;盯:What are you gazing at? 你在凝视什么? Ⅱ *n.* a steady fixed look 凝视:She turned her ~ to a strange man coming out of a car.她紧盯着一个从车里出来的陌生男人。

gazette /ɡəˈzet/

n. ❶ a newspaper 报纸 ❷an official publication containing announcements（政府）公报:an official ~ 正式公报

gear /gɪə(r)/

n. ❶ an apparatus, especially one consisting of a set of toothed wheels, that allows power to be passed from one part of a machine to another so as to control the power, speed, or direction of movement 齿轮,排挡:This is a car with five ~s.这是一辆五排挡的车。❷ clothing equipment, etc. for a particular purpose 工作服;工具:I'm sorry. I have left my ~ at home.很抱歉,我把工作服忘在家里了。

gearbox /ˈɡɪəbɒks/

n. a case enclosing a gear mechanism 齿轮箱,变速箱,变速器

gel /dʒel/

Ⅰ *n.* a jelly-like substance 凝胶,冻胶,胶滞体:hair ~ 发胶 Ⅱ *v.* (-ll-) ❶form into a gel 形成胶体:The mixture ~led at 7 degrees Celsius. 7 摄氏度时混合物变成了胶体。❷treat（the hair）with gel（往头发上）喷发胶

gelatin(e) /ˈdʒelətɪn/

n. a clear tasteless substance for making jelly as food, manufacturing photographic film, etc.骨胶;动物胶;明胶

gem /dʒem/

n. ❶a jewel; a precious stone 珠宝;宝石:Diamonds and emeralds are two kinds of ~s.钻石和绿宝石是两种不同的宝石。❷anything of great value 珍贵之物;精华

gender /ˈdʒendə/

n. ❶ the class into which a noun or pronoun is placed in the grammar of some languages, e.g. masculine, feminine, or neuter（名词、代词的）性 ❷a person's sex 性别:issues of class, race and ~ 阶级、种族和性别问题

gene /dʒiːn/

n. any of several small parts of the material at the nucleus of a cell, that controls the development of all the qualities in a living thing which have been passed on from its parents 基因,遗传因子

genealogy /ˌdʒiːnɪˈælədʒi/

n. ❶ the history of the members of a family from the past to the present 系谱学,宗谱学,家谱学 ❷ an account of this for one particular family, especially when shown in a drawing with lines and names spreading like the branches of a tree 系谱,家谱,宗谱

general /ˈdʒenrəl/

Ⅰ *adj.* ❶common;universal 普遍的;全体的:The General Assembly of the United Nations will be held in New York next month.联合国大会将于下月在纽约举行。/Rainy weather is ~ in Canada in the autumn.加拿大的秋天总是多雨。❷ applying to all or most members of a cat-

G

egory or group 总的；首要的：～ secretary 总书记 ❸ not specialized or limited to the main things only 大体的；笼统的：The teacher worked out a ～ outline of a teaching scheme. 教师订出了教学计划大纲。Ⅱ *n.* a senior army officer of very high rank 将军：Under the leadership of General Peng we defeated the enemy troops. 在彭将军的领导下我们打败了敌军。‖ ～ly *adv.* 一般地/ ～ity *n.* 一般性；普遍性

generate /ˈdʒenəreɪt/
v. produce; bring into; bring about 产生；发生；繁殖；引起；造成：～ electricity 发电/a generating plant (station) 发电站

generation /ˌdʒenəˈreɪʃn/
n. a period of time in which a human being can grow up and have a family (about 25 or 30 years) 世代；一代；一代人：There is a gap between the older ～ and the younger ～ in idea. 在观念方面，老一辈和年轻一代之间有代沟。/Four ～s live in their house. 他们家四世同堂。

generative /ˈdʒenərətɪv/
adj. having the power to produce or generate 生产的；有生产力的；生殖的

generator /ˈdʒenəreɪtə(r)/
n. a machine which generates electricity, etc. 发电机：The ～ has started up. 发电机已开动。

generic /dʒəˈnerɪk/
adj. ❶ of a genus 属的；类的：The Latin term "Vulpes" is the ～ name for the various types of fox. 拉丁术语"Vulpes"是不同种类狐狸的属名。❷ shared by or typical of a whole class of things 一般的；普通的；通用的 ❸ not offering legal protection because of not having a trademark 未注册的；无注册商标保护的；非专利的：a ～ drug 无注册商标的药品

generosity /ˌdʒenəˈrɒsəti/
n. ❶ the quality of being generous 宽大；慷慨；大方：show ～ 表示宽大 ❷ a generous act 慷慨行为；宽大行为：We thanked him for his generosities. 我们对他的慷慨行为表示感谢。

generous /ˈdʒenərəs/
adj. ❶ showing readiness to give money, help, kindness, etc. 慷慨的；大方的；不吝啬的：He's ～ and always ready to give the poor a lot of money. 他很慷慨，乐意给穷人许多钱。❷ plentiful 大量的，丰富的：a ～ meal 丰盛的一餐

genetic /dʒəˈnetɪk/
adj. ❶ to do with genes or heredity 基因的；遗传的：～ abnormalities 基因异常 ❷ to do with genetics 遗传学的 ‖ ～ally *adv.* 从遗传学角度；从基因方面

genetics /dʒəˈnetɪk/
n. the science which studies how heredity works 遗传学

genial /ˈdʒiːnɪəl/
adj. cheerful and cheering; kindly; pleasant 高兴的；友善的；令人愉快的：in ～ company 跟友善的朋友在一起/～ neighbours 友善的邻居

genie /ˈdʒiːni/
n. (*pl.* ～s) a spirit or goblin with strange powers in Arab fairy stories（神话中的）神怪，妖怪

genius /ˈdʒiːnɪəs/
n. (*pl.* ～es or genii /ˈdʒiːnɪaɪ/) ❶ great ability or skill in a particular subject 天才；才华：a man of ～ 有才华的人 ❷ (usually singular) unusual natural ability（常用单数）天资；天赋：have a ～ for music 有音乐天赋 ❸ someone who has exceptional intellectual ability and ori-ginality 天才人物；天才：Newton was a ～ in physics. 牛顿是一位物理学天才。

genome /ˈdʒiːnəʊm/
n. the complete set of an individual's chromosomes 基因组，染色体组

gent /dʒent/
n. ❶ gentleman 男士，绅士 ❷（Gents）a public lavatory for men 公共男厕：Where's the Gents? 男厕在哪里？

gentle /ˈdʒentl/
adj. ❶ mild, calm and kind 温和的；温柔的：The teacher is always ～ with her pupils. 这位老师对她的学生总是很温柔。❷ not rough or severe; soft and mild 轻柔的；柔和的：In spring the wind is ～ and warm. 春天，风儿温暖而柔和。

gentleman /ˈdʒentlmən/
  n.(pl.gentlemen) ❶a man who is kind, polite,and honest 绅士；有教养的人；品行端正的人 ❷ a polite word for any man (尊称)先生：Tod, you will send these things to the ～'s home.托德，你得把这批订货送到这位先生的住处去。

gently /ˈdʒentli/
  adv. ❶ in a gentle manner；with little weight or force 柔和地；轻轻地，温和地：Hold it ～.小心地拿着它。❷in a gradual manner 慢慢地；渐渐地：The road slopes ～ to sea.那条路逐渐向海边倾斜下去。

genuine /ˈdʒenjuɪn/
  adj.❶not fake or counterfeit 真正的；地道的：a ～ diamond 真钻石/a ～ friend 真正的朋友 ❷honest or frank；sincerely felt or expressed 诚恳的；真诚的；衷心的：a ～ person 诚恳的人/He seems ～ but can I trust him? 他似乎很诚实，但我可以信赖他吗？

genus /ˈdʒiːnəs/
  n.a division of animals or plants，below a family and above a species (动植物的)属

geocentric /ˌdʒiːəʊˈsentrɪk/
  adj.having, or measured from, the earth as the central point 以地球为中心的；由地球中心测量的：In former times,people thought the universe was ～.从前人们认为宇宙以地球为中心。

geographer /dʒɪˈɒɡrəfə/
  n.an expert in geography 地理学家

geography /dʒɪˈɒɡrəfi/
  n. the science of the earth surface, climate, people, countries, plants, etc. 地理学：book on ～ 地理书/ ～ of Africa 非洲地理/ physical ～ 自然地理

geology /dʒɪˈɒlədʒi/
  n.the study of the materials(rocks, soil, etc.) which make up the Earth, and of their changes during the history of the world 地质学：He studied ～ all his life and discovered a lot.他终生研究地质学，发现了许多东西。‖ geologic(al) adj.地质学的/geologist n.地质学家

geometry /dʒɪˈɒmətri/
  n.the study in mathematics of the angles and shapes formed by the relationships of lines, surfaces, and solids in space 几何(学)：Geometry is an ancient science. 几何是一门古老的科学。‖ geometric(al) adj.几何学的；几何图形的

geopolitics /ˌdʒiːəʊˈpɒlətɪks/
  n. the study of the effect of a country's position, population, etc., on its politics 地缘政治学,地理政治学

geostationary /ˌdʒiːəʊˈsteɪʃənəri/
  adj.of or being a spacecraft or satellite that goes round the Earth at the same speed as the Earth moves, so that it always stays above the same place on the Earth (宇宙飞船、卫星)与地球旋转同步的,对地静止的

geriatric /ˌdʒerɪˈætrɪk/
  adj.of or for geriatrics 老年医学的；老年病学的：～ medicine 老年病医学/a ～ hospital 老年病科医院

geriatrician /ˌdʒerɪəˈtrɪʃn/
  n.a doctor who specializes in geriatrics 老年病科医师

geriatrics /ˌdʒerɪˈætrɪks/
  n. the medical treatment and care of old people 老年医学；老年病学

germ /dʒɜːm/
  n. ❶a disease-producing bacterium；microbe 细菌；病菌：Peaceful people all over the world denounce indignantly the ～ warfare.全世界爱好和平的人民愤怒声讨细菌战。❷the portion of a living organism capable of becoming a new organism 胚芽：It's the ～ of a grain.这是谷粒的胚芽。

germinate /ˈdʒɜːmɪneɪt/
  v.(of a seed) begin to grow and put out shoots；cause (a seed) to sprout in such a way (种子)发芽；使(种子)发芽 ‖ germination n.发芽

germane /dʒɜːˈmeɪn/
  adj.relevant,or pertinent in an important way 关系密切的；有重要关联的；贴切的：a remark hardly ～ to the question 不大切题的话/The statement was ～ to the argument.这句话与论点有密切关系。

G

gestation /dʒe'steɪʃən/

n. ❶ the process of carrying or being carried in the womb between conception and birth 怀孕，妊娠 ❷ the period of this process 怀孕期，妊娠期 ❸ the development of a plan or idea over time 形成，孕育：Various ideas are in the process of ～.各种想法都在酝酿之中。

gesture /'dʒestʃə(r)/

n. a movement of the hand or other part of the body to indicate or illustrate an idea, feeling, etc. 手势；姿势：The mute expressed himself with ～s.哑巴用手势表达意思。

get /get/

v. (got; gotten) ❶ come into the possession of sth. 有，得到：I'll come and see you if I ～ time. 如果有时间，我会来看你。 ❷ buy 买；搞到：Where did you ～ that hat? 你在哪儿买的那顶帽子？ ❸ fetch 接人；取物：After a while she intended to ～ her daughter from the kindergarten. 过一会儿，她打算把女儿从幼儿园接回来。 ❹ receive 收到；接到：Jenny got plenty of presents for her birthday. 珍妮收到了大量生日礼物。 ❺ catch (an illness) 感染（疾病）：It's easy for children to ～ flu in spring. 春天，孩子们很容易患流感。 ❻ understand 理解；懂：Sorry, I don't ～ your meaning. 对不起，我不懂你的意思。 ❼ become 变得；成为：I'm ～ting hot, please turn on the electric fan. 我热起来了，请把电风扇打开。 ❽ arrive at or reach a place or point 到；抵达：We'll ～ to Shaoshan at 5 p.m. 下午五点我们将抵达韶山。 ❾ bring into or cause to be in a certain state 移动；弄来(去)：The wind is blowing outside. Get the door shut please. 外面起风了，请把门关上。 ‖ ～ **along**, ～ **on** 进展；过活：How are you ～ting along? 你好吗？/ How are you ～ting on with your study? 你的学习进展如何？/ ～ **in** 到达；收进：The farmers got in the crops in time. 农场主及时割了庄稼。/ ～ **off** 脱下；下车：I got off the bus at the bus-stop. 我在汽车停靠站下了车。/ ～ **on** 上车；I helped a blind man to ～ on the bus. 我帮

助一位盲人上了汽车。/ ～ **through** (考试)及格；完成：Did you ～ through your exam? 你的考试及格了吗？/ ～ **up** 起床；起立：When did you ～ up this morning? 今天早晨你何时起床的？ ‖ ～-**together** *n.* 聚会；联欢会

getaway /'getəweɪ/

n. an escape 逃跑，逃走：The burglar made his ～ across the roof. 小偷从屋顶上逃跑了。/ As the thieves ran out of the bank, the ～ car was waiting with its engine running. 窃贼从银行跑出来时，逃走用的汽车没有熄火正在等着他们。

getup /'getʌp/

n. a set of clothes, especially unusual clothes (尤指不寻常的)装束，穿戴：She looks ridiculous in that ～.她那套装束看起来十分可笑。

ghastly /'gɑːstli/

adj. ❶ shockingly repellent; horrible 骇人听闻的；可怕的：It was a ～ murder.这是一宗骇人听闻的谋杀。 ❷ pale and miserable, like a dead person 惨白的；形同死人的：You look ～; are you all right? 你脸色很难看，是不舒服吗？

ghost /gəʊst/

n. the spirit of a dead person who appeared again 鬼；幽灵：The room is said to be haunted by a ～ last year.据说这房间去年闹过鬼。 ‖ ～**ly** *adj.* 鬼的；鬼一样的

giant /'dʒaɪənt/

Ⅰ *n.* (in fairy tales) an imaginary person of very great size and strength (神话故事中虚构的)巨人：The huge building, like a ～ stands by the bridge. 这座高大的楼房，像巨人一样，耸立在桥旁。 Ⅱ *adj.* much larger than most others 巨大的：A ～ tower looked down over the whole city. 巨塔俯瞰全城。

gibber /'dʒɪbə(r)/

v. talk very fast, especially because of fear or shock, in a way that is meaningless for the hearer (由于害怕、震惊而)急促不清地说；叽里咕噜地说：What on earth are you ～ing about? Pull yourself together and speak calmly! 你到底在叽里咕噜地说

说些什么? 冷静下来,慢慢讲!

gibberish /ˈdʒɪbərɪʃ/
n. meaningless or unintelligible talking 无意义的话;胡言乱语

gibbon /ˈgɪbən/
n. an ape with long arms and no tail that lives in southern Asia 长臂猿

gibbous /ˈgɪbəs/
adj. (of the moon) having the bright part filling more than half a circle (月球)凸圆的

gibe /dʒaɪb/
n. an aggressive remark directed at a person and intended to have a telling effect 嘲弄,讥笑:He could not bear the ~s of the other boys.他忍受不了其他男孩的讥笑。

giblets /ˈdʒɪblɪts/
n. the parts of a fowl, such as the heart and liver, which are taken out before the bird is cooked, but may themselves be cooked and eaten (家禽可食用的)内脏,杂碎

gift /gɪft/
n. ❶ sth. which is given willingly; a present 礼物:Susan accepted lots of birthday ~s.苏珊收到了许多生日礼物。 ❷ a natural ability to do sth.; talent 天赋;才能:She has a ~ for art.她有艺术天赋。

gifted /ˈgɪftɪd/
adj. having great natural ability 有天赋的;有才华的:~ children 天才儿童

gigantic /dʒaɪˈgæntɪk/
adj. exceedingly large or extensive 巨大的;庞大的;:He has a ~ appetite and eats ~ meals.他的食量很大,能吃很多食物。

giggle /ˈgɪgl/
Ⅰ *n.* a silly laugh 痴笑:When she saw a boy, like her son, the mad woman broke into a ~.这个疯女人看到了一个像她儿子的男孩,突然痴笑起来。 Ⅱ *v.* laugh in a silly way 格格地笑:She ~d her appreciation of my silly joke.她格格地笑表示欣赏我愚蠢的笑话。

gild /gɪld/
v. cover thinly with gold or gold paint 镀金;涂以金色

gill[1] /gɪl/
n. (usually *pl.*) the part of the head of a fish through which it breathes 鳃 ‖ **to the ~s** (完全)满了,饱了;满满当当

gill[2] /dʒɪl/
n. a unit for measuring liquids that equals a quarter of a pint 及耳(等于 1/4 品脱)

gilt /gɪlt/
n. a thin covering of gold or gold paint 镀金的薄层;金色涂层:a ~ brooch 镀金的胸针

gimlet /ˈgɪmlət/
n. a tool which is used to make holes in wood so that screws may enter easily 螺丝锥;(木工)手钻:He has eyes like ~s.他的眼光锐利得像锥子。

ginger /ˈdʒɪndʒə(r)/
Ⅰ *n.* a hot-tasting root which is used as spice 生姜,姜 Ⅱ *v.* make more vigorous or lively 使更有生气,更有活力 Ⅲ *adj.* reddish-brown in colour 姜黄色的

gingerly /ˈdʒɪndʒəli/
Ⅰ *adv.* with great care and caution 小心谨慎地;战战兢兢地:She ~ picked the delicate flower.她小心翼翼地摘下那朵娇嫩的花朵。 Ⅱ *adj.* careful and cautious 小心的;谨慎的:in a ~ fashion 小心翼翼/The subject was handled in a ~ way.那问题处理得极为谨慎。

ginseng /ˈdʒɪnseŋ/
n. a medicine obtained from a plant root to be believed to help stay young and healthy 人参;西洋参

gipsy, gypsy /ˈdʒɪpsi/
n. a member of a people with dark skin and hair who traditionally live by seasonal work and fortune telling 吉卜赛人:a ~ girl 吉卜赛女郎

giraffe /dʒəˈrɑːf/
n. an African animal with a very long neck and long legs 长颈鹿:A ~ eats leaves from trees.长颈鹿吃树叶子。

gird /gɜːd/
v. (~ed or girt /gɜːt/) ❶ prepare oneself for a military confrontation 装备,佩带(兵器):~ on one's sword (~ sb. with a

sword) 佩剑 ❷encircle or surround 围绕；围起：～ castle with a moat 以壕沟围起一城堡

girder/ˈgɜːdə(r)/
*n.*a wood, iron or steel beam used in the framework of buildings and bridges（建筑物或桥梁的）大梁，桁

girdle/ˈgɜːdl/
Ⅰ *n.*❶a cord or belt fastened round the waist to keep clothes in position 腰带；带 ❷an encircling or ringlike structure 带状物；环形物 Ⅱ *v.*encircle 束住；环绕：a lake ～d with trees 四周植树的湖泊/a satellite girdling the moon 绕月球飞行的人造卫星

girlhood/ˈgɜːlhʊd/
*n.*a state or time of being a girl 少女时期；少女时代：in her ～ 在她的少女时期

girl/gɜːl/
*n.*❶ a female child；daughter 女孩，少女，姑娘；女儿：The ～ is a secretary.那姑娘是个秘书。❷a female servant 女仆 ❸a woman worker, especially in a shop, office, etc.（商店、办公室等的）女店员，女职员：factory ～s 女工人 ‖ ～-**friend** *n.*女朋友，女伴，情人：Mary is Tom's ～-friend.玛丽是汤姆的女朋友。

gist/dʒɪst/
n. the central meaning or theme of a speech or literary work 要点；要旨：the ～ of a question 问题的要点/Tell me the ～ of what he said.告诉我他所说的要点。

give/gɪv/
v.(gave, given)❶cause someone to have, hold, receive, or own 递给；给予：I gave David a book.我给了大卫一本书。❷pay in order to buy；pay in exchange(for sth.) 付出：How much will you ～ me for my old car? 你愿意出多少钱买我的旧车？❸cause to experience 引起：The old car is giving a lot of trouble.这辆旧摩托车老出故障。❹ provide or supply 产生；供给：The sun ～s light and heat.太阳发出光和热。❺perform or carry out(an action) 出声；做……动作：He gave a long sigh and shut his eyes.他长叹了一声闭上了双眼。❻allow to have 允许：Before

dictation the teacher gave the students 2 minutes to be ready.听写前老师给学生两分钟做准备。❼ set aside(time, thought, strength, etc.) for a purpose 献出：She gave her life to education.她将自己的一生献给了教育事业。❽be the cause of 传染给：Thomas gave her his Aids.托马斯把艾滋病传染给她了。❾collapse or break under pressure 坍塌；断裂 The branch gave but it did not break.这树枝弯了，但没有断。‖ ～ sb. **away** 出卖；泄密：I'm going to hide from my little sister behind the door. Please don't ～ me away.我要藏在门后让小妹妹找，请你别说出去。/ ～ **in** 屈服；让步：Tod always gave in to his big brother.托德总是屈从于他的大哥。/ ～ **out** 分发：Please ～ out the exercise books.请你分发这些练习本。/ ～ **up** 放弃；认输：The doctor asked the patient to ～ up smoking.医生要这位病人戒烟。/ ～ **way** 让步；退让：After a long argument, the representative gave way.经过长时间的辩论后，这位代表让步了。

given /ˈgɪvn/
Ⅰ *adj.*❶specified or stated 规定的；指明的 all the people in a ～ area 指定地区的所有人 ❷having a certain tendency 倾向于……的；有……特定习惯的：He is ～ to swearing.他总是爱发誓。Ⅱ *prep.*taking into account 考虑到：Given her ability, it's surprising she hasn't won more trophies.考虑到她的能力，她没赢得更多奖牌有点出人意料。

giver/ˈgɪvə(r)/
*n.*a person or organization that gives or supplies a particular thing 给予者；施赠者：a generous ～ 慷慨的赠送者

gizzard/ˈgɪzəd/
n. the second stomach of a bird, where food is broken up with the help of small stones the bird has swallowed（鸟等的）砂囊，胗

glace/ˈglæseɪ/
adj.(of fruits) preserved by coating with sugar（水果）糖渍的；蜜饯的：～ cherries 糖渍樱桃

glacial/ˈgleɪsɪəl/

*adj.*❶ of ice or glaciers 冰的；冰河（川）的 ❷ of an ice age 冰河期的：Two thirds of the continent was covered in ice during ~ periods.在冰河期有三分之二的陆地被冰覆盖。❸ very cold 极冷的：He gave me a ~ smile.他对我冷冷地笑了一下。

glacier/ˈɡlæsɪə(r)/
n. a big mass of ice that moves slowly down a mountain 冰川；冰河：An iceberg is a part of a ~ that has reached the sea. 冰山是冰川进入海洋的那一部分。

glad/ɡlæd/
adj. (-dd-) ❶ pleased and happy about sth. 高兴的；乐意的：I'm very ~ that you have made great progress in English learning.你们的英语有很大的进步,我非常高兴。❷ causing happiness 令人高兴的：Have you heard the ~ news? 你听到那喜讯没有?

gladden/ˈɡlædn/
v. make glad or happy 使高兴,使快乐：The sight of the child running about after his long illness ~ed his father's heart.父亲看到久病后的孩子到处奔跑,心里非常高兴。

gladly/ˈɡlædli/
adv. very willing;eagerly 乐意地;渴望地：I'll ~ come and help you; why didn't you ask me before? 我十分乐意来帮助你,以前你为什么不向我求助呢?

glamorize/ˈɡlæməraɪz/
v. make (sth.) appear better, more attractive, more exciting, etc. than it really is 使有魅力,使更吸引人：Television tends to ~ acts of violence.电视往往在渲染暴力。

glamorous/ˈɡlæmərəs/
adj. full of glamour 富有魅力的：~ film stars 富有魅力的电影明星

glamour /ˈɡlæmə/
*n.*❶an attractive and exciting quality that sth. has, often because it involves famous and successful people 吸引力,魅力,诱惑力：the ~ of Hollywood 好莱坞的魅力 ❷physical attractiveness 性感美;魔力

glance/ɡlɑːns/
I *v.*❶ take a quick look 扫视；一瞥：He ~d at the newspaper headlines.他浏览了

报上的标题。❷ flash 闪烁：Their helmets ~d in the sunlight.他们的钢盔在阳光下闪闪发光。II *n.* a quick or hurried look 瞥：She took a ~ at the letter and set fire to it.她浏览了这封信,然后把它点着了。

gland/ɡlænd/
n. an organ of the body that can make and give out some substance 腺：the sweat (tear) ~s 汗(泪)腺

glare/ɡleə(r)/
I *v.*❶ shine with a strong light or in a way that hurts the eyes 炫耀；发出强光：The sun ~d down on the Sahara Desert. 阳光强劲地照射着撒哈拉大沙漠。❷ look in an angry way 怒视；瞪眼：The old man ~d at the naughty boy.老人瞪了那淘气的男孩一眼。II *n.*❶ a hard unpleasant effect given by a strong light 闪耀；炫目：the ~ of the sun on the water 水面上刺目的阳光 ❷ an angry look or stare 愤怒的目光；瞪视：I intended to go but his fierce ~ stopped me.我打算走,但是他那凶狠瞪视的目光使我停住了脚步。

glaring/ˈɡleərɪŋ/
*adj.*❶very bright; dazzling 耀眼的,刺眼的,过于鲜艳的：This ~ light hurts my eyes.这种刺目的光线会伤害我的眼睛。❷very easily seen 显然的,明显的：a ~ mistake 明显的错误 ‖ ~ly *adv.*耀眼地;显眼地

glass/ɡlɑːs/
*n.*❶ a hard, transparent substance which can be seen through 玻璃：Glass is transparent, you can see through it.玻璃透明,隔着它能看见东西。❷ collection of objects made of this (总称)玻璃器皿：There's plenty of ~ in the store.商店里有大量的玻璃器皿。❸ a container made from glass which you can drink from; the contents of a glass 玻璃杯;一杯(的量)：Every morning I drink a ~ of milk.每天早晨我都喝一杯牛奶。❹ a mirror made of glass 镜子：She likes to look at herself in the ~.她爱照镜子。❺ (*pl.*) spectacles 眼镜：She can't read without ~es.不戴眼镜,她便无法阅读。‖ ~ful *adj.*一

杯(的容量)/ ~house *n*.温室/ ~y *adj*.玻璃般的

glassware /'glɑːsweə/
n.ornaments and articles made from glass 玻璃饰品,玻璃制品

glaze /gleɪz/
Ⅰ *v*. ❶ furnish with glass 装玻璃:~ a window 给窗户配玻璃 ❷ cover with a glass-like surface 上釉于;上光:~ pottery 给陶器上釉 ❸(of the eyes) become dull and lifeless (目光)变得呆滞无神:Her eyes ~d (over) and she fell unconscious.她的眼睛变得呆滞,接着便不省人事。Ⅱ *n*.a thin layer of liquid which is put on a piece of pottery and becomes hard and shiny when the pottery is heated in a very hot oven 釉;釉面:a vase with a fine crackle ~ 饰有上等纹釉的花瓶

gleam /gliːm/
Ⅰ *v*.give out a gentle light;shine softly 闪烁;发微光:The cat's eyes are ~ing in the dark.猫的眼睛在黑暗中闪闪发光。Ⅱ *n*. ❶ a gentle light, especially one that is small or shines for a short time 微光;闪光:On the horizon appear the first ~s of the morning sun.地平线上绽出晨曦。❷ a sudden showing of a feeling or quality for a short time 闪念:A ~ of pity came into his eyes.他眼里闪现出怜悯的光芒。

glean /gliːn/
v. ❶ gather facts or information in small amounts and often with difficulty 一点点地搜集(事实,信息):From what I was able to ~,it appears they don't intend to take any action yet.根据我所收集到的资料分析,他们看来还不打算采取任何行动。❷ collect grain that has been left behind after crops have been cut (收割后)拾穗

gleanings /'gliːnɪŋz/
n. ❶ small amounts of information or news, often gathered with difficulty 收集的零星资料 ❷ the grain gathered in the fields after the crops have been cut 拾得的落穗

glee /gliː/
n.a feeling of joy caused by success or triumph 高兴;欣欣;狂欢:full of ~ 高兴得不得了/She was in high ~ when she learnt the news.她获悉这个消息高兴极了。

gleeful /'gliːful/
adj. exuberantly or triumphantly joyful 兴高采烈的;欣快的:She gave a ~ chuckle.她发出了欢快的笑声。

glib /glɪb/
adj.(of a person, what he says or how he says it) ready and smooth, but not sincere;spoken too easily to be true (指人,言语,说话方式)伶牙俐齿的;油腔滑调的;油嘴滑舌的:a ~ tongue 三寸不烂之舌/~ excuses 油腔滑调的托词

glide /glaɪd/
Ⅰ *v*. move along smoothly and continuously 滑行;滑动;滑翔:The boat ~d over the river.船在河面上滑行。/Fish were gliding about in the lake.鱼儿在湖里游来游去。Ⅱ *n*. the act of moving smoothly along a surface while remaining in contact with it movement 滑动;滑行:The dancers crossed the floor in a series of ~s.舞者在地板上飘然而过。

glider /'glaɪdə/
n.an aircraft without an engine that flies by floating on warm air currents called thermals 滑翔机

glimmer /'glɪmə(r)/
Ⅰ *v*.give a very faint unsteady light 发出微光:A star ~ed in the dark sky.黑暗的天空中一颗星星发出微光。Ⅱ *n*.a faint unsteady light 微光;闪光:There's a ~ of hope about the near future.对于近来的事尚有一线希望。

glimpse /glɪmps/
Ⅰ *n*.a very quick sight 一瞥:I just caught a ~ of the plane as it flew over.当飞机飞过时我恰好瞥见了它。Ⅱ *v*. see very quickly 瞥见:He ~d his friend in the crowd.他在人群中一眼就看见了他的朋友。

glint /glɪnt/
Ⅰ *v*.send out a quick flash of light 闪耀,闪亮:The sun is ~ing through the

clouds. 太阳透过云层发出光芒。/His eyes ~ed with anger.他的眼睛闪耀着愤怒的光芒。Ⅱ n.a quick flash of light 闪光：He had an evil ~ in his eyes. 他的眼睛里有一种邪恶的光芒。

glisten /ˈɡlɪsn/
v.(usually of sth. wet or polished) shine （常指湿的或磨光擦亮的东西）闪耀，闪亮：Her eyes ~ed with tears.她的眼睛里有泪光闪耀。

glitter /ˈɡlɪtər/
Ⅰ v.shine with a bright sparkling light 发光：All that ~s is not gold.发光的并非全是金子。Ⅱ n.a brilliant light 光辉，光泽：the ~ of diamonds 钻石的光泽

glitterati /ˌɡlɪtəˈrɑːti/
n. fashionable, rich and famous people whose social activities are widely reported 知名人士；名流：Hollywood's ~ 好莱坞的知名人士

glittering /ˈɡlɪtərɪŋ/
adj.❶shining with a shimmering or sparkling light 发出微光的；闪烁的：~ jewels 璀璨的宝石 ❷impressively successful or elaborate 非常显赫的；非常精美的：a ~ military career 非常显赫的军旅生涯

glitz /ˈɡlɪts/
n.sth. that is exciting and attractive in a showy way 浮华，华丽 ‖ ~y adj.浮华的，华丽的：one of the year's glitziest parties 年度最浮华的盛会之一

gloaming /ˈɡləʊmɪŋ/
n.the time of day immediately following sunset 黄昏，薄暮

gloat /ɡləʊt/
v.look at or gaze sth.with great self-satisfaction 得意地看；幸灾乐祸地盯视：~ over another's misfortune 对别人的不幸幸灾乐祸/It's nothing to ~ about.没有什么可幸灾乐祸的。

global /ˈɡləʊbl/
adj.❶ of or concerning the whole world 全球的；全世界的：events of ~ importance 世界性的重要事件 /Global climatic changes may have been responsible for the extinction of the dinosaurs. 全球性的气候变化也许是造成恐龙灭绝的原因。

❷taking account of or including (almost) all possible considerations 整体的，总括的，全面的：The report takes a ~ view of the company's problems.报告对该公司的问题作了综合性的论述。

globalize /ˈɡləʊbəlaɪz/
v.develop or be developed so as to make possible international influence or operation （使）全球化：Communication ~s capital markets.通讯使得资本市场全球化。

globalism /ˈɡləʊbəlɪzəm/
n.the quality of being concerned with causes and effects over the whole world 全球性；全球观念 ‖ globalist adj.全球性的；全球观念的：globalist economic policies 全球性的经济政策

globe /ɡləʊb/
n. ❶ the planet we live on；an object shaped like a ball；the earth 球状物；地球：From space the earth looks like a huge blue ~.从宇宙空间看地球，它像一个巨大的蓝色圆球。❷ an object shaped like a ball with a map of the earth on it 地球仪：Our geography teacher told us how to use the ~.我们的地理老师教我们如何使用地球仪。

globular /ˈɡlɒbjələ/
adj.shaped like a globe 球形的，球状的

gloom /ɡluːm/
n.❶ darkness 黑暗；阴暗：I couldn't see the road in the ~.我在黑暗中看不见路。❷ a feeling of deep sadness or hopelessness 忧愁；忧郁：The future seems to be filled with ~.前途似乎很黯淡。

gloomy /ˈɡluːmi/
adj.(gloomier, gloomiest) ❶dark, poorly lit 黑暗的；昏暗的；光线不好的 ❷ sad and without hope 忧伤的；沮丧的；无望的：a ~ expression 沮丧的表情 ❸without much hope of success or happiness in the future 前景黯淡的；悲观的：a ~ picture of the country's economic future 该国经济前景的黯淡景象 ‖ gloomily adv.沮丧地；阴沉的/ gloominess n.黑暗；沮丧

glorify /ˈɡlɔːrɪfaɪ/
v.❶praise or make sth. seem better than

G

it is;worship 赞美,崇拜:The book glorified the war.这本书赞美了那场战争。❷ give fame to 表扬:He was glorified for his bravery.他因勇敢而受到表扬。

glorious /ˈɡlɔːrɪəs/
*adj.*❶splendid and impressive 辉煌的,壮丽的:They won a ~ victory.他们取得了辉煌的胜利。❷ having great fame or success;honourable 显赫的,光荣的:We should keep our ~ tradition.我们要保持光荣的传统。

glory /ˈɡlɔːri/
*n.*❶ the fame and honour won by great achievements 光荣;荣誉:Our soldiers returned from the front with ~.我们的士兵从前线凯旋。❷ the quality of being beautiful or magnificent 瑰丽;壮观:I saw the ~ of a sunrise at the top of Mount Tai.我在泰山之巅看到了瑰丽的日出。

gloss[1] /ɡlɒs/
*n.*a bright shine on the surface of sth. 光泽;光彩:In the photo we can see the ~ on her hair.我们能从照片上看到她头发上的光泽。

gloss[2] /ɡlɒs/
Ⅰ *n.*an explanation or definition of a word in a text 注释;注解 Ⅱ *v.*provide explanations for words or phrases 注解;释义

glossary /ˈɡlɒsəri/
*n.*a list of glosses;a list of words needing special explanation 词汇表;术语汇编:All the technical terms are shown in the ~ at the back of the book.所有术语都列入书后的词汇表。

glossy /ˈɡlɒsi/
*adj.*shiny and smooth 光滑的;有光泽的:Our cat has ~ black fur.我们的猫长着光滑的黑毛。

glove /ɡlʌv/
n. a covering for the hand and wrist (usually with a separate place for each finger) 手套(通常指分指手套)

glow /ɡləʊ/
Ⅰ *v.*❶give out heat and soft light without flames or smoke 发光;发热:A piece of iron ~ed in the furnace.一块铁在炉子里烧得通红。❷show redness and heat,especially in the face,e.g.after hard work or because of strong feelings (身体)发热;(面色)发红:He ~ed with pride.他得意扬扬。Ⅱ *n.*❶ a dull,steady light from sth. burning without flames or smoke 余晖;暗淡的光:the ~ of the sky at sunset 落日余晖 ❷ a strong feeling 强烈的感情:She is always in a ~ of enthusiasm.她总是热情洋溢。‖ ~worm *n.*萤火虫

glower /ˈɡlaʊə(r)/
*v.*look angrily at 怒目而视;瞪眼:She sat ~ing at her opponent.她坐在那里怒视着对手。

glowing /ˈɡləʊɪŋ/
*adj.*❶showing strong approval 热烈赞扬的 ❷highly enthusiastic 热情洋溢的:She gave a ~ description of the film,which made me want to see it for myself.她非常赞赏地描述这部影片,使我真想亲自去看看。/The director referred to your work in ~ terms.经理用非常赞赏的话提到了你的工作。

glue /ɡluː/
Ⅰ *n.*a sticky substance which is made chemically or obtained from animal or fish bones and is used for joining things together 胶;胶水:This kind of ~ sticks fast.这种胶水粘得很牢。Ⅱ *v.*join or stick sth. with glue 黏合;粘贴:The boy ~d two boxes together.男孩把两个盒子粘贴起来。

glum /ɡlʌm/
adj.(-mm-)in low spirits;gloomy 闷闷不乐;抑郁:She looks ~.她显得闷闷不乐。‖ ~ly *adv.*抑郁地/ ~ness *n.*闷闷不乐;愁容满面

gluten /ˈɡluːtn/
*n.*a sticky protein substance that is found in flour made from wheat 麸质;面筋

glutinous /ˈɡluːtənəs/
*adj.*very sticky 黏的;胶状的:a bowl of ~ rice 一碗糯米

gnash /næʃ/
*v.*grind one's teeth together in anger or pain (因愤怒或痛苦)咬牙:~ one's teeth 咬牙切齿

gnaw/nɔ:/

　　v. ❶ bite sth. repeatedly 咬；啃；嗑：He was ~ing his fingernails. 他在咬手指甲。/ The rats had ~ed away some of the woodwork.老鼠将一些木器咬坏。/ The dog was ~ing at a bone.那只狗在啃一块骨头。 ❷ torment; cause to keep worrying 因……苦恼；折磨：Grief ~s my heart.忧愁折磨着我的心。

gnawing/'nɔ:ɪŋ/

　　*adj.*painful or worrying 痛苦的；苦恼的：~ hunger(anxiety) 折磨人的饥饿(焦虑)

gnu/nu:/

　　n. a large antelope having a head with horns like an ox in Africa 角马，牛羚（产于非洲的一种大羚羊）

go/gəʊ/

　　Ⅰ *v.*(went, gone) ❶leave a place(so as to reach another) 去：Go and get your hat. 去拿你的帽子。 ❷ pass into a different state, either by a natural change or by changing on purpose;become 变为；成为：The dish has gone bad. 这菜已经坏了。 ❸ be placed where sth. is usually placed 安放；放置：This dictionary ~es on the top shelf.这本字典该放到架子的顶层。 ❹become weak, damaged, or worn out 衰退；垮；断：The casement went in the storm.窗扉被暴风雨刮坏了。 ❺（of a machine,etc)work (properly) （机器等）运转；开动：I dropped my compass with carelessness and now it doesn't ~.我粗心大意把指南针掉到地上，现在不走了。 ❻happen in a certain way 进行：How's his work ~ing? 他的工作情况怎么样？ ❼be got rid of 送走；扔掉：Her bike is no good—it must ~.她的单车不行——该扔了。 ‖ be ~ing to do sth.将要做某事/ ~ ahead 开始干；先走：Here is the novel,now ~ ahead and read it.小说在这儿，开始读吧。/ ~ all out 鼓足干劲/ ~ in for参加(考试、竞赛)；爱好/ ~ off 爆炸；变坏/~ on 发生；继续/ ~ out 熄灭/ ~ over 仔细看/ ~ round 够分配/ through 仔细检查/ ~ up 攀登；涨价/ without 没有(也得就) Ⅱ *n.*❶one's turn (especially in a game) 机会；轮次：Give

the bat to me—it's my ~.把球拍给我吧——轮到我了。 ❷ an attempt to do sth.尝试：It's not a difficult riddle—have a ~ at it.这谜语不难——试一试吧。 ❸（on the ~）be busy and active 忙碌：My sister is on the ~ all day.我姐姐整天都忙忙碌碌的。

goad/gəʊd/

　　Ⅰ *n.*❶a sharp stick for driving cattle（赶牛用的）刺棒 ❷sth.driving a person to do sth. 刺激物 Ⅱ *v.*urge; drive forward 激励；驱使：Their laughter ~ed him to try it again.他们的笑声促使他再试一次。/ The teacher was ~ed into fury by their stupid mistakes.他们愚蠢的错误使教师发怒。

goal/gəʊl/

　　*n.*❶ the posts between which the ball has to pass in football and other games 球门：The ~ keeper jumped and caught the ball tightly.守门员跳起来，紧紧地抓住了球。 ❷the point made by doing this 进球得分：Our team won by four ~s to one. 我们的足球队以四比一获胜。 ❸one's aim or purpose 目标：Her ~ is to be a singer.她的目标是当歌星。

goalkeeper/'gəʊlki:pə(r)/

　　*n.*a player who stands in the goal and tries to keep the ball out 守门员

goat/gəʊt/

　　n. a horned animal about the size of a sheep , whose hairs on their chin resemble a beard 山羊

goatherd/'gəʊthɜ:d/

　　n. a person who looks after a flock of goats 牧羊人，羊倌

goatskin/'gəʊtskɪn/

　　*n.*the hide of a goat 山羊皮

gobble/'gɒbl/

　　*v.*❶eat in lumps, quickly and noisily 狼吞虎咽地吃：Because they were late they ~d (down) their food.因为已经迟了，他们把食物猛吞下去。 ❷make a gurgling sound,characteristic of a male turkey 发出火鸡般的咯咯叫声

goblet/'gɒblət/

　　*n.*a drinking cup with a stem and no handle（无柄）高脚酒杯

goblin/'gɒblɪn/
n. a small, ugly supernatural creature that makes trouble for human beings 小鬼,小妖精

god/gɒd/
n. ❶ one of the spirits or beings that are believed to have power over the world or nature 神：Those people worship many ~s.那些人崇拜诸神。❷ the supernatural being conceived as the perfect originator and the ruler of the universe of the universe 上帝；造物主：God bless you! 愿上帝保佑你!

goddess/'gɒdes/
n. a female god, especially in Greek and Latin mythology 女神：Diana, the ~ of hunting 黛安娜,狩猎女神

godfather /'gɒdfɑːðə(r)/
n. ❶ a male godparent 教父；代父 ❷ the mastermind behind an illegal organization （犯罪组织的）头面人物,首领

godless/'gɒdləs/
adj. ❶ not having belief in God；not recognizing God 不信神的 ❷ wicked 邪恶的：~ behaviour 邪恶的行为

godlike/'gɒdlaɪk/
adj. like or suitable to God or a god 如神的；神圣的；庄严的：~ beauty(calm) 美若天仙(宁静如神)

godly/'gɒdli/
adj. showing great reverence or obedience to God 虔诚的；敬神的

godparent/'gɒdpeərənt/
n. the person who makes promises to help a Christian newly received into the church at a special ceremony 教父；教母

goggle/'gɒgl/
v. stare with the eyes wide open or moving around, usually in great surprise （常指非常惊讶地）瞪视：The children ~d in amazement at the peculiar old man.孩子们睁大眼睛瞪着这个很特别的老头儿。

goggles/'gɒglz/
n. (a pair of) large round glasses with an edge which fits against the skin so that dust and wind or water cannot get near

the eyes 护目镜；防风镜；防水镜；motorcycle ~ 骑摩托车用的风镜 /ski ~ 滑雪用的护目镜

gold/gəʊld/
Ⅰ *n.* ❶ a shining, bright-yellow valuable metal 金；黄金：Her necklace is made of ~.她的项链是金的。❷ a bright, yellow colour 金色：The ~ field stretches for miles.金色的田野连绵好几英里。❸ money or wealth 财富：The criminal ran away with lots of ~.罪犯携巨款逃走了。❹ a gold medal 金质奖章：Jack won the ~ in the long jump. 杰克在跳远比赛中获得了金牌。Ⅱ *adj.* bright yellow in colour；like gold 金色的；金制的：The company name was spelled out in ~ letters.该公司的名称用烫金字母拼成。

golden/'gəʊldən/
adj. ❶ of gold or like gold in value or colour 金制的；金黄色的；黄金般的：~ hair 金发 /the ~ age 黄金时代 /a ~ watch 金表 ❷ precious；excellent；important 极好的；贵重的；重要的：a ~ chance 大好机会 /~ remedy 灵丹妙药 /~ saying 金玉良言

goldfish/'gəʊldfɪʃ/
n. small gold or orange fishes kept in bowls or ponds as pets 金鱼

goldmine/'gəʊldmaɪn/
n. ❶ a place where gold is mined 金矿；金山 ❷ sth. produces large profits 宝库；大财源：This shop is a regular ~.这家商店日进斗金

goldsmith/'gəʊldsmɪθ/
n. a person who makes articles of gold 金饰工人；金匠

golf/gɒlf/
n. a game played with a small hard ball and a set of clubs 高尔夫球：play (at) ~ 打高尔夫球

gondola/'gɒndələ/
n. ❶ a long narrow flat bottomed boat with high points at each end, used only on the waterways (canals) in Venice in Italy （意大利威尼斯运河中的）平底船；贡多拉船 ❷ a hanging framework for workmen to stand in when they are painting or

repairing high walls and windows 吊篮，吊舱

gondolier /ˌɡɒndəˈlɪə(r)/
n. a man who guides and drives a gondola （意大利威尼斯的）贡多拉船船夫

gone /ɡɒn/
adj. ❶ moved away 已去的，离去的：The family of robins has ～ for the winter. 知更鸟都过冬去了。❷ used up; weak 用完的；耗尽的；筋疲力尽的；虚弱的：It's all ～. 完全用完了。/He's so ～. 他累坏了。❸ dead 死了的：Poor Tom is ～. 可怜的汤姆死去了。❹ lost 遗失了的：He was surprised to find his wallet ～. 他吃惊地发现钱包不翼而飞了。

gong /ɡɒŋ/
n. a round metal plate that is hit with a stick to make a sound 锣；铜锣：Gongs vary in size, tone, and pitch. 锣的大小、音调和音频各不相同。

goo /ɡuː/
n. ❶ any sticky material 黏性物质："What's all that ～ at the bottom of this bag?" "The chocolate must have melted." "是什么东西粘在袋子下面？" "一定是巧克力糖融化了。" ❷ words which seem to express unnaturally sweet feelings 故作多情的话；做作的甜言蜜语

good /ɡʊd/
Ⅰ *adj.* (better, best) ❶ of a high quality, level 好的；质量高的；水准高的：His son is a ～ student. 他儿子是个好学生。/I have the best education. 我得到了最好的教育。❷ happy and enjoyable 愉快的：Do you have a ～ time at the weekend? 周末过得愉快吗？❸ strong; healthy 强健的；起作用的：You really have ～ eyes. 你的视力真好。❹ having the ability to do sth. 熟练的：He's ～ at driving. 他是一名熟练的司机。❺ thorough; complete 完全的：She had a ～ wash after finishing her work. 工作完毕之后她痛痛快快地洗了个澡。‖ be ～ at 善于；长于：He's ～ at learning. 他善于学习。/ as ～ as 差不多：This bike I bought one year ago looks as ～ as new. 一年前我买的这辆自行车看去还和新的一样。/ ～ for 有益于：Fresh air and clean water are ～ for your health. 新鲜空气和清洁的水对人的身体有好处。Ⅱ *n.* that which is pleasing or valuable or useful 好事；好处；用处；利益：In society the retired old man does a lot of ～. 在社会上，这位退休老人做了许多好事。‖ for ～ 永久地；永远：She left the city for ～. 她永远地离开了这座城市。/ no ～ 没有用处‖ ～-natured *adj.* 心肠好的/ ～-tempered *adj.* 脾气好的

goodbye /ɡʊdˈbaɪ/
Ⅰ *int.* a saying to someone when you or they are leaving or at the end of a telephone conversation 再见：Good-bye, see you later. 再见，回头见。Ⅱ *n.* a farewell remark 再见，告别：They waved ～. 他们挥手告别。

goodlooking /ˈɡʊdˈlʊkɪŋ/
adj. handsome or beautiful 美貌的；好看的；漂亮的：Joe Hill was a tall, thin, ～ man. 乔·希尔是个瘦高型的美男子。

goodness /ˈɡʊdnəs/
n. ❶ the quality of being good; virtue 善良；美德：～ of heart 心地善良/ Her ～ is shown by the many good deeds she does. 她做的许多好事证明了她的美德。❷ the best part of sth. 精髓；精华：All the ～ has been boiled out of the meat. 肉中有的精华都煮掉了。

goods /ɡʊdz/
n. ❶ things which you can buy or sell 商品：There are lots of ～ for sale in this shop. 这家商店有许多货物出售。❷ possessions which can be moved, as opposed to houses, land, etc. 动产：The boss died and left lots of ～ after him. 老板死了，留下许多财物。

goodwill /ˌɡʊdˈwɪl/
n. ❶ a friendly attitude toward others 好意；亲善；友好：a ～ mission 友好代表团 ❷ good reputation which increases the value of the business 商业信誉：the ～ of a business 商号信誉

goody¹ /ˈɡʊdi/
n. ❶ sth. pleasant to eat 可口的食物：She had got us all sorts of delicious goodies for tea. 她给我们准备了各式各样可口的食品作茶点。❷ sth. particularly attrac-

G

tive, pleasant, or desirable 特别吸引人的东西；人人喜欢的东西：They had all the goodies — new cars, a big house, holidays abroad — that a higher income brings. 他们已经拥有一切令人向往的东西——新汽车、宽敞的住宅、海外度假——这些都是较高收入才拥有的东西。

goody² /ˈɡʊdi/
int. an expression of pleasure and approval, used especially by children 好啊！太好啦！（儿童用语，表示开心和赞同）

goose /ɡuːs/
n. (*pl.* geese /ɡiːs/) ❶ a large water bird that has a long neck and webbed feet 鹅 ❷ the goose's meat as food 鹅肉：We have roasted ~ for dinner. 我们晚餐吃烤鹅肉。 ❸ a man who is a stupid incompetent fool 傻瓜；笨蛋：You silly ~! 你这个笨蛋！

gorge /ɡɔːdʒ/
Ⅰ *n.* ❶ the passage between the pharynx and the stomach 咽喉 ❷ sth. which has been swallowed 咽下物；胃中物 ❸ a deep narrow valley 峡谷：the Sanmen Gorge 三门峡 Ⅱ *v.* eat greedily 狼吞虎咽：~ on rich food 贪婪地吃着油腻的食物

gorgeous /ˈɡɔːdʒəs/
adj. richly coloured; magnificent 华丽的；绚丽的；灿烂的；豪华的：a ~ sunset 绚丽的落日

gorilla /ɡəˈrɪlə/
n. a very large animal which has long arms, black fur and a black face 大猩猩：Two ~s have escaped from the zoo. 两只大猩猩逃出了动物园。

gosh /ɡɒʃ/
int. an exclamation of surprise（表示惊讶）哎呀！天哪！

gossamer /ˈɡɒsəmə(r)/
n. ❶ very thin threads of spider's web 蛛丝 ❷ a gauze fabric with a fine texture 薄纱

gossip /ˈɡɒsɪp/
Ⅰ *n.* ❶ idle talk about the affairs of others 闲话，流言：I often hear the ~ about her. 我经常听到有关她的闲话。 ❷ a person fond of idle talk 爱讲闲话的人：The old woman is a ~. 这老妇是一个爱讲闲话的人。 Ⅱ *v.* talk about the affairs of others and reveal their secrets 说闲话；搬弄是非：They are ~ing about you. 他们正在说你的闲话。

gouache /ɡʊˈɑːʃ/
n. a method of painting using colours that are mixed with water and thickened with a sort of gum 水粉画

gouge¹ /ɡaʊdʒ/
n. a tool for cutting out hollow areas in wood 半圆凿

gouge² /ɡaʊdʒ/
v. press or dig out with force 用力挖出；掘出；挤出：They tortured him and then ~d his eyes out. 他们拷打他，随后挖出了他的双眼。

gourd /ɡʊəd/
n. ❶ a large fruit of a climbing or spreading type of plant 葫芦 ❷ the dry, hard skin of this fruit as a container 葫芦瓢

govern /ˈɡʌvn/
v. ❶ be officially in charge of a country or a place and have responsibility for making laws, managing the economy and controlling public services 统治；治理：Britain is ~ed by parliament. 英国由议会治理。 ❷ direct or strongly influence the behaviour of 影响；支配：The climate is ~ed by the ocean. 气候受海洋的影响。

governess /ˈɡʌvənəs/
n. a woman who is employed to teach children in a private family 家庭女教师

government /ˈɡʌvənmənt/
n. ❶ the ruling of a country, etc. 统治；治理：What the country needs is strong ~. 这个国家所需要的是有力的统治。 ❷ the method or system by which a community or other political unit is governed 体制；政体：They prefer democratic ~. 他们喜欢民主政体。 ❸ the organization that is the governing authority of a political unit 内阁，政府：The Prime Minister has formed a ~. 首相已组阁。

governor /ˈɡʌvənə(r)/
n. ❶ the official who governs a province or colony or a state 省长；总督；州长：the

Governor of Washington State 华盛顿州州长 ❷a member of the governing body of an institution（such as school，hospital，etc.）（学校、医院等机构的）管理人员，理事

gown/gaʊn/
n. ❶ a woman's dress 女式长袍：She looked very beautiful in a wedding ~.她穿着结婚礼服非常漂亮。❷ a long，loose outer garment worn by members of a university，judges，etc.礼服；法衣：He went to the platform wearing a university ~.他穿着大学礼服走向讲台。

grab/græb/
Ⅰ *v.* (-bb-) take hold of sth. suddenly；snatch 强夺：The dog ~bed the bone and ran off with it.那狗抢了骨头就跑。Ⅱ *n.* a sudden snatch 抓取；攫取：The child made a ~ at a cricket，but it jumped away.小孩去抓一只蟋蟀，但它跳走了。

grace/greɪs/
Ⅰ *n.* ❶elegance and beauty of movement or manner 优美；雅致：She dances with ~.她舞姿优美。❷the ways of behaving and doings thing which are considered polite and well-mannered 风度 ❸a short prayer before or after a meal giving thanks to God（饭前或饭后）感恩祷告：Before a meal we always read ~s.饭前我们总是先念祷告。Ⅱ *v.*give grace or honour to 使增光：We were ~d by the presence of the Queen.女王光临，不胜荣幸。

graceful/ˈgreɪsfl/
adj. having or showing grace 优美的；雅致的：~ manners 文雅的风度

graceless/ˈgreɪsləs/
adj. awkward in movement or form；lacking in good manners 不优美的；不懂礼貌的；不通情理的：~ behavior 粗野的行为

gracious/ˈgreɪʃəs/
adj. pleasant and kind；polite 和蔼可亲的；好心的；有礼貌的：in a ~ manner 态度和蔼可亲

gradation/grəˈdeɪʃn/
*n.*a stage in a set of changes or degrees of

development 等级；阶段；层次

grade/greɪd/
Ⅰ *n.* ❶ the degree of rank or quality 等级：This ~ of refrigerator can be sold at higher price.这个等级的冰箱能卖较高价格。❷ a group of classes in which all the students are of a similar age 年级：An elementary school in China has six ~s.中国小学有六个年级。❸ the mark 分数：He got a ~ A in the exam in English.英语考试他的成绩是 A。Ⅱ *v.* sort things into sizes，kinds，etc.分级；分类：They ~ pears by size.他们按大小把梨子分类。

gradient/ˈgreɪdiənt/
*n.*the degree of a slope 坡度：On that hill the road has a ~ of 1 in 6.那座山上公路的坡度是每六米升高一米。

gradual/ˈgrædʒʊəl/
adj. happening a little at a time rather than suddenly 逐渐的；缓慢的：There's a ~ increase in the cost of living in recent years.近年来，生活费用逐渐增高。‖ ~ly *adv.*逐渐地

graduate
Ⅰ/ˈgrædʒʊeɪt/*v.* get a university degree，complete a course at an educational institution 大学毕业；获得学位：I ~d from Peking University. 我毕业于北京大学。Ⅱ/ˈgrædʒʊət/*n.* a person who has a university degree 大学毕业生：He was a ~ of Tsinghua university.他是清华大学毕业生。Ⅲ/ˈgrædʒʊət/*adj.*postgraduate 毕了业的；研究生的：She is a ~ student.她是研究生。

graduation/ˌgrædʒʊˈeɪʃn/
n. the act of completing a university degree；a ceremony at which degrees are given（大学）毕业；〈美〉授学位典礼，毕业典礼：After ~，he went to work.毕业后，他便去工作。/The ~ will be held in the large hall.毕业典礼将在大厅里举行。

graft/grɑːft/
Ⅰ *v.* transfer a part of one living thing to another（e.g. buds or branches from one tree to another；skin or bones from one part of the body to another or from one person to another）嫁接；移植：He ~ed

the branch onto the apple tree. 他把枝条嫁接到苹果树上。/His hands were so badly burned that the doctors had to ~ new skin onto them. 他的双手烧伤如此严重,医生只得为他植上新皮。Ⅱ *n.* the act of grafting sth. onto sth. else 嫁接;移植(手术)

grain /greɪn/
n. ❶ a small, hard seed of food plants such as wheat and rice 谷粒: Farmers produce millions of tons of ~ every year. 农民每年都生产千万吨谷物。❷ a tiny piece of sand, sugar or salt, etc. 细粒;颗粒: In the river there are numberless ~s of sand. 这条河里有无数的沙粒。

grammar /ˈgræmə(r)/
n. ❶ a study of the right way to put words together when we speak and write 语法: Grammar is very difficult for us in English. 对我们来说,英语语法很难。❷ a book containing contents of rules for a particular language 语法书: I have been reading a German ~ since last week. 自上周开始,我一直在看一本德语语法书。❸ the way in which someone obeys the rules of language when they write or speak 语言(语法)的运用: I'm trying to improve my ~. 我在努力提高语言能力。‖ ~ian *n.* 语法学家/**grammatical** *adj.* 语法上的/**grammatically** *adv.* 语法上

gram(me) /græm/
n. a metric unit of weight equal to one thousandth of a kilogram 克(重量单位): There are 1,000 ~s in a kilogram. 1 公斤等于 1 000 克。

gramophone /ˈgræməfəʊn/
n. a machine on which records can be played, so that you can hear the music or words 留声机;唱机

granary /ˈgrænəri/
n. a storehouse for grain 谷仓;产粮区: a natural ~ 天然粮仓;鱼米之乡

grand /grænd/
adj. ❶ very big, or impressive in size or appearance 雄伟的;富丽堂皇的: a ~ piano 大型平台钢琴 ❷ of most or greatest importance 主要的;重要的: a ~ stand (体育场的)正面看台 ❸ very enjoyable 有趣的;愉快的: All of us had a ~ time during the Spring Festival. 春节期间我们都过得非常愉快。‖ ~iose *adj.* 宏伟的;堂皇的/ ~ly *adv.* 显赫地;高贵地

grandchild /ˈgrændtʃaɪld/
n. (*pl.* -children) a child of one's son or daughter (外)孙子;(外)孙女

granddaughter /ˈgrændɔːtə(r)/
n. a daughter of one's son or daughter 孙女;外孙女

grandeur /ˈgrændʒə(r)/
n. greatness; magnificence 宏伟;壮观;威严;伟大;崇高: The ~ of Niagara Falls is impressive. 尼亚加拉瀑布的景色极为壮观。

grandfather /ˈgrændˌfɑːðə/
n. the father of one's father or mother (外)祖父

grandma /ˈgrænmɑː/
n. grandmother 奶奶;姥姥,外婆

grandmother /ˈgrænmʌðə/
n. the mother of one's father or mother (外)祖母

grandpa /ˈgrændpɑː/
n. grandfather 爷爷;外公

grandparent /ˈgrænpeərənt/
n. a parent of one's father or mother; a grandmother or grandfather 祖父母;祖父;祖母

grandson /ˈgrænsʌn/
n. one's son's or daughter's son 孙子;外孙: She has many ~s though she is quite young. 她虽然很年轻,可有不少孙子(外孙)。

grandstand /ˈgrænstænd/
n. a set of seats, arranged in rising rows and sometimes covered by a roof, from which people watch sports matches, races, etc. (比赛场地的)正面看台;大看台

grange /greɪndʒ/
n. a large country house with farm buildings 农庄;庄园: They want to buy the old ~ and turn it into a hotel. 他们要买下这座古老的庄园,并把它改建为旅馆。

granite /ˈgrænɪt/

n. a kind of hard grey stone used for building 花岗岩；花岗石：buildings built of ～用花岗石建造的建筑物

granny/ˈgræni/
n. grandmother (外)祖母

grant/grɑːnt/
Ⅰ *n.* an amount of money given by a state or other institution for a particular purpose, such as to a university or to a student during a period of study (政府或机构的)拨款，补助金：The government gives a ～ to every poor student so that he can continue his learning at school. 政府给每个贫困生拨款，使他们能继续上学。Ⅱ *v.* ❶ agree to fulfil or allow to be fulfilled 准予；允许 ❷ admit that sth. is true 承认(某事是对的)：She ～ed my honesty. 她认为我是诚实的。‖ ～ed(or ～ing) that ... 假定……即使……/take sth.for ～ed 认为某事是理所当然的

granular/ˈgrænjələ(r)/
adj. made of, full of, or covered with granules 颗粒状的；含颗粒的；由颗粒构成的

granule/ˈgrænjuːl/
n. a small bit like a fine grain 小粒，细粒：a ～ of sugar 小颗粒白糖/instant coffee ～s 速溶咖啡(晶)

grape/greɪp/
n. a small green or purple fruit which grows in bunches and can be eaten raw or, used for making wine 葡萄：a cluster of ～s 一串葡萄/～ juice 葡萄汁

grapefruit/ˈgreɪpfruːt/
n. a round yellow fruit with a thick skin, like a very large orange but with a more acid taste 西柚，葡萄柚

graph/grɑːf/
n. a diagram which shows the relationship between two or more sets of numbers or measurements 图表；图形；图解：directed ～ 定向图

graphic/ˈgræfɪk/
adj. ❶ of writing or drawing 书写的；图示的 ❷ clear and vivid 鲜明的；生动的：He gave a ～ account of his adventures. 他生动地叙述了他的奇遇。

graphics/ˈgræfɪks/
n. (*pl.*) designs, drawings or pictures that are used especially in the production of books, magazines, etc. 图样；图案；绘图：computer ～ 计算机制图

graphite/ˈgræfaɪt/
n. a form of carbon used in pencils and electrical equipment 石墨

grapple/ˈgræpl/
v. ❶ seize or struggle with 抓住；与……扭打：He ～d with the thief. 他跟小偷扭打了起来。❷ try to deal with (a problem, etc.) 设法对付：They are grappling with the problem. 他们正在尽力解决这个问题。

grasp/grɑːsp/
Ⅰ *v.* ❶ hold tightly in the hand；take a firm hold of；seize 抓住；抓紧：I ～ed the boy's hand and pulled him out of the water. 我紧紧抓住男孩的手，把他从水里拉出来。❷ understand 理解；掌握：He ～ed the teacher's meaning at once. 他立即领会了老师的意思。Ⅱ *n.* ❶ a firm hold of the hand 紧握：I kept her hand in my ～. 我紧紧地握住她的手。❷ the understanding of the nature or meaning or quality or magnitude of sth. 掌握；了解：She has a profound ～ of the practical work. 她对实际工作有一个深刻的了解。

grasping/ˈgrɑːspɪŋ/
adj. eager for more, especially more money, and often ready to use unfair or dishonest methods (尤指对钱)贪心的；贪婪的：Don't let those ～ taxi drivers overcharge you. 不要让那些贪心的计程车司机敲你的竹杠。

grass/grɑːs/
n. ❶ a very common, wild, green plant (青)草 ❷ a land covered by grass 草地：Keep off the ～! 请勿践踏草地！

grasshopper/ˈgrɑːsˌhɒpə(r)/
n. a terrestrial plant-eating insect with strong back legs for jumping 蚱蜢；蝗虫；Grasshoppers feed on plants. 蚱蜢以植物为食。

grassland/ˈgrɑːslænd/
n. a stretch of land covered mainly with

grass,especially wild open land used for cattle to feed on 牧场;草原

grassy/ˈɡrɑːsi/

*adj.*covered with growing grass 草多的;草长得茂盛的

grate/ɡreɪt/

Ⅰ *n.*a metal frame work where a fire is lit 炉格;炉栅;壁炉;I put a log on the ～.我在壁炉上放了一块木头。Ⅱ *v.*rub into small thin pieces with a special instrument 磨碎;～ cheese 磨碎干酪

grateful/ˈɡreɪtfl/

*adj.*❶ feeling or showing gratitude 感激的;感谢的:We're ～ to you for your help.谢谢你的帮助。❷ affording comfort or pleasure 令人愉快的;宜人的:The ～ rain has done the crops a lot of good. 这场雨对庄稼非常有益。‖ ～ly *adv.*感激地

grater/ˈɡreɪtə(r)/

*n.*an instrument for grating things into small pieces,often one consisting of a metal surface full of sharp-edged holes 磨碎东西的工具;(将食物等擦成碎块的)擦子:a cheese ～ 干酪磨碎器

gratify/ˈɡrætɪfaɪ/

*v.*make happy or satisfied 使满足;使高兴:He was gratified to learn you could come.他得知你能来非常高兴。‖ ～ing *adj.*使人满意的:It was ～ing for him to learn this.令人高兴的是他已经知道了这件事。/gratification /ˌɡrætɪfɪˈkeɪʃn/ *n.* 满足;满意;喜悦:I had the gratification of seeing him win.看到他赢了,我很高兴。

grating/ˈɡreɪtɪŋ/

*n.*a flat frame made of bars blocking a passage but admitting air 栅栏

gratitude/ˈɡrætɪtjuːd/

n. a feeling of thankfulness and appreciation 感谢,感激:I wish to express my ～ to you for your cooperation.我要对你的合作表达感激之意。

gratuitous/ɡrəˈtjuːɪtəs/

*adj.*❶not deserved or unnecessary 不值得的;不必要的:I was given plenty of ～ information .我得到了许多不必要的信息。❷given or done without payment 无

偿的:～ service 免费服务 ❸without reason or cause 没有理由的:a ～ insult 无理的侮辱

grave[1]/ɡreɪv/

*adj.*❶requiring careful consideration;important 重大的;严重的:The leader made a ～ mistake.那个领导人犯了一个严重的错误。❷ serious 严肃的:He looked ～.他表情严肃。‖ ～ly *adv.*严重地;严肃地

grave[2]/ɡreɪv/

n. the place in the ground where a dead person is buried 坟墓

gravel/ˈɡrævl/

*n.*a mixture of sand and small stones,often used for making garden paths 砾石;砂砾:The workers put ～ on the road.工人们把沙砾铺在道路上。

gravelly/ˈɡrævəli/

*adj.*❶ of, containing, or covered with gravel 碎石的;铺满碎石的;含有碎石的:This ～ soil is well drained and good for growing root crops.这块沙地利于排水,适于种植块根作物。❷(of a voice) low, rough, and harsh (声音)粗重沙哑的:a ～ voice 沙哑的嗓音

gravestone/ˈɡreɪvstəʊn/

*n.*a stone put up over a grave bearing the name,dates of birth and death,etc.of the dead person 墓碑,墓石

graveyard/ˈɡreɪvjɑːd/

*n.*a piece of ground, sometimes around a church,where people are buried;a cemetery 墓地,坟场,公墓:The area had become a ～ for old cars.这块地方已变成了堆放废弃汽车的场地。

gravitate/ˈɡrævɪteɪt/

*v.*move or tend to move under the influence of gravitational force;be strongly attracted 受吸引;被吸引:The earth ～s toward(s) the sun.地球受太阳的吸引。

gravitation/ˌɡrævɪˈteɪʃn/

*n.*the force of mutual attraction between all masses in the universe, especially the attraction of the earth's mass for bodies near its surface 万有引力;地心引力;吸引力:the law of ～(万有)引力定律

gravity/ˈɡrævəti/

　n. ❶ the quality of being serious 严肃;庄重:He could hardly keep his ~.他几乎无法保持严肃。❷ the force which attracts objects towards the centre of the earth 重力;地球引力:Anything that is dropped to the ground, pulled by the force of ~.任何跌落的物体均被地心引力所吸引而落向地面。

gray/ɡreɪ/

　n. = grey

graze/ɡreɪz/

　v. ❶(of an animal) feed on growing grass 吃草;放牧:The cattle are grazing in the field.牛群在地里吃草。❷ touch (sth.) lightly while passing 擦碰;掠过:A swallow ~d the surface of the river.一只燕子掠过河面。❸break the surface of sth.especially the skin by rubbing against sth.轻擦;擦破:The bullet ~d his cheek.子弹擦伤了他的面颊。

grease/ɡriːs/

　Ⅰ *n.* ❶animal fat;that has been made softer by heating(炼过的）动物油脂:We use ~ for cooking food.我们用动物油烹调食物。❷any thick, oily substance 油脂;axle ~ 轴用润滑脂 Ⅱ*v.*put grease or fat on 在……上涂油(或抹油、擦油):Before a long journey we must ~ the wheels of our car.长途旅行前,我们必须给车轮擦油。

greasy/ˈɡriːsi/

　adj. ❶ covered with or containing grease 油腻的,含油脂的: ~ food (skin, hair) 含油脂多的食物(皮肤、头发) ❷ slippery 滑溜溜的:The roads are ~ after the rain.雨后路滑。❸ insincerely polite; smarmy 油滑的;逢迎拍马的:I detest his ~ smile.我嫌恶他谄媚的微笑。

great/ɡreɪt/

　adj. ❶of excellent quality or importance 伟大的;重要的:He is a ~ painter.他是一位伟大的画家。❷ unusually good; very enjoyable 很好的:He's my ~ friend.他是我亲密的朋友。‖ a ~ many 许许多多/a ~ deal 大量

greatly/ˈɡreɪtli/

　adv. very much 大大地;非常: I am ~ surprised to see him! 见到他我非常吃惊!

greed/ɡriːd/

　n. ❶a strong desire to have a lot of sth., especially food,money,or power,often in a way that is selfish or unfair to other people 贪婪;贪心:His ~ made him rob a man of his money.贪心使他去抢人钱财。❷a strong desire for food, especially when one is not hungry 贪食(尤指某人不饥饿时) ‖ ~y *adj.* 贪婪的/ ~ily *adv.*贪婪地/ ~iness *n.*贪婪

green/ɡriːn/

　Ⅰ *adj.* ❶of the colour between yellow and blue,which is the colour of leaves or grasses 绿色的;青的:The fields are ~ in spring.春天,田野一片青绿。❷not ripe; not completely grown 未熟的;生的:Green oranges are not good to eat.没有熟的橘子不好吃。❸not trained or experienced 无经验的:I'm a ~ hand in work.在工作方面我是一个生手。Ⅱ*n.* ❶ the colour of grass or many other plants 绿色:She likes to be dressed in ~.她爱穿绿色衣服。❷ (*pl.*) green vegetables 绿叶蔬菜:Greens are rich in vitamins.青菜富含维生素。‖ ~ish *adj.*浅绿色的/ ~wood *n.*绿林

greenery/ˈɡriːnəri/

　*n.*the green leaves or plants 青枝绿叶;绿色植物:Add some ~ to that vase of flowers.给那瓶花加上些绿叶。

greengrocer/ˈɡriːnˌɡrəʊsə(r)/

　n. a shopkeeper selling vegetables and fruit 蔬菜水果商;菜贩

greenhorn/ˈɡriːnhɔːn/

　n. an inexperienced and easily deceived person 无经验的人;年轻易受欺骗的人

greenhouse/ˈɡriːnhaʊs/

　*n.*a building with sides and roof of glass, used for growing plants that need protection from the weather (玻璃)温室;花房;暖房:~ plants 温室植物

greet/ɡriːt/

　v. ❶say hello to sb.or to welcome them; say words of welcome to 问候;致意;欢

迎;向……致欢迎词:He ~ed her with a loving kiss.他用深情的一吻来欢迎她。/ She ~ed us by shouting a friendly "Hello".她友好地叫着"哈罗"来迎接我们。 ❷receive or acknowledge sth. in a specified way (以特定的方式)接受;对……做出反应:His speech was ~ed with cheers.他的演说受到热烈的喝彩。

greeting/ˈɡriːtɪŋ/

n.the words or actions used to welcome or address sb.问候;寒暄;致意;祝贺;祝词:He gave me a warm and friendly ~.他热情友好地向我问好。/We sent a card with birthday ~s.我们送了一张生日卡,表示祝贺。

gregarious/ɡrɪˈɡeərɪəs/

adj.living in groups;fond of company 群居的;爱交际的:Man is very ~.人类喜爱群居。

grenade/ɡrəˈneɪd/

n.a small bomb thrown by hand or shot from a rifle 手榴弹;枪榴弹:a hand ~ 一颗手榴弹

grey/ɡreɪ/

adj.❶of black mixed white 灰色的;灰白的:~ eyes 灰色的眼睛/His face was as ~ as ashes.他的脸色发灰。❷(of the skin of the face)of pale colour because of sudden fear or illness (脸色)苍白的:Her face turned ~ as she heard the bad news. 听到这个坏消息,她的脸变得惨白。❸having grey hair 有花白的头发的:He's gone ~ within a few weeks.他的头发在几星期内就变白了。❹half dark;cloudy 阴暗的;阴沉沉的:It's very ~ outside.外面天很阴沉。

grid/ɡrɪd/

n.❶a frame with bars;grating 格子;格栅 ❷numbered squares printed on a map to give exact positions 地图上的坐标方格 ❸a network of main power lines for distributing electricity 输电网

grief/ɡriːf/

n.❶great sadness caused by trouble or loss;heavy sorrow 悲伤;忧伤:When her mother died, she was almost mad with ~.她母亲去世时,她几乎悲伤得发狂。

❷a cause of sorrow or sadness 伤心事;悲痛事:His having no children was a great ~ to his parents.他没有孩子是他父母的一大伤心事。

grievance/ˈɡriːvəns/

n.sth. that you think is unfair and that you complain or protest about 委屈;怨愤,不满:He was nursing a ~.他心里滋生着怨恨。

grieve/ɡriːv/

v.❶feel sorrow or sadness 感到悲痛;伤心:We ~d over the death of the hero.我们为英雄的死感到非常悲痛。❷cause grief to;make very unhappy 使悲痛;使伤心:She's ~d for you.她为你悲伤。

grievous/ˈɡriːvəs, ˈɡrɪvəs/

adj.extremely serious 极其严重的,剧烈的:a ~ error 严重错误 ‖ ~ly *adv*.极其痛苦地

grill/ɡrɪl/

Ⅰ*v*.cook sth. under or over strong heat 在烤架上烤:The cook is ~ing chops.厨师正在烤牛排。Ⅱ*n*.an arrangement of a metal shelf under a gas flame or electric heat, used to cook food quickly 烤架:She hung a fat goose in the ~.她把一只肥鹅挂在烤架上。

grille/ɡrɪl/

n.a frame of upright metal bars filling a space in a door or window, such as one in a bank or post office separating a clerk from the customers (银行或邮局柜台上的)铁栅栏

grim/ɡrɪm/

adj.❶unpleasant and depressing 令人不快的;令人沮丧的:The ~ news came at last from the hospital.令人不安的消息终于从医院里传来了。❷looking or sounding very serious 严肃的;严厉的 ❸determined in spite of fear or great difficulty 艰苦的;不屈的:This is a ~ fight for peace.这是一场争取和平的艰苦斗争。 ‖ ~ly *adv*.严峻地;严厉地

grin/ɡrɪn/

Ⅰ*n*.a very wide smile 咧嘴笑;露齿笑:When I made a face to her, she had a big ~ on her face.当我向她做鬼脸时,她咧

嘴大笑。Ⅱ v.(-nn-) smile broadly so as to show the teeth 咧嘴笑：The boy ～ned from ear to ear when I gave him a gift.我给那男孩礼物时,他笑得合不拢嘴。

grind/graɪnd/

v.(ground) ❶ crush or make into small pieces or powder 磨碎；碾(碎)：They ～ the wheat into flour.他们把麦子磨成粉。❷polish or sharpen by rubbing on a hard surface 磨光；磨快：He ～s the knives and scissors from door to door.他挨家挨户磨刀磨剪。❸ rub harshly together 磨牙：The boy often ～s his teeth in his sleep.这男孩在睡梦中常磨牙。

grinder/'graɪndə(r)/

n.a machine or person that grinds 碾磨工人；研磨机；磨床：a coffee ～ 咖啡研磨器/a knife ～ 磨刀人

grindstone/'graɪndstəʊn/

n.❶ a round stone which is turned to sharpen tools, knives, etc. 磨石；砂轮 ❷(one's nose to the ～)in a state of continuous hard work 埋头苦干；不停地工作：He's got to keep his nose to the ～ to feed his six children.他必须不停地埋头干活才能养活六个孩子。

grip/grɪp/

Ⅰ v.(-pp-) ❶ seize or hold firmly in hand; grasp 紧握；抓紧：When there is lightning across the dark sky, she ～ped my hands in fear.当闪电划过夜空,她害怕得紧握我的手。❷ attract the attention of sb. 吸引(某人的)注意力：The new published novel ～ped my attention.新出版的小说吸引了我的注意力。Ⅱn.a very tight forceful hold 紧握：The patient took a ～ on his daughter's hand and murmured.病人紧握他女儿的手,喃喃自语。/The king has the power in his ～.这个国王大权在握。‖ ～ping adj.吸引人的；扣人心弦的

gristle/'grɪstl/

n.a rough substance like white elastic, found in meat 软骨

grit/grɪt/

Ⅰ n.❶ very small pieces of stone, sand, etc.沙砾；沙粒：I have a piece of ～ in my eye.我眼睛里有一粒沙子。❷ courage and endurance 毅力；勇气：It requires ～ to accomplish the task.完成这项工作需要勇气和毅力。Ⅱ v.(-tt-)❶ spread grit and often salt on the icy road 在(结冰的路面)上撒沙子和盐：They ～ the slippery roads in winter.冬天,他们在湿滑的公路上撒沙子和盐。❷(～ one's teeth)keep the jaws together to show courage 咬紧牙关

grizzle/'grɪzl/

v.❶(especially of a young child)cry continually as though tired or worried (尤指幼儿)烦躁地哭 ❷ complain in a self-pitying way 哀诉；诉苦

groan/grəʊn/

Ⅰ v.make a deep sound in response to pain or despair(因痛苦或失望而)呻吟；叹气：～ out a reply 呻吟着答复/He ～ed with pain.他因疼痛而呻吟。Ⅱn.a deep sound made in groaning 呻吟声；叹气声：the ～s of the injured men 受伤者的呻吟/He gave a ～ of despair.他失望地叹了口气。

groats/grəʊts/

n. grain, especially oats, from which the outer shell has been removed, and which may also have been broken into pieces 去壳的谷粒；燕麦粒

grocer/'grəʊsə(r)/

n.a man who sells food, and things for the house, usually in tins and packets 杂货商；食品商：You can buy biscuits, sugar, soap and tea at the ～'s.你可以在杂货商店买到饼干、糖、肥皂和茶叶。

grocery/'grəʊsəri/

n.❶(usually pl.) things sold by a grocer 杂货 ❷the shop or trade of a grocer 杂货店；杂货业：We buy our flour at the nearest ～.我们在最近的那家杂货店买面粉。

groom/gruːm/

Ⅰ n.❶a servant in charge of horses 马倌；马夫 ❷ bridegroom 新郎 Ⅱ v. keep (horses); brush and clean (horses) 养(马)；刷洗(马)

groove/gruːv/

*n.*a long narrow hollow cut in the wood, etc.槽；辙；纹：The needle moves along a ～ in the record.唱针沿着唱片上的纹道走。

grope/grəʊp/

Ⅰ*v.*❶feel or search about as one does in the dark 摸索：I had to ～ in the darkness for the candle and matches. 我只好在黑暗中摸索蜡烛和火柴。❷ search with uncertainty of success for an idea or fact 探索：They are groping after the truth.他们正在探寻真理。Ⅱ*n.*an act of groping 摸索：She was in an aimless ～ for her flashlight in the dark room. 她在黑暗的房间里漫无目标地摸她的手电筒。

gross/grəʊs/

*adj.*❶visible to the naked eye 显然的：You made a ～ mistake.你犯了一个显而易见的错误。❷ (especially of a person or his manner) rough, impolite, and offensive 粗鲁的；无礼的：His manner is too ～ for a gentleman.作为绅士，他的态度太粗鲁了。❸(of income, profit, or interest) without deduction of tax or other contributions；total（收入、利润或利息）毛的；总的：The ～ industrial output value of the country last year was over one hundred million dollars.去年该国的工业总产值超过一亿美元。

grotesque/grəʊˈtesk/

adj. extremely wily in a strange way; strange in a way that is unpleasant 奇形怪状的；怪诞的；荒唐的：These designs are ～.这些设计构思奇特。/His face has a ～ appearance.他的面部表情特别怪。

grotto/ˈgrɒtəʊ/

n.(*pl.*～es or ～s) a small cave, especially an imitation one in a park or garden 洞穴；（尤指园林中的）人工洞穴

grouch/graʊtʃ/

Ⅰ*v.*complain or grumble 发牢骚；发脾气：He's always ～ing. 他总是发脾气。Ⅱ*n.*❶a complaint or a grumble 抱怨；牢骚：I'm tired of his ～es.我受够了他的牢骚。❷a sulky discontented person 常发牢骚的人

ground/graʊnd/

Ⅰ*n.*❶ soil；on the surface of the earth 土地；土壤：After the rain the ～ is wet and soft.这场雨后，土地既潮湿又松软。❷ the solid surface of the earth 地面：I dropped my cup to the ～.我把杯子掉到地上摔破了。❸a piece of land for a special purpose 场地：There's a football ～ in our school. 我们学校有一个足球场。❹a large garden or small park around a building（建筑物周围的）场地花园，庭园：The pretty villa stands in lovely ～s. 这幢漂亮的别墅矗立在可爱的庭园中。❺(*pl.*) a good or true reason for sth. 记分的理由；根据：There are no ～s for complaint. 没有抱怨的理由。❻ background 背景：This is a design of white flowers on a red ～.这是红底白花的图案。Ⅱ*v.*❶lay on place（sth.）on the ground 把……放在地上：The enemy was forced to ～ arms. 敌人被迫放下武器。❷base 把……基于：You can only ～ your conclusions on the facts.你们只能根据事实得出结论。❸prevent（a plane or pilot）from flying 使停飞；阻止……起飞：The thunder storm has ～ed many planes at the airport.雷雨使许多飞机停在飞机场不能起飞。

groundless/ˈgraʊndlɪs/

*adj.*not based on any good reason 无理由的；无根据的：Our fears are quite ～.我们的担忧是没有理由的。

groundwater/ˈgraʊndwɔːtə(r)/

*n.*water held underground in the soil or in pores and crevices in rock 地下水（指地下土壤或岩石裂缝中的水）

groundwork/ˈgraʊndwɜːk/

*n.*the work that lays the basis for sth. 准备工作，基础工作：The inquiry's findings are expected to lay the ～ for a complete reform.调查结果预计将为全面改革打下基础。

group/gruːp/

Ⅰ*n.*❶a number of people, things, or organizations gathered, placed together or connected in a particular way 群；批：The students are playing games in ～s.学生们正在三五成群做游戏。❷a number of people that work together or share certain beliefs 小组;团体:They organized a study ~.他们组建了一个学习小组。Ⅱ *v.*form into or gather in a group or groups 集合;聚集:People in all walks of life ~ed together.各行各业的人们聚集在一起。/The students ~ed themselves to discuss the problem.学生们分组讨论问题。

grove/grəʊv/
*n.*a small group of trees;a small wood 小树林;树丛

grovel/ˈɡrɒvl/
v.(-ll- or -l-) lie or crawl on the ground with one's face downwards 匍匐(前进);趴;爬行:The slaves ~led before their master.奴隶们匍匐在主人面前。

grow/grəʊ/
v.(grew,~n)❶ live and develop naturally in a certain place 生长;发育:The wheat is ~ing fine in the field.地里的麦子长得不错。❷ raise by planting seeds and caring for 种植;栽:He ~s vegetables in the garden.他在菜园里种蔬菜。❸ become gradually (逐渐)变得:In spring it's ~ing warm.春天,天气渐暖。‖ ~ out of 长大后穿不下 / ~ up 长大成人 ‖ ~er *n.*栽培者

growing/ˈɡrəʊɪŋ/
*adj.*increasing in size, amount or degree 增加的;增长的;增强的:A ~ number of people are returning to full-time education.越来越多的人重返学校接受全日制教育。

growl/ɡraʊl/
*v.*make a low, angry sound 嗥叫;咆哮:The dog ~ed at the stranger.狗向生人吠叫。/He ~ed (out) a reply.他咆哮着回答。

grown-up/ˈɡrəʊnʌp/
Ⅰ*adj.*mature;arrived at full growth 成长的;成熟的;成人的:He has a ~ daughter.他有一个成年的女儿。Ⅱ*n.*a grown man;an adult 成年人;大人:There were no ~s there, only children.那里没有大人,只有孩子。

growth/ɡrəʊθ/
*n.*❶development;the process of growing 生长;发展;增长:the rapid ~ of our economy 我国经济的迅速发展/There has been a sudden ~ in membership of the club.俱乐部的会员人数突然之间大大增加。❷ sth. that has grown 种植物;栽培物:apples of foreign ~ 外国产的苹果

grub/ɡrʌb/
v.(-bb-)❶ turn over the soil, especially by digging with the hands or paws (尤指用手或爪)挖土,掘土:The dog was ~bing (about) under the bush, looking for a bone.狗在灌木丛下面刨土,寻找骨头。❷ dig up by the roots 连根挖起

grubby/ˈɡrʌbi/
*adj.*rather dirty 肮脏的;污秽的:~ hands 肮脏的手/That white shirt's looking rather ~.那件白衬衫看上去很脏。

grudge/ɡrʌdʒ/
Ⅰ *v.* feel resentful that someone has achieved (sth.) 忌妒;怨恨:I don't ~ him his success.我不忌妒他的成功。 Ⅱ *n.*a feeling of ill-will or resentment 妒忌;不满;嫌隙:I bear him no ~.我对他没有怨恨。

grudging/ˈɡrʌdʒɪŋ/
*adj.*unwilling;reluctant 不情愿的;勉强的:She was very ~ in her thanks (praise).她的道谢(称赞)十分勉强。/his ~ acceptance of our decision 他勉强接受我们的决定 ‖ ~ly *adv.*勉强地:He ~ly gave his permission.他勉强表示许可。

gruel/ˈɡruːəl/
n. a thin liquid food made by boiling crushed oats in milk or water 燕麦粥;麦片粥

gruelling/ˈɡruːəlɪŋ/
adj. extremely exhausting and demanding 使极度疲劳的;折磨人的:a ~ walk 让人走得精疲力竭的一段路

gruesome/ˈɡruːsəm/
*adj.*causing repulsion or horror 可憎的;可怕的:The injured man, with blood all over his face, was a ~ sight.受伤的人满脸是血,看来十分可怕。

grumble/ˈɡrʌmbl/
Ⅰ*v.*express discontent or dissatisfaction;complain in a quiet but bad-tempered way

抱怨；发牢骚：She never ～s about her unhappy fate.她从不抱怨她的不幸命运。Ⅱ*n.*a complaint or expression of dissatisfaction 牢骚：Her husband is always full of ～s.她丈夫总是怨天尤人。‖ ～r *n.* 爱抱怨的人

grunt/grʌnt/
Ⅰ *v.* ❶ (especially of a pig) make short deep rough sounds in the throat,as if the nose were closed（尤指猪）发出呼噜声 ❷ (of people)make a similar sound（人）咕哝：The old woman ～ed (out) an answer without raising her head.老妇人头也不抬地咕噜着回答。Ⅱ *n.* a short, deep,rough sound made by a pig or a person(猪发出的)呼噜声；(人发出的)咕哝声：The pig's ～s are troublesome for me.猪的呼噜声使我感到恼火。

guarantee/ˌɡærən'tiː/
Ⅰ *v.*❶promise to do sth.or sth.will happen 保证；保障 ❷ give a promise to replace or repair a product free if it goes wrong（免费）保修,保换（有问题的产品）：The colour TV set is ～d for two years.这台彩电保修两年。Ⅱ*n.*a promise that certain conditions will be fulfilled 保证：Unity is the ～ of victory.团结是胜利的保证。‖ **guaranty** *n.*保证书

guarantor/ˌɡærən'tɔː/
*n.*a person who gives a guarantee 担保人；保证人

guard/ɡɑːd/
Ⅰ *n.* ❶ a person,especially a soldier,policeman,or prison officer,who watches over people or places to prevent escape, danger,attack,etc.卫兵；哨兵；看守；警卫员 ❷ the act or duty of protecting property,places or people from danger or attack 守卫；警戒；保卫；看守：All the prisoners are under close ～.所有囚犯都受到严密的监守。❸ a person in charge of a train〈英〉列车员：At midnight the ～ waked me up,and told me that the train would soon arrive at the terminal.半夜里列车员把我叫醒,告诉我火车将很快到达终点站。‖ **keep or stand ～** 站岗/**on ～** 戒备着；提防Ⅱ*v.*❶watch over in order to control or,protect 看守,保卫；保护：

The soldiers ～ed the large bridge day and night.士兵们日夜守卫大桥。❷（～ **against**）take precautions against 预防；防范：I hid the TV set to ～ against being stolen.我把电视机藏起来以防被盗。

guarded/'ɡɑːdɪd/
adj. cautious and having reservations 谨慎的；有保留的：He gave a ～ reply.他做了审慎的回答。

guardhouse/'ɡɑːdhaʊs/
*n.*a building for military guards,especially at the entrance to a camp,sometimes also used for imprisonment of soldiers 卫兵室；禁闭室

guardian/'ɡɑːdɪən/
*n.*a person with the duty of looking after someone（especially young children）who cannot look after himself（尤指年幼儿童的）保护人,监护人：When their father died,I became their ～.他们的父亲去世后,我成为他们的监护人。

guer(r)illa/ɡə'rɪlə/
*n.*a person engaged in fighting in small secret groups 游击队员：～ warfare 游击战

guess/ɡes/
Ⅰ *v.*❶ give an answer that you feel may be right 猜；猜测：Can you ～ my weight? 你能猜出我的体重吗? ❷ suppose；consider 想；认为：I ～ so.我认为是这样的。Ⅱ *n.*an attempt to guess 猜测：Have a ～ at the riddle.猜一下这个谜语。

guesstimate/'ɡestɪmət/
*n.*an inexact judgment,especially of quantity,made by guessing 大概估计；约略的估计

guesswork/'ɡeswɜːk/
*n.*the act of or results of guessing,推测；猜测；猜测的结果：She arrived at the right answer by pure ～.她得出的正确答案纯粹是猜出来的。

guest/ɡest/
n. a person who is invited to visit the home of another or to a particular event 客人；来宾：a state ～ 国宾/We are expecting ～s this weekend.我们本周末要来客人。

guesthouse/'gesthaus/

*n.*a private house where visitors can stay and have meals for payment;a small hotel 宾馆;家庭供膳旅馆;小旅馆

guest room/'gestrum/

*n.*a bedroom in a private house which is kept for visitors to sleep in (私人住宅的)客房;留给宾客用的寝室

guidance/'gaɪdns/

*n.*advice or information aimed at resolving a problem or difficulty 指引;指导:I did the work with my teacher's ～.我在老师的指导下做作业。

guide/gaɪd/

Ⅰ *n.*❶a person who shows others the way 向导:a tourist ～ 导游 ❷a thing that helps someone to form an opinion or make a decision 有指导意义的事物;有助于形成观点(或做出决定)的事物:Instinct is not always a good ～.本能并不永远是好的指导者。❸a book ,document or display of information 指南;手册:a gardening ～ 园艺手册 ❹a member of an association for training girls in character and self-help 女童子军:She is a Girl-Guide.她是一个女童子军。Ⅱ *v.*❶show (sb.) the way by leading 引导;指引:The girl student ～ed a blind man across the busy street.那个女学生领着一位盲人穿过繁华的街道。❷direct or have an influence on the course of action of 领导;影响;指导:You must be ～d by your sense of what is right and just.你必须受正义感的引导。‖ ～book *n.*旅行指南

guideline/'gaɪdlaɪn/

*n.*a general rule,principle,or piece of advice 指导方针,准则:The government has drawn up ～s on the problem 政府制定了解决这一问题的指导方针。

guild/gɪld/

*n.*a society of craftsmen or businessmen 行会;同业公会:There were many ～s in London during the Middle Ages. 中世纪时伦敦有不少行会。

guile/gaɪl/

*n.*sly or cunning intelligence 狡猾;奸诈:a

man of ～ 诡计多端的人

guileless/'gaɪlləs/

*adj.*innocent ;honest and kind 单纯的;厚道的

guilt/gɪlt/

*n.*❶a feeling of shame for having done wrong or failed in an obligation 内疚;不安 ❷the fact of having committed an implied offence or crime 犯罪;过失:In the court the judge was sure of his ～.在法庭上法官肯定他有罪。‖ ～less *adj.*无罪的

guilty/'gɪlti/

*adj.*❶having broken a law 犯罪的;有罪的:The man was declared ～.这人被宣布有罪。/He is ～ of murder.他犯了杀人罪。❷conscious of or affected by a feeling of guilt 自知有罪的;内疚的:I still feel ～ about that error in the accounts. 我对账上的那个差错依然感到内疚。‖ guiltily *adv.*有罪地;内疚地

guinea-pig/'gɪnɪpɪg/

*n.*❶a kind of small rodent with no tail, often used in experiments 豚鼠;天竺鼠 ❷person or thing used in experiments 供做实验的人(或物):We are the ～s for his new ideas about overseas investment. 我们是他的关于海外投资新想法的试验品。

guise/gaɪz/

*n.*an external form or appearance , typically concealing the true nature of sth. (尤指掩饰本性的)外观;外表;形式;伪装:They got into the school in the ～ of inspectors.他们伪装成视察员进了学校。

guitar/gɪ'tɑː/

*n.*a musical instrument with six strings plucked with the fingers 吉他,六弦琴: play the ～弹吉他

gulf/gʌlf/

*n.*a deep inlet of the sea with land on three sides of it 海湾:the Persian Gulf 波斯湾

gull/gʌl/

*n.*a large long-winged sea bird 鸥;海鸥: Gulls are graceful fliers and plunge into the water for their food.海鸥是很漂亮的

鸟,能钻进水中捕食。

gullet /ˈɡʌlɪt/

n. the passage by which food passes from the mouth to the stomach 食道;食管: The dog had something stuck in its ～.那只狗的食管被什么东西哽住了。

gully /ˈɡʌli/

n. ❶ a small, narrow valley 小溪谷 ❷ a deep, narrow ditch caused by rainwater running down a slope (雨水冲击成的)沟渠

gulp /ɡʌlp/

Ⅰ *v.* ❶ swallow down food or drink quickly in large amounts 吞;吞咽;大口地喝: ～ (down) a drink 一饮而尽/Don't ～ your food. 吃东西不要狼吞虎咽。 ❷ make a sudden swallowing movement as if surprised or nervous 抑制;硬塞;强制: ～ down one's sobs 忍气吞声 Ⅱ *n.* the amount swallowed at a single time;a large mouthful 一大口:a ～ of water 一大口水

gum /ɡʌm/

Ⅰ *n.* ❶ a sticky substance obtained from certain trees 树脂;树胶: Some ～ trees are growing very well in the botanical garden.在这座植物园里一些橡胶树长势很好。 ❷ chewing gum 口香糖: The boy is always chewing ～.这男孩老是在嚼口香糖。 Ⅱ *v.* (-mm-) stick two things together with glue 黏合;用胶粘: He ～med a butterfly down. 他用胶粘住了一只蝴蝶。

gumboot /ˈɡʌmbuːt/

n. a long rubber boot 长筒胶靴

gumdrop /ˈɡʌmdrɒp/

n. a hard jelly-like sweet 橡皮糖

gummy /ˈɡʌmi/

adj. sticky 黏性的;粘的:a ～ substance 黏性物质

gun /ɡʌn/

n. firearm which sends out bullets very fast,used for hunting or killing animals or people 枪;炮: Our soldiers fired a ～ and the enemy ran away.我们的士兵开了炮,敌人逃跑了。 ‖ ～boat *n.* 炮舰/ ～cotton *n.* 火棉/ ～powder *n.* 火药/ ～-ship *n.* 武装直升机

gunman /ˈɡʌnmən/

n. (*pl.* -men) a man who uses a gun to commit a crime or terrorist act 持枪歹徒:a gang of masked gunmen 一伙蒙面持枪歹徒

gunner /ˈɡʌnə/

n. a serviceman who operates or specializes in guns 炮手

gunpoint /ˈɡʌnpɔɪnt/

n. (at ～) while threatening someone or being threatened with a gun 在枪口的威胁下: Two robbers held a family at ～ while they searched their house.在他们搜索屋子时,两个劫匪用枪指着这家人。

gunshot /ˈɡʌnʃɒt/

n. a shot fired from a gun (射出的)枪弹(或炮弹)

gurgle /ˈɡɜːɡl/

n. a sound like water flowing quickly through a narrow space (流水的)潺潺声,汩汩声: The water ～d as it ran down the plughole.水汩汩地从塞孔中流下去。

guru /ˈɡuruː/

n. ❶ an Indian religious leader or teacher of religious practices, especially those that produce peace of mind 古鲁(印度教的宗教导师或领袖) ❷ a greatly respected person whose ideas are followed (受人崇敬的)权威;大师: J. M. Keynes was the great ～ of economics.凯恩斯是经济学权威。/one of the president's foreign policy ～s 总统的外交政策智囊团之一

gush /ɡʌʃ/

Ⅰ *v.* ❶ pour or flow suddenly and quickly 涌出,喷出: His nose was ～ing (out) blood. 他的鼻子在大量出血。/Clear water ～ed into the irrigational channel. 清澈的水涌进了灌溉渠道。 ❷ talk continuously 滔滔不绝地讲: ～ over one's baby 大谈特谈自己的婴儿 Ⅱ *n.* ❶ a sudden flow (of a liquid, words, etc.) 涌出,喷出:a ～ of oil 油的突然喷出 ❷ a sudden strong expression of feeling (感情的)迸发,爆发:a ～ of anger 一阵突发的愤怒

gusher /ˈɡʌʃə(r)/

n. an oil-well from which oil rushes out strongly without pumping (自动喷油的)

喷油井,自喷井

gushing /ˈgʌʃɪŋ/

adj. expressing admiration, pleasure, etc. too strongly and perhaps without true feelings 信口开河的;装腔作势的;过分动感情的:a ～ account of the two presidents'meeting 一篇有关两位总统会见的夸大的报道 /She's rather ～.她颇有些装腔作势。

gust /gʌst/

n. ❶ a sudden strong rush of wind 一阵强风,一阵狂风:A ～ of wind broke several apricot trees.一阵狂风刮断了几棵杏树。❷ a burst of anger or other strong feelings (感情等的)爆发:In a ～ of anger she tore her own dress.在一阵狂怒中她撕破了自己的衣服。‖ ～y *adj.*阵风的;起大风的

gut[1] /gʌt/

n. ❶ the stomach or belly 腹部;肚子:I have a pain in my ～s. 我肚子痛。❷ courage and determination 胆量;勇气;毅力:You haven't the ～s to do it.你没有做这事的胆量。

gut[2] /gʌt/

v. (-tt-) ❶ remove the inside organs of a fish 取出鱼的内脏 ❷ destroy the contents of a building 损毁房屋的内部设备:The factory was ～ted by fire.工厂被大火焚烧后徒剩四壁。

gutless /ˈgʌtləs/

adj. lacking courage and determination 怯懦的;缺乏勇气的;无毅力的

gutsy /ˈgʌtsi/

adj. brave and determined 有勇气的,有决心的:That young boxer is a ～ fighter.那个年轻的拳击手是一位勇敢的斗士。

gutter /ˈgʌtə(r)/

n. ❶ an open metal pipe used at the edge of a roof to carry away rainwater 檐槽;天沟 ❷ a channel at the side of a road to carry away rainwater 路旁排水沟;阴沟:The ～ is too narrow to empty the rainwater after the heavy rain. 路边沟渠太窄,大雨后,雨水排不出去。❸ a poor district 贫民区:Living in the ～,the children didn't receive proper education.生活在贫民区的孩子没有接受过正规的教育。

guy /gaɪ/

n. a man or fellow 人;家伙:a nice ～ 好小伙子/He's a great ～.他是个了不起的小伙子。

gym /dʒɪm/

n. ❶ a gymnasium 体育馆:The teams practice in the ～.运动队在体育馆中锻炼。❷ gymnastics 体操:do ～ 做体操

gymkhana /dʒɪmˈkɑːnə/

n. an event in which people riding horse take part in various competitions 赛马会;马术比赛

gymnasium /dʒɪmˈneɪziəm/

n. a room or building for gymnastics, games,and other physical exercise 健身房;体育馆:After school we often go to the ～ to do gymnastic exercises.放学后我们常去体育馆做体操。

gymnast /ˈdʒɪmnæst/

n. a person trained in or skilled in gymnastics 体操运动员;体操教练

gymnastic /dʒɪmˈnæstɪk/

adj. of or relating to gymnastics 体操的;体育的:～ apparatus 体操用具

gymnastics /dʒɪmˈnæstɪks/

n. exercises for that develop and show the body's strength and ability to move and bend easily,often does as a sport in competitions 体操

gypsum /ˈdʒɪpsəm/

n. a soft white mineral from which plaster of paris is made,used in the building industry,also used as a fertilizer 石膏(可用于建筑中,也可用作肥料)

G

Hh

ha/hɑ:/

int.used to express surprise,interest,etc.
（表示吃惊、兴趣等）哈！

habit/'hæbɪt/

n.❶ a tendency to behave in a particular
way or do particular things，especially
regularly and repeatedly over a long period 习惯：form the ～ of analysis 养成分
析的习惯/Habit cures ～.〈谚〉新习惯可
以改掉旧习惯。/Habit is second nature.
习惯是第二天性。❷ general shape or
mode of growth，especially of a plant（尤
指植物的）习性：a shrub of spreading ～
有蔓生习性的灌木 ‖ be in the ～ of 有
……的习惯/break away from a ～ 尽快
改掉一个习惯/break sb.of a ～ 使某人改
掉某习惯/fall（get）into the ～ of 养成
……习惯/make a ～ of sth.经常做某事/
out of（from，by）～ 出于习惯

habitable/'hæbɪtəbl/

adj.able to be lived in 可居住的：Al-
though the house is very old，it is quite
～.这屋子虽然很旧，还可以住人。

habitat/'hæbɪtæt/

n.the natural home or surroundings of animals and plants（动物的）栖息地；（植物
的）产地：The natural ～ of the tiger is
Asia，not Africa.老虎的自然栖息地在亚
洲，而不是在非洲。

habitation/ˌhæbɪ'teɪʃn/

n.❶ the state or process of living in a
place 居住：The North Pole is not suitable for human ～.北极不适于人类居住。
❷a house or home 住处；家

habitual/hə'bɪtʃuəl/

adj.❶regular；usual 惯常的，通常的：a ～
greeting 通常的致意 ❷having a regular
habit 习惯的：He's a ～ thief.他是一个惯
偷。

habituate/hə'bɪtʃueɪt/

v.make or become used to（使）习惯于：
become ～d to a drug 吸毒成瘾/Over the
centuries，these animals have become ～d
to living in such a dry environment.经过
几个世纪，这些动物已经习惯于生活在
这样干燥的环境里。

habitué/hə'bɪtʃueɪ/

n.a regular attender to a particular place
常客：a ～ of the nightclub 夜总会的常客

hack/hæk/

v.❶ cut roughly or carelessly 劈；（乱）砍：
～ sth.into pieces 把东西劈碎/～ at sth.
乱砍某物 ❷ give a short，dry coughs 短
促地干咳：a ～ing cough 一阵猛烈的干
咳

hacker/'hækə(r)/

n.someone who is able to use or change
the information in other people's computer systems without their permission 黑客
（私自侵入或篡改他人计算机资料的人）

hackles/'hæklz/

n.❶ the erectile feathers or hairs on the
back of the neck of certain birds and animals which rise when they are angry or
alarmed（鸟、兽等遇危险时能竖起的）颈
背毛，细长颈羽 ❷ the hairs on the back
of a person's neck，thought of as being
raised when the person is angry or hostile
（想象中人在发怒或有敌对时竖起的）颈
背部毛发：His insensitive remarks about
foreigners made her ～ rise.他对外国人
冷漠的言语得她怒发冲冠。

haggard/'hægəd/

adj.looking tired or worried 疲倦的；焦虑
的：His face was ～ from lack of sleep.因
为没有睡好，他面容憔悴。

haggle/'hægl/

v. bargain over the price of sth. 讨价还价：In many countries you have to ~ before you buy anything. 在许多国家买东西之前都得讨价还价。

hail¹ /heɪl/

Ⅰ *n.* ❶ frozen rain drops which fall as little hard balls of ice 冰雹：Hail fell with such violence that it broke windows. 冰雹落得很猛，打破了窗户。❷ a number of things which strike at sb. with violence, causing pain or damage （像冰雹般落下的）一阵：a ~ of bullets 一阵弹雨/a ~ of blows 一阵打击/a ~ of curses 一阵咒骂　Ⅱ *v.* small balls of ice fall like rain from the sky 下冰雹：It ~ed in the late afternoon. 傍晚时下了冰雹。‖ ~（**sth.**）**down on**（**sb.**）（指打击等）猛烈迅速地落下‖ ~**storm** *n.* 雹暴

hail² /heɪl/

v. ❶ call to sb. to （say hello or attract attention）向……呼唤；跟……招呼：An old friend ~ed me from the other side of the street. 一位老朋友从街对面跟我打招呼。❷ acclaim as being a specified thing or person 认可；称誉：He was ~ed as a hero. 他被大家视为英雄。‖ ~ **a taxi** 叫计程车/ ~ **from** 来自……/**within** ~ 在可以招呼的距离内

hair /heə(r)/

n. any of the fine thread-like strands growing on the skin of animals and humans 毛；头发：The cat has left her ~s all over my clothes. 猫身上脱落的毛沾满了我的衣服。/My ~ has grown very long. 我的头发长得很长了。‖ **let one's** ~ **down** 态度随便，不拘礼节/**make sb.'s** ~ **stand on end** 令人毛骨悚然/**not turn a** ~（面对困难）毫无惧色；泰然自若/**split** ~s（尤指在争论中）吹毛求疵/**tear one's** ~ 气恼；焦急‖ ~**brush** *n.* 发刷/ ~**cut** *n.* 理发；发型/ ~ **do** *n.* 做头发；（女人的）发型/ ~ **dye** *n.* 染发剂/ ~ **net** *n.* 发网/ ~ **piece** *n.* 假发/ ~ **pin** *n.* 发夹/ ~ **restorer** *n.* 生发剂‖ ~**less** *adj.* 秃头的

haircut /ˈheəkʌt/

n. ❶ an act of cutting someone's hair 理发❷ the style in which someone's hair is cut 发式，发型

hairdresser /ˈheədresə(r)/

n. a person whose job is to cut and arrange other's hair 美发师；理发师

hairdryer /ˈheədraɪə/

n. an electrical device for drying the hair with warm air （吹干头发用的）吹风机

hairline /ˈheəlaɪn/

n. ❶ the edge of a person's hair especially at the front face 发际线（尤指前额头发轮廓线）❷ a very thin line 极细的线：a ~ fracture 细小的裂纹

hair-raising /ˈheəˌreɪzɪŋ/

adj. extremely alarming, astonishing, or frightening 令人毛骨悚然的；惊险的：~ adventures 惊心动魄的冒险

hairstyle /ˈheəstaɪl/

n. a particular way in which a person's hair is cut or arranged 发式，发型

hairy /ˈheəri/

adj. covered with hair, especially thick or long hair 盖满毛的；多毛的，毛茸茸的

hajj /hædʒ/

n. a pilgrimage to Mecca made during Ramadan, which all Muslims aim to make at least once in their lifetime （伊斯兰教徒去麦加的）麦加朝觐

hale /heɪl/

adj. （especially of an old person）very healthy and active （尤指老人）精神矍铄的，老当益壮的

half /hɑːf/

Ⅰ *n.*（*pl.* halves /hɑːvz/）❶ either of the two equal parts into which sth. is or could be divided 半；一半：the first ~ of the football match 足球赛的上半场/two pounds and a ~ of rice 两磅半大米 ❷ a half-price fare or ticket, especially for a child （尤指儿童的）半价票：One and two halves to the zoo. 请买去动物园的一张全票，两张半票。Ⅱ *pron.* an amount equal to a half 半数，一半：Half（of）the fruit was bad. 水果坏了一半。/Half the boys are absent. 有半数男孩缺席。Ⅲ *adv.* partly；not completely 部分地；不完全地：Don't leave the work ~ done. 工作不要

半途而废。/She's ～ French and ～ English.她是英法混血儿。‖ by halves 不完全地/ ～-and -～ 两种成分各半地/ not ～（very much）很；非常/（be）not ～ bad 不错；相当好 ‖ ～back n.（足球）中卫/ ～-brother n.异父（或异母）兄弟/ ～-blood n.混血儿/ ～-hearted adj.半心半意的/ ～-heartedly adv.马虎地/ ～-mast n.（表示哀悼）半旗；v.降半旗/ ～-sister n.异父（或异母）姐妹/ ～-time n.（足球比赛）中场休息/ ～-wit n.弱智者

halfway /ˈhɑːfˈweɪ/
adv. ❶at a point between and equally distant from two others 在中途,半路上 ❷to some extent 一定程度上；部分地

hall /hɔːl/
n. ❶a big room or building for meetings, concerts, etc.大厅；会堂：a banquet ～ 宴会厅/a concert ～ 音乐厅/the City Hall 市政厅 ❷the room or space（inside the front entrance）of a house, with doors of other rooms 过道；门厅 ❸a large room for meals；a building for university students to live in（大学的）学生宿舍；食堂：We eat in the ～.我们在食堂吃饭。/ I live in ～.我住在学生宿舍里。‖ dance ～ n.舞厅/ ～stand n.衣帽架/ ～way n. 〈美〉门厅；过道

hallelujah /ˌælɪˈluːjə/
*n.*a shout of praise to God 哈利路亚（赞美上帝语）

halo /ˈheɪləʊ/
n.（*pl.* ～es or ～s）❶ circle of light round the sun or moon（日月等的）晕,晕圈 ❷（in paintings）a circle of light round the head of sacred figure（绘画中画于神像头上的）光圈

halt /hɔːlt/
Ⅰ *v.*（cause to）stop abruptly（使）突然停止：The officer ～ed his troops for a rest. 军官令军队停止行进,休息一下。Ⅱ *n.*a stop or pause 停止；暂停：The train came to a ～ just in time to prevent an accident.火车及时停下,避免了一场事故。‖ bring to a ～ 使停止/call（cry）a ～ 命令停止/come to a ～ 停下来/grind to a ～ 慢慢停下来

halter /ˈhɔːltə(r)/
n. ❶a rope or leather band fastened round a horse's head for holding it 缰绳,（马的）笼头 ❷a rope for hanging a person 绞刑索

halting /ˈhɔːltɪŋ/
adj. stopping and starting especially through lack of confidence 迟疑不决的,踌躇的；吞吞吐吐的：a ～ voice 吞吞吐吐的话音/～ steps 迟疑不决的步伐

halve /hɑːv/
v. ❶divide sth. into two equal parts 二等分,平分,对分：Let's ～ the expenses.让我们平均分担费用。❷lessen or reduce by half 减半：The new railway will ～ the time needed for the journey.这条新铁路将使旅行所需要的时间减少一半。

ham /hæm/
*n.*the upper part of a pig's leg that was salted, dried and smoked 火腿：a ～ 一只火腿 /a ～ sandwich 一个火腿三明治 /a slice of ～ 一片火腿

hamburger /ˈhæmbɜːgə(r)/
*n.*a round patty of minced beef, fried or grilled and typically served in a bread roll 汉堡牛排饼,牛肉汉堡包

hammer /ˈhæmə(r)/
Ⅰ *n.*a tool with a handle and a heavy metal head used for hitting nails 锤子,榔头：The only tools in the box are a ～ and a screwdriver.这盒子中仅有的工具是一把锤子和一把改锥。Ⅱ *v.* hit with a hammer 锤击,敲打：She ～ed the nail in the wood. 她把钉子锤进木头里。/The boy ～ed at door.男孩使劲敲门。

hammock /ˈhæmək/
*n.*a bed made of cloth and ropes and hung between two posts 吊床

hamper /ˈhæmpə(r)/
v. hinder；get in the way of 阻碍,妨碍：The snow ～ed my movements.积雪阻碍了我运动。

hamster /ˈhæmstə(r)/
*n.*an animal like a large mouse with cheek pouches for carrying grain 仓鼠

hand /hænd/

Ⅰ n.❶ the part of the body of the end of the arm, including the fingers 手；I had a key in my ～. 我手里拿着一把钥匙。/I can't carry you；my ～s are full. 我不能抱你,我双手都拿着东西。❷ a person who is employed to do manual work 人手；体力劳动者；All ～s on deck! 全体船员到甲板上集合! /We are short of ～s. 我们正缺人手。❸ a pointer on a clock, watch, instrument, etc. (钟表或仪器的)指针；The minute ～ is bigger than the hour ～.分针比时针长。❹ a set of playing cards held by one person in a card game (纸牌游戏中)一手牌 ❺ a person's handwriting 字迹；书法；He writes a good ～. 他的字写得好。❻ side or direction (左、右)边；At the left ～ stood two men. 在左边站着两个男的。❼ (a ～)help in doing sth. 帮助；Do you need a ～? 要帮忙吗? ‖ ask for sb.'s ～ 向(某人)求婚/give one's ～ 接受求婚/at first ～ 直接地/at second ～ 间接地/at ～ 在手边；在附近/at the ～s of 在……手中(受折磨等)/bind(tie) sb. ～ and foot 捆住手脚/by ～ 手工(做的)/change ～s(物)转手；易手/fall(come, get) into the ～s of 落到……手中/from ～ to ～ 从一个人(传到)另一个人/get(gain, have) the upper ～ of 压倒；占上风/give(lend) a ～ 帮一下忙/in ～ 手拉手地/have a ～ in 参与；插手/in ～ 手上(的)/in the ～s of 由……照管/join ～s 携手合作/keep one's ～s off 不要管；不要碰/on ～ 手头(有……);在跟前/on the other ～ (可是)另一方面/out of ～ 失去控制/play into the ～s of (因失算)做了对(对手)有利的事/put one's ～ to 着手；开始做/shake ～s with (和……)握手/wash one's ～s of 不再管(某事)/with a high ～ 专横地；用高压手段/with an iron ～ 以铁的手腕/with clean ～s 廉洁地 Ⅱ v.❶ give；pass 交给；传递；Please ～ me the hammer. 请把榔头递给我。❷hold the hands of sb. in order to help them move 搀扶；He ～ed his wife out of the bus. 他扶他的太太下车。‖ ～ back 交还/ ～ down 传下来；传给；宣布/ ～ in 交上去(给老师等)/ ～ it to

承认(某人的)优点；赞扬/ ～ on 传给另一人/ ～ out 散发/ ～ over 移交/ ～ round(around) 分发(食品等) ‖ ～arm n.(手)枪/ ～ bag n.(女用)手提包/ ～ball n.手球/ ～bill n.传单/ ～book n.手册/ ～brake n.手煞车 / ～cart n.手推小车/ ～drill n.手钻/ ～loom n.手织机/ ～made adj.手工制；n.手工制品/ ～-to-mouth adj.勉强糊口的/ ～-gun n.手枪/ ～ shake n.握手；礼金,外快

handcuff /ˈhændkʌf/
Ⅰ n.(pl.) a pair of linked metal rings for fastening a prisoner's wrists together 手铐 Ⅱ v. to put handcuffs on someone 给……戴上手铐

handful /ˈhændfʊl/
n.❶a quantity as much as can be held in one hand 一把；a ～ of rice 一把米 ❷a small number of amount 少数,一些；a ～ of students 少数几个学生

handicap /ˈhændɪkæp/
Ⅰ n.❶a condition that markedly restricts a person's ability to function physically, mentally or socially 生理(或智力、交际功能)缺陷,残疾；Blindness is a great ～. 失明是很大的视力缺陷。❷a circumstance that make it difficult for sb. to do sth. 障碍,阻碍 ❸(in a race or other sport or game) a disadvantage given to the stronger competitors, such as carrying more weight or starting from a worse position (在赛跑等运动中强手的)让步；(在赛马中强马的)负磅 Ⅱ v.(-pp-)❶(of a quality or situation) cause (sb.) to have a disadvantage (使)不利；(使)受妨碍；Lack of money ～ped him badly. 缺乏资金对他十分不利。❷(of a physical or mental disability) prevent (sb.) from acting and living as most people do (身心因疾病而)受阻碍；He is ～ped by bad eyesight. 他因视力不好而障碍重重。

handicraft /ˈhændɪkrɑːft/
n. a skill which needs careful use of the hands 手艺,手工艺；～ workshops 手工艺作坊

handiwork /ˈhændɪwɜːk/
n.❶sth. made by hand 手工制品 ❷sth.

done or made by a person（某人的）做的东西，作品

handkerchief /ˈhæŋkətʃif/

n.（*pl.* ～s or -chieves /ˈhæŋkətʃiːvz/）a small piece of cloth or paper for wiping the nose, eyes, etc. 手帕；纸巾：dry one's tears on a ～ 用手帕把眼泪擦干

handle /ˈhændl/

Ⅰ *n.* a part of a tool or instrument that you hold in the hand 柄；把手 Ⅱ *v.* ❶ touch or move by hand 触摸；搬动：Handle with care! 小心轻放! ❷ deal with; control 处理；控制：He ～d a difficult argument skillfully. 他巧妙地应付了一场艰难的辩论。❸ buy and sell 经营；买卖：This shop does not ～ imported goods. 这家商店不经销进口货。‖ give a ～ for(to) 使人有可乘之机 ‖ ～able *adj.* 可处理的/ ～r *n.* 处理者；驯养动物者/ handling *n.* 处理；管理

handlebar /ˈhænd(ə)lbɑː/

n.（*pl.* ～s）the bar with a handle at each end, that steers a bicycle or motorcycle（自行车或摩托车的）把手，车把

handler /ˈhændlə/

n. ❶ a person who handles or deals with articles or things 物品的操作者；事情的处理者：a baggage ～ 一位行李搬运工 ❷ a device which handles certain articles or substances 操作装置；处理器 ❸ a police officer in charge of a dog 警犬训练员

handover /ˈhændəuvə/

n. an act or instance of handing sth. over 移交

handsaw /ˈhæn(d)sɔː/

n. a wood saw worked by one hand 手锯

handsome /ˈhænsəm/

adj. ❶（of men）good-looking; of attractive appearance（指男人）英俊的；有吸引力的 ❷（especially of women）strong-looking; attractive with a firm, large appearance rather than a delicate one（尤指女人）健美的，有风韵的 ❸ generous; plentiful 慷慨大方的；可观的：～ reward 数目可观的报酬/a ～ contribution 可观的捐款/a ～ fortune 不小的家产 ‖

treatment 优待 ‖ Handsome is as ～ does. 〈谚〉行为漂亮才是真。‖ ～ly *adv.* 漂亮地；慷慨地

handwriting /ˈhænd,raitiŋ/

n. ❶ writing done by hand with a pen or pencil 手写，书写 ❷ a person's style of writing 笔迹，写字风格：Her ～ was small and neat. 她的字迹小巧工整。

handy /ˈhændi/

adj. ❶（of things）convenient to handle; used easily 方便的，便利的：This is a ～ little box. 这是一个方便的小盒子。❷ skilled with the hands 手巧的：She is very ～ with her needle. 她很善于女红。❸（of places）located near to sb. or sth. or in a convenient place 手边的；便利的；附近的：The shops are quite ～. 商店就在附近。‖ come in ～ 迟早会有用处：A few more traveller's cheques may come in ～ on holiday. 多几张旅行支票，假期中可能有用场。‖ handily *adv.* 方便地/handiness *n.* 轻便灵巧

hang /hæŋ/

Ⅰ *v.*（hung /hʌŋ/ or ～ed）❶ fix sth. at the top so that the lower part is free 悬挂：Hang your coat (up) on the hook. 把你的外套挂在钩子上。/The curtains ～ well. 窗帘挂得很好。❷ show (a painting) publicly 陈列（画）：His pictures were hung in an important gallery. 他的画陈列在一个重要的画廊里。❸ stick (wallpaper) to a wall （在墙上）贴墙纸 ❹（cause to） kill sb. as a punishment a for a crime, by dropping with a rope around the neck 绞死；吊死：He was ～ed for murder. 他因杀人而被绞死。‖ ～ about 跟在身边；待在附近/ ～ around 闲待着(不走)；等/ ～ back 踌躇不前；迟疑(不肯做某事)/ ～ behind 迟迟不离开；落在后面/ ～ between life and death 生命垂危/ ～ by a thread (生命)危在旦夕/ ～ in the balance 安危未卜/ ～ off(～ back) 犹豫/ ～ on 紧抓着不放手；坚持下去；赖着不走；(电话用语)不挂断；(用于祈使句中)等一等；取决于/ ～ on to 抓住……不放/ ～ out 挂出去/ ～ over 威胁；遗留下来/ ～ round 闲逛，老找(某人)/ ～ up 挂起

来;挂断电话;搁置/ ～ **upon**（**on**）专注 Ⅱ *n*.the shape or way sth. hangs 挂样;挂 的方式:I don't like the ～ of this coat at the back.我不喜欢这件外套背后的剪裁。 ‖ ～**tag** *n*.（商品上）使用保养说明标签 / ～**up** *n*.障碍;大难题/ ～**wire** *n*.炸弹保 险丝

hanger/ˈhæŋə(r)/
n. a frame with a hook and crosspiece which is put inside the shoulders of clothes,so that it can be hung up and will keep their shape 衣架;挂钩,悬挂工具

hanging/ˈhæŋɪŋ/
n.❶ the practice in which death is caused by hanging a person from a rope round the neck as a form of punishment 绞刑: When was ～ abolished here? 这里是什 么时候废止绞刑的? /a ～ offence 死罪 ❷ a decorative piece of fabric or curtain hung on the wall of a room or around a bed（挂在墙上或床周围的装饰用的）墙 幔;帷幔

hangout/ˈhæŋaʊt/
n.a place that a person lives in or often visits 住处;常去的地方;聚集处:one of my favourite ～s 我最爱去的地方之一

hangover/ˈhæŋəʊvə(r)/
n.❶ the feeling of headache, sickness, etc.,caused by drinking too much alcohol 宿醉 ❷ a thing or effect resulting from an earlier event or situation 遗留物,遗留 影响: The licensing laws is a ～ from wartime.执照法是战时遗留下来的问题。

hank/hæŋk/
n.a bunch of thread ,wool,or other mate- rial 一束,一卷(纱线、毛线等)

hanker/ˈhæŋkə(r)/
v. have a strong desire for; want very much 渴望:～ after success 渴望成功

haphazard/hæpˈhæzəd/
adj.by chance;without design 随意的;偶 然的;:a ～ choice 随意的选择

happen/ˈhæpən/
v.❶ take place;occur 发生:How did the accident ～? 这事故是怎样发生的? ❷ have the luck or chance（to do sth.）碰

巧:I ～ed to be out when he called.他来 电话时我碰巧出去了。❸ find or meet by chance 偶然发现:We ～ed on him in the street.我们在街上偶然碰见了他。 ‖ **as it ～s** 偶然/ ～ **along** 恰好来了/ **whatever ～s** 不管发生什么情况 ‖ ～**ing** *n*.发生的 事情

happy/ˈhæpi/
adj.❶ full of joy; feeling pleasure 快乐 的;幸福的:This is a ～ child.这是个快乐 的孩子。/My parents have a ～ mar- riage.我父母的婚姻很美满。❷ (of be- haviour, thoughts, etc.) suitable and ap- propriate (行为、思想等)适当的,合适 的:That was not a ～ remark.那不是很 恰当的话。❸willing or glad to do sth.乐 意的:I'll be ～ to meet him when I have time.有空的时候,我很乐意同他见面。 ‖ **the**（**a**）～ **medium** 折中办法;中庸之 道 ‖ **happily** *adv*.幸福地;幸运地/**happi- ness** *n*.幸福;幸运;快乐

harass/ˈhærəs/
v.❶ trouble;worry 使烦恼;使忧虑:～ed by the cares of a large family 为照顾一个 大家庭而发愁 /～ed-looking housewives 愁容满面的家庭主妇 ❷ make repeated attacks on 反复袭击;骚扰: In old days the coasts of England were ～ed by the Vikings.过去英国沿海一带一再受到北 欧海盗的侵扰。

harbo（**u**）**r**/ˈhɑːbə(r)/
Ⅰ *n*.❶an area of water by a coast which is sheltered from rougher waters so that ships are safe inside it 港;港口:a deep water ～ 深水港 /an ice free ～ 不冻港 / a good ～ 良港 /a natural ～ 天然港 /an artificial ～ 人工港 ❷a place of safety or shelter 安全的地方;避难所 Ⅱ *v*.come to anchor (in a harbour) 停泊(于港内) ‖ **make** ～ 进港停泊 ‖ ～ **dues** *n*.港务费/ ～-**master** *n*. 港务长 ‖ ～**age** /ˈhɑːbə- rɪdʒ/ *n*.停泊处

hard/hɑːd/
Ⅰ *adj*.❶ firm; solid; not easily broken, bent or cut 坚硬的;坚固的:The ice is as ～ as rock.冰像石头一样硬。 ❷ difficult to do or understand 难的;困难的:It's ～

to know what he's really thinking.难以知道他真正在想什么。❸ needing a great deal of physical or mental effort 辛苦的：～ work 辛苦的工作 ❹ full of difficulty and trouble 艰苦的：a ～ life 艰苦的生活/He gave me a ～ time.他给我苦头吃。❺ strict; not kind; unfeeling 严厉的；冷酷的：She is a ～ woman. 她是个冷酷的女人。/My boss is very ～ on me.我的老板对我十分严厉。Ⅱ adv.❶ with great effort; with strength 努力地：Look ～ at this picture.用心多看看这张图。❷ with a great deal of force; violently 猛烈地：It was a winter night and raining ～.那是一个冬天的夜晚，天正下着大雨。❸ near; close to 靠近地；紧随地：Their house is ～ by the station. 他们的房子靠近车站。/The child held ～ to her mother's hand.孩子紧紧拉着她妈妈的手。‖ be ～ on 对……很苛刻/drive a ～ bargain 拼命讨价还价/give a ～ time 使……难受/～ of hearing 有点儿聋的/be ～ hit 受到很大损失/be ～ up 经济上困难,缺钱/come ～ to ……是困难的/go ～ with 难以忍受/～ at hand 就在眼前,迫在眉睫/～ at it 使劲干,用功/～ going 进展困难/take(it) ～ 难受；耿耿于怀‖ ～ back n.精装本(书)/～-bitten adj.(蛋)煮得老的；不动感情的/～ bound adj.(书)精装的/～ cash n.现款/～ currency n.不易贬值的货币/～ drinker n.酒量大的人/～ earned adj.辛苦挣得的/～-faced adj.其貌不扬的/～-headed adj.讲究实际的,现实的/～-hearted adj.冷酷的/～-mouthed adj.倔强的/～ nosed adj.(狗等)嗅觉不灵的；顽强的/～ ware n.金属制品/～-wearing adj.耐穿的/～-working adj.努力工作的；勤劳的

harden/'hɑːdn/

v.(cause to)become hard (使)变硬,(使)坚固：Frost ～ed the water of the puddles into ice.严寒使水坑里的水结成了冰。/The snow ～ed until ice was formed.雪渐渐变硬直到结成了冰。

hardly/'hɑːdli/

adv.❶ almost not; scarcely 几乎不：I could ～ wait to hear the news.我迫不及待地要听消息了。❷ only a very short time before 刚……就：Hardly had we started our journey when the car got a flat tyre.我们刚出发,车胎就破了。❸ not at all; not reasonably 一点也不；不合时宜：I can ～ ask him directly for more help.我不能直接向他要求更多的帮助。❹ severely 严厉地：He was ～ treated.他受到苛刻的对待。‖ ～ anybody(anything, anywhere) 简直没有什么人(什么东西,什么地方)/～ ever 几乎从不；很少：I ～ ever see him nowadays.近来我很少见到他。

hardship/'hɑːdʃɪp/

n.❶ a circumstance that causes discomfort or suffering 困苦,苦难：He went through all kinds of ～s.他吃尽了苦头。/He is the first to bear ～s, the last to enjoy comforts.他吃苦在前,享受在后。❷ severe suffering 痛苦,受苦：fear neither ～ nor death 一不怕苦,二不怕死

hardware/'hɑːdweə/

n.❶ heavy military equipment such as tanks and missiles 重型军事装备(如坦克,导弹) ❷ the mechanical and electronic parts of a computer as opposed to the software 硬件(计算机的机械和电子部件,相对于软件) ❸ tools and household implements, etc. used in home life and activities 五金器具

hardy/'hɑːdɪ/

adj.robust; able to endure hardship 强壮的；能吃苦的：a few ～ men 几个壮汉/～ settlers 能吃苦耐劳的拓荒者

hare/heə(r)/

n.a field mammal like a rabbit that has long ears and long back legs 野兔：First catch your ～(then cook him).〈谚〉先捕兔,后烹调(勿谋之过早)。/If you run after two ～s, you will catch neither.〈谚〉脚踏两只船,必然落空。

harm/hɑːm/

Ⅰ n.damage; injury 损害,伤害：He meant no ～.他并没有恶意。/There is no ～ in trying.不妨一试。Ⅱ v.hurt; damage 损害;伤害;有害于：Getting up early won't ～ you.早起对你没有害处。‖ come to ～

遭不幸/do sb. ~（do ~ to sb.）损害某人/out of ~'s way 在安全的地方

harmful/'hɑːmfl/

adj. causing or likely to cause harm（对……)有害的；致伤的：Smoking is ~ to health. 吸烟有害健康。

harmless/'hɑːmləs/

adj. unable or unlikely to cause harm 无害的；不致伤的：The dog seems fierce but it's ~. 这狗看起来很凶，但它不伤人。

harmonic /hɑːˈmɒnɪk/

Ⅰ *n.* a note that sounds together with the main note being played and is higher and quieter than that note 和声 Ⅱ *adj.* to do with or of harmony in music（与）和声（有关）的

harmonica/hɑːˈmɒnɪkə/

n. a small musical instrument played by being held to the mouth, moved from side to side, and blown into or sucked through 口琴

harmonious /hɑːˈməʊnɪəs/

adj. ❶combining together in a pleasant and attractive way 协调的；和谐的 ❷ free from disagreement or ill feeling 和睦的，一致的 ❸ sweet-sounding, tuneful 悦耳的；音调优美的 ‖ ~ly *adv.* 和谐地

harmonize/'hɑːmənaɪz/

v. make consistent 使协调：These colours ~ beautifully. 这些色彩调和得很好看。

harmony/'hɑːməni/

n. ❶ a state of complete agreement（in feelings, ideas, etc.）（感情、意见等的）协调，和睦：My cat and dog live together in perfect ~. 我的猫和狗和睦相处。/This article lacks ~. 这篇文章的论点不协调。 ❷ the combination of simultaneously sounded music notes to produce chords in a pleasant sounding way 和声 ‖ be in ~ with 与……协调一致/be out of ~ with 与……不协调一致/live in ~ 和睦相处

harness/'hɑːnɪs/

Ⅰ *n.* straps used to tie a horse to a cart, etc. 马具，挽具：put a harness on a horse 套马 Ⅱ *v.* ❶ put a harness on 上马具；~

a horse to a carriage 把马套到车上 ❷ control and use（a river, etc.）to produce electric power 利用（水力发电）；治理（河流）：~ a river 治河

harp/hɑːp/

Ⅰ *n.* a kind of stringed musical instrument played with fingers 竖琴 Ⅱ *v.* ❶play the harp 弹竖琴 ❷ talk or write repeatedly and tediously about sth. 唠叨；啰唆：She is always ~ing on my faults. 她老是数落我的缺点。

harrier/'hærɪə(r)/

n. ❶ a kind of dog used for hunting 猎兔犬 ❷ a cross-country runner 越野赛跑者 ❸ a kind of hawk with long wings and a slender body and long legs 鹞

harrow/'hærəʊ/

Ⅰ *n.* an implement with metal teeth for breaking up ground after ploughing 耙 Ⅱ *v.* ❶pull a rake over（the ground）；break up with a rake 用耙耙（地）❷cause distress to 使痛苦；使伤心 ‖ ~ing *adj.* 悲痛的；伤心的：a ~ing experience 惨痛的经验

harry/'hæri/

v. ❶raid and ravage; attack frequently 蹂躏；劫掠；不断侵袭：The soldiers harried the enemy out of their country. 士兵们不断进行袭击，把敌人赶出他们的国境。 ❷harass（sb.）frequently 不断骚扰（某人）：He never pays his debts unless you ~ him. 除非你缠着他，否则他绝不会还债。

harsh/hɑːʃ/

adj. ❶ rough and unpleasant to the senses 刺耳的；刺眼的；刺鼻的：a ~ voice 刺耳的声音 ❷ stern or cruel 残酷的；无情的：~ terms 苛刻的条件/a ~ judge（judgement, punishment）严厉的法官（判决、处罚）‖ ~ly *adv.* 严厉无情地/~ness *n.* 严厉

harvest/'hɑːvɪst/

Ⅰ *n.* ❶ the act or time of gathering the crops 收获；（收割、收获）季节：We all helped with the ~. 我们都一起帮忙收割。 ❷ the amount of the crops gathered

收成;产量:a good ～ 丰收/a large ～ 大丰收 ❸the result of past work or action 成果: This is the ～ of ten years' research. 这是十年的研究成果。Ⅱ v. ❶ gather (a crop) 收割(庄稼): ～ rice with combines 用联合收割机割稻。❷ receive (the result of past work or action) 获得(成果) ‖ make a long ～ for a little corn 小题大做 ‖ ～er n. 收获者;收割机

hash/hæʃ/
n. ❶ a dish containing meat cut into small pieces, and re-cooked 回锅肉末 ❷ sth. done badly or unsuccessfully; a mess 弄得乱七八糟的事;一团糟: I made a complete ～ of my driving test. 我的驾驶考试考得一塌糊涂。

hasp/hɑːsp/
n. a metal fastener for a box, door, etc., which is fitted over a hook and secured by a padlock (盒、门等的)(金属)搭扣,锁搭

hassle/ˈhæsl/
Ⅰ n. ❶ difficulty or annoyance; irritating inconvenience 困难;麻烦;斗争: It's a real ～ to get the children to eat 让孩子们吃饭确实麻烦。/I came by bus because I couldn't be bothered with the ～ of parking. 我是乘公共汽车来的,因为我受不了停放汽车的麻烦。❷ an argument or a quarrel 争论,争吵 Ⅱ v. ❶ annoy sb. continuously; harass 不断打扰,使烦恼: I wish you would stop hassling me (about stopping smoking). 我希望你别再烦扰我(有关戒烟的事)。❷ argue 争论,争吵: hassling with the umpire over a disputed point 为有争议的得分同裁判员争吵

haste/heɪst/
n. hurry; quickness of movement 匆忙,急速: He went off in great ～. 他匆匆离去。/More ～, less speed. 〈谚〉欲速则不达。

hasten/ˈheɪsn/
v. ❶ move or act quickly 急忙;赶快: a-way to the office 急忙到办公室 /～ home 急忙回家 /～ to correct a mistake 赶快改正错误 ❷ cause (sb.) to hurry; cause (sth.) to be done or to happen

quickly or earlier 催促(某人);促进(某事);～ sb. to do sth. 催促某人做某事 / Artificial heating ～s the growth of plants. 人工加热法能促进植物的生长。/ He ～ed everyone off to bed. 他催促每个人赶快睡觉。

hasty/ˈheɪsti/
adj. ❶ done in a hurry 匆忙的;仓促的: make a ～ meal 匆匆地做了一顿饭/eat a ～ meal 仓促地吃了一餐 ❷ too quick in acting or deciding, often with bad or unwanted results; rash 草率的;性急的: His ～ decision was a mistake. 他的草率决定是一次错误。/I'm sorry I've been ～. 真抱歉,我太性急了。

hat/hæt/
n. covering made to fit the head, usually with a brim, worn out of doors (有边的)帽子: a bowler ～ 礼帽/a straw ～ 草帽/a leaf ～ 斗笠 ‖ at the drop of a ～ 马上,很快/hang one's ～ 停止不干(长期以来干的事)/I'll eat my ～ if ... 我决不……(表示不相信)/keep under one's ～ 保密,不告诉(人)/take one's ～ off to (sb.) 佩服/talk through one's ～ 瞎说;说傻话 ‖ ～ful n. 一帽子所容的量

hatch/hætʃ/
Ⅰ v. ❶ (cause to) break out of an egg 孵蛋;孵鸡;(小鸡等)出壳: Three eggs have already ～ed. 有三个蛋孵出了小鸡。/ Don't count your chickens before they are ～ed. 蛋未孵出,先别数鸡(过早乐观)。❷ think out and produce (a plot, etc.) 图谋;策划: They ～ed a plan to murder the king. 他们策划了一次杀害国王的阴谋。Ⅱ n. an opening in a wall, floor, etc., through which people or things can pass (墙、地板等上的)开口

hatchery/ˈhætʃəri/
n. (pl.-ies) a place for hatching eggs, especially of fish (尤指鱼的)孵化场: a trout ～ 鳟鱼孵化场

hatchet/ˈhætʃɪt/
n. a light short-handed axe 手斧;短柄小斧

hate/heɪt/

I *v.* ❶ feel hatred towards (sb. or sth.); dislike very strongly 恨;憎恨:I ∼ violence.我憎恨使用暴力。❷ regret; be reluctant 遗憾;不愿意:I ∼ troubling (to trouble) him.我真不愿去麻烦他。Ⅱ *n.* the feeling of extreme or violent dislike or ill-will 怨恨;厌恶:She looked at her opponent with ∼ in her eyes.她用仇恨的目光望着她的对手。‖ ∼**less** *adj.* 不憎恨的/ ∼**r** *n.* 怀恨者

hateful /'heɪtfl/
　adj. arousing or evoking hatred 引起仇恨的;可恨的

hatred /'heɪtrɪd/
　n. the emotion of extreme dislike or hate 仇恨:racial ∼ 种族仇恨

haughty /'hɔːti/
　adj. having or showing arrogant superiority to and disdain of those one views as unworthy 傲慢的,骄傲的;目中无人的:A ∼ girl is always unpopular at school. 骄傲的女孩子在学校里总是不受人欢迎。

haul /hɔːl/
　I *v.* ❶ pull with effort or force 用力拖;拉;曳:∼ logs 拖木头 ❷ force to appear before an official body, especially a court of law 硬拖;押送(到法庭等):The police have ∼ed him (up) before the court on a charge of robbery.警方以抢劫的罪名把他押送到法庭。Ⅱ *n.* ❶ the act of pulling sth. with effort or force 拖;拉:The village's fishing vessels are making night ∼s.村里的渔船在夜晚撒网捕鱼。❷ the amount of fish caught when fishing with a net 一网捕得的鱼:The fishermen had a good ∼.渔民捕了满满一网鱼。‖ ∼ **down one's flag** 投降/ ∼ **off** 退却,撤退/ ∼ **over the coals** 严厉批评;斥责/ ∼ **up** 把……拉来责问;弄去受审 ‖ ∼**er** *n.* (货物)承运人

haunt /hɔːnt/
　I *v.* ❶ visit (a place) regularly 常去(某处):He ∼ed the art galleries. 他常去美术陈列室。❷ (of a spirit, especially of a dead person) visit (a place), appearing in a strange form (鬼和幽灵)常出没于:A

headless man is said to ∼ the castle.据说一个无头鬼在这古堡出没。❸ (especially of sth. unpleasant) be always in the thoughts of (someone) (尤指不愉快的事)萦绕心头:The thief is constantly ∼ed by fear of discovery.小偷经常提心吊胆,怕被人发觉。Ⅱ *n.* a place which a particular person visits frequently 常去的地方:The inn on the seashore is a ∼ of sailors.海岸边的客栈是水手常到的地方。‖ ∼**ing** *adj.* 萦绕心头的,耿耿于怀的

haunted /'hɔːntɪd/
　adj. ❶ frequented by a ghost or ghosts 幽灵出没的,闹鬼的:a ∼ house 鬼屋 ❷ looking anxious or troubled 忧心忡忡的;痛苦的:her ∼ eyes 她痛苦的双眼

have /hæv, həv/
　I *v.* (had) ❶ possess, own; hold; keep 拥有;有:—Do you ∼ any time? —No, I ∼n't any today.—你有时间吗? —不,我今天没有。❷ take; receive; get; drink 拿;受;取得;吃,喝:Which do you ∼, tea or coffee? 你要喝茶还是喝咖啡? ❸ experience; enjoy 经历;享有:I had much difficulty in reading Dickens in the original.我读狄更斯原著有很大困难。❹ suffer from an illness or a disease 得病,患病 ❺ want; wish; make; let 叫;让;使;被:I had my daughter go instead.我让我女儿替我去。❻ allow; permit 容忍,允许:I won't ∼ bad behaviour.我不能容忍恶劣行为。Ⅱ *aux. v.* used to form the perfect tenses 用以构成完成时态:I have (I've) been to Beijing. 我去过北京。/He has (He's) gone.他走了。/Had I (If I had) known...如果我知道……

haven /'heɪvn/
　n. harbour; a place of safety 港口;避难所;安全地方

haversack /'hævəsæk/
　n. a canvas bag for provisions or equipment, usually carried on the back 帆布背包;挎包

havoc /'hævək/
　n. widespread damage; great disorder and confusion 大破坏;浩劫:Wars cause great

~.战争造成了严重的破坏。

hawk¹ /hɔːk/

n. ❶ a large with a short, hooked beak, sharp claws, and very good eyesight, which catches small animals and birds for food 鹰 ❷ a person who believes in strong action or the use of force and, violence especially one who supports warlike political ideas (政治上主张使用强硬手段或武力的)鹰派人物 ‖ ~**-eyed** *adj.* 目光锐利的/ ~**ish** *adj.* 似鹰的；带点鹰派味道的/ ~**-nosed** *adj.* 长着鹰钩鼻子的

hawk² /hɔːk/

v. ❶ sell (goods) on the street or at the doors of houses, especially while moving from place to place 沿途叫卖：~ one's wares from door to door 挨家挨户叫卖货物 ❷ spread (information, ideas, etc.) around, especially by speech (用言语)散布；传播：~ one's ideas around 四处宣扬自己的主张

hay /heɪ/

n. dried grass as food for cattle, horse or other animals (作为动物饲料的)干草：make ~ 翻晒干草 ‖ hit the ~ 上床睡觉/look for a needle in a bundle of ~ 大海捞针/make ~ of 使混乱/make ~ out of 使对自己有利/Make ~ while the sun shines. 抓紧时机，趁热打铁。

hayfork /ˈheɪfɔːk/

n. a long-handled fork with two points (prongs), used for turning over hay in the field or for gathering it 干草叉

haystack /ˈheɪstæk/

n. a stack of hay 干草堆

hazard /ˈhæzəd/

‖ *n.* sth. likely to cause damage or loss; a danger or risk 冒险，危险：a life full of ~s 充满冒险的一生/a ~ to health (a health ~) 对健康有危险 ‖ *v.* ❶ risk；put in danger 冒……险，使置身危险中：He ~ed all his money in the attempt to save the business. 他孤注一掷，拿出所有的钱来挽救企业。 ❷ offer (a suggestion, a guess, etc.) when there is a risk of being wrong or unwelcome 冒险做出：~ a guess 做无把握的猜测/ ~ a remark 妄下评论(可能是错的) ‖ at all ~s 冒着一切危险/at (in) ~ 处在危急中；冒险/by ~ 偶然；碰运气

hazardous /ˈhæzədəs/

adj. risky or dangerous 冒险的，危险的 ‖ ~**ly** *adv.* 危险地/ ~**ness** *n.* 危险

haze /heɪz/

n. light mist；air that is not clear 霾；薄雾：The sun shone through the ~. 阳光照过薄雾。/a ~ of smoke 一片轻烟

hazel /ˈheɪzl/

‖ *n.* a type of small tree found in cool, northern regions, which has a small, round nut which can be eaten 榛树 ‖ *adj.* (usually used to describe the colour of eyes) having a brown colour like the nut of a hazel (通常指眼睛的颜色)淡褐色的；红褐色的

hazelnut /ˈheɪzlnʌt/

n. the round brown nut of the hazel 榛子

hazy /ˈheɪzi/

adj. (hazier, haziest) ❶ filled or abounding with fog or mist 有雾的 ❷ vague or indistinct in outline 朦胧的，不清楚的：a ~ recollection 朦胧的记忆 ❸ feeling confused or uncertain 困惑的；不确定的 ‖ **hazily** *adv.* 模糊地；朦胧地/**haziness** *n.* 模糊；混浊性，混浊度

he /hiː/

‖ *pron.* ❶ a male person or animal 他(男性或雄性动物第三人称单数)：Where is your father? He is at home. 你爸爸在哪里？他在家。 ❷ (in combination) a male (用于复合词)雄性；男性：~-goat 公羊，雄山羊/~-man 具有男性魅力的人 ❸ a person without saying whether that person is a man or a woman 一个人；任何人：He who laughs last laughs longest. 最后笑的人笑得最久。/Everyone should do what ~ considers best. 每个人都应he 认为最该做的事。 ‖ *n.* a male person or animal 男性；雄性动物：Is your dog a ~ or a she? 你的狗是公的还是母的？/Is it (the baby) a ~ or a she? 婴儿是男的还是女的？

head /hed/

Ⅰ *n.* ❶ the top part of your body, where eyes, ears, nose and mouth are 头，头部：She hit Tom on the ～.她打了汤姆的头（部）。/I'm taller than you by a ～.我比你高一个头。❷ person 人：Let's count ～s.让我们清点一下人数。❸ (*pl.* head) the unit of a herd or flock（表示牧群的数目）头：five ～ of cattle 五头牛/a large ～of game 很多猎物/one hundred ～ of sheep 一百头羊 ❹ a ruler or leader 首脑；首长；领头：the ～ of state 国家元首/～s of government 政府首脑/the ～ workman 工头 ❺ the mind or brain；mental abilities 心头；头脑：Can't you get these facts into your ～? 你难道不能把这些事实记在脑子里吗？❻ the top part of some plants, as when several leaves or flowers grow together（植物顶端的）头状叶丛；花冠：two ～s of cabbage 两棵白菜/a ～ of lettuce 一根莴苣头 ❼ the top of a page（一页纸的）顶端；上端：at the ～ of the page 在这页的顶端 ❽ the front of people, vehicles, etc.（人群或车辆的）前面，前部：at the ～ of the procession 在游行行列的前排 ‖ above one's ～ 超过……的理解力/at the ～ of 居……的首位，在最前头/be light in the ～ 头晕；头脑简单/be off (out of) one's ～ 神志不清；昏了头/be weak in the ～ 不大聪明/cry (talk) one's ～ off 没完没了地哭（说）/from ～ to foot 浑身/go to one's ～（酒）使有醉意；使冲昏头脑/hang one's ～（因害羞）垂下头/have a cool ～ 有冷静的头脑/have a good ～ for 有……的才能/have a (good) ～ on one's shoulders 有见识；有能力/～ over heels 倒栽葱；深深陷入/hit the nail on the ～ 说到点子上；切中要害/hold one's ～ up 抬起头来/lose one's ～ 惊惶失措；失去理智/(can't) make ～ or tail of 搞（不）清头绪；弄（不）清是怎么回事/on one's ～ 倒立/put (lay) our (your, their) ～s together 碰头（会）；集思广益/take it into one's ～ (to do sth.) 突然想到（做某事）/turn sb.'s ～ 使自负；use one's ～ 动动脑筋 Ⅱ *v.* ❶ lead；be at the front of 带领，为首：He ～ed a dele-gation.他率领一个代表团。/His name ～s the list.他是名单上的第一名。❷ be in charge of 主持；管理：Who ～s the u-nit? 谁是这单位的领导人？❸ be at the top of；provide a heading for 在……的顶端，给……提供标题：His address ～ed the letter.他的地址在信的顶端。❹ go or come toward 使朝……方向移动：～ for Nanjing 朝南京进发/be ～ing for col-lapse 走向崩溃 ‖ ～ for (～ed for) 朝……而去/～ off 赶在……前面；截住；回避/～ out 开出；出发/～ up 走在前头，领头 ‖ ～ship *n.* 领导地位（身份）/ ～band *n.* 束发带/ ～chair *n.* 有头靠的椅子

headache /ˈhedeɪk/

n. ❶ a pain in the head 头痛：I am tired and have a ～.我累了，而且头痛。❷ a person or thing that causes difficulty or worry 头痛的人（或问题）；伤脑筋的人（或事）：Trying to make the child eat is a big ～! 想让这孩子吃饭是大伤脑筋的事！

headed /ˈhedɪd/

adj. ❶ having the name and address of a person, an organization, etc. printed at the top 顶端印有名称和地址的；有信头的：～ notepaper 有信头的便笺纸 ❷ (often using in combination) having a head of a specified kind of anything that serves as a head(用于复合词)有……头的；有……个头的：his bold-～ grandpa 他的秃顶爷爷

heading /ˈhedɪŋ/

n. a word or words put at the top of a sec-tion of printing or writing as a title 标题；信头

headline /ˈhedlaɪn/

n. ❶ a heading in a newspaper, especially the largest one at the top of the front page 报纸的标题(尤其是头版顶端的最大标题) ❷ (the ～) a summary of the main items of news 重要消息；头条新闻，要闻

headmaster /ˈhedˈmɑːstə(r)/

n. the principle master of a school 校长

headquarters /ˈhedˌkwɔːtəz/

　　n. the place that serves as the administrative center of an enterprise 总部；指挥部

headship /ˈhedʃɪp/

　　n. ❶ the position of a head teacher in a school 校长的职位 ❷ the position of a head 领导的地位

headstrong /ˈhedstrɒŋ/

　　adj. determined to have one's own way 任性的，倔强的

heal /hiːl/

　　v. ❶ (usually of injuries and wounds) become well (通常指伤口) 愈合：The cut on my leg has ~ed. 我腿上的伤口已经痊愈。❷ cure；restore to health 治愈；康复：The wound has been ~ed. 创伤已治好了。

healing /ˈhiːlɪŋ/

　　n. the process of becoming or making sb. or sth. healthy again；the process of getting better after an emotional shock 康复；治疗；(情感创伤的) 愈合

health /helθ/

　　n. ❶ the condition of body or mind 身体状况，健康状况：mental ~ 心理健康/ be in good ~ 身体好/ be in bad (poor) ~ 身体不好 ❷ the state of being well in the body and mind, and free from disease 健康；健全：restored to ~ 恢复健康 ‖ drink sb.'s ~，drink a ~ to sb. 祝酒；举杯祝人健康/ Your (good) ~! (敬酒) 祝您健康！为您的健康干杯！

healthy /ˈhelθi/

　　adj. ❶ physically strong and not suffering from illness；usually in good health 健壮的；健康的 ❷ good for mind or character 有益心灵和品格的：That book is not ~ reading. 那本书不是健康读物。❸ natural 自然的；天生的：He has a ~ dislike of school. 他天生不喜欢上学念书。❹ showing good health 显示健康的：a ~ appetite 健康的胃口/a clear ~ skin 白皙、健康的皮肤 ‖ **healthily** *adv.* 健康地/ **healthiness** *n.* 健康，健全

heap /hiːp/

　　Ⅰ *n.* ❶ a pole of things arranged in a rather messy way 堆：a ~ of sand 一堆沙/in ~s 一堆堆的 ❷ a lot 很多；大量：We have ~s of time. 我们有很多时间。‖ *v.* ❶ put things in a large pile 堆积：~ (up) stones 堆积石头 ❷ load or place sth. in a pile 装满：He ~ed the plate with food. 他把食物堆满在盘子上。‖ a ~ of，~s of 很多，大量/ ~s more (longer …) 多 (长……) 得多/ ~ up wealth (riches) 积累财富/~ praises on (sb.) 极力赞美 (某人)

hear /hɪə(r)/

　　v. (heard) ❶ take in sound through the ears；listen to (music, a lecture, etc.) 听；听见：I ~d her say so. 我听她这样说的。/He was ~d to cry. 有人听见他哭。❷ be told and get to know, usually accidentally 听说，得知：I ~d that he was ill. 我听说他病了。❸ listen to and try a case in the court (指法官) 审理 (案件)：Who will ~ the case? 谁将审理这案子？‖ ~ about 听说 (某事)/ ~ from 接到……的来信；收到……的消息/ ~ of 听人说起，听说 (某事)/(will not) ~ of 不同意，不允许：I won't ~ of such a thing. 我不同意这样的事。/ ~ out 听完 (某人的话)/ ~ tell (of) 听说：I've often ~ tell of such happenings. 我常听说发生这类事情。‖ ~able /ˈhɪərəbl/ *n.* 听得见的/ ~er /ˈhɪərə(r)/ *n.* 听的人，旁听者

hearing /ˈhɪərɪŋ/

　　n. ❶ the sense which makes it possible for them to be aware of by sounds 听觉；听力：She has acute ~. 她听觉灵敏。❷ the distance within which one can hear 听力可以达到的距离：She said so in my ~, so that I could hear. 她当着我的面说的这番话。

hearsay /ˈhɪəseɪ/

　　n. information which you have been told but do not know to be true；rumour 风闻；传闻，流言

hearse /hɜːs/

　　n. a large carriage or car for carrying a coffin 柩车，灵车

heart /hɑːt/

　　n. ❶ the organ inside the chest, which controls the flow of blood by pushing it round the body 心，心脏：His ～ stopped beating.他的心脏停止了跳动。❷ deep feelings and beliefs 内心；心地 ❸ courage；strength of mind 勇气；意志：I lost my ～ when she has gone away. 她离去后，我就心灰意冷了。❹ the most central and important part of sth.核心；中心部分：get to the ～ of the subject 抓住问题的中心/the ～ of the matter 事情的实质/the ～ of a cabbage 卷心菜的菜心 ❺ a beloved person 心爱的人；dear ～ 心肝宝贝儿/sweet ～ 情人，爱人 ❻the mood 心情：with a light ～ (心情)轻松愉快地/with a heavy ～ (心情)沉重地，忧愁地 ‖ a change of ～ 改变主意，变心/after one's (own) ～ 完全合自己的心意/at ～ 在内心上，本质上/break sb.'s ～ 使某人很伤心(心碎)/cross one's ～ 在胸口画十字(表示说的是真话)/from the (bottom of one's) ～ 从心里(内心深处)，诚心诚意地/get to the ～ of 抓住……中心内容/have a ～ 行行好，发善心/have one's ～ in 心在(某方面)，用心/have sth. in one's ～ 把……放在心上，想着/have the ～ (to do sth.) 忍(做某事)，有勇气/～ and soul 全心全意地，完全地/～ in one's mouth 提心吊胆，胆战心惊/learn (know) by ～ 记熟，非常熟悉/lose ～ 灰心，泄气/lose one's ～ to 爱上，喜欢上/open one's ～ to 向……谈心里话/put one's ～ into 把全部心思放在……里面/set one's ～ on (sth.or doing sth.) 决心要(某物或做某事)/take sth.to ～ 对某事耿耿于怀/with all one's ～ 真心诚意地/with half a ～ 半心半意地 ‖ ～breaking adj.令人心碎的/～felt adj.衷心的/～sick adj.沮丧的，闷闷不乐的/～-stirring adj.振奋人心的/～-stricken，～-struck adj.伤心的，痛心的/～-string n.心弦/～warming adj.暖人心房的/～-whole adj.真诚的，全心全意的

heartache /ˈhɑːteɪk/
　　n.deep sorrow or grief 悲痛；伤心

heartbeat /ˈhɑːtbiːt/
　　n.the pulsation of the heart 心脏的搏动

heartbreak /ˈhɑːtbreɪk/
　　n.overwhelming sorrow caused by loss of

a loved one 心碎：an unforgettable tale of joy and ～ 快乐和悲伤的难忘故事

heartbroken /ˈhɑːtbrəʊk(ə)n/
　　adj.suffering from overwhelming sorrow 悲伤的；心碎的：She was ～ at the thought of leaving the house.一想到离开这所房子她都碎了。

hearten /ˈhɑːtn/
　　v.make a person feel cheerful or encouraged 振奋；鼓舞 ‖ ～ing adj.鼓舞人心的，令人振奋的

heartland /ˈhɑːtlænd/
　　n.the central or most important part of an area or country (国家或地区的)中心区域，心脏地带

heartless /ˈhɑːtlɪs/
　　adj.not feeling any pity or sympathy 无情的；狠心的：Heartless thieves stole the pushchair of a two-year-old child.狠心贼连两岁孩子的婴儿车都要偷。‖ ～ly adv.无情地；冷酷地/ ～ness n.冷酷，无情

hearty /ˈhɑːti/
　　adj.❶friendly and sincere；warmhearted 热情友好的；热诚的：a ～ greeting 热诚的问候/give sb.a ～ welcome 竭诚欢迎某人 ❷(of a person) strong and healthy；full of vigour 强健的；精神饱满的：He's still hale and ～ at eighty-five.他八十五岁仍很健壮。❸(of meals) large and very satisfying 大的，丰盛的：a ～ meal 丰盛的一餐/a ～ appetite 食欲很好，胃口大 ❹loud and (too) cheerful 喧闹而(过分)快活的：a ～ laugh 纵情大笑 ‖ heartily adv.由衷地；很，十分

heat /hiːt/
　　Ⅰ n.❶ the quality or quantity of being warm or cold；the degree of hotness；temperature of sth. 热度；温度：What is the ～ of the water in the swimming pool? 游泳池的水温是多少? ❷ the very hot weather 热天，酷热：She's suffering from the ～.她深受炎热天气之苦。❸ the intense feeling, especially of anger or excitement 冲动：He said it was all done in the ～ of the moment 他说所有这一切都

是在一时冲动下干的。Ⅱ *v*. make or become hot 加热;使暖和:We'll ～ some milk for the baby. 我们会为这婴儿热一些牛奶。‖ a dead ～ 不分胜负的赛跑/at a ～ 一口气地/in the ～ of 在……最激烈的时候/put the ～ on sb. 使某人为难;迫使某人付款(或干活等)‖ ～proof *adj*. 抗热的/ ～rash *n*. 痱子/ ～spot *n*. 雀斑/ ～stroke *n*. 中暑/ ～treat *n*. 热处理/ ～unit *n*. 热(量)单位/ ～wave *n*. (气象)热浪

heated /ˈhiːtɪd/
adj. (of a discussion) marked by emotional heat (讨论)激烈的:a ～ argument 一场激烈的争论 ‖ ～ly *adv*. 加热地;激昂地,热烈地

heater /ˈhiːtə/
n. a device for heating sth. 加热器

heating /ˈhiːtɪŋ/
n. the system and equipment used to provide heat to a building 供暖系统;供暖设备:We have no ～ in our bedrooms. 我们的卧室里没有供暖设备。

heatstroke /ˈhiːtstrəʊk/
n. illness caused by too much exposure to heat or sun 中暑

heave /hiːv/
Ⅰ *v*. (～d or hove) ❶ lift or pull sth. with difficulty 举起;拖;拉:～ a heavy box onto a truck 把重箱子搬上卡车 / ～ a hammer 举起铁锤 / I ～d the heavy box up the steps. 我把沉重的箱子拖上台阶。❷ rise and fall regularly;move up and down (强烈而有节奏地)起伏:The sea was heaving. 大海波涛起伏。/His chest ～s with every breath. 他的胸脯随着呼吸起伏。❸ throw with great effort 扔,抛,投,掷:～ a brick through the window 向窗外扔砖块 Ⅱ *n*. an act of heaving 拉;拖;举;扔;抛;起伏:with a mighty ～ 用力拉(抛)

heaven /ˈhevn/
n. ❶ the place where God or the angels are said to live, and where good people are believed to go after they die 天堂,天国:go to ～ 死去,进天国 ❷ (often *pl*.) the sky 天空,苍天;sail the blue ～s 在蓝天中翱翔/the starry ～s 星空 ❸ a place or state of complete bliss and happiness 极乐,极乐世界:I was in ～ when I heard the good news. 听到那好消息,我有点飘飘欲仙的感觉。❹ (Heaven) God;Providence 上帝;老天爷;神:It was the will of Heaven. 这是天意。‖ move ～ and earth 竭尽全力/to ～(s) 极度地/under ～ (用于加强语气)究竟,到底 ‖ ～sent *adj*. 天赐的;极巧的/ ～ward *adv*.&*adj*. 向天空(的)

heavy /ˈhevɪ/
adj. ❶ hard to lift or carry;having great weight or density 重的,沉重的:It is too ～ for me to lift. 这箱子太重了,我举不起来。/a ～ metal 重金属 ❷ of greater than usual;great in amount or force 大的;大量的;过量的;过度的:～ rain 大雨/a ～ blow 重击/a ～ punishment 重罚/ ～ fighting 激烈的战斗/ ～ traffic 拥挤的交通/ ～ smoking and drinking 抽烟和喝酒过多 ❸ clumsy;slow 迟钝的,笨拙的:My head is ～. 我的头脑反应迟钝。/a ～ sleeper 酣睡者 ‖ be ～ with 大量的/be ～ with child 怀孕了,大肚子/find sth. ～ going 发现……很难(枯燥)/hang ～ on one's hands (时间)过得很慢而沉闷无聊:Times hangs ～ on his hands. 他觉得时间过得慢而无聊。‖ ～buying *adj*. 大量买进的/ ～footed *adj*. 行动迟缓的/ ～handed *adj*. 笨手笨脚的,手拙的/ ～headed *adj*. 反应迟钝的/ ～hearted *adj*. 心情沉重的

heavyweight /ˈhevɪweɪt/
Ⅰ *n*. ❶ a person of more than average weight 特别重的人 ❷ a boxer of the heaviest class 重量级拳击手 ❸ a person of great influence or importance 有影响的人物;要人 Ⅱ *adj*. ❶ of more than average weight 超重的 ❷ having great influence or importance 重要的,有影响的

heck /hek/
Ⅰ *int*. used to show a slight annoyance or surprise 该死;见鬼(表示稍感恼怒、吃惊等):Oh ～! I've lost my keys again! 唉,我又把钥匙丢了! Ⅱ *n*. ❶ (a ～ of)

emphasis on the bigness or quantity of sth.(表示强调)极大;极多:～ of a lot of money 很多钱 ❷(the ～)an emphasis of a question, especially when you are puzzled or annoyed 到底;实况:The question was, where the ～ was she? 问题是,她到底哪儿去了?

hectare/'hekteə(r), 'hektɑ:(r)/
n.a unit for measuring an area of land (equal to 10,000 square metres) 公顷(等于10 000平方米)

hedge/hedʒ/
Ⅰ *n*.a fence of bushes or low trees, usually along the edge of a lawn, garden, or field 树篱:a dead ～ 用树枝编成的篱笆/a quick-set ～ 由活树围成的树篱 Ⅱ *v*.❶put fence around 用树篱围住(或隔开):～ a field(garden) 用树篱围住田地(花园) ❷avoid answering questions directly 回避问题;不正面答复:Answer "yes"or "no"—don't ～! 回答"是"或"不是"——不要回避问题! ‖ be (sit)on the ～ 骑墙,要两面派/～ off 用树篱把……隔断/～ out 用障碍物把……隔开 ‖ ～r *n*.种植(或修剪)树篱的人

hedgehog /'hedʒhɒg, 'hedʒhɔ:g/
n.a small insect-eating animal with a pig-like snout and a back covered in stiff spines, able to roll itself up into a ball when attacked 刺猬

heed/hi:d/
Ⅰ *v*.pay attention to 注意:Please ～ what the teacher says.请注意老师说的话。Ⅱ *n*.attention; notice 注意,留意:He took no ～ of what I said.他完全把我的话当成了耳边风。‖ ～ful *adj*.注意的,留心的/～less *adj*.不注意的,掉以轻心的

heel/hi:l/
Ⅰ *n*.❶ the back part of the foot 脚后跟,踵 ❷ the back part of the bottom of a shoe, sock, etc.(鞋、袜等的)后跟:There's a hole in the ～ of my stocking.我的长袜子后跟有一个破洞。/ shoes with high ～s 高跟鞋 ❸ an unpleasant or dishonourable man 卑鄙的小人;无赖 Ⅱ *v*.❶ put a heel on 补鞋跟,钉后掌;sole and ～ a pair of shoes 给一双鞋上鞋底及后跟

❷move along at the heels of someone (狗)紧跟在后:～ sb.upstairs 跟某人上楼 ‖ at ～ 跟在后面/at (on or upon) sb.'s ～s 紧跟在某人后面,紧追某人/bring sb. to ～ 使某人紧跟/come to ～ (狗)紧跟在主人后面,(人)顺从/cool one's ～s(让人)久等,空等/down at (the)～ 穿破鞋跟的,邋遢的/kick up one's ～s 高兴得跳起来/turn on one's ～ 急转身/under the ～ of 被……践踏,被蹂躏/take to your ～s 逃走,溜走 ‖ high-～ed *adj*.高跟的(鞋)/well-～ed *adj*.很富有的 ‖ ～ed *adj*.有鞋后跟的/～er *n*.政客的追随者/～less *adj*.没有后跟的

hegemony /hɪ'geɪməni/
n.a situation in which one country, organization, or group has more power or importance than others 霸权

height/haɪt/
n.❶distance from the base of sth. to the top or from a person's head to foot 高,高度;身高:This basketball player is two meters in ～.这个篮球运动员有两米高。❷the highest degree 极度,极点:It's the ～ of stupidity to have a picnic this weather.这样的天气去野餐真是愚蠢到了极点。/in the ～ of (the) summer 在盛夏时节 ❸a high place 高处,高地:climb the ～s of science and technology 攀登科学技术的高峰/ The soldiers are holding Height 302.战士们正坚守着302高地。‖ at (in) the ～ (of) 处于最厉害的阶段:The storm was at its ～.暴风雨达到最猛烈的程度。

heighten/'haɪtn/
v.make or become higher or greater 提高,增高:～ a building with an additional storey 在一幢建筑物上加高一层楼/ As she waited, her fears ～ed.她越等越害怕。

heir/eə(r)/
n.a person who has the legal right to get money or goods when someone dies 继承人:He is ～ to a large fortune.他是一大笔财产的继承者。‖ ～ess /'eərɪs/ *n*.女继承人/～ship *n*.继承权

helicopter/'helɪkɒptə(r)/
n. a kind of aircraft with horizontal revolving blades, able to take off and land in a very small space and remain stationary in the air if necessary 直升机

heliport/'helɪpɔːt/
n. a usually small airport for helicopters 直升机机场

helix/'hiːlɪks/
n. a spiral, especially a three-dimensional one, either like a corkscrew or flat like a watch spring 螺旋；螺旋状物

hell/hel/
Ⅰ *n.* ❶ (in some religions) a place where the souls of bad people are said to be punished after death（某些宗教里的）地狱，阴间 ❷ a place or condition of pain and turmoil 痛苦的地方；苦境：make sb.'s life a ~ 使某人的生活像地狱般的苦/ ~ on earth(or a living ~) 人间地狱/ suffer ~ 吃苦头 Ⅱ *int.* a swear word, used in anger or to give force to an expression（用于咒骂或加强语气）该死，见鬼：Go to ~! 滚开！见鬼去吧！ /To ~ with it! 让它见鬼去吧！ /What the ~ do you want? 你到底要什么？ ‖ a ~ of a …极度的/in ~ 究竟/like ~ 拼命地

hellish/'helɪʃ/
adj. ❶ very bad or unpleasant 很坏的；很讨厌的：~ weather 很坏的天气/I've had a ~ day at work. 我干了一天的重活儿，累坏了。 ❷ of or like hell 地狱似的 ‖ ~ly *adv.* 可怕地：a ~ly difficult exam 一次困难的考试

hello/he'ləʊ/
int. & *n.* an expression of greeting said when you meet someone or at the beginning of a telephone conversation 喂（唤起注意的呼声）；问候：Hello, how are you! 嘿，你好吗？ / Say ~ to him for me. 代我问候他。

helm/helm/
n. a long handle or wheel, used for turning the rudder of a ship 舵，舵柄，舵轮 ‖ ~s-man *n.* 舵手

helmet/'helmɪt/
n. a covering to protect the head 钢盔，头

盔：The policeman was wearing a ~. 那警察戴着一顶钢盔。

help/help/
Ⅰ *v.* ❶ do sth. or part of sth. for sb. 帮助：May I ~ you with your luggage? 我帮你拿行李好吗？ /His friend ~ed him(out) with money when he needed it. 当他缺钱时，他的朋友资助他摆脱了困境。 ❷ encourage, improve, or produce favourable conditions for (sth.) 促进：This medicine ~s digestion. 这种药是助消化的。 /Crying won't ~ (you). 哭（对你）于事无补。 /What have you got that will ~ a cold? 你有什么可治感冒的药吗？ ‖ can't ~（it）没有办法，控制不了/(it) can't be ~ed（这）是没法避免的，只好这样/can't ~ doing sth. 情不自禁做某事/can't ~ but(do sth.) 不由得不……，不能不/ ~… in sth. 在……方面帮助某人/oneself(sb.) to 给自己（别人）夹菜（斟酒等）；擅自享用：Help yourself. 请自便。 / ~ out 帮助（做事，克服困难）Ⅱ *n.* ❶ the act of helping 帮助；救助：You gave me a lot of ~. 你给了我很大帮助。 ❷ a person or thing that helps 助手，帮手：You're a good ~ to me. 你是我的得力帮手。 ‖ with the ~ of 在……帮助下，借助…… ‖ ~er *n.* 帮手，起帮助作用的东西/ ~ing *adj.* 帮助人的，辅助的；*n.*（食物的）一份：Please give me another ~ing. 请给我再来一份。 / ~mate *n.* 良伴，配偶

helpful/'helpfʊl/
adj. giving help 有用的，有帮助的：You have been very ~. 你帮了（我们）很多忙。

helpless/'helplɪs/
adj. without help; unable to help oneself 无助的；不能自助的：He was almost ~ without his glasses. 不戴眼镜他几乎寸步难行。 / as ~ as a baby 像婴儿一样无助

hem/hem/
Ⅰ *n.* a lap made by folding over cloth; the border on a shirt, etc.（衣服或台布类的）折边：take the ~ up 将衣服的边折起来 Ⅱ *v.* (-mm-) ❶ fold over and sew down the edge 缝边；镶边：~ a table cloth 给台布锁边 ❷ surround 包围：~ in (about, round)包围；围绕 ❸ make a sound like a

cough 哼一声;清嗓子

hemisphere/'hemɪsfɪə(r)/
*n.*one half of the earth 半球;地球的半面:
the Northern(Southern) ~ 北半球(南半
球)/the Eastern(Western) ~ 东半球(西
半球)

hen/hen/
*n.*a farm bird that lays egg and that can
be eaten as food;adult female chicken 母
鸡:They're big and fat ~s.它们是又大
又肥的母鸡。

hence/hens/
*adv.*❶ from here;from now 从此;今后;
此后:a week ~ 一周以后 /a kilometre
~ 由此一公里的距离 ❷ for this reason
因此,所以:My mother is by herself ~ I
must go home now.我母亲独自一人在
家,所以现在我该回家了。

henceforth/ˌhens'fɔːθ/
*adv.*from this time on 今后,从此以后

heptagon/'heptəgən/
*n.*a polygon with seven sides 七边形,七
角形

her/hɜː/
pron. ❶ (the object form of she) a
woman;girl or female animal (she 的宾
格)她:Can you see ~? 你能见到她吗?
❷(the possessive form of she) of or belonging to her (she 的所有格)她的:This
is ~ book, not yours.那是她的书,不是
你的。

herald/'herəld/
Ⅰ*n.* a person or thing foretelling the
coming of sth. 前驱;先兆;预示:Early
flowers are ~s of spring.早开的花预示
春天的来临。 Ⅱ*v.* be a sign of (sth.
coming or about to happen) 预示……的
到来:The first buds ~ spring. 嫩芽报春
到。

herb/hɜːb/
*n.*any plant used for medicine or for giving a special taste to food 草本植物,药
草,香草:a ~ prescription 草药方 / ~
beer 草药制的饮料/ ~ tea,~ water (草
药煎成的)水药

herbal/'hɜːbl/

Ⅰ*adj.* of herbs used in medicine or for
flavouring 药草的;芳草的:~ remedies
药草治疗法。 Ⅱ*n.*a book containing descriptions of herbs 草本植物志;药草书

herbage/'hɜːbɪdʒ/
*n.*grass and other field plants 草本植物群

herbicide/'hɜːbɪsaɪd/
*n.*a substance that is poisonous to plants,
used to destroy unwanted vegetation 除
草剂

herbivore/'hɜːbɪvɔː(r)/
n. animals that feed on grass and other
plants 食草动物

herd/hɜːd/
Ⅰ*n.* ❶ a group of animals of the same
kind 兽群,牧群:a ~ of cattle 一群牛/a
~ of elephants(deer) 一群象(鹿)❷
(used in compounds) a person who looks
after a herd (构成复合词)放牧人:a cow-
~ 放牛的人/sheep(goat) ~ 牧羊人 ❸a
large number of people;mob 民众,百姓,
人群:follow the ~ 随大流/the common
~ 小百姓 Ⅱ*v.*drive animals as a herd 驱
赶牧群:The farmer ~ed the cows into
the field.农民把那些牛一起赶到田野里。

herder/'hɜːdə(r)/
*n.*a person who cares for or drives herds
of cattle or flocks of sheep,especially on
an open range 牧人

herdsman/'hɜːdzmən/
*n.*a person who keeps or tends a herd 牧
人;牧主

here/hɪə(r)/
*adv.*❶ at, in or to this place 这里,在这
里:Come ~. 到这里来。❷at this point
在这点上,这时:Here the speaker paused
for a while. 讲到这里发言人停了一下。
❸(used for drawing attention to sth. or
sb.)(用以引起对某人或某事的注意):
Here the bus is coming! 瞧,公共汽车来
了。/Here is the news...现在报告新闻
…… ‖ Here! (点名时的回答)到! 有! /
~ and now 此时此地/ ~ and there 四
处/ Here's to …(祝酒)向……敬一杯/~
there and everywhere 到处/ Here you are.
这就是你要的东西。/ neither ~ nor

there 不中肯，不重要，与……无关的 ‖
~about(s) *adv.*在这附近/ ~from *adv.*
由此

hereafter/ˌhɪər'ɑːftə(r)/
*adv.*from now on, in the future 今后，将
来：She should have died ~.今后她就不
在人世了。

hereby/ˌhɪə'baɪ/
*adv.*by this means 以此，特此：I ~ declare that I will not be responsible for
any of her debts.我特此声明，我将不负
责她所欠的任何债务。

hereditary/hɪ'redɪtri/
*adj.*passed from one generation to another 遗传的：~ diseases 遗传病/ a ~ chief
世袭的首领

heredity/hɪ'redəti/
*n.*the passing of certain qualities from one
generation to another; the qualities passed in this way 遗传；遗传的特征：The
colour of our skin is due to ~.我们的肤
色是由于遗传。

herein/ˌhɪər'ɪn/
adv. in or into this place, thing, document,etc.此中，于此，在此处中：Herein
lies the answers.这里包含着答案。

heresy/'herəsi/
*n.*a belief which is not considered to be
correct; any belief not considered to be
correct 异教；异端邪说

heretic/'herətɪk/
*n.*a person who supports a heresy 异教
徒；信奉异端邪说的人 ‖ ~al *adj.*异端
的；异教的

hereto/'hɪətuː/
*adv.*to this place, thing matter or document 于此，至此，对于此事：the written
consent of each of the parties ~ 各方对
于此事的书面允诺

herewith/ˌhɪə'wɪð/
adv. with this letter 与此信，随信：A
cheque is enclosed ~.随信附上支票一
张。

heritage/'herɪtɪdʒ/
*n.*any attribute or immaterial possession
which has been or may be inherited from

ancestors 遗产，世袭财产，继承物：a
splendid historical ~ 一件优秀的历史遗
产/the country's artistic ~ 国家的文化
艺术遗产

hermit/'hɜːmɪt/
*n.*a person who lives alone (often in order
to lead a religious life) 隐士；修道者

hero/'hɪərəʊ/
n.(*pl.*~es)❶a man who does sth. great
or brave 英雄，英雄人物：a battle ~ 战斗
英雄/an unsung ~ 无名英雄 ❷ the chief
man in a poem, story, play, etc.(诗歌、小
说、戏剧等中)主人公，主角

heroic/hɪ'rəʊɪk/
*adj.*❶showing the qualities of a hero; extremely courageous 英雄的；英勇的：~
deeds 英雄的事迹 ❷of or concerning heroes 史诗的，歌颂英雄的：~ poems 英
雄诗篇/ ~ poetry 史诗 ‖ ~ally *adv.*英
雄地；超人地

heroin/'herəʊɪn/
n. a powerful drug which some people
take for pleasure, but which they can become highly addictive 海洛因

heroine /'herəʊɪn/
*n.*❶a woman who is admired for her
brave or noble deeds 女英雄 ❷the chief
female character in a story, play, or poem
(故事、戏剧或诗歌中的)女主角，女主人
公

heroism/'herəʊɪzəm/
*n.*very great courage 英勇，大无畏；英雄
气概：an act of great ~ 充满大无畏精神
的行动

heron/'herən/
*n.*a type of bird with long legs, neck and
beak, which walks in the water 苍鹭

hers/hɜːz/
*pron.*sth. belonging to a woman, girl or
female animal 她的：—Is the pen ~? —
Yes,it's her pen.—钢笔是她的吗? —是
的,这是她的钢笔。

herself/hɜː'self/
*pron.*❶(the reflexive form of she) a
woman, girl or female animal (反身代词)
她自己：She said to ~.她自言自语。❷

emphasize the person or thing that you are referring to (加强语气)她亲自,她本人:She ~ cooked the meal.她亲自做了这顿饭。❸(in) her usual state of mind or body(用于 be,become,come to 等后)她的正常情况(指健康、情绪):She is not quite ~ today.她今天不大舒服(她今天情绪有点反常)。/She has come to ~.她的心态恢复正常了。

hertz/hɜːts/

n.(the unit of frequency)one time each second(频率单位)赫(兹):These radio waves are transmitted at a frequency of 15,000 cycles per second, that's 15 kilohertz or 15,000 ~.这些无线电波发射频率为每秒一万五千波数,即十五千赫或一万五千赫。

hesitancy/ˈhezɪtənsɪ/

*n.*the state or quality of being slow or uncertain in doing or saying sth.犹豫;踌躇;迟疑不决

hesitant/ˈhezɪtənt/

adj. showing uncertainty or slowness about deciding to act; tending to hesitate 犹豫(不决)的;迟疑的;有疑虑的:She's ~ about making new friends.她在结交新朋友上有疑虑。/his ~ attempts to speak English 他那想说英语而又吞吞吐吐的犹豫态度

hesitate/ˈhezɪteɪt/

*v.*❶ stop for a moment before speaking or acting; be slow in deciding 犹豫;踌躇;迟疑:I ~ at nothing.我对什么都毫不迟疑。/I ~d to go in.我犹豫着不想进去。❷ be unwilling 不愿意,勉强:I ~ to ask you.But will you lend me some money? 我真不好意思向你开口,你能借些钱给我吗? ‖ **hesitating** *adj.*犹豫的/**hesitatingly** *adv.*犹豫地/**hesitation** *n.*犹豫;犹豫的事

heterodox/ˈhetərədɒks/

adj.(of beliefs, opinions, or ideas, etc.)against accepted or official ones(信仰、意见或思想等)异端的,非正统的

heterogeneous/ˌhetərəˈdʒiːnɪəs/

*adj.*consisting of parts or members that are very different from one another; not homogeneous 由不同的成分(或成员)组成的;混杂的;不等同的:a ~ mix of nationalities 多民族的混合体

heterosexual/ˌhetrəˈsekʃʊəl/

*n.*a person who is sexually attracted to persons of the opposite sex 异性恋者

heuristic/hjʊəˈrɪstɪk/

*adj.*❶(of education)based on learning by one's own personal discoveries and experiences(教育)启发式的 ❷ helping one in the process of learning or discovery(对学习或发现)有启发作用的,探索(性)的

hew/hjuː/

v.(~ed or ~n)chop or cut(sth.or sb.)with an axe, sword, etc.劈;砍;削:~ down a big tree 砍倒一棵大树 /~ branches from a tree 砍掉树枝 /Quite a few trees were ~n down by the storm.相当多的树被风暴吹倒了。

hexagon/ˈheksəgən/

*n.*a figure with six sides and angles 六角形,六边形

hey/heɪ/

*int.*used to call attention, or express surprise or interrogation 嘿,嗨(用以唤起注意或表示惊讶、询问):Hey, monkey! Would you like some bananas? 嘿,猴子! 要来些香蕉吗?

heyday/ˈheɪdeɪ/

*n.*a period of time of greatest power or prosperity 全盛时期:The country was then in its ~.当时这个国家正在其全盛时期。/He was a great singer in his ~.他在自己的黄金时代是个了不起的歌唱家。/ in the ~ of its power 在其权力鼎盛时期

hi/haɪ/

*int.*used as a greeting(问候用语)嗨,喂:Hi! How are you? 喂,你好吗?

hiatus/haɪˈeɪtəs/

*n.*❶ a break or interruption 间隙,间断:Talks between the two countries have resumed after a six year ~.在中断了六年之后,两国之间的谈判已经恢复。❷ a space or gap where sth. is missing, espe-

H

cially in a piece of writing（尤指文稿中的）脱漏

hibernate /ˈhaɪbəneɪt/

v.（of certain animals）be or go into a state like a long sleep during the winter（某些动物）冬眠，蛰伏：Some bears ～.有些熊冬眠了。‖ hibernation *n.*冬眠；过冬

hiccup /ˈhɪkʌp/

Ⅰ *n.* ❶ a high gulping sound made when your breath is briefly interrupted 打嗝 ❷ a brief hitch or setback 暂时的困难和挫折 Ⅱ *v.*make the sound of a hiccup 打嗝

hidden /ˈhɪdn/

*adj.*difficult to see or find 难以发现的，隐藏的：His words had a ～ meaning.他的话有隐藏的意义。

hide[1] /haɪd/

*v.*❶put or keep out of sight；prevent from being seen or found；conceal 把……藏起来，隐藏：A fox cannot ～ its tail. 狐狸尾巴是藏不住的。❷keep（facts，feelings，etc.）from being known 掩饰，隐瞒：Don't ～ your feelings；say what you think.不要掩饰你的感情，想什么就说什么。❸place oneself or be placed so as to be unseen 躲藏：You'd better ～.你最好躲起来。

hide[2] /haɪd/

n. an animal's skin，especially when removed to be used for leather（尤指用作皮革的）兽皮

hide-and-seek /ˌhaɪdnˈsiːk/

*n.*a children's game in which one player looks for others who are hiding 捉迷藏

hideaway /ˈhaɪdəweɪ/

*n.*a place，such as a house，where one can go to hide or avoid other people 躲藏处，藏匿处

hiding /ˈhaɪdɪŋ/

*n.*❶a beating 痛打，鞭打：I'll give you a good ～ when we get home! 到了家我要狠狠揍你一顿。❷a defeat 打败：The English team got quite a ～ in Paris.英国队在巴黎遭到惨败。

hierarchy /ˈhaɪərɑːki/

n. the organization of people at different ranks in an administrative body 阶层，等级制度

hieroglyph /ˈhaɪərəglɪf/

n. pictures or symbols representing a word，syllable，or sound，used by the ancient Egyptians and others 象形文字

hi-fi /ˈhaɪfaɪ/

n.（the short form of high fidelity）reproduction of sound using electronic equipment that gives faithful reproduction with little or no distortion 高保真度

high /haɪ/

Ⅰ *adj.* ❶ having a long way from the bottom to the top when it is upright 高的：a ～ mountain 高山/It's four metres ～.它有四米高。/That table is too ～ for the little girl.这桌子太高，小女孩够不着。❷ close to the top of a particular range of notes（音调）高声的；高音调的：～ notes 高音符 / speak in a ～ voice 尖声讲话 ❸ costing a lot of money 昂贵的；上流的：～ prices 高价 /the upper classes ～ society 上流社会 / the ～ life 豪华生活 ❹ morally good 高尚的，崇高的：a woman of ～ character 品德高尚的女子 / ～ ideals（aims）崇高的理想（目标）❺ senior；important 高级的，高等的：a ～ commander 高级指挥员 / ～er education 高等教育/ leather goods of ～ quality 高质量的皮革制品 ❻（of time）far advanced（时机）正盛的；（时间）成熟的：～ summer 盛夏/ ～ noon 正午/ It's ～ time we went.我们该走了。❼（of food，especially meat）slightly tainted，beginning to go bad（食物，尤指肉）不新鲜的，变质的：～ game 有点变质的野味 Ⅱ *adv.*in or to a high point，place，amount or degree 高地；高度地；高额地；高层次地；climb ～ 向高处攀登/pay ～ 付高价/ live ～ 过奢侈生活 ‖ be in ～ spirits 情绪高昂/have a ～ opinion（of）对……有很高评价/aim ～ 目标高，雄（野）心大/fly ～ 胸怀大志/～ and low 到处（寻找）/run ～（情绪）激昂 ‖ ～born *adj.*出身高贵的/ ～-flyer *n.*好高骛远者/ ～ grade *adj.*优质的/ ～-handed *adj.*高压的，专横的/ ～-minded *adj.*品格高尚的/ ～-

power(ed) adj.大功率的;精力充沛的/ ~-pressure adj.高压的/ ~-priced adj. 高价的/ ~-ranking adj.高级的(官员)/ ~-school n.〈美〉中学/a junior(senior) ~-school 初(高)中/ ~ seas n.公海/ ~ way n.公路

high-class/'haɪ'klæs/
adj.of a high standard, quality(标准、质量)高等的,一流的

highland /'haɪlənd/
n.(also ~s) mountainous land 高原;山地

high-level/ˌhaɪ'levl/
adj.❶involving important or high-ranking people 高水平的,高级的:~ negotiations 高层谈判 ❷(of a computer language) designed for convenience in programming, often by resembling ordinary language(计算机语言)高级的(设计用于编程,常与普通语言相似)

highlight /'haɪlaɪt/
Ⅰn.❶the most interesting or outstanding feature of sth. 最显著(或重要)的部分: the ~ of the tour 旅行最精彩的部分 ❷a light or bright area in a painting, picture, etc.(画、照片等)强光部分 ❸a light-coloured streak in a person's hair(头发的)亮彩 Ⅱv.❶draw special attention to sth. 使显著,使突出;强调 ❷emphasize a section of text using a highlighter pen 用荧光笔标记号

highly/'haɪli/
adv.❶to a high degree 高度地:He spoke very ~ of her. 他高度赞扬了她。/a ~ paid official 高薪官员 ❷very 很,非常:~ competitive 非常有竞争力

high-powered /'haɪ'paʊəd/
adj.❶(of a machine or device) having greater than normal strength or capabilities(机器、装置)大功率的,动力强的,高性能的:a ~ rifle 威力大的步枪 ❷dynamic and capable 精力充沛的,能力强的:a ~ delegation 一个阵容强大的代表团

highway /'haɪweɪ/
n.❶a public road 主干道,大路 ❷a main route by land, sea, or air(陆海空的)主要

路线

hijack/'haɪdʒæk/
v.❶take control of (a vehicle or aircraft) by force of arms 劫持,绑架:The plane was ~ed soon after it took off.那架飞机起飞后不久被劫持了。 ❷stop and rob 拦路抢劫

hike/haɪk/
Ⅰv.❶go on a hike 徒步旅行,远足:They ~d out to the forest.他们徒步旅行去森林。 ❷increase suddenly and steeply 急剧提高:The landlord was trying to ~ rents.房东企图提高租金。 Ⅱn.a long walk in the country, especially over rough ground, and taken for pleasure 徒步旅行,远足,行军:go out for a ~ 去远足,行军 ‖ ~r n.徒步旅行者

hill/hɪl/
n.❶an area of land that is higher than the land that surrounds it 小山;丘陵:go up (down) a ~ 上(下)山 ❷a small heap (of earth) 小土堆;堆:a ~ of potatoes 一小堆土豆

hilt/hɪlt/
n.the handle of a sword or dagger (剑、匕首等的)柄

him/hɪm/
pron.(the object form of he) a man, boy or male animal(he 的宾格)他:I like ~. 我喜欢他。/ Mr Smith is in town; I saw ~ yesterday.史密斯先生在城里,我昨天看见了他。

himself/hɪm'self/
pron.❶ the same male person as the one the sentence is about(反身代词)他自己:Did he hurt ~ when he fell? 他跌倒时伤了自己吗? ❷(used for emphasis)(加强语气)他本人,亲自:I want the manager ~, not his secretary.我找经理本人,不是他的秘书。 ❸(in) his usual state of mind or body 他(身心)的正常状况,健康:He's not quite ~.他今天不大舒服。 ‖(all) by ~ 独自,单独

hind/haɪnd/
adj.belonging to the back part 后面的,在后的:a ~ leg 后腿/ the ~ wheels of a

cart 车的后轮

hinder

Ⅰ /ˈhɪndə(r)/ v. keep back; delay; be an obstacle 阻碍, 阻止, 妨碍: That ~ed him from going further. 这使他不能继续向前了。/You're ~ing my work. 你在妨碍我的工作。Ⅱ /ˈhaɪndə(r)/ adj. located at or of the back part 后面的, 后部的, 在后的

hindmost /ˈhaɪndməʊst/

adj. furthest back; last 最后面的

hindquarters /ˌhaɪndˈkwɔːtəz/

n. the back part of an animal, including the legs (动物的)后臀及后腿

hindrance /ˈhɪndrəns/

n. a person or thing that makes it more difficult for you to do sth. 障碍; 妨碍者: Children are a ~ when you wish to work quietly. 在你想安静工作的时候, 孩子总是妨碍。

hindsight /ˈhaɪndsaɪt/

n. the ability to understand the nature of an event after it has happened 后见之明, 事后聪明

hinge /hɪndʒ/

Ⅰ n. the joint on which a lid, door, etc. turns and swings 铰链: The door swings on ~s. 这门靠铰链开关。/oil the ~s 给铰链加油 Ⅱ v. attach with a hinge; turn or depend on 给……装上铰链; (使)依靠: The door should ~ upon this post. 这门应该在这根门柱上装铰链。/The result ~s upon his reply. 结果取决于他的答复。

hint /hɪnt/

Ⅰ n.❶ a statement or action that gives a small or indirect suggestion 暗示: take a ~ 接受别人的暗示: give(drop)a ~ 给人暗示, 露口风 ❷ a slight indication 迹象: There is a ~ of summer in the air, although it's only May. 虽然才到五月, 空气里就散发着一点夏天的气息。❸ (usually pl.)a useful advice 忠告: helpful ~s 有益的忠告 Ⅱ v. suggest or mention indirectly 暗示, 示意: Ⅰ ~ed (to him) that he ought to work harder. 我向他暗示他应该

更努力地工作。/He ~ed at his anxiety. 他暗示别人自己很着急。

hinterland /ˈhɪntəlænd/

n. the inner part of a country, beyond the coast or the banks of an important river 内地, 腹地

hip /hɪp/

n. the fleshy part of either side of the human body above the legs 臀; 髋部: He put his hands on his ~s. 他两手叉腰。

hippopotamus /ˌhɪpəˈpɒtəməs/

n. a very large African animal live in and near rivers and lakes 河马

hire /ˈhaɪə(r)/

Ⅰ v.❶ pay for the use of; rent 租: ~ a horse for two days 租借一匹马使用两天 ❷ employ sb. or pay them for working 雇用: ~ three girls for the Children's Day rush 雇佣三个姑娘来应付儿童节的购买热潮 Ⅱ n. the act of hiring sth. or sb. 租用, 雇用: bicycles on(for) ~ 供出租的自行车/work for ~ 做雇工/fight for ~ 当雇佣兵 ‖ ~ oneself (out) to 受雇于 ‖ ~r n. 雇主, 租借者

his /hɪz/

pron.❶ belonging to a man, boy or male animal 他的: My uncle took ~ children to school. 我叔叔送他的孩子上学。❷ (a possessive pronoun)that or those belonging to a man, boy (物主代词)他的: That pen is my brother's; I know it is ~. 那支钢笔是我兄弟的; 我知道是他的。/It is not hers. 那是他的, 不是她的。

hiss /hɪs/

Ⅰ v.❶ make a sound like a long "s" 发嘶嘶声: Geese and snakes ~. 鹅和蛇发嘶嘶声。/The iron ~ed as it pressed the wet cloth. 熨斗在湿布上发出了嘶嘶声。❷ show disapproval and dislike of 发嘘声(表示反对): Have you ever been ~ed at (in the middle of) a speech? 你在讲演中有没有被人嘘过? Ⅱ n. a hissing sound 嘶嘶声; 嘘声: The speaker was received with a mixture of applause and ~es. 那演说者同时得到了喝彩声和嘘声。

hist /hɪst/

int. an exclamation used for getting attention or asking for silence（用于引起注意或要求肃静的声音）嘘

historian/hɪˈstɔːrɪən/

n. a person who studies history 历史学家：He is a ～.他是一个历史学家。

historic/hɪˈstɔːrɪk, hɪˈstɒrɪk/

adj. important in history 有历史意义的；历史性的：a congress of ～ significance 有历史意义的大会 /a ～ mission 历史使命 /～ spot（scene）古迹 /a ～ building 有历史意义的建筑 /a ～ year 有历史意义的一年

historical/hɪˈstɒrɪkl/

adj. ❶of or relating to the study of history 有关历史的：～ studies 历史研究 ❷which represents a fact or facts of history 史实的,依据历史的：a ～ novel 历史小说 / a ～ event 历史事件

history/ˈhɪstri/

n. ❶ (the study of) events in the past, especially events concerning the rulers and government of a country, social and trade conditions, etc.历史；历史学：It's rare in ～.这在历史上很罕见。❷ a written account of history 过去事件的叙述,历史记载：a short ～ of the last war 上次战争的简史 ❸ series of past events or experiences connected with an object, a person or a place 地方或人物的历史；经历：a long ～ of heart trouble 长期的心脏病史 /her life ～ 她一生的经历 ‖ make ～ 创造历史

histrionic/ˌhɪstrɪˈɒnɪk/

adj. ❶ behaving or done in a too theatrical way, especially in showing feelings that are insincere or pretended 演戏似的；装腔作势的, 做作的 ❷ concerning the theatre or acting 戏剧的,表演的；剧院(场)的

histrionics/ˌhɪstrɪˈɒnɪks/

n. the behaviour which is like a theatrical performance, showing strong but insincere feelings 矫揉造作,装腔作势

hit/hɪt/

Ⅰ*v.*(hit)❶give a blow to；strike 打击,击

中：The little boy ～ him hard.那个小男孩使劲打他。/He ～ me on the head.他打了我的头。/I ～ the target（mark）.我击中了目标。❷ come against sth. with force（使）碰撞：The ship ～ a rock.轮船撞在一块岩石上。/The child ～ his head on the table.孩子的头在桌子上碰了一下。❸reach 到达,达到：We ～ the main road two hours later.两小时后,我们才到达大路上。❹find sth. by accident or after searching 偶然碰上,找到：The ship ～ fog on its voyage.船在航行时碰上了雾。/The peasants ～ water at thirty metres.农民们在 30 米深处找到了水。‖ ～ at 打击/ ～ back 灵机一动；回击/ ～ on（upon）偶然发现,无意中遇见：I hope someone will ～ on a way out of our difficulty soon.我希望有人会很快想出个摆脱困难的办法。Ⅱ*n.* ❶ a blow; a stroke 一击,击中：score a ～ 命中 ❷a successful attempt or performance；a conspicuous success 成功的尝试(或表演)；轰动一时的人(或物)：The play was quite a ～ in London.这出戏在伦敦曾轰动一时。/The song is a ～ all over the world.这首歌风靡全球。/That is a ～ tune.那是流行曲调。‖ make a ～ 成功,受欢迎

hitch/hɪtʃ/

Ⅰ*v.*❶pull up with a quick movement 急拉,猛拉：He ～ed up his trousers.他很快系上了长裤。❷ fasten with a rope, hook, etc.拴住；钩住；套住：They ～ed the horses to the wagon.他们把马套上车。Ⅱ*n.* ❶a sudden pull or push 急拉；急推 ❷a type of knot made in a rope 索结,绳结 ❸an unforeseen obstacle；temporary difficulty or problem 障碍,阻碍：There has been a ～ in the discussions.讨论中存在着障碍。

hitchhike/ˈhɪtʃhaɪk/

v. go on a journey by getting rides in other people's cars 搭乘别人便车旅行：He ～d through France to Spain.他搭便车经过法国到达西班牙。

hitherto/ˌhɪðəˈtuː/

adv. until this time 直到此时；迄今为止

hive /haɪv/

n. ❶a box (of wood, straw, etc.) for bees to live in 蜂箱, 蜂巢: The ～ is made of wood.这蜂箱是用木材做的。❷a swarm of bees 蜂群: The whole ～ was busy.整个蜂群都在忙碌。❸a place where there is a lot of activities or people are busy working 热闹的场所; 繁忙的地方: The construction site was a ～ of activity.建筑工地上一片繁忙景象。

hoard /hɔːd/

Ⅰ*n.*a secret store, especially of sth. valuable to the owner 隐藏, 贮藏; 贮藏物, 秘藏物: a squirrel's ～ of nuts 松鼠储藏的坚果 Ⅱ*v.* store secretly, especially more than is needed or allowed 贮藏; 囤积; 隐藏: The miser ～ed (up) the gold under his bed.守财奴把金子藏在床下。

hoarding /'hɔːdɪŋ/

n. ❶ a temporary wooden fence round a house or piece of land 临时围篱, 临时围板 ❷a very large board on which advertisements are stuck 招贴板, 广告牌

hoarse /hɔːs/

adj. ❶(of sound) rough and harsh sounding (声音)粗糙刺耳的: a ～ cry 嘶哑的叫喊声 ❷having a hoarse voice 嗓门嘶哑的: I am ～ because I have a bad cold.我得了重感冒, 因此嗓音嘶哑。

hoary /'hɔːri/

adj. ❶(of hair) grey or white with age (头发)花白的, 灰白的 ❷very old 古老的; 陈旧的: a ～ joke that we'd all heard many times before 我们都已听过多次的老掉牙的笑话

hoax /həʊks/

Ⅰ*n.*a trick, intended to deceive; a deliberate trickery 骗局; 戏弄, 欺骗: A telephone caller said there was a bomb in the hotel but it was just a ～.打电话的人说旅馆里有一颗炸弹, 但这只不过是一场恶作剧。Ⅱ*v.* play a trick on (someone) 戏弄, 欺骗: ～ sb.into believing sth.骗某人相信某事

hobble /'hɒbl/

*v.*walk in an awkward way and with diffi-culty, especially as a result of damage to the legs or feet 跛行; 蹒跚: The old man ～d along with a stick.老人拄着拐杖蹒跚而行。/The wounded man had to ～ home.这受伤的男人, 只好一拐一拐地走回家。

hobby /'hɒbi/

*n.*sth. you do for pleasure in your spare time 业余爱好

hockey /'hɒki/

n. ❶ a team game played on a field with a ball and curved sticks 曲棍球 ❷ a game played on an ice between two teams of 11 players who try to knock a flat round puck into the opponents' goal with angled sticks 冰球

hoe /həʊ/

*n.*a tool for digging the soil and clearing weeds 锄头

hoist /hɔɪst/

Ⅰ*v.*lift up and put in a higher position 扯起, 升起: A flag was ～ed on the ship.船上升起一面旗子。Ⅱ*n.* ❶ an upward push 升起, 扯起, 举起 ❷an apparatus for lifting heavy goods 起重机; 卷扬机

hold /həʊld/

Ⅰ*v.*(held) ❶ grasp and keep; take in the hands or arms 拿着, 握住, 抱: The mother is ～ing her baby.母亲抱着婴儿。❷ put or keep in a certain position 使保持(某种姿势或状态): They held their heads up. 他们抬起头。/She held the child still. 她让孩子别动。❸ bear the weight of; support 夹住, 支撑: She held her hair back with a pin.她用发夹把头夹住。❹ keep back or control 阻止, 控制: Hold your tongue! 住嘴! /We held our breath in fear.我们害怕得大气不敢出。❺ contain; have room for 容纳, 装得下, 包含: The room could ～ thirty people.这个房间能容纳三十个人。❻ possess (money, land or a position) 拥有, 占有: He ～s a half share in the business.他拥有该企业一半的股份。❼arrange and take part in 举行: ～ a meeting (a debate, talks) 举行会议(辩论, 会谈) ❽ have a belief or an opinion about sb. or sth.怀有,持有(信念、意见);认为:The experts held that the drug was dangerous.专家们认为麻醉药品是危险的。❾ have a particular job or position;own or have sth.担任(职位);拥有,持有:~ a leading post 担任领导工作/ ~ power 掌权/ ~ office 执政 ‖ ~ back 阻止;踌躇,犹豫不定/ ~ by 坚持(意见)/ ~ down 压制,垂下(头部)/ ~ forth 滔滔不绝地讲/ ~ hard 停止/ ~ in 约束/ ~ off 不接近,拖延/ ~ on 继续/ ~ out 维持(多久)/ ~ over 将……延迟/ ~ to 坚持(原则、方向等)/ ~ together (使)团结一致/ ~ up (使)团结一致/ ~ up 阻碍;(使)停止 ‖ n.❶ the act of grasping 抓,握:catch(take, get, lay, seize) ~ of sth. 抓住某物 ❷sth. which can be held,especially in climbing 支撑点(可手攀或脚踏的东西):Can you find a ~ for your hands so that you can pull yourself up? 你能抓住什么东西攀登上来吗? ❸the part of a ship (below deck) where goods are stored 货舱;底层舱 ‖ have ~ of the wrong end of the stick 完全误解/let go (leave, lose) ~ of 松手放开…… ‖ ~ back n.阻碍物,暂时停顿/ ~down n.(费用等)缩减/ ~ man n.舱内装卸工人/ ~out n.(谈判中)坚持,不让步

holdall /ˈhəʊldɔːl/
n.a large bag with handles and a shoulder strap (有肩带的)大手提包

holder /ˈhəʊldə(r)/
n.a person or thing that holds sth. 支持物,持有者:a record ~ 纪录保持者/ a cigarette ~ 烟嘴

holding /ˈhəʊldɪŋ/
n.❶an area of land held by lease 租用的土地 ❷(pl.) financial assets 金融资产

hole /həʊl/
Ⅰn.❶ a hollow place in sth.洞,孔,窟窿:There's a ~ in the wall.墙上有个洞。 ❷ a burrow of an animal (动物的)洞穴,窝:a rabbit ~ 兔子窝 ❸hollow or clarity into which a ball,etc,must be hit in various games 球洞;孔穴:a nine-~ golf course 九个洞的高尔夫球场 ‖ be in a ~ 处于困境/be in the ~ (经济上)亏空,短缺/

~ up 躲藏;离群独居/every ~ and corner 每个角落,到处/make a ~ in 在……中花费了一大笔钱;凿洞/make ~ 钻油井/pick a ~ (~s) in 在……中找岔子 Ⅱv.❶ make or dig a hole in or through 穿孔,撞破:~ a ship 撞破船只 ❷(in golf)hit the ball into a hole (高尔夫球)打(球)入洞中:~ (out)in one 一杆进洞 ‖ ~r n.挖洞者

holiday /ˈhɒlədeɪ/
Ⅰn.❶ a day of festival or recreation 假日:25 December is a ~ in many countries.12 月 25 日在很多国家是假日。 ❷(pl.)a period of rest from work or study 假期:the school ~s 学校的假期 Ⅱv. spend one's holiday 度假 ‖ make ~ 度假/on ~ 在休假中,在度假/take a ~ 休假 ‖ ~er n.度假者/~s adv.在假日,每逢假日

holidaymaker /ˈhɒlədɪˌmeɪkə(r)/
n.a person on holiday 度假者

holiness /ˈhəʊlɪnɪs/
n.❶ the state or quality of being holy 神圣 ❷(Holiness) a title given to the Pope 陛下(对教皇的尊称):Your ~ 陛下,圣座/His ~ Pope John Paul 约翰·保罗教皇陛下 /His ~ the Pope 教皇陛下

hollow /ˈhɒləʊ/
Ⅰadj.❶ having an empty space inside 空的,中空的:The pillar is ~.那根柱子是空心的。 ❷(of parts of the body) lacking flesh so that the skin sinks inwards 凹陷的:~ cheeks 深陷的脸颊 ❸(of sounds) having a ringing sound like the note when an empty container is struck (声音)空洞的:a ~ voice 空洞的声音 ❹ (of feelings, words) not real; empty of real meaning (感觉、话语)不真实的,空虚的,虚假的:~ words 空话/ ~ promises 虚伪的诺言 Ⅱn.a wide, shallow hole 洞;穴;谷地:a ~ in the ground 地上的坑 / a wooded ~ 多树木的小山谷 Ⅲv.make a hollow or hollows in 挖空,使成中空:~ out a log 把圆木挖空/ ~ a canoe out of a log 挖空圆木造独木舟 ‖ wear ~ 损耗成空壳 ‖ ~-eyed adj.眼睛凹陷的/ ~-hearted adj.不真诚的,虚伪的 ‖ ~ly

*adv.*空心地；不诚实地/ ～ness *n.*空旷；空虚

holly/'hɒli/

n. a type of evergreen tree with sharp pointed leaves and red or yellow berries, used as decoration at Christmas 冬青树（可做圣诞节装饰用）

holster/'həʊlstə(r)/

n. a leather case in which a pistol or revolver is carried (usually over the hip)手枪皮套

holy/'həʊli/

adj. ❶connected with God and religion; sacred 上帝的；神圣的；神的：the Holy Bible《圣经》/ ～ water 圣水 ❷devoted to the service of God or religion（对上帝或宗教）虔诚的：a ～ man 献身于宗教的人 ‖ a ～ terror 可怕的人；淘气的孩子

homage/'hɒmidʒ/

n. the act of respect to sb. famous (and usually dead)（对名人，通常是死者的）崇敬：We all paid ～ to the great man. 我们都崇敬这位伟人。

home/həʊm/

I *n.* ❶ the place where one lives with one's family 家，家庭：He left his ～ at sixteen. 他十六岁离家。❷ the place where one was born 家乡，祖国：He left India for ～. 他离开印度回国。❸ a place where people who are homeless, poor, old or sick may live 养育院，疗养院，收容所：a children's ～ 儿童保育院 / nursing ～ 疗养所 / a ～ for the aged 敬老院 ❹a place where sth. originates or where an animal or plant is native or exists 发源地；产地：America is the ～ of baseball. 美国是棒球的发源地。 II *adv.* ❶ to or at one's home 到家，回家，在家：He will be ～ in half an hour. 他将在半小时内到家。/ on one's way ～ 在回家的路上 ❷ at, in, or to one's native country 回本国，在本国：call an ambassador ～ 召大使回国 ❸ as far as possible or to the right place 击中要害地，深入地：hit(strike) ～ 击中要害/ strike(drive) a nail ～ 把钉子深深敲入 III *adj.* ❶ of or connected with one's home 家的，家庭的：～ life 家庭生

活/ ～ joys 家庭生活的欢乐 ❷ in one's native country; inside the country; domestic 本国的，国内的：～ products 本国产品/ ～ affairs 内政/ the ～ trade (market) 国内贸易（市场）❸ (of a game) playing in one's own ground（比赛)本地进行的：the ～ team 主队/ a ～ game 在本地举行的比赛 ‖ (be) at ～ 在家，见客，国内/be (feel) at ～ 随便，无拘束,(在……方面)熟悉/make oneself at ～ 如同在自己家一样，无拘束/drive ～ 讲透彻/(hit) ～ 打中(目标)，击中要害/one's long (last) ～ 坟墓 ‖ ～bird *n.*喜欢待在家里的人/ ～born *adj.*土生土长的/ ～grown *adj.*本国产的，土生的/ ～made *adj.*家里做的，国产的/ ～maker *n.*家庭主妇

homeland /'həʊmlænd/

n. a person's native land 家乡；祖国

homeless /'həʊmləs/

adj. having no home 无家可归的 ‖ ～ness *n.*无家可归

homely/'həʊmli/

adj. ❶simple and plain 简朴的，家常的：～ meal 一顿家常便饭 ❷ not good-looking; unattractive 不好看的：The mother is beautiful, but the daughter is ～.母亲漂亮，可女儿长得难看。 ‖ homeliness *n.*朴素；寻常；粗野

homesick /'həʊmsɪk/

adj. upset because you are away from home 想家的，思乡的 ‖ ～ness *n.*乡愁

homestead/'həʊmsted/

n. a place, especially a farm, where a family makes its home, including the land, house, and outbuildings 家宅(包括田地、房屋和库房、畜棚等)

hometown /'həʊmtaʊn/

n. the place where you were born or lived as a child 家乡，故乡

homework /'həʊmwɜːk/

n. ❶school work that has to be done at home 家庭作业 ❷preparatory work that you need to do before discussing sth., making a speech, etc.(在讨论某事，做演讲等之前需要做的)准备工作

homicide /ˈhɒmɪsaɪd/
n. ❶the illegal killing of a person；murder 谋杀，杀人 ❷a murderer 谋杀者 ‖ **homicidal** *adj.*杀人的；行凶的；杀气腾腾的

homogeneity /ˌhɒməʊdʒeˈniːɪti/
n. the quality of being homogeneous 同种；同质

homogeneous /ˌhɒməˈdʒiːniəs/
adj. of the same kind 同种的；同类的：The people of this country are ～.该国居民属于同一种族。/a ～ group 同类型的群体

homogenize /həˈmɒdʒənaɪz/
v. ❶cause to become equal or homogeneous by mixing 使匀质，使均质；使类同 ❷treat（milk）so that fat droplets are emulsified and cream does not separate；make（a mixture）become evenly spread 使（牛奶的）油脂粒均匀分布；使（混合物）均质：～d milk 均脂牛乳

homosexual /ˌhəʊməˈsekʃʊəl/
Ⅰ *adj.* sexually attracted to members of the same sex 同性恋的 Ⅱ *n.*a person who is sexually attracted to people of the same sex 同性恋者

honest /ˈɒnɪst/
adj. ❶ not lying or deceiving；truthful 诚实的，老实的，正直的：an ～ man 诚实的人/an ～ attitude 老实的态度 ❷(of actions,appearance,etc.) typical of an honest person（行为、外表等）老实的，真诚的：an ～ face 诚实坦率的脸/an ～ opinion 坦诚的意见 ❸(of wages,,etc.) fairly earned（指工资等）以正当手段挣得的：She makes a ～living by herself.她靠自己的正当收入生活。❹(of actions,,etc.) sincere but undistinguished（指行为等）真挚却平凡的 ‖ be quite ～ about it（常作插入语）老实说 ‖ ～ly *adv.*诚实地，正当地

honesty /ˈɒnəsti/
*n.*the quality of being honest 诚实，正直，坦诚：We've never doubted her ～.我们从未怀疑过她的诚实。/I must tell you, in all ～,that your chances of passing the test are not very high.我必须坦诚地告诉

你,你通过考试的机会不大。

honey /ˈhʌni/
n. ❶ the sweet sticky usually golden-brown substance produced by bees,which can be eaten 蜂蜜，蜜 ❷（used when speaking to someone you love）darling；sweetheart（爱称）宝贝，亲爱的：Come here,my ～.到这儿来,亲爱的。/I love you,～.我爱你,宝贝。 ‖ ～bee *n.*蜜蜂/～comb *n.*蜂窝,蜂巢/～dew *adj.*甘汁,蜜露 ‖ ～ed *adj.*加了蜜的；甜如蜜的

honeymoon /ˈhʌnɪmuːn/
*n.*the holiday taken by a husband and wife immediately after their marriage 蜜月

honk /hɒŋk/
Ⅰ *n.* ❶the cry of a goose 似鹅的叫声 ❷any noise like this（especially the noise made by the horn of a motorcar）似鹅叫的声音；汽车喇叭声 Ⅱ *v.*make a honk 发出鹅叫声；按汽车喇叭

honorary /ˈɒnərəri/
adj. ❶working without payment 名誉的；义务的：the ～ secretary of our club 本俱乐部的义务秘书 ❷given as an honour 荣誉的：an ～ degree of the university 大学的荣誉学位

honour /ˈɒnə(r)/
Ⅰ *n.* ❶ good name；fame；glory 荣誉，名誉，光荣：win ～ for one's motherland 为祖国赢得荣誉,为祖国争光 ❷ great respect,often publicly expressed 尊敬,敬意：hold sb.in ～ 尊敬某人/show ～ to sb.向某人表示敬意 ❸ sth. special and desirable（in polite formulas）荣幸（客套话）：I have the ～ to inform you that.我荣幸地通知您。❹a person or thing that brings honour 引以为荣的人（或物）：He's an ～ to his parents.他父母以他为荣。❺a title to some judges or people of importance 大人（对法官或高级官员的尊称）：Your（His）Honour 阁下，先生 ❻a tangible symbol signifying approval or distinction or mark of respect 荣誉的标志（如奖品、勋章、绶带等）Ⅱ *v.* ❶ show respect for；give public praise and distinction to sb.尊敬；敬重；给……以荣誉；使增光：They were ～ed with the title of

Advanced Collective.他们被授予"先进集体"的光荣称号。/Will you ~ me with a visit? 可否请您光临？/ an ~ed guest 贵宾/ ~ one's father and mother 尊敬父母 ❷ accept and pay when due 承兑；兑现：~ a bill(cheque,draft) 承兑票据(支票、汇票) ‖ do ~ (to) 表示敬意,纪念/do one the ~ (of) 请屈驾……/have the ~ (of) 有幸……;荣幸地/in ~ of 为了(纪念或表敬意而举行某种活动)/give one's word of ~ (请……)以人格担保/~ roll 光荣榜/with ~s 以优异成绩

honourable/'ɒnərəbl/
　adj. deserving or satisfying honour 荣誉的,光荣的；体面的：He has done ~ work.他做了体面的工作。

hood/hʊd/
　n. ❶ a piece of clothing that covers the head and neck,often fastened to a coat 头巾；兜帽：cover one's head with a ~ 头上包着头巾 ❷ the covering of an open car 车篷：It's raining.Put the ~ up.下雨了,把车篷支起来吧。

hoof/huːf/
　n. (*pl*.~s or hooves) the hard lower parts of the foot of certain animals, as of the horse (马等动物的)足,蹄：A horse has ~s.马有蹄。

hook/hʊk/
　Ⅰ *n*. ❶ a bent piece of metal or plastic, for catching hold of sth.or for hanging sth.on 钩,挂钩：a fish ~ 钓鱼钩 ❷ a curved tool for cutting 弯刀,镰刀：a reap-ing ~(收割用的)镰刀 / a bill~ 砍树枝的弯刀 ❸ (in boxing) a blow given with the elbow bent (拳击)钩拳,钩击：a left ~ 左钩击 Ⅱ *v*. ❶ attach sth.with a hook 用钩钩住：~ a fish 用钩钓鱼 ❷fasten with a hook 用钩连接；扣住：Hook my dress up.把我的连衣裙钩扣拉上来(扣起来)。‖ by ~ or by crook 千方百计,不择手段/ ~, line, and sinker 全部地(相信)/ ~ up 通电；联播

hooked/hʊkt/
　adj. ❶ shaped like a hook 钩形的：a ~ nose 鹰钩鼻子 ❷addicted to sth.上了瘾的 ❸(of a rug) made by looping yarn

through canvas with a hook (小地毯)用钩针编织的

hookworm/'hʊkwɜːm/
　n. a worm, the male of which has hook-like spines, that can infest the intestines of people and animals 钩虫(寄生于人和动物的肠道)

hooligan/'huːlɪɡən/
　n. a man or boy making disturbances in the streets or other public places (小)流氓,恶棍

hoop/huːp/
　n. a thin ring of metal, wood, plastic, etc. 箍：Wooden barrels are fitted with iron ~s.木桶上装着铁箍。

hooray/hʊ'reɪ/
　int.&*n*.(also **hurray**) an exclamation of joy or approval 好哇,好；万岁(用于表示喜悦、赞成)

hoot/huːt/
　Ⅰ *n*.❶the cry made by an owl 猫头鹰的叫声 ❷a loud high-pitched noise showing anger, disapproval, amusement, etc.(表示愤怒、不赞成或逗乐的)尖叫 ❸ noise made by the horn of a motorcar, factory whistle, etc.汽车喇叭声；工厂汽笛声 Ⅱ *v*.❶utter the characteristic sound of owls (猫头鹰)鸣叫；发出像猫头鹰似的叫声；发嘟嘟声：I heard an owl ~ing.我听见了猫头鹰在叫。❷make a loud noise 喊叫；大叫：He ~ed with laughter.他狂笑。/They ~ed him down.他们给他喝倒彩。/At the corner I ~ed my horn.在拐弯处我按了喇叭。

hooter/'huːtə(r)/
　n.❶a siren or steam whistle used as a signal (用作信号的)警报声,汽笛声 ❷a vehicle's horn 车辆的喇叭

hop/hɒp/
　Ⅰ *v*.(-pp-)❶ (of person) jump on one foot only；(of birds or other smd)jump with all feet together (人)单足跳；(鸟或小动物)齐足跳：The squirrel ~ped up and down.松鼠蹦蹦跳跳。/The bird ~ped onto my finger.鸟跳到我的手指上。❷ move quickly or suddenly 快速移

动：She ～ped on her bike（into a car）and rushed off.她迅速跳上自行车（跳进汽车）匆匆离去。II *n.* ❶ an act of hopping；an act of jumping upward or forward（单足或齐足）跳跃：With one ～ the frog was back in the pond.青蛙一跳就回到了池塘里。❷ the distance travelled by a plane before landing；a short, quick trip by plane（飞机降落前的）一段航程；（飞机的）短途快速旅行：It's a short ～ from Chengdu to Chongqing.从成都到重庆是短途飞行。‖ be ～ping mad 气得跳脚, 怒不可遏/ catch（sb.）on the ～ 出其不意抓住（某人）, 趁人不备/ ～ it 走开/ ～, skip（step）and jump 三级跳/ ～ to it 开始做事/on the ～ 到处奔忙 ‖ ～scotch *n.*跳房子(一种儿童游戏)/ ～per *n.*跳跃的昆虫；袋鼠

hope/həʊp/

I *v.*wish for and expect 希望, 盼望：After this dry weather everyone ～s for rain.干燥的天气后, 大家都盼着下雨。II *n.* ❶ the feeling that one desires and expects 希望, 期望：hold out a ～ of victory 抱着胜利的希望/ live up to the people's ～s 不辜负人民的期望/ There's not much ～ that he is still alive.他仍然活着的希望不大。❷ a person, thing, on which hope is based on 被寄托希望的人（或物）：You're my only ～（last ～）.你是我唯一的希望（最后的希望）。‖（a）forlorn ～ 微乎其微的希望/beyond（past）～ 没有希望/ ～ against ～ 抱一线希望/ ～ chest 女子的嫁妆, 装嫁妆的箱子/in ～s of, in the ～ of, in the ～ that 怀着……的希望/live in ～(s) 仍然希望情况好起来/lay(pin) one's ～(s) on 把希望寄托在……上/raise(sb.'s) ～s 引起（某人的)希望

hopeful/ˈhəʊpfl/

I *adj.* ❶（of people）having or feeling hope（人）抱有希望的；be (feel) ～ about the future 对未来抱有希望/feel ～ of success 对成功充满希望 ❷ giving cause for hope of success；promising 有希望的, 有前途的：He's the most ～ man in poli-

tics.他在政界是最有希望的人。/ He's quite a ～ pupil.他是很有发展前途的学生。II *n.*a person who wants to succeed or seems likely to succeed 有希望成功的人：a presidential ～ 可望当上总统的人 ‖ ～ness *n.*抱有希望

hopeless/ˈhəʊpləs/

adj. ❶ feeling no hope；giving or promising no hope 不抱希望的, 绝望的, 无希望的：～ tears 绝望的眼泪 /She had a ～ look on her face.她脸上露出绝望的神色。❷incurable 不可救药的；无法医治的：～ illness 绝症 ❸ useless 无用的, 无效的, 白费的：Your work is ～.你的工作是无用的。

horde/hɔːd/

*n.*a great number of；a crowd of 大帮；大群：Hordes of people tried to get into the hall.乱纷纷的人群试图拥入大厅。

horizon/həˈraɪzn/

n.（usually *pl.*）❶ the limit of one's view across the surface of the earth, where the sky seems to meet the earth or sea 地平线：The sun sank below the ～.太阳落到地平线以下了。❷the limit of one's ideas, knowledge, or experience 眼界；见识；阅历：Meeting new friends widened the young man's ～s.与新朋友们相识使这个年轻人扩大了眼界。

horizontal/ˌhɒrɪˈzɒntl/

*adj.*parallel to the horizon 水平的, 横向的 ‖ ～ity *n.*水平状态；*adj.*水平的；地平的

hormone/ˈhɔːməʊn/

*n.*a type of chemical substance made by certain glands of the body 荷尔蒙；激素

horn/hɔːn/

n. ❶ the hard, curved outgrowths on the head of cattle, deer, and some other animals（牛、羊、鹿等的）角：A bull has two ～s.公牛有两只角。❷ a substance made of this 角质, 角质物：a ～ knife 角柄小刀/a ～ spoon 角质调羹 ❸ a musical wind instrument that makes a loud noise when you blow through it 号角；喇叭；号；管：a hunting ～ 猎号/ a French ～ 法

国号 ❹ the device on a car, bus, etc. which makes a noise as a signal 汽车喇叭: The driver blew (sounded) his ~ when the child stepped in front of his car. 当那孩子走到他车前时，司机按响了喇叭。‖ blow (toot) one's own ~ 自吹自擂/draw (haul, pull) in one's ~s 退缩，克制自己/lift up one's ~ 趾高气扬，盛气凌人/show one's ~s 露出凶相/take the bull by the ~s 不畏艰险‖ ~er n.制角器者，吹号角者/ ~ed adj.有角的/ ~less adj.无角的

hornbill /ˈhɔːnˌbɪl/
n. a bird with a horn-like growth on its beak 犀鸟

hornet /ˈhɔːnɪt/
n. a large wasp which lives in nests and have a powerful sting 大黄蜂

horoscope /ˈhɒrəskəʊp/
n. a written or spoken description of someone's character, life, and future, which is gained by knowing the positions of the stars or planets at the time of his or her birth and the effects these are said to have 占星(根据星象算命)

horrible /ˈhɒrəbl/
adj. ❶causing great shock, fear and disgust 可怕的；令人恐惧的: Murder is a ~ crime. 谋杀是一种可怕的罪行。❷very unkind or unpleasant; awful 讨厌的；糟透的；难看的: What ~ weather! 这鬼天气! /What a ~ meal! 真难吃的一顿饭! ‖ ~ness *n.*可怕的事或物/horribly *adv.*可怕地；非常地.

horrid /ˈhɒrɪd/
adj. very unpleasant; disgusting 令人极不愉快的；讨厌透顶的: Why are you so ~ to him? 为什么你这么讨厌他?

horrific /həˈrɪfɪk/
adj. causing or intended to cause horror; horrifying 令人恐惧的，可怕的: The film showed the most ~ murder scenes. 那部影片有极恐怖的谋杀场面。

horrify /ˈhɒrɪfaɪ/
v. fill someone with horror, or shock someone 使恐怖；使惊骇: the horrified

spectators 惊骇万分的观众 ‖ horrified *adj.*惊骇的；带有恐怖感的

horror /ˈhɒrə(r)/
n. ❶a feeling of extreme fear or dislike 恐怖；恐惧；憎恶: When I had read it I was filled with ~.我读过它后，心里充满了恐惧。/She sat motionless with ~.她吓得一动也不动地坐着。/His dreams were full of ~s.他做梦梦见的尽是些恐怖的东西。❷a naughty child 顽皮的孩子: The little ~ never stops playing tricks on his parents.这个小淘气总是不停地作弄他父母。‖ give (sb.) the ~s(使某人吓得)发抖/have a ~ of (sth.) 讨厌，害怕(某事)/in ~ 恐惧地/to one's ~ 使感到惊恐的是…… ‖ ~ fiction (films, comics) *n.*恐怖小说(电影、连环画)/ ~-struck *adj.*受惊吓的

horse /hɔːs/
n. ❶a large strong four-legged animal with hard feet (hooves), which people ride on and use for pulling and carrying heavy things 马: mount (dismount) a ~ 上(下)马/ ride a ~ 骑马 ❷soldiers riding on horses; cavalry (总称)骑兵: and foot 骑兵和步兵/ light ~ 轻骑兵 ❸an exercise apparatus for jumping over; vaulting horse 跳(鞍)马(体操器械) ‖ bet on the wrong ~ (赛马中)下错赌注，支持错了人/be on one's high ~ 趾高气扬/change ~s 换主持人；换(领导)班子/eat like a ~吃得很多/lock the barn door after the ~ is stolen 亡羊补牢/talk ~ 说大话/work like a ~ 辛苦地干活 ‖ ~back *n.*马背; *adv.*在马背上/ ~ box *n.*有篷的运马货车/ ~ doctor *n.*马医；蹩脚医生/ ~ faced *adj.*马脸的；脸长而难看的/ ~laugh *n.*纵声大笑，哄笑/ ~play *n.*粗鄙而喧闹的游戏，胡闹/ ~racing (~ race) *n.*赛马/ ~-sense *n.*常识/ ~ whip *n.*马鞭; *v.*用马鞭抽打

horseman /ˈhɔːsmən/
n. (*pl.* horsemen) a rider on horseback, especially a skilled one 骑马者(尤指有技巧的) ‖ ~ship *n.*马术；骑术

horsepower /ˈhɔːsˌpaʊə/
n. a unit for measuring the power of an

engine (550 foot-pounds per second, about 750 watts) 马力(在英制里,1 马力等于每秒钟做 550 英尺磅力的功,约 750 瓦特)

horseshoe /ˈhɔːsʃuː/
n. ❶ a U-shaped strip of metal nailed to a horse's hoof 马蹄铁,马掌 ❷ anything shaped like this 马蹄铁形之物：The seats were arranged in a ～ around the stage.那些座位被排列成马蹄形围着舞台。

hors(e)y /ˈhɔːsi/
adj. ❶ to do with or like a horse 马的；似马的 ❷ interested in horses and horse racing 对马(或赛马)感兴趣的

horticulture /ˈhɔːtɪkʌltʃə(r)/
n. gardening; the growing of flowers, fruits and vegetables 园艺

hose /həʊz/
Ⅰ *n.* a long, flexible pipe made of rubber, canvas, or plastic for directing water on to fires, watering gardens, etc. (橡皮、帆布或塑料制成的用于救火、浇花等的)软管：a fire ～ 救火水管 / ～s for watering the garden 花园洒水用的水管 Ⅱ *v.* water or wash with a hose 用水管冲洗：～ the car 用软管输水洗汽车

hospitable /hɒˈspɪtəbl, ˈhɒspɪtəbl/
adj. friendly, generous and kind to guests 好客的；殷勤的

hospital /ˈhɒspɪtl/
n. a place where people are treated for illness or injuries 医院：a field ～ 野战医院 / a mental ～ 精神病医院 / be in ～ 在住院 / walk the ～s 当实习医生 ‖ ～ism *n.* 医疗制度 / ～ize *v.* 把……送入医院治疗

hospitality /ˌhɒspɪˈtæləti/
n. friendly and generous reception and entertainment towards guests 好客,盛情款待：Many thanks for the ～ you showed me.多谢你对我的款待。

host /həʊst/
Ⅰ *n.* ❶ the person who invited the guests and entertains them; a country city or organization provides the facilities for an e-vent to take place 主人；东道主：act as ～ 做东道主 / a ～ country 东道国 ❷ the keeper of a hotel 旅馆主人 ❸ a large number (of) 一大群；许多：a ～ of friends 许多朋友 / ～s of trouble 许多麻烦 / a ～ of ideas 许多念头 ❹ a compere of a television program, , etc. (电视节目等的)主持人：Who will be the ～ of tonight's show? 今晚演出的主持人是谁? ❺ people, animal or plant where a people or parasite lives 寄主,宿主：a family 寄宿家庭 Ⅱ *v.* act as a host or hostess of an activity or to a person 主办(某活动)；招待(某人)：Which company is ～ing the carnival next year? 明年的嘉年华由哪个公司主办?

hostage /ˈhɒstɪdʒ/
n. a person who is kept as a prisoner by an enemy so that the other side will meet what the enemy demands 人质,抵押品：be held as a ～ 被扣作人质

hostel /ˈhɒstl/
n. ❶ a building in which board and lodging are provided (for students, workmen in training, etc.) (为学生、受培训的工人等提供的)旅馆,招待所：a young men's ～ 青年招待所 ❷ an inn 旅店

hostess /ˈhəʊstəs/
n. ❶ a female host 女主人：act as ～ 做女主人 / She will be ～ to party of seven this evening.今晚她将做七人聚会的女主人。❷ a woman inn-keeper 旅馆女主人

hostile /ˈhɒstaɪl/
adj. ❶ showing extreme dislike or disapproval; unfriendly 怀有敌意的；敌对的：be ～ to 对……怀有敌意 / ～ looks 敌视的神色 ❷ belonging to an enemy 敌人的,敌方的：a ～ army 敌军 / ～ forces 敌方兵力 ‖ ～ly *adv.* 敌对地

hostility /hɒˈstɪləti/
n. ❶ enmity; a hostile disposition 敌对,敌视,敌意：show ～ to sb.对某人表示敌意 ❷ (*pl.*) acts of fighting in war 战斗,战争：Hostilities have broken out between the two countries.两国之间爆发了战争。

hot /hɒt/

H

adj.(-tt-)❶ having a lot of heat;not cold 热的: ～ weather 炎热的天气/a ～ bath 热水浴/like a cat on ～ bricks 像热锅上的蚂蚁 ❷ having a strong,burning taste 辣的:Pepper makes food ～.胡椒使食物变辣。❸ (of news) fresh,very recent and usually sensational (新闻)最近的,最新的: ～ news 最新消息 /The book is ～ off the press.这本书是最新出版的。❹ full of strong feeling;easy and quick to get angry 强烈的,急躁的:a ～ temper 急躁的脾气/a ～ argument 激烈的争论/be ～ for reform 迫切要求改革 ❺gifted;knowledgeable 有天赋的;有丰富知识的 ‖ blow ～ and cold 犹豫不定,变化无常/ ～ air 空话,胡说八道/～ dog 热狗(一种面包)/ ～ and heavy 激烈的/(be) ～ on sb.'s trail(track) 紧紧跟踪(紧追)某人/ ～ up 加热,加剧,激化/ ～ water 热水;麻烦/ make it ～ for 惩治 ‖ -blooded *adj.*易激动的,热切的/—foot *adv.*火速地,匆忙地/v.急匆匆地走/ ～-shot *n.*快车(船或飞机)/～ spring *n.*温泉/ ～-water bottle (bag) *n.*热水袋/ ～-water heating *n.*暖气设备/ ～wire *n.*(好)消息 ‖ ～ness *n.*热烈;炎热

hotbed /'hɒtbed/
*n.*❶a bed covered with glass and heated by rotting manure to promote the growth of plant (用草覆盖用以发酵的)温床 ❷ an environment favorable to the growth of sth. (促使某事物发展的环境)温床

hotdog /'hɒtˌdɒg/
*n.*a hot sausage served in a long,soft roll 热狗

hotel /həʊ'tel/
*n.*a building where meals and rooms are provided 旅社,旅馆:We put up at a ～ for the night.我们在旅馆过夜。

hothead /'hɒthed/
*n.*an impetuous person 冲动的人;急躁的人 ‖ ～ed *adj.*暴躁的;易怒的;急性子的

hothouse /'hɒthaʊs/
*n.*a heated building made of glass, for growing plants in a warm temperature 温室

hotline /'hɒtlaɪn/
*n.*a telephone line for direct,instant communication between the public and an organization or,between the heads of state in different countries(公众与机构之间的)热线;(两国首脑间的)热线

hotly /'hɒtli/
*adv.*❶ with anger or other strong feelings 生气地;强烈地;激动地:The rumour was ～ denied.这个流言遭到强烈的否认。/a ～ debated issue 一个备受争论的问题 ❷ closely and eagerly 热切地

hotplate /'hɒtpleɪt/
n. an electric appliance for heating or cooking or keeping food warm 电炉;电热锅

hound /haʊnd/
Ⅰ *n.*a type of dog used for hunting 猎狗:A ～ hunts by scent.猎狗靠嗅觉捕猎。Ⅱ *v.*chase, hunt or worry continually 追逐;追逼;追猎:be ～ed by reporters 被记者纠缠

hour /'aʊə(r)/
*n.*❶a period of 60 minutes 小时;钟头:hire a horse by the ～ 按钟头租用一匹马 ❷a time of day when a new hour starts 每小时开始,某时零分:She arrived on the ～. 她准时到达。❸ the distance travelled or work done in an hour 一小时所走的距离:It's only an ～ away.那儿离这儿只有一小时的路程。❹(*pl.*)a fixed point or period of time, especially one that is set aside for a particular purpose or activity 固定的时间(尤指工作时间):The office (bussiness) ～s are(from) 8 a.m.to 5 p.m.办公(营业)时间从上午八点到下午五点。❺an important moment or period 重要时刻:in the ～ of danger 在危急时刻 ‖ after ～s下班后,打烊后/at all ～s 在任何时间,一直不断地/at the eleventh ～ 在最后时间,在危急之时/by the ～ 按钟点(计)/～ after ～ 一小时又一小时,连续地/keep early (late) ～s 早(晚)睡早(晚)起/off (out of) ～s 业余时间(办公时间以外)/serve the ～ 随波逐流/the rush ～ (交通)拥挤时间,高峰时间/～ hand (钟表的)时针

hourglass /'aʊəglɑːs/

n. a glass container for measuring time, which is narrow in the middle like a figure 8 so that the sand inside can run slowly from the top half to the bottom, taking exactly one hour (计时用的)沙漏

hourly /ˈauəli/

Ⅰ *adj.* ❶done or occurring every hour 每小时一次的:an ～ service of trains 一小时一班的火车 ❷continual 不断的,经常的:He lives in ～ fear of discovery. 他时时刻刻都怕被人发现。Ⅱ *adv.* ❶every hour;once every hour 每小时,每小时一次:The medicine should be taken ～. 此药应每小时服一次。❷at any hour 时时,随时:We are expecting news ～. 我们时时盼望新消息。

house

Ⅰ /haus/*n.* ❶ a building where people live 房屋,住宅:from ～ to ～ 挨家挨户地 ❷ all the people who live together in such a building 一家人;同住一幢房子的人:The whole ～ was waken up. 全家人都被叫醒了。❸a building for animals or goods (动物或放货物的)棚舍:a hen ～ 鸡舍/ a store ～ 仓库 ❹ a business firm,controlled by a family or one in the business of publishing 商号;出版社;所:the wholesale ～ 批发商行/ a publishing ～ 出版社/ a printing ～ 印刷所 ❺ an important family,especially noble or royal 名门;家族;王室:the House of Windsor 英国王室 ❻assembly 立法机关,议院:the Upper(Lower) House (议会的)上(下)议院/the House of Lords(Commons)(英国的)上(下)议院 ❼a theatre or audience in a theatre 剧院;(剧院)观众:a full ～ 满座(客满) Ⅱ /hauz/ *v.* ❶ provide with a house 提供住处,给……房子住:～ the flood victims 给(水灾)灾民提供住房 ❷ store (goods) 收藏,存放:～ farm tools in a shed 把农具放在小屋里 Ⅲ /haus/*adj.* used by or intended for people working in a particular firm or industry 内部传阅的:a ～ magazine 内部发行的杂志 ‖ **bring down the ～** 使全场为之倾倒(博得满场喝彩)/**get on like a ～ on fire** 一见如故/**keep ～** 管理家务,

当家/**put(set) one's ～ in order** 把事情安顿好/**under ～ arrest** 被软禁 ‖ ～**boat** *n.* 可供住家的船,水上住家/ ～**bound** *adj.* 闭门不出的/*n.* 入室行/ ～ **dog** *n.* 看家狗/ ～**father(mother)** *n.* (孤儿院的)男(女)监护人(代行父母职责)/ ～ **man** *n.* 实习医生/ ～**master** *n.* (学生宿舍的)舍监

housebreaking /ˈhausbreikiŋ/

n. breaking into a building to commit a crime 侵入家宅;破门入户罪 ‖ **housebreaker** *n.* 强盗,侵入家宅者;拆屋者

household /ˈhaushəuld/

n. all the people living together in a house 同住在一家的人;全家人;户:a peasant ～ 农户/ ～ expenses 家庭开支/ The whole ～ was(were) up early. 全家人都起得早。 ‖ ～ **name** (**word**) 家喻户晓的人(或物) ‖ ～**er** *n.* 房主,户主;占有房子的人

housekeeper /ˈhauskiːpə(r)/

n. a person, typically a woman, employed to look after a household (多指妇女)管家

housekeeping /ˈhauskiːpiŋ/

n. ❶ management of household affairs 料理家务,管家 ❷money set aside for this 家用开支 ❸routine work such as record-keeping and administration 内务处理;管理工作

housewife /ˈhauswaif/

n. (*pl.* housewives) a married woman whose main occupation is looking after the household 家庭主妇,家庭妇女 ‖ ～**ly** *adj.* 家庭主妇的;节俭的

housework /ˈhauswɜːk/

n. the regular work done in housekeeping, such as cleaning and cooking 家务劳动;家事

housing /ˈhauziŋ/

n. ❶houses and flats;accommodation 房屋,住宅 ❷a rigid cover enclosing a piece of machinery 外套;外壳;外罩 ❸ a shallow trench or groove cut in a piece of wood to allow another piece to be attached to it (木块上的)槽;柄穴

hover /ˈhɒvə(r)/

*v.*❶ (of birds) remain in the air at one place (指鸟)翱翔;盘旋:a hawk ~ing over head 在头上翱翔的鹰 /a helicopter ~ing over the lawn 盘旋于草地上空的一架直升机 ❷ (of persons) wait about; remain at or near (指人)徘徊,逗留:~ between life and death 处于生死关头 / The boys kept ~ing and interrupting her.男孩子们老是在旁边打扰她。

hovercraft /ˈhɒvəkrɑːft/
*n.*a vehicle that travels over land or water on a cushion of air thrust downwards from its engines 气垫车;气垫船

how /haʊ/
Ⅰ *adv.*❶ (used in questions to ask) in what way (用于疑问句中)怎样,如何: How do you know that? 你怎么知道的? ❷ used to ask about health (用于询问身体健康状况)好: How are you? 你好吗? /How's your father? 你爸好吗? ❸ used in questions about time, amount, or size (用于疑问句中)多久;多少;什么程度: How long have you learned English? 你学英语有多久了? ❹ used to express exclamation (表示感叹)多么: How pleased I am to see you! 我见到你们多么高兴啊! Ⅱ *n.*the way sth. can be done (做某事的)方法:the ~ and the why 方法和理由

however /haʊˈevə(r)/
Ⅰ *adv.*❶ in whatever degree 无论如何,不管怎样: However hard he tried, he can't win the game.不管他如何努力,他仍无法赢得这场比赛。 ❷ in spite of this;nevertheless 可是,然而,仍然: I'd like to go with you,~,my hands are full.我很想和你一道去,可是我忙不过来。 ❸ (showing surprise)how (表示惊讶)怎么: However did you find it? 你究竟怎么找到的? Ⅱ *conj.*in whatever way 不管用什么方法: However I cook eggs, she still refuses to eat them.不管我用什么方法煮鸡蛋,她还是不肯吃。

howl /haʊl/
Ⅰ *n.*a long, loud cry of dogs, wolves, etc. (狼、狗等的)嚎叫,嗥鸣 Ⅱ *v.*❶ give a long, loud crying sound 号叫:The wolf ~ed all night.那只狼整夜嚎个不停。/The wind ~ed in the trees.风在林中呼啸。 ❷ give a long loud cry expressing pain, anger or unhappiness (人因痛苦、愤怒、不愉快等)号叫:号啕大哭,大声哭:The baby's ~ing.婴儿在大声啼哭。 ❸ utter in a very loud voice 大声说出(或发出):He ~ed (out) my name.他大声叫出了我的名字。

hub /hʌb/
*n.*❶ the central part of a wheel (轮)毂 ❷ a central and important part of activity or transportation;a focal point around which events revolve 中心;活动中心: This office is the ~ of the whole company.这个办公室是全公司的中心。

hubbub /ˈhʌbʌb/
n. loud and confused noise from many sources 吵闹声;喧哗声:I could not hear myself speak above the ~.在一片喧闹声中我听不见自己的讲话声。

huddle /ˈhʌdl/
Ⅰ *v.*(cause to)crowd together, in a group or in a pile (使)挤成一堆,缩成一团:The children ~d together like a flock of sheep.孩子们像羊群一样挤在一起。/~ things together 把东西乱堆在一起 Ⅱ *n.*a crowd of people or things, close together and not in any ordered arrangement (杂乱的)一堆东西;一群人‖ go into a ~ 聚集在一起(磋商、密谈)

hue /hjuː/
*n.*❶ a colour 颜色,色彩:the ~s of the woods in autumn 林中秋色 ❷the quality of a colour as determined by its dominant wavelength 色调;色度;色泽

huff /hʌf/
*n.*a state of irritation or annoyance 生气;发怒:He walked away in a ~.他怒气冲冲地走了。

huffy /ˈhʌfi/
*adj.*❶ in a huff;sulky 怒气冲冲的;气鼓鼓的 ❷ easily offended;touchy 容易生气的;爱发脾气的

hug /hʌg/
Ⅰ *v.*(-gg-)❶ hold (sb.) tightly in the

arms, especially as a sign of love 紧抱, 搂抱：She ~ged her daughter when she saw her. 她一见到女儿就紧紧拥抱着她。❷ hold on to（an idea）with a feeling of pleasure or safety 坚持(意见)：He smiled and ~ged the thought to himself. 他笑着, 内心坚持着自己的想法。❸go along while staying near 靠近……走：The boat ~ged the coast. 船紧靠海岸行驶。Ⅱ *n.* a tight embrace 紧紧拥抱：She gave her little boy a ~ before he went to school. 孩子上学前, 她紧紧拥抱了他一下。‖ ~ **oneself** 沾沾自喜, 得意, 暗暗高兴

huge /hjuːdʒ/
adj. very large; very big; very great 巨大的; 极大的; 庞大的：The elephant is a ~ animal. 象是庞大的动物。

hugely /hjuːdʒli/
adv. very much; extremely 巨大地; 非常地：a ~ expensive house 十分昂贵的房子

huh /hʌ/
int. used for asking a question or for expressing surprise or disapproval 哼, 嘿, 呵（用于发问或表示惊讶、异议)：It's pretty big, ~? 那东西真大, 嘿？

hulk /hʌlk/
n. ❶a ship that is too old to be used at sea 废船 ❷a big, clumsy person 巨大笨重的人 ‖ ~ing *adj.* 笨重的; 庞大的

hum /hʌm/
Ⅰ *v.* (-mm-) ❶ make a low continuous sound as bees do 发连续低沉的声音; 嗡嗡作响 ❷ utter with the lips closed; not using words （人)发哼哼声; 哼(曲调)：~ a song 哼歌曲 ❸ (of work being carried out) be active; move fast 活跃, 忙碌：Things are starting to ~ (with activity). 气氛变得活跃起来。❹ smell unpleasantly 发出臭味：What is it which is ~ing in the kitchen? 厨房里的什么在发出臭味？Ⅱ *n.* the sound of humming 嗡嗡声

human /ˈhjuːmən/
Ⅰ *adj.* ❶ of or concerning people, especially as opposed to animals, plants, or machines 人的, 人类的：~ race 人类/~

behaviour 人的行为/~ nature 人性 ❷ showing the feelings, especially those of kindness, which people are supposed to have 有人情味的; 通人性的：a story with lots of ~ interest 一个很有人情味的故事/ He is quite ~, actually. 事实上, 他是很有人情味的。Ⅱ *n.* any living or extinct member characterized by superior intelligence, articulate speech, and erect carriage 人; 人类 ‖ ~ness *n.* 为人; 人情味

humane /hjuːˈmeɪn/
adj. ❶compassionate or merciful 仁慈的, 同情的 ❷inflicting as little pain as possible, especially in killing animals（尤指杀动物时)使少受痛苦的 ‖ ~ly *adv.* 人道地; 富有人情味地; 慈悲地

humanism /ˈhjuːmənɪzəm/
n. an outlook or system of thought attaching prime importance to human rather than divine or supernatural matters 人道主义; 人本主义

humanitarian /hjuːˌmænɪˈteərɪən/
Ⅰ *n.* a person concerned with working for all the welfare of all human beings 人道主义者, 慈善家; Ⅱ *adj.* ❶marked by humanistic values and devotion to human welfare 博爱的; 仁慈的; 慈善的 ❷of or relating to or characteristic of humanitarianism 人道主义的：These plays are ~. 这些戏是关于人道主义的。

humanity /hjuːˈmænəti/
n. ❶ the quality of being humane or human 仁爱; 人情; 人性; 人道：They treated the prisoners with ~. 他们对囚徒很人道。❷human beings generally 人, 人类：This new technology will help all ~. 这种新技术将有益于全人类。❸(**humanities**) learning or literature concerned with human culture, especially literature, history, art, music and philosophy 人文科学（尤指文学, 历史, 艺术, 音乐和哲学)

humankind /ˈhjuːmənkaɪnd/
n. human beings collectively（总称)人类：the origin of ~ 人类的起源

H

humanly /'hju:mənli/

adv. ❶ in a human way, from a human point of view 从人类角度；以人类方式 ❷ by human means, with human limitations 依靠人力；在人力所及的范围：We did all that was ～ possible. 我们做了所有人力所能及的事情。

humble /'hʌmbl/

Ⅰ *adj.* ❶ having or showing a modest opinion of oneself, one's position, etc. 谦卑的, 恭顺的：in my ～ opinion 依本人愚见 / a ～ man 一个谦卑的人 ❷ low in rank or position; unimportant 地位低下的, 卑贱的：men of ～ birth 出身卑微的人 / a ～ home 简陋的家 Ⅱ *v.* cause to feel shame; lower the rank or self importance of 使差辱；卑残；压低（地位、身份等）：～ oneself 自卑, 低声下气 / ～ sb.'s pride 压下某人气焰 ‖ ～ness *n.* 谦逊；恭顺 / humbly *adv.* 谦恭地

humdrum /'hʌmdrʌm/

adj. dull, ordinary or boring 单调的；索然寡味的：Life in a small village can be very ～. 小村子里的生活可能是平淡无趣的。

humid /'hju:mɪd/

adj. (usually of an atmosphere or climate) damp and usually very hot（通常指环境或气候）湿润的, 潮湿的 ‖ ～ity /hju:'mɪdəti/ *n.* 潮湿；湿气；湿润

humiliate /hju:'mɪlɪeɪt/

v. make ashamed; hurt the pride of 羞辱；伤……的自尊：They ～d us by laughing at everything we said. 他们对我们的每一句话都加以嘲笑, 使我们出丑。 ‖ humiliating *adj.* 丢脸的；羞辱性的 / humiliation /hju:ˌmɪlɪ'eɪʃn/ *n.* 丢脸；蒙羞

humility /hju:'mɪləti/

n. being humble or modest 谦逊

hummingbird /'hʌmɪŋbɜ:d/

n. a small tropical bird that vibrates its wings rapidly, producing a humming sound 蜂鸟（一种热带小鸟, 快速扇动翅膀, 发出嗡嗡声）

humo(u)r /'hju:mə(r)/

Ⅰ *n.* ❶ an ability to cause to feel amusement; a quality in sth. that makes you laugh 幽默；幽默感；幽默性：They have a good (keen, no sense of) ～. 他们很有（有很强的、缺乏）幽默感。/ His reports are famous for their ～. 他的报告以幽默著称。 ❷ temper or mood 脾性；情绪, 心情：He was in a good (bad) ～. 他兴致勃勃（兴致索然）。 Ⅱ *v.* make sb. happy by doing what he wants 逗……高兴；迁就……以使高兴：They ～ed him by agreeing they were wrong. 他们用承认自己不对的办法来哄着他。 ‖ ～ous *adj.* 幽默的；有趣的/ ～ist *n.* 谈吐幽默风趣的人；幽默作家

hump /hʌmp/

n. a round lump, e.g. on a camel's back or on a person's back 驼背；驼峰；圆形隆起的：Camels have ～s. 骆驼有驼峰。

hunch /hʌntʃ/

Ⅰ *n.* ❶ a hump 肉峰, 驼背 ❷ an idea or belief based on intuition and not on evidence 直觉, 预感：It seems that the policeman's ～ is right. 看起来这个警察的直觉是对的。 Ⅱ *v.* arch one's back 弯成弓状：He sat ～ed up on a chair. 他弓着背坐在椅子上。 ‖ ～back *n.* 驼背的人

hundred /'hʌndrəd/

num. the number 100 百, 百个（人或物）：(one) ～ men 一百个人 ‖ a cool ～ 百镑巨款, 巨款 / a ～ and one 许多 / one percent 百分之百, 完全 / by the ～ (by ～s) 数以百计, 大批大批地 / like a ～ of bricks 以压倒的势力, 来势猛烈的 ‖ ～fold *adj. & adv.* 一百倍的（地）

hundredth /'hʌndrədθ/

n. ❶ the one that you count as number one hundred in a series 第一百：his ～ birthday 他的百岁诞辰 ❷ each of one hundred equal parts of sth. 百分之一

hunger /'hʌŋgə(r)/

Ⅰ *n.* ❶ the feeling of being hungry 饥饿：die of (from) ～ 饿死 / satisfy one's ～ 充饥 ❷ a strong desire 渴望, 欲望：a ～ for excitement(adventure) 寻求刺激（冒险）的欲望 / have a ～ for knowledge 渴望（得到）知识 ❸ a lack of food 缺粮, 饥荒：There is ～ in the flooded area. 洪灾区在闹饥荒。 Ⅱ *v.* ❶ have a strong desire

or craving for 渴望,渴求 ❷starve 挨饿:
try to ～ sb.into surrender 企图以断粮迫
使某人投降

hungry /ˈhʌŋgri/
*adj.*❶having an uncomfortable or painful
feeling in stomach and wanting to eat
food 饿的;显出饥饿样子的:The orphan
had a ～ look.那孤儿面带饥色。❷cau-
sing hunger 引起饥饿的:Haymaking is
～ work.晒干草是容易使人肚子饿的工
作。❸ having a strong desire 渴望的:
We're ～ for news of our brother.我们渴
望得到弟弟的消息。‖ as ～ as a hunter
非常饥饿的‖ **hungrily** *adv.*饥饿地/**hun-
griness** *n.*荒漠;饥饿

hunk /hʌŋk/
*n.*❶ a thick piece,especially of food,bro-
ken or cut off (食物等的)一大块,一大
片:a ～ of bread 一块大面包 ❷ a strong
man with big muscles (肌肉发达的)壮汉

hunt /hʌnt/
Ⅰ *v.*❶ go after wild animals for food or
as a sport 打猎,猎杀:go out ～ing 去打
猎 ❷search for someone in order to catch
or harm them 追捕(罪犯、敌人等):The
police have been ～ing him for a year.一
年来,警方一直在追捕他。❸ search
carefully 搜索,搜寻:He went through
the whole house ～ing for his glasses.他
在整个屋子里到处寻找他的眼镜。❹
drive away 驱赶:～ the cat out of the
kitchen 把猫赶出厨房 Ⅱ *n.*❶the act of
hunting 打猎;追捕;搜寻:It was an exciting ～,but the hare escaped.这真是一
场扣人心弦的追猎,可惜野兔还是逃跑
了。❷the people who regularly hunt foxes together (经常一起猎狐的)猎队:
ride with the ～ 随猎队骑马打猎‖ ～
down 穷追……直至捕获/ ～ **out** 搜寻
出/～ **through** 涉猎,找遍/ ～ **up** 搜寻‖
～ing *n.*狩猎

hunter /ˈhʌntə(r)/
*n.*❶a person who hunts wild animals for
food or as a sport 猎手,猎人:A famous
～ came to Altorf with his little son.一位
著名的猎手和他的小儿子来到阿尔托
夫。❷ the animal such as a dog,a horse,

etc.that is used by people who hunt 猎
犬;猎马

hurdle /ˈhɜːdl/
*n.*❶a light movable barrier used to jump
over in a certain race (赛跑用的)栏:He
won the 120 yards ～ race.他在 120 码跨
栏比赛中获胜。❷a problem or difficulty
that may prevent you from achieving sth.
难关;障碍;困难:We soon got over that
particular ～.我们很快就克服了那非此
寻常的困难。❸the act of jumping over
an obstacle 跨栏;跳栏

hurl /hɜːl/
*v.*❶throw with great force 用力投掷:He
～ed himself at the door.他向门猛扑过
去。❷utter sth.with force; shout; yell
愤慨地说出;叫喊;叫嚷:He ～ed insults
at the man who ran him down.他厉声辱
骂撞倒他的人。

hurrah /həˈrɑː/
*int.*expressing joy,welcome,approval,etc.
(欢呼声或赞同声)好哇:Hurrah for the
Queen! 女王万岁! /We've done it!
Hurrah! 我们做到了! 好哇!

hurricane /ˈhʌrɪkən/
*n.*❶a storm with a violent wind,especial-
ly a tropical cyclone in the Caribbean 飓
风(尤指加勒比海的热带旋风) ❷a wind
of force 12 on the Beaufort scale (蒲福风
级)12 级狂风

hurry /ˈhʌri/
Ⅰ *v.*❶ (cause to) move or do sth.quickly
(使)赶快;(使)加快;催促:Hurry him,or
he'll be late.催他一下,不然他要迟到了。
❷ send or bring quickly 急派,急运:Doc-
tors and nurses were hurried to the acci-
dent.医生和护士被立即派往事故现场。
Ⅱ *n.*a condition of urgency making it necessary to hurry 匆忙;仓促;急切:In his
～ he forgot to leave his address.匆忙中
他忘了留下地址。‖ ～ **up** (使)赶紧,加
快,赶快/**in a** ～ 仓促地,急切地,(常用
于否定)轻易地/ ～ **with** 加紧(进行某
事)‖ **hurried** *adj.*仓促的,急速的/**hurriedly** *adv.*匆忙地;仓促地

hurt/hɜːt/

Ⅰ v.(hurt) ❶ cause physical pain or damage to（especially a part of the body）(使)受伤,(使)疼痛,伤害：He ～ his back when he fell.他跌倒时伤了背部. / These shoes are too tight.They ～ (me). 这双鞋太紧,使我有点脚痛. ❷ cause（a person）to suffer pain of the mind upset 伤……的感情；使伤心：She was ～ to find that no one admired her performance.她因发现无人赞赏她的表演而感到伤心. Ⅱ n.harm or damage especially to feelings 伤害；损害；创伤：I intended no ～ to his feelings.我不想伤害他的感情. ‖ ～ful adj.伤害人的,有害的;造成伤痛的

hurtle/'hɜːtl/

v.rush or fly with great speed 猛冲;急飞：The spears ～d through the air.长矛在空中嗖嗖飞过。

husband/'hʌzbənd/

n.a man to whom a woman is married 丈夫

hush/hʌʃ/

Ⅰ v. ❶ make or become silent or quiet (使)不作声,(使)静下来：～ a baby to sleep 哄婴儿安静入睡 /Hush up! 别作声! ❷ prevent sth. from becoming generally known, especially sth. shameful 防止某事(尤指丑闻)张扬出去：The government ～ed the affair up to avoid a great social panic. 当局对此事秘而不宣,以免引起社会恐慌。Ⅱ n.tranquil silence 寂静,宁静：There was a sudden ～.四周突然肃静下来。

husk/hʌsk/

n.the dry outer covering of a grain or a seed (种子的)外壳,皮

husky[1]/'hʌski/

adj.(especially of the voice) hoarse (尤指声音)沙哑的：His voice is ～ because he has a cold.他感冒了,声音有些沙哑。

husky[2]/'hʌski/

n.a type of dog used for pulling sledges over snow 雪橇犬

husky[3]/'hʌski/

adj.big and strong 高大强壮的：a fine,～ fellow 一个很壮实的人

hustle/'hʌsl/

Ⅰ v. ❶ cause to move furtively and hurriedly 催促;(使)赶快行动：I ～ed the children off to school.我催促孩子们赶快去上学. /I don't want to ～ you into a decision.我不想催促你做决定. ❷ sell to or gain from (sb.) by force,especially deceitful activity 硬逼,强卖(尤指用欺骗手段)：He ～d me into buying the car.他硬逼着我买下那辆汽车. Ⅱ n. the busy, noisy activity 忙碌;熙熙攘攘：a scene of ～ and bustle 熙熙攘攘的场景 ‖ ～r n. 催促者;乱挤乱推的人;非法攒钱的人

hut/hʌt/

n.a small wooden or stone house with one room 棚屋,小屋：In the evening they returned to their ～.晚上,他们回到自己的棚屋。

hybridize / 'haɪbrɪdaɪz/

v.cross-breed (individuals of two different species or varieties)杂交

hydrant/'haɪdrənt/

n.a water pipe to which a hose can be attached usually found in streets and beside large buildings, such as factories and schools, so that fires can be put out quickly 消防龙头;消防栓

hydrate / 'haɪdreɪt/

Ⅰ n.a chemical compound of water with another compound or element 水化物 Ⅱ v. combine chemically with water; to cause a substance to absorb water 使水化;使成水化物

hydraulic/haɪ'drɔːlɪk/

adj.moved or worked by the pressure of water or some other liquids 水力的,水压的：a ～ press 水压机/ a ～ station 水力发电站

hydrocarbon /ˌhaɪdrə'kɑːbən/

n. a substance formed of hydrogen and carbon 碳氢化合物

hydrogen/'haɪdrədʒən/

n.gas without colour,taste, or smell, that combines with oxygen to form water 氢

hyena /haɪ'iːnə/

*n.*a flesh-eating animal like a wolf, with a howl that sounds like wild laughter 鬣狗

hygiene/ˈhaɪdʒiːn/

n. ❶ the study and practice of how to keep good health, especially by paying attention to cleanliness 卫生学 ❷ the practice of keeping yourself and your living and working areas clean 卫生: mental ～ 心理卫生/public ～ 公共卫生

hygienic /haɪˈdʒiːnɪk/

*adj.*❶ according to the principles of hygiene 符合卫生原则的 ❷ clean and not likely to cause disease 卫生的 ‖ ～ally *adv.*卫生地

hymn/hɪm/

Ⅰ *n.*a song of praise, especially to God, usually one of the religious songs of the Christian church which all the people sing together during a service 圣歌, 赞美诗, 赞歌 Ⅱ *v.*sing a hymn; praise by singing a hymn 为……唱赞美诗: They ～ed their thanks to God.他们唱感谢上帝的赞美诗。 ‖ ～al /ˈhɪmnəl/ *n.*赞美诗集; *adj.*赞美诗的/～ist /ˈhɪmnɪst/ *n.*赞美诗作者

hyphen/ˈhaɪfn/

*n.*the mark (-) used to divide one word into syllables (e.g. Mon-day) or join two words (e.g.self-help) 连字符(-)

hypnosis/hɪpˈnəʊsɪs/

n. a sleep-like state in which a person's mind and actions can be influenced by the person who produced the state (受)催眠状态, 催眠: Under ～ the patient described her early childhood in great detail.这个病人在催眠状态下十分详细地描述了她的童年。

hypnotism/ˈhɪpnətɪzəm/

*n.*the practice of hypnosis 催眠(术)

hypnotist/ˈhɪpnətɪst/

*n.*a person who practises hypnotism and can produce hypnosis 施行催眠术的人; 催眠师

hypnotize/ˈhɪpnətaɪz/

*v.*put a person into a type of deep sleep during which he can be made to do things without his own knowledge 催眠; 使进入催眠状态

hypochondriac/ˌhaɪpəˈkɒndrɪæk/

n. a person who worries unnecessarily about his health 忧郁症患者; 疑病症患者

hypocrisy/hɪˈpɒkrəsi/

*n.*the act of pretending to believe, feel, or be sth. very different from, and usually better than, what one actually believes, feels, or is; extreme insincerity 伪善; 虚伪; 两面派做法

hypotenuse/haɪˈpɒtənjuːz/

n. the side of a right-angled triangle that is opposite the right angle (直角三角形的)斜边, 弦

hypothesis/haɪˈpɒθəsɪs/

*n.*sth. which is assumed in order to argue or explain 假设, 假说: His theory is based on the ～ that all men are born equal.他的理论是基于人人生来平等的假设之上的。

hypothetical/ˌhaɪpəˈθetɪkl/

*adj.*based only on a suggestion that has not been proved or shown to be real; imaginary (基于)假设的, 假定的; 臆想的: She asked me how I would deal with the problem if I were the president, but that is a purely ～ situation.她问我, 我要是总统的话将如何处理这个问题, 但那纯粹是一种假设的情况。

hysteria/hɪˈstɪərɪə/

*n.*❶ nervous excitement causing feelings and behaviour that cannot be controlled 歇斯底里, 癔症: mass ～ 群体歇斯底里, 人群的过度兴奋 ❷ an extremely excited and exaggerated way of behaving 大肆鼓吹; 大惊小怪 ‖ **hysterics** /hɪˈsterɪks/ *n.*歇斯底里症发作; 狂野情绪爆发: She always has hysterics at the sight of blood.她一见到血就会歇斯底里发作。

hysterical /hɪsˈterɪkl/

*adj.*❶ in a state of hysteria 歇斯底里的: a crowd of ～ fans 一群歇斯底里的粉丝 ❷ extremely funny 极为有趣的 ‖ ～ly *adv.*歇斯底里地

Ii

I/aɪ/

pron. the person who is speaking or writing 我：He wants bananas, but ～ want oranges.他想要香蕉，而我想要橘子。/ I'm(I am) very glad to see you. 见到您，我很高兴。/I've(I have) been waiting a long time.我已经等了很长时间了。/I'll (I will or I shall) wait a little longer.我要再等一会儿。/ When I'd(I had) written the story, I read it to my friend.我写完那部小说后，就把它读给我的朋友听。/I thought that I'd(I would or I should) miss the bus, but I didn't.我原以为赶不上那趟车了，但是却赶上了。

ibid. /'ɪbɪd/

abbr. in the same place, usually in a (part of a) book already mentioned 出处同上（同前），在同一处（章、节、段）

ICBM/ˌaɪ siː biː 'em/

abbr. intercontinental ballistic missile; a missile that is capable of traveling from one continent to another 洲际弹道导弹

ice/aɪs/

I n. ❶ frozen water 冰：There is ～ on the lake in winter. 冬天湖面上有冰。/ Her hands were as cold as ～.她两手冰冷。❷ frozen sweet of various kinds (一个)冰激凌：Two ～s, please. 请给我来两个冰激凌。‖ break the ～ 打破沉默，开个头；使气氛活跃起来/cut no ～ 不起作用，无效/on thin ～ 如履薄冰，处境极危险/skate over thin ～ 谈论棘手的问题 Ⅱ v. ❶ make very cold 冰冻，冷藏：～d drinks 冰冻饮料，冷饮 ❷ put ice on or put on ice 用冰覆盖 ‖ ～ age n.冰河时代/～-boat n.冰上滑行船/ ～-bound adj.冰封的/ ～box(～ chest) n.冰箱/ ～ fall n.冰崩/ ～-free adj.不冻的/ ～ hockey n.冰球，冰上曲棍球/ ～ house n.冰窖，制

冰场所/ ～man n.卖冰人/ ～show n.冰上表演/ ～-skate v.溜冰/（an）～ sucker n.棒冰，冰棍

iceberg /'aɪsbɜːɡ/

n. a huge mass of ice floating in the sea with the greater part under water 冰山

icebreaker /'aɪsbreɪkə(r)/

n. ❶ a ship designed for breaking a channel through ice 破冰船 ❷ a thing that serves to relieve inhibitions or tension between people, or start a conversation 打破僵局（或展开话题）的事物

ice cream/ˌaɪs'kriːm/

n. a soft frozen food made with sweetened and flavored milk fat 冰激凌

iced /aɪst/

adj. ❶ (of drink or other liquid) cooled in or mixed with pieces of ice (饮料等液体)冰镇的；掺冰的：jugs of ～ water 几罐冰水 ❷ (of a surface or object) covered or coated with ice (表面、物体)结冰的，覆冰的；被冰包裹的：I've played ice hockey on rivers, ponds, and ～ barnyard.我曾在河上、池塘上和结冰的谷仓空场上玩冰球。❸ (of a cake or biscuit) decorated with icing (蛋糕、饼干)撒有糖霜的

icon/'aɪkɒn/

n. ❶ an important person or thing who or which is a symbol of a particular thing 象征物；偶像 ❷ a picture on a computer screen which represents a special function 图标

icy/'aɪsi/

adj. ❶ extremely cold 冰冷的：My hands are ～.我双手冰冷。/an ～ wind from the north 来自北方的寒风/She gave me an ～ look.她冷冷地看了我一眼。❷ covered with ice 冰封的，结满冰的：Icy roads are dangerous.结满冰的道路很危险。❸

very cold and unfriendly in manner 态度冷漠的,冷冰冰的,不友好的:He talked with me in ~ voice.他跟我说话时态度冷淡。‖ **icily** *adv.* 冷冰冰地/**iciness** *n.* 冰冷

I'd/aɪd/

abbr. ❶I had 我已经:~ gone. 我已经走了。/~ no time left.我没有剩余的时间了。❷I would 我愿意:I decided ~ go. 我决定了要去。

id/ɪd/

n. (in Freudian psychology) the one of the three parts of the mind that is completely unconscious,but has needs and desires (弗洛伊德心理学中的)伊德,本我(指人潜意识的最深层,是构成人类人格的三个基本力量之一)

idea/aɪˈdɪə/

n. ❶ an opinion or a belief about sth. 意见,想法:What's your ~? 你觉得怎么样? ❷ a plan or suggestion,especially about what to do 计划,建议,主意:What a good ~! Let's do it.好主意! 我们干吧。❸a thought in the mind 思想,概念:You have no ~ how anxious we have been.你不知道我们多着急。❹the aim or purpose of sth.目标;意图:What's the ~ of all his words? 他说这些话的目的是什么? ‖ **give an ~ (of)** 使了解……(的情况)/**have an (the) ~** 感到,觉得,认为/**have any ~** (多用于问句)知道,了解/**have no ~** 不知道,不了解 ‖ **-less** *adj.*没想头的,没主意的

ideal/aɪˈdiːəl/

Ⅰ *adj.*perfect in every aspect 理想的,完善的:~ weather for a holiday 理想的假日天气 Ⅱ *n.*❶(a belief in) high principles or perfect standards 理想;理想的东西:the high ~s of the Party 党的崇高理想 ❷ a perfect example 完美的典型:She's looking for a husband but hasn't found her ~ yet. 她正在找老公,但还未找到一位理想的人选。‖ **-ist** *n.*理想主义者,空想家,唯心主义者,唯心论者 & *adj.*唯心主义的/ **~ly** *adv.*理想地那样,按理想说

idealism/aɪˈdiːəlɪzəm/

n. ❶the practice of forming or pursuing ideals,especially sth.unrealistic 理想主义 ❷the representation of things in ideal or idealized form 理想化 ❸ any of various systems of thought in which the objects of knowledge are held to be in some way dependent on the activity of mind 唯心主义,唯心论

idealize /aɪˈdiːəlaɪz/

*v.*regard or represent a person or thing as perfect,or as better than they are 使理想化 ‖ **idealization** *n.*理想化;理想化的事物

identical/aɪˈdentɪkl/

*adj.*❶the same 同一(个)的:This is the ~ place where we stopped before.这就是我们以前停留过的地方。❷ exactly alike 完全相同的,完全一样的:The fingerprints of no two persons are ~.没有两个人的指纹是完全一样的。‖ **be ~ with** 和……完全相同 ‖ **~ly** *adv.*同一地;相等地

identification/aɪˌdentɪfɪˈkeɪʃn/

*n.*❶the process of showing who or what sb. or sth. is 认出,识别,鉴定,验明:Identification of the jewels was made by the owner.珠宝的识别是由它的拥有者做出的。❷sth. used to identify a person or thing 身份的证明,身份证:A driver's license is adequate ~.司机的驾驶执照足以用作其身份的证明。

identify/aɪˈdentɪfaɪ/

*v.*❶say,show,prove who or what sb.or sth.is (身份、物件等)认明,鉴定:I identified the umbrella at once,it was mine.我一下认出了那把雨伞,它是我的。❷consider to be the same 等同于;使成为一致;认为……一致:He identifies her happiness with his own.他认为她的幸福就是他自己的幸福。‖ **~ oneself with** 和……打成一片,参加到……中去;和……有联系;支持 ‖ **identifiable** /aɪˌdentɪˈfaɪəbl/*adj.*可看作是相同的;可辨认的/**identifier** /aɪˈdentɪfaɪə(r)/*n.*鉴定人,检验人

identity/aɪˈdentəti/

*n.*❶sameness;exact likeness 同一(性),

一致：～ of thinking and being 思维与存在的同一性 ❷who or what a particular person or thing is 身份；正身；本体；特性：prove sb.'s ～ 证明某人的身份/an ～ certificate(card) 身份证

ideogram/ˈɪdɪəɡræm/
n. the graphic symbol representing an object or idea without expressing the sounds of words 表意文字

ideology/ˌaɪdɪˈɒlədʒi/
n. ❶a system of ideas and ideals which forms the basis of economic or political theory and policy, etc. 思想；思想体系：the socialist ～ 社会主义思想 ❷the ideas and beliefs of particular class or individual(团体、社会阶层或个人的)意识形态

idiocy/ˈɪdɪəsi/
n. ❶the state of being an idiot 白痴（状态）❷the stupid action 愚蠢行动

idiolect/ˈɪdɪəlekt/
n. a particular person's use of language 个人言语方式

idiom/ˈɪdɪəm/
n. ❶a phrase which means sth. different from the meanings of the separate words from which it is formed 习语；成语：Hard up is an English ～ meaning to lack money. "hard up"是英语中的一个习语，意为缺钱。❷the way of expression typical of a person or a people in their use of language (语言的)习惯用法，特有的表达方式：This expression is against ～. 这种表达方式不符合习惯用法。‖ ～atic /ˌɪdɪəˈmætɪk/ *adj.* 符合语言习惯的；成语的；地道的

idiot/ˈɪdɪət/
n. ❶a person born with such a weak mind that he can never learn to read or count 白痴 ❷a very stupid or foolish person 愚蠢的人

idle/ˈaɪdl/
I *adj.* ❶not in use 闲置的；不工作的：machines 闲置的机器 ❷(of time) not spent in doing sth. (时间)空闲的：He spent many ～ hours during the holidays.

他在假期里度过了很多悠闲的时光。❸(of persons) lazy (人)懒散的：an ～ fellow 游手好闲的家伙 ❹useless 无用的：an ～ dream 空想 II *v.* ❶ spend in an idle manner 虚度，浪费：Don't ～ away your precious time. 不要把宝贵的时间浪费掉（不要虚度光阴）。❷ close a factory, etc. (暂时)关闭工厂 ‖ ～ness *n.* 懒惰；闲散；～r *n.* 游手好闲者，懒汉；空转轮/ **idly** *adv.* 无所事事地；懒惰地

idol/ˈaɪdl/
n. ❶an image in wood, stone, etc. of a god 神像：They prayed to an ～. 他们向神祈祷。❷a person or thing greatly loved 偶像：The football player was the young boys' ～. 那个足球运动员曾是男孩子们的偶像。

idolatry/aɪˈdɒlətri/
n. ❶the worship of idols 偶像崇拜 ❷the great admiration of sb. or sth. 盲目崇拜：He supports his local team with a fervour that borders on ～. 他是本地队的球迷，狂热到了近乎盲目崇拜的程度了。

idolize/ˈaɪdəlaɪz/
v. treat as an idol；admire or love sb. deeply 把……当偶像崇拜；极度敬慕；宠爱：He ～s his father. 他十分崇拜自己的父亲。

if/ɪf/
conj. ❶on condition that；supposing that 假使，如果：If you ask him, he will help you. 如果你请求他，他会帮助你的。❷ used with a past tense for imaginary situations (与过去时态连用表示假想的情况)如果，要是：If John were(was) here, he would know what to do. 要是约翰在这里的话，他会知道该怎么做的。❸accepting that；although 虽然；即使：If too old to work much, the retired worker is very enthusiastic about neighbourhood affairs. 虽然年老不能多操劳，但这个退休工人对邻里工作非常热心。❹whether (用在 ask, know 等动词后)是否：Do you know ～(whether) she's coming? 你知道她来吗？❺when；whenever (每)当，无论何时：If you mix red and white, you get pink. 当你把红色和白色混合就会得到粉

红色。❻ used like that after words expressing surprise,sorrow,or pleasure（用于表示感情的词语后,用法如 that）:I'm sorry ~ she's annoyed.她要是生气了,我很抱歉。❼ expressing a wish（表示愿望）:If only I were rich.我要是有钱就好了。‖ as ~ 仿佛,就像……似的/even ~ 即使/ ~ any 如果说有的话/ ~ anything 更可能的是,相反/ ~ need be 如果必要的话/ ~ only 只要;要是……就好了/ ~ you like（please）（客气话）如果你愿意

iffy /ˈɪfi/

　　adj. full of uncertainty 未确定的;有问题的:Until the contract is signed,we're in a rather ~ situation. 只要合同还没有签字,我们就一直处于前途未卜的境地。

ignite /ɪgˈnaɪt/

　　v. catch fire;set on fire 着火;点燃:Dry grass ~ easily. 干草容易着火。 ‖ ignition /ɪgˈnɪʃn/ *n.* 点火;(汽车引擎的)点火装置

ignoble /ɪgˈnəʊbl/

　　adj. ❶ dishonourable;shameful 不光荣的;可耻的:an ~ man（action）可耻的人(行为) ❷ of low birth 出身卑微的

ignorance /ˈɪgnərəns/

　　n. the lack of knowledge,information,or consciousness,especially of sth.one ought to know about 无知,无学识,愚昧:If he did wrong,it was from（through） ~.要是他做错了,那是出于无知。 ‖（be）in ~ of（sth.）不知(某事),对……不了解

ignorant /ˈɪgnərənt/

　　adj. ❶（of persons）knowing little or nothing;not aware 无知的,缺乏知识的,愚昧的:be ~ of conditions at the lower levels 不了解下情 ❷ caused by or showing ignorance 显示无知的;由无知引起的:an ~ error 出于无知的错误 ❸ rude or impolite,especially because of lack of social training（缺乏社交训练造成的)粗鲁的,失礼的 ‖ be ~ of（about）对……不了解

ignore /ɪgˈnɔː(r)/

　　v. pay no attention to;not notice 忽视;不注视;不管;不理:~ the fact 不顾事实/

~ sb.不理某人/Never ~ the law.不要无视法律。

ill /ɪl/

　　Ⅰ *adj.* ❶ sick;in bad health;not well（常作表语)有病的,不健康的:fall(be taken) ~ 得病 ❷ bad;harmful;evil（作定语)坏的,不良的,有害的,恶劣的: ~ news 坏消息/ ~ health 不健康/an ~ wind 歪风/ ~ will 恶意 ‖ be ~ off 贫困;不幸/(be) ~ at ease 不安,不自在 Ⅱ *adv.* ❶ badly 坏地;不利地;使人不愉快地:speak(think) ~ of sb.把某人说(想)得很坏 ❷ scarcely 几乎不;不容易;不充分:I can ~ afford the time.我恐怕难以抽出这点时间。Ⅲ *n.* ❶（usually *pl.*）difficulty;trouble;misfortune 不幸,灾难: the various ~s of life 人生的种种不幸 ❷ evil;harm 邪恶;伤害: do ~ 作恶,为害 ‖ ~-advised *adj.* 没脑筋的,鲁莽的/ ~-bred *adj.* 教养不好的/ ~-favo(u)red *adj.* 其貌不扬的,凶相的/ ~-gotten *adj.* 非法获得的/ ~-judged *adj.* 判断失误的/ ~ness *n.* 疾病/ ~-suited(to) *adj.* 与……不适合的/ ~-timed *adj.* 不适时的,不合时宜的

illegal /ɪˈliːgl/

　　adj. forbidden by law;unlawful 违法的;不合法的 ‖ ~ly *adv.* 非法地;违法地

illegible /ɪˈledʒəbl/

　　adj. not able to be read 难读的,难以辨认的:Your writing is ~.你的字迹不易辨认。

illegitimate /ˌɪləˈdʒɪtɪmət/

　　adj. ❶ not allowed by the rules 非法的;违反条例的,不合规定的:In this sentence the writer uses an ~ construction. 在这个句子里,作者用了一个不合规范的结构。❷ born to parents who are not married 私生的:an ~ child 私生子 ‖ ~ly *adv.* 私生地;非法地;不合理地/illegitimacy /ˌɪləˈdʒɪtəməsi/ *n.* 非法;违法;不合理;私生

illicit /ɪˈlɪsɪt/

　　adj. forbidden by law,rules or custom 违禁的,违法的;不正当的

illiterate /ɪˈlɪtərət/

　　adj. ❶ uneducated;unable to read or write

文盲的, 目不识丁的, 未受教育的: About half the population is still ~. 大约一半人口仍是文盲。❷badly written, especially by uneducated people 语言错误的, 文字不通的: an ~ letter 一封错误百出的信

illness /'ɪlnəs/
n.(a) disease; unhealthy state of the body or mind 病, 疾病; (身体或精神)不适: There seems to be a lot of ~ in that family. 那一家人似乎病痛很多。/physical and mental ~ 身体和精神方面的疾病 / Tuberculosis is a very serious ~. 结核病是一种非常严重的疾病。

illogical /ɪ'lɒdʒɪkl/
*adj.*❶contrary to the principles of sound reasoning; not logical 不合逻辑的: an ~ reason 一个不合逻辑的理由 ❷not reasonable 不合常理的: Many children have an ~ horror of the dark. 许多小孩对黑暗有一种毫无理由的恐惧。

ill-treat /ɪl'triːt/
v. treat sb. or sth. badly or cruelly 虐待(人、动物等) ‖ ~ment *n.* 虐待

illuminate /ɪ'luːmɪneɪt/
*v.*❶give light to; fill (especially a room) with light 照亮, 照明: The room was ~d by candles. 这间房用蜡烛照明。❷decorate (buildings, streets, etc.) with lights for a special occasion 用灯装饰: The whole city was ~d in celebration of National Day. 全市灯火辉煌庆祝国庆。❸cause to understand; explain; make clear 阐明, 使明白; 启发: ~ a statement with many examples 用许多实例阐明一个论点 ‖ **illuminating** *adj.* 有启发性的

illumination /ɪˌluːmɪ'neɪʃən/
*n.*❶the lighting or light 照明; 光亮: Higher levels of ~ are needed for reading. 阅读时需要更高的照明度。❷(*pl.*) lights used in decorating a building or other structures 灯饰, 灯彩 ❸the spiritual or intellectual enlightenment (精神、智力上的)启迪, 启发 ❹clarification 澄清, 阐明, 解释

illusion /ɪ'luːʒn/
*n.*❶ sth. that a person wrongly believes to exist 错觉, 幻觉: The lake in the desert was just an optical ~ that a person wrongly believes to exist. 沙漠中的湖泊只是一种视力错觉。❷a false idea or belief 幻想; 错误的观念, 不切实际的想法: I have no ~s about his ability. 我对他的能力不抱幻想。‖ be under an ~ 有……的错觉, 误认为……/give the ~ 给人以假象/have no ~s about 对……不存幻想 ‖ ~al, ~ary *adj.* 错觉的, 幻影的/ ~ism *n.* 引起错觉的艺术手法/ ~ist *n.* 幻术师, 魔术师

illustrate /'ɪləstreɪt/
*v.*❶make the meaning of sth. clearer by giving related examples 举例说明, 阐明: His story ~s her true generosity very clearly. 他所讲的事很清楚地说明她确实慷慨大方。❷add pictures to (sth. written) 加插图于(文字作品等): an ~d magazine 带插图的杂志 ❸show that sth. is true or a situation exists 表明……真实; 显示……存在 ‖ **illustration** /ˌɪlə'streɪʃn/ *n.* 举例说明; 插图; 例证/ **illustrative** /'ɪləstrətɪv/ *adj.* 用作说明的; 解释性的; 作为例证的/ **illustrator** *n.* 插图画家; 说明者

image /'ɪmɪdʒ/
*n.*❶ a picture formed of an object in front of a mirror or lens, such as the picture formed on the film inside a camera or one's reflection in a mirror 影像, 图像: An ~ of a country garden came into my mind. 一幅乡村花园的景象浮现在我脑海里。❷ the general opinion about a person, an organization, etc. that has been formed or intentionally created in people's minds 形象: the splendid ~ of Lei Feng 雷锋的光辉形象 ❸a copy; a similar people or thing 翻版; 相像的人; 相似物: She is the very ~ of her mother. 她活像她妈。❹ an object made to represent a god or a person to be worshipped 神像; 偶像 ❺ metaphor or simile 明喻, 暗喻 ‖ be the ~ of 极像, 酷似/in the ~ of 按照……的形象

imagery /'ɪmɪdʒəri/
n. images (image generally, especially as

used in literature)（尤指用于文学修辞中的）意象

imaginable/ɪˈmædʒɪnəbl/
adj. that can be imagined possibly 可想象的；想象得出的：We tried every ~ means, but we couldn't wake her up.我们用了一切想得出的方法，但就是没能叫醒她。

imaginary/ɪˈmædʒɪnəri/
adj. not real, but produced from pictures or ideas in someone's mind；existing only in imagination 想象中的；假想的；虚构的：All the characters in this book are ~.此书中的所有人物都是虚构的。/My little daughter has an ~ friend.我的小女儿有个想象中的朋友。

imagination/ɪˌmædʒɪˈneɪʃ(ə)n/
n. ❶ the ability to imagine 想象；想象力：have a good(poor) ~ 想象力好(差) ❷ sth. that is imagined 想象(虚构)的事物：You didn't really see a ghost—it was only ~.你并没有真正看到鬼——那不过是你想象中的东西。

imaginative/ɪˈmædʒɪnətɪv/
adj. ❶ having or showing the imagination 富于想象力的；爱想象的；运用想象力的：~ writing 虚构的作品 /an ~ design 富有想象力的设计 ❷ good at inventing imaginary things or artistic forms, or at producing new ideas 想象力强的；想象力丰富的：an ~ child 想象力丰富的孩子

imagine/ɪˈmædʒɪn/
v. ❶ form a picture in the mind；think of (sth.) as possible 想象；设想：Can you ~ life without electricity and other modern conveniences? 你能想象出在没有电和其他现代化设备时的生活情景吗？ ❷ suppose or have an idea about (sth. that is false or does not exist) 误以为；猜测：He ~s that people don't like him.他总以为人们不喜欢他。 ❸ think that sth. is possibly true 认为；料想

imaging /ˈɪmɪdʒɪŋ/
n. the process of capturing, storing and showing an image on a computer screen 成像

imaginings/ɪˈmædʒɪnɪŋz/
n. thoughts or fantasies 思想；幻想

imbalance /ɪmˈbæləns/
n. a situation in which two or more things are lack of balance or proportion 不均衡，不平衡；失衡，失调

imbecile/ˈɪmbəsiːl/
Ⅰ *adj.* mentally weak；stupid 低能的；愚笨的 Ⅱ *n.* a person who is mentally weak or stupid 低能者；笨蛋

imbecility/ˌɪmbəˈsɪləti/
n. ❶ the state of being an imbecile 愚笨；低能 ❷ an act of great foolishness 愚蠢行为

imbed /ɪmˈbed/
v. (-dd-) fix sth. firmly and deeply in a surrounding mass 埋置；把……嵌入

imbibe/ɪmˈbaɪb/
v. ❶ drink or take in (especially alcohol) 喝，饮(尤指酒精饮料等) ❷ listen to and accept ideas, etc. 吸收(想法等)：~ knowledge at his mother's knee 孩提时在母亲膝前吸收知识

imbue/ɪmˈbjuː/
v. (usually with reference to feelings) fill in with (通常指感情)使充满；灌输：The speech ~d us with a desire to help.这次演说灌输我们乐于助人的思想。

imitate/ˈɪmɪteɪt/
v. ❶ copy the behaviour of；take as an example 模仿，效法；仿效：~ sb.'s way of doing things 效法某人做事的方式 ❷ be like；make a likeness of 仿造，制成……的样子，做得像……：The floors are painted to ~ marble.地板漆得像大理石。

imitation/ˌɪmɪˈteɪʃən/
n. ❶ the act or an action of copying sb. or sth. 模仿，效法；仿造：set sb. a good example for ~ 为某人树立一个可以效仿的榜样 ❷ a copy of the quality goods 仿制品，伪造物：an ~ of leather 仿皮制品/ beware of ~s 谨防假冒 ‖ in ~ of 仿效

imitative /ˈɪmɪtətɪv/
adj. that imitating sb. or sth.模仿的；仿效的 ‖ ~ly *adv.* 模仿地；伪造地/ imita-tiveness *n.*模仿性；模拟性

immaculate /ɪˈmækjʊlət/

adj. ❶pure, faultless 纯洁的，无瑕疵的；无斑点的：～ conduct 纯洁的行为 ❷ right in every detail 无缺点的，无过失的，清白无辜的

immaterial /ˌɪməˈtɪərɪəl/

adj. not important; not relevant 不重要的；无关的：What you say is ～ to the discussion. 你说的话与本讨论无关。

immature /ˌɪməˈtjʊə(r)/

adj. not yet fully grown or developed 发育未完全的；未成熟的

immeasurable /ɪˈmeʒərəbl/

adj. too big or great to be measured 不可估量的；无限的：This scandal has done ～ damage to the company's reputation. 这件丑闻对该公司的声誉已造成不可估量的损害。

immediacy /ɪˈmiːdɪəsi/

n. the quality of bringing one into direct and instant involvement with sth., giving rise to a sense of urgency or excitement 直接性；即刻性，即时性

immediate /ɪˈmiːdɪət/

adj. ❶done or needed at once and without delay 立即的，即刻的：I want an ～ reply. 我需要立即答复。 ❷ nearest in time, space, or degree; next 直接的；最接近的：the ～ cause 直接原因/the ～ superior 上一级领导，顶头上司/sb.'s ～ neighbo(u)rs 某人的近邻 ‖ **immediacy** /ɪˈmiːdɪəsi/ *n.* 直接(性)；刻不容缓/～**ness** *n.* 即刻；直接

immediately /ɪˈmiːdɪətli/

I *adv.* at once, without any delay 立刻，立即，马上 II *conj.* as soon as 一……就……：I came ～ you called. 你一叫我，我就过来了。

immense /ɪˈmens/

adj. very large or great 极大的；巨大的 ‖ ～**ly** *adv.* 非常；极大地：I enjoyed myself ～ly. 我玩得很高兴。

immensity /ɪˈmensəti/

n. unusual largeness in size, extent or number 广大；巨大；无限，无穷：the ～ of space 太空的浩瀚无际

immerse /ɪˈmɜːs/

v. ❶put deep under water 浸(入)，泡：～ one's head in water 把头浸入水里 ❷ cause(oneself) to enter deeply into an activity; absorb 使沉浸于，使陷入：The capital was ～d in a festival atmosphere. 首都沉浸在一片节日气氛中。 ‖ **be ～d in** 聚精会神从事(某工作)，陷入……之中/～ **oneself in** 专心从事(某事)，沉溺于……之中 ‖ **immersion** *n.* 沉浸；专心

immigrant /ˈɪmɪgrənt/

n. a person who comes into a foreign country or region to live 移民，侨民：California has many ～s from other countries. 加利福尼亚州有许多来自其他国家的移民。

immigrate /ˈɪmɪgreɪt/

v. come into a country to make one's life and home there 移居；移居国外

immigration /ˌɪmɪˈgreɪʃn/

n. the process of coming to live in a foreign country forever 移民入境：the ～ office at the airport 机场的移民局办事处 / There are strict controls on ～ into this country. 移民到这个国家有严格的限制。

imminent /ˈɪmɪnənt/

adj. (of events, especially dangers) likely to come or happen soon (指危险等)临头的；即至的，逼近的：A storm is ～. 暴风雨即将来临。 / He was faced with ～ death. 他死到临头。 ‖ **imminence** *n.* 逼近

immobile /ɪˈməʊbaɪl/

adj. not able to move or be moved 不能移动的；不动的；固定的 ‖ **immobility** /ˌɪməˈbɪləti/ *n.* 固定；稳定

immobilize /ɪˈməʊbəlaɪz/

v. prevent sb. or sth. from moving 使不动，使固定：Heavy snow ～d all traffic. 大雪使得全部交通停顿。 ‖ **immobilization** *n.* 固定(化)

immoderate /ɪˈmɒdərət/

adj. beyond what is proper; too much 不适中的；过多的，无节制的：He is ～ in his drinking. 他饮酒过多。

immodest /ɪˈmɒdɪst/

adj. not decent; rude and not socially acceptable 不正经的；不庄重的；无礼的；粗

鲁的：Her skirt is so short that it is ～.她的裙子短得有失体统。

immoral/ɪˈmɒrəl/

adj. wrong; evil; not conforming to accepted standards of morality 不道德的；邪恶的；猥亵的，淫荡的：the ～ earnings of a prostitute 娼妓赚得的肮脏钱 ‖ ～ity/ˌɪməˈræləti/ *n*.不道德的行为；不道德

immortal/ɪˈmɔːtl/

adj. living and lasting forever; having fame for all time 不朽的，不死的，流芳百世的：The heroes of the people are ～.人民英雄永垂不朽。‖ ～ity *n*.不朽，永存/～ly *adv*.不朽地，永久地；非常，很

immovable/ɪˈmuːvəbl/

adj. impossible to move or cannot move 不可移动的，坚定不移的：The entrance is blocked by an ～ rock.入口被一块无法移动的岩石堵住了。/The government is ～ on the open policy.政府坚定不移地贯彻执行开放政策。‖ **immovably** *adv*.固定不动地，确定地；冷静地

immune/ɪˈmjuːn/

adj.❶ free from (punishment) 免除（惩罚）的：He would be ～ from punishment if he helped the police.如果他协助警方，就可以免受惩罚。❷ unable to be harmed because of special qualities in oneself 安全的，有免疫力的：～ to disease (infection) 对疾病（传染病）有免疫力❸ not affected by sth.; not susceptible to sth.不受某事物影响的；对事物不敏感的：Peter is a strong-willed man and he is ～ to criticism and abuse. 皮特意志坚定，他从不为批评和漫骂所动摇。

immunity/ɪˈmjuːnɪti/

n.❶ the ability to resist infection 免疫力❷ the state of being protected from an obligation or penalty 免除义务；免除责罚

immunize/ˈɪmjʊnaɪz/

v.make someone immune to infection 使免疫 ‖ **immunization** *n*.免疫

impact/ˈɪmpækt/

n.❶ the force of one object hitting another 冲击（力），碰撞：the ～ of the swift current against the shore 激流对海岸的

冲击❷ a strong or powerful influence or effect, especially caused or produced by an idea, invention, event, etc. 强烈影响：make (have)a great ～ on the readers 对读者产生很大的影响

impair/ɪmˈpeə(r)/

v.weaken; damage 减少；削弱；损害：You need spectacles if your eyesight is ～ed. 要是你的视力减弱了，就需要配眼镜。

impaired/ɪmˈpeəd/

adj.having a disability of a specified kind 有残障的：hearing ～children 听力残障儿

impairment /ɪmˈpeəmənt/

n.the state or fact of being impaired, especially in a specified faculty (尤指某种功能的)损伤，削弱：a speech ～言语障碍

impale/ɪmˈpeɪl/

v.pierce through with a sharp-pointed object 刺穿：a butterfly ～d by a pin 用大头针钉住的蝴蝶

impart/ɪmˈpɑːt/

v.give, pass on qualities, knowledge, etc. to other people 给予；授予；传授：A teacher's aim is to ～ knowledge.教师的目的就是传授知识。

impartial/ɪmˈpɑːʃl/

adj.just; fair to both sides 公平的；不偏袒的：A judge must be completely ～.法官必须绝对公平无私。

impassable/ɪmˈpɑːsəbl/

adj.not possible to travel on, go over or through 不能通行的；不可逾越的：This road is ～ during the rains.下雨期间这条路不能通行。/ ～ mountains 不可逾越的山脉/ an ～ forest 无路可走的森林地带

impasse/æmˈpɑːs/

n.a situation at which further movement or development is blocked 僵局；绝境，死路：The negotiations have reached an ～.谈判已陷入僵局。/break (end) the ～打破(结束)僵局

impassioned/ɪmˈpæʃnd/

adj.full of passion or strong feelings 热情

洋溢的；激动的：an ～ request for help 恳切请求帮助

impassive /ɪmˈpæsɪv/

adj. showing no sign of feelings；unmoved 无表情的；冷淡的：～ faces 毫无表情的面孔

impatience /ɪmˈpeɪʃns/

n. ❶ lack of patience 不耐烦，急躁 ❷ eagerness 渴望，期望

impatient /ɪmˈpeɪʃnt/

adj. ❶ not patient；irritated 不耐烦的，急躁的：Don't be ～ with your children. 对孩子们不要急躁。 ❷ eager；expecting sth. to happen soon 急切的，渴望的：The children are ～ for the arrival of the Children's Day. 孩子们盼望儿童节的到来。‖ be ～ of（sth.）对……不耐烦；为……着急

impeach /ɪmˈpiːtʃ/

v. ❶ raise doubts about 怀疑：～ someone's motives（character）怀疑某人的动机（品格）❷ say that（someone）is guilty of a serious crime, especially against the state 控告（某人）；犯有（严重罪行，尤指危害国家罪）；检举 ❸（especially in the U.S.）charge（a public official）with serious misbehaviour in office（尤指在美国）弹劾（政府官员）

impedance /ɪmˈpiːdəns/

n. a measure of the power of a piece of electrical apparatus to stop the flow of an alternating current 全电阻，阻抗

impede /ɪmˈpiːd/

v. get in the way of or slow down the movement or development of；hinder 阻碍，妨碍；阻止：The rescue was ～d by bad weather. 营救因坏天气而受阻。

impediment /ɪmˈpedɪmənt/

n. ❶ a fact or an event which makes action difficult or impossible 阻碍，妨碍，障碍：The main ～ to development is the country's huge foreign debt. 发展的主要障碍是该国的大量外债。❷ a physical difficulty which prevents a person from speaking clearly 口吃，结巴：a speech ～ 讲话结巴

impel /ɪmˈpel/

v. (-ll-) drive，force，urge 驱使，迫使；促成，推动，推进；激励：～ sb. to do sth. 推动某人做某事 / ～ sb. to greater efforts 促使某人做出更大努力 / be ～led by necessity 迫不得已 / fell ～led to speak 觉得非说不可 ‖ ～lent *adj.* 推动的，促使的 / ～ler *n.* 推动者；推动器

impending /ɪmˈpendɪŋ/

adj. soon to happen；imminent 迫近的，即将发生的：～ departure 即将到来的离别

impenetrable /ɪmˈpenɪtrəbl/

adj. not able to be passed through 不能通过的；不能穿过的

imperative /ɪmˈperətɪv/

adj. ❶ very urgent or important and needing actions right now；necessary 紧急的；绝对必要的；迫切的：Is it really ～ for them to have six cars? 他们真的迫切需要六辆汽车吗？❷ not to be disobeyed 必须服从的，强制的，专横的：The duke's orders were ～. 公爵的命令必须服从。❸ of the verb form that expresses a command（句子）表示命令的，祈使的：the ～ mood(sentence) 祈使语气（句）‖ ～ly *adv.* 命令式地 / ～ness *n.* 命令式之事

imperceptible /ˌɪmpəˈseptəbl/

adj. difficult or impossible to see，feel，hear，etc. 难以察觉的；察觉不到的：He gave an almost ～ nod. 他极轻微地点了点头。

imperfect /ɪmˈpɜːfɪkt/

adj. ❶ not perfect；not complete；faulty 不完善的；不完全的；有缺点的 ❷ tense of the verb expressing an action not yet completed（e.g. I was walking along the street.）（动词时态）未完成的（例如：我正沿着街道走。）

imperial /ɪmˈpɪərɪəl/

adj. ❶ of an empire or its ruler 帝国的，皇帝的：the Imperial Palace 故宫 / an ～ envoy 钦差大臣 ❷ (of weights and measures) of the British standard（度量衡）英制的，法定标准的：an ～ pint 英国法定一品脱 ‖ ～ly *adv.* 帝王般地；威严地

imperialism /ɪmˈpɪərɪəlɪzəm/

n. (a belief in the) policy of extending a country's power and influence in the world through diplomacy or military force, and especially by acquiring colonies 帝国主义；帝国主义政策：Imperialism is the monopoly stage of capitalism. 帝国主义是资本主义的垄断阶段。‖ **imperialistic**/ɪmˌpɪərɪə'lɪstɪk/ *adj.* 帝国主义的/ **imperialize**/ɪm'pɪərɪəlaɪz/ *v.* 使帝国主义化，使成帝国

imperialist /ɪm'pɪərɪəlɪst/

Ⅰ *adj.* of, relating to, supporting, or practising imperialism 帝国主义的；拥护帝制的；实行帝制的 Ⅱ *n.* a person who supports or practises imperialism 帝制拥护者；帝国主义者

imperil /ɪm'perɪl/

v. (~ed or ~led) endanger sb. or sth. 使处于危险中

imperious /ɪm'pɪərɪəs/

adj. expecting people to obey you; domineering or bossy 专横的，傲慢的，盛气凌人的：his ~ demands 他专横的要求 ‖ ~ly *adv.* 专制地；妄自尊大地

impersonal /ɪm'pɜːsənl/

adj. ❶not influenced by personal feeling; showing no emotion 非个人的；不受私人感情影响的 ❷not referring to a particular person 不特指某个人的 ❸having no existence as a person 客观的：nature's ~ forces 大自然的客观力量 ‖ ~ity *n.* 非人格性；无人情味/~ly *adv.* 与个人无关地；客观地

impersonate /ɪm'pɜːsəneɪt/

v. pretend to be another person, either for entertainment or fraudulently 扮演，模仿，假冒（某人）：It's a very serious offence to ~a police officer. 假冒警官是重罪。

impersonator/ɪm'pɜːsəneɪtə(r)/

n. a person who impersonates other people （模仿他人的）演员；扮演他人的人

impertinent/ɪm'pɜːtɪnənt/

adj. ❶rude, especially to older people 无礼的；粗鲁的（尤指对长者）：She scolded her son for being ~. 她责骂儿子粗鲁。 ❷not pertinent; not pertaining to the matter in hand 不对题的；不相干的；无关联的：a point ~ to the question 与问题无关的要点

imperturbable/ɪmpə'tɜːbəbl/

adj. not able to be made angry or excited easily 沉着的；冷静的

impervious/ɪm'pɜːvɪəs/

adj. ❶ not allowing anything to pass through 不可渗透的，透不过气的：~ to gases and liquids 气体和液体都透不过的 ❷ not easily influenced or changed, especially in one's opinions 无动于衷的，不受影响的，不受干扰的：be ~ to the sugar-coated bullets 不受糖衣炮弹的侵蚀 ‖ ~ly *adv.* 透不过地/~ness *n.* 不渗透性；不透水性

impetuous/ɪm'petʃuəs/

adj. moving quickly or violently; acting or inclined to act energetically but with insufficient thought or care; done or said hastily 急促的；猛烈的；冲动的；急躁的：an ~ charge 猛攻/an ~ wind 狂风/an ~ young man 急躁的青年

impetus/'ɪmpɪtəs/

n. ❶a force which makes sth. happen or progress more quickly 动力；推动力：This is really the main ~ for the reform. 这确实是改革的主要动力。 ❷the act of applying force 刺激；促进：give an ~ to trade 促进贸易

impious/'ɪmpɪəs/

adj. not showing respect, especially for God; not pious 不敬神的；不虔诚的

impish/'ɪmpɪʃ/

adj. naughty; mischievous 顽皮的，淘气的：an ~ grin 顽皮的露齿笑/a charmingly ~ child 可爱的小淘气

implacable/ɪm'plækəbl/

adj. that cannot be appeased; relentless 不能平息的；毫不容情的；不可调和的：an ~ enemy 死敌；不可调和的敌人

implant/ɪm'plɑːnt/

v. fix in deeply usually into the body or mind 嵌入；灌输；注入：~ the new ideas in the minds of the youth 把新思想灌输

到青年的心中

implement

Ⅰ/'ɪmplɪmənt/*n*. tool; instrument 工具，用具：farming (gardening) ～s 农具（园艺工具）/ household ～s 日用器具 Ⅱ/'ɪmplɪment/ *v*. complete; perform; carry out 贯彻，执行，履行（契约、诺言）：～ the decisions 贯彻执行决议 ‖ ～**al** /ˌɪmplɪ'mentəl/ *adj*. 器具的；做器具用的；起作用的，有助的

implicate/'ɪmplɪkeɪt/

v. show that (someone else) is concerned (in sth. bad, especially criminal activity) 使牵连（于罪行等中），牵涉：The detective found an evidence which ～d him in the murder. 侦探发现了一件证据，使他牵连到谋杀案中。 ‖ **implication** /ˌɪmplɪ'keɪʃn/*n*. 牵连；含意，暗示/**implicative** /ɪm'plɪkətɪv/ *adj*. 含蓄的，言外之意的；牵连的

implicit/ɪm'plɪsɪt/

adj. ❶ not said openly but suggested or implied 暗示的；含蓄的：It was ～ in your statement that I was wrong. 你话中的含意是我错了。 ❷ without questioning; complete 无疑的；全然的，绝对的：He has an ～ belief in democracy. 他绝对信仰民主政治。

implore/ɪm'plɔː(r)/

v. ask (for) in a begging manner; entreat 恳求，乞求：She ～d the doctor to save her sick child. 她恳求医生救救她生病的孩子。

imply/ɪm'plaɪ/

v. ❶ express indirectly; suggest 暗示；含有……的意思：Silence sometimes implies consent. 沉默有时表示同意。/ Their nodding implied that they had agreed to the plan. 他们的点头表示他们已赞同这项计划。❷ make sth. seem to be true 说明；表明：The survey implies that more and more people want to buy a car. 调查显示，想买车的人越来越多。

impolite/ˌɪmpə'laɪt/

adj. not polite 不礼貌的：Don't speak in an ～ way. 说话要讲礼貌。

impolitic/ɪm'pɒlətɪk/

adj. not politic; not expedient 不高明的；失策的；不利的：It would be ～ to ask him now, because he is very angry. 现在去问他是失策的，因为他正在生气。

imponderable/ɪm'pɒndərəbl/

adj. not able to be measured or estimated 无法衡量的；无法估计的

import

Ⅰ/ɪm'pɔːt/*v*. bring in from a foreign country 进口；输入：～ sth. from Japan 从日本进口某物/～ed goods 进口货/～ raw silk into a country 把生丝输入某国/We ～ machinery that we cannot make in our country. 我们进口国内不能制造的机械。Ⅱ/'ɪmpɔːt/ *n*. sth. that is imported 进口货；输入品：Machinery is one of our ～s. 机械是我国的进口货物之一。

important/ɪm'pɔːtnt/

adj. ❶ of great effect or value; very serious and significant 重要的：It is very ～ to keep your teeth in good condition. 保持牙齿健康是很重要的。/It is ～ that we (should) master a foreign language. 对我们来说掌握一门外语是很重要的。❷(of people) powerful; having influence（人）显要的，有权力的，有影响力的：The prime minister is a very ～ man. 首相是一个很显要的人物。 ‖ **importance** *n*. 重要，重大

importation/ˌɪmpɔː'teɪʃn/

n. ❶ the act or business of importing 进口（业），输入 ❷ sth. brought in from another place or country, especially an object or way of behaviour typical of another place 进口货，舶来品；从外国引进的事物，输入物

importer /ɪm'pɔːtə/

n. a person, company, etc. that buys goods from another country to sell them in their own country 从事进口的人（或公司）；进口商

importune/ˌɪmpɔː'tjuːn/

v. make repeated requests to, often in an annoying or troubling way 纠缠不休地要求：We were ～d with request for assistance.有人纠缠不休地要求我们给予帮助。

impose/ɪmˈpəʊz/

*v.*❶ lay or place (a tax,duty,etc.)on 征收(税等),使缴纳(罚款):～ new duties on tobaccos and wines 征收烟酒新税 ❷ force sth.on 把……强加给,强迫……接受:Don't try to ～ your wishes on us.不要企图把你的愿望强加给我们。❸ take advantage of 利用,占(人)便宜;欺骗:I'm not to be ～d upon.我是不会受骗上当的。

imposing/ɪmˈpəʊzɪŋ/

*adj.*grand in appearance or large in size; impressive 气势雄伟的,壮观的;威严的:an ～ view across the valley 山谷的壮丽景色/an ～ building 一座气势雄伟的建筑

imposition /ˌɪmpəˈzɪʃən/

*n.*❶ the act of imposing sth.强加 ❷ a burden or obligation that has been imposed 强加的负担(或义务)❸ an unfair burden;inconvenience 不公平的负担;不便:I hope my visit won't be an ～.希望我的来访不会给您带来不便。

impossible/ɪmˈpɒsəbl/

*adj.*❶not possible 不可能的,做不到的:It's all ～ to me.这对我来说完全是不可能的。❷ that cannot be endured or dealt with 难以忍受的;难处理的:You're ～! 你真是令人难以忍受! ‖ **impossibility** /ɪmˌpɒsəˈbɪləti/ *n.*不可能;不可能的事

impotent/ˈɪmpətənt/

*adj.*weak;without power to change 虚弱的;无力的

impound/ɪmˈpaʊnd/

v. take possession of by law 扣留;扣押:Cattle found wandering on a road can be ～ed.发现牛在公路上走来走去可以把它们关起来。/The judge ordered the documents to be ～ed.法官下令扣留这些文件。

impracticable/ɪmˈpræktɪkəbl/

*adj.*not able to be carried out;(with reference to roads or paths) not passable 不能实行的;(指道路)不能通行的

impractical /ɪmˈpræktɪkl/

*adj.*not practical;unwise;not realistic 不能使用的;行不通的;不明智的;不切实际的:his ～ romanticism 他那不切实际的浪漫主义 ‖ ～ity *n.*不切实际的事

imprecise /ˌɪmprɪˈsaɪs/

*adj.*not precise;not clear 不精确的;不严密的;不确切的 ‖ ～ly *adv.*不严密地

impregnate/ˈɪmpreɡneɪt/

*v.*❶ make fertile or pregnant 使受精;使怀孕 ❷ fill or soak with sth.使充满;灌注;使浸透:The wood is ～d with chemicals which are antiseptic 这块木头正用防腐的化学药品浸泡。

impress/ɪmˈpres/

*v.*❶ press (one thing on another);make a mark,etc.by doing this 盖(印),压印:～ the words on a metal plate 在金属板上压印出字样 ❷ have a strong influence on; fill (sb.) with admiration 使(人)留下深刻印象:I was very ～ed by(with) their hospitality.他们的殷勤好客给我留下了深刻印象。❸ make the importance of (sth.) clear to (sb.) 铭刻;使铭记:My father ～ed on me the necessities of education.我父亲向我强调了教育的必要性。 ‖ ～ed *adj.*受到触动的;印象深刻的

impression/ɪmˈpreʃn/

*n.*❶ a mark left by pressure 印记,压痕:the ～ of a seal on wax 盖在蜡上的印记 ❷ an effect produced in the mind;feelings 印象;感觉:What's your ～ of the city? 你对这座城市的印象如何? ❸ all the copies of sth.(such as a book)made at one time 印刷,印数,印版:the third ～ of the second edition 再版的第三次印刷 ‖ (**be**)**under the** ～(**that**)有……这样的印象;认为,以为 ‖ ～al *adj.*印象(上)的/ ～ism *n.*(绘画等)印象主义,印象派/ ～ist *adj.*印象主义的 & *n.*印象派艺术家

impressive/ɪmˈpresɪv/

*adj.*causing admiration,especially by giving sb. a feeling of size, importance, or great skill; making a strong or good impression 给人深刻印象的;感人的:an ～

speech(speaker, scene) 令人难忘的演说(演讲者、场面) ‖ ～ness *n.*令人难忘；印象性/～ly *adv.*令人难忘地；感人地

imprint/ɪmˈprɪnt/

*v.*fix firmly in the mind 铭刻；牢记：The terrible accident is still ～ed on my memory.那起可怕的事故至今仍深深地留在我的记忆中。

imprison/ɪmˈprɪzn/

*v.*put or keep in prison；shut up closely 关押，监禁束缚：He was ～ed for life.他受到终身监禁。‖ ～ment *n.*监禁，徒刑；关押；束缚

improbable/ɪmˈprɒbəbl/

*adj.*not likely to be true or to happen 不大可能的，未必会的：Rain seems ～ on such a clear day.这样晴朗的天气，下雨似乎不大可能。

impromptu/ɪmˈprɒmptjuː/

adj.& *adv.*without preparation 无准备的(地)；即席的(地)；临时的(地)：an ～ lesson 无准备的课/play a tune ～ 即席演奏一曲

improper/ɪmˈprɒpə(r)/

*adj.*❶ not suitable for morality or honesty 不合适的，不恰当的：Your conduct here has been very ～.你在这里的行为是很不合适的。❷ not correct 不正确的，错误的：an ～ diagnosis of disease 对疾病的错误诊断 ‖ **impropriety** *n.*不适当(行为)

improve/ɪmˈpruːv/

*v.*❶ make better 改进，改善，提高：I want to ～ my English.我想提高我的英语水平。/～ farming methods 改进耕作方法 ❷ become better 变得更好，增进：His health is improving.他的身体正在康复。❸increase the value of (land or property) by farming, building, etc.(靠耕作或修建筑以)提高(土地、地产)的价值 ‖ ～ on 把……改得更好，把……加以提高 ‖ ～r *n.*改进者，改进物；学徒

improvement/ɪmˈpruːvmənt/

*n.*❶the act of making sth. better 改进，改善：Your work shows considerable ～.你的工作显示出相当大的改进。/There

has been a slight (significant) ～ in the company's trading position. 这家公司的贸易地位有所(有很大的)提高。❷sth. which improves, which adds to beauty, usefulness, value, etc. 改良的事物；增加美、用途、价值等的事物：carry out home ～s 进行住宅装修

improvident/ɪmˈprɒvɪdənt/

adj.(especially of someone who wastes money) not preparing for the future；spending money casually (尤指浪费金钱的人)不顾未来的，无远见的；挥霍的

improvise/ˈɪmprəvaɪz, ˌɪmprəˈvaɪz/

*v.*❶ do or make sth. (one has not prepared for) owing to an unexpected situation, sudden need, etc. 即席而作，临时凑成，临时准备：I forgot the words of my speech, so I had to ～.我忘了演讲词，所以只得临时凑台。❷make up (music) as one is playing 即席作曲：～ an accompaniment to the song 为那首歌作即兴伴奏

imprudent/ɪmˈpruːdnt/

*adj.*thoughtless；rash；unwise 不谨慎的；轻率的；不明智的：It was ～ of you to lend money to a stranger.你借钱给一个陌生人是欠考虑的。

impudent/ˈɪmpjʊdənt/

*adj.*rude；insolent；disrespectful 粗野的；无礼的；冒失的：That ～ boy put his tongue out at me.那个粗野的男孩子对我伸舌头。

impulse/ˈɪmpʌls/

*n.*❶ an impetus；a driving force 推动，冲力：give an ～ to the development of the friendly relations between the two countries 促进两国友好关系的发展 ❷ a sudden wish to do sth.；sudden urge 冲动，刺激：a man of ～ 易冲动的人 ‖ ～buy *n.*(未经考虑或计划的)购买，冲动购买

impulsive/ɪmˈpʌlsɪv/

*adj.*having or showing a tendency to act suddenly without thinking about the suitability, results, etc. of one's acts 冲动的，凭冲动办事的：He has been criticized for his ～ action.他由于太感情用事而受到批评。

impure/ɪm'pjʊə(r)/

adj. ❶ not pure, but mixed with sth. else 不纯洁的,掺杂的:~ motives 不纯的动机 ❷ morally bad,especially with regard to sexual behaviour 不道德的;肮脏的:~ thoughts 邪念

impurity/ɪm'pjʊərəti/

n. ❶ the state of being not pure 不纯洁 ❷ an impure thing or element 杂质,混杂物:Filtering the water can remove its impurities.过滤可除去水中的杂质。

impute/ɪm'pju:t/

v. consider as the act,quality,or outcome of sth. 把……归咎(归因)于:How can they ~ such dishonourable motives to me? 他们怎么能把这种卑鄙的动机强加到我头上来呢?

in/ɪn/

Ⅰ *prep.* ❶ contained by (sth. with depth, length,and height)(表示地点或部位)在……里,在……中,在……处:~ the room 在房间里 ❷ showing direction of movement (表示方向)进入,朝向:jump ~ (into) the water 跳入水中 ❸ at some time;during;at the time of (表示时间)在……期间:~ May 在五月/ ~ my youth 在我年轻时 ❹ during not more than (the space of)(表示时间长度)在……(时间)内,在……(时间)之后(之末):I'll be ready ~ an hour.我一小时以内准备好。❺ showing the condition of a person or thing 在……情况中,处于……状态:~ good health 身体好/ ~ tears 在哭泣/ ~ danger 处于危险中 ❻ indicating occupation,activity, etc.(表示职业)从事……(工作);在……方面:He's ~ business(politics,insurance).他是经商的(从政的、从事保险业的)。❼(of dress) wearing (表示服饰)穿,戴:a girl ~ red (a fur coat) 穿红衣服(穿皮大衣)的姑娘/a wolf ~ sheep's skin 披着羊皮的狼 ❽ indicating the method (tool,medium, material,etc.)(表示方式)以……方式,用……(语言等):Write it ~ pencil(ink, English).用铅笔(用墨水、用英文)写。/ ~ secret 秘密地;私下地 ❾ indicating surroundings (表示环境)在……环境下:

sleep ~ the shade(~ the open) 睡在树荫(在露天)下 ❿(showing division and arrangement) so as to be (表示划分与安排)划分为,安排成:~ groups 成群地/ stand ~ a circle 围成一圈站着 ⓫(showing relation or proportion) per (表示关系或比例)每:pay a tax of 40 penny ~ the pound 每英镑要付四十便士的税 Ⅱ *adv.* ❶ used with many verbs in different meanings (与动词连用,意义不同):Come ~! 进来! / give ~ 屈服 ❷(used with verb be) present,especially at home 在场,在家,在室内:Were you ~ or out! 你在家还是出去了? ❸ from a number of people,or from all directions to a central point 聚拢,集中:Letters have been coming(pouring) ~.信件蜂拥而至。❹ fashionably 流行,时髦:Mini skirts came ~ last year.去年流行迷你裙。Ⅲ *adj.* ❶ used for sending sth. to one 交来的(文件等):I took the letters from my ~ tray.我从收件盘上取下信件。❷ fashionable 时髦的:the ~ thing to wear 赶时髦穿戴的东西‖ be ~ for 免不了遭受;参加(竞争等)/be ~ for it 骑虎难下;势必受罚/be ~ on 参与/be ~ on it 熟悉内情/be (keep) ~ with sb. 与某人友好相处/day ~,day out(year ~,year out) 日复一日(年复一年)/the ~s and outs (of sth.) 里里外外;详情

in-/ɪn/

pref. ❶ showing the way sb. is coming, etc.表示"在内","进","入","向","朝":~coming 进来的/ ~vasion 侵犯/ ~land 向(在)内地 ❷not 表示"不","非", "无":~active 不活跃的/~action 无行动,不活跃

inability/ˌɪnə'bɪləti/

n. the state of being unable to do sth. 无能;无力,无能为力:~ to do sth. 无能力做某事

inaccessible/ˌɪnæk'sesəbl/

adj. not accessible to reach or get 不能接近的;不能进入的;不能达到的:an ~ person 令人难以亲近的人/The lake is ~ to motorists.汽车无法开到湖边。

inaccurate /ɪnˈækjərət/

adj.not accurate or exact 不准确的;不精确的:an ～ account 不准确的报道/The thermometer is ～.这温度计不准。

inaction /ɪnˈækʃn/

n.the lack of action or activity;the quality or state of doing nothing 无行动;无作为;不活跃;懒散

inactive /ɪnˈæktɪv/

adj.❶not active;idle 不活跃的,懒散的:He is ～ and dreamy by nature.他生性懒散,又好梦想。❷no longer working 停止活动的:an ～ machine 闲置的机器

inadequacy /ɪnˈædɪkwəsi/

n.❶the quality of being not enough or qualified 不适当,不够格;不充分;不胜任:a feeling of personal ～ 个人不胜任的感觉 ❷an example of incompleteness or poor quality;shortcoming 不完善,不足之处;缺陷,弱点:several inadequacies in your report 你报告中的几点不足之处 ‖ **inadequate** *adj*.不适当的;不充分的

inadvisable /ˌɪnədˈvaɪzəbl/

adj.unwise;not sensible 不明智的;不妥当的

inanimate /ɪnˈænɪmət/

adj.❶lifeless,not alive 无生命的:an ～ object 无生命物 ❷spiritless;dull 无生气的;单调的:～ conversation 沉闷的谈话

inapplicable /ɪnˈæplɪkəbl/

adj.not applicable or suitable 不适用的:The rule is ～ to this situation.这个规定不适用于这种情况。

inappropriate /ˌɪnəˈprəupriət/

adj.not proper;not suitable;not correct for a particular purpose 不适当的;不相宜的

inapt /ɪnˈæpt/

adj.not suitable or fitting 不适当的;不合适的:an ～ remark (question,translation) 不恰当的言语(问题、翻译)

inattention /ˌɪnəˈtenʃn/

n.the lack of attention to sb.or sth.不注意;漫不经心

inattentive /ˌɪnəˈtentɪv/

adj.not attentive;not paying attention to sb.or sth. 不注意的 ‖ ～**ly** *adv*.不注意地;疏忽地/～**ness** *n*.注意迟钝

inaudible /ɪnˈɔːdəbl/

adj.not loud enough to be heard 听不见的

inaugural /ɪˈnɔːgjʊrəl/

adj.of or for the beginning of sth.important 就职的;就任的:an ～ ceremony 就职典礼

inaugurate /iˈnɔːgjʊreɪt/

v.❶introduce (a new official,professor,etc.) at a special ceremony 为(重要人物)举行就职典礼:He was ～d as professor.他就任了教授(职位)。❷open with a ceremony 为……落成(或通车)举行仪式,为……举行开幕式:The Export Commodities Fair was ～d yesterday.出口商品交易会于昨日开幕。❸open;begin 开创,开辟,创始:～ a new era 开创新纪元 ‖ **inauguration** /ɪˌnɔːgjʊˈreɪʃn/ *n*.就职;就职典礼;开幕式;落成典礼/**inaugurator** *n*.主持就职(或开幕)仪式者;开创者

inborn /ˌɪnˈbɔːn/

adj.(of a quality) possessed (by a person or animal) at birth;implanted by nature 生来的;天生的;先天的:an ～ talent for art 天生的艺术才能

inbred /ɪnˈbred/

adj.❶possessed when born 天生的:～ courage 天生的勇气 ❷having ancestors who were closely related to each other 近亲繁殖的

inbuilt /ˈɪnbɪlt/

adj.existing as an original or essential part of sth.or sb.原有的,内在的,本质的:the body's ～ability to heal itself 人体自我修复的内在能力

incalculable /ɪnˈkælkjʊləbl/

adj.too great to be measured or counted 不可胜数的;数不清的

incapable /ɪnˈkeɪpəbl/

adj.not capable 无能力的;不能的,不会的;(be) ～ of doing the work 没有能力做这工作

incense¹ /ɪnˈsens/

v.make sb.angry 激怒(某人)

incense² /ɪnˈsens/

n. a substance which gives off a sweet-smelling smoke when burnt（usually used for religious purposes）香（通常为宗教目的而使用）

incentive /ɪnˈsentɪv/

n. sth. which makes sb. do sth.（especially work harder）刺激；动机：The best ~ in business is the chance of making more money. 商业上最好的刺激就是有机会赚更多的钱。

incessant /ɪnˈsesnt/

adj. continual；never stopping 连续不断的；不停的：a week of ~ rain 一星期来连绵不断的雨

inch /ɪntʃ/

Ⅰ *n.* ❶ a unit of length equal to 2.54cm or one twelfth of a foot 英寸（等于 2.54 厘米，一英尺的十二分之一）：six ~es of rain in one day 一天的雨量达六英寸 ❷ a small amount or distance（数量、距离等的）少许，一点儿：I can't see an ~ before me in the dense fog. 在浓雾中我一点也看不见。‖ by ~es 刚刚（仅）；一点一点地/every ~ 完全（彻底）地/not yield an ~ 寸步不让/to an ~ 精确地/within an ~ of one's life 差点儿丧命 Ⅱ *v.* move by inches（使）慢慢移动，渐进：The mountaineers ~ed their way up the peak. 登山队员一步一步登上了顶峰。

incidence /ˈɪnsɪdəns/

n. ❶ the rate at which sth. happens or exists 发生率：a high ~ of tuberculosis 结核病的高发病率 ❷ a way or scope in which sth. affects things 影响的方式；影响的范围：The ~ of a tax is limited if only a few people pay the tax. 如果只有少数几个人缴税，税收的范围就会受到限制。

incident /ˈɪnsɪdənt/

Ⅰ *n.* ❶ an event（especially in a story）小事件，发生的事情：On the very day before I left, an ~ occurred. 正是在我离开前那天，发生了一件事。 ❷ a political event（that includes violence, such as fighting or explosions）（含有战斗、爆炸

等暴力行为的）事件，事变：the Xi'an Incident 西安事变/border ~s 边境事件 Ⅱ *adj.* forming a natural or expected part of；naturally connected with 伴随而来的；（与……）有关的：new duties ~ to increased tasks 伴随新增加的任务而来的新职责

incidental /ˌɪnsɪˈdentl/

adj. happening or existing in connection with sth. else that is more important 附带的；伴随的；次要的：~ music to a film 电影的配乐 ‖ ~ly *adv.* 附带地；偶然地

incinerate /ɪnˈsɪnəreɪt/

v. destroy sth., especially waste material by burning it completely 焚毁（某物，尤指废料）‖ incineration *n.* 焚化

incinerator /ɪnˈsɪnəreɪtə(r)/

n. a container or furnace in which rubbish is burnt（垃圾等的）焚化炉

incipient /ɪnˈsɪpɪənt/

adj. just beginning 刚开始的；初发的；初期的：an ~ disease 初发的病症

incise /ɪnˈsaɪz/

v.（often with reference to surgical operations）cut into（常指外科手术）切入；切割 ‖ incision /ɪnˈsɪʒn/ *n.* 切口，切割

incisive /ɪnˈsaɪsɪv/

adj.（with reference to thoughts and words）sharp；acute（指思想、言语）敏锐的；锋利的；尖刻的：He refused the request in a few ~ words. 他用几句尖刻的话拒绝了这种要求。

incite /ɪnˈsaɪt/

v. urge sb. to do sth.（usually sth. wrong）激励；鼓动；煽动：He is inciting them to go on strike. 他在煽动他们举行罢工。‖ ~ment *n.* 煽动；鼓动

inclement /ɪnˈklemənt/

adj.（usually with reference to the weather）cold or stormy；not mild；severe（通常指天气）寒冷的；狂风暴雨的；严酷的

inclination /ˌɪnklɪˈneɪʃn/

n. ❶ a natural tendency to act in a certain way（人的）自然倾向 ❷ an interest or a liking for sth. 兴趣，爱好 ❸ a slope or slant 斜坡，倾斜 ❹ a leaning or bending movement, usually of a head（倾斜或弯曲的动作）点头；弯腰

incline /ɪnˈklaɪn/

I v. ❶ (cause to) slope（使）倾斜，（使）成斜坡：The road ~s to the right. 这条路向右边倾斜。❷ cause to move downwards 低下来，垂下：My grandfather ~d his head. 我祖父低下头去。Ⅱ n. a slope or a sloping surface 斜坡；斜面：The house is built upon an ~. 那幢房子建在一个斜坡上。

inclined /ɪnˈklaɪnd/

adj. ❶ wanting to do；feeling a wish（to）想要……的：The news makes me ~ to change my mind. 这消息使我想改变主意。❷ likely；tending（to）易于……的，趋向（常）……的：I'm ~ to get tired easily. 我很容易疲倦。

include /ɪnˈkluːd/

v. ❶ have as a part of the whole；contain 包括，包含：The price of this book ~s postage. 本书定价包括邮费在内。❷ regard as a member of a group；take into account 使列入，算入：I ~d books on the list of things to buy. 我把书列入了购物单中。‖ **inclusion** /ɪnˈkluːʒn/ n. 包含；内含物

including /ɪnˈkluːdɪŋ/

prep. containing as part of the whole 包括

inclusive /ɪnˈkluːsɪv/

adj. ❶ including；taking in；counting in 包括的，包含的：a household of ten persons, ~ of the servants 一家十口人，包括仆人在内 ❷ including everything concerned 包括一切在内的：made an ~ list of your expenses 列一个包括你所有花费的单子

incoherent /ˌɪnkəʊˈhɪərənt/

adj.（especially with reference to speeches, thoughts, ideas and explanations, etc.）not fitting together；not easy to understand（尤指言语、思想、观点、解释等）不连贯的；无条理的；语无伦次的；难理解的

income /ˈɪnkʌm/

n. money which is regularly received for work done, from trade, etc. 收入；收益；所得：He has an ~ of ￡3,000 a year. 他一年收入 3 000 镑。‖ ~ **tax** n. 所得税

incoming /ˈɪnkʌmɪŋ/

adj. ❶ coming in 进来的，到来的 ❷ about to take over from someone else 接替别人的：the ~ chairman 继任的主席

incomparable /ɪnˈkɒmprəbl/

adj. ❶ without an equal；matchless 无比的：~ beauty 无比的美 ❷ not able to be compared；unsuitable for comparison 不能比较的，不适于比较的：This one is ~ with that on. 这个不能与那个相比。

incompatible /ˌɪnkəmˈpætəbl/

adj. not able or suitable to go together 不相容的；不能和谐共存的：Those two people are ~. 这两人合不来。

incompetent /ɪnˈkɒmpɪtənt/

adj. not having the ability or power to do sth. 无能力的；不适合的：He is ~ at working with his hands. 他不适合用双手干活。

incomplete /ˌɪnkəmˈpliːt/

adj. not complete；not having all the necessary parts 不完全的；不完善的：The financial system is ~. 金融制度不完善。

incomprehensible /ˌɪnkɒmprɪˈhensəbl/

adj. not able to be understood 不能理解的；不可思议的

inconceivable /ˌɪnkənˈsiːvəbl/

adj. difficult to believe；that cannot be thought of or imagined 不可思议的；无法想象的

inconclusive /ˌɪnkənˈkluːsɪv/

adj. without a definite decision or result 非决定性的；不充分的；无确定结果的：~ evidence 不能使人信服的证据

incongruous /ɪnˈkɒŋgruəs/

adj. not having anything in common；not in agreement with 不调和的；不相称的；不一致的：They are an ~ couple. 他们是不相称的一对。/ an ~ remark 自相矛盾的话 ‖ **incongruity** /ˌɪnkɒŋˈgruːəti/ n. 不协调之物；不相称之物；不调和；不相称；不一致

inconsequential /ˌɪnkɒnsɪˈkwenʃl/

adj. **❶** not following what happened before 不连贯的；前后不一的 **❷** not important 不重要的

inconsiderate/ˌɪnkənˈsɪdərət/

adj. not thinking of other people's feelings；thoughtless 不替别人着想的，不体谅人的：He's ～ to his family. 他不体谅家里人。

inconsistent/ˌɪnkənˈsɪstənt/

adj. **❶** (of ideas, opinions, etc.) not in agreement with each other or with sth. else (想法、意见等)不一致的，前后矛盾的：Those remarks are ～ with what you said yesterday. 那些话与你昨天说的不一致。**❷** tending to change 反复无常的，常变的：The weather here is very ～. 这儿的天气反复无常。

inconstant/ɪnˈkɒnstənt/

adj. (especially with reference to feelings) changing easily (尤指感情)多变的；反复无常的

incontestable/ˌɪnkənˈtestəbl/

adj. that cannot be disputed or denied 无可争辩的；无可否认的

incontinence /ɪnˈkɒntɪnəns/

n. the lack of ability to control the bladder and bowels 失禁：Many patients in that hospital have been diagnosed with ～. 那家医院的很多病人都被诊断为尿失禁。

incontinent/ɪnˈkɒntɪnənt/

adj. not having control over one's feelings and behaviour (especially control over feelings of sexual desire or control over urine, etc.) 无节制的；纵欲的；(小便等)失禁的

inconvenience/ˌɪnkənˈviːnɪəns/

Ⅰ *n.* discomfort or trouble 不便(之处)；麻烦(的事)：Your visit caused him great ～. 你的来访给他带来很多麻烦。/the ～ of having to travel a long way to work 上班路远的不便之处(或困难) Ⅱ *v.* cause inconvenience to 使感到不便；使感到困难：I hope my visit will not ～ you. 我希望我的来访不会打扰你。

inconvenient/ˌɪnkənˈviːnɪənt/

adj. causing difficulty or trouble (引起)

不便的；麻烦的：Saturday is an ～ day to see him. 星期六去看他有所不便。

incorporate/ɪnˈkɔːpəreɪt/

v. **❶** make (sth.) a part of sth. else；join 结合；合并：～ fertilizer with soil 将化肥和泥土混合/mix ingredients until they ～ 搅拌配料直到它们混合均匀 **❷** set up a legal company 组建公司：They will ～ a company as soon as they have a little more capital. 他们的资本一旦再多一点他们就将组建公司。‖ ～d *adj.* 结合的，合并的，混合的

incorrect/ˌɪnkəˈrekt/

adj. not correct or true；wrong 不正确的；错误的

incorrigible/ɪnˈkɒrɪdʒəbl/

adj. (of people or behaviour) very bad and unable to be changed or improved 无可救药的；难以纠正的；固执的：She's an ～ liar. 她是个永不悔改的撒谎者。‖ **incorrigibility** *n.* 难以纠正；不能改进

incorruptible/ˌɪnkəˈrʌptəbl/

adj. **❶** that cannot decay or be destroyed 不易腐蚀的，不易败坏的 **❷** that cannot be corrupted, especially by being bribed 收买不了的，不贪污受贿的，廉洁的：as ～ as an English judge 像英国法官一样廉洁 ‖ **incorruptibility**/ˌɪnkəˌrʌptəˈbɪləti/ *n.* 清廉/**incorruptibly** *adv.* 廉洁地

increase

Ⅰ /ɪnˈkriːs/ *v.* make or become large in amount or number 增加，增大，增多，增殖：～ production and practise economy 增产节约 Ⅱ /ˈɪnkriːs/ *n.* a rise in amount, numbers, etc. 增加，增长，增进，增殖：The technical cooperation and cultural exchanges between the two countries are daily on the ～. 两国之间的技术合作和文化交流正与日俱增。‖ **on the ～** 正在增加，不断增长 ‖ **increasingly** /ɪnˈkriːsɪŋli/ *adv.* 渐增地，逐渐地，日益，越来越

incredible/ɪnˈkredəbl/

adj. **❶** too strange to be believed；unbelievable or very hard to believe 不可相信的，难以置信的：The plot of the book is

~.这本书里的情节难以置信。❷ wonderful;unbelievably good 好极了的,难以相信的好:She has an ~ house.她有一幢极好的房子。‖ **incredibility** /ɪnˌkredə'bɪləti/ n.不可信的事物/**incredibly** adv.难以置信地;极为

incredulous /ɪn'kredjʊləs/
adj.not believing someone,showing disbelief 不相信的,不轻信的 ‖ **incredulity** n.怀疑,不轻信/~**ly** adv.不轻信地

incriminate /ɪn'krɪmɪneɪt/
v.show a person to have been involved in a crime 显示……有罪;控告 ‖ **incrimination** n.控告;连累

incubate /'ɪnkjʊbeɪt/
v.❶hatch eggs by keeping them warm 孵(卵) ❷keep (eggs,cells,bacteria,embryos,etc.) at a suitable temperature so that they develop (尤指在实验室内)培养(卵、细胞、细菌、胚胎等)

inculcate /'ɪnkʌlkeɪt/
v.fix (ideas,principles,etc.) in the mind of (someone) 反复灌输(想法、原则等),谆谆教诲:The professor ~d his pupils with the love of truth.教授谆谆教导他的学生要热爱真理。‖ **inculcation** /ˌɪnkʌl'keɪʃn/ n.谆谆教诲/**inculcator** n.反复灌输者,谆谆教诲者

incumbency /ɪn'kʌmbənsi/
n.the period in office of an incumbent 任期:during his ~ as president 在他担任总统期间

incumbent[1] /ɪn'kʌmbənt/
n.❶a priest in the Church of England who is in charge of a church and its parish (英国国教的)教区牧师 ❷the holder of an official position,especially a political one (尤指担任政治职位的)现任者,在职者

incumbent[2] /ɪn'kʌmbənt/
adj.❶ necessary as part of the duty or responsibility (of someone) 成为责任的,义不容辞的:It's ~ on the purchaser to check the contract before signing.在签字之前买主有责任核对合同。❷ holding the stated office 现任的,在职的:the ~

priest 在职牧师/~ president 现任总统

incur /ɪn'kɜː(r)/
v.(-rr-) bring upon oneself 招致;蒙受:He has ~red many debts.他负债累累。/You will ~ your father's disapproval.你会遭到你父亲的反对。

incurable /ɪn'kjʊərəbl/
adj.that cannot be cured 不能治疗的,不可救药的

incurious /ɪn'kjʊərɪəs/
adj.lacking natural interest;not curious to know more 不感兴趣的;不好奇的:~ about the outside world 对外部世界不感兴趣

incursion /ɪn'kɜːʃn/
n.a sudden attack or invasion 侵袭;突然袭击

indebted /ɪn'detɪd/
adj.very grateful to (someone) for one's help 感激的;受惠的,欠人情的:I am greatly ~ to you for your help.我非常感激你的帮助。

indecent /ɪn'diːsnt/
adj.(especially with reference to talk and behaviour) not decent;morally offensive;improper (尤指言谈、行为等)下流的;猥亵的;粗鄙的 ‖ **indecency** n.粗野,非礼;下流,猥亵;粗鄙

indecisive /ˌɪndɪ'saɪsɪv/
adj.❶giving an uncertain result;inconclusive 非决定性的:an ~ battle (answer) 非决定性的战役(非结论性的答复) ❷ having or showing inability to make decisions 犹豫不决的,不定的:a man with an ~ manner 一个优柔寡断的人 ‖ ~**ly** adv.优柔寡断地

indeed /ɪn'diːd/
adv.❶ truly,really,certainly 的确,真正地:I am very glad ~ to hear that you are better.听说你身体好些了,我的确非常高兴。❷used to intensify(加强语气)确实,实在:Thank you very much ~.确实很感谢你。❸ used as a comment to show interest or surprise,etc.(表示兴趣、惊讶等)真的,真是:"He spoke to me about you.""Oh,~!"他对我谈起了你。"噢"

真的！"

indefensible/ˌɪndɪˈfensəbl/

adj. ❶ too bad to be excused or defended 不可原谅的；无可辩解的：～ behaviour 不可原谅的行为 ❷ which cannot be defended 无法防御(保卫)的：The enemy's position is ～.敌人的阵地是守不住的。

indefinable/ˌɪndɪˈfaɪnəbl/

adj. that cannot be defined；vague 难下定义的；模糊不清的：an ～ air of mystery 不可言状的神秘气氛

indefinite/ɪnˈdefɪnət/

adj. ❶ not clear or exact 模糊的；不明确的；不确定的 ❷ lasting for an uncertain time 无限期的 ‖ ～ly *adv.* 模糊地；不确定地；无限期地

indelible/ɪnˈdeləbl/

adj. that cannot be rubbed out 擦不掉的；不可磨灭的：an ～ pencil 笔迹擦不掉的铅笔

indelicate/ɪnˈdelɪkət/

adj. (with reference to speech or behaviour) rude；coarse (指言行)粗鄙的；不雅的；粗鲁的

indemnify/ɪnˈdemnɪfaɪ/

v. pay for loss or damage；protect against future loss or damage 赔偿，补偿；保障，保护：The company indemnifies you against any injuries you may suffer while at work.该公司保障你免受工作中可能遭受的伤害。

indent/ɪnˈdent/

Ⅰ *v.* ❶ make notches in 把……刻成锯齿状 ❷ make an order on(source or supply) or for (sth.) 订货 ❸ set back (beginning of line) farther from margin to mark new paragraph,etc.缩进；缩排(以示新的段落) Ⅱ *n.* ❶ a notch or cut in an edge 凹口，锯齿形 ❷ an order form, especially one used in foreign trade (尤指外贸)订单 ❸ a contract or sealed agreement between two or more parties 合同，契约 ❹ the space left between a margin and the start of an indented line 空格，(印刷的)缩进

indenture[1]/ɪnˈdentʃə(r)/

n. a contract，especially one in former times between an apprentice and his master (尤指旧时的)师徒契约

indenture[2]/ɪnˈdentʃə(r)/

v. cause to enter employment on conditions stated in indentures 以师徒契约雇用(学徒等)：an ～d bricklayer 签署了师徒契约的砌砖工人

independent/ˌɪndɪˈpendənt/

Ⅰ *adj.* ❶ not governed by another country；self-governing 独立的，自治的：an ～ country 独立国家 ❷ not dependent on (other persons or things) 自主的，不仰仗人的：～ thinking 独立思考 Ⅱ *n.* a person who does not belong to the same political party 独立派人士，无党派者 ‖ (be) ～ of … 独立于……之外的，不受……支持的；与……无关的，不依赖……的 ‖ independence *n.* 独立；自立

in-depth/ˈɪnˈdepθ/

adj. detailed and thorough 全面深入的：～ analysis of the figures 对数据全面深入的分析

indescribable/ˌɪndɪsˈkraɪbəbl/

adj. too good or bad to be described 难以描述的，难以形容的

indeterminate/ˌɪndɪˈtɜːmɪnət/

adj. not clearly seen，or not fixed 看不清楚的；不肯定的，未决定的：Our holiday plans are still at an ～ stage.我们的度假计划仍处于未定阶段。

index/ˈɪndeks/

Ⅰ *n.* (*pl.* ～es or indices/ˈɪndɪsiːz/) ❶ a thing that is a sign of sth. else. 指标，标志，表示……的东西：The increasing sale of luxuries was an ～ of the country's prosperity.奢侈品销售的增加显示出这个国家的繁荣。 ❷ a list of names，subjects，etc. in ABC order, at the end of a book，etc.索引 ❸ the system of numbers by which prices，costs，etc. can be compared to a former level 指数(用于价格、费用等的今昔比较)：the cost of living ～ 生活费用指数 ‖ the ～ finger *n.*食指/ ～ number(figure) *n.*(物价、工资等的)指数 Ⅱ *v.* provide with or include in an index

（为书等）编索引；把（字或参考指示）编入索引中：The book is not well ~ed.这本书的索引编得不好。‖ ~er n.编索引者

Indian /ˈɪndɪən/
adj. & n. ❶ (someone) belonging to or connected with India 印度的；印度人 ❷ (someone) belonging to or connected with any of the original peoples of North, Central, or South America except the Eskimos 美洲印第安人的；印第安人 ‖ **West** ~ adj. & n.西印度群岛的，西印度群岛的人/~ **club** n.瓶状棒（体育器具）/~ **corn** n.玉蜀黍，玉米/~ **ink** n.(写毛笔字用的)墨，墨汁/~ **red** n.印度红

indicate /ˈɪndɪkeɪt/
v. ❶ state or show briefly 指出，表示：I ~d that the interview was over.我表示会见结束了。❷ show (the direction in which one is turning in a vehicle) with hand signals, lights, etc.(用手势、灯光等)指示，指向：A road sign ~d the right road for us to follow.路标指示了我们应走的路。❸ show a need for; suggest 表示需要；建议：In this weather, a fire is ~d.这种天气需要生火。❹ make a sign (for) 暗示：He ~d that we could leave. 他暗示我们可以离开。

indication /ˌɪndɪˈkeɪʃn/
n. ❶ the act or sign that shows sth.is happening 指示，表示：A thermometer gives ~ of changes in temperature.温度计表示温度的变化。❷ a thing that indicates; a sign 象征，指示之物：There was no ~ that the house was occupied.没有迹象表明这房子有人住。

indicative /ɪnˈdɪkətɪv/
adj. ❶ showing or suggesting sth.指示的；标示的；暗示……的；象征……的：His presence is ~ of his willingness to help. 他的出席表明他愿意帮忙。❷ stating a fact 陈述的，直陈的：an ~ verb (form) 陈述语气的动词(形式)

indicator /ˈɪndɪkeɪtə(r)/
n. ❶ a needle or pointer on a machine showing a measurement, e.g. of tempera-ture, pressure, amount of petrol, etc.(仪器上显示温度、压力、耗油量等的)指针，指示器，记录器 ❷ the lights on a car which flash to show which way it is turn-ing (车辆上的)转弯指示灯

indict /ɪnˈdaɪt/
v. charge with a crime 控告；对……起诉：He was ~ed for murder.他被控告谋杀。‖ **~able** adj.可提出控告的；可起诉的：an ~able offence 刑事罪 ‖ **~ment** n.起诉书；控告

indifferent /ɪnˈdɪfrənt/
adj. ❶ not interested in; not caring about or noticing 漠不关心的，不在乎的，冷淡的：How can you be so ~ to the suffer-ings of these people? 你怎能对这些人的疾苦漠不关心呢？❷ not very good; medi-ocre 平常的，不大好的，欠佳的：an ~ book 一本很平常的书/a very ~ foot-baller 技术欠佳的足球运动员 ‖ **indif-ference** n.不关心，不在乎

indigenous /ɪnˈdɪdʒɪnəs/
adj. born in or belonging to a country; native 本土的；土生土长的：the ~ peo-ples of South America 南美洲的土著人

indigestible /ˌɪndɪˈdʒestəbl/
adj. difficult or impossible to digest 难消化的，不能消化的 ‖ **indigestibility** n.难消化；难理解

indigestion /ˌɪndɪˈdʒestʃ(ə)n/
n. an illness or a pain caused by the stom-ach being unable to deal with the food which has been eaten 消化困难，不消化，消化不良(症)

indignant /ɪnˈdɪɡnənt/
adj. (especially with reference to what is thought to be wrong or unjust) angry (尤指对错误或不公平行为)愤怒的，愤慨的：They are ~ about the increased prices.他们对物价上涨愤愤不平。

indignation /ˌɪndɪɡˈneɪʃən/
n. the anger at sth.unjust or wicked 愤愤不平，愤慨，义愤：The letter filled her with ~.这封信使她义愤填膺。

indignity /ɪnˈdɪɡnəti/
n. a rude treatment causing sb.to lose dig-

nity and feel ashamed 轻蔑；伤自尊，屈辱：He suffered the ～ of being kept waiting for three hours. 让他等三小时,他觉得是不给他面子。

indirect /ˌɪndɪˈrekt, ˌɪndaɪˈrekt/
adj. not straight；not directly connected 曲折的；间接的,迂回的：an ～ answer to a question 对一问题的间接答复 ‖ ～ **object** 间接宾语／～ **question** 间接问句 ‖ ～**ly** *adv*. 间接地,迂回地／～**ness** *n*. 间接

indiscreet /ˌɪndɪˈskriːt/
adj. careless in behaviour；telling secrets to other people；going beyond the limits of what is proper or sensible 不慎重的；泄露秘密的；轻率的；不得体的

indiscretion /ˌɪndɪsˈkreʃən/
n. ❶ the act of doing sth. indiscreet 轻率；草率 ❷ an indiscreet action or statement 轻率的言行

indiscriminate /ˌɪndɪˈskrɪmɪnət/
adj. without taking the trouble to choose or to find out 不加选择的；不加区别的；不分青红皂白的：～ punishment 不分青红皂白的惩罚

indispensable /ˌɪndɪˈspensəbl/
adj. that cannot be dispensed；necessary 不可缺少的；必需的：Books are ～ to a scholar. 对一个学者来说,书是必不可少的。

indisposed /ˌɪndɪˈspəʊzd/
adj. ❶ unwell；slightly ill 有病的；不舒服的：I stayed at home because I was ～. 我待在家里,因为我身体不舒服。 ❷ unwilling 不愿意的：She is ～ to go. 她不想去。

indisputable /ˌɪndɪˈspjuːtəbl/
adj. that cannot be argued about or disagreed with 不容置疑的,无可争辩的

indistinct /ˌɪndɪˈstɪŋkt/
adj. not clearly seen, heard, etc. 不清楚的；模糊的；不清晰的：Your voice is ～. 你的声音模糊不清。

individual /ˌɪndɪˈvɪdʒʊəl/
Ⅰ *adj*. ❶ of or for one person 个人的,个体的：combine collective leadership with ～ responsibility 集体领导与个人负责相结合 ❷(often with each) single；particular；separate 特殊的；单独的；个别的：Each ～ leaf on the tree is different. 树上每片叶子都不相同。 ❸(of a manner, style, or way of doing things) particular to the person, thing, etc. concerned (and different from others)；distinctive 独特的,个性的：She wears very ～ clothes. 她的穿着与众不同。 Ⅱ *n*. ❶ a single person or thing, considered separately from the class or group to which he, she, or it belongs to 个人,个体；独立单位：We serve the people instead of serving the selfish interests of ～s. 我们为人民服务而不是为个人私利服务。 ❷ a person(一个) 人：What a bad tempered ～ you are! 你这人脾气真坏! ‖ ～**ist** *n*. 个人主义者,利己主义者

individualism /ˌɪndɪˈvɪdjʊəlɪz(ə)m/
n. ❶ the habit or principle of being independent and self-reliant 个人自立主义 ❷ a self-centered feeling or conduct；egoism 自我中心,自我主义；利己主义 ❸ a social theory favoring freedom of action for individuals over collective or state control 个人主义；个人自由主义

individuality /ˌɪndɪˌvɪdjuˈælɪti/
n. the special qualities or characters that a person or thing has 个性；个体特征

individualize /ˌɪndɪˈvɪdʒʊəlaɪz/
v. give an individual character to sb. or sth. to satisfy the needs of sb., etc. 使具有个性,使有个人特色,使适应个别需要

indoor /ˈɪndɔː(r)/
adj. done or situated inside a building 室内(进行)的,户内(用)的：(an) ～ antenna(swimming bath) 室内天线(室内游泳池)／～ games(photography) 室内游戏(室内摄影)

indoors /ˌɪnˈdɔːz/
adv. in a house or building；not in the open air；into a house 在室内；在户内；进入室内：play ～ 在屋里玩／keep (stay) ～ 待在家里；闭门不出／go ～ 进屋里／You should not spend all your time ～. 你不该花那么多时间待在家里。

induce /ɪnˈdjuːs/

v. ❶ persuade or influence sb. to do sth. 劝,诱导,促使(某人干某事):What ~d you to do such a thing? 什么促使你做这种事的？ ❷ bring about 导致,招惹,产生:Too much food ~s sleepiness.吃得过饱会产生睡意。

inducement /ɪnˈdjuːsmənt/

n. sth. which provides encouragement to do sth.诱因;刺激物;鼓励:They offered her a share in the business as an ~ to stay.他们提出在生意中给她一份股份以鼓励她留下。

induct /ɪnˈdʌkt/

v. (especially with reference to introducing a clergyman formally to his work) bring in;introduce (尤指牧师)使正式就职;引入;介绍

induction /ɪnˈdʌkʃn/

n. ❶ the act of inducting sb. to a new job, party, etc.就职;接纳会员;征召 ❷ the act of inducing a pregnant woman 人工引产;诱导 ❸ a ceremony in which a person is inducted into a position or organization 就职仪式;入会仪式 ❹ (an) introduction into a new job, company, etc. (雇员参加新工作、加入新公司等的)入门:an ~ course 入门课程 ❺ the production of electricity in one object by another which already has electrical (or magnetic) power (电磁)感应 ❻ (an example or result of) a process of reasoning using known facts to produce general rules or principles 归纳(法)

inductive /ɪnˈdʌktɪv/

adj. using induction; reasoning from known facts to produce general principles 使用归纳法的;归纳的:~ reasoning 归纳推理

indulge /ɪnˈdʌldʒ/

v. ❶ allow (oneself or someone else) to have or do what they want,especially sth. bad 放纵,迁就:He ~d his children.他纵容他的孩子。 ❷ let oneself or someone else have (their wish to do or have sth., etc.)使(自己)纵情享受,沉溺:He's not really a drinker, but he ~s at parties.他

并不真会喝酒,但在宴会上却恣意狂饮。 ❸ satisfy (a perhaps unwarranted or illicit desire) 满足(可能不正当的或不应有的愿望):She ~s her boyfriend's every whim.她对她男朋友的怪念头有求必应。 ‖ ~ in (sth.) 沉溺于,喜欢,尽情享受

indulgence /ɪnˈdʌldʒ(ə)ns/

n. ❶ the action or fact of doing or having what you want 沉湎,沉迷,沉醉:~ in self-pity 对自哀自怜的沉醉 ❷ the state or attitude of being indulgent or tolerant 纵容,迁就,娇惯,放任 ❸ a thing that sb. is indulged in;a luxury 嗜好;乐趣

indulgent /ɪnˈdʌldʒənt/

adj. ❶ allowing someone to have whatever they want, often in a way that is not good for them 纵容的;放纵的 ❷ tolerant or lenient 宽容的;宽大的 ‖ ~ly *adv.* 溺爱地;放任地

industrial /ɪnˈdʌstrɪəl/

adj. ❶ connected with industry; used by industries 工业的;产业的;用于工业的:the ~ areas of England 英国工业区 ❷ having highly developed industries 工业高度发达的:Japan is an ~ nation.日本是一个工业发达国家。 ‖ ~ dispute 劳资纠纷/~ estate 工业用地,工业区/ ~ relations 劳资关系/Industrial Revolution (十八世纪六十年代英国开始的)工业革命,产业革命/take ~ action 罢工 ‖ ~ism *n.* 工业主义/ ~ist *n.* 工业家,实业家

industrialize /ɪnˈdʌstrɪəlaɪz/

v. (cause to) become industrially developed (使)工业化:China must increase foreign trade to ~.中国必须增加对外贸易来实现工业化。 ‖ industrialization /ɪnˌdʌstrɪəlaɪˈzeɪʃn/ *n.* 工业化

industrious /ɪnˈdʌstrɪəs/

adj. hard-working 勤劳的 ‖ ~ly *adv.* 勤奋地,努力地

industry /ˈɪndəstri/

n. ❶ a particular branch of trade or manufacture which produces goods from raw material 工业:The country is supported by ~.这个国家以工业为支柱。 ❷ a particular sort of work, usually employing lots of people and using machinery and (or) modern methods 制造业；行业；产业：the clothing ～ 服装工业/the hotel ～ 旅馆业 ❸a quality of being hard-working；being always employed usefully 勤奋；勤勉：His success was due to ～ and thrift.他的成功是由于勤劳和节俭。

inedible /ɪnˈedɪbl/
adj.not suitable for eating 不可食用的；不宜食用的

ineffective /ˌɪnɪˈfektɪv/
adj.❶that does not produce any result；of little use 无效力的：～ efforts 无效的努力 ❷(of a person) unfit for work；incapable (人) 无能力的：He is ～ in an emergency.他不能随机应变。

inefficient /ˌɪnɪˈfɪʃənt/
adj.not able to work well and produce good results 效率低的；无效的 ‖ **inefficiency** *n*.效率低；无能

inelegant /ɪnˈelɪɡənt/
adj.❶not having very good manners；not graceful 不雅的；粗俗的 ❷not beautiful in appearance or not well-made 不精致的；粗糙的

ineligible /ɪnˈelɪdʒəbl/
adj.not fit to be chosen (for some reason) 无资格的；不适当的

inept /ɪˈnept/
adj.not suitable；not skillful 不适当的；笨拙的：an ～ remark 不恰当的话 ‖ ～itude *n*.不合适，不称职

inequality /ˌɪnɪˈkwɒləti/
n.the state of not being equal 不平等；不平均；不相同

inert /ɪˈnɜːt/
adj.❶without active chemical properties 惰性的；不起化学作用的：an ～ gas 惰性气体 ❷not moving；slow 不动的；不活泼的；迟钝的：He lay ～ly on the ground.他在地上一动不动地躺着。

inescapable /ˌɪnɪˈskeɪpəbl/
adj.not to be escaped from；inevitable 逃避不了的；不可避免的

inevitable /ɪnˈevɪtəbl/
adj.❶that cannot be avoided or prevented from happening；certain to happen 不可避免的，必然（发生）的：It's the ～ course of history.这是历史必由之路。❷that always happens or is always present with someone or sth.else 照例必有的，老一套的：a tourist with his ～ camera 一个照例带着照相机的游客 ‖ **the ～** 必然的事

inexact /ˌɪnɪɡˈzækt/
adj.not correct in every way；having mistakes 不精确的；不正确的

inexcusable /ˌɪnɪkˈskjuːzəbl/
adj.that cannot be excused or forgiven 不可原谅的，不可宽恕的；无法辩解的

inexhaustible /ˌɪnɪɡˈzɔːstəbl/
adj.that cannot be exhausted or used up 无穷无尽的，用不完的

inexpensive /ˌɪnɪkˈspensɪv/
adj.not expensive；cheap 不贵的；便宜的

inexperience /ˌɪnɪkˈspɪərɪəns/
n.the lack of experience 缺乏经验；无经验

inexplicable /ˌɪnɪkˈsplɪkəbl/
adj.that cannot be explained and understood 无法解释的；费解的

inexpressible /ˌɪnɪkˈspresəbl/
adj.that cannot be described or expressed in words 无法形容的；言语无法表达的

inexpressive /ˌɪnɪkˈspresɪv/
adj.lacking expressions or meanings 无表情的；无意义的：an ～ face 无表情的脸

inextinguishable /ˌɪnɪkˈstɪŋɡwɪʃəbl/
adj.(of fire and feelings) which cannot be destroyed or put out (指火和感情)不能扑灭的；不能遏制的：～ hope 不能遏制的希望/the ～ flame of liberty 扑不灭的自由之火

in extremis /ˌɪnɪkˈstriːmɪs/
adv.(as if) at the moment of death (似乎)在弥留之际；在绝望中；在危急关头：The government's incomes plan was saved in ～ by some last-minute concessions to the unions.由于在最后时刻对工会做出让步，政府的工资计划才在危急情况下得到了挽救。

inextricable /ɪnˈekstrɪkəbl/
adj.that cannot be solved or made simple

不能解决的；解不开的；不能摆脱的：He was in ～ difficulties.他处于无法摆脱的困境之中。

infallible/ɪnˈfæləbl/

adj.❶not able to do wrong or be wrong 不会做错事的；不会错的：He is so proud that he thinks himself ～.他太骄傲了,自认为不会做错事。❷always effective 可靠的；确实的：This is an ～ way to get good results.这是获得好成绩的可靠方法。

infamous/ˈɪnfəməs/

adj.well known for wicked behaviour 声名狼藉的,臭名昭著的：an ～ swindler 臭名昭著的骗子

infamy/ˈɪnfəmi/

n.❶the quality of being well know for sth.bad；public dishonour 臭名昭著,声名狼藉；hold sb.up to ～ 使某人名誉扫地 ❷an infamous act 可耻的行为；恶行

infancy/ˈɪnfənsi/

n.❶a period when one is an infant；early childhood 幼稚状态；幼儿期：in early ～ 在婴儿期 ❷an early stage of development or growth（发展或成长）初期：the ～ of a nation 建国初期/when aviation was still in its ～ 当航空事业仍在起步阶段时

infant/ˈɪnfənt/

n.❶a child during the first few years of his life 婴儿；幼儿：～s, older children and adults 幼儿,大孩子和成人/an ～ teacher 幼儿教师/an ～ school (for children under 7) 幼儿园/～ voices 童声 ❷a person under the age of 18 未成年人（18 岁以下者）

infect/ɪnˈfekt/

v.cause to get a disease；cause to have a certain feelings 传染；感染：If you do not keep away from the children, you will ～ them with your cold.如果你不远离孩子,你会把感冒传染给他们。/His sadness ～ed us all.他的悲伤感染了我们所有的人。

infection/ɪnˈfekʃn/

n.the act or result of causing a disease；a disease spread by infecting 传染,感染；传

染病：a lung(chest) ～ 肺部(胸部)感染/Sterilize the needle to prevent ～.把注射针消毒以防感染。

infectious/ɪnˈfekʃəs/

adj.infecting with disease；(of disease) that can be spread by means of germs carried in the atmosphere or in water（疾病)传染性的；(尤指)通过空气传染的：Colds are ～.感冒是可以传染的。

infer/ɪnˈfɜː(r)/

v.(-rr-)find out by reasoning；come to believe after thinking；conclude 推断,臆测：～ an unknown fact from a known fact 从已知推断出未知的事/I ～ from your attitude that you like her very much.我从你的态度推断你很喜欢她。

inference/ˈɪnfərəns/

n.❶the process of inferring 推理；推断,推论：by ～ 根据推理 ❷sth. which is inferred；a conclusion 推断的结果；结论

inferior/ɪnˈfɪərɪə(r)/

Ⅰ*adj*.❶ lower in position 下级的,下级的：an ～ officer 下级军官/ ～ in social position 社会地位低的 ❷not good or less good in quality or value 低劣的,差的,次的：His works is ～ to mine.他的作品比我的差。Ⅱ*n*.a person who has a lower rank or position（地位)较低的人,下级：A good leader always gets on well with ～s.一个好领导总是与下级相处得很好。

inferiority/ɪnˌfɪərɪˈɒrəti/

n.the state of being not as good as sb.or sth. else 地位低；下级；下等,劣等,差,次：have a sense of ～ 有自卑感

infernal/ɪnˈfɜːnl/

adj.❶of hell；devilish 地狱的；魔鬼似的 ❷nasty；annoying 令人厌恶的；讨厌的：an ～ noise 令人厌烦的声音

infertile/ɪnˈfɜːtaɪl/

adj.not fertile；barren 不肥沃的；贫瘠的：～ ground 不毛之地

infest/ɪnˈfest/

v.(of rats, insects, etc.)be present in large numbers（老鼠、昆虫等)大批出现于,侵扰：Mice ～ed the old house.一大群老鼠在旧房子中横行骚扰。‖ infestation/

ˌɪnfeˈsteɪʃn/ *n.*感染,侵扰

infidelity/ˌɪnfɪˈdeləti/

　　*n.*the act or state of being unfaithful（especially to one's husband or wife）（尤指夫妻间的）不忠实行为;不贞

infinite/ˈɪnfɪnət/

　　*adj.*❶without limits or end 无穷的,无限的,无止境的:be of ~ power 具有无穷的力量/ ~ space 浩瀚无际的太空 ❷very great;not able to measure 极大的;无法计量的:Such ideas may do ~ harm. 这类思想可能会造成极大的危害。‖ ~**ly** *adv.* 无限地;极其

infinitive/ɪnˈfɪnətɪv/

　　n. a form of the verb without person, number or tense used with or without to, e.g."let him go", "allow him to go" 不定式

infinity /ɪnˈfɪnəti/

　　*n.*❶an infinite number or amount（数目、数额的）大宗,大量 ❷a number greater than any countable number, having the symbol ∞ 无穷大（符号∞）

infirm/ɪnˈfɜːm/

　　adj.(especially with reference to old persons) weak;not in good health（尤指老人）虚弱的;体弱的 ‖ ~**ity** *n.*虚弱;体弱

inflame/ɪnˈfleɪm/

　　*v.*make red or angry 使红(肿),使发炎,使愤怒:The dust ~d my eyes.灰尘弄得我双眼红肿。/The people were ~d by the news.人民被这则消息激怒了。

inflammable/ɪnˈflæməbl/

　　*adj.*❶ easily set on fire 易燃的 ❷easily excited 易激动的;易激怒的;性情暴躁的

inflate/ɪnˈfleɪt/

　　*v.*❶cause to swell with air or gas（用空气或气体）使膨胀:I had to ~ the tyre.我得给轮胎打气。 ❷ cause prices to increase by increasing the amount of money in use 使通货膨胀

inflation/ɪnˈfleɪʃn/

　　*n.*❶the act of swelling or state of being inflated 充气;膨胀;夸大;自满 ❷a rise in prices caused by the expansion of the supply of money, etc.通货膨胀:The rate

of ~ was 5% this year.今年的通货膨胀率为百分之五。‖ ~**ary** *adj.*膨胀的,通货膨胀引起的,由(通货)膨胀引起的/ ~**ism** *n.*通货膨胀政策/ ~**ist** *n.*通货膨胀政策的支持者

inflexible/ɪnˈfleksəbl/

　　*adj.*❶firm;unyielding;steadfast 坚定的;不屈的:~ determination 坚定的决心 ❷that cannot be changed 不可变的:The law is ~.法律是不可更改的。❸not easily bent;stiff 不易弯曲的;呆板的:an ~ rod 一根又硬又直的棒子

inflict/ɪnˈflɪkt/

　　*v.*give a blow 予以(打击):~ a fatal blow upon(on) the enemy 给敌人以致命的打击 ‖ ~ **oneself(one's company) on sb.** 打扰某人 ‖ ~**ion** /ɪnˈflɪkʃn/ *n.*施加,处罚

influence/ˈɪnfluəns/

　　Ⅰ *n.* ❶ the power to affect a person's character or actions 影响,作用:He's an ~ for good in the village.他在村子里有使人向善的影响力。❷ the power to shape policy or ensure favourable treatment from sb.势力,权势:a man of great ~ 权势很大的人/have ~ over... 有左右……的力量,对……有影响 ❸ a person who has power or effect on others 有影响的人,有权势的人:an ~ in politics 在政界有影响的人/He is one of the ~s in the company.他是公司里有势力的人物之一。‖ **a good（bad）~** 好(坏)影响/ **under the ~ of** 在……的影响下 Ⅱ *v.* have an effect on; affect 影响;左右;对……有作用:Don't be ~d by bad examples.不要受坏榜样的影响。

influential/ˌɪnfluˈenʃl/

　　*adj.*having great influence on sb.or sth.有影响的;有权势的:~ politicians 有势力的政客们/opinions which are ~ in reaching a decision 对于做决定有影响的意见/an ~ speech 有说服力的演说

influenza/ˌɪnfluˈenzə/

　　*n.*an illness which causes fever, headache, and other discomfort 流感

influx /ˈɪnflʌks/

n. the arrival or movement inwards usually of large numbers or quantities 流入；注入：an ～ of water（light）水（光）的流（射）入/an ～ of wealth 财富的涌入

inform /ɪnˈfɔːm/

v. ❶ give information to 告知，通知：Have you ～ed them of your intended departure? 你通知了他们你想离开了吗? ❷ give evidence or make an accusation against sb.（to the police）告发，告密：He went to the police and ～ed against（on）the criminals. 他去警局告发了罪犯。❸ give sth. its essential feature or character; pervade 赋予（某事物）特征；弥漫（品质或特征）：I love the sense of justice which ～s all her writings. 我喜欢贯穿她所有作品的那种正义感。❹ find out information about sb. or sth. 了解，熟悉 ❺ have effect on 对……有影响

informal /ɪnˈfɔːml/

adj. not formal；without ceremony 不拘礼仪的；非正式的：an ～ meeting of heads of the state 非正式的国家首脑会议/an ～ dinner 便餐/～ clothes 便服

informant /ɪnˈfɔːmənt/

n. a person who gives information, especially someone who gives details of their language, social customs, etc., to a person who is studying them 提供信息或情报的人（尤指为研究者提供语言、风俗资料的人）

information /ˌɪnfəˈmeɪʃn/

n.（sth. which gives）knowledge in the form of facts, news, etc. 消息；情报；资料：Could you give me some ～ about flights to Cairo, please? 请告诉我一些有关飞往开罗的航班的情况。/an interesting piece of ～ 一则有趣的消息/This book gives all sorts of useful ～ on how to repair cars. 这本书提供了有关怎样修理汽车的各种有用的资料。/According to ～ received, the police have arrested two suspects. 根据得到的情报，警方已拘捕了两名可疑分子。/According to my ～, he is no longer here. 据我所知，他现已不在此地。

informative /ɪnˈfɔːmətɪv/

adj. providing useful facts or ideas 提供资料的；增进知识的：an ～ television documentary 使人增长见闻的电视纪录片

informed /ɪnˈfɔːmd/

adj. ❶ having or showing knowledge; having information 有知识的；见闻广的；了解情况的：well-～ 消息灵通的/ill-～ 消息闭塞的/Please keep me ～ of any developments in the situation. 请让我随时了解形势的发展情况。❷ using one's knowledge of a situation 基于对情况的了解的；有根据的：I don't know exactly how many votes he will get, but I can make an ～ guess. 我说不准他会得到多少选票，但我能做个有根据的猜测。

informer /ɪnˈfɔːmə(r)/

n. a person who informs against someone else 告发者，告密者，检举者

infraction /ɪnˈfrækʃn/

n. the breaking of a rule or law 违规；违法：Any ～ of the regulations will be punished. 任何违犯法规的行为都将受到惩罚。

infrequent /ɪnˈfriːkwənt/

adj. not happening often 不常的；少有的；罕见的

infringe /ɪnˈfrɪndʒ/

v. ❶ break a law or rule 违反（法规）：People who drive without a licence ～ the law. 无驾驶执照开车的人违反了交通法规。❷ go beyond what is right; violate; interfere with 侵犯；侵害：You must not ～ the copyright of this article. 你决不可侵犯这篇文章的版权。/He has ～d our privacy. 他侵犯了我们的隐私。

infuse /ɪnˈfjuːz/

v. ❶ fill（someone）with（a quality）向（某人）注入（灌输）（某种素质）；使（人）充满：His speech ～d the men with a desire to win. 他的演说使人们充满取胜的欲望。❷ pour（hot）liquid on（tea leaves, etc.）to extract the taste, smell（使）浸泡（在热水中）；泡（茶等）：Let the tea ～ for a few minutes. 让茶泡上几分钟。

infusion /ɪnˈfjuːʒn/

n. ❶ the act of soaking 浸泡 ❷ a liquid

made by infusing, often for medical use 浸液;浸(泡)剂: The old woman recommended an ~ of special herbs for my cold. 那位老妇人推荐了一种能为我治好感冒的特殊草药泡剂。❸the act of mixing or filling with sth. new 注入,灌输: an ~ of new ideas into the department 灌输新观念到那个部门中去/This company needs an ~ of new blood. 这家公司需要注入新的血液。

ingenious /ɪnˈdʒiːnɪəs/

adj. showing cleverness at making or inventing things (人)机灵的,足智多谋的;有发明天赋的: an ~ mind 机灵的头脑/ an ~ person(idea)足智多谋的人(有独创性的见解) ‖ ~ly *adv.* 贤明地,有才能地

ingenuity /ˌɪndʒɪˈnjuːəti/

n. the quality of being clever, original, and inventive 机灵;独创性;创造力

ingrained /ɪnˈɡreɪnd/

adj. (with reference to habits, beliefs, etc.) firmly fixed for a long time (指习惯、信仰等)根深蒂固的

ingratitude /ɪnˈɡrætɪtjuːd/

n. the absence of thankfulness or gratitude 忘恩负义

ingredient /ɪnˈɡriːdɪənt/

n. ❶one of the parts of a mixture (混合物的)成分: The ~s of a cake usually include eggs, sugar, flour, and flavoring. 蛋糕的成分通常包括蛋、糖、面粉和调味品。❷a component or element of sth. 因素,要素: all the ~s of the mystery 谜团的所有要素

inhabit /ɪnˈhæbɪt/

v. live in 居住;栖息: ~ a city 住在城市/ The islands were ~ed by fishermen. 这些岛是渔民居住之地。/Whales ~ the sea. 鲸栖于海中。

inhabitant /ɪnˈhæbɪtənt/

n. a person or an animal that lives in a certain place 居民;栖息动物: a town of 20,000 ~s 两万居民的城镇/The village has thirteen thousand ~s. 这个村子有 1.3 万居民。

inhere /ɪnˈhɪə(r)/

v. (with reference to qualities) naturally belong to or exist in (性质或特性)原有,自然存在于 ‖ inherent *adj.* 天生的: Love of their children is ~ in all parents. 爱孩子是所有父母的天性。

inherit /ɪnˈherɪt/

v. ❶receive property, a title, etc. as heir 继承(财产、头衔等): She ~ed a large amount of money from her father. 她从父亲那里继承了一大笔财富。❷ derive (qualities, etc.) from ancestors (从父母等)遗传所得(品格等): She ~ed her mother's good looks. 她继承了母亲的美貌。‖ ~ance /ɪnˈherɪtəns/ *n.* 继承,遗传;继承物,遗产/ ~or *n.* 继承人,后继者

inhibit /ɪnˈhɪbɪt/

v. ❶hinder, restrain 禁止;抑制;阻碍: His bad English ~s him from speaking freely. 由于他英语不好,他不能自由地进行交谈。❷ make sb. nervous and embarrassed 使拘束;使尴尬

inhibition /ˌɪnhɪˈbɪʃən/

n. ❶ the process of preventing sth. 抑制;压抑 ❷a feeling of restraint that makes a person unwilling to act naturally 拘谨;拘束感: He has no ~s about speaking French. 他讲法语没有心理障碍。

inhospitable /ˌɪnhɒˈspɪtəbl/

adj. not hospitable; not friendly or ready to welcome 不殷勤的;冷淡的;不好客的

inhuman /ɪnˈhjuːmən/

adj. not human; cruel 无人性的;不人道的;残忍的

inhumane /ˌɪnhjuːˈ(ː)meɪn/

adj. without pity for suffering; not humane 残忍的;无人情味的

inhumanity /ˌɪnhjuː(ː)ˈmænəti/

n. extremely cruel and brutal behaviours 不人道;残暴

inimitable /ɪˈnɪmɪtəbl/

adj. too good to be imitated; better than or different from any other 无法模仿的;无双的;无与伦比的: his ~ way of making his students interested in their work 他使学生对工作感兴趣的独特方法

iniquity /ɪˈnɪkwəti/
n.(*pl.*-ies) great injustice or wickedness 不道德行为;不公正行为

initial /ɪˈnɪʃl/
I *adj.* that is (at) the beginning 开始的, 最初的,起初的: the ～ stage 开始阶段/ the ～ issue of a magazine 杂志的创刊号 Ⅱ *n.* a capital letter at the beginning of a name,especially when used alone to represent a person's first name(s) and last name 姓名(或组织名称)起首的字母 Ⅲ *v.* write one's initials on (a piece of writing),usually to show approval or agreement 签姓名的首字母于: ～ a note or document 用 (姓名)缩写签署便条或文件 ‖ ～ly *adv.* 最初,开始

initiate /ɪˈnɪʃieɪt/
I *v.*❶ be the first one to start; begin 开始,发动: ～ a new plan 开始实行一项新计划 ❷ admit (a person) by special forms or ceremonies into a group or society 介绍某人加入: The old members ～d the new members. 老成员介绍新成员入会。❸ explain sth. to sb. and help to get a first understanding 传授知识: ～ pupils into the principles of grammar 教授学生基本的语法规则 Ⅱ *n.* a person who is or has been initiated 被传授知识的人;新入会的人

initiation /ɪˌnɪʃiˈeɪʃn/
n. the act of starting sth.; being made acquainted with the rules of a society,etc. 开始,着手;加入组织;传授知识;熟悉社会等的规则: ～ ceremonies 入会仪式

initiative /ɪˈnɪʃətɪv/
*n.*❶ the first movement or act which starts sth. 主动;初步行动,率先,发端: win ～ 赢得主动 ❷ the willingness to act without consulting others 主动性,积极性;(表现)首创精神,创造性,进取心: He's got no ～.他没有主动性。‖ (act or do sth.) on one's own ～ 主动地(做某事)/ have the ～ 处于主动地位/take the ～(in doing sth.) 采取主动,主动做某事

inject /ɪnˈdʒekt/
v. put (liquid) into (someone) with a spe-

cial needle (syringe) 注射: The doctor ～ed the drug into my arm. 医生给我的手臂注射了这种药。‖ ～or *n.* 注射者;注射器,喷射器

injection /ɪnˈdʒekʃn/
n. an act of injecting sb. with a drug,etc. 注射: hypodermic ～ 皮下注射 ‖ fuel ～ 燃料喷射,注油/ ～ pump 喷射泵,喷油泵

injunction /ɪnˈdʒʌŋkʃən/
n. a command given with authority,especially an order from a law court 警告;命令(尤其是法令)

injure /ˈɪndʒə(r)/
*v.*❶ hurt sb., especially in an accident 伤害: She was ～d badly in the accident. 她在这次事故中受了重伤。❷ damage sb.'s feelings,reputation,etc. 损害(感情、名誉等): I hope I didn't ～ her(feelings).我希望我没有伤到她的感情。‖ ～d *adj.* 受伤的;受损害的;感情受损的

injurious /ɪnˈdʒʊəriəs/
*adj.*❶ causing or likely to cause injury 有害的;致伤的 ❷ (of language) maliciously insulting;libelous (语言)伤人的;中伤的;诽谤的

injury /ˈɪndʒəri/
*n.*❶ a harm or damage (to sb.'s feeling, reputation, etc.) 伤害,毁坏: insurance against ～ at work 工伤保险 ❷ a place (in the body) that is hurt or wounded;an act that hurts 受伤之处;伤害的行为: do sb.an ～(do an ～ to sb.) 伤害某人/He suffered serious injuries to the arms and legs.他的双臂和双腿严重受伤。‖ add insult to ～ 伤害之外再加侮辱;落井下石

injustice /ɪnˈdʒʌstɪs/
*n.*❶ the lack of justice 非正义;不公正,不公道,不公平: Justice will triumph over ～.正义必将战胜非正义。❷ an unjust act or thing 非正义的行为;不公平的事: You're doing a good man an ～.你在冤枉一个好人。‖ do sb.an ～ 冤枉某人,使某人受委屈;对某人做不公平的判断

ink¹ /ɪŋk/
n. a coloured liquid used for writing,printing,or drawing 墨水;油墨;墨汁: written

in ～ 用墨水书写的/a bottle of ～ 一瓶墨水/a selection of different-coloured ～s 一套不同颜色的墨水

ink² /ɪŋk/

v. put ink on 涂墨水(油墨)于：He ～ed the printing plate. 他给印版上了油墨。

ink-pad /'ɪŋkpæd/

n. a small box containing ink on a thick piece of cloth or other material, used for putting ink onto a marker that is to be pressed onto paper (打)印台

inkstand /'ɪŋkstænd/

n. a stand for pens, ink-bottles, etc., usually kept on a desk (通常放在桌上的)墨水台,墨水瓶架

inkwell /'ɪŋkwel/

n. an ink container which fits into a hole in a desk (嵌在桌上的)墨水池

inky /'ɪŋki/

adj. ❶ marked with ink 染上墨水的：～ fingers 沾上墨水的手指 ❷ very dark 漆黑的：I stared out into the ～ blackness of the night. 我凝视着外面漆黑的夜色。

inlaid /ˌɪn'leɪd/

adj. ❶ decoratively set into another substance 镶入的；嵌入的：gold ～ in (to) wood 镶嵌进木材中的黄金/～ gold 嵌金 ❷ having another substance set in it 有嵌饰的；镶嵌着……的：wood ～ with gold and precious stones 镶嵌着黄金和宝石的木材/～ wood 有嵌饰的木材

inland

Ⅰ /'ɪnlənd/ *adj.* away from the border or the coast; carried on within a country 内地的；内陆的；国内的：an ～ city 内陆城市/～ trade 国内贸易/an ～ sea 内海/an ～ river 内河/an ～ town 内地城市/～ transportation 内地运输 Ⅱ /ˌɪn'lænd/ *adv.* towards or in the heart of the country 在内地；到内地：go ～ 到内地去/live ～ 住在内地

inlay /ˌɪn'leɪ/

n. ❶ an inlaid pattern, surface, or substance 镶嵌图案；镶嵌物(料)；wood with an ～ of gold 镶金的木材 ❷ a filling of a metal or another substance used in the

inside of a decayed or damaged tooth 补牙用的填充料,(镶填牙洞的)镶体

inlet /'ɪnlet/

n. ❶ a strip of water extending into the land from a large body of water (the sea, a lake), or between islands 海湾,水湾,小港 ❷ sth. let in or inserted 插入物；镶入物 ❸ a way in for (water, liquid, etc.) (水、液体等)进入的通路；流入的渠道：～ and outlet channels 流入、流出水道

inmate /'ɪnmeɪt/

n. one of a number of persons living together (especially in a hospital, prison or other institutions) 同住者(尤指医院、监狱或其他机构中)

inn /ɪn/

n. a small hotel 旅店；小旅馆；客栈：put up at an ～ 住旅馆/a country ～ 乡村客栈/Towards evening, the travellers stopped at an ～ to rest. 临近傍晚,这些旅游者在一个小旅店停下来休息。

innards /'ɪnədz/

n. the inner parts, usually of the stomach 内部结构(尤指内脏)：a pain in her ～ 她肚子里面痛/He'd spread the ～ of the engine all over the kitchen floor. 他在厨房地板上摊满了发动机里的部件。

innate /ɪ'neɪt/

adj. (of a quality, etc.) possessed from birth 生来的；固有的；天生的：man's ～ desire for happiness 人类天生渴求幸福的愿望

inner /'ɪnə(r)/

adj. ❶ towards or close to the middle 在内的,内部的：an ～ room 内室/the ～ ear 内耳 ❷ close to the centre of a place or sth. 中心的,核心的：Inner London 伦敦中心区 ‖ the ～ man 灵魂(与 body 相对)；肚子

innermost /'ɪnəməʊst/

adj. ❶ furthest in, closest to the centre 最深处的；最内部的 ❷ (of thoughts or feelings) most private and deeply felt (思想、感情)内心深处的

innocence /'ɪnəsns/

n. the quality or state of being naive 天真

无邪;清白无辜;无知;无罪;单纯：He
protested his ～. 他申明自己无罪。/
Children lose their ～ as they grow older.
随着年龄的增长,孩子们将失去纯真。

innocent/'ɪnəsnt/
adj. ❶ not guilty (of wrongdoing) 无罪
的,清白的,无辜的：He was ～ of the
crime. 他没有犯罪。❷ harmless 无害的：
～ amusements(pleasures) 无害的娱乐
❸ knowing nothing of evil or unpleasant
things 单纯的,天真无邪的：Don't be so
～ as to believe everything they say. 不要
天真得竟然相信他们所说的一切。

innovate/'ɪnəveɪt/
v. change by bringing in sth. new 创新;革
新：The young teachers wish to ～. 青年
教师希望革新。

innovation/ˌɪnə'veɪʃn/
n. the act of bringing in sth. new 革新,创
新：the young teachers' ～s in classroom
work 这位青年教师在课堂工作方面的
革新

innumerable/ɪ'njuːmərəbl/
adj. too many to be counted 无数的;数不
清的;非常多的：～ stars 无数的星星/an
～ throng of people 人山人海

inoperable/ɪn'ɒpərəbl/
adj. ❶ (said about a disease) not able to
be cured by surgical operation;not able to
be suitably operated on (疾病)不宜动手
术的 ❷ impractical;unworkable 行不通
的;不能实行的

inoperative/ɪn'ɒpərətɪv/
adj. not valid;not functioning correctly 不
起作用的;无效果的;运转不正常的

inopportune/ˌɪn'ɒpətjuːn/
adj. unsuitable for the time; not convenient 不合时宜的;不方便的

inordinate/ɪn'ɔːdɪnət/
adj. not under control;excessive 无节制
的;过度的：～ pride 过分骄傲

inorganic/ˌɪnɔː'gænɪk/
adj. not having a living physical structure
of animals or plants (e.g. metals or
rocks) 无机的(例如:金属或岩石)

inpatient/'ɪnˌpeɪʃnt/

n. a person who stays in hospital while receiving treatment 住院病人

input/'ɪnput/
n. ❶ an action of putting sth. in 输入;置
入,放入 ❷ things or an amount of things
put in or supplied 输入物;输入量

inquest/'ɪnkwest/
n. an official inquiry to learn facts, especially concerning a death which may not
be the result of natural causes 审问;审
讯;验尸：An ～ was held to determine
the cause of his death. 进行验尸以确定其
死因。

inquire/ɪn'kwaɪə(r)/
v. ❶ ask for information 询问：We ～d
about the trains to Beijing. 我们打听了去
北京的火车。❷ look into 调查;查问：We
must ～ into the matter. 我们必须调查此
事。‖ ～ after 问起(某人的)健康或(生
活)情况 ‖ ～r /ɪn'kwaɪərə(r)/ *n.* 询问
者,调查人/inquiring *adj.* 爱打听的;显得
好奇的/inquiringly *adv.* 探询地,好奇地

inquisitive/ɪn'kwɪzətɪv/
adj. fond of inquiring into other people's affairs 好管闲事的;好问的;好奇的：Our
neighbours are very ～ about our friends.
我们的邻居很喜欢打听有关我们朋友的
事。

inroad/'ɪnrəʊd/
n. ❶ a sudden invasion or raid 突然侵犯;
突然袭击 ❷ any injurious encroachment
损害：make ～s on sb.'s health 使某人的
健康受到损害

inrush/'ɪnrʌʃ/
n. the sudden arrival or entry of sth. 涌入;
闯入

insane/ɪn'seɪn/
adj. (of people and their acts) not sane;
mad;senseless (人或其行为)神志不正常
的,疯狂的：an ～ person 疯子/go ～ 发
疯 ‖ ～ly *adv.* 疯狂地,荒唐地/insanity
/ɪn'sænəti/ *n.* 精神错乱,疯狂;愚行

insanitary/ɪn'sænɪtri/
adj. not sanitary,dirty and unhealthy 不
卫生的;有害健康的

inscribe/ɪn'skraɪb/

v. write or cut words in or on sth. 在……上题写；铭刻：He ~d his name in the book. 他在这本书中题名了。/Their names are ~d on the stone above their grave. 在他们的墓碑上刻上他们的名字。

inscription/ɪnˈskrɪpʃn/

n. sth. inscribed；words on a coin, monument, etc. 题字；碑文：the ~ on a monument 纪念碑上的题字

inscrutable/ɪnˈskruːtəbl/

adj. that cannot be discovered or understood 高深莫测的；不可理解的；不可思议的：His face was ~. 他的脸部表情令人费解。

insect/ˈɪnsekt/

n. a small creature with no bones, six legs, a body divided into three parts（the head, thorax, and abdomen）and usually two pairs of wings, such as an ant or a fly 昆虫，虫：Ants, flies and wasps are ~s. 蚂蚁、苍蝇和黄蜂都是昆虫。‖ ~ **powder** *n.* 杀虫粉/~**ology**/ˌɪnsekˈtɒlədʒ/ *n.* 昆虫学

insecticide/ɪnˈsektɪsaɪd/

n. a substance for killing insects 杀虫剂

insecure/ˌɪnsɪˈkjʊə(r)/

adj. not properly fastened；not safe 不牢靠的；不稳固的；不安全的；有危险的：These boxes are ~. 这些箱子不坚固。/I feel ~ in this lonely house. 在这偏僻的房子里我感到不安全。

insensible/ɪnˈsensəbl/

adj. ❶ not able to feel or notice 无知觉的；不能察觉的：A blind man is ~ to colors. 盲人对颜色没有感觉。 ❷ not aware of；without knowledge of 不知的：The boys in the boat were ~ of the danger. 那船上的孩子不知道这有危险。 ❸ unconscious 失去知觉，昏迷的：The man hit by the truck was ~ for four hours. 那个被卡车撞了的人昏迷了四小时。 ❹ not easily felt；too slow to be noticed 不易被感觉到的：~ motion 不易被感觉到的动作

insensitive/ɪnˈsensətɪv/

adj. ❶ not sensitive；without feeling 无感

觉的：~ to light 对光没有感觉 ❷ slow to feel or notice 感觉迟钝的：~ to the power of music 对音乐的力量感觉迟钝

inseparable/ɪnˈseprəbl/

adj. that cannot be separated 不能分离的；分不开的

insert

Ⅰ/ɪnˈsɜːt/ *v.* put, fit, place（sth. in, into, between, etc.）others 插入；嵌入；刊登：The book would be better by ~ing another chapter. 这本书再插进一章会更好。 Ⅱ/ˈɪnsɜːt/ *n.* sth. added or put into sth. else 插入物；嵌入物

insertion/ɪnˈsɜːʃən/

n. ❶ the action of putting sth. inside sth. else 插入；嵌入；塞入 ❷ a thing that is inserted 插入物

inset/ˈɪnset/

Ⅰ *v.*（inset or -tt-）decorate sth. with sth. set into its surface 镶嵌，插入：The crown is ~ with jewels. 那顶皇冠镶嵌着宝石。 Ⅱ *n.* ❶ sth. set into a larger thing 嵌入物 ❷ a small map printed within the frame of a larger one（套印在大地图中的）小地图

inshore/ˌɪnˈʃɔː(r)/

adj. & *adv.* near, toward the shore 近海岸的（地）；向海岸的（地）

inside/ɪnˈsaɪd/

Ⅰ *n.* ❶ the inner side or surface；the part(s) within 里面，内部，里边，内侧：proceed from the outside to the ~ 由表及里 ❷ belly；stomach and bowels 肚子，肠胃：feel a pain in one's ~ 感觉肚子痛 Ⅱ *adj.* ❶ forming the inner part of sth.；not on the outer side 在内部的，里面的：the ~ front(back)（杂志等的）封面(底)的背面 ❷ told or performed by sb. who is in a building, a group or an organization 内幕的，秘密的：~ information 内部消息/an ~ story 内情 Ⅲ *adv.* ❶ on or to the inside 在里面，在内部；往里面：There's nobody ~. 里面没人。 ❷ in prison 在狱中，在坐牢：Jones sits ~ for three years. 琼斯入狱服刑三年。 Ⅳ *prep.* on the inner side of 在……里边；在……

之内;向……内;~ a social club 在社团之内 ‖ ~ of 在……之内,不超过……时间/ ~ out 内外翻转地,里朝外地;完全地,彻底地/ on the ~ 在(或从)里面;知内情的;在内心深处/~ job 内部人作案 ‖ ~r n.(组织等)内部的人,知内情者

insidious /ɪnˈsɪdɪəs/

adj. causing harm or damage without being seen or felt 暗中为害的;阴险的;诡诈的

insight /ˈɪnsaɪt/

n. ❶ the power of using one's mind to see or understand the true nature of a situation 洞察力,见识:a man of deep ~ 有深远见识的人 ❷ an example or the understanding of this 洞悉;领悟:gain an ~ into sb.'s mind 看透某人心思/a book full of remarkable ~s 一本很有真知灼见的书

insignificant /ˌɪnsɪgˈnɪfɪkənt/

adj. not of value and importance 无意义的;无价值的;无关紧要的:an ~ amount 区区小数/~ talk 废话

insincere /ˌɪnsɪnˈsɪə(r)/

adj. not sincere 不真诚的;不诚恳的

insist /ɪnˈsɪst/

v. ❶ declare or maintain a statement firmly 坚持,坚持认为:I ~ed on my correctness.我坚持认为我是对的。❷ demand or order sth.strongly 坚持要,坚持主张:I ~ed on him going.我坚决要他去。

insistence /ɪnˈsɪstəns/

n. the act of demanding or saying sth. firmly 坚决主张,坚持认为;坚决要求;强调:At the director's ~ the new product was kept secret.由于董事的坚决要求,这种新产品对外保密。/the government's ~ on a price stability 政府实行物价稳定的坚决主张 ‖ **insistency** /ɪnˈsɪstnsi/ *n.* 坚持;强调

insistent /ɪnˈsɪstənt/

adj. ❶ repeatedly insisting one's demand or idea (人)坚持的,强求的:at sb.'s request 在某人的一再要求下 ❷ needing to be done, answered, or dealt with;ur-

gent (行为)迫切需要的,紧急的:the ~ demands for more troops 对增加军队的迫切要求

in situ /ˌɪnˈsɪtjuː/

adv. in its original place 在原地,在原来位置

insolent /ˈɪnsələnt/

adj. insulting, offensive; contemptuous (to) 傲慢的,目空一切的;无礼的;蛮横的;侮辱的:an ~ reply 无礼的答复/He was ~ to his parents.他对父母蛮横无理。

insoluble /ɪnˈsɒljʊbl/

adj. ❶ (of substances) that cannot be dissolved;not soluble 不溶解的:~ salts 不能溶解的盐类 ❷ that cannot be solved or explained 不能解决的,难以解释的:an ~ problem 不能解决的问题/an ~ mystery 难以解释的谜

inspect /ɪnˈspekt/

v. examine the details of sth.;make an official visit to judge the quality of;review (troops) 检查,调查;检阅:~ goods 检查货物/~ a plane 检查飞机/~ a factory 视察工厂/The general is ~ing the troops.将军正在检阅军队。

inspection /ɪnˈspekʃn/

n. an act of looking closely at sb. or sth.; an official visit to a place 检查,检验;视察:On ~, the notes proved to be forgeries.经过检验,那些钞票证明是伪造的。/ carry out two ~s a week 每周检查两次/ quality ~ 质量检查 ‖ **Inspection declined!** 谢绝参观!

inspector /ɪnˈspektə(r)/

n. ❶ an official who inspects 检查员,监察员:an ~ of taxes 税务稽查员 ❷ a police officer of middle rank (警察)巡官 ‖ ~ general 监察主任/the Inspector General's Department 监察署 ‖ ~al /ɪnˈspektərəl/ *adj.* 检查员的

inspectorate /ɪnˈspektərət/

n. a body that ensures that the official regulations applying to a particular type of institution or activity are obeyed 检查员的辖区;检察团;监察团

inspiration /ˌɪnspəˈreɪʃn/

n. ❶ sth. or sb. which gives a person the urge or the ability to do sth., especially to produce works of the imagination 灵感: Many poets and artists have drawn their ～ from love.许多诗人和艺术家从爱情中获得他们的灵感。❷a person or thing that inspires 鼓舞人心的人(或事): Doctor Bethune's glorious life will always be an ～ to us.白求恩大夫光辉的一生对我们将永远是一个鼓舞。❸a sudden good idea 好主意,妙想: have a sudden ～ 灵机一动(计上心来)

inspire /ɪnˈspaɪə(r)/

v. ❶ give sb. the desire or ability to act, especially with a good result 鼓舞,激起,激励: ～ sb. with courage (enthusiasm, confidence) 鼓起某人的勇气(热情、信心) ❷ be the force which produces (usually a good result) 促成;导致: The life living in the forest for three years ～d him to compose some lovely music. 在森林里的三年生活经历促使他写出了一些优美的乐曲。

inspired /ɪnˈspaɪəd/

adj. so clever or good as to seem to show inspiration, especially from God 凭灵感的;受神启示的: an ～ guess 凭灵感的猜测

inspiring /ɪnˈspaɪərɪŋ/

adj. that inspires sb. to do sth. 鼓舞人心的: ～ music (leadership) 激励人心的音乐(鼓舞人心的领导)

instability /ˌɪnstəˈbɪləti/

n. (usually with reference to behaviour or character) the lack of stability, firmness or determination (通常指行为或性格)不稳定性;不坚决;三心二意

install /ɪnˈstɔːl/

v. ❶ set (an apparatus) up, ready for use 安放: He ～ed an air-conditioner in the parlo(u)r.他在客厅里安放了一台空调。❷settle in a place 安顿,安置: He ～ed himself in a front-row seat.他在前排的一个位子上就座。❸ settle (someone) in an official position, especially with cere-

mony (常以仪式)使就职,任命: The new president was ～ed last week.新总统已于上星期就职。

installation /ˌɪnstəˈleɪʃn/

n. ❶a formal entry into an organization, position or office 就任,就职 ❷the act of installing sth.; sth. that is installed 设置;安装;装置;设备: a heating ～ 暖气装置

instal(l)ment /ɪnˈstɔːlmənt/

n. ❶a single payment of a set which will complete full payment in time 分期付款: I'm paying for my new house in ten yearly ～s.我买这新房子需要十年内分期付完款。❷a single part of a book, play, or television show which appears in regular parts until the story is completed (连续播放或刊载的)部分;一集,一期,一段: The novel will appear in ～s.这部小说将分期连载。/Did you watch the last ～? 你看了上一集吗? ‖ buy on the ～ plan 用分期付款办法购买

instance /ˈɪnstəns/

Ⅰ *n.* an example 例子,事例,实例: He's a greedy boy. Yesterday, for ～, he ate all our biscuits! 他是个贪吃的孩子——比如:昨天,他就把我们的饼干全都吃了! ‖ at the ～ of 应……之情,经……的提议 /for ～ 例如 /in the first ～ 首先,起初 Ⅱ *v.* give as an example 举……为例,用例子说明: His meaning is well ～d in the passage quoted.他的意思在那节引文中已有充分的说明(例示)。

instant /ˈɪnstənt/

Ⅰ *adj.* ❶ happening or working at once 立即的,立刻的: He gave an ～ answer to my question.他立刻回答了我的问题。❷ urgent; pressing 紧迫的,刻不容缓的: a patient in ～ need of first aid 急需抢救的病人 ❸(of food) that can be made ready for use quickly (食品)速食的,速溶的: ～ coffee 速溶咖啡 Ⅱ *n.* a precise point of time 片刻,瞬间,刹那: I'll be with you in an ～.我一会儿就来。

instantly /ˈɪnstəntli/

adv. at once; immediately 立即,马上: I'm leaving for Beijing ～.我马上就去北京。

instead/ɪnˈsted/

adv. ❶ in place of or as an alternative to 代替,顶替:He is tired,let me go ~.他累了,让我去(顶替)吧。❷ on the contrary 而不是……:He will go ~ of you.他去而不是你去。

instep/ˈɪnstep/

n. ❶ the upper surface of the foot between the toes and the ankle 脚背,足背 ❷ the part of a shoe,sock,etc.,which covers the instep 鞋面;袜背

instigate/ˈɪnstɪɡeɪt/

v. urge sb. to do sth.;cause sth. to happen by urging (usually sth. bad) 唆使某人做某事;教唆,煽动:They ~d the crime.他们教唆犯罪。

instill/ɪnˈstɪl/

v. put (ideas,feelings,etc.) into someone's mind by a continuous effort;train sb. to behave in a particular way gradually 逐渐灌输(思想、感情等);逐步培养:We ~ed the need for discipline and obedience into the new recruits.我们逐渐使新兵懂得遵守纪律和服从命令的必要性。

instinct/ˈɪnstɪŋkt/

Ⅰ *n.* a natural way of doing things;an ability that seems to come naturally 本能,直觉,天性:Birds learn to fly by ~.鸟儿学习飞翔是出于本能。‖ **have an ~ for** … 生性爱好,生来就…… Ⅱ *adj.* filled with 充满的:be ~ with confidence (passion) 充满信心(热情)

instinctive/ɪnˈstɪŋktɪv/

adj. based on instinct,not coming from training or teaching 凭本能的;天生的:Animals have an ~ dread of fire.动物天生怕火。/ A baby's cry is ~.婴儿的啼哭是天生的。

institute/ˈɪnstɪtjuːt/

Ⅰ *n.* a society or an organization formed to do special work or for a special purpose 学会;协会;学院;(研究)所,院:the Chinese People's Institute of Foreign Affairs 中国人民外交学会/an ~ of foreign languages 外国语学院 Ⅱ *v.* set up (a society,rules,actions in law,etc.) for the first time 建立,设立,制定:~ a sound system of meetings 建立健全的会议制度/ ~ rules 制定规定

institution/ˌɪnstɪˈtjuːʃn/

n. ❶ the act of instituting or setting up sth.建立,设立,制定:the ~ of customs 风俗的形成/the ~ of regulations 条例的制定 ❷ a large society or organization,usually set up to do sth.for others 团体;公共机构:public ~s 公共机构(指孤儿院、医院、学校等) ‖ ~**al** *adj.* 惯例的,社会事业性的/ ~**alize**/ˌɪnstɪˈtjuːʃənəlaɪz/ *v.* 使制度化;使成为惯常的行为

instruct/ɪnˈstrʌkt/

v. ❶ teach;train;educate 教,教育,指导:~ a class in history 教授一个班的历史 ❷ order;command;direct 指示,命令:He ~ed me to start early.他命令我提早动身。❸ tell;inform 通知,向……提供情况:I have been ~ed by my agent that you still owe me $500.我的代理人通知我,你还欠我五百美元。

instruction/ɪnˈstrʌkʃn/

n. ❶ teaching;education 教育,训练;讲授;教导:give ~ in English 讲授英语/All children must have ~.儿童都要接受教育。❷ directions;orders 指令;指示;命令:~s to computer 下达给计算机的指令 ❸ detailed information which tells you how to use or operate sth.使用(操作)说明

instructive/ɪnˈstrʌktɪv/

adj. giving useful information that increases knowledge or understanding 有教益的;增进知识的;有启发性的:a most ~ lecture(visit) 极富启发性的演讲(访问)

instructor/ɪnˈstrʌktə(r)/

n. a person whose job is to teach sb. sth. useful;a trainer 教师;教练:an experienced ~ in English 有经验的英语教师

instrument/ˈɪnstrʊmənt/

n. ❶ an object used to help in work 仪器,器具,工具:optical ~s 光学仪器/medical (surgical) ~s 医疗(外科)器械 ❷ an object,such as a piano,horn,drum,etc.,played to give musical sounds 乐器

instrumental/ˌɪnstrʊˈmentl/

adj. ❶ helpful (in); being (part of) the cause of 有帮助的；作为工具或手段的：This technical innovation is ～ in improving the qualities of our living.这项技术革新有助于提高我们的生活质量。❷ (of music) for instruments, not voices 乐器(上)的；供乐器用的：～ music 器乐/an ～ ensemble 器乐重奏曲 ‖ ~ity/ˌɪnstrumen'tæləti/ *n.* 工具，媒介/~ly *adv.* 仪器地；有帮助地

instrumentalist /ˌɪnstrə'mentəlɪst/
n. a musician who plays a musical instrument 乐器演奏者

instrumentation /ˌɪnstrʊmen'teɪʃən/
n. ❶ the arrangement or composition of music for particular instruments (乐曲的)配器方式 ❷ the provision or use of mechanical or scientific instruments 仪器化；仪表化

insubordinate /ˌɪnsə'bɔːdɪnət/
adj. disobedient; refusing to obey orders 不服从的；反抗的 ‖ **insubordination** /ˌɪnsəbɔːdɪ'neɪʃn/ *n.* 反抗

insubstantial /ˌɪnsəb'stænʃəl/
adj. ❶ not existing in reality; imaginary 非实体的，非真实的；虚构的 ❷ lacking strength or force 不牢固的，不牢靠的

insufferable /ɪn'sʌfrəbl/
adj. too difficult or unpleasant to bear; unbearable 不可容忍的；难以忍受的：～ conduct 令人难以忍受的行为

insufficient /ˌɪnsə'fɪʃnt/
adj. not enough 不够的，不足的 ‖ ~ly *adv.* 不充足地

insulate /'ɪnsjʊleɪt/
v. ❶ cover (sth.) so as to prevent electricity, heat, or sound from getting out or in 使绝缘；使绝热；使隔音：～ an electric wire with rubber 用橡皮使电线与外界绝缘 ❷ set apart; separate from others; isolate 使孤立，隔离：The English Channel ～s Great Britain from France and Belgium.英吉利海峡把英国与法国和比利时隔开了。‖ **insulation** /ˌɪnsjʊ'leɪʃn/ *n.* 绝缘；绝热；隔离；绝缘材料；绝热材料/**insulator** *n.* 绝缘体，绝热器

insult
Ⅰ /'ɪnsʌlt/ *n.* words or action that hurt another's feelings 侮辱；侮辱的言行：I could not stand his ～s.我受不了他的侮辱。Ⅱ /ɪn'sʌlt/ *v.* speak or behave rudely to sb.; speak or act in a way that hurts sb.'s feelings 侮辱；冒犯；辱骂：He ～ed me by saying that.他说那样的话是对我的侮辱。/He ～ed her by calling her a stupid fool.他侮辱了她，把她说成是个笨蛋。

insurance /ɪn'ʃɔːrəns/
n. ❶ an agreement by contract to pay money, especially in case of a misfortune, such as illness, death, or an accident 保险：Labour(life) ～ 劳动(人寿)保险/fire (marine) ～ 火(水)险/an ～ company 保险公司 ❷ money paid to an insurance company in order to make or keep such a contract 保险费，保险金：When her husband died, she received $20,000 ～.她丈夫去世后，她得到两万美元的保险金。❸ sth. you do to protect against future loss 预防措施；保护(措施)：I have one lock but I bought another as an additional ～ against thieves.我(现在)有一把锁，但我又买了一把以加强防盗。❹ the business of providing people with insurance 保险业

insure /ɪn'ʃɔː(r)/
v. ❶ make a contract that promises to pay a sum of money in case of accident, loss, death, etc. 给……投保(以防损失)：～ one's house against fire 给自己的房屋保火险/have one's life ～d 给自己保人寿险 ❷ be careful or certain to do sth. 确保；保证：Carefulness ～s you against errors.细心可确保你不出差错。‖ **the ～d** 受保人，被保险人/**the ～r** 承保人；保险公司

intact /ɪn'tækt/
adj. not having been touched; not damaged; complete 未动过的；未受损的；完整的：The parcels I sent by post arrived ～ly.我邮寄的包裹完好无损地到达了。

intake /'ɪnteɪk/
n. the quantity, number, etc. entering or

taken in 纳入量；吸入量：This college has an ~ of 200 students each year.这所学院每年招收 200 名学生。

intangible/ɪn'tændʒəbl/

adj. that cannot be touched; that cannot be clearly understood 触摸不到的；无形的；难以理解的；不可捉摸的，模糊的：an ~ sensation of fear 一种莫名其妙的恐惧感

integer/'ɪntɪdʒə(r)/

n. the whole number(e.g.2,4,7,etc.),not a fraction 整数(例如:2,4,7 等)

integral/'ɪntɪɡrəl/

adj. necessary to make sth.whole or complete 构成整体所必需的：Your help is an ~ part of our plan.你的帮助是我们计划中不可缺少的一部分。

integrate/'ɪntɪɡreɪt/

v. ❶combine two or more things together 使结合：Theory should be ~d with practice.理论应当结合实际。❷bring sb.into a group from other groups 使并入：We must ~ people who come to live here into the community.我们必须把来这里居住的人都纳入社区。

integrated/'ɪntɪɡreɪtɪd/

adj. showing a usually pleasing mixture of qualities,groups,etc.融合的；各组成部分相互协调的；综合的；完整的：an ~ school with children of different races and social classes 兼收不同种族及社会阶层儿童的学校

integrity/ɪn'teɡrəti/

n. ❶a state of being whole and undivided; completeness 完整，完全，完善：The old Roman walls may still be seen,but not in their ~.古代罗马人修筑的城墙仍然可见,但是已不完整了。❷honesty; trustworthiness 正直；诚实：a man of complete ~ 十分正直的人/commercial ~ 商业上的诚实

intellect/'ɪntəlekt/

n. ❶the ability to use the power of reasoning and understanding (rather than to feel or take action)（与感觉和行动相对而言的）智力；推理能力；思维能力；领悟

力；理解力：a woman of superior ~ 一位聪颖过人的妇女/Intellect distinguishes humans from other animals. 人类与其他动物之别在于人具有思维能力。❷a person of high intelligence and reasoning power 智力发达的人

intellectual/ˌɪntɪ'lektʃuəl/

Ⅰ*n.* a person who works and lives by his mind,and who is interested in activities which includes thinking and understanding rather than feeling and labouring 知识分子：The candidate was considered an ~ by most voters.大多数投票人认为该候选人是个知识分子。Ⅱ*adj.* ❶of, using,or needing the use of the intellect 智力的,理智的：~ education 智力教育/the ~ faculties 智能 ❷having a high intellect；well educated 有极高智力的；有才智的：Newton was an ~ giant.牛顿是一个智力超群的伟人。

intelligence/ɪn'telɪdʒəns/

n. ❶a good ability to learn and understand 理解力；智力 ❷information gathered,especially about an enemy country 军事情报；谍报：The general had secret ~ of the plans of the enemy.将军有敌人计划的情报。

intelligent/ɪn'telɪdʒənt/

adj. ❶clever; wise 聪明的，明智的：an ~ student 聪明的学生/an ~ plan 明智的计划 ❷able to take action in response to different situation 智能的

intelligible/ɪn'telɪdʒəbl/

adj. that can be understood or comprehended 易理解的；清楚明白的：an ~ explanation 明白易懂的解释/make oneself ~ 讲得使人清楚明白

intemperate/ɪn'tempərət/

adj. not controlled; excessive 无节制的，过度的：an ~ rage 狂怒/~ drinking 暴饮

intend/ɪn'tend/

v. ❶plan or mean (to do sth.) 打算,想要（做某事）：What do you ~ to do next? 你下一步打算做什么？❷mean to be 意指：The seat was ~ed for you, but she took it. 那个座位原来是给你的，可是她占了。

intended /ɪnˈtendɪd/

adj. that you are planning or meaning to do or have 计划中的，预期的

intense /ɪnˈtens/

adj. ❶ very great; strong; extreme 非常的；强烈的；极端的：～ heat 酷热/～ cold (pain, hatred) 严寒(剧痛、痛恨) ❷ ardent; showing strong feelings 热心的；热切的；热情的：～ longing 热望/an ～ worker 工作勤奋的人

intensify /ɪnˈtensɪfaɪ/

v. make or become more intense 加剧；加强；强化：～ colours 加强色彩/～ hatred 加深仇恨

intensity /ɪnˈtensəti/

n. ❶ the state or quality of being intense 强烈，剧烈，紧张：The poem shows great ～ of feelings. 这首诗表达了强烈的感情。/ He spoke with great ～. 他讲话慷慨激昂。❷ strength or depth 强度；深度

intensive /ɪnˈtensɪv/

adj. ❶ concentrating all one's efforts on a specific area 密集的；精深的：～ farming 精耕细作/～ reading 精读/make an ～ study of a subject 对一问题做精深的研究/an ～ bombardment 密集的炮火 ❷ giving force and emphasis 加强语气的；加强语义的：～ adverb 加强语义的副词 ❸ extremely thorough 彻底的；全面的：an ～ search 彻底的搜寻

intent /ɪnˈtent/

I *adj*. ❶ (of looks) eager; earnest (神情) 急切的 ❷ showing fixed attention (in doing or wishing to do) 专心致志的：He's ～ on his studies. 他专心致志地学习。Ⅱ *n*. purpose; intention 目的；意图：with murderous ～ behind one's smiles 笑里藏刀 ‖ **to all ～s (and purposes)** 实际上，实质上 ‖ ～**ly** *adv*. 专心地，一心一意地/～**ness** *n*. 热心，专心

intention /ɪnˈtenʃn/

n. plan; aim; purpose 打算；目的；意图；动机：I had no ～ of breaking the law. 我并不想触犯法律。/ His ～s are good. 他的

动机是好的。

intentional /ɪnˈtenʃənəl/

adj. done on purpose, deliberate and not accidental 故意的，有意的

interact /ˌɪntərˈækt/

v. ❶ act upon, have effect on each other 相互作用，相互影响：All things are interrelated and ～ed on each other. 一切事物都是互相联系、互相影响的。❷ (of people) act together or co-operatively (人) 一起活动，互相合作；互动：She is a social girl who loves ～ing with each other at parties. 她热爱社交活动，喜欢在聚会中和他人互动。❸ communicate with others; exchange ideas with each other 沟通，交流 ‖ ～**ive** *adj*. 一起活动或互相合作的；交互式的；人机对话的

intercede /ˌɪntəˈsiːd/

v. try to settle an affair; ask a favour for sb. 从中调停；代为求情；代为恳求：He ～d in the argument. 他在这场争论中进行调解工作。/ I ～d with the headmaster for (on behalf of) the boys who were to be punished. 我替那些要受处罚的男生向校长求情。

intercept /ˌɪntəˈsept/

v. stop or catch (sb. or sth.) between the starting-point and the destination 中途阻止；拦截：～ a letter (a messenger) 中途截取书信(拦阻信差)/Can our fighter planes ～ the enemy's bombers? 我们的战斗机能拦截敌人的轰炸机吗？

interchange

Ⅰ /ˌɪntəˈtʃeɪndʒ/ *v*. ❶ put each of two things in the other's place 相互易位：～ the front and rear tyres of a car 把汽车的前后轮胎对调 ❷ make an exchange 交换；互换：～ letters 交换信件/～ opinions 交换意见 ❸ (cause sth. to) alternate 交替；轮流：～ severity with indulgence 时而严时而宽 Ⅱ /ˈɪntətʃeɪndʒ/ *n*. ❶ (an example of) the act or action of interchanging or exchanging 交换，交替：an ～ of personnel 人事更迭/an ～ of views 交换意见 ❷ (on a motorway) a system of smaller roads by which two main roads are connected (高速公路) 立体交叉道；交通枢纽

intercom/'ɪntəkɒm/
　　n. a radio system used by a group of people in a building, plane, etc. for talking to each other (楼内、机上等工作人员的)内部通话装置；对讲装置，对讲机

intercourse/'ɪntəkɔːs/
　　n. communication between people, businesses, schools, or governments, such as exchange of thoughts, services, or feelings 交往，交际，交流：social ～ 社交

interdependent /ˌɪntədɪ'pendənt/
　　adj. dependent on each other 互相依赖的，互相依存的 ‖ **interdependence** *n.* 互相依赖

interest/'ɪntrəst/
　　Ⅰ *n.* ❶ the condition of wanting to know or learn about sth. or sb. 兴趣；关心；注意：This lecture has no ～ for(to) me.这个讲座对我来说没什么趣味。❷ sth. with which one concern oneself 感兴趣的事，爱好：Football and pop music are his two great ～s.足球和流行音乐是他的两大爱好。❸ (*pl.*) advantage or profit for sb.利益，利害关系：the ～s of the individual(collective) 个人(集体)利益 ❹ money paid for the use of money 利息：rate of ～ 利率 ‖ **in the ～(s) of** 为了……的利益，**of ～** （作表语)有兴趣的；(作定语)有意思的，使人感兴趣的/**to one's ～** 对……有利，对……有好处/**with ～** 怀着兴趣地；加倍地 Ⅱ *v.* ❶ cause (someone) to have a feeling of interest 使(某人)感兴趣：Football doesn't ～ me at all. 足球一点都提不起我的兴趣。❷ make (someone) want to buy, eat, or do sth. 引起(某人)购买、吃或做某事的)意愿：Can I ～ you in this question? 我可以请你注意这个问题吗？

interested/'ɪntrɪstɪd/
　　adj. ❶ concerned; having or showing interest 关心的；有兴趣的，感兴趣的：He became very ～ in science. 他对科学很感兴趣。❷ in a position to obtain an advantage (from sth.); not impartial 有利害关系的；不公平的；偏私的：～ motives 不纯的动机

interesting/'ɪntrɪstɪŋ/

　　adj. causing interest; catching the attention 有趣味的；引起兴趣的：an ～ film 有趣的影片/The story is very ～.这个故事很有趣。

interfere/ˌɪntə'fɪə(r)/
　　v. ❶ concern oneself with other person's affairs without invitation or being interfered with 干涉，干预，多管闲事：Please don't ～ in my private life.请不要干涉我的私生活。❷ touch or move (sth.) in a way that is annoying or not allowed 乱动，擅自使用：Don't ～ with the machine. 别乱动这台机器。❸ obstruct sth. wholly or partially; prevent sth. from being done or carried out properly 妨碍，干扰：The noise ～d with my sleep.那吵闹声妨碍了我睡觉。

interference/ˌɪntə'fɪərəns/
　　n. ❶ the act or fact of interfering or being interfered with 干涉，干预，妨碍：We will stop ～ from outside.我们要阻止外来干涉。❷ (radio and television, etc.) the signals interfering (无线电、电视等)干扰：～ wave 干扰波

interior/ɪn'tɪərɪə(r)/
　　Ⅰ *adj.* inside, or furthest from the edge or outside (在)内的，内部的：～ trade 国内贸易 Ⅱ *n.* ❶ the part which is inside, or farthest from the edge or outside 内部，内景：the ～ of a house 房子的内部 ❷ the inside of a country or the part of a country which is away from the coast 内地：travel in the ～ 内地旅行 ‖ ～**ize**/ɪn'tɪərɪəraɪz/ *v.* 使(观念、看法等)深入内心/ ～**ly** *adv.* 在内部；在国内

interlace/ˌɪntə'leɪs/
　　v. join or be joined by weaving or lacing together one with another; cross as if woven 交织；交错：interlacing branches 交错的树枝/～ with (与)交错

interlink/ˌɪntə'lɪŋk/
　　v. join or connect (two or more things) together 把……互相连接(或联结)起来

interlock/ˌɪntə'lɒk/
　　v. lock or join firmly together (使)连锁；(使)联结：The different parts of this puz-

zle should ~.这个拼图的不同部分应拼合在一起。

interlude/'ɪntəluːd/

n. a period of time between two events during which sth. else happens or is done (e.g. between two acts of a play) (两件事之间的)间歇;穿插事件;(戏剧的)幕间,幕间插入的戏

intermarry/ˌɪntə'mæri/

v. become connected by marriage 通婚: For many years these people have intermarried with foreigners. 多年来这些人和外国人通婚。‖ **intermarriage**/ˌɪntə'mæridʒ/ *n.* 联姻,通婚

intermediary/ˌɪntə'miːdiəri/

n. a person who maintains contact between people; a go-between 中间人;调解人;媒人

intermediate/ˌɪntə'miːdiət/

adj. being between two things (in time, space, degree, etc.) 中间的;中级的;中等的: ~ trade 中间贸易/an ~ class 中级班

intermission/ˌɪntə'mɪʃn/

n. interval; pause; rest 暂停,中断;休息: They worked all night without ~.他们通宵达旦地工作。

intern[1]/ɪn'tɜːn/

v. (especially with reference to people of another country during a war) put together in a certain place for some political reasons; imprison 拘留(尤指战时的外国人);监禁: During the last war all Germans living in Great Britain were ~ed.在上次战争期间住在英国的所有德国人都被拘留了。

intern[2]/ɪn'tɜːn/

n. a doctor who is competing his training by residing in a hospital and acting as an assistant physician or surgeon there 实习医生

internal/ɪn'tɜːnl/

adj. ❶ of or in the inside, especially of the body 内部的;体内的: the ~ relations of things 事物的内在联系/~ bleeding 内出血/~ organs 内脏 ❷ inside of a country;

of the home affairs of a country; domestic 国内的;内政的: ~ trade 国内贸易

international/ˌɪntə'næʃənl/

adj. having to do with more than one nation 国际的,世界的: ~ trade 国际贸易/ ~ agreement 国际协定/~ conventions 国际惯例/English is one of the working languages at ~ meetings. 英语是国际会议上使用的工作语言之一。/The United Nations is an ~ organization.联合国是一个国际组织。

Internet /'ɪntənet/

n. an international computer network that allows users throughout the world to communicate and exchange information with one another 因特网

interpersonal/ˌɪntə'pɜːsənl/

adj. being, relating to, or involving relations between persons 人与人之间的;人与人之间的关系的

interplay/'ɪntəpleɪ/

n. the action or effect of (two) things on each other 相互作用;相互影响: the ~ of light and sound 光与声的相互作用

interpret/ɪn'tɜːprɪt/

v. ❶ put sth. spoken in one language into the words of another language 翻译,口译;当译员 ❷ understand the likely meaning of (statement, action, etc.); consider to be the meaning of 把……理解为;把……看作: I ~ his silence as a refusal.我把他的沉默理解为拒绝。❸ show, make clear ideas of the meaning of either in words or by artistic performance 解释,说明,阐明: ~ a difficult passage in a text.解释课文中一段难懂的文字。‖ ~**able** *adj.* 可以解释的/ ~**ation** /ɪnˌtɜːprɪ'teɪʃn/ *n.* 解释,翻译;演出/ ~**er** *n.* 译员,口译者,解释者;翻译器/ ~**ress** /ɪn'tɜːprɪtrɪs/ *n.* 女译员

interrelate/ˌɪntərɪ'leɪt/

v. connect with each other (使)相互关联: These matters are ~d.这些问题是相互关联的。/Many would say that crime and poverty ~ (with one another).很多人都说犯罪与贫穷是密切相关的。

interrogate/ɪnˈterəgeɪt/

v. question sb. thoroughly for a long time to get some information 讯问;审问: The police ~d him for two hours.警察审问了他两小时。‖ **interrogator** *n.*审问者;讯问者/ **interrogation** /ɪnˌterəˈgeɪʃn/ *n.* 讯问;审问

interrogative/ˌɪntəˈrɒgətɪv/

Ⅰ *adj.* ❶asking a question 疑问的: in an ~ tone of voice 用疑问的声调 ❷ used in asking questions (e. g. "why" is an inter-rogative adverb） 表示疑问的（例如: "why"是疑问副词）Ⅱ *n.* an interrogative word 疑问词

interrupt/ˌɪntəˈrʌpt/

v. ❶break the flow of (sth.continuous)for a short time 中断,阻断: Traffic was ~ed by a snowstorm.交通被暴风雪所中断。❷break the flow of speech or action of (someone) by saying or doing sth.打断（某人）讲话,打岔,打扰: Don't ~ (me) while I'm speaking. 在我讲话时不要打岔。‖ ~ion/ˌɪntəˈrʌpʃn/ *n.*中断,打断,打扰;使中断的事物/ ~ive *adj.*中断的,打扰的

intersect/ˌɪntəˈsekt/

v. cross one another; divide by cutting across 相交;交叉;横断: The two lines ~ at point X.这两条线相交于 X 点。/This line ~s the other at point X.这条线与另一条线于 X 点相交。‖ ~ion *n.* 交叉路口;十字路口

intersperse/ˌɪntəˈspɜːs/

v. scatter among or put in sth. here and there 散置;散布;点缀: The trees are ~d with grass.树林里长满青草。

interval/ˈɪntəvl/

n. ❶ a period of time (between two events or two parts of an action）; the time between two acts of a play, two parts of a concert,etc.间隔时间,间歇;幕间休息: There is a two hours' ~ to the next train.离下一班火车还隔两小时。❷ a space between two objects or points 空间的间隔,空隙: arranged at ~s of ten feet 以十英尺的间隔排列 ‖ **at** ~**s** 不时;

相隔一定的距离/**at long** ~s 间或/**at reg-ular** ~s 每隔一定时间;每隔一定距离/**at short** ~s 常常

intervene/ˌɪntəˈviːn/

v. ❶ occur between other events or be-tween certain points of time 介于其间: A week ~s between Christmas and New Year's Day.圣诞节与元旦相距一个星期。❷ come between persons or groups to help settle a dispute; act as intermediary 干涉;调停: The president was asked to ~ in the strike.总统被要求出面调停罢工事件。

interview/ˈɪntəvjuː/

Ⅰ *n.*❶a meeting with sb.for discussion or conference 接见,会见,面谈: I thank you very much for this ~.我非常感谢您这次接见。❷a meeting at which a reporter, etc.asks sb.questions in order to find out his views (记者的)采访 ❸a meeting at which someone is asked questions to find out if they are suitable for a job or school 面试: a job ~ 求职面试Ⅱ *v.*❶conduct an interview in television, newspaper, and radio reporting 访问,采访: The news-paper reporter ~ed the famous singer.报界记者采访了那位著名歌手。❷ask someone questions to find out if they are suitable for a job, etc. 对……面试: The headmaster ~ed five people for this job.校长为这份工作面试了五个人。

intimacy/ˈɪntɪməsi/

*n.*❶ the state of being close 亲密,密切: His claims to (an) ~ with (to be on terms of ~ with)the president are some-what exaggerated.他声称自己与总统关系密切,这有点言过其实。❷a remark or action that happens only between people who know each other very well 亲昵的言语(或行为): exchanging intimacies with one's close friends 和密友们亲热地交谈

intimate[1]/ˈɪntɪmət/

Ⅰ *adj.*❶having an extremely close rela-tionship 亲密的,密切的: the most ~ friend 至交/be on ~ terms with sb.与某人关系密切 ❷personal; private 个人的,私人的,秘密的:an ~ diary 私人日记 ❸

detailed and thorough; resulting from a close study 详尽的；仔细研究而得的：He has an ~ knowledge of the city. 他对这个城市了如指掌。❹ having a sexual relationship with sb. 有性关系的；暧昧的 ‖ n. a very close friend 挚友，知己

intimate² /'ɪntɪmeɪt/
v. make known indirectly; suggest 提示，暗示，隐约地表示：He ~d a wish to go by saying that it was late. 他说时间不早了，暗示他想走了。 ‖ **intimation** /ˌɪntɪ'meɪʃn/ n. 告知，通知；通行；暗示，提示

intimidate /ɪn'tɪmɪdeɪt/
v. make sb. do, or not do sth. by frightening him 威胁；恐吓：The thieves ~d the boy into not telling the police. 小偷威胁这孩子不要报告警察。 ‖ **intimidation** /ɪnˌtɪmɪ'deɪʃn/ n. 恐吓，威胁

into /'ɪntə/
prep. ❶ to the inside of 进入……内部，到(向)……里：Throw it ~ the fire. 把它丢入火中。❷ so as to be in 进入其中：went ~ the law and then went ~ business 先进法律界然后进商界 ❸ expressing the change of state 成为，转入：When it is very cold, water turns ~ ice. 天冷时，水变成冰。❹ used when dividing one number by another 除：5 ~ 20 is 4.5 除 20 等于 4。 ‖ be ~ sth. 牵扯，与……有关

intolerable /ɪn'tɒlərəbl/
adj. that cannot be tolerated 无法忍受的

intolerant /ɪn'tɒlərənt/
adj. not tolerant of others' ideas, behaviours, etc. 不容忍的，不宽容的；不能忍受的；不能宽恕的：He is ~ of fools. 他不宽容愚人。 ‖ **intolerance** n. 不宽容

intonation /ˌɪntə'neɪʃn/
n. the rise and fall of the voice in speaking 语调；音调

intone /ɪn'təʊn/
v. say (a poem, prayer, etc.) in an almost level voice (以几乎平板的语调)吟诵(诗歌、祈祷文等)；吟咏：The priest ~d the blessing. 神父吟诵祈福词。

in toto /ɪn 'təʊtəʊ/
adv. totally; as a whole 全然；完全，全部：They accepted the plan ~. 他们完全接受了这个计划。

intoxicant /ɪn'tɒksɪkənt/
n. sth. which intoxicates, especially an alcoholic drink 致醉物(尤指酒精饮料)

intoxicate /ɪn'tɒksɪkeɪt/
v. make drunk; make very excited, as if one were drunk 使喝醉；使陶醉；使极度兴奋：They were ~d by their victory. 他们陶醉在胜利之中。 ‖ **intoxication** /ɪnˌtɒksɪ'keɪʃn/ n. 陶醉；醉酒

intransitive /ɪn'trænsətɪv/
adj. with reference to verbs which do not have a direct object (指动词)不及物的

intricate /'ɪntrɪkət/
adj. complicated; puzzling; difficult to follow or understand 错综复杂的；难懂的：an ~ instrument 复杂的仪器/a novel with an ~ plot 一部情节复杂的小说

intrigue /ɪn'triːg/
Ⅰ v. ❶ make and carry out secret plans or plots 策划阴谋；捣鬼：~ with Smith against Robinson 与史密斯密谋对付罗宾逊 ❷ arouse the interest or curiosity of 激起……的兴趣(或好奇心)：The news ~d all of us. 这消息引起了我们大家的兴趣。 Ⅱ n. ❶ a secret plan 阴谋诡计：political ~s 政治阴谋 ❷ a secret love affair 私通

introduce /ˌɪntrə'djuːs/
v. ❶ make known for the first time to each other or someone else, especially by telling two people each other's names 介绍：He ~d me to his parents. 他把我介绍给他的父母。❷ bring (sth.) into use or operation for the first time 引进，采用；传入：Potato was ~d into Europe from South America. 土豆是由南美洲传入欧洲的。❸ be a sign that sth. is about to happen 作为(某事物)的开头：This song ~s the most important part of the play. 这首歌引出了这出话剧最重要的部分。❹ carry out or put forward a plan, an order, etc. for the first time 推行，实施 ‖ ~r n. 介绍人，传入者，创始人，提出人

introduction /ˌɪntrəˈdʌkʃn/
n. ❶ the act of bringing in sth. or the fact of being introduced 介绍，提倡，采用：a letter of ～ 介绍信 ❷ an occasion of telling people each others' names 介绍；引见：It was necessary to make ～s all round. 需要将大家一一互相介绍。 ❸ a written or spoken explanation at the beginning of a book or speech（书或演讲的）前言，引言，引论，序(论)

introductory /ˌɪntrəˈdʌktəri/
adj. serving as an introduction to a subject 引导的，介绍的

introspect /ˌɪntrəˈspekt/
v. examine or be concerned with one's own thoughts and feelings 内省；反省 ‖ ～ion *n.* 内省，反省/～ive *adj.* 内省的；好反省的

intrude /ɪnˈtruːd/
v. ❶ introduce without invitation 强加：～ one's views upon others 把自己的意见强加于人 ❷ enter a place where sb. is unwanted or unasked 擅自进入，侵入，闯入；打扰：I hope I am not intruding. 我希望不致打扰(你)。

intrusion /ɪnˈtruːʒən/
n. the action of entering a place, etc. in an unpleasant way 侵入，闯入；打扰，侵扰：She was furious about this ～into her private life. 对她私生活的侵扰让她大为恼火。

intuition /ˌɪntjuːˈɪʃn/
n. ❶ the ability to understand sth. quickly without having to think about it carefully 直觉 ❷ the knowledge gained by this ability 直觉知识

intuitive /ɪnˈtjuːɪtɪv/
adj. using knowledge, etc. that is believed to be true 直觉的；直观的；由直觉判断的：an ～ guess 直观猜测

invade /ɪnˈveɪd/
v. ❶ enter (a country) with armed forces in order to attack 侵略，侵犯 ❷ crowd into a place in large numbers 蜂拥而至，进入：Visitors ～d the seaside in summer months. 在夏季，游客涌到海边 ❸ attack or affect (body, etc.) in an unpleasant way 侵扰，侵害：Disease germs had ～d his body. 病菌侵害了他的身体。

invalid[1] /ɪnˈvælɪd/
adj. not correct or correctly expressed, especially in law; not (any longer) suitable for use 无效的，作废的：an ～ contract (cheque) 无效的契约(支票)

invalid[2]
Ⅰ /ˈɪnvəlɪd/ *n.* a person who is disabled or suffers from ill health 病人；伤残者 Ⅱ /ˈɪnvəliːd/ *v.* allow (someone) to leave, especially the armed forces because of ill health 允许(某人)离开：He was ～ed out of the army when he lost the sight of one eye. 他一只眼睛失明后获准退役。

invalidate /ɪnˈvælɪdeɪt/
v. make (sth.) invalid; show that (sth.) is not correct 使无效；使作废；证明(某事)不正确：The fact that there is almost no critical discussion of his paintings ～s this book's claims to be the standard work on Blake. 书中对布莱克的绘画几乎未做评论，这就使该书自称为研究布莱克之权威著作一说难以成立。

invalidity /ˌɪnvəˈlɪdəti/
n. ❶ the state of being not legally acceptable 无效；无价值：the ～ of her arguments 她的论据无法成立 ❷ the state of being an invalid because of illness 伤残；病弱：an ～ pension 病残抚恤金

invaluable /ɪnˈvæljuəbl/
adj. of value too high to be measured 无法估计的；无价的；极宝贵的：Thank you for your ～ help. 感谢你宝贵的帮助。

invariable /ɪnˈveəriəbl/
adj. never changing; always the same 永远不变的；恒定的

invariant /ɪnˈveəriənt/
adj. never changing 永远不变的，始终如一的，恒定的：The pattern of cell divisions was found to be ～. 人们发现细胞分裂的方式是不变的。

invasion /ɪnˈveɪʒn/
n. an act of entering another country, especially an attack in war when the enemy spreads into and tries to control a coun-

try,city,etc.入侵,侵犯,侵略：the ～ of Normandy 对诺曼底的入侵/Opening my letter was an inexcusable ～ of privacy. 拆看我的信件是一种不可原谅的侵犯个人隐私的行为。

invective/ɪn'vektɪv/
adj.blaming or criticizing in very rude or unpleasant language；cursing 猛烈抨击的；痛骂的

inveigh/ɪn'veɪ/
v.attack strongly with words 猛烈抨击；痛骂：The speaker was ～ing against the evils of drinking.那位演讲者在猛烈抨击喝酒的坏处。

invent/ɪn'vent/
v.❶make or produce sth. which did not exist before 发明；创造：We do not know who ～ed the wheel. 我们不知道谁发明了车轮。❷make up 编造；虚构；杜撰：He ～ed a story to explain why he was late.他编造了一个故事来解释他为什么迟到。‖ ～or n.发明者

invention /ɪn'venʃən/
n.❶the process of inventing sth.发明,创造 ❷sth. that has been invented 发明物

inventive /ɪn'ventɪv/
adj.skilled at inventing things,especially ideas 有创造才能的；有创意的(尤指思想方面)

inventory/'ɪnvəntri/
n.(usually with reference to the contents of a house,shop,store,etc.) complete list (通常指房子、商店、仓库等里面东西的)完整的清单；财产目录；存货清单：take (make,check) an ～ 编制财产目录或开清单

inverse/ˌɪn'vɜːs/
Ⅰadj.exactly opposite；reversed in position, direction, or tendency（位置、方向等）倒转的,逆向的：DCBA is the ～ order of ABCD.DCBA 是 ABCD 的颠倒顺序。Ⅱn.the exact opposite of sth.倒置；颠倒

inversion /ɪn'vɜːʃn/
n.❶the process of inverting or reversing 倒转,倒置,颠倒 ❷sth. that is inverted 倒

转物；倒置物 ❸a form of a chord in which the root is not the lowest note 转位

invert/
Ⅰ/ɪn'vɜːt/v. put upside down or in the opposite order, position or arrangement 使反向,使颠倒：He ～ed the glass and the water ran out.他把杯子倒过来,结果水流了出来。 Ⅱ/'ɪnvɜːt/ n. sth. inverted 颠倒的事物

invest/ɪn'vest/
v.❶ put money (in) 投资(于)：～ one's savings in a enterprise 将储蓄投资于一家企业 ❷ spend a lot of time or energy on sth.that you think it will be useful 投入(时间、精力) ❸ buy (sth. considered useful) 购买(认为有用之物)：～ in a new kettle 买一把新水壶 ❹ decorate；surround with qualities 使……着衣；使带有,使笼罩：It is ～ed with romance.它带有传奇色彩。‖ ～or n.投资人

investigate/ɪn'vestɪgeɪt/
v.try to find out more information about；examine the reasons for (sth.),the character of (someone),etc.调查,侦查,审查：～ the causes of the accident 调查事故的原因 ‖ **investigator** n.调查者,审查者,侦查员

investigation /ɪnˌvestɪ'geɪʃn/
n.❶ the action of investigating sth. or sb.；a formal or systematic examination or research 调查,审查：He is under ～ for receiving illicit funds.他因收受非法资金而被审查。❷a formal inquiry or systematic study 调查研究

investigative /ɪn'vestɪgeɪtɪv/
adj.involving investigation or making inquiries,especially as distinct from merely reporting what is known 调查的,审查的：～ news 调查性新闻

investment /ɪn'vestmənt/
n.❶ the process of investing money in sth.投资：a debate over private ～in road-building 一场关于私人投资修路的争论 ❷an amount of money invested 投资额 ❸sth.worthwhile in which money, time,

or effort is invested 值得投资的东西

invigorate /ɪnˈvɪgəreɪt/
v. make vigorous; give strength or courage to 使有生气；使精力充沛；鼓舞：~ the national spirit 振奋民族精神

invincible /ɪnˈvɪnsəbl/
adj. not able to be defeated 不可征服的；不可战胜的

inviolate /ɪnˈvaɪəlɪt/
adj. not violated, attacked or destroyed; secure; pure 未被破坏的；未受侵犯的；无损的；纯洁的

invisible /ɪnˈvɪzəbl/
adj. that cannot be seen; hidden from sight 看不见的；无形的：~ stars 看不见的星星/X ray is ~. X射线是不可见的。

invitation /ˌɪnvɪˈteɪʃn/
n. ❶ a written or spoken request made to someone, asking them to come to an event, such as a meal or a meeting, or take part in an activity, etc. 邀请；accept ~ 接受邀请 ❷ a paper or sth. else used to invite sb. 请柬，请帖 ❸ sth. tempt sb. to do sth., especially sth. bad 引诱；招致 ‖ ~al adj. 邀请的，应邀参加的

invite
Ⅰ /ɪnˈvaɪt/ v. ❶ ask sb. politely to come somewhere or to take part in sth. 邀请，招待：She ~d me to her birthday party. 她邀请我参加她的生日晚会。❷ ask for 请求，征求：~ suggestions from sb. 征求某人的建议 Ⅱ /ˈɪnvaɪt/ n. a colloquial expression for invitation 邀请 ‖ ~r n. 邀请者

inviting /ɪnˈvaɪtɪŋ/
adj. attracting you to do sth. pleasant and tempting 诱人的；有魅力的 ‖ ~ly adv. 诱惑地；动人地

invoice /ˈɪnvɔɪs/
Ⅰ n. a bill for goods received 发票；发货单 Ⅱ v. make an invoice for (foods) 开发票，列账单：~ our company for two typewriters 给我们公司开一张两部打字机的发票

invoke /ɪnˈvəuk/
v. ❶ call upon (God; the power of the law,

etc.) for help or protection 祈求（上帝、法律的力量等）帮助（或保护）：~ the gods 求助于神灵 ❷ request earnestly 恳求；迫切地需求：~ sb.'s help 恳求某人帮助 ❸ summon up (by magic) （以法术）召唤：~ evil spirits 召唤恶鬼

involuntary /ɪnˈvɒləntəri/
adj. not controlled by the will; done without intention 非意志控制的；本能的；非本意的：When I touched his arm he gave an ~ jump. 我碰到他手臂时，他本能地跳了起来。‖ involuntarily adv. 无心地；不自觉地

involve /ɪnˈvɒlv/
v. cause (someone) to become connected or concerned 牵涉，牵连，拖累，使卷入：This problem ~s us all. 这个问题牵涉到我们所有人。‖ ~ment n. 牵连，包含

involved /ɪnˈvɒlvd/
adj. ❶ complicated and difficult to understand 难懂的；复杂的 ❷ concerned or sharing in sth. 有牵扯的，有关联的

invulnerable /ɪnˈvʌlnərəbl/
adj. that cannot be wounded or harmed 不能伤害的，无懈可击的

inward /ˈɪnwəd/
adj. ❶ on the inside 里面的，内部的：the ~ organs of the body 身体内部的器官 ❷ moving towards the inside 向内的；输入的：~ charges 入港费 ‖ ~ly adv. 在（向）内部，在心灵深处，暗自地/ ~ness n. 本质；灵性；思想（感情）的深度

iodine /ˈaɪədiːn/
n. a type of chemical substance found in sea water used for cleaning wounds and in photography, etc. 碘

ion /ˈaɪən/
n. an electrically charged particle in certain substances 离子

ionize /ˈaɪənaɪz/
v. change or become changed into ions （使）电离；（使）电离成离子

irate /aɪˈreɪt/
adj. very angry 发怒的；愤怒的

iron /ˈaɪən/
Ⅰ n. ❶ a hard and heavy metal from

which steel is made 铁：an ～ determination 钢铁般的决心 ❷ a tool made of iron，heated and used for smoothing clothes 熨斗：an electric ～ 电熨斗 ❸ (*pl.*)chains for a prisoner's hands or feet 镣铐：put sb.in ～s 给某人戴上镣铐 Ⅱ*v.* make (clothes) smooth with an iron（用熨斗）熨平，烫平（衣物）：I've been ～ing all day.我熨衣服熨了一整天。‖ **have many ～s in the fire** 同时有很多的事，同时要参加的活动太多/ ～ **out** 烫好，熨平；消除 ‖ ～**er** *n.*熨衣工；轧布机/ ～**monger** *n.*五金商/ ～**mongery** *n.*五金店/ ～**smith** *n.*铁匠/ ～**ware** *n.*（总称）铁器/ ～**works** *n.*（用作单或复）钢铁厂

ironic(al)/aɪˈrɒnɪk(l)/
*adj.*expressing your meaning is the opposite of what you have said 反语的，讽刺的，嘲讽的：an ～ smile 讥讽的笑，冷笑/ ～ remarks 讽刺的言语，冷言冷语 ‖ ～(**al**)**ly** *adv.*讽刺地，冷言冷语地

irony/ˈaɪərəni/
*n.*❶a way of speaking or writing in which the ordinary meaning of the words is the opposite of the thought in the speaker's mind 反语 ❷an event which is the opposite of what would naturally be expected 反常的事

irradiate/ɪˈreɪdɪeɪt/
*v.*❶ make bright by throwing light on 照亮；使发光；使生辉：His little face was ～d by happiness. 他那张小脸蛋高兴得容光焕发。❷ treat with X-rays,etc.用 X 射线等治疗：The surgeons ～d the tumour.外科医生用 X 射线照射那个肿瘤。❸ treat (food) with X-rays to kill bacteria and preserve it 照射（用 X 射线处理食品以便贮藏）

irrational/ɪˈræʃənl/
*adj.*not controlled by reason 不理性的：～ behaviour 不理性的行为

irregular/ɪˈreɡjʊlə(r)/
*adj.*❶ not inflect in the normal way 不规则的，无规律的：～ verbs 不规则动词 ❷ not belonging to the regular armed forces 非正规的：～ troops 非正规军 ❸ uneven；not regular in shape，arrangement，

etc.不整齐的，不平坦的：～ teeth 不整齐的牙齿 ‖ ～**ity**/ɪˌreɡjʊˈlærəti/ *n.*不规则，无规律/ ～**ly** *adv.*不规则地；不整齐地

irrelevant/ɪˈreləvənt/
*adj.*having nothing to do with the subject 不相关的；离题的：Your answer to my question is ～.你对我的问题的回答是不切题的。‖ **irrelevance** *n.*不相关；离题

irreligious/ˌɪrɪˈlɪdʒəs/
*adj.*against，or not interested in religion 反宗教的；对宗教无兴趣的；无宗教信仰的

irreparable/ɪˈrepərəbl/
*adj.*that cannot be repaired or put right 不可弥补的；无法挽回的：He has suffered ～ losses.他蒙受了无法挽回的损失。

irrepressible/ˌɪrɪˈpresəbl/
*adj.*not able to be controlled 不能抑制的；控制不住的：～ delight at hearing the good news 听到好消息时欣喜若狂

irreproachable/ˌɪrɪˈprəʊtʃəbl/
*adj.*without fault or blame 无过失的；无可非议的

irresistible/ˌɪrɪˈzɪstəbl/
*adj.*not able to be resisted；too strong to stop 不能抵抗的；不能压制的；强烈的：I had an ～ desire to run away.我有强烈的离家出走的愿望。

irresolute/ɪˈrezəluːt/
*adj.*not able to decide what to do；hesitating 无决断的；犹豫不决的；优柔寡断的

irrespective/ˌɪrɪˈspektɪv/
adj. without regard for；without paying attention to 不考虑……的；不顾……的：He is going to buy it ～ of what you say. 不管你说什么，他还是要把它买下。

irresponsible/ˌɪrɪˈspɒnsəbl/
adj. ❶（of persons）not responsible for their actions（指人）（对其行为）不需负责的：By law babies are ～.根据法律婴儿是不需负责的。❷not having a proper sense of responsibility 无责任感的；不负责任的：Your ～ refusal to help your friends surprised me.你不负责任地拒绝

帮助你的朋友使我感到惊讶。‖ **irresponsibility**/ˌɪrɪˌspɒnsə'bɪləti/ *n.*无责任感；不负责任的行为

irreversible /ˌɪrɪ'vɜːsəbl/

*adj.*not reversible；unable to be altered or revoked 不可逆转的；不可改变的；不可撤销的 ‖ **irreversibly** *adv.*不可逆地

irrigate/'ɪrɪgeɪt/

*v.*❶supply water to land in order to help crops grow 灌溉：The Changjiang River ~s vast stretches of farmland along its course.长江灌溉着两岸的大片农田。❷wash (a wound) with a flow of liquid 冲洗(伤口) ‖ **irrigation** *n.*灌溉

irritate/'ɪrɪteɪt/

*v.*❶make angry or annoyed 激怒；使烦躁：Your poor work ~d him.你工作不好使他很恼火。❷make sore or inflamed；cause discomfort to part of the body 使疼痛；使不舒服：Thick clothes ~ my skin.厚衣服使我的皮肤怪难受的。‖ **irritation**/ˌɪrɪ'geɪʃn/ *n.*激怒；烦躁／ **irritable** /'ɪrɪtəbl/ *adj.*易怒的；烦躁的 /**irritability**/ˌɪrɪtə'bɪləti/ *n.*烦躁

is/ɪz/

aux.v. the singular form of the present tense of "be" and used with "he, she or it"是(be 的现在时单数形式,同 he, she 或 it 一起连用)：Who ~ he? 他是谁? / Tom ~ not at home.汤姆不在家。/ She ~ singing.她在唱歌。/It ~ Sunday, today.今天是星期日。

Islam/'ɪz'lɑːm/

*n.*❶the religion of the Muslims 伊斯兰教 ❷the countries where Islam is the main religion 伊斯兰教国家

island/'aɪlənd/

*n.*❶a piece of land surrounded by water 岛：There are some banana trees on that ~ over there.那边岛上有些香蕉树。❷sth. resembling an island, because it is isolated 似岛之物：Platforms in the middle of crowded streets are safety ~s.交通繁忙的街道中心的平台是安全岛。

isle/aɪl/

*n.*an island (usually used in poetry except in the names of places e. g. the British Isles) 岛(有时用于地名,通常用于诗歌中)

isolate/'aɪsəleɪt/

*v.*❶separate, put, or keep apart from others 使隔离；使孤立；使隔绝：When a person has an infectious disease, he is usually ~d.当一个人患传染病时,他通常被隔离起来。❷separate (a substance, germ, etc.) from its combinations or surroundings 分解(物质等)；使(细菌)分离；离析：A chemist can ~ oxygen and hydrogen in water.化学家能将水中的氧与氢分解。/ We have ~d the bacterium in its pure form.我们已经把这细菌的完整形式分离出来了。

isolated /'aɪsəleɪtɪd/

*adj.*❶far away from other places, buildings, or people；remote and difficult to reach 远离(其他地方、建筑物或人群)的；遥远的，偏僻的 ❷having little contact or little in common with others 与世隔绝的；独自的：He lived a very ~life.他过着与世隔绝的生活。❸single；exceptional 个别的；例外的

isolation/ˌaɪsə'leɪʃn/

*n.*❶a state of separating between persons or groups 隔离；隔绝：an ~ hospital (ward) 隔离医院(病室) ❷(in chemistry) setting sth. apart from others(化学中的) 离析 ❸a feeling of being alone 孤立；孤独

issue/'ɪʃuː, 'ɪsjuː/

Ⅰ *v.*❶come, go or flow out 放出；流出：Smoke was issuing from the chimney. 烟囱在冒烟。❷ give out or provide officially 提供,发给：Please ~ everyone with a card.请给每人发一张卡片。Ⅱ *n.*❶the act of coming out or being produced 发出；流出：the place of ~ 发出地点 ❷publication；sending out 发行；出版：the ~ of a newspaper(a new coin) 报纸(新钱币)的发行 ❸sth. which is produced so as to be publicly sold or given out 发行物：new ~s of banknotes 新发行的钞票 ❹a question that arises for discussion 引起讨论的问题：raise a new ~ 提出新问

题/argue political ～s 争论政治问题 ‖ **join**(**take**) ～ **with sb.**(**on** /**about sth.**) 与某人争辩(讨论)某事/**the point**(**matter**) **at** ～ 争论点

it/ɪt/

pron. ❶ used to refer to lifeless things or animals (指无生命的事物或动物) 它：Where is my pen? I can't find ～.我的笔在哪里? 我找不着。❷ used to identify a person or thing (指人或事物)：Who's ～ at the door? It is me.谁在门外? 是我。❸used as the subject of "be"to say what the time,day,or date is (用作动词 be 的主语,指时间、日期等)：It is two to ten.差两分十点。❹ used to emphasize one part of a sentence (用以强调句中的某一部分)：It was work that exhausted him.使他疲惫不堪的是工作。‖ **that is** ～ ❶ 这(那)是要点(或重要原因等);正是这样 ❷这(那)就是终结：I'm afraid that's ～—we've lost.我看完了——我们输了。

italic/ɪ'tælɪk/

Ⅰ *adj.* (of printed letters) sloping (印刷字)斜体的：This is ～ type.这是斜体。Ⅱ *n.* (usually *pl.*) italic letters 斜体字：That sentence was printed in ～s.那个句子是用斜体字印刷的。

itch/ɪtʃ/

Ⅰ *n.* ❶ the feeling of irritation on the skin,causing a desire to scratch 痒：have (suffer from) an ～ 觉得痒 ❷ a strong desire or longing 强烈的欲望,渴望：have an ～ for writing(money) 很想写作(发财) Ⅱ *v.* ❶ have an itch 发痒：Are your mosquito bites still ～ing? 你被蚊子咬的地方还痒吗? ❷ long for 渴望：～ for sth.渴望得到某物/ ～ to have a try 跃跃欲试 ‖ **have an** ～**ing palm** 贪财 ‖ ～**y** /'ɪtʃi/ *adj.*发痒的;渴望的

item/'aɪtəm/

Ⅰ *n.*❶ a single thing among a set or on a list 条,项;条款;项目：～ by ～ 逐条(地)/the first ～ on the programme 节目中的第一项 ❷ a piece or paragraph (of news) (新闻的)一条,一则：Are there any interesting news ～s(～s of news) in the paper this morning? 今日晨报上有

什么有趣的新闻吗? Ⅱ *adv.* (used when listing or enumerating items) also (列举项目时)又,亦：One chair, ～, two carpets.椅子一把,又地毯两块。‖ ～**ize** *v.* 分项列举;分条列明

iterate/'ɪtəreɪt/

*v.*say sth.again and again;make (an accusation,a demand,etc.) repeatedly 重复地说,反复地控诉(要求)：～ a warning 反复予以警告

iterative /'ɪtərətɪv/

adj. ❶ relating to or involving iteration,especially of a mathematical or computational process 重复的,反反复复的 ❷denoting a grammatical rule that can be applied repeatedly (语法规则)反复的,多次的

its/ɪts/

*pron.*of it;belonging to it 它的(it 的所有格)：the stool and ～ legs 凳子和凳腿/Turn the box on ～ side.把箱子侧着立起来。/The dog hurt ～ foot.那条狗的腿受了伤。

itself/ɪt'self/

*pron.*❶ (the reflexive form of "it") the same thing,animal or baby as the one that the sentence is about (it 的反身格) 它自己,它本身,自身：The baby is too young to feed ～.那婴儿太小,他自己还不能吃饭。/The house stands by ～ (alone) outside the village.那所房子孤零零地坐落在村外。/ Did the bowl break ～? 难道碗是自己打破的吗? ❷used to emphasize an animal or a thing (用以加强语气)本身：the bicycle ～ 自行车本身

ivory/'aɪvəri/

n. ❶ a hard, creamy-white substance of which an elephant's tusks are made 象牙(质)：artificial ～人造象牙 ❷ the colour of this substance; a creamy-white colour 象牙色,乳白色：an ～skin(complexion) 乳白色的皮肤(肤色) ‖ ～ **tower** 象牙塔 (与世隔绝的境界)

ivy/'aɪvi/

*n.*a climbing plant, with shiny three-or-five-pointed leaves 常春藤

Jj

jab /dʒæb/

I v.(-bb-)❶push, usually with sth. sharp 猛捅,猛戳,猛刺:I ～bed the needle into my finger.我的手指被针猛刺了一下。/ He kept ～bing his finger into my back until I turned round. 他不停地用手指戳我的后背,直到我转过身来。❷ give short,quick blow with the fist 用拳猛击: The fighters ～bed away each other for a long time.打架者彼此猛击了很久。II n. a sudden,rough thrust or blow 刺;戳;猛击:get a ～ in the arm 胳膊被捅了一下

jabber /'dʒæbə(r)/

v. talk quickly and in a way not easy to understand 快而含糊地说: He is always ～ing.他总是含含糊糊地说话。/ He ～ed to me.他叽里咕噜地对我说了些话。

jack /dʒæk/

n. ❶ an apparatus for lifting off the ground anything of heavy weight,such as a car, etc. 千斤顶;起重器 ❷ a playing card bearing a representation of a soldier, page, or knave,normally ranking next below a queen 纸牌中的"J"牌

jackass /'dʒækæs/

n.❶ a person who behaves foolishly 笨蛋,傻瓜:Don't be a ～, come down off the roof! 别犯傻了,快从房顶上下来! ❷a male ass 公驴

jackboot /'dʒækbuːt/

n.❶a military boot which covers the leg up to the knee 长筒军靴 ❷the cruel rule of military men 军人的残酷统治:living under the ～ 生活在残暴的军人统治之下

jacket /'dʒækɪt/

n.❶ a short coat with sleeves 短外衣;夹克衫:He wore a brown ～ and grey trou-sers.他穿着棕色夹克和灰裤子。❷ pa-per wrapper;record sleeve 书籍护封;唱片套 ❸ the skin of potatoes 马铃薯皮: potatoes baked in their ～s 带皮烤的马铃薯

jackpot /'dʒækpɒt/

n.the biggest amount of money to be won in a game of cards or in any competition decided by chance (扑克牌或其他比赛中可赢得的)最大赌注

jade /dʒeɪd/

n. a type of hard, green stone used to make ornaments,etc.翡翠;玉

jaded /'dʒeɪdɪd/

adj.tired and unhappy 疲惫不堪的;厌倦的

jag /dʒæg/

I v.(-gg-) cut or tear roughly 把……切得参差不齐,把……撕(或割)成锯齿状:I ～ed my finger on a rusty nail.我的手指被生锈的铁钉割破了。 II n. sth. rough and sharp which jags;a cut caused by this 尖锐的突出物;锯齿状的缺口

jagged /'dʒægɪd/

adj.rough and sharp;with sharp edges 粗糙而尖锐的;锯齿状的:the ～ pieces of a broken bottle 破瓶子参差不齐的碎片

jaguar /'dʒægjʊə(r)/

n.a type of large, spotted wild animal of the cat family, found in South America and central America 美洲虎

jail /dʒeɪl/

I n.a prison 监狱:He spent the rest of his life in ～.他在狱中度过了余生。II v. put in jail 监禁;使……下狱:He was ～ed for robbery.他因犯抢劫罪被关进监狱。

jailbreak /'dʒeɪlbreɪk/

n. an escape from prison, especially by more than one person (尤指多人的)越狱,大逃狱

jam¹/dʒæm/

I *v.* (-mm-) ❶ push (things) tightly together 塞进 ❷ get stuck; become unable to work because the moving parts have got stuck 堵塞,卡住: The brakes ～med and the car went into a wall. 刹车发生故障,汽车朝一堵墙冲去。 ❸ block(radio or telephone signals) by broadcasting noise 干扰: The broadcast was ～med by the enemy. 广播受到了敌人的干扰。 II *n.* ❶ a number of things or people crowded together, preventing movement 拥挤,堵塞: She was delayed by a traffic ～. 她因交通拥堵迟到了。 ❷ an awkward position; a difficult situation 困境: He got himself into a ～ with the tax people. 他和税务人员之间有了麻烦。

jam²/dʒæm/

n. a food made by boiling fruit with sugar to a thick mixture 果酱

jamb/dʒæm/

n. a side post of a door or window (门、窗的)侧柱,边框

jamboree/ˌdʒæmbəˈriː/

n. ❶ a large, friendly meeting (especially of Boy Scouts from many nations)(尤指来自许多国家的)童子军大会 ❷ a merry meeting 欢乐的聚会

jammed/dʒæmd/

adj. ❶ not able to move 动弹不得的;卡住了的 ❷ very full; crowded 塞满的;拥挤不堪的

jammy/ˈdʒæmi/

adj. ❶ easy 容易的: That was a really ～ examination. 那次考试真是太容易了。 ❷ lucky, especially in a way that makes other people annoyed (尤指使其他人气恼的)运气好的: The ～ bugger passed the exam without doing any work! 那个走运的家伙没花一点工夫就通过了考试!

jangle/ˈdʒæŋɡl/

v. (cause to) make an unpleasant noise like pieces of metal striking one another

(使)发出如金属撞击般刺耳的声音

January/ˈdʒænjʊəri/

n. the first month of the year 一月

jar¹/dʒɑː(r)/

n. a tall vessel with a wide mouth made of glass, stone, clay, etc. 坛子;罐子;广口瓶: a ～ of wine 一坛酒

jar²/dʒɑː(r)/

v. ❶ have an unpleasant effect 使产生不愉快的感觉: Your screams ～ on my ears. 你的尖叫声很刺耳。 ❷ be out of harmony 与……不和谐: The two colours ～. 这两种色调不和谐。

jargon/ˈdʒɑːɡən/

n. (especially with reference to the special and technical words used by experts) the language which is difficult for ordinary people to understand (尤指专家使用的)专门术语;行话: When engineers talk about their work, they use a lot of ～s. 工程师们在谈论工作时使用很多专门术语。

jasmine/ˈdʒæzmɪn/

n. a shrub plant with sweet-smelling, white or yellow flowers 茉莉,素馨

jaunt/dʒɔːnt/

I *n.* a short trip for pleasure 短途旅游: They are off for a day's ～ to the beach. 他们到海边玩了一天。 II *v.* take a short trip or excursion 短途旅游: We ～ed through the Summer Palace. 我们游览了颐和园。

jaunty/ˈdʒɔːnti/

adj. ❶ (showing that one feels) satisfied with oneself and pleased with life 自信的;得意扬扬的 ❷ lively 快活的,活泼的: The happy boy walked with ～ steps. 这快乐的孩子迈着轻快活泼的步子往前走。

javelin/ˈdʒævlɪn/

n. a light spear for throwing, now used mostly in sport (现多用于田径运动的)标枪

jaw/dʒɔː/

I *n.* the lower part of the face 下巴 II *v.* ❶ talk in a boring way; gossip 闲谈,唠

J

叨：I got tired of him ～ing away all the time.他总是唠叨个没完，真烦人。❷ scold or lecture (a person) 责骂，教训：The teacher ～ed the lazy boys.老师责骂了那些懒惰的孩子。

jawbone/'dʒɔːbəʊn/
n.either of the big bones of the jaws,especially the lower jaw 颌骨（尤指下颌骨）；颚骨

jaywalk/'dʒeɪwɔːk/
v.cross streets in a careless and dangerous way, especially in the wrong place or without paying attention to the traffic lights (不遵守交通规则而)乱穿马路

jazz/dʒæz/
Ⅰ*n*.a popular music,originally created by African American musicians 爵士音乐，爵士舞曲 Ⅱ*v*.❶ play or dance jazz 奏爵士乐；跳爵士舞 ❷play (music) as jazz 将(乐曲)奏成爵士乐：～ classical tunes 把古典乐曲奏成爵士音乐 ❸make lively 使有生气,使活泼

jazzy/'dʒæzi/
adj.❶attracting attention,as with (too) bright colours 绚丽的，花哨的：a very ～ dress 一件非常花哨的衣服 ❷ like jazz music 似爵士乐的

jealous/'dʒeləs/
adj.❶ envious; feeling unhappiness because of the better fortune,etc.of others 妒羡的；嫉妒的；妒忌的：They are ～ of your wealth. 他们嫉妒你的财富。❷ wanting to keep what one has;possessive 珍惜的；唯恐失掉的：He is ～ of his girl friend.他唯恐失去他的女朋友。

jean/dʒiːn/
n.❶a strong,cotton cloth 斜纹布 ❷(*pl*.) overalls or trousers made of this cloth 斜纹布工装裤；牛仔裤：The cowboy wore blue ～s.那个牛仔穿着蓝牛仔裤。

jeep/dʒiːp/
n.a type of small car,suitable for travelling over rough ground 小型越野车,吉普车

jeer/dʒɪə(r)/
Ⅰ*v*.laugh rudely (at);make fun of 嘲笑，

嘲讽：Don't ～ at the foolish act of the poor child.不要嘲笑那个可怜的孩子的愚蠢行为。Ⅱ*n*.sarcastic remarks 嘲弄的言语：He spoke to her with lots of ～. 他对她极尽嘲弄。‖ ～ing *adj*. 嘲弄的,奚落的

jejune/dʒɪ'dʒuːn/
adj.❶childish; naive 孩子气的，天真的：～ political opinions 幼稚的政治观点 ❷ (especially of written material) dull; uninteresting (尤指文章)单调的,枯燥无味的：～ lectures 索然无味的演讲

jell/dʒel/
v.❶(of a liquid) become firmer,like jell (液体)凝成胶状，冻结 ❷(of ideas, thoughts,etc.) take a clear shape (意见、想法等)定形,成形：I found the film confusing—a lot of different ideas that didn't really ～.我觉得这部片子很混乱——许多不同观点都不够清楚。

jellied/'dʒelɪd/
adj.cooked and served in jelly 做成胶冻状的：～ eels 鳗鱼冻

jelly/'dʒeli/
n.❶a soft food made from gelatine,fruit juice and sugar 果冻：My mother is making apple ～.我的母亲在做苹果冻。/Children like ～ and ice cream.孩子们喜欢果冻和冰激凌。❷ any almost solid substance like this 似冻子之物；胶状物

jellyfish/'dʒelɪfɪʃ/
n.(*pl*.～ or ～es)a sea animal with a jelly-like body and stinging tentacles 水母；海蜇

jemmy/'dʒemi/
n.a type of iron bar used by thieves to open doors and windows (盗贼用来撬门窗的)铁棒

jerk/dʒɜːk/
Ⅰ*n*. a sudden pull, push, start, stop, twist,lift,or throw 急拉；急推；急动；急停；急扭；急抬；急投：The car stopped with a ～.车子猛然停住。Ⅱ*v*.move with a jerk or jerks 急摆；颠簸；猛推：He ～ed the door open.他猛然推开了门。

jerkin/'dʒɜːkɪn/

n. a short coat with or without sleeves (usually made of leather and worn by men) (通常为皮制、男子穿的)短上衣

jerky /ˈdʒɜːki/

adj. with jerks, not smooth in movement; with sudden starts and stops 颠簸的；不平稳的，忽开忽停的：We had a very ~ ride in the back of the old truck. 我们坐在那辆旧卡车的后部，一路上给颠得真够呛。

jerry-built /ˈdʒerɪbɪlt/

adj. built quickly, cheaply, and badly 仓促草率建成的，偷工减料盖成的：a ~ house 一座草草盖成的房子

jersey /ˈdʒɜːzi/

n. a tight-fitting garment with sleeves and few or no buttons in front (usually made from wool or cotton) (前面很少或没有纽扣的)紧身上衣(通常为羊毛或棉的)；运动衫：In cold weather he wears a ~ under his jacket. 在寒冷的天气他外穿一件短上衣，里面穿一件运动衫。

jest /dʒest/

Ⅰ *n.* a thing said or done to cause amusement; a joke 笑话；玩笑：make a ~ of sb. 愚弄某人 Ⅱ *v.* speak without serious intention; joke 开玩笑；讲笑话；取笑：Don't ~ with me. 不要跟我开玩笑。 ‖ ~**er** *n.* (旧时宫廷里的)弄臣

jet /dʒet/

n. ❶ a fast, narrow stream of liquid, gas, etc., coming out of a small hole 喷射：A fountain sends up a ~ of water. 喷泉喷出水。 ❷ an aircraft with a jet engine 喷气式飞机：Several silver ~s flew over the sea. 几架银白色的喷气式飞机飞过海洋上空。

jetsam /ˈdʒetsəm/

n. ❶ goods thrown from a ship in order to lighten it in distress (为使船减轻重量确保安全而从船上)抛弃的货物 ❷ goods of this kind washed on the shore 冲至岸上的投弃货物

jettison /ˈdʒetɪsn/

v. ❶ throw (goods) overboard to lighten a ship 抛弃船上货物 ❷ abandon or reject

放弃：~ a plan (an idea) 放弃计划(想法)

jetty /ˈdʒeti/

n. a long, narrow structure, built into the sea for getting into or out of a boat, or to protect a harbour 码头；防波堤

Jew /dʒuː/

n. a member of the people and cultural community whose traditional religion is Judaism and who come from the ancient Hebrew people of Israel; a person who believes in and practises Judaism 犹太人；犹太教徒：Albert Einstein was a ~. 阿尔伯特·爱因斯坦是个犹太人。 ‖ ~**ish** *adj.* 犹太人的

jewel /ˈdʒuːəl/

n. ❶ a precious stone such as a diamond, etc. 宝石；珠宝首饰：She is wearing her finest ~s today. 她今天戴上了她最好的首饰。 ❷ an important or valuable person or thing 珍贵的人(物) ‖ ~**ry**, ~**lery** *n.* 珠宝(总称)；珠宝饰物

jewel(l)ed /ˈdʒuːəld/

adj. decorated or fitted with jewels 镶有宝石的：a ~ bracelet 镶嵌宝石的手镯

jewel(l)er /ˈdʒuːələ(r)/

n. businessmen who buy and sell jewel or watches 宝石商；钟表商

jib¹ /dʒɪb/

n. the small front sail 船首小帆

jib² /dʒɪb/

v. (-bb-) (with reference to horses) stop and refuse to go further (指马)停下来不肯往前走，退缩

jibe /dʒaɪb/

Ⅰ *n.* an insulting or mocking remark 讥讽，嘲笑；嘲弄 Ⅱ *v.* say sth. rude or sth. that is intended to make another person look foolish 嘲讽

jiffy /ˈdʒɪfi/

n. moment of time 瞬间；片刻：I'll be ready in a ~. 我马上就好了。

jig /dʒɪg/

n. a lively dance; the music for it 吉格舞(曲)；快步舞(曲)

J

jigger/'dʒɪgə(r)/

n. ❶ a small measure for alcoholic drinks（通常为金属的）量酒的小量器 ❷ any small piece of apparatus 小器具，小玩意儿：Have you seen that ～ I fix the radio with? 你看见我用来修理收音机的那个小玩意了吗？

jiggered/'dʒɪgəd/

adj. ❶ very surprised 非常惊讶的：Well, I'll be ～. 啊！还有这种事。 ❷ very tired 筋疲力尽的：I'm completely ～ after that game of football. 踢完那场足球，我真是累极了。

jiggery-pokery/ˌdʒɪgərɪ 'pəukərɪ/

n. a secret and dishonest behaviour 阴谋，骗局：By the look of these election results, there's been some ～. 从这些选举结果来看，这当中是有一些弄虚作假。

jiggle/'dʒɪgl/

v. (cause to) move from side to side with short, quick and light jerks （使）轻摇，（使）左右摆动：～ the key in the lock 用钥匙在锁里轻轻左右摆动

jigsaw/'dʒɪgsɔː/

n. ❶ a type of narrow saw driven by a machine 线锯；锯曲线机 ❷ (also jigsaw **puzzle**) a picture on card board or wood and cut in irregularly shaped pieces to be fitted together again 七巧板，拼图玩具

jilt/dʒɪlt/

v. refuse to marry sb. after having promised to do so; end a relationship with a lover （女子）抛弃（情人）：She ～ed him the day before they were to be married. 在他们就要结婚的前一天她抛弃了他。

jingle/'dʒɪŋgl/

Ⅰ *n.* a metallic clinking or ringing sound (as of coins, keys or small bells) （金属的）叮当声（如钱币、钥匙、小铃发出的声音） Ⅱ *v.* make a light ringing sound 叮当；使叮当作响：I ～d my keys. 我把钥匙弄得叮当地响。/The money in his pocket ～d. 他口袋里的钱叮当响。

jitters/'dʒɪtəz/

n. (*pl.*) feeling of being anxious and nervous, especially before an important event

极度紧张不安：I have got the ～ about the examination next week. 我对下星期的考试极为紧张不安。‖ **jittery** *adj.* 神经过敏的；害怕的

jive[1]/dʒaɪv/

n. ❶ (a style of very fast dancing performed to) a kind of popular music with a strong regular beat （一种快节奏的）摇摆乐；摇摆舞 ❷ a deceiving or foolish talk 假话，蠢话

jive[2]/dʒaɪv/

v. dance to jive music 跳摇摆舞

job/dʒɒb/

n. ❶ a piece of work or task that you have to do（一件）工作：My ～ is to take care of patients. 我的工作是照料病人。 ❷ a paid position of regular employment 职位；工作岗位 ❸ a duty or responsibility 义务；责任 ‖ **do a good ～** 好好干；干好/**make a good ～ of sth.** 干得不错；干好/**be out of a ～** 失业/**on the ～** 在上班；在忙着

jobbing/'dʒɒbɪŋ/

adj. doing separate small jobs for various people 做零工的，干散活的：a ～ gardener 打零工的园丁

jobless/'dʒɒbləs/

adj. without a job; unemployed 无职业的，失业的

jockey/'dʒɒki/

n. the professional rider in horse-race 赛马的职业骑师

jockstrap/'dʒɒkstræp/

n. a tight-fitting undergarment for supporting the male sex organs, worn while doing sports （男运动员用的）下体松紧护身

jocular/'dʒɒkjulə(r)/

adj. fond of making people laugh; amusing 喜开玩笑的；诙谐的；打趣的：a ～ fellow 爱开玩笑的家伙

jodhpurs/'dʒɒdpəz/

n. (*pl.*) long trousers worn for horse riding, fitting closely from knee to ankle 马裤（膝至踝部分为紧身的长裤）

jog/dʒɒg/

v. (-gg-) ❶ push or knock slightly with

the arm, hand, etc. 轻推；轻撞：Jog his elbow to call his attention. 碰碰他的肘，引起他注意。❷move slowly, also shake up and down or from side to side 颠簸；摇晃：The cart ～ged along on the uneven country road. 大车在崎岖不平的乡间大道上颠簸行进。❸run slowly and steadily, especially for exercise（体育锻炼中的）慢跑：I go ～ging in the morning. 我每天早晨都要去慢跑。‖ ～ one's memory 唤起某人的记忆；提醒某人记起

joggle /'dʒɒgl/

v. (cause to) shake or move slightly（使）轻摇

join /dʒɔɪn/

v. ❶take part in 加入；参加：Will you ～ us in the game? 你加入我们的比赛吗？❷fasten or bring together; connect; unite 汇合；连接；联合：The two rivers ～ at the town. 这两条河在那个镇汇合在一起了。‖ ～ **battle** 交战；开战/ ～ **forces** (**with**) 联合行动；会师/ ～ **hands** (**with**) 互相合作，携手/ ～ **in** 参加（活动）/ ～ **up** 参军；把……连接起来

joiner /'dʒɔɪnə(r)/

n. a skilled workman who makes the inside woodwork of buildings, etc. 细木木匠

joinery /'dʒɔɪnəri/

n. the trade or work of a joiner 细木工行业（手艺）

joint /dʒɔɪnt/

Ⅰ *n.* ❶ the place at which two things or parts are connected 连接处 ❷a large piece of meat 大块肉 ❸ a place or part where two bones or corresponding structures are connected 关节 Ⅱ *adj.* shared and done by two or more persons 共有的，联合的：take ～ action 采取联合行动 Ⅲ *v.* fasten together by a joint or joints; give a joint or joints 连接，以接头连接

jointed /'dʒɔɪntɪd/

adj. having joints, especially movable ones 有关节（接头）的：a ～ doll 关节能活动的洋娃娃

joist /dʒɔɪst/

n. the beam to which the boards of a floor

or the laths of a ceiling are fixed at right angles 托梁，搁栅，小梁

joke /dʒəʊk/

Ⅰ *n.* ❶ sth. said or done to cause amusement, laughter, etc. 笑话；玩笑：She often tells us ～s. 她常给我们讲笑话。❷a person or thing that is ridiculous or annoying 荒唐的人（事）‖ a **practical** ～ 恶作剧/ **make** (**crack**) a ～ 开玩笑/ **play a** ～ **on** 开（某人）的玩笑/ **in** 闹着玩的/ **no** ～ 不是儿戏的 Ⅱ *v.* make jokes; not speak seriously, or not seriously enough 说笑话，开玩笑：He ～d with me about it. 这件事他跟我开了个玩笑。

joker /'dʒəʊkə(r)/

n. ❶a person who likes to make jokes 爱开玩笑的人 ❷ a person who is not serious or who should not be taken seriously 不正经的人；不必认真对待的人 ❸an additional card with no fixed value, used in certain games（某些牌戏中不带固定点数的）百搭牌

jolly /'dʒɒli/

Ⅰ *adj.* full of high spirits; cheerful 欢乐的，高兴的，快活的 Ⅱ *v.* (informal) encourage sb. in a cheerful way; try to keep someone cheerful（非正式）鼓励（某人）；劝（某人）高兴

jolt /dʒəʊlt/

Ⅰ *v.* shake while moving; shake suddenly; give a shock to 颠簸而行；震摇；（使）震惊：The car ～ed along the rough road. 汽车沿着崎岖不平的路颠簸行驶。/The train ～ed us from our seats by stopping suddenly. 火车突然停车把我们震离了座位。Ⅱ *n.* a sudden shake or shock 震摇；震惊：The bad news gave us a ～. 这坏消息让我们很震惊。

joss /dʒɒs/

n. a Chinese god worshipped in the form of an idol（中国的）神像；菩萨

jostle /'dʒɒsl/

v. push roughly against (usually where there is little room e.g. in a crowd) 推搡；挤（通常指几乎没有空间的地方，例如在拥挤的人群中）：We had to ～ through the crowd to reach the gate. 我们不得不挤过人群到达大门。/The crowd ~d against us. 人群推撞着我们。

jot /dʒɒt/
  Ⅰ *n.* a very small amount; a bit 一点儿, 少量: not a ~ of truth in it 没有一点真实性 Ⅱ *v.* (-tt-) write down quickly, especially without preparation 草草写上: ~ down sb.'s name and address 草草记下某人的名字和地址

jotter /'dʒɒtə(r)/
  n. a number of pieces of paper joined together, used for writing notes on 便条本, 便笺簿

jotting(s) /'dʒɒtɪŋ/
  n. a short note, usually written quickly 匆匆写下的小条子; 便条: It's not really an article, just a few preparatory ~s. 这实际上不是一篇文章, 只是些草稿而已。

joule /dʒuːl/
  n. a unit of energy or work 焦耳(能量或功的单位)

journal /'dʒɜːnl/
  n. ❶ a newspaper or periodical which deals with a particular subject 报纸; 杂志: a monthly ~ 月刊/He used to write articles for this ~. 他过去常为这家期刊撰写文章。❷ a daily record of sth. you do, see, etc. 日志; 日记

journalese /ˌdʒɜːnl'iːz/
  n. the language considered to be typical of newspapers, especially that full of hackneyed expressions (尤指陈词滥调的)新闻用语

journalism /'dʒɜːnlɪzəm/
  n. the profession of writing for newspapers and magazines 新闻业; 新闻工作

journalist /'dʒɜːnəlɪst/
  n. a person whose occupation is journalism; a reporter; a news editor, etc. 新闻记者, 新闻工作者

journey /'dʒɜːni/
  n. a trip from one place to another, especially by land over quite a long distance (尤指陆路长途的)旅行; 旅程: I dream to have a ~ around the world. 我梦想进行

一次环球旅行。‖ have a good (pleasant) ~ 一路顺风; 旅途愉快/make a ~ to 到(某处)旅行/start on a ~ 出发; 动身/take a ~ (to) 前往(某处)

journeyman /'dʒɜːnɪmən/
  n. (*pl.* -men) ❶ a trained workman who works for another person and is often paid by day (常按天计酬的)短工, 熟练工人: a ~ printer 一名熟练的印刷短工 ❷ an experienced person whose work is good, but not the very best 熟手, 熟练工: an example of the ~ work of this painter produced in his later years 这位画家在晚年所画的相当老练的作品实例

jovial /'dʒəʊvɪəl/
  adj. cheerful; friendly 快活的; 友好的: a ~ greeting (old man) 友善的问候(老人)

jowl /dʒaʊl/
  n. the lower part of the side of the face, especially loose skin and flesh near the lower jaw 下颌, 下巴; (尤指)下颌垂肉 ‖ ~ed /dʒaʊld/ *adj.* 有⋯⋯下颌的: a heavy-~ed dog 一条下颌宽厚的狗

joy /dʒɔɪ/
  n. ❶ great pleasure; happiness; gladness 欢乐; 喜悦; 乐趣: My heart was filled with ~ and gratitude. 我内心充满了喜悦和感激之情。❷ a thing that cause you to feel happy or pleasant 乐事; 乐趣 ‖ for ~ 高兴地/to the ~ of 使(某人)高兴的是/with ~ 高兴得; 高兴地

joyful /'dʒɔɪfl/
  adj. full of joy; causing great pleasure or happiness 快乐的; 令人高兴的: a ~ heart 愉快的心情/ a ~ event 令人兴奋的事情

joyless /'dʒɔɪləs/
  adj. without joy; unhappy 不快乐的, 不高兴的

joyous /'dʒɔɪəs/
  adj. full of or causing joy (充满)欢乐的, (令人)高兴的: a ~ heart (song, occasion) 愉快的心情(歌曲、场合)

joyride /'dʒɔɪraɪd/
  n. a ride for pleasure in a vehicle, especially a stolen car, often with careless driving (尤指用偷来的车)驾车兜风

joystick/ˈdʒɔɪˌstɪk/

*n.*an upright handle moved to control the operation of sth., especially the movement of an aircraft（尤指飞机的）操纵杆：the ～ of video game 电子游戏机的操纵杆

jubilant/ˈdʒuːbɪlənt/

*adj.*filled with or expressing great joy, especially at a success 喜气洋洋的；兴高采烈的：The people of the whole nation are ～.全国人民喜气洋洋。‖ **jubilation** *n.*欣喜；欢欣庆祝

jubilee/ˈdʒuːbɪliː/

n.(a special occasion marking) the return of the date of some important events（纪念某件大事的）欢庆日；欢乐的佳节：gold (silver) wedding ～ 金婚(银婚)纪念日

Judaism/ˈdʒuːdeɪɪzəm/

*n.*the religion of the Jewish people, based mainly on the Bible and the Talmud 犹太教

judas/ˈdʒuːdəs/

*n.*a person who secretly helps the enemies of his friends；traitor 出卖朋友的人；叛徒：You ～! 你这个叛徒！

judder/ˈdʒʌdə(r)/

*v.*shake violently 剧烈振动：The driver pulled the emergency brake and the train ～ed to a halt. 司机拉动紧急刹车，火车在剧烈摇晃中停了下来。

judge/dʒʌdʒ/

Ⅰ *v.*❶act as a judge in a court 审判 ❷decide the results of a competition（竞赛中）裁判；评判 ❸form an opinion or conclusion about sth.判断，判定 ‖ ～ **by** 以……来判断/ ～ **from** 根据……可以看出/ ～ **of** 判断 Ⅱ *n.*❶ an officer appointed to hear and try cases in a court of law 法官；审判员：The prisoner was taken before the ～.犯人被带到了法官面前。❷ a person who decides the winner in a sport contest or competition 裁判员：Who is the ～ in the long-jump competition? 跳远比赛的裁判是谁？

judgement /ˈdʒʌdʒmənt/

n. ❶ the ability to judge wisely；a good sense 判断力：He lacks ～.他缺乏判断力。❷an opinion or conclusion 意见；结论 ❸the decision of a judge or law court（法官或法庭的）裁决 ❹judging, or being judged 审判；被审判

judicial/dʒuːˈdɪʃl/

*adj.*of or by a court of law；of a judge or judgement 法庭的；司法的；法官的；审判的：～ proceedings 审判程序，诉讼手续

judiciary/dʒuːˈdɪʃəri/

*n.*the judges and system of law courts in a country；judicial departments（总称）法官；法院系统；司法部门：The ～ has (have) been consulted.已向司法部门咨询过。

judicious/dʒuːˈdɪʃəs/

*adj.*having or showing the ability to form sensible opinions；making sensible decisions, etc.明智的；明断的：Judicious parents will not encourage their children to be dependent on them.明智的家长不会鼓励孩子依赖他们。

judo/ˈdʒuːdəʊ/

*n.*a sport of wrestling and self-defence between two people who try to throw each other to the ground 柔道：a black belt at ～ 柔道中的黑腰带级/～ lessons 柔道课程

jug/dʒʌg/

Ⅰ *n.*a deep vessel with a handle and a lip for holding and pouring liquids 大壶；罐；缶：a ～ of water 一大壶水 /a ～ of milk 一瓶牛奶 Ⅱ *v.*(-gg-) stew or boil in a jug or jar 在壶或广口瓶里煨炖：～ged hare 用壶烧炖的野兔

juggle/ˈdʒʌgl/

*v.*keep (several objects) in the air at the same time by throwing them up quickly and catching them again 玩杂技；要把戏：He can ～ three balls, keeping them in the air at one time.他能在空中同时要三个球。

juggler /ˈdʒʌglə/

*n.*a person who juggles, especially an entertainer 玩杂耍的人；要把戏的人；变戏法的人

jugular /ˈdʒʌɡjʊlə(r)/

n. ❶ the veins of the neck that return blood from the head 颈静脉 ❷ an attack which causes as much hurt or damage as possible 致命的打击：When threatened with the dismissal he really went for the ～, accusing his boss of lying and corruption. 在受到解雇的威胁后，他对老板毫不含糊地迎头痛击，指控他欺骗和贪污。

juice /dʒuːs/

n. ❶ the liquid from fruits, vegetables, and meat（水果、蔬菜、肉等的）汁液：a mixture of fruit ～s 混合果汁/meat ～肉汁 ❷ (*pl.*) the liquid in a certain part of the body, especially the stomach, that helps people and animals to digest food 体液；(尤指)胃液：digestive ～s 消化液

juicy /ˈdʒuːsi/

adj. ❶ containing a lot of juice 多汁(液)的：a ～ orange 多汁的橙子/a ～ steak 一份多汁的牛排 ❷ interesting, especially that providing information about bad behaviours 有趣的，绘声绘色的(尤指有关不良行为的丑闻)：I want to hear all the ～ details of the scandal! 我想要听听那件丑闻的全部有趣的细节！❸ desirable, especially that is likely to produce a lot of money 合算的，上算的(尤指可赚大钱的)：a fat ～ contract that will make us all rich 一份能使我们都富起来的，优厚并有利可图的合同

ju-jitsu /dʒuːˈdʒɪtsuː/

n. a Japanese art of self-defence from which judo was developed 柔术，柔道

jukebox /ˈdʒuːkbɒks/

n. a type of record player which plays music when coins are put in it（投入硬币即放唱片的）自动电唱机

July /dʒuːˈlaɪ/

n. the seventh month of the year 七月

jumble /ˈdʒʌmbl/

Ⅰ *v.* be mixed or mix in an untidy way 混杂；混合；乱堆：His books and mine were ～d together. 他的书和我的书混杂在一起。Ⅱ *n.* a confused mixture of sth. 混乱的一堆；一团糟：a ～ of books 一堆书 ‖

～ sale *n.* 旧杂货拍卖(尤指义卖)

jumbo /ˈdʒʌmbəʊ/

adj. unusually big 特大的；巨大的 ‖ ～ jet *n.* 大型喷气式客机

jump /dʒʌmp/

Ⅰ *v.* ❶ spring from the ground; bound 跳，跳跃；跳过：Hearing the good news, I ～ed with joy. 听到这个好消息，我高兴地跳了起来。❷（especially of prices or quantities）rise suddenly and sharply（价格或数量）猛增；暴涨：The price of food ～ed. 食品价格大幅度上涨。❸ move suddenly and quickly 突然快速移动：He ～ed to his feet. 他一跃而起。‖ ～ at 欣然接受；立即抓住/ ～ down one's throat 斥责某人/ ～ out of one's skin 大吃一惊/ ～ the gun 起步过早；抢跑/ ～ the queue 插队/ ～ to a conclusion 匆忙下结论 Ⅱ *n.* an act of jumping 跳跃；一跳：long ～ 跳远/high ～ 跳高

jumper /ˈdʒʌmpə(r)/

n. ❶ a person or animal that springs 跳跃者，跳跃的人(动物) ❷ a woollen garment for the top half of the body 套头毛衣 ❸ a dress without sleeves, usually worn over a blouse（穿在女衬衫外的）无袖连衣裙

jumpsuit /ˈdʒʌmpˌsuːt/

n. a one-piece garment of jacket and trousers 连裤衫

jumpy /ˈdʒʌmpi/

adj. nervously excited, often before sth. bad happens 心惊肉跳的

junction /ˈdʒʌŋkʃn/

n. ❶ the act or process of joining 连接，接合：the ～ of two rivers 两条河的连接 ❷ a place or point of joining or crossing, as of highways or rail roads（河流、铁路等）会合处，交叉点：This railway station is a busy ～ for lines from all over the country. 该火车站是通向全国各地铁路线的繁忙的交汇处。

juncture /ˈdʒʌŋktʃə(r)/

n. a particular point in time or in a course of events（关键）时刻：At this ～, our troops arrived. 在这个关键时刻，我们的

部队赶到了。

June/dʒuːn/

　n.the sixth month of the year 六月

jungle/'dʒʌŋgl/

　n.❶a tropical forest which is too thick to walk through easily（热带）丛林,密林: Jungles are hot and humid regions with many kinds of plants and wild animals.热带丛林热而湿,有各种植物和野兽。❷ any confused and disordered mass of things 一堆杂乱的东西:a ～ of wrecked automobiles 一堆破旧汽车

junior/'dʒuːnɪə(r)/

　Ⅰ*adj*.❶（of a person）younger 较年幼的;年少的:She is ～ to me.她比我小。❷ lower in rank than another（等级、职位）较低的:He is the ～ partner in the firm.他是这公司地位较低的股东。❸ connected with young people below a particular age 青少年的 ❹ of or for students in the third year of a course which last for four years in college or high school 三年级（学生）的 Ⅱ*n*.the younger 较年幼者:She is my ～ by two years.她比我小两岁。

junk/dʒʌŋk/

　n.❶old things of no value 旧货;破烂货: Get all this ～ away.把这堆废物全搬走。❷a flat-bottomed Chinese sailing ship 平底船;舢板 ❸things that are thought useless or of little value 无用的（或无价值的）东西:There are lots of ～ in her paper which was handed in last week. 她上个星期上交的论文中有许多无用的内容。‖ ～ **food** *n*.垃圾食品,不利于健康的小吃

junket/'dʒʌŋkɪt/

　n.❶ a trip,especially one made by a government official and paid for with government money 旅行;（尤指政府官员的）公费旅游 ❷a dish of milk curdled by adding an acid, sweetened curds, and often given a particular taste 乳冻甜食,凝乳食品

junkie/'dʒʌŋki/

　n.a person who habitually takes the drug heroin and is dependent on it（海洛因）毒瘾者

junta/'dʒʌntə/

　n.a small political ruling group 小的政治统治集团:a country ruled by a military ～ 军政府统治的国家

Jupiter/'dʒuːpətə(r)/

　n.❶the god ruling over all other gods and all people 朱庇特（罗马神话中的主神）❷ the largest planet of the solar system and the fifth in distance from the sun 木星

juridical/dʒʊə'rɪdɪkl/

　adj.of or related to the law or judges 法律上的,司法上的

jurisdiction/ˌdʒʊə'rɪsdɪkʃn/

　n.the right to use the power of an official body, especially in order to make decisions on questions of law 司法权,审判权;管辖权:The prisoner refused to accept the ～ of the court.那囚犯拒绝接受法院的判决。/That area does not fall within the ～ of the city health bureau.那一地区不在该市卫生局管辖之内。/The U.N.court has no ～ over non-members. 联合国法庭对非成员国无管辖权。

jurist/'dʒʊərɪst/

　n.a person with a thorough knowledge of law;a legal expert 法学家,法律学者

juror/'dʒʊərə(r)/

　n.a member of a jury 陪审员;评判员

jury/'dʒʊəri/

　n.the persons（usually twelve）chosen to sit in a court of law and decide whether the accused person is guilty or not（通常由十二人组成的）陪审团:The ～ found the prisoner guilty.陪审团认定该囚犯有罪。

just/dʒʌst/

　Ⅰ*adj*.❶morally right and proper;fair 正义的;公正的;正直的:They are fighting for a ～ cause.他们正在为正义事业而斗争。❷deserved or appropriate in a particular situation 应得的;恰当的:a ～ punishment 应有的惩罚 Ⅱ*adv*.❶exactly 正好;恰好:It's ～ what I want to know.这

正是我想要知道的。❷only；no more than 仅仅，只是：He is ～ a child.他还只是个小孩。❸only a short time ago；only now and not sooner 刚才；刚刚：I've seen him.He has ～ left.我刚刚看见他了，他刚离开。❹at this（that）very moment 正要；刚要：I'm ～ about to leave.我刚要走。❺really；absolutely 真正地；绝对地：That's ～ great.那真不错。‖ ～ about 几乎；差不多/ ～ as 正如；就像/～ now 刚才/ ～ the same 照样/～ then 那时候；就在那时

justice /ˈdʒʌstɪs/
n.❶ the quality of being fair and just 正义，公正；公平：Everyone should be treated with ～. 每个人都应受到公正对待。/Judge treats all men with ～.法官公平对待所有的人。❷ the administration or authority of the law 审判；司法：The criminals were finally brought to ～. 罪犯们最终受到了法律制裁。❸ judge of the Supreme Courts 高等法院法官；最高法院法官：Mr. Justice Smith has been made Chief Justice.法官史密斯先生当了首席法官。

justifiable /ˈdʒʌstɪfaɪəbl/
adj.able to be shown to be right or reasonable；defensible（可证明为）正当或合理的，情有可原的，无可非议的；能辩护的 ‖ **justifiably** adv.正当地

justification /ˌdʒʌstɪfɪˈkeɪʃ(ə)n/
n.a good reason why sth.exists or is done 正当理由 ‖ in ～（of sb.or sth.）作为对……的辩护（或解释）：All I can say in ～ of her actions is that she was under a lot of pressure at work.我唯一能为她的行为辩解的理由是她的工作压力很大。

justified /ˈdʒʌstɪfaɪd/
adj.❶ having，done for，or marked by a good or legitimate reason 正当的，有理由的，合理的 ❷ having been adjusted so that the print fills a space evenly or forms a straight line at the margin 排列整齐的；对齐的

justify /ˈdʒʌstɪfaɪ/
v.show that sth.is right or reasonable 证明……是正当的（合理的）：How can you ～ your rude behaviour? 你怎么能认为你的粗暴行为是正当的呢？ /Do you think he was justified in saying that? 你认为他那样说是对的吗？

jut /dʒʌt/
v.(-tt-)（with out）stick out；stretch out（与 out 连用）突出；伸出：The rocks ～ out above the trees.岩石在树林的上方突出来。

juvenile /ˈdʒuːvənaɪl/
Ⅰ n.a youth person who is not yet an adult 青少年 Ⅱ adj.of，connected with or for young people 青少年的；适于青少年的：～ delinquent 少年犯/～ books 青少年读物

Kk

kaleidoscope/kə'laɪdəskəup/
  n. the tube containing mirrors and small pieces of coloured glass, turned to produce changing patterns 万花筒

kangaroo/ˌkæŋgə'ruː/
  n. (*pl.* ~s) an Australian animal that jumps along on its powerful hind legs(the female has a pouch in which its young are carried) 袋鼠

kapok/'keɪpɒk/
  n. a cotton-like substance, obtained from a tropical tree and used for filling pillows, etc. 木棉

kaput/kə'put/
  adj. broken; no longer useful 坏了的; 再也不能使用的: The TV's ~. 那台电视机坏了。

karaoke /ˌkærɪ'əuki/
  n. a form of entertainment in which people sing well-known songs over a pre-recorded backing tracks 卡拉OK; 自动伴奏录音

karat/'kærət/
  n. a unit of measurement of the purity of gold, pure gold being 24 karats 开(黄金纯度单位, 纯金为24开)

karate/kə'rɑːti/
  n. a Japanese method of unarmed combat in which the hands, feet, etc. are used as weapons 空手道

kayak/'kaɪæk/
  n. a type of covered canoe, used by the people who live in the Arctic; any canoe of this shape (住在北极区的人使用的) 独木舟; 小划艇

keel/kiːl/
  I *n.* a long piece of wood or steel along the bottom of a ship, to which the sides of the ship are fixed (船的)龙骨 II *v.* turn over; fall over 翻身; 倾覆: The ship ~ed over in the storm. 这只船在暴风雨中倾覆了。

keen/kiːn/
  adj. ❶ eager; desiring; very fond of 热心的; 渴望的: He is very ~ to revisit his birthplace. 他渴望重访他的出生地。❷ sharp; with a fine cutting edge 锋利的 ❸ very clever and aware of what is happening 敏锐的; 理解力强的: The old man still has ~ sight. 那位老人的目光仍很锐利。

keep/kiːp/
  v. ❶ have for some time or more time 保管; 保存; 保留: How long can I ~ this book? 这本书我可以借(保存)多久? ❷ cause to remain or continue in a particular state or situation (使)保持; 继续: Keep quiet. 保持安静。/Keep clean! 保持清洁! / ~ sb. waiting 让某人久等 ❸ take care of and provide with food, money, etc. 照管; 经营; 维持; 喂养: ~ a shop 经营商店/ ~ pigs 养猪/ ~ one's family 养活家庭 ❹ fulfill what you have promised to do 遵守; 履行: ~ one's word (promise) 守信用(遵守诺言)/ ~ the law 守法 ❺ write down details of sth. so that they can be referred to later 记录: ~ a diary 记日记/ ~ accounts(books) 记账 ❻ not let others know, not make known 不让别人知道: ~ secrets 保守秘密 ❼ prevent 阻止; 防止: Nothing can ~ us from marching forward. 没有什么能阻止我们前进。❽ continue (doing sth.); do sth. continuously, frequently or repeatedly 坚持做; 不断做: The news of victory kept coming. 胜利的消息不断传来。❾ own and manage 经营; 开设: ~ a shop, restaurant, etc. 开商店、饭馆等 ❿ own and take care of (farm animals) in order to

use or make money from 饲养(家畜自用或赚钱)：~ pigs, hens, bees, etc.(饲)养猪、鸡、蜂等 ‖ ~ a close watch on 密切注视/ ~ a firm hold (grip) on 牢牢控制/ ~ abreast of 与……并驾齐驱/ ~ an eye on 照看；照管/~ at 坚持(干某事)/ ~ away(from) 避开，(使)不接近/ ~ back 阻止；抑制；隐瞒/ ~ company (with) 和……结交/ ~ doing sth. 坚持做；老是做/ ~ down 控制；压制/~ faith with 对……守信用/~ from 隐瞒；使……不做某事/ ~ hold of 把握；抓住/ ~ in mind 记住/ ~ in touch with 保持……关系/ ~ off 使避开/ ~ on 继续(干)；坚持(干)/ ~ on at(sb. to do) 一再纠缠/ ~ one's chin (pecker) up 不泄气；鼓起勇气/ ~ one's distance 避免亲近/ ~ one's head 保持冷静/ ~ one's head above water 不欠债/~ one's mind on 把注意力(心思)集中于/ ~ one's temper 忍住性子；不发脾气/ out of 不牵涉/ ~ pace 跟上；不落后/ to 遵守；坚持/ ~ to oneself 保守秘密/ ~ under (control) 控制；压制/ ~ under one's hat 保密/ ~ up 保持；继续；跟上/ ~ up with 跟上；保持联系

keeper /'ki:pə/
n. ❶ a person who keeps or looks after sth. 管理人，看管者 ❷ a goalkeeper or wicketkeeper 门将，守门员 ❸ a gamekeeper 猎场看守人 ❹ a person in charge of animals in a zoo (动物园的)动物管理员

keeping /'ki:pɪŋ/
n. the act of caring and protecting sth. 照料；保护；保管：I'll leave these keys in your safe ~. 我要把这些钥匙放在你的保险箱里保管。‖ in ~ with 符合；与……一致：This modern furniture is not in ~ with such an old house. 这个新式家具不适合放在这样的老房子里。/ out of (with sth.) 与……不协调，不一致：The painting is out of ~ with the rest of the room. 这幅画和这间房其他东西不相称。

keepsake /'ki:pseɪk/
n. sth. kept in memory of the giver 纪念品：This ring is a ~ from my grandmother. 这戒指是我祖母留给我的纪念品。/ Please have it as a ~. 请收下做个纪念

吧。

kelvin /'kelvɪn/
n. the basic unit of thermodynamic temperature 开，开尔文(开氏温标的计量单位)

ken[1] /ken/
v. (~ned or ~t) know 知道

ken[2] /ken/
n. range of knowledge 知识范围：beyond one's ~ 不能理解；在某人的知识范围之外

kennel /'kenl/
n. a small hut in which a dog is kept 狗窝

kerb /kɜ:b/
n. the stone edge of a pavement 人行道的石边：Please park your car close to the ~. 请把车子停在靠近人行道石边的地方。

kernel /'kɜ:nl/
n. ❶ the inner, softer part of a nut, or seed 核，仁 ❷ the central or most important part of sth.；core；essence 中心，要点：the ~ of the argument 辩论的要点

ketchup /'ketʃəp/
n. a type of sauce, usually made from tomatoes 番茄酱，番茄沙司

kettle /'ketl/
n. a metal pot with a lid, a handle and a long curved mouth for boiling water 水壶：Will you put the ~ on? 请你把水壶放在炉火上好吗？/ The ~'s boiling. 壶里的水开了。

key /ki:/
I *n.* ❶ a metal instrument used to fasten or unfasten a lock 钥匙：He turned the ~ in the lock and opened the door. 他用钥匙开锁，打开了门。 ❷ a set of answers to questions；explanations on a map 答案；图例：This is the ~ to the exercises. 这是练习的答案。 ❸ sth. that controls the entrance to a place 关键：What is the ~ to the problem? 问题的关键在哪里？ ❹ one of a set of parts pressed in playing a piano, in typewriting, etc. (钢琴、打字机等的)键：Typewriters have a ~ for each letter of the alphabet. 打字机上每个字母都有一个键。 ❺ a set of musical notes

based on a particular note 音调；主音调：play the music in the ~ of C 用 C 调弹唱这首曲子 Ⅱ adj. essential；basic；chief；crucial 必要的；基本的；主要的；关键的：a ~ factor 关键因素 ‖ a ~ role 主要（关键）作用

keyboard¹ /ˈkiːbɔːd/
n. a row or several rows of keys on a musical instrument or a machine（乐器或机器上的）键盘：the ~ of a piano（a typewriter，a computer）钢琴（打字机、计算机）键盘

keyboard² /ˈkiːbɔːd/
v. ❶ work the keyboard of（especially a computer）操作（尤指计算机的）键盘 ❷ provide a machine with（information）by working a keyboard 操作键盘把（信息）输入机器

keyhole /ˈkiːhəʊl/
n. a hole for the key in a（door）lock, a clock, etc. 锁眼，钥匙孔

keynote /ˈkiːnəʊt/
n. ❶ the central theme of a speech, book, etc. 主旨，要旨；基调：The ~ of the discussion was concerning for the jobless. 讨论的基调是对于失业者的关切。/ We'd invited a world-famous expert to give the ~ speech at the conference. 在这次研讨会上，我们邀请了一位世界著名的专家来做主旨演说。❷ the particular note on which a musical key is based 主音

keypad /ˈkiːpæd/
n. a small keyboard, which is of numbered buttons 按钮式键盘

keystone /ˈkiːstəʊn/
n. ❶ the stone in the top of an arch, which keeps the other stones in position 拱顶石 ❷ an idea, belief, etc., on which everything else depends 主旨，基础；基本原则：Social justice is the ~ of their political programme. 社会公正是他们政治纲领的基础。

kick /kɪk/
Ⅰ v. ❶ strike or hit with the foot 踢：The baby was ~ing and screaming. 那婴儿又踢又叫。❷ score（a goal）by a kick 踢球得分 ❸ strike out with the foot 踢腿：He ~ed out at the boy. 他向那个男孩踢去。‖ ~ off（足球）开球 / ~ oneself 后悔；埋怨自己 / ~ out（of）踢出去；开除 / ~ upstairs（downstairs）明升暗降（踢下楼，降职）Ⅱ n. a blow or forceful thrust with the foot 踢：give sb.（or sth.）a ~ 踢了……一脚

kickback /ˈkɪkbæk/
n. ❶ a sudden forceful recoil 后坐力 ❷（informal）a payment made to someone for help they have given, especially in doing sth. dishonest（非正式）（尤指非法的）回扣

kicker /ˈkɪkə/
n. ❶ a person or animal that kicks 踢……的人（或动物）❷ an extra clause in a contract 合同中的附加条款：Smith added a ~ to the mortgage. 史密斯在抵押合同上加了一条。

kid /kɪd/
n. ❶ a young goat 小山羊：a goat with three young ~s 一只山羊和三只小山羊 ❷ a child or a young person 少年，孩子 ❸ the leather made from skin of a kid 小羊皮：~ gloves 小羊皮手套

kidnap /ˈkɪdnæp/
v.（-pp-）take sb. away and ask for money in return for bringing them back safely 绑架：He was ~ped in Paris a year ago and hasn't been set free now. 他一年前在巴黎被人绑架，至今仍未放回来。

kidney /ˈkɪdni/
n. ❶ one of the pair of organs in the body of animals, birds, etc. that separate waste from the blood 肾 ❷ the kidney of an animal, cooked for food（动物的）腰子（用作食物）❸（of a person）nature；disposition；temperament（人的）性格，气质

kill /kɪl/
v. put to death；cause the death of 杀死；弄死：Two persons were ~ed in the traffic accident. 在这次交通事故中，两人丧生。

killer /ˈkɪlə(r)/
n. a person, animal, or thing that kills 杀手；凶手；杀人者；杀生的人：This disease is a ~. 这种病是致命的。/ There's a ~

at large.有一个凶手还没有捉拿归案。

killjoy/ˈkɪldʒɔɪ/

n. a person who spoils the pleasure of other people 令人扫兴的人

kilo/ˈkiːləʊ/

n.(*pl.*~s) kilogram 公斤,千克:I weigh 52 ~s.我体重五十二公斤。/A ~ of apples, please.劳驾,我要一公斤苹果。

kilobyte /ˈkɪləʊbaɪt/

n. a unit of memory or data, equal to 1,024 bytes 千字节

kilogram(me)/ˈkɪləgræm/

n. a measure of weight, equal to 1,000 grams 千克;公斤:Several years ago the world's use of paper was about one ~ for each person a year. 几年前,世界上平均每人每年用纸大约 1 千克。

kilometre(-ter)/ˈkɪləˌmiːtə(r)/

n. a measure of length, equal to 1,000 metres 千米;公里:They ran at the speed of five ~s per hour.他们以每小时 5 公里的速度奔跑。/ It is three hundred and eight ~s away.那儿有 308 公里远。

kilowatt /ˈkɪləwɒt/

n. a unit of electrical power, equal to 1,000 watts 千瓦(功率单位)

kilter/ˈkɪltə(r)/

n. the good working order 良好状态:out of ~/off ~ (身心)不正常状态;(机器)出毛病,失常,失调

kimono/kɪˈməʊnəʊ/

n. a type of loose coat with a broad belt worn by the Japanese; dressing gown of this type (日本人穿的)和服;和服式女晨衣

kin/kɪn/

Ⅰ*n.* family; relations 家属,亲戚:What ~ is she to you? 她与你是什么亲戚关系? /All his ~ were at the wedding.他的家人和亲戚都参加了婚礼。Ⅱ*adj.* related by blood 有亲戚关系的:Your cousin is also ~ to me.你的堂兄与我也有亲戚关系。‖ ~ship *n.* 血缘关系,亲属关系;深切的同情;相似的性格 /~sman *n.* 男亲属 /~swoman *n.* 女亲属

kind/kaɪnd/

Ⅰ*n.* a group of people or things which share similar type 种;类:we have to overcome all ~s of difficulties.我们必须克服各种各样的困难。‖ a ~ of 某种……;一种(不明确的东西)/in ~ 同样的;照样(对待)/ ~ of 有一点;有几分 of a ~ 同类的/sth. of the ~ 类似的事物;……之类的东西 Ⅱ*adj.* in a gentle, caring and helpful way toward other people 和蔼的;友爱的;仁慈的:The teacher is very ~ to us.老师对我们很和蔼。‖ be ~ enough to (do) 劳驾……/it's ~ of you…你太好了;太难为了你‖ ~-hearted *adj.*好心肠的;仁慈的

kindergarten/ˈkɪndəgɑːtn/

n. the school for very young children, who is below the age of compulsory education 幼儿园

kindle/ˈkɪndl/

v. ❶ (cause to) start to burn; make sth. burn 着火;点燃:The wood is too wet to ~.木柴太湿了,不能燃烧。❷ rouse or stimulate (strong feelings, interest, etc.) 引起;激起;煽动:His report ~d our interest.他的报告激起了我们的兴趣。

kindling/ˈkɪndlɪŋ/

n. materials for lighting a fire, especially dry wood, leaves, grass, etc.引火物(尤指干的木柴、树叶、草等)

kindly/ˈkaɪndli/

Ⅰ*adj.* friendly; good-natured 好心的,仁慈的:~ people 和蔼的人 Ⅱ*adv.* ❶ in a kind or friendly way 和善地,亲切地:He spoke very ~.他说话非常和蔼。❷ please 请:Will you ~ put that book back? 请把那本书放回去好吗? ❸naturally 自然地,容易地:He does not take ~ to criticism.对待批评他不能泰然处之。

kindness/ˈkaɪndnɪs/

*n.*❶the quality or habit of being friendly 仁慈,亲切,友好:We admire his ~.我们钦佩他的与人为善。❷the kind act or treatment 仁慈的行为:They showed me many ~es during my visit.我拜访期间,他们帮了我很多忙。

kindred/ˈkɪndrɪd/

Ⅰ*n.*❶the relationship by blood 血亲关

系；claim ～ with sb. 声称与某人有血亲关系 ❷one's relatives or family 亲戚；家庭成员：Most of his ～ are still living in Ireland.他的大部分亲戚现在仍住在爱尔兰。Ⅱ adj. ❶ related; having a common source 同宗的，同源的：～ languages 同源的语言/～ tribes (races) 同族的部落 ❷similar 类似的；相似的：～ natures 相似的性质

kinetic/kɪˈnetɪk/
adj.connected with, or caused by motion 运动的；由运动引起的：～ energy 动能

king/kɪŋ/
n.❶the male ruler of a country 国王；He was ～ for only a short time.他当国王的时间不长。❷a person of great influence 有权力者；大王：an oil ～ 石油大王/ He is the ～ of popular music.他是流行音乐之王。❸ a principal in the game of chess; a court card with a picture of a king (国际象棋等的)王；(纸牌的)K：He had the ～ of hearts.他有一张红心 K。

kingdom/ˈkɪŋdəm/
n.❶a country headed by a king or queen 王国：the Kingdom of England 英格兰王国 ❷a realm regarded as being under the control of sb.or sth.领域：the ～ of poetry 诗歌界

kingfisher/ˈkɪŋfɪʃə(r)/
n.a small bird that feeds on fish in rivers, lakes, etc.翠鸟(一种食鱼鸟)

kingly/ˈkɪŋli/
adj.belonging to or suitable to a king 国王的；适合于君主身份的：a ～ manner (feast) 君王般的态度举止(豪华盛大的宴会)

kingpin/ˈkɪŋpɪn/
n.the most important person in a group, upon whom the success of the group depends 最重要的人物；领袖：Sir George was the ～ of the steel industry.乔治爵士是钢铁工业界的巨子。

kingship/ˈkɪŋʃɪp/
n. the condition or official position of a king 王位；王权：the responsibilities of ～ 王权的责任

king-sized/ˈkɪŋsaɪzd/
adj.(especially of a commercial product) of a larger size than the standard; very large (尤指商品)大号的，大的

kink/kɪŋk/
n.❶ an (unwanted) sharp turn or twist in hair, a rope, a chain, a pipe, etc.(头发、绳、链、管等的)扭结；纠缠：The water isn't coming out because there's a ～ in the hosepipe.水流不出来是因为水龙软管发生扭结。❷ a peculiarity of the mind or character 怪念头；怪癖；奇想

kinship/ˈkɪnʃɪp/
n.❶a family relationship 家属关系；亲属关系 ❷a close feeling between people who have similar attitudes or origins (因出身或态度相似而产生的)亲切感

kinsman/ˈkɪnzmən/
n.(pl.kinsmen) a male relative 男亲属：Brothers and uncles are kinsmen.兄弟、叔叔伯伯都是男亲属。

kinswoman/ˈkɪnzˌwʊmən/
n.(pl.kinswomen) a female relative 女亲属：Sisters and aunts are kinswomen.妹妹、伯母姨母都是女亲属。

kiss/kɪs/
Ⅰ v.touch with the lips to show affection or as a greeting 吻，接吻：Mary ～es her father and goes out.玛丽吻了她的父亲，然后走了出来。Ⅱ n.an act of kissing 吻，亲吻：She gave him a ～.她吻了他一下。

kit/kɪt/
n.❶ a set of articles or tools needed for a particular purpose 全套工具；应用器具：a carpenter's ～ 一套木工用具/ plumber's ～ 水管工人的工具 ❷ a set of clothes and other articles needed for daily life, especially by soldiers, sailors, etc. or for playing a particular sport (士兵、水手或其他旅行者所需的)全部装备(尤指衣物用具)：camping ～ 野营装备

kitchen/ˈkɪtʃɪn/
n.the room used for cooking 厨房　‖ ～ garden n.菜圃；菜园

kitchenware /ˈkɪtʃɪnweə(r)/
n.the utensils used in a kitchen 厨房用具

kite/kaɪt/
n.❶a toy with a light frame covered with

K

paper or cloth which flies in the air on the end of a long string 纸鸢；风筝：They are flying a ~.他们在放风筝。❷a bird of prey of the hawk family 鸢

kith and kin/ˌkɪθ ən ˈkɪn/

n. friends and relations 亲属；亲友；同族人：You can't refuse to help them；they're your own ~.你不能拒绝帮助他们，他们是你的亲属。

kitsch/kɪtʃ/

n. the popular decorative objects, writing, etc.that pretend to be art but are silly and worthless 庸俗文学（艺术）作品：She's decorated her flat with all kinds of plastic ~.她的屋内摆满了各式各样俗气的塑料装饰品。/His new film is pure ~.他的新影片完全是一部花里胡哨的作品。

kitten/ˈkɪtn/

n. a very young cat 小猫：Look at the lovely ~s.看这些可爱的小猫。

kitty/ˈkɪti/

n. ❶ money which is gambled for in various games 赌注 ❷a kitten 小猫

kiwi /ˈkiːwiː/

*n.*❶a New Zealand bird that does not fly, with a long beak, short wings, and no tail 几维鸟，无翼鸟 ❷(informal) a New Zealander, especially a soldier or member of a national sports team （非正式）新西兰人（尤指士兵或国家运动队队员）

kleptomania/ˌkleptəˈmeɪnɪə/

n. the strong desire to steal caused by mental illness 偷窃狂；盗窃癖 ‖ ~c *n.*有偷窃癖的人

knack/næk/

n. a special skill or ability, usually as the result of practice 技巧；诀窍，窍门，妙诀；本事：There's a ~ in it, you have to learn by doing it.这里面有技巧，你必须做方能学会。/It is quite easy when I have the ~ of it.我有了诀窍便容易多了。

knacker /ˈnækə/

n. a person who buys and slaughters useless horses, for the purpose of selling the meat and hides 屠马业者

knapsack/ˈnæpsæk/

n. a small bag with straps, carried on the back（especially by soldiers and travellers）（尤指士兵和旅行者用的）背包

knead/niːd/

v. mix together by pressing and squeezing with the hands（e.g. flour and water to make bread, or soft clay to make pots）揉；捏；捏制（例如揉面粉和水做面包，或捏陶土制陶器）

knee/niː/

n. the middle joint of the leg, where it bends 膝；膝盖：You have to bend your ~s to sit down.你要屈膝才能坐下。‖ be(go down, fall)on one's ~ 跪下/bow the ~s 屈膝，下跪/(bend) one's ~s before 向……跪下；屈服于/bring sb. to his ~s 使屈服‖ ~-cap *n.*膝盖骨/ ~- deep *adj.*齐膝深的/ ~ pad *n.*护膝

kneel/niːl/

v. (knelt) go down or remain on one's knees 跪着；跪下：She knelt down to scrub the floor.她跪下来擦地板。/Everyone in the church knelt when praying.教堂里的每个人都跪着祈祷。

knell/nel/

n. ❶the sound of a bell rung slowly after a death or at a funeral 丧钟：toll the ~ 敲丧钟 ❷signs of the end or death of sth.结束（或死亡）的征兆：the ~ of her hopes 她的希望破灭的征兆

knickers/ˈnɪkəz/

n. (*pl.*) pants, undergarment worn by women and girls 女用内裤；灯笼裤

knife/naɪf/

n.(*pl.* knives) a blade fixed in a handle, used for cutting as a tool or weapon（带柄）小刀；匕首：We eat with chopsticks, but the westerners use knives and forks.我们用筷子吃饭，但西方人用刀叉。‖ before you can say ~ 突然（说时迟那时快）/under the ~ 接受外科手术 ‖ ~ board *n.*磨刀板/ ~edge *n.*刀口

knight/naɪt/

I *n.*❶a noble soldier who has a duty to fight for his king 骑士，武士 ❷a man who is given a title by the Queen of England, and whose name has "Sir" in front of it 爵士（名字前加 Sir）：Sir James Hill was made a ~ for his service to his country.詹姆斯·希尔先生由于效忠祖国被封为爵士。❸a person who represented a shire or country in Parliament 郡选议员 ❹a piece in the game of chess, usually made with a horse's head（国际象棋中的）马 Ⅱ v. make（sb.）a knight 授予爵位,封为爵士;Sir George（Smith）has been ~ed by the Queen.乔治(史密斯)先生被女王封为爵士。

knightly /'naɪtli/
adj. consisting of knights ; typical of a knight 由爵士(或骑士)组成的;侠义的

knit /nɪt/
v. (knit or -tt-) make(thing to wear) by joining woollen threads into a close network with long needles(knitting needles) 编织;针织;My mother ~ted me a sweater.我妈妈给我织了一件毛衣。

knitting /'nɪtɪŋ/
n. the action or process of knitting;sth. being knitted 编织;编织物;keep one's ~ in a bag 把编织物放在包里

knitwear /'nɪtweə/
n. knitted garments 针织品,针织衣物

knob /nɒb/
n. ❶ a handle, usually round, or control button of a door,drawer,etc.(门、抽屉等的)圆形把手,旋钮;the ~ of an umbrella 雨伞的把手/ the ~ on the dial of a television set 电视调盘上的旋钮 ❷an isolated,rounded hill or mountain 圆丘 ❸a round-shaped swelling or mass on the surface of sth.(e.g.a tree trunk)圆形突出物;(树干等的)节,树疙瘩

knobbly /'nɒbli/
adj. having round,knoblike lumps 似球形突出物的;多节的:his ~ knees 他那突出的膝盖骨

knock /nɒk/
Ⅰ *v.* ❶ strike or hit a surface, especially when waiting to be let in through a door 敲;击:Someone is ~ing at the door.有人在敲门。❷ collide with sb. or sth. with a hard blow 撞, 碰:Lucy ~ed my water flying.露西把我的水打翻了。❸make (a hole or dent) in sth. by striking

it forcefully 打,凿(洞、坑)❹injure by striking 碰伤 ‖ ~down 击倒;拆除;(使)降价/ ~ off 停工;扣除/ ~ out 淘汰;击倒;使昏迷/ ~ over 打翻/~ up 敲门叫醒;使筋疲力尽 Ⅱ *n.* a blow; a short and sharp sound of a blow 敲击;碰撞;短促的敲打声;There's a ~ at the door.有人敲门。/He got a ~ on the head.他头上挨了一棒。

knockabout /'nɒkəbaʊt/
adj. ❶ suitable for rough use 耐磨的 ❷boisterous 喧闹的:~ comedy 喧闹的喜剧

knocker /'nɒkə/
n. ❶ a hinged metal flap for knocking against a door to summon a person 门环 ❷（informal）a person who continually criticizes（非正式）吹毛求疵的人

knockout /'nɒkaʊt/
Ⅰ *adj.* ❶（about a competition）in which the loser in the next stage has to drop out 淘汰赛的 ❷that knocks a boxer out（拳击中）击倒对手胜的 Ⅱ *n.* ❶a blow that knocks a boxer out 击倒对手取胜的一拳 ❷a competition in which the loser in each round is eliminated 淘汰赛 ❸（informal）an extremely attractive or outstanding person or thing（非正式）异常动人的人(或物);给人留下深刻印象的人(或物)

knoll /nəʊl/
n. a small hill or mound 小山

knot /nɒt/
Ⅰ *n.* a join made by tying a piece or pieces of rope, string, cord, etc.（绳索等打的）结:Put the string around the parcel and make a ~.用这根绳子捆包裹,然后打个结。Ⅱ *v.* form a knot in（rope, etc.）; tie with knots 打结;捆扎:Knot the end of the thread before you begin sewing.先将这根线的线头打个结,然后开始缝吧。

knotty /'nɒti/
adj. ❶（of wood）containing knots（木头）多节的 ❷full of difficulties 难于解决的;困难重重的:a ~ problem 棘手的问题

know /nəʊ/
v. (knew,~n) ❶ have sth. clearly in the

mind or memory; have knowledge or information 知道; 懂得: He ～s everything. 他什么都知道。❷ be acquainted with 认识; 熟悉: We've known each other since 1980.我们从 1980 年就认识了。❸ recognize or distinguish sb. or sth. 认出; 分辨: You will ～ him at once by his red hair.根据他的红头发,你一下就可以认出他。❹ have personal experience with 经历; 体验: He knew bitter days in his childhood.他童年时代曾过过苦日子。‖ be ～n as 以……著称; 称为/be ～n for 因……出名/～ about 了解; 知道……的情况/～ better than to 很懂得(而不至于)/～ by heart 记住; 背熟/～ of 听说; 知道/～ one's job (business) 懂行/～ one's own mind 有主见/make oneself known to 对……作自我介绍 ‖ ～-all *n.*万事通/～-how *n.*实际知识; 技能

knowing /'nəʊɪŋ/
adj. ❶ showing that you know or are aware of sth. 会意的, 心照不宣的: a ～ smile 会意的微笑 ❷done in full awareness or consciousness 明知的, 故意的 ‖ ～ly *adv.*故意地; 蓄意地

know-it-all /'nəʊɪtɔːl/
*n.*one who claims to know everything 万事通

knowledge /'nɒlɪdʒ/
*n.*❶ the state of understanding sth.知道; 了解; 理解: I have no ～ of where he is. 我不知道他在哪里。❷ what a person knows; the facts, information, skills, and under-standing that one has gained, especially through learning or experience 知识; 学问; 学识: He has a wide range of ～.他知识渊博。/Knowledge is power. 知识就是力量。❸familiarity with; information about 熟悉; 知道: He has a good ～ of the Summer Palace.他对颐和园很熟悉。‖ come to the ～ of 被……知道;

据……了解/to(the best of) one's ～ 据……所知/without the ～ of 在……不知道的情况下; 没告诉……就……‖ common ～ *n.*常识; 人所共知的事 ‖ ～able *adj.*有知识的; 有见识的

known /nəʊn/
*adj.*generally recognized by a lot of people 闻名的, 大家都知道的: a nationally ～ advanced unit 全国闻名的先进单位

knuckle /'nʌkl/
*n.*the finger joint 指关节: graze one's ～s 擦伤指关节

koala /kəʊ'ɑːlə/
*n.*an Australian tree-climbing animal with thick grey fur and large ears, feeding on eucalyptus leaves 树袋熊,考拉

kowtow /kaʊ'taʊ/
*v.*touch the ground with the forehead (as a sign of respect, submission, etc.); obey without question; be too humble 叩头; 磕头; 低三下四; 卑躬屈膝: Be polite, but don't ～.讲礼貌,但不是低三下四。

krone /'krəʊnə/
*n.*the standard coin in the money system of Denmark and Norway 克朗(丹麦、挪威的货币单位)

kudos /'kjuːdɒs/
n. the praise and honor received for an achievement 荣誉,声誉

kumquat /'kʌmkwɒt/
*n.*❶an orange-like fruit related to the cit-ruses, with an edible sweet rind and acid pulp.It is eaten raw or used in preserves 金橘 ❷ the East Asian shrub or small tree which yields this fruit, and which hy-bridizes with citrus trees 金橘树

kung fu /ˌkʌŋ'fuː/
n. a primarily unarmed Chinese martial art, resembling karate 中国功夫,中国拳术

Ll

label/'leɪbl/

I *n*.❶ a small piece of paper, cloth, etc. fixed on sth. to show what it is or where sth. is to go 标签:All the sale items usually have special ~s.凡销售物品一般都有特别的标签。❷ a word or phrase applied to describe a person, group, etc.(用以描述人、组织等的)称号,外号,绰号: Tom called her "the little fairy", and the ~ has spread quickly. 汤姆叫她"小仙女",之后这个美称便传开了。II *v*.❶ put a label on 贴标签:She ~led the luggage with her name and address. 她在行李上贴上自己姓名地址的标签。❷ describe or classify sb. or sth. 描述某人或某事物;将某人或某事物归类: His works are in different shapes; it's difficult to ~ them accurately. 他的作品形态各异,很难准确归类。‖ ~ …as… 把……说成是:Quite a few people ~led the boy as a thief.不少人说那男孩是个贼。

labial/'leɪbɪəl/

n. & adj. (a speech sound) made with one or both lips 唇音(的)

laboratory/lə'bɒrətəri, 'læbərətɔːri/

n. a room or building used for scientific experiment or test, especially on chemistry 实验室(尤指化学实验室)

laborious/lə'bɔːrɪəs/

adj. requiring hard work; not easy 困难的;费力的:They had the ~ task of cutting down the huge tree. 他们接受砍大树的艰苦工作。‖ ~ly *adv*. 费力地;辛苦地

labo(u)r/'leɪbə(r)/

I *n*.❶ work, especially physical work 劳动;(尤指)体力劳动:Both manual ~ and mental ~ are important in pushing production forward. 体力劳动和脑力劳动对促进生产的发展都很重要。❷ workers, especially manual workers 劳动者,劳工: a shortage of ~ 劳动力短缺 ❸ the British Labour Party 英国工党:He always votes Labour. 他老是投工党的票。II *v*. work, especially work hardly 辛勤地劳动:The farmers ~ed in the fields all day long.农民成天辛勤地在田间劳动。

labo(u)red/'leɪbəd/

adj.showing signs of effort and difficulty 吃力的,费劲的:You could tell from the ~ way he read out his speech that he didn't know much English.从他宣读演说稿的费力劲儿,可以看出他不大懂英语。

labo(u)rer/'leɪbərə(r)/

n. a worker whose job needs strength rather than skill, especially one who works outdoors 体力劳动者;工人;苦力

labo(u)ring /'leɪbərɪŋ/

n. a hard physical work needs strength rather than skill 体力劳动

labyrinth/'læbərɪnθ/

n.a network of winding paths, roads, etc. through which it is difficult to find one's way without help; entangled state of affairs 迷宫;迷津;错综复杂的事物

lace/leɪs/

n.❶ a string or cord put through small holes in shoes to draw edges together 鞋带:Tie your shoe ~s.把鞋带系上。❷ a netlike decorative cloth made of fine thread (带有装饰图案、网眼的)蕾丝;花边:a ~ collar 镶着花边的衣领

lack/læk/

I *v*.❶ be without; not have 缺乏:You ~ both experience and courage. 你既缺乏经验,又没有勇气。❷ have less than enough of need 不足;需要:He seems to ~ some courage to do it.他看来还缺少点勇气去做这件事情。II *n*. the state of being without or not having enough of sth. 缺乏，不足：The children grew weak for ~ of food.这些小孩子由于缺乏食物而长得很瘦弱。‖ ~ **for** 缺少；需要：He does not ~ for money.他并不缺钱。/**be ~ing in** 缺乏：Their reception of us was ~ing in warmth.他们接待我们不热情。

lacking /ˈlækɪŋ/
adj. ❶having not enough of sth.；missing 缺少的；不足的；没有的：We can't confirm these rumours because accurate information is ~.由于缺乏准确的信息，我们不能证实这些传闻。❷not present or not available 不在场的；得不到的

lacklustre /ˈlækˌlʌstə(r)/
adj. ❶(of eyes) lacking brightness；dull (指眼睛）无光泽的：He looked into space with ~ eyes.他目光呆滞地望着空中。❷lifeless；unexciting 毫无生气的；枯燥乏味的：a ~ speech (performance) 枯燥的演讲(表演)

laconic /ləˈkɒnɪk/
adj. saying sth. in the fewest possible words；brief 说话简短的；简洁的；简明的：He gave ~ answers to all our questions.他对我们提出的所有问题作了简短的答复。

lactate /ˈlækteɪt/
v. (said of a female mammal) produce milk(雌性哺乳动物）泌乳 ‖ **lactating** *n.* 泌乳；哺乳中的女性

lactation /lækˈteɪʃn/
n. ❶the production of milk for babies by a human or animal mother 泌乳 ❷the time that this lasts 泌乳期，哺乳期

lactic /ˈlæktɪk/
adj. of or obtained from milk 乳的；乳汁的：~ acid 乳酸

lactose /ˈlæktəʊs/
n. a sugary substance found in milk，sometimes used as a food for babies and sick people 乳糖

lacy /ˈleɪsi/
adj. made of or looking like lace 网眼织物的；网眼状的；有花边的；(似)带子的

lad /læd/
n. a boy or a young man 男孩，少年，青年男子，小伙子

ladder /ˈlædə(r)/
Ⅰ *n.* ❶ two lengths of wood，metal or rope，with cross pieces，used in climbing up and down walls，a ship's side，etc. 梯子：Jim went up the ~ to mend the roof. 吉姆从梯子爬上去修理屋顶。❷ the fault in a stocking caused by stitches becoming undone so that there is a vertical ladder-like flaw（袜子因脱线而成的）梯状滑丝，抽丝 Ⅱ *v.* (of stockings，etc.) develop ladders（指袜子等）抽丝：a pair of stocking that will not ~ 一双不会脱丝的长袜

laden /ˈleɪdn/
adj. carrying sth. heavy；loaded 负重的；载满的：The bushes were ~ with fruit.灌木丛里果实累累。/They arrived ~ with luggage.他们满载行李到达了。

ladle /ˈleɪdi/
n. a large，deep spoon with a long handle，used for serving liquids 长柄勺

lady /ˈleɪdi/
n. ❶ a polite word for any woman 女士（对一般女子的尊称）：Ladies and Gentlemen！女士们，先生们！❷ a woman of good manners or education or of good social position 有教养和社会地位的淑女：Her bearing and appearance indicated that she was a ~.她的举止和外表都说明她是个有教养的淑女。❸（Lady）a title for the wife and daughter of some noblemen（对英国某些贵族的妻女的尊称）……夫人，……小姐：Lady Jones 琼斯夫人 ❹（Ladies）a women's public lavatory 女厕所：Is there a Ladies near here? 附近有女厕所吗?

ladybird /ˈleɪdɪbɜːd/
n. a small flying beetle，usually red with black spots 七星瓢虫

ladylike /ˈleɪdɪlaɪk/
adj. suitable for a lady；well-mannered and refined 如淑女的；贤淑高贵的

ladyship /ˈleɪdɪʃɪp/
n.（Her or Your Ladyship）a title used in speaking about or to a woman of the rank of Lady（对贵族妇女的敬称）夫人

lag/læg/

　　v.(-gg-) walk or move too slowly; stay or fall behind 行动太慢,落后: We must help those who have ～ged behind. 我们应当帮助那些落后的人。

lagging/'lægɪŋ/

　　n. a material used to lag a water pipe or container (覆盖水管或容器的)隔热材料;罩壳

lagoon/lə'guːn/

　　n. a stretch of salt water (usually shallow) separated from the sea by a sandbank or coral reef 咸水湖

lair/leə(r)/

　　n. a place where a wild animal lives (野兽的)巢穴,窝

lake/leɪk/

　　n. a large area of water, surrounded by land 湖

lam¹/læm/

　　v.(-mm-) beat; thrash; flog 打;鞭打;抽打: ～ into sb. 鞭打某人

lam²/læm/

　　Ⅰ n. a sudden flight or escape〈美〉突然潜逃,逃走: on the ～ 在潜逃中/take it on the ～ 潜逃 Ⅱ v.(-mm-) escape or flee 逃走,潜逃

lamb/læm/

　　Ⅰ n.❶a young sheep 小羊,羔羊 ❷meat from a young sheep 羔羊肉: roast ～ 烤羊肉 Ⅱ v.give birth to lambs 生小羊

lambast(e)/læm'beɪst/

　　v. beat or attack fiercely, usually with words or blows 鞭抽,狠揍;粗暴地责骂;抨击: Her new play was really ～d(～ed) by the critics. 实际上她的新剧本受到评论家的抨击。

lambskin/'læmˌskɪn/

　　n.leather made from the skin of a lamb, especially with the wool on it (尤指带羊毛的)羔羊皮;羔皮革

lame/leɪm/

　　adj.❶ not able to walk properly because one's leg or foot is hurt or has some sort of weakness 跛的,瘸的: The ～ man needs a stick when he walks.那个瘸子走路需要拐棍。❷ not easily believed;

weak (议论等)站不住脚: I don't believe his story, it sounds a bit ～.我不相信他讲的那一套,那些听起来有点站不住脚。

lamely/'leɪmli/

　　adv. in a way that does not sound very confident; that does not persuade other people (听起来)信心不足地;不具说服力地

lament/lə'ment/

　　v.express or feel great sorrow; weep 感到悲伤;哀悼: He ～ed the death of his friend.他为朋友的去世而伤感。‖ ～able /'læməntəbl/ adj. 可悲的;令人惋惜的

lamented/lə'mentɪd/

　　adj.❶mourned or grieved for 被哀悼的 ❷regretted 令人遗憾的

lamp/læmp/

　　n. Ⅰ a device for giving light 灯: an electric ～ 电灯 Ⅱ ❶supply with lamps; illuminate 照明;照亮 ❷hit sb. or sth. hard 重击: He ～ed me.他打我打得不轻。

lampoon¹/læm'puːn/

　　n. a piece of writing fiercely attacking a person, government, etc., by making them seem foolish 讽刺文章;讽刺的作品

lampoon²/læm'puːn/

　　v.attack in an amusing way 用讽刺文抨击;嘲讽: In his essays he ～ed all the major political figures of the time.他在文章中讽刺了当时所有的主要政治人物。

lamp post/'læmpˌpəʊst/

　　n. a tall post for a lamp which lights a street or other public area 灯杆,路灯柱

lamprey/'læmpri/

　　n. a snakelike fish with a sucking mouth 七鳃鳗,八目鳗

lampshade/'læmpʃeɪd/

　　n.a usually decorative cover placed over a lamp, especially to soften or screen its light 灯罩

lance¹/lɑːns/

　　n.a type of spear with a very long handle once used in war by soldiers on horses (从前骑兵用的)长矛 ‖ ～ corporal n.上等兵,一等兵

lance²/lɑːns/

　　v.cut open with a lancet 用柳叶刀切开:

L

The doctor ~d the boil on his hand.医生用柳叶刀切开他手上的水泡。

lancet /ˈlɑːnsɪt, ˈlænsɪt/

n. ❶ a pointed two-edged knife used by surgeons 手术刀 ❷ a tall, narrow pointed arch or window 尖拱；尖头窗

land /lænd/

Ⅰ *n.* ❶ the ground used for a special purpose 土地：Land prices have risen quickly.地价上涨很快。❷ the solid, dry part of the earth's surface 陆地：About a third of the earth's surface is ~, the rest is water.地球表面约三分之一是陆地，其余是海洋。❸ a county or nation 国家：a native ~ 故国，祖国 Ⅱ *v.* ❶ come or put on land (from a ship, an aircraft, etc.) 上岸；着陆：The spaceship ~ed safely on the moon.宇宙飞船在月球安全着落了。❷ bring to, reach a position or situation 使……陷入：Fishing without permission will ~ you in trouble.未经允许钓鱼会使你招惹麻烦。

landform /ˈlændfɔːm/

n. a natural feature of the earth's surface 地形，地貌

landing /ˈlændɪŋ/

n. ❶ the act of coming or bringing to ground 登陆，着陆：The airplane made a safe ~.那飞机安全着陆了。❷ a place where persons or goods are landed 登陆处；(船等的)卸货处 ❸ a platform between flights of stairs 楼梯的平台

landlord /ˈlændlɔːd/

n. ❶ a person who lets land or a house or room, etc. to tenants 地主；房东 ❷ a person who runs a public house 出租屋房东

landmark /ˈlændmɑːk/

n. ❶ a conspicuous and easily recognized object in or feature of a landscape 地标，城镇标志性建筑 ❷ an event that marks an important stage or development in the history of sth. 重要事件；里程碑事件 ❸ a building or a place that is important for its history 有历史意义的建筑(遗址)

landmine /ˈlændaɪn/

n. an explosive mine laid on or just under the surface of the ground 地雷

landscape /ˈlændskeɪp/

Ⅰ *n.* ❶ a picture showing view of the countryside 风景画 ❷ the art of painting such scenes 山水绘画艺术 ❸ all the visible features of an area of land 风光，风景：an urban ~ 都市景观 Ⅱ *v.* make (land) more pleasant to look at by arranging trees, flowers, etc. 使美化：beautifully ~d motels with swimming pools 带有游泳池的美化了的汽车旅馆

landslide /ˈlændslaɪd/

n. ❶ the sliding down of a mass of earth or rock from a mountain or cliff 山崩，崩坍；泥石流 ❷ an overwhelming majority of votes for one side in an election (选举中)压倒性多数票

landward /ˈlændwəd/

Ⅰ *adv.* towards the land 朝陆地，向陆地 Ⅱ *adj.* facing towards land as opposed to sea 朝向陆地的

lane /leɪn/

n. ❶ a narrow country road 乡村小道 ❷ a narrow street 小巷；里弄；胡同 ❸ a route regularly used by ships or aircraft 航道；航线；航路 ❹ a marked division of a road, running track, etc. 车道；跑道：a three-~ motorway 三车道的高速公路/The world champion is in ~ four.那个世界冠军在第四跑道。

language /ˈlæŋɡwɪdʒ/

n. ❶ words that are spoken or written 语言：the spoken (written) ~ 口语(书面语)/Language is an instrument for communication.语言是交流的工具。❷ a form of speech used by a certain nation or race (某国或民族的)语言：He can speak several ~s.他会说好几国语言。❸ special words and terms used in a certain field 术语：the ~ of science (law) 科学(法律)用语 /medical ~ 医学用语 ❹ any way of expression 起语言作用的东西：finger (sign) ~ 手语 /computer ~ 计算机语言

languid /ˈlæŋɡwɪd/

adj. without strength or any show of effort; slow-moving 无精打采的，疲倦的，慢吞吞的：She stretched out a ~ arm to brush the cigar ash off the couch.她伸出懒洋洋的手臂拭去沙发椅上的雪茄烟灰。

languish/ˈlæŋgwɪʃ/

*v.*❶be or become languid 变得没精打采，衰弱无力：He told me about it with ~ing looks.他露出一副没精打采的神情，向我讲述了这件事情。❷ become weak or unhappy through desire 感到忧郁；苦苦思念：The mother ~ed for her son in the army.母亲十分思念她参军的儿子。

languor/ˈlæŋgə(r)/

*n.*❶ the state of tiredness of mind or body；the state of lack of strength or will 身心倦息 ❷ the pleasant or heavy stillness 清静；沉闷：the ~ of a hot summer's afternoon 炎炎夏日午后的沉闷 ❸a feeling or state of mind of tender sadness and desire 淡淡的抑郁；柔情：the ~s of a lovesick poet 一个害相思病的诗人的抑郁心情 ‖ ~ **ous** *adj.*无力的/-**ously** *adv.*疲倦地；郁闷地

lank/læŋk/

adj.(with reference to hair) straight and soft (指头发)平直的，柔软的

lanky/ˈlæŋki/

adj.(with reference to persons) tall, thin and rather clumsy (指人)瘦长而难看的：a ~ youth 一个瘦长难看的年轻人

lantern/ˈlæntən/

*n.*a light in a transparent case which will stay bright in wind or rain 提灯；灯笼：the Lantern Festival 灯节；元宵节 /a ~ slide 幻灯片

lap/læp/

Ⅰ *v.*(-pp-) ❶drink by taking up with the tongue, as a cat does 舔：The cat ~ped up all the milk in the bowl.那只猫舔光了碗里的牛奶。❷ (of water) move or hit with little waves and soft sounds (浪)拍打，(水)泼溅：The water of the river was ~ping on (against) the rocks of the bank.河水拍打着岸边的岩石。Ⅱ *n.*❶ one circuit of a track (跑道的)一圈 ❷a piece of or a section of sth.一段

lapdog/ˈlæpdɒg/

*n.*❶a small pet dog 宠物狗 ❷a person

completely under the control of another (usually important) person 趋炎附势(仰人鼻息)的人

lapel/ləˈpel/

*n.*the part of the front of a coat or jacket folded back and joined to the collar (大衣或上衣的)翻领：He wore a badge in(on) the ~ of his jacket.他在夹克衫的翻领上佩戴了一枚徽章。

lapse/læps/

Ⅰ *n.*❶a slight error in speech or behaviour 微小差错：a ~ of the tongue or pen 口误或笔误 ❷ a failure in correct behaviour, belief, duty, etc. 失检，偏离：His ~ of (from) virtue is unforgivable.他在道德上的失检不可原谅。❸ (of time) passing away (时间)流逝，过去：The country became very strong and powerful after a ~ of about 200 years.这个国家经过大约两百年的时间后已经变得非常强盛。Ⅱ *v.*❶ (of time) pass(时间)过去：Several hours ~d before he came back.过了几个钟头他才回来。❷ fail to keep one's position；fall from good ways into bad ways 陷入，堕落：The boy soon ~d into a bad habit of smoking.那孩子不久后染上了抽烟的恶习。

laptop/ˈlæptɒp/

*n.*a portable computer for use while traveling 笔记本电脑，便携式电脑

larch/lɑːtʃ/

*n.*a tall, upright tree with bright green, needle-like leaves and hard-skinned fruit (cones) 落叶松

lard/lɑːd/

Ⅰ *n.*the fat of pigs or hogs prepared for use in cooking 猪油 Ⅱ *v.*❶put pieces of fat on or in 涂猪油于 ❷ insert strips of fat or bacon in(meat) before cooking(烹调前)嵌肥肉(咸肉)于其他(肉)中 ❸ polish(speech or writing) with sth. 夹杂某内容；润色：The professor gave us a wonderful lecture ~ed with vivid examples. 教授的演讲精彩绝伦，夹杂着许多生动的事例。

larder/ˈlɑːdə(r)/

*n.*a place where food is kept；pantry 食物

储藏室,食品橱

large /lɑːdʒ/

adj. ❶ of considerable size, extent or capacity 大的,巨大的：I want a ～ room.我要一个大房间。❷ of greater size than the ordinary, especially with reference to size of clothes (衣服等)大号的 ❸ of wide range or scope 大范围的,大规模的：This is a ～ company which produces cars.这是一家大型汽车生产企业。‖ at ～ 逍遥法外;一般说来 /by and ～ 总的说来

largely /'lɑːdʒli/

adv. ❶ to a great extent; mainly 大部分,主要地：Success depends ～ on working hard.成功主要靠勤奋。❷ much; in great quantity 大量地：drink ～ 大量地饮酒

lark /lɑːk/

n. a small songbird, especially the skylark 小鸣禽,(尤指)云雀

larva /'lɑːvə/

n. the wormlike young of an insect between leaving the egg and changing into a winged form (昆虫的)幼虫,幼体

laryngitis /ˌlærɪn'dʒaɪtɪs/

n. a painful, swollen condition of the larynx 喉炎：suffering from (acute) ～ 患(急性)喉炎

larynx /'lærɪŋks/

n. (*pl.* larynges) the hollow boxlike part at the upper end of the throat in which the sounds of the voice are produced by the vocal cords 喉(头)

laser /'leɪzə(r)/

n. ❶ a narrow and very intense beam of light that can be used to cut metal, help medical operation, etc. 激光 ❷ an instrument that produces this kind of light 激光器

lash /læʃ/

Ⅰ *v.* ❶ strike with or as if with a whip 鞭打;狠击;猛甩：The big raindrops were ～ing against the windowpanes.大滴大滴的雨点猛烈地敲打在窗玻璃上。❷ tie firmly, especially with rope 捆绑：They ～ed the thief to a tree so that he would not run away.大家把小偷紧紧地绑在树干上使他不能逃走。Ⅱ *n.* ❶ the flexible part of a whip 鞭子 ❷ a blow given with or as with a whip, etc. 鞭：He gave the thief quite a few ～es.他抽了那个小偷好几鞭。❸ an eyelash 眼睫毛 ‖ ～ out at (against) 猛击,猛踢,揍

lashing(s) /'læʃɪŋz/

n. a large amount, especially of food and drink 许多,大量(尤指食物和饮料等)：apple pie with ～ of cream 有大量奶油的苹果馅饼

lass /læs/

n. a girl; a sweetheart 小姑娘;少女;情人：All the young ～es were there in their finest dresses.所有年轻的姑娘都在那儿,穿着她们最好的衣服。

last /lɑːst/

Ⅰ *adj.* ❶ final; the only remaining 最后的;唯一剩下的：The stress falls on the ～ syllable.重音在最后一个音节上。❷ coming immediately before the present 刚过去的,上一个：Did you see him ～ week? 你上周见过他吗？❸ the lowest in importance or rank 最差的,最低的：He came ～ in the race.这次比赛他跑了末尾。❹ the least likely or suitable 最不可能的;最不合适的：The ～ thing you need is a box.你最不需要的是一个盒子。Ⅱ *adv.* ❶ on the occasion nearest in the past; most recently 最近一次,上一次：When did you meet ～? 你们上次是什么时候见的面？❷ after anything else; after the others 最后：He laughs best who laughs ～.谁笑到最后就笑得最好。Ⅲ *n.* the person, thing, or group after all others 最后的人(或物)：He is often the first to come and the ～ to leave.他常常是最先到最后走。Ⅳ *v.* continue for the stated length of time; go on 持续,延续：This war ～ed four years.这场战争延续了4年。‖ at ～ 最后,终于

lasting /'lɑːstɪŋ/

adj. able to last for a long time 持久的,长久的：a ～ peace 持久的和平

lastly /'lɑːstli/

adv. in the last place; finally 最后：Lastly, I would like to thank my parents.最后,我要感谢我的父母。

latch /lætʃ/

n. ❶a small piece of wood or iron used to fasten a door 门闩 ❷a type of simple door lock opened by a latch key 闩锁,弹簧锁

latchkey/'lætʃkiː/

　*n.*a key for opening a lock on an outside door of a house or flat（住所大门的）碰簧锁钥匙;公寓门上的钥匙

late/leɪt/

　Ⅰ*adj.* ❶ after the right, fixed or usual time 迟的;晚的: The farmers finished harvesting the rice in ～ autumn. 晚秋时农民们收割完了稻子。❷ former（and now dead）已故的: her ～ husband 她的亡夫 ❸ former（and still living）前任的;已卸任的(现在在世): the ～ prime minister 前首相 ‖ of ～ 近来/till（until）～ 直到很晚 Ⅱ*adv.*❶after the usual, right, fixed or expected time 迟;晚: You shouldn't sit up too ～ at night.你不应当睡得太晚。❷toward the end of a period 在晚期,末期 ❸at a time in the near future 不久以后: I will see you ～r. 回头见。‖ ～r on 以后;后来/sooner or ～r 迟早 ‖ ～st *adj.*最近的;最新的

lately/'leɪtlɪ/

　*adv.*not long ago; in the recent past; recently 不久前,近来,最近: Have you seen him ～? 你最近见过他吗?

latent/'leɪtnt/

　*adj.*present but not yet noticeable, active, or fully developed 潜伏的;潜在的;不易察觉的: a ～ infection 潜伏性传染病/～ aggression 潜在的侵略

later/'leɪtə(r)/

　Ⅰ*adj.*the comparative degree of the word late（late 的比较级）: He was happy in his ～ years.他晚年幸福。Ⅱ*adv.*after that time you are talking about 其后,随后: I met him two years ～.两年后我遇见了他。

lateral/'lætərəl/

　*adj.*relating to the sides of sth.; sideways 侧面的;旁边的;横的: ～ buds 侧芽/～ position 侧翼位置

latest/'leɪtɪst/

　*n.*the most recent news, fashion, or exam-ple 最新消息,最时髦的东西: He told me the ～ about the book.他告诉了我这本书的最新消息。‖ at the ～ 最迟,至迟: Hand in your exercise books tomorrow morning at the ～.最迟明天上午交练习本。

latex /'leɪteks/

　n. ❶ a milky fluid produced by certain plants, e.g. the rubber tree（植物)胶乳,乳液;橡胶 ❷a synthetic product resembling this, used to make paints and coatings（制造油漆及涂层等用的)人造乳胶

lathe/leɪð/

　*n.*an apparatus which makes a piece of wood or metal turn round quickly while it is cut and shaped 车床,机床

lather/'lɑːðə(r), 'læðə(r)/

　Ⅰ*n.*the foam made from soap or deter-gent and water, or from sweat 肥皂泡沫;汗沫: To shave properly you need a good ～ on your face.要把脸刮得干净,你需要在脸上涂上足量的肥皂泡沫。/After the race the horse was in a ～.比赛后这匹马满身汗水。Ⅱ*v.*❶form a frothy white mass of bubbles 起泡沫: This soap does not ～ easily.这肥皂不易起泡沫。❷cov-er with lather 涂肥皂泡沫: You must ～ your face before shaving.在刮脸之前,你必须在脸上涂肥皂沫。

Latin/'lætɪn/

　Ⅰ*n.*the language of ancient Rome and its empire 拉丁语 Ⅱ*adj.*of the Latin lan-guage; of peoples speaking language de-scended from Latin 拉丁语的,拉丁语系民族的: Those languages belong to the ～ family.那些语言属于拉丁语系。

latitude/'lætɪtjuːd/

　*n.*the angular distance in degrees from the equator 纬度;纬线

latter/'lætə(r)/

　*adj.*nearer to the end or to the present time 近期的;末尾的: the ～ part of the year 一年中的后一段时期 ‖ the ～ 后者: Of pigs and cows, the ～ are more valuable.猪和牛相比,后者更值钱。

laud/lɔːd/

　*v.*praise sb. or sth. 称赞;赞美: Don't ～

him to the sky.不要把他捧上天了。

laudable /ˈlɔːdəbl/

adj. worthy of high praise 值得称赞的：a ～ attempt to save the environment 为拯救环境做的值得称赞的努力

laudatory /ˈlɔːdətəri/

adj. expressing praise or admiration 表示赞美的，颂扬的，褒扬的：～ comments 赞美性的评论

laugh /lɑːf/

v. show pleasure, amusement or contempt by expressions and sounds 发笑；大笑；嘲笑：His story was so funny that the people present couldn't help ～ing.他讲的故事真有趣，在场的人都忍不住大笑起来。‖ ～ at 笑，嘲笑(某人)/ ～ away 一笑置之/ ～ off 对……一笑置之/ ～ one's head off 放声大笑/have the ～ of sb.反笑，羞辱某人/have the last ～ (开始被人嘲笑)最后取得胜利 ‖ ～able *adj.* 可笑的；愚蠢的/～ingstock *n.* 笑柄；笑料

laughter /ˈlɑːftə(r)/

n. an act or a sound of laughing 笑；笑声：inward ～ 内心的微笑 /roar with ～ 哄然大笑 /burst (break out) into ～ 失声而笑；哈哈地笑起来 /a burst of ～ 一阵笑声

launch /lɔːntʃ/

Ⅰ *v.* ❶ send (a rocket) into the air 发射火箭 ❷ send into the water 使(船)下水 ❸ throw 投掷：～ an arrow into the air 把箭射入空中 /～ a spear 投矛 ❹ start or set up an activity, or enterprise, etc. 发起；开创；发动；开展：～ an attack against (upon) 向……发起进攻 /～ into politics 开始从政；投身政界 /～ (out) into an argument 热心地加入辩论 Ⅱ *n.* ❶ an act of launching 开办；发射；下水：the ～ of a space shuttle 航天飞机的发射 /the ～ of a new passenger liner 新客轮的下水 ❷ an open motorboat used for pleasure 游艇：a motor ～ 汽艇

launcher /ˈlɔːntʃə(r)/

n. a structure that holds a rocket or missile during launching 火箭发射装置

launder /ˈlɔːndə(r)/

v. ❶ wash, or wash and iron (clothes, sheets, etc.) 洗(衣服等)；洗烫(衣服等)：We must have these bedclothes ～ed.我们必须让人把这些床上用品洗一洗。❷ give (sth., especially money obtained illegally) the appearance of being legal 洗(黑钱)

laund(e)rette /ˈlɔːndəˈret/

n. a shop where the public can wash their clothes in machines that work when coins are put in them (装有投币洗衣机的)自助洗衣店

laundry /ˈlɔːndri/

n. ❶ a place or business where clothes, sheets, etc. are washed and ironed 洗衣业；洗衣店，洗衣房 ❷ clothes, sheets, etc. needing washing or that have just been washed (or washed and ironed) 所洗的衣服，待洗的衣服：Has the ～ been sent back yet? 洗的衣服送回来了吗？

laureate /ˈlɔːriət/

n. someone who has won a particular high honour 戴桂冠的人；奖金(荣誉)获得者：a Nobel ～ in physics 诺贝尔物理学奖获得者

laurel /ˈlɔːrəl/

n. a type of small tree with evergreen leaves, used in ancient times as a sign of honour or victory；bay tree 月桂树(古代用作荣誉或胜利的象征)

lava /ˈlɑːvə/

n. the melted rock coming out of a volcano and becoming hard when cool 熔岩

lavatory /ˈlævətri/

n. ❶ a toilet 厕所 ❷ a room for washing the hands and face in 盥洗室

lavender /ˈlævəndə(r)/

n. ❶ a type of plant with small, sweet-smelling, pale purple flowers which can be dried and used as a scent 薰衣草 ❷ the colour of lavender flowers 淡紫色

lavish /ˈlævɪʃ/

Ⅰ *adj.* giving or producing freely, liberally, or generously 慷慨大方的；不吝惜的；滥用的：He is ～ with money.他用钱大手大脚。Ⅱ *v.* give abundantly and generously 慷慨给予；大量花费；挥霍：The parents ～ed care on their only son. 父母

对他们的独生儿子太溺爱了。

law/lɔ:/

　　n.a rule made by the government for all the people of a country;a rule in science, art or a game 法规;法律;规则;守则;定律;规律:obey the ～ 守法/break the ～ 犯法,违法/maintain ～ and order 维持法治与社会秩序/criminal ～ 刑法/the ～ of gravity 万有引力定律 ‖ be a ～ unto oneself 我行我素;无法无天;为所欲为/go to ～ 诉诸法律,打官司/lay down the ～ 发号施令;严格规定/take the ～ into one's own hands 私自治罪,用私刑

lawful/ˈlɔ:fl/

　　adj.allowed by law;according to law;recognized by law 合法的,法定的,依法的:the ～ heir 合法的继承人

lawless/ˈlɔ:lɪs/

　　adj.❶(of a country or place) not governed by laws (国家、地方)没有法律的;法纪所不及的:～ frontier towns 没有法律的边境城镇 ❷uncontrolled;wild 失去法律控制的;无法无天的:～ frontiersmen 没有法律控制的边疆居民

lawn/lɔ:n/

　　n.an area of grass kept closely cut and smooth;such an area of grass used for a game 草地,草坪,草场:～ tennis 草地网球

lawsuit/ˈlɔ:su:t/

　　n.a claim or complaint against sb. in a court of law 诉讼;起诉:The victims have started a ～ to get compensation for their injuries.受害者已经开始起诉,要求得到损害赔偿。

lawyer/ˈlɔ:jə(r)/

　　n.a person who is trained and qualified in legal matters,especially a solicitor 律师

laxative/ˈlæksətɪv/

　　Ⅰ*adj*.causing the contents of the bowels to move easily 通便的 Ⅱ*n*.the medicine which does this 通便剂;轻泻剂

lay/leɪ/

　　v.(laid)❶ put sth.carefully in a particular position;place 放置;搁:Lay your hands smoothly on your knees.将双手平放在膝上。❷(of a bird, insect, etc.) produce eggs (鸟、虫)下蛋,产卵:Hens ～ eggs. 母鸡下蛋。❸put down sth. and set it in position 铺设;安放 ❹put forward an idea or suggestion,etc.提出(想法、建议等) ‖ ～ about sb.乱打;使劲地打/ ～ aside 搁置;积蓄/ ～ bare 暴露;揭发/ ～ by 存蓄/ ～ down 规定;制定;说明/ ～ down one's arms 放下武器/ ～ down one's life 牺牲/ ～ for 暗中等待(伺机攻击);等候/（one's）hands on 拿到,找到,抓到/ ～ hold of 抓住/ ～ in 储存/ ～ on 涂上;准备好/ ～ one's cards on the table 摊牌,亮底/ ～ out 设计,布局,编排,制定/ ～stress(emphasis) on 强调/ ～ the blame on 责怪,埋怨/～ the foundation (base) 打基础/ ～ to 归咎于/ ～ up 储存,放置不用/ ～ waste 损毁;荒废

layer/ˈleɪə(r)/

　　Ⅰ*n*.❶a quantity or thickness of some material laid over a surface 层:a ～ of rock 一层岩石 ❷a person or thing that lays sth.铺设者;铺设机:a brick ～ 砌砖者 ❸a bird, especially a hen, that lays eggs 生蛋的鸡(鸟):a good(bad) ～ 生蛋多(少)的鸡 ❹a plant stem that has been fastened partly under the ground, in order to grow roots and so become a separate plant 压条,压枝 Ⅱ*v*.fasten a stem down (and cover with soil)压条

layman/ˈleɪmən/

　　n.(*pl*. laymen /ˈleɪmən/) a person who does not have specialized knowledge of a subject 外行人;门外汉:Where the law is concerned,I am only a ～.谈到法律我不过是个外行人。

layout/ˈleɪaʊt/

　　n.❶the planned arrangement of a town, garden, building, etc., especially as shown in a drawing 布局,设计;安排:In the new ～ for the conference hall, the platform is to be placed at the western end.按照会议厅的新设计,主席台将位于西端。/The robbers studied the ～ of the bank. 这伙强盗研究了银行的布局。❷the way in which printed matter is set out on paper 版面编排(设计):The book designer will have to redo the page ～s.新书设计者将不得不重做版面设计。

laze¹ /leɪz/

v.do nothing;be lazy;rest lazily 混日子，懒洋洋地虚度光阴：He spent the afternoon lazing in a hammock.他在吊床上消磨了整个下午。

laze² /leɪz/

n.a short period of restful and lazy inactivity 懒散度过的片刻

lazy /'leɪzi/

adj. not wanting to work;doing little work;not diligent;idle 懒惰的；懒散的；缓慢的；The man seemed ~ all day.这人整天显得懒洋洋的。 ‖ ~ bones n.懒骨头；懒汉

leach /liːtʃ/

v.make liquid,especially rainwater,percolate through soil or ore,etc. in order to remove a soluble substance（从土壤、矿石等中）淋洗；过滤

lead /liːd/

Ⅰ v.(led) ❶guide a person by the hand, etc.带领；引导：The policewoman led the blind man across the road.女警察领着盲人过了马路。❷act as chief;direct 领导；率领：He led the nation in the struggle against the foreign invaders.他领导了全国人民反抗外国侵略者。❸influence; have sth.as a result 使得，导致（某人做某事）：What led you change your mind suddenly? 什么东西使你突然改变了主意？❹have a certain kind of life 过着（生活）：He led a quiet life.他过着安静的生活。❺show the way,especially by going in front 引路；带路：The guide led the tourists to a hotel.导游把游客带到宾馆。❻be a way to a particular place 通往：All roads ~ to Rome.条条道路通罗马。‖ ~ astray 引入歧途/ ~ sb.by the nose 牵着某人的鼻子走/ ~ the way 带路，带头/ ~ to 导致，造成/ ~ up to 导致；是导致……的原因 Ⅱ n.❶ the position ahead of all others 领导；引导；领先；带头：follow the ~ of sb.效法（某人）/give a ~ 起带头作用，引导；提示/in the ~ 在前头 ❷ a length of rope, leather, chain, etc., fastened to an animal,usually a dog,to control it（牵引动物的）绳索或皮带：Please keep your dog on a ~.请牵好你的狗。

leaded /'ledɪd/

adj.❶covered or framed with lead 加铅框的，盖铅板的 ❷（said about petrol）containing a lead compound 含铅的

leaden /'ledn/

adj.❶of the colour of lead;dull grey 铅（灰）色的：a ~ sky 灰暗的天空 ❷without cheerfulness or excitement 沉闷的，沉重的；郁郁寡欢的：With a ~ heart she opened the income tax envelope.她怀着沉重的心情打开了交纳所得税的信封。/a rather ~ performance 相当沉闷的演出

leader /'liːdə(r)/

n.❶ a person who guides or directs a group, team, organization, etc. 领袖，首领，领导者：the ~ of the miners' union 矿工工会的领导人/He's always been a follower rather than a ~.他一直是一个追随者，而不是领导者。/a born ~ 天生的领袖 ❷ a person or thing that is ahead of others 引导者，领先的人（或物）：Liverpool is the current ~ in the football championship.目前利物浦队在足球锦标赛中领先。❸the chief violin player of an orchestra 首席小提琴手，乐队首席 ❹the strongest stem or branch of a tree 树的主干（顶枝）

leadership /'liːdəʃɪp/

n.❶the position of leader 领导地位 ❷the ability to lead 领导能力

lead-in /'liːdɪn/

n.remarks made by someone to introduce a radio or television show（介绍广播或电视节目的）开场白；介绍

leading /'liːdɪŋ/

adj.❶most important;chief;principal 最重要的，主要的，第一位的：the ~ men of the day 今日的领导人物 ❷guiding;directing 领导的，指导的：the ~ cadre 领导干部 ❸playing the main part 扮演主角的：a ~ lady 演主角的女演员

leading light /,liːdɪŋ 'laɪt/

n.a person of importance or influence 有影响的重要人物：Bill is one of the ~s of the local dramatic society.比尔是当地戏剧社很有影响的人物之一。

leading question/ˌliːdɪŋ ˈkwestʃn/

　　n. a question formed in such a way that it suggests the expected answer 诱导性问题；暗示性问题

lead time/ˌliːd ˈtaɪm/

　　n. the time taken in planning and producing a new product, before it is actually ready for sale 新产品从设计到制成成品之间的时间

leaf/liːf/

　　n.（*pl.* leaves /liːvz/）❶ one of the green flat parts on trees or plants 叶；叶子：sweep up dead leaves in autumn 扫掉秋天的枯叶 ❷ a single piece of paper in a book forming two pages（书的）一页（两面）：I tore a ～ out of my note book. 我从笔记本上撕下一页。‖ come into ～ 长叶/take a ～ out of one's book 仿效某人/turn over a new ～ 改过自新；重新开始

leaflet/ˈliːflɪt/

　　n. ❶ a small young leaf 小叶，嫩叶 ❷ a small sheet, often folded, of printed matter, usually given free to the public 传单，活页

leafy/ˈliːfi/

　　adj. covered with leaves; having many leaves 多叶的；叶茂的：a very ～ bush 树叶相当茂盛的灌木丛

league/liːg/

　　n. ❶ an agreement made between persons, groups or nations for their common welfare, e.g. to work for peace; the parties that make such an agreement 盟约；同盟；联盟：The five nations formed a defense ～ after the First World War. 第一次世界大战后，这五个国家结成了防御联盟。 ❷ a group of sports clubs or players that play matches between themselves（运动竞赛）联合会，联赛：This game is a ～ match. 这场比赛是联赛。 ❸ a class or category of quality or ability（品质、能力）水平，类别 ‖ in ～（with）（与……）结盟；勾结在一起

leak/liːk/

　　Ⅰ *n.* a hole, crack, etc., caused by wear, injury, etc., may wrongly get in or out 漏洞，漏隙：There is a ～ in the gas pipe. 煤气管上有个漏洞。Ⅱ *v.* let（a liquid, gas, etc.）in or out of a hole or crack 漏水；漏气；泄漏（消息、秘密等）：The rain is ～ing in. 漏雨了。‖ ～ out 漏出来，泄漏出去

leakage/ˈliːkɪdʒ/

　　n. ❶ the act and process of fluid or gas escaping through a hole or crack 漏，泄漏，漏出：a ～ of information 消息的走漏 ❷ an instance of this; sth. which leaks in or out; the amount of such a leak 泄漏的实例；漏出物；泄漏量

leaky/ˈliːki/

　　adj.（leakier, leakiest）having a leak 漏的，有漏隙的，有漏洞的：a ～ bottle 一个有漏洞的瓶子

lean[1]/liːn/

　　v.（～ed or ～t）❶ slope or bend from an upright position 屈身；倾斜：The teacher ～ed forward to hear what the student was saying. 老师屈身向前倾听学生的讲话。 ❷ support or rest oneself in a bent or sloping position 倚；靠：He felt tired and sleepy and kept ～ing his head against my shoulder. 他感到困倦欲睡，不住地把头靠到我肩膀上。‖ ～ on（upon）依靠/～ towards 倾向于

lean[2]/liːn/

　　adj. producing or having little value 贫瘠的；瘦的：a ～ year 歉收年

leaning/ˈliːnɪŋ/

　　n. a tendency to prefer sth. or believe in sth. 倾向，倾斜：He has a ～ towards socialism. 他倾向于社会主义。

leap/liːp/

　　Ⅰ *v.*（～ed or ～t）❶（cause to）jump over（使）跳（跃）过：～ a horse over a fence 纵马跃过栅栏/～ on a horse 跃上马/～ for joy 高兴得跳起来/～ a ditch 跳过一条沟 ❷ seize a chance eagerly 抓住机会：He ～t at the opportunity. 他立刻抓住了这个机会。Ⅱ *n.* a forceful jump or quick movement 跳跃：take a ～ over an obstacle 跃过障碍物 ‖ ～ to conclusions 匆忙下结论/～ out of one's skin 大惊；大喜/by ～s and bounds 迅速地；飞跃地 ‖ ～-frog *n.* 跳背游戏

learn/lɜːn/

v.(～ed or ～t)❶ gain knowledge of（a subject）or skill in（an activity），especially through experience or through being taught 学习；学会：He ～ed to swim.他学会了游泳。❷ become informed（of）获悉；了解；明白：I ～ed from his letter that he had married.我从他的信中得知他已结婚了。‖ ～ **from** 向……学习；从……学习/ ～ **of(about)** 听说；了解……的事/ ～ **by heart** 记熟；默诵 ‖ **～-er** *n.*学生；学习者

learned/lɜːnd/

*adj.*❶ having or showing much knowledge，especially of the humanities 有学问的，博学的（尤指在人文科学方面）：a ～ professor 一位学识渊博的教授 ❷ of，for，or concerning advanced study 学术上的：～ books 学术性的书籍

learning/ˈlɜːnɪŋ/

*n.*❶ the process of learning 学习：She is good at ～.她善于学习。❷ the advanced knowledge gained by careful study 学问，学识，知识：The professor is a man of ～.这位教授学识渊博。

lease/liːs/

Ⅰ *n.*a written legal agreement by which the use of a building or piece of land is given by its owner to someone for a certain time in return for rent 租约；契约：When does the ～ expire? 租约何时期满? Ⅱ *v.*give or take the use of（land or buildings）on a lease（按租约）出租或租用：I have ～d the house for one month.我已租用这房屋一个月了。

leaseback/ˈliːsbæk/

*n.*an arrangement by which one sells or gives sth. to sb.，but he continues to have the use of it in return for rent 售后回租（租用已出售的东西）

leasehold/ˈliːshəʊld/

n.& *adj.*(land)(to be)held for a term of years on lease 租用的土地；租用的

leaseholder/ˈliːshəʊldə(r)/

n. someone who lives in a leasehold house，flat，etc.租借人；承租人

leash/liːʃ/

*n.*a string or strip of leather for holding a dog（usually fastened to a collar）（拴狗的）皮带，项圈：Dogs must be kept on the ～ in this public park.在这个公园里，狗必须用皮带拴住。

least/liːst/

Ⅰ *adj.* smallest in size，amount，or degree；fewest in number 最小的；最少的；最不重要的：the ～ distance 最小的距离/the ～ important meeting 最不重要的会议/He hadn't the ～ thought of his own interests.他丝毫不考虑个人利益。Ⅱ *adv.*in the smallest degree 最小；最少，最没(有)：the ～ angry man 最没脾气的人/He works hardest and is being paid ～.他干活最艰苦，得到的报酬最少。/It happened just when we ～ expected it.事情发生在我们最料不到的时候。Ⅲ *n.* the smallest number or amount 最小；最少，最少量：Buy the one that cost the ～.买最便宜的一个。/That's the ～ of it.那是最不重要的一点。

leather/ˈleðə(r)/

n. treated animal skin used for making shoes，bags，etc.皮革：a ～ coat 皮外套/This sofa is covered in real ～.这沙发是用真皮做的。

leatherette/ˌleðəˈret/

n. a cheap material made to look like leather 人造革，人造皮：a ～ sofa 一张人造革沙发

leathery/ˈleðəri/

*adj.*like leather；hard and stiff 似皮革的；坚韧的：～ meat(skin) 嚼不烂的肉(粗糙的皮肤)

leave/liːv/

Ⅰ *v.*(left)❶ go away(from) 离开；离去：The man has left his hometown.男子已离开了他的家乡。❷ cause to remain or to be in a certain place or condition 剩下；留下；丢下；遗留：He left his book on his desk.他把他的书丢在他的书桌上了。❸ abandon your wife，husband or partner 抛弃(配偶、伙伴)❹ entrust sth. to be kept，collected，etc.寄存；留给：She left a postcard for me.她留给我一张明信片。‖ ～ **about** 乱扔，乱放/ ～ **alone** 撇下；不管/ ～ **aside** 搁置/ ～ **behind** 留下；遗忘/

for 动身到(某处)/ ～ **much to be desired**
不够好;不理想/ ～ **no stone unturned** 千
方百计;竭尽全力/ ～ **off** 停止/ ～ **out**
遗漏;删掉/ ～ **over** 使剩余;遗留/ ～ **it
to chance**(**fate**) 碰运气,听天由命/ ～
word 留下话,留口信 Ⅱ *n*. the permission
(to be absent from duty or work);a period of such absence 准许;准假;假期:He
asked for three days' ～.他请了三天假。
‖ **on** ～ 休假/**take**(**one's**) ～ 告辞,告别

leaven[1]/'levn/
n.❶a substance that is added to flour and
water mixture to make it swell and make
bread 酵母,面肥 ❷ an influence that
causes a gradual change in character 潜移
默化的影响;促使性格渐变的因素

leaven[2]/'levn/
v.❶add leaven to (a cooking mixture,es-
pecially flour and water);cause to puff up
with a leaven 加发酵剂(酵母)于(面粉和
水的混合物);使发酵 ❷ influence or
change gradually 使渐变;改变

leavening/'levnɪŋ/
n.❶ a substance used to produce fermentation in dough or a liquid 发酵剂;发酵
物 ❷a thing which makes sth. different,
especially more cheerful 引起改变的因
素;添趣(增色)的东西:a ～ of humour in
an otherwise serious book 在一本原本严
肃的书中添加一些幽默色彩

leavings/'liːvɪŋz/
n.things that are left or unwanted,espe-
cially food after a meal (尤指食物的)剩
余物,残余

lecture/'lektʃə(r)/
Ⅰ *n*. ❶a talk to a group of people for the
purpose of teaching 讲演;讲课:The professor gives ～s to us once a week. 教授
每周给我们做一次讲演。❷a long angry
talk,especially one given as a reprimand
训斥;教训:The teacher gave the boys in
the class a ～ for smoking.班上的男孩子
因抽烟受到了老师的训斥。Ⅱ *v*.❶give a
lecture (course)演讲;讲课:The professor will ～ on Chinese literature tomor-
row.教授明天讲中国文学。❷scold;re-
prove 责备;批评:She ～d her son for being untidy.她训斥儿子不讲整洁。

lecturer/'lektʃərə(r)/
n.❶a person who gives lectures,especial-
ly at a university or college (大学或学院
中的)讲课者,讲授者 ❷a person who
holds the lowest teaching rank at a
British or American university or college
(英美大学中的)讲师

lectureship/'lektʃəʃɪp/
n.the position of a lecturer 讲师职位:a ～
in mathematics 数学讲师职位

ledger/'ledʒə(r)/
n.a book in which accounts of money are
written 账簿,总账

lee/liː/
n.a place on the side away from the wind,
which gives shelter 背风处:The ship
stayed in the ～ of the island during the
storm.这艘船暴风雨期间停泊在岛后避
风处。

leech/liːtʃ/
n.a type of worm which fastens itself to
the skin and sucks blood 水蛭,蚂蟥

leer/lɪə(r)/
v.look in a cunning or evil way (狡猾地或
不怀好意地)睨视,斜眼瞧:The old man
～ed at the girl.这老头色眯眯地睨视这
姑娘。

leeward/'liːwəd/
Ⅰ *adj*.in the direction towards which the
wind blows 顺风的;在下风方向的 Ⅱ *n*.
the side or direction towards which the
wind blows 下风,下风方向

leeway /'liːweɪ/
n.❶the amount of freedom that is available to move or act 余地:These instructions give us plenty of ～.这些指令给了
我们足够的余地。❷a ship's sideways
drift to leeward of its proper course 偏
航,风压差 ‖ **make up** ～(尤指以挽回失
去时间的方法)摆脱困境

left/left/
Ⅰ *adj*. &*adv*. of, in, on the side of the
body that usually contains the heart 左边
的;在左边:Turn ～ at the crossing.走到
十字路口,朝左拐。/He can write with
the ～ hand.他能用左手写字。/She sits
on my ～ side.她坐在我的左边。Ⅱ *n*.the

location near or the direction toward the side to the north when a person or object faces east 左边 ‖ ～handed *adj*.使用左手的；笨手笨脚的 ‖ ～wards *adv*.在左边；向左边

leftover/leftəurə/

Ⅰ *n*.the food not finished at a meal 吃剩的饭菜 Ⅱ *adj*.remaining after the rest has been used or finished 剩下的，多余的

leg/leg/

n.❶ one of the parts of an animal's or a person's body used for walking；the part of body from hip to ankle 腿：A man has two ～s, but most animals have four.人有两条腿，而多数动物却有四条腿。❷ the support of a chair, table, etc.(家具的)腿：This round table has only three ～s.这张圆桌只有三条腿。‖ on one's last ～s 将死，将失败/have not a ～ to stand on 没有道理；站不住脚/pull one's ～ 开玩笑；愚弄/stand on one's own ～s 自立/stretch one's ～s 散步，溜达 ‖ ~-gings *n*.(*pl*.)护膝；裹腿；绑腿；女式紧身裤/ ～less *adj*.无腿的；醉醺醺的

legacy/'legəsi/

n.❶the money or property left by sb. on his death to sb. else 遗产 ❷anything left from the past 遗留物；传代物：One of the legacies of the war was famine. 战争的后遗症之一是饥荒。

legal/'liːgl/

adj.of or connected with the law；permitted by the law；required by the law 法律(上)的；合法的：We'd better get a ～ adviser.我们最好找一位法律顾问。/one's ～ right 某人的合法权利/a ～ successor 合法继承人/ ～ age 法定年龄/a ～ holiday 法定假日

legalistic/ˌliːgə'lɪstɪk/

adj.placing great importance on keeping exactly to what the law says, rather than trying to understand and act in accordance with its true meaning and intention 墨守法规的；条文主义的

legality/liː'gæləti/

n.the condition of being allowed by law 合法性，法律性：I would question the ～

of the government's decision.我要对政府所做决定的合法性提出质疑。

legalize/'liːgəlaɪz/

v.make sth. legal 使合法化，使得到法律认可：Will the government ～d hemp? 政府要使大麻合法化吗？/～d abortion 人工流产合法化

legation/lɪ'geɪʃn/

n.a group of government officials and diplomats work in a foreign country；the building in which a legation works in a foreign country 公使馆全体人员；公使馆

legend/'ledʒənd/

n.❶ an old story about great deeds and men of ancient times having slight possible base in truth 传说，传奇：the Greek ～s 希腊传说 ❷ the literature of such stories 传奇文学：famous heroes in ～ 传奇文学中的著名英雄 ❸ the inscription on a coin or medal；words on a map, below a picture, etc.(钱币或奖章)的刻印文字；地图的图例；插图说明

legendary/'ledʒəndri/

adj.❶of, like, or told in a legend 传说(中)的，传奇(中)的；传奇式的：～ characters 传奇人物 ❷very famous 非常有名的，大名鼎鼎的：the ～ Elvis Presley 传奇人物埃维斯·普雷斯利/This restaurant is ～ for its fish.这家餐馆以它烹制的鱼而闻名。

leggings/'legɪŋz/

n.coverings, usually made of wool or of strong cloth, leather, etc., worn to keep the lower legs warm, or to protect them 绑腿，裹腿；护腿

leggy/'legi/

adj.(especially of a child, a young animal, or a woman) having long rather thin legs, especially in comparison with the rest of the body (尤指小孩子、小动物或女人)腿细长的：a ～ blonde 两腿修长的金发碧眼女人

legible/'ledʒəbl/

adj.(with reference to handwriting, print, etc.) that can be read easily；clear (指笔迹、印刷字体等)易读的；清楚的：In an examination your handwriting must be

～.在考试中,你的字迹必须清楚易读。

legislate/'ledʒɪsleɪt/
　v.make laws 制定法律,立法:The Senate has ～d against the importation of dangerous drugs.参议院制定法律禁止危险药物的进口。

legislation/ˌledʒɪs'leɪʃn/
　n.the act of making laws;the laws made 立法;法律:Congress has the power of ～.国会有立法权。

legislative/'ledʒɪslətɪv/
　adj.connected with having the power and duty to make laws 有立法权的;制定法律的:a ～ assembly 立法议会

legislator/'ledʒɪsleɪtə(r)/
　n.a maker of laws or a member of a lawmaking body 立法者;议员;立法机关成员

legislature/'ledʒɪsleɪtʃə(r)/
　n.a body of people who have the power to make and change laws 立法机关

legit/lɪ'dʒɪt/
　adj.legitimate;legal 合法的:I promise you,the deal is strictly ～.我向你保证这笔交易绝对合法。

legitimate/lɪ'dʒɪtɪmət/
　adj.correct or allowable according to the law 合法的;正当的;合理的:a ～ government 合法政府/a ～ seat 合法席位/a ～ conclusion 合理的结论/a ～ reason 正当理由 ‖ **legitimacy** n.合法性

legless/'leglɪs/
　adj.❶without legs 无腿的 ❷very drunk 烂醉如泥的

legroom/'legrʊm/
　n.the room enough to position one's legs comfortably when seated 坐下来时放脚处,供伸腿的空间:There's not much ～ in the back of this car.车子后座伸腿的空间不够宽。

legume/'legjuːm/
　n.(the seed of) a plant of the bean family that has its seeds in a pod which breaks in two along its length 豆科植物;荚果;豆荚

legwork/'legwɜːk/
　n.the work that needs much walking or

tiring effort 跑腿活;跑外工作:He leaves someone else to do all the ～ of gathering information while he sits in the office and collates it.他让别人做所有搜集资料的跑腿活,而自己坐在办公室里核对整理这些资料。

leisure/'leʒə(r)/
　n.the time when you are not working and can do what you want 闲暇;空闲时间:I have more ～ on Saturday afternoon.我星期六下午比较空闲。 ‖ at one's ～ 当其空闲的时候 ‖ ～ time (hours) 闲暇时光

leisured/'leʒəd/
　adj.having plenty of free time to do what you enjoy 有空闲的,悠闲自在的:the ～ man 悠闲的男子

leisurely[1] /'leʒəli/
　adj.moving,acting,or done at leisure 从容不迫的;悠闲的;不慌不忙的:a ～ stroll 悠闲的散步/I had a ～ glass of beer.我慢悠悠地品了一杯啤酒。/a ～ affair 一件从容的事

leisurely[2] /'leʒəli/
　adv.without haste or hurry 从容不迫地;悠闲地

lemon/'lemən/
　n.❶a fruit with a light yellow skin and sour juice 柠檬 ❷ the colour of this fruit;the light bright yellow 柠檬色:～ yellow 柠檬色;柠檬黄

lemonade/ˌlemə'neɪd/
　n.a soft drink with a lemon flavour 柠檬汁

lend/lend/
　v.(lent)❶give sth.to sb.for a limited time 借出;把……借给:Banks ～ money and charge interest.银行贷款收息。/Reluctantly I agreed to ～ it to her.我勉强答应把这借给她。 ❷ add or give sth.,especially a quality 增添,给予(品质) ❸provide sb.with help,support,etc. 提供(帮助、支援等) ‖ ～ a hand 帮忙/ ～ an ear to 倾听/ ～ itself 适合/～ oneself to 参与;帮助

length/leŋθ/
　n.the measurement from end to end (in space or time) (空间或时间的)长,长度:

the ～ of a road 道路的长度 ‖ at ～ 最后；终于；详细地/go to all (great) ～s 竭尽全力/go (to) the ～ of 走到……这样的极端；甚至会……

lengthen/'leŋθən/
v.make or become longer 变长；使延长；延伸：～ a skirt 将裙子加长/ The days are ～ing.白天在变长。

lengthways/'leŋθweɪz/
adv.from end to end; along the longest part 纵长地；直地

lengthy /'leŋθi/
adj. (lengthier, lengthiest) very long in time and size (尤指时间)过长的，冗长的 ‖ lengthiness n.冗长

lenient/'liːnɪənt/
adj.not severe in judgment or punishment; gentle 不严的；宽大的；宽厚的：a ～ punishment 轻的处罚/give sb. a ～ sentence 对某人从轻判决/ ～ judges 宽大的法官 ‖ leniency n.宽大；宽厚

lens/lenz/
n.a piece of glass or substance like glass, with one or both sides curved (used in binoculars, cameras, glasses or telescopes, etc.) 透镜(用于双筒望远镜、照相机、眼镜、望远镜等)：He has broken one of the ～es in his glasses.他打破了他眼镜的一个镜片。

lentil/'lentl/
n.❶a type of plant with a small bean 小扁豆(植物)❷the seed of this plant 小扁豆

leopard/'lepəd/
n.a large animal of the cat family which has a yellowish coat with many black spots 豹

leper/'lepə(r)/
n.a person who has the disease of leprosy 麻风病患者

leprosy/'leprəsi/
n.a type of disease which slowly destroys the skin, the flesh underneath and the nerves 麻风病

lesbian/'lezbɪən/
n. a woman who sexually prefers other women to men; homosexual woman 同性恋女子

less/les/
Ⅰ det.not so much; to a smaller quantity of 较小的；较少的：Eat ～ food, or you'll become fat.少吃点，不然你会发胖的。Ⅱ adv.to a smaller extent; not so much 更小地；较少地：You should speak ～ and listen more.你应当少说多听。‖ in ～ than no time 马上，一眨眼工夫/no ～ than 和……一样；不少于；不亚于/still (much, even) ～ 更不必说；何况

lessen/'lesn/
v.❶make or become less, weaker, etc.减少；变少；减轻：～ production costs 减少生产成本/ The symptoms ～ed.症状减轻了。❷cause (sth.) to appear smaller, less important 使变小；贬低：～ the differences between the city and the countryside 缩小城乡差别

lesser/'lesə(r)/
adj.& adv. (not used with than) not so great or so much as the other (of two) in worth, degree, size, etc.更小(的)，更少(的)，较轻(的)：the ～ of two evils 两害之较轻者/one of the ～-known modern poets 比较鲜为人知的现代诗人之一

lesson/'lesn/
n.❶ sth.to be learnt or taught; a period of time given to learning or teaching; a unit of teaching; a part of a subject to be taught or studied at one time 功课；课程；一节课：Everyday you should prepare and review your ～s.你们每天都应当预习和复习功课。❷ sth.learnt from experience 经验；教训：The driver learned a ～ in blood from this traffic accident.司机从这次交通事故中得到了一次血的教训。

lessor/'lesɔː(r)/
n.a person who gives the use of a house, building, or land by a lease to someone else (the lessee) for a certain time, in return for payment 出租人

lest/lest/
conj.❶ for fear that; in order that...not 以免；免得；唯恐：He dare not play jokes on her ～ she should become angry.他不敢跟她开玩笑，因为怕她会生气。❷

that(used after fear, be afraid, be anxious)用于上述词后陈述事件：I fear ～ she decides to leave me.我害怕她会决定离开我。/We were afraid ～ he should arrive too late.我们担心他会到得太迟。

let¹ /let/

v.(let) ❶ allow(to do or happen) 让；允许；听任：His brother didn't ～ him go.他哥哥不许他去。/Open the window and ～ in some fresh air.打开窗户，让新鲜空气进来。❷（used with first and third person pronouns to supply an in-direct imperative 与第一和第三人称的代词连用，形成间接的祈使句）：Let's go for a picnic.我们去野餐吧。/Let her do it at once.让她马上做此事。‖ **～ alone** 更不用说/ ～ … **be** 不打扰；听任/～ **go** 放开；放手/**let it go** 算了/ ～ **in** 放进/ ～ **off** 宽恕；放掉/ ～ **out** 放出，泄露

let² /let/

v. give the use of (a room, a building, land, etc.) in return for rent 出租：This house is to be ～.这幢房屋可供出租。/The flat ～s ＄200 a month.这套房屋出租，每月租金 200 美元。

let-down /'letdaʊn/

n. sth. that is disappointing 失望；令人失望的事：We were going out today, but now it's raining so we can't；what a ～! 我们原打算今天外出，可现在正下着雨使我们无法出去，多叫人失望啊!

lethal /'li:θl/

adj.causing, able to cause death 致命的；可致命的：a ～ blow 致命的打击

lethargy /'leθədʒi/

n. the lack of energy；the feeling of not wanting to do anything 无生气，嗜睡，懒洋洋

letter /'letə(r)/

n. ❶ a written or printed message sent usually in an envelope 书信：There's a ～ for you.你有封信。/a ～ of thanks 感谢信 ❷ any of the signs in writing or printing that represent a speech sound 字母：There are 26 ～s in the English language.英语有 26 个字母。‖ **to the** ～ 不折不扣地 ‖ **red** ～ **day** n.喜庆的日子/～ **box** n.

信箱，邮筒

lettering /'letərɪŋ/

n.❶ the act of writing or drawing letters or words 字母图案绘制术；印字；刻字；烫印：Lettering is this designer's speciality.字母图案的绘制是这位设计师的专长。❷ written or drawn letters, especially of the stated style 手写、印刷或雕刻等的字体：ornate old-fashioned ～ 华丽的老式字体

letterpress /'letəpres/

n. a method of printing in which the words, pictures, etc. to be printed stand a raised area on the printing machine 凸版(活版)印刷

letters /'letəz/

n. literature in general literary knowledge, ability or learning 文学；知识；文化修养：He was one of the foremost figures of(in) English ～ at the turn of the century.他是本世纪初和上世纪末英国文学的重要人物之一。

letting /'letɪŋ/

n.a house or flat that is (to be) rented (要)出租的房屋(公寓)：unfurnished ～s 不配备家具的出租房屋

lettuce /'letɪs/

n.a type of vegetable with green leaves(usually eaten uncooked) 莴苣(通常生吃)

let-up /'letʌp/

n.(a) stopping or lessening of activity 停止；中止；减弱：It rained for twelve hours without (a) ～.雨不停地下了十二个小时。

leucocyte /'lu:kəsaɪt/

n.white blood cell 白细胞

leuk(a)emia /lu:'ki:mɪə/

n. a serious disease in which the blood contains too many white cells 白血病

levee /'levi/

n. ❶ an embankment alongside a river constructed to prevent flooding 防洪堤：the ～s along the Mississippi 密西西比河大堤 ❷a quay 〈美〉码头

level /'levl/

I adj. ❶ flat；smooth；even 平的；水平的：a ～ floor 平整的地板/ ～ ground 平

坦的地面 ❷ equal in height, degree, value, etc. 同高度的；同水平的；同程度的：The tree top is ～ with the roof. 树顶和屋顶一样高。Ⅱ v. (-ll- or -l-) make or become level or flat 使平(坦)；变平：The bulldozer ～ed the mound of earth. 推土机把土堆推平了。/The fire ～ed the buildings to the ground. 这场大火把这些建筑物夷为了平地。Ⅲ n. ❶ the line or surface parallel to the horizon, especially with reference to its height 水平线；水平面；水平高度：3,000 metres above sea ～ 海拔 3 000 米 ❷ a relative position in rank, class or authority 级别；水平：high (low) ～ negotiations 高级别(低级别)谈判 ❸ a particular standard 标准；水准：the advanced world ～s in science and technology 世界先进的科技水平 ‖ do one's ～ best 全力以赴/draw ～ with 与……拉平；同……相齐/find one's own ～ 找到相称的位置/ ～ off 弄平, 整平；变平/on a ～ with 和……同一水准；和……相等/on the ～ 公平地, 坦率地 ‖ ～-headed adj. 头脑冷静的/ ～ crossing n. 道口；(铁路和公路)平面交叉处 ‖ ～(l)er n. 水准测量员；校平器

lever /ˈliːvə(r)/
　Ⅰ n. a bar or other tool turned on a fulcrum to lift sth. or to force sth. open, e.g. a window or drawer 杠杆；撬棍 Ⅱ v. move (sth. up, along into, out of position, etc.) with a lever 用杠杆移动；撬动：The workers ～ed the huge stones into the cavern. 工人们用杠杆将这些巨石撬进了地穴。

leverage /ˈliːvərɪdʒ/
　n. ❶ the action, power, or use of a lever 杠杆作用, 杠杆的力量：We'll have to use ～ to move this huge rock. 我们不得不借助杠杆之力来移动这块巨石。❷ influence; power 力量, 影响：She used political ～ to get that top job. 她利用政治影响获取那项最好的工作。

levitate /ˈlevɪteɪt/
　v. (cause to) rise and float in the air as if by magic (使)轻轻浮在空中, (使)悬浮空中

levity /ˈlevəti/
　n. the behaviour treating serious or important matters lightly or without respect 轻浮, 轻率

levy /ˈlevi/
　Ⅰ v. demand and collect officially 征收, 征集(税等)：The government levies a tax on tobacco. 政府征收烟草税。Ⅱ n. an official demand and collection, especially of a tax 征税, 收税；税款：There were all kinds of taxes and levies in the past. 在过去要征收各种各样的苛捐杂税。

lexical /ˈleksɪkl/
　adj. ❶ to do with the words of a language (与)词汇(有关)的 ❷ to do with a lexicon or dictionary (与)词汇(有关)的, (与)字典(有关)的

lexicography /ˌleksɪˈkɒɡrəfi/
　n. the writing of dictionaries 词典编纂 ‖ lexicographer n. 词典编纂者/lexicographical adj. 词典编纂的

lexicon /ˈleksɪkən/
　n. ❶ the vocabulary of a person, language, or branch of knowledge (个人、语言或学科的)词汇 ❷ a dictionary 词典

liability /ˌlaɪəˈbɪləti/
　n. ❶ the state of being responsible for sth. 责任 ❷ a debt or obligation 负债, 债务 ❸ a handicap or disadvantage 障碍；不利因素：Our goalkeeper is proving a ～. 我们的门将是个不利因素。

liable /ˈlaɪəbl/
　adj. ❶ obliged by law to pay for 有(法律)责任的；应付的：He is ～ for all the damage done by his workmen. 他有责任赔偿他的工人所造成的全部损失。❷ be subject to 易于……的；易患……的：In winter I am ～ to bad colds. 在冬天, 我常患重伤风。

liaise /liˈeɪz/
　v. (especially in the army or in business) make, have, or keep connection, especially so that information can be passed 与……建立(保持)联系：My job is to ～ with foreign clients. 我的工作是与外国客户建立联系。

liaison /liˈeɪzn/
　n. the process of keeping the different

parts of a large organization（especially an army or armies）in touch with each other 合作；（尤指军队或军队间的）联络：Victory depended on close ~ between the American and British armies.胜利取决于美、英军间的密切合作。

liar/ˈlaɪə(r)/
  *n.*a person who tells lies 说谎者

lib/lɪb/
  n.（the abbreviation for liberation）（a movement for）social equality and the removal of disadvantages suffered by particular social groups（liberation 的简写）解放（运动）：women's ~ 妇女解放运动/gay ~ 同性恋解放运动 ‖ ~ber *n.*解放运动者

libel/ˈlaɪbl/
  I *n.*sth. printed or written, etc., which accuses sb. wrongly and so harms him；anything that harms sb. wrongly 诽谤人的图片或文章；诽谤，中伤：Editors of newspapers must be very careful that they do not publish ~s.报纸的编辑必须非常谨慎，不发表诽谤人的文章。II *v.*(-ll- or -l-)publish a libel about sb. (发表文章等)诽谤

liberal/ˈlɪbərəl/
  I *adj.* ❶ favouring some change, as in political or religious affairs 赞成改革的；自由主义的：the Liberal Party of Great Britain 英国自由党 ❷ willing to understand and respect the ideas and feeling of others 宽容的；尊重他人意见的：a ~ thinker 开明的思想家 ❸ willing to give；generous 慷慨的，大方的：He is ~ with his money.他用钱很大方。II *n.*a person with wide understanding, who is in favour of change 开明的人；自由主义者 ‖ ~ist *n.*自由主义者/~istic *adj.*自由主义的/~ize *v.*自由化

liberalism/ˈlɪbərəlɪzəm/
  *n.*liberal opinions and beliefs, especially in politics 自由主义

liberality/ˌlɪbəˈræləti/
  n. ❶ the respect for political, religious or moral views, even if you do not agree with them 开放；开明 ❷ the quality of being generous 慷慨；大方

liberalize/ˈlɪbərəlaɪz/
  *v.*make sth. less strict 使自由化；放宽对……的限制 ‖ liberalization *n.*自由化

liberate/ˈlɪbəreɪt/
  *v.*set free（from control, prison, etc.）解放；释放；获得自由：~ slaves 解放农奴 / ~ the mind from prejudice 解除思想上的偏见

liberation/ˌlɪbəˈreɪʃn/
  *n.*the state of setting free or being set free 解放；获得自由：a war of ~ 解放战争

liberty/ˈlɪbəti/
  *n.*the state of being free from conditions that limit one's actions, so that one can do what one likes without the permission of others；the right or power to do as one chooses 自由；自由权：We will fight to defend our ~.我们将为捍卫自由而斗争。/Liberty or death.不自由，毋宁死。‖ at ~ 自由；有权；有空/take ~（liberties）with 随意对待/take the ~ to do(of doing) 擅自做；冒昧做(某事)

librarian/laɪˈbreərɪən/
  *n.*a person who is in charge of or helps to run a library 图书馆长；图书馆员，图书管理员

library/ˈlaɪbrəri/
  n.（a room or building for）collection of books for reading or borrowing 藏书；图书馆，图书室：a public ~ 公共图书馆/a ~ card 借书证/He has a ~ of over 3,000 books.他有三千多册的藏书。

licence(-se)/ˈlaɪsns/
  I *n.*❶ an official document showing that permission has been given to own, use or do sth.执照；特许证：a ~ to drive a car（a driving ~）驾驶执照 /a ~ to practise as a doctor 医师执照 ❷ formal or official permission to do sth. 许可；准许：marry by special ~ 特许结婚 ❸ the wrong use of freedom 放肆；放纵：The ~ shown by the troops disgusted everyone. 那些部队所表现的放肆使人厌恶。II *v.*give official permission to or for 准许；许可；发给许可证：~ sb.to do sth.准许某人干某事

licensed /ˈlaɪsənst/

adj. ❶ having an official licence 特许的，获得执照的 ❷ (of places) having a licence for the sale of alcoholic liquor（场所）获特许权可出售酒精类饮料的

lick /lɪk/

Ⅰ *v.* ❶ pass the tongue over or under 舔：The cat ~ed the bowl clean. 猫把碗舔干净了。❷ (especially of flames or waves) pass lightly or with rapid movements over or against (a surface)（火焰）卷过，吞没；(波浪) 轻轻拍打：The flames ~ed up the church. 火焰将教堂吞没了。❸ defeat sb.; exceed; surpass 打败某人；超过，超越：Our class ~ed class 3 in a football match. 在一场足球赛中，我们班打败了3班。Ⅱ *n.* ❶ an act of licking with the tongue 舔：He gave the ice cream cone a ~. 他舔了一下蛋卷冰激凌。❷ speed 速度 ❸ a slight use (of paint,, etc.)（颜料等的）施加：The picture will look better with a ~ of paint. 这幅画稍加颜色便会更好看。

licking /ˈlɪkɪŋ/

n. ❶ a severe beating 狠狠的一顿打，痛打 ❷ a heavy defeat 挫折；失败：The other team gave us quite a ~. 另一个队把我们打得惨败。

lid /lɪd/

n. ❶ a top or cover for closing the opening of a box, pot, jar, etc. 盖子：the ~ of a kettle 水壶盖 ❷ an eyelid 眼皮：the upper (lower) ~ 上(下)眼皮

lie[1] /laɪ/

v. (lay, lain) ❶ have or put one's body in a flat or resting position on a horizontal surface 平躺；躺：You are tired. Lie down for a while. 你累了，躺下休息一会儿。❷ (of things) be at rest on a surface 平放：The book was lying open on the desk. 书打开着放在桌上。❸ be situated 位于：The city ~s on the coast. 这个城市位于海边。❹ extend or spread out in a particular place 展现：The valley lay before us. 那个山谷展现在我们的面前。❺ be found; exist 存在；在于：The cure for stress ~s in learning to relax. 消除紧张的方法在于学会放松。‖ ~ behind 是……的含义(动机、原因等)/~ down（on the job）躺下不干；偷懒/ ~ in 在于/ ~ with 取决于/take lying down 甘心接受（失败等）

lie[2] /laɪ/

Ⅰ *v.* (~d) make an untrue statement in order to deceive 说谎，撒谎：Don't ~ to me. 不要对我撒谎。Ⅱ *n.* an untrue statement purposely made to deceive 谎话；谎言：The boy has a bad habit of telling ~s. 那孩子有扯谎的坏习惯。‖ ~ through your teeth 满口谎言 ‖ liar /ˈlaɪə(r)/ *n.* 说谎者

lieu /ljuː/

n. (in ~ of) instead (of) 代替……，作为……的替代：They accept a cheque in ~ of cash. 他们接受支票代替现金。

lieutenant /lefˈtenənt/

n. an army officer below a captain; a junior officer in the navy 陆军中尉；海军上尉

life /laɪf/

n. ❶ the quality that people, animals or plants have when they are not dead 生命；性命；一生：He devoted his ~ to the just cause. 他为正义事业献出了自己的生命。❷ activities and experiences that are typical of a way of living 生活：They are living a quiet ~ in the countryside. 他们在乡下过着安静的生活。❸ living things 生物(总称)：Is there any animal or vegetable ~ on the moon? 月球上有动植物吗？❹ spirit; liveliness; cheerfulness 活力；生气：The children are full of ~. 这些孩子生气勃勃。‖ between ~ and death 生命垂危/a matter of ~ and death 生命攸关的事情/bring to ~ 使苏醒/come to ~ 苏醒过来/for dear ~ (or for one's ~)（为）逃命；拼命地/take one's ~ in one's hand 冒生命危险，冒大险/to the ~ 逼真地/true to ~ 逼真的 ‖ ~belt *n.* 救生带；安全带/~guard *n.* 卫兵；救生员；禁卫军/ ~line *n.* 生命线；命脉/ ~long *adj.* 终身的；一辈子的

lifeblood /ˈlaɪfblʌd/

n. ❶ a person's or animal's blood which is necessary to life 血液 ❷ an influence or force that gives strength and vitality to sth. 生命线；命根子

lifeboat /ˈlaɪfbəut/

*n.*❶a boat specially constructed for going to help people in danger at sea along a coast 救生船(从陆地上下水的特种船只，用于海上救助)❷a small boat carried on a ship for use if the ship has to be abandoned at sea 救生艇

lifebuoy /ˈlaifbɔɪ/
*n.*a device to keep a person afloat in the water 救生圈

lifeless /ˈlaiflɪs/
*adj.*❶without life;not living 死的;无生命的 ❷unconscious 无意识的;失去知觉的;不省人事的 ❸lacking vitality or excitement 无生气的;死气沉沉的 ‖ ~ly *adv.*无生命地

lifelike /ˈlaiflaɪk/
*adj.*looking exactly like a real person or thing 栩栩如生的;逼真的

lifestyle /ˈlaifstaɪl/
*n.*a person's way of living 生活方式

lifetime /ˈlaiftaɪm/
*n.*❶the duration of a person's life (人的)一生;平均寿命 ❷of a thing's existence or usefulness (事物的)存在期;有效期;使用寿命 ❸(informal)a very long time (非正式)漫长的一段时间

lift /lɪft/
Ⅰ *v.*raise to a higher level or position 举起;提升;抬起：～ weights 举重/～ one's head 抬起头/ ～ up one's eyes 抬头;向上看/ ～ up one's voice 提高声音;高呼 Ⅱ *n.*❶ a movement in which sth.is lifted up 举;提升：a ～ in costs 费用的增加 ❷ a boxlike apparatus in a building for taking people up or down to another floor 电梯 ‖ give sb.a ～ 让人搭便车 ‖ ~boy, ~man *n.*开电梯的工人/ ~-off *n.*(飞机等的)起飞/ ~er *n.*举重者;起重机

ligament /ˈlɪɡəmənt/
*n.*a band of strong tissues in the body that holds bones together 韧带

light /laɪt/
Ⅰ *n.*❶the energy from the sun,lamp,etc. that makes things visible 光;光线;光亮：The sun gives ～ and heat.太阳发出光和热。❷sth. that gives light;the source of light,especially an electric lamp 发光体;光源(尤指电灯)：turn (switch) the ～s on(off) 开(关)灯/a traffic ～ 交通灯 ‖ **bring to ～** 让人知道;公之于世/**come to ～** 显露出来,暴露/**in the ～ of** 根据;按照;考虑到/**throw(cast) ～ on** 提供线索;帮助弄清楚 Ⅱ *adj.*❶ having light 明亮的：a ～ room 明亮的房间 ❷ not deep or dark in colour;pale 淡色的;浅色的：a ～ green dress 浅绿色的连衣裙 ❸not heavy 轻的：～ industry 轻工业 ❹gentle 轻柔的：～ touch 轻触 ❺not serious;for amusement 轻松愉快的：～ music 轻音乐 Ⅲ *v.*❶ (cause to) start to burn 点燃;点亮：～ a candle 点蜡烛 / ～ a cigarette 点燃香烟 ❷ give light to 照亮;使亮;变亮：Electricity ～s our houses. 电灯照亮了我们的房屋。 ‖ ～ up 照亮;亮起来;变得高兴起来/**make ～ of** 低估;轻视;小看 ‖ ~hearted *adj.*心情轻松的

lighten /ˈlaitn/
*v.*❶ make or become less heavy;reduce the weight of 使轻;变轻;减轻：～ a ship's cargo 减轻船上的载货 /～ taxes 减轻税收 /Her heart ～ed when she heard the news.她听到这个消息心情变轻松了。 ❷ make light or bright 使亮;使光明：A full moon ～ed our path to the hotel.一轮明月照亮了我们到旅馆去的路。 ❸ become light or bright 变亮;变光明：The eastern sky ～ed.东方的天空亮了。 ❹ send out lightning 闪电：It's thundering and ～ing.雷电交加。

lighter /ˈlaitə(r)/
*n.*a device for lighting cigarettes or cigars;a person or thing that lights 点火者;打火机;引燃器

lighting /ˈlaitɪŋ/
*n.*❶an equipment for providing light to a room,building or street,etc.照明设备 ❷ the effect of lights 灯光效果

lightly /ˈlaitli/
*adv.*❶with little weight or force;gently 轻盈地;轻巧地：leap ～ over a bench 轻巧地跳过板凳 ❷to a slight or little degree;not much 轻微地;少许;不多 ❸with little effort;easily 轻而易举地：It is impossible to get off ～.轻易逃脱是不可

能的。❹without careful thought or reasoning 轻率地,轻浮地:Don't take it ~. 可不能等闲视之。

lightning/'laɪtnɪŋ/

*n.*a flash of bright light produced by natural electricity between clouds in the sky and clouds on the ground, often with thunder 闪电:The ~ has struck a house. 闪电击中了一所房子。

light year/'laɪtjɜː/

*n.*❶a unit of distance equivalent to the distance that light travels in one year, 9.46trillion kilometers 光年 ❷great difference;a long distance 极大差异;极远距离

like[1] /laɪk/

*v.*❶regard with pleasure or fondness; have good feelings about;enjoy 喜爱;喜欢;爱好:He ~s fish. 他喜欢鱼。❷be willing (to) 愿意;想要:I'd ~ you to go with me.我想要你和我一起去。/I don't ~ to disturb you. 我不想麻烦你。‖ do as one ~s 爱怎样就怎样/ if you ~ 如果你愿意

like[2] /laɪk/

Ⅰ*prep*. with the same qualities as 像; 像……一样;与……相似:He climbed the tree ~ a monkey.他像猴子一样爬上了树。‖ feel ~ 想要/ ~ anything 使劲地; 极其/ ~ hell(mad) 拼命地;……得要命/ look ~ 像是……的样子;看来好像/ nothing ~ 什么也不如;完全不像/something ~ 大约;有点 Ⅱ*adj*.similar to another person or thing 很相像的;相似的:The two brothers are very ~.这两兄弟非常相像。

likelihood/'laɪklɪhʊd/

*n.*probability;the chance of sth.happening 可能性:There is a strong ~ of rain tomorrow.明天很可能要下雨。

likely/'laɪkli/

*adj.*❶ that is expected;probable 可能的; 有希望的;合适的:Is he ~ to win the game? 他有可能赢得比赛吗?❷seeming suitable 看上去合适的:He seems the most ~ man for this job.他似乎是这项工作最合适的人选了。

liken/'laɪkən/

*v.*show or say that sth. is like sth. else; compare one to another 把……比作;比喻为:Teachers are often ~ed to gardeners.教师常常被比作园丁。

likeness/'laɪknɪs/

*n.*❶ the fact of being like;resemblance 相似;相像:I can't see much ~ between them.我看不出他们有多相似。❷an instance of being like;a point of resemblance 相似的实例;相似点:a family ~ 一家人的相似处 ❸a portrait, picture or photograph of sb.肖像,画像,相片:You'd better have his ~ painted.你最好把他的照片画出来。

likes/laɪks/

*n.*❶things that one likes 爱好,喜欢的东西:~ and dislikes 好恶;爱憎 ❷(the ~ of) people of the stated type 类似……的人;……的一类人:High-class restaurants aren't for the ~ of us.高级餐厅不是为我们这类人开的。

likewise/'laɪkwaɪz/

*adv.*❶ in the same way; similarly; the same 同样,照样:They went by bike and we did ~.他们骑车去,我们也骑车。❷ also; in addition 也;又:A: Pleased to meet you.B: Likewise.甲:见到你很高兴。乙:我也是。

liking/'laɪkɪŋ/

*n.*a feeling of regard or fondness 喜好: for one's ~ 合……的口味,合……的意

lily/'lɪli/

*n.*a plant growing from a bulb,with large white or reddish flowers 百合,百合花

limb/lɪm/

*n.*❶a leg,an arm,or a wing 肢,臂,手足,翼:escape with life and ~ 逃出而未受重伤 ❷a large branch (of a tree) (树的)大枝

limber/'lɪmbə/

*adj.*flexible or supple 柔软的,易弯曲的 ‖ ~ up *v.*做体操使肌肉柔软;做柔软运动;做准备活动;热身:The runners ~ed up before the race.赛跑者在赛前做准备动作。

limbo/'lɪmbəʊ/

*n.*the state of uncertainty 不稳定,不确定的状态:The plan is in ~ until I decide what to do.这个计划暂搁一旁,等我决定怎么办。

lime/laɪm/

Ⅰ *n.*a white substance used in making cement and mortar 石灰:quick ~ 生石灰 Ⅱ *v.*add or put lime on (fields, etc.) 撒石灰于(田地等中):He drained the land and ~d it.他将地里的水排干,然后再撒上石灰。

limelight/ˈlaɪmlaɪt/

*n.*❶the centre of public attention 公众注意的中心:stay out of the ~ 避免引人注目 ❷ a bright white light produced by heating lime in a strong flame, which was formerly used in theatres to light the stage (舞台照明用的)石灰光(灯),聚光灯

limerick/ˈlɪmərɪk/

*n.*an amusing poem of five lines and having a special rhythm 五行打油诗

limit/ˈlɪmɪt/

Ⅰ *n.*a line or point that may not be passed 边界;界线;限度;极限:Our creative power knows no ~s.我们的创造力是无穷无尽的。Ⅱ *v.* keep below or at a certain point or amount 限制;限定;减少:Limit the expense to what we can afford. 限制开销不超出我们经济能力的范围。‖ go beyond the ~ 超过限度/set a ~ to 限制/there is a ~ to ……是有限的/to the ~ 到了最大限度/without ~ 无限(制)地 ‖ ~less *adj.*无限的

limitation/ˌlɪmɪˈteɪʃn/

*n.*❶ the condition of limiting and being limited 限制,受限制 ❷(*pl.*) the condition, fact, or circumstance that limits;disability or inability 限制的条件、事实或环境;无能力,能力上的缺陷:know one's ~s 知道自己能力有限(有自知之明)

limited/ˈlɪmɪtɪd/

*adj.*small in amount, power, etc., and not able to increase;restricted;narrow 少的;有限制的;(智力方面)狭窄的;有限的:This child has only a ~ intelligence.这个小孩智力有限。

limousine/ˈlɪməziːn, ˌlɪməˈziːn/

n. a large, luxurious motorcar (usually with a separate compartment for the driver) 大型贵重轿车(通常带有司机隔间)

limp/lɪmp/

Ⅰ *adj.*not stiff or firm;lacking strength 柔软的;软弱的;无力的:A starched collar gets ~ if the wearer sweats.如果穿衣的人出汗,浆过的衣领就会变软。Ⅱ *v.* walk lamely or unevenly when one leg or foot is hurt or stiff 跛行,一瘸一拐地走:Wilma ~ed off to school.威尔玛一瘸一拐地上学去了。

line/laɪn/

Ⅰ *n.*❶ a long, narrow mark made by a pen, pencil, etc.线;线条:a straight ~ 直线/a curved ~ 曲线/draw a ~ 画一条线 ❷ a long piece of rope, cord or wire 线;绳;索;金属丝等:a clothes ~ 晒衣绳/a fishing ~ 钓鱼线/a telephone ~ 电话线 ❸ a row of persons or things 行;排:The students stood in several ~s outside the cinema.同学们在电影院外排了几行。❹ a system of railroads, buses or airplanes that carries passengers 线路;(尤指空中或海上的)运输系统:a main (branch) ~ 铁路干线(支线)/an air~ 空中航线;航空公司 Ⅱ *v.*❶ mark with line;draw a line on 画线:Signs of worry ~d her face.忧虑的痕迹刻画在她的脸上。❷ form a line along (sth.) 沿(某物)排成行:Many workers ~d the gate to welcome their new factory director.许多工人都在大门两旁夹道欢迎他们的新厂长。‖ in (out of) ~ with (不)符合;与……(不)一致/in(out of)one's ~ 对……(不)在行/come(fall) into ~ (with……)一致/draw a ~ between 区分;区别开/read between the ~s 从字里行间看出/ ~ up 排队

lineage /ˈlɪniɪdʒ/

*n.*the line of descendants from an ancestor 血统;家族谱系

lineal /ˈlɪniəl/

*adj.*in a direct line of descent or ancestry 直系的:a ~ descendant 直系后代 ‖ ~ly *adv.*直系地;嫡系地

L

linear/ˈlɪnɪə(r)/

adj. ❶of or in a line or lines 线的；直线的：~ design 线形设计 ❷of length 长度的：~ measure 长度；长度单位

linen/ˈlɪnɪn/

n. ❶a type of cloth made from flax 亚麻布 ❷tablecloths, shirts, sheets, handkerchiefs, etc. made from linen or some other cloth (亚麻布或其他布的)桌布、衬衫、被单、手帕等：We must change the ~ on the bed 我们得换床单了。

liner[1]/ˈlaɪnə(r)/

n. ❶a large passenger ship of a steamship company 班轮 ❷an aircraft of a line 班机 ❸ a pencil, brush or material used around the eyes to give a usually dark line 眼线笔

liner[2]/ˈlaɪnə(r)/

n. sth. used for lining; a piece of material used inside another to protect it 衬里，衬垫

lines/laɪnz/

n. ❶ the words learnt by an actor to be said in a play (演员的)台词 ❷a usually stated number of written lines to be copied by a pupil as a punishment (用于惩罚学生抄写的)几行字：The teacher gave me 100 ~. 老师罚我抄写一百行字。 ❸ a poem 诗：Lines on the Death of Nelson 纳尔逊的挽诗

linesman/ˈlaɪnzmən/

n. ❶(in sport) an official helping the referee in certain games, especially in deciding whether or where a ball crosses one of the lines 巡边员；司线员；边线裁判 ❷a man who takes care of railway lines or telephone wires 铁路巡道员；电话线保养员

lineup/ˈlaɪnʌp/

n. ❶ an arrangement of people, especially side by side in a line looking forward 列队；(排列的)一行(排)人 ❷ a line of this sort organized by the police, containing a person thought to be guilty of a crime and looked at by a witness who tries to recognize the criminal (为识别疑犯)警方安排有待辨认的一列人 ❸the (arrange-ment of) players or competitors at the beginning of a race or game (上场运动员)站好位置：There are seven horses in the ~.起跑线上并排着七匹马。 ❹a set of events, following one after another 接连发生的一系列事件：What's next on the ~? 这一系列事件中的下一件又是什么呢？

linger/ˈlɪŋgə(r)/

v. stay for a long time; be late or slow in going away 逗留；徘徊：A stranger ~ed around the house last evening.昨天黄昏时，有个陌生人在这房子周围徘徊。 ‖ ~ing *adj.* 拖延的；留恋的

linguist/ˈlɪŋgwɪst/

n. ❶a person skilled in languages 通晓数国语言的人 ❷a person who makes a scientific study of language(s) 语言学家

linguistic/lɪŋˈgwɪstɪk/

adj. of (the study of) languages 语言的；语言学的，语言研究的

lining/ˈlaɪnɪŋ/

n. (a piece of) material covering the inner surface of a garment, box, etc. (衣服、盒子等的)(一块)衬里，里子：a coat with a silk ~ 绸子衬里的外套

link/lɪŋk/

Ⅰ *n.* ❶ a person or thing that unites or connects to others 联系；联系的人或物；环节：Scientists say that there is a certain ~ between smoking and lung cancer.科学家说吸烟和肺癌之间有某种联系。 ❷ one ring of a chain 链环 ❸the relationship between two countries, organizations, etc.关系，纽带 ❹a means of travelling between two place (道路之间的)连接线 Ⅱ *v.* join or connect 联系；连接；结合：The railway ~s the two cities.这条铁路把这两个城市连接起来了。

linkage/ˈlɪŋkɪdʒ/

n. ❶a system of links or connections 连接；连合；接合 ❷ a connecting relationship (between things or ideas) (事物、思想等的)关联，联系：a ~ between wages and prices 工资和价格之间的联系

linkman/ˈlɪŋkmən/

n. a person whose job is to introduce all

the separate parts of a television or radio broadcast (电视、广播节目的)主持人

links/lɪŋks/

n. a piece of ground on which golf is played 高尔夫球场

link-up/ˈlɪŋkʌp/

n. a connection or joining formed between two things 连接,接合,会合:a live TV ～ between studios throughout Europe 全欧电视实况联播

linocut/ˈlaɪnəʊkʌt/

n. ❶the art of cutting a pattern on a block of linoleum 油毡浮雕艺术 ❷a picture printed from such a block 油毡浮雕印出的图样

linoleum/lɪˈnəʊliəm/

n. a covering for a floor made of canvas, cork and oil 油地毡

linseed/ˈlɪnsiːd/

n. the seed of flax 亚麻子;亚麻仁:～ oil 亚麻子油

lint/lɪnt/

n. a linen fabric with the nap raised on one side, used for covering cuts and wounds (裹伤用的)亚麻布;软麻布

lion/ˈlaɪən/

n. a sort of big, wild animal of the cat family found in Africa and parts of Southern Asia, and also is called the king of beasts 狮:as brave as a ～ 勇猛如狮 ‖ a ～ in the way 拦路虎/the ～'s share 最大或最好的部分/put one's head into the ～'s mouth 置身险境 ‖ ～ess *n.* 母狮/ ～et *n.* 幼狮

lip/lɪp/

n. either of the two fleshy edges of the opening of the mouth 嘴唇:the upper (lower) ～ 上(下)唇/be as close as the ～'s are to the teeth 唇齿相依 ‖ bite one's ～(s) 咬紧嘴唇;欲言又止/button（up）one's ～ 闭嘴/保守秘密/on one's ～s (of) 挂在嘴边;在……中流传/hang on the ～s of 仔细地倾听/pay ～ service to 口头支持

lipstick/ˈlɪpstɪk/

n. a small stick of cosmetic paste, which is set in a case for colouring the lip 口红;唇

膏:She was wearing red ～.她涂着红色唇膏。

liquefy/ˈlɪkwɪfaɪ/

v. become or make liquid (使)液化

liquid/ˈlɪkwɪd/

I *n.* ❶ one of the three main forms of matter;a substance that is neither a solid nor a gas 液体;液态:Water is both a fluid and a ～.水既是流体也是液体。/ Most matter has three states:solid, ～ and gas.大多数物质都有三态:固态、液态、气态。❷ either of the consonants [r] or [l] 流音(如 r,l) II *adj.* ❶ in the form of a liquid;not gaseous or solid 液体的;液态的:～ gas 液态气体 /～ food 流质食品 ❷ clear and clean;like water 清澈的,明亮的;水汪汪的:～ eyes 明亮的眼睛 /a ～ sky 明朗的天空 ❸ (of sounds) clear,pure and flowing (指声音)清脆的;纯正的;流畅的:the ～ song of a wood thrush 画眉的清脆叫声 ❹ easily converted into cash 流动的,易变为现金的:one's ～ assets 某人的流动资产 ❺ not fixed 易变的;不稳的:～ opinions 易变的意见

liquidate/ˈlɪkwɪdeɪt/

v. settle the affairs of a bankrupt business company by selling its property to pay its debts;(with reference to the business) be settled in this way 清盘;清理,清算(破产的公司);了结(债务);结束(业务)

liquidator/ˈlɪkwɪdeɪtə(r)/

n. an official who ends the trade of a particular business,especially so that its debts can be paid 公司资产清理(盘)人

liquidity/lɪˈkwɪdɪti/

n. ❶ the state of having money in one's possession, or goods that can easily be sold for money 流动资产的拥有程度;资产变现能力 ❷the state of being liquid 流动性

liquidize/ˈlɪkwɪdaɪz/

v. crush (especially fruit or vegetables) into a liquid-like form 将(水果、蔬菜等)榨成汁

liquor/ˈlɪkə(r)/

n. ❶ (an) alcoholic drink 酒;酒类;malt

～ 麦芽酒 ❷ liquid produced by boiling or fermenting a food substance 煮汁；发酵而成的汁液

lisp/lɪsp/

Ⅰ *v.* speak incorrectly（especially by saying "th" instead of "s" e.g. "thip" instead of "sip"）口齿不清地说话（尤指将"s"说成"th"例如：将"sip"说成"thip"）Ⅱ *n.* the habit of lisping 口齿不清：The boy speaks with a ～（has a ～）.那男孩说话口齿不清。

list/lɪst/

Ⅰ *n.* a set of names of things written one after the other, so as to remember them or keep them in order that they can be found 名单；目录；一览表；名册：make（draw up）a ～ 造表，列表 Ⅱ *v.* make a list of；put on a list 造表，列于表上，列举：Please ～ my name.请将我的名字列在表上。

listen/'lɪsn/

v. ❶ try to hear；pay attention to 听；倾听：I ～ed but heard nothing.我听了，但没听见什么。❷ tell sb. to notice what you are saying 听着，注意听：Listen, I'm going.听着，我要走了。‖ ～ for 等着听（……的声音）/ ～ in（to…）收听；监听/ ～ to reason 听劝；听讲道理

listener/'lɪsnə(r)/

n. a person who listens 倾听者，收听者

listing /'lɪstɪŋ/

n. a list or catalogue 一览表

listless /'lɪstlɪs/

adj. not having enough energy or interest to do sth. 没精打采的；漠不关心的

literacy /'lɪtərəsi/

n. the ability to read and write 识字，读写能力

literal/'lɪtərəl/

Ⅰ *adj.* ❶ corresponding exactly to the original 完全按照原文的：a ～ translation 直译 ❷ taking words in their usual and obvious sense 按照字义的：a ～ meaning 字面意思 Ⅱ *n.* a mistake in printed matter 印刷错误

literally /'lɪtərəli/

adv. in a literal manner or sense；exactly 按照字面地，逐字地；确切地

literary/'lɪtərəri/

adj. of literature or authors 文学的，作家的：～ works 文学作品

literate/'lɪtərət/

adj. able to read and write 能读能写的

literature/'lɪtrətʃə(r)/

n. a written works which are of artistic value；all the writings of a country or a period 文学作品；(一国或一个时代的)文学：～ and art 文学艺术/We must read a great amount of ～.我们必须阅读大量的文学作品。

litigate/'lɪtɪgeɪt/

v. go to law 诉讼；提出诉讼

litigation/ˌlɪtɪ'geɪʃn/

n. the process of making and defending claims in a court of law 诉讼，起诉

litmus/'lɪtməs/

n. a type of blue substance which is turned red by an acid and then blue again by an alkali, and so used to indicate the presence of these substances 石蕊：～ paper 石蕊试纸

litre/'li:tə(r)/

n. a unit of liquid measure, equal to approximately 1 and 3/4 pints 公升(约合 1 又 3/4 品脱)

litter/'lɪtə(r)/

Ⅰ *n.* ❶ things（to be）thrown away, especially paper scattered untidily 杂物，纸屑等凌乱的东西；废弃物：Pick up the ～ on the ground after the picnic.野餐后把散落一地的杂物收拾好。❷ a group of young animals born at the same time to one mother 一胎所生的许多小动物：a ～ of little pigs 一窝小猪 ❸ straw, etc. used as bedding for animals.动物铺窝的草等 *v.* ❶ scatter；spread；cover untidily 乱丢，乱放：Newspapers and magazines ～ed the floor.报纸杂志丢满一地。❷ supply straw, etc. as bedding for animals. 给(动物的窝)铺草等 ❸ bring forth young 下崽，产仔：The cow is about to ～.这只母牛要产崽了。‖ ～-bin, ～-basket *n.* 垃圾箱

litterbin/'lɪtəˌbɪn/

n. a container for objects to be thrown away, especially in a public place（公共场所的）废物箱

little/ˈlɪtl/

Ⅰ*adj.* ❶ young 幼小的；年轻的：the ～ girl 小女孩 ❷ short（in time, distance, stature）短的：There's ～ time to go. 剩下的时间很少了。❸ small 小的：the ～ finger 小指 Ⅱ*adv.* ❶ not at all；not much 很少；毫不：I ～ know him. 我完全不了解他。/He knows ～ English. 他不懂英语。❷ rarely 很少：I go there very ～. 我很少去那里。Ⅲ*n.* a small amount or duration 少许；少量；一点：You eat very ～. 你吃得太少了。‖ ～ by ～ 一点点地；慢慢地；逐渐地/ ～ or nothing 简直没有/make ～ of 不重视；不以为然；不领会/think ～ of 不重视；对……没多加思索

live¹/lɪv/

v. ❶ be alive 生存；活着：Now many people can ～ to a great age. 现在许多人都可以活到高龄了。❷ have one's home at a place 居住：They ～ under the same roof. 他们住在同一幢房子里。❸ spend or experience sth. in a particular way 过；度过：～ a happy life 过快乐的生活 ‖ ～ and learn 活到老，学到老/ ～ by 靠……维持生活/ ～ from hand to mouth 挣一点吃一点/ ～ in 住校；在工作地方吃住/ ～ off 靠……生活/ ～ on 以……为主食，靠……生活/ ～ through 度过；经受/ ～ up to 做到……；使行为与……相符/ ～ with 与（异性）同居；接受某种局面

live²/laɪv/

adj. ❶ alive；living；full of energy 活的；有生命的；精力充沛的；充满活力的：a ～ fish 一条活鱼/a ～ young man 生气勃勃的年轻人 ❷（of a broadcast）transmitted while actually happening, not recorded or edited 实况转播的；现场直播的：～ TV coverage of the World Cup 世界杯现场直播

liveable/ˈlɪvəb(ə)l/

adj. ❶ worth living 活得有价值的 ❷ suitable for living in 适于居住的；可住的

livelihood/ˈlaɪvlɪhʊd/

n. a means of living；a way in which one earns money 生计；谋生之道：earn（gain,

make）a ～ 谋生

lively/ˈlaɪvɪli/

adj. ❶ gay；full of life and spirit 愉快的，有生气的，活泼的：a ～ imagination 丰富的想象力 ❷（of colour）bright and strong 鲜明的，明快的，艳丽的 ❸ lifelike；realistic；as if real；vivid 生动的；真实的：a ～ description 生动的描述

liven/ˈlaɪvn/

v. become or make lively（使）活泼起来；（使）活跃起来：He ～ed up the class by telling an interesting story. 他讲了个有趣的故事使班级活跃起来。

liver/ˈlɪvə(r)/

n. ❶ a large organ of the body near the stomach 肝；肝脏 ❷ animal's liver as food 肝（食物）：pig's ～ 猪肝

liverish/ˈlɪvərɪʃ/

adj. feeling slightly ill, especially after eating and drinking too much 患病的（尤指暴饮暴食之后）

livestock/ˈlaɪvstɒk/

n. farm animals；domestic animals kept as a source of food and other products 家畜

livid/ˈlɪvɪd/

adj. ❶ of the colour of lead, blue-grey 铅色的；蓝灰色的：a ～ bruise 青肿 ❷（of a person or his looks）furiously angry（指人或面容）狂怒的；怒气冲冲的：～ with rage 气得脸色发青

living/ˈlɪvɪŋ/

Ⅰ*adj.* ❶ alive 活着的；有生命的：a ～ creature 生物 ❷ of or for life；for living in 生活的；维持生活的：They are in poor ～ conditions. 他们的生活条件不好。❸ existing in use 现存的；现代的：～ language 现行的语言 Ⅱ*n.* ❶ a way of life 生活；生活方式：How is their standard of ～ there? 他们在那里的生活水平如何？❷ a means of keeping alive 生存之道；生计：He earns（gains, gets, makes）a ～ as a salesman. 他以当推销员谋生。

lizard/ˈlɪzəd/

n. a type of small, four-legged reptile with a long tail and dry scaly skin 蜥蜴；石龙子

load/ləud/

I *n*.❶ an amount which a cart, etc. can take (车、船装载的)货物;运载量:carry a ～ of wood 运载一车木头/two truck- loads of coal 两卡车煤炭 ❷sth. which is carried or supported;a feeling of care, re- sponsibility,etc.负担;重任:take a ～ off one's mind 消除某人的思想负担 II *v*.❶ put (a load) on or in (a vehicle, struc- ture,etc.) 把……装上车(船等);使承 载;使负荷:They ～ed a cart with coal.他 们把煤装上了车。❷put bullets,etc.into (a gun) or film into (a camera) 装子弹; 装胶卷:He quickly ～ed his pistol and fired.他迅速将手枪装上子弹,开了枪。

loaded/'ləudɪd/

adj.❶ unfairly;favouring one side 偏袒 的;不公正的;有利于一方的:a ～ state- ment 偏袒的说法/The argument was ～ in his favour. 这种说法是偏袒他的。❷ (of a question) put in such a way as to suggest a particular answer (问题)暗示 性或诱导性的 ❸ having lots of money 有很多钱的:Let him pay;He's ～! 让他 付账吧,他有的是钱! ❹ drunk 喝醉了的

loadstar/'ləudstɑːr/

n.❶ the star used as a guide in naviga- tion,especially the polar star 用以指示航 向的星;北极星; ❷a guiding principle 指 导(准则)

loadstone/'ləudstəun/

n.a kind of iron ore that is magnetic 天然 磁石

loaf[1] /ləuf/

n.(*pl*.loaves) a bread shaped and baked in one piece,usually fairly large 一条面包

loaf[2] /ləuf/

v.spend time idly;waste time,especially by not working when one should 浪费时 间,虚度光阴:Don't ～ about. 别到处游 荡。‖～er *n*. 虚度光阴者,游手好闲者, 无业游民

loam/ləum/

n.a good-quality soil made of sand, clay, and decayed plant material 壤土;沃土

loan/ləun/

I *n*.❶ sth. which is lent,especially money 借

出物,尤指贷款:a bank ～ 银行贷款/a long-term ～ 长期贷款 ❷ the act of lending 借出:the ～ of a bike 借出一辆 自行车 II *v*.give (sb.) the use of (sth.); lend 借出,把……借给(某人)使用:The bank only ～s to creditworthy customers. 银行只向信用良好的顾客贷款。

loath/ləuθ/

adj.unwilling (to do sth.) 不愿意的

loathe/ləuð/

v.feel great hate or strong dislike for sth. 厌恶;讨厌;不喜欢:I ～ this job.我讨厌 这个工作。/He ～s travelling by bus.他 不喜欢坐公共汽车旅行。

loathsome/'ləuðsəm/

adj.causing or able to cause nausea;high- ly offensive 讨厌的;令人恶心的

lobby[1] /'lɒbi/

n.❶ a wide hall or passage which leads from the entrance to the rooms inside a public building (公共场所入口处的)大 厅,通道:the hotel ～ 旅馆的大堂 ❷(in the British Parliament) a hall where members of parliament and the public meet (英国议院中的)民众接待厅 ❸a group of people who try to persuade a member of a parliament or public official to support or oppose certain actions (游 说议员或政府官员支持或反对某项行动 的)议院外活动集团:The minister was met by a ～ of industrialists.部长和产业 界院外活动集团见了面。❹a group of people who unite for or against a planned action in an attempt to persuade those in power to change their minds (企图劝说 当权者改变主意以支持或反对某项既定 行动的)群众团体:The clean air ～ is (are) against the plans for the new factory.空 气清洁运动组织反对开办新工厂的计划。

lobby[2] /'lɒbi/

v.meet or attempt to influence (someone with political power) in order to persuade them to support one's actions, needs, or beliefs (向政治上的掌权者)进行游说: They are ～ing for a reduction in defence spending.他们正在进行游说,以期削减 国防开支。

lobe/ləub/

n. ❶the round fleshy piece at the bottom of the ear 耳垂 ❷ a rounded division of an organ, especially of the brain or lungs (脑、肺等的)叶

lobster/ˈlɒbstə(r)/
n. ❶ a shellfish with eight legs and two claws, bluish-black before and scarlet after being boiled 龙虾 ❷ its flesh as food 龙虾肉

local/ˈləʊkl/
adj. of or in a certain place or area, especially the place one lives in 当地的: the ～ news 当地新闻/ ～ government 地方政府 ‖ ～ism *n.* 地方主义;地方观念

locality /ləʊˈkæləti/
n. ❶the position or site of sth. 位置 ❷a district or neighbourhood 地区;地盘;邻近社区

localize /ˈləʊkəlaɪz/
v. ❶restrict sth. to a particular area 使局部化: a ～d infection 局部感染 ❷assign (sth.) to a particular place 定位

locate/ləʊˈkeɪt/
v. ❶ find the place of 找出……的位置: He soon ～d the city on the map.他很快在地图上找到了这个城市。 ❷ place in a certain place; situate 放在某地点;使位于: The university is ～d at the foot of the hill.这所大学位于小山脚下。

location/ləʊˈkeɪʃn/
n. ❶ the act of finding the position of or state of being located 定位,测位 ❷a place or position 位置,地方: It is a suitable ～ for our new school.这是适合我们盖新学校的地方。 ❸a place away from a film studio, where one or more scenes are made for a cinema picture (电影的)外景拍摄地

lock/lɒk/
Ⅰ *n.* an apparatus for closing and fastening sth., usually by means of a key 锁: open (fasten) a ～ 开锁(锁上) Ⅱ *v.* fasten with a lock 锁;锁上: The room wasn't ～ed.房间未锁。 /The box ～s easily.这口箱子容易锁。 ‖ ～, stock and barrel 彻底地;全部地/ ～ away 把……锁起来/～ oneself in 把自己锁在屋里;闭门谢客/ ～

out(of) 锁在外面/ ～ up 锁好;锁上/under ～ and key 妥善地锁藏着;严密监禁着 ‖ ～-chain *n.*锁车链条/ ～smith *n.*锁匠

locker/ˈlɒkə(r)/
n. a box with a lid which can be locked (usually fixed to a wall and used in places where there are many people each of whom can have his own for his clothes, books, etc.) 有锁的小橱柜(通常固定在墙上在公共场所供个人存放衣服、书籍等用): In this school pupils keep their books in ～s.在这所学校里,学生把书存放在有锁的小橱柜里。

locket/ˈlɒkɪt/
n. a small flat box (usually made of gold or silver and hung round the neck on a thin chain) in which there is a picture or some of the hair of a person one loves (装有心爱的人的相片或头发的)小平盒(通常是金或银做的,挂在脖子上)

locus/ˈləʊkəs/
n. ❶ the position or point where sth. happens 位置;地点 ❷ set of points or lines whose location satisfies or is determined by one or more specified conditions 轨迹

locust/ˈləʊkəst/
n. ❶a type of insect which flies from place to place in large groups, often destroying almost all crops 蝗虫 ❷(kinds of)tree, especially carob 洋槐,刺槐

lodge/lɒdʒ/
v. ❶ give or find (someone) a home for a time, usually for payment 提供住宿: The shipwrecked sailors were ～d in the school.那些遭遇海难的船员暂住在学校里。 ❷ stay, usually for a short time in return for paying rent 寄宿: The student ～d at a farmhouse.这个学生寄宿在一户农户家。 ‖ ～r *n.*房客,寄宿者/lodging *n.*寄宿/lodg(e)ment *n.*住宿;寄存;沉积

lodgings/ˈlɒdʒɪŋz/
n. one or more rented furnished rooms 带家具及其他设备的公寓或房间: stay in ～ 住在公寓里

loft/lɒft/
n. the room at the top of a building just

under the roof 阁楼；顶楼

lofty /ˈlɒfti/

adj. ❶ very high and impressive 极高的；高耸的；巍峨的：a ～ mountain (tree, building) 高山（大树、高楼）❷ noble; grand; very proud 高尚的；伟大的；高傲的：a ～ smile 高傲的微笑

log /lɒg/

n. ❶ a long piece of the trunk that has been cut down 原木；木材：a ～ cabin 小木屋/Put another ～ on the fire. 往炉子里再添一段木柴。❷ a daily record of what happens during a ship's voyage 航海日志 ❸ an instrument telling the speed of a ship 测程仪

logarithm /ˈlɒgərɪðəm/

n. the number put in a form which makes calculating easier by using addition and subtraction instead of multiplication and division 对数

loggerheads /ˈlɒgəhedz/

n. (be at ～) an argue or quarrel with someone 与（某人）争辩；与（某人）不和：She and her husband are always at ～. 她和丈夫总是争吵。

logic /ˈlɒdʒɪk/

n. the science and methods of reasoning 逻辑；推理：dialectical ～ 辩证逻辑/formal ～ 形式逻辑/Might is right—that is the ～ of imperialism. 强权即公理——这是帝国主义的逻辑。

logical /ˈlɒdʒɪkl/

adj. ❶according to the rules of logic 符合逻辑的：a ～ argument 合乎逻辑的论点 ❷having or showing good clear reasoning; sensible 推理正确的；合理的：the ～ thing to do 按理应做的事/It's ～ that people who earn more money should pay higher taxes. 挣钱多的人应该缴纳更多的税，这是合情合理的。

logically /ˈlɒdʒɪkli/

adv. ❶in a logical way 在逻辑上；合理地：Think ～. 按逻辑推想。❷according to what is reasonable or logical 按照逻辑，按理而论：Logically, one should become wiser with experience, but some people never do! 照理来说，一个人应该经验越多就越聪明，可有的人就不是这样！

logician /ləˈdʒɪʃn/

n. a person who studies or is skilled in logic 逻辑学家

logistics /ləˈdʒɪstɪks/

n. ❶the planning and organization that is needed to carry out any large and difficult operation 后勤（工作）；（大规模复杂行动的）计划和组织：The ～ of supplying food to all the famine areas were very complex. 为向所有遭受饥荒的地区提供食物而作的计划和后勤工作是非常复杂的。❷the study or skill of moving soldiers, supplying them with food, etc. （部队的）调动（供应等）技巧；后勤学

logjam /ˈlɒgdʒæm/

n. ❶ tightly-packed mass of floating logs on a river （河流输送木材时出现的）木材堵塞 ❷ a difficult situation that prevents one from continuing；an impasse 僵局

logo /ˈlɒgəʊ/

n. a symbol or other small design adopted by a company or an organization to identify its products, uniform, vehicles, etc. （公司或机构的）徽标，标志

logrolling /ˈlɒgˌrəʊlɪŋ/

n. the practice of giving praise or help to someone's work in return for receiving the same 相互吹捧（支援）

logy /ˈləʊdʒi/

adj. of or being a dull heavy feeling that produces a lack of activity 迟钝的，无精打采的：I'm feeling rather ～ after all that eating and drinking last night. 在昨天夜里那样吃喝之后，我感到无精打采，一点力气也没有。

loin /lɔɪn/

n. (usually *pl.*) ❶ the lower part of the back between the hipbones and the ribs 腰 ❷the front part of the hindquarters of beef, lamb, veal, etc.（牛、羊、小牛等的）腰肉

loiter /ˈlɔɪtə(r)/

v. go slowly and stop frequently on the way somewhere；stand about；pass (time) thus 闲逛；徘徊；无所事事：Two men were ~ing near your house.有两个人在你家附近徘徊。/Don't ~ your time away.不要虚度光明。‖ ~er n.闲逛的人；混日子的人/ ~ingly adv.懒散地；吊儿郎当地

lollipop/'lɒlɪpɒp/
　n.a type of sweet at the end of a stick 棒棒糖：The child was licking a ~.那孩子在舔吃棒棒糖。

lone/ləʊn/
　adj.❶without other person or things 独自的；孤独的；孤单的 ❷without a husband or wife 单亲的：She is a ~ mother.她是一位单亲母亲。‖ ~some adj.感到寂寞的；渴望伴侣的，孤单的

lonely/'ləʊnli/
　adj.❶ by oneself；by itself；without others near 独自的；孤独的：He was ~ because there were no other boys to play with.他感到孤独，因为没有其他男孩和他玩。❷ (of places) not often visited；far from inhabited places （地方）偏僻的；偏远的：He lives in a ~ house far away from the village.他住在远离村子的一栋孤立的房子里。

long[1]/lɒŋ/
　I adj.❶ (of extent in space) measuring much from end to end （指空间）长的；远的：How ~ is the Nile River? 尼罗河有多长？/ He has come a ~ way.他远道而来。❷having a great or specified duration or extent in time （时间上）长的；久的：How ~ are the holidays? 假期有多长？/He has been ill for a ~ time.他病了很久了。‖ adv.a long time 长时间地；长久地：stay ~ 久留/wait ~ 久等 ‖ n.a long time 长时间：It won't take ~ to get there.到那里用不了多长时间。‖ as ~ as 长达……；只要/before ~ 不久以后/ ~ after 很久以后/in the ~ run 长远来说；最后，最终/no ~ er (not any ~ er) 不再/(put on) a ~ face 不高兴的样子/so ~ 再见/the ~ and the short of it 事情的原本本；总之 ‖ ~bow n.大弓/ ~-distance adj.远程的；长途的/ ~-legged adj.长腿的/ ~-range adj.远程的；长远的/ ~-term adj.长期的/ ~-tested adj.久经考验的/ ~-tongued adj.

长舌的；话多的

long[2]/lɒŋ/
　v.want sth. very much 渴望；极想：The people are ~ing for peace.人民渴望和平。/I'm ~ing to see you.我想想见你。

longevity/lɒn'dʒevɪti/
　n.long life 长寿，长命

longing/'lɒŋɪŋ/
　I n.a feeling of wanting sth.；a strong wish 渴望：have a ~ for sth.渴望某物 II adj.showing a strong wish 露出渴望的：with ~ eyes 以渴望的眼神

longitude/'lɒndʒɪtjuːd/
　n.the position on the earth east or west of a meridian, usually measured in degrees, from Greenwich 经度：the east(west)~ 东(西)经

longitudinal/lɒndʒɪ'tjuːdɪnl/
　adj.❶measured lengthways 纵向的 ❷to do with longitude （与）经度（有关）的 ‖ ~ly adv.长度上，经向；经度上

longlived/lɒŋ'lɪvd/
　adj.living or lasting a long time 长寿的；历时长久的，经久耐用的：a ~ family 长寿家庭/a ~ friendship 永恒的友谊

longsighted/lɒŋ'saɪtɪd/
　adj. able to see objects or read things clearly only when they are far from the eyes 远视的

longstanding/lɒŋ'stændɪŋ/
　adj.having existed in the same form for a long time 持续长时间的；耐久的：a ~ trade agreement between the countries 两国之间的长期贸易协定/the ~ rivalry between these two football clubs 两个足球俱乐部之间的长期竞争

long-suffering/lɒŋ'sʌfərɪŋ/
　adj.patient in spite of continued difficulty, especially bad or annoying treatment from another person（长期）耐心忍受的：Although he keeps leaving her, his ~ girlfriend always takes him back.尽管他屡次离开她，但耐心的女友总是把他接回来。

longwinded/lɒŋ'wɪndɪd/
　adj. (of a person, speech, piece of writing, etc.) going on too long and using too

L

many words（人）唠叨的；（演讲、文章）冗长的：That was the most ~ speech I've ever had to sit through! 那是我迄今为止不得不勉强听完的最冗长的一次演讲！

look/lʊk/
I v.❶ turn or fix one's eyes in order to see；try to see 看；望：The teacher asked us to ~ at the blackboard.老师要我们看着黑板。/Look before you leap.三思而后行。❷ appear to be；seem 看上去；似乎：They ~ healthy and strong.他们显得健康强壮。❸ search for；try to find 搜寻；寻找：I'm ~ing for my pen.我在找我的钢笔。❹ pay attention to 注意，留心：Look! It's dangerous.小心！这很危险。II n.❶ an act of looking 看：Let me have a ~ at your garden.让我看看你的花园。❷ the appearance of sb. or sth.；an expression on the face 外表；外观；脸色；眼神：Our hometown has taken on a new ~.我们的家乡换上了新貌。‖ ~ about 四下环顾/ ~ at 看；看待/ ~ back（to or upon）回顾（……）/ ~ down 向下看，俯视/ ~ down upon 看不起；轻视/ ~ for 寻找；期待/ ~ forward to 盼望/ ~ in（on sb.）顺便看望（某人）/ ~ into 向……里面看；调查/ ~ on（as）观看；看待；视为/ ~ out 留神；提防/ ~ over 察看；检查/ ~ through 看穿；仔细查看/ ~ up 向上看；仰望；（在词典等）查寻/ ~ to 照管；注意；指望

lookout/'lʊk'aʊt/
n.❶ a place from which you can keep watch 观察所；瞭望台 ❷ a person whose job is to keep watch 守望员 ❸ looking out or watching for sth. 注意；观察：Be on the ~ for pickpockets.小心扒手。❹ a future prospect 前景 ❺（informal）a person's own concern（非正式）自己的考虑，自己的事：If he wastes his money, that's his ~.如果他浪费他的钱，那是他自己的事。

loom/luːm/
I n. a machine for weaving cloth 织布机：a hand ~ 手工织布机 II v. appear indistinctly or in a threatening way 隐约出现；赫然临近：A figure ~ed（up）out of the

mist.一个人影在薄雾中隐约出现了。/War ~s ahead.战争迫在眉睫。

loop/luːp/
I n.❶ a shape produced by a curve（crossing itself）环；圈：enclose with a ~ 围成圈 ❷ a railway or telegraph line that separates from the main line farther on（铁轨或电报线之间）环状侧线；回车道；回线 II v. form or bend into a loop or loops 打环；结成圈：~ the curtains up 把窗帘卷起来

loophole/'luːphəʊl/
n. the way of escaping from a law, restriction, etc.漏洞：Wealthy people often look for ~s in the tax laws.富人常常寻找税法中的漏洞。

loose/luːs/
adj.❶ free；not held, tied up, fastened, packed, or contained in sth.松开的；未受束缚的：The dog is too dangerous to be left ~.那狗太危险，不可放开。❷ moving more freely than usual 不牢；松弛的：~ tooth 松动的牙齿 ❸（of clothes）not tight 不紧；宽松的：~ collar 宽松的衣领 ‖ get ~ 松开了/break ~ 挣脱/let ~ 释放；放出/cut ~ 不受控制；摆脱约束/play fast and ~ with 玩弄（感情）；对……不负责任/turn ~（螺丝等）松掉 ‖ ~-leaf n.活页/ ~-tongued adj.饶舌的；随口乱说的

loosely/'luːsli/
adv.❶ in a way that is not firm or tight 宽松地；松散地：Tom fastened the belt ~ around his waist.汤姆把皮带松松地系在腰上。❷ in a way that is not exact 不精确地

loosen/'luːsn/
v.❶ become or make loose 变松；放松；放宽：The screw has ~ed.这颗螺钉松了。❷ make sth. weaker 使变弱，减轻：This medicine may ~ your cough.这种药可以减轻你的咳嗽。

loot/luːt/
I n. the property which is stolen or taken illegally by force 赃物；掠夺物：The thieves were caught with their ~ by the police.警察抓住小偷并缴获赃物。II v.

steal things from 掠夺；强夺：The angry crowd ~ed the shops.愤怒的人群洗劫了商店。

lop/lɒp/

v.(-pp-)(with **off** or **away**) cut easily(especially the end or top of sth.)（与 off 或 away 连用）砍去（尤指某物的末端或顶端）：He ~ped off the small branches of the tree.他砍掉了树的小分枝。

lord/lɔːd/

n.❶ a peer；a nobleman 贵族；贵族的尊称：the House of Lords (英国)贵族院；上议院；live like a ~ 过上贵族似的奢华生活 ❷a supreme male ruler 君主；最高统治者：our sovereign ~ the King 国王陛下 ❸(**Lord**) God；Christ 上帝；基督：Lord bless me! 老天保佑! ‖ ~**ly** n.贵族的；气派十足的；高傲的/ ~**ship** n.贵族身份

lore/lɔː(r)/

n.learning or knowledge（especially passed by the older people to the younger）（尤指老人传给年轻人的）学问，知识：In the past every young man learnt the ~ of his tribe.过去每个青年人都学习本部落先辈传下的知识。

lorry/ˈlɒri/

n.a large motor vehicle for carrying big goods 运货汽车，卡车

lose/luːz/

v.(lost) ❶ have sth. or sb. taken away from one by accident, misfortune, old age, death, etc.失去，遗失，丧失：The man lost his job. 这人失业了。 ❷ fail to win 输：They lost the game. They lost to Italy.这场比赛他们输了，他们输给了意大利队。 ❸ be or become worse off 减少；损失；亏本：He has lost a lot of money on the transaction. 他在这场交易上亏了很多钱。 ‖ **be lost in** 消失；陷入(沉思等)/ ~ **face** 丢脸/ ~ **heart** 灰心；泄气/ ~ **no time** 立即/ ~ **one's head** 惊惶失措；失去控制/ ~ **one's heart to** 爱上/ ~ **one's temper** 发脾气/ ~ **one's way** 迷路/ ~ **oneself** 迷失方向/ ~ **oneself in** 迷上；陷入；聚精会神（做……）/ ~ **out** 输掉；失败/ ~ **sight of** 看不见了/ ~ **touch**(**contact**) **with** 和……失去联系/ ~ **track of**

不知……的情况或下落/ ~ **weight** 减轻体重

loser/ˈluːzə/

n.❶ a person or thing that loses or has lost sth.，especially a game or contest（尤指游戏或竞赛）失败者 ❷a person or thing that is put at a disadvantage by a particular situation or course of action.处于不利地位的人（物）

loss/lɒs/

n.❶ the act or fact of losing possession (of sth.) 丧失；遗失，丢失：~ of health 丧失健康 /~ of money 丢钱 ❷ a person, thing, or amount that is lost or taken away 失去的人（物）；损耗量：His death was a great ~ to his friends.他的去世对他的朋友来说是个重大损失。 ❸ the money that has lost by a business 亏损：profit and ~ 盈利和亏损

lost/lɒst/

adj.❶no longer possessed；that cannot be found 丢失的；失去的，丧失的：~ paradise 失去的天堂 ❷not used，obtained，or won 错过的；未获得的；输掉的：~ time 浪费掉的时间 ❸ destroyed；ruined；killed；drowned，etc.遭难的，死了的：a ~ ship 沉没了的船 ❹having gone astray 迷途的：She is like a ~ lamb.她像一只迷途的羔羊。

lot[1]/lɒt/

n.a great quantity，number，or amount 很多，许多：a ~ of time（money，people，etc.）很多时间(钱、人等) /~s of clothes (food，goods) 很多衣服(食品、货物)

lot[2]/lɒt/

n.any of a set used for making a choice or decision by chance 抽签；抓阄：draw (cast) ~s 抽签/It was settled by ~.这事就靠抽签解决了。

lotion/ˈləʊʃn/

n.a type of liquid rubbed on the skin or hair to cure a disease or improve one's appearance 洗液，洗剂；护肤液；护发剂：Women use many kinds of skin ~.妇女们使用多种护肤液。

lottery/ˈlɒtəri/

n.an arrangement to give prizes to holders

of numbered tickets previously bought by them and drawn by lot 抽彩给奖法：～ tickets 彩票/～ wheel 摇奖机

lotus /ˈləʊtəs/
n. any of several water lilies of tropical Africa and Asia（热带非洲和亚洲的）莲，荷花

loud /laʊd/
adj. having or producing great strength of sound; not quiet or soft; easily heard 高声的，吵闹的: a ～ voice 一个高昂的声音/ The machine was too ～. 这台机器的声音太吵了。‖ ～-hailer n. 扩音器

loudspeaker /ˈlaʊdˈspiːkə/
n. a device that converts electrical signals into audible sound, especially one used as part of a public address system 扬声器，喇叭

lounge /laʊndʒ/
I n. ❶ a comfortable room for sitting in, as in a house or hotel 休息室；接待室 ❷ a sitting-room, with comfortable chairs, in a private house（私宅中的）起居室 Ⅱ v. stand, sit in a lazy manner; pass time doing nothing 懒洋洋地站（坐）；吊儿郎当地混时间: ～ on a sofa 懒洋洋地靠在沙发上 ‖ ～r n. 闲逛的人；懒洋洋的人

louse /laʊs/
n.（pl. lice）any of several types of small insect that live on the skin and in the hair of people and animals, especially when they are dirty 虱

lousy /ˈlaʊzi/
adj. ❶ very bad, unpleasant, useless, etc. 非常糟糕的，令人作呕的；无用的: What ～ weather! 糟透的天气! ❷ filled (with) 充满（满是）……的: The town was ～ with tourists. 镇上挤满了游客。❸ having plenty of（especially money）（尤指钱）多的 ❹ covered with lice(louse) 多虱的，布满虱子的

louvre (-er) /ˈluːvə(r)/
n. an arrangement of narrow sloping bands of wood, plastic, metal, etc., fixed in a frame that swings across a window, doorway, etc., especially to allow some light in but keep rain or strong sunlight out 百叶板窗，固定百叶窗，通气窗

love /lʌv/
I v. ❶ have a strong affection for 爱；热爱: We ～ our country. 我们热爱祖国。/ Love me, ～ my dog. 爱屋及乌。❷ like very much; take pleasure in 喜爱；很喜欢: The girl ～s playing the piano. 这女孩爱弹钢琴。Ⅱ n. ❶ a strong emotion of regard and affection 爱；爱情: He fell in ～ with the girl. 他爱上了那女孩。❷ a person or thing that you like very much 心爱之人（物）: Football is his first ～. 足球是他的第一爱好。‖ be in (out of) with 跟……恋爱（不爱……）/ fall in ～ with 爱上/ for the ～ of 看在……面上/ give(send) one's ～ to 向……问好/ make ～ to 向……求爱/ for ～ or money 无论如何

lov(e)able /ˈlʌvəbl/
adj. deserving, causing, or worthy of love; pleasant; attractive 可爱的，惹人爱的

lovely /ˈlʌvli/
adj. ❶ beautiful; attractive; pleasant 美丽的，动人的，可爱的: a ～ woman 一位美丽的女人 ❷ enjoyable; amusing 令人愉快的，有趣的: What a ～ joke! 这个笑话多有趣!

lover /ˈlʌvə(r)/
n. ❶ a person who is fond of or devoted to (sth.) 爱好者: a ～ of horses 马匹的爱好者 ❷ man and woman in love 相爱中的男女，情侣: a pair of ～s 一对情侣 ❸ a man in love with or having a sexual relationship with a woman outside of marriage（指男性）情人，情夫

lovers /ˈlʌvəz/
n. two people in love with and (or) having a sexual relationship with each other 爱侣，情侣: They met in June and became ～ soon after. 他们在六月相遇，不久就成了情侣。

lovesick /ˈlʌvˌsɪk/
adj. sad or ill because of unreturned love 害相思病的，因失恋而悲伤（憔悴）的: a ～ poet 害相思病的诗人

lovey /ˈlʌvi/
n. a word used to address a person friend-

ly,especially a woman or child（尤用作对妇女或儿童的称呼语）亲爱的；宝贝：Come here,～!到这里来,宝贝!

loving/ˈlʌvɪŋ/

adj.showing or expressing love 表示爱意的,钟爱的:a ～ look 钟爱的一瞥/a ～ father 慈爱的父亲 ‖ ～**ly** *adv*.亲切地;钟爱地:They were looking at each other ～ly.他们充满爱意地对望着。/He polished his new sports car ～ly.他十分爱护地擦亮他那辆新跑车。

low/ləʊ/

Ⅰ *adj*.❶ not high;not extending far upwards 低的;矮的:a ～ house 低矮的房屋/a ～ price 低廉的价格 ❷ (of sounds) not loud;not high in pitch（声音）低的,小的:speak in a ～ voice 低声地讲话 ❸ below others in status,etc.低下的,次要的 ❹ weak and depressed 沮丧的,消沉的:Lucy is in ～ spirits today.露西今天精神不佳。Ⅱ *adv*.in or to a low position,point,degree,manner,etc.向下;在下面:bow ～ to sb.向某人深深地鞠躬 ‖ bring ～ 使跌落;使恶化/feel ～ 情绪不高/lay ～ 使倒下;打死;卧床/lie ～ 躲藏/run ～ 快用完了

lower/ˈləʊə(r)/

v.❶ (cause to) become less high;bring down（使）降低,（使）减低;降下,落下,放下:They ～ed the flag at sunset.他们在日落时将旗子降下。/This shop has ～ed its prices.这家商店已降低了价格。❷ make less or lower 减少;使减弱,削弱:You must ～ your voice.你必须把声音放低。/I ～ed the pressure in the tyre.我把轮胎的压力减小了。

lowly/ˈləʊli/

adj.low in social position;not proud;simple 社会地位低的;谦逊的;平凡的;简单的

loyal/ˈlɔɪəl/

adj.true and faithful（to）忠诚的;忠贞的:She was a true pioneer and my ～ friend.她是一个真正的探险家——我忠诚的朋友。

loyalty/ˈlɔɪəlti/

n.the quality or conduct of being loyal;

loyal conduct 忠诚;忠心

lozenge/ˈlɒzɪndʒ/

n.❶ a four-sided figure in the shape of a diamond 菱形 ❷ a small tablet containing medicine which is sucked（usually to cure a sore throat）供含食的小药片（通常用于治疗咽喉炎）

lubricant /ˈluːbrɪkənt/

n.a substance such as oil or grease for lubricating an engine,,etc.润滑剂;润滑油

lubricate/ˈluːbrɪkeɪt/

v.put oil or grease into（machine parts）加润滑油:～ the gears of a car 在车的齿轮上加润滑油

lucid/ˈluːsɪd/

adj.❶ clear;easily understood 清楚的;易懂的:He gave a ～ description of what happened.他对所发生的事情做了清晰的描述。/He has a ～ brain.他头脑清楚。❷ sane;fully conscious（usually between periods of insanity or unconsciousness）神志正常的;完全清醒的（通常指神经错乱或昏迷之间的清醒时间）:in his ～ moments 在他神志清醒的时候。/He was ～ for a few minutes before he lost his senses again.他清醒了几分钟后又昏迷了过去。 ‖ ～**ly** *adv*.透明地;清晰地;/ ～**ity** *n*.明朗;清澈;清醒

luck/lʌk/

n.chance;fortune（good or bad）;sth. that is considered to come by chance 运气;侥幸:Wish you good ～! 祝你好运! ‖ be down on one's ～ 运气不佳;倒霉/for ～ 为了带来好运/in(out of) ～ 运气好(不好)/try one's ～ 碰运气

lucky/ˈlʌki/

adj.❶ having a good luck 好运气的,走运的:You're ～ to own a car.你有一辆小汽车,真走运。❷ bringing good luck 带来好运的;吉祥的,吉利的:a ～ number 吉利数字

lucre/ˈluːkə(r)/

n.money or profit 钱财;利润:filthy ～不义之财

luff/lʌf/

v.bring the front of a sailing boat closer to or directly facing the wind 转船首迎风

行驶,抢风行驶

lug/lʌg/
v.(-gg-) pull with force；drag roughly or with effort 用力拉,使劲急拖：They ~ged the boxes across the field.他们吃力地把箱子拖过场地。

luggage/ˈlʌgɪdʒ/
n.boxes, bags, etc. for travelling；baggage 行李：three pieces (articles) of ~ 三件行李 /personal ~ 随身行李；小件行李 / check one's ~ 存行李；打行李票

lull/lʌl/
Ⅰ v.(cause to) become quiet slowly（使）慢慢安静下来,（使）缓和：During the night the wind ~ed.风在夜间逐渐停了下来。/She ~ed the baby to sleep.她哄婴儿入睡。Ⅱ n.a period of quietness in a storm or when there is noise and activity（风暴、喧嚣、活动的）停歇时期,间歇,暂停：There was a ~ in the storm.风暴已暂停了。/During the holidays there was a ~ in business.假日期间生意暂时停歇。

lullaby/ˈlʌləbaɪ/
n.a song sung to a child to lull it to sleep 摇篮曲,催眠曲

lumber/ˈlʌmbə(r)/
Ⅰ n.❶useless or unwanted articles stored away or taking up space（e.g. old furniture）无用的杂物（如旧家具）❷roughly prepared wood；wood that has been sawn into planks, boards, etc.木材,木料,木板 Ⅱ v.cut trees or wood into timber 伐木,制材

luminous/ˈluːmɪnəs/
adj.giving light；shining；clear 发光的,发亮的；照耀着的；清楚的：The clock has a ~ face .这时钟有夜光钟面。

lump/lʌmp/
Ⅰ n.❶ a piece of hard or solid mass 团；块：a ~ of clay（rock, ice, sugar）一块泥土（石头、冰、糖）❷ a hard swelling in part of the body 肿块；疮：a ~ on one's head 头上的疱 Ⅱ v.❶ form into a lump（使）成块（团）：The milk powder has ~ed.奶粉成坨了。❷ walk or move along in a heavy way 笨重地走或动：The bear ~ed its huge bulk about.那只熊挪

动笨拙的身子来回走动。

lumpy/ˈlʌmpi/
adj.filled or covered with pieces 多块的：This sauce is rather ~.这种酱汁里面的结块不少。/a ~ mattress 疙疙瘩瘩的褥垫

lunar/ˈluːnə(r)/
adj.of, for, or to the moon 月亮的；与月亮有关的；阴历的：a ~ eclipse 月食/ calendar 阴历/the Lunar New Year 阴历新年

lunatic/ˈluːnətɪk/
Ⅰ adj.mad, crazy or stupid 疯的,疯狂的 Ⅱ n.a person who is mad 疯子；狂人

lunch/lʌntʃ/
n.a meal between breakfast and supper；midday meal 中餐,午饭：They were at ~ when I called.我去喊他们的时候他们正在吃午饭。‖ ~time n.午餐时间

luncheon/ˈlʌntʃən/
n.a rather formal lunch 午餐（较为正式）

lung/lʌŋ/
n.one of the two organs of breathing in animals and humans 肺

lunge/lʌndʒ/
Ⅰ n.a quick, forward movement of the arm and body（especially with a sword or other weapons）（身体或手臂一起的）向前猛冲；（尤指用剑或其他武器的）刺,戳 Ⅱ v.make a sudden forward movement 冲刺；猛击：He ~d at me with his stick.他用手杖向我猛戳过来。

lurch/lɜːtʃ/
v.stagger；lean or roll suddenly 突然倾斜；蹒跚而行：The bus ~ed.汽车突然偏向一边。/The drunken man ~ed across the road.那醉汉摇摇摆摆地穿过了马路。

lure/lʊə(r)/
Ⅰ v.attract or tempt, especially away from what one should do into sth. one should not 引诱,诱惑：~ sb. away from（work, home, etc.）引诱某人离开（工作、家等）/ ~ sb.into（a trap）引诱某人落入（陷阱、圈套）Ⅱ n.a piece of equipment, such as a plastic bird or fish, to attract animals into a place where they can be caught；decoy 吸引人的东西；诱惑物,诱

饵：the ～ of money 金钱的诱惑

lurid/ˈlʊərɪd/

*adj.*❶brightly coloured（especially light yellow like a flame）颜色鲜明的（尤指似火焰的淡黄色）❷shocking and unpleasant 惊人的；恐怖的；令人不愉快的：He told us many ～ stories about the war.他跟我们讲了许多有关战争的恐怖故事。

lush/lʌʃ/

*adj.*❶（of plants, especially grass）growing very well；thick and healthy（植物，尤指草）茂盛的，葱翠的：～ meadows 青草繁茂的草原 ❷ luxurious and making you feel comfortable 豪华舒适的：a ～ hotel 豪华舒适的旅馆

lust/lʌst/

Ⅰ *n.*❶ strong sexual desire 色欲，淫欲：curb one's ～ 节欲 ❷ intense desire for sth.or enjoyment of sth.渴望；贪求：a ～ for power 对权力的欲望 Ⅱ *v.* feel a strong desire for sb.or sth.贪求；渴望：～ for gains 贪利 /～ after a woman 好色

lustre(-er)/ˈlʌstə(r)/

n. the shining quality of sth.（e.g. of polished metal, smooth cloth, etc.）（抛光的金属、平滑的布料等的）光泽，光亮

lustrous/ˈlʌstrəs/

*adj.*shining；brilliant 光亮的，有光泽的：～ black hair 光亮的黑发

lusty/ˈlʌsti/

*adj.*strong；vigorous 强壮的；精力充沛的

luxuriant/lʌɡˈʒʊərɪənt/

*adj.*growing thickly in great quantity 茂盛的；大量的：After the rains the grass is ～.雨后青草长势茂盛。

luxurious/lʌɡˈzjʊərɪəs/

*adj.*supplied with luxuries；very comfortable 奢侈的，豪华的；极其舒适的

luxury/ˈlʌkʃərɪ/

*n.*❶ the great comfort, as provided by wealth 奢侈；豪华：He lives in ～.他过着奢侈的生活。/a ～ car 豪华轿车 ❷ a pleasant and often expensive thing that is not necessary 奢侈品：Rings or necklaces are luxuries.戒指或者项链都是奢侈品。

lymph/lɪmf/

n. an almost colourless fluid, containing chiefly white blood cells, that is collected from the tissues of the body 淋巴；淋巴液

lyric/ˈlɪrɪk/

*adj.*like a song or expressing strong personal feelings 为歌唱而作的，抒情的：a ～ poet 抒情诗人/～ poetry 抒情诗/～ drama 歌剧

lyricist/ˈlɪrɪsɪst/

*n.*a writer of song lyrics 歌词作者

L

Mm

ma/mɑː/

　　*n.*a short form for mamma;mother 妈

ma'am/mæm/

　　*n.*a short form of madam（madam 的缩略形式）夫人;女士;太太;小姐

macabre/məˈkɑːbrə/

　　*adj.*causing fear or horror 骇人的,令人毛骨悚然的：The film I saw last night frightened me, it had some very ～ scenes.昨晚我看的电影把我吓坏了,影片中有一些非常骇人的镜头。

mace/meɪs/

　　*n.*a kind of rod carried in the presence of a high official（e.g.the mayor of a town）to show the importance of his position（持于高级官员例如市长的面前,作为职位标志的）权杖

machine/məˈʃiːn/

　　n. ❶ instrument with many parts that move together to do work 机器;a sewing ～ 缝纫机 ❷ persons organized to control（part of）an organization,a group,etc.机构;（控制政党的）核心小集团;the state ～ 国家机器 ‖ ～building *n.*机器制造/～ gun *n.*机枪/ ～ language *n.*计算机语言/～-made *adj.*机制的;机械的;刻板的/～ code *n.*机器代码

machinery/məˈʃiːnəri/

　　*n.*❶machines collectively 机器（总称）❷ moving parts of a machine（机器的）运转部分 ❸methods;the organization of sth.方法;组织;机构

machinist /məˈʃiːnɪst/

　　*n.*a person who operates a machine,especially a machine tool 机械工人;机械师

macrocosm /ˈmækrəkɒzəm/

　　n. the universe that contains smaller structure 宏观世界;宇宙

macroeconomics /ˌmækrəuˌiːkəˈnɒmɪks/

　　n.(*pl.*) the part of economics concerned with large-scale or general economic factors,such as interest rates and national productivity 宏观经济学

mad/mæd/

　　*adj.*❶ crazy;sick in mind 疯的：She went ～ after the death of her son.儿子死后她就疯了。❷ very angry 生气的：She is ～ about him.她对他很生气。 ‖ ～-brained *adj.*狂热的;鲁莽的/ ～house *n.*疯人院/ ～ man *n.*疯子,狂人/ ～ woman *n.*女疯子 ‖ ～ly *adv.*发狂地;极端地;非常地/～ness *n.*疯狂;癫狂

madam/ˈmædəm/

　　*n.*the polite word that you say when you speak to a woman who is a stranger or when you write a business letter to a woman（对妇女的尊称）夫人,太太：～ Curie 居里夫人/I began my letter with "Dear Madam".我在书信的开头写上"亲爱的夫人"。

made/meɪd/

　　*adj.*❶ formed with sth. particular 形成的,做成的：The cup is ～ of wood.这只杯子是木制的。❷assured of success 保证会成功的：When you find gold you're ～.找到金子,你就会发迹。❸ fictitious or imaginary 虚构的：They were all moved by the ～ story.他们都被那个编造的故事打动了。

made-up /ˈmeɪdˈʌp/

　　*adj.*❶wearing make-up 化过妆的 ❷invented;not true 编造的;虚构的：a ～ story 编造的故事

Madonna/məˈdɒnə/

　　*n.*Mary,Mother of Jesus Christ 圣母玛利亚（耶稣的母亲）

maestro/ˈmaɪstrəʊ/

　　n.(*pl.* ～s) ❶a distinguished musician,

especially a conductor or performer of classical music 音乐大师（尤指古典乐曲指挥家或演奏家）❷a great or distinguished figure in any sphere 大师，名家：a movie ~ 电影大师

magazine/ˌmæɡəˈziːn/
*n.*❶a paper book with different articles，which appears usually every week or month 期刊；杂志：We have that ~ in the library.我们图书馆里有那本杂志。❷a store for arms，ammunition，explosives，etc.(武器、弹药、炸药等的)仓库；军火库

maggot/ˈmæɡət/
n. a soft-bodied legless larva of a fly or other insect，often found in bad meat 蛆（苍蝇或昆虫的幼虫，常存在于腐败的肉中）

magic/ˈmædʒɪk/
Ⅰ *n.*❶ strange powers that make wonderful or unusual things happen 魔法，魔力：The fairy changed her into a frog by ~.仙人用魔法把她变成了青蛙。❷an art or skills of getting mysterious results by tricks 魔术，戏法：The man used ~ to produce a lot of flowers from his hat.那个人耍魔术，从他帽子里变出了无数花朵。Ⅱ *adj.* having or apparently having supernatural powers 魔术的；有魔力的；奇异的：~ carpet 魔毯/a ~ weapon 法宝

magical /ˈmædʒɪkl/
*adj.*❶containing magic；used in magic 有魔力的；魔法的 ❷resembling magic；produced or working as if by magic 似有魔法的；似由魔力产生的

magician /məˈdʒɪʃən/
*n.*❶a person who can do magic tricks 魔术师 ❷a person with magical powers 会施魔法者；巫师

magistrate/ˈmædʒɪstreɪt/
n. a person who judges people in a local court 地方行政官；地方法官：the county ~ 县长

magma/ˈmæɡmə/
n.(*pl.*~s or magmata /ˈmæɡmətə/) hot melted rock found below the solid surface of the earth 岩浆；熔岩

magnanimous/mæɡˈnænɪməs/
*adj.*generous and noble 宽宏大量的，慷慨的；高尚的：After winning the war，the ~ victor set all his prisoners free.在赢得战争胜利以后，宽宏大量的胜利者释放了所有的俘虏。

magnate/ˈmæɡneɪt/
*n.*sb. who is rich or important(especially in business) 阔人；权贵；(尤指工商界的)巨头，大亨：He started poor but he eventually became an oil ~.他开始时很穷，但是最后成了石油大王。

magnesium /mæɡˈniːzjəm/
n. the chemical element of atomic number 12，a silver-white metal of the alkaline earth series. It is used to make strong lightweight alloys，especially for the aerospace industry，and is also used in flash bulbs and pyrotechnics，as it burns with a brilliant white flame（Symbol：Mg）镁（符号 Mg）

magnet/ˈmæɡnɪt/
*n.*a piece of iron，often shaped like a horseshoe，which is able to attract iron 磁铁

magnetic/mæɡˈnetɪk/
*adj.*❶having the properties of magnet 磁的，有磁性的；磁化的：~ field 磁场/~ needle 磁针❷attractive to sb.or sth.有吸引力的：He has a ~ personality.他的个性很有魅力。

magnetism/ˈmæɡnɪtɪzəm/
*n.*❶the quality of strong personal charm；the power to attract，etc.(人的)魅力；吸引力 ❷ the physical property of being magnetic 磁性；磁力

magnification /ˌmæɡnɪfɪˈkeɪʃən/
*n.*❶ the action or process of magnifying sth. or being magnified，especially visually 放大 ❷the degree to which sth. is or can be magnified 放大的程度

magnificent/mæɡˈnɪfɪsnt/
adj. extremely splendid or grand；noble；greatly nice 华丽的，宏伟的，堂皇的；高尚的；美好的，极好的：a ~ hall 富丽堂皇的会堂/a ~ palace 宏伟的宫殿/a ~ ceremony 盛大隆重的典礼

M

magnifier /'mægnɪfaɪə/

n. a piece of equipment that is used to make things look larger 放大器;放大镜

magnify /'mægnɪfaɪ/

v. ❶ make（sth.）appear larger than in reality 放大,扩大: The microscope can ～ the object 100 diameters. 这架显微镜能把物体放大一百倍。❷ make sth. seem more important, etc. that it really is 夸大,夸张: ～ facts 夸大事实/the difficulties 夸大困难

magnitude /'mægnɪtjuːd/

n. ❶ greatness of size or importance 巨大;重大;重要: an affair of the first ～ 头等重要的事情 ❷ size 大小: the ～ of current 电流量/the ～ of traffic flow 交通流量 ❸ the degree of brightness of a star 星等(星的亮度): a star of the first ～ 一等星

magpie /'mægpaɪ/

n. a black and white bird of the crow family, which sometimes is thought to steal small bright objects 喜鹊

maid /meɪd/

n. ❶ a girl or（young）woman who is not married 年轻未婚女子,少女;姑娘: ～ of honour 宫女/old ～ 老处女 ❷ a woman servant 侍女,女仆: nurse ～ 保姆/house ～ 女清洁工/a ～ of all work 什么活儿都干的女仆 ‖ ～ish *adj.* 少女的;老处女的/ ～y *n.* 小女孩

maiden /'meɪdn/

Ⅰ *n.* a girl or unmarried woman 姑娘;少女,年轻未婚女子 Ⅱ *adj.* ❶ of a girl or woman 少女的,未婚女子的: ～ modesty 少女的质朴/a ～ aunt 未婚的姑妈(或姨妈) ❷ first or earliest 首次的: a ～ work 处女作 ❸ not used before; fresh 未使用过的;新鲜的: ～ land 未开垦过的处女地 ‖ ～ish *adj.* 处女似的/ ～-like *adj.* 处女般的;柔和的/ ～-aunt *n.* (未婚的)姑,孃

maidenhood /'meɪdnhʊd/

n. the state of being a maiden; the period when one is a maiden 处女身份,处女时代;童贞

maidenly /'meɪdnli/

adj. ❶ like or suitable to a young unmarried girl 少女似的,适合少女的: ～ mod-esty 少女似的谦虚 ❷ in a gentle or modest manner 温柔的;文雅的;端庄的

maidservant /'meɪdˌsɜːvənt/

n. a female servant 女佣人,女仆

mail /meɪl/

Ⅰ *n.* ❶ the postal system of carrying and delivering letters and parcels 邮政: This is a letter by air ～. 这是一封航空信件。❷ letters and anything else sent or received by post, especially those travelling or arriving together 邮件: The ship sank and the ～s were lost. 船沉没了,邮件全丢了。/She received a lot of ～s last week. 她上周收到了很多信。Ⅱ *v.* post 邮寄 ‖ ～bag *n.* 邮袋/ ～ carrier, ～man *n.* 邮递员/ ～ cart *n.* 邮车/ ～ clerk *n.* 邮务员/ ～-day *n.* 邮件截止日

mailbox /'meɪlbɒks/

n. a letter box 邮筒;信箱

main /meɪn/

Ⅰ *n.* ❶ principal pipe bringing water or gas, wire transmitting electricity into a building（自来水、煤气的）总管道;（电的）干线 ❷ sea, especially a wide expanse of sea 大海,沧海 Ⅱ *adj.* the most important; chief 主要的;最重要的: the ～ street of a town 市镇主干道/the ～ course of a meal 一餐的主菜 ‖ ～line *n.* 主线,（铁路的）干线

mainframe /'meɪnfreɪm/

n. ❶ a large high-speed computer, especially one supporting numerous workstations or peripherals 主计算机,大型计算机 ❷ the central processing unit and primary memory of a computer 计算机中央处理机

mainland /'meɪnlænd/

n. the main area of land of a country, without its islands 大陆;国土的主体

mainline /'meɪnlaɪn/

v. take an illegal drug into one of the chief veins of the body, either for pleasure or because one is dependent on it, not for medical reasons 静脉注射(毒品)

mainly /'meɪnli/

adv. for the most part; mostly 主要地,大部分地: I don't know what her interests are,because ～ we talk about work when we meet.我不知道她的兴趣是什么,因为我们见面时主要在谈论工作。

mainmast/'meɪmɑːst/
n. the largest or most important of the masts which hold up the sails on a ship (船的)主桅,大桅

mains/meɪnz/
n. a supply of electricity produced centrally and brought to houses,etc.by wires 总输电线:Does your radio work off the ～ or from a battery? 你的收音机是输电线还是用电池供电? / a ～ radio 输电线供电的收音机

mainsail/'meɪnsl,'meɪnseɪl/
n. the chief sail on a ship,usually the one on the mainmast 主帆

mainspring/'meɪnsprɪŋ/
n. ❶ the chief spring in a watch 主发条 ❷ the chief force or reason that makes sth. happen 主要原因,动机:His belief in liberty was the ～ of his fight against slavery.他对自由的信仰是他反抗奴隶制度的主要原因。

mainstay/'meɪnsteɪ/
n. sb. or sth. which provides the chief means of support 主要靠山,主要支持者;支柱:Agriculture is still the ～ of the country's economy.农业仍然是这个国家经济的主要支柱。

mainstream/'meɪnstriːm/
n. the main or most widely accepted way of thinking or acting in relation to a subject (思想或行为的)主流:Their views lie outside the ～ of current medical opinion.他们的观点不属于当今医学界观点的主流。

maintain/meɪn'teɪn/
v. ❶ keep up;continue 保持;继续:～ balance 保持平衡 ❷ support 供给,赡养:He is too poor to ～ his family.他太穷了,无法养家糊口。❸ claim to be true 坚持,主张:He ～ed that it was wrong. 他坚持认为是这样的。❹ keep in safety and protect from harm,etc.维护:～ one's rights 维护自己的权利 ❺ keep sth.in good condition by regularly checking and repairing

it 保养:～ the roads 保养道路 ‖ ～able *adj.*可维持的;可维修的

maintenance/'meɪntənəns/
n. ❶ the act of maintaining or being maintained 维持或被维持;保养,保持 ❷ what is needed to support life 生活费用,赡养费

maize/meɪz/
n. a kind of grain plant 玉米,玉蜀黍

majestic/mə'dʒestɪk/
adj. having or showing majesty 雄伟的,壮丽的;威严的,庄严的 ‖ ～ally *adv.* The great ship sailed slowly and ～ally into harbour.这艘大船缓慢而庄严地驶进了港口。

majesty/'mædʒɪsti/
n. ❶ sth. that is magnificent;nobility 雄伟,庄严,威严;崇高:the ～ of the mountains 山峦的雄伟气势 ❷ supreme power of authority 最高权威:the ～ of the law 法律的至高权力 ❸(**Majesty**) a title used to refer to the king or queen 陛下:His (Her,Your) Majesty 陛下

major/'meɪdʒə(r)/
Ⅰ *adj.* greater or more important of two (parts,etc.);older of two brothers (两部分中)比较大的,比较重要的;(两兄弟中)较长的:the ～ portion 大部分/Smith ～ 大史密斯(史密斯兄弟中的哥哥) Ⅱ *n.* ❶ a chief or special subject at a university 主修课程,主科:the ～ subjects 主修(专业)课程 ❷ an army officer between a captain and a colonel 陆军少校 Ⅲ *v.* study as the chief subject(s) when doing a university degree 主修,专攻(大学里某一科目):He ～ed in English. 他主修英文。

major general/ˌmeɪdʒə'dʒenrəl/
n. an army officer ranking between a brigadier and a lieutenant-general 陆军少将

majority/mə'dʒɒrəti/
n. ❶ the greater number or part (of) 大多数,大部分:The ～ of doctors believe smoking is harmful to health.大多数医生相信吸烟有害健康。/The ～ were(was) in favour of the proposal.多数人赞成这个意见。❷ the number by which votes for one side exceed those for the other

M

side（选举中）超过对方的票数；多数：win by a ~ of 20 以 20 票的多数获胜 ❸a legal age of reaching manhood or womanhood（达到成年的）法定年龄：reach (attain) one's ~ 达到法定年龄/He will reach his ~ next month. 下个月他将达到法定的年龄。

make/meɪk/

Ⅰ v.(made) ❶produce by work or action 做，制造：~ paper 造纸/ ~ cloth 织布 ❷ used with a large number of nouns in various special senses（与名词连用构成各种特定含义）：~ the bed 铺床/ ~ a fire 生火 /~ tea 泡茶 ❸cause to be or cause to do sth. 使成为；使发生：~ sb. happy 使某人愉快/ ~ the fire burn up 使火烧起来/He made her his wife. 他娶她为妻。/Newton was made president of the Royal Society. 牛顿被选为皇家学会会长。❹force or cause（a person to do sth. or a thing to happen）使得；迫使：Make yourself at home. 请不要客气。/ Make him repeat it. 叫他背诵。❺earn or gain money；win 赚，赢得：~ money（a profit, one's fortune, success）赚钱（获利，发财，成功）❻ arrive at or reach a place 到达 ❼reckon or consider 推断，认为：What do you ~ the total? 你认为总数是多少？❽have the qualities of（especially sth. good）有……的性质：The hall would ~ a good theatre. 这会堂很适合作剧场。❾travel（a distance）or at a speed 行走一段距离；以……速度行进：The train was making 70 miles an hour. 火车以每小时七十英里的速度前进。❿ turn out to be；result in 形成；结果是：One swallow does not ~ a summer. 一燕不成夏。（不能单凭微小的迹象而下定论）⓫ equal with or add up to；amount to；come to 等于；合计，总计：Two and two ~s four. 二加二等于四。⓬establish（a law）立法：~ laws 制定法律 ⓭be about（to）正要：I made to speak, but she stopped me. 我正要发言，但是她阻止了我。⓮eat or have（a meal）吃饭，进餐：He ~s a hasty breakfast every day. 他每天都很忙地吃早饭。⓯write, compose or prepare with：写作，创作，准备：She

has made several novels. 她已经写了好几部小说。⓰cause sth. happen or be done 引起，产生：~ trouble 捣乱，制造麻烦 ‖ ~ after 追逐，跟随/ ~ as if (as though) 假装，装作/ ~ away oneself 自杀/ ~ certain（把……）弄确实/ ~ do and mend 修修补补将就过去/ ~ down 改小（衣服）/ ~ for 走向；有利于；向……猛攻/ ~ from 由……制造/ ~ fun of sb. 和……开玩笑/ ~ into 把……制成，使转为/ ~ it 规定时间；办成功，做到/ ~ love(to)（向……）求爱/~ much of 重视，充分利用/ ~ of 用……制造；明白；对待，重视/ ~ off 离开/ ~ or break 或成之或毁之/ ~ out 填写；拼凑；证明；理解；辨认出；设法应付/ ~ the most of 尽量利用；极为重视/ ~ up 弥补；赔偿；补(考)；配制；虚构；缝制；组成；和解；化装/ ~ use of 利用 Ⅱ n. a type of product, especially as produced by a particular maker; a method or style of manufacture 制造的方法；样式：Is this your own ~? 这是你们自己制造的吗？‖ **making**/'meɪkɪŋ/ n. 制造；成功的原因（或手段）；素质，材料/ ~r /'meɪkə(r)/ n. 创造者，制作者

make-believe/'meɪkbɪˌliːv/
n. the act of imagining that sth. is real; pretence 假装；托词；口实

makeover /'meɪkəʊvə(r)/
n. a complete transformation or remodelling of sth., especially a person's hairstyle, make-up, or clothes（尤指发型、化妆或衣服）完全改变；重做

makeshift/'meɪkʃɪft/
adj. used as a substitute for the real thing 权宜之计的；临时凑合代用的：They used the boxes as ~ chairs. 他们暂时用木箱当椅子坐。

malady /'mælədi/
n. a disease or ailment 病，疾病：an incurable ~ 不治之症

malaria/mə'leərɪə/
n. a disease with fever caused by the bite of a certain kind of mosquito 疟疾

male/meɪl/
Ⅰ adj. ❶ of the sex that does not give birth to young 男性的；雄性的：a ~ mon-

key 公猴 ❷ (of a flower or plant) not producing fruit (花或植物)不结果的；只有雄蕊的 Ⅱ *n.* a person or animal, etc. who or which belongs to the sex that can't have babies 男人；雄性动物

malevolent /məˈlevələnt/
adj. wanting to do harm to other people 怀有恶意的，恶毒的：He gave me a ~ look.他恶狠狠地看了我一眼。

malformation /ˌmælfɔːˈmeɪʃn/
n. ❶ the condition of being formed or shaped wrongly 畸形 ❷ a shape, structure, or part (especially of the body) that is formed badly or wrongly (尤指身体的)畸形部分，畸形构造，畸形物

malformed /ˌmælˈfɔːmd/
adj. made or shaped badly 畸形的，变形的

malfunction /mælˈfʌŋkʃn/
n. a fault in operation 故障，障碍：Results have been delayed owing to a ~ in the computer.由于电脑发生故障，计算结果被推迟了。

malign[1] /məˈlaɪn/
v. say or write bad or unkind things about sb. or sth., especially falsely 诽谤，中伤：She was ~ed by the newspapers. 她受到报纸的诽谤。/This much-~ed novel is in fact remarkable in many ways. 这部受到猛烈抨击的小说事实上在许多方面是很出色的。

malign[2] /məˈlaɪn/
adj. (of a thing) harmful；causing evil 有害的；邪恶的：a ~ influence 有害的影响

malignancy /məˈlɪgnənsi/
n. ❶ the state of being malignant 恶毒；恶性 ❷ a dangerous growth of cells；tumour of a malignant kind 恶性肿瘤

malignant /məˈlɪgnənt/
adj. ❶ (of persons or their actions) filled with or showing a desire to hurt (指人及其行为)恶毒的；恶意的：~ fairies 恶毒的妖怪/~ glances 凶恶的目光 ❷ (of diseases) harmful to life；violent (指疾病)致命的；恶性的：~ cancer 恶性的癌症/a ~ tumour 恶性瘤

malleable /ˈmælɪəbl/
adj. ❶ (of a metal) that can be beaten, pressed, rolled, etc. into a new shape (金属)可锻压的，有延展性的 ❷ (of people or their character) easily influenced, changed, or trained (人或性格)可塑的，易改变的；可训练的

mallet /ˈmælɪt/
n. a hammer with a wooden head 木槌

malnourished /ˌmælˈnʌrɪʃt/
adj. suffering from malnutrition 营养不良的

malnutrition /ˌmælnjuːˈtrɪʃn/
n. (of persons) the poor state of health caused by the lack of enough food or the right kind of food (指人)营养不良：The people in this area suffer from ~.这个地区的人营养不良。/children suffering from severe ~ 严重营养不良的儿童

malpractice /ˌmælˈpræktɪs/
n. a careless, improper or illegal behaviour while in a professional job 玩忽职守；渎职：The doctor who had neglected his patient was found guilty of ~.这个医生因对病人疏忽大意被裁定为渎职。

malt /mɔːlt/
n. grain (e.g. barley, oats) specially treated in making beer or spirits 麦芽(经过特殊处理的谷物，如大麦、燕麦，用于酿造啤酒或酒精)

maltreat /mælˈtriːt/
v. behave cruelly towards someone 虐待：This man is accused of ~ing his children. 这个人被指控虐待他的孩子。

mammal /ˈmæml/
n. an animal of a class that give birth to live babies and feeds its young on milk 哺乳类动物：Dogs and cats are ~s.狗和猫是哺乳类动物。

mammy /ˈmæmi/
n. (a child's word for) mother (儿语)妈妈

man /mæn/
Ⅰ *n.* ❶ (*pl.* men) an adult male human 男子：be only half a ~ 不像个男子汉 ❷ a human being 人：Any ~ could do that.谁都能那样做。 ❸ the human race 人类：

M

Man's knowledge of things constantly develops. 人类的认识总是不断发展的。❹ a husband, lover, or other adult male with whom a woman lives 丈夫：～ and wife 夫妇 ❺ an adult male under the authority of another or in employment (男性的)下属：masters and men 主人和仆人/ officers and men 军官和士兵 ❻ used for addressing an adult male, especially when the speaker is excited or angry (用作对成年男子的呼喊语)：Hurry up ～! 嗨，赶快! ‖ a ～ of iron 意志坚强的人；严酷无情的人/a ～ of letters 学者；文人/a ～ of mark 名人/a ～ of men 杰出的人物/a ～ of word 守信的人/a ～ of the world 深通世故的人/as a ～, as one ～ 一致地/ ～ for 以一个人对一个人/the inner ～ 人的灵魂(或精神)/the right in the right place 人地相宜/to the last ～, to a ～ 全体无例外地 Ⅱ❶ v. (-nn-) strengthen one's spirits or courage 振作精神, 增强勇气：You should ～ yourself and not lose heart. 你应该鼓起勇气, 不要灰心。❷ provide with men for operation 配备人员：～ the machine 给机器配备人手 ‖ ～-eating adj. 食人的/ ～-like adj. 男子似的, 有男子气概的/ ～-made adj. 人造的, 人工的/ ～power n. 人力 ‖ ～ful adj. 勇敢的, 果断的/～less adj. 无男人的

manacle/ˈmænəkl/
Ⅰ n. (usually pl.) a metal band, chain for the hands or feet 手铐；足镣 Ⅱ v. ❶ fetter with manacles 上手铐；加足镣 ❷ restrain 束缚；妨碍；拘束：Grief can ～ the mind. 忧能伤人。

manage/ˈmænɪdʒ/
v. ❶ control or guide (especially a business) 控制；处理：～ a horse 驭马/～ a car 驾车/～ a shop 管理店铺/～ a business 经营事业 ❷ succeed in dealing with (a problem) 完成, 设法：We finally ～d to get there in time. 最后我们及时赶到了。❸ succeed in taking or using 能吃；能用：Can you ～ another slice of cake? 你能不能再吃一块蛋糕? ‖ ～able /ˈmænɪdʒəbl/ adj. 能处理的；容易管理的

management/ˈmænɪdʒmənt/
n. ❶ the act of managing, especially a business or other organizations 管理, 处理；经营；支配：bad ～ 管理不善 ❷ delicate contrivance；skillful treatment (周密的、巧妙的)处理手段 ❸ the people who are in charge of a firm, industry, etc., considered as one body 经营者；管理部门；资方；厂方：The workers are having talks with the ～. 工人们正在和厂方谈判。

manager/ˈmænɪdʒə(r)/
n. ❶ a person who controls a business 经理 ❷ a person who conducts business or manages household affairs 当家人；管理业务者：a good ～ 一位善于理财的人 ❸ a person dealing with the business of an entertainer, a sportsman, , etc. (演员、运动员等的)经理人, 经纪人：Tom is the ～ of that movie star. 汤姆是那个电影明星的经纪人。

manageress/ˌmænɪdʒəˈres/
n. a woman who controls a business, especially a shop or restaurant；a female manager 女经理

managerial/ˌmænəˈdʒɪəriəl/
adj. of or concerning a manager or management 经理的；管理的：a ～ position 经理职位 / ～ responsibilities 经营责任

mandarin/ˈmændərɪn/
n. ❶ (in former times) important Chinese official (旧时)中国政府高级官吏 ❷ a small kind of orange 橘子

mandate/ˈmændeɪt/
n. ❶ an instruction or a permission (especially from a superior official) (尤指上级下达的)命令；指令, 许可：The magistrate was given a ～ on how to deal with the case. 地方法官接到如何处理这一案件的命令。❷ the right and power given to a government, or any body of people chosen to represent others or to act according to the wishes of those who voted for it 授权, 权限：The country gave the Prime Minister a ～ to carry out new policies. 国家授权首相执行新的政策。

mandatory/ˈmændətəri/
Ⅰ adj. of, containing a command which

must be obeyed; compulsory, obligatory 命令的, 指令的; 强制性的; 义务性的: a ～ payment 一笔必须支付的款项/the ～ power 受委托统治的国家, 托管国 Ⅱ *n.* a person or state to whom a mandate has been given 受托者; 受委托统治的国家

mandible/'mændəbl/

n. ❶ a jaw which moves, especially the lower jaw of an animal or fish, or a jawbone 颌, 下颌 ❷ the upper or lower part of a bird's beak 鸟喙的上下部 ❸ either of the two biting or holding parts in insects and crabs (昆虫、螃蟹的) 上 (下) 颚

mane/meɪn/

n. long hair on the back of the neck of some animals (e.g. horse, lion) (马、狮子等动物颈部上的) 鬃毛

manganese/'mæŋgəniːz/

n. a hard, brittle, light-grey metal used in making steel, glass, etc. 锰

manger/'meɪndʒə(r)/

n. a long open box that cattle and horses feed from (牛、马的) 饲料槽

mango/'mæŋgəʊ/

n. (*pl.* ～es or ～s) ❶ a kind of tropical fruit which has yellow skin when ripe 杧果 ❷ a tree bearing this fruit 杧果树

mangy/'meɪndʒi/

adj. ❶ suffering from the disease of mange 患疥癣的 ❷ of bad appearance because of loss of hair 脱毛后很难看的: a ～ carpet 脱毛的破旧地毯

manhandle/'mænhændl/

v. ❶ move (sth. heavy or awkward) by using the strength of men, not machines 以人力搬动 (笨重物体) ❷ treat sb. or sth. roughly 粗暴地对待

manhole/'mænhəʊl/

n. a hole, with a cover, through which a man can go down to look at or repair pipes, sewers, etc. under the ground 人孔 (检查或修理地下管道、排水管、下水道等的出入口)

manhood/'mænhʊd/

n. ❶ the condition or period of time of being a man 成年, 成人: reach ～ 成年 ❷

the good qualities of a man, such as courage, strong will, etc. 男人的气质 ❸ all the men of a nation, considered together as one body (一国的) 男人的总称

man-hour/'mænaʊə(r)/

n. (a measure of) the amount of work done by one person in one hour 一人一小时内完成的工作量, 人时, 工时

manhunt/'mænhʌnt/

n. a search for a wanted person, especially a criminal 搜捕, 追捕: The police are conducting an extensive ～ for the murderer. 警察正在广泛搜查杀人犯。

mania/'meɪnɪə/

n. ❶ a mood disorder which causes the sufferer to respond excessively and sometimes violently 躁狂症: Kleptomania is a ～ for stealing things. 盗窃癖是一种爱偷东西的躁狂症。 ❷ a desire or interest so strong that it seems mad 狂热; 热衷: She has a ～ for (driving) fast cars. 她有开快车的癖好。/ He's got motorcycle ～. 他爱摩托车爱得发狂。/ disco ～ 迪斯科迷

maniac/'meɪnɪæk/

n. ❶ a person (thought to be) suffering from mania 躁狂者 ❷ a wild thoughtless person 疯疯癫癫的人: Don't drive so fast, you ～ ; you'll kill us all! 别开得这样快, 你这个疯子, 你要让我们都送死啊!

maniacal/mə'naɪəkl/

adj. of or like a maniac 狂躁的, 发狂的: ～ laughter 狂笑

manic/'mænɪk/

adj. ❶ of or suffering from mania 躁狂的, 癫狂的 ❷ very excited; wild in behaviour 非常激动的, 狂热的

manifest/'mænɪfest/

Ⅰ *adj.* plain to see or clear to the mind 明白的, 明显的: This principle should be ～ to all of you. 这条原则应是你们全体都明白的。 Ⅱ *v.* ❶ show(sth.) plainly 明白显示, 清楚表示: These newly unearthed cultural objects ～ the intelligence of the working people of ancient China. 这些新出土的历史文物显示了古代中国劳动人民的聪明才智。 ❷ give signs of 显露

M

(……的征象)：She doesn't ～ much desire to marry him.她没显露出很想嫁给他的样子。‖ ～ation/ˌmænɪfesˈteɪʃn/ n.显示，表明

manifesto /ˌmænɪˈfestəʊ/
n. a public declaration of principles, policy, purpose, etc. by a ruler, political party, etc.宣言，声明，布告：an election ～ 竞选宣言

manipulate /məˈnɪpjʊleɪt/
v. ❶ handle or control（a tool, mechanism, etc.）, typically in a skilful manner（尤指熟练地）操作，使用（工具、机械装置等）❷control or influence（a person or situation）cleverly, unfairly, or unscrupulously 操纵，控制（人或局势）❸examine or treat（a part of the body）by feeling or moving it with the hand 推拿（身体部位）

mankind
n. ❶ /ˌmænˈkaɪnd/the human race 人类：They hope to find new resources for ～.他们希望为人类找到新的资源。❷ /ˈmænkaɪnd/men in general（泛指）男人

manly /ˈmænli/
adj. ❶ having the qualities suitable to a man 有男子气概的；雄赳赳的；果断的：a ～ act 有男子气概的行为 ❷（of things, qualities, etc.）right for a man（指物品、性质等）适合于男人的：～ jobs 适合于男子的工作 ❸（of a woman）having a man's qualities（指女人）有男子气概的

manner /ˈmænə(r)/
n. ❶ the way in which sth. is done or happens 方式，方法：Do it in this ～.用这种方法做。❷（only singular）person's way of behaving toward others（仅用单数）态度，举止：He has an awkward ～.他举止笨拙。❸（pl.）the habits and customs of a particular group of people 习惯，风俗：a novel of ～s 一本社会风俗小说 ❹（pl.）social behaviour that is considered to be polite 礼貌：He has no ～s at all.他毫无礼貌。❺a style in literature or art（文学或艺术的）风格，文体：a ～ of one's own 自成一家的风格 ❻ a kind or sort 种类：What ～ of man is he? 他是哪种人?

mannered /ˈmænəd/
adj. having an unnatural way of behaving 做作的，不自然的：a ～ way of speaking 矫揉造作的说话方式

mannerism /ˈmænərɪzəm/
n. ❶ a particular and especially odd way of behaving, speaking, etc. that has become a habit 习气：She has this strange ～ of pinching her ear when she talks.她谈话时有掐耳朵的奇怪习气。❷the use of unnatural ways of representing things in art, according to a set of styles（艺术的）独特风格

mannish /ˈmænɪʃ/
adj.（of a woman）like a man in character, behaviour, or appearance 似男人的，男子气的

manoeuvre /məˈnuːvə(r)/
Ⅰ n. ❶ planned movement（of armed forces）；（pl.）large-scale exercises by troops or ships（军队的）调遣，机动部署；大规模演习：carry out（perform）grand ～s 举行大规模演习/troops on ～s 参加演习的部队 ❷a skillful move or clever trick 策略，巧计；花招：the despicable ～s of some politicians 政客的卑鄙策略/resort to political ～s 玩弄政治花招 Ⅱ v.（cause to）perform manoeuvre（使）调遣；演习；调动；实施机动：～ a car into the garage 把车驶进车库/～ the secretary out of the office 把秘书喊出办公室/The fleet will ～ in the Mediterranean.舰队将在地中海演习。

manor /ˈmænə(r)/
n.❶（in medieval Europe）an area of land owned by a person of high birth（中世纪欧洲的）采地；采邑 ❷the estate with a large house called the manor house 古老的大宅第，宅邸，庄园

manpower /ˈmænpaʊə/
n. the number of people working or available for work 人力，劳动力：a ～ shortage 劳动力短缺

mansion /ˈmænʃn/
n.❶a large and stately house 大厦，巨宅；官邸：the Mansion House 伦敦市长官邸 ❷（pl.）（in proper names）block of flats

（用于专有名词中）公寓，大厦：Victoria Mansions 维多利亚公寓

mantle/'mæntl/

Ⅰ *n.* a loose sleeveless cloak; a layer of sth. that covers a surface 披风，斗篷；覆盖物：a ~ of snow 一层雪/the ~ of night 夜幕/hills with a ~ of snow 覆着一层雪的山　Ⅱ *v.*❶ cover in or as in a mantle （用披风等）盖，罩，覆盖：Snow ~d the hills. 白雪覆盖了山峦。❷ flow into the blood vessels of;(of the face)flush （指血液）流入……的血管；(指脸)涨红，发红：Blushes ~d (over) her cheeks. 她的两颊绯红。

manual/'mænjuəl/

Ⅰ *adj.* of or using hands 手工的，手操作的，手工做的：~ training （学校等的）手工课；手工训练/a ~ fire engine 手压灭火机/a sign ~ 亲笔签名　Ⅱ *n.*❶ a handbook or textbook 手册；教科书；便览，指南：a shorthand ~ 速记手册 ❷ a keyboard of an organ, played with the hands 风琴键盘

manufacture/ˌmænju'fæktʃə(r)/

Ⅰ *v.*❶ make(goods, etc.)on a large-scale by machinery 制造，(用机器大量)生产：~d goods 机制商品/A lot of cars are ~d in Europe. 很多汽车是在欧洲制造的。❷ invent(evidence, an excuse, etc.), make up 捏造，虚构：~ a story(an account) 编造故事(假账)　Ⅱ *n.* the act of making 制造，生产：Thousands of people are employed in the ~ of shoes. 制鞋工业雇用了成千上万的人。

manuscript/'mænjuskrɪpt/

n. a book or article in handwriting or typewritten form 手稿；打字稿；底稿，原稿：~ notes 手写的笔记/in ~ 尚未付印的 / send a ~ to the printer 将一份原稿送厂排版/poems still in ~ 尚未付印的诗章(稿)

many/'meni/

Ⅰ *adj.* (more, most)a large number(of) 许多的，多的：Many people think so. 许多人都这样想。　Ⅱ *n.* (the ~) the majority of people 大多数人：The ~ of us have seen the film. 我们中许多人都看过这电

影了。‖ a good ~ 很多，相当多/a great ~ 许许多多/as ~ 一样多的/ ~ a(an, another) (后接单数名词)许多的 ‖ ~-angled *adj.* 多角的/ ~-headed *adj.* 多头的/ ~-sided *adj.* 多边的

map/mæp/

Ⅰ *n.* a flat drawing of a large surface 地图：a ~ of China 中国地图/a ~ of the world 世界地图/In the library there are ~s of towns, countries, and the world. 图书馆藏有许多城镇、国家和世界的地图。　Ⅱ *v.* show in the form of a map; make a map of 用地图表示；绘制……的地图：~ the South Pole 绘制南极地图

maple/'meɪpl/

*n.*❶ trees with five-pointed leaves grown for wood or shade 枫树 ❷ wood of this tree 枫木

mar/mɑː(r)/

v. (-rr-) damage or spoil sth. good 破坏，损坏：His essay was ~red by careless mistakes. 粗心大意的错误损害了他的文章。

marathon/'mærəθən/

Ⅰ *n.*❶ (in athletics) running race of 26 miles (体育)马拉松赛跑(全程 26 英里) ❷ any long race, journey or activity 长距离的比赛；长途旅行(或活动)　Ⅱ *adj.* very long 很长的，很久的：a ~ speech 马拉松式的长篇演说

marble/'mɑːbl/

*n.*❶ a hard sort of limestone used for building, sculpture, gravestones, etc. when cut and polished, and usually showing an irregular pattern of colours 大理石 ❷ a small ball of glass, clay, or stone used in games 玻璃弹子，泥制弹子

march/mɑːtʃ/

Ⅰ *v.*❶ walk with regular steps 行进，行军，齐步前进：~ from victory to victory 从胜利走向胜利/Time ~es on. (比喻)时间不停前进。❷ make sb. walk quickly 使前进：They ~ed the prisoner away. 他们把犯人押走了。　Ⅱ *n.*❶ way of walking with regular steps 行进，行军：on the ~ 在行进中，进军中 ❷ a piece of music to which soldiers march 进行曲：military

~es 军乐进行曲

March/mɑːtʃ/

n. the third month of the year 三月：A windy ~ and a rainy April makes a beautiful May.三月多风,四月多雨,造就五月好风光。

mare/meə(r)/

n. a female horse or donkey 母马；母驴：Money makes the ~ go.有钱能使鬼推磨。‖ a grey ~ 胜过丈夫的妻子/**win the ~ or lose the halter** 孤注一掷/~'s **nest** 骗人的东西；乱糟糟的地方

margin/'mɑːdʒɪn/

n. ❶ the extreme edge or limit of a place 边,边缘 ❷ the space at each edge of a page without writing or printing 页边的空白；栏外：make notes on the ~ 在页边做注释 ❸ an amount beyond the minimum necessary 余裕：The schedule leaves a wide ~ of time for self-study.时间表留有充裕的自学时间。❹the condition near the limit or borderline below or beyond which sth. is impossible 边际,有限的余地：He escaped defeat by a narrow ~.他差一点儿失败了。❺ the difference between the cost and the selling price of a product 成本与售价的差额,利润空间：a narrow ~ of profit 微利

marginal /'mɑːdʒɪnəl/

adj. ❶written in a margin 记在页边的：~ notes 旁注 ❷of or at an edge 与(或在)……边缘的 ❸very slight in amount 微小的：The difference is only ~.差别是微小的。❹(said about a parliamentary seat) having a very small majority in the previous election (指议会席位)占微弱多数的 ‖ ~**ly** *adv.*有限地；微小地

marigold /'mærɪɡəʊld/

*n.*an orange or yellow garden flower 金盏花,万寿菊：There are many ~ in our school graden.我们学校花园里有许多万寿菊。

marijuana/ˌmærə'wɑːnə/

*n.*a type of intoxicating drug made from dried hemp 大麻,大麻烟

marinate/'mærɪneɪt/

*v.*keep (meat or fish) in a marinade before cooking 将(鱼、肉于烹调前)浸泡在腌泡汁中

marine/mə'riːn/

Ⅰ *adj.* ❶of, by, found in or produced by the sea 海的；海路的；海中的；海产的：~ products 海产品 ❷ of ships, sea-trade, the navy, etc. 船舶的；航海的；海上贸易的；海军的：~ insurance 海上保险,水险 Ⅱ *n.*❶(only the merchant marine, all the merchant) ships of a country (一个国家的)船舶；海运业：the merchant ~ 商船 ❷ a soldier who serve for a naval ship 海军陆战队士兵

mariner/'mærɪnə(r)/

n. a sailor, especially one who assists in navigating a ship 水手,海员：a ~'s compass 航海罗盘/a master ~ 商船船长

marionette/ˌmærɪə'net/

n. a small wooden figure which can be moved by strings 提线木偶

marital/'mærɪtl/

*adj.*of a husband；of marriage 丈夫的；婚姻的：~ obligations 丈夫的责任

maritime/'mærɪtaɪm/

*adj.*❶of the sea or navigation 海上的；海中的；海运的：~ law 海商法/a ~ court 海事法庭 ❷near the sea 沿海的；近海的：~ countries 沿海国家

mark/mɑːk/

Ⅰ *n.* ❶ line, scratch, cut, stain, etc., that spoils the appearance of sth. 痕迹；污点；斑点：the ~ of a wound 伤痕 ❷a noticeable spot on the body by which a person or animal may be recognized (人或动物身上可供识别用的)记号,特征,标志：a birth ~ 胎记,痣 ❸ a figure or printed or written sign which shows sth. 符号；标点；标记：trade ~s 商标/punctuation ~s 标点符号 ❹ a figure, letter, or sign which represents a judgment of the quality of someone's work, behaviour, performance in a competition, etc. 分数：give sb.a good ~ 给某人以好的评分/gain full ~s for English 英语得了满分 ❺ the object or place one aims at as target；指标：(miss) hit the ~ (没有)打中目标；达到目的 ❻ an acceptable level of quality 正

常水平,标准:up to (below) the ～ 达到 (低于) 正常标准 ‖ beside the ～ 没有打中目标;不切题/beyond the ～ 越出界限;过分/get off the ～ 起跑;开始/make one's ～ 使自己出名/not feel up to the ～ (口) 身体有点不舒服/On your ～s! (赛跑出发前的口令) 各就各位! /over the ～ 超过限度 Ⅱ v. ❶ make a mark or marks on appearance 留痕迹于;做记号于:The hot cups have ～ed the table badly.热杯子把桌子弄得都是印痕。/Mark the parcel "Fragile".在包裹上标明"易碎品"。 ❷ give marks to 打分数,评成绩:～ examination papers 评阅考卷 ❸ pay attention (to);watch or listen to carefully 注意,留心:Mark my words! 你(留心)听着! ‖ ～ down 记下/～ off 划分出/～ up 把……标出 ‖ ～er /'mɑːkə(r)/ n.(比赛中的)记分员;记分器;书签

marked /mɑːkt/
adj. clearly noticeable 明显的,显然的:a ～ improvement 明显的改进 ‖ ～ly *adv.*明显地,显然地

marker /'mɑːkə/
*n.*❶sth. that serves to mark a position 标志;指示 ❷a pen with a broad felt tip 记号笔 ❸a person who records the score in games 记分员

market /'mɑːkɪt/
Ⅰ *n.* ❶ a place where people can bring goods to sell 市场,集市:There are numerous small ～s in the town.镇里有许多小市场。 ❷ trade in a certain class of goods 行业(市场):the money ～ 金融市场 ❸ the state of trade as shown by prices or the rate at which things are bought and sold (某种货物的)交易情况;行情:a rising(falling) ～ 上涨的(下跌的)行情 ❹the demand to purchase goods and services 需求;销路:There's not much ～ for down jacket in tropical areas.在热带地区,羽绒服的需求量不大。 Ⅱ*v.*buy or sell in a market 买,卖:go ～-ing 去市场买东西或卖东西 ‖ ～able /'mɑːkɪtəbl/ *adj.* 畅销的;有销路的

marketeer /ˌmɑːkɪ'tɪə(r)/

*n.*a person who works in a certain sort of market 销售商;市场经营者

marketer /'mɑːkɪtə(r)/
*n.*a person or firm that sells a product 货商

marketing /'mɑːkɪtɪŋ/
*n.*the commercial process involved in promoting,selling and distributing a product or service 销售;营销:a job in ～ 市场销售工作 /～ strategies 销售策略;营销策略/ the ～ director 销售经理

marketplace /'mɑːkɪtpleɪs/
n. ❶ an open area,especially a square, where a market is held 集市 ❷ the area of business activity in which buying and selling are done 交易场所;市场:We don't know if this new product will be successful until we test it out in the ～.这种新产品是否畅销,只有拿到市场上试销之后才能知道。

marking /'mɑːkɪŋ/
n.(any of a set of) coloured marks on an animal's skin,fur,or on a bird's feathers (兽皮、鸟羽的)斑纹;斑点:The leopard has beautiful ～s.豹身上有美丽的斑纹。

marksman /'mɑːksmən/
*n.*a person who can shoot well with a gun 神枪手,神射手

marksmanship /'mɑːksmənʃɪp/
n. the quality of ability of a marksman; skill in shooting 射击术

markup /'mɑːkʌp/
*n.*the amount by which a price is raised by a seller to pay for costs and allow for profit 提价幅度,商品价格的上涨金额:a ～ of 20% on cigarettes in the hotel shop 旅馆商店的香烟 20%的提价幅度

marl /mɑːl/
*n.*a soil formed of clay and lime 泥灰

marmot /'mɑːmət/
n. a small European plant-eating animal that lives in holes in the ground 旱獭,土拨鼠

maroon[1] /mə'ruːn/
*v.*leave(someone) alone in a place where no one lives,with no means of getting

M

away 使陷入孤立无援的地方：Our boat sank and we were ~ed on a small island. 我们的船沉了，我们被困在一个荒凉的小岛上。

maroon² /məˈruːn/

adj. a small rocket that explodes high in the air, used as a signal, especially at sea（尤用于海上的）警报鞭炮

marquise /mɑːˈkiːz/

❶the wife or widow of a marquis 侯爵夫人（或遗孀）❷a woman holding the rank of marquis in her own right 女侯爵

marriage /ˈmærɪdʒ/

n. a legal union of a man and woman as husband and wife; the state of being married 结婚；婚姻：freedom of ~ 婚姻自由 ‖ give sb. in ~ 把某人嫁出去/take sb. in ~ 娶某人 ‖ ~ licence *n.* 结婚登记证 / ~ portion *n.* 嫁妆 ‖ ~able /ˈmærɪdʒəbl/ *adj.* 达到结婚年龄的

married /ˈmærɪd/

adj. ❶having a husband or wife 已婚的；已有配偶的：Are you ~? 你结婚了吗？❷of the state of marriage 婚姻的；夫妇的：~ couple 夫妇/~ life 婚姻生活

marry /ˈmæri/

v. ❶ take sb. as a husband or wife 结婚；嫁娶：They are going to be married on New Year's Day. 他们将于元旦结婚。/ He married both his daughters to rich directors. 他把两个女儿都嫁给了富有的董事。❷（of a priest or official）perform the ceremony of marriage for（two people）（指牧师、官员）主持……的婚礼；使……正式结为夫妇：The priest married them. 牧师主持了他们的婚礼。

marsh /mɑːʃ/

n.（an area of）low-lying wet land 沼泽（地带）；湿地：miles and miles of ~ 湿地连绵/We had to cross the ~es. 我们不得不穿过沼泽地带。

marshal /ˈmɑːʃl/

Ⅰ *n.* ❶an officer of the highest rank in certain army and air force 元帅，最高级军官 ❷an official responsible for important public events or ceremonies 司仪，典礼官，司礼官 ❸an official with the func-

tions of a sheriff 法院执行官 Ⅱ *v.* (-ll- or -l-) ❶ arrange in good or correct order 排列；安排；整理：~ troops 集结部队 ❷ lead（a person）to the correct place, especially on a ceremonial or important occasion（尤指在正式或重要场合）带领；引导：He ~led the minister into the presence of her. 他领这位部长去见她。

martial /ˈmɑːʃl/

adj. having to do with war 战争的；军事的：~ music 军乐/~ law 军事管制法；戒严令

martyr /ˈmɑːtə(r)/

Ⅰ *n.* one who dies because of his religion or who is badly treated because of his beliefs 烈士，殉难者：die a ~ at one's post 以身殉职 Ⅱ *v.* put sb. to death; cause to suffer as a martyr 使殉难；折磨 ‖ ~ize /ˈmɑːtəraɪz/ *v.* 折磨；使殉难

marvel /ˈmɑːvl/

Ⅰ *n.* sth. that is wonderful and surprises people 奇迹；奇观：the ~s of nature 自然奇观/the ~s of modern science 近代科学奇迹/It's a ~ to me that he escaped unhurt. 他没受伤而逃脱了，在我看来是件奇事。Ⅱ *v.* (-l- or -ll-) be greatly surprised at（对……）感到惊讶；惊叹；惊异：~ at one's courage 惊叹某人的勇气/~ at sb.'s deed 对某人的举动感到惊异

marvel(l)ous /ˈmɑːvələs/

adj. wonderful; surprisingly good 奇迹的；妙极的；了不起的：a ~ film 一部极好的电影/~ weather 极好的天气/That was a ~ show. 那是一场绝妙的表演。

Marxism /ˈmɑːksɪzəm/

n. the political and economic theories of Karl Marx and Friedrich Engels, later developed by their followers to form the basis for the theory and practice of communism 马克思主义（马克思和恩格斯创立的政治经济理论，经后人发展成为共产主义理论和实践的基础）

mascara /mæsˈkɑːrə/

n. a substance used to make the eyelashes darker 睫毛膏；睫毛油

mascot /ˈmæskət/

n. sth. or sb. that is supposed to bring

good luck（被认为会带来好运的）吉祥人；吉祥物

masculine /ˈmæskjulɪn/

adj. ❶like or of a man 男人的；有男子气概的：a ～ fellow 男子汉/a ～ voice 男子般的嗓音/ ～ courage 男子汉的勇气 ❷ of male gender 阳性的："He"and "him" are ～ pronouns. He 和 him 都是阳性代名词。

masculinity /ˌmæskjuˈlɪnɪti/

n. the quality of being masculine 男子气概；男性

mash /mæʃ/

Ⅰ *n.* any kind of soft mixture（任何捣成糊状的）混合物；泥；浆 Ⅱ *v.* compress (food) with violence so that it forms a soft mass 把……捣成糊状：～ed potatoes 马铃薯泥

mask /mɑːsk/

Ⅰ *n.* ❶a covering for the face to hide or protect it 面具；口罩：People in the north wear ～s in winter. 北方人冬天戴口罩。❷a false face worn by an actor or actress （演员所戴的）假面具 ❸the head of a fox 狐狸的头 Ⅱ *v.* ❶conceal 隐蔽；遮掩：～ one's real purpose 掩饰真实目的/～ one's enmity 隐藏某人的敌意 ❷ cover (the face) with a mask 戴假面罩；参加化装舞会：go ～ing 去参加化装舞会

masked /mɑːskt/

adj. wearing a mask 戴面具的：The robbery was carried out by a gang of ～ men. 一伙蒙面人进行了抢劫。/ a ～ ball 化装舞会

mason /ˈmeɪsn/

n. ❶a stone-cutter；a worker who works or builds with stone 石匠；泥瓦匠；砖石匠 ❷freemason 互助会会员

Masonic /məˈsɒnɪk/

adj. of or connected with Freemasons or their beliefs，practices，etc. 共济会会员的：～ rituals 共济会会员的例行仪式/ a ～ lodge 共济会支部的会员集会处

masonry /ˈmeɪsnri/

n. ❶bricks or stones from which a building，wall，etc.，is made 砖石建筑：She was hurt by a piece of falling ～. 她被掉下来

的一块建筑用的石块砸伤。❷ freemasonry 共济会的制度

mass¹ /mæs/

Ⅰ *n.* ❶ a lump or quantity of matter，without regular shape 团；堆；块：A ～ of snow and rock broke away and fell on the climbers. 一块积雪和岩石突然崩落到登山者身上。/There are ～es of dark clouds in the sky. 天空乌云密布。❷a large number 大批；大量：She's got ～es of Christmas cards this year. 她今年已收到了很多圣诞卡。/a ～ of data 大批资料/a ～ of information 大量情报 ❸the amount of a material in a body measured by its resistance to change of motion 物体的质量 ❹ the mass of the majority of (people) 大多数（人）：The ～ of workers do not want this strike. 大多数工人不愿举行这次罢工。Ⅱ *v.* gather together in large numbers 集合，集结：Troops are ～ing on the frontier. 军队正在边境集结。‖ be a ～ of 遍布着…… /in the ～ 总体上 /the（great）～ of 大多数

mass² /mæs/

n. (used in the Catholic and Orthodox churches) the ceremony of the eucharist 弥撒（尤指罗马天主教的圣餐礼）

massacre /ˈmæsəkə(r)/

Ⅰ *n.* the killing of a large number of (usually defenceless) people 大屠杀（通常指屠杀手无寸铁的人群）Ⅱ *v.* kill in this way 大屠杀：When the soldiers captured the town，they ～d all the inhabitants. 士兵攻占该城镇时屠杀了全镇居民。

massage /ˈmæsɑːʒ/

Ⅰ *v.* take away stiffness or pain by rubbing and pressing parts of the body 按摩：The doctor recommended ～ for my back pain. 医生建议我做按摩医治背痛。Ⅱ *n.* the action of rubbing and pressing parts of the body 按摩 ‖ ～r *n.* 按摩师

masses /ˈmæsɪz/

n. the body of common people in society 群众：He spent his life trying to improve the living conditions of the ～. 他毕生为改善劳动群众的生活条件而努力。

M

masseur/mæˈsɜː(r)/

　　*n.*someone who gives massages 按摩师

massif/ˈmæsiːf/

　　*n.*a group of mountains 山岳；山群

massive/ˈmæsɪv/

　　*adj.*of great size, especially strong, solid, and heavy 大而重的；庞大的：a ～ monument 一块巨大的纪念碑

mast/mɑːst/

　　*n.*❶a long, upright pole of wood or metal that supports the sails on a ship 船桅；桅杆：The ～ on a ship holds the flags and sails.船上的桅杆挂着旗子和航帆。❷a tall pole for a flag 旗杆 ❸a tall steel structure for the aerials of a radio or television transmitter（无线电或电视发射机的）天线塔 ❹the fruit of beech, oak, and other forest trees（as food for pigs）（山毛榉、橡树等的）果实（做猪的饲料）

master/ˈmɑːstə(r)/

　　Ⅰ*n.*❶ a chief person；the person who controls sb.or sth.主人；有控制力的人 ❷ the captain of a merchant ship（商船的）船长 ❸ the master of a house 户主（男）❹ a male teacher in a school 男教师，校长 ❺ a person that is extremely skilled at a particular activity 专家 Ⅱ*v.*❶ become the master of 征服，控制 ❷ control；become skilled in 掌握，精通 ‖ ～hand *n.*能手 /～piece,～work *n.*杰作，名作 ‖ ～less *adj.*无主人的/ ～hood *n.*主人（或师傅等）的身份

masterful/ˈmɑːstəfʊl/

　　*adj.*❶（said about a person）powerful or domineering（人）有权力的，有支配力的 ❷very skilful 技艺高超的，精湛的 ‖ ～ly *adv.*好支配人地；技艺高超地

masterly/ˈmɑːstəli/

　　*adj.*having or revealing supreme skills 熟练的；技巧高超的

mastermind/ˈmɑːstəmaɪnd/

　　Ⅰ*n.*a person with superior brain 英才；老手 Ⅱ*v.*plan or direct a scheme 策划：～ a crime 策划一次犯罪活动

masterpiece/ˈmɑːstəpiːs/

　　*n.*a very good piece of work or art 杰作；名著：It's Behrman's great ～.那就是贝尔曼的伟大的作品。/We consider this novel his ～.我们认为这部小说是他的代表作。

mastery/ˈmɑːstəri/

　　*n.*❶complete control over sb. or sth. 控制，统治 ❷ thorough knowledge or skill 精通，熟练：his ～ of Arabic 他精通阿拉伯语

mat/mæt/

　　Ⅰ*n.*❶a floor covering made of woven straw, wood, etc. 席垫，地席，席子：a straw ～ 草席/ spread a ～ on the bed 在床上铺席子 ❷a small piece of material placed under objects on a table（桌上用的）垫：Put the hot dish down on the ～, so you don't spoil the table.把碟子放在垫子上，这样就不会烫坏桌子。❸anything thickly tangled or twisted together 丛，簇，团：a ～ of weeds 一簇野草 Ⅱ*v.*(-tt-)(cause to) become thickly tangled or knotted (使)缠结：As the fibers dry they ～ together to form a sheet.随着纤维的干燥，它们就缠结在一起，构成板状物。

match/mætʃ/

　　Ⅰ*n.*❶ a game or contest 比赛，竞赛：a football ～ 足球赛 ❷ a person equal in strength, ability, etc. 对手，敌手：find (meet) one's ～ 找(碰)到对手 ❸ marriage 婚姻：They decided to make a ～ of it.他们决定结婚。❹a person or thing combining well with another 相匹配的人（或物）：The chairs and the desk are a good ～.这些椅子和这张书桌很相配。‖ make a ～ of it 结婚/play off a ～ （平局后）再赛以决胜负 Ⅱ*v.*❶ put in competition 与……比赛：～ one's strength with that of another 与另一人较量 ❷ find an equal for；be equal to 是……的对手；与……匹敌：This hotel can't be ～ed for good service and food.这家旅馆在服务及饮食方面是无可匹敌的。❸correspond with (quality, colour, etc.) 相称，相配：The curtains and the carpets ～ perfectly.窗帘和地毯很协调。‖ Let beggars with beggars.龙配龙，凤配凤。‖ ～able *adj.*敌得过的，相配的/ ～maker *n.*媒人

matching/ˈmætʃɪŋ/

adj. having the same colour, pattern, style, etc. and therefore looking attractive together (颜色、模式、款式等)相同的；相称的,相配的

matchless /'mætʃləs/

adj. so good that nothing can be compared with it 无比的；无双的；无敌的：~ courage 无比的勇气

mate /meɪt/

Ⅰ *n*. ❶ a fellow workman or friend; a way of addressing a man 同事,伙伴,朋友；(打招呼) 老兄,老弟：Where have you been,~? 老兄,你上哪去了? ❷ a ship's officer in command after the captain 船长的副手：the chief (first) ~副船长;大副/ the second ~ 二副 ❸ the partner of an animal (especially a sexual partner) (常指动物的)配偶 Ⅱ *v*. (cause to) form a couple, especially of animals for sexual union and the production of young (使)配对;(使)交配(尤指动物)：They ~d a horse with a donkey. 他们使驴子和马交配。/Birds ~ in the spring. 鸟在春天交尾。

material /mə'tɪərɪəl/

Ⅰ *n*. ❶ anything from which sth. is or can be made 材料;原料：raw ~s 原料/writing ~ 文具/dress ~ 衣料 ❷ knowledge of facts from which a (written) work is produced 素材;题材;资料：teaching ~ 教材 Ⅱ *adj*. ❶ made or connected with matter or substance 物质构成的,物质的：the ~ world 物质世界 ❷ of the body; of physical needs 身体的;身体所需的：~ comforts and pleasures 物质享受 ❸ important; essential 重要的;主要的：a ~ difference 本质上的区别 ‖ ~ly *adv*. 大大地;实质性地;重大地

materialism /mə'tɪərɪəlɪzəm/

n. ❶ the theory that everything in the world is made up of matter or depends on matter 唯物主义：dialectical ~ 辩证唯物主义/historical ~ 历史唯物主义 ❷ the tendency to value, valuation of material things too much and spiritual and intellectual things (wealth, bodily comforts, etc.) too little 物质主义;实利主义

materialist /mə'tɪərɪəlɪst/

Ⅰ *n*. a believer in materialism 唯物主义者 Ⅱ *adj*. of materialism 唯物主义的

materialistic /mə,tɪərɪə'lɪstɪk/

adj. of materialism or materialists 唯物主义的;唯物主义者的：the ~ interpretation (conception) of history 唯物史观

materialize /mə'tɪərɪəlaɪz/

v. ❶ appear or become visible 显形,出现 ❷ become a fact or happen 实现;发生：The threatened strike did not ~. 那场威胁性的罢工没有发生。 ‖ **materialization** *n*. 物质化;实体化;具体化

maternal /mə'tɜːnl/

adj. ❶ of or like a mother 母亲的,似母亲的：~ care (instincts) 母爱(母性) ❷ related through the mother's part of the family 母方的;母系的：my ~ aunt 我的姨母

maternity /mə'tɜːnəti/

n. being a mother 母性：~ ward(hospital) 产科病房(医院)

mathematician /,mæθəmə'tɪʃən/

n. a person who is skilled in mathematics 数学家

mathematics /,mæθə'mætɪks/

n. the study or science of numbers 数学：His ~ is weak. 他的数学不好。/Mathematics is his weak subject. 数学是他比较差的科目。

mating /'meɪtɪŋ/

n. sex between animals 交尾;交配

matriarch /'meɪtrɪɑːk/

n. a woman, especially a mother or grandmother, who rules a family or a group of people 女家长;女族长

matriarchal /,meɪtrɪ'ɑːkl/

adj. (of a society or system) controlled by women rather than men; passing power, property, etc. from mother to daughter rather than from father to son 母系的;母权的

matriarchy /'meɪtrɪɑːki/

n. a social system in which the oldest woman is the head of the family, and passes power and possessions on to her

M

daughters 母权制；母系制

matriculate /məˈtrɪkjʊleɪt/

v. enter a college or university as a student，usually after passing an examination (准许)进入大学；录取；被录取

matriculation /məˌtrɪkjʊˈleɪʃn/

n. ❶ the act of matriculating 录取入学 ❷ an examination held by colleges or universities which must be passed before a student can be admitted (学院或大学的)入学考试

matrix /ˈmeɪtrɪks/

n. (*pl.* matrices) ❶ a mould or framework in which sth. is made or allowed to develop 模板 ❷ an array of quantities or expressions in rows and columns that is treated as a single quantity 矩，矩阵 ❸ an interconnected array of circuit elements that resembles a lattice or grid 矩阵连接

matron /ˈmeɪtrən/

n. ❶ a woman in charge of nurses in a hospital 护士长 ❷ a woman in charge of the feeding，medical care，etc. in a school (学校的)女总管；女舍监 ‖ ～ly *adj.* 尊严的，高贵的，庄重的；与女总管有关的：～ly appearance 庄重的仪表/～ly duties 女总管的责任

matter /ˈmætə(r)/

Ⅰ *n.* ❶ the physical material of which everything that we can see or touch is made，as opposed to thought or mind 物质，物体 ❷ sth. printed or written 印刷之物；书写材料 ❸ a subject to which one gives attention；situation or affair 事情；问题：money ～s 金钱的事/They had important ～s to discuss. 他们有些重要的问题要讨论。❹ (a ～ of) used to emphasize how small an amount is or how short a period of time is 仅仅(表示强调)：a ～ of ten days 仅仅十天 ❺ importance 要紧；重要：No ～. 不要紧。/It makes (It's) no ～ whether you come early or late. 不论你早来迟来，都不要紧。/No ～ what he says，you should listen carefully. 不管他说什么，你都应该仔细听。❻ a trouble or a cause of pain，illness，etc. 困难；毛病；麻

烦：What's the ～ with you? (你)出了什么事？怎么啦？‖ Ⅱ *v.* be important or have an important effect on sb. or sth. 对(某人)很要紧：It doesn't ～. 这不碍事。‖ a ～ of course 理所当然的事/a ～ of life and death 生死攸关的事情/a ～ of record 有案可查的事/as ～ s stand (as the ～ stands) 照目前的情况/for that ～ (for the ～ of that) 就此而言/in the ～ of 就……而论/no ～ how(what，when，where，who，whether)……不管怎样(什么、何时、哪里、谁、是否)‖ ～-of-course *adj.* 当然的/ ～-of-fact *adj.* 注重事实的；平淡无味的

matting /ˈmætɪŋ/

n. a rough material used for covering floors，etc. 地席

mattress /ˈmætrɪs/

n. a large flat bag full of soft material on which we sleep 褥子：Mattresses are filled with feathers，cotton，or straw. 褥子里填充的东西是羽毛，棉花或稻草。

mature /məˈtjʊə(r)/

Ⅰ *adj.* ❶ fully grown and developed 成熟的：a ～ age 成熟的年龄 ❷ careful；perfected 慎重的，周密的：after ～ deliberation 经过周密的考虑 Ⅱ *v.* (cause to) become mature (使)成熟；(使)成长：His character was ～d by age. 他的性格因年龄而成熟。‖ **maturity** /məˈtjʊərəti/ *n.* 成熟，完成；到期

mauve /məʊv/

n. a lilac colour；lavender 淡紫色

max /mæks/

Ⅰ *n.* (informal) a maximum amount or degree (非正式)最大，最高 Ⅱ *adv.* (informal) at the most (非正式)至多，最多：The trip takes about 35 minutes ～. 这段路程最多花 35 分钟。 Ⅲ *v.* (informal) reach or cause to reach the limit of capacity or ability (非正式)达到最大，达到最高限度

maxi- /ˈmæksi/

pref. large；long 长的；大的：maxiskirt 长裙

maxim /ˈmæksɪm/

n. a widely accepted rule of conduct or

general truth which is briefly expressed 箴言,格言:an established ～ 公认的格言

maximal /'mæksɪməl/

adj. greatest or largest possible; being a maximum 最大的,最高的 ‖ ～ly *adv.* 最大地;最高地

maximum /'mæksɪməm/

Ⅰ *n.* the largest amount, number, or size 最大量;最大数;最大限度:achieve the ～ of efficiency with the minimum of labour 以最少的劳动取得最高的效率 Ⅱ *adj.* as large, fast, etc. as possible 最大的;最高的: ～ speed 最高速度

May /meɪ/

n. the fifth month of the year 五月:～ Day "五一"节,劳动节

may /meɪ/

aux. v. ❶ (used to show possibility) be likely to (表示可能性)或许:That ～ or ～ not be true.那件事可能是真的,也可能不是真的。❷used to express or to indicate permission or request for permission (表示许可或请求许可)可以:May I come in? 我可以进来吗? ❸used to indicate the purpose (表示目的)(以便)能;(使⋯⋯)可以:Sit here, so that I ～ have a chat with you. 坐这儿吧,我们好讲话。/ May you have a good luck! 祝你好运! ‖ as the case ～ be 看情况,根据具体情况/ ～ as well 是⋯⋯的好/ ～ as well... as... (做)⋯⋯与(做)⋯⋯一样

maybe /'meɪbi/

adv. perhaps; possibly 或许;大概:Maybe it is right.这可能是对的。/Maybe somebody took it by mistake. 也许有人拿错了。

mayor /meə(r)/

n. the head of a town or city government 市长:The ～ gave a speech at the opening.市长在开幕式上讲了话。‖ ～al *adj.* 市长的

mayoralty /'meərəlti/

n. the position of mayor or the time during which it is held 市长的职位;市长的任期

mayoress /'meəres/

n. the wife of a mayor or a woman mayor 市长夫人;女市长

maze /meɪz/

n. ❶a complex system of paths or tunnels in which it is easy to get lost; labyrinth 迷宫;迷魂阵:He was lost in the ～ for several hours.他在迷宫里兜了好几个小时出不来。❷sth. jumbled or confused; the state of being confused 错综复杂,混乱;迷惘,困惑:be in a ～ 弄糊涂了

me /miː/

pron. the object form of I 我(I的宾格):I need that book, so please give it to ～.我需要那本书,请交给我吧。/Give ～ the book.给我那本书。

mead /miːd/

n. an alcoholic drink made of honey, spices, and water 蜂蜜酒

meadow /'medəʊ/

n. ❶grassland on which cattle, sheep, etc. may feed 草地,牧场 ❷a low land by the bank of a river, lake or stream (河、湖或溪边的)低洼地

meagre(-er) /'miːɡə(r)/

adj. ❶thin; lacking flesh 瘦削的;皮包骨的:a ～ face 清瘦的脸 ❷ not enough in quantity, quality, strength, etc. 量不足的;质量不高的;力量不够的;贫弱的:a ～ income 微薄的收入

meal /miːl/

n. ❶the food taken at one time 一餐;一顿饭:a light ～ 便餐/a square ～ 丰盛的一餐/three ～s a day 一日三餐/make a ～ of noodles 吃一顿面条/between ～s 在两餐之前/Jack has just had an excellent ～. 杰克刚用完一顿美餐。❷ food that is eaten 膳食:have a good ～ 饱餐一顿 ‖ ～ ticket 餐券/～ time 进餐时间

mean¹ /miːn/

v. (meant) ❶ represent or express (a meaning) 意谓;意指:What does this word ～? 这个词做什么解释。❷ have sth. as a purpose or intention 意欲,计划:He ～s mischief. 他存心捣乱。/He ～s his son to succeed.他想要儿子获得成功。❸be determined about; act on 决定做:I ～ what I say. 我是言出必行。❹ be a sign of 是⋯⋯的征兆:Does this incident

~ war? 这事件是否会引起战争？❺ be of importance or value to 具有意义；重要：Your cooperation ~s much to us. 你们的协助对我们帮助很大。

mean²/miːn/
adj. ❶ （especially of a place）poor or poor-looking（指地方）简陋的；难看的：a ~ house in a ~ street 陋巷上的一所旧房子 ❷ unwilling to give or share what one has; ungenerous 自私的；吝啬的：be ~ about（over）money matters 在金钱问题上很小气 ❸（of behaviour）unkind; nasty（指行为）卑鄙的；下贱的：He took a ~ advantage of me. 他用卑鄙的手段欺骗了我。❹ （of the understanding, the natural powers）inferior; poor（指智力等）低劣的：a man of no ~ ability 一个能力很强的人 ‖ ~ly *adv.* 吝啬地；简陋地/~ness *n.* 卑鄙；吝啬

mean³/miːn/
Ⅰ *adj.* of an average amount, figure, or value（数量、数字、价值等）中间的，平均的：the ~ temperature 平均温度 Ⅱ *n.* a state or way of behaviour or course of action which is not too strong or too weak, too much or too little, but in between or in the middle position 中间，中庸：take the golden(happy) ~ 采取中庸之道

meander/miˈændə(r)/
v. ❶wander here and there 漫游：We ~ed through the park. 我们在公园里散步。❷ speak in an aimless way 漫谈；闲聊 ❸（of a stream）follow a winding course, flowing slowly and gently（指河流）缓缓蜿蜒而流：A brook ~s through the meadow. 一条小溪从草地中蜿蜒流过。

meaning/ˈmiːnɪŋ/
Ⅰ *n.* what is meant or intended 企图；意思；意义；含义：Do you know the ~ of this word? 你知道这个单词的意思吗？/What is the ~ of life? 人生的意义是什么？ Ⅱ *adj.* rich in significance or implication 有意义的；意味深长的：a ~ look 意味深长的表情

meaningful/ˈmiːnɪŋfl/
adj. significant; full of meaning 富有意义的；意味深长的

means/miːnz/
n. ❶the method, process or way by which a result may be obtained 方法，手段：a ~ to an end 达到目的的方法/the ~ of transport 运输工具 ❷ money, income, or wealth, especially large enough for comfort 金钱；收入；财富：a man of ~ 一个富人 ‖ by all ~ 尽一切办法；一定；务必；by any ~ 无论如何/by fair ~ or foul 用正当或不正当的手段/by ~ of 用，依靠/by no ~ 决不/by some ~ or other 用某种方法

meantime/ˈmiːntaɪm/
Ⅰ *adv.* in the time that sth. else is happening 同时；当时；在那当中：I'll finish the work ~. 同时我就可干完这工作。/We will leave at five ~ I will take a nap. 我们5点动身，现在这段时间(在动身前)我要睡一会儿。/Class is over at three, but you can start doing your homework. 下午3点下课，在那时你们可以开始做家庭作业。Ⅱ *n.*（= meanwhile）the period of time between two events; at the same time 期间；同时

meanwhile/ˈmiːnwaɪl/
Ⅰ *n.*（= meantime）the period of time before sth. happens or while sth. else is happening 当时；同时：You get the table ready and in the ~ I'll cook the fish. 你把桌子摆好，与此同时，我去烹鱼。Ⅱ *adv.* during this time; in the same period of time 在此期间；同时：They'll arrive in a few minutes; ~, we'll have a cup of tea. 他们将在几分钟后到达——我们将在这几分钟去喝茶。

measles/ˈmiːzlz/
n. an illness, which can be caught from another person, causing fever with red spots appearing on the skin 麻疹

measurable/ˈmeʒərəbl/
adj. able to be measured, or large enough to be measured 可测量的，可计量的：Objectives should be ~ and achievable. 目标应该是可度量、可实现的。

measure/ˈmeʒə(r)/
Ⅰ *n.* ❶the size, quantity, degree, weight, etc. as found by a standard or unit 大小、

数量；度量：give full(short) ～ 给足(不给足)分量 ❷ an unit, standard, or system used in stating size, quantity, or degree (大小、数量、度量的)单位；标准；制度：A metre is a ～ of length. 米是长度单位。 ❸ sth. with which to test size, quantity, etc. (测量大小、数量等的)量具：a ～ for liquids 液体量器 ❹ a sign of the size or the strength of sth. 程度：in some ～ 某种程度上 ‖ beyond(above, out of) ～ 无可估量，极端，过分/for good ～ 加重分量/in(a) great(large) ～ 大部分/in a (some) ～ 一部分，有几分/keep ～s with 宽大对待/know no ～ 无止境；极度/ ～ oneself against(with) 同……较量/ ～ up to(with) 符合，达到/set ～s to 限制；约束/take sb.'s ～(take the ～ of sb.) 给某人量尺寸，估量某人/without ～ 过度 Ⅱ *v*. ❶ find the size, extent, volume, degree, etc. of sth. or sb. 测量；量度：～ the distance 测量距离/ ～ sb. for a new suit 给某人量尺寸做一套新衣服 ❷ assess; gauge 估量，衡量：～ oneself by a high standard 以高标准要求自己 ‖ ～d *adj.* 量过的；(言语)有分寸的；整齐的/ ～ment *n*. 衡量，测量，(复)(量得的)尺寸，大小，长度；度量制/measuring /'meʒərɪŋ/ *n*.&*adj.* 测量；测量用的

meat/miːt/
n. ❶ the flesh of animals, apart from fish and birds, which is eaten 食用肉类(不包括鱼和鸟类) ❷ (of fruits, eggs, nut, etc.) the part that can be eaten (水果、蛋、坚果等)食用部分 ❸ valuable matter, ideas, etc. 重要内容，实质，要点：There was no real ～ in his speech. 他的演说里没有实质性内容。

meatball/'miːtbɔːl/
n. a small round ball of finely cut-up meat 肉丸

meaty/'miːti/
adj. ❶ full of meat 多肉的 ❷ full of valuable ideas 内容丰富的：a ～ lecture 内容丰富的演讲

mecca/'mekə/
n. a place that many people wish to reach 众人渴望去的地方；胜地：Lord's cricket ground is the cricketer's ～. 洛德板球场是板球运动员都想去的地方。/This resort is a ～ for tourists in the summer. 这个度假胜地是夏季旅游者向往之地。

mechanic/mɪ'kænɪk/
n. a person who has been trained to work with machines 技工；机械工；机修工；机械化

mechanical/mɪ'kænɪkl/
adj. ❶ of, connected with machinery or produced by machinery 机械的；用机械的；机制的 ❷ (of people or their acts) as if moved by machinery or habit, not by will (指人或其动作)机械似的；呆板的：～ answers 机械的回答

mechanics/mɪ'kænɪks/
n. ❶ the science of motion and force; the science of machinery 力学；机械学：Mechanics is taught by Mr. Smith 力学由史密斯先生执教。 ❷ the ways in which sth. works, produces results, etc. 技巧：the ～ of playwriting 编剧的技巧

mechanism/'mekənɪzəm/
n. ❶ working parts of a machine, etc. 机械装置；机件：the firing ～ of a rifle 步枪的射击装置 ❷ parts of an organism or system which work together 结构；机构；机制：the ～ of the body 身体结构/ the ～ of government 政府机构 ❸ the way in which sth. works or is constructed 机械作用；结构方式

mechanize/'mekənaɪz/
v. finish the production or work with machinery instead of manual labour 机械化 ‖ mechanization *n*. 机械化

medal/'medl/
n. a piece of metal with a design or words on it given to sb. to show that he has done sth. special 奖章；勋章；纪念章：award sb. with a ～ 授予某人奖章

medallion/mɪ'dæljən/
n. a round medal like a large coin, usually worn round the neck for decoration 圆形奖章；大奖牌

medallist/'medəlɪst/
n. a person who has won a medal, especially in sport 奖牌获得者：He was the silver

～ in the 800-metre race. 他是八百米赛跑的银牌获得者。

meddle /'medl/

v. take too much interest in, or take action about other people's private affairs; interfere (with) 干涉; 干预: Don't ～ in the internal affairs of other countries. 不要干涉别国内政。‖ ～some/'medlsəm/ *adj.* 好干涉的, 爱管闲事的

media /'miːdɪə/

n. a means or instrumentality which convey information to the public 媒体, 传媒

medial /'miːdɪəl/

adj. ❶ situated in the middle 中间的, 中央的, 居中的: ～ station 中间站 ❷ of average size 中等的; 一般的; 普通的: ～ earnings 一般的收入/ ～ temperature 平均温度

median /'miːdɪən/

Ⅰ *adj.* situated in or passing through the middle 在中间的; 通过中点的 Ⅱ *n.* ❶ a middle point or line 中点; 中线: The ～ duration of this treatment was four months. 这种治疗的平均疗程为四个月。❷ a medial number or point in a series 中位数; 中间点

mediate /'miːdɪeɪt/

v. act as a peacemaker between opposing sides 调解; 调停: ～ between two quarrelling persons 在两个争吵的人中间进行调停 ‖ mediation/miːdɪ'eɪʃn/ *n.* 调停; 调解/mediator/'miːdɪeɪtə(r)/ *n.* 调停者

medical /'medɪkl/

adj. ❶ of the art of medicine; of curing disease 医学的; 医疗的: ～ and health work 医疗卫生工作/a ～ certificate 健康证明书; 诊断书 ❷ of the treatment of disease by medicine than by operation 医药的; 内科的: a ～ compound 药剂/ a ～ ward 内科病房/ ～ examination 体格检查/ ～ inspection 检疫 ‖ ～ly *adv.* 医学上地; 医药上地

medicated /'medɪkeɪtɪd/

adj. containing a medicinal substance 掺入药物的: ～ shampoo 药物洗发剂

medication /medɪ'keɪʃn/

n. a medical substance, especially a drug; medicine 药物; 药剂: She's on ～ for her heart. 她因心脏病正在吃药治疗。

medicinal /mə'dɪsɪnl/

adj. used to treat and cure illnesses 药用的; 治疗的: ～ alcohol 药用酒精/He drinks it for ～ purposes. 他为了治病而喝这个药。

medicine /'medsn/

n. ❶ the science of treating and understanding illnesses 医学; 医术: practise ～ 行医 ❷ things which we drink or eat when we are ill to help us to get better 内服药: a ～ for colds 感冒药 ‖ take one's ～ 忍受不愉快的事情; 受到惩罚; 饮酒 ‖ ～ chest *n.* 药箱; 药柜

medieval /medi'iːvl/

adj. relating to or belonging to the Middle Ages (about A.D.476-1500) 中古的; 中世纪的(约在公元 476 年至 1500 年之间): ～ history 中世纪史/Medieval Greek 中世纪希腊语

mediocre /miːdɪ'əukə(r)/

adj. not very good; neither very good nor very bad; second rate 平庸的; 普通的; 第二流的; 中等的: a person of ～ abilities 平庸之才

Mediterranean /medɪtə'reɪnɪən/

adj. of the sea surrounded by Europe, Asia Minor and Africa 地中海的: the ～ (Sea) 地中海/ ～ climate 地中海气候

medium /'miːdɪəm/

Ⅰ *n.* (*pl.* ～s or media/'miːdɪə/) ❶ means by which sth. is expressed or communicated 媒介; 方法, 手段: Newspapers are a ～ for advertising. 报纸是广告的媒介。❷ sth. that is in the middle between two extremes 中等, 中庸: the happy ～ 中庸之道 ❸ a substance or surroundings in which sth. exists or moves or is transmitted 中间物, 介质, 传导体: Air is the ～ of sound. 空气是声音传播的媒介。Ⅱ *adj.* in the middle between two amounts, extremes, etc.; average 中庸的, 不极端的, 中等的: a man of ～ height 中等身材的人 ‖ ～ frequency (无线电)中频/～ wave (无线电)中波

meet /miːt/

Ⅰ v.（met）❶ come face to face with; come across by chance 遇见;相逢:I met him in the street. 我在街上碰见他。❷ go to a place and await the arrival of 迎接:Will you ～ her at the airport? 你到机场去接他吗? ❸ make the acquaintance of 引见;结识:I'd like you to ～ my husband. 我想把你介绍给我的丈夫。❹ satisfy(a demand,etc.) 满足;适合;符合:～ the requirements of the consumers 满足消费者的需要 ❺ pay sth. 支付:The cost will be met by the company. 费用将由公司支付。❻ undergo or experience 遭受;经历:～ the danger calmly 沉着应变/～ with misfortunes 遭受不幸 Ⅱ n. coming together of a number of people for a purpose 聚会,集会:a sports ～ 运动会‖ ～ one's end (fate) 死,送命/～ sb.halfway 在半路上迎接(或迎战)某人;迎合某人/～ trouble halfway 自寻烦恼/～ up with 偶尔碰见/～ with (偶尔)遇见,碰到

meeting/'miːtɪŋ/

*n.*❶ the coming together of two or more people by chance or arrangement 聚合;会合;会见:at the first ～ 在初次见面时 ❷ a gathering of people for a purpose 会议;集会:call a ～ 召集一次会议‖ ～ of minds 意见一致‖～place *n.*会场

mega /'meɡə/

*adj.*❶very large;huge 极大的;巨大的 ❷ excellent 优秀的;极佳的:It will be a ～ film.它会是一部优秀的电影。‖ ～ly *adv.*十分,极度

megabyte /'meɡəbaɪt/

n. a unit of information,namely one million bytes 兆字节

megalithic/ˌmeɡə'lɪθɪk/

*adj.*❶of megaliths 巨石的,巨石建成的:a ～ circle 巨石圈 ❷of the time when these stones were put up 巨石时代的

megaphone/'meɡəfəʊn/

n. a metal horn for speaking through to make the voice sound louder 传声筒;喇叭筒;扩音器

melancholy /'melənkɒli/

Ⅰ *adj.*sad;depressed;low-spirited 忧郁

的;消沉的;悲伤的 Ⅱ *n.*feeling of sadness 忧郁;悲哀

mellow/'meləʊ/

Ⅰ *v.*（cause to）become mellow as time passes （使）成熟;（使）柔和;（使）圆满 Ⅱ *adj.*❶ soft,pure and rich in colour or sound （颜色或声音）柔和的;丰富的 ❷ fully ripe in flavour or taste 熟透的;香醇的 ❸genial,cheerful,etc.,especially as a result of being slightly drunk 欢乐的;欢快的(尤因有酒意) ❹（of people or behaviour) wise and gentle through age or experience （人因年龄和经验而)成熟的;老练的:a ～ attitude to life 对生活的成熟看法

melodrama/'melədrɑːmə/

*n.*a play in which there are a lot of exciting and emotional events and in which people's emotions are very exaggerated 传奇剧;情节剧

melodramatic/ˌmelədrə'mætɪk/

*adj.*behaving in a very emotional and excited way;intended to arouse emotions 非常激动人的;激起感情的:a ～ speech 激起(听众)情感的演说

melody/'melədi/

*n.*❶ the arrangement of music in a tuneful way;melodiousness 美妙的音乐;和谐的声调音律 ❷a song or tune 歌曲;曲调 ❸ the part which forms a clearly recognizable tune in a larger arrangement of notes 主调;旋律‖ melodious /mɪ'ləʊdɪəs/ *adj.*旋律优美的,悦耳的

melon/'melən/

n. any of a few kinds of fruit which are large and rounded,with very juicy flesh inside and a firm skin 瓜,甜瓜

melt/melt/

*v.*❶ reduce or cause to be reduced from a solid to a liquid state usually by heating （使）融化;（使）熔化:～ ice(snow) 使冰(雪)融化/～ iron 使铁熔化/The ice has ～ed in the hot water. 冰在热水中融化了。/Iron ～s at a high temperature. 铁在高温下溶化。❷(of a solid in a liquid) (cause to) dissolve （使）(液体中的固体)溶解:Salt ～s in water. 盐在水中溶解。

❸(of a person, heart, feelings) soften or be softened (指人、心、感情)(使)感动;(使)软化:Pity ~ed his heart. 怜悯使他心软了。❹gradually disappear (逐渐)消散:The mist ~ed away. 雾渐渐消散了。

meltdown /'meltdaʊn/
n. the melting of the material inside an atomic pile, so that it burns through its container and allows dangerous radioactivity to escape (核反应堆)熔毁

melting /'meltɪŋ/
adj. (especially of a voice) gentle, soft, and pleasant (尤指声音)优美的;柔和的;悦耳的

member /'membə(r)/
n. a person belonging to a group, club, society, etc. 成员;会员:He is a ~ of a musical society. 他是音乐协会的会员。/a ~ of the delegation 代表团成员 ‖ ~-ship *n.* 资格;会员身份

memento /mɪ'mentəʊ/
n. (*pl.* ~s or ~es) sth. which one keeps to remember a person or a special occasion 纪念品;令人回忆的东西

memo /'meməʊ/
n. a short form of memorandum 备忘录 (memorandum 的缩略形式)

memoir /'memwɑ:(r)/
n. ❶ a record of events, especially by sb. with first-hand knowledge 传记 ❷ (*pl.*) the person's own written account of his life or experiences 回忆录:the flood of war ~s by generals and politicians 将军和政治家们所写的多如潮涌的战争回忆录 ❸ an essay on a learned subject, especially studied by the writer 研究报告;学术论文:He has published a ~ on the subject of his investigation. 他已发表了有关他的调查重点的学术论文。

memorable /'memərəbl/
adj. worthy to be remembered 值得纪念的;难忘的:a ~ day 值得纪念的日子

memorandum /ˌmemə'rændəm/
n. (*pl.* ~s or memoranda /ˌmemə'rændə/) ❶ a note or record for future use; a brief informal note or report 备忘录:make a ~ of sth. 记录某事 ❷ an informal busi-ness communication, usually unsigned 非正式商业文件

memorial /mə'mɔːrɪəl/
Ⅰ *n.* sth. made to remind people of an event, person, etc. 纪念物;纪念馆;纪念碑:a war ~ 战争纪念碑 Ⅱ *adj.* in honour of someone who has died so that they will be remembered 记忆的;纪念的;追悼的:~ meeting 追悼会

memorize /'meməraɪz/
v. learn by heart; commit to memory 默记;记住:He ~d these sentence patterns. 他记住了这些句型。

memory /'meməri/
n. ❶ the ability to remember things 记忆力;记性:have a good (bad) ~ 记性好(坏) ❷ the time during which things happened which someone can remember 记忆力所及的时期:be still within living ~ 还被令人所记忆 ❸ sth. that you remember from the past 记住的事情;记忆:a ~ of one's childhood 童年的回忆 ‖ beyond (within) the ~ of men 有史以前(以来)/commit sth. to ~ 把某事记住/in ~ of 纪念/slip sb.'s ~ 使某人一时想不起来/to the best of one's ~ 就记忆力所及

mend /mend/
Ⅰ *v.* ❶ repair; make sth. torn or broken good again 修理;修补;缝补:~ a road 修路 ❷ be free from faults or errors 改善,改进;改正:~ one's ways 改过自新 ❸ recover or heal 恢复健康;愈合:The patient is ~ing nicely. 病人正在日益好转。‖ It's never too late to ~. 改过不嫌晚。/Least said, soonest ~ed. 多说反坏事。/ ~ or end 不改则废/ ~ or mar 或成之或毁之 Ⅱ *n.* the part mended after breaking; a patch or darn 修补好的地方;修理部分:The ~ is almost invisible. 修理的部分几乎看不出来。‖ on the ~ (on the ~ing hand) (病情或事态)在好转中 ‖ ~able *adj.* 可修补的,可改正的/ ~er *n.* (常用以构成复合词)修补者/ ~ing /'mendɪŋ/ *n.* 修补工作;需修补的东西

menstruate /'menstrueɪt/

*v.*produce monthly blood from the uterus 来月经；行经

menstruation/ˌmenstrʊˈeɪʃn/

　n. woman's monthly discharge of blood from the womb 月经 ‖ **menstrual** /ˈmenstrʊəl/　*adj.*月经的；每月一次的

mental/ˈmentl/

　*adj.*❶ of or in the mind 心理的；智力的；精神的：～ labour 脑力劳动 / ～ faculties 智力/ ～ outlook 精神面貌 ❷ concerning illness of the mind 精神病的：a ～ patient 精神病人 /a ～ specialist 精神病专家 ‖ ～ly *adv.*精神上；智力上；在内心

mentality /menˈtæləti/

　*n.*a person's mental ability or attitude of mind 智能；心态

mention/ˈmenʃn/

　Ⅰ *v.*speak or write about sth. briefly 简短地提及；说到；写到：I must just ～ that everyone has been very kind to us here. 我得提一提大家对我们实在太好了。Ⅱ *n.*brief reference to sb. or sth. 提及：He made no ～ of his work.他根本没提他的工作。

menu/ˈmenjuː/

　*n.*❶a list of different kinds of food that can be obtained in a hotel, restaurant, etc. (旅馆、餐馆等)菜单：What's on the ～ tonight? 今晚的菜单上有什么菜？❷a list of options from which a user can choose which is displayed on a computer screen 项目单，选择单，命令

merchandise/ˈmɜːtʃəndaɪz/

　*n.*products that are bought, sold or traded 商品

merchant/ˈmɜːtʃənt/

　*n.*a person who buys and sells goods, especially in large amount in foreign countries 商人(通常指批发商,尤指与外国通商者)：a coal ～ 煤炭商 ‖ ～able *adj.*可销售的；有销路的

merciful/ˈmɜːsɪfl/

　*adj.*having or showing mercy 仁慈的；宽大的：a ～ man 仁慈的人 / be ～ to sth. (sb.) 对某物（某人）仁慈

merciless/ˈmɜːsɪlɪs/

　*adj.*cruel；without mercy 残忍的；冷酷无情的：～ blows 无情的打击 / be ～ to sth.(sb.) 对某物（某人）残酷

mercury/ˈmɜːkjʊri/

　n. a silver-coloured metal, usually liquid 水银；汞

Mercury/ˈmɜːkjʊri/

　n. a small planet that is the closest to the sun in the solar system, sometimes visible to the naked eye just after sunset 水星

mercy/ˈmɜːsi/

　*n.*willingness to forgive, not to punish；kindness and pity 怜悯；宽恕；仁慈：throw oneself on sb.'s ～ 请求某人的宽容 ‖ at the ～ of 在……支配中；任凭……摆布/be left to the tender ～（mercies) of 任凭虐待/have ～ on(upon) 对……表示怜悯/without ～ 毫不容情地；残忍地

mere/mɪə(r)/

　*adj.*not more than；no better than；only 仅仅；不过；几乎就是；只：a ～ child 仅仅是个小孩子

merely/ˈmɪəli/

　*adv.*only；simply 仅仅；只，不过：I ～ suggested you should do it again；there's no need to get annoyed. 我只是建议你应该重新做；你不需要为此而不高兴。/She's ～ a child.她只不过是个小孩。

merge/mɜːdʒ/

　*v.*combine or cause(two or more things) to combine, especially gradually, so as to become a single thing (使)兼并,吞并,合并：～ a company into another 把一家公司并入另一家公司/That group ～d many smaller enterprises.那个集团吞并了许多较小的企业。‖ ～r *n.*(企业等的)合并；并吞；合并者/ ～nce/ˈmɜːdʒəns/ *n.*合并；结合；消失

meridian/məˈrɪdiən/

　*n.*❶an imaginary circle of the earth passing through the geographical poles and any given point on the earth's surface 子午圈,子午线：All places on the same ～ have the same longitude.在同一子午线上的地方都有相同的经度。❷ the highest point; the highest point of power, success, etc. 顶点;(权力、成就等的)全盛时期:He is now at the ～ of his intellectual power. 他现在正值智力最盛期。

merit/'merɪt/

　I n.❶ sth. that is good in sth. or sb.; excellence; good quality 长处,优点:～s and demerits 优缺点 ❷the quality or fact of deserving reward 功劳,功绩:a certificate of ～ 奖状 Ⅱ v. be worthy of; deserve; have a right to 值得,应受赏(罚):It ～s our attention. 这事值得我们注意。

meritorious /ˌmerɪ'tɔːrɪəs/

　adj. having merit; deserving praise 应受奖赏的;值得称赞的 ‖ ～ly adv. 值得称颂地

mermaid/'mɜːmeɪd/

　n. an imaginary creature supposed to live in the sea, with a woman's body but a fish's tail instead of legs (传说中的)美人鱼

merrily /'merɪli/

　adv.❶in a cheerful way 欢快地,兴高采烈地 ❷in a brisk and lively way 轻快地,活跃地

merriment/'merɪmənt/

　n. laughter and sounds of fun and enjoyment 欢乐;欢笑;快活:His strange new hairstyle was the cause of much ～. 他新奇的发型引来一片笑声。

merry/'meri/

　adj. cheerful; full of lively happiness, fun, etc. 高兴的;快乐的;活跃的:Merry Christmas! 祝圣诞节快乐! ‖ as ～ as a cricket 非常快活/make ～ at another's expense 以取笑别人为乐/make ～ over 嘲弄,嘲笑

mesh/meʃ/

　I n.❶ a piece of material woven in a fine network with small holes between the threads (一张)网;网状物:a net with half-inch ～es 半英寸孔的网 ❷ (pl.)the threads in such a network 网丝:the ～es of a spider's web 蜘蛛网系/ The fish were caught in the ～es of the net. 鱼落入网中。 Ⅱ v. connect; be held together 相联结;相啮合:The teeth on the gears ～

as they turn round. 转动时齿轮上的齿与齿相啮合。

mess/mes/

　I n. a state of disorder or untidiness 混乱;肮脏:make a ～ of sth. 把某事弄得一团糟/ get into a ～ 陷入困境 Ⅱ v. put (sth.) into an untidy state 弄糟;搞乱;弄脏:The boy's clothes are all ～ed. 这男孩的衣服都弄脏了。 ‖ ～ about (around) 浪费时间,混日子/ ～ up 搞乱;弄糟;粗暴地处理 ‖ ～y/'mesi/ adj. 凌乱的;混乱的;肮脏的

message/'mesɪdʒ/

　n. a spoken or written piece of information passed from one person to another 音信,消息:a ～ of greeting 贺电,贺信 ‖ a ～ centre 文件收发所/a New Year ～ 新年祝贺/run ～s for sb. 为某人送信跑腿/verbal(oral) ～ 口信/send a person on a ～ 差人出去/an international ～ 国际电报

messenger/'mesɪndʒə(r)/

　n. a person who takes message 报信的人,信差

metabolism/mə'tæbəlɪzəm/

　n. the process by which living cells change to gain energy 新陈代谢

metabolic/ˌmetə'bɒlɪk/

　adj. of or relating to metabolism 新陈代谢的

metal/'metl/

　I n.❶ a hard substance such as iron, tin, gold, etc. 金属:Copper and sliver are both ～s. 铜和银都是金属。 ❷ small broken stones for making roads 铺路用的碎石 Ⅱ v. cover (a road) with small broken stones 用碎石修补道路 ‖ ～lic /mɪ'tælɪk/ adj. 金属的;似金属的

metaphor/'metəfə(r)/

　n. (the use of) a word or phrase which describes one thing by stating another thing with it can be compared without using the words "as" or "like" 隐喻;暗喻 ‖ ～ical/ˌmetə'fɒrɪkl/ adj. 隐喻的;隐喻般的;含有许多隐喻的

metaphysical/ˌmetə'fɪzɪkl/

　adj.❶of metaphysics 形而上学的;玄学的 ❷ (based on abstract general reasoning or thinking) difficult to understand; based on abstract general reasoning 深奥难懂的;抽象的 ❸ (of British poetry) a 17th century style which combined strong feelings with clever arrangements of words 玄学派诗体的(17 世纪英国的一种诗体)

metaphysics /metə'fɪzɪks/
n. a branch of philosophy dealing with the nature of existence, truth and knowledge 形而上学;玄学

mete /miːt/
v. give, punish or reward sb. 给予,加以(惩罚、奖励等): ~ out punishment to the offenders 对犯罪的人施行处罚

meteor /'miːtɪɔː(r)/
n. a piece of rock or metal travelling through space which glows with heat when it enters the earth's atmosphere 流星

meteoric /ˌmiːtɪ'ɒrɪk/
adj. ❶ to do with meteors 与流星有关的;陨石的 ❷ like a meteor in brilliance or sudden appearance 迅疾的,流星似的: a ~ career 迅速成功的事业

meteorite /'miːtɪəraɪɪ/
n. a piece of rock or metal that has fallen to earth as a meteor 陨石

meteorology /ˌmiːtɪə'rɒlədʒi/
n. the science of the conditions in the earth's atmosphere (especially with regard to forecasting future weather) 气象学(尤指有关天气预报) ‖ **meteorological** /ˌmiːtɪərə'lɒdʒɪkl/ *adj.* 与气象有关的,气象的

meter /'miːtə/
Ⅰ *n.* a device that measures and indicates the quantity or rate of sth., such as the amount of electricity used or the distance travelled 仪表;计量器: a water ~ 自来水表/ an electricity ~ 电表/ a gas ~ 煤气表 Ⅱ *v.* measure the use of sth. by means of a meter 用仪表测量

method /'meθəd/
n. ❶ a way or manner of doing sth. 方法,办法: the deductive(inductive) ~ 演绎法(归纳法) ❷ the order or system in doing

things or thinking 条理,秩序: If you had used more ~, you wouldn't have wasted so much time. 要是你安排得更有条理些,就不会浪费那么多时间了。

methodical /mɪ'θɒdɪkl/
adj. doing things carefully, using an ordered system 细心的,有条不紊的: a ~ person 办事有条不紊的人 ‖ ~ly *adv.* 有条不紊地

methodology /ˌmeθə'dɒlədʒi/
n. the set of methods used for study or action in a particular subject, as in science or education 方法学,方法论;一套方法: a new ~ of teaching 一套新的教学方法

metre(-er) /'miːtə(r)/
n. ❶ a unit for measuring length, equal to 100 centimetres 公尺,米(长度单位,合100 厘米) ❷ any arrangement of words in poetry into strong and weak beats (诗的)韵律,格律 ‖ **metric** /'metrɪk/ *adj.* 米制的,公制的/**metrical** /'metrɪkl/ *adj.* 韵律的,格律的

metric /'metrɪk/
adj. ❶ based on the metric system 米制的;公制的 ❷ made or measured using the metric system 按公制制作的

metrication /ˌmetrɪ'keɪʃn/
n. a change from standards of measurement used before (such as the foot and the pound) to metres, grams, etc. (度量衡的)公制化

metricize /'metrɪsaɪz/
v. change to the metric system 把……改为公制;把……改为十进制

metro /'metrəʊ/
n. (*pl.* ~s) an underground railway system in cities in France and various other countries (法国及其他一些国家的)地下铁道系统;地铁: the Paris Metro 巴黎地下铁道系统 /Can you get there by ~? 你能乘地铁到那里吗?

metropolis /mə'trɒpəlɪs/
n. ❶ a chief city or the capital city of a country 一个国家的大都会;首都 ❷ an important centre of a particular activity (某特定活动的)重要中心: a business ~ 商业中心

M

metropolitan /ˌmetrə'pɒlɪt(ə)n/

　　adj. to do with or belonging to a metropolis 大都会的，大城市的

mettle /'metl/

　　n. the will to continue bravely in spite of difficulties 奋斗精神；勇气：The runner fell and twisted his ankle badly, but he showed his ～ by continuing in the race. 赛跑者跌倒了，他的足踝扭伤得很厉害，但他继续赛跑，表现了他的奋斗精神。‖ be on one's ～ 鼓起勇气 / put someone on their ～ 鼓起勇气；鼓励；奋发

mew /mjuː/

　　Ⅰ *n.* the sound made by a cat 猫叫的声音 Ⅱ *v.* make the sound as a cat makes 作猫叫声；猫叫

mews /mjuːz/

　　n. a back street in a city, where horses were once kept, now partly rebuilt so that people can live there, cars can be stored there, etc. (城市中偏僻的)小街，小巷，街道：They live at 6, Camden Mews. 他们住在卡姆登小街六号。

mezzo /'metsəʊ/

　　Ⅰ *adv.* quite；not very 中，适中，半 Ⅱ *n.* a voice that is not so high as a soprano's nor so low as a contralto's 女中音(歌手)

miaow /miː'aʊ/

　　v. make the crying sound as a cat makes 猫叫，喵喵叫

mickey /'mɪki/

　　n. ❶(also ～ finn) an alcoholic drink to which a drug has been added which will make the drinker unconscious 蒙汗酒(一种混有麻醉药的酒) ❷(take the ～ out of)make someone feel foolish by copying them or laughing at them 取笑，嘲弄

microbe /'maɪkrəʊb/

　　n. a living thing that is so small that it cannot be seen without a microscope, and that may cause disease；bacterium 微生物；细菌

microcomputer /ˌmaɪkrəʊkəm'pjuːtə(r)/

　　n. the smallest type of computer, used especially in the home, in schools, or by small businesses 微型(电子)计算机，微型电脑

microcosm /'maɪkrəʊkɒzəm/

　　n. sth. small and self-contained that represents all the qualities, activities, etc., of sth. larger；miniature representation (of) 微观世界，微观宇宙：In this fish tank is a ～ of life on the sea bed；it shows the sea bed in ～. 这个鱼缸是海底生活的一个缩影，它显示出微观中的海底情景。

microfilm /'maɪkrəʊfɪlm/

　　Ⅰ *n.* photographic film on which documents, books, etc. are recorded much smaller than actual size 微型胶卷，缩影胶片 Ⅱ *v.* photograph (sth.) using microfilm 把……摄成缩微胶片：～ old historical records 将过去的历史纪录拍摄成缩微胶片

microphone /'maɪkrəfəʊn/

　　n. an instrument which can change sound waves into electric waves, and can therefore be used in recording people's voices, etc. 话筒，麦克风，传声器

microprocessor /ˌmaɪkrəʊprəʊsesə(r)/

　　n. a small electronic device containing a silicon chip and used in calculators, computers, etc. 微信息处理机

microscope /'maɪkrəskəʊp/

　　n. an instrument with lenses which makes very small things appear bigger 显微镜

microscopic /ˌmaɪkrə'skɒpɪk/

　　adj. ❶to do with a microscope 与显微镜有关的 ❷too small to be visible without the aid of a microscope 用显微镜才可见的 ❸(informal) extremely small (非正式)极小的，微小的

microwave /'maɪkrəʊweɪv/

　　n. ❶an electromagnetic wave of length between 0.001 － 0.3 m 微波(波长通常为 0.001 － 0.3 米的电磁波) ❷the short form for microwave oven 微波炉

mid /mɪd/

　　adj. in the middle of；middle 在中间的；中间的：～ June 六月中旬 ‖ ～stream *n.* 中流 / ～summer *n.* 仲夏 / ～winter *n.* 仲冬，冬至 / ～year *n.* 年中；学年中期

midday /ˌmɪd'deɪ/

n. 12 o'clock of the day; in the middle of the day 中午; 正午: at ～ 在正午 / the ～ meal 午餐

middle /'mɪdl/

I *adj.* ❶ of the same distance from each end or side 中部的, 中间的, 当中的: a ～ road 中间道路 ❷ in the middle; intermediate 中等的, 中级的: a ～ school 中学 Ⅱ *n.* ❶ a point or part which is at the same distance from each side or end 中间, 中部, 当中: the ～ of a month 月中 ❷ waist 腰部: He is thirty-five inches round the ～. 他腰围三十五英寸。‖ in the ～ of 在……当中, 在……的途中 /in the ～ of nowhere 在偏僻的地方 ‖ ～-aged *adj.* 中年的 /Middle Ages *n.* 中世纪 / ～-of-the-road *n.* 中间道路 / ～ of-the-roader *n.* 走中间道路的人 ‖ middling /'mɪdlɪŋ/ *adj.*& *n.* 中号的, 中等的; 中级品, 中等货

middleman /'mɪd(ə)lmæn/

n. ❶ a person who buys from producers of goods and sells to consumers 中间商 ❷ a go-between or intermediary 经纪人; 中间人

middling /'mɪdlɪŋ/

I *adj.* ❶ moderate or average in size or quality (大小或质量)中等的; 普通的; 一般的 ❷ neither very good nor very bad 凑合的; 一般的 Ⅱ *adv.* fairly or moderately 中等程度地: The family is ～ rich. 这个家庭中等富裕。

midfield /ˌmɪd'fiːld/

n. ❶ the central part of a football pitch away from the goals (足球)中场 ❷ the players on a team who play in a central position between attack and defence 中场队员

midnight /'mɪdnaɪt/

n. the middle of the night; 12 o'clock at night 午夜, 半夜: at ～ 在半夜 / the ～ hours 半夜三更 / burn the ～ oil 工作到深夜, 开夜车

midst /mɪdst/

n. the middle part 中部, 中央, 中间 ‖ first, ～, and last 彻头彻尾, 始终 /from (out of) the ～ of 自……之中 /in the ～ of 在……之中 /into the ～ of 入……之中

midterm /'mɪdtɜːm/

n. the middle of a period of office, an academic term, or a pregnancy (任期、怀孕中)中期; (学期)期中

might /maɪt/

n. great power, strength or force 势力; 权力; 力量, 力气: work with all one's ～ 全力以赴地工作 ‖ with ～ and main 尽全力

mightily /'maɪtɪli/

adv. ❶ with power or strength 强有力地, 猛烈地 ❷ to a great extent or degree 非常, 很: He struck it ～ with his sword. 他用剑狠狠地击了它一下。 / It pleased him ～. 那使他非常高兴。

mighty /'maɪti/

I *adj.* ❶ having great power or strength 强大的, 强有力的 ❷ very great 伟大的, 非凡的: a ～ nation 一个强大的国家 / high and ～ 趾高气扬, 神气活现 Ⅱ *adv.* very 非常, 很: It is ～ easy. 这容易极了。 ‖ mightiness *n.* 强大, 有力; 高官, 高位

migraine /'miːɡreɪn/

n. a repeated severe headache, usually with disorder of the eyesight 偏头痛

migrant /'maɪɡrənt/

n. a person or animal, especially bird that migrates 移民; 候鸟: Summer ～s nest here. 夏天候鸟来这里筑巢。 /Migrant workers move from country to country in search of work. 流动工人为寻找工作从一个国家迁移到另一个国家。

migrate /maɪ'ɡreɪt/

v. ❶ move from one place to another to live 迁移, 迁居 ❷ (of birds and fishes) come and go with the seasons (指鸟类或鱼类)随季节迁徙 ‖ migration /maɪ'ɡreɪʃn/ *n.* 迁居; 移居外国; (候鸟等的)定期迁徙 /migratory /maɪ'ɡreɪtəri/ *adj.* 迁移的, 移居的, 移栖的; 流动的

mild /maɪld/

adj. ❶ gentle; not violent 温柔的, 温和的: be ～ of manner 态度温和 ❷ (of food, drink, etc.) not strong or bitter in taste (指食物、饮料等)柔和的; 清淡的: ～ beer 淡啤酒 ‖ as ～ as a dove 非常温和 /draw it ～ 说(做)得适度 ‖ ～ly *adv.*

温和地;轻微地;适度地/ ～ness *n*. 温和;清淡

mildew/'mɪldjuː/

　Ⅰ *n*. (usually destructive) growth of tiny fungi forming on plants, leather, food, etc. in warm and damp conditions（通常指破坏性的）霉：roses ruined by ～ 被霉菌弄死了的玫瑰 Ⅱ *v*. affect or become affected with mildew（使）发霉：～ed fruit 发了霉的水果

mile/maɪl/

　n.❶ a unit of distance, equal to approximately 1.6 kilometres 英里（1 英里等于约 1.6 千米）❷ a race over this distance 一英里的赛跑 ‖ not a hundred ～s from 离……不远,离……不久 / ～post *n*. 里程标志 ‖ ～r *n*. 参加一英里赛跑者

milestone/'maɪlstəʊn/

　n.❶ a stone set beside a road to mark the distance between places 里程碑 ❷an important event or stage in life or history 里程碑式事件,里程碑：The visit is being hailed as a ～ in the relations between the two countries. 这次访问被赞为两国关系的里程碑。

militant/'mɪlɪtənt/

　adj. (especially of a person or a political group) ready to fight or use force; taking an active part in a struggle（指人或政治团体）好斗的;战斗性的：a ～ call 战斗的号召 ‖ ～ly *adv*. 好战地;强硬地/ ～ness *n*. 好战;交战

military/'mɪlɪtri/

　adj. having to do with the army or war 军事的;军队的,军人的;战争的：～ uniform 军服,军装/ ～ life 军队生活/ ～ police 宪兵/ ～ service 服兵役期

militate/'mɪlɪteɪt/

　v. stop or hinder; have a negative effect on 妨碍;对……有不利影响：The fact that he'd been in prison ～d against him when he applied for jobs. 他曾坐过牢这一事实对他求职很不利。/ The high risks involved in such a business venture ～ against finding backers. 这样的企业投资所冒的巨大风险有碍于找到赞助者。

milk/mɪlk/

　Ⅰ *n*. white liquid produced by female mammals as food for their young 乳,奶;牛奶 Ⅱ *v*.❶ take milk from e.g. a cow 挤奶 ❷ take away the poison from（a snake）取出（蛇）的毒液 ❸ get money, knowledge, etc. from sb. or sth. by clever or dishonest means 榨取：～ sb. dry 对某人进行敲骨吸髓的压榨 ‖ ～powder *n*. 奶粉 ‖ ～er *n*. 挤奶的人;挤奶器;乳牛/ ～man *n*. 卖(送)牛奶的人

milky/'mɪlki/

　adj.❶ of or like milk; mixed with milk 牛奶的;像牛奶的;掺奶的：a ～ food 加了奶的食物/ I like my coffee ～. 我喜欢加牛奶的咖啡。❷(of a jewel or a liquid) not clear; cloudy（指珠宝或液体）白而混浊的：～ gems 乳白色的宝石/ ～ water 混浊的水 ‖ Milky Way 银河/ the Milky Way galaxy 银河系

mill/mɪl/

　Ⅰ *n*.❶ a building or place where grain is made into flour 碾磨厂,磨坊 ❷ a factory where things are made by machinery 工厂：a paper (cotton, steel, saw, silk) ～ 造纸(棉纺、钢材、锯木、丝)厂 ❸ a small machinery for grinding grain into flour 小型碾磨机 ‖ go through the ～ 经受磨炼/ No ～, no meal. 不磨面,没饭吃。 Ⅱ *v*. put through a machine for grinding 碾,磨：～ grain (flour) 碾米(磨面粉)

millennium/mɪ'leniəm/

　n.❶a period of 1,000 years 一千年 ❷the point at which one period of a thousand years ends and another begins 千禧年 ❸ a period of great happiness and prosperity 太平盛世;黄金时代

miller/'mɪlə(r)/

　n. a man who owns or works a mill that produces flour 磨坊主;面粉厂主;磨坊工人

millet/'mɪlɪt/

　n. a cereal crop bearing grain in the form of very small seeds; the seeds (as food) 粟,小米

milligram(me)/'mɪlɪɡræm/

　n. one thousandth part of a gram in the metric system 毫克(千分之一克)

millimeter /ˈmɪlɪmiːtə(r)/
　n. one thousandth of a metre 毫米

milliner/ˈmɪlɪnə(r)/
　n. a person who makes or sells women's hats 女帽商(制造或销售女帽的人)

millinery/ˈmɪlɪnəri/
　n. ❶ women's hats 女帽 ❷ the business of making or selling women's hats, etc. 女帽制造业；女帽销售业

million/ˈmɪljən/
　num. & n. one thousand thousand 百万：hundreds of ～s of people 亿万人 /～s of people 几百万人 / Millions of other stars are even bigger and brighter than the sun. 千千万万颗其他星星比太阳更大更亮。

millionaire/ˌmɪljəˈneə(r)/
　n. a person who has a million dollars, pounds, etc.; an extremely rich man 百万富翁；大富豪 ‖ ～ss/ˌmɪljəˈneəres/ *n.* 女百万富翁

mime/maɪm/
　Ⅰ *n.* actions done without words, often as an entertainment (通常作为娱乐的)哑剧表演 Ⅱ *v.* do actions of this kind 作哑剧表演

mimic/ˈmɪmɪk/
　Ⅰ *adj.* imitated or pretended; done in play 模仿的；模拟的：～ warfare 模拟战 Ⅱ *v.* ❶ copy sb.'s speech or actions to make people laugh (尤指为逗笑而)模仿：～ sb.'s voice, gestures and manners 模仿某人的声音、姿势和举止 ❷ (of things) resemble closely 酷似：In a mirage the desert will ～ a lake. 在海市蜃楼中，沙漠时会现出湖泊的景象。‖ ～y *n.* 模仿；仿制品

mince/mɪns/
　Ⅰ *v.* ❶ cut meat or other food into very small pieces 将(肉或其他食物)切碎，剁碎 ❷ walk with short steps in a manner that is meant to be elegant but only looks foolish 扭扭捏捏地小步走 Ⅱ *n.* meat which has been cut into very small pieces 剁碎的肉，碎肉

mind/maɪnd/
　Ⅰ *n.* ❶ an ability to remember; a person's memory 记忆；回忆：bear(keep) sth. in ～ 记住某事物 ❷ a person's way of thinking or feeling; thoughts; opinion; intention 心思，想法，看法，意见；目的：make up one's ～ 下决心，决定/change one's ～ 改变主意 ❸ the ability to think and reason 才智：be in one's right ～ 脑子正常，清醒 ‖ absence of ～ 心不在焉/an open ～ 虚心/apply one's ～ to 专心于/a sound ～ in a sound body 有健全的身体才有健全的精神/be of the same ～ 意见相同；保持原来的意见/be out of one's ～ 精神不正常，发狂/bring(call) to ～ 使被想起，想起/give one's ～ to 专心于/have a (good, great) ～ to do sth. (很)想做某事/have half a ～ to do sth. 有点想做某事/have little(no) ～ to do sth. 不想做某事/have sth. in ～ 记得某事，想到某事，想要做某事/have sth. on one's ～ 为某事担忧/keep one's ～ on 专心于/never ～ 不要紧，没关系/open one's ～ to 把心里话透露给/pass(go) out of ～ 被忘却/presence of ～ 镇定，沉着/set one's ～ on 决心要，很想要/sink into the ～ 留在心头，被铭记在心/take sb.'s ～ off(sth.) 移开某人(对某事)的注意 Ⅱ *v.* ❶ take care of sb. or sth. 照顾，留心：Who is ～ing the baby? 谁在照顾那个婴儿？/ Mind your own business. 少管闲事。❷ dislike; object to 介意；反对：Do you ～ my smoking? 你介意我抽烟吗？❸ (not ～ doing sth.) be willing to do sth. 愿意：Lucy doesn't ～ helping me with my homework. 露西很乐意帮助我做家庭作业。❹ used to tell sb. to be careful about sth. or warn them about danger 当心；注意：Mind that step! 注意台阶！ ‖ ～ful /ˈmaɪndfl/ *adj.* 留心的，记住的/ ～less *adj.* 没头脑的；不注意的，忘却的

minded /ˈmaɪndɪd/
　adj. ❶ having a mind of a certain kind 具有……头脑的；有……思想的；有……观念的：independent-～ 有独立思想的 ❷ having certain interests 对……有兴趣的，热衷于……的：conservation-～ citizens 热衷于交际的公民

mine¹ /maɪn/

　*pron.*that or those belonging to me（物主代词）我的（东西或有关的人）：This book is ~.这是我的书。/He's a friend of ~.他是我的朋友。

mine² /maɪn/

　Ⅰ *n.* ❶ a big hole in the ground that people make when they are looking for coal, metal, etc.矿，矿山，矿井 ❷a rich source of knowledge 知识的源泉：a ~ of the raw materials for literature and art 文学艺术素材的源泉 ❸explosive device that explodes on contact 地雷，水雷：lay ~s 布雷 Ⅱ *v.*dig out sth.from a mine 开矿：~ (for) coal 采煤 ‖ ~r *n.*矿工

mineral /ˈmɪnərəl/

　Ⅰ *n.* any of various especially solid substances that are formed naturally in the earth, such as stone, coal, and salt, especially that obtained from the ground for human use 矿物，矿石 Ⅱ *adj.*of the class of minerals; containing or mixed with minerals 矿物的；矿质的，混有矿物质的 ‖ ~ **acid** 无机酸/ ~ **black** 石墨/ ~ **water** 矿泉水

minesweeper /ˈmaɪnswiːpə(r)/

　*n.*a naval ship fitted with apparatus for taking mines out of the sea 扫雷舰

mingle /ˈmɪŋɡl/

　*v.*bring or combine together or with sth. else（使）混合；（使）混在一起：They ~d with the other people at the party.他们与聚会上的其他人混在一起。

mini- /ˈmɪni/

　*pref.*of small size, length, etc.小，短，微（型）：minibus 小型公共汽车/miniskirt 超短裙

miniature /ˈmɪnətʃə(r)/

　Ⅰ *adj.*copied on a small scale 小型的：~ railway 小型铁路 Ⅱ *n.*❶a very small picture of someone 小画像，袖珍画 ❷any very small thing 极小之物，微型物

minibus /ˈmɪnɪbʌs/

　*n.*a small bus with seats for between six and twelve people 小型公共汽车，小巴，迷你巴士：The children go to school in a ~.孩子们乘坐小型公共汽车去上学。

minicab /ˈmɪnɪkæb/

　*n.*a taxi that can be called by telephone, but not stopped in the street（用电话叫但不能在街上叫停的）小型计程车

minimal /ˈmɪnɪml/

　*adj.*as little as possible 最小的；极少的：The storm did only ~ damage.暴风雨只造成极轻微的损失。/Her clothing was ~.她穿的衣服少得不能再少。

minimize /ˈmɪnɪmaɪz/

　*v.*❶ reduce to the least possible amount or degree 减到最少；缩到最小：~ the risk 把风险降到最低限度 ❷put the value, importance, effect, etc. of sth. at the lower possible amount 贬低（价值、重要性、影响等）：He doesn't want to ~ your services.他不想贬低你的贡献。

minimum /ˈmɪnɪməm/

　Ⅰ *n.*（*pl.*~s or minima /ˈmɪnɪmə/）the smallest amount of sth. that is possible or has actually been recorded 最小量，最少数：That is the very ~ that I shall accept.那就是我能接受的最低数额。 Ⅱ *adj.*the smallest or lowest that is possible or recorded 最小的；最少的；最低的：~ rainfall 最低降雨量

mining /ˈmaɪnɪŋ/

　*n.*the action or industry of getting minerals out of the earth by digging 采矿（业）：coal ~ 采煤/ a ~ company 采矿公司

minion /ˈmɪnɪən/

　n. an employed person or helper who is too obedient 忠实的奴才；特别驯服听话的雇员：He'll probably send one of his ~s to buy the tickets.他大概会派一个老实听话的人去买票。

minister /ˈmɪnɪstə(r)/

　Ⅰ *n.*❶a person who is in charge of a particular government department 部长，大臣：a prime ~ 总理，首相 ❷ a person who is sent to a foreign country to represent his own government 外交使节 ❸ a person who performs the services in a church 牧师 Ⅱ *v.*perform duties to help sb. 伺候，照顾；给予帮助：~ to a sick man's wants 照顾病人需要 ‖ ~ial /ˌmɪnɪˈstɪərɪəl/ *adj.*部长的；部的；公使的；代理的；牧师的，教士的

ministry/'mɪnɪstri/

n. ❶ a government department led by a minister 部：the Ministry of National Defence 国防部 ❷ a building where such a department works（政府的）部的办公楼 ❸ the office, duties or position of a minister 部长的职位；部长的职责

mink/mɪŋk/

n. ❶ a type of small animal like a stoat 水貂 ❷ the expensive fur from this animal 貂皮 ❸ the coat made from this fur 貂皮大衣

minor/'maɪnə(r)/

Ⅰ *adj.* smaller or less；less important 较小的；次要的：~ problems 小问题/a ~ part in a film 电影中的配角/a ~ operation 小手术 Ⅱ *n.* a person under the legal age（法律上）未成年者

minority/maɪ'nɒrəti/

n. ❶ the smaller number or part；less than half a total 少数，未过半数；少数派：The ~ is subordinate to the majority. 少数服从多数。 ❷ a group of people who which are different from a larger group in race, religion, etc. 少数民族：the ~ nationalities 各少数民族 ❸ any age prior to the legal age 未成年：They are in the ~. 他们尚未成年。

minster/'mɪnstə(r)/

n. a large or important church, especially one that formed part of an abbey 大教堂：York ~ 约克大教堂

mint/mɪnt/

Ⅰ *n.* a place where money is made 造币厂 Ⅱ *v.* ❶ make（a coin）铸造硬币：~ five-cent pieces 铸造五分钱的硬币 ❷ invent（a new word, phrase, etc.）创造（新词、短语等）：a newly-~ed phrase 一个新创造出来的短语

minus/'maɪnəs/

Ⅰ *prep.* being subtracted from another by（the stated quantity）减，减去：Four ~ two is two. 4 减 2 等于 2。 Ⅱ *adj.* (of a number or quantity) less than zero（数字或数量）负的：a ~ sign 负号；减号/a ~ quantity 负数 Ⅲ *n.* a sign（一）used for showing that a number is less than zero,

or that the second number is to be taken away from the first 负号；减号

minute¹/'mɪnɪt/

n. ❶ one of the sixty parts of an hour（时间上的）分 ❷ a short length of time 片刻：see you in a ~. 一会儿见。 ❸（*pl.*）the written records of the things that are discussed or decided at a meeting 会议记录：read the ~s of the last meeting 宣读上次会议记录 ‖ half a ~ 片刻/in a ~ 立刻/to the ~ 一分不差，恰好

minute²/maɪ'njuːt/

adj. ❶ very small 非常小的，细微的：~ particles of gold dust 金粉的细小微粒 ❷ very detailed；careful and exact 详细的；精确的；准确的：a ~ description 细致的描写

miracle/'mɪrəkl/

n. ❶ a surprising and wonderful event；wonder；a remarkable example 奇迹；不平凡的事：work (do) a ~ 创造奇迹 ❷ a wonderful or amazing affair 奇事；不可思议的事

miraculous/mɪ'rækjʊləs/

adj. wonderful；surprising；like a miracle 神奇的，令人惊讶的，奇迹般的，不可思议的：It has entered Britain's history in the story of an almost ~ escape. 它已经以一个近乎奇迹的脱险故事载入了英国史册。

mirage/'mɪrɑːʒ, mɪ'rɑːʒ/

n. an illusion caused by air conditions in hot areas（especially deserts）in which things which are actually far away seem to be near, or in which one seems to see sth. which is not actually there 海市蜃楼，幻景（尤见于沙漠地区）

mire/'maɪə(r)/

Ⅰ *n.* a soft wet area of low-lying land that sinks underfoot 沼泽，泥坑：be in the ~ 陷入困难之中 Ⅱ *v.* cover with mud；cause to be fast in deep mud（使）溅满污泥；（使）陷入泥坑 ‖ drag sb.（sb.'s name）through the ~ 把某人搞臭/find oneself in the ~ 发现自己陷入困境

mirror¹/'mɪrə(r)/

n. ❶ a piece of glass, or other shiny or pol-

ished surface, that reflects images 镜子：
The driver saw the police car in his driving ~.司机从反光镜中看到了警车。❷
an exact or close representation（of sth.）
真实的反映：This newspaper claims to be the ~ of public opinion. 这家报纸声称是忠实反映舆论的镜子。

mirror² /ˈmɪrə(r)/
v. reflect as in a mirror 反映：Do these opinion polls really ~ what people are thinking? 这些民意调查真实地反映了人民的想法吗？/This is a novel that ~s modern society.这是一部反映现代社会的小说。

mirth /mɜːθ/
n. laughter and fun 欢笑；欢乐

misapprehension /ˌmɪsæprɪˈhenʃn/
n. an understanding of sth. that is not correct 误解；误会：be under a ~ 处于误解的情况中

misappropriate /ˌmɪsəˈprəʊprɪeɪt/
v. take sth. and use it for a wrong purpose；use what belongs to another for one's own purposes 滥用；盗用；挪用，私吞：The treasurer ~d the society's funds. 财务主管挪用了协会的公款。

misbehave /ˌmɪsbɪˈheɪv/
v. behave badly 行为不当，举止不端 ‖ misbehaviour /ˌmɪsbɪˈheɪvə(r)/ *n.* 不良的行为；不规矩的举动

miscalculate /ˌmɪsˈkælkjuleɪt/
v. ❶ calculate sth. incorrectly 误算，算错 ❷ assess (a situation) wrongly 错误估计（或判断）‖ miscalculation *n.* 误算，算错

miscarriage /ˌmɪsˈkærɪdʒ, ˈmɪskærɪdʒ/
n. ❶ mistake in judgement or in punishment；failure 错误；差错；失败：~ of justice 判决不公，误判 ❷ an untimely delivery (of woman)；abortion 小产，流产

miscarry /ˌmɪsˈkærɪ/
v. ❶ (of a woman) have a miscarriage (妇女）流产，小产 ❷ (of an intention, plan, etc.) be unsuccessful；fail to have the intended result（意图、计划等）失败；没有得到预期效果

miscast /ˌmɪsˈkɑːst/

v. (miscast) ❶ give an unsuitable part in a play, film, etc.给（戏剧、电影等的演员）分配一个不适当的角色：He was badly ~ as Julius Caesar.分配他扮演恺撒，太不恰当了。❷ put an unsuitable actor or actors into (a part, play, etc.) 分配不适当的演员去演（某剧或某个角色）：The play is ~.戏中角色分配不当。

mischance /ˌmɪsˈtʃɑːns/
n. bad luck 不幸；灾祸；坏运气：by some ~ 由于不幸

mischief /ˈmɪstʃɪf/
n. ❶ damage or harm, especially on purpose（故意的）伤害，损害：make ~ between 挑拨离间 ❷ behaviour, especially of children that causes trouble and possible damage, but no serious harm（尤指）恶作剧，胡闹：boys who are always getting into (up to) ~ 总是胡闹的男孩子们 ‖ ~-maker *n.*挑拨离间的人

mischievous /ˈmɪstʃɪvəs/
adj. ❶ (said about a person) behaving badly in a troublesome way（人）好捣乱的，爱捣鬼的 ❷ (said about an action) causing trouble or harm（行为或事情）有害的；恶意中伤的

misconceive /ˌmɪskənˈsiːv/
v. understand wrongly；have a wrong conception (of) 误解；对……有错误观念：~ the nature of a problem 误解问题的性质

misconception /ˌmɪskənˈsepʃn/
n. failure to understand；a wrong idea 误解；错误的看法，错误的观念

misconduct /ˌmɪsˈkɒndʌkt/
Ⅰ *v.* ❶ behave badly or improperly 行为不端正，行为轻佻 ❷ manage badly 管理不善；处置不当：~ a business 业务经营不当 Ⅱ *n.* ❶ bad behaviour, especially improper sexual behaviour 不规矩的行为（尤指性行为）❷ bad management 处置不当；经营不善：He was charged with ~ of the war.他被指控对这场战争指挥不当。

miscount /ˈmɪskaʊnt/
Ⅰ *v.* count wrongly 算错，数错：The teacher ~ed the number of boys. 老师数

错了男生的人数。Ⅱ *n.* a wrong reckoning of the total number of sth. 误算;数错:a ~ in the election results 选举结果的误算

misdeed/ˌmɪsˈdiːd/
n. a wicked or illegal act 罪行;恶行;违法行为:He will pay for his ~s. 他必将因恶行而受到惩罚。

misdiagnose /ˌmɪsˈdaɪəgnəʊz/
v. make an incorrect diagnosis of (a particular illness) 误诊(疾病)

miser/ˈmaɪzə(r)/
n. a person who loves money for its own sake and spends or gives away as little as possible 守财奴;吝啬鬼,小气鬼‖ ~ly *adj.* 吝啬的,小气的

miserable/ˈmɪzrəbl/
adj. ❶ very unpleasant 悲惨的;不幸的:~ life 悲惨的生活 ❷ poor in quality 劣质的:a ~ dinner 菲薄的饭食 ❸ making people unpleasant 很糟的;使人难受的:~ weather 糟糕的天气‖ miserably *adv.* 悲惨地;糟糕地

misery/ˈmɪzəri/
n. ❶ a state or feeling of great distress or discomfort of mind or body 悲惨;痛苦:be in ~ from the toothache 受牙痛之苦 ❷ (*pl.*) painful happenings;great misfortunes 痛苦的事,苦难:a book about one's own frustrations and miseries 一本有关某人自己挫折和磨难的书 ❸ a person who is always unhappy and complaining 总是抱怨的人,老发牢骚的人:I've heard enough of your complaints, you little ~! 我已经听够了你的抱怨,你这个小唠叨鬼!

misfire/ˌmɪsˈfaɪə(r)/
v. ❶ (of a gun, etc.) fail to fire properly (指枪等)射失,不发火:The engine ~d. 发动机发动不起来。 ❷ fail to have the intended result 不奏效;失败:His plans ~d. 他的计划失败了。

misfit/ˈmɪsfɪt/
n. someone who is unsuitable for a position or for his surroundings 不适合其职位的人;不适应环境的人

misfortune/ˌmɪsˈfɔːtʃuːn/
n. ❶ bad luck 不幸;厄运:suffer ~ 遭受不幸/ companions in ~ 患难之交 ❷ an unlucky accident, or event 灾难,灾祸;不幸事故:She bore her ~s during the war. 战争期间她忍受着所遭到的灾难。/Her ~ was that she'd never had any children. 她的不幸就是她从未生过孩子。

misgiving/ˌmɪsˈgɪvɪŋ/
n. (usually *pl.*) feelings of fear, doubt and distrust 害怕;疑虑;不信任:I had some ~s about lending him the money.借给他钱,我有些担心。

misguided/ˌmɪsˈgaɪdɪd/
adj. having or showing faulty judgement or reasoning 判断或推理错误的;误入歧途的:a ~ attitude 错误或愚蠢的态度/ His untidy clothes give one a ~ impression of him. 他衣冠不整往往给人一种假象。

mishap/ˈmɪshæp/
n. an unfortunate accident or event(usually not serious)(通常指不严重的)不幸事件:a slight ~ 小小的不幸

mishear/ˌmɪsˈhɪə(r)/
v. (~d) hear sb.'s words wrongly or mistakenly 听错(人)的话;听错

misinform/ˌmɪsɪnˈfɔːm/
v. give (sb.) wrong information 向(某人)提供错误信息;向……误报:I'm sorry, I thought they had already been sent; I must have been ~ed. 很抱歉,我以为它们早已被送去了,一定是我得到的消息不正确。

misinterpret/ˌmɪsɪnˈtɜːprɪt/
v. explain wrongly; not understand correctly 误解,曲解;解释错误:I think you ~ed my meaning.我想你误解了我的意思。‖ ~ation/ˌmɪsɪntɜːprɪˈteɪʃn/ *n.*误解

misjudge/ˌmɪsˈdʒʌdʒ/
v. ❶ form a wrong opinion of sb. or sth. 对……判断错误;错看 ❷ estimate an amount or distance incorrectly 错误判断(或估计)‖ ~ment *n.*错误判断

mislay/ˌmɪsˈleɪ/
v. (mislaid) put a thing somewhere and be unable to find it later (将某物随便放置,后来找不到)误置;丢失

mislead/mɪsˈliːd/

　　v. (misled) ❶ lead or guide wrongly 把
……带错路，引错方向：be misled by a
guide 被向导领错路 ❷cause to be or do
wrong；give a wrong idea to 使误入歧途；
使误解：be misled into thinking that... 被
误导以为…… /The information is rather
～ing to give a wrong impression. 这些信
息很容易引起误解。

mismanage/mɪsˈmænɪdʒ/

　　v. manage or deal with (sth.) badly, unskillfully, etc. 管理不善，经营不当：It's
not surprising the company's in debt —
It's been completely ～d. 这家公司欠了
债是不足为奇的——它早就被经营得一
团糟。

mismatch/ˌmɪsˈmætʃ/

　　v. match wrongly or unsuitably, especially
in marriage 误配；错配：a ～ed couple 一
对错配的夫妻

misnomer/ˌmɪsˈnəʊmə(r)/

　　n. a wrong or unsuitable name given to sb.
or sth. 错误（或使用不当）的名字；名字
的误用：To call it a hotel is a ～—it's
more like a prison! 把这个地方叫作旅
馆是用词不当，它更像一座监狱！

misplace/ˌmɪsˈpleɪs/

　　v. ❶ (of love, trust, etc.) give to an unde-
serving person or thing 把（爱情、信任等）
给错对象；不该给：Your trust in him is
～d；he'll cheat you if he can. 你对他信任
错了，他一有机会就会欺骗你的。❷ put
sth. in the wrong place and unable to find
it temporarily (因错放) 暂时丢失：I've
～d my glasses again. 我又忘记把眼镜搁
在什么地方了。❸ put sth. in an unsuitable or wrong place 把……放错位置：
She's ～d in that job, she ought to be doing something more creative. 她被不恰当
地安排在那个工作岗位上，她应该去从
事一些更有创意的工作。

misprint/mɪsˈprɪnt/

　　n. mistake in printing 印刷错误

misquote/ˌmɪsˈkwəʊt/

　　v. make a mistake in quoting (a person's
words) 错误地引述（一个人的话语）；误
引：The minister complained that the

newspapers had ～d him. 部长抱怨报纸
错误地引用了他的讲话。

misread/ˌmɪsˈriːd/

　　v. (misread) read or understand sth.
wrongly 读错；误解：～ an instruction 误
解指示 / This book has been ～ by us. 这
本书我们没有读懂。

misrepresent/ˌmɪsˌreprɪˈzent/

　　v. give a wrong idea of 曲解，歪曲；理解错
误：You are ～ing my views on this matter. 你是在歪曲我对此事的看法。

miss¹ /mɪs/

　　n. (Miss) used before the first and family
name of a woman who is not married 小
姐；女士（用于未婚女子或女孩的姓氏或
姓名前）

miss² /mɪs/

　　v. ❶ fail to hit, hold, catch , see, etc. 未打
中；未抓住；未赶上；未看见：～ one's
way 迷路 / ～ a train 没赶上火车 ❷ feel
sadness or regret at the absence of sb. or
sth. 惦念，想念：I ～ you terribly! 我多么
惦记你呀! ❸ fail to put in or say 遗漏，
缺少：You've ～ed out one word. 你漏掉
了一个词。❹ keep away from；escape 逃
脱，躲避：He just ～ed being struck. 他险
些儿被打着。

misshapen/ˌmɪsˈʃeɪpən/

　　adj. not having the normal or natural
shape or form 畸形的：a ～ body 畸形的
身体

missile/ˈmɪsaɪl/

　　n. any object or weapon that is thrown or
projected 投掷物，发射物；导弹，飞弹：
The angry crowd threw stones and other
～s at the players. 愤怒的人群朝运动员
投掷石块和其他东西。/an air-to-air ～
空对空导弹/ a cruise ～ 巡航导弹

missing/ˈmɪsɪŋ/

　　adj. out of its usual place；not to be
found；lost；gone 不在的；找不到的；失踪
的；丢失的：The ～ ring was found under
the dresser. 那丢失的戒指在梳妆台上找
到了。/the ～ child 失踪的孩子

mission/ˈmɪʃn/

　　n. ❶ a number of people sent abroad with
special work (通常派至国外的)使团，代

表团：a trade ～ 贸易代表团 ❷ an important assignment that a person or group of people is given to do，especially when they are sent abroad 使命；使团的任务 ❸ one's duty in life 任务，天职：a historic ～ 历史使命 ‖ ～er *n.*传教士

missionary /ˈmɪʃənəri/
*n.*a person who is sent to another country to spread a religious faith 传教士

misspent /ˌmɪsˈspent/
adj. spend time or money in a careless rather than a useful way；used foolishly 浪费掉的；乱用的：a ～ youth 虚度的青春年华

misstate /ˌmɪsˈsteɪt/
*v.*state wrongly；give a false account of 误述；错误地说明：Be careful not to ～ your case.小心点，别把你的情况讲错了。

misstep /ˌmɪsˈstep/
*n.*❶a wrong step 失足，错步 ❷a mistake in judgement or action 失策；错误

mist /mɪst/
*n.*a cloud of tiny drops suspended in the air just above the ground，that makes it difficult to see 薄雾，霭：hills hidden in ～ 薄雾笼罩着的小山 ‖ ～y *adj.*有雾的；模糊的

mistake /mɪˈsteɪk/
Ⅰ *n.*a wrong opinion，judgement or action 错误：It's easy to make a ～.犯错误很容易。Ⅱ *v.*(mistook，～n) ❶be wrong or have a wrong idea about 弄错；误会：～ sb.'s meaning 误解某人的意思 ❷fail to recognize 错认：He mistook me for my brother.他把我错认为我的弟弟了。

mistaken /mɪˈsteɪkən/
*adj.*wrong；incorrect 错误的；弄错的：～ identity 认错了人 /You are ～ about it.这件事你弄错了。

mister /ˈmɪstə(r)/
n. ❶ used for addressing a man whose name is unknown（用作陌生男子的称呼）先生："What's the time,～?" Asked the little boy.小男孩问："先生，几点钟了?" ❷ (Mister)Mr.先生

mistime /ˌmɪsˈtaɪm/
*v.*do or say at a wrong time 做（或说）……不合时宜：～ one's remarks 说话不合时宜/～ one's arrival 到得不是时候/With the election only three days away，the government badly ～d its announcement of tax increases.大选只差三天就要举行，政府却非常不合时宜地宣布加税。

mistreat /mɪsˈtriːt/
v. treat sb. or sth. badly 虐待；不公平对待 ‖ ～ment *n.*虐待

mistress /ˈmɪstrɪs/
*n.*❶a woman as the head of a household or family 女主人，主妇：a ～ of the situation 一个能控制局面的女人 ❷a woman teacher 女教师：the English ～ 女英语教师 ❸a woman with a good knowledge or control of sth.有专长的妇女；女能手：a ～ of needlework 做针线活的能手

mistrust /ˌmɪsˈtrʌst/
*v.*feel no confidence in 不信任，不相信：～ one's own power 不相信自己的力量 ‖ ～ful *adj.*疑惑的，疑心的

misunderstand /ˌmɪsˌʌndəˈstænd/
v.(misunderstood) understand wrongly；put a wrong meaning on 误解，误会；曲解：I am misunderstood.我被误会了。/They have simply misunderstood what rock and roll is.他们完全误解了摇滚乐是什么。

misunderstanding /ˌmɪsˌʌndəˈstændɪŋ/
*n.*❶a failure to understand sth. correctly 误解；误会；曲解：There must have been some kind of ～.肯定产生了某种误会。❷a disagreement or quarrel 不和；争执

misuse
Ⅰ /ˌmɪsˈjuːz/*v.* ❶ use（sth.）in a wrong way or for a wrong purpose 误用；滥用：～ a word 滥用词语/～ public funds 滥用公款 ❷ treat（sb.or sth.）badly 虐待：She felt ～d by the boss.她感受到老板的虐待。Ⅱ /ˌmɪsˈjuːs/ *n.*（an example of）bad，wrong，or unsuitable use 误用；滥用：a ～ of word 误用字词 / a ～ of power 滥用权力

mix /mɪks/
Ⅰ *v.* ❶ put different things together to make sth.new；join together 混合，掺和：～ flour and sugar 把面和糖混在一起 ❷

(of persons) come or be together in society（指人）相处，交往：He doesn't ～ well.他不善与人相处。Ⅱ n. the combination of different substances, prepared to be ready,or nearly ready,for the stated use 混合物：cake made from a packaged ～ 由包装好的混合材料制成的糕饼‖ be (get) ～ed up in sth.(with sb.) 与某事(或某人)有(发生)牵连/～ up 拌和；混淆

mixed /mɪkst/
adj. ❶ consisting of different kinds of things or people 混合的；掺和的；混杂的 ❷ involving people from different races or social classes 不同种族(或阶层)混合的 ❸ for people of both sexes 男女混合的

mixer /'mɪksə/
n. ❶ a machine or device for mixing or blending things 搅拌器：a food ～ 食品搅拌器 ❷ a person who gets on in a certain way with others 交际家：He is a good ～. 他是一个擅长交际的人。❸ a soft drink for mixing with an alcoholic drink 调酒用的软饮料

mixture /'mɪkstʃə(r)/
n. ❶ sth. made by mixing 混合物；混合体；混合料：Air is a ～,not a compound of gases.空气是几种气体的混合物,不是化合物。❷ (a mixture of) a combination of different qualities,things or emotions 混合；混杂；混合状态：a ～ of grief and comfort 悲喜交加

moan /məʊn/
Ⅰ *n.* a low sound of pain or sorrow 呻吟声；呜咽声：the ～s of the wounded 受伤者的呻吟/the ～ of the wind on a winter evening 冬夜寒风的呼啸声 Ⅱ *v.* make a low sound of pain or sorrow 呻吟；呜咽；以呻吟声说出：～ for the dead 哀悼死者‖ ～ful *adj.* 呻吟的；悲伤的

mob /mɒb/
Ⅰ *n.* ❶ a disorderly crowd of people 暴民；乌合之众 ❷ a criminal gang 犯罪团伙：We were attacked by a ～ of armed fugitives.我们遭到一群武装逃亡团伙的袭击。Ⅱ *v.*(-bb-)(of people) crowd round

in great numbers, either to attack or to admire 围攻；围观：The angry crowd ～bed the unpopular mayor.愤怒的群众纷纷围攻那位不受欢迎的市长。

mobile /'məʊbaɪl/
adj. ❶ movable；not fixed in one position 可移动的；非固定的：a ～ missile launcher 可移动的火箭发射台 ❷ changing quickly,as of a person's face that quickly shows changes in his feelings or thoughts 易变的；常变的：a ～ face 表情多变的脸 ‖ mobility /məʊ'bɪləti/ *n.* 流动性；变动性；灵活性

mobilize /'məʊbɪlaɪz/
v. ❶ organize troops for active service in war 动员(部队) ❷ bring people or resources together for a particular purpose 动用；利用 ‖ mobilization *n.* 动员；调动

mock /mɒk/
Ⅰ *v.* ❶ mimic to laugh at sb.or sth. 嘲讽地模仿：They ～ed his way of walking.他们模仿他走路的样子。❷ laugh at；make fun of 嘲笑；取笑：～ at sb. 嘲笑某人 / a plan 嘲笑一项计划 ❸ cause to become useless 使徒劳：be ～ed with false hopes 抱着空头希望；落得一场空 Ⅱ *adj.* not real；false 假的；不真实的；模拟的：a ～ battle 模拟战 / a ～ examination 模拟考试/ ～ modesty 假谦虚 Ⅲ *n.* mockery 嘲笑；取笑：make a ～ of sb. 嘲弄某人 / Don't take to heart what was said in ～. 别把别人的嘲笑放在心里。‖ ～er *n.* 嘲弄者；嘲笑者

mocking /'mɒkɪŋ/
adj. showing that you think sb. or sth. is ridiculous 嘲笑的；嘲弄的；愚弄的：His voice was faintly ～.他的声音里略带一丝嘲弄。

modal /'məʊdl/
adj. ❶ of the mood of a verb 语气的；情态的 ❷ of or written in a musical mode 调式的

mode /məʊd/
n. ❶ a way in which sth. is done 方法，方式：civilized ～s of living 文明的生活方式 ❷ a fashion or style of dress；most usual fashion or custom （服饰)式样；风

尚;时尚;out of ~ 过时,不流行

model/'mɒdl/

　　Ⅰ *n*. ❶ a small copy of sth. 模型,模样:a ~ of an aeroplane 飞机模型 ❷ a person or thing used as an example 模范,典范:a labour ~ 劳动模范 ❸ a person who takes up a certain position for a painter, etc. 模特儿:stand ~ 做模特儿　Ⅱ *v*. (-ll- or -l-) ❶ fashion or shape a figure in a malleable material(用可塑材料)塑造:~ sb.'s head in clay 用黏土制作某人头部的塑像 ❷ make from a model;take as a copy or an example 仿造;模仿:She ~ed herself on her mother.她模仿母亲的一举一动。 ❸ work as a fashion model 做模特儿:She ~s for a painter.她为一个画家当模特儿。

moderate

　　Ⅰ/'mɒdərət/*adj*. average in degree, amount, quality, etc. 中等的;一般的;平庸的;适中的:~ prices 公道的价格/a ~ appetite 有节制的食欲　Ⅱ/'mɒdərət/*n*. a person who holds moderate opinions 不偏激的人　Ⅲ/'mɒdəreɪt/*v*. make or become less in force, degree, rate, etc. 减轻;缓和;降低:~ one's demands 降低自己的要求

moderation/ˌmɒdə'reɪʃn/

　　n. ❶ the quality of being moderate; the avoidance of excess or extreme 适度;温和;中庸:His doctor has advised ~ in eating and drinking. 他的医生劝告他节食。/Will alcoholic drinks be harmful taken in ~? 酒喝得适度有没有害处? ❷ (*pl*.)the first public examination for the degree of the B.A.degree(at Oxford University)(牛津大学)文学士学位初试

modern/'mɒdn/

　　adj. ❶ of the present or recent times 现代的;近代的:~ history 近代史 ❷ new and up-to-date 新的,时兴的:~ fashions 时尚 ‖ ~ization *n*.现代化

modernize/'mɒdənaɪz/

　　v. make modern; bring up to the present ways or standards (使)现代化:Every business is in danger of losing money if it can't ~.如果经营不能现代化,每一个行业都有亏本的危险。 / We should ~ the

transport system.我们应该使运输系统现代化。

modest/'mɒdɪst/

　　adj. ❶ not making oneself noticed or talking too much about one's own abilities or possessions 谦逊的;谦虚的:be ~ about one's achievements 对自己的成就非常谦虚 ❷ moderate;not large in size, degree or amount 适度的;适中的:I'm ~ in my requirements.我不过分要求。

modesty/'mɒdɪsti/

　　n. the state of being modest 谦虚;节制;适度:Her ~ prevented her from making her feelings known to him.她的羞怯使她不敢向他表露感情。

modification/ˌmɒdɪfɪ'keɪʃn/

　　n. ❶ the action of modifying sth. 修改,更改;改型,改装;改变 ❷ a change made 修改,改型,改变

modifier/'mɒdɪfaɪə(r)/

　　n. a word or group of word that give additional information about another word 修饰词

modify/'mɒdɪfaɪ/

　　v. ❶ make partial or minor changes to sth. in order to improve it 调整;修改;变更:~ the terms of a contract 修改合同条款 ❷ make sth. less severe or extreme 减轻,缓和:~ one's tone 缓和语气 ❸ qualify the sense of (another word) 修饰:adjective ~ noun 形容词修饰名词

modular/'mɒdjulə/

　　adj. consisting of independent units or modules 组合式的;组件的

modulate/'mɒdjuleɪt/

　　v. ❶ adjust or regulate sth. 调节;调整 ❷ vary the tone or pitch of your voice 变调;转调 ❸ change from one key to another 变化音调,音高 ❹ alter the amplitude, frequency, or phase of a carrier wave so as to convey a particular signal(改变振幅、频率或载波的相位)调制 ‖ modulation *n*.调整;调制

module/'mɒdjuːl/

　　n. ❶ each of a set of standardized parts or units used to make sth. more complex 组件,模件,预制件 ❷ a section of a course of study（课程）单元 ❸a self-contained unit attached to a spacecraft（航天器的）舱

moist/mɔɪst/

*adj.*slightly wet；damp or humid 潮湿的；湿润的：Winds from the sea are usually ～.海上吹来的风通常都是湿润的。

moisten/ˈmɔɪsn/

*v.*make or become moist 使湿润；弄湿：～ the lips 使嘴唇湿润 / ～ a sponge 把海绵沾湿

moisture/ˈmɔɪstʃə(r)/

*n.*condensed vapour on a surface；liquid in the form of vapour 潮气；湿气；水汽：The sun dries the ～ on the ground. 太阳晒干地面上的潮气。/Keep it from ～.不要让它受潮。

molecule/ˈmɒlɪkjuːl/

*n.*a smallest unit into which a substance could be divided without a change in its chemical nature 分子；摩尔：Molecules are so small that they are invisible under the most powerful microscopes.分子小到在最高倍的显微镜下都看不见。

moment/ˈməʊmənt/

*n.*❶a very short time；a brief period of time 顷刻；瞬间：Please wait（for）a ～.请等一下。 ❷（formal）importance（正式）重要，重大：a matter of ～ 重大的事/men of ～ 要人 ‖ at the ～ 此刻；那时/for the ～ 暂时；目前/Half a ～! 稍等片刻! /have one's ～ 走红；得意/in a ～ 立即，立刻/in one's extreme ～s 在临终时刻/of the ～ 此刻；现在/on（upon）the ～ 立刻，马上/to the ～ 恰好，不差片刻 ‖ ～ary *adj.*顷刻的；短暂的/ ～ly *adv.*时刻地，随时；一会儿

momentous /məʊˈmentəs/

*adj.*very important or significant 重大的，重要的

momentum/məˈmentəm，məʊˈmentəm/

*n.*the quantity of motion of a moving body 动量；冲量：The truck gained ～ as it rolled down the steep road.卡车驶下陡峭的路时，速度愈来愈快。

monarch/ˈmɒnək/

*n.*a sovereign head of state，especially a king，queen or emperor 君主；国王；女皇；皇帝：an absolute ～ 专制君主

monarchy/ˈmɒnəki/

*n.*a form of government rule by a king or queen 君主政体；君主制度：an absolute ～ 君主专制制度 / a constitutional ～ 君主立宪制度

Monday/ˈmʌndi，ˈmʌndeɪ/

*n.*the day of the week after Sunday 星期一：on ～（morning）在星期一（早晨）

money/ˈmʌni/

*n.*coins or paper notes 钱币；（硬币和纸币）；small ～ 零钱 ‖ **earn good ～** 赚大钱/**easy ～** 来得容易的钱/ **～ talks** 金钱万能/**put ～ into** 投资于……/**spend like water** 挥金如土/**splash one's ～ about** 大肆挥霍/**Time is ～.** 一寸光阴一寸金。 ‖ ～ed *adj.*有钱的，金钱的/～less *adj.* 没钱的/ ～wise *adv.*在金钱方面；财政上

monitor/ˈmɒnɪtə(r)/

Ⅰ *n.*❶a pupil given disciplinary or other duties over his fellows 级长；班长 ❷a person whose job is to check that sth. is done fairly，especially in a foreigner country（尤指派往国外的）监督员 ❸an apparatus for testing transmissions by radio or TV，for detecting radioactivity，for tracing the flight of missiles，etc.监测器；监控器 Ⅱ *v.*❶keep under systematic review 检测；监测 ❷listen to and report on（a foreign radio broadcast）监听（外国广播）

monk/mʌŋk/

n. one of a religious community of men living under vows of poverty，chastity and obedience 修道士；僧侣

monkey/ˈmʌŋki/

Ⅰ *n.*❶ a tree-climbing animal with a long tail and with paws that look like human hands 猴子 ❷ a child who is fond of mischief 淘气鬼，顽童：You little ～! 你个小顽皮! Ⅱ *v.* behave in a foolish way 胡闹：Stop ～ing about with the machine! 不要瞎弄机器! ‖ ～ around 闲荡捣蛋/make a ～ of a person 戏弄某人 ‖ ～ish *adj.*猴子似的；顽皮的，胡闹的

mono-/ˈmɒnəʊ/

pref.one ;single 单一 :monosyllable 单音节词

monologue/'mɒnəlɒg/
n.a long talk or speech by one person 独白(词)

monoplane/'mɒnəpleɪn/
n.an aircraft with one wing on each side of the fuselage 单翼飞机

monopolize /mə'nɒpəlaɪz/
v.❶control or use sth.so that other people are excluded 垄断;专卖:My uncle always seems to ～ the conversation.我的叔叔似乎总是垄断谈话。❷get or keep exclusively to oneself 独占;全部占有,完全控制 ‖ **monopolization** *n*.垄断;专卖;独占

monopoly/mə'nɒpəli/
n.❶the exclusive possession or control of trade,talk,etc.垄断;独占: ～ capital 垄断资本/the ～ of a conversation (使别人插不上嘴的)滔滔不绝的谈话❷the sole right to supply or trade in some commodity or service 专卖权;专利权;垄断权: gain(hold) a ～ 获得(持有)专利权❸a commodity or service controlled in this way 垄断商品;专利品;专营服务:make a ～ of some commodity 独家经销某种商品 ‖ **monopolism** /mə'nɒpəlɪzəm/ *n*.垄断主义;垄断制度/**monopolist**/mə'nɒpəlɪst/ *n*. & *adj*.垄断者(的)

monotonous/mə'nɒtənəs/
adj.not varying; unchanging 单调的;千篇一律的,缺乏变化的:He spoke in a ～ voice.他用单调的腔调说话。/ ～ food 单调的食物

monsoon/ˌmɒn'suːn/
n.❶a seasonal wind(mainly in Southeast Asia) blowing from the Southwest for part of the year and from the north-east for another part 季风(主要在东南亚,一年中部分时间吹西南风,部分时间吹东北风)❷a rainy season caused by the south-west monsoon (西南季风带来的)雨季

monster/'mɒnstə(r)/
n.❶a large imaginary creature that looks very ugly and has a strange or unusual shape,often very big 怪物,妖怪:ghosts and ～s 妖魔鬼怪❷an animal,plant, that is abnormal in form 畸形的动物(或植物)❸a person who is remarkable for some bad or evil quality 恶人,极残忍的人:a ～ of cruelty 一个非常残忍的人

monstrous /'mɒnstrəs/
adj.❶huge and ugly 巨大而丑陋的 ❷outrageously wrong or unjust 骇人听闻的;极不公正的 ‖ ～ly *adv*.邪恶地;骇人听闻地

month/mʌnθ/
n.one of the twelve periods of time which make a year 月;一个月的时间:this(last, next) ～ 本(上、下)月 ‖ for ～s 好几个月以来/ ～ after ～ 一月又一月/by ～ 逐月/ ～ in, ～ out 月月/this day ～ 上或下个月的今天

monthly/'mʌnθli/
Ⅰ *adj*.done every month; once a month 每月的;按月的;每月一次的:a ～ examination 月考/a ～ salary 月薪 Ⅱ *adv*.every month; once a month 每月,按月地: They pay ～.他们按月付钱。Ⅲ *n*.a magazine issued once a month 月刊(杂志)

monument/'mɒnjumənt/
n.a building, statue, etc. in memory of a person or event 纪念馆;纪念碑;纪念像: the Monument to the People's Heroes 人民英雄纪念碑 ‖ ～ al /ˌmɒnjuˈmentl/ *adj*.不朽的;纪念的;雄伟的

mood/muːd/
n.❶ the state of mind or spirits 心境;情绪:put sb.in a happy ～ 使某人情绪很好 / He is in a bad ～ now.他现在的心情很不好。❷ one of the groups of forms that a verb may take to show whether things are regarded as certain,possible or doubtful 语气: the indicative (imperative, subjunctive) ～ 陈述(祈使、虚拟)语气

moody/'muːdi/
adj. ❶having moods that change often and quickly 喜怒无常的,情绪多变的:a ～ child 喜怒无常的孩子 ❷ sad; gloomy 令人感伤的;忧郁的

moon/muːn/
n. ❶ the object which goes around the

earth and can be seen at night 月球,月亮：a half (full) ~ 半(满)月 ❷ the satellite of other planets (行星的)卫星 ‖ (a) blue ~ 不可能的事/below the ~ 在月下(的)/once in a blue ~ 千载难逢(地)/promise sb.the ~ 对某人做无法兑现的许诺 ‖ ~beam n.(一道)月光/ ~-blindness 夜盲/ ~cake 中秋月饼/ ~calf n.傻瓜/ ~-down, ~-set 月落(时)/ ~-eyed n.患夜盲症的；(因惊奇等)圆睁着双眼的/ ~flower n.月光花/ ~head n.笨蛋/ ~light n.月光/ ~lit adj.月照的/ ~rise n.月出(时)/ ~shine n.月光；空谈 ‖ ~less adj.没有月亮的/ ~y adj.月亮的；月照的；精神恍惚的

mop/mɒp/

I n. a piece of cleaning implement for washing floors or dishes 拖把；洗碗刷 II v.(-pp-) clean with, or as if with a mop 用拖把拖；擦拭：~ the floor 拖地板 ‖ ~ up 抹去，擦去；结束 ‖ ~py adj.拖把似的；(头发)蓬乱的

mope/məʊp/

I v.be in low spirits,often without trying to become more cheerful 闹情绪；丧气；抑郁；闷闷不乐：~ one's time away 闷闷不乐地过日子 II n. ❶ a person who mopes 闷闷不乐的人；忧郁的人 ❷ (the ~s) the state of moping 忧郁；烦闷；沮丧：He suffers from the ~s.他闷闷不乐。

moped/ˈməʊped/

n. a bicycle which has a small engine；a small motorcycle 机动脚踏两用车；机动自行车

moral/ˈmɒrəl/

I adj. ❶ concerning principles of right and wrong 道德(上的)：~ standards 道德标准 ❷good and virtuous 有道德的；品行端正的：a ~ person 有道德的人 ❸ teaching good behaviour 道德教育的：a ~ story 有教育意义的故事 ❹based on the sense of what is right or just rather than on what the law says should be done 道义上的 ❺ psychological rather than physical or tangible in effect 精神上的：give a person ~ support 给某人精神支持 II n.(pl.) moral habits；standards of be-

haviour 道德,品行：a high standard of ~s 高的道德标准

morale/məˈrɑːl/

n. the state of discipline and spirit in an army,a nation,etc.；the temper state of mind,as expressed in action (军队的)士气；(国家等的)风气,精神；(表现于行为的)性情；心境：The army recovered its ~ and fighting power.这支军队恢复了士气和战斗力。

moralist/ˈmɒrəlɪst/

n. ❶a teacher of moral principles 道德家；德育家,德育工作者 ❷ a person who tries to control other people's morals 说教者；卫道士

moralistic/ˌmɒrəˈlɪstɪk/

adj. having convention and narrow ideas about right and wrong behaviour 道德观念上因循守旧的；善恶观念狭隘的

morality/məˈræləti/

n. rightness or pureness of behaviour or an action 道德；(行为等的)道德性：One sometimes wonders if there's any ~ in politics.人们有时怀疑政治这东西是否有道德可言。/question the ~ of someone's actions 对某人行为的道德性提出疑问/public (private) ~ 公共(个人)道德

moralize/ˈmɒrəlaɪz/

v.express one's thoughts on the rightness or,more usually,the wrongness of behaviour 教化；说教

morally/ˈmɒrəli/

adv. ❶ with regard to moral principles 道义上；道德上：What you did wasn't actually illegal,but it was ~ wrong.你所做的算不上犯法,但在道义上是错的。❷in a moral way 有道德地；品行端正地：He behaves ~.他行为端正。❸ most probably 很可能：It's ~ certain that she'll be the next Minister of Education.她非常可能当选下一任教育部长。

morass/məˈræs/

n. a low-lying area of soft, wet ground；marshy area 潮湿低洼的地区；沼泽地

morbid/ˈmɔːbɪd/

adj.❶connected with disease 疾病的：a

〜 growth 疾病的生长 /〜 anatomy 病理解剖学 ❷（of sb.'s mind or ideas）unhealthy（指人的思想或观念）不健全的，病态的：a 〜 imagination 病态的想象

more /mɔː(r)/

Ⅰ *adj*. greater in number, size, amount, degree, etc. 更多的，更高程度的：More than one person have made the suggestion. 不止一人提过这个建议。Ⅱ *adv*. ❶ in a greater quantity; to a greater degree 更多；更：He works 〜 and better than he used to. 他的工作做得比过去更多更好。❷ again 再；另外：Count it once 〜, please. 请再数一遍。Ⅲ *n*. a greater amount of sth. than before or than sth. else or than average 更多：Give me some 〜. 再多给我一些。‖（and）what is 〜 更重要的是 /all the 〜 更加，越发 /〜 and 〜 越来越（多）/ 〜 or less 或多或少 / much 〜 更加 /never 〜 决不再 /no 〜 不再 /no（not any）〜 than 仅仅，至多，不比……更

moreover /mɔːˈrəʊvə(r)/

adv. in addition; besides 此外，并且：The price is too high, and 〜, the house isn't in a suitable position. 这房子价格太高，而且它的位置也不合适。

morning /ˈmɔːnɪŋ/

n. an early part of the day; the time between sunrise and noon 早晨；上午：on Sunday 〜 星期日上午 ‖ from 〜 till night 从早到晚 /〜 dress（男式）晨礼服 /〜 glory 牵牛花 /〜 paper 晨报 / 〜 sickness 孕妇晨吐

morsel /ˈmɔːsl/

n. a small piece of food; a bite of food 一小块食物；一口食物：not a 〜 left 一点儿食物也没剩下

mortal /ˈmɔːtl/

Ⅰ *adj*. ❶ which must die; which cannot live for ever 终归要死的：Man is 〜. 人终有一死。❷ causing death; fatal 致命的：〜 wound 致命伤 ❸ lasting until death; marked by great hatred 直至死亡的；不共戴天的：a 〜 enemy 不共戴天的敌人 ❹ accompanying death 垂死的；临终的：〜 agony 临死的痛苦 ❺ extreme or in-tense 极度的；极端的：in a 〜 fear of death 对死亡的极度恐惧 Ⅱ *n*. an ordinary person 凡人；普通人 ‖ 〜ly *adv*. 致命地；非常

mortar[1] /ˈmɔːtə(r)/

n. a mixture of lime or cement or both with sand and water, used in building to hold bricks, stones, etc. in place 灰泥，灰浆（石灰或水泥或两者和水、沙的混合物，用以黏合砖头、石块等）

mortar[2] /ˈmɔːtə(r)/

n. a short gun which fires shells high into the air 迫击炮

mortgage /ˈmɔːɡɪdʒ/

Ⅰ *n*. the conditional conveyance of property as security for the payment of a loan 抵押：We must pay off the 〜 this year. 我们今年必须付还抵押借款。Ⅱ *v*. give a person a claim on one's house, etc. as a security for payment of a loan 抵押：He 〜d his car to the bank for five thousand dollars. 他把汽车抵押给银行，借款五千美元。

mortify /ˈmɔːtɪfaɪ/

v. hurt the feelings of; make sb. feel ashamed or embarrassed 伤害……感情；使感到羞耻；使感到难为情：We were mortified by his silly behaviour. 我们因他的愚蠢行为感到羞耻。

mosque /mɒsk/

n. a building where Muslims worship 清真寺

mosquito /məsˈkiːtəʊ/

n.（*pl*. 〜es）small flying insects that sucks blood and can carry malaria from one person to another 蚊子：a 〜 net（curtain）蚊帐 / a 〜 screen 纱窗

moss /mɒs/

n. a green or yellow plant growing in thick masses on the wet surface 苔藓；地衣：〜-covered rocks 生了青苔的岩石

most /məʊst/

Ⅰ *adj*. greatest in number, amount, etc. 最多的；最高程度的：Who has the 〜 need of help? 谁最需要帮助？Ⅱ *n*. the biggest number, amount, part, etc. 最大量；最多数：Do the 〜 you can. 尽你最大的力量去

做。Ⅲ*adv.*❶ used to form the superlative of adj.'s and adv.'s of two or more syllables（用于多音节的形容词或副词前表示最高级）最；最高程度地：Which do you like the ～, dancing, reading or swimming? 跳舞,阅读和游泳三者中你最喜欢哪一样? ❷ very much 很,非常：It is a ～ dangerous trick to play with fire. 玩火是非常危险的把戏。❸almost 几乎：He goes to the bookstore ～ every week. 他差不多每周都去书店。‖ at (the) ～ 至多/ ～ and least 统统;毫无例外

mostly/'məustli/
adv. mainly or chiefly; in large part 主要地;大部分地;基本地;多半：They are ～ visiting scientists.他们大多数是短暂访问的科学家。/The earth here is ～ clay. 这里的土地大都是黏土。

motel/məu'tel/
n. a hotel which makes special arrangements for customers who have cars（附有旅客停车场所的）汽车旅馆

moth/mɒθ/
*n.*❶a winged insect, similar to the butterfly flying chiefly at night 蛾：a brain ～ 谷蛾 ❷a type of moth whose larva feed on cloth, fur, etc., and make holes 蛀虫：a clothes ～ 蛀衣服的蛀虫

mother/'mʌðə(r)/
Ⅰ*n.* a woman who has given birth to a child or a term of address to her 母亲：Failure is the ～ of success. 失败是成功之母。Ⅱ*v.* care for as a mother does（如母亲般地）照看：Ruth ～s her baby sister.露丝对她襁褓中的妹妹尽母职。‖ Mother's Day（美国、加拿大等的）母亲节（五月份的第二个星期日）/ ～ tongue 本国语言 ‖ ～hood *n.*母性;母亲身份;（总称）母亲/ ～less *adj.*没有母亲的/ ～like *adj.*母亲般的/ ～ly *adj.*母亲的;慈母般的;慈爱的/ ～-in-law *n.*岳母;婆婆

motherland/'mʌðəlænd/
n. one's own or one's ancestors' native country 祖国

motion/'məuʃn/
Ⅰ*n.* ❶ a natural event that involves a change in the position or location of sth. 运动：～ and rest 运动和静止 ❷ a particular movement, especially of the hands to communicate 手势;特殊的动作：graceful ～s 优美的动作 ❸ a proposal to be discussed at a meeting 提议：The ～ was adopted.提议通过了。Ⅱ*v.* direct by a motion or gesture（以动作或手势）示意：He ～ed me in. 他示意叫我进去。‖ go through the ～s（of）装（……的）样子/set sth.in ～ 开动某物,使某物运转 ‖ ～picture 电影 ‖ ～al/'məuʃənl/ *adj.*运动的,动的

motionless/'məuʃnləs/
adj. without any movement; completely still 静止的,一动不动的：The cat remained ～, waiting for the mouse to come out of its hole.猫一动不动地等着老鼠出洞。

motivate/'məutɪveɪt/
*v.*❶ provide sb. with a（strong）reason for doing sth. 激发,激励,使……产生动机：He was ～d by love, and expected nothing in return.他完全是出于爱,不期望任何回报。/ We've got to try and ～ our salesmen. 我们得设法调动推销员的积极性。❷be the reason why sth. is or was done 出于……的动机：This murder was ～d by hatred.这宗谋杀案是出于仇恨。

motivation/ˌməutɪ'veɪʃn/
n. the state of being motivated; need or purpose 动力;动机;诱因：The stronger the ～, the more quickly a person will learn a foreign language.动力愈强,外语学得愈快。/ His parents give him so much money that he's got no ～ to get a job.他的父母给他的钱太多,以致他不想找工作做。

motive/'məutɪv/
Ⅰ*n.* the cause of or reason for action; that which urges a person to act in a certain way 动机;目的：the unity of ～ and effect 动机与效果的统一 Ⅱ*adj.* causing or able to cause motion 发动的;运动的：the ～ power（force）动力 ‖ ～less *adj.*没有动

机的;无目的的

motor/ˈməʊtə(r)/

Ⅰ *n.* a machine that changes power into movement;engine 马达,发动机 Ⅱ *adj.* driven by a motor 机动的: ～ power 原动力 ‖ ～**bike** *n.* 机动脚踏两用车,摩托车/ ～**boat** *n.* 汽船 ‖ ～**ist** *n.* 驾驶汽车的人;乘汽车旅行的人

motorcar/ˈməʊtəkɑː(r)/

n. a vehicle on wheels, driven by an engine, that you can travel in car 汽车: drive a ～ 开汽车

motorcycle/ˈməʊtəˌsaɪkl/

n. a bicycle worked by an engine 摩托车;机动脚踏车

mottled/ˈmɒtld/

adj. marked with spots of different sizes and colours 杂色的;斑点的;斑驳的:～ leaves 斑驳的叶子

motto/ˈmɒtəʊ/

n. (*pl.* ～es or ～s) a saying, phrase, or word used as a rule or guide of life 箴言;座右铭;格言:"Think before you speak" is a good ～."想好再说"是一条很好的座右铭。

mo(u)ld/məʊld/

Ⅰ *n.* ❶loose soil rich in organic matter 土壤;松软沃土;leaf ～ 腐殖土 ❷a hollow container which shapes whatever was poured into 铸模;模子: a cake ～ 糕饼模子 Ⅱ *v.* ❶ become covered with a greenish-white substance which grows on food and clothes if they are left in warm wet air 发霉: Cake ～s easily in warm wet weather.在温暖潮湿的天气里糕饼很容易发霉。❷make sth. into the shape you want it to be 塑造;铸造: We ～ clay with our fingers.我们用手指把黏土捏成某种形象。❸shape or influence sb. or sth.使形成(性格): I don't think the climate has ～ed its character.我并不认为气候形成了它的性格。

moult/məʊlt/

Ⅰ *v.* ❶ (of birds) lose feathers before a new grows (指鸟类)换羽 ❷(of dogs, cats,etc.) lose hair (指狗、猫等)脱毛 Ⅱ *n.* the process or time of unhairing 换羽;

脱毛;换羽期;脱毛期

mound/maʊnd/

n. a large, rounded pile of earth; a small hill 土堆;小山: Your dog has dug up a ～ of earth.你的狗刨了一个土堆。

mount/maʊnt/

Ⅰ *n.* (abbr. Mt.) mountain, used before proper names (略作 Mt.)(用于山名前)山;峰: Mount Everest 珠穆朗玛峰/Mt. Tai 泰山 Ⅱ *v.* ❶climb up sth.; get on a horse or bicycle 登;爬上;骑马;骑车:～ a hill 爬上小山 / ～ stairs 上楼 / ～ a ladder 上梯/～ a bicycle 骑上自行车 ❷ become greater in amount; rise 增长;上升: The temperature has ～ed up.温度升高了。/The cost of living is steadily ～ing.生活费用不断上涨。❸put and fix in position 安放;安置;镶嵌:～ a photo 给照片装镜框/～ stamps in an album 将邮票插进邮集/～ some guards 设些岗哨 ❹ prepare or begin (an attack)发动攻势;准备攻击 ❺ put (a play)on the stage 上演(剧本):～ an opera 上演歌剧

mountain/ˈmaʊntɪn/

n. ❶a very high hill, usually of bare or snow-covered rock 山丘;山脉: the Rocky Mountains 落基山脉 ❷a very large amount;sth.immense 大堆,大量;巨大之物:～ of work 一大堆工作/a ～ of flesh 巨人/overcome ～s of difficulties 克服重重困难 ‖ **make a ～ out of a molehill** 小题大做/**remove ～s** 移山倒海,创造奇迹/**run ～s high** (波浪等)汹涌澎湃/**the ～ in labo(u)r** 费力大收效小 ‖ ～ **group** 山群/～ **man** 山地人/～ **range** 山脉/～ **sickness** 高山病 ‖ ～**side** *n.*山腰/～**top** *n.* 山顶 ‖ ～**y** *adj.*多山的;山区的

mountaineer /ˌmaʊntɪˈnɪə/

*n.*a person who climbs mountains or who is skilful at climbing mountains 爬山能手,登山者

mountaineering /ˌmaʊntɪˈnɪərɪŋ/

n. the sport or activity of climbing mountains 登山运动: go ～ 去爬山

mountainous/ˈmaʊntɪnəs,ˌmaʊntɪnəs/

adj. ❶having many mountains 有山的;多山的:～ country 多山的国家 ❷huge;

rising like mountains 巨大的；山似的：～ waves 巨浪

mourn /mɔːn/
v. feel or show sorrow or regret for the loss of sth. or sb. (为某事)哀痛；(向某人)致哀：～ the loss of sb. 为失去某人而哀痛/ ～ for(over) the dead 哀悼死者

mourner /'mɔːnə(r)/
n. a person who attends a funeral 参加葬礼者；送葬者

mournful /'mɔːnfl/
adj. causing a sad feeling or expressing sorrow 哀痛的,悲哀的；令人伤心的：a ～ occasion 令人伤心的场合/ a ～ expression on her face 她脸上的悲痛表情

mourning /'mɔːnɪŋ/
n. ❶ (the expression of) grief, especially for a death 哀痛,哀悼,悲痛(的表情)：All the flags were all half-masted, as a sign of ～ for the dead president. 全国降半旗为已故总统致哀。 ❷ the clothes, black in some countries, worn to show grief at the death of someone (黑色的)丧服：The royal court went into ～ when the queen died. 女王逝世后,王宫里的人都穿上了丧服。

mouse /maʊs/
n. (*pl.* mice /maɪs/) a small furry animal with a long tail that lives in houses and in fields, related to but smaller than a rat 鼠,耗子：When the cat's away, the mice will play. 猫儿一跑耗子闹。 ‖ (as) poor as a church ～ 一贫如洗 ‖ ～hole *n.* 鼠洞/ ～proof *adj.* 防鼠的/ ～trap *n.* 捕鼠器 ‖ ～er /'maʊzə(r)/ *n.* 捕鼠动物；探头探脑打听的人/ mousy *adj.* 胆小如鼠的

mousse /muːs/
n. ❶ a creamy light pudding of fruit or chocolate whipped with cream or egg white 慕斯 ❷ a savoury dish of meat or fish purée mixed with cream and shaped in a mould 奶油冻 ❸ a frothy creamy substance used for styling the hair 摩丝

mouth
Ⅰ /maʊθ/ *n.* ❶ the opening through which people and animals take in food 口,嘴：take the bread out of sb.'s ～ 口中夺食；

抢某人的饭碗 ❷ opening or outlet 口状物：the ～ of a volcano 火山口 ❸ the place where a river flows into the sea 河口 Ⅱ /maʊð/ *v.* speak (words) with too much movements of the jaws 装腔作势地说(话)：An actor who ～s his words is a poor actor. 装腔作势背诵台词的演员不是好演员。 ‖ button up one's ～ 保持缄默/ down in(at) the ～ 垂头丧气/ from ～ to ～ 口口相传,广泛流传/ give it ～ 滔滔不绝地讲/ in everyone's ～ 大家都如此说/ in the ～ of 出于……之口/ make a ～ 做鬼脸/ run at the ～ 流口水/ shoot off one's ～ 信口开河/ stop sb.'s ～ 用贿赂塞住某人的口/ the lion's ～ 狮窝,虎穴(指极危险处)/ with open ～ 张着口；张口结舌 ‖ ～ organ 口琴 *n.*/ ～-to-～ method *n.* 口对口人工呼吸法

mouthful /'maʊθfʊl/
n. ❶ a quantity of food or drink that fills the mouth 满口；一口 ❷ a long or awkward word or phrase that is difficult to say 长而拗口的词；难读的词组

mouthy /'maʊði/
adj. inclined to talk a lot, especially in a cheeky way 饶舌的,嘴碎的,话多的

movable /'muːvəbl/
adj. ❶ that can be moved 可移动的,活动的：～ antenna 移动式天线 ❷ varying in date from year to year (指日期)逐年不同的；不固定的：a ～ feast 不固定的节日

move /muːv/
Ⅰ *v.* ❶ (cause to) change place or position (使)改变位置；搬动；移动：Move the table here. 把桌子搬过来。 ❷ arouse the feeling of 感动,激动：be ～d to tears 感动得流出眼泪 ❸ (cause to) be in motion；go, walk, run, etc., especially in a particular way (使)开动；走；跑等：The train began to ～ on time. 火车准时开动了。 ❹ cause sb. to do sth. 鼓动,促使：What ～d you to do this? 什么力量鼓动你干这件事呢？ ❺ put forward sth. for discussion and decision (at a meeting) 动议,提议：I ～ (that) the meeting be adjourned. 我提议休会。 ❻ change residence 迁居,搬家：They've ～d to Shanghai. 他

们已迁居上海。‖ *n.* ❶ the act of going from one place to another; a change of position 移动,搬动;改变位置:make a ~ 开始行动;搬家 ❷ (in games such as chess) an act of taking a piece from one square and putting it on another (象棋等)走棋:Whose ~ is it? 轮到谁走了? ❸ an action that you do or need to do to achieve sth. 行动:This latest ~ by the company has aroused fierce opposition.公司最近采取的行动引起了强烈反对。‖ get a ~ on 行动起来,赶快/~ about 走来走去/ ~ heaven and earth 竭尽全力/ ~ out 搬出,搬走;(军)开始行动/ ~ (sb.) back (使某人)退缩/ ~ up 提前;上升;(被)提升/~ upon 进逼/on the ~ 在活动中,在进展中 ‖ mov(e)able *adj.* & *n.* 可移动的(东西);活动的

movement/'muːvmənt/

n. ❶moving or being moved 移动,运动,活动:He lay there without ~.他躺在那里不动。❷ the act of changing position 移动,迁移 ❸united actions and efforts of a group of people for a special purpose (一群人为某个目的联合起来的)运动:the local trade union ~ 当地工会运动 ❹ the whole of the activities of a person, especially when he is at a distance 动向,动态:He was watching their ~s carefully. 他密切注视他们的动向。

mover /'muːvə/

n. ❶a person or thing in motion, especially an animal 活动中的人或物(尤指动物) ❷a person whose job is to remove and transport furniture from one house to another 搬家工人 ❸a person undertaking or undergoing a move or change in a particular aspect of their life 接受(或经受)生活中某方面变化的人

movie/'muːvi/

n. a cinema picture; a film 影片;电影:the ~s(总称)电影;电影放映 / go to the ~s 去看电影/ ~ fan 影迷

moving /'muːviŋ/

adj. ❶in motion 行进的;活动的:a fast-~ river 流速很快的河流 ❷arousing strong emotions, especially of sorrow or sympathy 动人的:It was a very ~ story. 这是一个感人的故事。

mow/məʊ/

Ⅰ *v.* (~ed, ~n or ~ed) cut grass short 割(草、麦等):~ grass 割草/ The field has been newly ~ed (mown).这块地新近割过草。Ⅱ *n.* a place in a barn where hay, grain, etc.is piled 谷仓内的草;谷堆

Mr./'mɪstə(r)/

n. a title used before a man's name(用于男子的姓名前)先生:~ Jones 琼斯先生/ ~ Chairman 主席先生

Mrs./'mɪsɪz/

n. a title used before a married woman's name (用于已婚女子的姓名前)夫人:~ Henry Jones 亨利·琼斯夫人

Ms./mɪs/

n. a title for any woman, instead of "Miss" or "Mrs."女士

much/mʌtʃ/

Ⅰ (more, most) *adj.* great in quantity, amount, etc.许多,大量的:There isn't ~ food left. 没剩下多少食物了。Ⅱ *n.* a great quantity; a great deal 许多,大量:Much of what you say is true.你的话有许多是对的。Ⅲ *adv.* ❶to a great degree; greatly 非常;很:Thank you very ~. 多谢。❷almost; nearly 差不多,几乎:The two children are ~ of an age.这两个孩子的年龄差不多。‖ as ~ 同样多少的;同样的事物/as ~ as 有……那样多;差不多/be too ~ for 非……力所能及/ how ~ 多少;什么价钱;到什么程度/make ~ of 重视,充分利用/ ~ as …虽然很……/ ~ at one 几乎相同/ ~ less 更不/ ~ more 更加/ ~ of a …(常用于否定句或疑问句)了不起的/not so ~ …as 与其……不如/not think ~ of 对……估价不高/that (this) ~ 那(这)样多,那(这)些/too ~ 太多;(估价)太高/too ~ of a good thing 好事过头反成坏事/without so ~ as 甚至于不……

muchness /'mʌtʃnɪs/

n. greatness in quantity or degree 大量;(程度)大 ‖ (much) of a ~ 十分相似,差不多,相差无几

muck /mʌk/

Ⅰ n. ❶ waste matter dropped from animal's bodies, especially when used for spreading on the land; manure 粪肥 ❷ dirt 污秽；污物 Ⅱ v. ❶ make dirty 弄脏，搞糟：～ up a plan 把计划搞乱 ❷ live in an aimless way; waste time in valueless activity 鬼混；混日子；虚度光阴：The mother shouted at the boy, "stop ～ing about and finish your homework!"那位母亲对男孩叫道："别混时间了，把作业做完吧！" ‖ throw ～ at sb.中伤某人 ‖ ～y adj.肮脏的

mud /mʌd/

n.the soft, wet earth 泥；泥浆：After the rain, the roads were covered in ～.雨后道路泥泞。

muddle /'mʌdl/

Ⅰ v.put into disorder; mix up; confuse 使混乱；弄糟；迷惑：If your mind is ～d, you can't think clearly. 如果你脑子乱糟糟的，你就不可能清楚地思考。Ⅱ n.a state of confusion and disorder 混乱；糊涂；杂乱无章：She was in a ～, she couldn't even remember what day it was. 她稀里糊涂，甚至不记得那是星期几了。

muddling /'mʌdlɪŋ/

adj.causing confusion; difficult to understand 引起困惑的；使人糊涂的；难以理解的

muddy /'mʌdi/

Ⅰ adj.❶ full of mud 泥泞的；多泥的：～ shoes 沾满泥巴的鞋 ❷ mud-coloured (颜色)似泥土的：a ～ stream 浑浊的小溪 Ⅱ v.make sth. dirty with mud 使沾上污泥，把……弄脏：He is ～ing my clothes.他正往我衣服上扔污泥。

mudguard /'mʌdɡɑːd/

n.a cover over the wheel of a bicycle, etc. to keep the mud from flying up（脚踏车的）挡泥板

muffle /'mʌfl/

v.❶ wrap or cover for warmth or protection 包裹（以保暖或保护）：～ one's throat 围着脖子 ❷ make the sound less easily heard, especially with a material（尤指借助某种材料）压低声音：There are ～d voices coming from the next room.有一些压低了的声音从隔壁房间传来。

mugger /'mʌɡə(r)/

n.a person who attacks someone violently in a street in order to rob them of their money 行凶抢劫者

muggins /'mʌɡɪnz/

n.a simpleton, especially when used humorously to refer to oneself 傻子，白痴（尤用于自嘲）：Everyone disappeared after dinner, leaving ～ to do the washing-up.吃完饭后大家都走得无影无踪了，只有我这个傻子留下来洗碗碟。

muggy /'mʌɡi/

adj.(of weather) oppressively warm and damp（天气）闷热的；湿热的：～ days during the rainy season 雨季的闷热天

mulberry /'mʌlbri/

n.❶ a tree whose leaves are used for feeding silkworms 桑树 ❷ the fruit of this kind of tree 桑椹果 ❸ purplish red colour 紫红色

mule /mjuːl/

n.❶ an animal whose parents are a donkey and a horse 骡子；马骡：The ～ is a cross between a horse and an ass. 骡子是马和驴的杂种。❷ a stubborn person 倔强的人；顽固的人

mull /mʌl/

v.think carefully about sth. 仔细考虑，深思熟虑：I'll give you time to ～ it over.我会给你时间好好考虑。

multi- /'mʌlti/

pref.more than one; many 多的；许多

multicultural /ˌmʌltɪˈkʌltərəl/

adj.made up of people of different races and cultures 多种文化的；融合多种文化的：a ～ society 多元化社会

multilateral /ˌmʌltɪˈlætərəl/

adj.❶ having many sides 多边的：a ～ figure 多边形 ❷ involving many groups, countries, etc. 涉及多方面的，多国参加的：～ aid 多方援助，多国援助

multiple /'mʌltɪpl/

adj.including many different parts, types, etc.复合的；多样的；多重的：a ～ job holder 有多样职业的人 ‖ ～**choice** n. 多项选择,复式选择

multiplicity/ˌmʌltɪˈplɪsəti/
n. a large number or great variety 大量;多样:a ～ of ideas 多种多样的观念/ the stars in all their ～ 众多的繁星

multiply/ˈmʌltɪplaɪ/
v. ❶ combine by multiplication 乘;使相乘:～ 2 by 3 用 3 去乘 2 / to ～ two numbers together 使两数相乘 ❷ greatly increase in number or amount (使)大大增加:～ one's chances of success 使某人成功的机会大大增加 /Spending on military equipment has multiplied in the last five years. 过去五年中军事装备的开支大大增加。❸ reproduce in large numbers 繁殖,增殖:When animals have more food, they generally ～ faster. 动物在有较多的食物时,一般繁殖得较快。

multiracial/ˌmʌltɪˈreɪʃl/
adj. consisting of or including several races of people 多种族的:a ～ community 多种族的社区

multistorey/ˌmʌltɪˈstɔːri/
adj. (of a building) having several levels or floors (建筑物)多层的:a big ～ car park 一所大型的多层停车场

multitude/ˈmʌltɪtjuːd/
n. ❶ a great number (especially of people gathered together) 大批,大群,多数(尤指集结的人群):a great ～ of people 一大群人/a ～ of thought 各种想法/vast ～s of birds 成群结队的鸟 ❷ greatness of number 大量:in ～ as the stars in the sky 多得像繁星一样 ❸ the masses;the common people 群众;人群

mum[1]/mʌm/
Ⅰ int. Silence! 别出声! 安静! :Mum's the word! 别多话! Ⅱ adj. silent 沉默的,缄默的,不出声的

mum[2]/mʌm/
n. mummy 妈妈

mumble/ˈmʌmbl/
v. speak or say sth. unclearly 含糊不清地说:He ～d a few words and went off. 他咕哝了几句就走了。

mummy[1]/ˈmʌmi/
n. a dead body treated in a special way so that it does not decay 木乃伊:an Egyptian ～ 一具埃及木乃伊

mummy[2]/ˈmʌmi/
n. (used by and to children) mother (小孩使用及向小孩说话时用的)妈咪;母亲

mumps/mʌmps/
n. an infectious disease which causes painful swelling in the neck 腮腺炎

municipal/mjuːˈnɪsɪpl/
adj. concerning or belonging to a town or city, under its own government 市的,市政的:a ～ university 市立大学 ‖ ～ity/mjuːˌnɪsɪˈpæləti/ n. 自治市,自治地区;市政当局/～ize/mjuːˈnɪsɪpəlaɪz/ v. 把……归市所有;把……归市管

munitions/mjuːˈnɪʃnz/
n. military weapons, ammunition, equipment and stores 军需品,军火(尤指枪炮、弹药):～ factories 军火工厂

mural/ˈmjʊərəl/
n. a painting done on a wall, sometimes on the outside wall of a building 壁画

murder/ˈmɜːdə(r)/
Ⅰ n. the crime of killing a human being intentionally 谋杀:willful ～ 蓄意谋杀(罪) Ⅱ v. kill (sb.) unlawfully and on purpose 谋杀;犯杀人罪 ‖ **Murder will be out**,杀了人终究要败露;纸包不住火。‖ ～er/ˈmɜːdərə(r)/ n. 杀人犯,凶手/ ～ous adj. 杀人的,行凶的;凶恶的

murmur/ˈmɜːmə(r)/
Ⅰ n. a low continuous sound as that of a stream, wind or talk 低沉连续的声音:the ～ of a distant brook 远方溪水潺潺声/ a ～ of conversation 一阵轻轻的谈话声 Ⅱ v. make a low continuous sound; speak or say in a low voice 发低沉连续的声音;低声说:～ a secret to sb. 低声告诉某人一个秘密 ‖ ～ous/ˈmɜːmərəs/ adj. 低声的

muscle/ˈmʌsl/
n. ❶ a band or bundle of fibrous tissue in a human or animal body that can be tightened or loosened to produce movement 肌肉:develop one's arm ～s by playing tennis 借打网球来锻炼手臂的肌肉

❷ the bodily strength 力量,体力：Put some ～ into your work.加把劲工作。‖ not move a ～ 一点不动弹；毫不动容 ‖ ～less adj.无肌肉的；无气力的

muscular /'mʌskjulə/

adj.❶of or affecting the muscles 肌肉的；影响肌肉的 ❷having well-developed muscles 肌肉发达的；强壮的：His arms are strong and ～.他的手臂强壮有力。

muse /mjuːz/

v.think deeply,ignoring what is happening around 沉思,冥想：～ over past memories 缅怀往事/ Her words set his mind musing.她的话使他陷入沉思。

museum /mjuː'ziəm/

n.a building in which objects of art,history,science,etc.are kept and shown 博物馆：art (science) ～ 美术(科学)博物馆 / ～ piece 美术品；古董 /the Palace Museum in Beijing 北京故宫博物院/the British Museum 大英博物馆

mush /mʌʃ/

n.❶a soft,thick mixture or mass 糊状物 ❷the thick maize porridge 玉米粥；糊状物；粥状物：～ for the cattle 牲口的糊状饲料

mushroom /'mʌʃrum,'mʌʃruːm/

Ⅰ *n*.❶fungus of which some kinds can be eaten 蘑菇 ❷anything that grows and develops rapidly 迅速增长(或发展)的事物：the ～ of new housing 新式住房的迅速发展 Ⅱ *v*.grow and spread rapidly 迅速增长；迅速发展：New buildings have ～ed in the city these years.这几年城市的新建筑物拔地而起。

music /'mjuːzɪk/

n.❶the art of making pleasing combinations of sounds in rhythm and harmony 音乐；音乐艺术：a ～ teacher 音乐教师/study ～ 学习音乐 ❷the sounds and composition so made 乐曲；音乐作品：compose ～ 作曲/piano ～ 钢琴曲/play a piece of ～ 演奏一曲 ❸written or printed signs representing these sounds 乐谱：The little girl can read ～.这个小女孩会识乐谱。‖ ～ book 乐谱/ ～ case 乐谱夹/ ～ hall 杂耍剧场；音乐厅

musical /'mjuːzɪkl/

Ⅰ *adj*.❶of or relating to music 音乐的；与音乐有关的：a ～ instrument 乐器 / a ～ voice 悦耳的嗓音 ❷fond of music；skilled in music 爱好音乐的；擅长音乐的：a very ～ child 很有音乐才能的孩子 Ⅱ *n*.a play or film with songs and dances 音乐剧,音乐

musician /mjuː'zɪʃn/

n.a person skilled in the art of music；a performer or composer of music 音乐家；乐师；作曲家：An orchestra is composed of many ～s.交响乐团由许多乐师组成。

musk /mʌsk/

n.❶a reddish-brown substance with strong smell got from the male deer 麝香 ❷kinds of plant with a similar smell 麝香植物

Muslim /'muzlɪm/

n.a follower of the religion of Islam 穆斯林

must /mʌst,məst/

Ⅰ *aux.v*.❶have to 必须，得：I ～ go now.我现在得走了。❷be likely or certain to 必定：You ～ be tired after your long walk.你走了这么远的路一定累了。❸be necessary 需要；应当：The house ～ be clean if there are guests.如果来客人,房子应当是干净的。❹should or ought to 应该：We ～ think about this very seriously.这件事我们应该慎重考虑一下。❺indicating insistence(表示坚持)一定要：He said he ～ see you.他说他一定要见你。❻indicating the occurrence of sth. perverse or sth. contrary to what was wanted (表示与说话人愿望相反或不耐烦)偏要：Why ～ you be so stubborn? 为什么你偏要这么固执呢? Ⅱ *n*.sth. which it is necessary or very important to have or experience 必需的东西；必须做的事：This rule is a ～.这条规则必须执行。

mustard /'mʌstəd/

n.❶ a plant with yellow flowers and seeds 芥菜 ❷ a hot-tasting yellow or brown paste made from the crushed seeds of this plant 芥末；芥末酱 ❸ a dark yellow colour 暗黄色,芥末色

muster¹ /'mʌstə(r)/

　v. ❶ assemble(troops, etc.), especially for battle; collect 集合(部队等); 集中, 召集 ❷ summon up (a feeling, attitude or response)激起(某种情感、态度或反应): Muster up your courage. 鼓起勇气来。‖ pass (cut the) ～ 及格; 符合要求

muster² /'mʌstə(r)/

　n. ❶ assembling of troops for inspection (部队的)集合 ❷ persons or things assembled (被)集合的人(或物) ❸ commercial samples 样品

musty /'mʌsti/

　adj. with an unpleasant smell as if old 霉的, 发霉的, 霉臭的: a ～ room 霉臭的房间 ‖ mustiness *n.* 发霉; 冷淡

mute /mjuːt/

　Ⅰ *adj.* ❶ not speaking; making no sound 缄默的, 不出声的: He kept ～. 他保持沉默。❷ (of a letter) not pronounced (字母)不发音的 Ⅱ *n.* a dumb person 哑巴

mutilate /'mjuːtɪleɪt/

　v. ❶ cut off a part of the body 使(肢体)残缺不全; 残害 ❷ severely damage 严重毁坏: The book was ～d through someone tearing out the pages. 这本书因被人撕去几页而受到了严重的损坏。

mutinous /'mjuːtɪnəs/

　adj. rebellious or disobedient 任性的; 固执己见的; 不服从的; 桀骜不驯的

mutter /'mʌtə(r)/

　Ⅰ *v.* speak in a low voice 低声地说, 咕哝: ～ to oneself 喃喃自语 Ⅱ *n.* a quiet sound or words that are difficult to hear 轻声低语, 咕哝的话

mutton /'mʌtn/

　n. meat from a sheep as food 羊肉: roast ～ 烤羊肉 ‖ be (as) dead as ～ 已僵死了的; 被彻底废弃(或遗忘)的/eat ～ cold 受人白眼, 被冷待/to return to one's ～ (用作插入语)回到本题, 言归正传 ‖ ～-head *n.* 笨蛋, 呆子/～y *adj.* 羊肉味的

mutual /'mjuːtʃuəl/

　adj. ❶ (of a situation, feeling or action) experienced, felt or done by both of two people mentioned (处境、感情或行动)彼此的; 相互的: ～ support 相互支持/by ～ consent 经双方同意 ❷ (of love, respect, etc.) shared 共同的: our ～ friend 我们共同的朋友 ‖ ～ly *adv.* 相互; 共同

muzzle /'mʌzl/

　Ⅰ *n.* ❶ the front part of an animal's face, with the nose and mouth (动物)凸出的口鼻 ❷ a covering round an animal's mouth to prevent it from biting 口套; 口络 ❸ the open end or mouth of a firearm 枪口; 炮口: a ～ loading gun 前膛装填的炮 Ⅱ *v.* ❶ put a muzzle on 戴口络于; 给……戴上口套 ❷ prevent (a person, society, newspaper, etc.) from expressing opinions freely 禁止(人、社会、报纸等)自由发表意见: ～ the press 钳制新闻

my /maɪ/

　pron. ❶ belonging to the speaker 我的; 属于我的: ～ friends 我的朋友们 ❷ as a part of a form of address (用于称呼中)我的: Tell me, ～ little boy. 告诉我,(我的)好孩子。❸ used in various expresses of surprise (用于各种表示惊讶的表达中): My, what a downpour! 哎呀, 好大的雨呀!

myopic /maɪ'ɒpɪk/

　adj. unable to see clearly things which are far away; short-sighted 近视的; 缺乏远见的

myriad /'mɪrɪəd/

　Ⅰ *n.* a very great number 极大数量; 无数: a ～ a stars 无数的星星 /～s of changes 千变万化 Ⅱ *adj.* of very great number 无数的; 数不清的: ～ events 众多的事件

myself /maɪ'self/

　pron. ❶ (the reflexive form of I) used when the speaker or writer is also the person affected by an action(I 的反身形式)我自己: I often criticize ～. 我经常进行自我批评。❷ I or me personally (used to emphasize the speaker)我本人(表示强调): I saw it ～. 这是我亲眼所见的。‖ (all) by ～ (我)独自, 单独; 独立地: I can do it (all) by ～. 我能独立做这件事。/I live by ～. 我一个人住。

mysterious /mɪ'stɪərɪəs/

　adj. difficult to understand or explain; full

of mystery 难以理解的；神秘的：He is a
～ person.他是个神秘的人。

mystery/ˈmɪstəri/

　　*n.*❶sth. which cannot be explained or understood 神秘的事物；难以理解的事物：
It's a ～ to me.这对我来说是个谜。❷a
strange secret nature or quality 神秘；奥
妙：an air of ～ 神秘的气氛

mystic/ˈmɪstɪk/

　　*adj.*of hidden meaning or spiritual pow-
er；causing a feeling of wonder 神秘的；不
可思议的：～ rites and ceremonies 神秘
的仪式 / ～ teachings 神秘的教训

mysticism/ˈmɪstɪsɪzəm/

　　*n.*the attempt to gain, or practice of gaining a knowledge of real truth and union
with God by prayer and meditation 神秘
主义；玄想

mystify/ˈmɪstɪfaɪ/

　　*v.*puzzle or bewilder (someone) 使迷惑；
使困惑：I'm completely mystified about
what happened.我对所发生的事迷惑不解。
‖ **mystification**/ˌmɪstɪfɪˈkeɪʃn/*n.*神秘化；神
秘的事物

mystique/mɪˈstiːk/

　　*n.*❶a feeling of mystery connected with a
person, institution, etc., caused by popular devotion and veneration 神秘感；神秘

性：the ～ of the monarchy in Great Britain 英国君主政治的神秘色彩 ❷a secret
skill that cannot be taught (技艺的)秘诀

myth/mɪθ/

　　❶ a story, handed down from old times,
especially one that was told to explain
some natural or social phenomenon and
typically involving supernatural beings or
events 神话；神话故事：ancient Greek ～
古希腊神话 ❷ such stories collectively
(总称)神话 ❸a person, thing, etc., that
is imaginary, fictitious, or invented 虚构
的人(或事物)：Her wealth is a ～.她的
财富是骗人的鬼话。‖ ～ologist/mɪˈθɒlə-
dʒɪst/ *n.*神话研究者；神话学家

mythological /ˌmɪθəˈlɒdʒɪkəl/

　　*adj.*connected with ancient myths 神话
的：～ stories 神话故事

mythology /mɪˈθɒlədʒi/

　　*n.*❶a collection of myths, especially one
belonging to a particular religious or cultural tradition (尤指属于特定宗教或文
化传统的)神话 ❷a set of stories or beliefs about a particular person, institution, or situation, especially when exaggerated or fictitious 虚夸不实之词；不符
合事实的看法；荒诞无稽之谈 ❸ the
study of myths 神话学

Nn

nab/næb/

　　v.(-bb-) ❶ catch (someone) in an act of wrongdoing 当场抓住；逮住 ❷ get or catch quickly 猛然抓住；快速追上

nadir/ˈneɪdɪr/

　　n.(usually singular) the lowest point of hope or fortune (常用单数)最低点；最不幸的时刻

nag/næg/

　　v.(-gg-) ❶ criticize continuously；annoy by scolding 唠唠叨叨责骂；不断地找岔子：She ～ged (at) him all day long. 她整天唠唠叨叨地责骂他。❷ worry or annoy 恼人：The noise in the street kept ～ging at me. 街上的噪音使我不安宁。‖ ～ger *n.*爱唠叨的人；尽找岔子的人/～gish *adj.*有些爱唠叨的

nagging /ˈnægɪŋ/

　　*adj.*❶continuing for a long time and difficult to cure or remove 纠缠不休的；难以摆脱的 ❷ complaining 唠叨的；抱怨的：He dislikes his mother's ～ voice. 他不喜欢妈妈唠唠叨叨的声音。

nail/neɪl/

　　I *n.*❶ a layer of hard substance over the outer tip of a finger or toe (手或脚的)指甲：finger ～ 手指甲/toe ～ 脚指甲 ❷a thin piece of metal with a sharp point at one end and a flat head at the other for hammering into a piece of wood, usually to fasten the wood to sth. else 钉；fasten sth.with ～s 用钉子把某物钉牢 ‖ *v.*make secure with a nail or nails 钉，将……钉牢：～ lid on a box 给箱子钉上盖子 ‖ hard as ～s 强硬的；冷酷无情的/ a ～ in the coffin 致命一击/hit the (right) ～ on the head 说得中肯；打中要害；做得恰到好处/ ～ down 用钉钉住；束缚/on the ～ 立即；当场；在讨论中/to the ～ 极

其；完全 ‖ ～-biting *n.*咬指甲；束手无策/ ～ clippers *n.* 指甲刀/～hole *n.*钉眼/ ～ puller *n.* 起钉钳 ‖ ～er *n.*敲钉者；自动敲钉机/～less *adj.*没指甲的；不用钉的

naive/naɪˈiːv/

　　*adj.*simple and innocent in what one says and does because of lack of experience or ability 天真的；幼稚的；无知的；缺乏经验的：～ girl 天真烂漫的女孩 ‖ ～ly *adv.*天真烂漫地；无邪地/ ～ty *n.*天真；朴素

naked/ˈneɪkɪd/

　　*adj.*❶ without clothes on 裸体的，光身的：be stark ～ 一丝不挂 ❷ without the usual covering or protection 无掩饰的，无保护的：a ～ sword 出鞘的剑/a～bulb 无罩灯泡 ❸not hidden, especially by false statements 未隐藏的；不掩饰的：～ facts 赤裸裸的事实/the ～ truth 真相 ‖ as ～ as when one was born 赤条条/(with) the ～eye (用)肉眼(看) ‖ ～ly *adv.*裸体地；露出地/ ～ness *n.*赤裸；明显

name/neɪm/

　　I *n.*❶ a word or words by which a person, animal, place, thing, etc. is called or known by 姓；姓名；名字；名称：What's your ～? 你叫什么名字？/What's the ～ of this machine? 这台机器叫什么？❷ (only singular) reputation；the opinion that people have about sb.or sth.(只用单数) 名誉；名声；名气：a good (an ill) ～ 好(坏)名声 ❸a well-known person 名人：the great ～s of history 历代名人 ‖ *v.*❶ give a name to 给……取名：They ～d the child Mary.他们给这个孩子取名玛丽。❷ tell the name(s) of 叫出……的名字：Can you ～ these plants? 你叫得出这些植物的名称吗？❸ choose or appoint 任命；提名：～ a person as chairman 提

名某人为主席‖ by ～ 名叫；用名字，凭名字/call sb.'s ～谩骂某人/drag sb.'s ～ through the mire 把某人搞臭/get（make）a ～（for oneself）成名；得到名声/have one's ～ up 成名；扬名/in the ～ of ……的名义；代表……；凭……/keep one's ～ on the books 保留学籍（会籍等）/～ it 讲出来/not to be ～d on（in）the same day with 与……不可同日而语，比……差得多/of ～ 有名的/take a ～ in vain 滥用名字/take one's ～ off the books 退学（退会等）/without a ～ 无名的；名字说不出的 ‖ ～ board n.名牌 ‖ ～d adj. 被指名的；指定的

nameless /'neɪmlɪs/
adj.❶having no name or no known name 没有名字的；不知其名的 ❷whose name is kept secret；anonymous 隐名的；匿名的：There are others who shall be ～.应该有其他人是匿名的。❸difficult or too bad to describe 不可名状的；难以表达的：Nameless misfortunes hit the village. 不可名状的灾难袭击了这个村庄。

namely /'neɪmli/
adv. that is to say；specifically 即，那就是：My two best subjects，～ French and German.我最好的两门科目就是法语和德语。

namesake /'neɪmseɪk/
n.a person or thing with the same name as another 同名者；同姓者；同名同姓者；同名物

nanny /'næni/
n.a woman who looks after children as a job（照看小孩的）保姆

nap /næp/
Ⅰ n.a short sleep, especially during the day（白天的）小睡；打盹；瞌睡：have（take，get）a ～ 稍睡片刻，打盹，睡午觉 Ⅱ v.(-pp-) sleep for a short time, especially during the day（白天）小睡；打盹：He ～ped in the chair after lunch.午饭后他在椅子上小睡。‖ catch sb. ～ping 使人措手不及；乘其不备

napkin /'næpkɪn/
n.a piece of cloth used at meals for protecting one's clothes and for cleaning one's hands and lips 餐巾：a paper ～ 餐巾纸

nappy /'næpi/
n. a piece of cloth or soft paper folded round a baby's bottom to absorb urine, etc.尿布

nark[1] /nɑːk/
n.a person who mixes with criminals and secretly reports on them to the police；a stool pigeon（混于罪犯中向警方提供情报的）密探，线人，卧底

nark[2] /nɑːk/
v.make sb.angry or annoyed 使……生气，使发火：I was rather ～ed at(by) what she said.我听到她所讲的话很生气。

narrate /nə'reɪt/
v.tell（a story）；give an account of 叙述；讲故事：～ one's adventures 叙述奇遇 ‖ narration n.讲述；故事；记叙体/narrator n.讲述者

narrow /'nærəʊ/
Ⅰ adj.❶ of small width from one side to the other 窄的，狭窄的：a ～ road 狭路 ❷ limited in extent, amount or scope（在程度、数量或范围等方面）有局限的：move in a ～ circle of friends 生活在狭小的朋友圈子中 ❸ almost not enough or only just successful 勉强的：a ～ majority 勉强的多数 ❹ having little sympathy for the ideas, etc.of others 心胸窄的，度量小的：a ～ mind 小心眼儿 ❺ careful and thorough 仔细而彻底的：a ～ search 彻底地搜查 Ⅱ v. make or become narrow (使)变窄：～ the gap between 缩小两者间的差距 ‖ a ～ escape 九死一生 ‖ ～-minded adj.气量狭窄的；有偏见的

narrowly /'nærəʊli/
adv.❶ only just；hardly 仅仅；勉强：The boy ～ escaped drowning.那孩子险些淹死。❷ closely；carefully 严密地；仔细地：examine the machine ～ 仔细检查那台机器

nasal /'neɪzl/
Ⅰ adj.❶ of or related to the nose 鼻的：a ～ discharge 鼻涕 /the ～ opening 鼻孔

❷ (of sound) made through the nose 鼻音的：a ～ sound 鼻音（如 /ŋ/） Ⅱ n. a speech sound made through the nose 鼻音

nasty /'nɑːsti/

adj. ❶ very unpleasant especially to the senses 恶心的；令人厌恶的：a ～ smell 臭味，难闻的气味 ❷ showing ill will and spite 恶意的：a ～ remark 恶毒的话 ❸ causing difficulty or danger 麻烦的；危险的；险恶的：a ～ storm at sea 海上的狂风暴雨 ❹ immoral；wicked 缺德的；邪恶的：a person with a ～ mind 思想肮脏的人 ‖ a ～ **piece of work** 讨厌的家伙；恶意行为 ‖ **nastily** *adv.* 不洁地；讨厌地/ **nastiness** *n.* 不洁；污秽

nation /'neɪʃn/

n. people associated with a particular country under one government 民族；国家 ‖ a most favoured ～ 最惠国/the United Nations（organization） 联合国（组织）‖ ～hood *n.* 作为一个国家的地位/ ～wide *adj.* 全国性的

national /'næʃnəl/

Ⅰ *adj.* ❶ typical of the people or customs of a particular country or nation 国家的；民族的；国民的：the ～ anthem 国歌 / National Day 国庆节 /the ～ debt 国债 / ～ defence 国防 /a ～ flag 国旗 /the ～ economy 国民经济 /～ income 国民收入 /the ～ independence and liberation movement 民族独立和解放运动 /～ spirits 民族精神 ❷ owned or controlled by the central government of a country 国有的；国立的：～ bank 国家银行 /a ～ enterprise 国有企业 /a ～ park 国立公园 /a ～ university 国立大学 Ⅱ *n.* citizens of a particular nation 公民，国民：American ～s in China 在华的美国侨民 /Foreign ～s were forced to leave the country. 外国侨民被迫离开了那个国家。

nationalism /'næʃnəlɪzəm/

n. a feeling of love for and pride in one's own nation 爱国心；民族主义，国家主义

nationality /ˌnæʃəˈnæləti/

n. ❶ being a member of a nation 国籍：What's your ～? 你是哪国人? ❷ a large group of people with the same race, origin, language, etc. 民族：the Chinese people of all nationalities 中国各族人民

nationalize /'næʃənəlaɪz/

v. put an industry or business under the state ownership or control 把……收归国有；使国有化

native /'neɪtɪv/

Ⅰ *adj.* ❶ of the place of one's birth 出生地的；本土的：one's ～ country 某人的祖国 ❷ of one's native country（land） 祖国的 ❸ belonging to someone from birth without having to learn 天生的；与生俱来的：～ ability 天赋才能 ❹ growing, living, produced, found, etc., in a place, not brought in from another place 原产于某地的；土产的；当地的：plants ～ to America 原产于美洲的植物 Ⅱ *n.* ❶ a person born in a place, country, etc. 出生于某国（或某地）的人：He is a ～ of Beijing. 他是北京人。❷ an animal or plant natural to a certain area 原产于某地的动物（或植物）：The kangaroo is a ～ of Australia. 袋鼠是产于澳大利亚的动物。‖ ～-born *adj.* 本地生的；本国生的 ‖ **nativism** *n.* 本土主义，排外主义；天性论/ **nativist** *n.* 本土主义者，排外主义者；天性论者/ **nativity** /nəˈtɪvəti/ *n.* 出生；出生地

natural /'nætʃrəl/

adj. ❶ existing in or caused by nature 自然的；天然的：～ resources 天然资源/～ forces（e. g. storms） 自然力（如风暴等）❷ born with certain qualities or powers 生来的；天生的：a ～ orator 天生的演说家 ❸ occurring as a matter of course and without debate；inevitable 必然的；自然如此的：die a ～ death 寿终正寝 ‖ **come ～ to sb.** 对某人来说是轻而易举的 ‖ ～-born *adj.* 生来的

naturalism /'nætʃərəlɪzəm/

n. （in art and literature） the theory or practice of drawing, painting, or describing things as they are in nature （艺术和文学中的）自然主义 ‖ **naturalistic** *adj.* 自然主义的

naturalist /'nætʃərəlɪst/

n. someone who studies natural history 自

然主义者;博物学者 ‖ ～ic *adj.*自然主义的;模仿自然的;根据自然的

naturalize /ˈnætʃərəlaɪz/

v. ❶ give a person of foreign birth the right of citizenship of a country 接受(侨民)入籍,使入籍 ❷ adopt a foreign word or custom,often adapting it so that it fits local practice 使(外来词语或习俗)归化 ❸ cause a plant or animal to grow or live naturally in a country where it is not native 使(植物)自然化;使(动物)驯化(或归化) ‖ **naturalization** *n.*归化;移入;移植

naturally /ˈnætʃərəli/

adv. ❶ by nature 天然地;天生地:He speaks ～. 他说起话来很自然。❷ of course 当然;必然:"Did you answer her letter?""Naturally!""你回过信给她吗?""当然!"

naturalness /ˈnætʃərəlnɪs/

n. ❶ the state or quality of being like real life 自然状态;逼真 ❷ the quality of behaving in a normal,relaxed or innocent way 自然;大方:Adults lose their childhood simplicity and ～.成年人就不像童年时那么淳朴天真了。❸ the style or quality of happening in a normal way that you would expect 当然;必然性

nature /ˈneɪtʃə(r)/

n. ❶ the world including plants,animals,the landscape,and other features and products of the earth 自然界,大自然;天地万物:a law of ～ 自然法则 ❷ qualities naturally belonging to a person or thing 性格;性质:the ～ of gases 气体的性质/a girl with a kind ～ 性情善良的女孩 ❸ force(s) controlling the physical world 自然力;控制物质世界的力量:Man is engaged in a constant struggle with ～.人类不断地与大自然作斗争。‖ a call of ～ 要去厕所/against ～ 违反自然的(地);奇迹般的(地)/(be) true to ～ 逼真/by ～ 生性,本性上/ease(relieve) ～ 大便;小便/in ～ 性质上;实际上/in(of) the ～ of 具有……的性质的/in(by, from) the ～ of things(of the case) 必然地/nature's engineering 天工之作/pay the debt of ～

(pay one's debt to ～) 死/second ～ 第二天性 ‖ good-～d *adj.*好心肠的/ill-～d *adj.*坏心肠的

naught /nɔːt/

Ⅰ *n.*the number 0 零 Ⅱ *pron.*nothing 无;没有什么:bring sth. to ～ 使某事成泡影 ‖ all for ～ 徒然,无用/a thing of ～ 无用之物/care ～ for 对……不感兴趣/set at ～ 蔑视

naughty /ˈnɔːti/

adj. ❶ (of children)disobedient; causing trouble (指孩子)顽皮的;不听话的;淘气的:a ～ child 顽皮的孩子 /You ～ boy! I told you not to pull the cat's tail.你这个淘气的孩子! 我告诉过你不要拉那只猫的尾巴。❷ immorally, especially because related to sex 不道德的;淫秽的;下流的:an amusing and ～ book 一本低级趣味的书

nauseous /ˈnɔːsjəs/

adj. ❶ feeling as if you want to vomit 恶心的,想呕吐的:She felt dizzy and ～.她觉得头晕、恶心。❷ causing a feeling of vomit 使人恶心的:The smell was ～.那味道让人恶心

naval /ˈneɪvl/

*adj.*of a navy;of warships 海军的;军舰的:a ～ battle 海战 /a ～ captain 海军上校 /～ forces 海军部队/a ～ base 海军基地 /a ～ officer 海军军官

navigable /ˈnævɪɡəbl/

adj. ❶ (of a body of water) deep and wide enough to allow ships to travel (水域)可航行(通航)的:The St Lawrence River is ～ from the Great Lawrence Lakes to the Atlantic Ocean.圣劳伦斯河自五大湖区至大西洋的整阔河道都可通航。❷ (of a ship, aircraft, etc.) able to be guided; steerable(船舶、航空器等)可领航的;可操纵的

navigate /ˈnævɪɡeɪt/

v. ❶ (cause to) sail or travel on the water or in the air 航行:～ up a river 向上游航行 ❷ direct the course of (a ship, plane, etc.) 导航:～ by the stars 以星导航 ‖ **navigation** /ˌnævɪˈɡeɪʃn/ *n.* 航行;航

海;航空;导航;领航/**navigator** *n.*航行者;
(船舶、飞机等的)驾驶员;领航员

navy/'neɪvi/

  n. the organization, including ships, people, buildings, etc., which makes up the
power of a country for war at sea 海军:
the PLA Navy 中国人民解放军海军 /He
is an officer in the ～.他是个海军军官。

near/nɪə(r)/

  Ⅰ *adv.*to or at a short distance 接近,近:
A bosom friend afar brings a distant land
～.海内存知己,天涯若比邻。Ⅱ *prep.*
close to (in space, time, etc.) 接近,靠近:
She's ～ twenty.她接近二十岁。Ⅲ *adj.*
❶ not far (in time or space) (时间或空
间)近的:in the ～ future 在不久的将来
❷ close in relation 关系近的,亲密的:a
～ relation 近亲 Ⅳ *v.*come closer (to) in
space or time (空间或时间上)接近:The
harvest season ～s.收获季节快到了。‖
～ **and dear** 极亲密的/ ～ **upon** (时间)将
近‖～**-sighted** *adj.*近视眼的;眼光短浅
的

nearby/ˌnɪə'baɪ/

  Ⅰ *adv.*close by 在附近:They live ～.他们
住在附近。Ⅱ *adj.*near;not far away 附
近的:a ～ village 附近的村庄 Ⅲ *prep.*at
a short distance from 在……的附近:
build a pumping station ～ the reservoir
在水库附近建一个抽水站

nearly/'nɪəli/

  *adv.*❶almost;not quite 几乎;差不多:
I'm ～ ready. 我差不多准备好了。/It's
～ twelve o'clock.差不多十二点钟了。/
Nearly everyone has heard about it.几乎
每个人都听说此事了。❷ closely 密切
地;亲近地:They are ～ related. 他们是
近亲。‖ **not** ～ 相差很远;远远少于:
There isn't ～ enough time to learn all
these English new words. 要把这些英语
新词都学会了,时间远远不够。

neat/niːt/

  *adj.*❶ tidy and clean;in good order 简洁
的;整齐的;整洁的:a ～ room 整洁的房
间/a ～ speech 简练的演说/a ～ handwriting 工整的笔迹 ❷ cleverly said or
done 熟练的;灵巧的:a ～ worker 做事

干净利落的人/a ～ answer 巧妙的回答
❸ (of alcoholic drinks) without ice or
water or other liquid(酒)纯的(不加冰、
水或其他酒的):I like my whisky ～.我
喜欢喝纯威士忌。

necessary/'nesəsəri/

  Ⅰ *adj.*❶ that is needed or essential 必要
的;必需的;必须做的:Physical exercise
is ～ to health.体育锻炼对健康是必要
的。❷ which cannot be avoided;which
must be;determined or fixed by the nature of things 不可避免的;必然的:the
～ outcome of the affair 事情的必然结局
Ⅱ *n.*(usually *pl.*)the basic requirements
for living 必需品:the necessaries of life
生活必需品‖ **if** ～ 如果必需的话‖ **necessarily**/'nesəsərəli/*adv.*必定,必然

necessitate/nɪ'sesɪteɪt/

  *v.*cause a need for;make necessary 使成
为必需;需要:Lack of money ～s a
change of plan.由于缺乏资金,就有必要
改变计划。/This change would ～ starting all over again.有了这一变动,就得从
头干起。

necessity/nɪ'sesəti/

  *n.*❶ need;the state of being necessary 需
要;必要性:We should understand the ～
to get a good education.我们应该懂得接
受良好教育的必要性。❷ sth. that is
necessary 必需品:daily necessities 日常
必需品‖ **be under the** ～ **of doing sth.**必
须做某事/**bow to** ～ 屈服于需要/Neces-
sity is the mother of invention.需要是发明
之母。/Necessity knows no law.需要面前
无法律。/**of** ～ 必然地,势必

neck/nek/

  *n.*❶ the part of the body between the
head and shoulders 颈,脖子:Giraffes
have very long ～s.长颈鹿的脖子很长。
❷ the part of a garment for this part of
the human body (衣服的)领圈,领口:a
V ～ V 字领圈,尖领圈 ❸ a narrow part
of sth.like a neck in shape or position 颈
状部位;细长部分:the ～ of a bottle 瓶颈
‖ **a stiff** ～ 硬脖子;固执;固执的人/
break one's ～ 折颈致死/**break the** ～ **of**
做完(工作等)的最难部分/**by a** ～ (在竞

赛中)以些微之差(得胜或输去)/harden the ～ 变得顽固/ ～ and crop 干脆,彻底/～ and ～ (在竞赛中)并驾齐驱/ or nothing 铤而走险/on the ～ of 紧跟在……后面/risk one's ～ 冒生命危险/save one's ～ 免受绞刑;免于遭殃/talk through(the back of) one's ～ 吹牛/tread on the ～ of 骑在……头上;压迫/up to one's ～ in 深陷于……中 ‖ ～band n.(装饰用的)领圈,领巾;领口;衬衫领子

necklace /'neklɪs/
 n. an ornamental string of beads or precious stones worn round the neck 项链

need /niːd/
 I n.❶ the condition in which sth. is necessary 需要,必要:There is a great ～ for (of) a new dictionary. 急需一本新词典。❷(pl.)a thing that is wanted or required 要求;需要之物,必需品:My ～s are few.我的要求很少。❸ the state of poverty or misfortune 贫穷;不幸;逆境:A friend in ～ is a friend indeed.患难朋友才是真正的朋友。 II v. want or require sth. 需要,必需:～ help 需要帮助 III aux.v.(with negative or in questions) have to; be necessary (用于疑问句和否定句中) 必要,必须:Need I go? 我必须去吗? / He ～n't be told.不必告诉他。 ‖ at ～ 紧急时/be(stand) in ～ of 需要/do one's ～ 解大(小)便/have ～ of(for) 需要……/ have ～ to do sth.必须做某事/if ～ be 如果需要的话 ‖ ～ful /'niːdfl/ adj.需要的,必要的

needle /'niːdl/
 I n.❶ a thin, pointed piece of metal used in sewing, knitting, etc.针:～ work 针线活/thread a ～ 穿针 ❷ a thin (usually metal) pointer on a dial, e.g. of a compass, meter, etc.(罗盘或仪表盘上的)指针:a magnetic ～ 磁针 ❸ a very thin hollow pointed tube, at the end of a hypodermic syringe, which is pushed into someone's skin to put a liquid (especially medicine) into the body 注射针 II v. push through sth. with or as if with a needle 用针缝;刺穿;穿过:～ one's way through a crowd 在人群中穿过 ‖ as sharp

as a ～ 非常机敏,非常敏锐/hit the ～ 击中要害/look for a ～ in a bottle (bundle) of hay 大海捞针 ‖ ～point n.针尖;针绣花边

needless /'niːdlɪs/
 adj. unnecessary; not needed 不需要的;不必要的:～ trouble 不必要的麻烦 / Needless to say, he kept his promise.不必说,他已遵守了他的承诺。

needlewoman /'niːdlˌwʊmən/
 n. a woman or girl who has sewing skills or who sews for a living 会缝纫的妇女;女裁缝:a good ～ 针线活做得很好的妇女/ I'm not a ～.我不会做针线活。

needlework /'niːdlwɜːk/
 n. sewing and embroidery work, especially fancy work, done with needle and thread 缝纫;刺绣;针线活:tired eyes from doing fine ～ 由于做精细刺绣活而疲劳的眼睛/ chairs with ～ cushions 有刺绣靠垫的椅子

needs /niːdz/
 adv. in a way that cannot be avoided 必定;必须:If those are his commands we must ～ obey.如果这些是他的命令,我们就一定要服从。

needy /'niːdi/
 adj. not having enough money, food, clothing, etc.贫穷的;贫困的:a ～ family 一个贫穷的家庭/ money to help the ～ 用来帮助穷人的钱

negate /nɪ'geɪt/
 v.❶ cause to have no effect 取消;使无效:This burst of terrorist activity could completely ～ our efforts to expand tourism here.恐怖活动的突然爆发会使我们在这儿扩展旅游业的努力完全白费。 ❷ disapprove the truth or fact of; deny 否定;否认

negation /nɪ'geɪʃən/
 n. the contradiction or denial of sth. 否定;否认;对立面

negative /'negətɪv/
 I adj.❶(of words and answers) showing no or not (指言语和回答)否定的:a ～ answer 否定的回答 ❷ without any positive character 消极的:～ attitude 消极

的态度 ❸less than zero 负的,负数的 ❹ (of electricity) of the type that is carried by electrons (电)阴性的,负的 Ⅱ *n*.❶ a word or statement that denies 否定语,否定词;否定的观点: He gave us a ~ answer.他给了我们否定的答复❷ a number less than zero 负数 ❸ a film with lights and shades reversed 负片,底片 Ⅲ *v*.refuse to accept;say no to 驳斥;否定: Practical experience ~d this theory.实践的经验驳斥了这一学说。 ‖ in the ~ 否定地 ‖ ~ly *adv*.否定地,消极地/ ~ness *n*. 否定性,消极性

neglect/nɪˈɡlekt/

Ⅰ *v*.❶ give no or too little attention or care to 疏忽;忽视: ~ one's meals and sleep 废寝忘食 ❷ fail or forget to do sth. that should be done 遗漏;疏漏: ~ one's duties 玩忽职守 Ⅱ *n*. the state or fact of being uncared for or not receiving enough attention 忽略;疏忽:in a state of ~ 处于无人管理的状态 ‖ ~ed *adj*.被忽视的

neglectful/nɪˈɡlektfəl/

adj.forgetful or careless 疏忽的,不注意的,不留心的: He was ~ of his appearance when he was young.年轻时他不太注意自己的仪表。

negligence/ˈneɡlɪdʒəns/

n.the failure to give sb.or sth.enough care or attention 粗心大意,疏忽,不注意,不留心: The fire was caused by ~.这次火灾是由于疏忽而引起的。

negligent/ˈneɡlɪdʒənt/

adj.not taking or showing enough care 疏忽的,粗心大意的,不留心的:a man who is ~ in his work 一位工作马虎的人/~ officials 不负责任的官员

negligible/ˈneɡlɪdʒəbl/

adj.so small or insignificant as to be not worth taking into account 可忽略不计的;无关紧要的 ‖ negligibly *adv*.可忽视地

negotiable/nɪˈɡəʊʃɪəbl/

adj.❶able to be changed after being discussed 可谈判的,可磋商的: The salary is ~.工资可以商议。 ❷ (said about a cheque) able to be converted into cash or transferred to another person (支票)可兑现的,可转让的

negotiate/nɪˈɡəʊʃɪeɪt/

v.❶ discuss in order to come to an agreement 谈判;协商: The boss has decided to ~ with the labour about the wage claims.老板已决定就工资要求和劳工谈判。 ❷arrange by discussion 商订,议定;谈妥: ~ a peace treaty 商订和约 ❸succeed in dealing with or getting past (sth.difficult) 处理,解决(难题);通过(障碍等): The car ~d the small corner. 小车顺利通过了那个小弯角。

negotiation/nɪˌɡəʊʃɪˈeɪʃn/

n.an act of negotiating 谈判,协商:Price is a matter of ~.价格是可以商议的事。 / be in ~ with sb.over sth.与某人协商某事

neigh/neɪ/

Ⅰ *n*.a long loud cry that a horse makes 马嘶声 Ⅱ *v*.(of a horse) make such a sound (马)嘶叫

neighbour/ˈneɪbə(r)/

Ⅰ *n*.a person,thing or country that is near another 邻居;邻人;邻国;邻近的东西: next-door ~s 隔壁邻居 Ⅱ *v*.be near or next to 邻接,邻近 ‖ ~ing *adj*.邻近的;接壤的/ ~less *adj*.无邻居的

neighbo(u)rhood/ˈneɪbəhʊd/

n.❶ a group of people and their homes forming a small area within a larger place such as a town 邻居,四邻,街坊:The fire alarmed the whole ~.火灾惊动了整个街坊。 ❷ the area around a point or place 邻近地区,附近:There is some beautiful scenery in our ~.我们附近有一些美丽的景色。 ❸a district especially one forming a community 地区;社区:a wealthy ~ 富人区

neighbourly/ˈneɪbəli/

adj.kind and friendly to the people living near you 友邻的,邻人似的;友善的,睦邻的

neither/ˈniːðə(r)/,/ˈnaɪðə(r)/

Ⅰ *pron*.not one and not the other of two

两者都不(的);两者中无一(的):Neither of them is in good temper.他们两人脾气都不好。Ⅱ *adv.* also not 也不:The first one was not bad and ～ was the second.第一个不坏,第二个也不坏。Ⅲ *conj.* (～…nor …) used to show that a negative statement is true of two things (否定的陈述适用于两方面) 既不……也不……,……和……都不:Neither you nor I could do it.你和我都不能做这件事。

nephew/ˈnevjuː, ˈnefjuː/

n. the son of one's brother or sister 侄子,外甥

nerve/nɜːv/

n. ❶ threadlike parts in the body which carry feelings and messages to and from the brain 神经 ❷ (*pl.*) the state of being easily excited or anxious 神经过敏,神经质:suffering from ～s 患神经过敏症 ‖ get on sb.'s ～s 使某人心烦/have iron ～s (have ～s of steel) 有胆量/lose one's ～ 变得慌张/ ～ oneself 鼓起勇气/regain one's ～ 恢复镇静/strain every ～ 竭力/ ～ cell 神经细胞/ ～ centre 神经中枢 ‖ ～-racking, ～-wracking *adj.* 伤脑筋的

nerveless /ˈnɜːvlɪs/

adj. ❶ lacking strength or feeling 麻木的;无生气的;无力气的 ❷ not nervous and confident 自信沉着的;镇静的

nervous/ˈnɜːvəs/

adj. ❶ of the nerves 神经的:the ～ system of the human body 人体的神经系统 ❷ tense and anxious; easily excited or worried 神经紧张的;紧张不安的;易激动的:feel ～ about (at) sth.因某事而心中忐忑不安 /I got a little ～ at the examination.考试时我有点紧张不安。/ Don't be ～.别紧张。

nest/nest/

Ⅰ *n.* ❶ a place or structure built or chosen by a bird for its eggs 鸟巢 ❷ the home thought of as the safe place 家;安乐窝:The husband and wife built themselves a comfortable ～.夫妻共筑了一个安乐窝。Ⅱ *v.* build or make a nest 筑巢 ‖ a mare's ～ 幻想的东西/bring (raise, arouse) a ～ of hornets 捅马蜂窝;惹麻烦/feather

one's ～ 营私/foul one's own ～ 家丑外扬/ take a ～ 摸鸟巢 ‖ ～ful *n.* 满巢/ ～ling *n.* 雏鸟;婴儿

nestle/ˈnesl/

v. ❶ settle comfortably and warmly (舒适而温暖地)安顿:He ～d down in bed shortly after he got home.他到家后不久便上床休息了。❷ press (oneself) closely to 依偎:The child ～ (his head) up against to his mother.小孩(将头)紧紧地依偎着他的母亲。

net[1] /net/

Ⅰ *n.* material of strings, wires, threads, etc.twisted, tied, or woven together for a special purpose 网:fishing ～ 渔网 Ⅱ *v.* (-tt-)catch(fish, bird, etc.) with a net 用网捕(鱼、鸟等);用网覆盖:～ fruit trees 用网覆盖果树 ‖ ～full *n.* 满网/ ～like *adj.* 网状的

net[2] /net/

Ⅰ *adj.* remaining when nothing further is to be subtracted 净的,纯净的:～ profit 净利,纯利 Ⅱ *v.* (-tt-)gain (sth.) as a net profit 净得,净赚:The sale ～ted $3,000.这笔买卖净赚三千美元。/What do you earn, ～ of tax? 你完税后净得多少?

network /ˈnetwɜːk/

n. ❶ an arrangement or pattern of intersecting lines or parts 网状物;网状系统:a railway ～ 铁路网络 ❷ a chain of interconnected people or operations 人际网;网络 ❸ a group of radio or television stations which broadcast the same programmes 广播电视网 ❹ a set of computers which are linked to one another 计算机网络

neural /ˈnjuərəl/

adj. to do with a nerve or the nervous system (与)神经(有关)的;(与)神经系统(有关)的

neuron /ˈnjuərɒn/

n. a cell that is part of the nervous system and sends impulses to and from the brain 神经细胞;神经元

neurotic/njuəˈrɒtɪk/

adv. abnormally sensitive; easily excited

神经不正常的;神经过敏的

neuter /ˈnjuːtə(r)/

adj. ❶ neither male nor female 无雌雄之别的;无性的 ❷ (with reference to words) neither masculine nor feminine (e.g. boy is masculine, but stone is neuter) (指字、词) 中性的(例如:boy 是阳性,而 stone 是中性)

neutral /ˈnjuːtrəl/

Ⅰ *adj.* ❶ taking neither side in a quarrel or a war 中立的:a ～ position 中立立场/ be ～ 保持中立 /He was absolutely ～. 他完全不偏不倚。❷ belonging to an impartial party, state or group 中立国的;中立团体;中立党派的:～ ships 中立国船只/ ～ territory 中立国领土 Ⅱ *n.* an impartial person or country 中立者;中立国

neutralize /ˈnjuːtrəlaɪz, nuːˈtrəlaɪz/

v. ❶ make sth. ineffective by applying an opposite force or effect 使无效;抵消 ❷ make a substance chemically neutral 使化学物质中和 ‖ neutralization *n.* 中和;中立

neutron /ˈnjuːtrɒn/

n. a tiny particle that is neutral electrically and has about the same mass as a proton 中子

never /ˈnevə(r)/

adv. ❶ not ever; at no time 从不;永不:I've ～ met him and I hope I ～ will meet him. 我从未见过他,我也希望永远不会见到他。❷ not at all 决不:Never forget to lock the door at night. 晚上千万别忘了锁门。/You ～ left the key in the lock! 你总不会把钥匙留在锁上吧! ‖ Better late than ～. 迟做总比不做好/ ～ a one 没有一个(人)/Never say die. 不要失望。/ ～ so 非常/ ～ so much as 甚至不/ ～ the (后接比较级) 毫不(更……) ‖ ～-ending *adj.* 永远不会完结的/ ～-failing *adj.* (友谊、恩惠等) 永远不变的/ ～-～-land *n.* 世外桃源/ ～-to-be-forgotten *adj.* 永远不会被遗忘的

nevertheless /ˌnevəðəˈles/

adv. however; in spite of that; all the same 然而;不过;尽管如此;仍然:This sounds strange;～, it is true. 这听起来很奇怪,然而是真实的。/He was very sleepy;～ he went on reading. 他尽管很困倦,却继续看书。

new /njuː/

adj. ❶ never known or used before; invented or discovered recently; seen or heard of for the first time 新的:～ fashions 新款式 ❷ only recently found or known 新发现的:the discovery of a ～ star 一颗新星的发现 ❸ unfamiliar with 不熟悉的:I'm ～ to this town. 我不熟悉这个城镇。❹ first picked of a crop 首次摘采的;时鲜的;新上市的:～ potatoes 新上市的马铃薯 ‖ ～ blown *adj.* (花) 新开的/ ～ born *adj.* 新生的;再生的/ ～-coined *adj.* (尤指词) 新造出来的/ ～ comer *adj.* 新来的人;移民;新手/ ～ fashioned *adj.* 新式的;新流行的/ ～ found *adj.* 新发现的/ ～ made *adj.* 新做的/ ～-rich *n.* 新发迹的人/ ～-type *adj.* 新型的/ ～ wave *n.* 新浪潮 ‖ ～ ish /ˈnjuːɪʃ/ *adj.* 有些新的

newly /ˈnjuːli/

adv. ❶ recently 新近,最近:a ～ built house 新建的房子 ❷ in a new way 以新的方式;重新:The room has been ～ painted. 这房间已重新油漆过了。

news /njuːz/

n. new information; report of a recent event or events 新闻;消息:the latest ～ 最新消息 ‖ be in the ～ 被报道/break the ～ to sb. 把坏消息告诉某人/Good ～ goes on crutches. 好事不出门。‖ ～ agency *n.* 通讯社/ ～ analyst *n.* 新闻分析员,评论员/ ～ boy *n.* 报童/ ～ cast 新闻广播/ ～ caster *n.* 新闻广播员/ ～ casting *adj. n.* 新闻广播的/ ～ conference *n.* 记者招待会/ ～ flash *n.* 简短的新闻报道/ ～ magazine *n.* 新闻杂志/ ～ man *n.* 卖报人;送报人;新闻记者/ ～ monger *n.* 传播新闻的人;饶舌的人/ ～ reel *n.* 新闻短片/ ～ room *n.* 新闻编辑室/ ～ stall, ～ stand *n.* 报摊,报刊柜/ ～ vendor *n.* 卖报人/ ～ window *n.* 新闻图片栏/ ～ worthy *adj.* 有新闻价值的 ‖ ～ less *adj.* 没有新闻的/

N

~iness /'njuːzɪnɪs/ *n.*多新闻；饶舌/ ~y /'njuzi/ *adj.*新闻多的

newspaper /'njuːspeɪpə/
*n.*❶a daily or weekly publication printed on large sheets of paper, containing news reports, articles and features, advertisements, etc.报纸；报 ❷the sheets of paper from old newspapers 旧报纸：Wrap it in ~.用旧报纸将它包起来。

next /nekst/
Ⅰ *adj.*❶ coming immediately after, in order or space 紧接着的；下一个：Let's take the ~ train. 我们赶下一班火车吧。/What's the ~? 下一个是谁？/the woman in the ~ room 隔壁房间里的女子❷ (of a day of the week) following；nearest (一周中的一天)接着的：We are going ~ Monday. 我们下星期一走。Ⅱ *adv.*just afterwards；after this or that 在这(那)以后，然后：When you have finished this, what are you going to do ~? 你做完这件事之后做什么？Ⅲ *prep.*beside；at the side of 靠近，贴近：My seat is ~ to the door.我的座位在门旁边。‖ in the ~ place 其次，第二点/ ~ to 贴近；次于；几乎/the ~ best 仅次于最好的/What ~? (表示惊讶)下一步怎么样？

nibble /'nɪbl/
Ⅰ *v.* take tiny bites 啃；一点一点地咬：The fish is ~ (at) the bait.那鱼在啃咬鱼饵。/The mice have ~d a hole in the bread. 老鼠在面包上啃了个洞 。Ⅱ *n.*❶ an act of nibbling (at) sth. 啃，轻咬 ❷ a very small amount of food 一小口的量；少量

nice /naɪs/
*adj.*❶ good, fine, pleasant or agreeable 令人愉快的；令人喜悦的；美好的：~ weather 好天气/ a ~ face 悦人的面容 ❷ needing care and exactness；fine or subtle 微妙的；细致的，细微的：~ shades of meaning 意义的微妙区别 ❸ kind；friendly 好的，和蔼的，友好的：He's a really ~ guy. 他真是个好人❹ hard to please or showing delicate tastes 难以取悦的；讲究的：very ~ in one's dress 穿着讲究 ‖ more ~ than wise 因爱面子而损

害自己的实际利益/ ~ and 令人满意地；恰到好处的：It's ~ and warm in here.这里温暖怡人。‖ ~ looking *adj.*好看的，漂亮的‖ ~ly *adv.*恰好地；令人愉快地

nick /nɪk/
Ⅰ *n.*a small often accidental cut in a surface or edge 刻痕；槽口 Ⅱ *v.*cut a nick in 刻痕于；割伤：~ a tree as signal 在树上刻痕作为记号 ‖ in the ~ (of time) 正是时候，正在关键时刻

nickel /'nɪkl/
*n.*❶ a hard, silver white metal used in alloys (symbol Ni) 镍(化学符号 Ni) ❷ a coin of the US and Canada worth five cents (美国和加拿大的)5 分镍币，5 分钱

nickname /'nɪkneɪm/
Ⅰ *n.*a name used informally instead of sb.'s own name 绰号；诨号："Fatty" is a ~ for a very fat person."胖子"是一个胖人的绰号。Ⅱ *v.*give sb. a nickname 给……起绰号；给……加诨名：They ~d him "Hurry".他们给他起了个"匆忙"的绰号。

niece /niːs/
*n.*the daughter of one's brother or sister 侄女；外甥女

niggle /'nɪgl/
*v.*❶ cause slight but persistent annoyance, discomfort, or anxiety 使隐隐不安，使烦躁 ❷ find fault with (someone) in a petty way 对……吹毛求疵，挑剔：I don't react anymore when the teacher tries to ~ me.当老师试图对我吹毛求疵时，我不再回应了。

night /naɪt/
*n.*❶ the time of darkness between evening and morning 夜，夜晚：on Sunday ~ 在星期日夜里 ❷a sad period or experience 黯淡的时期(或经历)：through the ~ of doubt and sorrow 经过疑惑及悲伤的黯淡时期 ‖ a dirty ~ 雨夜/all (long) 整夜/as black (dark) as ~ 漆黑；天黑时；在夜里/a white ~ 失眠之夜/by ~ 在夜间；趁黑夜/Good ~! 晚安！再会！(晚上分别时用语)/have a good (bad) ~ 一夜睡得好(不好)/have a ~

out (off) 在外玩一晚上；一个晚上不上班/make a ～ of it 痛快地玩一晚上/after ～ 一夜又一夜地/ ～ and day 夜以继日地/turn ～ into day 以黑夜当白昼/under ～ 乘黑夜；秘密/What is done by ～ appears by day. 若要人不知，除非己莫为。‖ ～-bell n.夜间用的门铃/ ～ cap n.睡帽/ ～clothes n.睡衣/ ～ club n.夜总会/ ～dress n.妇女（或孩子）穿的睡衣/ ～ flower n.夜里开的花/ ～gown n.睡袍；长睡衣/ ～ life n.夜生活/ ～ long adj.& adv.通宵的(地)/ ～man n.掏粪工(一般在夜里工作)/ ～mare n.噩梦/ ～stick n. 〈美〉警棍/ ～stool n.便桶/ ～ suit n.(一套)睡衣/ ～time n.夜间/ ～walker n.梦游病患者；晚上行窃者；妓女/ ～ watch 守夜；值夜的人们；值夜时间/ ～ watchman n.(专职的)守夜人 / ～wear n.(总称)睡衣/ ～work n.夜间工作

nightfall /'naɪtfɔːl/
　n.the beginning of darkness at the end of the day 黄昏；傍晚；日暮

nightingale /'naɪtɪŋɡeɪl/
　n. a small bird known for its beautiful singing, heard mostly at night 夜莺

nightly /'naɪtli/
　adj.❶happening or done in the night 夜间发生的；晚上的，夜间的 ❷happening or done every night 每晚的

nil /nɪl/
　n. nothing (often used in giving scores) 无，零(通常用于记分)：win by two goals to ～ 以二比零的得分获胜

nimble /'nɪmbl/
　adj.❶able to move quickly and easily 敏捷的，迅速的：a ～ leap 敏捷的一跃 ❷sharp；quick to understand 敏锐的；聪明的：have a ～ tongue 能说会道/a ～ reply 巧妙的回答‖ as ～ as a squirrel 身手灵活，举动轻捷

nine /naɪn/
　num.the number 9 九‖ A cat has ～ lives. 猫有九条命。(指生命力强)/a ～ day's wonder 轰动一时的事物/ ～ tenths 十之八九，几乎全部/ ～ times out of ten 几乎每次，十之八九，常常/to the ～s 完美

nineteen /ˌnaɪn'tiːn/
　num.the number 19, one more than eighteen 十九；十九个：talk ～ to the dozen 喋喋不休

ninety /'naɪnti/
　num.the number 90, equal to nine times ten 九十；九十个

ninth /naɪnθ/
　num.❶next after eighth 第九 ❷one of nine equal parts of a thing 九分之一

nip[1] /nɪp/
　I v.(-pp-)❶ give sb.or sth.a quick painful bite or pinch 夹；钳；捏；咬：～ a child between one's knees 把孩子夹在双膝当中 ❷go quickly or go for a short time 快走；急忙离去；离开一会儿：I'll ～ out and buy a newspaper. 我要出去一下买份报纸。Ⅱ n.❶the act of nipping；pinch 夹；钳；捏 ❷ coldness 严寒：There's a ～ in the air today. 今天的风有点阴冷刺骨。‖ ～ and tuck 势均力敌/ ～ in 飞快地跑进来；插嘴‖ ～per n.钳子，镊子/～-ping adj.(空气、冷风)刺骨的，讽刺的/ ～py adj.刺人的；寒冷刺骨的；刺鼻的；尖锐的

nip[2] /nɪp/
　n. a small amount of a strong alcoholic drink,(not beer or wine) 一小口(酒)，一呷：take a ～ of whisky 呷一口威士忌酒

nitrogen /'naɪtrədʒən/
　n. a gas without colour, taste or smell, forming about four-fifths of the air 氮，氮气

no /nəʊ/
　I adj.not a；not any 没有：I had ～ money.我没有钱。Ⅱ int. as a short reply, expressing refusal or disagreement, opposite to "Yes"(用于否定的回答或拒绝) 不，不是："Are you busy?" "No, I'm not." "你忙吗?" "不，我不忙。" Ⅲ adv.(with comparatives)(置于比较级形容词前) 毫不，一点也不：I'm feeling ～ worse than yesterday.我并不觉得比昨天差。Ⅳ n.(pl.～es or ～s)❶an answer or decision of no 否定；拒绝：Two ～es make a yes.否定的否定就是肯定。/a clear ～ to my request for money 明确地拒绝我要钱

的要求 ❷(usually *pl.*) a vote or voter a-gainst a question to be decided, especially in a parliament 反对票；投反对票者：The ～es won and the idea was dropped.反对的人赢了，这意见也就搁置下来了。‖ say ～(to)拒绝……，不批准……，否认……‖ ～-account,～-count *adj.& n.*无价值的(人)，微不足道的(人)/ ～-being *n.*不存在/ ～-good *adj.& n.*无价值的，无用的；无用的人(或物)/ ～man *n.*惯常反对别人意见(或拒绝别人要求)的人/ ～man's land *n.*荒地；无主土地/ ～-nonsense *adj.*不胡闹的；严肃的

nobility/nəʊˈbɪləti/
n. the quality of being noble; the noble birth or rank; the noble as a class 高贵；贵族(阶层)：the ～ of one's mind 某人的崇高思想/a member of the ～ 贵族阶层的一员

noble/ˈnəʊbl/
Ⅰ *adj.* ❶ (of character and quality) good; fine 高尚的，高贵的：a ～ leader 伟大的领袖/ ～ sentiments 高尚的情操 ❷ of high rank or title, usually by birth 显贵的，贵族的 ❸ grand, great or excellent in size or quality 卓越的；辉煌的：～ buildings 宏伟的建筑/ a ～ horse 骏马 Ⅱ *n.*a person of noble birth 出身高贵的人；贵族 ‖ **nobly**/ˈnəʊbli/ *adv.*高贵地；高尚地；壮丽地/ ～ness *n.*高贵；高尚

nobleman /ˈnəʊbəlmən/
*n.*a person of noble birth or rank 贵族

nobody/ˈnəʊbədi/
pron. ❶ no one; no person; not anybody 无人；无一人；谁也不：Nobody is at home.没有人在家。/I know ～ there.那些人我谁也不认识。❷ an unimportant person 不重要的人；小人物；无名小卒：She is married to a ～.她嫁给了一个小人物。/He is (a) ～.他是个无名小卒。

nod/nɒd/
Ⅰ *v.*(-dd-)❶ bend (one's head) slightly to express agreement or greet to sb. 点头(表示同意或招呼)：He ～ded approval.他点头表示赞成。❷ let one's head drop forward when sleepy or asleep, while sitting 打盹，打瞌睡：She sat ～ding by the fire.她坐在火炉边打盹。Ⅱ *n.*the act of nodding to express agreement or greet to sb. 点头(表示同意或打招呼)：He gave me a ～ as he passed.他走过时对我点头。‖ A ～ is as good as a wink.心有灵犀一点通。/be at sb.'s ～(be dependent on sb.'s ～)依某人而定；受某人支配/have a ～ding acquaintance with 和……有点头之交，对……略知一二/Homer sometimes ～s.智者千虑，必有一失。/ ～ to its fall 摇摇欲坠/the Land of Nod(the land of Nod)梦乡

noise/nɔɪz/
Ⅰ *n.*a loud and unpleasant sound 声音；噪声；嘈杂声：Don't make so much ～! 不要这么吵闹！Ⅱ *v.*make much noise 喧闹 ‖ make a ～(about sth.)(为某事而)吵吵嚷嚷/make a ～ in the world 名噪一时 ‖ ～maker *n.*发出噪声的人；噪音器/ ～-proof *adj.*防杂音的；隔音的 ‖ ～ful *adj.*喧闹的/ ～less *adj.*无声的；声音很轻的

noisy/ˈnɔɪzi/
*adj.*❶ making much noise 吵闹的，聒噪的：～ children 吵吵闹闹的孩子们 ❷ full of noise 喧哗的；充满噪声的：a ～ classroom 喧闹的教室

nomad/ˈnəʊmæd/
*n.*members of a tribe which wanders from one place to another seeking pasture, etc. 游牧部落的人

nominal/ˈnɒmɪnl/
*adj.*❶ in name or form but usually not in reality 名义上的：The young man is only the ～ head of the business; his father makes the decisions.那个年轻人只是这家公司名义上的主人，做决定的是他的父亲。❷ of or used as a noun 名词的；名词性的：a ～ phrase 名词短语 ❸(of an a-mount of money) very small; negligible (款额)很小的：a ～ sum 极小的款项

nominate/ˈnɒmɪneɪt/
*v.*suggest for election to a position 提出(某人为候选人)，提名：～ sb. for the presidency 提名某人为总统候选人 ‖ **nominator**/ˈnɒmɪneɪtə(r)/ *n.*提名者；任命者/**nominee**/ˌnɒmɪˈniː/*n.*被提名者；被任命者

nomination/ˌnɒmɪˈneɪʃn/

*n.*an instance of nominating 提名,任命: How many ～s have there been so far? 到现在为止有多少人已被提名?

nominative /ˈnɒmɪnətɪv/

Ⅰ*n.* the case used for the subject of a verb,etc.主格 Ⅱ*adj.* ❶ relating to or denoting a case of nouns,pronouns,and adjectives in Latin,Greek,and other inflected languages,used for the subject of a verb 主格的 ❷of or appointed by nomination as distinct from election（被）任命的

non-committal/ˌnɒnkəˈmɪtl/

adj. not giving any clear decision on a matter 不表态的;不明朗的

none/nʌn/

Ⅰ*pron.* not any,not one 一个也没有: None of them have(has)come yet.他们都还没来呢。Ⅱ*adv.*by no means;not at all 绝不;毫不: He spent three weeks in hospital but he's ～ the better for it.他在医院待了三个星期,但一点也没好转。‖ ～ but 只有/ ～ the less 仍然,依然

nonsense/ˈnɒnsns/

n. meaningless words;foolish statements or ideas 废话;胡扯,谬论:talk ～ 胡说八道

noodle/ˈnuːdl/

n.（usually *pl.*）paste of flour and eggs prepared in long,narrow strips and used in soups,etc.面条

noon/nuːn/

n. the middle of the day 中午,正午: at high ～ 在正午时 ‖(as) clear as ～ 一清二楚/the ～ of night 午夜 ‖ ～-tide *n.*中午,正午;最高点/ ～time *adj.*中午的,正午的

nor/nɔː(r)/

conj. ❶（neither … ～ …）and not 也不: Neither a flower ～ even a blade of grass will grow in this desert.这沙漠上既没有一朵花也没有一片草。❷（used at the beginning of an expression just before a verb）and also not（用在词句之首、动词之前）也不: He can't do it;～ can I.他不能这事,我也不能。

norm/nɔːm/

*n.*❶ a standard,model or pattern considered as typical 准则;标准;规范 ❷an amount of work required or expected in a working day in a factory,etc.定额;工作量:Our ～ is forty machines per day.我们的定额是每日 40 台机器。

normal/ˈnɔːml/

Ⅰ*adj.* usual;regular;ordinary 正常的,常态的;平常的;正规的: the ～ temperature of the human body 人体的正常温度 Ⅱ*n.*sth.regarded as a normative example 通常情况;通常的标准:return to ～ 恢复正常 ‖ ～ity/nɔːˈmæləti/ *n.*正常状态

normalize /ˈnɔːməlaɪz/

v. make sth. normal,or to become normal（使）正常化;恢复正常 ‖ **normalization** *n.*正常化;标准化

normally /ˈnɔːməli/

*adv.*under normal or usual conditions;as a rule 通常;正常地;常规地

north/nɔːθ/

Ⅰ*n.* the direction which is on your left when you face the rising sun 北方:a cold wind from the ～ 北方吹来的寒风 Ⅱ*adv.*in towards the north 北方的,朝北的;在北方,向北方:a ～ window 北窗/sail ～ 向北航行 ‖ **too far ～** 精明的,不会受骗的/ ～ light 北面来的光线/North Pole 北极/North Star 北极星 ‖ ～ward, ～wards *adv.*向北方/ ～western *adj.*西北的

northern/ˈnɔːðən/

adj. of, in or from the north part of world,a country,etc.北方的;北部的:～ habits and customs 北方的风俗习惯

nose/nəʊz/

Ⅰ*n.* ❶ the part of the face above the mouth for breathing and smelling 鼻子: the bridge of the ～ 鼻梁 ❷ the sense of smell 嗅觉:a dog with a good ～ 嗅觉灵敏的狗 ❸ sth.like a nose in shape or position 鼻形物:～ wheel 前轮 Ⅱ*v.* ❶ smell;discover by smelling 闻出,探出,侦察出:The dog ～d out a rat.那只狗嗅到一只老鼠的气味。❷push sth.with the nose 用鼻子推：The dog ～d the door open.狗用鼻子顶开了门。‖ a ～ of wax 没有主意的人/(as) plain as the ～ in your face 一清二楚/bite sb.'s ～ off 气势汹汹地回答某人/by a ～ 以些微之差/cannot see beyond one's ～ 鼠目寸光/count(tell) ～s 数人数/follow one's ～ 笔直走；凭本能行事/fuddle one's ～ 酩酊,烂醉/keep one's ～ clean 不喝酒/keep one's (sb.'s) ～ to the grindstone 使自己(某人)埋头从事辛苦的劳动/lead sb.by the ～ 牵着人的鼻子走,完全支配某人/look down one's ～ at 瞧不起/make a long ～ 做蔑视的手势/ ～ to ～ 面对面地/pay through ～ 被敲竹杠/poke (或 push, thrust) one's ～ into 探听；干涉(别人的事情)/put sb.'s ～ out of joint 打乱某人的计划；挤掉某人(使自己得宠)/run at the ～ 流鼻涕/speak through one's ～ 带鼻音说话/thumb one's ～ (at)(对……)做蔑视的手势/turn up one's ～ at 对……嗤之以鼻,瞧不起/under sb.'s ～ 就在某人眼前；当着某人的面‖ ～d adj.有……鼻子的/ ～less adj.无鼻子的

nostalgia/nɒˈstældʒə/
　n.homesickness；a desire for sth.that has known in the past 思乡病；怀旧：the ～ of one's childhood 怀念童年

nostril/ˈnɒstrɪl/
　n.each of the two openings in the nose through which air is admitted 鼻孔

nosy/ˈnəʊzi/
　adj. inquisitive；too interested in things that do not concern you 好奇的；好问的，爱打听的 ‖ **nosily** adv.爱管闲事地；好打听地

not/nɒt/
　adv. ❶ (often contracted to -n't, as in hasn't) used to make a negative (用以构成否定式,常略作-n't,如hasn't) 不 ❷ used in front of word referring to a distance,length of time,or other amount to say that the actual distance, time or amount is less than the one mentioned (用于表示距离、时间或其他数量的词之间)不到：～ fifty metres away 不到 50 米远 ❸used to represent the negative of a

word,group or clause that has just been used (用于表示对前面出现过的单词、词组或从句的否定)不："Thank you very much""Not at all.""非常谢谢你。""不必啦。"‖ as likely as ～ 很可能/ ～ a 一个也不/ ～ all that 不那么……(地)/ ～ only...but(also)...不但……而且……/ ～ that 并不是说/ ～ but…that that...不是(因为)……而是(因为)……/Not that I know of.据我所知并不是那样。

notable/ˈnəʊtəbl/
　Ⅰ adj.worthy of notice；remarkable；eminent 值得注意的；显著的；著名的：a ～ lawyer 著名的律师 Ⅱ n.notable person 名人；要人；达官显贵 ‖ notability/ˌnəʊtəˈbɪləti/ n.显著；著名；名人,显要人物/notably adv.显著地；著名地

notation/nəʊˈteɪʃn/
　n.a set of signs or symbols representing numbers,musical notes,etc.(一组)符号；记数法；记谱法：musical ～ 音乐符号/the Arabic ～ 阿拉伯记数法

notch /nɒtʃ/
　Ⅰ n.❶a small cut or indentation in a surface or on the edge of sth. (物体边缘或表面上的)槽口；凹痕；切口 ❷each of a row of holes into which the tongue of a buckle fits (皮带上搭扣插入的)凹口，槽口 ❸a point or level in a graded system or scale 刻度分 Ⅱ v.❶ make a notch or notches in the surface or an edge of sth. 刻凹痕 ❷ score or achieve a success in a sports contest (体育比赛)得分；赢得：The team ～ed up another win.该队获得了又一次胜利。

note/nəʊt/
　Ⅰ n.❶ a written record or reminder 笔记；记录：the ～s of a journey 旅行笔记 ❷ a short letter 便笺；短信：a ～ of thanks 感谢函 ❸a remark added to a piece of writing and placed outside the main part of the writing, e.g. at the side or bottom of a page, especially to give more information 评注,注解：～ on an article 文章的注解 ❹a formal letter between governments (外交上的)照会：a ～ of protest 抗议照会 ❺ a piece of pa-

per money 期票;钞票;bank ～s 纸币/a promissory ～ 期票 ❻ a single musical sound of a particular length and degree of highness or lowness 音符;音调;鸣声:the blackbird's merry ～ 画眉快乐的鸣声 ❼ a stated quality or feeling 声调,语气:A ～ of self-satisfaction in his speech. 他讲话中有自满的口气。❽ fame or importance 名望;重要性:a family of ～ 有名望的家庭 ❾ notice;attention 注意:worthy of ～ 值得注意 Ⅱ v.❶ notice or pay careful attention to sth.注意;觉察:I failed to ～ that he had left.我没有注意到他已经走了。❷ call attention to;remark 特别提到;说起;指出 ‖ compare ～s 对笔记;交换意见/make（take）a ～（～s）of 把……记下来/strike the right ～ 说（做）得恰当/strike the false ～ 说（做）得不恰当/take ～ of 注意（到）……/take(make) ～s 记笔记 ‖ ～book n.笔记本;期票簿/ ～paper n.信纸,便条纸 ‖ ～less adj.不被注意的,不著名的;音调不和谐的/ ～r n.做笔记的人

noted /ˈnəʊtɪd/
adj.famous or well-known 著名的;显著的:She is a ～ dancer. 她是著名的舞蹈家。

noteworthy /ˈnəʊtwɜːðɪ/
adj.worth noting;remarkable 值得注意的;显著的

nothing /ˈnʌθɪŋ/
Ⅰ n.❶not anything;no things 没有东西,无物:Nothing in the world is difficult for one who sets his mind to it.天下无难事,只怕有心人。❷sb. or sth. of no importance 微不足道的人（或事物）:"Sorry to have interrupted you.""Oh,it's ～.""打扰了你真是对不起。""没有什么。"Ⅱ adv.in no way;not at all 一点也不,并不:It's ～ surprising.这毫不奇怪。 ‖ all to ～ 百分之百的/be ～ to 对……来说无足轻重;不能与……相比/come to ～ 失败,没有结果/for ～ 免费;徒然,没有理由/have ～ in one 不足道;没有个性/have ～ to do with 和……无关;和……不往来/have ～ to show for 在……没有成绩可言/leave ～ to be desired 完美无缺/like

～ on earth 珍奇的/make ～ of 对……等闲视之;不能理解;不能解决/no ～ 什么也没有/ ～ but 除了……以外什么也不;只有;只不过/ ～ if not 极其/ ～ less than 和……一模一样,完全是/ ～ like 没有什么能比得上……/ ～ much 很少/Nothing succeeds like success.一事成功,事事顺利。/Nothing venture,～ have.不入虎穴,焉得虎子。/There is ～ in it.里面没有什么内容;这是不真实的;这是不重要的。/think ～ of 把……看成平常/to say ～ of 更不必说 ‖ ～ness n.无,不存在;无价值(的事物);死

notice /ˈnəʊtɪs/
Ⅰ n.❶ information;news about sth. to happen 通告,布告;通知:Notice is hereby given that.特此布告。❷ warning or information about sth. that to happen 预告;提前通知:Will you allow us ten minutes' ～? 请你在十分钟前通知我们好吗? ❸ a statement of opinion,especially in a newspaper,about a new book,play,etc.(期刊中对新书、剧作等的)评论:book ～ 书评 ❹the act of noticing or paying attention 注意:bring sth.into public ～ 使某事为公众所注意 Ⅱ v.pay attention to 注意:Please ～ the regulations overleaf.请注意本页反面的规章(或使用须知)。 ‖ at short ～ 一俟通知(马上就……)/bring sth.to sb.'s ～ 使某人注意某事/come into ～ 引起注意/come to sb.'s ～ 引起某人的注意/give ～ 通知/have ～ 接到通知/take ～ 注意/take sb.'s ～ 得到某人的通知/till(until) further ～ 在另行通知以前/without ～ 不预先通知地;不另行通告地/ ～board 布告栏

noticeable /ˈnəʊtɪsəbl/
adj.easily seen or noticed 显而易见的,显著的;值得注意的 ‖ noticeably adv.显著地,明显地;引人注目地

notify /ˈnəʊtɪfaɪ/
v.inform（sb.）about sth. officially 通知;通告:～ the police of a robbery 向警方报告一次抢劫案 /～ sb.of one's new telephone number 告诉某人自己新的电话号码 /We have been notified that the meeting was put off.已经通知我们会议延期

N

了。

notion/ˈnəʊʃn/

　n. ❶ an idea, opinion or belief about sth. 想法, 见解: Her head is full of silly ～s. 她一脑袋糊涂想法。❷ a desire or intention 打算; 意图: I have no ～ of resigning. 我没有辞职的意思。‖ ～al *adj.* 概念的; 想象的; 表意的

notorious/nəʊˈtɔːrɪəs/

　adj. well-known for sth. bad（因坏事而）著名的; 臭名昭著的; 声名狼藉的: a ～ cheat 声名狼藉的骗子

notwithstanding/ˌnɒtwɪθˈstændɪŋ/

　prep. in spite of 尽管; 虽然: They finished the task, ～ the heavy rain. 尽管下大雨, 他们还是把工作做完了。

nought/nɔːt/

　n. ❶（the figure）0; zero（数字）零: ～ point six 零点六 ❷ used in particular phrases to mean nothing 无: come to ～ 落空

noun/naʊn/

　n. a word that is the name of a person, thing, place, etc. 名词: an abstract（a material）～ 抽象（物质）名词/a collective（an individual）～ 集体（个体）名词/a common（proper）～ 普通（专有）名词/a countable（an uncountable）～ 可数（不可数）名词

nourish/ˈnʌrɪʃ/

　v. ❶ keep alive, well or strong by giving food, water, etc. 养育; 给以营养: ～ the soil 给土地施肥 ❷ have（certain feelings）怀有（某种感情）: ～ feelings of hatred 怀恨在心 ‖ ～ing *adj.* 滋养的/～ment *n.* 滋养品; 营养情况

novel/ˈnɒvl/

　Ⅰ *n.* a long written story in prose printed as a book 小说: a popular ～ 流行小说/a historical ～ 历史小说 Ⅱ *adj.* new; strange 新的; 新奇的: a ～ experience 新奇的经历

novelty/ˈnɒvlti/

　n. ❶ the quality of being new, different and interesting 新鲜; 新奇: The ～ of his surroundings soon wore off. 他对环境的新奇感很快消失了。❷ sth. new and strange 新奇的事物: Snow is ～ to people from Africa. 对非洲人来说, 雪是新奇的事物。❸ a small toy, decoration, etc. of low value 廉价的小玩意儿（或小装饰品）: The poor mother tried to find some ～ inside the garbage can for her son. 那位可怜的母亲想在垃圾桶里找一些廉价的小玩意儿给她儿子。

November/nəʊˈvembə(r)/

　n. the 11th month of the year 十一月

now/naʊ/

　Ⅰ *adv.* ❶ at the present time; at this moment 现在; 此刻: He ～ lives in Paris. 他现在住在巴黎。❷ at once; without delay 立刻, 马上: You must go ～. 你必须马上走。❸ used by the speaker to continue a narrative, request, warning, etc.（用于表示说话者的语气, 如解释、请求、警告等）暂且; 现在: Now listen to me. 且听我讲。Ⅱ *conj.* since 既然; 由于: Now（that）you mention it, I do remember. 你这样一提, 我就记起来了。Ⅲ *n.* the present time or moment 现在; 此刻: I suppose he has arrived in Beijing by ～. 我想他现在已到北京了。Ⅳ *adj.* at this time 现时的, 现在的: the ～ chairman of the association 现任协会主席 ‖（every）～ and again 时而, 不时/from ～ on 从现在开始/just ～ 刚才; 眼下; 立即/Now or never! 机不可失! / ～ then（用于句首, 表示警告、抗议或引起注意）喂/up to ～ 到目前为止

nowadays/ˈnaʊədeɪz/

　adv. at the present time 现在; 现今: Nowadays people seldom go to the cinema. They watch TV at home. 现在人们很少去电影院了, 他们在家看电视。

nowhere/ˈnəʊweə(r)/

　Ⅰ *adv.* in, at or to no place 任何地方都不: The book is ～ to be found. 到处找不到这本书。Ⅱ *n.* no place; an insignificant or unexpected place 无处; 无名之地; 不知道的地方: There is ～ to sit in the crowded room. 房间里人很挤, 无处可坐。/A tiger appeared from ～. 蓦地出现了一只老虎。‖ be ～ 一无所得; 一事无成;（在比赛等中）未得名次

nuclear/ˈnjuːklɪə(r)/

adj. ❶ of a nucleus 核心的；中心的：the ～ part of a city 城市的中心部分 ❷ of, concerning, or using atomic energy 原子能的；核动力的：～ weapons 核武器/a ～ war 核战争 ‖ ～-armed *adj.*用核武器装备的/ ～ energy *n.*核能/ ～-free zone *n.*无核区

nucleus/ˈnjuːklɪəs/

n.(*pl.*nuclei/ˈnjuːklɪaɪ/ or ～es) ❶ a central part, around which other parts are grouped or collected 中心；核心：The fortress was the ～ of the ancient city.这个堡垒是这个古城的中心。❷ the central part of an atom 原子核 ❸ the central part of a living cell 细胞核

nude/njuːd/

I *adj.*not wearing any clothes, especially of a human figure in art 裸体的：～ trees of winter 冬天光秃秃的树 II *n.*❶ a person not wearing any clothes 裸体者 ❷ a painting of a naked human figure（especially in art）裸体人像（尤指艺术的）‖ in the ～ 赤身裸体的，公开的，赤裸裸的

nuisance/ˈnjuːsns/

*n.*a person, thing or act that annoys or causes trouble 讨厌的人；讨厌的东西；讨厌的事情（或行为）：The mosquitoes are a ～.蚊子是讨厌的东西。/What a ～ that child is! 那个孩子真讨厌！

null/nʌl/

*adj.*having no effect or force 无效力的；无约束力的 ‖ ～ and void 无法律效力的；无效的：Their marriage was declared ～ and void.他们的结婚被宣布为无效。

nullify /ˈnʌlɪfaɪ/

*v.*❶ make sth. null and void 使无法律效力；使无效；否定 ❷ cancel or neutralize the effect of sth.使无用；使无价值；抵消 ‖ nullification *n.*无效；废弃；取消

numb/nʌm/

I *adj.*unable to feel or move 失去知觉的；麻木的：My fingers were ～ with cold.我的手指冻僵了。 II *v.*make numb 使麻木：feet ～ed with cold 冻麻了的脚

number/ˈnʌmbə(r)/

I *n.*❶ a word or sign that shows how many 数；数字：an even(odd) ～ 偶(奇)数/a known(unknown) ～ 已知(未知)数 ❷ a number used to show the position of sth. in an ordered set or list 号码：the room ～ 房间号 ❸ the series of numbers that you dial when you are making a telephone call 电话号码 ❹ issue of a periodical, newspaper（杂志的）期：a back ～ 过期期刊 ❺ a quantity or amount 若干；数目；数量：A ～ of accidents always occur on such days.在这种日子里常常有许多事故发生。❻ a change in the form of words, especially nouns and verbs, depending on whether one or more than one thing is talking about（名词和动词的）数：the singular (plural) ～ 单(复)数 II *v.*❶reach as a total；be in number 总计：The students in our class ～ thirty.我们班总共有三十名学生。❷give a number to 编号：Let's ～ them from 1 to 10.给他们从一到十编号。❸ include or be included as one of a particular group 把……算作；认为：～ sb. among one's friends 认为某人是朋友 ‖ any ～ of 许多/beyond ～ 多得数不清/in ～ 在数字上；总共/in round ～ s 以整数表示；以约数表示/～ one 头号人物；最重要的人/to the ～ of 达到……的数目，合计数为……/without ～ 多得数不清的 ‖ ～ing machine *n.*号码机/ ～ plate *n.*号码牌

numberless /ˈnʌmbələs/

*adj.*too many to count 无数的；数不清的

numeral/ˈnjuːmərəl/

I *adj.*of number 数的；示数的 II *n.*a sign that represents a number 数字：the Roman ～s 罗马数字/the Arabic ～s 阿拉伯数字 ‖ numerable/ˈnjuːmərəbl/*adj.*可数的

numerator/ˈnjuːməreɪtə(r)/

*n.*❶ the number above the line in a vulgar fraction（分数的）分子：The ～ of the fraction 2/3 is 2.分数 2/3 的分子是 2。❷a person or thing that numbers 计算者；计算器

numerical/njuːˈmerɪkl/

*adj.*of a number；having sth. to do with

numbers 数字的，用数字表示的，数值的：~ symbols 数字符号‖~ly adv. 用数字或数值表示地

numerous /ˈnjuːmərəs/

adj. ❶ many；large in number 许多的：~ books 许多书籍 ❷ made up of a large number 由多数人组成的：a ~ class（人数很多的）大班 /a ~ army 一支庞大的军队 /a ~ family 子女众多的家庭

nurse /nɜːs/

Ⅰ *n.* ❶ a woman who takes care of the sick，the old，babies or small children，etc. as a job 保姆 ❷ a person，typically a woman，who is trained to take care of sick，hurt，or old people，especially as directed by a doctor in a hospital 护士；看护：a hospital ~ 医院的护士 Ⅱ *v.* ❶ take care of as or like a nurse 护理，看护：~ sb. back to health 护理某人使恢复健康 ❷ (of a woman) feed (a baby) with milk from the breast 喂奶 ❸ give special care to 细心照看：~ young plants 培育幼苗‖put ... (out) to ~ 将……寄养于人‖~r *n.* 培育者；奶瓶/ ~ry /ˈnɜːsəri/ *n.* 托儿所，保育室；苗圃/nursing/ˈnɜːsɪŋ/ *n.* 保育，护理

nursing home /ˈnɜːsɪŋhəʊm/

n. a small private hospital，especially which provides the elderly with health care 小型私人医院，疗养院

nurture /ˈnɜːtʃə(r)/

Ⅰ *v.* care for and educate；nourish；encourage the growth of 教养；养育；培育：

She ~d the child as if he had been her own. 她把那个孩子当作自己的孩子来养育。Ⅱ *n.* education，training，and development 教养；训练；培育：the ~ of new talent 对新人的培育

nut /nʌt/

n. ❶ the fruit with a hard shell enclosing a kernel that can be eaten 坚果 ❷ a small piece of metal with a threaded hole for screwing on to the end of a bolt 螺母；螺帽‖a hard ~ to crack 棘手的问题；难对付的人/not care a (rotten) ~ 毫不在乎‖~let /ˈnʌtlɪt/ *n.* 小坚果，果核/ ~-brown *adj.* 深棕色的，栗色的/ ~-tree *n.* 坚果树

nutrition /njuːˈtrɪʃən/

n. the process of providing or being provided with nourishment；nourishing food 营养(物)；滋养(物)：Good ~ is important for good health. 良好的营养对良好的身体是很重要的。

nutritious /njuːˈtrɪʃəs/

adj. valuable to the body as food；nourishing 有营养的；滋养的：Apples and bread are ~. 苹果和面包有营养。

nutritive /ˈnjuːtrətɪv/

adj. of or providing nourishment 滋养的；有营养的；有关营养的：What is the ~ value of that? 那东西有什么营养价值？

nylon /ˈnaɪlɒn/

n. a strong light synthetic fibre or fabric 尼龙；尼龙制品

Oo

oaf/əuf/

n. a stupid or clumsy fellow 蠢人；呆子；笨蛋：Careful, you great ~! 小心, 你这十足的蠢货!

oak/əuk/

n. a large tree with hard wood; the wood of this sort of tree 橡树；橡树木：an ~ door 橡木门

oar/ɔ:(r)/

n. a long pole with a flat blade, used for rowing a boat 桨；橹：bend to the ~s 用力划桨

oasis/əuˈeɪsɪs/

n. (*pl.* oases) ❶ a place with water and trees in a desert 沙漠中的绿洲：The travellers in the desert stopped at an ~ for the night. 那些沙漠旅行者们在一个绿洲停下来过夜。 ❷ a place or situation that is different from its surroundings usually in a pleasant or comforting way 宜人的地方：This is my only ~ in life. 这是生活中唯一一令我感到宜人的地方。

oat/əut/

n. an erect annual grass, Avena sativa, grown in temperate regions for its edible seed 燕麦：Oats can be grown further north than wheat. 燕麦比小麦生长区的纬度更高。 /There are a lot of wild ~s in the fields. 地里长了许多野燕麦。

oath/əuθ/

n. (*pl.* ~s/əuðz/) a solemn promise 誓言；誓约：Every U.S. president must take an ~ to uphold the Constitution. 每一任美国总统都要宣誓捍卫宪法。 ‖ on (upon) ~ 发誓/ put sb. on ~ 使某人立誓/ take an ~ 宣誓；发誓

oatmeal/ˈəutmiːl/

n. crushed oats used for making cakes and porridge 燕麦片(粉)；燕麦

obedient/əˈbiːdiənt/

adj. willing to do what one is told to do 服从的；顺从的；听话的；恭顺的：an ~ child 听话的小孩/ a very well-trained and ~ dog 一只受过严格训练、绝对服从(命令)的狗

obese/əuˈbiːs/

adj. very fat 极为肥胖的：an ~ old man 非常肥胖的老人 ‖ obesity *n.* 肥胖

obey/əˈbeɪ/

v. do what one is asked or ordered to do 服从；顺从；听从：~ the law 遵守法律／~ orders 服从命令 ‖ obedience /əˈbiːdɪəns/*n.* 顺从；听话

obituary/əˈbɪtʃuəri/

n. a printed notice, especially in a newspaper, that presents someone has died, usually with a short account of his life 讣告；讣闻

object[1]/ˈɒbdʒɪkt/

n. ❶ a thing that can be seen or touched 实物；物体：There are three ~s on my desk. 我桌上有三件东西。 ❷ an aim or a purpose 目标；目的：Everyone should have a clear ~ in his life. 每个人都应该有明确的人生目标。 ❸ the word(s) towards which the action of the verb is directed or to which a preposition shows some relation (动作的对象)宾语：direct ~ 直接宾语/ indirect ~ 间接宾语

object[2]/əbˈdʒekt/

v. be opposed (to) 反对，不赞成：I ~ to the proposal. 我反对这个提议。 /Do you ~ to smoking? 你反对吸烟吗?

objection/əbˈdʒekʃn/

n. ❶ the action or feeling of disliking, opposing or disapproving 厌恶；反对，不赞成：He has a strong ~ to getting up early. 他强烈反对早起。 ❷ the reason of protesting 反对的理由：He presented his ～s in a formal report.他在正式报告中提出了他的反对意见。

objective/əb'dʒektɪv/

Ⅰ *adj*.not influenced by personal feelings or opinions；fair 客观的；真实的；无偏见的：This is an ～ fact.这是客观事实。Ⅱ *n*. an aim，especially one that must be worked towards over a long period；goal 目标；目的：The climber's ～ is the top of that mountain.登山者的目标就是那座山顶。

obligate/'ɒblɪgeɪt/

v. make（sb.）feel it necessary（to do sth.），especially because of a sense of duty 使（某人）负起……义务：He felt ～d to visit his parents.他觉得有义务去探望双亲。

obligation/ˌɒblɪ'geɪʃn/

n. promise，duty，or condition that indicates what action ought to be taken 义务；职责；责任：Every citizen has the ～ to perform military service.每个公民都有服兵役的义务。/Every one owes a certain ～ to society.每个人对社会都负有一定的责任。

obligatory/ə'blɪgətri/

adj. that is necessary，required by rule，law or custom；compulsory 必须履行的；义不容辞的；强制的：Attending school is ～.上学是强制性的。

oblige/ə'blaɪdʒ/

v.❶ make sb.do sth.迫使：They were ～d to give up this plan.他们被迫放弃这项计划。❷ do（sb.）a favour 施恩惠于：Could you ～ me with some money? 请借给我一些钱行吗? ‖ ～d *adj*.❶受恩惠而感激（某人）：I'm much ～d to you for your help.对于你的帮助我深表感激。❷多谢："Much ～d," he said as I got an apple for him.我给他一个苹果时他说了一声"多谢"。/ **obliging** *adj*.愿意帮助的

oblique/ə'bliːk/

adj.❶slanting；having a sloping direction or position 倾斜的；歪斜的：an ～ angle 斜角/ an ～ plane 斜面 ❷not expressed or done in a direct way 间接的；迂回的：

an ～ remark 拐弯抹角的话/ ～ hints 间接的暗示

oblivion/ə'blɪvɪən/

n.the state of having forgotten，or of being forgotten 忘却；被忘却：Those songs are now fallen into ～.那些歌现在已经被忘却了。

oblivious /ə'blɪvɪəs/

adj.completely unaware of what is happening around you 遗忘的；健忘的；不注意的；不知道的：She seemed ～ to the danger.她似乎忘记了危险。/I was ～ of my surroundings.我忘记了我所处的环境。

oblong/'ɒblɒŋ/

Ⅰ *n*.a shape which has two long sides and two short sides and two short sides and in which all the angles are right angles 长方形 Ⅱ *adj*.shaped like an oblong 长方形的

oboe/'əʊbəʊ/

n.a type of woodwind 双簧管

obscene/əb'siːn/

adj. connected with sex in a way that most people find offensive 猥亵的；淫秽的；令人厌恶的：an ～ book 淫秽书籍 ‖ **obscenity**/əb'senəti/ *n*. 猥亵；淫秽；猥亵淫秽的事物(尤指淫秽的语言)

obscure/əb'skjʊə(r)/

adj.dark，not clear；hard to understand 阴暗的；隐蔽的；模糊不清的：an ～ meaning 隐含的意思/an ～ corner 昏暗的角落/an ～ answer 含糊的答复 ‖ **obscurity**/əb'skjʊərəti/ *n*.阴暗；含糊；晦涩

observable/əb'zɜːvəbl/

adj.that can be seen or noticed 看得见的，观察得出的；显著的：no ～ improvement 没有显著的改进

observance/əb'zɜːvəns/

n.❶ the practice of acting in accordance with a law，ceremony，or custom（对法律、仪式或风俗的）遵守，奉行：strict ～ of the rules 对规则的严格遵守/ the ～ of Christmas 奉行过圣诞节的习俗 ❷act performed as a part of a religious ceremony 宗教典礼；ritual ～ 例行的宗教仪式

observant/əb'zɜːvənt/

adj. ❶quick at noticing things 观察力敏锐的;机警的:Luckily an ～ passerby noticed the fire.幸亏一位机警的路人发现了火灾。❷ acting in accordance with especially religious law or custom 严格遵守宗教法律或习俗的

observation/ˌɒbzəˈveɪʃn/
n. ❶ observing or being observed 观察;监视:～ of natural phenomena 对自然现象的观察 ❷ power of noticing things 观察力:a man of keen ～ 观察力敏锐的人 ❸ report on things observed 观察报告;～s on social life 有关社会生活的观察报告

observatory/əbˈzɜːvətri/
*n.*a place from which the stars and other heavenly bodies may be observed 天文台;气象台

observe/əbˈzɜːv/
v. ❶ see and notice;watch carefully 看到;注意到;观察;观测:You must ～ everything carefully.你们必须仔细观察一切事物。❷obey;pay attention to (rules,etc.) 遵守(规则等):～ the discipline 遵守纪律/ ～ the law 遵守法律 ❸ say;make a remark 说;评论:He ～d that our work was well done.他说我们的工作做得很好。

observer/əbˈzɜːvə(r)/
n. ❶one who observes 遵守者,观察者:He is an astronomical ～.他是一个天文观察者。❷a person who attends a conference,etc. only to listen,not to speak (出席会议的)观察员:He'll attend the conference in the capacity as an ～.他将以观察员的身份出席会议。

obsess/əbˈses/
*v.*fill (someone's) mind continuously 使痴迷;使在脑海中萦绕:～ed by the fear of unemployment 被失业的恐惧所困扰 ‖ ～**ion** *n.* 使人痴迷的人(或物);With him,gambling is an ～ion. 对于他来说,赌博是无法摆脱的。

obsessional/əbˈseʃənl/
*adj.*thinking too much about a particular person or thing,in a way that is not normal 痴迷的;迷恋的;摆脱不了的:That lady is ～ about cleanliness.那位女士有

洁癖。

obsessive/əbˈsesɪv,ɒbˈsesɪv/
*adj.*causing or showing obsession 强迫性的;着迷的;分神的 ‖ ～ly *adv.*强迫地;着迷地

obsolete/ˈɒbsəliːt/
*adj.*not now in use;out-of-date 已不用的,已废弃的;过时的:～ weapons 旧式武器

obstacle/ˈɒbstəkl/
*n.*sth. in the way that prevents action or progress 障碍(物);妨害;阻碍:clear away ～s to progress 排除进步的障碍/ Courage knows no ～.有勇气便无障碍。

obstinate/ˈɒbstənət/
*adj.*not easily giving way to persuasion;not easily defeated 固执的;不易说服的;不易击败的;顽强的:an ～ person 一个固执的人 /～ resistance 顽强的抵抗

obstruct/əbˈstrʌkt/
*v.*get in the way of;block 挡住;堵塞;阻碍:～ a road 阻塞道路/ ～ the traffic 堵塞交通/～ one's view of 挡住……的视线/ ～ one's work 妨碍工作

obstruction/əbˈstrʌkʃən/
n. ❶ obstructing or being obstructed 障碍;阻碍;妨碍 ❷a thing that obstructs 障碍物,妨碍物

obstructive/əbˈstrʌktɪv/
*adj.*causing or intended to cause obstruction 阻碍的;妨碍的;阻塞的

obtain/əbˈteɪn/
*v.*get sth.,especially by making an effort 获得;得到;买到:He ～ed the information easily.他轻而易举地获得了情报。/ He ～ed a prize at the sports meet.他在运动会上得了奖。

obtainable/əbˈteɪnəbl/
*adj.*that can be obtained 能得到的;能达到的;可买的:I'm sorry,sir,that type of camera is no longer ～.对不起,先生,那种照相机已买不到了。

obtrude/əbˈtruːd/
v. ❶ (cause to) stick out (使)伸出;(使)凸出:The snail's horns ～.这蜗牛的触角伸了出来。/The snail ～d its horns.这蜗

牛伸出了它的触角。❷（cause to）be noticed especially when unwanted（使）强行进入；强加：Unfortunately, in this essay his personal opinions keep obtruding（themselves）.不幸的是,他在这篇论文中处处强加个人的观点。

obtrusive/əbˈtruːsɪv/
*adj.*❶sticking out very much 非常突出的 ❷fond of pushing oneself, or one's ideas,etc.forward 爱突出自己的；爱出风头的；爱强迫人接受己见的；炫耀（自己想法等）的

obvious/ˈɒbvɪəs/
*adj.*clear; easy to see or understand 明显的；明白的；清楚的：It is ～ that you are telling a lie.很明显,你在撒谎。‖ ～ly *adv.*显然；很明显

occasion/əˈkeɪʒn/
Ⅰ*n.*❶ the time when sth.（usually special）happens 时刻；场合；盛事：on a formal ～ 在正式场合/a great ～ 盛大的场面/A wedding is a big family ～.婚礼是家庭中的一件大事。❷a suitable time for sth.时机；机会：He seized the ～ to visit the Summer Palace.他抓住机会参观了颐和园。❸a reason or need 理由；需要：You had no ～ to hit him.你没有理由打他。Ⅱ*v.* cause sth. 引起：He ～ed me much worry.他使我很担心。‖ on ～ 间或；有时/take ～（to）利用机会；乘机

occasional/əˈkeɪʒənl/
*adj.*❶fortuitous；not regular 偶然的，非经常的：He pays me ～ visits.他偶尔来看看我。/There will be ～ showers during the night.今晚有阵雨。/He is an ～ visitor.他是稀客。❷written or intended for a special event, purpose,etc.适应特殊场合或目的的：～ driver 临时驾驶员/～ music for a royal wedding 皇家婚礼上的应景音乐

Occident/ˈɒksɪdənt/
n.（the countries of）the West Europe and America, contrasted with the Orient 西方,西洋；欧美

occupancy/ˈɒkjupənsi/
*n.*the action or fact of occupying a place 居住；占用

occupant/ˈɒkjuːpənt/
*n.*a person who resides or is present in a house, vehicle, seat, place, etc. at a given time 居住者；（车辆的）乘坐者；（座位的）占有者；（地方的）占用者

occupation/ˌɒkjuˈpeɪʃn/
*n.*❶a person's job or profession 工作；职业 ❷a way of spending time 消遣 ❸capturing a country or region by military force（被）占领,（被）占领期间

occupational/ˌɒkjuˈpeɪʃənl/
*adj.*to do with or caused by your occupation 工作的；职业的：an ～ disease 职业病

occupy/ˈɒkjupaɪ/
*v.*❶ capture; hold possession of 占领；占有；占据：Our troops quickly occupied the town.我军很快就占领了该城。❷ fill（a position, space or time）占（时间、空间）；担任（职位等）：My books ～ a lot of space.我的书籍占用了很多地方。/He once occupied an important position in the Ministry of Education.他曾在教育部担任要职。❸ keep oneself busy doing sth.使从事；忙于：I occupied myself in（with）editing this dictionary.我忙于编纂这本词典。❹live in 住进；居住：He is going to ～ this room.他打算住这间房。‖ be occupied with(in) 忙于；正在做……/ ～ oneself with(in) 忙于

occur/əˈkɜː(r)/
v.(-rr-)❶ happen; take place 发生：When did the accident ～? 这场事故什么时候发生的? ❷come into（sb.'s mind）突然想到；想起：A good idea ～red to me.我突然想到了一个好主意。❸exist or be found somewhere 存在；出现：Errors ～ on every page.每一页都有错误。

occurrence/əˈkʌrəns/
*n.*❶ sth. that happens or exists 发生；事件：Her arrival was an unexpected ～.她的到来是一件出乎意料的事。/It was a disastrous ～.这是一次灾难性的偶然事件。❷fact or process of occurring 发生的事实或过程：Violent storms are of frequent ～ here.这里经常有风暴。

ocean/ˈəʊʃn/

n. **❶** a great mass of water that surrounds the landmass 海洋；an ~ voyage 海洋航行 **❷** one of the main divisions of this mass 世界上的大洋之一；the Atlantic (Pacific) Ocean 大西洋(太平洋)

ochre /ˈəʊkə(r)/

n. a yellowish-brown colour 赭色；黄褐色

o'clock /əˈklɒk/

adv. (used in telling time) exactly the hour (用于表示时间)……点钟(只用于整点)：—What ~ is it? —It's ten ~.—现在几点钟？—十点。/ He usually gets up at six ~.他通常六点钟起床。

octagon /ˈɒktəgən/

n. a plane figure with eight sides and eight angles 八边形；八角形 ‖ ~al /ɒkˈtægənl/ *adj.* 八边形的

October /ɒkˈtəʊbə(r)/

n. the tenth month of the year 十月(略作 Oct.)：the ~ Revolution 十月革命/ on ~ 1st 在十月一日

ocular /ˈɒkjʊlə(r)/

adj. of, for or by the eyes; of seeing 眼睛的；视觉的；适于用眼睛的；用眼睛的；凭视觉的；an ~ disease 眼病 / an ~ proof 显而易见的证据 / an ~ witness 目击者

oculist /ˈɒkjʊlɪst/

n. an eye doctor 眼科医生：He is an ~.他是一个眼科医生。

odd /ɒd/

adj. **❶** not even; that cannot be divided exactly by two 奇数的；单数的：These are ~ numbers. 这些是奇数。 **❷** strange, peculiar or unusual 奇特的；古怪的：an ~ man 古怪的人/ ~ behaviour 奇特的行为 **❸** not regular; occasional 临时的；偶尔的：He made a living by doing ~ jobs.他靠打零工生活。 ‖ ~ly *adv.* 奇怪地；古怪地：~ly enough 说来奇怪

odds /ɒdz/

n. (*pl.*) the chances in favour of or against 可能的机会；失败的可能性：The ~ are in your favour.你们有成功的可能。/ The ~ are against us.我们成功的机会很小。 ‖ at ~ 争执；不合/ by all ~ 肯定地；远远地/ ~ and ends 残余；零星杂物/ the ~ are (that) 很可能/ It makes no ~.没有关

系；没有差别。

odo(u)r /ˈəʊdə(r)/

n. **❶** pleasant or unpleasant smell 气味；香气；臭气：I find the ~ of hay especially pleasing.我觉得干草气味特别宜人。 **❷** reputation 名誉，声誉：an ~ of sanctity 崇高的声誉

odourless /ˈəʊdəlɪs/

adj. without a smell 无气味的：an ~ gas 无臭的气体

of /ɒv, əv/

prep. **❶** belonging to sb. or sth. 属于……的：a friend ~ mine 我的一个朋友/ the secret ~ success 成功的秘诀 **❷** containing 包含(内容)：a cup ~ tea 一杯茶/ a bag ~ potatoes 一袋马铃薯 **❸** (showing a part in relation to a whole) (表示部分或数量)：some ~ our comrades 我们有些同志/ most ~ the students 大部分学生 **❹** made from 由……制成：The desk is made ~ wood. 这桌子是木制的。 **❺** about; having as a subject 关于：I told them ~ what I had seen and heard.我给他们讲了我的所见所闻。 **❻** coming from 出身于；来自：He came ~ a noble family. 他出身于贵族门第。 **❼** by; through 因为；由于：die ~ hunger and cold 饥寒交迫而死 **❽** from among 在其中：He is the best ~ teachers.他是最好的老师。 ‖ ~ course 当然/ ~ late 最近；近来/ ~ oneself 自动地/ what ~ (it) (这)有什么关系呢？

off /ɒf/

Ⅰ *prep.* **❶** not on; away from; down from 从；从……离开：The boy fell ~ the tree and hurt his leg.那男孩从树上掉下来跌伤了腿。 **❷** branching from (a larger one) 从(主道)分岔：a lane ~ the main street 大街分出的一条小胡同 **❸** in the near 在……附近；靠近：an island ~ the coast 靠近海岸的岛 Ⅱ *adv.* **❶** not being used 中断；脱落；分开：Is the light on or ~? 灯是开着还是关着的？/ Turn ~ the radio, please.请关收音机。 **❷** away from a place 离开：I must be ~ now.我现在必须走了。/ The bird flew ~.鸟儿飞走了。 **❸** indicating completion 完；光；结

束：pay ～ the debts 还清债务/drink it ～ 喝光；干杯 ❹（of food）no longer fresh（指食物）坏了，变质了：The fish is going ～.这鱼不新鲜了。‖ well（badly）～ 富裕（贫困）/～ with 去；去掉/～ and on 断断续续地 ‖ ～shore adj.& adv.～ 离岸（的）；向海（的）/～side n.后面；反面；（足球）越位/～stage adv.& adj.台后（的）；幕内（的）/～-street adj.不靠街面的

offal/'ɒfl/
n.❶waste matter 废物；垃圾 ❷ the internal parts of an animal for food 内脏；下水：Offal is now thought to be very nutritious.现在人们认为动物的内脏很有营养。

offence(-se)/ə'fens/
n.❶sth. unpleasant 令人讨厌、不快或生气的事物：That dirty old house is an ～ to the neighbourhood.那幢又脏又旧的房子令附近邻居感到讨厌。❷a wrong or crime 犯法行为；罪过；过错：The police charged him with several ～s.警察指控他多次犯罪。❸ the hurting of sb.'s feeling；the state of being hurt in feelings 冒犯，触怒；不悦：He is quick to take ～.他易于动怒。❹the act of attacking 攻击：They say that the most effective defence is ～.据说最有效的防御就是进攻。

offend/ə'fend/
v.❶ hurt the feelings of；make unhappy or angry；annoy 冒犯；触怒；得罪；伤害……的感情：I'm sorry if I've ～ed you.如有冒犯，请你原谅。❷ do wrong；commit an offence 犯错；违反/～ against the law 犯法/～ against customs and habits 违反风俗习惯 ❸cause unhappiness or annoyance to（sb.or sth.）使（某人）不快，不适，恼怒：There are sounds that ～the ear at a construction site.建筑工地不时传来刺耳的声音。‖ ～er n.冒犯者；犯规者；犯罪者，犯人

offender/ə'fendə(r)/
n.someone who offends，especially a criminal 冒犯者；（尤指）罪犯：They don't usually imprison first ～s.他们通常不监禁初次犯罪的人。

offending/ə'fendɪŋ/
adj. causing displeasure，discomfort，or inconvenience 使人生气的；引起不便的：I had bad toothache and decided to have the ～ tooth removed.我牙疼得很厉害，决定把这颗讨厌的牙拔掉。

offensive¹/ə'fensɪv/
adj.❶causing offence to the mind or senses；unpleasant 讨厌的；令人不快的；冒犯的：～ remarks(smells) 令人不快的话（气味）/I found him extremely ～.我发现他非常令人讨厌。/ crude jokes that are ～ to women 冒犯女士的粗鲁笑话 ❷ of or for attacking 进攻（性）的，攻击的：～ weapons 攻击性武器/ The troops took up ～ positions.部队已准备发起攻击。

offensive²/ə'fensɪv/
n.a continued military attack 进攻；攻势：The enemy launched a full-scale ～.敌人发起了全面进攻。‖ take the ～ 采取攻势；先发制人

offer/'ɒfə(r)/
Ⅰ v.❶make sth. available or provide the opportunity for sth.给；提供：He ～ed me his help. 他给予我帮助。/No hint was ～ed. 没有人提供任何线索。❷ express willingness（to do sth.）表示要：They ～ed to help us.他们表示愿意帮助我们。❸put forward 提出：He ～ed a very good suggestion.他们提出了一个很好的建议。Ⅱ n.❶a statement offering（to do）sth. 提出；提供；提议：make an ～ of help 提出愿意帮忙 ❷ an amount of money offered 出价：He made an ～ of $100,000 for this house.他出价十万美元购买这栋房子。

offering/'ɒfərɪŋ/
n. sth. offered，especially to God 赠品；供品；祭品

offhand/ˌɒf'hænd/
Ⅰ adv. at once；without preparation 立即；事先无准备地：decide ～ 临时决定 / speak ～ 即席发言 Ⅱ adj.without preparation 临时的；即席的；未经准备的：～ remarks 随口说出的话

office/'ɒfɪs/
n.❶the room where business is done 办

公室;办事处;事务所:I work in the ~. 我在办公室工作。❷a government department 政府的部；局；处：the Home Office 内政部/post ~ 邮政局/~ of information 新闻处 ❸ important position 高级职位：hold (enter, leave) ~ 在职(上任，辞职)/in (out of) ~ 在位（下野）/take(assume) ~ 就职 ‖ ~-bearer n.官员；公务员/ ~-boy n.(办公室)勤杂员

officer /'ɒfɪsə(r)/
　n.❶a person in command in the armed forces, police force, etc.军官；警官：a naval ~ 海军军官 ❷ a person with authority 高级官员；高级职员；干事：the ~s of the club 俱乐部的高级职员

official /ə'fɪʃl/
　Ⅰ n. a person holding public office or working in government 官员；官吏：government ~ 政府官员/bank ~s 银行高级职员 Ⅱ adj. of or from the government；of a position of trust or authority 官方的；正式的：an ~ letter 公函/an ~ report 一则官方报道/ ~ duties 公务/an ~ visit 正式访问 ‖ ~ly adv.正式地；按官方说法

officious /ə'fɪʃəs/
　adj. too anxious to help; interfering; too eager to show one's authority 过分殷勤的；多管闲事的；爱显示权力的

offing /'ɒfɪŋ/
　n.(in the ~) (with reference to an event) about to happen（指事件）即将发生：Is there anything exciting in the ~? 有什么激动人心的事即将发生吗?

offload /ɒf'ləʊd/
　v.❶unload goods 卸货 ❷get rid of sth. that you don't need or want 脱手；转让

offset /'ɒfset/
　v.(offset) balance; make up for 抵消；补偿：~ the loss 弥补损失 / The gains ~ the losses.收支相抵。

offshoot /'ɒ(ː)fʃuːt/
　n.❶a side shoot on a plant（植物的）旁枝，分枝 ❷sth. that develops from sth. else 衍生事件

offshore /ɒf'ʃɔː(r)/
　adj.❶at sea not far from the land 近海

的；离岸近的：~ fisheries 近海渔业 ❷ blowing seawards from the land 由陆地吹向海洋的：~ breezes 离岸微风

offside /ɒf'saɪd/
　adj.❶ (in certain sports) in a position in which play is not allowed（在某些运动中)越位的，犯规的：That player is ~.那个运动员越位了。/She's two yards ~. 她越位两码。❷ on the right-hand side, especially of an animal, a car or a road（尤指动物、汽车、公路等）右边(的)，右侧(的)：the ~ rear light of a car 汽车右边的尾灯

offspring /'ɒfsprɪŋ/
　n. (pl. offspring or ~s) child; children; descendants of animals 儿女；子孙；后代；（动物的）仔；崽：a mother of numerous ~ 一位多子女的母亲 / limit one's ~ 节育

offstage /ɒf'steɪdʒ/
　adv.& adj. not on the open stage; out of sight of those watching a play 不在舞台上(的)；台后(的)；幕后(的)：He ran ~. 他跑进后台。

off-white /ɒf'waɪt/
　Ⅰ n. a colour that is not pure white but with some grey or yellow in it 米黄色；灰白色 Ⅱ adj. not pure white, but with a very pale grey or yellow tinge 米黄色的；灰白色的：~ paint 灰白色的涂料

often /'ɒfn, 'ɒftən/
　adv. many times; in a large proportion of the instances 时常，常常：The children ~ help her to do housework on Sundays.孩子们经常在礼拜天帮她做家务。/He ~ watches TV at eight in the evening.他常常在晚上八点看电视。/How ~ do the buses run? 公共汽车多久开一趟? ‖ every so ~ 时常，不时/as ~ as not 通常，往往

oh /əʊ/
　int. an exclamation of surprise, fear, etc. 啊；噢；呀：Oh, what a clever boy! 哦，多么聪明的孩子!

oil /ɔɪl/
　n.a fatty liquid used for burning, for making machines work smoothly, or for cook-

ing 油；石油：an ～ worker 石油工人/
mineral ～s 矿物油/vegetable and animal
～s 植物和动物油 ‖ **burn the midnight ～**
开夜车/**paint in ～s** 画油画/**strike ～** 发
现石油；发大财 ‖ **～ cloth** *n.* 油布/
colour *n.* 油画颜料；油漆/ **～paper** *n.* 油纸

oily /ˈɔɪli/
　adj. (oilier, oiliest) ❶containing, covered,
or soaked in oil 含油的；被油覆盖的；被
油浸没的 ❷like oil 似油的 ❸behaving in
an insincerely polite and smooth way；
trying to win favour by flattery（人或行
为）油腔滑调的，讨好的 ‖ oiliness *n.* 含
油；油质；浸油；滑腻

ointment /ˈɔɪntmənt/
　n. a substance（often medicinal）with oil
or fat to be rubbed on the skin 药膏；软
膏；油膏

OK /əʊˈkeɪ/
　Ⅰ *adv.* & *adj.* all right；correct 好；行；
对：—Let's go there.—～.—我们去那里
吧。—好的。/—Can I use your pen？—
～.—我可以用一下你的钢笔吗？—可
以。/I hope the children are ～.我希望
孩子们都很好。 Ⅱ *n.* agreement 同意；
get an ～ on a proposal 提案获得同意 Ⅲ
v. agree to 同意；赞成

old /əʊld/
　adj. ❶having lived a long time；not young
年老的：an ～ man 一位老人/ an ～ uni-
versity 一所古老的大学 ❷of age ……岁
的：The baby is one year ～.这婴儿一岁
了。/How ～ are you？你几岁了？ ❸
belonging to past times；in use for a long
time；not new 旧的：～ habits 旧习惯/an
～ book 一本旧书 ❹ known for a long
time or familiar 熟悉的：an ～ friend 老
朋友/the same ～ story 老一套 ‖ **of ～**
古时；从前/ **～ and young** 老老少少 ‖
～time *adj.* 过去的；旧式的

old-fashioned /ˌəʊldˈfæʃənd/
　adj. ❶ old in style 旧式的；老式的：an ～
house 老式的房子 ❷ keeping to old
ways，ideas，customs，etc. 守旧的：an ～
person 守旧的人

olive /ˈɒlɪv/
　n. ❶（tree of Europe with a）small oval

fruit，green when unripe and black when
ripe，used for food and for oil 橄榄（树）
❷a yellowish-green colour of an unripe
olive 橄榄绿 ‖ ～ **branch** 橄榄枝（和平的
象征）：They held out an ～ branch to
their opponents.他们向对手伸出了橄榄
枝。

Olympic /əˈlɪmpɪk/
　adj. of Olympia 奥林匹亚的：the ～
Games（the ～s）奥林匹克运动会；奥运
会 / The ～ Games are held once every
four years.奥运会每四年举行一次。

ominous /ˈɒmɪnəs/
　adj. being an omen，especially of sth. bad
预兆的；预示的；不祥的；不吉的：an ～
silence 一阵不祥的寂静 /It was ～ of his
downfall.这预示着他要垮台。

omission /əˈmɪʃn/
　n. ❶ the act of omitting；neglect 省略；删
除；遗漏；忽略：state without ～ 毫无遗
漏地叙述 ❷ sth. omitted or neglected 省
略之物；遗漏之物：supply the ～ 补入遗
漏之物

omit /əʊˈmɪt/
　v. (-tt-) ❶ fail to do；leave undone 疏忽；
遗忘：I ～ted to warn him.我忘记提醒他
了。/She ～ted making her bed. 她忘了
铺床。 ❷ leave out 省略；删去；漏掉：
You have ～ted a word in this sentence.
在这句话中你漏掉了一个单词。

omnibus /ˈɒmnɪbəs/
　n. ❶ a large book containing several works
选集；文选：a Dickens ～ 狄更斯选集 ❷
a former name for bus 公共汽车：a hotel
～（载运旅客往返于车站和旅馆之间的）
客车

omnivorous /ɒmˈnɪvərəs/
　adj. ❶（especially of animals）eating eve-
rything，especially both plant and animal
food 杂食的，肉草兼食的 ❷ interested in
everything especially in all books 对任何
事物都感兴趣的；（尤指）什么书都看的：
an ～ reader 什么书都读的人

on /ɒn/
　Ⅰ *prep.* ❶（showing position）in relation
to a surface or supported by a surface 用
来表示地点：～ the desk 在桌上/ ～ the

wall 在墙上/ ～ the floor 在地上 ❷during;at the time of 表时间(用于星期几与日期)：～ May Day 在五一节/ ～ Sunday 在星期日/ ～ Monday morning 在星期一上午/ ～ April 4.1993 在 1993 年 4 月 4 日 ❸with regard to;about 关于：a book ～ the current international situation 一本论述当前国际形势的书 ❹to;towards;in the direction of 向着；对着：make an attack ～ the enemy 向敌人进攻 ❺directly after (and often as a result of) 凭；因；根据；按照：～ account of 因为/～ what ground(fact) 凭什么理由(根据什么事实) ❻in a state or process of 从事……活动,行动;处于……情况等：～ business 因公;办事;出差/ ～ holiday 度假/～ tour 在旅行/ ～ one's way 在途中/ ～ fire 着火 Ⅱ *adv.* ❶ further in space or time; forward 向前：They walked ～ without speaking.他们一声不响地向前走着。❷continuously;not stopping 连续地,不间断地:The war still went ～.战争仍在继续。❸(especially of a machine or electrical apparatus) working;operating 开着:Turn the light ～.开灯。❹You must put your coat ～.你必须穿上外衣。‖ and so ～ 等等/ ～ and ～ 继续不断地/ ～ one's own 独立地/ ～ time 准时/ ～ to 到……上面去

once/wʌns/

Ⅰ *adv.* ❶ one time 一次：I come home ～ a week.我每周回家一次。 ❷ at a time in the past; formerly 从前：He ～ lived and worked there.他曾一度在那里生活和工作过。 Ⅱ *conj.*when;as soon as 一旦；当……(就)：Once you understand this rule,you will have no further difficulty.你一旦了解了这条规则,就不会再有困难。‖ (all)at ～ 突然,同时/at ～ 立即;马上/ ～ (and) for all 一劳永逸地;永远地/ ～ in a while (way) 偶尔;间或/～ a time 从前

one/wʌn/

num.& pron. ❶the number 1 一;一个：There was only ～ student in the classroom.教室里只有一个学生。❷a certain 某一(个)：One day he will go home.有一天他会回家的。❸any person 任何人：

One should never lose heart.任何人都决不要气馁。❹ a particular example or type (of) (同类中的)一个(人或物)：One (of them) went North, the other went South.(他们之中)一个朝北走,另一个向南行。❺ the same 同一：The birds all flew away in ～ direction.鸟儿都朝一个方向飞了。❻(the) only necessary and desirable 唯一：She's the ～ person for this particular job.她是做这项工作的唯一人选。‖ at ～ 一致/be all ～ 都一样/by ～s and twos 三三两两地/for ～ 例如/for ～ thing 一个原因是,一则是/number ～ 最好的;头等的/ ～ and all 所有的人;全都/ ～ and the same 同一个;完全一样/ ～ another 互相/ ～ by ～ 一个一个地/ ～ of these days 有一天,总有一天/ten to ～ 十之八九;很有可能 ‖ ～-eyed *adj.*独眼的/ ～-handed *adj.*单手的/ ～-ideaed *adj.*想法单一的,思想狭隘的/ ～-legged *adj.*独脚的;单方面的/ ～-sided *adj.*一边的;片面的;单方面的/ ～-time *adj.& adv.* 从前(的);一度的/ ～-way *adj.*单程的;单行的

onerous/ˈɒnərəs/

*adj.*needing effort;troublesome 繁重的;麻烦的:～ work 繁重的工作

oneself/wʌnˈself/

pron. one's own self 自己;自身;亲自：One shouldn't always praise ～.一个人不应该总是自夸。/To do something ～ is often easier than getting someone else to do it.亲自做往往要比叫别人做容易。

ongoing/ˈɒŋɡəʊɪŋ/

adj. continuing; still in progress 不间断的,进行的;前进的：～ negotiations 进行中的谈判

onion/ˈʌnɪən/

n. a round white vegetable with a strong smell,which is made up of one skin inside another 洋葱：He likes to eat ～s.他喜欢吃洋葱。

online/ˌɒnˈlaɪn/

adj. directly connected to and or controlled by a computer 联机的;在线的：an ～ printer 联机打印机/ an ～ database 联机数据库/Nowadays, more and more people like ～ shopping. 如今，越来越多的人喜欢网上购物。

onlooker/ˈɒnlʊkə(r)/

　n. a person who watches something that is happening; spectator 旁观者

only/ˈəʊnlɪ/

　Ⅰ *adj.* single and isolated from 唯一的：the ～ way out 唯一的出路/an ～ son 独生子　Ⅱ *adv.* ❶ nothing more than; with no one or nothing else added or included 只是；仅仅：Only five people went home. 只有五个人回家了。❷ no more interesting, serious, etc. than; merely 只是；才：He is ～ a child. 他只不过是个孩子。Ⅲ *conj.* but; except that 可是；不过：I'll do it with pleasure, ～ I'm too busy. 我很乐于做这事，只不过是太忙了一点。‖ not ～…but（also）不仅……而且……/ ～ too 非常

onrush/ˈɒnrʌʃ/

　n. a strong movement forward 猛冲，直冲；急流：There was a sudden ～ of demonstrators, and the police withdrew. 示威者突然向前猛冲，于是警察后退了。

onset/ˈɒnset/

　n. the beginning 开始：the ～ of some disease 某种疾病的发病（或发作）

onshore/ˈɒnʃɔː(r)/

　adj. moving towards the shore; on the land 向着海岸的；陆上的

onslaught/ˈɒnslɔːt/

　n. a fierce, strong attack 猛攻；猛袭

on-stream/ˈɒnstriːm/

　adv. & *adj.* (of an industrial process, a piece of equipment, etc.) in operation or ready to go into operation（工序、设备等）投入生产（的），处于开工状态（的）

onto/ˈɒntə, ˈɒntuː/

　prep. to a position on 到……上：jump ～ the roof 跳上屋顶 / The pencil slipped ～ the floor. 铅笔滑到了地上。/an ～ march（movement）前进（前进运动）

ontology/ɒnˈtɒlədʒɪ/

　n. the branch of philosophy concerned with the nature of existence 实体论，本体论

onus/ˈəʊnəs/

　n. the burden or responsibility for sth. 义务，担子；责任：The ～ of the proof is on us. 提出证据的责任落在我们身上。

onward(s)/ˈɒnwəd/

　adj. & *adv.* forward; on from here 向前的（地）；前进的（地）：an ～ march（movement）前进（前进运动）/move ～ 向前走动；向前移动；向前进/from now ～ 从现在起

oof/uːf/

　int. (an exclamation like the sound that people make when hit in the stomach) 哎哼！

oops/ʊps/

　int. a word said when someone has fallen, dropped sth., or made a mistake（跌倒、掉了东西或出差错时的用语）啊呀，哎哟：～! I nearly dropped my cup of tea! 啊呀！我差点把这杯茶掉了！

opaque/əʊˈpeɪk/

　adj. ❶ not allowing light to pass through; that cannot be seen through 不透光的；不透明的：His eyes were light, large, and bright, but it was that kind of brightness which belongs to an ～, and not to a transparent body. 他那眼睛闪着光，大而且亮，但那是属于一种不透明的亮，而不是透明物体的亮。❷ hard to understand 难以理解的，难懂的：How ～ and incredible the past seems to us. 对我们来说，过去的事情看来是多么的难以理解和难以置信。

open/ˈəʊpən/

　Ⅰ *adj.* ❶ not closed or shut 开着的：～ door 开着的门 ❷ ready for business 在营业的：This shop is ～ around the clock. 这家商店二十四小时营业。❸ sincere; frank 公开的；坦率的：Let's be ～ with each other. 让我们坦诚相见吧。❹ not covered 无遮盖的：in the ～ air 在户外；在野外 ❺ not enclosed, fenced in, barred, or blocked 空旷的；开阔的：the ～ country 旷野/the ～ sea 公海 ❻ not settled or decided 未解决的；未决定的：an ～ question 未解决的问题　Ⅱ *v.* ❶ (cause to) become open 开；打开；张开

展开：Open your book. 打开书。 ❷ cause to start (使)开业；the bank ~s at eight o'clock. 银行八点开始营业。 ‖ in the ~ 在户外；在野外/into the ~ 公开化/keep one's eyes ~ 留心；注意/lay ~ 摊开；揭露/ ~ fire 开火/ ~ into (on, onto) 通往/ ~ out 打开；展开；展现；畅谈/ ~ one's eyes to 使人看清/ ~ one's heart to 向……讲心里话；同情/ ~ up 打开；开放；展现；开辟 ‖ ~ing n. 开口；孔隙；开端；空缺 ‖ ~ly adv. 公开地；直率地

opener /ˈəʊpənə(r)/
　n. ❶ a device for opening tins or bottles 开启物 ❷ a person or thing that opens sth. 开球员

opening /ˈəʊpnɪŋ/
　Ⅰ n. ❶ a clear space or gap 空地；洞；孔；穴；空隙：They got it through an ~ in the wall. 他们使那个东西穿过墙上的一个洞。 ❷ an opportunity; a position in a firm that is to be filled 机会；(厂商中职位的)空缺：new ~ in industry 新开放行业 ❸ the start or beginning 开始；开端：the ~ of your speech 你演说的开始部分 Ⅱ adj. first; beginning 开始的；开头的：his ~ words 他的开场白

openly /ˈəʊpənli/
　adv. without secret; frankly or honestly 公开地；坦白地；公然

openness /ˈəʊpənnɪs/
　n. ❶ the quality of being honest and not hiding information or feelings 诚实；坦率 ❷ the quality of not being confined or covered 公开；开放

opera /ˈɒpərə/
　n. a musical play, in which the words are sung 歌剧：~ house 歌剧院 / Beijing ~ 京剧

operable /ˈɒpərəbl/
　adj. (of a disease or medical condition) able to be treated by means of an operation (疾病或医疗情况)可施手术的，可开刀的

operate /ˈɒpəreɪt/
　v. ❶ produce effects 起作用；运转；操作：Can you ~ car? 你们会开这辆车吗？ ❷ cut the body in order to set right or re-move a diseased part 做手术：The doctor will ~ on his leg next week. 下周医生要为他的腿做手术。 ❸ have or produce an effect 有效；起作用：The medicine began to ~ at once. 药立刻开始见效了。

operation /ˌɒpəˈreɪʃn/
　n. ❶ working; the way sth. works 工作；运作(方式)：the ~ of a machine 机器运转 / The elevator is in ~. 电梯在工作。 ❷ a cutting into the body to cure a certain disease (外科)手术：perform an ~ on a patient 对病人进行手术 ❸ the state in which effects can be produced 作用；效力：the ~s of nature 大自然的作用 / mental ~s 精神作用 / the ~ of the medicine 药物的效力/When does the law come into ~? 这条法律何时生效？

operational /ˌɒpəˈreɪʃənl/
　adj. ❶ ready to be used 可以使用的：The new machines are not yet fully ~. 这些新机器还不能全面投入使用。 ❷ of or about operations 操作的；经营的：~ costs 经营成本

operative[1] /ˈɒpərətɪv/
　adj. ❶ (of plans, laws, etc.) in operation; producing effects (计划、法律等)实施中的，起作用的 ❷ most suitable 最适合的："We should push him for a decision." "Yes, 'push' is the ~ word!" "我们要催促他做出决定。" "对，用'催促'这个词正合适！"

operative[2] /ˈɒpərətɪv/
　n. a worker or mechanic 工人；技工

operator /ˈɒpəreɪtə(r)/
　n. ❶ a person who works a machine, appa-ratus, etc. (机器、设备等的)操作员 ❷ a person who works a telephone switch-board 电话接线员：Operater, I've been cut off. 接线员，我的电话被挂断了。

opinion /əˈpɪnjən/
　n. a view or idea one holds about sth. 意见；看法；主张；见解：ask the ~ of sb. 征求某人的意见 / express (give) one's ~ on... 对……发表意见 / public ~ 舆论/ be of the ~ that... 觉得……；相信……；认为…… / stick to one's ~ 坚持己见 / They are divided in ~. 他们的意见有分

歧。/What's your ～ of the new teacher? 你对新来的老师看法如何？

opium/ˈəʊpɪəm/

　　*n.*a substance prepared from poppy seeds, used as a drug 鸦片

opponent/əˈpəʊnənt/

　　*n.*a person who takes the opposite side in a game,a fight,an argument,etc.对手;敌手;反对者:He defeated his ～ in the election.他在选举中击败了敌手。

opportune/ˈɒpətjuːn/

　　*adj.*❶（of time）suitable,favourable; good for a purpose（指时间）合适的;恰好的;及时的:You've arrived at a most ～ moment.你来得正是时候。/Time is ～ for doing that.现在正是做那件事的时候。❷（of an action or event）done, coming at the right time（行为或事件等）适时的;及时的:He made an ～ remark at the meeting.他在会上做了一次合乎时宜的讲话。

opportunism/ˌɒpəˈtjuːnɪzəm/

　　*n.*the tendency to take advantage of every chance for success now,without regard for what will happen later 机会主义;投机取巧

opportunist/ˈɒpətjuːnɪst,ˌɒpətuːnɪst/

　　*n.*a person who is quick to take advantage of opportunities,often in an unprincipled way 机会主义者

opportunity/ˌɒpəˈtjuːnəti/

　　*n.*a favourable time or chance for sth.机会;良机:I'm glad to have this ～ to speak(of speaking)to you.我很高兴有这个机会给大家讲话。

oppose/əˈpəʊz/

　　*v.*be against;act against 反对;反抗:They ～d this idea bitterly.他们强烈反对这个主意。‖ **as ～d to** 和……相对;相反:This is a book about business practice as ～d to theory.这是一本讲商业实务,而不是讲理论的书。

opposed/əˈpəʊzd/

　　*adj.*❶ in opposition to（a policy or an attitude,etc.）相反的;对立的:Their opinions are diametrically ～.他们的看法截然相反。/Truth is ～ to falsehood.真

理是谬误之对立面。❷against（a person,activity,plan,etc.）反对的;对抗的:I am strongly ～ to your suggestion.我坚决反对你的建议。/Our members are definitely ～ to making concessions on the health and safety question.我们的成员绝对反对在保健和安全问题上做出让步。

opposing/əˈpəʊzɪŋ/

　　*adj.*❶ in conflict or competition with a specified or implied subject 对抗的,对手的 ❷facing;opposite 对面的;相对的

opposite/ˈɒpəzɪt/

　　Ⅰ *adj.*❶ facing 对面的:on the ～side of the street 在马路对面 ❷contrary;different 相反的;对立的:in the ～ direction 向相反的方向/ ～ ideas 对立的看法,相反的意见 Ⅱ *prep.* on the other side of a space from sth. 在……对面:There is a small restaurant ～ the bank.在银行对面有家小餐馆。Ⅲ *n.*a person or thing that is entirely different from another 对立者;对立面;对立物:I thought quite the ～.我的想法完全相反。‖（be）～ **to** 在……对面;和……相反

opposition/ˌɒpəˈzɪʃn/

　　*n.*❶the state of being opposite or opposed 反对,敌对,相对:There is a lot of ～ to his ideas.对于他的想法有不少反对意见。/The enemy met with ～ everywhere.敌人到处遭到对抗。❷ political parties opposing the government 反对党:Last election saw considerable strengthening of the ～.在上次大选中,反对党的实力明显增强。

oppress/əˈpres/

　　*v.*❶ rule in a hard and cruel way 压迫;压制:The tyrant ～ed the people cruelly.那个暴君残酷地压迫人民。❷ cause to feel troubled,uncomfortable 使忧郁,压抑:She felt ～ ed.她忧心忡忡。‖ ～**ive** *adj.*压迫的;沉重的;难以忍受的/～**or** *n.*压迫者

opt/ɒpt/

　　*v.*choose to take or not to take a particular course of action 选择,挑选(某事物):Choosing between a high salary and a secure but lowly-paid job, he ～ed for the high salary. 当他在高薪水和可靠但工资低的职位之间做出选择时，他选择了高薪水。

optic /ˈɒptɪk/

adj. of or belonging to the eyes or the sense of sight 眼的；视觉的：the ～ nerve 视（觉）神经

optical /ˈɒptɪkl/

adj. ❶ of the sense of sight 视觉的：an ～ illusion 光幻觉，错视 ❷ for looking through; to help eyesight 用于使人看得清楚的；帮助视力的：A telescope is an ～ instrument. 望远镜是有助于视力的工具。

optimism /ˈɒptɪmɪzəm/

n. the belief that everything will come right or end well 乐观；乐观主义：They expressed ～ about the development of the situation. 他们对形势的发展表示乐观。

optimist /ˈɒptɪmɪst/

n. a person who always expects good things to happen or things to be successful 乐观的人；乐天派

optimistic /ˌɒptɪˈmɪstɪk/

adj. showing optimism; hopeful 乐观的；乐观主义的 ‖ ～ally *adv.* 乐观地；乐天地

optimum /ˈɒptɪməm/

adj. best; most profitable 最好的；最有益的；最有利的：What would you say was the ～ age for retirement? 你认为最佳的退休年龄是多大年纪？

option /ˈɒpʃn/

n. ❶ the freedom to choose 选择自由：Everyone has his ～ in the marriage. 人人都有婚姻自由。 ❷ the thing that is or may be chosen; choices 可供选择的事物；选择：The staff of the amusement park have made a list of the various ～s at the tickets. 游乐园的员工在门票上列出了可供选择的娱乐项目。 ‖ ～al *adj.* 可任意选择的；选修的

opus /ˈəupəs/

n. (*pl.* ～es or opera /ˈɒpərə/) a chief work of a composition (especially musical) 作品（尤指乐曲）：Beethoven Opus 106 贝多芬作品第 106 号

or /ɔː(r)/

conj. ❶ (either … ～ …) (used before the last of a set of possibilities) 或；还是：Which do you prefer, coffee ～ tea? 你喜欢喝咖啡还是茶？ /Either he comes here, ～ I go there. 不是他来，就是我去。 ❷ if not; otherwise 要不；否则：Hurry up ～ (else) you'll be late. 快点，要不然你就会迟到了。 ‖ ～ else 否则 / ～ rather 倒不如说 / ～ so 约莫；左右 / rain ～ shine 不管怎样；无论天晴下雨

oracle /ˈɒrəkl/

n. a prophecy revealed by a priest or priestess 神谕；预言

oral /ˈɔːrəl/

adj. ❶ spoken rather than written 口头的；口述的：an ～ examination 口试 / ～ instruction 口授 ❷ of or by the mouth 口的；口部的；口腔发出的：the ～ cavity 口腔

orange /ˈɒrɪndʒ/

n. ❶ a round, juicy fruit with thick, yellow-red skin 橙子；橘子：～ juice 橘子汁 ❷ the colour of an orange 橙色；橘黄色：an ～ hat 橘黄色的帽子

orangeade /ˌɒrɪndʒˈeɪd/

n. a drink containing orange, orange juice 橘子水，橙汁饮料

oration /ɔːˈreɪʃn/

n. a formal public speech 演说；演讲：deliver an ～ 发表演说

orator /ˈɒrətə(r)/

n. a person who makes a speech (especially a good speaker) 演说者；演说家；雄辩家

oratory[1] /ˈɒrətri/

n. ❶ the art of making good speeches 演讲术 ❷ the language highly decorated with long or formal words (用长词或正式词语的)华丽的言辞

oratory[2] /ˈɒrətri/

n. (especially in the Catholic Church) a small room or building for prayer (尤指天主教的)祈祷室，小礼拜堂

O

orb /ɔːb/

　　n. ❶a ball standing for the sun or another heavenly body, especially one carried by a king or queen on formal occasions as a sign of power and justice（国王或女王在正式场合作为王位标志携带的）宝球 ❷ an eye, especially the eye of a beautiful lady 美女的眼睛，眼珠

orbit /'ɔːbɪt/

　　Ⅰ *n.* the path of one heavenly body round another 运行轨道：How many earth satellites are now in ～? 现在有多少地球卫星在轨道上运行？Ⅱ *v.* move in an orbit 在轨道上运行：The spaceship ～（round）the earth. 飞船绕地球运行。

orbital /'ɔːbɪtl/

　　adj. ❶（said about a road）passing round the outside of a city（道路）环城的，绕城的 ❷to do with an orbit（与）轨道（有关）的

orchard /'ɔːtʃəd/

　　n. the field where fruit trees grow 果园：an apple ～ 苹果园

orchestra /'ɔːkɪstrə/

　　n. a group of people who play musical instruments together 管弦乐队；管弦乐团：a symphony ～ 交响乐队

orchid /'ɔːkɪd/

　　n. a type of plant with flowers, many of which have bright colours and unique but beautiful shapes 兰科植物；兰花

order /'ɔːdə(r)/

　　Ⅰ *n.* ❶ the way in which people or things are placed or arranged in relation to one another 顺序；次序：Please enter the hall in ～. 请大家按次序进入大厅。❷ a condition in which things are carefully and neatly arranged 秩序；条理；整齐：The police kept ～. 警察维持了秩序。❸ a command 命令；指令：Soldiers must obey ～s. 军人必须服从命令。❹ a request to supply goods 订货；订单；订购的货物：an ～ of 100 tons of sugar 一张一百吨白糖的订单 Ⅱ *v.* ❶ use your position of authority to tell sb. to do sth. or say that sth. must happen 嘱咐；命令；指令：The regiment was ～ed to the front. 该团奉命开往前线。❷ give an order for 订货；订

购：I have ～ed a new suit. 我订购了一套新衣。‖ by ～ of 奉……之命/call to ～ 宣布开会；叫人安静/in ～ 整齐；秩序井然；状况良好；合适，符合规定/in ～ that（in ～ to）为了；以便/on ～ 已定购/out of ～ 坏了；不合规定/place an ～ for sth. with 向……定购某物/the ～ of nature 自然的规律/the ～ of the day 议事日程；风气/under the ～ of 受……指挥；奉……之命

orderly /'ɔːdəli/

　　adj. ❶well arranged, tidy 整齐的；有条理的 ❷methodical 有系统的；有方法的 ❸ well-behaved and obedient 规矩的，遵守秩序的：an ～ crowd 守秩序的人群

ordinal /'ɔːdɪnl/

　　Ⅰ *adj.* showing order or position in a series 序数的；顺序的；依次的：First, second and third, etc. are ～ numbers. 第一、第二、第三等是序数词。Ⅱ *n.* the number designating place in an ordered sequence 序数词

ordinarily /'ɔːdɪnərɪli/

　　adv. ❶usually 通常地，惯常地 ❷in a normal way 一般地；正常地

ordinary /'ɔːdənri/

　　adj. normal; not unusual or different in any way 普通的；平常的；平凡的：They are ～ people. 他们是普通人。‖ in an（the）～ way 在一般情况下/out of the ～ 不寻常；特殊的

ore /ɔː(r)/

　　n. a kind of rock or earth in which metal is found 矿石：He picked up a piece of ～ from the ground. 他从地上拾起一块矿石。/We live in a district rich in ～s. 我们住在矿产丰富的地区。

organ /'ɔːgən/

　　n. ❶ a part of an animal or plant that serves a special purpose 器官：the ～s of speech 发音器官 ❷ an official organization 官方机构，机关：the government ～s 政府机关 ❸ a musical instrument made of many pipes through which air is forced 风琴：play an ～ 弹风琴 ‖ ～ic /ɔː'gænɪk/ *adj.* 器官的；有机的；有组织的

organism /'ɔːgənɪzəm/

n. living being with parts which work together; individual animal or plant; any system with parts dependent upon each other 生物；有机体；组织：the social ～ 社会组织/ The nation is not merely the sum of individual citizens at any given time, but it is a living ～.国家在任何时候都不仅仅是单个公民的总和，而且是一个活的有机的整体。

organization /ˌɔːɡənaɪˈzeɪʃn/
n. ❶ the arrangement of parts so as to form an effective whole 组织；构成：Only with ～ can the wisdom of the collective be given full play.只有组织得当，才能充分地发挥集体的智慧。❷ a group of people with a special purpose 组织；团体：Party ～s at all levels 各级党组织

organize /ˈɔːɡənaɪz/
v. form into a whole; arrange 组织；编组；筹备：～ a political party 组织一个政党/ ～ the masses 组织群众 /～ an army 编组军队

organized /ˈɔːɡənaɪzd/
adj. having good and effective organization 有组织的：Organized crime has been highly emphasized in all states.有组织犯罪已引起了世界各国的高度重视。

orient /ˈɔːrɪənt/
Ⅰ *n.* Asia; the (Far) East 亚洲；东方；远东：The ship sailed for the ～.轮船向东方航行。Ⅱ *adj.* ❶ eastern 东方的 ❷(of the sun) rising (指太阳)上升的：the ～ sun 初升的太阳 Ⅲ *v.* ❶make a building, etc. face a direction 使朝某方向 ❷ find out one's position in relation to sth. else 确定方位：You can ～ yourself by remembering that the tower is due north. 只要记住那座塔位于正北方，你就能确定自己所在的方位。❸ get (oneself) used to unfamiliar surroundings, conditions, etc. 使适应环境：We must ～ our work to the needs of the people.我们必须使我们的工作适应人民的需要。/We'll help freshmen to ～ themselves to college life.我们将帮助新生适应大学生活。

oriental /ˌɔːrɪˈentl/
Ⅰ *n.* a person or thing of or from the Orient 东方人；亚洲人（或事物）Ⅱ *adj.* of or from the Orient（来自）东方的；（来自）亚洲的

orientalist /ˌɔːrɪˈentəlɪst/
n. a specialist in the languages, civilizations, etc., of the countries of the Orient（研究东方国家语言、文化等的）东方学专家，东方通

orientate /ˈɔːrɪənteɪt/
v. ❶ arrange or direct with a particular purpose 按……调整，为……设计；使适应：an English language course that is ～d towards the needs of businessmen 为适应商人的需要而设置的英语课程/ an export-～d company 一家以出口为主的公司 ❷establish the position of (oneself or sth. else) especially in relation to a map or compass（根据地图或指南针而）确定……的位置，定……的方位：The climbers stopped to ～ themselves before descending the mountain.登山者先停下来确定所在的位置，然后开始下山。

orientation /ˌɔːrɪenˈteɪʃən/
n. ❶an act or the state of orienting or being oriented 定向，定位；确定方向 ❷the position relative to surroundings 方向，方位 ❸ the direction of a person's attitude or interest, especially sexual or political（尤指政治或性方面的）倾向

orienteering /ˌɔːrɪənˈtɪərɪŋ/
n. a sport in which competitors use a map and a compass to find their way over rough country（参赛者自带地图和罗盘的）越野识途赛

origin /ˈɒrɪdʒɪn/
n. ❶the country, race or living conditions of one's parents or ancestors 出身；血统：He is a Dane by ～.他原籍丹麦。/He is a college student of worker ～.他是一位工人出身的大学生。❷a starting point 起源；开端：The book *The Origin of Species* was written by Charles Darwin.《物种起源》这本书是查尔斯·达尔文所著。

original /əˈrɪdʒənl/
Ⅰ *adj.* ❶existing at the beginning of a particular period, process or activity 最初

的;最早的;原始的:the ～ settlers 最早的移民 / an ～ edition 原版 ❷ new;not copied 新颖的;非抄袭的:～ ideas 新思想 ❸ able to produce new ideas;creative 独创的;有独到见解的:an ～ thinker 有创见的思想家 Ⅱ n.❶ the earliest form of sth.(from which copies can be made) 原作;原物:This is not ～;it's only a copy. 这不是原物;这不过是复制品。❷ a document,a work of art or a piece of writing that was first written 原件;原作;原文:read Homer in the ～ 读荷马作品的原文

originality /əˌrɪdʒɪˈnælɪti/
n.❶ the ability to think independently and creatively 独创能力 ❷ the quality of being novel or unusual 新颖;独创性

originally /əˈrɪdʒənəli/
adv.❶ from or in the beginning;at first 一开始,起初;原来 ❷ in a novel and inventive way 独创地;新颖地

originate /əˈrɪdʒɪneɪt/
v.(cause to) begin;bring about;create 开始;引起;发起;创始:～ a new style of dancing 开创一种新的舞蹈风格 / The quarrel ～d in a misunderstanding. 这次口角由误解而起。/All theories ～ from (in) practice. 所有的理论都来源于实践。/The scheme ～d with him. 这计划是他提出来的。

ornament /ˈɔːnəmənt/
Ⅰ n.❶ things which is added to make sth. richer in style or more beautiful 装饰;装饰品:add a painting by way of ～ 增加一幅画作为装饰 ❷ an object possessed beautiful rather than useful 装饰品:She was wearing earrings,a necklace and other ～. 她戴着耳环、项链及其他装饰物。❸ a thing or a person that adds honour, importance,or beauty to sth. 增添光彩的人或物:He was an ～ to his country. 他是为国争光的人。Ⅱ v. add ornament to 装饰:They were ～ing the walls with paintings.他们正在用画装饰墙壁。

ornamental /ˌɔːnəˈmentl/
Ⅰ adj. serving or intended as an ornament;decorative 装饰用的;装饰的 Ⅱ n. a plant grown for its attractive appear-ance 观赏植物

ornamentation /ˌɔːnəmenˈteɪʃən/
n.❶ things added to sth. to provide decoration 装饰物 ❷ the action of decorating sth. or making it more elaborate 装饰;点缀

ornate /ɔːˈneɪt/
adj.❶ richly ornamented 装饰华丽的:furniture 装饰华丽的家具 ❷ not simple in style or vocabulary (文体)华丽的;(修辞上)极考究的

orphan /ˈɔːfən/
n. a child whose parents are dead 孤儿:He became an ～ when he was very young. 他很小时就成了孤儿。‖ ～age /ˈɔːfənɪdʒ/ n.孤儿院

orthodox /ˈɔːθədɒks/
adj.generally accepted or approved;holding ideas that are generally accepted(especially in religion) 正统的;公认的;传统的;持正统思想的(尤指在宗教上):～ behaviour 拘于习俗的行为/an ～ believer 正统的信徒

ostrich /ˈɒstrɪtʃ/
n. a very large African bird with a long neck,unable to fly,but run fast 鸵鸟:an ～ policy 鸵鸟政策(无视现实或自我陶醉)/try to play ～ 想实行鸵鸟政策/an ～ egg 鸵鸟蛋/～ farm 鸵鸟养殖场

other /ˈʌðə(r)/
Ⅰ adj. remaining;more as well 另外的,其他的(人或物);其余的:Come some ～ day. 改日再来吧。/Where are the ～ students? 其他学生到哪里去了? /Each of them helps the ～.他俩互相帮助。Ⅱ adv.(otherwise) in a different way 用别的办法;不同地:I can't do it ～ slowly.我只能慢慢地做这件事。‖ each ～ 互相/none ～ than 不是别人,而是……/one after the ～ 相继;一个接一个地/～ than 除了

otherwise /ˈʌðəwaɪz/
Ⅰ adv.❶ differently;in another way 不同地;别样:But I think ～.但我想法不同。/You mustn't do ～.你不能另搞一套。❷ in other respects or conditions 此外;在别的方面:The room is small, but

~ it is comfortable.房间小是小，但是很舒适。Ⅱ *conj.* if not; or else 否则；不然：Do it now, ~ it will be too late.这事现在就要做，否则来不及了。

ouch/aʊtʃ/
int. an exclamation of pain（用来表示痛苦）哎哟!

ought/ɔːt/
aux. v. ❶（usually indicate duty or obligation）used to say what is the right thing to do（用来表示责任或义务）应该：It ~ not to be done.此事决不应当做。❷ will probably（表示可能性）可能会：He ~ to be here soon, I think.我想他大概不久就会到了。

ounce/aʊns/
n.（abbr. oz.）an unit of weight, one sixteenth of a pound avoirdupois, equal to 28.35 grams or one twelfth of a pound troy, namely 31.1 grams 盎司，英两（常衡为 1/16 磅即 28.35 克；金衡为 1/12 磅即 31.1 克）

our/'aʊə(r), ɑː(r)/
pron. of or belonging to us 我们的：Our country is a great socialist one.我们的祖国是一个伟大的社会主义国家。

ours/ɑːz, 'aʊəz/
pron. the one or ones belonging to us possessive 我们的（东西）；我们的家属（或有关的人）：This farm is ~.这个农场是我们的。/Ours is a great country.我们的国家是一个伟大的国家。/He is a friend of ~.他是我们的一个朋友。

ourselves/ɑː'selvz, aʊə'selvz/
pron. ❶ used instead of us as the object of a verb or preposition for emphasis（替代us 做动词或介词的宾语，用以强调）我们自己：We must not deceive ~.我们不可以欺骗自己。/We teach ~ English.我们自学英语。❷（used for referring to the people rather than anyone else）（用于加强语气）我们亲自；我们自己：We ~ have often done the same thing.我们自己常做这样的事情。/We have to do every thing ~.我们不得不亲自做每件事。❸ our usual state of mind or body 我们的正常情况：We were not ~ for some time.我们半

天不能恢复常态。

oust/aʊst/
v. drive or push sb. out（e. g. from a position, job, etc.）驱逐；撵走；把……逐出（例如：从职位，工作等撵走某人）：He was ~ed from his post.他被撤职。

ouster/'aʊstə(r)/
n. ❶ the ejection from a freehold or other possession; the deprivation of an inheritance 对不动产（或遗产）的剥夺 ❷ the dismissal or expulsion from a position 撤职；罢黜

out/aʊt/
adv. ❶ not at home or at a place of work 不在：I'm afraid he is ~.恐怕他不在家。❷ to or at an end 到尽头；完结了；完全地：I am tired ~.我筋疲力尽了。❸（of a fire or light）not burning（火，灯）熄灭：The fire went ~.火灭了。❹ clearly and loudly so that people can hear 大声地：speak ~ 大声讲话/cry ~ 高声叫喊 ❺ away from a place, the usual condition, etc. 离去；在外：go ~ 出去/dine ~ 在外吃饭/live ~ 住在外面 ❻ on strike 罢工：The workers are ~ again.工人又罢工了。❼ far away 遥远：He lives ~ in the country.他住在乡下。❽ so as to be clearly seen, shown, understood, etc. 显现；清晰可见；理解等：The sun is（comes）~.太阳出来了。/Think it ~ properly.请适当考虑。‖ be ~ for 力图要；一心为；企图追求/ ~ and away 大大地；远远地/ ~ and ~ 十足地；彻头彻尾地；不折不扣地/ ~ of 从……出来；出于；由于；缺乏；没有；失去；用完/ ~ of date 过时/ ~ with 说出；拿出；赶出

outback/'aʊtbæk/
Ⅰ *adj.* of the back country 内陆的 Ⅱ *adv.* to the back country 向内陆地 Ⅲ *n.* the back country 内地

outboard/'aʊtbɔːd/
adj.（usually in ~**motor**）an engine which can be attached to the outside of a boat 装于小船外侧的马达；艇外推进机

outbreak/'aʊtbreɪk/
n. ❶ the sudden start of sth. unpleasant, especially violence or disease 爆发，突然

发生：The ～ of war was in 1983.战争爆发于 1983 年。❷an uprising 暴动，起义：The famine led to ～ in many cities.在许多城市中饥饿引发了暴动。

outbuilding/'aʊtˌbɪldɪŋ/
*n.*a small building(e.g.a shed) near a larger one 附属小建筑物(例如：棚、车库)

outburst/'aʊtbɜːst/
*n.*a burst of steam, energy, laughter, anger, etc. (蒸汽、能量、笑声、怒气等的)爆发，突发：an ～ of affection 感情的爆发/an ～ of fever 发烧

outcast/'aʊtkɑːst/
*n.*a person without a home or friends 无家可归的人；无亲友的人；流浪者

outclass/aʊt'klɑːs/
*v.*be much better than 远远胜过(或超过)；远优于：He ～es everyone else at running.在赛跑上他遥遥领先于别人。

outcome/'aʊtkʌm/
*n.*an effect or result 结果；后果：the ～ of scientific experiments 科学研究成果/a final ～ 最后结果/ This book is the ～ of some 30 years of travel, study and observation.这本书是约 30 年的旅游、探讨和观察的结果。

outcry/'aʊtkraɪ/
*n.*❶a loud shouting or crying 大声喊叫；呐喊 ❷ a public show of anger 公愤：a great ～ all over the country against the government's actions 反对政府行动的强烈怒火烧遍全国

outdated/ˌaʊt'deɪtɪd/
*adj.*old-fashioned；not modern 老式的；过时的

outdistance/aʊt'dɪstəns/
*v.*go further or faster than(especially in a race) (尤指在竞赛中)遥遥领先于；超过

outdo/ˌaʊt'duː/
*v.*do better than 胜过；优于

outdoor/'aʊtdɔː(r)/
adj. done, existing, happening, or used outside 户外的；野外的：～ sports 户外活动/ ～ life 野外生活

outdoors[1] /ˌaʊt'dɔːz/
*adv.*outside；in the open air 在户外；在野外：I haven't been ～ all day.我整天没有外出。/children playing ～ 在户外玩耍的孩子们

outdoors[2] /ˌaʊt'dɔːz/
n. the open air, especially far away from any buildings 户外；野外：hunting in the great ～ 在野外打猎

outer/'aʊtə(r)/
*adj.*of the outside；farther from the centre 外部的；外面的；外侧的；远离中心的：～ garment 外衣 / the ～ world 外界；世间 / the ～ suburbs 郊外

outermost/'aʊtəməʊst/
*adj.*furthest outside or furthest from the middle 最外面的，离中心最远的：the ～ stars 最远的星球

outerwear /'aʊtəweə(r)/
n. the clothing worn over other clothes, especially outdoors (尤指在户外穿的)外衣

outface/ˌaʊt'feɪs/
*v.*❶meet and deal with bravely 勇敢地面对，面对……而无惧色 ❷ cause (someone) to look away by looking at steadily 逼视(某人)直至其目光移开；盯得(某人)局促不安

outfall/'aʊtfɔːl/
*n.*❶an outlet of a river, drain, etc.；river mouth (河流沟渠等的)排水口；河口 ❷ sortie 出击；突围

outfit/'aʊtfɪt/
*n.*all the clothes or tools that are needed for a certain job or occasion (某一工作或场合所需的)全部衣服；全套工具；整套装备：an ～ for school 上学的用品/ a camping ～ namely tent, pegs, etc.露营的装备即帐篷、帐篷桩等 ‖ ～ter *n.* 出售衣服或运动器械的商人

outflow /'aʊtfləʊ/
*n.*❶an outward flow 流出量；流出物 ❷ an amount of liquid, money or people that flows out (液体、金钱或人员的)大量外流

outgo/ˌaʊt'gəʊ/
Ⅰ *v.*(outwent, ～ne) go beyond or faster than；excel 走得比……远或快；优于 Ⅱ

n.(*pl.*~es) money paid out;expenditure 支出;开支

outgoing /ˈaʊtɡəʊɪŋ/
*adj.*❶sociable and friendly 友好的;愿与人交际的 ❷leaving an office or position, especially after an election or term of office (尤指选举结束或任期届满后)即将离任的:the ~ chairman 即将离任的主席

outgrow /ˌaʊtˈɡrəʊ/
v. (outgrew,~n) ❶ grow too big for clothes,etc.长大而不适于(原有衣服等):~ one's clothes 因长大穿不下衣服 ❷ become older to stop doing sth.长大不再做(某事):He has ~ his interest in toys.他已长大,对玩具已没有兴趣。

outing /ˈaʊtɪŋ/
*n.*a short pleasure trip 远足,郊游:go on (have) an ~ 去远足,去郊游

outlaw /ˈaʊtlɔː/
Ⅰ *n.*a criminal;a person punished by being placed outside the protection of the law 歹徒;罪犯;被剥夺公民权的人:Gangs of ~s lived in the forest.一伙伙的亡命歹徒栖身于森林中。Ⅱ *v.* declare sth.unlawful;ban 宣布某事非法;禁止:~ the sale of guns 禁止贩卖枪支

outlay /ˈaʊtleɪ/
*n.*an amount of money spent on sth. 花费;费用:Our total ~ on repairing the house was eighty pounds.我们修房子的全部费用是八十镑。

outlet /ˈaʊtlet/
*n.*❶ an opening that permits escape or release for water,etc. 出口;排泄口:the ~ of a river 河流的出口 ❷ a way of expressing or releasing sth. 发泄途径;表达方法:an ~ for one's energy(anger) 发泄精力(愤怒)的途径

outline /ˈaʊtlaɪn/
Ⅰ *n.*❶lines showing shape 轮廓;外形:the ~ of a temple 一座寺庙的外观 ❷ main facts;chief points;a general idea 大纲;提纲;概要:an ~ of one's speech 某人讲话的要点 Ⅱ *v.* draw in outline;give an outline of 绘出轮廓;提出要点;概述

outlive /ˌaʊtˈlɪv/
*v.*live longer than;live until sth.is forgotten 比……活得长久;活到(某事)被忘却:Nowadays,women ~ men by about 5 to 6 years.现今,女人平均比男人长寿五到六年。

outlook /ˈaʊtlʊk/
*n.*❶ a view from a particular place;future probabilities 视野;景色;景物:a pleasant ~ over the valley 山谷的宜人景色 ❷ a way of thinking 观点;看法:a correct ~ on life 正确的人生观 ❸the future probabilities;a prospect 前景;展望:The ~ for world peace is bright.世界和平的前景是光明的。

outlying /ˈaʊtlaɪɪŋ/
*adj.*far from the centre(of a town,etc.); distant 远离(城镇等)中心的;边远的:several ~ farms 几个边远的农场

outmoded /ˌaʊtˈməʊdɪd/
*adj.*old fashioned;not modern 老式的;过时的

outnumber /ˌaʊtˈnʌmbə(r)/
v. be more in number than 比……多:They ~ed us three to one.他们在人数上以三比一胜过我们。

outpatient /ˈaʊtpeɪʃnt/
*n.*a person who gets treatment at a hospital but does not live there during treatment 门诊病人:the ~ department 门诊部

outplay /ˌaʊtˈpleɪ/
*v.*defeat in a game (比赛中)打败,胜过

outpoint /ˌaʊtˈpɔɪnt/
*v.*defeat (an opponent in boxing) by gaining more points (拳击赛中)以得分多而战胜(对手)

outpost /ˈaʊtpəʊst/
*n.*❶(soldiers in an) observation post at a distance from the main body of troops 前哨;哨兵:an ~ area 警戒地区 ❷any distant settlement 边远地区

output /ˈaʊtpʊt/
n. the amount of goods,etc.produced 产量:The factory must increase its ~.工厂必须提高产量。

outrage/'aʊtreɪdʒ/
Ⅰ *n*.(an act of) extreme violence or cruelty 暴行；残暴；凌辱：a terrible ～ 可怕的暴行 Ⅱ *v*.do sth. which shocks people；act cruelly towards someone 引起……的愤怒；虐待：an act that ～s public 违反民意的行为/～ one's sense of justice 伤害某人的正义感 ‖ ～ous /aʊt'reɪdʒəs/ *adj*.令人震惊的；极不道德的：an ～ous crime 骇人听闻的罪行

outright/'aʊtraɪt/
adv.❶in a direct way and without trying to hide anything 直率地；无保留地：I told him ～ about it.我毫无保留地将此事告诉了他。❷completely and totally 完全地；彻底地：He denied it ～.他断然否认此事。

outset/'aʊtset/
n.the beginning 开始；开端：I warned you at the ～ not to trust him.我从一开始就警告你不要相信他。‖ at（from）the ～ 从一开头

outside/ˌaʊt'saɪd/
Ⅰ *n*.the outer part of sth.外部；外面：The ～ of the building is magnificent.这栋大楼的外观很宏伟。 Ⅱ *adv*.on or to the outside 在外面；向外面：He is waiting for you ～.他在外面等你。 Ⅲ *prep*.at or on the outer side of 在(向)……外边：A man stood ～ the door.有个人站在门外。 Ⅳ *adj*.of the outside；from elsewhere 外面的：We need ～ help.我们需要外来的帮助。 ‖ at the ～ 至多；充其量

outsider/ˌaʊt'saɪdə(r)/
n.❶ a person who is not accepted as a member of a particular social group 局外人；外人；非成员：The ～ sees the best (the most) of the game.旁观者清。❷ a person or animal not expected to win a race or competition 不大可能获胜的人：The woman who actually got the job was a rank ～.事实上得到这份工作的女士是大家都没有想到的人。

outsize/'aʊtsaɪz/
adj.larger than the usual size 特大号的：～ skirt 特大号的裙子

outskirts/'aʊtskɜːts/
n.(*pl*.) the outer parts of a town,etc.(城镇等的)郊区；市郊

outspoken/ˌaʊt'spəʊkən/
adj.saying openly what one thinks 直言不讳的；坦率的：～ criticism 坦率的批评

outstanding/ˌaʊt'stændɪŋ/
adj.❶ excellent；easily seen 杰出的；显著的；突出的：an ～ leader 杰出的领导人 ❷ still to be done 未完成的；未偿付的：some ～ works 一些未完成的工作

outstay/ˌaʊt'steɪ/
v.stay longer than 比……住得久；住得超过(限度)：～ the other visitors 比其他来宾逗留更久 /～ one's welcome 因住得(逗留)太久而讨人厌恶

outstretched/ˌaʊt'stretʃt/
adj.stretched out to full length 伸开的；展开的：lie ～ on the grass 手脚伸开地躺在草地上/ He welcomed his friend with ～ arms.他伸开双臂欢迎他的朋友。

outward/'aʊtwəd/
Ⅰ *adj*.of or towards the outside 外面的；外表的；向外的；外出的：the ～ appearance of things 事物的外观/ an ～ voyage 出航 Ⅱ *adv*.(also ～s) towards the outside 向外：open ～ 往外开

outweigh/ˌaʊt'weɪ/
v.be more in weight, value, importance, etc.than 在重量(价值、重要性等)上超过……：His love for her ～s everything else.他爱她胜过一切。

outwit/ˌaʊt'wɪt/
v.defeat by being more clever than 以智胜过：～ the enemy 斗智克敌

oval/'əʊvl/
Ⅰ *adj*.egg-shaped；elliptic 卵形的；椭圆形的：an ～ ball 椭圆形球 Ⅱ *n*.a shape like an egg 卵形；椭圆形

ovary/'əʊvəri/
n.❶one of the pair of organs in a female in which eggs are produced 卵巢 ❷ the part of a plant enclosing the young seeds (植物的)子房

oven/'ʌvn/
n.a device that is like a box with a door heated for baking, roasting, etc.烤箱；烤炉：Bread is baked in an ～.面包是在烤炉

里烘烤成的。

over/ˈəʊvə(r)/

Ⅰ *prep.* ❶ directly above;in or to a position higher than but not touching 在······上方;在······之上:The sky is ～(above) our heads.天空在我们的头上。❷ resting on and covering 在······上边;覆盖:She put a blanket ～ the floor.她在地上铺了一条毛毯。❸ to the other side of 越过:He jumped ～ the wall.他跳过了那堵墙。❹ more than 超过;多于:I have been here ～ three years.我到这里三年多了。❺ in or on all or most parts of sth.遍及;all ～ the world 全世界 Ⅱ *adv.* ❶ across (a distance,etc.) 横过;从一处到另一处:Can you jump ～? 你能跳过去吗? ❷ down 向下;翻倒:Don't knock the vase ～.别把花瓶打翻了。❸ finished;ended 结束;完毕:The war was ～.战争结束了。❹ through;again 从头至尾;自始至终;再:I read the article ～.这篇文章我通读了一遍。❺ remaining;more 剩下;还有:Is there any money ～? 还有多余的钱吗? ❻in all parts of;everywhere 遍布;到处:He was sweaty all ～.他浑身是汗。❼ too 太;过分地:He was ～ excited.他太兴奋了。❽upwards and downwards 满溢:The milk boiled ～.牛奶煮沸溢出来了。❾more;in addition 超过;加之:children of nine and ～ 九岁及九岁以上的儿童 ‖ ～ again 再一遍;重新/ ～ against 在······对面;与······相反/ ～ and ～(again)反复;再三

overact/ˌəʊvərˈækt/

v. act a part in a play in an unnatural or exaggerated fashion 表演过火,演得过火

overall[1]/ˌəʊvərˈɔːl/

adj.& adv. ❶including everything 全面的(地);综合的(地):The ～ situation is encouraging.总的形势令人鼓舞。❷ on the whole;generally 总体上(的);总的说来:Overall,the film is good.总的说来,这部影片是好的。

overall[2]/ˌəʊvərˈɔːl/

n. a loose-fitting coat-like garment worn over other clothes to protect them 宽大罩衫

overawe/ˌəʊvərˈɔː/

v. fill with fear and respect 把······吓住;使敬畏:The children were ～d by the presence of the headmaster.孩子们被校长的出现吓住了。

overbalance/ˌəʊvəˈbæləns/

v. fall over;(cause to) lose balance 跌倒;翻倒:He ～d and fell into the water.他失去平衡跌入水中。

overbearing/ˌəʊvəˈbeərɪŋ/

adj. forcing others to obey one's will 专横的;跋扈的:No one liked her ～ attitude.谁都不喜欢她那盛气凌人的态度。

overboard/ˈəʊvəbɔːd/

adv. over the side of a ship or boat into the water 向船外;从船上落(或抛)入水中;fall ～ 从船上跌入水中

overcast/ˌəʊvəˈkɑːst/

adj. cloudy;full of dark clouds 多云的;阴暗的:an ～ sky 阴云密布的天空;多云的天空

overcharge/ˌəʊvəˈtʃɑːdʒ/

v. charge too much 对······索价太高;要价太高:I was ～d for my ticket.我的入场券买贵了。

overcoat/ˈəʊvəkəʊt/

n. a long coat worn over other clothes in cold weather 大衣

overcome/ˌəʊvəˈkʌm/

v. (overcame,overcome) ❶ fight successfully (against);defeat 战胜:We soon overcame the enemy.我们很快就战胜了敌人。❷be victorious;triumph 获胜;得胜:We shall ～.我们一定会胜利。

overdo/ˌəʊvəˈduː/

v. (-did,-done) do too much;cook (meat, etc.)too much 做过头;表演过火;煮(肉类等)过久或过熟:The meat was overdone.肉煮得过久了。

overdone/ˌəʊvəˈdʌn/

adj. cooked too much 煮得过度的,烧得太久的

overdose/ˈəʊvədəʊs/

n. too much of a drug taken at one time 剂量过大;过量用药;an ～ of sleeping pills 过量的安眠药

overdraft/ˈəʊvədrɑːft/
*n.*a deficit in a bank account caused by drawing more money than the account holds 透支(额)：We are paying off a large ~.我们正在偿还一大笔透支的钱。

overdraw/ˌəʊvəˈdrɔː/
v.(overdrew, ~n) ❶ draw more money (from a bank account) than the amount that is in it 透支(存款账户) ❷ exaggerate 夸张；言过其实：~ the dangers 夸大危险

overdress/ˌəʊvəˈdres/
v.(cause to)dress in clothes that are too formal (使)穿着过于正式；(使)打扮得太考究：I feel rather ~ed in this suit—everyone else is wearing jeans! 我觉得这身西服太讲究了——别人全都穿牛仔裤。

overdrive/ˈəʊvədraɪv/
*n.*a type of high gear in a car, in addition to the ordinary gears, which allows it to cruise at a fast speed 超速转动装置；超速档

overdue/ˌəʊvəˈdjuː/
*adj.*later than the arranged time(for payment, arrival, etc.) (付款、到达等)晚于规定时间的；过期未付的：This bill is ~. 这账单已过期尚未付清。

overestimate/ˌəʊvərˈestɪmeɪt/
*v.*❶ have too high an opinion of 过高评价：~ her work 过高地评价了她的工作 ❷ give too high a value for (an amount) 过高估计：We ~d the distance, so we still have some time left after our walk. 我们过多地估计了距离，因此步行之后我们还有一些时间剩下来。

overgrown/ˌəʊvəˈɡrəʊn/
*adj.*❶covered 覆盖的；长满的：garden ~ with weeds 长满了杂草的花园 ❷ having grown fast 生长太快：an ~ boy 长得太快的男孩

overhaul/ˈəʊvəhɔːl/
Ⅰ *v.*❶examine thoroughly and perhaps repair if necessary 彻底检修；大修：We are going to ~ the car.我们打算把这辆汽车彻底检修一次。❷come up to from behind and pass; overtake 赶上；追上：

The police soon ~ed them.警察不久就追上了他们。 Ⅱ *n.*a complete examination followed by any necessary repairs 彻底检修；大修：The workers have taken all the typewriters for an ~.工人已把所有打字机拿去彻底检修了。/Mary is going to the doctor for her annual ~tomorrow. 玛丽明天要到医生那里做年度身体检查。

overhead/ˌəʊvəˈhed/
adv. & *adj.*above one's head 在头上(的)；在空中(的)；在高处(的)：an ~ bridge 天桥/ an ~ railway 高架铁路/A helicopter flies ~.直升机在头顶上飞。

overhear/ˌəʊvəˈhɪə(r)/
v.(~d) ❶hear what one is not intended to hear; hear by chance 无意中听到；偶然听到：I ~d him saying that he was closing down his shop.我无意中听到他说他要关闭他的店铺。 ❷ hear without the knowledge of the speaker(s) 偷听

overjoyed/ˌəʊvəˈdʒɔɪd/
*adj.*very glad; delighted 非常高兴的；极为快乐的：be ~ at the news 听到消息非常高兴

overland/ˈəʊvəlænd/
*adj.*going by land 经由陆路的：an ~ route (journey, etc.)陆上路线(旅程等)

overlap/ˌəʊvəˈlæp/
v.(-pp-) partly cover and extend beyond one edge (of sth.) 部分重叠；搭接：a roof made of ~ping tiles 用相互搭接的瓦片铺成的屋顶：Our holidays ~.我们的假期有部分时间重叠/The language of science ~s with that of everyday life.有些科学用语也用于日常生活。

overload/ˌəʊvəˈləʊd/
*v.*❶ load too heavily 使超载，使负荷过量：Don't ~ your students with assignment.不要让你的学生负担过重。 ❷ cause to produce too much electricity 使超负荷供电：~ a circuit 使一条电路超负荷

overlook/ˌəʊvəˈlʊk/
*v.*❶ have or give a view of from a higher position 俯视；俯瞰：From the tower on the hilltop, we can ~ the whole city. 从山

顶的塔楼上,我们能俯瞰全城。❷ fail to notice;miss 忽视;忽略;看漏:You ～ed some serious problems.你忽视了几个严重问题。

overnight /ˌəʊvəˈnaɪt/
adj.& adv. ❶ sudden(ly) 突然(的):an ～ success 突然的成功/He became famous ～.他一下子就名扬四海了。❷ on the night before 在前一天晚上(的):You must get everything ready for the journey ～.你必须在前一天晚上为旅行做好一切准备。

overpower /ˌəʊvəˈpaʊə(r)/
v. be too strong for 压服;制服:～ an opponent 压倒对手 ‖ ～ing *adj.* 非常强大的;太强烈的:an ～ing feeling of hatred 非常强烈的憎恨

overrate /ˌəʊvəˈreɪt/
v. value sth.or sb. too highly 过高估计(某事或某人),对……评价过高:His work is greatly ～d.他的工作受到过高的评价。

overrule /ˌəʊvəˈruːl/
v. decide against 驳回,否决,不准:The judge ～d the lawyer's objections.法官宣布律师的反对意见无效。/Our suggestions were ～d by the committee.我们的建议被委员会否决了。

overseas /ˌəʊvəˈsiːz/
adj.& adv. to,from or situated in places across the sea (向、来自、在)海外(的):～ countries 海外国家/～ trade 海外贸易;对外贸易 /come from ～ 从海外来,从国外来

oversee /ˌəʊvəˈsiː/
v. (-saw,-seen) look after,control (e.g. work or workers);supervise 监视;监督(工作或工人)

overshadow /ˌəʊvəˈʃædəʊ/
v. cause to seem less important 使相形见绌;使黯然失色:My success ～ed his.我的成功远远超过他的成功。

oversight /ˈəʊvəsaɪt/
n. failure to notice or do sth. 忽略;疏忽:Your essay was not marked through an ～ on my part.由于我的疏忽没有给你的文章打分数。

oversleep /ˌəʊvəˈsliːp/
v. (overslept) sleep too long or too late 睡过头;睡太久:He overslept (himself) and didn't go to work.他睡过头了而未去上班。

overspill /ˈəʊvəspɪl/
n. things that spills over,especially excess population 溢出物;(尤指)过剩的人口:～ towns 为过剩人口而设的城镇

overstate /ˌəʊvəˈsteɪt/
v. say sth. in a way that makes it seem more important than it really is 把……说过头;把……讲过火;夸大:～ one's case 对自己的事情言过其实

overtake /ˌəʊvəˈteɪk/
v. (overtook,～n) ❶ catch up with and pass(e.g. in a vehicle) 追上;赶上;追过(例如乘坐车辆):Only one car overtook us.只有一辆车追(上并超)过我们。❷ come to suddenly and unexpectedly 突然降临:On his way home he was overtaken by a storm.他在回家的路上遭遇了暴风雨。/Disaster overtook the project.突发的灾难阻碍了这项工程。

overthrow /ˌəʊvəˈθrəʊ/
v. (overthrew,～n) put an end to;defeat;destroy 打倒;摧毁;推翻;颠覆:～ the king 推翻国王

overtime /ˈəʊvətaɪm/
Ⅰ *n.* the time beyond the usual time,especially working time 额外时间;加班时间 Ⅱ *adv.* beyond the regular time 超时地:They are working ～ to finish their task.他们加班加点以完成他们的任务。

overtone /ˈəʊvətəʊn/
n. (usually *pl.*) a suggestion or hint 联想;含意;暗示:The ceremony had ～s of sadness 仪式带有悲哀的气氛。

overturn /ˌəʊvəˈtɜːn/
v. turn over;cause sth. to turn over 打翻;翻倒;(使)倾覆;推翻:The car ～ed and the driver was killed. 汽车翻倒,司机死亡。/They ～ed the boat.他们翻了船。

overweight /ˌəʊvəˈweɪt/
adj. weighing too much 超重的:an ～ letter 超重的信件 /If your luggage is ～, you'll have to pay extra.假如你的行李超重了,你得付额外的运费。

overwhelm/ˌəʊvəˈwelm/

*v.*❶(of water) cover completely and suddenly (指水)泛滥;淹没:A great mass of water ~ed the city.大水淹没了村庄。❷ defeat sb.completely 击败;征服:The enemy was ~ed by the reinforcements who came later.敌军被随后赶来的援军击败了。❸(of feeling) overcome completely; greatly affect the emotion of (指感情上)制服;影响:be ~ed with fear (excitement,sorrow) 极为恐惧(兴奋、悲痛)/feel ~ed by someone's kindness 对某人的好意不胜感激

overwrought/ˌəʊvəˈrɔːt/

*adj.*tired out by too much work,excitement,etc.;very nervous (因过度工作、兴奋等而)过分劳累的;过度紧张的:She is not to be disturbed in her present ~ condition.她精疲力竭,不能受到打扰。

ovum/ˈəʊvəm/

n.(*pl.*ova /ˈəʊvə/) a female cell or egg from which animals develop 卵;卵细胞

owe/əʊ/

*v.*❶ have to pay 欠(某人的)债:I still ~ you a lot of money.我还欠你很多钱。❷ feel grateful 感激:We ~ our parents and teachers a lot.我们很感激自己的父母和老师。❸ be indebted to as the source of 归功于;由于:He ~s his success to good luck more than to ability. 他认为他的成功是靠运气而不是自己的能力。

owing/ˈəʊɪŋ/

*adj.*still to be paid 欠着的,未付的:There is £10 ~ (to you).欠(你)10 英镑。‖ ~ to 由于:She had to stay at home ~ to her illness.由于生病她只好待在家里。

owl/aʊl/

*n.*a bird with large eyes which hunts mice and small birds (usually at night) 猫头鹰;枭;鸱鸮

own/əʊn/

Ⅰ *adj.*belonging to oneself 自己的:my ~ house 我自己的房屋 Ⅱ *v.*❶ possess 有;拥有:Many people now ~ cars and houses.现在许多人都拥有汽车和房子。❷ admit that sth.is true 坦白;承认:He ~s that you are right.他承认你是对的。‖ come into one's ~ 得到自己名分应得的东西/get one's ~ back 报复/hold one's ~ 稳住;坚持住;保持局面/of one's ~ 自己的/of one's ~ accord (free will) 自愿地;主动地/on one's ~ account 为自己/on one's ~ 独自;靠自己

owner /ˈəʊnə/

*n.*a person who owns sth.物主;所有人

ownership /ˈəʊnəʃɪp/

*n.*the fact of owning sth.所有权;物主身份

ox/ɒks/

n.(*pl.*oxen /ˈɒksn/) an animal of the cattle family kept for milk or meat;a cow or bull 牛;母牛;公牛

oxide/ˈɒksaɪd/

n. a compound of oxygen with another element 氧化物:iron ~ 氧化铁

oxidize /ˈɒksɪˌdaɪz/

*v.*❶combine or cause a substance to combine with oxygen 使氧化 ❷form or make sth. form a layer of metal oxide,as when sth. becomes rusty 使生锈 ‖ oxidization *n.*氧化,氧化作用

oxygen/ˈɒksɪdʒən/

*n.*a chemical element or a gas present in the air, without colour, taste, or smell, but necessary for all forms of life on earth 氧;氧气:Fish have gills through which ~ is absorbed from the water.鱼是通过鳃从水中来吸收氧气的。

oyster/ˈɔɪstə(r)/

*n.*a flat shell-fish used for food 蚝;牡蛎:Pearls are sometimes found in ~shells.有时在牡蛎壳里会发现珍珠。

ozone /ˈəʊzəʊn, əʊˈzəʊn/

*n.*❶a colourless gas which is a form of oxygen 臭氧 ❷the invigorating air at the seaside (海滨的)清新空气

Pp

pa/pɑː/

n. the short for papa（papa 的缩略）爸：Pa, can I borrow your car tonight? 爸, 今晚我能借你的车吗?

pace/peɪs/

I *n*.❶ a step in walking or running 步; 一步：Take one ～ forward! 向前一步走! ❷ the rate or speed in walking or running 步速; 速度：quicken the ～ 加快步伐 Ⅱ *v*.❶ walk with slow regular steps 踱步; 慢步：He ～d up and down the room anxiously. 他焦急不安地在屋里踱来踱去。❷ measure by taking steps of an equal and known length 步测：She ～d out the length of the room. 她步测了房间的长度。‖ **keep ～ with** 跟上/**put through one's ～s** 考查……的性能或能力/**set the ～** 定步调(速度); 树榜样

pacific/pəˈsɪfɪk/

adj.❶ making or loving peace; peace-loving 和平的; 爱好和平的 ❷ showing calmness 平静的; 温和的 ❸ of the Pacific Ocean 太平洋的：the Pacific countries 太平洋沿岸国家

pacifier/ˈpæsɪfaɪə(r)/

n. a person who pacifies 抚慰者; 平定者; 调停者

pacifist/ˈpæsɪfɪst/

n. a person who believes that all wars are wrong and refuses to fight in them 和平主义者; 反战主义者

pacify/ˈpæsɪfaɪ/

v.❶ calm or quieten 镇定; 安定; 抚慰：Try to ～ the baby, he has been crying for hours. 试着哄哄那个婴儿, 他已经哭了几个小时了。❷ bring the state of peace to sth. 平定; 平息

pack/pæk/

I *v*.❶ put（things）into（a case, box, etc.）打包; 包装; 收拾(行李)等：Please ～ your bags quickly and we are leaving in an hour. 请赶快打包好行李, 我们一小时后就出发了。❷ crowd together into a place 挤满; 填塞：Over a hundred people ～ed into a small classroom. 一百多个人挤在一间小小的教室里。Ⅱ *n*.❶ a bundle of things tied or wrapped together for carrying 包; 捆; 包裹：a ～ of cloth 一捆布 ❷ a group of wild animals that hunt together（动物）群 ❸ a group of similar people or things（人或东西）帮, 批：a ～ of wolves 狼群 ‖ ～ **in** 停止/～ **off** 打发走/～ **up** 打包/**send sb. ～ing** 叫人卷铺盖走人; 撵走

package/ˈpækɪdʒ/

I *n*. a parcel, bale or bundle of things which are packed together 捆; 束; 包; 包裹：a ～ of books 一捆书 Ⅱ *v*. make into or tie up as a package 包成一包; 把……扎成一捆：She ～d up the old books. 她把旧书捆起来了。

packaging/ˈpækɪdʒɪŋ/

n. materials used for packing products 包装材料：Complicated ～ increases the price of food. 复杂的包装材料提高了食品的价格。

packed/pækt/

adj.（of a room, building, etc.）full of people; crowded（房间、大楼等）挤满人的; 拥挤的：a ～ theatre 满座的戏院

packer/ˈpækə(r)/

n.❶ a person or thing that packs, such as a person who works at a place where food is put into tins, etc. for preserving 包装工; 打包机; 装罐头食品的工人 ❷ a person employed to pack the furniture, clothing, etc. of people moving from one house to another（受雇为搬家的人打捆家具、衣物等的)捆扎工

packet/'pækɪt/

*n.*a paper or cardboard container in which goods are packed for selling（商品的)小包装纸袋；小硬纸板盒：a ～ of needles and thread 一个针线包

packing /'pækɪŋ/

*n.*the action or process of putting clothes, possessions,etc.into bags or boxes 打包；包装

pact/pækt/

*n.*a formal agreement between individuals or parties 协定；公约；条约：trade ～ 贸易协定/ a non-aggression ～ 互不侵犯条约

pad/pæd/

Ⅰ *v.*(-dd-) ❶ fill with soft material in order to protect,shape,or make more comfortable（用柔软的材料)填塞，衬垫：a coat with ～ded shoulders 带垫肩的外套 ❷ make (a sentence,speech,story,etc.) longer by adding unnecessary words or sentences（用废话等把文章)拉长：～ a story 把故事拉得冗长 /I made my speech longer by ～ding it with a few jokes.我用了几个笑话来拉长演说。Ⅱ *n.* ❶ anything filled with a soft material used to protect,give comfort or improve the shape of sth.衬垫；护垫：a shoulder ～ 垫肩 /Put a clean ～ of cotton over the wound.把一块干净的纱布敷在伤口上。❷ sheets or paper fastened together,used for writing letters 本子；信笺：a ～ of writing paper 一本便笺

paddle/'pædl/

Ⅰ *n.*a short pole with a wide, flat blade at one or both ends, used for pushing a small boat,especially a canoe through the water 桨；短桨 Ⅱ *v.*❶ move a small boat through water, using one or more paddles 划桨：We ～d the small boat across the river. 我们划着小船过河。❷ walk, jump, run, etc. barefeet in shallow water 涉水；戏水：The baby is paddling about in the water.小孩在水里玩。‖ ～**one's own canoe** 独立自主；自立

paddy（field）/ˌpædi'fiːld/

*n.*a field where rice is grown 稻田

padlock/'pædlɒk/

*n.*a detachable lock hung by a hook to the object 挂锁；扣锁

page/peɪdʒ/

*n.*❶ one or both sides of a sheet of paper in a book,newspaper,etc.页(书籍、报纸的一面)或一张(两面)：on ～ forty-seven 第 47 页 /turn to ～ thirty-two 翻到 32 页/Someone has torn a ～ out of this book.有人把这本书撕了一张。❷ an event written in history book (历史上的)事件：a fine ～ in China's history 中国历史上的光辉一页 ‖ **on the same ～** 目标一致/**turn the ～** 开始新生活

pagoda/pə'ɡəʊdə/

*n.*a tower built with several floors or levels, often with an ornamental roof at each level 宝塔；塔：There is a ～ in front of our school.我们学校前面有一座宝塔。

paid /peɪd/

*adj.*❶（of work or leave) for or during which one receives pay (工作)有报酬的；(假期)照常领取工资的 ❷(of a person in a specified occupation) in receipt of pay 受雇用的；支取薪金的：a ～,anonymous spy 受雇的匿名间谍

pain/peɪn/

Ⅰ *n.*❶ feelings of suffering of the body or mind；a feeling of hurting 疼痛；痛苦：His bad behaviour caused his parents much ～.他的不良行为使他父母很痛苦。/I feel a ～ in my breast.我感觉胸部有些疼。❷（*pl.*) great trouble；careful effort 劳苦；辛苦：No ～s, no gains. 不劳则无获。‖ **at ～s (to do)**,**at the ～s (of doing)** 尽力；下苦功/**go to great ～s to** 努力；下功夫/**spare no ～s** 不遗余力；全力以赴/**take ～s** 尽力；费苦心 Ⅱ *v.*make sb. unhappy；cause pain to 使痛苦；使疼痛：His foot is still ～ing him. 他的脚还在痛。

painful/'peɪnfl/

*adj.*causing pain or distress 使痛的；使痛苦的：Her failure in the experiment was ～ to her.实验失败使她感到痛苦。

painkiller/ˈpeɪnˌkɪlə(r)/

n. a medicine which lessens or removes pain 止痛药

painless/ˈpeɪnləs/

adj. ❶ causing no pain 无痛的：～ childbirth 无痛分娩 ❷ needing no effort or hard work 不费力的：a ～ way of learning a foreign language 一种轻松的外语学习方法

painstaking/ˈpeɪnzˌteɪkɪŋ/

adj. very careful and thorough 精心的；仔细的：～ care 无微不至的关心 / She is not very clever but she is ～.她并不很聪明但肯下苦功。

paint/peɪnt/

Ⅰ*n.* a liquid coloring matter which can be spread on a surface to make it a certain color 油漆；涂料；颜料：The ～ on the wall is wet.墙上的油漆还没干。Ⅱ*v.* ❶ put paint on 油漆；粉刷；涂色：He ～ed the window yellow.他将窗子漆成了黄色。❷ make a picture using paint 用颜料绘画：～ flowers(a landscape, a portrait)画花卉(风景、肖像) ❸ describe vividly in words 生动地描写：In his letter he ～s a vivid picture of life in Africa.他在信中生动地描写了他在非洲的生活。❹(pl.) a set of small tubes or cakes of paint of different colors, usually in a box (paint box), used for making pictures (绘画用的)颜料：a set of oil ～ 一套绘画颜料

painter/ˈpeɪntə(r)/

n. a person whose job is painting, either pictures or things like houses 画家；油漆工：He is a famous ～.他是一位著名的画家。

painting/ˈpeɪntɪŋ/

n. ❶ the process of using paint; the occupation of a painter 油漆；绘画；油漆业；绘画业 ❷ a painted picture 图画；油画：traditional Chinese ～ 中国画

paintwork/ˈpeɪntwɜːk/

n. a painted surface 漆面：some damage to the ～ on my car 对我小汽车的漆面(造成)的一些毁坏

pair/peə(r)/

Ⅰ*n.* ❶ a single article with two parts always joined 由两部分合在一起的单件物品：a ～ of scissors 一把剪刀/a ～ of spectacles 一副眼镜 ❷ two things of the same kind used together or regarded as a unit 一双；一对：a ～ of shoes 一双鞋/ a ～ of gloves 一副手套 ❸ two people closely connected or doing sth. together 关系密切或共做某事的两人：a ～ of dancers 一对舞伴/the happy ～ 一对快乐的新婚夫妇/The pupils practise English conversation in ～s.学生们成对地练习英语对话。Ⅱ*v.* form a pair or pairs 成对；配合：She's ～ed with Hunter.他和亨特是搭档。/Their parents try to ～ the two young people off.他们的父母想撮合这对年轻人。

pairing/ˈpeərɪŋ/

n. an arrangement or match resulting from organizing or forming people or things into pairs 配对；搭配

pal/pæl/

n. a friend 朋友：He is a ～ of mine.他是我的一个朋友。

palace/ˈpælɪs/

n. ❶ a very large, grand house of king or other rulers 宫；宫殿：The Queen of England lives in Buckingham Palace.英国女王住在白金汉宫。/the Summer Palace 颐和园 ❷ any large and splendid building (for entertainment) 华丽的(娱乐)大厦；宏伟的建筑物：the Cultural Palace of Nationality 民族文化宫/the Workers' Cultural Palace 工人文化宫

palatable/ˈpælətəbl/

adj. ❶ pleasant to taste 美味的；可口的：a ～ meal 一顿美餐 ❷ agreeable to the mind; pleasant 合意的；惬意的：She didn't find my suggestion ～ at all.她觉得我的建议不合心意。

palate/ˈpælɪt/

n. ❶ the roof of the mouth 上颚：hard (soft)～ 硬(软)腭 ❷ a sense of taste 味觉：have a good ～ for wines 精于品评酒类

pale/peɪl/

　　adj. ❶ with little colour in the face; having skin that is rather white 苍白的；灰白的：He looks ～.他脸色苍白。❷ (of colours) not bright or vivid（指颜色）暗淡的，浅淡的：～ blue 淡蓝色 ❸ (of light) dim, faint（指光）暗淡的，微弱的：the ～ light of the moon 微弱的月光

palette/ˈpælət/

　　n. a thin board with a hole for the thumb at one end, on which an artist mixes his colours（画家用的）调色板

paling/ˈpeɪlɪŋ/

　　n. ❶ a pointed piece of wood used with others in making a fence 尖木桩 ❷ (usually *pl.*) a fence made out of palings 木栅；栅栏；围篱：He jumped over the ～.他跳过了木栅栏。

palisade/ˌpælɪˈseɪd/

　　n. a fence of strong wooden stakes pointed at the top, used as a means of defence（用顶部削尖的粗木桩做成，作为防御之用的）栅栅，木栅

pall[1]/pɔːl/

　　n. ❶ a heavy cloth which is put over a coffin, tomb, etc. 柩衣；棺罩；墓布 ❷ any kind of dark, heavy covering（暗色而厚重的）遮盖物：a ～ of smoke 一片烟幕

pall[2]/pɔːl/

　　v. become uninteresting because there is too much of it（因过多而）厌倦，生厌，感到乏味：His stories ～ed on me after a while.他的故事不久便使我感到厌倦。

pallet[1]/ˈpælɪt/

　　n. ❶ a mattress stuffed with straw 草垫 ❷ a simple or makeshift bed 简陋床

pallet[2]/ˈpælɪt/

　　n. a large tray or platform for carrying goods that are being lifted, stacked, or stored, especially one that can be raised by a forklift truck（用于移动或堆存货物的）托盘，集装架（尤指借助叉车使用的货板）

palm/pɑːm/

　　n. the inner surface of the hand 手掌；掌心：read one's ～ 看手相 ‖ grease one's ～ 买通；行贿/have an itching ～ 贪财；贪钱

palmist/ˈpɑːmɪst/

　　n. a person who claims to be able to tell what someone is like or what his future is by examining the lines on his palm 看手相者

palmistry/ˈpɑːmɪstri/

　　n. the art or practice of being a palmist 手相术

palmy/ˈpɑːmi/

　　adj. (especially of a period in the past) flourishing and successful（尤指过去一段时期）兴旺的，兴盛的，成功的

palpable/ˈpælpəbl/

　　adj. ❶ easily seen; obvious 显而易见的；明显的：a ～ mistake 明显的错误 ❷ that can be felt or touched 可触知的；摸得出的：a thing that is ～ 摸得出的东西

palpitate/ˈpælpɪteɪt/

　　v. ❶ beat very quickly 急速地跳动：His heart was palpitating.他的心脏直扑腾。❷ tremble 发抖；颤动：palpitating with fear 吓得直发抖 ‖ palpitation /ˌpælpɪˈteɪʃn/ *n.* 心脏急速跳动；心悸

paltry/ˈpɔːltri/

　　adj. almost worthless; of no importance 几乎无价值的；微不足道的；不重要的：be offered with a ～ sum of money 得到一笔少得可怜的钱

pamper/ˈpæmpə(r)/

　　v. be too kind to; indulge too much 娇养；溺爱；纵容：～ a child 溺爱小孩

pamphlet/ˈpæmflɪt/

　　n. a small paper book that collects information about a particular subject 小册子：The article was first issued in ～ form.这篇文章最初是以小册子形式发表的。

pamphleteer/ˌpæmfləˈtɪə(r)/

　　n. a person who writes pamphlets, especially political ones（尤指政论性）小册子的作者

pan/pæn/

　　n. ❶ a metal plate used for cooking 平底锅：pots and ～s 缸子和锅子 ❷ sth. shaped like a pan 锅形物

pancreas/ˈpæŋkrɪəs/

n. a gland near the stomach, discharging a juice which helps digestion 胰;胰腺

panda/ˈpændə/

n. a large black and white animal like a bear 熊猫:giant ～ 大熊猫 /lesser ～ 小熊猫

pandemic /pænˈdemɪk/

Ⅰ *adj.* (of a disease) occurring over a whole country or the whole world (疾病) 在全国(或世界)流行的,泛流行的 Ⅱ *n.* an outbreak of such a disease 流行病

pander/ˈpændə(r)/

v. do what sb. wants, or try to please them, especially when this is not acceptable or reasonable 迎合;奉迎;投其所好: Films sometimes ～ to the public by showing violence and immorality. 电影有时以反映暴力和伤风败俗的行为来迎合观众。

pane/peɪn/

n. a piece of glass used in window 窗玻璃: He broke this ～ of glass. 他打破了这块玻璃。

panel/ˈpænl/

Ⅰ *n.* ❶ a separate part of the surface of a door, wall, ceiling, etc. (门、墙、天花板等的)嵌板,镶板 ❷ a piece of material of a different kind or colour inserted in a dress (衣服上的缝缀的不同质料或颜色的)布块 ❸ a board on which controls or instruments of various kinds are fixed 控制板;操纵盘;仪表盘 ❹ a group of speakers, especially chosen to speak, answer questions, take part in a game before audience (e.g.of listeners to a broadcast) (广播等中的)座谈小组,答问小组,游戏小组 ❺ a list of names of people chosen to form a jury 陪审员名单 Ⅱ *v.* divide into or decorate with panels 装镶板;用嵌板装饰: They are ～ing a wall with wood. 他们正在用木头镶嵌墙壁。

pang/pæŋ/

n. a sharp, sudden pain or feeling 突发的剧痛;突发的悲痛:the ～s of hunger 饥饿的疼痛;饿得发痛/ a ～ of anxiety 忧虑的折磨

panic/ˈpænɪk/

Ⅰ *n.* a sudden, uncontrollable fear or terror 恐慌;惊慌:be seized with ～ 惊慌失措 /There was (a) ～ in the theater when fire started. 剧院失火的时候,一片惊慌混乱。 Ⅱ *adj.* resulting from a sudden terror 由恐慌引起的;莫名其妙的:a ～ fear 莫名恐惧 /a ～ price 恐慌价格 Ⅲ *v.* be affected with sudden fear or terror 受惊;惊慌:Don't ～!不要惊慌!

pansy/ˈpænzɪ/

n. a small garden plant with brightly coloured flowers 三色堇;蝴蝶花

pant/pænt/

Ⅰ *n.* the acting of gasping 喘气:speak between ～s 气喘喘地说话 Ⅱ *v.* ❶ take short, quick breaths 喘气 ❷ have a strong wish for sth. 渴望;热望:He ～ed to be wealthy. 他渴望致富。

pantheon/ˈpænθɪən/

n. ❶ a temple dedicated to all the gods;all the gods of a people 万神殿;(一个民族信奉的)众神 ❷ a building in which the famous dead person of a nation are buried or given honour 伟人祠

panther/ˈpænθə(r)/

n. ❶ a leopard, especially a black one 豹;黑豹 ❷ a large American feline resembling a lion 美洲狮

panties/ˈpæntɪz/

n. (*pl.*) an item of underclothing worn by women, covering the lower part of the body above the legs 妇女穿的紧身短内裤

pantry/ˈpæntrɪ/

n. a small room in which food is kept 食品贮藏室:A ～ adjoins the kitchen. 食品贮藏室与厨房毗连。

pants/pænts/

n. (*pl.*) ❶ a piece of clothing worn under other clothes from the middle of the body to the top of legs 三角裤;短衬裤 ❷ trousers 裤子:I bought a pair of ～ yesterday. 昨天我买了一条裤子。

pap/pæp/

n. ❶ a soft almost liquid food, especially for babies or sick people（婴儿、病人吃的）软食，半流质食物 ❷ a reading matter or entertainment intended only for amusement, which does not instruct or contain ideas of any value 消遣性读物；娱乐节目

papa/pə'pɑ:/

n. an informal term for children to address their father 爸爸

papal/'peɪpl/

adj. connected with a pope or to the papacy 教皇的；教皇职位的

papaya/pə'paɪə/

n. a tropical fruit with yellow and green skin, sweet orange or red flesh and round black seeds 木瓜

paper/'peɪpə(r)/

n. ❶ the material made in the form of sheets from very thin threads of wood, used for writing, printing, etc. 纸：a sheet of ～ 一张纸 ❷ a newspaper 报纸：a morning ～ 晨报 ❸ official documents; documents establishing the identity of the bearer 文件；证件：a white ～ 白皮书 ❹ a set of printed examination questions 试卷；考卷：The English ～ was easy. 英语试题很容易。‖ on ～ 在名义上；理论上；以书面形式/send in one's ～s 辞职/set a ～ 出考题 ‖ ～back *n.* 平装本/ ～ cut *n.* 剪纸/ ～ clip *n.* 回形针；曲别针

par/pɑ:(r)/

n. ❶ an average or normal amount or condition 平均数量；常态：below ～ 低于票面价值；在标准以下 ❷ the value of a bond, share, etc., that is printed on it（债券或票证的）面值：Your shares are above ～. 你的股份高于票面价值。 ❸ （golf）the score which is considered as a standard for a particular golf course（高尔夫球赛中）标准杆数 ‖ be on a ～ with sb. or sth. 跟某人或某物同样好，不分伯仲：I don't think his ability is on a ～ with yours. 我认为他的能力跟你不同。

parabola/pə'ræbələ/

n. a curve like the line made by a ball when it is thrown in the air and falls to the ground 抛物线

parachute/'pærəʃu:t/

Ⅰ *n.* ❶ a large umbrella-shaped device for a jump from an aircraft or for dropping supplies 降落伞：a ～ jump 跳伞 ❷ any of various unpowered devices similar to a parachute 像降落伞的东西 Ⅱ *v.* jump or drop from an aircraft by parachute 用降落伞降落；空投：He enjoys parachuting. 他喜欢跳伞运动。/Supplies were ～d into the earthquake zone. 大量必需品被空投到地震地区。

parade/pə'reɪd/

Ⅰ *v.* ❶ gather together for a formal display; march through or around 集合训练；列队行进；游行：The people ～d through the square. 人们游行通过广场。❷ display; show off 炫示；夸耀：He likes to ～ his knowledge. 他喜欢炫耀他的知识。 Ⅱ *n.* ❶ a ceremonial review of troops 阅兵；游行：Let's go and watch the May Day ～. 我们去看五一节的阅兵吧。❷ an act of showing one's skill, knowledge, feelings, etc., with the intention of attracting people's attention or gaining admiration 展示；夸耀；炫耀：make a ～ of one's virtues 夸耀自己的优点

paradigm/'pærədaɪm/

n. ❶ a very clear or typical example of sth. 范例；示例 ❷ an example or pattern of a word, showing all its forms in grammar 词形变化："Child, child's, children, children's", is a ～. "Child, child's, children, children's"是词形变化的形式。

paradigmatic/ˌpærədɪg'mætɪk/

adj. of, like, or by means of a paradigm 示范的；例证的；词形变化的

paradise/'pærədaɪs/

n. a place of complete happiness; heaven 乐园；天堂：He who will enter into ～ must have a good key. 谁要进入天堂，谁就得有一把好钥匙。

paradox/'pærədɒks/

n. a saying which at first may seem to be nonsense but may actually contain some truth 似是而非的隽语

paraffin /ˈpærəfɪn/

　　n. a type of oil used as a fuel for lamps, heating, cooking stoves, etc. 煤油

paragon /ˈpærəgən/

　　n. an example of goodness which should be imitated; sb. or sth. which seems to have no faults 模范, 典型; 完美的人或物: a ～ of virtue 美德的典型

paragraph /ˈpærəɡrɑːf/

　　I *n*. ❶ a piece of writing that begins on a new line（文章的）段, 节: Read the first ～, please. 请读第一段。 ❷ a small item of news in a newspaper（报纸上新闻的）小节　II *v*. divide into paragraphs 将……分段: This book is much better ～ed than that one. 这本书的段落划分远比那本书要好。

parallel /ˈpærəlel/

　　I *adj*. ❶ being the same distance apart at every point 平行的: be ～ to (with) 与……平行 /～ line 平行线 /The highway runs ～ to the river. 这条公路和河流平行。 ❷ very familiar 相似的; 类似的: a ～ case 相同的例子 /～ hobbies 类似的爱好 /a rather ～ history 十分相像的历史 /My experience in this matter is ～ to yours. 在这个问题上我的经历与你差不多。 ❸ marking a circuit connected in parallel 并连的: ～ circuit 并联电路 /～ connection 并联　II *n*. ❶ similar features 相似的特征 ❷ a person, situation, event, etc. that is exactly similar to another 极相似的人（事或物）: a great event without ～ in history 史无前例的伟大事件　III *v*. ❶ be parallel to 与……平行 ❷ be similar to 与……类似: His experiences ～ mine in many instances. 他的经历在许多方面和我的相似。 ❸ be compared with 与……比较: Nothing can ～ that discovery. 没有什么能和那一发现相比。

parallelogram /ˌpærəˈleləɡræm/

　　n. a flat four-sided figure with its opposite sides parallel to each other 平行四边形

paralyse(-ze) /ˈpærəlaɪz/

　　v. cause sb. unable to feel or move his body 使麻痹; 使瘫痪; 使无能为力: His left arm was ～d. 他的左臂瘫痪了。

paralysis /pəˈrælɪsɪs/

　　n. a loss of feeling in, and loss of control of all or some of the body muscles 麻痹; 瘫痪

paramedic /ˌpærəˈmedɪk/

　　n. a person who is trained to do medical work, especially the first aid, but is not a fully qualified doctor 护理人员; (尤指做急救工作的)医疗辅助人员　‖ ～al *adj*. 辅助医务的

parameter /pəˈræmɪtə/

　　n. ❶ a quantity that is constant in the case in question but varies in different cases 参数 ❷ a numerical or other measurable factor forming one of a set that defines a system or sets the conditions of its operation 参(变)数; 参(变)量 ❸ a limit that defines the scope of sth. 范围; 界限: We are working within the ～s of time and money. 我们在时间和金钱的限定范围内工作。

paramount /ˈpærəmaʊnt/

　　adj. most important; most powerful 最重要的; 至高无上的: of ～ importance 最重要的 /the ～ chief 最高首领

paranormal /ˌpærəˈnɔːməl/

　　adj. beyond what is normal and can be rationally explained; supernatural 超出正常范围的; 超自然的

parapet /ˈpærəpɪt, ˈpærəpet/

　　n. a low protective wall at the edge of a bridge, flat roof, etc. (桥梁、平屋顶等边缘的)低矮挡墙

paraphrase /ˈpærəfreɪz/

　　I *n*. a reexpression of sth. written or said in different words, especially the words that are easier to understand 释义; 意译: plays which are not ～s from the Greek 不是从希腊文意译过来的剧本　II *v*. make or give an explanation of (sth. written or said) 意译; 转述; 释义: The stories will have to be ～d by mother. 这些故事还要由母亲来解释。

parasite/'pærəsaɪt/

n. ❶ an animal or plant living on or in another and getting its food from it 寄生虫；寄生植物：a ～ on cattle 牛身上的寄生虫 ❷ a useless person who is supported by the wealth or efforts of others 靠他人为生的人：a court society ridden with ～s 寄生虫充斥的宫廷社会

parasol/'pærəsɒl/

n. an umbrella which gives protection from the rays of the sun 遮阳伞

paratrooper/'pærətruːpə(r)/

n. a soldier who is trained to drop by parachute 伞兵；空降兵

parcel/'pɑːsl/

Ⅰ *n.* things wrapped and tied up for carrying 包裹；小包：I'm just going to take this ～ to the post office. 我正要去邮局寄包裹。Ⅱ *v.* wrap sth. up and make it into a parcel for carrying 打包：Please ～ up these books. 请把这些书打包。

parch/pɑːtʃ/

v. ❶ make hot or very dry 使焦干；烘干：earth ～ed by the sun 被太阳晒焦的大地 ❷ roast slightly by exposing to heat 烘烤：～ed peas 炒豆 ❸ make very thirsty 使极度口渴：be ～ed with thirst 渴得唇干舌燥

parchment/'pɑːtʃmənt/

n. a writing material made from the skin of a sheep, goat, etc. 羊皮纸

pardon/'pɑːdn/

Ⅰ *v.* excuse; forgive 原谅；宽恕：Please ～ me for coming late. 请原谅我来晚了。Ⅱ *n.* the act of forgiving sb. 原谅；宽恕：I beg your ～. 请原谅，请再说一遍。

pardonable/'pɑːdnəbl/

adj. that can be forgiven 能原谅的，可宽恕的：a ～ mistake 可原谅的错误

pare/peə(r)/

v. ❶ cut away the thin outer covering, edge, or skin of sth., usually with a sharp knife 削（某物的覆盖物、边或皮）：～ one's fingernails 修指甲 ❷ reduce the size or amount 缩减：We must ～ down costs to improve our profitability. 我们必须削减成本以使利润增加。

parent/'peərənt/

Ⅰ *n.* ❶ a person's father or mother 父亲；母亲：～s 双亲/a ～s' meeting 家长会 / Either ～ may write the reason for an absence. 父亲或母亲都可以写缺席的原因。❷ an organism that produces another 动植物亲本；母体 Ⅱ *adj.* referring to a progenitor 母（体）的；作为起源的：a ～ company 母公司

parentage/'peərəntɪdʒ/

n. the identity and origins of one's parents 父母的身份和家系

parental/pə'rentl/

adj. connected with parent or parents 父亲的；母亲的；父母的；双亲的

parenthesis/pə'renθəsɪs/

n.(*pl.*) a pair of the brackets ( ) used to separate part of a sentence from the rest 圆括号

parenting/'peərəntɪŋ/

n. the process of caring for your child or children 养育；抚养；教养：～ skills 教养子女的技巧

parish/'pærɪʃ/

n. an area looked after by one christian priest or served by one church 教区

parity/'pærəti/

n. being equal; being at par 平等；同等：struggle for ～ of treatment 为同等的待遇而斗争

park/pɑːk/

Ⅰ *n.* a large, usually grassy, enclosed piece of land in a town, used by the public for pleasure and rest 公园：There are some beautiful ～s in the city. 这个城市里有几座美丽的公园。Ⅱ *v.* put or place (a car or other vehicle) in a particular place for a time 停放（汽车等）：You can ～ your car here. 你可以把车停在这儿。 ‖ ～ing meter *n.* 停车计时器

parking/'pɑːkɪŋ/

n. ❶ the act of stopping a vehicle at a place and leaving it there for a period of time 停车；泊车 ❷ a space or an area for leaving vehicles 停车场；停车位

parliament/'pɑːləmənt/

n.(in some countries) the main law-making body, made up of members wholly or partly elected by the people of the country 议会；国会：The British Parliament consists of the House of Lords and the House of Commons. 英国议会包括上院和下院。‖ ～ary /ˌpɑːləˈmentri/ *adj.* 议会的；国会的

parlo(u)r /ˈpɑːlə(r)/

n. a sitting room in a house 客厅；会客室

parole /pəˈrəʊl/

n. ❶ a solemn promise on the part of a prisoner not to misuse his privileges 犯人的宣誓 ❷ release from prison, under certain conditions, before one's full sentence (term of imprisonment) is complete（在刑期届满前）假释出狱：He was on six months' ～. 他获得了六个月的假释。

parrot /ˈpærət/

Ⅰ *n.* ❶ a sort of birds with a hooked beak and usually brightly-coloured feathers that can be taught to imitate human speech 鹦鹉 ❷ a person repeating, often without understanding the words or action of another 人云亦云者 Ⅱ *v.* repeat the words or actions of someone else without thinking or understanding 鹦鹉学舌般地复述，模仿：They confined themselves to ～ing textbooks. 他们仅限于模仿教科书。

parsley /ˈpɑːsli/

n. a garden plant of which curly leaves are used for flavouring food or decorating food when it is served 香菜；芫荽

parson /ˈpɑːsən/

n. a minister or priest in charge of a parish 教区牧师

part /pɑːt/

Ⅰ *n.* ❶ one of the pieces into which a thing is divided 部分：Only ～ of his story is true. 他的故事只有一部分是真实的。❷ a person's duty 本分；作用；职责：Everyone must do his ～. 人人都须尽职尽责。❸ a character in a play 角色 ❹ a component of a machine 零件；部件：I'll buy some car ～s. 我要购买一些汽车零

件。❺ (*pl.*) a general area or division of a country, without fixed limits（一个国家的）地区，区域：We don't have much rain in these ～. 这一带没有多少雨水。/She lives in foreign ～. 她住在国外。Ⅱ *v.* separate；make people leave each other 分离；分开：～ the hair 分开头发 ‖ for one's ～ 对本人来说 /for the most ～ 大部分；大体上 /in ～ 部分地；在某种程度上 /on one's ～ 就……而言；在……方面 /play a...～（in）起……的作用 /take ～ in 参加 /take ～ with（take the ～ of）站在……一边；支持

partial /ˈpɑːʃl/

adj. ❶ not complete；not all；in part 不完全的；部分的：a ～ success 部分成功 /a ～ loss 部分损失 ❷ favoring one side over another；biased 片面的；不公平的：a ～ opinion 偏见 ❸ having a particular liking for sth. 癖好的；偏爱的：She is ～ to sweets. 她偏爱甜食。

partiality /ˌpɑːʃiˈæləti/

n. ❶ being partial；bias 偏袒；不公平 ❷ a special liking or fondness for sth. 偏爱；特殊爱好；癖好：a ～ for cream cakes 对奶油蛋糕的偏爱

partially /ˈpɑːʃəli/

adv. ❶ not completely；partly 不完全地；部分地：He was（only）～ to blame for the accident. 他对事故（只）应负部分责任。❷ in a partial way 偏袒地；不公平地

participant /pɑːˈtɪsɪpənt/

n. a person who participates in an activity or event 参与者；参加者：a ～ in the table-tennis tournament 乒乓球锦标赛参赛者

participate /pɑːˈtɪsɪpeɪt/

v. have a share；take part in 分享；参与：actively ～ in the mass sports activities 积极参加群众性体育活动 /～ in an international exposition 参加国际博览会

participle /ˈpɑːtɪsɪpl/

n. a verbal adjective qualifying nouns but retaining some participles of a verb 分词：Rewrite the following sentences using present or past ～s. 用现在分词或过去分

词改写下列句子。

particle/'pɑːtɪkl/

*n.*❶ a very small piece of matter 微粒;粒子:dust ~s 尘埃 ❷ a very small amount or degree 极小量:She has not a ~ of feelings.她没有丝毫的感情。

particular/pə'tɪkjʊlə(r)/

*adj.*❶ different from others;special;unusual 特殊的;特别的;特定的:a ~ friend 一位特殊的朋友 ❷ hard to satisfy 讲究的;苛求的;挑剔的:She is ~ about what she wears.她对衣着十分讲究。‖ in ~ 特别;尤其

particularity /pə,tɪkjʊ'lærɪti/

*n.*❶ the quality of being individual or unique 个性;独特性❷an attention to detail;being exact 考究;准确

particularly /pə'tɪkjʊləli/

*adv.*❶to a higher degree than is usual or average 特别;尤其;异乎寻常地:Traffic is bad,~ in the downtown.交通状况很差,尤其是在市中心。❷ used to single out a subject to which a statement is especially applicable 详细地;清楚地 ❸ so as to give special emphasis to a point;specifically 具体地;明确地

parting /'pɑːtɪŋ/

*n.*❶the action of leaving or being separated from someone 离别;分别 ❷a line where hair is combed away in different directions 头发的分线

partition/pɑː'tɪʃn/

Ⅰ *n.*❶ the action or state of dividing or being divided into parts 分开;分割 ❷ sth.that separates 分隔物 Ⅱ*v.*divide into two or more parts 分开:~ a house into rooms 把房子隔成几个房间

partitive/'pɑːtɪtɪv/

*n.*a word or a phrase which expresses a part of a whole 表示部分的词(或词组):"Some" is a ~ word,as in the phrase "Some of the cake".在"some of the cake"中,some 是表示部分的词。

partly/'pɑːtli/

*adv.*to some degree;not completely 一定程度上;部分地;不完全地:We are all ~ to blame.我们都得负一部分责任。/ a ~ finished building 部分完工的大楼/What you say is ~ true.你所说的有几分是真实的。

partner/'pɑːtnə(r)/

*n.*❶a person who takes part in an undertaking with another or others,especially in a business with shared risks and profits 合伙人;伙伴;合作者:He is my business ~.他是我的生意合伙人。❷ the person that you are married 配偶:a marriage ~ 配偶 ❸ an organization or a country which shares an agreement with another 伙伴:a trade ~ 贸易伙伴

partnership/'pɑːtnəʃɪp/

*n.*❶the state of being a partner,especially in business 合伙关系:We've been in ~ for five years.我们合伙已经五年了。❷ a business owned by two or more partners 合伙企业;合股公司

part-time/'pɑːt-taɪm/

*adj.*for only part of the usual working day or week 非全日的;兼职的:~ job 兼职工作

party/'pɑːti/

*n.*❶ a group of people who have the same political ideas 政党:the Communist Party 共产党 ❷ a group of people travelling or working together 一批;一行;一伙:a ~ of Japanese tourists 一批日本旅游者 ❸a social gathering attended by the people invited 聚会:a birthday ~ 生日聚会

pass/pɑːs/

Ⅰ *v.*❶ go by (a person or place);go through 经过;穿过:Let me ~,please.请让我过去。❷ give (especially by hand) 递给;传递:~ the ball 传球 ❸ succeed in an examination (考试)及格:All the students in the class ~ed the final examinations.班上所有的同学期终考试都及格了。❹ (of time) go by;spend time (时间)流逝;度过(时间):Where did you ~ the summer holidays? 你在什么地方过的暑假? Ⅱ*n.*❶ a narrow way through mountains 山路;关口 ❷ a ticket or a written permission to pass 许可证;通行证 ‖ ~ **away** 死亡;终止;消磨(时间)/

P

～ by 经过/ ～ for 被认为是/ ～ out 失去知觉;昏倒;分发/ ～ over 不注意;忽略/ ～ through 穿过;通过;经历/ ～ up 错过,放弃(机会等)

passage/'pæsɪdʒ/

n. ❶ an act of passing movement from one place to another 通过;经过:the ～ of time 时间的推移 /force a ～ through the crowd 从人群中挤过去 ❷ a voyage 航行;have a smooth ～ 航行顺利 ❸ a narrow way in a building that leads to other rooms;a corridor 通路;过道;走廊 ❹ a piece of a speech or writing 一段话;一节:a ～ from *Capital*《资本论》的一节 ❺ the passing of a bill (法案的)通过

passbook/'pɑːsbʊk/

n. a book in which a record of the money one puts into and takes out of a building society or a bank (建房互助会存款)存折;银行存折

passenger/'pæsɪndʒə(r)/

n. a person travelling in a train, bus, plane,etc. or in a car in addition to the driver 旅客;乘客

passer-by/ˌpɑːsə'baɪ/

n. a person who (by chance) is walking, driving,etc. past a place 过路人:A few passers-by saw the accident. 有几个过路人目击了那次事故。

passing/'pɑːsɪŋ/

Ⅰ *adj.* moving by;not lasting very long; going by 经过的;暂时的;逝去的:with each ～ day 日益/She watched the ～ cars.她注视着路过的汽车。 Ⅱ *n.* the act of going by 逝去;经过:the ～ of the old year 旧年的逝去

passion/'pæʃn/

n. ❶ a very strong feeling of love,anger, etc.强烈的感情;激情;热情:They always work with ～.他们总是满怀热情地工作。 ❷ an activity, sports, etc. that you like very much 酷爱,喜爱的活动(运动等): She has a ～ for music.她酷爱音乐。 ‖ ～ate *adj.*热情的;激昂的

passive/'pæsɪv/

*adj.*acted upon but not acting 消极的;被动的:～ resistance 消极抵抗/play a ～ role in a marriage 在婚姻中扮演被动的角色

passport/'pɑːspɔːt/

*n.*a document to be carried when visiting foreign countries,with details concerning oneself and showing that one has the protection of one's government 护照

password/'pɑːswɜːd/

*n.*❶a secret word or phrase used to distinguish friends from enemies 暗语;密码 ❷a word you need to gain access to certain computer files (进入计算机文件的)口令,密码

past/pɑːst/

Ⅰ *n.* ❶ the time gone by 过去;从前:in the ～ 在过去 ❷ the life in earlier time or history 往事;经历:Do you know anything about his ～? 你对他过去的情况了解吗? Ⅱ *adj.* passed;gone by 以往的; 过去的 Ⅲ *prep.* beyond in time (space, number,degree) 超过:It's a quarter ～ eight.现在是八点过一刻。

pasta /'pɑːstə/

n. an Italian food consisting of a dried paste made with flour and produced in various shapes 意大利面制品;意大利面食

paste/peɪst/

Ⅰ *n.* ❶ a mixture used for sticking two things together 糨糊:a bottle of ～ 一瓶糨糊 ❷ any soft, smooth mixture 糊状物;tooth ～ 牙膏 Ⅱ *v.*stick with paste 用糨糊粘贴:～ a stamp 贴邮票 /～ a wall with paper 用纸糊墙

pasteboard/'peɪstbɔːd/

*n.*a flat stiff cardboard made by pasting sheets of paper together 纸板

pastel/pæs'tel/

Ⅰ *n.*❶a chalk-like crayon 蜡笔 ❷a drawing made with this 蜡笔画 ❸a light delicate shade of a colour 柔和的淡色彩 Ⅱ *adj.*of a soft and delicate shade of colour 淡的;柔和的

pastime/'pɑːstaɪm/

n. anything done to pass time pleasantly

P

消遣；娱乐；游戏：She often plays the piano as a ~.她常以弹钢琴作为消遣。

pasting/ˈpeɪstɪŋ/

　*n.*❶a hard beating 痛打；毒打：You'll get a real ~ if the teacher finds out what you've done! 如果老师发现你所干的事，你会挨一顿痛打的。❷ (in sport or other sorts of competition) a severe defeat (体育或其他竞赛的)惨败

pastor/ˈpɑːstə(r)/

　*n.*a minister in charge of a church 牧师

pastoral/ˈpɑːstərəl/

　*adj.*❶ connected with a clergyman 牧师的：~ letter 牧师写给他教区人民的公开信 ❷ (literature, music, painting) having to do with shepherds and country life (文学、音乐、绘画)田园式的,牧歌式的

pastry/ˈpeɪstri/

　*n.*❶ a small cake of flour, fat, etc. baked in an oven (用面粉和油脂烤成的)点心，馅饼 ❷ an article of food made wholly or partly of this (全部或部分地用这些原料制成的)食物

pasture/ˈpɑːstʃə(r)/

　Ⅰ *n.*❶ the grass considered or used as food for cattle 牧草 ❷ grassland for cattle 牧场 Ⅱ *v.*put (farm animals) to graze 放牧：The sheep are pasturing on the mountain slope.羊群在山坡上吃草。

pasty[1]/ˈpeɪsti/

　*adj.*pale and unhealthy 苍白的；不健康的：a ~ complexion 苍白的脸色

pasty[2]/ˈpæsti/

　*n.*a pastry baked with meat in it 肉馅饼

pat/pæt/

　Ⅰ *v.*(-tt-) touch gently with the hand several times; tap lightly with the open hand 轻拍；轻打：The little boy ~ted the dog.小男孩轻轻地拍那条狗。/ I ~ted him on the shoulder.我轻轻拍了拍他的肩膀。Ⅱ *n.*a gentle blow with the open hand 轻拍；轻打：a ~ on her arm 在她手臂上轻拍了一下

patch/pætʃ/

　Ⅰ *n.*❶ a piece of cloth that you put over a hole in sth.补丁；补片；补块 ❷ a small

piece of ground 小块地 Ⅱ *v.*mend, put a patch(patches) on 补；修补：He ~ed the hole in the bicycle tyre with a small round ~ of rubber.他用一小块圆橡胶补片来修补自行车轮胎上的洞。

patchwork/ˈpætʃwɜːk/

　n.(a piece of) sewn work made by joining together a number of pieces of cloth of different colours, patterns, and shapes 缝缀而成的各色布片；补缀的手工：a ~ quilt (blanket) 百衲被(毯子) /From the aircraft we could see a ~ of fields of different shapes and colours.从飞机上我们能看见由不同形状和颜色田野拼缀而成的图案。

patchy/ˈpætʃi/

　*adj.*❶made up of or appearing in patches 斑驳的：The sun has faded the curtains so the colours are rather ~.窗帘被阳光晒得褪了色,显得斑斑驳驳。/There will be ~ fog at dawn.拂晓将有零星薄雾。❷ incomplete 不完整的：My knowledge of science is ~.我对科学的了解不是很全面。❸only good in parts 只有部分好的：The concert was ~.这场音乐会只有一部分很出彩。

pate/peɪt/

　*n.*the top of the head 头顶：his bald ~ 他的秃头顶

patent

　Ⅰ *n.*/ˈpætnt/❶ an authority from the government to manufacture sth. and also to prevent it from being imitated 专利；专利权：get a ~ for a new kind of car 获得一种新型汽车的专利 ❷ sth. that is protected by a patent 专利品 ‖ ~ **leather** *n.*漆皮 Ⅱ *v.*/ˈpeɪtnt/get a patent for 获得……的专利：He ~ed his invention.他获得了他的发明专利。Ⅲ *adj.*/ˈpeɪtnt/❶ plain; easily seen 明白的；显而易见的：It is ~ that a country must educate her people to make progress.显而易见,一个国家必须教育她的人民追求进步。❷ protected by a patent 专利的：~ medicines 专利药品 ‖ ~**ly** *adv.*毫无疑问；显然：He is ~ly a fool.他显然是个笨蛋。

paternal/pəˈtɜːnl/

adj. ❶ of (like) father 父亲(似)的：~ love 父爱 ❷ related through the father's side 父方的：my ~ grandmother 我的祖母

path/pɑːθ/

n. ❶ a narrow way made by the passing of people or animals 小径；小路：a ~ in the park 公园里的小路 ❷ a way along which an object moves 运行路线：The moon has a regular ~ round the earth. 月球绕地球运行有一定的轨道。‖ set sb.on the right ~ 使某人走上正路/break（blaze）a new ~ 开辟新路 ‖ ~-breaker *n.* 开拓者；闯将/~way *n.* 路径；途径

pathetic/pəˈθetɪk/

adj. ❶ sad; pitiful 可怜的；悲哀的：This was a ~ scene. 这是一个悲惨场面。❷ weak; not successful 无力的；不成功的：a ~ attempt 徒劳的尝试

patience/ˈpeɪʃns/

n. the capacity to accept or tolerate delay, trouble, or suffering without getting angry or upset 容忍；忍耐；耐心；耐性；忍耐力：I haven't the ~ to hear your complaints again. 我没有耐心再听你的抱怨。/I have no ~ with people who are always grumbling. 我不能容忍那些常发牢骚的人。

patient/ˈpeɪʃnt/

Ⅰ *n.* a sick person who is being treated by a doctor 病人；患者：Any doctor will say some words to please his ~s. 任何大夫都会说些话来安慰患者。Ⅱ *adj.* having or showing patience 耐心的；容忍的：be ~ with...对……有耐心 / be ~ of sufferings 忍受痛苦

patio/ˈpætɪəʊ/

n. an open courtyard within a house; an open part outside a house (usually paved and used for dining, etc.) 房子中的内院；(常用作就餐等的地方)房子外的凉台

patriarch/ˈpeɪtrɪɑːk/

n. ❶ the father and ruler of a family or tribe 家长；族长 ❷ a man of great age and dignity; a founder 元老；创始人 ❸ (in Eastern Churches) the bishop of the highest honour (东正教中的)大主教

patriot/ˈpætrɪət/

n. a person who loves and loyally defends his country 爱国者；爱国主义者：He is a true ~. 他是位真正的爱国主义者。‖ ~ism *n.* 爱国主义；爱国心

patriotic/ˌpætrɪˈɒtɪk/

adj. having or expressing the qualities of a patriot 爱国的：Mr. Liu is a ~ overseas Chinese. 刘先生是一位爱国华侨。

patrol/pəˈtrəʊl/

Ⅰ *v.* walk or ride around an area with the purpose of guarding it 巡查；巡视：Some soldiers are ~ling the streets. 一些士兵在街上巡逻。Ⅱ *n.* ❶ an act of making sure a place is safe 巡逻 ❷ a person or a group of person, ships or airplanes on patrol duties 巡逻兵；巡逻队

patron/ˈpeɪtrən/

n. ❶ a person who supports a person with money or encouragement 资助人 ❷ a famous or important person who takes an honorary position in a charity (慈善事业的)赞助人 ❸ a regular customer of a restaurant, hotel, shop, etc. (饭店、商店或商店等的)老主顾

patronage/ˈpætrənɪdʒ/

n. ❶ the support, encouragement from sb. 支持；赞助；资助 ❷ a customer's support (顾客的)光顾，惠顾 ❸ the manner of treating sb. as if he were an inferior person 恩赐的态度：the air of ~ 施恩于人的那副神态

patronize/ˈpætrənaɪz/

v. ❶ buy regularly at a shop 光顾：I always ~ this shop. 我常常光顾这家商店。❷ treat sb. in a friendly way while showing one thinks he is lower than oneself 屈尊俯就：The rich man ~d his poor friends. 这富人对他的穷朋友屈尊俯就。

patter[1] /ˈpætə(r)/

Ⅰ *n.* a sound of a series of quick, light blows or steps 急速的轻拍声：the ~ of rain on a roof top 屋顶上淅沥的雨声 Ⅱ *v.* make this sound 啪嗒啪嗒地响

patter² /'pætə(r)/

n. a quick and clever way of talking 急口词；不间断说话

pattern /'pætn/

n. ❶ an excellent example 模范；典型：He is a ~ of the selfless spirit. 他是大公无私精神的典范。 ❷ a model, style or design 模型；式样：sentence ~s 句型 ❸ a regular decorative design on cloth, material, carpets, etc. 图案；图样

paunch /pɔːntʃ/

n. a fat stomach on a man（男人的）大肚子，啤酒肚

pause /pɔːz/

Ⅰ *n.* a short period of stopping doing sth. 暂停；中止：He made a ~ and then went on reading. 他略停了一下，然后又继续读下去。 Ⅱ *v.* stop for a time 暂停；中止；停留：He ~d and looked about. 他停下来朝四周看看。

pave /peɪv/

v. cover（street, sidewalk）with stones, bricks, etc.（用石块、砖头等）铺砌（道路等）：~ a path with sand and cobbles 用沙子和圆石子铺路 ‖ ~ **the way for** 为……铺平道路

pavement /'peɪvmənt/

n. a path at the side of a road for people to walk on（马路边的）人行道

pavilion /pə'vɪlɪən/

n. ❶ a building at the side of a sports ground for the use of players and spectators 看台 ❷ a decorated building for concerts, dancing, etc.（舞会、音乐会等的）华美建筑

paving /'peɪvɪŋ/

n. ❶ the material used to pave a surface 铺筑材料；铺面材料 ❷ a paved surface of any sort 铺过的道路 ❸ a piece of paving stone 铺路石

paw /pɔː/

Ⅰ *n.* foot that has claws 脚爪；爪子：Cats and dogs have ~s. 猫和狗都有爪子。 Ⅱ *v.* ❶（of animals）scratch with the paws（动物）用脚爪抓（扒）：He was ~ed by a cat. 他被猫抓了一下。/ The horses ~ed

the dust of the street. 马群踢起了街上的尘土。 ❷（of persons）touch with the hands awkwardly（人）用手笨拙地摸：The little girl doesn't like being ~ed about. 这个小姑娘不喜欢被人乱摸。

pawn¹ /pɔːn/

n. one of the persons or things that are least important; a piece of the smallest size and value in chess 无足轻重的人或物；卒（国际象棋中最不重要的棋子）

pawn² /pɔːn/

v. get money by leaving sth. of value（e.g. jewellery, clothes）which will be returned to one only when the money is paid back 典当；抵押

pay /peɪ/

Ⅰ *v.*（paid）❶ give money to sb. in exchange for goods that one has bought, services that have been provided, or work that has been done 付钱；付款：I've paid for the goods. 我已付了货款。 ❷ distribute wages 发工钱；付酬：The workers are paid at the end of the month. 工人月底发工资。 ❸ give（money that is owed）; settle（a bill, debt, etc.）付债；还钱：~ a debt 还债 ‖ ~ **a call**（**visit**）**to** 访问；拜访/~ **a compliment to** 恭维；赞扬/~ **attention**（**heed**）**to** 注意（倾听）/~ **back** 偿还；报复/~ **down** 付头款/~ **for** 为……付钱，付出代价/~ **lip service to** 口头支持/~ **off** 付清/~ **one's respects to** 向……表示敬意/~ **out** 付款；报复/**through the nose** 付出高昂代价/~ **up** 付清 Ⅱ *n.* the money received in exchange for work 工钱；工资；薪水 ‖ ~**check**, ~**cheque** *n.* 薪水支票；薪金；工资/~**day** *n.* 发薪日/~**roll** *n.* 薪水册；工资单 ‖ ~**ee** /peɪ'iː/ *n.* 受款人；收款人/~**er** *n.* 付款人

payable /'peɪəbl/

adj. ❶ needing to be paid 需支付的 ❷ able to be paid 可支付的；能支付的

payment /'peɪmənt/

n. ❶ the action or process of paying sb. or sth. or of being paid 支付；付款 ❷ the money given in return for work, goods, or services 报酬；报偿；酬劳

pea /piː/

*n.*a plant with seeds in pods, used for food 豌豆：I bought some fresh ～s.我买了一些新鲜豌豆。‖ **as alike as two ～s, two ～s in a pod** 一模一样

peace/piːs/

*n.*the state of freedom from war and disturbance 和平；安宁；太平；宁静：the world ～世界和平/I want ～.我需要安静。‖ **at ～** 处于和平（和睦、平服）状态/**keep（hold）one's ～** 保持缄默/**keep the ～** 维持治安/**make one's ～ with** 同……解决纷争；言归于好/**make ～ with** 与……谈和 ‖ **～breaker** *n.*破坏和平者/**～-loving** *adj.*爱好和平的

peaceful/'piːsfl/

*adj.*❶ calm and quiet 安详的；宁静的：spend a ～ day in the garden 在花园里度过平静的一天 ❷ liking peace 爱好和平的：～ nations 爱好和平的国家

peacemaker/'piːsˌmeɪkə(r)/

*n.*a person who restores friendly relations 调停人；和事佬

peach/piːtʃ/

*n.*❶ a round fruit with yellowish-red skin and a rough stone-like seed 桃子；桃树 ❷ the color of the skin of this fruit；yellowish-red 桃色；桃红色

peacock/'piːkɒk/

*n.*a large bird with beautiful green, blue and gold feathers 雄孔雀

peak/piːk/

Ⅰ *n.*❶ the top of a hill or a mountain 山顶；山峰：The mountain ～ was covered with snow. 山顶覆盖着白雪。❷ the pointed front part of a cap 帽檐；帽的鸭舌 ❸ the highest point or level of an amount, rate, etc.高峰；最高点 Ⅱ *v.*come to the highest point 达到高峰

peaked/piːkt/

*adj.*having a peak 有帽檐的：a ～ cap 有帽檐的帽子

peaky/'piːki/

*adj.*rather pale or ill；uncomfortable 有病容的；苍白的；不舒服的：I'm feeling a bit ～ this morning.今天上午我感觉有点不舒服。/ She's been looking rather ～

lately.她最近显得有点憔悴。

peal/piːl/

Ⅰ *n.*❶ a loud and continuous sound 响亮而持久的声音：～s of laughter 一阵哄笑 ❷ the ringing of bells 铃声；钟声 Ⅱ *v.*sound or cause to sound loudly；ring 使响；使鸣；鸣

peanut/'piːnʌt/

*n.*a nut that grows underground in a thin shell 花生

pear/peə(r)/

*n.*a sweet juicy fruit, narrow at the stem end and wide at the other 梨：Do you prefer ～s or apples? 你喜欢吃梨还是吃苹果？

pearl/pɜːl/

*n.*❶ a smooth, round, hard ball formed inside some oysters 珍珠 ❷ the color of this；silvery-white 珍珠色；银白色 ❸ sth. or sb. very precious 珍品；杰出的人：She is a ～ among women.她是妇女中的杰出者。

peasant/'peznt/

*n.*a farmer who owns and lives on a small piece of land 农民；小农：workers and ～s 工人和农民

peasantry/'pezntri/

*n.*all the peasants of a particular country （某国家的）农民（总称）

pebble/'pebl/

*n.*a small, roundish smooth stone 卵石；小圆石：There are many ～s on the seashore.海边有许多卵石。

peck/pek/

*v.*strike sth. with the beak 啄：The woodpecker ～ed a hole in the tree.啄木鸟在树上啄了一个洞。

peculate/'pekjʊleɪt/

*v.*take money（for which one is responsible, e.g. because of one's job）and use it for one's own purposes 挪用，盗用（公款）

peculiar/pɪ'kjuːlɪə(r)/

*adj.*odd, strange or unusual, especially in a way that is unpleasant 奇异的；罕见的；不寻常的：He was a ～ man.他是古怪的人。‖ **～ity**/pɪˌkjuːlɪ'ærəti/ *n.*特征，特

点;怪癖;奇异的事物

pedagogy/'pedəɡɒdʒi/

*n.*the practice of teaching or the study of teaching methods 教学法;教育学

pedal/'pedl/

Ⅰ*n.*a bar-like part of a machine which can be pressed with the foot in order to control the working of the machine or to drive it 踏板;脚蹬:the ～ of a bicycle 自行车的踏脚板 Ⅱ*v.*work the pedals of 用脚踩踏板;蹬:He ～led the bicycle up the hill.他踩着自行车上山。

pedant/'pednt/

*n.*a person who pays too much attention to small details and unimportant rules 拘泥于细节和不重要的规则的人;学究;迂夫子 ‖ ～ic *adj.*迂腐的;学究气的

pedantry/'pedntri/

*n.*❶the quality of being a pedant 迂腐 ❷a pedantic expression or action 呆板的话语或行为

peddle/'pedl/

*v.*go from house to house trying to sell small articles 沿街叫卖

peddler/'pedlə(r)/

*n.*❶a person who sells dangerous or illegal drugs 贩卖危险或非法药品的人;毒品贩子 ❷a pedlar 小贩

pedestal/'pedɪstl/

*n.*the base(raised piece of stone, etc.) on which a column or statue stands;the base of a lamp, tall vase, etc.基座;灯座;大花瓶底座

pedestrian/pə'destriən/

Ⅰ*n.*a person who goes on foot along roads or streets;a walker 步行者;行人 Ⅱ*adj.*❶connected with walking;for pedestrians 徒步的;行人使用的 ❷dull;without imagination;uninspired 乏味的;缺乏想象力的;没趣的:a ～ novel 一部枯燥无味的小说 ‖ ～ crossing 人行横道

pedigree/'pedɪɡriː/

*n.*the recorded history of a person or family 家谱;系谱

pedlar/'pedlə(r)/

*n.*a person who goes from place to place

trying to sell small articles 流动小贩;货郎

pee /piː/

Ⅰ*v.*pass waste liquid from your body 撒尿;小便 Ⅱ*n.*an act of urinating 撒尿;小便

peek/piːk/

Ⅰ*n.*a quick or secret look 匆忙看过;偷看 Ⅱ*v.*look quickly or secretly 偷看:～ at the girl over there 偷看那边的小女孩

peel/piːl/

Ⅰ*n.*the skin of fruits or vegetables （水果或蔬菜的）皮:orange ～ 橘皮 Ⅱ*v.*take the skin off 削皮;剥皮:～ a banana 剥香蕉皮 ‖ ～ing *n.*果皮;剥下来的皮

peep/piːp/

Ⅰ*v.*❶ look at secretly and quickly;look through a crack 偷看;窥视:He ～ed at the answer at the back of the book.他偷看了书后的答案。 ❷ come gradually into view;appear partly 显露出来;隐约可见 Ⅱ*n.*a quick, incomplete, or secret look 一瞥;偷看

peer/pɪə(r)/

Ⅰ*v.*look at carefully;stare at 凝视;盯着看:She ～ed through the mist, trying to find the right path.她在雾中仔细张望,设法寻找该走的路径。 Ⅱ*n.*❶ a person of the same age, social status, ability as another person 同龄人;（身份或地位）相同的人 ❷a member of the nobility in Britain or Ireland, comprising the ranks of duke, marquess, earl, viscount, and baron（英国或爱尔兰）有爵位的贵族

peerage/'pɪərɪdʒ/

*n.*❶ the rank of a peer 贵族爵位:After ten years in the government she was given a ～.她在政府工作十年后,被授予贵族爵位。 ❷ all the peers, considered as a group 贵族的总称 ❸ a book containing a list of peers and the families from which they are descended 贵族名册

peeress/'pɪərɪs/

*n.*❶a female peer 女贵族 ❷ the wife of a peer 贵族夫人

peerless/'pɪələs/

adj. without an equal; better than any other 无比的；绝世的：～ beauty 绝代佳人

peevish/'pi:vɪʃ/
adj. easily annoyed; always complaining 易怒的；爱抱怨的 ‖ ～**ness** *n*. 爱发牢骚

peg/peg/
n. a short piece of wood, metal, etc. used for fastening things, hanging things on, etc. 木钉；木栓；金属钉：a hat ～ 挂帽钩

Pekinese/ˌpi:kɪ'ni:z/
n. a type of small dog with long hair and a flat face 哈巴狗；小狮子狗

pellet/'pelɪt/
n. ❶ a little ball made from sth. soft (e.g. mud or bread) 软物做成的小丸，小球（例如：泥球、面包球）❷ a little ball of lead to be fired from a gun 小弹丸

pelt[1] /pelt/
v. ❶ attack by throwing things at 投掷：The crowd ～ed him with stones. 人群向他掷石头。❷ (with reference to rain, hail, etc.) come down heavily (雨、冰雹等) 猛降：The rain is ～ing down. 雨下得很大。

pelt[2] /pelt/
n. the skin of an animal with the fur still on it 毛皮

pen[1] /pen/
n. a tool used for writing with ink 钢笔：I write with a ～. 我用钢笔写字。‖ ～**craft** *n*. 书法；笔法；写作／～**holder** *n*. 笔杆；笔架／～**knife** *n*. 铅笔刀；小刀

pen[2] /pen/
n. a small yard or enclosure for cattle, etc. (牛等的)圈，栏：a sheep ～ 羊圈

penalty/'penlti/
n. ❶ a punishment for breaking a rule or a law; sth. that is ordered as a punishment 刑罚；处罚；惩罚：under (on) ～ of 违者受……处罚／Fishing in this river is forbidden, and the ～ is $25. 此河禁止钓鱼，违者罚款 25 美元。❷ a disadvantage suffered by a player for breaking a rule 犯规处罚；罚球

penance/'penəns/

n. a punishment which one gives to oneself (often on the advice of a priest) because of some wrong things that one has done 自我惩罚；苦行：do ～ for one's sins 对罪过的自我惩罚

pencil/'pensl/
Ⅰ *n*. a writing instrument made of wood with graphite in it which marks the paper 铅笔：The little boy bought a dozen ～s. 这小男孩买了一打铅笔。Ⅱ *v*. write or draw with a pencil 用铅笔写(或画)：He ～ed a house. 他用铅笔画了一幢房子。

pendant/'pendənt/
n. a hanging ornament (e.g. sth. hanging from a necklace, etc.) 垂环；垂饰

pending/'pendɪŋ/
Ⅰ *adj*. waiting to be decided or settled 未决定的；待解决的：Your case is still ～. 你的事仍未决定。Ⅱ *prep*. until sth. happens 直到；在……之前：～ the judge's decision 在法官决定之前

pendulum/'pendjʊləm/
n. a weighted rod hung from a fixed point so that it swings freely, especially one to regulate the movement of a clock 钟摆：The ～ of the clock stopped moving. 这钟摆停止了摆动。

penetrate/'penɪtreɪt/
v. make a way into or through sth. 刺入；穿过；渗透：A bullet can ～ a wall. 子弹能穿过墙壁。

penetrating/'penɪtreɪtɪŋ/
adj. ❶ able to make a way into or through sth. 有穿透力的；有渗透力的 ❷ (of a voice or sound) loud, clearly heard above or through other sounds (话音或声音)响亮的，尖锐的

penetration/ˌpenɪ'treɪʃn/
n. the act or process of making a way into or through sth. 穿透；渗透；进入

penguin/'peŋgwɪn/
n. a seabird of the Antarctic with wings used for swimming 企鹅

penicillin/ˌpenɪ'sɪlɪn/
n. a substance used as a medicine to destroy certain bacteria in people and ani-

mals 盘尼西林,青霉素:Penicillin can kill germs.青霉素能杀死细菌。

peninsula/pɪˈnɪnsjʊlə/
n. an area of land almost surrounded on three sides by water 半岛: the Italian Peninsula 意大利半岛

penis/ˈpiːnɪs/
n. the male sex organ 阴茎

pennant/ˈpenənt/
n. a long,narrow flag (usually like a triangle in shape) to give signals (常呈三角形的)信号旗,小旗

penny/ˈpeni/
n. a British bronze coin and monetary unit equal to one hundredth of a pound 便士 (英国铜硬币和货币单位,100 便士等于 1 英镑) ‖ **penniless** *adj.* 不名一文的

pension/ˈpenʃn/
n. an amount of money paid to an officer or a worker who has completed his service,from the time he gives up work to his death 养老金;退休金;抚恤金: live on a ～ 靠养老金生活 /receive a ～ 领取养老金

pensive/ˈpensɪv/
adj. deep in thought;anxious 沉思的;焦虑的:look rather ～ 显得比较焦虑

pentagon/ˈpentəgən/
n. a figure with five sides and five angles 五角形

penthouse/ˈpenthaʊs/
n. ❶ an apartment or house on the top of a building 阁楼:luxury ～ 豪华的阁楼 ❷ a kind of hut built against a wall with its roof sloping down from the wall 遮檐;披屋

pent-up/ˌpentˈʌp/
adj. shut-in;not released 关闭的;压抑的:～ emotions 压抑的情绪

people/ˈpiːpl/
n. ❶ persons in general;the citizens of a country,especially when considered in relation to those who govern them 人(们),人类;人民,国民;民众:the broad masses of the ～ 广大人民群众 ❷ all the persons in a society, especially those common ones 平民;百姓:～ of all walks of life 各行各业的人 ❸ race;nation 种族;民族:a great ～ 一个伟大的民族 /the ～s of Asia 亚洲各民族(各国人) ❹ one's family;one's near relations 家人;亲属: Please come home with me and meet my ～.请跟我一起回家见见我的家人。

pepper/ˈpepə(r)/
Ⅰ *n.* a powder made from the crushed seeds of certain plants and used to give food a hot taste 胡椒粉:Please add some ～ to the dish.请给这个菜加些胡椒粉。
Ⅱ *v.* put pepper on food(在食物上)撒胡椒粉于:We often ～ a stew.我们常常在炖菜上撒胡椒粉。

peptic/ˈpeptɪk/
Ⅰ *adj.* ❶ digestive; promoting digestion 消化的;助消化的 ❷ of or relating to pepsin 胃液的 Ⅱ *n.* a substance promoting digestion 消化剂

per/pɜː(r), pə(r)/
prep. for each 每:We work eight hours ～ day.我们每天工作八小时。

per capita/pə ˈkæpɪtə/
adv. & *adj.* for each person;in relation to people taken individually 每人(的);按人计算地(的):The city has fewer parks ～ than elsewhere.按人头计算,这个城市拥有的公园数要比其他地方少。

perceive/pəˈsiːv/
v. have or come to have knowledge of sth. through one of the senses or through the mind 察觉;看出;领悟;理解:Can't you ～ this obvious truth? 这个明显的道理难道你还看不出吗? /I ～d that he failed to grasp the meaning of my words.我觉得他并没有明白我的意思。

percent/pəˈsent/
n. one part in every hundred 百分之……: Thirty ～ of the students in our class are League members.我们班百分之三十的学生是共青团员。

percentage/pəˈsentɪdʒ/
n. ❶ an amount or rate in each hundred 百分比;百分率:The higher the income,the larger is the ～ saved.收入越高,储蓄的

百分率就越大。❷ proportion 部分：a large ～ of the earth surface 地球表面的大部分

perceptible/pə'septəbl/

*adj.*that can be perceived or noticed 可感觉到的；可看见的：a barely ～ difference 几乎察觉不出的差别

perception/pə'sepʃn/

*n.*❶ the ability to perceive 洞察力：keen ～ 敏锐的洞察力 ❷ an act of being aware of sth.感觉：sense ～ 感觉

perceptive/pə'septɪv/

*adj.*having or connected with perception 有知觉的；与感觉有关的；有理解力的；有悟性的：This is a good ～ article.这是一篇富有洞察力的好文章。

perch/pɜːtʃ/

Ⅰ *n.*a bar, branch or anything on which a bird can rest (禽鸟的)栖木；栖息地 Ⅱ *v.* fly down and rest on sth.栖息；停歇：The birds ～ed upon the television aerial.鸟栖息在电视天线上。

percipient/pə'sɪpɪənt/

*adj.*quick to notice and understand 洞察力强的

percolate/'pɜːkəleɪt/

*v.*❶ pass slowly through a material that has small holes in it 滤出；渗透：The water gradually ～d down through the rock.水渐渐从岩石中渗漏下来。/News from the war eventually ～d through to us.战争的消息终于慢慢地传到我们这里。❷ (of coffee) be prepared in a percolator (咖啡)(在渗滤式咖啡壶中)滤煮

perennial/pə'renɪəl/

Ⅰ *adj* ❶ lasting for a very long time 永久的；不断的；长久的：a ～ source of pleasure 永久的快乐源泉 ❷ (with reference to flowers, etc.) lasting more than two years (指花等)多年生的 Ⅱ *n.*a perennial plant 多年生植物

perfect

Ⅰ /'pɜːfɪkt/*adj.* excellent; having no faults; completely correct 完美的；极好的；无瑕的：The weather here is ～.这里的天气十分好。Ⅱ /pə'fekt/ *v.*make per-fect 使完美；使完善

perfection/pə'fekʃn/

*n.*❶ the best possible state 完美；十全十美：bring a work to ～ 把工作做得尽善尽美 /attain (arrive at, reach, achieve) ～ 达到完美程度 /It makes ～ more perfect.这是锦上添花。❷ being perfected 完成：the ～ of the plan 这项计划的完成 ❸ a perfect example 完美的典型：As an actress, she is ～ itself.就一个女演员来说，她是完美的化身。

perfectly/'pɜːfɪktli/

*adv.*❶ extremely well 极好地；完美地：Janet sings ～.珍妮特唱得好极了。❷ totally 完全地；全然：He is ～ happy in his new job.他对他的新工作非常满意。

perforate/'pɜːfəreɪt/

*v.*make a hole or holes through(especially through a piece of paper so that it can easily be torn off) 打洞，穿孔(尤指在纸上打洞，便于撕开)

perforation/ˌpɜːfə'reɪʃn/

*n.*❶ a hole made in sth. 孔 ❷ a line of holes made on paper (e.g. on a sheet of stamps so that each stamp can be easily torn off) 排孔；接缝孔(例如：邮票上的接缝孔，便于撕开)

perform/pə'fɔːm/

v. ❶ act, play, sing or dance, etc. before the audience 表演；演出：He ～ed a part in the play. 他在戏中扮演了一个角色。❷ do; carry out; accomplish 做；执行；完成：～ an operation on sb. 给某人做手术 ❸ work well or badly 运转(好、不好)

performance/pə'fɔːməns/

*n.*❶ the action or process of carrying out an action, task or function 履行；执行：～ of one's duties 履行义务 ❷ result; score 成绩 ❸ (of machines) the ability to do sth.(机器)性能：the car's ～ on corners 汽车拐弯的性能 ❹ an act of presenting a play, concert, etc.表演；演奏：give (see) an acrobatic ～ 表演(观看)杂技 /two ～s a day 一天两场演出

performer/pə'fɔːmə(r)/

*n.*a person who performs, especially an

actor, a musician, etc. 表演者 (尤指演员、音乐家等): The audience bored some of the ~s. 观众对某些演员喝了倒彩。/He's their star ~. 他是他们的明星演员。

perfume /'pɜːfjuːm/
I n. ❶ a sweet smell 香气;香味;芳香: the ~ of flowers 花朵的香味 ❷ a liquid having the sweet or pleasant smell of flowers 香水;香料: sell ~s 出售香水 II v. ❶ (of flowers, etc.) give a fragrant smell to (sth.) (指花) 散发香味;使有香气: The roses ~d the room. 玫瑰花使房间散发香味。 ❷ put perfume on (sb. or sth.) 洒香水于: ~ a handkerchief 往手帕上洒香水

perfunctory /pə'fʌŋktəri/
adj. ❶ done carelessly and without real interest 草率的;敷衍的: give someone only a ~ glance 对某人不屑一顾 ❷ acting in a careless, uninterested manner 行为草率的;不关心的

perhaps /pə'hæps, præps/
adv. probably; possibly 大概;可能;也许: Perhaps you could get better results in this way. 这样做效果可能更好一点。

peril /'perəl/
n. ❶ serious danger (严重的) 危险: He was in ~ of death. 他面临死亡的危险。 ❷ sth. that causes danger 危险的事物: lessen the ~s of the streets 减少街道上的险情

perilous /'periləs/
adj. full of risk or danger 充满危险的 ‖ ~ly adv. 危机四伏地;充满危险地

perimeter /pə'rimitə(r)/
n. ❶ the outside boundary of a surface or figure 边缘 ❷ the length of such a boundary 周长

period /'piəriəd/
n. ❶ a length of time with a beginning and an end 时期;一段时间: She has had several long ~s of work aborad. 她在国外长期工作过几次。 ❷ one of the set divisions of the day in a school allocated to a lesson or other activities 学时;课时 ‖ put a ~ to 结束

periodic /ˌpiəri'ɒdik/
adj. occurring or appearing at regular intervals 定期的;周期的: ~ elections of public officers 官员的定期选举

periodical /ˌpiəri'ɒdikl/
I adj. ❶ happening, appearing again and again at regular times 周期的;定期的 ❷ published at regular times 定期出版(发行)的: the ~ publications 期刊 II n. a magazine, newspaper, etc. published at regular times 期刊;杂志: a monthly ~ 月刊 /a weekly ~ 周刊

perish /'periʃ/
v. ❶ destroy completely 毁坏 ❷ die, especially in a sudden violent way 死亡;暴死: Several people ~ed in the fire. 有几个人在这次大火中丧生。 ‖ ~able adj. 容易腐烂的

perjury /'pɜːdʒəri/
n. an act of swearing on an oath (usually in a court of law) that sth. is true when it is not (通常用于法院) 伪证;伪证罪

perk /pɜːk/
v. (always with up) ❶ become lively and gay (after being depressed or ill, etc.) (常与 up 连用) (病后或沮丧之后等) 快活起来,振作起来: The child soon ~ed up when he saw his mother. 孩子看到他母亲时精神马上振作起来。 ❷ raise quickly 竖起: The dog ~ed up its ears. 狗竖起了它的耳朵。 ‖ ~y adj. 活泼的;伶俐的

permanent /'pɜːmənənt/
adj. never changing; lasting for a long time 永久的;持久的: a ~ committee 常设委员会/ a ~ magnet 永久磁铁/ I have a ~ job here. 我在这里有份固定的工作。

permeate /'pɜːmieit/
v. spread through; pass through 渗透;弥漫: Water ~s the soil. 水渗入泥土中。 ‖ **permeable** adj. 有渗透性的;可渗透的

permissible /pə'misəbl/
adj. allowable or permitted according to laws or rules 容许的;许可的;可准许的 ‖ **permissibly** adv. 获准地;得到许可地

permission /pə'miʃ(ə)n/

n. the right to do sth., given by someone in authority 同意;许可;准许: They had entered the nature reserve area without ～. 他们未经许可就进入了那个自然保护区。

permit /pə'mɪt/

Ⅰ *v*. (-tt-) allow sb. to do sth. 准许;允许: Smoking is not ～ted here. 不准吸烟。 Ⅱ *n*. a formal written order giving permission to do sth.;a license 许可证;执照

perpetual /pə'petʃuəl/

adj. ❶ lasting forever or for a long time 永恒的;永久的;持久的: ～ motion 恒动;永动 /the ～ snow on the mountain 山上的终年积雪 ❷ happening often or uninterruptedly 不间断的: I'm tired of her ～ complaints. 我厌烦了她那没完没了的抱怨.

perplex /pə'pleks/

v. puzzle;cause to feel confused 困惑;使迷惑不解: The problem even ～ed the teacher. 这个问题甚至难倒了老师。 ‖ ～ity *n*. 困惑;茫然

persecute /'pɜːsɪkjuːt/

v. ❶ cause to suffer, usually for religious or political beliefs (因政治、宗教信仰不同) 迫害: He was ～d by the reactionary government. 他受到反动政府的迫害。 ❷ annoy sb. persistently 烦扰;困扰: ～ someone with questions 以提问题来为难某人 /We ～d him with questions. 我们给他出了一些难题。

persecution /ˌpɜːsɪ'kjuːʃn/

n. the act of persecuting or being persecuted 迫害;残害: They suffered serious ～ ten years ago. 十年前他们遭受了严重的迫害。

perseverance /ˌpɜːsɪ'vɪərəns/

n. the quality of doing constant effort to achieve sth. 坚持;毅力;坚韧不拔: By ～ the crippled boy learned how to swim. 依靠毅力,那跛腿男孩学会了游泳。

persevere /ˌpɜːsɪ'vɪə(r)/

v. continue firmly in spite of difficulties 坚持;不屈不挠: ～ in one's efforts 坚持努力 /～ with one's task 百折不挠地进行

工作 /～ to an end 坚持到底

persist /pə'sɪst/

v. continue firmly;refuse to stop or be changed 坚持;固执;持续: He ～ed in his belief. 他坚持自己的信念。

persistence /pə'sɪstəns/

n. the state of continuing firm or obstinate attempt in a course of action in spite of difficulty or opposition 坚持不懈;执意

persistent /pə'sɪstənt/

adj. continuing firmly or obstinately in a course of action in spite of difficulty or opposition 坚持不懈的;执意的

person /'pɜːsn/

n. ❶ a human regarded as an individual 人;个人 ❷ a human, especially one who is not identified 人;某人: Some ～s are waiting to see you. 一些人等着要见你。 ‖ in ～ 亲自;身体上;外貌上 /in the ～ of 以……的身份;代表……

personage /'pɜːsənɪdʒ/

n. an important or distinguished person 要人;大人物

personal /'pɜːsənl/

adj. ❶ private;of a single person 私人的;个人的: a ～ letter 私人信件 /～ needs 个人需要 ❷ done in person;directly by oneself 亲自的;亲身的: a ～ call 亲自访问 /～ service 亲自服务 ❸ of the body or appearance 身体的;容貌的: ～ beauty 形体美 /～ cleanliness 身体的清洁 ❹ (of remarks) directed against a particular person 人身的;针对个人的: make ～ abuse 进行人身攻击 ❺ showing the person 人称的: a ～ pronoun 人称代词

personality /ˌpɜːsə'næləti/

n. ❶ a famous person, especially in sport or entertainment(尤指体育或娱乐界的)名人 ❷ the qualities of a person which make him different from others 个性;性格;人格: I like a woman with a strong ～. 我喜欢个性鲜明的女人。

personally /'pɜːsənəli/

adv. ❶ in person, not through someone else 亲自;本人直接地: The chairman showed us round ～. 主席亲自带我们参

观。❷as a person;in a personal capacity 作为个人 ❸from one's personal standpoint or according to their particular nature;in a subjective way 从个人立场;从个人本性;主观地:Don't take it ~.不要主观地看问题。❹as regards yourself 就个人而言;就本人而言:Personally, I like it.就我个人而言,我喜欢它。

personify /pə(:)'sɒnɪfaɪ/
v.(-ies,personified,~ing) ❶ represent an idea in human form or a thing as having human characteristics 把……人格化;把……拟人化:In this book the bird is personified.在这本书中鸟儿被拟人化了。❷embody a quality in your life or behaviour (生活或行为的)体现 ‖ **personification** n.人格化;化身;拟人法;象征

personnel /ˌpɜːsə'nel/
n.❶staff;all the people employed in any business service or public institution 全体人员;职员;员工:engineering and technical ~ 工程技术人员 ❷the department in a company that deals with (the complaints and difficulties of) these people 人事部:the ~ department 人事部

perspective /pə'spektɪv/
n.❶the art of picturing objects on a flat surface so as to give the appearance of their relative height, width, depth, distance,etc.透视画法;透视:We had a lesson in drawing class on ~.在绘画课上,我们学过透视画法。❷ a picture in perspective 透视画;透视图 ❸ a view 景色;远景 ❹a point of view 观点;看法:a distorted ~ of the nation's history 对国家历史的歪曲看法

perspiration /ˌpɜːspə'reɪʃən/
n.❶the process of sweating 出汗 ❷drops of sweat 汗(珠)

perspire /pə'spaɪə(r)/
v.(used more of human beings than animals) sweat (多用于指人)流汗

persuade /pə'sweɪd/
v.cause to do sth. by reasoning, arguing, etc.说服;劝服:I ~d him not to go.我劝他不要去。‖ **persuasive** adj.有说服力

的;令人信服的

pertain /pə'teɪn/
v.belong to; have connection with 属于;关于;有关:the enthusiasm ~ing to youth 属于年轻人的热情 /The letter does not ~ to politics.这封信与政治无关。

pertinent /'pɜːtɪnənt/
adj.having to do directly with what is being discussed,etc.;very suitable 有关的;中肯的;恰当的:a ~ question 有关的问题

pervade /pə'veɪd/
v.spread through; get into every part of 遍及;弥漫:An unpleasant smell ~s the house.整个房子弥漫着一股难闻的气味。

perverse /pə'vɜːs/
adj.❶ refusing to do what is right or what one is told 任性的;固执的:a ~ child 任性的孩子 ❷ deliberately wrong; unnatural 错误的;荒谬的;反常的:~ behaviour 反常的行为 / ~ beliefs 荒谬的信仰 ‖ ~ly adj.倔强地

perversion /pə'vɜːʃn/
n.the alteration of sth. from its original course, meaning, or state to a distortion or corruption of what was first intended 错乱;反常;歪曲;曲解;误用;颠倒

pervert
Ⅰ /pə'vɜːt/ v.❶ turn sb.or sth. away from what is right and normal 使堕落;引入邪路,使变坏:He was ~ed by his evil companions.他被他的坏伙伴引入邪路。❷ use sth. for a bad purpose 滥用:He was accused of ~ing the law.他被控告滥用法律。Ⅱ /'pɜːvɜːt/ n.a perverted person (especially one with a sexual perversion) 行为反常的人(尤指性变态者)

pessimism /'pesɪmɪzəm/
n.❶ a tendency to believe that the worse thing is most likely to happen 悲观;厌世 ❷ a belief that evil will always triumph over good 悲观主义

pessimist /'pesɪmɪst/
n.a person subject to pessimism 悲观主义者

pessimistic /ˌpesɪˈmɪstɪk/
adj. showing pessimism; gloomy 悲观的
‖ ~ally *adv*.悲观地

pest /pest/
n. ❶ an insect or animal that eats or damages crop 害虫;有害的动物:a garden ~ 植物害虫 /Mosquitoes are ~s.蚊子是害虫。❷ a person or thing that causes trouble, harm or destruction 讨厌的人或事

pester /ˈpestə(r)/
v. annoy sb. by repeated asks for sth. 使烦恼;纠缠:~ed by people asking for money 被讨钱的人所纠缠

pesticide /ˈpestɪsaɪd/
n. a substance for killing harmful insects and other pests 杀虫剂

pet /pet/
Ⅰ *n*. ❶ an animal kept at home as a companion 宠物:She keeps a dog as a ~.她养了条狗供玩赏。❷ a delightful or lovely person 宠儿;宝贝儿:make a ~ of a child 宠爱小孩 Ⅱ *adj*. favorite; lovely 宠爱的;亲昵的:a ~ name 昵称 Ⅲ *v*. fondle; treat with affection 抚摸;爱抚:~ a little cat 抚摸一只小猫

petal /ˈpetl/
n. a coloured leaf-like part of a flower 花瓣:the red ~s of a rose 玫瑰花的红花瓣

peter /ˈpiːtə(r)/
v. (always with *out*) become gradually smaller in amount, size and finally end (常与 out 连用)逐渐减少;逐渐枯竭:Our supply of food has ~ed out. 我们的食物供应已经终止。

petition /pɪˈtɪʃn/
n. ❶ a request or demand made to a deity or a superior by a solemn one 请愿 ❷ a formal written request, typically one signed by many people, appealing to authority in respect of a particular cause 请愿书:Many people signed the ~ for a new school in the village.许多人都在请愿书上签名,要求在村子里新建一所学校。

petitioner /pəˈtɪʃənə(r)/
n. ❶ someone who makes or signs a petition 请愿人;请求人 ❷ someone asking for the ending of their marriage (尤指离婚诉讼的)原告,上诉人

petrel /ˈpetrəl/
n. a black and white seabird 海燕

petrify /ˈpetrɪfaɪ/
v. ❶ turn into a stone; change (plant or animal, etc.) into a substance like stone 石化;(使)变成化石:There is a petrified forest in Arizona.亚利桑那州有一个石化森林。❷ make sb. unable to think or to move because of fear, surprise, etc. (因恐惧、惊慌等而)使发呆:The warning whistle petrified him.警报声把他吓呆了。

petrochemical /ˌpetrəʊˈkemɪkl/
Ⅰ *n*. a chemical substance derived from petroleum oil or natural gas 石油化学产品 Ⅱ *adj*. of or having to do with petrochemicals or petrochemistry 石油化工的;石油化学的:the ~ industry 石油化学工业

petrol /ˈpetrəl/
n. a liquid used as a fuel for motor vehicles 汽油:a ~ station 加油站

petroleum /pəˈtrəʊlɪəm/
n. mineral oil found under the surface of the earth or under the sea bed 石油:the ~ industry 石油工业 /~ jelly 凡士林

pettish /ˈpetɪʃ/
adj. impatiently angry; showing childish bad temper, especially over sth. unimportant 易怒的;使性子的

petty /ˈpeti/
adj. ❶ unimportant; on a small scale 次要的;小规模的:a ~ quarrel 小争吵 ❷ having or showing a narrow mind; mean 气量小的;卑鄙的:It was ~ of her not to accept the apology.她不接受道歉是心胸狭窄的表现。

petulant /ˈpetjʊlənt/
adj. easily made angry over small things; bad-tempered 爱发脾气的;暴躁的

pharaoh /ˈfeərəʊ/
n. a ruler of ancient Egypt 法老(古埃及统治者)

pharmacist /'fɑːməsɪst/

 n. a person who is trained to prepare and sell medicines 药剂师

pharmacology /ˌfɑːmə'kɒlədʒi/

 n. the scientific study of medicinal drugs and their effects on the body 药理学；药物学

pharmacy /'fɑːməsi/

 n. ❶ the study of how to prepare drugs and medicines 制药学；药剂学：student of ～ 药学学生 ❷ a place where drugs and medicines are sold 药房；药店

phase /feɪz/

 Ⅰ *n.* ❶ a stage of development 阶段；时期：a ～ of history 历史阶段 / the highest ～ of art 艺术的最高阶段 ❷ an aspect；a side 方面；侧面：This is only one ～ of the whole matter. 这只是整个事情的一个侧面。/ The problem has many ～s. 这个问题是多方面的。❸ (of the moon) amount of bright surface visible from the earth (new moon, full moon, etc.)（指月亮的）相位；盈亏（新月、满月）：the ～s of the moon 月相 Ⅱ *v.* plan or carry out sth. in stages 分期计划；按阶段执行：a ～d troops 军队的分期撤出

phenomenal /fə'nɒmɪnl/

 adj. ❶ very unusual 非凡的；很不一般的：～ strength 超人的力气 / a ～ memory 非凡的记忆力 ❷ known through the senses 从感官认识到的：a ～ experience 从感觉得到的经验

phenomenon /fə'nɒmɪnən/

 n. (*pl.* phenomena) ❶ sth. that happen or exist in nature or society 现象：Magnetic attraction is an interesting ～. 磁性吸引是一种有趣的现象。❷ an outstanding person or impressive thing 杰出的人(物)

phew /fjuː/

 int. a quick short whistling breath, either in or out (expressing tiredness, shock, or relief) 呼! 啊! 唉!（表示疲倦、惊讶或松一口气）

philanthropic /ˌfɪlən'θrɒpɪk/

 adj. of or showing philanthropy 慈善的：a ～ attitude 慈善的态度 / our ～ institu-

tions 我们的慈善机构

philanthropy /fɪ'lænθrəpi/

 n. ❶ love of mankind 善心 ❷ the help given to people, especially those who are unfortunate in some way 乐善好施 ‖ **philanthropist** *n.* 慈善家

philately /fɪ'lætəli/

 n. the collecting of postage stamps as a hobby 集邮 ‖ **philatelist** *n.* 集邮者

philosopher /fɪ'lɒsəfə(r)/

 n. ❶ a person studying or teaching philosophy 哲学家：Rousseau was a famous ～. 卢梭是一位著名的哲学家。❷ a person governed by reason and calmness, especially in times of difficulty (逆境中)泰然自若的人：You're quite a ～. 你是一个相当豁达的人。

philosophy /fɪ'lɒsəfi/

 n. ❶ the study or creation of theories about basic things such as the nature of existence or how people should live 哲学 ❷ calmness and quiet courage, especially in spite of difficulty or unhappiness 达观；沉着：accept bad news with ～ 泰然接受坏消息 / a particular system of ～ theories 哲学(理论)体系

phlegm /flem/

 n. a thick liquid coming from the nose and throat(especially when one has a cold) 痰

phlegmatic /fleg'mætɪk/

 adj. not easily excited or agitated 沉着冷静的 ‖ ～ally *adv.* 沉着冷静地

phobia /'fəubɪə/

 n. a strong, unnatural, and usually unreasonable fear and dislike of sth. 恐惧症；憎恶感：She has a ～ about water and won't learn to swim. 她怕水，所以不想学游泳。

phoenix /'fiːnɪks/

 n. a magic bird of the Arabian desert, said to live for hundreds of years and then burn itself on a funeral pyre, rising from its ashes young again to live for another cycle (神话中的)长生鸟，凤凰

phone /fəun/

 Ⅰ *n.* a machine used for talking to people

over a long distance 电话：You are wanted on the ～.你有电话。Ⅱ v.make a call to sb.给……打电话：Phone the doctor at once.马上打电话给医生。/I'll ～ you the news.我将打电话把消息告诉你。

phonetic/fə'netɪk/

adj.❶ of or concerning the sounds of human speech 语音的：～ exercises 语音练习 ❷ using signs to represent the actual sounds of speech 表示语音的：～ symbols 音标 /the international ～ alphabet 国际音标

phonetics/fə'netɪks/

n.the study and science of speech sounds 语音学：Phonetics deals with speech sounds.语音学是研究语言声音的。

phoney/'fəʊni/

Ⅰ adj.false；untrue；insincere 假的；伪造的；不诚恳的 Ⅱ n.a false or insincere person 冒充者；虚伪的人：This man is a ～.这男人是个骗子。

phonograph/'fəʊnəɡrɑːf/

n.an instrument for reproducing sounds which have been recorded on flat disks (called records) 〈美〉留声机

photo/'fəʊtəʊ/

Ⅰ n.a short，informal form of photograph 相片；照片：take a ～ 拍照 Ⅱ v.take a photo of 拍照；拍摄：He ～ed the library.他把这座图书馆拍下来了。

photocopy/'fəʊtəʊkɒpi/

Ⅰ n.a copy of (a document，etc.) by a photographic method 复印件；影印本：I made two photocopies of the report.我将此报告复印了两份。Ⅱ v.make a photocopy of 复制；复印：Will you ～ this article for me? 你可以为我复印这篇文章吗?

photogenic/ˌfəʊtəʊ'dʒenɪk/

adj. having an appearance that would make a good photograph 上镜头的；适于拍照的：a very ～ face 一张上镜的面孔

photograph/'fəʊtəɡrɑːf/

Ⅰ n.a picture made with a camera 照片：a ～ album 照相簿 /a ～ studio 照相馆/take a ～ 照相 /have a ～ taken (请别人给自己)照相 Ⅱ v.take a photo (picture) of 摄影；照相：～ the castle 把城堡照下来

photographer/fə'tɒɡrəfə/

n.a person who takes photographs 摄影师；照相师

photographic/ˌfəʊtə'ɡræfɪk/

adj.❶ connected with photography 摄影的：expensive ～ equipment 昂贵的摄影器材 ❷(of a person's memory) able to remember things in great detail after having seen them 能原原本本地把所见事物记住的：She has a ～ memory for details.她对细节有惊人的记忆力。

photography/fə'tɒɡrəfi/

n.the art or process of taking photographs 摄影术；摄影：He's very keen on ～.他非常喜欢摄影。

photosynthesis/ˌfəʊtəʊ'sɪnθəsɪs/

n.the process by which green plants use sunlight to turn carbon dioxide, which is taken from the air, and water into complex substances, giving off oxygen 光合作用

phrase/freɪz/

n.❶ a group of words that gives a particular idea 短语；词组：a set ～ 固定词组 /a prepositional ～ 介词短语 ❷ an idiomatic expression 习惯用语：There are a lot of ～s in English.英语中有很多习惯用语。

phrasebook/'freɪzbʊk/

n.a book giving and explaining phrases of a particular (foreign) language, for people to use when they go abroad (供游客到国外旅行时用的)常用语手册

phraseology/ˌfreɪzi'ɒlədʒi/

n.the way in which words are chosen, arranged, and/or used, especially in the stated subject or field 专门用语；术语：I don't understand all this scientific ～.我不明白这些科学术语。

physical/'fɪzɪkl/

adj.❶ of the body rather than the mind 身体的；肉体的：～ training 体育锻炼 ❷ of matter，material；of the laws of nature

P

物质的；自然规律的：the ～ world 物质世界 ❸connected with physics，studying mechanics，heat，light，etc.物理学的

physically /ˈfɪzɪk(ə)li/

*adv.*❶in a way that is connected with a person's body rather than their mind 身体上；肉体上：He felt ～ sick before the college entrance examination.高考前他感到身体不适。❷according to the laws of nature or what is probable 依据自然规律；根本上

physician /fɪˈzɪʃn/

*n.*a doctor，especially one who treats diseases with medicines (内科)医生：a chief ～ 主任医生

physicist /ˈfɪzɪsɪst/

*n.*a person who studies physics 物理学家：a famous ～ 一位著名的物理学家

physics /ˈfɪzɪks/

n. the science dealing with the study of matter and natural forces 物理学：Physics studies mechanics，heat，light，sound，electricity，etc.物理学研究力学、热学、光学、声学和电学等。

physiology /ˌfɪzɪˈɒlədʒi/

*n.*the study of the way in which the body of a living thing works under normal conditions 生理学

physiotherapy /ˌfɪzɪəʊˈθerəpi/

*n.*the treatment of disease by physical exercises，heat，etc.物理疗法

physique /fɪˈziːk/

*n.*the way in which the body is formed or developed 体格：a person of strong ～ 一个体格强壮的人

pianist /ˈpɪənɪst/

*n.*a person who plays the piano 钢琴家；钢琴演奏者

piano /pɪˈænəʊ/

n. a large musical instrument played by striking keys 钢琴：a grand ～ 大钢琴 /a ～ player 钢琴演奏者 /She plays (on) the ～ well.她钢琴弹得好。

pick /pɪk/

Ⅰ *n.*❶an act of choosing sth. 选择：You can take your ～ of the apples. 这些苹果

你可以任意挑选。❷sb. or sth. that has been chosen 选中的人(物)：You are the teacher's ～ to give a speech next.你是老师选中下一个演讲的人。Ⅱ *v.*❶ take (what one likes or considers best or most suitable) from a group or number of sb. or sth.；choose 挑选；选择：It took her an hour to ～ a dress that suited her. 她花了一个钟头才挑选到一件合身的衣服。❷take (part of a plant) from a tree or plant；gather 采；摘；捡，拾：～ flowers 采花 ❸ steal or take from，especially in small amounts 扒窃 ‖ have a bone to ～ (with) 有争论/～ a hole (holes) in 挑毛病/～ a quarrel (fight) with 找人吵(打)架/～ and choose 仔细挑选；挑剔/～ at 啄食；拉扯；挑毛病/～ one's way 小心前进/～ oneself up 爬起来/～ to pieces 拆开；批得体无完肤/～ up 拾起；(无意中)学会

picket /ˈpɪkɪt/

Ⅰ *n.*a person who is posted near a factory during a strike to prevent other workers from going in 罢工纠察员 Ⅱ *v.*❶ put pickets near a place 监视：～ a factory 监视工厂 ❷ act as a picket 当纠察员

pickings /ˈpɪkɪŋz/

*n.*additional money or profits taken dishonestly 不义之财：There are some easy ～ to be made in this job.这工作可赚到一些易得的外快。

pickle /ˈpɪkl/

Ⅰ *v.*put meat，vegetables，etc.in salt water or vinegar，etc.腌制：～d meat 腌肉 Ⅱ *n.*vegetables which have been pickled 腌菜

pickpocket /ˈpɪkˌpɒkɪt/

*n.*a person who steals things from people's pockets or handbags in public places 扒手：Because he knew there would be ～s in the crowd，he kept his wallet in his hand.因为他知道人群中会有扒手，所以他把钱包抓在手里。

pickup /ˈpɪkʌp/

*n.*❶a small open truck or van 小卡车；轻型货车 ❷the part of a record player that holds the stylus (唱机的)收唱器(包括唱头、唱针等)

picky/ˈpɪki/

*adj.*choosy;difficult to please 挑剔的;难讨好的:She's such a ~ eater.她是个对饮食十分挑剔的人。

picnic/ˈpɪknɪk/

*n.*a pleasure trip with a meal in the open air 野餐:have a ~ in the forest 在森林中举行野餐 /go on (for) a ~ 去野餐

pictorial/pɪkˈtɔːrɪəl/

Ⅰ*adj.*of, having, represented in picture 图画的;有图的;用图片表示的:a ~ record of the wedding 婚礼的图片记录 Ⅱ*n.* a newspaper or magazine made up mainly of photographs 画报;画刊:a copy of *China Pictorial* 一本《中国画报》

picture/ˈpɪktʃə(r)/

Ⅰ*n.*❶ a drawing,painting or photograph 图画;照片:There are many ~s in the book.书里有很多图画。❷ a movie or film 影片;电影:go to the ~s去看电影 ❸an image on a television screen (电视)图像 ❹a portrait 画像,肖像:Lucy wants to have her ~ painted.露西想找人给她画像。Ⅱ*v.*paint or draw;imagine 绘画;描述;想象:The speaker ~d the suffering of the poor.演讲人生动地描述了穷人的困苦。‖ ~ book *n.*图画书

picturesque/ˌpɪktʃəˈresk/

*adj.*❶ charming;having the quality of being like a picture 似画的;美丽如画的:a ~ village 风景秀丽的村庄 ❷(of language) unusually clear,vivid and descriptive (指语言)有趣的,生动的,逼真的,形象的:~ language 生动的语言

pie/paɪ/

*n.*meat,fruit or vegetables baked in a dish with pastry 馅饼:a meat ~ 肉馅饼

piebald/ˈpaɪbɔːld/

adj.(with reference to a horse)with large black and white patches (指马)黑白斑纹的

piece/piːs/

*n.*❶ a portion of an object or of material, produced by cutting, tearing or breaking the whole 块;张;片;段;碎块;断片:a ~ of cake 一块蛋糕 ❷ a single item 一件;

一条;一个:a ~ of furniture 一件家具 ❸ parts of sth.that has broken up 碎片:The glass has smashed into ~s.玻璃杯摔成碎片了。❹ an article of a magazine, news,etc.一则报道 ‖ **break into (to) ~s** 打碎/**give sb.a ~ of one's mind** 对某人直言不讳/**go to ~s** 崩溃;身体(或精神上)垮下来‖ **~work** *n.*计件工作

pier/pɪə(r)/

*n.*❶ a landing place for ships that extends over the water (凸式)码头:a ship lies alongside a ~ 船停靠在码头 ❷ a pillar supporting a span of a bridge 桥墩 ❸ a brickwork between windows 窗间壁;户间壁

pierce/pɪəs/

*v.*❶ make a hole in or through sth.with a sharp object 刺穿;穿(孔):Her ears were ~d.她扎了耳环孔。❷ force or break a way into or through 穿透 ❸pass into or through 刺入;突破:The knife did not ~ very deeply.那刀子刺得不是很深。

piercing/ˈpɪəsɪŋ/

*adj.*❶(of wind) very strong and cold (风)刺骨的,凛冽的 ❷(of sound) very sharp and clear,especially in an unpleasant way (声音)刺耳的,尖的:A ~ cry rang out across the moor.一声尖叫掠过荒野。/a very ~ voice 非常刺耳的声音 ❸ going straight to the centre or the main point 直指要害的;深刻的:a ~ look (question) 锐利的目光(直指要害的问题)

piety/ˈpaɪəti/

*n.*the quality of being pious 虔诚

pig/pɪg/

*n.*a fat, short-legged animal with a usually curly tail and thick skin with short stiff hairs,often kept for its meat 猪:raise ~s 养猪 ‖ **drive one's ~s to market** 打鼾/**make a ~ of oneself** 狼吞虎咽 ‖ **~pen** *n.*猪圈/**~skin** *n.*猪皮/**~tail** *n.*辫子

pigeon/ˈpɪdʒɪn/

*n.*a fat bird with a small head,short legs.and cooing voice, typically having grey and white plumage 鸽子:a homing ~ 信

鸽

piggery /ˈpɪgəri/

n. a place where pigs are bred or kept 养猪场；猪栏；猪圈

piggy /ˈpɪgi/

Ⅰ *n.* a pig or piglet （儿）猪；小猪 Ⅱ *adj.* like a pig 似猪的；像猪一样的

pig iron /ˈpɪg aɪən/

n. crude iron, as it comes from the blast furnace 生铁

pigment /ˈpɪgmənt/

n. ❶ a colouring matter which is used to make paints, dyes, etc. （粉状）颜料 ❷ a substance which gives the hair, skin of animals and the leaves of plants their colour （天然）色素

pile /paɪl/

Ⅰ *n.* a mass of sth. lying one upon another 堆；堆积物：We put the old newspapers in ~s on the floor. 我们把旧报纸一叠叠地堆在地板上。Ⅱ *v.* make into a pile; heap up 堆放；堆积：He ~d his books in the corner. 他把他的书堆放在角落里。‖ ~ in (into) 挤进；塞进／~ it on 夸张；吹嘘

piles /paɪlz/

n. an illness in which there is a painful swelling around the anus 痔疮

pilgrim /ˈpɪlgrɪm/

n. a person who travels to a sacred place as an act of religious devotion 往圣地朝拜者；香客；游历者：~s to Mecca 去麦加的朝圣者

pill /pɪl/

n. a small ball or tablet of medicine for swallowing whole 药丸：a sleeping ~ 安眠药片

pillage /ˈpɪlɪdʒ/

v. plunder; steal things, with violence, from a place that has been captured in war 掠夺；抢劫

pillar /ˈpɪlə/

n. ❶ a tall vertical structure, usually made of stone, used as a support or ornament 柱子；支柱；墩 ❷ sth. resembling this in shape 柱状物：a ~ of rock 石柱 ❸ a person or thing regarded as one of the chief support of sth. 栋梁；台柱；主要支持者：He is a ~ of the local community. 他是当地社区的台柱。‖ ~ box *n.* 邮筒

pillion /ˈpɪliən/

n. the pad or seat behind the driver's on which a passenger can sit 摩托车的后座：ride ~ 骑在后座

pillow /ˈpɪləʊ/

Ⅰ *n.* a cloth bag filled with soft material, used for supporting head in bed 枕头：~ case 枕头套 Ⅱ *v.* rest or support (sth.) on or as if on a pillow 搁在枕头上：~ one's head on one's arm 把头枕在手臂上

pilot /ˈpaɪlət/

n. ❶ a person who flies an airplane 飞行员：The boy wants to be a ~ when he grows up. 这男孩长大后想当飞行员。❷ a person who steers a big ship into (out of) a harbor 领航员；领港员

pimp /pɪmp/

n. a man who finds customers for prostitutes 拉皮条的男人

pimple /ˈpɪmpl/

n. a small, inflamed spot on the skin 丘疹；粉刺

pin /pɪn/

Ⅰ *n.* a short thin piece of metal that looks like a small nail, used for fastening together pieces of cloth, paper, etc., used e.g. when making clothes 大头针：a safety ~ 别针 ‖ on ~s and needles 坐立不安，如坐针毡 Ⅱ *v.* (-nn-) fasten or join with a pin or pins 钉住；别住：He ~ned the notice on the wall. 他把通知钉在墙上。‖ ~ on 把……加在某人身上／~ one's faith (hopes) on 信赖(指望)；把信心(希望)寄托在

pincer /ˈpɪnsə/

n. (*pl.*) a tool for gripping things and holding them tight (e. g. to take nails out of wood, etc.) 钳子

pinch /pɪntʃ/

Ⅰ *v.* ❶ squeeze between the thumb and forefinger 捏；拧：He ~ed the boy's cheek. 他捏了捏那男孩的面颊。❷ hurt being too tight 轧痛；夹痛：These shoes

~.这双鞋子会夹脚。❸ steal sth. that is not valuable 盗窃:Who ~ed my watch? 谁偷了我的表? Ⅱ *n*.❶ an act of pinching 捏;拧;夹:give someone a ~ in the leg 在某人腿上拧一下 ❷ a very small amount 一撮;少量:a ~ of salt 一撮盐

pine/paɪn/

Ⅰ *v*.❶ waste away with hunger, pain or deep sorrow 消瘦;憔悴:be pining from (away, with) hunger 饿瘦了 ❷ have a desire to do sth. 渴望:He is pining to go to the army. 他渴望从军。Ⅱ *n*. one of several kinds of (mostly) evergreen trees with needle-shaped leaves and cones 松树;针叶松

pineapple/'paɪnæpl/

n. a large oval fruit that grows in tropical area;a plant which bears this fruit 菠萝,凤梨;菠萝树

ping-pong/'pɪŋpɒŋ/

n. table tennis 乒乓球:Can you play ~? 你会打乒乓球吗?

pink/pɪŋk/

Ⅰ *n*.❶ light or pale red 淡(粉)红色:rose ~ 玫瑰红 ❷ a garden plant with sweet-smelling white, pink, crimson flowers 石竹 Ⅱ *adj*.of pale red color 淡(粉)红色的

pinnacle/'pɪnəkl/

n.❶ a pointed rock or high peak 尖岩石;尖峰 ❷ the highest point (e.g. of someone's career, achievements, etc.) (某人的事业、成就等)的顶点,极点

pint/paɪnt/

n. a unit of liquid or dry capacity, equal to one eighth of a gallon, in Britain equal to 0.568 litre and in US equal to 0.473 litre (for liquid measure) or 0.551 litre (for dry measure)品脱(一种液量或干液单位,相当于1/8加仑,在英国相当于0.568升,在美国液量相当于0.473升,干量相当于0.551升):a ~ of milk 一品脱牛奶

pioneer/ˌpaɪə'nɪə(r)/

Ⅰ *n*.❶ one who is first or among the first to explore or settle a region 拓荒者;开辟者;log cabin built by the ~s 拓荒者建的小木屋 ❷ one who is first or among the first to open up or develop an area of thought, inquiry or endeavor 先驱;创始人;a ~ of photography 摄影术的创始人 Ⅱ *v*.explore or develop sth.new 开辟;倡导:~ adult education 开办成人教育

pioneering/ˌpaɪə'nɪərɪŋ/

adj.involving new ideas or methods 创造性的;开拓性的

pious/'paɪəs/

adj ❶ devoutly religious and moral 虔诚的;敬神的:a ~ woman 一个虔诚的妇女 ❷ pretending to have deep respect and sincere feelings 虚伪的:one's ~ expression of regret 虚伪的歉疚

pip/pɪp/

n.❶ a small seed in an apple, orange, etc. (苹果、橘子等的)小粒种子 ❷ a note of the time signal on the telephone or radio (电话或收音机的)尖音信号

pipe/paɪp/

Ⅰ *n*.❶ a tube through which liquids or gases can flow 管子;导管:Water comes to the tap through a ~.水由管子通到龙头。❷ a small bowl attached to a hollow stem, used for smoking 烟斗:The old man was smoking a long ~.那位老人用一根长烟袋抽烟。❸ a musical instrument in the shape of a pipe 管乐器 Ⅱ *v*.❶ carry sth. by means of pipes;supply with pipes 用管子输送 ❷ play on a pipe 用笛袋吹奏 ‖ ~ down 停止说话;安静下来/~ up 开始说话;开始吹奏

pipeline/'paɪpˌlaɪn/

n.❶ a pipe for carrying oil, gas, water, etc. over long distances (长距离输送油、气、水等的)管道,管线 ❷ a channel of supplying goods or information (供应货物、信息等的)渠道、途径;线路

piping/'paɪpɪŋ/

n.❶ lengths of pipe made of metal, etc.管件;管子 ❷ a decorative line of icing or cream piped on a cake or dessert (糖衣、奶油等做成的)食物花饰 ❸ a long narrow pipe-like fold, often enclosing a cord, decorating edges or seams of clothing or upholstery（衣服、室内陈设品的）滚边

pirate/ˈpaɪrət/

Ⅰ*n*.❶ a sea robber 海盗 ❷ one who appropriates the work, invention, or ideas of another without permission or authorization 剽窃者；盗印者：pop music ～ 非法翻录流行歌曲的人 Ⅱ*v*.use or reproduce a book, a recording, another's work, etc. without authorization 非法翻印：～ a book 盗印一本书

pistol/ˈpɪstl/

n.a small gun held in one hand 手枪：Bob's ～ 鲍勃的手枪

piston/ˈpɪstən/

n.a piece of metal（usually cylindrical）which moves to and fits inside a hollow tube（called a cylinder）as part of the mechanism of engines, pumps, etc. 活塞（常用于汽缸内）

pit/pɪt/

Ⅰ*n*.❶a hole in the ground 坑；洼；地洞：～s in the road 道路上的坑坑洼洼 ❷ a coal mine 煤窑 ❸ a covered hole as a trap for wild animals, etc. 陷阱：dig a ～ for someone 给某人设陷阱 Ⅱ*v*.match against in a fight 使相斗；使对立

pitch/pɪtʃ/

Ⅰ*n*.❶（in sport）a special marked-out area of ground on which football, hockey, netball, etc. are played 球场 ❷ a degree of highness or lowness of tone 音调 ❸ the highest point of sth.（事物的）最高点：Excitement rose to the highest ～.兴奋已达极点。Ⅱ*v*.❶ set up; fix firmly in the ground 搭（帐）；扎（营）：They ～ed a tent in the field.他们在田间搭起了帐篷。❷（cause to）fall heavily or suddenly forwards or outwards 栽倒；摔下 ❸ throw sb.or sth. with force 掷；抛：He ～ed the ball out of the field.他把球掷出了场外。

pitcher/ˈpɪtʃə(r)/

n.❶（in baseball）a player who throws the ball towards the person who is batting（棒球）投手 ❷ a large container for holding liquids with a handle and a lip for pouring; a jug（带柄和倾口的）大水罐；水壶

piteous/ˈpɪtiəs/

adj.making one feel pity; deserving pity 令人怜悯的；值得同情的

pith/pɪθ/

n.❶ a soft substance inside the stem, etc. of some plants（植物茎内的）木髓 ❷ the most necessary, essential part of sth. 要点，精髓 ‖ ～y *adj*. 简练的；有力的；中肯的：a ～y speech 简练的讲话

pitiless/ˈpɪtɪlɪs/

adj.showing no pity 冷酷的；无情的 ‖ ～ly *adv*.无情地；冷酷地

pity/ˈpɪti/

Ⅰ*n*.a feeling for the sorrow of others 怜悯；同情：Her eyes were full of ～.她的眼神中充满了同情。Ⅱ*v*.feel sorrow for 同情；可怜；怜悯：He pitied the poor.他同情穷人。‖ have（take）～ on 可怜；同情/out of ～ 出于同情 ‖ pitiful *adj*.可怜的；令人怜悯的

pixel /ˈpɪksəl/

n.one of the tiny illuminated dots on a computer display screen from which the image is composed（电子）像素

pixie/ˈpɪksi/

n.a type of fairy 小仙子，小精灵

pizza /ˈpiːtsə/

n.an Italian dish consisting of a layer of dough baked with meat, vegetables, etc. on top 比萨饼

placard/ˈplækɑːd/

n.a public notice put up where it can be easily seen 广告；布告，招贴

placate/pləˈkeɪt/

v. take away someone's anger; make peaceful 安抚，抚慰；使和解：We tried to ～ them with gifts.我们尽量用礼物来抚慰他们。

place/pleɪs/

Ⅰ*n*.❶ a particular position, point, or area 位置；地点；场所：I can't remember the ～ where it is.我不记得它的位置了。❷a particular city, town, etc.城镇 ❸a building or area used for a specified purpose or activity 有某用途的建筑（或土地）❹a person's home 家;住所 ❺ a portion of space occupied by sb. 座位;位子:The manager has set a ～ for you in the office. 经理已经在办公室给你安排了位子。❻ a person's rank or status 等级;地位 ❼ the role played by or the importance to (sb. or sth.) 作用;重要性 ❽ a position in a sequence, especially in sporting contest (尤指体育比赛的)排名 II v. ❶ put in a particular position 放置;安排 ❷ cause to be in a particular situation 使处于特定情景 ❸ find a home or employment for 安家;就业 ❹ dispose of sth. 处置 ❺ give instructions about sth. or make a request for sth. to happen 下指示;请求 ❻ achieve a specified position in a race 取得名次

placed /pleɪst/

adj. ❶ in the stated situation 处于某种情况的:How are you ～ for money? 你的经济情况怎么样? ❷ be placed (especially of a horse) to be one of the first three to finish a race (尤指马)赛跑名列前三名的

placement /'pleɪsmənt/

n. the act or an example of placing sb. or sth. in position 安置;就业安排:The university offers a ～ service for its graduates. 这所大学为毕业生提供就业服务。

placenta /plə'sentə/

n. a thick mass of flesh containing many blood tubes, which forms inside the womb to join an unborn child to its mother 胎盘

placid /'plæsɪd/

adj. peaceful;not easily made angry 平和的,宁静的;不易生气的:a ～ scene 宁静的景色/someone having a ～ nature 生性平和的人 ‖ ～ity /plə'sɪdəti/ *n.* 平和,宁静

plagiarism /'pleɪdʒərɪzm/

n. ❶ the action of plagiarizing 剽窃;抄袭 ❷ sth. that has been plagiarized 剽窃作品:an article full of ～s 满篇剽窃他人著作的文章

plagiarize /'pleɪdʒəraɪz/

v. take (words, ideas, etc.) from (someone else's work) and use them in one's own work without permission 剽窃,抄袭

(别人的作品):Half the ideas in his talk were ～d from an article I wrote last year. 他讲话中有一半的观念是从去年我写的一篇文章中剽窃来的。

plague /pleɪg/

I *n.* ❶ a very dangerous infectious disease 瘟疫:catch a ～ 染上瘟疫 ❷ a disaster 灾害;祸患:a ～ of rats 鼠灾 ❸ annoyance;trouble 苦恼;麻烦:What a ～ that child is! 那小孩多么讨厌! II *v.* annoy with repeated requests or questions 折磨;烦扰:be ～d to death 烦得要死

plain /pleɪn/

I *adj.* ❶ clear;easy to understand;easily seen or heard 明白的;清楚的;易懂的:The meaning is quite ～. 意思很清楚。❷ simple;ordinary 朴素的;普通的:She's in ～ clothes. 她穿着朴素。❸ honest;sincere;frank 坦率的;诚实的:I must be ～ with you. 我必须坦白地告诉你。 II *n.* a flat stretch of land 平原;平地:a vast ～ 辽阔的平原

plainly /'pleɪnli/

adv. ❶ in a plain way;easily seen or heard 简单地;清楚地;直率地:Their conversation could be quite ～ heard by the neighbours. 他们的谈话能够被邻居清楚地听到。/ I told her ～ what I thought of her scheme. 我直率地告诉她我对她的计划的看法。❷ in a clear and obvious way 很清楚地;显然地:The door's locked, so ～ they must be out. 门已上锁,他们显然外出了。

plainspoken /ˌpleɪn'spəʊkən/

adj. speaking in a direct and honest way, sometimes in a rude way 直言不讳的;坦率的;不客气的

plaint /pleɪnt/

n. an expression of great sorrow 悲叹;哀怨;哀叹

plaintiff /'pleɪntɪf/

n. a person who brings a charge against sb. in court 原告:The ～ accused the defendant of fraud. 原告控诉被告犯欺诈罪。

plaintive/ˈpleɪntɪv/
*adj.*sounding sad and mournful 悲哀的；哭诉的：a ~ voice 哭诉的声音

plan/plæn/
Ⅰ *n.*❶ an arrangement for carrying out some future activities；a design；a scheme 计划；规划；设计；方案：I have made a ~ for overcoming the difficulties. 我已制订了克服困难的计划。❷ an outline drawing of a house，machine，etc. 设计图：the ~s of a house 房屋的图样 Ⅱ *v.*❶make an arrangement for 计划；打算；规划：What do you ~ to do this afternoon? 你今天下午打算干什么？❷design sth. 设计

plane/pleɪn/
Ⅰ *n.*❶ an airplane 飞机：You can go there by ~.你可以坐飞机到那儿去。❷ a flat or level surface 平面：a horizontal ~ 水平面/an inclined ~ 斜面 ❸ a carpenter's tool for making a wood surface smooth 刨子 Ⅱ *v.* use a plane on sth. 刨平：The carpenter ~d the wood smooth. 木匠把木头刨平。Ⅲ *adj.* flat or level 很平的；平面的：a ~ figure 平面图形

planet/ˈplænɪt/
*n.*❶ one of the heavenly bodies which move round a star，such as the sun 行星：The earth is a ~.地球是个行星。❷ the earth 地球

planetarium/ˌplænɪˈteərɪəm/
*n.*a building containing an apparatus that throws spots of light onto the inside of a curved roof to show the movements of planets and stars 天文馆；太空馆

plankton/ˈplæŋktən/
*n.*a mass of small plants and animals drifting on or near the surface of seas or lakes 浮游生物

planner/ˈplænə(r)/
*n.*a person who plans，especially one who plans the way in which towns develop （城市）规划者，策划人

planning/ˈplænɪŋ/
*n.*the process of making plans for sth. 计划过程

plant/plɑːnt/
Ⅰ *n.*❶ living things that have leaves and roots，and grow from the ground，especially the kind smaller than trees 植物：All ~s need water and light.所有植物都需要水分和阳光。❷ a factory 工厂 ❸ the large equipment for industrial purposes 设备 Ⅱ *v.* put in the ground to grow 栽培；种植：We ~ rice in the south.我们在南方种植水稻。

plantation/plænˈteɪʃn，plɑːnˈteɪʃn/
*n.*❶ a large piece of land on which crops such as tea，sugar and rubber are grown 种植园 ❷ a large group of growing trees planted especially to produce wood 人造林；植树造林

plaque/plɑːk/
*n.*a flat piece of metal，etc. used as an ornament or in remembrance of sth. 匾；饰板

plasma/ˈplæzmə/
*n.*a liquid part of blood 血浆

plaster/ˈplɑːstə(r)/
Ⅰ *n.*❶ a soft mixture of lime，sand，water，etc.used for coating walls and ceilings （涂墙等用的）灰泥 ❷ a similar quick drying substance used for supporting broken limbs，making models，etc. 石膏：a ~ figure 石膏像 ❸a kind of sticky material used for covering small cuts or sores 膏药；膏：put a ~ on a sore 贴膏药于患处 Ⅱ *v.*❶cover a wall，etc.with plaster 涂灰泥于（墙上等）：~ a wall 用灰泥抹墙 ❷cause to adhere or lay flat （使）粘贴：The downpour ~ed his shirt to his body.倾盆大雨使他的衬衫湿淋淋地贴在身上。

plasterboard/ˈplɑːstəbɔːd/
*n.*a board made of large sheets of cardboard held together with plaster，used instead of plaster to cover walls 灰泥板；石膏板

plastered/ˈplɑːstəd/
*adj.*drunk 喝醉了的

plasterer/ˈplɑːstərə(r)/
*n.*a person whose job is to plaster walls 泥水匠；抹灰工

plastic/ˈplæstɪk/

I *n.* substances made of the light material that are produced chemically from oil or coal, and then are manufactured into various articles, especially synthetic resinous substances 塑料: Plastics don't rust like metal. 塑料不像金属那样生锈。**II** *adj.* ❶ (of goods) made of plastic 塑料的: ~ cups 塑料杯 /~ raincoats 塑料雨衣 ❷ (of materials) easily shaped or moulded 可塑的; 可塑性的‖~s *n.* 塑料学

plate /pleɪt/
I *n.* ❶ a flat round dish 盘子; 盆子: a dinner ~ 菜盘 /a paper ~ 纸盘 ❷ the amount of food that this will hold 一盘 (菜): a ~ of fish 一盘鱼 / two ~s of meat 两盘肉 ❸ metal articles made of gold or silver; a common metal with a thin covering of gold or silver 金的或银的餐具; 镀金或镀银器皿: a piece of ~ 一件金(银)餐具 /gold ~ 镀金餐具 ❹ a colored picture in a book, printed on different paper from the written part (书的) 图版, 插图 ❺ a large piece of metal or glass (金属或玻璃的) 板: steel ~s 钢板 /photographic ~s (照相) 感光板 **II** *v.* ❶ coat thinly with gold, silver or other metal 给……镀(金、银等): ~ copper with silver 用银镀铜 ❷ cover with metal plate (以薄金属板) 覆盖

plateau /ˈplætəʊ/
n. (*pl.* ~s or plateaux) a large area of high and fairly flat land 高原

plateful /ˈpleɪtful/
n. the amount that a plate will hold 一盘的量

platelet /ˈpleɪtlɪt/
n. a small colourless disc, found in the blood and involved in clotting 血小板

platform /ˈplætfɔːm/
n. ❶ a raised level surface on which people or things can stand; a raised floor of boards for speakers, performers, etc. 平台; 讲台; 舞台: on the concert ~ 在音乐台上 /launching ~ 发射台 ❷ a raised flat surface built along the side of the track at a railway station 站台; 月台: Platform One 一号站台 ❸ a statement

of main ideas and plans set forth by a party or group (政党、团体的) 政纲, 党纲

plating /ˈpleɪtɪŋ/
n. a thin coating of gold, silver, or other metal (金、银或其他金属的) 镀层

platinum /ˈplætɪnəm/
n. a soft, white, valuable metal (Pt) 铂, 白金

platitude /ˈplætɪtjuːd/
n. a statement of sth. obvious or of sth. which has often been said before, but now used by a speaker as if it were sth. new 陈词滥调: His speech was full of ~s. 他的讲话全是陈词滥调。

platonic /pləˈtɒnɪk/
adj. (of a relationship between a man and woman) just friendly, not sexual (男女间关系) 柏拉图式的

platoon /pləˈtuːn/
n. a small number of soldiers organized as a single unit (军队的) 排

platypus /ˈplætɪpəs/
n. a small furry Australian animal that has a beak and feet like ducks, lays eggs, and gives milk to its young 鸭嘴兽

plausible /ˈplɔːzəbl/
adj. ❶ appearing to be true or reasonable 似乎合理的; 似真实的; 有理的: a ~ excuse 有理的借口 ❷ good at making up sounding honest and sincere excuses, etc. 花言巧语的

play /pleɪ/
I *n.* ❶ sth. done for amusement 玩耍; 游戏: It's time for ~. 是玩的时候了。 ❷ a work written to be acted on the stage 戏剧; 剧本; 表演: He went to a ~ every Saturday night. 他每周星期六晚上都去看戏。 ❸ the influence of sth. on sb. or sth. else 影响 **II** *v.* ❶ do sth. for pleasure, especially using toys; have fun 玩; 做游戏: Children like to ~. 小孩子爱玩。 ❷ take part in a sport or game 参加比赛: ~ basketball 打篮球 /~ a friendly match 举行友谊赛 ❸ perform (musical instruments); produce or give out music 演奏: He ~s the violin. 他演奏小提琴。 ❹

perform or act 扮演；演出；起……作用：She ~ed the heroine in the film. 她在影片中扮演女主角。 ❺make；carry out 做；实行：He ~ed a joke on me. 他开了我一个玩笑。

player/'pleɪə(r)/

n. ❶ a person who takes part in a sport or game 运动员；游戏者：a football ~ 足球选手 ❷an actor；a person playing a musical instrument 演员；演奏者：a bit ~ 饰演小角色的演员

playful /'pleɪfʊl/

adj. ❶fond of fun and amusement 爱玩耍的；嬉戏的 ❷done in fun；not meant seriously 开玩笑的；闹着玩的；不当真的：He gave his pal a ~ punch on the arm. 他开玩笑地在他伙伴的膀子上打了一拳。

playground /'pleɪɡraʊnd/

n. a piece of ground for children to play on 运动场；操场；游乐场

playing card/'pleɪɪŋkɑːd/

n. one of the 52 cards used for various games and for telling fortunes 扑克牌；纸牌

playing field/'pleɪɪŋfiːld/

n. a field used for outdoor team games 运动场

plaything/'pleɪθɪŋ/

n. ❶a toy 玩具 ❷ a person who is treated without seriousness or consideration by another 玩物；被玩弄的人：He was just her ~. 他只是她的玩物。/ Are we the ~s of fate? 我们是被命运捉弄的人吗？

playtime/'pleɪtaɪm/

n. a (short) period of time，especially at a school，when children can go out to play （尤指学校的）游戏、娱乐时间

playwright/'pleɪraɪt/

n. a writer of plays 剧作家

plaza/'plɑːzə/

n. ❶a public square or marketplace，especially in towns in Spanish-speaking countries （尤指讲西班牙语国家的城市中的）广场，集市场所 ❷ a group of public buildings in a town 城市中的一系列公共建筑物：a shopping ~ 购物中心

plc/ˌpiː el 'siː/

abbr. public limited company 公共有限公司：Marks & Spencer PLC 马莎公共有限公司

plea/pliː/

n. ❶ a statement by a person in a court of law，saying whether or not he is guilty of a charge 抗辩；答辩：a ~ of guilty 服罪 ❷ an earnest request 请求；恳求：He made a ~ for forgiveness. 他恳求宽恕。 ❸ an excuse；a reason offered for wrongdoing 借口；托词：He refused the invitation to dinner on the ~ of being too busy. 他以太忙为借口拒绝了晚宴的邀请。

plead/pliːd/

v. (~ed or pled) ❶ offer reasons for（为……）辩护；抗辩：Everyone should have a lawyer to ~ his case. 每个人都应有个律师为他的案件辩护。 ❷ beg or request earnestly 恳求；祈求：~ for mercy 恳求宽恕 /~ with someone for pity 求某人怜悯 ❸ offer as an excuse 以……为借口：He ~ed illness as the reason for his absence. 他以生病作为缺席的理由。

pleasant/'plezənt/

adj. ❶giving pleasure；agreeable 舒适的；愉快的：a ~ news 令人愉快的消息 ❷ friendly and polite 友爱的

please/pliːz/

v. ❶ be used when asking politely for sth. 请：Please be quiet. 请安静。 ❷ give pleasure or happiness to；satisfy 使高兴（愉快）；使满意：It's hard to ~ all. 很难做到使人人都满意。 ❸ like sth. or be willing to do sth. 喜欢；愿意：Go where you ~. 你愿意到哪儿去就到哪儿去。

pleased/pliːzd/

adj. glad；feeling or showing satisfaction 高兴的；满意的：be ~ to travel 乐意去旅行 /Her father was ~ with her. 她父亲对她很满意。

pleasing /'pliːzɪŋ/

adj. that gives you pleasure or satisfaction 令人高兴的；令人满意的 ‖ ~ly *adv.* 高兴地；令人满意地

pleasure/'pleʒə(r)/

n. ❶ a state of being delighted and satisfied 快乐;愉快;满足: I'll do it with ~. 我很乐意做这事。❷ sth. that pleases you 乐事;乐趣: It is a ~ to work with you.和你一起工作是件乐事。/the ~s of friendship 友谊的乐趣 ‖ **have the ~ of** 有幸能……/**take (a) ~ in** 喜欢;以……为乐 ‖ **~ ground** *n.* 游乐场;娱乐场 ‖ **pleasurable** *adj.* 愉快的;令人高兴的

pleat /pliːt/
Ⅰ *n.* a fold made by doubling cloth on itself (衣服上的)褶:a shirt with ~s in the front 前面有褶的衬衣 Ⅱ *v.* make pleats in 打褶;使打褶:a ~ed skirt 百褶裙

pledge /pledʒ/
Ⅰ *n.* ❶ a solemn promise 誓言;保证: be under ~ of secrecy 誓不泄密 ❷ sth. given as a sign of love, approval, etc.信物;保证物:a ~ of love 爱的象征 ❸ sth. valuable left with someone else as proof that one will fulfil an agreement or pay back money you owe 抵押(品);典当(品):goods lying in ~ 作抵押的货物 Ⅱ *v.* ❶ promise solemnly or formally 发誓;保证:~ one's honour 保证荣誉/~ to help someone 保证帮助某人/They have ~d that they will always remain faithful.他们发誓将永远忠贞不渝。❷ give as security 抵押;典当:~ one's house 抵押房子

plenary /ˈpliːnəri/
adj. ❶ (of a meeting) attended by every-one who has the right to attend (会议)全体出席的: Will you be at the ~ session of the conference? 你将出席该大会的全体会议吗? ❷ complete; without limit 全权的;无限制的: The envoy was given ~ powers to negotiate with the rebels.该特使被授予全权同反叛者谈判的权利。

plentiful /ˈplentɪfl/
adj. in large amounts or numbers 丰富的;众多的:~ food 充裕的食品

plenty /ˈplenti/
Ⅰ *n.* a large number or quantity of sth. 丰富;大量;充足:We have ~ to eat.我们有足够的东西吃。/There are ~ of books on the shelf. 书架上有许多书。Ⅱ *adv.* quite; very 十分;非常:It's ~ big enough.

这足够大的了。

pliable /ˈplaɪəbl/
adj. easily bent 易弯曲的;柔韧的: ~ piece of metal 易曲的金属片 ‖ **pliability** /ˌplaɪəˈbɪlɪti/ *n.* 柔软;易曲折

pliant /ˈplaɪənt/
adj. easily influenced; accepting the wishes or commands of others 易受影响的;听命于人的

pliers /ˈplaɪəz/
n. (*pl.*) a tool for holding things tightly or for bending or twisting them (often **pair of pliers**) 钳子(常用 pair of pliers)

plight /plaɪt/
n. a bad or sorrowful situation or condition (恶劣的或悲伤的)处境,情况,情势: The homeless family was in a terrible ~.这无家可归的一家人处境很悲惨。

plimsoll /ˈplɪmsəl/
n. a type of shoe made of canvas, with a rubber sole 胶底帆布鞋

plinth /plɪnθ/
n. a square block, usually of stone, which forms the base of a pillar or statue (石柱或雕像的)柱脚,底座

plod /plɒd/
v. (-dd-) ❶ walk slowly and heavily 慢步走;重步走: You could see he was tired by the way he ~ded along the road. 从他一路上拖着沉重的步子走,你可看出他太累了。❷ work slowly but without resting 孜孜不倦;辛苦工作:~ away at a task 孜孜不倦地工作

plodder /ˈplɒdə(r)/
n. a person who works slowly and steadily but without imagination 沉闷苦干者

plonk¹ /plɒŋk/
Ⅰ *n.* a sound like sth. dropping onto or into a metal object 砰的声音(物体掉落到金属上或掉入金属制品中的声音) Ⅱ *v.* put down heavily or with force 沉重地放下: Just ~ those parcels down over there.把那些包裹放在那里就行了。/ She ~ed herself in the chair and refused to move. 她咚的一声坐在椅子上就不肯动了。

plonk² /plɒŋk/

*n.*a cheap wine 廉价酒

plop/plɒp/

Ⅰ *n.*a noise made by a falling stone into water（石头落入水中的）扑通声 Ⅱ *v.* make a plop 发出落水声：The stone ～ped into the water.石头扑通一声落入水中。

plot/plɒt/

Ⅰ *n.*❶ a small piece of ground 小块土地：Tomatoes will grow well on this ～.这块地上的西红柿会长得很好。❷ an outline of the events of a story or drama 情节 ❸ a secret plan 密谋；阴谋：Two men formed a ～ to rob the bank.二人合谋抢劫这家银行。Ⅱ *v.*(-tt-)❶make a secret plan 密谋；阴谋策划：They ～ted to kill the king.他们密谋杀害国王。/ ～ a rebellion 阴谋反叛 ❷write the plot of 设计情节

plough/plaʊ/

Ⅰ *n.*a tool used in farming for turning up soil 犁头 Ⅱ *v.* use a plough upon to dig and turn over a field or other area of land 犁地；耕地：The farmer ～ed the field before he planted the corn.农民先把地耕了，然后再种上玉米。‖ ～ back 把（利润）再投资/～ the sand 做无用功；徒劳无功

ploy/plɔɪ/

*n.*an idea or action which is often used to gain some advantages 手法；花招：His favourite ～ is to pretend to be stupid and then people try to help him.他爱用的花招是装傻，使人尽力帮助他。

pluck/plʌk/

Ⅰ *v.*❶ pick 采摘：Please don't ～ the flowers.请不要摘花。❷show bravery in spite of fear 鼓起勇气；振作精神：Pluck up your courage.鼓起勇气来。Ⅱ *n.*courage and will 勇气；精神；毅力：Mountain climbers need a lot of ～.登山者需要有很大的勇气。‖ ～y/'plʌki/ *adj.*勇敢的

plug/plʌg/

Ⅰ *n.*❶ a small, usually round, piece of rubber, wood, metal, etc., used for blo-

cking a hole, especially in sth. that contains liquid 塞子 ❷a small plastic object with two or three metal pins that are pushed into an electric socket to connect an apparatus with the electricity supply 插头：put the ～ in the socket 把插头插入插座 Ⅱ *v.*(-gg-)❶block, close, or fill with a plug 塞住；堵住：The pipe is ～ged up with dirt.管子被脏物堵住了。❷ connect to a supply of electricity with a plug 插入（电源）；接通电源

plum/plʌm/

*n.*a round, juicy fruit with a large seed in it which grows in cool dry areas 梅子；李子：～ pudding 李子布丁

plumage/'pluːmɪdʒ/

*n.*bird's feathers（鸟的）羽毛：a bird with bright ～ 羽毛鲜艳的鸟

plumb/plʌm/

Ⅰ *n.*a small heavy object at the end of a line, used to find out how deep water is, or whether a wall, etc. is straight（用以测量水深或墙壁是否垂直的）铅锤：The wall was out of ～.这堵墙不垂直。Ⅱ *adv.*exactly 准确地：His shot was ～ on the target.他的射击准确地打中了目标。‖ ～ line 锤线；铅锤线；测深线

plumber/'plʌmə(r)/

*n.*a person who fits and repairs pipes for water, gas, etc. in buildings 管子工

plumbing/'plʌmɪŋ/

*n.*❶ the work of a plumber 修理水管的工作 ❷ the system of pipes and tanks having to do with water and gas supply in a building 管路系统：a house with very poor ～ 一座管路系统很糟的房子

plume/pluːm/

Ⅰ *n.*❶feather especially a large one used as a decoration（尤指做装饰用的）羽毛 ❷ ornament of feathers 羽毛饰物 ❸ a thing that rises into the air in the shape of a feather 羽状物：a ～ of smoke 一缕烟 Ⅱ *v.*(of a bird) smooth (its feathers)（鸟）整理（羽毛）

plumed/pluːmd/

*adj.*having or decorated with plume 用羽

毛装饰的：a ～ hat 饰有羽毛的帽子

plummy/ˈplʌmi/

　*adj.*❶ having or being an unattractively, full-sounding and rich voice, of a type considered typical of the upper class 故作浑厚的；上层阶级腔调的 ❷ desirable; very good 称心的；极好的：a ～ part in the play 这出戏的最精彩部分

plump/plʌmp/

　adj. rather fat; fat in a pleasant-looking way 圆胖的；丰满的：a ～-faced boy 脸蛋胖乎乎的男孩

plunder/ˈplʌndə(r)/

　Ⅰ*v.* rob（people），especially during war or civil disorder（尤指在战争或内乱中）抢劫，掠夺：The invading troops ～ed the town. 入侵军队抢劫了那个城镇。/The enemy ～ed the village.敌人抢劫了村庄。Ⅱ*n.* ❶ the stolen goods 抢夺物：carloads of ～ 整车整车劫掠来的财物 ❷ the act of plundering 掠夺

plunge/plʌndʒ/

　Ⅰ*v.* ❶ push（sth.）into, or go suddenly and with force into（使）陷入，插入，突入：～ one's hands into one's coat pockets 将手插入大衣口袋/be ～d into poverty 陷入贫困 ❷ move quickly or suddenly forwards or downwards 猛冲：～ up a staircase 冲上楼梯/The car ～d forward. 汽车蓦地向前开。Ⅱ*n.* an act of plunging，especially head first into water 跳水；扎入：a thirty-five feet ～ 一次35英尺高的跳水

plural/ˈplʊərəl/

　Ⅰ*adj.* ❶more than one in number 多于一个的；多的 ❷（of a word or form）denoting more than one（词或形态的）复数的 Ⅱ*n.*❶a plural word or form 复数词；复数形式 ❷the plural number 复数

plurality /plʊəˈrælɪti/

　*n.*❶the fact or state of being plural 复数；复数形式 ❷the number of votes cast for a candidate who receives more than any other but does not receive an absolute majority〈美〉（选举中的）相对多数（票）

plus/plʌs/

　Ⅰ*prep.*with the addition of 加：Two ～ two is four.2 加 2 等于 4。❷adj.positive 正的：a ～ growth rate 正增长率 Ⅲ*n.*❶ the sign"＋" 正号；加号 ❷ a positive quality 增益；好处：be a ～ for 对……有好处

ply¹ /plaɪ/

　n. ❶ a thin layer of wood（夹板）层：three-～ wood 三层夹板 ❷ a strand of rope,wool,etc.（绳、毛线等的）股：three-～ rope 三股绳

ply² /plaɪ/

　*v.*❶ work at 从事：someone who plies a trade 从事贸易的人 ❷ go regularly between 经常来往于：a ship that plies between London and New York 一艘经常来往于伦敦和纽约之间的船 ❸ ask often 常问：～ someone with questions 常问某人问题

plywood/ˈplaɪwʊd/

　n. material made of thin layers of wood glued and pressed together 胶合板；夹板

p.m.,**P.M.**/ˌpiː ˈem/

　abbr. post meridiem；after midday 下午；午后：5 ～ 下午 5 点

pock/pɒk/

　*n.*a mark on the skin caused by smallpox 麻点；痘疱‖～marked *adj.* 有痘疮的

pocked /pɒkt/

　*adj.*having holes or hollow marks on the surface（表面）有洞的，有坑的

pocket/ˈpɒkɪt/

　n. a small bag sewn in clothing for carrying things 衣袋；口袋‖ pick one's ～ 扒窃‖～book *n.*笔记本/～money *n.*零用钱

pod/pɒd/

　*n.*a long seed vessel containing the seeds of some plants,e.g.peas or beans 豆荚

poem/ˈpəʊɪm/

　*n.*a piece of writing in verse 诗；韵文：Often a ～ has words that rhyme.诗的词语常常是押韵的。

poet/ˈpəʊɪt/

　*n.*a writer of poems 诗人：a realistic ～ 现实主义诗人

poetic/pəʊˈetɪk/

　　*adj.*of, like, or connected with poetry 诗的;诗歌的:~ genius 诗歌方面的天才

poetry/ˈpəʊɪtri/

　　*n.*❶ the art of a poem;poems in general 作诗法;诗(总称):a collection of ~ 一本诗集 ❷ the quality of beauty,grace,and deep feeling 诗意:the ~ of dance 舞蹈中的诗意

point/pɔɪnt/

　　Ⅰ *v.*direct to;show the position of 指;指向;指出:The signpost ~s to the hospital.路牌指向那家医院。 Ⅱ *n.*❶ a tip;a sharp end 尖;尖端 ❷ a position(real or imagined)in space or time 地点;时刻:a ~ of departure 出发点/a turning ~ 转折点 ❸ a score;a mark or unit on a scale of measurement 分数;刻度;点:the boiling ~ 沸点 ❹ the main idea in sth. that is said or done 要点;目的:You've missed the whole ~.你没有抓住整个要点。 ❺ the purpose or aim of sth.目的 ‖ a ~ of view 观点/beside(off)the ~ 离题;不中肯/in ~ of 就……而言;关于/keep to the ~ 扣住主题/make a ~ of doing 重视;特意/on the ~ of 正要……的时候/to the ~ 中肯;扼要

pointed/ˈpɔɪntɪd/

　　*adj.*❶having a sharp end 尖的:a ~ jaw 尖下巴 ❷directed clearly against a particular person or his behaviour 尖锐的;明确的:a ~ criticism 尖锐的批评/ a ~ remark 一针见血的话

pointer/ˈpɔɪntə(r)/

　　*n.*❶a stick used to point to things on a map,etc.指示棒;教鞭 ❷an indicator on a dial or balance(标度盘或天平上的)指针 ❸ a hint;a suggestion 暗示;建议:I can give him a ~ or two.我可以给他一两点提示。

pointless/ˈpɔɪntlɪs/

　　*adj.*❶having no meaning or purpose 无意义的;无目的的 ❷not having scored any points 无得分的 ‖ ~ly *adv.*不相干地;漫无目标地;不得要领地

poise/pɔɪz/

　　Ⅰ *v.*keep balanced;hold lightly in a position of being steady (使)平衡;保持平衡:He ~d the bottle on the edge of the shelf.他把瓶子稳稳地放在架子边上。/ The little girl ~d herself on her toes.小女孩踮着脚尖使身体保持平衡。 Ⅱ *n.*❶ balance 平衡;均衡:~ of the body 身体的平衡 ❷ the way of holding one's head or body(头部或身体的)姿态,体态 ❸ good self-control and self-possession 沉着;泰然自若:a woman of great ~ 一位泰然自若的妇女

poised/pɔɪzd/

　　*adj.*having a composed and self-assured manner 镇定的;镇静的

poison/ˈpɔɪzn/

　　Ⅰ *n.*❶ a drug or other substance very dangerous to life and health 毒;毒药;毒物:take ~ 服毒/One man's meat is another man's ~.各有所好。 ❷ harmful thoughts,feelings,etc.有害的思想(感情)等 Ⅱ *v.*harm or kill with poison;put poison into(onto)毒害;毒杀;下毒:He tried to ~ the dog.他想毒死这只狗。

poisonous/ˈpɔɪzənəs/

　　*adj.*❶ containing poison;having the effect of poison 有毒的;有害的:~ weeds 毒草 ❷ morally injurious 败坏的;恶毒的:a ~ lie 歹毒的谎言

poke/pəʊk/

　　v. push(a pointed thing)into sth.(sb.)戳;刺;插;捅:~ a hole in the paper 在纸上戳个洞/~ the fire with a stick 用棍子拨火 ‖ ~ fun at 嘲笑;取笑/~ one's nose into 管闲事

poker[1] /ˈpəʊkə(r)/

　　n. a long, metal rod for stirring up the coals, wood, etc. in a fire 拨火棒 ‖ ~-faced *adj.* 面无表情的

poker[2] /ˈpəʊkə(r)/

　　*n.*a card game which is usually played for money 扑克牌游戏

polar/ˈpəʊlə(r)/

　　*adj.*❶ of or near the North or South Pole 极地的;近极地的:the ~ circles 南极圈和北极圈 ❷directly opposite 截然相

反的：～ viewpoints 截然对立的观点

polarity /pəʊˈlærɪti/

　　n. the property of having poles or being polar 极性

polarize /ˈpəʊləraɪz/

　　v. ❶ restrict similar vibrations of (a light wave or other transverse wave) to a single direction or plane 使产生偏振 ❷ (in physics) cause sth. to have polarity (物理中的)使产生极性,使极化 ❸ separate into two extremes of opinion 使(观点)形成对立的两派：The debate has become ～d.那场辩论形成了对立的两派。‖ **polarization** *n.* 极化;偏振;两极分化

pole /pəʊl/

　　n. ❶ a tall,slender piece of wood,etc. that stands on the ground to hold sth. up 杆;柱;棒：the telephone ～ 电线杆 /a flag ～ 旗杆 /a bean ～ 豆架 ❷ either the north or south end of the earth's axis 极(点)：the North (South) Pole 北(南)极 /the ～ star 北极星 ❸ either of the two ends of a magnet;either of the two points of an electric battery 磁极;电极：the negative ～ 阴极;负极 /the positive ～ 阳极;正极

polemic /pəˈlemɪk/

　　n. ❶ a fierce attack on or defence of an opinion 争论;辩论;论战 ❷ the art or practice of attacking or defending opinions,ideas,etc. 辩论术;辩论法

polemical /pəˈlemɪkl/

　　adj. written or said with the main purpose of attacking or defending opinions,ideas, etc. as if in an argument,rather than simply expressing or explaining them 争论的;论战的

police /pəˈliːs/

　　Ⅰ *n.* (*pl.*) (the ～) the civil force of a state,responsible for the prevention and detection of crime and the maintenance of public order 警察部队;警察;警方：several hundred ～ 数百名警察 /～ station; office of a local ～ force 警察分局;派出所 /The drunken driver was taken to the ～ station.那位醉酒的司机被带进了警察

局。Ⅱ *v.* keep order in a place with police or as with police;control 维持……的治安;控制：～ a lawless place 维持闹事地点的治安

policy /ˈpɒləsi/

　　n. ❶ a general plan of a political party, government,business company 方针;政策：a foreign ～ 对外政策 /the educational ～ 教育方针 /carry out (implement) a ～ 执行(落实)政策 ❷ a wise and sensible conduct;the art of government 权谋;策略;治术：Honesty is the best ～.诚实是上策。 ❸ terms of a contract of insurance 保险单：insurance ～ 保险单

polio /ˈpəʊliəʊ/

　　n. a type of disease which causes paralysis (short for **poliomyelitis** /ˌpəʊliəʊˌmaɪəˈlaɪtɪs/) 小儿麻痹症

polish /ˈpɒlɪʃ/

　　Ⅰ *v.* ❶ make or become smooth and shiny by rubbing 擦亮;打磨：～ one's shoes with a brush 用刷子把皮鞋擦亮 ❷ improve sth. by making changes,modifying, etc. 润色;修改：He ～ed the paper before handing in it for the teacher.把论文交给老师之前,他进行了仔细的修改润色。Ⅱ *n.* a substance used to give smoothness or shine 擦光剂;擦光油：shoe ～ 鞋油

polished /ˈpɒlɪʃt/

　　adj. ❶ elegant or refined 优雅的;有教养的 ❷ accomplished and skillful 完美的;精湛的：The singers gave a ～ performance.这些歌唱家进行了一场完美的表演。

polite /pəˈlaɪt/

　　adj. having or showing good manners; courteous 有礼貌的;客气的：It is ～ to say "Please" when you ask for a thing.当你向别人要东西的时候,说声"请"才有礼貌。

politic /ˈpɒlətɪk/

　　adj. wise;prudent 精明的;有智慧的;有策略的：a ～ action 有策略的行动

political /pəˈlɪtɪkl/

　　adj. ❶ relating to politics 政治的;政治上的：～ economy 政治经济学 /～ power

政权 ❷connected with different parties 政党的;党派的

politician/ˌpɒlɪ'tɪʃn/
n.a person taking part in politics or much interested in politics;one who is skilled in maneuvering 从政者;政治家;政客:a professional ～ 职业政治家

politicize/pə'lɪtɪsaɪz/
v.❶ give a political character to 使政治化;使具有政治性 ❷ cause to develop an interest in politics 使对政治有兴趣 ‖ politicization *n*.政治化

politicking/'pɒlətɪkɪŋ/
n.a political activity,especially for personal advantage 政治活动;(尤指)拉拢活动

politico/pə'lɪtɪkəʊ/
n.a politician or other person who is active in politics 政客

politics/'pɒlətɪks/
n.the science of political affairs 政治学:I'm very interested in ～.我对政治很感兴趣。

polity/'pɒləti/
n.an organized society;a state as a political entity 政治组织;政体;国体

poll/pəʊl/
Ⅰ *n*.❶the giving of votes at an election 选举投票:be successful at the ～ 选举投票中获胜 ❷ the number of votes recorded at an election 投票数:head the ～ 选票最多 Ⅱ *v*.vote at an election 投票

pollard/'pɒləd/
Ⅰ *n*.❶a tree from which the top has been cut in order to make the branches below the cut place grow more thickly 截去了树梢的树;截头木 ❷ a hornless kind or sheep,goat,etc.无角的动物;无角兽 Ⅱ *v*.cut the top off (a tree) in order to make lower branches grow more thickly 截去(树的)树梢(以使枝叶更繁茂)

pollen/'pɒlən/
n.fine powder (usually yellow) which is found on flowers and which makes other flowers fertile when it is brought to them (e.g.by the wind,bees,etc.) 花粉

pollinate/'pɒləneɪt/
v.cause (a flower or plant) to be able to produce seeds by adding or bringing pollen 给(花、植物)传播花粉:Flowers are often ～d by bees.花常常由蜜蜂传播花粉。

polling/'pəʊlɪŋ/
n.the act of voting 投票:Polling was quite heavy.投票很踊跃。

pollster/'pəʊlstə(r)/
n.a person who carries out, or who explains the meaning of the results of polls 民意调查者

pollutant/pə'lu:tənt/
n.a substance, especially a waste product of an industrial process, that pollutes sth. 污染物质:Pollutants are constantly being released into the atmosphere.污染物质正在不断地被排放到大气中去。

pollute/pə'lu:t/
v.make dirty or impure 污染;弄脏:Many rivers and lakes have been ～d by industrial waste.许多河流湖泊都已被工业物污染。

pollution/pə'lu:ʃn/
n.❶the act or process of making air,water,etc.dirty or being polluted 污染;玷污:industrial ～ 工业污染/ cultural ～ 文化污染 ❷ a substance that pollutes water,air,or atmosphere 污染物:the ～ on the beach 海滩上的污染物

polygamy/pə'lɪɡəmi/
n.the act or custom of having more than one wife 一夫多妻制

polygon/'pɒlɪɡən/
n.a plane figure having more than four angles and four sides 多角形;多边形

polysyllable/ˌpɒlɪ'sɪləbl/
n.a polysyllabic word 多音节词

polytechnic/ˌpɒlɪ'teknɪk/
n.an institution(usually for adults)where many different subjects are taught,especially practical subjects (尤指教授应用学科)理工学院

pomp/pɒmp/
n.a solemn, magnificent display 盛况;大场面:The queen was greeted at the town

hall with much ～ and ceremony. 女王在市政厅里受到隆重的欢迎。‖ ～ous *adj.* 傲慢的;自大的:a ～ous official 傲慢的官僚 /～ously *adv.* 傲慢地;自大地

pond/pɒnd/
n. a small area of water that is smaller than a lake 池塘:the village ～ 乡村池塘

ponder/'pɒndə(r)/
v. consider; think over 考虑;沉思: He ～ed the problem for a long time.这个问题他考虑很久了。‖ ～ation *n.*考虑;沉思

ponderous/'pɒndərəs/
*adj.*❶ very heavy 沉重的;笨重的:a ～ item 沉重的物品 ❷ slow and clumsy 粗笨的;笨拙的:～ movements 粗笨的动作 ❸(with reference to a person) dull and slow (指人)呆板的,沉闷的

pool/puːl/
Ⅰ *n.*❶ a small area of still water 水池;池塘;水坑:a swimming ～ 游泳池 ❷ a small amount of any liquid on a surface 一小摊液体:lie in a ～ of blood 躺在血泊中 ❸ the total of money staked by a number of gamblers 赌注总额 ❹ an arrangement by business firms to share business and divide profits, to avoid competition and agree on prices 合伙经营;联营 ❺ a common fund or service provided by or shared among many contributors 公共基金或服务:a typing ～ 联合打字服务 /a car ～ 汽车互助组 ❻a game on a billiard table with six pockets 台球 Ⅱ *v.*put money or other assets into a common fund 集中(钱或其他资金等)共同使用:～ our ideas 把我们大家的想法集中起来 /They ～ed their money to buy a gift.他们共同出钱买礼物。

poor/pɔː(r)/
*adj.*❶ having little or no money 贫穷的:a ～ country 穷国 ❷ unfortunate; needing pity or sympathy 不幸的;可怜的:The ～ little girl began to cry.那个可怜的小女孩开始哭起来。❸ bad in quantity 劣质的;差的:in ～ health 健康不佳‖ as ～ as a church mouse 一贫如洗 ‖ ～house *n.*救济院

poorly/'pɔːli/
Ⅰ *adj.* unwell 身体不适的:She is feeling ～ today.她今天感到身体不舒适。Ⅱ *adv.*in a way or at a level which is considered inadequate 不足地;欠佳地:The boy is ～ fed.那男孩经常吃不饱。

poorness/'pɔːnɪs/
n. lowness of quality; lack of a desired quality 粗劣;低劣:the ～ of the quality of the materials 材料质量的低劣

pop[1]/pɒp/
n. a modern popular music of a simple kind with a strong beat and not of lasting interest, liked especially by younger people 流行音乐:a ～ star 流行歌手

pop[2]/pɒp/
Ⅰ *n.*a sound like that of a slight explosion 砰的一声;爆破声:The cork came out of the bottle with a ～.塞子砰的一声从瓶子里飞出来了。Ⅱ *v.*(-pp-)❶(cause to) make a short sharp explosive sound 发出砰的一声;(使)发爆裂声 ❷go or come quickly 疾走;迅速行动:I've just ～ped in to say goodbye to you.我匆匆进来向你告别。‖ ～ off 急速离去;死掉/～ up 突然出现

pope/pəʊp/
n.(often the Pope) the head of the Roman Catholic Church 教皇

poplar/'pɒplə(r)/
*n.*a tall, thin tree that grows very quickly 白杨树

poppy/'pɒpi/
*n.*❶ a plant with large red, white or yellow flowers 罂粟 ❷ the flower of this plant 罂粟花

popular/'pɒpjulə(r)/
*adj.*❶ liked or enjoyed by the general public 流行的;受欢迎的:a ～ song 流行歌曲 ❷ suited to the understanding or needs of the general 大众的,通俗的 ❸ of the ordinary people 民众的:～ support 民众的支持

popularity/ˌpɒpjuˈlærəti/
n. the quality of being liked, favoured, or admired by the ordinary people 大众性;

普及；流行：win ～ 得人心 /the ～ of table tennis 乒乓球运动的流行

popularize /'pɒpjʊləraɪz/
v. ❶ cause to be well known and generally liked or used 普及；推广：Reggae music was ～d by Bob Marley in the 1970s. 雷鬼音乐是鲍勃·马利在 20 世纪 70 年代推广开来的。❷ make（a difficult subject or idea）easily understood to ordinary people 使通俗化；使易懂

popularly /'pɒpjʊləli/
adv. generally；by most people 一般地；广泛地：It's ～ believed that taking large amounts of vitamin C cures colds. 一般认为大剂量服用维生素 C 可以治疗感冒。

populate /'pɒpjʊleɪt/
v. (usually passive) inhabit in an area（常用被动）居住于：a densely ～d area 人口稠密地区

population /ˌpɒpjʊ'leɪʃn/
n. ❶ people living in a place, country, etc. 人口：the ～ of London 伦敦的人口 /a fall（rise）in ～ 人口的减少（增加）/ What's the ～ of China? 中国的人口有多少？❷ the total number of people who live there 人口数

populist /'pɒpjʊlɪst/
n. ❶ a person who claims to believe in the wisdom and judgment of ordinary people, especially in political matters 平民主义者；平民论者 ❷ (especially in the US) a member of a political party that claims to represent ordinary people（尤指美国的）平民党党员

populous /'pɒpjʊləs/
adj. (of a place) having a large population, especially when compared with its size 人口稠密的：London is the most ～ area of Britain. 伦敦是英国人口最稠密的地区。

porcelain /'pɔːsəlɪn/
n. a hard, shiny substance made by heating clay and used for making delicate cups and decorative objects；objects that are made of this 瓷；瓷器：That figure is made of ～. 那个人像是瓷制的。

pore /pɔː(r)/
n. a tiny opening（especially in the skin）through which fluids（especially sweat）may pass 毛孔；小孔：～s in the human skin 人皮肤上的毛孔

pork /pɔːk/
n. meat from a pig（usually fresh and not smoked or salted）猪肉：～ chop 猪排

porous /'pɔːrəs/
adj. allowing liquid to pass through 可渗透的：～ soil 可渗透的土壤

porridge /'pɒrɪdʒ/
n. a thick, sticky food made from oats cooked in water or milk 粥；麦片粥

port /pɔːt/
n. ❶ a harbour 港口：close a ～ 封港 ❷ a town or a city with a harbour 港市；口岸：a trading ～ 通商口岸

portable /'pɔːtəbl/
adj. able to be easily carried 手提式的；轻便的：a ～ typewriter 手提式打字机

portend /pɔː'tend/
v. be a sign or warning that sth. is going to happen 预兆；预示

portent /'pɔːtənt/
n. a sign that sth. important or calamitous will happen 前兆；预示；迹象

porter /'pɔːtə(r)/
n. ❶ a doorkeeper；a gatekeeper 守门人：a hospital ～ 医院看门人 ❷ a person whose job is to carry things 脚夫；挑夫：a railway station ～ 火车站搬运工

portfolio /pɔːt'fəʊliəʊ/
n. ❶ a flat, portable case for carrying papers, etc. 公事包；文件夹 ❷ the position and duties of a minister of state or a member of a cabinet 部长职；阁员职

portion /'pɔːʃn/
Ⅰ *n.* ❶ a part；a share 一部分；一份：a large ～ of the products 大部分产品 ❷ the amount of food given to one person at a meal（食物的）一份：Two ～s of salad, please. 请来两份色拉。Ⅱ *v.* divide into parts or shares 把……分成多份：She ～ed out the pie so everyone had a piece. 她把馅饼切开给每人一块。

portly/ˈpɔːtli/

　*adj.*fat 肥胖的：a ～ old gentleman 肥胖的老绅士

portrait/ˈpɔːtreɪt, -trət/

　n. ❶ a picture of a person 肖像；画像：A ～ of his grandfather hung in the hall. 厅里挂着他祖父的画像。❷ a very clear description in words of a person's appearance and character 生动描写；人物描写

portray /pɔːˈtreɪ/

　v. ❶make a picture of a person or animal 描述；刻画 ❷ describe sb. or sth. in words or represent them in a play or film（演员在戏剧或电影中）表现；扮演

pose/pəʊz/

　v. ❶(cause to) sit or stand in a particular position, especially in order to be photographed, painted, etc. 摆好姿势；作好姿势 ❷ask（a question that is difficult or needs to be carefully thought about）提出(问题等)：He ～d a very strange question at the meeting. 他在会上提出了一个非常奇怪的问题。

position/pəˈzɪʃn/

　n. ❶ a place where a thing or person is 位置；地方：Can you show me the ～ of your factory on this map? 你能在这张地图上给我指一指你们工厂的位置吗？❷ a certain way of holding body; a posture 姿势：Are you sitting in a comfortable ～? 你坐的姿势舒服吗？❸a condition; a situation 情况；状况；处境‖ in a ～ to do sth. 能够(做某事)/in (out of) ～ 在(不在)适当的位置

positive/ˈpɒzətɪv/

　adj. ❶ definite and clear 明确的；肯定无疑的：a ～ proof 确证/a ～ fact 无可怀疑的事实 ❷ practical and constructive 有效的；建设性；确有助益的 ❸ showing pleasing progress 积极的：bring all ～ factors into play 调动一切积极因素

positively/ˈpɒzətɪvli/

　adv. ❶in a positive way 有把握地 ❷with certainty; so as to leave no room for doubt 明确地；毋庸置疑地

possess/pəˈzes/

　v. ❶ own or have sth. 有；拥有：He ～es a lot of money. 他拥有很多钱。❷ own or have a particular quality 具有(特质) ❸ have influence on sb.'s feelings 控制(情感)‖ be ～ed of 有；拥有；享有/be ～ed with 被(某种想法)迷住心窍

possession/pəˈzeʃn/

　n. ❶ the state of holding or having sth. 占有；拥有；具有；持有：countries in ～ of nuclear weapons 拥有核武器的国家 / The house is in my ～. 这栋房子归我所有。❷（usually *pl.*) sth. possessed; personal property 所有物；财产：personal ～s 个人财产 ❸ ownership 所有权

possessive/pəˈzesɪv/

　adj. ❶of possession or ownership 所有(权)的 ❷ showing that sth. belongs to sb. or sth. 所属关系的；所有格的：～ pronouns 所有格代词

possibility/ˌpɒsəˈbɪləti/

　n. ❶ sth. that is possible 可能的事：There are three possibilities. 有三种可能。❷ the state of being possible;（degree of）likelihood 可能；可能性：There is a ～ that the train may be late. 火车有晚点的可能性。

possible/ˈpɒsəbl/

　adj. ❶that can exist, happen, or be done 可能的；可行的：finish the task as soon as ～ 尽早完成任务 ❷that can be reasonable or acceptable 合理的；可接受的：There are two ～ explanations of the matter. 这件事有两种合理的解释。

possibly/ˈpɒsəbli/

　adv. ❶ used to emphasize that someone has or will put all their effort into sth. 尽可能地：I'll do all I ～ can. 我将尽一切能去做。❷ perhaps 也许；或者：He may ～ recover. 他也许会恢复健康。

post¹ /pəʊst/

　Ⅰ *n.* a strong thick upright pole or bar made of wood, metal, etc., fixed into the ground or some other base, especially as a support 柱；支柱；标杆：gate～ 门柱 Ⅱ *v.* display（a notice）in a public place 张贴(通知)‖ ～ up 张贴出去；公布‖ ～er *n.*

招贴；海报

post² /pəʊst/

I *n.* ❶ the official system for carrying letters, parcels, etc., from the sender to the receiver 邮寄：I'll send the book by ～.我将把这本书邮寄出去。❷ letters and parcels delivered 邮件 II *v.* send (a letter, parcel, etc.) by post 邮寄：I ～ed the letter a week ago.这封信我已寄出一周了。‖ ～man *n.* 邮差；邮递员/～master *n.* 邮政局长

postage /'pəʊstɪdʒ/

n. the money charged for carrying a letter, parcel, etc. by post 邮资；邮费：～ due 欠(邮)资

postal /'pəʊstl/

adj. ❶ connected with the public letter service 邮政的；邮局的：Postal charges have gone up again. 邮资又涨价了。❷ sent by post 邮寄的：a ～ vote 邮寄投票

postbag /'pəʊstbæg/

n. ❶ a postman's bag for carrying letters 邮袋 ❷ all the letters received by someone at one particular time 一次收到的邮件：The magazine's advice column always gets a big ～.杂志的意见栏经常收到大批来信。

postbox /'pəʊstbɒks/

n. an official metal box in a public place, fixed to the ground or on a wall, into which people can put letters to be collected and sent by post (投寄信件用的)邮箱，邮筒

postcard /'pəʊstkɑːd/

n. ❶ a card of a fixed size for sending messages by post without an envelope 明信片 ❷ a card like this with a picture or photograph on one side (印有图画或照片的)明信片

postcode /'pəʊstkəʊd/

n. a group of letters and/or numbers that mean a particular small area, and can be added to a postal address so that letters, etc. can be delivered more quickly 邮政编码

postdate /'pəʊst'deɪt/

v. ❶ write a date later than the actual date of writing on (a letter, cheque, etc.) 把……的日期填迟；在……上填事后日期：My rent's due on Monday and I'm not paid until Friday — I'll have to ～ the rent cheque.我的房租应在星期一交，但我要到星期五才领工资——所以我得把交租金的支票日期填迟一些。❷ occur or come at a later date 发生在……之后

poster /'pəʊstə(r)/

n. a large notice or picture stuck on a wall or notice board for advertisement 海报；广告；招贴画：～ paper 广告纸

posterity /pɒ'sterəti/

n. ❶ a person's descendants 子孙 ❷ people who will be living at some future time 后代：discoveries which will be of great benefit to ～ 对后代极有益的发现

postgraduate /ˌpəʊst'grædʒʊət/

I *adj.* (of studies, etc.) done after taking a first academic degree 研究生的：a ～ course 研究生课程 II *n.* a person engaged in postgraduate studies 研究生

posthumous /'pɒstjʊməs/

adj. after the death of someone 死后的：a ～ child 遗腹子/a ～ book 遗著

postpone /pə'spəʊn/

v. put off to a later time 延迟；延期：We are postponing our trip until the weather grows warmer.我们打算把旅行推迟到天气暖和一些的时候再进行。/～ sending an answer 暂缓答复

postscript /'pəʊstskrɪpt/

n. sth. added at the end of a letter, after the signature (usually introduced by the letters P.S.) 附言，又及，再者(通常用P.S.表示)

posture /'pɒstʃə(r)/

I *n.* ❶ the position of the body；a way of holding the body 姿势；姿态：a sitting ～ 坐姿 ❷ a particular way of dealing with or considering sth.；an approach or attitude (处理或考虑问题的)方式，方法，态度 II *v.* ❶ put in a certain position；pose 使作出某种姿势：～ a model 让模特儿摆出某种姿势 ❷ behave in a way that is intended to impress or mislead others 故作姿态：He enjoys posturing in front of an audience.他喜欢在观众面前故作姿态。

post-war /ˌpəʊstˈwɔː(r)/

adj. existing after a war，especially the Second World War 战后的（尤指二战后的）：a ～ building 一座战后建筑

posy /ˈpəʊzi/

n. a small bunch of flowers 小花束：The little girl was holding a ～.小姑娘正拿着一束花。

pot /pɒt/

I *n.* a round vessel of earthenware，metal or glass for holding liquids or solids，for cooking things in 锅；壶；罐；瓶；盆：a tea ～ 茶壶 /a flower ～ 花盆 /a watering ～ 喷壶 /make a ～ of tea 沏壶茶 /a salt ～ 盐罐 /a ～ of sugar 一罐糖 /a ～ of soup 一锅汤 II *v.*(-tt-) put into a pot 罐藏；装罐：～ted meat 罐头肉

potassium /pəˈtæsiəm/

n. a soft，silver-white，metallic chemical element 钾

potato /pəˈteɪtəʊ/

n. a roundish root plant with white flesh，commonly used as a vegetable 马铃薯

potency /ˈpəʊtənsi/

*n.*❶power or influence 威力；影响 ❷ the extent of the contribution of sb.or sth.to affect sth.潜能；潜力

potent /ˈpəʊtnt/

*adj.*❶ having a strong and rapid effect on the body or mind 强有力的；有效力的：a ～ cure 有效的治疗 ❷ strongly persuasive；convincing 有说服力的；使人信服的：～ arguments 使人信服的论点 ❸ (of a male) able to have sexual relations （指男性）有性交能力的 ❹ having great power，especially politically （尤指政治上）强有力的，有势力的：a ～ effect on ……产生很大的影响

potential /pəˈtenʃl/

I *adj.* existing in possibility；that may come into action 可能的；潜在的：～ resources 潜在的资源 /～ enemy 潜在的敌人 /She is seen as a ～ leader of the party.她被看作是该党的未来领袖。II *n.* ❶ the possibility for developing or being developed 潜力；可能性：industrial ～ 工业潜力 /war ～s 军事潜力 /tap the ～ of production 挖掘生产潜力 ❷ electromotive force expressed in volts 电势，电位

potion /ˈpəʊʃn/

n. a drink of medicine，or poison 药水；毒液

potted /ˈpɒtɪd/

*adj.*❶ (of a piece of writing) shortened or abridged from a longer version （作品）简洁的 ❷(of food) preserved in a pot (食物)罐(坛)装保存的：～ shrimps 罐装虾

potter /ˈpɒtə/

I *n.* a person who makes clay pots by hand 陶工 II *v.*occupy oneself in a desultory but pleasant manner，doing a number of small tasks or not concentrating on any-thing particular 闲散地做琐事

pottery /ˈpɒtəri/

n. ❶ vessels and other objects made of baked clay 陶器 ❷the craft or profession of making pottery，or the place where it is made 制陶工艺；制陶业；陶器工厂；陶器作坊

pouch /paʊtʃ/

*n.*❶ a small bag 小袋子：tobacco ～ 烟袋 ❷ a part of the body coming out to form a bag on the stomach for carrying their young，or in the cheeks for storing food 育儿袋；(动物藏食物的)颊袋：kangaroo's ～ 袋鼠的育儿袋

poultry /ˈpəʊltri/

n. (*pl.*) any domestic fowl as chickens，turkeys，geese，and ducks，usually raised for their meat or eggs 家禽：Their ～ are kept in the yard.他们的家禽关在院子里。

pound¹ /paʊnd/

*n.*❶ the standard unit of money in Britain，divided into 100 pence 英镑（一镑等于 100 便士）：A ～ is made up of 100 pence or pennies.一英镑有一百便士。❷ a unit of weight equal to 0.454 kilograms 磅(重量单位，等于 0.454 千克)

pound² /paʊnd/

　v. ❶ strike heavily and repeatedly 连续重击：He ~ed the table angrily. 他愤怒地捶着桌子。❷ move with noisy steps 咚咚地走 ❸ beat quickly and loudly（心脏）狂跳 ❹ hit sth. many times to break it into smaller pieces 捣碎；击碎

pour /pɔː(r)/

　v. ❶（cause to）flow from a container（使）流；倒；流出；涌出：~ the milk from the pitcher into the glass 把牛奶从壶里倒入杯里 /~ out tea 倒茶 /The people ~ed out of the hall. 人们涌出大厅。❷ express one's ideas, etc. freely 倾诉：~ out words 侃侃而谈 ❸（of rain）fall heavily（雨）倾盆而下：The rain ~ed down during the storm. 暴风雨期间大雨倾盆。

poverty /ˈpɒvəti/

　n. the condition of being poor 贫穷：Many people in the world are still living in ~. 现在世界上还有很多人仍然生活在贫困之中。

powder /ˈpaʊdə(r)/

　Ⅰ *n.* ❶ a dry mass of very small fine pieces or grains 粉末；粉：grind into ~ 磨成粉 /baking ~ 发酵粉 /soap ~ 肥皂粉 /face ~ 定妆粉 ❷ gunpowder 火药：~ and shot 弹药 Ⅱ *v.* ❶ crush or grind into powder 把……磨成粉 ❷ cover with powder; use powder on the face 撒（擦）粉于；搽香粉：~ one's face 往脸上搽粉

power /ˈpaʊə(r)/

　Ⅰ *n.* ❶ the ability to do or act 能力：It is not within my ~ to help. 我没有能力相助。❷（*pl.*）the faculty of the body or mind 体力；智力；精力：the ~ of vision 视力 ❸ energy of force that can do work, especially electrical energy 动力：wind ~ 风力 ❹ the right or authority 权力；政权：organs of state ~ 国家权力机关 ❺ the right to act, given by law, rule, or official position 权限：the ~s of the president 总统的职权 ❻ a person, group, nation, etc. that has influence or control 当权者；有影响的机构；强国：The great ~s held an international conference. 强国召开了国际会议。❼ the num-ber of times that an amount is to be mul-tiplied by itself; the result of this multiply-ing 乘方；幂：The third ~ of 2 is 8.2 的 3 次方是 8。Ⅱ *v.* provide with power 给……提供动力：All these training aids are ~ed by electricity. 所有这些教具都是电动的。

powerful /ˈpaʊəfl/

　adj. having or producing great power 强的；强大的；强有力的：a ~ nation 强国 / a ~ voice 一个洪亮的声音

practical /ˈpræktɪkl/

　Ⅰ *adj.* ❶ having to do with action or practice rather than thought or theory 实际的；实践的：~ work 实际工作 /~ ex-perience 实际经验 /~ activities 实践活动 /~ difficulty 实际困难 /take (adopt) ~ measures 采取实际措施 ❷ engaged in actual work; experienced 实际从事的；经验丰富的：a ~ engineer 有经验的工程师 ❸ fit for actual practice; workable 实用的；可行的：a ~ dictionary 实用词典 /~ chemistry 应用化学 Ⅱ *n.* an exam or a les-son in which theories are applied to do sth. or make things 实用知识考试；实用知识教学

practicality /ˌpræktɪˈkæləti/

　n. ❶ the quality or state of being practical 实际性；实用性；实践性 ❷ the aspects of a situation that involve the actual doing or experience of sth. rather than theories or ideas 实际事物；实例；实用之物

practically /ˈpræktɪkli/

　adv. ❶ in a practical way 实际上：He was ~ a dictator. 他实际上是个独裁者。❷ nearly; almost 几乎：He knew ~ no Eng-lish. 他几乎不懂英语。

practice /ˈpræktɪs/

　Ⅰ *n.* ❶ actual use; actual doing of sth. 实践；实施；实行：They put the plan into ~. 他们把计划付诸实施。❷ repeated exer-cise or training of doing sth. 练习；实习 ❸ the business of a doctor or a lawyer（医生或律师的）业务：The doctor has a ~ in Changsha. 这位医生在长沙工作。‖ in ~ 在实践中；实际上 /make a ~ of 经常进行 /out of ~ 久不练习；荒疏 /put

in（into）～ 实行；实施 Ⅱ v.＝practise ‖
practicable adj.可实行的；行得通的

practise /ˈpræktɪs/
　　v.❶ do sth. repeatedly or regularly in order to become skilful; do sth. actively 练
习；实习；训练：～ criticism and self-crit-
icism 进行批评与自我批评/～（at）
shooting 练习射击 ❷ do the work of a
doctor or a lawyer, etc. 从事（医务、法律
专业等）：He ～s medicine. 他开业行医。

practised /ˈpræktɪst/
　　adj. expert and skillful, typically as the
result of much experience（尤指由于经
验丰富而）内行的,熟练的,娴熟的

practitioner /prækˈtɪʃənə/
　　n. a person actively engaged in art, discipline, or profession, especially medicine
（艺术、学科或职业,尤指医药）开业者,
从业人员

prairie /ˈpreəri/
　　n. a very large area of flat, grassy land, especially in North America（尤指北美）大
草原

praise /preɪz/
　　Ⅰ v. speak well of; express admiration of;
applaud 表扬；称赞：The teacher ～d the
child for his honesty. 老师称赞这孩子诚
实。Ⅱ n. an expression of admiration 称
赞；颂扬；赞美之词：This is a book in ～
of country life. 这是一本赞美乡村的书。
‖ **sing one's own** ～s 自吹自擂/**sing the** ～s
of 歌颂；颂扬 ‖ ～**ful** adj.赞美的；赞不绝
口的/～**worthy** adj.值得称赞的

pray /preɪ/
　　v. ❶ speak to God with love and worship
祷告；祈祷：～ to God for help 向上帝祈
祷求助 ❷ ask earnestly 请求；恳求：I ～
you to think again. 我请求你再考虑一下。
❸ please 请（正式请求）：Pray don't
speak so loud. 请不要这样大声说话。/
Pray be quiet! 请安静！

prayer /preə(r)/
　　n. ❶ the act of praying to god; a form of
church worship 祈祷；祷告；祈祷式：Eve-
ning Prayer 晚祷 ❷ a fixed form of
words used in praying 祈祷文

preach /priːtʃ/
　　v. ❶ give religious talk（sermon）espe-
cially as a part of service in church 讲道；
说教；劝诫 ❷ advise or urge others to accept or believe sth. 鼓吹；倡导：He often
～es the value of cold bath. 他经常鼓吹冷
水浴的好处。‖ ～**er** n.传道士；说教者；
鼓吹者

precarious /prɪˈkeəriəs/
　　adj. dangerous; uncertain 危险的；不肯定
的：a ～ life 危险的生活 ‖ ～**ly** adv.不安
全地；不确定地

precaution /prɪˈkɔːʃn/
　　n. ❶ caution or care taken beforehand 预
防：as a ～ 为了预防 ❷ a measure taken
beforehand to avoid danger, failure, loss
or harm 预防措施：take all the ～s against
accident 采取一切措施预防意外事故

precede /prɪˈsiːd/
　　v. come or go just in front of or before in
time 居先；在前；优于：It is the stillness
that ～s a storm. 这是暴风雨前的平静。

precedence /ˈpresɪdəns/
　　n. the right of sth. to be put first, or of sb.
to go first, because they are more important or urgent the condition of being considered more important than sb. or sth.
else; the priority in importance, order, or
rank 优先权；（重要性、顺序、头衔）领先；
居前：take ～ 有优先权

precedent /prɪˈsiːdənt/
　　Ⅰ n. a previous action or decision that is
taken as an example to be followed in
other cases of the same kind 先例；前例
Ⅱ adj. preceding in time, order, or importance 在前的；在先的；前面的：a ～ case
一个先例

precious /ˈpreʃəs/
　　adj. ❶ having great value 贵重的；宝贵
的：～ time 宝贵的时间 /～ knowledge
宝贵的知识 ❷ highly valued; dear 珍爱
的；可爱的：Her children are very ～ to
her. 她极珍爱孩子。❸（of language,
style, etc.）overrefined; unnatural（指语
言、风格等）过于讲究的；矫揉造作的：po-
etry full of ～ images 充满了矫揉造作的

P

比喻的诗歌 ❹ considerable 相当的；十足的：a ～ fool 大傻瓜

precipice/'presɪpɪs/
n. a very steep cliff or face of a rock, mountain,etc.悬崖：The climber fell over a ～.那个登山者跌下悬崖。

precipitate/prɪ'sɪpɪteɪt/
Ⅰ *v.* make sth. happen at once, or more quickly than it might have done 加速；突然引起：The killing of the prime minister ～d a war.杀害总理突然引发一场战争。Ⅱ *adj.* done very quickly; done without thinking carefully 匆忙的；鲁莽的：a ～ departure (decision,etc.)匆忙的离开(决定等)

precipitation /prɪˌsɪpɪ'teɪʃən/
n. ❶ the action or process of precipitating a substance from a solution 沉淀(反应)；淀析(作用)；沉降作用 ❷ rain, snow or hail that falls to or on the ground (雨、雪、雹等)降落；降水

precipitous/prɪ'sɪpɪtəs/
adj. very steep 陡峭的

precise/prɪ'saɪs/
adj. ❶ strictly accurate; definite 精确的；明确的：～ measurements 精确的尺寸 ❷ strictly observant, as of rules or standards 严格的；严谨的：He was very ～ in his manner.他说话做事都有板有眼。❸ particular; exact; very 恰好的：At the ～ moment the train started. 就在这时候火车开动了。

precisely /prɪ'saɪsli/
adv. ❶ in a precise manner; exactly 准确地；精确地；毫不含糊地 ❷ used to express agreement with what someone has said 准确地；正好

precision /prɪ'sɪʒən/
n. the quality of being precise, accurate and exact 准确度；精密度；准确性；确切性

preclude/prɪ'kluːd/
v. make sth. impossible; prevent 使不可能；阻止：The condition of the roads ～s us from driving anywhere tonight.道路的情况使我们今晚不可能开车到别处去。

predatory/'predətri/
adj. living by killing and eating other animals 食肉的：a ～ bird 食肉鸟

predecessor/'priːdɪsesə(r)/
n. a person who had a job or position before another person 前任

predestine/ˌpriː'destɪn/
v. (usually with reference to fate or God) decide in advance (通常指命运或上帝)预定，注定：He believed that the time of his death was ～d.他相信他死亡的时间是命中注定的。‖ predestination /priːˌdestɪ'neɪʃn/ *n.*命运；预先注定

predetermine/ˌpriːdɪ'tɜːmɪn/
v. decide before an event occurs 预先决定；预先确定

predicate
Ⅰ /'predɪkət/ *n.* the part of a sentence which makes a statement about the subject 谓语 Ⅱ /'predɪkeɪt/ *v.* declare to be true or real 论断；断言：～ a motive to be good 断言某一动机是好的

predict/prɪ'dɪkt/
v. tell or declare beforehand 预言；预示；预测：He ～ed that war would soon break out.他预言战争很快就会爆发。‖ ～able *adj.*可预测的；可预料的

prediction/prɪ'dɪkʃn/
n. ❶ sth. predicted 预言之事：the weather ～ for the day 当天的气象预报 ❷ the action of predicting sth.预言；预计

predominance /prɪ'dɒmɪnəns/
n. the state or condition of being greater in number or amount (数量等的)优势；普遍；显著：There is a ～ of female teachers.女教师占多数。

predominant/prɪ'dɒmɪnənt/
adj. most powerful, noticeable, or important 占支配地位的；显著的：Wheat is the ～ crop here.小麦是这里的主要农作物。

predominate/prɪ'dɒmɪneɪt/
v. ❶ have or exert control (over) 占支配地位：In his mind a wish to become rich has always ～d.他心目中最大的愿望一直是发财致富。❷ surpass others, as in number or amount (在数量等方面)占优

势：a forest in which oak trees ～ 一个以橡树为主的森林

pre-eminent/ˌpriːˈemɪnənt/

*adj.*most outstanding；best 卓越的；杰出的；最优秀的

preface/ˈprefɪs/

Ⅰ *n.*a note written at the beginning of a book；foreword 序言；前言；绪言 Ⅱ *v.* provide with a preface 为……写序言；作为……开端：He ～d his speech with an amusing story.他以一个有趣的故事作为他演说的开场白。

prefer/prɪˈfɜː(r)/

*v.*choose one thing rather than another；like better 宁愿；更喜欢：I ～ tea to coffee.我喜欢茶而不喜欢咖啡。

preferable/ˈprefrəbl/

*adj.*worthy of being chosen；more desirable 更可取的；更好的：Poverty is ～ to ill health.贫困总比体弱多病好。

preference/ˈprefrəns/

*n.*❶a desire for one thing rather than another 偏爱；优先：He has a ～ for fruit over vegetables.他喜欢吃水果胜过蔬菜。❷the thing preferred 偏爱物：Which is your ～，tea or coffee? 你喜欢喝茶还是咖啡? ❸ a special favour or consideration shown to a person，group，etc. 优先权：～ stock 优先股

preferential /ˌprefəˈrenʃəl/

*adj.*showing or based on a preference 优先的；优待的；优惠的：～ treatment 优惠待遇‖ ～ly *adv.*优先地；优待地；优惠地

prefix

Ⅰ/ˈpriːfɪks/ *n.*❶ syllable(s) put at the beginning of a word to change its meaning 前缀；词头："Semi-" is a ～ that means "half"."Semi-"是意为"一半"的前缀。❷ a word used before a person's name (e.g. Mr.Dr.，etc.) 人名前的尊称(如：Mr.，Dr.等) Ⅱ/ˌpriːˈfɪks/ *v.*add a prefix to；add at the beginning of sth.给……加前缀；放在……之前：～ a new paragraph to Chapter Nine 在第九章前新加一段

pregnancy /ˈpregnənsi/

*n.*the condition or period of being pregnant 怀孕，妊娠；怀孕期，妊娠期

pregnant/ˈpregnənt/

*adj.*❶ (of woman) having a child in the womb 怀孕的 ❷ full of meaning 深意的：a ～ remark 意味深长的话

prehistoric/ˌpriːhɪˈstɒrɪk/

*adj.*belonging to the time before recorded history 史前的：～ man 史前时期的人

prejudice/ˈpredʒudɪs/

*n.*an opinion formed before looking at the facts 偏见；成见：Some people have a ～ against all foreigners.有些人对所有外国人抱有偏见。‖ ～d *adj.*怀偏见的；有成见的

preliminary /prɪˈlɪmɪnəri/

Ⅰ *adj.*coming before an important action or event and preparing for it 初步的；起始的；预备的 Ⅱ *n.*(*pl.*-ies)a preliminary action or event 初步做法；起始行为

prelude/ˈpreljuːd/

Ⅰ *n.*❶ sth.that comes before and acts as introduction to sth.more important 序言；序幕 ❷ a short piece of music that introduces a large musical work 序曲；前奏 Ⅱ *v.*serve as a prelude to 作为……的序言；作序曲；奏序曲：He ～d with some banal remarks.他用一些老生常谈的话作开场白。

premature/ˈpremətjuə(r)/

*adj.*too early；done or happening before the proper time 过早的；早熟的：a ～ decision 过早的决定 ‖ ～ly *adv.*早熟地；过早地

premeditate/ˌpriːˈmedɪteɪt/

*v.*plan or think over sth.before doing it 预谋：a ～d murder 谋杀 ‖ **premeditation**/ˌpriːmedɪˈteɪʃn/ *n.*预谋；预先设想

premier/ˈpremɪə(r)/

Ⅰ *n.*the head of the government in certain countries 总理；首相：Premier of the State Council 国务院总理 Ⅱ *adj.*first in position，importance，etc.首位的；首要的：of ～ importance 头等重要的

premiere/ˈpremɪeə(r)/

*n.*the first performance of a play，film，

etc.(戏剧、影片等的)首次公演

premise/ˈpremɪs/

n.❶a statement which is taken to be true and from which certain conclusions are drawn 前提 ❷(pl.) a house or building, including the lands,etc.belonging to it 房屋连四周土地

premium/ˈpriːmɪəm/

n.an amount paid in or for insurance 保险费：I have insured my house for £5,000 at a ～ of only £10 per year.我为我的房子投保 5 000 英镑,每年的保险费仅 10 英镑。

premonition/ˌpriːməˈnɪʃn, ˌpremˈnɪʃn/

n.a feeling that sth.(usually sth. unpleasant)is going to happen (通常指不祥的)预感,前兆：a ～ of danger 危险的前兆

preoccupy/priːˈɒkjupaɪ/

v.take up so much of someone's attention that he does not notice what is going on around him 使全神贯注于；使出神：look preoccupied 看起来心不在焉/preoccupied by (with) family troubles 由于家庭的麻烦而心事重重‖ **preoccupation** /ˌpriːɒkjuˈpeɪʃn/ n. 全神贯注；出神

prep/prep/

n. preparation for school lessons; homework 预习；家庭作业

preparation/ˌprepəˈreɪʃn/

n.❶ things or work done to get ready for sth.准备工作；准备措施：make ～s for the examination 为考试做准备 /My ～s complete.我的准备工作做完了。❷ the act of getting (making) ready 准备；预备：mental ～ 精神准备/pack things in ～ for a journey 收拾东西准备旅行 ❸ the act of preparing school lessons 预习(功课) ❹ a kind of medicine which is specially prepared 特别的药剂；配制品

preparatory /prɪˈpærətəri/

adj.preparing for an event or activity 预备性的；准备性的：～ training 预备训练

prepare/prɪˈpeə(r)/

v.❶make ready for use, work or a purpose 准备：～ one's lessons 准备功课 ❷ make food ready to be eaten 做饭,准备

饭菜：My mother is preparing supper at home.我的妈妈正在家里准备晚饭。

preposition/ˌprepəˈzɪʃn/

n.a word used with a noun or pronoun to show its relation to another(e. g. to, by, with, from, etc. can be used as prepositions) 介词(例如：to, by, with, from 等)

prequel /ˈpriːkwəl/

n.a story or film containing events which precede those of an existing work (根据已问世作品的情节凭想象上溯创作的)先行篇,前篇

prerequisite/ˌpriːˈrekwɪzɪt/

n.a thing required before one can have or do sth. else 先决条件：A good pass in the school certificate is a ～ for (the) university.以优良的成绩获得中学毕业证书是进入大学的先决条件。

prerogative/prɪˈrɒɡətɪv/

n.a special power or right which no one else has 特权：It was the ～ of the king to pardon criminals. 宽赦犯人是国王的特权。

prescribe/prɪˈskraɪb/

v.❶ order; give as a rule; state 命令；规定；指示：Do what the law ～s.按照法律的规定办事。❷ give medical advice; order the use of (a medicine or treatment) (医生)嘱咐；开药方：The doctor ～d long rest for him. 医生嘱咐他长期休息。/ The doctor ～d some tablets for her.医生给她开了些药片。

prescription/prɪˈskrɪpʃn/

n.❶an act of prescribing a medicine or treatment 开处方❷ a medicine or remedy that is prescribed 处方药：give a ～ for an ailment 为一种疾病开处方药

presence/ˈprezns/

n.❶ the state of being present in a place 出席；在场；光临：Your ～ is requested.敬请光临。/She was so quiet that her ～ was hardly noticed. 她一声不响,几乎没有人注意到她在场。❷ the fact of being present 存在：all foreign military ～ 一切外国的军事存在 ❸ a person's impressive appearance and manner 仪容；风度：a man of great ～ 风度翩翩的人

present¹ /ˈpreznt/

  Ⅰ *adj*. ❶ being in the place 出席的；在场的；在座的 ❷ existing or being considered now 现在的；目前的；现存的：The ～ situation is excellent. 目前的形势大好。Ⅱ *n*. the time now 现在；现在时态：I don't need the book at ～. 我现在还不需要这本书。‖ **for the** ～ 暂时；暂且/ **up to the** ～ 直到现在；至今

present²

  Ⅰ /prɪˈzent/ *v*. ❶ give (sth.) away, especially at a ceremonial occasion 给予；赠送：～ a gift 赠送礼物 ❷ introduce sb. to someone else formally; take part in (a television or radio show) 引见；介绍；参加(电视或广播节目)：Allow me to ～ Mr. Wang to you. 请允许我把王先生介绍给你。Ⅱ /ˈpreznt/ *n*. a gift 礼物：birthday ～s 生日礼物/ exchange ～s 互赠礼物 ‖ **make a ～ of sth. to sb.** 把某物送给某人/ **make sb. a ～ of sth.** 送给某人某样东西

presentable /prɪˈzentəbl/

  adj. fit to be presented to other people; of good appearance 像样的；体面的；摆得出去的：She did her best to make herself look ～. 她尽量把自己打扮得像样些。

presentation /ˌprezənˈteɪʃən/

  n. ❶ the process of presenting sth. 赠送；授予 ❷ sth. that is presented 提供；展示 ❸ an exhibition or performance 上演；演出；表演

present-day /ˌpreznt ˈdeɪ/

  adj. current 当今的；现代的：～ society 当今社会

presently /ˈprezntli/

  adv. ❶ after a short time; soon 不久；一会儿 ❷ at the present time; now 目前；现在

preservation /ˌprezəˈveɪʃn/

  n. the act of preserving sth. 保护；维护：the ～ of wildlife 野生动物保护/ a building worthy of ～ 一座有保存价值的建筑

preservative /prɪˈzɜːvətɪv/

  Ⅰ *n*. a substance that preserves food, wood, or other perishable substances 防腐剂；保护剂 Ⅱ *adj*. acting to preserve

sth. 保护的；保存的

preserve /prɪˈzɜːv/

  v. keep safe; keep from harm; maintain 保护；保存；维持：You can ～ fish or meat in salt. 你可以用盐来保存鱼或肉。

preside /prɪˈzaɪd/

  v. be in charge or lead a meeting, etc. 主持；当会议主席：～ at a meeting 主持会议 / He ～s over all the workshops. 他负责所有车间。

president /ˈprezɪdənt/

  n. ❶ the head of government in many modern states 总统：The ～ took office after the election. 选举后总统就职。❷ the head of a club, society, etc. (俱乐部、协会等的)负责人：the President of the U.N. General Assembly 联合国大会主席 ‖ **presidency** *n*. 总统职位；主席、会长等职务

presidential /ˌprezɪˈdenʃəl/

  adj. of or concerning a president 总统(或校长等)的：a ～ airplane 总统座机

press /pres/

  Ⅰ *v*. ❶ push, use force on (sth.) with the hand or finger 压；按；推：Please ～ this button to start the radio. 请按这个按钮打开收音机。❷ smooth with an iron 熨平(衣服等)：He was ～ing a shirt. 他正在熨衬衣。❸ urge; keep asking earnestly 逼迫；催促；紧迫 ‖ **be ～ed for** 缺少/ ～ **ahead(forward on)with** 加紧(做……)/ ～ **for** 迫切要求；敦促/ ～ **forward** 奋力向前/ ～ **on(upon)** 敦促接受；强加 Ⅱ *n*. ❶ an act of pressing or pushing 按；压：Give the doorbell a ～. 按一下门铃。❷ a business of printing; printing machines 印刷业；印刷机：an oil ～ 榨油机 ❸ (the ～) a business publishing and selling books, magazines, etc.; a collection of newspapers and magazines 新闻界；报刊(总称)：We read news in the daily ～. 我们从每天的报刊上看新闻。‖ ～ **man** *n*. 新闻记者；报界人士

pressing /ˈpresɪŋ/

  Ⅰ *adj*. (of a problem, need, or situation) requiring quick or immediate action or attention（问题、需求、情况）紧迫的,急迫的,迫切的 Ⅱ n. a thing made by the application of force or weight, especially a record 模压制品,冲压件(尤指唱片)

pressure /'preʃə(r)/
n. an action of weight or the force; the force per unit of area 压力;压强:the ～ of atmosphere 大气压力 ‖ under ～ 受到压力;被迫/under the ～ of 在……的压力下/bring ～ to bear on 对……施加压力

prestige /pre'stiːʒ/
n. respect that results from the good reputation (of a person, nation, etc.) (人或国家等的)声望,威望:build up one's ～ 树立威望

prestigious /pre'stɪdʒəs/
adj. having or bringing prestige 有威信的;有声望的:the most ～ school in this country 这个国家最有声望的学校

presume /prɪ'zjuːm/
v. ❶ take for granted; suppose 认定;假定;推想:I ～ you are very busy. 我想你很忙。/Let's ～ that he is right. 我们假定他是对的。❷ dare to do sth. 敢于;冒昧 ～ on (upon) 指望;滥用 ‖ presumption /prɪ'zʌmpʃn/ n. 假定;设想;大胆;冒昧/presumably /prɪ'zjuːməbli/ adv. 可能;或许

presumptive /prɪ'zʌmptɪv/
adj. ❶ presumed when no further information is available 以推测为根据的;假定的;设想的:a ～ diagnosis 推测性诊断 ❷ giving grounds for a particular inference 可据以推定的

pretend /prɪ'tend/
v. show a false appearance of; claim falsely 假装;伪称:He ～ed friendly with me. 他假装跟我友好。‖ pretence n. 假装;做作;借口:make a pretence of 假装/under pretence of 在……的借口下

pretension /priː'tenʃən/
n. ❶ a claim or aspiration, especially a false one 要求;抱负 ❷ pretentious behaviour 矫饰;造作

pretentious /prɪ'tenʃəs/
adj. trying to impress by claiming greater importance or merit than is actually the case 自命不凡的;炫耀的;做作的 ‖ ～ly adv. 做作地

pretext /'priːtekst/
n. a false reason given for doing sth. 借口:He was absent from school on the ～ that he was ill. 他借口生病,没有来上课。

pretty /'prɪti/
Ⅰ adj. ❶ (especially of a woman, a child) charming and attractive without being very beautiful or good-looking (尤指女子、小孩)可爱的;漂亮的:a ～ girl 漂亮的姑娘 ❷ pleasing to look at, listen to, etc. 赏心悦目的;动听的 Ⅱ adv. to some extent; rather 颇为;相当:Your work is ～ good. 你的工作相当不错。‖ ～ well 几乎;差不多

prevail /prɪ'veɪl/
v. ❶ gain control or victory; win a fight 胜过;占优势:Truth will ～. 真理必胜。❷ (continue to) exist or be widespread 盛行;流行;普遍 ‖ ～ing adj. 流行的;盛行的;占主要地位的

prevalent /'prevələnt/
adj. widespread in a particular area or at a particular time 流行的;盛行的;普遍的 ‖ prevalence n. 风行;流行

prevent /prɪ'vent/
v. keep from happening 阻止;制止;防止:He stopped the car quickly and ～ed an accident. 他迅速刹住了车,避免了一起事故。‖ ～ion n. 防止;预防(措施)

preventive /prɪ'ventɪv/
adj. designed to keep sth. undesirable such as illness, harm, or accidents from occurring 预防的;防止的;防病的

preview /'priːvjuː/
n. a private performance of a film or play, before it is shown to the public (影片或戏剧正式公演前的)预演

previous /'priːvɪəs/
adj. existing or occurring before a particular time 以前的;先前的:on the ～ day (afternoon) 在前一天(头天下午) /in a ～ letter 在前一封信中 /a ～ illness 从前的病 /a day ～ to Christmas 圣诞节的

前一天

prey /preɪ/

Ⅰ *n*.❶ an animal that is hunted and eaten by another animal;a person or thing easily injured or taken advantage of 猎物;牺牲品:be (fall or become) a ～ to 成为……的牺牲品 ❷ a way of life based on killing and eating other animals 捕食(习性);掠食:The tiger is a beast of ～.老虎是食肉的野兽。Ⅱ *v*.(～ on) ❶ hunt and eat another animal for food 捕食;掠食:～ on small birds 捕食小鸟 ❷ trouble greatly 使苦恼;折磨:This problem has been ～ing on my mind all day.这个问题让我伤了整整一天脑筋。

price /praɪs/

n.❶ the amount of money for sth.that is sold;the cost in money 价格;价钱;物价:Prices are going up.物价在上涨。 ❷ the unpleasant thing that you must experience as a result of what you have gotten 代价:You must pay a high ～ for this.你必须对此付出高昂的代价。‖ at a ～ 花大钱;付代价/at any ～ 不惜任何代价;无论如何

priceless /'praɪslɪs/

adj.too valuable to be priced;invaluable 无价的;极贵重的:～ paintings 贵重的名画

prick /prɪk/

v.make a little hole or holes in the skin or surface of sth.with a sharp-pointed object 刺;扎;戳:She ～ed her finger with a needle.她用针刺伤了手指头。

prickle /'prɪkl/

n.(especially of a plant,animal,etc.) a sharp point (尤指植物的)棘,刺;(动物的)皮刺:the ～s on a thorn 荆棘上的刺

prickly /'prɪkli/

adj.❶ covered with prickles 多刺的 ❷ causing a prickling feeling 针刺般的,刺痛的 ❸(of a person) irritable or touchy (人)易生气的,易动怒的

pride /praɪd/

Ⅰ *n*.❶ a feeling of deep pleasure or satisfaction that you get when you or people who are connected with you have done sth.well or own sth.that other people admire 自豪;得意;骄傲:He looked at his garden with ～.他得意地看着他的园地。 ❷ a feeling of confidence in you ability,etc.自尊(心):I take (a) great ～ in your success.我为你的成功感到非常骄傲。 ❸ a person or thing that gives people a feeling of pleasure or satisfaction 值得自豪的人(或事物):The fine picture is the ～ of my collection.这张名画是我收藏物当中的珍品。Ⅱ *v*.(～ oneself on/upon) be proud of sth.为……感到自豪(骄傲):He ～s himself on being a member of the class.他以身为这个班的一员而自豪。

priest /priːst/

n.a person empowered to perform the rites of a non-christian religion,especially one who performs sacrificial rites or other public religious acts (非基督教的)神职人员

primary /'praɪməri/

adj.❶ earliest in time or order of development;elementary 最初的;基础的:the ～ reason 基本的理由 ❷chief;main 首要的;主要的:one's ～ goal in life 一生的主要目标 ❸ original 原始的:the ～ forest 原始森林

primate¹ /'praɪmeɪt/

n.archbishop 大主教

primate² /'praɪmeɪt/

n.one of the highest classes of animals,containing men,apes,monkeys,etc.灵长类(包括人类、猩猩、猴子等)

prime /praɪm/

Ⅰ *adj*.❶ first in rank;chief 第一的;首要的:the ～ minister 总理;首相 /～ cost 主要成本 /of ～ importance 最重要的 ❷ of the best quality;first-rate 最好的;第一流的:～ quality 优质 /a ～ cut of beef 一块上等牛肉 ❸ primary 基本的;原始的:a ～ mover 原动力 Ⅱ *n*.❶the earliest or first part 最初;初期:the ～ of the moon 新月 ❷ the best part;the state of greatest perfection 最好部分;精华:in the ～ of life 壮年 /He has passed his ～.他的盛年已过。Ⅲ *v*.❶ get ready for 预先

P

准备好：~ a pump 将水灌入水泵（以便抽水）❷ fill（a person）with food or drink 使人吃饱喝足：~ someone with liquor 使某人喝足酒

primer/'praɪmə(r)/

n. the first book in a subject used by a child at school 初学读物；入门书

primeval/praɪ'miːvl/

adj. belonging to the earliest times in the history of the world；very ancient 原始的；太古的：~ forests 原始森林

primitive/'prɪmɪtɪv/

adj. ❶ of the earliest time；of an early stage of social development 原始的；早期的：~ societies 原始社会/Living conditions in the camp were pretty ~.营地的生活条件甚为原始。❷ simple；having undergone little development 简单的；未开化的：~ technology 简陋的技术

prince/prɪns/

*n.*❶a son or other near male relation of a king or queen 王子；王孙 ❷ a ruler, usually of a small country or of a state protected by a bigger country（小国的）君主，诸侯 ❸ a very great, successful, or powerful man of some stated kind 巨头；名家：a banking ~ 银行巨头/ a ~ of artists 艺坛名家

princess/prɪn'ses/

*n.*a daughter or other near female relation of a king or queen；the wife of a prince 公主；君王的女性近亲属；王妃

principal/'prɪnsəpl/

Ⅰ *adj.*chief；most important 首要的；主要的：the ~ food 主食 Ⅱ *n.* ❶ heads of colleges and of some other organizations 校长；负责人：a lady ~ 女校长 ❷ a person directly responsible for a crime 主犯 ❸money lent or invested on which interest is paid 本金；资本：How much interest will there be on a ~ of 5,000 dollars? 5 000美元的本金可产生多少利润?

principality/ˌprɪnsɪ'pæləti/

*n.*a small country, ruled by a prince 公国；封邑

principle/'prɪnsəpl/

*n.*❶a moral rule or belief that influences your action 行为准则；规范 ❷a law, rule or theory that sth. is based on 法则；原则；原理 ❸a belief that is accepted as a reason for acting or thinking in a particular way 观念；（行动、思想的）信条 ❹a general or scientific law that explains how sth. works or why sth. happens, especially that applied across a wild field 定律；工作原理

print/prɪnt/

Ⅰ *v.*❶produce books, newspapers, etc. by printing them in large quantities 印刷 ❷publish text or picture in such a way 刊登；发表 ❸produce a paper copy of (information stored on a computer)打印（电脑存储的信息）❹produce a photograph from a film 洗印；冲洗 ❺write (text) clearly without joining the letters together 用印刷体 Ⅱ *n.*❶the business of producing newspapers, magazines and books 印刷行业；出版界 ❷letters, words, numbers, etc. that have been printed onto paper 印刷字体 ❸a mark left by your finger, foot, etc. on the surface of sth. 指纹；手印；脚印 ❹ a photograph produced from film(用底片洗印的)相片

printer/'prɪntə(r)/

n. ❶ a person employed in the trade of printing 印刷工 ❷an owner of a printing business 印刷商 ❸ a machine for making copies, especially one printing text 打印机

printing/'prɪntɪŋ/

*n.*❶the process, business or art of printing press 印刷（术、业）：the ~ industry 印刷工业 ❷all the copies of a book or other matter printed at one time（书等的)一次印数

prior/'praɪə(r)/

adj.（~to)❶earlier in time, order, etc.较早的；在先的；先前的：have a ~ engagement 有约在先 ❷ existing already and therefore more significant 优先的；较重要的 ❸before a period of time 在……前面的：~ to the meeting 在开会前

priority/praɪ'ɒrəti/

*n.*❶the right or need to receive attention before other people or things 优先权;优先考虑:You must give this matter ~.你必须优先考虑这件事。❷ a person or thing given priority 优先处理的人或事

prise/praɪz/
*v.*open sth. by force (usually with a lever of some kind) 撬开:I ~d open the lid of the box.我撬开了这个箱子的盖子。

prism/'prɪzəm/
*n.*❶a solid figure with similar, equal, and parallel ends and with sides which are parallelograms 棱柱;柱体 ❷a transparent solid, often of glass, having the shape of a prism, usually with three sided ends, which will separate white light passing through it into the colours of the rainbow 棱镜

prison/'prɪzn/
*n.*a place where people who break the law are locked up 监狱;监牢:be in ~ 在坐牢;在狱中 /come out of ~ 出狱 /go to ~ 入狱

prisoner/'prɪznə(r)/
*n.*❶a person who is put into prison 囚犯;拘留犯 ❷a person who is not free to move 受禁锢的人;行动不自由的人:a ~ of war (POW) 战俘 /take someone ~ 俘虏某人

privacy /'praɪvəsi/
n. a state of being private and not disturbed by other people 清静;隐私,私密

private/'praɪvɪt/
*adj.*❶personal 私人的;私有的;个人的:~ affairs 私事 ❷that you don't want other people to know about 内心的;隐秘的 ❸owned or managed by an individual person or an independent company rather than by the state 私立的;民营的 ❹not likely to be disturbed;quiet 不受打扰的;僻静的 ‖ in ~ 私下地;在不公开场合 ‖ ~ly *adv.*私下地;单独地

privilege/'prɪvəlɪdʒ/
*n.*a special right, advantage, or immunity granted or available only to a particular person or group 特权;优惠: In some

countries education is a ~.在一些国家里受教育是一种特权。

privileged /'prɪvɪlɪdʒd/
*adj.*having privileges or advantages over other people 有特权的;优惠的;特免的

privy/'prɪvi/
*adj.*secret;private 秘密的;私下的 ‖ **Privy Council** *n.*枢密院

prize/praɪz/
Ⅰ*n.*❶ sth. won in a contest;an award 奖;奖品;奖金:win the Nobel Peace Prize 获诺贝尔和平奖(金) /~ for physics 物理奖 ❷ anything struggled for or worth struggling for (值得)奋斗争取的东西;(竞争)目标:the ~s of life 人生的目标 ❸ sth. (a ship or its cargo) captured at sea during a war 战利品;捕获物 Ⅱ*adj.*❶ given as an award 作为奖品的:a ~ cup (medal) 奖杯(章) ❷ worthy of a prize 值得奖励的:a ~ student 应该奖励的学生 ❸ having won a prize 已得奖的:a ~ painting 获奖油画 /a ~ novel 获奖小说 Ⅲ*v.*❶ value or treasure sth. highly 珍视:I ~ honour above money.我珍视荣誉胜过金钱。❷ use force to get (a box, lid, etc.) open or up 把……撬开;撬起:~ the door open 撬开门

probability/ˌprɒbə'bɪləti/
*n.*❶the quality or state of being probable;likelihood 可能性:There is little ~ of his success. 他不大可能成功。❷a probable event or result 可能的事或结果:The ~ is that she will come. 她很可能会来。

probable/'prɒbəbl/
*adj.*most likely to happen or exist, etc. 可能的;大概的:It is ~ that most of the boys will pass the examination.大概多数男孩子都能及格。

probably/'prɒbəbli/
*adv.*most likely;almost certainly 或许;大概:He will ~ refuse the offer.他或许会拒绝这个建议。

probe/prəʊb/
Ⅰ*n.*❶a slender surgical instrument for exploring a body cavity, wound, or similar

probing 探针 ❷a thorough investigation or examination 探查；调查：a ～ into suspected drug dealing 对涉嫌毒品交易事件的调查 Ⅱ *v.* investigate, examine, explore thoroughly；examine with a surgical probe 调查；(用探针)探查：The doctor ～d the cut on my leg. 医生探查我腿上的伤口。/～ into the essence of things 探索事物的本质

probing /ˈprəʊbɪŋ/
adj. ❶intended to discover the truth 探查性的；追根究底的 ❷examining sb. or sth. closely 逼视的；仔细观察的

problem /ˈprɒbləm/
n. a question to be worked out；sth. that is difficult to be solved 问题；难题；疑难之事：Pollution has become a serious social ～. 污染已成为一个严重的社会问题。

procedure /prəˈsiːdʒə(r)/
n. ❶an established or official way of doing sth. 程序 ❷a series of actions conducted in a certain order or manner 手续；步骤：legal ～法律程序/It's just a matter of ～. 那只不过是手续问题。

proceed /prəˈsiːd, prəʊ-/
v. move forward；go on after having stopped 前进；(继续)进行：Please ～ with your story. 请继续讲你的故事吧。‖ ～ **against** 对……起诉；控告/～ **from** 由……发出/～ **to** 继续下去/～ **with** 继续进行 ‖ ～s *n.* 收益

proceeding /prəˈsiːdɪŋ/
n. ❶a course of actions 程序；进程：during the whole ～ 在整个进程中 ❷sth. done；a piece of conduct 行为；行动：suspicious ～s 可疑的行径

process /ˈprəʊses/
Ⅰ *n.* a connected series of actions, changes,, etc. 过程；工序：He explained the ～es of building a boat. 他解释了造船的工序。Ⅱ *v.* treat or prepare by some special methods 加工；处理：～ leather 加工皮革/～ polluted water 处理污水

procession /prəˈseʃn/
n. ❶a line of people, cars, etc. following one another；persons who are marching (列队)行进；行进的队伍：form a ～ 排成行列 /We marched in ～ along the main street. 我们沿着主要街道列队行进。❷ a lot of people coming one after the other (一个接一个的)一队人

proclaim /prəˈkleɪm/
v. make known publicly and officially 公布；公告；宣布：He ～ed the founding of the republic. 他宣布了共和国的成立。‖ **proclamation** *n.* 宣布；布告；宣言

procure /prəˈkjʊə(r)/
v. ❶ obtain, especially with care or effort (努力)得到；(设法)获取：～ a success 努力获得成功 /Our school ～d a famous scientist to talk to us. 学校请到一位著名科学家给我们讲话。❷ bring about；cause 实现；达成：～ an agreement 达成协议

prod /prɒd/
Ⅰ *v.* push with sth. pointed；stimulate 刺；戳；刺激：～ an animal with a stick 用棍子戳动物 Ⅱ *n.* the act of prodding 刺；刺激

prodigy /ˈprɒdɪdʒi/
n. someone who is unusually clever, intelligent, etc. 不凡的人：a child ～ 神童

produce
Ⅰ /prəˈdjuːs/ *v.* ❶ make or manufacture things to be sold 生产；制造；出产：This factory ～s computers. 这家工厂生产计算机。❷ take out；bring out 拿出；展示；出示：Now ～ your identity card. 请出示身份证。/～ evidence 拿出证据 ❸give birth to；lay (eggs) 生殖；生育；生产：The cat ～d six kittens. 这只猫下了六只小猫。❹ bring about, cause to happen 产生；导致：His joke ～d great deal of laughter. 他的笑话引起哄堂大笑。 Ⅱ /ˈprɒdjuːs/ *n.* things that have been produced or grown, especially by farming(尤指农产品)产品；物产：The ～ in this market is always cheap. 这个市场的农产品价格一向很便宜。

producer /prəˈdjuːsə(r)/
n. ❶ a person or company that produces goods, foods, or materials 生产者；制造

商：～'s price 出厂价 ❷ a person in charge of producing a play, film, or similar entertainment 制片人；监制人；舞台监督

product/'prɒdʌkt/
n. ❶ anything that is produced 产品；产物：industrial ～s 工业产品 ❷ the result or consequence of actions, etc. 结果；成果：the ～ of one's labour 劳动成果 ❸ a number or algebraic expression obtained by multiplication 乘积：40 is the ～ of 8 and 5. 40 是 8 与 5 的乘积。

production/prə'dʌkʃn/
n. ❶ the act or process of producing 生产（过程）：an efficient method of ～ 有效的生产方法 ❷ the amount produced 产量：a fall in ～ 产量下降

productive/prə'dʌktɪv/
adj. ❶ producing a large number of goods, crops, etc. 多产的；富饶的：～ fishing waters 鱼产丰富的水域 ❷ tending to produce 生产（性）的：～ labour 生产劳动 ‖ productivity *n.* 生产率

profess/prə'fes/
v. ❶ claim (sth.) often falsely 声称；自称；冒充：～ to be a learned man 自称学者 ❷ state openly 公开承认；声明：～ oneself an idealist 承认自己是唯心主义者 ❸ publicly declare one's faith in (a religion) 表示信仰（宗教）：～ Christianity 信仰基督教

profession/prə'feʃn/
n. ❶ an occupation that requires special education and training, as law, medicine, etc. 职业：the ～ of (a) doctor 医师的职业 ❷ a declaration (of one's belief, opinion or feeling) 声明；表白：a ～ of loyalty 效忠宣言 ❸ the whole people in a particular occupation 同业；同行：The teaching ～ favours this law. 教师们赞成此项法令。

professional/prə'feʃənl/
Ⅰ *adj.* ❶ of a profession 职业（上）的：～ etiquette 行规 ❷ doing sth. as a profession rather than as a hobby 职业性的：a ～ boxer 职业拳击手 Ⅱ *n.* a person who

does sth. for payment rather than pleasure 以特定职业谋生的人；专业人员：The band consists of a ～ and three amateurs. 此乐队由一名职业乐师和三名业余人员组成。

professor/prə'fesə(r)/
n. ❶ a teacher of the highest rank in a college, university, or other institution of higher education 大学教授：associate ～ 副教授 ❷ any teacher in a university 〈美〉大学老师

proficient/prə'fɪʃnt/
adj. highly skilled; expert 熟练的；精通的：be ～ in management 精通管理工作

profile/'prəufaɪl/
n. ❶ a side view (e.g. of someone's face) 侧面（例如：某人的脸）❷ the edge or outline of sth. seen against a background 轮廓；外形 ❸ a summary of a person's character and career in a newspaper or on television（报纸或电视上的）人物简介

profit/'prɒfɪt/
n. the advantage or money obtained from doing sth. 利润；赢利；好处；得益：He gained a lot of ～ from his visit. 他从这次访问中获益匪浅。

profitable/'prɒfɪtəbl/
adj. bringing profit; beneficial 有利的；有益的：a ～ business 有利可图的企业

profound/prə'faund/
adj. ❶ deep, far-reaching 深的；深远的：a ～ sleep (sigh, bow) 酣睡（深深的叹息、深深的鞠躬）/～ significance 深远的意义 /～ silence 寂静 ❷ having great knowledge; showing deep understanding 渊博的；造诣高的：～ knowledge 渊博的知识 /a ～ mind (theory) 深刻的思想（理论）❸ very strongly or deeply felt 深刻的；深厚的：～ feelings 深厚的感情 /～ lessons 深刻的教训 /read the novel with ～ interest 极感兴趣地阅读小说 /～ sympathy 深切的同情

profuse/prə'fjuːs/
adj. ❶ in large amounts; abundant 非常丰富的；大量的：～ thanks 千谢万谢 /～ tears 泪如泉涌 ❷ expressing or giving

sth. freely or generously, lavishing with sth.浪费的；挥霍的：They are ～ of their money.他们挥金如土。

program(me) /ˈprəʊɡræm/

Ⅰ n.❶ a list of items, events, etc. as for a concert, or to be broadcast for radio or TV, or for a sports meeting 节目单：a concert ～ 音乐会节目单 ❷ a plan of what to be done 计划；方案：an employment ～就业计划 /a political ～ 政治纲领 ❸ a coded collection of information, data, etc. fed into an electronic computer (电脑)程序 ❹ sth. that people watch on TV or listen to on the radio 节目 Ⅱ v. make a programme of or for; supply (a computer) with a program(me); plan 为……安排节目；(为电脑)编程序；制订计划：The broadcasters interpret this to mean their freedom to ～ whatever they want to ～.广播员们把这理解为他们可以随心所欲地安排节目。

programming /ˈprəʊɡræmɪŋ/

n.❶ the action or process of writing computer programs (计算机)程序编制 ❷ the action or process of scheduling sth., especially radio or television programmes (尤指广播、电视)节目安排

progress

Ⅰ /ˈprəʊɡres/ n. the process of advancing or developing 前进；进步；进展：Study well and make ～ every day.好好学习，天天向上。‖ in ～在进行中；在举行/make ～ with 在……(方面)取得进步 Ⅱ /prəˈɡres/ v. move forward; make progress 前进；进行；进步；进展：The work is ～ing steadily.工作在继续进行中。‖ ～ion /prəˈɡreʃən/ n.前进；进步；进展；发展

progressive /prəˈɡresɪv/

Ⅰ adj.❶ moving forward 前进中的：～ motion 向前的运动 ❷ progressing steadily or step by step 渐次的：～ reduction 逐渐减少 ❸ that favours or is eager for change, especially in politics or education 进步的；革新的：～ ideas 先进思想 ❹ denoting action in progress 进行(时)的：the ～ tense 进行时 Ⅱ n. one who favors or advocates progress or reform, as in po-litical, social or educational matters 进步人士；革新主义者

prohibit /prəˈhɪbɪt/

v. forbid formally sth. by law, rule, or sth. else (通过法律、条例等)禁止：Smoking is ～ed in the theatre. 戏院里禁止抽烟。‖ ～ive adj.禁止的；昂贵得让人出不起

prohibition /ˌprəʊhɪˈbɪʃn/

n.❶ the act of stopping sth. being done 禁止：call for a total ～ on alcohol 要求全面禁酒 ❷ a law, order, or rule that forbids sth. 禁令；禁律

project

Ⅰ /ˈprɒdʒekt/ n.❶ a plan or scheme that to be carried out 方案；计划；规划：They will carry out a new ～.他们将实行一项新计划。❷ an individual or collaborative enterprise that is carefully planned and designed to achieve a purpose 工程；项目 Ⅱ /prəˈdʒekt/ v.❶ make plans for 计划；设计：They are ～ing a new machine.他们正在设计一种新机器。❷ cause a shadow (an outline, a picture from a film or slide) to fall on a surface, etc.投映：The tree ～s a shadow on the ground. 树投影到地上。❸ stick out 突出 ‖ ～ion n.投影；放映；突出(之物)；投影图

projector /prəˈdʒektə(r)/

n. an apparatus that projects images, as from a film or printed page, onto a screen or other surface 放映机；幻灯机；投影仪

proletarian /ˌprəʊlɪˈteəriən/

Ⅰ n. a member of the proletariat 无产者 Ⅱ adj. of or relating to the proletariat 无产阶级的

proletariat /ˌprəʊlɪˈteəriət/

n. the working class or workers, regarded collectively 无产阶级，工人阶级(总称)

prolific /prəˈlɪfɪk/

adj. producing much or many 多产的：a ～ author 多产的作家

prologue /ˈprəʊlɒɡ/

n. an introductory part of a poem or play 开场白；序幕

prolong /prəˈlɒŋ/

v. make longer 延长：～ one's life 延长寿

命 /The visit will be ～ed for a few days. 访问的时间将延长几天。

prominent /ˈprɒmɪnənt/

adj. easily seen; important; famous 突出的;重要的;卓越的;著名的:a ～ nose 突出的鼻子/a ～ thinker 著名的思想家 ‖ **prominence** *n.* 卓越地位;名望

promise /ˈprɒmɪs/

Ⅰ *v.* ❶ tell sb. that one will certainly do sth. 许诺;答应:They ～d to help us. 他们答应帮助我们。❷ give reason to expect;give hope of 给人以……的指望;有……的希望:It ～s to be a fine day. 今天看来是晴天。Ⅱ *n.* a written or spoken undertaking to do, or not to do sth. 诺言:If you make a ～, you must keep it; never break a ～. 如果你许下诺言,就必须遵守,决不要违背诺言。

promising /ˈprɒmɪsɪŋ/

adj. showing signs of future success 有指望的;有希望的;有出息的;有前途的:a ～ singer 前途无量的歌手

promote /prəˈməʊt/

v. ❶ help in the growth of; help the progress of 促进;鼓励;支持:～ peace 促进和平/～ health 增进健康 ❷ raise in rank or position 提升:He was ～d to the position of manager. 他被提升任经理之职。

promotion /prəˈməʊʃn/

n. ❶ an advancement on rank, position, honor or grade 提升:block his ～ 阻挠他的提升 ❷ the action to help sth. develop or succeed 促进;发扬:the ～ of friendship 友谊的增进 ❸ a set of advertisements of a product or commercial enterprise 宣传;推销:a ～ worker 推销员

prompt /prɒmpt/

Ⅰ *adj.* quick in action; done without delay; on time 敏捷的;迅速的;即时的:a ～ reply 迅速的回答/～ aid 急救 /～ carry out an order 立即执行命令 /be ～ in responding 立即响应 Ⅱ *adv.* punctually 准时地;整:at six o'clock ～ 六时整 Ⅲ *v.* cause sb. to do sth. 促使;推动:He was ～ed by patriotism. 他为爱国心所鼓舞。

promptly /ˈprɒmptli/

adv. ❶ without delay 迅速地;立即 ❷ exactly at the correct time or at the time mentioned 及时地;准时地:They arrived ～ at six o'clock. 他们于六点钟准时达到。❸ immediately 立即;马上

prone /prəʊn/

adj. ❶ lying flat with face downwards 俯卧的:He was lying ～ on the ground. 他正俯卧在地上 ❷ inclined to do sth.; likely to suffer sth. 易于……的:be ～ to anger 易于生气

pronoun /ˈprəʊnaʊn/

n. a word used in place of a noun or a noun phrase 代词:a relative ～ 关系代词

pronounce /prəˈnaʊns/

v. ❶ make the sound of 发音:You must ～ these words correctly. 你必须把这些单词的音发正确。❷ declare formally 宣布:～ a sentence (or judgment) on the criminal 对罪犯宣布判决 ‖ ～ment *n.* 正式宣布

pronounced /prəˈnaʊnst/

adj. definite or noticeable 显著的;明显的:The man had a ～ limp. 那个男子有明显的跛足。

pronunciation /prəˌnʌnsiˈeɪʃn/

n. the way in which a word or a language is usually pronounced 发音:This word has two ～s. 这个词有两种读法。

proof /pruːf/

Ⅰ *n.* ❶ an evidence that is sufficient to show, or helps to show, that sth. is a fact 证据:supply ～ of a statement 对供述提供证据 /Is there any ～ of her honesty? 有什么证据可以证明她的诚实吗? ❷ the process of testing whether sth. is true 证明:give ～ of 证明…… /He did that in ～ of his sincerity. 他那么做是为了证明他的诚意。❸ a test, trial or an examination 检验;考验:stand a severe ～ 经受严峻的考验 Ⅱ *adj.* able to resist or withstand 能抵挡的;防……的:be ～ against fire 耐火 Ⅲ *v.* make sth. waterproof 使……不透水;使……防水

prop¹ /prɒp/

Ⅰ *n.* a support used to hold sth. up 支撑

物;支架;pit ~s 坑道支架 Ⅱ v.(-pp-) help;keep in position 支持;支撑:The house was ~ped up with planks of wood. 这房子是用木板支撑的。

prop² /prɒp/

n.(usually *pl.*) a thing used on the stage when a play is being performed (but not including the scenery) 舞台道具

propaganda /ˌprɒpəˈɡændə/

n.(usually disapproving) ideas or statements that may be false or exaggerated and that are used to gain support for a political leader,party,etc.宣传;鼓吹

propagate /ˈprɒpəɡeɪt/

v.❶ increase the number of plants or animals by reproduction 繁殖 ❷ spread news,opinions,etc. 传播;传送:~ scientific ideas 传播科学的思想 ‖ **propagation** /ˌprɒpəˈɡeɪʃn/ n. 传播:the propagation of new ideas 新思想的传播

propel /prəˈpel/

v.❶ drive forward 推动;推进:The wind ~led the sailing boat. 风推动这只帆船前进。❷ force sb. to move or take actions 驱使;迫使 ‖ ~ler n.(飞机、轮船上的)螺旋桨;推进器

proper /ˈprɒpə(r)/

adj.❶ suitable;fitting;right 合适的;适当的:be ~ for 适合于 /at ~ time 在适当的时间 /a ~ tool 合适的工具 /~ clothes for such an occasion 适合这种场合的衣服 ❷ belonging particularly;relating distinctively 专门的;特有的:a ~ noun 专有名词 /be ~ to 是……所特有的 /feelings ~ to mankind 人类特有的感情 ❸ strictly so called;according to the exact meaning of 严格意义上的/the building ~ 大楼本身 ❹ thorough;complete 彻底的;完全的:in a ~ mess 一团糟

properly /ˈprɒpəli/

adv.❶ correctly or satisfactorily 正确地;满意地 ❷ in a way that is socially or morally acceptable 得体地;恰当地;符合习俗地:Tom should learn to behave ~ in class.汤姆应当学着在课堂上规矩些。

❸ in the strict sense; exactly 严格意义上;恰好

property /ˈprɒpəti/

n.❶ things owned; possessions 所有物;财产;资产:This bicycle is my ~.这辆自行车是我的财产。❷ a special quality that belongs to sth.性质;特性:Soap has the ~ of removing dirt.肥皂有去污的特性。

prophecy /ˈprɒfəsi/

n. the power of telling what is going to happen;a statement about the future 预言能力;预见;预言

proportion /prəˈpɔːʃn/

n.❶ a part or share, especially when measured and compared with the whole 部分;份:A large ~ of the earth surface is covered with water.地球表面的大部分为水覆盖。❷ the compared relationship between two things in regard to size, amount, importance, etc. 比;比率;比例:The ~ of boys to girls in our school is 2 to 5.我校男女学生的比例是 2 比 5。 ‖ ~(to)(和……比较)成比例/in the ~ of 按……的比例/out of ~ 不成比例;不相称

proportional /prəˈpɔːʃənl/

adj.corresponding in degree or amount 相称的:Payment will be ~ to the amount of work done.支付的工资将与所干的工作量相称。

proposal /prəˈpəʊzl/

n.❶ sth. proposed; a plan or scheme 提议;计划;提案:put forth cease fire ~s 提出停火建议 ❷ an offer of marriage 求婚:She has had a ~.已经有人向她求婚。

propose /prəˈpəʊz/

v.❶ put forward; suggest 提议;建议:The chairman ~d that they should stop the meeting and the members agreed to his proposal.主席提议休会,会员们同意他的建议。❷ make an offer of marriage to sb. 求婚:He ~d to her.他向她求婚。

proposition /ˌprɒpəˈzɪʃn/

n.❶ a proposal or a suggestion 提议;建议:an attractive ~ 引人注目的建议 ❷

question with the answer or without the solution;a statement in which a judgment is expressed 命题;主题:a major(minor) ～ 大(小)主题

propound /prə'paʊnd/

　v. put forward an idea, problem, etc. for consideration 提出(主意、问题等)供考虑

proprietary /prə'praɪətri/

　adj. owned by a private person or company 专卖的;私有的;专利的:～ medicine 专卖药品

proprietor /prə'praɪətə(r)/

　n. the owner of a business (especially of land or a shop)(尤指土地和商店的)所有人,业主

pro rata /ˌprəʊ'rɑːtə/

　Ⅰ *adj.* in proportion 按比例的;成比例的: If costs go up, there will be a ～ increase in prices.如果成本增加,价格就会相应上涨。Ⅱ *adv.* proportionally 按比例;成比例

prose /prəʊz/

　n. writing that is not in verse form 散文: He writes very clear simple ～.他写的散文相当明快质朴。

prosecute /'prɒsɪkjuːt/

　v. ❶ persist in so as to complete;carry on 彻底进行;从事;经营:The detective ～d his search for the murderer.侦探对凶手进行了彻底侦查。❷ start legal proceedings against 检举;对……起诉:He was ～d for stealing.他因偷窃而被起诉。

prosecution /ˌprɒsɪ'kjuːʃən/

　n. ❶ the process of starting legal proceedings against someone(就刑事指控的)起诉,告发,检举 ❷ the party prosecuting someone in a lawsuit 起诉方;原告

prosecutor /'prɒsɪkjuːtə/

　n. a law officer conducting prosecutions on behalf of the state or in the public interest 检察官;公诉人

prospect /'prɒspekt/

　n. sth. expected, hoped for or looked forward to 期望;前景;前程:The young man has good ～s in business. 这个年轻人的事业前程无量。‖ ～ive /prə'-spektɪv/ *adj.*预期的;将来的;未来的

prospectus /prə'spektəs/

　n. a printed document which advertises a school, business, etc. by giving details of how it is run, etc.章程;简介

prosper /'prɒspə(r)/

　v. cause to prosper or do well;be successful;develop well 成功;繁荣;兴旺:Our school is beginning to ～.我们学校现在开始兴旺起来。

prosperity /prɒ'sperɪti/

　n. the state of being successful 繁荣;昌盛;成功

prosperous /'prɒspərəs/

　adj. financially successful 成功的;富足的 ‖ ～ly *adv.* 繁荣地;幸运地

prostitute /'prɒstɪtjuːt/

　n. a woman who engages in sexual intercourse for money 妓女;娼妓

prostrate

　Ⅰ /'prɒstreɪt/ *adj.* ❶ lying stretched out on the ground, usually face downward 俯卧的:lie ～ at the foot of someone 拜倒在某人脚下 ❷ physically or emotionally exhausted;beaten;defeated 精疲力竭的;打败了的;屈服的:a ～ enemy 被征服的敌人 Ⅱ /prɒ'streɪt/ *v.* ❶ make(oneself) kneel down in humility;throw down 使俯卧;弄倒:trees ～d by the wind 被风刮倒的树木 ❷(usually passive)overcome;make incapacitated(常用被动式)克服;使无能为力:He was ～d with grief.他无能为力,悲痛不已。

protagonist /prə'tæɡənɪst/

　n. the main person in a story or play;a leader(in a contest, etc.)(戏剧或小说中的)主人公,主角;(比赛中的)主将:The struggle between the two ～s lasted one hour.两个主将之间的争斗持续了一小时。

protect /prə'tekt/

　v. keep safe;make sure sb. or sth. is not harmed, etc.保卫;保护:They were fighting to ～ their country.他们在为保卫祖国而战斗。‖ ～ against(from) 保护……使不……;防御 ‖ ～or *n.* 保护人;防护性

东西

protection/prəˈtekʃn/

n. ❶ the action of protecting sb. or sth. or the state of being protected 保护；警戒；受到保护：under the ～ of 在……保护下/These trees have grown up under the ～ of the students. 这些树在学生们的保护下长大了。❷ a person or thing that protects 保护者；防护物：a ～ from the wind 防风设施 /various ～s against fire 各种防火装置 /He is wearing an overcoat as a ～ against the cold. 他身穿大衣御寒。

protective/prəˈtektɪv/

adj. giving or showing a desire of protection 保护的：～ packaging 保护性包装 / ～ trade 保护性贸易

protein/ˈprəʊtiːn/

n. a body-building substance essential to good health in food, such as milk, eggs, meat 蛋白质

protest

I /prəˈtest/ *v.* object to; say sth. against 对抗；抗议：The workers ～ed about their pay. 工人就他们的工资问题提出抗议。 II /ˈprəʊtest/ *n.* a statement of objection or disapproval 抗议；反对：The people made a ～ about the rise in the price of bread. 人们对面包涨价表示抗议。‖ ～ against 抗议；反对/in ～（against）抗议/under ～ 不愿意地/without ～ 乖乖地；毫无反对表示地

protocol/ˈprəʊtəkɒl/

n. the rules of behaviour, especially between officials of different governments 外交礼节；官方礼节：Everything was arranged according to ～. 一切都按外交礼节安排。

proton/ˈprəʊtɒn/

n. a positively charged particle forming part of an atomic nucleus 质子

prototype/ˈprəʊtətaɪp/

n. a first or trial model of sth. (e. g. a machine, etc.) which is later to be made in larger numbers（尤指机器的）原型，样机

protrude/prəˈtruːd/

v. stick out; stand out 突出；伸出：stone protruding from the wall 从墙上伸出的石头

proud/praʊd/

adj. ❶ arrogant; having or showing too much pride 骄傲的；自高自大的：～ as a peacock 非常高傲/It's nothing to be ～ of. 没什么可骄傲的。❷ having or showing a proper pride or dignity 自豪的；有自尊心的；a ～ day 令人自豪的日子 /～ achievement 值得夸耀的成就/Our team feels ～ that it has won every match this year. 我们队为今年每场比赛都获胜而感到自豪。

prove/pruːv/

v.（～d, proven）❶ show that sth. is true; supply proof of 证明；证实：He has ～d his courage in battle. 他在战斗中证明了自己的英勇。/Who can ～ it? 谁能证实这件事？❷ test the validity of sth. by an example or experiment 检验；考验；试验：～ a new tool 试验一种新工具 /～ her honesty 考验她的诚实 /The truth can only be ～d through practice. 真理只能通过实践才能得到检验。❸ turn out to be; be found to be 证明是；发现是：That dictionary ～d quite useful. 那本词典证明是十分有用的。/All my efforts ～d a failure. 结果证明我的一切努力均告失败。

proverb/ˈprɒvɜːb/

n. a short, pithy saying expressing popular wisdom 谚语："Practice makes perfect" is a ～. "熟能生巧"是一句谚语。

provide/prəˈvaɪd/

v. ❶ make ready; supply; furnish 提供；供应：The sun ～s us with light and heat. 太阳供给我们光和热。❷ stipulate in a will or other legal document（遗嘱等法律文件中）规定 ‖ ～ against 为……做好准备；预防/～ for 养活；防备/～ … with 给……提供 ‖ providing（that）*conj.* 假使，倘若

provided /prəˈvaɪdɪd/

conj. on the condition that 假如；以……为条件；若是：They can stay ～ that they help. 他们若能提供帮助就留下来。

providence/ˈprɒvɪdəns/

n. God; God's care for human beings 上帝;上帝保佑:leave it to ～ 让上帝保佑

province /ˈprɒvɪns/

n. any of the main divisions of some countries, and formerly of some empires that forms a separate whole for purposes of government control 省: Hunan Province 湖南省/We come from all parts of the ～.我们来自全省各地。

provincial /prəˈvɪnʃl/

adj. of a province 省的:a ～ governor 省长

provision /prəˈvɪʒn/

n. ❶ an amount or sth. provided 供应量;供给物 ❷ the action of providing sth. 提供:You must make ～ for the future.你们必须为将来做准备。❸ (usually *pl.*) food (stored) or food supplies 食品:They took plenty of ～s on their trip. 他们在旅行中带了充足的食物。❹ a condition or regulation (in an agreement or law) (协议或法律的) 条款,规定:Both sides have to act according to the ～s of the agreement.双方都应按照协议的条款办事。

provisional /prəˈvɪʒənl/

adj. provided for a present or temporary need; for the time being 临时的;暂时的:～ regulations 暂行条例

proviso /prəˈvaɪzəʊ/

n. a condition attached to an arrangement 附文;附带条款:with the ～ that 以……为条件

provocative /prəˈvɒkətɪv/

adj. ❶ arousing or likely to arouse anger or other strong feelings 挑衅的;煽动的;激怒的 ❷ intended to arouse sexual desire or interest 性挑逗的 ‖ ～ly *adv.* 煽动地;挑拨地

provoke /prəˈvəʊk/

v. make angry; cause or arouse anger 触怒;挑起;引起;激发:This attitude of his ～d his father to anger.他的这种态度激怒了他父亲。

proximity /prɒkˈsɪməti/

n. nearness in space, time, or relationship 接近;附近

prude /pruːd/

n. a person who is too concerned about small things 过分拘谨的人

prudent /ˈpruːdnt/

adj. sensible; careful 敏感的;慎重的;谨慎的:You should be ～ with your money. 你应该慎重花钱。 ‖ ～ly *adv.* 谨慎地;慎重地/ prudence *n.* 审慎

pry /praɪ/

v. (～ into) look into; investigate (especially other people's affairs) 打听;侦查(尤指别人的私事):～ into things which do not concern one 打听跟某人无关的事

psalm /sɑːm/

n. ❶ a song or poem to God 赞美歌;赞美诗;圣诗 ❷ a song or poem from *the Book of Psalms* in *the Old Testament* 《圣经·旧约》中的《诗篇》

pseudo- /ˈsjuːdəʊ/

pref. not real; pretending to be 假的;伪的;冒充的

pseudonym /ˈsjuːdənɪm/

n. a name used by a writer instead of his real name (作家的)假名,笔名:write under a ～ 用笔名写作

psychological /ˌsaɪkəˈlɒdʒɪkəl/

adj. ❶ do with or affecting the mind and its working 心理的,精神的:The victim had sustained physical and ～ damage.受害人遭受了身心伤害。❷ to do with psychology 心理学的 ‖ ～ly *adv.* 心理上地;心理学地

psychologist /saɪˈkɒlədʒɪst/

n. a specialist or expert in psychology 心理学家

psychology /saɪˈkɒlədʒi/

n. ❶ the science of the mind and its processes 心理学:abnormal ～ 变态心理学 ❷ the mental nature, processes, etc. of a person 心理(活动)

pub /pʌb/

n. a place where people go to drink and meet friends 酒馆

puberty /ˈpjuːbəti/

n. the age at which a person is physically

P

able to become a parent 青春期;发育期

public/'pʌblɪk/

I *adj.* ❶ of, for, connected with, or owned by people in general 公共的;公众的:～ affairs 公众事务/～ health 公共卫生 ❷ known to people in general 公开的 ❸ provided, especially by the government for people in general 公立的:～ schools 公立学校 ❹ where there are lots of people 公开场合的 Ⅱ *n.* people in general 民众;众人:This book attracts a large ～.这本书的读者很多。‖ in ～ 公开地;当众/make ～ 公布;公开 ‖ ～ly *adv.* 公开地;公然地

publican/'pʌblɪkən/

n. the owner of a public house 酒吧老板

publication/ˌpʌblɪ'keɪʃn/

n. ❶ anything that is published(e.g. book, newspaper, magazine) 出版物(例如:书报和杂志) ❷ the act of publishing sth. 出版;发行

publicity/pʌb'lɪsɪti/

n. ❶ the public attention directed upon a person or thing 公众的注意;名声 ❷ the process of drawing public attention to a person or thing; the spoken, written, or other material by which this is done 宣传;广告;宣传品

publicize/'pʌblɪsaɪz/

v. make publicly known; advertise sth. 宣传;公布;做广告

publish/'pʌblɪʃ/

v. ❶ make known to the public 宣布;发表:～ a plan 公布计划/～ the news 宣布消息/～ an article in the newspaper 在报上发表文章 ❷ print and offer for sale; issue 发行;刊印:When are you going to ～ this book? 你打算什么时候出版这本书? ‖ ～er *n.* 出版者;出版商/～ing *n.* 出版;发行/～ing house 出版社

pudding/'pudɪŋ/

n. (dish of) food, usually a soft, sweet mixture, served as part of a meal, generally eaten after the meat course 布丁(西餐中一种松软的甜点心):milk ～s 牛奶布丁

puff/pʌf/

I *v.* ❶ breathe rapidly and with effort, usually during or after hurried movement 喘气:He ～ed as he ran up the stairs.他跑上楼梯时气喘吁吁。 ❷ breathe in and out while smoking a cigarette, pipe, etc. 吹气;喷烟:The engine ～ed out of the station.机车喷着烟驶出了车站。 Ⅱ *n.* ❶ a short, explosive burst of breath or wind 一阵(气息或风):A sudden ～ of wind blew his hat off.突然刮来一阵风吹掉了他的帽子。 ❷ breath 呼吸 ❸ a hollow piece of light pastry filled with cream, etc.泡芙

pull/pul/

v. ❶ draw (sth.) along behind one while moving 拉;拖;牵:The horse was ～ing a cart.这匹马拉着一辆大车。 ❷ remove sth. from a place by pulling 拔出 ❸ damage a muscle, etc. by using too much force 拉伤 ❹ open or close curtains, etc. 拉上 ❺ attract sb. sexually 吸引异性 ‖ ～ a face (faces) 做鬼脸/～ a long face 拉长脸;不高兴/～ about (around)粗暴对待/～ apart 拆开;严厉批评/～ at 用力拉;深吸/～ away 脱身;离开/～ back 撤退;后撤/～ down 拆(房子);拆毁;使身体虚弱/～ oneself together 振作起来/～ round 痊愈;恢复健康/～ through 渡过难关;恢复健康/～ together 齐心协力

pulley/'puli/

n. grooved wheel(s) for ropes or chains, used for lifting things 滑轮:a fixed ～ 定滑轮

pullover/'puləuvə(r)/

n. a knitted outer garment, with or without sleeves, pulled on over the head 套衫(如羊毛套衫等)

pulp/pʌlp/

n. ❶ the soft part of a fruit or vegetable 蔬果的肉质部分 ❷ a soft, wet mass of wood or cloth, used for making paper (用于造纸的)纸浆

pulse/pʌls/

I *n.* ❶ the regular beating of blood in the main blood vessels carrying blood from the heart 脉搏；feel one's ～ 诊脉 /His ～ raced.他的脉搏跳得很快。❷ regular or rhythmical beating（有规律的）跳动，波动：the ～ in music 音乐节奏 ❸transient amplification or intensification of a wave characteristic 脉冲：～ frequency 脉冲频 Ⅱ v. beat or throb with regular movements 搏动；跳动：pulsing with excitement 因兴奋而脉搏加速跳动

pump/pʌmp/

Ⅰ n. a machine for forcing liquids or gas into or out of things 抽水机；泵；打气筒：an air ～ 气泵，打气筒 Ⅱ v. ❶ remove or raise by a pump；use a pump on 用泵抽出或打进：～ water from the well 从井中抽水 /～ a flat tyre 给瘪轮胎打气 /～ a pail of water 抽一桶水 ❷ tire out；put out of breath 使（人）精疲力竭；使气喘 ❸ keep on questioning 盘问；追问：～ someone for information 向某人探问消息

pumpkin/'pʌmpkɪn/

n. a large, round, orange-coloured vegetable with a thick skin 南瓜

pun/pʌn/

Ⅰ n. a type of joke in which words have more than one meaning or in which two expressions sound the same 双关语 Ⅱ v. make such a joke 用双关语开玩笑

punch/pʌntʃ/

Ⅰ v. ❶ force nails beneath a surface；make holes in by using a punch 冲孔；打洞；穿孔：～ a hole in the cardboard 在硬纸板上打孔 /The attendant ～ed my ticket.列车员给我的车票打了孔。❷ hit with the fist 用拳（猛）击；用力打：He ～ed me in the chest.他用拳头猛打我的胸。/He ～ed the man on the jaw.他用拳头打那人的下巴。Ⅱ n.❶a tool or machine for cutting holes in leather, paper, etc.穿孔机（器）❷a tool for forcing nails beneath a surface 钻凿器；冲压机 ❸a blow given with a fist 拳击：give someone a ～ on the nose 在某人的鼻子上打了一拳 ❹energy or power 力量；活力：a team with a terrific ～ 实力强大的队伍 ❺a drink made of wine or spirits mixed with

hot water, sugar, lemons, etc.（酒、柠檬、糖等）混合的饮料

punctual/'pʌŋktʃʊəl/

adj.neither early nor late；be on time 准时的；守时的：He is ～ to the minute.他严守时间。‖ ～ity /ˌpʌŋktʃʊ'æləti/ n.严守时间；准时/～ly adv.准时地

punctuation/ˌpʌŋktʃʊ'eɪʃn/

n. the marks used in writing that divide sentences and phrases；the art or practice of punctuating 标点；标点法

punish/'pʌnɪʃ/

v.❶cause pain, loss or trouble to a person for wrongdoing 惩罚；处罚：The boy was ～ed for being late.这孩子因迟到而受罚。❷blame sb., especially oneself 责怪

punishment/'pʌnɪʃmənt/

n.❶an act or a way of punishing sb.处罚：physical ～ 体罚 ❷the penalty inflicted for wrongdoing 受到的处罚：make the ～ fit the crime 依罪量刑

punitive/'pjuːnətɪv/

adj. concerned with punishment；done in order to punish 惩罚的；刑罚的

pupil/'pjuːpl/

n. ❶ a young person who is learning in school or from a private teacher 小学生；学生：a ～ of grade six 六年级的学生 ❷a circular opening in the center of the iris of the eye, regulating the passage of light 瞳孔

puppet/'pʌpɪt/

n.❶a toy-like jointed wooden or cloth figure of a person or animal, that is made to move by some one pulling wires or strings that are fixed to it 木偶；玩偶：a ～ show 木偶戏 ❷a person or group whose actions are not independent, but controlled by someone else 傀儡：～ government 傀儡政府

puppy /'pʌpi/

n.a young dog 小狗；幼犬

purchase/'pɜːtʃəs/

Ⅰ v.buy sth.购买：～ a car 购买一辆汽车 /I've just ～d a new house in the country.我刚在乡下买了一栋新房子。Ⅱ n.❶an act of buying 采购 ❷ sth. that has been bought 购买的东西：Have you paid for your ~s? 你买的东西付了钱吗？‖ **make a** ~买东西

pure/ˈpjʊə(r)/
adj. ❶ unmixed with any other substance 纯的；纯净的：~ gold 纯金／~ alcohol 纯酒精／~ water 纯净水／~ white 纯白色 ❷ without evil or sin 纯洁的；贞洁的：Her motives on this matter are ~. 在这件事上，她动机纯正。 ❸ complete，thorough 完全的；彻底的；纯粹的：What you said is ~ nonsense. 你讲的全是胡说八道。‖ ~ **and simple** 纯属；完全是

purely/ˈpjʊəli/
adv. ❶ in a pure way 纯粹地 ❷ entirely；only 全然；完全地；专门地：We came ~ out of interest. 我们完全不是为了兴趣而来。

purify/ˈpjʊərɪfaɪ/
v. make sth. pure or cleanse it of impurities 使纯净；净化：The air in the room was purified. 房间里的空气被净化了。

purity/ˈpjʊərəti/
n. the quality or condition of being pure 纯净；纯正：~ of style 风格纯正

purple/ˈpɜːpl/
Ⅰ *n.* a color of red and blue mixed together 紫红；紫色 Ⅱ *adj.* ❶ of such a color 紫色的：turn ~ with rage 气得脸色发紫 ❷ over written 辞藻华美的；华而不实的：~ prose 辞藻华美的散文

purpose/ˈpɜːpəs/
n. ❶ the reason for which sth. is done or created or for which sth. exists 目的；意图：What is the ~ of your journey? 你此行的目的是什么？ ❷ the function of sth. 用途：There is a credit card for all ~s. 有一种通用的信用卡。 ❸ determination；the power of forming plans and keeping to them 意志；决心：He is firm in ~. 他意志坚定。‖ **on** ~ 有意地；故意地／**to the** ~ 中肯 ‖ ~**ful** *adj.* 有目的的；有决心的／~**ly** *adv.* 故意地；有意地；特意地

purse/pɜːs/
Ⅰ *n.* ❶ a small bag for money 钱包；钱袋：

a plastic ~ 塑料钱夹 ❷ money；funds 资金；财力；a common ~ 公共资金 Ⅱ *v.* draw together 缩拢：She ~d her lips to show her dislike. 她撅起嘴表示反感。

purser/ˈpɜːsə(r)/
n. an officer on a ship who is in charge of stores and money（船上的）事务长

pursue/pəˈsjuː/
v. ❶ go after in order to catch up with；capture 追赶；追捕：The police are pursuing an escaped prisoner. 警方正在追捕一个在逃的犯人。 ❷ try to achieve sth. in a particular time 追求；贯彻

pursuit/pəˈsjuːt/
n. ❶ the act of pursuing sb. or sth. 追赶；追捕；寻求 ❷ an activity to which you devote time 事业；爱好

push/pʊʃ/
Ⅰ *v.* ❶ use force on（sth. or sb.）to cause forward movement 推；推动；推进：You ~ and I'll pull. 你来推，我来拉。 ❷ compel or urge sb. to do sth.，especially to work hard 催逼；促使：We always have to ~ him to do his homework. 我们总要催促他做作业。‖ be ~ed for 困于／~ along（forward）继续前进／~ around 支使；对……发号施令／~ aside 推开；推向一边／~ off 出发；走开／~ on 奋力前进／~ one's luck 轻率冒险／~ one's way 挤着前进 Ⅱ *n.* an act of pushing 推；推动；推进；促进：He gave me a ~ and I fell. 他推了我一下，我就跌倒了。

put/pʊt/
v. ❶ lay or place sth. in a particular place 放；搁：~ the book on the desk 把书放在书桌上／~ the thief in prison 把小偷关进监狱 ❷ bring into a certain condition 使变成……样子；使处于……状态：~ the books in order 把书整理好 ❸ express in words；say 用言语表达；说：I don't know how to ~ it. 我不知道如何表达。 ❹ mark or write sth. on sth. 写上；标上：Please ~ your name and address on the card. 请将你的姓名和地址写在卡片上。‖ ~ **an end to** 结束；制止

puzzle/ˈpʌzl/

Ⅰ*v.*confuse;cause uncertainty 使迷惑;使困惑:The question ～d me.这个问题把我难住了。/I'm ～d what to do.我不知道怎样做才好。Ⅱ*n.*❶ a problem to be solved 难题:No one has yet succeeded in explaining this ～.至今还没有人成功地解释这个难题。❷ a toy or problem for testing cleverness,skill,or ingenuity(测验智力的)玩具或问题:a book of ～s 一本智力测验书

pyramid/ˈpɪrəmɪd/

*n.*❶a solid having triangular sides meeting in a point 角锥体 ❷a large building with a square or triangular base and sloping sides that meet in a point at the top(埃及)金字塔:One of the ～s,the Great Pyramid,is more than four hundred feet high.金字塔之一的大金字塔有 400 多英尺高。

python/ˈpaɪθən/

*n.*a type of large snake which kills the animals by winding itself very tightly round them 蟒蛇

P

Qq

quack/kwæk/

Ⅰ *n.*❶the harsh sound made by a duck 鸭声 ❷a person who pretends to be a doctor 江湖医生；庸医 ❸a person dishonestly claiming to have knowledge and skill 冒充内行的人；骗子 Ⅱ *v.*❶(of duck) make this sound (鸭子)嘎嘎叫 ❷boast or tout loudly 大肆吹嘘

quadrilateral/ˌkwɒdrɪˈlætərəl/

*n.*a flat, four-sided figure 四边形

quadruple

Ⅰ/ˈkwɒdrʊpl/*adj.* made up of four parts；including four people 由四部分(包括四人)组成的：a ～ agreement 四方协议 Ⅱ/kwɒˈdrʊpl/*v.*make or become four times greater 使成四倍或变成四倍

quail /kweɪl/

*n.*a small brown bird with a short tail, related to the partridge 鹑；鹌鹑

quaint/kweɪnt/

adj. attractive or pleasing because unusual or old-fashioned；whimsical 离奇的；古怪的；奇妙的：a ～ old man 一个古怪的老头

quake/kweɪk/

Ⅰ*v.*(of the earth) shake 震动；颤动：The ground ～d under our feet.地在我们脚底下震动。Ⅱ*n.*an earthquake 颤动；地震：The ～ caused much damage.地震带来了巨大的损害。

qualification/ˌkwɒlɪfɪˈkeɪʃn/

*n.*❶any quality, skill knowledge, experience, etc. that fits a person for a position, office, profession, etc. 资格；条件：a teacher's ～s 教师资格 ❷limitation to sth.限制条件：We can accept his statement without ～.我们可以不附带任何条件接受他的声明。

qualified/ˈkwɒlɪfaɪd/

*adj.*❶having the necessary or desirable qualities；fit or competent for sth.有资格的；合格的；胜任的：He's not ～ to teach French.他没有资格教法语。❷limited in some way 限制的

qualify/ˈkwɒlɪfaɪ/

v. give the necessary qualities to；make fit；obtain the knowledge, skill to perform certain acts 使合格；使有合法资格；(使)有条件；取得资格：Two years of experience qualified him for the job.他有两年工作经验，能够胜任这一工作。

quality/ˈkwɒləti/

*n.*❶ the standard of sth. as measured against other things of a similar kind；the degree of excellence of sth.质量；品质；优质：I want to buy a piano of superior ～.我想买一架质量上乘的钢琴。❷ a distinctive attribute or characteristic possessed by sb.or sth.特性；性质；才能：The man has the ～ of leadership.此人有领导才能。

quandary/ˈkwɒndəri/

*n.*the state of doubt；a feeling of difficulty 困惑；进退两难：be in a ～ about what to do 不知道该做什么

quantify /ˈkwɒntɪfaɪ/

v. express sth. as a quantity 表示(或测量)……的数量；量化 ‖ quantifiable *adj.*可以计量的

quantity/ˈkwɒntəti/

*n.*❶an amount or a number of sth.数量；数目：He can only eat a small ～ of rice.他只能吃少量的饭。❷ the measurement of sth. by saying how much of it there is 量；数量：I prefer quality to ～.我重质不重量。‖ a ～ of, quantities of 大量的；许多的/in ～, in(large) quantities 大量地

quantum /ˈkwɒntəm/

n. ❶ a minimum amount of a physical quantity (such as energy) which can exist in a given situation(动量或电荷等物理值的)量子 ❷ the amount required or allowed 定额;定量

quarantine/ˈkwɒrəntiːn/

n. separation from others so that disease is not spread 隔离;检疫:People coming from an infected area must be kept in ~. 来自传染病区的人们必须进行隔离。

quarrel/ˈkwɒrəl/

Ⅰ *v.* (-ll-) have or take part in a quarrel; disagree by using angry words 争吵;争辩:He ~led with me about the prize.他为奖金的事和我争吵。‖ ~ **with** 抱怨;挑毛病;对……提出疑义 Ⅱ *n.* ❶ an angry argument;a violent disagreement 吵;吵架:I had a ~ with him yesterday.昨天我和他吵了一架。❷ the cause of a quarrel 争吵的原因(理由):I have no ~ with him.我没有和他争吵的理由。‖ **pick a** ~(**with sb.**)(向某人)寻衅 ‖ ~**some** *adj.* 爱争吵的

quarry/ˈkwɒri/

Ⅰ *n.* ❶ a place where stone is cut,dug or blasted 采石场 ❷(usually singular) an animal,bird,etc.,which is hunted(常用单数)猎物:birds in search of ~ 寻觅猎物的鸟 ❸ anything eagerly pursued 追求物 Ⅱ *v.* ❶ get stone or sth. else from a quarry 采(石);凿(石):~ limestone 开采石灰石 ❷ get from a productive source 发掘(资料):~ in old manuscripts 在旧手稿中寻找资料

quart/kwɔːt/

n. a unit for measuring liquids,equal to 2 pints or about 1. 136 litres in the UK and Canada,and 0. 946 of a litre in the US 夸脱(液量单位,在英国和加拿大等于 2 品脱或 1. 136 升,在美国等于 0. 946 升):There are two pints in a ~.一夸脱有二品脱。‖ **put a** ~ **into a pint pot** 做不可能的事

quarter/ˈkwɔːtə(r)/

Ⅰ *n.* ❶ one of four equal parts;one fourth 四分之一:A ~ of the class supported her.全班有四分之一的人支持她。❷ a period of 15 minutes before or after any hour 刻钟;刻:It's a ~ to nine.时间是九点差一刻。❸ one fourth of a year;one of four terms into which a school or university year may be divided 季(度);学期:pay one's rent every ~ 按季付房租/the second ~第二个四期制学期 ❹ a special part of a town;a section;a district(市镇)区;居民区(常为某种特定区):the student ~学生区/the manufacturing ~ 工厂区 ❺(*pl.*)a place where one lives 住所;营房;军营:The captain sent the soldiers back to their ~s.上尉送士兵回营房去。❻ a source of supply,help,information,etc. 来处;供给者;来源:Foreign friends are arriving from all ~s of the earth.外国朋友正从世界各地陆续到来。Ⅱ *v.* ❶ divide into four parts 四等分;切成四块;She ~ed the apple.她将苹果切成四块。❷ provide quarters for soldiers 为人(尤指部队)找住处;~ troops in the village 把部队扎在村中

quarterly/ˈkwɔːtəli/

Ⅰ *adj.*(happening, appearing, etc.)every three months 季度的;按季的:a ~ review(评论性的)季刊 Ⅱ *adv.* once a quarter of a year 一季一次地;按季:The committee meets ~.该委员会每季开一次会。

quash/kwɒʃ/

v. ❶ officially refuse to accept (sth. already decided)取消;废除;宣布无效:The court ~ed the previous ruling on the case.法庭取消了以前对案件做的裁决。❷ bring to an end by force;crush 镇压;平息:~ a revolt 平息叛乱

quasi-/ˈkweɪzaɪ, ˈkweɪsaɪ/

pref. seemingly;not really 类似的;假的

quaver/ˈkweɪvə(r)/

Ⅰ *v.* shake;tremble(指声音)震颤,发抖 Ⅱ *n.* ❶ a trembling sound 颤音 ❷ a type of musical note that is half as long as a quarter note 八分音符

quay/kiː/

n. a place(often built of stone)where ships are loaded or unloaded 码头

queasy/'kwɪzi/
adj. ❶ having a feeling of sickness 令人作呕的;不舒服的:feel rather ~ 感到很不舒服 ❷ easily made sick 易呕吐的

queen/kwiːn/
n. ❶ the wife of a king;a woman ruler in her own right 王后;女王:When a lady is made ~ of a country,a crown is placed on her head. 当一位夫人被立为国家的女王时,就把王冠戴在她头上。❷ any of the four playing cards with a picture of a queen 王后(牌) ❸ the large leading female insect of a group (一窝昆虫中的)后:the ~ ant (bee)蚁后(蜂王) ‖ **beauty ~** *n.* 选美皇后/~ **mother** *n.* 皇太后;母后 ‖ ~**ly** *adj.* 女王般的;适于女王的;威严的

queer/kwɪə(r)/
adj. ❶ strange;odd;peculiar 奇特的;古怪的:He often has some very ~ ideas.他常有一些很奇特的想法。❷ unwell;faint (身体)不舒服;情绪不好:feel ~感到不舒服 ‖ ~**ly** *adv.*奇特地;古怪地

query/'kwɪəri/
Ⅰ *n.* ❶ a question 问题;询问;质问:raise a ~ 提问 ❷ the mark ? put after a question or beside sth.to show doubt 问号 Ⅱ *v.* ❶ ask about 询问;质问 ❷ express doubt about 质疑;表示怀疑:~ if (whether) it is true 怀疑它是否真实

quest/kwest/
*n.*a long search for sth.找寻:a ~ for gold 找黄金/a ~ for knowledge 对知识的探求 ‖ **in ~ of** 探求/**in ~ of adventure** 探险

question/'kwestʃən/
Ⅰ *n.* ❶a sentence that asks sth.;a request for information,which demands an answer 问句;询问;疑问:He did not answer my ~.他没回答我的问题。❷a matter or topic that need to be settled or dealt with 待解决的事;存在的问题:The ~ is who will do it.问题是谁来做。❸a doubt 疑问:There is no ~ about her honesty. 她的诚实无可怀疑。Ⅱ *v.* ❶ ask a question or questions of;examine 询问;提问;盘问:You can ~ the whole class on the

stories they have read.你可就班上学生读过的故事向他们提问。❷ express or feel doubt about 怀疑;对……表示(感到)怀疑:I ~ his leadership.我对他的领导能力表示怀疑。

questionnaire /ˌkwestʃə'neə(r)/
*n.*a list of questions seeking information from people for use in a survey or statistical study 问题单;调查表;问卷

queue/kjuː/
Ⅰ *n.*a line of people,vehicles,etc.waiting for sth.or to do sth.(人或车辆等的)长列,行列 ‖ **jump the ~**插队;加塞 Ⅱ *v.*wait in a line of people,vehicles,etc.for sth.or to do sth.排队等候:We ~d (up) for the bus.我们排队等候公共汽车。‖ ~ **up** 排队等候

quick/kwɪk/
adj. ❶ moving fast;done in a short time 快的;迅速的:Be ~! 快! /He is ~ about his work.他工作干得快。❷keenly perceptive;alert 敏锐的;灵敏的:a ~ ear for music 乐感敏锐的耳朵

quicken/'kwɪkən/
v. ❶make or become quicker;increase the speed of 加快;加速:~ one's steps 加快步伐/The spring rain ~ed the vegetables.春雨使蔬菜长得更快了。❷ make or become more lively,vigorous or active 活跃;(使)恢复生机:Good literature ~s the imagination.好的文学作品能激发想象力。

quickly /'kwɪkli/
adv. ❶ fast 迅速地;很快地: The lady walked ~away.那位女士迅速走开了。❷soon;after a short time 不久;立即:He replied to his girl friend's letter very ~. 他很快回复了他女朋友的信。

quickness /'kwɪknəs/
n. the quality of being fast,especially at thinking,etc.机智;敏捷:The little boy amazes me with his ~ and eagerness to learn.那个小男孩机智好学,令我惊讶。

quicksilver/'kwɪksɪlvə(r)/
*n.*mercury 水银,汞

quid/kwɪd/
n. (*pl.* quid) one pound or one hundred

pence 一英镑；一百便士：She earns at least 50 ~ a week. 她一周至少赚 50 英镑。

quiet /ˈkwaɪət/

I *adj.* ❶ with little or no movement or sound 安静的；平静的；不动的：Everyone must keep ~ in the library. 在图书馆人人必须保持安静。❷ calm，free from trouble or anxiety 平和的；（心神）宁静的：I want to lead a ~ life. 我想过一种宁静的生活。❸ secret 隐蔽的 II *n.* quietness；calmness 安静；宁静；平静：We need a few hours of ~ after the day's work. 一天工作之后我们需要有几小时安静的休息。III *v.* make or become calmer （使）变平静；（使）镇定：The riot ~ed down. 骚乱平息下来了。/~ a child 安抚小孩 ‖ **keep sth.** ~ 对某事保密 / **on the** ~ 悄悄地；偷偷地 ‖ **-en** *v.* 使平静（镇定）；平静（镇静）下来 / ~ **ly** *adv.* 静静地；静悄悄地；平静地 / ~ **ness** *n.* 安静；平静；宁静

quilt /kwɪlt/

I *n.* a bed covering made of two pieces of clothes with soft material kept in （装有棉花、羽绒的）被子 II *v.* make such a cloth cover for a bed 缝被子

quip /kwɪp/

I *n.* a clever saying；a witty remark 妙语；俏皮话 II *v.* make a clever saying 说俏皮话

quirk /kwɜːk/

n. a peculiar or odd event，saying or action 奇行；怪癖；怪事

quit /kwɪt/

v. (-tt-) ❶ go away from；leave；give up 离开；离职；辞退：He ~ted his job to start his own business. 他辞去了工作，自己做生意。❷ stop doing sth. 停止：~ working 停止工作

quite /kwaɪt/

adv. ❶ to the greatest possible degree 完全地；十分地：You are ~ right. 你完全正确。/ I feel ~ well. 我感觉（身体）好得很。❷ to some degree 相当地；颇为：It's ~ warm today. 今天天气相当暖和。❸ really 确实地；真正地：She's ~ a beauty.

她真是个美人儿。

quiver /ˈkwɪvə(r)/

I *v.* shiver，shake or tremble slightly （使）微微颤动：The moth ~ed its wings. 飞蛾颤动双翼。II *n.* a light，quick，trembling motion 微微的颤动：I felt a ~ of excitement. 我感到一阵兴奋地颤抖。

quiz /kwɪz/

I *n.* ❶ a short oral or written test （简短的）口试或笔试：We have a ~ in maths today. 今天我们要测验数学。❷ a competition or game 比赛；游戏：a TV ~ program 电视比赛节目 II *v.* (-zz-) ❶ ask questions 提问：The teacher ~zed the students on history. 老师向学生提问了几个历史问题。❷ give students an informal test 测验（学生）

quota /ˈkwəʊtə/

n. an amount of sth. that one must give or receive 定量；配额；限额：exceed one's ~ 超过限额

quotation /kwəʊˈteɪʃn/

n. ❶ a passage or group of words from a book or speech that is repeated by someone other than the original writer or speaker 引文；引语；语录 ❷ the process of quoting or being quoted 引用；引证 ❸ a statement or estimation of a price 估价单；报价单；行情表

quote /kwəʊt/

v. ❶ repeat （in speech or writing） the words of 引用；摘引：He ~d a few lines of Marx to support his own point of view. 他引用了马克思的一段话来支持他的观点。❷ mention an example of sth. to give force to one's argument 引证；举例说明：He ~d his own experience. 他引证自己的经验。❸ give a price 报价：This is the best price I can ~ you. 这是我能给您报的最优价。

quotient /ˈkwəʊʃnt/

n. （in mathematics） a number of times，as the result，one number can be divided by another （e.g. if you divide 21 by 3，the quotient is 7）（数学中的）商（例如：21÷3＝7，7 是商数）‖ **intelligence** ~ 智商

Q

Rr

rabbit/ˈræbɪt/
n. ❶ a common small long-eared animal of the hare family that lives in holes 兔子 ❷ the fur or meat of this animal 兔皮；兔肉：John's collar is made of ～.约翰的领子是兔毛皮的。‖ like（as think as）～s in a warren 挤得水泄不通 ‖ ～y *adj.* 像兔子的；胆小的

rabble/ˈræbl/
n. a mob；a rough, disorganized crowd 暴民；乌合之众

rabid/ˈræbɪd/
adj. ❶ very angry and violent 狂怒的；过激的 ❷（of dogs, etc.）affected by rabies 患狂犬病的；疯的

rabies/ˈreɪbiːz/
n. a disease which causes madness（especially in dogs）狂犬病

race[1] /reɪs/
Ⅰ *n.* a competition in speed 竞赛；赛跑：Wilma set a new world record on the 100-metre ～.威尔玛刷新了一百米跑的世界纪录。Ⅱ *v.* compete against sb. or sth. to see who can go faster or fastest, and who can do sth. first, etc.；take prat in a race or races（和……）比赛；参加比赛：They ～d to the second runners. 他们向第二棒运动员跑去。‖ ～ against time 争取时间

race[2] /reɪs/
n. a group of people descended, or believed to be descended, from the same ancestors；a section of mankind different from others in colour, etc. 种族；种类：the human ～ 人类 ‖ racialist /ˈreɪʃəlɪst/ *n. &. adj.* 种族主义者（的）

racial/ˈreɪʃl/
adj. relating to race 种族的；民族的：a ～ problem 种族问题 /～ customs 民族习俗

racially/ˈreɪʃəli/
adv. from the point of view of race 从种族观点来看；在种族上：a ～ mixed population 种族混杂的人口

racing/ˈreɪsɪŋ/
Ⅰ *n.* ❶ the sport of racing horses 赛马；跑马：watching the ～ on TV 在电视上看赛马 ❷ any sport that involves competing in races 速度比赛 Ⅱ *adj.* designed or bred for racing 专为比赛而设计或饲养的；比赛用的：～ pigeons 赛鸽 /a ～ yacht 赛艇

racialism/ˈreɪʃəlɪzəm/
n. ＝racism

racism /ˈreɪsɪzəm/
n. ❶ the belief that there are characteristics, abilities, or qualities specific to each race 种族主义 ❷ discrimination against or hostility towards people of other races 种族歧视；种族偏见；种族对抗 ‖ racist *n.* 种族主义者

rack/ræk/
Ⅰ *n.* ❶ a frame with shelves, bars or hooks used for holding sth. 挂物架 ❷ an overhead shelf on a coach, train, or plane for stowing luggage 行李架；搁板 Ⅱ *v.* cause to suffer physical or mental pain 使……难受：Jim has been ～ed with a bad cough these days.吉姆这几天咳嗽得难受。‖ ～ one's brains 苦苦思索

racket/ˈrækɪt/
n. ❶ a light bat used for hitting the ball in tennis, badminton, etc.球拍 ❷ an uproarious, loud noise 吵闹；喧嚷：What a ～! 多么大的吵闹声! ❸ a dishonest way of getting money, e. g. by threatening or cheating people 勒索；敲诈；诈骗：be in

on a ～ 参与敲诈勒索/Police investigating the fraud suspected him of being in on the ～.警方调查这一诈骗案时怀疑他涉嫌参与诈骗活动。

radar/'reɪdɑ:(r)/

*n.*an instrument for determining the distance and direction of unseen objects by the reflection of radio waves 雷达；无线电探测器：a marine ～ 船用雷达 /～ installations 雷达装置

radiant/'reɪdɪənt/

*adj.*❶ sending out rays of light; shining 光芒四射的；绚丽的：the ～ sun 光芒四射的太阳 ❷ (of a person or his appearance) showing love and happiness 喜悦的；容光焕发的：wear a ～ face 红光满面

radiate/'reɪdɪeɪt/

*v.*❶ send out (light or heat, etc.) 发射（光、热等）：The sun ～s light and heat.太阳发出光和热。❷ clearly emanate a strong feeling or quality through their expression or bearing 散发；流露：a woman who ～s happiness 一位洋溢着幸福的妇女 ❸ spread out in all directions 辐射；向各方伸展：streets radiating from the central square 从中央广场伸展出去的各条街道

radiation/ˌreɪdɪ'eɪʃn/

*n.*❶ the emission of energy as electromagnetic waves or as moving subatomic particles, especially high-energy particles which cause ionization 辐射；辐射作用：nuclear ～ 核辐射 ❷ the energy transmitted in this way 放射物；辐射线；辐射能：～s emitted by an X-ray apparatus X 光装置所放射出来的辐射线

radiator/'reɪdɪeɪtə(r)/

*n.*❶ a type of apparatus for heating a room 暖气设备；发热器 ❷ an apparatus which keeps the engine of a motor vehicle cool (汽车的)冷却器

radical/'rædɪkl/

Ⅰ*adj.*❶ of the root or base; fundamental 基本的；根本的：a ～ change 根本的变化 /a ～ principle 基本原理 ❷ (of politics) favoring fundamental reforms; advanced in opinions and politics (政治方面)激进的：～ opinions 激进的观点 /in ～ language 用过激的语言 ❸ relating to the root of a number or quantity 根号的：the ～ sign 根号 Ⅱ*n.*❶ a person with radical opinions; a member of the Radical Party 激进分子；激进党员 ❷ (in mathematics) the radical sign (数学中的)根号

radio/'reɪdɪəʊ/

*n.*❶ use of a wireless telegraph or telephone 无线电：They got in touch by ～.他们通过无线电取得联系。❷ an apparatus for receiving programmes 收音机 ❸ radio programmes 无线电广播节目 ‖ by ～ 通过广播

radioactive/ˌreɪdɪəʊ'æktɪv/

*adj.*having the quality of giving off rays which pass through the solids 放射性的：Radium is a ～ element.镭是一种放射性元素。

radioactivity/ˌreɪdɪəʊæk'tɪvəti/

*n.*the state of being radioactive 放射性；放射现象：artificial ～ 人工放射

radish/'rædɪʃ/

*n.*a small vegetable, of which red or white root is eaten raw 小萝卜：a bunch of ～es 一堆小萝卜

radium/'reɪdɪəm/

*n.*a radioactive metallic element used in the treatment of some diseases e.g.cancer 镭：Radium is used in treating cancer.镭被用来治疗癌症。

radius/'reɪdɪəs/

n.(*pl.* radii/'reɪdɪˌaɪ/) ❶ a straight line from the centre of a circle to its circumference 半径：The ～ of a circle is half its diameter.圆的半径是直径的一半。❷ a circular area measured from its centre point 半径范围；半径距离：a ～ of action 活动半径

raft/rɑːft/

*n.*a flat boat made from large pieces of wood which is bound together 木筏

rafter/'rɑːftə(r)/

*n.*one of the sloping beams which helps to

support a roof 椽

rag/ræg/

*n.*❶a piece of old cloth 破布：He cleaned the car with an oily ～(a piece of oily ～).他用一块沾满油污的旧布擦汽车。❷(*pl.*) old and torn clothes 破旧衣服：The beggar was in ～s.那乞丐衣衫褴褛。‖ chew the ～ 聊天/glad ～s 盛装；晚礼服

rage/reɪdʒ/

Ⅰ*n.*a feeling of furiousness and wild anger 暴怒：He jumped with ～ at the news.听到这消息他气得暴跳如雷。‖ be all the ～ 风行一时/fly into a ～ 勃然大怒 Ⅱ*v.*❶be violently angry 发怒❷(of illness, disaster, etc.) spread quickly 迅速扩散(蔓延)：A great storm was raging in the south last year.去年南方狂风肆虐，暴雨滂沱。‖ ～ at 对⋯⋯生气/through (狂风)从⋯⋯经过

ragged/ˈrægɪd/

*adj.*❶ (with clothes) badly torn 穿破的：a ～ coat 破了的外套 ❷ (with clothes) in rags 衣着破烂的：a ～ man 衣衫褴褛的人 ❸ having rough or irregular outlines or surfaces 高低不平的；外形参差不齐的：a sleeve with ～ edges 毛边袖筒/～ rocks 凹凸不平的岩石 ❹ lacking uniformity or smoothness；imperfect 不协调的；粗糙的；不完善的：row a ～ stroke 桨划得不协调

raging/ˈreɪdʒɪŋ/

*adj.*❶showing violent, uncontrollable anger 狂怒的；盛怒的 ❷(of natural forces) continuing with overpowering force (自然力)狂暴的，凶猛的，肆虐的

raid/reɪd/

Ⅰ*n.*a surprise attack made by troops, ships or aircraft 突然袭击：The enemy made a ～ on the village.敌人突袭了这个村子。Ⅱ*v.*make a raid on or into；carry out a raid 突然袭击(搜查)：The police ～ed the gambling house.警察出其不意地搜查了赌场。

rail/reɪl/

*n.*❶ a bar of wood or metal placed level between two posts 栏杆：wooden ～s round a field 围着一块地的木栏杆 ❷ a steel line laid on the ground as one side of a track for trains or trams 铁轨：off the ～s (火车)出轨，越轨 ‖ by ～ 乘火车

railing/ˈreɪlɪŋ/

*n.*a fence of rails supported on upright metal bars 栅栏；屏障

railroad/ˈreɪlrəud/

*n.*a track for trains 〈美〉铁路

railway/ˈreɪlweɪ/

*n.*a track with rails on which trains run 铁路：the Beijing-Guangzhou Railway 京广铁路/work on the ～ 在铁路上工作

rain/reɪn/

Ⅰ*n.*❶ water falling in drops from the sky 雨：We have plenty of ～ this year.今年雨水充足。❷ (*pl.*)the season in tropical countries when rain falls continually (热带国家的)雨季：The ～ have started early this year.今年雨季来得早。Ⅱ*v.* fall in drops of water；fall or pour down rain 下雨：It ～ed heavily.雨下得很大。‖ ～ or shine 不管天晴还是下雨/It never ～s but pours.祸不单行。/～ cats and dogs 下倾盆大雨

rainbow/ˈreɪnbəu/

*n.*an arch of different colours that sometimes appears in the sky opposite the sun, especially after rain 彩虹：After a storm, a ～ appeared.大雨过后，出现了彩虹。

raincoat/ˈreɪnkəut/

*n.*a light coat of waterproof 雨衣：You'd better take the ～ with you.你最好随身带着雨衣。

rainfall/ˈreɪnfɔːl/

*n.*❶a fall of rain 降雨 ❷ the amount of rain falling within a given area in a given time 降雨量：That area has a large ～.那个地区降雨量很大。

rainproof/ˈreɪnpruːf/

*adj.*able to keep rain out 防雨的；防水的：The roof is no longer ～.这屋顶已经漏雨了。

rainy/ˈreɪni/

adj.(rainier, rainiest) having much rain 多雨的;下雨的:～ weather 多雨的天气/ the ～ season 雨季

raise/reɪz/

v.❶ lift up;hold up 举起;抬起:The boy stood there with his right hand still ～d. 男孩站在那儿,右手仍抬着。❷ cause to rise or appear 使升起;使出现:The price of rice has been ～d. 大米价格提高了。❸ bring forward for consideration;present;offer 提出:He ～d the problem of pollution at the meeting.在会议上他提出了关于污染的问题。❹ bring up (a child);breed or grow(animals or plants) 养大;饲养:This is how the Chinese people began to ～ silk worms.这就是中国人怎样开始养蚕的。‖ ～ **a glass to** 为……祝酒/～ **a row** 争吵/～ **an objection to** 对……表示反对/～ **hell** 大吵大闹/～ **one's hand to** 打人/～ **one's voice against** 反对/～ **the devil** 大吵大闹/～…**with** 和(向)……提出

raiser/'reɪzə(r)/

n.❶a person who raises especially money or animals (款项等的)筹集者;(牲畜的)饲养者:a fund-～ 基金筹集者 ❷ a person who causes sth. 提出者:A fire-～ is someone who sets fire to buildings on purpose.纵火者是故意放火烧建筑物的人。

raisin/'reɪzn/

n. a dried grape (sometimes put into bread,cakes,etc.) 葡萄干

rake/reɪk/

Ⅰ *n*.a long-handled tool having a bar at one end with teeth in it 耙 Ⅱ *v*.use a rake upon 耙(土):Please ～ the garden path. 请把花园的小路耙平。‖ ～ **in** 赚大钱/～ **it in** 大捞一笔/～ **off** 提取 /～ **out** 找出来/～ **over** 寻找 /～ **through** 搜索

rally/'ræli/

Ⅰ *v*.❶ come or bring together (again) for a shared purpose or effort (重新)集合:The general rallied the fleeing troops.将军把溃军重新集合起来。❷return to a former good state,e.g.after illness or difficulty 恢复(体力、健康等):He rallied after a short rest.他休息了一会儿便恢复了体力。Ⅱ *n*.a large,especially political public meeting 集合;集会:a political ～ 政党集会

ramble/'ræmbl/

v. ❶ wander about;walk for pleasure, with no special destination 漫步;闲逛:The boys were rambling in the street.孩子们在街上闲逛。❷ wander in one's talk,not keeping to the subject 闲聊:The housewives were rambling there.家庭主妇们在那边闲聊。‖ ～**r** /'ræmblə(r)/ *n*.漫步者/*rambling adj*.漫无边际的

ramification/ˌræmɪfɪ'keɪʃn/

n.a part of sth.(especially an idea,argument,set of rules,etc.)that is very complicated 分支;细节;门类:I have never got to know all the ～ of his business.我从来没弄清楚他的业务的全部细节。

ramify/'ræmɪfaɪ/

v.(cause to) branch out in all directions; form (into) a network (使)分支;(使)汇合成网状

rampage/ræm'peɪdʒ/

Ⅰ *v*.rush about wildly or angrily 狂暴地乱冲 Ⅱ *n*.a period of violent and uncontrollable behaviour 横冲直撞;暴怒 ‖ **be on the** ～ 暴怒;狂跳

rampant/'ræmpənt/

adj.❶ growing or spreading without being controlled 蔓延的;猖獗的:Crime was ～.犯罪很猖獗。❷ standing up on the hind legs (as animals are sometimes shown on coats of arms)(臂章上所画的动物的)后足直立的

rampart/'ræmpɑːt/

n.a wide bank of earth,sometimes with a wall on top of it,built around a fort,castle,etc.to defend it 土堤;壁垒;城墙

ramshackle/'ræmʃækl/

adj.almost falling down 快倒塌的;摇摇欲坠的:a ～ house 摇摇欲坠的房子

ranch/rɑːntʃ/

n.❶a very large farm 大牧场 ❷ any kind of farm 农场:a chicken ～ 养鸡场 ‖ ～**er** *n*. 牧场主

rancid/ˈrænsɪd/

adj. gone bad; stale; not fresh 败坏的;陈腐的;不新鲜的:~ butter(fat,etc.)坏掉的黄油(脂肪等)

random/ˈrændəm/

Ⅰ *n*. the state of being aimless 随便;偶然:at ~ 随便/shoot at ~无的放矢 Ⅱ *adj*. done, made, etc. aimlessly; without purpose 随便的;任意的:make a ~ choice 任意选择 /a ~ guess 瞎猜

range/reɪndʒ/

Ⅰ *n*.❶ a row or line; a continuous series 一列(行);一连串;一系列:a ~ of pictures 一排画 /a ~ of bicycles 各种型号的自行车 /a mountain ~ 一条山脉 /~ of houses 一排房屋 /a complete ~ of gardening tools 一整套园艺工具 ❷ the distance between certain limits 距离;射程:be out of (in) ~ 在射程以外(内) ❸ an area where shooting is practised 靶场;射击场 ❹ extent; the distance between two things 幅度;范围;区域:a wide ~ of knowledge 广博的知识 /the ~ of vision 眼界 /a subject outside one's ~ 不属于某人研究范围的题目 /Physics is out of my ~. 物理我一窍不通。 Ⅱ *v*.❶ put in order; arrange 排列;分类;调整:~ books by size on the shelf 按大小将书排在书架上 /~ soldiers in line 让战士排成横队 ❷ stretch; extend 延绵;伸展:a boundary ranging north and south 绵亘南北的边界 /The Himalayas ~ from west to east. 喜马拉雅山脉自西向东绵亘。 ❸ vary or extend between specified limits (在一定幅度或范围内)变动,变化,延伸:Its prices ~ from ten to twenty yuan. 价钱从十元到二十元不等。

ranger/ˈreɪndʒə(r)/

n.❶ the keeper of a forest; a forest guard 森林管理员;护林员 ❷(in North America) a policeman who rides through country areas to see that the law is kept (北美的)巡逻骑警 ❸(in the US) a commando (美国陆军中的)突击队员,特别行动队队员 ❹(Ranger) an older member of the Girl scouts aged from 14 to 19 高年级女童子军队员(14 至 19 岁)

rank/ræŋk/

Ⅰ *n*.❶ a line (row) of persons or things 排;列:Soldiers stood in ~s for inspection. 士兵们列队等候检阅。 ❷ a position in the hierarchy of the armed forces 军衔:What is your ~? 你担任什么军衔? ❸ (*pl*.) the stated class or group 阶级;阶层:She's joined the ~s of the unemployed. 她加入了失业大军。 ‖ the ~s 普通士兵:He was reduced to the ~s as a punishment for drinking. 作为对他酗酒的惩罚,他被降级为普通士兵。 Ⅱ *v*.❶ hold a certain grade or position 占……地位:He ~ed low. 他地位低下。 ❷ take precedence over 分属某类

ranking/ˈræŋkɪŋ/

n. a position in a scale of achievement or status; a classification 地位;等级;品类

ransack/ˈrænsæk/

v.❶ search thoroughly (often causing great untidiness or disorder) 彻底搜查:~ a room for important documents 为寻找重要文件把房间搜遍 ❷ steal everything from 洗劫;抢光:Thieves ~ed the house. 小偷们把屋里洗劫一空。

ransom/ˈrænsəm/

n. an amount of money that has to be paid to set sb. free 赎金 ‖ **hold someone to** ~ 绑票;抓了某人勒取赎金

rap/ræp/

Ⅰ *n*.❶ a light, quick blow 轻敲;轻拍 ❷ a rebuke or criticism 指责;批评 ‖ **take the** ~ 受责备;背黑锅 Ⅱ *v*.(-pp-)❶pat or hit sb. or sth. gently 轻拍:The teacher ~ped him on the shoulder. 老师轻轻地拍了拍他的肩膀。 ❷blame sb. severely 批评

rape/reɪp/

Ⅰ *v*.❶have sex with sb. against one's will 强奸 ❷ seize and carry off by force 强夺;抢劫 Ⅱ *n*. the act of raping 强夺;抢劫;强奸

rapid/ˈræpɪd/

adj. quick, fast; moving or occurring with great speed 迅速的:He made ~ progress in English. 他在英语方面取得了迅速的进步。 ‖ ~**ly** *adv*. 迅速地/~**ity** /rəˈpɪdəti/ *n*.快速

rapids /'ræpɪdz/

n.(*pl*.) a part of a river where the water flows very fast, usually over rocks (河的)急流

rapture /'ræptʃə(r)/

n.a feeling of great joy and delight 极高兴;狂喜:He was filled with ～.他欣喜若狂。

rare /reə(r)/

adj.not often seen or happening 稀少的:She wanted to buy her husband a ～ gift. 她想要为她丈夫买一件珍贵的礼物。

rarefied /'reərɪfaɪd/

adj.❶(of air in high places) light, thin; with less oxygen than usual (空气在高处)变稀薄的,缺氧的 ❷ limited to people who are special·in some way 只限于小圈子内的:He moves in very ～ circles;his friends are all lords.他只在非常小的圈子里交际,他的朋友都是有爵位的人。

rarely /'reəli/

adv.seldom;not often 很少;难得:He visits us ～ nowadays. 如今他很少来看我们。

raring /'reərɪŋ/

adj.very eager 渴望的;极想的:The children were ～ to get out into the snow.孩子们渴望着到外面雪地里去。/They were ～ to go.他们极想动身。

rarity /'reərəti/

n.❶ the state or quality of being rare 稀罕;罕见:These stamps have great ～ value.这些罕见的邮票非常珍贵。 ❷ sth. uncommon,especially one having particular value 罕见事物;珍奇的东西:People who bake their own bread have become a ～.自己动手烘制面包的人已经很少。

rash /ræʃ/

adj.overbold;not thinking enough of the results 鲁莽的;轻率的:It is ～ of you to do that.你那样做太鲁莽了。‖ ～ly *adv*. 鲁莽地;轻率地

rat /ræt/

Ⅰ *n*. ❶ a big mouse 老鼠;耗子:A ～

crossing the street is chased by all.老鼠过街,人人喊打。 ❷ a low,worthless or dishonest person 讨厌鬼;可耻的人;叛徒 Ⅱ *v*.(-tt-) ❶ trap rats 捕鼠:go ～ting 去捕鼠 ❷ act in a disloyal way; break a promise 变节;违背誓言:～ on an agreement 背弃协议

ratbag /'rætbæg/

n.an unpleasant or disliked person 讨厌的家伙

rate /reɪt/

Ⅰ *n*.❶ the speed with which sth.moves, etc.速度:The train ran at the ～ of 60 km an hour. 火车以每小时 60 千米的速度运行。 ❷ a price which is paid for sth. 价格:He was paid at the ～ of one dollar an hour.他按每小时一美元的价格收费。 ❸ a rank or class in an organization, a country,etc.等级:She received a first-～ education.她接受了第一流的教育。 Ⅱ *v*. regard as 认为:He was ～d the richest man in the village.他被认为是村里最富的人。

rather /'rɑːðə(r)/

adv.❶ more willingly; by preference or choice 宁愿:I would ～ you came tomorrow than today.我宁愿你明天来,而不是今天来。 ❷ in or to some degree;somewhat 相当;有点:She felt ～ tired.她感到相当累。 ❸ more truly, accurately or precisely 更真实地;更正确地;更精密地:He arrived very late last night or ～ in the early hours this morning.他昨晚深夜才到,或者更精确地说,今天清晨才到。

ratify /'rætɪfaɪ/

v.confirm (an agreement) by signature or other formality 批准;认可:The heads of the two governments met to ～ the treaty.两国政府首脑会晤批准该条约。

rating /'reɪtɪŋ/

n.a class to which sth. (e.g. a ship) belongs (船的)等级

ratio /'reɪʃɪəʊ/

n.(*pl*.～s) the relation in degree or number between two similar things 比;比率;比值:the ～ between industry and agri-

R

culture 工农业的比率 /They're in the ～ of 3：5.他们是三对五之比。

ration/'ræʃn/

Ⅰ n. a fixed allowance served out to, e.g. members of the armed forces; the fixed quantity, especially of food allowed to one person（军队每日）口粮, 给养; 配给量, 定量: a daily ～ of grain 每天的粮食定量 /the rice ～s for the month 每月的大米定量 Ⅱ v. limit (sb.) to a fixed ration 配给; 定量供应: ～ meats 配售肉类 /～ water 限制用水

rational/'ræʃnəl/

adj.（of ideas and behaviour, etc.）sensible; according to reason（思想、行为等）合理的: ～ explanations 合理的解释 /a ～ act 合理的行为

rationale/ˌræʃə'nɑːl/

n. the principles or reasons for a course of action 基本原理; 理论基础

rationalism /'ræʃənəlɪzəm/

n. the belief that all behaviours, opinions, etc. should base on reason rather than on religious belief or emotions 理性主义; 唯理论 ‖ **rationalist** n. 理性主义者, 唯理主义者

rattan/ræ'tæn/

n. ❶ a climbing palm with long, slender and tough stems 藤 ❷ these stems, used in making wicker work, etc. 藤条

rattle/'rætl/

Ⅰ v. make a number of short sounds when shaken 嘎嘎响: The boy ～d the coins in his tin. 男孩把罐子里的硬币摇得叮当响。 Ⅱ n.（a toy or an instrument that makes）a rattling noise 嘎嘎声 ‖ ～ off 一口气说完 /～ on 喋喋不休地讲话

rattlesnake/'rætlsneɪk/

n. a poisonous American snake that makes a rattling noise with its tail when it is angry 响尾蛇

rattletrap/'rætltræp/

n. a noisy old vehicle, especially a car 破旧车辆; 老爷车

rattling/'rætlɪŋ/

adv. very good 非常好: a ～ story 一个非

常好的故事

ratty/'ræti/

adj. ❶ bad-tempered and irritable 爱发脾气的; 易怒的 ❷ in bad condition and untidy 破旧的; 邋遢的: a ～ old coat 一件邋遢的旧外套 ❸ like or full of rats 老鼠似的; 老鼠多的

ravage/'rævɪdʒ/

v. ❶ rob or plunder with violence 掠夺: The invaders ～d the whole village. 侵略者蹂躏了整个村庄。 ❷ destroy sth. badly 严重损害; 破坏: The crops were ～d. by the snowstorm. 庄稼被暴风雪毁坏了。

ravages/'rævɪdʒɪz/

n.（pl.）the damage caused (as if) by ravaging; destroying effects 破坏的结果;（遭破坏的）残迹: the ～ of fire (war, inflation) 火灾（战争、通货膨胀）造成的破坏性后果

ravel/'rævl/

Ⅰ v.(-ll- or -l-) ❶ be twisted or knotted together; make confused 使纠缠, 使混乱: ～(l)ed wool 纠缠在一起的毛线 ❷ disentangle ropes, etc. 拆开（绳索等）: ～ a rope's end 拆开绳子的一头 ❸ clarify by separating the aspects of sth. 使明白; 解决: The difficulty will soon ～ out. 困难不久即可解决。 ❹ become tangled or confused 使错综复杂: ～ and complicate the meaning 把意思搞得扑朔迷离 Ⅱ n. a broken, discarded thread 拆开的绳索（线头）

ravine/rə'viːn/

n. a long, deep and narrow valley 峡谷; 深谷

raving/'reɪvɪŋ/

adj. ❶ talking or behaving wildly 语无伦次的; 疯狂的: a ～ lunatic 胡言乱语的疯子 ❷ very great; attracting great admiration 极好的; 出色的: a ～ beauty 绝色美女 /The concert was not a ～ success. 音乐会不是很成功。

ravings/'reɪvɪŋz/

n. wild uncontrolled talks 胡言乱语; 疯话: the ～ of a madman 疯子的胡言乱语

ravish/'rævɪʃ/

v. ❶ fill with delight and pleasure 使陶醉；使狂喜：I was ～ed by her beauty.她的美貌使我倾倒。 ❷ seize or rob with violence 抢劫；掠夺 ❸ force sb. to have sex against their will 强奸

ravishing /'rævɪʃɪŋ/

adj. very beautiful；causing great delight 非常美丽的；令人陶醉的：a ～ sight 令人陶醉的景色 ‖ ～**ly** *adv.* 令人陶醉地

raw /rɔː/

adj. ❶ uncooked 生的：You can't eat ～ meat.你不能吃生肉。 ❷ in the natural state；not yet treated for use 天然的；未加工的：～ cotton 原棉 /the ～ material of industry 工业原料 ❸ (of persons) untrained, unskilled (指人)未受训练的，不熟练的

ray /reɪ/

n. ❶ a thin light or narrow beam of radiant light, heat or energy 光线；(热或其他能量的)辐射线：the ～s of the sun 日光/X ～s X 光射线 ❷ any one of a number of lines coming out from a center 辐射状的直线

rayon /'reɪɒn/

n. a fibre made from cellulose；a smooth material made from this，used for making clothes 人造丝；人造丝织品：a ～ shirt 人造丝衬衫

raze /reɪz/

v. destroy houses, towns, etc. by levelling them to the ground (把房子、城镇等)夷为平地：The village was completely ～d during the battle.这个村庄在交战中被完全夷为平地。

razor /'reɪzə(r)/

n. a sharp tool for cutting hair from the skin 剃刀：He shaved with an electric ～. 他用电动剃须刀刮胡子。 ‖ ～ **blade** *n.* 剃须刀片

reach /riːtʃ/

v. ❶ get to；arrive at (in) 到达：Your letter didn't ～ me until today. 直到今天我才收到你的来信。 ❷ hold out (one's hand) 伸出：He ～ed for the book on the shelf.他伸手去书架上拿书。 ‖ ～ **down** 把……拿下来/～ for 伸手拿/～ out for 设法抓住/～ out to 和……联系/～ to (声音)传到

reachable /'riːtʃəbl/

adj. that is possible to reach 可及的；可到达的；够得到的：The lake is only ～ by car.那个湖只能开车去。

react /rɪ'ækt/

v. ❶ act as a result of another happening 反应：How did he ～ to our plan? 他对我们的计划有何反应？ ❷ act in chemical way 化学反应：Hydrogen ～s with oxygen to form water.氢和氧起化学反应生成水。 ‖ ～ **against** 反抗/～ **on** (**up on**) 对……产生影响/～ **to** 对……作出反应

reaction /rɪ'ækʃn/

n. ❶ an action performed in response to a situation or event 反应：What was your ～ to the news? 你对这条新闻有什么反应？ ❷ an action set up by one substance in another；a change within the nucleus of an atom 化学反应；核反应：chain ～s 连锁反应 ❸ opposition to political or social progress 反动：The forces of ～ were defeated in the end. 反动势力最终被击败了。

reactionary /rɪ'ækʃənri/

Ⅰ *adj.* strongly against or preventing (especially political) changes in society 反动的：clear out the ～ elements 肃清反动分子 Ⅱ *n.* an opponent of progress, reform or changes 反动分子：All reactionaries are paper tigers.一切反动派都是纸老虎。

reactivate /ˌriː'æktɪveɪt/

v. make or become active again (使)恢复活动；(使)重新活跃起来：We ～d the machine.我们使这台机器重新开动。/ The chemicals ～ when heated.这些化学药物加热后会再度活化。

reactive /rɪ'æktɪv/

adj. (of chemical substance) having a tendency to react (化学物质)反应性的，能起化学反应的

reactor /rɪ'æktə(r)/

n. ❶ a large machine for the controlled production of atomic energy 核反应堆 ❷

a container for a chemical reaction 反应器

read/riːd/

v. (read/red/) ❶ look at and get the meaning of；repeat with the voice 阅读；朗读：He could hardly ～ and write. 他几乎不会读书写字。❷ understand (a foreign language) when it is written；understand the nature of sth. by observation 看懂：There was such an expression on his face that she could not ～. 他脸上有一种使她捉摸不透的表情。❸ understand sth. in a particular way 懂得；理解 ❹ show a particular weight，pressure，，etc. 显示；读数为

readable/ˈriːdəbl/

adj. ❶ easy or enjoyable to read 易读的；有趣味的 ❷ able to be read 可读的

readdress/ˌriːəˈdres/

v. write a different address on (a letter that has been delivered to one's own address) 更改(邮件上的)地址(再转寄)：I asked them to ～ my letters (to the new house). 我要求他们转寄我的信件(到新住址)。

reader/ˈriːdə(r)/

n. ❶ a person who reads，especially one who spends much time in reading 读者：the ～s of a newspaper 一家报纸的读者 ❷ a textbook for reading in class；a book with selections for reading by students of a language 读物；读本；文选：an English ～ 英语读本 ❸ (Reader) a university lecturer of the highest grade below professor 〈英〉(大学的)高级讲师

readership/ˈriːdəʃɪp/

n. ❶ the particular number or type of people who read a newspaper or magazine (报纸、杂志的)读者人数：The paper has a ～ of 80,000. 这份报纸有八万读者。❷ the position of a Reader at a university 高级讲师的职位

readily/ˈredɪli/

adv. ❶ willingly 乐意地：He ～ promised to help. 他很乐意地答应帮忙。❷ with no difficulty 容易地：These data are ～

available. 这些资料很容易弄到。❸ quickly 迅速地

readiness/ˈredɪnɪs/

n. ❶ willingness to do sth. 愿意；乐意 ❷ the state of being ready 准备就绪 ❸ immediacy，quickness，or promptness 迅速；敏捷

reading/ˈriːdɪŋ/

n. ❶ an act of one who reads 读；阅读；朗读：intensive ～ 精读 /extensive ～ 泛读 ❷ knowledge，especially of books 学识：a man of wide ～ 博览群书的人 ❸ selections or materials for reading 读物；阅读材料：～s from English literature 英国文学选读 /～s for children 儿童读物 ❹ a figure of measurement，etc.，as shown on a dial，scale，etc. (仪表等的)读数：the ～s on the thermometer 温度计读数

readjust/ˌriːəˈdʒʌst/

v. get or put back into the proper state or position 再整理；再调整：Readjust the driving mirror. 重新调整一下汽车的后视镜。/It's hard to ～ (oneself) to school life after the holidays. 假日之后，(自己)一时还很难适应学校生活。‖ ～ment n. 调整时期：The mechanic made a few minor ～ments. 机修工重新作了一些细小的调节。

read-out/ˈriːdaʊt/

n. a display of information，e.g. in printed form or on a screen，that has been processed by a computer 信息输出：Using this program，you can get a ～ of all the areas where sales have increased. 利用这种计算机程序，你能得到各个地区销售额增长的信息。

ready/ˈredi/

adj. ❶ prepared 准备好的：We're always ～ to give our lives to the country. 我们时刻准备为国捐躯。❷ willing to do sth. 乐意的：He is always ～ to help others. 他总是乐于助人。❸ in need of 需要的 ❹ likely to do sth. 可能的 ❺ quick or prompt 迅速的；及时的

reaffirm/ˌriːəˈfɜːm/

v. declare again；in answer to a question or

doubt 重申；再次确定：The statement ~ed that the government would never make concessions to terrorists.该声明重申，政府永远不会向恐怖分子让步。

reafforest /ˌriːəˈfɒrɪst/

v. plant (land) again with forest trees 重新造林

real /rɪəl/

adj. ❶ not false；genuine 正宗的；真的：He was eager to get a ~ gun. 他渴望得到一杆真枪。❷ actually existing；not imagined or supposed 真实的；实在的 ❸ true or actual 真的；实际的 ❹ complete 完全的；十足的

realism /ˈrɪəlɪzəm/

n. (art and literature) showing of real life, facts, etc. in a true way（艺术、文学）写实主义，现实主义：revolutionary ~ 革命的现实主义

realist /ˈrɪəlɪst/

n. a person whose social, political, and artistic ideas are based on realism 现实主义者；写实主义者

realistic /rɪəˈlɪstɪk/

adj. ❶ showing realism 现实主义的：a ~ novel 一本现实主义小说 ❷ (of art or literature) lifelike（文艺作品）逼真的：Their acting was ~.他们演得逼真。❸ having or showing a sensible and practical idea of what can be achieved or expected 现实的；实际可行的

reality /rɪˈæləti/

n. ❶ the state of being real or true 真实（性）；现实（性）：I doubted the ~ of what I had seen. 我怀疑我所见到的真实性。❷ the true state of affairs；the true nature；a real thing 真相；本性；实物：an objective ~ 客观现实 /It is sometimes hard to face ~.有时很难面对现实。/My dream has become a ~.我的梦想已变成现实。

realization /ˌrɪəlaɪˈzeɪʃn/

n. ❶ the process of becoming aware of sth. 认识；领会：The ~ of her mistake came too late.她认识自己的错误太迟了。❷ the achievement of sth. desired 实现：

the ~ of the four modernizations 实现四个现代化

realize /ˈrɪəlaɪz/

v. ❶ see clearly；understand 明白；领悟：You'll ~ your mistakes sooner or later. 你迟早会意识到你的错误。❷ bring into actual existence；make real；accomplish 实现：At last she ~d her intention of being a singer.她终于实现了当一名歌唱家的愿望。‖ ~ on 从……赚得(一笔钱)

really /ˈrɪəli/

adv. ❶ truly；in fact；actually 真正地；实际地；确实地：reflect things as they ~ are 如实地反映事物 /He is ~ a very kind person.事实上他是一个很善良的人。❷ used to express surprise or interest, etc.(用来表示惊异、感兴趣等)真的：I'm going to China next year.—Really! 我明年要到中国去。——真的!

realm /relm/

n. ❶ a kingdom that has a king or queen 王国：an independent ~ 独立王国 /the laws of the ~ 王国的法律 ❷ a field or domain of activity or interest 领域；范围：the ~ of science 科学领域 /the ~ of literature and art 文学艺术领域 /within the ~ of possibility 在可能的范围之内

reap /riːp/

v. ❶ cut (grain)；gather (crops) 收割：It is time to ~ the crops.收割庄稼的时候到了。❷ obtain as a result of effort 获得(成果)：He ~ed the teacher's praise for his good behavior. 他的良好行为受到了老师的赞扬。

reaper /ˈriːpə/

n. a person or machine that harvests crops 收割者；收割机

rear¹ /rɪə(r)/

Ⅰ *n.* the back 后部；后面：The kitchen is in the ~ of the house.厨房在房子的后部。Ⅱ *adj.* in or at the back 后部的；后面的：the ~ lamps of a car 小车的后灯

rear² /rɪə(r)/

v. ❶ help to grow；bring up 抚养；养育：~ children 抚养孩子 ❷ (of a horse or other animals) raise itself upright on its hind legs（马或其他动物）用后脚直立：The horse ~ed.这匹马后腿直立起来了。❸ breed and raise 饲养

rearing/ˈrɪərɪŋ/

n. ❶ the process of caring for children as they grow up, teaching them how to behave as members of society 养育；抚养；培养 ❷ the process of breeding animals or birds and caring for them as they grow 饲养

rearm/ˌriːˈɑːm/

v. provide（oneself or others）with weapons again, or with new weapons 重新武装；重整军备：They ~ed their allies with modern missiles.他们用现代化导弹重新武装他们的盟国。

rearmost/ˈrɪəməust/

adj. furthest back; last 最后（面）的：the ~ carriage of the train 火车的最后一节车厢

rearrange/ˌriːəˈreɪndʒ/

v. put into a different order 重新布置：Let's ~ the room.我们来重新布置房间吧。

reason/ˈriːzn/

Ⅰ *n.* an explanation; a cause 原因；理由：Do you know the ~ why the sun rises in the east and sets in the west? 你知道太阳从东方升起从西方落下的原因吗？‖ **beyond** ~ 没有道理/**by** ~ **of** 由于……的缘故/**for this（that）** ~ 为此/**in** ~ 有道理地/**listen to** ~ 讲道理，听劝告/**lose one's** ~ 失去理智/**out of** ~ 不合理/**with** ~ 有道理 Ⅱ *v.* ❶ say by way of argument（that）讲道理：He ~ed but nobody listened to him.他陈述他的理由，但没人听他的。❷ make use of one's reason 推断；推理：~ clearly 推理清楚 ❸ persuade（someone）to do or not to do 劝说：He tried to ~ people out of the false belief. 他试图说服人们放弃这一错误信念。

reasonable/ˈriːznəbl/

adj. ❶ fair, practical and sensible 公平合理的；有理由的；明智的：a ~ explanation（demand, price）合理的解释（要求、价格）❷ not too expensive 不太贵的

reasonably/ˈriːznəbli/

adv. ❶ sensibly 合理地：behave ~ 行为态度得体 ❷ quite; fairly 相当地：The car is in ~ good condition.这车性能相当好。/They live ~ close.他们住得相当近。

reasoned/ˈriːznd/

adj.（of a statement, an argument, etc.）clearly thought out; based on reason（陈述、论点等）合乎逻辑的，经过缜密思考的：a ~ statement 有条有理的说明

reasoning/ˈriːzənɪŋ/

n. the use of one's reason 推理；推论：According to their ~, lower oil prices will stimulate business activity in the poorer countries.根据他们的推论，低油价将会促进穷国的商业活动。

reassemble/ˌriːəˈsembl/

v. ❶ assemble again 再集合；重新聚集 ❷ put sth. back together 重新装配

reassure/ˌriːəˈʃuə(r)/

v. say some words or do sth. to make sb. feel less doubted or worried 安慰；宽慰：No matter how we ~d him, he did not believe us.不管我们怎样安慰，他都不相信。

rebate/ˈriːbeɪt/

n. the return of part of the money one has paid 折扣；回扣：a ~ of one's income tax 所得税的折扣部分

rebel

Ⅰ /rɪˈbel/ *v.*（-ll-）fight against and refuse to obey 造反：Shortly after Lincoln took office, the Southern States ~led.林肯就职后不久，南部各州就起来造反。‖ ~ **against** 强烈反对/~ **at** 对……反感 Ⅱ /ˈrebl/ *n.* a person who fights against authority instead of obeying 叛逆者

rebellion/rɪˈbeljən/

n. ❶ an act or the state of rebelling 造反；反叛：They raised a ~ against the king.他们奋起反叛国王。❷ a refusal to obey orders or accept rules, etc.反抗；对抗：~ against fate 与命运对抗

rebellious/rɪˈbeljəs/

adj. disobedient and hard to control 反叛的；难控制的：~ troops 叛军/~ temper 倔强的脾气

rebirth/ˌriːˈbɜːθ/

　n. a renewal of life or existence 再生；新生；复兴：The firm had gone bankrupt, but the following year saw its ～ under a new name. 这家公司已经破产，可是第二年用一个新的名字恢复营业了。

reborn/ˌriːˈbɔːn/

　adj. as if born again 再生的；新生的；复兴的：Our hopes of success were ～. 我们又有了成功的希望。

rebound

　Ⅰ /rɪˈbaʊnd/*v.* ❶ fly back after hitting sth. 弹回；跳回：The ball ～ed from the wall and I caught it. 这球从墙上弹了回来，我把它接住了。 ❷（especially of prices, amounts, etc.）move quickly back to a former level after falling（尤指价格、数量等跌后）回升：Share prices ～ed today after last week's falls. 股票价格在上周下跌之后今天又回升了。 Ⅱ /ˈriːbaʊnd/*n.* ❶ a movement back from an impact 弹回；反冲：I caught the ball on the ～. 在球弹回时，我接住了它。 ❷ an unsettled state of mind as a result of unhappiness or a disappointment（失意或失望后）情绪波动；心灰意冷：He married Mary on the ～, only a few weeks after his previous girlfriend left him. 在他以前的女朋友离开他几个星期之后，他失望之余便和玛丽结婚了。

rebuild/ˌriːˈbɪld/

　v. ❶（rebuilt）build again or build new parts to 重建；重新组装：They ～ the bridge. 他们重建了大桥。 ❷ make sb. or sth. recover again 恢复，复原：The government has attempted to ～ its economy. 政府试图恢复经济。

rebuke/rɪˈbjuːk/

　Ⅰ *v.* reprove; speak severely to 指责；非难：The girl was ～d by her mother for telling a lie. 这女孩因撒谎受到妈妈的责备。 Ⅱ *n.* a few severe words or scolding 指责；训斥：be without ～ 无可非议

rebus/ˈriːbəs/

　n. a word game or puzzle in which words have to be guessed from pictures or let-

ters that suggest the sounds that make them（用图画或字母代表声音的）字谜，画谜：“R U 18” is a ～ for “Are you 18?”. “R U 18”是“Are you 18?”的字谜。

rebut/rɪˈbʌt/

　v. prove the falseness of（a statement or charge）反驳；驳斥

recall/rɪˈkɔːl/

　Ⅰ *v.* ❶ bring back to the mind 想起：He often ～ed his bitter childhood. 他经常想起他苦难的童年。 ❷ call back 召回：He was ～ed to settle the problem. 他被召回解决这一问题。 ❸ take back 收回：The library will ～ all the books. 图书馆将收回所有书籍。 Ⅱ *n.* the power of remembering 记忆力：Do you have any ～ of him? 你还记得他吗？

recant/rɪˈkænt/

　v. say that one no longer believes in something one used to believe in 宣布改变或放弃（信仰）

recapture/ˌriːˈkæptʃə(r)/

　v. ❶ get into one's power again 重获；夺回；收复：The police ～d the escaped criminal. 警察重新捕获了逃犯。 ❷ bring back into the mind; cause to be experienced again 再现；使再次经历：a book that ～s perfectly the flavour of the period 一本出色地再现那个时期情趣的著作

recast/ˌriːˈkɑːst/

　v. ❶ give a new shape to 重铸；再铸：～ a stature 重铸塑像 ❷ change the actors in（a play）更换（剧中的）演员：The cabinet has been completely ～ in the latest government changes. 新近的政府更迭中，内阁官员完全更换。

recede/rɪˈsiːd/

　v. ❶（appear to）go back from an earlier position 退却；后退 ❷ pull back or move away 撤销；撤回：He ～d from the agreement. 他撤回了协议。 ❸ slope backwards 向后倾斜：a receding chin 向后缩去的下巴

receipt/rɪˈsiːt/

　Ⅰ *n.* ❶ the action of receiving sth. or the fact of its being received 接收；收到：on

～ of the news 当收到消息时 /I am in ～ of your letter. 我收到了你的来信。 ❷ (*pl.*) money received during a particular period by a firm, etc. 收入；进款；收益：Their expenses were less than their ～s. 他们的开支小于收入。 ❸ a written statement that sth. has been received 收据；收条：sign a ～ 在收据上签字 Ⅱ *v.* write out and sign or stamp a receipt 开收据

receivable/rɪˈsiːvəbl/
adj. ❶ able or fit to be received 可收到的；可接受的 ❷ (of a bill or debt) for which money is to be received (票据或债务)应收的

receive/rɪˈsiːv/
v. ❶ come into possession of (sth. that is given or sent to one); get 收到：He ～d many gifts, but he didn't accept them. 他收到了很多礼物，但他没有接受。 ❷ suffer, experience, or be subject to 遭受；经受：It was a knife wound, ～d from twenty to twenty four hours before. 那是一处在 20 至 24 小时之前受的刀伤。 ❸ welcome or entertain 接见

receiver/rɪˈsiːvə(r)/
n. ❶ the person who receives 接收人：the ～ of a letter 收信人 ❷ the part of a radio or TV set that produces sound and pictures (无线电、电视)接收器；收音机；电视机 ❸ the part of a telephone through which one hears 听筒 ❹ the person officially appointed to take charge of the property and affairs of a bankrupt 破产产业管理人

recent/ˈriːsnt/
adj. done or made not long ago; fresh 近来的；新近的：He wanted to know the most ～ news about his homeland. 他想要知道关于他祖国的最新消息。 ‖ ～ly/ˈriːsntli/ *adv.* 近来

reception/rɪˈsepʃn/
n. ❶ the way of receiving or being received 接待；欢迎：The winning team got a wonderful ～ in their hometown. 这获胜的球队在他们的家乡受到了热烈的欢迎。 ❷ a party or gathering to entertain visitors 招待会；欢迎会：a wedding ～ 婚宴 ❸ people in a hotel whose job is to receive guests, etc; the place where such people work (旅馆的)接待员；接待部门；接待处 ‖ ～ist *n.* 接待人员；招待员 /receptive/rɪˈseptɪv/ *adj.* 易接受的；愿接受的

recess/rɪˈses/
n. ❶ a period of time during which work stops 休息时间；休假期，休会期：a ～ of thirty minutes 三十分钟的休息时间 ❷ a hollow space in a wall for a bed, cupboard, etc. 壁凹 ❸ a remote or secret place 深处；隐蔽处：the dark ～es of a cave 洞穴乌黑的深处

recipe/ˈresɪpi/
n. a set of instructions on how to prepare a certain kind of food 食谱；烹饪法：a ～ for a cake 蛋糕的做法

recipient/rɪˈsɪpiənt/
n. a person who receives sth. 接受者；收受者

recital/rɪˈsaɪtl/
n. a performance of music by one person 独奏会：He is going to give a piano ～. 他打算举行一场钢琴独奏会。

reckless/ˈrekləs/
adj. not caring about danger; very careless 不顾危险的；鲁莽的：a ～ driver 鲁莽的驾驶员

reckon/ˈrekən/
v. ❶ calculate sth. approximately 计算；估算：She ～ed how much she had saved. 她数了数共储蓄了多少钱。 ❷ guess or have an opinion about sth. 猜想；认为：I ～ that he'll be here on time. 我猜他会准时来的。

reclaim/rɪˈkleɪm/
v. ❶ make (land) fit for use 开垦；开拓：～ wasteland 开垦荒地 ❷ ask for the return of 收回；收复：～ lost territory 收复失地

recline/rɪˈklaɪn/
v. ❶ lie down 横卧：～ on a couch 横卧在长沙发上 ❷ lean or lie back in a relaxed position with the back supported; put in a

resting position 斜倚;倚靠:～ one's head 斜倚着头

recognition/ˌrekəɡˈnɪʃn/

n. ❶ the action or process of recognizing or being recognized 认出;认识:The place has changed beyond ～.这地方已变得认不出来了。❷ the state of being acknowledged 承认:The school hopes for ～ by the Department of Education. 这所学校希望得到教育部的承认。

recognize/ˈrekəɡnaɪz/

v. ❶ know again (sb. or sth. one has seen,heard,or experienced before) 认出;辨认出:He ～d her at last.他终于认出了她。❷ accept as being legal or real,or as having value 承认:His labour has been ～d by all.他的劳动得到了大家的承认。

recoil/rɪˈkɔɪl/

Ⅰ *v.* ❶ draw back in fear, disgust, etc. 畏缩;退却:～ from the sight of a snake 看到蛇就退缩 ❷ spring back 反弹;弹回:The rifle ～ed when it was fired.步枪射击时就弹回了。Ⅱ *n.* an act of moving back 退缩;弹回

recollection/ˌrekəˈlekʃn/

n. ❶ an act or power of recollecting or recalling 回忆;追忆;记忆力:beyond (past) ～ 已无法被回忆起 /to the best of someone's ～ 就某人记忆所及 /It is my ～ that he said that.我记得他是那么说的。❷ sth. recollected or remembered;a memory 回忆的事;往事;回忆录:happy ～s 愉快的往事 /He is writing his ～s.他正在写回忆录。

recommend/ˌrekəˈmend/

v. ❶ advise;suggest 建议:He ～ed me to read more.他建议我多看书。❷ speak in favour of 推荐:Will you ～ me to the manager? 你能向经理推荐我吗? ❸ make sb. or sth. attractive 使有吸引力:This restaurant has nothing to ～ it except cheapness. 这家饭馆除便宜外没有什么吸引人的地方。‖ ～ for 推荐……作某种用途 /～ to 向……推荐

recommendation/ˌrekəmenˈdeɪʃn/

n. ❶the act of suggesting sb.or sth. should be used,etc. 推荐;介绍:speak in ～ of someone 口头推荐某人 ❷ a statement that recommends sb.or sth. 推荐书;介绍信 ❸ a suggestion 建议

recompense/ˈrekəmpens/

Ⅰ *v.* give money to someone for some loss,injury,etc. that he has suffered 赔偿;酬答 Ⅱ *n.* reward; payment 报酬;酬金:work hard without ～ 不计报酬地辛勤工作

reconcile/ˈrekənsaɪl/

v. ❶ cause to become friends after having an argument or a disagreement 和解:The couple quarrelled but now they are ～d. 两口子虽吵过架,但现在已和好如初。❷ bring into harmony with; cause to agree with 使一致:She tried to ～ the expense with the income each month. 她尽量使每月收支平衡。

reconsider/ˌriːkənˈsɪdə(r)/

v. think again and change one's mind about (a subject) 重新考虑:Won't you ～ your decision to leave the club? 退出俱乐部的决定你可以重新考虑一下吗?

reconstruct/ˌriːkənˈstrʌkt/

v. ❶ rebuild after damage 重建;再建:～ a city after the war 战后重建城市 ❷ build up a complete description or picture of (sth. only partly known) 重现;重整:～ a crime from known facts 从已知事实设想出犯罪经过

record

Ⅰ /rɪˈkɔːd/ *v.* ❶write down (a description or piece of information) so that it will be known in the future 记录:Please ～ what I say. 请把我说的记录下来。❷ preserve (sound or a television broadcast) so that it can be heard and/or seen again 录下(声音,形象等):The recorder ～ed his voice and the camera ～ed his features. 录音机录下了他的声音,照相机录下了他的容貌。Ⅱ /ˈrekɔːd/ *n.* ❶ a written statement of facts,events,etc. 记录:Thus he kept a ～ of all his students. 这样他把所有的学生都记录下来了。❷ the best yet done, especially in sport; the highest (lowest) figure ever reached 运动纪录:She set a

R

new world ～ in high jump.她刷新了世界跳高纪录。

recorder/rɪˈkɔːdə(r)/
n. ❶ a person who makes or keeps records 记录员；书记员 ❷ a device for recording sounds 录音机：a tape ～ 磁带录音机

recount¹/rɪˈkaʊnt/
*v.*give an account of；tell 叙述；讲述：He ～ed the story of his adventures in Mexico to them.他向他们讲述了他在墨西哥的冒险经历。

recount²
Ⅰ /ˈriːkaʊnt/ *n.*a second count 再数；重新计算 Ⅱ /riːˈkaʊnt/ *v.*count again 重新计算；再数

recourse/rɪˈkɔːs/
*n.*a person or thing that is turned to for help, etc. 求助的人或物：have ～ to parents 向父母求助

recover/rɪˈkʌvə(r)/
*v.*get back (sth.lost)；get back the use of 挽回；恢复：He has ～ed his strength after his fever.他退烧后已经恢复体力。‖ ～y/rɪˈkʌvəri/ *n.*恢复；痊愈

recreation/ˌrekrɪˈeɪʃn/
*n.*a way of occupying free time pleasantly 娱乐；消遣：Reading books is one kind of ～.读书是一种消遣。‖ **recreate** *v.*再现；再创造/**recreative** *adj.*娱乐的；消遣的

recruit/rɪˈkruːt/
Ⅰ *n.*a new member of an organization；a person newly joined in the armed forces 新成员；新兵：All the ～s have got their uniforms.所有新兵都领了制服。Ⅱ *v.*get (recruits) for the armed forces 招募新兵：It is the duty of every citizen to be ～ed.应征入伍是每个公民的职责。

rectangle/ˈrektæŋgl/
n. a four-sided figure with the opposite sides equal and four right angles 长方形；矩形

recur/rɪˈkɜː(r)/
v.(-rr-) ❶ happen again；be repeated 再发生；复发：If the pain should ～, take the medicine.如果再疼，服这种药。❷ go

back (to sth.) in words or thought 重新提起：～ to what was said before 提到以前说过的话 ❸ (of passed events) come back (往事) 重新浮现：Old memories constantly ～red to him.往事常常浮现在他脑海里。

recycle/ˌriːˈsaɪkl/
*v.*treat (waste material) so that it can be used again 回收利用

red/red/
Ⅰ *n.*the colour of blood 红色 Ⅱ *adj.*of the colour of blood 红色的：Have you ever read *Red Star over China*? 你看过《西行漫记》这本书吗？ ‖ catch sb. ～handed 当场抓住某人/～ carpet treatment 热情招待/～ hot 热情的/～ letter day 特别高兴的日子

redeem/rɪˈdiːm/
v. ❶ buy back；get back by payment or doing sth.赎回：～ a watch from (out of) pawn 赎回典当的表 /She ～ed her gold ring.她赎回了金戒指。❷ perform (a promise or pledge) 履行诺言、承诺 ❸ compensate；make up for 补救；弥补：～ a mistake 弥补错误 /We had to work on weekends to ～ the lost time.我们不得不在周末也工作以弥补丢失的时间。

redo/riːˈduː/
*v.*❶do sth. again or differently 再做；重做 ❷redecorate a room, etc. 重新装饰：The house is being redone to suit her taste.正在重新装饰房子，以满足她的品味。

redouble/ˌriːˈdʌbl/
*v.*increase greatly 激增；加倍：～ one's efforts 加倍努力

reduce/rɪˈdjuːs/
*v.*make less or smaller 减少：The population of that area has been ～d.那个地区的人口已经减少。‖ ～ to order 整顿/～ to silence 使安静下来/～ sb. to tears 使哭起来

reduction/rɪˈdʌkʃn/
*n.*❶ the act of making sth. less or smaller；the state of being made less or smaller 减少；减小；缩减：～ of armament 裁

军 ❷ sth. on a smaller scale（e.g. a map or price）缩小的东西（如缩图、低价等）❸ the amount reduced 缩减的量 ❹（in mathematics）the cancelling of common factors in the numerator and denominator of a fraction（数学中的）简化

reed/riːd/

n. ❶（the tall strong hollow stem of）any of various grasslike plants that grow in wet places 芦苇 ❷ a thin piece of cane or metal in a musical instrument（乐器的）簧

re-educate/ˌriːˈedjukeɪt/

v. train or educate（someone）again 对……再教育：We should ～ young criminals to take their place in society. 我们应当对年轻的罪犯进行再教育使他们在社会上立足。

reedy/ˈriːdi/

adj. ❶（of a sound）thin and high in tone（声音）高而尖的：a ～ voice 高而尖的声音 ❷（of a place）full of reeds 芦苇丛生的：a ～ lake 芦苇湖

reef/riːf/

n. a line of sharp rocks or bank of sand, at or near the surface of the sea 礁；暗礁：The ship was wrecked on a ～. 那条船触礁而沉。

re-elect/ˌriːɪˈlekt/

v. elect again 重选：He has been ～ed to Parliament. 他被重新选入了议会。‖ ～ion *n.* 重选；再选：She is seeking ～ion for a third term of office. 她正在争取第三次连续当选。

re-entry/riːˈentri/

n. ❶ the action or process of reentering sth. 重新进入 ❷ the return of a spacecraft or missile into the earth's atmosphere（航天器、导弹）重返大气层

reface/riːˈfeɪs/

v. put a new surface on（a building）整修（建筑物）表面：The worn stonework on this building must be ～d. 建筑物上破损的石雕必须加以整修。

refer/rɪˈfɜː(r)/

v.（-rr-）❶ concern, mention; speak about or of 提到；谈到：The book you ～red to is not here. 你提到的那本书不在这儿。❷ make reference 查阅：I ～red to a history book in order to find out the date of the event. 为了弄清楚那一事件的日期我查阅了历史书。‖ ～ **back to** 重提

referee/ˌrefəˈriː/

n. ❶ a judge to keep the rules of a game 裁判员 ❷ a person who is asked to settle disagreement 仲裁者

reference/ˈrefərəns/

n. ❶ the use for help or information 参考；参阅：～ material 参考材料 / ～ frequency 参考频率 / make constant ～ to dictionaries 经常查字典 /Reference to a map will make the position clear. 参照地图会把位置弄清楚。❷ a note in a publication referring the reader to another source 参考书目：cross ～ 相互参照 ❸ the action of mentioning or alluding to sth. 提及；涉及：make ～s to this point 提到这一点 /make ～s to the heroic deeds of the frontier guards 提到边防战士的英勇事迹 ❹ a submission of a case to sb. 提交；委托：the ～ of a bill to a committee 向委员会提交议案 ❺ a statement about a person's character or ability（品格、能力）介绍，证明

referendum/ˌrefəˈrendəm/

n. a direct vote by all the people to decide about sth. on which there is strong disagreement，instead of the government making the decision（以表决政治、法律等问题的）全民投票，公民投票：The government will hold a ～ on whether the electoral system should be changed. 选举制度是否应当改变，政府将举行全民投票。/The question was decided by ～. 这问题是由全民投票决定的。

refill

Ⅰ/ˌriːˈfɪl/*v.* fill again 再填满；再注满：I'll ～ my teapot. 我要把茶壶再灌满。Ⅱ /ˈriːfɪl/*n.*（a container holding）a quantity of ink, petrol, etc. to fill sth. 添补物；新补充物：I bought two ～s for my pen. 我买了两支圆珠笔芯。/I can see your glass is empty；would you like a ～? 我看到你的

杯子空了；你还想再来一杯吗？‖ ~able adj. 适于再装的

refine/rɪˈfaɪn/

v. purify；make or become pure 精炼：Oil must be ~d before it is used. 石油在使用之前必须提炼。

refined/rɪˈfaɪnd/

adj. ❶ made pure 精炼的；精制的：~ salt 精盐 ❷elegant and cultured 优美的；文雅的：~ manner 文雅的举止/Her tastes are very ~. 她的趣味十分高雅。

refinement/rɪˈfaɪnmənt/

n. ❶ the act of making pure 精制；提炼：the ~ of metals 金属的提炼 ❷the quality of being elegant and cultured 优美；文雅：a lady of ~ 一位娴雅的女士 ❸small changes that improve sth. 改进：introduce ~s into a machine 对机器作精心的改进

refinery/rɪˈfaɪnəri/

n. a place, building, etc., where sth. is refined 精炼厂；提炼厂：a sugar ~ 炼糖厂

refit/ˌriːˈfɪt/

Ⅰ v. (especially of a ship) be made ready for further use (尤指船) 整修，重新装配：We sailed into port to ~. 我们驶入港口整修。Ⅱ n. the process of being refitted 整修；重新装备：The yacht needs a ~. 这艘游艇需要整修。

reflate/ˌriːˈfleɪt/

v. increase the supply of money (in a money system) to a former or desirable level 使(通货)再膨胀

reflation/ˌriːˈfleɪʃn/

n. a government policy of increasing the amount of money being used in a country, usually leading to more demand for goods and more industrial activity 通货再膨胀

reflect/rɪˈflekt/

v. ❶ throw back (light or sound)；send back an image of 反射；反照：The mirror ~s my face. 镜子照出我的脸。❷ show the nature of sth. 反映；表达：~ the objective external world 反映客观外界 / Their actions ~ their thoughts. 他们的行为反映了他们的思想。❸ bring back as a result 招致；导致：~ upon... 对……产生不良影响 /His behavior will ~ seriously upon his future. 他的行为会给他自己的未来带来严重后果。❹ think deeply 深思：~ on a problem 考虑问题

reflection/rɪˈflekʃn/

n. ❶ the throwing back by a body or surface of light, heat, or sound without absorbing it (光、热或声音的)反射，反映：the ~ of heat 热的反射 ❷ deep and careful thought 考虑；沉思：On ~, we decided to change our plan. 经过审慎的考虑，我们决定改变计划。❸ sth. reflected 被反射或反映之物：the ~ of trees in a lake 倒映在湖中的树影

reflex/ˈriːfleks/

Ⅰ adj. performed without conscious thought as an automatic response to a stimulus 本能反应的：a ~ action 本能反应动作 Ⅱ n. an action which is automatic or not controlled 本能反应

reflexive/rɪˈfleksɪv/

adj. denoting a pronoun that refers back to the subject of the clause in which it is used (代词)反身的：~ verb 反身动词

reform/rɪˈfɔːm/

Ⅰ v. make or become better；improve the condition, character, etc. 改革；改进；改过：He has completely ~ed. 他已完全改过自新。Ⅱ n. the action or process of reforming an institution or practice 改革；修订

reformation/ˌrefəˈmeɪʃn/

n. improvement；the act of reforming or state of being reformed 改进；改革；改善：a complete ~ in his character 他性格大变

refract/rɪˈfrækt/

v. (of water, glass, etc.) cause (light) to change direction when passing through at an angle (水、玻璃等)使(光)折射 ‖ ~ion n. 折射：Refraction makes a straight stick look bent if it is partly in water. 光的折射使一根部分浸在水中的木棒看来像是弯曲的。

refrain/rɪˈfreɪn/

*v.*hold oneself back 忍住；抑制：～ from laughing 忍住不笑／～ from smoking 戒烟

refresh /rɪˈfreʃ/

*v.*make fresh again；give new strength to 使消除疲劳：The hot bath ～ed him.热水澡使他消除了疲劳。‖ ～ one's memory 恢复记忆

refreshing /rɪˈfreʃɪŋ/

*adj.*❶restoring strength and energy 使人恢复活力的，提神的，凉爽的：The morning air was so ～.早晨的空气真清新。❷ welcome and interesting because it is new or different (因新颖)宜人的；刺激的

refreshment /rɪˈfreʃmənt/

*n.*❶ the state of refreshing or being refreshed (精力或精神上的)恢复；爽快；feel ～ of mind and body 身心均感爽快 ❷(usually *pl.*) light food and drinks 茶点；点心：take some ～s 吃些点心

refrigerate /rɪˈfrɪdʒəreɪt/

*v.*make (food, liquid, etc.)cold as a way of preserving it 冷冻，冷藏(食物等)：～d meat 冻肉 ‖ **refrigeration** *n.*制冷；冷藏：The meat is kept under refrigeration. 这块肉在冷藏。

refrigerator /rɪˈfrɪdʒəreɪtə(r)/

*n.*a fridge；an ice box；a machine which keeps food or drink at a low temperature 冰箱；冷冻机：There's some milk in the ～.冰箱里有些牛奶。

refuel /ˌriːˈfjuːəl/

v.(especially with reference to an aeroplane) get or provide with more fuel (尤指给飞机)加油，加燃料

refuge /ˈrefjuːdʒ/

n.(a place that provides) protection or shelter from danger 庇护；避难；庇护所；避难处：When the storm came, they found ～ in a cave.当暴风雨来临时，他们在山洞里躲避。

refugee /ˌrefjuˈdʒiː/

*n.*a person who has been forced to flee from danger, e. g. from floods, war, political persecution 避难者；难民：a political ～ 政治难民

refund

Ⅰ /riːˈfʌnd/ *v.*pay back money 退款；退还；偿付 Ⅱ /ˈriːfʌnd/ *n.*the paying back of money；the money paid back 退款；退回的款；When the concert was cancelled, many people demanded a ～.音乐会被取消时，许多人要求退款。

refusal /rɪˈfjuːzl/

*n.*an act of saying no 拒绝；谢绝：My offer met with a cold ～.我的建议遭到冰冷的拒绝。‖ first ～ 优先取舍权

refuse /rɪˈfjuːz/

*v.*turn down；say no to；decline to accept 拒绝：Einstein once ～d to speak on the radio for ＄1,000 a minute. 爱因斯坦曾经拒绝了每分钟 1000 美元作为报酬在电台发表讲话。

refute /rɪˈfjuːt/

*v.*prove sb. to be wrong or sth. to be untrue 驳斥；反驳：I ～d him easily.我轻易地驳倒了他。

regain /rɪˈgeɪn/

*v.*❶ get back again 收回；复得：The army has ～ed the town.军队收回了这个城镇。❷ reach again；get back to 再到；重回：～ the shore 重回岸边

regard /rɪˈgɑːd/

*v.*❶ consider；think of 认为；看作：The American people ～ Lincoln as one of the greatest of all American presidents. 美国人民认为林肯是美国最伟大的总统之一。❷ gaze at steadily in a specified fashion 凝视：They ～ed each other appreciatively.他们非常感激地对视着。

regarding /rɪˈgɑːdɪŋ/

*prep.*with reference to；concerning 关于：He knew nothing ～ the case.关于这个案子他一无所知。

regardless /rɪˈgɑːdləs/

*adv.*without paying attention to the present situation；despite the prevailing circumstances 不管怎样；无论如何：Everything's been done ～.不管怎样，一切都已做好了。

regenerate /rɪˈdʒenəreɪt/

*v.*❶give new life or strength to sth. 再生；重新生长 ❷reform someone spiritu-

ally or morally 使(精神)重生;使新生 ❸
grow new tissues or organs to replace
damaged ones (器官或组织)再生,重长
‖ **regeneration** n.再生;重生;重建

region/ˈriːdʒən/
n.❶ a division or area with or without
definite boundaries 地区;区域:the autonomous ～ 自治区/forest ～s 森林地
带/mountainous ～ 山区 ❷ a field of interest or activity 范围;领域:the ～ of art
艺术领域 /the ～ of physics 物理界 ❸a
part of the body 身体的某一部分:the ～
of the heart 心脏部分 /abdominal ～ 腹
部

regional /ˈriːdʒən(ə)l/
adj.of, relating to, or characteristic of a
region (与)地区(有关)的;区域性的:～
variations 地区性差异 ‖ ～ly adv.地域
性地;地方地

register/ˈredʒɪstə(r)/
Ⅰ v.❶ write down in a list;record officially 登记;注册 :Is your bicycle ～ed?
你的单车登记了吗? ❷make sth. known
publicly,especially your opinion 公开发
表意见‖ n.❶ a list or record of names,
facts,etc.名单 ❷(a book containing) an
official record or list 登记;登记本 ‖ re-
gistration /ˌredʒɪˈstreɪʃn/ n.登记;注册

regret/rɪˈɡret/
Ⅰ v.be sorry for the loss of 为……感到
遗憾(惋惜): How he ～ted the hours
that he had wasted! 他多么惋惜那些浪
费的时光啊! Ⅱ n.❶ a feeling of sadness
at the loss of sth.;a feeling of sorrow 懊
悔 ❷ a feeling of annoyance because of
sth.done;a polite reply to refuse an invitation 遗憾 ‖ ～ to say (tell,etc.) 遗憾地
说(告诉等)/much to my ～ 非常抱歉 ‖
～ful /rɪˈɡretfʊl/ adj. 懊 悔 的/～fully
/rɪˈɡretfʊli/ adv.懊悔地

regrettable /rɪˈɡretəbl/
adj.that is to be regretted that you are
sorry about 使人后悔的;令人遗憾的;可
惜的,可悲的:a ～ incident 令人遗憾的
事件

regular/ˈreɡjʊlə(r)/
adj.coming,happening or done again and
again at even intervals every time 经常
的;有规律的:He keeps ～ hours.他生活
有规律。

regularity/ˌreɡjʊˈlærəti/
n.the state or quality of being regular 规
则性;规律性;经常性:The same exam
questions cropped up with unfailing ～.同
样的试题经常一再出现。

regularly/ˈreɡjʊləli/
adv.at regular times 按时地;定期地:I
have a physical examination ～.我定期作
体格检查。

regulate/ˈreɡjʊleɪt/
v. keep at some standard;adjust;control
by rule,principle or system 调整;调节;
校正;管制;使遵守规章:～ prices 调整
价格 /～ temperature 调节温度 /～ a
clock 对准时间

regulation/ˌreɡjʊˈleɪʃn/
n.❶ the act of controlling sth. by rule,
principle or system of affairs 管理;控制:
the ～ of affairs 事务管理 ❷an official
rule or order 规则;规章;法规:traffic ～s
交通规则/We should follow the school
～s.我们应该遵守学校的规章制度。

rehearsal/rɪˈhɜːsl/
n.❶the action or process of rehearsing 排
练;排演 ❷a trial performance of a play
预演;试演 ‖ dress ～ n.彩排

rehearse/rɪˈhɜːs/
v. practise for public performance 排演:
They ～d the play again and again before
putting it on.上演这个剧之前,他们排练
了一遍又一遍。

reign/reɪn/
Ⅰ v.hold office as a monarch 统治 Ⅱ n.
the period of dominance 统治时期:in
(during) the ～ of King George 在乔治
王统治时期

reigning/ˈreɪnɪŋ/
adj.holding a particular title currently 本
届的:the ～ Miss World 本届世界小姐

rein/reɪn/
n.a long narrow band usually of leather,
by which a horse,or sometimes a young

child, is controlled and guided 缰绳 ‖ **draw ~走慢一点/give（free）~ to 让自由活动；充分发挥（想象）/keep a tight ~ on 严格控制/take（hold）the ~s 负责管理**

reindeer/'reɪndɪə(r)/
*n.*a kind of large deer with horns,found in Arctic regions (e.g.Lapland) 驯鹿

reinforce/ˌriːɪn'fɔːs/
v. ❶ make stronger by adding or supplying more men or materials 增援；支援：~ the army at the front 增援前线部队 /~ a fleet 增援一支舰队 ❷ increase the amount, size or the thickness of sth.so that it supports more weight 加强；增加……数量（尺寸或厚度）：a ~d platoon 加强排 /~ a bridge 加固一座桥 /~ a wall with mud 用泥土加固墙

reinforcement/ˌriːɪn'fɔːsmənt/
*n.*❶the act of making sth.stronger 增援；加固；强化：This roof needs some ~.这屋顶需要加固。❷(*pl.*) more men sent to strengthen an army 援军：receive ~s of 30,000 men 得到三万人的增援

reinstate/ˌriːɪn'steɪt/
*v.*put back into a former position or condition 使复原位；恢复原职；恢复原状：The manager was dismissed, but he was ~d later.经理被解雇，但不久他恢复了原职。

reject/rɪ'dʒekt/
*v.*❶ refuse to take,accept or believe 拒不接受：He ~ed my suggestion. 他拒不接受我的建议。❷ throw away, cast aside as useless 扔掉：Choose the good apples and ~ the bad ones.挑好的苹果，把坏的剔出来。

rejection/rɪ'dʒekʃn/
*n.*the act of refusing to accept 拒绝；丢弃：the ~ of the manuscript 退稿

rejoice/rɪ'dʒɔɪs/
*v.*feel great joy；show signs of great happiness 感到高兴：They ~d at the news. 听到这个消息他们感到非常高兴。 ‖ **~ with 分享……的快乐/~ in 享有** ‖ **rejoicing**/rɪ'dʒɔɪsɪŋ/ *n.*喜庆；欢庆

rejoin[1]/ˌriː'dʒɔɪn/
*v.*❶join sth. together again 重新接合；使再结合 ❷return to sth.；join sb.or sth. again after leaving it 重返；重新加入：The soldiers were returning from leave to ~ their unit.休假后士兵正在返回部队。

rejoin[2]/rɪ'dʒɔɪn/
*v.*answer；reply 回答；答复

relapse/rɪ'læps/
Ⅰ *n.*the fact of falling back (especially into illness) (疾病)复发，恶化：He seemed to recover for a short time, but then he had a ~. 他好像短时间恢复了，但后来又复发了。 Ⅱ *v.* suffer deterioration after a period of improvement 重新恶化；复发

relate/rɪ'leɪt/
*v.*❶ tell；give an account of 讲述：He ~d his adventure.他讲述了他的历险经过。 ❷ show or make a connection between two or more things 把……联系起来：We should ~ what we learn in books with practice.我们应该把书本知识同实践联系起来。

related /rɪ'leɪtɪd/
*adj.*❶connected with sb.or sth. 关联的；有关系的 ❷connected by birth or marriage 同一家族的；有亲属关系的

relation/rɪ'leɪʃn/
*n.*❶ the connection between two or more people,etc. 关系；联系：have friendly ~s with someone 与某人有友好关系 /break off all ~s with someone 与某人绝交 / Your statement had no ~ to the subject of our discussion.你的话与我们讨论的事毫无关系。 ❷ a person who is connected to another by blood or marriage；relative；kinship 家属；亲属；亲属关系：a near ~ of mine 我的一个近亲 ❸ the action of telling a story；sth.narrated 叙述；叙述的事(故事)

relationship/rɪ'leɪʃnʃɪp/
*n.*❶the state of being related 关系；联系：The ~ between the army and the people is as close as fish to water.军民关系就像鱼和水的关系。 ❷ a family connection 家属关系；亲属关系

R

relative/ˈrelətɪv/

  Ⅰ *adj*.❶ having relation with each other 相关的；有关系的：the facts ～ to this problem 与此问题有关的事实 ❷ referring to an earlier noun, clause or sentence 相关的；有关系的：a ～ pronoun (adverb) 关系代(副)词 ❸ comparative; compared with another 相对的；比较的：～ speed 相对速度 /a ～ truth 相对真理 Ⅱ *n*.a person connected by blood or marriage 亲戚：Aunts, uncles and cousins are all my ～s. 姑妈、姨妈、伯父、叔叔、堂(表)兄弟姐妹都是我的亲戚。

relatively/ˈrelətɪvli/

  adv. quite; compared to other people or thing 相当地；相对地；比较地：The matter is unimportant, ～ speaking. 相对来说，此事不重要。

relativity/ˌreləˈtɪvəti/

  n.❶ the state or quality of being relative 相对性；相关性 ❷ the relationship between time, size and mass, which is said to change with increased speed 相对论：Einstein's Theory of Relativity 爱因斯坦的相对论

relax/rɪˈlæks/

  v.make tenser; cause to become tighter 放松：We should ～ ourselves after work. 工作之余，我们应当放松下来。

relaxation/ˌriːlækˈseɪʃn/

  n.❶ the act of resting and enjoying oneself 松弛；放松 ❷ sth.done for rest and amusement 消遣；娱乐：Fishing is his favourite ～. 钓鱼是他最喜爱的消遣。

relaxed/rɪˈlækst/

  adj.❶ free from tension and anxiety easy in manner 轻松的；自在的；无拘无束的：He was lying in the sun looking very ～ and happy. 他躺在阳光下，看来十分自在和愉快。 ❷ (especially of a group, situation or surroundings) comfortable and informal; restful (尤指环境)舒适的，随便的，使人感到悠闲的：a ～ atmosphere 轻松的气氛

relaxing/rɪˈlæksɪŋ/

  adj.making one feel relaxed 使人懒洋洋的：a ～ afternoon in the garden 花园中度过的一个懒洋洋的下午

relay/ˈriːleɪ/

  Ⅰ *v*.pass (a message) from one person to another 传递：Could you ～ the letter for me? 你能帮我转交这封信吗？ Ⅱ *n*. a part of a team or organization, that takes its turn in keeping an activity going continuously, a fresh group replacing a tired one 传递：Wilma and her team mates won the first prize in the ～ race.威尔玛和她的队友赢得了接力赛冠军。 ‖ in ～s 一批批的人轮番(工作)

release/rɪˈliːs/

  Ⅰ *v*.set free; liberate 释放：The prisoners were ～d after the war.战后犯人获释了。 Ⅱ *n*. the state of releasing or being released 释放：After their ～, they made up their minds to turn over a new leaf.获释后，他们决心重新做人。

relegate/ˈrelɪgeɪt/

  v.put into a lower position, rank, etc.使降级；使降位：The football team was ～d to the lowest division.这支足球队被降到最低级的队。

relent/rɪˈlent/

  v.become less severe 变温和：The next morning, the storm ～ed.第二天早上，暴风雨减弱了。 ‖ ～less/rɪˈlentlɪs/ *adj*.严酷无情的；残酷的

relevant/ˈreləvənt/

  adj.connected with what is being discussed 有关的：a ～ question 有关的问题

reliable/rɪˈlaɪəbl/

  adj.that can be trusted or relied on 可靠的；可信赖的 ‖ reliably *adv*.可靠地；可信赖地/ reliance *n*. 信任；信赖；依靠

relic/ˈrelɪk/

  n.❶ sth. belonging to a saint and kept after his death as a mark of respect 圣人遗物；圣骨 ❷ sth. which still exists to remind us of the past 遗物；遗迹；遗俗：～s of an ancient civilization 古代文明的遗迹 ❸ (*pl*.)all that is left of sth.残留物；废墟

relict/ˈrelɪkt/

  n.a thing which has survived from an earlier period or in a primitive form 遗物；残遗物

relief /rɪˈliːf/

n. ❶ the feeling of happiness that you have when sth. unpleasant has stopped and will not happen again（忧虑、痛苦）解除，宽慰，免除：sigh with ～ 宽慰地松口气 /This medicine will give (bring) the patient some ～.这种药将会减轻病人一些痛苦。/To my great ～, he was already out of danger.使我感到宽慰的是，他已经脱险了。❷ money or food given to people in need of them 救济金；救济品：send ～ 发送救济品 /～ fund (food) 救济金(粮) /provide ～ for refugees 向难民提供救济品 ❸ a person appointed to go on duty 换班的人：a ～ driver 接班的司机 /a ～ bus 加班车 ❹ a method of carving or moulding in which a design stands out from a flat surface 浮雕法；浮雕：～ map 立体地图 /in bold (sharp) ～ against 在……衬托下形象鲜明

relieve /rɪˈliːv/

v. ❶lessen(pain or trouble) 减轻；解除；宽慰：The medicine will ～ your headache.这药可治好你的头痛。❷ bring aid to; help 救援；帮助：The soldiers hastened to ～ the fortress.战士们火速赶去增援要塞。❸ take one's turn on duty 换班；接替：The guard will be ～d at five.该哨兵将在五点换班。

relieved /rɪˈliːvd/

adj. feeling relief; no longer worried 宽慰的；不再忧虑的：She had a ～ look on her face.她脸上现出宽慰的表情。/I was ～ to (to hear) that they were safe.（听说）他们平安无事，我就放心了。

religion /rɪˈlɪdʒən/

n. ❶the belief in one or more gods 宗教；宗教信仰：He does not believe in ～.他不信仰宗教。❷a particular system of belief and the worship and, behaviour, etc.宗教；教派：state ～国教

religious /rɪˈlɪdʒəs/

adj. ❶of or concerning religion 宗教的；宗教上的：a ～ believer 一个宗教信徒 ❷ much interested in religion; devoted to the worship of god or gods 虔诚的；信奉宗教的：The old man is very ～.那位老人笃信宗教。

religiously /rɪˈlɪdʒəsli/

adv. ❶in a careful and thorough way 认真彻底地：They followed the instructions quite ～.他们一丝不苟地遵循这些指示。❷connected with religion in a way 与宗教有关的

reline /ˌriːˈlaɪn/

v. put a new lining into 给……换衬里：She ～d the old coat.她给这件旧上衣换衬里。

relish /ˈrelɪʃ/

Ⅰ *n.* great enjoyment, especially of food; pleasure and satisfaction 享受；滋味；乐趣：He was eating with great ～.他正津津有味地吃着。Ⅱ *v.* enjoy; be pleased and satisfied with 喜欢：The old lady doesn't ～ pop music.那老太太不喜欢流行音乐。

relive /ˌriːˈlɪv/

v. experience again, especially in the imagination 再次体验；重温：She ～d her school days in conversation with an old friend.她在同老友的谈话中重温了在校时的生活。

reload /ˌriːˈləʊd/

v. load (a gun) again 再装填(枪炮等)

relocate /ˌriːləʊˈkeɪt/

v. move to or establish in a new place 重新安置；迁徙：The factory has been ～d in the Bristol area.工厂已迁到布里斯托尔地区。/We're relocating in the Bristol area.我们要搬到布里斯托尔地区。

reluctant /rɪˈlʌktənt/

adj. unwilling; offering resistance 不愿的；勉强的：He seemed ～ to help us.他似乎不愿帮助我们。‖ reluctance *n.*不情愿/～ly *adv.*不情愿地

rely /rɪˈlaɪ/

v. ❶ depend on; look to (sb.) for help 依靠；依赖：Nowadays, a lot of people ～ heavily on computers to make a purchase.如今，很多人很大程度上依靠电脑来购物。❷ trust sb. or sth. 信任，信赖：We should ～ on ourselves.我们应该相信自己。‖ **reliant** *adj*.依靠的

remain/rɪˈmeɪn/

v.❶ be left after sth.has been removed, taken, etc. 剩下：How much ～s if we take five from ten? 如果我们从 10 里面减去 5 还剩多少？ ❷ stay；last without changing；continue 继续（保持） ‖ ～**ing**/rɪˈmeɪnɪŋ/ *adj*.剩下的

remainder/rɪˈmeɪndə(r)/

n.❶ the remaining things, people or time 剩余物；其他人员；剩余时间：the ～ of his life 他的余年 /the ～ of the feast 宴会剩下的饭菜 /Twenty people came in and the ～ stayed outside.进来了 20 人，其余的还在外面。❷ (in mathematics) the number which is left over in a division in which one quantity does not exactly divide another（数学中的）余数：If you take 4 from 10, the ～ is 6.10 减 4 等于 6。

remains/rɪˈmeɪnz/

n.❶ the part or parts that is/are left 残余；遗物：the ～ of ancient Rome 古罗马的遗迹 /The ～ of the meal are in the refrigerator. 剩饭在冰箱里。❷ a dead body 遗体：His ～ are buried here.他的遗体被葬于此。❸ historical or archaeological relics 遗迹

remake

Ⅰ/ˌriːˈmeɪk/ *v*. make (especially a film) again 重新制作；重新摄制（电影） Ⅱ/ˈriːmeɪk/ *n*.a thing remade 重制之物；改制品：They're doing a ～ of *Gone with the Wind*.他们正在重拍影片《飘》。

remand/rɪˈmɑːnd/

v.send back to prison until a trial is held 还押（候审）

remark/rɪˈmɑːk/

Ⅰ*v*.❶ explicit notice or observe 注意：He ～ed the difference between these two words.他注意到了这两个单词的不同。❷ say sth.by way of comment；give view 说起；议论 Ⅱ*n*.❶ explicit notice or observation 注意：The problem is not worthy of ～.这个问题不值得注意。❷

comment or sth.that you say about sth.评论

remarkable/rɪˈmɑːkəbl/

adj.worth mentioning, especially because unusual or noticeable 值得注意的；十分不平常的；出众的：a most ～ sunset 非常壮观的日落（景象）/Finland is ～ for the large number of its lakes.芬兰以它的众多湖泊著称。

remarkably/rɪˈmɑːkəbli/

adv.(used especially with adjectives and adverbs) unusually；noticeably（尤与形容词和副词连用）不寻常地；突出地：He sings ～ well.他唱得特别好。/a ～ fine day 特别晴朗的一天

remarry/ˌriːˈmæri/

v.marry again 再婚：He decided to ～ after his wife's death. 他妻子死后，他决定再娶。

remedial/rɪˈmiːdiəl/

adj.curing or helping；providing a remedy 治疗的；矫正的；修补的；补救的：He had to do ～ exercises for his weak back.他必须为衰弱的背部做矫正运动。/～ teaching (classes)辅助教学；补习班

remedy/ˈremɪdi/

Ⅰ*n*. a treatment or sth.else to cure a disease, etc.such as medicine 治疗；办法；药方：The doctor found a ～ for cancer.医生找到了治疗癌症的办法。 ‖ be past (beyond) ～ 无法弥补（挽救）Ⅱ*v*.❶ cure a disease or relieve pain 治疗：The pills remedied his headache.这些药片治好了他的头痛。❷ correct or improve sth. 改正；纠正

remember/rɪˈmembə(r)/

v.❶ keep in mind 记住：Madame Curie will be ～ed as the discoverer of radium.居里夫人将作为镭的发现者被人们记住。❷ bring back to mind；recall 记得：I could not ～ his name at that time. 当时我不记得他的姓名。

remind/rɪˈmaɪnd/

v.❶ bring sth. to the attention of sb. 提醒：If I forget to post the letter, please ～ me. 要是我忘了寄信，请提醒我一下。/

Remind me to buy some envelopes. 提醒我买一些信封。❷ cause sb. to remember 使某人想起：The picture ~s me of a story I heard. 这幅画使我想起我听过的一个故事。/The sight of the clock ~ed me (that) I was late. 一看见钟使我想起我迟到了。

reminder /rɪˈmaɪndə(r)/
n. sth. that makes one remember 提醒人记忆之物；起提醒作用的东西：He hadn't paid the bill, so the shop sent him a ~. 他还没有付账，所以商店寄给他一封催款信。

remiss /rɪˈmɪs/
adj. ❶ careless of duty；negligent 不负责任的；疏忽的；懈怠的：That was very ~ of you. 你那样做太粗心大意了。❷ showing slackness 无精打采的；懒洋洋的

remission /rɪˈmɪʃn/
n. ❶ pardon or forgiveness（of sins；by God）赦免；宽恕（罪孽）❷ freeing（from debt, punishment, etc.）（债务、处分等的）免除：~ of one's debts 免除债务 ❸ lessening of（pain, etc.）（病痛等的）减轻，缓和：~ of a fever 发烧减退

remit /rɪˈmɪt/
v. ❶ send（money, etc.）to a person or place, especially by post 汇款：He ~s the money to his son monthly. 他每月给儿子汇款。❷ free sb. from 免掉

remittance /rɪˈmɪtəns/
n. ❶ the sending of money to a person 汇款 ❷ the money sent 汇款额

remnant /ˈremnənt/
n. ❶ a small part that is left 残余；剩余：the ~s of a defeated army 溃军的残余 ❷ a small piece of cloth left over and sold at a cheaper price（常减价出售）零头布：a ~ sale 零头布拍卖

remote /rɪˈməʊt/
adj. ❶ far off in distance or time 遥远的；偏僻的：~ control 遥控 /the ~ future 遥远的将来 /a ~ village 偏僻的乡村 ❷ being distantly related by blood or marriage 关系远的；远亲的：a ~ relative 远房亲戚 ❸ cold and unfriendly；aloof 冷淡

的；疏远的：Her manner was ~. 她的态度很冷淡。❹ slight；not very great 很少的：You haven't the ~ idea. 你毫无概念。

removal /rɪˈmuːvl/
n. ❶ the state of removing, or being removed 除去；消除 ❷ the transfer of furniture, etc. when moving house（家具等）搬迁：A van came for the ~ of our furniture. 搬ısını卡车开来为我们搬家具。

remove /rɪˈmuːv/
v. take away；take off 拿走；脱掉：~ one's hat 脱帽 /~d to a hospital 给送去医院

remuneration /rɪˌmjuːnəˈreɪʃn/
n. an amount of money that is paid to sb. for his work, etc. 报酬；酬劳 ‖ **remunerative** /rɪˈmjuːnərətɪv/ *adj.* 报酬高的：a very remunerative job 报酬很高的工作

renaissance /rəˈneɪsəns/
n. ❶（the Renaissance）the revival of art and literature in Europe in the 14th – 16th centuries, influenced by classical forms 文艺复兴 ❷ revival of sth. 复兴；再生

renal /ˈriːnl/
adj. of or relating to the kidneys（与）肾脏（有关）的

rename /riːˈneɪm/
v. give a new name to 给……重新命名；给……以新名：The street has been ~d Silver Lane. 这条街已重新命名为银巷。

rend /rend/
v. ❶ divide by force；split（用力）把……分开；把……撕开：She wept and rent her garments. 她哭着把衣服撕了。/A terrible cry rent the sky. 一阵可怕的哭声划破长空。❷ pull violently 猛拉；扯：She was ~ing her hair out in anger. 她气得直扯自己的头发。

render /ˈrendə(r)/
v. ❶ give sb. sth. in return or exchange 归还；报答：~ thanks 致谢 ❷ offer sb. sth. 给予：~ service to the people 为人民服务 /~ help to those students in difficulty 给予困难的学生以帮助 ❸ send in（an account for payment）提出（账单）：~ a

R

bill for payment 报账 ❹ give a performance of 演出；演奏：The piano solo was well ~ed.钢琴独奏曲弹得很好。/They ~ed *Othello* very successfully.他们演出《奥赛罗》非常成功。❺ express in another language 翻译；表达：~ a sentence in English 将一个句子译成英文 /I've ~ed my meaning clearly.我已经把意思表达得很清楚了。❻ cause to be；make 使成为；使得：~ every customer happy 使每个顾客高兴 /An accident ~ed him helpless.一次意外事故使他不能自理。❼ melt down（fat），typically in order to clarify it（尤指将脂肪）熬油：~ lard 熬猪油

renew /rɪˈnjuː/
v. ❶ make new or fresh again 更新；恢复：Everything has been ~ed at the beginning of the new year.新年伊始万象更新。❷ begin again 再开始：They ~ed their friendship.他们重新开始了他们的友谊。❸ obtain a further period of lending for sth. 续借：You may ~ your book if you can't finish it on time.如果你不能按时看完这本书，你可以续借。‖ ~able *adj.*可更新的；可继续的

renown /rɪˈnaʊn/
n. fame and respect 名望；声誉 ‖ ~ed *adj.* 著名的

R

rent /rent/
Ⅰ *v.* ❶ pay a sum of money for the use of property or goods 租用：The Greens ~ed a cottage in the country for the holidays. 格林一家在乡间租了所房子度假。❷ allow the use of property or goods in return for a sum of money 出租：He has a house to ~.他有一所房子出租。Ⅱ *n.* a regular payment for the use of property 租金：How much ~ do you pay for your flat? 你那套房子的租金是多少?

reorganize(-se) /ˌriːˈɔːɡənaɪz/
v. organize again or in a new way 改组；改编；整顿：~ an army 改编军队

repair /rɪˈpeə(r)/
Ⅰ *v.* ❶ return（restore）to good condition；fix or mend 修复；修补；修理：I'll have my bicycle ~ed. 我得把单车修一

下。❷ put right again；make up for 使重归于好；弥补：I'll try my best to ~ the damage I've caused.我将尽力挽回我所造成的损失。Ⅱ *n.* the action of mending sth. 修理 ‖ beyond ~ 无法修理/in good ~ 处于完好状态/in bad ~ 年久失修/out of ~ 坏了/under ~ 正在修理

reparation /ˌrepəˈreɪʃən/
n. ❶ the act of making amends or paying for damage or loss 补偿；赔偿 ❷（*pl.*）compensation for war damage paid by the defeated nation（战败国的）赔款

repay /rɪˈpeɪ/
v. ❶ pay back（money）偿还：He repaid all the money he borrowed.他偿还了所有债务。❷ make a return for sth. or to sb.；give in return 报答：How can I ~ for your kindness? 我怎样才能报答你的恩情? ‖ ~able *adj.*可偿还的；必须回报的

repayment /riːˈpeɪmənt/
n. the act of paying back money that you have borrowed from a bank, etc.归还借款；偿还债务

repeal /rɪˈpiːl/
Ⅰ *v.* do away with；make（a law）no longer valid 撤销；废止（法令等）Ⅱ *n.* the action of revoking or annulling a law or an act of parliament 撤销；废止

repeat /rɪˈpiːt/
v. ❶ say, do, make or perform again 重说；重做；重复：Would you ~ what you said? 请把你说的重复一遍好吗? ❷ say over from memory；recite 背诵：The pupils were ~ing their lessons at the top of their voices.学生们在高声背诵课文。

repeatedly /rɪˈpiːtɪdli/
adv. again and again 反复地；再三地：He ~ pointed out that...他再三指出……

repel /rɪˈpel/
v.(-ll-) ❶ drive away（as if）by force 击退：They ~led another attack.他们又击退了一次进攻。❷ cause strong feelings of dislike 使感到厌恶：His long dirty hair ~led her.他那又长又脏的头发使她恶心。

repellent /rɪˈpelənt/

Ⅰ*adj.*❶causing disgust or distaste 令人反感的；令人厌恶的 ❷not able to be penetrated by a specified substance 抗……的；防……的：The fabric is water-~.这种纤维是防水的。Ⅱ*n.*a substance that repels sth. 防护剂：insect ～ 驱虫剂 ‖ **repellence** *n.*抵抗性；反击性；排斥性

repent/rɪˈpent/
*v.*feel sorry for；regret 懊悔；后悔：～ and start anew 悔过自新 /～ of one's carelessness 对自己的粗心大意表示后悔 / too late to ～ 悔之莫及 /He will soon ～ (of) what he did.他很快就会悔恨自己所做的事。

repentance /rɪˈpentəns/
*n.*the fact of showing that you are sorry for sth.wrong that you have done 悔改；后悔

repentant/rɪˈpentənt/
*adj.*sorry for wrongdoing 懊悔的；后悔的：If you are truly ～ you will be forgiven.假如你真的后悔，你会得到原谅的。

repetition/ˌrepɪˈtɪʃn/
*n.*❶ the fact of doing or saying the same thing many times 重复；重做；重说：learn by ～ 经过重复而学会 ❷ sth.repeated 重复的事物 ❸ a copy；an imitation 副本；仿效：a ～ of a previous talk 前一次会谈的副本

repetitious/ˌrepɪˈtɪʃəs/
*adj.*containing parts that are said or done too many times 重复的；反复的：a ～ speech 内容重复的演说/ a ～ job 翻来覆去老一套的工作

repetitive /rɪˈpetɪtɪv/
*adj.*characterized by repetition 重复的 ‖ ～**ly** *adv.*重复地

rephrase/ˌriːˈfreɪz/
*v.*express (sth.) in different words，especially so as to make the meaning clearer 换言；重新表述(使意思更清楚)

replace/rɪˈpleɪs/
v. ❶ put back in its former or proper place again 放回原处：Please ～ the book on the shelf.请将书放回书架。❷ take

the place of；fill the place with another 代替：Plastics has ～d wood in many ways.塑料在很多方面代替了木头。

replacement/rɪˈpleɪsmənt/
*n.*❶the action or process of replacing sb. or sth. 代替；替换：Your worn-out tyres need ～.你的破轮胎需要换掉。❷ sb.or sth.that takes the place of another 替换者；替换物：get a ～ while one is away on holiday 外出度假时找一位代理工作的人

replay/ˌriːˈpleɪ/
*v.*play again 重赛；重播：The game would have to be ～ed.这次比赛非重赛不可。

replicate /ˈreplɪkɪt/
*v.*❶make or be an exact copy of sth. 复制；重制 ❷reproduce itself 自我繁殖；自我复制：a computer virus that ～s itself 计算机病毒进行自我复制 ❸repeat a scientific experiment to obtain a consistent result satisfactorily 重现，证实(实验或试验) ‖ **replicable** *adj.*能复现的；可复制的

reply/rɪˈplaɪ/
Ⅰ*v.*give an answer；answer 回答；答复：～ a letter 回信 /～ to a question 回答问题 /～ by a blow 回以一击 /She didn't ～.她没回答。Ⅱ*n.*an act of replying 答复；回答：make no ～ 不作答复 /the letter under ～ 本函所答复的来信 /in ～ to a remark 为答复批评 /I write this in ～ to your letter.我写此文以回复你的来信。

report/rɪˈpɔːt/
v. give a spoken or written account of (sth.seen，heard，done，etc.) 报告；报道：The TV reporter from BBC ～ed what he saw in China in the newspaper.那位来自BBC的电视记者在报上报道了他在中国的见闻。

reportage/ˌrepɔːˈtɑːʒ，rɪˈpɔːtɪdʒ/
*n.*❶the act of reporting news 报道(新闻) ❷ the style in which this is usually done 报道文体 ❸writing，photographs，or film in this style，intended to give an exciting account of an event 报道文学(作品)；报道体裁的摄影或电影等

R

reportedly /rɪˈpɔːtɪdli/

adv. according to what is said 据报道；据传说：He is ~ not intending to return to this country. 据说，他无意返回这个国家。

reporter /rɪˈpɔːtə(r)/

n. a person who reports for a newspaper, for radio or TV 记者；通讯员：a sports ~ 一位体育新闻记者

repose /rɪˈpəʊz/

Ⅰ *n.* ❶ (a state of) calm，rest or peace 休息；安宁 ❷ calmness of manner 安详；镇静 Ⅱ *v.* ❶ lie or be placed (on) 躺着休息 ❷ lie dead 长眠；安息：His body ~d in state in the cathedral. 他的遗体安放在大教堂里以供瞻仰。 ❸ place (an object or part of the body) on 安放（物件）；把（身体某部位）放在……上休息

repossess /ˌriːpəˈzes/

v. regain possession of (property)，especially when necessary payments have not been made 重新获得；收回（财产）：The rental company are threatening to ~ the television. 这家出租公司警告说要收回电视机。‖ ~ion *n.* 收回：The landlord has applied for a ~ion order. 地主已（向法院）申请土地收回令。

reprehend /ˌreprɪˈhend/

v. express disapproval of 谴责；申斥；责难：His conduct deserves to be ~ed. 他的行为应受谴责。

reprehensible /ˌreprɪˈhensəbl/

adj. deserving blame 应受谴责的；应加非难的

represent /ˌreprɪˈzent/

v. ❶ act or speak for 代表：They ~ed their government. 他们代表政府。 ❷ stand for；symbolize 表示：The stars in the flag of the Untied States ~ states. 美国国旗上的星表示每一个州。

representation /ˌreprɪzenˈteɪʃn/

n. ❶ the act or condition of representing or being represented 代表；表示 ❷ sth. that represents 绘画；演出 ❸ (usually *pl.*) a strong appeal；arguments or protest 呼吁；申述；抗议：make ~ to the government 向政府提抗议

representative /ˌreprɪˈzentətɪv/

Ⅰ *adj.* ❶ being an example；typical 有代表性的；典型的：a ~ Chinese city 一个典型的中国城市 ❷ carried out by elected people 代表的；代理的：a ~ government 代议制政府 Ⅱ *n.* a person who represents others 代表：The old man is a ~ of the people. 这位老人是一位人民代表。

repress /rɪˈpres/

v. ❶ bring under control 抑制：I ~ed a desire to hit him. 我抑制住要揍他一顿的念头。 ❷ put down 镇压：~ a rebellion 镇压叛乱 ‖ ~ive *adj.* 抑制的；镇压的/ ~ion *n.* 抑制；镇压

reprieve /rɪˈpriːv/

Ⅰ *v.* say that the execution of someone condemned to death will take place later or not take place at all 暂缓处刑；缓期处死：The president ~d the condemned man. 总统下令暂缓处决此犯人。 Ⅱ *n.* an order of stopping an execution；the act of postponing punishment 死刑缓行令；缓刑：The condemned murderer was granted a ~. 此杀人犯获准暂缓处决。

reprimand /ˈreprɪmɑːnd/

Ⅰ *v.* blame severely 申斥：~ a naughty child 训诫一个顽童 Ⅱ *n.* a statement of blaming or scolding 申斥；叱责：give someone a ~ 狠狠教训某人一顿

reproach /rɪˈprəʊtʃ/

Ⅰ *v.* find fault with sb. 责备：His wife ~ed him with cowardice. 他的妻子责怪他怯懦。 Ⅱ *n.* ❶ the expression of disapproval or disappointment 指责；责备：heap ~es on a person 痛责某人 ❷ the state of disgrace or discredit 耻辱；丢脸：bring ~ upon oneself 给自己带来耻辱

reprocess /ˌriːˈprəʊses/

v. treat (sth. that has been used) so that it can be used again 对……进行再加工：nuclear fuel ~ing 核燃料的后处理

reproduce /ˌriːprəˈdjuːs/

v. ❶ bring about a natural increase；give birth to 繁殖：This kind of insect ~s rapidly. 这种昆虫繁殖很快。 ❷ cause to be heard，seen，etc. again 使重现：This instrument can ~ man's voice. 这种仪器能

复制人的声音。

reproduction/ˌriːprəˈdʌkʃn/

　　n. ❶the process of reproducing 复制；再生 ❷sth. reproduced; a copy of sth. 再生物；复制品：The painting is a ~.这幅画是一件复制品。

reproof/rɪˈpruːf/

　　n. blame; words of blame 责备；训斥；斥责的话

reprove/rɪˈpruːv/

　　v. blame; find fault with; rebuke 责备；指责；责骂：~ a child for coming to school late 指责孩子上学迟到

republic/rɪˈpʌblɪk/

　　n. a country that is governed by a president and politicians elected by the people and where there is no king or queen 共和国；共和政体：The People's Republic of China was founded on Oct. 1, 1949. 中华人民共和国成立于 1949 年 10 月 1 日。

republican/rɪˈpʌblɪkən/

　　adj. belonging to a republic 共和国的；共和政体的：the Republican Party 共和党

repulse/rɪˈpʌls/

　　v. ❶ drive back by force 击退：~ an enemy attack 击退敌人的进攻 ❷ refuse to accept; treat with coldness 拒绝接受；冷淡对待：~ someone's friendship 拒绝某人的友谊 ‖ **repulsion** *n.* 厌恶 /**repulsive** *adj.* 令人厌恶的

reputation/ˌrepjuˈteɪʃn/

　　n. ❶ the beliefs of opinions that are generally held about sb. or sth. 名誉；名声：of high ~ 名誉很好的 /of no ~ 默默无闻的 ❷ the state of being held in high repute 好名声；声望：live up to one's ~ 不负盛名 /lose one's ~ 失去声望

repute/rɪˈpjuːt/

　　Ⅰ *v.* be generally said or considered to be sb. or sth. 被认为；被当作：She is ~d to be very wealthy. 她被认为很富有。/He is ~d as an advance.他被称为先进工作者。Ⅱ *n.* reputation; the opinion that people have of sb. or sth. 名声，名誉：a man of good ~ 名誉好的人 /be held in high ~ 声望很高

reputed/rɪˈpjuːtɪd/

　　adj. generally supposed or considered (to be), but with some doubt 一般认为(但不无怀疑)的；号称的：She is ~ to be extremely wealthy.据说她十分富有。

reputedly/rɪˈpjuːtɪdli/

　　adv. according to what people say 据说：Reputedly, she is very rich. 据说她很有钱。

request/rɪˈkwest/

　　Ⅰ *v.* ❶politely or formally ask for 请求；要求 ❷politely ask sb. to de sth.请求(某人)做某事 Ⅱ *n.* ❶an act of asking politely or formally for sth. 要求；请求 ❷a thing that is asked for 要求(或请求)的内容 ❸ an instruction to a computer to provide information or to perform another function 指令；要求

require/rɪˈkwaɪə(r)/

　　v. ❶ need; want; call for 需要：My watch ~s cleaning now.我的表要洗了。❷ demand; order 要求；命令：All the drivers are ~d to observe traffic lights.所有司机都要遵守交通规则。

requirement/rɪˈkwaɪəmənt/

　　n. sth. that is needed or that is demanded as necessary 必需品；要求之物：The refugees' main ~s are food and shelter. 难民的主要必需品是食物和住所。/Can this computer handle the ~s of the wages department? 这台计算机能处理工资部门的要求吗？

requisite/ˈrekwɪzɪt/

　　Ⅰ *adj.* needed for a purpose; necessary 需要的；必要的：He hasn't got the ~ qualifications for this job. 他不具备这项工作所需的资格。Ⅱ *n.* (used especially in shops) sth. needed for or used in connection with the stated thing 必需品：toilet ~s 卫生间必需品

requisition/ˌrekwɪˈzɪʃn/

　　n. an official demand or request, especially one made by a military body 正式要求；需要；征用：The school authorities have made a ~ for more computing equipment.学校当局提出要求，说需要更多的

R

计算设备。/fill in a ～ form 填写申请领取表格

requite /rɪ'kwaɪt/

v. ❶ give sth. in return for sth. else; repay sth. 报答；回报；酬谢：The charms of travel more than ～ its inconvenience. 旅行的乐趣补偿了旅途中的不便。❷ take vengeance on sb. 报复；报仇：～ sb. for evils 对某人的恶行进行报复

rerun /ˌriːˈrʌn/

Ⅰ *v.* ❶ show a film or recorded broadcast, etc. again 重播；重放（影片、广播等）：They ～ so many old films on television. 他们在电视上重放许多旧影片。❷ arrange for (a race or competition) to be held again 重跑；重赛：One of the competitors was found to have cheated, so the race had to be ～. 由于发现参赛者当中有一人作弊，所以这次赛跑不得不重新开始。Ⅱ *n.* ❶ a film or recorded broadcast that is shown again 再次放映的影片；重播节目 ❷ sth. that happens again in the same way as before (旧事的) 重演

reschedule /ˌriːˈʃedjuːl/

v. ❶ arrange (a loan or debt) to be paid back at a later time than was originally agreed 推迟还款，延期还款 ❷ change the time of (a planned event) 改变……的时间；重订……的时间表

rescue /'reskjuː/

Ⅰ *v.* save from danger or harm 营救；救援：He ～d a baby from the fire. 他从大火中救出了一个婴儿。Ⅱ *n.* an act of saving or being saved from danger or distress 救援；被救援

research /rɪ'sɜːtʃ, 'riːsɜːtʃ/

Ⅰ *n.* a careful study or investigation 研究：He was quite successful in his scientific ～ work. 他的科研工作相当成功。Ⅱ *v.* do study or investigation 研究：He began to ～ into the cause of cancer. 他开始研究癌症的起因。

resemblance /rɪ'zembləns/

n. the fact of being similar 相似，类似：There's very little ～ between them. 他们之间相似之处很少。

resemble /rɪ'zembl/

v. be like; be similar to 相似；像；类似：～ each other in appearance or nature 外表或本质上彼此相像 /Her voice ～s her mother's. 她声音像她母亲。

resent /rɪ'zent/

v. feel angry or bitter at 愤恨，不满，怨恨：I strongly ～ your remarks. 我对你的评论表示强烈不满。/Does he ～ my being here? 他对我待在此地感觉不满吗？

resentful /rɪ'zentfʊl/

adj. feeling bitter and indignant about sth. 气愤的，感到愤愤不平的；表示愤恨的 ‖ ～ly *adv.* 充满愤恨地

reservation /ˌrezə'veɪʃn/

n. ❶ the act of reserving sth.; a limiting condition 保留，保护；限制条件：I accept your offer completely and without ～. 我无条件地接受你的报价。❷ a room, etc. in a hotel to be kept for you 预定：Have you made your ～s? 你已预订好了吗？❸ an area of land reserved for a special purpose 专用地，保留地：an Indian ～ 印第安人居留地

reserve /rɪ'zɜːv/

Ⅰ *v.* ❶ store; keep back unused, but available if needed 储备；保存：～ one's strength for the next battle 养精蓄锐 ❷ have or keep for sb. (or sth.) 保留；留给；留出：～ some cakes for tomorrow 留一些饼到明天吃 /These seats are ～d for foreign guests. 这些座位是给外宾保留的。/I'll ～ my opinion on this question. 在这个问题上我保留自己的观点。❸ order; book 预订；登记：～ tickets 订票 Ⅱ *n.* ❶ sth. that has been stored for later use 储备（物），保存（物）：the gold ～ 黄金储备 /war ～s 军需储备品 ❷ a feeling that you do not want to accept or agree to sth. 谨慎，保留；限度：without ～ 毫无保留

reservoir /'rezəvwɑː(r)/

n. ❶ a natural or artificial lake for keeping water 水库，蓄水池：Most of our city's water comes from this ～. 我市大部分用水自该水库。❷ a large supply (of facts or knowledge)（事实、知识的）储藏

reside/rɪˈzaɪd/
*v.*❶ live in 住（在某处）：He ~s in the country.他住在乡下。❷（of qualities）be present in(性质）存在于：Her success ~s in her diligence.她的成功在于她的勤奋。

resident/ˈrezɪdənt/
Ⅰ*n.*a person who resides in a place 居民：He is a ~ of London.他是伦敦居民。Ⅱ*adj.*living in a particular place（在某地）居住的，居留的：the ~ population of the town 该镇的居民人口

residue/ˈrezɪdjuː/
*n.*what is left of anything after some of it has been taken away 剩余；残渣；剩余财产

resign/rɪˈzaɪn/
*v.*❶ give up (a job or claim) 辞职；放弃（权利）：~ from a committee 辞去委员会里的职务 /~ one's position as manager 辞去经理职务 /~ one's job 辞去工作 / I've ~ed all my hope.我已经放弃了一切希望。❷ submit oneself passively; accept as inevitable 听从；忍受 ‖ ~ oneself to 听从；听任：You must ~ yourself to wait a bit longer.你得忍耐着再等待一会儿。

resignation/ˌrezɪɡˈneɪʃn/
*n.*❶ an act of resigning; a written statement that one resigns 辞职；辞职书，辞呈：The company accepted his ~.公司接受了他的辞职。❷ the state of being resigned 听任，顺从：accept one's fate with ~ 听天由命

resist/rɪˈzɪst/
*v.*❶ fight back when attacked 反抗；抵抗：This country is too weak to ~ the invasion.这个国家太弱无法抵抗外来侵略。❷ refuse to accept sth. and try to stop it from happening 顶住；抵制：He could no longer ~ the temptation of the nice food.他再也经不住美食的诱惑了。

resistance/rɪˈzɪstəns/
*v.*❶ the act of opposing sb. or sth. 抵抗：break down the enemy's ~ 粉碎敌人的抵抗 ❷ the force that stops sth. moving or makes it move more slowly 阻力：An aircraft has to overcome the ~ of the air.飞机必须克服空气的阻力。❸ the power or ability not to be affected by sth. 抗力；抵抗力：She has little ~ to germs so she is often ill.她对病菌缺乏抵抗力，所以经常生病。

resistant/rɪˈzɪstənt/
Ⅰ*adj.*not affected by sth.; able to resist sth.抵抗的，反抗的，有抵抗力的：The transplanted seedlings are ~ to cold weather.那些移植的秧苗有抗寒力。Ⅱ*n.*a person who resists 反对者，抵抗者

resolute/ˈrezəluːt/
*adj.*fixed in determination or purpose 坚决的，刚毅的：a ~ man 有决心的人/ He was ~ in carrying out his plan.他坚决执行他的计划。

resolution/ˌrezəˈluːʃn/
*n.*❶ the quality of being resolute or determined 坚决，决心，果断：She lacks ~.她不够果断。❷ a formal decision made by a group vote 决议，提案：The committee have passed a ~ to build a new library.委员会通过了建一幢新图书馆的决议。❸ the act of solving or settling a doubt, question, discord, etc. 解决，消除（疑惑、问题、不和等）

resolve/rɪˈzɒlv/
Ⅰ*v.*❶make a determined decision; decide firmly 决心：He ~d to catch up with others.他决心赶上别人。❷（of a committee or public body）to make a resolution 通过决议：This resolution was ~d by the representatives.这项决议由代表们投票表决。❸ find a satisfactory way of dealing with (a difficulty); settle 解决 Ⅱ*n.*strong determination to achieve sth. 决心：make a ~ to do sth.决意要做某事

resonant/ˈrezənənt/
adj.(of sound) deep, clear and continuing for a long time (声音）洪亮的，悠扬的；回响的：a ~ voice 洪亮的嗓音/~ walls 回音壁

resort/rɪˈzɔːt/

Ⅰ v.❶ make use of sth. as a means of achieving sth. 诉诸；求助于：She had nothing to do but ～ to the law.她只有求助于法律。❷ go (to a place, etc.) often 常去（某地）：They ～ed to the seashore to spend their holidays.他们常去海滨度假。Ⅱ n.❶ the act of using sth.诉诸；求助 ❷ a place which people often go to for rest or pleasure 度假的地方：a summer (health)～ 避暑胜地（疗养地）

resound/rɪˈzaʊnd/

v. fill a place with sound；be filled with sound 回响；回荡；回荡着声音：The hall ～ed with the shouts of the people.大厅里回荡着人们的叫喊声。‖ ～ing adj.响亮的；轰动的

resource/rɪˈsɔːs, rɪˈzɔːs/

n.❶ any of the possessions or qualities of a person, an organization, or a country 资源：Oil is the most important natural ～s in Kuwait.石油是科威特最重要的自然资源。❷ cleverness in finding a way to avoid difficulties；the practical ability 机智：He is a man of great ～.他是个足智多谋的人。

respect/rɪˈspekt/

Ⅰ v.❶ honour or admire sb. or sth.尊重；尊敬：Students should ～ teachers. 学生应该尊敬老师。❷ agree to recognize and abide by 遵守：Everyone must ～ the law.人人都要遵纪守法。Ⅱ n.❶ the feeling of admiration for sb. or sth.尊重；尊敬：We should show ～ to the old.我们应该尊敬长者。❷ (pl.) regards；polite greetings 敬意：Please give my ～s to your parents.请代我向你父母致意。‖ ～ oneself 自重/hold in (great)～ 很尊敬/in ～ of (to) 关于/pay ～ to 考虑/with ～ to 至于/without ～ to 不管

respectable/rɪˈspektəbl/

adj.❶ deserving respect；that should be respected 可敬的；值得尊敬的；应受尊重的：a ～ old cadre 一位可敬的老干部 ❷ of good character and good social position；having the qualities associated with such positions 正派的；高雅的；体面的：a

～ address 像样的演说 /a ～ coat 雅观的上装 /a ～ girl 正派的女孩 /～ motives 高尚的动机

respecting/rɪˈspektɪŋ/

prep.concerning；with respect to 关于；就……而言

respective/rɪˈspektɪv/

adj. belonging separately to each one mentioned 各自的，分别的：We went off to our ～ rooms.我们各自回到自己的房间。

respectively/rɪˈspektɪvli/

adj.separately or in turn, and in the order mentioned 分别的；各自的：We shall discuss the two questions ～.我们将分别讨论这两个问题。/Joe and Jane went back to their rooms ～.乔和珍妮回到了各自的房间。

respiration/ˌrespəˈreɪʃn/

n.the act of breathing 呼吸

respirator/ˈrespəreɪtə/

n.❶ a device worn over the nose and mouth to filter or purify the air before it is inhaled 口罩；防尘面罩 ❷ an apparatus for giving artificial respiration（人工）呼吸器，呼吸机

respire/rɪsˈpaɪə/

v.❶ breathe 呼吸 ❷（said about plants）perform the process of respiration（植物）呼吸

respond/rɪˈspɒnd/

v.act in answer to the action of another；reply 做出反应：I don't know how to ～ to your help.我不知道怎样才能感激你的帮助。‖ ～ to 响应

response/rɪˈspɒns/

n.an answer and a reaction to sth.that has been said, etc. 回答；回报；反应：They made a quick ～ to my inquiry.他们对我的询问很快做了答复。

responsibility/rɪˌspɒnsəˈbɪləti/

n.（pl.-ies）❶ the condition of being responsible 责任，职责：I take full ～ for this action.我对这次行动负完全责任。❷ sth.for which a person is responsible；duty 职责，任务：undertake fresh responsibilities 担负起新任务

R

responsible /rɪ'spɒnsəbl/

adj.(of a person) legally or morally liable for carrying out a duty;in charge of 负责的;对……有责任的：You must be ～ for what you have done. 你要对你所做的负责。

responsive /rɪ'spɒnsɪv/

*adj.*❶ given or made as an answer 回答的;应答的：a ～ smile 报以微笑 /a ～ gesture 应答的手势 ❷ reacting quickly or positively 积极反应的;反应快的;灵敏的：These brakes should be more ～.这些制动器应该更灵敏些。

rest¹ /rest/

*n.*what is left; the ones that still remain 其余,剩余部分：Three of us will go; the ～ are to stay here.我们去三个人,其余的人将留在这里。

rest² /rest/

Ⅰ *n.*(a period of) freedom from activity or from sth. tiring or worrying 休息 Ⅱ *v.* relax, sleep or do nothing after a period of activity or illness 放松;休息

restaurant /'restrɒnt/

*n.*a place where meals can be bought and eaten 饭馆,餐厅：Is there a ～ in the hotel? 这旅馆里有餐厅吗?

restful /'restfl/

*adj.*❶ peaceful; giving a feeling of rest 悠闲的,安宁的;使人得到休息的：He spent a ～ evening watching television.他悠闲地看了一晚电视。❷(of colour, music,etc.) causing a person to feel calm or pleasant（色彩、音乐等）使(感到)平静（宁静、愉快）：a ～ scene 宁静的景色/ a color ～ to the eye 悦目的颜色

restless /'restlɪs/

*adj.*❶ without rest or sleep 得不到休息的：a ～ night 不眠之夜 ❷never quite; unwilling or unable to stay still 好动的; 不安的,焦虑的;烦躁的：The audience was getting ～.听众开始不耐烦了。

restore /rɪ'stɔ:(r)/

*v.*❶ give back; return 归还：～ a magazine to its place 将杂志放归原处 /～ a book to the library 将书归还图书馆 /

The stolen article was ～d to its owner. 失窃物件已归还原主。❷ bring back to a former condition or place 恢复;复原：～ our national economy 恢复我国的国民经济 /～ order 恢复秩序 /His health is entirely ～d.他的健康完全恢复了。❸ repair or reconstruct 修补;修复;重建：～ an old building 修建老建筑

restrain /rɪ'streɪn/

*v.*prevent sb.from doing sth.克制：He was too excited to ～ himself. 他太激动了无法克制自己。

restrict /rɪ'strɪkt/

*v.*put a limit on sb.or sth.限制：The football team is ～ed to twenty.足球队以 20 人为限。‖ ～ **to** 仅限于;仅限……知道

restriction /rɪ'strɪkʃn/

*n.*the act of limiting or controlling sb. or sth.限制,限定;约束：～ of expenditure 限制费用 /A person's behaviour must be subject to certain ～s.一个人的行为举止必须受到一定的限制。

restrictive /rɪ'strɪktɪv/

*adj.*restricting; tending to restrict 限制的,约束的：～ sight distance 受到限制的视距 /～ practices in industry 工业方面的限制性措施

result /rɪ'zʌlt/

Ⅰ *n.*❶ a consequence, an effect, or an outcome of sth.结果;成果;后果;效果：obtain good ～s 获得优良结果 /What was the ～ of the game? 比赛结果如何? /As a ～, the discussion was adjourned.结果,讨论中止了。/I was late as a ～ of the snow.由于下雪我迟到了。❷ sth. found by calculation; answer to a mathematical problem, etc.答案;(计算)结果 Ⅱ *v.*❶be a result of; have as a result (from,in) 产生;起于：Sickness often ～s from eating.疾病常因吃东西而引起。/My failure ～ed from not working hard enough.我的失败是由于工作不够刻苦而造成的。/His success ～ed from hard work.他的成功是努力工作的结果。❷ bring about; have as a consequence 终致;归于;引起(某结果);使获得(某成果)：～ in failure 终致失败 /The experiment ～ed in the discovery of a cure for cancer.实验结果发现一种治疗癌症的药物。/The accident ～ed in five deaths.这次事故造成了 5 人死亡。

resume/rɪˈzjuːm/
v. ❶ go on after stopping for a time；begin again 继续，重新开始：Now let's ～ our work.我们继续工作吧。❷ take or occupy again 重获：He ～d his office.他复职了。‖ **resumption**/rɪˈzʌmpʃn/ *n.*重新开始(做某事)

retail/ˈriːteɪl/
Ⅰ *v.* ❶ sell goods in small quantities 零售：These shoes ～ at 20 yuan a pair.这些鞋子零售 20 元一双。❷ repeat to others in turn 转述；传播：～ a rumour 传播流言 Ⅱ *n.* the sale of goods to customers in small quantities 零售，零卖：sell goods by ～ 零售货物/～ prices 零售价格 Ⅲ *adv.* being sold in such a way 以零售方式：Do you buy wholesale or ～? 你按批发价还是按零售价购买? ‖ ～**er** *n.*零售商

retain/rɪˈteɪn/
v. ❶ keep；continue to have or hold 保持：The people there ～ the custom.那里的人们仍保留着这一习俗。❷employ (especially a lawyer or adviser) to act for one by paying in advance 付定金聘请(律师或顾问)

retell/ˌriːˈtel/
*v.*tell again；tell in a different way or in a different language 重述，复述：Retell the story,please.请把故事复述一遍。

retire/rɪˈtaɪə(r)/
v. ❶ give up or cause to leave one's work or position 退休 ❷ go to bed 就寝：He ～d early because he was tired.他因疲劳很早就睡觉了。❸ (of an army) retreat from an enemy or an attacking position (军队)撤退

retired/rɪˈtaɪəd/
*adj.*having stopped working, usually because of old age 退职的；退休的；退役的：a ～ civil servant 一个退休的公务员

retirement/rɪˈtaɪəmənt/
n. ❶ a case or the act of retiring 退休；退

职；退役：His boss gave him a gold watch on his ～.他的老板在他退休时给了他一块金表。❷ the period of the life after a person has stopped work at a particular age 退休生活：go into ～开始退休生活

retort/rɪˈtɔːt/
Ⅰ *v.*reply quickly and sharply 回嘴；反驳；反击："It's your fault." I ～ed.我反驳道："这是你的错。" Ⅱ *n.*a sharp reply 回嘴；反驳：say a few words in ～ 反驳几句

retrace/rɪˈtreɪs/
*v.*go back over 折回；回顾；追溯：～ one's steps from where one started 沿原路返回/ ～ past events in one's memory 回顾记忆中的往事

retract /rɪˈtrækt/
v. ❶ pull sth. or be pulled back or in 缩回，缩进 ❷withdraw a statement or accusation 撤回，收回(声明或指控) ❸go back on an agreement or promise 收回，违背(保证，诺言) ‖ ～**able** *adj.*可取消的,可收回的;伸缩自如的

retraction /rɪˈtrækʃən/
*n.*❶a statement saying that sth. you previously said or wrote is not true 撤销；收回❷the act of pulling sth. back 收回；拉回: the ～ of a cat's claws 猫爪子的回缩

retreat/rɪˈtriːt/
Ⅰ *v.*go back,or fall back in face of danger or an attack 撤退：The wounded ～ed from the front.伤员从前线撤下来了。Ⅱ *n.*an act of moving away from a place or an enemy 撤退

retrieve/rɪˈtriːv/
v. ❶ regain；find and bring back 再获得，找回，恢复：～ a lost piece of luggage 找回一件遗失的行李/He ～d his spirits.他的精神恢复了。❷set or put right；make amends for 纠正,修补,补偿,挽回：～ one's honour 挽回名誉/ ～ an error 纠正错误

retrograde/ˈretrəɡreɪd/
*adj.*moving backwards or making worse 后退的；倒退的；恶化的：a ～ action 退步的行动

retrospect/ˈretrəspekt/

n. an act of looking at past events 回顾 ‖ in ～ 回顾

retrospective /ˌretrəˈspektɪv/

adj. having an effect on sth. already done 有追溯效力的：～ legislation 追溯法

return /rɪˈtɜːn/

Ⅰ *v.* ❶ come or go back to a former place 回来：He found everything had changed when he ～ed home. 当他返回时他发现一切都变了。❷ give or send back；repay 归还，报答：Don't ～ evil for good. 不要以怨报德。 Ⅱ *n.* ❶ the act or an example of coming back 返回，回来 ❷ the act of giving, putting, or sending sth. back 归还；回报

reunion /ˌriːˈjuːnɪən/

n. ❶ a gathering of old friends, former colleagues, etc. after separation 重聚，团聚，联欢会：We have a family ～ every new year. 每逢新年，我们全家都会团聚。❷ the state of being brought together again 再结合，再会合

reunite /ˌriːjuːˈnaɪt/

v. bring or come together again 重新统一；再联合：Don't you think the two parts of the country will ～？ 难道你不认为该国的两部分会再联合吗？

reveal /rɪˈviːl/

v. ❶ allow to be seen；display 使露出：He ～ed great interest in science when he was small. 他很小就对科学感兴趣。❷ make known 泄露：Don't ～ the secret. 不要泄露这一秘密。

revelation /ˌrevəˈleɪʃn/

n. ❶ the act of making known of sth. secret 揭露，透露，展现：a ～ of the true facts 揭露事实真相 ❷ a fact that is made known 被暴露的真相：The ease of his driving was a ～ to me. 我没有想到他居然能驾驶自如。

revenge /rɪˈvendʒ/

Ⅰ *v.* inflict hurt or harm on sb. for an injury or wrong done to oneself 报复；复仇：～ a defeat 雪失败之耻 /I will ～ that insult. 我要对那个侮辱进行报复。/Hamlet ～d his dead father. 哈姆雷特为他死

去的父亲报了仇。 Ⅱ *n.* the action of inflicting hurt or harm on someone in return for a wrong, injury, etc.；the desire for doing this 报复；复仇；复仇心：I'll have my ～ on you for what you did. 我要为你所干的事对你进行报复。

revenue /ˈrevənjuː/

n. money coming in (especially to the government from taxes, etc.) 收入（尤指政府的税收等）

revere /rɪˈvɪə(r)/

v. feel deep respect or（especially religious）veneration for sb. or sth. 崇敬：They wrote a letter to the ～d heroes. 他们给可敬的英雄们写信。 ‖ ～nce *n.* & *v.* 崇敬/～nd *adj.* 值得崇敬的/～nt *adj.* 崇敬的；虔诚的

reverie /ˈrevəri/

n. daydream；the state of thinking pleasant thoughts 白日梦；美好幻想：lost in ～ 想入非非

reversal /rɪˈvɜːsl/

n. ❶ a change to an opposite direction, position, or course of action 反向，反转，倒转，颠倒 ❷ an adverse change of fortune（运气）逆转

reverse /rɪˈvɜːs/

Ⅰ *n.* a complete change of direction or action 逆向；逆转 Ⅱ *v.* ❶ move backwards 倒退 ❷ change sth. completely so that it is the opposite 颠倒；彻底转变 Ⅲ *adj.* opposite 反面的

reversible /rɪˈvɜːsəbl/

adj. ❶ that can be reversed 可逆的：a ～ chemical reaction 可逆化学反应 ❷（of clothes）able to be worn on either side out（衣服）正反两面可穿的：This coat is ～. 这大衣正反两面都可穿。

revert /rɪˈvɜːt/

v. return to a former state 恢复；复归：When the ground was not cultivated, it ～ed to jungle. 这块地不耕种时，又恢复成丛林。

review /rɪˈvjuː/

Ⅰ *v.* ❶ look again at sth. you have studied 复习：They are busy ～ing their lessons.他们正忙于复习功课。❷ think about past events 回顾 Ⅱ n. an act of thinking about past events 复习；回顾：a careful ～ of political events 仔细回顾一连串政治事件

revise/rɪˈvaɪz/
v.❶ read carefully in order to correct errors 校订：The dictionary has been ～d. 这本字典已经修订。❷ change opinions or plans 改变，更改(意见或计划)：She ～d her opinion about him. 她改变了对他的看法。‖ **revision** n.修改／**revisionist** n. & adj.修正主义者(的)；修正主义(的)

revive/rɪˈvaɪv/
v.❶ come and bring back to life 复苏：The snake gave the farmer a bite after reviving.那条蛇苏醒后咬了农夫一口。❷ come or bring back to a fresh condition 恢复：The old custom has been ～d quietly.这一旧的习俗又悄然兴起。‖ **revival** n.复苏；恢复

revoke/rɪˈvəʊk/
Ⅰ v. repeal or cancel sth. so that it is no longer valid 撤回；撤销；取消；废除：～ an order 撤销命令／～ a driving licence 吊销驾驶执照 Ⅱ n.failure to follow suit in a card game (纸牌戏)有牌不跟

revolt/rɪˈvəʊlt/
Ⅰ v.❶ rebel；rise in rebellion 反叛：The people ～ed against the cruel governor.人民起来反抗暴君。❷ fill with disgust or horror 使憎恶：The bad smell ～ed him. 怪味使他恶心。Ⅱ n.a protest against authority, etc.；the state of being revolted 叛乱：two ～s in three years 三年两次叛乱

revolution/ˌrevəˈluːʃn/
n.❶ an overthrow of an established government or political system 革命：Do you know the American Revolution? 你知道美国革命吗？❷a movement around some point in a circle 旋转，绕转：One ～ of the earth around the sun takes a year.地球绕着太阳旋转一周要一年时间。❸ a complete change 改革：～ in the means of communication 交通工具的大改革

revolutionary/ˌrevəˈluːʃənəri/
Ⅰ adj.❶ of a revolution；connected with a revolution 革命的，与革命有关的：～ organizations 革命组织 ❷ bringing or causing great changes 引起大变革的：Radio and television were two ～ inventions of 20th century.无线电和电视是 20 世纪两项重大发明。Ⅱ n.a person who works for or engages in political revolution 革命者

revolve/rɪˈvɒlv/
v.❶ (cause to) go round in a circle 使旋转；使绕转：The moon ～s around the earth.月亮绕着地球旋转。／The earth ～s on its own axis.地球绕轴自转。❷ turn over in the mind；think about all sides of (a problem) 细想；默想；沉思；反复思考：～ a scheme 反复思考一方案 /Ideas ～ in his mind.他思考再三。❸ recur at periodic intervals 周期性地(或间断地)出现：Season ～s.季节周期性转换。

revolver/rɪˈvɒlvə(r)/
n. a type of pistol which can be fired quickly 左轮手枪

reward/rɪˈwɔːd/
Ⅰ n.a return made for sth. done；payment offered 报酬：He got a ～ for his invention.他因一项发明获得了奖金。Ⅱ v. give sth.to sb.for services, efforts, or successes 酬报；报答：You'll be well ～ed.你将得到优厚的报酬。

rewrite/ˌriːˈraɪt/
v.write again；write in a different form 重写；改写：Rewrite the sentence! 重写这句话!

rhetoric/ˈretərɪk/
n.❶the art of using words in speaking or writing so as to influence others 修辞学：Do you know something about ～? 你懂修辞学吗？❷ the exaggerated language used especially by politicians 花言巧语，虚夸：the exaggerated ～ of presidential campaigns 总统竞选活动中夸张的辞令

rhetorical/rɪˈtɒrɪkl/
adj.❶ of or having rhetoric 修辞的：The speaker showed great ～ skill.演讲者显示出了杰出的演说技能。❷expressed in

terms intended to persuade or impress 虚夸的;空洞华丽的

rhinoceros /raɪˈnɒsərəs/

n. a type of large, thick-skinned animal with a horn on its nose, found in Africa and Asia 犀牛

rhombus /ˈrɒmbəs/

n. a four-sided figure with equal sides, and angles which are not right angles 菱形;斜方形

rhyme /raɪm/

Ⅰ *n.* ❶ a short poem where lines end in the same sounds 押韵的短诗 ❷ a word that has the same sound as another 同韵词,押韵词:"Pain" and "gain" are ～s. "Pain" 与 "gain" 两词同韵。❸ correspondence of sound between words or the endings of words 韵;押韵:The poem is written in ～. 这首诗押韵。Ⅱ *v.* put together to form a rhyme; be in rhyme 押韵:"Duty" ～s with "beauty". Duty 和 beauty 押韵。

rhythm /ˈrɪðəm/

n. the movement with regular repetition of a beat, accent, rise and fall; repetition of musical beats; the arrangement of syllables or cadences in a line of poetry 节奏,节拍,韵律:She played in quick ～. 她用快节奏演奏。

rib /rɪb/

n. ❶ one of a set of bones round the chest 肋骨;肋:a false ～ 假肋 /a true ～ 真肋 ❷ a piece of meat from the ribs of an animal 肉排:a ～ of beef 一块牛排 ❸ a curved rod used for strengthening a framework 骨架:the ～ of an umbrella 伞骨

ribbon /ˈrɪbən/

n. a long narrow strip of silk material used in decorating clothes, tying hair, etc. 缎带,丝带:She wrapped the gift in paper, tying it in yellow ～. 她将礼物用纸包好,再用黄色缎带扎好。

rice /raɪs/

n. a plant growing in water as a source of food; the grains of this plant 稻;稻米;米饭:every grain of ～ 每一粒米 /coarse ～ 糙米 /polished ～ 精米 /paddy (upland) ～ 水(旱)稻 /broken ～ 碎米 /middle-season ～ 中稻 /cook ～ 烧饭 /cut ～ 割稻 /grow ～ 种稻 /Rice is an important food in India, China and Japan. 稻米在印度、中国和日本是重要食物。/We live on ～. 我们以稻米为主食。

rich /rɪtʃ/

adj. ❶ having much money, land, goods, etc.; wealthy 有钱的;富有的;富的:grow ～ 富起来 /a ～ man 富人 /the ～ 富人(们) /make our country ～ and strong 使我国富裕强大 ❷ containing and producing much; abundant 多产的;丰富的;富饶的:～ soil 沃土 /a ～ harvest 丰收 /a country ～ in oil 石油丰富的国家 /He is ～ in experience. 他经验丰富。❸ fine; splendid; costly 珍贵的;华美的;贵重的:～ jewels 珍贵的首饰 /～ furniture 富丽堂皇的家具 ❹ (of food) containing a large proportion of fat, spices, sugar,, etc. (食物)油腻的;味浓的;特甜的 ❺ (of colours, sounds, etc.) full; deep; mellow (色彩)鲜艳的;(声音)低沉洪亮的:a ～ dark red 深红色 /a ～ tone 洪亮圆润的音调 ❻ (informal) highly entertaining; giving opportunities for humor (非正式)有趣的;可笑的;荒唐的:That's ～! 真可笑! 真荒唐!

rickshaw /ˈrɪkʃɔː/

n. a small, two-wheeled carriage pulled by a man 人力车,黄包车

rid /rɪd/

v. make free from 摆脱;除去:～ a house of rats 消灭屋内的老鼠 ‖ get ～ of ❶ 摆脱:try to get ～ of unwelcome visitors 设法摆脱不受欢迎的客人 ❷ 去掉;废除

riddle¹ /ˈrɪdl/

Ⅰ *n.* a puzzling question, situation, person, etc. 谜;谜一般的人(或事):Can you answer this ～? 你能解答这个谜吗? / That man is a ～ to me 此人对我来说是个谜。Ⅱ *v.* solve or explain (a riddle) to (sb.) 猜(某人)出的(谜)

riddle² /ˈrɪdl/

v. make many holes in (在……上面)打许

多洞；The door was ～d with bullets. 门被子弹打得尽是窟窿。

ride/raɪd/

Ⅰ v.❶ sit on and control the movement of an animal（especially a horse）or a bicycle,or motor cycle 骑(马)；骑(自行车,摩托车)；Can you ～ a bike? 你会骑自行车吗? ❷ take part in as a passenger 乘坐；They ～ in a bus to work every day. 他们每天乘公共汽车上班。Ⅱ n.a journey on horseback,a bicycle,etc.,or in public conveyance 骑马；乘车；It was an hour's ～ from here to the zoo.从这里去动物园乘车只需一小时。

rider/'raɪdə(r)/

n.a person who rides 骑马(或自行车,摩托车)的人；乘客；He is no ～.他不善于骑马。

ridge/rɪdʒ/

n.❶ a raised line where two sloping surfaces meet 脊；垄；the ～ of a roof 屋脊 ❷ a long narrow hilltop, mountain range, or watershed 山脊,岭；分水岭

ridicule/'rɪdɪkjuːl/

Ⅰ v.laugh unkindly at sb. 嘲笑；奚落；讥讽；Don't ～ him.不要嘲笑他。Ⅱ n.unkind comments that make fun of sb. or sth. 嘲笑；奚落；讥讽

ridiculous/rɪ'dɪkjuləs/

adj.deserving ridicule；laughable 荒谬的；可笑的；It would be ～ to walk backward all the time.老向后走是荒谬的。

rifle/'raɪfl/

n.❶ a gun with a long rifled barrel,to be fired from the shoulder 步枪；来复枪 ❷ troops armed with rifles 步枪队

rift/rɪft/

n.a large crack in rocks,etc. 裂缝；隙缝；裂口；cause a ～ between two friends 使两个朋友龃龉不和

rig/rɪg/

Ⅰ v.(of an election,etc.)bring about the result that one wants by dishonest means (指选举等)操纵；舞弊 ‖～sth. up 赶忙拼凑；～ up a shelter 匆匆搭起一个遮蔽所 Ⅱ n. ropes,etc. used to support the

masts and sails of a ship（支撑船桅帆的）索具 ‖ oil ～ n.海上钻油平台

right/raɪt/

Ⅰ adj.❶ morally good, justified , or acceptable 正当的,正义的；理所当然的 ❷ true or correct as a fact 正确的；对的 ❸ according to what is correct for a particular situation or thing 对头的；符合要求的 ❹ in a satisfactory or normal state 令人满意的；正常的 ❺ of, on or towards the side of the body that is towards the east when a person faces north 右边的 Ⅱ n.❶ the right side 右边 ❷ sth. that is good, just, etc. 正义,正当,公正 Ⅲ adv.❶ completely 完全地 ❷ correctly 正确地 ❸ on or to the right 在右边；向右 ❹ properly；satisfactorily 恰当地；令人满意地

rightly /'raɪtli/

adv.❶correctly or properly 正确地；准确地 ❷in accordance with justice or what is morally right 公正地,正当地

rigid/'rɪdʒɪd/

adj.❶ stiff, unbending 僵直的；She was ～ with fear.她吓得全身僵直。❷ strict；not to be changed 坚决的；He is ～ in his idea.他坚持他的观点。

rigour/'rɪɡə(r)/

n.❶severe or difficult conditions 艰苦的条件 ❷the state or quality of firmness, severity or strictness 坚定；严厉,严格 ‖ **rigorous**/'rɪɡərəs/ adj.艰苦的；严厉的

rim/rɪm/

n.(usually of sth.round) the edge of sth. (通常指圆形物体的)边,缘；the ～ of a cup (wheel) 杯缘(轮缘)

ring¹/rɪŋ/

Ⅰ v.❶cause (a bell) to sound(使)发出铃声；The boy was too short to ～ the door bell.男孩太小按不到门铃。❷be filled with sound 回响；The teacher's words are still ～ing in my ears.老师的话仍在我耳边回响。❸ telephone (someone) 打电话；Please ～ me up.请打电话给我。Ⅱ n.❶the sound of a bell or a bell-like sound 铃声；铃声般的响声 ❷a certain quality that words，sounds，，etc. have（言语、声音等的）特性

ring^2 /rɪŋ/

n. ❶ a small circular band worn on a finger as an ornament or a token of marriage or authority 戒指；指环 ❷ a circular band of any material 圆环；圆圈：fried onion ～s 油炸洋葱圈

rinse /rɪns/

Ⅰ *v.* wash with clean water to remove soap，dirt，etc. 以清水冲洗；漂洗：～ the soap off 漂掉肥皂 /～ a shirt 漂清衬衫 /～ cups 冲洗茶杯 /Rinse your mouth before you eat.吃东西前先漱一下口。Ⅱ *n.* ❶ an act of rinsing 冲洗；漂洗：Give the shirts at least two ～s.这些衬衫至少要清洗二遍。❷ a solution for tinting or conditioning the hair 染发液；护发液：a blue ～ 蓝色染发液

riot /ˈraɪət/

Ⅰ *n.* ❶ a violent public disturbance；disorder 骚乱；暴动：put down a ～ 平息骚乱 /～ police 防暴警察 /A ～ broke out.骚乱发生了。❷ noisy or uncontrolled behaviour 狂闹；放荡；放纵：run ～ 胡闹；肆无忌惮 ❸ (of colour) profusion；luxuriance（色彩的）丰富：a ～ of colour 五彩缤纷 ❹ a play of wild enthusiasm 轰动的演出：I hear the new show is a ～ —let's go and see it.听说这出新戏轰动一时，咱们一定要去看看。Ⅱ *v.* take part in violent actions in public place 参加暴乱；聚众闹事

rip /rɪp/

Ⅰ *v.* (-pp-) divide or make a hole in (sth.) by pulling sharply 撕开；扯开；扯破：～ open a letter 撕开一封信 /I ～ped my stocking on a nail.我的袜子被钉子扯破了。Ⅱ *n.* an uneven or ragged tear or cut 裂口；裂缝；破绽：There's a big ～ in my sleeve.我的衣袖上有一个大裂口。

ripe /raɪp/

adj. ❶ full-grown and ready to be gathered or eaten；mature 成熟的，熟的：～ fruit 成熟了的水果 /～ vegetable 可以采摘的蔬菜 ❷ ready or suitable for sth. to happen 时机成熟的；适宜的：a ～ plan 一

个时机成熟的计划 ❸ (of cheese or wine) full matured or developed（干酪或酒）成熟的；醇美可口的

ripen /ˈraɪpən/

v. become ripe；make ripe 变成熟；使成熟：The sun ～s the crops.太阳使庄稼成熟。/The crops will grow and ～.庄稼会生长成熟。

ripple /ˈrɪpl/

Ⅰ *n.* a very little wave on the surface of liquid 微波，涟漪：Throw a stone into still water and watch the ～s spread in rings.朝静水里扔一块石头，观看一圈一圈展开的涟漪。Ⅱ *v.* cause to move in small waves 使引起微波（涟漪）：The lake ～d gently.湖水轻轻泛起微波。/The wind ～d the surface of the lake.风把湖面吹得泛起微波。

rise /raɪz/

Ⅰ *v.* (rose，～n) ❶ appear above the horizon；move upward；go (come) up 上升，升起：Steam can be seen rising from the wet clothes.可以看到蒸气从湿衣上冒出。❷ increase；go higher in price，quality，sound，degree，etc. 上涨；(价格、质量、音量、程度等)增加，提高：The price will ～.价格可能会上涨。❸ get up from a lying，sitting，kneeling position 站起：Tom rose from the chair.汤姆从椅子上站起。❹ get out of bed 起床：Early to bed and early to ～ makes a man healthy.早睡早起身体好。Ⅱ *n.* an upward movement；increase 上涨；上升

risen /ˈrɪzn/

adj. having moved to a higher position 升起的：the ～ moon 升起的月亮

risk /rɪsk/

Ⅰ *v.* expose in a dangerous situation 冒……风险；面临危险：I would ～ climbing the tall tree for our soldiers.我愿为我们自己的战士冒险爬上那棵大树。Ⅱ *n.* the possibility of loss，harm or danger 危险；风险：There is a great ～ of doing that.那样做很危险。

risky /ˈrɪski/

adj. full of risk；dangerous 有风险的；危

R

险的：a ～ undertaking 危险任务

rite/raɪt/

　　Ⅰ n. a ceremony, especially a religious ceremony (尤指宗教的)仪式，典礼：the marriage ～s 婚礼 Ⅱ adj. connected with rites (宗教)仪式的：a ～ dance 祭神舞蹈

ritual/ˈrɪtjʊəl/

　　Ⅰ n.❶ a series of actions used in a religious or other ceremony；a particular form of this (宗教等)庄严仪式 ❷ a procedure that is regularly followed ritual 例行公事；老规矩；习惯 Ⅱ adj. to do with or done as a ritual (与)仪式(有关)的

rival/ˈraɪvl/

　　Ⅰ n. a person who competes with another 对手 Ⅱ adj. of competitor or competition 竞争的 Ⅲ v. compete with 和……竞争：The two players ～ed each other for the gold medal. 双方队员为夺金牌奋力拼搏。

rivalry/ˈraɪvəlri/

　　n. a competition for the same objective or for superiority in the same field 竞争；对抗，对立：commercial～ 商业竞争

river/ˈrɪvə(r)/

　　n. a large stream of water 江；河：the Changjiang River 长江/the Yellow River 黄河/the River Nile 尼罗河/a boundary ～ 国境河/a dry ～ 干水道/the Thames River 泰晤士河

road/rəʊd/

　　n. a way between places；highway；a specially prepared way, publicly or privately owned 路；道路；公路；大道：go by ～ 赶路/take the socialist ～ 走社会主义道路

roam/rəʊm/

　　v. go about with no special plan or aim；wander 漫步，漫游，徘徊：They ～ed from town to town. 他们从一个城镇漫游到另一个城镇。/He used to ～ the street for hours on end. 过去他往往要连续逛几小时大街。‖ ～er n. 徘徊者；漫游者

roar/rɔː(r)/

　　Ⅰ v. make or utter a loud deep and prolonged sound 吼叫；呼啸；轰鸣：The north wind ～ed. 北风呼啸。Ⅱ n. a loud, deep and prolonged sound 怒吼声：The ～ of lion was frightening. 狮子的吼叫令人恐惧。

roast/rəʊst/

　　Ⅰ v.❶ cook with dry heat, as in an oven or near hot coals (用烤炉)烤；炙(肉等)：～ meat (potatoes) 烤肉(土豆)/The meat is ～ing nicely. 肉烤得恰到火候。/She ～ed the beef in the oven. 她把牛肉放在烤炉中烤。❷ dry by exposing to heat 烘干，烙 Ⅱ n.❶ a joint of meat roasted 烤好的肉：order a ～ 订一份烤肉 ❷ an outdoor picnic at which food is roasted 烤肉野餐会

rob/rɒb/

　　v. (-bb-)❶ take away by force；steal 抢劫，盗取：～ a bank 抢劫银行/～ (the) jewels 盗窃珠宝/That thief ～bed me of my wallet. 那贼抢走了我的钱包。❷ deprive a person of (what is legally due to him) 非法剥夺：～ one's rights 非法剥夺某人的权力

robber/ˈrɒbə/

　　n. a person who commits robbery 抢劫者，强盗，盗贼

robbery/ˈrɒbəri/

　　n. the act of stealing money or goods from a person, shop, etc. 抢劫，盗取，抢劫案：He was charged with a bank ～. 他被指控与一次银行抢劫案有关。

robe/rəʊb/

　　n.❶ (usually pl.) a long loose outer garment worn for official or ceremonial occasions 礼服；官服；制服：a judge's black ～s 法官的黑色长袍 ❷ a dressing gown 〈美〉晨衣，浴衣 ❸ a long, loose outer garment 长袍：Many Arabs still wear ～s. 许多阿拉伯人仍然穿着长袍。

robot/ˈrəʊbɒt/

　　n. a machine made in imitation of a human being；a mechanical device that does routine work in response of commands 机器人；自动机：These cars were built by ～. 这些汽车是机器人造的。

robust/rəˈbʌst/

　　adj. strong and healthy 强壮的：a ～ man

壮汉

rock/rɒk/

I *n.*(a type of) stone forming part of the Earth's surface 岩石：The ship hit a ～ and sank.船触礁沉没了。 II *v.*(cause to) move regularly backwards and forwards or from side to side （使）摇动：She likes to sit in a ～ing chair.她喜欢坐摇椅。

rocket/'rɒkɪt/

I *n.* ❶ an engine with long round sides that pushes a spacecraft up into the space 火箭 ❷ a firework for aerial display 烟火 II *v.* increase very rapidly 飞涨；快速前进：Prices ～ed after the war.战后物价飞涨。

rocky /'rɒki/

*adj.*❶of, like or made of rock 岩石的；像岩石的；岩石构成的 ❷full of rocks 多岩石的

rod/rɒd/

n. ❶ a thin, straight piece of wood or metal 杆；棒；棍：fishing ～ 钓竿 /a calculation ～ 计算尺 /a lightening ～ 避雷针 ❷（the ～）a stick used for punishing (拷打用的)刑条；棍棒：give the ～ 鞭打 /The ～ is not allowed in the school. 学校不许处罚学生。

rodent/'rəʊdnt/

*n.*a small animal of the kind that has special teeth for gnawing things (e. g. rats, rabbits, etc.) 啮齿动物(如鼠、兔等)

role/rəʊl/

*n.*❶ a character in a play 角色：play the leading ～ in a film 在一部电影中扮演主角 ❷ the part played in activities；a task or duty in an undertaking 作用；任务：play an important ～ in developing agriculture 在发展农业中起重要作用

roll/rəʊl/

I *v.* ❶ move along by turning over and over （使）滚动：The old goat ～ed over, dead.老山羊翻下去死了。 ❷ wrap or rotate sth.around and around upon itself, or around sth. else 卷，卷拢：Please ～ the wool into a ball.请把毛线卷成团。 II *n.* ❶a rolling movement, over and over or

to and for sideways 打滚 ❷a list of names 名单

roller/'rəʊlə(r)/

n. ❶ a cylinder-shaped object of wood, metal, rubber, etc. usually part of a machine, for pressing, smoothing, crushing, printing, etc.滚子；滚筒；辊，辗子；滚轴：a road ～压路机 ❷a long swelling wave 巨浪：The great Atlantic ～s surged high.大西洋巨浪波涛汹涌。 ‖ ～-skate *n.*（轮式）溜冰鞋

Roman/'rəʊmən/

I *adj.*connected with Rome 罗马的：～ Empire 罗马帝国 II *n.* someone from Rome 罗马人 ‖ ～ numerals 罗马数字/～ Catholic 罗马天主教徒

romance/rəʊ'mæns/

I *n.* ❶ an exciting and adventurous story 传奇故事 ❷ a love story；a love affair （男女间的）罗曼史；情事：How is your little ～with you girlfriend? 你和女朋友爱情进展如何？ II *v.*carry on a love affair 求爱；求婚

romantic/rəʊ'mæntɪk/

*adj.*❶showing a strong feeling of love 热恋的：a very ～ love story 一个非常浪漫的爱情故事 ❷ dealing with or suggesting adventure or love 传奇的；富有浪漫色彩的：She has a dreamy ～ nature.她有令人喜爱的浪漫的性格。 ❸fanciful；not practical 空想的，不切实际的，虚幻的：She has ～ ideas about becoming a famous actress. 她幻想成为一名著名演员。/～ views 不切实际的看法

roof/ruːf/

I *n.* the top covering of a building or vehicle 屋顶，房顶；车顶：a flat ～ 平顶/the ～ of a car 汽车的车顶 II *v.* cover with a roof 加屋顶；盖屋顶：a house ～ed with wood 用木头做屋顶的房屋

room/ruːm/

I *n.* ❶ a division of a building, with its own walls, floor and ceiling 房间 ❷ space that could be filled, or that's enough for any purpose 空间：Please make ～ for the old lady.请给这位老太太让个地方。 II

R

v. occupy a room or rooms of other persons' house;lodge 住（一个或一套房间）;寄宿:They ～ed together at college. 他们在大学同住一个房间。

roost/ruːst/

Ⅰ *n.*a bar,pole on which birds rest（鸟类的）栖架,栖息处:a hen on a ～ 栖架上的一只母鸡 Ⅱ *v.*sleep or rest on a roost 栖息 ‖ ～er *n.* 公鸡

root/ruːt/

Ⅰ *n.*❶ the part of a plant that grows beneath the ground 根:New bamboo shoots will come up around the ～.新的竹根将从竹根周围长出来。❷ the part from which sth. grows and develops;the basic cause of a thing 根源:Money is the ～ of all evil.金钱是万恶之源。 Ⅱ *v.*cause to send out roots and begin to grow （使）生根

rooted/ˈruːtɪd/

*adj.*❶（～ **in sth.**）developing from or being strongly influenced by sth.根源在于;由……产生 ❷fixed in a place;not moving or changing 固定在某地的;根深蒂固的

rope/rəʊp/

Ⅰ *n.*❶ a thick,strong cord made by twisting finer cords or wires together 绳索:twist a ～ 搓绳 /two pieces of ～ 两条绳 /He tied the horse to the tree with ～s. 他用绳子把马拴在了树上。❷（**the ～**）the cord used in hanging;punishment by hanging 绞索;绞刑 ❸ a number of things strung together（用绳索串联某物的）一串:a ～ of pearls 一串珍珠 Ⅱ *v.*tie or fasten with a rope 捆;扎;缚;绑;用绳系住;用绳拖:～ a box 用绳捆住箱子

rose/rəʊz/

Ⅰ *n.*a kind of brightly-coloured, usually sweet-scented flower 玫瑰花:a bunch of red ～s 一束红玫瑰 Ⅱ *adj.*pinkish-red; pink in colour 玫瑰色的:Her dress is ～. 她的衣服是玫瑰色的。

rosemary/ˈrəʊzməri/

*n.*an evergreen shrub with fragrant leaves,used as a herb in cooking 迷迭香

roster/ˈrɒstə(r)/

*n.*a list of people's names showing what jobs they must do and when 勤务簿;值勤表

rosy /ˈrəʊzi/

adj.(rosier,rosiest)❶rose-coloured,deep pink 玫瑰色的;（面色）红润的;深粉色的:～ cheeks 红润的面颊 ❷promising or hopeful 乐观的;有希望的:a ～ future 锦绣前程 ‖ **rosily** *adv.*乐观地

rot/rɒt/

Ⅰ *v.*(-tt-)（cause to）decay, go bad or spoil（使）腐烂:Some of the rubbish will ～ away.有些垃圾会腐烂掉。 Ⅱ *n.*the process or condition of decaying 腐败: They tried their best to stop the ～ in the government.他们尽了最大努力在政府内阻止腐败。

rotate/rəʊˈteɪt/

*v.*❶ move round a central point 旋转: The earth ～s around the sun.地球绕太阳旋转。/The moon ～s rather slowly. 月球旋转得十分缓慢。❷ take turns or come in succession 循环;顺序轮流;更迭:The seasons ～.四季循环。/The two guards ～d between the day and night shifts.这两个卫兵日夜班轮换。

rotation /rəʊˈteɪʃən/

*n.*❶the action of rotating 旋转,转动 ❷ the practice of growing a different crop each year on a plot of land in a regular order to avoid exhausting the soil 轮作,换茬

rotten/ˈrɒtn/

*adj.*❶ decayed;having gone bad 腐烂的;腐败的:～ wood 朽木 ❷very bad;very unpleasant 糟糕的,非常讨厌的:The film was pretty ～.那部影片相当糟糕。

rough/rʌf/

Ⅰ *adj.*❶ not smooth;not level 粗糙的;高低不平的:The road is ～.道路崎岖不平。❷ not gentle;rude 粗暴的:Don't be so ～ to her.不要对她那么粗暴。 Ⅱ *n.*a violent,noisy man 粗野好斗的人 Ⅲ *v.*make untidy or uneven 使变粗糙:Ten years of hard work ～ed Mathilde's hands.十年艰苦的劳作使玛蒂尔德的双手变粗糙了。

roughly /ˈrʌfli/
adv. ❶ in a rough manner 粗暴地;凶暴地 ❷ approximately 粗略地;大体上,大约

round /raʊnd/
Ⅰ *prep.* so as to enclose,surround,etc. 在周围:They sat ~ the fire. 他们围坐在火旁。Ⅱ *adv.* on all sides;in circular motion 在四周:The Emperor turned ~ and ~ before the mirror. 皇帝在镜子前转了一圈又一圈。Ⅲ *adj.* shaped like a ball,circle or ring 圆形的:Her face is ~. 她的脸圆圆的。Ⅳ *v.* make round 使成圆形:He ~ed his lips and gave a sharp whistle. 他撮起嘴唇使劲吹了一声口哨。

roundabout /ˈraʊndəbaʊt/
Ⅰ *n.* a circular piece of ground where several roads meet, and round which traffic must travel 道路交叉处的环行路 Ⅱ *adj.* not direct 间接的,兜圈子的:I heard the news in a ~ way. 这条消息我是间接听到的。

rouse /raʊz/
v. ❶ wake up;cause to be more active,interested or excited 唤醒;叫醒;激励;激动:~ someone to action 鼓励某人行动起来 /rousing cheers 令人激动的欢呼声 ❷ stop being inactive and start doing sth. 使振作:~ up 奋起;打起精神

route /ruːt/
Ⅰ *n.* a way or course to travel from one place to another 路线;路程;航线:the shortest ~ 最短的路线 /an air ~ 航空路线 /My ~ lay through a forest. 我的路线经过森林。Ⅱ *v.* plan a route for 给……定路线:We were ~d to France by way of Dover. 我们被指定要经过多佛前往法国。

routine /ruːˈtiːn/
Ⅰ *n.* a fixed regular way of doing sth. 惯例:According to ~, you should come at 8. 按惯例你应该 8 点钟赶到。Ⅱ *adj.* usual;ordinary 例行的

row¹ /rəʊ/
n. a number of things or people arranged

a line 一行,一排:two ~s of houses 两排房子/They were sitting in a ~. 他们坐成一排。

row² /rəʊ/
Ⅰ *v.* ❶ move (a boat) using oars 划船:~ to the island 划到岛上去 /We ~ed a boat in the river. 我们在河里划船。❷ carry in a rowboat 摆渡:Shall I ~ you home? 我划船送你回家好吗? Ⅱ *n.* (a ~) a trip in a rowing boat 划船游览:Come for a ~! 来坐船游览吧!

royal /ˈrɔɪəl/
adj. ❶ of or concerning a king or queen 皇家的,王室的:the ~ family 王室/His Royal Highness Prince Charles 查尔斯王子殿下 ❷ magnificent;splendid 盛大的,极大的,庄严的:a ~ feast 盛大宴会

royalty /ˈrɔɪəlti/
n. ❶ people of the royal family 王族,皇亲:The commands of ~ must be obeyed. 皇亲的命令必须遵守。❷ a payment made to a writer, recording artist, etc. for every book, record, etc. 专利权税,版税:The writer gets a 10% ~ on each copy of his book. 作者可以从每本书中得到 10% 的版税。

rub /rʌb/
Ⅰ *v.* (-bb-) ❶ move one thing back and forth against another, or on the surface; make clean or dry by doing this 擦;搓;摩擦:~ one's face with a towel 用毛巾擦脸 /~ the glasses with a cloth 用布擦玻璃杯 /~ one's hands together 搓手 ❷ cause irritation by rubbing 擦伤;擦破:~ a hole in one's elbow 胳膊肘上磨出一个洞 /get one's arm ~bed sore 手臂擦痛了 Ⅱ *n.* ❶ the act of rubbing a surface 摩擦;磨损:give the table a good ~ 把桌子好好擦一擦 ❷ difficulty; a point at which doubt arises 难点;要点:Here is the ~. 难点就在这里。

rubber /ˈrʌbə(r)/
n. ❶ a strong elastic substance made from the juice of certain plants 橡胶:Tyres are made of ~. 轮胎是用橡胶制成的。❷ a piece of rubber used to remove pencil marks, etc. 橡皮擦:Rub out the pencil

marks with a ～.用橡皮擦把这些铅笔字迹擦掉。

rubbish/'rʌbɪʃ/

*n.*❶waste stuff of no use 垃圾,废物:Our ～ is taken away twice a week.我们的垃圾一周清运两次。❷ silly words or thoughts;nonsense 废话;无聊的想法:Don't talk ～! 别讲废话!

ruby/'ru:bi/

*n.*❶ a clear,hard and red precious stone 红宝石:She is wearing a ring set with rubies.她戴着一枚镶有红宝石的戒指。❷ the colour of this stone;a deep red colour 红宝石色:a ～ dress 一件红宝石色衣服

rucksack/'rʌksæk/

n. a bag carried on the back, used when walking long distances,etc.(远足用的)背包

rudder/'rʌdə(r)/

n. a movable flat piece of wood or metal at the back of a boat,used to guide or steer it (船)舵

ruddy/'rʌdi/

adj. looking red and healthy 红润的;气色好的:～ cheeks 红润的面颊

rude/ru:d/

*adj.*❶ rough;impolite 粗鲁无礼:It's bad manners to be ～ to others.对人粗鲁是不礼貌的。❷ primitive;roughly made;simple;in the nature state 粗陋的;简陋的:He made a ～ bed for the night. 他搭了一个简陋的床准备过夜。

rudiment/'ru:dɪmənt/

n. (usually *pl.*) first things to be learnt in a subject 初阶;基础;入门:the ～s of chemistry 化学入门 ‖ ～ary/ˌru:dɪ'mentəri/*adj.*初步的;简单的;基本的:a few ～ary facts 一些基本事实

ruffle/'rʌfl/

Ⅰ*v.* move the smooth surface and make uneven 使不平整;弄皱:The wind ～d the surface of the lake.风使湖面出现了波纹。Ⅱ*n.* a strip of material gathered into folds, used to ornament a garment at the wrist,neck or breast 皱褶

rug/rʌg/

*n.*❶ a piece of covering for a floor(usually made of wool or animal skin)(通常为毛织或兽皮制的)地毯 ❷ a thick,warm piece of material which can be put over the legs when travelling, etc.(旅行等时候围膝用的)围毯

rugby/'rʌgbi/

n. a kind of football in which the ball, which is oval-shaped, can be touched by the hands as well as the feet 英式橄榄球

rugged/'rʌgɪd/

*adj.*❶ uneven,rough;having furrows or wrinkles 崎岖不平的;有皱纹的:～ hills 起伏的群山 /a ～ path through the mountains 崎岖的山路 ❷ not gentle or refined 粗鲁的;粗暴的;严肃的:～ manner 粗鲁而朴实的态度 ❸ (of a person or his character) rough but strong 结实的;强壮的:a ～ good looking man 彪形大汉 ❹ (of sound) unpleasant to hear (声音)刺耳的;难听的 ❺ (of climate) stormy (气候)恶劣的

ruin/'ru:ɪn/

Ⅰ*v.* destroy or damage sth. that it loses its value,etc. 毁坏,毁掉:The flood ～ed the crops.洪水毁掉了庄稼。Ⅱ*n.* an extreme damage;the state of being decayed,destroyed or collapsed 毁灭;破坏;没落:Drugging led to his ～.吸毒导致了他的毁灭。

rule/ru:l/

Ⅰ*n.*❶ a law or statement which guides or controls behavior or action 规则:We must obey the ～.我们应该遵守规则。❷ the government or control of a country or a group of people,etc.管理;统治:Under the cruel ～ of the governor, people lived a miserable life.在统治者的残酷统治下,人们过着悲惨的生活。Ⅱ*v.*❶ control;govern;have authority (over) 统治:An emperor is a monarch who ～s over an empire.皇帝是统治一个帝国的君主。❷(especially in law) give an official decision (on) (尤指在法律上)判定,裁定

ruler/'ru:lə/

*n.*❶a person who governs 统治者;管理者;支配者 ❷a straight strip of wood or metal, etc. used for measuring or for drawing straight lines 尺,直尺;刻线板

ruling/ˈruːlɪŋ/

Ⅰ *adj.* ❶ exercising control or authority 统治的;主导的;支配的:the ～ class 统治阶级 /the ～ ideas 主导思想 ❷ predominant 主要的;普遍的:the ～ price 市价 Ⅱ *n.* an official decision 裁定;裁决:give (make) ～s 做出判决 /accept the ～ 接受判决

rumble/ˈrʌmbl/

Ⅰ *v.* (cause to) make rumbling sounds (使)发出隆隆的响声:gunfire rumbling in the distance 远方发出隆隆的炮火声 Ⅱ *n.* a rumbling sound 隆隆声:the ～ of thunder 雷声隆隆

rumo(u)r/ˈruːmə(r)/

Ⅰ *n.* a story which people are repeating, which may not be true 谣言;传闻:Rumour has it that the president is coming to visit our school.据传闻,总统要来访问我们的学校。/ I have heard some ～s that you are going to leave.我听到一些谣传,说你打算离开。 Ⅱ *v.* (usually passive)be reported as a rumour (常用被动语态)谣传:It is ～ed that you are going to leave.听说,你打算离开。

run/rʌn/

Ⅰ *v.* (ran, run) ❶ go on with quick steps 跑:He ran as fast as he could to the station.他尽快向车站跑去。 ❷ go away in a hurry;escape 逃,逃跑:As soon as the hunter appeared,the hare ran off.猎人一露面,野兔都逃跑了。 ❸ (of a car,train,ship,etc.) be moved or driven 行驶:The train ～s at a speed of 60 kilometres an hour.火车以每小时 60 千米的速度行驶。 ❹ be in charge of or organize a business or an activity 经营:He ～s a big company in Hong Kong.他在香港经营一家大公司。 Ⅱ *n.* ❶ an act or period of running on foot 跑;跑步:go for a ～去跑步 ❷ the instance or period of travelling by car,train,etc.路程;短期旅行:It's a long ～ from here to Shenzhen.从这里到深圳路途挺远。 ❸ a space for domestic animals,fowls 饲养场:a chicken ～ 养鸡场

❹ a point scored in the game of cricket or baseball (板球或棒球)一分:score (make) 10 ～s 得十分

runaway/ˈrʌnəweɪ/

n. a person,horse,etc.that runs away 逃跑者;脱缰的马

runner/ˈrʌnə(r)/

n. ❶ a person who runs;an animal or vehicle that runs 赛跑的人(或动物、车辆):a long-distance ～ 长跑运动员 ❷ a messenger;a salesperson 通信员;使者;推销员 ❸ a person who operates machines (机器的)操作者 ❹ the blade of a skate (溜冰鞋的)冰刀 ❺ (of curtain) part on which sth. slides or moves along (窗帘的)滑圈 ❻ one of the stems with which a plant (like the strawberry) spreads itself along the ground 蔓藤植物:strawberry ～s 草莓匍茎

running/ˈrʌnɪŋ/

Ⅰ *n.* an act of sb. or sth. that runs 跑;奔跑 Ⅱ *adj.* ❶ done while running 边跑边做的 ❷ without a break;continuous 连续的;不断的:give a ～ commentary 连续评说/for three nights ～ 连续三夜 ❸ flowing 流动的:hot and cold ～ water 冷热自来水

runway/ˈrʌnweɪ/

n. an area of hard surface in an airfield on which planes land and take off (机场)跑道

rupture/ˈrʌptʃə(r)/

Ⅰ *n.* the state of being torn or burst open 断裂;破裂:What caused the ～ of the friendship between the two nations? 是什么使得两国间的友谊破裂? Ⅱ *v.* cause to break or tear 使破裂:What ～d their friendship? 什么东西使他们的友谊破裂了?

rural/ˈruərəl/

adj. connected with the country 农村的;乡村的:a ～ area 农村地区

rush/rʌʃ/

Ⅰ *v.* ❶ move suddenly and hastily in the stated direction 冲,猛跑:Fools ～ in where angels fear to tread.蠢人爱鲁莽行

事。/Out ～ed the boy.那男孩冲了出来。❷ do（sth.）as soon as possible 急着做，赶忙做：Don't ～,we have plenty of time.别急，我们还有足够的时间。❸take sb.or sth. to a place quickly 迅速送往：They ～ed some medical workers to the front.他们急忙把医务人员送往前线。Ⅱ n.❶ a rapid, headlong movement；a sudden swift advance 冲：He made a ～ for the ball.他向球猛冲过去。❷ a situation in which you need to go somewhere or do sth. very quickly 匆忙：He was always in a ～.他总是匆匆忙忙的。Ⅲ adj.hasty or busy 忙碌的

rust /rʌst/

Ⅰ n. reddish-brown coating formed on iron by the action of water and air；the colour of this 锈：The machine was covered with ～.机器上生满了锈。Ⅱ v. become covered with rust 生锈：The lock has ～ed.这把锁生锈了。

rustic /'rʌstɪk/

Ⅰ adj.❶ connected with countryside 农村的 ❷ simple；unaffected 质朴的：～ simplicity 淳朴 ❸ backward and provincial 落后的；土气的：～ manner 土头土脑的样子 ❹ of rough workmanship 制作粗糙的：a ～ bridge 质量不好的桥 Ⅱ n.a peasant；a countryman 庄稼人；乡下人

rustle /'rʌsl/

Ⅰ n.a soft sound, like the sound leaves make in the wind（似风吹动叶子的）沙沙响声：the ～ of leaves 树叶的飒飒声/the ～ of a skirt 裙子的窸窣声 Ⅱ v.❶ make this sound 发出沙沙声 ❷ cause sth. to make this sound 使发出沙沙声：～ papers 把文件弄得沙沙作响

rusty /'rʌsti/

adj.❶affected with rust 生锈的 ❷rust-coloured 铁锈色的 ❸weakened by lack of use or practice 荒废的；生疏的：My French is a bit ～.我的法语有些生疏了。❹(of a voice) croaking（声音）沙哑的 ‖ **rustiness** n.生锈；声音嘶哑

rut /rʌt/

n.a track made in soft ground by a wheel 车辙；车印 ‖ get into a ～ 因循守旧：If you stay in the same place too long, you can get into a ～.如果你老待在一个地方,那你可能会因循守旧。

ruthless /'ruːθlɪs/

adj.without mercy or kind feelings；having no pity 残忍的；冷酷的；无情的：a ～ enemy 残酷的敌人

R

Ss

sabre(-er) /ˈseɪbə(r)/

　　n. ❶a heavy military sword with a curved blade used in former times（刀身微弯的）马刀，军刀 ❷a light sharp-pointed sword with one sharp edge used in fencing（击剑用的）长剑，佩剑

sac /sæk/

　　n. a bag-like cavity in an animal or plant, especially filled with liquid 囊；液囊

sack[1] /sæk/

　　Ⅰ *n.* ❶ a large bag made of strong material 麻袋；袋：a ~ of potatoes 一袋土豆 ❷dismissal from employment 解雇；give sb. the ~ 解雇某人／get the ~ for being lazy 因懒惰被解雇 Ⅱ *v.* ❶dismiss sb. from employment 解雇；开除：If he is late again，~ him. 他要是再迟到，就开除他。❷ place in a bag 把……装袋：~ rice 把大米装入袋中

sack[2] /sæk/

　　n. the act of stealing or destroying sth. 洗劫；抢夺：The citizens lost everything they had during the ~ of the town. 在城市被洗劫时，市民们失去了他们所有的一切。

sackful /ˈsækful/

　　n. (*pl.* ~s) the amount that a sack will hold 一大袋（的量）：a ~ of rice 满满一袋大米

sacred /ˈseɪkrɪd/

　　adj. ❶ of God；connected with religion 神圣的；宗教的：a ~ thing 宗教圣物 ❷ solemn 严肃的；郑重的：The local people regard cattle as a ~ animal. 当地人将牛视为一种神圣的动物。‖ **hold a promise** ~ 信守诺言‖~**ly** *adv.* 神圣地；庄重地／~**ness** *n.* 神圣；受人尊敬

sacrifice /ˈsækrɪfaɪs/

　　Ⅰ *n.* the offering of sth. precious to a god or the thing offered 供奉；献祭，牺牲：Quite a few people would rather give their life as a ~ for their motherland. 不少人愿意为自己的祖国而献出自己的生命。Ⅱ *v.* give up sth. that is important to you for another person 献祭；牺牲：Anyhow，I'd like to ~ money for fame. 不管怎样，我愿舍利求名。

sacrilege /ˈsækrɪlɪdʒ/

　　n. an act of being disrespectful to a holy person or thing 亵渎神圣：guilty of ~ 犯亵渎神圣的罪／It is (a) ~ to steal a crucifix from an altar. 从圣坛窃取耶稣受难像是亵渎神灵的行为。

sad /sæd/

　　adj. unhappy；causing unhappy feelings 悲哀的；忧伤的；引起悲伤的：Tom was ~ because he didn't pass the examination. 汤姆很伤心，他的考试没及格。

sadden /ˈsædn/

　　v. make sb. sad 使悲伤，使伤心；使难过：Fans were ~ed to see their team play so badly. 看到自己的球队表现如此差劲，球迷感到难过。

saddle /ˈsædl/

　　n. ❶ a seat for a rider on a horse, donkey, bicycle, etc. 鞍座 ❷ a line or ridge of high land rising at each end to a high point 鞍状地形

saddlebag /ˈsædlbæg/

　　n. ❶either of a joined pair of bags placed over an animal's back so that one hangs on each side below a saddle 鞍囊，马褡子 ❷a bag fixed to bicycle, motorcycle, etc., behind the seat or in a pair over the back wheel（脚踏车、摩托车等车座后的）挂包，工具包

saddler /ˈsædlə(r)/

　　n. a maker of saddles and other leather articles for horses 鞍匠；马具工

saddlery /'sædləri/

n. ❶ goods made by a saddler 马具；鞍具 ❷ a saddler's shop 马具店

sadness /'sædnɪs/

n. the feeling of being sad 悲伤；悲痛；难过：I felt a deep ～. 我感到深深的悲痛。

safe /seɪf/

Ⅰ *adj.* ❶ free from or protected from danger 安全的：You're quite ～ in your uncle's. 在你叔叔那里你会很安全的。 ❷ of very little risk of loss or failure 风险小的；稳妥的：a ～ investment 小风险投资 Ⅱ *n.* a strong box in which money and other valuables are kept 保险箱

safeguard /'sefgɑːd/

Ⅰ *n.* anything that serves as a protection from harm, risk or danger 防护措施；防护器：Keeping clean is a ～ against disease. 保持清洁是一种防病措施。 Ⅱ *v.* protect; keep safe; guard against hurt, danger or attack 保护，保卫，防护：They will press for international action to ～ the ozone layer. 他们将竭力要求国际行动来保护臭氧层。

safety /'seɪfti/

n. the state of being safe; the state of freeing from danger 安全；保险；平安；稳妥：～ measures 安全措施／～ in production 安全生产／She led the children to a place of ～. 她把孩子们带到安全的地方。

sage /seɪdʒ/

Ⅰ *n.* a very wise man 哲人，贤人，智者 Ⅱ *adj.* having or showing wisdom or good judgement 睿智的；贤明的；精明的 ‖ ～**ly** *adv.* 贤明地／～**ness** /'seɪdʒnɪs/ *n.* 贤明

sail /seɪl/

Ⅰ *n.* ❶ a sheet of large cloth used to catch the wind and move a boat 帆 ❷ a sailing ship 船 ❸ a voyage by ship 航行：go for a ～ 乘船游玩 Ⅱ *v.* ❶ move over the sea, a lake, , etc. 横渡（海或湖等）❷ direct a boat with sails 驾船；扬帆航行：There are five seamen ～ing the ship. 有五个海员驾驶着这条船。

sailboard /'seɪlbɔːd/

n. a flat floating board with a sail fixed to

it which is used by one person standing up in the sport of windsurfing （滑浪用的）风帆滑水板，帆板

sailing /'seɪlɪŋ/

n. ❶ the skill of directing the course of a ship 航海术 ❷ the sport of riding in or directing a small boat with sails 帆船运动 ❸ an occasion of a ship leaving a port 开船，起航，出航：When is the next ～ to Ostend? 下一班开往奥斯坦德的轮船什么时候起航？

sailor /'seɪlə(r)/

n. a member of a ship's crew; seaman 船员，水手，海员：I want to be a ～. 我想当一名水手。 ‖ good ～ *n.* 不晕船的人：I'm not a good ～. 我晕船。

saint /seɪt, sənt/

n. a person acknowledged as holy or virtuous, because of the way they have lived and died 圣人，道德高尚的人

sake /seɪk/

n. cause; aim; purpose 理由；目的：for your ～ 为了你／for the ～ of convenience 为了方便起见

salad /'sæləd/

n. a dish usually consisting of raw green vegetables tossed with a dressing 沙拉（西餐中的一种凉拌菜）：vegetable ～ 蔬菜沙拉／chicken ～ 凉拌鸡肉

salary /'sæləri/

n. a fixed payment for regular work 薪水：He is now working in a firm with a good ～. 他现在在一家公司工作，薪水很高。

sale /seɪl/

n. ❶ the act of selling things 出售：Winter clothes will be on ～ next week. 下周将进行冬季服装展销。 ❷ the act of selling at lower prices 廉价出售；贱卖：Sales of art books have been down recently. 最近艺术类书籍一直销售量很低。

salient /'seɪliənt/

adj. easily seen or noticed; most important 显著的；惹人注目的；最重要的：the ～ points of a speech 一篇演说的要点

saliva /sə'laɪvə/

n. a liquid that comes into the mouth to help chewing, etc. 唾液

sallow/'sæləʊ/

adj.(of complexion) pale yellowish colour (肤色)灰黄的

sally/'sæli/

Ⅰ *n.* ❶ a sudden breakout by soldiers who are surrounded by the enemy (被围士兵的)突围,出击:a successful ～ 发动一次成功的突围 ❷ a lively, witty remark, especially one that is a good-humoured attack on sb.or sth.俏皮话;妙语(尤指善意批评某人或某事的话语):She continued her story undisturbed by the merry sallies of her hearers.她继续讲她的故事,毫不为听众的笑谈所扰乱。Ⅱ *v.* ❶ break out from a defensive position suddenly 突围:～ out against the besiegers 出击围攻者 ❷ go out on a journey or for a walk 外出散步;外出:～ forth at dawn 拂晓出发

salmon/'sæmən/

n.(*pl.* salmon or ～s) ❶ a large silver-coloured fish, valued for food 鲑鱼;大马哈鱼:Many ～ were hovering.许多鲑鱼游来游去。 ❷ the colour of its flesh;orange-pink 粉橙色;橙红色

salon/'sælɒn/

n. ❶ an elegant drawing room 豪华大客厅 ❷ an assemblage of persons, usually of social or intellectual distinction, who frequent the home of a particular person (社交家或知识界名人的)联谊会,沙龙:a literary ～ 文学沙龙

saloon/sə'luːn/

n. ❶ a room for social use in a ship, hotel, etc.(轮船、旅馆等的)大厅,会客室:the ship's dining ～ 轮船上的餐厅 / the ～ bar 酒店或客栈的卖酒处 ❷ a public room for a specified use (有特殊用途的)公共大厅:a dancing ～ 跳舞场 / a hairdressing ～ 理发厅 ❸ a place where alcoholic drinks may be bought and drunk 〈美〉酒馆 ❹ a car with wholly enclosed seating space for 4～7 passengers (可供4到7人乘坐的)大轿车

salt/sɔːlt/

Ⅰ *n.* ❶ a kind of white powder which has the taste of sea water 盐:common (ta-

ble)～ 食盐(精盐)/ rock ～ 岩盐 / Pass me the ～ and pepper,please.请把盐和胡椒递给我。 ❷ a chemical compound of a metal and an acid 金属和酸的化合物;盐化物 ❸ an experienced sailor 有经验的水手:a ～ 有经验的海员 / an old ～ 老水手 Ⅱ *v.*give salt to;preserved with salt 给……加盐;用盐腌:～ed meat 腌肉 Ⅲ *adj.*containing,full of or tasting of salt;salty 盐的,含盐分的:～ water 盐水

saltcellar/'sɔːltselə(r)/

*n.*a container for salt at meals,especially a small pot with usually one hole in the top for shaking salt out (盖子上有小孔的)盐瓶

saltpan/'sɔːltpæn/

*n.*a natural or artificial hollow place from which salt water dries up leaving a surface of salt (天然或人工的)盐田,晒盐池

saltwater/'sɔːltwɔːtə(r)/

*adj.*of or living in salty water or the sea 咸水的;海水的;生于海水中的:～ plants 咸水中生长的植物

salty/'sɔːlti/

adj. ❶of, containing, or tasting of salt 盐的;含盐的;咸的:This soup's too ～.这汤太咸了。 ❷(of talk, stories, etc.) slightly improper in an amusing or exciting way;racy(讲话、故事等)略带猥亵意味的;不大正经的;粗俗的:～ humour 有点儿下流的幽默

salute/sə'luːt/

Ⅰ *n.*a formal greeting of respect 行礼;致敬:Salute to those who have made great contributions to our country's modernization.向那些为我们国家现代化做出巨大贡献的人致敬。Ⅱ *v.*❶greet in a friendly way 致意;打招呼 ❷ show or state the admiration for sb. or their achievements 对……表示敬意

salvage/'sælvɪdʒ/

Ⅰ *n.*❶the act of saving things from damage or danger 海上抢救;打捞:There is little hope of her ～.她获救的希望甚微。 ❷ the property be saved 抢救出的财物:a sale of ～ from the wreck 拍卖由沉船打捞得到的货物 ❸waste material that can be used again after being processed（加工后可再用的）废品 Ⅱ *v.* save a sick or wounded person, etc. 救治；抢救：The doctors succeeded in salvaging the patients.医生们成功地抢救了病人。

salvation/sæl'veɪʃn/
*n.*❶ the act of saving; the state of having been saved from sin and its consequences 超度；拯救；救世：Salvation Army 救世军 ❷ the state of being saved or preserved from harm, loss, disaster, etc.解救；拯救；救助：You must work out your own ～.你必须谋求自救之道。

salve/sælv/
Ⅰ *n.* an oily substance used on wounds, sores, or burns 药膏；软膏：lip ～ 唇膏 Ⅱ *v.*❶ put salve to 敷药膏 ❷ soothe 安慰；缓和：～ one's conscience by giving stolen money to charity 把偷来的钱用于救济以安慰良心

salver/'sælvə(r)/
n. a large metal plate for serving food, drink, etc., especially at a formal meal（尤指正式宴会时用的）金属托盘；大盘子：a silver ～ 银制托盘

samba/'sæmbə/
n.（a piece of music for）a quick dance of Brazilian origin（源自巴西的）桑巴舞（曲）

same/seɪm/
Ⅰ *adj.* being one person or thing; alike in every way 同一的；同样的：We have the ～ kind of bicycles.我们的自行车是同种类型的。Ⅱ *pron.* the same thing 同一事物：You must do the ～.你必须照样做。

sameness/'seɪmnɪs/
n. ❶ the state of being the same; very close likeness; similarity 同一；同样；相似 ❷ the quality of wearisome constancy, routine, and lack of variety 千篇一律，单调：Don't you ever get tired of the ～ of the work in this office? 你难道对这办公室的单调工作从不感到厌倦吗？

samey/'seɪmi/
adj. dull because lacking in variety 单调乏味的，无变化的：His novels tend to be very ～.他写的小说往往非常单调乏味。

sampan/'sæmpæn/
n. a light flat-bottomed boat used along the coasts and rivers in China and Southeast Asia（中国或东南亚沿海和内河地区用的）舢板

sample/'sɑːmpl/
Ⅰ *n.* a part to show what the whole is like 标本；样品：This is a ～ car, it is not for sale.这是样品车，不出售。Ⅱ *v.* take a sample（samples）of; taste a small amount of food or drink 品尝：You can ～ it before you buy the chocolate.买巧克力之前，你可以先品尝一下。

sampling /'sɑːmplɪŋ/
*n.*❶ the taking of a sample or samples 取样，抽样，采样 ❷ a sample 样板，试样

sanctify/'sæŋktɪfaɪ/
v. make holy by means of religious rites 使神圣；使圣洁

sanction/'sæŋkʃn/
*n.*❶ the right or permission given by authority to do sth. 许可；批准：You cannot do it without the ～ of the manager.未得经理允许，你不能做这件事。❷（usually *pl.*）measures taken by countries to restrict trade and official contact with a country that has broken international law 制裁

sanctity/'sæŋktəti/
n. the state or quality of being holy or sacred 神圣；圣洁：His life was famous for ～.他的一生以圣洁闻名。

sanctuary/'sæŋktʃʊəri/
*n.*❶ a holy or sacred place, especially a church or temple 圣所；圣地；（尤指）教堂，寺院 ❷ a place of refuge 庇护所；避难所：a ～ of political refugees 政治犯的庇护所 ❸ an area where birds are protected by law 鸟类保护区

sand/sænd/
Ⅰ *n.*❶ tiny grains of crushed or worn-down rock 沙，沙子 ❷（*pl.*）a wide area of sand 沙滩；沙地：playing on the ～s 在沙滩上玩 Ⅱ *v.* cover or sprinkle with sand 撒沙于；铺沙于：The roads were ～ed after the storm.暴风雨过后路面上铺满了沙子。

sandal/ˈsændl/

*n.*open shoes that can be put on easily 凉鞋;草鞋;便鞋:plastic ～s 塑料凉鞋/straw ～s 草鞋

sandwich/ˈsænwɪdʒ/

Ⅰ *n.* two slices of bread with meat,cheese,etc.between them 三明治;夹心面包:ham ～ 火腿三明治 / chicken ～ 鸡肉三明治 Ⅱ *v.* put sth.between two others 紧夹(某物)于中间;插入(某物):I was ～ed (in) between two fat men.我被夹在两个胖子之间。

sandy/ˈsændi/

adj.(sandier, sandiest)❶ containing sand;filled or covered with sand 沙的,含沙的,多沙的:～ land 沙质地 ❷ yellowish red 黄中带红的,沙色的:She is a ～ haired girl.她有着一头沙色头发。

sane/seɪn/

*adj.*❶ healthy in mind;not mad 精神健康的;神志清楚的:He seemed perfectly ～.他看起来心智非常健全。❷ reasonable and sensible 理智的;合乎情理的:a ～ policy 理智的政策/a ～ proposal 合情合理的建议

sanitary/ˈsænɪtri/

*adj.*❶clean 清洁的:～ conditions 清洁状况 ❷ of,concerned with the protection of health 卫生的;保健的:a ～ inspector 卫生检查官员 /～ engineering 卫生工程学

sanitation/ˌsænɪˈteɪʃn/

*n.*arrangements to protect health 卫生;卫生设备(尤指下水道设备)

sanity /ˈsænɪti/

*n.*the state of being sane 明智;理智;通情达理

Santa Claus/ˌsæntə ˈklɔːz/

*n.*a person who, small children are told, puts toys in their stockings by night at Christmas 圣诞老人

sapphire/ˈsæfaɪə(r)/

*n.*a clear,blue and precious stone 蓝宝石

sarcasm/ˈsɑːkæzm/

*n.*❶ bitter remarks often intended to hurt someone's feelings 讽刺话;挖苦话 ❷ an act of making this kind of remark 讽刺;挖苦

sardine/sɑːˈdiːn/

*n.*a type of small sea fish (often preserved in oil in a tin and eaten as food) 沙丁鱼(常用油浸泡做成罐头食品)

sardonic/sɑːˈdɒnɪk/

*adj.*scornful;mocking 嘲笑的;冷笑的:a ～ smile 冷笑

sash/sæʃ/

n. a broad strip of cloth worn over the shoulder or round the waist 肩带;腰带

Satan/ˈseɪtn/

*n.*the Evil One;the Devil 撒旦,恶魔

satellite/ˈsætɪlaɪt/

*n.*❶a smaller body that revolves around a planet 卫星:The Moon is a ～ of the Earth.月球是地球的卫星。❷ a man-made object fired into space round the Earth 人造地球卫星:China launched a communications ～ yesterday. 中国昨天发射了一颗人造通信卫星。❸a state controlled by a more powerful neighbouring 卫星国 ❹a follower or attendant upon a person of importance 仆从

satin/ˈsætɪn/

Ⅰ *n.*a type of cloth with a smooth shiny surface 缎:figured ～ 花缎 Ⅱ *adj.*of satin;smooth like satin 缎子做的;光滑如缎的:a ～ bed cover 一床缎质床罩

satire/ˈsætaɪə(r)/

*n.*❶(a work of) literature,theatre,etc.intended to show the foolishness or evil of some person,organization,or practice in an amusing way 讽刺作品;讽刺文学:There is always sharp ～ in his writing. 他的作品中总有一种尖锐的讥刺。❷ a piece of writing that does this 讽刺文

satisfaction/ˌsætɪsˈfækʃn/

*n.*❶ the act of satisfying or the state of being satisfied 满足:The ～ of hunger requires food.充饥需要食物。❷pleasure or contentment 满意,称心:Your success gives me great ～.你的成功让我非常满意。

satisfactory/ˌsætɪsˈfæktəri/

*adj.*good enough for a purpose;giving satisfaction 良好的;令人满意的;圆满的:a ～ result 令人满意的结果 /His re-

S

ply was not ~.他的答复不令人满意。/ We want a ~ reason for your failure to help.我们要知道你未能协助的合理理由。

satisfied /'sætɪsfaɪd/
adj. contented or pleased because you have got or achieved sth.满意的;满足的: ~ customers 满意的顾客/ I was very ~ with the results.我对这结果非常满意。

satisfy /'sætɪsfaɪ/
v.make contented;give sb. what he wants or needs 使满意;使满足: The teacher is satisfied with your homework. 老师对你的家庭作业感到满意。

saturate /'sætʃəreɪt/
v.❶ put as much liquid as possible into; make completely wet 湿透: be ~d with history 精通历史 ❷put as much of a solid substance as possible into (a chemical solution) 饱和 ‖ ~d *adj*.饱和的

Saturday /'sætədi/
n.the day after Friday and before Sunday in a week 星期六: We have no school on ~.星期六我们不上学。

Saturn /'sætən/
n.the 6th planet from the sun 土星: the ~'s rings 土星环

sauce /sɔːs/
Ⅰ*n*.❶liquid preparation served with food to give flavor 酱油;调味汁;brandy ~ 白兰地调味汁/tomato ~ 番茄酱/ soy (soybean) ~ 酱油/apple ~ 苹果酱/ roast lamb and mint ~ 烤小羊肉和薄荷酱 ❷ talk or behaviour that is annoying or impudent 无礼;莽撞;None of your ~,my girl! 我的孩子,不要无礼。Ⅱ*v*. be impudent to 对……无礼: How dare you ~ your grandfather! 你怎么敢对爷爷无礼!

saucer /'sɔːsə(r)/
n.a small,curved plate on which a cup is placed 茶杯托;茶碟

sauna /'sɔːnə,'saʊnə/
n.❶ a small room used as a hot-air or steam bath for cleaning and refreshing the body 桑拿浴室 ❷ a steam bath in such a room 蒸汽浴,桑拿浴

saunter /'sɔːntə(r)/
Ⅰ*v*.walk leisurely 闲逛;漫步: ~ along Oxford Street looking at the shop windows 沿牛津街漫步,看商店的橱窗 /~ through life 逍遥一生 Ⅱ*n*.a quiet, unhurried walk or pace 闲逛;漫步;come at a ~ 漫步走来 /Let's go for a ~ in the park.咱们去公园走走吧。

sausage /'sɒsɪdʒ/
n.chopped meat cooked in a tube of thin skin 香肠;腊肠: ~ roll 腊肠卷

savage /'sævɪdʒ/
Ⅰ*adj*.❶in an uncivilized state 野蛮的;未开化的: ~ people 野蛮人 /~ customs 野蛮的习俗 / a ~ tribe 野蛮部落 ❷ fierce;cruel 凶猛的;残酷的:a ~ dog 凶犬/ ~ criticism 猛烈的批评 / a ~ blow 猛烈的打击/ make a ~ attack on sb. 猛烈攻击某人 ❸ out of temper 愤怒的:as ~ as a meat axe 暴跳如雷 / Her rudeness really made me ~.她的无礼使我大怒。Ⅱ*n*.❶ a person who belongs to a tribe that is simple and not developed;a cruel person 野蛮的人;残酷的人: He killed two persons,he was a real ~.他杀死两人,真是个残酷的人。❷a member of a people regarded as primitive and uncivilized 原始人;未开化的人;野蛮人

save /seɪv/
Ⅰ*v*.❶ make or keep safe from loss,injury, etc. 挽救;拯救: The young man plunged into the river to ~ the drowning boy.那个年轻人跳入河中去救那个快被淹死的小男孩。❷ store up;keep for future use 储存: He worked hard to ~ enough money for travelling. 他努力工作,以存足钱去旅游。❸ avoid wasting or using more than necessary 省去;节省 Ⅱ*prep*.except 除……之外:All people ~ the teacher went there.除老师外,所有的人都去了那里。

saving /'seɪvɪŋ/
n.❶ an act or way of using less money, time,etc. 节约,节省:It's a great ~ to be able to make one's own clothes. 自己会做衣服可以节省一大笔。❷ the amount of money saved up 存款:The ~s deposits rise steadily.储蓄存款稳步上升。

savio(u)r/'seɪvɪə(r)/

n. ❶ a person who rescues or saves sb. from danger or loss 拯救者；救助者 ❷ (in the Christian religion) Jesus Christ (基督教中) 救世主；耶稣基督

savo(u)r/'seɪvə(r)/

Ⅰ *n.* a taste or smell；a flavor 味道：have a strong ~ of pepper 有很重的胡椒味 Ⅱ *v.* taste or smell with pleasure 品味；品尝……味道：Would you like to ~ this dish? 你愿尝尝这道菜吗？

saw/sɔː/

Ⅰ *n.* a type of tool with toothed edge, used for cutting wood, metal, etc. 锯；锯机 Ⅱ *v.* (sawed, sawn) use a saw to cut sth. 锯：~ wood 锯木 ‖ **~dust** *n.* 锯屑，锯末

saxophone/'sæksəfəʊn/

n. a metal musical instrument, played by blowing through reed and pressing finger keys 萨克斯管

say/seɪ/

Ⅰ *v.* (said) ❶ pronounce；speak；utter 说，讲：He said "yes". 他说了一声"是"。 ❷ express in words；tell；state；declare 用语言表达；告诉；陈述；宣称：He said nothing about it. 对这件事他什么也没有说。/She said that I was standing on her toe. 她说我踩着了她的脚趾。 ❸ indicate；show 表明；说明：What do these figures ~? 这些数字表示什么？/Her eyes said she was not satisfied with his answer. 她的眼神表明她对他的回答不满意。 ❹ suppose；assume 假设；比如说：Shall we meet again, ~, Sunday? 我们是不是再碰一次头，星期天怎么样？ ‖ **go without ~ing** 不言而喻，理所当然：It goes without ~ing that he will attend the meeting. 他当然会参加会议。/**not to ~** 近乎，甚至可以说：He sounded annoyed, not to ~ furious. 听起来他是生气了，甚至可以说是大发雷霆。/**that is to ~** 换句话说，即：She invited us to her birthday party on May Day, that is to ~, next Monday. 她邀请我们五一节，即下星期一，参加她的生日晚会。/**to ~ nothing of** 更不用说：She is a beautiful young woman, to ~ nothing of her kindness and generosity. 她是一位貌美的少妇，她的仁慈大方就更

不用说了。 Ⅱ *n.* the right or opportunity to state one's opinion 发言权，说话机会：Let him have his ~. 让他把话讲完。/Who has the final ~ in your family? 你家谁说了算？

saying/'seɪɪŋ/

n. ❶ a well-known statement that most people believe is wise；a proverb 名言，格言，谚语：As the ~ goes, "There's no smoke without fire." 正如谚语所说，"无风不起浪"。 ❷ the act of making a statement 说话：Saying and doing are two things. 说和做是两回事。

scab/skæb/

n. ❶ a crust that forms over a wound while it is healing 痂；疮疤 ❷ (informal) a person who works when other workers are on strike (非正式) 拒绝参加罢工的工人 ‖ **~by** *adj.* 结痂的

scabbard/'skæbəd/

n. a sheath for the blade of a sword or dagger (剑或匕首的) 鞘

scaffold/'skæfəʊld/

n. a high platform on which criminals are put to death 断头台；绞架

scaffolding/'skæfəldɪŋ/

n. a structure made up of poles put up at the side of a building which is being built, repaired, knocked down, etc. so that workmen can reach the different parts of the building easily (建筑用的) 脚手架

scalar/'skeɪlə(r)/

Ⅰ *adj.* ❶ in, on or of a scale 梯状的；分等级的 ❷ designating or of a quantity that has magnitude but no direction in space 纯量的；标量的；无向量的 Ⅱ *n.* a scalar quantity 无向量；标量；纯量

scald/skɔːld/

Ⅰ *v.* ❶ burn with hot liquid or stream 烫伤：He ~ed his hand with the hot water. 热水烫伤了他的手。 ❷ heat (a liquid, e.g. milk) almost to the point of boiling 加热，烫热：~ milk 加热牛奶 Ⅱ *n.* a burn from hot liquid or steam 烫伤：~s and burns 烫伤和烧伤

scale/skeɪl/

n. ❶ a set of regularly spaced marks made on sth. for use as a measure; a system of measurement 分度, 刻度, 标度, 尺度: This ruler has ～s in centimeters. 这把尺有厘米的刻度。❷ a set of numbers or standards for measuring or comparing 级别, 等级: a salary ～ 工资级别 ❸ a group of notes going up or down in order 音阶: The boy practises his ～s on the piano every day. 这男孩天天在钢琴上练习音阶。❹ the size of measurements on a map, etc. compared with the real size of sth. shown by it 比例, 缩尺: In a map drawn to the ～ of 1 : 50,000, one centimeter represents half a kilometer. 在一张按1 : 50000 的比例画的地图上, 1 厘米表示 0.5 千米。❺ the size of an activity 规模, 程度: They are making "patriot" missiles on a large ～. 他们正在大规模制造"爱国者"导弹。

scallop/'skɒləp/

Ⅰ *n.* ❶ a kind of edible shellfish with two deeply grooved and curved shells (一种壳上有深槽的可食用的) 扇贝 ❷ a single valve from the shell of a scallop 扇贝壳 ❸ (*pl.*) any of a series of curves, etc. forming an ornamental edge (装饰用的) 扇形边, 荷叶边 Ⅱ *v.* ❶ ornament with scallops 用扇形 (或荷叶) 边装饰 ❷ bake with sauce and bread crumbs (加酱汁和面包屑) 烘烤

scalp/skælp/

Ⅰ *n.* ❶ the skin of the head 头皮 ❷ used with reference to the defeat of an opponent 击败 Ⅱ *v.* ❶ cut the scalp off 剥去……头皮 ❷ buy and sell in order to make small profits on quick returns 〈美〉转手倒卖

scalpel/'skælpəl/

n. a small knife used by a surgeon 手术刀, 解剖刀

scamper/'skæmpə(r)/

v. run about quickly, as children or small animals do (孩子、小动物) 蹦蹦跳跳地跑, 奔跑: The children ～ed home. 孩子们蹦蹦跳跳地跑回家。/ The mouse ～ed away when it saw the cat. 老鼠看见猫就奔

逃了。

scan/skæn/

v. (-nn-) ❶ look at closely; examine with care 细看, 审视: The radar ～ned the sky for enemy planes. 雷达仔细搜索天空以便发现敌机。❷ look at quickly without careful reading 浏览, 粗略地看: He ～ned the newspaper while having his breakfast. 他一边吃早饭一边浏览报纸。❸ fit into a particular rhythm or metre 符合格律, 顿挫合拍: The verse ～s very well. 这首诗很合格律。

scandal/'skændl/

n. ❶ an unkind talk about sb. 诽谤; 中伤; 诋毁: You shouldn't spread ～. 你不应该散布流言蜚语。/ I heard a bit of ～ about your friend. 我听到一些关于诋毁你朋友的话。❷ an event or action that is thought morally or legally wrong and causes general public outrage 丑事, 丑闻: a bribery ～ 贿赂丑闻 ❸ the outrage or anger caused by such an event or action (由丑闻引起的) 反感, 愤慨: There was a tremendous ～ when it was revealed that some policemen had been accepting bribes. 一些警察接受贿赂的消息披露出来时, 激起极大的公愤。‖ ～ous *adj.* 可耻的; 恶劣的/ ～ize *v.* 震惊; 使反感; 使感到愤慨

scanner/'skænə/

n. a device for examining, reading or monitoring sth. using beams of light sound 扫描器; 扫描仪

scant/skænt/

adj. hardly any; not very much 不足的, 欠缺的: There has been a ～ supply of water recently. 最近供水一直不足。

scanty/'skænti/

adj. (scantier, scantiest) ❶ small in amount or extent 少量的, 不足的 ❷ barely enough 暴露的; 近乎裸露的 ‖ scantily *adv.* 缺乏地; 不充足地

scar/skɑːr/

Ⅰ *n.* a mark left by a healed cut, wound, burn, or sore 疤, 疤痕: He has a ～ on his arm. 他手臂上有一块疤。Ⅱ *v.* (-rr-) ❶ mark with a scar 使留下疤痕: He recovered from the accident but his face was badly ～red.他虽然从事故中救过来了，但脸上却留下了可怕的疤痕。❷form a scar 结疤：His wound is ～ring well.他伤口上的疤结得很好。

scarce/skeəs/

*adj.*❶ not enough；not plentiful 不充足的；缺乏的：Nowadays pandas are very ～.现在，大熊猫数量很少。❷ rare；seldom 稀有的：a kind of ～ resource 一种稀有资源

scarcely/'skeəsli/

*adv.*❶ barely；not quite 不足地：There were ～ a hundred people present.到场的不足一百人。❷almost not 几乎没有；简直不：I ～ know him.我几乎不认识他。/ He was so frightened that he could ～ speak.他吓得几乎说不出话来。

scarcity/'skeəsəti/

*n.*the state of being scarce；insufficient or limited supply 缺乏；不足；稀少：a ～ of water 缺水

scare/skeə(r)/

Ⅰ *v.* frighten；be frightened；cause to do sth.by frightening 惊吓；使恐慌；使受惊；恐吓：Scaring a child is wrong.吓唬小孩是不对的。/His warning ～d her into obeying him.他的警告吓得她顺从他。Ⅱ *n.*a (sudden) fright；a frightened condition 惊吓；受惊：I had a sudden ～ when I saw a dog running toward me.我看见一条狗向我奔来，吓了一跳。

scarf/skɑ:f/

n.(*pl.*scarves/skɑ:vz/ or ～s) a piece of cloth，worn about the neck，shoulders，or head 围巾；披肩；领巾：a red ～ 红领巾 / a woolen ～ 羊毛围巾

scarlet/'skɑ:lɪt/

Ⅰ *n.*a very bright red colour 鲜红色；猩红色：Scarlet is a colour often used for royal robes.帝王的长袍常是猩红色的。Ⅱ *adj.* very bright red 鲜红的；深红的：～ drops of blood 鲜红的血滴 / a ～ dress 一套颜色鲜红的服装

scathing/'skeɪðɪŋ/

adj. severe；harsh 尖锐的；苛刻的：The newspapers direct much ～ comment on the current policy.报纸对目前政策进行了许多尖锐的评论。

scatter/'skætə(r)/

*v.*❶ throw here and there 散播；撒：～ sand on an icy road 把沙子撒在结冰的路面上 ❷ send，drive in different directions 使分散；驱散：～ a crowd of children 驱散一群孩子 ❸ go in different directions 分散；四散：The mob ～ed.那群暴民四处散开。‖ ～ing *n.* 散落；三三两两；零零星星：a ～ing of farms on the hillside 疏疏落落地散布在山坡上的农庄

scattered/'skætəd/

*adj.*situated at various points apart from each other 分散的；零散的；疏落的：There were ～ huts down the hillside.小木屋零散地分布在山坡下。

scavenger/'skævɪndʒə/

*n.*❶ a person who scavenges 拾荒者；拾垃圾的人；捡破烂的人 ❷ bird or animal that eats refuse and decaying organic matter 食腐鸟类；食腐野兽；食腐动物

scene/si:n/

*n.*❶ the setting or place of an incident 场景；出事地点：The ～ of this novel is in the south.该小说的故事发生在南方。❷ view，landscape 风景：Scenes in the mountain are particularly beautiful.山里的风景尤其漂亮。

scenery/'si:nəri/

*n.*❶ landscape；general natural features of a district 天然景色；风景：mountain ～ 山景/ The ～ of Spain is beautiful.西班牙风光美丽。❷ the printed backdrop on a theatrical stage 舞台布景：The ～ for this play must have been very expensive.该剧的布景一定很费钱。

scenic/'si:nɪk/

*adj.*having fine natural scenery 风景优美的：the ～ route along the coast 海边风景优美的路线 ‖ ～ally *adv.*风景优美地

scent/sent/

*n.*❶ a distinctive odor 气味；香味：This flower has no ～ at all.这种花没有一点香味。❷ a liquid having a nice smell；perfume 香精；香水：He uses some ～ every day.他每天都要用一些香水。

sceptic，skeptic/ˈskeptɪk/

n. a person who usually doubts the truth of 惯持怀疑态度的人；怀疑论者 ‖ **scepticism，skepticism**/ˈskeptɪsɪzəm/ *n.* 怀疑（态度）；怀疑主义

sceptical，skeptical/ˈskeptɪkəl/

adj. inclined to question or disbelieve things 不轻易相信的；持怀疑态度的：The public were deeply ～ about some of the proposals.公众对某些提议深表怀疑。‖ ～**ly** *adv.*怀疑地

sceptre(-er)/ˈseptə(r)/

*n.*a rod or staff carried by a ruler to show his authority 权杖；节杖：a king's ～ 王杖

schedule/ˈʃedjuːl/

Ⅰ *n.*❶a planned list or order of things to be done，dealt with，etc. 计划表，程序表；议事日程：The teacher posted the ～ of classes.老师把课程表贴出来了。❷ a formal list of prices，details，etc. 价格表；明细表：a ～ of freight 运费表/ a train ～ 火车时刻表 ‖ **ahead of** ～ 提前；早于预定计划：They finished their work ahead of ～.他们提前完成了工作。/ **behind** ～ 晚于预定时间（或计划）：The train arrived behind ～.火车晚点到达。Ⅱ *v.*plan or arrange sth.for a definite time or date 计划，安排：～ a meeting 安排一次会议/ The plane is ～d to take off at 9 am. 飞机定于上午 9 点起飞。

scheme/skiːm/

Ⅰ *n.*❶ a plan or arrangement 计划，规划；方案：There are various ～s for improving the roads. 改进这些道路有各种不同的方案。❷ a secret and dishonest plan 阴谋，诡计：His ～ to steal the money was discovered.他企图偷钱的阴谋被揭穿了。Ⅱ *v.*make dishonest plans 搞阴谋；策划：He was scheming to rob the bank.他正在策划抢劫银行。

scholar/ˈskɒlə(r)/

*n.*❶ a person with much knowledge 学者：He went to America as a visiting ～.他是以访问学者的身份去的美国。/A ～ will give us a lecture this afternoon.今天下午一位学者将给我们搞一次讲座。❷ a university student holding a scholar-

ship 大学奖学金获得者：a British Council ～ 获英国文化协会奖学金的学生

scholarly/ˈskɒləli/

*adj.*❶involving or relating to serious academic study 学术的：～ journals 学术期刊 ❷ having or showing knowledge and learning；devoting to academic pursuits 博学的；勤奋好学的

scholarship/ˈskɒləʃɪp/

n. ❶ a grant of money to pay for a person's education，usually awarded on the basis of academic achievement 奖学金 ❷the work of scholars，advanced academic work 学问；学术；学术研究：a magnificent work of ～ 学术巨著

school/skuːl/

*n.*❶ an institution for educating children 学校：He goes to ～ at eight every morning. 他每天早晨 8 点钟去上学。❷ lessons；the time when teaching is given 上课时间；上课：School begins in September. 九月份开学。❸ a group of people who share the same or similar ideas in their works，etc.流派；学派❹a department in college or university that teach a particular subject （高等院校的）学院，系

science/ˈsaɪəns/

n. knowledge learned from research and arranged in an ordered system 科学；科学研究：The development of modern society depends on ～.现代社会的发展依赖于科学。

scientific/ˌsaɪən'tɪfɪk/

*adj.*❶ of science 科学的：～ books 科学书籍/ ～ instruments 科学仪器 ❷ following the rules of science 符合科学规律的：a ～ arrangement 科学的安排/ a ～ method 科学的方法

scientist/ˈsaɪəntɪst/

*n.*a person who has expert knowledge of some branch of science 科学家：He is a very famous ～.他是一位很有名的科学家。

scissors/ˈsɪzəz/

n. a cutting instrument with two blades and two handles fastened together 剪刀：a pair of ～ 一把剪刀

scoff/skɒf/

Ⅰ *n.*❶ the act of mocking；mocking remarks 嘲笑;嘲弄的话:vicious ～s 不怀好意的嘲笑 ❷ an object of ridicule; laughing-stock 笑柄;笑料:He was the ～ of the town.他是镇上的笑料。Ⅱ v.speak contemptuously;mock at 嘲笑;嘲弄:～ at a person 嘲弄人 / ～ at religion 嘲弄宗教 /～ at dangers 蔑视危险

scold/skəuld/

　Ⅰ n. a woman who blames with angry words 好骂人的女人:His big wife is a ～.他粗壮的老婆是个好责骂人的女人。Ⅱ v.rebuke angrily and often noisily 骂;斥责;责骂:～ a child for being lazy 责备孩子懒/ She's always ～ing.她总是骂骂咧咧。

scoop/sku:p/

　Ⅰ n.a kitchen tool like a small shovel 铲子:This ～ is easy to handle.这把铲子很好使。Ⅱ v.take up or hollow up with a scoop 用勺取出

scooter/'sku:tə(r)/

　n.❶ a type of children's toy on wheels, which can be moved along by using one foot 踏板车 ❷ a type of small motorcycle 小型摩托车

scope/skəup/

　n.❶ the range of action or observation 眼界;范围;领域:The college offers a wide ～ of subjects.这所大学开了很多课程。❷ the opportunity or possibility·to do or achieve sth.机会;可能

scorch/skɔ:tʃ/

　Ⅰ v.❶ cause to dry up;burn or discolour the surface of sth.by dry heat 使枯萎;使烤焦:The sun ～ed the flowers.太阳把花晒枯了。/It is likely to ～.它似乎要焦了。❷ (informal) travel very fast (非正式)飞驰:The car ～ed down the road at 90 miles an hour.这辆汽车以每小时90英里的速度飞驰而去。Ⅱ n.a mark made by burning on a surface 焦痕:～ marks 焦痕

score/skɔ:(r)/

　Ⅰ n.❶ a record of points made in a game or test,etc.得分;比分:The ～ is six to four.比分是六比四。❷ a cut,scratch or mark made on a surface 划痕;刻痕 Ⅱ v.

gain (a point) in a game (比赛中)得分:～ a goal 进一球

scorn/skɔ:n/

　Ⅰ n.a feeling that sb. or sth. deserves no respect 轻蔑:The hero smiled at the enemies with ～.那个英雄向敌人露出轻蔑的微笑。Ⅱ v.feel or show contempt for 表示出轻蔑:I ～ your words.我对你说的话表示蔑视。‖ hold in ～ 藐视;瞧不起/ laugh sb.to ～ 嘲笑某人/think it ～ to 不屑做/think ～ of 貌视 ‖ ～ful adj.轻蔑的;嘲笑的

scorpion/'skɔ:piən/

　n.a small creature with a sting in its tail, which is a member of the spider family 蝎子

scout/skaut/

　Ⅰ n.❶ a person,aircraft,etc. sent out to get information,etc.侦察兵;侦察机:The ～s reported that there were enemies ahead.侦察兵报告说前面有敌人。❷ members of an association for training boys and girls in character and various useful skills 童子军:Boy Scouts 男童子军/ Girl Scouts 女童子军 Ⅱ v.go about looking for sth. 探索,寻找:We ～ed around for the lost sheep.我们到处寻找丢失的绵羊。

scramble/'skræmbl/

　Ⅰ v.❶move or climb hurriedly 爬行;攀爬:～ up a hill 爬上山 /～ up the side of a cliff 爬上峭壁 /He ～d up the steep bank.他爬上陡的河堤。❷ struggle for sth.desired also by others 争夺;抢夺:～ for the ball (power) 争抢球(权力) / They ～d for the best seats.他们争夺最佳座位。❸ cook (eggs) while mixing and stirring together 炒(蛋) Ⅱ n.❶climb or walk over rough ground,etc.攀登;爬行 ❷ an eager struggle to obtain or a-chieve sth.抢夺;争夺:a ～ for the best seats 抢最好的座位

scrap/skræp/

　Ⅰ n.❶ a small piece of sth., especially cloth,paper,etc.碎片;碎屑;小块:There were some ～s of paper on the floor.地板上有些纸屑。/There's not a ～ of truth in what he says.他的话没有一点真实的。

❷ bits of uneaten food 剩余的食物,残食:They gave the ~s to their dog.他们用剩饭剩菜喂狗。 ❸ a picture or paragraph cut from a periodical,etc.for a collection 剪报,剪贴:My ~s of newspapers are all on that shelf.我的剪报全部在那个书架上。 ❹ any waste articles or material 废品,废料:Men in the village go out collecting ~ in winter.这村里的男人冬天外出收破烂。 Ⅱ v. throw away or discard sth.that is no longer practical or useful 抛弃;废弃:We had to ~ the whole plan.我们不得不放弃整个计划。

scrape/skreɪp/
Ⅰ v.❶ rub (a surface) with considerable pressure 刮;擦;刮落;擦去:~ one's boots 刮去靴底泥 /~ the rust off sth.刮去某物上的锈/~ off the paint from the wall 刮掉墙上的油漆 /~ scales off fish 刮鱼鳞 ❷ injure or damage by harsh rubbing,etc.擦伤;刮坏:~ one's knee on the stone 在石头上擦伤膝盖 / He ~d his hand on a rock.他的手在石头上擦伤。 ❸ manage to win or get sth. with difficulty 艰难取得;勉强获得:~ together a little sum 好不容易积几个钱 /~ a living 勉强维持生活 /~ through an exam 考试勉强及格 Ⅱ n.❶an act or sound of scraping 刮;擦;刮擦发出的声音:the ~ of a pen on paper 钢笔在纸上的摩擦声 ❷ a place that is scraped 擦伤;刮痕:a ~ on the leg 腿上的擦伤 ❸ an awkward situation resulting from foolish or thoughtless behaviour 困境;窘境:get into ~s 陷入困境 / get someone out of (his) ~s 使某人摆脱窘境

scratch/skrætʃ/
Ⅰ v.❶ make lines on or in a surface;hurt with sth.pointed or sharp 抓;划破;抓伤:This cat ~es.这只猫会抓人。 ❷ rub to relieve itching 搔(痒):He ~es his ear when he can't answer the teacher's questions.他回答不出老师的问题时总是搔耳朵。 ❸withdraw from a game,competition,etc.退出(比赛):I hope you are not going to ~ at the last moment.我希望你不会在最后一刻退出比赛。 ❹ score or mark the surface of sth.with a sharp or

pointed object 刮,擦:He ~ed his name in the wall with a knife.他用小刀把他的名字刻在墙上。 Ⅱ n.a mark, injury or sound made by scratching 抓伤;刮擦痕;刮擦声:There was a deep ~ on the desk.桌子上有一道很深的刮痕。 ‖ from ~ 从起跑线开始;从零开始:Let's see who get there first if we start from ~.从起跑线开始看看我们谁先到达那儿。

scrawl/skrɔːl/
Ⅰ v.write or draw quickly or carelessly 乱涂;潦草地写:Don't ~ on the wall. 别在墙上乱涂。/He ~ed a few words to his friend.他潦草地给朋友写了几句话。 Ⅱ n.a piece of bad writing;a shapeless and untidy writing 潦草的笔迹;涂鸦:What a ~! 多么潦草的字!

scream/skriːm/
Ⅰ v. cry out loudly and shrilly, as from pain or fear (因痛苦或害怕)尖叫,大叫:The woman ~ed at the sight of the car accident.看到车祸的场面,那个妇女尖叫了起来。 Ⅱ n.a loud, shrill cry or noise 尖叫:They heard a ~ in the middle of the night.半夜时,他们听到了一声尖叫。

screech/skriːtʃ/
v.make a harsh piercing sound 发出尖叫声:Monkeys are ~ing in the trees. 猴子在树丛中发出尖叫声。

screen/skriːn/
Ⅰ n.❶ the white or silver surface on which a picture is projected for viewing 银幕:It does harm to the eyes looking at the TV ~ for a long time.长时间盯着电视屏幕对眼睛有害。 ❷ sth. that serves to divide, conceal, or protect, as a movable room partition 屏风,隔板:under ~ of night 在夜幕的掩护下 Ⅱ v.conceal or protect sth. from view 遮掩;隐藏:The soldiers ~ themselves behind the bushes.士兵们在灌木丛中隐蔽了起来。

screw/skruː/
Ⅰ n.a nail with a ridge around its length 螺钉:drive in a ~ 把螺钉旋进去 Ⅱ v. fasten with one or more screws 用螺钉钉紧

scribe/skraɪb/

n. a person whose profession is to write copies of things 抄写员

script/skrɪpt/

n. ❶ a handwriting as distinguished from a print 手稿；原文：The ～s of the listening are at the back of the book.听力原文在书的后面。❷ a writing done by hand, especially as in English with the letters of words joined 笔迹

scripture/'skrɪptʃə(r)/

n. ❶ sacred writings that are regarded as holy in a religion（宗教）圣典；经文：the Buddhist ～ 佛经 ❷（the S-）the Bible 圣经

scrub/skrʌb/

Ⅰ *v.* rub hard at sth. in order to clean, e.g. with a stiff brush 擦洗，擦净：The students are ～bing the windows.学生们正在擦洗窗户。Ⅱ *n.* low trees and bushes; a land covered with low trees and bushes 矮树丛；丛林地

scruffy/'skrʌfi/

adj. rather dirty and untidy in appearance 不整洁的；褴褛的；邋遢的

scrunch/skrʌntʃ/

v. ❶ make a loud crunching noise 发出咔嚓声；发出嘎吱声 ❷ crush or crumple sth. 挤压成团：He ～ed the paper into a ball.他把纸揉成一团。

scruple/'skruːpl/

Ⅰ *n.* hesitation caused by uneasiness of conscience 自责；良心的不安：have ～s about doing sth.对做某事有所顾虑/ remove one's ～s 排除疑虑 / stand on ～ 顾虑重重 / He will tell lies without ～.他毫无顾忌地说谎。Ⅱ *v.* hesitate to do sth.犹豫；顾忌：She would not ～ to tell a lie.她对撒谎无所忌惮。

scuffle/'skʌfl/

Ⅰ *n.* a brief confused struggle or fight at close quarters 厮打，扭打 Ⅱ *v.* take part in a fight or struggle 厮打；扭打：The teacher noticed two pupils scuffling in the corridor.老师注意到两个学生在走廊里扭打。

sculpt/skʌlpt/

v. make figures or sth. else by carving wood, stone, etc. 雕刻；雕塑：She was learning how to ～.她正在学习雕塑方法。

sculptor/'skʌlptə(r)/

n. an artist who makes works in stone, wood, clay, metal, etc. by carving or modelling 雕刻家，雕塑家：He turned out to be a ～, while he was poor at drawing at school.读中学时他的绘画并不怎么好，后来他却成了一位雕塑家。

sculpture/'skʌlptʃə(r)/

Ⅰ *n.* ❶ the making of three-dimensional works of art in stone, clay, metal, wood, etc.雕塑：He spends lots of time on ～.他很多时间都花在了雕塑上。❷ works created in this manner 雕塑作品：This piece of ～ is marvelous.这件雕塑作品棒极了。Ⅱ *v.* make or represent（a form）by carving, casting, or other shaping techniques 雕塑

scurvy/'skɜːvi/

Ⅰ *n.* a disease resulting from a deficiency of vitamin C in the body 坏血病 Ⅱ *adj.* of the most contemptible kind 卑鄙的；下流的

sea/siː/

n. ❶ the continuous body of salt water that covers most of the surface of the earth 海洋：Ships sail on the ～.船在海上航行。/Most people go there by ～.大多数人是乘船去那儿的。❷ a vast number, expanse or extent 大量：a ～ of flame 一片火海/There is a ～ of information.信息浩如烟海。

seal¹/siːl/

Ⅰ *v.* close or fasten sth. tightly 封口；贴：The letter must be ～ed before it is posted.信寄出之前必须封好。Ⅱ *n.* a piece of wax, soft metal or paper that is placed across the opening of sth. to stop people from opening it without permission（防止任意开启的）封条，封蜡，封印

seal²/siːl/

n. a large animal with a rounded body and flat legs called flippers, living in and near the sea 海豹

seam/siːm/
n. ❶ a line formed by sewing two pieces of cloth, leather, etc. 缝缝口；接缝处：the ~s of a coat 外套的接缝 / The ~ has split. 接缝处开了。❷ a layer of coal, etc. 煤层；矿层；层 ❸ a scar or wrinkle of the skin 伤痕；皱纹：~s on the face 脸上的皱纹

sear/sɪə(r)/
v. ❶ burn the surface of 烧……的表面；炙；烧灼：~ing iron 烙铁 / He ~ed his hand on a hot steam pipe. 灼热的蒸汽管烫伤了他的手。❷ make someone's heart or feelings insensitive 使失去同情心；使变冷酷；麻木；无情：a ~ed conscience 麻木的良心 / His soul had been ~ed by injustice. 不公道使他变得冷酷无情了。

search/sɜːtʃ/
Ⅰ *v.* make a thorough examination in order to find sth. 搜寻；搜查：~ the pocket for money 在袋里搜钱 Ⅱ *n.* an act of looking for sth. 寻找：He came here in ~ of a rare plant. 他来这里是为了寻找一种稀有的植物。

seashore/'siːʃɔː/
n. an area of sandy, stony, or rocky land bordering and level with the sea 海岸；海滩

seasick/'siːsɪk/
adj. suffering from sickness or nausea caused by the motion of a ship at sea 晕船的 ‖ ~ness *n.* 晕船

season/'siːzn/
Ⅰ *n.* ❶ one of the four equal divisions of the year according to the weather 季：the dry (rainy) ~ 干（雨）季 / at all ~s 一年到头 / Spring, summer, autumn and winter are the four ~s. 春、夏、秋、冬是四季。/ Autumn is a busy ~. 秋季是繁忙的季节。❷ a special time of the year suitable or normal for sth. 季节，时期：the harvest ~ 收获季节 / the busy (off) ~ 旺（淡）季 / the football ~ 足球季节 / Christmas ~ 圣诞节前后 Ⅱ *v.* ❶ improve the flavour of food (with salt, pepper, etc.) 给……加味；调味：highly ~ed dishes 调味浓的菜 / mutton ~ed with garlic 用大蒜调味的羊肉 ❷ soften；moderate 使温和；缓和；调剂 ❸ make more acceptable or suitable by adding sth. else 使适应；使缓和

seasonable/'siːznəbl/
adj. suitable for a particular season 合时令的，应时的：Hot weather is ~ in summer. 夏天天气炎热是合时令的。‖ seasonably *adv.* 应时地

seasonal/'siːzənl/
adj. ❶ happening or needed during a particular season；varying with the seasons 季节性的；随季节变化的：~ fresh fruit 时鲜水果 ❷ typical of or suitable for the time of year, especially Christmas 节令性的；适应节日需要的；(尤指)圣诞节的：~ decorations 圣诞节装饰品

seasoned/'siːznd/
adj. experienced and competent because of training and practice 富有经验的；训练有素的：a ~ soldier 一位训练有素的士兵

seasoning/'siːznɪŋ/
n. a substance used to season food 调味品，佐料

seat/siːt/
Ⅰ *n.* ❶ sth. that may be sat on as a chair 座；座位：There are no ~s in the theatre now. 剧场里已经没有座位了。❷ an official position as a member of a committee, organization, etc. 席位：a Labour ~ 工党席位 Ⅱ *v.* sit down in a place 坐下：Now please be ~ed, every one of you. 现在请各位坐下来。

secede/sɪ'siːd/
v. withdraw formally from membership in an organization, association, or union 脱离，退出（联盟、组织等)：~ from a church 脱离教会 / He ~d from a political party. 他退出了一个党派。

seclude/sɪ'kluːd/
v. set apart from others 使隔离；使孤立；keep women ~d 使妇女们深居 / a ~d garden 与外面隔离的花园 / ~ oneself from society (world) 隐退；与世隔绝

second/'sekənd/
Ⅰ *adj.* next after the first 第二的：He is the ~ person to make this kind of mis-

takes. 他是第二个犯这类错误的人。Ⅱ n. ❶ a person or thing that comes next to the first 第二：the ~ of April 4月2日 ❷ a length of time equal to 1/60 of a minute(一)秒 Ⅲ v. give support or one's approval to 赞成；支持：Many officials ~ed this project. 许多官员赞成这项计划。

secondary/'sekəndri/
Ⅰ adj. ❶ immediately derived from what is primary 第二的；中级的：~ education (schools) 中等教育(学校)/No. 3 Secondary School 第三中学 ❷ inferior；less important than 次要的；副的；从属的：a ~ cause 次要原因 /~ product 副产品 / a ~ stress 次重音 Ⅱ n. a person that acts in an auxiliary or subordinate capacity 副手；次要人物；代表

second-hand/'sekənd'hænd/
adj. ❶ not new, already owned by someone else 旧的；用过的；属于他人的：a ~ books (store) 旧书(店)/~ furniture 旧家具 ❷ obtained from others, not based on personal observation, etc. 间接的；第二手的：~ news 第二手消息 /~ ideas 非本人想法 / get information ~ 获得转述的信息

secondly/'sekəndli/
adv. in the second place (used to introduce a second point or reason) 第二，其次(用于引出第二条观点、原因)：Firstly, it's expensive, and ~, it's too slow. 首先是价格贵，其次，速度太慢。

secret/'si:krit/
Ⅰ adj. kept or hidden from the knowledge of others 秘密的：We should keep this news ~ from the old woman. 我们必须保守秘密，不把这个消息告诉老妇。Ⅱ n. sth. known by few persons or hidden 秘密：It is a ~. 那是一个秘密。

secretariat/ˌsekrə'teəriət/
n. ❶ an office or position of secretary or secretary-general 秘书(或秘书长)的职位；书记的职位 ❷ a department, including staff, buildings, etc., controlled by a secretary or secretary-general 秘书处；书记处；书记处的全体人员：the United Nations ~ 联合国秘书处

secretary/'sekrətri/

n. ❶ a person employed to handle correspondence and do clerical work 秘书；书记：a private ~ 私人秘书/ She is the ~ to the general manager. 她是总经理的秘书。❷ an officer of an organization 书记；干事：a chief ~ 总干事 / the ~ of a party branch 党支部书记 / an honorary ~ 名誉干事 ❸ the minister in charge of a government office 大臣；部长：the Secretary of State for Foreign Affairs 外交部长 / the Secretary of State 国务大臣；国务卿/ Secretary of the Treasury 财政部长

secrete/sɪ'kri:t/
v. ❶ produce a liquid substance 分泌：This type of insects ~s a kind of honeydew. 这类昆虫分泌出一种蜜露。❷ hide；put into a secret place 躲藏；藏匿，隐藏：The dog ~d itself behind the door. 那只狗躲在门后。

secretion/sɪ'kri:ʃən/
n. ❶ the process of secreting substances 分泌 ❷ a substance secreted by an organ or cell of the body 分泌物

sect/sekt/
n. a group of people united by beliefs or opinions that differ from those more generally accepted 派；宗派；教派：Each religious ~ in the town has its own church. 这个镇上每一个教派都有自己的教堂。

section/'sekʃn/
Ⅰ n. ❶ a part, division or slice that result from cutting a solid along a plane 切断；断面；切片：the ~ of a bone 骨头的切片 / a cross ~ 横断面 / the ~s of an orange 橘子的各片 ❷ one of a number of parts that can be put together as a whole 零件；一部分：a ~ of a pipe 管子的一段 / the ~s of a machine 机器的各部分 / a hut consisting of five ~s 由五部分构成的棚屋 ❸ a distinct part of a community, country, etc. 区域；地区：the industrial ~ of the nation 那个国家的工业区 / a rural ~ 乡村地区 Ⅱ v. separate or divide into parts 切开；分开

sector/'sektə(r)/
n. ❶ the part connected with that specified type of industry of a country's

economy（经济的）部门；the public ~ 国营部门 ❷ an area or portion that is distinct from others 区域；部分

secular/ˈsekjʊlə(r)/

adj. concerned with this world, material things, not with religious or spiritual matters 现世的；世俗的；物质的；非宗教的；非精神的：~ matters 世俗问题

secure/sɪˈkjʊər/

Ⅰ *adj.* ❶ free from danger; feeling confident and safe 无虑的；安心的：She never feels ~ about her children. 她总是对孩子放心不下。❷ certain and sure（to happen or succeed）确定的；可靠的：Our victory is ~. 我们的胜利是有把握的。Ⅱ *v.* cause to be firmly attached 使牢固；紧闭：Be sure to ~ the door at night. 晚上一定要把门关牢。

security/sɪˈkjʊərəti/

n. sth. that provides to protect sb. from danger or anxiety; measures or actions that take to make secure 安全（感）；安全措施：He saw the children cross the street in ~. 他看见孩子们安全地穿过了街道。/Tight ~ was in force during the president's visit. 总统视察期间采取了严格的安全措施。

sedan/sɪˈdæn/

n. ❶ an enclosed chair carried on poles by two men 轿子 ❷ a saloon car for four or more persons 轿车

sedate/sɪˈdeɪt/

adj. quiet and rather dignified 沉静的；庄重的：a ~ little girl 娴静的少女/behave in a ~ manner 举止庄重

sedation/sɪˈdeɪʃn/

n. the condition of quietness which is brought about by drugs（服用镇静剂后的）镇静状态

sedative/ˈsedətɪv/

n. a medicine which makes people calm 镇静剂；安定片：take a ~ before going to bed 睡前服用镇静剂

sedentary/ˈsedntri/

adj. requiring sitting or little activity 久坐不动的：a ~ occupation 久坐不动的工作

sediment/ˈsedɪmənt/

n. a matter that settles to bottom of a liquid 沉积物：The ~ of coffee will settle. 咖啡渣会沉淀下去。

sedition/sɪˈdɪʃn/

n. a speech, writing or behaviour that incites others to rebel against the state 煽动性言论；煽动性文章；煽动性行为：stir up a ~ 煽起暴动

seduce/sɪˈdjuːs/

v. ❶ persuade a person to have sexual intercourse with 诱奸 ❷ persuade sb. to do sth. wrong 诱使……干坏事

seduction/sɪˈdʌkʃn/

n. ❶ an act of seducing or being seduced 诱奸；引诱；诱惑 ❷ sth. attractive 魅力；吸引力：the ~s of modern life 现代生活的魅力

seductive /sɪˈdʌktɪv/

adj. tending to seduce sb.; temptingly attractive or alluring 诱人的；迷人的；有吸引力的 ‖ ~ly *adv.* 有吸引力地/ ~ness *n.* 诱惑；吸引力

see/siː/

v. ❶ perceive with the eye; have the power of sight 看；看见：What did you ~? 你看见了什么？❷ understand sth. 领会；明白：I can ~ he does not agree with her. 我可以看得出（领会，知道），他不同意她的意见。❸ receive（a person）；call on；visit sb. 会见；访问；拜访：You'd better go to ~ the doctor. 你最好去看一下医生。

seed/siːd/

n. the small, hard part of a plant from which another plant can grow 种子：a packet of ~s 一包种子 ‖ ~less *adj.* 无籽的/~y *adj.* 多（种）子的

seek/siːk/

v.（sought）❶ look for or try to find 寻觅，寻找：We were ~ing shelter from the rain. 我们当时正在找地方避雨。❷ ask for; go to request 请求，征求：You should ~ your parents' advice on this matter. 在这件事情上你应该征求一下你父母亲的意见。❸ try; attempt 试图，企图：They sought to cheat him out of his money. 他们企图骗取他的钱。‖ **sought after** 供不应求的：Air-conditioners are much sought after this summer. 今年夏天空调供不应求。

seem /siːm/

v. have or give the impression or appearance of being or doing 似乎是；好像：He ~s to know everything. 他好像什么都知道。

seeming /'siːmɪŋ/

adj. apparent but perhaps not real or genuine 表面上的；似乎的；仿佛的：his ~ loyalty 他在表面上的忠诚 / her ~ friendliness 她表面上的友好 / the ~ acceptance of the invitation 对邀请很不情愿的接受

seemingly /'siːmɪŋli/

adv. ❶ so as to give the impression of having a certain quality；apparently 表面上；显得：a ~ well-organized person 一个表面上有条有理的人 ❷ according to the facts as one knows them；as far as one knows 好像：It's touch and go, ~, and she's asking for you. 好像还不一定，她正找你呢。

seemly /'siːmli/

adj. ❶ proper or suitable for a particular social situation 端庄的；合适的；大方的：It's not ~ to praise oneself. 自夸是不适宜的。❷ of pleasing appearance；decent 体面的；正经的：Striptease is not a ~ occupation for any girl. 脱衣舞对任何女孩而言都不是正经的职业。

seep /siːp/

v. flow slowly or pass gradually through or as if through small openings 渗漏：water ~ing through the roof of the tunnel 从隧道顶部渗出的水 / Rain ~ed through the roof. 雨水透过屋顶渗入。

seesaw /'siːsɔː/

Ⅰ *n.* a plank balanced on support at its centre 跷跷板：lay at ~ 玩玩跷跷板 Ⅱ *v.* move up and down or to and from 上下来回摇动；玩跷跷板

seethe /siːð/

v. be in an agitated emotional state 激昂；发怒：seething with anger 大发雷霆 / a place seething with people 人群沸腾的地方

segment

Ⅰ /'segmənt/ *n.* a part cut off or marked off；section 切片；部分：a few ~s of orange 几瓣橘子 Ⅱ /seg'ment/ *v.* divide or be divided into different parts 分割，使分开：Orange may be ~ed into 10 or 12 pieces. 橘子可分成10瓣或12瓣。

segregate /'segrɪgeɪt/

v. keep separate from others 隔离；分开：~ people of different races 对不同种族实行隔离 ‖ **segregation** /ˌsegrɪ'geɪʃn/ *n.* 隔离

seismograph /'saɪzməgrɑːf/

n. an instrument for recording the direction, intensity, and duration of earthquakes or other movements of the earth's crust 地震仪

seize /siːz/

v. ❶ take hold of sth. or sb. suddenly and forcibly 抓住；逮捕：~ a rope 抓住一条绳子 / He ~d my arm. 他抓住了我的胳膊。/The spy has been ~d. 特务被逮捕了。❷ take possession of（property, etc.）by law（依法）扣押，没收，查封：~ sb.'s goods for payment of debt 扣押某人货物以偿还债务 ❸ see cleverly and use 了解并利用；掌握：~ an opportunity 趁机 / ~ a point 抓住要点 ❹ have a sudden effect upon；overwhelm 夺取；占据；占领：~ an enemy fortress 占领敌人要塞 / Panic ~d him. 恐慌击倒了他。

seldom /'seldəm/

adv. not often, rarely 很少；不常；罕见：She ~ goes out. 她不常外出。/Seldom have I met him. 我很少碰到他。/He ~, if ever, goes to the theatre. 他差不多不上戏院。/He is ~ or never ill. 他几乎不生病。

select /sɪ'lekt/

v. choose from among a group of people or things；pick out 选择；挑选：You can ~ a book as a gift. 你可以挑选一本书来作为礼物。

selection /sɪ'lekʃn/

n. ❶ the act of choosing；a choice 选择，挑选：Her ~ of a hat took a long time. 她挑选帽子花了很长时间。❷ sth. to choose

S

from 待选物：The shop has a good ～ of hats.这家商店有许多帽子可供选择。❸ a collection of things that have been selected 选集：a ～ of poems 诗集

selective /sɪˈlektɪv/
*adj.*❶chosen or choosing carefully 认真挑选的；严格筛选的：The admissions policy is very ～.录取政策非常严格。❷ involving or allowing a choice 选择性的；有选择的 ‖ ～**ly** *adv.*严格挑选地；选择性地/**selectivity** *n.*选择；选择性

self /self/
*n.*❶ the total being of one person；the individual 本性；本质；自我：He has found a new ～ after that happening.自发生那件事之后,他找到一个新的自我。❷ one's own interests,welfare,or advantage 私利

self-control /ˈselfkənˈtrəʊl/
*n.*the ability to control oneself,in particular one's emotions and desires or the expression of them in one's behaviour,especially in difficult situations 自控,自制

selfish /ˈselfɪʃ/
*adj.*caring too much for oneself and too little for others 自私的,自利的：A ～ person puts his own interests first.一个自利的人先替自己打算。

selfless /ˈselflɪs/
*adj.*thinking of other people；unselfish 无私的；不自私的：an act of ～ devotion 无私奉献的行为 ‖ ～**ly** *adv.*无私地 /～**ness** *n.*无私

sell /sel/
v. (sold) ❶ give in exchange for money 卖,出售：～ books 卖书/ I sold my brother my bicycle for 50 dollars.我以50美元的价格把自行车卖给了我哥哥。❷ be on sale 销售：The book ～s well here.这书在此地很畅销。‖ ～ **off** 廉价出售：The store sold off its summer stock to be ready for the winter goods.那家商店廉价出售夏季存货,准备进冬季货物。/ ～ **out** 卖光：The books you ask for are all sold out.你要的书都卖光了。

seller /ˈselə(r)/
*n.*❶a person who sells sth.售货人；出售者：a book ～ 书商/ a ～'s market 销售

者市场；供不应求 ❷ sth.that is sold 出售之物：This novel is a best ～.这本小说是畅销书。

semantics /sɪˈmæntɪks/
*n.*the study of meaning and development of meaning in words 语义学

semester /sɪˈmestə(r)/
n. a half of a school or university year 一学期；半学年

semi- /ˈsemɪ/
*pref.*half；partly 半；部分：～circle 半圆/ ～tone 半音；半程音

semicolon /ˌsemɪˈkəʊlən/
*n.*a mark of punctuation,used in writing and printing,between a comma and a full stop in value 分号(即；)

semiconductor /ˌsemɪkənˈdʌktə(r)/
*n.*any of a group of material having an electrical conductivity between that of metals and insulators 半导体：～ electronics 半导体电子学

semifinal /ˌsemɪˈfaɪnl/
*n.*a match or round immediately preceding the final,as in a series of competitions 半决赛；准决赛

seminar /ˈsemɪnɑː(r)/
*n.*a small group of advanced students engaged in special study 研习班；研讨会

senate /ˈsenɪt/
*n.*the upper house of the Congress (of the United States of America) or of a state legislature (美国)参议院,上议院：a US Senate subcommittee 美国参议院的一个小组委员会

senator /ˈsenətə(r)/
*n.*a member of a senate 参议员

send /send/
v. (sent) ❶ cause sth.to be carried to a place 送,传递：～ a message 送个口信/ ～ someone a letter 给某人寄信 ❷ tell sb.to do sth.or to go to a place 派遣,打发：～ a person for the doctor 叫人去请医生 ❸ cause to become or behave in a particular way 使变成,使处于：～ someone mad 使某人发疯/ The news sent me into panic.这消息使我恐慌。‖ ～ **away** ❶使离去,送走：She sent her son away

for the summer vacation in the country-side.她送孩子到农村去过暑假。❷ 驱逐,开除: I sent him away because I was tired of his idle chatter.我把他赶走了,因为他那无聊的扯淡使我厌烦。/ ～ **for** 派人去请,派人去叫: He is very ill; you must ～ for a doctor.他病得很重,你必须派人去请医生。/ ～ **off** ❶ 派遣,发送: Her mother sent her off to her aunt.她母亲打发她到她姨妈家去。❷送别: We all went to the airport to ～ him off.我们都到机场去送他。/ ～ **out** ❶分发: ～ out a letter of invitation 发出邀请信 ❷放射,放出: The sun ～s out light and heat.太阳发出光与热。‖ ～**er** *n.* 送信人,发送人

senile /'si:naɪl/
   adj. characteristic of or proceeding from old age; mentally and physically weakness because of old age 衰老的;年老的: ～ decay 年老体衰 /She keeps forgetting things; I think she's getting ～.她总是忘事,我看她是老了。

senior /'si:nɪə(r)/
   Ⅰ *adj.* older; higher in rank or status 年长的;地位较高的;资深的: ～ students 高年级学生 /I'm six years ～ to her.我比她大六岁。Ⅱ *n.* a student in the final year in a university or high school (大学或高中的)毕业班学生

seniority /ˌsi:nɪ'ɒrɪti/
   n. ❶the fact of being older or of a higher rank than others 年长;级别高: a position of ～ 高级职位 ❷the rank that you have in a company because of the length of time you have worked there 资历: a lawyer with five years' ～ 有五年从业经验的律师

sensation /sen'seɪʃn/
   n. ❶ a physical feeling that you have when sth. happens to your body 知觉;感觉: He has a ～ of coldness in the room.他感到房间里有一股寒冷的感觉。❷ a feeling of deep interest and excitement 激动;感动

sensational /sen'seɪʃənl/
   adj. ❶causing excitement 轰动的;令人激动的: ～ news 轰动性的新闻 / a ～ mur-der 耸人听闻的谋杀案 ❷ of or relating to sensation (与)感觉(有关)的

sense /sens/
   Ⅰ *n.* ❶ any of the functions of hearing, sight, smell, touch, and taste 官能;感觉;知觉: ～ of smell 嗅觉 ❷ the ability to understand and appreciate 领悟,赏识: This work requires a ～ of duty.做这项工作需要责任感。❸ a consciousness to the presence or importance of sth. 意识: have no ～ of shame 没有羞耻感 ❹ the ability to judge external conditions 辨别力: There is a lot of ～ in what he said.他的话颇有见地。Ⅱ *v.* feel sth. or be aware of sth. 感觉到: I can ～ the pain in her heart.我可以感觉到她内心的痛苦。

senseless /'senslɪs/
   adj. ❶not showing good sense; foolish 不明智的;愚蠢的 ❷unconscious; having no sensation 失去知觉的: The attack left a policeman beaten ～.袭击中一名警察被打昏。‖ ～**ness** *n.* 无意义;无知觉

sensibility /ˌsensə'bɪləti/
   n. ❶the ability to feel or perceive 感觉能力;感受性;敏感性: the ～ of the skin 皮肤的感觉 /～ to kindness 对仁慈的感觉 / the ～ of a poet 诗人的敏感 ❷ (usually *pl.*) a person's feelings, especially delicate feelings 情感: a man of strong sensibilities 有强烈情感的人/ Her sensibilities are easily hurt.她的情感容易地受到伤害。

sensible /'sensəbl/
   adj. ❶ showing reason or sound judgement 明智的;明白事理的: a ～ idea 明智的想法 / a ～ person 理智的人/ How ～ of you! 你真懂事! ❷ able to feel or perceive 发觉的;察觉的: I am ～ of his mistakes.我察觉到他的错误。/He is ～ of the danger of his position.他发觉他处境的危险。❸reasonable; practical 切合实际的;合理的;实用的: a ～ plan 合理的计划

sensitive /'sensɪtɪv/
   adj. ❶quick to receive impressions 敏感的;易感的: be ～ to light (cold) 对光(冷)敏感/ A ～ skin is easily hurt by too much sunshine.敏感的皮肤晒太阳过多

S

易受伤害。❷(of photographic film, paper, etc.) affected by light (胶片、纸等) 易感光的:~ paper 感光纸 ❸ easily hurt in the spirit; easily offended 神经过敏的;易受伤害的:~ to criticism 对批评神经过敏 / be ~ to ridicule 对别人的嘲笑容易生气 / He is very ~ about his ugly appearance.他因丑陋的外表而神经过敏。❹ able to respond to a very slight change 灵敏的;灵敏度高的:an ~ instrument 灵敏的仪器 /~ scales 反应灵敏的天平 / The stock exchange is ~ to political disturbances.证券交易对于政治风波很敏感。

sensitivity/ˌsensəˈtɪvəti/

n.the quality or degree of being sensitive 敏感;敏感性;感光;感光度:The dentist gave her an injection to reduce the ~ of the nerves.牙医为她注射以减少神经的敏感。

sensor/ˈsensə(r)/

n.a device that detects and responds to a signal or stimulus 传感器

sensory/ˈsensəri/

adj.of the senses or sensation 感觉的;知觉的:~ organs 感觉器官

sensual/ˈsenʃʊəl/

adj.connected with the feelings of the body rather than of the mind or spirit 肉体上的:~ pleasures 感官上的愉悦

sentence/ˈsentəns/

Ⅰ*n*.❶ a grammatical unit comprising a word or group of words that usually consists of at least one subject and a finite verb or verb phrase 句子:This ~ is wrong.这个句子是错误的。❷ the statement of a judicial decision to punish; the penalty which forms a part of such a statement 判决;宣判:a ~ of three years 三年的徒刑 Ⅱ*v*.state the penalty to be paid 判决:The criminal is ~d to death.这个罪犯被判了死刑。

sentiment/ˈsentɪmənt/

n.❶an attitude which is based on thoughts and feelings 情操;情绪:a person of noble ~ 有高尚情操的人 /the ~ of pity 怜悯的情绪 ❷(usually *pl*.)an opinion about a specific matter; view 观点;意见:express one's ~s 表示意见/ The ambassador explained the ~s of his government on the question.

大使就该问题解释其政府的意见。❸ thought or attitude based on emotion rather than reason 伤感;多愁善感:There's no place for ~ in business.做生意不可感情用事。

sentimental/ˌsentɪˈmentl/

adj.❶characterized by excessive emotional show 感情的;言情的;激发感情的:~ poetry 言情诗 /~ comedy 言情喜剧 ❷ influenced by feeling rather than reason 多愁善感的;感情用事的:a ~ girl 多愁善感的女孩 / do sth. for ~ reasons 因感情用事而做某事

separate

Ⅰ/ˈseprət/*adj*.not joined to sth.else 分开的:The two parcels are kept in ~ rooms.两个小包分开放在不同的房间里。Ⅱ/ˈsepəreɪt/*v*.move apart; (cause to) become disconnected physically or in the mind 使分离;分开:Don't ~ the children from their parents.不要让孩子们与他们的父母分开。

separation/ˌsepəˈreɪʃən/

n.❶ the process of separating, or of being separated 分开;分离:They were reunited after a ~ of 10 years.他们离别 10 年后重又聚首。❷a legal arrangement by which a couple live apart while remaining married (夫妻)分居

September/sepˈtembə(r)/

n.the ninth month of the year 九月:in ~ 在九月

septic/ˈseptɪk/

adj.infected or poisoned by germs 受感染的;脓毒性的:a ~ wound 受到感染的伤口

sequel/ˈsiːkwəl/

n.❶ sth. that follows, as a result of sth. or after sth.else 结局;结果;后果 ❷ a book, film, , etc. which carries on the story of a previous one 续集;续篇

sequence/ˈsiːkwəns/

n.❶ the order of sth. 连续;顺序:arrange the names in alphabetical ~ 按字母顺序排列名字 ❷ a connected line of events, ideas, etc.(事件、观念等)系列,一连串:a ~ of bumper harvest 连续大丰收

serene/sɪˈriːn/

adj.❶(of the weather) clear and calm (指

天气）晴朗的,风和日丽的:a ～ sky 晴朗的天空 / a ～ weather 晴朗的天气 ❷(of a person) peaceful,calm (指人)安静的,从容的:a ～ smile 安静的微笑 / a ～ look 宁静的神情 ❸(of a place,etc.) quiet (指地方等)宁静的,安静的:a ～ mountain landscape 宁静的山区景色 / a ～ life 宁静的生活

serf/sɜːf/

n.(in the past) a person who is not allowed to leave the land on which he works;a slave (旧时的)农奴;奴隶

sergeant/'sɑːdʒənt/

*n.*❶ a non-commissioned army officer above a corporal and below a sergeant-major 士官;军士;中士:staff ～〈英〉陆军上士 ❷ a police officer with rank below that of an inspector 警官;警佐;巡佐

serial/'sɪərɪəl/

n. a story appearing in parts once weekly, monthly,etc.连载小说;电视连续剧:A new ～ is starting on television tonight. 今晚电视开播一部新的电视连续剧。‖ ～ize *v.* 分期刊载;连载;连续广播

series/'sɪəriz/

*n.*❶a group of events related by order of occurrence 连续;系列:a ～ of questions 一系列问题/ a ～ of natural disasters 一连串自然灾害 / a ～ of lectures on American politics 一系列关于美国政治的演讲 ❷ a group of related books stamps,etc. 丛书;(邮票)套: the first ～ 第一辑 / a ～ of stamps 一套邮票/ the World History ～ 世界历史丛书

serious/'sɪərɪəs/

*adj.*❶ causing fear or anxiety by threatening great harm 严重的;危急的 ❷ concerned with work or important matters rather than play or trivialities 严肃的;认真的;不闹着玩的:Our radio offers ～ programmes.我们电台播送一些严肃的节目。

sermon/'sɜːmən/

*n.*❶ a religious talk delivered as part of a church service 布道;讲道:deliver (preach) a ～ 布道 ❷ (informal) lengthy and tedious reproof or exhortation (非正式)训诫;唠叨的教训:treat someone.to a ～ 对某人进行说教

serrated/sɪ'reɪtɪd/

*adj.*shaped like the teeth of a saw 锯齿形的:a ～ edge 有锯齿的刀口

serum/'sɪərəm/

n. a watery liquid taken from the blood of an animal which has had a certain disease,and put into the blood of a person to prevent him from having that disease (防疫)血清

servant/'sɜːvənt/

*n.*❶ a person paid to wait on another or others,especially to do work in or around a house 仆人;佣人:keep a ～ 雇佣仆人 / have a large staff of ～s 仆人众多 ❷ a person employed in the service of government or a company 公务员;雇员:a public ～ 公仆 ❸ a person devoted to sb. or sth.忠实的门徒(信徒):a ～of Jesus Christ 耶稣基督的忠实信徒/ a faithful ～ of the Church 教会忠实的仆人

serve/sɜːv/

*v.*❶ be a servant to;work for 做仆人;为……服务:～ the people 为人民服务 ❷ perform duties 尽责;履行义务:My brother ～d in the army for four years.我的兄弟在部队里服役了四年。❸ provide people with sth.that they need 供应,提供;招待:I'll ～ you chicken.我将用鸡肉款待你。❹ be satisfactory for a need or purpose 用作;适合:Our table also ～s as a bed.我们的桌子也做床用。

service/'sɜːvɪs/

*n.*❶ sth.done to help or benefit another or others 服务:I'm always at your ～.我永远听候你的吩咐。❷ benefit or advantage 利益;好处:Can I be of ～ to you? 我能给你帮得上忙吗? ❸sth.that the public needs, such as hospitals, parks, etc. which is supplied in an organized way 公共服务系统 ❹ an examination,test,etc.of sth.to make sure it keeps working or operating 检修,维修

serviceman/'sɜːvɪsmən/

*n.*❶ a member of the armed forces 军人 ❷ a person whose work is serving or repairing sth.维修人员:an automobile ～ 汽车修理工

servile/'sɜːvaɪl/
adj. showing too much respect as a slave would 阿谀的;奴性的:~ flattery 阿谀奉承/a ~ attitude 一副奴才相

serving /'sɜːvɪŋ/
n.a portion of food at a meal 一份食物:a large ~ of noodle 一大份面条

session/'seʃn/
n.❶ a formal meeting of an organization,especially a law-making body or court 正式会议;一届会议;(尤指)开庭:go into secret ~ 开秘密会议/ have a long ~ 开庭(会)期长/ between ~s 休会期间 / in ~ 在开会(庭)/ an emergency ~ of the United Nations Security Council 联合国安理会紧急会议 ❷ the part of a year or of a day during which a school holds classes 学期;上课时间:the summer ~ 夏季学期/ the morning ~s 上午的课 ❸a meeting or period of time used especially by a group for a particular purpose (从事某项活动的)一段时间:a recording ~ 录音时间

set/set/
Ⅰ*v*.(set,set)❶ bring into or cause to be in a special state or relation 使处于,使达到(某种状态):~ the ladder straight 将梯子放正 ❷ disappear below the horizon,as the sun, etc.降至地平线以下:The sun ~s.太阳正下山。 ❸ put,place or lay sth.in a particular place 放;搁置:Set the books on the table, please.请把书放到桌子上。 ❹ cause (sb.) to do sth.使某人开始做某事:The situation ~ everyone thinking.形势促使每一个人深思。 Ⅱ*n*.a number of things that belong together or that are thought of as a group 套,系列:a ~ of furniture 一套家具/a ~ of books 一套书

setback /'setbæk/
n.sth. that stops or slows progress 退步,挫折:a serious ~ for the process 进程中的严重挫折

setting /'setɪŋ/
n.❶ a framework in which sth.is fixed or fastened (安装、固定东西的)架;框:the ~ of a jewel 镶嵌珠宝的底座 ❷ jewelry mounting (珠宝)镶嵌 ❸ a piece of vocal or choral music composed for particular words 配曲 ❹ a particular place or type of sur-roundings where sth.is or takes place 背景;环境:the social ~ 社会环境

settle/'setl/
v.❶place (sb. or oneself) so as to be comfortable 安放,安身:She ~d (herself) in the armchair and closed her eyes.她坐在扶手椅里闭上了眼睛。❷ make an agreement about;decide 调停;解决,决定:~ disputes 调解争端/ ~ on a plan 决定计划 ❸ make or become calm or untroubled (使)镇定,平静:He took some medicine to ~ his stomach.他吃了一些药以防闹肚子。❹ pay 支付,结算:~ a bill 付账,结账/ Will you ~ for all of us? 你愿为我们大家付账吗? ❺ make one's home in a place permanently (使)定居,安居:~ in London 在伦敦定居 ‖ ~ down ❶停落在地上:The airship ~d down in a field.飞艇降落在原野上。❷ 定居下来,安家落户:He has ~d down in the countryside.他已在乡村安家落户了。❸ (使)平静下来,(使)安静下来:The chairman tried to ~ the audience down. 会议主席试图让听众安静下来。/Wait until his excitement has ~d down.一直等到他激动的情绪平静下来。❹ 舒服地坐或躺,休息:He ~d down in his armchair to read a new novel.他安坐在扶手椅里看一本新小说。

settlement/'setlmənt/
n.❶the act of settling a dispute,debt,etc. 解决;和解;清偿:the ~ of the differences 分歧的解决 / come to (reach) a ~ 达成和解 / The terms of ~ seem just.和解的条件似乎很公道。/I enclose a check in ~ of your account.我寄上一张支票以清偿你的账目。 ❷ the property given 赠予的财产:a mar-riage ~ 赠予妻子的财产 / a handsome ~ 一笔可观的钱 ❸ a place where people have come to live and have built homes 定居地:the ~ of California 在加利福尼亚的定居地

set-up /'setʌp/
n.❶a way of organizing sth.;a system 组织;机构;建制;体制:I've only been here sever-al days and I don't really know the ~.我刚来几天,对这里的组织情况不大了解。❷a set of equipment needed for a particular ac-tivity or purpose (用于特定活动或用途的)一套设备,装置:I have a recording ~ in

my house.我有一套录音设备。

seven/'sevn/

num.the number 7 七

seventeen /ˌsevən'tiːn/

num.one more than sixteen, or seven more than ten 17 十七

seventeenth /ˌsevn'tiːnθ/

num.being number 17 in a series; being one of the 17 equal parts of anything 第十七; 十七分之一

seventh/'sevnθ/

num.being number 7 in a series; being one of the 7 equal parts of anything 第七; 七分之一

seventieth/'sevntɪɪθ/

num.being number 70 in a series; being one of the 70 equal parts of anything 第七十; 七十分之一

seventy /'sevnti/

num.the number equivalent to the product of seven and ten; ten less than eighty 70 七十; 七十个

sever/'sevə(r)/

v.❶cut right through sth.割断; 切断: ~ a rope in two sth.割断绳子为两截/ His leg was ~ed from his body in the accident.他的腿在事故中断了。❷break off 中断; 断绝: ~ one's connections with someone 与某人断绝关系 /~ a friendship 断绝友谊/ ~ diplomatic relations 断绝外交关系 / The rope ~ed under the strain.绳在拉紧后断了。

several/'sevərəl/

Ⅰ*adj*.❶three or more; some 三个或更多的; 几个的; 整个的: ~ times 几次 / for ~ days 数天 / He makes ~ visits each year to China.他每年都去几次中国。/You will need ~ more.你还需要几个。❷ separate; individual 个别的; 单独的: ~ different students 个别不同的学生 / They went their ~ ways.他们各走各的路。Ⅱ*pron*.a few; some 几个; 整个: I already have ~.我已经有几个。/Several of us decided to walk home.我们中有几个人决定步行回家。

severe/sɪ'vɪə(r)/

adj. ❶ intensely or extremely bad or un-

pleasant in degree or quality 严重的, 剧烈的: ~ pain 剧痛❷ stern; strict 严厉的: He speaks to the prisoners in a ~ way.他对罪犯说话严厉。

sew/səʊ/

v.work with a needle and thread 缝纫, 缝制; 缝: She has been ~ing all morning.她早上一直在做针线活。/ ~ a coat 缝制上装/ ~ two pieces of cloth together 把两块布缝在一起/Doctor ~ed up the wound.医生把伤口缝合了。

sewer/'sjuːə(r)/

n.an underground pipe or tunnel that carries off waste matter from houses in a town 阴沟; 污水管; 下水道

sewing /'səʊɪŋ/

n.the activity of making, repairing or decorating things made of cloth using a needle and thread 缝纫: knitting and ~ 编织和缝纫

sex/seks/

n.❶being male or female 性; 性别: without distinction of age or ~ 不分男女老幼 / What is its ~? 它的性别是什么? ❷ males or females as a group (总称)男, 女: both ~es 男人们和女人们/ the equality of ~es 男女平等

sexless/'sekslɪs/

adj.❶without sex 无性的; 无性别的 ❷ lacking normal sexual desire or attractiveness 缺乏性欲(感)的

sexual/'sekʃuəl/

adj.of sex or sexes 性的; 两性的: ~ organs 性器官 /~ behaviour 性行为

sexy /'seksi/

adj. (sexier, sexiest) sexually attractive or stimulating 性感的; 迷人的; 刺激的: ~ underwear 性感的内衣/ He has climbed most of the really ~ west coast mountains. 他已攀登过绝大多数十分迷人的西海岸山峰。

shabby/'ʃæbi/

adj.❶ poorly dressed; looking badly worn 破旧的; 褴褛的: My coat is getting ~.I must buy a new one.我的外衣已破旧, 得买一件新的。❷ mean or shameful in a petty way 吝啬的; 卑鄙的

S

shackle/'ʃækl/

*n.*one of a pair of iron rings joined by a chain for fastening a prisoner's wrists or ankles 手铐;脚镣;镣铐

shade/ʃeɪd/

Ⅰ*n.*comparative darkness caused by the cutting off of direct rays of light 背阴(处);阴凉(处):People like to stand in the ～ when it is hot.天气热的时候,人们喜欢站在阴凉的地方。Ⅱ*v.*keep direct rays of light from 遮蔽:～ the face with a hat 用帽遮住脸

shadow/'ʃædəʊ/

Ⅰ*n.*❶ the region of relative darkness caused by the interception of the light 影子;阴影:in the ～ of a tree 在树影里 / the ～ of a person 人影 / throw a ～ on the ground 在地上投下影子 ❷ sth.unsubstantial or unreal 不实之物;幽灵:catch at ～s 捕风捉影 / worn to a ～ 虚弱得不成人形 ❸ darkness in a place or on sth.黑暗;背阴:the ～s of evening 暮色 ❹a slight trace 微量;少许:a ～ of doubt (difficulty) 丝毫怀疑(一点困难) Ⅱ*v.*❶ darken;cover sth. with a shadow 遮蔽;使阴暗:The square was ～ed by the trees.广场有树荫。❷follow after, especially in secret 秘密尾随;盯梢:He was ～ed by a plain-clothes detective.他被便衣侦探盯梢了。

shady/'ʃeɪdi/

*adj.*❶ sheltered from bright sunlight by trees or buildings 阴凉的;成荫的;多荫的:～ trees 成荫的树 / the ～ side of the street 街道阴凉的一边 ❷questionable;of doubtful honesty 成问题的;可疑的;不老实的:a ～ person 形迹可疑的人 / a ～ looking fellow 可疑的家伙 /Politics has its ～ side.政治有其阴暗面。

shaft/ʃɑːft/

*n.*❶ a long stem of an arrow or spear 箭杆;矛杆:～s of satire 一支支讽刺的利箭 ❷ a handle of an axe or other tool 柄:the ～ of an axe 斧柄 ❸ a long,vertical passage,e.g. for descending into a coal mine 矿井;竖井

shaggy/'ʃægi/

adj.(of hair) rough and coarse;covered with rough,coarse hair (毛发)浓粗蓬松的;长满粗毛的:～ eyebrows 粗眉 / a ～ dog 粗毛狗

shake/ʃeɪk/

Ⅰ*v.*(shook/ʃʊk/, shaken/'ʃeɪkən/) ❶move or cause to move up and down and to and from with short jerky movements (使)摇动;挥动;使震动;(使)抖动:～ up a bottle of medicine 摇动药瓶 /～ fruit from a tree 把果子从树上摇落下来/～ one's head 摇头 /～ hands with sb. 同某人握手/ ～ one's fist at sb. 对某人挥拳 ❷ shock or quiver 使震惊;发抖:be ～n by the news 对消息感到震惊 / He was shaking in his shoes.他吓得发抖。/His voice was shaking.他的声音在震颤。❸weaken(belief or confidence) 动摇;减弱(信仰、信心):～ sb.'s courage 减弱某人的勇气 /～ sb.'s faith 动摇某人的信念 Ⅱ*n.*❶ an act of shaking 摇动;颤抖:a ～ of head 摇头 ❷ a moment 片刻:in two ～s 一会儿 / in half a ～ 几乎立刻地

shaky /'ʃeɪki/

adj.(shakier, shakiest) ❶ shaking or unsteady 摇动的;不平稳的:a dangerously ～ table 一张摇摇晃晃随时要倒的桌子 ❷unsafe or unreliable 不安全的;不可靠的:thoroughly ～ evidence 完全站不住脚的证据 ‖ **shakily** *adv.*颤抖着;摇动着

shall/ʃæl, ʃəl/

*aux.v.*❶sometimes used with I and we to express the future tense (与第一人称连用表将来时)将:I ～ do it tomorrow.我明天做这件事。❷used to show a promise,command,or obligation,etc.(用于表示承诺、命令、义务等)应;必须;必将:You ～ stay at home.你应该待在家里。

shallow/'ʃæləʊ/

Ⅰ*adj.*❶of little depth 浅的:a ～ stream 浅溪/a ～ dish 浅盘 ❷ lacking depth of intellect or knowledge;concerned only with what is obvious 浅薄的;肤浅的 Ⅱ*n.*a shallow part of a body of water 浅水处;浅滩 Ⅲ*v.*become shallow 变浅

shamble/'ʃæmbl/

*v.*walk in an unsteady way 蹒跚;踉跄:The tired old beggar was just shambling along the street.那疲倦的老乞丐正沿着街道踉跄而行。

shambles/'ʃæmblz/

n.(informal)(**a ～**) any scene of violence; the state of disorder (非正式)任何暴力

场所;混乱:The room was in a ~ after the explosion.发生爆炸后,房内一片混乱。

shame/ʃeɪm/

Ⅰ n.❶ a painful emotion resulting from the loss of self-respect caused by doing sth.wrong 羞愧,惭愧:feel ~ at having told a lie 因撒谎而感到羞愧 ❷ a state of dishonour 羞辱,耻辱:bring ~ on oneself 给自己带来耻辱 ❸(a ~) sth. that make you feel ashamed 遗憾的事:It's a ~ you can't come with us. 你不能与我们一起来,太遗憾了。Ⅱ v.cause to be ashamed 使蒙受耻辱,使丢脸:My silly mistakes ~d me.我犯的愚蠢错误使我抬不起头来。/He was ~d out of his bad habits. 他感到难为情从而改掉了不良习惯。

shameful /ˈʃeɪmful/

adj.causing shame;disgraceful 可耻的;丢脸的:a ~ behaviour 可耻的行为 ‖ ~ly adv.可耻地;丢脸地

shameless /ˈʃeɪmlɪs/

adj. having or showing no feeling of shame 无耻的:~ hypocrisy 无耻的虚伪 ‖ ~ly adv.无耻地

shampoo/ʃæmˈpuː/

Ⅰ n.❶a special kind of soap,liquid,powder,etc.for washing the hair 香波;洗发剂;洗发粉:creamy ~ 乳状洗发剂 ❷ an act of washing the hair 洗头,洗发:give sb.a ~ 给某人洗发 Ⅱ v.wash the hair 洗头,洗发

shape/ʃeɪp/

Ⅰ n.❶ an outer form;a total effect produced by a thing's outlines 外形:the ~ of the building 建筑的外形 ❷ the physical condition of sb. or sth. 情况;状况:The team are now in good ~ for the match.队员们比赛状态良好。Ⅱ v.give a shape or form to 塑造;使……变型:Such education ~d his life.这样的教育塑造了他的一生。

shapeless /ˈʃeɪplɪs/

adj.not having a distinct or an attractive shape 无定形的;不成形的;样子不好看的:a ~ suit 样子难看的套装 ‖ ~ly adv.不成形地

share/ʃeə(r)/

n.a part or division 一份;一部分:He has a large ~ in the profit.这利润中他占有很大的份额。

shark/ʃɑːk/

n.❶ a large fish that eats other fish and sometimes attacks people 鲨(鱼) ❷ a person clever at getting money from others in dishonest ways 敲诈勒索者;骗子

sharp/ʃɑːp/

Ⅰ adj.❶ having a fine point or a thin edge for cutting;pointed 锋利的:a ~ knife 利刃/keep tools ~使工具保持锋利 ❷ quick aware of things;acute 敏锐的;警觉的:keep a ~ look 警惕地守望 ❸ severe or harsh 尖刻的;严厉的:~ reprimand 严厉的斥责 ❹ changing direction suddenly 急转的:a ~ turn 急转弯 Ⅱ adv.punctually 准时地:He always comes at four o'clock ~.他总是在四点钟准时到。

sharpen/ˈʃɑːpən/

v.❶ make or become sharp (使)变锋利;弄尖:~ a pencil 削铅笔/~ a knife 磨刀 ❷ become better at noticing sb.'s thinking or doing sth.使敏锐;增强:~ one's vigilance 提高警惕/The walk has ~ed my appetite.散步增进了我的食欲。

shatter/ˈʃætə(r)/

v.❶ break suddenly into small pieces 粉碎,砸碎:The glass was ~ed to pieces.玻璃被砸得粉碎。❷ destroy or damage sth.破坏,破灭:Our hopes were ~ed.我们的希望破灭了。

shave/ʃeɪv/

v.❶ cut (hair) off the chin,etc.修面;刮胡:My father ~s every day.我父亲每天都要修面。❷ pare off (a thin layer,etc.) 削,刮:The carpenter's shop ~s hundreds of boards everyday.木工厂每天要刨几百块木板。

shawl/ʃɔːl/

n. square pieces of material worn about the shoulders 披肩:Grandmother wears a ~ on cool days.祖母在天冷时戴披肩。

she/ʃiː , ʃi/

Ⅰ pron.(主格)❶ a female person already

referred to（已提及的女人）她：My sister says ～ is going for a walk.我姐（妹）说她要去散步。❷ a female animal or thing, such as a ship, the moon, nation, etc.（表示雌性动物或指船、月亮、国家等）女性；雌性：a～ goat 雌山羊 / a ～ ass 母驴 / a ～ cat 雌猫 Ⅱ n. a female 女性；雌性：Is the baby a "he" or a "～"? 婴儿是男孩还是女孩?

sheaf/ʃiːf/
n.（pl. sheaves/ʃiːvz/）❶ cut stalks of grain bundled together in an orderly way（收割后的小麦等的）束；捆：a ～ of wheat 一捆小麦 / tie the straw into sheaves 把麦秸捆成捆 ❷ a collection of things put together（文件等的）束；扎：a ～ of papers 一叠文件

shear/ʃɪə(r)/
Ⅰ v.（～ed, shorn/ʃɔːn/ or ～ed）❶ remove (the wool, hair, etc.) by cutting or clipping with a sharp instrument 剪（羊）毛；修剪（树木等）：～ a sheep 剪羊毛 /～ a lawn 修剪草坪 ❷（～ of）deprive or divest 剥夺；诈取：be shorn of one's right 被剥夺权利 /She came home shorn of everything. 她被骗得精光回来。Ⅱ n. a pair of large sized scissors 大剪刀；Mother uses ～s to cut cloth. 妈妈用大剪刀裁布。

shed¹/ʃed/
n. a small structure for storage or shelter 棚；小屋：coal ～ 煤棚 / tool ～ 工具房 / bicycle ～ 自行车棚

shed²/ʃed/
v.（shed; shedding）❶ pour forth or cause to pour forth（使）流出；（使）落下：～ tears 流泪 /～ blood 杀戮/～ one's blood 流血牺牲 ❷ loose by a natural process 脱落：～ leaves 树落叶 /～ one's clothes 脱衣服 /～ hair 脱毛 /A snake is ～ding its skin.一条蛇正在蜕皮。❸ give off 散发；发射：～ light 发出光 /～ warmth 散热 / a lamp that ～s a soft light 发射柔光的灯

sheep/ʃiːp/
n.（pl. sheep）❶ a farmed animal with heavy wool（绵）羊：a black～ 害群之马 / a flock of ～ 一群羊 ❷ a person who is

gentle or timid 害羞而忸怩的人；胆小鬼

sheepish/'ʃiːpɪʃ/
adj.❶ awkwardly self-conscious 腼腆的；害羞的：a ～ looking boy 样子腼腆的男孩 ❷ timid and stupid like a sheep 绵羊似的；怯懦而愚笨的

sheer/ʃɪə(r)/
adj.❶ complete; thorough; absolute 完全的，彻底的，绝对的：by ～ chance 纯属偶然 / ～ nonsense 胡说八道 ❷ straight up and down; very steep 垂直的，陡峭的：The rock rises ～ from the water.礁石垂直地从水中伸出水面。

sheet/ʃiːt/
n.❶ a large piece of cloth used on a bed 床单；被单：put clean ～s on the bed 在床上铺干净床单 / get between the ～s 睡；就寝 ❷ a broad, flat piece of some thin material（一）张；（一）片；薄板：a ～ of paper 一张纸/ a ～ of glass 一片玻璃 / ～ copper 薄铜片 /～ music 散页乐谱 / This book is in ～s.这书尚未装订。❸ wide expanse 大片；广大：a ～ of water 一片汪洋/ The rain fell in ～s.大雨倾盆。

shelf/ʃelf/
n.（pl. shelves/ʃelvz/）❶ a flat piece of wood or metal used for holding books or dishes, etc. 架子；搁板：put the book on the ～ 把书放在书架上 / a store ～ 商品陈列架 / replace the books on the shelves 把书放回架上 ❷ sth. like a shelf 搁板状物；岩棚：a continental ～ 大陆架

shell/ʃel/
n.❶ the hard outside covering of sth., such as a fruit, seed, egg, etc.壳；贝壳；果壳；蛋壳：After the fire, only the ～ of the building was left.火灾后大楼只剩下外壳了。❷ a metal case, filled with explosive, to be fired from a large gun 炮弹

shelter/'ʃeltə(r)/
Ⅰ n.❶ sth. that gives safety or protection 庇护所，躲避处 ❷ the condition of being kept safe 庇护；保护 Ⅱ v. give protection to 保护

shelve/ʃelv/
v.❶ put sth. on a shelf 把……置于架上；

~ books 把书放在架子上 ❷ postpone dealing with 搁置；暂缓：~ someone's plan 将某人计划暂时搁下 ❸ cease to employ a person 解雇；辞退：~ an official 辞退官员 ❹（of land）slope gently（土地）渐次倾斜：The shore ~s down to the sea. 海岸向海渐次倾斜。

shepherd/'ʃepəd/
　Ⅰ n. a person who takes care of sheep 牧羊人 Ⅱ v. take care of; guide or direct (people) like sheep 照料；带领，引导：He spent lots of time ~ing the sick. 他花了大量时间去照看病人。

shield/ʃiːld/
　Ⅰ n. ❶ a piece of metal carried by a soldier to protect the body in battle 盾；护板；盾牌：a spear and a ~ 矛和盾 ❷ a person or thing that protects sb. or sth. 保护人；保护物：He's our help and ~. 他是我们的帮手和保护神。Ⅱ v. protect sb. or sth. from a danger, risk or unpleasant experience 保护；防护：~ one's eyes with one's hand 用手保护眼 /~ a friend from censure 使朋友不受责难 /~ a country from invasion 保护国家不受侵略

shift/ʃɪft/
　Ⅰ n. ❶ a change of position, direction, condition, etc. 变更；转变：a ~ of crops 庄稼轮作/a ~ of duties 转换职责 ❷ one of two or more recurring periods in which different groups of workers do the same jobs in relay 轮班：She hates the night ~. 她不喜欢上夜班。Ⅱ v. change opinion, attitude, etc. to another（观点、态度等）转变，改变：His interest ~s easily. 他的兴趣容易改变。

shilling/'ʃɪlɪŋ/
　n. a former British coin worth twelve pennies, one twentieth of a pound 先令（原英国货币单位；20 先令为 1 镑，12 便士为 1 先令）：eight ~s ten pennies 8 先令十便士

shimmer/'ʃɪmə(r)/
　v. shine with an unsteady light 微微发光；闪烁：a lake ~ing in the moonlight 在月光下粼粼发光的湖水

shine/ʃaɪn/
　Ⅰ v. ❶ give out or reflect light; be bright 发光；反光；照耀：Her clothes ~s brightly in the sun. 她的衣服在阳光下闪闪发光。❷ be brilliant or excellent at sth. 表现卓越，表现出众：He ~s in mathematics. 他在数学方面显示出卓越才能。Ⅱ n. high polish or sheen; luster 光泽

shiny/'ʃaɪni/
　adj. polished or rubbed bright 磨光的；擦亮的：~ shoes 锃亮的鞋/~ hair 有光泽的头发

ship/ʃɪp/
　Ⅰ n. a seagoing vessel of considerable size 船；海轮：Now it's time to board the ~. 是上船的时候了。Ⅱ v. (-pp-) transport (goods or people) on a ship 用船运：These equipment will be ~ped to New York in five days. 这些设备将在五天内用船运往纽约。

shipment/'ʃɪpmənt/
　n. ❶ the act of sending goods from one place to another 装船；航运：We are going to effect ~ by the end of this month. 我们将于本月底装船。❷ the goods sent at one time to a person or a company 装载的货物：a ~ to Europe 运往欧洲的货物

shipwreck/'ʃɪprek/
　n. ❶ the loss or destruction of a ship at sea 船只失事，海难：Only two people survived the ~. 这次船只失事只有两人幸免于难。❷ a wrecked ship 沉船，船骸：We found the ~ near the island. 我们在该岛附近找到了失事船只的残骸。

shire/'ʃaɪə(r)/
　n. one of the areas into which Britain is divided 郡

shirt/ʃɜːt/
　n. a garment for the upper part of a man's body (usually of thin cloth)（男式）衬衫 ‖ lose in one's ~ 丧失全部财产

shiver/'ʃɪvə(r)/
　Ⅰ v. tremble, especially from cold or fear 发抖，颤抖，哆嗦：A sudden gust of cold wind made me ~. 一阵突然刮来的寒风使我浑身发抖。Ⅱ n. a trembling that cannot be controlled 冷战，战栗：The sights gave me the ~s. 那景象使我不寒

而栗。

shivery /ˈʃɪvəri/
adj. shaking with cold, fear, illness, etc. (因寒冷、恐惧、患病等)颤抖的,战栗的,哆嗦的

shock /ʃɒk/
Ⅰ *n.* ❶ a violent force from a hard blow, crash, explosion, etc. 摇动;震动 ❷ a state or feeling caused by a sudden, unexpected, and usually very unpleasant event or situation that severely upsets the mind and feelings 震惊;休克:The news was a great ～ to him. 那个消息对他是一个打击。 Ⅱ *v.* surprise and upset sb. 使震惊,使吃惊:Your words ～ed all of us. 你的话使我们大家都很吃惊。

shocking /ˈʃɒkɪŋ/
adj. ❶ causing indignation or disgust 引起愤慨的;令人憎恶的;讨厌的:～ behaviour 骇人听闻的行为 ❷ very bad 非常糟糕的:～ weather 非常糟糕的天气 ‖ ～ly *adv.* 非常地;骇人地

shoddy /ˈʃɒdi/
adj. poorly made or done 劣质的:a ～ piece of work 一件劣质品

shoe /ʃuː/
Ⅰ *n.* a covering of leather, rubber, etc. that you wear on your foot 鞋:put on (take off) one's ～s 穿鞋(脱鞋)/ a pair of ～s 一双鞋/ high-heeled ～s 高跟鞋/ ～ horn 鞋拔/～ string (lace) 鞋带 Ⅱ *v.* (shod /ʃɒd/ or ～d) ❶ be wearing shoes of a specified kind 穿鞋(或靴) ❷ fit (a horse) with a shoe or shoes 给(马)钉蹄铁 ❸ protect sth. with a metal shoe 用金属片包覆:an iron-shod stick 装有铁包头的手杖

shoot /ʃuːt/
v. ❶ hurt or kill a person or animal with a bullet or arrow 射击:Don't ～ the birds. 不要打鸟。 ❷ pass quickly by or along 迅速通过,穿过 ❸ photograph (a scene) 拍照;照相

shop /ʃɒp/
Ⅰ *n.* a building or part of a building where goods are shown and sold 商店:The ～ will not be open until nine o'clock. 商店要

到九点钟才开门。 Ⅱ *v.* (-pp-) visit one or more shops in order to buy things 购物,采购:She goes ～ping every week. 她每周都要去商店买东西。/～ for food 去商店买食物

shore /ʃɔː(r)/
n. the land along the edge of a sea, lake, etc. 岸;滨:walk along the ～ 沿岸散步 / on ～ 在陆上 / go on ～ (从船)上岸 / 2,000 miles off ～ 离岸两千英里 / Then he made his way down to the ～. 然后他走向岸边。

short /ʃɔːt/
Ⅰ *adj.* ❶ not long 短的:The time for us to stay here is very ～. 我们能在这里的时间很短。 ❷ not having enough of sth. 短缺的 ❸ small in height 矮的:Lucy is ～ and dumpy. 露西又矮又胖。 ❹ lasting a small amount of time 短暂的:have a ～ break 短暂休息 Ⅱ *adv.* abruptly; suddenly 唐突地;突然地:stop ～ 突然停止

shortage /ˈʃɔːtɪdʒ/
n. the condition of having not enough 不足;缺乏:food ～s 粮食缺乏 / a ～ of cloth 布匹缺乏 / owing to ～ of staff 由于人员的缺少 / cover the ～ 弥补不足

shortcoming /ˈʃɔːtˌkʌmɪŋ/
n. fault; failure to reach a required standard 缺点;不足:Despite all his ～s, he makes a good friend. 尽管有种种缺点,他仍然是个不错的朋友。

shorten /ˈʃɔːtn/
v. make or become shorter 缩短;变短:The days ～ in November in this country. 这个国家从十一月开始白日渐短。/The new highway ～s the trip. 新的高速公路缩短了旅程。

shorthand /ˈʃɔːthænd/
n. a system of rapid writing using special signs 速记:write (in) ～ 做速记

shortlist /ˈʃɔːtlɪst/
Ⅰ *n.* a list of selected candidates from which a final choice is made 决选名单 Ⅱ *v.* put (sb. or sth.) on a shortlist 把……列入决选的名单:The novel was ～ed for the Booker Prize. 这本小说列入图书奖的决选名单。

short-lived/ˌʃɔːtˈlɪvd/

*adj.*living or lasting only for a short time 短命的；短暂的：a ～ triumph 短暂的胜利

shortly/ˈʃɔːtli/

*adv.*❶in a short time；soon 立刻，马上；不久：They will be here ～.他们很快就会到达这儿。/I'll be ready ～.我马上就准备好了。❷in a few words 简短地；扼要地 ❸in an impolite or curt manner 唐突地；简慢地；草率地

shorts/ʃɔːts/

*n.*trousers which stop above the knees 短裤：a pair of ～ 一条短裤

shot/ʃɒt/

*n.*❶the firing of a gun or cannon 开枪；开炮；射击：I can hear ～s outside.我听到外面有枪声。❷taking of a drug or injection into the bloodstream through a needle 注射；打针

should/ʃʊd, ʃəd/

aux.v. ❶ought to 应该：Why ～n't I say what I think? 为什么我不该把我心里所想的说出来？❷ probably happen 可能：If you leave now, you ～ arrive there by ten o'clock.如果你现在就走，十点钟就能到达那里。❸used in conditional sentences（用在条件句中表假设）应,应该；将要：If it ～ happen, what shall we do? 如果发生那种事，我们怎么办？❹used in that clauses after adjectives and verbs like anxious, intend, desire, demand, etc.（用在形容词 anxious 等，动词 intend, desire, demand 等之后的 that 从句中）应该；必须：I demand that Tom ～ go there at once! 我要求汤姆马上到那里去！

shoulder/ˈʃəʊldə(r)/

Ⅰ *n.*the part of the body at each side of the neck where the arms are connected 肩：shrug one's ～ 耸肩/with a box on the ～ 肩上有一个箱子 Ⅱ *v.*push sb. or sth. with the shoulder 用肩推：Someone is ～ing me.有人在用肩膀推我。

shout/ʃaʊt/

Ⅰ *n.*a loud call or cry 大叫 Ⅱ *v.*say or utter in a loud voice 大声说（喊）：～ at someone 对某人大喊 ‖ ～ sb. down 大声

喊，压过某人的声音

shovel/ˈʃʌvl/

Ⅰ *n.*a tool for lifting and moving loose material 铁锹；铲："Why are a pick and a ～ here?" he asked."这儿怎么会有镐和锹呢？"他问。Ⅱ *v.*(-ll- or -l-) take up and throw with a shovel 用锹铲；把……铲干净：～ the earth into the truck 用锹将土装进汽车 /～ a path through the snow 在雪中铲出一条小路 /～ the snow away from the garden path 铲去公园小路上的雪

show/ʃəʊ/

Ⅰ *n.*❶ sth. that is shown；exhibition 展览：a ～ of oil paintings 油画展/Is there any good ～ tonight? 今晚有什么好节目（表演）吗？❷ an act of showing 表演：There will be a ～ tonight.今晚有演出。Ⅱ *v.*❶ allow to look at；permit sb. to see 出示；上映：Please ～ me your passport. 请出示通行证。❷ display；exhibit 看得出；显示：It ～s that he does not like it.这表明他不喜欢。❸ point out；guide 引导；引领：～ him out 带他出去 ‖ ～ sb. the way 指路/～ sb. (sth.) off 显示优点/on one's own ～ing 诚如某人自己所承认的

shower/ˈʃaʊə(r)/

Ⅰ *n.*❶ a brief fall of rain 阵雨：He was caught in a ～.他淋了一场雨。❷a bath in which water pours down on the body from above in small jets 淋浴：take a ～ 洗淋浴 Ⅱ *v.*❶wash oneself in a shower 淋浴 ❷ fall or be thrown in a shower 雨点般落下

showing/ˈʃəʊɪŋ/

*n.*❶the presentation of a cinema film or television programme 放映 ❷ the evidence or quality that someone shows 表现：On today's ～, he will succeed. 从今天的表现来看，他将会成功。

showy/ˈʃəʊi/

*adj.*having a striking appearance or style, typically by being excessively bright, colourful 引人注目的；显眼的：～ flowers 鲜艳的花

shred/ʃred/

Ⅰ *n.*❶ a small piece of sth.；fragment 碎

条;碎片;tear that piece of cloth to ～s 把那块布撕成碎片 / tear an argument to ～s 把一番议论驳得体无完肤 ❷ a small amount;particle 少量;一点点;not a ～ of reason 没一点道理 / without a ～ of evidence 没有丝毫证据 Ⅱ v.(-dd-) tear or scrape into small pieces 撕成碎片;～ the cloth 把布撕成碎片 /～ded suet 切成细条的板油

shrewd/ʃruːd/
adj. ❶ sharp;smart or clever at making judgements about a situation 敏锐的;精明的;机灵的;a ～ businessman 敏锐的;精明的生意人 / a ～ lawyer 头脑敏锐的律师 / ～ arguments 明智的辩论 / The woman is ～ at a bargain.那位妇女精于讨价还价。❷ showing good judgement and likely to be right 判断得准的;高明的;make a ～ guess 做有眼光的猜测 / a ～ blow 有效的一击

shriek/ʃriːk/
Ⅰ v.❶ make a high loud cry 尖声喊叫;～ in fear 吓得尖声喊叫 ❷ utter in a screaming voice 以尖叫声说出;～ out a warning 厉声警告 Ⅱ n.a loud,high shout 尖叫;～s of girlish laughter 女孩的尖锐笑声 / the ～ of a railroad engine 铁路机车的尖鸣声

shrill/ʃrɪl/
Ⅰ *adj.*(of sounds) sharp,piercing (指声音)尖锐的,刺耳的;a ～ whistle 尖锐的汽笛声 / a ～ complaint 哀诉 Ⅱ v.make a loud,usually unpleasant noise 尖叫

shrimp/ʃrɪmp/
Ⅰ n.a small shellfish 小虾;虾 Ⅱ v.catch shrimps 捕虾;go ～ing 去捕虾

shrine/ʃraɪn/
n.a holy place 神龛;圣地;the ～ of liberty 自由的圣地

shrink/ʃrɪŋk/
v.❶ draw together;contract 收缩;皱缩;Cotton clothes ～ in washing.棉质衣服洗的时候缩水。❷ draw back;turn away 畏缩;退缩;A shy man ～s from meeting strangers. 羞怯的人怕见生人。❸ become or make smaller in size or amount 变小;减少

shrinkage/ˈʃrɪŋkɪʤ/
n. ❶ the process of shrinking, or the amount by which sth. has shrunk 收缩;皱缩;收缩量;Give long curtains to allow for ～.考虑到会缩水,窗帘要做长一些。❷an allowance made for loss of income in business due to theft or wastage 损耗容许量

shrivel/ˈʃrɪvl/
v.(-ll-)make or become twisted and dried up (使)皱缩;(使)枯萎;a plant ～led with heat 遇热皱缩的植物/a person ～led with age 年老萎缩的人

shrub/ʃrʌb/
n. a small low plant that have several woody stems 灌木

shrug/ʃrʌg/
Ⅰ v.(-gg-) lift and drop the shoulders to show that you do not know or do not care (为表示不知道、冷漠)耸肩;～ one's shoulders 耸耸肩 Ⅱ n.a movement involving raising one's shoulders 耸肩;a ～ of despair 失望地耸肩/ with a ～ of the shoulders 耸肩地 / smile with a ～ 耸耸肩笑了

shudder/ˈʃʌdə(r)/
Ⅰ v. tremble of shiver with fear, horror, cold or disgust, etc.(因恐惧、寒冷、厌恶等)发抖,战栗;～ with cold (horror) 寒冷(恐怖)得发抖/～ at the sight of blood 看见血而发抖/ He ～s to think of it.他一想到它就打起颤来。Ⅱ n. an act of shaking that you make for fear, cold, etc. 发抖;战栗;give someone the ～s 使某人吓得发抖/ A ～ passed over him.他不由自主地发抖。

shuffle/ˈʃʌfl/
Ⅰ v.❶ drag one's feet along the ground when walking 拖着脚走;Don't ～ along! 别拖着脚走路。❷ mix up the order of (playing cards) 洗(牌);It's your turn to ～.轮到你洗牌了 。Ⅱ n.❶ a slow dragging walk 曳行;曳步 ❷ an act of shuffling cards 洗牌;Here are the cards; it's your ～.牌在这里,该你洗牌了。

shut/ʃʌt/
v. keep from entering or leaving; enclose

S

关：Shut your mouth! 闭住你的嘴！/Don't ～ the door.不要关门。‖～ **sth.off** 停止供应/～ **sb.(sth.) out** 把某人(物)排除在外/～ **down** 关掉

shutdown /'ʃʌtdaʊn/
n. ❶ the closing of a factory or business (尤指工厂或公司的)关闭,倒闭 ❷ the turning off of a computer or other device (计算机或其他装置的)关闭

shutter/'ʃʌtə(r)/
*n.*a movable cover made of wood, metal, etc. which can be put over a window to keep out sunlight, cold, thieves, etc. 百叶窗(遮光、御寒、防贼等用)

shuttle/'ʃʌtl/
Ⅰ*n.* ❶ a device used in weaving to carry the thread back and forth 梭子;梭 ❷ the regular service to and from by air, bus, etc.between two places 来往于两地之间的航班(或班车等);a space ～ 定时往返的航天飞机 Ⅱ*v.*move back and forth by or as if by a shuttle (使)往返如梭

shy/ʃaɪ/
*adj.*not at ease in front of strangers;easily frightened 怕羞的;害羞的:a ～ look 羞怯的一瞥/a ～ girl 怕羞的女孩

sick/sɪk/
*adj.*❶ ready to throw up food 翻胃的;作呕的 ❷ suffering from disease; ill; not well 病的:He's been ～ for a long time. 他已经生病很长时间了。‖ ～ **at heart** 深为悲伤/～ **at (about) sth.** 对……感到不快

sickbed/'sɪkbed/
*n.*the bed on which a sick person is lying 病床;床榻:lie on one's ～ 躺在病床上

sicken/'sɪkən/
v. ❶ become ill; be in the first stages of (an illness) 生病;初步发出症状:The child is ～ing for something.这孩子怕是生了什么病了。 ❷ cause to feel disgusted 使厌恶:Cruelty ～s most of us.我们大多数人厌恶残酷。 ❸ feel sick 作呕;恶心欲吐:～ed at the sight of blood 看到血而欲吐

sickening /'sɪknɪŋ/
*adj.*❶disgusting or appalling 引起呕吐的;令人厌恶的:a ～ stench of blood 令人恶心的血腥味 ❷annoying or irritating 令人恼怒的;烦恼的

sickle/'sɪkl/
*n.*a tool used for cutting grass and grain 镰刀

sickly /'sɪkli/
adj. (sicklier, sickliest) ❶ often ill or in poor health 常生病的;多病的;体弱的: a ～ child 爱闹病的孩子 ❷ causing poor health 引起疾病的;有碍健康的:a ～ climate 对健康不利的气候 ❸causing sickness or nausea 令人反胃的;令人不适的:a ～ smell 令人反胃的气味

sickness /'sɪknɪs/
*n.*❶the state of being ill 生病;患病: She was absent because of ～.她因患病没来。 ❷ the act of vomiting 恶心;呕吐:Symptoms include ～ and diarrhea.症状包括呕吐和腹泻。

side/saɪd/
Ⅰ*n.* ❶ one of the parts of sth. that is not the top, bottom, back, or front 边 ❷ the right or left half of the body (人的)侧边:on the right ～ 在右侧 ❸ an area separated from another by some intervening line, barrier, or other feature 一部分 ❹ a part to be considered, usually in opposition to another; an aspect 不同方面(观点):There are two ～s to everything. 任何事物都有其两面性。‖ **on (from) all ～s, on (from) every ～** 从各方面;到处/**take sb.on one ～** 把某人带到一边/**put sth.on one ～** 将某物搁置一旁/**be on sb.'s ～** 支持某人 Ⅱ*v.* support on a person or group in a quarrel, fight, etc. a-gainst another (在争吵,争斗等中)站在……一边;偏袒…… ‖ ～ **view** *n.*侧景/～ **walk** *n.*人行道

sideways/'saɪdweɪz/
Ⅰ*adv.*to, towards or from the side; with the side or edge first 斜着;侧着;横着: look ～ at someone 斜视某人/walk ～ through a narrow opening 侧着身子走过狭窄的通道 Ⅱ*adj.* toward one side 横的;斜的:a ～ glance 斜视

siege/siːdʒ/

　　n.(a period of) operations of armed forces to capture a fortified place 围困；围攻；围城；围攻期间：lay a ～ to a town 围攻一城 / raise the ～ 解围/ a ～ of 60 days 六十天的围困期

sigh/saɪ/

　　Ⅰ *v.*let out a very long, deep breath because one is sad, tired, or relieved 叹息；叹气：We heard her ～ing.我们听见她在叹气。Ⅱ *n.*the act or sound of sighing 叹息声；叹气：draw a ～ 叹一口气

sight/saɪt/

　　Ⅰ *n.*❶ the power of seeing 视力；视觉：a good eye ～ 很好的视力 ❷ the action or fact of seeing sb. or sth. 看，看见：She cried at the ～ of the accident.看到事故现场，她叫了起来。❸ sth. seen；a remarkable view 情景；风景：～ seeing 观光‖**know by** ～ 面熟/**catch** ～ **of, have (get) a** ～ **of** 发现；看到/**keep** ～ **of, keep sb.(sth.) in** ～ 监视/**lose** ～ **of** 看不见/**at first** ～ 初见/**in (within)(out of)** ～ **of sth.**看得见(看不见)/**keep out of** ～ 待在看不见的地方 Ⅱ *v.*see sth. suddenly, especially sth. you have been looking for 看到；发现：After days of voyage, they at last ～ed an island.经过数日的航行，他们终于看见了一个小岛。‖～ **less** *adj.*盲目的；无视力的

sightseeing /ˈsaɪtsiːɪŋ/

　　*n.*the act of visiting interesting places in a town, etc. 观光；游览：go ～ 去观光‖**sightseer** *n.*观光客

sign/saɪn/

　　Ⅰ *n.*a mark, symbol or word which has a message for the person who sees it or them 符号；标志：a ～ of strength 力量的象征 Ⅱ *v.* write one's name on 签名：Please ～ your name here.请在这儿签上你的名字。‖～ **sth. away** 签字让出(财产等)/～ **sb.on (up)** 签约雇佣

signal/ˈsɪɡnəl/

　　Ⅰ *n.*any kind of mark, light, sound, movement, etc. which gives an idea to someone, or controls his actions in some way 信号；暗号：traffic ～s 交通信号 Ⅱ *v.* make a signal or signals 发信号

signature/ˈsɪɡnətʃə(r)/

　　*n.*❶the writer's name at the end of a letter 签名；署名：put one's ～ to a letter 签名于信件 ❷the act of signing 签字

significance/sɪɡˈnɪfɪkəns/

　　*n.*the meaning or importance of sth.意义；含义；重要性：a matter of ～ 重大的事情/ understand the ～ of the idiom 了解这个成语的意义 / political ～ 政治意义 / a look of deep ～ 富于表情的脸色 / the ～ of a remark 一句话的含义

significant/sɪɡˈnɪfɪkənt/

　　*adj.*having a special meaning；important 有特殊含义的；重要的：a ～ glance 意味深长的一瞥/ a ～ day 有意义的日子 / a ～ event 重大的事件 / His smile is ～ of acceptance.他的微笑表示了答应。

signify/ˈsɪɡnɪfaɪ/

　　*v.*❶mean；be a sign of 意味；表明：What does that ～? 那意味着什么？ /He signified his agreement (that he agreed) with a nod.他点头表示同意。/His wife signified her approval.他的妻子表示赞同。❷ be matter；be of importance 有关系；有重要性：It does not ～.这没有什么意义。/It signifies much (little).那甚为重要(不太重要)。

signing /ˈsaɪnɪŋ/

　　*n.*❶the action of writing one's signature on an official document（在正式文件上）签署 ❷the action of recruiting someone, especially to a professional sports team or record company（尤指专业运动队、唱片公司的）签约

silence/ˈsaɪləns/

　　Ⅰ *n.*❶ the absence of sound；stillness 无声；寂静：The teacher asked for ～.老师要求大家安静。❷ the state of being or keeping silent 沉默；缄默：keep ～ 保持缄默/break ～ 打破沉默 Ⅱ *v.*make silent and quiet 使安静；使沉默：The mother ～d the baby's crying.母亲使婴孩止住了哭。

silent/ˈsaɪlənt/

　　*adj.*❶with no sound；quiet 安静的；无声的：a ～ night 一个寂静的夜晚/a ～ prayer 默祷/ with ～ footsteps 脚步寂静地 ❷ saying nothing；giving no answer 不

作声的；不搭腔的：～ for a while 沉默一会/ a ～ film 无声电影/ You'd better be ～ about what happened.你对所发生的事最好不开口。

silicon/'sɪlɪkən/

n. a non-metallic chemical element which is often used in making glass（非金属元素）硅‖ ～ **chip** *n.*（用作微机电路等的）硅片

silk/sɪlk/

n.（smooth soft cloth made from）fine thread which is produced by a silkworm 丝；丝织品：China is famous for its ～.中国以其丝绸而闻名。‖ ～**en** *adj.*柔软光滑的

silky /'sɪlki/

adj.（silkier, silkiest）soft, fine, or smooth like silk 丝绸一样的；柔软光洁的：～ fur 像丝绸一样的毛皮

sill/sɪl/

n. a piece of wood or stone across the bottom of a door or a window 门槛；窗台

silly/'sɪli/

Ⅰ *adj.*absurd and foolish 愚蠢的；傻的；糊涂的：say ～ things 说蠢话/ a ～ talk 糊涂话/ Don't be ～! 别傻！/What a ～ question! 多么愚蠢的问题。Ⅱ *n.*（chiefly used to or by children）a foolish person（主要用于指小孩或由小孩所用）傻瓜；笨蛋：Don't be a ～! 别当傻瓜！/ Go away, you little sillies! 走开，你们这些小傻子！

silt/sɪlt/

n. fine earth and sand which is left by a river 淤泥；淤沙

silver/'sɪlvə(r)/

*n.*❶a soft whitish precious metal that is a simple substance（element）, carries electricity very well, can be brightly polished, and is used in jewellery, coins, and knives, forks, etc. 银 ❷ a shiny greyish-white colour 银色；银白色‖ **be born with a ～ spoon in one's mouth** 生来就有钱‖ ～ **paper** *n.*锡纸/～ **smith** *n.*银匠/～ **wedding** *n.*银婚‖ ～**n** *adj.*似银的

silvery /'sɪlvəri/

*adj.*❶like silver in colour or appearance；

shiny and grey-white 似银的；有银色光泽的：shoals of ～ fish 一群群银色闪亮的鱼 ❷（of a sound）gentle, clear, and melodious（声音）清脆的，银铃般悦耳的：a little ～ laugh 清脆的笑声

similar/'sɪmɪlə(r)/

*adj.*like or alike；of the same kind；almost but not exactly the same in nature or appearance 类似的；相像的：Gold is ～ in colour to brass.金和黄铜的颜色相似。

similarity /ˌsɪmɪ'lærɪti/

n.（*pl.*-ies）the state or fact of being like 相似性；类似性：There is some ～ in the way they sing.他们的演唱风格有点像。

simple/'sɪmpl/

*adj.*❶easy to understand；not complicated 易于理解的；简单的：This question is very ～.这个问题十分简单。❷basic and plain without anything extra 简朴的，朴素的 ❸ordinary；not special 普通的，平凡的：a ～ teacher 平凡的教师‖ **pure and ～** 绝对的；无疑的

simplicity /sɪm'plɪsɪti/

*n.*the quality of being simple 简单（性）；容易（性）：the relative ～ of the new PC 新型个人电脑的相对简易

simplify /'sɪmplɪfaɪ/

v.（simplified, simplifying） make sth. simple or simpler 简化；精简；使简明：a simplified version of the story for young children 供小朋友阅读的故事简写本‖ **simplification** *n.*简化；简化的事物

simply/'sɪmpli/

*adv.*❶in a simple manner 简单地；简朴地：He is ～ dressed.他衣着简朴。❷absolutely；completely 简直；完全：～ hopeless 简直毫无希望 ❸ merely；only 仅仅，只不过：He is ～ a teacher.他只是一名教师。

simulate/'sɪmjʊleɪt/

*v.*pretend to be or to have 假装；冒充；模仿：～ enthusiasm 假装热情‖ **simulation**/ˌsɪmjʊ'leɪʃn/ *n.* 假装；模仿

simultaneous/ˌsɪml'teɪnɪəs/

*adj.*happening or done at the same time（with）同时的；同时发生的：This was ～ with that.这件事跟那件事同时发生。

S

sin/sɪn/

  Ⅰ *n*. an evil act; an act against God's teaching 罪(恶);罪孽:commit ～ 犯罪 / a ～ against good manners 违反礼节的过错 / ask for one's ～s to be forgiven 请求赦罪 Ⅱ *v*.(-nn-) commit a sin; do wrong 犯罪;犯过失:We are all liable to ～.我们都易于犯罪。/Have you ever ～ned against propriety? 你曾违背过礼仪吗?

since/sɪns/

  Ⅰ *adv*. before now; ago 之前;以前:He left home ten years ago and has never returned home ～.他十年前离开了家,以后就从来没回来过。Ⅱ *conj*.(used with the present perfect or past perfect tenses) from an event in the past until a later past event, or until now 自从;自从……以后:It is two years ～ I came to live in Beijing.自从我到北京生活以来,已有两年了。‖ **ever ～** 此后一直

sincere/sɪnˈsɪə(r)/

  adj.(of a person, feelings, or behaviour) without any deceit or falseness; real, true, or honest; genuine 真诚的;不虚假的:He's ～ in doing that.他做那件事是诚心的。/～ thanks 真诚的谢意 ‖ **～ly** *adv*.真诚地:Yours ～ly 用于书信末的套语

sine/saɪn/

  n. the ratio between the side opposite a given acute angle in a right-angled triangle and the hypotenuse 正弦

sing/sɪŋ/

  v.(sang/sæŋ/, sung /sʌŋ/) ❶make music with the voice 唱;歌唱:～ in chorus 合唱 /～ to the piano 和着钢琴唱 / Will you ～ a song for me? 给我唱一支歌好吗? /He ～s well. 他唱得很好。/You are not ～ing in tune.你唱得不合调子。❷(of a bird)make characteristic melodious whistling and twittering sounds (鸟)啼,鸣:The birds were ～ing.鸟在啼叫。❸ make or be filled with a ringing sound 作响;发出嗡嗡声:The kettle ～s.水壶响了。/My ears are ～ing. 我在耳鸣。❹ celebrate in verse 歌颂;吟咏:～ the praises of 歌颂…… / ～(of) someone's exploits 歌颂某人的功勋

singe/sɪndʒ/

  v. burn the surface of sth. slightly 烧焦:Singe a shirt while ironing it.熨衬衫时,把一件衬衫烫焦了

singer /ˈsɪŋə/

  n. a person who sings, or whose job is singing, especially in public 唱歌的人;歌唱家;歌手

single/ˈsɪŋɡl/

  Ⅰ *adj*.❶ one only; one and no more 唯一的;单一的:a ～ bird 仅仅一只鸟/～-handed 独自的/～ minded 一心一意的 ❷ not married 未婚的;单身的:remain ～ 仍然单身 Ⅱ *n*.(tennis and golf) a game with one person on each side 单打:play a ～单打比赛 Ⅲ*v*.pick out; select 单独挑出:Why did you ～ me out for praise? 为什么要单单表扬我一个人?

singly/ˈsɪŋɡli/

  adv.❶ one by one 逐一地;一个一个地;依次地:deal with the questions ～ 一个一个地处理问题 ❷ alone 单独地;独自地:Some guests came ～,others in groups.有的客人是自己个别前来的,有的则成群结队而来。

singular/ˈsɪŋɡjʊlə(r)/

  adj.❶very unusual or strange; out of the ordinary 奇特的;非凡的;异常的 ❷of or being a word or form representing exactly one 单数的:"One book" is ～;"two books" is plural."一本书"是单数,"两本书"是复数。

sinister/ˈsɪnɪstə(r)/

  adj.❶ suggesting evil or the likelihood of coming misfortune 不吉祥的;凶兆的:a ～ beginning 不吉祥的开始 ❷ showing ill will 险恶的;邪恶的;凶恶的:a ～ face 凶恶的脸 /～ looks 阴险的表情 ❸ (in heraldry) on the left side of the shield (盾形徽章的)左上方的

sink/sɪŋk/

  Ⅰ *v*.(sank, sunk) ❶ go down, especially below the horizon or the surface of water or other liquid 沉:The ship sank with twenty people dead.船沉没了,有二十个人死亡。❷ make by digging 挖;掘:～ a hole here 在这里挖一个洞 Ⅱ *n*.a basin fixed to a wall or floor and having a drainpipe and a piped water supply 水槽 ‖ ～ or swim 沉浮全凭自己/～ in;～ into sth.渗入 ‖ ～ing n.虚弱无力的感觉

Sino-/'saɪnəʊ/

pref. Chinese (e. g. Sino-Japanese trade) 中国(的)(例如中日贸易)

sip/sɪp/

Ⅰ *v*.(-pp-) drink little by little 啜;小口地喝:～ (at) the wine 啜饮酒/～ tea 啜茶 Ⅱ *n*.(quantity taken in a) sipping 啜;一啜之量:take a ～ 啜饮/ drink brandy in ～s, not gulps 细品白兰地酒,不是牛饮

sir/sɜː(r), sə(r)/

n. ❶ a respectful form of address to a man (对男人的尊称)先生,阁下,君:Yes,～.是的,先生。/Good morning,～.早安,先生。/Dear Sir(s).(商务信函中的称呼) ❷ a prefix to the name of a knight or baronet 爵士或男爵地尊称(置于名或姓名前,不能只用于姓前):Sir Walter Scott 沃尔特·斯科特爵士/ Sir Winston Churchill 温士顿·丘吉尔爵士

siren/'saɪərən/

n. ❶ a kind of whistle that makes a loud, sharp sound 警报器;汽笛:a ship's ～ 船上的号笛 ❷ a dangerous and beautiful woman 女妖;危险的美女

sister/'sɪstə(r)/

n.❶a female relative with the same parents 姐妹 ❷(a title for) a nurse (usually a female) in charge of a department (WARD) of a hospital 护士长 ‖ ～ -in-law *n*. 嫂;弟媳/younger ～ *n*.妹妹

sit/sɪt/

v.(sat) ❶ rest on the bottom of the back 坐:Sit down, please. 请坐下。❷ (of bird) settle;rest (鸟)落;栖 ❸ cause to take a seat 使坐:Don't ～ the baby by the fire. 不要让婴儿坐在火边。‖ ～ down under 无怨言地忍受/～ on (upon) sth.做陪审员;调查

site/saɪt/

Ⅰ *n*.❶ a place where sth.of special interest existed or happened 场所;遗址:historic ～s 史迹 ❷the place where there is

a building or where one may be placed 基地;位置;地址:a construction ～ 建筑工地/I do not like this ～ for a school.我不喜欢把这个地点作为学校校址。Ⅱ *v*. place in a position; locate 定址; 位于: Where have they decided to ～ the new factory? 他们已经决定新厂址了吗?

sitting-room/ˌsɪtɪŋ'rʊm/

n.a room in a house where we can sit during the day;a lounge 客厅;起居室

situate/'sɪtjʊeɪt/

v.place in a certain stop;locate 使位于;使处于:The village is ～d in a valley.这村庄坐落于山谷中。/I'm awkwardly ～d just now.我目前处境困难。

situation/ˌsɪtʃʊ'eɪʃn/

n.❶ the position or condition at the moment 处境;局面:the international (domestic) ～ 国际(国内)形势/ be in an embarrassing ～ 处于尴尬的境地 / the political ～ in China 中国的政局 ❷a job; a position of employment 工作;职位:～s vacant (报纸广告)招聘 /apply for a ～ 申请工作 / be in (out of) a ～ 受雇(未受雇)

six/sɪks/

num. the number 6 六;六个 ‖ at sixes and sevens 乱七八糟

sixteen/'sɪks'tiːn/

num.six more than ten 十六(个)

sixteenth/'sɪks'tiːnθ/

num.next after the fifteenth;one of sixteen equal parts 第十六;十六分之一:An ounce is one ～ of a pound.一盎司是十六分之一磅。

sixth/sɪksθ/

num.next after the fifth;one of six equal parts 第六;六分之一:a ～ share 六分之一份

sixtieth/'sɪkstɪəθ/

num.next after the fifty-ninth;one of sixty equal parts 第六十;六十分之一

sixty/'sɪksti/

num.the numbr 60 六十:～-two 六十二

size/saɪz/

n.❶ the degree of largeness or smallness 大小;规模:He is about your ～.他身材

S

和你差不多。❷ each of the classes, typically numbered, into which garments or other articles are divided according how large they are(衣服或其他物品的)尺码，号

skate/skeɪt/

Ⅰ*n.*a sharp-edged steel blade fastened to a boot for moving over ice 冰鞋：a pair of ～s 一双冰鞋 Ⅱ*v.*move on skates 滑冰；溜冰：～ over the lake 在湖面上滑冰/ go skating 去滑冰 ‖ ～r *n.* 滑冰者

skeleton/ˈskelɪtən/

*n.*the framework of all the bones in a human or animal body 骨骼 ‖ **reduced to a ～** 因(疾病、饥饿)而皮包骨/**a ～ in the cupboard** 家丑

sketch/sketʃ/

Ⅰ*n.*❶ a rough, quickly-made drawing 草图；素描；速写：made a ～ of a building 作一建筑物的略图 / a rough ～ 草图 / ～ book 素描簿 ❷ a short account or description；a rough draft or general outline 概略；大纲：He gave me a ～ of his plan. 他对我简述他的计划。❸ a short, humorous play or piece of writing 幽默的短剧或短文 Ⅱ*v.*make a rough drawing or brief description of 画素描；略述：～ (out) a plan 草拟计划 /～ from nature 写生

ski/skiː/

Ⅰ*n.*(*pl.*ski or ～s) one of a pair of long, narrow strips of wood, strapped under the feet for moving over snow 滑雪履：a pair of ～(s) 一副滑雪履/bind on one's ～(s) 缚在滑雪履上 Ⅱ*v.*(skied；skiing) move over snow on ski(s) 滑雪：go ～ing at New Year 新年时去滑雪 / go in for ～ing 爱好滑雪

skill/skɪl/

*n.*❶ the ability to do sth. well 技能；技巧：The girl plays the piano with great ～.那小女孩钢琴弹得很娴熟。❷a particular kind of ability (某种)技能，技艺：master the carpenter's ～ 掌握木工技能

skilled /skɪld/

*adj.*❶having or showing the knowledge, ability, or training to perform a certain activity or task well 有技能的；有技巧的：a ～ draughtsman 专业制图员 ❷ based on such training or experience；showing expertise 熟练的；显示技巧的：～ legal advice 专业的法律意见

skil(l)ful/ˈskɪlfl/

*adj.*❶having or showing skill 有技巧的；灵巧的；熟练的：be ～ at painting 善于绘画 / be ～ in teaching 善于教书 / be ～ with a tool 善于使用工具 ❷ done with skill 制作精巧的：～ handicrafts 精巧的手工艺品

skim/skɪm/

v.(-mm-)❶ read quickly, noting only the chief points 略读；快读：A good reader should be skillful at ～ming.一个善于读书的人必须善于略读。❷ glide or pass quickly and lightly over 轻轻掠过

skin/skɪn/

*n.*❶ the outer covering of a person, animal or plant 皮肤；皮❷ an outer layer or covering 外层 ‖ **～ and bone** 瘦成皮包骨/**by the ～ of one's teeth** 侥幸/**get sb.on one's ～** 迷恋某人/**have a thin (thick) ～** 薄(厚)脸皮/**save one's ～** 安然逃脱

skip/skɪp/

*v.*❶ jump (over) lightly 轻快地跳：The girls were playing with a ～ping rope.女孩子们在跳绳。❷ pass over or omit what you should do, read, etc.next 跳过；跳读

skipper/ˈskɪpə(r)/

*n.*the captain of a small ship (小船的)船长

skirt/skɜːt/

Ⅰ*n.*❶a garment for a woman or girl that hangs from the waist 裙子：divided ～s 裤裙 /A woman's suit consists of a coat and a ～.一套女装指一件上衣和一条裙子。❷ the part of a dress or other garment that hangs below the waist 衣服的下身；下摆 ❸(*pl.*) border；extreme parts (复数)边界；边缘；边：on the ～s of the town 在城郊 ❹a (young) woman (年轻)女性 Ⅱ*v.*❶go along the border (edge) of 沿……边缘而行：We ～ed the town to get away from the heavy traffic.我们环城

走以避开拥挤的车辆。❷avoid 回避：She ~ed round the subject of her family.她回避她的家庭问题。

skull /skʌl/

n. the bones of the head 头盖骨：The ~ can take a hard blow without injury to the brain.头盖骨能经受重击而脑子不受伤。

sky /skaɪ/

n. the upper air; the space above the Earth where clouds and the sun, moon, and stars appear 天；天空：~ lark 云雀/ There are millions of stars in the ~.天空中有成千上万颗星星。

slack /slæk/

adj. ❶ giving little care or attention to one's work 马虎的；懒散的：He is ~ in his work.他工作马虎。❷ inactive; dull 呆滞的；萧条的：Business is ~ this week. 本周生意清淡。❸ not stretched tight; loose 松的；宽松的：He tightened a few ~ screws.他把几个松了的螺丝拧紧了。

slacken /'slækən/

v. make or become slower, looser, less active, etc.放慢；放松；萧条：~ speed 减速/ ~ the reins 放松缰绳/ Slacken away (off)! 放开! 放松!

slam /slæm/

v. (-mm-) shut with a bang; bang 使劲关；砰地关上：My little brother always ~s the door.我的弟弟总是把门关得砰砰响。

slander /'slɑːndə(r)/

Ⅰ *n.* a false statement that damages a person's reputation 诽谤，诋毁：a wicked ~ 恶毒的诽谤 Ⅱ *v.* talk falsely about 造谣中伤，诽谤：He ~ed me in front of my friends.他在我的朋友面前诽谤我。

slang /slæŋ/

Ⅰ *n.* words, phrases, etc.often used in conversation but not suitable for formal occasions 俚语；行话：army ~ 军队俚语/ schoolboy ~ 学童俚语/ "Brass" is ~ for "money". "铜"是"钱"的俚语。Ⅱ *v.* use violent language to; abuse 对……讲粗话；漫骂：Stop ~ing him. 别骂他。/ I won't take part in a ~ing match.我不会

用粗话与人吵架。

slant /slɑːnt/

Ⅰ *v.* slope, or cause to be at an angle from straight up and down across (使)倾斜；斜放：His handwriting ~s from right to left.他的字体是从右向左倾斜。/ It ~s 14 feet 10 inches at the present time. 目前，它倾斜 14 英尺 10 英寸。Ⅱ *n.* ❶ a sloping position 斜面；倾斜：on the (a) ~ 倾斜着 ❷ a point of view when considering sth.意见；看法：get a new ~ on the political situation 获知对政治形势的新观点

slap /slæp/

v. strike with the open hand or with sth. flat 用手掌击：Slap him on the face.打了他一个耳光。‖ ~ sth.down 重重地放下某物/ get (give) sb.a ~ in the face 严拒；奚落

slash /slæʃ/

Ⅰ *v.* ❶ cut with a violent, sweeping movement 挥砍；挥击：~ grass 砍草 ❷ cut down or reduce severely 削减；大幅度减少：~ expenditure 大幅度削减开支 Ⅱ *n.* a cut or wound made by sharp movement with a knife, etc. 砍痕；砍伤

slaughter /'slɔːtə(r)/

Ⅰ *v.* ❶ kill (especially many people) cruelly or wrongly; massacre 屠杀；残杀：people needlessly ~ed 被无辜杀戮的人们 ❷ kill (animals) for food 屠杀；屠宰 ❸ defeat severely in a game 使惨败 Ⅱ *n.* ❶ killing of animals (especially for food) 屠宰 (尤指为食物) ❷ killing of many people at once 屠杀；杀戮：the ~ on the roads 道路车祸造成的死亡

slave /sleɪv/

n. a person who is legally owned by someone else; a servant without personal freedom 奴隶：This ~ is forced to work 20 hours a day.这个奴隶被迫每天干二十小时的活。‖ ~ry /'sleɪvəri/ *n.* 奴役；奴隶制

sledge /sledʒ/

Ⅰ *n.* ❶ a vehicle on long runners, used for transporting loads across snow and ice 橇；雪橇 ❷ a heavy hammer with a long handle, used by black smith (铁匠用的)

S

大锤 Ⅱ v.travel or carry on a sledge 乘雪橇;用雪橇装运:go sledging 乘雪橇去

sleek /sliːk/

  Ⅰ *adj.* ❶ (of fur and hair, etc.) smooth, soft and shiny (毛发等)柔滑的,有光泽的:~ hair 有光泽的头发 ❷ smooth in speech and action (人)圆滑的,花言巧语的:A ~ salesman never argues with a customer. 圆滑的店员从来不同顾客争辩。 Ⅱ *v.* make soft, smooth, and glossy 使柔滑发亮;使光滑:~ a cat's fur 使猫的皮毛光滑

sleep /sliːp/

  Ⅰ *n.* the natural resting state of unconsciousness of the body 睡眠 Ⅱ *v.* rest in the condition of sleep; be or fall asleep 睡:The baby ~s well every night.这个婴儿每天晚上都睡得很好。 ‖ **get to** ~ 睡着;入眠/**go to** ~ 睡着/**put sb.to** ~ 使某人入睡/~ **like a log** 睡得很沉/~ **the clock round** 连续睡十二个小时/~ **sth.off** 借睡眠消除……

sleepless /'sliːplɪs/

  adj. ❶ characterized by or experiencing lack of sleep 失眠的;不眠的:a ~ night 不眠之夜 ❷ unable to sleep 睡不着的,不能入睡的:feeling ~ 睡不着 ‖ ~**ly** *adv.*/~**ness** *n.*失眠

sleepwalk /'sliːpwɔːk/

  v. walk around while you are asleep 梦游 ‖ ~**er** *n.* 梦游者

sleepy /'sliːpi/

  adj. ❶ needing or ready for sleep 欲睡的;困乏的:feel (look) ~ 觉得(看起来)很困 ❷ quiet;inactive 寂静的;不活动的:a ~ little village 寂静的小村 / those ~ rural towns 那些寂静的乡村城镇

sleet /sliːt/

  n. rain which is frozen or partly frozen 冻雨;雨夹雪

sleeve /sliːv/

  n. a part of a garment for covering (part of) an arm 衣袖 ‖ **wear one's heart on one's** ~ 对真情毫无掩饰 ‖ ~**less** *adj.*无袖的

slender /'slendə(r)/

  adj. ❶ (of a person or the body) thin in an attractive and graceful way 细长的,纤细的:a ~ figure 苗条的身材 / a ~ girl 苗条的少女 / a ~ hand 纤细的手 ❷ slight; scanty; inadequate 微小的;微薄的;不足的:a ~ income 微薄的收入 /~ prospects 渺茫的前景

slice /slaɪs/

  Ⅰ *n.* ❶ a thin, flat piece cut off sth., especially bread or meat 片;(尤指面包、肉)薄片:a ~ of bread (meat) 一片面包(肉)/ a tissue ~ 组织切片 ❷ a part or share of sth. 部;份:a ~ of territory 一部分领土 / a ~ of good luck 一份好运气 / a ~ of life 人生的片段 ❸ a knife with a broad, thin and flexible blade 薄刀 Ⅱ *v.* cut into slices 切成片;切下:~ an apple 把苹果切成薄片 /~ off a piece of meat 切下一块肉

slick /slɪk/

  Ⅰ *adj.* smooth; clever (perhaps too clever) 圆滑的;聪明的;滑头的:~ move 滑头的行动 Ⅱ *n.* an amount of oil, etc. on the surface of the sea 海面上的浮油:Many birds are being killed by the oil ~s near our beaches. 许多鸟正被我们海滩附近的浮油毒死。

slide /slaɪd/

  Ⅰ *n.* an act of sliding 滑行 Ⅱ *v.* (slid) move smoothly over a surface 滑行:The book slid off my knee.书从我膝盖上滑落了。 ‖ **let things** ~ 顺其自然

slight /slaɪt/

  Ⅰ *adj.* ❶ slim; slender; frail-looking 细长苗条的 ❷ small in size or degree; of no importance 微小的;轻微的;不重要的:His plan is of ~ importance.他的计划不太重要。 Ⅱ *v.* insult sb. by treating or speaking of them without proper respect or attention 轻视;对人冷落 Ⅲ *n.* an insult caused by a failure to show sb. proper respect or attention 轻视;冷落;冒犯

slightly /'slaɪtli/

  adv. ❶ slenderly 细长地:a ~ built boy 瘦长的男孩 ❷ to a slight degree; somewhat 些许;稍稍:The patient is ~ better today.病人今天稍稍好一点了。/I know her ~.我略略知道他。

slim /slɪm/

adj. ❶attractively thin;not fat 苗条的：a ～ girl 窈窕少女 ❷(of chance,etc.) very small（机会等）小的,少的：The chance of success is very ～.成功的可能性很小。

slip/slɪp/
　Ⅰ *v.*(-pp-) fall or almost fall as the result of losing one's balance 滑；滑倒：Quite a few old people ～ped on the icy road. 不少的老人在结冰的道路上滑倒了。Ⅱ *n.* an act of shipping 滑；溜；失足

slipper/'slɪpə(r)/
　n.(usually *pl.*) a loose-fitting shoe worn in the house 拖鞋,便鞋：She has a pair of comfortable bedroom ～s.她有一双舒服的卧室拖鞋。

slippery/'slɪpəri/
　adj. ❶(of a surface)smooth,wet,difficult to hold or move on 滑的；湿滑的：～ roads 湿滑的道路 /～ under foot 脚下滑溜溜的 ❷(of person) unreliable;unscrupulous（指人）狡猾的,靠不住的：a ～ customer 老滑头/ She's as ～ as an eel.她非常狡猾。

slit/slɪt/
　Ⅰ *v.*（slit；slitting）cut or tear in a straight line 切开；撕开：Slit the envelope open. 把这信封撕开。/ ～ cloth into strips 把布撕成细条 Ⅱ *n.* a narrow cut,tear or opening 裂缝；狭缝：the ～ in a letter box 信箱的投信口

slither/'slɪðə(r)/
　v. ❶ slide unsteadily 不稳地滑动：He was ～ing about on the icy surface.他摇摇晃晃在滑冰。❷ slide like a snake 蜿蜒地滑行

slobber/'slɒbə/
　*v.*dribble a lot from the mouth 流涎；流口水 ‖ ～ over sb.or sth. 对……垂涎欲滴；毫不掩饰地表示喜爱

slog/slɒg/
　Ⅰ *v.*(-gg-) ❶ hit sth. hard 猛击：The fighters were ～ging away.拳手们挥拳猛击。❷work hard for a long period（长时间）艰苦地干,努力苦干：They were ～ging away to meet a deadline.他们在截止日期前拼命干活。❸walk with great effort over a long distance；跋涉；艰难行进 Ⅱ *n.* ❶a hard hit 猛击 ❷a spell of hard tiring work or walking 一段时间的艰苦努力；跋涉 ‖ ～ger *n.*苦干者

slogan/'sləʊgən/
　*n.*a word,phrase or sentence used to advertise sth.or to make clear the aim(s) 标语；口号：political ～s 政治口号 / shout ～s 喊口号/ under this ～ 在这个口号下

slop/slɒp/
　Ⅰ *v.*(-pp-) spill over the edge;flow over 溢出；溅出：The tea ～ped over into the saucer.茶水溢出流到碟子里。Ⅱ *n.* dirty waste water from kitchen,etc.（厨房等处）污水

slope/sləʊp/
　Ⅰ *v.*go up or down at an angle 倾斜：The land ～s toward the sea.陆地向海洋倾斜。Ⅱ *n.* ❶a surface that slopes;a piece of ground going up or down 斜面；斜坡：mountain ～s 山坡 ❷ a degree of sloping 坡度；斜度：a hill with a ～ of 30 degrees 一座斜度为30°的小山

slow/sləʊ/
　Ⅰ *adj.* ❶ not fast;taking a long time 缓慢的；费时的：a ～ bus 慢车 ❷ dull;not quick to learn 笨的：He is ～ in learning chemistry.他化学学得慢。Ⅱ *v.*（cause to) go at a slower speed（使）缓慢；减慢：Slow down at the corner.在拐弯处要减速。

sluggish/'slʌgɪʃ/
　adj. ❶slow-moving or inactive 缓慢的；迟缓的；不活跃的：a ～ economy 停滞的经济 ❷lacking energy or alteration 缺乏活力的,迟钝的：I felt very heavy and ～ after the meal.饭后我感觉身子很沉,不想动。‖ ～ly *adv.*缓慢地；迟钝地 /～ness *n.*迟缓；迟钝

slum/slʌm/
　Ⅰ *n.*a street of dirty and crowded houses,especially in an area of a city that is very poor 陋巷；贫民窟；陋室：the ～s 贫民区/ live in a ～ 居于陋巷 Ⅱ *v.*(-mm-) live very cheaply 过贫苦生活

slumber/'slʌmbə(r)/
　Ⅰ *v.*sleep 睡眠：～ away a hot afternoon 以睡眠打发一个炎热的下午 Ⅱ *n.*(usual-

ly *pl.*) sleep 睡眠：fall into a ～ 入睡／disturb one's ～(s) 打扰某人的睡眠

slump/slʌmp/

Ⅰ*v.*❶ sit down heavily 扑通一声坐下：Tired from his walk,he ～ed into a chair. 由于走路太累了,他一下倒在椅子里。❷ go down in number or strength (数量或体力等)暴跌,下降,衰退：Sales have ～ed recently.销售额近来下降了。Ⅱ*n.*a sudden depression in prices,value,etc. 不景气,萧条

slur/slɜː(r)/

Ⅰ*v.*(-rr-) say sth. in an unclear way 含糊不清地说：The drunk man ～red his words.那醉汉含糊不清地说话。Ⅱ*n.*❶ sth. said against someone；insult 诽谤；中伤；侮辱：a ～ on his character 对他人格的侮辱 ❷ an act of slurring 含糊不清地说话

sly/slaɪ/

*adj.*having or showing a deceitful nature 狡猾的；狡诈的：The murderer was ～.凶手很狡猾。

smack/smæk/

*v.*strike with an open hand 掴；拍

small/smɔːl/

*adj.*❶not large in degree,size,etc.小的：a ～ room 一间小房间／This box is too ～, have you got a larger one? 这只盒子太小,你有大一点的吗? ❷ young 年幼的 ❸ not important 不重要的 ❹ little；not much 极少的；不多的

smart/smɑːt/

*adj.*❶ bright；new-looking；clean and well-dressed 鲜明的；新奇的；衣冠楚楚的：He looks very ～.他看上去很帅。❷ intelligent；clever；quick in mind 聪明的；有技巧的；很棒的：a ～ student 一位出色的学生 ❸ beautiful and fashionable 漂亮的；时髦的：The general praised the soldiers for their ～ appearance.将军赞扬士兵们外表漂亮。

smash/smæʃ/

Ⅰ*v.*❶break violently into small pieces 打碎；粉碎：～ a window 打破窗户／～ up furniture 打碎家具 ❷ defeat or destroy 击毁；击溃；瓦解：～ an enemy's attack 粉碎敌人的进攻 ❸ rush,force a way violently (into,through,etc.) 猛冲；猛撞；撞入：The car ～ed into a wall.汽车撞在墙壁上。❹ (tennis) powerful, usually overhand stroke (网球等)扣杀：He ～ed the lob.他猛扣高球。Ⅱ*n.*❶(a sound of) smashing or breaking into pieces 粉碎(声)；重击(声)：The teapot fell with an awful ～.茶壶落下,发出极大的破裂声。❷ car crash 车辆相撞：There has been a terrible ～ (up) on the railroad.铁道上发生了一次可怕的撞车(事件)。❸ (tennis) a stroke in which the ball is brought swiftly down (网球) 扣球：violent ～es 大力劈杀

smattering/'smætərɪŋ/

n.(usually with a) slight knowledge (常与 a 连用)一知半解；肤浅的知识：have a ～ of Greek 懂得一点希腊语

smear/smɪə(r)/

Ⅰ*v.*❶cover or spread with sth.sticky or greasy 涂抹：hands ～ed with blood 沾有血迹的双手 ❷make dirty marks on sth. 弄脏；涂污：～ the table with jam 用果酱把桌子弄脏 ❸ damage sb.or sb.'s reputation 中伤；诽谤：get ～ed by one's opponents 受到对手的诋毁中伤 Ⅱ*n.*❶ a mark made by smearing 污点；污迹；污斑：There are ～s of paint on the wall paper.壁纸上有油漆的污点。❷ a suggestion or accusation that damages sb.'s reputation 诽谤；污蔑：a vile ～ 卑鄙的诽谤 ❸ a specimen of a substance spread on a slide to be examined under a microscope 涂片；涂料：a cervical ～子宫颈涂片

smell/smel/

Ⅰ*v.*get the odour or scent of sth. through the nose；sniff at 闻：This kind of food ～s terrible.这种食物非常难闻。Ⅱ*n.*❶ the sense of smelling 嗅觉 ❷ an odour or scent 气味 ‖ ～ round (about) 到处探听消息／～ sth.out 察觉 ‖ ～y *adj.*有气味的

smile/smaɪl/

Ⅰ*n.*a pleased,happy,or amused expression on the face 笑；微笑：He greeted me with a ～.他微笑着向我打了招呼。Ⅱ*v.* give a smile；have a smile on the face 微

笑：The baby ～s at everyone.这个婴儿对谁都笑。

smirk /smɜːk/

　Ⅰ *v.* smile in a silly or self-satisfied way 傻笑；自得其乐地笑　Ⅱ *n.* this type of smile 傻笑；得意的笑

smite /smaɪt/

　v. (smote, smitten) hit hard; strike 重击，打：He smote the ball into the grandstand.他把球打进了看台。

smith /smɪθ/

　n. a worker in iron or other metals 铁匠；锻工：Instead of iron, some ～s worked with gold or silver. 有些铁匠不是锻造铁，而是加工金或银。

smog /smɒg/

　n. fog or haze intensified by smoke or other atmospheric pollutants （由烟或其他大气污染物混合而成的）雾，阴霾；烟雾

smoke /sməʊk/

　Ⅰ *n.* the cloud of gas and tiny solid particles that rise from anything burning 烟：There is thick ～ in the kitchen.厨房里烟很大。‖ **end up in** ～ 化为乌有　Ⅱ *v.* ❶ give out smoke 起烟 ❷ draw in and let out the smoke of burning tobacco or other substance 吸烟：My father ～s twenty cigarettes a day.我父亲每天要吸二十支烟。‖ ～**less** *adj.* 无烟的／～**r** *n.* 吸烟者

smoky /ˈsməʊki/

　adj. (smokier, smokiest) ❶ giving off much smoke 产生大量烟的 ❷ covered or filled with smoke 烟雾弥漫的：a ～ pub 烟雾弥漫的酒吧 ❸ having the taste or smell of smoked food 有熏制食物味道的：～ bacon 熏肉

smooth /smuːð/

　Ⅰ *adj.* ❶ having a surface like that of glass; free from roughness 平滑如镜的；光滑的：a ～ road 平坦的路 ❷ having an even or gentle motion 稳的；不摇晃的：a ～ landing 平稳着陆　Ⅱ *v.* make smooth 使平滑：You should ～ down your dress before you wear it.衣服穿之前你必须将它弄平整。‖ **take the rough with the ～** 逆来顺受 ‖ ～**ly** *adv.* 平稳地

smother /ˈsmʌðə(r)/

　v. stop air from reaching a person or thing 使……窒息；闷住：We can ～ a fire by covering it with a heavy floor covering.我们可以用一条厚地毯把火闷熄。

smoulder /ˈsməʊldə(r)/

　Ⅰ *v.* burn slowly without a flame 用文火焖烧；熏烧：The mat was ～ing where the burning log had fallen.燃烧的木棒落下的地方垫子慢慢燃烧起来。　Ⅱ *n.* smoke coming from a fire which is burning slowly without a flame 焖烧；文火：The ～ became a blaze.文火变为烈焰。

smug /smʌg/

　adj. showing satisfaction with oneself 自满的；沾沾自喜的：a ～ smile 自满的笑 ／～ young man 沾沾自喜的年轻人 ／～ optimism 自鸣得意的乐观

smuggle /ˈsmʌgl/

　v. ❶ take (goods) into or out of a country secretly and illegally 偷运；私运；走私：～ goods into (out of) a country 向（自）一国走私 ／～ Swiss watches into England 走私瑞士表到英国 ❷ take (sth. or sb.) secretly and in defiance of rules and regulations 不按规章地偷带（人或物）：～ a letter into a prison 偷带一封信到监狱

snack /snæk/

　Ⅰ *n.* a light meal (of sandwiches, etc.), usually eaten between meals 小吃；点心；快餐：I only have a ～ at lunch time.午饭我通常只吃一份快餐。　Ⅱ *v.* eat snacks between or instead of main meals 吃快餐；吃点心

snail /sneɪl/

　n. a soft creature without bones or legs, but with a round shell on its back, which eats plants 蜗牛：walk at a ～'s space 慢吞吞地走

snake /sneɪk/

　Ⅰ *n.* ❶ any of various kinds of long legless crawling reptile, some of which are poisonous 蛇：Some ～s are poisonous. 有些蛇是有毒的。 ❷ a treacherous person who pretends to be a friend 阴险而装作友善的人：a ～ in the grass 潜伏的敌人　Ⅱ *v.* move in a snake-like manner 蜿蜒前进；曲折滑行：The river ～d away into

S

the distance.那条河蜿蜒曲折流向远方。

snap/snæp/

v. (-pp-) ❶ bite fiercely and suddenly 猛咬,突然咬:A dog ～s at another dog.一条狗猛咬另一条狗。 ❷ break with a sharp sound,as a stick breaks 折断:The rope ～ped.绳子突然断了。 ❸ suddenly lose one's self-control 突然失去控制 ❹ take a snap shot of 拍快照

snare/sneə(r)/

Ⅰ *n.* ❶ a trap to catch birds or animals 陷阱;圈套:lay a ～ 设陷阱/ fall into a ～ 落入圈套 ❷ sth. that tempts one to expose oneself to defeat,disgrace,loss,etc. 诱惑物;圈套:His promises are a ～.他的诺言是一种圈套。 Ⅱ *v.* catch sth. in a snare (用罗网)捕捉

snarl/snɑːl/

Ⅰ *v.* ❶ (of dogs, etc.) show teeth and growl angrily (指狗等)吠,嗥叫:The dog ～ed at me.这狗对我嗥叫。 ❷ (of people) speak in an angry, bad-tempered voice 咆哮着说;厉声地说:～ a threat 咆哮着威胁/"I will kill you." he ～ed."我要杀死你,"他咆哮道。 Ⅱ *n.* an act or sound of an animal's snarling 嗥叫;咆哮:the sudden ～ of the dog 狗的突然吠叫声 / answer with a ～ 咆哮着回答

snatch/snætʃ/

Ⅰ *v.* ❶ put out the hand suddenly and take 突然伸手拿取;攫取;抓住:It is rude to ～.攫夺是粗野的。/He ～ed the letter from me.他从我手中抢去了那封信。 ❷ get quickly or obtain when a chance occurs 迅速获得;趁机获取:～ a kiss 趁机一吻 / ～a rest 抽空休息/ ～ a meal 趁机吃一顿饭 /～ at a chance 抓住机会 Ⅱ *n.* ❶ an act of snatching 抢;夺;攫取:make a ～ at sth. 攫取某物 ❷ a short outburst of or a period of sth. (物的)片段;短时间;一阵:work in (by) ～es 断断续续地工作 / short ～es of verse 片段的诗

sneak/sniːk/

Ⅰ *v.* ❶ go quietly and secretly 潜行,潜逃 ❷give information, especially to a teacher about the wrongdoings of others 打小报告 Ⅱ *n.* (used by schoolchildren) some-

one who gives information 告状人:She is a ～. She told mother I had not cleaned my teeth this morning.她是个爱告状的人,她告诉母亲说我今天早上没刷牙。

sneer/snɪə(r)/

Ⅰ *v.* express dislike and disrespect by a kind of unpleasant smile 嘲笑;讥笑:He ～ed at my clothes.他嘲笑我的衣服。 Ⅱ *n.* scornful expressions, words, etc. that express contempt 鄙视,冷语:She replied with a ～.她回之以冷笑。

sneeze/sniːz/

Ⅰ *n.* a sudden, uncontrollable outburst of air through the nose and mouth 喷嚏 Ⅱ *v.* make a sneeze at 打喷嚏:I think I am getting a cold. I have ～d several times this morning.我想我感冒了,今天早上我已经打了几次喷嚏了。

sniff/snɪf/

Ⅰ *v.* take air in through the nose in short breaths;see what the air smells of 以鼻吸气;嗅;闻:When she had stopped crying she ～ed and dried her eyes.当她停止哭泣时,她吸了吸鼻子,擦干了眼泪。 Ⅱ *n.* an act or sound of sniffing 嗅;气息声:get a ～ of sea air 吸一口海上空气

snigger/ˈsnɪgə(r)/

Ⅰ *n.* a type of quiet laugh, often showing disrespect 窃笑;暗笑 Ⅱ *v.* laugh in this way 窃笑;暗笑

snob/snɒb/

n. a person who cares only for people who are rich or of high birth 势利小人;趋炎附势的人

snobbish /ˈsnɒbɪʃ/

adj. of, characteristic of, or like a snob 势利的;自命不凡的:The speaker takes a rather ～ tone.发言人的口吻很是自命不凡。

snooze/snuːz/

Ⅰ *v.* sleep for a short time 小睡;打盹;瞌睡:He was snoozing by the table.他在桌子旁打瞌睡。 Ⅱ *n.* a short sleep 小睡:have a ～ after lunch 午饭后小睡

snore/snɔː(r)/

Ⅰ *v.* breathe roughly and noisily when sleeping 打呼噜;打鼾:How frightful to have a husband who ~s! 有一个发鼾声的丈夫多讨厌啊! Ⅱ n. the sound of snoring 呼噜,鼾声:His ~s woke me up.他的鼾声吵醒了我。

snort/snɔ:t/
Ⅰ v. force air violently out through the nose (to show impatience, contempt, etc.) 喷鼻息(以表示不耐烦、轻蔑等):~ with rage 发怒地喷鼻息 Ⅱ n. an act or sound of snorting 喷鼻息,鼻息声:give a ~ of contempt 作轻蔑的鼻息声

snow/snəʊ/
Ⅰ n. frozen water falling in soft white flakes 雪;雪花:There is much ~ on the ground this morning. 今天早上地上有很多雪。 Ⅱ v. snow comes down from the sky 下雪:Will it ~ tomorrow? 明天会下雪吗?

snowdrift/'snəʊˌdrɪft/
n. a bank of snow heaped up by the wind (被风吹成的)雪堆:The train ran into a ~.火车开进了雪堆。

snowfall /'snəʊfɔ:l/
n. a fall of snow;the amount of snow that falls 降雪;降雪量

snowflake /'snəʊfleɪk/
n. a flake of snow 雪花

snowy/'snəʊi/
adj. (snowier, snowiest) ❶ full of snow 多雪的:I went to see him on one ~ day. 一个下雪天我去看了他。 ❷ of or like snow 雪的;似雪的:~ hair 雪白的头发

snub/snʌb/
Ⅰ v. refuse to notice 不理睬;冷落;怠慢 Ⅱ n. the act of treating sb. or sth. in this way 不理睬;冷落;怠慢 Ⅲ adj. short and turned up at the end 短而翘的

snuggle/'snʌgəl/
v. (usually with up) come close to sb. or sth. for warmth and comfort (常与 up 连用)偎依;蜷伏:The boy ~d up to his mother.那男孩偎依在母亲身旁。

so/səʊ/
Ⅰ adv. ❶ to such a great degree 这么;那么:It is ~ hot.I cannot stand it.天气这么热,我忍受不了。 ❷ in this way;in that way 这样;那样:So, you can do it now.这

样,你现在可以做了。 ❸ extremely;very much 极为;非常 ❹ that is the case 是那样的 ❺ the truth 事实 ❻ similarly 同样地 ❼ expressing agreement 的确 Ⅱ conj. with the result that 因此:She is not at home, ~ I must go back.她不在家,所以我必须回去。 ‖ ~ far 至此/~ far as 到某种程度/~ far ~ good 到目前为止,一切都好/~ far from 非但不……反而……/~ much 完全;这么多/~ much ~ that 到这种程度以至……/~ that 为的是;以便/~ as to 以便/and ~ on (and ~ forth) 等等;诸如此类/just ~ 正是如此/~ to say (speak) 可以说;打比方说

soak/səʊk/
Ⅰ v. ❶ (let) stay in water or other liquid 浸(泡):~ the clothes in water 把衣服泡在水中/~ it in cold water 把它泡在冷水中/Just leave it to ~.就让它泡在水里。 ❷ penetrate; enter or pass 渗入;透过:be ~ed to the skin 浑身湿透 / The rain had ~ed through his overcoat.雨淋透了他的外衣。 ❸ absorb, take up (liquid) 吸;吸收:Blotting paper ~s up ink. 吸墨纸吸墨水。/Sponge ~s up water.海绵吸水。 ❹ extract money from charging or taxing too much 敲竹杠;征重税:a town where people enjoy ~ing the tourists 一个喜欢敲旅游者竹杠的城镇 Ⅱ n. an act of soaking 浸;泡;渍:Give the sheets a good ~.把床单好好泡一下。

soap/səʊp/
Ⅰ n. a substance people use for washing 肥皂:Wash your hands with ~ and water.用肥皂和水洗手。 Ⅱ v. wash with soap 用肥皂洗:~ oneself down 用肥皂擦身子

soar/sɔ:(r)/
v. ❶ (of birds) fly or go up high in the air (指鸟)高飞,翱翔:a ~ing eagle 高飞的鹰/ Birds are ~ing over the hills.鸟儿正在群山上空飞翔。 ❷ rise high 高涨;猛增:Prices are ~ing.物价飞涨。

sob/sɒb/
Ⅰ v. (-bb-) ❶ weep or sigh with short quick breaths 哭泣;啜泣:The child started to ~ when he couldn't find his mother.孩子因为找不到妈妈,哭起来了。/

She ～bed herself to sleep. 她啜泣着睡了。❷tell while doing this 哭诉；呜咽地说：She ～bed out the story of her son's death.她哭诉着她儿子的死。Ⅱ *n*.the act or sound of sobbing 呜咽(声)：She nodded with a ～.她抽泣着点了点头。

sober/'səʊbə(r)/
adj.❶ not drunk；in control of oneself 没喝醉的；清醒的：Robert knew he had to stay ～ to drive home.罗伯特知道他必须保持清醒以便开车回家。❷thoughtful, serious or solemn 严肃的；沉着的：He was a ～ man and seldom smiled.他是个严肃的人，他很少笑。❸plain and rather dull 朴素的；不耀眼的：a pair of ～ shoes 一双朴素的鞋

so-called/'səʊkɔːld/
adj.❶ used to show that sth. or sb. is commonly designated by the name or term specified 如此称呼的；号称……的 ❷used to express one's view that such a name or term is inappropriate（表示不认同）所谓的：the opinion of a ～"expert"一个所谓的"专家"的意见

soccer/'sɒkə(r)/
n.a type of football in which the ball may not normally be touched by the hands, except by the goalkeeper 足球(运动)

sociable/'səʊʃəbl/
adj.friendly；fond of meeting other people 友善的；好交际的

social/'səʊʃəl/
adj.❶having to do with human beings in a group where people meet each other for pleasure 社会的；群居的：～ activities 社会活动 ❷relating to the society 社会的

socialism/'səʊʃəlɪzəm/
n.a political and economic theory of social organization which advocates that the means of production, distribution, and exchange should be owned or regulated by the community as a whole 社会主义：scientific ～ 科学社会主义

socialist/'səʊʃəlɪst/
n.a person who believes in socialism 社会主义者：the Socialist Party 社会党 /～ country 社会主义国家

society/sə'saɪəti/
n.❶ the system by which people live together in an organized community 社会：a ～ full of love and friendship 一个充满爱和友谊的社会 ❷ people in general, considered with regard to the structure of laws, organizations, etc.that makes it possible for them to live together 群体生活

sociology/ˌsəʊsɪ'ɒlədʒɪ/
n.the science of the nature and growth of society 社会学

sock/sɒk/
n.❶ a piece of clothing covering for the foot, inside the shoe 短袜：a pair of clean ～s 一双干净的短袜 ❷ a loose sole used inside a shoe 鞋垫

socket/'sɒkɪt/
n. ❶a hollow in which sth. fits or turns 孔；穴 ❷an electrical device receiving a play or light bulb to make a connection 插座：a ～ for an electric light bulb 电灯灯泡座 / a wall ～ 墙上的插座 / the eye ～s 眼窝

soda/'səʊdə/
n.❶a substance used to make soap, glass, etc.苏打：～ biscuit 苏打饼干 / washing ～ 洗涤用苏打 / baking ～烹调用的苏打 ❷the water containing a gas to make it bubble 苏打水

sodden/'sɒdn/
adj.❶very wet；wet through 很湿的；湿透的：～ clothes 湿透的衣服 ❷ having drunk an excessive amount of a particular alcoholic drink 喝多了，喝醉了

sodium/'səʊdɪəm/
n.a silver-white metal that is found naturally only in compounds（symbol Na）钠（符号 Na）

sofa/'səʊfə/
n.a long seat with raised ends and back, on which several persons can sit 沙发：This ～ served me as a bed.我把这沙发当床使用。

soft/sɒft/
adj.❶ not hard；not firm 柔软的：a ～ seat 柔软的座位 ❷ mild；gentle 温文尔雅的 ❸smooth and pleasant to touch 柔

滑的：～ hair 柔顺的头发 ❹(of sound or voice) quiet and gentle 轻柔的：～ music 轻音乐 ‖ ～ drinks *n.*软饮料/～-headed *adj.*笨的

soften/'sɒfn/

*v.*cause to become soft, gentle, less stiff, or less severe（使）变软；变柔和；I'm waiting for the icecream to ～.我正在等冰激凌软化。/You need to ～ the light. 你需要把光线变柔和。

software/'sɒftweə/

n. programs for databases, word processing, and other tasks a computer performs, as distinct from the machinery in which these are loaded（called hardware）软件（与硬件相对）

soggy/'sɒgi/

*adj.*extremely wet and soft 极度湿软的

soil¹/sɔɪl/

*n.*❶ the top layer of the earth in which plants, trees, etc. grow 土（壤）：rich ～ 沃土/sandy ～ 沙质土 ❷a country; an area of land 国土；领土；土地

soil²/sɔɪl/

*v.*make or become dirty 弄脏；变脏：～ a clean shirt 弄脏一件干净衬衣

solar/'səʊlə(r)/

*adj.*concerning the sun 太阳的：The earth is a part of the ～ system.地球是太阳系的一部分。

soldier/'səʊldʒə(r)/

*n.*❶ a member of an army 军人；士兵：The ～s will fight bravely.士兵们将勇敢地作战。 ❷ a person who works for a cause 战士

sole/səʊl/

Ⅰ *adj.*one and only; single 唯一的；独一的：She is the ～ girl in the class. 她是班上唯一一个女生。Ⅱ *n.*the bottom of the foot or shoe（脚、鞋的）底部

solemn/'sɒləm/

*adj.*❶ (of a person) not happy or smiling 表情严肃的 ❷ formal and dignified; characterized by deep sincerity 正式的；庄严的，郑重的 ‖ ～ity *n.*庄重；严肃

solicit/sə'lɪsɪt/

*v.*❶ ask (for) earnestly; make request(s) for

恳求；请求；乞求：～ for someone's vote 求某人投一票 /～ a person for help 请人帮忙 / ～ contributions for a person 向人征稿 ❷(of a prostitute) speak to men in public places（指娼妇）拉客：A prostitute was ～ing on the street.一名妓女正在街上拉客。

solid/'sɒlɪd/

Ⅰ *adj.*❶ not liquid or gas 固体的 ❷ that can be depended on 可靠的：～ reason 充分的理由 Ⅱ *n.* a solid object; sth. that does not flow 固体：Steel is a ～.钢是一种固体。

solidarity/ˌsɒlɪ'dærɪti/

*n.*unity resulting from common interests or feelings 团结：national ～ in the face of danger 全国团结一致面对危险

solidify/sə'lɪdɪfaɪ/

*v.*make or become solid; make or be made into a hard mass（使）凝固；（使）固体化，（使）硬化：Freezing solidifies water into ice.冷冻使水凝结成冰。

solidity/sə'lɪdɪti/

*n.*❶the state or quality of being solid 坚实性；固体性 ❷firmness or strength 坚（稳）固

solitary/'sɒlɪtəri/

*adj.*❶ habitually done or existing alone 独居的；孤独的：a ～ person 孤独的人 ❷(of a place) alone or isolated 孤零零的；荒凉的：a ～ farm 荒凉的农场

solitude/'sɒlɪtjuːd/

*n.*❶being without companions; a solitary state 独居；孤独；单独：in ～ 独居 / not fond of ～ 不喜欢孤独 ❷a solitary place 荒僻的地方；人迹罕至的地方：in the ～s of the Antarctic 在南极人迹罕至之处

solo/'səʊləʊ/

Ⅰ *n.*a piece of music performed by one person; any musical performance by one person 独奏曲；独奏曲；独唱；独奏：a violin ～ 小提琴独奏曲 Ⅱ *adj.*of a musical solo 独唱的；独奏的：She has a good ～ voice.她有一副好的独唱歌喉。

soloist/'səʊləʊɪst/

*n.*a person who performs a solo 独奏（或独唱）演员

S

soluble/ˈsɒljəbəl/
adj.able to be dissolved in a liquid 可溶的：Salt is ~ in water.盐可溶于水。

solution/səˈluːʃən/
n.❶a way of solving problems or difficulties 解决方法：I think this is the only ~ to the problem.我认为这是解决问题的唯一办法。❷ the process of dissolving a solid in liquid 溶解 ❸a liquid or mixture formed by dissolving 溶液

solve/sɒlv/
v.find the answer to（a problem）；find a way out of（a difficulty）解答：We found it difficult to ~ the problem.我们发现难以解决这个问题。

solvent/ˈsɒlvənt/
Ⅰ*n*.a substance that can dissolve another substance 溶剂 Ⅱ*adj*.❶ able to dissolve 有溶解力的：grease ~ 脂油溶剂 ❷able to pay all one's debts 有还清债务能力的：A bankrupt firm is not ~.宣告破产的商行是不能偿清债务的。

sombre(-er)/ˈsɒmbə(r)/
adj.❶ dark；dull 昏暗的：~ colours 暗淡的颜色 ❷ sad and serious 忧郁的：~ expression 忧郁的表情

some/sʌm,səm/
Ⅰ*det*.❶an unspecified amount or number of 若干；一些：Please give me ~ money（apples）.请给我一些钱（苹果）。/ Would you please give me ~ books? 您能给我一些书吗? ❷used to refer to sb. or sth. that is unknown or specified 某个 ❸approximately 大约 ❹a large number or amount of sth. 大量的；可观的 ❺a small number or amount of sth. 少量的；不多的 Ⅱ*pron*.❶an unspecified number or amount of people or things 一些人；一些东西 ❷a part of the whole number or amount being considered 部分；有些 Ⅲ*adv*.to some extent；quite a lot 在某种程度上；大量地

somebody/ˈsʌmbɒdi/
Ⅰ*pron*.some person；someone 某人；有人：There's ~ at the door. 门口有个人。/Somebody lost his umbrella.有人把伞弄丢了。Ⅱ*n*.a person of some impor-tance 重要人物：If you study hard at col-lege you may become（a）~.如果你在大学时努力学习，你将来可能成为（一位）重要人物。

someday/ˈsʌmˌdeɪ/
adv.at some future time 将来某一天

somehow/ˈsʌmhaʊ/
adv.❶ by some means；in some way not yet known or stated 以某种方法或方式：We must find the lost child ~.我们必须设法找到丢失的孩子。❷ for some rea-son that is not clear 以某种理由

someone/ˈsʌmwʌn/
pron.❶an unknown or unspecified per-son；some person 某人；有人：There's ~ at the door.有个人在门口。❷a person of importance or authority 重要的人；有权力的人

somersault/ˈsʌməsɔːlt/
Ⅰ*n*.the act of jumping and turning over completely and landing on the feet again 翻筋斗：turn a ~ 翻筋斗 Ⅱ*v*.turn a somersault 翻筋斗

something/ˈsʌmθɪŋ/
Ⅰ*pron*.❶ a thing not named or known；some thing 某物：There is ~ in the box.盒子里有什么东西。❷ an amount or description,etc. that is not exact 表不十分肯定：His father is a teacher or ~.你父亲是教师或什么的。Ⅱ*adv*.sth. like；somewhat 颇似：It is ~ like a house.那个东西很像一间房子。

sometime/ˈsʌmtaɪm/
adv.& adj.❶ at some time 在某一时间，在任何时候：I saw him ~ in May.我在五月某一个时候看见过他。/I hope you will come ~ soon.我希望你早些来看我。❷former(ly) 以前；从前：my ~ teacher 我从前的老师 /the ~ president 前总统

sometimes/ˈsʌmtaɪmz/
adv.at times；now and then 有时；不时：I ~ go for a walk after lunch,but not al-ways.我有时在午饭后去散步,但并不是天天如此。/She likes ~ the one and ~ the other.她有时喜欢这个,有时喜欢那个。

somewhat/ˈsʌmwɒt/

adv. rather; in some degree 颇为；稍微：Your article is ~ long. 你的文章稍有点长。

somewhere/ˈsʌmweə(r)/

adv.❶ in some place 在某地；在某处：It must be ~ near here. 它一定在附近某处。/She lost the key ~ between her office and the station. 她在办公室与车站之间的路上遗失了钥匙。❷ at some point in amount, degree, time, etc. 大约；在某种程度：He is ~ about 60. 他大约六十岁左右。

son/sʌn/

n.❶ a male child of a person 儿子：They have two ~s and two daughters. 他们有两个儿子和两个女儿。❷ a male descendant 子孙，后裔：the ~s of Abraham 亚伯拉罕的子孙 ❸ (used as a form of address for a boy or young man by an elder person) my son 我的孩子

song/sɒŋ/

n.a piece of music with words for singing 歌曲：We love this ~. 我们特喜欢这首歌。‖ **buy sth.for a (an old)** ~ 贱价买

sonic/ˈsɒnɪk/

adj.❶ of or concerning sound or sound waves 声音的；声波的：~ speed 音速❷ denoting or having a speed equal to that of sound 声速的 ‖ ~ **boom** *n*.音爆

sonnet/ˈsɒnɪt/

n.a kind of poem containing 14 lines, each of 10 syllables, and with a formal pattern of rhymes 十四行诗；商籁体：Shakespeare wrote a lot of ~s.莎士比亚写了许多十四行诗。

soon/suːn/

adv.❶ in a short time 不久；很快：I will ~ come back. 我很快就会回来的。❷ quickly; early 快；早：How ~ can it be ready? 准备好要多久？‖ **as (so)** ~ **as** —……就；当……就；**no** ~ **er... than** —……就；刚……就/~ **er or later** 或早或晚；迟早/~ **after** 不久

soot/sʊt/

n.a black powdery substance rising in smoke and deposited by it on surfaces 烟灰；煤烟：The table was soon covered with ~.桌面上很快布满了烟灰。

soothe/suːð/

v.❶ quiet, calm or comfort sb.who is upset or anxious 使安静；安抚；使舒适：~ a crying baby 抚慰哭叫的孩子 /~ someone's anger 使某人息怒 ❷ make less painful; relieve 缓和；减轻：~ an aching tooth 减轻牙痛 / a soothing lotion for the skin (皮肤用)镇痛剂

sophist/ˈsɒfɪst/

n.❶ a person practising clever but fallacious reasoning 诡辩者；诡辩家：Many politicians are cunning ~s.许多政客都是狡猾的诡辩家。❷ (often **Sophist**) in ancient Greece, any of a group of teachers of rhetoric, philosophy, etc.(常用大写)古希腊修辞学(哲学的)教师；诡辩学者

sophisticated/səˈfɪstɪkeɪtɪd/

adj.❶ wise in the ways of the world; cultured; elegant 世故的；老练的；有教养的；优雅的：~ person 老于世故的人 ❷ advanced; developed to a high degree 高级的；尖端的：~ techniques 先进技术

sophomore/ˈsɒfəmɔː(r)/

n.a student in his second year of high school or college (美国高中或大学)二年级学生

soporific/ˌsɒpəˈrɪfɪk/

adj.causing sleep 催眠的：~ drug 催眠药

sordid/ˈsɔːdɪd/

adj.❶ dirty and unpleasant 肮脏的；污秽的：live in ~ circumstances 生活在肮脏的环境里 ❷ immoral or dishonest 卑鄙的；恶意的：~ act 卑鄙的行动

sore/sɔː(r)/

Ⅰ *adj*.(of a part of one's body) painful 痛的；疼痛的：My feet were ~ after the walk.我走路走得脚都痛了。Ⅱ *n*. a painful or injured place 痛处；患处：The animal's back was covered with ~.那头牲畜的背部尽是伤肿。

sorely/ˈsɔːli/

adv.seriously; very much 严重地；非常：I was ~ tempted to complain. 我大发牢骚。

sorrow/ˈsɒrəʊ/

Ⅰ *n*.a feeling of deep sadness or regret 悲

伤;悲痛;遗憾:feel ～ at the news 听到那消息很悲伤 / to my great～ 使我极为悲哀地 /The whole nation was in deep ～ at this news.当全国人民听到这个噩耗时,都沉浸在深切的悲痛之中。Ⅱ v.feel sadness(at,for,over sth.)感到悲伤:～ for someone's death 为某人的去世而悲痛 /～ at (for,over) a misfortune 因遭遇不幸而悲伤

sorry /'sɒri/
int. ❶used when you are apologizing for sth.(道歉时用)很抱歉,请原谅:Sorry I'm late! 对不起,我来晚了! ❷used for asking sb. to repeat sth. that you have not heard clearly (请某人重复你没听清的话)你说什么,请再说一遍:Sorry? Could you repeat the question? 你说什么? 能不能把你的问题再说一遍? ❸ filled with compassion for 对……感到同情 ❹feeling regret or penitence 感到遗憾(或后悔)

sort /sɔːt/
Ⅰ *n.*a kind or a group of people or things that are the same 类;群:Do keep away from this ～ of persons.跟这一类的人要离远一点。Ⅱ *v.*arrange in groups;separate things of one kind from things of other kinds 分类:Sort good oranges from the bad ones.将好橙子与坏橙子分开。‖ ～ sth.out 整理好 /～ well (ill) with 配得(不)上

SOS /ˌes əʊ 'es/
*n.*a short term for "save our souls" or "save our ships",an international signal calling for help,used especially by ships in trouble (尤指船只遇难时所发出的)呼救信号

so-so /'səʊsəʊ/
*adj.*neither very good nor very bad 一般的;普通的;中等的;不好也不差的:"How are you?" "So-so." "最近怎么样?""还可以。"

soul /səʊl/
n. ❶ the spiritual part of a person that thinks,feels and makes the body act 灵魂 ❷ a central,most important or most active part 核心人物 ‖ ～ful *adj.*深情的/ ～fully *adv.*感情深切地

soulless /'səʊllɪs/
*adj.*❶lacking human feelings 不懂感情的;淡漠的 ❷ dull;uninteresting 没有生气的;呆板的;乏味的:～,non-productive work 枯燥乏味、没有前途的工作

sound /saʊnd/
Ⅰ *adj.* ❶ healthy;not damaged,hurt, etc. 健全的;完好的:He has a ～ mind in a ～ body. 他身心健康。 ❷ reliable; wise;reasonable 可靠的;明智的;合理的:a ～ judgement 可靠的判断 ❸ thorough and good 彻底的;完全的:be in ～ sleep 酣睡 Ⅱ *n.*a thing that can be heard; noise;voice;tone 声音:～ film 有声影片/ ～ wave 声波 ‖ ～proof *adj.*隔音的 Ⅲ *v.* ❶ convey a specified impression when heard 听起来:It ～s impossible.那听起来不可能。 ❷ (cause to) make a voice 使发声

soup /suːp/
*n.*a liquid food made by cooking meat, vegetables,etc.in water 汤:tomato ～ 西红柿汤 / a thick ～ 浓汤

sour /'saʊə(r)/
Ⅰ *adj.*❶ having a sharp taste (like that of vinegar,lemon,etc.) 酸的;有酸味的: The fruit is still green and eats ～.这水果还是青的,吃起来是酸的。 ❷ made sour by fermentation 发酸的;酸腐的: This milk has gone ～.这牛奶变酸了。 ❸ bad-tempered and unpleasant 脾气不好的:He gave me a ～ look.他气愤地看了我一眼。/a ～ fellow 脾气不好的人 ‖ ～ grapes *n.*酸葡萄(表示某人表面贬低某事物,实则是忌妒) Ⅱ *v.*become sour 变酸:Milk ～s quickly in summer. 夏天牛奶易变酸。

source /sɔːs/
*n.*❶ the beginning of a river;a place of origin 水源;源头 ❷ a place from which sth.comes or is got 来源:The funds come from many ～s.资金来于多个渠道。

south /saʊθ/
Ⅰ *n.*❶ one of the four main points of the compass,the direction which is on the right of a person facing the rising sun 南方:Mexico is to the ～ of the USA.墨西

哥在美国南面。❷ the southern part of a country or continent, etc. (国家或地区的) 南部: The South of this country is warmer than the North. 这个国家的南部比北部暖和。Ⅱ *adj*. lying towards or situated in the south; facing south 南方的; 朝南的: the South Pole 南极 Ⅲ *adv*. towards the south 向南方: travel ～ 向南旅行

southwest /ˌsaʊθˈwest/

Ⅰ *n*. the direction halfway between south and west; a district in that direction 西南; 西南部: in the ～ of the USA 在美国的西南部 Ⅱ *adj*. ❶ lying in or directed towards the southwest 位于西南部的; 朝西南的: a ～ city 西南部的城市 ❷ blowing from the southwest 西南方吹来的: a ～ wind 西南风 Ⅲ *adv*. towards the southwest 向西南: sailing ～ 向西南航行

souvenir /ˌsuːvəˈnɪə(r)/

n. sth. that reminds one of a person or place 纪念物 (品): Tourists often buy ～s to remind them of the places they have visited. 游客常买纪念品, 纪念他们所游历过的地方。

sovereign /ˈsɒvrɪn/

Ⅰ *adj*. ❶ (of power) highest; without limit (指权力) 最高的; 无限的: ～ power 最高权力 ❷ (of a nation, state or ruler) having great power 有主权的; 独立的: become a ～ state 成为主权国家 ❸ excellent; effective 极好的; 有效的: a ～ remedy 特效药 (补救办法) Ⅱ *n*. ❶ a sovereign ruler 统治者; 君主; 王: King George, the late ～ of England. 乔治王, 已故的英国国王。❷ a British gold coin (旧时) 英国金币

sow /səʊ/

v. (sowed, sown /səʊn/ or sowed) put (seed) on or in soil; plant (a piece of land) with seed 播 (种); 在 (一块地) 播种: ～ wheat in the field 在地里播小麦 / ～ grass 种植青草 / ～ the seeds of hatred 散布仇恨的种子

soya /ˈsɔɪə/

n. protein derived from the beans of an Asian plant, used as a replacement for animal protein in certain foods 大豆; 黄豆

soy(a) sauce /ˈsɔɪəsɔːs/

n. a sauce made in China and Japan from soya beans (在中国、日本用大豆制成的) 酱油

spa /spɑː/

n. ❶ a spring, the water of which can be used as a medicine (有疗效作用的) 矿泉, 温泉 ❷ a place where there is a spring like this 矿泉或温泉疗养地

space /speɪs/

n. ❶ the physical universe beyond the earth's atmosphere 空间; 太空: ～ship 太空船 / ～helmet 太空帽 / ～rocket 太空火箭 ❷ the interval or distance between two or more objects 间隔; 距离: the ～s between the printed words 印刷文字之间的距离 ❸ a period of time 时期: a ～ of five years 5 年的时间

spacious /ˈspeɪʃəs/

adj. having much space; roomy 宽大的; 宽阔的; 广大的: a ～ room 宽敞的房间

spade /speɪd/

Ⅰ *n*. ❶ a tool for digging 铲; 锹: dig the ground with a ～ 用锹挖地 ❷ (one of a) suit of playing cards (纸牌中) 黑桃 Ⅱ *v*. dig with a spade 以锹挖; 铲: ～ up the garden 把花园的土掘翻一下

span /spæn/

Ⅰ *n*. ❶ the distance or part between the supports of an arch 跨度 ❷ the length in time, from beginning to end 一段时间: the ～ of life 一生的时间 Ⅱ *v*. extend across (from side to side) 横跨; 架: The bridge ～s the river. 桥横跨河面。

Spanish /ˈspænɪʃ/

Ⅰ *adj*. of or belonging to Spain, its people, or language 西班牙的; 西班牙人的; 西班牙语的: the ～ government 西班牙政府 Ⅱ *n*. ❶ the people of Spain 西班牙人 ❷ the language of Spain 西班牙语

spanner /ˈspænə(r)/

n. a tool for loosening and tightening nuts on screws and bolts 扳钳; 扳头; 扳手

spare /speə(r)/

Ⅰ *adj*. ❶ additional to what is usually needed 多余的; 备用的 ❷ (of time) not occupied, available to do sth. you want rather than work 空闲的；空余的：～ time 空闲时间　Ⅱ *v.* ❶ be able to give (time, money, etc.) 匀出；分出：Can you ～ some time for me? 你能为我匀出一些时间吗？ ❷ show mercy to 不伤害：～ his life 饶他一命

spark /spɑːk/

　Ⅰ *n.* a tiny particle of fire 火花；火光：the ～ of love 爱情的火花　Ⅱ *v.* send out little sparks or flashes 发出火花

sparkle /'spɑːkl/

　Ⅰ *n.* a shiny flash of light 闪亮；光芒：the ～ of a diamond 钻石的光芒　Ⅱ *v.* ❶ shine in small flashes 闪光；闪烁：Her eyes ～d with excitement. 她的眼睛闪耀着兴奋的光芒。 ❷ send out little sparks 发出火花，冒火星：The fireworks ～d. 爆竹喷射出火花。

sparrow /'spærəu/

　n. a small, gray-brown bird 麻雀：Sparrows chirp. 麻雀喳喳叫。

sparse /spɑːs/

　adj. spread widely and in small numbers 稀少的；稀疏的：The trees on the hill were ～. 山上的树木稀稀拉拉的。

spasm /'spæzəm/

　n. a short and sudden movement of the muscles which you can't control; any short and sudden movement or feelings 痉挛；抽筋；一阵突发动作或情感：A ～ of coughing stopped him speaking. 一阵咳嗽使他说不下去。

spatter /'spætə(r)/

　Ⅰ *v.* ❶ splash and scatter in all directions 溅；洒；泼：～ grease on one's clothes (～ one's clothes with grease) 把油溅在衣服上 ❷ fall or spread out in drops 溅出水滴；滴落：We heard the rain ～ing down on the roof. 我们听到雨滴落在屋顶上。　Ⅱ *n.* a spray or splash of sth. 溅；洒；滴落；纷落：a ～ of rain (bullets) 一阵雨（子弹）

spawn /spɔːn/

　Ⅰ *n.* eggs of fish, frogs, etc. (鱼、蛙等的)卵　Ⅱ *v.* produce eggs 产卵

speak /spiːk/

　v. (spoke, spoken) ❶ say words with your own voice 说；说话：He always ～s very slowly. 他说话总是慢条斯理。 ❷ be able to use a particular language 讲某种语言 ❸ talk to sb. about sth. 交谈：Can I ～ to Lucy? 我能和露西讲话吗？ ❹ give a speech to sb. 演讲：～ in public 公开演讲 ‖ ～ for oneself 以自己的方式说明自己的见解 / nothing to ～ of 不值一谈；无足陈述 / so to ～ 可以说；可谓 / ～ one's mind 坦率地表白自己 ‖ ～er *n.* 说话者

spear /spɪə(r)/

　Ⅰ *n.* a weapon with a long stem and a sharp-pointed head 矛；枪；梭镖；鱼叉：antelopes killed with ～s 用矛刺杀的羚羊　Ⅱ *v.* pierce, wound, make (a hole) in sth. with a spear 用矛刺；伤害；戳洞：They were standing in the river ～ing fish. 他们站在水中用矛叉鱼。/ The warriors ～ed the man to death. 那些武士用矛将那个男子刺死了。

special /'speʃl/

　adj. ❶ unusual; out of the ordinary; not common ; different from others 特别的；特殊的 ❷ designed or organized for a particular person, purpose, or occasion 专门的；特设的：～ treatment 特殊治疗

specialist /'speʃəlɪst/

　n. a person who is very skillful on a particular subject; an expert 专家：an eye ～ 眼科专家

speciality /ˌspeʃɪ'ælɪti/

　n. ❶ a special field of work or study 专业，专业研究：Her ～ is ancient Greek poetry. 她的专业是研究古希腊诗歌。 ❷ a type of food or product that a restaurant or place is famous for 特色菜；特产：Baked fish is the ～ of this restaurant. 烤鱼是这家餐馆的特色菜。

specialize /'speʃəlaɪz/

　v. ❶ study a subject with special intensity; become a specialist 专攻；专门研究；成为专家：She ～d in the economics. 她专攻经济学。 ❷ have a product, etc. to which you devote special attention 专营：The shop ～s in sports goods. 这家商店专营运动类商品。 ‖ specialization *n.* 专业化；专门化；专营

species /'spiːʃiːz/

n. a group of animals or plants having similar characteristics（生物）种：the human ～ 人类 /*the Origin of Species*《物种起源》(达尔文著)/ In the struggle for life, some ～ had not been successful. 在争取生存的斗争中，一些物种并没获得成功。

specific/spə'sɪfɪk/
adj. ❶ connected with one particular or fixed thing only 特种的；特殊的：a ～ purpose 特定的目的 ❷ detailed and exact; clear in meaning or explanation 详细而精确的

specification/ˌspesɪfɪ'keɪʃn/
n. ❶ the action of specifying 指明；指定 ❷ (usually *pl.*) any of the parts of a detailed plan or set or descriptions or directions 详细说明书，清单：～s for building a ship 造船说明书

specify/'spesɪfaɪ/
v. mention or name clearly; tell or state in detail 指明；载明；详述：The contract specifies red tiles, not slates, for the roof. 合约载明屋顶用红瓦，并非石板瓦。

specimen/'spesɪmən/
n. ❶ a single typical thing or example 标本；样品；范例：He collected many ～s of insects. 他收集了许多昆虫标本。 ❷ a piece or amount of sth. to be shown, tested, etc. 抽样；取样：The doctor will need a ～ of your blood. 医生需要取你的血样。 ❸ (informal) an odd or peculiar kind of person（非正式）怪人

specious/'spi:ʃəs/
adj. not good or correct, although appearing to be so 貌似有理的；似是而非的；华而不实的：He gave a ～ reason for being late. 他说了一个似是而非的迟到理由。

speck/spek/
n. a very small spot or dirty mark; a tiny bit 微粒；斑点；污点；一点点：a ～ of dust 一粒灰尘 / clean the ～s on the wall 清除墙上的污点 / a ～ of cloud 一丝云彩 / not a ～ of truth 没有一点真实的东西 / The boat was a ～ in the sea. 小船在海里宛如小黑点一般。/ I have not a ～ of interest in the novel. 我对这部小说没有一点兴趣。

speckle/'spekl/
Ⅰ *n.* a small spot; a speck（尤指皮肤或羽毛上的）小斑点；斑：This hen is gray with white ～s. 这只母鸡是灰色带白色斑点的。Ⅱ *v.* mark or cover with or as if with speckles 使染斑点；沾上；点缀：The boy's legs were ～d with mud. 那男孩的腿上沾上了点点污泥。/ The land is ～d with small ponds. 地面上小池塘星罗棋布。/ Cars ～d the parking lot. 汽车停满了停车场。

spectacle/'spektəkl/
n. ❶ sth. seen; sth. taking place before the eyes, especially sth. fine or remarkable 景象；场面；奇观；壮观：a fine ～ 极为壮观的景象 / A quarrel is an unpleasant ～. 争吵场面令人不快。 ❷ a visually striking display or performance 壮观；惊人的展示（表演）：The marching soldiers made a fine ～. 行军士兵形成了壮观的景象。 ❸ (*pl.*) a pair of eye glasses 眼镜：a pair of ～s 一副眼镜 / a man in (with) ～ 一个戴眼镜的人

spectacular /spek'tækjələ/
Ⅰ *adj.* striking or impressive 壮观的；壮丽的；令人印象深刻的：It was a ～ achievement. 这是一项了不起的成就。Ⅱ *n.* an event or performance produced on a large scale and with striking effects 场面恢宏的事件（或表演）

spectator/spek'teɪtə(r)/
n. a person who watches, especially an event or sport without taking part in 参观者；旁观者：Many ～s stood round the football field to watch the game. 许多观众站在足球场周围观看比赛。

speculate/'spekjuleɪt/
v. ❶ consider; form opinions; guess 沉思；默想；构思；思索；推测：～ about the future 思索未来/～ about the reasons for their visits 推测他们来访的原因 ❷ engage in risk business ventures that offer the chance of large profits 投机买卖：～ in oil shares（wheat）做石油股票(小麦)的投机买卖

speech/spiːtʃ/

　　n. ❶ a talk or address given in public 演说：He made a ～ to thousands of people. 他向成千上万的人做了一次演讲。❷ the power, act or manner of speaking 语言；说话 ‖ ～**less** *adj.* 说不出话来的

speed/spiːd/

　　Ⅰ *n.* ❶ the rate of movement 速度：at a high ～ 以高速…… ❷ quickness of movement 迅速；快捷：～way 高速道 ‖ **more haste less ～** 欲速则不达 ‖ ～ **limit** *n.* 最高限速 Ⅱ *v.* (cause to) move along, go quickly 速进；速行：The bus is ～ing up now. 汽车此时正在加速。

speedy /ˈspiːdi/

　　adj. (speedier, speediest) ❶ moving quickly 快速移动的 ❷ done or coming without delay 迅速完成的；迅速到来的：a ～ recovery 迅速恢复 ‖ **speedily** *adv.* 迅速地，快速地 / **speediness** *n.* 快速；迅速

spell/spel/

　　Ⅰ *v.* name or write the letters (of a word) in their proper order 拼出（写出）字母：How do you ～ your name? 你的名字怎么写？ Ⅱ *n.* a short period 一段时间：a long ～ of rain 下了很长时间的雨 ‖ **sth.out** 费力而缓慢地写

spend/spend/

　　v. ❶ pay money for sth. 花；用（钱）：～ much money on clothes 将很多钱花在衣服上 ❷ give time, energy, etc. to sth. 耗尽：They ～ a lot of time on their work. 他们把许多时间花在了工作上。

sperm/spɜːm/

　　n. (*pl.* sperm or ～s) ❶ a cell that is produced by the male sex organs and that can combine with a female egg to produce young 精子：He has a low ～ count. 他的精子很少。❷ the liquid that is produced by the male sex organs that contains these cells 精液

sphere/sfɪə(r)/

　　n. ❶ globe；ball 球形；球：geometry of ～s 球面几何学 ❷ one of the heavenly bodies；star or planet 天体；恒星或行星 ❸ range；field；extent 范围；领域：a ～ of influence 势力范围 / in economic ～ 在经济领域里 / He is famous in many ～s.

他在许多方面都很出名。

spice/spaɪs/

　　Ⅰ *n.* sorts of substance used to flavour food 香料；调味品 Ⅱ *v.* add flavour to (sth.) with spice, or as with spice 加香料于（某物）：Their food is highly ～d. 他们的食物中调味的作料加得很重。

spicy /ˈspaɪsi/

　　adj. flavoured with spice 加香料的：People who live in eastern countries like ～ food. 东方国家的人喜欢吃加了调味作料的食物。

spider/ˈspaɪdə(r)/

　　n. a kind of small animal with eight legs, which makes webs to catch insects for food 蜘蛛：a ～ web 蜘蛛网

spill/spɪl/

　　Ⅰ *v.* ❶ (of liquid or powder) (allow to) run over the side of the container（指液体或粉末）溢出，(使)洒出，(使)溅出；泼：～ water over them 把水泼在他们身上 / ～ sugar on the ground 把糖洒到地上 / Be careful not to ～ the milk. 小心别让牛奶溢出来。/ The soup spilt on my clothes. 汤溅到我的衣服上。❷ fall from a horse, etc.；cause to fall（从马上等）摔下；使跌下：be spilt from a horse 从马上摔下来 Ⅱ *n.* a fall from a horse, out of a carriage, etc.（从马、车等上）落下；摔下；跌下：have a nasty ～ 被摔得很重

spin/spɪn/

　　Ⅰ *v.* (spun/spʌn/；spinning) ❶ form (thread) by twisting wool, cotton, etc.（纱）纺（线）；纺织：～ning thread (yarn) 纺纱(线) ❷ form by means of threads 以丝或线做成；编结：Spiders ～ webs. 蜘蛛结网。/ Silkworms ～ cocoons. 蚕做茧。❸ compose (a story) 编造（故事）：～ a yarn 讲故事 ❹ (cause sth. to) go round and round (使某物)旋转：～ a top 抽陀螺 / ～ a coin 抛钱币 Ⅱ *n.* ❶ a turning movement 旋转：The bowler gave (a) ～ to the ball. 投球手使球旋转。❷ a short ride in a motorcar 乘汽车短途旅行；乘车兜风：go for a ～ in a car 乘汽车去兜风

spinach/ˈspɪnɪdʒ/

　　n. a plant with dark green leaves, used as a

vegetable 菠菜

spine/spaɪn/

n. ❶ the backbone of an animal or person 脊椎；脊柱：The football player injured his ～.那个足球运动员的脊椎受了伤。❷ hard, sharp-pointed parts like needles on some plants and animals 尖刺：The cactus has ～s.仙人掌有刺。

spinster/ˈspɪnstə(r)/

n. an unmarried woman；an old maid 未婚女子；老处女：bachelors and ～s 未婚男女

spiral/ˈspaɪərəl/

Ⅰ *adj.* circling about a centre；winding 盘旋的；盘旋上升的；螺旋：A snail's shell is ～.蜗牛的壳是螺旋形的。Ⅱ *n.* a spiral curve 螺旋；螺纹：The rocket went up in a ～.火箭盘旋着上升。Ⅲ(-ll- or -l-) *v.* move in continuous circles 盘旋移动；螺旋状移动：The smoke ～(l)ed up.烟盘旋而升。

spire/ˈspaɪə(r)/

n. a pointed structure like a tall cone or pyramid 尖塔；(建筑物的)尖顶：the ～ of the church 教堂的尖顶

spirit/ˈspɪrɪt/

n. ❶ the part of a person that includes their soul or mind 心灵；精神 ❷ courage，determination or energy 勇气；志气；意志；活力：They work with a high ～.他们的工作热情很高。❸ feelings；the state of mind 心境；心情 ‖ ～ sb.(sth.) away(off) 迅速或神秘地带走；诱拐

spirited /ˈspɪrɪtɪd/

adj. ❶ full of liveliness and courage 生气勃勃的；精力充沛的；勇猛的：a ～ response 热烈的回应 ❷ having a character or mood of a specified kind 有某种性格(或情绪)的：a generous-～ person 慷慨大方的人 ‖ ～ly *adv.* 活泼地；有精神地

spiritless /ˈspɪrɪtlɪs/

adj. lacking courage or vigour 无精打采的；缺乏活力的

spiritual /ˈspɪrɪtʃʊəl/

Ⅰ *adj.* ❶ of the spirit or soul；not of material things；of God 精神的；心灵的；上帝的：one's ～ life 精神生活 ❷ of spirits 灵魂的；超自然的 ❸ caring much for things of the spirit 脱俗的；崇高的：a ～ mind 崇高的精神 ❹ connected with the religion 宗教的 Ⅱ *n.* a religious song sung originally by the black slaves of the US 灵歌(宗教歌曲，最初为美国黑人奴隶所唱)

spit/spɪt/

Ⅰ *v.*(spit or spat/spæt/；spitting)❶ send out (saliva) from the mouth 吐痰；吐：～ blood 吐血 /Spitting in public places is not allowed.公共场所禁止吐痰。❷ utter sharply or angrily 尖刻地说；气愤地说：She spat (out) curses at him.她尖刻地咒骂他。❸ (of rain or snow) fall lightly (雨或雪)微降：It's not raining heavily，only ～ting.雨下得不大，只是小雨而已。Ⅱ *n.* ❶ an act of spitting 吐痰 ❷ saliva 唾液 ❸ a long thin piece of land that sticks out into the sea，a lake，etc.山甲；沙嘴

spite/spaɪt/

n. an unreasonable dislike for or desire to annoy another person 恶意；怨恨：out of ～ 出于恶意/in ～ of 尽管，不顾

spittle/ˈspɪtl/

n. the liquid in the mouth；saliva 口水；唾沫

splash/splæʃ/

v. ❶(of a liquid) fall or be scattered in irregular drops (液体)滴下，泼落，散落 ❷ print (a story，etc.) in a prominent place in a newspaper，etc.刊登在(报纸等)显著位置

splendid/ˈsplendɪd/

adj. ❶ glorious；brilliant；grand 灿烂辉煌的；雄伟壮观的：a ～ victory 辉煌的胜利 / a ～ house 豪华的房子 ❷ worthy of honour or fame；distinguished 卓越的；高超的：～ talents 卓越的才能 ❸ very good；fine；excellent 极佳的；优秀的；精彩的：a ～ idea 极好的主意 /That's ～! 那可太好了！

splendo(u)r/ˈsplendə(r)/

n. ❶ magnificence；brightness 华丽；壮丽；光亮：the ～ of the jewels 珠宝的灿烂 ❷ glory 堂皇；光辉，荣耀：the ～ of the sun 太阳的光辉

splinter /'splɪntə(r)/

Ⅰ *n.* a thin sharp piece of wood or metal (木、金属的)薄片,尖片,碎片:I have got a ~ in my finger. 我指头上扎了一块碎片。Ⅱ *v.* (cause sth. to) break into pieces 使裂成碎片;碎裂:This wood ~s easily. 这裂木头易碎。/A shot ~ed the window. 一颗子弹打碎了窗户。

split /splɪt/

v. break into two or more parts, especially from end to end 裂开;劈开 ‖ ~ **the difference** 让步;妥协/~ **one's sides** 捧腹大笑

splutter /'splʌtə(r)/

v. ❶ talk quickly in an excited manner (usually with liquid thrown from the mouth) 急促而激动地说(通常口沫横飞) ❷ make a hissing or spitting sound 发嘶嘶声;作噼啪声;发爆裂声:The rain caused the lamp to ~. 雨水打得油灯噼啪响。

spoil /spɔɪl/

v. ❶ make useless or unsatisfactory 破坏;损坏:The soup will ~ the food. 汤会搞坏这个食物的。❷ harm the character of (children) by lack of discipline 娇惯;惯坏

spoke /spəʊk/

n. one of the thin rods connecting the centre of a wheel to its outside edge (车轮的)辐条

spoken /'spəʊkən/

adj. ❶ speaking in a certain way 以……为说话特点:soft ~ 说话温柔的 ❷ expressed with the mouth 口述的;口头的:~ English 英语口语

spokesman /'spəʊksmən/

n. a person who speaks on behalf of a group or an organization 发言人:a police ~ 警方发言人

sponge /spʌndʒ/

Ⅰ *n.* ❶ a type of sea animal with a body full of holes to allow water to enter 海绵动物 ❷ a substance full of holes used for cleaning and wiping 海绵状的东西(用于清洁擦拭):rubber ~ 橡皮海绵 ❸ a type of very soft and light cake 松软蛋糕 Ⅱ *v.* clean or wipe with a sponge 用海绵揩抹、擦拭:She ~d the cut on my head. 她用海绵擦拭我头上的伤口。‖ ~ **off**(**on**) **sb.** 白吃;揩油;蹭(饭等) ‖ **spongy** *adj.* 像海绵的;柔软多孔的

sponsor /'spɒnsə(r)/

Ⅰ *n.* ❶ a person who promises to be responsible for another person 保证人 ❷ a person or business company that gives financial support to a radio or television programme, a concert, an exhibition, etc. (usually in return for publicity and the right to advertise goods) (广播、电视节目、音乐会、展览会等的)赞助人,赞助商 Ⅱ *v.* be sponsor for 主办;发起;赞助:I ~ed the first proposal. 我领衔提出第一个建议。/The company ~ed several television programmes. 这家公司赞助了几套电视节目。

spontaneous /spɒn'teɪnɪəs/

adj. at one's own wish; not forced; natural 自动的;自发的;自然的:They made a ~ decision to work for an extra half hour. 他们自发作出决定,加班半小时。

spoon /spuːn/

Ⅰ *n.* a utensil with a shallow bowl on a handle, used for taking up food 勺;匙;调羹:salt ~ 盐勺 / a ~ of tea 一匙茶 Ⅱ *v.* take (up, out) with a spoon 用勺舀:She ~ed out bowls of porridge. 她用勺舀了几碗粥。

sporadic /spə'rædɪk/

adj. happening one by one or here and there 个别发生的;散发的:There have been ~ fighting in the city during the last few days. 近日来,这座城市已出现零星的战斗。

sport /spɔːt/

n. ❶ an athletic game or outdoor amusement 运动:Do you like ~s? 你喜欢体育活动吗? ❷ amusement or plaything 娱乐;玩耍 ‖ ~**s man** *n.* 运动员

sporting /'spɔːtɪŋ/

adj. ❶ connected with or interested in sport 运动的;喜爱运动的:a major ~ event 一场重大的体育赛事 ❷ fair and generous in one's behaviour or treatment

S

of others, especially in a game or contest (尤指在竞赛中)公正慷慨的, 有君子之风的 ‖ ~ly *adv.* 公正地

spot/spɒt/

Ⅰ *n.* ❶ a particular place or area 地点; 场所: This is the ~ where the murder happened. 这就是谋杀案发生的地方。❷ a personal fault or defect 缺陷; 弱点 ❸ a small dirty mark or stain on sth. 污渍; 污迹 ‖ on the ~ 在现场/put sb. on the ~ 置某人于困境中/put one's finger on sb.'s weak ~ 找出某人的弱点 / knock ~s off sb. 轻易地超越或胜过某人 Ⅱ *v.* make dirty 弄脏

spotlight/'spɒtlaɪt/

Ⅰ *n.* ❶ a beam of light directed on to a small area, or a lamp giving this 聚光灯 ❷ the public attention 公众焦点: She is not used to being in the ~. 她还不习惯成为公众关注的焦点。Ⅱ *v.* (~ed or spot-lit) ❶ direct a spotlight on sth. 用聚光灯照明 ❷ draw attention to sth. 关注: The programme ~s financial problems. 节目突出报道了财政问题。

spouse/spaʊs/

n. a husband or wife 配偶

spout/spaʊt/

Ⅰ *n.* ❶ a pipe or tube of a container through which liquid is poured (容器的)嘴: The ~ is chipped, so it doesn't pour very well. 这水管壶边上有个缺口, 因此出水不畅。❷ a jet of liquid coming out with great force 喷水; 水柱 Ⅱ *v.* ❶ throw out liquid; shoot or pour out in stream 喷; 涌; 喷出: A whale ~s water. 鲸能喷水。/The well ~s oil. 这口井喷出油来。❷ speak lengthily and loudly 夸夸其谈; 滔滔不绝地说: ~ nonsense 喋喋不休地说无聊话 / Stop ~ing about all the rubbish. 别夸夸其谈那些废话。/Our teacher is always ~ing the works of Lu Xun. 我们的老师总是侃侃而谈论鲁迅的作品。

sprain/spreɪn/

v. damage a joint of your body by turning it suddenly 扭伤(关节或筋等): He ~ed his ankle when he fell. 他摔倒时扭伤了踝部。

sprawl/sprɔːl/

Ⅰ *v.* ❶ stretch out (oneself or one's limbs) awkwardly in lying or sitting 伸开手足躺或坐: She ~ed on the sofa. 她懒散地躺在沙发上。❷ spread ungracefully 蔓延 Ⅱ *n.* ❶ a sprawling position or movement (伸开四肢)躺卧的姿势或动作: He lay in a ~ on the bed. 他手脚摊开躺在床上。❷ a widespread untidy area, especially covered with buildings 大片杂乱拓展建筑的地区

spray/spreɪ/

Ⅰ *n.* ❶ water in very small drops blown from sea, a waterfall, etc. 水珠; 水雾; 浪花: the ~ of a waterfall 瀑布的水雾 ❷ kinds of liquid preparation, such as perfume, disinfectant or insecticide, etc. 液体制剂(如香水、消毒剂、杀虫剂等) ❸ an atomizer, etc. used for applying such a liquid 喷雾器 Ⅱ *v.* scatter or be scattered in small drops under pressure 喷射; 溅散: ~ paint on a wall 在墙上喷漆

spread/spred/

Ⅰ *v.* ❶ open sth. so as to show an extended surface 展开; 铺开: ~ the map out on the floor 在地板上摊开地图 ❷ make sth. be known by more people 传播; 散步: ~ the news 传播消息 Ⅱ *n.* ❶ a variety or range of sb. or sth. 广泛; 多样: a broad ~ of opinion 各种各样的意见 ❷ an increase in amount, number or area 传播; 扩展; 蔓延

sprightly/'spraɪtli/

adj. lively; brisk 活泼的; 轻快的: a ~ dance 轻快活泼的舞蹈

spring/sprɪŋ/

Ⅰ *n.* ❶ the first season of the year 春季 ❷ an act of leaping or jumping 跳; 跳跃 ❸ a flow of water from the ground; fountain 泉; 泉水 Ⅱ *v.* leap; jump; bound 跳跃: After hearing it, she sprang up from her seat. 听了之后, 她从座位上跳了起来。

sprinkle/'sprɪŋkl/

Ⅰ *v.* scatter in drops or tiny bits 撒; 洒: ~ water on the flowers 浇花 /~ the street with water 将水洒在街上 / ~ salt on fish 往鱼上撒盐 Ⅱ *n.* ❶ light rainfall 小雨: It was just a ~. 这只是一场小雨。❷ a tiny amount 少量: a ~ of students 一些学生 / The cook put a ~ of nuts on the cake.厨师在糕点上放了一点点果仁。

sprint/sprɪnt/

　Ⅰ v.run a short distance at full speed 短距离快跑 Ⅱ n. an act of running in a short distance at full speed 冲刺;短距离比赛:He won the hundred yard ～.他在百码短跑中获胜。‖ ～er n. 短路选手

sprout/spraʊt/

　Ⅰ v.start to grow 开始生长;发芽:These seeds have ～ed—you can see little green leaves above the earth.这些种子已经发芽了——你可以看到地面上露出的小绿叶。/David has ～ed a beard since we last saw him.我们上次见到大卫后,他长出了胡子。Ⅱ n.a newly sprouted part of a plant 植物的苗;芽:The gardeners were setting out ～.园丁们正在移种秧苗。

spruce[1]/spruːs/

　adj.neat in dress;smart 衣着整洁的;漂亮的

spruce[2]/spruːs/

　n.a type of tall, cone-shaped, evergreen tree with pointed leaves on every side of the twig 针枞;云杉

spur/spɜː(r)/

　Ⅰ n.❶ sth.that urges a person on to greater activity 刺激;驱策 ❷ a sharp toothed instrument attached to a rider's heels used to urge the horse forward 踢马刺;靴刺 Ⅱ v.(-rr-)❶ ride fast or hard 疾驰;疾驱 ❷ urge on with,or as with spurs 以马刺等刺激:The riders ～red (on) their horses.骑手们用马刺驱马前进。

spurious/ˈspjʊərɪəs/

　adj.false;not genuine 假的;伪造的;乱真的:～ coin 假钱币

spurn/spɜːn/

　v. kick or drive away; refuse to accept sth.,especially in a proud way (尤指傲慢地)一脚踢开;拒绝接受:They ～ed all our offers of help.他们拒绝接受我们提出的一切援助。

spurt/spɜːt/

　Ⅰ v. (with reference to liquids, flame, etc.)(cause to) come out suddenly (指液体、火焰等)喷出;(使)涌出;(使)进出:Water ～ed from the broken pipe.水从破裂的水管中喷出。/ Their guns ～ed fire.他们的枪喷射出火焰。Ⅱ n.❶ a sudden flow from an opening 喷出;涌出;进出:～s of water from the broken pipe 水从破裂的水管中喷出 ❷an increase of one's speed for a short time to get somewhere faster 冲刺;(短暂地)加速前进:Mary ～ed past her classmate to get to the line first.玛丽冲刺超过了她的同学率先抵达终点线。

spy/spaɪ/

　Ⅰ n.a person who tries to get secret information about the enemy or another country 特务;间谍 Ⅱ v.act as a spy (upon); watch secretly 做侦探;侦察 ‖ ～ into (on, upon) sth.,～ sth.out 侦探;窥视

squabble/ˈskwɒbl/

　Ⅰ n.a noisy quarrel about a small matter (为小事的)争吵;口角 Ⅱ v.engage in a petty or noisy quarrel 口角;争吵;争论:Tom was squabbling with his sister.汤姆跟他的妹妹在争吵。

squander/ˈskwɒndə(r)/

　v.(with reference to money, possessions, etc.)waste;spend carelessly (指钱、财产等) 浪费;乱花:He ～s all the money which his father gives him.他挥霍了他父亲给他的全部钱财。/A country which ～s its talented people cannot grow rich.浪费人才的国家不可能富裕起来。

square/skweə(r)/

　Ⅰ adj.❶ having the shape of a square 正方形的;方形的:a piece of ～ land 一块方地 ❷ of or being quantity multiplied by itself 平方的:200 ～ miles 200 平方英里 Ⅱ ❶ n. a figure having four equal straight sides and a right angle at each corner 正方形 ❷an open area in a place 广场:Thousands of people gathered in the ～.成千上万的人聚集在广场上。‖ get ～ with sb.和某人算账/get (give) sb.a ～ deal 公平交易

squash/skwɒʃ/

　Ⅰ v.❶crush;become crushed (使)压扁;压挤:We all ～ed into the car.我们全挤进了这辆小汽车。/The fruits at the bottom of the box has been ～ed.箱子底部的水果已被压烂了。❷ subdue(a rebellion) 镇压(反叛);压制:The police ～ed the riot.警察平息了暴乱。II n.❶crowd of people in a small space 拥挤的人群:a ～ in the train 火车上拥挤的人群 ❷ fruit-drink 果汁饮料:lemon ～ 柠檬汽水

squat/skwɒt/

I v.sit on one's heels,or on ground with knees drawn up 蹲;蹲坐:He ～ted down on the ground.他蹲坐在地上。II adj. ungracefully short or low and thick 矮胖的;粗短的:a ～ man 矮胖的人

squawk/skwɔːk/

I n.(especially with reference to a bird when frightened)a short and harsh cry (尤指鸟受惊时)尖厉的叫声:The hen gave a ～ when it saw the cat.母鸡见到猫时略略叫了起来。II v.give a short, harsh cry 发出尖厉的叫声;略略地叫:The hen ～ed.母鸡略略地叫。

squeak/skwiːk/

I v.make a high,short and thin sound 发出短促的尖锐叫声;吱吱叫声:Rats ～. 老鼠吱吱叫。II n.a short, thrill cry or sound 短促刺耳的尖叫声;吱吱声:a startled ～ 受惊吓的尖叫声

squeal/skwiːl/

I v.make a long and high cry 发出长而尖的叫声:Pigs ～.猪长声尖叫。II n.a shrill cry or sound,longer and louder than a squeak 长而尖锐的叫声

squeeze/skwiːz/

v.❶ press on from the opposite side or from all sides;change the shape,size,etc. of sth.by doing this 挤压:You should ～ water out of the clothes.你应该将衣服中的水拧出来。❷ get or force out by squeezing 挤推:He tried to ～ his way through the crowd but failed.他想在人群中挤出一条路来,但没有成功。‖ ～ **sth. out of sth.(sb.)**敲诈;榨取

squid/skwɪd/

n.a type of sea creature with ten arms, which sends out a black substance when attacked 乌贼;鱿鱼

squint/skwɪnt/

I v.look in a different direction with each eye because of a defect 斜视:The doctor

says that the child ～s.医生说这个小孩斜视。II n.a condition of the eye muscles which causes each eye to look in a different direction 斜视:The boy was born with a ～.那个男孩生下来就斜视。

squirm/skwɜːm/

v.move like a snake;twist the body like one(often through embarrassment,etc.) (常因困窘等)蠕动;扭曲身体;局促不安:The little boy ～ed with shame.这个男孩因羞愧而局促不安。

squirrel/ˈskwɪrəl/

n.❶a small grey,or brown animal with a big furry tail,which lives in trees 松鼠: Red ～s are now very rare in Britain.红松鼠在英国很珍贵。❷ the fur of squirrel 松鼠毛皮

squirt/skwɜːt/

v.(with reference to liquids or powder) push out or be pushed out with force through a small hole (指液体或粉末)喷出;喷射:She ～ed water from the hose onto the flowers.她通过软管将水喷洒到花上。/The oil from the engine ～ed into my face.发动机里的机油喷了我一脸。

stab/stæb/

I v.(-bb-) ❶wound with a pointed weapon 以尖物刺伤;戳:～ at sb.向某人刺去 / He ～bed the woman with a knife and she died.他用刀子刺向那个妇女,之后她死了。❷ hurt one's feelings,reputation, etc.伤害(感情、声誉等):～ sb. to the heart 伤害某人的心 / The bitter words ～bed her.激烈的言语深深地伤了她的心。/Tom's lack of respect ～ bed his mother to the heart.汤姆的不孝敬使他母亲很伤心。II n.❶an act of thrusting or jabbing 刺;戳 ❷a wound made by sth. pointed 刺伤的伤口:a ～ in the arm 臂部刺伤的伤口 ❸a sudden painful feeling;a pang 突然的剧痛;一阵剧痛:a ～ of guilt 因罪责而内疚 ❹an attempt to do sth.尝试;企图:make(have) a ～ at (on) solving the problem 试图(努力)去解决问题

stable/ˈsteɪbl/

I adj.firmly fixed; steady 坚定的;固定不变的:a ～ belief 坚定的信念/What we need is a ～ government.我们需要的是一

个稳定的政府。Ⅱ *n.* a building in which horses are kept 马厩；～boy 马童；马夫

stack/stæk/
Ⅰ *n.* ❶ a pile of hay or straw（干草）堆；垛：Stacks of hay were in the field after the harvest. 收获以后，一堆堆干草堆在田里。❷ an orderly pile 整齐的一堆：a ～ of papers 一叠文件 ❸ a large amount or number 大量；许多：～s of work to do 要做的大量工作 ❹ a chimney 烟囱：Smoke poured out of the ～s of the factory. 烟从工厂的烟囱中喷出来。Ⅱ *v.* make into a neat pile；arrange in a stack 堆起；堆积；堆放：～ hay 堆干草 / ～ arms 架枪

stadium/'steɪdɪəm/
n.（*pl.*～s or stadia /'steɪdɪə/）an enclosed area of land for games，sports，etc. usually with stands（通常有看台的）体育场：I'm going to watch a volleyball match in the Capital Stadium. 我要去首都体育场观看一场排球赛。

staff/stɑːf/
n. ❶ a group of assistants working together under a manager 全体职员：～ of a company 一家公司的全体职员 ❷ a strong stick used as a support when walking 棍；拐杖

stage/steɪdʒ/
Ⅰ *n.* ❶ a raised floor in a hall where the actors or performers stand 舞台：This play will be put on the ～ next month. 这出戏下个月上演。❷ time or step in a long event 时期：at the early ～ of human history 在人类历史的早期阶级 Ⅱ *v.* put on the stage；put before the public 上演：The new play will be ～d next week. 这个新剧将在下星期搬上舞台。

stagger/'stægə(r)/
Ⅰ *v.* ❶（cause to）walk or stand unsteadily（使）蹒跚；（使）摇晃：The drunk man ～ed across the road. 醉汉蹒跚地穿过公路。/The blow on the head ～ed me. 头上挨了一拳使我摇摇欲倒。❷ surprise greatly；shock 使惊愕；使震惊：The bad news ～ed me. 这坏消息使我很震惊。❸ cause to happen at different times 使发生在不同一时间；错开时间：The manager

～s the holidays of those working in the factory so that everybody is not away at one time. 经理把工厂公休日错开，以便在同一时间内不至于大家都休假。Ⅱ *n.* an act of walking with weak unsteady steps 蹒跚；摇晃

staggered /'stægəd/
adj.（～ at/by sth.）very surprised and shocked at sth. you are told or at sth. that happens 震惊的；大吃一惊的：I was ～ at the price of the dress. 这套衣服的价格令我非常吃惊。

stagnant/'stægnənt/
adj. ❶（with reference to water）not moving，therefore dirty（指水）不流动的；停滞的；污浊的：The old pot was full of ～ rainwater. 这个旧陶罐里积满了污浊的雨水。❷（with reference to business，work，etc.）not changing，growing or developing（指生意、工作等）不景气的；萧条的；呆滞的；不发展的：Trade with other countries was ～. 没有发展和其他国家的贸易往来。

stagnate /'stægneɪt/
v. ❶ become stagnant 不流动；停滞；变臭 ❷（said about a person）become dull through lack of activity，variety，or opportunity（指人）不发展，变得死气沉沉，变呆滞：be stagnating in the job 工作上没有长进 ‖ **stagnation** *n.* 停滞；呆滞

staid /steɪd/
adj.（with reference to persons）too quiet and well-behaved（指人）过于沉静而有礼貌的；严肃呆板的

stainless/'steɪnləs/
adj. ❶ without stains；not liable to stains 没有污点的 ❷ resisting rust 不锈的：～ steel 不锈钢

stair/steə(r)/
n. ❶（usually *pl.*）a set of steps one above the other on which one can go up or down in a building 楼梯；阶梯：I went up the ～s to my room. 我上楼梯去我的房间。❷ one of these steps 楼梯（阶梯）的一级：He was standing on the top ～. 他站在楼梯的最上面一级上。

staircase /'steəkeɪs/

S

*n.*a set of stairs and its surrounding walls or structure 楼梯；楼梯间

stairway /ˈsteəweɪ/

*n.*a set of steps or stairs and its surrounding walls or structure 楼梯；阶梯

stake /steɪk/

I *n.* ❶ a pointed piece of wood for driving into the ground as a mark 标桩；木柱 ❷ a post to which a person was tied to be burnt to death 火刑柱 ❸ money，etc.wagered on an event 赌注；赌金：play for high ~s 下大赌注赌钱 ❹ money offered as prize in a horse race （赛马等的）奖金 ❺ interest or concern，especially financial ones 利润；利害关系 ‖ **at ~** 处于危险之中；在危急关头：The life of the sick man is at ~.这病人的生命危在旦夕。II *v.* ❶ secure or support with stakes 以柱支撑：~ vines 用柱支撑葡萄藤 ❷ risk money，etc.on an event 以（钱等）为赌注：I've ~d all my hopes on you.我已把所有的希望都寄托在你身上了。

stale /steɪl/

adj. ❶ not fresh；tasting old and dry 不新鲜的；干而瘪的；走了味的：~ bread 陈面包 /~ beer 走了气的啤酒 /~ water 死水 /Running water never gets ~.流水不腐。❷ uninteresting because sth.that has been spoken or talked about many times before 陈旧的；陈腐的：~ news 过时的消息 /~ jokes 陈旧的笑话

stalemate /ˈsteɪlmeɪt/

n.(in chess)a state in which neither player can win or lose because no other moves can be made （棋）和；（棋）僵局；相持不下的状态

stalk /stɔːk/

*n.*the main upright part of a plant that is not a tree；the long part that supports leaves or flowers （植物的）茎；叶柄；花梗：~s of celery 芹菜梗 / Flowers have ~s.花有花梗。

stall /stɔːl/

n. ❶ a compartment for an animal in a stable （畜舍内的）分隔栏 ❷ a small open shop，especially one in a market 棚店摊子；货摊：There were several fruit ~s in

the market.市场上有几处水果摊。

stalwart /ˈstɔːlwət/

I *adj.*strong，brave and loyal 健壮的；勇敢的；忠实的 II *n.*a person who is stalwart 坚定忠实的人；高大健壮的人

stammer /ˈstæmə(r)/

I *v.* speak with difficulty，repeating the same sounds 口吃；结巴地说话："Th-th-thank you"，he ~ed. 他口吃地说，"谢、谢，谢谢你。"/He ~s when he feels nervous.他一感到紧张就口吃起来。/ She ~ed out an apology.她结结巴巴地道歉了一番。II *n.*a tendency to stammer 口吃；口吃的倾向：He had a nervous ~.他有紧张就说口吃的病。

stamp /stæmp/

I *v.* ❶ put （one's foot） down with force 用力踩：~ a letter on the ground 在地上用脚踩出一个字母来 ❷ put a stamp on 贴邮票 II *n.* ❶ a small piece of paper stuck on a letter or parcel to show how much money has to be paid to send it 邮票；印花：He has a hobby of collecting ~s.他有集邮的爱好。❷ an act of putting the foot down hard 踏；踩

stand /stænd/

I *n.* ❶ stopping of motion or progress 停止；停顿：come to a ~ 停了下来 ❷ an attitude toward sth.；a position 立场；位置 ❸ a small article of furniture，support on or in which things are placed 架；货架 II *v.* ❶ be on one's feet or legs 站；站立：Who is the man ~ing there? 站在那儿的那个人是谁？ ❷ be in a certain place condition or state 位于；坐落：~ by a river 坐落在一条河边 ❸ go through；bear；endure 忍受：I cannot ~ the hot weather. 这么热的天气我受不了。‖ **~ one's ground** 固执己见/**~ one's trial** 受审/**~ sb.sth.** 忍受某人做某事/**~ a good(poor) chance** 有很大（很小）成功的机会/**~ to win(gain，lose) sth.** 很有可能会赢（获利，亏损）/**~ aside** 不活跃，不做事/**~ back** 退缩；退后/**~ by** 袖手旁观/**~ by sth.** 信守……/**~ down** 离开证人席/**~ for sth.** 代表；代替/**~ in(with sb.)** 参加；分担/**~ off** 远离；避开/**~ over** 延缓/**~ over sb.** 监督/**~ to** 保持警戒/**~ up for sb.** 支

持某人/～ **well with sb.** 与某人相处甚佳/ **take one's** ～ 表明自己的立场

standard/ˈstændəd/
n. a level or degree of quality that is considered proper or acceptable 标准；准则：the ～ **of living** 生活水平(标准) ‖ **be up to**（**below**）～ 达于(低于)标准 ‖ **～ize** *v.* 使符合标准

standing/ˈstændɪŋ/
Ⅰ *adj.* without change; permanent 不变的；永久的：His long beard is a ～ joke.他的长胡须是个老笑话。/ She has a ～ order for ten pounds of sugar at the shop. 她在这家商店里有十磅糖的长期订单。/～ **army** 常备军 Ⅱ *n.* ❶ a period of time 期间：He is an engineer of long ～. 他长期以来是一名工程师。❷ the position in society; rank 社会地位；身份：Doctors have a high ～ in our country. 在我们国家医生享有很高的地位。

staple/ˈsteɪpl/
Ⅰ *n.* ❶ a chief sort of article or goods produced or traded in 主要商品；土产；名产；主要产品：Cotton is the ～ in many southern states.棉花是南方各州的主要产品。❷ a chief material or element (of sth.) 主要原料；主要成分：the ～ of their conversation 他们谈话的主题 / Rice is the ～ of their diet.大米是他们的主食。❸ fibre 纤维：The best cotton has a long ～.最好的棉花纤维长。Ⅱ *adj.* forming the chief element or material 主要的；重要的：the ～ product of China 中国的主要产品 / a ～ subject of conversation 主要的话题

star/stɑː(r)/
n. ❶ a very large mass of burning gas in space, especially one that can be seen as a small bright point of light in a clear sky at night 星；恒星：countless ～s in the sky 天空中数不清的星星 ❷ a famous or very skilful performer 明星人物：The young people got very excited when they saw the film ～.看到那个电影明星时，那些年轻人十分激动。

stare/steər/
v. look fixedly with wide open eyes, as in wonder, fear, or deep thought 盯；凝视：

Don't ～ at me.不要盯住我看。‖ **make sb.** ～ 使某人惊愕/～ **sb. out** 把某人盯得局促不安/～ **one in the face** 注视某人的面孔

stark/stɑːk/
Ⅰ *adj.* stiff; bleak 僵硬的；荒凉的；不毛的；裸露的 Ⅱ *adv.*（～ **naked**）completely naked 一丝不挂的；赤裸裸的

start/stɑːt/
Ⅰ *v.* ❶ begin a journey, activity, etc.开始；着手：～ **to work** 开始工作/If you are ready, we will ～ our work.如果你准备好了，我们就开始工作。❷ begin to move or travel 动身：～（**out**）**early** 早点出发 ❸（cause to）come into existence（使)出现；(使)发生：How did the trouble ～? 这麻烦事是怎么发生的？❹ make sth. begin to exist 发起；开创；建立 Ⅱ *n.* an act of setting out or leaving on a journey 启程；动身；着手 ‖ ～ **back** 开始回归/～ **out**（**to do sth.**）开始；动工/～ **up** 惊起；跳起/**to** ～ **with** 首先；第一

startle/ˈstɑːtl/
v. surprise; give shock to 使惊愕；使吃惊：You ～d me when you shouted.你大叫时我大吃一惊。/The knocking at the window ～d me. 有人敲窗使我大吃了一惊。/She was ～d at the sight.见此情景她吓了一跳。/Babies ～ easily.婴儿容易受惊吓。

startling/ˈstɑːtlɪŋ/
adj. surprising or alarming 令人吃惊的；非常惊人的：a ～ discovery 惊人的发现

starve/stɑːv/
v. not have enough to eat; suffer or die from hunger（使)饿；饿死：Many people ～d to death at that time.有许多人在那个时候被饿死了。‖ **be** ～**d of,** ～ **for** 迫切需要 ‖ **starvation**/stɑːˈveɪʃn/ *n.* 饥饿；饿死

state/steɪt/
Ⅰ *n.* ❶ the condition of a person or thing 状况；状态：be in a good ～ 良好状态/The field is in a very muddy ～.原野上到处是烂泥。❷ the body of people living under a single independent government; a nation 国家 ❸ an organized political com-

munity forming part of a country 州；邦
Ⅱ v. express in words, especially carefully, fully, and clearly 阐述；陈述：It was ～d that no government has ever done it before. 据称以前从未有政府这样做过。

stately /ˈsteɪtli/
adj. impressive; dignified 庄严的；高贵的；堂皇的：a ～ pace 庄严的步子 / with ～ grace 壮丽而温雅地

statement /ˈsteɪtmənt/
Ⅰ n. stating orally or on paper 表述；陈述：Clearness of ～ is more important than beauty of language. 叙述清楚比用词优美更重要。Ⅱ v. ❶ sth. stated; a single declaration or remark 陈述；声明：issue a ～ 发表声明 / an official ～ 正式声明 ❷ a summary of a financial account 财务报表

statesman /ˈsteɪtsmən/
n. (pl. statesmen) a person taking an important part in the management of state affairs 政治家；国务活动家：a great ～ 一位伟大的政治家

station /ˈsteɪʃn/
Ⅰ n. a building or place used for a certain purpose 站；台；所：a police ～ 警察局/a railway ～ 火车站/bus ～ 公共汽车站 Ⅱ v. place in a certain spot 驻扎；安置：The soldiers were ～ed at Hai-nan. 那些士兵曾驻扎在海南。

stationer /ˈsteɪʃnə(r)/
n. a dealer in writing materials, etc. 文具商：go to the ～'s 去文具店

statistics /stəˈtɪstɪks/
n. ❶ numbers that give information about a subject 统计：according to official ～ 根据官方统计 / Statistics show that... 统计表明…… ❷ the science that deals with collecting and using such facts 统计学：Statistics is a rather modern branch of mathematics. 统计学是数学相当现代化的分支。

statue /ˈstætʃuː/
n. a figure of a person or animal carved in wood, stone, metal or other material 雕像；塑(铸)像：the Statue of Liberty (美国纽约的) 自由女神像 / a ～ to Lu Xun 鲁迅塑像

stature /ˈstætʃə(r)/
n. ❶ the height of the body 身高；身材：short of ～ 矮身材 ❷ the quality or position gained by proved worth 德行；成就：a woman of (high) ～ 一位德行很高的妇女

status /ˈsteɪtəs/
n. ❶ the rank or social position in relation to others 地位；身份：class ～ 阶级成分 ❷ a superior social position 重要地位；要人身份 ❸ the situation at a particular time 情况；状况

statute /ˈstætʃuːt/
n. a law passed by Parliament or other lawmaking body 成文法；法规：public ～ 公法

stay /steɪ/
Ⅰ v. ❶ remain in a place 停留；待：I ～ed in the classroom until 7：00 p.m. 我在教室里一直待到下午 7 点。❷ remain in a certain condition 保持；维持：You should do running every day to ～ healthy. 为保持健康，你必须每天跑步。Ⅱ n. an act of staying; the time spent in one place as a guest 停留；做客 ‖ ～ for, ～ to (a meal) 留下来(吃饭)/～ in 待在家里/～ out 停在外面/～ up 不睡觉；熬夜/come to ～ 来小住

stead /sted/
n. (in sb.'s/sth.'s ～) instead of sb. or sth. 代替某人(某事)：If you can't come, send him in your ～. 如果你不能来，叫他替你来。/ He became the manager in Mr. Brown's ～. 他取代布朗先生成为经理。

steady /ˈstedi/
Ⅰ adj. (steadier, steadiest) ❶ firm in position; not shaking; balanced 稳固的；平衡的；不动摇的：make a table ～ 使桌子平衡 ❷ regular in movement, speed, direction, etc. (动作、速度、方向等)有规律的；稳定的：a ～ speed 稳定的速度 / keep ～ 保持稳定 ❸ regular in behavior, habits, etc. (行为、习惯等)规则的；稳健的；可靠的：a ～ young man 一个忠实的青年 ❹ constant; unchanging 不变的；永恒的：a ～ purpose 永恒的目标 Ⅱ v. make

or become stable, regular, or less changing 使稳定：～ a table 使桌子稳定/Prices are ～ing.物价渐渐稳定。

steak /steɪk/
n.❶a slice of meat or fish for cooking 大块肉片(或鱼片)❷beef steak 牛排；扒：ham ～ 火腿扒

steal /stiːl/
v.(stole, stolen)❶take away unlawfully or without permission 偷窃：Someone stole my bike.有人把我的自行车偷去了。/～ information 窃取情报/～ sb.'s heart 巧妙地博取某人的欢心 ❷move secretly or quietly 溜；偷偷地行动：She stole quietly into her room.她轻轻地溜进了她的房间。‖ ～ **a match on sb.** 占先；抢先一步

stealth /stelθ/
Ⅰ n.the fact of doing sth.in a quiet or secret way 偷偷摸摸；秘密行动 Ⅱ adj.(said about aircraft, missiles, etc.) designed using advanced technology that makes detection by radar or sonar difficult (飞机、导弹等)隐形的：a ～ bomber 隐形炸弹

stealthy /'stelθi/
adj.doing things quietly or secretly；done quietly or secretly 偷偷摸摸的；不声张的；秘密的

steam /stiːm/
Ⅰ n.water in the form of vapour 蒸汽：The glass is covered with much ～.玻璃上有很多蒸汽。/a ～ boat 蒸汽船 Ⅱ v.give out (off) steam 蒸发 ‖ **full ～ ahead** 全速前进/**get up (raise) ～** 增加蒸汽压力/**run out of ～** 变得精疲力竭/**under one's own ～** 全凭自己努力

steamer /'stiːmə/
n.❶a boat or ship driven by steam 汽船；轮船❷a type of saucepan in which food can be steamed 蒸锅；汽锅

steel /stiːl/
Ⅰ n.❶iron mixed with carbon so that it is very hard, strong and rough 钢：make ～ 炼钢/ Wood is harder than rubber, but softer than ～.木头比橡胶硬，但是比钢软。❷ sword；a steel weapon 刀；剑；

钢制武器：cold ～ 利器；刀剑；白刃/an enemy worthy of one's ～ 强敌；好对手 Ⅱ v. harden 使坚硬：～ oneself (one's heart) (against pity) to do sth.硬着心肠(不同情)地做某事 / ～ oneself for a shock 使自己坚强起来经受住打击

steep /stiːp/
adj.❶ (of a slope) rising or falling sharply (指斜坡)陡峭的，险峻的：a ～ roof 陡峭的屋顶 ❷ unreasonable；excessive 不合理的；过分的：That story is rather ～.那个故事不太合情理。

steer /stɪə(r)/
v.direct the course of (a ship, car, etc.) 驾驶：It's hard to ～ a ship in a storm.大风暴中很难驾驶船。/～ north 向北行驶 ‖ ～**age** n.驾驶

stem /stem/
Ⅰ n.the part of a plant coming up from the roots；the part of a leaf, flower or fruit that joins it to the main stalk or twig 茎；杆；柄 Ⅱ v.❶ arise (from) 来自：This custom ～s from its culture.这一习俗源自它对应的文化。❷ remove the stems from sth.去掉……的干(或茎、梗)❸(of a boat) make headway against the tide or current (船)逆流而行

stenographer /stə'nɒɡrəfə(r)/
n. a person whose job is to write down what sb.else says, using a quick system of signs or abbreviation 速记员

step /step/
Ⅰ v.(-pp-) lift one's foot and move it in a particular direction；walk into 走步；踏入：～ into the room 步入房间/Step this way, please. 请这边走。Ⅱ n.❶ one movement forwards and backwards when you walk, dance, etc.；the sound of walking, etc.步；举步：He walks in large ～s. 他大踏步地走。❷ one in a list of things that you must do 措施；步骤：What's your next ～? 下一步你怎么办？❸ a place for the foot in going up or coming down；stair 梯：Mind the ～s when you go downstairs.下楼时当心梯级。‖ ～ **on the gas** 加大油门/～ **aside** 站到一边/～ **down** 辞职/～ **out** 快步行进/**watch one's ～** 谨慎；小心/～ **by** ～ 逐渐地/**keep ～**

with 步调一致

stereo /ˈsterɪəʊ/

　　n. a record player, radio, etc. which gives out sound from two places by means of two speakers 立体声录放机 ‖ ~**scope** *n.* 立体镜

stereoscopic /ˌsterɪəˈskɒpɪk/

　　adj. giving a three-dimensional effect, e.g. in photographs 有立体效果的: ~ vision 立体视觉

stereotype /ˈstɪərɪəʊtaɪp/

　　Ⅰ *n.* ❶ an over-simplified image or idea of a type of person or thing that has become fixed through being widely held 陈规; 老套; 旧框框 ❷ a relief printing plate cast from a mould 铅版; 铅版浇铸; 铅版印刷 Ⅱ *v.* represent or view sth. as a stereotype 使成为老一套; 使成为陈规; 对……有成见: The film is weakened by its ~d characters. 这部电影人物刻板, 因而效果受到削弱。

sterling /ˈstɜːlɪŋ/

　　Ⅰ *adj.* ❶ (with reference to gold and silver) of fixed value and purity (指金和银)标准成分的: These spoons are made of ~ silver. 这些调羹是用标准成分的银制成的。❷ reliable; of good quality 可靠的; 质量好的 Ⅱ *n.* British money 英国货币: They wish to be paid in ~ not dollars. 他们希望对方用英镑而非用美元支付。/ £1 ~ 一英镑 ‖ **the ~ area** *n.* 英镑地区(用英镑作为货币的国家)

stern[1] /stɜːn/

　　adj. severe; strict 严厉的; 严格的; 严肃的: He has a ~ face. 他面孔严肃。/ We have a very ~ headmaster. 我们有一位很严厉的校长。‖ ~**ly** *adv.* 严厉地 /~**ness** *n.* 严厉

stern[2] /stɜːn/

　　n. the back end of a ship 船尾

stew /stjuː/

　　Ⅰ *v.* cook or be cooked slowly and gently in liquid 煨; 炖; 焖 Ⅱ *n.* a dish consisting usually of meat and vegetables cooked together in liquid 炖肉: Mother put all the vegetables into the ~. 母亲把所有蔬菜都放在炖肉里了。‖ **let sb. ~ in his own**

juice 让某人自作自受

stick /stɪk/

　　Ⅰ *n.* ❶ a thin piece of wood; sth. like this 小树枝; 柴枝 ❷ such a piece of wood shaped for a special use 杖; 棍; 棒 Ⅱ *v.* (stuck) ❶ fasten or fix with glue, paste, etc. 粘着; 贴: ~ a stamp on a letter 把信贴上邮票 ❷ push a pointed thing into; prick 插进去; 刺: She stuck a pin through the papers to keep them together. 她用大头针把文件别在一起。‖ ~ **in one's throat** 难以接受; 难以启齿 /~ **around** 徘徊; 停留 /~ **at sth.** 迟疑; 犹豫 ‖ ~ **sth. down** 放下 /~ **on sth.** 停留住 /~ **to sb. (sth.)** 忠于某人(坚持某事) /~ **up** 直立; 竖立 /~ **up for sb. (sth.)** 维护某人(某物) /give sb. the ~ 惩罚某人 /get hold of the wrong end of the ~ 弄迷惑

sticker /ˈstɪkə/

　　n. ❶ an adhesive label or notice, which is generally printed or illustrated 有粘胶的标签 ❷ a determined or persistent person 坚定不移者; 坚持不懈者

stickler /ˈstɪklə(r)/

　　n. (~ **for**) a person who pays great attention to sth. so that it is done properly 坚持做……的人: My father is a ~ for neatness and honesty. 我父亲是个坚持整洁和诚实的人。

sticky /ˈstɪki/

　　adj. (stickier, stickiest) ❶ able or tending to stick to things 黏的; 黏性的: ~ tape 黏性胶带 ❷ (said about weather) hot and humid (天气)湿热的, 闷热的: hot and ~ summer 极其湿热的夏天 ❸ difficult or awkward 困难的; 难对付的 ‖ **to come to a ~ end** 遭到报应; 落得悲惨下场 / **have ~ fingers** 好偷东西的; 有顺手牵羊的毛病 ‖ **stickily** *adv.* 黏糊糊地

stiff /stɪf/

　　adj. ❶ not easily bent; hard to move 坚硬的; 不易弯曲的: a ~ hand 僵硬的手 ❷ difficult or strict 艰难的; 严厉的 ❸ not friendly; rigid 不友好的; 刻板的 ‖ **keep a ~ upper lip** 咬紧牙根

stiffen /ˈstɪfn/

　　v. make sth. stiff, or become stiff (使)僵

直；(使)挺直：My back ～s up and I can't bend.我的后背僵硬，因此我弯不下腰。

stifle/ˈstaɪf(ə)l/

*v.*❶give or have the feeling that breathing is difficult(使)窒息；(使)窒闷：The heat was stifling. 热气闷人。❷suppress；put down；keep back 镇压；遏制；抑制：～ a rebellion 镇压叛乱 / ～ a yarn 抑制呵欠

still/stɪl/

Ⅰ*adj.* without motion；motionless 静止的，一动不动的：Keep ～，don't move. 别作声，不要动。Ⅱ*adv.*❶continuing until a particular time 仍：Those people are ～ in the building. 那些人仍然在大厦里头。❷even；more 更；愈：It is ～ hotter today. 今天更加炎热。

stilt/stɪlt/

*n.*long sticks for walking high above the ground 高跷：walk on ～s 踩高跷

stilted/ˈstɪltɪd/

adj.(with reference to behaviour，writing，etc.)stiff；artificial；not natural (指行为，写作等)生硬的；呆板的；做作的；不自然的

stimulant/ˈstɪmjʊlənt/

*n.*a drink，drug，etc. that increases bodily or mental activity 兴奋剂；刺激物：Coffee and beer are ～s.咖啡与啤酒是刺激物。

stimulate/ˈstɪmjʊleɪt/

v. encourage by exciting the mind or interest 激励；刺激：The good news ～s us to go on.这个好消息激励我们继续前进。‖ **stimulating** *adj.*激励人心的/**stimulation** *n.*刺激；激励

stimulus /ˈstɪmjʊləs/

n.(*pl.*stimuli)❶sth.that produces a reaction in an organ or tissue of the body 刺激(器官、组织)的事物；刺激：areas of the brain which respond to auditory stimuli 会对听觉刺激做出反应的大脑区域 ❷sth. that rouses a person or thing to activity or energy 刺激物，激励物

sting/stɪŋ/

Ⅰ*n.* a sharp，often pointed，pointed organ of some insects 毒刺；针 Ⅱ*v.*prick or stab with the sharp，pointed organ of

some insects and other animals 刺；蜇伤：Look out，the bees will ～ you.小心点，蜜蜂会蜇伤你的。

stingy/ˈstɪndʒi/

*adj.*not generous；unwilling to spend or give 小气的；吝啬的：a ～ boss 吝啬的老板 / Don't be so ～ with the butter！不要那么吝啬黄油！

stink/stɪŋk/

Ⅰ*v.*(stank/stæŋk/ or stunk/stʌŋk/，stunk) have a very bad smell 发臭味；有臭味：Rotten meat ～s.腐肉散发臭味。/ The place stank of decayed fish.这地方发出烂鱼的臭气。Ⅱ*n.*a very bad smell 臭味；臭气

stint/stɪnt/

Ⅰ*v.*give too small an amount (of) 限制；节制；吝啬：Don't ～ the food.不要舍不得吃。/We should ～ on administrative expenses.我们应该节约行政开支。Ⅱ*n.*a fixed amount，especially of work 定额工作；定量：do one's daily ～ 做每天的定额工作

stipulate/ˈstɪpjʊleɪt/

v. make sth. as a part of an agreement；make certain conditions 要求以……作为协议的条件；讲明；规定：They say they will repair the door but they ～ that they must be paid as soon as they have finished.他们说愿意修理这扇门，不过要求一修理完，就得马上给他们钱。

stir/stɜː(r)/

v.(-rr-)❶ mix by moving round with a stick or spoon 搅动；摇动：Stir up the mixture.把混合物搅动一下。❷ excite；be roused 激励：The picture ～red his interest.这张照片激起了他的兴趣。❸ be moving；cause to move 动，移动，走动；摆动：Not a boy ～red when the headmaster came into the room. 校长走进房间时，没有一个孩子走动。

stitch/stɪtʃ/

Ⅰ*n.*one movement of a threaded needle；the method of making stitches 缝纫的一针；针法；缝法：a cross ～ 十字针法 / put a few ～es in a coat 在外衣上缝几针 / drop a ～ 漏一针 / make long (neat) ～-

es 缝长（平整）的针脚 II v. join using needle and thread 缝：She ~ed the two pieces of cloth together. 她把两块布缝在一起。

stock/stɒk/

I n. ❶ a supply or store of goods that is available for sale 存货：The store still has a large ~ of sugar. 商店还有大量的食糖存货。❷ the capital of a company divided into shares 公债；股票：~ broker 债券经纪人/~ exchange 证券交易所/~ holder 股票经纪商 II v. supply or equip with；keep in stock 提供；供应 ‖ **be in (out of)** ~ 有（缺）存货/**take** ~ 清点存货

stockade/stɒˈkeɪd/

n. a fence made of upright poles（usually put round a building to defend it）栅栏，围栏（通常围住建筑物用以保护）：~ building 用栅栏围起来的建筑物

stocking/ˈstɒkɪŋ/

n. a covering of wool，cotton，silk，nylon，etc. which fits the leg and foot tightly and reaches to the knee or to the top of the leg 长袜

stocky/ˈstɒki/

adj.（with reference to persons，animals and plants）short and strong（指人或动植物）粗短而结实的；矮而壮的

stomach/ˈstʌmək/

n. ❶ a bag-like organ in the body where food is digested 胃 ❷ the front part of the body below the chest；abdomen 腹部；肚子 ❸（usually negative）appetite；an inclination or liking for things（常用否定）食欲；兴趣；爱好：I have no ~ for football. 我对足球不感兴趣。

stony/ˈstəʊni/

adj.（stonier，stoniest）❶ having or covered with many stones 多石的：a ~ road 多石的路 ❷ hard；cruel；showing no pity or feelings 冷酷的；无情的；铁心肠的：a ~ heart 铁石心肠

stoop/stuːp/

v. bend the upper part of the body forward and downward 屈身；俯身；弯腰：She ~ed to talk to the little child. 她弯下身来对那小孩说话。

stop/stɒp/

I n. ❶ an act or the state of stopping or being stopped 停止：The car came to a sudden ~. 车突然停了下来。❷ a place where a bus or tram stopped regularly 车站 II v. ❶（cause to）cease（使）停止：The water ~s running. 水停止了流动。❷ prevent from 阻止：Nothing can ~ us from marching on. 没有什么能阻止我们继续前进。‖ ~ **short at sth.** 突然停做某事/**put a** ~ **to sth.**；**bring sth. to a** ~ 停止做某事

stopcock/ˈstɒpkɒk/

n. a device for stopping the flow of a liquid or gas on or off；valve；tap 管闩；柱塞；活栓；旋塞阀；龙头

storage/ˈstɔːrɪdʒ/

n. ❶ the act of storing；the state of being stored 贮藏；储藏：keep fish in cold ~ 把鱼冷藏起来 ❷ a place for storing goods 贮藏室；仓库：an oil ~ 一个油库

store/stɔː(r)/

I n. ❶ a place where goods are kept 仓库；商店：a grocery ~ 杂货商店 ❷ the quantity or supply of sth. kept for use as needed 储备物：winter ~s 冬季储备用品 II v. keep goods for later use 储蓄备用：Some animals ~ much food for the winter. 有些动物要储备足够多的食物用来过冬。

storey/ˈstɔːri/

n.（pl. ~s or stories）a floor or level in a building 楼层：a house of six ~s 六层楼的房子

storm/stɔːm/

I n. ❶ bad weather with strong wind，heavy rain，thunder，lightning，etc. 暴风雨：The ~ caused damage to the village. 暴风雨给这个村庄造成了巨大的损失。❷ a violent outburst of feelings 强烈的情感：a ~ of applause 暴风雨般的掌声 II v. capture（a place）by sudden and violent attack 闯入；突击（某地）；攻占：The men ~ed（their way）into the fort. 士兵们猛攻后进入那座堡垒。‖ **a** ~ **in a tea cup** 大惊小怪

stormy/'stɔːmi/
adj.(stormier, stormiest)❶ having a lot of strong wind, heavy rain, etc.多风暴的；有暴风雨的：a ～ night 暴风雨之夜 ❷ noisy and angry 激昂的；激烈的：a ～ quarrel 激烈的争吵

story/'stɔːri/
n.❶ a description of events and people telling people sth. that are true or untrue 故事；小说：a ghost ～ 鬼故事 / a children's ～ book 儿童故事书 / an adventure ～ 冒险故事 / true stories 真实的故事 / a short ～ 短篇小说 / Tell me a ～.给我讲个故事。❷ an account of past events 历史；事迹：stories of ancient Greece 古希腊史 / the ～ of Columbus 哥伦布的事迹 ❸ an untrue statement 谎言；虚话：He's a liar; he tells stories.他是一个说谎者，他总是说谎。❹＝storey

stout/staut/
I *adj*.❶ strong, thick; not easily broken or worn out（东西）结实的；牢的：a ～ ship 坚固的船 / a ～ cloth 结实的布 / a ～ rope 粗绳 ❷ determined and brave 坚决的；刚勇的：a ～ fellow 刚勇的人 / a ～ heart 勇气 / offer a ～ resistance to the enemy 对敌人做顽强的抵抗 ❸（of a person）rather fat; tending to fatness （人）矮胖的；肥胖的：The woman is too ～ for her clothes.那妇女太胖了，衣服穿不下了。II *n*.a strong kind of dark beer 烈性黑啤酒

stove/stəuv/
n.a structure or device used for cooking or heating 火炉：a gas ～ 煤气炉 / an oil ～ 煤油炉 / a coal ～ 煤炉/ an electric ～ 电炉

straggle/'stræɡl/
v. fall behind the others while going somewhere 落后；落伍：The young children ～d behind the older ones.年幼的小孩落在大一点的小孩后面。‖ ～r *n*. 落后者；落伍者

straight/streit/
I *adj*.❶ not bent or curved 直的：a ～ line 一条直线 ❷ honest, frank and upright 坦诚的；正直的：a ～ response 坦率

的回答 II *adv*.directly 直地；笔直地：Go ～ ahead.一直往前走。‖ come ～ to the point 开诚布公；开门见山/keep a ～ face 板起面孔/～ out 直言地；未犹豫地‖ ~-way *adv*.立即；马上

straightforward/ˌstreit'fɔːwəd/
adj.simple; without difficulties 简单的；易懂的：The first question he asked me was quite ～.他向我提出的第一个问题很简单。

strain/strein/
I *n*.❶ a condition of being stretched 拉紧；扯紧：The floor collapsed under the ～.楼被压垮了。❷ exhaustion 劳累；疲劳：Quite a few people fall ill under much ～.不少人因疲劳过度而病倒。II *v*.draw or stretch 用力拉紧：～ a rope 拉紧绳子

strait/streit/
I *n*.❶ a narrow passage of water connecting two large bodies of water 海峡：the Bering Strait 白令海峡/ the ～s of Dover 多佛海峡 ❷（usually *pl*.）difficult position 困难；困境；窘迫：in financial ～s 在经济困难中 / He is in great ～s for money.他手头极为拮据。/She has been in great ～s since her husband died.自从她丈夫死后，她的处境一直很困难。II *adj*. narrow 狭窄的

strand/strænd/
I *n*.❶ a sandy shore of a lake, sea, or river（湖、海、河的）沙岸；滨 ❷ any of the threads, hairs, wires, etc. twisted together into a rope or cable（线、绳等的）股；缕；串：a rope of three ～s 一根三股的绳子 / a ～ of pearls 一串珍珠 II *v*.❶ make a boat or fish be left on the shore and unable to return to the water 使搁浅：The ship was ～ed on the rocks.这船在礁石上搁浅。❷（of a person）be left in difficulties, helpless, without money, friends, etc.（指人）使处于困境；使束手无策：be ～ed in the strange country 流落在陌生的国家里一筹莫展

strange/streindʒ/
adj.❶ unusual; peculiar 不为所知的；奇怪的：a ～ person 一个陌生人 ❷ unknown or not familiar 不熟悉的：I am ～ with her.我和她不熟。

stranger/'streɪndʒə(r)/

n. ❶ a person not known, seen or heard before 陌生人：They never talk to ～s.他们从不跟陌生人谈话。❷ a person in an unfamiliar place 外人：He's a ～ in this city.他对这个城市很陌生。❸ a person without experience 门外汉；无经验者 ‖ **be no ～ to sth.**熟悉某事：We are no ～s to this kind of thing.我们对于这类事是有亲身体会的。

strangle/'stræŋgəl/

v. ❶ kill by pressing round the throat 扼杀；勒死；绞死；使窒息：～ in the cradle 扼杀在摇篮里 ❷ restrict or prevent 抑制；扼制；束缚：～ a bill 压制一项议案

strap/stræp/

Ⅰ *n.* a strong narrow piece of material, such as leather, used as fastening 带子；皮带；铁皮条；窄带条：a watch ～ 表带 / a purse ～ 钱包带 Ⅱ *v.*(-pp-) ❶ fasten or hold in place with a strap 用带子束住：～ on a watch 带上手表 ❷ beat with a strap 用皮带打：The slave was ～ped to death. 奴隶被鞭打致死。

strategic /strə'ti:dʒɪk/

adj. ❶ relating to the identification of long-term or overall aims and interests and the means of achieving them 战略（上）的：～ planning 战略规划 ❷ carefully designed or planned to serve a particular purpose or advantage 认真谋划的；仔细策划的；关键的：Alarms are positioned at ～ points around the building. 警报器被设置在建筑物四周关键的地方。

strategy/'strætɪdʒi/

n. the art of planning operations in war, etc.战略；策略；谋略：～ of trading space for time 以空间换时间的战略/By careful ～ she negotiated a substantial pay rise. 她精心策划后，谈妥了大幅增加工资的事。

straw/strɔ:/

n. dry, cut stalks of wheat, barley, etc. 稻草；麦秆 ‖ **make bricks without ～** 做无米之炊/**catch**(**clutch,grasp**)**at a ～** 抓住稻草，依靠完全靠不住的东西/**not care a ～** 毫不介意/**not worth a ～** 一文不值

strawberry/'strɔ:'bri/

*n.*a plant having a juicy red fruit with tiny seeds on its surface 草莓：We grow strawberries in our garden.我们在园子里种草莓。

stray/streɪ/

Ⅰ *v.* move away (from the right path, etc.) 偏离正道；迷路；走失：They ～ed from the path and lost their way. 由于走岔了道，他们迷路了。Ⅱ *adj.* lost from home；having no home 迷路的；离群的：We found a ～ dog at the door. 在门边我们发现了一条迷路的狗。

stream/stri:m/

Ⅰ *n.* ❶ the running water, as a small river, or brook 小河；溪流：a mountain ～ 山涧/cross a ～ 横跨小溪/go with the ～ 顺潮流 / go against the ～ 逆潮流 ❷ anything flowing forth like a stream 流动；流出：a ～ of cars 一长串汽车 Ⅱ *v.* flow freely；move continuously and smoothly in one direction 流；流出；涌：Tears ～ed down her cheeks.热泪从她脸上流下。/ The students ～ed into the dining hall.学生们络绎不绝地走进餐厅。

street/stri:t/

n. a town or village road with houses on one side or both 街道：The ～ is empty. 街上空无一人。‖ **the man in the ～** 典型公民/**not in the same ～** 难以与……相比

strength/streŋθ/

n. the quality of being strong in body or mind 力量；强壮：He is a man of much ～.他是一个力气很大的人。

strengthen /'streŋθən/

v. make sth. stronger, or become stronger 加强；巩固；使坚强；变强：The wind won't ～ until tomorrow.风在明天才会变强。

strenuous/'strenjʊəs/

adj. ❶ needing or using great effort 奋发的；费力的；艰辛的：make ～ efforts 尽全力 / ～ work 艰苦的工作 / lead a ～ life 过奋斗生活 ❷ energetic 精力充沛的：～ workers 努力的工作者

stress/stres/

Ⅰ *n.* ❶ the condition causing depression, mental illness, etc. 压力；忧郁：the ～ of work 工作的压力 ❷an extra force used in speaking,on a particular word or syllable 重音 Ⅱ*v.*put extra force to a word or syllable when speaking or emphasis on 重读;强调:He ~ed the point again.他又强调了这一点。

stretch/stretʃ/

v. ❶ make wider, longer or tighter by pulling; be or become wider, etc. when pulled 张开;拉长;拉紧:~ one's arm 伸臂 ❷ extend or spread over an area of land 延伸:The grassland ~es hundreds of miles.草原绵延数百英里。

stricken/'strɪkən/

adj. struck by; affected by 受……侵袭的:They were ~ with terror.他们受恐怖的折磨。

strict/strɪkt/

adj. stern; demanding obedience or exact observance 严厉的;严格的:They are very ~ with their children.他们对孩子要求十分严格。‖~ly *adv.* 严厉地;严格地 /~ness *n.* 严格;严重

stride/straɪd/

Ⅰ *v.* (strode/strəud/, stridden/'strɪdn/) walk with long steps 大步行走:He strode angrily about the room.他怒气冲冲地在房间里走来走去。Ⅱ *n.*(distance covered in) one long step 大步;阔步 ‖ **make great** ~**s** 突飞猛进/**take sth.in one's** ~ 轻易地做某事/~ **over (across) sth.**跨过某物

strident/'straɪdnt/

adj.(of sound)loud and harsh;shrill (指声音)粗大的;尖锐的:the ~ notes of the cicadae 蝉的尖锐鸣叫声

strike/straɪk/

Ⅰ *n.*the act of stopping working for more money or sth. else 罢工:The workers have been on ~ for several days.工人们已连续罢工几天了。Ⅱ *v.* ❶ hit;give a blow or blows to;aim a blow (at) 击;打:~ one's face 打某人的脸 ❷stop working because of disagreement 罢工 ❸ (cause to) sound 发声;鸣:The clock has just struck 5.钟刚敲过 5 点。‖ ~ **for (a-gainst)** 因……而罢工/**be (go on)** ~ 进

行罢工/~ **sb.down** 把某人打倒在地/~ **sth.off** 删除/~ **on (upon)sth.**突然得到或发现

striking/'straɪkɪŋ/

adj. ❶ that draws the attention 显著的;引人注目的:a very ~ woman 一位很吸引人的女子 ❷on strike 罢工的;罢课的

string/strɪŋ/

Ⅰ *n.*❶a thick thread or very thin cord 细绳 ❷ the thin cord or wire of some musical instruments (乐器的)弦 ❸a number of things in a line or row (一)行;(一)列:a ~ of beads 一串珠子/a ~ of questions 一连串问题 Ⅱ *v.*put strings on 上弦;装上线 ‖ **have sb.on a** ~ 置某人于控制之下/**pull the** ~**s** 操纵某事/~ **sb. along** 欺骗;吊胃口

strip/strɪp/

Ⅰ *v.*remove parts of or the covering from sth., especially by pulling or tearing 脱去;剥去 Ⅱ *n.*a narrow long piece of metal,wood,etc.长条;条块 ‖ ~ **off;**~ **sth. (sb.) (off);**~ **sth.from (off) sth.**夺去/ ~ **sth.down** 分解;拆开/~ **sb.of sth.**剥夺某人某物

stripe/straɪp/

Ⅰ *n.*❶narrow lines of different colour to each other 条纹;条子:the Stars and Stripes 星条旗(美国国旗) / a white shirt with green ~s 有绿色条纹的白衬衫 ❷(usually v-shaped) a mark showing rank 级别臂章;袖章(通常为 V 字形):get (lose) one's ~s 升(降)级 ❸ a blow with a whip 鞭打(现用 stroke) Ⅱ *v.*mark … with stripes 给……划上条纹:a ~d shirt 一件有条纹的衬衫

strive/straɪv/

v.(strove/strəuv/ or ~d,striven /'strɪvn/ or ~d) ❶ struggle with or against sb. or sth.抗争;奋斗:~ against (with) difficulties 与困难作斗争 ❷make great efforts (for sth.or to do sth.) 努力;奋斗:~ for freedom 争取自由 / ~ to be a useful member of the society 争取成为社会的有用人才 / ~ to complete the task ahead of time 争取提前完成任务

stroke/strəuk/

Ⅰ*n.*❶ an act of hitting or blowing 打击；(一)打；(一)击；(一)挥：I killed three flies at one ～.我一下打死了三只苍蝇。❷a line made by a single movement of a pen or brush in writing or painting 笔画：He writes with firm ～s.他笔力遒劲。Ⅱ*v.*rub gently with the hand 抚摸：It's a cute kitten.Can I ～ it? 这只小猫好可爱,我能摸一摸吗?

stroll/strəʊl/

Ⅰ*n.*a quiet,unhurried walk 漫步；闲逛：Let us go for a ～ in the park.我们去公园散步吧。Ⅱ*v.*walk slowly for pleasure 漫步

strong/strɒŋ/

*adj.*❶ not weak；powerful 强壮的：a ～ wind 一股强大的风 ❷(of a drink,drug, etc.) having a lot of material which gives taste,produces effects,etc.(指物)强烈的；效力大的 ❸ having great power of body or mind 坚定的；坚强的 ❹ hard to break or knock down 坚固的；牢固的 ‖ as ～ as a horse 健壮如马；力大如牛/one's ～ points 一个人的长处 ‖ ～-minded *adj.*有主见的；坚持己见的

structure/'strʌktʃə(r)/

*n.*❶ the way in which parts are formed into a whole 结构；构造：the ～ of a building 一幢房屋的结构 ❷ sth.built；a building 建筑物：a wooden ～ 木制建筑物

struggle/'strʌgl/

Ⅰ*v.*fight；make great efforts 抗争；搏斗：～ against difficulties 与困难作斗争 Ⅱ*n.* a strong effort；a hard attempt 抗争：It's a long and hard ～.这是一场长期而艰巨的斗争。

strum/strʌm/

v.(-mm-) run the fingers over the strings of a stringed musical instrument,often without skills 乱弹；不熟练地弹奏弦乐器：He was ～ming (on) his guitar.他正在乱弹吉他。/ He was ～ming a popular tune on his guitar.他正用吉他乱弹着一着流行曲。

stub/stʌb/

Ⅰ*n.*a short part of anything remaining after use 残余部分；残端：He threw away the ～ of his cigarette.他扔掉了烟蒂。/ He was writing with the ～ of a pencil.他正用铅笔头写字。/～ of a cheque book 支票簿存根 Ⅱ*v.*(～ out) extinguish (a lighted cigarette) by pressing the lighted end 掐灭；捻熄 ‖ ～by *adj* 粗短的

stubborn/'stʌbən/

adj. obstinate；unwilling to yield, obey, etc.顽固的；固执的：As he is a ～ child, he won't listen to his parents.他是一个固执的小孩,他不会听父母的话。

student/'stjuːdnt/

*n.*❶ a person who is studying,especially at college or university；anyone who is at school (大、中学的)学生：a high school ～ 中学生 / a college ～ 大学生 / a music ～ 学音乐的学生 ❷anyone who studies or who is devoted to learning knowledge 学者；研究者：a ～ of bird life (nature,theology) 研究鸟类生活(自然、神学)的学者

studied/'stʌdɪd/

*adj.*carefully considered or planned；done on purpose 精心策划的；故意的；有意的：a ～ insult 有意的侮辱

studio/'stjuːdɪəʊ/

*n.*❶ a workroom of a painter or photographer (画家、摄影家等的)画室；摄影室；工作室 ❷ a place where cinema films or recordings are made or from there television or radio programmes are made or produced 摄影棚；制片厂；演播室,播音室

studious/'stjuːdɪəs/

adj. ❶ having or showing the habit of learning 好学的；用功的：a ～ boy 勤勉好学的男孩 ❷painstaking 努力的；用心的：be ～ of one's business 兢兢业业 ❸deliberate 故意的：with ～ politeness 故作有礼貌地

study/'stʌdi/

Ⅰ*n.*❶ the activity of learning or gaining knowledge, either from books or by examining things in the world 学习；研究 ❷ the room (in one's home) used for reading,writing,etc.书房 Ⅱ*v.*spend time

S

in learning;examine 学习;研究:He was ~ing to be a doctor.他在读医科。

stuff /stʌf/

Ⅰ v.fill tightly with 塞满:The box is ~ed with paper.盒子里塞满了纸。Ⅱ n.material of which sth.else is made from 素材;资料

stuffy /ˈstʌfi/

adj.(stuffier, stuffiest) ❶ (of a room, etc.) too warm and lacking fresh air (房间等)闷热的,不通气的:a ~ room 闷热的房间 ❷ dull;stopped up 呆板的;迟钝的 ❸ (informal) sulky;ill-tempered (非正式)不高兴的;愠怒的

stumble /ˈstʌmbl/

v.hit the foot against sth.and almost fall 绊一下脚;绊跌;绊倒:I ~d over a stump.我的脚在树桩上绊了一下。

stump /stʌmp/

Ⅰ n.❶ the part of a tree or plant that is left after the main part has been cut off 树桩;残干;残桩:a tree ~ 树桩 ❷anything remaining after the main part has been cut or broken off or has worn off 残余部分:a cigarette ~ 香烟蒂 / the ~ of a limb 残肢 Ⅱ v.❶walk with stiff, heavy movements 笨重地行走;沉重地走:He ~ed angrily up the stairs.他踏着沉重的脚步气呼呼地上楼去。/The man ~ed along.那人迈着沉重的步子行走。❷ make unable to answer;leave at a loss 难倒:The problem ~ed the professor.这个问题难倒了那位教授。The committee was ~ed as to what decision to make.委员会犯难了,不知道作出什么决定才好。❸ go about (a district, the country)making stump speeches 做巡回演说

stun /stʌn/

v.(-nn-) ❶make senseless or unconscious 打昏;使不省人事;使失去知觉;使昏迷:The robber ~ned the guard.强盗把守卫打晕了。❷ shock deeply;astonish 使震惊;使惊呆:I was ~ned by so many questions.他这么多的问题,把我问得张口结舌。/The beauty of the garden ~ned the visitors.花园的美景使参观者惊叹不已。

stunning /ˈstʌnɪŋ/

adj.extremely good and attractive 极好的;极吸引人的:The girl looks ~.那姑娘看起来非常漂亮。‖ ~ly adv.极好地

stunt[1] /stʌnt/

v.stop the growth 阻碍……的发育(或成长):The children have been ~ed by disease.孩子们因病发育不良。

stunt[2] /stʌnt/

n.sth.done deliberately to get attention or publicity 故意引人注目的行动;花招;噱头

stupid /ˈstjuːpɪd/

adj.foolish;slow-thinking 愚蠢的;鲁钝的:It's ~ to do that.那样做是愚蠢的。

sturdy /ˈstɜːdi/

adj.(sturdier, sturdiest) ❶ strong and healthy 强壮的;结实的:We need several ~ men to push this car.我们需要几个壮汉推这辆车。❷ firm;not yielding 坚定的;不退让的:~ defenders 坚强防御者

stutter /ˈstʌtə(r)/

v.repeat the same sound in an effort to speak 结巴地说;口吃:~ an apology 结结巴巴地道歉

style /staɪl/

n.❶the manner, method or way of speaking, writing, doing or building 风格 ❷a general manner of doing sth.which is typical or representative of a person or group,a time in history, etc.作风;格调 ❸ fashion 款式;时尚:The ~ of your dress is very fashionable.你的衣服款式十分时髦。

stylish /ˈstaɪlɪʃ/

adj.fashionable;elegant and attractive 时髦的;新潮的;高雅的;雅致的:a ~ restaurant 雅致的餐馆

stylist /ˈstaɪlɪst/

n.❶ a designer of fashionable styles of clothing 时装设计师 ❷a hairdresser 发型师

sub- /sʌb/

pref.under;less than;almost 在……之下;低于;少于;几乎:subaltern 下级的,低级的/subnormal 低于正常的/subtropical 亚热带的

subconscious /ˌsʌbˈkɒnʃəs/

Ⅰ *adj.* to do with mental processes of which we are not fully aware but which influence our actions 下意识的,潜意识的: ~ fear 下意识中的恐惧 **Ⅱ** *n.* the part of the mind in which these processes take place 下意识;潜意识 ‖ ~ly *adv.* 下意识地;潜意识地

subcontract /sʌbˈkɒntrækt/
v. hire a company or person outside your company to do a particular part of your work 分包;转包: We would ~ the work out. 我们会把这工作转包出去。

subdivide /ˌsʌbdɪˈvaɪd/
v. divide again into more parts (把……)再分;(把……)细分: The country is divided into provinces and the provinces are ~d into districts. 国分为省,省又细分为地区。

subdivision /ˌsʌbdɪˈvɪʒn/
n. the act or state of subdividing 重分;再分;细分: A district is the ~ of a province. 地区是省细分而成的。

subdue /səbˈdjuː/
v. ❶ conquer;overcome 征服;克服;使屈服: ~ an enemy 使敌人屈服 / ~ nature 征服自然 / Napoleon once ~d much of Europe. 拿破仑曾一度征服了欧洲的大部分地域。 / He ~d his anger. 他克制住了愤怒。 ❷ make milder;soften 使柔和;减弱: a ~d voice 压低了声音 / a ~d lights 减弱的光 / a tone of ~d satisfaction 满足的语气

subdued /sʌbˈdjuːd/
adj. ❶ (said about a person) quiet, shy, or slightly depressed (人)克制的;低沉的;抑郁的 ❷ not loud, harsh, or bright 柔和的;减弱的;缓和的: ~ lighting 柔和的灯光

subject /ˈsʌbdʒɪkt/
Ⅰ *n.* ❶ an area of knowledge discussed or studied in school, college, etc. 学科;题目: We now have seven ~s at school. 现在我们在学校学七门功课。 ❷ individual that experiences sth. or is subjected to sth. 对象 **Ⅱ** *adj.* (~ to sb. or sth.) under the authority of sb. or sth. 服从于: All citizens in this nation are ~ to the law. 这个国家

的全体公民都必须服从法律。 ‖ ~ion *n.* 服从

subjective /səbˈdʒektɪv/
adj. giving the thoughts or feelings of one particular person 主观的: The writer of the book has a very ~ view of modern life. 该书作者对现代生活持非常主观的观点。

subjunctive /səbˈdʒʌŋktɪv/
adj. expressing a condition of possibility, etc. 假设语气的,虚拟语气的: the ~ mood 虚拟语气

sublet /sʌbˈlet/
v. rent to sb. else property which one has rented from a landlord 转租,分租(房屋或土地)

sublime /səˈblaɪm/
Ⅰ *adj.* ❶ of the greatest and highest sort or quality 崇高的;庄严的;卓越的: a ~ thought 崇高的思想 / a ~ thinker 卓越的思想家 / ~ building 雄伟的建筑 ❷ astounding;extreme 极端的;异常的: ~ conceit 极端的骄傲 / ~ enthusiasm 异常的热情 **Ⅱ** *n.* the sublime that fills one with awe or reverence 卓越;崇高: from the ~ to the ridiculous 由崇高到荒诞

submarine /ˈsʌbməriːn/
Ⅰ *n.* a ship that can go under water 潜水艇: a nuclear-powered ~ 核潜艇 **Ⅱ** *adj.* existing or living underwater 水下的;海底的;海生的: a ~ mine 水雷 / ~ plants 海底的植物 / a ~ cable 海底电缆

submerge /səbˈmɜːdʒ/
v. ❶ put under water;cover with liquid 淹没;浸没;沉没;埋没: The flood ~d the small village. 洪水淹没了小村庄。 / He ~d the bowls and dishes in the basin. 他将碗碟浸在脸盆里。 / His talent was ~d in the past. 他的才华过去一度被埋没。 ❷ sink out of sight;go down under the surface 沉没;潜入水中;潜航

submission /səbˈmɪʃn/
n. ❶ an act of being controlled by sb. else and surrendering power, etc. to others 归顺;投降;降服: ~ to the president 向总统投降 ❷ obedience;humility 服从;忠顺: with all due ~ 毕恭毕敬地 ❸ sugges-

S

tion or opinion 建议；意见；看法：In my ~, the witness is lying.依我看，这证人在说谎。❹ the act of presenting sth. for consideration 提出；递交；呈交：the ~ of the essay 论文的上交 / the ~ of his report for the newspaper 把报告交报纸发表

submissive /səb'mɪsɪv/

adj.gentle and willing to obey orders 服从的；顺从的；谦恭的：~ to advice 听从忠告

submit /səb'mɪt/

v.(-tt-) ❶ put (oneself) under the control of another 使归顺；使降服；使服从：~ oneself to discipline 服从纪律 / refuse to ~ to a wrong decision 拒绝服从错误的决定 / He refused to ~ himself to their criticism.他拒绝接受他们的批评。/She did not ~ herself of the insult. 她无法忍受这种侮辱。/The enemy ~ted to our troops.敌人向我军投降了。❷ put forward for opinion, discussion, decision, etc. (为评析、讨论、决定等而)提交；提出：~ a proposal 提出一项建议 / I ~ted the problem to the committee.我向委员会提出了这个问题。❸ suggest；argue 建议；认为；声辩：I ~ that he is wrong.我认为他错了。

subnormal /sʌb'nɔːml/

adj.below normal 低于正常的；比正常少的；低能的：~ intelligence 智力低能

subordinate

Ⅰ /sə'bɔːdɪnət/ *adj*.junior in rank or position；less important 下级的；次要的；从属的：a ~ officer 下级军官 / be in a ~ position 处于从属地位 / a ~ clause 从句 / a ~ conjunction 从属连接词 / The factory is ~ to that company.这厂是从属那个公司的。/The minority is ~ to the majority.少数服从多数。Ⅱ /sə'bɔːdɪnət/ *n*.a person in a subordinate position；a person working under another 属下；部下；居下位者 Ⅲ /sə'bɔːdɪneɪt/ *v*.treat as less important than sb. or sth. else；make less important than sb. or sth. else 使屈从于；使服从

suborn /sə'bɔːn/

v.get (a person) by bribery or other means to commit perjury or other unlawful act 贿买；贿赂；使作伪证；唆使：~ a witness 买通证人

subscribe /səb'skraɪb/

v.❶ contribute 捐献(助)；认捐：The old man ~d 2,000 yuan to the foundation.那位老人给基金会捐赠了 2 000 元钱。❷ order in advance and pay 预订；订购：~ to a magazine 订阅杂志 ❸ agree；approve 同意；赞同：~ to his opinion 赞同他的观点 ❹ write (one's name, etc.) at the foot of a document 签(名字等)；签署：~ one's name to a petition 在请愿书上签名

subscription /sʌb'skrɪpʃən/

n.❶ an act of subscribing 订购；认购；认捐；捐赠 ❷ a payment to subscribe to sth. 订购款；认购款；认捐款；捐赠款 ❸ a fee for membership of a society, etc. 会费

subsequent /'sʌbsɪkwənt/

adj.following or coming after 随后的；继起的：The first ticket cost 10 dollars, but all ~ ones were 8 dollars.第一张票花了 10 美元，但以后的票都是 8 美元。‖ **to** 以后：She became ill ~ to the event.这事发生以后她生病了。

subside /səb'saɪd/

v.❶ fall or sink lower 沉降；下陷；凹陷；消退：The river ~d when the rain stopped.雨停后河水消退。❷ become quieter；grow less 平静；平息；减退：The wind has ~d. 风平息了。/ His anger soon ~d.他的愤怒很快就平息了。‖ **~nce** /səb'saɪdns, 'sʌbsɪdns/ *n*. 沉降；塌陷；消退；平息

subsidiary /səb'sɪdɪəri/

Ⅰ *adj*.giving help or support to sb. (sth.) more important；secondary 辅助的；补助的；次要的；副的；附属的：My work as an assistant is ~ to the work of the senior staff.作为助手，我的工作是辅助高级职员。/ study French with German as a ~ subject 学法语而把德语作为次要课程 Ⅱ *n*.a person or thing which is owned or controlled by others 辅助者；辅助物；附属机构

subsidy /'sʌbsɪdi/

n. money paid (especially by a government) to help an industry or another country to keep prices up or down, etc. (尤指政府向企业或别国提供以调节物价等的）补助金；津贴；资助：In Britain and the USA, farmers receive subsidies from the government to grow certain crops.在英国和美国,农民种植某些作物得到政府的补助金。‖ subsidize/'sʌb-sɪdaɪz/ *v.* 发补助金或津贴给……；资助

subsist/səb'sɪst/
v. exist; be kept in existence 生存；存在；维持生活：~ on charity 靠施舍维持生活 / ~ the troops 供部队给养

subsonic/ˌsʌb'sɒnɪk/
adj. (of speed) less than that of sound 亚音速的：a ~ plane 亚音速飞机

substance/'sʌbstəns/
n. ❶ material of which a thing is made; matter 物质：Ice, snow and water are the same ~ in different forms. 冰、雪和水是不同形式的同一种物质。/Soils consist of various chemical ~s.土壤含有各种不同的化学物质。❷ the real element or part of a thing 实质；要旨：in ~ 实质上；基本上/The speech lacks ~.该讲话缺乏实质性的东西。/Please tell me the ~ of your speech.请把你讲话的要旨告诉我。❸ money; property 钱；财产；资产：a man of ~ 有大量资产的人 / waste one's ~ 浪费钱 ❹ firmness; solidity 牢固；坚实：This material has some ~.这材料相当坚实。

substandard/ˌsʌb'stændəd/
adj. less good than usual or than the average 标准以下的；不合格的；不够平均水准的

substantial/səb'stænʃl/
adj. ❶ made of good substance; strong; solid; firm 质地良好的；结实的；坚固的：a ~ table 结实的桌子 / a man of ~ build 身体壮实的人 / a ~ wall 坚固的墙 ❷ having real existence; actual 现实的；实在的；实质性的：the ~ world 现实世界 / ~ understanding of politics 对政治的现实理解 / the ~ truth of the report 那份报告的基本事实 / We are in ~ agreement.我们实质上是一致的。❸ large in

amount or value; important 大量的；巨大的：~ salary 高额薪金 / a ~ profit 高额利润 / a ~ progress 重大进步 / a ~ improvement 重大改进 / a ~ change 巨大变化 / ~ help 极大帮助 ❹ possessing considerable property; well-to-do 富裕的；殷实的；富足的：a ~ tobacco crop 烟草大丰收 / a ~ meal 丰盛的餐食 / a ~ supply of food 食品的丰足供应 /a ~ farmer 富裕的农民

substitute/'sʌbstɪtjuːt/
Ⅰ *n.* a person or thing act or used in place of another 替代人；替代品 Ⅱ *v.* act as a substitute; be used instead of sth. 替代；用于：I'll ~ for the teacher who is in hospital.我代替生病住院的老师。

subtend/səb'tend/
v. be opposite to 对着；对向：The side AC ~s the angle ABC. 斜边 AC 对着角 ABC。

subtense/səb'tens/
v. the chord of an arc or any other subtending line 弦；角的对边

subtitle/'sʌbtaɪtl/
Ⅰ *n.* ❶ a secondary title 副标题；小标题 ❷ the translation of a foreign language film, printed on the film （外国影片上的）译文字幕：a Russian film with French ~ 附有法文字幕的俄国影片 Ⅱ *v.* give a subtitle or subtitles to (sth.) 给……加副标题；给……加小标题

subtle/'sʌtl/
adj. ❶ delicate; hardly noticeable 微妙的；细微的：~ differences in meaning 意思上细微的差别 ❷ ingenious; complex 巧妙的；错综复杂的：a ~ design 巧妙的设计 ❸ quick and clever at seeing or making delicate differences; sensitive 敏锐的；精明的；敏感的：a ~ observer 敏锐的观察者

subtract/səb'trækt/
v. take (a number, quantity) away from (another number, etc.) 减去；减除；扣除：~ three from five 5 减去 3/3 ~ed from 5 is 2.5 减 3 等于 2。

subtropical/ˌsʌb'trɒpɪkl/
adj. near the tropics; almost tropical 亚热

带的

suburb/ˈsʌbɜːb/

n. an outlying district of a town or city 城郊：I do not live in downtown. I live in the ～s. 我不是住在市中心，而是住在市郊。‖ ～**an** *adj.* 城郊的

subvert/səbˈvɜːt/

v. overthrow sth. (e.g. a government or set of beliefs) by destroying people's faith or confidence in it 颠覆（政府）；破坏（信念）

subversive/səbˈvɜːsɪv/

adj. trying or likely to destroy or damage a government or political system by attacking it secretly or indirectly 颠覆性的；起破坏作用的：He was arrested for making a ～ speech to the soldiers. 他因向士兵做策反演说而遭拘捕。

subway/ˈsʌbweɪ/

n. ❶ an underground passage or tunnel 地下通道 ❷ an underground railway in a town 地下铁路

succeed/səkˈsiːd/

v. ❶ turn out well; do well 成功；完成：～ in life 发迹 / ～ in passing an examination 通过考试 ❷ follow another; come next in order 跟着；接着：The storm died down, and a great calm ～ed. 风暴止息了，继之而来的是非常平静。 ❸ take place of another; become the successor 继位；继承：Who will ～ when the king dies? 国王驾崩之后谁继位？ ❹ take the place of; follow 继位；继任：Mr. Smith ～ed Mrs. Jones as our teacher. 继琼斯太太之后史密斯先生任我们的老师。

success/səkˈses/

n. the achievement of one's aim 成功：Work hard and you'll meet with ～. 只要努力干，你就会成功。

successful /səkˈsesfʊl/

adj. ❶ accomplishing an aim or purpose 成功的：He was ～ in getting the job. 他成功得到了那份工作。 ❷ having achieved popularity, profit, or fruit 受欢迎的；赚了钱的；有成就的：a ～ actor 一个受欢迎的演员

succession/səkˈseʃn/

n. ❶ the coming of one thing after another in time or order 继续；连续：Her words came out in quick ～. 她的话像连珠炮一样脱口而出。 ❷ the act, right, or process of succeeding to an office, property, or rank; a person who has this right 继承；继承权；有继承权的人：Who is first in ～ to the throne? 谁是王位的第一继承人？ / a number of things in ～ 接二连三的事 / a ～ of accidents 一连串的故事

successive/səkˈsesɪv/

adj. coming one after the other 接连的；连续的；一个连一个的：five ～ matches 接连五次比赛 / four ～ days 接连四天 / ～ years of good harvests 连年的丰收 / the fourth ～ victory 连续第四次获得的胜利

successor/səkˈsesə(r)/

n. a person who succeeds another 接班人；继承人：a ～ to the manager (the manager's ～) 经理的接班人 / the ～ to the king 王位的继承者

such/sʌtʃ/

Ⅰ *adj.* of that sort 这样的；同类的：Such a person is hard to get along with. 这样的人很难相处。 Ⅱ *adv.* of that kind; of the same kind; like that 这样；那样：He had never seen ～ a large lake. 他从未见过这么大的湖。 Ⅲ *pron.* such person(s) or thing(s) 这样的人(事)：Such are his parents. 他的父母就是这样的人。 ‖ ～ **as to** 如此……以致 / ～ **that**, ～ … **that** 如此……以致

suck/sʌk/

v. ❶ draw (liquid) into the mouth by the action of lips and breathing 用嘴吸；吸 ❷ take liquid, etc. out of 吸收：the earth ～s rainwater 土地吸收雨水

sucker/ˈsʌkə(r)/

n. ❶ an organ by which some animals can stick to sth. （动物的）吸盘 ❷ a device made of rubber, leather, etc. which sticks to sth. by suction （橡胶、皮革等做的）吸板 ❸ a person who is easily cheated 容易受骗的人

suckle/ˈsʌkl/

v. (especially of animals) feed (the young) with milk from the mother's breast 给……喂奶；哺乳：The cat ~s her young.这只猫正在给她的小猫喂奶。

sudden/'sʌdn/

adj. happening or done quickly or unexpectedly 突然的；出人意料的：They heard a ~ cry and wondered what was the matter.他们听见突如其来的叫喊声，不知道出了什么事。‖ **all of a ~** 忽然 ‖ **~ly** *adv.* 突然地：An idea ~ly occurs to me.我突然有了办法。

suds/sʌdz/

n. (*pl.*) masses of bubbles caused by a mixture of soap, air and water 肥皂泡沫

sue/sjuː/

v. bring a lawsuit 起诉；控告；上诉：~ a person for damages 控告某人要求赔偿损害

suffer/'sʌfə(r)/

v. feel or have pain, loss, etc. 受苦；受损失：~ from illness 受疾病之苦 ‖ **~able** *adj.* 可忍受的；能容许的 / **~ance** *n.* 默许；容许

suffering/'sʌfərɪŋ/

n. ❶ pain of body or mind （身体或心灵的）痛苦；苦难：How much ~ is there in the world? 世上有多少苦难? ❷ (usually *pl.*) misery; distress 各种苦恼；折磨：They laughed at the prisoner's ~s.他们嘲笑那囚犯所受的折磨。

suffice/sə'faɪs/

v. be enough or sufficient 足够：Will this food ~ for you? 这点食物足够你吃了吗?

sufficient/sə'fɪʃnt/

adj. enough for a particular purpose 足够的；充分的：~ food 足够的食物 / a ~ reason 充分的理由 / be ~ for sb.'s needs 足够满足某人的需要

suffix/'sʌfɪks/

Ⅰ *n.* an addition made to the end of a word 后缀；词尾 Ⅱ *v.* add as a suffix 加后缀于：~ a syllable to a word 在词后附加一个音节

sugar/'ʃʊgə(r)/

Ⅰ *n.* a sweet substance made from sugar-cane or sugar beets （尤指用甘蔗或甜菜制的）糖：a lump of ~ 一块方糖 Ⅱ *v.*

make sweet with sugar 加糖于：~ one's milk 给牛奶加糖

suggest/sə'dʒest/

v. ❶ put forward for consideration; propose 提议；建议：What can you ~ to me? 你能向我建议什么? ❷ bring (an idea, possibility) into the mind 使想起；提醒：His words ~ that he didn't tell her.他的话表明他没有告诉她。

suggestible/sə'dʒestəbl/

adj. easily influenced by people's suggestions 耳根软的；易受影响的：He was young and highly ~.当时他年轻，很容易听信他人。‖ **suggestibility** *n.* 被暗示性

suggestion/sə'dʒestʃən/

n. ❶ an act of suggesting, or being suggested 建议；提议 ❷ sth. suggested 建议；意见 ❸ a slight trace 细微的迹象：a ~ of a French accent 一丝法国口音

suggestive/sə'dʒestɪv/

adj. ❶ tending to suggest an idea 提示的；暗示的；引起联想的：There were various ~ pieces of evidence.有各种使人产生联想的证据。❷ indicative or evocative 指示的；唤起的：flavours ~ of coffee 有点咖啡的味道 ‖ **~ly** *adv.* 提示地；暗示地

suicide/'suːɪsaɪd, 'sjuːɪsaɪd/

n. ❶ the action of killing oneself 自杀：commit ~ 自杀 / a ~ bomber 自杀式爆炸袭击 / three ~s last week 上周的三件自杀案 ❷ a person who commits suicide 自杀者 ❸ an action destructive to one's interests or welfare 自毁；自暴自弃：political ~ 政府前途的自毁

suit/suːt/

Ⅰ *n.* ❶ a set of clothes 一套（衣服）❷ a lawsuit 诉讼；控告 Ⅱ *v.* look well; be appropriate 使合适；满意：The clothes ~ me very well.这件衣服我穿很合适。‖ **~ sb. down to the ground** 非常适合某人 / **~ the action to the word** 言行一致

suitable/'suːtəbl/

adj. right for the purpose or occasion; fitting; proper 适合的；适宜的；恰当的：clothes ~ for cold weather 适于寒冷天气穿的衣服 / a ~ place for a picnic 适合于野餐的地方

suite/swiːt/

n. ❶a set of rooms or furniture（一套）房间；（一套）家具：a ～ of rooms 一套房间 / a bedroom ～ 一套寝室用家具 ❷a company of followers（一批）随从人员：The queen travelled with a ～ of twelve. 皇后带着十二名随从旅行。❸an orchestral composition made up of three or more related parts 组曲

sulphur/'sʌlfə/

n. a pale-yellow non-metallic element used in medicine and industry 硫；硫黄

sultan/'sʌltən/

n. the title given a Muslim prince or ruler 苏丹（某些伊斯兰教国家统治者的称号）

sum/sʌm/

Ⅰ *n.* the total obtained by adding 总数：a large ～ of money 一大笔钱 Ⅱ *v.* add up; give the total of 总计；合计：Let me ～ up all we have said. 我来总结一下我们所说的话。

summary/'sʌməri/

Ⅰ *n.* a short account giving the main points 摘要；概略 Ⅱ *adj.* brief; giving the main points only 简明的；扼要的：a ～ account 简要说明

summation /sʌ'meiʃən/

n. ❶the process of adding things together 求和：The ～ of numbers of small pieces of evidence. 许多细小的证据汇集在一起。❷a summary 总结

summer/'sʌmə(r)/

Ⅰ *n.* the warmest season of the year coming between spring and autumn 夏天；夏季：in ～ 在夏季 /～ heat 暑热 /～time 夏令时 /～ house 凉亭；避暑别墅 Ⅱ *v.* spend the summer 过夏天；避暑：～ at the seaside 在海滨度夏

summit/'sʌmit/

n. the highest point; the top, especially of mountain 顶点；绝顶；最高峰：～ meeting 最高级会议 / reach the ～ of a mountain 到达顶峰 / the ～ of his ambition (power) 野心（权力）的巅峰 / talks at the ～ (～ talks) 最高层会谈

summon/'sʌmən/

v. ❶demand the presence of; call or send for 召唤；召集；传唤：be ～ed as a witness 被传唤作证 / ～ sb. to one's presence 把某人召唤来 / ～ sb. to be in readiness 号召某人做好准备 / The debtor was ～ed to appear in the court. 债务人被传出庭。❷ gather together; make a great effort to have a particular quality in yourself 鼓起；唤起；振作：I ～ed my courage for the task. 我鼓起勇气接受了任务。/He ～ed up all his strength to jump the stream. 他使出浑身的力气跳过了溪流。/Mr. Smith ～ed up the nerve to speak his mind. 史密斯先生鼓起勇气说出了自己的心里话。

summons /'sʌmənz/

Ⅰ *n.*（*pl.* ～es）❶an order to appear in a law court, or a document containing this 传唤；传票 ❷a command to do sth. or appear somewhere 召唤；召见令：obey a royal ～ 听从国王的召唤 Ⅱ *v.* serve sb. with a summons 用传票传唤：He has been ～ed to appear in court next week. 他已经被传唤下星期出庭。

sumptuous/'sʌmptʃʊəs/

adj. costing a large amount of money; very splendid 奢侈的；豪华的：He lives in a ～ house. 他住在豪华的住宅里。

sun/sʌn/

n. the burning star in the sky around which the Earth moves and from which it receives light and heat 太阳 ‖ rise with the ～ 黎明即起/under the ～ 在太阳下/give sb.(have) a place in the ～ 处顺境 ‖ ～bathe *v.* 做日光浴/～burnt *adj.* 太阳晒黑的/～flower *n.* 向日葵/～glasses *n.* 太阳镜 ‖ ～less *adj.* 无阳光的；阳光照不到的

Sunday/'sʌndei/

n. the day of the week before Monday and after Saturday 星期日；星期天：Many people work on ～s. 许多人星期天工作。‖ one's ～ clothes 最好的衣服

sundry/'sʌndri/

Ⅰ *adj.* separate; various 个别的；各种的：～ things 零星杂物 Ⅱ *n.*（*pl.*）sundry items; miscellaneous things 杂项；杂事；杂物；杂货 ‖ all and ～ 各种各样的人；所有人：All and ～ agree. 所有人都同意。/He

was known to all and ～ as David. 人人都
叫他大卫。

sunflower /'sʌnflaʊə/

n. a very tall plant with large yellow flowers, grown in gardens for its seeds and oil
that are used in cooking 向日葵；葵花

sunken /'sʌŋkən/

adj. ❶ below the surface of water; under
the sea, etc. 水面下的；沉没的：～ treas-
ure 沉在水底的财宝 ❷ below the level
of sth. else 低于周围平面的；凹陷的：～
garden 低地公园

sunny /'sʌni/

adj. (sunnier, sunniest) ❶ having much
sunshine 向阳的；晴朗的：a ～ room 向阳
的房间 / ～ days 晴朗的日子 ❷ cheerful
and happy 欢乐的；愉快的：a ～ smile 愉
快的微笑

sup /sʌp/

Ⅰ *v.* (-pp-) drink a little at a time 啜饮：
He ～ped up his broth with a spoon. 他用
汤匙喝肉汤。/ He that ～s with the devil
must have a long spoon. 与恶人交往，须
特别留意。Ⅱ *n.* a small quantity (of liquid) 小量；一饮；一啜：a ～ of tea 一口茶

super /'suːpə(r)/

Ⅰ *adj.* excellent; splendid; wonderful 优等
的；特级的；极好的 Ⅱ *n.* an article of superior quality 特级品

superb /sjuːˈpɜːb, suːˈpɜːb/

adj. of the finest quality; excellent; grand
极佳的；最好的；宏伟的；壮丽的；壮观
的；华美的：a ～ palace 壮丽的宫殿 / a
～ performance 极好的表演 / ～ food 上
好的食物

superficial /ˌsuːpəˈfɪʃl/

adj. ❶ of or on the surface only 表面(性)
的：a ～ wound 表皮上的伤 ❷ not thorough or profound 肤浅的；浅薄的：～
knowledge 浅薄的知识 / a ～ book 立论
肤浅的书 / a ～ mind 浅薄的智力

superfluous /suːˈpɜːfluəs, sjuː-/

adj. more than that is needed or wanted
过多的；多余的；不必要的：～ food
(money) 多余的食物(钱) / ～ worries
不必要的忧虑

superhighway /ˌsuːpəˈhaɪweɪ, sjuː-/

n. a divided highway for high-speed traffic
高速公路；超级公路

superhuman /ˌsuːpəˈhjuːmən, ˌsjuː-/

adj. having much greater power, knowledge, etc. than is normal 超出常人的；非
凡的

superintendent /ˌsuːpərɪnˈtendənt, ˌsjuː-/

n. ❶ a person who directs, controls or
manages; manager 主管人；监督人；经营
者 ❷ a senior police officer 公安局长；督
察长

superior /suːˈpɪərɪə(r)/

adj. ❶ better or greater in quality 优良
的；超群的：This cloth is ～ to that one.
这种布比那种好。❷ higher in rank,
class or position (级别、阶层、职位)更高
的：～ status 更高的地位 ❸ showing confidence that you are better than others 高
傲的：Tom always behaves in a ～ manner. 汤姆总是神气活现的样子。‖ ～ity
n. 优秀；卓越

superlative /suːˈpɜːlətɪvs, sjuː-/

Ⅰ *adj.* ❶ of the highest kind or degree；
above all others 最高的；无上的：～ skills
卓越的技巧 / a man of ～ wisdom 聪明
绝伦的人 / a ～ actor 演技高超的演员
❷ of adjectives or adverbs expressing the
highest or a very high degree (形容词、副
词的)最高级："Happiest" is the ～ form
of "happy". Happiest 是 happy 的最高级
形式。Ⅱ *n.* the superlative form of an adjective or adverb (形容词、副词的)最高
级

supermarket /'suːpəˌmɑːkɪt/

n. a big shop where you collect things in a
basket and pay when you leave 超级市
场；自选商品市场：Buy the meat and the
other things at the ～. 在超级市场买肉和
其他东西。

supernatural /ˌsuːpəˈnætʃrəl, ˌsjuː-/

adj. of that which is not controlled or explained by physical laws 超自然的；神奇
的；不可思议的：～ beings 不可思议的存
在物

superpower /'suːpəˌpaʊə(r), sjuː-/

n. a powerful and influential nation 超级
大国：an economic ～ 经济超级大国

S

supersonic/ˌsuːpəˈsɒnɪk/
　*adj.*faster than the speed of sound 超音速的;超声波的:a ～ plane 超音速飞机 / ～ wave 超声波

superstition/ˌsuːpəˈstɪʃn/
　n. a belief resulting from ignorance of what really exists 迷信:break down(do away with)～s 破除迷信 / Many people have the ～ that 13 is an unlucky number.许多人都迷信地认为 13 是个不吉利的数字。

supertanker/ˈsuːpətæŋkə(r),ˈsjuː-/
　n. a very large, fast tanker for carrying oil,etc.超级油船;大型快速油船

supervise/ˈsuːpəvaɪz/
　*v.*watch over and direct(work,workers) 监督(工作、工人);管理;指导

supper/ˈsʌpə(r)/
　*n.*the evening meal 晚餐:have a big ～ 吃一顿丰盛的晚餐/ have very little ～ 晚餐吃得很少

supplant/səˈplɑːnt/
　*v.*take the place of;supersede 代替;取代:Trams in London have been ～ed by buses.伦敦的电车已被公共汽车取代。

supple/ˈsʌpl/
　*adj.*easy to bend or move 柔软的;易弯曲的;灵活的:A dancer has a ～ body.舞蹈演员身体柔软。‖ ～ness *n.* 柔软;易弯曲

supplement/ˈsʌplɪmənt/
　Ⅰ *n.*sth.added to a book or newspaper to give further information 补遗;附录;副刊;增刊:Sunday ～s 星期天副刊 Ⅱ *v.* make an addition or additions to 增补;补充:～ one's wages 增加工资

supply/səˈplaɪ/
　Ⅰ *v.*furnish;provide;satisfy the needs of 提供;供应:The school supplied us with knowledge.学校给我们提供了知识。Ⅱ *n.*an act of supplying 供应:There is a good ～ of all kinds of goods during the festival.节日期间,各种商品供应充足。‖～ and demand 供与求/in short ～ 供应不足/～ sb.with sth.;～ sth.to sb.向某人提供某物

support/səˈpɔːt/

　Ⅰ *v.*❶ hold up or keep in place;bear the weight of 支撑;支持:I don't think this pole can ～ the roof.我认为这根柱子是支撑不了房顶的。❷ take the side of;help 支持;拥护:I'll ～ you at any time. 在任何时候,我都支持你。❸ provide everything necessary, especially money, so that sb.or sth. can live or exist 养活;维持:He ～s his family by writing.他靠写作维持他一家人的生活。Ⅱ *n.*the state of supporting or being supported 支持;被支持‖in ～ 预备的;支援的/be in ～ of sb.(sth.)支援某人(某事)‖～able *adj.*可维持的

supporting/səˈpɔːtɪŋ/
　*adj.*❶a supporting actor in a play or film (movie) has an important part but not the leading one(演员、角色)次要的;配角的:He is featured in the movie in a ～ role.他在这部电影中担任配角。❷carrying the weight of sth.支承的;支撑的;承重的:a ～ wall 承重墙

suppose/səˈpəʊz/
　*v.*❶ take it a fact that 假定;假设:Suppose he is dishonest, what will you do? 假设他弄虚作假,你将怎么办? ❷ guess;think 推测:I ～ he won't come.我想他不会来。‖ be ～d to 被期望;应该 ‖supposition *n.*假设;假定

supposed/səˈpəʊzd/
　*adj.*believed to exist or to have a certain character or identity 误以为的;误信的;所谓的:his ～ brother 他那所谓的兄弟

supposedly/səˈpəʊzɪdli/
　adv. according to what is generally assumed or believed(often used to indicate that the speaker doubts the truth of the statement)一般说来;根据推测;据称;可能(常用来暗示说话人对此有怀疑):The adverts are aimed at women,～ because they do the shopping.这些广告是针对妇女做的,据称是因为总是她们在购物。

suppress/səˈpres/
　*v.*put an end by force;put down 镇压;平定:～ the slave rising 镇压奴隶起义/He could hardly ～ his feelings.他几乎难以控制自己的感情。‖ ～ion *n.* 镇压

supremacy /sjuˈpreməsi/

*n.*being supreme;the position of supreme authority or power 至高无上;最高权威;最高地位

supreme/suːˈpriːm/
*adj.*highest in rank or authority 最高的:Supreme Court 最高法院 ‖ ～**ly** *adv.*至高无上地

surcharge/ˈsɜːˈtʃɑːdʒ/
Ⅰ*n.*an extra charge 附加费 Ⅱ*v.*take an extra charge 收取额外费用

sure/ʃʊə(r)/
Ⅰ*adj.*certain to do sth.or confident that sth.will happen 必定的;确信的:I'm not ～ why he wants that book.我不太知道他为何需要那本书。Ⅱ*adv.*certainly 事实上 ‖ be (feel) ～ about sth.有把握;确信/be ～ to do sth.肯定会干某事/to be ～ 诚然/～ enough 事实上/for ～ 确切地/as ～ as 千真万确地

surely/ˈʃʊəli/
*adv.*❶ with certainty 当然;必然;一定:He will ～ fail.他必然会失败。❷ express strongly one's hope or belief 必定;必然:Surely I've met you before somewhere.我一定在什么地方见过你。❸(in answers) certainly;of course (用于答语中) 当然:"Would you be willing to help?""Surely!""你愿意帮忙吗?""当然!"

surety/ˈʃʊəti, ˈʃɔːti/
n.(*pl.*-ies)❶a person who promises to pay a debt or fulfil a contract,etc.if another person fails to do so 保证人;担保人 ❷money given as a guarantee that someone will do sth.保证金

surf/sɜːf/
Ⅰ*n.*waves of the sea breaking on the shore 拍岸的海浪:The ～ is high just after a storm.暴风雨过后风浪大。Ⅱ*v.*engage in surfing 做冲浪运动:go ～ing 去冲浪

surface/ˈsɜːfɪs/
*n.*the outside of any objects 表面;最上层:the ～ of the ocean 海洋表面/ the ～ of the land 地面

surfeit/ˈsɜːfɪt/
n.(with a)(especially with reference to food and drink) too much of sth.(与 a 连用)(尤指饮食)过量;过多:a ～ of cakes 过多的蛋糕

surge/sɜːdʒ/
Ⅰ*v.*❶ move forward, roll on, in or like waves 汹涌;澎湃:The waves ～d high.波涛汹涌。/The crowd ～d out of the hall.人群拥出了大厅。❷(of a feeling) arise powerfully (感情)激动;激烈:Anger ～d (up) within him.他怒火中烧。Ⅱ*n.*❶ forward or upward movement 巨浪;波涛;汹涌;澎湃:～s of enthusiasm 热情的洋溢 / a ～ of people 一大群人 / the ～ of the sea 海水的汹涌 ❷ an onrush of a strong feeling 波动;激动:a ～ of anger (pity) 一阵怒气(怜悯)

surgeon/ˈsɜːdʒn/
*n.*❶ a doctor who treats patients by operations 外科医师:a dental ～ 口腔科医师 ❷ a medical officer in the armed forces 军医

surgery/ˈsɜːdʒəri/
*n.*❶ the science and practice of treating injuries and disease by manual and instrumental operations 外科;外科手术 ❷ a doctor's or dentist's room where patients come to consult him 诊疗室;应诊室

surmount/səˈmaʊnt/
*v.*❶overcome;get over 越过;克服:～ a fence 越过围墙 / ～ every difficulty 克服每个困难 ❷(passive) be surmounted by (with);have on or over the top (用被动语态)在顶上有;顶上覆盖着:a spire ～ed by a weather vane 装有风向标的尖顶 / The tower is ～ed with snow.塔顶上覆盖着白雪。

surname/ˈsɜːneɪm/
*n.*a family name;a last name 姓;姓氏:Smith is the ～ of John Smith.史密斯是约翰·史密斯的姓。

surpass/səˈpɑːs/
*v.*rise above;go beyond 超过;胜过:Her ability ～ed my expectation.她的能力超过了我的预想。‖ ～**ing** *adj.*非凡的;卓越的

surplus/'sɜːpləs/

n. the amount of money that remains after needs have been supplied 剩余；节余：There is still a large ～ of food after the distribution. 分配之后，还节余有许多的食品。

surprise/sə'praɪz/

Ⅰ*n.* ❶a feeling caused by sth. unexpected 惊讶；惊愕：His action was a great ～ to all of us. 他的行为使我们大家大吃一惊。❷an event or sth. else that is unexpected 意想不到的事：I have a ～ for you. 我要告诉你一件出人意料的事 Ⅱ*v.* give a feeling of surprise; astonish 使惊讶；使……大吃一惊：The result ～d us. 结局使我们大吃了一惊。‖ ～ sb. into doing sth. 冷不防地促使某人做某事 ‖ **surprising** *adj.* 令人吃惊的/～d *adj.* 吃惊的/～dly *adv.* 吃惊地；惊愕地

surrender/sə'rendə(r)/

v. give up or yield to the power (especially of an enemy), as a sign of defeat (尤指向敌人)投降；(向……)自首；屈服(于)：The enemy ～ed at last. 敌人最后还是投降了。‖ ～ oneself to 屈服于

surround/sə'raʊnd/

Ⅰ*v.* be all around on every side 包围：a city ～ed by mountains 四面环山的城市 Ⅱ*n.* a usually decorative edge or border 覆盖物；框，边

surrounding/sə'raʊndɪŋ/

Ⅰ*adj.* encircling; around and nearby 周围的；环绕的：York and the ～ countryside 约克城和周围的乡村 Ⅱ*n.* (*pl.*) everything around and about a place; conditions that may affect a person 周围的事物；环境：The hotel stands in picturesque ～s. 宾馆四周的环境优美如画。

survey

Ⅰ/sə'veɪ/*v.* ❶ take a general view of 眺望；纵览：～ the city below 纵览下方的城市 ❷ examine the general condition of 检查 Ⅱ/'sɜːveɪ/ *n.* a piece of study, examination, etc. of a particular group; a map or record of this 测量；检查；鉴定：We had better make a ～ of the market. 我们最好做个市场调查。

survival/sə'vaɪvl/

n. ❶the fact or likelihood of continuing to live 生存：～ of many rare animals 许多稀有动物的生存 ❷sth. which has continued to exist from an earlier time, especially when similar ones have disappeared 残存物；遗迹；遗风

survive/sə'vaɪv/

v. remain alive; live longer than 幸存；比……活得久：Only a few soldiers ～d the battle. 那次战斗中且只有少数士兵幸存。/ My father has ～d all his brothers and sisters. 我父亲所有的兄弟姐妹都先他去世。‖ **survivor** *n.* 幸存者

susceptible/sə'septəbl/

adj. easily impressed; sensitive 易受感动的；敏感的：Children are more ～ than adults. 儿童要比大人更容易受外界影响。/ I am ～ to colds. 我易患感冒。‖ **susceptibility**/səˌseptə'bɪləti/ *n.* (身、心的)弱点；敏感点

suspect/sə'spekt/

v. feel doubt about 怀疑；猜疑：He ～ed it was a trick. 他怀疑那是一个骗局。/ I ～ his motives. 我对他的动机表示怀疑。

suspend/sə'spend/

v. ❶ hang sth. from above 悬吊：a box ～ed from the roof 吊在房顶下的一个盒子 ❷ stop for a time; delay; keep in an undecided state for a time 悬而未决：a ～ed case 一个悬而未决的案件

suspense/səs'pens/

n. the state of great fear, worry, uncertainty, etc. about the outcome of an event (对事件结果的)担心；悬而未决；焦虑：Their next step is still in ～. 他们的下一个步骤尚未决定。/ Don't keep me in ～ any longer. 不要再让我焦虑了。

suspicion/sə'spɪʃn/

n. ❶a feeling that a person has when he suspects; the state of suspecting or being suspected 猜疑；怀疑；嫌疑；疑心：I have a ～ that he is dishonest. 我怀疑他不诚实。/ He was looked upon with ～. 他被人猜疑。❷a small amount of; a little; slight 些微；一点点；一丝：There was a ～ of sadness in her voice. 她的声音中有点悲伤意味。

suspicious /səˈspɪʃəs/

adj. having, showing or causing suspicion; not trusting 怀疑的；表示怀疑的；引起怀疑的，可疑的：a ～ character 可疑人物/ The affair looks ～ to me.这事在我看来很可疑。/The policeman became ～ of his movement.那警察对他的行动表示怀疑。

sustain /səˈsteɪn/

v. ❶ hold up; support 支撑；承受：Will this light shelf ～ all these books? 这个轻便的书架承受得住所有这些书吗？❷ (enable to) keep up; maintain （使能）维持；支持：～ a family 持家/ food sufficient to ～ life 足够维持生命的食物 ❸ suffer; undergo 蒙受；遭受：～ a defeat 遭受失败/ ～ serious injuries 受重伤 ❹ uphold; give a decision in favour of 确认；准许：The court ～ed his claim. 法庭准许了他的要求。

sustainable /səˈsteɪnəbl/

adj. ❶ able to be maintained at a certain rate or level 能保持一定速度（或水平）的；能持续的；能保持的：～ reactions 持续的反应 ❷ (especially of development, exploitation, or agriculture) conserving an ecological balance by avoiding depletion of natural resources（尤指发展、开采、农业）可持续性的

sustenance /ˈsʌstɪnəns/

n. ❶ food and drink that sustains life 生活资料；食物；营养 ❷ the process of sustaining life by food 支撑；维持

swagger /ˈswæɡə(r)/

v. walk in a proud way; behave in this way 昂首阔步，大摇大摆地走；狂妄自大

swallow /ˈswɒləʊ/

Ⅰ *v.* ❶ cause or allow to go down the throat 吞；咽：～ sth.吞下某物/ ～ one's breakfast 急匆匆地吃早饭 ❷ take back; retract 收回：～ one's words 食言 ❸ believe without question 轻信：～ a story 轻信一故事 / ～ the bait 陷入罗网；上当 ❹ suffer or experience 忍耐；忍受：～ an insult 忍辱/ ～ rude remarks 忍受粗话 ❺ take in; exhaust; cause to disappear; use up 吞没；淹没；耗尽：His earnings

were ～ed up.他的收入全耗尽了。/The plane was ～ed (up) in the clouds. 飞机没入云中。Ⅱ *n.* ❶ an act of swallowing; the amount swallowed at one time 吞；咽；一次吞的量：take a ～ of water 饮一口水 ❷ a kind of small swift-flying insect-eating bird with a forked tail 燕子：～ dive 燕子式跳水 / ～-tailed 燕尾状的 /One ～ does not make a summer. 一燕不成夏。(不能光凭一个事例就下判断)

swamp /swɒmp/

Ⅰ *n.* an area of soft wet land; marsh 沼泽地；湿地：tropical ～s 热带沼泽 Ⅱ *v.* ❶ fill with water, especially causing to sink 淹没；浸入水中；(尤指)使下陷：A big wave ～ed the boat.一个巨浪淹没了那只小船。❷ overwhelm sb.or sth.with great quantity of things 使不知所措；使应接不暇；使忙得不可开交：We are ～ed with work. 我们忙得一塌糊涂。

swan /swɒn/

n. a large, long-necked bird that is usually white 天鹅：a black ～ 黑天鹅；珍品

swap /swɒp/

Ⅰ *v.* (-pp-) exchange one thing for another 交换：I've finished this magazine. Can I ～ with you? 这本杂志我看完了。我能跟你交换一下吗？ Ⅱ *n.* ❶ an act of exchanging one thing for another 交换：Let's do a ～.我们做个交换吧。❷ a thing suitable for swapping 适合交换的东西

swarm /swɔːm/

Ⅰ *v.* move, be present in large numbers 蜂拥：The hall is ～ed with people. 大厅里挤满了人。Ⅱ *n.* a large number of insects, etc. 大群；大量：a ～ of bees 一群蜜蜂

sway /sweɪ/

Ⅰ *v.* ❶ swing; (cause to) move from side to side (使)摇摆；(使)动摇：The grasses and trees ～ed in the wind.草及树在风中摇动。❷ control or influence; govern the direction of 影响；支配：～ed by one's feelings 受自己感情的支配 / Nothing can ～ our determination.什么也不能动摇我们的决心。Ⅱ *n.* ❶ a swaying movement 摇晃；摇摆；摇动：The ～ of the

S

ship made him fall over.船的摇晃使他跌倒。❷a rule or control 统治;控制;支配:under the ～ of 在……统治下

swear/sweər/
*v.*say solemnly or emphatically 发誓;郑重说明:He swore he would never do that again.他发誓他再也不会做那件事了。‖ ～ sb.to secrecy 使某人誓守秘密/～ a witness 使证人发誓/sworn enemies 不共戴天之敌/sworn friends（brothers）莫逆之交/～ to sth.强调地说

sweat/swet/
Ⅰ *n.*moisture that is given off by the body through the skin 汗 Ⅱ *v.*(cause to) give out sweat（使）出汗:In summer,we always ～ a lot.在夏天,我们通常要出很多的汗。

sweater/'swetə(r)/
*n.*a woollen jersey or jacket 羊毛衣;厚运动衫

sweep/swi:p/
Ⅰ *v.*clear away（dust,dirt,etc.）with a brush or broom;clean by doing this;push away 清扫;扫除:You must ～ the room tomorrow.你们必须明天清扫房间。Ⅱ *n.*an act of cleaning 清扫 ‖ **all before one** 所向披靡/**be swept off one's feet** 被弄得神魂颠倒

sweeping/'swi:pɪŋ/
*adj.*❶wide-ranging 面广的;大幅的 The new manager made ～ changes.这位新任经理进行了大刀阔斧的改变。❷（said about a statement）making no exceptions or limitations;too general（言语）笼统的;概括的:～ generalizations 笼统的概括

sweet/swi:t/
Ⅰ *adj.*❶ tasting like sugar or honey 甜的 ❷pleasing to the senses 悦耳的;惬意的;芬芳的;令人感觉愉快的:～ music 悦耳的音乐 Ⅱ *n.*candy;dessert 甜食;糖果 ‖ ～heart *n.*爱人 ‖ ～ly *adv.*甜地;悦耳地/～ness *n.*甜味;美妙/～ish *adj.*甜得发腻的/～en *v.*使变甜;使变得可爱

swell/swel/
v.(cause to) become great in volume,thickness,or force 增大;膨胀:The plas-

tic bag ～s up after it is stuffed with vegetable.这个塑料袋子在里边塞满蔬菜后胀大了。

swelling/'swelɪŋ/
*n.*a swollen place on the body（身体上的）肿胀处

swift/swɪft/
*adj.*fast;rapid 快的;迅速的:a ～ answer 迅速做出回答 ‖ ～ly *adv.*快速地 /～ness *n.*迅速

swim/swɪm/
Ⅰ *v.*(-mm-) ❶ move the body through water by using arms,legs,fins,the tail,etc.游泳:We go ～ming every other day.我们每隔一天要去游一次泳。❷ have a dizzy feeling 头晕;目眩 Ⅱ *n.*an act or period of swimming 游泳 ‖ ～ with the tide（stream)顺大流/～suit *n.*(女式)游泳衣

swindle/'swɪndl/
*v.*cheat;deceive 行骗 ‖ ～ sth.out of sb,～ sb.out of sth.从某人身上榨取某物:You cannot ～ anything out of me.你从我身上榨取不了任何东西。

swine/swaɪn/
n.(*pl.*swine) ❶pigs 猪:a herd of ～ 一群猪 ❷a disgusting person 讨厌的人;混账:You ～! 你这猪猡!

swing/swɪŋ/
*v.*move back and forth regularly 摇摆 ‖ ～ for sb.(sth.)被处绞刑/no room to ～ a cat in 场地十分狭小/～ the lead 轻快地走或跑

swipe/swaɪp/
Ⅰ *v.*❶ hit with a wide,heavy blow 猛击;重击:He ～d me on the shoulders with his stick.他用手杖猛击我的肩膀。❷ steal 偷:～ $100 worth of goods 偷窃了价值 100 美元的商品 Ⅱ *n.*the act of hitting sth.拍打;击打:He took a ～ at the fly on the wall.他猛拍墙上的苍蝇。

swirl/swɜ:l/
Ⅰ *v.*move with a twisting motion;whirl 旋转;回旋;打旋:dust ～ing about the streets 在街上旋转的尘土 Ⅱ *n.*a twisting movement;a whirl or eddy 旋转;回旋;旋涡:a ～ of dust 一阵旋涡的尘土

swish/swɪʃ/

Ⅰ *n.* a sound made by a stick or sth. thin moving very quickly through the air; a sound made by cloth moving over a surface (棍子等挥动的)嗖嗖声;(衣服摩擦的)沙沙声: ~ of a whip 鞭子挥动的嗖嗖声/~ of their long robes over the floor 他们的长袍拖过地板时发出的沙沙声 Ⅱ *v.* move and make a sound like this 嗖地挥动,嗖嗖作响;发沙沙声: The animal ~ed its tail. 那头牲口嗖嗖地挥动尾巴。

switch /swɪtʃ/

Ⅰ *n.* a device for turning on or off an electrical equipment 开关;闸 Ⅱ *v.* ❶ turn on or turn off 接通;切断 ❷ change 转变;改变: Later, his interest ~ed to playing football. 后来,他的兴趣转移到了踢足球上面。‖ ~ **sth. on** (**off**) 打开(关闭)/~ **over to** 转向

swollen /ˈswəʊlən/

adj. larger than normal, especially as a result of disease or an injury 肿大的;肿胀的: a ~ ankle 肿胀的脚踝

swoop /swuːp/

Ⅰ *v.* (with **down on**) attack suddenly from above (与 down on 连用)俯冲攻击;猛扑;突然袭击: The hawk ~ed down on the chickens. 那只鹰猛地扑向小鸡。Ⅱ *n.* an act of attacking or hitting suddenly 扑击;袭击

sword /sɔːd/

n. a weapon with a long sharp blade 剑;刀 ‖ **cross** ~**s with sb.** 与……争论/**put to the** ~ 杀死/**at the point of the** ~ 在暴力威胁下

syllable /ˈsɪləbl/

n. a unit of pronunciation consisting of a vowel alone or of a vowel with one or more consonants 音节: America is a word of four ~s. America 是一个四音节词。

symbol /ˈsɪmbl/

n. ❶ a sign, mark, object, etc. representing sth. 代表;象征: Now this building has become a ~ of peace. 现在,这幢房子已成为和平的象征。❷ a sign, number, etc. that has a fixed meaning 符号,记号 ‖ ~**ically** *adv.* 象征性地

symbolic /sɪmˈbɒlɪk/

adj. to do with, using, or used as a symbol 象征主义的;作为象征的;使用象征的: The dove is ~ of peace. 鸽子是和平的象征。

symbolism /ˈsɪmbəlɪzəm/

n. the use of symbols to represent things 符号使用;象征主义;象征手法

symbolize /ˈsɪmbəlaɪz/

v. ❶ be a symbol of sth. 象征;是……的象征: The use of light and dark ~s good and evil. 用光明与黑暗来象征善与恶 ❷ represent sth. by means of symbols 用象征的方法代表

sympathetic /ˌsɪmpəˈθetɪk/

adj. feeling or showing sympathy 有同情心的;表示同情的: The president is very ~ with the poor people. 那位总统十分同情穷人。

sympathize /ˈsɪmpəθaɪz/

v. ❶ feel or express sympathy (with) 同情;表示同情: We ~ heartily with you. 我们由衷地同情你。❷ agree; share or understand another's feeling 同感;赞同;共鸣: ~ with sb. in his point of view 赞同某人的观点

sympathy /ˈsɪmpəθi/

n. ❶ having the same feeling as another 同情;同感;慰问: have no ~ with (for) 不同情 / Yet the other children felt a genuine and profound ~ for the little girl. 但别的孩子对这个小姑娘怀有真切的、深深的同情。/ I have ~ with (for) the sick. 我对病人表示同情。/ My sympathies are with you. 我同情你。❷ agreement with or approval of an opinion or aim 同感;赞同;一致: be in (out of) ~ with a plan 赞同(不赞同)某一计划

symphony /ˈsɪmfəni/

n. a musical composition in three or four parts for orchestra 交响乐: a ~ orchestra 交响乐团 / A new ~ was being played for the first time. 一首新的交响曲正在首次演奏。

symposium /sɪmˈpəʊziəm/

n. a meeting of several persons to discuss and exchange ideas; a number of essays by several persons about one subject 专题

S

讨论会;专题论文集

symptom/ˈsɪmptəm/

　　n. ❶a sign of illness,etc.征候;病症;症状:a ～ of malaria 疟疾的症状 / ～s of smallpox 天花的症状 / Fever is a ～ of illness.高烧是生病的症状。❷a sign of the existence of sth.bad 征兆;征候:a ～ of despair 绝望的征兆 / Bad behaviour is often a ～ of unhappiness.不得体的举止常常是心里不高兴的表现。

syn-/sɪn/

　　pref. together;with;at the same time as 共;同;同时

synchronize/ˈsɪŋkrənaɪz/

　　v. (cause to) agree in time;(cause to) happen at the same time (使)同步;(使)同时发生;对准(钟表):Before the attack,the army officers ～d their watches.进攻开始之前,军官们对准了表。

syndrome/ˈsɪndrəum/

　　n. a number of symptoms of an illness occurring together 综合症状;综合征

synonym/ˈsɪnənɪm/

　　n. word that means the same or nearly the same as another word 同义词;近义词:"Diligent" is a ～ of "industrious"."Diligent"是"industrious"的同义词。

synopsis/sɪˈnɒpsɪs/

　　n. (*pl.*synopses/sɪˈnɒpsiːz/) an outline or a brief summary of sth.大意;纲要;梗概:a ～ of a story 故事的梗概

syntax/ˈsɪntæks/

　　n. (rules for) building sentences 句法;造句(法):bad ～ 错误的句法

synthesis/ˈsɪnθɪsɪs/

　　n. the combining of separate things ideas,etc.,into a complete whole 综合;合成

synthetic /sɪnˈθetɪk/

　　Ⅰ *adj.* ❶made by chemical synthesis;artificially made,not natural 合成的;人造的:～ rubber 合成橡胶 ❷not genuine or natural 不诚恳的;虚假的;不自然的:Their words are a bit ～.他们的话有点虚伪。Ⅱ *n.* a synthetic substance or fabric,e.g.nylon 合成物;合成纤维(如尼龙)

syrup/ˈsɪrəp/

　　n. thick sweet liquid made from sugarcane juice or by boiling sugar with water 糖浆;糖水:lemon ～ 柠檬糖水 / chocolate ～ 巧克力糖浆/ corn ～ 玉米糖浆

system/ˈsɪstɪm/

　　n. a set of things or parts forming a whole 系统:A good ～ leads to efficiency.优良的体系会带来高效率。‖ ～atic *adj.*有方法的;系统的

systemic /sɪsˈtemɪk/

　　adj. affecting or connected with the whole of sth.,especially the human body 涉及全系统的;系统的;影响全身的;全身的:The disease is localized rather than ～.这种疾病是局部性的而非全身性的。

S

Tt

tab/tæb/

*n.*a small piece of cloth or paper fixed to a garment,etc.(钉在服装等物品上的)标签,悬挂牌:To open,pull ～.开启时请拉环。

table/'teɪbl/

*n.*❶ a piece of furniture consisting of a flat top 桌子:a dining ～ 餐桌/a kitchen ～ 厨房用桌/a billiard ～ 台球桌 ❷ a list (of facts or figures) 表;目录 ‖ lay sth.on the ～ 将某物搁置一旁/turn the ～s on sb.扭转形势

tablecloth/'teɪblklɒθ/

*n.*a cloth for covering a table,especially during a meal (尤指用餐时覆盖餐桌的)桌布,台布

table mat/'teɪblmæt/

*n.*a small mat made of material that will not let heat pass,placed under hot dishes to protect a table's surface (放在热食碟下,防止桌面烫坏的)桌垫

tablet/'tæblɪt/

*n.*❶ pill;a small piece of medicine 药片:throat ～s 润喉片 /a ～ of aspirin 一片阿司匹林 /take two ～s 服两片药 ❷ a lump of hard soap,etc.小片;小块:a ～ of soap 一块肥皂 ❸ a flat piece of stone or metal that has words written on it 石板;金属板 ❹ a flat sheet of wood,stone,etc. for cutting words on 写字板

taboo/tə'buː/

Ⅰ *n.* sth. which is forbidden by religious belief or custom (宗教或习俗的)禁忌,忌讳,避讳:This tribe has many ～s about the kinds of food women may eat.这个部落对于妇女的食物有多种禁忌./The top of that sacred hill is under a ～.那座圣山的山顶属禁忌之列。Ⅱ *adj.*strongly forbidden by social custom, especially be-cause offensive or likely to cause social discomfort (社会习俗方面)禁忌的;忌讳的:Eating eggs is a ～ in this tribe.这个部落忌讳吃蛋。/Arguments about politics are ～s in many countries.在许多国家避讳辩论政治。

tabular/'tæbjʊlə(r)/

*adj.*arranged in the form of a table 列成表的;表格式的:The information is shown in ～ form.该资料以表格形式列出。

tabulate/'tæbjʊleɪt/

v. arrange facts or figures shortly and clearly in a list 将(事实或数字)列表

tachograph/'tækəɡrɑːf/

*n.*an instrument fitted to a vehicle to record its speed and the distance travelled, etc.(车辆的)速度计,里程表

tachometer/tæ'kɒmɪtə(r)/

n. (especially in vehicles) an apparatus which record how an engine turns (尤指车辆的)速度表;(汽车引擎的)转速表

tacit/'tæsɪt/

*adj.*accepted or understood without anything being said 默认的;心照不宣的:By sitting quietly at the meeting,he gave his ～ approval to the plan.开会时他静静地坐着,表示对这项计划已默认。

tack[1]/tæk/

Ⅰ *n.*❶ a type of small,sharp nail with a flat head 图钉;平头钉 ❷a type of stitch made quickly with needle and thread to fasten pieces of cloth together until closer and more permanent stitches are made (固定布片用的)粗缝;假缝 Ⅱ *v.* fasten with tacks (用平头钉)钉住;粗缝:We ～ed the map on the board.我们把地图钉在板上。/She ～ed up the hem of her dress.她用线粗缝衣服的折边。

tack² /tæk/

n. ❶ the course of a sailing ship in relation to the wind (跟风向相关的)帆船航向：The yacht left the harbour on the starboard ~.游艇离港时作右舷抢风行驶。❷a method of dealing with a situation or problem；a course of action for policy (解决问题的)方法，方针；策略

tackle /'tækl/

Ⅰ *v.* try to deal with or solve 处理；解决：This is a difficult problem to ~.这是一个难以解决的问题。 Ⅱ *n.* the equipment used in sports (运动)器械 ‖ ~ sb. about (over) sth.坦白地向某人谈某事

tacky /'tæki/

adj. (with reference to glue, paint, etc.) sticky；not quite dry (指胶水、颜料、油漆等)黏的；未干的

tact /tækt/

n. the ability to do or to say the right thing at the right time；the skill in handling people without causing offence 机智；老练；圆滑：having great ~ in dealing with people 与人交往极为圆滑

tactful /'tæktful/

adj. having or showing the ability to deal with difficult situation without annoying others 机智的；灵活的；圆通的；得体的：They need a ~ assistant.他们需要一个机智灵活的助手。‖ ~ly *adv.* 机智灵活地；圆通地

tactical /'tæktɪkəl/

adj. ❶to do with tactics，especially as distinct from strategy 战术上的；策略上的：a ~ officer 精通战术的军官 ❷ (said about weapons) intended to support the immediate needs of a military operation (武器)战术的；短程的 ❸(of a person or their actions) showing adroit planning；aiming at an end beyond the immediate action (人或行为)有策略的 ‖ ~ly *adv.* 战术上；策略上

tactics /'tæktɪks/

n. ❶ (usually singular) the art of arranging military forces for battle and moving them during battle (常用单数)战术；兵法：a grand ~ 大兵团作战术 ❷the art of handling a situation，of gaining advantage or success 策略；手法：win by surprise ~ 出奇制胜

tactless /'tæktlɪs/

adj. having or showing a lack of adroitness and sensitivity in dealing with others or with difficult issues (处世或处理问题)不圆通的，不灵活的：a ~ remark 不得体的话

tadpole /'tædpəʊl/

n. a young frog after it has left its egg and before it is fully grown 蝌蚪

tael /teɪl/

n. ❶ any of various units of weight of East Asia，especially liang (old Chinese unit of weight) (亚洲东部的)衡量单位，尤指中国的旧衡量单位)两 ❷ a former Chinese unit of money originally a tael，in weight of silver (中国旧时的货币单位)银两：100 ~s of silver 一百两银子

tag /tæg/

n. ❶a label attached to sb. or sth. for the purpose of identification or to give other information 标签；标牌 ❷a nickname or description popularly given to someone or sth. 绰号 ❸a character or a set of characters appended to an item of data in order to identify it 标识符；标记 ❹a small piece or part that is attached to a main body (主体上的)一小部分

tail /teɪl/

Ⅰ *n.* a movable rear end of an animal's body 尾巴 Ⅱ *v.* follow closely behind 尾随 ‖ turn ~ 逃走 / ~s up 心情好；兴致勃勃 / at the ~ end 末端；尾部 / ~ after a person 紧随某人

tailor /'teɪlə(r)/

Ⅰ *n.* a person whose business is making clothes 裁缝：go to the ~'s 去缝衣店 / The ~ makes the man.人靠衣装。 Ⅱ *v.* cut out and sew 缝制；剪裁：a well ~ed coat 一件裁制得合身的上衣 /a material that ~s well 容易缝制的布料

taint /teɪnt/

Ⅰ *v.* make or become infected 使感染；使腐败；变污；使道德败坏；腐蚀：be ~ed with bad habit 沾染上坏习气 /The meat was ～ed. 这肉坏了。Ⅱ *n.* a trace of some bad quality, decay or infection 污点;堕落(或耻辱)的迹象;感染;腐坏

take/teɪk/

v.(took, ～n)❶ get into one's hand 拿;握:Take me by the arm. 抓住我的胳膊。❷ carry to a place; go carrying 拿走:Please ～ the dog home. 请把这条狗带回家。❸ avail oneself of; use; use or borrow without permission; steal 擅自取用:I don't know who has ～n my umbrella. 不知道是谁拿了我的伞。❹ spend; use up; need 需要;花费:It took him two hours to get to the train station. 他花了两小时才到达火车站。‖ ～ sb.'s fancy 令某人喜欢/～ sb. at a disadvantage 乘人之危/～ sb. by surprise 冷不防出现/～ one's chance 碰运气/～ down 记录下来/～ sb. (sth.) for…;～ sb. (sth.) to be… 推断为……;～ sb. (sth.) for granted 习惯地认为……;认为……理所当然/～ account of sth. (～ sth. into account) 对某事加以考虑/～ advantage of sb. (sth.) 利用某人(某物)/～ part in 参加/～ place 发生/～ the place of 取代/～ sth. back 收回/～ sth. off 带走/～ one's mind off sth. 分心;转移注意力/～ on 激动;激昂/～ to sth. 从事某事/～ sth. up 拿起/be ～n up with sb. (sth.) 对某人或某物感兴趣/～ sth. upon (on) oneself 承揽某事 ‖ ～r *n.* 拿取的人或物

take-off/ˈteɪkˌɒf/

*n.*❶ the process by which an aircraft becomes airborne; the action of becoming airborne 起飞:The plane accelerated down the runway for ～. 飞机沿着跑道加速起飞。❷ an act of mimicking 模仿:The film is a ～ of *Star Wars*. 这部电影模仿了《星球大战》。

takeover/ˈteɪkəʊvə(r)/

n. the act of taking control of sth., especially of one business company by another 收购;接收;接管(尤指一家公司收购了另一家公司)

tale/teɪl/

n. ❶ a story, especially ones involving magic or exciting events 传说;故事:a fairy ～ 童话 /～s of adventure 探险故事

❷ a report or account; a trivial lie 报告;记述;传闻;谎言:You hear all sorts of ～s. 你可以听到各种编造的传闻。

talent/ˈtælənt/

*n.*❶ a natural ability to do sth. well 天才;才能;才干;本事:a man of ～ 有才能的人 /have a ～ for organization 有组织才能 /He has a ～ for music. 他有音乐才能。❷ people with a natural ability to do sth. well (总称)有才能的人;人才:athletic ～ 体育人才 /artistic ～ 艺术人才

talented/ˈtæləntɪd/

adj. having a natural talent or skill 有才能的;天才的;有才干的:a ～ player 天才运动员

talk/tɔːk/

Ⅰ *n.* a conversation 谈话;讨论:give a ～ to the students 给学生做一次演讲 Ⅱ *v.* say things; speak to give information 说话;谈论:Please ～ to your parents about this. 请跟你的父母谈一下这件事。‖ be (get oneself) ～ed about 成为话柄/～ away 继续谈话/～ sb. down 高声压倒某人/～ sth. over 讨论某事/～ sb. into (out of) doing sth. 说服某人做(不做)某事

talkative/ˈtɔːkətɪv/

adj. talking a lot; full of trivial conversation 爱说话的,健谈的;多嘴的

talker/ˈtɔːkə(r)/

*n.*❶ a person who talks, especially one who talks a lot or in a persuasive way 谈话者;(尤指)健谈的人,说话娓娓动听的人:What a ～ that man is—no one else can get a word in! 那人可真健谈,别人都插不进嘴! /She's a good ～. 她是一个很会讲话的人。❷ a bird that can copy human speech 会说(人)话的鸟

talkie/ˈtɔːki/

n. a cinema film with sounds and words, rather than a silent film 有声电影

talks/tɔːks/

n. a formal exchange of opinions and views (正式的)会谈:The two presidents met for ～. 两位总统晤面进行会谈。/ peace ～ 和谈

tall/tɔːl/

*adj.*❶ having a greater height than is

normal or average 高的；高大的：a ～ man (house) 高个子男人(高大的房屋) /How ～ are you? 你有多高? / I'm 5 feet 8 inches ～.我身高 5 英尺 8 英寸。/ She's ～ and thin with black hair.她又高又瘦,一头黑发。❷ hard to believe；excessive 夸大的；过分的：a ～ order 无理(过分)的要求；难题 /a ～ price 高价 / That's a ～ story.那故事太夸张了。

tally/ˈtæli/

v. agree；be the same 符合；吻合；一致：Your story does not ～ with mine.你所说的跟我所说的不一样。/The expenditure and the receipts should ～.支出与收入应当相符。

tame/teɪm/

Ⅰ *adj.*❶ not wild；accustomed to living with human beings 驯服的：～ animals 驯服的动物 ❷ (of a person) spiritless；submissive (指人)没精打采的；顺从的：a ～ man 温顺的人 ❸ dull or not exciting 平淡的；沉闷的；乏味的：a ～ football match 一场乏味的足球赛 /The film has a ～ ending.那电影的结局乏味。Ⅱ *v.*make sth.tame 使顺从；使驯服：～ a lion 驯狮

tamper/ˈtæmpə(r)/

v. interfere；change；damage 干扰；窜改；损害：Someone has ～ed with the lock on the door.有人撬过门上的锁。/He was accused of ～ing with the examination papers.他被指责窜改考卷。

tan/tæn/

Ⅰ *n.*the yellowish brown colour 棕黄色；黄褐色：I would like some shoes in ～.我想要黄皮鞋。Ⅱ *adj.* yellowish brown 黄褐色的：～ leather shoes 黄褐色的皮鞋 Ⅲ *v.*(-nn-) ❶ make (skin of an animal) into leather 制成皮革 ❷ (cause sth.to) become brown by exposure to the sun (使)晒成褐色：My skin ～s easily.我的皮肤很容易晒黑。

tandem/ˈtændəm/

*n.*a type of bicycle with two seats,one behind the other,and two sets of pedals (有前后座位并有两套踏板的)双人自行车

tangent/ˈtændʒənt/

*n.*a straight line which touches a curve at one point only 切线；正切线

tangential/ˌtænˈdʒenʃl/

*adj.*❶ having only indirect connection with sth.；peripheral 间接相关的；次要的；外围的；略为触及题目的：～ comments 略为触及题目的评论 ❷ moving or going out in different directions；showing divergence 漫射开去的；表现出分歧的 ❸ (having the nature) of a tangent 切线的

tangerine/ˌtændʒəˈriːn/

*n.*a type of small,slightly flat orange with loose skin 红橘；柑橘

tangible/ˈtændʒəbl/

*adj.*able to be touched；real 可触摸的；真实的：The plan has produced ～ results. 这项计划确有成效。

tangle/ˈtæŋgl/

Ⅰ *n.*❶ (with reference to thread,string, hair,etc.) mixed-up and untidy mass (指线、绳子、头发等)缠结：Her hair was full of ～s.她的头发缠结成团。/All the ropes were in a ～.所有的绳子都乱成一团。❷ a state of confusion or disorder 混乱；杂乱：His affairs are in a ～.他的事务一片混乱。Ⅱ *v.*(cause to) become confused or disordered (使)纠缠；(使)混乱；弄乱

tango[1] /ˈtæŋgəʊ/

n.(a piece of music for) a lively dance originated in South America (起源于南美洲的)探戈舞(曲)

tango[2] /ˈtæŋgəʊ/

v. dance the tango 跳探戈舞 ‖ it takes two to ～ 两者要为所做的事负责；一个巴掌拍不响：She says he led her astray, but it takes two to ～.她说是他把她引入歧途,可是一个巴掌拍不响,双方都有责任。

tank/tæŋk/

*n.*❶ a large container for liquid or gas (装液体或气体的)大容器,大桶,大箱：the petrol-tank of a car 汽车的油箱/ a hot-water tank 热水箱 ❷ an enclosed heavily armed and armoured vehicle that moves on two endless metal belts 坦克 ‖ ～er *n.* 油轮；油车；水车

tantalize/'tæntəlaɪz/

　　v. cause to hope or wish for sth. that is not possible, or not easily obtained (以不可能实现或很难实现的希望)逗引；逗弄：They ～d the poor prisoner with promises of freedom.他们以允诺给予自由来逗弄那个可怜的囚犯。‖ **tantalizing** *adj.* 逗引性的；干着急的

tantamount/'tæntəmaʊnt/

　　adj.（with **to**）equal in meaning to; the same as（与 to 连用）意义相等的；相同的：His silence was ～ to saying that he disagreed.他的沉默等于说他不同意。

tap/tæp/

　　Ⅰ *n.* ❶ a sort of handle that you turn to let water, gas, etc., come out of a pipe 开关；龙头：turn on (off) the ～ 打开(关上)龙头/leave the ～ running 让龙头开着 ❷ a quick, light blow 轻快的敲打；轻拍；轻踏；轻叩：There was a ～ on the window.有人轻敲窗户。❸ a sound made by a light blow 轻敲(拍)声 Ⅱ *v.*(-pp-) ❶ strike lightly 轻拍；轻敲；轻踏：He ～ped me on the shoulder.他拍拍我的肩膀。/Someone is ～ping at (on) the door.有人在轻轻敲门。❷ make a hole in sth. so as to let out or draw off a liquid 在……上开孔(引出液体或使之流出)：～ a cask of cider 打开酒桶的活塞取酒/～ rubber trees 切开橡树树皮汲取树液 ❸ furnish (a cask, etc.) with a tap (为木桶等)装上龙头(或塞子) ❹ extract or obtain 引出；获取：～ a man for money (or information) 利用某人获得钱(或消息)/～ the telephone wires 私接电话以窃听

tape/teɪp/

　　Ⅰ *n.* ❶ a length of narrow material, used for tying up parcels, packets, etc. 带；线带：Please tie the bundle of letters with a tape.请用带子把这札信捆起来。❷ a string stretched between the winning posts on a race track（系在跑道终点的）终点线；breast the ～ 冲线 ❸（a length of）narrow plastic material covered with a special magnetic substance on which sounds or pictures can be recorded 磁带；录音带；录像带：I recorded the song on a

～.我把这支歌录下来。Ⅱ *v.* ❶ record (sounds, pictures, etc.) on tape 录音；录像：You can ～ the concert.你可以把这场音乐会录下来。❷ fasten or tie (a parcel, packet, etc.) with tape 用带子捆扎：Have you finished taping all the presents up yet? 你把所有礼物都包扎好了吗？‖ ～-record *v.* 录音；录像/ ～-recorder *n.* 录音机/ ～-recording *n.* 录音

taper¹ /'teɪpə(r)/

　　v.（cause to）become thinner at one end（使）一端逐渐变细：The pencil ～s to a sharp point.铅笔的一端细成笔尖。/He ～ed the stick with a knife.他用小刀把棍子的一端削尖。

taper² /'teɪpə(r)/

　　n. a type of thin candle 极细的蜡烛

taproot/'tæpruːt/

　　n. the main root of a plant, which grows straight down and produces smaller side roots（植物的）主根；直根

tar/tɑː(r)/

　　Ⅰ *n.* a black substance, hard when cold, thick and sticky when warm, obtained from coal, etc. used to preserve timber in making roads, etc. 柏油；木焦油；沥青：It takes a lot of ～ to build this road.修这条路要很多柏油。Ⅱ *v.*(-rr-) cover with tar 铺柏油：This road has just been ～red.这条路刚铺上柏油。

tardy/'tɑːdi/

　　adj. ❶ delayed beyond the proper or expected time; late 迟到的；晚了的；误了规定时间的：We apologize for our ～ response to your letter.来函迟复，谨表歉意。/a ～ arrival 晚来 ❷ acting or moving slowly; sluggish 行动缓慢的；拖拖拉拉的

tare¹ /teə(r)/

　　❶ the weight or wrapping material in which goods are packed 皮重；包装重量 ❷ the weight of an unloaded goods vehicle 车身重量；空车重量 ❸ the amount subtracted when weighing a loaded truck, in order to calculate the actual weight of the goods（称量载重货车时）车身重量的扣除

tare² /teə(r)/

n. an unwanted plant growing among corn; weed 莠草；杂草

target /'tɑːgɪt/

Ⅰ *n.* ❶ an object to be aimed at in shooting 靶心 ❷ an objective to be achieved 对象；指标；目标；目的：~ date 预定完成的日期 / the ~ of the new plan 新计划的目标 / the ~ of complaints 抱怨的对象 / the ~ of criticism 批评的对象 / set a ~ for production 制订生产指标 Ⅱ *v.* aim sth. 把……作为目标（对象）：He is already ~ed as the first victim. 他已被定为第一个牺牲品。

tariff /'tærɪf/

n. ❶ a list of rates or fees; a price list （旅馆或公用事业的）收费表；价目表：a postal ~ 邮费表 / the ~ at a hotel 旅馆的价目表 ❷ a list or system of duties imposed on imported or exported goods 关税；关税率；关税表：raise the customs ~ 提高关税税率

tarnish /'tɑːnɪʃ/

Ⅰ *v.* ❶ lose, cause the loss of, brightness （使）无光泽：Salt ~es silver. 盐可使银失去光泽。 ❷ stain or blemish（a reputation, etc.）损坏（名誉）；玷污：His reputation is ~ed. 他的名誉受到玷污。 Ⅱ *n.* dullness; loss of polish 晦暗；无光泽：Rub the spoon well to remove the ~! 认真擦这个勺子使它发亮。

tarry¹ /'tæri/

v. ❶ delay; linger; lodge 停留；逗留；住：He tarried a few days at an inn. 他在客栈住（或逗留）了几天。 ❷ stay for a time, especially longer than intended; be tardy 耽搁；迟延：Why do you ~ so long? 你为什么耽搁这么久？ ❸ wait 等候：~ for a person 等候一个人

tarry² /'tɑːri/

adj. ❶ of or like tar 柏油的；像柏油的 ❷ covered or smeared with tar 涂有柏油的；被柏油弄脏的

tart¹ /tɑːt/

adj. ❶ having a sour taste 酸的 ❷ sharp; severe 尖刻的；严厉的：He gave a ~ reply. 他给出了一个尖刻的答复。

tart² /tɑːt/

n. a type of pie containing fruit or jam 果馅饼

tart³ /tɑːt/

n. (informal) an immoral woman; prostitute （非正式）轻佻的女人；妓女

tartar /'tɑːtə(r)/

n. a hard deposit on the teeth 牙垢；牙石

task /tɑːsk/

n. a piece of work which has to be done 任务；工作：I was given the ~ of cleaning the room. 给了我打扫房间的任务。 ‖ ~ force 特遣部队；特遣舰队；执行特别任务的小组 / take sb. to ~ 严厉地责备；申斥；盘问：The little boy's father took him to ~ about his dirty hands. 那个小男孩的父亲因他手脏而严厉地责备他。

taskmaster /'tɑːskmɑːstə(r)/

n. a person who gives sb. tasks to do and keeps him busy 工头；监工：Their team leader is a hard ~. 他们的队长要求很严格。

tassel /'tæsl/

n. a number of threads fastened together at one end and used as an ornament, e.g. on cushions 缨；流苏（作为坐垫、靠垫的装饰用）

taste¹ /teɪst/

v. ❶ have a particular flavour in the mouth 有某种味道：The tea ~d sweet. 这茶有甜味。 /Some oranges ~ bitter. 有些橘子吃起来是苦的。 /This soup ~s too much of salt. 这汤太咸了。 ❷ feel or try the flavour of sth. in the mouth 尝；品尝：Can you ~ the sugar in your coffee? 你能尝出咖啡的甜味吗？ /She ~d the pudding to see if it was sweet enough. 她尝了尝布丁，看看够不够甜。 ❸ have experience of; meet 体验；领略；遇到；经历：They ~d defeat for the first time. 他们初次尝到失败的滋味。

taste² /teɪst/

n. ❶ (with a or the) a sense or feeling given by sth. in the mouth （与 a 或 the 连用）味觉；味道：Children like the ~ of sugar. 孩子们喜欢糖的味道。 /Some oranges have a bitter ~. 有些橘子有苦

味。/Food which is cooked too much has no ～.煮得太久的食物吃起来没有味道。❷(with a) small quantity for sample（与 a 连用）一口；一点；少量：May I have a ～ of your pudding? 我可以尝一尝你的布丁吗? /He gave us a ～ of his bad temper.他让我们领教了一下他的坏脾气。/Just have a ～ this cookie.尝一点儿这种饼干吧。❸ a liking（or preference）for sth.爱好：She has a ～ for expensive hats.她爱好戴昂贵的帽子。/His ～ in music is not the same as mine.他在音乐方面的爱好跟我的爱好不同。❹ the choice or judgment in the things' appreciation 品味；判断力；鉴赏力：Their house is furnished in very good ～.他们的房子布置得雅致大方。/His reply to their question was in bad ～.对于他们的问题,他的回答不得体。/We all admire your ～ in art.我们都钦佩你的艺术鉴赏力。‖ ～ful adj.雅致的；有鉴赏力的：The furniture in their house is very ～ful.他们家的家具非常雅致。/～fully adv.雅致地；高雅地

tasteless/'teɪstləs/
    adj.❶without taste in the mouth having no or little flavour 无味的；不好吃的：The food is ～.这种食物吃起来毫无味道。❷ having or showing bad taste 庸俗的：a ～ colour scheme 庸俗的配色

tasty/'teɪsti/
    adj.having a pleasant taste in the mouth 美味的；可口的：a ～ cake 一块美味的蛋糕

tattered/'tætəd/
    adj.old and torn；in bad condition 破烂的；破旧的；褴褛的：He was wearing a ～ coat.他穿着一件破烂的外套。

tatters/'tætəz/
    n.torn pieces of cloth,paper,etc.破烂的衣服；破布条；碎纸片：His coat was in ～.他衣衫褴褛。

tattle/'tætl/
    Ⅰ n.an idle talk；a gossip 闲谈；聊天；闲话：endless ～ about dress 关于服装的无休止的闲谈 Ⅱ v.talk about sth.unimportant incessantly and foolishly 闲谈；饶舌；搬弄是非：She's always tattling about her

neighbours.她老是喜欢对邻居说三道四。

taunt/tɔːnt/
    v.say cruel or insulting words to sb.嘲讽；嘲弄：He ～ed me for being weak.他嘲讽我的软弱。/He ～ed me with my weakness.他嘲讽我的弱点。

taut/tɔːt/
    adj.tight；fully stretched 紧的；绷紧的：The skin of the drum is ～.鼓皮绷得很紧。

tawdry/'tɔːdri/
    adj.bright and showy but of poor quality 花哨低级的；俗气的：She was wearing a ～ hat.她戴着一顶花哨低级的帽子。

tawny/'tɔːni/
    adj.yellow-brown in colour 黄褐色的

tax/tæks/
    Ⅰ n.money which has to be paid to the government of a country by those who live in it 税：The government has increased the ～ on motorcars.政府已提高了汽车税。/People who refuse to pay ～ can be put in prison.拒绝纳税者会被送进监狱。Ⅱ v.❶ put a tax on；make sb. pay a tax 对……征税；使纳税：He wants all liquor to be heavily ～ed.他想让所有酒类都被课以重税。/Governments do not usually ～ children.政府通常不向孩子们收税。❷ test severely 严峻地考验：The war ～ed the soldiers' courage.战争考验士兵的勇气。‖ ～-free adj.免税的

taxation/tæk'seɪʃn/
    n.❶money taken by taxes；an act of taxing 税收；课税：The new government has increased ～.新政府已提高了税收。❷ the imposition or payment of tax 征税；课税

taxi/'tæksi/
    Ⅰ n.a motorcar,especially one with a meter,which maybe hired for journeys 出租车；计程车：come by ～ 乘出租车来 / take a ～ to the hotel 乘出租车去旅馆 Ⅱ v.❶ ride in a taxi 乘出租车：The visitor has been ～ed to the hotel.已用出租车将客人送到旅馆。❷ move on wheels along the ground slowly（指飞机）滑行：The plane was ～ing along the runway.飞机在

跑道上滑行。

taximeter/ˈtæksiˌmiːtə(r)/
n. a small machine fitted in taxis to calculate the charge for each journey（出租车上安装的）计程表，自动计费器

taxing/ˈtæksɪŋ/
adj. needing great effort; physically or mentally demanding 累人的；费力的：Such a long rough journey would be very ～ for an old man. 这么长而难走的路程对一个老年人来说是非常费力的。

taxman/ˈtæksmən/
n. ❶ a tax collector 收税员，税务员 ❷ the government department that collects taxes 税务部门

taxpayer/ˈtækspeɪə(r)/
n. any person or organization that has a legal duty to pay tax 纳税人；纳税的机构：The opposition parties have condemned the new airport as a waste of ～s' money. 各反对党指责修建新机场是浪费纳税人的金钱。

tea/tiː/
n. ❶ the leaves of a small low bush which are dried and prepared for use as a drink 茶叶 ❷ a drink made by adding boiling water to tea leaves or tea bags 茶，茶水：Would you like a cup of ～? 喝一杯茶吗？/make ～ 沏茶 ‖ not my cup of ～ 不是我喜爱之物/～ bag 茶袋/a storm in a ～ cup 小题大做/～ room 茶室/high ～ 下午茶

teach/tiːtʃ/
v. instruct or give lessons to sb. to show how to do sth. 教；教授：The teacher is ～ing his pupils to swim. 那个老师正在教他的学生学游泳。‖ ～able *adj.* 可以施教的

teacher/ˈtiːtʃə(r)/
n. a person who teaches, especially as a profession 老师；教师；教育者：He is my history ～. 他是我的历史老师。

teaching/ˈtiːtʃɪŋ/
n. ❶ the work of a teacher 教学；教书：I've been in ～ for 10 years. 我教书已经十年了。❷ sth. that is taught 教导；学说；教诲：They try to follow their teachers' ～.

他们尽力遵循他们老师的教诲。

tea garden/ˈtiːˌɡɑːdn/
n. ❶ an outdoor restaurant where drinks and light meals are served 露天茶座 ❷ a large area of land on which tea is grown; a tea plantation 茶园；茶圃；茶叶种植场

teahouse/ˈtiːhaʊs/
n. a restaurant in China or Japan where tea is served（中国及日本的）茶馆，茶楼，茶室

team/tiːm/
Ⅰ *n.* a group of people who play sports together on one side 比赛队：a football ～ 足球队/ The guy in yellow is in our ～. 那个穿黄衣服的小伙子是我们队的。Ⅱ *v.* work together (with sb.), especially for a common purpose 协作，合作

teamster/ˈtiːmstə(r)/
n. a person who drives a truck（大）卡车司机

teamwork/ˈtiːmwɜːk/
n. the ability of a group of people to work together effectively; the work done through combined effort 团队协作能力；协力进行的工作；联合作业

teapot/ˈtiːpɒt/
n. a container with a handle and a spout, in which tea is made and served 茶壶

tear[1]/tɪə(r)/
n. a drop of salty water coming from the eyes 眼泪：Tears are running down her face. 她泪流满面。

tear[2]/teə(r)/
Ⅰ *v.* ❶ pull sharply apart or to pieces; make a rough hole in sth. by pulling sharply 撕碎：～ the contract into pieces 将合同撕成碎片 ❷ remove sth. from sth. else by pulling it roughly or violently 撕掉；拔掉 ‖ ～ sth. up 把某物撕碎/～ oneself away from 离开；停止做某事/～ sb. (sth.) apart 彻底毁灭

tearful/ˈtɪəful/
adj. ❶ crying or inclined to cry 流泪的；哭泣的；爱哭的：a ～ girl 一个爱哭的姑娘 ❷ causing tears; sad or emotional 使人流泪的；催人泪下的；令人伤心的：a ～ farewell 令人伤心的告别

tease/tiz/

*v.*make fun of（a person）取笑；揶揄：Don't ~ him about his deformed foot.不要拿他畸形的脚来取笑他。‖ ~r *n.*嘲弄者；难题

teaspoon /'tiːspuːn/

*n.*a small spoon for stirring tea 茶匙；小匙 ‖ ~ful *n.*一茶匙（的量）

teat/tiːt/

*n.*❶ a point of the breast through which milk comes；nipple 乳头，奶头 ❷ a rubber mouthpiece of child's feeding bottle 奶瓶嘴

technical/'teknɪkl/

*adj.*❶ of special，practical knowledge 技术的；技能的：a ~ school 技术学校 /~ knowledge 技术知识 ❷ of or connected with a particular craft science 工艺的；专门的：~ terms 专门术语 /This book is too ~ for me.这本书对我来说专业性太强了。

technician/tek'nɪʃn/

*n.*a skilled worker or expert，especially a scientific or industrial subject 技术人员；技工；技师；技术专家

technique/tek'niːk/

*n.*the technical or mechanical skill in art，music，science，etc. 技术；技巧：Modern life depends on good ~.现代生活依赖良好的技术。/We should further improve our science and ~.我们应该进一步提高我们的科学技术水平。

technological/ˌteknə'lɒdʒɪkl/

*adj.*of or related to technology 工艺的；技术上的：~ advances 工艺的进步

technologist/tek'nɒlədʒɪst/

*n.*a specialist in technology 工艺学家；技术专家

technology/tek'nɒlədʒi/

*n.*the science of the mechanical and industrial arts 科技；工艺学：the ~ of computers 电脑的工业技术

tedious/'tiːdɪəs/

*adj.*long and tiring；dull 乏味的；沉闷的：It is no more than a ~ speech.那只不过是一次沉闷的演讲。‖ ~ness *adj.*沉闷；单调

teem/tiːm/

*v.*have in great numbers 充满；到处都是；有很多：The forest ~ed with wild animals.森林里到处都是野生动物。/His mind is ~ing with ideas.他脑子里充满了各种想法。

teenage/'tiːneɪdʒ/

*adj.*of or for people in their teens 十几岁的；少年的：a ~ boy 一个十几岁的男孩

teenager/'tiːneɪdʒə(r)/

*n.*a person in his or her teens 十几岁的少年

teens/tiːnz/

*n.*the period of one's life from the age of 13 to 19 十几岁（13 至 19 岁之间）：She is in her ~.她现在十几岁。

telecast/'telɪkɑːst/

Ⅰ *n.*a television broadcast or programme 电视广播；电视节目 Ⅱ *v.*broadcast by television 电视广播：The news was ~ed yesterday.昨天电视广播了这条新闻。

telecommunications/ˌtelikəmjuːnɪ'keɪʃnz/

*n.*the process or business of receiving or sending messages by telephone，radio，television，or telegraph 电信，电讯：Technological developments in ~ 电信技术的发展/the ~ industry 电信业

telegram/'telɪgræm/

n.(a piece of paper with) a message sent by telegraph （一份）电报：We informed them by ~ that we would be arriving early.我们打电报通知他们，我们将在早上到达。

telegraph/'telɪgrɑːf/

Ⅰ *n.*an apparatus for sending messages by the use of electric current along wires or by wireless 电报机 Ⅱ *v.*send a telegram to 发电报：He ~ed (to) his wife after arrived.到达之后，他给妻子发了电报。‖ ~er *n.*电报员

telepathy/tɪ'lepəθi/

n. the passing of thoughts and feelings from one person to another without using the normal senses of sight，sound，touch or smell 心灵感应；传心术

telephone/'telɪfəun/

Ⅰ *n.*a system for sending the human voice

by electric current through wires or by radio;a machine used for this 电话;电话机:Who is on the ~? 谁在打电话？ Ⅱ v. send (a message to sb.),speak (to sb.)by telephone 打电话:You should ～ your mother.你必须给你母亲打电话。

telephony /tɪˈlefəni/
n.the system or use of telephones 电话通讯

telephoto/ˌtelɪˈfəutəu/
Ⅰ adj.having pictures taken in a distance 远距离摄影的;摄远景的;a ～ lens 远距离摄影镜头 Ⅱ n.❶ a camera lens that help you to take a picture of a distant object 远距离摄影镜头 ❷ a picture sent from one place to another by radio,etc.传真照片;传真电报

telephotography/ˌtelɪfəˈtɒɡrəfi/
n.photography of distant objects by using a special lens 远距离摄影 ‖ **telephotographic**/ˌtelɪfəutəˈɡræfɪk/ adj.用远距镜头照相的;摄远的(通常写作 telephoto,例如 a telephoto lens 长焦距镜头)

teleprinter/ˈtelɪprɪntə(r)/
n.an electrical machine which automatically sends and receives typed messages by telegraph 电传打字机

telerecording/telɪrɪˈkɔːdɪŋ/
n.a programme recorded for television(e. g.in video tape)电视录像(例如录制于录像带上的节目)

telescope/ˈtelɪskəup/
n.a tubelike instrument with special glass that makes distant objects appear bigger and nearer 望远镜:Galileo built a ～ through which he could study the skies. 伽利略制作了一架望远镜用以研究天空。

television/ˈtelɪvɪʒən/
n.the sending of pictures from a distance and their reproduction on a screen by means of radio waves 电视;电视机:Nowadays,children spend too much time in front of ～.现在,孩子们花在看电视上的时间太多了。

telex/ˈteleks/
Ⅰ n.❶a telegraphic method of sending printed messages 电传:We'll answer you by ～.我们会用电传答复你。 ❷a message received or sent in this way 一份电传:A ～ has just arrived from Paris.刚从巴黎发来一份电传。 Ⅱ v.send a message to a person or a place by telex 发电传:Telex your parents when you get the news.一得到消息,就向你父母发电传。

tell/tel/
v.❶ make known;give information to sb. by speaking or writing 告诉;述说:Someone told me you were not at home.有人告诉我你不在家。 ❷ distinguish one thing from another 区别:Can you ～ John from his brother? 你能把约翰和他的兄弟区别开来吗？ ‖ **you can never** 你永远都不知道/～ **tales about (on)** sb. 搬弄某人的是非/～ **the time** 看钟表时间

teller/ˈtelə(r)/
n.❶a person employed to receive and pay out money in a bank 银行出纳员 ❷a person who counts votes 选票清点人;点票员

telling/ˈtelɪŋ/
adj.having a great or important effect; significant 有力的;有效的;有重大影响的;重要的:The most ～ factor in their defeat was their lack of reliable supplies. 他们战败的一个最重要因素是他们缺乏可靠的供应。/ a ～ argument 有说服力的论点

telltale[1]/ˈtelteɪl/
adj.that makes a fact known,especially an unpleasant fact 导致真相(坏事)被揭露的;显示出某事的:The murderer was given away by a few ～ bloodstains on his car seat.凶手是因汽车座位上留下的几滴血迹露了马脚而被揭发出来的。/～ signs of a slowdown in business activity 显示商业活动放缓的若干迹象

telltale[2]/ˈtelteɪl/
n. a person who informs about other people's secrets,wrong actions,etc. 泄露他人隐私的人;告发者;告密者

temp/temp/
n.a temporary employee 临时雇员

temper/ˈtempə(r)/

n. the condition of the mind and emotions 心情；脾气：If you go on like this, he will surely lose his ~.如果你继续这样下去，他肯定会发脾气的。‖ **get (fly) into a** ~ 发怒/**keep one's** ~ 忍住不发脾气/**out of** ~ (**with**) 发脾气

temperament /'temprə mənt/

n. sb.'s character as shown by his behaviour and feelings 性格；性情；气质：He has a happy ~.他性格开朗。/James doesn't have the ~ for working in an office.詹姆士的性格不适合在办公室工作。/She and I have similar ~s.她跟我有相似的性格。‖ ~**al** /ˌtemprə'mentl/ *adj.* 易激动的；喜怒无常的：Many great artists are ~al.许多伟大的艺术家都易激动。

temperance /'tempərəns/

n. control over oneself in behaving, eating, etc. and especially in drinking 节制；克制；节食；戒酒：~ society 禁酒会

temperate /'tempərət/

adj. ❶ showing or behaving with temperance 有节制的；节欲的；适中的：He is ~ in his eating habits.他的饮食习惯是很节制的。/He is a ~ man.他是个有节制的人。❷ (of climate) free from extremes of heat or cold (气候)温和的：the ~ areas of the world 世界上气候温和的地区 / a ~ climate 温和的气候 / the north ~ zone 北温带

temperature /'temprətʃə(r)/

n. ❶ the degree of heat or coldness 温度；体温：What's the average ~ in Beijing in winter? 北京冬天的平均气温是多少？/ The nurse took the boy's ~.护士给这男孩量了体温。❷ a body temperature above the normal 发烧：The child has a ~, perhaps he has caught cold.这孩子有点发烧，可能是着凉了。

tempest /'tempɪst/

n. a violent storm 暴风雨

tempestuous /tem'pestʃʊəs/

adj. stormy；violent 有暴风雨的；猛烈的：~ sea 波涛汹涌的海洋/~ argument 激烈的争论

temple /'templ/

n. ❶ a building for the worship of a god or gods 神殿；庙宇；寺院：Greek ~s were beautifully built.希腊的庙宇建得很漂亮。❷ the flat area on either side of the forehead 太阳穴

tempo /'tempəʊ/

n. the speed at which music is played (音乐进行的)速度；节奏：The tune has a fast (slow) ~.该曲调节奏快(慢)。

temporal /'tempərəl/

adj. ❶ of time 时间的 ❷ of this world；not spiritual 此世的；现世的；世俗的

temporary /'tempərəri/

adj. lasting only for a short time；not permanent 暂时的；临时的：I got a ~ work before graduation.毕业前，我找到了一个临时工作。‖ **temporarily** *adv.* 暂时地；临时地：The manager is temporarily busy；he will be able to see you in a few minutes.经理一时没有空，他要待一会儿才能见你。

tempt /tempt/

v. try to make sb. do sth. wrong or foolish 吸引；引诱：The warm weather ~s us for an outing.暖和的天气吸引我们去郊游。

temptation /temp'teɪʃn/

n. the act or state of tempting or being tempted 引诱；诱惑：resist ~ 抵制诱惑/fall into ~ 受诱惑

ten /ten/

num. the number 10 十 ‖ ~**th** /tenθ/ *num.* 第十

tenable /'tenəbl/

adj. ❶ able to be held or occupied 可保有的：The position as chairman is ~ for three years.主席职位任期 3 年。❷ able to be defended or justified 无懈可击的；站得住脚的：Do you think his argument is ~? 你认为他的论点站得住脚吗？

tenacious /tə'neɪʃəs/

adj. ❶ holding firmly；giving nothing away 紧握的 ❷ determined；strong 坚韧不拔的；顽强的：~ defence against the enemy 顽强抵御敌军

tenancy /'tenənsi/

n. ❶ the length of time during which someone uses a room, land, building, etc., for which they have paid rent（住房、土地、建筑物等的）租赁期限：a six-month ～ 六个月的租赁期 ❷the possession and use of a room, land, building, etc., for which rent is paid 租赁；租用：rights of ～ 租用权利/ a ～ agreement 租约

tenant/ˈtenənt/

I n.a person who pays rent for the use of a house or land 房客；佃户：He was a ～ before 1949.1949 年前他是个佃户。 II v. (usually passive) occupy as a tenant（常用被动语态）租借：These houses are all ～ed by workers.这些房子都被工人租用了。

tend/tend/

v.❶move or turn in a certain direction 倾向；有某种趋势：Temperature ～s to go up in May.五月份气温会上升。 ❷ take care of；look after；attend to 照料

tendency/ˈtendənsi/

n.a trend or inclination towards a particular action,etc.趋势；倾向：a ～ to rain 下雨的势头/My business is showing a ～ to improve.我的生意有好转的趋势。

tender/ˈtendə(r)/

I adj.❶ easily hurt or damaged；quickly feeling pain 脆弱的；易受伤害的：She is a ～ girl. 她是一个脆弱的女孩子。 ❷ showing kindness or gentleness 温柔的；亲切的 II n.❶ a small boat for carrying passengers, supplies, etc. between the shore and a larger boat（来往于大船和岸边,运送乘客、补给品等的）驳运船；补给船 ❷ a vehicle carrying coal or water, pulled behind a railway engine（蒸汽机车后的）煤车,水车

tenderfoot/ˈtendəfʊt/

n.❶a person who has recently arrived in a rough place, such as the western US, where life is hard（艰苦地区的）新来者；还没吃过苦的新手 ❷an inexperienced beginner 无经验者；初学者：a political ～ 政界的新手

tenderhearted/ˌtendəˈhɑːtɪd/

adj.easily made to have feelings of love, pity,or sorrow 软心肠的：She was too ～

to refuse.她心肠太软,不好意思拒绝。

tenderize/ˈtendəraɪz/

v.make（meat）tender by special preparation（通过特殊处理）使（肉）变得软嫩

tenner/ˈtenə(r)/

n.￡10 or a ten-pound note 十英镑；十英镑面值的钞票：It costs a ～.这个价值十英镑。 /I've only got a ～.我只有一张十英镑的钞票。

tennis/ˈtenɪs/

n.a game played between two people（singles）or two pairs of people（doubles）who use rackets to hit a small ball backwards and forwards across a low net on a specially marked area 网球：Do you like playing ～? 你喜欢打网球吗?

tension/ˈtenʃn/

n.❶ the state of being stretched tight 拉紧状态；张力；拉伸：His ～ on the rope made it break.他拉紧绳子将绳子拉断了。 ❷a feeling of nervous anxiety, worry,or pressure 紧张,不安：I am suffering from nervous ～.我很紧张。

tent/tent/

I n.a shelter of cloth over poles, which can be put up and taken down quickly 帐篷：pitch a ～ 搭帐篷 /strike a ～ 拆帐篷 II v.stay or live in a tent 住帐篷；宿营：These boys ～ed in a small village in the summer holiday.这些男孩子暑假在一个小村庄里宿营。

tentacle/ˈtentəkl/

n.a long,boneless limb which grows from the head of certain sea animals, used for feeling and holding things,and moving 触手；触角；触须

tentative/ˈtentətɪv/

adj.made or done to find out what may happen；experimental；not yet decided 试探性的；试验的；尝试性的：I can only give a ～ opinion.我只能提出尝试性的意见。

tenuous/ˈtenjʊəs/

adj.very thin and fine 纤细的

tenure/ˈtenjə(r)/

n.the length of time or condition under which a job is held or land is occupied, etc.(职位的)任期;任职条件;(土地的)占有期限,占有条件:his four-year ～ as President 他四年的总统任期

term/tɜːm/
n. ❶ a period of time when schools, universities, etc. hold classes 学期:We'll have five subjects in this ～.这个学期我们有五门课。❷ a word or phrase used as the same of sth., especially connected with a particular type of language 术语;措辞 ‖ come to ～s 达成协议/do sth. on one's own ～ 照自己的意愿行事/be on good (friendly) ～s (with sb.) 关系良好

terminal/'tɜːmɪnl/
Ⅰ *adj.* ❶ of or taking place each term 每期的;定期的;学期的:～ examinations 学期考试 /～ accounts 按期结账 ❷ of the end 末端的;终点的:～ cancer 后期癌症 /a ～ station 终点站 Ⅱ *n.* ❶ the end of a railway line, bus route, etc.; the centre (in a town) for passengers using an airport (铁路、公路等的)终点站;(城市中的)航空集散站:an air ～ 航空终点站 ❷ a connection in an electric circuit (电路的)接头:the ～s of a battery 电池的接头

terminate/'tɜːmɪneɪt/
v. bring or come to an end 终止;结束:The chairman ～d the meeting by knocking on the table.董事长敲敲桌子,宣布会议结束。

termination/ˌtɜːmɪ'neɪʃn/
n. ❶ an act of ending sth.结束;终止;停止 ❷ the last part or last letter of a word 词尾(词的最后一部分或最后一个字母)

terminology/ˌtɜːmɪ'nɒlədʒi/
n. words with a special or definite meaning, especially those used in a particular branch of knowledge 术语;专门用语:engineering (medicine) ～ 工程学(医学)术语

terminus/'tɜːmɪnəs/
n. the last stop where a journey by air, bus or railway, etc. ends(航空、公共汽车或铁路等行程的)终点,终点站

termly/'tɜːmli/
adj. happening each term 每学期的:～

exams 每学期都举行的考试

terms/tɜːmz/
n. ❶ the conditions of an agreement, contract, etc.(协议、合约等中的)条件,条款:a contract specifying the ～ of employment 具体规定了各项雇用条件的合约 / According to (Under) the ～ of the agreement, British ships will be allowed to take a limited quantity of fish each year.按协议的条款,英国渔船将被允许每年捕捞一定数量的鱼。❷ the stated conditions concerning payment, prices, etc.费用;价格,价钱;付款条件:We sell furniture at very reasonable ～.我们以非常合理的价格出售家具。/to negotiate a loan on favourable ～ 商洽一笔优惠条件的贷款/He bought the car on easy ～.他以分期付款的方式买了一辆车。❸ a relationship of the stated quality(某种相处的)关系:I'm not on very good ～ with her at the moment.我和她目前的关系不太好。/We met on equal ～.我们以平等的地位会晤。❹ a way of expressing yourself or of saying sth.表达方式;措辞:I'll try to explain in simple ～.我会尽量讲得通俗易懂。‖ come to ～ with sth. 与……妥协;对……让步;勉强接受(不愿接受的某事):It's hard to come to ～ with going blind.要接受失明这个事实是很难的。/in ～ of …(in …～) 至于;关于;从……观点来看:The book has been well reviewed, but in ～ of actual sales, it hasn't been very successful. 这本书获得了好评,但是从实际销售情况来看,它并不太成功。

terrace/'terəs/
Ⅰ *n.* ❶ a porch or balcony 露台;屋顶平台;阶梯看台 ❷ a raised bank of earth with vertical or sloping sides and a flat top 梯台;台地,阶地:Vines are grown on ～s on the hillside.葡萄种在山坡的梯田里 Ⅱ *v.* form into a terrace 使形成梯田:～d fields 梯田

terrain/tə'reɪn/
n. an area of land (especially with reference to its use in war) 地带;地势,地形:Before the battle the general studied the ～.战斗前将军研究地形。

terrestrial /təˈrestrɪəl/

adj. ❶ relating to the Earth rather than to the moon, space, etc. 地球的：～ life forms 地球上的生命形态 ❷ of, living on, or being land rather than water 陆地的；陆上的；陆栖的；陆生的：～ animals 陆栖动物

terrible /ˈterɪbl/

adj. ❶ causing great fear or horror 可怕的；吓人的：It's a ～ car accident. 那是一场可怕的车祸。❷ very bad or of very poor quality 糟糕的；劣质的：She said her English was ～. 她说她的英语很糟糕。

terribly /ˈterɪbli/

adv. ❶ very；extremely 非常；很：I'm ～ sorry. 我非常抱歉。/They were beat ～. 他们被痛打了一顿。❷ in a terrible manner 可怕地；可怖地

terrific /təˈrɪfɪk/

adj. ❶ very good；enjoyable；excellent 极好的，极棒的：a ～ book 一本极好的书 ❷ very great in amount, value, etc. 极大的：She drove at a ～ speed. 她把车开得飞快。❸ causing terror；terrifying 可怕的；恐怖的：a ～ hurricane 可怕的飓风

terrify /ˈterɪfaɪ/

v. fill with fear 使恐惧：be terrified out of one's wits 吓得魂不附体 ‖ ～ing *adj.* 令人恐惧的；骇人的

territorial /ˌterəˈtɔːrɪəl/

adj. of or being land or territory 领土的；土地的：～ integrity 领土完整/ ～ demands 领土要求

territory /ˈterɪtəri/

n. (*pl.*-ies) ❶ an area of land under the control of a ruler or state 领土；版图；领地 ❷ an area for which a person has responsibility or in which a person conducts an activity 属地；辖地 ❸ a special sphere of thought or experience (思想、经验的) 领域，范围：Criminal law was not her ～. 刑法不是她负责的领域。❹ an area which an animal defends against others of the same species 领域，地盘

terror /ˈterə(r)/

n. ❶ a great fear 恐怖；惊骇：a feeling of ～ 恐怖感/ run away in ～ 慌慌张张地

逃走 ‖ in ～ of 对⋯⋯感到提心吊胆 / have a ～ of sth. 对某物感到恐怖 ❷ sth. or sb. that causes great fear 可怕的人；恐怖的事：the war on ～ 反恐战争/have a ～ of fire 害怕火 /This added to our ～. 这增加了我们的恐怖。❸ a troublesome person (usually a child) 讨厌鬼；小捣蛋：That boy is a perfect ～. 那个男孩是个讨厌鬼。

terrorist /ˈterərɪst/

n. a person who is in favour of the practice of using violence to obtain political demands 恐怖主义者；恐怖分子：The ～s killed two workers. 那些恐怖分子杀了两个工人。

tertiary /ˈtɜːʃəri/

adj. of the third rank, order, formation, etc.；third 第三位的；第三级的；第三系的；第三期的；第三的：He must have come to know those philosophers through secondary or ～ sources. 他一定是通过第二手或第三手资料了解那些哲学家的。‖ The Tertiary Period 第三纪

test /test/

n. an examination or trial (of sth.) to find its quality, value, composition, etc. 测试；考验：He passed the English ～. 他通过了英语测验。‖ put sth. to the ～ 使某物接受考验 ‖ a driving ～ 驾驶考试/ ～ tube 试管/ ～-tube baby 试管婴儿

testament /ˈtestəmənt/

n. ❶ (often in last will and ～) the most recent will that sb. has made, especially the last will that is made previous to sb.'s death 临终遗嘱 ❷ one of the two main parts of *the Bible* 圣约书(《圣经》的两个主要部分之一)：*Old Testament*《旧约全书》/*New Testament*《新约全书》

testicle /ˈtestɪkl/

n. either of the two glands that produce sperm in male mammals, contained in the scrotum behind the penis 睾丸

testify /ˈtestɪfaɪ/

v. ❶ say as a witness；give testimony in a court of law (在法庭上)作证；提供证据：Several eyewitnesses testified for him. 几个目击者为他作证。❷ give evidence of；

serve as evidence of 表明；证明：Her tears ～ her grief.她的眼泪表明她很伤心。

testimonial/ˌtestɪˈməʊnɪəl/

*n.*❶a written statement about sb.'s character and abilities（有关某人品格和能力的）推荐书；证明书；鉴定书：When I left school, the headmaster gave me a good ～.我毕业离校时，校长给我一份很好的证明书。❷ a written statement together with a gift presented to sb. by a group of persons 褒扬状；感谢信；纪念品

testimony/ˈtestɪməni/

*n.*a solemn statement；an evidence 证词；证明

testy/ˈtesti/

*adj.*quick-tempered；impatient 暴躁的；性急的

tetra-/ˈtetrə/

*pref.*four 四：tetragon 四边形/tetrahedron 四面体

text/tekst/

*n.*❶ the main body of writing in a book 正文；课文：too much ～ and not enough pictures 正文太多，图画不够 ❷ the words written by the author；the original words of a writer 原文：a corrupt ～ 有错误的原文 /the original ～ of *David Copperfield*《大卫·科波菲尔》的原文

textbook/ˈtekstbʊk/

*n.*a standard printed book for the study of a subject，especially used in schools 教科书；课本：a history ～ 历史课本

textile/ˈtekstaɪl/

Ⅰ *n.*any material made by weaving 纺织品：a ～ factory 纺织厂/We need to produce more ～, especially silk and cotton.我们要生产更多的纺织品，特别是丝和棉花的。 Ⅱ *adj.*❶woven or capable of being woven 纺织的；可纺织的：～ fibers 纺织纤维 ❷of or having sth. to do with textile 纺织的；与纺织有关的：the ～ industry 纺织工业

texture/ˈtekstʃə(r)/

*n.*❶ the way that a substance feels when touching it（织物）质地：This is a cloth with a fine ～.这块布质地很好。 ❷ the

structure of（food or soil, etc.）组织；结构：the ～ of a mineral 矿物的构造

than/ðæn, ðən/

*conj.*❶introducing the second part of a comparison 比：John is taller ～ his twin brother.约翰比他的孪生兄弟要高一些。❷（of number, quantity, etc.）above or below another 多于；少于：It takes more ～ an hour to walk there.走路去那儿要一个多小时。‖ **no other** ～ 就是/**nothing else** ～ 完全是；无异于/**rather** ～ 宁愿

thank/θæŋk/

Ⅰ *v.* express gratitude to 致谢；道谢：Thank you for your assistance.感谢你的帮助。 Ⅱ *n.*a grateful feeling；an expression of this 感谢：Thanks (No, ～s).谢谢（不必了，谢谢）。‖ ～**s to** 由于；因为/**Thanksgiving Day** 感恩节

thankful/ˈθæŋkfl/

*adj.*feeling or expressing thanks；grateful 感谢的；感激的：He is ～ for her good care.他感激她的悉心照料。‖ ～**ly** *adv.*感激地/～**ness** *n.*感懑

thankless /ˈθæŋklɪs/

*adj.*unpleasant or difficult to do and unlikely to bring you any rewards or thanks from anyone 让人不领情的；徒劳无益的；吃力不讨好的

thanks/θæŋks/

int. used to show that you are grateful to sb. for sth. they have done（表示感激）谢，谢谢：—How are you? ——你好吗？—Fine, ～.——好，谢谢。

thanksgiving/ˌθæŋksˈɡɪvɪŋ/

*n.*❶an expression of gratefulness, especially to God（尤指对上帝的）感谢，感恩：He offered a ～ to God for his escape.他因脱险而感谢上帝。❷a festival for giving thanks to God（in USA, the fourth Thursday in November；in Canada, the second Monday in October）感恩节（在美国是十一月第四个星期四，在加拿大是十月的第二个星期一）

that/ðət/

Ⅰ *pron.*❶ referring to a person or thing that is not near the speaker（指较远的人或事物）那，那个：That tastes nice.那东西

味道不错。❷ used to identify a specific person or thing observed or heard by the speaker(指已看到或听到的人或事)那，那个：That's her husband over there.那边那个人是她的丈夫。❸(*pl.*that)used as a relative pronoun used to introduce a defining clause,especially one essential to identification（引导限定性定语从句）：Where's the newspaper ～ came yesterday? 昨天来的报纸在哪儿？❹ instead of "which""who"或"whom"替代"which" "who""whom"：The man ～ is standing there is my cousin.站在那里的那个人是我的表兄。Ⅱ *conj.* used after some verbs,adjectives and nouns to introduce a new part of the sentence（用于某些动词、形容词和名词后,引出从句）：Peter said (that) the story was true.彼得说这件事是真的。‖ so … that … 如此……以至……Ⅲ*adv.*to such a degree;so 那样;那么:Her little son can't walk ～ far.她的小儿子走不了那么远。

thaw/θɔ:/
Ⅰ *n.* a period of warmer weather when snow and ice melt,usually at the end of winter（冬末的）解冻期 Ⅱ *v.* become or cause to become soft or liquid（使）融化;（使）解冻:The snow has begun to ～ and the roads will soon be muddy.雪已开始融化,路面很快就会泥泞不堪。

the/ðə,ði/
Ⅰ *art.*❶used for mentioning a particular thing,either because you already know which one is being talked about or because only one exists（用于对方已知的名词前或用于独一无二的事物前面）:Would you please open ～ window for me? 请你替我把窗子打开,好吗？❷ used with an adjective to make it into a noun meaning all members of a group or class（用于形容词前,表一类）:～ old 老年人/～ rich 富人 Ⅱ *adv.*❶used with the superlative（与最高级连用）:Jane is ～ tallest in our class.珍妮是我们班个儿最高的。❷used in comparisons,to show that two things happen together（与比较级形容词、副词连用）越,愈:The sooner you take your medicine ～ better you will

feel.服药愈早,好得愈快。

theatre(-er)/'θɪətə(r)/
*n.*❶ a building for the performance of plays,for dramatic spectacles,etc. 戏院;剧场:go to the ～ 去看戏 /a ～ ticket 戏票 /Has the play been put on at this ～? 那个剧在这个剧场演出过吗？❷ a hall or room with seats in rows rising one behind another 会场;礼堂❸ a scene of important events 重大事件发生的场所;现场:a ～ of war 战场

theft/θeft/
*n.*❶ the act of stealing 偷盗;盗窃:commit a ～ 行窃❷ an instance of this 偷窃案件:There have been several ～s in this area.这一地区已发生了几起偷盗案。❸ sth.stolen 被盗物

their/ðeə(r),ðə(r)/
*adj.*of or belonging to them (they 的所有格)他们的;她们的;它们的:They have lost ～ dog.他们的狗丢了。/They have a house of ～ own. 他们有一幢自己的房子。

theirs/ðeəz/
*pron.*sth.belonging to them (they 的物主代词)他(她、它)们的东西:Our house is white;～ is brown.我们的房子是白色的;他们的是棕色的。/It's a habit of ～.那是他们的习惯。

them/ðem,ðəm/
*pron.*the object form of they (they 的宾格)他(她、它)们:Give the books to ～.把这些书给他们。

theme/θi:m/
*n.*❶ the subject of a talk,book,etc.题目;主题:The ～ for tonight's talk is education.今晚讲座的主题是教育。❷ repeated melody in a symphony,etc.主题曲;主旋律:～ song 主题歌

themselves/ðəm'selvz/
*pron.*❶a reflexive form of they (they 的反身代词)他(她、它)们自己,他(她、它)们本身:The kids are enjoying ～.孩子们玩得正开心。❷a strong form of they（加强语气）他(她、它)们本身,亲自:They did it ～.这事是他们自己干的。❸ (informal) their real selves (非正式)(他

们的)常态;正常情况:They are not quite ～ today.他们今天不太舒服。

then/ðen/

*adv.*❶ at that time (in the past or future) 当时;其时:We were all in the classroom ～.当时我们还都在教室里。❷ next;after that;afterwards 其后;继之:We had our supper, ～ we did our homework.我们吃了晚饭,然后我们做家庭作业。❸ if that so;in that case 那么;因此:Then what do you want? 那么,你想要什么呢? ❹besides;also 另外;还有;而且;再者:Then there's his mother——she is in the sitting room.还有他母亲——她在起居室里。‖ now and ～ 不时;时常

theology/θɪ'ɒlədʒi/

*n.*the science of the nature of God and of religion 神学;宗教学

theorem/'θɪərəm/

n. a statement which has to be proved by reasoning 定理;命题

theoretical/ˌθɪə'retɪkl/

*adj.*❶ based on theory,not on fact 理论的;抽象的:The work is still ～.这项工作还处在理论阶段。❷ existing only in theory,not in practice 理论上的;推测的;假设的:～ possibility 理论上的可能性

theoretically/ˌθɪə'retɪkli/

*adv.*❶in a theoretical way;not practically 在理论上;从理论上说:First I'll explain how it works ～,then I'll give you a practical demonstration.我先从理论上说明它的工作原理,然后再向你们做实际操作示范。❷according to theory but not really 按道理讲:Theoretically he's in charge,but in fact his secretary takes all the decisions.按道理讲他是主管,但事实上所有的决定都是由他的秘书做出的。

theorist/'θɪərɪst/

*n.*a person who forms or studies the theory of a subject 理论家;理论研究者:a leading political ～ 一名重要的政治理论家

theorize/'θɪəraɪz/

*v.*form a theory or theories;speculate 创建理论,建立学说;推理;从理论上说明:It's easy to ～ about the reasons for the crisis,but we don't have the facts.从理论上说明危机的原因是不难的,但我们没有事实依据。

theory/'θɪəri/

n. general principles,put forward to explain certain facts 原理;理论:Your conclusion is reasonable in ～.从理论上来说,你的结论是有道理的。

therapy/'θerəpi/

*n.*a medical treatment 治疗;疗法

there/ðeə(r)/

Ⅰ *adv.*❶in,at,or to that place or position 在那里;往那里;到那里:We went to Yunnan and stayed ～ 12 days last year.我们去年去了云南,并在那里待了 12 天。/People ～ usually have two meals a day.在那里,人们通常一天吃两餐。❷ existing or available 存在;现有:Mr Chen went to see if his old school was still ～.李先生去看过母校是否依然存在。/There are a few houses in the picture.那幅图上有一些房子。❸in that respect;on that issue 在那个方面;在那个问题上:I don't agree with you ～.在那个问题上我不同意你的看法。‖ be ～ for sb.(在逆境中)支持或安慰某人;与某人在一起/been ～,done that 早就知道,没什么稀奇/～ and then 当时当地/～ and back 往返 Ⅱ *int.*❶used to call attention, usually stressed (用于引起注意,常重读) 瞧,喂:There! I told you he wouldn't mind! 你瞧! 我告诉过你他不会在意的! ❷used to praise or encourage small children (用于夸奖或勉励幼儿):There's a good boy (girl)! 乖孩子!

thereabouts/'ðeərəbaʊts/

*adv.*❶near that place 在那附近 ❷somewhere near that number or quantity or time,etc.(数量、时间等)大约;左右;上下:in 2001 or ～ 2001 年左右

thereby/ˌðeə'baɪ/

*adv.*by that means;because of that 因此;由此;从而:Regular exercise strengthens the heart, ～ reducing the risk of heart attack.经常锻炼可以增强心脏机能,从而减少心脏病发作的危险。

therefore /ˈðeəfɔː(r)/

adv. for this or that reason; on this or that account 因此；所以：I was ill，～ could not come. 我当时病了，所以没能来。/It rained，～ the outing was postponed. 下雨了，所以出游延期了。

therein /ˌðeərˈɪn/

adv. ❶ in that place, time or thing; into that place or thing 在那里；在那时；在那点上；在其中：the case and the books found ～ 箱子和放在箱子里的书 ❷ in that matter; in that way 在那件事上；那样：The captain thought all danger was past，～ he made a mistake. 队长认为危险全都过去了，在那件事上他犯了个错误。

thereof /ˌðeərˈɒv/

adv. of that; from that source 由此；因此；从那个来源：the diseases and the remedies ～ 疾病及其治疗 /All citizens of the United Kingdom are ruled by the laws ～. 英国的全体国民都受其法律的约束。

thereon /ˌðeərˈɒn/

adv. on that or it 在其上；就此：I read the report and wrote some remarks ～. 我读了该报告，并在上面写了几句批语。

thereto /ˌðeəˈtuː/

adv. to that (agreement or piece of writing，etc.) 加于 (协议、作品等) 之上；随附：any conditions attached ～... 附加在……上的任何条件

thereunder /ˌðeərˈʌndə(r)/

adv. ❶ under that，it，or them (在) 其下：the land，with any minerals found ～ 土地以及在它下面发现的一切矿物 ❷ below，following，or in accordance with (sth. written) 以下；依照 (书面文件等)：the items listed ～ 以下所列的各项

thereupon /ˌðeərəˈpɒn/

adv. ❶ as a result of that; about that matter 因此；关于此事 ❷ without delay after that; happening immediately after sth. else has happened 随即；随后；于是：Thereupon she asked me to marry her. 她随即要我娶她。

thermal /ˈθɜːml/

adj. of，producing，or caused by heat 热的；热量的；由热造成的：a ～ spring 温泉 / a ～ power station 热电站

thermometer /θəˈmɒmɪtə(r)/

n. an instrument used for measuring and showing temperature 寒暑表；体温表：Celsius ～ 摄氏温度计 /Fahrenheit ～ 华氏温度计

thermonuclear /ˌθɜːməʊˈnjuːklɪə(r)/

adj. concerned with hydrogen bombs or other bombs of that type 热核的：～ war 热核战争

thermos /ˈθɜːməs/

n. a bottle having two thin glass walls to keep sth. inside at its original temperature 热水瓶，保温瓶：There is nothing in the ～. 热水瓶里什么东西也没有。

thesis /ˈθiːsɪs/

n. (*pl.* theses) ❶ an opinion or statement that is supported by reasoned argument to prove it is true 论题；命题；论点：He argued his ～ well. 他为他的论点进行了有力的辩论。 ❷ a long piece of writing done for a higher university degree 毕业论文：a ～ on the works of Shakespeare 评论莎士比亚作品的论文

they /ðeɪ/

pron. the subject form or plural of he，she，it (主格形式，he、she、it 的复数) 他们；她们；它们：My brother and sister are coming for their holiday. They arrive on Sunday. 我的弟弟和妹妹要来度假，他们星期日到。

thick /θɪk/

adj. ❶ of great depth from one surface to the opposite 厚的；粗的：a ～ wall 厚厚的墙 /a ～ coat 厚外套 ❷ growing closely together in small area 稠密的，茂密的：a ～ forest 茂密的森林 ❸ relatively dense in consistency 浓的，黏稠的：～ soup 浓汤 ‖ as ～ as thieves 非常亲密 /through ～ and thin 不顾艰难险阻；在任何情况下 /lay it on ～ 拼命恭维；过分赞备 ‖ ～-headed *adj.* 愚笨的 /～-skinned *adj.* 脸皮厚的

thicken /ˈθɪkən/

v. ❶ make or become thick or thicker (使) 变厚；(使) 变粗；(使) 变浓密：The cook often ～s his soup by adding some flour.厨师常常在汤里添加一些生粉,使汤变稠。❷become more closely grouped together or more solid than it was before 变密集:The mist is ～ing.雾越来越浓了。‖～er n.增稠剂/～ing n.增厚(或变粗、变密、变浓)

thickness/'θɪknɪs/

n.❶ the state or degree of being thick 厚(度);粗:a ～ of four centimeters 4 厘米的厚度 /The length of nails you need depends on the ～ of the planks.钉子的长度依木板的厚度而定。❷a layer of sth. 层:one ～ of cotton wool 一层棉绒

thief/θiːf/

n.a person who steals or robs secretly and without violence 小偷;窃贼:Once a ～, always a ～? 做过一次贼,就永远是贼吗?

thieve/θiːv/

v.steal things;rob people;act as a thief 偷东西;行窃;做贼

thieving/'θiːvɪŋ/

n.the act of stealing things 偷窃,行窃:Those ～ children keep stealing our apples.那些偷东西的小孩一直在偷我们的苹果。

thievish/'θiːvɪʃ/

adj.of or like a thief 贼(似)的;有偷窃行为的:～ habits 有偷窃习性

thigh/θaɪ/

n.the top part of the human leg between the knee and the hip 股;大腿

thin/θɪn/

adj.❶ with little space from one side to the opposite side;not thick 薄的:a ～ sheet of paper 一张薄纸/～ air 稀薄的空气;子虚乌有 ❷ not having much flesh 瘦的:Why are you so ～? 你为什么这么瘦? ❸(especially of sth. said or written) not having the necessary qualities the intended result;unsatisfactory 贫乏的:a ～ excuse 不能令人信服的托词/a ～ story 乏味的故事

thing/θɪŋ/

n.❶ any material object 东西;物体:She's very fond of sweet ～s.她非常喜欢吃甜食。❷ sth.that is nonmaterial 非物质的事物:～ of the mind 心灵之物 ❸ a circumstance or an event;the course of an action 情况;事件:What you said made ～s worse.你把事情弄得更糟了。‖ taking one ～ with another 考虑各方面的情况/have a ～ about 被……困扰

think/θɪŋk/

v.❶ form in the mind;have in the mind as an idea 思索;考虑:Use your mind and ～ about it.动脑筋考虑一下。❷ consider;be of the opinion 认为;以为:I ～ it will rain.我想天会下雨的。‖ ～ about sth.思量;考虑某事/～ of sth.思索/～ nothing of sth.轻视;看不起/～ nothing of it不必客气/～ better of sb.看重某人/～ sth.over 仔细地想/～ sth.up 想出 ‖ ～able adj.可想象的

thinker/'θɪŋkə(r)/

n.a person who thinks 思考者;思想家:a great (shallow) ～ 伟大的(肤浅的)思想家

thinking/'θɪŋkɪŋ/

Ⅰ adj.thoughtful;reasoning 深思熟虑的;有思考力的;思想的:the ～ people 好思考的人 Ⅱ n.❶ thought;reasoning 思想;思考;思维:It is man's social being that determines his ～.人们的社会存在决定其思想。❷ opinion;judgement 想法;见解:You are of my way of ～.你和我的想法一样。

third/θɜːd/

num.❶ next after the second 第三:the Third World 第三世界 /the ～ month of the year 三月份 ❷ one of three equal parts 三分之一:one ～ 三分之一 /two ～s 三分之二

thirdly/'θɜːdli/

adv.in the third place 第三:Firstly, I haven't enough money;secondly, I'm too old;and ～, it's raining.第一,我没有足够的钱;第二,我太老了;第三,天又在下雨。

thirst/θɜːst/

n.the feeling caused by a desire or need to drink;suffering caused by this 渴:They could not stand the ～.他们干渴难熬。‖ ～y adj.渴的:～y for knowledge 渴望

知识

thirteen /ˌθɜːˈtiːn/

num. the number 13 十三

thirty /ˈθɜːti/

num. the number 30 三十；～ years ago 30 年前 ‖ the thirties 30 年代 ‖ **thirtieth** *num.* 第三十

this /ðɪs/

(*pl.* these) Ⅰ *pron.* ❶ used to refer to a person or thing that is near you 这个（用于指附近或最近的人或物）：This is the table you want. 这就是你要的那个桌子。❷ used to introduce sb. or sth. that you are going to talk about 这（用于引出将要谈论的人或物） Ⅱ *adv.* to this extent；so 到如此程度；这样：My book is not ～ small. 我的书没有这么小。

thong /θɒŋ/

n. a thin piece of leather 皮带；皮条

thongs /θɒŋz/

n. a type of open shoe which is held on by the toes and loose at the back 平底人字拖鞋

thorax /ˈθɔːræks/

n. ❶ the chest in human or animals' body （人的）胸，胸部；动物的胸腔 ❷ the middle of three main sections in an insect's body （昆虫的）胸

thorn /θɔːn/

n. ❶ a sharp pointed part on the stem of a plant 荆棘；刺：the ～ of a rose 玫瑰的刺 ❷ sth. that causes irritation and annoyance 引人生气（或苦恼）的事；令人烦恼的事

thorny /ˈθɔːni/

adj. ❶ prickly；having thorns 多刺的；有刺的 ❷ difficult to deal with；causing worry or trouble 棘手的；难处理的；伤脑筋的：a ～ problem 棘手的问题

thorough /ˈθʌrə/

adj. complete in every way 完全的；彻底的：The doctor gave me a ～ examination. 医生对我进行了彻底的检查。

thoroughbred /ˈθʌrəbred/

n. ❶ an animal of pure breed 纯种动物 ❷ a well-bred person 受过严格训练的人 ❸ a particular breed of racing horse 纯种赛马

thoroughfare /ˈθʌrəfeə(r)/

n. a road or street which is open at both ends to allow traffic to pass through 大道；大街 ‖ no ～（用于告示）此路不通

thoroughgoing /ˌθʌrəˈɡəʊɪŋ/

adj. ❶ very thorough；complete in every way 彻底的：a ～ search 彻底的搜查 ❷ complete；utter 十足的；完全的：a ～ fool 十足的傻瓜

those /ðəʊz/

pron. & adj. plural of that that 的复数形式

thou /ðaʊ/

pron. used as the subject of a sentence with special old forms of verbs such as art, canst, didst, etc. （用作句子的主语，与 art, canst, didst 等古体动词连用）汝；尔：Thou shalt not kill. (from *the Bible*) 汝不可害人性命。（源自《圣经》）

though /ðəʊ/

Ⅰ *conj.* in spite of the fact that 虽然：Though it is raining hard, we'll still go out. 虽然雨下得很大，我们还是要出去。Ⅱ *adv.* however 然而；不过：He said he would come, he didn't ～. 他说过他要来，不过他没来。‖ even ～ 即使 / as ～ 好像

thought /θɔːt/

n. ❶ the process of thinking 思索；思考：lost (deep) in ～ 陷入沉思之中 ❷ an idea, opinion, or intention formed by thinking 思想；观点：Different people have different ～s. 不同的人有着不同的见解。‖ on second ～s 经过进一步的考虑

thoughtful /ˈθɔːtfl/

adj. ❶ full of thought；showing thought 深思的；思索的：～ looks 沉思的表情 ❷ considerate；thinking of or showing thought for the needs of others 体谅的；体贴的；关切的；考虑到旁人需要的：It was ～ of you to let me know of your arrival. 你考虑得真周到，来之前就事先通知我。

thoughtless /ˈθɔːtlɪs/

adj. ❶ careless；unthinking；showing lack of thought 欠考虑的；粗心的；疏忽的；不

注意的:It was ~ of you to forget your sister's birthday.你真粗心,居然忘记了你姐姐的生日。❷ selfish; inconsiderate (of others) 自私的;不顾及别人的:a ~ action 自私的行为

thousand/ˈθaʊznd/
adj.& *num.*& *n.* (of) the number 1000 千(的);千个(的):~s of times 几千次(遍) /It's three hundred and eighty ~ kilometres away.它离我们有三十八万公里。

thrash/θræʃ/
*v.*❶ beat with a stick, whip, etc.抽打;鞭打:Don't ~ that dog! 别抽打那条狗! ❷ win a victory over in a contest 胜过;击败 ❸ (cause to) toss or move violently (使) 颠簸;扭动:~ about (around) in bed 在床上翻来覆去(辗转反侧)

thread/θred/
Ⅰ *n.*❶ a line, thin piece of cotton, wool, etc.for sewing or weaving (棉、毛等的)线:cotton ~ 棉线 /pass a ~ through the eye of a needle 把线穿过针眼 ❷ sth.very thin, suggesting a thread 丝;丝状体:the ~s of a spider web 蛛网丝 ❸ a chain or line 线索;脉络:gather up the ~s of a story 综合一个故事的脉络 ❹ a spiral ridge round a screw 螺纹:This screw has a worn ~.这个螺丝的螺纹磨损掉了。Ⅱ *v.*❶ pass one end of a thread through 穿针;引线;纫针;穿成串:~ a needle 纫针 ❷ make (one's way) through 穿过:They ~ed the paths of the forest at dawn.他们在拂晓时穿过了森林小路。

threadbare/ˈθredbeə(r)/
*adj.*❶ (of material, clothes, etc.) very thin because of a lot of use; very worn (材料、衣服等)穿旧的;(衣料等)磨得很薄的 ❷ having been so much used as to be no longer interesting or effective 陈旧的:~ excuses 老一套的托词

threat/θret/
*n.*❶ an expression of an intention to inflict pain, injury, or evil 恐吓;威胁:It's nothing but a ~.那只不过是恐吓而已。❷ the possibility of trouble, danger or disaster 凶兆;征兆

threaten/ˈθretn/
*v.*❶ utter threats against 恐吓;威胁:They ~ed to revenge him.他们扬言要报复他。/He ~ed me. 他威胁我。/She ~ed that she would leave home. 她扬言要离家出走。❷ give signs or warning of; be a menacing indication of sth.预示;(坏事)可能发生:The clouds ~s rain. 乌云预示有雨。/The fighting is ~ing to turn into full-scale war.这次冲突可能要演变成全面战争。❸ give the danger or threat to; likely to harm, spoil, ruin, etc. 危及;威胁到:Noisy traffic ~s our peaceful life.交通的噪音威胁着我们的安静生活

threatening /ˈθretənɪŋ/
*adj.*❶ having a hostile or deliberately frightening quality or manner 威胁的;恐吓的:The manager received a ~ letter. 经理收到了一封恐吓信。❷ (of a person or situation) causing someone to feel vulnerable or at risk (人、形势)构成威胁的;具有威胁性的:He was a type she found ~.她发现他是具有威胁性的那种人。❸ (of the sky, clouds, etc.) showing that bad weather is likely (天空、云等)阴沉沉的;乌云密布:black ~ clouds 滚滚乌云

three/θri:/
*num.*the number 3 三

threshold/ˈθreʃhəʊld/
*n.*❶ a piece of wood or stone fixed beneath the door into a house 门槛 ❷ the point just before a new start or beginning 入口;开端;开始:He was on the ~ of his career.他的事业刚刚起步。

thrift/θrɪft/
*n.*the quality and practice of being careful in the use of money or goods 节约;节俭 ‖ ~y *adj.*节俭的:a ~y housewife 节俭的家庭主妇

thrill/θrɪl/
Ⅰ *v.*feel excitement; make greatly excited 使激动;激励:The news ~ed all the people present.这个消息使在场的每一个人激动不已。Ⅱ *n.* a strong feeling caused by great excitement 激动;狂喜:a ~ of joy 一阵狂喜

T

thriller/'θrɪlə(r)/

n. a book, play, or film that tells a very exciting story, especially of crime and violence (尤指描述犯罪与暴力的)惊险小说(戏剧、电影)

thrilling/'θrɪlɪŋ/

adj. exciting and enjoyable 惊险的；紧张的；扣人心弦的；令人兴奋不已的：a ～ experience 激动人心的经历

thrive/θraɪv/

v. (throve /θrəʊv/ or ～d, ～n /'θrɪvən/) prosper; succeed; grow strong and healthy 兴盛；成功；长得健壮 ‖ **thriving** *adj.* 兴盛的；繁荣的；蒸蒸日上的：a ～ business 兴旺的生意

throat/θrəʊt/

n. ❶ the front part of the neck 喉头：grip sb. by the ～ 抓紧某人的喉头 ❷ the passage in the neck through which food passes to the stomach and air to the lungs 咽喉：clear one's ～ (开始说话前)清嗓咙 / He had a sore ～. 他嗓子痛。

throb/θrɒb/

v. (-bb-) ❶ (with reference to the heart) beat more strongly (指心脏)剧烈跳动：Her heart ～bed with excitement. 她兴奋得心怦怦地跳。❷ beat or work regularly like the heart 悸动；律动；颤动：My head was ～bing with pain. 我的头疼得怦怦直跳。/ The engine ～bed all night. 那台发动机彻夜颤动。

throne/θrəʊn/

Ⅰ *n.* ❶ (the ～) the seat of a king, queen, bishop, etc. (国王、女王、主教等的)宝座；御座 ❷ the power or authority of a king 王位；王权：obey the ～ 服从王权 /seize the ～ 篡夺王位 Ⅱ *v.* place upon a throne; occupy a throne (使)即王位；使登基：The new king will be ～d today. 新国王将于今天登基。

throng/θrɒŋ/

Ⅰ *n.* a large crowd of people 群；人群：A ～ of people is (are) here. 这里聚集了一大群人。Ⅱ *v.* go (as if) in a crowd 群集；拥挤：People ～ed to see the play. 人们争先恐后去看这出戏。/ The street is ～ed with people. 街上挤满了人。

through/θru:/

prep. ❶ from one end or side of sth. to the other (opening, channel, or location) 穿过：go ～ the doorway 走过门道/ The river flows ～ London. 这条河流经伦敦。/making the way ～ the crowd 在人群中穿行 ❷ so as to make a hole or opening in (a physical object) 破开；穿：The lorry smashed ～ a wall. 货车把墙撞出了个洞。❸ continuing in time towards completion of a process (or period) 一直到底；达到……的末尾；(直至)完成：The goal came midway ～ the second half. 下半场进行到一半时踢进了球。❹ from the beginning to the end of (an experience or activity, typically a tedious or stressful one) 从头至尾；从开始至结束；在整个期间：We sat ～ a very boring movie. 我们坐着从头到尾看完了一部极其乏味的电影。❺ by means of; because of 以；凭借；因为；由于：You can only achieve success ～ hard work. 你得努力工作才能获得成功。

throughout/θru:'aʊt/

Ⅰ *adv.* in every part; in, into or during every part 到处；始终；彻头彻尾：Prices remain stable ～. 物价始终保持稳定。/ The house is painted ～. 这房子到处都刷上了漆。Ⅱ *prep.* during the whole period of time 自始至终；贯穿整个时期：It rained ～ the night. 雨下了一整夜。/ The disease spread ～ the country. 这种疾病蔓延到全国各地。/ ～ one's life 终生

throw/θrəʊ/

v. go through the air, usually with a force, by a movement of the arm or by mechanical means 投；扔：He can ～ a stone a hundred yards. 他能把石头扔一百码远。‖ ～ **cold water on sth.** 向……泼冷水；使灰心/ ～ **sth. about** 散布；乱扔/ ～ **oneself at** 拼命讨好/ ～ **sth. away** 丢弃；抛掉/ ～ **oneself down** 倒下/ ～ **oneself on** (upon) sb. (sth.) 依赖于；委身于/ ～ **up one's hands** 绝望；认输

thrush/θrʌʃ/

n. one of various types of small songbird (especially one with a speckled chest) 画眉鸟

thrust/θrʌst/

Ⅰ *v.* push suddenly or violently 用力推；挤：The two people are ~ing themselves into the bus.这两个人正用力挤进汽车。Ⅱ *n.* the act of pushing suddenly or violently 推；挤

thud/θʌd/

Ⅰ *n.* a dull sound as of a blow on sth. soft 沉闷声；fall with a ~ to the carpet 倒在地毯上，发出一声闷响 Ⅱ *v.* (-dd-) fall or hit sth. with a low dull sound 砰地落下；重击：The dictionary ~ded onto the floor.那本词典砰地掉在地板上。

thumb/θʌm/

Ⅰ *n.* the short thick finger at the side of the hand, slightly apart from the other four 拇指 Ⅱ *v.* ❶ turn over pages with or as if with one's thumb 翻阅：~ the pages of a book 翻阅书本 ❷ hitchhike 搭便车旅行：~ one's way 搭便车

thunder/'θʌndə(r)/

Ⅰ *n.* ❶ the loud noise which usually follows a flash of lightning 雷声；roll of ~ 雷声隆隆 ❷ a loud sound like a thunder 似雷的声音；轰隆声：~s of applause 雷鸣般的掌声 Ⅱ *v.* make a noise like thunder 发出雷一般的声音：Don't ~ at me. 不要对我大吼大叫。‖ ~**ous** *adj.* 轰声如雷的

thunderstorm/'θʌndəstɔːm/

n. a storm with thunder and lightening, usually with heavy rain 雷阵雨

Thursday/'θɜːzdeɪ/

n. the day of the week after Wednesday and before Friday 星期四

thus/ðʌs/

adv. ❶ in this way 像这样；如此：He spoke ~.他是这样说的。❷ consequently; hence 因此；从而：She worked hard, ~she finished the work in time. 她努力工作，因而及时完成了工作。❸ to a stated degree or extent 至此：We have managed all right ~ far.迄今为止，我们一切都十分顺利。

tick/tɪk/

Ⅰ *n.* ❶ a light and regularly repeated sound, especially of a clock or watch（钟表的）滴答声 ❷ a mark（√）used to

show that sth. is correct 钩号；对号 ❸ a moment; a second〈英〉刹那；瞬间：I'll be down in a ~.我一会儿就下来。Ⅱ *v.* ❶ (of a clock, watch, etc.) make a regularly repeated short sound（钟表）滴答滴答响：Your watch ~s very loudly.你的表滴答响。❷ mark with a tick 打钩号：She ~ed off an item on the list.她在表上勾出了一项。‖ **make sb. or sth.** ~（机器等）运转；（工作等）进行；（人）发生行为；起作用：We are trying to find out what makes him ~.我们正设法找出他那样做的动机。

ticker/'tɪkə(r)/

n. the heart 心脏：She's got a weak ~.她的心脏很弱。

ticker tape/'tɪkəteɪp/

n. very long narrow lengths of paper on which information is printed by a special machine, and which is often thrown in the US to greet famous people who are visiting a town（电报、电传机等用的）纸带；（供欢迎名人时抛用的）彩色纸带：The astronauts were given a ~ welcome in New York.太空飞行员在纽约受到抛彩带的热烈欢迎。

ticket/'tɪkɪt/

n. a written or printed piece of card or paper, giving the holder right to do sth. 票；票证：Have you bought a ~? 你买好了票吗？/ roundtrip ~ 来回票/~ of leave 假释许可证

ticking/'tɪkɪŋ/

n. the thick strong cloth, usually cotton, used for making mattress and pillow covers, etc.（用于制作床垫套、枕套等的）结实的厚棉布

tickle/'tɪkl/

v. touch sb. lightly so as to cause laughter 搔痒 使发笑：We can ~ a person by touching him under the arms or on the bottom of his feet.挠腋下或脚底可使人发笑。

ticklish/'tɪklɪʃ/

adj. ❶(of a person or part of their body) sensitive to being tickled（某人或其身体某部分）怕痒的 ❷(of a problem, situation, etc.) difficult; needing special care and attention (问题、形势等)棘手的,难应付的

tidal/ˈtaɪdl/

adj.of or having a tide (有关)潮汐的;涨潮的: ~ currents 潮流/The river is ~ up to this bridge.河水涨到这座桥了。

tide/taɪd/

n.❶ a rise and fall of the level of the sea, caused by the attraction of the moon 潮汐: Every year, thousands of people come to watch the wonderful ~.每年,成千上万的人来观看壮观的潮汐。❷ a flow or tendency 潮流;趋势

tidemark/ˈtaɪdmɑːk/

n.❶ a mark round the inside of an emptied bath that shows the level to which the bath had been filled (浴缸水位所留下的)垢痕 ❷ a dirty mark on the skin left by incomplete washing (皮肤上未洗净的)污点,垢痕

tidewater/ˈtaɪdˌwɔːtə(r)/

n.❶water that flows onto the land when the tide is very high (涨大潮时涌上陆地的)潮水 ❷the water in the tidal parts of rivers and streams (江河中的)潮水

tideway/ˈtaɪdweɪ/

n.❶a narrow stretch of water through which the tide flows 潮路 ❷a strong current running through a tideway (经潮路流过的)劲流;强潮流

tidings/ˈtaɪdɪŋz/

n. news; information 音信;消息: The messenger brought ~ of the battle.使者带来了战斗的消息。/glad ~ 佳音

tidy/ˈtaɪdi/

Ⅰ *adj*.❶ in good order; arranged neatly 整齐的;整洁的;打扮得整整齐齐的: a ~ person 爱整洁的人 /a ~ room 整洁的房间 /~ habits 爱整洁的习惯 ❷ considerable; fairly large 相当好的;相当多的: a ~ sum of money 相当大的一笔钱 /cost a ~ penny 花费相当多的钱 Ⅱ *v*.make (a place) neat 使整齐,使整洁: ~ up a room 收拾房间 /I must ~ myself.我必须梳洗一下。

tie/taɪ/

Ⅰ *v*.❶ fasten or bind 绑;拴;捆: ~ the feet together 将双脚缚在一起 ❷ be equal in points, marks, etc.(在比赛中)不分胜负,打成平局 Ⅱ *n*. a long, narrow piece of cloth that a man wears round the neck of his skirt 领带 ❷a piece of string or wire used for tying sth.绳子 ‖ ~ sb. down 限制某人的自由/~ sb.down to sth. 置某人于约束之下/be (get) ~d with sb. (sth.)为某人(某物)所缠

tiebreak(er)/ˈtaɪˌbreɪk(ər)/

n.(in tennis) a number of quickly-played points (not part of a standard game), played to decide the winner of a set in which each side has won six games (网球)各胜六局后的加赛;决胜局;平局决胜赛

tiepin/ˈtaɪˌpɪn/

n.a small decorative clip, often of silver or gold, for holding a tie in place 领带别针

tier/tɪə(r)/

n.(especially of seats arranged above and behind another row) 一排;一列(尤指阶梯式的座位): The ~s in the theatre were full.剧院里一排排的座位都坐满了人。

tiger/ˈtaɪgə(r)/

n.a type of very large, fierce, wild animal that has yellowish fur with black lines across and lives in Asia 老虎,虎: paper ~ 纸老虎/ ride the ~ 骑虎难下

tight/taɪt/

adj.fastened, fixed, or held firmly 紧的: The drawer is too ~ to open.抽屉太紧,打不开。‖ in a ~ corner 处于困境/~ schedule 紧迫的日程

tighten/ˈtaɪtn/

v.make or become tight or tighter (使)变紧;(使)绷紧: ~ the ropes 绷紧绳索/ ~ (up) the screws 旋紧螺钉/It needs ~ing up.(它)需要再拉紧一点。

tightfisted/ˌtaɪtˈfɪstɪd/

adj. very ungenerous, especially with money; stingy 非常小气的;吝啬的: a ~ old skinflint 一个非常小气的老守财奴

tightrope/ˈtaɪtrəʊp/

n.a tightly stretched rope or wire, high

above the ground, on which performers walk along (供走索者表演用的)绷索,钢丝: An actor is walking a ~ in a circus.一个马戏团演员正在表演走钢丝。

tights/taɪts/
n. ❶ a very close fitting garment, made of thin material, covering the legs and lower part of the body, as worn by girls and women (女用)连裤袜 ❷ a similar garment, covering the legs and body, worn by acrobats, ballet dancers, etc.(杂技演员、芭蕾舞演员等穿的)紧身衣裤

tigress/'taɪɡrəs/
n. a female tiger 母虎,雌虎

tile/taɪl/
I *n.* a thin piece of baked clay for covering roofs, walls, etc. 瓦;瓷砖;砖瓦: a ~ roof 瓦屋顶 II *v.* cover (a surface) with tile 铺瓦;贴砖: ~ a floor 铺地砖

till/tɪl/
I *conj.* up to the time when; up to; down to 直到……之时;在……以前: They didn't get the answer ~ I gave them some help. 直到我帮忙,他们才找到答案。 II *prep.* until 直到: I waited ~ 5 o'clock. 我一直等到5点钟。

tiller/'tɪlə(r)/
n. a bar by which the rudder of a boat is moved (小船的)舵柄

tilt/tɪlt/
v. lean, cause to lean, so as to be no longer level or upright (使)倾斜: When he ~ed the desk the books fell off. 他掀斜书桌时,书桌上的书掉到了地上。/Her hat is ~ed to one side of her head. 她的帽子歪向脑袋的另一边。/The boat ~ed in the storm. 船在风暴中倾斜了。‖ at full ~ 全速地;猛烈地: He ran into the wall at full ~. 他猛地撞在墙上。

timber/'tɪmbə(r)/
n. ❶ wood used for building and making things 木料;木材: a ~ industry 木材工业 ❷ a large piece of shaped wood or beam, forming a support 栋木;梁木;横木: The ~s are weak. 这些横木不结实。

timbre/'tɪmbə(r)/
n. the quality in a sound which allows one

to tell the difference between sounds of the same level and loudness when made by different musical instruments or voices 音品;音色;音质

time/taɪm/
n. ❶ all the days of the past, present and future 时间;时光: Remember not to waste your ~. 记住不要浪费光阴。/a two-week period of ~ 一段为期两周的时间 ❷ the point of time stated in hours and minutes of the day 时刻: What ~ is it? 几点钟了? /It's dinner ~. 该是吃饭的时候的。 ❸ an occasion when sb. do sth. or when sth. happens 次数: this ~ 这次/next ~ 下一次 ‖ ahead of one's ~ 超越时代/behind the ~s 过时的;落伍的/have a good ~ 自得其乐 ‖ ~ limit *n.* 时限/~-saving *adj.* 节约时间的

timeless/'taɪmlɪs/
adj. not affected by the passage of time or by changes of taste or fashion 不受时间影响的;永恒的;永不过时的: her ~ beauty 她的永恒的美丽

timely/'taɪmli/
adj. occurring at a suitable or useful time 及时的;适时的: a ~ warning 及时的警告 ‖ timeliness *n.* 及时

timer/'taɪmə(r)/
n. ❶ a device for timing things 计时器 ❷ a device for activating sth. at a preset time 定时器

times
v. (informal) multiply (a number) (非正式)乘(以): You ~ eight by four to get thirty-two. 你用4乘以8得到32。

timetable/'taɪmteɪb(ə)l/
I *n.* a list showing the time at which certain events will happen, e.g. when buses or trains leave and arrive, or when lessons take place in a school 时刻表;时间表;课程表: a train ~ 火车时刻表 / We have a new ~ each term. 我们每个学期都有新的课程表。 II *v.* organize events in a timetable 为……订时间表;为……安排时间: English lessons are ~d on every morning. 英语课被排在每天上午。

timid/ˈtɪmɪd/
adj. easily frightened; nervous 易受惊的；胆怯的：as ～ as a rabbit 胆小如兔 ‖ ～ly *adv.* 胆怯地／～ity/tɪˈmɪdəti/ *n.* 胆怯

timing/ˈtaɪmɪŋ/
n. the choosing of exactly the right moment to do sth. so as to get the best effect 时间的选择；时机的掌握：I don't think much of their ～——introducing a new brand of suntan oil in November. 我认为他们时间选得并不好——竟然在十一月份推出一种新牌子的防晒油。／The dancer's ～ is perfect. 这名舞蹈演员对时间的把握真是恰到好处。

timorous/ˈtɪmərəs/
adj. easily frightened; nervous and lacking confidence 胆小的；易受惊的；畏怯的

tin/tɪn/
Ⅰ *n.* ❶ a type of soft metal 锡；马口铁；镀锡钢板 ❷ a container (usually airtight) made of tinplate〈英〉(通常指密封的)罐头：We bought five ～s of fruit and two ～s of soup. 我们买了五听水果罐头和两听汤罐头。Ⅱ *v.* (-nn-) put food, etc. in an airtight tin〈英〉把(食物等)装于罐中：～ned fruit 罐头水果 Ⅲ *adj.* like tin; making a sound like tin when struck 像锡的；(声音)不响亮的 ‖ ～ **opener** 开罐器；罐头刀

tinder/ˈtɪndə(r)/
n. material that burns easily, used especially for lighting fires (尤指用于引火的)易燃物；引火物(如火线、火绳等)：The plants are as dry as ～ after the long hot summer. 在漫长的炎夏之后，草木干燥得如同火绒一般。

tinderbox/ˈtɪndəbɒks/
n. ❶ a box containing tinder, flint, and steel, used in former times instead of matches for providing a flame (旧时取火用的，内装火绒、打火石和击石钢片的)火绒盒 ❷ a very dangerous, uncontrollable place or situation) 危机四伏的地区(形势)

tine/taɪn/
n. a point or narrow pointed part of a fork, a deer's antlers, etc. (叉、耙等的)尖齿；(鹿角的)分叉

tinfoil/ˈtɪnfɔɪl/
n. a very thin sheet of tin like paper used for packing food, etc. (用于包装食品等的)锡箔纸

ting/tɪŋ/
Ⅰ *v.* (cause to) make a high clear ringing sound (使)发叮当声；(使)叮当作响 Ⅱ *n.* a high clear sound such as that made by a small bell 叮当声；叮叮声：The glass went "～" as I tapped it with my knife. 当我用小刀轻敲玻璃杯时，它便发出"叮"的声音。

tinge/tɪndʒ/
Ⅰ *v.* ❶ colour slightly 微染；着淡色：be ～d with pink 染成粉红色 ❷ affect slightly 使带有……意味的：admiration ～d with jealousy 含有忌妒意味的赞美 Ⅱ *n.* a slight colouring; a small amount of sth. 微染；淡色；少许；微量：water with a ～ of dull green 带一点儿淡绿色的水／a ～ of sadness (irony) 略带哀伤(讥讽)

tingle/ˈtɪŋɡl/
Ⅰ *v.* ❶ have a slight pricking, stinging feeling in the skin 感到刺痛：My fingers were tingling with cold. 我的手指冻得刺痛。❷ be affected by an emotion 震颤；激动：～ with excitement 兴奋地激动起来 Ⅱ *n.* (a ～) a tingling feeling 刺痛感：The cold caused a ～ in my ears. 严寒使我的耳朵有刺痛感。

tinker/ˈtɪŋkə(r)/
Ⅰ *n.* a person who repairs pots and pans (especially one who travels from place to place) (尤指流动的)补锅匠 Ⅱ *v.* try to repair (usually in a clumsy way) (通常指笨拙地)修补，修理：He likes ～ing with broken clocks. 他喜欢修理钟表。

tinkle/ˈtɪŋkl/
Ⅰ *v.* make, cause to make, small quick sounds like those made by a small bell (使)发出叮当声：The glasses on the tray ～d. 盘里的玻璃杯叮当作响。Ⅱ *n.* a light clear sound as of a small bell 叮当声：～ of a bell 铃儿的叮当声

tinnitus/ˈtɪnɪtəs/
n. an illness in which one hears noises, such as ringing, that are not there 耳鸣

（症）

tinny/'tɪni/

adj. ❶ of, like, or containing tin（含）锡的；似锡的 ❷ having a thin metallic sound 发尖细金属声的：a cheap stereo that gives a ～ sound 发出尖细刺耳声音的廉价立体声音响 ❸（especially of sth. metal）cheap and badly made（尤指金属制品）廉价粗制的

tint/tɪnt/

n. a quality of a given colour that differs slightly from a primary colour 淡色；浅色：She likes wearing ～ glasses in summer. 她夏天喜欢戴浅色眼镜。

tiny/'taɪni/

adj. very small in size or amount 极小的；微小的：a ～ box 小盒

tip/tɪp/

Ⅰ *n.* ❶ the pointed or thin end of sth. 尖；尖端：the ～ of your nose 鼻尖/the ～s of your fingers 指尖 ❷ a gift or money to a porter, waiter, etc. for personal services 小费 Ⅱ *v.* ❶ touch or strike slightly 轻击 ❷ knock over or upset；topple 使倾斜

tiptoe/'tɪptəʊ/

Ⅰ *n.* the tip of the toe 脚趾尖：She is standing on her ～s. 她踮起脚尖站着。‖ on ～(s) ❶ 踮着脚 ❷ 焦急；兴奋：She was on ～ in the morning of her wedding. 她结婚那天早晨很兴奋。Ⅱ *v.* walk on the front parts of your foot 踮着脚走：She ～d to the bedside of the sleeping child. 她踮着脚走到酣睡的孩子床边。

tire/'taɪə(r)/

v. make or become weary, or uninterested（使）疲倦；（使）厌倦：The housework ～s me. 家务把我累坏了。‖ ～d out 精疲力竭的

tired/'taɪəd/

adj. ❶ needing to rest or sleep 疲劳的；累的：I'm ～ to death. 我累得要死。/He was a ～ man when the long race was over. 跑完长跑他累极了。❷ no longer interested in；annoyed with 厌倦的；厌烦的：I'm ～ of your stupid remarks. 你的那些蠢话我听厌了。‖ ～ness *n.* 疲倦；疲劳

tireless/'taɪələs/

adj. not tiring easily；having a lot of energy 不知疲倦的；不觉疲劳的；精力充沛的：a ～ campaigner 坚持不懈的活动家 ‖ ～ly *adv.* 不知疲倦地；不屈不挠地

tiresome/'taɪəsəm/

adj. troublesome；making you feel annoyed；causing to be tired 令人厌倦的；使人疲倦的；讨厌的：He is a ～ man. 他是个令人讨厌的人。

tiring/'taɪərɪŋ/

adj. making tired；causing fatigue 引起疲劳的；令人厌倦的：a ～ argument 令人厌倦的争论

tissue/'tɪʃuː/

n. ❶（any kind of）woven fabric 织物 ❷ a collection of cells that from different parts of humans, animals and plants 组织：the organs and ～s of the body 人体的器官和组织 ❸ a piece of soft absorbent paper 纸巾：disposable ～s 一次性（使用）纸巾 /face ～s 面巾纸 /Have you got a ～? 你有纸巾吗？

titan/'taɪtn/

n. a person of great strength, importance, size, cleverness, etc. 巨人；大力士；泰斗；大师；巨子

titanic/taɪ'tænɪk/

adj. of great size, strength, power, importance, etc. 巨人（般）的；极大的；力大无比的；强大的：a ～ struggle 大搏斗

titanium/taɪ'teɪniəm/

n. a silvery grey light strong metal that is a simple substance（element）, used especially for making compounds with other metals（Ti）钛（一种金属元素，符号 Ti）

titbit/'tɪtˌbɪt/

n. a very pleasant or interesting piece of sth. 珍品；珍闻：～ of cake 精美的糕点/～s of news 令人愉快而有趣的新闻

title/'taɪtl/

n. ❶ an identifying name given to a book, painting, etc. 书名；题目；标题：The ～ of the painting is *A Summer Evening*. 这幅画的题名为《夏日的黄昏》。❷ a claim or right, especially a legal right to ownership 所有权；权利：have ～ to do sth. 有权做某事 ❸ a name that describes the rank

or office 头衔；称号；职位名称：She has a
~.她有个头衔. ❹ championship 冠军：
win the world ~ 获得世界冠军 /the
woman's singles ~ 女子单打冠军

to/tuː/

Ⅰ*prep*.❶ in the direction of；toward 向；
朝……方向：go ~ school 去上学/It is
five minutes ~ four.现在是四点差五分。
❷ (indicating comparison, ratio and reference) (引导间接受词)：Whom did you
give the key ~? 你把钥匙给了谁? ❸ (of
time) before 在……之前：from morning
~ night 从早到晚 ❹ so as to cause (especially a feeling) 使：~ my surprise 使
我感到惊讶的是 Ⅱ*infinitive marker* 用
于动词前构成不定式：To see is ~ be-
lieve.眼见为实。Ⅲ*adv*.into a shut position 在关上的位置：The wind blew the
door ~.风把门吹得关上了。

toad/'təud/

n.a small animal like a frog but with a dry
skin 蟾蜍，癞蛤蟆

toast/'təust/

Ⅰ*n*.❶ sliced bread heated and browned
烤面包(片)：a slice of ~ 一片面包 /a
poached egg on ~ 烤面包加一个荷包蛋
❷ the act of drinking in honor of sb. or
sth.干杯；祝酒：drink a ~ to sb.'s health
为某人的健康干杯 /At the feast I proposed a ~ to our friendship.在宴会上，我
提议为我们的友谊干杯。Ⅱ*v*.wish hap-
piness, success, etc. to sb. (or sth.) while
raising a glass of wine 祝酒；敬酒：~ the
bride and bridegroom 举杯祝贺新娘和新
郎 /I ~ to your health.我为你的健康干
杯。

toaster /'təustə(r)/

n.an electrical device for toasting bread 烤
面包炉；烤面包片机

tobacco/tə'bækəu/

n.a plant or its large leaves, prepared for
smoking in cigarettes, pipes, etc.烟草；烟
叶：He used to smoke ~ in a pipe.他过去
常用烟斗吸烟。

today/tə'dei/

n.❶ on this day 今天：Your son will come
~.你儿子今天会来的。❷ at the present

time；nowadays 现在；现今；现代：Some
children of ~ have too much money.现在
有些儿童手上的钱太多了。

toddle/'tɒdl/

v.walk with short, unsteady steps as a baby does when learning to walk (如学走路
的婴儿般) 蹒跚而行；摇摇晃晃地移动脚
步 ‖ ~r *n*.初学走路的婴儿

to-do/tə'duː/

n. excitement；fuss 吵闹；骚动；纷扰：
There was a great ~ about the money
which was stolen.为款项被盗发生了一场
激烈的争吵。/He made quite a ~ about
it.他为此大吵大闹一番。

toe/təu/

n.each of the five divisions of the front
part of the foot；the similar part of an
animal's foot 脚趾 ‖ **from top to** ~从头
到脚；完全

toffee/'tɒfi/

n.a type of hard sweet made from sugar
and butter 乳脂糖；太妃糖

together/tə'geðə(r)/

adv.in company；with or near each other
共同地；在一起：We went to the cinema
~.我们一起去看了电影。 ‖ **put your
heads** ~ 一起商量一下

toil/tɔil/

v.work long or hard；move with difficulty
辛劳工作：~ at one's research 艰辛地进
行研究 ‖ ~some *adj*.辛苦的

toilet/'tɔilit/

n.❶ the process of dressing, arranging
the hair, etc.梳妆；打扮：~ articles 化妆
品 /She started making her ~.她梳妆打
扮起来。❷ a room with receptacle for
waste matter from the body 盥洗室；厕
所：go to the ~ 去厕所

tolerable/'tɒlərəbl/

adj.fairly good or acceptable；that can be
tolerated 尚好的；过得去的；可接受的；
可以忍受的

tolerably/'tɒlərəbli/

adv.to a limited degree；fairly 在一定程
度上；过得去：I feel ~ well today.今天我
觉得身体还可以。

tolerance/'tɒlərəns/

n. the ability to suffer pain, hardship, etc., without being damaged 忍受力;忍耐:He has no ~ to cold. 他一点也不耐寒。

tolerant/'tɒlərənt/

adj. having or showing tolerance 宽容的;容忍的:He is not very ~ of criticism. 他不大能容忍批评。

tolerate/'tɒləreɪt/

v. allow or endure with protest 容忍;忍受:No one will ~ his foolishness. 没有人能容忍他的愚蠢。

toleration/tɒlə'reɪʃən/

n. the quality of allowing people to behave in a way that may not please one, without becoming annoyed 容忍;宽恕:We should try to show ~ to other people. 我们应尽量宽以待人。

toll¹ /təʊl/

n. ❶ money paid to use a bridge, ferry, road, etc. (过桥、摆渡、过路等的)费;税 ❷ damage; loss 损害;损失:~ of malaria in tropical countries 疟疾在热带国家造成的损失

toll² /təʊl/

v. (with reference to a bell) ring slowly and deeply (指钟)缓慢而低沉地响;缓慢低沉地鸣钟报时

tollbooth/'təʊlbuːθ/

n. a place where tolls are collected 通行费(使用费)征收站;收费亭

tomato/tə'mɑːtəʊ, tə'meɪtəʊ/

n. (*pl.* ~es) ❶ a soft red fruit eaten as a vegetable 番茄, 西红柿 ❷ the plant on which this fruit grows 番茄苗

tomb/tuːm/

n. a grave, especially a large decorated one 坟;冢;墓;陵:There are a lot of ~s on the hillside. 山坡上有很多墓。

tomboy/'tɒmbɔɪ/

n. a spirited young girl who likes to be rough and noisy 野丫头;假小子

tombstone /'tuːmstəʊn/

n. a memorial stone set up over a grave 墓碑;墓石

tomorrow/tə'mɒrəʊ/

Ⅰ *n.* ❶ the day after today 明天,明日:Tomorrow is (will be) Saturday. 明天是

星期六。 ❷ the future 将来,未来:~'s world 未来的世界 Ⅱ *adv.* during or on the day after today 在明天:We're going to a party ~. 明天我们要去参加一个聚会。

ton/tʌn/

n. (*pl.* ~s or ton) ❶ a measure of weight, or the internal capacity of a ship 吨;(船的)吨位 ❷ a large weight, quantity, or number 许多;大量:~s of fruit 大量水果 /~s of people 许许多多的人

tonal/'təʊnl/

adj. relating to tones of sound or colour 音质的;音调的;色调的

tonality/təʊ'næləti/

n. ❶ the character of a tune depending on the musical key in which it is played 调性 ❷ a musical key 音调;调子

tone/təʊn/

Ⅰ *n.* ❶ the quality of a sound, especially with reference to its quality, feeling, etc. 音调;声调;腔调;语气:the rising (falling) ~ 升(降)调 /take a kind ~ 口气友好 /an encouraging ~ 一种鼓励人的口气 /a piano with a better ~ 一架音色较好的钢琴/the four ~s of Chinese (汉语的)四声 ❷ the shade of colour; the degree of light 色调;光度:the soft green ~ 浅绿色调 /a photograph in warm ~s 暖色调的相片 ❸ (only singular) the general spirit, character, morale of a community, etc. (只用单数)(社会等的)特性;风纪;风气;气氛:the ~ of a school 校风 /the moral ~ 道德风气 ❹ a proper and normal condition of the body 健康状况:lose (recover) ~ 失去(恢复)健康 Ⅱ *v.* give a particular tone of sound or colour to 带上调子;调色;上色

tongs/tɒŋz/

n. (*pl.*) an instrument with two movable arms, used for holding or lifting 钳;镊;夹子:She used the ~ to add coal to the fire. 她用钳子加煤。

tongue/tʌŋ/

n. ❶ the movable part in the mouth, used in talking, tasting, licking, etc. 舌头:The doctor asked me to put out my ~ and see what was wrong with me.医生要我把舌头伸出来,看我有什么毛病。❷ a particular language 语言:What is your mother ~? 你的母语是什么? ‖ **have sth. on the tip of one's ~** 话到嘴边/**find one's ~** 恢复说话能力/**speak with one's ~ in one's cheek** 说说而已;半开玩笑地/**have lost one's ~** 说不出话来/**have a ready ~** 能言善道/**hold one's ~** 缄默

tonic/'tɒnɪk/

Ⅰ *n.*❶a medicine giving strength and energy 滋补品;补药:The doctor gave me a special ~.医生给我开了一种特殊的补药。❷ anything which increases health or strength 强身健体之物:Country air is a good ~.乡村空气对身体很有益处。❸ the keynote; the first note of a musical scale 主音 Ⅱ *adj.* ❶ giving strength or energy 滋补的;激励的:a ~ medicine 补药;强身剂/ the ~ quality of sea air 海上空气使人振奋的特性 ❷ of or based on the keynote 主音的

tonight/tə'naɪt/

Ⅰ *adv.*on this present night 在今晚,在今夜:What's on TV ~? 今晚有什么电视节目? Ⅱ *n.*the night of today 今晚,今夜: ~'s radio news 今晚的广播新闻

tonsil/'tɒnsl/

*n.*one of the two small organs at the back of the throat which sometimes become diseased and have to be taken away 扁桃体

too/tuː/

*adv.*❶ also;as well;in addition 也;加之:My brother has such a shirt,~.我兄弟也有一件这样的衬衫。❷ in a higher degree that is allowable,required,etc.(表程度的副词,修饰形容词、副词)过于;太:The young man is ~ reckless.这个年轻人太鲁莽了。‖ **all ~ soon (quickly)** 太早(快)/**none ~ soon** 恰逢其时/**one ~ many** 多余的一个;多余的

tool/tuːl/

*n.*❶ any instrument used in doing work,especially with the hands 工具;器具:farm ~s 农具 /a machine ~ 机床 ❷ means 工具;手段:Languages are ~s in communication.语言是交流的工具。❸ a

person used by another for dishonest purposes 爪牙;傀儡;走狗:He was a ~ of the secret agent.他是特务的傀儡。

toot/tuːt/

Ⅰ *n.*a short but loud sound (e.g.one made by the horn of a motorcar,a ship's siren) (如汽车、船等发出的)短促的鸣笛声 Ⅱ *v.*make or cause to make this sound (使)发出短促的鸣笛声

tooth/tuːθ/

n.(*pl.*teeth) one of the white bony objects which grow in the mouth 牙齿:Smoking will make your teeth yellow.吸烟会使你的牙齿变黄。‖ **armed to the teeth** 武装到牙齿/**cast sth. in a person's teeth** 以某事责备某人/**escape by the skin of one's teeth** 幸免于难/**get one's teeth into sth.** 奋力干/**lie in one's teeth (throat)** 无耻地说谎

toothpaste /'tuːθpeɪst/

*n.*a paste for cleaning the teeth 牙膏

toothpick /'tuːθpɪk/

*n.*a small pointed piece of wood,etc.for removing bits of food from between the teeth 牙签

top/tɒp/

*n.*❶ the highest part of sth. 顶部:We could not see the ~ of the tree.我们看不见树顶。❷(the ~) the highest or most important rank or position 最高的级别;最重要的职位 ‖ **from ~ to bottom** 完全地/**blow one's ~** 气炸了‖ ~s *n.*最优秀的人;最好的东西

topic/'tɒpɪk/

*n.*a subject for conversation,talk,writing,etc.题目;话题;论题;主题:They discussed the weather and other ~s.他们讨论天气和其他话题。

topical /'tɒpɪkəl/

*adj.*❶(of a subject) of immediate relevance,interest,or importance owing to its relation to current events (主题)有关时事的;时下关注的:a ~ affairs programme 一栏时事节目 ❷ relating to a particular subject;classified according to subject 专题的;按专题分类的:~ stamps 专题邮票

topography /təˈpɒɡrəfi/

n. the arrangement of the features of a place or district, including the position of its rivers, mountains, roads, and buildings 地形；地貌；地势；地形学：a map showing the ~ of the island 这个岛的地形图 ‖ **topographical** *adj.* 地志的；地形学的

topping /ˈtɒpɪŋ/

n. a layer of food poured or spread over a base of a different type of food to add flavour （添味的）菜肴浇头；糕点装饰配料

torch /tɔːtʃ/

n. a piece of wood, twisted flax, etc., treated with oil, soaked in tallow, etc., for carrying or using as a flaming light 火炬；火把：~ light 火炬光 / ~ race 火炬接力跑 ‖ **carry a ~ for sb.** 单恋某人

torment /ˈtɔːment/

Ⅰ *n.* the severe bodily or mental pain or suffering 煎熬；痛苦：the ~ of jealousy 忌妒之苦 Ⅱ *v.* cause severe suffering to; annoy 使痛苦：The decision ~ed him. 这一决定使他感到痛苦。

tornado /tɔːˈneɪdəʊ/

n. a violent wind which goes round and round 龙卷风；飓风

torpedo /tɔːˈpiːdəʊ/

Ⅰ *n.* (*pl.* ~es) a weapon which is fired through the water from a ship to destroy another ship 鱼雷；水雷：~ boat 鱼雷艇 / launch ~es 发射鱼雷 Ⅱ *v.* attack or destroy with or as with a torpedo 以鱼雷袭击或摧毁；破坏：~ a plan 破坏一个计划 / The ship was ~ed. 舰艇被鱼雷击中。

torrent /ˈtɒrənt/

n. ❶ a violently rushing stream 奔流；急流；洪流；激流：It rains in ~s. 大雨倾盆。/ mountain ~s 山洪 ❷ a violent outpouring 爆发；迸发；狂潮：a ~ of bad language 破口大骂 / a ~ of eloquence 滔滔不绝的口才 / a ~ of speculative buying 抢购狂潮

tortoise /ˈtɔːtəs/

n. a slow-moving land animal with a hard shell 龟，乌龟

tortuous /ˈtɔːtʃʊəs/

adj. ❶ having many bends and twists 弯弯曲曲的：~ road over the hills 弯弯曲曲的盘山路 ❷ difficult to understand; dishonest 难以理解的；转弯抹角的；不正直的：He has a ~ mind. 他的思想令人难以捉摸。

torture /ˈtɔːtʃə(r)/

Ⅰ *v.* cause severe suffering to 使受剧烈痛苦；折磨；拷问：~ a man to make him confess sth. 拷打某人使其承认某事 / He was ~d with heart trouble. 他受到心脏病的折磨。Ⅱ *n.* severe physical or mental suffering; the act of causing sb. great pain 痛苦；折磨；拷打：put a man to the ~ 折磨某人 / instruments of ~ 刑具 / I suffered ~ from headache. 我受到头痛的折磨。

Tory /ˈtɔːri/

n. a member of the Conservative Party in British politics 英国的保守党党员

toss /tɒs/

v. ❶ throw into or through the air 投；掷；抛：The horse ~ed its rider. 那匹马将骑手掀翻（在地）。/ He ~ed the beggar a coin. 他丢给那乞丐一个铜板。❷ (cause to) move about violently and rapidly （使）摇摆，颠簸，动荡：He ~ed about in his sleep. 他睡觉时辗转反侧。/ The waves ~ed the boat. 波浪使那条船摇摆不定。❸ mix lightly （轻轻地）搅拌：~ a salad 拌色拉 ❹ produce quickly with little effort 轻而易举地完成：She ~ed off a few suggestions. 她即席提了几条建议。

tot[1] /tɒt/

n. ❶ a small child 小孩子 ❷ a small amount of alcoholic liquor 少量烈酒

tot[2] /tɒt/

v. (with **up**) add 把……加起来：~ up the bill 结账

total /ˈtəʊtl/

Ⅰ *adj.* complete; entire 完全的；全部的：Can you give me the ~ number? 你能向我提供总数吗？Ⅱ *v.* find the total; reach the total of; amount to 总计 Ⅲ *n.* the whole amount 总数

totality /təʊˈtæləti/

n. the whole of sth. 全部；整体：the ~ of their current policies 他们的全部现行政

策

totally /ˈtɒt(ə)li/

adv. completely；absolutely 完全地；绝对地：The building was ～ destroyed by the fire. 大楼完全被焚毁了。

totem /ˈtəʊtəm/

n. an animal or plant believed by some primitive people to belong to their group and to have special powers in it 图腾：a thick pole on which a ～ is carved 刻有图腾的粗木桩

totter /ˈtɒtə(r)/

v. move or walk as if about to fall 摇摇晃晃地行走

touch /tʌtʃ/

I *v.* ❶ bring a part of the body (especially the hand) into contact with 触摸：Don't ～ the samples. 不要触摸展品。 ❷ tap or nudge lightly 碰及：The skyscraper seems to ～ the sky. 摩天大楼好像要擦到天空似的。 II *n.* the act or fact of putting your hands or fingers onto sb. or sth. 接触：A ～ on the key will produce sound. 这个键盘一下就会发出声音。‖ in (out of) ～ (with) 跟……有牵连 (无关系) /lose ～ (with) 失去联络 ‖ ～able *adj.* 可触知的

touched /tʌtʃt/

adj. caused to feel sympathy or gratitude 感激的；受感动的；激动的：I was ～ by their warm welcome. 他们的热烈欢迎使我十分感动。

touching /ˈtʌtʃɪŋ/

adj. rousing kind feelings, sympathy or pity 令人同情的；令人感激的：It was a ～ story that moved many of us to tears. 那是一个让我们许多人落泪的动人故事。‖ ～ly *adv.* 难以取悦地；动人地

touchy /ˈtʌtʃi/

adj. (touchier, touchiest) ❶ (of a person) oversensitive and irritable (人) 过于敏感的；易怒的：I was a little ～ about his words. 我对他的这番话感到有点儿生气。 ❷ (of an issue or situation) requiring to be dealt with carefully (问题、情况) 需谨慎处理的；棘手的：a ～ topic 一个棘手的话题

tough /tʌf/

adj. ❶ (of meat) hard to cut or to get one's teeth into (肉) 硬的；咬不动的：a ～ piece of meat 一块硬肉 ❷ difficult；demanding effort 棘手的：Mr. Jones is a very ～ person to deal with. 琼斯先生是一个十分难对付的人。

toughen /ˈtʌfn/

v. become or make tough (使) 变坚韧 (坚强、强硬)：～ed glass 钢化玻璃/Three years in the army ～ed him up. 三年的军队生活使他变坚强了。

tour /tʊə(r)/

I *n.* a journey made for pleasure during which several places are visited 旅行；周游：George is now on a ～ to Europe. 乔治正在欧洲旅游。 II *v.* travel around a place 漫游；旅行：I ～ed Beijing many years ago. 许多年前我就到北京旅游过。

tourism /ˈtʊərɪzəm/

n. the business of providing entertainment，hotels，etc. for tourists 旅游业；观光业：The country depends on ～ for much of its income. 该国的很大一部分收入依靠旅游业。

tourist /ˈtʊərɪst/

I *n.* a person travelling for pleasure 旅游者；游览者；观光者：London is full of ～s in summer. 夏天伦敦有很多观光者。 II *adj.* of or for a tour 旅行的；观光的：a ～ agency 旅行社/ a ～ ticket 游览票 / a cheap ～ hotel 收费低廉的旅馆

tournament /ˈtʊənəmənt/

n. a number of contests 锦标赛；联赛；比赛：a tennis (chess) ～ 网球 (国际象棋) 比赛

tout[1] /taʊt/

v. ❶ try repeatedly to persuade people to buy (one's goods)，use (one's services)，etc. 招徕 (顾客)；兜售，推销 (商品、服务等)；拉生意：At one time，solicitors were not allowed to advertise，it is regarded as ～ing for business. 有一段时期，律师是不允许刊登广告的，这被视为拉生意。 ❷ praise greatly，especially as a form of advertising 高度赞扬，吹捧 (尤指以广告形式)：This show is being widely ～ed in the press as the greatest ever on Broadway.这部戏被新闻界吹捧为百老汇有史以来最好的。

tout² /taʊt/

n. a person who offers tickets that are in short supply for sale at a price higher than usual 票贩子;卖黄牛票者:A ticket ～ offered me a £5 Cup Final ticket for £60.一个票贩子向我索价 60 英镑,兜售原价为 5 英镑的决赛杯门票。

tow /təʊ/

Ⅰ*v.* pull along by a rope or chain 拖;拉;牵引:～ sb.along 拖着某人走 /The lifeboat ～ed them to safety.救生艇把他们拖到了安全处所。Ⅱ*n.* the act of towing or being towed 拖;拉:Give him a ～.拉他一把。/My car has broken down. Can you have a ～,please? 我的汽车抛锚了,你能帮我拖一拖吗?

toward(s) /təˈwɔːd(z)/

prep. ❶ in the direction of 朝……的方向:People moved ～ the government building.人们走向政府大楼。❷ near in time (时间上)接近:～ the end of a meeting 接近会议尾声的时候

towel /ˈtaʊəl/

Ⅰ*n.* a piece of cloth for drying sth.wet 毛巾;手巾;抹布:a bath ～ 浴巾 Ⅱ*v.* (-ll- or -l-) dry or rub (oneself) with a towel 用毛巾擦干

tower /ˈtaʊə(r)/

n. a tall building, either standing alone or forming part of a church, castle or other large building 塔:We could hear the bells ringing in the church ～.我们听得见教堂钟楼里的钟在响。‖ a ～ of strength 可依赖的人;中流砥柱

towering /ˈtaʊərɪŋ/

adj. ❶very tall 高大的;高耸的:～ trees (skyscrapers)参天的树木(屹立的摩天大楼)❷of great importance;outstanding 极为重要的;杰出的:one of the ～ intellects of our time 当代最杰出的英才之一 ❸very great; intense 极度的;强烈的:She was in a ～ rage.她怒气冲天。

town /taʊn/

n. a centre of population, larger than a vil- lage but smaller than a city 市镇;镇:I was born in a small ～ in the north of the country.我出生在这个国家北部的一个小镇上。/～ centre 市镇中心 ‖ **man about ～** 花花公子 ‖ ～**ship** *n.* 镇区

toxic /ˈtɒksɪk/

adj. poisonous or caused by poisonous substances 有毒的;中毒的:a ～ plant 一种有毒的植物

toxicity /tɒkˈsɪsɪti/

n. the quality of being poisonous;the extent to which sth. is poisonous 毒性;毒力:substances with high levels of ～ 毒性大的物质

toxin /ˈtɒksɪn/

n. a poisonous substance of animal or vegetable origin, especially one formed by micro-organisms in the body 毒素

toy /tɔɪ/

Ⅰ*n.* sth.for amusement;an object for children to play with 玩具:He is very pleased like a child with a new ～.他像小孩子得到新玩具一样非常开心。Ⅱ*v.* amuse oneself 自娱:～ with dolls 玩洋娃娃

trace /treɪs/

Ⅰ*n.* a mark, sign, etc. of the former presence or passage of some person, thing, or event 踪迹;痕迹:The police cannot find any ～ of the criminal.警方找不到罪犯的任何痕迹。Ⅱ*v.* mark out;outline 描绘出……轮廓

tracing /ˈtreɪsɪŋ/

n. a copy of a map or drawing made by tracing it 描摹;摹图;描图

track /træk/

n. ❶ a line or route along which sth. travels or moves 轨道;路线:the ～ of a storm 风暴的路线 ❷ a railway line 铁轨 ❸ marks left on sth.足迹;踪迹 ‖ **be on sb.'s ～** 追踪 / **cover up one's ～s** 隐藏行踪 / **keep (lose) ～ of sb. (sth.)** 保持(失去)联系

tract /trækt/

n. ❶ a short printed essay on sth.especially a moral or religious subjects(尤指以道德、宗教为题材的)小册子;短文:a

philosophical ～ 一本哲学方面的小册子
❷ a stretch or an area（of forest，farmland，etc.）（森林、土地等的）一片；一片土地；地带：a wooded ～ 一片森林地带 / a ～ of desert 一片沙漠 ❸ a system of related parts in an animal body 系统；道：the digestive ～ 消化道 /the respiratory ～ 呼吸道

tractable /ˈtræktəbl/
　adj. easily controlled，worked，or persuaded 易控制的；易处理的；温顺的

traction /ˈtrækʃn/
　n. ❶ the act of drawing or pulling a heavy load over a surface 拖；拉；牵引 ❷ the form or type of power used for this 牵引（动）力：steam ～ 蒸汽牵引（力）❸ the force that prevents a wheel from slipping over the surface on which it runs（防止车轮在路面滑动的）附着摩擦力：Wet or muddy surfaces can cause a loss of ～.潮湿或泥泞的路面会使车辆失去附着摩擦力。❹ the process of being pulled by a special medical apparatus in order to cure a broken bone or similar injury（治疗骨折等用的）牵引（疗法）：Her leg's in ～.她的脚正在接受牵引治疗。

tractor /ˈtræktə(r)/
　n. a vehicle for pulling heavy loads（e.g. machinery used in agriculture）牵引机；拖拉机

trade /treɪd/
　Ⅰ *n.* ❶ buying and selling of goods；an exchange of goods for money or other goods；a particular branch of this 交易；买卖：We should try our best to promote the ～ between the two countries.我们必须尽最大的努力,促进两国的贸易发展。❷ occupation；a way of making a living；employment of any kind；handicraft 职业；谋生手段；手艺：—What ～ is your brother learning? —He is going to be a carpenter.——你哥哥在学什么手艺？——他打算当木工。Ⅱ *v.* buy and sell 做买卖：～ with foreign countries 跟外国做生意 ‖ ～ **sth. for sth.** 交换；交易 / ～ **sth. in** 折价购物

trademark /ˈtreɪdmɑːk/
　n. a company's legally registered name or emblem，used to identify its products or services 商标

tradition /trəˈdɪʃn/
　n. a custom，habit and belief handed down from generation to generation 传统；因袭：We should keep our good ～s.我们国家应该保持好传统。‖ ～**al** *adj.* 传统的 / ～**alism** *n.* 传统主义 / ～**alist** *n.* 传统主义者

traffic /ˈtræfɪk/
　Ⅰ *n.* ❶（the movement of）people，vehicles，etc. along a street，road，etc.（街上来往的）行人，车辆；交通，运输；通行：a ～ accident 交通事故 /～ regulations 交通规则 /～ lights 交通灯 /a ～ policeman 交通警察 /a ～ police box 交通警岗亭 / ～ jam 交通阻塞 ❷ the business done by a railway line，steamship line or airline 运输业 ❸ trading；commerce 买卖；交易：the illegal drug ～ 非法的毒品交易 Ⅱ *v.*（～ked；～king）trade（in）（especially illegal）买卖；交易；做……买卖（尤指非法进行的）：They are ～king in wheat with us.他们正在我们做小麦生意。

tragedian /trəˈdʒiːdiən/
　n. ❶ a person who writes tragedies 悲剧作家 ❷ an actor in tragedies 悲剧演员

tragedy /ˈtrædʒədi/
　n. a play for the theatre，a film play of a serious or solemn kind，with a sad ending 悲剧：It is the driver's carelessness that leads to this ～.是司机的粗心大意导致了这场悲剧。

tragic /ˈtrædʒɪk/
　adj. ❶ of or related to tragedy 悲剧的：a ～ actress 悲剧女演员 ❷ very sad，unfortunate，etc. 悲惨的；不幸的：a ～ tale 悲惨故事 /～ event 悲惨事件 /It was ～ when our football team lost the match. 我们的足球队输了，真惨。

tragicomedy /ˌtrædʒɪˈkɒmədi/
　n. ❶ a play that is both funny and sad 悲喜剧 ❷ an event that is both funny and sad 悲喜交加的事情

trail /treɪl/
　n. a line，a mark or series of marks，drawn or left behind by sb. or sth. that has pas-

sed by 踪迹；a ～ of smoke 一道烟 ‖ **hot on the** ～ 紧跟在后

trailer/'treɪlə(r)/
*n.*❶ a vehicle pulled by another vehicle (挂在另一辆车子后面的)拖车，挂车：He transports his boat by putting it on a ～ behind his car.他把小船放在他自己汽车后面的拖车上运走。❷an advertisement for a new film or TV show, usually consisting of small pieces taken from it (影片、电视片等的)新片预告；预告片

train/treɪn/
Ⅰ *n.*❶ a line of railway carriages pulled by an engine 火车，列车：I'll take a ～ there.我会乘火车去那里。/get on (off) a ～ 上（下）火车 ❷a series or chain of sth.连续；连串：a ～ of events 一系列的事件 Ⅱ *v.* teach; drill; bring up 训练；教育：The ～ing of animals is a hard work. 训练动物是一件难事。 ‖ **go into** ～**ing** 参加训练

trainee /treɪ'niː/
*n.*a person who is being trained for a particular job or profession 受培训者；学员；实习生

trainer /'treɪnə/
*n.*❶a person who trains people or animals 教员；教练；驯兽师 ❷an aircraft used to train pilots, or a machine simulating an aircraft 教练机；飞行练习器

training/'treɪnɪŋ/
*n.*the act or process of learning the skills 训练；培训；锻炼；教育：flight ～ 飞行训练/ go into ～ 参加训练

trait/treɪt/
*n.*a special feature (especially of sb.'s character) 特性；特点；品质：One of his ～s is complete honesty.他的特点之一是十分诚实。

traitor/'treɪtə(r)/
*n.*a person who betrays his friend or is disloyal to his country 叛徒；卖国贼：turn ～ 成为叛徒；叛变/ a hidden ～ 内奸/ a ～ to one's country 叛国分子

traitorous/'treɪtərəs/
*adj.*of or like a traitor; giving away secrets about your friend, country, etc.叛徒

(似)的；卖国贼(似)的；叛变的；卖国的；奸诈的

tram/træm/
*n.*a public vehicle, driven by electricity, that runs along metal lines set in the road 有轨电车

tramlines/'træmlaɪnz/
*n.*❶ the metal tracks, set in the road, along which a tram runs 有轨电车的轨道 ❷either of the pairs of lines on the edges of a tennis court, marking additional space used only when four people are playing (网球双打时使用的)网球场两侧的加道

tramp/træmp/
Ⅰ *v.*walk with heavy steps 重步走；踩踏：They ～ed away.他们迈着沉重的步伐离开了。Ⅱ *n.*❶ a long walk 步行；徒步旅行 ❷a person with no home or job, who wanders from place to place and usually begs for food or money 流浪者；流浪乞丐

trample/'træmpl/
Ⅰ *v.*❶ beat down with the feet so as to injure or destroy 践踏；踩坏；踩蹦：～ down the grass 践踏草地 /～ out the fire 把火踏灭 ❷ tread heavily (on); treat harshly or ruthlessly 踩；踩蹦；虐待：～ on sb.虐待某人 Ⅱ *n.*an act or the sound of trampling 践踏；踩蹦；践踏声

trampoline/'træmpəliːn/
n. a strong frame covered with canvas used by acrobats and gymnasts to jump high in the air (杂技演员和体操运动员用以跳高的)蹦床，弹簧垫

trance/trɑːns/
*n.*a state of unconsciousness during which a person seems to be asleep but is aware of what is said to them 出神；恍惚；昏睡状态：The holy man fell into a ～.这个圣徒进入昏睡状态。

tranquil/'træŋkwɪl/
*adj.*quiet and peaceful 安静的；宁静的；平静的；安宁的 ‖ ～**ity** /træŋ'kwɪləti/ *n.* 宁静；平静

tranquil(l)ize/'træŋkwəlaɪz/
v.(said about a drug)make someone feel calm (药)使镇静，使安静 ‖ ～**r** *n.* 镇静

剂;安定药

trans- /træns,trænz/

pref. across;beyond;on the other side of 横过;超越;在……的另一边:~ pacific 横渡太平洋的

transact /træn'zækt/

v. conduct, carry through (business, etc. with sb.) 办理;处理;处理事物:~ business 处理事务

transaction /træn'zækʃən/

n. ❶ the process of doing sth.办理;处理 ❷ a piece of business carried out (一笔) 交易,业务 ❸ a published report of the proceedings of a learned society (学术团体会议的)议事录,公报 ‖ ~al *adj.* 交易型的;事务性的

transatlantic /ˌtrænzət'læntɪk/

adj. across or on the other side of the Atlantic 横越大西洋的;在大西洋彼岸的

transcend /træn'send/

v. go or be beyond or outside the range of 超出;超越 ‖ ~ent *adj.* 超越的;超凡的

transcendental /ˌtrænsen'dentl/

adj. belonging to a spiritual or visionary world 精神的;非物质领域的

transcribe /træn'skraɪb/

v. (especially with reference to writing out in full notes taken in shorthand) write out again 抄写(尤指将速记符号转写成文字)

transcript /'trænskrɪpt/

n. a written or printed version of sth. originally in a different medium 抄本;誊本;打印本

transect /træn'sekt/

v. cut cross;divide by passing across 横切;横断

transection /træn'sekʃn/

n. an act or the process of transecting; cross section 横切;横断面

transfer

Ⅰ /træns'fɜː(r)/ *v.* (-rr-) change position; move from a thing or a place to another thing or place 转换;调动:His interest has ~red to sports.他的兴趣已转移到体育上。Ⅱ /'trænsfɜː(r)/ *n.* an act of moving from a place, etc. to another one 转

移;转换:Preparations should be made for a ~.要转换一下,必须有所准备。

transform /træns'fɔːm/

v. change the shape, appearance, quality, or nature of sth.改变(形状、外形、品质): ~ into 转变成/That happening ~ed his personality.那件事改变了他的个性。

transformation /ˌtrænsfə'meɪʃn/

n. the act or state of changing shape, etc. 变化;变形;变质;转变:His character has undergone a ~ since his brain operation. 自从动过脑部手术后,他的性格就变了。

transfuse /træns'fjuːz/

v. take blood from one person and put it into another 给……输血

transfusion /træns'fjuːʒn/

n. the process of putting new blood into a person or an animal 输血:The doctor gave him a blood ~ after the accident.事故发生后医生给他输了血。

transient /'trænzɪənt/

adj. not lasting or staying long;short in time 一时的;短暂的;片刻的:~ pleasures 片刻的快乐

transistor /træn'zɪstə(r)/

n. ❶ a small electrical apparatus, especially used in radios, televisions, etc.晶体管 ❷ a radio that has these instead of valves 晶体管收音机;半导体收音机:The old man took his ~ radio with him everyday. 那老人每天都带着半导体收音机。

transit /'trænsɪt/

n. an act of moving or being moved across or through 通过;穿过;运送;运输:Transit by ship through the canal is expensive.乘船通过运河费用昂贵。/His luggage was lost in ~.他的行李在运输途中丢失了。

transition /træn'zɪʃn/

n. an act of changing or passing from one state, subject, or place to another 过渡;转变;变迁:They hope there will be a peaceful ~ to the new system.他们希望能够和平过渡到新制度。/Adolescence is the period of ~ between childhood and adulthood.青春期是童年与成年之间的过渡期。

transitive /ˈtrænsətɪv/
adj. (of a verb) taking a direct object 及物的; In that dictionary the mark T shows a ~ verb. 在那本词典中用符号 T 表示及物动词。

transitory /ˈtrænsɪtri/
adj. not lasting long; short in time 暂时的; 短暂的; 瞬间的

translate /trænsˈleɪt/
v. give the meaning of words of one language in another language 翻译; ~ English into Chinese 将英语译成中文 ‖ **translatable** *adj.* 可翻译的

translation /trænsˈleɪʃn/
n. ❶ translating 翻译; I've only read Tolstoy's books in ~. 我只读过托尔斯泰作品的译本。❷ sth. translated 译文; ~ of *the Bible* 《圣经》译本 / make (do) a ~ into French 译成法文

translator /trænsˈleɪtə(r)/
n. a person who translates (especially sth. written) 译员; 翻译者 (尤指笔译); an English ~ 英语翻译 / a ~ into French 把其他语言译成法语的翻译者

transmission /trænzˈmɪʃn/
n. the act of transmitting or state of being transmitted 传送; 传播

transmit /trænzˈmɪt/
v. (-tt-) ❶ pass or hand on; send on 传播; 遗传; 传送; 传达; ~ a letter by hand 派专人递送信件 / ~ an order to sb. 把命令传达给某人 / ~ a disease 传播疾病 / Messages are often ~ted by radio. 人们常用无线电传送信息。❷ allow through or along 传导; ~ electricity 导电 / Iron ~s heat. 铁能传热。

transmitter /trænzˈmɪtə/
n. a device or set of equipment for transmitting radio or television signals (尤指广播或电视信号的) 发射机; 发射台

transparency /trænsˈpeərənsi/
n. (*pl.* -ies) ❶ a state of being transparent 透明; 透明性; 透明度 ❷ a positive photograph printed on film or glass; a slide 透明正片; 幻灯片

transparent /trænsˈpeərənt/
adj. ❶ clear and capable of being seen through 透明的; ~ windowpanes 透明的窗玻璃 / ~ silk 透明的绸子 ❷ easily discovered or found out 显然的; 易识破的; a ~ lie 显而易见的谎言 / a man of ~ honesty 非常忠诚的人 ❸ clear; easily understood 明晰的; 易了解的; a ~ style of writing 明晰的文体

transplant /trænsˈplɑːnt/
Ⅰ *v.* ❶ plant sth. again in a different place 移植; 移栽; 移种; ~ young cabbage plants 移栽白菜幼苗 / Some plants do not ~ well. 有些植物不宜移植。❷ transfer (tissue or an organ) from one body to another 移植 (组织或器官等); ~ a heart 移植心脏 ❸ (of people) move from one place to another (指人) 迁移, 迁徙; He wished to ~ his family to Guangdong Province. 他想举家迁往广东。Ⅱ *n.* ❶ sth. transplanted 被移植物 ❷ an act or operation of transplanting 移植; 移植手术; do a heart ~ 做心脏移植手术

transport /ˈtrænspɔːt/
Ⅰ *v.* carry from one place to another 运输; 运送; You should ~ the goods by lorry. 你们必须用卡车运货。Ⅱ *n.* conveying or being conveyed; means of conveyance 运输; 运输工具 ‖ ~**er** *n.* 运送者

transpose /trænˈspəʊz/
v. ❶ change the usual or relative order or position of (two or more things); interchange 改换……的位置; 改变次序; 调换; 变换; Transpose the two colours to make a better design. 把这两种颜色的位置互换一下, 使图案更加好看。❷ change the key of (a composition) 使换调; 使变调; be ~d from G to B 从 G 调变为 B 调 ❸ (in mathematics) transfer (a term) to the other side of an algebraic equation, changing plus to minus or minus to plus (数学中的) 移 (项)

transposition /ˌtrænspəˈzɪʃn/
n. ❶ the act of transposing or condition of being transposed 调换; 变换; 互换位置 ❷ a composition transposed into a different key 变调; 换调; 变调曲 ❸ (in mathematics) the transfer of a term of an algebraic equation from one side to the other

with a change of sign（数学中的）易位；移项：～ of terms of an equation 方程式的移项

transversal/trænz'vɜːsəl/
Ⅰ*adj*.lying or passing a cross；transverse 横向的；横断的；横截的 Ⅱ*n*.a line intersecting two or more other lines 截断线；横断线

transverse/'trænzvɜːs/
Ⅰ*adj*.lying or passing across；placed crosswise；crossing from side to side 横向的；横放的；横截的；横切的；横贯的：～ axis 横截轴/～ beams 横梁/～ current 横向电流/～ nerve 横神经/～ section 横断面/～ stress 横向应力；弯曲应力 Ⅱ*n*.
❶a transverse part，beam，etc.横向物；横向部分；横梁 ❷horizontal axis；the longer axis of an ellipse 横轴；椭圆的长轴 ❸ muscle which is transverse to other part of the body 横肌

trap/træp/
Ⅰ*n*.a device used to capture animals 陷阱：Be careful，it's just a ～ for you.小心点，那只不过是为你设的陷阱。Ⅱ*v*.
(-pp-)set a trap；catch with trap 设圈套：His sweet words ～ped quite a few girls.他的甜言蜜语使不少女孩上了当。

trapezium/trə'piːzɪəm/
n. a four-sided shape in which only one pair of sides is parallel 梯形

trapper/'træpə(r)/
n.a person who traps wild animals，especially for their fur（尤指为获取毛皮而）设陷阱捕兽者

trappings/'træpɪŋz/
n.ornaments；signs of a rank or military rank 装饰物；（等级或军衔的）标志：He was wearing the ～ of an army general.他身着陆军将军的服饰。

trash/træʃ/
n.❶ useless things；rubbish 废物；废料；垃圾：Throw it away！It's just ～.把它扔掉！那纯粹是垃圾。❷ a worthless material，writing，or person 无价值的东西；拙劣的作品；无用的人：That book is mere ～.那本书毫无价值。

trashcan/'træʃkæn/

n.a dustbin or a public litterbin 垃圾桶；公用垃圾箱

trashy/'træʃi/
adj.of extremely low quality or value，especially of low artistic quality（尤指艺术上）毫无价值的；没有一点用处的：～ novels 无价值的小说

trauma/'trɔːmə/
n. the condition of the body or mind caused by severe injury or shock 外伤；损伤；精神创伤

traumatize/'trɔːmətaɪz/
v.❶shock deeply and unforgettably 使受精神创伤 ❷wound 使受外伤

travail[1] /'træveɪl/
n.❶very hard work 艰苦的努力；苦活 ❷ the pains of giving birth to a child 分娩的阵痛：a woman in ～ 正在分娩阵痛中的妇女

travail[2] /'træveɪl/
v.work very hard 艰苦努力；努力工作

travel/'trævl/
v.❶ make（especially long）journeys 旅行：He has ～ed a lot these years.这些年来，他去过很多地方。❷ move or run along 沿……运动；移动：Light ～s very fast.光的传播速度很快。‖ ～ agent *n*.旅游代理商 ‖ ～led *adj*.富有旅游经验的；游历广泛的

travel(l)er/'trævlə(r)/
n.a person on a journey 旅行者；旅客：The hotel was full of ～s.旅馆里住满了旅客。

travel(l)ing/'trævlɪŋ/
adj. ❶ performing in different places around an area or a country 巡回演出的：a ～ theatre company 巡回剧团 ❷carried by or used by a traveller 旅行用的：a ～ alarm clock 旅行用闹钟 /a ～ rug 旅行用毛毯 ❸of or connected with travel 旅行的；与旅行有关的；When she returned to England，she claimed her ～ expenses from her company.她回到伦敦时，向公司报销差旅费。

travelogue/'trævəlɒg/
n.a film or talk describing travel in a particular country，a person's travels，etc.旅

行纪录片;游记

travel-sick/ˈtrævlˌsɪk/

　*adj.*feeling sick because of the movement of a vehicle 晕车的;晕船的;晕飞机的 ‖ ～ness *n.*晕车;晕船;晕机

traverse/trəˈvɜːs/

　*v.*pass across 通过;穿过;横越:The main road ～s the plain from north to south.这条主干道由北向南穿越平原。

trawl/trɔːl/

　Ⅰ *n.* a type of very large fishing net shaped like a bag,dragged along the bottom of the sea (海上捕鱼用的)拖网 Ⅱ *v.* fish with a trawl 用拖网捕(鱼) ‖ ～er *n.* 拖网渔船

tray/treɪ/

　*n.*a flat piece of wood or metal with raised edges,used for carrying small articles 盘;托盘;碟:a ～ of glasses 一托盘玻璃杯/There are three ash ～s on the table.桌上有三只烟灰缸。

treacherous/ˈtretʃərəs/

　*adj.*unfaithful;not to be trusted or relied upon 背叛的;叛逆的;不忠实的;不可信的;靠不住的:The ～ soldier told the enemy where his friends were.那个背叛的士兵把朋友们所在的地方告诉了敌人。

treachery/ˈtretʃəri/

　*n.*❶great disloyalty and deceit;unfaithfulness 不忠;背信弃义;背叛;欺诈 ❷a disloyal or deceitful action 背叛行为;欺诈行为

treacle/ˈtriːkl/

　*n.*thick,dark and sweet liquid made from sugar 〈英〉糖浆;糖蜜

treacly/ˈtriːkli/

　*adj.*❶ thick and sticky;like treacle 黏(稠);似糖浆的:～ black mud 黑黏土/a story full of ～ sentiment 充满柔情蜜意的小说 ❷(of a drink or liquid food) too thick and sweet (饮料、流质食物)太稠的;太甜的

tread/tred/

　*v.*put the foot down while walking 践踏:～ on the lawn 践踏草坪 ‖ ～ **on air** 得意忘形/～ **on sb.'s corns (toes)** 触怒某人

treason/ˈtriːzn/

　n.(the crime of) disloyalty to one's country 叛国;叛国罪

treasure/ˈtreʒə(r)/

　Ⅰ *n.*❶ valuable things as gold,silver,jewels,etc.;wealth 财宝:The millionaire has many ～s. 这个百万富翁有许多珍宝。❷ a highly valued object or person 极受珍爱的人(或物):～s of American literatures 美国文学之精华 Ⅱ *v.* keep sth.or care for sth.carefully 珍惜:～ our friendship 珍惜我们的友谊 ‖ **the Treasury** *n.*财政部

treasurer/ˈtreʒərə(r)/

　*n.*a person in charge of money 司库;掌管财务的人

treat/triːt/

　*v.*❶ act or behave towards 对待;看待:It's a pity that her mother ～s her badly. 遗憾的是她母亲对她不好。❷try to cure by medical means 治疗:The doctor will ～ him this afternoon.医生今天下午给他治疗。❸ regard or consider 视为;以为:We all ～ed it as a trick of him.我们就都认为那是他的一个诡计。‖ ～ **with sb.** 磋商;谈判

treatment/ˈtriːtmənt/

　*n.*❶ (a particular way of) dealing with sb.or sth.;what is done to obtain a desired result 对待;待遇;治疗:most favoured nation trade ～ 最惠国贸易待遇/heat ～ 热处理 ❷ sth.that is done to relieve or cure an illness or a defect,etc.治疗;疗法:be under ～ 在治疗中/a new ～ for cancer 一种治疗癌症的新方法

treaty/ˈtriːti/

　*n.*❶ an agreement made and signed between nations (国家之间缔结的)条约;协议;协定:sign a peace ～ 签订和平条约/Treaty of Friendship between China and Japan《中日友好条约》❷ the agreement or negotiation between persons 协商;谈判:be in ～ with sb.与某人谈判

treble[1]/ˈtrebl/

　Ⅰ *adj.* three times as much as 三倍的:Clothes are ～ the price (that) they used to be.服装的价格是以前的三倍。‖ *v.* become or cause to become three times bigger（使）成为三倍；（使）增加两倍：Why have the prices ~d? 为什么物价增加了两倍？

treble² /ˈtrebl/

n. the highest notes in music；a child's voice which can sing the highest notes 最高音部；唱最高音部的童声

tree /triː/

n. a tall plant with a wooden trunk and branches，that lives for many years 树：We plant a lot of ~s every spring. 每年春天我们都要植很多的树。‖ at the top of the ~ 居某行业最高位置/family ~ 家谱

treeline /ˈtriːlaɪn/

n. ❶ the height above sea level beyond which trees will not grow 树木生长线（按海拔标示的树木生长上限）❷ the northern or southern limit in the world beyond which trees will not grow（南极或北极的）树木生长线

tremble /ˈtrembl/

‖ *v.* ❶ shake because of fear，cold，etc. 颤抖；战栗：~ with cold 冷得发抖 /Her voice ~d with anger. 她气得声音发抖。❷ move and shake slightly 摇晃；微微摆动：The leaves ~ in the wind. 树叶在风中摇晃。/The ground ~d under our feet. 地面在我们的脚下晃动。❸ be in a state of agitation 振奋；激动；焦虑；担忧：~ for sb.'s safety 为某人的安全担忧 /I ~ to think what's going to happen. 我一想到将要发生的事就担心极了。‖ *n.* shudder；uncontrollable shaking 战栗；震颤；身不由己的发抖：a ~ in one's voice 声音发抖

tremendous /trɪˈmendəs/

adj. ❶ very great in size，amount，or degree 巨大的；极大的；惊人的：travel at a ~ speed 以惊人的速度行进/a ~ difference 极大的差别 ❷ wonderful；extremely good 了不起的；极好的：We went to a ~ party last night. 我们昨晚参加了一个很精彩的聚会。

tremolo /ˈtremələʊ/

n. a special slightly shaking effect produced by rapidly varying the sound of a musical note，especially when played on a stringed instrument，or when sung（音乐中的）颤音，震音

tremor /ˈtremə(r)/

n. a very short，shaking movement；quiver 震动；震颤；发抖

trench /trentʃ/

‖ *n.* a long narrow hole cut in the ground；ditch 深沟；地沟；堑沟；壕沟：dig ~es for drainage 挖排水沟 ‖ *v.* surround with a trench；fortify with a trench or trenches；make trenches in 以沟围绕；筑壕以防御；挖壕沟于：~ a field 在地里挖沟

trenchant /ˈtrentʃənt/

adj. (of language) forceful，effective and direct；not minding about giving offence（语言）锋利的；尖锐的；直言不讳的：a hard hitting speech with some ~ comments about the government's failures 一次用词严厉且对政府的失误作了尖刻批评的演说/~ criticism 一针见血的批评

trend /trend/

‖ *n.* the general direction；tendency 走向；倾向；趋势：The ~ of the coastline is to the south. 此海岸线向南延伸。/The ~ of prices is still upwards. 物价仍呈上涨趋势。/ the latest ~s in women's clothes 女装的最新潮流 ‖ *v.* have a certain trend 倾向：The road ~s towards the west. 这条路通向西部。/His opinion ~ed towards yours. 他倾向于你的意见。

trendsetter /ˈtrendˌsetə(r)/

n. a person who starts or popularizes the latest fashion（在服装式样等方面）创新风的人；创新潮流者；标新立异者

trendy¹ /ˈtrendi/

adj. very fashionable；deeply influenced by the latest fashions 时髦的；赶时髦的；追随时髦的：a ~ dress（restaurant，girl）时髦服装（餐馆、女郎）/These ideas are typical of the ~ middle-class liberals. 这些都是时髦的中产阶级自由派的典型想法。

trendy² /ˈtrendi/

n. a trendy person 时髦人物；赶时髦的人：a restaurant full of young trendies 一家坐满时髦年轻人的餐馆

trespass/ˈtrespəs/

v. ❶ go on to sb.'s land or building without permission 未经许可进入他人土地或建筑物；非法侵入：You must not ~ on (upon) government land. 你不能非法侵入政府的土地。❷ take too much advantage of 过分利用：They are always ~ing upon his kindness. 他们老是利用他心地善良占他便宜。

trestle/ˈtresl/

n. ❶ a wooden frame made of two pairs of legs, each pair joined at the top to horizontal bar (used to support planks, platforms or tables) (用以支撑木板、台面或桌子的)支架；台架 ❷ a table with its top resting on a bar of trestles 搁板桌；台桌

tri-/traɪ/

pref. three 三：triangle 三角形/tricycle 三轮车

triad/ˈtraɪæd/

n. a group of three related people or things 三个一组；三件一套

trial/ˈtraɪəl/

n. ❶ a process of testing or proving 试验；考验，证明：give sb. a ~ 试一试某人/have a ~ of strength with sb. 与某人较量力气 ❷ examination in a law court before a judge 审讯；审判：bring sb. to ~ 审讯某人 ‖ **stand ~ for** 因……而受审/~ **and error** 反复试验；尝试错误法

triangle/ˈtraɪæŋgl/

n. ❶ a flat shape with three straight sides and three angles 三角形：The angles of a ~ total 180°. 三角形内角之和为 180 度。❷ a thing shaped like this 三角形物体：a ~ of grass beside the path 小路边的三角形草地 ❸ the situation involving three people, ideas, opinions, etc. 涉及三个人(三种主意、三种看法)的情况：the uneasy ~ of forces 不稳定的三角均势 /a love ~ 三角关系；三角恋爱

triangular /traɪˈæŋgjulə/

adj. ❶ shaped like a triangle 三角形的 ❷ involving three people, groups, opinions,

etc. 三人之间的；三方的：a ~ contest 三方较量

tribe/traɪb/

n. a group of people of the same race, language, customs, etc. 部落；部族：the India ~s of America 美洲的印第安部落 ‖ **tribal** *adj.* 部落的

tribulation/ˌtrɪbjuˈleɪʃn/

n. great trouble or hardship 忧患；苦难；灾难；艰辛

tributary/ˈtrɪbjutəri/

Ⅰ *n.* ❶ a small stream or river that joins a larger river 支流：the tributaries of the Rhine 莱茵河的支流 ❷ a state, ruler, etc. paying tribute to another 进贡国；附属国 Ⅱ *adj.* ❶ (of a stream or river) flowing into another (指河川)支流的：a ~ stream 支流 ❷ (of a person, country, etc.)paying tribute to another 进贡的；纳贡的

tribute/ˈtrɪbjuːt/

n. ❶ the payment which one government or ruler exacts from another 贡金 ❷ sth. done, said, or given to show respect or admiration for someone 致敬；歌颂：At Mr. Li's funeral, his old friend paid ~ to his life and work. 在李先生的葬礼上，他的老朋友对他的一生和工作给予了高度赞扬。

trice/traɪs/

n. (in a ~)in an instant；very quickly：马上；立刻；转眼之间；弹指一挥间

trick/trɪk/

Ⅰ *n.* ❶ sth. done to deceive, outwit, or outdo sb.；sth. done to make a person appear ridiculous 阴谋；诡计：Anyone can see through your ~. 任何人都能看穿你的阴谋。❷ a mischievous act；a practical joke 顽皮的行为，玩笑：play a ~ on sb. 开某人的玩笑 Ⅱ *v.* make sb. believe that sth. is true 欺骗：~ sb. out of his money 骗某人的钱 ‖ **get (learn) the ~ of** 学会诀窍

trickery /ˈtrɪkəri/

n. (*pl.*-ies)the practice of deception 欺骗；哄骗：The dealer made the deal resorting to ~. 那个商人采取欺骗手段做成那笔交

易。

trickle/ˈtrɪkl/

Ⅰ v.(cause to)flow in drops or in the thin stream 滴;淌;细流:Blood ~d down his face.血从他脸上一滴滴流下。/He ~d oil into the gear.他把油滴入传动装置。Ⅱ n.weak or thin flow 滴;淌;细流:a ~ of rain 少量流淌的雨水 /a ~ of blood 沁出的血

trickster/ˈtrɪkstə(r)/

n.a person who deceives or cheats people 骗子;欺诈者

tricky/ˈtrɪki/

adj.❶(of a situation,piece of work,etc.) difficult to handle or deal with;full of hidden or unexpected difficulties（形势、工作等）复杂的;棘手的;微妙的:I'm in a rather ~ position,can you help me out? 我处境十分尴尬,你能帮我摆脱困境吗? /This problem may prove rather ~ for the government.这个问题可能会使政府感到十分棘手。❷deceitful;clever in cheating;crafty 狡猾的;会耍花招的;诡计多端的:Be careful how you deal with him.He's a ~ customer.同他打交道要小心,他是个狡猾的家伙。

tricolour/ˈtrɪkələ(r)/

n.❶the national flags of France and Irish 法国和爱尔兰的国旗 ❷a flag with three equal bands of different colours 三色旗

tricycle/ˈtraɪsɪkl/

n.a cycle with three wheels（often used by young children instead of a bicycle）三轮(脚踏)车

trier/ˈtraɪə(r)/

n.a person who tries hard;someone who always does their best,even if they do not often succeed 工作尽心尽力的人;埋头苦干的人

trifle/ˈtraɪfl/

Ⅰ n.❶ a thing having no value;matter,affair of small importance 无价值的东西;琐事:Don't worry over such ~s! 别为那些小事而烦恼! ❷ a small amount 少量;少许;一点点:a ~ of salt 一点点盐 /It costs only a ~.这只花费一点儿钱。❸（a ~）somewhat;a little 稍微;有点:

This dress is a ~ too short.这衣服有点太短了。/Isn't the meat a ~ tough? 肉不是稍微有点硬吗? ❹ a sweet dish made of cream,jam,etc.甜食;布丁;蛋糕;松糕:I'm making a ~ for dessert.我在做甜食蛋糕。Ⅱ v.❶ play idly with; behave lightly or insincerely towards 嘲弄;轻视;闹着玩:~ with sb.'s affections 玩弄某人的感情 /One does not ~ with history.可不能跟历史开玩笑。❷ waste 浪费:Don't ~ away your time.别浪费你的时间。

trifling/ˈtraɪflɪŋ/

adj.trivial or unimportant 琐碎的;微不足道的;无足轻重的;不重要的:~ details 琐碎细节

trigger/ˈtrɪgə(r)/

n.the part of a gun pulled with the finger to fire it 扳机 ‖ have one's finger on the ~ 完全控制/~ sth.off 引发;引起

trillion /ˈtrɪljən/

num.❶ one million million 万亿;兆 ❷（pl.）a very large number or amount 极多:the yammering of ~s of voices 无数的哀号声

trilogy/ˈtrɪlədʒi/

n.a group of three books or plays about the same subject 三部曲

trim/trɪm/

Ⅰ adj.in good order;neat and tidy 整齐的;整洁的:a ~ garden 整洁的花园 Ⅱ v.cut (sth.) to make it tidy 修剪整齐:~ the beard 修剪胡须

trinity/ˈtrɪnɪti/

n.❶a group of three 三个一组;三件一套 ❷（the Trinity）the Father,Son and Holy Ghost,considered as one in the Christianity（基督教中,圣父、圣子和圣灵）三位一体

trio/ˈtriːəʊ/

n.a group of three persons（especially people playing music together）;a piece of music for three players 三人一组;三重奏;三部合奏曲

trip/trɪp/

Ⅰ n.a journey,especially a pleasure excursion 旅行;远足:on a ~ to Europe 去欧

洲旅行 Ⅱ *v.* walk, run, or dance with quick, light steps 轻快地走(跑)

triple/ˈtrɪpl/
　Ⅰ *adj.* made up of three parts or parties 三倍的；三方的；三部分的；三重的：He received ~ wages for all his extra work. 他因加班加点得到了三倍的工资。Ⅱ *v.* make, become or be three times bigger 三倍(于某数)，增至三倍，增加两倍：~ the output 使产量增加两倍(即增至三倍) / ~ one's efforts 做出三倍的努力

triplet/ˈtrɪplɪt/
　n. one of three children born at the same time to the same mother 三胞胎中的一个

triplicate/ˈtrɪplɪkət/
　n. (especially with reference to papers which are typed) one of three copies (尤指打出的文件)一式三份中的一份 ‖ in ~ 一式三份：Please type this letter in ~. 请把这封信打成一式三份。

tripod/ˈtraɪpɒd/
　n. a table with three legs; a stand with three legs on which sth. can be rested (e.g. blackboard or camera) 三脚桌；(黑板或摄影机等的)三脚架

trite/traɪt/
　adj. (with reference to sth. said or written) used too often; not new (指话语或文章)陈词滥调的；陈旧的

triumph/ˈtraɪəmf/
　Ⅰ *n.* a complete victory or success 成功；胜利 Ⅱ *v.* gain victory or success, especially in dealing with a very difficult situation or opponent 获胜；成功：~ over difficulties 战胜困难

triumphant/traɪˈʌmfənt/
　adj. ❶ feeling or showing great happiness because you have won sth. 胜利的；成功的：a ~ army 获胜的部队 ❷ wild excited because of victory (因胜利而)喜悦的；狂欢的；得意扬扬的：a ~ shout 胜利的欢呼

trivial/ˈtrɪvɪəl/
　adj. ❶ of small value or importance 不重要的；琐屑的；无价值的：Why do you get angry over such ~ matters? 你何必为这种琐事生气？ / a ~ loss 轻微的损失 ❷

ordinary; commonplace 平常的；平凡的：the ~ round 平凡的日常事务

trolley/ˈtrɒli/
　n. ❶ a two or four-wheeled handcart (两轮或四轮的)手推车 ❷ a small table on small wheels used for serving food 装有脚轮的小台 ❸ an electric car; a streetcar 〈美〉电车

trombone/trɒmˈbəʊn/
　n. a type of musical instrument played by pushing a sliding tube in and out (一种乐器)长号，拉管

troop/truːp/
　n. ❶ (*pl.*) a group of soldiers 一群士兵；部队：The ~s are marching towards the city. 部队正向那个城市进军。 ❷ a large group of persons or animals 人群；动物群：a ~ of ducks 一群鸭子

trophy/ˈtrəʊfi/
　n. ❶ a prize for winning a competition in sport (体育比赛中)奖品；奖杯：a table tennis ~ 乒乓球赛奖杯 /The ~ for winning the game was a gold medal. 赢得比赛的奖品是一枚金质奖章。 ❷ sth. kept in memory of a victory or success 胜利纪念品；战利品：hang the deer's head as a ~ 挂出鹿头为纪念品 /a ~ of war 战利品

tropic/ˈtrɒpɪk/
　n. one of the two circles round the earth about 23° 26′ north or south of the equator. (The one north of the equator is the Tropic of Cancer; the one south of it the Tropic of Capricorn) 回归线 (赤道以北的为北回归线；赤道以南的为南回归线) ‖ the ~s *n.* 热带

tropical /ˈtrɒpɪkl/
　adj. ❶ to do with or located in the tropics (与)热带(有关)的；位于热带的：~ countries 热带国家 / a ~ rainforest 热带雨林 ❷ (said about the climate) hot and humid (气候)热而潮湿的

trot/trɒt/
　Ⅰ *v.* (-tt-) ❶ run with short steps 小跑；疾走：I must be ~ting along now or I'll miss the train. 现在我得赶紧走了，要不就赶不上火车了。/She ~ted along the

street. 她在街上匆匆地走。❷ cause to run or walk fast 使疾走;使快跑:~ sb. round 领着某人四处走 II *n.* ❶a trotting pace 疾走;小跑:go a steady ~ 一路以快步走去❷a period of ~ting 疾走或小跑的期间:go for a 做跑步运动

trotter /'trɒtə(r)/
*n.*❶an animal that trots 踏着小步的动物 ❷a pig's foot used as food（用作食物的）猪蹄

trouble /'trʌbl/
I *v.*cause worry, discomfort or anxiety to 麻烦;使苦恼:I'm very sorry to have ~d you so much. 很抱歉麻烦了你这么多。II *n.* ❶ a mental disturbance, worry, problem, etc. 忧虑;苦恼;不适;困难:The little boy is always making ~s. 这个小男孩总是惹是生非。❷（political or social）disorder or violent situation（政治或社会的）不安,纷争:There are still a lot of ~s in the world today. 当今世界仍然是动荡不安。‖ be in ~ 处于麻烦之中/ask（look）for ~ 自找苦吃/get into ~ 陷入困境/make ~ 闹事

troublemaker /'trʌblmeɪkə(r)/
*n.*someone who constantly causes trouble 惹是生非者

troublesome /'trʌblsəm/
*adj.*❶ causing trouble or anxiety 令人烦恼的;讨厌的:a ~ child 惹人心烦的小孩/ The cough is quite ~. 咳嗽真讨厌。❷difficult to deal with 麻烦的,困难的:a ~ problem 难题;棘手的问题

trough /trɒf/
*n.*❶a long, narrow container which holds food or water for animals 饲料槽;（牲口喝水的）水槽 ❷ a low area between two waves（两浪间的）波谷 ❸（with reference to weather）decrease in the pressure of the atmosphere（指天气）低压槽:a ~ of low pressure over the British Isles 不列颠群岛上空的低压槽

troupe /tru:p/
*n.*a group of singers, actors, dancers, etc. 剧团;戏班;歌舞团;杂技团;马戏团:a ballet ~ 一个芭蕾舞剧团/ a chorus ~ 合唱团

trouper /'tru:pə(r)/
*n.*someone who has worked at the same thing for a long time, especially in the entertainment business（多年从事同一工作,尤指演艺团的）同事,成员:a veteran Hollywood ~ 资深的好莱坞电影演员

trouser /'traʊzə(r)/
*adj.*of trousers 裤子的:There's a tear in your ~ leg. 你裤腿上有个破口。/a ~ pocket 裤袋

trousers /'traʊzəz/
*n.*a two-legged outer garment, reaching from the waist to the ankles 裤子:a pair of ~ 一条裤子

troy /trɔɪ/
*n.*a system of weights for gold, silver, precious stones, etc. in which one pound equals twelve ounces 金衡,金衡制（金、银、宝石等的衡量制度,每金衡磅等于十盎司）:weigh 3 lb 5 oz ~ 计重金衡制 3 磅 5 盎司

truancy /'tru:ənsi/
n. the practice of staying away from school without permission 旷课;逃学

truant /'tru:ənt/
I *n.* a pupil who purposely stays away from school without permission 逃学者;旷课者 ‖ play ~ 逃课;逃学;旷课:Anyone who plays ~ will be punished. 逃学者都要受罚。II *v.*stay away from school without permission 逃学;旷课:Several pupils of that class have been ~ing regularly. 那个班上的几个小学生经常旷课。

truce /tru:s/
*n.*an agreement to stop a war, fighting, etc. for a period of time 休战协定

truck /trʌk/
I *n.*❶an open cart used on a railway for carrying heavy goods 敞篷货车 ❷ a motor lorry 货车;卡车:Heavy ~s aren't allowed to cross this bridge. 此桥禁止载重卡车通行。❸ a railway porter's barrow （火车站脚夫的）手推车 II *v.*carry on a truck 用货车运

trudge /trʌdʒ/
I *v.*walk wearily or heavily 跋涉;吃力地走:We ~d wearily up the hill. 我们吃力

地朝山上爬去。/They had to ～ through deep snow.他们不得不走过深深的积雪。Ⅱ n.a long tiring walk 跋涉；费力的步行：a long ～ up the hill 费力的上山长途爬行 /a hard ～ 艰苦跋涉

true/truː/
　adj.❶ real；in agreement with the fact 真实的：It is ～ that she's going to Rome next month.她下个月去罗马，这是真的。❷ behaving loyal and faithful as promised 忠诚的；忠实的：be ～ to one's words 信守诺言

trueborn/ˌtruːˈbɔːn/
　adj.actually so by birth 生来就是的；天生的；地道的：a ～ Scot 地道的苏格兰人

truelove/ˈtruːlʌv/
　n. the person one loves；a sweetheart 爱人；恋人；心上人

trug/trʌg/
　n.a broad flattish basket used in gardens to carry flowers, tools, etc.(用于盛放鲜花、小工具等的)浅篮，浅筐

truism/ˈtruːɪzəm/
　n.a statement that is clearly true, especially one that is too plain to need mentioning 自明之理；不言而喻的话；天经地义的事

truly/ˈtruːli/
　adv. ❶ exactly；in accordance with the truth 确实地；准确地；严格地 a ～ memorable occasion 的确值得纪念的盛事 ❷ really 真正地：There was a ～ beautiful view from the window. 从这个窗户向外看景色真美。❸ sincerely 诚挚地；真诚地：I am ～ grateful for all your help. 我衷心感谢你所给予的一切帮助。/He is ～ sorry. 他是真心地感到抱歉。❹ (**Yours** ～) used at the end of a formal letter, just before the signature, when addressing someone as Sir, Madam, etc.(用于正式书信签名前)你的忠诚的；谨启；谨上

trump/trʌmp/
　Ⅰ *n*.❶ each card of a suit that has, for the time being, higher value than the other three suits 王牌 ❷ an excellent fellow；a person who is intelligent, generous, etc.

老好人；有智慧的人；慷慨的人 Ⅱ v.❶ play a ～ card(on)出王牌；以王牌取胜 ❷ invent(an excuse, a false story, etc.) in order to deceive sb.(为欺骗而)捏造；假造：She had ～ed up a charge against him.她对他的控告纯属捏造。

trumpet/ˈtrʌmpɪt/
　Ⅰ *n*.❶ a brass wind instrument 喇叭；号角；小号：play the ～ 吹小号 ❷ sound (as) of a trumpet 喇叭声；似喇叭声 ❸ sth.suggesting a trumpet in shape or use 喇叭状的东西；用作喇叭的东西 Ⅱ v.❶ proclaim, make known by the sound of trumpets(似)吹号宣布；鼓吹：～(forth) sb.'s heroic deeds 宣扬某人的英勇事迹 ❷ make loud sounds 高声鸣叫

trunk/trʌŋk/
　Ⅰ *n*.❶ the main stem of a tree 树干 ❷ the long nose of an elephant 象鼻：The elephant sucked up water into its ～.那头象把水吸进鼻子。❸ a large box with a hinged lid for clothes, etc.大衣箱；行李箱：pack one's ～ 收拾好衣箱 ❹ the body with head, arms, or legs 躯干；身躯：the ～ of a dead man 一具男尸 ❺ the main part of any structure(任何结构的)主要部分；骨干部分 ❻(～s)man's shorts worn by athletes, acrobats,, etc. for swimming 运动短裤；游泳裤 Ⅱ *adj*. main；chief 主要的

trust/trʌst/
　Ⅰ *v*.believe sb.is sincere, etc.and that they will not try to harm you 信任；相信：I have no reason to ～ him.我没有理由相信他。Ⅱ *n*.a confidence, strong belief in the goddess, strength, reliability of sth.or sb.信赖；信任；依靠：We should have ～ in each other.我们应该互相信赖。‖ ～ **in sb.** 对某人有信心/～ **to sth.** 依赖/～ **sth. to sb.** 委托

trustee/trʌsˈtiː/
　n.❶a person or firm that holds and controls property or money for the advantage of someone else 受托人；信托公司 ❷a member of a group appointed to control the affairs of a company, college, or other organizations(公司、学院等的)理事，董事；管理机构的成员：a ～ of the National Theatre

国家剧院的理事

trusteeship/trʌˈstiːʃɪp/

n. ❶ the position of trustee 受托人(理事)的职位 ❷ the government of an area by a country appointed by the United Nations 托管(联合国委托某国对某一地区进行管理)

trusting/ˈtrʌstɪŋ/

adj. (too) ready to trust others (太)容易相信别人的;充满信任的;无疑心的: the ~ nature of a small child 小孩容易相信他人的天性

trust territory/trʌst terɪt(ə)ri/

n. an area under this form of government 托管地

trustworthy/ˈtrʌstwɜːði/

adj. worthy of trust; dependable 值得信赖的;可靠的

trusty[1]/ˈtrʌsti/

adj. that can be trusted; dependable; faithful 可依赖的;可靠的;忠诚的: my ~ sword 我这把可靠的剑/My ~ old car will get us home safely. 我那辆可靠的旧车会把我们安全送回家的。

trusty[2]/ˈtrʌsti/

n. a prisoner given special rights because of good behaviour in prison (因表现好而享有特权的)模范囚犯,信得过的犯人

truth/truːθ/

n. ❶ sth. that is true; the true facts 真实;真相;实际情况: There is not a word of ~ in what he says. 他没说一句真话。/The ~ is that he didn't come. 实际上他没来。 ❷ the quality or state of being true 真实性;忠实性: I don't doubt the ~ of his information. 我不怀疑他那情报的真实性。 ❸ a fact, belief, principle, etc. accepted as true 真理;真义: universal ~s 普遍真理/the ~s of religion 宗教的真义 ‖ **in ~** 事实上;的确: In ~, she was not happy. 实际上,她很不高兴。/**to tell the ~** 坦率地说;说老实话;实话实说(坦白陈述时所用的套语): To tell the ~, I forgot all about your request. 说实话,我完全忘了你的要求。

truthful/ˈtruːθful/

adj. ❶ (said about a person) always telling the truth 诚实的;讲真话的: Are you being completely ~ with me? 你跟我讲的全是真话吗? ❷ true or accurate 真实的;准确的: a ~ account of what happened 对发生事件准确的陈述 ‖ ~**ly** *adv.* 诚实地;深信不疑地/~**ness** *n.* 真实;坦率;正当

try/traɪ/

I *v.* ❶ make an effort to do; attempt to do 试图得到;争取: He did ~ very hard but failed. 他确实做了很大的努力,但没成功。 ❷ use sth. or do sth. as an experiment or test, to see whether it is effective 试验;试用: Would you please ~ this new medicine and see if it is effective? 请你试一下这种新药,看是否有效,好吗? II *n.* an attempt or effort 尝试: Let me have a ~. 让我试一下。 ‖ ~ **sth. on** 试穿

trying/ˈtraɪɪŋ/

adj. distressing; annoying; embarrassing; causing strain; hard to endure or bear 难受的;难堪的;费力的;恼人的: a ~ person to deal with 一个难以对付的人 /a ~ situation 尴尬的局面

tsunami /tsjuːˈnɑːmi/

n. (*pl.* tsunami or ~s) a long high sea wave caused by an underwater earthquake 海啸

tub/tʌb/

I *n.* ❶ a round, open, flat-bottomed vessel used for packing, storing, or washing 盆;桶: a rainwater ~ 盛雨水的桶 ❷ the contents of such a container 一盆(桶): a ~ of water 一盆(桶)水 ❸ bath tub 浴盆;沐浴: have a cold ~ 洗冷水澡 ❹ a clumsy slow boat 笨拙缓慢的船 II *v.* (-bb-) have a bath in a tub 盆浴

tuba/ˈtjuːbə/

n. a type of large, brass musical instrument 大号;低音号

tubby/ˈtʌbi/

adj. (with reference to persons) short and fat (指人)矮胖的

tube/tjuːb/

n. ❶ a long pipe of metal, glass, rubber, etc. used to carry liquid or gas 管;筒: boiler ~s 锅炉管 /the inner ~ of a bicycle tyre 自行车内胎 ❷ a soft metal container with a screw-cap, used for pastes, paints, etc.(装膏、颜料等的)软金属桶：a ～ of toothpaste 一管牙膏 ❸ (in London) underground railway (伦敦)地下铁道：I go to work on the ～ (by ～).我坐地铁上班。❹ electron tube or vacuum tube 电子管；真空管：the ～s of a TV set 电视机的电子管

tuberculosis /tjuːˌbɜːkjʊˈləʊsɪs/
　n.(*abbr*. TB) a serious infectious disease that usually attacks the lungs (略作 TB) 结核病，肺结核

tuck /tʌk/
　I *v*.❶ put or push into a narrow or hidden place 夹；塞；裹：～ a baby up in bed 把婴儿裹在床上 /I ～ed the letter in a dictionary.我把信夹进词典里。❷ gather up in a fold or folds 折起；卷起；挽起：He ～ed up his sleeves. 他卷起了袖子。❸ put in an out-of-the-way and snug place (使)蜷曲；(使)隐藏：a small village ～ed away in the hills 隐藏在群山中的小村 / He sat with his legs ～ed up under him. 他把双腿蜷曲坐在屁股下面。/The bird ～s its head under its wing. 鸟把头藏在翅膀下。II *n*. flattened pleat or fold 褶皱；裥：make a ～ 打个裥

Tuesday /ˈtjuːzdeɪ/
　n.the third day of the week, after Monday 星期二：He will arrive (on) ～.他将于星期二到达。/We have a music lesson on ～s.我们每周星期二上音乐课。

tuft /tʌft/
　n.a bunch of sth. soft (e.g. hair, grass, etc.)(头发、草等的)一束，一簇，一丛

tug /tʌg/
　I *v*.pull hard (at) 用力拖；使劲拉：We ～ged so hard that the rope broke.我们用力拖，把绳子拉断了。/The child was ～ging her toy car.那孩子正拖着她的玩具车。II *n*.a sudden hard pull 猛拉；猛拖；猛扯：The naughty boy gave his sister's hair a ～.那个顽皮的男孩用力扯了一下姐姐的头发。‖ ～ of war 拔河比赛

tuition /tjuːˈɪʃn/
　n.❶ teaching or instruction 教学；讲授；教诲：receive careful ～ from sb.得到某人的细心教诲 ❷ the money that you pay to be taught 学费：How much did you pay for the ～? 你交了多少学费？

tulip /ˈtjuːlɪp/
　n.a garden plant that grows from a bulb and has large colorful cup-shaped flowers 郁金香

tumble /ˈtʌmbl/
　I *v*.(cause to) fall, especially quickly or violently 跌倒；跌落：The old man ～d off the bicycle. 老人从自行车上摔了下来。II *n*.a sudden drop from a position 跌落；摔落

tumbler /ˈtʌmblə(r)/
　n.❶ a drinking glass with a flat bottom 平底无脚酒杯：a ～ of whisky 一杯威士忌酒 ❷ acrobat or gymnast 杂耍艺人；杂技演员

tummy /ˈtʌmi/
　n.(*pl*.-ies) the stomach 胃；肚子：a ～ upset 肚子不舒服

tumour /ˈtjuːmə/
　n.a swelling in the body, caused by an abnormal growth of tissue 肿瘤；肿块：a benign (malignant) ～ 良性(恶性)肿瘤

tumult /ˈtjuːmʌlt/
　n.❶ uproar; disturbance 喧嚣；扰乱；吵闹：The ～ and the shouting died. 喧闹的声音消逝了。❷ a confused and excited state of mind 激昂；烦乱：in a ～ 激动的

tuna /ˈtjuːnə/
　n.a type of very large sea fish, related to the mackerel, used for food 金枪鱼

tundra /ˈtʌndrə/
　n.a vast, nearly level, treeless plain in the arctic regions (北极地区不生树木的) 苔原，冰原，冻土地带

tune /tjuːn/
　n.the succession of notes forming a melody (of a song, hymn, etc.) 曲；调子：Wherever he is, he always singing a popular ～.不管在什么地方，他总是哼着一个流行曲子。‖ **in**（**out of**）～ 和调(不和调)/**change one's ～, sing another ～** 改变自己的论调(或行为)

tunnel /'tʌnl/

Ⅰ *n.* a large hole dug for a road or railway through a hill or under a river, town, or mountain 隧道；地道；坑道；隧洞：a railway ~ 铁路隧道 /~ warfare 地道战 /an undersea ~ 海底隧道 Ⅱ *v.* (-ll- or -l-) make a tunnel (through or into) (掘)隧道；(挖)地道：~ under the sea 在海底挖隧道 / They ~led for weeks before they reached the other side of the hill. 他们用了几个星期才开凿到山那边。

turbid /'tɜːbɪd/

adj. (with reference to liquid) muddy；not clear (指液体)浑浊的，不清的

turbulence /'tɜːbjʊləns/

n. ❶ a violent or unsteady movement of air or water, or of some other fluid (空气、水等的)紊流，湍流 ❷ conflict；confusion 冲突；混乱：a time of political ~ 政治动乱时期

turbulent /'tɜːbjʊlənt/

adj. ❶ (said about air or water) moving violently and unevenly (气流)湍流的；(水)湍急的：the ~ river 汹涌的江水 ❷ confused or unruly 动荡的；混乱的；失控的

turf /tɜːf/

Ⅰ *n.* ❶ the soil surface with grass roots growing in it 草皮；草根土；草泥：He covered the pit with ~. 他在那坑上覆盖了一层草皮。 ❷ a horse racing 赛马：He is very interested in the ~. 他对赛马很感兴趣。 Ⅱ *v.* ❶ cover (a piece of land) with turf 用草皮铺盖：We are going to ~ that part of the garden. 我们要给花园的那部分铺上草皮。 ❷ throw out 赶走；扔：We ~ed him out of the house. 我们把他从房子里赶了出去。 /He ~ed out all his old books. 他把他所有的旧书都扔出去了。

turgid /'tɜːdʒɪd/

adj. foolishly solemn；pompous 煞有介事的；浮夸的：He writes in ~ prose. 他的文章华而不实。

turkey /'tɜːki/

n. ❶ a large bird with a red featherless head and big flaps under the chin 火鸡 ❷ the meat of this bird, eaten as food 火鸡肉

turmoil /'tɜːmɔɪl/

n. the state of great confusion or disorder 混乱；动乱；骚乱

turn /tɜːn/

Ⅰ *v.* ❶ (cause to) move around a point；(cause to) move so as to face in a different direction 转动；翻转：She ~ed her back on me. 她转过身去不理我。 ❷ (cause to) change in nature, quality, condition, etc. (使)改变：Her hair has ~ed grey. 她的头发已变得灰白。 ‖ ~ one's mind (attention) to sth. 把自己的心思(注意力)放到某物上面 /~ one's hand to sth. 从事；担任 /~ a deaf ear to sb. 拒绝听取某人的意见或忠告 /~ sb. adrift 驱逐某人 /~ against sb. 反抗 /~ aside 避开 /~ back 折回 /~ in on oneself 隐居 /~ sb. in 把某人交给警方 /~ off 改变方向；离开 /~ sth. off 关掉 /~ sth. on 打开 /~ on sb. 突然某人 /~ out 结果为；生产 /~ sth. over 压过；打翻 /~ sth. over in one's mind 再三考虑 /~ round 转向 /~ ~ to sb. 求助于某人 /~ up 出现 /~ up one's nose at sth. 轻视 Ⅱ *n.* ❶ a turning；a change in direction or condition 旋转；转动：the ~ of the wheel 轮子转动 ❷ an occasion or opportunity for doing sth., especially in one's proper order among others 时机；次序：It's your ~ to answer the question. 现在轮着你来回答问题了。 ‖ on the ~ 即将改变 /done to a ~ (食物)恰到好处 /at every ~ 不时地 /by ~s 轮流地 /in ~ 依次 /out of ~ 不按次序 /do sb. a good ~ 为某人做好事

turnabout /'tɜːnbaʊt/

n. a sudden and complete change or reversal of policy, opinion, or situation (政策、观点、情况的)突变：The move was a significant ~ for the company. 此举是这家公司意义重大的转变。

turning /'tɜːnɪŋ/

n. a place where one road meets another, forming a corner 岔路口；拐弯处；转弯处：Take the second ~ on the left. 在第二个路口向左拐。

turnip /'tɜːnɪp/

*n.*a type of plant with a round root used as food and to feed animals 萝卜

turnover /ˈtɜːnɪˌəʊvə/

n. ❶ the amount of money a business takes in a particular period（一定时期内的）营业额；成交量 ❷ the rate at which goods are sold 货物周转率；销售比率 ❸ the rate at which workers leave and are replaced 人事变更率；人员调整率

turnpike/ˈtɜːnpaɪk/

*n.*❶ a road, especially expressway, for the use of which a toll is charged 征收通行税的道路；（尤指）征收通行税的高速公路 ❷a gate across a road, which was opened when the traveller paid a toll（昔日的）收费门；收取通行税的关卡

turntable/ˈtɜːnˌteɪbl/

*n.*❶the round, revolving platform of a record player upon which records are played 唱机的转盘 ❷a circular revolving platform for reversing engines（转换机车方向的）转车台

turquoise/ˈtɜːkwɔɪz/

*n.*a greenish-blue colour 蓝绿色；天蓝色；湖蓝色

turret/ˈtʌrɪt/

*n.*a small tower on a building 塔楼；角塔

turtle/ˈtɜːtl/

*n.*a big tortoise which lives in the sea 大海龟；海鳖

tusk/tʌsk/

*n.*a long, pointed tooth which sticks out of the mouth of certain animals（e. g. elephant, walrus, boar, etc.）（象、海象、野猪等露出口外的）长牙

tut/tʌt/

Ⅰ*int.*a sound made to show disapproval 啧（表示不赞成的声音）Ⅱ*v.*(-tt-) make this noise 发"啧"声

tutor/ˈtjuːtə(r)/

Ⅰ*n.*❶ a private teacher of a single pupil 私人教师；家庭教师：His parents employed a ～ to teach him Greek.他的父母请了位家庭教师教他希腊语。 ❷a university teacher who guides the studies of a number of students〈英〉导师；指导教师Ⅱ*v.*❶ teach as a tutor（作为家庭

教师）个别教授；个别指导：She ～ed the child in math.她对那个孩子的数学进行个别辅导。 ❷ train or exercise restraint over 养成；管制；约束：～ oneself 自我克制 /～ one's passions 抑制激情

tweak/twiːk/

*v.*❶ take hold of, pull, and twist（especially the ear or nose）with a sudden movement 拧；扭；捏 ❷make small changes to sth.（such as a car engine or computer program）in order to improve its performance 对（汽车引擎或电脑程序等）做小小的改良

tweezers/ˈtwiːzəz/

*n.*a pair of small pincers used for picking up very small things or pulling out hairs 镊子；小钳子：eyebrow ～ 修眉钳

twice/twaɪs/

*adv.*two times 两倍；两次：Remember, you have made the same mistakes ～.记住，同样的错误你已经犯了两次了。‖ think ～ about doing sth.三思而行

twiddle /ˈtwɪdl/

Ⅰ*v.*turn or fiddle with sth. aimlessly（无聊地）旋弄，摆弄，捻弄（物件）：She began twiddling with the ring on her finger.她开始无聊地旋弄着手指上的戒指。 ‖ ～ your thumbs 闲得无聊；闲着没事 Ⅱ*n.*❶a slight twirl 旋弄；捻弄；摆弄 ❷a rapid series of musical notes 急促（或复杂）的乐音

twig / twɪg/

*n.*a small shoot on a branch or stem of a tree or shrub 细枝；小枝；嫩枝

twilight/ˈtwaɪlaɪt/

Ⅰ*n.*❶ the faint half-light or the period of time after sunset 黄昏；傍晚；暮色：at ～ 黄昏（黎明）时分 /go out for a walk in the ～ 在暮色下外出散步 /The ～ came on.傍晚即至。/The ～ is deepening.暮色渐浓。/Can you see clearly in the ～? 暮色下你能看清楚吗？ ❷ a remote period about which little is known 遥远而不为人知的时代：in the ～ of history 在远古时代 Ⅱ*adj.*❶ of or happening at twilight 黄昏的；微明的；昏暗的：a ～ storm 黄昏时的暴风雨 ❷ of or like the time of twilight 暮年的；晚年的；the ～ years 晚年

twin/twɪn/

Ⅰ *n.*one of two children born at the same time to the same mother 孪生儿之一；双胞胎之一 Ⅱ *adj.*❶ used to describe one of a pair of twins 孪生儿之一的；双胞胎之一的；～ sisters 孪生姊妹 ❷ used to describe two things that are used as a pair 成对的；成双的；a ship with ～ propellers 有双螺旋桨的船 ❸ used to describe two things that are connected 双重的；双联的

twine/twaɪn/

Ⅰ *v.*twist or wind sth.编结；缠绕；蜿蜒；捻：The vine ～s around the tree.藤缠绕着树。/A snake ～d over the ground.蛇在地上蜿蜒爬行。/She ～d flowers into a wreath.她把花儿编成花环。/She ～d her arms round her mother's neck.她用双臂搂住母亲的脖子。Ⅱ *n.*a thin string 细绳；合股线：He tied the parcel with ～.他用细绳扎包裹。

twinkle/'twɪŋkl/

Ⅰ *v.*shine with unsteady light 闪烁；闪耀：Stars are twinkling in the sky.繁星在天空中闪烁。Ⅱ *n.* ❶ an expression in your eyes that shows you are happy（眼睛的）闪亮；欣喜的神情 ❷the twinkling of a light 闪光；闪烁

twirl/twɜːl/

Ⅰ *v.*❶（cause to）turn round and round quickly（使）迅速旋转；快速地转动：The dancers ～ed gaily.跳舞的人欢快地旋转着。❷（cause to）curl 扭转；卷曲：She ～ed her hair round her finger.她用手指卷弄她的头发。Ⅱ *n.*a rapid circular motion 快速地旋转；扭曲：She did a quick ～ to show off her dress.她快速转了一圈来炫耀她的衣服。

twist/twɪst/

Ⅰ *v.*❶ wind or turn one around the other 绞；搓：She ～ed her hair round her fingers.她把头发卷在手指上。❷ turn and curve in different directions；change position or direction 盘旋；曲折：A small road ～s towards the summit.一条小道盘旋着通向山顶。‖ ～ sth.off 拧断；扭断 Ⅱ *n.*

the action of twisting or being twisted 扭曲；弯曲：There are too many ～s on the way to the village.去村庄的那条路上迂回曲折太多。

twitch/twɪtʃ/

Ⅰ *v.*❶ move suddenly and quickly without control 抽搐；抽动：He felt his lip ～.他感到嘴唇在抽搐。❷ give a sudden quick pull or jerk to 急拉；扯：The wind ～ed the paper out of my hand.风吹走了我手中的纸。/She ～ed the curtain into place.她把窗帘拉好。Ⅱ *n.*❶ a sudden, quick, usually uncontrollable movement of a muscle（肌肉的）痉挛；抽动：a muscle ～ 肌肉痉挛 ❷a sudden quick pull 急拉；扯

twitter/'twɪtə(r)/

Ⅰ *n.*a sharp, short sound made by birds when they are excited；an excited talk 鸟兴奋时的吱喳叫声；兴奋的谈话 Ⅱ *v.*make this sound；talk in this way 吱吱地叫；兴奋地讲

two/tuː/

*num.*the number 2 二 ‖ **break（cut）sth.in ～** 分其为二／**by ～s and threes** 三三两两 ‖ **～-edged** *adj.*正反两面的；双刃的

tycoon/taɪ'kuːn/

*n.*a very rich and powerful businessman 有钱有势的商人；大亨；(实业界)巨头

type/taɪp/

Ⅰ *n.*❶a particular kind, class, or group；a group or class of people or things that share certain qualities and are different from those outside the group or class 类型；型号：This ～of persons is fit for the job.这一类人适合这种工作。❷a person or thing that has all the characteristics of a particular group or class；a standard example 典型；模范；表率：a ～ of good students 优秀学生的典型 Ⅱ *v.*write with a typewriter or using a word processor 打字：Can you ～? 你会打字吗?

typewriter/'taɪpˌraɪtə(r)/

*n.*a typing machine with keys for printing letters on a piece of paper 打字机

typhoid /'taɪfɔɪd/

n. an infectious bacterial fever with an

eruption of red spots on the chest and abdomen and severe intestinal irritation 伤寒

typhoon /ˌtaɪˈfuːn/

n. a violent tropical storm with very strong winds 台风：They were caught in a ～ in the China seas. 他们在中国海域遭到了台风袭击。

typical /ˈtɪpɪkl/

adj. ❶having or showing the usual qualities of a people, thing, etc. 代表性的；象征性的：This is a ～ Chinese dish. 这是一道典型的中国菜。❷behaving in the way that sb. expected 一贯的；不出所料的

typicality /ˌtɪpɪˈkælɪti/

n. the quality or character of being typical 典型性；特征

typically /ˈtɪpɪkəli/

adv. ❶ used to say that sth. usually happens in the way that you are stating 通常；一般：The factory ～ produces 100 chairs a day. 这家工厂通常每天生产 100 把椅子。❷in a way that shows the usual qualities or features of a particular type of person, thing or group 典型地；具有代表性地：～ American hospitality 美国人典型地好客

typify /ˈtɪpɪfaɪ/

v. be a representative specimen of sb. or sth. 作为……的典型；具有……的特点：clothes that ～ the 1980s 20 世纪 80 年代典型的服装

typist /ˈtaɪpɪst/

n. a person whose job is to type or who uses a typewriter 打字员：She is a ～. 她是一个打字员。

tyranny /ˈtɪrəni/

n. ❶ the cruel or unjust use of power to rule a person or country 残暴；专横；暴虐 ❷ a government ruled by a cruel ruler with complete power 施行暴政的国家；专制国家

tyrant /ˈtaɪərənt/

n. a person who rules or uses authority harshly or cruelly 暴君；专制君主

tyre /ˈtaɪə(r)/

n. a band of solid rubber on the rim of a wheel, especially the kind on bicycle and motorcar wheels 轮胎；车胎；轮箍：a flat ～ 瘪轮胎 /People would like to use a jack when changing a ～. 人们换轮胎时喜欢用千斤顶。

T

Uu

U- /juː/

pref. shaped like a U U 字形的：U-bend U 形弯头/U-bolt U 形螺栓/U-turn U 形转弯；180°转弯

ugly /ˈʌgli/

adj. unpleasant to look at 难看的；丑恶的：He is born very ～. 他生来就丑。‖ make ～ faces 做鬼脸

ulcer /ˈʌlsə(r)/

n. an open sore producing poisonous matter（皮肤上或体内的）溃疡：a stomach ～ 胃溃疡/mouth ～s 口腔溃疡

ulcerate /ˈʌlsəreɪt/

v.（cause to）turn into or become covered with one or more ulcers（使）生溃疡；（使）溃烂：Some medicines can ～ the stomach. 一些药能造成胃溃疡。

ulterior /ʌlˈtɪərɪə(r)/

adj. ❶ situated on the further side 较远的 ❷（often in ～ **motive**）that different from the one actually stated 不可告人的：He says that he is doing this to help me, but I suspect an ～ motive. 他说他这样做是为了帮助我，但我怀疑他别有用心。

ultimate /ˈʌltɪmɪt/

adj. ❶ being or happening last, final or farthest 最终的；最后的；最远的：This is my ～ decision, and no other changes will be considered. 这是我最后的决定，不会再做其他任何的变动。 ❷ the best or greatest 极端的；最好的；最伟大的：the ～ in sth. 最好（或最先进的）事物；精华

ultimately /ˈʌltɪmətli/

adv. ❶ in the end; finally 最终；最后；终归：Ultimately, I'll have to do it myself. 最终我还是得自己完成。 ❷ at the most basic and important level 最基本地；根本上：All life depends ～ on oxygen and water. 一切生命归根到底都要依靠氧气和水。

ultimatum /ˌʌltɪˈmeɪtəm/

n.（*pl*. ～s or ultimata /ˌʌltɪˈmeɪtə/）a final statement of sth. that must be accepted without discussion 最后通牒：He gave me an ～ to pay the money back in ten days. 他给我下了一道最后通牒，要我在十天内还款。

um /ʌm/

int.（used when one cannot decide what to say next）啊，嗯（用以表示说话时迟疑不定、犹豫不决）：And then he... ～... just seemed to... ～... disappear! 那么他……嗯……似乎……嗯……不见了!

umber /ˈʌmbə(r)/

adj. having a yellowish or reddish brown colour, especially as used in painting 棕土色的；赭色的

umbrage /ˈʌmbrɪdʒ/

n. offence or annoyance 不快 ‖ take ～（at)（对……）表示不高兴；（因……）见怪；（为……）生气

umbrella /ʌmˈbrelə/

n. a cover with a handle used to shelter one from rain or sun 伞；雨伞；阳伞：Take an ～ with you in case it rains. 带上伞，以防下雨。 ‖ under the ～ of 在……的保护下；在……的庇护下

umpire /ˈʌmpaɪə(r)/

Ⅰ*n*. a judge in a game; a judge in a dispute 裁判员；仲裁人；裁决者 Ⅱ*v*. act as umpire 仲裁；裁判；任公断人；当裁判：～ a dispute 公断一项争论 / He ～d in the tennis match. 他在网球比赛中担任裁判。

un- /ʌn/

pref. ❶（before an adjective, adverb and noun）not（用于形容词、副词或名词前）不：unable 不能的/unaffected 不装腔作势的；未受影响的 ❷（before a verb）do the opposite of (用于动词前)做相反的动作:undress 脱衣服/unchain 替……解开锁链

unabashed/ˌʌnəˈbæʃt/

adj.fearless;not embarrassed or ashamed 泰然自若的;不怕难为情的;不害臊的;脸皮厚的:He lost his trousers but was quite ~.他丢了裤子但仍泰然自若。

unabated/ˌʌnəˈbeɪtɪd/

adj.(usually with reference to noise, pain, suffering, etc.) not becoming less (通常指噪声、疼痛、苦难等)不减弱的:The storm continued ~ for several hours.暴风雨持续数小时未见减弱。

unable/ʌnˈeɪbl/

adj.not able to do sth.不能的;不会的;无能为力的:The boy was ~ to go to the school because he was sick.这孩子因病不能去上学。

unacceptable/ˈʌnəkˈseptəbl/

adj.that you cannot accept, allow or approve of 不能接受(或允许、同意)的:Noise from the factory has reached an ~ level.工厂的噪声达到了难以容忍的地步。

unaccompanied/ˌʌnəˈkʌmpənɪd/

adj.❶ not accompanied;travelling alone (旅行时)无人做伴的 ❷(of a song) sung without the help of a musical instrument (唱歌时)无伴奏的

unaccountable/ˌʌnəˈkaʊntəbl/

adj.not able to be explained 无法解释的;不可理喻的;莫明其妙的

unaccustomed/ˌʌnəˈkʌstəmd/

adj.❶ not accustomed;not used to sth.不习惯的:Polar bears are ~ to hot weather.北极熊不习惯炎热的天气。 ❷ not familiar;unusual or strange 不熟悉的;反常的;奇怪的:He was ~ to the routine of his new job.他不熟悉他的新工作的程序。

unadvised/ˌʌnədˈvaɪzd/

adj.not sensible;done without thinking or taking advice 不审慎的;轻率的;未曾受到劝告的;未经商量的:an ~ haste 未经商量而仓促行事

unaffected/ˌʌnəˈfektɪd/

adj.❶ not affected;not influenced;unchanged 未受影响的;未改变的:Many of these birds seem ~ by climate.似乎这些鸟许多都多未受到气候的影响。 ❷ natural;without affectation 自然的;非矫揉造作的:an ~ smile 会心的一笑

unanimous/juːˈnænɪməs/

adj.agreed by all 一致同意的;无异议的;全体一致的:The meeting was ~ in support of his suggestion.会议一致同意支持他的建议。

unashamed/ˌʌnəˈʃeɪmd/

adj.feeling no guilt or embarrassment 不害臊的;不感觉难为情的:an ~ emotionalism 毫无顾忌的感情表达 ‖ ~ly *adv*.不害臊地;不觉羞耻地

unassuming/ˌʌnəˈsjuːmɪŋ/

adj.modest;not proud or overbearing 谦逊的;不傲慢的;不专横的

unattached/ˌʌnəˈtætʃt/

adj.❶ not attached 非隶属的 ❷ not connected or associated with a particular body, group, organization, etc.;independent 与(组织、团体、机构等)无关系的;无联系的;独立的:an ~ organization 一个独立的组织 ❸ not engaged or married 未婚的;未订婚的

unattended/ˌʌnəˈtendɪd/

adj.❶without attendants 无随员的;无同伴的:an ~ visit 一次无随员的访问 ❷ not taken care of;not attended to 无人照看的;没人照顾的:Don't leave your bike ~ there.别将你的自行车丢在那儿不管。

unavailable/ˈʌnəˈveɪləbl/

adj.not able to be used or obtained;not at someone's disposal 不可用的;不可获得的;达不到的:material which is ~ to the researcher 研究者无法获得的材料

unavoidable/ˌʌnəˈvɔɪdəbl/

adj.not able to be avoided 不可避免的:~ delay 不得已的耽搁

unaware/ˌʌnəˈweə(r)/

adj.not having knowledge or consciousness (of sth.) 不知道的;没有觉察的;没有意识到的:She was ~ of the danger.她没有意识到这种危险。 ‖ ~s *adv*.不知不觉地;无意地

U

unbalanced /ˌʌnˈbælənst/
adj. ❶ not keeping or showing an even balance 不平衡的：~ development of the economy 经济发展不平衡 ❷ made slightly mad 精神错乱的；精神失常的

unbearable /ʌnˈbeərəbl/
adj. too annoying or unpleasant to deal with or accept 不堪忍受的；承受不了的：~ suffering 无法忍受的痛苦／~ burden 承受不了的负担

unbeaten /ˌʌnˈbiːtn/
adj. not beaten；not defeated 未受打击的；未被击败的：Our football team was ~ last year. 我们的足球队去年保持不败。

unbecoming /ˌʌnbɪˈkʌmɪŋ/
adj. not suitable；unseemly 不恰当的；不相称的；不得体的：an ~ dress 一件不合身的衣服／~ behaviour 有失体统的举止

unbeknown /ˌʌnbɪˈnəʊn/
adj. (with **to**) without the knowledge of 不为⋯⋯所知的：They arrived ~ to us. 他们到了，我们还不知道。

unbelievable /ˌʌnbɪˈliːvəbl/
adj. very surprising；difficult to believe 难以置信的：~ but true 虽然难以相信，却是真实的

unbend /ˌʌnˈbend/
v. behave in an informal manner，especially when usually formal；relax 松弛，放松：~ one's mind 放松心情

unbias(s)ed /ʌnˈbaɪəst/
adj. without bias；not prejudiced；fair 不偏心的；没有偏见的；公平的

unbolt /ʌnˈbəʊlt/
v. open by drawing a bolt 拉开闩：~ a door 拔闩开门

unbounded /ʌnˈbaʊndɪd/
adj. without limit；excessive 无限的；过多的

unbroken /ʌnˈbrəʊkən/
adj. ❶ without a break；continuous 未中断的；继续不断的：They had a life of ~ happiness. 他们的生活一直很幸福。 ❷ (with reference to records) not beaten (指纪录)未被打破的：His time for the mile is still ~. 他跑一英里的时间纪录仍未被打破。 ❸ (with reference to a horse，etc.) not tamed or trained (指马等)未驯服的，未受训练的

unburden /ˌʌnˈbɜːdn/
v. get rid of a burden；make easier 使卸去负担；使轻松：He ~ed his mind by telling me everything that was worrying him. 他把烦恼的事情全部告诉了我，解除了思想负担。／He ~ed himself to me. 他向我倾诉衷肠。

unbutton /ˌʌnˈbʌtn/
v. open the buttons of 解开⋯⋯的纽扣：~ a shirt 解开衬衫的纽扣

uncalled /ʌnˈkɔːld/
adj. (with **for**) not necessary；not justified 不必要的；没有理由的：His anger was ~ for when everybody was being very friendly to him. 在大家都对他非常友好时，他生气是没有道理的。

uncertain /ʌnˈsɜːtn/
adj. ❶ not known with certainty；unable to decide；not certain 不能确定的；不能断定的，不肯定的：I'm ~ of his age. 我不能确定他的年龄。／We are ~ if the candidate will win. 我们不能断定这个候选人是否会赢。 ❷ changeable；not reliable 多变的；靠不住的：~ situation 不稳定的时局

uncertainty /ʌnˈsɜːtnti/
n. (*pl.* -ies) ❶ the state of being uncertain 不确定性；不确信；靠不住：situation of ~ and danger 不确定而危险的处境 ❷ the state of being uncertain 犹豫；迟疑；无把握：He had an air of ~ about him. 他显出将信将疑的神情。

uncharted /ˌʌnˈtʃɑːtɪd/
adj. not shown on a map；not explored so as to be shown on a map 地图上未标明的；未经探查的

unchecked /ˌʌnˈtʃekt/
adj. not checked；not controlled or stopped 未受制止的；未加控制的；未被阻挡的：the enemy's ~ advance 敌人的长驱直入

uncivilized /ˈʌnˈsɪvɪlaɪzd/
adj. rough，cruel and ignorant in behaviour，etc. 粗鲁的；残酷的；愚昧无知的；未开化的

unclassified /ʌnˈklæsɪfaɪd/

adj.not classified 未分类的；无类别的：
Many texts remain 〜.很多文本尚未归
类。

uncle/ˈʌŋkl/
n.❶the brother of one's father or mother 伯
父；叔父；舅父 ❷ the husband of one's
aunt 姑父；姨父

unclean/ˌʌnˈkliːn/
adj.not clean 不洁的；肮脏的

uncomfortable/ʌnˈkʌmf(ə)təbl/
adj.not comfortable；uneasy 不舒适的；不
安的；不自在的：an 〜 seat 不舒适的座
位/ feel 〜 with strangers 和陌生人在一
起感到不自在

uncommon/ʌnˈkɒmən/
adj.unusual；remarkable 不普通的；罕见
的；不平凡的；显著的：an 〜 word 一个罕
见的字

uncompromising/ʌnˈkɒmprəmaɪzɪŋ/
adj.not ready to make any compromise；
refusing to come to an agreement or to
change any of one's opinions 不妥协的；
不肯通融的；不让步的：He is an 〜 de-
fender of freedom.他是一个坚定的自由
卫士。

unconcerned/ˌʌnkənˈsɜːnd/
adj.not concerned；not worried or anxious
漠不关心的；无忧无虑的；淡漠的：He is
〜 with school affairs.他对学校的事务漠
不关心。

unconscious/ʌnˈkɒnʃəs/
adj.not conscious about what is happening 失去知觉的；昏迷的；不自觉的：He
was 〜 for two days after the accident.事
故发生后，他昏迷了两天。‖ be 〜 of 没
有意识到……

uncountable/ʌnˈkaʊntəbl/
adj.that cannot be counted or used with a
or an 不可数的：The 〜 noun is marked
in that dictionary.在那本词典中，不可数
名词已被标明。

uncouple/ʌnˈkʌpl/
v.separate（especially joined railway car-
riages）；free from being fastened together
解开（尤指连接的火车车厢的）挂钩；使
分离；放开；松开

uncover/ʌnˈkʌvə(r)/
v.❶remove a cover from sth.移去……的
盖子（或覆盖物）：〜 a kettle 揭开水壶的
盖子 ❷ make known 揭露：〜 a plot 揭
露一项阴谋

uncritical/ˌʌnˈkrɪtɪkl/
adj.not willing to criticize 不加批评的；
不置可否的

uncurl/ˌʌnˈkɜːl/
v.straighten sth. out or be straightened
out from a curled state 弄直（卷曲状态）；
使（卷曲物）伸直；变直：The new leaves
〜 in spring.春天新叶伸展开来。

uncut/ˌʌnˈkʌt/
adj.❶（of a film or story）not made shorter,e.g.by having violent or sexually improper scenes removed（电影或故事）未
加删节的，未剪辑的：the 〜 version of
Lady Chatterley's Lover 影片《查泰莱夫
人的情人》的未剪辑版本 ❷（of a dia-
mond or other precious stone）not shaped
and formed for wearing（钻石、宝石等）
未经琢磨的；未切割雕琢的

undaunted/ˌʌnˈdɔːntɪd/
adj.not at all discouraged or frightened
by danger or difficulty 无畏的；勇敢的；
不泄气的

undeceive/ˌʌndɪˈsiːv/
v.inform（someone）of the truth,espe-
cially when they are mistaken 使不受迷
惑；使醒悟；使明白真相：She thought he
was a famous film director,but I had to
〜 her.她以为他是一位著名的电影导
演,但我得把真相告诉她。

undecided/ˌʌndɪˈsaɪdɪd/
adj.❶not having made a decision 迟疑不
决的；拿不准的：He was 〜 whether to
go or stay.他决定不了是去是留。❷not
settled or resolved 未定的；未决的

undeniable/ˌʌndɪˈnaɪəbl/
adj.clearly and certainly unable to be denied 无可否认的；确实的：〜 ability 无可
否认的能力

under/ˈʌndə(r)/
prep.❶ in or to a lower position than 在
……下面：There's a man 〜 the tree.树
下有个人。❷ less than 少于；低于：chil-
dren of ten and 〜 十岁及十岁以下的儿

童/Children ～ six are not allowed to go to school in many countries.在许多国家,六岁以下的儿童不能入学。❸ used to express dominance or control 在……的控制下;在……管理下;受制于:～ the control (rule,leadership,etc.) of 在……的控制(统治、领导等)下 ❹ undergoing (a process)在(过程)中:～ discussion 正在讨论/～ construction 正在修建 ‖ go ～ 失败;屈服/keep (bring) ～ 控制;压制

underachieve/ˌʌndərəˈtʃiːv/
*v.*perform worse than one could,especially at one's school work 未能充分发挥(学习等的)能力;学习成绩不理想

underact/ˌʌndərˈækt/
*v.*act (a part in a play) with very little force 表演(角色)不充分;未尽情表演

underage/ˌʌndərˈeɪdʒ/
*adj.*done by people who are too young by law 未成年的;未及法定年龄的;年龄太小的

underarm/ˈʌndərɑːm/
*adj.*of the armpit 腋下的:～ pass in basketball 腋下传球

underbrush/ˈʌndəbrʌʃ/
*n.*low trees growing among taller ones 矮树丛;下层林丛

undercarriage/ˈʌndəˌkærɪdʒ/
*n.*the landing gear of an aircraft (飞机的)起落架;飞机脚架

undercharge/ˌʌndəˈtʃɑːdʒ/
*v.*not charge enough in price 对……少算了价钱;对……少要价

underclass /ˈʌndəˌklɑːs/
*n.*the lowest social group in a community,consisting of the poor and the unemployed 下层社会

underclothes/ˈʌndəkləʊðz/
*n.*underwear 内衣裤:Have you packed my vest and other ～? 你收了我的背心和其他内衣吗?

undercoat /ˈʌndəkəʊt/
*n.*❶ a layer of paint under a finishing coat;the paint used for this 底涂层;内涂层;底层涂料 ❷ (of animals) a coat of hair under another (动物)下层绒毛

undercover/ˌʌndəˈkʌvə(r)/
*adj.*working or done in secret 秘密进行的:The jeweler was an ～ agent of the police.这个珠宝商是警察的暗探。

undercurrent/ˈʌndəkʌrənt/
*n.*a hidden movement or feeling 暗流;潜流;潜在的情绪:There is an ～ of anger in their behaviour.他们的举止中有一种潜在的愤怒情绪。

undercut/ˌʌndəˈkʌt/
*v.*sell goods or services more cheaply than (a competitor) 削价与(竞争者)抢生意;低于(竞争者)的价格出售(商品或服务)

underdeveloped/ˌʌndədɪˈveləpt/
*adj.*not yet fully developed 不够发达的;发育不全的:～ countries 欠发达国家

underdog/ˈʌndədɒg/
*n.*a person who usually loses;one neglected or oppressed by others 常输的人;输家;被忽视的人;受压迫的人

underdone/ˌʌndəˈdʌn/
*adj.*not completely cooked 半生不熟的

underestimate/ˌʌndərˈestɪmeɪt/
*v.*guess too low a value for (an amount) 低估:It's wrong to overestimate the enemy and ～ the people.过高估计敌人的力量,低估人民的力量都是错误的。

underfeed/ˌʌndəˈfiːd/
v.(underfed) ❶ feed too little;not give enough food or fuel to 不给吃饱;不给足燃料:The scientist ～ the mice.那科学家不让那些老鼠吃饱。 ❷ stoke with coal or other fuel from the bottom 从底部加燃料:～ the boiler with coal 从下部给锅炉加煤

undergo/ˌʌndəˈgəʊ/
v. have an unpleasant experience;suffer from 经历;遭受:China has ～ne great changes in the past twenty years.中国在过去二十年经历了重大的变化。

undergraduate/ˌʌndəˈgrædʒuət/
n. a student who is doing a university course for a first degree 大学本科生;尚未毕业的大学生:All the ～s in the university will be taking their final exams next week.下周,这所大学的所有在校学生都要参加期终考试。

underground

I /'ʌndəgraund/ *adj.* ❶ under the ground 地（面）下的：～ passage 地下通道/an ～ tunnel 地道/～ railroad（railway）地下铁道 ❷ secret 秘密的；地下的：～ activities 秘密活动/～ newspaper 地下报纸 II /ˌʌndə'graund/ *adv.* ❶ under the surface of ground 在地下：Coal miners work ～.煤矿工人在井下工作。❷ secretly 秘密地：Under such conditions they had to go ～.在这种情况下，他们不得不转入地下工作。

undergrowth /'ʌndəgrauθ/

n. smaller trees or bushes growing among taller trees（长在大树下的）小树，灌木丛

underhand(ed) /ˌʌndə'hænd(ɪd)/

adj. secret；deceitful；sly 秘密的；欺诈的；阴险的：an ～ action 诡秘的行动/an ～ scheme 阴险的计划/～ methods 卑鄙的手段

underlie /ˌʌndə'laɪ/

v. form the basis of a theory, conduct, behaviour, etc. 构成……的基础：The principles which ～ our foreign policy are sound.我们外交政策基础的原则是健全的。

underline /ˌʌndə'laɪn/

v. draw a line under；emphasize sth. 在……下面画线；强调：He ～d the importance of unity in his speech. 他在讲话中强调了团结的重要性。

underlying /ˌʌndə'laɪɪŋ/

adj. ❶ existing under or beneath sth. else 位于……之下的；下层的：～ strata 下层 ❷ basic；fundamental 基本的，根本的：～ principles 基本原则

undermine /ˌʌndə'maɪn/

v. weaken or destroy gradually 逐渐损坏；破坏：The enemy tried to ～ our friendship.敌人竭力破坏我们的友谊。

underneath /ˌʌndə'niːθ/

prep. & adv. to or at a lower position than...；under；below 到或处于比……低的位置；在……之下：We can sit ～ this tree.我们可以坐在这棵树下面。/Someone was pushing up from ～.有人从下面往上推。

underpants /'ʌndəpænts/

n. underclothes especially for men, covering the lower part of the body and sometimes the top part of the legs（尤指男人的）衬裤，内裤

underpass /'ʌndəpɑːs/

n. a passage, path, or road built beneath a road or railway line（在铁路或公路下面建造的）地下通道；下穿交叉道；高架桥下通道

underpay /ˌʌndə'peɪ/

v. pay（someone）too little for his or her work 少付（某人）工资；付给……低于正常的工资：They're overworked and underpaid! 他们超额工作，可是所得工资却不足额！

underpin /ˌʌndə'pɪn/

v. ❶ support（especially a wall）from below, e.g. by means of a solid piece of material 加强地下基础；用东西支撑（墙等）❷ give strength or support to（especially an argument）支持；加强（尤指论点）：A solid basis of evidence ～ned her theory. 有力的证据证实了她的论点。

underplay /ˌʌndə'pleɪ/

v. ❶ make sth. appear less important than it really is；play down 淡化（贬低）重要性；轻描淡写 ❷ underact 表演（角色）不充分；有节制地表演 ‖ ～ one's hand 小心行事，不露锋芒

underrate /ˌʌndə'reɪt/

v. have too low an opinion of the quality of；underestimate 对……评价过低；低估；看轻；轻视：It would be dangerous to ～ his ability.低估他的能力是危险的。/ a much ～d film 一部被评价过低的影片

undersecretary /ˌʌndə-'sekrətri/

n. ❶ a person who is in charge of the daily work of a government department, either a member of parliament of the governing party or a civil servant, and who helps and advises a minister in the UK（英国的）职位较低的大臣，政务次官 ❷（in other countries）a very high official in a government department（其他国家的）副部长

U

undersell/ˌʌndəˈsel/

　　v. (undersold) ❶ sell goods at a lower price than (a business competitor) 以低于(竞争者)的价格出售 ❷ put too low a value on the good qualities of (a person or thing), especially when persuading or selling (尤指在推荐或出售时)过低评价(人或物): I think he undersold himself at the job interview. 我认为他在求职面谈时对自己的评价太低了。

underside/ˈʌndəsaɪd/

　　n. the part below; the lower side or surface 下侧；下面；底部: The ~ of the rock was covered with seaweed. 岩石的下面布满了海草。

undersigned/ˌʌndəˈsaɪnd/

　　n. a person whose signature appears beneath the writing (信函、文件等末尾的)签字人；署名人: Both the ~ are bound by the contract. 签约双方都必须遵守合同。

understand/ˌʌndəˈstænd/

　　v. (understood) ❶ get the meaning (of) 懂；了解；理解: I wish you could ~ me. 但愿你能理解我。 ❷ know or believe sth. because you have been told 据信；获悉；听说: I understood from him that you were going to study abroad. 我从他那里获悉你打算出国留学。 ❸ assume to be the case; take for granted 认为……理所当然；视……不言而喻: It is understood that he has the ability to do it. 谁都相信他有能力干这事。 ‖ give sb. to ~ 让某人认为/make oneself understood 清楚表达自己的意思/~ one another (each other) 相互了解 ‖ ~able *adj.* 可以理解的

understanding/ˌʌndəˈstændɪŋ/

　　Ⅰ *adj.* good at knowing how other people feel; sympathetic 善解人意的；有同情心的: She was helpful and ~ about what happened. 对所发生的事她既乐于相助又善于体谅。 Ⅱ *n.* ❶ the power of abstract thought 思维能力；理解力 ❷ the capacity for sympathizing 同情心: Her kindness and ~ were a great comfort to him. 她的仁慈和善解人意给了他很大安慰。 ❸ an informal agreement 非正式的协议: reach an ~ 达成默契 ‖ on the ~ that … 在……条件下

understate/ˌʌndəˈsteɪt/

　　v. not state strongly or fully enough 轻描淡写；不充分地陈述

understatement/ˈʌndəˈsteɪtmənt/

　　n. a statement that makes sth. seem less important, impressive, serious, etc. than it really is 轻描淡写的陈述；不充分的陈述: It is an ~ to say they are not very pleased. They are furious. 说他们不太高兴是把话说轻了，他们正怒不可遏呢。

understudy/ˈʌndəstʌdi/

　　Ⅰ *v.* study the part in play taken by another actor in case he is absent; act in the place of another actor 学习(某角色)准备当替角；代替(别的演员)演出 Ⅱ *n.* a person who has learned another's part in a play so as to act the part if necessary 预备演员；替角

undertake/ˌʌndəˈteɪk/

　　v. (undertook, ~n) ❶ start sth. or be responsible for sth. 着手；从事；承担: It's the most difficult job I've ever ~n. 这是我所从事的最困难的工作。 ❷ promise; agree 答应；同意: John undertook to get here by eight o'clock. 约翰答应8点前到达这里。 ‖ undertaking *n.* 从事的事情；承诺/~r *n.* 承办者

undertone/ˈʌndətəun/

　　n. a quiet voice or sound 低调；低音；小声: He spoke in an ~. 他低声说话。

underwater/ˌʌndəˈwɔːtə/

　　Ⅰ *adj.* situated, used, or done beneath the surface of water 水下的；供水下用的；水下生长的；水下操作的: ~ creatures 水生动物/an ~ camera 水下摄影机 Ⅱ *adv.* beneath the surface of water 在水下；在水中: The hippo spent a lot of time ~. 那头河马在水中待了很长时间。

underwear/ˈʌndəweə(r)/

　　n. clothes worn under outer garments, especially next to the skin 内衣: She washed her skirt, blouse and ~. 她洗了裙子、衬衫和内衣。

underworld/ˈʌndəwɜːld/

　　n. ❶ the place of departed spirits of the dead 阴间；地狱 ❷ the criminal world 黑社会；下流社会: In the west most of the gambling houses and brothels are controlled by the ～.在西方，赌场和妓院大多都由黑社会控制。

undesirable /ˌʌndɪˈzaɪərəbl/

I *adj.* not wanted, not welcomed; unpleasant 令人不快的；不受欢迎的；讨厌的：The result is ～.结果令人不快。II *n.* an unwanted person, especially someone regarded as immoral, criminal, or socially unacceptable 不受欢迎的人；讨厌的人；不良分子：Pickpockets are ～s.扒手都是些讨厌的家伙。

undeveloped /ˌʌndɪˈveləpt/

adj. not developed;(usually of a place) in its natural state（地区）不发达的；未发展的；未开发的：an ～ child 一个发育不全的孩子 / ～ natural resources 未开发的自然资源 / ～ land 未开发的土地

undistinguished /ˌʌndɪˈstɪŋgwɪʃt/

adj. not marked by good qualities;with no excellent ability,character,etc.不出色的；平凡的：～ record of service 平凡的服役记录

undivided /ˌʌndɪˈvaɪdɪd/

adj. complete 完整的：give ～ attention to sth.专心致力于某事

undo /ʌnˈduː/

v. ❶ untie or unfasten 解开；松开：Help me ～ this knot.请帮我解开这个结。❷ remove the effects of 消除；破坏；毁掉：What is done cannot be undone.覆水难收。‖ ～ing *n.*失败的原因

undone /ʌnˈdʌn/

adj. ❶ not tied or fastened 解开的；松开的：The top few buttons of his shirt were ～.他衬衫最上面几粒纽扣松开了。❷ not done or finished 未做的；未完成的：Most of the work was left ～.大多数工作还未完成。

undoubted /ʌnˈdaʊtɪd/

adj. certain; accepted as true 确定的；无疑的；真正的：There is an ～ improvement in his condition.他的情况有明显的好转。

undress /ʌnˈdres/

v. ❶ take the clothes off 脱去……的衣服：He ～ed his little son.他给小儿子脱去了衣服。❷ take one's clothes off 脱衣服：～ and get into bed 宽衣就寝

undue /ˌʌnˈdjuː/

adj. improper;too much 不适当的；过度的；过分的：～ emphasis on sth.过分强调某事 / ～ behaviour 不适当的行为

unearth /ʌnˈɜːθ/

v. dig up 发掘；发现：～ a treasure buried in the earth 挖出埋在地下的宝藏/ ～ a secret 揭开秘密

unearthly /ʌnˈɜːθli/

adj. not of this world; very strange and frightening 非尘世的；不属于现世的；怪异的；可怕的 ‖ at an ～ hour 过早地；在很不方便的时刻

uneasy /ʌnˈiːzi/

adj. not easy in body or mind;anxious 心神不安的；不舒服的；担心的：I feel ～ about his future.我对他的未来很担心。

uneducated /ʌnˈedʒʊkeɪtɪd/

adj. showing a lack of (good) education 没有教育的；缺乏教养的：They are poor because they are ～.他们贫穷是因为没有受到良好的教育。

unemployed /ˌʌnɪmˈplɔɪd/

adj. not having a job 未受雇用的；失业的

unemployment /ˌʌnɪmˈplɔɪmənt/

n. ❶ the state of being unemployed 失业：The closure of the factory will mean ～ for 200 workers.关闭这家工厂意味着将有 200 名工人失业。❷ the number of unemployed workers 失业人数：～ has increased 失业人数增加了

unequal /ʌnˈiːkwəl/

adj. not equal or balanced 不平等的；不均衡的：They do the same job but get ～ pay.他们同工不同酬。‖ be ～ to 不能胜任；干不了

uneven /ˈʌniːvən/

adj. ❶ not level or smooth 不平坦的；崎岖的；不平滑的 ❷ not regular or uniform 不规则的；不稳定的；不平均的：an ～ rhythm 不规则的节奏 ❸ not equally balanced 非势均力敌的：an ～ contest 一场实力悬殊的比赛 ‖ ～ly *adv.*不平坦地/ ～ness *n.*不均匀；参差不齐

unexceptional /ˌʌnɪkˈsepʃənl/
adj.not interesting or unusual 乏味的；平常的；不突出的；普通的

unexpected /ˌʌnɪksˈpektɪd/
adj. not expected or anticipated; not planned 出乎意料的；始料不及的；不在计划的：an ～ result 意想不到的结果/an ～ visitor 不速之客 ‖ ～**ly** *adv*.出乎意料地；没想到地

unfailing /ʌnˈfeɪlɪŋ/
adj.constant; that can be relied on 永恒的；忠实可靠的：～ interest 一贯的兴趣/an ～ friend 忠实可靠的朋友

unfair /ʌnˈfeə(r)/
adj.not just,reasonable,or honest 不公平的；不公正的；不正直的：～ treatment 不公平的待遇

unfaithful /ˌʌnˈfeɪθfl/
adj.not true to a promise; not faithful to marriage vows 不忠实的；(对婚姻)不忠贞的：an ～ friend 不忠实的朋友

unfavo(u)rable /ˌʌnˈfeɪvrəbl/
adj.❶expressing or showing a lack of approval or support 反对的；不赞同的：an ～ comment 负面的评论❷ adverse; inauspicious 不利的；有害的：The remarks were ～ for unity.这些话不利于团结。

unfeasible /ʌnˈfiːzəbl/
adj.inconvenient or impractical 不方便的；无法实现的：It is ～ here to put most finds from excavations on public display. 在这里公开陈列大部分出土文物是行不通的。

unfortunate /ʌnˈfɔːtʃənɪt/
adj.❶having bad luck; unlucky 倒霉的；不幸的：It was an ～ accident.那是一次不幸的事故。❷unsuitable or regrettable 不合适的；不当的：a most ～ position 十分可悲的处境

ungrateful /ʌnˈgreɪtfl/
adj. not expressing thanks, especially when thanks are deserved; not grateful 不感激的；忘恩负义的：He is an ～ man.他是个忘恩负义的人。

unguarded /ˌʌnˈgɑːdɪd/
adj. unwisely careless, especially in speech (尤指讲话)不留神的；粗心大意的；无防备的：I agreed to do it in an ～

moment, and I've regretted it ever since. 我一时轻率答应做这事，之后一直很后悔。/an ～ remark 不小心说漏的话

unhappily /ʌnˈhæpɪli/
adv.❶in an unhappy way 不高兴地❷unfortunately 遗憾地；不幸地：Unhappily, she was not able to complete the course.很遗憾，她不能修完这门课程。

unhappy /ʌnˈhæpi/
adj.not happy; sad and depressed 不愉快的；不高兴的；痛苦的；不幸福的：He thought of his ～ life in the past.他回忆起了他过去的痛苦生活。

unhealthy /ʌnˈhelθi/
adj.not in good health; likely to cause poor health 不健康的；有害健康的：an ～ person 有病的/an ～ habit 不良习惯

unheard /ʌnˈhɜːd/
adj.not listened to; not heard 没人理会的；没听到的：His complaints went ～.他的抱怨没人听。 ‖ ～**-of** *adj*.闻所未闻的；空前的

unidentified /ˌʌnaɪˈdentɪfaɪd/
adj.of which the name, nature or origin has not been found or given 身份不明的；来历不明的；无从辨识的：an ～ man 身份不明的人/～ flying object (UFO) 飞碟；不明飞行物

uniform /ˈjuːnɪfɔːm/
Ⅰ *adj*.the same; not changing 相同的；一致的；始终如一的：～ temperature 恒温/a ～ size 大小一样/a ～ pace 整齐的步伐/～ friendship 始终如一的友谊 Ⅱ *n*. clothes worn by all members of a group 统一的服装；制服：They must go to school in ～.他们必须穿制服上学。 ‖ ～**ity** /ˈjuːnɪfɔːmɪti/ *n*.完全一致

unify /ˈjuːnɪfaɪ/
v.make parts into one whole (使)统一；使一致：～ a country 统一一个国家/～ all the money systems 统一所有的货币制度 ‖ **unified** *adj*.统一的；一致的/**unification** /ˌjuːnɪfɪˈkeɪʃn/ *n*.统一

unilateral /ˌjuːnɪˈlætrəl/
adj.done by or having an effect on only one side, especially one of the political groups in an agreement 单方面的；片面

的：～ disarmament 单方面裁军/a ～ withdrawal of troops 单方面撤军

unimportant /ˌʌnɪmˈpɔːtənt/

adj. not important 不重要的；次要的；无足轻重的：～ details 细枝末节

uninformed /ˌʌnɪnˈfɔːmd/

adj. showing a lack of knowledge or enough information 未被告知的；无知的：He was absent from the meeting because he was ～ of it. 他未到会是因为他没得到通知。

uninterested /ʌnˈɪntrəstɪd/

adj. having or showing no interest in sb. or sth. 不感兴趣的；漠不关心的：I'm ～ in computer games. 我对电子游戏不感兴趣。

uninteresting /ʌnˈɪntrɪstɪŋ/

adj. not interesting 无趣味的；没意思的：The story was very interesting, but he told it in a very ～ way. 这故事本来很有趣，但他讲出来就索然无味了。

union /ˈjuːnjən/

n. ❶ the act or state of uniting or joining 团结；联合；合并：In ～ there is strength. 团结就是力量。 ❷ an association for a group of people 联合会；协会：A trade ～ is a group of workers who have joined together. 工会是由工人组织的团体。

unique /juːˈniːk/

adj. ❶ having no equal; being the only one 唯一的；独一无二的：The writer has his own ～ style. 那位作家有他自己独特的风格。 ❷ often considered nonstandard; unusual 稀罕的；不寻常的：～ dress 奇装异服/a ～ animal 珍稀动物

unison /ˈjuːnɪsn, ˈjuːnɪzn/

n. the doing of sth. by everyone in agreement or at the same time 和谐；一致：sing in ～ 齐唱/act in ～ 一致行动/answer in ～ 齐声回答

unit /ˈjuːnɪt/

n. ❶ an individual thing or person regarded as single and complete, especially for purposes of calculation 单位；单元：The family is the basic ～ of society. 家庭是社会的基本单位。 ❷ an amount or quantity used as a standard of measurement (计

量)单位：An ounce is a ～ of weight. 盎司是重量的单位。

unite /juːˈnaɪt/

v. ❶ join together into one 联合；团结；合并；统一：These two companies are planning to ～. 这两家公司打算合并。 ❷ act together for a purpose 协力；一致行动：Let's ～ to overcome the present difficulty. 让我们齐心协力共渡难关。 ‖ ～d *adj.* 联合的；团结一致的；共同的：the United Nations 联合国

unity /ˈjuːnəti/

n. ❶ concord between two or more persons; harmony 协调；和谐：The argument spoilt their ～. 争吵伤了他们的和气。 ❷ the state of being one, or the condition of being united 统一；团结；联合；一致：A nation has more ～ than a group of tribes. 一个国家比一群部落更为统一。/ Unity is strength. 团结就是力量。

universal /ˌjuːnɪˈvɜːsəl/

adj. ❶ of the whole world 全世界的；宇宙的：a ～ peace 世界和平 / ～ gravitation 万有引力 ❷ affecting all; general; of or for all 影响全体的；普遍的；普通的；全体的：a ～ rule 普遍规律 / ～ applause 全场的喝彩/～ misery 普遍的苦难

universally /ˌjuːnɪˈvɜːsəli/

adv. by everyone; in every case 普遍地；无一例外地：Reform is not always ～ welcomed. 并非人人都一直欢迎改革。

universe /ˈjuːnɪvɜːs/

n. everything that exists everywhere; the whole of space and all the stars, planets and other forms of matter 宇宙；天地万物：Our world is but a small part of the ～. 我们的世界只是宇宙的一小部分。

university /ˌjuːnɪˈvɜːsɪti/

n. (*pl.*-ies) an educational institution that provides instruction and facilities for research in many branches of advanced learning, and which awards degrees 大学：My sister is at ～. 我妹妹正在读大学。

unjust /ˌʌnˈdʒʌst/

adj. not right or fair, not just 不公平的；不公道的；非正义的：It's ～ to punish a person who has done nothing wrong. 去惩罚一个毫无过错的人是不公道的。

unkind/ˌʌnˈkaɪnd/

adj. not kind; cruel 不亲切的；无情的；残酷的：It's not right to be ~ to the beggar. 对那乞丐不仁慈是不对的。

unknown/ˌʌnˈnəʊn/

adj. ❶ not known; not familiar; strange 不知道的；不熟悉的；陌生的：an ~ helper 暗中帮忙的人/an ~ language 不熟悉的语言 ❷ not famous; not well known 不出名的；知名度不高的：an ~ singer 一位不出名的歌手

unless/ʌnˈles/

conj. ❶ if not; except; if it were not that 除非：We shall go there ~ it rains. 我们会去那儿，除非下雨。❷ except when… 除……时之外：The directors usually have a meeting every Friday, ~ there is nothing to discuss. 经理们通常每周五开一次会，无事讨论时除外。

unlike/ʌnˈlaɪk/

Ⅰ *prep*. not like; different from 不像……；和……不同：His son is ~ him in every respect. 他的儿子没有一处像他。/ This photo is quite ~ her. 这张照片一点儿不像她。Ⅱ *adj*. different; not the same 不同的；不相似的：~ poles 异极/These two cases are quite ~. 这两种情况完全不同。

unlikely/ʌnˈlaɪkli/

adj. improbable; not likely to happen or be true 未必可能的；靠不住的：an ~ story 不像是真的故事 / He is ~ to come to the meeting. 他未必可能来参加会议。/That he will win the race is ~. 他不见得会在比赛中获胜。

unload/ʌnˈləʊd/

v. ❶ remove (a load) from 从……卸下（货物）：~ a truck 从卡车上卸下货物 / The ship will ~ tomorrow. 这只船明天卸货。❷ get rid of (sth. not wanted or the responsibility) 解除……的拖累；甩掉……的包袱：~ one's mind 解脱心头的焦虑 /Unload your trouble onto me. 把你的烦恼告诉我。

unlock/ʌnˈlɒk/

v. use a key to open the lock of 开……的锁：~ a door 开门上的锁

unmoved/ʌnˈmuːvd/

adj. showing no pity or sympathy 不受感动的；无动于衷的；镇静的：No matter what happens, he always remains ~. 无论发生什么事，他总是很冷静。

unnatural/ʌnˈnætʃrəl/

adj. not natural; unusual 不自然的；不正常的：give an ~ laugh 不自然地笑/an ~ reaction 不正常的反应

unnecessary/ʌnˈnesəsri/

adj. not necessary or wanted 不必要的；多余的；无用的：cut out ~ words 删掉不必要的字 / with ~ care 怀着不必要的顾虑

unpack/ʌnˈpæk/

v. remove (possessions) from (a container) 从（包裹或箱子等）拿出东西；打开（包裹或行李等）取出东西：~ one's clothes（开箱等）取出衣服 /~ a trunk 开箱取物

unpick/ˌʌnˈpɪk/

v. take out the stitches from 将……的针线拆开：Her mother ~ed the dress and sewed it again. 她母亲拆开了衣服的针线，再重新缝上。

unpleasant/ʌnˈpleznt/

adj. causing dislike; not enjoyable; disagreeable 使人不愉快的；不合意的；讨厌的：an ~ sight 令人不快的情景

unprecedented/ʌnˈpresɪdentɪd/

adj. never happened before 没有先例的；空前的：We have achieved an ~ great victory. 我们取得了一次史无前例的伟大胜利。

unqualified/ʌnˈkwɒlɪfaɪd/

adj. not having suitable knowledge or qualifications 不合格的；没有资格的：He's quite ~ for his work. 他的工作是非常不合格的。

unquestionable/ʌnˈkwestʃənəbl/

adj. which cannot be doubted; certain 不容置疑的；确实的：The fact is ~. 事实不容置疑。

unquestioning/ʌnˈkwestʃənɪŋ/

adj. without any doubt, delay, or argu-

ment 无异议的;毫无疑问的;不犹豫的:
～ obedience 无条件的服从

unquiet/ˌʌnˈkwaɪət/

adj.not calm or at rest 不平静的;不安的

unquote/ˌʌnˈkwəʊt/

adv. a word used in speech for showing that one has come to the end of a quotation (说话中用以表示引语结束):The figures given are (quote) "not to be trusted"(～),according to this writer.根据这位作家所说,所提供的数字(引语开始) "是不可信的"(引语结束)。

unreadable/ˌʌnˈriːdəbl/

adj.❶too dull to be read;not worth reading 不值一读的;无可读性的;不能读的 ❷illegible 难辨认的;字迹不清的

unreal/ˌʌnˈrɪəl/

adj.seeming more like a dream than reality 不真实的;想象的;虚假的:It's quite wrong to think everything is ～.认为一切东西都是虚假的是十分错误的。 ‖ ～**ity**/ˌʌnrɪˈælɪti/ *n*.不真实;空想;虚构的事物

unreasonable/ˌʌnˈriːznəbl/

adj.unfair in demands;not sensible 无理的;不合理的;过分的:Don't make any ～ demands on me.不要向我提任何无理的要求。

unreasoning/ˌʌnˈriːznɪŋ/

adj.not using or influenced by the power of reason 不理智的;无理性的;不讲理的:～ anger 盲目冲动的怒火

unrelenting/ˌʌnrɪˈlentɪŋ/

adj. continuous; without decreasing in power or effort 持续不断的;不松懈的;不屈不挠的:a week of ～ activity 一个星期的紧张不懈的活动

unrelieved/ˌʌnrɪˈliːvd/

adj.(of sth.bad) not varied in any way; continuous or complete (不好的事物)未减轻的,未得到缓解的,未解除的;无变化的:～ anxiety (gloom,hardship) 未消除的忧虑(未减轻的忧郁、未减轻的困苦)

unremitting/ˌʌnrɪˈmɪtɪŋ/

adj.(of sth. difficult) never stopping; continuous (困难的事物)不间断的,不停

的,持续的:～ activity 不间断的活动

unreserved/ˌʌnrɪˈzɜːvd/

adj.without limits or reservations;frank 毫无保留的;坦白的:You can have my ～ support.我会毫无保留地支持你。/～ nature 坦率的性格

unseasonable/ʌnˈsiːznəbl/

adj.(of weather) unusual for the time of year,especially bad (气候)不合时令的,不合季节的

unseat/ʌnˈsiːt/

v.❶ (of a horse) throw off (a rider) (马)把(骑手)摔下来;使坠马 ❷remove from a position of power,e.g.a seat in a parliament 夺去(议员等)的席位;革除(职位)

unseeded/ˌʌnˈsiːdɪd/

adj.not chosen as a seed,especially in a tennis competition (尤指网球赛中)未被选为种子选手的;(球员)非种子的

unseeing/ˌʌnˈsiːɪŋ/

adj.not noticing anything;(as if) blind 视而不见的;不注意的;(似)看不见的:She stared out of the window with ～ eyes.她以视而不见的目光凝望着窗外。

unseemly/ʌnˈsiːmli/

adj. not proper or suitable (in behaviour);likely to attract disapproval (举止)不得体的;不合时宜的;易遭非议的:They left with ～ haste.他们不合乎礼仪地急匆匆离去。

unshakable/ʌnˈʃeɪkəbl/

adj.firm,especially in belief or loyalty 坚定不移的;不可动摇的:We have an ～ confidence in our bright future.我们对光辉灿烂的前途有着坚定不移的信心。

unsound/ˌʌnˈsaʊnd/

adj.not in good condition 不健康的;不健全的;不稳固的:The foundation of the building is ～.那幢大楼的根基不牢固。

unspeakable/ʌnˈspiːkəbl/

adj. ❶ that cannot be expressed or described in words 不能用言语表达的;无法形容的:～ joy 无法形容的快乐 / ～ wickedness 无法形容的邪恶 ❷ terrible 极恶劣的:His manners are ～.他的态度非常恶劣。

U

unthinkable/ʌnˈθɪŋkəbl/
adj.that cannot be considered;inconceiva-
ble 难以想象的;难以相信的;不可考虑
的;It would be ～ for him to resign now.
很难想象他现在要辞职。

untidy/ʌnˈtaɪdi/
adj.in disorder;not tidy 凌乱的;不整洁的;
不修边幅的;an ～ room 不整洁的房间

untie/ʌnˈtaɪ/
v.❶ loosen or unfasten a knot,etc.解开;
松开:～ a knot 解开一个结 ❷ make
free;release 释放;使自由:Untie the
prisoners and set them free.释放囚犯,让
他们自由。

until/ʌnˈtɪl/
prep & *conj*.❶up to a certain time or event
直到……为止:We work ～ 10 o'clock.我们
工作到 10 点钟。/He laughed ～ tears
rolled down his face.他一直笑到流出了
眼泪。❷（in negative）before a certain
time or event（用于否定句）在……之前:
He didn't get up ～ 8 o'clock.他一直睡
到 8 点钟才起床。

untimely/ʌnˈtaɪmli/
adj.not suitable for the occasion;inoppor-
tune 不适时的;不合时宜的;～ remarks
不合时宜的话/an ～ visit 不合时宜的访
问

untiring/ʌnˈtaɪrɪŋ/
adj.never stopping or showing tiredness,
especially in spite of hard work 孜孜不倦
的;不知疲倦的;坚持不懈的:feel ～ 不
知疲倦/～ efforts 坚持不懈的努力

untold/ʌnˈtəʊld/
adj.❶ not told or expressed 未说的;没
有讲出来的:His story remained ～.他的
故事还是没有讲出来。❷ too great to be
counted or measured;limitless 数不尽
的;无数的;无限的:～ wealth 无数的财
富/～ suffering 说不尽的苦难

untrue/ʌnˈtruː/
adj.false;not true 虚假的;不真实的:be
～ to sb.对某人不忠实 ‖ **untruth** *n*.谎言;
假话

unusual/ʌnˈjuːʒʊəl/
adj.not usual;rare;strange 不寻常的;少
有的;独特的:It is ～ for girls to play

football.女孩子踢足球很少见。

unusually/ʌnˈjuːʒəli/
adv.❶very;more than is usual 非常:It's
～ hot today.今天天气非常热。❷in an
unusual way 不寻常地

unutterable/ʌnˈʌtərəbl/
adj.of the greatest or worst kind;terrible
（大得或坏得）无法用言语表达的;十足
的,彻头彻尾的;糟透的:in ～ pain 处于
极其疼痛的状态/an ～ fool 十足的蠢货

unvarnished/ʌnˈvɑːnɪʃt/
adj.plain;without additional description
未加修饰的;未加渲染的;率直的:Just
give me the plain ～ truth.直截了当地告
诉我事实好了。

unveil/ˌʌnˈveɪl/
v.remove a covering from;show sth.to
the public 除去面纱;揭开覆盖物;揭露;
公开:He ～ed himself finally as a traitor
to his country.他自己最终暴露出来是国
家叛徒。

unwind/ʌnˈwaɪnd/
v.wind off;become unwound 打开;解开;
旋开;放松:～ a bandage 打开绷带/～
oneself 使自己放松

unwrap/ʌnˈræp/
v.(-pp-)❶ open sth.wrapped or folded 打
开(包好或折叠好的东西):She ～ped the
parcel.她打开了包裹。❷ disclose sth.,
especially sth.unpleasant 揭示:The
newspaper ～ped the case in great detail.
报纸详细地披露了案情。

up/ʌp/
Ⅰ *prep*.❶ to or in a higher position 向,
在(较高位置):The tide's ～.潮水上涨
了。❷ along 沿着;顺着:We walked ～
the highway.我们顺着公路走。Ⅱ *adv*.❶
to or in a higher place or position 向上;
向较高处:stand ～ 站起来/get ～ 起床
❷to the place where sb.or sth.is 朝(某人
或某物)的方向;向……地方:walk
(come) ～ 走上前来 ❸at or in a higher
position;above 在高处:The plane is flying ～ in the sky.飞机在高空飞行。❹ so
as to be completely finished 彻底地;完全
地:use ～ 用光/eat ～ 吃光/Time is ～.
时间到了。❺at or towards a higher lev-

el,e.g.in price or quantity;from a smaller to a larger amount（价格、数量等）由低到高;上升:The price of food was ～.食品价格上涨了。❻ at or to a higher level of intensity（强度等）由弱到强;由低到高:Speak ～.讲大声点。/Turn the radio ～.把收音机开大声些。‖ be ～ to（do）打算做……/be ～ to sb.to（do）应由某人做;由某人决定/bring … ～ to date 使……现代化/be ～ to the mark（standard, etc.）达到要求（标准等）/be well ～ in（on）通晓,对……很熟悉/～ and down 来回;上下/～ to（till）直到;到……为止

upbringing/ˈʌpbrɪŋɪŋ/

　　n. the care, training, and education that someone receives, especially from their parents,when they are growing up（对儿童的)教育;培养:Many parents are very concerned about the ～ of their children.许多父母很关心孩子的教育和培养。

upcoming/ˈʌpˌkʌmɪŋ/

　　*adj.*about to happen 即将来临的;即将发生的;the ～ elections 即将举行的选举

update/ˌʌpˈdeɪt/

　　Ⅰ *v.*❶ make more modern or up-to-date 更新;使现代化;使不过时:an ～d model of this popular car 这种流行轿车的最新型号 ❷ supply with the latest information 为……提供最新的情况（信息）:The minister's advisers ～ her on the situation.部长的顾问们给她讲了最新的形势。Ⅱ*n.*an act of modernizing and providing with the most recent information 更新;现代化:a computer file ～ 计算机文件更新;电脑档案更新

upend/ʌpˈend/

　　*v.*❶cause to stand on end or on any part that does not usually stand on the floor 使倒立;倒放;颠倒 ❷ knock down 击倒;打倒:He ～ed his opponent with a single punch.他一拳就打倒了对手。

upfront/ˌʌpˈfrʌnt/

　　*adj.*very direct and making no attempt to hide one's meaning 坦率的;无保留的:He's very ～ about his political views.他毫不隐瞒自己的政治观点。

upgrade/ˌʌpˈgreɪd/

*v.*put in a higher grade 使升级;提升

uphill/ˌʌpˈhɪl/

　　Ⅰ*adj.*❶sloping upwards 向上的;上坡的 ❷ difficult; needing lots of effort 困难的;费力的:～ work 困难的工作 Ⅱ*adv.*on an upward slope 上坡

uphold/ˌʌpˈhəʊld/

　　v.（upheld) ❶ hold up; support 支撑:Walls ～ the roof.墙壁支撑着屋顶。❷ give support to;maintain 支持;维持:The principal upheld the teacher's decision.校长支持老师的决定。❸ confirm 确认;批准:The higher court has upheld the decision of the lower court.上级法院批准了下级法院的判决。

upkeep/ˈʌpkiːp/

　　*n.*the cost or process of keeping sth.in good condition and working order 保养;维修;维修费;保养费:You can buy a car but you may not afford the ～ of it.你能买一辆车,但你很可能维修不起它。

upon/əˈpɒn/

　　prep.＝on 根据;接近;在……之上:rest ～ 依靠

upper/ˈʌpə(r)/

　　*adj.*higher in rank; situated above 较高的;上面的;上层的;上首的:～ lip 上唇/the Upper House（英国议会的)上议院/the ～ class 上流社会

upright/ˈʌpraɪt/

　　Ⅰ*adv.*in or into a vertical position 笔直地;stand ～ 笔直地站着 Ⅱ*adj.*❶vertical;erect 挺直的,竖立的;an ～ post 一根直立的杆子 ❷ just;honest 正直的;诚实的:It's a pleasure to work with ～ people.与正直的人一起共事令人愉快。

uprising/ˈʌpˌraɪzɪŋ/

　　*n.*an act of the ordinary people suddenly and violently opposing those in power;rebellion 起义;暴动:There were many ～s against the slavery in history.在历史上曾发生过无数次反抗奴隶制的起义。

uproar/ˈʌprɔː(r)/

　　n.（usually with **an**) a loud and impassioned noise and shouting（通常与 an 连用）喧闹（声）;鼓噪（声）;喧嚣（声）:There was an ～ when he told them they had all

U

failed in the examination. 他告诉他们说他们考试都不及格,此时爆发出一阵鼓噪声。‖ ~**ious**/ʌpˈrɔːrɪəs/ *adj.* 爆笑如雷的;闹哄哄的

uproot/ˌʌpˈruːt/
v. pull up by the roots; get rid of 连根拔起;根除;去除

upset/ʌpˈset/
Ⅰ *v.* ❶ knock (sth.) over; be turned over 打翻;弄翻: ~ a glass 打翻杯子/ The boat will ~. 船会翻的。❷ make sb. unhappy or worried or make sth. go wrong 使烦恼;使不安;使不适;扰乱;打乱: ~ one's plan 打乱某人的计划/~ one's stomach 使胃不舒服 Ⅱ *adj.* worried; anxious; feeling unhappy about sth. 不安的;不快的;感到不适的: He felt ~ about losing the money. 丢了钱,他感到难过。

upshot/ˈʌpʃɒt/
n. (with **the**) the final result (与 the 连用) 结果;结局: What was the ~ of the official investigation? 官方调查的结果如何呢?

upside/ˈʌpsaɪd/
n. the upper side; the top part; the top surface 上边;上部;上面: The ~s of all the pictures should be at the same height. 所有画的上边应在同一高度上。

upstairs/ˌʌpˈsteəz/
Ⅰ *adv.* to or on the upper floor 往楼上;在楼上 Ⅱ *adj.* situated on or of upper floors of a building 楼上的: an ~ room 楼上的房间

upstart/ˈʌpstɑːt/
n. a person who has suddenly become rich or powerful 暴发户;新贵

upstream/ˌʌpˈstriːm/
adv. against the flow of water in a river, stream, etc. 逆流地: It is much more difficult to row a boat ~ than downstream. 逆流划船要比顺流划船困难得多。

upsurge/ˈʌpsɜːdʒ/
n. ❶ a sudden rise 突然的高涨;急剧上升: the recent ~ in the number of people buying video recorders 买录像机的人数最近突然增多 ❷ a sudden appearance of strong feelings (情绪的)激发,(突然)迸

发: an ~ of joy 突然喜出望外

upswing/ˈʌpˌswɪŋ/
n. an improvement or increase in an amount or level 进步;改进;提高;上升: an ~ in the president's popularity rating 总统支持率的提高

uptake/ˈʌpteɪk/
n. ❶ the action of taking up or making use of sth. that is available 利用;采用 ❷ the act of taking in or absorbing of a substance by a living organism or bodily organ 摄入;摄取;吸收 ‖ **be quick**(**slow**) **on the ~** 理解快(慢);领悟快(慢)

up-to-date/ˌʌptəˈdeɪt/
adj. of the latest kind; right up to the present 新式的;时新的;直到最近的;最新的: ~ clothes 时髦的衣服/~ information 最新消息

upward/ˈʌpwəd/
Ⅰ *adj.* moving or directed up 向上的;上升的: an ~ movement 上升运动 Ⅱ *adv.* (also **upwards**) towards what is higher 向上地;上升地: He climbed ~. 他向上爬。‖ ~(**s**) **of** 超过……;……多: The dress cost ~ of ＄50. 买这件衣服花了 50 多美元。

upwards/ˈʌpwədz/
adv. ❶ towards a higher level, position 向上;朝上;上升: He looked ~ at the sky. 他朝着天空看。/She lay on the bed, face ~. 她仰面朝天躺在床上。❷ towards a higher amount or price (数量、价格)上升,上涨: Costs are moving ~. 费用在上涨。/The budget has been revised ~. 预算已经上调。

upwind/ʌpˈwɪnd/
adj. & *adv.* in the direction from which the wind is blowing 迎风的(地);顶风的(地)

uranium/jʊˈreɪnɪəm/
n. a type of radioactive metal that can be used to produce nuclear energy (U) 铀(放射性金属,符号 U)

urban/ˈɜːbən/
adj. of a town or city 城市的;都市的: ~ districts 市区/~ life 城市生活 ‖ ~**ize** *v.* 使都市化

urbane /ɜːˈbeɪn/
adj.very polite;refined 有礼貌的;温文尔雅的;文雅的

urge /ɜːdʒ/
Ⅰ*v*.force or push forward sb.to do sth.敦促;驱策;恳求;力劝;强调:Her parents ~d her to study harder.她的父母敦促她更加努力地学习。 Ⅱ*n*.a strong desire 迫切的要求;强烈的愿望:They have an ~ to visit China.他们极想访问中国。 ‖ ~ **for** 要求做出/~ **on** 促使加紧干/~ **to** 促使采取/~ **sth. upon sb.** 向……强调;竭力主张

urgent /ˈɜːdʒənt/
adj.that must be dealt with immediately 紧急的;紧迫的:an ~ letter 紧急信件/an ~ appeal (for) 紧急呼吁……

usable /ˈjuːzəbl/
adj.❶ that can be used;capable of use 可用的;能用的:Are any of these tools ~? 这些工具有能用的吗? ❷ suitable for use 适用的:This tool is ~.这件工具适用。

usage /ˈjuːzɪdʒ/
n.❶the generally accepted way of using a language;the customary use 习惯用法:*Contemporary English Usage*《当代英语惯用法》❷habitual or customary practice 常规做法;习惯:Travelers should learn many of the ~s of the countries they visit.旅行者应了解他们参观的国家的许多习俗。❸the act of using 使用;利用;对待:The paint came off the surface because of much ~.由于长期使用,表面上的漆脱落了。

use
Ⅰ /juːz/*v*.❶ cause to act or serve a purpose 用;使用;运用:May I ~ your pen? 我可以用一下你的钢笔吗? ❷ consume;finish 用掉;消耗:This machine ~d too much electricity.这台机器耗电太多。❸ treat in the stated manner 对待:They ~d the prisoners cruelly.他们残酷地对待犯人。 Ⅱ /juːs/*n*. ❶ the action of using or being used 使用;运用;利用:This reading room is for the ~ of teachers only.这个阅览室只供教师使用。❷ a purpose for which sth.is used 用处;作用;好处;用法:Can you find a ~ for this old dictionary? 你认为这本旧词典有什么用处吗? ‖ be ~d to 习惯于/(be) in ~ 在使用/(be) of no ~ 没有用/be (go)out of ~ 不再使用/bring into ~ 把……使用起来/come into ~ 开始使用/have ~ for 需用;派上用场/make ~ of 利用/put (turn) to ~ 加以利用/~ up 用完;用光

useful /ˈjuːsfl/
adj.❶ effective in use;bringing help or advantage 有用的;有益的;有帮助的:a ~ idea (tool,piece of advice) 有用的主意(工具、忠告)/The minister said that an inquiry would serve no ~ purpose.部长说调查不会有多大的用处。❷ satisfactory 令人满意的:The England cricket team scored quite a ~ total.英格兰板球队得分总数很令人满意。 ‖ ~ly *adv*.有用地;有效地/~ness *n*.有用;有效性;有益:This old radio has outlived its ~ness.这台旧收音机早已不能用了。

useless /ˈjuːsləs/
adj.having no use;worthless;having no effect 无用的;无价值的;无效的:A television set would be ~ without electricity.没有电,电视机就没有用。

user /ˈjuːzə(r)/
n.a person who uses or operates sth.使用者;用户:The factory is one of the biggest ~s of oil in the country.这家工厂是这个国家使用石油的大户之一。/road ~s 道路使用者

usher[1] /ˈʌʃə(r)/
n.❶someone who shows people to their seats,especially on an important occasion (尤指重要场合的)引座员;迎宾员;招待员 ❷someone who keeps order in a law court (法庭)庭警

usher[2] /ˈʌʃə(r)/
v.bring or show sb.to a place,especially by showing the way 引;领,接入;迎接:She ~ed the visitor into the room.她把来访者引进屋里。/I ~ed him to a seat.我领他入座。

usual /ˈjuːʒʊəl/
adj.in common use;that happens in most

cases;ordinary 通常的;惯例的;普通的:
the ～ bedtime 通常的睡觉时间/as ～ as
has happened before 像过去一样/ It is
～ for him to be late.他经常迟到。/ We
met as ～,on the way to school.跟以往一
样,我们在上学路上相遇了。‖ ～ly *adv.*
通常地;一般地;经常地

utensil/juːˈtensl/
*n.*a container or an instrument of any kind
used in the home（especially in the kitchen）(尤指厨房的)器皿,器具

utilitarian/ˌjuːtɪlɪˈteərɪən/
*adj.*of practical use only 功利的;实用的;
功利主义的;实用主义的

utility/juːˈtɪləti/
*n.*❶the degree of usefulness 有用;使用;
效用:We do not deny the ～ of grammatical research for the teaching of foreign
languages.我们并不否认语法研究对外语
教学的作用。❷a useful service for the
public,such as supplies of water to the

home,the bus service,etc.公用事业:Supplying water,electricity,gas,and bus or
railway services,etc.,are public utilities.
水、电、气的供应,公共汽车或火车服务
设施 等 都 属 于 公 用 事 业。‖ **utilize**
/juːˈtɪlaɪz/ *v.*使用;利用;发挥

utmost/ˈʌtməʊst/
adj.& *n.*of the greatest degree;most extreme 最大的;极度的(努力);an event of
the ～ importance 最重要的事件/ in the
～ danger (处于)极度危险中

utter¹/ˈʌtə(r)/
*adj.*complete,total 完全的;彻底的:Utter nonsense! 纯粹是一派胡言! /in ～
darkness (处于)漆黑一片

utter²/ˈʌtə(r)/
*v.*send out (a sound);say 说,讲;发出(声
音):The first word a baby ～s is usually
"ma".婴儿说的第一个词通常是"妈"。
‖ ～ance/ˈʌtərəns/ *n.*发声;表达

U

Vv

vacancy/ˈveɪkənsi/

　n. ❶ an unfilled place, such as a hotel room that is not being used 空位;(旅馆中的)空房 ❷ an unfilled job in a factory,office, etc. (职位的)空缺;空职 ❸ a lack of interest or ideas 无兴趣;无主意;空虚

vacant/ˈveɪkənt/

　adj. ❶ empty;not occupied or filled (地方)空的:a ～ room 空房间/a ～ piece of land 一块空地 ❷ (of a job) not filled at present (职位)空缺的:Are there any positions ～ in your firm? 你们公司有空缺的职位吗? ❸ empty of thought 空虚的;茫然的;没有表情的:a ～ expression 一种茫然的表情

vacate/vəˈkeɪt/

　v. leave empty or unoccupied;give up 使空出;空出(房屋、职务等);离开:～ a room 腾出房间 /～ a professorship 辞去教授职位 /All civilians ～d from the city.所有老百姓都离开了那座城市。

vacation/vəˈkeɪʃn/

　n. a holiday;a period of rest from work, school or court 假期:summer ～ 暑假/winter ～ 寒假/take a ～ 休假

vaccinate/ˈvæksɪneɪt/

　v. put a vaccine into a human or animal body 接种牛痘;接种疫苗:The children were all ～d against smallpox. 小孩子都种了牛痘,预防天花。‖ **vaccine** /ˈvæksiːn/ *n.* 牛痘苗;疫苗/**vaccination** *n.* 种痘;接种

vacuous/ˈvækjuəs/

　adj. ❶ empty 空的;空洞的 ❷ stupid;foolish 愚蠢的;傻的:the ～ smile of an idiot 白痴的傻笑 ❸ senseless;idle;indolent 无意义的;懒散的;无所事事的:～ life 无聊的生活

vacuum/ˈvækjuəm/

　n. a space completely empty of substance or gas;a space from which air or other gas has been removed 真空;真空状态 ‖ ～ **cleaner** *n.* 吸尘器/～ **flask** *n.* 保温瓶;热水瓶

vagary/ˈveɪɡəri/

　n. (usually *pl.*) an act or thought for which there is no clear reason 奇思遐想;变幻莫测:It is difficult to explain the vagaries of a child's mind.很难解释儿童的奇怪念头。

vagrant/ˈveɪɡrənt/

　Ⅰ *adj.* going from place to place with no fixed purpose 过着流浪生活的;生活无定居的:a ～ life 流浪生活/a ～ tribe 游牧部落/～ thoughts 飘忽不定的思想 Ⅱ *n.* a person who has no home or job 流浪者;漂泊者;游民

vague/veɪɡ/

　adj. not clear in shape or not definite in form,meaning;unable to express oneself clearly 含糊的;模糊的;表达不清的:His ～ statement confused us.他那含糊不清的声明把我们弄糊涂了。

vain/veɪn/

　adj. ❶ without value, use or result 无用的;徒劳的:It is ～ to tell him.告诉他也无用。 ❷ thinking too highly of oneself 自负的;自视过高的;爱慕虚荣的:He is a ～ man.他是个虚荣心很重的人。

valentine/ˈvæləntaɪn/

　n. ❶ a letter or card expressing love,sent on St.Valentine's Day i.e.14 February,to a person one loves (2 月 14 日)圣瓦伦廷节情人卡 ❷ a person to whom such a letter or card is sent (收受圣瓦伦廷节情人卡的)情人

valiant/ˈvæliənt/
adj. very brave, especially in war; heroic 勇敢的;英勇的:a ～ soldier 一个勇敢的战士 ‖ **valo(u)r**/ˈvælə(r)/ *n*.勇敢;英勇

valid/ˈvælɪd/
adj.well based; effective according to law (法律上)有效的;站得住脚的;有充分根据的:The contract is still ～.这个合同仍然有效。 ‖ **~ate** *v*.使有效;使成立/**~ity**/vəˈlɪdəti/ *n*.有效性;正确性

validate/ˈvælɪdeɪt/
v. make valid, especially legally 使合法化;使生效:In order to ～ the agreement, both parties sign it.为使协议有效,双方都在上面签了字。

valley/ˈvæli/
n.❶an area of lowland between hills or mountains and usually having a river or stream flowing along its bottom 山谷;峡谷:In spring the ～ is covered with green grass.春天,这峡谷里长满了青草。❷a wide region of flat, low country drained by a great river system 流域:the Mississippi Valley 密西西比河流域

valuable[1]/ˈvæljuəbl/
adj.❶worth a lot of money 贵重的;值钱的;珍贵的;名贵的:a ～ painting(property) 名贵绘画(贵重财物) ❷having great usefulness or importance 宝贵的;有价值的;极有用的:years of ～ service 多年的宝贵服务/～ advice 有益的劝告/a waste of my ～ time 浪费我的宝贵时间

valuable[2]/ˈvæljuəbl/
n.(*pl*.)sth., especially sth.small such as a piece of jewellery, that is worth a lot of money 贵重物品(尤指珠宝等小件物品):Guests may deposit their ～s in the hotel safe.客人可将贵重物品寄存在旅馆的保险柜里。

valuation/ˌvæljuˈeɪʃn/
n.❶the action or business of calculating how much money sth.is worth 估价:We asked an expert to make a ～ of the painting.我们请了一位专家给这幅画估价。❷a value or price decided on 定价;估值;估定的价格:The ～ (put) on the house was ￡90,000.这所房子估定的价格是 9 万英镑。

value/ˈvæljuː/
Ⅰ *n*.❶the material or monetary worth of sth.(物质或货币)价值 ❷the importance or preciousness of sth.重要性:Her suggestion can be of great ～.她的建议很有价值。❸ the usefulness of sth.益处;用处:You'll find that book of little ～ in helping you to learn English.你会发现那本书对你学习英语没有什么帮助。Ⅱ *v*.❶ think highly of 重视;高度评价:The media highly ～d they visit to China.媒体高度评价他们的这次来华访问。❷ estimate the value, price or worth of 估算……的价值或价格:He ～d the necklace at about＄500.他估计这条钻石项链的价值为 500 美元左右。

valuer/ˈvæljuə(r)/
n.a person whose work is to decide how much money things are worth 估价者

values/ˈvæljuːz/
n.standards or principles; ideas about the worth or importance of certain qualities, especially those generally accepted by a particular group 标准;准则;价值观:moral ～ 道德标准

valve/vælv/
n.❶ a device for allowing liquid or gas to pass through an opening in one direction only 阀门;气门;闸门 ❷ a structure in the heart or in a vein that lets blood flow in one direction only (心脏或血管的)瓣,瓣膜 ❸ the hard shell of certain soft creatures 软体动物的外壳;甲 ❹ a type of electronic tube with no air in it 真空电子管

van/væn/
n.❶a covered truck (大)篷车:a police ～ 警车 ❷a covered railway carriage 铁路货车

vane/veɪn/
n.❶ a piece of metal, or some other device, fixed upon a spire or other high objects in such a way as to move with the wind and indicate its direction 风向标 ❷ a blade of a windmill, fan, etc.(风车、风扇等的)翼,叶片,轮叶

V

vanguàrd/'væŋɡɑːd/

n. ❶ the front part of an advancing army 先头部队:The ~ is under attack.先头部队遭到了袭击。❷ the foremost leading position,usually in intellectual and political movement or social reforms（知识、政治运动或社会改革的）先锋:In the 19th century Britain was in the ~ of industrial progress.在 19 世纪,英国是工业发展的先锋。

vanish/'vænɪʃ/

v. ❶ disappear;become invisible 消失:The sun ~ed behind a cloud.太阳消失在云层之中了。/His anger ~ed and he burst into laughter.他的怒气烟消云散了,并哈哈大笑起来。❷ stop existing 不复存在;消亡

vanity/'vænɪti/

n. ❶ too much pride in one's looks,ability,or accomplishments 骄傲;自负:Vanity is her chief fault.自负是她的主要弱点。❷ a lack of real value;worthlessness 无价值:Fame,power,wealth,all is ~.名利财势都是空的。

vanquish/'væŋkwɪʃ/

v. conquer or defeat sb. completely in a war,match,etc. 征服;击败;克服;抑制:~ all enemies 战胜一切敌人/~ fear 克服恐惧心理

vantage/'vɑːntɪdʒ/

n. a better chance or an advantage 较好的机会;优势:The hill was a good ~ point to watch the soldiers passing.这座山是个有利地势,可以观望士兵走过。

vapo(u)r/'veɪpə(r)/

n. ❶ moisture that can be seen,such as steam from boiling water,fog or mist 蒸气;雾气:the ~ of the morning mist 早晨的雾气 ❷ sth.without substance;empty fancy 空想的东西;幻想

variable/'veərɪəbl/

Ⅰ *adj.* ❶ changeable;uncertain 易变的:The weather is ~.天气是变化无常的。❷ that can be varied by the user 可调整的;可变的:The temperature inside the room is ~.室内温度可以调节。❸ uneven 不均衡的:The team's perform-

ance this year has been ~.该队今年的比赛成绩时好时坏。Ⅱ *n.* changeable factors 可变因素:There are several ~s that could change our plan.有几个可变因素可能会改变我们的计划。

variance/'veərɪəns/

n. difference which causes argument;disagreement 意见不同,分歧;争论;不和:He has been at ~ with his parents for years.他多年来一直与父母不和。

variant/'veərɪənt/

Ⅰ *adj.* different from a norm or standard 不同的 Ⅱ *n.* a form or version of sth. that is a slightly different form of sth. else 变种;变体;变形

variation/ˌveərɪ'eɪʃn/

n. ❶ a change or difference in condition,amount,or level 变化;变动;变更:a principle without ~ 不变的方针 /~ of temperature 温度的变化 ❷ a simple melody repeated in a different form 变奏曲;变奏:~s on a theme by Mozart 莫扎特所作某一曲子的变奏 ❸ the occurrence of change from what is usual in the form of a group or kind of living things 变种;变异

variegated/'veərɪɡeɪtɪd/

adj. ❶ marked with patches or spots of different colours;many-coloured 杂色的;斑驳的:The flowers of pansies are usually ~.蝴蝶花通常是杂色的。❷ having varieties 多样化的

variety/və'raɪəti/

n. ❶ the quality or state of being different 多样化;变化:a life full of ~ 变化多端的生活 /give ~ to the programme 使节目丰富多彩 ❷ kind or sort 种类:every ~ of form 各种形式 /a new ~ of rice 新的水稻品种

various/'veərɪəs/

adj. ❶ differing from one another;different in kind 不同的;不同种类的:There are ~ opinions as to the best way to raise children.关于养育小孩的最佳方法有多种多样的意见。❷ several;many 几个;许多:We have looked at ~ houses,but have decided to buy this one.我们看了许

多房子,但决定买这一栋。

varnish/'vɑ:nɪʃ/

Ⅰ *n*. a type of liquid which gives a hard, shining surface to wood, metal, etc. when dry 清漆;罩光漆;凡立水 Ⅱ *v*. put varnish on 给……涂清漆

vary/'veəri/

v. (cause to) be different; change 变化;使变化: The weather varies from hour to hour. 天气时刻在变化。‖ ~ between … and 由……到……情况不等 ‖ ~ from 不同于/~ from … to … 由……到……情况不等

vase/vɑ:z/

n. a holder or container used chiefly for ornament or for holding flowers 装饰瓶;花瓶: a ~ of flowers 一瓶花

vassal/'væsl/

n. ❶ a person in the feudal system who held land in return for loyalty, military help, etc. to an overlord (封建时代的)诸侯;封臣;家臣 ❷ a person or country in a subordinate position to another 附庸(国);部属;仆人;邑从

vast/vɑ:st/

adj. large and wide; great in number or amount 巨大的;广阔的: a ~ sea 浩瀚的海洋/a ~ plain 辽阔的平原

vastly/'vɑ:stli/

adv. very greatly 很大地;巨大地: This is ~ superior to his previous film. 这部电影比他过去的好得多。/a ~ over-rated actress 一位被大大高估的女演员

vastness/'vɑ:stnɪs/

n. a greatly empty area 空旷无际的地区: the ~ of space 广阔无垠的空间

vault/vɔ:lt/

Ⅰ *v*. jump over using the hands or a pole (用手或杆支撑)跳越;跳跃: He ran towards the wall and ~ed over. 他向墙跑去,飞越而过。Ⅱ *n*. a jump made in this way 撑物跳跃;一跃而过: He went over the gate in a single ~. 他纵身一跳,跃过大门。‖ **pole** ~ 撑竿跳/~ing horse 鞍马

vector/'vektə(r)/

n. ❶ a quantity, such as a force or veloci- ty, which has both force and magnitude and which can be represented by a straight line, such as an arrow 矢量;向量 ❷ a mosquito or other organism that transmits disease germs 传染病介体(如蚊子等) ❸ the course of an aircraft 飞机航线

veer/vɪə(r)/

v. turn; (especially with reference to the wind) change direction 转变;(尤指风)转向

veg/vedʒ/

n. vegetable 蔬菜: meat and two ~ 肉和两份蔬菜

vegan/'vi:gən/

n. a person who does not eat meat, fish, eggs, cheese or drink milk 纯素食者(肉、鱼、蛋、乳酪、牛奶均不吃的人)

vegetable/'vedʒ(ɪ)təbl/

n. plants grown for food 蔬菜;植物: Lettuce, beans, tomatoes, beets are ~s. 莴苣、豆子、西红柿、甜菜都是蔬菜。‖ **vegetarian**/ˌvedʒɪ'teəriən/ *n*. 素食者;吃斋的人

vegetate/'vedʒɪteɪt/

v. ❶ grow as a plant does 植物似地生长 ❷ live an idle, uninteresting life 过呆板乏味的生活;过单调的生活

vegetation/ˌvedʒɪ'teɪʃn/

n. plants in general (泛指)植物;草木: Deserts have very little ~. 沙漠几乎没有植物。

vehicle/'vɪəkl/

n. ❶ sth. that can carry people and things (客运和货运的)车辆;运载工具: Cars, buses, and lorries are all ~s. 轿车、公共汽车和卡车都是车辆。❷ means of conveying thoughts, and feelings 传播工具;媒介物: Language is the ~ of thought. 语言是传达思想的工具。‖ **vehicular**/vi:'hɪkjʊlə(r)/ *adj*. 车辆的;交通工具的

veil/veɪl/

Ⅰ *n*. a covering of light, thin cloth or net for a woman's face (妇女戴的)面纱: draw a ~ over 隐瞒 Ⅱ *v*. put a veil over; hide 戴面纱;以面纱遮掩;掩盖: ~ the face 用面纱蒙脸/~ the facts 掩盖事实

‖ ～ed *adj.*蒙上面纱的;掩饰的;含蓄的

vein/veɪn/

　n. ❶ a vessel along which blood flows to the heart 血管;静脉:He was so angry that the ～s stood out on his forehead.他气得额头上青筋直暴。❷ one of the lines in leaves or the wings of insects 叶脉;(昆虫)翅脉 ❸ a (written or spoken) style or mood (写作或讲话的)风格,语气:He often talks in a humorous ～.他讲话常常很幽默。

veined/veɪnd/

　*adj.*having veins or thin lines 有叶脉的;有翅脉的;有纹理的:a ～ leaf 有叶脉的叶子/the many ～ wings of the bee 有许多翅脉的蜜蜂翅膀/～ marble 有纹理的大理石

velar/ˈviːlə(r)/

　Ⅰ *n.*a consonant (such as /k/ or /g/) made with the back of the tongue against or near the soft plate 软腭音(例如/k/或/g/) Ⅱ *adj.* ❶ of or relating to velum 膜的;软腭的 ❷ produced with the back of the tongue against or near the soft palate 软腭音的

velvet/ˈvelvɪt/

　*n.*a fine closely-woven material made of silk,nylon,cotton,etc.,with a soft furry surface on one side only 天鹅绒;丝绒;立绒:～ curtains 丝绒窗帘/a ～ jacket 丝绒短上衣

velveteen/ˌvelvəˈtiːn/

　*n.*a cheap material made of cotton but having the appearance of velvet 平绒;棉天鹅绒

velvety/ˈvelvɪti/

　adj. ❶ (of a thing which is soft to the touch) looking or feeling like velvet (指有柔软触感的物体)天鹅绒般的;柔软光滑的:the kitten's ～ fur 小猫那柔软光滑的毛皮 ❷ (of a colour) having a soft deep look (颜色)深而柔和的:～ brown 深而柔和的棕色 ❸ (especially of wine) very smooth to the taste;not acid (尤指酒)醇和的

venal/ˈviːnl/

　adj. ❶ ready to behave in an unfair or dis-honest way, especially by using one's power or position to help other people in return for money or other reward 贪赃的;贪污的:～ judges 贪赃枉法的法官 ❷ (of an action) done in order to gain money, rather than for the proper or honest reasons (行为)腐败的;为钱而干的;受贿而为的

vend/vend/

　*v.*sell or bring to market 出售;叫卖;贩卖:The little girl lived by ～ing flowers in the street.那小女孩靠在街上卖花维持生活。‖ ～**ing machine** *n.*售货机

venerable/ˈvenərəbl/

　*adj.*deserving respect(because of age or experience)(尤指因年高历深)值得尊敬的;令人崇敬的

venerate/ˈvenəreɪt/

　*v.*admire or respect greatly 崇拜;尊敬 ‖ **veneration** *n.*崇拜;尊敬

venetian blind/vəˌniːʃnˈblaɪnd/

　*n.*a type of blind made of thin horizontal pieces of plastic,etc.which can be moved to allow air and light to pass through 软百叶帘;活动百叶帘

vengeance/ˈvendʒəns/

　*n.*the act of taking revenge 报仇;复仇:He swore ～ on his enemy.他发誓要向他的敌人报仇。

vent/vent/

　Ⅰ *n.* ❶ a hole, opening, or pipe serving as a means by which air, gas, or liquid can enter or escape from 通风口;排放口 ❷ express (a strong feeling) freely (感情的)发泄;吐露:find ～ in 从……中得到发泄 Ⅱ *v.* ❶ allow or cause fresh air to enter and move around inside (a room, building, etc.), thus driving out bad air, smoke, gas, etc.排出(气体等):～ smoke from the kitchen 排出厨房的烟雾 ❷ express feelings forcefully 发泄感情

ventilate/ˈventɪleɪt/

　v. ❶ cause fresh air to enter;change the air in 使通风;通风:We ～ the room by opening the windows.我们打开窗户让房间通风。❷ make known publicly;discuss openly 公开;公开讨论:～ one's complaints 发牢骚

ventilator/ˈventɪleɪtə(r)/

　　*n.*❶an apparatus for ventilating a room, building, etc. 通风装置；排气风扇；送风机：a ～ shaft 通风井 ❷an apparatus for pumping air into and out of the lungs of someone who cannot breathe properly 人工呼吸机：The patient is on a ～.这个病人要使用人工呼吸机。

ventricle/ˈventrɪkl/

　　*n.*❶either of the two lower chambers of the heart 心室：left (right) ～ of the heart 左(右)心室 ❷ small cavity in the brain (脑)室：～ of the brain 脑室

venture/ˈventʃə(r)/

　　Ⅰ *n.*a project or activity in which there is a risk 冒险；冒险行动；(成败难测的)事业：a joint ～ 合资企业 Ⅱ *v.*❶ take the risk of going or doing sth.冒险去；冒险干；Don't ～ into the forest.You might be lost.不要冒险进入这个大森林，你会迷路的。❷ do sth.that requires courage 大胆(做)；敢于(做)：No one ～d to interrupt him.没有人敢打断他的话。❸ take the risk of harming or losing；put at risk 冒失去……的危险；把……置于危险之中：The gambler ～d all his money on the final try.那赌徒孤注一掷，把钱全部押上了。‖ **Nothing ～, nothing have.** 不入虎穴,焉得虎子。/～ **on** (**upon**) 冒险进行(某事) ‖ ～**some** *adj.*大胆的；危险的；有风险的

venue/ˈvenjuː/

　　*n.*a place where an event happens (事件的)发生地点,现场;举办场所

veranda(**h**)/vəˈrændə/

　　*n.*an open area with a floor and a roof at one side of a house 阳台(房子外侧有顶的敞廊)：She sat in the shade on the ～.她坐在阳台上的遮阴处。

verb/vɜːb/

　　*n.*a word or group of words that is used in describing an action, experience, or state 动词(表示动作行为、事情发生或存在状态的词)：transitive and intransitive ～s 及物动词和不及物动词

verbal/ˈvɜːbl/

　　*adj.*❶ spoken；not written 口头的；非书面的；a ～ promise 口头的诺言 /～ confession 口供 ❷ of or in words 言辞的；字句的：a ～ error 用字的错误 /have a good ～ memory 善于记忆字句 ❸ word for word 逐字的；照字面的：～ translation 逐字翻译；直译 ❹ of verbs 动词的

verbalize/ˈvɜːbəlaɪz/

　　*v.*express your feelings or ideas in words 用言语(或文字)表述

verdant/ˈvɜːdnt/

　　adj.(of land) covered with freshly growing green plants or grass (土地)长满青翠草木的：the ～ landscape of spring 大地一片青翠的春景

verdict/ˈvɜːdɪkt/

　　*n.*a decision or judgment made after the evidence (especially by a jury in a court of law) (尤指法庭陪审团的)评决,裁决,决定：The ～ of the jury is that you are guilty.陪审团裁决你有罪。

verdure/ˈvɜːdʒə(r)/

　　n. the fresh green colour of growing grass, plants, trees, etc.(草木的)青翠色

verge/vɜːdʒ/

　　Ⅰ *n.*a region marking a boundary (especially the grass edge at the side of a road or bed of flowers) 边,边缘(尤指路边植草边沿,花坛边沿) ‖ **be on the ～ of** 濒于；行将：He was on the ～ of telling him the truth. 他差点儿告诉他真相。Ⅱ *v.* (with **on** or **upon**) come near the edge of；be very close to (与 on 或 upon 连用)接近；濒于：His behaviour ～s on madness. 他的行为近于发疯。

verify/ˈverɪfaɪ/

　　*v.*test or prove the truth of 证明；证实；核对；查实：～ a theory 证明一个理论 /～ a figure 核实一个数字 ‖ **verifiable** *adj.*可核实的；可查实的

veritable/ˈverɪtəbl/

　　*adj.*used to emphasize that sb.(sth.) can be compared to sb.(sth.)else that is more exciting, more impressive, etc. 名副其实的；不折不扣的

vermillion/vəˈmɪlɪən/

　　Ⅰ *n.* ❶ bright red pigment 朱砂 ❷a

bright red or scarlet colour 朱红色 Ⅱ *adj.* of a bright red or scarlet colour 朱红色的 Ⅲ *v.* colour or paint with vermillion 涂成朱红色

vermin/'vɜːmɪn/
n. (*pl.*) small animals or birds that destroy crops, spoil food, or do other damage, and are difficult to control 害兽；害鸟；害人虫；寄生虫：Fleas, lice, and bedbugs are very unpleasant ~.跳蚤、虱子和臭虫都是非常令人讨厌的寄生虫。

verminous/'vɜːmɪnəs/
adj. ❶ full of vermin 长满害虫的：the tramp's ~ old coat 流浪汉那长满虱子的旧外套 ❷(of a person) very unpleasant; nasty (指人) 讨厌的；令人作呕的；极脏的

vernacular/və'nækjʊlə(r)/
Ⅰ *adj.* of the local language or dialect 本国语的；方言的，本地话的：the ~ press 当地语报刊 Ⅱ *n.* the language or dialect that is most widely spoken by ordinary people in a region or country 本国语；本地话，方言

vernal/'vɜːnl/
adj. of, like, or appearing in the spring season 春天的；春天似的；在春季出现的

versatile/'vɜːsətaɪl/
adj. interested in and clever at many different things 有多方面才能的；多才多艺的

verse/vɜːs/
n. ❶ a writing in regular lines and with rhythm 诗；诗体；韵文：blank ~ 无韵诗/free ~ 自由诗/lyrical ~ 抒情诗 ❷ a group of lines of this kind forming a unit in rhyme scheme 诗句，诗行；诗节：a poem of six ~s 一首有六个诗节的诗歌 ❸ any of the numbered (groups of) sentences that together form one numbered division (chapter) of a holy book, especially *the Bible* or *the Koran*（《圣经》、《古兰经》的）节；短句

version/'vɜːʃn/
n. ❶ a form of a written or musical work that exists in more than one form (不同的)版本；变形；变体：the English ~ of

Lu Xun's works 鲁迅作品的英译本 ❷ an interpretation of a matter from a particular viewpoint (由于不同的观点面对事件的)说法，解释

versus/'vɜːsəs/
prep. against 对：England ~ Wales 英格兰队对威尔士队

vertex/'vɜːteks/
n. ❶ the highest point of sth.; the top 顶；顶点：the ~ of a hill 山的顶点 ❷ the top or crown of a head 头顶 ❸ the point in the heavens directly overhead 天顶 ❹ the point opposite to and farthest from the base of a triangle, pyramid, or other figure having a base; the point where the two sides of an angle meet (三角形、角锥形等与底线相对的)顶点；角顶：~ angle 顶角/~ of a cone 锥顶/~ of a triangle 三角形的顶点

vertical/'vɜːtɪkl/
adj. straight up and down; upright 垂直的：The cliff rose in a ~ wall from the sea.这悬崖像一道垂直的墙立在海面上。

very/'veri/
Ⅰ *adv.* in a high degree; extremely 很，甚；非常；格外：a ~ interesting story 极其有趣的故事 Ⅱ *adj.* exact; this and no other 正是的；恰好的；同一的；真正的：That's the ~ thing I need.这正是我所需要的东西。

vespers/'vespəz/
n. the evening service in a church 晚间礼拜，晚祷

vessel/'vesl/
n. ❶ a container for holding liquids (盛液体的)容器 ❷ a ship or large boat 船；舰：a sailing ~ 帆船/a fishing ~ 渔船 ❸ a tube, such as a vein, that carries blood or other liquid through the body, or plant juice through a plant 血管；脉管；导管：blood ~s 血管

vest[1]/vest/
n. ❶ a garment worn next to the skin on the upper part of the body 〈英〉汗衫；内衣 ❷ a short garment fastened with buttons up the front but without sleeves, worn beneath a jacket 马甲；背心

vest² /vest/

v.(with **in** or **with**) give the right to use (与 in 或 with 连用) 给予；授予；赋予 (某人使用某权利)：The government has ~ed great powers in the Minister of Agriculture.政府已把大权授予农业部长。‖ ~ed **interest** ❶ 既得利益 ❷ 自私；利己：Those employers have a ~ed interest in keeping workers' wages low.那些雇主们压低工人的工资，这有其私利。

vestige /'vestɪdʒ/

*n.*a mark or sign left by sth.that once existed 遗迹；形迹；痕迹

vet /vet/

Ⅰ *n.*a trained animal doctor 兽医 Ⅱ *v.*(-tt-) ❶ treat (an animal) medically 诊疗（兽类）❷ examine carefully 仔细检查：~ motorcars 检查汽车

veteran /'vetərən/

*n.*❶a person who has had much experience in some position or occupation 老手；He is a ~ in the printing trade.他是印刷行业中的老手。❷a person who has served any length of time in the armed forces 退伍军人

veterinary /'vetərinəri/

Ⅰ *adj.*of or relating to veterinarians or veterinary medicine of animals 兽医的 Ⅱ *n.*a doctor who practices veterinary medicine 兽医

veto /'viːtəu/

Ⅰ *n.*❶the power or right to refuse or forbid 否决权；否认权：The president has the power of ~es.总统有否决权。❷ any such rights or powers 行使否决权：Mother put a ~ on (upon) our staying out late.母亲不允许我们在外面待到很晚才回来。Ⅱ *v.*reject or forbid；refuse to consent to 否决；不同意：My father ~ed my plan.我父亲不同意我的计划。

vex /veks/

*v.*make sb.feel annoyed；troubled 烦恼；苦恼：Her continuous chatter vexes me. 她的喋喋不休使我烦透了。

via /'vaɪə/

*prep.*❶by way of 经过；途经：He is going home ~ Shanghai.他打算途经上海回家。

❷by means of；using 用，通过（……手段）：I sent a message to Mary ~ her sister.我托玛丽的妹妹带信给她。

viable /'vaɪəbl/

*adj.*able to exist or develop；that will be successful 能生存的；能发展的；行得通的：The economy of the country is not ~.这个国家的经济是行不通的。

viaduct /'vaɪədʌkt/

*n.*a high bridge carrying a road or railway over a valley 高架桥；跨线桥；旱桥

vibrate /vaɪ'breɪt/

*v.*❶ move，cause to move very quickly from side to side or up and down （使）颤动；（使）振动；（使）震动；（使）摆动：The skin of a drum ~s when it is struck.鼓面受击时就会颤动。❷make a throbbing sound 发出颤动声：The speaker's voice ~d with emotion.讲演人的声音激动得颤抖了。

vice /vaɪs/

n.(an example of) badness of character 邪恶；坏事；不道德；坏习惯：Laziness is thought to be the source of all the ~s.人们认为，懒惰乃是一切恶习之源。

vice versa /ˌvaɪs 'vɜːsə/

*adv.*the other way round 反过来（也是这样）：You sent my letter to John，and ~ you also sent John's letter to me.你把我的信送给约翰，反过来也是这样，你也把约翰的信送给我。

vicinity /vɪ'sɪnəti/

*n.*❶nearness；being close 近；接近；密切：He is in the ~ of 60.他六十岁左右。❷ a neighbourhood or local area 附近；邻近：There is no hotel in the ~.附近没有旅馆。

vicious /'vɪʃəs/

*adj.*❶full of bad habits or behaviour 堕落的；品行不端的：a ~ life 堕落的生活 ❷ cruel；having or showing the desire to hurt 残酷的；狠毒的：He gave the dog a ~ blow with his stick.他朝着那只狗狠狠地打了一棍子。

victim /'vɪktɪm/

*n.*a person who suffering pain，death，loss，injury，destruction，etc.受害者；牺牲

者;遇难者：There are always countless innocent ～s in a war.发生一场战争,总有无数无辜的受害者。‖a ～ of a swindler 受骗者/fall ～ to 成为……的受害者 ‖～ize v.使受害;欺骗

victor/ˈvɪktə(r)/

*n.*a person who defeats an enemy in battle;a person who wins 战胜者;胜利者

Victorian/vɪkˈtɔːrɪən/

Ⅰ *adj.* of or connected with the time when Queen Victoria ruled 维多利亚时代的：～ manners 维多利亚女王时代的风俗 Ⅱ *n.* a person living in Queen Victorian's reign 维多利亚时代的人

victorious/vɪkˈtɔːrɪəs/

*adj.*having won a victory;ending in a victory 胜利的;取胜的:a ～ army 一支凯旋的部队/a ～ war 一场以胜利告终的战争

victory/ˈvɪktəri/

*n.*a success in a struggle,war or competition 战胜;胜利:Our team has had two defeats and eight victories.我们队八胜二负。/The general won a ～ over the army of the enemy.将军战胜了敌军而赢得了胜利。

video/ˈvɪdɪəʊ/

adj. ❶ connected with or used in the showing of pictures by television 电视的;视频的 ❷using videotape 电视录像的 ‖～**tape** *n.*录像磁带/～ **recorder** *n.*录像机

videophone/ˈvɪdɪəʊfəʊn/

*n.*a type of telephone with a screen that enables you to see the person you are talking to 可视电话;电视电话

vie/vaɪ/

v.(vied;vying) (with **with**) try to do better than sb. else; compete with sb. (与 with 连用)争,竞争:They ～d with each other in wealth.他们在财富方面互相竞争。

view/vjuː/

Ⅰ *n.*❶the ability to see or be seen from a particular place 视力;视野;眼界:A stranger came into our ～.我们看见了一个陌生人。❷sth. seen from a particular place, especially a stretch of pleasant

country;a scene 风景;风光;景色:The ～ here is very beautiful.这儿的风景很美。❸a personal opinion, belief, idea, etc., about sth. 见解;信念;观点;看法:What are your ～s on this subject? 你对这一题目有何高见? ‖ have (get) a bird's eye ～ of 鸟瞰……的全景/come in ～ of ……尽收眼底/come into ～ 进入视野/get a ～ of 看到,观看到/give a ～ of 使看到;使了解/have a ～ of 能看到/have... in ～ 打算;心中想到/in full ～ of 在大家面前;在众目睽睽之下/in one's ～ 据某人看来/in ～ 在视野范围内;在考虑中的/in ～ of 由于;考虑到/keep in ～ 监视;一直瞧(想)着/on ～ (在)展出/out of ～ 看不见了/point of ～ 观点;看法/take a ～ of 对……持某种看法/take the long ～ 看得远;有长远观点/with a ～ to 为了;为的是;打算/with...in ～ 想到……/within ～ 可以看得见 Ⅱ *v.*❶examine; look at thoroughly 查看;观看:They will come to ～ the workshops.他们要来查看车间。❷consider,regard;think about 考虑;看待:How do you ～ the present situation? 你如何看待当前的形势? ‖～**er** *n.*观察者/～**point** *n.*观点;看法

vigil/ˈvɪdʒɪl/

*n.*an act of remaining watchful for some purpose, especially while staying awake during the night 看守;警戒;(尤指)守夜,值夜:She kept an all-night ～ by the sick woman's bedside.她整夜守在病妇床边。/his lonely ～ 他独自一人的守夜

vigilance/ˈvɪdʒɪləns/

n. watchful care; continual attentiveness 警惕;警戒:Thanks to their constant ～, a crisis was averted.多亏他们经常保持警惕,危机才得以避免。

vigilant/ˈvɪdʒɪlənt/

*adj.*continually watchful of;on guard;always prepared for possible danger 警惕的;戒备的

vile/vaɪl/

adj. shameful; hateful; disgusting; very bad 可恨的;可耻的;极坏的:a ～ crime 卑劣的罪行/a ～ TV programme 糟糕的电视节目/～ weather 恶劣的天气/a ～

smell 臭味

vilify/'vɪlɪfaɪ/

 v. say bad things about (sb. or sth.) without good cause, especially in order to influence others unfavourably 诽谤, 中伤, 诬蔑(某人或某事)

villa/'vɪlə/

 n. ❶ a pleasant country house in its own garden, often used for only part of the year for holidays, especially in southern Europe (尤指南欧的)乡间别墅, 度假别墅: We're renting a ~ in the south of France for the summer. 我们在法国南部租了一栋暑假用的别墅。❷ (often use capital, as a part of the name of a house, a large house on the edge of a town, usually with a garden〈英〉常用大写, 用作邸宅名)城郊有花园的大住宅: fine old 19th century ~ 优雅的十九世纪旧式住宅 ❸ a large ancient Roman country house with the buildings and belongings to it 古罗马的庄园, 乡间宅邸

village/'vɪlɪdʒ/

 n. ❶ a group of houses in a country area, smaller than a town 村; 村庄 ❷ people of a village 全村人: The whole ~ was in deep sorrow at the news. 听到这个消息全村人陷入深深的悲痛之中。

villain/'vɪlən/

 n. ❶ a bad or wicked person 坏人; 恶棍; 歹徒: Some ~s robbed the bank. 一些歹徒抢劫了银行。❷ a main bad character in a play, film, etc. 反面人物, 反派角色: play the ~ 扮演反面角色

villainous/'vɪlənəs/

 adj. evil; threatening great harm 邪恶的; 凶恶的: He was brandishing a knife with a ~ face. 他挥舞着一把刀子, 杀气腾腾。

villainy/'vɪləni/

 n. an evil or wicked behaviour 恶行, 罪恶的行为

vindicate/'vɪndɪkeɪt/

 v. show or prove the truth, justice, etc. of 证明……正确; 为……辩白: I will go to the court and ~ my friend. 我将出庭作证, 为我的朋友辩护。‖ **vindication** *n.* 辩护

vindictive/vɪn'dɪktɪv/

 adj. wanting revenge; spiteful 报复性的; 怀恨的

vinegar/'vɪnɪɡə(r)/

 n. a liquid with sour taste made from malt or wine, etc. and used to flavour or preserve food 醋

vinegary/'vɪnɪɡəri/

 adj. ❶ of or like vinegar; very sour 醋(似)的; 酸的: This wine has a ~ taste. 这酒有酸味。❷ unkind; bitter; sharp-tempered 尖酸的; 刻薄的; 乖戾的: She has a ~ tongue. 她说话尖酸刻薄。

vinous/'vaɪnəs/

 adj. of, relating to or coloured like wine 葡萄酒的; 有葡萄酒颜色的 ‖ ~ excitement 酒后兴奋

vintage/'vɪntɪdʒ/

 Ⅰ *n.* ❶ the time of year when grapes are gathered to make wine 葡萄收获期 ❷ the wine made in a particular year (特定年份酿造的)葡萄酒: Last year's ~ is not yet ready for drinking. 去年酿的葡萄酒还不能喝。 Ⅱ *adj.* typical of a period in the past and of high quality (过去某个时期)典型的; 优质的: This is a ~ wine. 这是佳酿。/ a ~ car 老式的名贵汽车

viola/vɪ'əʊlə/

 n. a type of stringed musical instrument, larger than a violin 中提琴

violate/'vaɪəleɪt/

 v. break or act against an agreement, a rule, etc. 违背; 违反: The company player ~d some terms of the contract. 那公司违反了合同的某些条款。

violation/ˌvaɪə'leɪʃn/

 n. an act that disregards an agreement or a right 违反; 冒犯; 侵害: the ~ of traffic laws 违反交通规则

violent/'vaɪələnt/

 adj. ❶ forceful; fierce, severe 强暴的; 强烈的; 猛烈的; 严重的: a ~ wind 暴风 / ~ attack 猛攻 / lay ~ hands on sb. 对某人施暴行 ❷ caused by damaging force 暴力引起的: die a ~ death 死于暴力

violet/'vaɪələt/

n. ❶ a type of very small flower, usually blue or purple 紫罗兰 ❷ the blue or purple colour 蓝紫色

violin /ˌvaɪəˈlɪn/

n. a musical instrument with four strings played with a bow 小提琴：She played the ～ in the school orchestra. 她在学校管弦乐队中是拉小提琴的。‖ ～ist *n.* 小提琴手

VIP(**V.I.P.**) /ˌviː aɪ ˈpiː/

abbr. a very important person 要人；重要人物；大人物

viper /ˈvaɪpə(r)/

n. ❶ a small poisonous snake 蝰蛇（一种小毒蛇）❷ a wicked or ungrateful person who does harm to others 阴险毒辣的人

virago /vɪˈrɑːɡəʊ/

n. ❶ a fierce-tempered complaining woman with a loud voice 嗓门很大的泼妇，悍妇 ❷ a woman of great strength and courage 力大而勇敢的妇女

viral /ˈvaɪrəl/

adj. of or caused by a virus 病毒(性)的；病毒引起的：～ pneumonia 病毒性肺炎

virgin /ˈvɜːdʒɪn/

Ⅰ *n.* a girl or woman who has not experienced sexual intercourse 处女 Ⅱ *adj.* ❶ in a state of sexual virginity 童贞的；贞洁的 ❷ in sth.'s original pure or natural condition 纯洁的；未被玷污的；原始的；未开发的：Within 100 years there will be no ～ forest left. 不到一百年，原始森林将所剩无几。

virginal /ˈvɜːdʒɪnl/

adj. of or suitable for a virgin；maidenly 处女般的；纯洁的：～ pureness 处女般的纯洁

virtual /ˈvɜːtʃuəl/

adj. being actual or nearly sth. 实际上的；真正的：The battle was won with such a great loss of soldiers that it was a ～ defeat. 那次战斗牺牲了很多战士才取胜，实际上是打败了。

virtue /ˈvɜːtʃuː/

n. ❶ a good quality of a person's character 德行；高尚品德；优良品质：～ and vice 善

与恶 ❷ an advantage 优点；长处：Patience is but one of his ～s. 耐心只是他的一个优点。

virtuous /ˈvɜːtʃuəs/

adj. ❶ having or showing virtue 品德高尚的；有美德的 ❷（too）satisfied with one's own good behaviour, and expressing this in one's manner towards those who have done wrong 自命清高的；自以为高尚的 ‖ ～ly *adv.* 合乎道德地；品性正直地

virulent /ˈvɪrʊlənt/

adj. ❶ very poisonous；deadly 剧毒的；致命的：a ～ disease 致命的病 ❷（with reference to feelings, etc.）full of hate and anger（指情绪等）仇恨的；恶毒的：He made a ～ speech against that organization. 他发表了一次对那个组织充满仇恨的讲话。

virus /ˈvaɪərəs/

n. a living thing even smaller than bacteria which causes infectious disease in the bodies, plants, etc. 过滤性病原体；病毒：the ～ of infection 流行性感冒病毒

visa /ˈviːzə/

Ⅰ *n.* an official mark put onto a passport to show that it has been examined and approved by the officials of a country, giving a foreigner permission to enter, pass through, or leave that country 签证：an entrance（exit）～ 入境（出境）签证 Ⅱ *v.* provide a visa for（a passport）签准护照

viscount /ˈvaɪkaʊnt/

n. the title of nobility, lower in rank than an earl 子爵 ‖ ～ess /ˈvaɪkaʊntɪs/ *n.* 子爵夫人

visible /ˈvɪzəbl/

adj. able to be seen；noticeable, obvious（to the eye）看得见的；可见的；明显的；显然的：～ stars 看得见的星星 /with impatience 显然不耐烦的 /There is no ～ cause. 没有明显的原因。‖ **visibility** /ˌvɪzəˈbɪləti/ *n.* 能见度

vision /ˈvɪʒən/

n. ❶ the ability to see；the visual faculty 视力 ❷ a vivid mental dream；sth.

imagined 幻想；梦幻：As a boy he had ~s of being a great man. 他小时候就有着要当大人物的各种梦想。

visit/ˈvɪzɪt/

I v. go to see (sb.); go to (a place) for a time 参观，访问（某地）；拜访，探问（某人）；逗留；作客：Have you ever ~ed the Summer Palace? 你参观过颐和园吗？ II n. the act of going to (a place, etc.) 参观；访问；探望；拜访：I have invited him for a ~ to my hometown next month. 我已邀请他下月到我家乡去访问。‖ on a ~ (to …)（到某地）访问/pay a ~ (to) 访问，去（某地）/make a ~ (to)（对……）做一次访问；拜访

visiting/ˈvɪzɪtɪŋ/

adj. ❶ (of a person) on a visit to a person or place（人）访问的；参观的 ❷ (of an academic) working for a fixed period of time at another institution（学者）访问的；客座的

visitor/ˈvɪzɪtə(r)/

n. ❶ a person who visits or is visiting; a guest 访问者；参观者；游客：~s not admitted 游客止步（谢绝参观） ❷ a bird that frequents certain areas at regular seasons 候鸟

visor/ˈvaɪzə(r)/

n. the part of a helmet which can be lift-ed to show the face（头盔的）面罩，面甲

vista/ˈvɪstə/

n. a view especially from a distance and in a particular direction 远景；（尤指从远处或特定方向看到的）景色：We enjoyed the ~ of the mountain as seen from the north. 我们欣赏了由北望去的山的远景。

visual/ˈvɪʒʊəl/

adj. ❶ connected with or having an effect on the sense of sight 视觉的；视力的：~ art 视觉艺术 /~ field 视野 /the ~ nerve 视神经 ❷ able to be seen; gained by seeing 看得见的；凭视力的：~ object 可见物体 /~ colours 可见色

vital/ˈvaɪtl/

adj. necessary (for life); very important 生命必需的；极其重要的：The heart is the ~ part of the body. 心脏是身体的命

门。‖ ~ity /vaɪˈtæləti/ n. 活力；生命力/ ~ize v. 赋予生命力；赋予活力

vitamin/ˈvɪtəmɪn/

n. any of a group of substances necessary for healthy life, different ones occurring in different natural things such as raw fruit, dairy products, fish, meat, etc. 维生素：Oranges contain ~ C. 橘子含有维生素 C。

vivid/ˈvɪvɪd/

adj. ❶ strong and very bright 鲜艳的；明亮的：a ~ colour 鲜艳的颜色 /~ red 鲜红色 ❷ full of life; lively; active 清晰的；生动逼真的：a ~ description 生动的描述

viz. /vɪz/

adv. and it is (they are); that is to say 那就是；即是说：Great Britain consists of four parts, ~, England, Scotland, Wales and Northern Ireland. 英国包括四部分，即英格兰、苏格兰、威尔士和北爱尔兰。

vocabulary/vəˈkæbjʊləri/

n. ❶ all the words of a language 词汇；语汇 ❷ a list of words in alphabetical order with meaning e.g. added as a supplement to a book dealing with a particular subject 词汇表

vocal/ˈvəʊkl/

adj. using or connected with the voice 声音的；发音的；口头表达的：The tongue is one of the ~ organs. 舌头是发音器官之一。‖ ~ist n. 声乐家；歌唱者

vocation/vəʊˈkeɪʃn/

n. ❶ occupation; employment 行业；职业：She chose teaching as her ~. 她选择教书为职业。 ❷ a particular fitness or ability for a certain kind of work, especially of a worthy kind（适合做某事的）能力，条件，禀赋，才能：He has a real ~ for writing. 他在写作方面具有真正的才能。

vogue/vəʊg/

n. a current fashion; sth. in current fashion; a popular favour 时髦；时髦品；流行：the ~s of the 18th century 十八世纪的流行物 /The novel has had a great ~ in its day. 这部小说在当时风行一时。

voice/vɔɪs/

I n. ❶ the sound produced when speaking or singing 说话声音；嗓音；嗓子：raise (lower) one's ～ 提高(放低)声音 ❷ the opinion on a particular topic 意见；看法：the ～ of reason 理智的呼声 ‖ be of one's ～ 众口一词；意见一致/at the top of one's ～ 高声地/be in (good) ～ 嗓音正常(良好)/give ～ to 表达/have ～ in 在……有发言权/lose one's ～ 嗓子哑了/raise one's ～ 放大声音讲话；表示意见/with one ～ 异口同声；一致地 Ⅱ v. put into words 表示；表达；说出：He ～d his opinions at the meeting. 他在会上发表了他的看法。

void /vɔɪd/
adj. completely empty; that can't be used any longer 空的；没有的；无用的；缺乏的；无效的：You cannot declare the contract ～ unilaterally. 你不能单方面宣布合同无效。 ‖ be ～ of 没有；缺乏

volatile /ˈvɒlətaɪl/
adj. ❶ (with reference to a liquid) evaporating easily; changing easily into a gas (指液体)易挥发的；挥发性的 ❷ (with reference to a person) changing moods easily (指人)心情变化快的，反复无常的

volcanic /vɒlˈkænɪk/
adj. ❶ of, from, produced by, or caused by a volcano 火山的；由火山作用引起的：～ rocks 火山岩/～ activity 火山活动 ❷ violently forceful 暴烈的；猛烈的：a ～ temper 火暴脾气

volcano /vɒlˈkeɪnəʊ/
n. (*pl.* ～s or ～es) a hill or mountain with an opening through which melting rock, ashes, gases, steam, etc. come out 火山：an active ～ 活火山 /an extinct ～ 死火山 /The village was destroyed when the ～ erupted. 这个村庄在火山爆发时被毁了。

vole /vəʊl/
n. a small thick-bodied, short-tailed animal of the rat and mouse family, which lives in fields, woods, banks of rivers, etc. 田鼠

volition /vəˈlɪʃn/
n. the power of choosing sth., making a decision, etc. by yourself 自愿选择；自行决定

volleyball /ˈvɒlɪbɔːl/
n. a game in which a large ball is struck by hand backwards and forwards across a net without being allowed to touch the ground 排球

volt /vəʊlt/
n. the unit for measuring the force of electric energy 伏特(电压单位)

voltage /ˈvəʊltɪdʒ/
n. the electrical force measured in volts 伏特数；电压：～ divider 分压器

voluble /ˈvɒljʊbl/
adj. speaking quickly and easily with great energy and enthusiasm 流畅的；健谈的；口若悬河的

volume /ˈvɒljuːm/
n. ❶ a book, especially one of a set of books 书本；(尤指一套书中的)一册，一卷：a library of a million ～s 藏书 100 万册的图书馆 ❷ the amount of space filled by sth. 容积；容量；体积：the ～ of a container 一个容器的容积 ❸ the degree of loudness of sound 音量；响度：the ～ of a radio 收音机的音量 ❹ the amount produced by some kind of activity 量；数量：the ～ of trade 贸易额 ‖ speak ～s (for) 雄辩地 说 明；充分表明 ‖ **voluminous** /vəˈluːmɪnəs/ *adj.* 大量的；长篇的；冗长啰唆的

voluntary /ˈvɒləntəri/
adj. (of a person or action) acting or done willingly; without being forced 自愿的；主动的；自发的：a ～ helper 主动帮忙者/～ contributions 自愿捐助

volunteer /ˌvɒlənˈtɪə(r)/
Ⅰ *n.* ❶ a person who offers his service or help, etc. without payment 志愿者；自愿参加者：～s for the post 自愿担任这一职位的人 ❷ a person who offers to enter the armed services 志愿兵；义务兵：the Chinese People's Volunteers 中国人民志愿军 Ⅱ *v.* do sth. as a volunteer 自愿(做、提供、参加等)：～ for service 自愿参军 / He ～ed his opinion on the plan. 他主动提出对这个计划的意见。/She ～ed to search for the missing child. 她自告奋勇去寻找那个失踪的孩子。

V

vomit/'vɒmɪt/

　I *v.* ❶ bring up (the contents in the stomach) through the mouth 呕吐: ～ one's dinner 把吃的饭都吐出来 /The mixture of drinks made him ～.喝了混合饮料之后他吐了出来。 ❷ send out with force and in great quantity 大量喷出: Volcanoes ～ lava.火山喷出大量岩浆。 Ⅱ *n.* sth. vomited 呕吐物: His bed was covered with ～.他的床上到处都是吐出来的东西。

vortex/'vɔːteɪks/

　n. ❶ a powerful circular moving mass of water or wind that can draw objects into its hollow centre, as in a whirlpool or whirlwind (尤指水或风形成的)涡流,涡旋;旋涡;旋风 ❷ a situation so powerful that one is helpless against it 无法抗拒的形势(处境): Against their will they were drawn into the ～ of war.他们不由自主地被卷进了战争的旋涡。

votary/'vəʊtəri/

　n. a regular worshipper 信徒;崇拜者: Roman soldiers were often votaries of Mars, the god of war.古罗马军人一般都信奉战神马尔斯。

vote/vəʊt/

　I *v.* pass or determine by marking a piece of paper or holding up hands 选举;投票;表决: ～ for (against) 投票选举(不选);投票赞成(反对)/～ by ballot (show of hands) 投票(举手)表决 Ⅱ *n.* a choice made by voting 投票;表决;选票: They called for a ～.他们要求投票表决。

vow/vaʊ/

　I *v.* make a serious promise or decision that you will do it 立誓;发誓: He ～ed revenge.他发誓要报复。 Ⅱ *n.* a serious promise or decision to do sth.誓言;誓约: All the court officials made a ～ of loyalty to their new Emperor.所有朝臣都宣誓效忠于他们的新皇上。 ‖ be under a ～ 发过誓/take ～s (as) 立誓(修行)

vowel/'vaʊəl/

　n. ❶ any one of the human speech sounds, in which the breath is let out without any stop or any closing of the air passage in the mouth or throat that can be heard 元音: front ～ 前元音/ central ～ 中元音 ❷ a letter that stands for such a sound 元音字母: The ～s in the English alphabet are a, e, i, o, u.英语字母表中元音字母有 a、e、i、o、u。

voyage/'vɔɪɪdʒ/

　I *n.* a long journey, often by sea 航海;航行: We shall go on a long sea ～.我们要做一次长途海上旅行。 Ⅱ *v.* make a long journey by sea 航海;航行: Columbus ～d across the Atlantic Ocean in 1492.哥伦布于 1492 年进行了横越大西洋的航行。

vulgar/'vʌlgə(r)/

　adj. rude or likely to offend sb.; not showing good judgement about sth. appropriate 粗鄙的;庸俗的;低级趣味的: ～ life 平庸生活/～ taste 低级趣味/～ language 粗鄙言语 ‖ ～ity/vʌl'gærəti/ *n.* 庸俗;粗俗

vulnerable/'vʌlnərəbl/

　adj. (of a place or thing) not well protected; able to be easily attacked; sensitive (地方或事物)未保护好的;易受攻击的;敏感的: Most girls are ～ to criticism.大多女孩子对批评很敏感。 ‖ be ～ to 易受攻击;易受害;对……敏感

V

Ww

wad /wɒd/

n. a thick collection of things, such as pieces of paper, which is folded, pressed, or fastened together 一卷;一叠;一捆;一团;一束(东西):a ~ of banknotes 一叠纸币/a ~ of letters 一叠信件

waddle /ˈwɒdl/

I *v*. walk like a duck, swaying from side to side 如鸭子般行走;摇摆着走;蹒跚 II *n*.a walk with unsteady steps 摇摆的步伐

wade /weɪd/

v. walk with an effort (through water, mud, etc.)(从水、泥等)趟,走过;跋涉;艰难前进:~ (across) a river 蹚水过河 / ~ through sand (the marshland, the long grass) 走过沙地(沼泽地、高草丛) / ~ through a dull book 啃完一本枯燥乏味的书

wafer /ˈweɪfə(r)/

n.a very thin, dry biscuit, which is often eaten with ice cream 威化饼;薄脆饼干

waffle[1] /ˈwɒfl/

n. a type of cake made of batter and cooked in an iron mould (用面粉、蛋、牛奶等混合成,在铁模里烘出的)蛋奶饼

waffle[2] /ˈwɒfl/

I *v*.talk nonsense;talk too much 胡扯;唠叨;What is he waffling on about? 他在唠叨些什么? II *n*.a foolish, unnecessary talk or writing 胡扯;夸夸其谈;空话:There is too much ~ in this essay. 这篇散文的空话太多了。

waft /wɑːft/

I *v*.carry or move lightly (through air or over water) 吹送;漂送;(使)浮动;(使)飘荡:A distant song was ~ed to our ears by the breeze. 远处的歌声随风飘到我们耳中。/The waves ~ed the boat to shore. 波浪将船漂送到岸边。 II *n*.a smell carried through the air 气味;一阵气味:a ~ of perfume 一阵香气 / ~ s of cigar smoke 一阵阵雪茄烟味

wag /wæg/

I *v*.(-gg-)❶ cause to shake quickly and repeatedly from side to side 使摇摆:The dog ~ged its tail with pleasure.那条狗得意地摇着尾巴。❷move from side to side 摇摆:~ back and forth 前后摆动 II *n*. (usually singular) a wagging motion (常用单数)摇摆:with a ~ of one's head 头一摇

wage /weɪdʒ/

n. the payment received for labour or service 工资;工钱 ‖ ~ earner 靠工资为生的人;雇佣劳动者/~ freeze 工资冻结/~ scale 工资等级(表)/~(s) fund 工资基金/~ packet 工资袋;工资/~ pattern 标准工资等级

waggle /ˈwægl/

v.(cause to) move up and down or from side to side quickly (使)摇摆;(使)摆动;(使)上下移动:The bird ~d its tail to shake the water off.那只鸟摆动着尾巴把水抖掉。

wag(g)on /ˈwægən/

n.❶ a four-wheeled carriage for heavy loads 四轮运货马车 ❷ an open railway truck 铁路货车

waif /weɪf/

n. ❶ a homeless person, especially an abandoned child 无家可归的人;弃儿;流浪儿童:The ~ was left on the steps of the orphanage.那个弃儿被丢在孤儿院的台阶上。❷ an object without an owner 无主的东西

wail /weɪl/

I *v*. make a prolonged cry showing sadness or pain 恸哭;哀号:The women ~ed over the war victims.妇女们为战争中的死难者号啕大哭。Ⅱ *n.*a prolonged cry of sadness or pain 号啕声 ‖ ~ful *adj.*悲叹的;恸哭的

waist/weɪst/

*n.*❶ the part of a person's body between the ribs and the hips 腰,腰部:She has a very small ~.她的腰部很苗条。❷ the part of an article of clothing which goes round one's waist 衣服的腰部,腰身:Can you take in the ~ of the trousers? 你能将这条裤子的腰缩小一点吗?

wait/weɪt/

*v.*❶ stay in a place until sb. comes or sth. happens 等;等候;等待:Time and tide ~ for no man. 岁月不等人。❷ serve meals,especially as a regular job 招待进餐,当侍者:The king had many people to ~ upon him.那位国王有无数的人来服侍他。 ‖ ~ and see 等着瞧/~ at table 伺候进餐/~ on (upon) 服侍;伺候;招待/~ on sb.hand and foot 像佣人一样地伺候 ‖ ~ing *n.*等待;等候;服侍;伺候;~ing room 候车室;候诊室,等候室/~er *n.*服务员,招待员/~ress *n.*女服务员;女招待员

waive/weɪv/

v.(with reference to a claim or right) give up;not insist on (指要求、权利)放弃;不坚持

wake[1]/weɪk/

v.(cause to) stop sleeping 醒来;唤醒;叫醒:He woke to find himself in the hospital.他醒来发现自己在医院里。

wake[2]/weɪk/

*n.*a track left by a ship in water or an aircraft in air (船的)航迹,尾波;(飞机的)尾流 ‖ in the ~ of 尾随;接踵而来:The storm left a trail of destruction in the ~ of it.暴风雨过处满目疮痍。

wakeful/'weɪkfl/

*adj.*not sleeping or in which one cannot sleep;sleepless 没有睡觉的;不眠的;失眠的;a ~ baby (night) 不睡觉的婴儿;不眠之夜 ‖ ~ly *adv.*没有睡觉地;失眠地/~ness *n.*失眠

waken/'weɪkən/

v.(cause to) wake 醒来;唤醒;(使)觉醒:I ~ed (up) at five.我 5 点钟就醒了。/Please ~ me at five.请在五点钟叫醒我。

walk/wɔːk/

Ⅰ *v.*move along on foot in a natural way,in such a way that one foot is always touching the ground 走;步行;散步 Ⅱ *n.*❶ a natural way of moving on foot in which a person's feet are lifted one at a time,in such a way that one foot is always touching the ground 步行;散步;go for a ~ 出去散步 ❷ a place, path, or course for walking 走道;行走路线:There is a very beautiful ~ up the hill.有一条美丽的小径上山去。 ‖ ~ away with 轻易赢得/~ into 走进;陷入(圈套)/~ off with 携走;偷走;(比赛中)赢得/~ on air 飘飘然;得意扬扬/~ out (of) 罢工;退出/~ out on 遗弃;放弃/~ over 欺侮;轻易取胜

walkaway/'wɔːkəweɪ/

*n.*an easily won competition 轻易取胜的比赛:That race was just a ~ for my horse.我的马在那场赛马中轻易取胜。

walker/'wɔːkə(r)/

*n.*❶ a person who walks, especially for pleasure or exercise (经常)散步的人;步行者:a fast ~ 走路走得快的人 ❷an apparatus for helping sb. to walk,especially a frame used by babies or people who cannot walk properly (帮助幼儿或病人练习走路的)助行架

walkies/'wɔːkɪz/

n.(used to dogs) a walk 散步(用于对狗发话):Come along,Spot;Let's go ~! 快来,斯波特,咱们散步去!

walkie-talkie/ˌwɔːki 'tɔːki/

*n.*a two-way radio that can be carried,allowing one to talk as well as listen 步话机,无线电对讲机

walking/'wɔːkɪŋ/

*adj.*❶used in the process of moving on foot 用于步行的:~ shoes 轻便鞋 ❷consisting of or done by travelling on foot 徒步旅行的:a ~ holiday(tour) 徒步旅行的假日;徒步旅行,远足 ❸ used to describe a human or living example of the thing mentioned 似人的，活的：She knows so many words that she's a ～ dictionary! 她知道的词非常多，她真是部活词典！

walkout/'wɔːkaʊt/

n. **❶** the action of leaving a meeting or organization as an expression of disapproval（表示抗议的）退席，退会：a ～ by (of) the Russian delegation 俄罗斯代表团的退席 **❷** a strike, especially at its start（尤指开始时的）罢工：The ～ was caused by a disagreement over pay and working conditions. 罢工是由于在工资和劳动条件等问题上发生争论而引起的。/The union staged a ～ over the issue. 工会针对这个问题发动了罢工。

walkover/'wɔːkəʊvə(r)/

n. **❶** an easy victory 轻易取得的胜利 **❷** an advance from one part of a competition to the next without having to compete against anyone, because of the sickness or withdrawal of one's opponent 幸运晋级，幸运出线（由于对手有病或主动弃权而顺利进入下一轮比赛）

wall/wɔːl/

n. a side of a house or room; a vertical solid structure made of stone or brick enclosing a piece of land 墙；围墙；城墙：the Great Wall 长城 ‖ **beat (knock) one's head against a ～** 白费劲/**go to the ～** 失败；破产 ‖ **～paper** *n.* 护墙纸

wallet/'wɒlɪt/

n. a small flat leather case which can be folded for holding papers and paper money 钱夹；皮夹：He has lost his ～. 他把钱夹弄丢了。

wallop/'wɒləp/

Ⅰ *v.* hit hard; beat 重击；猛打：He ～ed the ball (for) miles. 他把球打出很远很远。Ⅱ *n.* a hard blow 重击；痛打

wallow/'wɒləʊ/

v. **❶** roll about in mud or dirty water（在泥、污水中）打滚；翻滚 **❷** indulge too much in sth. 沉迷于：～ in money 沉迷于金钱

walnut/'wɔːlnʌt/

n. **❶** the nut containing an eatable kernel

with a rough shell which can be easily divided into two parts 核桃；胡桃 **❷** the tree on which this nut grows 核桃树；胡桃树 **❸** wood of this tree 核桃木

waltz/wɔːls/

n. **❶** a smooth, and elegant dance with three beats to the measure 华尔兹舞：I can't dance the ～. 我不会跳华尔兹舞。**❷** the music for the dance 华尔兹舞曲：They're playing a ～ by Strauss. 他们正在演奏施特劳斯的华尔兹舞曲。

wan/wɒn/

adj. **❶**（with reference to a person）looking tired or ill; pale（指人）有倦容的，病态的，苍白的 **❷**（with reference to light）pale and weak（指光）暗淡的，微弱的

wand/wɒnd/

n. a thin stick carried in hand, especially by a magician 棒；棍；竿；杖；指挥棒；魔杖：The magician waved his ～. 魔术师挥动他的魔棒。

wander/'wɒndə(r)/

v. go from place to place without special purpose 漫游；闲逛；徘徊 ‖ ～away(back) 走神；神态恍惚；(思想)开小差 ‖ ～er *n.* 漫游者；流浪汉/～ing *adj.* 漫游的；闲逛的；漂泊的；流浪的

wane/weɪn/

v. become less, weaker, etc. 缩小；减弱；衰落：His strength is waning. 他的精力在衰退。

wangle/'wæŋgl/

Ⅰ *v.* get sth. by a clever talk or a trick（以花言巧语或诡计）骗取：He ～d free tickets to the concert. 他用计骗取音乐会免费入场券。Ⅱ *n.* an act or an instance of getting sth. in such a way 欺诈行为；哄骗：Be careful! This is one of his ～s. 小心！这是他的一个小把戏。

want/wɒnt/

Ⅰ *v.* **❶** have a desire to or for; wish for 要；想要：I ～ some tea. 我想要喝点茶。**❷** say that sth. needs to be done 需要：Plants ～ water. 植物需要水分。**❸** a lack of sth. 缺乏：He doesn't ～ courage. 他有的是勇气。Ⅱ *n.* need; sth. needed 需要；

W

必需之物：Are you in ～ of money? 你需要钱吗？‖ (be) ～ing in 缺乏/(not) ～ for（不）缺乏/～ some doing 需要费大劲/for（from）～ of 因为缺乏/in ～ 穷困；生活困难/in ～ of 缺乏/～ out of 不想参与某事

war /wɔː(r)/

n. an armed conflict（between countries）战争：the First World War 第一次世界大战/a civil ～ 内战/prisoners of ～ 战俘/cold ～ 冷战 ‖ be at ～（with）（同……）作战；交战/declare ～ on（upon）向……宣战/go to ～ 开战；上战场打仗/make（wage）～ on 和……开战 ‖ ～cry *n.*（作战时鼓舞士气的）呐喊声/～fare *n.* 战争；作战；交战；战事/～like *adj.* 好战的；尚武的；准备作战的/～lord *n.* 军阀/～monger *n.* 战争贩子/～plane *n.* 军用飞机/～ship *n.* 军舰/～time *n.* 战时

ward /wɔːd/

n. a separate room in a hospital 病房；牢房：a medical（surgical）～ 内科（外科）病房

warden /ˈwɔːdn/

n. a person who is in charge of a building or has particular duties 看守人；保管员；管理员：the ～ of a students' hostel 学生宿舍的管理员 ‖ traffic ～ *n.* 交通执勤人员

warder /ˈwɔːdə(r)/

n. a man who guards those in prison；jailer 狱吏；（监狱）看守

wardrobe /ˈwɔːdrəub/

n. ❶ a room, closet, or piece of furniture for holding clothes 衣柜；衣橱；藏衣室：Hang your suit in the ～. 把你的衣服挂在衣柜里。❷ a person's entire collection of clothes（个人）全部服装：She is shopping for her spring ～. 她正在选购春装。

ware /weə/

n. articles for sale；goods 货物；商品：This shop sells a great variety of ～s. 这家商店出售许多不同的商品。‖ ～house *n.* 贮藏室/house～ *n.* 家庭用品/silver～ *n.* 银器/iron～ *n.* 铁器

warm /wɔːm/

Ⅰ *adj.* ❶ neither hot nor cold；of medium heat（between hot and cool）温暖的；暖和的：The climate is ～ in the south. 南方的气候很温暖。❷ friendly；hearty 热烈的；热情的；亲切的：We received a ～ welcome. 我们受到了热烈的欢迎。Ⅱ *v.* make or become warm（使）温暖；（使）暖和；变热：The fire soon ～ed the room. 炉火很快使房子暖和起来了。‖ ～-blooded *adj.* 热血的；热情的

warmth /wɔːmθ/

n. the condition of being warm or kind 温暖，热情：She greeted me with ～. 她热情地向我致意。

warn /wɔːn/

v. tell in advance（of sth. bad or dangerous）警告；告诫；提醒注意：The doctor ～ed the patient not to smoke. 医生告诫病人不要抽烟。

warning /ˈwɔːnɪŋ/

Ⅰ *n.* a statement or an event that indicates sth. bad or dangerous 警报；警告；告诫；预告：He gave her a ～ against driving too fast. 他告诫她不要开快车。/Let this experience be a ～ to you to be more careful. 以这次经历作为告诫，以后你要更加小心。Ⅱ *adj.* giving a warning 警告的；预示的：She gave me a ～ look. 她对我使了一个警告的眼色。

warp /wɔːp/

Ⅰ *v.* ❶（cause to）become bent or twisted 弄弯；变弯；（使）翘起：The sun ～ed the boards. 阳光把木板晒得翘起了。/The cover of the book has ～ed. 这本书的书皮翘起来了。❷（cause to）become biased, distorted or perverted（使）有偏见；歪曲；反常：a ～ed account 歪曲真相的叙述/Prejudice ～s our judgment. 偏见歪曲了我们的判断。Ⅱ *n.* a twist out of a true level or straight line 弯曲；扭曲：There is a ～ in the board. 这块板有些弯曲。

warrant /ˈwɒrənt/

Ⅰ *n.* ❶ a proper reason or justification for sth. 正当理由；正当：He left without ～. 他没有正当理由就离开了。/She had no ～ for thinking thus. 她这样想是没有正当理由的。❷ a written order giving official authority for sth. 授权；委任状；许可证；搜查令：You can't search my house without a ～.没有搜查令你不能搜查我的房子。Ⅱ v.❶ give authority to; cause to appear reasonable 授权给; 批准; 使有(正当)理由: Nothing can ～ such insolence. 这等无礼毫无道理。❷ guarantee; ensure 担保; 保证: I ～ you that I'm telling the truth. 我向你保证我说的是实话。/I ～ him to be honest. 我担保他为诚实的。

warranty/ˈwɒrənti/
n. a written guarantee 保证书; 保单: The manufacturers will have to repair the car without charge because it's still under ～. 厂家非得免费修理这辆车不可, 因为现在它还在保修期内。

warring/ˈwɔːrɪŋ/
adj. at war; in conflicting with each other 交战的; 冲突(中)的; 敌对的: ～ factions (families) 敌对的派别(家族)/～ beliefs 互相冲突的信念

warrior/ˈwɒrɪə(r)/
n. a soldier who fights in a battle 武士; 勇士; 战士

warship/ˈwɔːʃɪp/
n. a naval ship used for war 军舰

wartime/ˈwɔːtaɪm/
n. a period of time when a nation is at war 战时: rationing in ～ 战时的定量配给/France 战时的法国

wary/ˈweəri/
adj. careful; looking out for danger 谨慎的; 谨防的; 小心翼翼的: wild animals ～ of traps 提防着陷阱的野生动物/a ～ old politician who never says too much 从不多说话的、谨慎小心的老政客

wash/wɒʃ/
Ⅰ v.❶ make sth. clean with water or other liquid 洗; 洗涤: ～ the clothes clean 把衣服洗干净 ❷ carry away in the moving water or liquid 流过; 冲击; 拍打; 卷走: The waves ～ (against) the shore. 波浪拍打海岸。Ⅱ n.❶ an act of washing or being washed 洗; 洗涤; 冲洗: dry ～ 干洗 ❷ clothes to be washed or being washed 待洗的衣服; 洗好的衣服 ‖ ～ **against** (**on**) 拍击; 冲刷/～ **away** 冲走; 洗刷掉; 洗掉/～ **clean** 洗干净/～ **down** 冲洗/～

off 洗掉/～ **one's hands of** 不再管(参与)某事/～ **out** 洗掉; 冲走; 打消; 消除/～ **o-ver** 从上面冲刷过去/～ **overboard** (波浪)把……打到海里/～ **up** 洗(盘子); 洗手; 洗脸 ‖ ～**ing** *n.* 洗涤; 洗的衣服: a ～**ing machine** 洗衣机

wasp/wɒsp/
n. a kind of winged insect, having a sting and a slender waist 黄蜂; 马蜂: a waist like a ～'s 蜂腰; 细腰

wastage/ˈweɪstɪdʒ/
*n.*❶ loss or destruction of sth., especially wasteful loss of the valuable (尤指贵重物的)浪费, 损耗 ❷ a reduction in numbers because of leaving, dying, etc. (退职、死亡等非人为裁减引起的)减员: We expect to lose over 50 people from our work force every year by natural ～. 我们预计我们的劳动力每年的自然减员为 50 人。

waste/weɪst/
Ⅰ v. use wrongly; make no use of 浪费; 滥用; 挥霍: ～ one's time and money 浪费时间和金钱 Ⅱ n.❶ the act of using sth. wrongly or carelessly 浪费; 滥用: It's a ～ of time to wait any longer. 再等下去是白费时间。❷ waste material or sth. else that is not needed 废物; 废料: Throw the ～ away. 把这些废物扔掉。Ⅲ *adj.* (of land) that cannot be used; ruined (指土地)荒芜的; 贫瘠的;(指东西)无用的; 废弃的: ～ paper 废纸 ‖ ～ one's breath (words) 白费口舌/go to ～ 浪费掉/lay ～ 损坏; 蹂躏/lie ～ (土地等)荒芜 ‖ ～**basket** *n.* 废纸篓/～**bin** *n.* 废纸箱; 垃圾桶/～**land** *n.* 荒地/～**ful** *adj.* 浪费的; 挥霍的; 耗费的

watch/wɒtʃ/
Ⅰ v.❶ look at sb. or sth. continuously; observe carefully; keep the eyes on 观看; 注视: He was ～ing TV. 他在看电视。❷ look after 看护; 守护; 照管 ❸ be careful of sb. or sth. 注意; 监视: The man is being ～ed by the police. 警方正监视那个人。‖ ～ **for** 注意等候/～ **one's time** 等待时机/～ **out** (**for**) 当心; 注意; 提防/～ **over** 照看; 守护; 监视 Ⅱ n. the act of watching sb. or sth. in case of possible danger or problems 看守; 监视; 照管: Keep close ～

over the enemy.密切注意敌人的行动。‖ be on the ～ for 提防;警惕;当心;留心/go on ～ 值勤;上夜班/keep ～ for 提防;警惕;注意等候/keep ～ on 监视;密切注视/keep ～ over 照看;注意/keep ～ 站岗;守夜/on ～ 站岗;值勤守夜/set a ～ on 布置监视人 ‖ ～dog n.看门狗;警犬;监察人/～man n.看守人;警卫员;更夫/～word n.暗语;暗号;口号 ‖ ～able adj.值得注意的/～er n.看守人;守夜者;护理者

water/'wɔːtə(r)/
I n.a liquid without colour,smell or taste that forms the seas,lakes,rivers and rain 水 ‖ in deep ～(s) 在不幸(困难)中;处于困境/be under ～ 被水所淹/go through fire and ～ 赴汤蹈火/by ～ 乘船/fish in troubled ～ 浑水摸鱼/hold ～ 站得住脚;能成立/in smooth ～ 处境顺利/keep one's head above ～ 勉强维持;不负债/make (pass) ～ 小便/of the first ～ 一流的;头等技术的/spend money like ～ 挥霍;挥金如土/throw cold ～ on 给……浇冷水/Still ～s run deep.〈谚〉静水流深,大智若愚。II v.❶ put water on 洒水;浇水;灌溉 ❷ (of the eyes or mouth) fill with water;have mouth liquid 流泪;淌口水:The thick smoke made my eyes ～.浓烟熏得我直流泪。‖ ～ closet (WC)n.厕所;抽水马桶/～colour n.水彩颜料;水彩画/～course n.河道;水道/～fall n.瀑布/～front n.水边;滩;滨水区/～ing place n.矿泉;疗养地/～line n.(船的)吃水线/～mark n.(纸张上的)水印/～melon n.西瓜/～proof n.& adj.防水(的)/～shed n.分水线;分水岭/～works n.自来水厂

waterski/'wɔːtəˌskiː/
v.travel over water on skis 滑水:If you ～,you ski on water while you are pulled along by a boat.假如你滑水,你就是由船拖着在水面上滑行。

watertight/'wɔːtətaɪt/
adj.made or fastened so that water cannot get in or out 不透水的;防水的:～ boxes 不漏水的盒子

watery/'wɔːtəri/
adj.like water;of water;full of water 似水的;水的;多水的:～ fluid 稀流质

watt/wɒt/
n.a unit of electrical power 瓦特;瓦(电功率单位):My lamp is 100 ～s.我的灯是100瓦的。

wattage/'wɒtɪdʒ/
n.an amount of electrical power in watts 瓦(特)数:an electric heater with a ～ of three kilowatts 瓦数为三千的电热器

wave/weɪv/
I v.❶ (cause to) move the hand or arm from side to side or up and down 晃动;挥臂;挥手:He ～d his hand to me.他向我挥手。❷ move freely and gently while remaining fixed to one point 飘动;飘扬;波动;起伏:The red flag is waving in the breeze.红旗迎风招展。II n.❶ curving lines of water, especially on the sea, which rise and fall 浪;波浪;波涛:A big ～ turned our boat over.一个大浪打翻了我们的小船。❷ the act of waving, especially of sth., as a signal 挥手;招手;挥臂;摇摆;挥动:He gave us a friendly ～ as he passed.他走过时,向我们友好地挥了挥手。❸ a form in which some types of energy move, such as light and sound (热、光、音、电的)波:radio ～s 无线电波/long (short) ～s 长 (短)波 ‖ ～length n.波长 ‖ wavy adj.波动的;起伏的;波状的;动摇的

waver/'weɪvə(r)/
v.❶ move unsteadily 摇摆;摇晃:The old man ～s a little as he walks.那位老人走路时有些摇晃。/The flame ～ed and went out.火焰摇晃了几下就熄灭了。❷ tremble 颤抖:His hands were ～ing as he talked.他说话时手在颤抖。❸ hesitate or be uncertain, especially when making choice 犹豫不决:She ～ed between going and staying.她在去留之间举棋不定。❹ begin to give away 动摇;开始退让:They showed a sign of ～ing.他们表现出动摇的迹象。

wax/wæks/
n.a solid material made of fats or oils which changes to a thick liquid when melted by heat 蜡;蜂蜡:sealing ～ 封蜡;火漆/～ candle 蜡烛/～ cloth 蜡布

waxen/'wæksn/

adj. ❶very pale;looking ill and sick 蜡黄的,苍白的;a ～ face 苍白的脸 ❷made of wax 蜡制的

waxwork /ˈwæksˌwɜːk/
n. ❶a model of human being made in wax 蜡像 ❷a place where one can see wax models 蜡像(陈列)馆

waxy /ˈwæksi/
adj. looking or feeling like wax 蜡质的;似蜡的

way /wei/
n. ❶ a road,path or street 路;道路;街道:the ～ to the station 到车站的路/ask the ～ 问路 ❷ a route or road you take to some place 路线:He is on his ～ home.他在回家的途中。❸the distance from one place to another 路程;距离:The church is a long ～ off.教堂距此很远。/The post office is only a short ～ away. 邮局隔得很近。❹a method or manner of doing sth. 方式;方法;手段:the best ～ to do sth.做某事的最好方法 ❺an aspect of sth.方面:He has changed in every ～.他已经彻底改变了。‖ all the ～ 一直地/be one's ～ 就是这个习惯(脾气)/by the ～ 顺便说一句/by ～ of 取道、经由;为了/cut both ～s 对人对己均不利/get into (out of) the ～ of 变得习惯于(不习惯于)/give ～ to 让位给;听任/go out of one's ～ 特意;专门/have (get, go, take) one's own ～ 自主行动;一意孤行/in a big(small) ～ 大(小)规模地/in a (one)～ 在某种程度上;就某个意义来说/in every ～ 在各方面,无论从哪方面说/in many ～s 在多方面/in no ～ 一点也不;决不/in one ～ or another 以各种方式/(in) one's own ～ 按自己特有的方式/in the family ～ 怀孕/in the ～ 碍事;妨碍/lead the ～ 带路;引路/lose one's ～ 迷路/make one's ～ 到某地;上进;成功/make ～ (for) 让路/on the ～ (to...) 在……途中/out of the ～ 不挡道;不碍事/pave the ～ for 为……铺平道路/pick one's ～ 费劲地走/put in the (one's) ～ (of) 帮助得到/put out of the ～ 除掉;处置掉/show the ～ 指明道路/stand in one's ～ 阻挠;妨碍/to one's ～ of thinking 照……看来/under ～ 在进行中

waylay /weiˈlei/
v. wait in order to attack,or speak to sb. passing by (为了袭击或谈话而)拦住,拦截

wayward /ˈweiwəd/
adj. not easily controlled or predicted 任性的;倔强的:a child with a ～ disposition 性格倔强的孩子/She is obstinate and ～.她既固执又任性。

we /wiː/
pron. ❶the plural form of I (I 的复数形式)我们 ❷people in general 人们

weak /wiːk/
adj. ❶ lacking in strength 弱的;虚弱的:He felt very ～ after illness.他病后觉得很虚弱。❷ not good at 差的;不擅长的:He's ～ in grammar.他的语法很差。❸ containing a lot of water 淡的;稀薄的:～ tea 淡茶/The coffee is too ～.这咖啡太淡了。

weaken /ˈwiːkən/
v. make weak or weaker 使减弱;使变淡:You can ～ tea by adding water.你可以加水把茶冲淡一些。

weal /wiːl/
n. a raised usually red mark on the skin where one has been hit (皮肤上被打过的)红肿;隆起的伤痕,条痕

wealth /welθ/
n. ❶ many valuable possessions; much money or property;riches 财富;财产:He is a man of great ～.他是一位富翁。❷ a large quantity; abundance 大量;丰富:a ～ of words 大量的词汇

wealthy /ˈwelθi/
adj. (especially of a person, family, or country) rich (尤指人、家庭或国家)富有的,富裕的

weapon /ˈwepən/
n. ❶a tool used for fighting or attacking sb.武器;兵器:the most modern ～ of war 最现代化的战争武器 / nuclear ～ 核武器 ❷ means of attack or defence (攻击或防御)手段:Humour is her only ～ against their hostility.幽默是她对付他们敌意的唯一一手段。

W

wear/weə(r)/

Ⅰ*v.*❶ have sth. on one's body, especially as clothing, but sometimes also for protection, decoration or other purposes 穿；戴；佩带：A policeman ～s a blue uniform. 警察穿蓝色制服。❷ have (a particular expression) on the face (脸上)显出，呈现：The people wore a happy smile. 人们脸上露出了愉快的笑容。❸ be reduced, weakened, or damaged by continued use, rubbing, etc. 变旧；磨损；穿烂；用坏：His shoes have started to ～. 他的鞋已开始磨坏了。❹ have one's hair or beard arranged in a specific style 留，蓄（头发、胡须）‖ ～ away 磨损；磨掉；慢慢过去；日益憔悴/～ down 磨薄；使逐渐虚弱/～ off 磨掉；慢慢消失掉/～ on 缓缓进行；(时间)慢慢过去/～ out 穿破；用旧；使疲惫不堪；耗尽；消磨掉/～ through 磨穿/～ well 经穿；耐用 Ⅱ*n.*❶ the act of wearing, especially clothes 使用；穿；戴；损耗；磨损；用坏；穿破：The carpet shows signs of ～. 地毯有磨损的迹象。❷ clothes of the stated type, or for the stated purpose 衣服；穿戴之物：The store sells children's ～. 这家商店卖童装。

wearing/'weərɪŋ/

adj. mentally or physically tiring 使人疲乏的；令人厌倦的：I find him very ～ when he talks on and on. 他说个没完的时候，我真觉得他很烦。

wearisome/'wɪərɪsəm/

adj. that makes one feel tired, bored, or annoyed 令人厌倦的；令人厌烦的；讨厌的：a ～ day 累人的一天/a ～ task 乏味的任务

weary/'wɪərɪ/

Ⅰ*adj.* feeling or showing tiredness 疲倦的；劳累的；令人厌烦的：I was ～ after a day of hard work. 辛勤工作一天之后，我感到疲惫不堪。Ⅱ*v.* cause to become tired 使疲乏，使疲倦：The trip wearied me. 旅行使我感到疲劳。‖ (be) ～ of 对……(感到)厌烦 ‖ **weariness** *n.* 疲乏

weasel/'wiːzl/

n. a small fierce animal with a thin body, short legs and a long tail, which kills and eats chickens, rabbits, etc. 鼬鼠，黄鼠狼

weather/'weðə(r)/

n. the condition of rain, wind, sunshine, etc. in a particular area and at a specific time 天气：What's the ～ like today? 今天的天气怎么样？/fine ～ 晴天；好天气/bad ～ 坏天气 ‖ be (feel) under the ～ 不舒服 ‖ -beaten *adj.* 饱经风霜的；(皮肤)粗糙的；晒黑的/～man *n.* 气象播音员

weave/wiːv/

v. (wove, woven) ❶ make (threads, etc.) into cloth, etc. 纺织；编；织：～ a rug 织地毯/～ straw into hats 把草编成帽子/It is woven of silk. 这是用丝织成的。❷ put together；compose (a story, etc.) 编排；撰写(故事等)：～ facts into a story 把事实编成故事/～ a plot 编一个情节

weaver/'wiːvə(r)/

n. a person whose job is to weave cloth 织布工；织布者

web/web/

*n.*❶ a thin net woven by a spider 蜘蛛网：spider's ～ 蜘蛛网 ❷ a system of interconnected elements (相互关联因素组成的)网状物，网络：a ～ of railways 纵横交错的铁路网

wed/wed/

v. (-dd-) marry 娶；嫁；结婚：He ～ded a girl from America. 他与一个美国女孩结婚了。/He ～ded his daughter to an artist. 他将女儿嫁给了一位艺术家。

wedding/'wedɪŋ/

n. a marriage ceremony 婚礼：～ day 婚礼日 / golden ～ 金婚 / silver ～ 银婚

wedge/wedʒ/

Ⅰ*n.*❶ a piece of wood or metal shaped like a "V" which is driven into wood, etc. to split it, or is used to keep two things firm or separate 楔子；三角木 ❷ sth. which is V shaped 楔形物，V形物：a ～ of cake 一块切成楔形的糕饼 Ⅱ*v.*❶ keep firm or separate with a wedge 用楔木使牢固；用楔木劈开 ❷ push in like a wedge 楔入；挤进：The little boy ～d himself between the two big ones. 这小孩挤在两个大孩子中间。

Wednesday/'wenzdeɪ/

n. the day of the week after Tuesday and

before Thursday 星期三

weed /wiːd/

I *n.* the unwanted wild plant, especially one which prevents crops or garden flowers from growing properly 野草;杂草 II *v.* remove weeds from (a place where crops or flowers grow) 除草,锄草,拔草:~ a garden 除去花园里的杂草‖~ **out** 除去;淘汰

weedy /ˈwiːdi/

adj. ❶ thin and physically weak 瘦弱的 ❷ weak in character 性格软弱的 ❸ full of weeds 杂草丛生的:a ~ garden 长满杂草的园子

week /wiːk/

n. a period of seven days (and nights), from Sunday to Saturday or from Monday to Sunday 周;星期:He goes to the cinema once a ~.他每周去看一次电影。

weekday /ˈwiːkdeɪ/

n. any day except Saturday and Sunday 工作日:Our store is open only on ~s.我们店只在工作日开门。

weekend /ˈwiːkˌend/

n. Saturday and Sunday 周末:They spent a ~ in Paris.他们在巴黎过的周末。

weekly /ˈwiːkli/

I *adv.* once a week 每周一次:be published ~ 每周出版一次 II *adj.* of, for a week 每周的;每周一次的:a ~ magazine 周刊 / a ~ visit 每周一次的访问 III *n.* a newspaper or magazine that is published once a week 周报;周刊:Is this newspaper a ~ or daily? 这种报纸是周报还是日报?

weep /wiːp/

v. cry; let tears fall from the eyes 哭;哭泣;流泪:~ for joy 由于高兴而落泪/~ at the sad news 听到悲伤的消息而哭泣/~ tears of joy 流出兴奋的眼泪/~ one's life away 终日以泪洗面

weeping /ˈwiːpɪŋ/

adj. (of a tree) with the branches hanging down (树枝)低垂的:a ~ willow 垂柳

weepy /ˈwiːpi/

adj. ❶ tending to cry, or crying often; tearful 要哭的;常哭的;泪汪汪的:not

very well, and feeling ~ 觉得身体不舒服,想哭 ❷ (of story, film, etc.) that makes one sad (故事、电影等)使人伤心的

weigh /weɪ/

v. ❶ measure how heavy sth. is 称(重量):Do you often ~ yourself? 你常称体重吗? ❷ have a weight of 重量为:The luggage ~s twenty kilograms.行李重 20 千克。 ❸ consider the importance of sth., especially before a decision or action 考虑,权衡‖~ **anchor** 起锚/~ **against** 对……不利;与……权衡/~ **down** 压下;压倒;压得低垂/~ **in** 过秤;(赛前)称重量/~ **in one's favour** 对……有利/~ **on** (**upon**) 压在肩上;成为负担/~ **one's words** 推敲;斟酌;估量‖~**er** *n.* 过磅员/~ **bridge** *n.* 台秤;桥秤/~ **house** *n.* 过秤处;计量所/~**ing machine** *n.* 衡器/~ **man** *n.* 过秤员;称货员

weight /weɪt/

n. ❶ the heaviness of a person or thing 重量;分量:He was at least 70 kilograms in ~.他的体重至少有 70 千克。 ❷ the ability to influence sb.'s actions and decisions 影响力 ❸ the great responsibility 重压,重担

weighty /ˈweɪti/

adj. ❶ heavy; having much weight 重的;沉重的:weightier than Mount Tai 比泰山还重 ❷ important 重要的:a ~ speaker 一位重要的发言人

weir /wɪə(r)/

n. a wall built across a river to control but not stop the flow of water (拦河而筑以控制水流的)堰堤,拦河坝,水栅

weird /wɪəd/

adj. strange; unnatural 奇异的;非自然的:~ clothes 奇装异服 / a ~ idea 古怪的想法

welcome /ˈwelkəm/

I *v.* ❶ greet in a friendly way; show pleasure at the arrival of 欢迎;迎接:We were warmly ~d.我们受到了热烈欢迎。 ❷ accept or receive sth. happily 欣然接受:I ~ your criticism. 对你的批评我欣然接受。 II *adj.* that one is glad to have, receive,see,etc.受欢迎的：You are ～ to our school.欢迎你到我们学校来。‖ **make sb.** ～ 款待某人 Ⅲ *n*.an instance or manner of greeting sb.欢迎；迎接：They will give you a warm ～.他们将热烈欢迎你。

weld/weld/

v. join（pieces of metal）by pressure （when the metal is hot）焊接；熔接；锻接：～ a broken rod 焊接一根断了的杆子/Iron ～s.铁可以焊接。

welfare/'welfeə(r)/

n. the condition of being well or doing well；health，happiness and prosperity 幸福；康乐：We are concerned about his ～.我们关心他的幸福。

well/wel/

Ⅰ *adj*. in good health 健康的；痊愈的：You don't look ～.你的脸色不大好。Ⅱ *adv*.❶in a good way；satisfactorily，kindly，successfully，etc.好地；令人满意地：It is ～ written.写得好。❷much；quite 很；极；非常：I like it ～.我很喜欢它。❸ thoroughly and completely 充分地；彻底地；完全地：Shake the bottle ～ before you take the medicine.服药前将瓶充分摇动。‖ **as** ～ 也；又/**be** ～ **out of sth.**幸亏没卷入/**just as** ～ 还是……好；不妨/**come off** ～ 结局很好/**do** ～ 工作得好；进行得好；生长得好/**do** ～ **out of** 从中得到好处/**as** ～ 还/**speak（think）** ～ **of** 称颂；赞扬/～ **off** 富裕的/～ **up in** 很了解；很懂行 Ⅲ *int*. used for introducing an expression of surprise，doubt，acceptance，etc.(表示惊讶、怀疑、接受等)：Well，who would have guessed it! 真的，谁会想到呢! ‖ ～**-being** *n*. 幸福；康乐/～**born** *adj*.出身名门的/～ **connected** *adj*.出身望族的/～**disposed** *adj*.怀有好意的；乐于助人的/～**doing** *n*.善事；善行/～**intentioned**，～**meaning**，～ **meant** *adj*.善意的；好意的；好心的/～**-nigh** *adv*.几乎；将近/～ **timed** *adj*.适时的；合时的/～**-to-do** *adj*.富裕的

well advised/ˌweləd'vaɪzd/

adj.prudent；wise 审慎的；明智的：a ～ action 审慎的行为

well-appointed/ˌweləˈpɔɪntɪd/

adj.having all the necessary objects，apparatus or furniture 装备完善的；配备齐全的：a ～ hotel 装备完善的旅馆/ a ～ office 设备完善的办公室

well-dressed/wel'drest/

adj.fashionably dressed 穿着入时的：I met a very ～ woman.我遇到一位穿着十分入时的女人。

well-known/wel'nəun/

adj.famous；widely known 著名的；闻名的；众所周知的：a ～ scientist 一位著名的科学家 /He was ～ some years ago.他几年前就出名了。/Guilin is ～ for its scenery.桂林以风景优美而闻名。

welterweight/'weltəweɪt/

n.a boxer heavier than a lightweight but lighter than a middleweight 次中量级拳击手

wend/wend/

v.（～ one's way）move or travel over a distance，especially slowly（尤指缓慢地）行；走：We ～ed our way across the street after supper.晚饭后我们慢悠悠地走过街道。

west/west/

n.❶ the direction in which the sun goes down 西；西方 ❷ the western part of a country，region，etc.西部地区：a ～ wind 西风/the ～ of Europe 欧洲西部/The sun sets in the ～.太阳在西方落下。‖ **go** ～ 完蛋了/～ **of** 在……以西 ‖ ～**erly** *adj*.& *adv*.向西方(的)；(风)来自西方(的)

western/'westən/

adj.toward the west；from the west；of or in the west 西方的：～ customs 西方习俗/ a ～ wind 西风

westerner/'westənə(r)/

n.❶someone who lives in or comes from the west 西方人 ❷someone who lives in or comes from the west of America（美国的)西部人

westernize/'westənaɪz/

v.cause or influence sb. or sth. (especially African or Asian people and countries) to have or copy the customs and behaviour typical of America and Europe 使西方化；

使西化

westernmost/ˈwestənməʊst/

　adj.in or of the furthest west 最西的：the ～ parts of Scotland 苏格兰最西的部分

westward/ˈwestwəd/

　Ⅰ *adj*.that towards the west 向西的：on the ～ slope of the hill 在西山坡 Ⅱ *adv*.(also ～s) towards the west 向西地：They travelled ～(s).他们向西而行。

wet/wet/

　Ⅰ *adj*.covered or soaked with liquid；rainy 湿的；潮的；多雨的：Her eyes were ～ with tears. 她两眼泪汪汪。 Ⅱ *v*.cause sth.to be wet 把……弄湿：Don't ～ your feet.不要打湿脚。‖ ～ nurse *n*.乳娘

whale/weɪl/

　n.a very large animal living in the sea and looking like a fish 鲸

whaler/ˈweɪlə(r)/

　n.❶someone who hunts whales at sea 捕鲸者 ❷a ship or boat from which whales are hunted 捕鲸船

whaling/ˈweɪlɪŋ/

　n. the business of hunting whales and treating them in order to obtain oil and other materials 捕鲸业；鲸加工业

wharf/wɔːf/

　n.a structure built into the water where ships can load and unload 码头

what/wɒt/

　pron. ❶ used in questions about an unknown thing or person，or kind of thing or person 什么：What do you want? 你想要什么? ❷the thing or things that …… 的事物；无论什么：What he said is true. 他所讲的话都是真的。‖ I know ～.我有一个主意。/So ～? 那又怎么样呢? /What about...? (征求意见) …… 怎么样? /～ if 假设；如果；该怎么样/～ is called 所谓/～'s ～ 事情的真相 Ⅱ *int*.used in exclamations to emphasize sth.surprising or remarkable 多么(用于感叹)：What lovely weather! 多好的天气啊! /What a pity! 多可惜!

whatever/wɒtˈevər/

　Ⅰ *pron*.❶ anything that 不论什么：You can eat ～ you like.你愿意吃什么就吃什

么。❷ no matter what 无论什么：Whatever happens，he is safe.无论发生什么事，他总是平安无事。Ⅱ *adj*.any that；no matter what 任何的；无论什么的：Whatever excuse he makes will not be believed.无论他找什么借口也没有人相信。

wheat/wiːt/

　n.a plant producing grain from which flour is made 小麦：We drove past endless fields of ～.我们驾车驶过无边无际的麦田。/He grows a lot of ～.他种了很多小麦。

wheaten/ˈwiːtn/

　adj.made from wheat (flour) 小麦做的；面粉做的：～ bread 面包

wheel/wiːl/

　n.a circular object with an outer frame which turns round an inner part the hub to which it is joined，used for turning machinery，making vehicles move，etc.轮子；车轮；机轮：the ～ of history 历史的车轮 ‖ go (run) on ～s 顺利进行/put one's shoulder to the ～ 使劲干；全力以赴/set the ～s in motion 干起来；实施起来/take the ～ 负责管理/～s within ～s 复杂的结构；中间还有奥妙 ‖ ～barrow *n*.独轮手推车/～wright *n*.车轮匠

wheelbase/ˈwiːlbeɪs/

　n.the distance between the front and back axle on a vehicle (车辆前、后轴的)轴距：This truck is the long-～ model. 这种卡车是长轴距的型号。

wheelchair/ˈwiːltʃeə(r)/

　n.a chair with large wheels which can be turned by the user，used especially by people who are unable to walk 轮椅：The injured pilot spent the rest of his life in a ～.这个受伤的飞行员在轮椅上度过了余生。

wheeled/wiːld/

　adj.having wheels 有轮子的：～ vehicles 带轮的运载工具/a two-～ cart 两轮大车

wheelhouse/ˈwiːlhaʊs/

　n. the place on a ship where the captain stands at the wheel 操舵室；舵手室；(船上的)驾驶室

W

wheels/wi:lz/
n.a car or similar vehicle 汽车;小型车辆:
Are these your new ～,man? 老兄,这是
你的新车吗?

when/wen/
Ⅰ adv. at what time 什么时候;何时:
When will you come? 你什么时候会来?
Ⅱ conj.❶ at or during the time that 当
……时;在……时候:It was dark ～ we
arrived.我们抵达时天色已晚。❷ al-
though 虽然;尽管;既然:He usually
walks ～ he might ride.虽然有车可坐,他
通常总是步行。❸ just after which 一
……就:He had just been home when the
phone rang.他刚到家电话铃就响了。

whenever/wen'evə(r)/
adv. & conj. when; at whatever time; at
any time that 随时;无论何时:Please
come ～ you wish.你无论什么时候想来
就请来。/He played chess ～ possible.他
一有可能就下棋。

where/weə(r)/
adv.at, to, or from what place, position, or
situation; at or to the place that 在哪里;
往哪里:Where is he? 他现在在哪里?
‖～fore adv. & conj.为何;何故;因此;
～upon adv. 因此/～withal /'weəwɪðɔ:l/
n.必要的资金

whereabouts/'hweərəbauts/
Ⅰ adv.where;near what place 在哪里;靠
近哪里:Whereabouts can I find a doctor?
我在哪里可以找到医生? Ⅱ n. the place
where a person or thing is 下落,行踪;所
在:I've forgotten the ～ of his present
home.我忘记了他现在的家庭地址。

whereas/ˌweər'æz/
conj.❶ on the contrary; but; while 相反;
然而 ❷（especially in legal preambles）
considering that; since（尤指在法律序文
中）考虑到;鉴于:"Whereas the people of
the colonies have been grieved and bur-
dened with taxes…""鉴于殖民地人民在
繁重租税的压迫下一直过着痛苦的生活
……"

whereby/weə'baɪ/
adv. by which; by what 凭此;凭什么:
There is no other way ～ he can be saved.

没有其他方法可以救他。/Whereby
shall we know him? 我们如何才可以认
识他?

wherever/ˌweər'evə(r)/
Ⅰ adv.used in questions to mean where,
expressing surprise（用于问句,表示惊
讶）究竟何处:Wherever did you put it?
你究竟把它放在哪里了? /Wherever did
you get the two tickets? 你究竟是在哪
儿弄到的这两张票? Ⅱ conj. to or in any
place;no matter where 在(到)任何地方;
无论在哪里:Go ～ you like.你愿意去哪
里就去哪里。/Wherever he may be, he
will be happy.他无论在什么地方都很快
乐。

whether/'weðə(r)/
conj.❶ expressing a doubt or choice（of-
ten used in indirect questions）是否（常用
于间接引语中）:I asked him ～ he would
go there.我问他是否愿意到那里去。❷
used to show that sth. is true in either of
two cases（表示两种情况都真实）无论;
不管……(还是):Whether you like it or
not, I'm going.无论你是否愿意,我都要
走了。

which/wɪtʃ/
pron.❶（used in questions, when a choice
is to be made）what particular one or ones
（用于疑问句中）哪一个,哪一些（人或
物）:Which way shall we take? 我们要走
哪一条路? ❷ used to refer to sth. previously mentioned when introducing a
clause（用于引导定语从句）那个;那些:
The book ～ you want is on my desk.你
要的那本书在我桌子上。

whichever/wɪtʃ'evə(r)/
pron. & adj.❶ any one(s) that; any one
无论哪个;无论哪些:You may choose ～
you like.你喜欢哪一个,就可以选哪一
个。/Take ～ seat you like.你愿意坐哪
个座位就坐哪一个。❷ regardless of
which 不论哪个;不论哪些:Whichever
you choose, make sure that it is a good
one.不论你选哪一个,都要确保是个好的。

whiff/wɪf/
n.a slight breath or smell of sth. 一阵气
味;a ～ of cigarette smoke 一股香烟味

whiffy/'wɪfi/

adj. having an unpleasant smell; smelly 有臭味的; 发出臭味的: The dog is a bit ~. 这条狗有点儿臭。

while/waɪl/

I *conj*. ❶ during the time that sth.is happening 当……的时候; 和……同时: We should strike ~ the iron is hot.我们要趁热打铁。 ❷ although 虽然; 尽管: While I like the colour of the hat, I do not like its shape.我虽然喜欢这帽子的颜色, 可我不喜欢它的样子。 ❸ whereas; however 而……; 然而: One apple is big, ~ the other is small.一个苹果很大, 而另一个很小。 II *n*.a short period of time 一段时间; 一会儿: Wait for a ~. 稍等片刻。/I saw him a short ~ ago.刚刚我就看到他了。

whim/wɪm/

n. a sudden idea (usually one without a good reason) 忽起的念头; 一时的兴致

whimper/'wɪmpə(r)/

v.❶ (especially of a frightened animal or person) make small weak cries (尤指人或动物因受惊) 发出微弱的叫声; 啜泣; 呜咽: The sick baby was ~ing in its cot. 生病的婴儿在摇篮里哭泣。 ❷ speak or say in a weak trembling voice as if about to cry 啜泣地说; 呜咽地说: "Don't beat me!"The child ~ed. "不要打我了!"这孩子哭着说。

whine/waɪn/

I *v*.❶make a long moaning or screaming sound 哀号: The bullets ~d through the air.子弹在空中呼啸而过。 ❷ complain in a voice like this 哀诉; 诉怨 II *n*.a sound or complaint of this kind 哀号声; 哀诉

whiner/'waɪnə(r)/

n.a person who complains, especially habitually and in an unnecessarily sad voice 嘀嘀咕咕地哀诉的人

whinny/'wɪni/

v. make the sound which horses make gently (马) 嘶叫

whip/wɪp/

I *n*.a long piece of leather or rope fastened to handle, used for urging a horse on or for punishing 鞭子; 皮鞭: wield a ~ 挥鞭/strike sb.with a ~ 用鞭子抽打某人 II *v*.(-pp-) hit or drive with a whip 鞭笞; 抽打: ~ a horse 鞭打马/People used to be ~ped for offending officials. 在过去, 如有人冒犯官差, 就会遭到鞭笞。 ‖ ~ on 扬鞭催马; 促使前进/~ out 猛地抽出

whipping/'wɪpɪŋ/

n. the beating, especially as punishment (尤指作为惩罚的) 鞭打, 鞭笞

whippy/'wɪpi/

adj.(of a rod, stem, etc.) which bends or springs back easily (杆、茎等) 富于弹性的, 柔韧的

whirl/wɜː(r)/

I *v*. (cause to) move fast round and round (使) 回旋; 旋转; 急转: The fallen leaves ~ed in the air. 落叶在空中回旋。 II *n*. the act or sensation of whirling 旋转; 回旋; 急旋: The snow is falling in a ~.大雪纷飞。 /a ~ of dust 尘土飞扬 ‖ be in a ~ 头晕; 脑子乱/give a ~ 尝一尝; 试一试 ‖ ~pool *n*.旋涡/~wind *n*.旋风; 一片忙乱

whirr/wɜː/

I *n*.the sound made by sth.moving quickly in or through the air (快速移动或旋转的) 呼呼声, 飕飕声 II *v*.make this kind of noise 发出飕飕声, 作呼呼声

whisk/wɪsk/

I *v*.❶(cause to) move lightly and quickly (使) 轻快地移动; 拂; 掸; 扫; 挥动: The horse stood ~ing its tail.那匹马站着挥动尾巴。 /He ~ed the dust off his desk with a cloth.他用一块布把桌上的灰尘掸掉。 /She was ~ed away by her friends before I could speak to her.我还来不及跟她说话, 她的朋友就把她带走了。 ❷mix by stirring lightly and quickly 轻快地搅拌, 打 (蛋): She ~ed the eggs and milk together.她把蛋和牛奶搅拌在一起。 II *n*.a device for stirring eggs, etc.搅拌器; 打蛋器

whisker/'wɪskə(r)/

n.❶ the hairs growing on a man's face 连鬓胡子; 髯: His face was full of gray ~s. 他一脸灰色的连鬓胡子。 ❷ the long, stiff hairs or bristles growing near the mouth of a cat, rat, etc.(猫、鼠等的)触须；the cat's ～s 猫的触须

whisper/ˈwɪspə(r)/

Ⅰ v. speak or say in a soft and low voice 悄悄地说；低语；耳语；He ～ed the news to me.他低声告诉了我这个消息。Ⅱ n. a soft or low voice or sound；sth. said secretly 低语；耳语；She spoke in a ～, so I could not hear what she said.她讲话声音很低，我听不见她说了些什么。

whistle/ˈwɪsl/

Ⅰ n. ❶ an instrument for producing a clear, shrill sound, especially as a signal 汽笛；哨子；叫声；The referee blew his ～ to end the match.裁判员吹哨，宣布比赛结束。❷ a high sound made by forcing air or steam through a whistle, the lips, or bird's beak 哨子声；口哨声；笛声；He gave a long ～ for the students to gather.他吹了一声长哨，要求学生集合。Ⅱ v. make a sharp, clear sound by blowing through lips or teeth 吹哨子；吹口哨；The policeman ～d for the car to stop.警察吹哨令汽车停下来。‖ blow the ～ on 制止/～ for 空想；别想得到/～ in the dark 假装不怕；给自己壮胆/wet one's ～ 喝一盅

whit/wɪt/

n. a small amount 少量；丝毫；He cares not a ～ for public opinion.他对舆论毫不关心。

white/waɪt/

Ⅰ adj. ❶ of the colour of milk, salt, and snow 白色的；白的；雪白的；Her face was ～ with fear.她的脸色吓得苍白。❷ morally pure；innocent 纯真的；清白的 ❸ very pale 苍白的 ❹(coffee or tea) added with milk or cream (咖啡、茶)加牛奶的 ‖ as ～ as a sheet 苍白如纸/White House (美国)白宫/～ paper 白皮书 Ⅱ n. white colour；white clothes or material 白色；白色衣服，白布；be dressed in ～ 穿着白色的衣服 ‖ in black and ～ 用白纸黑字写下来‖ ～-collar adj.白领阶层的/～-hot adj.白热的；激烈的/～smith n.锡匠；铁匠；镀铁匠/～wash v.粉刷/～wood n.白木

whiz(z)/wɪz/

Ⅰ n. a whistling sound made by sth. moving quickly in (through) the air 呼呼声；嗖嗖声 Ⅱ v. make such a sound 发嗖嗖声；He ～ed past us on his bicycle.他骑着自行车嗖嗖地从我们身边经过。

who/huː/

pron. ❶ (used in questions) what or which person or people 谁，什么人；Who are you? 你是谁? ❷ used to show what person or people is(are) meant (关系代词)……的人；I don't know the man ～ lives next door.我不认识住在隔壁的那个人。

whoever/huːˈevə(r)/

pron. any person that；no matter who 任何人；无论是谁；Whoever wants the book may have it.无论是谁想要这本书都可以得到它。/Whoever makes mistakes must correct them.无论是谁犯了错误都必须改正。

whole/həʊl/

Ⅰ adj. complete；total 全部的；完全的；整个的；He told me the ～ story.他把事情的原委都告诉我了。Ⅱ n. a complete amount of sth.；all of sth. 全部；全数；整个；整体；He lost the ～ of his money.他丢了他全部的钱。‖ as a ～ 整个看来；就全体而论/on the ～ 总的说来；大体上；基本上 ‖ ～hearted adj.全心全意的；全神贯注的/～-length adj.全长的；全身的 Ⅲ adv.completely different or new 完全不同地；全新地；That's a ～ other story.那完全是另一回事。

wholesale/ˈhəʊlseɪl/

Ⅰ n. the selling of goods in large quantities to shopkeepers and traders who then sell them to the public 批发 Ⅱ adj. of wholesale as a method of trade 批发的；They own a ～ business in clothes.他们经营服装批发生意。Ⅲ adv. on a large scale；including almost everybody, everything 大规模的(地)；大批的(地)；全部的(地)；During the war houses were destroyed ～.战争期间，大批的房子被摧毁了。

wholesome/ˈhəʊlsəm/

W

*adj.*be good for health;healthy 有益于健康的;健康的:~ climate 有益于健康的气候 / a ~ youth 精神饱满的青年 /~ food 有益于健康的食物

whom/huːm/

*pron.*the object form of who（who 的宾格）谁;哪个人;什么人:Whom are you looking for? 你在找谁? /Tell me ~ they are talking about.告诉我他们在谈论谁。/The man with ~ I shook hands just now is one of my old friends.我刚才与他握手的那个人是我的一个老朋友。

whoop/huːp,wuːp/

Ⅰ*n.*❶a loud cry 大叫;呼喊:give a ~ of anger 发出一声怒吼 / give a ~ of joy 欢呼一声 ❷a gasping cough 哮喘声;喘息声 Ⅱ*v.*make a loud cry or yell 高声呼叫;呐喊:~ with joy 欢呼

whoosh¹/wuʃ/

*n.*a soft sound,like air rushing out of sth.（空气从容器中逸出时的）嘶嘶声、嗖的一声;呼的一声

whoosh²/wuʃ/

*v.*move quickly with a rushing sound 嗖嗖地飞快移动:The express train ~ed past.特快列车嗖嗖地飞驰而过。

whop/wɒp/

*v.*beat or defeat 打败;重击

whopper/'wɒpə(r)/

*n.*❶sth. unusually or surprisingly big 巨大的东西;特大的东西;庞然大物:Did you catch that fish? What a ~! 你抓住那条鱼了吗? 多大的家伙啊! ❷a big lie 弥天大谎:He told a real ~ to excuse his lateness.他为迟到撒了个弥天大谎来作借口。

whopping/'wɒpɪŋ/

*adj.*very large 异常大的;巨大的:a ~ (great) lie 弥天大谎

whose/huːz/

pron. belonging to or associated with which person 谁的,……的:Whose book is this? 这是谁的书? /Hand me the book ~ cover is broken.把那本封面破了的书给我。/The dog ~ bark is loud is new.那只叫得很响的狗是只新来的狗。

why/waɪ/

Ⅰ*adv.*for what reason 为什么;为何:Why didn't you tell them the good news? 你为什么不把那个好消息告诉他们? /Why so early? 为什么(来) 这么早? / I wonder ~ he failed in the examination.我感到奇怪,他为什么考试没有及格。 Ⅱ*int.* expressing surprise, protest, approval, hesitation,etc.（表示惊异、抗议、赞成、犹豫等）啊,哎呀,嗨,哟,呃:Why, it's already ten o'clock.哎呀,已经十点钟了。/ Why,it's you! 啊,是你呀!

wicked/'wɪkɪd/

*adj.*❶very bad; evil; morally wrong 坏的;邪恶的;不道德的;恶劣的:~ weather 恶劣的天气 ❷behaving badly;mischievous 淘气的;恶作剧的:~ boy 好恶作剧的男孩/ You ~ child—go to bed at once.你这个小淘气——马上上床睡觉。

wicker/'wɪkə(r)/

*n.*twigs or canes woven together 枝条;柳条:a ~ chair 柳条椅 / a ~ basket 柳条篮子

wide/waɪd/

Ⅰ*adj.*❶of great width from side to side or edge to edge 宽的;宽阔的:a door three feet ~ 3 英尺宽的门 ❷fully open 充分张开的;敞开的:He stared at me with ~ eyes.他睁大眼睛盯着我。❸including a great variety of sb.or sth.广泛的 ‖ by a ~ margin 比分悬殊地/give a ~ berth 避免;回避/be ~ apart 张得很开;相距很远/be ~ of the mark 没击中目标;不正确 Ⅱ*adv.*❶to a great distance from side to side 广大地;广阔地 ❷(in sport) far away from the right point 相距很远:The arrow fell ~ of the mark.箭落在距离目标很远的地方。 ‖ far and ~ *adv.*到处 ‖ ~n/'waɪdn/*v.*加宽;扩大/ ~-spread*adj.*分布广泛的;遍及的

widow/'wɪdəʊ/

Ⅰ*n.*a woman whose husband is dead 寡妇;遗孀:George's ~ has married again.乔治的遗孀又结婚了。 Ⅱ*v.*cause to become a widow or widower 使丧偶:She was ~ed by war in 1943.由于战争 1943 年她丧偶了。

widower/'wɪdəʊə(r)/

n. a man whose wife is dead and who

hasn't married again 鳏夫

width/wɪdθ, wɪtθ/

n.❶the size form side to side 宽度;阔度;广度: What is its ~? 它的宽度是多少? /The garden is six metres in ~.这个花园 6 米宽。❷a piece of material of the full width that the material had when it was actually made (某种宽度的)一幅料子: We need four ~s of curtain material to cover the windows.我们需要四幅窗帘布来做这些窗子的窗帘。

wield/wiːld/

v.use in the hand;hold (a weapon, tool, or power) 挥舞;使用;支配;掌握;行使: He was ~ing a knife. 他挥舞着一把刀。/ The president ~s great power. 总统行使很大的权力。

wife/waɪf/

n.(pl. wives/waɪvz/) a married woman considered in relation to her husband 妻子;夫人;太太: She is a good ~ and mother. 她是一位贤妻良母。

wifely/ˈwaɪfli/

adj.typical of a wife;having qualities that are thought to be a good wife 妻子特有的;贤惠的;贤淑的;具备好妻子美德的: ~ concern 妻子的关怀/~ duties 妻子的责任

wig/wɪg/

n. an artificial covering of hair for the whole head, used to hide one's real hair or conceal one's baldness 假发: The bald man wore a ~.那个秃头的人戴着一顶假发。‖ **pull** ~s 扭打;吵架/~s **on the green** 纠纷;争执

wiggle/ˈwɪgl/

Ⅰv.(cause to) move quickly up and down or from side to side (使)快速扭动;(使)摆动: He sat wiggling his toes. 他坐着扭动脚趾。Ⅱn. the movement of this kind 扭动;摆动

wild/waɪld/

adj.❶ living or growing in natural conditions; untamed; uncultivated 野生的;野的:~ plants 野生植物/~ animals 野兽 ❷ (scenery or region) in its natural state 无人烟的;天然的;荒芜的 ❸ very an-

gry, excited, passionate, etc. 发怒的;狂暴的: He was ~ with joy.他欣喜若狂。‖ **beyond sb.'s ~est dreams** 做梦都没想到/**be ~ with** …… 得发狂/**run** ~ 失去控制/胡闹/**sow one's ~ oats** 干荒唐事;过放荡的生活/~ **goose chase** 白费力气的追逐 ‖ ~**ly** adv.疯狂地;胡乱地;狂热地

wilderness/ˈwɪldənɪs/

n.a large, bare and uninhabited land; desert 荒野;沙漠

wilful/ˈwɪlfl/

adj.❶(with reference to a person) determined to do what one wants, whether it is good or bad; having a strong will (指人)任性的;倔强的 ❷ (with reference to an act) done on purpose, not by accident (指行为)蓄意的;故意的: The ~ killing of a person is murder. 故意杀人便是谋杀。

will¹/wɪl/

v.❶used for expressing the simple future tense (用在将来时里)将,会: He ~ come tomorrow.他明天会来。❷ be willing to; be ready to 愿意(做): I ~ do my best to help you.我愿尽力帮助你。❸used when asking someone to do sth.(用于表示请求): Will you open the window? 请打开窗户好吗? ❹shows what always happens (用于表示习惯或某事经常发生): Boys ~ be boys. 小孩子总归是小孩子。❺ used like can to show what is likely (用法同 can,表示可能性)可,能: This car ~ hold fifteen people.这辆车可坐 15 个人。

will²/wɪl/

n.❶the power of the mind to make decisions and acts in accordance with them, sometimes in spite of difficulty or opposition 意志;意志力: He has a strong ~.他有很强的意志。❷what is wished or intended (by the stated person) 决心;意向;目的: The ~ to live helps a patient to recover.求生的决心有助于病人的康复。❸an official statement of the way someone wants his property to be shared out after his death 遗嘱: make a ~ 立遗嘱 ‖ **against one's** ~ 违心地;不情愿地/**at** ~ 任意;随意/**by force of** ~ 靠毅力/**have one's** ~ 达到自己的愿望;自行其是/**of**

one's own (free) 〜 出于自愿/with a 〜
热情地；起劲地/with the best 〜 in the
world 尽管做了很大努力 ‖ 〜power n.意
志力

willow/'wɪləʊ/
n.a tree with long, thin branches 柳树；柳
木：a weeping 〜 垂柳

willy-nilly/ˌwɪli'nɪli/
adv.❶in a careless way；in a mess 杂乱无
章地；乱七八糟地：She threw the books
〜 into the cupboard. 她把书往壁橱里乱
扔。❷ whether sb. is willing or unwillingly 不管愿意不愿意：He'll have to do
it 〜.不管愿意不愿意，他都得做此事。

wilt/wɪlt/
v. lose strength and hang down loosely
(使)凋谢；枯萎：The flowers 〜ed in the
hot sun.花儿在炎炎烈日下凋谢了。

win/wɪn/
v.(won；winning)❶ get or gain (victory,
a stated place, prize, etc.) in competition,
etc.获胜；赢：Who won the race? 谁赢了
这场比赛？❷ gain or receive as a result
of victory or success in any kind of competition 获得；赢得：He won a lot of
money at cards.他打牌赢了很多钱。‖
〜 sb.'s heart 赢得某人的爱/〜 or lose 无
论输赢/〜 sth.or sb.back 重新获得 ‖ 〜
ner n.得胜者；获奖者

wind[1]/wɪnd/
n. moving air；a current of air, especially
one moving strongly or quickly 风：The
〜 blew my hat off. 风吹落了我的帽
子。/He ran like the 〜.他跑得像风一样
快。‖ before the 〜 顺风/between 〜 and
water 在危险中/break 〜 放屁/cast
(throw)...to the 〜s 不理睬；不顾/get 〜
of 得到……的风声；获得……的线索/in
the 〜 (某事)即将发生；在筹划中/like
the 〜 飞快地/in the eye of the 〜 (in the
teeth of the 〜) 逆风/off the 〜 顺风/
straw in the 〜 迹象(预示即将发生某
事)/take the 〜 out of one's sails 先发制
人而占上风/杀……的威风；使某人难
堪/under the 〜 在背风处/up the 〜 顶着
风 ‖ 〜breaker n.防风外衣/〜 break n.防
风林/〜fall n.被风吹落的果实；意外收
获/〜 instrument n.管乐器/〜mill n.风

车/〜pipe n.气管/〜screen n.挡风玻璃/
〜ward adj.顶风的；向风的 & n.向风
面；迎风面/〜y adj.有风的；多风的

wind[2]/waɪnd/
v.❶ follow a twisting course, with many
changes of direction 蜿蜒；绕行：The river 〜s (its way) through the plain. 这条
河流蜿蜒流经平原。❷ turn or twist
(sth.) repeatedly, especially round an object 卷绕：The vine 〜s round a pole. 藤缠
绕柱子生长。❸ tighten the working
parts of sth. by turning round and round
上弦；上发条：〜 a clock (watch) 上钟
(表)‖ 〜 around one's little finger 使听
自己摆布/〜 back 倒片，倒磁带/〜 down
把(车窗)摇低；干劲逐渐降低；结束/〜
into 缠成(一团)/〜 on 把……缠上去；绕
上去/〜 one's way 蜿蜒前行/〜 one's
way (oneself) into 巧妙地赢得(感情)/〜
through 贯穿/〜 up 缠好；上好发条；结
束；处理完；使振奋

window/'wɪndəʊ/
n.an opening in the wall, etc.to let in light
or air 窗；窗户：The eyes are the 〜s of
the mind.眼睛是心灵之窗。‖ 〜 dressing n.商店橱窗摆设/〜-shopping n.观看
橱窗商品/〜pane n.窗玻璃/〜sill n.窗台

wine/waɪn/
n. an alcoholic drink made from grapes,
fruit, etc.葡萄酒；果酒：red (white) 〜 红
(白)葡萄酒 ‖ good 〜 needs no bush 酒
好客自来

wing/wɪŋ/
n.a movable limb which a bird, insect, etc.
uses for flying 翼；翅膀：A bird has two
〜s.鸟有双翅。‖ clip one's 〜s 无用武之
地/lend 〜s (to) 使快走；加快……的速
度/take 〜(s) 展翅飞走；迅速逃离/under
the 〜 of 在……保护之下

winged/wɪŋd/
adj.having wings for flight 有翅的；有翼
的

winger/'wɪŋə(r)/
n.❶(in games like football) a player in
the area on the far left or right of the
field (足球等运动中的)边锋队员 ❷ a
person who belongs to the stated group

(right wing or left wing) in a political party (党派之中的)……翼分子：Republican right-~s 共和党中的右翼分子

wings/wɪŋz/

n. ❶(either of) the sides of a stage, where an actor is hidden from view 舞台的两侧；舞台侧面 ❷a sign which a pilot can wear to show he or she can fly an aircraft 飞行胸章(表示有飞行资格的胸章)：Have you got your ~ yet? 你得到飞行胸章了吗? ‖ in the ~ 在等待之中的；已准备就绪的

wingspan/ˈwɪŋspæn/

n. the distance from the end of one wing to the end of the other, when both are stretched out (两翼展开时的宽度)翼展；翼幅：the eagle's huge ~ 老鹰巨大的翼展/an aircraft with a ~ of 50 metres 翼展为五十米的飞机

wink/wɪŋk/

Ⅰ*v.* ❶ close and open (the eye) quickly 眨眼 ❷ (of star, light, etc.) shine or flash quickly (星星、灯光等)闪烁；闪耀：The stars ~ed in the sky. 星星在空中闪烁。Ⅱ*n.* a winking movement of the eye 眨眼：give sb.a ~ 向某人眨眼 ‖ ~ at 向某人使眼色/forty ~s 小睡一会儿

winner/ˈwɪnə(r)/

n. a person, animal, or thing that wins 获胜者：The ~ of the contest got a prize. 这次比赛的获胜者得了奖。

winning/ˈwɪnɪŋ/

adj. ❶very pleasing or attractive; charming 可爱的；迷人的：His ~ ways made him popular with everyone. 他富有魅力的待人处事方式使他深受大家喜爱。/a ~ smile 迷人的微笑 ❷that wins or has won sth.in a race or competition 获胜的；赢的：a ~ horse 获胜的马

winnings/ˈwɪnɪŋz/

n. money which has been won in a game, by betting in a game, horse race, etc.(在比赛、赛马等下注)赢得的钱

winnow/ˈwɪnəʊ/

v. blow the outer part (husks) from (grain) 扬，簸(谷物)

winsome/ˈwɪnsəm/

adj. pleasant and attractive, especially in a fresh, childlike way 天真烂漫的；令人愉快的；迷人的：a ~ girl 讨人喜欢的女孩 ‖ ~ly *adv.* 讨人喜欢地；楚楚动人地

winter/ˈwɪntə(r)/

n. a season between autumn and spring when it is cold 冬季；冬天：We often have snow in ~. 我们这儿的冬季经常下雪。‖ ~less *adj.* 无冬天(气候)的/~ly *adj.* 冬天的；冷淡的

wipe/waɪp/

v. ❶ make clean or dry by rubbing with a cloth, etc. 擦净；擦干；抹：~ the table 擦桌子 / ~ one's eyes 擦干眼泪 ❷remove by wiping 擦掉：~ one's tears 擦掉眼泪 / ~ the ink off one's hands 擦去手上的墨水

wire/ˈwaɪə(r)/

n. ❶ a thin, flexible thread of metal 金属丝；金属线；电线：telephone ~ 电话线/iron ~ 铁丝 ❷ telegraph 电报：send (receive) a ~ 发(收到)电报 ‖ by ~ 通过发电报/pull ~s 暗中操纵；利用私人关系(走后门) ‖ ~man *n.* 架线工；(电路)检修员/~photo *n.* 有线传真(照片)/~pull *v.* 牵线；幕后操纵/~work *n.* 金属丝制品

wireless/ˈwaɪəlɪs/

Ⅰ*adj.* having or requiring no wires 无线的：~ telephone 无线电话 Ⅱ*n.* broadcasting or telegraphy using radio signals 无线电广播：listen to a concert over the ~ 通过收音机收听音乐会

wiretap/ˈwaɪətæp/

Ⅰ*v.* secretly listen to other people's telephone conversations by attaching a device to the telephone line 搭线窃听 Ⅱ*n.* an act of wiretapping 窃听电话的行为

wiring/ˈwaɪərɪŋ/

n. the arrangement of wires that form the electrical system in a building; network of wires 配线；布线；(建筑物供电的)线路系统：We're having this old ~ replaced. 我们正在更换旧的电线线路。/faulty ~ 出了毛病的线路

wiry/ˈwaɪəri/

adj. rather thin, but with strong muscles 瘦而结实的：his ~, athletic body 他那精

瘦结实的身体

wisdom/ˈwɪzdəm/

n. ❶ the quality of being wise; a good sense and judgment 智慧；才智；明智：a man of great ~ 才智超群的人/I would question the ~ of borrowing such a large sum of money. 借这么一大笔钱，我怀疑是否明智。❷ knowledge gained through learning or experience 知识；学问：the ~ of the ancients 古人(流传下来)的知识/folk ~ 民间流传的知识/According to the received ~ in these matters, the voters usually make their choices on the basis of domestic issues. 按一般人在这些问题上的看法，选民常常着眼于国内问题来选择候选人。

wise/waɪz/

adj. having or showing good sense and judgment, and the ability to understand and decide on the right action 明智的；聪明的；有智慧的；博学的 ‖ be (get) ~ to 了解；觉察/be ~ after the event 事后聪明；马后炮 ‖ ~crack *n.* & *v.* (说)俏皮话，妙语/~ly *adv.* 明智地；明白地

wish/wɪʃ/

Ⅰ *v.* ❶ want to do sth.; express a desire to do sth. 想要；需要：Do you ~ to visit the Great Wall? 你想去看看长城吗? ❷ have a desire that is impossible to be satisfied at present 但愿：I ~ I would be young again. 但愿我可以返老还童。❸ hope that (sb.) has (sth.) 祝；祝愿：I ~ you a good journey. 祝你一路平安。Ⅱ *n.* ❶ a desire or hope for sth. to happen; sth. wished for 希望；打算；想：a ~ for peace 希望和平 ❷ an invocation or recitation of a hope or desire 愿；愿望(的事物)：My ~ came true. 我的愿望实现了。❸ an attempt to make a particular desired thing or situation expressed in a special way or silently; an act of wishing 祝愿；致意：With best ~es. 祝好。‖ ~ful *adj.* 渴望的；表示愿望的；怀有希望的：~ful thinking 如意算盘

wishy-washy/ˈwɪʃiˌwɒʃi/

adj. watery; thin; weak; uninteresting 稀稀拉拉的；稀薄的；淡的；乏味的

wisp/wɪsp/

n. a small amount of grass, hair, smoke, etc. 一小束(草)；一绺(头发)；一缕(烟)等

wistful/ˈwɪstfl/

adj. wanting sth. but sad because it is not likely to be obtained 渴望的；惆怅的；怅惘的；依依不舍的：There was a ~ look on the child's face when he saw all the toys in the shop window. 那孩子看见商店橱窗里陈列的玩具，脸上露出了渴望又怅然的神情。

wit/wɪt/

n. ❶ keen intelligence; quickness of the mind 头脑；理智；聪明；机智：A fall into the pit, a gain in your ~. 吃一堑，长一智。❷ the ability to express ideas in a clever and humorous manner 妙语；风趣：The conversation was full of ~. 这次谈话情趣横溢。‖ be at one's ~s' end 智穷计尽；不知所措/frighten (scare) one out of one's ~s 吓坏了/have (keep) one's ~s about one 机警；警觉/live by one's ~s 靠耍小聪明混日子/out of one's ~s 脑子不清醒

witch/wɪtʃ/

n. a woman who is believed to have evil magic powers 巫婆；女巫 ‖ ~craft *n.* 魔法；巫术/~ doctor *n.* 巫医；巫师

with/wɪð/

prep. ❶ in the presence or company of; near, beside, or among 和……一起：work and study ~ you 同你们一起工作和学习 ❷ having or possessing 具有；带有：a girl ~ a long pigtail 长辫子姑娘 ❸ by means of; using 用；通过；凭借：We cut meat ~ a knife. 我们用刀切肉。❹ because of or considering the fact of 因为：He jumped ~ joy. 他高兴得跳了起来。❺ concerning; in regard to or in the case of 对于；关于：I don't agree ~ you. 我不同意你的意见。❻ indicating the manner 表示方式：I will come ~ pleasure. 我很乐意来。❼ in support of; in favour of 支持；赞成；在：The people voted ~ the government. 人民投票支持政府。❽ against 反对：fight ~ the enemy 对敌斗争 ❾ at the same time and rate as 随着；与……一样；与……同时：The shadow moves ~ the sun.

阴影随着太阳移动。❿in spite of 尽管；虽然：With all my efforts, I failed in the exam.尽管我做了很大的努力,但考试还是没有及格。⓫indicating separation 表示分离：break ～ the past 与过去一刀两断/part ～ sb.与某人分手

withdraw/wɪð'drɔː,wɪθ'drɔː/
v.❶ (cause to) move away or back（使）撤退；撤回；后退：The army withdrew.军队撤退了。❷go away 离开；退出：He withdrew from the teaching work a year ago.他一年前离开了教学工作。❸ take away or back 取出；提取：I'll ～ some money from the bank.我将从银行提取一些钱。

withdrawal/wɪð'drɔːəl/
n.the act of withdrawing or state of being withdrawn 收回；取回；撤回；撤退；撤走；退出：～ of financial support for his scheme 取消对他那项计划的财务援助/He's made several ～s from his account recently.最近他已经多次从银行提取存款。/a gradual ～ of troops from the war zone 逐步从战区撤军

wither/'wɪðə(r)/
v.(cause to) become dry, faded or dead（使）枯萎；（使）干枯；（使）凋谢：These flowers will soon ～.这些花不久就会凋谢。/His hope ～ed.他的希望破灭了。/The heat ～ed some plants.炎热使一些植物枯萎了。

withhold/wɪð'həuld/
v.(withheld) hold or keep back；refuse to give 抑制；制止；忍住；不给：～ from doing sth.忍着不做某事 / That thing withheld me from making a decision.那件事使我不能做出决定。/Don't ～ information from the police.不要对警察隐瞒消息。

within/wɪð'ɪn/
I prep.❶inside sb.or sth.在……之内：the city 在城内 ❷during a particular period of time 在(某段时间)之内：～ two hours 在两小时内 ❸not further than a particular distance 在（某段）距离之间：Our school is ～ three miles of the post office.我们学校离邮局不出三英里。❹ inside the range of sth.在……范围之内：This task is ～ my powers.这项工作是我

所能胜任的。II adv.inside；inwardly 在内；在室内；在内部：The house has been painted ～ and without.这所房屋里外都油漆过了。/He is pure ～.他心地纯洁。

without/wɪð'aut/
I prep.❶ in the absence of 没有；缺乏：A cat walks ～ noise.猫走路没有声音。❷ not doing sth.mentioned 没有；不（做某事）：He drove away ～ saying goodbye.他没有说再见就开车走了。II adv.outside 在外面：The house is clean within and ～.这座房子里里外外都很干净。

withstand/wɪð'stænd/
v.(withstood /wɪð'stud/) resist；continue in good condition in spite of 抵抗；抵挡；经得起：～ the enemy 挡住敌人 /～ fire 耐火 /～ temptation 经得起诱惑

witless/'wɪtlɪs/
adj.(as if) lacking in ability to think；silly （好像）缺乏思考能力的；无才智的；愚蠢的：He was scared ～.他被吓蒙了。/a ～ idea 愚蠢的主意 ‖ ～ly adv.无知地；愚蠢地

witness/'wɪtnɪs/
I n.❶ a person who was present at an event,especially sth.bad 目击者：a ～ of an incident 事件的目击者 ❷ a person giving sworn testimony to a court of law or the police 证人：The accused had many ～es to say that he was not guilty.被告有很多证人声称他是无罪的。II v.❶ see an event,especially sth.bad take place 目击；目睹：He ～ed the accident.他目睹了这场事故。❷ give evidence of 作证；证明：My teacher will ～ that I was in the classroom all the morning.我的老师可以作证,我整个上午都在教室里。‖ ～ against 证明……有罪/～ for 作证为……辩护/bear ～ to（against）为……作证；证明（有罪）

witty/'wɪti/
adj. full of wit；clever and amusing 机智的；机敏的；诙谐的：a ～ person 一个机智的人/ ～ remarks 妙语；有趣的话

wizard/'wɪzəd/
n.❶(especially in stories) a man who has magic powers（尤指故事中的）男巫,术

士 ❷ a person with unusual,almost magical abilities 有特殊才干的人;奇才: He's a real ～ at playing the piano.他是个演奏技术高超的钢琴家。/a computer ～电脑奇才/a financial ～ 高明的理财家

wizardry/'wɪzədri/
*n.*❶ the performing of magic 魔术;法术 ❷ the wonderful ability 杰出才能: his football ～ 他在足球方面的杰出才能

wizened/'wɪzənd/
adj. smaller in size and dried up, with lines in the skin,especially as a result of age（尤指因年岁大了而）干瘦的,干瘪的,皱巴巴的:～ apples 干瘪了的苹果/a ～ old lady 形容枯槁的老妇人

woe/wəʊ/
n. great sorrow 悲哀;苦恼:a tale of ～ 悲哀的故事/share weal and ～ 同甘共苦

woebegone/'wəʊbɪgɒn/
adj. very sad in appearance 满面愁容;愁眉苦脸的

woeful/'wəʊfl/
*adj.*❶ very sad;mournful or pathetic 悲哀的;忧愁的;可怜的;可悲的:～ eyes 忧郁的眼神 ❷（of sth.bad）very great;deplorable（坏事情）糟糕透顶的;非常不幸的;可叹的:a ～ lack of understanding 非常的缺乏理解 ‖ ～ly *adv.*悲伤地;不幸地;严重地: The education service has been ～ly neglected.教育工作已经被严重忽视了。

wog/wɒg/
n. a foreigner,especially of a dark-skinned race（considered extremely offensive）外国佬(尤指深肤色的人;带有强烈冒犯的意味)›

wolf/wʊlf/
n. a wild animal of the dog family which hunts other animals in a group 狼:a ～ in sheep's clothing 披着羊皮的狼/ cry ～ 喊叫"狼来了";发假警报 ‖ ～-like *adj.*似狼的/～ling *n.*狼崽;小狼

woman/'wʊmən/
n. a fully grown human female 成年女子;妇女:men,women,and children 男人,妇女和儿童 ‖ ～hood *n.*女性的成年阶段;妇女的总称/～ish *adj.*女子气的;像女性

的/～ly *adj.*＆ *adv.*富有女性气质的(地);适合女子的(地)

womb/wuːm/
n. an organ of a woman or female animal inside which a baby grows before it is born 子宫

wonder/'wʌndə(r)/
Ⅰ *n.*❶ a feeling of strangeness,surprise, etc., usually combined with admiration that is produced by sth.unusually fine or beautiful,or by sth.unexpected or new to one's experience 惊异;惊叹: The little boy looked at the beautiful rainbow in great ～.这个小男孩惊奇地看着那美丽的彩虹。❷ sth. that causes this feeling, especially a wonderfully made object 奇迹;奇观;奇事: the seven ～s of the world 世界七大奇观 ‖ it's a ～（that）真是令人惊奇;真奇怪 Ⅱ *v.*❶ be surprised and want to know（why）感到惊奇:I ～ that he didn't criticize you. 我感到很惊奇,他竟然没有批评你。❷ express a wish to know, in words or silently 想知道:I ～ who she is.我想知道她是谁。

wonderful/'wʌndəfl/
*adj.*❶ causing wonder;surprising 令人惊奇的;奇妙的:～ memory 惊人的记忆力/～ patience 惊人的耐性 ❷ very good; excellent 极好的;精彩的:～ weather 非常好的天气 / a ～ game 一场精彩的比赛

wood/wʊd/
n. ❶ the substance of which the trunks and branches of trees are made,which is cut and used for various purposes,such as burning,making paper or furniture,etc. 木;木材:chop ～ for the fire 劈柴生火 ❷ a place where trees grow thickly,smaller than a forest 林地;小树林: go through the ～s 穿过树林 ‖ out of the ～(s) 摆脱困境/in the green ～处于佳境 ‖ ～en *adj.* 木制的/～land *n.* 林地/～work *n.*木制品;木工活/～cut *n.*木刻/～cutter *n.*樵夫;木版雕刻师

wooden/'wʊdn/
*adj.*❶made of wood 木制的:a ～ box 木箱子 ❷ stiff, clumsy 呆板的;笨拙的:a ～ face 呆板的面孔 /～ motions 笨拙的

动作

woodpecker/ˈwʊdpekə(r)/

n. a bird that can make holes in the wood of trees and pull out insects 啄木鸟

wool/wʊl/

n. ❶ soft hair of sheep, goats and some other animals 羊毛 ❷ thread, cloth or clothes made from wool 毛线；毛料：This suit is made of ～.这套西装是毛料的。‖ lose one's ～ 生气/pull the ～ over one's eyes 瞒过某人 ‖ ～gathering *adj.* 心不在焉的；胡思乱想的

wool(l)en/ˈwʊlən/

Ⅰ *adj.* made of wool; relating to the production of wool 羊毛的；羊毛制的；毛织的；毛料的：～ cloth 毛料 / a ～ mill 毛纺厂/～ blankets 毛毯 Ⅱ *n.* wool(l)en clothes 毛织物；毛料织物

word/wɜːd/

n. ❶ a written, printed or spoken unit of a language 字；词；单词 ❷ a short remark or statement 简短的话：I have a ～ with you.我有话对你说。❸ a promise 诺言；保证：I will keep my ～.我一定遵守诺言。❹ a message; a piece of news 消息；音讯：Send me ～ as soon as you get there.你一到达那里就给我个信。‖ a man of few ～s 沉默寡言的人/a man of his ～ 说话算数的人/as good as one's ～ 说话算数；信守诺言/beyond ～s 无法用言语形容/break one's ～ 失信；不遵守诺言/eat one's ～s 收回前言；认错道歉/give one's ～ 保证/give the ～ 说一声 / have the last ～ 下结论；有决定权/in a ～ 总之/in other ～s 换句话说/keep one's ～ 遵守诺言/put ～s into one's mouth 把话强加在某人的头上/send ～ 带信(话)来/take one at one's ～ 完全相信某人的话/take one's ～ (for it) 相信……的话/take the ～s right out of one's mouth (抢先)讲出了某人要讲的话/too...for ～s 太……无法形容/upon my ～ (表示惊奇)的确/～ came 有信来；有话传来/～ for ～ 逐字逐句地 ‖ ～ing *n.* 措辞/～y *adj.* 多言的；啰唆的

wordless/ˈwɜːdlɪs/

adj. without words; unable to speak; speechless 无言的；哑的；沉默的：a ～ man 沉默的人

work/wɜːk/

Ⅰ *n.* ❶ an activity which uses bodily or mental powers 干活；劳动：Let's get to ～.大家开始干活吧。❷ employment or occupation 生计；职业；工作：A teacher's ～ is teaching.教师的工作是教书。❸ a task or tasks to be undertaken 任务；手头的活：I'm taking some ～ home from the office this evening.今晚我要从办公室带点工作回去做。❹ what is produced by work, especially of the hands 成果；产品；工艺品：This mat is my own ～.这席子是我自己制作的。❺ the product of an artist, composer, writer, etc. 著作；作品：～s of literature and art 文艺作品/the ～s of Shakespeare 莎士比亚的著作 Ⅱ *v.* ❶ do work; do physical or mental activity 工作；干活；做：He often ～s long hours.他经常长时间地干活。❷ do work; engage in physical or mental activity 工作；从事……职业：He ～s in a bank.他在银行工作。/She ～s as a bus driver.她是公共汽车司机。❸ make (a machine) operate 开动；使运转：Do you know how to ～ this machine? 你知道如何开动这台机器吗？❹ produce a particular effect or result 起作用；行得通；有效：Does the switch ～? 这个开关还起作用吗？‖ ～ as 担任……；做……工作/～ at 从事；在……上下功夫/～ away (on) 干下去；继续干/～ off 渐渐除去；消除/～ on 从事；对……施加影响/～ out 制订；算出；弄懂/～ through 解决；干完/～ up 努力取得；渐渐造成(发展成)；激起(兴趣、热情等)/at ～ 在工作；在上班/get (set) to ～ 着手；开始工作/make light ～ of 轻而易举地/make short ～ of 快速完成

workable/ˈwɜːkəbl/

adj. that can be worked or operated; that will work 可使用的；可操作的；可运转的；可实行的；可经营的：The scheme is ～.这个计划可行。

workaday/ˈwɜːkədeɪ/

adj. of one's work or job; ordinary or dull 日常的；平凡的；乏味的：～ concerns 平常的事

workbag/ˈwɜːkbæg/

*n.*a bag for holding things, especially for sewing 针线袋;工具袋

worker/'wɜːkə(r)/

*n.*a person who works 工人;工作者;劳动者:an industrial ~ 产业工人 / a mental ~ 脑力劳动者 / a manual ~ 体力劳动者 / office ~s 办公室工作人员

workman/'wɜːkmən/

n.(*pl.*workmen) a man who works, especially with his hands 工人;工作者;劳动者

workmanship/'wɜːkmənʃɪp/

*n.*the skill in making things 手艺;技艺:Good ~ deserves good pay.好手艺该得高报酬。

workshop/'wɜːkʃɒp/

*n.*a room or place where things are made or repaired 工厂;车间;工场:The workers are working very hard in the ~.工人们在车间里辛勤地工作着。

world/wɜːld/

*n.*❶the body in space on which we live; the earth 世界;地球 ❷all the people on the earth 世人;人类 ❸a part or an aspect of human life or of the natural features of the Earth (人类活动的)领域;界:the Third World 第三世界/the ~ of literature and art 文艺界/the animal ~ 动物世界 ❹a large number or amount 大量;无数:Sunshine will do you a ~ of good.阳光对你会大有益处。‖ for all the ~ like (as if) 酷似;完全像(简直就像)/give the ~(to do) 不惜一切代价……/in the ~(加强语气)天下;到底/make the best of both ~s 两全其美/not for (all) the ~ 怎样也不(想)/out of this ~ 好极了;太妙了/rise in the ~ 飞黄腾达/set the ~ on fire 轰动一时;非常成功/think the ~ of 非常喜欢;钦佩 ‖ ~-class *adj.*世界一流水平的/~-famous *adj.*震撼世界的;惊天动地的/~wide *adj.& adv.*世界范围的(地);全世界的(地)/~ly *adj.& adv.*尘世间的(地);老于世故的(地)

worm/wɜːm/

Ⅰ*n.*a small, thin creature with no bones or limbs, like a round tube of flesh, especially an earthworm 虫;蠕虫;蚯蚓;寄生虫 Ⅱ*v.*move gradually by twisting or wriggling (使)蠕动 ‖ ~ one's way into 逐渐取得;逐渐地(或迂回地)钻进/~ one's way to 悄悄地爬到/~ out (of) 设法了解;钻出来;摆脱 ‖ silk~ *n.*蚕/earth~ *n.*蚯蚓/book~ *n.*书呆子/hook~ *n.*钩虫/glow~ *n.*萤火虫/tape~ *n.*绦虫

worn/wɔːn/

adj.(~ out) ❶ used until no longer fit for use 用旧了的;穿破了的:~ out shoes 穿破了的鞋/~ out equipment 破旧的设备 ❷ physically exhausted; very tired 精疲力竭的;累极了的:He was ~ out after three sleepless nights. 三天三夜没睡觉,他已疲惫不堪了。

worry/'wʌri/

Ⅰ*v.*(cause to) feel anxious or troubled (使)烦恼;(使)担忧;(使)发愁:Don't ~ about your future. 你不要为前途担忧。‖ be worried about 为……发愁(着急)/~ oneself 自寻烦恼/~ out 绞尽脑汁解决(想出)Ⅱ*n.*❶ a feeling or state of anxiety 烦恼;焦虑;担忧:His face showed signs of ~.他脸上显出不安的神色。❷ a source of anxiety 令人烦恼(或发愁)的人(或事):Life is full of worries. 人生充满着烦恼的事情。‖ worried *adj.*担忧的/worrisome *adj.*使人烦恼(焦虑)的/~ing *adj.*使人烦恼的;忧虑重重的

worse/wɜːs/

Ⅰ*adj.*❶less good or desirable 更坏的;更糟的;更差的 ❷more serious or severe 更严重的;更严厉的:The crisis is getting ~ and ~.危机越来越严重了。❸becoming more ill or sick (病情)更严重的,恶化的 Ⅱ*adv.* less well or more seriously 更坏地;更糟地;更差地;更严重地 Ⅲ*n.*a more serious or unpleasant event or condition 更严重的情况;更令人不快的事 ‖ change (turn) for the ~ 恶化/for better or (for) 好歹;不管怎样/none the ~ 并不更差;没有受到损害/so much the ~ 那就更糟 ‖ ~n/'wɜːsn/ *v.*(使)变坏;(使)恶化;加剧

worship/'wɜːʃɪp/

Ⅰ*v.*❶show respect or great honour (to) 崇拜;尊敬;敬仰:Children usually ~ their first teachers.小孩子对他们的启蒙

老师一般都很崇拜。❷attend a church service 做礼拜：This is the church where we used to ～．这是我们过去常去做礼拜的那个教堂。Ⅱ n.❶ the practice of showing respect for God or a god（对上帝或神的）崇拜，敬仰，礼拜 ❷a strong feelings of love and respect 崇拜，崇敬；爱戴

worst/wɜːst/
Ⅰ adj.& adv.most bad or ill；most badly 最坏的（地）；最差的（地）；最糟的（地）；最恶劣的（地）：the ～ enemy 最凶恶的敌人/Who suffered ～? 谁受苦最深？Ⅱ n. the worst thing or condition 最坏的事；最坏的情况：You must be prepared for the ～．你必须做最坏的打算。‖ at ～ 在最坏的情况下/get the ～ of（打）输/比不过某人/bring out the ～ in sb.使原形毕露/if ～ comes to 如果最坏的事发生/make the ～ of 对……做最坏的打算

worth/wɜːθ/
Ⅰ adj.❶deserving；valuable or useful for sb.值得……的；有价值的：This book is ～ reading.这本书值得一读。❷having a value in money，etc.有……价值；值……钱：How much is the dress ～? 这件连衣裙值多少钱？‖ for all one is ～ 拼命地/for what it is ～ 不论好坏；姑且这么说/be ～ the name 名副其实 Ⅱ n.price or value 价值：the true ～ of friendship 友情的真正价值 ‖ ～less adj.毫无价值的；无用的/～ful adj.有价值的；可贵的/～while adj.值得花时间（或花钱等）的；令人愉快的

worthy/'wɜːði/
Ⅰ adj.❶ having worth 有价值的：a ～ life 有价值的生活 ❷deserving 值得……的：a teacher ～ of respect 值得尊敬的老师 / This new film is ～ to be seen.这部新电影值得一看。Ⅱ n.a person of importance 知名人物；杰出人物：The mayor and some other worthies took part in the ceremony.市长和一些其他名人都参加了这个典礼。

would/wʊd/
v.❶used instead of will to describe what someone has said，asked，etc.（will 的过去式）将：He said he ～ help me. 他说他会

帮助我。❷if only 愿；想：I couldn't find one who ～ take the job.我找不到一个愿意接受这项工作的人。❸shows that sth. always happens or is typical（表示过去经常发生）总是；经常：We used to be good friends.He ～ come to my home on Sundays.我们过去是好朋友，每逢星期日他总要到我家来玩。❹ expressing a polite request（用于婉转语气，有礼貌的请求）：Would you please lend me a hand? 请帮我一把好吗？

wound/wuːnd/
Ⅰ v.❶deliberately damage the body by cutting，striking，shooting at it，etc. 使受伤；伤害：He fired his gun and ～ed the thief in the leg.他开了枪，打伤了那个贼的腿。/ In the battle ten soldiers were ～ed.在交战中，十个士兵受了伤。❷ cause a person to have an unpleasant feelings 伤害（人的感情）：Your remarks have ～ed his pride.你的话伤了他的自尊心。/We must not ～ his feelings.我们不应伤他的感情。Ⅱ n.❶ a deliberate damage done to the body（故意造成的）伤，创伤 ❷a painful feeling 痛苦的感觉：The defeat was a ～ to his pride.那次失败伤了他的自尊心。

wow/waʊ/
Ⅰ int. expressing surprise or admiration（表示惊讶、羡慕等）哇 Ⅱ n.a great success 巨大的成功：The new play is a ～.新剧获得了成功。

wrap/ræp/
v.(-pp-) cover sth.in a material folded around 包；捆；裹：He ～ped up the new books in paper.他用纸把那些新书包了起来。‖ be ～ped up in 埋头于；沉陷在……中

wrapper/'ræpə(r)/
n.a piece of paper which forms a loose cover 包装纸；封皮；封套：a book's ～ 书套

wrapping/'ræpɪŋ/
n.the material used for folding round and covering sth.用于包裹的材料：I undid the ～(s) and looked inside.我拆开包装材料往里边看。

wrath/rɒθ/

*n.*great anger 暴怒;愤怒;burn with ～ 怒火中烧 / A soft answer turns away ～.好言好语能消除怒气。

wreak/riːk/

*v.*do (violence) or express (strong feelings) violently 诉诸(武力),施行(暴力);泄(怒),发(脾气):We shall ～ a terrible vengeance on our enemies.我们要向敌人进行无情的报复。/These floods are ～ing in low-lying areas.洪水正在地势低洼地区肆虐。

wreath/riːθ/

*n.*a ring of flowers or leaves twisted together 花环;花圈:Many people hang ～s in the windows at Christmas.圣诞节时许多人在窗户上挂上花环。

wreck/rek/

Ⅰ*v.*destroy;cause to be destroyed 破坏;毁灭:The ship was ～ed on the rocks.船因触礁被撞毁。 Ⅱ*n.*a ship, car, building, etc.which has been destroyed 损毁的船(汽车、建筑物等):The divers found a ～ on the seabed.潜水员在海底发现了一艘沉船。

wreckage/ˈrekɪdʒ/

*n.*the broken parts of a destroyed thing (被毁物的)残余,碎片,残骸:The ～ of the aircraft was spread over a five-mile area.飞机的残骸散布在 5 英里的区域内。/trying to put together the ～ of my life (of our marriage) 试图把我人生(我们婚姻)的残局收拾起来

wrecker/ˈrekə(r)/

*n.*❶a person who destroys,especially one who tried to cause a ship to be caught on rocks in order to be able to steal from it 利用残骸船谋利者;毁船打劫者 ❷a person whose job is to bring out goods from ships which have been wrecked, so that they will not be lost (职业的)抢救失事船货物的人,打捞货物者 ❸ a vehicle used for moving other vehicles when these have stopped working,or after accidents (将抛锚或交通事故中的汽车拖走的)拖吊车,救险车,清障车

wrench/rentʃ/

*v.*❶ pull suddenly and violently 猛拉;猛扭:He ～ed the stick from me.他从我这里夺走了拐杖。 ❷ twist suddenly and painfully 扭伤:When I fell I ～ed my ankle.我跌倒时扭伤了脚踝。 Ⅱ*n.*❶a sudden and violent pull or twist 猛拉;猛扭 ❷ a tool for holding and twisting nut and bolts,etc.;spanner 扳手;扳钳

wrestle/ˈresl/

*v.*fight or compete with sb.by seizing him and trying to throw him to the ground (与……)搏斗;摔跤;角力;格斗

wretch/retʃ/

*n.*❶an unfortunate or unhappy person 可怜的人;不幸的人:The poor ～ has no relatives or friends.这个可怜的人无亲无友。 ❷a bad or annoying person 可恶的人;卑鄙的人:That ～ has stolen my bike! 那个可恶的家伙偷了我的自行车! ‖ ～ed /ˈretʃɪd/ *adj.*悲惨的;倒霉的;糟糕的;可恶的

wriggle/ˈrɪgl/

v.(cause to) move the body or part of the body from side to side (使)扭动;(使)蠕动:The snake ～ through the grass.蛇蠕动着穿过草丛。/He ～d himself out of my grip.我紧抓住他,他却扭动着挣脱了。

wright/raɪt/

n.(now usually in combinations)a maker of sth. (现在通常用以构成复合名词)工人,匠,制造者:a ship～ 造船工人/ a wheel～ 制造车轮的工人/ a play～ 剧作家

wring/rɪŋ/

v.(wrung) ❶ hold firmly and twist 扭;拧;绞:He is ～ing the hoodlum's arm in order to subdue him.他正在拧歹徒的手臂以便将其制服。 ❷remove water from clothes,etc.in this way 拧掉(湿衣服的水);拧干,绞干(衣服):My socks were so wet that I had to ～ them (out).我的短袜太湿了,我得把它拧干。/ I had to ～ the water out of my socks.我得把袜子的水拧掉。 ‖ ～ing wet 湿淋淋的,湿得能拧出水来的/ ～ one's hands 搓着双手(表示悲哀或忧伤) ‖ ～er *n.*(尤指衣服洗用后的)绞干器

wrinkle/'rɪŋkl/

Ⅰ *n.*a small fold or line in the skin（especially of the kind produced by age）or on the surface of sth.皱纹；皱褶：The man's face has ～s.这个男人的脸上有皱纹。Ⅱ *v.*have wrinkles；become full of wrinkles 有皱纹；起皱纹；起皱褶；皱起：This shirt will not ～. 这件衬衫不起皱。‖ ～d *adj.*布满皱纹的：his ～d face 他那布满皱纹的脸

wrist/rɪst/

*n.*the joint between the hand and the arm 腕；手腕：I took him by the ～.我握住了他的手腕。

write/raɪt/

v.（wrote，written）❶ make letters or words by using a pen，a pencil，etc. 书写；写字：The old man can't read or ～.那位老人不会阅读和写字。/You must ～ in ink.你必须用钢笔写字。❷put down in words 写；写下：Can the girl ～ her name? 那个女孩会写自己的名字吗？/I wrote what I saw and heard.我把自己的所见所闻都写下来了。❸ make up（a book，story，etc.）for publication 编写；写作；写：～ a novel 写小说 /～ a report 写报告 ❹produce and send a letter（to）写信（给）：He often ～s to me.他常给我写信。/I wrote to ask him to come.我写信叫他来。

wrong/rɒŋ/

Ⅰ *adj.* ❶ not correct；not in accordance with the facts or the truth 错误的；不对的；不正确的：You are taking the ～ way. 你走错了路。❷ evil；against moral standards 不好的；不正当的；邪恶的：It is ～ to cheat.欺骗是不道德的。❸ not good or normal in condition，health，results，work，etc. 失常的；有毛病的：What's ～ with the machine? 机器出了什么毛病？❹not suitable 不适当的：He's the ～ man for the job.他不适合这个工作。Ⅱ *adv.*with an incorrect result 错误地：He guessed ～.他猜错了。Ⅲ *n.*❶an action or behaviour that is not morally right or correct 错误；坏事；不道德：Know the difference between right and ～.辨是非，明善恶。❷a seriously bad or unjust action 不公正的行为；冤屈：She complained of her ～s.她诉说了她的冤屈。‖ **do** ～ 做错；作恶 Ⅳ*v.*act unjustly or dishonestly towards（sb.）不公正对待；冤枉：Do you really think I ～ed him? 你真的认为我冤枉他了吗？‖ ～**ly** *adv.*错误地；不对地/～**doer** *n.*做坏事的人/～**doing** *n.*坏事；不道德的行为

wrought/rɔːt/

v.（used only in the past tense）caused sth.to happen（仅用于过去时）造成；引起：The storm ～ great damage.暴风雨造成了巨大的破坏。

W

Xx

x/eks/

n. ❶ a quantity that is unknown until a calculation has been made 未知数 ❷ an unknown person, value, etc. 未知的人（价值等）

xerox/ˈzɪərɒks/

v. make copies by using Xerox or a similar process 复印；影印：We ~ed five copies of the letter. 我们将这封信复印了五份。

X-ray/ˈeks reɪ/

Ⅰ *n.* a powerful, unseen beam of light that can penetrate solids and makes it possible to see into or through them; photograph taken using this X 射线；X 光；X 光照片：an ~ examination X 光检查 Ⅱ *v.* examine, treat, photograph with X-rays 用 X 光检查（治疗或照相）：They ~ed his arm to find whether the bone was broken. 他们用 X 光检查了他的胳膊以查明是否骨折。

xylophone/ˈzaɪləfəʊn/

n. a musical instrument made up of wooden bars of different length, which is played by striking the bars with little hammers 木琴

X

Yy

yacht/jɒt/

　　n. a boat for pleasure trips or racing, equipped with sails or engines, or both of them 快艇：a racing ～ 一艘竞赛快艇/ I spent a day on my friend's ～. 我在朋友的游艇上玩了一天。

yak/jæk/

　　n. a long-haired ox of Central Asia（产于中亚的）牦牛

yank/jæŋk/

　　Ⅰ *v.* pull sharply and suddenly 拽；猛拉；拔：He ～ed away the chair before I could sit on it. 我还没有坐下来，他就猛地把椅子拉走了。 Ⅱ *n.* an action of pulling away sharply 突然的猛拉：give the chair a ～ 突然猛拉椅子

yap/jæp/

　　Ⅰ *v.* (especially of small dogs) utter short sharp barks（尤指小狗）狂吠 Ⅱ *n.* (especially of small dogs) short sharp barks（尤指小狗的）狂吠声

yard/jɑːd/

　　n. ❶ an area outside a building, usually with a hard surface and a surrounding wall 院子：The children are playing in the ～ at the front of the house. 孩子们正在房前的院子里玩。❷ a unit of length equal to 3 feet 码（长度单位，1 码＝3 英尺或 36 英寸）

yarn/jɑːn/

　　n. ❶ a type of thread used for knitting; thick thread from which a rope is made 纱；纱线，毛线：cotton ～ 棉纱 ❷ a story 故事；奇谈：spin a ～ 编故事；摆龙门阵

yashmak/ˈjæʃmæk/

　　n. (in some Muslim countries) a type of veil worn over the face by women（某些伊斯兰教国家中妇女所戴的）面纱

yawn/jɔːn/

　　v. open the mouth wide and take a breath when tired or bored 打呵欠：He was so tired that he ～ed and fell asleep. 他太疲劳了，打声呵欠就睡着了。

year/jɪə(r), jɜː(r)/

　　n. the period of time of about 365 days from January 1 to December 31 年；历年；年岁；年度：this ～ 今年/last ～ 去年/ He is 50 ～s old. 他 50 岁了。‖ all the ～ round 一年到头/～ after ～ 年复一年/ in ～ out 一年又一年

yearly/ˈjɪəli/

　　adj. & *adv.* once a year; every year 一年一度（的）；每年（的）：a ～ income 年收入/He is paid ＄6,000 ～. 他每年收入 6 000 美元。

yearn/jɜːn/

　　v. have a strong or intense desire for sth. 强烈希望；渴望；向往：They ～ed to go home. 他们渴望回家去。/The people there ～ for freedom and liberation. 那里的人民渴望获得自由和解放。

yeast/jiːst/

　　n. a living substance used in the preparation of bread and beer and other alcoholic drinks 酵母；发酵粉：～ cake 发面饼/～ powder 发酵粉

yell/jel/

　　Ⅰ *n.* a strong, loud outcry 大叫；叫喊：a ～ of pain 疼痛时的叫喊声 Ⅱ *v.* cry out with a strong and loud sound 大叫，呼喊：He ～ed at her to be careful. 他向她大叫，要她小心。

yellow/ˈjeləʊ/

　　Ⅰ *adj.* having the colour like lemon or butter 黄的；黄色的：the ～ race 黄种人；黄色人种/Yellow Book 黄皮书/the

Yellow River 黄河 Ⅱ *n.* the colour like lemon or butter 黄色：The girl was dressed in ～.那女孩穿着黄衣服。

yelp/jelp/

v. cry out suddenly because of fear or pain （由于害怕或疼痛）突然叫喊，尖叫：The dog ～ed when he kicked it.他踢了狗一脚，狗便狂吠起来。

yes/jes/

Ⅰ *adv.* ❶ used to express agreement, affirmation, etc.（用于表示同意、肯定等的回答）是，是的："Do you like English?" "Yes, I do.""你喜欢英语吗？""是的，我喜欢。"/"This is an interesting book." "Yes, it is.""这是一本有趣的书。""是的。"❷ used to show that one has heard a call or command（表示应答呼唤）是；在；嗳；来了："Waiter!" "Yes." "服务员！""嗳，来了。"/"Go and open the door." "Yes, sir.""去把门打开。""是，先生。"/"Excuse me!" "Yes?""打扰一下！""什么事呀？"Ⅱ *n.* an affirmative answer or decision 同意；赞成；是：He said ～ to me.他同意我说的。

yes-man/ˈjesmæn/

n. a person who always agrees with his employer, leader, etc.（对上司）唯唯诺诺的人

yesterday/ˈjestədi, -deɪ/

Ⅰ *n.* ❶ the day before today 昨天：～'s newspaper 昨天的报纸 / the day before ～ 前天/～ morning 昨天上午 /Yesterday was my birthday.昨天是我的生日。❷ the time just past 最近：It was a thing of ～. 这是最近的事。Ⅱ *adv.* ❶ on the day preceding today 昨天，昨日：What did you do ～? 昨天你做了些什么？❷ in the recent past；only a short time ago 最近，新近：I was not born ～.我不是刚出生的孩子。（意指：你不要以为我什么都不懂）。

yet/jet/

Ⅰ *adv.* up until now or then；by a particular time；already 至今；到此时；仍然；尚还：I haven't finished my homework ～. 我还未完成作业。Ⅱ *conj.* in spite of that；but 但是；然而：He studied very

hard,～ he failed in the exam.他学习很努力,但考试还是没有及格。‖ as ～到现在或那时为止还（多用于否定句）/not just ～ 暂时还不能/not…nor ～ 不……也不/and（but）～ 但是

yield/jiːld/

v. ❶ produce, bear, or provide, especially as a result of work or effort 生产；生长出；结出（果实）：The trees ～ plenty of fruits each year.这些树每年硕果累累。❷ give up control（of）让步；屈服；投降：We shall never ～.我们决不投降。‖ ～ to 向……低头（让步、投降）；顺从；把……交给/～ up（to）生产出；让给；放弃给

yoga/ˈjəʊɡə/

n. a religious way of life（originally followed mainly by some Hindus）which includes prayer, deep breathing, physical exercise and fasting（主要始于印度教的）瑜伽，瑜伽修行法

yogh(o)urt/ˈjɒɡət/

n. a thick, liquid food made from sour milk 酸乳酪

you/juː/

pron. ❶ the person or people being spoken to 你；你们 ❷ a person；anyone；one 任何人；人们（泛指）：You can never tell what they will do next.谁也说不上他们下一步要干什么。

young/jʌŋ/

Ⅰ *adj.* in a early stage of life, growth, development, etc.；recently born or begun 年轻的；年幼的；初期的：a ～ man 年轻人/a ～ country 新成立的国家 Ⅱ *n.* young people considered as a group；any immature animal 年轻人；幼仔；雏：Both ～ and old like to see the film.无论是年轻人还是老年人都爱看这部影片。

youngster/ˈjʌŋstə(r)/

n. a young person；a child, especially a boy 年轻人；小孩；小伙子；男孩：When he was a ～, he was very naughty.他小时候很淘气。

your/jɔː(r)/

pron. of or belonging to you（you 的所有

格)你的；你们的：Wash ～ hands before meals! 饭前洗手! /Show me ～ new dictionary.把你的新词典给我看看。

yours/jɔːz/

*pron.*sth.belonging to you（you 的物主代词）你的东西；你们的东西：This pencil is ～.这支铅笔是你(你们)的。

yourself/jɔːˈself/

pron. ❶ used to emphasize the person that you are referring to（表示强调）你亲自；你本人：You told me so ～.你亲自对我这么说的。❷ refer to the person that a speaker or writer is talking or writing to 你自己；你们自己：Ask ～ what you really want.问问

你自己到底需要什么。❸ your real or true condition（你的）真实情况：You are ～ again.你又康复了。

youth/juːθ/

n. ❶ the state of being young；the period of life between childhood and maturity 青春；青少年时代 ❷ young people（总称）青年人；青年男女；青年

youthful/ˈjuːθfl/

*adj.*young；having the qualities of youth 年轻的；青年的；有青年气质的；显得年轻的：～ days 青年时代/～ energy 青春的活力/She's a very ～ 75.她已 75 岁了，却显得很年轻。

Y

Zz

zeal/ziːl/

  *n.*eagerness or enthusiasm in pursuit of sth.热心；热情；渴望；渴求：He showed great ~ for his work.他对他的工作很热心。

zealous/ˈzeləs/

  *adj.*full of zeal；actively enthusiastic 热心的；热情的；热忱的：We made ~ efforts to clean up the house for the party.为了开晚会我们积极努力地把房子收拾干净。/ a ~ supporter 一个热心的支持者

zebra/ˈziːbrə, ˈzebrə/

  n.(*pl.*zebra 或 ~s) a wild mammal of southern and eastern Africa, related to the horse and donkey but striped with dark or white bands 斑马

zero/ˈzɪərəʊ/

  I *num.*❶ the figure 0 零：The figure 200 has two ~s in it.数字 200 里有两个零。II *n.*❶ a freezing point on the centigrade and Celsius scale（摄氏）零度：The temperature fell to ~.温度降到了零度。❷ the quantity that registers a reading of zero on a scale（刻度表上的）零点，零位

zigzag/ˈzɪgzæg/

  I *n.*a line or course which turns sharply from side to side 锯齿形线条；之字形：go in ~s 作之字形 II *adj.*being looking like a zigzag 之字形的；弯曲的；曲折的：a ~ ruler 折叠尺/a ~ path up the hill 通往山上的弯曲小道 III *adv.*so as to move right and left alternately 之字形地；弯曲地；曲折地：He drove ~ across the city.他左弯右拐地驾车穿过城市。IV *v.*have or move along in a zigzag course 呈之字形移动；曲折行进：The path ~s between dry hills in the land.一条小径在这些干涸的小山丘间蜿蜒。

zinc/zɪŋk/

  I *n.*a bluish-white metallic element (Zn) 锌（符号 Zn）II *v.*coat or treat with zinc；

galvanize 在……上面镀锌；用锌处理；给……镀锌；电镀

zip/zɪp/

  I *n.*❶ the sound of sth. moving quickly and suddenly through the air, or of cloth tearing 尖啸声；撕裂声；嗖嗖声：the ~ of a flying bullet 子弹飞过的嗖嗖声 ❷ the device for bringing together or separating two rows of metal or plastic teeth by means of drawing together 拉链：The ~ on my bag has got stuck.我提包的拉链卡住了。II *v.*(-pp-) open or shut by means of a zipper 拉开（拉链）；扣上（拉链）：~ the bag open (shut) 把包的拉链拉开（拉上）/Zip up your jacket.把夹克的拉链拉上。

zone/zəʊn/

  *n.*❶ one of the five divisions of the earth's surface, marked by imaginary lines parallel to the equator（地球上的）带：frigid (temperate, torrid) ~ 寒（温、热）带 ❷ an area or a region with particular qualities 地区；区域：the cotton ~ 产棉区 /a war ~ 战区 /a business ~ 商业区

zoo/zuː/

  *n.*a place where animals are kept and shown for the public to see 动物园：There are often many tame animals in a children's ~.儿童动物园里往往有很多驯服了的动物。

zoology/zəʊˈɒlədʒi/

  *n.*the science of animals；the study of animals and animal life 动物学；动物研究

zoom/zuːm/

  I *n.*the low, deep humming sound of the sudden upward flight of an aircraft 飞机发出的嗡嗡声 II *v.*(of an aircraft) move upwards at high speed（飞机）急速上升；迅速移动

Z

附录一

英语度量衡单位对照表

1. 公　制

类别	英文名称	符号	中文名称	对主单位的比	折合市制
长度	kilometre	km	千米(公里)	1 000 米	2 市里
	metre	m	米	主单位	3 市尺
	decimetre	dm	分米	1/10 米	3 市寸
	centimetre	cm	厘米	1/100 米	3 市分
	millimetre	mm	毫米	1/1 000 米	3 市厘
	micron	μm	微米	1/1 000 000 米	
	nanometre	nm	纳米	1/1 000 000 000 米	
重量(或质量)	metric ton	t	吨	1 000 千克	
	kilogram(me)	kg	千克(公斤)	主单位	2 市斤
	gram(me)	g	克	1/1 000 千克	2 市分
	decigram(me)	dg	分克	1/10 000 千克	2 市厘
	centigram(me)	cg	厘克	1/100 000 千克	2 市毫
	milligram(me)	mg	毫克	1/1 000 000 千克	
容积	litre	L,l	升	主单位	1 市升
	decilitre	dL,dl	分升	1/10 升	1 市合
	centilitre	cL,cl	厘升	1/100 升	1 市勺
	millilitre	mL,ml	毫升	1/1 000 升	1 市撮
面积	square kilometre	km^2	平方千米(平方公里)	1 000 000 平方米	4 平方市里
	hectare	ha	公顷	10 000 平方米	15 市亩
	square metre	m^2	平方米	主单位	9 平方市尺
	square decimetre	dm^2	平方分米	1/100 平方米	9 平方市寸
	square centimetre	cm^2	平方厘米	1/10 000 平方米	9 平方市分
	square millimetre	mm^2	平方毫米	1/1 000 000 平方米	9 平方市厘

2. 英美制

(1) 度量表

类别	名　称	缩写	汉译	换　算	折合公制
长度	league		里格	3 miles	4.828 千米
	(statute) mile	m,mi	英里	8 furlongs	1.609 千米
	furlong	fur	浪	4 rods	201.17 米
	pole,rod	rd	杆	5½ yards	5.029 米
	yard	yd	码	3 feet	0.914 米
	foot	ft (或 ′)	英尺	12 inches	30.48 厘米
	inch	in (或 ″)	英寸		2.54 厘米
水程长度	nautical mile		海里	10 cable's lengths	1.852 千米
	cable's length		链	[英] 100 fathoms [美] 720 feet	[英] 185.2 米 [美] 219 米
	fathom	f,fm	英寻,拓	6 feet	1.829 米
	foot	ft	英尺		0.305 米
面积	square mile	mi²	平方英里	640 acres	2.59 平方千米
	acre	a	英亩	4 840 sq yd	40.469 公亩
	square rod	rd²	平方杆	30.25 sq yd	25.293 平方米
	square yard	yd²	平方码	9 sq ft	0.836 平方米
	square foot	ft²	平方英尺	144 sq in	929 平方厘米
	square inch	in²	平方英寸		6.452 平方厘米
干量	bushel	bu	蒲式耳	4 pecks	36.367 升
	peck	pk	配克	8 quarts	9.092 升
	quart	qt	夸脱	2 pints	[英] 1.136 升 [美] 1.101 升
	pint	pt	品脱,量磅		[英] 0.568 升 [美] 0.551 升
液量	gallon	gal	加仑	4 quarts	4.546 升
	quart	qt	夸脱	2 pints	[英] 1.136 升 [美] 0.946 升
	pint	pt	品脱,量磅	4 gills	[英] 0.568 升 [美] 0.473 升
	gill	gi	及耳		0.142 升

（2）衡制表

类别	名　　称	缩写	汉译	换　算	折合公制
常衡	ton	tn,t	吨	20 hundred weights	
	long ton［英］	lt	长吨	2 240 pounds	1 016.05 千克
	short ton［美］	st	短吨	2 000 pounds	907.18 千克
	hundredweight	cwt	英担	［英］112 pounds ［美］100 pounds	［英］50.80 千克 ［美］45.36 千克
	stone	st	英石	14 pounds	6.35 千克
	pound	lb	磅	16 ounces	0.454 千克
	ounce	oz	盎司	16 drams	28.35 克
	dra(ch)m	dr	打兰		1.772 克
金衡	pound	lb t	磅	12 ounces	373.24 克
	ounce	oz t	盎司	20 pennyweights	31.103 克
	pennyweight	dwt	本尼威特	24 grains	1.555 克
	carat	car	开	3 086 grains	0.2 克
	grain	gr	格令		0.0648 克
药衡	pound	lb ap	磅	12 ounces	373.24 克
	ounce	oz ap	盎司	8 drams	31.103 克
	dra(ch)m	dr ap	打兰,英钱	3 scruples	3.888 克
	scruple	scr ap	英分	20 grains	1.296 克
	grain	gr	格令		50 毫克

附录二

英文字母开头的词语

AA 制　Dutch treatment 指聚餐或其他消费结账时个人平摊出钱或各人算各人账的做法

ABC　1. the letters of the English alphabets as taught to children 儿童学习的字母表 2. the basic facts about a particular subject 基础知识，入门 3. American Broadcasting Corporation 美国广播公司

ABS　anti-lock braking system 防抱死制动系统

ADSL　symmetrical digital subscriber line 非对称数字用户线路

AI　artificial intelligence 人工智能

AIDS　acquired immune deficiency syndrome 获得性免疫缺陷综合征，即艾滋病

AM　amplitude modulation 调幅

AOL　American On-line（美国在线）

APC　aspirin, phenacetin and caffeine 复方阿司匹林（由阿司匹林，非那西丁和咖啡因制成的一种解热镇痛药）

APEC　Asia-Pacific Economic Cooperation 亚太经济合作组织

API　air pollution index 空气污染指数

AQ　adversity quotient 逆境商数

ASAP　as soon as possible 尽快

ATM　automated teller machine 自动柜员机

AV　audio-visual 音频和视频

B&W　black and white 黑白片

B2B　business to business 电子商务中企业对企业的交易方式

B2C　business to customer 电子商务中企业对消费者的交易方式

B.A.　Bachelor of Arts 文学士

BBC　British Broadcasting Corporation 英国广播公司

BBS　1. bulletin board system 电子公告牌系统 2. bulletin board service 电子公告牌服务

BD　Blue-ray Disc 蓝光光盘

BEC　Business English Certificate 商务英语证书

BP 机　beeper（BB）无线寻呼机

BRT　bus rapid transit 快速公交系统

B.S.　Bachelor of Science 理学士

B 超　type-B ultrasonic B 型超声诊断

C2C　consumer to consumer 电子商务中消费者对消费者的交易方式

CAD　computer-aided design 计算机辅助设计

CAI　computer-aided instruction 计算机辅助教学

CATV　cable TV 有线电视

CBA　Chinese Basketball Association 中国篮球协会

CBD　central business district 中央商务区

CCC　China Compulsory Certification 中国强制性产品认证（即 3C 认证）

CCD　charge-coupled device 电荷耦合器件

CCTV　China Central Television 中国中央电视台

CD　compact disc 激光唱盘

CDC　center for disease control and prevention 疾病预防控制中心（简称疾控中心）

CDMA　code division multiple access 码分多址（一种数字通信技术）

CD-R　compact disc-recordable 可录光盘

CD-ROM　compact disc read-only memory 只读光盘

CD-RW　compact disc-rewritable 可擦写光盘

CEO　chief executive officer 首席执行官

CET College English Test 大学英语考试

CFO chief finance officer 首席财务官

CI 1.corporate identity 企业标志 2.corporate image 企业形象

CIA Central Intelligence Agency 美国中央情报局

CIMS computer-integrated manufacturing system 计算机集成制造系统

CIP cataloguing in publication 在版编目;预版编目

CMMB China mobile multimedia broadcasting 手持电视;中国移动多媒体广播

CNN Cable News Network 美国有线电视新闻网

CPA certified public accountant 注册会计师

CPI consumer price index 消费者价格指数,居民消费价格指数

CPU central processing unit 中央处理器

CRT cathode-ray tube 阴极射线管

CT computerized tomography 计算机层析成像

DC digital camera 数字相机

DIY do it yourself 自己动手做

DJ disco jockey (迪厅、酒吧等场所的)音响调音师;电台音乐节目主持人

DNA deoxyribonucleic acid 脱氧核糖核酸

DOS disk operating system 磁盘操作系统

DSL digital subscriber line 数字用户线路

DV digital video 数字视频;数字摄像机

DVD digital video disc 数字激光视盘

EBD electronic brakeforce distribution 电子制动力分配系统

ED erectile dysfunction 男性勃起功能障碍

EDI electronic data interchange 电子数据交换

EMBA Executive Master of Business Administration 高级管理人员工商管理硕士

EMS express mail service 邮政特快专递

EQ emotional quotient 情商

ETC electronic toll collection system 电子不停车收费系统

EU European Union 欧洲联盟;欧盟

F-1 赛车 Formula One, motor vehicle races featuring the best drivers and the fastest vehicles 一级方程式赛车

FAQ frequently asked question 常见问题

FAX facsimile 传真件;传真系统

FBI Federal Bureau of Investigation 美国联邦调查局

FM frequency modulation 调频

FTA 1.free trade agreement 自由贸易协定 2.free trade area 自由贸易区

GATT General Agreement on Tariffs and Trade 关贸总协定

GDP gross domestic product 国内生产总值

GIS geographic information system 地理信息系统

GM genetically modified 基因改性的;转基因的

GMAT Graduate Management Admission Test (美国等国家)管理专业研究生入学资格考试

GMDSS global maritime distress and safety system 全球海上遇险与安全系统

GMP good manufacturing practice 药品生产质量管理规范

GMT Greenwich Mean Time 格林尼治标准时间

GNP gross national product 国民生产总值

GPS global positioning system 全球定位系统

GRE Graduate Record Examination (美国等国家)研究生入学资格考试

GSM global system for mobile communication 全球移动通信系统

HDMI high-definition multimedia interface 高清晰度多媒体接口

HDTV high-definition television 高清晰度电视

hi-fi high-fidelity 高保真度

HIV human immunodeficiency virus 人类免疫缺陷病毒;艾滋病病毒